ROGET'S
UNIVERSITY
THESAURUS

ROGET'S
UNIVERSITY
THESAURUS

EDITED BY

C. O. Sylvester Mawson, Litt.D., Ph.D.

THOMAS Y. CROWELL COMPANY

New York · Established 1834

Originally published as *Roget's International Thesaurus of English Words and Phrases*

Manufactured in the United States of America

Library of Congress Catalog Card No. 63-13469

ISBN 0-8152-0062-5

Apollo Edition, 1963

PREFACE
TO THE FIRST EDITION
(1852)

IT IS now nearly fifty years since I first projected a system of verbal classification similar to that on which the present work is founded. Conceiving that such a compilation might help to supply my own deficiencies, I had, in the year 1805, completed a classed catalogue of words on a small scale, but on the same principle, and nearly in the same form, as the Thesaurus now published. I had often during that long interval found this little collection, scanty and imperfect as it was, of much use to me in literary composition, and often contemplated its extension and improvement; but a sense of the magnitude of the task, amidst a multitude of other avocations, deterred me from the attempt. Since my retirement from the duties of Secretary of the Royal Society, however, finding myself possessed of more leisure, and believing that a repertory of which I had myself experienced the advantage might, when amplified, prove useful to others, I resolved to embark in an undertaking which, for the last three or four years, has given me incessant occupation, and has, indeed, imposed upon me an amount of labour very much greater than I had anticipated. Notwithstanding all the pains I have bestowed on its execution, I am fully aware of its numerous deficiencies and imperfections, and of its falling far short of the degree of excellence that might be attained. But, in a work of this nature, where perfection is placed at so great a distance, I have thought it best to limit my ambition to that moderate share of merit which it may claim in its present form; trusting to the indulgence of those for whose benefit it is intended, and to the candour of critics who, while they find it easy to detect faults, can at the same time duly appreciate difficulties.

P. M. ROGET

April 29, 1852.

PETER MARK ROGET

(1779–1869)

PETER MARK ROGET was the only son of John Roget, who hailed from Geneva and later had oversight of the French Protestant Church in Threadneedle Street, London, where Peter was born in 1779. His father died a few years later, and his mother removed to Edinburgh, where the son entered the university at the age of fourteen. He graduated M.D. from the medical school at the early age of nineteen and distinguished himself by valuable research work on such subjects as consumption and the effects of laughing gas. In 1802 he went to Geneva, his father's home, in company with the sons of a wealthy merchant of Manchester, to whom he acted as tutor. The disturbances caused by the breach of the Peace of Amiens interrupted their tour and Roget was for a time held a prisoner at Geneva. He succeeded in getting away, however, at the end of 1803 and became private physician to the Marquis of Lansdowne.

In 1805 he became physician to the Manchester Infirmary and made a name for himself there by giving courses of lectures on scientific subjects. He combined in an unusual degree exact knowledge with a power of apt and vivid presentation, and this work he continued for well-nigh fifty years after his removal to London in 1808. He became physician to the Northern Dispensary in 1810 and lectured assiduously on medical and other subjects in various parts of the metropolis. A testimony to his versatility is afforded by the fact that he was asked by the Government to make an inquiry into the water supply of London, and in 1828 he published a report on the subject. For three years he held the post of Fullerian Professor of Physiology at the London Institution.

Dr. Roget was made a Fellow of the Royal Society in 1815, and served as secretary of the organization for over twenty years. He was appointed Examiner in Physiology in the University of London. He wrote various papers on physiology and health, among them *On Animal and Vegetable Physiology*, a Bridgewater treatise, 1834; a work on phrenology in two volumes, 1838; and *Electricity, Galvanism*, 1848.

These activities would be more than enough for most men, but Roget's insatiable thirst for knowledge and his appetite for work led him into yet other fields. He was no high-and-dry scientist who thought that learning was the prerogative of the elect; his aim was to broadcast it as widely as possible. He was a founder of the Society for the Diffusion of Knowledge and wrote for it a series of popular manuals. He devised a slide rule and spent much time in attempting to perfect a calculating machine. He showed remarkable ingenuity in inventing and solving chess problems and designed a pocket chessboard called the "Economic Chessboard."

However, the work which extended and perpetuated his fame on two continents was one which he probably regarded as a mere avocation. In the year 1852 he brought out his *Thesaurus of English Words and Phrases Classified and Arranged so as to Facilitate the Expression of Ideas and Assist in Literary Composition*. A second edition followed the next year, a third two years later, and still others in the next few years. The work was extended and corrected by his son. In the present "University" edition, edited by C. O. Sylvester Mawson, this treasury of ideas has had an ever widening distribution.

Peter Mark Roget died in West Malvern, on September 12, 1869, at the advanced age of ninety.

PREFACE

In devising a book of synonyms two different methods are open to us: one is the so-called dictionary method, in which the synonymized words are given in alphabetical order; the other is the plan adopted by Roget, which today still stands preëminent. What the dictionary plan gains in facility of reference it loses in suggestiveness and comprehensiveness. It appeals to the novice rather than to the practiced writer.

ROGET'S UNIVERSITY THESAURUS, by means of its Index Guide and its prominent key words, combines the advantages of the dictionary plan with the masterly scheme conceived by Roget. In short, it is not an accretion but an organism, each word being related to its neighbors and each part to the whole.

The dictionary is the birthplace of the synonym: almost every definition supplies an affinitive term for the word defined. The making of dictionaries thus affords a rare training for the preparation of a book of synonyms and antonyms. The Thomas Y. Crowell Company has always applied such experience in its revisions of Roget.

Lexicography is not a prophetic science: it merely records the past and the present and plays an important part in the standardization of speech. It follows therefore that the dictionary and the thesaurus must constantly be kept abreast of present-day requirements. Not only is the language actually growing, but old words take on new senses, while others drift into desuetude. The scientist and the inventor are constantly adding to the linguistic store.

ROGET'S UNIVERSITY THESAURUS has been modernized and systematized and brought into line with the latest lexicographical science. Just as Noah Webster's epoch-making work has been merged in its vigorous descendants, so has the pioneer achievement of Roget been embodied in the UNIVERSITY THESAURUS.

The UNIVERSITY edition offers the user (1) a greatly enlarged list of synonyms and antonyms; (2) a special grouping of comparisons and associated terms; (3) the systematization of scientific and technical terminology; (4) a regrouping of synonyms, so that each paragraph consists of words more or less related and interchangeable; (5) characterization of all obsolete, obsolescent, rare, archaic, colloquial, dialectal, and slang words, as well as all British, foreign, and special terms, as is done in the best dictionaries; (6) plural forms, in all cases of unusual difficulty; (7) numerous phrases and idioms; (8) many citations from modern authors, felicitous and keen in phrase and thought; (9) a compilation of foreign words and phrases translated into English; (10) an alphabetical list of basic synonyms; (11) a separate thesaurus of basic scientific words.

The new words run well into the thousands and embrace every department of knowledge. Particular attention has been given to scientific and technical terms and the newer words of the schools and the street. The special needs of the student, the speaker, and the writer have been kept in view, and the aim has been not merely to supply a selection of synonyms but to suggest ideas and new turns of

PREFACE

thought. The parallel arrangement of synonyms and antonyms, peculiar to Roget's scheme, adds further to the usefulness of the book and gives a completeness to every page. Books on the dictionary plan usually cover the antonyms (if they give them at all) by cross-references to other groups of synonyms in the main vocabulary. Thus, under *goodness* they refer to *badness* as an antonym. Roget gives *goodness* and *badness* side by side.

Apart from the scientific and logical arrangement, the distinguishing feature of Roget is the inclusion of phrases. Not only does the use of phrases enlarge the group of synonyms for any particular word, but in many instances the phrase furnishes the only possible synonym. The improvement of this unique feature has received the most painstaking attention. The plays of modern dramatists have been searched for the pithy phrase, the apt expression, the well-turned aphorism — in short, for spoken English at its best. Scores of other modern writers have also been laid under contribution, while, as the quotations themselves will show, new and old alike have given of their choicest in thought and form.

The international character of the book is evidenced by the variant spellings and by the scope of the vocabulary. All Briticisms and Americanisms are labeled, and where the usage differs in the two countries such difference is pointed out. The English language marches with no frontiers; it is a world possession. Every race and country is reflected in its vocabulary. The UNIVERSITY THESAURUS is alive to this universality, and, to assist writers in giving local color, the home of every imported word is duly recorded.

C. O. SYLVESTER MAWSON

CONTENTS

INTRODUCTION

The present work is intended to supply, with respect to the English language, a desideratum hitherto unsupplied in any language; namely, a collection of the words it contains and of the idiomatic combinations peculiar to it, arranged, not in alphabetical order as they are in a dictionary, but according to the *ideas* which they express.[1] The purpose of an ordinary dictionary is simply to explain the meaning of words; and the problem of which it professes to furnish the solution may be stated thus:— The word being given, to find its signification, or the idea it is intended to convey. The object aimed at in the present undertaking is exactly the converse of this: namely, — The idea being given, to find the word, or words, by which that idea may be most fitly and aptly expressed. For this purpose, the words and phrases of the language are here classed, not according to their sound or their orthography, but strictly according to their *signification*.

The communication of our thoughts by means of language, whether spoken or written, like every other object of mental exertion, constitutes a peculiar art, which, like other arts, cannot be acquired in any perfection but by long-continued practice. Some, indeed, there are more highly gifted than others with a facility of expression, and naturally endowed with the power of eloquence; but to none is it at all times an easy process to embody, in exact and appropriate language, the various trains of ideas that are passing through the mind, or to depict in their true colors and proportions, the diversified and nicer shades of feeling which accompany them. To those who are unpracticed in the art of composition, or unused to extempore speaking, these difficulties present themselves in their most formidable aspect. However distinct may be our views, however vivid our conceptions, or however fervent our emotions, we cannot but be often conscious that the phraseology we have at our command is inadequate to do them justice. We seek in vain the words we need, and strive ineffectually to devise forms of expression which shall faithfully portray our thoughts and sentiments. The appropriate terms, notwithstanding our utmost efforts, cannot be conjured up at will. Like "spirits from the vasty deep," they come not when we call; and we are driven to the employment of a set of words and phrases either too general or too limited, too strong or too feeble, which suit not the occasion, which hit not the mark we aim at; and the result of our prolonged exertion is a style at once labored and obscure, vapid and redundant, or vitiated by the still graver faults of affectation or ambiguity.

It is to those who are thus painfully groping their way and struggling with the difficulties of composition, that this work professes to hold out a helping hand. The assistance it gives is that of furnishing on every topic a copious store of words and phrases, adapted to express all the recognizable shades and modifications of the general idea under which those words and phrases are arranged. The inquirer can readily select, out of the ample collection spread cut before his eyes in the following pages, those expressions which are best suited to his purpose, and which might not have occurred to him without such assistance. In order to make this selection, he scarcely ever need engage in any critical or elaborate study of the subtle distinctions existing between synonymous terms; for if the materials set before him be sufficiently abundant, an instinctive tact will rarely fail to lead him to the proper choice. Even while glancing over the columns of this work, his eye may chance to light upon a particular term which may save the cost of a clumsy paraphrase, or spare the labor of a tortuous circumlocution. Some felicitous turn

[1] See note on p. xx.

of expression thus introduced will frequently open to the mind of the reader a whole vista of collateral ideas, which could not, without an extended and obtrusive episode, have been unfolded to his view; and often will the judicious insertion of a happy epithet, like a beam of sunshine in a landscape, illumine and adorn the subject which it touches, imparting new grace and giving life and spirit to the picture.

Every workman in the exercise of his art should be provided with proper implements. For the fabrication of complicated and curious pieces of mechanism, the artisan requires a corresponding assortment of various tools and instruments. For giving proper effect to the fictions of the drama, the actor should have at his disposal a well-furnished wardrobe, supplying the costumes best suited to the personages he is to represent. For the perfect delineation of the beauties of nature, the painter should have within reach of his pencil every variety and combination of hues and tints. Now, the writer, as well as the orator, employs for the accomplishment of his purposes the instrumentality of words; it is in words that he clothes his thoughts; it is by means of words that he depicts his feelings. It is therefore essential to his success that he be provided with a copious vocabulary, and that he possess an entire command of all the resources and appliances of his language. To the acquisition of this power no procedure appears more directly conducive than the study of a methodized system such as that now offered to his use.

The utility of the present work will be appreciated more especially by those who are engaged in the arduous process of translating into English a work written in another language. Simple as the operation may appear, on a superficial view, of rendering into English each of its sentences, the task of transfusing, with perfect exactness, the sense of the original, preserving at the same time the style and character of its composition, and reflecting with fidelity the mind and the spirit of the author, is a task of extreme difficulty. The cultivation of this useful department of literature was in ancient times strongly recommended both by Cicero and by Quintilian, as essential to the formation of a good writer and accomplished orator. Regarded simply as a mental exercise, the practice of translation is the best training for the attainment of that mastery of language and felicity of diction which are the sources of the highest oratory, and are requisite for the possession of a graceful and persuasive eloquence. By rendering ourselves the faithful interpreters of the thoughts and feelings of others, we are rewarded with the acquisition of greater readiness and facility in correctly expressing our own; as he who has best learned to execute the orders of a commander, becomes himself best qualified to command.

In the earliest periods of civilization, translators have been the agents for propagating knowledge from nation to nation, and the value of their labors has been inestimable; but, in the present age, when so many different languages have become the depositories of the vast treasures of literature and of science which have been accumulating for centuries, the utility of accurate translations has greatly increased and it has become a more important object to attain perfection in the art.

The use of language is not confined to its being the medium through which we communicate our ideas to one another; it fulfills a no less important function as an *instrument of thought;* not being merely its vehicle but giving it wings for flight. Metaphysicians are agreed that scarcely any of our intellectual operations could be carried on, to any considerable extent, without the agency of words. None but those who are conversant with the philosophy of mental phenomena can be aware of the immense influence that is exercised by language in promoting the development of our ideas, in fixing them in the mind, and in detaining them for steady contemplation. Into every process of reasoning, language enters as an essential element. Words are the instruments by which we form all our abstractions, by which we fashion and embody our ideas, and by which we are enabled to glide along a series of premises and conclusions with a rapidity so great as to leave in the memory no trace of the successive steps of the process; and we remain unconscious how much we owe to this potent auxiliary of the reasoning faculty. It is on this ground, also, that the present work founds a claim to utility. The review of a catalogue of words of analogous signification, will often suggest by association other trains of thought, which, presenting the subject under new and varied aspects, will vastly expand the sphere of our mental vision. Amidst the many objects thus brought within the range of our contemplation, some striking similitude or appropriate image, some excursive flight or brilliant conception, may flash on the mind, giving point and force to our arguments, awakening a responsive chord in the imagination or sensibility of the reader, and procuring for our reasonings a more ready access both to his understanding and to his heart.

It is of the utmost consequence that strict accuracy should regulate our use of language, and that every one should acquire the power and the habit of expressing his thoughts with perspicuity and correctness. Few, indeed, can appreciate the real extent and importance of that influence which language has always exercised on human affairs, or can be aware how often these are determined by causes much slighter than are apparent to a superficial observer. False logic, disguised under specious phraseology, too often gains the assent of the unthinking multitude, disseminating far and wide the seeds of prejudice and error. Truisms pass current, and wear the semblance of profound wisdom, when dressed up in the tinsel garb of antithetical phrases, or set off by an imposing pomp of paradox. By a confused jargon of involved and mystical sentences, the imagination is easily inveigled into a transcendental region of clouds, and the understanding beguiled into the belief that it is acquiring knowledge and approaching truth. A misapplied or misapprehended term is sufficient to give rise to fierce and interminable disputes; a misnomer has turned the tide of popular opinion; a verbal sophism has decided a party question; an artful watchword, thrown among combustible materials, has kindled the flame of deadly warfare, and changed the destiny of an empire.

In constructing the following system of classification of the ideas which are expressible by language, my chief aim has been to obtain the greatest amount of practical utility. I have accordingly adopted such principles of arrangement as appeared to me to be the simplest and most natural, and which would not require, either for their comprehension or application, any disciplined acumen, or depth of metaphysical or antiquarian lore. Eschewing all needless refinements and subtleties, I have taken as my guide the more obvious characters of the ideas for which expressions were to be tabulated, arranging them under such classes and categories as reflection and experience had taught me would conduct the inquirer most readily and quickly to the object of his search. Commencing with the ideas expressing abstract relations, I proceed to those which relate to space and to the phenomena of the material world, and lastly to those in which the mind is concerned, and which comprehend intellect, volition, and feeling; thus establishing six primary Classes of Categories.

1. The first of these classes comprehends ideas derived from the more general and ABSTRACT RELATIONS among things, such as *Existence, Resemblance, Quantity, Order, Number, Time, Power.*

2. The second class refers to SPACE and its various relations, including *Motion,* or change of place.

3. The third class includes all ideas that relate to the MATERIAL WORLD; namely, the *Properties of Matter,* such as *Solidity, Fluidity, Heat, Sound, Light,* and the *Phenomena* they present, as well as the simple *Perceptions* to which they give rise.

4. The fourth class embraces all ideas of phenomena relating to the INTELLECT and its operations; comprising the *Acquisition,* the *Retention,* and the *Communication of Ideas.*

5. The fifth class includes the ideas derived from the exercise of VOLITION; embracing the phenomena and results of our *Voluntary and Active Powers;* such as *Choice, Intention, Utility, Action, Antagonism, Authority, Compact, Property,* &c.

6. The sixth and last class comprehends all ideas derived from the operation of our SENTIENT AND MORAL POWERS; including our *Feelings, Emotions, Passions,* and *Moral and Religious Sentiments.*[1]

The further subdivisions and minuter details will be best understood from an inspection of the Tabular Synopsis of Categories prefixed to the Work, in which are specified the several *topics* or *heads of signification,* under which the words have been arranged. By the aid of this table, the reader will, with a little practice, readily discover the place which the particular topic he is in search of occupies in the series; and on turning to the page in the body of the work which contains it, he will find the group of expressions he requires, out of which he may cull those that are most appropriate to his purpose. For the convenience of reference, I have designated each separate group or heading by a particular number; so that if, during the search, any doubt or difficulty should occur, recourse may be had to the copious alphabetical Index of words at the end of the volume, which will at once indicate the number of the required group.[2]

The object I have proposed to myself in this work would have been but imperfectly attained if I had confined myself to a mere catalogue of words, and had omitted the numerous phrases and forms of expression composed of several words, which are of such frequent use as to entitle them to rank among the constituent parts of the language.[3] Very few of these verbal combinations, so essential to the knowledge of our native tongue, and so profusely abounding in its daily use, are to be met with in ordinary dictionaries. These phrases and forms of expression I have endeavored diligently to collect and to insert in their proper places, under the general ideas that they are designed to convey. Some of these conventional forms, indeed, partake of the nature of proverbial expressions; but actual proverbs, as such, being wholly of a didactic character, do not come within the scope of the present work; and the reader must therefore not expect to find them here inserted.[4]

For the purpose of exhibiting with greater distinctness the relations between words expressing opposite and correlative ideas, I have, whenever the subject admitted of such an arrangement, placed them in two parallel columns in the same page, so that each group of expressions may be readily contrasted with those which occupy the adjacent column, and constitute their antithesis. By carrying the eye from the one to the other, the inquirer may often discover forms of expression, of which he may avail himself advantageously, to diversify and infuse vigor into his phraseology. Rhetoricians, indeed, are well aware of the power derived from the skillful introduction of antitheses in giving point to an argument, and imparting force and brilliancy to the diction. A too frequent and indiscreet employment of this figure of rhetoric may, it is true, give rise to a vicious and affected style; but

---

[1] It must necessarily happen in every system of classification framed with this view, that ideas and expressions arranged under one class must include also ideas relating to another class; for the operations of the *Intellect* generally involve also those of the *Will,* and *vice versâ;* and our *Affections* and *Emotions,* in like manner, generally imply the agency both of the *Intellect* and of the *Will.* All that can be effected, therefore, is to arrange the words according to the principal or dominant idea they convey. *Teaching,* for example, although a Voluntary act, relates primarily to the Communication of Ideas, and is accordingly placed at No. **537,** under Class IV, Division (II). On the other hand, *Choice, Conduct, Skill,* &c., although implying the coöperation of Voluntary with Intellectual acts, relate principally to the former, and are therefore arranged under Class V.

[2] If often happens that the same word admits of various applications, or may be used in different senses. In consulting the Index the reader will be guided to the number of the heading under which that word, in each particular acceptation, will be found, by means of *supplementary words* printed in Italics; which words, however, are not to be understood as explaining the meaning of the word to which they are annexed, but only as assisting in the required reference. I have also, for shortness' sake, generally omitted words immediately derived from the primary one inserted, which sufficiently represents the whole group of correlative words referable to the same heading. Thus the number affixed to *Beauty* applies to all its derivatives, such as *Beautiful, Beauteous, Beautifulness, Beautifully,* &c., the insertion of which was therefore needless.

[3] For example: — To take time by the forelock; — to turn over a new leaf; — to show the white feather; — to have a finger in the pie; — to let the cat out of the bag; — to take care of number one; — to kill two birds with one stone, &c., &c.

[4] See Trench, *On the Lessons in Proverbs.*

it is unreasonable to condemn indiscriminately the occasional and moderate use of a practice on account of its possible abuse.

The study of correlative terms existing in a particular language may often throw valuable light on the manners and customs of the nations using it. Thus, Hume has drawn important inferences with regard to the state of society among the ancient Romans from certain deficiencies which he remarked in the Latin language.[1]

In many cases, two ideas which are completely opposed to each other admit of an intermediate or neutral idea, equidistant from both; all these being expressible by corresponding definite terms. Thus, in the following examples, the words in the first and third columns, which express opposite ideas, admit of the intermediate terms contained in the middle column, having a neutral sense with reference to the former.

Identity,	*Difference,*	*Contrariety.*
Beginning,	*Middle,*	*End.*
Past,	*Present,*	*Future.*

In other cases, the intermediate word is simply the negative to each of two opposite positions; as, for example, —

Convexity,	*Flatness,*	*Concavity.*
Desire,	*Indifference,*	*Aversion.*

Sometimes the intermediate word is properly the standard with which each of the extremes is compared; as in the case of

Insufficiency,	*Sufficiency,*	*Redundance;*

for here the middle term, *Sufficiency,* is equally opposed, on the one hand, to *Insufficiency,* and on the other to *Redundance.*

These forms of correlative expressions would suggest the use of triple, instead of double, columns, for tabulating this threefold order of words; but the practical inconvenience attending such an arrangement would probably overbalance its advantages.

It often happens that the same word has several correlative terms, according to the different relations in which it is considered. Thus, to the word *Giving* are opposed both *Receiving* and *Taking;* the former correlation having reference to the *persons* concerned in the transfer, while the latter relates to the *mode* of transfer. *Old* has for opposite both *New* and *Young,* according as it is applied to *things* or to *living beings. Attack* and *Defense* are correlative terms; as are also *Attack* and *Resistance. Resistance,* again, has for its other correlative *Submission. Truth in the abstract* is opposed to *Error;* but the opposite of *Truth communicated* is *Falsehood. Acquisition* is contrasted both with *Deprivation* and with *Loss. Refusal* is the counterpart both of *Offer* and of *Consent. Disuse* and *Misuse* may either of them be considered as the correlative of *Use. Teaching,* with reference to what is taught,

[1] "It is an universal observation," he remarks, "which we may form upon language, that where two related parts of a whole bear any proportion to each other, in numbers, rank, or consideration, there are always correlative terms invented which answer to both the parts, and express their mutual relation. If they bear no proportion to each other, the term is only invented for the less, and marks its distinction from the whole. Thus, *man* and *woman, master* and *servant, father* and *son, prince* and *subject, stranger* and *citizen,* are correlative terms. But the words *seaman, carpenter, smith, tailor,* &c., have no correspondent terms, which express those who are no seamen, no carpenters, &c. Languages differ very much with regard to the particular words where this distinction obtains; and may thence afford very strong inferences concerning the manners and customs of different nations. The military government of the Roman emperors had exalted the soldiery so high that they balanced all the other orders of the state: hence *miles* and *paganus* became relative terms; a thing, till then, unknown to ancient, and still so to modern languages." — "The term for a slave, born and bred in the family was *verna.* As *servus* was the name of the genus, and *verna* of the species without any correlative, this forms a strong presumption that the latter were by far the least numerous: and from the same principles I infer that if the number of slaves brought by the Romans from foreign countries had not extremely exceeded those which were bred at home, *verna* would have had a correlative, which would have expressed the former species of slaves. But these, it would seem, composed the main body of the ancient slaves, and the latter were but a few exceptions." — HUME, *Essay on the Populousness of Ancient Nations.*

The warlike propensity of the same nation may, in like manner, be inferred from the use of the word *hostis* to denote both *a foreigner* and *an enemy.*

is opposed to *Misteaching;* but with reference to the act itself, its proper reciprocal is *Learning.*

Words contrasted in form do not always bear the same contrast in their meaning. The word *Malefactor,* for example, would, from its derivation, appear to be xactly the opposite of *Benefactor:* but the ideas attached to these two words are far from being directly opposed; for while the latter expresses one who confers a benefit, the former denotes one who has violated the laws.

Independently of the immediate practical uses derivable from the arrangement of words in double columns, many considerations, interesting in a philosophical point of view, are presented by the study of correlative expressions. It will be found, on strict examination, that there seldom exists an exact opposition between two words which may at first sight appear to be the counterparts of one another; for, in general, the one will be found to possess in reality more force or extent of meaning than the other with which it is contrasted. The correlative term sometimes assumes the form of a mere negative, although it is really endowed with a considerable positive force. Thus *Disrespect* is not merely the absence of *Respect;* its signification trenches on the opposite idea, namely, *Contempt.* In like manner, *Untruth* is not merely the negative of *Truth;* it involves a degree of *Falsehood.* *Irreligion,* which is properly *the want of Religion,* is understood as being nearly synonymous with *Impiety.* For these reasons, the reader must not expect that all the words which stand side by side in the two columns shall be the precise correlatives of each other; for the nature of the subject, as well as the imperfections of language, renders it impossible always to preserve such an exactness of correlation.

There exist comparatively few words of a general character to which no correlative term, either of negation or of opposition, can be assigned, and which therefore require no corresponding second column. The correlative idea, especially that which constitutes a sense negative to the primary one, may, indeed, be formed or conceived; but, from its occurring rarely, no word has been framed to represent it; for, in language, as in other matters, the supply fails when there is no probability of a demand. Occasionally we find this deficiency provided for by the contrivance of prefixing the syllable *non;* as, for instance, the negatives of *existence, performance, payment,* &c., are expressed by the compound words, *nonexistence, nonperformance, nonpayment,* &c. Functions of a similar kind are performed by the prefixes *dis-,*[1] *anti-, contra-, mis-, in-,* and *un-.*[2] With respect to all these, and especiaily the last, great latitude is allowed according to the necessities of the case; a latitude which is limited only by the taste and discretion of the writer.

On the other hand, it is hardly possible to find two words having in all respects the same meaning, and being therefore interchangeable; that is, admitting of being employed indiscriminately, the one or the other, in all their applications. The investigation of the distinctions to be drawn between words apparently synonymous forms a separate branch of inquiry, which I have not presumed here to enter upon; for the subject has already occupied the attention of much abler critics than myself, and its complete exhaustion would require the devotion of a whole life. The purpose of this work, it must be borne in mind, is, not to explain the signification of words, but simply to classify and arrange them according to the sense in which they are now used, and which I presume to be already known to the reader. I enter into no inquiry into the changes of meaning they may have undergone in the course of time.[3] I am content to accept them at the value of their present

---

[1] The words *disannul* and *dissever,* however, have the same meaning as *annul* and *sever; to unloose* is the same as *to loose,* and *inebriety* is synonymous with *ebriety.*

[2] In case of adjectives, the addition to a substantive of the terminal syllable *less,* gives it a negative meaning: as *taste, tasteless; care, careless; hope, hopeless; friend, friendless; fault, faultless;* &c.

[3] Such changes are innumerable: for instance, the words *tyrant, parasite, sophist, churl, knave, villain,* anciently conveyed no opprobrious meaning. *Impertinent* merely expressed *irrelative;* and implied neither *rudeness* nor *intrusion,* as it does at present. *Indifferent* originally meant *impartial; extravagant* was simple *digressive;* and *to prevent* was properly *to precede* and *assist.* The old translations of the Scriptures furnish many striking examples of the alterations which time has brought in the signification of words. Much curious information on this subject is contained in Trench's *Lectures on the Study of Words.*

currency, and have no concern with their etymologies, or with the history of their transformations; far less do I venture to thread the mazes of the vast labyrinth into which I should be led by any attempt at a general discrimination of synonyms. The difficulties I have had to contend with have already been sufficiently great, without this addition to my labors.

The most cursory glance over the pages of a dictionary will show that a great number of words are used in various senses, sometimes distinguished by slight shades of difference, but often diverging widely from their primary signification, and even, in some cases, bearing to it no perceptible relation. It may even happen that the very same word has two significations quite opposite to one another. This is the case with the verb *to cleave*, which means *to adhere tenaciously*, and also *to separate by a blow*. *To propugn* sometimes expresses *to attack;* at other times *to defend*. *To let* is *to hinder*, as well as *to permit*. *To ravel* means both *to entangle* and *to disentangle*. *Shameful* and *shameless* are nearly synonymous. *Priceless* may either mean *invaluable* or *of no value*. *Nervous* is used sometimes for *strong*, at other times for *weak*. The alphabetical Index at the end of this work sufficiently shows the multiplicity of uses to which, by the elasticity of language, the meaning of words has been stretched, so as to adapt them to a great variety of modified significations in subservience to the nicer shades of thought, which, under peculiarity of circumstances, require corresponding expression. Words thus admitting of different meanings have therefore to be arranged under each of the respective heads corresponding to these various acceptations. There are many words, again, which express ideas compounded of two elementary ideas belonging to different classes. It is therefore necessary to place these words respectively under each of the generic heads to which they relate. The necessity of these repetitions is increased by the circumstance, that ideas included under one class are often connected by relations of the same kind as the ideas which belong to another class. Thus we find the same relations of *order* and of *quantity* existing among the ideas of *Time* as well as those of *Space*. Sequence in the one is denoted by the same terms as sequence in the other; and the measures of time also express the measures of space. The cause and the effect are often designated by the same word. The word *Sound*, for instance, denotes both the impression made upon the ear by sonorous vibrations, and also the vibrations themselves, which are the cause or source of that impression. *Mixture* is used for the act of mixing, as well as for the product of that operation. *Taste* and *Smell* express both the sensations and the qualities of material bodies giving rise to them. *Thought* is the act of thinking; but the same word denotes also the idea resulting from that act. *Judgment* is the act of deciding, and also the decision come to. *Purchase* is the acquisition of a thing by payment, as well as the thing itself so acquired. *Speech* is both the act of speaking and the words spoken; and so on with regard to an endless multiplicity of words. Mind is essentially distinct from Matter; and yet, in all languages, the attributes of the one are metaphorically transferred to those of the other. Matter, in all its forms, is endowed by the figurative genius of every language with the functions which pertain to intellect; and we perpetually talk of its phenomena and of its powers, as if they resulted from the voluntary influence of one body on another, acting and reacting, impelling and being impelled, controlling and being controlled, as if animated by spontaneous energies and guided by specific intentions. On the other hand, expressions, of which the primary signification refers exclusively to the properties and actions of matter, are metaphorically applied to the phenomena of thought and volition, and even to the feelings and passions of the soul; and speaking of a *ray of hope*, a *shade of doubt*, a *flight of fancy*, a *flash of wit*, the *warmth of emotion*, or the *ebullitions of anger*, we are scarcely conscious that we are employing metaphors which have this material origin.

As a general rule, I have deemed it incumbent on me to place words and phrases which appertain more especially to one head, also under the other heads to which they have a relation, whenever it appeared to me that this repetition would suit the convenience of the inquirer, and spare him the trouble of turning to other parts of the work; for I have always preferred to subject myself to the imputation of redundance, rather than incur the reproach of insufficiency.[1] When, however, the divergence of the associated from the primary idea is sufficiently marked, I have contented myself with making a reference to the place where the modified signification will be found. But in order to prevent needless extension, I have, in general, omitted *conjugate words*[2] which are so obviously derivable from those that are given in the same place, that the reader may safely be left to form them for himself. This is the case with adverbs derived from adjectives by the simple addition of the terminal syllable *-ly;* such as *closely, carefully, safely,* &c., from *close, careful, safe,* &c., and also with adjectives or participles immediately derived from the verbs which are already given. In all such cases, an "&c." indicates that reference is understood to be made to these roots. I have observed the same rule in compiling the Index; retaining only the primary or more simple word, and omitting the conjugate words obviously derived from them. Thus I assume the word *short* as the representative of its immediate derivatives *shortness, shorten, shortening, shortened, shorter, shortly,* which would have had the same references, and which the reader can readily supply.

The same verb is frequently used indiscriminately either in the active or transitive, or in the neuter or intransitive sense. In these cases, I have generally not thought it worth while to increase the bulk of the work by the needless repetition of that word; for the reader, whom I suppose to understand the use of the words, must also be presumed to be competent to apply them correctly.

There are a multitude of words of a specific character which, although they properly occupy places in the columns of a dictionary, yet, having no relation to general ideas, do not come within the scope of this compilation, and are consequently omitted.[3] The names of objects in Natural History, and technical terms belonging exclusively to Science or to Art, or relating to particular operations, and of which the signification is restricted to those specific objects, come under this category. Exceptions must, however, be made in favor of such words as admit of metaphorical application to general subjects, with which custom has associated them, and of which they may be cited as being typical or illustrative. Thus, the word *Lion* will find a place under the head of *Courage,* of which it is regarded as the type. *Anchor,* being emblematic of *Hope,* is introduced among the words expressing that emotion; and in like manner, *butterfly* and *weathercock,* which are suggestive of fickleness, are included in the category of *Irresolution.*

With regard to the admission of many words and expressions, which the classical reader might be disposed to condemn as vulgarisms, or which he, perhaps, might stigmatize as pertaining rather to the slang than to the legitimate language of the day, I would beg to observe, that, having due regard to the uses to which this work was to be adapted, I did not feel myself justified in excluding them solely on that ground, if they possessed an acknowledged currency in general intercourse. It is obvious that, with respect to degrees of conventionality, I could not have attempted to draw any strict lines of demarcation; and far less could I have presumed to erect any absolute standard of purity. My object, be it remembered, is

---

[1] Frequent repetitions of the same series of expressions, accordingly, will be met with under various headings. For example, the word *Relinquishment,* with its synonyms, occurs as a heading at No. **624,** where it applies to *intention,* and also at No. **782,** where it refers to *property.* The word *Chance* has two significations, distinct from one another: the one implying the *absence of an assignable cause;* in which case it comes under the category of the relation of Causation, and occupies the No. **156:** the other, the *absence of design,* in which latter sense it ranks under the operations of the Will, and has assigned to it the place No. **621.** I have, in like manner, distinguished *Sensibility, Pleasure, Plain, Taste,* &c., according as they relate to *Physical,* or to *Moral Affections;* the former being found at Nos. **375, 377, 378, 390,** &c., and the latter at Nos. **822, 827, 828, 850,** &c.

[2] By "*conjugate* or *paronymous* words is meant, correctly speaking, different parts of speech from the same root, which exactly correspond in point of meaning." — *A Selection of English Synonyms,* edited by Archbishop Whately.

[3] [This rule was not in all cases rigorously observed by the author; and the present editor has used his discretion in including such words in the interest of the general writer. C. O. S. M.]

not to regulate the use of words, but simply to supply and to suggest such as may be wanted on occasion, leaving the proper selection entirely to the discretion and taste of the employer. If a novelist or a dramatist, for example, proposed to delineate some vulgar personage, he would wish to have the power of putting into the mouth of the speaker expressions that would accord with his character; just as the actor, to revert to a former comparison, who had to personate a peasant, would choose for his attire the most homely garb, and would have just reason to complain if the theatrical wardrobe furnished him with no suitable costume.

Words which have, in process of time, become obsolete, are of course rejected from this collection.[1] On the other hand, I have admitted a considerable number of words and phrases borrowed from other languages, chiefly the French and Latin, some of which may be considered as already naturalized; while others, though avowedly foreign, are frequently employed in English composition, particularly in familiar style, on account of their being peculiarly expressive, and because we have no corresponding words of equal force in our own language.[2] The rapid advances which are being made in scientific knowledge, and consequent improvement in all the arts of life, and the extension of those arts and sciences to so many new purposes and objects, create a continual demand for the formation of new terms to express new agencies, new wants, and new combinations. Such terms, from being at first merely technical, are rendered, by more general use, familiar to the multitude, and having a well-defined acceptation, are eventually incorporated into the language, which they contribute to enlarge and to enrich. *Neologies* of this kind are perfectly legitimate, and highly advantageous; and they necessarily introduce those gradual and progressive changes which every language is destined to undergo.[3] Some modern writers, however, have indulged in a habit of arbitrarily fabricating new words and a newfangled phraseology, without any necessity, and with manifest injury to the purity of the language. This vicious practice, the offspring of indolence or conceit, implies an ignorance or neglect of the riches in which the English language already abounds, and which would have supplied them with words of recognized legitimacy, conveying precisely the same meaning as those they so recklessly coin in the illegal mint of their own fancy.

A work constructed on the plan of classification I have proposed might, if ably executed, be of great value, in tending to limit the fluctuations to which language has always been subject, by establishing an authoritative standard for its regulation. Future historians, philologists, and lexicographers, when investigating the period when new words were introduced, or discussing the import given at the present time to the old, might find their labors lightened by being enabled to appeal to such a standard, instead of having to search for data among the scattered writings of the age. Nor would its utility be confined to a single language; for the principles of its construction are universally applicable to all languages, whether living or dead. On the same plan of classification there might be formed a French, a German, a Latin, or a Greek Thesaurus, possessing, in their respective spheres, the same advantages as those of the English model.[4] Still more useful would be a conjunction of these methodized compilations in two languages, the French and

---

[1] [An appreciable number of obsolete terms have nevertheless found their way into the *Thesaurus*, but these in the present edition have been specially characterized, thus rendering the book of enhanced value to the dramatist and *littérateur*. C. O. S. M.]

[2] All these words and phrases are printed in Italics.

[3] Thus, in framing the present classification, I have frequently felt the want of substantive terms corresponding to abstract qualities or ideas denoted by certain adjectives; and have been often tempted to invent words that might express these abstractions: but I have yielded to this temptation only in the four following instances; having framed from the adjectives *irrelative, amorphous, sinistral,* and *gaseous,* the abstract nouns *irrelation, amorphism, sinistrality,* and *gaseity.* I have ventured also to introduce the adjective *intersocial,* to express the active voluntary relations between man and man.

[4] [Similar works in other languages have since appeared, notably *Dictionnaire Idéologique* by T. Robertson (Paris, 1859); *Deutcher Sprachschatz* by D. Sanders (Hamburg, 1878), and *Deutscher Wortschatz, oder Der passende Ausdruck* by A. Schelling (Stuttgart, 1892). C. O. S. M.]

English, for instance; the columns of each being placed in parallel juxtaposition. No means yet devised would so greatly facilitate the acquisition of the one language, by those who are acquainted with the other: none would afford such ample assistance to the translator in either language; and none would supply such ready and effectual means of instituting an accurate comparison between them, and of fairly appreciating their respective merits and defects. In a still higher degree would all those advantages be combined and multiplied in a *Polyglot Lexicon* constructed on this system.

Metaphysicians engaged in the more profound investigation of the Philosophy of Language will be materially assisted by having the ground thus prepared for them, in a previous analysis and classification of our ideas; for such classification of ideas is the true basis on which words, which are their symbols, should be classified.[1] It is by such analysis alone that we can arrive at a clear perception of the relation which these symbols bear to their corresponding ideas, or can obtain a correct knowledge of the elements which enter into the formation of compound ideas, and of the exclusions by which we arrive at the abstractions so perpetually resorted to in the process of reasoning, and in the communication of our thoughts.

Lastly, such analyses alone can determine the principles on which a strictly *Philosophical Language* might be constructed. The probable result of the construction of such a language would be its eventual adoption by every civilized nation; thus realizing that splendid aspiration of philanthropists, — the establishment of a Universal Language. However utopian such a project may appear to the present generation, and however abortive may have been the former endeavors of Bishop Wilkins and others to realize it,[2] its accomplishment is surely not beset with greater difficulties than have impeded the progress to many other beneficial objects, which in former times appeared to be no less visionary, and which yet were successfully achieved, in later ages, by the continued and persevering exertions of the human intellect. Is there at the present day, then, any ground for despair, that at some future stage of that higher civilization to which we trust the world is gradually

[1] The principle by which I have been guided in framing my verbal classification is the same as that which is employed in the various departments of Natural History. Thus the sectional divisions I have formed, correspond to Natural Families in Botany and Zoölogy, and the filiation of words presents a network analogous to the natural filiation of plants or animals.

The following are the only publications that have come to my knowledge in which any attempt has been made to construct a systematic arrangement of ideas with a view to their expression. The earliest of these, supposed to be at least nine hundred years old, is the AMERA CÓSHA, or *Vocabulary of the Sanscrit Language,* by Amera Sanha, of which an English translation, by the late Henry T. Colebrooke, was printed at Serampoor, in the year 1808. The classification of words is there, as might be expected, exceedingly imperfect and confused, especially in all that relates to abstract ideas or mental operations. This will be apparent from the very title of the first section, which comprehends "*Heaven, Gods, Demons, Fire, Air, Velocity, Eternity, Much:*" while *Sin, Virtue, Happiness, Destiny, Cause, Nature, Intellect, Reasoning, Knowledge, Senses, Tastes, Odors, Colors,* are all included and jumbled together in the fourth section. A more logical order, however, pervades the sections relating to natural objects, such as *Seas, Earth, Towns, Plants,* and *Animals,* which form separate classes; exhibiting a remarkable effort at analysis at so remote a period of Indian literature.

The well-known work of Bishop Wilkins, entitled, *An Essay towards a Real Character and a Philosophical Language,* published in 1668, had for its object the formation of a system of symbols which might serve as a universal language. It professed to be founded on a "scheme of analysis of the things or notions to which names were to be assigned;" but notwithstanding the immense labor and ingenuity expended in the construction of this system, it was soon found to be far too abstruse and recondite for practical application.

In the year 1797, there appeared in Paris an anonymous work, entitled "PASIGRAPHIE ou *Premiers Eléments du nouvel Art-Science d'écrire et d'imprimer une langue de manière à être lu et entendu dans toute autre langue sans traduction,*" of which an edition in German was also published. It contains a great number of tabular schemes of categories; all of which appear to be excessively arbitrary and artificial, and extremely difficult of application, as well as of apprehension.

[2] "The Languages," observes Horne Tooke "which are commonly used throughout the world, are much more simple and easy, convenient and philosophical, than Wilkins's scheme for a *real character;* or than any other scheme that has been at any other time imagined or proposed for the purpose." —'Επεα Πτερόεντα, p. 125.

tending, some new and bolder effort of genius towards the solution of this great problem may be crowned with success, and compass an object of such vast and paramount utility? Nothing, indeed, would conduce more directly to bring about a golden age of union and harmony among the several nations and races of mankind than the removal of that barrier to the interchange of thought and mutual good understanding between man and man, which is now interposed by the diversity of their respective languages.

P. M. ROGET.

ABBREVIATIONS USED IN THIS BOOK

abbr. abbreviated, abbreviation
adj. adjective, adjectival expression
adv. adverb, adverbial expression
Afr. Africa
Am. *or* **Amer.** America, American
Am. hist. American history
anat. anatomy
anc. ancient
Anglo-Ind. Anglo-Indian
anon. anonymous
antiq. antiquities
Ar. Arabic
arch. architecture
archæol. archæology
arith. arithmetic
A.-S. Anglo-Saxon
astrol. astrology
astron. astronomy
Austral. Australian
Bib. Biblical
biol. biology
bot. botany
Brit. British
Can. Canada, Canadian
Can. F. Canadian French
Celt. Celtic
chem. chemistry
Chin. Chinese
Ch. of Eng. Church of England
Cic. Cicero
class. classical
colloq. colloquial
com. commerce, commercial
conj. conjunction
Du. Dutch
Dan. Danish
derog. derogatory
dial. dialect, dialectal
dim. diminutive
E. East
eccl. ecclesiastical
econ. economics
elec. electricity
Eng. English, England
erron. erroneous, -ly
esp. especially
exc. except
fem. feminine
fig. figurative, -ly
G. *or* **Ger.** German
Gr. Greek
gram. grammar
Gr. Brit. Great Britain
Heb. Hebrew
her. heraldry
Hind. Hindustani
hist. history, historical
Hor. Horace
Icel. Icelandic
Ind. Indian
Ir. Irish, Ireland

int. interjection
It. Italian
Jap. Japanese
Jew. Jewish
joc. jocular
Juv. Juvenal
l.c. lower case
L. L. L. *Love's Labor's Lost*
Luc. Lucretius
Mar. Martial
masc. masculine
math. mathematics
Meth. Methodist
Mex. Mexico, Mexican
M. for M. Measure for Measure
mil. military
M. N. D. Midsummer Night's Dream
M. of V. Merchant of Venice
Moham. Mohammedan
myth. mythology
N. North
n. noun
N. Am. North American
naut. nautical
N. E. *or* **New Eng.** New England
neut. neuter
Nfld. Newfoundland
NL. New Latin
Norw. Norwegian
N. W. Northwest, -ern
N. Z. New Zealand
obs. obsolete
obsoles. obsolescent
OE. Old English
opp. opposed
orig. original, -ly
parl. parliamentary
path. pathology
Per. Persian
Pg. Portuguese
pharm. pharmacy
philos. philosophy
physiol. physiology
P. I. Philippine Islands
pl. plural
P. L. Paradise Lost
Plut. Plutarch
pol. *or* **polit.** political
pop. popular, -ly
prep. preposition
Prot. Epis. Protestant Episcopal
prov. proverb, provincial
psychol. psychology
Quin. Quintilian
R. C. Ch. Roman Catholic Church
relig. religion
rhet. rhetoric, rhetorical
Russ. Russian
S. *or* **So.** South
S. Afr. South African
Sal. Sallust

ABBREVIATIONS USED IN THIS BOOK

S. Am. South American
Scand. Scandinavian
Scot. Scottish, Scotland
Sen. Seneca
sing. singular
Skr. Sanskrit
surg. surgery
Sw. Swedish
S. W. Southwest, -ern
S. W. U. S. Southwest United States
Tac. Tacitus
tech. technical
Ter. Terence

Tertul. Tertullian
theat. theatrical
theol. theology
theos. theosophy
Turk. Turkish
typog. typography
Univ. University
U. S. United States
v. verb
Ver. Vergil
W. West
W. Ind. West Indies
zoöl. zoölogy

Dashes and hyphens are used to avoid the repetition of some term common to each word or phrase in the same group. For example: —

"over –, above- the mark;" = "over the mark," "above the mark"

"on the -verge, – brink, – skirts- of;" = { "on the verge of," "on the brink of," "on the skirts of " }

"brush –, whisk –, turn –, send- -off, – away;" = { "brush off," "brush away," "whisk off," "whisk away," "turn off," "turn away," "send off," "send away " }

"quick-, keen,- clear-, sharp- -eyed, -sighted, -witted;" = { "quick-eyed," "quick-sighted," "quick-witted," "keen-eyed," "keen-sighted," "keen-witted," "clear-eyed," "clear-sighted," "clear-witted," "sharp-eyed," "sharp-sighted," "sharp-witted " }

"away from –, foreign to –, beside- the -purpose, – question, – transaction, – point;" = { "away from the purpose," "away from the question," "away from the transaction," "away from the point," "foreign to the purpose," &c., "beside the purpose," &c. }

"fall, – to the ground;" = "fall," "fall to the gound "

"shortness &c. *adj.*;" "shortly &c. *adj.*;" "shortening &c. *v.*;" = { in a similar manner form other words from the groups of *adjectives* or *verbs* in the same category }

[See also *"How to Use the Book,"* p. xxiv.]

HOW TO USE THE BOOK

I. To find a synonym or antonym for any given WORD:

Turn to the Index Guide and find the particular word or any term of kindred meaning; then refer to the category indicated. Under the part of speech sought for [**N., V., Adj., Adv.**] will be found a wide choice of synonymous and correlative terms, with their antonyms in the adjoining column. For example, suppose a synonym is wanted for the word "rare" in the sense of "choice." Turn to the Index Guide, where the following references will be found: —

> **rare** *unique* 20
> *exceptional* 83
> *few* 103
> *infrequent* 137
> *underdone* 298
> *tenuous* 322
> *neologic* 563
> *choice* 648

The italicized words denote the general sense of the affinitive terms in the respective categories. Turning to No. **648** (the sense required) we select the most appropriate expression from the comprehensive list presented. To widen the selection, suggested references are given to allied lists; while in the parallel column, viz., **649**, are grouped the corresponding antonyms. The groups are arranged, not merely to supply synonyms for some special word, but to suggest new lines of thought and to stimulate the imagination.

The story-writer at a loss for some archaism, colloquialism, or even slang, will find the *University Thesaurus* a veritable mine, such terms being clearly indicated in the text.

II. To find suitable words to express a given IDEA:

Find in the Index Guide some word relating to the idea, and the categories referred to will supply the need. Thus, suppose a writer wishes to use some less hackneyed phrase than "shuffle off this mortal coil," let him look up "die" or even the phrase itself, and reference to No. **360** will immediately furnish a generous list of synonymous phrases.

III. To find appropriate words or new ideas on any given SUBJECT:

Turn up the subject or any branch of it. The Index Guide itself will frequently suggest various lines of thought, while reference to the indicated groups will provide many words and phrases that should prove helpful.

Thus, suppose "philosophy" is the theme, No. **451** will be found most suggestive. Or again, the subject may be "the drama" (**599**), "music" (**415**), "zoölogy" (**368**), "psychical research" (**992a**), or "mythology" (**979**). The writer may perhaps be hazy about the titles of the ruling chiefs of India. The Thesaurus (**875**) will prevent his applying a Hindu title to a Mohammedan prince. The subject may be such an everyday one as "food" (**298**), "automobiles" (**272**), "aviation" (**267** and **269a**), or various kinds of "amusements" (**840**); whatever it is, the Thesaurus will not prove altogether unprofitable as regards ideas. Writers and speakers who have acquired the "Roget habit" do not need to be reminded of this valuable aid.

N.B. To grasp the underlying principle of the classification, study the *Tabular Synopsis of Categories* (pp. 889–899). Reference may be made direct from this Synopsis to the body of the work; but it is usually found more convenient to consult the Index Guide first.

[See also "*Abbreviations Used in This Book*," pp. xxii and xxiii.]
The Guide numbers always refer to the *section numbers* in the text and *not to* pages.

THESAURUS OF ENGLISH WORDS AND PHRASES

CLASS I

WORDS EXPRESSING ABSTRACT RELATIONS

SECTION I. EXISTENCE

1. BEING, IN THE ABSTRACT

1. Existence.— N. EXISTENCE, being, entity, ens [*L.*], *esse* [*L.*], subsistence; quid, hypaxis [*rare*], automaton.

REALITY, actuality; positiveness &c. *adj.*; fact, matter of fact, sober reality; truth &c. 494; actual existence.

PRESENCE &c. (*existence in space*) 186; coexistence &c. 120.

STUBBORN FACT; not a dream &c. 515; no joke.

ESSENCE, inmost nature, center of life, inner reality, vital principle.

[SCIENCE OF EXISTENCE] ontology.

V. EXIST, be; have being &c. *n.;* subsist, live, breathe, stand, obtain, be the case; occur &c. (*event*) 151; have place, rank, prevail; find oneself, pass the time, vegetate.

come into existence &c. *n.;* arise &c. (*begin*) 66; come forth &c. (*appear*) 446.

BECOME &c. (*be converted*) 144; bring into existence &c. 161; coexist, postexist [*rare*], preëxist [*rare*].

CONSIST IN, lie in; be comprised in, be contained in, be constituted by.

ABIDE, continue, endure, last, remain.

Adj. EXISTING &c. *v.;* existent, subsistent, under the sun; in existence &c. *n.;* extant; afloat, on foot, current, prevalent; undestroyed.

REAL, actual, positive, absolute; factual, veritable, true &c. 494; substan-

2. Nonexistence. — N. NONEXISTENCE, nonsubsistence; inexistence; nonentity, *nil* [*L.*]; negativeness &c. *adj.;* nullity; nihility, nihilism; *tabula rasa* [*L.*], blank; abeyance; absence &c. 187; no such thing &c. 4; nonbeing, nothingness, oblivion, *non esse* [*L.*].

ANNIHILATION; extinction &c. (*destruction*) 162; extinguishment, extirpation, Nirvana, obliteration.

V. NOT EXIST &c. 1; have no existence &c. 1; be null and void; cease to exist &c. 1; pass away, perish; be *or* become extinct &c. *adj.;* die out; disappear &c. 449; melt away, dissolve, leave not a rack behind; go, be no more; die &c. 360.

ANNIHILATE, render null, nullify; abrogate &c. 756; destroy &c. 162; take away; remove &c. (*displace*) 185; obliterate, extirpate, deracinate [*rare*].

Adj. INEXISTENT, nonexistent &c. 1; negative, blank; null, minus, missing, omitted; absent &c. 187; insubstantial, shadowy, spectral, visionary.

UNREAL, potential, virtual; baseless, *in nubibus* [*L.*]; unsubstantial &c. 4; vain.

UNBORN, uncreated, unbegotten, unconceived, unproduced, unmade.

PERISHED, annihilated &c. *v.;* extinct, exhausted, gone, lost, departed; defunct &c. (*dead*) 360.

tial, substantive; self-existing, self-exist-ent; essential, beënt.

WELL-FOUNDED, well-grounded; un-ideal, unimagined; not potential &c. 2; authentic.

Adv. ACTUALLY &c. adj.; in fact, in point of fact, in reality; indeed; de facto [L.], ipso facto [L.].

FABULOUS, ideal &c. (imaginary) 515; supposititious &c. 514.

Adv. negatively, virtually &c. adj.

₊ non ens; "and what's her history? A blank, my Lord" [Twelfth Night].

₊ ens rationis; cogito ergo sum; "think'st thou existence doth depend on time?" [Byron]; "all is concenter'd in a life intense" [Byron]; "to live is not merely to breathe, it is to act" [Rousseau]; "the mainspring of life is in the heart" [Amiel]; "I came like Water, and like Wind I go" [Omar Khayyám — Fitzgerald].

2. Being, in the Concrete

3. Substantiality.— N. SUBSTANTIAL-ITY, hypostasis; person, thing, object, article; something, a being, an existence; creature, body, substance, flesh and blood, stuff, substratum; matter &c. 316; corporeity, element, essential na-ture, groundwork, materiality, substan-tialness, vital part.

[TOTALITY OF EXISTENCES] world &c. 318; plenum [L.].

Adj. SUBSTANTIVE, substantial; hy-postatic or hypostatical; personal, bod-ily, practical, effective; tangible &c. (material) 316; corporeal; right, sober.

Adv. SUBSTANTIALLY &c. adj.; bodily, essentially.

₊ "The heavy and the weary weight Of all this unintelligible world" [Wordsworth].

4. Unsubstantiality. — N. UNSUB-STANTIALITY, insubstantiality; nothing-ness, nihility; no degree, no part, no quantity, no thing.

NOTHING, naught, nil [L.], nullity, zero, cipher, no one, nobody; never a one, ne'er a one; no such thing, none in the world; nothing whatever, nothing at all, nothing on earth; not a particle &c. (smallness) 32; all talk, all moonshine, all stuff and nonsense; matter of no importance, matter of no consequence.

THING OF NAUGHT, man of straw, John Doe and Richard Roe, fagot (or faggot) voter [polit. cant, Eng.]; nominis umbra [L.], nonentity, cipher, nought, nothing, obscurity, lay figure; flash in the pan, vox et præterea nihil [L.].

PHANTOM &c. (fallacy of vision) 443; shadow; dream &c. (imagination) 515; ignis fatuus [L.] &c. (luminary) 423; "such stuff as dreams are made on" [Tempest]; air, thin air; bubble &c. 353; mockery.

BLANK; void &c. (absence) 187; hollowness.

INANITY, fatuity, fool's paradise.

V. VANISH, evaporate, fade, fleet, sink, fly, dissolve, melt away; die, die away, die out; disappear &c. 449.

Adj. UNSUBSTANTIAL; baseless, groundless; ungrounded; without foundation, having no foundation.

VISIONARY &c. (imaginary) 515; immaterial &c. 317; spectral &c. 980; dreamy; shadowy; ethereal, airy, gaseous, imponderable, tenuous, vague, vaporous, dreamlike, mushroom; cloud-built, cloud-formed; gossamery, illusory, insubstantial, unreal, unsolid [rare], slight, bodiless.

VACANT, vacuous; empty &c. 187; eviscerated; blank, hollow; nominal; null; inane [rare].

₊ there's nothing in it; "an ocean of dreams without a sound" [Shelley]; "the baseless fabric of this vision" [Tempest]; "this bodiless creation ecstasy Is very cunning in" [Hamlet]

3. Formal Existence

Internal conditions

5. Intrinsicality. — N. INTRINSICAL-ITY, intrinsicalness, inbeing, inherence, inhesion, immanence, indwelling; sub-jectiveness; ego; egohood; essence, quin-

External conditions

6. Extrinsicality. — N. EXTRINSICAL-ITY, objectiveness, non ego [L.]; extra-neousness &c. 57; accident.

Adj. EXTRINSIC, extrinsical; derived

tessence, elixir; essentialness &c. *adj.;* essential part, incarnation, quiddity, gist, pith, core, kernel, marrow, sap, lifeblood, backbone, heart, soul, life, substance, flower; important part &c. (*importance*) 642.

PRINCIPLE, nature, constitution, character, type, quality, crasis, diathesis.

TEMPER, temperament; spirit, humor, grain, nature, vein, mood, frame, cue; disposition; habit.

CAPACITY, endowment; capability &c. (*power*) 157.

from without; objective; extraneous &c. (*foreign*) 57; modal, adventitious; ascititious, adscititious; incidental, accidental, nonessential, unessential, accessory; contingent, fortuitous, casual, subsidiary.

IMPLANTED, ingrafted; inculcated, infused.

OUTWARD &c. (*external*) 220.

Adv. EXTRINSICALLY &c. *adj.*

*** "these but the trappings and the suits of woe" [*Hamlet*]; "the accident of an accident" [Thurlow] .

ASPECTS, moods, declensions, features; peculiarities &c. (*speciality*) 79; idiosyncrasy; idiocrasy &c. (*tendency*) 176; diagnostics.

V. be in the blood, run in the blood; be born so; be intrinsic &c. *adj.*

Adj. INTRINSIC, intrinsical; derived from within, subjective; idiocratic *or* idiocratical, idiosyncratic *or* idiosyncratical; fundamental, normal; implanted, inherent, essential, natural; innate, inborn, inbred, ingrained, indwelling, inwrought; coeval with birth, genetic, genetous, hæmatobious, syngenic; radical, incarnate, thoroughbred, hereditary, inherited, immanent; congenital, congenite [*obs.*]; connate, running in the blood; ingenerate, ingenit *or* ingenite [*obs.*], ingenita [*obs.*], indigenous; in the grain &c. *n.;* bred in the bone, instinctive; inward, internal &c. 221; to the manner born; virtual.

CHARACTERISTIC &c. (*special*) 79, (*indicative*) 550; invariable, incurable, ineradicable, fixed.

Adv. INTRINSICALLY &c. *adj.;* at bottom, in the main, in effect, practically, virtually, substantially, *au fond* [*F.*]; fairly.

*** "character is higher than intellect" [Emerson]; "the head is not more native to the heart" [*Hamlet*]; "come give us a taste of your quality" [*Hamlet*]; *magnos homines virtute metimur non fortunâ* [Nepos]; *non numero hæc judicantur sed pondere* [Cicero]; "vital spark of heavenly flame" [Pope]; "the all-important factor in national greatness is national character" [Roosevelt].

4. MODAL EXISTENCE

Absolute

7. State.—N. STATE, condition, category, estate, lot, case, trim, mood, temper; aspect &c. (*appearance*) 448.

DILEMMA, pass, predicament, quandary, corner, hole, *impasse* [*F.*], fix, pickle, plight.

FRAME, fabric &c. 329; stamp, set, fit, mold *or* mould; constitution, habitude, diathesis.

FORM, fettle, shape, kilter *or* kelter; tone, tenor, turn; trim, guise, fashion, light, complexion, style, character; build &c. 240; mode, modality, schesis [*obs.*]

V. be in –, possess –, enjoy– a state &c. *n.;* be on a footing, do, fare; come to pass.

Adj. CONDITIONAL, modal, formal; structural, organic.

Adv. CONDITIONALLY &c. *adj.;* as the matter stands, as things are; such being

Relative

8. Circumstance. — N. CIRCUMSTANCE, situation, phase, position, posture, attitude, place, point; terms; *régime* [*F.*]; footing, standing, status.

OCCASION, juncture, conjuncture; contingency &c. (*event*) 151.

PREDICAMENT; emergency; exigency, crisis, pinch, pass, plight, push; occurrence; turning point.

BEARINGS, how the land lies.

Adj. CIRCUMSTANTIAL; given, conditional, provisional; critical; modal; contingent, incidental; adventitious &c. (*extrinsic*) 6; limitative.

DETAILED, minute, full, fussy.

Adv. THUS, in such wise; in *or* under the circumstances &c. *n.*; in *or* under the conditions &c. 7.

ACCORDINGLY; that being the case; such being the case; that being so;

the case &c. 8; *quæ cum ita sint* [*L.*].

*** "it is a condition which confronts us — not a theory" [Grover Cleveland].

CONDITIONALLY, provided, if, in case; if so, if so be, if it be so; if it so happen, if it so turn out; in the event of; in such a contingency, in such a case, in such an event; provisionally, unless, without.

according to circumstances, according to the occasion; as it may happen, as it may turn out, as it may be; as the case may be, as the wind blows; *pro re natâ* [*L.*].

*** "yet are my sins not those of circumstance" [Lytton]; "the happy combination of fortuitous circumstances" [Scott]; "fearful concatenation of circumstance" [Daniel Webster]; "circumstances alter cases" [Haliburton].

SECTION II. RELATION

1. ABSOLUTE RELATION

9. Relation. — N. RELATION, bearing, reference, connection, concern, cognation, applicability, apposition, appositeness; correlation &c. 12; analogy; similarity &c. 17; affinity, homology, alliance, nearness, rapport, homogeneity, association; approximation &c. (*nearness*) 197; filiation &c. (*consanguinity*) 11; interest; relevancy &c. 23; dependency, relationship, relative position; correlation, interrelation, interconnection.

RATIO, proportion; comparison &c. 464.

LINK, tie, bond of union, privity [*law*].

V. BE RELATED &c. *adj.;* have a relation &c. *n.;* relate to, refer to; bear upon, regard, concern, touch, affect, have to do with; pertain to, belong to, appertain to; answer to; interest.

ASSOCIATE, connect; bring into relation with, bring to bear upon; draw a parallel; link &c. 43.

Adj. RELATIVE; correlative &c. 12; relating to &c. *v.;* relative to, in relation with, referable *or* referrible to; belonging to &c. *v.;* appurtenant to, in common with.

RELATED, connected; implicated, associated, affiliated; allied, allied to; collateral, connate [*rare*], cognate, congenerous, connatural, affinitive, paronymous; *en rapport* [*F.*], in touch with.

APPROXIMATIVE, approximating; proportional, proportionate, proportionable; allusive, comparable, equiparable [*obs. or rare*].

RELEVANT &c. (*apt*) 23; applicable,

sith [*obs. or archaic*], sithen [*obs.*], since, seeing that.

as matters stand; as things go, as times go.

10. [WANT OR ABSENCE OF RELATION.] **Irrelation. — N.** IRRELATION, dissociation; misrelation; inapplicability; inconnection; multifariousness; disconnection &c (*disjunction*) 44; inconsequence, independence; incommensurability; irreconcilableness &c. (*disagreement*) 24; heterogeneity; unconformity &c. 83; irrelevancy, impertinence, *nihil ad rem* [*L.*]; intrusion &c. 24; nonpertinence.

V. NOT CONCERN &c. 9; have no relation to &c. 9; have no bearing upon, have no concern with &c. 9; have no business with; have nothing to do with, have no business there; intrude &c. 24.

bring-, drag-, lug- in by the head and shoulders.

Adj. IRRELATIVE, irrespective, unrelated, disrelated, irrelate [*rare*]; arbitrary; independent, unallied; disconnected, unconnected, adrift, isolated, insular; extraneous, strange, alien, foreign, outlandish, exotic.

not comparable, incommensurable, heterogeneous; unconformable &c. 83.

IRRELEVANT, inapplicable; not pertinent, not to the purpose; impertinent [*legal*], unessential, inessential, accidental, inapposite, beside the mark, *à propos de bottes* [*F.*]; aside from-, away from-, foreign to-, beside the -purpose, -question, - transaction, - point; misplaced &c. (*intrusive*) 24; traveling out of the record.

REMOTE, far-fetched, out-of-the-way, forced, neither here nor there, quite another thing; detached, apart, segre-

equiparant; in the same category &c. 75; like &c. 17.

Adv. RELATIVELY &c. *adj.;* pertinently &c. 23.

THEREOF; as to, as for, as respects, as regards; about; concerning &c. *v.;* anent; relating to, as relates to; with relation to, with reference to, with respect to, with regard to; in respect of; speaking of, *à propos* [*F.*] of; in connection with; by the way, by the by; whereas; for as much as, in as much as; in point of, as far as; on the part of, on the score of; *quoad hoc* [*L.*]; *pro re natâ* [*L.*]; under the head of &c. (*class*) 75; in the matter of, *in re* [*L.*].

gated, segregate; disquiparant.

MULTIFARIOUS; discordant &c. 24.

INCIDENTAL, parenthetical, *obiter dictum* [*L.*], episodic.

Adv. PARENTHETICALLY &c. *adj.;* by the way, by the by; *en passant* [*F.*], incidentally, *obiter* [*L.*]; irrespectively &c. *adj.;* without reference to, without regard to; in the abstract &c. 87; *a se* [*L.*].

*** "remote, unfriended, melancholy, slow" [Goldsmith]; "she stood in tears amid the alien corn" [Keats]; "so she went into the garden to cut a cabbage-leaf to make an apple pie" [S. Foote].

*** "thereby hangs a tale" [*Taming of the Shrew*]; "but that's another story" [Kipling]; "a man is a bundle of relations, a knot of roots" [Emerson].

11. [RELATIONS OF KINDRED.]   **Consanguinity.** — **N.** CONSANGUINITY, relationship, kindred, blood; parentage &c. (*paternity*) 166; filiation, affiliation; lineage, agnation, connation [*obs.*], cognation, connection, alliance; people [as, my *people*], family, family connection, family tie; ties of blood, blood relation; nepotism.

KINSMAN, kinsfolk; kith and kin; relation, relative; connection; sib [*rare*]; next of kin; uncle, aunt, nephew, niece; cousin, cousin-german; first cousin, second cousin; cousin once removed, cousin twice removed &c.; near relation, distant relation; brother, sister, one's own flesh and blood.

FAMILY, fraternity; brotherhood, sisterhood, cousinhood.

RACE, stock, generation; sept &c. 166; stirps, side; strain; breed, clan, tribe.

V. BE RELATED TO &c. *adj.;* claim relationship with &c. *n.*

Adj. RELATED, akin, sib [*Scot. or archaic*], consanguineous, of the blood, family, allied, collateral; cognate, agnate, connate [*rare*]; kindred; affiliated; fraternal.

intimately related, nearly related, closely related, remotely related, distantly related; intimately allied, nearly allied, closely allied, remotely allied, distantly allied; affinal, german.

*** "A little more than kin and less than kind" [*Hamlet*]; "I'm all o'er sib to Adam's breed that I should bid him go" [Kipling]; "and so do his sisters and his cousins and his aunts" [Gilbert].

12. [DOUBLE OR RECIPROCAL RELATION.]   **Correlation.** — **N.** RECIPROCALNESS &c. *adj.;* reciprocity, reciprocality, reciprocation; mutuality, correspondence, correlation, interrelation, interconnection, interdependence; interchange &c. 148; exchange, barter, *quid pro quo* [*L.*].

ALTERNATION, seesaw, shuttle [*rare*], to-and-fro.

reciprocitist.

V. RECIPROCATE, alternate, interact; interchange &c. 148; exchange; counterchange.

Adj. RECIPROCAL, mutual, commutual [*rare*], correlative; correspondent, corresponding; alternate; interchangeable; international; complemental, complementary; equivalent.

Adv. *mutatis mutandis* [*L.*]; *vice versâ* [*L.*]; each other; by turns &c. 148; reciprocally &c. *adj.*

*** "happy in our mutual help" [Milton]; "my true love hath my heart and I have his" [Sidney].

13. Identity. — **N.** IDENTITY, sameness, identicalness, unity, selfsameness, coincidence, coalescence; convertibility;

14. [NONCOINCIDENCE.]   **Contrariety.** — **N.** CONTRARIETY, contrast, foil, antithesis, antipode, counterpole, counter-

equality &c. 27; selfness, self, oneself; identification.

CONNATURALITY, connature, connaturalness, homogeneity.

MONOTONY; tautology &c. (repetition) 104.

FACSIMILE &c. (copy) 21; homoousia; alter ego [L.] &c. (similar) 17; ipsissima verba [L.] &c. (exactness) 494; same; selfsame, very same, one and the same; counterpart; very thing, actual thing; no other.

V. BE IDENTICAL &c. adj.; coincide, coalesce.

treat as the same, render the same; treat as identical; render identical; identify; recognize the identity of.

Adj. IDENTICAL; self, ilk [archaic]; the identical same &c. n.; selfsame, homoousian, one and the same; ditto.

COINCIDENT, coinciding, coalescing, coalescent, indistinguishable; one; equivalent &c. (equal) 27; much the same, much of a muchness; unaltered.

Adv. IDENTICALLY &c. adj.; on all fours with; ibidem [L.], ibid.

₊ "Liberty and Union, now and forever, one and inseparable" [Webster]; "All one body we, One in hope, in doctrine, One in charity" [Baring-Gould]; "the selfsame flight, the selfsame way" [Merchant of Venice]; "another, yet the same" [Pope].

point; counterpart; complement; vis-à-vis [F.], oppositeness; contradiction; antagonism &c. (opposition) 708; clashing, repugnance, antipathy.

INVERSION &c. 218; the opposite, the reverse, the inverse, the converse, the antipodes, the other extreme.

V. BE CONTRARY &c. adj.; contrast with, oppose, antithesize [rare]; differ toto cœlo [L.].

INVERT, reverse, turn the tables; turn topsy-turvy, turn end for end, turn upside down; retrograde, transpose, invaginate, intussuscept.

CONTRADICT, contravene; antagonize &c. 708.

Adj. CONTRARY, contrarious [archaic], contrariant [rare], opposite, counter, dead against; adverse, averse, converse, reverse; opposed, antithetical, contrasted, antipodean, antagonistic, opposing; conflicting, inconsistent, contradictory, at cross purposes; negative; hostile, inimical &c. 703.

differing toto cœlo [L.]; diametrically opposite; as opposite as black and white, as opposite as light and darkness, as opposite as fire and water, as opposite as the poles; "Hyperion to a satyr" [Hamlet]; quite the contrary, quite the reverse; no such thing, just the other way, tout au contraire [F.].

Adv. CONTRARILY &c. adj.; contra, contrariwise, per contra [L.], on the contrary, nay rather; vice versâ [L.]; on the other hand &c. (in compensation) 30.

₊ "all concord's born of contraries" [B. Jonson]; "our antagonist is our helper" [Burke]; "woman's| at best a contradiction still" [Pope]; "the innate perversity of inanimate objects" [Gail Hamilton]; "opposition is the surest persuasion" [Cynic's Calendar].

15. Difference. — N. DIFFERENCE; variance, variation, variety; diversity, divergence, heterogeneity, discongruity, contrast, inconformity, incompatibility, antithesis, antitheticalness, discrepation [rare], dissimilarity &c. 18; disagreement &c. 24; disparity &c. (inequality) 28; distinction, dissimilitude [rare], distinctness, contradiction, contradictoriness, contrariety, contradistinction; alteration.

nice distinction, fine distinction, delicate distinction, subtle distinction; shade of difference, nuance [F.]; discrimination &c. 465; differentia.

DIFFERENT THING, something else, apple off another tree, another pair of shoes; this, that, or the other.

MODIFICATION, commutation [rare], moods and tenses.

V. BE DIFFERENT &c. adj.; differ, vary, ablude [obs.], mismatch, contrast; diverge from, depart from, deviate from, disaccord with, discrepate [rare]; divaricate; differ toto cœlo [L.], differ longo intervallo [L.].

VARY, modify &c. (change) 140.

DISCRIMINATE &c. 465.

Adj. DIFFERING &c. v.; different, diverse, heterogeneous; distinguishable; varied, variant, divergent, contrastive, incongruous, discrepant, dissonant, inharmonious, disparate, inconformable, differential, modified; diversified, various, divers [archaic], all manner of; variform &c. 81; dædal.

OTHER, another, not the same; unequal &c. 28; unmatched; widely apart.

DISTINCTIVE, characteristic; discriminative, differentiative, distinguishing; diacritic, diacritical; diagnostic.

Adv. DIFFERENTLY &c. *adj.*

*** *il y a fagots et fagots; tot homines tot sententiæ;* "a distinction without a difference" [Fielding]; "you must wear your rue with a difference" [*Hamlet*]; "But she is in her grave, and oh, The difference to me" [Wordsworth]; "not Lancelot, nor another" [Tennyson].

2. CONTINUOUS RELATION

16. Uniformity. — N. UNIFORMITY; homogeneity, homogeneousness; stability, continuity, permanence, consistency; connature [*rare*], connaturality [*rare*], connaturalness; homology; accordance; conformity &c. 82; agreement &c. 23; consonance, uniformness.

REGULARITY, constancy, evenness, sameness, unity, even tenor, routine; monotony.

V. BE UNIFORM &c. *adj.;* accord with &c. 23; run through.

BECOME UNIFORM &c. *adj.;* conform to &c. 82.

RENDER UNIFORM &c. *adj.;* assimilate, level, smooth, dress.

Adj. UNIFORM; homogeneous, homologous; of a piece, consistent, connatural; singsong, drear [*rare*], drearisome, dreary, monotonous, even, equable, constant, level; invariable; regular, unchanged, undeviating, unvaried, undiversified, unvarying; jog-trot.

Adv. UNIFORMLY &c. *adj.;* uniformly with &c. (*conformably*) 82; in harmony with &c. (*agreeing*) 23; in a rut.

ALWAYS, ever, evermore, perpetually, forever, everlastingly, invariably, without exception, never otherwise; by clockwork.

*** *ab uno disce omnes;* "Consistence, thou art a jewel!" [*Anon.*]; "a foolish consistency is the hobgoblin of little minds" [Emerson]; "Young Obadias, David, Josias, — All were pious" [*New England Primer*].

16a. [ABSENCE OR WANT OF UNIFORMITY.] **Nonuniformity. — N.** DIVERSITY, irregularity, unevenness; multiformity &c. 81; unconformity &c. 83; roughness &c. 256; dissimilarity, dissimilitude, divarication, divergence, heteromorphism, heterogeneity.

Adj. DIVERSIFIED, varied, irregular, checkered, dædal, uneven, rough &c. 256; multifarious; multiform &c. 81; of various kinds; all manner of, all sorts of, all kinds of.

Adv. in all manner of ways; here, there, and everywhere.

*** "I do desire we may be better strangers" [*As You Like It*]; "of every shape that was not uniform" [Lowell].

3. PARTIAL RELATION

17. Similarity. — N. SIMILARITY, resemblance, likeness, similitude [*rare*], semblance, consimilarity [*rare*]; affinity, approximation, parallelism; agreement &c. 23; analogy, analogicalness; correspondence, homoiousia, parity.

CONNATURALNESS, connature [*rare*], connaturality [*rare*]; brotherhood, family likeness.

ALLITERATION, rime *or* rhyme, pun.

REPETITION &c. 104; sameness &c. (*identity*) 13; uniformity &c. 16; isogamy.

ANALOGUE; the like; match, pendant, fellow, companion, pair, mate, twin, double, congener, counterpart, brother,

18. Dissimilarity. — N. DISSIMILARITY, dissimilitude; unlikeness, diversity, disparity, dissemblance; divergence, variation; difference &c. 15; novelty, originality; creativeness; oögamy.

V. BE UNLIKE &c. *adj.;* vary &c. (*differ*) 15; bear no resemblance to, differ *toto cœlo* [*L.*].

RENDER UNLIKE &c. *adj.;* vary &c. (*diversify*) 140.

Adj. DISSIMILAR, unlike, disparate; divergent, nonidentical, unidentical; of a different kind &c. (*class*) 75; unmatched, unique; new, novel; unprecedented &c. 83; original.

nothing of the kind; no such thing,

sister; one's second self, *alter ego* [*L.*], chip of the old block, *par nobile fratrum* [*L.*], *Arcades ambo* [*L.*], birds of a feather, *et hoc genus omne* [*L.*]; *gens de même famille* [*F.*].

SIMILE; parallel; type &c. (*metaphor*) 521; image &c. (*representation*) 554; photograph; close-, striking-, speaking-, faithful &c. *adj.* --likeness, - resemblance.

V. BE SIMILAR &c. *adj.;* look like, resemble, favor [*colloq.*], follow, echo, reproduce, bear resemblance; savor of, smack of; approximate; parallel, match, rime *or* rhyme with; take after; imitate &c. 19; span [*U. S.*]; hunt in couples, run in couples.

RENDER SIMILAR &c. *adj.;* assimilate, approximate, bring near; connaturalize, make alike; rime *or* rhyme, pun.

Adj. SIMILAR; resembling &c. *v.;* like, alike; twin.

ANALOGOUS, analogical; parallel, of a piece; such as, so; homoiousian.

CONNATURAL, correlative, corresponding, cognate, congeneric, congenerous, allied to; akin to &c. (*consanguineous*) 11.

APPROXIMATE, much the same, near, close, something like, near- [as *near*-silk, *colloq.*, *U.S.*], such like; a show of; mock, pseudo, simulating, representing.

EXACT &c. (*true*) 494; lifelike, faithful; true to nature, true to life; the very image of, the very picture of; for all the world like, *comme deux gouttes d'eau* [*F.*], as like as two peas, as like as it can stare; *instar omnium* [*L.*], cast in the same mold, ridiculously like.

Adv. AS IF, so to speak; as it were, as if it were; *quasi* [*L.*], just as, *veluti in speculum* [*L.*].

, *et sic de similibus; tel maître tel valet; tel père tel fils,* like father like son; "as lyke as one pease is to another" [Lyly]; "they say we are Almost as like as eggs" [*Winter's Tale*]; "Fair Portia's counterfeit" [*M. of V.*]; "so and no otherwise hill-men desire their hills" [Kipling].

quite another thing; far from it, other than, cast in a different mold, *tertium quid* [*L.*], as like a dock as a daisy, "very like a whale" [*Hamlet*]; as different as chalk from cheese, as different as Macedon and Monmouth; *lucus a non lucendo* [*L.*].

diversified &c. 16*a.*

Adv. OTHERWISE, elsewise; alias.

, *dis aliter visum;* "no more like my father Than I to Hercules" [*Hamlet*]; "it is a custom More honoured in the breach than in the observance" [*Hamlet*]; "agreed to differ" [Southey].

---

19. Imitation. — N. IMITATION; copying &c. *v.;* transcription; repetition, duplication, reduplication; quotation; reproduction; mimeography.

MOCKERY, apery, mimicking, mimicry.

SIMULATION, personation; parrotism, parrotry; representation &c. 554; semblance, pretense; copy &c. 21; assimilation.

paraphrase, parody &c. 21.

PLAGIARISM; forgery &c. (*falsehood*) 544.

IMITATOR, echo, cuckoo, parrot, ape, monkey, mocking bird, mimic; copyist.

V. IMITATE, copy, mirror, reflect, reproduce, repeat; do like, echo, reëcho, catch; transcribe; match, parallel.

MOCK, take off, borrow, mimic, ape, simulate, personate; act &c. (*drama*) 599; represent &c. 554; counterfeit, forge, parody, travesty, caricature, burlesque.

FOLLOW in the steps of, follow in the footsteps of; follow in the wake of; tread in the steps of, tread in the footsteps of; take pattern by; follow suit [*colloq.*], follow the example of; walk in the shoes of, take a leaf out of another's book, strike in with; take after, model after; emulate.

20. Nonimitation. — N. NONIMITATION, no imitation; originality; creativeness.

Adj. UNIMITATED, uncopied; unmatched, unparalleled; inimitable &c. 33; unique, original, archetypal, prototypal, prototypical, primordial, creative, untranslated; exceptional, rare, *sui generis* [*L.*], uncommon, unexampled, out-of-the-way, insitate [*rare*], unwonted, *recherché* [*F.*], unordinary [*rare*], supernormal.

, "wrapped in the solitude of his own originality" [Charles Phillips — *of Napoleon*].

Adj. IMITATED &c. *v.;* mock, mimic; modeled after, molded on.

PARAPHRASTIC; literal; imitative; secondhand; imitable; aping, apish, mimicking, borrowed, counterfeit, imitation, false, pseudo, near- [as, *near-*silk, *colloq., U. S.*].

Adv. LITERALLY, to the letter, verbatim, *literatim* [*L.*], *sic* [*L.*], *totidem verbis* [*L.*], word for word, *mot à mot* [*F.*], *verbatim et literatim* [*L.*]; exactly, precisely.

⁎ like master like man; "like — but oh! how different!" [Wordsworth]; "genius borrows nobly" [Emerson]; "pursuing echoes calling 'mong the rocks" [A. Coles]; "quotation confesses inferiority" [Emerson]; "the little actor cons another part" [Wordsworth]; "play the sedulous ape to men of letters" [Stevenson].

20a. Variation. — N. VARIATION; alteration &c. *(change)* 140.

MODIFICATION, moods and tenses; discrepance, discrepancy.

DIVERGENCY &c. 291; deviation &c. 279; aberration; innovation.

V. VARY &c. *(change)* 140; deviate &c. 279; diverge &c. 291; alternate, swerve.

Adj. VARIED &c. *v.;* modified; diversified &c. 16a; dissimilar &c. 18.

⁎ "variety is the very spice of life" [Cowper]; "age cannot wither her, nor custom stale Her infinite variety" [*Antony and Cleopatra*].

21. [RESULT OF IMITATION.] Copy.—

N. COPY, facsimile, counterpart, *effigies* [*L.*], effigy, form, likeness, similitude, semblance, cast, tracing, ectype, electrotype; imitation &c. 19; model, representation, adumbration, study; "counterfeit presentment" [*Hamlet*]; portrait &c. *(representment)* 554; resemblance.

duplicate; transcript, transcription; counterscript; reflex, reflexion; shadow, echo; chip of the old block; reprint, replica, offprint, transfer, reproduction; second edition &c. *(repetition)* 104; *réchauffé* [*F.*]; apograph, fair copy, revise, rewriting.

MATTER; manuscript, typescript *or* typoscript, flimsy [*cant*].

22. [THING COPIED.] Prototype. —

N. PROTOTYPE, original, model, pattern, precedent, standard, scantling [*rare*], type; archetype, antitype; protoplast, protoplasm, plasm [*obs.*], proplasm [*rare*], module, exemplar, example, ensample [*archaic*], paradigm; lay-figure; fugleman, guide.

COPY, text, design; keynote.

DIE, mold; matrix, last, mint, seal, punch, intaglio, negative; stamp.

V. be an example, set an example; set a copy.

⁎ "a precedent embalms a principle" [Disraeli]; *exempla sunt odiosa;* "I do not give you to posterity as a pattern to imitate, but as an example to deter" [*Letters of Junius*].

PARODY, caricature, burlesque, travesty, *travestie* [*F.*], paraphrase; cartoon. servile copy, servile imitation; counterfeit &c. *(deception)* 545; *pasticcio* [*It.*].

Adj. FAITHFUL; lifelike &c. *(similar)* 17; close, exact, strict, conscientious.

⁎ "nature's copy's not eterne" [*Macbeth*]; "follow the copy though it fly out of the window" [*Printers' Saying*]; "parody might indeed be defined as the worshipper's half-holiday" [Chesterton].

4. GENERAL RELATION

23. Agreement. — N. AGREEMENT,

accord, accordance; unison, harmony; concord &c. 714; concordance, concert; understanding, mutual understanding; gentleman's agreement, *entente cordiale* [*F.*], consortium; unanimity, consension [*rare*], concentus, consentaneity.

CONFORMITY &c. 82; conformance; uniformity &c. 16; assonance, consonance, consentaneousness, consistency; congruity, congruence *or* congruency; keeping; congeniality; correspondence, concinnity, parallelism, apposition, union.

24. Disagreement. — N. DISAGREE-

MENT; discord, discordance, discordancy; dissonance, dissidence, disunity, disunion, discrepancy; unconformity &c. 83; incongruity, incongruence; discongruity, *mésalliance* [*F.*]; jarring &c. *v.;* dissension &c. 713; conflict &c. *(opposition)* 708; bickering, clashing, misunderstanding, wrangle.

DISPARITY, mismatch, disproportion; dissimilitude, inequality; disproportionateness &c. *adj.;* variance, divergence, repugnance.

UNFITNESS &c. *adj.;* inaptitude, im-

FITNESS, aptness &c. *adj.;* relevancy; pertinence *or* pertinency; sortance [*obs.*]; case in point; aptitude, coaptation, propriety, applicability, admissibility, commensurability, compatibility; cognation &c. (*relation*) 9.

ADAPTATION, adaption, adjustment, graduation, accommodation; reconciliation, reconcilement; assimilation.

CONSENT &c. (*assent*) 488; concurrence &c. 178; consensus, *rapport* [*F.*], meeting of minds, coöperation &c. 709.

right man in the right place, very thing; quite the thing, just the thing.

V. BE ACCORDANT &c. *adj.;* agree, accord, harmonize; correspond, tally, respond; meet, suit, fit, befit, do, adapt itself to; fall in with, chime in with, square with, quadrate with, consort with, comport with; dovetail, assimilate; fit like a glove; fit to a tittle, fit to a T; match &c. 17; become one; homologate.

consent &c. (*assent*) 488.

RENDER ACCORDANT &c. *adj.;* fit, suit, adapt, accommodate; graduate; adjust &c. (*render equal*) 27; dress, regulate, readjust; accord, harmonize, reconcile; fadge, dovetail, square.

Adj. AGREEING, suiting &c. *v.;* in accord, accordant, concordant, consonant, congruous, consentaneous [*archaic*], answerable, correspondent, congenial; coherent; becoming; harmonious, reconcilable, conformable; in accordance with, in harmony with, in keeping with, in unison with &c. *n.;* at one with, of one mind, of a piece; consistent, compatible, proportionate; commensurate; on all fours with.

APT, apposite, pertinent, pat; to the point, to the purpose; happy, felicitous, germane, *ad rem* [*L.*], in point, bearing upon, applicable, relevant, admissible.

FIT, adapted, *in loco* [*L.*], *à propos* [*F.*], appropriate, seasonable, sortable, suitable, idoneous [*rare*], deft; meet &c. (*expedient*) 646.

at home, in one's proper element.

Adv. *à propos* of; pertinently &c. *adj.*

propriety; inapplicability &c. *adj.;* inconsistency, inconcinnity; irrelevancy &c. (*irrelation*) 10.

MISJOINING, misjoinder; syncretism, intrusion, interference.

fish out of water.

V. DISAGREE; clash, conflict, dispute, quarrel, jar &c. (*discord*) 713; interfere, intrude, come amiss; not concern &c. 10; mismatch; *humano capiti cervicem jungere equinam* [*L.*]

Adj. DISAGREEING &c. *v.;* discordant, discrepant; at variance, at war; hostile, antagonistic, repugnant, inaccordant, clashing, jarring, factious, dissentient, dissentious, dissident, inacquiescent, incompatible, irreconcilable, inconsistent with; unconformable, exceptional &c. 83; intrusive, incongruent, incongruous; disproportionate, disproportioned; unharmonious; unconsonant; divergent, repugnant to.

INAPT, unapt, inappropriate, malappropriate [*rare*], improper; unsuited, unsuitable; inapplicable; unfit, unfitting, unbefitting; unbecoming; ill-timed, illadapted, dissuitable [*rare*], infelicitous, unseasonable, *mal à propos* [*F.*], inadmissible; inapposite &c. (*irrelevant*) 10.

UNCONGENIAL; ill-assorted, ill-sorted; mismatched, misjoined, misplaced; unaccommodating, irreducible, uncommensurable; unsympathetic.

out of character, out of keeping, out of proportion, out of joint, out of tune, out of place, out of season, out of its element; at odds, at variance with.

Adv. in defiance of, in contempt of, in spite of; discordantly &c. *adj.; à tort et à travers* [*F.*].

** asinus ad lyram; "fill'd the air with barbarous dissonance" [Milton]; "all discord, harmony not understood" [Pope]; "I heard him speak disrespectfully of the equator" [Sydney Smith]; "the dissidence of dissent" [Burke].

** rem acu tetigisti; the cap fits; *auxilia humilia firma consensus facit* [Syrus]; *concordia discors* [Hor.]; "Be not the first by whom the new is tried, Nor yet the last to lay the old aside" [Pope].

Section III. QUANTITY

1. Simple Quantity

25. [Absolute quantity.] **Quantity.**
— **N.** quantity, magnitude; size &c.
(*dimensions*) 192; amplitude, mass,
amount, quantum, measure, measurement, substance, strength.

[Science of quantity] mathematics,
mathesis [*rare*].

[Logic] category, general conception, universal predicament.

[Definite or finite quantity] arm-
ful, handful, mouthful, spoonful, capful;
stock, batch, lot, dose; quota, quotiety
[*rare*], quotum, pittance, driblet, grist
[*U. S.*]; yaffle [*dial.*].

V. quantify, rate.

Adj. quantitative, some, any, more
or less.

Adv. to the tune of.

. "I waive the quantum o' the sin"
[Burns].

26. [Relative quantity.] **Degree.**—
N. degree, grade, step, extent, measure,
amount, ratio, stint *or* stent, standard,
height, pitch; reach, amplitude, range,
scope, caliber; gradation, shade; tenor,
compass; sphere, station, rank, standing; rate, way, sort.

point, mark, stage &c. (*term*) 71;
interval, line [*music*], space [*music*];
intensity, strength &c. (*greatness*) 31.

V. graduate, calibrate, measure; rectify.

Adj. comparative; gradual, grada-
tional, gradatory [*rare*], shading off;
within the bounds &c. (*limit*) 233.

Adv. by degrees, gradually, inasmuch, *pro tanto* [*L.*]; however, howso-
ever; step by step, bit by bit, little by
little, inch by inch, drop by drop; by
inches, by slow degrees, by little and
little; in some degree, in some measure;
to some extent; *di grado in grado* [*It.*].

. "the rank is but the guinea's stamp"
[Burns].

2. Comparative Quantity

27. [Sameness of quantity or degree.] **Equality.** — **N.** equality, parity, coextension, symmetry, balance,
poise; evenness, monotony, level.

equivalence; equipollence, equipoise, equilibrium, equiponderance; par,
quits; not a pin to choose; distinction
without a difference, six of one and
half a dozen of the other; identity &c.
13; similarity &c. 17; coequality, coevality [*rare*], isonomy, isopolity, isotropy, parallelism, owelty [*law*].

equalization, equation; equilibration,
coördination, adjustment, readjustment.

tie, dead heat; drawn game, drawn
battle; neck-and-neck race.

match, peer, compeer, equal, mate,
fellow, brother; equivalent.

V. be equal &c. *adj.*; equal, match,
reach, keep pace with, run abreast; come
to, amount to, come up to; be on a level
with, lie on a level with; balance; cope
with; come to the same thing, even off.

render equal &c. *adj.*; equalize,
level, dress, balance, equate, handicap,

28. [Difference of quantity or
degree.] **Inequality.**— **N.** inequality,
inequalness [*rare*]; disparity, imparity
[*rare*]; odds; difference &c. 15; unevenness; inclination of the balance,
partiality; shortcoming; casting weight,
makeweight; superiority &c. 33; inferiority &c. 34; inequation, inadequation
[*archaic*], inadequacy.

V. be unequal &c. *adj.*; countervail;
have the advantage, give the advantage;
turn the scale; kick the beam; topple,
topple over; overmatch &c. 33; not come
up to &c. 34.

Adj. unequal, inequal [*rare*], uneven,
disparate, partial, inadequate; over-
balanced, unbalanced; top-heavy, lop-
sided; disquiparant; unequaled, unparalleled, fellowless [*rare*], unmatched
[*rare*], unrivaled, unique, unapproached,
matchless, inimitable, transcendent,
peerless, nonpareil, unexampled, unpatterned [*rare*], unpeered [*rare*].

Adv. unequally &c. *adj.*; *haud passibus æquis* [Vergil].

give points, trim, adjust, poise; fit, accommodate; adapt &c. (*render accordant*) 23; strike a balance; establish equality, restore equality, establish equilibrium, restore equilibrium; readjust; stretch on the bed of Procrustes.

Adj. EQUAL, even, level, monotonous, coequal, symmetrical, coördinate; on a par with, on a level with, on a footing with; up to the mark; equiparant, equiparate [*rare*].

EQUIVALENT, tantamount; quits; homologous; synonymous &c. 522; resolvable into, convertible, much at one, as broad as long, neither more nor less; much the same as, the same thing as, as good as; all one, all the same; equipollent, equiponderant, equiponderous, equibalanced; equalized &c. *v.;* drawn; half and half; isochronal, isochronous; isoperimetric *or* isoperimetrical; isobath, isobathic.

Adv. EQUALLY &c. *adj.; pari passu* [*L.*], *ad eundem* [*L.*], *cæteris paribus* [*L.*], *in equilibrio* [*L.*]; to all intents and purposes.

*** it comes to the same thing, it amounts to the same thing; what is sauce for the goose is sauce for the gander; "the modern zeal for equality makes a counterpoise for Darwinism" [Amiel].

29. Mean. — N.
MEAN, medium, intermedium [*obsoles.*], average, balance, normal, rule, run; mediocrity, generality; golden mean &c. (*mid-course*) 628; middle &c. 68; compromise &c. 774; middle course, middle state; neutrality.

V. AVERAGE, split the difference; take the average &c. *n.;* reduce to a mean &c. *n.;* strike a balance, pair off.

Adj. MEAN, intermediate; medial, middle &c. 68; average, normal, standard; neutral.

MEDIOCRE, middle-class, *bourgeois* [*F.*], commonplace &c. (*unimportant*) 643.

Adv. ON AN AVERAGE, in the long run; taking one with another, taking all things together, taking it for all in all; *communibus annis* [*L.*], in round numbers.

IN THE MIDDLE, *in medias res* [*L.*], *meden agan* [*Gr. μηδὲν ἄγαν*].

*** *medium tenuere beati;* "keep the golden mean" [Publius Syrus]; *est modus in rebus* [Horace]; "give me neither poverty nor riches" [*Bible*].

30. Compensation. — N.
COMPENSATION, equation; commutation; indemnification; compromise &c. 774; neutralization, nullification; counteraction &c. 179; reaction; measure for measure; retaliation &c. 718; equalization &c. 27; redemption, recoupment.

SET-OFF, offset; makeweight, casting weight; counterpoise, ballast; indemnity, equivalent, *quid pro quo* [*L.*]; bribe, hush money; gift, donation &c. 784; amends &c. (*atonement*) 952; counterbalance, counterclaim, countervailing; cross debt, cross demand.

PAY, payment, reward &c. 973.

V. COMPENSATE, compense [*obs.*], make compensation, indemnify; counteract, countervail, counterpoise; balance; counterbalance, offset, outbalance, overbalance, set off; hedge, square, give and take; make up for, make leeway; cover, fill up, neutralize, nullify; equalize &c. 27; make good; recoup, redeem &c. (*atone*) 952; pay, reward &c. 973.

Adj. COMPENSATING, compensatory, compensative, amendatory, indemnificatory, reparative; countervailing &c. *v.;* in the opposite scale; equivalent &c. (*equal*) 27.

Adv. FOR A CONSIDERATION, in return, in consideration.

NOTWITHSTANDING, but, however, yet, still, nevertheless, natheless *or* nathless [*archaic*]; although, though; howbeit, albeit; mauger *or* maugre, at all events, in spite of, in despite of, despite, at any rate; be that as it may, for all that, even so, on the other hand, at the same time, *quoad minus* [*L.*], *quand même* [*F.*], however that may be; after all, after all is said and done; taking one thing with another &c. (*average*) 29.

*** robbing Peter to pay Paul; "light is mingled with the gloom" [Whittier]; *primo avulso non deficit alter* [Vergil]; *saepe creat molles aspera spina rosas* [Ovid].

QUANTITY BY COMPARISON WITH A STANDARD

31. Greatness. — N. GREATNESS &c. *adj.*; magnitude; size &c. (*dimensions*) 192; multitude &c. (*number*) 102; immensity, enormity, muchness; infinity &c. 105; might, strength, intensity, fullness.

GREAT QUANTITY, quantity, deal [*colloq.*], power [*colloq.*], sight [*colloq.*], pot [*colloq.*], volume, world; mass, heap &c. (*assemblage*) 72; stock &c. (*store*) 636; peck, bushel, load, cargo; cartload, wagonload, shipload; flood, spring tide; abundance &c. (*sufficiency*) 639.

principal part, chief part, main part, greater part, better part, major part, best part, essential part; bulk, mass &c. (*whole*) 50.

FAME, distinction, grandeur, dignity; importance &c. 642; generosity.

V. BE GREAT &c. *adj.*; run high, soar, tower, loom, tower above, rise above, transcend; rise to a great height, carry to a great height; bulk, bulk large; know no bounds; ascend, mount.

ENLARGE &c. (*increase*) 35, (*expand*) 194.

Adj. GREAT; greater &c. 33; large, considerable, fair, above par; big, bulky, huge &c. (*large in size*) 192; titanic, Atlantean, Herculean, cyclopean, voluminous; ample; abundant &c. (*enough*) 639; wholesale; many &c. 102; full, intense, strong, sound, passing [*archaic*], heavy, plenary, deep, high; signal, at its height, in the zenith.

WORLD-WIDE, widespread, far-famed, extensive.

GOODLY, noble, precious, mighty; sad, grave, serious; far gone, arrant, downright; uttermost; crass, gross, tall [*slang, U. S.*], mickle [*archaic*], arch, profound, intense, consummate; rank, unmitigated, red-hot desperate; glaring, flagrant, stark staring; thorough-paced, thorough-going; roaring, whacking [*colloq.*], magnitudinous [*rare*], thumping; extraordinary; important &c. 642; unsurpassed &c. (*supreme*) 33; complete &c. 52.

AUGUST, grand dignified, sublime, majestic &c. (*repute*) 873.

VAST, immense, enormous, extreme; inordinate, excessive, extravagant, exorbitant, outrageous, preposterous, unconscionable, swinging, monstrous, overgrown; towering, stupendous, prodigious,

32. Smallness. — N. SMALLNESS &c. *adj.*; littleness &c. (*small size*) 193; tenuity; paucity; fewness &c. (*small number*) 103; meanness, insignificance &c. (*unimportance*) 643; mediocrity, moderation.

SMALL QUANTITY, modicum, minimum; vanishing point; material point, atom, particle, electron, molecule, corpuscle, point, speck, dot, mote, jot, iota, ace; minutiæ, details; look, thought, idea, *soupçon* [*F.*], dab, dight [*dial.*], whit, tittle, shade, shadow; spark, scintilla, gleam; touch, cast; grain, scruple, granule, globule, minim, sup, sip, sop, spice, drop, droplet, sprinkling, dash, *morceau* [*F.*], screed [*Scot.*], smack, tinge, tincture; inch, patch, scantling, tatter, cantle, cantlet, flitter, gobbet, dole, mite, bit, morsel, crumb; scrap, shred, tag, splinter, rag; seed, fritter, shive; snip, snippet; snick, snack [*dial.*], snatch, slip; chip, chipping; shiver, sliver, driblet, clipping, paring, shaving, hair.

nutshell; thimbleful, spoonful, handful, capful, mouthful; fragment; fraction &c. (*part*) 51; drop in the ocean.

animalcule &c. 193.

TRIFLE &c. (*unimportant thing*) 643; mere nothing, next to nothing; hardly anything; just enough to swear by; the shadow of a shade.

FINITENESS, finite quantity.

V. BE SMALL &c. *adj.*; lie in a nutshell.

DIMINISH &c. (*decrease*) 36, (*contract*) 195.

Adj. SMALL, little; diminutive &c. (*small in size*) 193; minute, miniature, minikin; fine; inconsiderable, dribbling, paltry &c. (*unimportant*) 643; faint &c. (*weak*) 160; slender, light, slight, scanty, scant, limited; meager &c. (*insufficient*) 640; sparing; few &c. 103; low; soso *or* so-so *or* so so [*colloq.*], middling, tolerable, no great shakes [*slang*]; below par, under par, below the mark, under the mark; at a low ebb; halfway; moderate, modest; tender, subtle.

INAPPRECIABLE, evanescent, infinitesimal, homeopathic *or* homœopathic, very small; atomic, corpuscular, microscopic, molecular; skin-deep.

MERE, simple, sheer, stark, bare; near run.

astonishing, incredible, pronounced, fearful [*colloq.*], thundering [*slang*], terrible [*colloq.*], dreadful [*colloq.*], terrific [*colloq.*]; marvelous &c. (*wonder*) 870.

UNLIMITED &c. (*infinite*) 105; unapproachable, unutterable, indescribable, ineffable, unspeakable, inexpressible, beyond expression, fabulous.

UNDIMINISHED, unabated, unreduced, unrestricted.

ABSOLUTE, positive, stark, decided, unequivocal, essential, perfect, finished.

REMARKABLE, of mark, marked, pointed, veriest; notable, noticeable, noteworthy; renowned.

Adv. [IN A POSITIVE DEGREE] truly &c. (*truth*) 494; decidedly, unequivocally, purely, absolutely, seriously, essentially, fundamentally, radically, downright, in all conscience; for the most part, in the main.

[IN A COMPLETE DEGREE] entirely &c. (*completely*) 52; abundantly &c. (*sufficiently*) 639; widely, far and wide.

[IN A GREAT OR HIGH DEGREE] greatly &c. *adj.*; much, muckle [*archaic*], well, indeed, very, very much, a deal, no end of, most, not a little; pretty, pretty well; enough, in a great measure, no end [*colloq., U. S.*], passing, richly; to a large extent, to a great extent, to a gigantic extent; on a large scale; so; never so, ever so; ever so much; by wholesale, mighty [*colloq.*], mightily, powerfully; with a witness [*colloq.*], ultra, in the extreme, extremely, exceedingly, intensely, exquisitely, acutely, indefinitely, immeasurably; beyond compare, beyond comparison, beyond measure, beyond all bounds; out of sight [*colloq.*]; incalculably, infinitely.

[IN A SUPREME DEGREE] preëminently, superlatively &c. (*superiority*) 33.

DULL, petty, shallow, stolid, phlegmatic, unintelligent; Bœotian, ungifted &c. 499.

Adv. [IN A SMALL DEGREE] to a small extent, on a small scale; a little, a wee bit; slightly &c. *adj.*; imperceptibly; miserably, wretchedly; insufficiently &c. 640; imperfectly; faintly &c. 160; passably, pretty well, well enough.

[IN A CERTAIN OR LIMITED DEGREE] partially, in part; in a certain degree, to a certain degree; to a certain extent; comparatively; some, rather, middling [*colloq.*]; in some degree, in some measure; something, somewhat; simply, only, purely, merely; at least, at the least, at most, at the most; ever so little, as little as may be, *tant soit peu* [*F.*], in ever so small a degree; thus far, *pro tanto* [*L.*], within bounds, in a manner, after a fashion.

ALMOST, nearly, well-nigh, short of, not quite, all but; near upon, close upon; *peu s'en faut* [*F.*], near the mark; within an ace of, within an inch of; on the brink of; scarcely, hardly, barely, only just, no more than.

[IN AN UNCERTAIN DEGREE] about, thereabouts, somewhere about, nearly, say; be the same more or less, be the same little more or less.

[IN NO DEGREE] noway *or* noways, nowise, not at all, not in the least, not a bit, not a bit of it, not a whit, not a jot, not a shadow; in no wise, in no respect; by no means, by no manner of means; on no account, at no hand.

*** dare pondus idonea fumo** [Persius]; *magno conatu magnas nugas* [Terence]; "small sands the mountain, moments make the year" [Young].

[IN A TOO GREAT DEGREE] immoderately, monstrously, preposterously, inordinately, exorbitantly, excessively, enormously, out of all proportion, with a vengeance.

[IN A MARKED DEGREE] particularly, remarkably, singularly, curiously, uncommonly, unusually, peculiarly, notably, signally, strikingly, pointedly, mainly, chiefly; famously, egregiously, prominently, glaringly, emphatically, strangely, wonderfully, amazingly, surprisingly, astonishingly, incredibly, marvelously, awfully, stupendously.

[IN AN EXCEPTIONAL DEGREE] peculiarly &c. (*unconformity*) 83.

[IN A VIOLENT DEGREE] furiously &c. (*violence*) 173; severely, desperately, tremendously, extravagantly, confoundedly, deucedly [*slang*], devilishly [*colloq.*], with a vengeance, *à outrance* [*F.*], *à toute outrance* [*F.*].

[IN A PAINFUL DEGREE] painfully, sadly, grossly, sorely, bitterly, piteously, grievously, miserably, cruelly, woefully, lamentably, shockingly, frightfully, dreadfully, fearfully, terribly, horribly, distressingly, balefully, dolorously.

. *a maximis ad minima;* "greatness knows itself" [*Henry IV*]; "mightiest powers by deepest calms are fed" [B. Cornwall]; *minimum decet libere cui multum licet* [Seneca]; "some are born great, some achieve greatness, and some have greatness thrust upon them" [*Twelfth Night*]; "with Atlantean shoulders, fit to bear" [Milton].

Quantity by Comparison with a Similar Object

33. Superiority. [Supremacy.] — **N.** superiority, majority, plurality; greatness &c. 31; advantage; pull [*slang*]; preponderance, preponderation; vantage ground, prevalence, partiality; personal superiority; scepter, sovereignty, sovranty [*poetic*]; nobility &c. (*rank*) 875; Triton among the minnows, *primus inter pares* [*L.*], *nulli secundus* [*L.*]; superman, overman; captain; crackajack [*slang, U. S.*].

supremacy, supremeness, supremity [*rare*], primacy, paramountcy, preëminence; lead; maximum, record; crest, climax; culmination &c. (*summit*) 210; transcendence; *ne plus ultra* [*L.*]; lion's share, Benjamin's mess; excess, surplus &c. (*remainder*) 40; redundance &c. 641.

V. be superior &c. *adj.;* exceed, excel, transcend; outdo. outbalance, outweigh, outrank, outrival, out-Herod Herod; pass, surpass, get ahead of; overtop, override, overpass, overbalance, overweigh, overmatch; top, o'ertop, cap, beat, cut out [*colloq.*]; beat hollow [*colloq.*]; outstrip &c. 303; eclipse, throw into the shade, take the shine out of [*colloq.*], put one's nose out of joint [*colloq.*]; have the upper hand, have the whip hand of, have the advantage; turn the scale; play first fiddle &c. (*importance*) 642; preponderate, predominate, prevail; precede, take precedence, come first; come to a head, culminate; beat &c. all others, bear the palm; break the record; take the cake [*slang, U. S.*].

34. Inferiority. — **N.** inferiority, minority, subordinacy [*obs.*], subordinance [*obs.*]; shortcoming, deficiency; minimum; smallness &c. 32; imperfection; subjacency [*rare*]; lower quality, lower worth; meanness, poorness, baseness, shabbiness.

[Personal inferiority] commonalty &c. 876; juniority, subordinacy; subaltern, sub [*colloq.*].

V. be inferior &c. *adj.;* fall short of, come short of; not pass, not come up to; want.

become smaller, render smaller &c. (*decrease*), 36, (*contract*) 195; hide its diminished head, retire into the shade, yield the palm, play second fiddle, take a back seat [*colloq.*], kick the beam.

Adj. inferior, deterior [*rare*], smaller; small &c. 32; minor, less, lesser, deficient, minus, lower, subordinate, secondary, junior, humble; second-rate &c. (*imperfect*) 651; sub-, subaltern.

least, smallest &c. (*see* little, small &c. 193); lowest.

diminished &c. (*decreased*) 36; reduced &c. (*contracted*) 195; unimportant &c. 643.

Adv. less; under the mark, below the mark, under par, below par; at the bottom of the scale, at a low ebb, at a disadvantage; short of, under.

. * weighed in the balance and found wanting; not fit to hold a candle to; thrown into the shade.

become *or* render larger &c. (*increase*) 35, (*expand*) 194.

Adj. superior, greater, major, higher; exceeding &c. *v.;* great &c. 31; distinguished, ultra; vaulting; more than a match for.

supreme, greatest, maximal, maximum, utmost, paramount, preëminent, foremost, crowning, hegemonic [*rare*]; first-rate &c. (*important*) 642, (*excellent*) 648; unrivaled; peerless, matchless; second to none, *sans pareil* [*F.*]; unparagoned, unparalleled, unequaled, unapproached, unsurpassed; superlative, inimitable, *facile princeps* [*L.*], incomparable, sovereign, without parallel, *nulli secundus* [*L.*], *ne plus ultra* [*L.*]; beyond compare, beyond comparison; culminating &c (*topmost*) 210; transcendent, transcendental; *plus royaliste que le Roi* [*F.*].

increased &c. (*added to*) 35; enlarged &c. (*expanded*) 194.

Adv. beyond, more, over; over the mark, above the mark; above par; upwards of, in advance of; over and above; at the top of the scale, at its height.

[IN A SUPERIOR OR SUPREME DEGREE] eminently, egregiously, preëminently, surpassing, prominently, superlatively, supremely, above all, of all things, the most, to crown all, *par excellence* [*F.*], principally, especially, particularly, peculiarly, *a fortiori* [*L.*], even, yea, still more.

. "I shall not look upon his like again" [*Hamlet*]; *deos fortioribus adesse* [Tacitus]; "the doors of opportunity are marked 'push' and 'pull' " [*Cynic's Calendar*]; "Eclipse first and the rest nowhere" [*Annals of Sporting*]; "great men are the true men, the men in whom Nature has succeeded" [Amiel].

CHANGES IN QUANTITY

35. Increase. — N. INCREASE, augmentation, increasement [*rare*], addition, enlargement, extension; dilatation &c. (*expansion*) 194; increment, accretion; accession &c. 37; development, growth; aggrandizement, accumulation, reënforcement, redoubling, intensification, inflation, enhancement, aggravation; rise; ascent &c. 305; exaggeration, exacerbation; spread &c. (*dispersion*) 73; flood tide, spring tide.

GAIN, produce, product, profit, gettings [*archaic*], advantage, booty, plunder, superlucration [*rare*], clean-up [*U. S.*].

V. INCREASE, augment, add to, enlarge; dilate &c. (*expand*) 194; grow, wax, get ahead, gain strength; advance; run up, shoot up; rise; swell, mount, ascend &c. 305; sprout &c. 194.

AGGRANDIZE; raise, exalt; deepen, heighten, lengthen, greaten [*archaic*], thicken; eke [*archaic*], inflate; strengthen, intensify, enhance, magnify, redouble, double, triple, &c.; aggravate, exaggerate; exasperate, exacerbate; add fuel to the flame, *oleum addere camino* [*L.*]; superadd &c. (*add*) 37; spread &c. (*disperse*) 73.

Adj. INCREASED &c. *v.;* on the increase, undiminished; additional &c. (*added*) 37.

INCREASING, growing, crescent, crescive [*rare*], lengthening, multiplying, intensifying, intensive, intensitive [*rare*], incretionary [*rare*]; crescendo.

Adv. crescendo, increasingly.

. *vires acquirit eundo* [Vergil]; "they go from strength to strength" [*Bible*].

36. Nonincrease, Decrease. — N. DECREASE, diminution, decrescence, decrement, diminishment, lessening &c. *v.;* subtraction &c. 38, reduction, rebatement [*rare*], abatement, declension; shrinkage &c. (*contraction*) 195; coarctation [*obs.*]; curtailment, abridgment &c. (*shortening*) 201; extenuation.

SUBSIDENCE, wane, ebb, decline; ebb tide, neap tide, ebbing; descent &c. 306; reflux, depreciation, wear and tear, erosion, consumption; deterioration &c. 659; anticlimax; mitigation &c. (*moderation*) 174; catabasis [*med.*].

V. DECREASE, diminish, lessen; abridge &c. (*shorten*) 201; shrink &c. (*contract*) 195; drop off, fall off, tail off; fall away, waste, wear; wane, ebb, decline; descend &c. 306; subside; melt away, die away; retire into the shade, hide its diminished head, fall to a low ebb, run low, languish, decay, crumble, erode, consume away.

BATE, abate [*archaic*], dequantitate [*obs.*]; discount, belittle, minify [*rare*], minimize, minish [*rare*], depreciate; extenuate, lower, weaken, attenuate, fritter away; mitigate &c. (*moderate*) 174; dwarf, throw into the shade; reduce &c. 195; shorten &c. 201; subtract &c. 38; deliquesce, ease, remit [*rare*].

Adj. UNINCREASED &c. (*see* increase &c. 35); decreased, decreasing &c. *v.;* decrescent, reductive; deliquescent, contractive; decrescendo; on the wane &c. *n.*

Adv. decrescendo, decreasingly.

. "a gilded halo hovering round decay" [Byron]; "fine by degrees and beautifully less" [Prior].

3. Conjunctive Quantity

37. Addition. — N. ADDITION, annexation, adjection [*rare*], junction &c. 43; superposition, superaddition, superjunction, superfetation; accession, reënforcement; increase &c. 35; increment.

AFFIX, codicil, subscript, tag, rider, appendage, continuation, equation, postscript, adjunct, &c. 39; supplement; accompaniment &c. 88; interlineation, interposition &c. 228; insertion &c. 300.

COMPUTATION, footing, totaling, casting, summation.

V. ADD, annex, affix, superadd, subjoin, superpose; clap on, saddle on; tack to, append, tag, adject [*rare*], attach, postfix, adjoin [*rare*], ingraft; saddle with; sprinkle; introduce &c. (*interpose*) 228; insert &c. 300.

COMPUTE, foot up, total, cast, sum, count up.

BECOME ADDED, accrue; supervene, advene.

REËNFORCE or reinforce, restrengthen; strengthen, swell the ranks of; augment &c. 35.

Adj. ADDED &c. *v.;* additional; supplement, supplemental, supplementary; suppletive [*rare*], supervenient [*rare*], suppletory, subjunctive; adjectitious, adscititious, ascititious; additive, extra, further, fresh, more, new, ulterior, other, remanent [*rare*]; auxiliary, contributory, accessory; spare.

Adv. *au reste* [*F.*]; in addition, more, plus, extra; and, also, likewise, too, furthermore, further, item; and also, and eke [*archaic*]; else, besides, to boot; et cætera, &c.; and so on, and so forth; into the bargain, *cum multis aliis* [*L.*], over and above, moreover.

with, withal; including, inclusive, as well as, not to mention, let alone; together with, along with, coupled with, in conjunction with; conjointly; jointly &c. 43.

** *adde parvum parvo magnus acervus erit.*

38. Nonaddition. Deduction. — N. DEDUCTION, subtraction, subduction; retrenchment; removal; sublation [*rare*], ablation; abstraction &c. (*taking*) 789; garbling &c. *v.;* mutilation, detruncation; amputation; recision, abscision, excision; abrasion; curtailment &c. 201.

REBATE &c. (*decrement*) 40a; minuend, subtrahend; decrease &c. 36.

V. SUBDUCT, subtract, deduct, deduce; bate, retrench; remove, withdraw; take from, take away; detract; garble.

MUTILATE, amputate, detruncate; cut off, cut away, cut out; abscind, excise.

PARE, thin, prune, decimate, eliminate, rebate; bant [*colloq.*], reduce; abrade, scrape, file.

GELD, castrate, envirate [*rare*], cut, spay (*female*), capon *or* caponize (*a cock*), eunuchize [*rare*], unman, emasculate.

DIMINISH &c. 36; curtail &c. (*shorten*) 201; deprive of &c. (*take*) 789; weaken.

Adj. SUBTRACTED &c. *v.;* subtractive. TAILLESS, acaudal, acaudate.

Adv. IN DEDUCTION &c. *n.;* less; short of; minus, without, except, excepting, with the exception of, barring, bar, save, exclusive of, save and except, with a reservation, ablatitious [*rare*].

39. [THING ADDED.] Adjunct. — N. ADJUNCT; addition, additament; *additum* [*L.*], affix, appendage, annex *or* annexe; augment, augmentation; increment, reënforcement, supernumerary, accessory, item; garnish, sauce; accompaniment &c. 88; adjective, addendum (*pl.* addenda); complement, supplement; continuation.

rider, offshoot, episode, side issue, corollary, codicil &c. (*addition*) 37.

FLAP, lug, lapel, apron, tab, fly, tuck, lap, piece, lappet, skirt, embroidery,

40. [THING REMAINING.] Remainder. — N. REMAINDER, residue; remains, remanet [*rare*], relict [*rare*], remanence [*rare*], remnant, rest, relic; leavings, heeltap, odds and ends, cheeseparings, candle ends, orts; residuum; dregs &c. (*dirt*) 653; refuse &c. (*useless*) 645; stubble, result, educt; fag-end; ruins, wreck, skeleton, stump, rump; alluvium.

SURPLUS, overplus, excess; balance [*commercial slang*], complement; surplus [*obs. or Scot.*], surplusage; superfluity &c. (*redundance*) 641; survival,

trappings, cortege *or cortège* [*F.*]; tail, suffix &c. (*sequel*) 65; wing.

V. ADD, annex &c. 37.

Adj. ADDITIONAL &c. 37.

WINGED, alate *or* alated.

Adv. in addition &c. 37.

survivance [*rare*]; fossil, shadow, *caput mortuum* [*L.*].

V. REMAIN; be left &c. *adj.;* exceed, survive; leave.

Adj. REMAINING, left; left behind, left over; residual, residuary; over, odd; unconsumed, sedimentary; surviving; net; exceeding, over and above; outlying, outstanding; cast off &c. 782; superfluous &c. (*redundant*) 641.

*** "it is strange that men should see sublime inspiration in the ruins of an old church and see none in the ruins of a man" [Chesterton]. ·

40a. [THING DEDUCTED.] **Decrement.** — **N.** DECREMENT, discount, rebate, rebatement, tare, offtake, drawback, draft, reprise; defect, loss, deduction; afterglow; eduction; waste.

---

41. [FORMING A WHOLE WITHOUT COHERENCE.] **Mixture.** — **N.** MIXTURE, admixture, mixtion [*obs.*], · admixtion, commixture, commixtion *or* commixion [*obs.*], intermixture, immixture, minglement, eucrasy [*med.*], interfusion, intertanglement, interlacement, interlacery, intertexture, levigation, alloyage; matrimony; junction &c. 43; combination &c. 48; miscegenation.

IMPREGNATION; infusion, diffusion, suffusion, transfusion; infiltration; seasoning, sprinkling, interlarding; interpolation &c. 228; adulteration, sophistication.

[THING MIXED] tinge, tincture, touch, dash, smack, sprinkling, spice, seasoning, infusion, *soupçon* [*F.*].

[COMPOUND RESULTING FROM MIXTURE] alloy, amalgam; brass, chowchow, pewter; magma, half-and-half, *mélange*

42. [FREEDOM FROM MIXTURE.] **Simpleness.** — **N.** SIMPLENESS &c. *adj.;* purity, homogeneity.

ELIMINATION; sifting &c. *v.;* purification &c. (*cleanness*) 652.

V. RENDER SIMPLE &c. *adj.;* simplify.

SIFT, winnow, bolt, eliminate; exclude, get rid of; clear; purify &c. (*clean*) 652; disentangle &c. (*disjoin*, 44).

Adj. SIMPLE, uniform, of a piece, homogeneous, Attic, homespun, single, pure, clear, sheer, neat.

UNMIXED, unmingled, unblended, uncombined, uncompounded; elemental, elementary, undecomposed; unadulterated, unsophisticated, unalloyed, untinged, unfortified; *pur et simple* [*F.*]; incomplex, incomposite [*rare*].

free from, exempt from; exclusive.

Adv. SIMPLY &c. *adj.;* only.

[*F.*], *tertium quid* [*L.*], miscellany, ambigu [*obs.*], medley, mess, hash, hodgepodge, hotchpotch, hotchpot, *pasticcio* [*It.*], patchwork, odds and ends, all sorts; jumble &c. (*disorder*) 59; salad, sauce, mash, omnium-gatherum [*colloq.*], gallimaufry, olla-podrida, olio, salmagundi, potpourri, Noah's ark; texture; mingled yarn; mosaic &c. (*variegation*) 440.

HALF-BLOOD, half-breed, half-caste; mulatto; quarteron *or* quarteroon [*rare*], quintroon *or* quinteron, quadroon, octoroon, sambo *or* zambo; cafuzo; Eurasian; fustee *or* fustie [*W. Ind.*], mestee [*W. Ind.*], mestizo (*fem.* mestiza), griffe, ladino, marabou, sacatra [*U. S.*]; zebrule; catalo; mule; cross, hybrid, mongrel; cross-breed &c. (*unconformity*) 83.

V. MIX; join &c. 43; combine &c. 48; commix, immix, intermix; levigate, mix up with, mingle; commingle, intermingle, bemingle; shuffle &c. (*derange*) 61; pound together; hash up, stir up; knead, brew; impregnate with; interlard &c. (*interpolate*) 228; intertwine, interweave &c. 219; associate with; miscegenate.

BE MIXED &c.; get among, be entangled with.

IMBUE; infuse, suffuse, transfuse, instill *or* instil, infiltrate, dash, tinge, tincture, season, sprinkle, besprinkle, attemper, medicate, blend, cross; alloy, amalgamate, compound, adulterate, sophisticate, infect.

Adj. MIXED &c. *v.;* implex [*rare*], composite, half-and-half, linsey-woolsey,

medley, chowchow, hybrid, mongrel, heterogeneous; motley &c. (*variegated*)
440; miscellaneous, promiscuous, indiscriminate; miscible.

Adv. AMONG, amongst, amid, amidst; with; in the midst of, in the crowd.

43. Junction. — N. JUNCTION; joining &c. *v.*; joinder, union; connection, conjunction, conjugation; annexion, annexation, annexment [*rare*]; astriction, attachment, compagination [*rare*], subjunction, vincture [*obs.*], ligation, alligation; accouplement; marriage &c. (*wedlock*) 903; infibulation, inosculation, symphysis, anastomosis, confluence, communication, concatenation; meeting, reunion; assemblage &c. 72.

COITION, copulation; sexual congress, sexual conjunction, sexual intercourse.

JOINT, joining, juncture, chiasm, osculature, pivot, hinge, articulation, commissure, seam, gore, gusset, suture, stitch; link &c. 45; miter, mortise.

CONTINGENCY, emergency, predicament, crisis, concurrence.

CLOSENESS, tightness &c. *adj.*; coherence &c. 46; combination &c. 48.

annexationist.

V. JOIN, unite; conjoin, connect; associate; put together, lay together, clap together, hang together, lump together, hold together, piece together, tack together, fix together, bind up together; embody, reëmbody; roll into one.

ATTACH, fix, affix, immobilize [*rare*], saddle on, fasten, bind, secure, clinch, twist, make fast &c. *adj.*; tie, pinion, string, strap, sew, lace, stitch, tack, knit, button, buckle, hitch, lash, truss, bandage, braid, splice, swathe, gird, tether, moor, picket, harness, chain; fetter &c. (*restrain*) 751; lock, latch, belay, brace, hook, grapple, leash, couple, accouple, link, yoke, bracket; marry &c. (*wed*) 903; bridge over, span.

pin, nail, bolt, hasp, clasp, clamp, screw, rivet; impact, solder, braze; cement, set; weld together, fuse together; tighten, trice up, screw up; wedge, rabbet, mortise, miter, jam, dovetail, enchase; graft, ingraft, inosculate.

ENTWINE *or* intwine; interlink, interlace, intertwine, intertwist, interweave; entangle; twine round, belay.

BE JOINED &c.; hang together, hold together; cohere &c. 46.

Adj. JOINED &c. *v.*; joint; conjoint, conjunct; corporate, compact; hand in hand.

44. Disjunction. — N. DISJUNCTION, disconnection, disunity, disunion, disassociation, disengagement, dissociation, disjointure; discontinuity &c. 70; abjunction [*obs.*]; cataclasm; inconnection [*obs.*]; abstraction, abstractedness; isolation; insularity, insulation; oasis; island; separateness &c. *adj.*; severalty; *disjecta membra* [*L.*]; dispersion &c. 73; apportionment &c. 786.

SEPARATION; parting &c. *v.*; circumcision, detachment, segregation; divorce, sejunction [*obs.*], seposition [*obs.*], diduction [*rare*], diremption [*rare*], discerption; elision; cæsura, division, subdivision, break, fracture, rupture; compartition [*obs.*]; dismemberment, disintegration, dislocation; luxation; severance, disseverance; scission; rescission, abscission; laceration, dilaceration; disruption, abruption; avulsion, divulsion; section, resection, cleavage; fission; partibility, separability, separatism.

FISSURE, breach, rent, split, rift, crack, slit, incision.

DISSECTION, anatomy; decomposition &c. 49; cutting instrument &c. (*sharpness*) 253; buzz saw, circular saw.

separatist.

V. BE DISJOINED &c.; come off, come to pieces, fall off, fall to pieces; peel off; get loose.

DISJOIN, disconnect, disengage, disunite, dissociate, dispair [*obs.*]; divorce, part, dispart, detach, separate, cut off, rescind, segregate; set apart, keep apart; insulate, isolate; throw out of gear; cut adrift; loose; unloose, undo, unbind, unchain, unlock &c. (*fix*) 43, unpack, unravel; disentangle; set free &c. (*liberate*) 750.

SUNDER, divide, subdivide, sever, section, sectionize [*rare*], segment, dissever, abscind; circumcise; cut; incide [*obs.*], incise; saw, snip, nib [*obs.*], nip, cleave, rive, rend, slit, split, splinter, chip, crack, snap, break, tear, burst; rend &c., asunder, rend in twain; wrench, rupture, shatter, shiver, crunch, craunch *or* cranch, chop; cut up, rip up; hack, hew, slash; whittle; haggle, hackle, discind [*obs.*], lacerate, scamble [*obs.*], mangle, gash, hash, slice; cut up, carve,

FIRM, fast, close, tight, taut or taught, secure, set, intervolved [obs.]; insuparable, indissoluble, insecable [obs.], inseverable.

Adv. JOINTLY &c. adj.; in conjunction with &c. (in addition to) 37; fast, firmly, &c. adj.; intimately.

, tria juncta in uno; "in every union there is a mystery — a certain invisible bond which must not be disturbed" [Amiel].

PART, part company; separate, leave; alienate, estrange.

Adj. DISJOINED &c. v.; discontinuous &c. 70; bipartite, biparted [rare], multipartite, abstract; disjunctive; secant; isolated &c. v.; insular, separate, disparate, discrete, apart, asunder, far between, loose, free; lobate, lobulate, lobulated, lobulose, digitate; unattached, unannexed, unassociated, unconnected; distinct; adrift; straggling; rift [obs.], reft, cleft.

[CAPABLE OF BEING CUT] scissile, divisible, discerptible [rare], partible, separable, severable, dividuous [rare].

Adv. SEPARATELY &c. adj.; one by one, severally, apart; adrift, asunder, in twain; in the abstract, abstractedly.

, "separatism . . . is the abstraction of a negation, the shadow of a shadow" [Amiel].

45. [CONNECTING MEDIUM.] **Vinculum. — N.** VINCULUM, link; connective, connection; junction &c. 43; bond of union, copula, intermedium, hyphen; bracket; bridge, stepping-stone, isthmus.

bond, tendon, tendril; fiber; cord, cordage; ribband, ribbon, rope, guy, cable, line, halser [obs.], hawser, painter, moorings, wire, chain; string &c. (filament) 205.

FASTENING, tie; ligament, ligature; strap; tackle, rigging; standing rigging; running rigging; traces, harness; yoke; band, bandage; brace, roller, fillet; inkle; with, withe, withy; thong, braid; girder, tiebeam; girth, girdle, cestus, garter, halter, noose, lasso, surcingle, knot, running knot; cabestro [Sp. Amer.], cinch [U. S.], lariat, legadero [Sp. Amer.], oxreim [S. Africa]; suspenders.

PIN, corking pin, nail, brad, tack, skewer, staple, clamp; cramp, cramp iron, detent, larigo [Sp. Amer.], pawl, terret, screw, button, buckle, clasp, hasp, bar, hinge, hank, catch, latch, bolt, latchet, tag; tooth; hook, hook and eye; lock, holdfast, padlock, rivet, couple, coupler, ring; anchor, grappling iron, treenail or trennel, stake, post; prop &c. (support) 215.

CEMENT, glue, gum, paste, size, wafer, solder, lute, putty, birdlime, mortar, stucco, plaster, grout; viscum.

SHACKLE, rein &c. (means of restraint) 752.

V. BRIDGE OVER, span; connect &c. 43; hang &c. 214.

46. Coherence. — N. COHERENCE, cohesion, cohesiveness, adherence, adhesion, adhesiveness; concretion, accretion; conglutination, conglomeration, agglutination, agglomeration; aggregation; consolidation, set, cementation; sticking, soldering &c. v.; connection; dependence.

TENACITY, toughness; stickiness &c. 352; inseparability, inseparableness; bur or burr, remora.

CONGLOMERATE, concrete &c. (density) 321.

V. COHERE, adhere, coagulate, stick, cling, cleave, hold, take hold of, hold

quarter, dissect, anatomize; dislimb; take to pieces, pull to pieces, pick to pieces, tear to pieces; tear to tatters, tear piecemeal; divellicate; skin &c. 226.

DISINTEGRATE, dismember, disbranch, disband; disperse &c. 73; dislocate, disjoint; break up; mince; comminute &c. (pulverize) 330; apportion &c. 786.

PARTITION, parcel, demarcate [rare], graduate, district, chapter, canton.

47. [NONADHESION, IMMISCIBILITY.] **Incoherence. — N.** INCOHERENCE, nonadhesion; immiscibility; looseness &c. adj.; laxity; relaxation; loosening &c. v.; freedom; disjunction &c. 44; rope of sand.

V. MAKE LOOSE &c. adj.; loosen, slacken, relax; unglue &c. 46; detach &c. (disjoin) 44.

Adj. NONADHESIVE, immiscible; incoherent, detached, loose, baggy, slack, lax, relaxed, flapping, streaming; disheveled; segregated, like grains of sand; unconsolidated &c. 231; uncombined &c. 48; noncohesive.

fast, close with, clasp, hug; grow together, hang together; twine round &c. (*join*) 43.

stick like a leech, stick like wax, stick like the paper on the wall; stick closer than a brother; stick close; cling like ivy, cling like a bur; adhere like a remora, adhere like Dejanira's shirt.

glue; agglutinate, conglutinate; cement, lute, belute [*rare*], paste, gum; solder, weld; ferruminate [*archaic*]; cake, consolidate &c. (*solidify*) 321; agglomerate.

Adj. ADHESIVE, cohesive, adhering, cohering &c. *v.*; tenacious, tough; sticky &c. 352.

united, unseparated, sessile, inseparable, inextricable, infrangible; compact &c. (*dense*) 321.

** "Closer is He than breathing, Nearer than hands or feet" [Tennyson].

48. Combination. — N.

COMBINATION; mixture &c. 41; junction &c. 43; union, unification, synthesis, syniztesis, synæresis *or* syneresis, incorporation, amalgamation, embodiment, coalescence, crasis, fusion, coalescing, blend, blendure [*rare*], blending, absorption, centralization.

ALLOY, compound, amalgam, composition, *tertium quid* [*L.*]; resultant, impregnation.

V. COMBINE, unite, incorporate, inosculate, consubstantiate, alloy, intermix, interfuse, interlard, syncretize, interlace, agglutinate, amalgamate, embody, absorb, reëmbody, blend, merge, fuse, melt into one, consolidate, coalesce, solidify, commix [*archaic*], contemper, centralize, impregnate; put together, lump together.

LEAGUE, interleague [*rare*], federate, confederate, fraternize, club, associate, amalgamate, cement a union, marry, couple, pair, ally.

Adj. COMBINED &c. *v.*; wedded; indiscrete, conjunctive, conjugate, conjoint; inoculated.

49. Decomposition. — N.

DECOMPOSITION, analysis, diæresis *or* dieresis, dissection, resolution, catalysis, dissolution, break-up; dispersion &c. 73; disjunction &c. 44; disintegration.

DECAY, rot, putrefaction, putrescence, putridity, caries; corruption &c. (*uncleanness*) 653.

ELECTROLYSIS, electrolyzation, hydrolysis, proteolysis, thermolysis, catalysis.

V. DECOMPOSE, decompound [*rare*]; analyze, disembody, dissolve; resolve into its elements, separate into its elements; dissect, decentralize, break up; disintegrate, disperse &c. 73; unravel &c. (*unroll*) 313; crumble into dust.

CORRUPT [*archaic*], rot, decay, consume; putrefy, putresce.

ELECTROLYZE, hydrolyze, thermolyze, catalyze.

Adj. DECOMPOSED &c. *v.*; catalytic, analytical; resolvent, separative, solvent.

impregnated with, ingrained; imbued, inoculated.

ALLIED, amalgamated, federate, confederate, corporate, leagued.

** "and our spirits rushed together at the touching of the lips" [Tennyson].

4. CONCRETE QUANTITY

50. Whole. [PRINCIPAL PART.] — N.

WHOLE, totality, integrity; totalness &c. *adj.*; entirety, entire [*rare*], ensemble [*F.*], collectiveness; unity &c. 87; completeness &c. 52; indivisibility, indiscerptibility; integration, embodiment; integer, integral.

ALL, general [*archaic*], the whole, total, aggregate, one and all, gross amount, sum, sum total, the altogether [*humorous*], *tout ensemble* [*F.*], length and breadth of, Alpha and Omega, "be all

51. Part. — N.

PART, portion; dose, item, particular; aught, any; division; ward, parcel [*law or archaic*], count; sector, segment; fraction, fragment; cantle, cantlet; frustum [*rare*]; detachment, subdivision.

section, chapter, verse; article, clause, phrase, paragraph, passage, number, book, fascicle, fascicule *or* fasciculus, *livraison* [*F.*].

PIECE, lump, bit, snatch; cut, cutting; chip, chunk, collop, slice, scrap, crumb,

and end all"; complex, *complexus* [*L.*]; lock, stock, and barrel.

BULK, mass, lump, tissue, staple, body, compages; trunk, torso, bole, hull, hulk, skeleton; greater part, major part, best part, principal part, main part; essential part &c. (*importance*) 642; lion's share, Benjamin's mess; the long and the short; nearly all, almost all.

V. FORM A WHOLE, constitute a whole; integrate, embody, amass; aggregate &c. (*assemble*) 72; amount to, come to.

Adj. WHOLE, total, integral [*rare*], integrate [*rare*], entire; complete &c. 52; one, individual.

UNBROKEN, uncut, undivided, unsevered, unclipped, uncropped, unshorn; seamless; undiminished; undemolished, undissolved, undestroyed, unbruised.

INDIVISIBLE, indissoluble, indissolvable, indiscerptible.

WHOLESALE, sweeping; comprehensive.

Adv. WHOLLY, altogether; as a whole, one and indivisible; totally &c. (*completely*) 52; entirely, all, all in all, wholesale, in a body, collectively, all put together; in the aggregate, in the lump, in the mass, in the gross, in the main, in the long run; *en masse* [*F.*], on the whole, bodily, *en bloc* [*F.*], *in extenso* [*L.*], throughout, every inch; substantially.

⁎⁎* *tout bien ou rien;* "I am the Vine, ye are the branches" [*Bible*].

---

52. Completeness. — N. COMPLETENESS &c. *adj.;* completion &c. 729; integration; allness [*rare*], totality, integralness, totalness, integrality [*rare*], integrity.

ENTIRETY; perfection &c. 650; solidity, solidarity; unity; all; *ne plus ultra* [*L.*], ideal, limit; undividedness, intactness, universality.

COMPLEMENT, supplement, makeweight; filling up &c. *v.*

FILL; impletion; saturation, saturity [*obs.*]; high water; high tide, flood tide, springtide; load, bumper, bellyful; brimmer; sufficiency &c. 639.

V. BE COMPLETE &c. *adj.;* come to a head.

RENDER COMPLETE &c. *adj.;* complete &c. (*accomplish*) 729; fill, charge, load, stevedore, replenish; make up, make good; piece out, eke out; supply deficien-

scale; lamina &c. 204; small part; morsel, moiety, particle &c. (*smallness*) 32; installment, dividend; share &c. (*allotment*) 786.

ODDMENTS, *débris* [*F.*], odds and ends, detritus; *excerpta* [*L.*], excerpt.

MEMBER, limb, lobe, lobule, arm, wing, scion, branch, bough, joint, link, offshoot, ramification, twig, bush, spray, sprig; runner, tendril; leaf, leaflet; stump; component part &c. 56; sarmentum.

CUE, rôle, cast; lines, pageant [*archaic*].

COMPARTMENT; department &c. (*class*) 75; county &c. (*region*) 181.

V. PART, divide, break &c. (*disjoin*) 44; partition &c. (*apportion*) 786.

Adj. FRACTIONAL, fragmentary, portional [*rare*]; sectional, aliquot; divided &c. *v.;* in compartments, multifid; disconnected; incomplete, partial.

DIVIDED, broken, cut, severed, clipped, cropped, shorn; seamed.

DIVISIBLE, dissoluble, dissolvable, discerptible.

Adv. PARTLY, in part, partially; piecemeal, part by part; by installments, by snatches, by inches, by driblets; bit by bit, inch by inch, foot by foot, drop by drop; in detail, in lots.

⁎⁎* "a snapper-up of unconsidered trifles" [*Winter's Tale*].

---

53. Incompleteness. — N. INCOMPLETENESS &c. *adj.;* deficience [*rare*], deficiency, short weight, short measure; shortcoming &c. 304; want, lack, insufficiency &c. 640; imperfection &c. 651; immaturity &c. (*nonpreparation*) 674; half measures.

[PART WANTING] defect, deficit, defalcation, omission; caret; wantage [*rare*], ullage, shortage; interval &c. 198; break &c. (*discontinuity*) 70; noncompletion &c. 730; missing link.

V. BE INCOMPLETE &c. *adj.;* fall short of &c. 304; lack &c. (*be insufficient*) 640; neglect &c. 460.

Adj. INCOMPLETE; imperfect &c. 651; unfinished; uncompleted &c. (*see* complete &c. 729); defective, deficient, wanting, failing; bobtailed; in default, in arrear; short, short of; hollow, meager, jejune, poor, scarce, lame, half-and-half,

22

cies; fill up, fill in, fill to the brim, fill the measure of; satiate; saturate.

go the whole hog [*colloq.*], go the whole length; go all lengths; go the limit [*colloq.*].

Adj. COMPLETE, entire; whole &c. 50; perfect &c. 650; full, good, absolute, thorough, plenary; solid, undivided; with all its parts; all-sided.

EXHAUSTIVE, radical, sweeping, thorough-going; dead.

REGULAR, consummate, unmitigated, sheer, unqualified, unconditional, free; abundant &c. (*sufficient*) 639.

BRIMMING; brimful, topful; chock-full, choke-full; as full as an egg is of meat, as full as a vetch; saturated, crammed; replete &c. (*redundant*) 641; fraught, laden; full-laden, full-fraught, full-charged; heavy laden.

COMPLETING &c. *v.*; supplemental, supplementary; ascititious.

Adv. COMPLETELY &c. *adj.*; altogether, outright, wholly, totally, *in toto* [*L.*], quite; all out; over head and ears; effectually, for good and all, nicely, fully, through thick and thin, head and shoulders, out of sight [*slang, U. S.*]; neck and heel, neck and crop; in all respects, in every respect; at all points, out and out, to all intents and purposes; *toto cælo* [*L.*]; utterly; clean, clean as a whistle; to the full, to the utmost, to the limit, to the backbone; hollow, stark; heart and soul, root and branch, down to the ground.

to the top of one's bent, as far as possible, *à outrance* [*F.*].

THROUGHOUT; from first to last, from beginning to end, from end to end, from one end to the other, from Dan to Beersheba, from head to foot, from top to toe, from top to bottom; *de fond en comble* [*F.*]; *à fond* [*F.*]; *a capite ad calcem* [*L.*]; *ab ovo usque ad mala* [*L.*]; fore and aft; every whit, every inch; *cap-à-pie* [*F.*], to the end of the chapter; up to the brim, up to the ears, up to the eyes; as . . . as can be.

on all accounts; *sous tous les rapports* [*F.*]; with a vengeance, with a witness [*colloq.*].

⁎⁎ *falsus in uno falsus in omnibus; omnem movere lapidem; una scopa nuova spazza bene.*

perfunctory, sketchy; crude &c. (*unprepared*) 674.

MUTILATED, garbled, hashed, mangled, butchered, docked, lopped, truncated.

IN PROGRESS, in hand; going on, proceeding.

Adv. INCOMPLETELY &c. *adj.*; by halves.

⁎⁎ *cætera desunt; caret;* "And I smiled to think God's greatness Flowed around our incompleteness" [E. B. Browning].

---

54. Composition. — **N.** COMPOSITION, constitution; crasis, synizesis, synæresis *or* syneresis; confection [*rare*], synthesis, compaction [*rare*], make, make-up; combination &c. 48; inclusion, admission, comprehension, reception; embodiment; formation.

AUTHORSHIP, compilation, composition, *recueil* [*F.*], production, inditing *or* inditement, conflation, invention; writing &c. 590.

HYMNODY, hymnology, instrumentation; opus, aria &c. (*music*) 415.

PAINTING, scenography, etching, design &c. (*painting*) 556; relief, relievo &c. (*sculpture*) 557.

TYPESETTING, typography &c. (*printing*) 591.

V. BE COMPOSED OF, be made of, be formed of, be made up of; consist of, be resolved into.

INCLUDE &c. (*in a class*) 76; contain,

55. Exclusion. — **N.** EXCLUSION, nonadmission, omission, exception, rejection, repudiation; exile &c. (*seclusion*) 893; noninclusion, preclusion, debarrance [*rare*], debarment, lock-out, disfellowship [*rare*], ostracism, prohibition.

SEPARATION, segregation, seposition [*obs.*], elimination, expulsion; cofferdam.

V. be excluded from &c.

EXCLUDE, bar; leave out, shut out, bar out; reject, repudiate, blackball, ostracize; lay apart, lay aside, put apart, put aside, set apart, set aside; relegate, segregate; throw overboard; strike off, strike out; neglect &c. 460; banish &c. (*seclude*) 893; separate &c. (*disjoin*) 44.

pass over, omit; garble; eliminate, weed, winnow.

Adj. EXCLUDING &c. *v.*; exclusive, exclusory; excluded &c. *v.*; unrecounted, not included in; inadmissible, preclusive, preventive, prohibitive.

hold, comprehend take in, admit, embrace, embody; involve, implicate; drag into; synthesize.

COMPOSE, constitute, form, make; make up, fill up, build up; fabricate, weave, construct; compile, redact, collate, dash off, address, indite, score, scribble, draw, write; set (*in printing*); enter into the composition of &c. (*be a component*) 56.

Adj. containing, constituting &c. *v.*

Adv. exclusive of, barring; except; with the exception of; save; bating.

56. Component. — N. COMPONENT, integrant; component part, integral part, integrant part; element, constituent, ingredient, leaven; part and parcel; contents; appurtenance; feature; member &c. (*part*) 51; personnel.

V. ENTER INTO, enter into the composition of; be a component &c. *n.;* be *or* form part of &c. 51; merge in, be merged in; be implicated in; share in &c. (*participate*) 778; belong to, appertain to; combine, inhere in, unite.

FORM, make, constitute, compose, precompose, recompose; sonnetize [*rare*]; fabricate &c. 54.

Adj. FORMING &c. *v.;* inherent, intrinsic, essential.

INCLUSIVE, all-embracing, compendious, comprehensive, inclusory.

57. Extraneousness. — N. EXTRANEOUSNESS &c. *adj.;* extrinsicality &c. 6; exteriority &c. 220; alienage, alienism.

foreign body, foreign substance, foreign element.

ALIEN, stranger, intruder, interloper, foreigner, *novus homo* [*L.*], newcomer, new chum [*colloq., Australia*], jackaroo [*Australia*], griffin [*Anglo-Ind.*]; recruit, immigrant, emigrant; creole, Africander; outsider, outlander [*archaic*], barbarian, extern [*rare*], tramontane [*rare*], ultramontane; Guinea [*slang, U. S.*], Wop [*slang, U. S.*], Dago [*slang*], Chink [*slang*], kiˈke [*slang*], sheeny [*slang*], mick [*slang*], nigger [*colloq.*], Easterner [*U. S.*], Dutchman, tenderfoot [*slang*].

Adj. EXTRANEOUS, foreign, alien, ulterior, exterior, external, outlandish, outside, outland [*archaic*]; barbaric, barbarian, metic, oversea, tramontane [*rare*], ultramontane.

EXCLUDED &c. 55; inadmissible; exceptional.

Adv. ABROAD, in foreign parts, in foreign lands; beyond seas; oversea, overseas; on one's travels.

SECTION IV. ORDER

1. ORDER IN GENERAL

58. Order. — N. ORDER, regularity, uniformity, symmetry, *lucidus ordo* [*L.*]; harmony, music of the spheres.

GRADATION, progression; series &c. (*continuity*) 69.

COURSE, even tenor, routine; method, disposition, arrangement, array, system, economy, discipline; orderliness &c. *adj.;* subordination.

RANK, place &c. (*term*) 71.

V. FORM; be *or* become in order &c. *adj.;* fall in, draw up; arrange itself, range itself, place itself; fall into one's place, fall into rank, take one's place, take rank; rally round.

ADJUST, methodize, regulate, systematize, standardize, normalize; time, police.

Adj. ORDERLY, regular; in order, in

59. [ABSENCE OR WANT OF ORDER, &c.] Disorder. — N. DISORDER; derangement &c. 61; irregularity; deray [*archaic*], deordination [*rare*]; anomaly &c. (*unconformity*) 83; anarchy, anarchism; want of method; untidiness &c. *adj.;* disunion; discord &c. 24.

CONFUSION; confusedness &c. *adj.;* mishmash, mix; disarray, jumble, topsy-turvy, botch, huddle, litter, lumber; *cahotage* [*F.*]; farrago; mess, mash, muddle, muss [*colloq., U. S.*], hash, hodgepodge, hotchpotch, hotchpot; what the cat brought in [*colloq., U. S.*]; imbroglio, chaos, omnium-gatherum [*colloq.*], medley; mere mixture &c. 41; fortuitous concourse of atoms, *disjecta membra* [*L.*], *rudis indigestaque moles* [Ovid].

24

trim, in apple-pie order, in its proper place; neat, tidy, *en règle* [*F.*], well regulated, correct, methodical, uniform, symmetrical, shipshape, businesslike, systematic, systematical, normal, habitual; unconfused &c. (*see* confuse &c. 61); arranged &c. 60.

Adv. IN ORDER; methodically &c. *adj.*; in turn, in its turn; step by step; by regular steps, by regular gradations, by regular stages, by regular intervals; *seriatim* [*NL.*], systematically, by clockwork, gradatim; at stated periods &c. (*periodically*) 138.

⁎ *natura non facit saltum;* "order is heaven's first law" [Pope]; "order from disorder sprung" [*Paradise Lost*]; *ordo est parium dispariumque rerum sua loca tribuens dispositio* [St. Augustine].

COMPLEXITY; complexness &c. *adj.*; complexus, complication, implication; intricacy, intrication [*rare*]; perplexity; network, maze, labyrinth; wilderness, jungle; involution, raveling, entanglement, dishevelment; coil &c. (*convolution*) 248; sleave, tangled skein, knot, Gordian knot, wheels within wheels; kink, gnarl *or* knarl [*obs.*]; webwork.

TURMOIL; ferment &c. (*agitation*) 315; to-do [*colloq.*], trouble, pudder [*obs. or dial.*], pother, row [*colloq.*], disturbance, convulsion, tumult, uproar, riot, rumpus [*colloq.*], stour [*archaic*], scramble, fracas, embroilment, *mêlée* [*F.*], spill and pelt, rough and tumble; whirlwind &c. 349; bear garden, pandemonium, Babel, Saturnalia, Donnybrook Fair, confusion worse confounded, most admired disorder, *concordia discors* [*L.*]; Bedlam broke loose, hell broke loose; bull in a china shop; all the fat in the fire, *diable à quatre* [*F.*], Devil to pay; pretty kettle of fish; pretty piece of work, pretty piece of business.

SLATTERN, slut, drab, dowdy, trollop, sloven, draggle-tail [*colloq.*].

V. BE DISORDERLY &c. *adj.*; ferment, play at cross-purposes.

PUT OUT OF ORDER; botch, derange &c. 61; drag from under the bed [*colloq.*, *U. S.*]; ravel &c. 219; ruffle, rumple.

Adj. DISORDERLY, orderless; out of order, out of place, out of gear, out of kilter [*colloq.*]; irregular, desultory; anomalous &c. (*unconformable*) 83; acephalous; aimless; disorganized; straggling; unmethodical, immethodical; unsymmetric, unsystematic; untidy, slovenly, messy [*colloq.*], hugger-mugger, dislocated; out of sorts; promiscuous, indiscriminate; chaotic, anarchic, anarchical; unarranged &c. (*see* arrange &c. 60); confused; deranged &c. 61; topsy-turvy &c. (*inverted*) 218; shapeless &c. 241; disjointed, out of joint; gnarled *or* knarled [*obs.*].

COMPLEX, complexed; intricate, complicated, perplexed, involved, raveled, entangled, knotted, tangled, inextricable; irreducible.

TROUBLOUS, tumultuous, turbulent; riotous &c. (*violent*) 173.

Adv. IRREGULARLY &c. *adj.*; by fits, by fits and snatches, by fits and starts; pellmell; higgledy-piggledy; helter-skelter [*colloq.*], harum-scarum [*colloq.*]; in a ferment; at sixes and sevens, at cross-purposes; upside down &c. 218.

⁎ the cart before the horse; chaos is come again; "the earth was without form and void" [*Bible*]; "the wrecks of matter and the crush of worlds" [Addison].

60. [REDUCTION TO ORDER.] **Arrangement. — N.** ARRANGEMENT; plan &c. 626; preparation &c. 673; disposal, disposition, disposure; collocation, allocation; distribution; sorting &c. *v.*; assortment, allotment, apportionment, taxis, taxonomy, syntaxis, graduation, organization, ordination, grouping, groupage.

ANALYSIS, classification, division, systematization, categorization, codification, digestion.

[RESULT OF ARRANGEMENT] orderliness, form, lay, array, digest; synopsis &c. (*compendium*) 596, syntagma, table,

61. [SUBVERSION OF ORDER; BRINGING INTO DISORDER.] **Derangement.— N.** DERANGEMENT &c. *v.*; muss [*colloq.*] *U. S.*], mess, touse [*colloq.*], disorder &c. 59; evection, discomposure, disturbance; disorganization, deorganization; dislocation; perturbation [*rare*], interruption; shuffling &c. *v.*; inversion &c. 218; corrugation &c. (*fold*) 258; involvement; insanity &c. 503.

V. DERANGE; misarrange, disarrange, displace, misplace; mislay, discompose, disorder; disorganize; embroil, unsettle, disturb, confuse, trouble, perturb, jumble, tumble; huddle, shuffle, mud-

atlas; register &c. (*record*) 551; cosmos, schematism, organism, architecture; instrumentation, orchestration, score &c. (*music*) 415; stipulation, settlement, *bandobast* or *bundobust* [*Anglo-Ind.*].

[INSTRUMENT FOR SORTING] sieve, riddle, screen, bolter, colander, grate, grating.

FILE, card index.

V. REDUCE TO ORDER, bring into order; introduce order into; rally.

ARRANGE, dispose, place, form; put in order, set in order, place in order; put out, collocate, allocate, compose, space, range, pack, marshal, array, size, rank, group, parcel out, allot, distribute, deal; cast the parts, assign the parts; dispose of, assign places to; assort, sort; sift, riddle; put to rights, put into shape, put in trim, put in array, set to rights,

dle, toss, hustle, fumble, riot; bring into disorder, put into disorder, throw into disorder &c. 59; muss [*colloq., U. S.*], mess, touse [*obs. or dial.*]; break the ranks, disconcert, convulse; break in upon.

UNHINGE, dislocate, put out of joint, throw out of gear.

TURN TOPSY-TURVY &c. (*invert*) 218; bedevil; complicate, involve, perplex, confound; embrangle *or* imbrangle, tangle, entangle, ravel, tousle [*colloq.*], dishevel, ruffle; rumple &c. (*fold*) 258; dement, become insane &c. 503.

LITTER, scatter; mix &c. 41.

Adj. DERANGED &c. *v.;* syncretic, syncretistic; mussy [*colloq., U. S.*].

*** "a nice derangement of epitaphs" [Sheridan].

set into shape, set in trim, set in array; tidy [*colloq.*]; apportion.

CLASS, classify; divide; file, list, string together, thread; register &c. (*record*) 551; catalogue, tabulate, index, alphabetize, graduate, grade, codify; orchestrate, score, harmonize.

METHODIZE, regulate, systematize, coördinate, organize, brigade, echelon, seriate [*rare*], settle, fix.

UNRAVEL, disentangle, unweave, ravel, card; disembroil; feaze.

Adj. ARRANGE &c. *v.;* embattled, in battle array; cut and dried; methodical, orderly, regular, systematic, on file; tabular, tabulate.

2. CONSECUTIVE ORDER

62. Precedence. — N. PRECEDENCE; predecession [*rare*]; coming before &c. *v.;* the lead, *le pas* [*F.*]; superiority &c. 33; importance &c. 642; premise *or* premiss; antecedence *or* antecedency; anteriority &c. (*front*) 234; precursor &c. 64; priority &c. 116; precession [*rare*] &c. 280; anteposition; epacme; preference.

PREFIX, prefixture [*rare*], prelude, affix, preamble, overture, ritornel, *ritornello* [*It.*], voluntary.

V. PRECEDE, forerun, forego [*archaic*], prevene [*rare*]; come before, come first; head, lead, take the lead; lead the way, lead the dance; introduce, prologize [*rare*], usher in; have the *pas* [*F.*]; set the fashion &c. (*influence*) 175; open the ball, lead the cotillion [*U. S.*], lead the german [*U. S.*]; rank, outrank; take precedence, have precedence; have the start &c. (*get before*) 280.

PLACE BEFORE; prefix; premise, prelude, preface; affix.

Adj. PRECEDING &c. *v.;* precedent, antecedent; anterior; prior &c. 116;

63. Sequence. — N. SEQUENCE, train, coming after; pursuance, going after &c. (*following*) 281; consecution, succession; posteriority &c. 117.

CONTINUATION, prolongation; mantle of Elijah; order of succession; successiveness; paracme.

SECONDARINESS; subordinancy [*obs.*], subordinacy &c. (*inferiority*) 34.

AFTERBIRTH, afterburden, afterclap, aftercrop, afterglow, aftergrass, aftermath, afterpain, afterpiece, aftertaste; placenta, secundines; sequelæ.

V. SUCCEED; come after, come on, come next; follow, ensue, step into the shoes of; alternate.

FOLLOW, tag [*colloq.*], heel, dog, dodge, shadow, hound, bedog, hunt; trace, retrace.

PLACE AFTER, suffix, append, subjoin.

Adj. SUCCEEDING &c. *v.;* sequent; subsequent, consequent; sequacious, proximate, next; consecutive &c. (*continuity*) 69; alternate, amœbean.

before; former, foregoing; before mentioned, above mentioned, aforementioned; aforesaid, said; precursory, precursive; prevenient, preliminary, prefatory, introductory; prelusive, prelusory;
Adv. BEFORE; in advance &c. (*precession*) 280.

LATTER; posterior &c. 117.
    Adv. AFTER, subsequently; behind &c.
(*rear*) 235.

proemial, preparatory.

* *seniores priores; prior tempore prior jure.*

---

64. Precursor. — N.

PRECURSOR, antecedent, precedent, predecessor; forerunner, apparitor, vancourier [*obs.*]; pioneer, prodrome [*obs.*], prodromos [*Gr.*
πρόδρομος], prodromus [*rare*], outrider;
leader, bellwether; herald, harbinger;
dawn; bellmare, *avant-coureur* [*F.*], avant-
courier, *avant-courrier* [*F.*], forelooper *or*
foreloper *or* forelouper [*S. Afr.*], *voorlooper* [*Dutch*], *voortrekker* [*Dutch*].

PRELUDE, preamble, preface, prologue, foreword, *avant-propos* [*F.*], protasis, proemium, prolusion [*rare*], proem,
prolepsis, prolegomena, prefix, exordium, introduction; heading, frontispiece, groundwork; preparation &c.

65. Sequel. — N.

SEQUEL, suffix, suc-
cessor; tail, queue, train, wake, trail,
rear; retinue, suite; appendix, postscript, subscript, postlude, conclusion,
epilogue; peroration; codicil; continuation, sequela [*pl.* sequelæ]; appendage;
tailpiece, heelpiece; tag, more last
words; colophon.

FOLLOWER, successor, sectary, heeler
[*slang*], pursuer, adherent, partisan, disciple, client; sycophant, parasite.

AFTERCOME [*Scot.*], aftergrowth, after-
part, afterpiece, after course, after-
game, afterthought; *arrière pensée* [*F.*],
second thoughts; outgrowth.

673; overture, voluntary, ritornel, *ritornello* [*It.*], descant, symphony; premises.
    PREFIGUREMENT &c. 511; omen &c. 512.
    Adj. PRECURSORY; prelusive, prelusory, preludious; proemial [*rare*], intro-
ductory, preludial, prefatory, prodromous [*rare*], inaugural, preliminary;
precedent &c. (*prior*) 116.
    * "a precedent embalms a principle" [Disraeli].

---

66. Beginning. — N.

BEGINNING, incunabula [*pl.*], commencement, opening, outset, incipience, incipiency, inception, inchoation, inchoacy [*rare*]; introduction &c. (*precursor*) 64; alpha,
initial; inauguration, ingress [*archaic*],
début [*F.*], *le premier pas* [*F.*], embarkation, rising of tne curtain; curtain-
raiser, maiden speech; exordium; outbreak, onset, brunt; initiative, move,
first move; prelude, prime, proem,
gambit; narrow *or* thin end of the wedge,
fresh start, new departure.

first stage, first blush, first glance,
first impression, first sight.

ORIGIN &c. (*cause*) 153; source, rise;
bud, germ &c. 153; egg, embryo, rudiment; genesis, birth, nativity, cradle,
infancy; forefront, outstart, start, starting point &c. 293; dawn &c. (*morning*)
125.

HEAD, heading; title-page; van &c.
(*front*) 234; caption, *fatihah* [*Ar.*].

ENTRANCE, entry; inlet, orifice, mouth,
chops, lips, porch, portal, portico, propy-

67. End. — N.

END, close, termina-
tion; desinence [*rare*], conclusion, finis,
finale, period, term, terminus, last,
omega; extreme, extremity; gable end,
butt end, fag-end; tip, nib, point; tail &c.
(*rear*) 235; verge &c. (*edge*) 231; tag,
peroration, appendix, epilogue; bottom
dollar [*colloq.*], bitter end, tail end
[*colloq.*], terminal, apodosis.

CONSUMMATION, *dénouement* [*F.*]; finish &c. (*completion*) 729; fate; doom,
doomsday; crack of doom, day of Judgment, fall of the curtain; goal, destination; limit, stoppage, end-all, wind-up
[*colloq.*]; determination; expiration, ex-
piry; dissolution, death &c. 360; end of
all things; finality; eschatology.

BREAK UP, *commencement de la fin*
[*F.*], last stage, evening (*of life*); turning
point; *coup de grâce* [*F.*], deathblow;
knock-out, knock-out blow; sockdolager
[*slang, U. S.*], K. O. [*slang*].

V. END, close, finish, terminate, conclude, be all over; expire; die &c. 360;
come to a close, draw to a close &c. *n.*;

lon, door; gate, gateway; postern, wicket, threshold, vestibule; propylæum; skirts, border &c. (*edge*) 231; tee.

RUDIMENTS, elements, principia, outlines, grammar, protasis, alphabet, ABC.

V. BEGIN, commence, inchoate, rise, arise, originate, conceive, initiate, open, start, gin [*archaic*], dawn, set in, take its rise, enter upon, enter; set out &c. (*depart*) 293; embark in; incept [*rare*], institute.

USHER IN; lead off, lead the way, take the lead, take the initiative; inaugurate, auspicate, head; stand at the head, stand first, stand for; lay the foundations &c. (*prepare*) 673; found &c. (*cause*) 153; set up, set on foot, set agoing, set abroach, set the ball in motion; apply the match to a train; launch, broach; open up, open the door to; set about, set to work; make a beginning, make a start; handsel; take the first step, lay the first stone, cut the first turf; break ground, break the ice, break cover; pass the Rubicon, cross the Rubicon; open fire, open the ball; ventilate, air; undertake &c. 676.

perorate; have run its course; run out, pass away.

BRING TO AN END &c. *n.;* put an end to, make an end of; determine; get through; achieve &c. (*complete*) 729; stop &c. (*make to cease*) 142; shut up shop; hang up the fiddle [*colloq.*].

Adj. ENDING &c. *v.;* final, terminal, terminative [*rare*], conclusive, conclusory, determinative, definitive; crowning &c. (*completing*) 729; last, ultimate; hindermost; rear &c. 235; caudal; vergent [*rare*].

conterminate [*obs.*], conterminous, conterminable [*rare*].

ENDED &c. *v.;* at an end; settled, decided, over, played out, set at rest; conclusive.

penultimate; last but one, last but two, &c.

Adv. FINALLY &c. *adj.;* in fine; at the last; once for all.

₊ "as high as Heaven and as deep as hell" [Beaumont and Fletcher]; *deficit omne quod nascitur* [Quintilian]; *en toute chose il faut considérer la fin; finem respice; ultimus Romanorum.*

come into existence, come into the world; make one's *début* [*F.*], take birth; burst forth, break out; spring up, crop up.

RECOMMENCE; begin at the beginning, begin *ab ovo* [*L.*], begin again, begin *de novo* [*L.*]; start afresh, make a fresh start, shuffle the cards, resume.

Adj. BEGINNING &c. *v.;* initial, initiatory, initiative; inceptive, introductory, incipient; proemial [*rare*], inaugural, inauguratory; inchoate, inchoative [*rare*]; embryonic, rudimentary, rudimental; primal, primary, prime, premier [*rare*], primigenial, primigenious *or* primigenous, primogenial; primeval &c. (*old*) 124; aboriginal; natal, nascent.

FIRST, foremost, front, head, leading; maiden.

BEGUN &c. *v.;* just begun &c. *v.*

Adv. at *or* in the beginning &c. *n.;* first, in the first place, *imprimis* [*L.*], first and foremost; *in limine* [*L.*]; in the bud, in embryo, in its infancy; from the beginning, from its birth; *ab initio* [*L.*], *ab ovo* [*L.*], *ab incunabilis* [*L.*], *ab origine* [*L.*]; formerly, erst [*archaic*].

₊ *aller Anfang ist schwer; dimidium facti qui cœpit habet* [Cicero]; *omnium rerum principia parva sunt* [Cicero]; *il n'y a que le premier pas qui coûte.*

68. Middle.— N. MIDDLE, midst, mid [*rare*], thick, midmost, middlemost, [*rare*], mediety [*obs.*]; mean &c. 29; medium, middle term; center &c. 222, mid-course &c. 628; *mezzo termine* [*It.*], *mezzo cammin* [*It.*]; *juste milieu* [*F.*] &c. 628; halfway house, nave, navel, omphalos; nucleus, nucleolus.

EQUIDISTANCE- bisection, half distance; equator, diaphragm, midriff; interjacence &c. 228.

Adj. MIDDLE, medial, mesial, mesian, mean, mid, middlemost, midmost, midway [*rare*], midship, mediate [*rare*]; intermediate &c. (*interjacent*) 228; equidistant; central &c. 222; mediterranean, equatorial; homocentric.

Adv. MIDWAY, halfway; in the middle; midships, amidships, *in medias res* [*L.*] *meden agan* [*Gr.* μηδὲν ἄγαν.]

69. [Uninterrupted sequence.] **Continuity.** — **N.** continuity, continuousness, unbrokenness; consecution, consecutiveness &c. *adj.;* succession, round, suite, progression, series, train, catena, chain; catenation, concatenation; scale; gradation, course; ceaselessness, constant flow, unbroken extent; perpetuity.

procession, column; retinue, *cortège* [*F.*], cavalcade, parade; funeral, ovation, triumph; rank and file, line of battle, array.

pedigree, genealogy, lineage, history, tree, race; ancestry, descent, family, house; line, line of ancestors; strain.

rank, file, line, row, range, tier, string, thread, team; suit; colonnade.

V. form a series &c. *n.;* fall in; follow in a series &c. *n.*

arrange in a series &c. *n.;* string together, file, list, thread, graduate, tabulate.

Adj. continuous, continued; consecutive; progressive, gradual; serial, successive; immediate, unbroken, entire; linear; in a line, in a row &c. *n.;* uninterrupted, unintermitting; unremitting; perennial, evergreen; constant.

Adv. continuously &c. *adj.; seriatim* [*NL.*]; in a line &c. *n.;* in succession, in turn; running, gradually, step by step, gradatim, at a stretch; in file, in column, in single file, in Indian file.

*** "what! will the line stretch out to th' crack of doom?" [*Macbeth.*]

70. [Interrupted sequence.] **Discontinuity.** — **N.** discontinuity, discontinuousness, discreteness, disconnectedness; disjunction [*rare*] &c. 44; anacoluthon; interruption, break, fracture, flaw, fault, crack, cut; gap &c. (*interval*) 198; solution of continuity, cæsura; broken thread; parenthesis, episode, rhapsody, crazy quilt [*colloq.*], patchwork; intermission; alternation &c. (*periodicity*) 138; dropping fire.

V. be discontinuous &c. *adj.;* alternate, intermit.

discontinue, pause, interrupt; intervene; break, break in upon, break off; interpose &c. 228; break the thread, snap the thread; disconnect &c. (*disjoin*) 44; dissever.

Adj. discontinuous, unsuccessive, disconnected, broken, interrupted, *décousu* [*F.*]; disconnected, unconnected; discrete, disjunct [*rare*], disjunctive; fitful &c. (*irregular*) 139; spasmodic, desultory; intermitting &c. *v.*, intermittent; alternate; recurrent &c. (*periodic*) 138.

Adv. at intervals; by snatches, by jerks, by skips, by catches, by fits and starts; skippingly, *per saltum* [*L.*]; *longo intervallo* [*L.*].

*** like "angel visits, few and far between" [Campbell]; "it struggles and howls at fits" [Shelley].

71. Term. — **N.** term, rank, station, stage, step; degree &c. 26; scale, remove, grade, link, peg, round of the ladder, status, state, position, place, point, mark, *pas* [*F.*], period, pitch; stand, standing; footing, range.

V. hold a place, occupy a place, find a place, fall into a place &c. *n.;* rank.

3. Collective Order

72. Assemblage. — **N.** assemblage; collection, collocation, colligation; compilation, levy, gathering, ingathering, mobilization, meet, forgathering, muster, *attroupement* [*F.*]; team; concourse, conflux, congregation, contesseration [*obs.*], convergence &c. 290.

meeting, levee, reunion, drawing room, at home; *conversazione* [*It.*] &c. (*social gathering*) 892; assembly, congress, house, senate, legislature, convocation; caucus, séance, eisteddfod, gemot *or* gemote; convention, conventicle; con-

73. Nonassemblage. Dispersion. — **N.** dispersion; disjunction &c. 44; divergence &c. 291; aspersion; scattering &c. *v.;* dissemination, diffusion, dissipation, distribution; apportionment &c. 786; spread, respersion [*obs.*], circumfusion, interspersion, spargefaction [*obs.*], affusion.

waifs and estrays, flotsam and jetsam, *disjecta membra* [Hor.]; waveson.

V. disperse, scatter, sow, disseminate, diffuse, radiate, shed, spread, bestrew, overspread, dispense, disband,

clave &c. (*council*) 696; Noah's ark.

COMPANY, platoon, faction, caravan, claque, posse, *posse comitatus* [*L.*]; watch, squad, corps, troop, troupe; army, regiment &c. (*combatants*) 726; host &c. (*multitude*) 102; populousness.

MISCELLANY, *collectanea* [*L.*]; museum, menagerie &c. (*store*) 636; museology.

CROWD, throng; flood, rush, deluge; rabble, mob, rout, press, crush, *cohue* [*F.*], horde, body, tribe; crew, gang, knot, squad, band, party; swarm, shoal, school, covey, flock, herd, drove; kennel; *atajo* [*Sp. Amer.*]; bunch, drive, force, *mulada* [*U. S.*]; *remuda* [*Sp.*]; round-up [*U. S.*]; array, bevy, galaxy.

CLAN, brotherhood, association &c. (*party*) 712.

GROUP, cluster, Pleiades, clump, pencil; set, batch, lot, pack; budget, assortment, bunch; parcel; packet, package; bundle, fascine, bale, *seron* [*Sp.*], fagot,

disembody, dismember, distribute; apportion &c. 786; blow off, let out, dispel, cast forth, draft (or draught) off; strew, straw [*obs.*], strow [*archaic*]; ted; spurtle or spirtle [*obs.*], cast, sprinkle; issue, deal out, retail, utter; intersperse, resperse [*obs.*]; set abroach, circumfuse.

spread like wildfire, disperse themselves.

TURN ADRIFT, cast adrift; scatter to the winds; sow broadcast.

Adj. UNASSEMBLED &c. (*see* assemble &c. 72); diffuse, disseminated scattered, strown, strewn, dispersed &c *v.*, dispersive, dissipative, diffusive, dispellent [*rare*]; sparse, dispread, broadcast, sporadic, widespread; epidemic &c. (*general*) 78; adrift, stray; disheveled, streaming resolvent, discutient [*med.*].

Adv. *sparsim* [*L.*], here and there, *passim* [*L.*].

wisp, truss, tuft; grove, thicket, plump [*archaic*]; shock, rick, fardel, stack, sheaf, haycock, swath; fascicle, fascicule, fasciculus, gavel, hattock [*dial. Eng.*], stook [*dial.*].

volley, shower, storm, cloud.

ACCUMULATION &c. (*store*) 636; congeries, heap, lump, pile, rouleau, tissue, mass, pyramid; bing [*obs.*]; drift; snowball, snowdrift; acervation [*rare*], cumulation, amassment; glomeration, agglomeration; conglobation; conglomeration, conglomerate; coacervation [*rare*], coagmentation [*obs.*], aggregation, concentration, congestion, omnium-gatherum [*colloq.*], spicilegium [*L.*], Black Hole of Calcutta; quantity &c. (*greatness*) 31.

COLLECTOR, gatherer; whip, whipper-in.

V. [BE OR COME TOGETHER] assemble, collect, muster; meet, unite, join, rejoin; cluster, flock, swarm, surge, stream, herd, crowd, throng, associate; congregate, conglomerate, concentrate; center round, rendezvous, resort; come together, flock together, get together, pig together; forgather or foregather; huddle; reassemble.

[GET OR BRING TOGETHER] assemble, muster; bring together, get together, put together, draw together, scrape together, lump together; collect, collocate, colligate; get in, whip in; gather; hold a meeting; convene, convoke, convocate; rake up, dredge, heap, mass, pile; pack, put up, truss, cram; acervate [*rare*]; agglomerate, aggregate; compile; group, aggroup, concentrate, unite; collect into a focus, bring into a focus; amass, accumulate &c. (*store*) 636; collect in a dragnet; heap Ossa upon Pelion.

Adj. ASSEMBLED &c. *v.*, closely packed, dense, serried, crowded to suffocation, teeming, swarming, populous; as thick as hops; swarming like maggots; all of a heap, fasciculated; cumulative.

. the plot thickens; *acervatim; tibi seris tibi metis;* "in narrow room throng numberless" [Milton].

74. [PLACE OF MEETING.] **Focus. — N.** FOCUS; point of convergence &c. 290; corradiation [*rare*]; center &c. 222; gathering place, resort; haunt; retreat; venue, rendezvous; rallying point, headquarters, home, club; depot &c. (*store*) 636; tryst, trysting place; place of meeting, place of resort, place of assignation; *point de réunion* [*F.*] issue

V. bring to a point, bring to a focus, bring to an issue, focus, corradiate [*rare*].

. all friends round St. Paul's; "I have a rendezvous with Death" [Seeger].

4. Distributive Order

75. Class. — N. CLASS, division, subdivision, category, head, order, section; department, province, domain, sphere.

KIND, sort, estate, genus, species, variety, family, race, tribe, caste, sept, phylum, clan, breed; clique, coterie; type, kit, sect, set; assortment; feather [*rare*], kidney; suit; range; gender, sex, kin.

MANNER, description, denomination, persuasion, connection, designation, character, stamp; predicament; indication, particularization, selection, specification.

SIMILARITY &c. 17.

---

76. Inclusion. [COMPREHENSION UNDER, OR REFERENCE TO, A CLASS.] — **N.** INCLUSION, admission, incorporation, comprisal, comprehension, reception.

COMPOSITION &c. (*inclusion in a compound*) 54.

V. BE INCLUDED in &c.; come under, fall under, range under; belong to, pertain to; range with; merge in.

INCLUDE, comprise, comprehend, contain, admit, embrace, subsume, receive, inclose &c. (*circumscribe*) 229; incorporate, cover, embody, encircle.

reckon among, enumerate among, number among; refer to; place under, place with, arrange under, arrange with; take into account.

Adj. INCLUSIVE, inclusory; included, including &c. *v.;* congener [*rare*], congenerous; of the same class &c. 75; comprehensive, sweeping, all-embracing, liberal, unexclusive [*rare*].

⁎ *a maximis ad minima, et hoc genus omne; et cætera,* &c., etc.

77. Exclusion.[1] **— N.** EXCLUSION &c. 55.

---

78. Generality. — N. GENERALITY, generalization; universality; catholicity, catholicism; miscellany, miscellaneousness; dragnet; common run; worldwideness.

Pan-Americanism, Pan-Anglicanism, Pan-Hellenism, Pan-Germanism, Panslavism *or* Pansclavism.

EVERYONE, everybody, *tout le monde* [*F.*]; all hands [*colloq.*], all the world and his wife [*humorous*]; anybody, N or M, all sorts.

PREVALENCE, rifeness, run.

V. BE GENERAL &c. *adj.;* prevail, be going about, stalk abroad.

RENDER GENERAL &c. *adj.;* spread, broaden, universalize, generalize.

Adj. GENERAL, generic, collective; current, wide, broad, comprehensive, sweeping; encyclopedic *or* encyclopedical, panoramic; widespread &c. (*dispersed*) 73.

UNIVERSAL; catholic, catholical; common, worldwide, nationwide, statewide, heavenwide, ecumenical *or* œcumenical; prevalent, prevailing, rife, epidemic, besetting; all over [*colloq.*], covered with.

79. Speciality. — N. SPECIALITY, *spécialité* [*F.*]; individuality, individuity [*obs.*]; particularity, peculiarity; *je ne sais quoi* [*F.*], *nescio quid* [*L.*]; idiocrasy &c. (*tendency*) 176; personality, characteristic, mannerism, idiosyncrasy, physiognomic [*rare*], diagnostic; specificness &c. *adj.;* singularity &c. (*unconformity*) 83; reading, version, lection; state; trait; distinctive feature; technicality; differentia.

PARTICULARS, details, items, counts; minutiæ.

I, self, I myself; myself, himself, herself, itself.

V. SPECIFY, particularize, individualize, realize, specialize, designate, determine; denote, indicate, point out, select, differentiate, specificize [*rare*], come to the point.

ITEMIZE, detail, descend to particulars, enter into detail.

Adj. SPECIAL, particular, individual, specific, proper, personal, original, private, respective, definite, determinate, minute, especial, certain, esoteric, endemic, partial, party, peculiar, marked,

---

[1] The same set of words are used to express *Exclusion from a class* and *Exclusion from a compound.* Reference is therefore made to the former at 55. This identity does not occur with regard to *Inclusion,* which therefore constitutes a separate category.

Pan-American, Pan-Anglican, Pan-Hellenic, Pan-Germanic, Panslavic or Pansclavic, Panslavonic, Panslavonian; panharmonic.

EVERY, all; unspecified, impersonal, indefinite.

CUSTOMARY &c. (*habitual*) 613.

Adv. whatever, whatsoever; to a man, one and all.

GENERALLY &c. *adj.;* always, for better for worse; in general, generally speaking; speaking generally; for the most part; in the long run &c. (*on an average*) 29; by and large, roughly speaking.

intimate, appropriate, several, characteristic, diagnostic, exclusive, restricted; singular &c. (*exceptional*) 83; idiomatic; typical, representative.

this, that; yon, yonder.

Adv. SPECIALLY &c. *adj.;* in particular, *in propriâ personâ* [*L.*]; *ad hominem* [*L.*]; for my part.

EACH, apiece, one by one; severally, respectively, each to each; *seriatim* [*NL.*], in detail, bit by bit; *pro hac vice* [*L.*], *pro re natâ* [*L.*].

NAMELY, that is to say, *videlicet* [*L.*], viz.; to wit.

₊ *le style est l'homme même.*

5. ORDER AS REGARDS CATEGORIES

80. Rule. — **N.** REGULARITY, uniformity, constancy, clockwork precision; punctuality &c. (*exactness*) 494; even tenor, rut; system; routine &c. (*custom*) 613; formula; canon, convention, maxim, rule &c. (*form, regulation*) 697; keynote, standard, model; precedent &c. (*prototype*) 22; conformity &c. 82.

LAW, capitular *or* capitulary, gnomology [*rare*], *règlement* [*F.*], order of things; normality, normalcy; normal state, normal condition, natural state, natural condition, ordinary state, ordinary condition, model state, model condition; standing dish, standing order; Procrustean law; law of the Medes and Persians; hard and fast rule; nature, principle.

Adj. REGULAR, uniform, symmetrical, constant, steady; according to rule &c. (*conformable*) 82; normal, habitual, customary &c. 613; methodical, orderly, systematic, systematical.

₊ "Order is heav'n's first law" [Pope].

81. Multiformity. — **N.** MULTIFORMITY, omniformity; variety, diversity; multifariousness &c. *adj.;* varied assortment.

Adj. MULTIFORM, multifold, multifarious, multigenerous, multiplex; variform [*rare*], diversiform, amœbiform, manifold, many-sided; omniform, omnigenous, omnifarious; polymorphic, polymorphous, multiphase, metamorphotic, protean, proteiform, heterogeneous, motley, mosaic; epicene.

indiscriminate, desultory, irregular, diversified, different, divers; all manner of; of every description, of all sorts and kinds; *et hoc genus omne* [*L.*]; and what not?

₊ *de omnibus rebus et quibusdam aliis;* "harmoniously confused" [Pope]; "variety's the very spice of life" [Cowper].

82. Conformity. — **N.** CONFORMITY, conformance; observance; habituation; naturalization; conventionality &c. (*custom*) 613; agreement &c. 23.

EXAMPLE, instance, specimen, sample, quotation; exemplification, illustration, case in point; object lesson; elucidation.

PATTERN &c. (*prototype*) 22.

CONVENTIONALIST, formalist, bromide [*slang*], Philistine.

V. CONFORM TO, conform to rule; accommodate oneself to, adapt oneself to; rub off corners.

BE REGULAR &c. *adj.;* move in a

83. Unconformity. — **N.** NONCONFORMITY &c. 82; unconformity, disconformity; unconventionality, informality, abnormity, anomaly; anomalousness &c. *adj.;* exception, peculiarity; infraction–, breach–, violation–, infringement- of -law, -custom, -usage; teratism, eccentricity, *bizarrerie* [*F.*], oddity, *je ne sais quoi* [*F.*], monstrosity, rarity; freak of nature; rouser [*colloq.*], snorter [*slang, U. S.*].

INDIVIDUALITY, idiosyncrasy, singularity, selfness [*rare*], originality, mannerism.

groove, move in a rut, travel in a rut; follow –, observe –, go by –, bend to –, obey- -rules, – precedents; agree with, comply with, tally with, chime in with, fall in with; be guided by, be regulated by; fall into a custom, fall into a usage; follow the fashion, follow the multitude; assimilate to, shape, harmonize, conventionalize, pass muster, do as others do, *hurler avec les loups* [*F.*]; do at Rome as the Romans do; go with the -stream,– current,– tide; swim with the -stream,– current,– tide; pass current; tread the beaten track &c. (*habit*) 613; keep one in countenance.

EXEMPLIFY, illustrate, example, sample, type [*rare*], cite, quote, put a case; produce an instance &c. *n.;* elucidate, explain.

Adj. CONFORMABLE TO RULE; adaptable, consistent, agreeable, compliant; regular &c. 80; according to regulation, according to rule, according to Cocker, according to Gunter, according to Hoyle [*all colloq.*]; *en règle* [*F.*], *selon les règles* [*F.*], well regulated, orderly; symmetric &c. 242.

CONVENTIONAL &c. (*customary*) 613; of daily occurrence, of everyday occurrence; in the natural order of things; ordinary, common, habitual, usual, commonplace, prosaic, bromidic [*slang*], Philistine.

in the order of the day; naturalized.

TYPICAL, normal, formal; canonical, orthodox, sound, strict, rigid, positive, uncompromising, Procrustean.

secundum artem [*L.*], shipshape, point-device [*archaic*], technical.

EXEMPLARY, illustrative, in point.

Adv. CONFORMABLY &c. *adj.;* by rule; agreeably to; in conformity with, in accordance with, in keeping with; according to; consistently with; as usual, *ad instar* [*L.*], *instar omnium* [*L.*]; *more solito* [*L.*], *more majorum* [*L.*].

for the sake of conformity; of course, as a matter of course; *pro formâ* [*L.*], for form's sake, by the card.

invariably &c. (*uniformly*) 16.

FOR EXAMPLE, for instance; *exempli gratiâ* [*L.*]; *e. g.; inter alia* [*L.*].

⁎⁎⁎ cela va sans dire; ex pede Herculem; noscitur a sociis; ne e quovis ligno Mercurius fiat [Erasmus]; "they are happy men whose natures sort with their vocations" [Bacon].

ABERRATION; irregularity; variety; singularity; exemption; salvo [*rare*] &c. (*qualification*) 469.

NONCONFORMIST, bohemian, sulphite [*slang*], nondescript, character [*colloq.*], original, nonesuch *or* nonsuch [*rare*], freak, crank [*colloq.*], prodigy, wonder, miracle, curiosity, missing link, flying fish, black swan, monster, white blackbird, basilisk, salamander, *lusus naturæ* [*L.*], *rara avis* [*L.*], queer fish [*slang*].

MONGREL; half-caste, half-blood, half-breed &c. 41; metis, crossbreed, hybrid, mule, mulatto; *tertium quid* [*L.*], hermaphrodite.

MONSTER, phœnix, chimera, hydra, sphinx, minotaur; griffin *or* griffon; centaur; xiphopagus; hippogriff, hippocentaur; sagittary; kraken, cockatrice, wivern *or* wyvern [*obs.*], roc, dragon, sea serpent; mermaid; unicorn; Cyclops, "men whose heads do grow beneath their shoulders" [*Othello*]; teratology.

fish out of water; neither one thing nor another; neither fish, flesh, fowl, nor good red herring; one in a way, one in a thousand.

OUTCAST, outlaw, Ishmael, pariah.

V. BE UNCOMFORMABLE &c. *adj.;* abnormalize; leave the beaten track, leave the beaten path; infringe –, break –, violate - a -law,– habit,– usage,– custom; drive a coach and six through; stretch a point; have no business there; baffle all description, beggar all description.

Adj. UNCOMFORMABLE, exceptional; abnormal, abnormous; anomalous, anomalistic; out of order, out of place, out of keeping, out of tune, out of one's element; irregular, arbitrary; teratogenic, teratogenetic; lawless, informal, aberrant, stray, wandering, wanton; peculiar, exclusive, unnatural, eccentric, egregious; out of the beaten track, out of the common, out of the common run, out of the pale of; misplaced; funny [*colloq.*].

UNUSUAL, unaccustomed, uncustomary, unordinary, unwonted, uncommon; rare, singular, unique, curious, odd, extraordinary, strange, monstrous; wonderful &c. 870; unexpected, unaccountable; *outré* [*F.*], out of the way, remarkable, noteworthy, *recherché* [*F.*], queer, quaint, nondescript, *sui generis* [*L.*]; original, unconventional, super-

normal [*rare*], bohemian, sulphitic [*slang*], unfashionable; undescribed, unprecedented, unparalleled, unexampled, unheard of, unfamiliar;· fantastic, newfangled,
grotesque, bizarre; outlandish, exotic, *tombé des nues* [*F.*], preternatural; de-
naturalized.

HETEROGENEOUS, heteroclite, amorphous, mongrel, amphibious, epicene, half
blood, hybrid; androgynous, androgynal; unsymmetric &c. 243; adelomorphic
or adelomorphous, gynandrous, bisexual, hermaphrodite, androgynic, androgynous,
monoclinous.

Adv. UNCONFORMABLY &c. *adj.;* except, unless, save, barring, beside, without, save and except, let alone.

HOWEVER, yet, but.

Int. what on earth! what in the world!

** never was seen the like, never was heard the like, never was known the like; "not con-
ventionally unconventional" [Shaw].

Section V.   NUMBER

1. Number, in the Abstract

84. Number. — N. NUMBER, symbol, numeral, figure, cipher, digit, integer;
counter; round number; formula; function; series.

sum, difference, complement, subtrahend; product, total, aggregate; multiplicand, multiplier, multiplicator; coefficient, multiple; dividend, divisor, factor,
quotient, submultiple, fraction; mixed number; numerator, denominator; decimal,
circulating decimal, repetend; common measure, aliquot part; reciprocal; prime
number; totient; quota, quotum [*rare*].

figurate numbers, pyramidal numbers, polygonal numbers.

permutation, combination, variation; election.

RATIO, proportion; progression; arithmetical progression, geometrical progression,
harmonical progression; percentage.

POWER, root, radix, exponent, index, logarithm, antilogarithm; modulus.

differential, integral, fluxion, fluent.

Adj. NUMERAL, complementary, divisible, aliquot, reciprocal, prime, fractional,
decimal, figurate, incommensurable.

proportional, exponential, logarithmic, logometric, differential, fluxional, integral,
totitive.

positive, negative; rational, irrational; surd, radical, real, imaginary, impossible.

85. Numeration. — N. NUMERATION; numbering &c. *v.;* pagination; tale, tally,
telling [*archaic*], recension, enumeration, summation, reckoning, computation,
supputation [*obs.*]; calculation, calculus; algorithm [*obs.*], algorism, rhabdology,
dactylonomy; measurement &c. 466; statistics, logistics.

arithmetic, analysis, algebra, fluxions; differential calculus, integral calculus,
infinitesimal calculus; calculus of differences.

[STATISTICS] dead reckoning, muster, poll, census, capitation, roll call, recapitulation; account &c. (*list*) 86.

[OPERATIONS] notation, addition, subtraction, multiplication, division, proportion,
rule of three, practice, equations, extraction of roots, reduction, involution,
evolution, approximation, interpolation, differentiation, integration, indigitation
[*rare*].

[INSTRUMENTS] abacus, suan pan, logometer, sliding rule, tallies, Napier's bones,
calculating machine, difference engine; adding machine; cash register.

ARITHMETICIAN, calculator, geodesist, abacist; algebraist, geometrician, trigo-
nometrician, mathematician, actuary, statistician.

V. NUMBER, count, tell; call over, run over; take an account of, enumerate,
call the roll, muster, poll, recite, recapitulate; sum; sum up, cast up; tell off, score,
cipher, reckon, reckon up, estimate, make an estimate, furnish an estimate,

make up accounts, compute, calculate, suppute [obs.], add, subtract, multiply, divide, extract roots, algebraize, "tell his tale" [Milton].

CHECK, prove, demonstrate, balance, audit, overhaul, take stock.

PAGE, affix numbers to, foliate, paginate.

AMOUNT TO, come to, total.

Adj. NUMERAL, numerical; arithmetical, analytic, algebraic, statistical, countable, reckonable, numberable, computable, calculable, rhabdological; commensurable, commensurate; incommensurable, incommensurate.

86. List. — **N.** LIST, catalogue *or* catalog, inventory, schedule, calends [*rare*]; register &c. (*record*) 551; account; bill, bill of costs; syllabus; terrier, tally, file; calendar, index, table, atlas, contents; book, ledger; synopsis, *catalogue raisonné* [*F.*]; scroll, brief [*obs.*], screed, manifest, invoice, bill of lading; prospectus, program *or* programme; bill of fare, menu, carte; score, bulletin, *tableau* [*F.*], census, statistics, returns; Red Book, Blue Book, Domesday Book; directory, gazetteer.

almanac; army list, clergy list, civil service list, navy list; Statesman's Year-Book, Whitaker's Almanack, *Almanach de Gotha*, cadastre *or* cadaster, *cadre* [*F.*], card index; Lloyd's Register, Nautical Almanac, Who's Who.

DICTIONARY, lexicon, glossary, word-book, thesaurus, gloss [*rare*], gradus.

ROLL; check roll, checker roll, bead roll; muster roll, muster book; roll of honor; roster, slate, rota, poll, panel; chartulary *or* cartulary, diptych.

V. LIST, enroll, schedule, inventorize [*rare*], inventory, register, catalogue *or* catalog, invoice, bill, book, indent, slate, post, manifest, docket; matriculate, empanel, calendar, tally, file, index, tabulate, enter, score, keep score; census.

Adj. inventorial, cadastral; listed &c.v.

*** "How index-learning turns no student pale, Yet holds the eel of science by the tail" [Pope].

2. Determinate Number

87. Unity. — **N.** UNITY; oneness &c. *adj.*; individuality; solitude &c. (*seclusion*) 893; isolation &c. (*disjunction*) 44; unification &c. 48; completeness &c. 52.

ONE, unit, ace, monad; individual; none else, no other, nought beside.

INTEGER, item, point, module.

V. BE ONE, be alone &c. *adj.*

ISOLATE &c. (*disjoin*) 44.

RENDER ONE; unite &c. (*join*) 43, (*combine*) 48.

Adj. ONE, sole, only-begotten, single, solitary, companionless; individual, apart, alone; kithless.

UNACCOMPANIED, unattended; *solus* (*fem.*, *sola*) [*L.*], single-handed; singular, odd, unique, unrepeated, azygous, first and last; isolated &c. (*disjoined*); insular.

MONADIC, monadical; unific, uniflorous, unilobed, uniglobular, unifoliolate, unigenital, uniliteral, unilocular, unimodular, unitary; monospermous.

inseacable [*obs.*], inseverable, indiscerptible; compact, irresolvable.

LONE, lonely, lonesome; desolate, dreary.

88. Accompaniment. — **N.** ACCOMPANIMENT; adjunct &c. 39; context; appendage, appurtenance.

COMPANY, association, companionship; coexistence, concomitance; partnership, copartnership; coefficiency.

CONCOMITANT, accessory, coefficient; companion, attendant, fellow, associate, *fidus Achates* [*L.*], consort, spouse, colleague; partner, copartner; satellite, hanger-on, shadow; escort, *cortège* [*F.*], suite, train, convoy, follower &c. 65; attribute.

V. ACCOMPANY, coexist, attend, company [*archaic*], convoy, chaperon; hang on, wait on; go hand in hand with; synchronize &c. 120; bear company, keep company; row in the same boat; bring in its train; associate with, couple with.

Adj. ACCOMPANYING &c. *v.*; concomitant, fellow, twin, joint; associated with, coupled with; accessory, attendant, comitant [*rare*], obbligato.

Adv. WITH, withal; together with, along with, in company with; hand in hand, side by side; cheek by jowl (*or*

Adv. SINGLY &c. *adj.*; alone, by itself, *per se* [*L.*], only [*rare*], apart, in the singular number, in the abstract; one by one, one at a time; simply; one and a half, *sesqui-*.

✱ *natura il fece, e poi roppe la stampa; du fort au faible;* "two souls with but a single thought, two hearts that beat as one."

jole); arm in arm; therewith, herewith; and &c. (*addition*) 37.

TOGETHER, in a body, collectively, in conjunction.

✱ *noscitur a sociis; virtutis fortuna comes;* "into their inmost bower. Handed they went" [Milton].

89. Duality — N. DUALITY, dualism; duplicity; biplicity [*rare*], biformity; polarity.

two, deuce, couple, couplet, both, twain, brace, pair, cheeks, twins, Castor and Pollux, gemini, Siamese twins; fellows; yoke, conjugation; dispermy, doublets, dyad, duad, twosome [*rare*], distich, span.

V. [UNITE IN PAIRS] pair, couple, bracket, yoke; conduplicate; mate, span [*U.S.*]

Adj. TWO, twain; dual, dualistic; binary, binomial; twin, biparous; dyadic; conduplicate; duplex &c. 90; biduous, binate, binary, binal [*rare*], diphyletic, dispermic, paired, unijugate; *tête-à-tête* [*F.*].

COUPLED &c. *v.*; conjugate.

BOTH, both the one and the other.

90. Duplication. — N. DUPLICATION; doubling &c. *v.*; gemination, ingemination; reduplication; iteration &c. (*repetition*) 104; renewal.

DUPLICATE, facsimile, copy, replica, counterpart &c. (*copy*) 21.

V. DOUBLE; redouble, reduplicate; geminate [*rare*]; repeat &c. 104; renew &c. 660.

Adj. DOUBLE; doubled &c. *v.*; bicipital, bicephalous, bidental, bilabiate, bivalve, bivalvular, bifold, biform, bilateral, bifarious, bifacial; twofold, two-sided; disomatous; duple [*rare*], duplex; double-faced, double-headed; twin, duplicate, geminous [*rare*], geminate, ingeminate; second: dual &c. 89.

Adv. TWICE, once more; over again &c. (*repeatedly*) 104; as much again, twofold.

secondly, in the second place, again.

91. [DIVISION INTO TWO PARTS.] **Bisection. — N.** BISECTION, bipartition; dichotomy, subdichotomy [*rare*]; halving &c. *v.*; dimidiation.

BIFURCATION, furcation, forking, branching, ramification, divarication; fork, crotch, furculum, prong; fold.

HALF, moiety.

V. BISECT, halve, hemisect [*rare*], divide, split, cut in two, cleave, dimidiate, dichotomize.

GO HALVES, divide with.

SEPARATE, fork, bifurcate, furcate, divaricate; branch off *or* out; ramify.

Adj. BISECTED &c. *v.*; cloven, cleft; bipartite, dimidiate, divaricate, biconjugate, bicuspid, bifid; bifurcous [*rare*], bifurcate, bifurcated; bigeminate, distichous, distichal, dichotomous, furcular, furcate, lituate [*rare*]; semi-, demi-, hemi-.

92. Triality. — N. TRIALITY [*rare*], trinity,[1] triunity, Trimurti [*Hindu*], triplicity, trialism [*rare*].

THREE, triad, triplet, ternion, ternary, trine [*rare*], trey, trio, leash; shamrock, tierce, delta, spike-team [*U. S.*], trefoil; triangle, trident, triennium, trigon [*rare*], trinomial, trionym, triplopia *or* triplopy, tripod, trireme, triseme, triskelion *or* triskele, trisul *or* trisula, triumvirate.

third power, cube.

Adj. THREE; triform, trinal, trinomial; tertiary; triune; triarch, triadic.

✱ *tria juncta in uno.*

93. Triplication. — N. TRIPLICATION, triplicity; trebleness, terza, trine; trilogy.

94. [DIVISION INTO THREE PARTS.] **Trisection. — N.** TRISECTION, tripartition, trichotomy; third, third part.

[1] *Trinity* is hardly ever used except in a theological sense; *see* Deity 976.

V. TREBLE, triple, triplicate, cube.

Adj. TREBLE, triple; tern, ternary; ternate, tertiary; triplicate, threefold, trilogistic; triplasic; third; trinal, trine [*rare*].

Adv. THREE TIMES, thrice, in the third place, thirdly, threefold, triply, trebly &c. *adj.*

V. TRISECT, divide into three parts, third.

Adj. TRIFID; trisected &c. *v.;* tripartite, trichotomous, trisulcate; ternal, trident, tridental.

triadelphous, triangular, trichotomic, tricuspid, tricapsular, tridental, tridentate *or* tridentated, tridentiferous, trifoliolate, trifurcate *or* trifurcated, trigonoid, trigonous, trigonal, trigrammic *or* trigrammatic, tripedal, trilateral, tripetalous, tripodal, tripodic, triquetral, triquetrous.

95. Quaternity. — N. QUATERNITY [*rare*], four, tetrad, quartet *or* quartette, quatre [*rare*], quadruplet, quaternion, square, quadrilateral, quadrinomial, biquadrate, quarter, quarto, tetract, tetragon.

quadrangle, quadrature, quadruplet; quatrefoil; tetragram, tetragrammaton; tetrahedron, tetrapody, tetrology, quatrefoil *or* quadrefoil.

V. SQUARE, biquadrate, reduce to a square.

Adj. FOUR; quaternary, quaternal; quadratic; quartile, quartic, quadrifid, quadriform, quadric, biquadratic; tetract, tetractine, tetractinal [*zoöl.*], four-rayed; tetrad, quadrivalent; quadrangular, tetragonal, quadrilateral, tetrahedral.

96. Quadruplication. — N. QUADRUPLICATION.

V. QUADRUPLICATE, biquadrate, multiply by four.

Adj. FOURFOLD; quadrable, quadruple, quadruplex, quadruplicate, quadrible; fourth.

Adv. FOUR TIMES; in the fourth place, fourthly.

97. [DIVISION INTO FOUR PARTS.] **Quadrisection. — N.** QUADRISECTION, quadripartition; quartering &c. *v.;* fourth; quart, quarter, quartern; farthing (*i. e.*, fourthing).

V. QUARTER, divide into four parts, quadrisect.

Adj. QUARTERED &c. *v.;* quadrifid, quadripartite [*rare*]; quadrifoliolate *or* quadrifoliate, quadrigeminal, quadrigeminous, quadrigeminate, quadripennate, quadriplanar, quadriserial, quadrivial, quadrifurcate, quadrumanal, quadrumane, quadrumous.

98. Five, &c. — N. FIVE, cinque, quint, quincunx, quintet *or* quintette, quintuple [*rare*], quintuplet, quinary [*rare*], pentad; pentagon, pentagram, pentameter, pentapody, pentarchy, pentastich, Pentateuch.

SIX, sise *or* size [*rare*], hexad, sextuplet, hexagon, hexahedron, hexagram, hexameter, hexapod, hexapody, hexastich, Hexateuch, sextet, half-a-dozen.

SEVEN, heptad, septenary [*rare*], hep-

99. Quinquesection. &c. — N. QUINQUESECTION &c.; division by five &c. 98; decimation; fifth &c.

V. DECIMATE; quinquesect; decimalize.

Adj. QUINQUEFID, quinqueliteral, quinquepartite.

sexpartite; octofid; decimal, tenth, tithe; duodecimal, twelfth; sexagesimal, sexagenary; hundredth, centesimal; millesimal &c.

tagon, heptahedron, heptameter, heptarchy, Heptateuch.

EIGHT, octave, octonary, octad, ogdoad, octagon, octahedron, octameter, octastyle, octavo, octet.

NINE, novenary [*rare*], ennead, nonary [*rare*]; nonagon, three times three; *novena* [*R. C. Ch.*]

TEN, decad [*rare*], decade, dicker; decagon, decagram *or* decagramme, decahedron, decapod, decare, decastere, decastyle, decasyllable, decemvir, decemvirate, decennium.

eleven; twelve, dozen; thirteen; long dozen, baker's dozen; twenty, score; twenty-four, four and twenty, two dozen; twenty-five, five and twenty, quarter of a hundred; forty, twoscore; fifty, half a hundred; sixty, sexagenary, threescore; seventy, threescore and ten; eighty, fourscore; ninety, fourscore and ten.

HUNDRED, centenary, hecatomb, century, bicentenary, tercentenary; hundred-weight, cwt.; one hundred and forty-four, gross.

THOUSAND, chiliad, milliad [rare], millenary [rare], millennium; myriad, ten thousand; one hundred thousand, lac or lakh [India], plum [obs.], million; ten million, crore [India]; thousand million, billion, milliard.

billion, trillion &c.

V. quintuplicate, sextuple, centuplicate, centuriate [obs.].

Adj. FIVE, fifth, quinary, quintuple; quintuplicate, pentangular, pentagonal, pentastyle.

SIXTH, senary [rare], sextuple, hexagonal, hexangular, hexastyle, hexahedral, sextan.

SEVENTH, septuple, septenary, septimal [rare]; heptagonal, heptahedral, heptamerous, heptangular.

EIGHTH, octuple, octonary; octagonal, octahedral, octan, octangular, octastyle.

NINTH, ninefold, novenary [rare], nonary [rare], enneahedral, enneastyle.

TENTH, tenfold, decimal, denary, decuple, decagonal, decahedral, decasyllabic.

ELEVENTH, undecennial, undecennary.

TWELFTH, duodenary, duodenal.

in one's teens, thirteenth, &c.

TWENTIETH, vicenary, vicennial, vigesimal, vicesimal.

SIXTIETH, sexagesimal, sexagenary.

SEVENTIETH, septuagesimal, septuagenary.

CENTUPLE, centuplicate, centennial, centenary, centurial; secular, hundredth; thousandth, millenary, millennial &c.

3. INDETERMINATE NUMBER

100. [MORE THAN ONE.] **Plurality.** — N. PLURALITY; a number, a certain number; one or two, two or three &c.; a few, several; multitude &c. 102; majority.

Adj. PLURAL, more than one, upwards of, some, certain; not, not alone &c. 87.

Adv. et cetera, &c., etc.

*** non deficit alter.

102. Multitude. — N. MULTITUDE; multitudinousness, numerousness &c. adj.; numerosity, numerality [obs.]; multiplicity; profusion &c. (plenty) 639; legion, host; great number, large number, round number, enormous number; a quantity, numbers, array, sight, army, sea, galaxy; scores, peck, bushel, shoal, oodles [slang], pile [colloq.], heap [colloq.], power [colloq.], sight [colloq.], lot [colloq.], lots [colloq.], swarm, bevy, cloud, flock, herd, drove, flight, covey, hive, brood, litter, farrow, fry, nest; mob, crowd &c. (assemblage) 72; all the world and his wife [humorous].

[INCREASE OF NUMBER] greater number, majority; multiplication, multiple.

V. BE NUMEROUS &c. adj.; swarm with, teem with, be alive with, creep with; crowd, swarm, come thick upon;

100a. [LESS THAN ONE.] **Fraction.** — N. FRACTION, fractional part; part &c. 51.

Adj. FRACTIONAL, fragmentary, inconsiderable, partial, portional.

101. Zero. — N. ZERO, nothing; naught, nought; cipher, none, nobody; nichts [Ger.], goose egg [U. S.], duck [slang], nixie [slang], nix [slang]; not a soul; absence &c. 187; unsubstantiality &c. 4.

Adj. NO, not one, not any.

103. Fewness. — N. FEWNESS &c. adj.; paucity, scarcity, sparseness, sparsity, small number; only a few; small quantity &c. 32; rarity; infrequency &c. 137; handful; minority; exiguity.

[DIMINUTION OF NUMBER] reduction; weeding &c. v.; elimination, sarculation [obs.], decimation; eradication.

V. BE FEW &c. adj.

RENDER FEW &c. adj.; reduce, diminish, diminish the number, weed, eliminate, thin, decimate.

Adj. FEW; scant, scanty; thin, rare, scarce, sparse, thinly scattered, few and far between; exiguous; infrequent &c. 137; rari nantes [L.]; hardly any, scarcely any; to be counted on one's fingers, to be counted on the fingers of one hand; reduced &c. v.; unrepeated.

Adv. here and there.

outnumber, multiply; people; swarm like locusts, swarm like bees.

Adj. MANY, several, sundry, divers, various, not a few; Briarean; a hundred, a thousand, a myriad, a million, a billion, a quadrillion, a nonillion, a thousand and one; some ten or a dozen, some forty or fifty &c.; half a dozen, half a hundred &c.; alive with; very many, full many, ever so many; numerous; profuse, in profusion; manifold, multifold, multiplied, multitudinous, multiple, multinomial, teeming, populous, peopled, outnumbering, crowded, thick, studded; galore [*colloq.*].

thick coming, many more, more than one can tell, a world of; no end of, no end to; *cum multis aliis* [*L.*], thick as hops, thick as hail; plenty as blackberries; numerous as the stars in the firmament, numerous as the sands on the seashore, numerous as the hairs on the head; and what not, and heaven knows what; endless &c. (*infinite*) 105.

. their name is "Legion"; *acervatim; en foule;* "many-headed multitude" [Sidney]; "Thick as autumnal leaves that strow the brooks In Vallombrosa" [Milton]; "numerous as glittering gems of morning dew" [Young]; *vel prece vel pretio.*

104. Repetition. — **N.** REPETITION, iteration, reiteration, iterance [*rare*], reiterance [*rare*], alliteration, duplication, reduplication, ding-dong [*colloq.*], monotone, harping, recurrence, succession, run; battology, tautology; monotony, tautophony; rhythm &c. 138; diffuseness, pleonasm, redundancy.

chimes, repetend, echo, reëcho, encore, dilogy [*rare*], *ritornello* [*It.*], burden of a song, refrain, undersong; rehearsal; *réchauffé* [*F.*], *rifacimento* [*It.*], recapitulation.

cuckoo &c. (*imitation*) 19; reverberation &c. 408; drumming &c. (*roll*) 407; renewal &c. (*restoration*) 660.

TWICE-TOLD TALE, chestnut [*slang*], old stuff [*slang*], old story, old song; second edition, new edition; reappearance, reproduction; periodicity &c. 138.

V. REPEAT, iterate, reiterate, reproduce, echo, reëcho, drum, harp upon, battologize, tautologize, hammer, redouble.

RECUR, revert, return, reappear; renew &c. (*restore*) 660.

REHEARSE; do over again, say over again; ring the changes on; harp on the same string; din in the ear, drum in the ear; conjugate in all its moods, tenses and inflexions; begin again, go over the same ground, go the same round, duplicate, reduplicate, never hear the last of; resume, return to, recapitulate, reword.

Adj. REPEATED &c. *v.;* warmed up, warmed over, repetitional, repetitionary, repetitive, repetitious, reduplicatory [*rare*], reduplicative, recurrent, recurring; ever recurring, thick coming; frequent, incessant; redundant, pleonastic, tautological, tautologous, tautophonical; inexhaustible, unplumbed.

MONOTONOUS, ding-dong [*colloq.*], harping, iterative, unvaried; mocking, chiming; retold; habitual &c. 613; another.

AFORESAID, aforenamed; above-mentioned, said.

Adv. REPEATEDLY, often, again, anew, over again, afresh, once more; ditto, encore, *de novo* [*L.*], bis, *da capo* [*It.*].

again and again; over and over, over and over again; many times over; time and again, time after time; times without number; year after year; day by day &c.; many times, several times, a number of times; many a time, full many a time; frequently &c. 136; inexhaustibly, depth beyond depth.

. *ecce iterum Crispinus; toujours perdrix;* "cut and come again" [Crabbe]; "to-morrow and to-morrow and to-morrow" [*Macbeth*]; *cantilenam eandem canis* [Terence]; *nullum est jam dictum quod non dictum sit prius* [Terence].

105. Infinity. — **N.** INFINITY, infinitude, infiniteness &c. *adj.;* perpetuity &c. 112; inexhaustibility, immensity, boundlessness.

V. BE INFINITE &c. *adj.;* know no limits, know no bounds, have no limits, have no bounds; go on forever.

Adj. INFINITE; immense; numberless, countless, sumless, measureless, innumerable, immeasurable, incalculable, illimitable, interminable, unfathomable, unapproachable; exhaustless, indefinite; without number, without measure, without limit, without end; incomprehensible; limitless, endless, boundless, termless; untold, unnumbered, unmeasured, unbounded, unlimited, illimited; perpetual &c. 112.

Adv. INFINITELY &c. *adj.; ad infinitum* [*L.*].

** "as boundless as the sea" [*Romeo and Juliet*]; "a dark Illimitable ocean, without bound, Without dimension, where length, breadth, and height, And time, and place are lost" [Milton].

Section VI. TIME

1. Absolute Time

106. Time.— N. TIME, duration; period, term, stage, space, tide [*archaic*], span, spell, season; the whole time, the whole period; course &c. 109; snap.

INTERMEDIATE TIME, while, bit, breathing, interim, interval, pendency; intervention, intermission, intermittence, interregnum, interlude; respite.

ERA, epoch, Kalpa, eon, cycle; time of life, age, year, date; decade &c. (*period*) 108; point, bell, moment &c. (*instant*) 113; reign &c. 737.

glass of time, ravages of time, whirligig of time, noiseless foot of Time; scythe of Time.

107. Neverness.[1] **— N.** "NEVERNESS"; absence of time, no time; *dies non* [*L.*]; St. Tib's eve; Greek Calends (*or* Kalends).

Adv. NEVER, ne'er; at no time, at no period; on *or* at the Greek Calends (*or* Kalends); on no occasion, never in all one's born days [*colloq.*], *jamais de ma vie* [*F.*], nevermore, *sine die* [*L.*], in no degree.

** "Quoth the raven, 'Nevermore.'" [Poe].

V. CONTINUE, last, endure, stay, go on, remain, persist, subsist, abide, run, stand, dure [*archaic*], perdure [*rare*], perennate [*rare*], stick [*colloq.*]; intervene; elapse &c. 109; hold out.

take time, take up time, fill time, occupy time.

PASS TIME; pass away time, spend time, while away time, consume time, talk against time; tide over; use time, employ time; seize an opportunity &c. 134; linger on, drag on, drag along, tarry &c. 110; waste time &c. (*be inactive*) 683; procrastinate &c. 133.

Adj. CONTINUING &c. *v.*; on foot; permanent &c. (*durable*) 110; timely &c. (*opportune*) 134.

Adv. WHILE, whilst, during, pending; during the time, during the interval; in the course of; for the time being, day by day; in the time of, in the consulship of [*humorous*], when; meantime, meanwhile; in the meantime, in the interim; *ad interim* [*L.*], *pendente lite* [*L.*]; *de die in diem* [*L.*]; from day to day, from hour to hour &c.; hourly, always; for a time, for a season; till, until, up to, yet; the whole time, all the time; all along; throughout &c. (*completely*) 52; for good &c. (*diuturnity*) 110.

THEN, hereupon, thereupon, whereupon; *anno Domini* [*L.*], A.D.; *ante Christum* [*L.*], A.C.; before Christ, B.C.; *anno urbis conditæ* [*L.*], A.U.C.; *anno regni* [*L.*], A.R.; once upon a time, one fine morning.

** time runs, time runs against; *tempus fugit*.
ad calendas Græcas; "panting Time toileth after him in vain" [Johnson]; "'gainst the tooth of time and razure of oblivion" [*Measure for Measure*]; "rich with the spoils of time" [Gray]; *tempus edax rerum* [Horace]; "the long hours come and go" [C. G. Rossetti]; "the time is out of joint" [*Hamlet*]; "Time rolls his ceaseless course" [Scott]; "Time the foe of man's dominion" [Peacock]; "time wasted is existence, used is life" [Young]; *truditur dies die* [Horace]; *volat hora per orbem* [Lucretius].

[1] A term introduced by Bishop Wilkins.

108. [DEFINITE DURATION, OR POR-
TION OF TIME.] **Period.** — **N.** PERIOD;
second, minute, hour, day, week, month,
octave, *novena* [*L.*], semester, quarter,
year, decade, decennium, luster *or*
lustrum, indiction; cycle-, era- of indiction (*or* indictions); quinquennium, life-
time, generation; epoch, era, epact,
ghurry *or* ghari [*India*], lunation, moon.

century, age, millennium; *annus magnus* [*L.*], *annus mirabilis* [*L.*].

Adj. horary; hourly, annual, epochal
&c. (*periodical*) 13 ; *ante bellum* [*L.*].

108a. Contingent Duration. — Adv.
during pleasure, during good behavior;
quandiu se bene gesserit [*L.*].

Adv. IN TIME; in due time, in due season, in due course; in course of time, in
process of time, in the fullness of time.

⁎⁎⁎ labitur et labetur [Horace]; *truditur dies die* [Horace]; *fugaces labuntur anni* [Horace]; "to-
morrow and to-morrow and to-morrow Creeps in this petty pace from day to day" [*Macbeth*].

109. [INDEFINITE DURATION.] **Course.**
— **N.** corridors of time, sweep of time,
vista of time, halls of time, course of
time, progress of time, process of time,
succession of time, lapse of time, flow
of time, flux of time, stream of time,
tract of time, current of time, tide of
time, march of time, step of time, flight
of time; duration &c. 106.

[INDEFINITE TIME] æon *or* eon, age,
Kalpa; aorist.

V. ELAPSE, lapse, flow, run, proceed,
advance, pass; roll on, wear on, press on;
flit, fly, slip, slide, glide; crawl, drag;
run its course, run out; expire; go by,
pass by; be past &c. 122.

Adj. ELAPSING &c. *v.*; aoristic; transient &c. 111; progressive.

110. [LONG DURATION.] **Diuturnity.**
— **N.** DIUTURNITY [*rare*]; a long time,
length of time; an age, æon *or* eon, a
century, an eternity; slowness &c. 275;
coeternity, sempiternity, perpetuity &c.
112; blue moon [*colloq.*], coon's age
[*U. S.*], dog's age [*colloq.*].

DURABLENESS, durability; persistence,
eternalness, lastingness &c. *adj.*; continuance, standing; permanence &c.
(*stability*) 150; survival, survivance;
longevity &c. (*age*) 128; distance of
time.

PROTRACTION of time, prolongation
of time, extension of time; delay &c.
(*lateness*) 133.

V. LAST, endure, stand, remain, abide,
continue &c. 106; brave a thousand
years.

TARRY &c. (*be late*) 133; drag on, drag
its slow length along, drag a lengthening
chain; protract, prolong; spin out, eke
out, draw out, lengthen out; temporize;
gain time, make time, talk against time.

OUTLAST, outlive; survive; live to
ight again.

Adj. DURABLE, endurable [*rare*]; lasting &c. *v.*; of long duration, of long
standing; permanent, chronic, long-
standing; diuturnal [*rare*]; intransient,
intransitive; intransmutable, persistent;
lifelong, livelong; longeval [*rare*], lon-
gevous, endless, fixed, immortal, per-
durant [*rare*], perdurable, long-lived,

111. [SHORT DURATION.] **Transience.**
— **N.** TRANSIENCE, transiency, ephem-
erality, transientness [*rare*] &c. *adj.*;
evanescence, impermanence *or* imper-
manency, preterience [*rare*], volatility,
fugacity, caducity [*rare*], mortality,
span; nine days' wonder, bubble, May-
fly; spurt; temporary arrangement, interregnum, interim.

VELOCITY &c. 274; suddenness &c.
113; changeableness &c. 149.

EPHEMERON; transient, transient
boarder, transient guest, transient rates
[*all colloq., U. S.*].

V. BE TRANSIENT &c. *adj.*; flit, pass
away, fly, gallop, vanish, fleet, sink,
melt, fade, evaporate; pass away like
a -cloud, - summer cloud, - shadow,
- dream.

Adj. TRANSIENT, transitory, transitive; passing, evanescent, fleeting; flying
&c. *v.*; fugacious, fugitive; transeunt,
interim, shifting, slippery; spasmodic.

TEMPORAL, temporary; provisional,
provisory; cursory, short-lived, ephem-
eral, ephemerous [*rare*], preterient [*rare*],
caducous [*rare*], deciduous; perishable,
mortal, precarious; impermanent.

BRIEF, quick, brisk, fleet, cometary,
meteoric, volatile, extemporaneous, summary; pressed for time &c. (*haste*) 684;
sudden, momentary &c. (*instantaneous*)
113.

Adv. TEMPORARILY &c. *adj.*; pro tem-

macrobiotic, evergreen, perennial; sem-pervirent [*rare*], sempervirid; uninter-mitting, unremitting; perpetual &c. 112.

LINGERING, protracted, prolonged, spun out &c. *v.;* long-pending, long-winded; slow &c. 275.

Adv. LONG; for a long time, for an age, for ages, for ever so long, for many a long day; long ago &c. (*in a past time*) 122; *longo intervallo* [*L.*].

all the day long, all the year round; the livelong day, as the day is long, morning, noon and night; hour after hour, day after day &c.; for good, for good and all; permanently &c. *adj.; semper eadem* (Queen Elizabeth's motto) [*L.*], *semper et ubique* [*L.*].

pore [*L.*]; for the moment, for a time; awhile, *en passant* [*F.*], *in transitu* [*L.*]; in a short time; soon &c. (*early*) 132; briefly &c. *adj.;* at short notice; on the point of, on the eve of; *in articulo* [*L.*]; between cup and lip.

⁎⁎⁎ one's days are numbered; the time is up; here to-day and gone to-morrow; *non semper erit œstas; eheu! fugaces labuntur anni; sic transit gloria mundi;* "a schoolboy's tale, the wonder of the hour!" [Byron]; *dum loqui-mur fugerit invidia œtas; fugit hora.*

---

112. [ENDLESS DURATION.] **Perpetuity.** — **N.** PERPETUITY, eternity, everness,[1] aye, sempiternity, perenniality [*rare*], coeternity, immortality, athanasy, athanasia; everlastingness &c. *adj.;* per-petuation; continued existence, unin-terrupted existence; perennity [*obs.*].

V. HAVE NO END; last forever, endure forever, go on forever.

ETERNIZE, immortalize, eternalize, monumentalize, perpetuate.

Adj. PERPETUAL, eternal; everduring, everlasting, everliving, everflowing; continual, sempiternal, sempiternous [*rare*], eviternal [*rare*]; coeternal; end-less, unending; ceaseless, incessant, unin-terrupted, indesinent [*obs.*], unceasing; interminable, eterne [*poetic*], having no end; unfading, evergreen, amaranthine; never-ending, never-dying, never-fading; deathless, immortal, undying, imper-ishable.

Adv. PERPETUALLY &c. *adj.;* always, ever, evermore [*archaic*], aye; forever, for aye, forevermore, forever and a day, forever and ever; forever and aye, in all ages, from age to age; without end; world without end, time without end; *in secula seculorum* [*L.*]; to the end of time, to the crack of doom, to the "last syllable of recorded time" [*Mac-beth*]; till doomsday; constantly &c. (*very frequently*) 136.

⁎⁎⁎ esto perpetuum; labitur et labetur in omne volubilis œvum [Horace]; "but thou shalt flourish in immortal youth" [Addison]; "Eter-nity! thou pleasing, dreadful thought" [Addi-son]; "her immortal part with angels lives" [*Romeo and Juliet*]; *ohne Hast aber ohne Rast* [Goethe's motto]; *ora e sempre.*

[1] Bishop Wilkins.

113. [POINT OF TIME.] **Instantaneity.** — **N.** INSTANTANEITY, instantaneous-ness; suddenness, abruptness.

MOMENT, instant, second, minute; twinkling, flash, breath, crack, jiffy [*colloq.*], *coup* [*F.*], burst, flash of light-ning, stroke of time.

TIME; epoch, time of day, time of night; hour, minute; very minute &c., very time, very hour; present time, right time, true time, exact time, correct time.

V. BE INSTANTANEOUS &c. *adj.;* twinkle, flash.

Adj. INSTANTANEOUS, momentary, ex-tempore, sudden, instant, abrupt; subitaneous [*obs.*], hasty; quick as thought,[2] quick as lightning; rapid as electricity.

Adv. INSTANTANEOUSLY &c. *adj.;* in no time, in less than no time; presto, *subito* [*It. and L.*], instanter, forthright [*archaic*], eftsoon *or* eftsoons [*archaic*], in a trice, in a jiffy [*colloq.*], suddenly, at a stroke, like a shot; in a moment &c. *n.;* in the twinkling of an eye, in the twinkling of a bedpost [*humorous*]; in one's tracks; right away; *toute à l'heure* [*F.*]; at one jump, in the same breath, *per saltum* [*L.*], *uno saltu* [*L.*]; at once, all at once; plump, slap [*colloq.*]; "at one fell swoop" [*Macbeth*]; at the same instant &c. *n.;* immediately &c. (*early*) 132; extempore, on the moment, on the spot, on the dot [*colloq.*], on the spur of the moment; just then; slapdash &c. (*haste*) 684.

⁎⁎⁎ touch and go; no sooner said than done; "we shall all be changed, in a moment, in the twinkling of an eye" [*Bible*].

[2] See note on 264.

114. [ESTIMATION, MEASUREMENT, AND RECORD OF TIME.] **Chronometry. — N.** CHRONOMETRY, horometry, chronology, horology; date, epoch; style, era, age.

almanac, calendar, ephemeris; standard time, daylight-saving time; register, registry; chronicle, annals, journal, diary, chronogram, isochronon.

[INSTRUMENTS FOR THE MEASUREMENT OF TIME] clock, watch; chronometer, chronoscope, chronograph; repeater; timekeeper, timepiece; dial, sundial, gnomon, horologe, horologium [rare], hydroscope, pendule [F.], hourglass, clepsydra; ghurry or ghari [Hind.].

CHRONOGRAPHER, chronologer, chronologist, horologer; annalist.

V. FIX THE TIME, mark the time; date, register, chronicle, chronologize; measure time, beat time, mark time; bear date.

Adj. CHRONOLOGIC or chronological, chronometric or chronometrical, chronogrammatical; datal [rare], temporal, isochronous, isochronal, cinquecento, quattrocento, trecento.

Adv. o'clock.

₊ "we were none of us musical, though Miss Jenkins beat time, out of time, by way of appearing so" [Gaskell].

115. [FALSE ESTIMATE OF TIME.] **Anachronism. — N.** ANACHRONISM, metachronism, parachronism, prochronism; prolepsis, misdate; anticipation, antichronism [rare].

disregard of time, neglect of time, oblivion of time.

intempestivity [rare] &c. 135.

V. MISDATE, antedate, postdate, overdate; anticipate; take no note of time; anachronize [rare].

Adj. MISDATED &c. v.; undated; overdue; out of date, anachronous, anachronistic, intempestive, behind time.

2. RELATIVE TIME

1. Time with reference to Succession

116. Priority. — N. PRIORITY, antecedence, anteriority, precedence, preëxistence; precession &c. 280; precursor &c. 64; the past &c. 122; premises.

V. PRECEDE, come before; forerun; prevene [rare], antecede; go before &c. (lead) 280; preëxist; dawn; presage &c. 511; herald, usher in, announce.

be beforehand &c. (be early) 132; steal a march upon, anticipate, forestall; have the start, gain the start.

Adj. PRIOR, previous; preceding, precedent [rare]; anterior, antecedent; preëxistent; former, aforegoing, aforesighted, aforementioned, aforethought, fore [obs.], foregoing; before-mentioned, above-mentioned; aforesaid, said; introductory &c. (precursory) 64; prodromal.

Adv. BEFORE, prior to; earlier; previously &c. adj.; afore [obs.], aforehand [archaic], ere, theretofore, erewhile; ere then, ere now, before then, before now; already, yet, beforehand; or ever, aforetime; on the eve of.

₊ prior tempore prior jure; "When I was a king in Babylon And you were a Christian slave" [Henley].

117. Posteriority. — N. POSTERIORITY; succession, sequence; following &c. 281; subsequence, subsequency, supervention; continuance, prolongation; futurity &c. 121; successor; sequel &c. 65; remainder, reversion.

V. FOLLOW AFTER &c. 281, come after, go after; succeed, supervene; ensue, attend, emanate [rare], occur, result; step into the shoes of.

Adj. SUBSEQUENT, posterior, following, after, later, succeeding, sequacious [rare], successive, sequential [rare], ensuing, consecutive, attendant, sequent, postliminary [rare], postnate [obs.]; postdiluvial, postdiluvian; posthumous; future &c. 121; after-dinner, postprandial.

Adv. SUBSEQUENTLY, after, afterwards, since, later; at a subsequent period, at a later period; next, in the sequel, close upon, thereafter, thereupon, upon which, eftsoon or eftsoons [archaic]; from that time, from that moment; after a while, after a time; in process of time.

₊ "He smiled a sickly smile and he curled up on the floor, And the subsequent proceedings interested him no more" [Bret Harte].

118. Present Time. — N. THE PRESENT TIME, the present day, the present moment, the present juncture, the present occasion; the times, existing time, time being; twentieth century; crisis, epoch, day, hour.

age, time of life.

Adj. PRESENT, actual, instant, current, nonce, latest, existing, that is.

Adv. AT THIS TIME, at this moment &c. 113; at the present time &c. *n.*; now, at present; at hand.

at this time of day, to-day, now-a-days; already; even now, but now, just now; on the present occasion; for the time being, for the nonce; *pro hâc vice* [*L.*]; on the nail, on the spot; on the spur of the moment, on the spur of the occasion.

UNTIL NOW; to this day, to the present day.

*** "upon this bank and shoal of time" [*Macbeth*]; "unborn To-morrow and dead Yesterday" [Omar Khayyám — Fitzgerald]; "the present hour alone is man's" [Johnson].

119. [TIME DIFFERENT FROM THE PRESENT.] **Different time.** — N. different time, other time.

[INDEFINITE TIME] aorist.

Adj. aoristic; indefinite.

Adv. THEN, at that time, at that moment, at that instant; at which time, at which moment, at which instant; on that occasion, upon.

WHEN; whenever, whensoever; whereupon, upon which, on which occasion; at another time, at a different time, at some other time, at any time; at various times; some of these days, one of these days, some fine morning, one fine morning; some fine day, on divers occasions, sooner or later; some time or other.

ONCE, formerly, once upon a time.

120. Synchronism. — N. SYNCHRONISM; coexistence, coincidence; simultaneousness &c. *adj.*; concurrence, concomitance, unity of time, interim.

[HAVING EQUAL TIMES] isochronism.

CONTEMPORARY, coeval, coetanian [*obs.*].

V. COEXIST, concur, accompany, go hand in hand, keep pace with; synchronize, isochronize.

Adj. SYNCHRONOUS, synchronal, synchronic *or* synchronical, synchronistic *or* synchronistical, simultaneous, coexisting, coincident, concomitant, concurrent; coeval, coevous [*obs.*]; contemporary, contemporaneous; coetaneous [*rare*], coinstantaneous, coterminous, collateral, coeternal; isochronous.

Adv. AT THE SAME TIME; simultaneously &c. *adj.*; together, in concert, during the same time; in the same breath; *pari passu* [*L.*]; in the interim.

at the very moment &c. 113; just as, as soon as; meanwhile &c. (*while*) 106.

121. [PROSPECTIVE TIME.] **Futurity.** — N. FUTURITY, futurition [*rare*]; future, hereafter, time to come; approaching —, coming —, subsequent —, after- -time, -age, -days, -hours, -years, -ages, -life; morrow, to-morrow, by and by, the yet [*rare*]; millennium, chiliad [*rare*], millenary, doomsday, day of judgment, crack of doom, remote future.

APPROACH OF TIME, advent, time drawing on, womb of time; destiny &c. 152; eventuality.

HERITAGE, heirs, posterity, descendants.

PROSPECT, anticipation &c. (*expectation*) 507; foresight &c. 510.

V. LOOK FORWARDS; anticipate &c. (*expect*) 507, (*foresee*) 510; forestall &c. (*be early*) 132.

122. [RETROSPECTIVE TIME.] **Preterition.** — N. PRETERITION; priority &c. 116; the past, past time; heretofore [*rare*]; days of yore, days of old, days past, days gone by; times of yore, times of old, times past, times gone by; bygone days; old **times,** ancient times, former times; foretime [*rare*]; yesterday, the olden time, good old time; langsyne; eld [*obs. or poetic*].

ANTIQUITY, antiqueness, ancientness, *status quo* [*L.*]; time immemorial, distance of time; history, remote age, remote time; remote past; rust of antiquity.

paleontology, paleography, paleology; palætiology, archæology; archaism, antiquarianism, medievalism, Pre-Raphaelitism.

RETROSPECTION, looking back; memory &c. 505.

APPROACH, await, threaten; impend &c. (*be destined*) 152; come on, draw on; draw near.

Adj. FUTURE, to come; coming &c. (*impending*) 152; next, near; near at hand, close at hand; eventual, ulterior; anticipant, expectant, prospective, in prospect &c. (*expectation*) 507; millenary, millennial.

Adv. PROSPECTIVELY, hereafter, in future; on the knees of the gods; *kal* [*Hind.*], to-morrow, the day after to-morrow; in course of time, in process of time, in the fullness of time; eventually, ultimately, sooner or later; proximo; *paulo post futurum* [*L.*]; in after time; one of these days; after a time, after a while.

FROM THIS TIME; henceforth, henceforwards; thence; thenceforth, thenceforward; whereupon, upon which.

SOON &c. (*early*) 132; on the eve of, on the point of, on the brink of; about to; close upon.

⁎ *quid sit futurum cras fuge quœrere* [Horace]; "The Bird of Time has but a little way To flutter — and the Bird is on the Wing" [Omar Khayyám — Fitzgerald].

ANTIQUARY, antiquarian; paleologist, archæologist &c.; Oldbuck, Dryasdust; *laudator temporis acti* [*L.*]; medievalist, Pre-Raphaelite.

ANCESTRY &c. (*paternity*) 166.

V. BE PAST &c. *adj.*; have expired &c. *adj.*, have run its course, have had its day; pass; pass by, pass away, pass off; go by, go away, go off; lapse, blow over.

LOOK BACK, trace back, cast the eyes back; exhume.

Adj. PAST, gone, gone by, over, passed away, bygone, foregone [*archaic*]; elapsed, lapsed, preterlapsed [*rare*], expired, no more, run out, blown over, that has been, bypast, agone [*archaic*], whilom [*archaic*], extinct, never to return, exploded, forgotten, irrecoverable; obsolete &c. (*old*) 124.

FORMER, pristine, quondam, *ci-devant* [*F.*], late; ancestral.

FOREGOING; last, latter; recent, overnight, preterit *or* preterite, past, pluperfect, past perfect.

LOOKING BACK &c. *v.*; retrospective, retroactive; archæological &c. *n.*

Adv. FORMERLY; of old, of yore; erst [*archaic or poetic*], erstwhile [*archaic*], whilom [*archaic*], erewhile [*archaic*], time was, ago, over; in the olden time &c. *n.*; anciently, long ago, long since; a long while ago, a long time ago; years ago, ages ago; some time ago, some time since, some time back.

yesterday, the day before yesterday; last year, last season, last month &c.; *ultimo* [*L.*]; lately &c. (*newly*) 123.

RETROSPECTIVELY; ere now, before now, till now; hitherto, heretofore; no longer; once, once upon a time; from time immemorial; in the memory of man; time out of mind; already, yet, up to this time; *ex post facto* [*L.*].

⁎ time was; the time has been, the time hath been; *fuimus Troës* [Vergil]; *fuit Ilium* [Vergil]; *hoc erat in more majorum;* "O call back yesterday, bid time return" [*Richard II*]; *tempi passati;* "the eternal landscape of the past" [Tennyson]; *ultimus Romanorum;* "what's past is prologue" [*Tempest*]; "whose yesterdays look backward with a smile" [Young]; "the old days were great because the men who lived in them had mighty qualities" [Roosevelt].

2. Time with reference to a particular Period

123. Newness. — N. NEWNESS &c. *adj.;* novelty, recency; neology, neologism; immaturity; youth &c. 127; gloss of novelty.

INNOVATION; renovation &c. (*restoration*) 660.

MODERNIST, neoteric; neologist.

UPSTART, *narikin* [*Jap.*], start-up [*rare*], *nouveau riche* [*F.*], parvenu.

MODERNISM, modernness, modernity; modernization; *dernier cri* [*F.*]; latest fashion; mushroom.

V. RENEW &c. (*restore*) 660; modernize.

124. Oldness. — N. OLDNESS &c. *adj.;* age, antiquity, eld [*obs. or poetic*]; cobwebs of antiquity.

MATURITY, matureness, ripeness.

DECLINE, decay; senility &c. 128.

SENIORITY, eldership, primogeniture.

ARCHAISM &c. (*the past*) 122; thing of the past, relic of the past; megatherium; Babylonian, Assyrian, Sanskrit.

TRADITION, prescription, custom, immemorial usage, common law; folklore.

V. BE OLD &c. *adj.*; have had its day, have seen its day.

Adj. NEW, novel, recent, fresh, green; young &c. 127; evergreen; raw, immature; virgin; untried, unhandseled, unheard-of, untrodden, unbeaten; fire-new, span-new.

MODERN, late, neoteric, neoterical; new-born, new-fashioned, newfangled, newfledged; of yesterday; just out [colloq.], brand-new, up-to-date [colloq.]; fin-de-siècle [F.], vernal, renovated; sempervirent [rare], sempervirid [rare].

fresh as a rose, fresh as a daisy, fresh as paint [colloq.]; spick-and-span, spick-and-span-new, unhandled.

Adv. NEWLY &c. adj.; afresh, anew, lately, just now, only yesterday, the other day; latterly, of late.

not long ago, a short time ago.

₊ di novello tutto par bello; nullum est jam dictum quod non dictum est prius; una scopa nuova spazza bene; "an upstart crow decked in our feathers" [Peele — of Shakespeare].

BECOME OLD &c. adj.; age, fade.

Adj. OLD, ancient, olden [archaic], eldern [archaic], antique; of long standing, time-honored, venerable, hoary, vetust [obs.]; elder, eldest; firstborn.

PRIMITIVE, prime, primeval, primigenous, primigenial, primigenious; paleo-anthropic; primordial, primordiate [rare]; aboriginal &c. (beginning) 66; diluvian, antediluvian, protohistoric, prehistoric, dateless, patriarchal, preadamite; palæocrystic; fossil, paleozoic, preglacial, antemundane; archaic, Vedic, classic, medieval, Pre-Raphaelite, ancestral; black-letter.

IMMEMORIAL, traditional, traditive, traditionary [rare], prescriptive, customary, unwritten, whereof the memory of man runneth not to the contrary; inveterate, rooted.

ANTIQUATED, of other times, old as the hills, of the old school, after-age, obsolete; out-of-date, out-of-fashion; fusty, outworn, moth-eaten [humorous], gone out, gone by, passé [F.], extinct, time-worn; crumbling &c. (deteriorated) 659; secondhand.

stale, old-fashioned, old-fangled [rare], behind the age; old-world; exploded; dead, disused, past, run out; senile &c. 128; time-worn; crumbling &c. (deteriorated) 659; secondhand.

old as the hills, old as Methuselah, old as Adam, old as history.

Adv. since the world was made, since the year one, since the days of Methuselah.

₊ vetera extollimus recentium incuriosi [Tacitus]; "How weary, stale, flat, and unprofitable Seem to me all the uses of this world" [Hamlet.]

125. Morning. [NOON.] — **N.** MORNING, morn, matins [eccl.], morningtide [rare or poetic], forenoon, a.m., prime, dawn, daybreak; dayspring, foreday [chiefly Scot.], sun-up [U. S.], peep of day, break of day; aurora; first blush of the morning, first flush of the morning, prime of the morning; twilight, crepuscle or crepuscule, sunrise; daylight, daypeep, cockcrow, cockcrowing; the small hours, the wee sma' hours [Scot.].

NOON, midday, noonday, noontide, meridian, prime; nooning, noontime.

SPRING, springtide, springtime, seed-time; vernal equinox.

SUMMER, summertide, summertime, midsummer.

Adj. MATIN, matutinal, matinal, matutinary [rare]; crepuscular.

NOON, noonday, midday, meridional [rare in this sense].

SPRING, vernal, vernant [obs.].

SUMMER, æstival or estival.

126. Evening. [MIDNIGHT.] — **N.** EVENING, eve; decline of day, fall of day, close of day; candlelight, candle-lighting; eventide, evensong [eccl. or archaic], vespers [eccl.], nighttide [archaic], nightfall, curfew, dusk, twilight, eleventh hour; sunset, sundown; going down of the sun, cockshut [obs.], dewy eve, gloaming, bedtime.

AFTERNOON, post meridiem [L.], p.m.

MIDNIGHT; dead of night, witching hour of night, witching time of night, killing-time.

AUTUMN; fall, fall of the leaf; harvest, autumnal equinox; Indian summer, St. Luke's summer, St. Martin's summer.

WINTER, hiems [L.].

Adj. VESPER, vespertine, nocturnal; autumnal.

WINTRY, winterly, brumous, brumal.

₊ "midnight, the outpost of advancing day" [Longfellow]; "sable-vested Night" [Milton]; "this gorgeous arch with golden worlds inlay'd" [Young]; "the gradual dusky veil" [Collins].

Adv. AT SUNRISE &c. *n.;* with the lark, when the morning dawns.

. "at shut of evening flowers" [*Paradise Lost*]; *entre chien et loup;* "flames in the forehead of the morning sky" [Milton]; "the breezy call of incense-breathing morn" [Gray].

---

127. Youth. — N. YOUTH; juvenility, juvenescence [*rare*]; juniority; infancy; babyhood, childhood, boyhood, girlhood, youthhood [*archaic*]; incunabula; minority, boyage [*rare*], immaturity, nonage, teens, tender age, bloom.

CRADLE, nursery, leading strings, pupilage [*rare*], puberty, pucelage.

FLOWER of life, springtide of life, seedtime of life, prime of life, golden season of life; heyday of youth, school days; rising generation.

Adj. YOUNG, youthful, juvenile, juvenescent, green, callow, budding, sappy, puisne [*law*], beardless, under age, in one's teens, *in statu pupillari* [*L.*]; younger, junior; hebetic, unfledged, unripe.

. "youth on the prow and pleasure at the helm" [Gray]; "youth . . . the glad season of life" [Carlyle]; "*si jeunesse savait! si vieillesse pouvait!*" [*F. prov.*].

128. Age. — N. AGE; oldness &c. *adj.* old age, advanced age; senility, senescence; years, anility, gray hairs, climacteric, grand climacteric, declining years, decrepitude, hoary age, caducity [*rare*], eld [*archaic*], superannuation; second childhood, childishness; dotage; vale of years, decline of life, senectitude [*rare*], "sear and yellow leaf" [*Macbeth*]; threescore years and ten; green old age, ripe age; longevity; time of life.

SENIORITY, eldership; elders &c. (*veteran*) 130; firstling; *doyen* [*F.*], dean, father; primogeniture.

[SCIENCE OF OLD AGE.] nostology; gerocomy [*med.*].

V. BE AGED &c. *adj.;* grow old, get old &c. *adj.;* age; decline, wane; senesce [*rare*].

Adj. AGED; old &c. 124; elderly, eldern [*archaic*], senile; matronly, anile; in years; ripe, mellow, run to seed, declining, waning, past one's prime; gray, grayheaded; hoar, hoary; venerable, time-worn, antiquated, *passé* [*F.*], effete, decrepit, superannuated; advanced in life, advanced in years; stricken in years; wrinkled, marked with the crow's foot; having one foot in the grave; doting &c. (*imbecile*) 499; like the last of pea time.

years old; of a certain age, no chicken [*colloq.*], old as Methuselah; ancestral; patriarchal &c. (*ancient*) 124; gerontic.

OLDER, elder, oldest, eldest; senior; firstborn.

. "give me a staff of honor for my age" [Titus Andronicus]; *bis pueri senes; peu de gens savent être vieux;* plenus annis abiit plenus honoribus [Pliny the Younger]; "old age is creeping on apace" [Byron]; "slow-consuming age" [Gray]; "the hoary head is a crown of glory" [*Proverbs xvi*, 31]; "the silver livery of advised age" [*II Henry VI*]; to grow old gracefully; "to vanish in the chinks that Time has made" [Rogers].

---

129. Infant. — N. INFANT, babe, baby; nursling, suckling, yearling, weanling; papoose, *bambino* [*It.*]; vagitus.

CHILD, bairn [*Scot.*], tot, mite, scrap, chick, kid [*slang*], butcha or bacha [*Hind.*]; little one, brat, chit, pickaninny [*U. S.*], urchin; bantling, bratling elf.

YOUTH, boy, lad, laddie, slip, sprig, stripling, youngster, younker [*colloq.*], whipster [*rare*], youngling [*rare*], damoiseau [*archaic*], cub, callant [*Scot.*], whippersnapper [*colloq.*], whiffet [*U. S.*], schoolboy, hobbledehoy, hopeful, cadet, minor, master.

SCION, sapling, seedling; tendril, olive-branch, nestling, chicken, duckling,

130. Veteran. — N. VETERAN, old man, reverend sir, seer, patriarch, graybeard; grandfather, grandsire [*archaic*], grisard [*rare*], oldster [*colloq.*], pantaloon [*obs.*]; gaffer, sexagenarian, octogenarian, nonagenarian, centenarian; *doyen* [*F.*], old stager; dotard &c. 501.

GRANNY, grandam *or* grandame [*archaic*], gammer [*dial. Eng.*], crone, hag, oldwife, beldam *or* beldame.

preadamite, Methuselah, Nestor, old Parr; elders; forefathers &c. (*paternity*) 166; Darby and Joan, Philemon and Baucis, "John Anderson, my jo" [Burns].

Adj. VETERAN; aged &c. 128.

. "superfluous lags the veteran on the stage" [Johnson].

larva, chrysalis, tadpole, whelp, cub, pullet, fry, callow [*obs.*], codling *or* codlin; fœtus, calf, colt, pup, puppy, foal, kitten; lamb, lambkin; aurelia, caterpillar, cocoon, nymph, nympha, pupa, staddle.

GIRL, lass, lassie; wench [*dial.*], miss, damsel; damoiselle, damosel *or* damozel [*archaic*]; demoiselle; maid, maiden; virgin; nymph, colleen, girleen, flapper [*slang*], girly [*colloq.*], minx, missy, baggage, hussy; schoolgirl; hoyden, tomboy, romp.

Adj. INFANTINE, infantile; puerile; boyish, girlish, childish, babyish, kittenish; childly [*rare*], boylike, girllike, kiddish [*colloq.*], dollish [*colloq.*]; youngling, infant, baby; newborn, unfledged, newfledged, callow.

in the cradle, in swaddling clothes, in long clothes, in arms, in leading strings; at the breast; in one's teens; young &c. 127.

⁎ "first the infant Mewling and puking in the nurse's arms" [*As You Like It*].

---

131. Adolescence. — N. ADOLESCENCE, pubescence, majority; adultism; adulthood, adultness &c. *adj.*; manhood, virility; flower of age; full bloom; spring of life.

man &c. 373; woman &c. 374; adult, pubescent, no chicken [*colloq.*].

MIDDLE AGE, *mezzo cammin* [*It.*], maturity, full age, ripe age, prime of life, meridian of life.

V. COME OF AGE, come to man's estate, come to years of discretion; attain majority, put on long trousers, assume the *toga virilis* [*L.*]; have cut one's eyeteeth [*colloq.*], settle down, have sown one's wild oats.

Adj. ADOLESCENT, pubescent, of age; of full age, of ripe age; out of one's teens; grown up, full-blown, in full bloom, full-grown, manly, manlike, virile, adult; womanly, matronly; marriageable, marriable, nubile.

MIDDLE-AGED, mature, in one's prime; matronly.

⁎ "Yet ah, that Spring should vanish with the Rose! That Youth's sweet-scented manuscript should close!" [Omar Khayyám — Fitzgerald].

---

3. Time with reference to an Effect or Purpose

132. Earliness. — N. EARLINESS &c. *adj.*; morning &c. 125.

PUNCTUALITY; promptitude &c. (*activity*) 682; haste &c (*velocity*) 274; suddenness &c. (*instantaneity*) 113.

PREMATURITY, precocity, precipitation, anticipation, prevenience; a stitch in time.

V. BE EARLY &c. *adj.;* be beforehand &c. *adv.;* keep time, take time by the forelock, anticipate, forestall; have the start, gain the start; steal a march upon; gain time, draw on futurity; bespeak, secure, engage, preëngage.

ACCELERATE; expedite &c. (*quicken*) 274; make haste &c. (*hurry*) 684.

Adj. EARLY, prime, timely, seasonable, in time, punctual, forward; prompt &c. (*active*) 682; summary.

PREMATURE, precipitate, precocious; prevenient, anticipatory; rath *or* rathe [*obs. or poetic*].

SUDDEN &c. (*instantaneous*) 113; unexpected &c. 508; imminent, impending, near, near at hand; immediate.

Adv. EARLY, soon, anon, betimes,

133. Lateness. — N. LATENESS &c. *adj.;* tardiness &c. (*slowness*) 275.

DELAY, cunctation [*rare*] tarriance, moration [*rare*], delation [*archaic*], procrastination; deferring &c. *v.;* postponement, adjournment, prorogation, retardation, respite; protraction, prolongation; after-time; circumlocution office [*ridicule*], "circumlocution court" [Dickens], chancery suit, Fabian policy, *médecine expectante* [*F.*], moratorium; leeway; high time; truce, reprieve, demurrage; stop, stay, suspension, remand.

V. BE LATE &c. *adj.;* tarry, wait, stay, bide, take time; dawdle &c. (*be inactive*) 683; linger, loiter; bide one's time, take one's time; gain time; hang fire; stand over, lie over; hang, hang around *or* about [*colloq.*], hang back [*colloq.*], hang in the balance, hang in the hedge, hang up [*colloq.*], sit up for, stay up for.

PUT OFF, defer, delay, lay over, suspend; shift off, stave off; waive, retard,

rath *or* rathe [*poetic*]; eftsoon *or* eftsoons [*archaic*]; ere long, before long; punctually &c. *adj.;* to the minute; in time; in good time, in military time, in pudding time [*oos.*], in due time; time enough, on time, on the dot [*slang*].

BEFOREHAND; prematurely &c. *adj.;* precipitately &c. (*hastily*) 684; too soon; before its time, before one's time; in anticipation; unexpectedly &c. 508.

SUDDENLY &c. (*instantaneously*) 113; before one can say "Jack Robinson," at short notice, extempore; on the spur of the moment, on the spur of the occasion [Bacon]; at once; on the spot, on the instant; at sight; off hand, out of hand; *à vue d'œil* [*F.*]; straight, straightway, straightforth; forthwith, incontinently, summarily, instanter, forthright [*archaic*], immediately, briefly, shortly, erewhile [*archaic*], quickly, speedily, apace, before the ink is dry, almost immediately, presently, at the first opportunity, in no long time, by and by, in a while, directly.

₊ touch and go, no sooner said than done; *tout vient à point à qui sait attendre;* "misers get up early in the morning; and burglars . . . get up the night before" [Chesterton].

remand, postpone, adjourn; procrastinate; dally; prolong, protract; spin out, draw out, lengthen out; prorogue; keep back; tide over; push to the last, drive to the last; let the matter stand over; table, lay on the table, shelve; respite [*rare*], perendinate [*rare*]; reserve &c. (*store*) 636; temporize, filibuster [*U. S.*], stall [*slang*]; consult one's pillow, sleep upon it.

BE KEPT WAITING, dance attendance; kick one's heels [*colloq.*], cool one's heels [*colloq.*]; *faire antichambre* [*F.*]; wait impatiently; await &c. (*expect*) 507; sit up, sit up at night; lose an opportunity &c. 135.

Adj. LATE, tardy, slow, cunctatious *or* cunctative [*rare*], behindhand, serotine [*rare*], belated, postliminary [*rare*], posthumous, backward, unpunctual, impunctual [*rare*], overdue, moratory; dilatory &c. (*slow*) 275; delayed &c. *v.;* in abeyance.

Adv. LATE; backward, lateward [*obs.*], late in the day; at sunset, at the eleventh hour, at length, at last; ultimately; after time, behind time; too late; too late for &c. 135.

SLOWLY, leisurely, deliberately, at one's leisure; *ex post facto* [*L.*]; *sine die* [*L.*].

₊ *nonum prematur in annum* [Horace]; "against the sunbeams serotine and lucent" [Longfellow]; *è meglio tardi che mai; deliberando sæpe perit occasio* [Syrus]; "seven years, my lord, have now passed since I waited in your outward rooms, or was repulsed from your door" [Johnson].

134. Occasion. — N. OCCASION, opportunity, opening, room, scope, space, place, liberty, show [*colloq., U. S.*]; suitable time, suitable season, proper time, proper season; high time; opportuneness &c. *adj.;* tempestivity [*obs.*].

nick of time; golden opportunity, well-timed opportunity, fine opportunity, favorable opportunity; clear stage, fair field; *mollia tempora* [*L.*]; spare time &c. (*leisure*) 685.

CRISIS, turn, emergency, juncture, conjuncture; turning point, given time.

V. IMPROVE THE OCCASION; seize &c. (789) an opportunity *or* an occasion; use &c. (677) an opportunity *or* an occasion; give &c. (784) an opportunity *or* an occasion.

suit the occasion &c. (*be expedient*) 646.

strike the iron while it is hot, *battre le fer sur l'enclume* [*F.*], make hay while

135. Intempestivity. — N. INTEMPESTIVITY [*rare*]; unsuitable time, improper time; unreasonableness &c. *adj.;* evil hour; *contretemps* [*F.*], misventure [*archaic*], misadventure; intrusion; anachronism &c. 115.

V. BE ILL-TIMED &c. *adj.;* mistime, intrude, come amiss, break in upon; have other fish to fry; be busy, be occupied, be engaged.

LOSE AN OPPORTUNITY; throw away an opportunity, waste an opportunity, neglect &c. (460) an opportunity; allow *or* suffer the opportunity *or* occasion to -pass, – slip, – go by, – escape, – lapse; waste time &c. (*be inactive*) 683; let slip through the fingers, lock the stable door when the steed is stolen.

Adj. ILL-TIMED, mistimed; ill-fated, ill-omened, ill-starred; untimely, intrusive, unseasonable; out of date, out of season; inopportune, timeless [*archaic*],

49

the sun shines, seize the present hour, take time by the forelock, *prendre la balle au bond* [*F.*].

Adj. OPPORTUNE, timely, well-timed, timeful [*obs.*], seasonable, tempestive [*archaic*], timeous [*rare*].

lucky, providential, fortunate, happy, favorable, propitious, auspicious, critical; suitable &c. 23; *obiter dicta* [*L.*].

OCCASIONAL, accidental, extemporaneous, extemporary; contingent &c. (*uncertain*) 475.

Adv. OPPORTUNELY &c. *adj.;* in proper time, in proper course, in proper season; in due time, in due course, in due season;

inconvenient, intempestive [*rare*], untoward, *mal à propos* [*F.*], unlucky, inauspicious, unpropitious, unfortunate, unfavorable; unsuited &c. 24; inexpedient &c. 647.

unpunctual &c. (*late*) 133; too late for; premature &c. (*early*) 132; too soon for; wise after the event.

Adv. INOPPORTUNELY &c. *adj.;* as ill luck would have it, in an evil hour, the time having gone by, a day after the fair.

*** After meat mustard, after death the doctor.

for the nonce; in the nick of time, in the fullness of time; all in good time; just in time, at the eleventh hour, now or never.

BY THE WAY, by the by; *en passant* [*F.*], *à propos* [*F.*]; *pro re natâ* [*L.*], *pro hac vice* [*L.*]; *par parenthèse* [*F.*], parenthetically, by way of parenthesis; while on this subject, speaking of; *par exemple* [*F.*]; extempore; on the spur of the moment, on the spur of the occasion; on the spot &c. (*early*) 132.

*** *carpe diem* [Horace]; *occasionem cognosce;* one's hour is come, the time is up; that reminds me; *bien perdu bien connu; è sempre l'ora; ex quovis ligno non fit Mercurius; nosce tempus; nunc aut nunquam;* "there is a tide in the affairs of men Which taken at the flood, leads on to fortune" [*Julius Caesar*]; "The Moving Finger writes; and, having writ, Moves on" [Omar Khayyám — Fitzgerald].

3. RECURRENT TIME

136. Frequency. — N. FREQUENCY, frequence, oftness [*rare*], oftenness [*rare*], quotiety [*rare*]; repetition &c. 104.

V. KEEP, keep on; recur &c. 104; do nothing but.

Adj. FREQUENT, often [*archaic*], many, many times, not rare, thickcoming, incessant, perpetual, continual, constant, repeated &c. 104; habitual &c. 613; hourly &c. 138.

Adv. OFTEN, oft, ofttime [*archaic*], ofttimes, oftentimes; oftentime [*rare*], oftentide [*obs.*], not seldom, frequently; repeatedly &c. 104; unseldom, not unfrequently; in quick succession, in rapid succession; many a time and oft; oftly [*rare*], daily, hourly &c.; every day, every hour, every moment &c.

PERPETUALLY, continually, constantly, incessantly, unchangingly, steadfastly, without ceasing, at all times, daily and hourly, night and day, day and night, day after day, morning noon and night, ever and anon.

137. Infrequency. — N. INFREQUENCY, infrequence, unfrequency [*rare*], rareness, rarity; sparseness, fewness &c. 103; seldomness; uncommonness.

V. BE RARE &c. *adj.*

Adj. INFREQUENT, unfrequent [*rare*], seldseen [*archaic*], uncommon, sporadic; rare, rare as a blue diamond; few &c. 103; scarce; almost unheard of, scarce as hen's teeth [*colloq.*], unprecedented, which has not occurred within the memory of the oldest inhabitant, not within one's previous experience.

Adv. SELDOM, rarely, scarcely, hardly; not often, unfrequently, infrequently, uncommonly, sparsely, unoften; scarcely ever, hardly ever; once in a blue moon [*colloq.*].

once; once for all, once in a way; *pro hac vice* [*L.*].

*** *einmal keinmal;* "like angel visits, few and far between" [Campbell].

COMMONLY &c. (*habitually*) 613; most often.

SOMETIMES, occasionally, at times, now and then, from time to time, there being times when, *toties quoties* [*L.*], often enough, again and again.

*** "I'll do and I'll do and I'll do!" [*Macbeth*].

138. Regularity of recurrence. **Periodicity.** — **N.** PERIODICITY, intermittence; beat; oscillation &c. 314; pulse, pulsation; systole and diastole; rhythm; alternation, alternateness, alternacy [*rare*], alternativeness, alternity [*rare*].

ROUND, revolution, rotation, bout, turn, say.

ANNIVERSARY, biennial, triennial, quadrennial, quinquennial, sextennial, septennial, octennial, decennial; tricennial, jubilee, centennial, centenary, bicentennial, bicentenary, tercentenary; birthday, birthright, natal day, fête day, saint's day.

CATAMENIA, courses, menses, menstrual flux.

[REGULARITY OF RETURN] rota, cycle, period, stated time, routine; days of the week; Sunday, Monday &c.; months of the year; January &c.; feast, festival, fast &c.; Christmas, Yuletide, New Year's day, Ash Wednesday, Maundy Thursday, Good Friday, Easter; Allhallows, Allhallowmas, All Saints' Day; All Souls' Day; Candlemas, Dewali [*Hindu*], Holi *or* Hoolee [*Hindu*], Memorial *or* Decoration Day [*U. S.*], Independence Day [*U. S.*], Labor Day [*U. S.*], Thanksgiving [*U. S.*], ground-hog day [*U. S.*], woodchuck day [*U. S.*], Halloween, Hallowmas, Lady Day; leap year, bissextile; Bairam, Ramadan, Muharram [*Mohammedan*]; St. Swithin's Day; Midsummer Day; May Day &c. (*holiday*) 840; yearbook.

PUNCTUALITY, regularity, steadiness.

V. RETURN, revolve; recur in regular -order, – succession; come again, come in its turn; come round, – again; beat, pulsate; alternate; intermit.

Adj. PERIODIC, periodical; serial, recurrent, cyclic, cyclical, rhythmic *or* rhythmical; recurring &c. *v.;* intermittent, remittent; alternate, every other; every.

hourly; diurnal, daily, quotidian [*rare*]; tertian, weekly; hebdomadal, hebdomadary; biweekly, fortnightly; bimonthly; monthly, catamenial, menstrual; yearly, annual; biennial, triennial &c.; centennial, secular; paschal, lenten &c.

REGULAR, steady, constant, methodical, punctual, regular as clockwork.

Adv. PERIODICALLY &c. *adj.;* at regular intervals, at stated times; at fixed periods, at established periods; punctually &c. *adj.; de die in diem* [*L.*]; from day to day, day by day.

BY TURNS; in turn, in rotation; alternately, every other day, off and on, ride and tie, round and round.

139. Irregularity of recurrence. — **N.** IRREGULARITY, uncertainty, unpunctuality; fitfulness &c. *adj.;* capriciousness, ecrhythmus; acatastasia [*med.*].

Adj. IRREGULAR, uncertain, unpunctual, capricious, erratic, heteroclite, ecrhythmic, ecrhythmous, desultory, fitful, flickering; rambling, rhapsodical; spasmodic; immethodical, unsystematic, unequal, uneven, variable.

Adv. IRREGULARLY &c. *adj.;* by fits and starts &c. (*discontinuously*) 70.

Section VII. CHANGE

1. Simple Change

140. [DIFFERENCE AT DIFFERENT TIMES.] **Change.** — **N.** CHANGE, alteration, mutation, permutation, variation, novation [*rare*], modification, modulation, inflection *or* inflexion, mood, qualification, innovation, eversion, deviation, shift, turn; diversion; break.

TRANSFORMATION, transfiguration, transfigurement; metamorphosis; metabola *or* metabole [*med.*], transmorphism [*rare*], transmutation; deoxidization, deoxidation; transubstantiation; metagenesis, transanimation, transmigration,

141. [ABSENCE OF CHANGE.] **Permanence.** — **N.** PERMANENCE, permanency, fixity, persistence, endurance; durableness, durability, lastingness; standing, *status quo* [*L.*]; maintenance, preservation, conservation; conservatism; *laisser faire* [*F.*], *laisser aller* [*F.*]; law of the Medes and Persians; standing dish.

stability &c. 150; quiescence &c. 265; obstinacy &c. 606.

V. LET ALONE, let be; persist, remain, stay, tarry, rest; hold, hold on; last,

metempsychosis, version [*rare*]; metasomatism *or* metasomatosis, metathesis; metabolism, metastasis; transmogrification [*colloq.*]; avatar; alterative.

resolution, conversion &c. (*gradual change*) 144; revolution &c. (*sudden or radical change*) 146; inversion &c. (*reversal*) 218; displacement &c. 185; transference &c. 270.

CHANGEABLENESS &c. 149; tergiversation &c. (*change of mind*) 607.

V. CHANGE, alter, vary, wax and wane; modulate, diversify, qualify, tamper with; turn, shift, veer, gybe *or* jibe, jib, tack, chop, shuffle, swerve, warp, deviate, dodge, tergiversate, turn aside, evert, intervert [*obs.*]; pass to, take a turn, turn the corner, resume.

WORK A CHANGE, modify, vamp, patch, piece, vamp up, superinduce; transform, transfigure, transmute, transmogrify [*colloq.*], transume [*rare*], transverse [*rare*], transshape [*rare*], metabolize, convert, transubstantiate, resolve, revolutionize; chop and change; metamorphose, ring the changes.

innovate, introduce new blood, shuffle the cards; give a turn to, give a color to; influence, turn the scale; shift the scene, turn over a new leaf.

recast &c. 146; reverse &c. 218; disturb &c. 61; convert into &c. 144.

Adj. CHANGED &c. *v.;* newfangled; eversible; changeable &c. 149; transitional; modifiable; metagenetic; alterative.

Adv. *mutatis mutandis* [*L.*].

Int. *quantum mutatus!* [*L.*].

* "a change came o'er the spirit of my dream" [Byron]; *nous avons changé tout cela* [Molière]; *tempora mutantur nos et mutamur in illis; non sum qualis eram* [Horace]; *casaque tourner; corpora lente augescent cito extinguuntur* [Tacitus]; *in statu quo ante bellum;* "still ending and beginning still" [Cowper]; *vox audita perit littera scripta manet;* "all things are in perpetual flux and fleeting" [*Proverb*].

endure, bide, abide, aby *or* abye[*archaic*], dwell, maintain, keep; stand, – still, – fast, – pat [*colloq.*]; subsist, live, outlive, survive; hold – , keep one's ground, – footing; hold good.

Adj. PERMANENT; stable &c. 150; persisting &c. *v.;* established; fixed, irremovable, durable; pucka *or* pakka [*Hind.*]; unchanged &c. (change &c. 140); renewed; intact, inviolate; persistent; monotonous, uncheckered; unfailing, unfading.

UNDESTROYED, unrepealed, unsuppressed; conservative, *qualis ab incepto* [*L.*]; prescriptive &c. (*old*) 124; stationary &c. 265.

Adv. FINALLY; *in statu quo* [*L.*]; for good, at a stand, at a standstill, *uti possidetis* [*L.*]; without a shadow of turning; as you were!

* *esto perpetua; nolumus leges Angliæ mutari; j'y suis et j'y reste.*

---

142. [CHANGE FROM ACTION TO REST.] **Cessation.** — **N.** CESSATION, discontinuance, desistance, desinence.

intermission, remission; suspense, suspension; interruption; stop; hitch [*colloq.*]; stopping &c. *v.;* stoppage, halt; arrival &c. 292.

PAUSE, rest, lull, respite, truce, truce of God, armistice, stay, drop; interregnum, abeyance.

[IN DEBATE] closure, cloture, *clôture* [*F.*].

DEADLOCK, checkmate, backwater, dead water, dead stand, dead stop; end &c. 67; death &c. 360.

PUNCTUATION, comma, semicolon, colon, period, full stop, cæsura.

V. CEASE, discontinue, desist, stay; break off, leave off; hold, stop, pull up,

143. Continuance in action. — **N.** CONTINUANCE, continuation; run, pursuance, maintenance, extension, perpetuation, prolongation; persistence &c. (*perseverance*) 604a; repetition &c. 104.

V. CONTINUE, persist; go on, jog on, keep on, run on, hold on; abide, keep, pursue, stick to; take –, maintain its course; carry on, keep up, drag on, stick [*colloq.*], persevere, endure, carry on.

SUSTAIN, uphold, hold up, keep on foot; follow up, perpetuate, prolong, maintain; preserve &c. 604a; harp upon &c. (*repeat*) 104.

KEEP GOING, keep alive, keep the pot boiling [*colloq.*], keep up the ball [*colloq.*]; die in harness; plug at it *or* along [*slang*]; keep the field, keep the ball rolling,

stop short; check, check in full career, deadlock; stick, hang fire; halt; pause, rest.

come to a -stand, – standstill, – deadlock, – full stop; arrive &c. 292; go out, die away; wear away, wear off; pass away &c. (*be past*) 122; be at an end.

HAVE DONE WITH, give over, surcease, shut up shop; give up &c. (*relinquish*) 624.

hold –, stay- one's hand; rest on one's oars, repose on one's laurels.

INTERRUPT, suspend, interpel [*obs.*]; intermit, remit; put an end to, put a stop to, put a period to; derail; bring to a -stand,– standstill; stop, stall, cut short, arrest, stem the -tide, – torrent;

Int. STOP! hold! enough! avast! [*naut.*], have done! a truce to! soft! leave off! *tenez!* [*F.*], fade away! [*slang*], let up! [*slang*], cut it out! [*slang*].

⁂ "I pause for a reply" [*Julius Caesar*].

keep at it, keep up; hold on –, pursue -the even tenor of one's way.

LET BE; *stare super antiquas vias* [*L.*]; *quieta non movere* [*L.*]; let things take their course.

Adj. CONTINUING &c. *v.*; uninterrupted, unintermitting, unvarying, persistent, unceasing, unremitting, unshifting; unreversed, unstopped, unrevoked, unvaried; sustained; chronic; undying &c. (*perpetual*) 112; inconvertible.

Int. carry on! stand fast!

⁂ *nolumus leges Angliæ mutari; vestigia nulla retrorsum* [Horace]; *labitur et labetur* [Horace].

pull the check-string.

---

144. [GRADUAL CHANGE TO SOMETHING DIFFERENT.] **Conversion. — N.** CONVERSION, reduction, transmutation, resolution, assimilation; chemistry, alchemy; lapse, assumption, growth, progress; naturalization; transportation.

PROSELYTIZATION, regeneration, Catholicization, Protestantization.

PASSAGE, transit, transition, transmigration; shifting &c. *v.*; flux; phase; conjugation; convertibility.

LABORATORY &c. 691; crucible, alembic, caldron, retort, mortar; potter's wheel, anvil, lathe, blowpipe.

CONVERT, neophyte, catechumen, proselyte; pervert, renegade, apostate, turncoat.

V. BE CONVERTED INTO; become, get, wax; come –, turn- -to, –into; turn out, lapse, shift; run –, fall –, pass –, slide –, glide –, grow –, ripen –, open –, resolve itself –, settle –, merge- into; melt, grow, come round to, mature, mellow; assume the - form, – shape, – state, – nature, character- of; illapse [*rare*]; assume a new phase, undergo a change.

CONVERT INTO, resolve into; make, render; mold, form &c. 240; remodel, new-model, refound, reform, reorganize; assimilate to, bring to, reduce to.

Adj. CONVERTED INTO &c. *v.*; convertible, resolvable into; conversible [*rare*], chemical, transitional; naturalized.

Adv. gradually &c. (*slowly*) 275; *in transitu* [*L.*] &c. (*transference*) 270.

⁂ "But doth suffer a sea-change Into something rich and strange" [*Tempest*].

145. Reversion. – N. REVERSION, return; revulsion.

TURNING POINT, turn of the tide; *status quo ante bellum* [*L.*]; calm before a storm. alternation &c. (*periodicity*) 138; inversion &c. 219; recoil &c. 277; retrocession, retrospection, regression &c. 283; restoration &c. 660; relapse &c. 661; atavism, throwback; vicinism; escheat.

V. REVERT, reverse, return, turn back; relapse &c. 661; invert &c. 219; recoil &c. 277; retreat &c. 283; restore &c. 660; undo, unmake; turn the tide, turn the scale; escheat.

Adj. REVERTING &c. *v.*; revulsive, reactionary; retrorse.

Adv. REVULSIVELY, retrorsely, on the rebound, *à rebours* [*F.*].

146. [SUDDEN OR VIOLENT CHANGE.] **Revolution. — N.** REVOLUTION, revolt, *bouleversement* [*F.*], subversion, breakup; destruction &c. 162; sudden –, radical –, sweeping –, organic- change; clean sweep, debacle, *débâcle* [*F.*], overturn, overthrow, *coup d'état* [F.], rebellion, rising, uprising, mutiny, sansculottism, bolshevism, counter-revolution.

SPASM, convulsion, throe, revulsion; storm, earthquake, eruption, upheaval, cataclysm, transilience *or* transiliency [*rare*], jump, leap, plunge, jerk, start, dash; explosion.

LEGERDEMAIN &c. (*trick*) 545.

V. REVOLUTIONIZE, revolt, rebel, insurrect, rise; new-model, remodel, recast; strike out something new, break with the past; change the face of, unsex.

Adj. UNRECOGNIZABLE; transilient.

REVOLUTIONARY, catastrophic, cataclysmic, cataclysmal, convulsionary, insurgent, Red, insurrectional, insurrectionary, mutinous, rebellious, sansculottic, bolshevist *or* bolshevik.

---

147. [CHANGE OF ONE THING FOR ANOTHER.] **Substitution.** — **N.** SUBSTITUTION, commutation, subrogation [*law*], surrogation [*rare*]; supplanting &c. *v.*, supersession, supersedence, supersedure; metonymy &c. (*figure of speech*) 521.

[THING SUBSTITUTED] substitute, succedaneum, makeshift, temporary expedient; shift, apology, *pis aller* [F.], stopgap, jury mast, *locum tenens* [L.], alternate, warming pan [*colloq.*], dummy, scapegoat; double; changeling; *quid pro quo* [L.], alternative; representative &c. (*deputy*) 759; palimpsest.

PRICE, purchase money, consideration, equivalent.

V. SUBSTITUTE, put in the place of, change for; make way for, give place to; supply –, take- the place of; surrogate [*rare*], subrogate [*law*], supplant, supersede, replace, cut out [*colloq.*], serve as a substitute; step into the shoes of, stand in the shoes of; make a shift with, put up with; borrow of Peter to pay Paul; commute, redeem, compound for.

Adj. SUBSTITUTED &c. *v.*; vicarious, vicarial, substitutional, subdititious [*rare*].

Adv. INSTEAD; by proxy; in place of, in lieu of, in the stead of, in the room of; *faute de mieux* [F.].

. "Compound for sins they are inclined to
By damning those they have no mind to"
[Butler].

148. [DOUBLE OR MUTUAL CHANGE.] **Interchange.** — **N.** INTERCHANGE, exchange; commutation, permutation, intermutation; reciprocation, transposition, transposal, shuffle, shuffling; alternation, reciprocity; castling [at chess]; hocus-pocus; swap [*colloq.*].

barter &c. 794; a Roland for his Oliver; tit for tat &c. (*retaliation*) 718; cross fire, battledore and shuttlecock; *quid pro quo* [L.].

INTERCHANGEABLENESS, interchangeability.

V. INTERCHANGE, exchange, counterchange; bandy, barter, transpose, shuffle, change hands, swap [*colloq.*], permute, reciprocate, commute; interwork, give and take, return the compliment; play at -puss in the corner, – battledore and shuttlecock; take in one another's washing; retaliate &c. 718; requite.

Adj. RECIPROCAL, interactive, mutual, commutative, interchangeable; interchanged &c. *v.*; intercurrent [*rare*].

international, interstate, interurban, intercollegiate, intertribal, interdenominational, interscholastic.

Adv. IN EXCHANGE, *vice versa* [L.], conversely, *mutatis mutandis* [L.], backwards and forwards, forward and back, to and fro, back and forth, by turns, turn about, contrariwise, commutatively, turn and turn about; each in his turn, every one in his turn.

---

2. COMPLEX CHANGE

149. Changeableness. — **N.** CHANGEABLENESS &c. *adj.*; mutability, inconstancy; versatility, mobility; instability, unstable equilibrium; vacillation &c. (*irresolution*) 605; fluctuation, vicissitude; dysphoria; alternation &c. (*oscillation*) 314; transientness &c. 111.

150. Stability. — **N.** STABILITY; immutability &c. *adj.*; unchangeableness &c. *adj.*; constancy; stable equilibrium, immobility, soundness, vitality, stabiliment [*rare*], stabilization; stiffness, ankylosis, solidity, *aplomb* [F.]; coherence.

permanence &c. 141; obstinacy &c. 606.

[COMPARISONS] moon, Proteus, kaleidoscope, chameleon, quicksilver, shifting sands, weathercock, vane, weathervane, harlequin, turncoat, Vicar of Bray, Cynthia of the minute, April showers; wheel of Fortune.

RESTLESSNESS &c. *adj.;* fidgets, disquiet; disquietude, inquietude; unrest; agitation &c. 315.

V. FLUCTUATE, vary, waver, flounder, flicker, flitter [*archaic*], flit, flutter, shift, shuffle, shake, totter, tremble, vacillate, wamble [*dial.*], turn and turn about, ring the changes; sway –, shift– to and fro; change and change about; oscillate &c. 314; vibrate –, oscillate– between two extremes; alternate; have as many phases as the moon.

Adj. CHANGEABLE, changeful; changing &c. 140; mutable, variable, checkered, ever changing, kaleidoscopic; protean, proteiform; versatile.

INCONSTANT, unstaid, unsteady, unstable, unfixed, unsettled; fluctuating &c. *v.;* restless, uneasy; agitated &c. 315; erratic, fickle; mercurial, irresolute &c. 605; capricious &c. 608; touch and go; inconsonant, fitful, spasmodic; vibratory; vagrant, feathery [*rare*], lightheaded, wayward; desultory; afloat; alternating; alterable, plastic, mobile; transient &c. 111; wavering.

Adv. SEESAW &c. (*oscillation*) 314; off and on.

** "a rolling stone gathers no moss"; *pietra mossa non fa muschis; honores mutant mores; varium et mutabile semper femina* [Vergil].

FIXTURE, establishment; rock, pillar, tower, foundation, leopard's spots, Ethiopian's skin; law of the Medes and Persians.

standpatter [*U. S. politics*].

V. BE FIRM &c. *adj.;* stick fast; stand firm, keep firm, remain firm; stand pat; weather the storm.

ESTABLISH, settle, stablish [*archaic*], ascertain, fix, set, stabilitate [*obs.*], stabilize; stet [*printing*], retain, keep hold; make good, make sure; fasten &c. (*join*) 43; set on its legs [*colloq.*], set on its feet; float; perpetuate.

SETTLE DOWN; strike root, take root; take up one's abode &c. 184; build one's house on a rock.

Adj. UNCHANGEABLE, immutable; unaltered, unalterable; not to be changed, constant; permanent &c. 141; invariable, unyielding, undeviating; stable, durable; perennial &c. (*diuturnal*) 110.

FIXED, steadfast, firm, firm as Gibraltar, firm as a rock, on a rock; tethered, anchored, moored, at anchor, firmly –seated, – established &c. *v.;* deep-rooted, ineradicable; fast, steady, balanced; confirmed, inveterate, valid; fiducial; immovable, irremovable, riveted, rooted; stated, settled, stereotyped, established &c. *v.;* obstinate &c. 606; vested; incontrovertible, indeclinable.

STUCK FAST, transfixed, aground, high and dry, stranded.

INCOMMUTABLE, indefeasible, irretrievable, intransmutable, irresoluble, irrevocable, irreversible, reverseless, inextinguishable, irreducible; indissoluble, imperishable, indelible, indeciduous; insusceptible, – of change.

indissolvable; indestructible, undying, susceptible, – of change.

Int. stet [*L., printing*].

** *littera scripta manet;* "Come one, come all! this rock shall fly From its firm base as soon as I" [Scott]; *cælum non animum mutant qui trans mare currunt* [Horace].

Present Events

151. Eventuality. — N. EVENTUALITY, eventuation, event, occurrence, supervention, incident, affair, transaction, proceeding, fact; matter of fact, naked fact; phenomenon: advent.

CIRCUMSTANCE, particular, casualty, accident, happening, adventure, passage, crisis, pass, emergency, contingency; concern, business.

CONSEQUENCE, issue, result, termination, conclusion.

Future Events

152. Destiny. — N. DESTINY &c. (*necessity*) 601; future existence, postexistence; hereafter; foredoom, future state, next world, world to come, after life; futurity &c. 121; everlasting life, everlasting death; life beyond the grave, life to come, world beyond the grave; prospect &c. (*expectation*) 507.

V. IMPEND; hang over, lie over; threaten, loom, await, hover, come on, approach, stare one in the face; fore-

AFFAIRS, matters; the world, life, things, doings; things –, affairs- in general; the times, state of affairs, order of the day; course –, tide –, stream –, current –, run –, march- of -things, – events; ups and downs of life; chapter of accidents &c. (*chance*) 156; situation &c. (*circumstances*) 8; memorabilia.

V. HAPPEN, occur; take place, take effect; come, become of; come -off, – about, – round, – into existence, – forth, – to pass, – on; pass, present itself; fall; fall out, turn out; run, be on foot, fall in; befall, betide, bechance; prove, eventuate, draw on; turn up, crop up, spring up, cast up; supervene, survene, |*obs.*] issue, arrive, ensue, result, eventuate, arise, start, hold, take its course; pass off &c. (*be past*) 122.

EXPERIENCE; meet with; fall to the lot of; be one's -chance, – fortune, – lot; find; encounter, undergo; pass through, go through; endure &c. (*feel*) 821.

Adj. HAPPENING &c. *v.;* going on, doing, current; in the wind, afloat; on foot, on the carpet, on the tapis; at issue, in question; incidental.

EVENTFUL, stirring, bustling, full of incident; memorable, momentous, signal.

Adv. EVENTUALLY, ultimately, finally; in the event of, in case; in the course of things; in the natural *or* ordinary course of things; as things go, as times go; as the world -goes, – wags; as the tree falls, as the cat jumps [*colloq.*]; as it may -turn out, – happen.

***** the plot thickens; "breasts the blows of circumstance" [Tennyson]; "so runs the round of life from hour to hour" [Tennyson]; "sprinkled along the waste of years" [Keble]; "Life is our dictionary" [Emerson]; "A Moment's Halt — a momentary taste Of Being from the Well amid the Waste" [Omar Khayyám — Fitzgerald].

ordain, preorder; predestine, doom, foredoom, have in store for.

Adj. IMPENDING &c. *v.;* destined; about to be, about to happen; coming, in store, to come, going to happen, instant, at hand, near; near at hand, close at hand; overhanging, hanging over one's head, imminent; brewing, preparing, forthcoming; in the wind, on the cards [*colloq.*], in reserve; that will be, that is to be; in prospect &c. (*expected*) 507; looming in the -distance, – horizon, – future; postexistent, unborn, in embryo; in the womb of -time, futurity; on the knees of the gods, in the future; pregnant &c. (*producing*) 161.

Adv. IN TIME, in the long run; all in good time; eventually &c. 151; whatever may happen &c. (*certainly*) 474; as chance &c. (156) would have it.

***** "see future sons and daughters yet unborn" [Pope].

SECTION VIII. CAUSATION

1. CONSTANCY OF SEQUENCE IN EVENTS

153. [CONSTANT ANTECEDENT.] **Cause.** — **N.** CAUSE, origin, source, principle, element; prime mover, *primum mobile* [*L.*], primordium [*rare*]; *vera causa* [*L.*], ultimate cause, Great First Cause; author &c. (*producer*) 164; mainspring, agent; leaven; groundwork, foundation &c. (*support*) 215.

SPRING, fountain, well, font; fountain-head, springhead, reservoir, headspring, wellspring, wellhead; *fons et origo* [*L.*], genesis; descent &c. (*paternity*) 166; remote cause; influence.

PIVOT, hinge, turning point, lever; key; heart, nucleus, hub, focus; proximate cause, *causa causans* [*L.*]; last straw that breaks the camel's back.

154. [CONSTANT SEQUENT.] **Effect.** — **N.** EFFECT, consequence; aftercome [*Scot.*], aftergrowth, afterclap, aftermath, aftercrop, derivative, derivation; result; resultant; upshot, issue, outcome, resultance [*rare*], *dénouement* [*F.*], conclusion; falling action, catastrophe, end &c. 67; impress, impression; development, outgrowth; blossom, bud, ear, fruit, crop, harvest, product.

PRODUCTION, produce, work, handiwork, fabric, performance; creature, creation; offspring, offshoot; first fruits, firstlings; heredity, telegony; premices [*obs.*], primices [*obs.*].

V. BE THE EFFECT OF &c. *n.;* be due to, be owing to; originate in *or* from;

REASON, reason why; ground; why and wherefore [*colloq.*], rationale, occasion, derivation; final cause &c. (*intention*) 620; *les dessous des cartes* [*F.*]; undercurrents.

RUDIMENT, egg, germ, embryo, fetus *or* fœtus, bud, root, radix, radical, radication [*rare*], etymon, nucleus, seed, stem, stock, stirps, trunk, taproot, gemma, gemmule, radicle, semen, sperm.

NEST, cradle, nursery, womb, nidus, birthplace, breeding-place, hotbed.; CAUSALITY, causation; origination; causative; production &c. 161.

V. BE THE CAUSE OF &c. *n.*; originate; give origin to, give rise to, give occasion to; cause, occasion, sow the seeds of, kindle, suscitate [*obs.*]; bring on, bring to pass, bring about; produce; create &c. 161; set up, set afloat, set on foot; found, broach, institute, lay the foundation of; lie at the root of.

PROCURE, induce, draw down, open the door to, superinduce, evoke, entail, operate; elicit, provoke.

rise from, arise from, take its rise from, spring from, proceed from, emanate from, come from, grow from, bud from, sprout from, germinate from, issue from, flow from, result from, follow from, derive its origin from, accrue from; come to, come of, come out of; depend upon, hang upon, hinge upon, turn upon.

TAKE THE CONSEQUENCES, reap where one has sown, make one's bed and lie on it, sow the wind and reap the whirlwind.

Adj. OWING TO; resulting from &c. *v.*; resultant, firstling; derivable from; due to; caused by &c. 153; dependent upon; derived from, evolved from; derivative; hereditary; telegonous.

Adv. CONSEQUENTLY, of course, it follows that, naturally; as a consequence, in consequence; through, all along of [*dial.*], necessarily, eventually.

⁎ *cela va sans dire,* "thereby hangs a tale" [*Taming of the Shrew*].

CONTRIBUTE; conduce to &c. (*tend to*) 176; have a hand in; have a finger in the pie [*colloq.*]; determine, decide, turn the scale, have the deciding vote, have the final word; have a common origin; derive its origin &c. (*effect*) 154.

Adj. CAUSED &c. *v.*; causal, ætiological *or* etiological, original; primary, primitive, primordial; aboriginal; originative, generative, inceptive, productive, creative, constitutive, procreative, formative, demiurgic, protogenic, protogenal; radical; in embryo, embryonic, embryotic; *in ovo* [*L.*]; seminal, germinal; at the bottom of; connate, having a common origin.

Adv. FROM THE BEGINNING, in the first place, before everything; because &c. 155; behind the scenes.

⁎ *causa latet vis est notissima* [Ovid]; *felix qui potuit rerum cognoscerc causas* [Vergil]; "gentlemen, who made all that?" [Bonaparte].

155. [ASSIGNMENT OF CAUSE.] **Attribution.** — **N.** ATTRIBUTION, theory, ascription, assignment, reference to, rationale; accounting for &c. *v.*; ætiology *or* etiology, palætiology, imputation, derivation from.

FILIATION, affiliation; filiality; pedigree &c. (*paternity*) 166.

EXPLANATION &c. (*interpretation*) 522; reason why &c. (*cause*) 153.

V. ATTRIBUTE TO, ascribe to, impute to, refer to, lay to, point to, trace to, bring home to; put down to, set down to; blame; blame upon [*colloq.*]; charge on, ground on; invest with, assign as cause, lay at the door of, father upon, saddle; filiate, affiliate; account for,

156. [ABSENCE OF ASSIGNABLE CAUSE.] **Chance.**[1] — **N.** CHANCE, indetermination, accident, fortune, hazard, hap [*rare*], haphazard, chance-medley, random, luck, *raccroc* [*F.*], fluke [*cant*], casualty, fortuity, contingence, adventure, hit; fate &c. (*necessity*) 601; equal chance; lottery; tombola; lotto; toss-up [*colloq.*] &c. 621; turn of the -table, - cards; hazard of the die, chapter of accidents; cast -, throw- of the dice; heads or tails, wheel of Fortune; *sortes* [*L.*], *sortes Virgilianæ* [*L.*].

PROBABILITY, possibility, contingency, odds, long odds, run of luck; accidentalness, accidentalism, accidentality; main chance.

---

[1] The word *Chance* has two distinct meanings: the first, the absence of assignable *cause,* as above; and the second, the absence of *design* — for the latter see 621.

derive from, point out the reason &c. 153; theorize; tell how it comes; put the saddle on the right horse; find the real culprit.

Adj. ATTRIBUTED &c. *v.*; attributable &c. *v.*; referable *or* referrible; due to, derivable from; affiliate, derivate [*rare*]; owing to &c. (*effect*) 154; putative; ecbatic.

Adv. HENCE, thence, therefore, for, since, on account of, because, owing to; on that account; from this cause, from that cause; thanks to, forasmuch as; whence, *propter hoc* [*L.*].

WHY? wherefore? whence? how comes it? how is it? how happens it? how come? [*colloq.*, *esp. negro*], how does it happen? how so?

IN SOME WAY, in some such way; somehow, somehow or other.

₊ that is why; *hinc illæ lachrymæ* [Terence]; *cherchez la femme*.

theory of -Probabilities, – Chances; bookmaking; assurance; gamble, speculation, gaming &c. 621.

V. CHANCE, hap, turn up; fall to one's lot; be one's fate &c. 601; stumble on, light upon; blunder upon, hit, hit upon; take one's chance &c. 621.

Adj. CASUAL, fortuitous, accidental, chance, chanceable [*archaic*], chanceful [*archaic*], haphazard, random, casual, adventive, adventitious, causeless, incidental, contingent, uncaused, undetermined, indeterminate; possible &c. 470; unintentional &c. 621.

Adv. BY CHANCE, by accident; at random, casually; perchance &c. (*possibly*), 470; for aught one knows; as -good, – bad, – ill-luck &c. *n.*- would have it; as it may -be, – chance, – turn up, – happen; as the case may be.

₊ "grasps the skirts of happy chance" [Tennyson]; "the accident of an accident" [Lord Thurlow].

2. CONNECTION BETWEEN CAUSE AND EFFECT

157. Power. — **N.** POWER; potency, potentiality; jiva [*theos.*]; puissance, might, force; energy &c. 171; dint; right hand, right arm; ascendancy, sway, control; prepotency, prepollence *or* prepollency [*rare*]; almightiness, omnipotence; *carte blanche* [*F.*], authority &c. 737; strength &c. 159; predominance.

ABILITY; ableness &c. *adj.*; competency; efficiency, efficacy; validity, cogency; enablement; vantage ground; influence &c. 175.

PRESSURE, electromotive force, high pressure; conductivity; elasticity; gravity, electricity, magnetism, magnetoelectricity; galvanism, voltaic electricity; voltaism, electromagnetism, electrostatics, electrokinetics, electrodynamics; electromotion, electrification; magnetization, galvanization; attraction, pull; *vis inertiæ* [*L.*], *vis mortua* [*L.*], *vis viva* [*L.*]; potential –, dynamic- energy; friction, suction; live- circuit, – rail, – wire; volt, voltage.

[INSTRUMENTS] galvanometer, rheometer; variometer, magnetometer, magnetoscope, electrometer, electroscope, galvanoscope, electrophorus, electrodynamometer, voltameter, ammeter, voltammeter, voltmeter, wattmeter.

CAPABILITY, capacity; *quid valeant hu-*

158. Impotence. — **N.** IMPOTENCE; inability, disability; disablement, impuissance [*rare*], caducity, imbecility; incapacity, incapability; inaptitude, ineptitude; indocility; invalidity, inefficiency, incompetence, disqualification.

telum imbelle [*L.*], *brutum fulmen* [*L.*], blank cartridge, flash in the pan, *vox et præterea nihil* [*L.*], dead letter, bit of waste paper, dummy; Quaker gun; cripple.

INEFFICACY &c. (*inutility*) 645; failure &c. 732.

HELPLESSNESS &c. *adj.*; prostration, paralysis, palsy, apoplexy, syncope, sideration [*obs.*], vincibility, vincibleness, deliquium, collapse, exhaustion, softening of the brain, senility, superannuation, atony, decrepitude, imbecility, neurasthenia, invertebracy, inanition; emasculation, orchotomy; eunuch.

MOLLYCODDLE, old woman, muff [*colloq.*], tenderling [*rare*], milksop, molly [*colloq.*], sissy [*colloq.*], mother's darling.

V. BE IMPOTENT &c. *adj.*; not have a leg to stand on.

vouloir rompre l'anguille au genou [*F.*], *vouloir prendre la lune avec les dents* [*F.*].

COLLAPSE, faint, swoon, fall into a swoon, drop; go by the board; end in smoke &c. (*fail*) 732.

meri quid ferre recusent [*L.*]; faculty, quality, attribute, endowment, virtue, gift, property, qualification, susceptibility.

V. BE POWERFUL &c. *adj.;* gain power &c. *n.*

BELONG TO, pertain to; lie –, be- in one's power; can.

EMPOWER; give –, confer –, exercise-power &c. *n.;* enable, invest; indue, endue; endow, arm; strengthen &c. 159; compel &c. 744.

ELECTRIFY, magnetize, energize, galvanize, attract.

Adj. POWERFUL, puissant; potent, potential [*rare*]; capable, able; equal to, up to; cogent, valid; effective, effectual; efficient, efficacious, adequate, competent; multipotent [*rare*], plenipotent [*rare*], prepollent [*rare*], predominant; mighty, ascendent, prepotent, omnipotent, armipotent, mightful [*archaic*]; almighty.

forcible &c. *adj.* (*energetic*) 171; influential &c. 175; productive &c. 168.

ELECTRIC, electrodynamic, electrokinetic, electromagnetic, electrometric, electrometrical, electromotive, electronegative, electropositive, electroscopic; magnetic, magneto-electric *or* magneto-electrical, magnetomotive; voltametric, voltaic; galvanic, galvanometric, galvanoscopic, dynamo-electric *or* dynamo-electrical; dynamic, static, potential.

Adv. POWERFULLY &c. *adj.;* by virtue of, by dint of.

*** *à toute force;* δός μοι ποῦ στῶ καὶ κινῶ τὴν γῆν; *eripuit cælo fulmen sceptrumque tyrannis; fortis cadere cedere non potest.*

RENDER POWERLESS &c. *adj.;* depotentiate [*rare*], deprive of power; disable, disenable; disarm, incapacitate, disqualify, unfit, invalidate, disinvigorate [*rare*], undermine, deaden, cramp, tie the hands; double up, prostrate, paralyze, muzzle, cripple, becripple, maim, lame, hamstring, unsinew [*rare*], draw the teeth of; throttle, strangle, garrote *or* garrotte, ratten [*trade-union cant*], silence, sprain, clip the wings of, put *hors de combat* [*F.*], spike the guns; take the wind out of one's sails, scotch the snake, put a spoke in one's wheel; break the -neck, – back; unhinge, unfit; put out of gear.

UNMAN, unnerve, devitalize, effeminize, attenuate, enervate; emasculate, evirate [*rare*], spay, eunuchize [*rare*], caponize, castrate, geld, alter.

SHATTER, exhaust; weaken &c. 160.

Adj. POWERLESS, impotent, unable, incapable, incompetent; inefficient, ineffective; inept; unfit, unfitted; unqualified, disqualified; unendowed; doddering [*colloq.*], wambly [*Scot. and dial. Eng.*], inapt, unapt; crippled, disabled &c. *v.;* armless; senile, decrepit, superannuated.

harmless, unarmed, weaponless, defenseless, *sine ictu* [*L.*], unfortified, mightless [*archaic*], indefensible, vincible, pregnable, untenable.

paralytic, paralyzed; palsied, imbecile; nerveless, sinewless, marrowless, pithless, lustless; emasculate, disjointed; out of joint, out of gear; unnerved, unhinged; water-logged, on one's beam ends, rudderless; laid on one's back; done up [*colloq.*], done for [*colloq.*], done brown [*colloq.*], done [*colloq.*], dead-beat [*colloq.*], exhausted, shattered, atonic, demoralized; graveled [*colloq.*] &c. (*in difficulty*) 704; helpless, unfriended, fatherless; without a leg to stand on, *hors de combat* [*F.*], laid on the shelf.

NUGATORY, null and void, inoperative, good for nothing, invertebrate, ineffectual &c. (*failing*) 732; inadequate &c. 640; inefficacious &c. (*useless*) 645.

*** *der kranke Mann;* "desirous still but impotent to rise" [Shenstone]; "it has been well said that there is no surer way of courting national disaster than to be 'opulent, aggressive, and unarmed'" [Roosevelt].

159. [DEGREE OF POWER.] **Strength.** — **N.** STRENGTH; power &c. 157; energy &c. 171; vigor, force; main –, physical –, brute- force; spring, elasticity, tone, tension, tonicity.

[COMPARISONS] adamant, steel, iron, oak, heart of oak; iron grip; bone.

VIRILITY, vitality; stoutness &c. *adj.;*

160. Weakness. — N. WEAKNESS &c. *adj.;* debility, atony, relaxation, languor, enervation; impotence &c. 158; infirmity, effeminacy, feminality; fragility, flaccidity; inactivity &c. 683.

[COMPARISONS] reed, thread, rope of sand, house of cards, house built on sand.

lustihood, stamina, nerve, muscle, sinew *or* sinews, thews and sinews, physique; grit, pith, pithiness.

ATHLETICS, athleticism; gymnastics, acrobatism, agonistics, feats of strength.

ATHLETE, gymnast, pancratiast, acrobat; Atlas, Hercules, Antæus, Samson, Cyclops, Briareus, Colossus, Polyphemus, Titan, Brobdingnagian, Goliath; tower of strength; giant refreshed

STRENGTHENING &c. *v.;* invigoration, refreshment, refocillation [*obs.*].

[SCIENCE OF FORCES] dynamics, statics.

V. BE STRONG &c. *adj.*, be stronger; overmatch.

RENDER STRONG &c. *adj.;* give strength &c. *n.;* strengthen, invigorate, potentiate [*rare*], brace, nerve, fortify, buttress, sustain, harden, caseharden, steel, gird; screw up, wind up, set up; gird –, brace-up one's loins; recruit, set on one's legs [*colloq.*]; vivify; refresh &c. 689; refect [*archaic*], reinforce *or* reënforce &c. (*restore*) 660.

Adj. STRONG, mighty, vigorous, forcible, hard, adamantine, stout, robust, sturdy, husky [*colloq., U. S.*], doughty, hardy, powerful, potent, puissant, valid.

RESISTLESS, irresistible, invincible, proof against, impregnable, unconquerable, indomitable, inextinguishable, unquenchable; incontestable; more than a match for; overpowering, overwhelming; all-powerful, all-sufficient; sovereign.

ABLE-BODIED; athletic, gymnastic, carobatic, agonistic, palæstral [*rare*]; Herculean, Briarean, Brobdingnagian, Titanic, Cyclopean, Atlantean; muscular, brawny, wiry, well-knit, broad-shouldered, sinewy, sinewous [*rare*], strapping, stalwart, gigantic.

MANLY, manlike, manful; masculine, male, virile, in the prime of manhood.

UNWEAKENED, unallayed, unwithered, unshaken, unworn, unexhausted; in full force, in full swing; in the plentitude of power.

SOUND; stubborn, thick-ribbed, made of iron, deep-rooted; strong as -a lion, – an ox, – a horse – brandy; sound as a roach; in fine feather, in high feather [*both colloq.*]; like a giant refreshed.

ANÆMIA, bloodlessness, deficiency of blood, poverty of blood.

INVALIDATION; declension –, loss –, failure– of strength; delicacy, decrepitude, asthenia, adynamy [*rare*], cachexia *or* cachexy, sprain, strain.

WEAKLING; softling [*obs.*]; infant &c. 129; youth &c. 127.

V. BE WEAK &c. *adj.;* drop, crumble, give way, totter, dodder, tremble, shake, halt, limp, fade, languish, decline, flag, fail, have one foot in the grave.

RENDER WEAK &c. *adj.;* weaken, enfeeble, debilitate, invalidate, shake, deprive of strength, relax, enervate; unbrace, unnerve; cripple, unman &c. (*render powerless*) 158; cramp, reduce, sprain, strain, blunt the edge of; dilute, impoverish; decimate; extenuate; reduce in strength, reduce the strength of; *mettre de l'eau dans son vin* [*F.*].

Adj. WEAK, feeble, debile [*obs.*]; impotent &c. 158; relaxed, unnerved &c. *v.;* sapless, strengthless, powerless; weakly, unstrung, flaccid, adynamic, asthenic; nervous.

SOFT, effeminate, feminate [*obs.*], womanish.

FRAIL, fragile, shattery; flimsy, sleazy, gossamery, papery, unsubstantial, gimcrack, gingerbread; rickety, jerry-built, *kucha* or *kachcha* [*Hind.*], cranky; craichy [*dial. Eng.*], drooping, tottering, doddering [*colloq.*] &c. *v.;* broken, lame, withered, shattered, shaken, crazy, shaky, tumbledown; palsied &c. 158; decrepit.

UNSOUND, poor, infirm; faint, faintish; sickly &c. (*disease*) 655; dull, slack, evanid [*obs.*], languid; spent, short-winded, effete; weather-beaten; decayed, rotten, forworn [*archaic*], worn, seedy, languishing, wasted, washy, wishy-washy [*colloq.*], laid low, pulled down, the worse for wear.

UNSTRENGTHENED &c. 159, unsupported, unaided, unassisted; aidless, defenseless &c. 158.

on its last legs; weak as a -child, – baby, – chicken, – cat, – rat, – rag; weak as -water, – water gruel, – gingerbread,– milk and water; colorless &c. 429.

⁎⁎ *non sum qualis eram;* "at the hour when sick men mostly die and sentries on lonely ramparts stand to their arms" [Dunsany]; "to be weak is miserable, Doing or suffering" [Milton].

Adv. STRONGLY &c. *adj.;* by force &c. *n.;* by main force &c. *(by compulsion)* 744.

*** "our withers are unwrung" [*Hamlet*]. *Blut und Eisen; cœlitus mihi vires; du fort au diable; en habiles gens; ex vi termini; flecti non frangi;* "he that wrestles with us strengthens our nerves and sharpens our skill" [Burke]; "inflexible in faith, invincible in arms" [Beattie].

3. POWER IN OPERATION

161. Production. — N. PRODUCTION, creation, construction, formation, fabrication, manufacture; building, architecture, erection, edification; coinage; diaster; organization; *nisus formativus* [*L.*]; putting together &c. *v.;* establishment; workmanship, performance; achievement &c. *(completion)* 729.

FLOWERING, fructification, fruition; inflorescence.

BRINGING FORTH &c. *v.;* parturition, birth, birth throe, childbirth, delivery, confinement, *accouchement* [*F.*], travail, labor, midwifery, obstetrics; geniture [*obs.*]; gestation &c. *(maturation)* 673; assimilation; evolution, development, growth; entelechy; fertilization, gemination, germination, heterogamy, genesis, generation, histogenesis, breeding, begetting, isogamy, epigenesis, procreation, progeneration, propagation; fecundation, impregnation; albumen &c. 357.

spontaneous generation; archigenesis, archebiosis, abiogenesis, biogenesis, biogeny, dysmerogenesis, eumerogenesis, heterogenesis, oögenesis, merogenesis, metogenesis, monogenesis, parthenogenesis, homogenesis, xenogenesis.[1]

dissogeny, digenesis, physiogeny, phylogeny, ontogeny, ontogenesis, mitosis, xenogeny; theogony, tocogony, tocology, vacuolation, vacuolization.

PUBLICATION; works, *œuvres* [*F.*], opus *(pl.* opera) [*L.*]; authorship.

STRUCTURE, building, edifice, fabric, erection, pile, tower; flower, fruit, blossom.

V. PRODUCE, perform, operate, do, make, gar [*obs.*], form, construct, fabricate, frame, contrive, manufacture; weave, forge, coin, carve, chisel; build, raise, edify, rear, erect, put together; set up, run up; establish, constitute, compose, organize, institute; achieve, accomplish &c. *(complete)* 729.

flower, burgeon *or* bourgeon, blossom, bear fruit, fructify, teem, ean [*obs.*], yean, farrow, drop, pup, whelp, kitten, kindle [*obs.*], spawn, spat; bear, lay, bring forth, give birth to, lie in, be

162. [NONPRODUCTION.] Destruction — N. DESTRUCTION; waste, dissolution, breaking up; disruption; diruption [*obs.*], consumption; disorganization.

FALL, downfall, ruin, perdition, debacle, *débâcle* [*F.*], crash, *éboulement* [*F.*], smash [*colloq.*], havoc, *délabrement* [*F.*], breakdown, break-up; prostration, cave-in [*colloq.*]; desolation, *bouleversement* [*F.*], wreck, wrack [*archaic*], shipwreck, cataclysm; washout.

EXTINCTION, annihilation; destruction of life &c. 361; knock-out, K. O. [*slang*], knock-out blow, knock-down blow; doom, crack of doom.

DESTROYING &c. *v.;* demolition, demolishment [*rare*], overthrow, subversion, suppression; abolition &c. *(abrogation)* 756; biblioclasm; sacrifice; ravage, devastation, razzia; incendiarism; revolution &c. 146; extirpation &c. *(extraction)* 301; *commencement de la fin* [*F.*], road to ruin; dilapidation &c. *(deterioration)* 659; *sabotage* [*F.*].

V. BE DESTROYED &c.; perish; fall; fall to the ground; tumble, topple; go –, fall- to pieces; break up; crumble, – to dust; go to -the dogs, – the wall, – smash, – shivers, – wreck, – pot [*colloq.*], – wrack and ruin; go by the board, go all to smash [*colloq.*]; be all over with, be all up with [*colloq.*], go to glory [*colloq. or slang*], go to pieces, go under, go up the spout [*colloq.*], go bung [*slang*]. totter to its fall.

DESTROY; do –, make- away with nullify; annul &c. 756; sacrifice, demolish; tear up; overturn, overthrow, overwhelm; upset, subvert, put an end to; seal the doom of, do for [*colloq.*], dish [*slang*], undo; break up, cut up; break down, cut down, pull down, mow down, blow down, beat down; suppress, quash, put down; cut short, take off, blot out; efface, obliterate, cancel, erase, strike out, expunge, delete, dele; dispel, dissipate, dissolve; consume.

smash, crash, quell, squash [*colloq.*], squelch [*colloq.*], crumple up, shatter, shiver; batter; tear –, crush –, cut –;

[1]Huxley.

brought to bed of, evolve, pullulate, usher into the world.

MAKE PRODUCTIVE &c. 168; create; beget, get, generate, fecundate, impregnate; procreate, progenerate, propagate; engender; bring –, call- into -being, – existence; breed, hatch, develop, bring up.

INDUCE, superinduce; suscitate [obs.]; cause &c. 153; acquire &c. 775.

Adj. PRODUCED, PRODUCING &c. v., productive of; prolific &c. 168; creative; formative; procreant, generative, genitive, genetic, genial [rare], genital; pregnant; enceinte [F.], big with, fraught with; in the family way [colloq.], teeming, parturient, in the straw [colloq.], brought to bed of; lying-in; puerperal, puerperous [rare].

digenetic, heterogenetic, oögenetic, xenogenetic; ectogenous, gamic, hæmatobious, sporogenous, sporophorous.

ARCHITECTONIC or architectonical, constructive.

₊ ex nihilo nihil; fiat lux; materiam superabat opus [Ovid]; "he who hath put forth his total strength in fit actions has the richest return of wisdom" [Emerson].

shake –, pull –, pick -to pieces; laniate [rare]; nip; tear to -rags, – tatters; crush –, knock- to atoms; ruin; strike out; throw down, throw over, knock down, knock over, lay out [slang], lay by the heels, fell, sink, swamp, scuttle, wreck, shipwreck, engulf or ingulf, submerge; lay in ashes, lay in ruins; sweep away, raze; level, – with the -ground, – dust.

deal destruction, lay waste, ravage, gut; disorganize; dismantle &c. (render useless) 645; devour, swallow up, desolate, devastate, sap, mine, blast, confound; exterminate, extinguish, quench, annihilate; snuff out, put out, stamp out, trample out; lay –, trample- in the dust; prostrate; tread –, crush –, trample- under foot; lay the ax to the root of; make short work of, make a clean sweep of, make mincemeat of; cut up root and branch; fling –, scatter- to the winds; throw overboard; strike at the root of, sap the foundations of, spring a mine, blow up; ravage with fire and sword; cast to the dogs; eradicate &c. 301.

Adj. DESTROYED &c. v.; perishing &c. v.; trembling –, nodding –, tottering- n.; extinct; all-destroying, all-devouring, all-engulfing.

DESTRUCTIVE, subversive, ruinous, incendiary, deletory [obs.]; destroying &c. n.; suicidal; deadly &c. (killing) 361.

Adv. with crushing effect, with a sledge hammer.

₊ delenda est Carthago; dum Roma deliberat Saguntum perit; écrasez l'infâme [Voltaire]; "I would fain die a dry death" [Tempest].

---

163. Reproduction. — N. REPRODUCTION, renovation; restoration &c. 660; renewal; new edition, reprint &c. (copy) 21; revival, regeneration, palingenesis, revivification; apotheosis; resuscitation, reanimation, resurrection, resurgence, reappearance; regrowth; Phœnix.

generation &c. (production) 161; multiplication.

V. REPRODUCE; restore &c. 660; revive, renovate, renew, regenerate, revivify, resuscitate, reanimate, refashion, stir the embers, put into the crucible; multiply, repeat; resurge.

CROP UP, crop out, spring up like mushrooms.

Adj. REPRODUCED &c. v.; renascent, resurgent, reappearing; reproductive, proligerous [rare], progenitive, proliferous, gametal; hydra-headed; suigenetic.

---

164. Producer. — N. PRODUCER, originator, inventor, author, founder, generator, mover, architect, grower, raiser, introducer, deviser, constructor, begetter, creator; maker &c. (agent) 690; prime mover.

165. Destroyer. — N. DESTROYER &c. (destroy &c. 162); cankerworm &c. (bane) 663; assassin &c. (killer) 361; executioner &c. (punish) 975; biblioclast; eidoloclast, iconoclast, idoloclast; vandal, destructor [rare], Hun, nihilist.

166. Paternity. — N. PATERNITY; parentage; consanguinity &c. 11.

PARENT, father, sire, dad, papa, governor [*slang*], pater [*colloq.*], daddy [*colloq.*], paterfamilias, abba; genitor [*rare*], progenitor, procreator, begetter; ancestor; grandsire, grandfather; greatgrandfather; fathership, fatherhood; *mabap* [*Hind.*].

MOTHERHOOD, maternity, motherhead [*rare*], mothership; mother, dam, mamma *or* mama, mammy, mam [*colloq.*], motherkin, matriarch, materfamilias; grandmother.

STEM, trunk, tree, stock, stirps, pedigree, house, lineage, line, family, tribe, sept, race, clan; genealogy, family tree, descent, extraction, birth, ancestry; forefathers, forbears, patriarchs.

Adj. PARENTAL; paternal; maternal; family, ancestral, linear, patriarchal; racial, phyletic.

₊ *avi numerantur avorum;* "happy he with such a mother" [Tennyson]; *philosophia stemma non inspicit* [Seneca]; "thank God for the iron in the blood of our fathers" [Roosevelt].

168. Productiveness. — N. PRODUCTIVENESS &c. *adj.;* fecundity, fertilization, fertility, luxuriance, uberty [*obs.*].

[COMPARISONS] milch cow, rabbit, hydra, warren, seed plot, land flowing with milk and honey.

AFTERMATH, second crop, aftercrop, aftergrowth, arrish [*dial. Eng.*], eddish [*dial. Eng.*], rowen.

MULTIPLICATION, multiparity, propagation, procreation; superfetation, pregnancy, pullulation [*rare*], fructification.

V. MAKE PRODUCTIVE &c. *adj.;* fructify; procreate, pullulate, generate, fertilize, spermatize, impregnate; fecundate, fecundify; teem, spawn, multiply; produce &c. 161; conceive.

Adj. PRODUCTIVE, prolific, copious; teeming, teemful [*dial.*]; fertile, fruitful, frugiferous [*obs.*], fructuous [*rare*], plenteous, proliferous, fructiferous, fruitbearing; fecund, luxuriant; pregnant, uberous.

PROCREANT, procreative; generative, life-giving, spermatic, inceptive, originative; multiparous; omnific; propagable.

parturient &c. (*producing*) 161; profitable &c. (*useful*) 644.

167. Posterity. — N. POSTERITY, progeny, breed, issue, offspring, brood, litter, seed, farrow, spawn, spat; family, children, grandchildren, heirs; greatgrandchildren.

CHILD, son, daughter, bairn, baby, kid [*colloq.*], papoose [*Am. Ind.*], imp, brat, moppet [*archaic*], lambkin, cub, cherub, nestling, tot, innocent, urchin, chit [*colloq.*]; infant &c. 129; *butcha* or *bacha* [*Hind.*]; bantling, scion; acrospire, plumule, shoot, sprout, olive-branch, sprit, branch; offshoot, offset; ramification; descendant; heir, heiress; heirapparent, heir-presumptive; chip of the old block; heredity; rising generation.

LINEAGE, straight descent, sonship, line, filiation, primogeniture.

Adj. FILIAL; diphyletic.

₊ "the child is father of the man" [Wordsworth].

169. Unproductiveness. — N. UNPRODUCTIVENESS &c. *adj.;* infertility, sterility, infecundity; impotence &c. 158; unprofitableness &c. (*inutility*) 645.

WASTE, desert, Sahara, wild, karoo, wilderness, howling wilderness.

V. BE UNPRODUCTIVE &c. *adj.;* hang fire, flash in the pan, come to nothing.

Adj. UNPRODUCTIVE, acarpous, inoperative, barren, addle, unfertile, unprolific, arid, sterile, unfruitful, infecund, [*rare*], jejune, infertile; useless, otiose; *sine prole* [*L.*]; fallow; teemless, issueless, fruitless, infructuose [*rare*]; unprofitable &c. (*useless*) 645; null and void, of no effect.

₊ "no one can dam the Mississippi" [Roosevelt].

170. Agency. — N. AGENCY, operation, force, working, strain, function, office, maintenance, exercise, work, swing, play; interworking, interaction; procuration procurement.

CAUSATION &c. 153; mediation, intermediation, instrumentality &c. 631; conation, influence &c. 175; action &c. (*voluntary*) 680; *modus operandi* [*L.*] &c. 627.

quickening -, maintaining -, sustaining- power; home stroke.

V. BE IN ACTION &c. *adj.;* operate, work; act, act upon; perform, play, support, sustain, strain, maintain, take effect, quicken, strike.

come –, bring- into -operation, – play; have play, have free play; bring to bear upon.

Adj. OPERATIVE, operant [*rare*], efficient, efficacious, practical, exertive, conative, effectual.

at work, on foot; acting &c. (*doing*) 680; in operation, in force, in action, in play, in exercise; acted upon, wrought upon.

Adv. BY THE AGENCY OF &c. *n.;* through &c. (*instrumentality*) 631; by means of &c. 632.

₊ "I myself must mix with action lest I wither by despair" [Tennyson]; "the day is always his who works in it with serenity and great aims" [Emerson].

---

171. Energy. — N. ENERGY, physical energy, force; keenness &c. *adj.;* intensity, vigor, backbone [*colloq.*], vim [*colloq.*], mettle, *vis viva* [*L.*], *vis vitæ* [*L.*], pep [*slang*], ginger [*slang*], go [*colloq.*]; strength, elasticity; high pressure; fire; rush; human dynamo.

ACTIVITY, agitation, effervescence; ferment, fermentation; ebullition, splutter, perturbation, stir, bustle; voluntary energy &c. 682; quicksilver.

EXERTION &c. (*effort*) 686; excitation &c. (*mental*) 824; resolution &c. (*mental energy*) 604.

ACRIMONY, acridity, acritude [*obs.*]; causticity, virulence, poignancy; harshness &c. *adj.;* severity, edge, point; pungency &c. 392.

EXCITANT, stimulant; Spanish fly, cantharides; seasoning &c. (*condiment*) 393.

172. Inertness. — N. INERTNESS, physical inertness, inertia, *vis inertiæ* [*L.*], inertion, inactivity, torpor, languor; dormancy, *fainéance* [*F.*], quiescence &c. 265; latency, inaction; passivity; stagnation; dullness &c. *adj.*

mental inertness; sloth &c. (*inactivity*) 683; inexcitability &c. 826; irresolution &c. 605; obstinacy &c. 606; permanence &c. 141.

V. BE INERT &c. *adj.;* hang fire, smolder *or* smoulder.

Adj. INERT, inactive, passive; torpid &c. 683; sluggish, stagnant, *fainéant* [*F.*], dull, heavy, flat, slack, tame, slow, blunt; lifeless, dead, uninfluential.

LATENT, dormant, smoldering *or* smouldering, unexerted.

Adv. INACTIVELY &c. *adj.;* in suspense, in abeyance.

V. GIVE ENERGY &c. *n.;* energize, stimulate, kindle, excite, exert; activate, potentialize [*rare*], dynamize, doubleshot; sharpen, intensify; inflame &c. (*render violent*) 173; wind up &c. (*strengthen*) 159.

strike, – into, – hard, – home; make an impression.

Adj. ENERGETIC, strong, forcible, active, strenuous, forceful, mettlesome, enterprising; go-ahead [*colloq.*]; intense, deep-dyed, severe, keen, vivid, sharp, acute, incisive, trenchant, brisk.

rousing, irritating; poignant; virulent, caustic, corrosive, mordant, harsh, stringent; double-edged, double-shotted, double-distilled; drastic, escharotic; racy &c. (*pungent*) 392; excitant, excitative, excitatory.

potent &c. (*powerful*) 157; radio-active.

Adv. STRONGLY &c. *adj.; fortiter in re* [*L.*]; with telling effect.

₊ the steam is up; *vires acquirit eundo;* "the race by vigor not by vaunts is won" [Pope]; "like a steam-engine in trousers" [Sydney Smith — *of Daniel Webster*].

---

173. Violence. — N. VIOLENCE, inclemency, vehemence, might, impetuosity, furiosity [*rare*]; boisterousness &c. *adj.;* effervescence, ebullition; turbulence, bluster; uproar, callithump [*U. S.*], riot, row [*colloq.*], rumpus [*colloq.*], *le diable à quatre* [*F.*], devil to pay [*colloq.*], all the fat in the fire [*colloq.*].

FEROCITY, rage, fury; exacerbation,

174. Moderation. — N. MODERATION; lenity &c. 740; temperateness, temperance, passability, passableness, gentleness &c. *adj.;* sobriety; quiet; mental calmness &c. (*inexcitability*) 826.

MODERATING &c. *v.;* anaphrodisia; relaxation, remission, mitigation, tranquilization, assuagement, alleviation, contemporation [*obs.*], pacification.

exasperation, malignity; severity &c. 739.

FORCE, brute force; outrage; *coup de main* [*F.*]; strain, shock, shog [*rare*].

FIT, paroxysm, spasm, convulsion, throe; hysterics, passion &c. (*state of excitability*) 825; orgasm, aphrodisia.

OUTBREAK, outburst; debacle; burst, bounce, dissilience [*rare*], discharge, volley, explosion, blow-up, blast, detonation, rush, eruption, displosion [*obs.*], torrent.

TURMOIL &c. (*disorder*) 59; ferment &c. (*agitation*) 315; storm, tempest, rough weather; squall &c. (*wind*) 349; earthquake, volcano, thunderstorm.

FURY, berserk *or* berserker, dragon, demon, tiger, beldam *or* beldame, madcap, wild beast; fire eater [*colloq.*] &c. (*blusterer*) 887; Erinys (*pl.* Erinyes), Eumenides, Tisiphone, Megæra, Alecto.

V. BE VIOLENT &c. *adj.*; run high; ferment, effervesce; romp, rampage; run wild. run riot; break the peace; rush, tear; rush headlong, rush headforemost; run amuck, raise a storm, make a riot; make –, kick up- a row [*colloq.*]; rough-house [*slang*]; bluster, rage, roar, riot, storm; boil, boil over; fume, foam, come in like a lion, wreak, bear down, ride roughshod, out-Herod Herod; spread like wildfire.

EXPLODE, go off, displode [*obs.*], detonate, detonize, fulminate, let off, let fly, discharge, thunder, blow up, flash, flare, burst; shock, strain.

BREAK OPEN, force open, prize open, pry open; break out, fly out, burst out.

RENDER VIOLENT &c. *adj.*; sharpen, stir up, quicken, excite, incite, urge, lash, stimulate; irritate, inflame, kindle, suscitate [*obs.*], foment; accelerate, aggravate, exasperate, exacerbate, convulse, infuriate, madden, lash into fury; fan the flame, add fuel to the flame; *oleum addere camino* [*L.*].

Adj. VIOLENT, vehement; warm; acute, sharp, rough, tough [*colloq.*], vicious [*colloq.*], rude, ungentle, bluff, boisterous, wild; brusque, abrupt, waspish; impetuous; rampant.

TURBULENT; disorderly; blustering, towering, raging &c. *v.*; troublous, riotous; tumultuary, tumultuous; obstreperous, uproarious; extravagant; unmitigated, immitigable; ravening, tameless;

MEAN, measure, *juste milieu* [*F.*], golden mean, *meden agan* [*Gr.* μηδὲν ἄγαν]. *ariston metron* [*Gr.* ἄριστον μέτρον].

MODERATOR; lullaby, sedative, calmative, lenitive, palliative, demulcent, antispasmodic, carminative; laudanum; rose water, balm, poppy, chloroform, opium: soothing sirup, opiate, anodyne, milk.

V. BE MODERATE &c. *adj.*; keep within -bounds, – compass; sober down, settle down; keep the peace, remit, relent; take in sail.

MODERATE, soften, mitigate, temper, accoy [*obs.*]; attemper, contemper [*obs.*], mollify, lenify [*rare*], dulcify, dull, take off the edge, blunt, obtund, sheathe, subdue, chasten; sober down, tone down, smooth down, slow down; weaken &c. 160; lessen &c. (*decrease*) 36; check; palliate.

TRANQUILLIZE, assuage, appease, suage *or* swage [*dial.*], lull, soothe, compose, still, calm, cool, quiet, hush, quell, sober, pacify, tame, damp, lay, allay, rebate [*archaic*], slacken, smooth, alleviate, rock to sleep, deaden, smother; throw cold water on, throw a wet blanket over; slake; curb &c. (*restrain*) 751; tame &c. (*subjugate*) 749; smooth over; pour oil on the -waves, – troubled waters; pour balm into; *mettre de l'eau dans son vin* [*F.*].

go out like a lamb, "roar you as gently as any sucking dove" [*M. N. D.*].

Adj. MODERATE; lenient &c. 740; gentle, mild; cool, sober, temperate, reasonable, measured; tempered &c. *v.*; calm, unruffled, quiet, tranquil, still; slow, smooth, untroubled; tame; peaceful, peaceable; pacific, halcyon.

UNEXCITING, unirritating; soft, bland, oily, demulcent, lenitive, anodyne; hypnotic &c. 683; sedative, calmative, assuaging, assuasive, calmant; antiorgastic, anaphrodisiac.

mild as mother's milk, mild as milk, milk and water, gentle as a lamb.

Adv. MODERATELY &c. *adj.*; gingerly; piano; under easy sail, at half speed, in moderation; within bounds, within compass; in reason.

⁎⁎⁎ est modus in rebus [Horace]; "not poppy nor mandragora, Nor all the drowsy syrups of the world "[*Othello*].

frenzied &c. (*insane*) 503; desperate &c. (*rash*) 863; infuriate, furious, outrageous, frantic, hysteric, in hysterics.

FIERY, flaming, scorching, hot, red-hot, ebullient.

SAVAGE, fierce, ferocious, fierce as a tiger.

EXCITED &c. *v.;* unquelled, unquenched, unextinguished, unrepressed, unbridled, unruly; headstrong; ungovernable, unappeasable, unmitigable; uncontrollable, incontrollable; insuppressible, irrepressible; orgastic.

SPASMODIC, convulsive, explosive; detonating &c. *v.;* volcanic, meteoric; stormy &c. (*wind*) 349.

Adv. VIOLENTLY &c. *adj.;* amain; by storm, by force, by main force; with might and main; tooth and nail, *vi et armis* [*L.*], at the point of the -sword, – bayonet; at one fell swoop; with a high hand, through thick and thin; in desperation, with a vengeance; *à outrance* [*F.*], *à toute outrance* [*F.*]; headlong, headfirst, headforemost.

APHRODISIAC, aphrodisiacal, aphroditous.

*** *furor arma ministrat;* "blown with restless violence round about the pendent world" [*Measure for Measure*]; "*hysterica passio!* down, thou climbing sorrow!" [*King Lear*].

4. INDIRECT POWER

175. Influence. — **N.** INFLUENCE; importance &c. 642; weight, pressure, preponderance, prevalence, sway; predominance, predominancy; ascendancy; dominance, reign; control, domination, pull [*colloq. or slang*]; authority &c. 737; power, potency, capability &c. (*power*) 157; interest; spell, magic, magnetism.

FOOTING; purchase &c. (*support*) 215; play, leverage, vantage ground, advantage.

175a. Absence of Influence. — **N.** IMPOTENCE &c. 158; powerlessness; inertness &c. 172; irrelevancy &c. 10.

V. have no influence &c. 175.

Adj. UNINFLUENTIAL; unconducing [*rare*], nonconductive, unconductive; forceless, powerless &c. 158; irrelevant &c. 10.

TOWER OF STRENGTH, host in himself; protection, patronage, auspices; patron &c. (*auxiliary*) 711.

V. HAVE INFLUENCE &c. *n.;* be influential &c. *adj.;* carry weight, sway, bias, actuate, weigh, tell; have a hold upon, magnetize, bear upon, gain a footing, work upon; take root, take hold; strike root in.

PERVADE, run through; spread like wildfire, be rife &c. *adj.;* rage, gain head.

DOMINATE, subject, predominate; outweigh, overweigh; override, overbear; have –, get –, gain- -the upper hand, –full play; prevail.

BE RECOGNIZED, be listened to; make one's voice heard, gain a hearing; play a -part, – leading part- in; lead, control, rule, manage, master, get the mastery of, get control of, make one's influence felt; take the lead, pull the strings; wind round one's finger; turn –, throw one's weight into- the scale; set the fashion, lead the dance.

Adj. INFLUENTIAL, effective, effectual [*rare*], potent; important &c. 642; weighty; prevailing &c. *v.;* prevalent, rife, rampant, dominant, regnant, predominant, in the ascendant, hegemonical; authoritative, recognized, telling.

Adv. with telling effect, with authority.

*** *tel maître tel valet.*

176. Tendency. — **N.** TENDENCY; aptness, aptitude; proneness, proclivity, bent, turn, tone, bias, set, warp, leaning (*with* to *or* towards), predisposition, inclination, tendence [*rare*], propensity, susceptibility; conatus, conation [*obs.*], nisus; liability &c. 177; quality, nature, temperament; idiocrasy, idiosyncrasy; cast, vein, grain; humor, mood; trend; drift &c. (*direction*) 278; conduciveness, conducement; applicability &c. (*utility*) 644; subservience &c. (*instrumentality*) 631.

V. TEND, contribute, conduce, lead, influence, dispose, incline, verge, bend to, warp, turn, work towards, trend, affect, carry, redound to, bid fair to, gravitate towards; promote &c. (*aid*) 707.

Adj. TENDING &c. *v.;* conative, conducent [*obs.*], conducive, working towards, in a fair way to, likely to, calculated to; liable &c. 177; subservient&c. (*instrumental*) 631; useful &c. 644; subsidiary &c. (*helping*) 707; idiocratic, indiosyncratic, idiosyncratical.

Adv. for, whither; for the purpose of.

* "all men that are ruined are ruined on the side of their natural propensities" [Burke].

---

177. Liability. — N. LIABILITY, liableness; possibility, contingency; susceptivity, susceptiveness, susceptibility.

V. BE LIABLE &c. *adj.;* incur, lay oneself open to, be subjected to, run the chance, stand a chance; lie under, expose oneself to, open a door to.

Adj. LIABLE, subject, susceptive; in danger &c. 665; open to, exposed to, obnoxious to; answerable, responsible, accountable, amenable; unexempt from; apt to; dependent on; incident to.

CONTINGENT, incidental, possible, on the cards, within range of, at the mercy of.

5. COMBINATIONS OF CAUSES

178. Concurrence. — N. CONCURRENCE, coöperation, coagency; union; coadunation, coaction [*rare*], coworking [*rare*], synergy [*rare*], collaboration, conformity, conformableness, agreement &c. 23; consilience; consent &c. (*assent*) 488; alliance; concert &c. 709; partnership &c. 712.

V. CONCUR, conduce, conspire, contribute; agree, unite, harmonize, hitch [*colloq.*], jibe [*colloq., U. S.*], coadunate, combine; hang –, pull– together &c. (*coöperate*) 709; help to &c. (*aid*) 707.

keep pace with, run parallel; go with, go along with, go hand in hand with.

Adj. CONCURRING &c. *v.;* concurrent, conformable, corresponsive [*rare*], joint, coöperative, concomitant, coincident, concordant, harmonious, consentaneous [*archaic*]; coadunate, coadunative, consilient, in alliance with, banded together; of one mind, at one with.

Adv. with one consent.

179. Counteraction. — N. COUNTERACTION, opposition; contrariety &c. 14; antagonism, polarity; clashing &c. *v.;* collision, interference, resistance, renitency, friction; reaction; retroaction &c. (*recoil*) 277; counterblast; neutralization &c. (*compensation*) 30; *vis inertiæ* [*L.*]; check &c. (*hindrance*) 706.

voluntary opposition &c. 708; voluntary resistance &c. 719; repression &c. (*restraint*) 751.

V. COUNTERACT; run counter, clash, cross; interfere with, conflict with; contravene; jostle; go –, run –, beat –, militate– against; stultify; antagonize, frustrate, oppose &c. 708; traverse; overcome, overpower, withstand &c. (*resist*) 719; impede, hinder &c. 706; repress &c. (*restrain*) 751; react &c. (*recoil*) 277.

UNDO, neutralize, offset, cancel; counterpoise &c. (*compensate*) 30; overpoise.

Adj. COUNTERACTING &c. *v.;* antagonistic, conflicting, retroactive, renitent, reactionary; contrary &c. 14.

Adv. ALTHOUGH &c. 30; against; mauger *or* maugre, malgre *or* maulgre [*obs.*], malgrado [*obs.*], notwithstanding; in spite of &c. 708.

CLASS II

Words relating to SPACE

Section I. SPACE IN GENERAL

1. Abstract Space

180. [Indefinite space.] **Space.** —
N. space, extension, extent, superficial
extent, expanse, stretch; room, accommodation, capacity, scope, range, latitude, field, way, expansion, compass,
sweep, play, swing, spread.

spare room, elbowroom, houseroom;
leeway, seaway, headway, stowage,
roomage [obs.], tankage, margin; opening, sphere, arena.

open space, free space; void &c.
(absence) 187; waste, desert, wild; wild-
ness [obs.], wilderness; moor, down,
downs, upland, moorland; prairie,
steppe, llano [Sp. Amer.], campagna.

unlimited space; heavens, ether,
plenum, infinity &c. 105; world, wide
world; ubiquity &c. (presence) 186;
length and breadth of the land; abyss
&c. (interval) 198.

proportions, acreage; acres, - roods
and perches; square -inches, - yards
&c.; ares, arpents.

Adj. spacious, roomy, extensive, expansive, capacious, ample; widespread,
vast, world-wide, wide, far-flung, vasty
[rare], uncircumscribed; boundless &c.
(infinite) 105; shoreless, trackless, pathless; extended; beyond the verge, far
as the eye can see.

Adv. extensively &c. adj.; wherever;
everywhere; far and -near, - wide; right
and left, all over, all the world over;
throughout the -world, - length and
breadth of the land; under the sun, in
every quarter; in all -quarters, - lands;
here, there, and everywhere; from pole
to pole, from China to Peru [Johnson],
from Indus to the pole [Pope], from Dan
to Beersheba, from end to end; on the
face of the earth, in the wide world, on
the face of the waters, "from the four

180a. **Inextension.** — N. inextension, nonextension, point, dot, speck,
spot, pinprick, tittle; atom &c. (small,
ness) 32.

181. [Definite space.] **Region.** —
N. region, sphere, ground, soil, area,
realm, hemisphere, quarter, orb, circuit,
circle; pale &c. (limit) 233; compartment, department; clearing; domain,
tract, terrain, dominion, colony, commonwealth, territory, country, fatherland, motherland.

canton, county, shire, province, arrondissement [F.], mofussil [India], parish,
diocese, township, commune, ward,
wapentake [hist.], hundred, riding, lathe
[Kent, Eng.], soke [hist.], tithing,
bailiwick; principality, duchy, palatinate, archduchy, dukedom, kingdom,
empire.

precinct, arena, enceinte [F.], walk,
march, district, beat; patch, plot, inclosure, close, enclave, field, garth, court;
street &c. (abode) 189; paddock &c.
(inclosure) 232.

clime, climate, zone, meridian, latitude.

Adj. territorial, local, parochial,
provincial, regional, insular.

182. [Limited space.] **Place.** — N.
place, lieu, spot, whereabouts, point,
dot; niche, nook &c. (corner) 244; hole;
pigeonhole &c. (receptacle) 191; compartment; confine, premises, precinct,
station; area, courtyard, square, place
[F.], piazza [It.], plaza [Sp.], forum [L.],
agora [Gr.], hamlet, village &c. (abode)
189; pen &c. (inclosure) 232; country-
side, location, site, locality &c. (situation) 183.

corners of the earth" [*Merchant of Venice*], from all points of the compass; to the four winds, to the uttermost parts of the earth.

ins and outs; every hole and corner.

Adv. SOMEWHERE, in some place, wherever it may be, here and there, in various places, *passim* [*L.*].

2. RELATIVE SPACE

183. Situation. — N. SITUATION, position, locality, locale (*properly*, local), status, latitude and longitude; footing, standing, standpoint, post; stage; aspect, attitude, posture, set [*colloq.*], pose.

PLACE, site, situs, station, seat, venue, whereabouts, environment, ground; bearings &c. (*direction*) 278; spot &c. (*limited space*) 182.

topography, geography, chorography; map &c. 550.

V. BE SITUATED, be situate, be located; lie; have its seat in.

Adj. SITUATE, situated; local, topical, topographical &c. *n.*

Adv. *in situ* [*L.*], *in loco* [*L.*]; here and there, *passim* [*L.*]; hereabouts, thereabouts, whereabouts; in place, here, there.

in –, amidst- such and such- -surroundings, – environs, – *entourage* [*F.*].

---

184. Location. — N. LOCATION, localization; lodgment; deposition, reposition; stowage; collocation; packing, lading; establishment, settlement, installation; fixation; insertion &c. 300.

anchorage, roadstead, mooring, encampment.

SETTLEMENT, plantation, colony, cantonment; situation; quarters, barracks; habitation &c. (*abode*) 189; "a local habitation and a name" [*M. N. D.*].

DOMESTICATION, cohabitation, colonization; endenization [*obs.*], naturalization.

V. PLACE, situate, locate, localize, make a place for, put, lay, set, seat, station, lodge, quarter, post, install; house, stow; establish, fix, pin, root; graft; plant &c. (*insert*) 300; shelve, pitch, camp, lay down, deposit, reposit, store, store away, cradle; moor, tether, picket; pack, tuck in; embed, imbed; vest, invest in.

BILLET ON, quarter upon, saddle with.

LOAD, lade, stevedore, freight; pocket, put up, bag.

185. Displacement. — N. DISPLACEMENT, elocation [*obs.*], heterotopy, transposition.

EJECTMENT &c. 297; exile &c. (*banishment*) 893.

REMOVAL &c. (*transference*) 270; unshipment, transshipment *or* transhipment, unplacement [*rare*], moving, shift.

MISPLACEMENT, dislocation &c. 61; fish out of water.

V. DISPLACE, displant, dislodge, disestablish; misplace, unplace [*rare*], translocate [*rare*], unseat, disturb, disniche; exile &c. (*seclude*) 893; ablegate [*obs.*], set aside, remove; take away, cart away; take off, draft off; lade &c. 184.

UNLOAD, empty &c. (*eject*) 297; transfer &c. 270; dispel.

VACATE; depart &c. 293.

Adj. DISPLACED &c. *v.;* unplaced, unhoused, unharbored, unestablished, unsettled; houseless, homeless, harborless [*archaic*]; out of place, out of a situation.

MISPLACED, out of its element.

INHABIT &c. (*be present*) 186; domesticate, colonize, found, people; take root, strike root; anchor; cast –, come to an- anchor; sit down, settle down; settle; take up one's -abode, – quarters; plant –, establish –, locate- oneself; have one's legal residence at; hang out one's shingle [*colloq.*]; squat, perch, hive, *se nicher* [*F.*], bivouac, burrow, get a footing; encamp, pitch one's tent; put up -at, – one's horses at; keep house.

NATURALIZE, endenizen [*rare*], adopt.

PUT BACK, replace &c. (*restore*) 660.

Adj. PLACED &c. *v.;* situate, posited, ensconced, imbedded, embosomed, rooted; domesticated; vested in, unremoved.

MOORED &c. *v.;* at anchor.

3. Existence in Space

186. Presence. — N. presence, presentness, occupancy, occupation; attendance.

permeation, pervasion; diffusion &c. (*dispersion*) 73.

whereness, ubiety, ubiquity, ubiquitariness; omnipresence.

bystander &c. (*spectator*) 444.

V. be present &c. adj.; *assister* [*F.*]; make one -of, – at; look on, attend, remain; find –, present- oneself; show one's face; fall in the way of, occur in a place; exist in space, lie, stand; occupy.

inhabit, dwell, reside, stay, sojourn, live, abide, lodge, bunk, room [*U. S.*], nestle, roost [*colloq.*], perch; take up one's abode &c. (*be located*) 184; tenant; people.

frequent, resort to, haunt; revisit.

pervade, permeate; be diffused through, be disseminated through; overspread, overrun; fill, run through; meet one at every turn.

Adj. present; occupying, inhabiting &c. *v.;* moored &c. 184; resiant [*obs.*], resident, residential, residentiary; domiciled.

ubiquitous, ubiquitary; omnipresent; universally present.

peopled, populous, full of people, inhabited.

Adv. here, there, where, everywhere, aboard, on board, at home, afield; on the spot; here there and everywhere &c. (*space*) 180; in presence of, before; under the eyes of, under the nose of; in the face of; *in propriâ personâ* [*L.*].

⁎⁎⁎ nusquam est qui ubique est [Seneca].

188. Inhabitant. — N. inhabitant; resident, residentiary; dweller, indweller, habitant [*rare*]; addressee; occupier, occupant; householder, lodger, roomer [*U. S.*], inmate, tenant, incumbent, sojourner, *locum tenens* [*L.*], commorant; settler, squatter, backwoodsman, colonist; islander; denizen, citizen; burgher, oppidan, cockney, cit [*colloq.*], townsman, burgess; villager; cottager, cottier, cotter; compatriot; backsettler, boarder; hotel keeper, innkeeper; habitant; paying guest; planter.

native, indigene [*rare*], aborigines, autochthon (*pl.* autochthones), abo-

187. [Nullibicity.] **Absence. — N.** nullibicity, nullibiety [*rare*], absence; awayness [*rare*], cut [*colloq.*]; inexistence &c. 2; nonresidence, absenteeism; nonattendance, alibi.

emptiness &c. adj.; void, vacuum; vacuity [*rare*], vacancy, voidness [*rare*], *tabula rasa* [*L.*]; exemption; hiatus &c. (*interval*) 198; lipotype.

truant, absentee.

nobody; nobody -present, – on earth; not a soul; no man, nix [*slang*].

V. be absent &c. adj.; keep away, keep out of the way; play truant, absent oneself, stay away; slip off, slip out, slip away; keep –, hold- aloof.

withdraw, make oneself scarce [*colloq.*], retreat, retire, vacate; go away &c. 293.

Adj. absent, not present, away, nonresident, gone, from home; missing; lost; wanting; omitted; nowhere to be found; inexistent &c. 2.

empty, void; vacant, vacuous; blank, null; untenanted, unoccupied, uninhabited; tenantless; desert, deserted; devoid; unhabitable, uninhabitable.

exempt from, not having.

Adv. without, minus, nowhere; elsewhere; neither here nor there; in default of; sans; behind one's back.

⁎⁎⁎ the bird has flown; *non est inventus.*

"absence makes the heart grow fonder" [Bayley]; "absent in body but present in spirit" [*1 Corinthians v, 3*]; *absenti nemo ne nocuisse velit* [Propertius]; "Achilles absent was Achilles still" [Homer]; *aux absents les os; briller par son absence;* "conspicuous by his absence" [Russell]; "in the hope to meet shortly again and make our absence sweet" [B. Jonson].

189. [Place of habitation, or resort.] **Abode. — N.** abode, dwelling, lodging, domicile, residence, address, habitation, where one's lot is cast, local habitation, berth, diggings [*colloq.*], seat, lap, sojourn, housing, quarters, headquarters, resiance [*obs.*], tabernacle, throne, ark.

home, fatherland, motherland, country; homestead, home stall [*Eng.*], fireside; hearth, hearthstone; chimney corner, ingleside; harem, seraglio, zenana; household gods, *lares et penates* [*L.*], roof, household, housing, *dulce domum* [*L.*], paternal domicile; native

riginal; newcomer &c. (*stranger*) 57.

American; Briton, Englishman, Britisher, John Bull; Canadian, Canuck [*slang*]; downeaster [*U. S.*]; Scot, Scotchman, Scotsman, Caledonian; Hibernian, Irishman, Paddywhack, Paddy, Mick, Teague, Greek *or* Grecian [*slang*]; Welshman, Cambrian, Taffy; Frenchman, Parleyvoo, Froggy [*slang*]; Chinaman, Celestial; Uncle Sam, Yankee, Brother Jonathan.

PEOPLE &c. (*mankind*) 372; colony, settlement; household; mir [*Russia*]; garrison, crew; population.

V. INHABIT &c. (*be present*) 186; endenizen [*rare*] &c. (*locate oneself*) 184.

Adj. INDIGENOUS; native, natal; autochthonal, autochthonous; British, English; American; Canadian; Irish, Hibernian; Scotch, Scottish; Welsh, Cambrian; French, Gallic; Chinese, Celestial, Sinæan, Sinaic *or* Sinic [*rare*], Chink [*slang*], Chinee [*slang*]; domestic; domiciliated, domiciled; naturalized, vernacular, domesticated; domiciliary; colonial.

OCCUPIED BY, in the occupation of; garrisoned by.

⁎⁎⁎ "For he might have been a Roosian, A Frenchman, Turk or Proosian, Or perhaps Italian! But in spite of all temptations To belong to other nations, He remains an Englishman" [Gilbert].

soil, native land, "God's own country," down home [*colloq.*]

quarter, parish &c. (*region*) 181.

RETREAT, haunt, resort; nest, nidus, snuggery [*colloq.*], arbor, bower &c. 191; lair, den, cave, hole, hiding place, cell, sanctum sanctorum, aerie, eyrie *or* eyry, rookery, hive; habitat, covert, perch, roost; nidification; *kala jagah* [*Hind.*].

CAMP, bivouac, encampment, cantonment; castrametation; barrack, casemate, casern *or* caserne; tent &c. 223.

TENEMENT, messuage, farm, farmhouse, grange, hacienda [*Sp. Amer.*], toft [*Scot., and dial. Eng.*].

COT, cabin, hut, chalet *or* châlet [*F.*], croft, shed, booth, stall, hovel, bothy *or* boothy, shanty, dugout [*U. S.*], wigwam; pen &c. (*inclosure*) 232; barn, bawn [*obs.*], kennel, sty, doghole, cote, coop, hutch; byre, cowhouse, cowshed, cowbyre; stable, dovecote, columbary, columbarium, shippen [*dial.*]; igloo *or* iglu [*Eskimo*], jacal; lacustrine –, lake –, pile- dwelling; log cabin, log house; shack [*colloq.*], shebang [*slang*], tepee, topek.

HOUSE, mansion, place, villa, cottage, box, lodge, hermitage, *rus in urbe* [*L.*], folly, rotunda, tower, château [*F.*], castle, pavilion, hotel, court, manor-house, messuage, hall, palace; kiosk, bungalow, chummery [*esp. Anglo-Indian*], *casa* [*Sp., Pg. and It.*], country seat; apartment-, brownstone-, duplex-, frame-, shingle-, flat-, tenement- house; three-decker, monitor building [*U. S.*]; building &c. (*construction*) 161; room, chamber &c. (*receptacle*) 191; rents [*colloq. or cant, U. S.*], buildings, mews.

HAMLET, village, bustee *or* basti [*Hind.*], thorp *or* thorpe, dorp, kraal [*S. Africa*], rancho [*Sp. Amer.*].

TOWN, borough, burgh, ham [*now used only in compounds*], city, capital, metropolis; suburb; provincial town; county town, county seat; courthouse [*U. S.*]; ghetto.

STREET, place, terrace, parade, esplanade, *alameda* [*Sp.*], board walk, embankment, road, row, lane, alley, court, quadrangle, quad [*colloq.*], wynd [*dial.*], close, yard, passage.

square, polygon, circus, crescent, mall, piazza, arcade, colonnade, peristyle, cloister; gardens, grove, residences; block of buildings, market place, *place* [*F.*], plaza.

ANCHORAGE, roadstead, roads; dock, basin, wharf, quay, port, harbor.

ASSEMBLY ROOM, auditorium, concert hall, armory, gymnasium; cathedral, church, chapel, meetinghouse &c. (*temple*) 1000; parliament &c. (*council*) 696.

INN, hostel [*archaic*], hostelry [*archaic*], hotel, tavern, caravansary *or* caravanserai, xenodochium, dak bungalow [*India*], khan, hospice; public house, alehouse, pothouse, mughouse; gin palace; bar, barroom; barrel house [*slang, U. S.*] cabaret [*U. S.*], chophouse; club, clubhouse; cookshop, dive [*U. S.*], exchange [*euphemism, U. S.*]; grill room, saloon [*U. S.*], shebeen [*Irish and Scot.*]; coffeehouse, eating-house; canteen, restaurant, buffet, café, estaminet [*F.*], posada [*Sp.*]

ALMSHOUSE, poorhouse, townhouse [*U. S.*].

GARDEN, park, pleasure ground, pleasance *or* plaisance [*archaic*], demesne.

SANATORIUM. health resort, Hill station *or* the Hills [*India*], health retreat, sanitarium, spa, watering-place, pump room.

V. INHABIT &c. (*be present*) 186; take up one's abode &c. (*locate oneself*) 184.

Adj. URBAN, oppidan [*rare*], metropolitan; suburban; provincial, rural, rustic, agrestic, country, countrified, regional; domestic; cosmopolitan; palatial.

⁎ *eigner Herd ist goldes Werth;* "even cities have their graves" [Longfellow]; *ubi libertas ibi patria;* "the herds are shut in byre and hut" [Kipling]; "My wants are few, I only wish a hut of stone (A *very plain* brown stone will do) That I may call my own" [Holmes].

190. [THINGS CONTAINED.] **Contents. — N.** CONTENTS; cargo, lading, freight, shipment, load, bale, burden, jag [*colloq.*]; cartload, shipload; cup of, basket of &c. (*receptacle*) 191; inside &c. 221; stuffing.

V. LOAD, lade, ship, charge, weight, pile, fill, stuff.

191. Receptacle. — N. RECEPTACLE, container; inclosure &c. 232; recipient, receiver, reservatory [*obs.*].

COMPARTMENT; cell, cellule; follicle; hole, corner, niche, recess, nook; crypt, stall, pigeonhole, cove, oriel; cave &c. (*concavity*) 252; mouth.

CAPSULE, vesicle, cyst, pod, calyx, cancelli, utricle, bladder; pericarp, udder.

STOMACH, paunch, belly, venter, ventricle, ingluvies, crop, craw, maw, gizzard, breadbasket [*slang*], Little Mary [*slang*]; omasum, manyplies, abomasum, rumen, reticulum.

BAG, sac, sack, saccule, wallet, pocket, pouch, fob, sheath, scabbard, socket, cardcase, scrip [*archaic*], poke [*chiefly dial.*], knapsack, haversack, satchel, reticule, budget [*dial.*], net; ditty-bag, -box; housewife *or* hussif; saddlebags; portfolio; quiver &c. (*magazine*) 636.

CASE, chest, box, coffer, caddy, casket; pyx *or* pix, monstrance [*R. C. Ch.*]; caisson; desk, bureau, reliquary, shrine; trunk, portmanteau, bandbox, valise, grip *or* gripsack [*colloq., U. S.*], suitcase, handbag, Boston bag, school bag, brief case, travelingbag, Gladstone *or* Gladstone bag; skippet, vasculum; boot, imperial [*now rare*]; *vache* [*F.*]; cage, manger, rack.

VESSEL, vase, bushel, barrel; canister, jar; pottle, basket, pannier; buck basket, clothes basket, hopper, maund [*obs.*], creel, cran *or* crane [*Scot.*], crate, cradle, bassinet, whisket *or* wisket [*dial. Eng.*]; *jardinière* [*F.*], *corbeille* [*F.*], hamper, dosser *or* dorser, tray, hod, scuttle, utensil; brazier; cuspidor, spittoon.

[FOR LIQUIDS] cistern &c. (*store*) 636; vat, caldron *or* cauldron, barrel, cask, puncheon, keg, rundlet, tun, butt, firkin, kilderkin, carboy, amphora, bottle, jar, decanter, ewer, cruse, carafe, crock, kit [*dial. Eng.*], canteen, flagon; demijohn; flask, flasket; stoup *or* stoop, noggin, vial, phial, cruet, caster; urn, epergne, salver, patella, *tazza* [*It.*], patera, piggin; biggin, percolator, coffeepot, coffee urn, teapot, tea urn, samovar; tig *or* tyg [*dial. Eng.*], nipperkin [*now rare*], pocket pistol [*slang*], tub, bucket, pail, skeel [*dial.*], pot, tankard, jug, pitcher, mug, pipkin; gallipot; matrass *or* mattrass, receiver, retort, alembic, bolthead, capsule, can, kettle; bowl, basin, jorum [*colloq.*], punch bowl, cup, goblet, chalice, tumbler, glass, rummer, horn, saucepan, skillet, posnet [*obs.*], tureen, stein.

bail, beaker, billy [*Australia*], cannikin *or* canakin; catch basin, catch drain; chatti *or* chatty [*India*], lota *or* lotah [*India*], mussuk *or* mussuck [*India*]; schooner [*U. S.*], spider, terrine, toby, *urceus* [*L.*].

PLATE, platter, dish, trencher, calabash, porringer, potager [*obs.*], saucer, pan, crucible; glassware, tableware; vitrics.

LADLE, dipper, tablespoon, spoon; shovel, trowel, spatula.

CUPBOARD, closet, commode, cellaret, chiffonier *or* chiffonnier, *chiffonnière* [*F.*], locker, bin, bunker, buffet, press, clothespress, safe, sideboard, drawer, chest of drawers, till, escritoire, scrutoire [*obs.*], secretary, *secrétaire* [*F.*], davenport, bookcase, cabinet, canterbury; *étagère* [*F.*], vargueno, vitrine.

CHAMBER, apartment, room, cabin; office, court, hall, atrium; suite of rooms, apartment [*U. S.*], flat, story; saloon, *salon* [*F.*], parlor; by-room, cubicle; presence chamber; living-, sitting-, drawing-, reception-, state- room; best room [*colloq.*], keeping room [*dial. Eng.*]; gallery, cabinet, closet; pew, box; boudoir; adytum, sanctum; bedroom, dormitory; refectory, dining room, *salle-à-manger* [*F.*]; nursery, schoolroom; library, study; studio; billiard room, bathroom, smoking room; den; state room, tablinum, tenement.

attic, loft, garret, cockloft, clerestory; cellar, vault, hold, cockpit; cubbyhole; cook house; *entre-sol* [*F.*]; mezzanine *or* mezzanine floor; ground floor, *rez-de-chaussée* [*F.*], basement, kitchen, pantry, *bawarchi-khana* [*Hind.*], scullery, offices; storeroom &c. (*depository*) 636; lumber room; dairy, laundry, coach house; garage; hangar; outhouse, penthouse; lean-to.

PORTICO, porch, stoop [*U. S.*], veranda, lobby, court, hall, vestibule, corridor, passage; anteroom, antechamber; lounge; piazza [= veranda, *U. S.*].

BOWER, arbor, summerhouse, alcove, grotto, hermitage; conservatory, greenhouse.

LODGING &c. (*abode*) 189; bed &c. (*support*) 215.

CARRIAGE &c. (*vehicle*) 272.

Adj. capsular; saccular, sacculated; recipient; ventricular, cystic, vascular, vesicular, cellular, camerated, locular, multilocular, polygastric; gastric, stomachic, gasteral [*rare*]; marsupial; siliquose, siliquous.

SECTION II. DIMENSIONS

1. GENERAL DIMENSIONS

192. Size. — N. SIZE, magnitude, dimension, bulk, volume; largeness &c. *adj.*; greatness &c. (*of quantity*) 31; expanse &c. (*space*) 180; amplitude, mass; proportions.

CAPACITY; tonnage *or* tunnage; cordage; caliber *or* calibre; scantling [*obs.*].

CORPULENCE, obesity; plumpness &c. *adj.*; *embonpoint* [*F.*], corporation [*colloq.*], flesh and blood, lustihood; turgidity &c. (*expansion*) 194.

HUGENESS &c. *adj.*; enormity, immensity; monstrosity.

GIANT, Brobdingnagian, Antæus, Goliath, Polyphemus, Colossus, Titan, Titaness, Briareus, Norn, Hercules, Cyclops, Gog and Magog, Gargantua; monster, mammoth, cachalot, whale, porpoise, behemoth, leviathan, elephant, jumbo [*colloq.*], hippopotamus; colossus.

LUMP, bulk, block, loaf, mass, swad [*slang, U. S.*], clod, nugget, tun, cord, bushel; thumper [*slang*], whopper *or* whapper [*colloq.*], spanker [*slang*], strapper [*slang*]; "Triton among the minnows" [*Coriolanus*].

mountain, mound; heap &c. (*assemblage*) 72.

FULL-SIZE, life-size; largest portion &c. 50.

V. BE LARGE &c. *adj.*; become large &c. (*expand*) 194.

Adj. LARGE, big; great &c. (*in quan-*

193. Littleness. — N. LITTLENESS &c. *adj.*; smallness &c. (*of quantity*) 32; exiguity, inextension; parvitude [*rare*], parvity [*obs.*]; duodecimo; Elzevir edition, epitome; microcosm; rudiment; vanishing point; thinness &c. 203.

DWARF, pygmy *or* pigmy, Liliputian, Negrito, Negrillo; chit, fingerling [*rare*], Pigwiggen, pigwidgeon [*now rare*], urchin, elf; atomy, dandiprat [*archaic*], doll, puppet; Tom Thumb, hop-o'-my-thumb; manikin *or* mannikin; micromorph [*rare*], homunculus, dapperling.

MITE, insect, arthropod, ephemerid, ephemera, bug [*pop., U. S.*], larva, emmet, fly, midge, gnat, shrimp, minnow, worm, maggot, grub; tit, tomtit, runt, mouse, small fry; millet seed, mustard seed; barleycorn; pebble, grain of sand; molehill, button, bubble.

ATOM, monad, animalcule, animalculum (*pl.* animalcula), diatom, dyad, triad, tetrad, pentad, hexad, heptad, octad, molecule, microbe, germ, microörganism, bacterium (*pl.* bacteria), microphyte, microzyme, amœba, microzoa, entozoön (*pl.* entozoa), phytozoaria, infusoria.

PARTICLE &c. (*small quantity*) 32; point, micron; scintilla; fragment &c. (*small part*) 51; powder &c. 330; point of a pin, mathematical point; minutiæ &c. (*unimportance*) 643.

tity) 31; considerable, bulky, voluminous, ample, massive, massy; capacious, comprehensive, spacious &c. 180; mighty, towering, fine, magnificent.

STOUT, corpulent, fat, plump, squab, full, lusty, strapping [*colloq.*], bouncing; portly, burly, well-fed, full-grown; corn-fed, gram-fed [*Anglo-Ind.*]; stalwart, brawny, fleshy; goodly; in good -case, – condition; in condition; chopping, jolly; club-faced [*obs.*], chubby-faced.

large as life; plump as a -dumpling, – partridge; fat as -a pig, – a quail, – butter, – brawn, – bacon [*all colloq.*].

HULKY, hulking, unwieldy, lumpish, lubberly, gaunt, spanking [*slang.*], whacking [*colloq.*], whopping [*colloq.*], thumping [*colloq.*], thundering [*colloq.*], overgrown; puffy &c. (*swollen*) 194.

HUGE, immense, enormous, titanic, mighty; vast, vasty [*archaic*]; stupendous; monster, monstrous; gigantic; elephantine; giant, giantlike; colossal, Cyclopean, Brobdingnagian, Gargantuan; infinite &c. 105.

⁎⁎ "obesity is the mother of abstinence" [*Cynic's Calendar*]; "he was plump and he was chubby" [Gilbert].

MICROGRAPHY; micrometer, microscope, interferometer, vernier; scale.

V. BE LITTLE &c. *adj.*; lie in a nutshell; become small &c. (*decrease*) 36, (*contract*) 195.

Adj. LITTLE; small &c. (*in quantity*) 32; minute, diminutive, microscopic; inconsiderable &c. (*unimportant*) 643; exiguous, puny, runty [*U. S.*], tiny, wee [*colloq.*], petty, minikin [*obs.*], miniature, pygmy *or* pigmy, elfin; undersized; dwarf, dwarfed, dwarfish; spare, stunted, limited; cramp, cramped; pollard, Liliputian, Negritic, dapper, pocket; portative, portable; duodecimo; dumpy, squat; short &c. 201.

IMPALPABLE, intangible, evanescent, imperceptible, invisible, inappreciable, infinitesimal, homeopathic; rudimentary, rudimental; embryonic, vestigial.

ANIMALCULAR, amœbic, amœboid, diatomaceous, diatomic, microzoal, microbial, microbic, molecular, atomic, corpuscular.

SCANT, weazen [*obs.*], scraggy, scrubby; thin &c. (*narrow*) 203; granular &c. (*powdery*) 330; shrunk &c. 195; brevipennate.

Adv. in a small compass, in a nutshell; on a small scale.

---

194. Expansion. — N. EXPANSION, dilation, expansibleness; increase &c. 35 -of size; enlargement, extension, augmentation; amplification, ampliation; aggrandizement, spread, increment, growth, development, pullulation [*rare*], swell, dilatation, rarefaction; turgescence *or* turgescency, turgidness, turgidity; dispansion [*obs.*]; obesity &c. (*size*) 192; hydrocephalus, hydrophthalmus; dropsy, tumefaction, intumescence, swelling, tumor, diastole, distension; puffing, puffiness; inflation; pandiculation.

dilatability, expansibility.

GROWTH, upgrowth; accretion &c. 35; germination, budding, gemmation.

bulb &c. (*convexity*) 250; plumper; superiority of size.

OVERGROWTH, overdistension; hypertrophy, tympany.

V. BECOME LARGER &c. (large &c. 192); expand, widen, enlarge, extend, grow, increase, incrassate, swell, gather; fill out; deploy, take open order, dilate, stretch, spread; mantle, wax; grow up,

195. Contraction. — N. CONTRACTION, reduction, diminution; decrease &c. 36 -of size; defalcation, decrement; lessening, shrinking &c. *v.*; compaction [*rare*], tabes, collapse, emaciation, attenuation, tabefaction [*rare*], consumption, marasmus, atrophy; systole, syncopation, syncope; neck, hourglass.

COMPRESSION, condensation, constraint, astriction [*rare*], compactness; compendium &c. 596; squeezing &c. *v.*; strangulation; corrugation; constringency, astringency; astringents, sclerotics; contractibility, contractibleness, contractility, compressibility, compressibleness, coarctation.

inferiority in size.

V. BECOME SMALL, become smaller; lessen, decrease &c. 36; grow less, dwindle, shrink, contract, narrow, shrivel, syncopate, collapse, wither, lose flesh, wizen [*dial.*], fall away, waste, wane, ebb; decay &c. (*deteriorate*) 659.

BE SMALLER THAN, fall short of; not come up to &c. (*be inferior*) 34.

RENDER SMALLER, lessen, diminish,

spring up; bud, burgeon *or* bourgeon, shoot, sprout, germinate, put forth, vegetate, pullulate, open, burst forth; gain flesh, gather flesh; outgrow; spread like wildfire, overrun.

BE LARGER THAN; surpass &c. (*be superior*) 33.

RENDER LARGER &c. (large &c. 192); expand, spread, extend, aggrandize, distend, develop, amplify, spread out, widen, magnify, rarefy, inflate, puff, blow up, stuff, pad, cram, bloat; exaggerate; fatten.

Adj. EXPANDED &c. *v.;* larger &c. (large &c. 192); swollen; expansive; wide open, widespread; fan-shaped, flabelliform; overgrown, exaggerated, bloated, fat, turgid, tumid, hypertrophied, dropsical; pot-bellied, swagbellied [*obs.*]; œdematous *or* edematous, corpulent, obese, puffy, pursy, blowzy, distended; patulous; bulbous &c. (*convex*) 250; full-blown, full-grown, full-formed; big &c. 192; abdominous, enchymatous, rhipidate; tumefacient, tumefying.

*** "Her waist is ampler than her life, For life is but a span" [Holmes]; "the more waist the less speed" [*Cynic's Calendar*].

contract, draw in, narrow, pucker, cockle, coarct *or* coarctate [*rare*]; boil down; deflate, exhaust, empty; constrict, constringe; condense, compress, squeeze, corrugate, crush, crumple up, warp, purse, purse up, pack, stow; pinch, tighten, strangle; cramp; dwarf, bedwarf; shorten &c. 201; circumscribe &c. 229; restrain &c. 751.

PARE, reduce, attenuate, rub down, scrape, file, grind, chip, shave, shear.

Adj. CONTRACTING &c. *v.;* astringent, constringent, shrunk, shrunken, tabescent, tabetic, contractible, contracted &c. *v.;* strangulated, tabid, wizened, weazen, weazeny [*colloq.*], corky, stunted; waning &c. *v.;* neap, compact, compacted.

UNEXPANDED &c. (expand &c. 194); contractile; compressible; smaller &c. (small &c. 193).

196. Distance. — N. DISTANCE; space

&c. 180; remoteness, farness; far cry to; longinquity [*rare*], elongation; easting, westing, drift, offing, background; remote region; removedness; parallax; reach, span, stride.

outpost, outskirt; horizon, sky line: aphelion; foreign parts, *ultima Thule* [L.], *ne plus ultra* [L.], antipodes; jumping-off place [*colloq.*], long range, giant's stride.

DISPERSION &c. 73.

V. BE DISTANT &c. *adj.;* extend to, stretch to, reach to, spread to, go to, get to, stretch away to; range, outreach, outlie [*rare*].

remain at a distance; keep –, stand- -away, – off, – aloof, – clear of.

Adj. DISTANT; far off, far away; remote, telescopic, distal, wide of; stretching to &c. *v.;* yon, yonder; ulterior; transmarine, transpontine, transatlantic, transalpine; tramontane; ultramontane, ultramundane; hyperborean, antipodean; inaccessible, out-of-the-way, God-forsaken [*colloq.*]; unapproached, unapproachable; incontiguous [*obs.*].

Adv. FAR OFF, far away; afar, -off; off; away; a -long, – great, – good- way off; wide away, beyond range, aloof; wide

197. Nearness. — N. NEARNESS &c.

adj.; proximity, propinquity; vicinity, vicinage; neighborhood, adjacency, nighness [*archaic*], appropinquity [*rare*]; contiguity &c. 199.

short -distance, – step, – cut; earshot, close quarters, range, stone's throw; bowshot, gunshot, pistol shot; hair's breadth, span.

PURLIEUS, neighborhood, vicinage, environs, *alentours* [F.], suburbs, *faubourg* [F.], confines, *banlieue* [F.], borderland; whereabouts.

BYSTANDER, spectator; neighbor *or* neighbour, borderer.

APPROACH &c. 286; convergence &c. 290; perihelion.

V. BE NEAR &c. *adj.;* adjoin, abut, neighbor, hang about, trench on; border upon, verge upon; stand by, approximate, tread on the heels of, cling to, clasp, hug; huddle; hang upon the skirts of, hover over; burn [*colloq.*].

bring *or* draw near &c. 286; converge &c. 290; crowd &c. 72; place side by side &c. *adv.*

Adj. NEAR, nigh; close –, near- at hand; close, neighboring, vicinal, propinquent [*rare*]; bordering upon, contiguous, adjacent, adjoining; proximate,

of, clear of; out of -the way, – reach; abroad, yonder, farther, further, beyond; *outre mer* [*F.*], over the border, far and wide, "over the hills and far away" [Gay]; from pole to pole &c. (*over great space*) 180; to the -uttermost parts, – ends- of the earth; out of range, out of hearing, nobody knows where, *à perte de vue* [*F.*], out of the sphere of, wide of the mark; a far cry to.

APART, asunder; wide apart, wide asunder; *longo intervallo* [*L.*]; at arm's length.

** "distance lends enchantment" [Campbell]; "Across the hills and far away Beyond their utmost purple rim" [Tennyson].

proximal; at hand, warm [*colloq.*], handy; near the mark, near run; home, intimate.

Adv. NEAR, nigh; hard by, fast by; close to, close upon; hard upon; at the point of; next door to; within -reach – call, – hearing, – earshot, – range; within an ace of; but a step, not far from, at no great distance; on the -verge, – brink, – skirts- of; in the environs &c. *n.;* at one's -door, – feet, – elbow, – finger's end, – side; on the tip of one's tongue; under one's nose; within a stone's throw &c. *n.;* in sight of, in presence of; at close quarters; cheek by jowl, cheek to cheek, shoulder to shoulder; beside, alongside, side by side, *tête-à-tête* [*F.*]; in juxtaposition &c.

(*touching*) 199; yardarm to yardarm; at the heels of; on the confines of, at the threshold, bordering upon, verging to; in the way.

ABOUT; hereabout *or* hereabouts, thereabout *or* thereabouts; roughly, in round numbers; approximately, approximatively; as good as, well-nigh.

198. Interval. — N. INTERVAL, interspace; separation &c. 44; hiatus, cæsura; interruption, interregnum; interstice, intersection, lacuna.

parenthesis &c. (*interjacence*) 228; void &c. (*absence*) 187; incompleteness &c. 53.

CLEFT, break, gap, opening; hole &c. 260; chasm, mesh, crevice, chink, rime [*now rare*], creek, cranny, crack, chap, slit, fissure, scissure, rift, fault, flaw, breach, fracture, rent, gash, cut, leak, dike, ha-ha.

GORGE, defile, ravine, cañon, crevasse, abyss, abysm; gulf; inlet, frith, strait, gully, nullah [*India*]; pass; furrow &c. 259; *abra* [*Sp. Amer.*], *barranco* [*Sp.*]; clove [*U. S.*], gulch [*U. S.*], notch [*U. S.*], yawning gulf; *hiatus maxime deflendus* [*L.*], *hiatus valde deflendus* [*L.*].

V. GAPE &c. (*open*) 260; separate &c. 44.

199. Contiguity. — N. CONTIGUITY, contiguousness, contact, proximity, apposition, abuttal, juxtaposition, touching &c *v.;* abutment, osculation; meeting, appulse, appulsion, *rencontre* [*F.*], rencounter, syzygy, conjunction, conjugation, coincidence, coexistence; adhesion &c. 46.

BORDERLAND; frontier &c. (*limit*) 233; tangent; abutter.

V. BE CONTIGUOUS &c. *adj.;* join, adjoin, abut on, neighbor, border, march with; graze, touch, meet, osculate, come in contact, coincide; coexist; adhere &c. 46.

Adj. CONTIGUOUS; touching &c. *v.;* in contact &c. *n.;* conterminous, end to end, osculatory; pertingent [*obs.*]; tangential.

hand to hand; close to &c. (*near*) 197; with no interval &c. 198.

Adj. with an interval, far between; breachy, rimose, rimous, rimulose.
Adv. AT INTERVALS &c. (*discontinuously*) 70; *longo intervallo* [*L.*].

2. LINEAR DIMENSIONS

200. Length. — N. LENGTH, longitude, longness [*rare*], extent, span; mileage.

LINE, bar, rule, stripe, streak, spoke, radius.

LENGTHENING &c. *v.;* prolongation, production, protraction; tension, tensure [*obs.*]; extension.

201. Shortness. — N. SHORTNESS &c. *adj.;* brevity littleness &c. 193; a span.

SHORTENING &c. *v.;* abbreviation, abbreviature [*obs.*], abridgment, concision, retrenchment, curtailment, decurtation [*obs.*], epitomization, obtruncation [*rare*], condensation; reduction &c. (*con-*

[MEASURES OF LENGTH] line, nail, inch, hand, palm, foot, cubit, yard, ell, fathom, rood, pole, furlong, mile, knot, league; chain; arpent, handbreadth, *jornada* [*U. S.*], kos [*Hind.*], vara [*Sp. & Pg.*]; meter, kilometer, centimeter &c.

pedometer, odometer, odograph, viameter, viatometer, log [*naut.*], speedometer, telemeter, perambulator; scale &c. (*measurement*) 466.

V. BE LONG &c. *adj.;* stretch out, sprawl; extend to, reach to, stretch to; make a long arm, "drag its slow length along" [Pope].

RENDER LONG &c. *adj.;* lengthen, extend, elongate; stretch; prolong, produce [*now rare*], protract; let out, draw out, spin out; drawl.

ENFILADE, look along, view in perspective.

Adj. LONG, longsome [*archaic*]; elongate *or* elongated, longish, lengthy, wiredrawn, outstretched, extended; lengthened &c. *v.;* sesquipedalian &c. (*words*) 577; interminable, no end of [*colloq.*].

LINEAR, lineal; longitudinal, oblong.

LANKY, lank, slabsided [*slang, U. S.*], rangy; tall &c. 206; macrocolous, longlimbed.

as long as -my arm, – to-day and to-morrow; unshortened &c. (shorten &c. 201).

Adv. LENGTHWISE, at length, longitudinally, endlong [*archaic*], endways, endwise, along; tandem; in a line &c. (*continuously*) 69; in perspective.

from end to end, from stem to stern, from head to foot, from the crown of the head to the sole of the foot, from top to toe; fore and aft; over all.

₊ "And he is lean and lank and brown as is the ribbed sea-sand" [Wordsworth].

traction) 195; epitome &c. (*compendium*) 596.

elision, ellipsis; conciseness &c. (*in style*) 572.

ABRIDGER, epitomist, epitomizer, obtruncator [*rare*].

V. BE SHORT &c. *adj.;* RENDER SHORT &c. *adj.;* shorten, curtail, abridge, abbreviate, take in, reduce; compress &c. (*contract*) 195; epitomize &c. 596.

CUT SHORT, retrench, obtruncate [*rare*], scrimp, cut, chop up, hack, hew; cut down, pare down; clip, dock, lop, prune, shear, shave, mow, reap, crop; snub; truncate, pollard, stunt, nip, check the growth of; foreshorten [*drawing*].

Adj. SHORT, brief, curt; compendious, compact; stubby, pudgy, tubby [*colloq.*], squatty, squidgy [*rare*], scrimp; shorn, stubbed; stumpy [*colloq.*], thickset, pug; chunky [*U. S.*], curtate, curtal [*archaic*], decurtate; *retroussé* [*F.*], turned up; scrub, stocky; squab, squabby; squat, squattish, dumpy; little &c. 193; curtailed of its fair proportions; short by; oblate; abbreviatory; concise &c. 572; summary.

Adv. SHORTLY &c. *adj.;* in short &c. (*concisely*) 572.

---

202. Breadth, Thickness. — N.
BREADTH, width, latitude, amplitude; diameter, bore, caliber, radius; superficial extent &c. (*space*) 180.

THICKNESS, crassitude [*obs.*]; corpulence &c. (*size*) 192; dilatation &c. (*expansion*) 194.

V. BE BROAD &c. *adj.;* become *or* render broad &c. *adj.;* expand &c. 194; thicken, widen, calibrate.

Adj. BROAD, wide, ample, extended; discous, discoid; fanlike; outspread, outstretched; "wide as a church-door" [*Romeo and Juliet*]; latifoliate [*rare*], latifolious [*rare*].

THICK, dumpy, squab, squat, thickset, stubby &c. 201; thick as a rope.

203. Narrowness, Thinness. — N.
NARROWNESS &c. *adj.;* closeness, exility [*rare*]; exiguity &c. (*little*) 193.

line; hair's –, finger's- breadth; strip, streak, vein.

THINNESS &c. *adj.;* tenuity; emaciation, marcor [*obs.*], macilence *or* macilency [*rare*].

shaving, slip &c. (*filament*) 205; thread paper, skeleton, shadow, scrag, atomy [*obs. or joc.*], anatomy [*archaic*], study in anatomy [*humorous*], spindleshanks [*humorous or contemptuous*], barebone, lantern jaws, mere skin and bone.

MIDDLE CONSTRICTION, stricture, coarctation [*med.*]; neck, waist, isthmus, wasp, hourglass; ridge, ghât *or* ghaut [*India*], pass; ravine &c. 198.

NARROWING, angustation, tapering; contraction &c. 195.

V. be narrow &c. *adj.;* narrow, taper, contract, &c. 195; render narrow &c. *adj.*

Adj. NARROW, close; slender, gracile, thin, fine; thread-like &c. (*filament*) 205; finespun, taper, slim, slight-made; scant, scanty; spare, delicate, incapacious; contracted &c. 195; unexpanded &c. (*expand* &c. 194); slender as a thread.

LEAN, emaciated, meager *or* meagre, gaunt, macilent; lank, lanky; weedy [*colloq.*], skinny; scrawny [*U. S.*], slinky [*dial.*]; starved, starveling; attenuated, shriveled, pinched, poor, peaked [*colloq.*], lathy [*colloq.*], skeletal, flatsided [*colloq.*], slabsided [*slang*, *U. S.*]; spindle-legged, spindle-shanked, spindling; coarctate, angustate, tabic, tabelic, tabid, extenuated, marcid [*obs.*], rawboned; herring-gutted [*colloq.*]; worn to a shadow, "lean as a rake" [Chaucer]; thin as a -lath, – whipping post, – wafer; hatchet-faced; lantern-jawed.

****** "Pinch, a hungry, lean-faced villain, a mere anatomy" [*Comedy of Errors*].

204. Layer. — N. LAYER, stratum, course, bed, couch, coping, zone, substratum, floor, flag, stage, story, tier, slab, escarpment; table, tablet; dess [*Scot. & dial. Eng.*]; flagstone; board, plank; trencher, platter.

LEAF, lamina, lamella, sheet, flake, foil, wafer, scale, coat, peel, pellicle, membrane, film, lap, ply, slice, shive, cut, rasher, shaving, plate; overlay, integument &c. (*covering*) 223; eschar.

STRATIFICATION, lamination, delamination, foliation; scaliness, nest of boxes, coats of an onion.

V. SLICE, shave, pare, peel, skive; delaminate; plate, coat, veneer; cover &c. 223.

Adj. LAMELLAR, lamelliferous, lamellate *or* lamellated, lamelliform; laminate *or* laminated, laminiferous; micaceous; schistose, schistous; scaly, filmy, membranous, membranaceous, flaky, squamous; foliated, foliaceous; stratified, stratiform; tabular, discoid; spathic, spathose.

206. Height. — N. HEIGHT, altitude, elevation; eminence, pitch; loftiness &c. *adj.;* sublimity, celsitude [*rare*].

TALLNESS &c. *adj.*; stature, procerity [*rare*]; prominence &c. 250; apex, zenith, culmination.

COLOSSUS &c. (*size*) 192; giant, grenadier; giraffe, camelopard.

HEIGHT, mount, mountain; hill, *alto* [*Sp.*], butte [*U. S.*], monticule, monticle [*obs.*], fell [*obs. exc. in proper names*], knap; cape; headland, foreland; promontory; ridge, hogback *or* hog's-back, dune, rising –, vantage- ground; down; moor, moorland; Alp; uplands, highlands; heights &c. (*summit*), 210; knob, *loma* [*U. S.*], *pena* [*U. S.*], *picacho* [*Sp.*], tump

205. Filament. — N. FILAMENT, line; fiber, fibril; funicle, vein, hair, cobweb, capillary, ciliolum, capillament [*rare*], cilium, cirrus, barbel, strand, tendril, gossamer; hair stroke; veinlet, venula, venule.

beard &c. (*roughness*) 256; ramification.

THREAD, threadlet, harl, yarn, packthread, cotton, sewing silk.

STRING, twine, twist, whipcord, cord, rope, hemp, oakum, jute; tape, ribbon, wire.

STRIP, shred, slip, spill, list, tænia *or* tenia, band, fillet, fascia; ribbon, rib-band *or* riband [*archaic*], roll, lath, splinter, shiver, shaving; ligule *or* ligula.

Adj. FILAMENTOUS, filamentiferous, filaceous [*rare*], filiform; fibrous, fibrillous, fibrilliform, fibrilliferous; thread-like, wiry, stringy, ropy; capillary, capilliform; funicular, wire-drawn; anguilliform; flagelliform; barbate, hairy &c. (*rough*) 256; tæniate, tæniform, tænioid; venose, venous; ligulate *or* ligulated.

207. Lowness. — N. LOWNESS &c. *adj.;* debasement; prostration &c. (*horizontal*) 213; depression &c. (*concave*) 252; subjacency; lowlands.

GROUND FLOOR; *rez de chaussée* [*F.*]; street floor.

BASEMENT, basement floor, cellar; hold; base &c. 211.

[COMPARISONS] feet, heels; molehill.

LOW WATER; low –, ebb –, neap- tide.

V. BE LOW &c. *adj.;* lie low, lie flat; underlie; crouch, slouch, wallow, grovel; lower &c. (*depress*) 308.

Adj. LOW, neap, debased; lower, inferior, under, nether; lowest, nethermost, lowermost; flat, level with the ground; lying low &c. *v.;* crouched, sub-

[*dial.*]; knoll, hummock, hillock, barrow, mound; steeps, bluff, cliff, craig [*Scot.*], tor, peak, pike [*dial.*], clough [*obs.*]; escarpment, edge, ledge, brae [*Scot. & dial. Eng.*]; dizzy height.

TOWER, pillar, column, obelisk, monument, belfry, steeple, spire, minaret, campanile, turret, dome, cupola; pylon, *tourelle* [*F.*], barbican, martello tower; ceiling &c. (*covering*) 223; upstairs.

POLE, pikestaff, maypole, flagstaff; mast, mainmast, topmast, topgallant mast.

HIGH WATER; high -, flood -, spring-tide.

HYPSOGRAPHY, hypsometry, hypsometer, altimeter, altimetry &c. (*angle*) 244; hypsophobia.

V. BE HIGH &c. *adj.*; tower, soar, command; hover; cap, culminate; overhang, hang over, impend, beetle; bestride, ride, mount; perch, surmount; cover &c. 223; rise above, overtop &c. (*be superior*) 33; stand on tiptoe.

BECOME HIGH &c. *adj.*; grow, grow higher, grow taller; upgrow; rise &c. (*ascend*) 305.

RENDER HIGH &c. *adj.*; heighten &c. (*elevate*) 307.

Adj. HIGH, elevated, eminent, exalted, lofty; tall; gigantic &c. (*big*) 192; Patagonian; towering, beetling, soaring, mountained, hanging [gardens]; elevated &c. 307; higher, superior, upper, supernal; highest &c. (*topmost*) 210; high-reaching, insessorial, perching; hill-dwelling, monticoline, monticolous.

tall as a -maypole, - poplar, - steeple; lanky &c. (*thin*) 203.

UPLAND, moorland; hilly, knobby [*U. S.*]; mountainous, alpine, subalpine, heaven-kissing; cloud-topt, cloud-capt, cloud-touching; aërial.

OVERHANGING &c. *v.*; incumbent, overlying; superincumbent, supernatant, superimposed; prominent &c. 250.

HYPSOGRAPHIC, hypsographical, hypsometric, hypsometrical.

Adv. ON HIGH, high up, aloft, up, above, aloof, overhead; airward; upstairs, above stairs; in the clouds; on tiptoe, on stilts, on the shoulders of; over head and ears; breast high.

over, upwards; from top to bottom &c. (*completely*) 52.

*** *è meglio cader dalle finistre che dal tetto.*

jacent, squat, prostrate &c. (*horizontal*) 213; depressed.

Adv. UNDER; beneath, underneath; below; down, downwards; adown, at the foot of; underfoot, underground; downstairs, belowstairs; at a low ebb; below par.

pyramid, pagoda, mole [*Rom. antiq.*].

---

208. Depth. — N. DEPTH; deepness &c. *adj.*; profundity, depression &c. (*concavity*) 252.

PIT, shaft, hollow, well, crater; gulf &c. 198; deep, abyss, bowels of the earth, bottomless pit, hell.

209. Shallowness. — N. SHALLOWNESS &c. *adj.*; shoals; mere scratch.

Adj. SHALLOW, slight, superficial; skin -, ankle -, knee- deep; depthless, just enough to wet one's feet; shoal, shoaly.

SOUNDINGS, depth of water, water, draft *or* draught, submersion; plummet, sound, probe; sounding -rod, - line; lead; bathometer, bathymeter, bathymetry; benthos; submarine, U-boat; depth bomb.

V. BE DEEP &c. *adj.*; render deep &c. *adj.*; deepen.

SOUND, heave the lead, take soundings; dig &c. (*excavate*) 252; plunge &c. 310.

Adj. DEEP, deep-seated, deep-bosomed; profound, sunk, buried; submerged &c. 310; subaqueous, submarine, subterranean, subterrene [*obs.*], subterraneous; underground.

knee-deep, ankle-deep.

BOTTOMLESS, soundless, fathomless; unfathomed, unfathomable; abysmal; deep as a well; bathycolpian *or* bathukolpic *or* bathukolpian; deep-sea, benthal, benthopelagic; bathymetric, bathymetrical; bathypelagic, bathysmal; downreaching, yawning.

Adv. OUT OF ONE'S DEPTH; beyond one's depth; over head and ears.

*** "under the whelming tide Visit'st the bottom of the monstrous world" [Milton].

210. Summit. — N.

SUMMIT, top, vertex, apex, summity [obs.], zenith, pinnacle, acme, culmination, meridian, utmost height, ne plus ultra [L.], height, pitch, maximum, climax; culminating –, crowning –, turning- point; turn of the tide, fountainhead; watershed, water parting; sky, pole.

TIP, tiptop; crest, crow's nest, cap, truck, peak, nib; end &c. 67; crown, brow; head, nob [slang], noddle [colloq.], pate [now humorous or derog.]; capsheaf.

HIGH PLACES, heights.

topgallant mast, skyscraper; quarter deck, hurricane deck.

architrave, frieze, cornice, corona, coping, coping stone, zoöphorus, capital, epistyle, sconce, pediment, entablature; tympanum; ceiling &c. (covering) 223.

attic, loft, garret, housetop, upper story, roof.

V. CROWN, top, cap, crest, surmount; overtop &c. (be superior to) 33; culminate.

Adj. HIGHEST &c. (high &c. 206); top; topmost, overmost, uppermost; tiptop; culminating &c. v.; meridian, meridional; capital, head, polar, supreme, supernal, apical, culminant [rare], culminal [rare], topgallant, skyward.

Adv. ATOP, at the top of the tree; en flûte [F.]; à fleur d'eau [F.].

211. Base. — N.

BASE, basement; plinth, dado, wainscot; baseboard, mopboard [U. S.]; bedrock, hardpan [U. S.]; foundation &c. (support) 215; substructure, substratum, ground, earth, pavement, floor, paving, flag, carpet, ground floor, deck; footing, ground work, basis; hold, bilge, sump; culet.

BED, basin, channel, coulee [Western N. Amer.], cañon &c. (interval) 198.

BOTTOM, nadir, foot, sole, toe, hoof, keel, root; centerboard.

Adj. BOTTOM, undermost, nethermost; fundamental; founded on, based on, grounded on, built on.

headpiece, capstone, fastigium, larmier,

212. Verticality. — N.

VERTICALITY; erectness &c. adj.; perpendicularity, aplomb; right angle, normal; azimuth circle.

CLIFF, steep, crag, bluff, palisades; wall, precipice.

ELEVATION, erection; square, plumb line, plummet.

V. BE VERTICAL &c. adj.; stand -up, – on end, – erect, – upright; stick up, cock up.

RENDER VERTICAL &c. adj.; set up, stick up, raise up, cock up; erect, rear, raise, pitch, raise on its legs.

Adj. VERTICAL, upright, erect, perpendicular, unrecumbent [rare], plumb, normal, straight, bolt upright; rampant; straight up; standing up &c. v.; rectangular orthogonal.

Adv. VERTICALLY &c. adj.; up, on end; up –, right- on end; à plomb [F.], endwise; on one's legs; at right angles.

213. Horizontality. — N.

HORIZONTALITY; flatness; level, plane; stratum &c. 204; dead level, dead flat; level plane.

RECUMBENCY; lying down &c. v.; reclination, decumbence or decumbency, discumbency [obs.]; proneness &c. adj.; accubation, supination, resupination, prostration; azimuth.

[LEVEL SURFACES] plain, floor, platform, bowling green; cricket ground; croquet -ground, – lawn; billiard table; terrace, estrade [rare], esplanade, parterre, table-land, plateau, ledge.

V. BE HORIZONTAL &c. adj.; lie, recline, couch; lie -down, – flat, – prostrate; sprawl, loll; sit down.

RENDER HORIZONTAL &c. adj.; lay, lay down, lay out; level, flatten, even, raze, equalize, smooth, align or aline.

prostrate, knock down, floor, fell, ground, drop, grass [slang]; cut –, hew –, mow- down.

Adj. HORIZONTAL, level, even, plane, flush; flat &c. 251; flat as a -billiard table, – bowling green; alluvial; calm, – as a mill pond; smooth, – as glass.

RECUMBENT, procumbent, accumbent, decumbent [bot.]; lying &c. v.; prone, supine, couchant, jacent [rare], prostrate, recubant [rare], resupinate.

Adv. HORIZONTALLY &c. adj.; on one's back, on all fours, on its beam ends.

214. Pendency. — N.

PENDENCY, dependency; suspension, hanging &c. v.

PENDANT, drop, eardrop, tassel, tippet,

215. Support. — N.

SUPPORT, ground, foundation, base, basis; terra firma [L.], bearing, fulcrum, bait [U. S.], caudex,

lobe, tail, train, flap, skirt, queue, pigtail, pendulum; hangnail.

peg, knob, button, hook, nail, stud, ring, staple, tenterhook; fastening &c. 45; spar, horse.

CHANDELIER, gaselier, electrolier.

V. BE PENDENT &c. *adj.*; hang, depend, swing, dangle, lower, droop: swag [*dial.*]; daggle, flap, trail, flow; beetle, jut, overhang.

SUSPEND. hang, sling, hook up, hitch, fasten to, append.

Adj. PENDENT, pendulous, pendulant [*rare*], decumbent, penduline [*rare*], pensile; hanging &c. *v.*; beetle; beetling, jutting over, overhanging, projecting; dependent; lowering; suspended &c. *v.*; loose, flowing.

HAVING A PENDANT &c. *n.*; tailed, caudate.

crib; *point d'appui* [*F.*], *pou sto* [*Gr.* που στω], purchase, footing, hold, *locusstandi* [*L.*]; landing, – stage, – place; stage, platform; block; rest, resting place; groundwork, substratum, riprap, sustentation [*now rare*], sustention [*rare*], subvention; floor &c. (*basement*) 211.

SUPPORTER; aid &c. 707; prop, stand, anvil, fulciment [*obs.*]; cue rest, jigger [*slang*], monkey [*builders' slang*], hod; stay, shore, skid, rib, truss, bandage; sleeper; stirrup, stilts, shoe, sole, heel, splint, lap; bar, rod, boom, sprit, outrigger; ratline *or* ratlin *or* ratling.

PEDICLE, pedicel *or* pedicellus *or* pediculus, peduncle [*all bot.*], stalk.

board, ledge, shelf, hob, bracket, trivet, arbor, rack; mantel, mantelpiece, mantelshelf; slab, console; counter, dresser; flange, corbel; table, trestle; shoulder; perch; horse; easel, desk; clotheshorse, hatrack; retable, predella, teapoy.

STAFF, stick, crutch, alpenstock, baton, crosier, cross, crook, lituus [*Rom. antiq.*], caduceus, thyrsus, staddle; bourdon, cowlstaff [*archaic*], *lathi* [*Hind.*], maulstick *or* mahlstick.

POST, pillar, shaft, thill, column, pilaster; pediment, pedestal; plinth, shank, leg, socle *or* zocle; buttress, jamb, mullion, stile, abutment; baluster, banister, stanchion; balustrade; headstone.

FRAME, framework; scaffold, skeleton, beam, rafter, girder, lintel, joist, travis *or* traviss [*dial. Eng.*], trave, corner stone. summer, breastsummer *or* bressomer, summertree, transom; rung, round, step, sill; angle-rafter, hip-rafter; cantilever, modillion; crown-post, king-post; vertebra, modiolus.

columella, backbone; keystone; axle, axletree; axis; arch, mainstay.

trunnion, pivot, rowlock; peg &c. (*pendency*) 214; tiebeam &c. (*fastening*) 45; thole pin.

SEAT, throne, dais; divan, musnud *or* masnad [*Ar.*], guddee *or* gaddi [*Hind.*]; chair, bench, form, sofa, davenport, couch, day-bed, settee, stall; wingchair, armchair, easychair, elbow-chair, rocking-chair; *fauteuil* [*F.*], woolsack, ottoman, settle, squab, bench; long chair, long-sleeve chair [*Anglo-Ind.*], *chaise longue* [*F.*], morris chair; *lamba chauki* or *lamba kursi* [*Hind.*]; saddle, aparejo, panel *or* pannel, pillion; sidesaddle, packsaddle; pommel, horn.

STOOL, foldstool, *prie-dieu* [*F.*], hassock, footstool; tabouret; tripod.

BED, berth, pallet, tester-bed, crib, cot, hammock, shakedown, truckle-bed, trundle-bed, cradle, litter, stretcher, bedstead; four-poster, French bed; bunk, kip [*dial.*], *palang* [*Hind.*]; roost [*slang*]; bedding, *bichhana* [*Hind.*], mattress, paillasse; pillow, bolster; mat, rug, cushion.

Atlas, Herakles *or* Hercules; tortoise that supports the earth.

[IN ARCHITECTURE] atlas (*pl.* atlantes), telamon (*pl.* telamones), caryatid (*pl.* caryatids *or* caryatides).

V. BE SUPPORTED &c.; lie –, sit –, recline –, lean –, loll –, rest –, stand –, step –, repose –, abut –, bear –, be based &c. – on; have at one's back: bestride, bestraddle.

SUPPORT, bear, carry, hold, sustain, shoulder; hold up, back up, bolster up, shore up; uphold, upbear; brace, truss, cradle, pillow, prop; underprop, underpin, underset; riprap; bandage &c. 43.

give –, furnish –, afford –, supply –, lend- –support, – foundations; bottom, found, base, ground, embed, imbed.

MAINTAIN, keep on foot; aid &c. 707.

Adj. SUPPORTING, supported, &c. *v.*; Atlantean, columellar, columelliform; sustentative, sustentational; fundamental; dorsigerous.

HAVING A PEDICLE &c. *n.*; pedunculate, pedicellate.

Adv. STRADDLE, astride on.

*** "With Atlantean shoulders, fit to bear The weight of mightiest monarchies" [Milton].

---

216. Parallelism. — N. PARALLELISM, coextension, equidistance, concentricity; collimation.

V. BE PARALLEL &c. *adj.;* parallel, equal; collimate.

Adj. PARALLEL, coextensive, equidistant, collateral, concentric, concurrent; abreast, aligned, equal, even, alongside.

Adv. alongside &c. (*laterally*) 236.

217. Obliquity. — N. OBLIQUITY, in-clination, incline, slope, slant, skew, thrawnness [*Scot. & dial. Eng.*]; crooked-ness &c. *adj.;* slopeness; leaning &c. *v.;* bevel, ramp, pitch, bezel, tilt; bias, list, twist, swag [*prov. Eng.*], sag, cant, lurch; distortion &c. 243; bend &c. (*curve*) 245; tower of Pisa.

ACCLIVITY, rise, ascent, gradient [*chiefly Brit.*], grade [*U. S.*], khudd [*Hind.*], glacis, rising ground, hill, bank, declivity, downhill, dip, fall, devexity [*obs.*]; gentle –, rapid– slope; easy –ascent, – descent; shelving beach; talus; *montagne Russe* [*F.*]; *facilis descensus Averni* [*L.*].

steepness &c. *adj.;* cliff, precipice &c. (*vertical*) 212; escarpment, scarp; chevron.

[MEASURE OF INCLINATION] clinometer; sine, cosine, cotangent, angle, hypoth-enuse.

diagonal; zigzag.

V. BE OBLIQUE &c. *adj.;* slope, slant, skew, lean, incline, shelve, stoop, decline, descend, bend, keel, careen, sag, swag [*dial.*], seel [*obs.*], slouch, cant, sidle.

RENDER OBLIQUE &c. *adj.;* sway, bias; slope, slant; incline, bend, crook; cant, tilt; distort &c. 243.

Adj. OBLIQUE, inclined; sloping &c. *v.;* tilted &c. *v.;* recubant [*rare*], recumbent, clinal, skew, askew, slant, bias, aslant, plagihedral, indirect, wry, awry; agee *or* ajee, thrawn [*both Scot. & dial. Eng.*], crooked; sinuous, zigzag, zigzaggy, chev-rony; knock-kneed &c. (*distorted*) 243; bevel, out of the perpendicular; aslope; asquint, backhand *or* backhanded.

UPHILL, rising, ascending, acclivous.

DOWNHILL, falling, descending: hanging (as, *hanging* gardens), declining, declivitous, proclivous [*rare*], declivous, devex [*obs.*], synclinal, anticlinal.

STEEP, abrupt, precipitous, breakneck.

DIAGONAL; transverse, transversal; athwart, antiparallel; curved &c. 245; loxic, loxotic, loxodromic.

Adv. OBLIQUELY &c. *adj.;* on one side, all on one side; askew, askance *or* askant, awry, skew, skewed, edgewise, at an angle; sidelong, sideways, slopewise, slant-wise; by a side wind.

---

218. Inversion. — N. INVERSION, eversion, subversion, reversion, retroversion, introversion; retroflexion; contraposition &c. 237; contrariety &c. 14; reversal; turn of the tide &c. (*reversion*) 145.

OVERTURN; somersault *or* summersault, somerset *or* summerset; *culbute* [*F.*] eversion [*archaic*]; revulsion; pirouette.

TRANSPOSITION, transposal, anastrophy, metastasis, hyperbaton, anastrophe; hysterology, hysteron proteron; hypallage, synchysis, tmesis, parenthesis; metath-esis; palindrome; ectropion [*path.*]; invagination, intussusception.

pronation and supination.

V. BE INVERTED &c.; turn –, go –, wheel– –round, – about, – to the right-about [*colloq.*]; turn –, go –, tilt –, topple– over; capsize, turn turtle.

INVERT, subvert, retrovert, introvert; reverse; turn the cat in the pan [*obs*]; upturn, overturn, upset, overset, *bouleverser* [*F.*], evert [*archaic*]; turn topsy-turvy

&c. *adj.; culbuter* [*F.*]; transpose, put the cart before the horse, turn the tables; invaginate, intussuscept.

Adj. INVERTED &c. *v.;* wrong side -out, – up; inside out, upside down; bottom -, keel- upwards; supine, on one's head, topsy-turvy, *sens dessus dessous* [*F.*]; ectropic.

INVERSE; reverse &c. (*contrary*) 14; opposite &c. 237; palindromic *or* palindromical.

TOPHEAVY, unstable.

Adv. INVERSELY &c. *adj.;* hirdy-girdy; heels over head, head over heels.

219. Crossing. — N. CROSSING &c. *v.;* intersection, interdigitation; decussation, transversion; chiasm *or* chiasma; convolution &c. 248; level crossing [*Eng.*], grade crossing [*U. S.*].

NETWORK, reticulation, cancellation; inosculation, anastomosis, intertexture, mortise.

NET, plexus, plexure, web, mesh, twill, skein, Hippocrates's sleeve, sleave [*archaic*]; sieve, sifter, riddle rocker, screen, cradle; felt, lace; wicker; mat, matting; plait, trellis, wattle, lattice, grating, grille, gridiron, tracery, fretwork, filigree, reticle [*obs.*]; tissue, netting, moke [*dial. Eng.*]; rivulation.

cross, chain, wreath, braid, cat's cradle, knot; entanglement &c. (*disorder*) 59.

CRUCIFIX, cross, rood, crisscross, christcross, tau; crux.

[WOVEN FABRICS] cloth, linen, muslin, cambric, *toile* [*F.*], drill, homespun, silk, satin, broadcloth, tweed &c.

V CROSS, decussate; intersect, interlace, intertwine, intertwist, interweave, interdigitate, interlink, intercross [*rare*], crisscross, crossbar.

twine, entwine, weave, inweave, twist, wreathe; anastomose, inosculate, dovetail, splice, link.

MAT, plait, pleat, plat, braid, felt, twill; tangle, entangle, ravel; net, knot; dishevel, raddle.

Adj. CROSSING &c. *v.;* crossed, matted &c. *v.;* transverse; intersected, decussate *or* decussated; chiasmal.

CROSS, cross-shaped cruciform, crucial; netlike, retiform, reticular, reticulate; areolar, cancellate *or* cancellated, cancellous, latticed, grated, barred, streaked; textile; crossbarred, cruciate, secant; cruciferous; plexal, plexiform; anastomotic; web-footed, palmiped.

Adv. CROSS, thwart, athwart, transversely; at grade [*U. S.*]; crosswise, thwartwise [*rare*].

3. CENTRICAL DIMENSIONS[1]

1. General

220. Exteriority. — N. EXTERIORITY; outside, exterior; surface, superficies; skin &c. (*covering*) 223; superstratum; disk *or* disc; face, facet; extrados.

eccentricity; circumjacence &c. 227.

V. BE EXTERIOR &c. *adj.;* lie around &c. 227.

PLACE EXTERIORLY, place outwardly, place outside; put out, turn out.

EXTERNALIZE, objectize [*rare*], objectify, visualize, envisage, actualize.

Adj. EXTERIOR, external, extraneous; outer, outermost; outward, outlying, outside, outdoor, *alfresco* [*It.*]; round about &c. 227; extramural; extralimi-

221. Interiority. — N. INTERIORITY; inside, interior; interspace, subsoil, substratum; intrados.

contents &c. 190; substance, pith, marrow; backbone &c. (*center*) 222; heart, bosom, breast; abdomen.

vitals, viscera, entrails, bowels, belly, intestines, guts [*vulgar or tech.*], chitterlings, womb, lap [*obs.*], rectum, cæcum, ileum, duodenum, jejunum.

GLAND, glandule [*rare*], gland cell; thyroid, parotid, prostate; liver, kidney.

PENETRALIA, recesses, innermost recesses; cave &c. (*concavity*) 252.

ENTEROLOGY, enterotomy, enterop-

---

[1] That is, Dimensions having reference to a center.

tary, extramundane, extraterrene, extraterrestrial, extraterritorial, exterritorial;
extern [*rare*].

extraregarding; eccentric *or* eccen-
trical; outstanding; extrinsic &c. 6;
ecdemic, exomorphic.

SUPERFICIAL, skin-deep; frontal, discoid.

Adv. EXTERNALLY &c. *adj.;* out, without, over, outwards, *ab extra* [*L.*], out
of doors; *extra muros* [*L.*].

IN THE OPEN AIR; *sub Jove* [*L.*], *sub
dio* [*L.*]; *à la belle étoile* [*F.*], *alfresco* [*It.*].

athy, enteritis, splanchnology; peristalsis, vermiculation.

INMATE, intern, inhabitant &c. 188.

V. BE INSIDE &c. *adj.;* be within &c.
adv.

INCLOSE &c. (*circumscribe*) 229; intern
embed *or* imbed &c. (*insert*) 300; place
within, keep within.

Adj. INTERIOR, internal; inner, intern
[*archaic*], intraneous [*rare*], intimate.
inside, inward, intraregarding; inmost.
innermost; deep-seated; intestine, in-
testinal, visceral, rectal, duodenal,
splanchnic; subcutaneous; abdominal,

cœliac *or* celiac, endomorphic.

intracanal, intracellular, intralobular, intramarginal, intramolecular, intramundane, intraocular, intraseptal, intratelluric, intrauterine, intravascular, intravenous, intraventricular.

interstitial &c. (*interjacent*) 228; inwrought &c. (*intrinsic*) 5; inclosed &c. v
HOME, inland, domestic, family, indoor, intramural, vernacular; endemic.

Adv. INTERNALLY &c. *adj.;* inwards, within, in, inly; herein, therein, wherein,
ab intra [*L.*], withinside [*obs.* or *Scot.*]; indoors, within doors; at home, in the
bosom of one's family.

222. Centrality. — N. CENTRALITY, centricalness, centricality, center *or* centre;
middle &c. 68; focus &c. 74.

center of -gravity, – pressure, – percussion, – oscillation, – buoyancy &c.;
metacenter.

CORE, kernel; nucleus, nucleolus; heart, pole, axis, bull's-eye, nave, hub, navel,
umbilicus; marrow, pith; backbone; vertebra, vertebral column; hotbed.

CONCENTRATION &c. (*convergence*) 290; centralization; symmetry; metropolis.

V. BE CENTRAL &c. *adj.;* converge &c. 290.

RENDER CENTRAL, centralize, concentrate; bring to a focus.

Adj. CENTRAL, centrical; middle &c. 68; axial, pivotal, nuclear, nucleate, centric,
focal, umbilical, concentric; middlemost; rachial, rachidial *or* rachidian; spinal,
vertebral; metropolitan.

Adv. MIDDLE; midst; centrally &c. *adj.*

*** "Boston State-house is the hub of the solar system" [Holmes].

223. Covering. — N. COVERING, cover,
baldachin *or* baldaquin; canopy, *shamianah* [*Hind.*], tilt, awning, tent, marquee,
marquise, wigwam, tepee, *tente d'abri*
[*F.*], umbrella, parasol, sunshade; veil
(*shade*) 424; shield &c. (*defense*) 717.

ROOF, ceiling, thatch, tile, pantile,
tiling, slates, slating, leads, shingles;
dome, cupola, mansard, hip roof; barrack [*U. S.*], *plafond* [*F.*], planchment
[*U. S.*], tiling, shed &c. (*abode*) 189.

224. Lining. — N. LINING, inner coating; coating &c. (*covering*) 223; stalactite, stalagmite.

FILLING, stuffing, wadding, padding,
facing; bushing.

WAINSCOT, parietes, wall, brattice,
sheathing.

V. LINE, stuff, incrust, wad, pad, fill,
face, ceil, bush, wainscot, sheathe.

Adj. LINED &c. *v.*

TOP, lid, covercle [*obs.*], door, operculum; bulkhead [*U. S.*].

WRAPPING, bandage, plaster, lint, dossil, pledget, finger stall.

COVERLET, counterpane, sheet, quilt, blanket, rug, drugget; housing; tidy,
antimacassar, eiderdown quilt *or* eiderdown; comforter *or* comfortable *or* comfort [*all U. S.*] numdah [*Hind.*], pillowcase, pillowslip; linoleum, oilcloth; tar-
paulin; saddle blanket, saddlecloth; tilpah [*U. S.*], apishamore [*U. S.*], poncho.

TEGMEN (*pl.* tegmina), integument, tegument; skin, pellicle, fleece, fell, fur, leather, lambskin, sable, miniver, beaver, ermine, shagreen, hide, coat, buff, pelt, peltry [*collective noun*]; cordwain [*archaic*]; robe, buffalo robe [*U. S.*].

CUTICLE, cutis, dermis, corium, scarfskin, epidermis, derm [*rare*], derma; ectoderm, epithelium, ecderon, ecteron, enderon.

EXUVIÆ, desquamation, slough, cast, cast-off skin.

CLOTHING &c. 225; mask &c. (*concealment*) 530.

PEEL, crust, bark, rind, cortex, husk, shell, epicarp, testa; eggshell, glume.

CAPSULE; sheath, sheathing; pod, cod [*dial.*], casing, case, theca; elytron; elytrum; involucrum; wrapping, wrapper; envelope, vesicle; cornhusk, cornshuck [*U. S.*].

DERMATOGRAPHY, dermatology, dermatogen, dermoplasty, dermatopathy, dermatophyte; conchology; testaceology.

VENEER, facing; pavement; imbrication, scale &c. (*layer*) 204; anointing &c. *v.*; ointment &c. (*grease*) 356; inunction; incrustation, superposition, obduction [*obs.*]; coating, paint, stain, engobe; varnish &c. (*resin*) 356*a*; ground, enamel, whitewash, plaster, stucco, roughcast, plasterwork, scagliola, compo; cerement; cerecloth, shroud.

V. COVER; superpose, superimpose; overlay, overspread; wrap &c. 225; incase, encase, enchase, face, case, veneer, pave, paper; tip, cap, bind; bulkhead, bulkhead in; clapboard [*U. S.*], shingle; imbricate.

overlie, overarch; endome [*rare*]; conceal &c. 528.

COAT, paint, stain, varnish, flat, incrust, encrust, crust, cement, roughcast, stucco, dab, plaster, tar; wash; besmear; bedaub; anoint, do over; gild, plate, japan, lacquer, lacker, enamel, whitewash; parget; lay it on thick.

Adj. COVERING &c. *v.*; cutaneous, dermal, cortical, cuticular, tegumentary, tegumental, tegmental, integumentary, integumental, epidermal *or* epidermic, endermic, epicarpal, testaceous, dermatopathic, dermatological, dermoplastic, dermatophytic, subcutaneous, hypodermic.

SCALY, squamate, squamiferous, squamous; covered &c. *v.*; imbricate, imbricated, loricate, loricated, armored, encuirassed, armor-plated, ironclad, under cover.

HOODED, cowled, cucullate *or* cucullated, tectiform, rooflike; vaginate.

SKINLIKE, dermic, dermoid, dermatoid, epidermoid, skinny.

---

225. Investment. — N. INVESTMENT; covering &c. 223; dress, clothing, raiment, drapery, costume, attire, guise, toilet, toilette, trim; habiliment; vesture, vestment; garment, garb, palliament [*obs.*], apparel, wardrobe, wearing apparel, clothes, things.

ARRAY; tailoring, millinery; best bib and tucker [*colloq.*]; finery &c. (*ornament*) 847; full dress &c. (*show*) 882; garniture; theatrical properties.

OUTFIT, equipment, trousseau; uniform, khaki, olive-drab, regimentals; continentals [*Am. hist.*]; canonicals &c. 999; livery, gear, harness, turn-out, accouterment, caparison, suit, rigging, trappings, traps [*colloq.*], slops, togs [*colloq. or slang*], toggery [*colloq.*]; masquerade.

DISHABILLE *or* deshabille, morning dress, tea gown, wrapper, negligee *or* négligé [*F.*], dressing gown, undress; kimono; shooting coat; smoking jacket;

226. Divestment. — N. DIVESTMENT; taking off &c. *v.*

NUDITY; bareness &c. *adj.*; undress; dishabille &c. 225; altogether; *tout ensemble* [*F.*]; nudation [*rare*], denudation; decortication, depilation, excoriation, desquamation, slough &c. 223; molting *or* moulting, exuviation; exfoliation; trichosis.

BALDNESS, hairlessness, alopecia.

V. DIVEST; uncover &c. (*cover* &c. 223); denude, bare, strip; disfurnish; undress, disrobe &c. (*dress, enrobe* &c. 225); uncoif; dismantle; put off, take off, cast off; doff.

PEEL, pare, decorticate, desquamate, slough, excoriate, skin, scalp, flay, bark, husk, rind; expose, lay open; exfoliate, molt *or* moult, exuviate, mew [*archaic*]; cast the skin.

Adj. DIVESTED &c. *v.*; bare, naked, nude; undressed, undraped, unclad, ungarmented, unclothed, unappareled,

mufti [*chiefly Eng.*]; rags, tatters, old clothes; mourning, weeds; duds [*colloq. or slang*]; slippers.

ROBE, tunic, paletot, habit, gown, coat, frock, blouse, middy blouse *or* middy, jumper, shirt waist, suit; one-piece –, two-piece- suit; toga, smock, frock; Prince Albert coat [*colloq.*]; frock–, sack–, tail- coat.

DRESS SUIT, dress clothes, evening dress, swallow-tailed coat [*colloq.*], claw-hammer coat [*colloq.*]; dinner -coat, –jacket; Tuxedo coat *or* Tuxedo [*colloq., U. S.*]; glad rags [*slang, U. S.*].

CLOAK, pall [*archaic*], mantle, mantua, mantelet *or* mantlet, sagum, shawl, pelisse, wrapper; veil; cape, kirtle [*archaic*], plaid [*Scot.*], tippet, muffler,

unarrayed; exposed; in dishabille.

IN A STATE OF NATURE, in nature's garb, in buff, in native buff, in birthday suit; *in puris naturalibus* [*L.*]; with nothing on, stark-naked; bare as the back of one's hand.

out at elbows; threadbare, ragged, callow, roofless; barefoot; bareback, barebacked; leafless, napless, hairless.

BALD, hairless, depilous [*rare*], glabrous, glabrate, tonsured, beardless, bald as a coot.

EXUVIAL, sloughy, desquamative, desquamatory.

***** "unaccommodated man is no more but such a poor, bare, forked animal as thou art" [*King Lear*].

comforter, balaklava helmet, haik, huke [*obs.*], chlamys, mantilla, tabard, housing, horse cloth, burnoose *or* burnous, roquelaure; houpland [*hist.*]; surcoat, overcoat, greatcoat; surtout, spencer; oilskins, slicker [*U. S.*], mackintosh, waterproof, ulster, dreadnaught *or* dreadnought, wraprascal, poncho; pea-coat, pea-jacket; cardinal, pelerine; chuddar *or* chadar [*Hind.*], jubbah [*Hind.*], pyjamas *or* pajamas, pilot jacket, sweater, blazer, coatee, cardigan *or* cardigan jacket; Mackinaw coat *or* Mackinaw; talma.

JACKET, vest, jerkin [*hist. or dial.*], *chaqueta* [*Sp.*], sontag, waistcoat, doublet, gaberdine; stays, corsage, corset, *brassière* [*F.*], camisole, corselet, bodice; stomacher.

SKIRT, petticoat, farthingale, kilt, filibeg *or* philibeg, jupe, crinoline, bustle, panier, apron, pinafore; bloomer, bloomers; *tablier* [*F.*].

LOIN CLOTH, dhoti [*Hindu*], lungi [*Burmese*]; G string.

TROUSERS, breeches, pantaloons, inexpressibles [*humorous*], trews [*Scot.*], innominables [*humorous*], unmentionables [*humorous*], continuations [*slang*], kicks [*slang*]; overalls, smalls [*colloq. or archaic*], smallclothes [*archaic*]; pants [*colloq.*]; shintiyan; shorts; tights, drawers; knickerbockers, knickers [*colloq.*].

HEADDRESS, headgear, coiffure [*F.*], head, headcloths, chignon [*F.*]; chapeau [*F.*], crush hat, opera hat; kaffiyeh [*Ar.*]; taj, tam-o'-shanter, topee *or* topi [*India*], sola topi [*India*], puggree *or* pagri [*Hind.*]; sombrero, sundown [*U. S.*], cap, hat, beaver, castor, bonnet, tile [*slang*], wide-awake, panama, leghorn; derby [*U. S.*], bowler [*Eng.*], billycock [*Eng.*]; wimple; nightcap, skullcap; mobcap, boudoir cap, Dutch cap; Salvation-Army bonnet; hood, coif, capote, calash, kerchief, snood; crown &c. (*circle*) 247; pelt, wig, front, peruke, periwig; caftan, turban, fez, tarboosh, shako, busby; kepi, forage cap, campaign hat, overseas cap, bearskin; helmet &c. 717; mask, domino.

BODY CLOTHES; linen; hickory shirt [*U. S.*]; shirt, O.-D. (olive-drab) shirt; sark [*archaic or dial.*], smock, shift, chemise; nightgown, nightshirt; bed-gown, *sac de nuit* [*F.*]; jersey; underclothing, underwaistcoat, undershirt, undervest, chemisette, guimpe.

TIE, neckerchief, neckcloth; ruff, collar, cravat, stock, handkerchief, scarf; bib, tucker; boa; girdle &c. (*circle*) 247; cummerbund [*India*], rumal [*Hind.*], *rabat* [*F.*], rabato.

SHOE, pump, sneakers [*U. S.*], boot, slipper, sandal, galosh *or* galoshe, patten, clog; high-low; Blucher –, Wellington –, Hessian –, jack –, top- boot; Oxford -shoe, –tie; Balmoral; arctics, bootee, bootikin, brogan, brogue, *chaparajos* [*Mex. Sp.*], chaps [*colloq.*], chivarras *or* chivarros [*Sp. Amer.*]; gums [*U. S.*], larrigan [*N. Amer.*], rubbers; snowshoe, ski; stogy, *veldtschoen* [*Dutch*], legging, puttee *or* putty, buskin, greave, galligaskin [*dial.*], moccasin, gambado, gaiter, spatterdashes, spats, gamashes [*archaic or dial. Eng.*], *gamache* [*F.*]; antigropelos.

STOCKING, hose, gaskins [*obs. or dial.*], trunk hose, sock; hosiery.

GLOVE, gauntlet, mitten, mitt.

CUFF, wristband; sleeve.

BABY LINEN, swaddling clothes, layette.

[SUPPLIERS] clothier, tailor, snip [*slang*], tailoress, milliner. costumer, costumier, seamstress *or* sempstress, dressmaker, *modiste* [*F.*], habit-maker; breeches-maker; shoemaker, Crispin cordwainer, cobbler; hosier, hatter, glover, draper, linen draper, haberdasher, mercer; hairdresser, *friseur* [*F.*].

V. INVEST; cover &c. 223; envelop, lap, involve; inwrap *or* enwrap; wrap; fold up, wrap up, lap up, muffle up; overlap; sheathe, swathe, swaddle, roll up in, shroud, circumvest [*obs.*].

CLOTHE, vest [*rare*], array, dress, dight [*archaic*], bedight [*archaic*], drape, robe, enrobe, attire, apparel, tire [*archaic*], habilitate [*rare*], garb, enclothe, breech, coat, jacket, gown, accouter, rig, fit out; dizen, bedizen, deck &c. (*ornament*) 847; perk, equip, harness, caparison.

WEAR; don; put on, huddle on, slip on; mantle.

Adj. INVESTED &c. *v.*; habited; dight, dighted; barbed, barded; clad, *costumé* [*F.*], shod, *chaussé* [*F.*]; *en grande tenue* [*F.*] &c. (*show*) 882; *décolletée* [*F.*].

SARTORIAL, sartorian [*rare*].

. "the soul of this man is his clothes" [*All's Well*]; "a bird on a bonnet is worth ten on a plate" [*Cynic's Calendar*]; "clothes have made men of us; they are threatening to make clothes-screens of us" [Carlyle].

227. Circumjacence. — N. CIRCUMJACENCE *or* circumjacency, circumfluence [*rare*], circumambience environment, encompassment; atmosphere, medium; surroundings, *entourage* [*F.*].

OUTPOST; border &c. (*edge*) 231; girdle &c. (*circumference*) 230; outskirts, boulevards, suburbs, purlieus, precincts, *faubourgs* [*F.*], environs, environment, entourage, *banlieue* [*F.*], neighborhood, vicinage, vicinity.

V. LIE AROUND &c. *adv.*; surround, beset, compass, encompass, environ, inclose *or* enclose, encircle, encincture [*rare*], circle, girdle, ensphere, hedge, embrace, circumvent, lap, gird; belt; begird, engird; skirt, twine round; hem in &c. (*circumscribe*) 229; beleaguer, invest, besiege, beset, blockade.

Adj. CIRCUMJACENT, circumambient, circumfluent; ambient; surrounding &c. *v.*; circumferential, suburban.

Adv. AROUND, about; without; on every side, on all sides; right and left, all round, roundabout.

228. Interjacence. — N. INTERJACENCE *or* interjacency, intercurrence, intervenience *or* interveniency [*rare*], interlocation, interdigitation, interpenetration; permeation.

INTERJECTION, interpolation, interlineation, interspersion, intercalation; embolism.

INTERVENTION, interference, interposition, intromission, intrusion, obtrusion; insinuation; insertion &c. 300; dovetailing; infiltration.

INTERMEDIUM, intermediary; go-between, interagent, middleman, intervener, mean, medium, bodkin [*colloq.*], intruder, interloper; parenthesis, episode, flyleaf.

PARTITION, septum, interseptum, phragma, septulum, mediastinum, diaphragm, midriff; dissepiment; party wall, panel, bulkhead, brattice, *cloison* [*F.*], perpend, halfway house.

V. LIE BETWEEN, come between, get between; intervene, slide in, interpenetrate, permeate.

PUT BETWEEN, introduce, import; throw in, wedge in, edge in, jam in, worm in, foist in, run in, plow in, work in; interpose, interject, intercalate, interpolate, interline, interleave, intersperse, interweave, interlard, interdigitate; let in, dovetail, splice, mortise; insinuate, smuggle; infiltrate, ingrain.

INTERFERE, put in an oar, thrust one's nose in; intrude, obtrude; have a finger in the pie; introduce the thin end of the wedge; thrust in &c. (*insert*) 300.

Adj. INTERJACENT, intervenient [*rare*], intervening &c. *v.*; intercalary, intercolumnar, intercostal, intercurrent, interfacial, intergrowth, interlineal, interlobular, interlocular, intermedial, intermediary, intermediate, intermaxillary, intermolecular, intermurdane, internasal, interneural, internodal, interoceanic, interosseal, interosseous, interplanetary, interpolar, interradial, interrenal, interscapular, interseptal, interstellar, interstitial, intervalvular, intervascular, interventricular, intervertebral; septal, embolismal.

parenthetical, episodic; mediterranean; intrusive; embosomed; merged.

MEAN, medium, mesne, middle, median.

Adv. BETWEEN, betwixt; 'twixt; among or amongst; amid, amidst; 'mid, 'midst; in the thick of; betwixt and between [colloq.]; sandwich-wise; parenthically, obiter dictum [L.].

229. Circumscription. — N. CIRCUMSCRIPTION, limitation, inclosure; confinement &c. (restraint) 751; circumvallation; encincture; envelope &c. 232.

V. CIRCUMSCRIBE, limit, bound, confine, inclose or enclose; surround &c. 227; compass about; imprison &c. (restrain) 751; hedge in, wall in, rail in; fence round, hedge round; picket; corral.

ENFOLD, bury, incase, pack up, enshrine, inclasp or enclasp; wrap up &c. (invest) 225; embay, embosom.

Adj. CIRCUMSCRIBED &c. v.; begirt, circumambient, girt, cinct [rare], circumcinct [rare], lapt; buried in, immersed in; embosomed, in the bosom of, imbedded, encysted, mewed up; imprisoned &c. 751; landlocked, in a ring fence.

230. Outline. — N. OUTLINE, circumference; perimeter, periphery; ambit, circuit, lines, tournure [F.], contour, profile, silhouette, relief, lineaments; bounds; coast line.

ZONE, belt, girth, band, baldric, zodiac, girdle, tire or tyre, cingle [rare], clasp, girt, girth; cordon &c. (inclosure) 232; circlet &c. 247.

V. OUTLINE, contour, delineate, silhouette, block, sketch, profile; circumscribe &c. 229.

Adj. OUTLINED &c. v.; circumferential, perimetric, perimetrical, peripheral.

231. Edge. — N. EDGE, verge, brink, brow, brim, margin, border, confine, skirt, rim, flange, side, mouth; jaws, chops, chaps, fauces; lip, muzzle.

SHORE, coast, strand, bank; bunder, bund [both Oriental], quay, wharf, dock, mole, landing.

FRINGE, flounce, frill, list, trimming, edging, skirting, hem, selvage or selvedge, welt; furbelow, valance; frame; exergue.

THRESHOLD, door, porch; portal &c. (opening) 260.

V. EDGE, border, skirt, fringe, marginate.

Adj. BORDER, marginal, skirting; labial, labiated, marginated.

232. Inclosure. — N. INCLOSURE or enclosure, envelope; case &c. (receptacle) 191; wrapper; girdle &c. 230.

pen, fold, sty, penfold, sheepfold; paddock, croft, pasture, wood lot; pound; corral; yard, compound; net, seine net.

FENCE &c. (defense) 717; pale, paling, balustrade, rail, railing, quickset hedge, park paling, circumvallation, enceinte [F.]; ring fence; wall; hedge, hedgerow; espalier.

BARRIER, barricade; gate, gateway; weir; bent, dingle [U. S.]; door, hatch, cordon; prison &c. 752.

DIKE or dyke, ditch, fosse, trench, drain, dugout, tranchée [F.], coupure [F.], moat.

V. INCLOSE or enclose; circumscribe &c. 229.

233. Limit. — N. LIMIT, boundary, bounds, confine, enclave, term, bourn or bourne, verge, curbstone, but [Scot.]; pale; termination, terminus, terminal; stint, stent; frontier, precinct, marches; backwoods.

BOUNDARY LINE, landmark; line of -demarcation, - circumvallation; pillars of Hercules; Rubicon, turning point; ne plus ultra [L.]; sluice, floodgate.

V. LIMIT, bound, compass, confine, define, circumscribe, demarcate, delimit.

Adj. DEFINITE; conterminate [*obs.*], conterminable; terminable, limitable; terminal, frontier; bordering, border, limitary, boundary, limital [*rare*].

Adv. THUS FAR, – and no further.

*** "The undiscover'd country from whose bourn No traveller returns" [*Hamlet*].

2. Special

234. Front — N FRONT; fore, fore part *or* forepart; foreground, forefront; face, disk *or* disc, frontage, façade, proscenium, facia, frontispiece; priority, anteriority; obverse (*of a medal*).

VAN, vanguard; advanced guard; forerank, front rank; outpost; first line; scout.

BROW, forehead, visage, physiognomy, phiz [*colloq.*], features, countenance, mug [*slang*]; metoposcopy; chin, mentum; rostrum, beak, bow, stem, prow, prore, jib, bowsprit.

pioneer &c. (*precursor*) 64; metoposcopist, physiognomist

V. FRONT, face, confront, breast, buck [*slang, U. S.*], brave, dare, defy oppose, outbrazen; bend forwards; come to the front, come to the fore; be *or* stand in front &c. *adj.*

Adj. FORE, forward, anterior, front, frontal; metopic

Adv. BEFORE in front, in the van, in advance; ahead right ahead· foremost, headmost in the foreground, in the lee of; before one's -face, – eyes: face to face, *vis-à-vis* [*F.*]; *front à front* [*F.*].

*** *formosa facies muta commendatio est* [Syrus]; *frons est animi janua* [Cicero]; "human face divine" [Milton]; *imago animi vultus est indices oculi* [Cicero]; "sea of upturned faces" [Scott].

235. Rear. — N. REAR, back, posteriority; rear rank, rear guard, rearward [*archaic*]; background, hinterland. occiput, nape; heels.

SPINE, backbone, rachis, spinal column, chine.

TAIL, scut, brush, appendage [*humorous*].

RUMP, croup, buttock, posteriors, fundament, bottom [*colloq.*], stern [*colloq.*], seat, backside [*vulgar*], breech, dorsum, tergum, loin; dorsal –, lumbarregion; hind quarters; aitchbone.

STERN, poop, counter, mizzenmast, postern door, tailpiece, after-part, heelpiece, crupper.

WAKE; train &c. (*sequence*) 281.

REVERSE; other side of the shield.

V. BE BEHIND &c. *adv.*; fall astern; bend backwards; bring up the rear; heel, tag, shadow, follow &c. (*pursue*) 622.

Adj. BACK, rear; hind, hinder, hindmost, hindermost; sternmost; postern, posterior; dorsal, after; caudal, tergal, neural, spinal, vertebral, lumbar; mizzen.

Adv. BEHIND; in the -rear, – background; behind one's back; at the -heels, – tail, – back- of; back to back.

after, aft, abaft, baft, astern, aback, rearward, hindward, backward.

*** *ogni medaglia ha il suo rovescio.*

236. Laterality. — N. LATERALITY [*rare*]; side, flank, quarter, lee; hand; cheek, jowl *or* jole, wing; profile; temple, paries (*pl.* parietes), loin, haunch, hip; beam.

gable, gable-end; broadside; lee side.

points of the compass; East, sunrise, Orient, Levant; West, Occident, sunset; orientation.

V. FLANK, outflank; sidle; skirt, border, wing; orientate; be on one side &c. *adv.*

Adj. LATERAL, sidelong; collateral; parietal, flanking, skirting; flanked; sideling.

237. Contraposition. — N. CONTRAPOSITION, opposition; polarity; inversion &c. 218; opposite side; reverse, inverse; counterpart; antithesis.

ANTIPODES, opposite poles, North and South.

V. BE OPPOSITE &c. *adj.*; subtend.

Adj. OPPOSITE; reverse, inverse; converse; antipodal, diametrical, antithetic, counter, subcontrary; fronting, facing, diametrically opposite.

NORTHERN, north, northerly, northward, hyperborean, septentrional, boreal, polar, arctic.

SOUTHERN, south, southerly, meridi-

many-sided; multilateral, bilateral, trilateral, quadrilateral.

EASTERN, eastward, east, orient, oriental, auroral or aurorean; Levantine.

WESTERN, west, westerly, westward, occidental, Hesperian.

Adv. SIDEWAYS or sideway, sidewise, sideling, sidelong; broadside on; on one side, abreast, alongside, beside, aside; by, by the side of; side by side; cheek by jowl &c. (near) 197; to windward, to leeward; laterally &c. adj.; right and left; on her beam ends.

₊ "his cheek the map of days outworn" [Shakespeare].

onal, southward, Austral, antarctic.

Adv. OVER, over the way, over against; against; face to face, vis-à-vis [F.]; as poles asunder.

---

238. Dextrality. — N. DEXTRALITY; right, right hand; dexter, offside, starboard.

Adj. DEXTRAL, dexterous or dextrous, right-handed; dexter, dextrorsal, dextrorse.

AMBIDEXTER, ambidextrous, ambidextral.

Adv. DEXTRAD, dextrally; ambidextrously.

239. Sinistrality. — N. SINISTRALITY, sinistration; left, left hand, south paw [slang, U. S.]; sinistra or sinistra mano [music, It.]; nearside, larboard, port.

Adj. LEFT-HANDED, sinister-handed [obs.], sinister, sinistral, sinistrorsal, sinistrorse, sinistrous, ambilevous [rare]; sinistrogyrate, sinistrogyric.

Adv. SINISTRAD, sinistrally, sinistrously.

SECTION III.　FORM

1. GENERAL FORM

240. Form. — N. FORM, figure, shape; conformation, configuration; make, formation, frame, construction, cut, set, build, tournure [F.], outline, get-up [colloq.], trim, cut of one's jib [colloq.]; stamp, type, cast, mold or mould; fashion; contour &c. (outline) 230; structure &c. 329; plasmature [obs.].

FEATURE, lineament, turn; phase &c. (aspect) 448; posture, attitude, pose.

[SCIENCE OF FORM] morphology.

[SIMILARITY OF FORM] isomorphism; isomorph.

FORMATION, figuration, efformation [rare]; forming &c. v.; sculpture; plasmation [rare].

V. FORM, shape, figure, fashion, efform [rare], carve, cut, chisel, hew, cast; roughhew, roughcast; sketch; block out, hammer out; trim; lick –, put– into shape; model, knead, work up into, set,

241. [ABSENCE OF FORM.] Amorphism. — N. AMORPHISM, misproportion, informity [rare]; uncouthness; rough diamond; unlicked cub; rudis indigestaque moles [L.]; disorder &c. 59; deformity &c. 243.

DISFIGUREMENT, defacement; mutilation; deforming.

V. [DESTROY FORM] deface, disfigure, deform, mutilate, truncate; derange &c. 61; blemish, mar.

Adj. SHAPELESS, amorphous, formless; unshapely, misshapen, unsymmetrical, malformed, unformed, unhewn, unfashioned, unshapen; anomalous.

ROUGH, rude, Gothic, barbarous, rugged, scraggy, vandalic; in the rough.

₊ "If shape it might be call'd that shape had none Distinguishable in member, joint, or limb" [P. L.].

mold, sculpture; cast, stamp; build &c. (construct) 161.

Adj. FORMED &c. v.; structural, morphologic or morphological.

SHAPELY, well-proportioned, symmetrical, well-made, well-formed, comely, trim, neat.

[RECEIVING FORM] plastic, fictile; formative, impressible, creative.

[GIVING FORM] plasmatic, plasmic; protoplasmic.

[SIMILAR IN FORM] isomorphic, isomorphous.

242. [REGULARITY OF FORM.] **Symmetry.** — **N.** SYMMETRY, shapeliness, finish; beauty &c. 845; proportion, eurythmy *or* eurhythmy, eurythmics *or* eurhythmics, uniformity, parallelism; bilateral –, trilateral –, multilateral-symmetry; centrality &c. 222; radiation, regularity, evenness.

ARBORESCENCE, branching, ramification; arbor vitæ; peloria.

Adj. SYMMETRICAL, shapely, well set, finished; beautiful &c. 845; classic, chaste, severe.

REGULAR, uniform, radiate, radiated. balanced; equal &c. 27; parallel, co-extensive.

ARBORESCENT, arboriform; dendriform, dendroid *or* dendroidal; branching; ramous, ramose; fern-shaped, filiciform, filicoid; subarborescent; papilionaceous.

243. [IRREGULARITY OF FORM.] **Distortion** — **N.** DISTORTION, detortion [*rare*], contortion, contortuosity, knot, warp, buckle, screw, twist; crookedness &c. (*obliquity*) 217; grimace; deformity: malformation, malconformation; harelip; monstrosity, misproportion, want of symmetry, anamorphosy, anamorphosis; ugliness &c. 846; talipes, clubfoot; teratology.

V. DISTORT, contort, twist, warp, buckle, screw, wrench, writhe, gnarl, wrest, writhe, make faces, deform, misshape.

Adj. DISTORTED &c. *v.;* out of shape, irregular, unsymmetric, anamorphous, awry, wry, askew, crooked; not true, not straight; on one side, crump [*obs.*], deformed; harelipped; misshapen, misbegotten; misproportioned, ill-proportioned; ill-made; grotesque, crooked as a ram's horn; camelbacked, humpbacked, hunchbacked, bunchbacked, crookbacked; bandy; bandylegged, bowlegged; bowkneed, knockkneed; splayfooted, taliped *or* talipedic, clubfooted; round-shouldered; snub-nosed; curtailed of one's fair proportions; stumpy &c. (*short*) 201; gaunt (*thin*) &c. 203; bloated &c. 194; scalene; simous.

Adv. all manner of ways.

*** crooked as a Virginia fence [*U. S.*]; "Then, since the heav'ns have shap'd my body so, Let hell make crook'd my mind to answer it" [*Henry VI*].

2. SPECIAL FORM

244. Angularity. — **N.** ANGULARITY, angularness; aduncity; angle, cusp, bend; fold &c. 258; notch &c. 257; fork, furculum, bifurcation.

elbow, knee, knuckle, ankle, groin, crotch, crutch; crane, fluke, scythe, sickle; zigzag.

CORNER, nook, recess, niche, oriel, coign (*as in* "coign of vantage").

RIGHT ANGLE &c. (*perpendicular*) 212; obliquity &c. 217; angle of 45 degrees, miter; acute –, obtuse –, salient –, reëntering –, spherical- angle.

ANGULAR -MEASUREMENT, – elevation, – distance, – velocity; trigonometry, goniometry; altimeter, pantometer, altimetry; clinometer, graphometer, goniometer; theodolite; transit *or* transit theodolite, sextant, quadrant; dichotomy.

triangle, trigon, wedge; rectangle, square, lozenge, diamond; rhomb, rhombus, rhomboid, rhombohedron, quadrangle, quadrilateral; parallelogram; quadrature; polygon, pentagon, hexagon, heptagon, octagon, oxygon, decagon.

Platonic bodies; cube, rhomboid; tetrahedron, pentahedron, hexahedron, octahedron, dodecahedron, icosahedron; prism, pyramid; parallelepiped *or* parallelepipedon; curb –, gambrel –, French –, mansard- roof.

V. FORK, furcate, divaricate, branch, ramify, bifurcate, bend, crinkle.

Adj. ANGULAR, bent, crooked, aduncous, adunc *or* aduncal, aduncate *or* aduncated, uncinated, aquiline, jagged, serrated; falciform, falcated; furcal, furcate, furcated, forked, bifurcate, crotched, zigzag, furcular, hooked; dove-tailed; knockkneed, crinkled, akimbo, kimbo [*obs.*], geniculated; oblique &c. 217.

' wedge-shaped, cuneiform; cuneate, multangular, oxygonal; triangular, trigonal, trilateral; quadrangular –, quadrilateral, foursquare, rectangular, square; multilateral; polygonal &c. *n.;* cubical, rhombic *or* rhombical, rhomboidal, pyramidal.

245. Curvature. — N. CURVATURE, curvity [*rare*], curvation; incurvature, incurvity [*obs.*], incurvation; bend; flexure, flexion; conflexure [*obs.*]; crook, hook, bought [*obs.*], bending; deflexion, inflexion; concameration; arcuation, devexity [*obs.*], turn; deviation, detour *or détour* [*F.*], sweep; curl, curling; bough; recurvity [*rare*], recurvation [*rare*]; sinuosity &c. 248; aduncity.

CURVE, arc, arch, arcade, vault, bow, crescent, meniscus, half-moon, lunule, horseshoe, loop, crane neck; parabola, hyperbola; catacaustic, diacaustic; geanticline, geosyncline; catenarian, catenary, festoon; conchoid, cardioid; caustic; tracery; arched- ceiling, – roof; bay window, bow window.

V. BE CURVED &c. *adj.;* sweep, swag [*obs. or dial.*], sag; deviate &c. 279; turn; reënter.

RENDER CURVED &c. *adj.;* bend, curve, incurvate; deflect, inflect; crook; turn, round, arch, arcuate, arch over, embow, recurvate [*rare*], concamerate [*rare*]; bow, coil, curl, recurve, frizzle, friz *or* frizz.

Adj. CURVED &c. *v.;* curvate *or* curvated, lobiform; curviform, curvilineal *or* curvilinear; devex [*obs.*], devious; recurved, recurvous; crump [*obs.*]; bowed &c. *v.;* vaulted; geanticlinal, geosynclinal; bow-legged &c. (*distorted*) 243; oblique &c. 217; circular &c. 247.

BEAK-SHAPED, beaked, rostrate, rostriform, rostroid, rhamphoid.

BELL-SHAPED, campaniform, campanular, campanulous, campanulate.

BOAT-SHAPED, navicular, cymbiform, naviform, scaphoid.

BOW-SHAPED, arcuate *or* arcuated, arcual; arciform, arclike, embowed.

CRESCENT-SHAPED, crescent, crescentiform, crescentic, convexo-concave, sigmoid, semilunar, horned, meniscal, bicorn, bicornute *or* bicornuate, bicornuous [*rare*], bicorned *or* bicornous, semicircular.

HEART-SHAPED, cordiform, cardioid, cordate.

HELMET-SHAPED, galeiform, galeate, galeated, cassidiform.

HOOK-SHAPED, hooked, hooklike, unciform, uncate, uncinal, uncinate, hamulate, hamate, hamiform, hamose *or* hamous [*both rare*]; unguiform, unguiculate *or* unguiculated; curvated, aduncate, aduncous, adunc.

KIDNEY-SHAPED, reniform.

LENS-SHAPED, lenticular, lentoid, lentiform, meniscal, meniscoid.

MOON-SHAPED, lunar, lunate *or* lunated, luniform, lunular, lunulate *or* lunulated, crescent-shaped (*q. v.*); Cynthian.

OAR-SHAPED, remiform [*rare*].

PEAR-SHAPED, pyriform; obconic.

SHELL-SHAPED, conchate, conchiform, conchylaceous [*rare*], conchoidal [*min.*].

SHIELD-SHAPED, scutate, scutiform, peltate, clypeate *or* clypeated, clypeiform.

SICKLE-SHAPED, falcate, falciform, falculate [*rare*].

TONGUE-SHAPED, linguiform, lingulate, ligulate.

TURNIP-SHAPED, napiform.

246. Straightness. — N. STRAIGHTNESS, rectilinearity, rectilinearness; directness; inflexibility &c. (*stiffness*) 323; straight -, bee -, right -, direct- line; short cut.

V. BE STRAIGHT &c. *adj.;* have no turning; not -incline, – bend, – turn, -- deviate- to either side; go straight; steer for &c. (*direction*) 278.

RENDER STRAIGHT, straighten, rectify; set -, put- straight; unbend, unfold, uncurl &c. 248; unravel &c. 219, unwrap.

Adj. STRAIGHT; rectilinear, rectilineal; direct, even, right, true, in a line; virgate, unbent &c. *v.;* undeviating, unturned, undistorted, unswerving; straight-lined, straight as an arrow &c. (*direct*) 278; inflexible &c. 323.

PERPENDICULAR, plumb, vertical, upright, erect.

247. [SIMPLE CIRCULARITY.] **Circularity. — N.** CIRCULARITY, roundness; rotundity &c. 249.

CIRCLE, circlet, ring, areola, hoop, roundlet, annulus, annulet, bracelet,

248. [COMPLEX CIRCULARITY.] **Convolution. — N.** CONVOLUTION, involution, circumvolution; winding &c. *v.;* wave, undulation, tortuosity, anfractuosity; sinuosity, sinuation, sinuousness,

armlet; ringlet; eye, loop, wheel; cycle, orb, orbit, rundle, zone, belt, cordon, band; contrate –, crown- wheel; hub, nave; sash, girdle, cestus, cest *or* ceste, cincture, baldric, fillet, fascia, wreath, garland; crown, corona, coronet, chaplet, snood, necklace, collar; noose, lasso.

ELLIPSE, oval, ovule; ellipsoid, cycloid, epicycloid, epicycle.

semicircle; quadrant, sextant, sector.

V. MAKE ROUND &c. *adj.;* round.

GO ROUND; encircle &c. 227; describe a circle &c. 311.

Adj. ROUND, rounded, circular, annular, orbicular, orbiculate *or* orbiculated; oval, ovate, obovate, ovoid, ovoidal [*rare*], elliptic, elliptical, egg-shaped; pear-shaped &c. 245; cycloidal &c. *n.;* spherical &c. 249; fasciate *or* fasciated.

∗∗ "I watched the little circles die" [Tennyson].

flexuosity, tortility; meandering, circuit, circumbendibus [*humorous*], twist, twirl, windings and turnings, ambagiousness, ambages; torsion; inosculation; reticulation &c. (*crossing*) 219; rivulation.

COIL, roll, curl, buckle, spiral, helix, corkscrew, worm, volute, whorl, rundle; tendril; scollop, scallop, escalop *or* escallop; kink; ammonite, snakestone.

serpent, snake, eel; maze, labyrinth.

V. BE CONVOLUTED &c. *adj.;* wind, twine, turn and twist, twirl; wave, undulate, meander; inosculate; entwine *or* intwine; twist, coil, roll; wrinkle, curl, crisp, twill; frizz, frizzle; crimp, crape, indent, scollop, scallop; wring, intort; contort; wreathe &c. (*cross*) 219.

Adj. CONVOLUTED; winding, twisted &c. *v.;* tortile, tortive [*obs.*]; wavy; undate *or* undated [*rare*], undulatory; circling, snaky, snakelike, serpentine; serpentiform, anguilliform, anguiform, anguilloid, anguillous, vermiform, vermicular; mazy, tortuous, sinuose, sinuous, sinuate, flexuous; undulating, undulated, wavy; anfractuous, reclivate [*rare*], rivulose, scolecoid; sigmoid, sigmoidal; spiriferous, spiroid.

wreathy, frizzly, *crêpé* [*F.*], buckled; raveled &c. (*in disorder*) 59.

INVOLVED, intricate, complicated, perplexed; labyrinthic, labyrinthian, labyrinthine; circuitous, ambagious; peristaltic; Dædalian; kinky, curly.

SPIRAL, coiled, helical; cochlear, cochleate, cochleous [*rare*]; screw-shaped; turbinated, turbiniform, turbinoid, turbinal.

Adv. in and out, round and round.

249. Rotundity. — N. ROTUNDITY; roundness &c. *adj.;* cylindricity; sphericality, sphericity, spheroidicity *or* spheroidity, globoseness, globosity, globularity, annularity, orotundity, orbiculation.

CYLINDER, cylindroid; barrel, drum; roll, roller; rouleau, column, rolling-pin, rundle.

CONE, conoid; pear-shape, egg-shape, bell-shape.

SPHERE, globe, ball, bowlder *or* boulder; spheroid, geoid, globoid, ellipsoid; oblong –, oblate- spheroid; drop, spherule, globule, vesicle, bulb, bullet, pellet, clew, pill, marble, pea, knob, pommel, horn, knot; oval &c. 247.

V. RENDER SPHERICAL &c. *adj.;* form into a sphere, sphere, roll into a ball; give rotundity &c. *n.;* round.

Adj. ROTUND; round &c. (*circular*) 247; cylindric *or* cylindrical, cylindroid *or* cylindroidal, columnar, vermiform, lumbriciform; conic, conical; spherical, spheroidal; globular, globous, globose; gibbous; fungiform, bulbous; *teres atque rotundus* [*L.*]; round as -an orange, – an apple, – a ball, – a billiard ball, – a cannon ball.

BEAD-SHAPED, beadlike, moniliform, monilated.

BELL-SHAPED, campaniform, campanulate, campanulous, campanular.

EGG-SHAPED, ovoid, oviform, ovoidal, ovate, globoid, globate *or* globated; obovate, obovoid [*both bot.*].

PEAR-SHAPED, pyriform.

RICE-SHAPED, riziform.

∗∗ "she is spherical, like a globe." [*Comedy of Errors.*]

3. Superficial Form

250. Convexity. — N. CONVEXITY, prominence, projection, swelling, gibbosity, bilge, bulge, protuberance, protrusion, excrescency; camber, cahot [*N. Amer.*], thank-ye-ma'am [*U. S.*], swell.

INTUMESCENCE, tumidity; tumor *or* tumour; tubercle, tuberousness, tuberosity, carunculation, bubo.

EXCRESCENCE, hump, hunch, bunch; knob, knur, knurl, gnarl, knot; bow, boss, embossment, bump, mamelon, clump; bulb, node, nodule, nodosity.

tooth, molar; lip, flange; tongue; withers, shoulder, back, dorsum; elbow.

process, apophysis, condyle.

wheel, hub, hubble [*U. S.*].

peg; button, stud; ridge, rib, trunnion, snag; sugar loaf &c. (*sharpness*) 253.

PIMPLE, wen, whelk, papula, papule, pustule, pock, proud flesh, growth, sarcoma, caruncle, corn, wart, verruca, furuncle, polypus, fungus, fungosity, exostosis, bleb, blister, bulla, blain; boil &c. (*disease*) 655; air bubble, blob.

PAPILLA, nipple, teat, pap, breast, dug, mammilla.

PROBOSCIS, nose, olfactory organ, neb, beak, snout, nozzle.

BELLY, corporation [*colloq.*], paunch, epigastrium, abdomen.

ARCH, cupola, dome, vault, beehive; balcony; eaves.

RELIEF, relievo, cameo; low relief, bas-relief, basso-relievo *or basso-rilievo* [*It.*]; half relief, mezzo-relievo *or mezzo-rilievo* [*It.*]; high relief, alto-relievo *or alto-rilievo* [*It.*]; pilaster.

POINT OF LAND, hill &c. (*height*) 206; cape, promontory, mull; foreland, headland; hummock, ledge, spur; naze, ness; mole, jetty, jutty.

V. BE PROMINENT &c. *adj.;* project, bulge, protrude, bag, belly, carunculate, pout, bouge [*obs.*], bunch; jut out, stand out, stick out, poke out; stick up, bristle up, start up, cock up, shoot up; swell over, hang over, bend over; beetle.

RENDER PROMINENT &c. *adj.;* raise 307; emboss, chase.

Adj. PROMINENT, protuberant, protrusile, protrusive; undershot, underhung; projecting &c. *v.;* bossed, bossy, nodular, convex, bunchy; clavate, clavated, claviform; hummocky, *moutonné*

251. Flatness. — N. FLATNESS &c *adj.;* smoothness &c. 255.

PLANE; level &c. 213; plate, platter, table, tablet, slab.

V. FLATTEN; render flat; squelch [*colloq.*], squash [*colloq.*], fell; level &c 213.

Adj. FLAT, plane, even, flush, scutiform, discoid; complanate, flattish, homaloid; level &c. (*horizontal*) 213; flat as - a pancake, – a fluke, – a flounder, – a board, – my hand; smooth.

Adv. FLAT, flatly [*rare*], flatways, flatwise, lengthwise, horizontally.

252. Concavity. — N. CONCAVITY, depression, dip; hollow, hollowness; indentation, intaglio, cavity, vug *or* vugg *or* vugh, dent, dint, dimple, follicle, pit, sinus, antrum, alveolus, lacuna; honeycomb.

EXCAVATION, pit, sap, mine, shaft, colliery; caisson, *fougasse* [*F.*], countermine; trough &c. (*furrow*) 259; bay &c. (*of the sea*) 343.

cup, basin, crater, punch bowl; cell &c. (*receptacle*) 191; socket.

VALLEY, vale, dale, dell, dingle, coomb *or* combe, bottom, slade [*obs.*], strath [*Scot.*], gill *or* ghyll [*Scot. & dial. Eng.*], glade, grove, glen, donga [*S. Africa*], nullah [*India*], park [*U. S.*].

CAVE, subterrane, cavern, cove; grot, grotto; alcove, blind alley, *cul-de-sac* [*F.*], hole, burrow, kennel, tunnel; gully &c. 198; arch &c. (*curve*) 245.

EXCAVATOR, sapper, miner.

V. BE CONCAVE &c. *adj.;* retire, cave in.

RENDER CONCAVE &c. *adj.;* depress, dish, hollow; scoop, scoop out; gouge, dig, delve, excavate, dent, dint, mine, sap, undermine, burrow, tunnel, stave in.

Adj. DEPRESSED &c. *v.;* alveolate, alveolar, calathiform, cup-shaped, dishing; favaginous, faveolate, favose; scyphiform, scyphose; concave, hollow, vuggy, stove in; retiring; retreating; cavernous; porous &c. (*with holes*) 260; cellular, spongy, spongious; honeycombed; infundibular, infundibuliform, funnel-shaped, bell-shaped, campaniform, capsular; vaulted, arched.

[*F.*]; caruncular *or* carunculous, carunculate *or* carunculated; furuncular, furunculous, furunculoid; mammiform; papulous, papulose; hemispheric, bulbous; bowed, arched; bold; bellied; tuberous, tuberculous; tumorous; cornute, odontoid; lentiform, lenticular; gibbous; club-shaped, hubby [*U. S.*], hubbly [*U. S.*], knobby, papillose; saddle-shaped, selliform; subclavate, torose, ventricose, verrucose; excrescential.

SALIENT, in relief, raised, *repoussé* [*F.*]; bloated &c. (*expanded*) 194.

⁎ "the knobbes sittynge on his chekes". [Chaucer].

---

253. Sharpness. — N. SHARPNESS &c.
adj.; acuity, acumination, mucronation; spinosity.

POINT, spike, spine, spiculum; needle, pin; prick, prickle; spur, rowel, barb; spit, cusp; horn, antler; snag; tag; thorn, bristle; Adam's needle, bear grass [*U. S.*], tine, yucca.

nib, tooth, tusk; spoke, cog, ratchet.

254. Bluntness. — N. BLUNTNESS &c
adj.

V. BE *or* RENDER BLUNT &c. *adj.*; obtund, dull; take off the -point, – edge; unedge [*rare*], turn.

Adj. BLUNT, obtuse, dull, dullish, pointless, unpointed; unsharpened, bluff; edentate, toothless.

---

beard, cheval-de-frise (*pl.* chevaux-de-frise), porcupine, hedgehog, brier, bramble, thistle; comb; awn, beggar's lice, bur *or* burr, catchweed, cleavers *or* clivers, goose grass, hairif *or* hariff [*dial. Eng.*], flax comb, hatchel *or* hackle *or* heckle.

PEAK, crag, crest, *arête* [*F.*], cone, sugar loaf, pike, aiguille; spire, pyramid, steeple.

CUTTING-EDGE, knife-edge, blade, edge tool, cutlery, knife, penknife, whittle, razor; scalpel, bistoury, lancet; plowshare, colter; hatchet, ax *or* axe, pickax, mattock, pick, adz *or* adze, bill; billhook, cleaver, cutter; scythe, sickle, scissors, shears; sword &c. (*arms*) 727; wedge; bodkin &c. (*perforator*) 262; *belduque* [*F.*], bowie knife, paring knife; bushwhacker [*U. S.*]; drawing knife *or* drawknife, drawshave.

SHARPENER, hone, strop; grindstone, whetstone; novaculite; steel, emery.

V. BE SHARP &c. *adj.*; taper to a point; bristle with, acuminate.

RENDER SHARP &c. *adj.*; sharpen, point, aculeate, acuminate, whet, barb, spiculate, set, strop, grind.

CUT &c. (*sunder*) 44.

Adj. SHARP, keen; acute; acicular, aciform; aculeate *or* aculeated, acuminate *or* acuminated, pointed; tapering; mucronate *or* mucronated, mucronulate; spiked, spiky, peaked, salient; cusped, cuspidate *or* cuspidated; prickly, echinate *or* echinated, acanaceous, acanthophorous, spiny, spinous, spinulose, spinulescent, spinuliferous; apiculate *or* apiculated; thorny, bristling, muricate *or* muricated, corniculate, pectinate *or* pectinated, studded, thistly, briery; craggy &c. (*rough*) 256; snaggy, digitate *or* digitated, two-edged.

ARROW-SHAPED, arrowheaded, arrowy, sagittal, sagittate, sagittated, sagittiform.

BARBED, glochidiate, spurred, aristate, awned, awny, bearded, barbate, crestate, setarious, subulate, tetrahedral.

CONE-SHAPED, conic, conical, coniform [*rare*], pyramidal.

HORN-SHAPED, corniform, cornute *or* cornuted; crescent-shaped; horned, corniculate.

LANCE-SHAPED, lanceolate, lanciform.

REED-SHAPED, calamiform [*rare*], arundinaceous, reedy.

SCIMITAR-SHAPED, acinaciform.

SPEAR-SHAPED, hastate, hastiform [*rare*], lance-shaped (*q. v.*).

SPINDLE-SHAPED, fusiform.

STAR-SHAPED, stellate *or* stellated, stelliform, stellular, starlike, starry.

SWORD-SHAPED, gladiate, ensate, ensiform, xiphoid.

TOOTH-SHAPED, dentiform, toothlike, odontoid, dentoid.

KEEN-EDGED, cutting; sharp-edged, knife-edged; sharp –, keen- as a razor; sharp as a needle; sharpened &c. *v.*; set.

255. Smoothness. — N. SMOOTH-
NESS &c. *adj.;* polish, gloss; lubricity,
lubrication.

[SMOOTH SURFACES] bowling green &c.
(*level*) 213; glass, ice, slide; asphalt,
granolithic pavement, wood pavement,
flags; down, velvet, silk, taffeta, satin,
velveteen, velumen.

SMOOTHER; roller, steam roller; sandpaper, emery paper; flatiron, sadiron;
burnisher, chamois *or* shammy, tur-
pentine and beeswax.

V. SMOOTH, smoothen [*rare*]; plane;
file; mow, shave; level, roll; macadamize;
polish, burnish, sleek, planish, levigate,
calender, glaze; iron, hot-press, mangle;
lubricate &c. (*oil*) 332.

Adj. SMOOTH; polished &c. *v.;* leiodermatous, slick [*colloq.*], velutinous; even;
level &c. 213; plane &c. (*flat*) 251; sleek,
glossy; silken, silky; lanate, downy,
velvety; glabrous, slippery, glassy, lubricous, oily, soft; unwrinkled; smooth
as -glass, – ice, – monumental alabaster,
– ivory, – satin, – velvet, – oil; slippery
as an eel; woolly &c. (*feathery*) 256.

256. Roughness. — N. ROUGHNESS &c.
adj.; tooth, grain, texture, ripple; asperity, rugosity, salebrosity [*obs.*], corrugation, nodosity, nodulation; arborescence &c. 242; pilosity.

HAIR, brush, beard, shag, mane,
whiskers, moustache, imperial, tress,
lock, curl, ringlet, fimbria, eyelashes,
lashes, cilia, villi; lovelock; beaucatcher;
curl paper; goatee; papillote, scalp lock,
scolding locks [*colloq.*], elf locks, mop,
mat, thatch; fringe, toupee; hair shirt.

PLUMAGE, plumosity; plume, panache,
crest; feather, tuft.

NAP, pile, floss, velvet, plush, fur,
down, wool, fluff; byssus, moss, bur *or*
burr.

V. BE ROUGH &c. *adj.;* go against the
grain.

RENDER ROUGH &c. *adj.;* roughen,
knurl, crinkle, ruffle, crisp, crumple,
corrugate, engrail; roughcast; set on
edge, stroke the wrong way, rub the fur
the wrong way, rumple.

Adj. ROUGH, uneven; scabrous, knotted; rugged, rugose, rugous, rugulose;
nodose, nodular, nodulated; knurled,

cross-grained, knurly; asperous [*obs.*], crisp, salebrous [*obs.*], gnarled, gnarly,
scraggly, scragged, scraggy; jagged; unkempt, unpolished, unsmooth, roughhewn; craggy, cragged; crankling [*obs.*]; prickly &c. (*sharp*) 253; arborescent &c.
242; leafy, well-wooded.

FEATHERY, plumose, plumigerous.

HAIRY, bristly, hirsute, hispid, pappous *or* pappose, pileous, pilose, pilous;
trichogenous, trichoid; tufted, ciliated, filamentous; crinose, crinite; bushy;
villous, nappy; bearded, shaggy, shagged; setous [*obs.*], setose, setaceous, setiferous, setigerous, setiform; "like quills upon the fretful porcupine" [*Hamlet*];
rough as a -nutmeg grater, – bear.

DOWNY, velvety, flocculent, woolly, lanate, lanated, lanuginous, lanuginose;
tomentose; fluffy.

FRINGED, befringed, fimbriate, fimbriated, fimbricate, laciniate *or* laciniated,
laciniform, laciniose.

Adv. AGAINST THE GRAIN; the wrong way of the goods; in the rough; on
edge.

*** *cabello luengo y corto el seso;* "flesh like slag in a furnace, knobbed and withered and
grey" [Kipling].

257. Notch. — N. NOTCH, dent, nick, cut; dimple; scotch, indent, indentation, denticulation, serration, serrature.

saw, tooth, crenel *or* crenelle, scallop *or* scollop; rickrack, picot edge, vandyke;
depression; jag.

EMBRASURE, battlement, machicolation.

V. NOTCH, nick, pink, mill, score, cut, dent, indent, jag, scarify, scotch, crimp,
scallop *or* scollop, crenulate, crenelate *or* crenellate, vandyke.

Adj. NOTCHED &c. *v.;* crenate *or* crenated; dentate *or* dentated, denticulate *or*
denticulated, crenelated *or* crenellated, toothed, palmate *or* palmated, serriform,
serrate *or* serrated, serrulate-

258. Fold. — **N.** FOLD, plicature, plication, pleat, plait, ply, crease; knife-pleat, knife-plait, box-pleat, box-plait; accordion pleat, accordion plait; tuck, gather; flexion, flexure, joint, elbow, double, doubling, duplicature, gather, wrinkle, rimple, crinkle, crankle, crumple, rumple, rivel [*archaic*], ruck, ruffle, dog's-ear, corrugation, frounce [*obs.*], flounce, lapel; pucker, crow's-feet.

V. FOLD, double, plicate, pleat, plait, crease, wrinkle, crinkle, crankle, curl, smock, shrivel, cockle up, cocker [*dial.*], rimple, rumple, frizzle, frounce [*archaic*], rivel [*archaic*], twill, corrugate, ruffle, crimple [*obs.*], crumple, pucker; turn -, double- -down, - under; dog's-ear, tuck, ruck, hem, gather.

Adj. FOLDED &c. *v.*

*** "not tricked and frounced as she was wont" [Milton].

259. Furrow. — **N.** FURROW, groove, rut, sulcus, scratch, streak, striæ, crack, score, incision, slit; chamfer, fluting; corduroy road, cradle hole [*sleighing*].

TRENCH, ditch, dike *or* dyke, moat, fosse, trough, channel, gutter, ravine &c. (*interval*) 198; depression, tajo [*U. S.*], thank-ye-ma'am [*U. S.*].

V. FURROW &c. *n.;* flute, groove, chamfer, carve, corrugate, cut, chisel, plow; incise, engrave, etch, enchase, mezzotint, crosshatch, hatch, grave, bite in.

Adj. FURROWED &c. *v.;* ribbed, striated, sulcated, fluted, canaliculate *or* canaliculated; bisulcous *or* bisulcate *or* bisulcated; canaliferous; unisulcate; trisulcate; corduroy; costate, rimiform [*rare*].

260. Opening. — **N.** OPENING, aperture, apertness [*archaic*]; hiation [*rare*], yawning, oscitance *or* oscitancy, dehiscence, patefaction [*obs.*], pandiculation; chasm &c. (*interval*) 198.

outlet, inlet; vent, venthole, blowhole, airhole, spiracle; vomitory [*Rom. arch.*]; embouchure; orifice, mouth, sucker, muzzle, throat, gullet, weasand, wizen [*dial.*], nozzle; placket.

WINDOW, casement; embrasure, *abat-jour* [*F.*]; light; skylight, fanlight; lattice; bay window, bow window, oriel, dormer; lantern.

PORTAL, porch, gate, ostiary [*obs.*], postern, wicket, trapdoor, hatch, door; arcade; cellarway, driveway, gateway, doorway, hatchway, gangway; lich gate *or* lych gate [*archaic*].

WAY, path &c. 627; thoroughfare; channel, gully; passage, passageway.

TUBE, pipe, main; water pipe &c. 350; air pipe &c. 351; vessel, tubule, canal, gut, fistula; ajutage *or* adjutage; ostium; smokestack; chimney, flue, tap, funnel.

TUNNEL, mine, pit, adit, drift, shaft; gallery.

ALLEY, lane, mall, aisle, glade, vista.

BORE, caliber *or* calibre; pore; blind orifice; fulgurite, thunder tube.

HOLE, foramen; puncture, perforation; fontane *or* fontanelle; transforation; pinhole, keyhole, loophole, porthole, peephole, mousehole, pigeonhole; eye, eye of a needle; eyelet; slot.

POROUSNESS, porosity; sieve, strainer, colander *or* cullender; cribble, riddle, screen; honeycomb.

261. Closure. — **N.** CLOSURE, occlusion, blockade; shutting up &c. *v.;* obstruction &c. (*hindrance*) 706; embolism, embolus; contraction &c. 195; infarct, infarction; constipation, obstipation; blind -alley, - corner; keddah [*India*], *cul-de-sac* [*F.*]; cæcum; imperforation, imperviousness &c. *adj.;* impermeability; stopper &c. 263; operculum.

V. CLOSE, occlude, plug; block up, stop up, fill up, bung up, cork up, button up, stuff up, shut up, dam up; blockade; obstruct &c. (*hinder*) 706; bar, bolt, stop, seal, plumb; choke, throttle; ram down, dam, cram; trap, clinch; put to -, shut- the door; slam, clap, snap.

Adj. CLOSED &c. *v.;* shut, operculated; unopened, blank.

UNPIERCED, imporous, cæcal; embolic; infarcted, imperforate, impervious, impermeable; impenetrable; impassable, unpassable, invious [*obs.*]; pathless, wayless; untrodden.

TIGHT, unventilated, air-tight, watertight, hermetically sealed; snug.

PERFORATION, apertion [*archaic*]; piercing &c. *v.;* terebration, empalement, pertusion [*obs.*], puncture, acupuncture, penetration.

OPENER, key, master key, *passepartout* [*F.*], clavis, open-sesame.

V. OPEN, ope [*poetic*], gape, yawn, hiate [*rare*], dehisce, bilge; fly open.

PERFORATE, pierce, empierce [*obs.*], tap, bore, drill; mine &c. (*scoop out*) 252; tunnel; transpierce, transfix; enfilade, impale, spike, spear, gore, spit, stab, pink, puncture, lance; trepan, trephine; stick, prick, riddle, punch; stave in.

cut a passage through; make way for, make room for.

UNCOVER, unclose, unrip, rip; lay –, cut –, rip –, throw- open.

Adj. OPEN; perforated &c. *v.;* perforate; wide open, patulous, agape, dehiscent, ringent; ajar, unclosed, unstopped; oscitant, gaping, yawning; patent.

TUBULAR, cannular, fistulous; pervious, permeable; foraminous; vesicular, vascular; porous, follicular, cribriform, honeycombed, infundibular *or* infundibulate, riddled; tubulose *or* tubulous, tubulate *or* tubulated; piped, tubate, tubiform.

OPENING &c. *v.;* aperient.

Int. open sesame! gangway! passageway!

** "she open'd, but to shut Excell'd her power; the gates wide open stood" [*P. L.*].

262. Perforator. — **N.** PERFORATOR, piercer, borer, auger, chisel, gimlet, drill, wimble, awl, bradawl, scoop, terrier [*obs.*], corkscrew, dibble, trocar, trepan, trephine, probe, bodkin, needle, stylet, stiletto, broach, reamer, rimer, lancet; punch, puncheon; spikebit, gouge; spear &c. (*weapon*) 727; puncher; punching machine, punching press; punch pliers.

263. Stopper. — **N.** STOPPER, stopple; plug, cork, bung, spike, spill, spile, stopcock, tap, faucet; rammer; ram, ramrod; piston; stop-gap; wadding, stuffing, padding, stopping, dossil, pledget, sponge [*surg.*], tampion *or* tompion, tourniquet.

VALVE, vent peg, spigot, slide valve; cover &c. 223.

DOORKEEPER, gatekeeper, janitor, janitress [*fem.*], janitrix [*fem.*], *concierge* [*F.*], porter, portress [*fem.*], warder, beadle, tiler *or* tyler [*Freemasonry*], durwaun [*Hind.*], usher, guard, sentinel; beefeater, yeoman of the guard [*Eng.*]; Cerberus, watch dog, ostiary.

SECTION IV. M O T I O N

1. MOTION IN GENERAL

264. [SUCCESSIVE CHANGE OF PLACE.[1]] **Motion.** — **N.** MOTION, movement, motility, motivity; move; going &c. *v.;* mobility; movableness, motive power, motorium; laws of motion; mobilization.

stream, flow, flux, run, course, stir; conduction; evolution; kinematics; telekinesis.

RATE, pace, tread, step, stride, gait, port, footfall, cadence, carriage, velocity, angular velocity; clip [*colloq.*], progress, locomotion; journey &c. 266; voyage &c. 267; transit &c. 270.

RESTLESSNESS &c. (*changeableness*) 149; unrest.

V. BE IN MOTION &c. *adj.;* move, go,

265. Quiescence. — **N.** REST; stillness &c. *adj.;* quiescence; stagnation, stagnancy; fixity, immobility, catalepsy; indisturbance [*rare*]; quietism.

QUIET, tranquillity, calm; repose &c. 687; peace; dead calm, anticyclone; statue-like repose; silence &c. 403; not a breath of air, not a mouse stirring; not a leaf stirring; sleep &c. (*inactivity*) 683.

PAUSE, lull &c. (*cessation*) 142; stand, standstill; standing still &c. *v.;* lock; deadlock, dead stop, dead stand; full stop; fix; embargo.

RESTING PLACE; *gîte* [*F.*]; bivouac; home &c. (*abode*) 189; pillow &c. (*sup-*

---

[1] A thing cannot be said to *move* from one place to another, unless it passes in succession through every intermediate place; hence motion is only such a change of place as is *successive*. "Rapid, swift, &c., as thought" are therefore incorrect expressions.

hie, gang [*Scot. & dial. Eng.*], budge, stir, pass, flit; hover -round, – about; shift, slide, glide; roll, roll on; flow, stream, run, drift, sweep along; wander &c. (*deviate*) 279; walk &c. 266; change –, shift- one's -place, – quarters; dodge; keep going, keep moving.

PUT IN MOTION, set in motion; move; impel &c. 276; propel &c. 284; render movable, mobilize.

Adj. MOVING &c. *v.;* in motion; traveling, transitional, metabatic; motory [*rare*], motive; shifting, movable, mobile, motiferous, motile, motific [*rare*], motor, motorial, quicksilver, mercurial, unquiet; restless &c. (*changeable*) 149; nomadic &c. 266; erratic &c. 279.

telekinetic, kinematic *or* kinematical, evolutionary.

Adv. UNDER WAY; on the -move, – wing, – fly, – tramp, – march.

** *eppur si muove* [Galileo]; *es bildet ein Talent sich in der Stille, sich ein Charakter in dem Strom der Welt;* "she 'gan stir With a short uneasy motion" [Coleridge]; "pace came to him like a maiden with a lamp, a new and beautiful wonder" [Dunsany]; "those proud ones swaying home with mainyards backed and bows a cream of foam" [Masefield].

port) 215; haven &c. (*refuge*) 666; goal &c. (*arrival*) 292.

V. BE QUIESCENT &c. *adj.;* stand still, stand fast, stand firm, lie still; keep quiet, repose, rest one's bonnet on a chair [*dial., U. S.*], rest one's face and hands [*dial., U. S.*], hold the breath.

REMAIN, stay; stand, lie to, ride at anchor, remain *in situ*, tarry, mark time; bring to, heave to, lay to; pull up, draw up; hold, halt; stop, stop short; rest, pause, anchor; cast anchor, come to anchor; rest on one's oars; repose –, rest– on one's laurels; lie back on one's record; take breath; stop &c. (*discontinue*) 142.

VEGETATE, stagnate; *quieta non movere* [*L.*]; let alone, let well enough alone; abide, rest and be thankful; keep within doors, stay at home, go to bed, live the life of a clam.

dwell &c. (*be present*) 186; settle &c. (*be located*) 184; alight &c. (*arrive*) 292; stick, stick fast; stand, stand like a post; not stir a -peg, – step; stand like a stuck pig [*colloq.*]; be at a stand &c. *n.*

QUELL, becalm, hush, calm, still, stay, lull to sleep, lay an embargo on, put the brakes on.

Adj. QUIESCENT, still; motionless, moveless; fixed; stationary; immotile; at rest, at a stand, at a standstill, at anchor; stock-still; standing still &c. *v.;* sedentary, untraveled, stay-at-home; becalmed, stagnant, quiet; unmoved, undisturbed, unruffled; calm, restful; cataleptic; immovable &c. (*stable*) 150; sleeping &c. (*inactive*) 683; silent &c. 403; still as - a statue, – a post, – a stone, – a mouse, – death.

Adv. AT A STAND &c. *adj.; tout court* [*F.*]; at the halt.

Int. STOP! stay! avast! [*naut.*], halt! hold hard! whoa! hold! *sabr karo!* [*Hind.*], *arrêtez!* [*F.*], *halte!* [*F.*].

** *requiescat in pace; Deus nobis hæc otia fecit* [Vergill]; "the noonday quiet holds the hill" [Tennyson]; "the silence surged sottly backward When the plunging hoofs were gone" [De La Mare]; "There is not wind enough to twirl The one red leaf" [Coleridge].

---

266. [LOCOMOTION BY LAND.] **Journey.** — **N.** TRAVEL; traveling &c. *v.;* wayfaring, campaigning, nomadization.

EXCURSION, journey, expedition, tour, trip, grand tour, *Wanderjahr* [*Ger.*], circuit, peregrination, discursion [*obs.*], ramble, pilgrimage, hadj *or* hajj [*Ar.*], trek [*S. Africa*], course, ambulation, march, walk, promenade, constitutional [*colloq.*], stroll, saunter, hike [*colloq.*], tramp, jog trot, turn, stalk, perambulation; outing, ride, drive, airing, jaunt.

nightwalking, noctambulation, noctambulism; somnambulism, sleep walking, somnambulation.

267. [LOCOMOTION BY WATER OR AIR.] **Navigation.** — **N.** NAVIGATION; volatility; aquatics; boating, yachting, cruising; ship &c. 273.

oar, scull, sweep, pole; paddle, screw, turbine; sail, canvas.

natation, swimming; fin, flipper, fish's tail.

AËRONAUTICS, aërostatics, aërostation, aërodonetics, aërial navigation, aëronautism; aëromechanics, aërodynamics, balloonery; balloon &c. 273; ballooning; aviation, airmanship; flying, flight, volitation; volplaning, planing [*colloq.*], hydroplaning, volplane, glide, dive,

RIDING, equitation, horsemanship, manège or manege, manage [archaic], ride and tie.

ROVING, vagrancy, pererration [obs.]; marching and countermarching; nomadism; vagabondism, vagabondage; hoboism [U. S.]; gadding; flit, flitting; migration; emigration, immigration, demigration [obs.], intermigration; Wanderlust [Ger.].

ITINERARY, plan, guide; handbook, roadbook; Baedeker, Bradshaw, Murray.

PROCESSION, parade, cavalcade, caravan, file, cortège [F.], column.

[ORGANS AND INSTRUMENTS OF LOCOMOTION] cycle, automobile, motor car &c. (vehicle) 272; trolley, locomotive; palanquin or palankeen, litter, dandy or dandi [India], jinrikisha or jinricksha; roller skates, skates, skis, snowshoes; legs, shanks, feet; pegs, pins, trotters [colloq.].

TRAVELER &c. 268.

STATION, stop, stopping place, terminal [U. S.], terminus, depot [U. S.], railway station, gare [F.].

V. TRAVEL, journey, course; take –, go- a journey; railroad [U. S.]; flit, take wing; migrate, emigrate, immigrate; trek [S. Africa]; scour –, traverse- the country; peragrate [obs.]; perambulate, circumambulate; tour, peregrinate, itinerate [rare], nomadize.

motor, motorcycle, bicycle, cycle [colloq.], spin, speed, burn up the road; trolley [colloq.]; go by -car, – trolley, – automobile, – rail, – train &c.

MOTORIZE, electrify.

WANDER, roam, range, prowl, rove, jaunt, ramble, stroll, saunter, hover, go one's rounds, straggle; gad, gad about; expatiate [rare]; patrol, pace up and down, traverse; take a walk &c. n.; go out for a walk &c. n.; have a run, take the air; noctambulate; somnambulate.

TAKE HORSE, ride, drive, trot, amble, canter, prance, fisk [obs.], frisk, caracoler [F.], caracole; gallop &c. (move quickly) 274.

WALK, march, step, tread, pace, plod, wend [archaic]; promenade; trudge, track, hoof it [slang], hike [colloq.], tramp; stalk, stride, straddle, strut, foot it, stump, bundle, bowl along, toddle; paddle; tread –, follow –, pursue- a path.

peg on, jog on, wag on, shuffle on; stir one's stumps [colloq.]; bend one's -steps, – course; make –, find –, wend –, pick –, thread –, plow- one's way.

GLIDE, slide, coast, skim, skate.

FILE OFF, march in procession, defile.

GO TO, repair to, resort to, hie to, betake oneself to.

nose-dive, spin, looping the loop; wing' pinion, aileron.

VOYAGE, sail, cruise, passage, circumnavigation, periplus; headway, sternway, leeway; fairway.

MARINER &c. 269; AËRONAUT &c. 269a.

V. SAIL; put to sea &c. (depart) 293; take ship, weigh anchor, get under way; spread -sail, – canvas; gather way, have way on; make –, carry- sail; plow the -waves, – deep, – main, – ocean; ride the waves, ride the storm, buffet the waves, walk the waters.

NAVIGATE, warp, luff, scud, boom, kedge; drift, course, cruise, steam, coast; hug the -shore, – land; circumnavigate.

ROW, paddle, ply the oar, pull, scull, punt.

FLOAT, swim, skim, effleurer [F.], dive, wade.

[IN AËRONAUTICS] fly, soar, drift, hover, be wafted, aviate, volplane, plane [colloq.], glide, dive, fly over, nose-dive, spin, loop the loop, land; take wing, take a flight; wing one's flight, wing one's way.

Adj. SAILING &c. v.; seafaring, nautical, maritime, naval; seagoing, coasting; afloat; navigable; grallatorial or grallatory.

AËRONAUTIC, aëronautical, aërostatic or aërostatical, aëromechanic or aëromechanical, aërodynamic, aërial, volant, volitant, volatile, volitational.

AQUATIC, natatory, natatorial, natational.

Adv. UNDER -WAY, – sail, – canvas, – steam; on the wing.

₊ bon voyage; "spread the thin oar and catch the driving gale" [Pope]; "the waves bowed down before her like blown grain" [Masefield]; "like the eagle free Away the good ship flies" [Cunningham]; "As if it dodged a water-sprite, It plunged and tacked and reared" [Coleridge].

Adj. TRAVELING &c. *v.;* ambulatory, itinerant, peripatetic, perambulatory, mundivagant [*rare*], roving, rambling, gadding, discursive, vagrant, migratory, nomadic; circumforanean [*obs.*], circumforaneous.

NIGHT-WANDERING, noctivagant [*rare*], noctambulistic, noctivagous, somnambulistic *or* somnambular, somnambulant.

SELF-MOVING, automobile, automotive, locomotive, locomobile, automatic.

WAYFARING, wayworn; travel-stained.

Adv. on foot, on horseback, on Shanks's mare; by the Marrowbone stage; *in transitu* &c. 270; *en route* &c. 282.

Int. come along! step on it! [*automobile cant*].

⁎ "I will paddle it stoutly at your side With the tandem that nature gave me" [Holmes]; "I dislike feeling at home when I am abroad" [Shaw].

---

268. Traveler. — N. TRAVELER, wayfarer, voyager, itinerant, passenger, transient, commuter, straphanger [*colloq.*].

tourist, excursionist, explorer, adventurer, mountaineer, Alpine Club; peregrinator, wanderer, rover, straggler, rambler; landsman, landlubber, horse marine; bird of passage; gadabout [*colloq.*], gadling [*obs.*]; vagrant, scatterling [*obs.*], landlouper *or* landloper, waifs and estrays, wastrel, stray; loafer, swagman *or* swagsman [*Australia*], tramp, vagabond, nomad, Bohemian, gypsy, Arab, Wandering Jew, hadji *or* hajji [*Ar.*], pilgrim, palmer; peripatetic; comers and goers, immigrant; *émigré* [*F.*], emigrant; runagate, runaway, renegade, fugitive, refugee; beachcomber; booly [*Irish hist.*]; globe-girdler, globe-trotter [*colloq.*]; hobo [*U. S.*], runabout, trekker [*S. Africa*], camper, *zingaro* (*pl. zingari*) [*It.*].

SLEEPWALKER, somnambulist, somnambulator [*rare*], nightwalker, noctambulist.

COURIER, messenger, express, *estafette* [*F.*], runner; Mercury, Iris, Ariel; comet.

PEDESTRIAN, walker, foot passenger, hiker [*colloq.*], perigrinator [*rare*], tramper.

RIDER, horseman, horsewoman [*fem.*], equestrian, equestrienne [*fem.*], cavalier,

269. Mariner. — N. MARINER, sailor, navigator; seaman, seafarer, seafaring man, sea dog [*colloq.*], hand, water dog [*colloq.*], shellback [*slang*]; Ancient Mariner, Flying Dutchman; dock walloper [*slang*]; Jack, Jack Tar *or* jack-tar, tar, jacky (*pl.* jackies) [*landsman's term*], shipman [*obs. or poet.*], gob [*slang, U. S.*]; salt, able seaman, A. B.; man-of-war's man, bluejacket, galiongee *or* galionji, marine, devil-dog [*slang, U. S.*], jolly [*slang*]; midshipman, middy [*colloq.*]; lascar, *mangee* or *manjhi* [*Hind.*], *matelot* [*F.*], captain, commander, master mariner, skipper; mate; boatman, ferryman, waterman, lighterman, bargeman, longshoreman; bargee, gondolier; oar, oarsman; rower; boatswain.

STEERSMAN, coxswain *or* cockswain, cox [*colloq.*], helmsman, wheelman, pilot, *patron* [*F.*]; crew.

⁎ "the keen Eye-puckered, hard-case seamen, silent, lean" [Masefield].

269a. Aëronaut. — N. AËRONAUT, aviator, aëroplanist, airman, airwoman, flyer, birdman [*colloq.*], birdwoman [*colloq.*], aviatress *or* aviatrix, aërial navigator, man-bird [*colloq.*], wizard of the air, monoplanist; pilot, observer, spotter [*mil. cant*], scout, bomber, ace; balloonist, Icarus.

---

jockey, roughrider, trainer, breaker, huntsman, whip, postilion *or* postillion, postboy.

DRIVER, coachman, Jehu [*humorous*], charioteer, carter, wagoner, drayman; cabman, cabdriver; *voiturier* [*F.*], *vetturino* [*It.*], *condottiere* [*It.*], gharry-wallah *or* gari-wala [*Hind.*], hackman, syce [*India*], truckman.

[RAILROAD] engine driver [*Brit.*], engineer [*U. S.*], fireman, stoker, conductor, guard [*Brit.*], motorman.

[AUTOMOBILE] driver, chauffeur, chauffeuse [*fem.*], automobilist, motorist, truck driver, mechanician; scorcher [*slang*], speed maniac, road hog [*slang*].

⁎ "of the cannibals that each other eat, And anthropophagi, and men whose heads Do grow beneath their shoulders" [*Othello*].

270. Transference. — **N.** TRANSFER, transference; translocation, elocation [*obs.*]; displacement; metastasis, metathesis; removal; remotion; amotion; relegation; deportation, asportation, extradition, conveyance, draft; carrying, carriage; convection, conduction, contagion, infection; transfusion; transfer &c. (*of property*) 783.

TRANSIT, transition; passage, ferry, gestation; portage, porterage, freightage, carting, cartage; shoveling &c. *v.*; vection [*obs.*], vecture [*obs.*], vectitation [*obs.*]; shipment, freight, waftage; transmission, transport, transportation, transumption [*rare*], transplantation, translation; shifting, dodging; dispersion &c. 73; transposition &c. (*interchange*) 148; traction &c. 285; *portamento* [*music, It.*].

[THING TRANSFERRED] drift, alluvion, alluvium, detritus, deposit, moraine; deed, gift, bequest, legacy, lease; quitclaim; freight, cargo, mail, baggage, luggage [*Brit.*], goods [*Brit.*].

TRANSFEREE, grantee, assignee; donee, legatee, consignee, indorsee, devisee.

V. TRANSFER, transmit, transport, transplace, transplant, transfuse; convey, carry, bear, fetch and carry; carry over, ferry over; hand, pass, forward; shift; conduct, convoy, bring, fetch, reach; tote [*U. S.*].

SEND, delegate, consign, relegate, turn over to, deliver; ship, freight, embark; waft; shunt; transpose &c. (*interchange*) 148; displace &c. 185; throw &c. 284; drag &c. 285; mail, post.

LADLE, bail *or* bale, bucket, lade, dip, drip; shovel, decant, draft off.

Adj. TRANSFERRED &c. *v.*; drifted, movable; portable, portative; conductive, contagious, infectious; metastatic, metathetic *or* metathetical; transumptive [*rare*].

TRANSFERABLE, assignable, conveyable, devisable, bequeathable, negotiable, transmittible, transmissible; mailable [*U. S.*].

Adv. from hand to hand, from pillar to post; by freight, by rail, by steamer, by aëroplane, by trolley, by motor truck, by express, by mail, by special delivery.

on the way, by the way; on the road, on the wing; as one goes; *in transitu* [*L.*], *en route* [*F.*], *chemin faisant* [*F.*], *en passant* [*F.*], in mid-progress.

271. Carrier. — **N.** CARRIER, porter, red cap [*U. S.*], bearer, tranter [*obs.*], conveyer; *cargador* [*P.I.*], freighter, express, expressman; stevedore; coolie; conductor, chauffeur, truck driver; letter carrier, postman, man of letters [*humorous*], aërial mail-carrier.

BEAST OF BURDEN, beast, cattle, horse, steed, nag, palfrey, Arab, blood horse, thoroughbred, galloway, charger, courser, racer, hunter, jument [*obs.*], pony; Shetland, – pony; filly, colt, foal, barb, roan, jade, hack, bidet, pad, cob, tit [*dial.*], punch [*dial.*], roadster, goer; race –, pack –, draft –, cart –, dray –, post- horse; shelty *or* sheltie; garran *or* garron [*Brit.*], jennet *or* genet, bayard, mare, stallion, gelding; broncho *or* bronco, cayuse [*U. S.*]; creature, critter [*rural U. S.*]; cow pony, mustang, Narragansett, waler; stud.

ASS, donkey, jackass, burro [*S. W. U. S.*], cuddy [*Scot. & dial. Eng.*], moke [*slang*]; wild ass, onager.

mule, hinny; sumpter -horse, – mule; ladino [*U. S.*].

reindeer; camel, dromedary, llama, elephant; carrier pigeon.

Pegasus, Bucephalus, Rosinante *or* Rocinante, Alborak, Bayard, Incitatus, Kantaha, Veillantif, Vindictive, Black Bess, Kelpie *or* Kelpy.

[MEANS OF TRANSPORT] locomotive, motor, trolley, carriage &c. (*vehicle*) 272; ship &c. 273.

Adj. equine, asinine; electric, motor, express.

*** "I was not made a horse; And yet I bear a burthen like an ass" [*Richard II*].

272. Vehicle. — **N.** VEHICLE, conveyance, carriage, caravan, car, van; wagon *or* waggon, wain [*archaic*], dray, cart, lorry.

cariole *or* carriole; truck, tram; limber, tumbrel *or* tumbril, pontoon; barrow;

273. Ship. — **N.** SHIP, vessel, sail; craft, bottom.

NAVY, marine, fleet, flotilla.

SHIPPING, man-of-war &c. (*combatant*) 726; transport, tender, storeship; merchant ship, merchantman; packet, liner;

wheelbarrow, handbarrow; perambulator; Bath –, wheel- chair; chaise; police van, patrol wagon, black Maria [*colloq.*, *U. S.*]; conestoga wagon *or* wain; jinrikisha *or* jinricksha, ricksha [*colloq.*], dearborn [*U. S.*], dump cart, hack, jigger [*U. S.*, horse car; *New Eng.*, heavy cart; *Eng.*, light cart]; kittereen, mail stage, manumotor, rig, rockaway, prairie schooner [*U. S.*], shay [*colloq.*], sloven [*Can.*], team, tonga [*India*], Cape cart [*S. Africa*], hackery [*India*], ekka [*India*]; gharri *or* gharry *or* gari [*India*]; gocart.

EQUIPAGE, turnout [*colloq.*]; coach, chariot, phaëton, mail phaëton, wagonette, break *or* brake, drag, curricle, tilbury, whisky [*obs.*], landau, barouche, victoria, brougham, clarence, calash, *calèche* [*F.*], britzka, araba [*Oriental*], kibitka; berlin; sulky, *désobligeant* [*F.*], sociable, *vis-à-vis* [*F.*], *dormeuse* [*F.*], jaunting –, outside- car; runabout; *vettura* [*It.*].

post chaise; diligence [*F.*], stage, stagecoach; mail –, hackney –, glass-coach; stage wagon; car, omnibus, bus [*colloq.*]; fly [*Eng.*], cabriolet, cab, hansom, four-wheeler, growler [*slang, Eng.*], droshki *or* drosky.

dogcart, trap [*colloq.*], whitechapel, buggy, *char-à-bancs* (*pl. chars-à-bancs*) [*F.*], shandrydan *or* shandradan [*Scot., Ir.,* & *dial. Eng.*].

TEAM, pair, span, tandem, randem; spike team *or* spike [*U. S.*], unicorn; four-in-hand.

LITTER, palanquin *or* palankeen, sedan *or* sedan chair; palki, jampan, dandy *or* dandi, dooly *or* doolie, munchil [*all India*]; cacolet [*F.*]; tonjon [*Ceylon*], brancard, horse litter; stretcher, hurdle; ambulance.

SLED, bob, bobsled *or* bobsleigh [*U. S.*]; cutter [*U. S.*]; doubleripper, double-runner [*U. S.*]; jumper [*U. S.* & *Can.*], sledge, sleigh, toboggan, cariole *or* carriole [*Can.*], pung [*U. S.*]; ski (*pl. ski or* skis), snowshoes, skates, roller skates.

CYCLE, monocycle, bicycle, tricycle, quadricycle, hydrocycle, tandem; machine [*colloq.*], wheel [*colloq.*], bike [*slang*], safety bicycle *or* safety [*colloq.*], motor cycle *or* motorcycle; velocipede, hobby-horse, draisine *or* draisene.

AUTOMOBILE, motor car *or* motorcar, limousine, sedan, touring car, roadster,

whaler, slaver, collier, coaster, freight-steamer, freighter, lighter; fishing –, pilot- boat; trawler, hulk; yacht; baggala; floating -hotel, – palace; ocean greyhound [*colloq.*].

ship, bark *or* barque; shipentine, four-masted bark *or* barque; brig, snow, hermaphrodite brig; brigantine, barkentine *or* barquentine, schooner; topsail –, fore-and-aft- schooner; fore-and-after [*colloq.*]; three-, four-, five-, six- masted schooner; *chasse-marée* [*F.*], sloop, cutter, revenue cutter [*U. S.*], corvet *or* corvette, clipper, foist [*obs.*], yawl, dandy, ketch, smack, lugger, barge, hoy, cat, catboat, buss; sailer, sailing vessel; windjammer [*colloq.*]; steamer, steam-boat, steamship; mail –, paddle –, turbine –, screw- steamer; tug; line of steamers &c.

BOAT, pinnace, launch; lifeboat, long-boat, jolly-boat, bumboat, flyboat, cock-boat, ferry-boat, canal boat; ark, bully [*Nfld.*], bateau [*Can.*], broadhorn [*W. U. S.*], dory, drogher, dugout, Durham boat [*U. S.*], galiot *or* galliot, flatboat, shallop, gig, funny [*Eng.*], skiff, dinghy *or* dingey *or* dingy, scow, cockleshell, wherry, coble, punt, cog, lerret [*dial. Eng.*]; eight-, four-, pair- oar; randan; outrigger; float, raft, pontoon; ice-boat, ice-canoe, ice-yacht.

catamaran, coracle, gondola, caravel *or* carvel, felucca, caïque, canoe; galley, galley foist [*hist.*], bilander, dogger, hooker *or* howker [*obs.*]; argosy, carack *or* carrack [*hist.*], galleass *or* galliass, galleon; polacre *or* polacca, corsair, piragua, bunderboat [*India*], tartane, junk, lorcha, praam, proa *or* prahu, saic, sampan, xebec, dhow; dahabeah; nuggar; kayak, keel boat [*U. S.*], log canoe, pirogue; quadrireme, trireme; stern-wheeler [*U. S.*]; wanigan *or* wangan [*U. S.*], wharf boat; derelict.

[AËRONAUTICS] balloon; airship, aëroplane, airplane, aëro [*colloq.*], monoplane, biplane, triplane; *avion* [*F.*], aëronat, dirigible, zeppelin, zepp [*colloq.*]; air cruiser, battle –, bombing –, combat-plane; two-seater, *biplace* [*F.*]; single-seater, *monoplace* [*F.*], aëroboat, aëro-bus, aëro-hydroplane, aëroyacht, flying boat; aircraft; hydroplane, aërodrome [*obsoles.*], air –, pilot –, captive –, fire-balloon; aërostat, Montgolfier; kite, parachute.

coupé, motor [*colloq.*], machine [*colloq.*], car [*colloq.*], auto [*colloq.*], locomobile, autocar, steamer, electric, runabout, coupelet, racer, torpedo; truck, tractor; taxicab, taxi [*colloq.*], taxicoach, motor bus *or* motorbus; flivver [*slang*], jitney [*colloq.*], tacot [*F. mil. slang*].

[ALLIED AUTOMOBILE TERMS] tonneau, chassis, hood, top, ignition, spark plug, sparking plug [*Eng.*], generator, distributor, magneto, self-starter, gear, gear box, differential, cylinder, manifold, intake, exhaust, carburetor or carburettor; four -, six -, eight -, twelve- cylinder; twin six, ammeter, speedometer, oil gauge, primer, clutch, universal joint, crank shaft, transmission, tire *or* tyre [*Brit.*], rim; gasoline *or* gasolene, petrol [*Brit.*]; trailer; garage; chauffeur &c. 268.

[ALLIED AËRONAUTICAL TERMS] fuselage, gondola, wings, *ailes* [F.], controls, aileron, lifting power, camouflage, rudder; tail, *empennage* [F.]; cabane, hangar; aëronaut &c. 269a.

Adj. MARINE, maritime, naval, nautical, seafaring, ocean-going; A1, A1 at Lloyd's; seaworthy.

AËRONAUTIC *or* aëronautical, aërial; airworthy; volant &c. 267.

Adv. AFLOAT, aboard; on board, on ship board; hard-a -lee, – port, – starboard, – weather.

* "The hollow oak our palace is, Our heritage the sea" [Cunningham]; "all the marvelous beauty of their bows" [Masefield].

TRAIN; express, mail; accommodation –, passenger –, express –, special –, limited –, mail –, corridor –, parliamentary –, luggage [*Brit.*] –, freight –, goods [*Brit.*]- train; 1st-, 2d-, 3d-class- -train, – carriage, – compartment; rolling stock; cattle truck; car, coach, carriage [*Brit.*]; baggage –, freight –, chair –, drawing-room –, palace –, parlor –, Pullman –, sleeping- car; surface –, tram- car; trolley *or* trolley car [*U. S. & Can.*], electric car, electric [*colloq.*]; trollibus, trackless trolley; box car, box wagon; horse box [*Brit.*], horse car [*U.S.*]; lightning express; mail car, mail van [*Brit.*]; baggage car, luggage van [*Brit.*].

HAND CAR, trolley *or* trolly.

[UTENSILS & IMPLEMENTS] spoon, spatula, ladle, hod, hoe; spade, shovel, spaddle [*obs.*], loy [*Ir. & U. S.*]; spud; pitchfork.

Adj. VEHICULAR, curricular [*rare*], vehiculatory [*rare*]; ambulatory &c. (*traveling*) 266.

* "Now in building of chaises, I tell you what, There is always *somewhere* a weakest spot" [Holmes].

2. DEGREES OF MOTION

274. Velocity. — N. VELOCITY, speed, celerity; swiftness &c. *adj.*; rapidity, eagle speed, lightning speed; expedition &c. (*activity*) 682; pernicity [*obs.*]; acceleration; haste &c. 684.

SPURT, sprint, rush, dash, race, steeple chase; automobile race; Marathon race *or* Marathon; smart –, lively –, swift &c. *adj.* –, rattling [*colloq.*] –, spanking [*slang*] –, strapping [*colloq.*]- -rate, – pace; round pace; flying, flight.

PACE, gallop, canter, trot, round trot, run, scamper; hand –, full- gallop; swoop.

[COMPARISONS] lightning, light, electricity, wind; cannon ball, rocket, arrow, dart, hydrargyrum, quicksilver, Mercury; wireless, telegraph, express train; swallow flight; torrent.

eagle, antelope, courser, race horse, barb, gazelle, greyhound, hare, doe, squirrel, camel bird, swallow, chickaree, chipmunk, hackee [*U. S.*], ostrich.

275. Slowness. — N. SLOWNESS &c. *adj.*; languor &c. (*inactivity*) 683; drawl; creeping &c. *v.*, lentor [*rare*].

jog-trot, dog-trot; amble, rack, pace, single-foot, walk; mincing steps; dead march, slow march, slow time.

RETARDATION; slackening &c. *v.*; delay &c. (*lateness*) 133; claudication [*obs.*].

SLOW GOER, slow coach [*colloq.*]; lingerer, loiterer, sluggard, tortoise, snail; poke [*slang, U. S.*]; dawdle &c. (*inactive*) 683.

V. MOVE SLOWLY &c. *adv.*; creep, crawl, lag, slug [*dial.*], walk, drawl, linger, loiter, saunter; plod, trudge, stump along, lumber; trail, drag; dawdle &c. (*be inactive*) 683; grovel, worm one's way –, inch, inch along, steal along; jog on, rub on, toddle, waddle, wabble *or* wobble, wamble, traipse *or* trapes [*dial. or colloq.*], slouch, shuffle, halt, hobble, limp, claudicate [*obs.*], shamble; flag, falter, totter, stagger;

scorcher [*slang*], joy rider [*colloq.*], speed maniac.

Mercury, Ariel, Puck, Camilla, Harlequin.

[MEASUREMENT OF VELOCITY] velocimeter, speedometer, patent log, log, log line.

V. MOVE QUICKLY, trip, fisk [*obs.*]; speed, hie, hasten, spurt, sprint, post, spank, scuttle; scud, scuddle [*obs. or Scot.*], scurry, whiz; thunder -by, – on; scour, scour the plain; scamper; run, run like mad [*colloq.*], fly, race, run a race, cut away, shoot, tear, whisk, sweep, skim, brush; skedaddle [*colloq.*], cut and run [*colloq.*], cut along [*colloq.*], bowl along; scorch [*colloq.*]; rush &c. (*be violent*) 173; dash on, dash off, dash forward; bolt; trot, gallop, bound, flit, spring, dart, boom; march in -quick, – double- time; ride hard, get over the ground; give her the gas, step on her tail, run wide open [*all automobile cant*].

HURRY &c. (*hasten*) 684; bundle, bundle along; bundle on; accelerate, put on; quicken; quicken –, mend -one's pace; clap spurs to one's horse; make haste, make rapid strides, make forced marches, make the best of one's way; put one's best leg foremost, stir one's stumps [*slang*], wing one's way, set off at a score; carry sail, crowd sail; go off like a shot, go ahead, gain ground; outstrip the wind, fly on the wings of the wind.

KEEP UP WITH, keep pace with.

OUTSTRIP &c. 303; outmarch.

Adj. FAST, speedy, swift, rapid, quick, fleet; nimble, agile, expeditious; express; active &c. 682; flying, galloping &c. *v.*; light-footed, nimble-footed; winged, eagle-winged, mercurial, electric, telegraphic; light-legged, light of heel; swift as an arrow &c. *n.*; quick as lightning &c. *n.*; quick as thought.[1]

Adv. SWIFTLY &c. *adj.*; with speed &c.*n.*; apace; at a great rate, at full speed, at railway speed; full drive, full gallop; posthaste, in full sail, tantivy; like a shot [*colloq.*], like greased lightning [*colloq.*]; trippingly; instantaneously &c. 113.

under press of -sail, – canvas, – sail and steam; *velis et remis* [*L.*], on eagle's wing, in double-quick time; with rapid strides, with giant strides, *à pas de géant* [*F.*], in seven-league boots; whip and spur; *ventre à terre* [*F.*]; as fast as one's -legs, – heels- will carry one; as fast as one can lay feet to the ground, at the top of one's speed; by leaps and bounds; with haste &c. 684; in high (gear *or* speed) [*automobiling*].

∗ *tempus fugit; vires acquirit eundo;* "I'll put a girdle round about the earth In forty minutes" [*M. N. D.*]; "swifter than arrow from the Tartar's bow" [*M. N. D.*]; "he was the sworn companion of the wind" [Dunsany].

mince, step short; march in slow time, march in funeral procession; take one's time; hang fire &c. (*be late*) 133.

RETARD, relax, slacken, check, moderate, rein in, curb; reef; strike –, shorten –, take in- sail; put on the drag, brake, apply the brake; clip the wings; reduce the speed; slacken speed, slacken one's pace, backwater, back pedal, throttle down, lose ground.

Adj. SLOW, slack; tardy; dilatory &c. (*inactive*) 683; gentle, easy; leisurely; deliberate, gradual; insensible, imperceptible; languid, sluggish, apathetic, phlegmatic, lymphatic; moderate, slow-paced, tardigrade [*rare*], snail-like; creeping &c. *v.*; reptatorial *or* reptatory.

DULL, slow [*colloq.*], prosaic, unentertaining, boresome, wearisome, uninteresting &c. (*dull*) 843.

Adv. SLOWLY &c. *adj.*; leisurely; *piano* [*It.*], *adagio* [*It.*], *largo* [*It.*], *larghetto* [*It.*], at half speed, under easy sail; at a -foot's, – snail's, – funeral- pace; dead slow [*colloq.*]; slower than– death, – cold molasses [*colloq.*], – a funeral; in slow time; with mincing steps, with clipped wings; *haud passibus œquis* [Vergil]; in low (gear *or* speed) [*automobiling*].

GRADUALLY &c. *adj.*; gradatim; by degrees, by slow degrees, by inches, by little and little; step by step; inch by inch, bit by bit, little by little, *seriatim* [*L.*], consecutively.

∗ *dum Roma deliberat Saguntum perit;* "that, like a wounded snake, drags its slow length along" [Pope].

3. MOTION CONJOINED WITH FORCE

276. Impulse. — **N.** IMPULSE, impulsion, impetus; momentum; push, pulsion, thrust, shove, jog, jolt, brunt, boom, booming, boost [*U. S.*], throw; explosion &c. (*violence*) 173; propulsion &c. 284.

CLASH, collision, occursion [*obs.*], encounter, appulsion, appulse, shock, crash, bump; impact; *élan* [*F.*]; charge &c. (*attack*) 716; percussion, concussion; beating &c. (*punishment*) 972.

BLOW, dint, stroke, knock, tap, rap, slap, smack, pat, dab; fillip; slam, bang; hit, whack, thwack; cuff &c. 972; squash, douse *or* dowse, whap [*dial.*], swap [*obs.*], punch, thump, pelt, kick, punce [*obs.*], calcitration; *ruade* [*F.*]; arietation [*obs.*]; cut, thrust, lunge, yerk [*obs.*]; cannon [*billiards, Brit.*], carom *or* carrom, clip [*slang*], jab, plug [*slang*], sidewinder [*slang, U.S.*], sidewipe [*slang, U.S.*].

HAMMER, sledge hammer, mall, maul [*archaic*], mallet, flail; ram, rammer; ramrod; battering-ram, monkey, tamper, tamping iron, pile driver, pile-driving engine, punch, bat; cant hook [*U. S. or dial. Eng.*]; cudgel &c. (*weapon*) 727; ax &c. (*sharp*) 253.

[SCIENCE OF MECHANICAL FORCES] mechanics, dynamics; kinematics, kinetics; dynamograph, dynamometer; seismometer.

V. IMPEL, give an impetus &c. *n.*; push; start, give a start to, set going; drive, urge, boom; thrust, prod, foin [*archaic*]; cant; elbow, shoulder, jostle *or* justle, hustle, hurtle, shove, jog, jolt, encounter; run –, bump –, butt- against; knock –, run- one's head against; impinge; boost [*U. S.*]; bunt, carom *or* carrom, cannon [*billiards, Brit.*], clip [*slang*]; fan, -out; jab, plug [*slang*].

STRIKE, knock, hit, tap, rap, slap, flap, dab, pat, thump, beat, bang, slam, dash; punch, thwack, whack; hit –, strike- hard; swap [*obs.*], batter, douse *or* dowse [*obs.*], tamp, baste, paste [*slang*], pelt, patter, buffet, belabor; fetch one a blow; poke at, pink, lunge, yerk [*obs.*]; kick, calcitrate; butt, strike at &c. (*attack*) 716; whip &c. (*punish*) 972.

COLLIDE; come –, enter- into collision; foul; fall –, run- foul of; telescope. throw &c. (*propel*) 284.

Adj. IMPULSIVE, impellent, propulsive, pulsive [*rare*], booming; dynamic, dynamical; kinetic, kinematic *or* kinematical; impelled &c. *v.*; impelling &c. *v.*

⁎⁎ "a hit, a very palpable hit" [*Hamlet*].

277. Recoil. — **N.** RECOIL; reaction, retroaction; revulsion; rebound, ricochet, backlash, repercussion, recalcitration: kick, *contrecoup* [*F.*]; springing back &c. *v.*; elasticity &c. 325; reflexion, reflex, reflux; reverberation &c. (*resonance*) 408; rebuff, repulse; return.

ducks and drakes; boomerang; spring. REACTIONARY, reactionist, recalcitrant.

V. RECOIL, react; balk, jib; spring –, fly –, bound- back; rebound, reverberate, repercuss, recalcitrate; echo, ricochet.

Adj. RECOILING &c. *v.*; refluent, repercussive, recalcitrant, reactionary, revulsive, retroactive.

Adv. on the recoil &c. *n.*

4. MOTION WITH REFERENCE TO DIRECTION

278. Direction. — **N.** DIRECTION, bearing, course, set, trend, run, drift, tenor; tendency &c. 176; incidence; bending, trending &c. *v.*; dip, tack, aim, collimation; steering, steerage.

points of the compass, cardinal points; north, east, south, west; N by E, NNE, NE by N, NE, &c.

rhumb, azimuth, line of collimation.

LINE, path, road, range, quarter, line of march; alignment *or* alinement; air line, bee line; straight shot.

279. Deviation. — **N.** DEVIATION; swerving &c. *v.*; obliquation [*obs.*], warp, refraction; flection *or* flexion; sweep; deflection, deflexure; declination.

DIVERSION, digression, departure from, aberration, drift, sheer, divergence &c. 291; zigzag; detour &c. (*circuit*) 629; divagation, disorientation, exorbitation [*rare*].

[DESULTORY MOTION] wandering &c. *v.*; vagrancy, evagation [*obs.*]; bypaths and crooked ways; byroad.

V. TEND TOWARDS, bend towards, point towards; conduct to, go to; point -to, – at; bend, trend, verge, incline, dip, determine.

STEER FOR, steer towards, make for, make towards; aim at, level at; take aim; keep –, hold- a course; be bound for; bend one's steps towards; direct ‥, steer –, bend –, shape- one's course; align one's march; go straight, – to the point; make a bee line; march -on, – on a point.

ascertain one's direction &c. *n.*; *s'orienter* [*F.*], see which way the wind blows; box the compass; take the air line.

Adj. DIRECTED &c. *v.*, – towards; pointing towards &c. *v.*; bound for; aligned with; direct, straight; undeviating, unswerving; straightforward; north, northern, northerly, &c. *n.*

DIRECTABLE, steerable, leadable, dirigible, guidable, aimable, determinable.

Adv. TOWARDS; on the -road, – high road- to; *en avant* [*F.*]; *versus* [*L.*], to; hither, thither, whither; directly; straight, – forwards, – as an arrow; point-blank; in a -bee, – direct, – straight- line -to, – for, – with; in a line with; full tilt at, as the crow flies.

before –, near –, close to –, against- the wind; windward, in the wind's eye.

THROUGH, *viâ* [*L.*], by way of; in all -directions, – manner of ways; *quaquaversum* [*L.*], from the four winds.

[MOTION SIDEWAYS, OBLIQUE MOTION] sidling &c. *v.*; gybe *or* jibe, tack, yaw [*all naut.*]; passage, right passage, left passage [*manège*]; echelon [*mil.*]; knight's move at chess.

V. DEVIATE, alter one's course, depart from, turn, trend; bend, curve &c. 245; swerve, heel, bear off; gybe *or* jibe, break, yaw, wear, sheer, tack [*all naut.*].

DEFLECT; intervert [*obs.*]; divert, divert from its course; put on a new scent; shift, shunt [*Brit.*], switch [*U. S.*], draw aside, crook, warp.

STRAY, straggle; sidle, edge; diverge &c. 291; tralineate [*obs.*], digress, wander; wind, twist, meander; veer, divagate; go astray, go adrift; lose one's way; ramble, rove, drift.

SIDETRACK; turn aside, turn a corner, turn away from; wheel, steer clear of; dodge; step aside, ease off, make way for, shy, jib.

GLANCE OFF, fly off at a tangent; wheel about, face about; turn –, face- to the right-about; echelon [*mil.*]; waddle &c. (*oscillate*) 314; go out of one's way &c. (*perform a circuit*) 629.

Adj. DEVIATING &c. *v.*; aberrant, errant; excursive, discursive; devious, desultory, loose; rambling; stray, erratic, vagrant, undirected; circuitous, roundabout, crooked, sidelong, indirect, zigzag; crab-like.

Adv. ASTRAY FROM, round about, all manner of ways; circuitously &c. 629.

wide of the mark; to the right about; all manner of ways; circuitously &c. 629.
  OBLIQUELY, sideling, sidelong, like the knight's move [*chess*].
  ** "with Whom is no variableness, neither shadow of turning" [*Bible*].

280. [GOING BEFORE.] **Precession.** — **N.** PRECESSION, leading, heading; precedence &c. 62; priority &c. 116; the lead, *le pas* [*F.*]; van &c. (*front*) 234; precursor &c. 64.

V. PRECEDE, go before, go ahead, go in the van, go in advance; forerun, forego [*archaic*]; usher in, introduce, herald, head, take the lead; lead, lead the way, lead the dance; get –, have- the start; steal a march; get before, get ahead, get in front of; outstrip &c. 303; take precedence &c. (*first in order*) 62.

Adj. LEADING, precedent &c. *v.*; first, foremost.

Adv. IN ADVANCE, before, ahead, in the van; foremost, headmost; in front.

  ** *seniores priores.*

281. [GOING AFTER.] **Sequence.** — **N.** SEQUENCE; sequel; coming after &c. (*order*) 63, (*time*) 117; following; pursuit &c. 622; run [*cards*].

FOLLOWER, attendant, satellite, pursuer, shadow, dangler, train.

V. FOLLOW; pursue &c. 622; go after, fly after.

ATTEND, beset, dance attendance on, dog; tread in the steps of, tread close upon; be –, go –, follow- in the -wake, – trail, – rear- of; follow as a shadow, hang on the skirts of; tread –, follow- on the heels of; camp on the trail.

LAG, loiter, linger, get behind.

Adj. following &c. *v.*

Adv. BEHIND; in the rear &c. 235; in the train of, in the wake of; after &c. (*order*) 63, (*time*) 117.

282. [MOTION FORWARDS; PROGRESSIVE MOTION.] **Progression.** — N. PROGRESSION, progress, progressiveness; advancing &c. *v.*; advance, advancement; ongoing; flood tide, headway; march &c. 266; rise; improvement &c. 658.

V. ADVANCE; proceed, progress; get on, get along, get over the ground; gain ground; forge ahead; jog on, rub on, wag on [*obs.*], go with the stream; keep –, hold on– one's course; go –, move –, come –, get –, pass –, push –, press- -on, – forward, – forwards, – ahead; press onward *or* onwards, step forward; make –, work –, carve –, push –, force –, edge –, elbow- one's way; make -progress, – head, – way, – headway, – advances, – strides, – rapid strides &c. (*velocity*) 274; go ahead, shoot ahead; drive -on, – ahead; go full steam ahead; distance; make up leeway.

Adj. ADVANCING &c. *v.*; ongoing; progressive, profluent; advanced.

Adv. FORWARD, onward; forth, on, ahead, under way, *en route* for, on -one's way, – the way, – the road, – the high road- to; in progress, in mid-progress; *in transitu* [*L.*] &c. 270.

⁎ *vestigia nulla retrorsum;* "westward the course of empire takes its way" [Berkeley].

283. [MOTION BACKWARDS.] **Regression.** — N. REGRESSION, regress, retrocession, retrogression, retrogradation, retroaction; *reculade* [*F.*], retreat, withdrawal, retirement, remigration; recession &c. (*motion from*) 287; recess [*obs.*]; crab-like motion.

REFLUX, refluence, backwater, regurgitation, ebb, return; resilience, resiliency; reflexion (*recoil*) 277; *volte-face* [*F.*].

COUNTERMOTION, countermovement, countermarch; veering, tergiversation, recidivation [*obs. exc. in criminology*], backsliding, fall; deterioration &c. 659; recidivism *or* recidivity, relapse.

turning point &c. (*reversion*) 145; climax.

V. RECEDE, regrade, return, revert, retreat, remigrate, retire; retrograde, retrocede; back, back out [*colloq.*], back down [*colloq.*], balk; crawfish [*slang, U. S.*], crawl [*slang*]; withdraw; rebound &c. 277; go –, come –, turn –, hark –, draw –, fall –, break –, get –, put –, run- back; lose ground; fall astern, drop astern; backwater, put about [*naut.*], take the back track; veer, veer round; double, wheel, countermarch; ebb, regurgitate; jib, shrink, shy.

turn tail, turn round, turn upon one's heel, turn one's back upon; retrace one's steps, dance the back step; sound –, beat- a retreat; go home.

Adj. RECEDING &c. *v.*; retrograde, retrogressive; regressive, refluent, reflex, recidivous, resilient; crab-like; contraclockwise, counterclockwise; balky; reactionary &c. 277.

Adv. BACK, backwards; reflexively, to the right-about; *à reculons* [*F.*], *à rebours* [*F.*].

⁎ *revenons à nos moutons*, as you were.

---

284. [MOTION GIVEN TO AN OBJECT SITUATED IN FRONT.] **Propulsion.** — N. PROPULSION, projection; propelment; *vis a tergo* [*L.*], push &c. (*impulse*) 276; jaculation, ejaculation; ejection &c. 297; throw, fling, toss, shot, discharge, shy.

[SCIENCE OF PROPULSION] gunnery, ballistics, archery.

PROPELLER, screw, twin-screws, turbine.

MISSILE, projectile, ball, shot; spear, arrow; gun &c. (*arms*) 727; discus, quoit; brickbat.

285. [MOTION GIVEN TO AN OBJECT SITUATED BEHIND.] **Traction.** — N. TRACTION; drawing &c. *v.*; draft *or* draught, pull, haul; rake; "a long pull, a strong pull, and a pull all together"; towage, haulage.

V. DRAW, pull, haul, lug, rake, snake [*slang, U. S.*], trawl, draggle, drag, tug, tow, trail, train; take in tow.

WRENCH, jerk, twitch; yank [*U. S.*].

Adj. DRAWING &c. *v.*; tractile, tractive, tractional, ductile.

SHOOTER, shot; archer, toxophilite; bowman, rifleman, marksman, gun [*cant*], gunner, good shot, dead shot, crack shot; sharpshooter &c. (*combatant*) 726.

V. PROPEL, project, throw, fling, cast, pitch, chuck, toss, jerk, heave, shy, hurl; flirt, fillip.

dart, lance, tilt; ejaculate, jaculate [*rare*], fulminate, bolt, drive, sling, pitchfork.

SEND; send off, let off, fire off; discharge, shoot; launch, send forth, let fly; dash.

START; put –, set- in motion; set agoing, give a start to, give an impulse to; bundle, bundle off; impel &c. 276; trundle &c. (*set in rotation*) 312; expel &c. 297.

carry one off one's legs; put to flight.

Adj. propelled &c. *v.*; propelling &c. *v.*; propulsive, projectile, ballistic.

⁎ "When Ajax strives some rock's vast weight to throw" [Pope].

286. [MOTION TOWARDS.] **Approach.** — **N.** APPROACH, approximation, approximateness, appropinquation; access; appulse, appulsion; afflux, affluxion; advent &c. (*approach of time*) 121; pursuit &c. 622.

V. APPROACH, approximate [*archaic*], appropinquate [*rare*]; near; get –, go –, draw- near; come, – near, – to close quarters; move towards, set in towards; drift; make up to [*dial. or slang*]; gain upon; pursue &c. 622; tread on the heels of; bear up; make land; hug the shore, hug the land.

Adj. APPROACHING &c. *v.*; approximate, approximative; affluent; converging, connivent, convergent; impending, imminent &c. (*destined*) 152.

Adv. on the road.

Int. APPROACH! come hither! here! come! come near! forward!

288. [MOTION TOWARDS, ACTIVELY.] **Attraction.** — **N.** ATTRACTION, attractiveness; attractivity; pull, drawing to, pulling towards, attrahent, adduction, magnetism, gravity, attraction of gravitation.

LOADSTONE *or* lodestone, lodestar *or* loadstar, polestar, lode [*archaic*]; magnet, magnetite, siderite.

LURE, bait, charm, decoy.

V. ATTRACT, adduct; draw –, pull –, drag- towards; pull, draw, magnetize, bait, trap, decoy, charm; adduce.

Adj. ATTRACTING &c. *v.*; attrahent, attractive, adducent, adductive.

⁎ *ubi mel ibi apes* [Plautus]; "the cynosure of neighboring eyes" [Milton]; "and Beauty draws us by a single hair" [Pope].

290. [MOTION NEARER TO.] **Convergence.** — **N.** CONVERGENCE *or* convergency, confluence, concourse, conflux, congress, concurrence, concentration; appulse, meeting; corradiation [*rare*].

assemblage &c. 72; resort &c. (*focus*) 74; asymptote.

287. [MOTION FROM.] **Recession.** — **N.** RECESSION, retirement, withdrawal; retreat; regression, regress, retrogradation, retrocession &c. 283; departure, &c. 293; recoil &c. 277; flight &c. (*avoidance*) 623.

SWITCH, by-pass, shunt [*Brit.*].

V. RECEDE, go, move back, move from, retire, withdraw, retrograde, retrogress, regress, ebb; shrink; come –, move –, go –, get –, drift- away; depart &c. 293; retreat &c. 283; move off, stand off, sheer off, swerve from; fall back, stand aside; run away &c. (*avoid*) 623.

SWITCH, shunt [*Brit.*], sidetrack, turn, remove.

Adj. RECEDING &c. *v.*; recessive, retrogressive, regressive.

⁎ "remember Lot's wife" [*Bible*].

289. [MOTION FROM, ACTIVELY.] **Repulsion.** — **N.** REPULSION; driving from &c. *v.*; repulse, abduction, retrusion [*rare*].

V. REPEL; push from, drive from &c. 276; chase, dispel; retrude [*rare*]; abduce [*obs.*], abduct; send away; repulse; repercuss.

keep at arm's length, turn one's back upon, give the cold shoulder; send -off, – away- with a flea in one's ear [*colloq.*]; send about one's business; send packing.

Adj. REPELLENT, repulsive; repelling &c. *v.*; abducent, abductive, repercussive.

291. [MOTION FURTHER OFF.] **Divergence.** — **N.** DIVERGENCE *or* divergency, divarication, ramification, forking; radiation; separation &c. (*disjunction*) 44; dispersion &c. 73; deviation &c. 279; aberration, declination.

V. DIVERGE, divaricate, radiate; ram-

V. CONVERGE. concur; come together, unite, meet, fall in with; close with, close in upon; center *or* centre, center round, center in; enter in; pour in.

CONCENTRATE, bring into a focus; gather together, unite.

Adj. CONVERGING &c. *v.*; convergent, confluent, concurrent; centripetal; asymptotic *or* asymptotical; confluxible [*rare*].

ify; branch off, glance off, file off; fly off, fly off at a tangent; spread. scatter, disperse &c. 73; deviate &c. 279; part &c. (*separate*) 44.

Adj. DIVERGING &c. *v.*; divergent, divaricate, radiant, radial, centrifugal, aberrant; broadcast.

Adv. broadcast; *passim* [*L.*].

---

292. [TERMINAL MOTION AT.] **Arrival.**
— **N.** ARRIVAL, advent; landing; debarkation, disembarkation.

RECEPTION, welcome; *vin d'honneur* [*F.*].

DESTINATION, bourn *or* bourne, goal; landing -place,– stage; bunder *or* bandar [*Pers. & India*]; resting place; harbor, haven, port; terminus, terminal; halting -place, – ground; home, journey's end; anchorage &c. (*refuge*) 666; completion &c. 729.

RETURN, recursion [*obs.*], remigration, reëntry.

MEETING, joining, rencounter, encounter, rejoining.

V. ARRIVE; get to, come to; come; reach, attain; come up, – with, – to; overtake; make, fetch; come from, hail from; complete &c. 729; join, rejoin.

visit, pitch one's tent; sit down &c. (*be located*) 184; get to one's journey's end; be in at the death; come –, get- -back, – home; return; come in &c. (*ingress*) 294; make one's appearance &c. (*appear*) 446; drop in; detrain; outspan, offsaddle [*both S. Africa*].

LIGHT, alight, dismount.

LAND, make land, cast anchor, put in, put into; go ashore, debark, disbark [*rare*], disembark

MEET; encounter, rencounter [*rare*], come in contact; come to hand; come at, come across; hit; come –, light –, pop [*colloq.*] –, bounce [*colloq.*] –, plump [*colloq.*] –, burst –, pitch- upon.

Adj. ARRIVING &c. *v.*; homeward bound, terminal.

Adv. HERE, hither.

Int. WELCOME! hail! all hail! good-day! good-morrow! come in and rest your bonnet on a chair! [*Southern U. S.*], *bienvenu!* [*F.*].

⁎⁎ "Journeys end in lovers meeting, Every wise man's son doth know" [*Twelfth Night*].

293. [INITIAL MOTION FROM.] **Departure.** — **N.** DEPARTURE, decession [*rare*], decampment; embarkation; outset, start, headway, inspan [*S. Africa*], debouchment, debouch *or* débouché [*F.*]; removal; exit &c. (*egress*) 295; *congé* [*F.*], exodus, hegira, flight.

LEAVE-TAKING, valediction, adieu, farewell, good-by *or* good-bye, Godspeed, stirrup cup; valedictorian.

STARTING POINT, starting post; point –, place- of -departure, – embarkation; port of embarkation.

V. DEPART; go, go away, part [*urchaic*], take one's departure, set out; set –, march –, put –, start –, be –, move –, get –, whip –, pack –, go –, take oneself-off; start, boun [*archaic*], issue, march out, debouch; go forth, sally forth; sally, set forward; be gone.

leave a place, quit, vacate, evacuate, abandon; go off the stage, make one's exit; retire, withdraw, remove; "use your legs" [*Merchant of Venice*]; vamose *or* vamoose [*slang, U. S.*], mizzle [*slang*], skip [*slang*], cut [*colloq. or slang*], go one's way, go along, go from home; take flight, take wing; spring, fly, flit, wing one's flight; fly away, whip away; strike tents, decamp; break camp, break away, break ground [*naut.*] walk one's chalks [*slang*], cut one's stick *or* cut stick [*slang*], cut and run [*colloq.*]; take leave; say –, bid- good-by &c. *n.*; disappear &c. 449; abscond &c. (*avoid*) 623; entrain; saddle, bridle, harness up, hitch up [*colloq.*], inspan [*S. Africa*]; "speed the parting guest" [*Pope*].

EMBARK; go on board, go aboard; set sail; put to sea, go to sea; sail, take ship; hoist the blue Peter; get under way, weigh anchor.

Adj. DEPARTING &c. *v.*; valedictory, outward bound.

Adv. HENCE, whence, thence; with a foot in the stirrup; on the wing, on the move.

Int. BEGONE! &c. (*ejection*) 297; cut! cut away! cut off! [*all colloq.*], away! to horse! boot! saddle! all aboard! busk and boun ye! [*archaic*].

FAREWELL! adieu! good-by *or* goodbye! good-day! *au revoir!* [*F.*], *vale!* [*L.*], fare you well! God bless you! Godspeed! *auf Wiedersehen!* [*G.*], *au plaisir de vous revoir!* [*F.*], *bon voyage!* [*F.*], *glückliche Reise!* [*G.*], *vive valeque!* [*L.*], bye-bye! [*colloq.*], be good! [*slang*], so long! [*slang*], come again!

*** "See the shaking funnels roar, With the Peter at the fore" [Kipling]; "Boot! saddle! to horse and away!" [Browning].

---

294. [MOTION INTO.] Ingress. — N. INGRESS; entrance, entry; introgression, ingressiveness, influx, intrusion, inroad, incursion, invasion, irruption; ingression; penetration, interpenetration; illapse [*rare*], infiltration; insinuation &c. (*interjacence*) 228; insertion &c. 300.

IMMIGRATION, incoming, foreign influx; admission &c. (*reception*) 296.

IMPORT, importation; imports.

IMMIGRANT, visitor, incomer, newcomer, comeling [*archaic*], colonist, Buttinsky [*humorous*].

INLET; way in; mouth, door, &c. (*opening*) 260; barway; path &c. (*way*) 627; conduit &c. 350.

V. ENTER; go –, come –, pour –, flow –, creep –, slip –, pop –, break –, burst- -into, – in; have the entrée; set foot on; ingress [*obs.*]; burst –, break- in upon; invade, insinuate itself; interpenetrate, penetrate; infiltrate; find one's way –, wriggle –, worm oneself- into; intrude, butt in [*slang*] horn in [*slang, U. S.*].

give entrance to &c. (*receive*) 296, insert &c. 300

Adj. INCOMING, inbound, ingressive, inward, entrant [*rare*]; entering &c. *v.*

295. [MOTION OUT OF.] Egress. — N. EGRESS, exit, issue; emersion, emergence; outbreak, outburst, proruption [*rare*], eruption; emanation; egression; evacuation. disemboguement, exudation, transudation; extravasation, perspiration, sweating, leakage, percolation, lixiviation, leaching, distillation, seep, oozing; gush &c. (*water in motion*) 348; outpour, outpouring; effluence, effusion; efflux, effluxion; drain; dribbling &c. *v.*; defluxion; drainage; outcome, output; outflow, discharge &c. (*excretion*) 299.

EXPORT, exportation; exports, shipments.

EMIGRATION, exodus &c. (*departure*) 293; expatriation, remigration.

EMIGRANT, migrant, redemptioner [*U. S.*], colonist, *émigré* [*F.*].

OUTLET, vent, spout, tap, sluice, floodgate; vomitory, outgate, sallyport; debouch [*mil.*], *débouché* [*F.*]; way out; mouth, door &c. (*opening*) 260; path &c. (*way*) 627; conduit &c. 350; airpipe &c. 351; pore, emunctory.

V. EMERGE, emanate, issue; egress; go –, come –, move –, pass –, pour –, flow- out of; pass off, evacuate.

EXUDE, transude; leak; run, – out, – through; lixiviate, leach, percolate, transcolate [*obs.*]; egurgitate [*rare*]; strain; distill; perspire, sweat, drain, seep, ooze; filter, infiltrate, filtrate; dribble, gush, spout, flow out; well, – out; pour, trickle, &c. (*water in motion*) 348; effuse, extravasate, disembogue, discharge itself, debouch; come –, break forth; burst -out, – through; find vent; escape &c. 671.

Adj. EMERGENT, emerging, erumpent, eruptive, emanant, emanational, emanative, exudative, porous, pervious, leaky, sweaty, transudatory; effused &c. *v.*; outgoing, outbound, outward-bound.

PERCOLATIVE, oozing, gushing, transuding &c. *v.*; effluent, emunctory, effusive, excretory.

*** "Like a child from the womb, like a ghost from the tomb, I arise" [Shelley].

---

296. [MOTION INTO, ACTIVELY.] Reception. — N. RECEPTION; admission, admittance, entrée, importation; initiation, introduction, intromission; immission, ingestion, imbibition, introception,

297. [MOTION OUT OF, ACTIVELY.] Ejection. — N. EJECTION, emission, effusion, rejection, expulsion, eviction, extrusion, detrusion, trajection; discharge.

EGESTION, evacuation, vomition;

absorption, resorbence, engorgement, ingurgitation, inhalation; suction, sucking; eating, drinking &c. (*food*) 298; insertion &c. 300; interjection &c. 228; introit.

V. GIVE ENTRANCE TO, give admittance to, give the entrée; introduce, usher, admit, initiate, intromit [*rare*], receive, import, bring in, immit [*rare*], open the door, throw open, ingest, absorb, imbibe, instill, implant, infiltrate, induct, inhale; let in, take in, suck in; readmit, resorb, reabsorb; snuff up.

SWALLOW, ingurgitate; engulf, engorge; gulp; eat, drink &c. (*food*) 298.

Adj. INTRODUCTORY, introductive, initiatory, initiary [*rare*], preliminary, ingestive; imbibitory, introceptive, intromittent, intromissive; admissible; absorbent, resorbent; admitting &c. *v.*, admitted &c. *v.*

emesis, eruption, eruptiveness, eruptivity, voidance, disgorgement; ructation, eructation; bloodletting, venesection, phlebotomy, extravasation, paracentesis; expuition [*rare*], exspuition [*rare*]; tapping, drainage; emetic; vomiting; excretion &c. 299; clearance, clearage.

DISLODGMENT; deportation; banishment &c. (*punishment*) 972; rogue's march; relegation; extradition.

EJECTOR, bouncer [*slang*, *U. S.*], chucker-out [*slang*].

V. EJECT, reject; expel, discard; cut [*colloq.*], ostracize, send to Coventry, boycott; *chasser* [*F.*], banish &c. (*punish*) 972; bounce [*slang*, *U. S.*]; fire [*slang*], – out [*slang*]; throw &c. (284) -out, – up, – off, – away, – aside; push &c. (276) -out, – off, – away, – aside; shovel –, sweep- -out, – away; brush –, whisk –, turn –, send- -off, – away; discharge; bundle out; throw overboard; give the one's business, send to the right-about; turn out -neck and heels [*colloq.*], – head and shoulders, – neck and crop [*colloq.*]; pack off; send away with a flea in the ear [*colloq.*]; send to Jericho [*colloq.*]; bow out, show the door to.

send –, turn –, cast- adrift; turn out, sack to [*slang*]; send packing, send about strike off the roll &c. (*abrogate*) 756;

EVICT, oust, dislodge; turn out of -doors, – house and home; unhouse, unkennel; unpeople, dispeople; depopulate; relegate, deport.

LET OUT, give out, pour out, send out; dispatch *or* despatch, exhale, excern [*obs.*], excrete; embogue [*obs.*], disembogue; extravasate, shed, void, egest, evacuate; emit; open the -sluices, – floodgates; turn on the tap; give exit to, give vent to; extrude, detrude; effuse, spend, expend; pour forth; squirt, spurt *or* spirt, spill, slop; perspire &c. (*exude*) 295; breathe, blow &c. (*wind*) 349.

TAP, draw off; bale out, lade᾽ out; let blood, broach.

EMPTY; drain, – to the dregs; sweep off; clear, – off, – out, – away; suck, draw off; clean out, make a clean sweep of, clear decks, purge.

DISEMBOWEL, embowel [*rare*], disbowel [*rare*], eviscerate, gut.

ROOT OUT, root up, unearth; eradicate, averruncate [*obs.*]; weed out, get out; eliminate, get rid of, do away with, shake off; exenterate [*rare*].

VOMIT, spew, puke [*obs. or vulgar*], keck, retch; cast up, bring up; disgorge.

SALIVATE, ptyalize, expectorate, clear the throat, hawk, spit, sputter, splutter, slobber, drivel, slaver, slabber, drool.

BELCH, eruct, eructate.

UNPACK, unlade, unload, unship; break bulk; dump [*chiefly U. S.*].

EMERGE, ooze &c. 295; be let out.

Adj. EJECTIVE, emissive, extrusive; egestive; salivant; vomitive, vomitory; emitting, emitted &c. *v.*

Int. BEGONE! get you gone! get –, go- -away, – along, – along with you! go your way! away, – with! off with you! go! go about your business! be off ! avaunt! aroint *or* aroynt! [*archaic*], *allez-vous-en!* [*F.*], jao! [*Hind.*], *va-t'en!* [*F.*], scoot! [*colloq.*], shoo! "get thee behind me, Satan!" [*Bible*].

298. [Eating.] **Food.** — **N.** EATING &c. *v.*; deglutition, gulp, epulation [*rare*], mastication, manducation [*rare*], rumination; gastronomy, gastrology, pantophagy, hippophagy, carnivorism, carnivorousness, herbivority [*rare*], vegetarianism, ichthyophagy; gluttony &c. 957.

carnivore; herbivore, vegetarian.

MOUTH, jaws, gob [*slang*], mandible, mazard, chaps, chops.

DRINKING &c. *v.*; potation, draft *or* draught, libation; compotation, symposium; carousal &c. (*amusement*) 840; drunkenness &c. 959.

FOOD, pabulum; aliment, nourishment, nutriment; sustenance, sustentation; nurture, subsistence, provender, corn, feed, fodder, provision, ration, keep, commons, board; commissariat &c. (*provisions*) 637; prey, forage, pasture, pasturage; fare, cheer; diet, dietary; regimen; belly timber [*facetious, dial.*], staff of life; bread, – and cheese; liquid diet, spoon victuals.

EATABLES, comestibles, victuals, edibles, ingesta; grub [*slang*], prog, [*slang*], meat; bread, breadstuffs; cereals, viands, cates [*obs.*], delicacy, dainty, creature comforts, creature, contents of the larder, fleshpots; festal board; ambrosia; good cheer, good living.

[BREADSTUFFS AND DESSERTS] biscuit, cracker [*chiefly U. S.*], bun, cooky *or* cookie [*U. S.*], doughnut, cruller, hard-tack, pilot bread, sea biscuit, pilot biscuit, ship biscuit, hoecake [*U. S.*], ashcake, corncake, corndodgers [*U. S.*], corndabs [*U. S.*], shortbread, scone, rusk, matzo [*Jewish*], chupatty [*India*], damper [*Australia*], flapjack [*U. S. or dial.*], waffle, pancake, griddlecake, pastry, *pâtisserie* [*F.*], pie, *pâté* [*F.*], pasty, patty, turnover, *vol-au-vent* [*F.*], apple dumpling, apple slump, apple dowdy [*U. S.*], pandowdy [*U. S.*], mince pie, pudding, supawn [*U. S.*], apple pie, blueberry pie, custard pie, lemon pie, pumpkin pie, squash pie, charlotte russe, plum pudding, tart, compote, apple fritters, *beignets de pommes* [*F.*], banana fritters, macaroon, meringue, marchpane *or* marzipan, *massepain* [*F.*], whipped cream, *crème fouettée* [*F.*], cake, *gâteau* [*F.*], stewed prunes, *pruneaux* [*F.*], stewed apples, *compote de pommes* [*F.*], blancmange, cornstarch [*U. S.*], jam, *confiture* [*F.*], Bar-le-Duc, red currant jelly, *gelée de groseilles* [*F.*], ice cream, *crème glacée* [*F.*], college ice, sundae [*U. S.*]; vanilla –, strawberry –, chocolate –, coffee –, Neapolitan –, country club-ice cream; banana royal, water ice, sherbet [*U. S.*]; sweets &c. 396; see FRUIT.

[CEREALS] hominy [*U. S.*], oatmeal, mush, hasty pudding, porridge, gruel, crowdie *or* crowdy [*Scot. & dial. Eng.*], atole [*Mex. Sp.*], samp [*U. S.*], hulled corn, frumenty.

[SOUPS] *potage* [*F.*], pottage, broth, *bouillon* [*F.*], gravy soup, *consommé* [*F.*], thick soup, *purée* [*F.*], bisque, mulligatawny, turtle soup, mock-turtle soup, oyster stew, oyster chowder, clam chowder, fish chowder, *julienne* [*F.*], *potage à la julienne* [*F.*], vermicelli soup, *potage au vermicelle* [*F.*], chowder, spoon-meat, trepang, ox-tail soup, gumbo, okra soup, stock, *bouillabaisse* [*F.*].

[FISH] *poisson* [*F.*], salmon, *saumon* [*F.*], sole, fried sole, *sole frite* [*F.*], shad, plaice, bluefish, whiting, *merlan* [*F.*], trout, *truite* [*F.*], mackerel, *maquereau* [*F.*], herring, *hareng* [*F.*], bloater, kipper, kippered herring, cod, *morue* [*F.*], sturgeon ("Albany beef"), sardines, haddock, *aiglefin* [*F.*], finnan haddie *or* haddock, scrod [*U. S.*], sturgeon roe, caviar *or* caviare, shad roe, tarpon, tuna, lobster, *homard* [*F.*], lobster à la King, lobster Newburg, periwinkles, prawns, shrimps, crevettes [*F.*], oysters, *huitres* [*F.*], oyster stew, blue points, sea slug, *bêche de mer* [*F.*], clams, eel, *anguille* [*F.*], crab, crab meat, soft-shell crab, crawfish *or* crayfish, *écrevisse* [*F.*].

[MEATS] *rôti* [*F.*], joint, *pièce de résistance* [*F.*], *relevé* [*F.*], hash, *réchauffé* [*F.*], stew, ragout, fricassee, mince, chow mein, chop suey [*U. S.*], salmis, fatling, barbecue, kickshaws, mincemeat, forcemeat, meat balls, croquettes, goulash *or* Hungarian goulash; condiment &c. 393; haggis [*Scot.*], bubble and squeak, pilau *or* pilaw [*India*], curry, aspic jelly; turtle, terrapin, diamond-back terrapin.

BEEF, *bœuf* [*F.*], porterhouse steak, boiled beef, bouilli, beef à la mode, beefsteak, roast beef, *rosbif* [*F.*], *bifteck* [*F.*], sirloin, rump, chuck.

VEAL, *veau* [*F.*], fricandeau, calf's head, *tête de veau* [*F.*], tongue, *langue* [*F.*], fried brains, *cervelle frite* [*F.*], sweetbread, *ris de veau* [*F.*], calf's liver, *foie de veau* [*F.*].

MUTTON, *mouton* [*F.*], mutton chop, *côtelette de mouton* [*F.*], plain chop, *côtelette au naturel* [*F.*], *côtelette à la maître d'hôtel* [*F.*], *côtellette à la jardinière* [*F.*], broiled kidneys, *rognons à la brochette* [*F.*], lamb, *agneau* [*F.*], saddle, *selle* [*F.*].

PORK, *porc* [*F.*], pork chop, *côtelette de porc frais* [*F.*], sausage, *saucisson* [*F.*], Frankforter, hot dog [*slang, U. S.*], bacon, ham, *jambon* [*F.*], sucking pig, *cochon de lait* [*F.*], pig's knuckles, pig's feet, trotters, *pieds de cochon* [*F.*], crackling.

POULTRY, *volaille* [*F.*], capon, *chapon* [*F.*], poularde [*F.*], pigeon, fowl, broiler, chicken, *poulet* [*F.*], duck, *canard* [*F.*], muscovy duck, roast duck, *canard rôti* [*F.*], goose, *oie* [*F.*], turkey, *dinde* (*masc. dindon*) [*F.*], wing, *aile* [*F.*], leg, *cuisse* [*F.*], breast, *filet (of a goose)* [*F.*], *blanc (of a fowl)* [*F.*], drumstick.

GAME, venison, *chevreuil* [*F.*], hare, *lièvre* [*F.*], jugged hare, *civet* [*F.*], rabbit, *lapin* [*F.*], pheasant, *faisan* [*F.*], partridge, *perdrix* [*F.*], snipe, *bécasse* [*F.*], quail, *caille* [*F.*], wild duck, *canard sauvage* [*F.*], canvasback, teal, *sarcelle* [*F.*], grouse, ricebird [*Southern U. S.*], pigeon, squab.

[EGGS] *œufs* [*F.*], boiled eggs, *œufs à la coque* [*F.*], fried eggs, *œufs sur le plat* [*F.*], poached eggs, *œufs pochés* [*F.*], scrambled eggs, *œufs brouillés* [*F.*], new-laid eggs, *œufs frais* [*F.*], buttered eggs, dropped eggs, shirred eggs, stuffed eggs, omelet, *omelette* [*F.*], *soufflé* or *soufflée* [*F.*].

[CHEESE DISHES] cheese, *fromage* [*F.*], cheesecake, *talmouse* [*F.*], cheese-mold, *moule à fromage* [*F.*], Welsh rabbit *or* Welsh rarebit [*an erroneous form*], *rôtie au fromage* [*F.*], golden buck, cheese straws, cheese fondue; cream –, cottage –, Neuchatel –, Swiss (*Schweizerkäse* or *Schweizerkäse* or *Schweitzer*) –, Gruyère –, Emmenthaler –, Dutch –, Edam –, Roquefort –, Brie –, Limburg *or* Limburger –, Wensleydale- cheese.

[VEGETABLES] *légumes* [*F.*], greens, asparagus, *asperge* [*F.*], green peas, *petits pois* [*F.*], artichoke, *artichaut* [*F.*], cabbage, *chou* [*F.*], coleslaw, Brussels sprouts, *choux de Bruxelles* [*F.*], cauliflower, *chou-fleur* (*pl. choux-fleurs*) [*F.*], lettuce, *laitue* [*F.*], romaine, cos lettuce, *laitue romaine* [*F.*], lima beans, string beans, French beans, *haricots verts* [*F.*], kidney beans, *haricots blancs* [*F.*], baked beans, potatoes, *pommes de terre* [*F.*], yams, sweet potatoes, *patates* [*F.*], spinach, *épinards* [*F.*], endive, *chicorée* [*F.*], pumpkin, squash, sauerkraut, *choucroute* [*F.*], eggplant, oyster plant, salsify, *salsifis* [*F.*], tomato, *tomate* [*F.*], celery, *céleri* [*F.*], cress, *cresson* [*F.*], water cress, *cresson de fontaine* [*F.*], beets, beetroot [*Brit.*], *betterave* [*F.*], parsnips, *panais* [*F.*], turnip, *navet* [*F.*], radish, *radis* or *rave* [*F.*], horse radish, *raifort* [*F.*], onion, *oignon* [*F.*], scallion, shalot, *échalote* [*F.*], cucumber, *concombre* [*F.*], mushrooms, *champignons* [*F.*], rhubarb, truffles, succotash [*U. S.*].

[FRUIT] figs, *figues* [*F.*], raisins, nuts, *noisettes* [*F.*], almonds: *les quatres mendiants* [*F.*]; apple, *pomme* [*F.*], pear, *poire* [*F.*], alligator pear, avocado, apricot, *abricot* [*F.*], peach, *pêche* [*F.*], plantain, banana, breadfruit, grapefruit, mango, mangosteen, grapes, pineapple, *ananas* [*F.*], walnuts, *noix* [*F.*], orange, lemon, lime, cherries, *cerises* [*F.*], watermelon, currants, cranberry, loganberry, blueberry, blackberry, gooseberry, whortleberry, huckleberry, raspberry, strawberry.

TABLE, *cuisine*, bill of fare, menu, *table d'hôte* [*F.*], ordinary, *à la carte* [*F.*], cover, *couvert* [*F.*]; American plan, European plan.

MEAL, repast, feed [*archaic or colloq.*], spread [*colloq.*]; mess; dish, plate, course; side dish, *hors-d'œuvre* [*F.*], entrée, *entremets* [*F.*], remove, dessert [*in U. S., often includes pastry or pudding*]; regale; regalement, refreshment, entertainment; refection, collation, picnic, feast, banquet, junket; breakfast; lunch, luncheon; *déjeuner* [*F.*], *déjeuner à la fourchette* [*F.*]; bever [*dial.*], tiffin, dinner, supper, snack [*colloq.*], whet, bait [*dial.*]; potluck: hearty –, square –, substantial –, full- meal; blowout [*slang*]; light refreshment; *chota hazri, bara hazri, bara khana* [*all Hind.*].

MOUTHFUL, bolus, gobbet [*archaic*], tidbit, kickshaw, morsel, sop, sippet.

DRINK, beverage, liquor, broth, soup; potion, dram, draft *or* draught, drench, swill [*slang*]; nip, sip, sup, gulp.

[BEVERAGES] wine, spirits, liqueur, beer, ale, malt liquor, (Sir) John Barleycorn, stingo [*old slang*], heavy wet [*slang, Eng.*]; grog, toddy, flip, purl, punch, negus, cup, bishop, wassail; hooch [*slang, U. S.*], whisky *or* whiskey, the creature [*humorous*]; gin &c. (*intoxicating liquor*) 959; coffee, chocolate, cocoa, tea, "the cup that cheers but not inebriates"; bock –, lager –, Pilsener –, schenk –, near- beer; Brazil tea, cider, claret, ice water, maté, mint julep [*U. S.*].

RESTAURANT, eating house &c. 189.

V. EAT, feed, fare, devour, swallow, take; gulp, bolt, snap; fall to; dispatch *or* despatch, discuss [*colloq.*]; take –, get –, gulp- down; lay in, lick, pick, peck; tuck in [*slang*], gormandize &c. 957; bite, champ, munch, craunch *or* cranch, crunch, chew, masticate, nibble, gnaw, mumble.

live on; feed –, batten –, fatten –, feast- upon; browse, graze, crop, regale; carouse &c. (*make merry*) 840; lick one's chops [*colloq.*], make one's mouth water; eat heartily, do justice to, play a good knife and fork [*dial. Eng.*], banquet.

break bread, break one's fast; breakfast, lunch, dine, take tea, sup.

DRINK, – in, – up, – one's fill; quaff, sip, sup; suck, – up; lap; swig [*dial. or colloq.*], swill [*slang*], tipple &c. (*be drunken*) 959; empty one's glass, drain the cup; toss off, toss one's glass; wash down, crack a bottle [*colloq.*], wet one's whistle [*colloq.*].

CATER, purvey &c. 637.

Adj. EATABLE, edible, esculent, comestible, gustable, alimentary; cereal, cibarious [*rare*]; dietetic; culinary; nutritive, nutritious; gastric; succulent.

underdone, rare, *saignant* [*F.*]; well-done, *bien cuit* [*F.*]; overdone; with gravy, *au jus* [*F.*]; high [*of game*]; ripe [*of cheese*].

DRINKABLE, potable, potulent [obs.]; bibulous.

omnivorous, carnivorous, herbivorous, granivorous, graminivorous, phytivorous, phytophagous, ichthyophagous; omophagic, omophagous; pantophagous, xylophagous.

. "But hark! the chiming clocks to dinner call" [Pope]; "across the walnuts and the wine" [Tennyson]; "blesséd hour of our dinner!" [O. Meredith]; "now good digestion wait on appetite, and health on both!" [Macbeth]; "who can cloy the hungry edge of appetite?" [Richard II]; "sit down and feed and welcome to our table" [As You Like It]; "bachelor's fare: bread and cheese and kisses" [Swift]; "my dinner was noble and enough" [Pepys]; "we have met the enemy and they are ours" [Perry]; "the cry is still 'They come!'" [Macbeth]; "the stag at eve had drunk his fill" [Scott]; "my grief lies onward and my joy behind" [Shakespeare, Sonnets].

299. Excretion. — N. EXCRETION, discharge, emanation, ejection; exhalation, exudation, extrusion, secretion, effusion, extravasation, ecchymosis, evacuation, dejection, feces or fæces, defecation, cacation, excrement; bloody flux; cœliac (or celiac) flux; dysentery; perspiration, sweat; subation [obs.], exudation; diaphoresis; sewage; eccrinology.

hemorrhage, bleeding; outpouring &c. (egress) 295; menses, menstrual discharge, menstrual flow, catamenial discharge; leucorrhea or leucorrhœa, the whites.

EJECTA (pl.), saliva, spittle, sputum (pl. sputa); spit, rheum; ptyalism, salivation, catarrh; diarrhea or diarrhœa; egesta (pl.), excreta; lava; exuviæ &c. (uncleanness) 653

V. EXCRETE &c. (eject) 297; secrete, secern; emanate &c. (come out) 295.

Adj. EXCRETORY, fecal or fæcal, feculent, secretory.

EJECTIVE, eliminative, eliminant.

300. [FORCIBLE INGRESS.] Insertion. — N. INSERTION, infixion, implantation, introduction; embolism, interpolation, intercalation, interlineation, insinuation &c. (intervention) 228; planting &c. v.; injection, inoculation, importation, infusion; forcible ingress &c. 294; immersion; submersion, submergence, dip, plunge; bath &c. (water) 337; interment &c. 363.

ENEMA, clyster, glyster, lavage, lavement.

V. INSERT, introduce, intromit, put into, run into; import; inject; imbed, inlay, inweave; interject &c. 228; infuse, instill or instil, inoculate, impregnate, imbue, imbrue.

insert &c. itself; plunge in medias res [L.].

GRAFT, ingraft, engraft, bud, plant, implant; dovetail.

OBTRUDE; thrust in, stick in, ram in, stuff in, tuck in, press in, drive in, pop in, whip in, drop in, put in: impact; pierce &c. (make a hole) 260.

IMMERSE, immerge, merge; bathe, soak &c. (water) 337; dip, plunge &c. 310.
BURY &c. (inter) 363.
Adj. INSERTED &c. v.

301. [FORCIBLE EGRESS.] Extraction. — N. EXTRACTION; extracting &c. v.; removal, elimination, extrication, eradication, evulsion, extirpation, extermination; ejection &c. 297; export &c. (egress) 295; avulsion, wrench, forcible separation.

EXPRESSION, squeezing; distillation.

EXTRACTOR, corkscrew, forceps, pliers.

V. EXTRACT, draw; take out, draw out, pull out, tear out, pluck out, pick out, get out; wring from, wrench; extort; root -, weed -, grub -, rake- -up, - out; eradicate; pull -, pluck- up by the roots; averruncate [obs.]; unroot; uproot, pull up, extirpate, dredge.

EDUCE, elicit, evolve, bring forth, draw forth; extricate.

ELIMINATE &c. (eject) 297; eviscerate &c. 297; remove.

EXPRESS, squeeze out, press out, distill or distil.

Adj. EXTRACTED &c. v.

302. [MOTION THROUGH.] **Passage.** — **N.** PASSAGE, transmission; permeation; penetration, interpenetration; transudation, infiltration; exosmosis *or* exosmose; osmosis *or* osmose, endosmosis, endosmose; intercurrence; ingress &c. 294; egress &c. 295; path &c. 627; conduit &c. 350; opening &c. 260; journey &c. 266; voyage &c. 267.

V. PASS, pass through; perforate &c. (*hole*) 260; penetrate, permeate, thread, thrid [*archaic or dial.*], enfilade; go through, go across; go over, pass over; cut across; ford, cross; pass and repass, work; make –, thread –, worm –, force- one's way; make –, force- a passage; cut one's way through; find its -way, – vent; transmit, make way, clear the course; traverse, go over the ground.

Adj. PASSING &c. *v.*; intercurrent; endosmosmic, endosmotic, exosmotic *or* exosmic, osmotic.

Adv. *en passant* [*F.*] &c. (*transit*) 270.

303. [MOTION BEYOND.] **Overrun.** — **N.** OVERRUN, transcursion [*obs.*], transilience *or* transiliency [*rare*], transgression; trespass; inroad, advancement, intrusion, infraction, encroachment, infringement; extravagation [*obs.*], transcendence; redundance &c. 641.

V. SURPASS, transgress, pass; go beyond, go by; show in front, come to the front; shoot ahead of; steal a march upon, gain upon.

OVERSTEP, overpass, overreach, overgo, override, overleap, overjump, overskip, overlap, overshoot the mark; outstrip, outleap, outjump, outgo, outstep, outrun, outride, outrival, outdo; beat, beat hollow [*colloq.*]; distance; leave in the -lurch, – rear; throw into the shade; exceed, transcend, surmount; soar &c. (*rise*) 305.

encroach, trespass, infringe, intrude, invade, accroach [*rare*], advance upon, trench upon, intrench on; strain; stretch –, strain- a point; pass the Rubicon.

Adj. SURPASSING &c. *v.*

Adv. AHEAD, beyond the mark.

304. [MOTION SHORT OF.] **Shortcoming.** — **N.** SHORTCOMING, failure; falling short &c. *v.*; default, defalcation, delinquency; leeway; labor in vain, no go [*colloq.*]; fizzle [*colloq.*], dud [*slang*], slump [*colloq.*]; flash in the pan.

INCOMPLETENESS &c. 53; imperfection &c. 651; insufficiency &c. 640; noncompletion &c. 730; failure &c. 732.

V. FALL SHORT, – of; come short. – of; stop short, – of; not reach; want; keep within -bounds, –the mark, – compass.

COLLAPSE, fail, break down, stick in the mud, flat out [*U. S.*], come to nothing; fall down, slump, fizzle out [*all colloq.*]; fall through, fall to the ground; cave in [*colloq.*], end in smoke, miss the mark; lose ground; miss stays [*naut.*]; miss one's moorings.

Adj. UNREACHED; deficient; short, short of; minus; out of depth; perfunctory &c. (*neglect*) 460.

Adv. WITHIN THE MARK, within compass, within bounds; behindhand; *re infectâ* [*L.*]; to no purpose; far from it.

** the bubble burst; "Oh, the little more, and how much it is! And the little less, and what worlds away!" [Browning].

305. [MOTION UPWARDS.] **Ascent.** — **N.** ASCENT, ascension; rising &c. *v.*; rise, upgrowth, upward flight, upgrade; leap &c. 309; grade [*U. S.*], gradient [*Eng.*], ramp, acclivity, hill &c. 217.

STAIRWAY, staircase, stair [*esp. in Scot.*], stairs; flight of -steps, – stairs; ladder, scaling ladder; Jacob's ladder, companionway, companion, companion ladder [*all naut.*]; escalator, elevator &c. 307.

[COMPARISONS] rocket, skyrocket, lark, skylark; Alpine Club.

V. ASCEND, rise, mount, arise, uprise; go up, get up, work one's way up, start

306. [MOTION DOWNWARDS.] **Descent.** — **N.** DESCENT, descension [*rare*], inclination, declension, declination; decurrence [*rare*], downcome, comedown, downcast, setback, fall; falling &c. *v.*; slump [*colloq.*], drop, cadence; subsidence, lapse; downfall, tumble, slip, tilt, trip, lurch; *culbute* [*F.*], titubation, stumble; fate of -Icarus, – Phaëthon, – Lucifer.

AVALANCHE, debacle, *débâcle* [*F.*], landslip [*Eng.*], landslide [*U. S.*], slide, snowslip, snowslide, glissade.

DECLIVITY, dip, decline, pitch, drop, down-grade.

up, spring up, shoot up; aspire, aim high.
plane, swim, float.

CLIMB, shin [colloq.], swarm [colloq.],
clamber, ramp [rare], scramble, escalade,
surmount; wind upward; scale, - the
heights.

TOWER, soar, hover, spire, go-, fly-
aloft; surge; leap &c. 309.

Adj. RISING &c. v.; upcast; scandent,
buoyant; supernatant, superfluitant·
excelsior.

Adv. UP, upward or upwards, skyward. heavenward, toward the empyrean; upturned; uphill.

. "Hark! hark! the lark at heaven's gate
sings" [Shakespeare]; "they climbed the steep
ascent of heaven" [Heber]; "Higher still and
higher, From the earth thou springest"
[Shelley].

ELEVATOR &c. 307.
STAIRWAY &c. 305.

V. DESCEND; go -, drop -, comedown; fall, gravitate. drop, slip, slide,
settle; decline, set, sink, droop, come
down a peg [colloq.], slump [colloq.].

GET DOWN, dismount, alight, light;
swoop, souse; stoop &c. 308; fall prostrate, precipitate oneself; let fall &c.
308.

TUMBLE, trip, stumble, titubate [rare],
lurch, pitch, swag, topple; topple -,
tumble- -down, - over; tilt, sprawl,
plump, plump down; come -, fall -,
get- a cropper [colloq. or slang].

Adj. STEEP, sloping, declivitous, declivous; beetling &c. (high) 206; bottomless &c. (deep) 208.

DESCENDING &c. v.; down, downcast;
descendent; decurrent, decursive; labent [rare], deciduous; nodding to its
fall.

Adv. DOWNWARD or downwards, downhill.

. "from morn To noon he fell, from noon to dewy eve" [Milton].

---

307. Elevation. — N. ELEVATION;
raising &c. v.; erection, lift; sublevation,
upheaval; sublimation, exaltation;
prominence &c. (convexity) 250.

LEVER &c. 633; crane, derrick, wind-
lass, capstan, winch; dredge, dredger,
dredging machine.

ELEVATOR, ascenseur [F.], lift [chiefly
Eng.], dumb-waiter, escalator.

V. ELEVATE, raise, heighten, lift,
erect; set up, stick up, perch up, perk
up, tilt up; rear, hoist, heave; uplift,
upraise, uprear, upbear, upcast, uphoist, upheave; buoy, weigh, mount,
give a lift; exalt; sublimate; place -,
set- on a pedestal.

take up, drag up, fish up; dredge.

STAND UP, rise up, get up, jump up;
spring to one's feet; hold oneself up,
hold one's head up; draw oneself up to
his full height.

Adj. ELEVATED &c. v.; upturned,
retroussé [F.]; stilted, attollent, rampant.

Adv. on stilts, on the shoulders of, on
one's legs, on one's hind legs [colloq.].

. "He raised a mortal to the skies, She
drew an angel down" [Dryden].

308. Depression. — N. DEPRESSION;
lowering &c. v.; dip &c. (concavity) 252;
abasement; detrusion; reduction.

OVERTHROW, overset, overturn; upset; prostration, subversion, precipitation.

BOW; curtsy or curtsey, dip [colloq.],
bob, obedience [archaic], duck, genuflexion, kotow or kowtow [Chinese].
obeisance, salaam or salam.

V. DEPRESS, lower; let -, take- -down,
- down a peg [colloq.]; cast; let drop, let
fall; sink, debase, bring low, abase,
reduce, detrude, pitch, precipitate.

OVERTHROW, overturn, overset; upset,
subvert, prostrate, level, fell; down
[archaic or colloq.], cast down, take
down, throw down, fling down, dash
down, pull down, cut down, knock down,
hew down; raze, raze to the ground;
trample in the dust, pull about one's
ears; come off -, pull off- one's high
horse [slang]; come off -, get off- one's
perch [slang].

SIT, sit down, couch, squat; recline
&c. 213.

CROUCH, stoop, bend, cower.

BOW; curtsy or curtsey, genuflect,
bend -; bow- the -head, - knee; incline,
make obeisance, salaam or salam, prostrate oneself, bow down.

Adj. DEPRESSED &c. v.; at a low ebb; prostrate &c. (horizontal) 213; detrusive.

. facinus quos inquinat æquat [Lucan]; "with looks Downcast and damp" [Milton].

309. Leap. — N. LEAP, jump, hop, spring, bound, vault, pole vault, leaping, saltation [*rare*].

CAPER; dance, curvet, caracole *or* caracol; gambade, gambado, gambol, frisk, prance, dido [*colloq.*, *U. S.*], capriole, demivolt; buck, – jump; hop skip and jump; falcade.

[COMPARISONS] kangaroo, jerboa, chamois, goat, frog, grasshopper, flea; buckjumper; wallaby.

V. LEAP; jump -up, – over the moon; hop, spring, bound, vault, negotiate [*cant*], clear, ramp, trip, skip.

prance, dance, caper; buck, buckjump; curvet, caracole *or* caracol; foot it, bob, bounce, flounce, start; frisk &c. (*amusement*) 840; jump about &c. (*agitation*) 315; cut capers [*colloq.*], cut a dido [*colloq.*, *U. S.*]; trip it on the light fantastic toe, dance oneself off one's legs, dance the soles off one's feet.

Adj. LEAPING &c. *v.;* saltatorial, saltatoric *or* saltatory; frisky, lively.

Adv. on the light fantastic toe.

** *di salto in salto;* "From peak to peak, the rattling crags among, Leaps the live thunder" [Byron].

310. Plunge. — N. PLUNGE, dip, dive, nose dive [*aviation*], header [*colloq.*]; ducking &c. *v.*

SUBMERGENCE, submersion, immersion, engulfment [*rare*].

DIVER; diving bird, loon, auk, penguin, grebe, sea duck &c.

V. PLUNGE, dip, souse, duck; dive, plump; take a -plunge, – header [*colloq.*]; make a plunge; bathe &c. (*water*) 337; pitch.

SUBMERGE, submerse; immerse; douse *or* dowse, sink, engulf, send to the bottom; send to -Davy Jones's locker, – feed the fishes.

FOUNDER, welter, wallow; get out of one's depth; go to the bottom, go down like a stone.

Adj. PLUNGING &c. *v.;* submergible, submersible; soundable.

---

311. [CURVILINEAR MOTION.] **Circuition. — N.** CIRCUITION [*archaic*], circulation, volutation; turn, curvet; excursion; circumvention, circumnavigation, circumambulation, circumambience *or* circumambiency, circumflexion, circumfluence [*rare*], circummigration, circumvolation [*rare*]; Northwest Passage; wheel, gyre, ambit, compass, lap, circuit &c. 629.

turning &c. *v.;* wrench; evolution; coil, spiral, corkscrew.

V. TURN, bend, wheel; go about, put about [*both naut.*]; heel; go –, turn--round, – to the right-about; turn on one's heel.

CIRCLE, encircle, circumscribe; circuit; make –, describe- a -circle, – complete circle; go –, pass- through -180°, – 360°; circumnavigate, circumambulate, circumvent; "put a girdle round about the earth" [*M. N. D.*]; go the round, make the round of, circumvolate [*rare*], circumflex.

ROUND; turn –, round- a corner; double a point [*naut.*]; make a detour &c. (*circuit*) 629.

WIND, circulate, meander; whisk, twirl; twist &c. (*convolution*) 248.

WALLOW, welter, roll, volutate.

Adj. CIRCUITOUS; turning &c. *v.;* circumforaneous, circumfluent, roundabout; devious, deviatory; circumambient, circumflex, circumfluent, circumfluous, circumvolant, circumnavigable.

Adv. round about.

** "throws his steep flight in many an aery wheel" [Milton].

---

312. [MOTION IN A CONTINUED CIRCLE.] **Rotation. — N.** ROTATION, revolution, gyration, circulation, roll; circumrotation, circumvolution [*rare*], circumgyration; circumfusion, circina-

313. [MOTION IN A REVERSE CIRCLE.] **Evolution. — N.** EVOLUTION, unfolding, development; evolvement; unfoldment; eversion &c. (*inversion*) 218.

V. EVOLVE; unfold, unroll, unwind,

tion [obs.], turbination, pirouette, convolution.

EDDY, vortex, whirlpool, swirl, gurge
[rare]; verticity [obs.]; vertiginousness;
whir, whirl; countercurrent; cyclone,
tornado; surge; vertigo, dizzy round; maelstrom, Charybdis.

uncoil, untwist, unfurl, untwine, unravel; disentangle· develop.

Adj. EVOLUTIONAL, evolutionary;
evolving &c. v.; evolved &c. v.

Ixion; Wheel of Fortune.

[COMPARISONS] wheel, screw, propeller, turbine, whirligig, rolling stone, wind-
mill; treadmill, top, teetotum; roller; cogwheel, gear, gearwheel, flywheel; jack,
smokejack, turnspit; gyroplane, gyroscope, gyrostat, gyrocar; caster.

axis, axle, spindle, pivot, pin, hinge, pole, swivel, gimbals, arbor, bobbin, spool,
reel, mandrel.

[SCIENCE OF ROTATORY MOTION] trochilics, gyrostatics.

V. ROTATE; roll, roll along; revolve, spin; turn, turn round; circumvolve [rare],
circumgyrate [rare], circumvolute, circumfuse, turbinate [rare], encircle; circulate,
gurge [rare], swirl, gyre, gyrate, wheel, whirl, twirl, trundle, troll, bowl, roll up,
furl.

box the compass; spin like a -top, – teetotum.

Adj. ROTATING &c. v.; rotatory, rotary; circumrotatory, trochilic, vertiginous,
gyral, circumgyratory, circumvolutory, gyratory, gulfy; vorticular, vortical,
vorticose; gyrostatic, gyroscopic.

Adv. ROUND AND ROUND, head over heels, like a horse in a mill, in circles,
clockwise.

---

314. [RECIPROCATING MOTION, MOTION TO AND FRO.] **Oscillation.** — **N.** OSCILLA-
TION; vibration, vibratility, libration; motion of a pendulum; nutation, circumnutation; undulation; pulsation; pulse, beat, throb; seismicity, seismism,
seismology.

ALTERNATION; coming and going &c. v.; ebb and flow, flux and reflux, systole
and diastole; libration -of the moon, – in latitude; ups and downs; crossruff [in
cards].

FLUCTUATION; vacillation &c. (irresolution) 605.

SWING, wave, vibratiuncle [rare], beat, shake, wag, seesaw, teeter [U. S.]; dance,
lurch, dodge.

ROCKING STONE, logan (or loggan) stone.

[INSTRUMENTS] vibroscope, vibrograph; seismograph, seismoscope.

V. OSCILLATE; nutate, vibrate, librate; undulate, wave; rock, sway, swing;
pulsate, beat; wag, waggle; nod, bob, curtsy or curtsey, tick; play; wamble,
wabble; dangle, swag [obs. or dial.].

fluctuate, dance, curvet, reel, quake; quiver, quaver; shake, flicker; wriggle; roll,
toss, pitch; flounder, stagger, totter; move -, bob- up and down &c. adv.

ALTERNATE, pass and repass, shuttle, ebb and flow, come and go; vacillate &c. 605.
BRANDISH, shake, flourish; agitate &c. 315.

Adj. OSCILLATING &c. v.; oscillatory, undulatory, pulsatory, libratory; vibratory,
vibrative, vibratile; seismic or seismical, seismal, seismographic, seismological;
pendulous; shuttlewise.

Adv. TO AND FRO, up and down, backwards and forwards, back and forth, in and
out, seesaw, zigzag, wibble-wabble [colloq.], in and out, from side to side, like
buckets in a well.

---

315. [IRREGULAR MOTION.] **Agitation.** — **N.** AGITATION, stir, tremor, shake,
ripple, jog, jolt, jar, jerk, shock, succussion, trepidation, quiver, quaver, dance,
tarantella, tarantism; vellication, jactation, jactitation, quassation [rare]; shuffling
&c. v.; twitter, flicker, flutter.

DISQUIET, perturbation, commotion, turmoil, turbulence; tumult, tumultuation
[obs.]; hubbub, rout, bustle, fuss, racket.

TWITCHING, subsultus, floccillation, carphology *or* carphologia; staggers, megrims, epilepsy, fits; chorea, the jerks [*colloq.*], St. Vitus's dance, tilmus.

SPASM, throe, throb, palpitation, pitapatation [*humorous*], convulsion, paroxysm, seizure, grip, cramp.

DISTURBANCE &c. (*disorder*) 59; restlessness &c. (*changeableness*) 149.

FERMENT, fermentation; ebullition, effervescence, hurly-burly, *cahotage* or *cahotement* [*F.*], cahot [*Can.*]; tempest, storm, ground swell, heavy sea, whirlpool, vortex &c. 312; whirlwind &c. (*wind*) 349.

V. BE AGITATED &c.; shake; tremble, – like an aspen leaf; shake like a jelly, quiver, quaver, quake, shiver, twitter, twire [*obs.*], writhe, toss, jactitate [*rare*], shuffle, tumble, stagger, bob, reel, sway; wag, waggle; wriggle, – like an eel; dance, stumble, shamble, flounder, totter, flounce, flop, curvet, prance, cavort [*U. S.*]; squirm; bustle.

toss about, jump about; jump like a parched pea; shake like an aspen leaf; shake to its -center, – foundations; be the sport of the winds and waves; reel to and fro like a drunken man; move –, drive- from post to pillar and from pillar to post; keep between hawk and buzzard.

THROB, pulsate, beat, palpitate, go pitapat.

FLUTTER, flitter [*archaic*], flicker, bicker; twitch, vellicate.

FERMENT, effervesce, foam; boil, boil over; bubble, bubble up; simmer.

AGITATE, shake, convulse, toss, tumble, bandy, wield, brandish, flap, flourish, whisk, jerk, hitch, jolt; jog, joggle; jostle, buffet, hustle, disturb, stir, shake up, churn, jounce, wallop [*dial.*], whip.

Adj. AGITATED, tremulous; subsultory [*obs.*], desultory, successive, saltatorial, saltant, saltatoric *or* saltatory· quassative [*rare*]; shambling; giddy-paced, convulsive, jerky; effervescent, effervescive, vellicative, unquiet, restless, all of a twitter [*colloq.*], all of a flutter; shaking &c. *v.*

Adv. by fits and starts; subsultorily [*obs.*] &c. *adj.; per saltum* [*L.*]; hop, skip, and jump; in convulsions, in fits, in a flutter.

₊ *tempête dans un verre d'eau;* "the tempestuous petticoat" [Herrick]; "with many a flirt and flutter" [Poe]; "the waves were not like water: they were like falling city walls" [Chesterton]; "Let the ether go surging 'Neath thunder and scourging Of wild winds unbound" [E. B. Browning].

CLASS III

Words relating to MATTER

Section I. MATTER IN GENERAL

316. Materiality. — N. MATERIALITY, materialness; corporeity, corporality; substantiality, substantialness, materialization, material existence, incarnation, flesh and blood, plenum; physical condition.

MATTER, body, substance, brute matter, protoplasm, plasma, stuff. element, principle, parenchyma, material, substratum, hyle, *corpus* [*L.*], pabulum; frame.

object, article, thing, something; still life; stocks and stones; *matériel* [*F.*]; materials &c. 635.

[SCIENCE OF MATTER] physics; somatology, somatics; natural –, experimental- philosophy; physicism; physical science, *philosophie positive* [*F.*], materialism, hylism, hylicism, hylotheism, somatism, substantialism.

MATERIALIST; physicist; somatologist, somatist, corporealist [*rare*], hylicist, hylotheist, substantialist.

V. MATERIALIZE, incorporate, substantiate, substantialize, insubstantiate [*rare*], incorporate, embody, incarnate, corporify [*obs.*].

Adj. MATERIAL, bodily; corporeal, corporal; physical; somatic, somatoscopic; mundane &c. (*terrestrial*) 318; sensible, tangible, ponderable, palpable, substantial, somatologic *or* somatological; embodied, fleshly.

317. Immateriality. — N. IMMATERIALITY, immaterialness; incorporeity, dematerialization, insubstantiality, incorporality, decarnation [*obs.*], unsubstantiation, unsubstantiality, spirituality; inextension; astral plane.

PERSONALITY; I, myself, me.

ego, spirit &c. (*soul*) 450; astral body, etheric double, subliminal self, subconscious self, higher self.

IMMATERIALISM; spiritualism, spiritism, animism, Platonism; Platonic -Idea, – Ideal.

IMMATERIALIST, spiritualist, spiritist, animist, Platonist.

V. IMMATERIALIZE, dematerialize, unsubstantialize [*rare*]; disembody, spiritualize.

Adj. IMMATERIAL, immateriate, incorporeal, incorporal, incorporate, unsubstantial, insubstantial, immateriate [*obs.*], spiritistic, animistic; unfleshly; supersensible; asomatous, unextended; unembodied, discarnate, bodiless, decarnate *or* decarnated, disembodied; extramundane, unearthly; pneumatoscopic; spiritual &c. (*psychical*) 450; Platonistic.

SUBJECTIVE, personal, nonobjective.

*** "there is a natural body, and there is a spiritual body" [*Bib.*]; "the Thee in Me who works behind The Veil" [Omar Khayyám — Fitzgerald].

neuter, unspiritual, materialistic *or* materialistical, hylic, hylotheistic *or* hylotheistical, parenchymatous.

OBJECTIVE, impersonal, nonsubjective.

*** "and the Word was made flesh and dwelt among us" [*Bible*]; "this muddy vesture of decay" [*M. of Venice*].

318. World. — N. WORLD, creation, nature, universe; earth, globe, wide world; cosmos *or* kosmos; Midgard; terraqueous globe, sphere; macrocosm, megacosm; music of the spheres.

HEAVENS, sky, welkin [*archaic*], empyrean; starry -cope, – heaven, – host; firmament, *caelum* [*L.*], hyaline, supersensible regions; *varuna* [*Skr.*]; vault –, canopy- of heaven; celestial spaces.

HEAVENLY BODIES, luminaries, stars, asteroids; nebulæ; galaxy, Milky Way, galactic circle, *via lactea* [*L.*].

sun, orb of day, day-star [*poetic*], Helios, Apollo, Phœbus &c. (*sun god*) 423;

photosphere, chromosphere; solar system; planet, planetoid; Venus, Aphrodite Urania, Hyades; comet; satellite; moon, orb of night, Diana, Luna, Phœbe, Cynthia, Selene, "glimpses of the moon" [*Hamlet*], silver-footed queen; aërolite, meteor; falling –, shooting- star; meteorite, uranolite.

constellation, zodiac, signs of the zodiac; Charles's Wain, The Dipper; Great Bear, Ursa Major; Little Bear, Ursa Minor; Southern Cross, Orion's Belt, Cassiopeia's Chair, Pleiades.

colures, equator, ecliptic, orbit.

[SCIENCE OF HEAVENLY BODIES] astronomy; uranography, uranology; uranometry, cosmology, cosmography, cosmogony; eidouranion, orrery; geodesy &c. (*measurement*) 466; star-gazing; observatory; planetarium.

COSMOLOGIST, cosmographer, cosmogonist, geodesist, geographer; astronomer, star-gazer.

Adj. COSMIC *or* cosmical, mundane; terrestrial, terrestrious [*obs.*], terraqueous, terrene, terreous, [*obs.*]; fluvioterrestrial, geodesic *or* geodesical, geodetic *or* geodetical, cosmogonal, cosmogonic, cosmographic *or* cosmographical; telluric, earthly, under the sun; sublunary, subastral.

SOLAR, heliacal; lunar; empyreal, celestial, heavenly, sphery; starry, stellar, stellary, bespangled, sidereal; sideral, astral; nebular; uranic.

Adv. in all creation, on the face of the globe, here below, under the sun.

** *die Weltgeschichte ist das Weltgericht;* "earth is but the frozen echo of the silent voice of God" [Hageman]; "green calm below, blue quietness above" [Whittier]; "hanging in a golden chain this pendent World" [*Paradise Lost*]; "nothing in nature is unbeautiful" [Tennyson]; "silently as a dream the fabric rose" [Cowper]; "some touch of nature's genial glow" [Scott]; "this majestical roof fretted with golden fire" [*Hamlet*]; "through knowledge we behold the World's creation" [*Spenser*].

---

319. Gravity. — **N.** GRAVITY, gravitation; weight; heft [*U. S. & dial. Eng.*], heaviness &c. *adj.;* specific gravity; ponderation [*rare*], ponderousness, ponderance [*rare*], ponderosity, pressure, load; burden *or* burthen; ballast, counterpoise; mass; lump –, mass –, weight-of.

[COMPARISONS] lead, millstone, mountain; Ossa on Pelion.

WEIGHING, ponderation, trutination [*obs.*]; weights; avoirdupois –, troy –, apothecaries'- weight; grain, scruple, drachma, dram *or* drachm, ounce, pound, lb., arroba, load, stone, hundredweight, cwt., ton, quintal, carat, pennyweight, tod; gram *or* gramme, decagram, hectogram, kilogram *or* kilo, myriagram, decigram, centigram, milligram.

[WEIGHING INSTRUMENT] balance, scales steelyard, beam, weighbridge, spring balance.

[SCIENCE OF GRAVITY] statics.

V. BE HEAVY &c. *adj.;* gravitate, weigh, press, cumber, load.

[MEASURE THE WEIGHT OF] weigh, counterweigh, scale [*rare*], poise.

Adj. WEIGHTY; weighing &c. *v.;* heavy, – as lead; ponderous, ponderable; lumpish, lumpy, cumbersome, burdensome; cumbrous, unwieldy, massive; static *or* statical.

incumbent, superincumbent.

---

320. Levity. — **N.** LEVITY; lightness &c. *adj.;* imponderability, buoyancy, volatility; imponderables [*tech.*].

[COMPARISONS] feather, dust, mote, down, thistledown, flue, fluff, cobweb, gossamer, straw, cork, bubble; float, buoy; ether, air.

FERMENT, leaven, barm, yeast, zyme, enzyme, pepsin, diastase.

V. BE LIGHT &c. *adj.;* float, swim, be buoyed up.

RENDER LIGHT &c. *adj.;* lighten.

FERMENT, work, raise, leaven.

Adj. LIGHT, subtile, subtle, airy; imponderous, imponderable; astatic, weightless, ethereal, sublimated; gossamery; suberose *or* suberous, subereous; uncompressed, volatile; buoyant, floating &c. *v.;* foamy, frothy; portable.

light as -a feather, – thistledown, – air.

FERMENTING, fermentative, zymogenic, zymologic *or* zymological, diastatic, yeasty.

** "Trifles light as air" [*Othello*].

Section II. INORGANIC MATTER

1. Solid Matter

321. Density. — N. DENSITY, solidity; solidness &c. *adj.;* impenetrability, impermeability; incompressibility; imporosity; cohesion &c. 46; costiveness, constipation, consistence, spissitude.

specific gravity; hydrometer, areometer.

CONDENSATION; caseation; solidation [*obs.*], solidification, consolidation, concretion, coagulation; petrifaction &c. (*hardening*) 323; crystallinity, crystallizability, crystallization, precipitation; deposit, precipitate; inspissation; incrassation, crassitude; thickening &c. *v.*

INDIVISIBILITY, indiscerptibility, indissolvableness [*rare*], infrangibility, infrangibleness, indissolubility, indissolubleness.

322. Rarity. — N. RARITY; tenuity; absence of solidity &c. 321; subtility; subtilty; sponginess, compressibility.

rarefaction, rarefication [*rare*], expansion, dilatation, inflation, subtilization.

ether &c. (*gas*) 334.

V. RAREFY, expand, dilate, subtilize [*rare*], attenuate, thin.

Adj. RARE, subtile [*now rare*], subtle, thin, fine, tenuous, compressible, flimsy, slight; light &c. 320; cavernous, porous, spongy &c. (*hollow*) 252.

rarefied &c. *v.;* unsubstantial; uncompact, uncompressed; rarefiable, rarefactive, rarefactional.

*** "melted into air, thin air" [*Tempest*]; "I pass through the pores of the ocean and shores" [Shelley, *Cloud*].

SOLID BODY, mass, block, knot, lump; concretion, concrete, conglomerate; cake, stone, bone, gristle, cartilage.

CLOT, coagulum, casein, crassament [*obs.*], crassamentum, legumin, curd; clabber, bonnyclabber, clotted cream, Devonshire cream, grume.

SEDIMENT, lees, dregs, settlings.

V. BE DENSE &c. *adj.;* become *or* render solid &c. *adj.;* solidify, solidate; concrete, set, take a set, consolidate, congeal, coagulate; curd, curdle, cruddle [*dial.*], lopper; fix, clot, cake, candy, precipitate, deposit, cohere, crystallize; petrify &c. (*harden*) 323.

CONDENSE, thicken, inspissate, incrassate.

COMPRESS, squeeze, ram down, constipate [*rare*].

Adj. DENSE, solid; solidified &c. *v.;* caseate, caseous; pucka *or* pakka [*Hind.*], coherent, cohesive &c. 46; compact, close, serried, thickset; substantial, massive, lumpish; impenetrable, impermeable, imporous; incompressible; constipated, costive; crass, spiss [*obs.*], clabber, kern [*chiefly dial.*]; concrete &c. (*hard*) 323; knotted, knotty; gnarled; crystallitic, crystalline, crystallizable; thick, grumose, grumous, stuffy.

UNDISSOLVED, unmelted, unliquefied, unthawed.

INDIVISIBLE, indiscerptible, infrangible, indissolvable [*rare*], indissoluble, insoluble, infusible.

*** "O, that this too too solid flesh would melt" [*Hamlet*].

323. Hardness. — N. HARDNESS &c. *adj.;* rigidity; renitency *or* renitence; inflexibility, temper, callosity, durity [*obs.*].

INDURATION, petrifaction; lapidification, lapidescence [*rare*]; cornification, chondrification, vitrification, vitrescence, ossification; crystallization.

[COMPARISONS] stone, pebble, flint, marble, rock, fossil, crag, crystal, quartz, granite, adamant; bone, cartilage; calculus; hardware; heart of oak, block, board, deal board; iron, steel; cast –,

324. Softness. — N. SOFTNESS, pliableness &c. *adj.;* flexibility; pliancy, pliability; sequacity [*obs. in this sense*], malleability, ductility, ductibility, tractability, tractility, extensibility, extendibility; plasticity; inelasticity, flaccidity, laxity, flabbiness, flocculence; mollescence, mollification; softening &c. *v.*

[COMPARISONS] clay, alumina, argil; wax, putty, butter, dough, pudding; cushion, pillow, feather bed, down, eider down, padding, wadding.

decarbonized –, wrought- iron; nail;
brick, concrete; cement; osmiridium,
iridosmine *or* iridosmium.

V. HARDEN; render hard &c. *adj.;*
stiffen, indurate, petrify, temper, ossify,
vitrify, lithify, lapidify, cement.

Adj. HARD, rigid, stubborn, stiff, firm;
starch, starched; stark, unbending, unlimber, renitent, unyielding; inflexible,
tense; indurate, indurated; gritty,
proof.

adamantine, adamantean; concrete,
stony, rocky, granitic, calculous, lithic,
vitrescent, vitrifiable, vitrescible, vitreous; horny, cornified, callous, corneous; bony, ossipid, osseous, ossific;
cartilaginous; lapideous, lapidific *or*
lapidifical [*rare*]; crystallized, crystal-
loid; hard as a -stone &c. *n.;* stiff as
-buckram, – a poker.

V. SOFTEN; render soft &c. *adj.;*
mollify, mellow, milden, tender [*rare*],
gentle [*rare*], dulcify; relax, temper;
mash, knead, massage, squash [*colloq.*].

BEND, yield, relent, relax, give.

Adj. SOFT, tender, supple; pliant,
pliable; flexible, flexile; lithe, lithesome;
lissom, limber, plastic; ductile, ductible
[*rare*], tractile, tractable; malleable,
extensile, extensible, lax, sequacious
[*obs. in this sense*], inelastic; aluminous;
remollient [*obs.*], mollient, mollescent,
mollitious, mollified.

yielding &c. *v.;* flabby,| limp, flimsy.

flaccid, flocculent, downy; spongy,
œdematous *or* edematous, medullary,
doughy, clayey, argillaceous, mellow.

soft as -butter, – down, – silk, – putty,
– a feather bed; yielding as wax; tender
as a chicken.

⁎ "smoothing the raven down Of darkness till it smil'd" [Milton].

---

325. Elasticity. — N. ELASTICITY,
springiness, spring, resilience *or* resiliency, renitency, buoyancy, tensibility,
tensibleness, tensility, extensibility; recoil, rebound, reflex.

[COMPARISONS] India rubber *or* india-
rubber, caoutchouc, gum elastic, whalebone, baleen; turf, moss; balloon, battledore.

V. BE ELASTIC &c. *adj.;* spring back &c. (*recoil*) 277.

Adj. ELASTIC, tensile, tensible, springy, resilient, renitent, ductile, extensible,
buoyant.

326. Inelasticity. — N. INELASTICITY
&c. (*softness*) 324; want of –, absence
of- elasticity &c. 325; irresilience.

Adj. INELASTIC &c. (*soft*) 324; irresilient.

---

327. Tenacity. — N. TENACITY,
toughness, strength; cohesiveness, cohesion &c. 46; sequacity, sequaciousness
[*both obs. in this sense*]; stubbornness &c.
(*obstinacy*) 606; gumminess, glutinous-
ness, viscidity &c. 352.

[COMPARISONS] leather; white leather
or whitleather, tawed leather; gristle,
cartilage.

CLAW, talon, pincers, nippers, vise;
bulldog.

V. BE TENACIOUS &c. *adj.;* resist fracture.

Adj. TENACIOUS, cohesive, tough,
strong, resisting, adhesive, stringy,
viscid, gummy, glutinous, gristly, cartilaginous, leathery, coriaceous, tough as
whitleather; stubborn &c. (*obstinate*) 606.

328. Brittleness. — N. BRITTLENESS
&c. *adj.;* fragility, friability, frangi-
bility, fissility [*rare*], frailty, cold-short-
ness; house of -cards, – glass.

V. BE BRITTLE &c. *adj.;* live in a glass
house.

BREAK, crack, snap, split, shiver,
splinter, crumble, crash, crush, break
short, burst, fly, give way; fall to pieces;
fall to dust; crumble -to, – into- dust.

Adj. BRITTLE, brash [*U. S.*], frangible,
breakable, friable, delicate, shattery
[*rare*], fragile, frail, gimcrack, shivery,
fissile; splitting &c. *v.;* lacerable, splin-
tery, crisp, crimp, short, brittle as glass,
cold-short; crisp as celery.

⁎ "mistress of herself though china fall"
[Pope].

---

329. [STRUCTURE.] Texture. — N. STRUCTURE, organization, anatomy, frame,
mold *or* mould, fabric, construction; framework, carcass, architecture; stratification, cleavage.

substance, stuff, compages, parenchyma; constitution, staple, organism.

[SCIENCE OF STRUCTURES] organology, osteology, myology, splanchnology neurology, angiology, adenology ; angiography, adenography, organography.

TEXTURE, intertexture, contexture; tissue, grain, web, surface; warp and -woof, – weft; gossamer, homespun, linsey-woolsey, frieze, fustian; satin, velvet; tooth, nap &c. (*roughness*) 256; fineness –, coarseness- of grain; dry goods.

[SCIENCE OF TEXTURES] histology.

Adj. STRUCTURAL, organic; anatomic *or* anatomical; splanchnic, splanchnological, visceral, adenological.

TEXTURAL, textile; fine-grained, coarse-grained, ingrained, ingrain; fine, delicate, subtile, subtle, gossamer, gossamery, filmy; coarse; homespun, linsey-woolsey.

---

330. Pulverulence. — N. [STATE OF POWDER.] PULVERULENCE; sandiness &c. *adj.;* efflorescence; friability, friableness, arenosity, sabulosity.

PARTICLE &c. (*smallness*) 32; powder, dust, sand, shingle; sawdust; grit; meal, bran, flour, farina, rice, paddy, spore, sporule; crumb, seed, grain; limature [*obs.*], filings, *débris* [*F.*], detritus, scobs, magistery, fine powder; flocculi.

smoke; cloud of -dust, – sand, – smoke; puff -, volume- of smoke; sand storm, dust storm.

[REDUCTION TO POWDER] pulverization, comminution, attenuation, granulation, disintegration, subaction, contusion, trituration, levigation, abrasion, detrition, multure limation; tripsis; filing &c. *v.*

[INSTRUMENTS FOR PULVERIZATION] mill, arrastra, gristmill, grater, rasp, file, pestle and mortar, nutmeg grater, teeth, grinder, grindstone, kern [*dial.*], quern, quernstone, millstone.

[SCIENCE] koniology.

V. COME TO DUST; be disintegrated, be reduced to powder &c.

PULVERIZE, comminute, granulate, triturate, levigate; reduce *or* grind to powder; scrape, file, abrade, rub down, grind, grate, rasp, pound, bray, bruise, contuse, contund [*rare*]; beat, crush, craunch *or* cranch, crunch, scranch [*colloq.*], crumble, disintegrate; attenuate &c. 195.

Adj. POWDERY, pulverulent, granular, mealy, floury, farinaceous, branny, furfuraceous, flocculent, dusty, sandy, sabulous, psammous; detrital, arenaceous, arenose, arenarious, gritty; efflorescent, impalpable; lentiginous, lepidote, sabuline; sporaceous, sporous.

PULVERABLE *or* pulverizable; friable, crumbly, shivery; pulverized &c. *v.;* attrite; in pieces.

*** "Though the mills of God grind slowly, yet they grind exceeding small" [Longfellow — from von Logau].

---

331. Friction. — N. FRICTION, attrition; rubbing &c. *v.;* attriteness, attritus, erasure; confrication [*obs.*], contrition [*obs.*]; affriction [*obs.*], abrasion, arrosion [*obs.*], limature [*obs.*], anatripsis, anatripsology, frication, rub; elbow grease [*colloq.*]; rosin; massage.

MASSEUR (*fem. masseuse*) [*F.*], massagist, rubber.

V. RUB, abrade, scratch, scrape, scrub, fray, rasp, graze, curry, scour, polish, rub out, raze, erase, gnaw; file, grind &c. (*reduce to powder*) 330; rosin; massage.

set one's teeth on edge.

Adj. ABRASIVE, anatriptic; attrite [*rare*], attritive [*obs.*].

*** "let the galled jade wince" [*Hamlet*].

332. [ABSENCE OF FRICTION. PREVENTION OF FRICTION.] **Lubrication. — N.** LUBRICATION, lubrification [*rare*], lubricity; anointment; oiling &c. *v.*

smoothness &c. 255; unctuousness &c. 355.

LUBRICANT, lubricator, synovia; glycerin, oil &c. 356; saliva; lather; ointment, salve, balm, unguent, unguentum [*pharm.*], lenitive, unction.

V. LUBRICATE, lubricitate [*obs.*]; oil, grease, lather, soap; wax; anoint; salivate.

Adj. LUBRICATED &c. *v.;* lubricous, lubricant, lubric [*rare*]; lenitive, synovial.

*** "a dinner lubricates business" [Lord Stowell — quoted by Boswell].

2. FLUID MATTER

1. *Fluids in General*

333. Fluidity. — N. FLUIDITY, liquidity, liquefaction; liquidness &c. *adj.;* gaseity &c. 334; solution, chylifaction, serosity.

fluid, inelastic fluid; liquid, liquor; lymph, humor, juice, sap, serum, blood, gravy, rheum, ichor, sanies; chyle.

solubility, solubleness.

[SCIENCE OF LIQUIDS AT REST] hydrology, hydrostatics, hydrodynamics, hydrometry, hydrokinetics.

hydrometer, hydrophone, hydrostat, meter.

V. BE FLUID &c. *adj.;* flow &c. (*water in motion*) 348; liquefy &c. 335.

Adj. LIQUID, fluid, serous, juicy, succulent, sappy; ichorous; rheumy, chylous, sanious, lymphatic; fluent &c. (*flowing*) 348.

LIQUEFIED &c. 335; uncongealed; soluble.

HYDROLOGICAL, hydrostatic *or* hydrostatical, hydrodynamic *or* hydrodynamical, hydrometric *or* hydrometrical.

*** "that liquefaction of her clothes" [Herrick].

335. Liquefaction. — N. LIQUEFACTION; liquescence, liquescency; deliquescence; melting &c. (*heat*) 384; colliquation [*obs.*], colliquefaction [*obs.*]; thaw; solubleness, deliquation [*obs.*], liquation; lixiviation, dissolution.

SOLUTION, decoction, apozem [*rare*], infusion, flux; alloy; lixivium.

SOLVENT, diluent, resolvent, dissolvent, menstruum, alkahest.

V. RENDER LIQUID &c. 333; liquefy, run; deliquesce; melt &c. (*heat*) 384; solve; dissolve, resolve; liquate; hold in solution.

LEACH, lixiviate, percolate.

Adj. LIQUEFIED &c. *v.*, liquescent, liquefiable; deliquescent, soluble, dissoluble, dissolvable, colliquative; leachy, porous.

SOLVENT, diluent, resolutive, resolvent, dissolvent.

334. Gaseity. — N. GASEITY, gaseousness, vaporousness &c. *adj.;* flatulence *or* flatulency; volatility; aëration, aërification; gasification.

ELASTIC FLUID, gas, air, vapor *or* vapour, ether, steam, fume, reek, effluvium, flatus; cloud &c. 353; ammonia, ammoniacal gas; volatile alkali.

[SCIENCE OF ELASTIC FLUIDS] pneumatics, pneumatology, pneumatonomy, pneumatostatics; aërostatics, aërodynamics, aëroscopy, aërography, aërology, aëromechanics.

pneumatoscope, pneumatometer, gasometer, gas meter; air −, swimmingbladder, sound (*of a fish*).

V. GASIFY, aërify, aërate; emit vapor &c. 336.

Adj. GASEOUS, gasiform, aëriferous, aëriform, ethereal, aëry, aërial, airy, vaporous, volatile, evaporable, flatulent.

pneumatolytic, aërostatic *or* aërostatical, aërodynamic, aëromechanic.

336. Vaporization. — N. VAPORIZATION, volatilization; gasification; evaporation, vaporation [*rare*], vaporishness, vaporosity, atomization, distillation, cupellation, cohobation, sublimation, exhalation; volatility.

fumigation, steaming.

VAPORIZER, atomizer, spray, evaporator, cohobator, finestill, still, retort.

bay salt, chloride of sodium.

V. RENDER GASEOUS &c. 334; vaporize, volatilize, atomize, spray; distill, sublime, sublimate, evaporate, exhale, smoke, transpire, emit vapor, fume, reek, steam, fumigate; cohobate; finestill.

Adj. VOLATILE, evaporable, vaporizable, vaporific, vapory, vaporous, gaseous; volatilized &c. *v.;* reeking &c. *v.*

*** "and those who came to cough remained to spray" [*Cynic's Calendar*].

2. Specific Fluids

337. Water. — N. WATER, lymph; *aqua* [*L.*], *eau* [*F.*], flood, crystal [*poetic*], Adam's ale [*humorous*], *agua* [*Sp.*], *pani* [*Hind.*]; diluent, serum &c. 333.

WASHING &c. *v.;* immersion, mersion [*obs.*]; dilution, maceration, lotion; humectation, infiltration, spargefaction [*obs.*], affusion, irrigation, seepage [*U. S.*, *dial. Eng. & Scot.*], balneation, bath.

DELUGE &c. (*water in motion*) 348; high water, flood tide, springtide.

SPRINKLER, sparger, aspergillum *or* aspergill, shower *or* shower bath, douche, enema; nozzle; atomizer &c. 336.

V. BE WATERY &c. *adj.;* reek.

WATER, wet; moisten &c. 339; dilute, add water, dip, immerse; merge; soak, drouk [*Scot.*]; affuse [*rare*], immerge, douse *or* dowse, submerge; plunge, souse, duck, drown; steep, macerate, wash, sprinkle, sparge, humect *or* humectate [*rare*], lave, bathe, splash, swash, drench; dabble, slop, slobber, irrigate, inundate, deluge; infiltrate, percolate, seep [*dial. & U. S.*]; slosh; marinate *or* marinade, pickle.

INJECT, gargle; syringe, douche.

Adj. watery, aqueous, aquatic, hydrous, lymphatic; balneal; diluent, solvent, hydrotic *or* hydrotical; infiltrative, seepy; drenching &c. *v.;* diluted &c. *v.;* weak; wet &c. (*moist*) 339.

*** the waters are out; "men really know not what good water's worth" [Byron].

338. Air. — N. AIR &c. (*gas*) 334; common –, atmospheric- air; atmosphere; aërosphere [*rare*].

THE OPEN, – air; sky, lift [*archaic*], welkin [*archaic*], the blue, blue serene, blue sky; cloud &c. 353.

WEATHER, climate; rise and fall of the -barometer, – mercury.

isopiestic line, isobar.

exposure to the -air, – weather; ventilation.

[SCIENCE OF AIR] aërology, aërometry, aëroscopy, aërography; meteorology, climatology; pneumatics; aëronautics; eudiometry; eudiometer, barometer, vacuometer, climatometer, aërometer, aëroscope; aneroid, baroscope, weatherglass, weathergauge, barograph.

aërostation &c. (*aëronautics*) 267; aëronaut &c. 269*a*.

WEATHERVANE, weathercock, vane, cock.

V. AIR, ventilate, perflate [*rare*]; fan &c. (*wind*) 349.

FLY, soar, drift, hover; aviate &c. (*aëronautics*) 267.

Adj. CONTAINING AIR, flatulent, effervescent; windy &c. 349.

ATMOSPHERIC, airy; aërial, aëriform; aëry, pneumatic.

METEOROLOGIC *or* meteorological, aërological, aërometric, eudiometric *or* eudiometrical, barometric *or* barometrical, barographic, baroscopic *or* baroscopical; isobaric, isopiestic; aërographic

or aërographical; weatherwise.

Adv. IN THE OPEN AIR, *à la belle étoile* [*F.*], in the open, out of the blue, under the stars, out of doors, outdoors; *al fresco* [*It.*]; *sub Jove* [*L.*], *sub dio* [*L.*].

*** "heaven's sweetest air" [Shakespeare].

---

339. Moisture. — N. MOISTURE; moistness &c. *adj.;* humidity, humectation; madefaction [*obs.*], dew; serein [*F.*]; marsh &c. 345.

hygrometry, hygrometer.

V. MOISTEN, wet; humect *or* humectate [*rare*]; sponge, damp, bedew; imbue, imbrue, infiltrate, saturate; soak, sodden, seethe, sop, dampen; drench &c. (*water*) 337.

BE MOIST &c. *adj.;* not have a dry thread; perspire &c. (*exude*) 295.

Adj. MOIST, damp; watery &c. 337; madid [*now rare*], undried, humid, wet,

340. Dryness. — N. DRYNESS &c. *adj.;* siccity [*rare*], siccation, aridness, aridity, drought *or* drouth.

ebb tide, low water.

DESICCATION, exsiccation [*rare*], dehydration, insolation, anhydration, anhydromyelia [*med.*], evaporation, arefaction [*rare*], dephlegmation, drainage.

drier, desiccative, desiccator.

V. BE *or* RENDER DRY &c. *adj.;* dry; dry up, soak up; sponge, swab, wipe. drain, parch, sear.

BE FINE, hold up; be bright and fair.

DESICCATE, exsiccate, dehydrate, an-

dank, muggy, dewy; roric; roriferous, rorifluent [*both rare*], roral [*obs*], rorid [*obs.*]; roscid [*rare*]; juicy.

SATURATED &c. *v.;* wringing wet; wet through, wet to the skin.

SODDEN, swashy [*dial.*], soppy, soggy, dabbled; reeking, dripping, soaking, droukit [*Scot.*], soft, sloppy, muddy; swampy &c. (*marshy*) 345; irriguous.

⁎ "honest water, which ne'er left man i' the mire" [*Timon of Athens*]; "My lips were wet, my throat was cold, My garments all were dank" [Coleridge].

hydrate, evaporate, insolate, infumate, torrefy, siccate [*rare*], arefy.

Adj. DRY, arid; droughty, waterless, siccaneous [*rare*], siccate [*obs.*], aneroid, sear *or* sere, siccant [*rare*], siccific, desiccatory; adust, arescent; dried &c. *v.;* undamped; dephlegmatory; juiceless, sapless; corky; husky; rainless, without rain, fine; dry as -a bone, – dust, – a stick, – a mummy, – a biscuit; waterproof, watertight.

ANHYDROUS, desiccated, desiccate, anhydric, dehydrated, insolated.

⁎ "with throats unslaked, with black lips baked" [Coleridge].

---

341. Ocean. — N. OCEAN, sea, main, deep, blue, brine, salt water, waters, waves, billows, high seas, offing, great waters, watery waste, "vasty deep" "briny deep," "swan-bath" [*A.-S.*], "swan-road" [*A.-S.*], "whale-path" [*A.-S.*], mere [*archaic*], herring pond *or* pond [*humorous for Atlantic*], hyaline, the Seven Seas, *kala pani* [*Hind.*]; wave, tide &c. (*water in motion*) 348; ocean basin; ocean lane, steamer track.

Neptune, Poseidon, Oceanus, Thetis, Triton, Naiad, Nereid; sea nymph, Siren, mermaid, merman; trident, dolphin.

OCEANOGRAPHY, hydrography; oceanographer, hydrographer.

Adj. OCEANIC, marine, maritime; pelagic, pelagian [*rare*], pelagious [*obs.*]; seaworthy, seagoing; hydrographic *or* hydrographical, oceanographic *or* oceanographical; bathybic, cotidal.

Adv. at sea, on sea; afloat; over-sea *or* over-seas, oceanward *or* oceanwards.

⁎ "great Neptune's ocean" [*Macbeth*]; 'Listen! the mighty Being is awake! And doth with his eternal motions make A sound like thunder — everlastingly" [Wordsworth].

342. Land. — N. LAND, earth, ground, soil, dry land, *terra firma* [*L.*].

continent, mainland, main, peninsula, chersonese, delta; tongue -, neck- of land; isthmus, oasis; promontory &c. (*projection*) 250: highland &c. (*height*) 206.

REALTY, real estate &c. (*property*) 780; acres.

COAST, shore, scar *or* scaur, strand, beach; *playa* [*Sp.*]; bank, lea; seaboard, seaside, sea bank, seacoast, seabeach; seashore, rock-bound coast, iron-bound coast; loom of the land; derelict; innings; reclamation, made land, alluvium, alluvion; *ancon* [*S. W. U. S.*].

REGION &c. 181; home, fatherland &c. (*abode*) 189.

SOIL, glebe, clay, loam, marl, cledge [*dial. Eng.*], chalk, gravel, mold *or* mould, subsoil, clod, clot [*dial.*].

ROCK, crag, cliff.

GEOGRAPHY, geodesy, geology, geognosy, geogony, agriculture, agronomics, agronomy, geoponics, georgics.

GEOGRAPHER, geodesist, geologist, geognost.

LANDSMAN, landlubber, tiller of the soil; agriculturist &c. 371.

V. LAND, disembark, debark, come to land; set foot on -the soil, – dry land; come -, go- ashore.

Adj. EARTHY; continental, midland; terrene &c. (*world*) 318.

LITTORAL, riparian, riparial, riparious, ripicolous, ripuarian; alluvial.

LANDED, prædial *or* predial, territorial; geophilous.

GEOGRAPHIC *or* geographical, geodesic *or* geodesical, geodetic *or* geodetical, geognostic *or* geognostical, geologic *or* geological, geoponic; agricultural &c. 371.

Adv. ASHORE; on shore, on land, on dry land, on *terra firma* [*L.*].

343. Gulf. Lake. — N. GULF, gulph, bay, inlet, bight, estuary, arm of the sea, bayou [*U. S.*], fiord, armlet; frith *or* firth, ostiary [*obs.*], mouth; lagoon *or* lagune; indraft *or* indraught [*obs.*], cove, creek; natural harbor; roads; strait; narrows; euripus; sound, belt, gut, kyle [*Scot.*].

LAKE, loch [*Scot.*], lough, [*Ir.*], mere, tarn, plash, broad [*Eng.*], pond, pool, sump [*Scot. or dial. Eng.*], slab [*dial.*], linn *or* lin [*Scot.*], tank, puddle, well, artesian well; standing -, dead -, sheet of- water; fish -, mill- pond; ditch, dike *or* dyke, dam, race, mill race; reservoir &c. (*store*) 636; *alberca* [*Sp. Amer.*], hog wallow, buffalo wallow.

Adj. LACUSTRINE, lacustral.

344. Plain. — N. PLAIN, table-land, face of the country; open -, champaign-country; basin, downs, waste, weary waste, desert, wild, steppe, tundra, peneplain, pampas, savanna, prairie &c. (*grassland*) 367; heath, common, wold, veldt *or* veld, moor, moorland; bush plateau &c. (*level*) 213; campagna [*obs. as Eng.*], champaign, uplands, fell [*Brit.*]; reach, stretch, expanse; alkali flat, llano; mesa, mesilla [*U. S.*], *playa* [*Sp.*]; shaking -, trembling- prairie; *vega* [*Sp. Amer.*].

MEADOW, mead, haugh [*Scot. & dial. Eng.*], pasture, lea, ley *or* lay [*dial.*], pasturage, field.

LAWN, green, plat, plot. grassplat.

GREENSWARD, sward, turf, sod, grass; heather.

GROUNDS; *maidan* [*India*], park, common, campus [*U. S.*], *agostadero* [*Sp.*].

Adj. CHAMPAIGN, campestral, campestrial [*obs.*], campestrian, campestrine. ALLUVIAL, fluvio-marine.

Adv. in the bush.

345. Marsh. — N. MARSH, swamp, morass, marish [*archaic*], peat bog, moss, fen, bog, quagmire, slough, sump [*Scot. or dial. Eng.*], bottoms, holm [*Eng.*], wash; mud, squash, slush; baygall [*U. S.*], *ciénaga* [*Sp.*], *jhil* [*India*]. *vlei* [*S. Africa*].

Adj. MARSH, marshy, swampy, boggy, plashy, poachy, quaggy, soft; muddy, sloppy, squashy, spongy; paludal; moorish, moory; fenny, marish [*archaic*].

346. Island. — N. ISLAND, isle, islet, ait *or* eyot, holm, reef, atoll; archipelago; islander.

V. INSULATE, island, enisle [*rare*], isle [*rare*].

Adj. INSULAR, insulary [*rare*], seagirt; archipelagic.

3. Fluids in Motion

347. [FLUID IN MOTION.] **Stream.** —N. STREAM &c. (*of water*) 348, (*of air*) 349. V. FLOW &c. 348; BLOW &c. 349.

348. [WATER IN MOTION.] **River.** — N. running water.

jet, swash, spurt *or* spirt, squirt, spout, splash, rush, gush, *jet d'eau* [*F.*]; sluice.

waterspout, waterfall; fall, cascade, force *or* foss [*dial. Eng.*], linn *or* lin [*Scot.*], gill *or* ghyll; Niagara; cataract, catadupe [*obs.*], cataclysm; debacle, inundation, deluge; chute, washout.

RAIN, rainfall; *serein* [*F.*]; plash, shower, scud [*dial.*]; downpour; downflow, pour, cloudburst, drencher; driving -, drenching- rain; predominance of Aquarius, reign of St. Swithin; drisk [*U. S.*], brash [*dial.*], mizzle [*dial.*], drizzle, stillicidium, dropping &c. *v.;*

349. [AIR IN MOTION.] **Wind.** — N. WIND, draught, flatus, afflatus, sufflation [*rare*], insufflation, perflation, inflation, afflation, indraft *or* indraught, efflation; air; breath, - of air; puff, whiff, whiffet, zephyr, blow, drift; aura; stream, current; undercurrent.

Æolus *or* Eolus, Boreas, Euroclydon, Eurus, Notus [*rare*], Zephyr *or* Zephyrus, Favonius; cave of Æolus *or* Eolus; Wabun (east wind), Kabibonokka (north wind), Shawondasee (south wind), Mudjekeewis (west wind) [*all four from Hiawatha*].

GUST, blast, breeze, capful of wind, fresh breeze, stiff breeze, keen blast, squall, half a gale, gale.

TRADE WIND, trades, monsoon.

rains, rainy season, monsoon, *bursat* or *barsat* [*Hind.*]; falling weather [*colloq.*].

HYETOLOGY, hyetography; hyetograph, rain chart.

STREAM, course, flux, flow, profluence; effluence &c. (*egress*) 295; defluxion; flowing &c. *v.;* current, tide, race, mill race, tide race.

spring; fount, fountain; rill, rivulet, rillet; streamlet, brooklet; branch [*U. S.*]; runnel, runlet; sike, burn [*both dial. Eng. & Scot.*], beck [*Eng.*], brook, river; reach; tributary.

body of water, torrent, rapids, flush, flood, swash; spring –, high –, flood –, full- tide; bore, eagre *or* hygre; fresh, freshet; indraft *or* indraught; ebb, refluence, reflux, undercurrent, undertow, eddy, vortex, gurge [*rare*], whirlpool, Charybdis, Maelstrom (*also* maelstrom), regurgitation, overflow, alluvion; confluence, corrivation [*obs.*].

WAVE, billow, surge, swell, ripple, *anerithmon gelasma* [*Gr.* ἀνήριθμον γέλασμα]; beach comber, riffle [*U. S.*], tidal wave, comber, chop, choppiness, roll, rollers, ground swell, surf, breakers, white horses; rough –, heavy –, cross –, long –, short -, choppy –, chopping- sea.

[SCIENCE OF FLUIDS IN MOTION] hydrodynamics; hydraulics, hydrostatics, hydrokinetics, hydromechanics, pegology, pluviometry.

[MEASURES] hyetometer, hyetometrograph, hydrodynamometer, nilometer, fluviometer, fluviograph, marigraph, hydrometer, hydrometrograph, udometer, ombrometer, rain gauge *or* gage, pluviometer, pluviograph.

IRRIGATION &c. (*water*) 337; pump; watering- pot, – cart; hydrant, standpipe, syringe, siphon, *mussuk* [*Hind.*].

WATER CARRIER, bheesty *or* bheestie [*India*], Water Bearer, Aquarius.

V. FLOW, run; meander; gush, pour, spout, roll, jet, well, issue; drop, drip, dribble, plash, spirtle, trill, trickle, distill, percolate; stream, gurge [*rare*], surge, swirl, overflow, inundate, deluge, flow over, splash, swash; guggle, murmur, babble, bubble, purl, gurgle, sputter, spurt, regurgitate; ooze, flow out &c. (*egress*) 295.

FLOW INTO, fall into, open into, drain into; discharge itself, disembogue.

[CAUSE A FLOW] pour; pour out &c.

STORM, tempest, hurricane, whirlwind, tornado, samiel, cyclone, typhoon, simoom *or* simoon, harmattan, sirocco, mistral, *bise* [*F.*], *tramontana* [*It.*], tramontane, levant, levanter; blizzard, barber [*Can.*], *candelia* [*Sp. Am.*], chinook, foehn, khamsin, norther, northeaster, northeast gale, *vendaval* [*Sp.*], wuther [*dial.*], willy-willy [*Austral.*].

WINDINESS &c. *adj.;* ventosity [*obs.*]; rough –, dirty –, ugly –, wicked –, foul –, stress of- weather; dirty sky, mare's-tail, mackerel sky; cloud &c. 353; thick –, black –, white- squall.

ANEMOGRAPHY, anemology, anemometry, aërology, aërography, aërodynamics.

WIND-GAUGE, anemometer, anemoscope, anemograph, anemometrograph; weathercock, weathervane, vane.

BREATHING, respiration, inspiration, inhalation, expiration, exhalation; blowing, fanning, &c. *v.;* ventilation; sneezing &c. *v.;* errhine; sternutation; hiccup *or* hiccough, eructation, catching of the breath; inspirator, respirator, ejector.

air pump, lungs, bellows, pulmotor, blowpipe; branchiæ, gills.

FAN, punkah *or* punka [*India*], flabellum, thermantidote, electric fan; *ventilabrum* [*L.*].

VENTILATOR, louver, aërator [*rare*], transom; airpipe &c. 351; hygrometer, psychrometer.

V. BLOW, waft; blow -hard, – great guns, – a hurricane &c. *n.;* storm; wuther [*dial.*], stream, issue.

RESPIRE, breathe, inhale, exhale; inspire, expire; puff; whiff, whiffle; gasp, wheeze; snuff, snuffle; sniff, sniffle; sneeze, cough, hiccup *or* hiccough; belch, eruct [*rare*].

FAN, ventilate; inflate, pump, perflate [*obs.*]; blow up.

WHISTLE, scream, roar, howl, sing, sing in the shrouds, growl.

Adj. WINDY, airy, æolian *or* eolian, borean, favonian; ventilative; blowing &c. *v.;* breezy, gusty, squally.

STORMY, tempestuous, blustering, cyclonic, typhonic; boisterous &c. (*violent*) 173.

ANEMOGRAPHIC, anemological, anemometric *or* anemometrical, aërologic *or* aërological, aërographic *or* aërographical, aërodynamic.

PULMONIC, pulmonary, pulmonate.

(*discharge*) 297; shower down; irrigate, drench &c. (*wet*) 337; spill, splash.

[Stop a flow] stanch *or* staunch; dam, dam up &c. (*close*) 261; obstruct &c. 706.

RAIN, ~ hard, – in torrents, – cats and dogs, – pitchforks [*both colloq.*]; pour, shower, sprinkle, pour with rain, drizzle, spit [*colloq.*], set in; mizzle.

Adj. FLUENT, deliquescent, defluent, profluent [*rare*], diffluent, affluent; tidal; flowing &c. *v.;* meandering, meandrous, meandry [*obs.*], flexuous, fluvial, fluviatile; streamy, streamful; choppy, rolling; stillicidious [*obs.*], stillatitious [*rare*]; hydragogue [*med.*].

RAINY, showery, pluvial [*rare*], pluvious, pluviose [*rare*], drizzly, drizzling, mizzly, wet; pluviometric *or* pluviometrical.

*** "for men may come and men may go but I go on forever" [Tennyson]; "that mountain floods should thunder as before" [Wordsworth]; "the immense and contemptuous surges" [Kipling]; "the heave and the halt and the hurl and the crash of the comber wind-hounded" [*ibid.*]; "rivers are moving roads" [Pascal].

NASAL, errhine; sternutative, sternutatory.

FLATULENT, gassy, windy, ventose.

*** "lull'd by soft zephyrs" [Pope]; "the storm is up and all is on the hazard" [*Julius Cæsar*]; "the winds were wither'd in the stagnant air" [Byron]; "while mocking winds are piping loud" [Milton]; "winged with red lightning and tempestuous rage" [*Paradise Lost*]; "the headsail's low-volleying thunder" [Kipling]; "that gay companion, the loudly laughing wind" [Dunsany].

350. [Channel for the passage of water.] **Conduit. — N.** CONDUIT, channel, duct, watercourse, cañon *or* canyon, coulee *or* coulée [*geol.*], water gap, gorge, ravine, chasm; race; head –, tail– race; abito [*F. Amer.*], aboideau *or* aboiteau [*local Can.*], bito [*dial., U. S.*]; acequia [*Sp. Amer.*], acequiador [*Sp. Amer.*], arroyo; adit, aqueduct, canal, trough, gutter, pantile; flume, dike, main; gully, gullet [*rare*], gulch [*U. S.*], moat, ditch, drain, sewer, culvert, cloaca, sough [*dial. Eng.*], kennel, siphon; piscine, piscina; pipe &c. (*tube*) 260; funnel; tunnel &c. (*passage*) 627; water –, waste– pipe; emunctory, gully hole, spout, scupper; ajutage; hose; gargoyle *or* gurgoyle; penstock, pentrough, weir, lock weir, floodgate, water gate, sluice, lock, valve; rose, rosehead; waterworks.

[For metal] ingate, runner, tedge.

[Anatomy] artery, vein, *vena* [*L.*], blood vessel, lymphatic, pore; aorta; intestines, bowels; small intestine, duodenum, jejunum, ileum; large intestine, cæcum, colon, rectum; esophagus *or* œsophagus, gullet; throat.

Adj. VASCULAR &c. (*with holes*) 260.

EXCRETORY, eliminative.

351. [Channel for the passage of air.] **Air Pipe. — N.** AIR PIPE, air tube, air hole, blowhole, breathing hole, spiracle, touchhole, vent hole, spile hole, bung, bunghole; shaft, airway, air shaft, smokeshaft, flue, chimney, funnel, vent, ventage; ventiduct, ventilator; pipe &c. (*tube*) 260; blowpipe &c. (*wind*) 349.

nostril, nozzle, throat, weasand, bronchus (*pl.* bronchi), larynx, tonsils, windpipe, trachea.

LOUVER, Venetian blind, Venetian shutter, *jalousie* [*F.*], *jhilmil* [*India*].

3. Imperfect Fluids

352. Semiliquidity. — N. SEMILIQUIDITY; stickiness &c. *adj.;* viscidity, viscosity, mucidness, gummosis, emulsification, jellification; gummosity [*rare*], glutinosity [*rare*], mucosity; crassitude, spissitude; lentor [*now rare*]; pastiness; adhesiveness &c. (*cohesion*) 46; succulence *or* succulency; lactescence.

INSPISSATION, incrassation, crassamentum, coagulum; thickening.

[Comparisons] jelly, gelatin, carlock, ichthyocol. ichthyocolla, isinglass; mu-

353. [Mixture of air and water.] **Bubble, Cloud. — N.** BUBBLE; foam, froth, head, spume, scum, fume, lather, suds, spray, surf, yeast, barm, spoondrift *or* spindrift.

EFFERVESCENCE, fermentation; bubbling &c. *v.;* evaporation, exhalation, emanation.

CLOUDINESS &c. (*opacity*) 426; nebulosity &c. (*dimness*) 422.

CLOUD, vapor, fog, mist, haze, steam; scud, rack, nimbus; cumulus, nebula,

cus, pus, phlegm, pituite; lava; paste; library –, flour- paste; glair, starch, gluten, albumen, milk, cream, protein; treacle, rob, sirup *or* syrup, molasses; gum, size, glue, varnish, mastic, mucilage, fish glue; wax, beeswax; emulsion; gruel, porridge; *purée* [*F.*], soup.

SQUASH, mud, slush, slime, ooze; moisture &c. 339; marsh &c. 345.

V. INSPISSATE, incrassate; coagulate, gelatinate, gelatinize; jellify, jelly, jell [*colloq.*, *U. S.*]; emulsify, thicken; mash, squash, churn, beat up.

Adj. SEMIFLUID, semiliquid; half-melted, half-frozen; milky, muddy &c. *n.;* lacteal, lactean [*rare*], lacteous, lactescent, lactiferous; emulsive, curdled, thick, succulent, uliginose *or* uliginous.

GELATINOUS, albuminous, mucilaginous, glutinous; gummous, spissated [*rare*], crass, tremelloid, tremellose, amylaceous, ropy, clammy, clotted; viscid, viscous; sticky, tacky; slab [*dial.*], slabby; lentous [*obs.*], pituitous; mucid, muculent, mucous.

***** "lucent syrops tinct with cinnamon" [Keats].

354. Pulpiness. — **N.** PULPINESS &c. *adj.;* pulp, paste, dough, sponge, batter, clotted cream, curd, pap, jam, pudding, poultice, grume.

V. PULP, pulpify [*rare*], mash, squash [*colloq.*], masticate, macerate; coagulate &c. 352.

Adj. PULPY &c. *n.;* pultaceous, grumous; baccate; [*of fruit*] fleshy, succulent.

***** "crisp and juicy stalks Culled from the ocean's meadows" [Bryant].

meteor, woolpack, cirrus, curl cloud, thunderhead, stratus; cirro-stratus, cumulo-stratus; cirro-cumulus; mackerel sky, mare's-tail, colt's-tail, cat's-tail, cocktail, dirty sky; frost smoke.

[SCIENCE OF CLOUDS] nephology, nephelognosy, meteorology; nephoscope, nephelometer, nephograph.

V. BUBBLE, boil, foam, spume, froth, mantle, sparkle, guggle, gurgle; effervesce, pop, ferment, fizzle; aërate.

CLOUD, overcast, overcloud, befog, becloud, adumbrate [*rare*], mist, fog, overshadow, shadow.

Adj. BUBBLING &c. *v.;* frothy, nappy [*obs.*], effervescent, sparkling, *mousseux* [*F.*], fizzy, heady, with a head on, with a collar on [*slang*], up [*colloq.*].

CLOUDY &c. *n.;* cirrous, cirrose; nubiferous, cumulous, thunderheaded; vaporous, nebulous, overcast.

NEPHOLOGICAL, nepheloscopic, nephelometric, meteorologic *or* meteorological.

***** "the lowring element scowls o'er the darkened landscip" [*Paradise Lost*]; "stinging, ringing spindrift" [Kipling].

355. Unctuousness. — **N.** UNCTUOUSNESS &c. *adj.;* unctiousness [*rare*], unguent, unctuosity, lubricity; salve, cerate; ointment &c. (*oil*) 356; anointment; lubrication &c. 332.

V. OIL, anoint, lubricate &c. 332; smear, salve, grease, lard, pinguefy.

Adj. UNCTUOUS, unctious [*rare*], unguentary, unguentous, oily, oleaginous, adipose, sebaceous, unguinous, fat, fatty, greasy; waxy, butyraceous, soapy, saponaceous, pinguid, lardaceous; slippery.

356. Oil. — **N.** OIL, fat, butter, cream, grease, tallow, suet, lard, dripping, exunge [*obs.*], blubber; glycerin *or* glycerine, stearin, elain *or* elaine, olein, oleagine; coconut butter; soap; soft soap, wax, cerement; paraffin *or* paraffine, benzine, gasoline *or* gasolene, petrol, spermaceti, adipocere; petroleum, mineral –, rock –, crystal- oil; vegetable –, colza –, olive –, salad –, linseed –, cottonseed –, coconut –, palm –, nut- oil; animal –, neat's-foot –, train- oil; ointment, pomade, pomatum, unguent, liniment; amole, Barbados tar; fusel –, grain –, rape –, seneca- oil; hydrate of amyl, ghee *or* ghi [*India*], kerosene, naphtha.

356a. Resin. — **N.** RESIN, rosin, colophony, gum; lac, shellac *or* shell-lac, sealing wax; amber, ambergris; bitumen, pitch, tar; asphalt *or* asphaltum; camphor; varnish, copal, mastic, megilp *or* magilp, lacquer, japan, Brunswick black.

V. VARNISH &c. (*overlay*) 223; rosin, resin.

Adj. RESINOUS, resiny, rosinous [*rare*], lacquered, japanned, camphorated, tarred, tarry, pitched, pitchy, gummed, gummy, gummous, waxed; bituminous, asphaltic, asphaltite.

Section III. ORGANIC MATTER

1. Vitality

1. Vitality in general

357. Organization. — N. organization, organized world, organized nature,
living nature, animated nature; living
beings; organic remains; organism, bion
[*physiological individual*]; morphon [*morphological individual*]; biota, animal and
plant life, fauna and flora.

fossils, fossilization, lapidification,
petrification, petrifaction, paleontology
or palæontology, paleozoölogy *or* palæ-
ozoölogy; paleontologist *or* palæontologist.

[Science of living beings] biology,
natural history; [1]zoölogy &c. 368; botany

358. Inorganization. — N. mineral
kingdom, mineral world; unorganized –,
inorganic –, brute –, inanimate- matter.

[Science of the mineral kingdom]
mineralogy, geology, geognosy, geos-
copy, metallurgy, metallography, lithology, petrology, oryctology [*obs.*], oryc-
tography [*obs.*].

V. mineralize; pulverize, turn to
dust.

Adj. inorganic, inanimate, unorganized *or* inorganized, lithoid *or* lithoidal;
azoic; mineral.

&c. 369; physiology, anatomy, cytology, embryology, organic chemistry, morphology; promorphology, tectology; cell theory *or* cellular theory, evolution,
metabolism; abiogenesis, spontaneous generation; archigenesis &c. (*production*)
161; biotaxy, ecology *or* œcology, ontogeny, phylogeny, polymorphism, oxidation,
invagination, vertebration.

Darwinism, Lamarckism, neo-Lamarckism, Weismannism.

naturalist, biologist, zoölogist, botanist, bacteriologist, embryologist, Dar-
winian.

protoplasm, plasma *or* plasm, cytoplasm, metaplasm, karyoplasm, bioplasm, trophoplasm,
idioplasm; cell, proteid, protein, albumen, albumin, albuminoid; structure &c. 329; chromatin;
centrosome, nucleolus, karyosome, vacuole, chromosome; protoplast, protozoan, amœba;
karyaster, erythroblast, dysmeromorph, antherozoid.

ovum, oösperm, zygote, oösphere, oöcyte, oœcium, ovicell, oögonium; oöphyte, oöspore,
oögamy, heterogamy, isogamy, oögenesis; gamete, gametophore, gametophyte, sporophyte,
sporocyte, sporocyst, sporocarp, cystocarp, sporogonium, sporozoite, gametangium, antheridium
or antherid; macrospore, megasporangium; microspore, microsporangium; biophore; spermatozoid, zoöspore, macrogamete, microgamete, spermatozoön, spermatium, spermatia, sperma-
tocyte, spermatogenesis, spermatophore, spermatozoid, spermatozooid; spermogonium, spermary,
sperm gland, testis, testicle, ovary; germ cell, blastoderm, mesoblast *or* mesoplast, meroblast
(*opp.* to holoblast); germinal matter, biogenesis *or* biogeny, germ plasm *or* germ plasma, zoöglœa,
zooid.

V. organize, systematize, form, arrange, construct.

fossilize, petrify, lapidify, mummify.

Adj. organic, organized; biotic, zooid, zooidal.

fossilized, petrified, petrifactive, lapidified; paleontologic, paleontological *or*
palæontological, paleozoölogical *or* palæozoölogical.

protoplasmic, plasmatic *or* plasmic, cytoplasmic, metaplasmic, karyoplasmic,
bioplasmic, trophoplasmic, idioplasmic; cellular, cellulous; proteid, proteinaceous,
albuminous *or* albuminose, albuminoidal, structural; nuclear, nucleate, nucleolar,
nucleolate *or* nucleolated; vacuolar, protoplastic, protozoan, amœbic, amœboid.

ovarian, oviferous, oviparous (*opp.* to viviparous), ovicular; oöphytic, oösporic,
oösporous, oögamous, heterogamous (*opp.* to autogamous *or* isogamous); gamic,
sporogenous; spermatic, spermatogenetic, spermatoid, spermatophoral, sperma-
tozoal; blastodermic, mesoblastic (*opp.* to holoblastic), biogenetic, germinal;
zoöglœic, zoöglœoid; unsegmentic, diœcious *or* diecious (*opp.* to monœcious *or*
monecious).

---

[1] The term *natural history* is also used as relating to all the objects in Nature whether organic
or inorganic, and including, therefore, *mineralogy, geology, meteorology*, &c.

359. Life. — **N.** LIFE; vitality, viableness, viability; animation.

VITAL SPARK, vital flame, Promethean spark, lifeblood; respiration, wind; breath of life, breath of one's nostrils; Archeus or Archæus; anima [L.], anima bruta [L.], anima divina [L.], anima mundi [L.]; world -soul, – spirit, – principle; existence &c. 1.

VIVIFICATION; oxygen; vital -air, – force; life force; vitalization; revival; revivification &c. 163; Prometheus; Deucalion and Pyrrha; life to come &c. (destiny) 152.

"a short summer" [Johnson]; "a bubble" [Browne]; "a battle" [Aurelius]; "one dem'd horrid grind" [Dickens].

[SCIENCE OF LIFE] physiology, biology, ætiology or etiology, embryology; animal economy.

NOURISHMENT, staff of life &c. (food) 298.

V. LIVE; be alive &c. adj.; breathe, respire, suspire; subsist &c. (exist) 1; walk the earth; (a poor player that) "struts and frets his hour upon the stage" [Macbeth]; be spared.

BE BORN, see the light, come into the world; fetch –, draw- -breath, – the breath of life; breathe the vital air; quicken; revive; come to, – life.

GIVE BIRTH TO &c. (produce) 161; bring to life, put into life, vitalize; vivify, vivificate [rare]; reanimate &c. (restore) 660.

KEEP ALIVE, keep body and soul together, keep the wolf from the door; support life.

have nine lives like a cat.

Adj. LIVING, alive; in life, in the flesh, in the land of the living; on this side of the grave, above ground, breathing, quick, animated; animative; lively &c. (active) 682; alive and kicking [colloq.]; tenacious of life.

VITAL, vitalic; vivifying, vivified &c. v.; viable, zoëtic; Promethean.

Adv. vivendi causâ [L.].

. atqui vivere militare est [Seneca]; non est vivere sed valere vita [Martial]; "all that a man has will he give for his life" [Bible]; "our life is what our thoughts make it" [Aurelius]; "in short measures life may perfect be" [Jonson]; "all is concentr'd in a life intense" [Byron]; "as though to breathe were life!" [Tennyson]; "how good is man's life, the mere living!" [Browning]; "Life's but a walking shadow"

360. Death. — **N.** DEATH; decease, demise; mortality; dying; passing -away, – of the soul; dissolution, departure, obit, release, rest, eternal rest, quietus, fall; loss, bereavement.

end &c. 67 –, cessation &c. 142 –, loss –, extinction –, ebb- of life &c. 359.

DEATH-WARRANT, deathwatch, death rattle, deathbed; stroke –, agonies –, shades –, valley of the shadow –, summons –, jaws –, hand –, bridge –, river- of death; Jordan, Jordan's bank, "one more river to cross"; last -breath, - gasp, – agonies; dying -day, – breath. – agonies; swan song, chant du cygne [F.]; rigor mortis [L.]; Stygian shore· "crossing the bar" [Tennyson]; the great adventure.

euthanasia, euthanasy [rare]; happy release, bona mors [L.]; break-up of the system; natural -death, – decay; sudden –, violent- death; untimely end, taking off [colloq.], watery grave; debt of nature; mortification, heart failure, suffocation, asphyxia; fatal disease &c. (disease) 655; deathblow &c. (killing) 361.

ANGEL OF DEATH, death's bright angel, Azrael; King -of terrors, – Death; Death, doom &c. (necessity) 601; "Hell's grim Tyrant" [Pope].

NECROLOGY, bills of mortality, obituary.

DEATH SONG &c. (lamentation) 839.

V. DIE, expire, perish; meet one's -death, – end; pass away, pass over, be taken; yield –, resign- one's breath; resign one's -being, – life; end one's -days, – life, – earthly career; breathe one's last; cease to -live, – breathe; depart this life; be no more &c. adj.; go off [colloq.], drop off [colloq.], pop off [slang]; lose –, lay down –, relinquish –, surrender- one's life; drop –, sink- into the grave; close one's eyes; fall –, drop- -dead, – down dead; break one's neck; give –, yield- up the ghost; be all over with one.

pay the debt to nature, shuffle off this mortal coil, take one's last sleep; go the way of all flesh; hand –, pass- -in one's checks, – in one's chips [all slang]; go over to the –, join the- -greater number, – majority, – great majority; join the choir invisible; awake to life immortal; come –, turn- to dust; give an obolus to

[*Macbeth*]; "a little gleam of time between two eternities" [Carlyle]; "the vital warmth that feeds my life" [Otway]; "Life, like a dome of many-coloured glass, Stains the white radiance of eternity" [Shelley]; "Life, a beauty chased by tragic laughter" [Masefield].

Charon; cross the Stygian ferry; go to one's long account, go to one's last home, go to Davy Jones's locker, go to glory [*colloq. or slang*]; receive one's death warrant, make one's will, step out [*colloq.*], die a natural death, go out like the snuff of a candle; come to an untimely end; catch one's death; go off the twig, turn up one's toes [*all slang*]; die the hooks, kick the bucket, hop the a violent death &c. (*be killed*) 361.

die for one's country, make the supreme sacrifice, go West [*World War euphemism*].

Adj. DEAD, lifeless; deceased, demised, departed, defunct; late, gone, no more; exanimate [*rare*], inanimate; out of the world, taken off, released; bereft of life; stone dead; departed this life &c. *v.;* dead and gone; dead as -a doornail, − a doorpost, − mutton, − a herring, − nits [*all slang or colloq.*]; launched into eternity, gathered to one's fathers, numbered with the dead; born into a better world, born into the next world; gone to a better land; dying −, dead- in the Lord; asleep in Jesus; with the saints.

stillborn; mortuary; deadly &c. (*killing*) 361.

DYING &c. *v.;* moribund, morient [*obs.*]; Hippocratic; *in articulo* [*L.*], *in extremis* [*L.*]; in the -jaws, − agony- of death; going, − off; *aux abois* [*F.*]; on one's -last legs [*colloq.*], − deathbed; at the point of death, at death's door, at the last gasp; near one's end, given up, given over, booked [*slang*]; with one foot in −, tottering on the brink of- the grave.

Adv. *post obit* [*L.*], *post mortem* [*L.*].

*** Life -ebbs, − fails, − hangs by a thread; one's days are numbered, one's hour is come, one's race is run, one's doom is sealed; Death knocks at the door, Death stares one in the face; the breath is out of the body; the grave closes over one; *sic itur ad astra* [Vergil]; *de mortuis nil nisi bonum; dulce et decorum est p̦o patria mori* [Horace]; *honesta mors turpi vitâ potior* [Tacitus]; "in adamantine chains shall death be bound" [Pope]; *mors ultima linea rerum est* [Horace]; *omnia mors æquat* [Claudianus]; "spake the grisly Terror" [*Paradise Lost*]; "the lone couch of his everlasting sleep" [Shelley]; "the push of death has swung her into life" [Tagore]; "And Death is beautiful as feet of friend Coming with welcome at our journey's end" [Lowell]; "Why do we then shun Death with anxious strife? If Light can thus deceive, wherefore not Life?" [J. Blanco White].

361. [DESTRUCTION OF LIFE; VIOLENT DEATH.] **Killing. — N.** KILLING &c. *v.;* homicide, manslaughter, murder, assassination, trucidation [*obs.*], occision [*obs.*]; effusion of blood; blood, bloodshed; gore, slaughter, carnage, butchery; *battue* [*F.*]; bomb explosion, electrocution, shipwreck; gladiatorial combat; lapidation.

MASSACRE; fusillade, *noyade* [*F.*]; thuggism, thuggee, thuggery; saturnalia of blood, sacrifice to Moloch; organized massacre, *pogrom* [*Russia*].

WAR, warfare, "organized murder," *horrida bella* [*L.*], crusade, jihad *or* jehad [*Moham.*]; battle; war to the death &c. (*warfare*) 722; Armageddon; gigantomachy; deadly weapon &c. (*arms*) 727.

DEATHBLOW, finishing stroke, *coup de grâce* [*F.*], quietus; execution &c. (*capital punishment*) 972; judicial murder; martyrdom.

SUFFOCATION, strangulation, garrote *or* garrotte; hanging &c. *v.*

SLAYER, butcher, murderer, Cain, assassin, cutthroat, garroter *or* garrotter, bravo, Thug *or* thug, Moloch, matador, *sabreur* [*F.*]; *guet-apens* [*F.*]; gallows, executioner &c. (*punishment*) 975; man-eater, Apache, hatchet man [*U. S.*], highbinder [*U. S.*], gunman [*colloq., U. S.*], bandit, lapidator [*rare*].

regicide, parricide, fratricide, infanticide; feticide *or* fœticide, aborticide; uxoricide, vaticide [*these words ending in* -cide *refer to both doer and deed*].

SUICIDE, self-murder, self-destruction, *felo-de-se* (*pl. felos-de-se*), seppuku [*Jap.*], hara-kiri [*Jap.*], suttee, sutteeism, car of Jagannath *or* Juggernaut [*an erroneous assumption*]; immolation, holocaust.

FATAL ACCIDENT, violent death, casualty, disaster, calamity.

ACELDAMA (*often l.c.*), potter's field, field of blood.

[DESTRUCTION OF ANIMALS] slaughtering; phthiozoics;[1] sport, sporting; the chase, venery; hunting, coursing, shooting, fishing; pig-sticking.

sportsman, huntsman, fisherman; hunter, Nimrod.

shambles, slaughterhouse, *abattoir* [*F.*].

V. KILL, put to death, slay, shed blood; murder, assassinate, butcher, slaughter, victimize, immolate; massacre; take away –, deprive of-life; make away with, put an end to; dispatch *or* despatch; burke, settle [*colloq.*], do to death, do for [*colloq.*]; hunt.

shoot, – dead; blow one's brains out; brain, knock on the head, blackjack; drop in one's tracks; stone, lapidate; give –, deal- a deathblow; give the -quietus, – *coup de grâce* [*F.*].

STRANGLE, garrote *or* garrotte, hang, throttle, choke, stifle, suffocate, stop the breath, smother, asphyxiate, drown.

SABER *or* sabre; cut -down, – to pieces, – the throat; jugulate; stab, run through the body, bayonet; put to the -sword, – edge of the sword.

EXECUTE, behead, guillotine, hang, electrocute; bowstring &c. (*execute*) 972.

CUT OFF, nip in the bud, launch into eternity, send to one's last account, sign one's death warrant, strike the death knell of.

GIVE NO QUARTER, pour out blood like water; decimate; run amuck; wade knee-deep in blood; dye –, imbrue- one's hands in blood.

DIE A VIOLENT DEATH, welter in one's blood; dash –, blow- out one's brains; commit suicide; kill –, make away with –, put an end to- oneself; suicide [*colloq.*]; disembowel, commit hara-kiri.

Adj. MURDEROUS, slaughterous, sanguinary, sanguinolent, blood-stained, blood-thirsty; killing &c. *v.;* homicidal, red-handed; bloody, bloody-minded; ensanguined, gory, sanguineous.

MORTAL, fatal, lethal; deadly, deathly; mortiferous [*obs.*], lethiferous; unhealthy &c. 657; mutually destructive, internecine; suicidal.

SPORTING; piscatorial, piscatory.

Int. thumbs down! *habet! hoc habet!* [*L.*], let him have it!

* dead men tell no tales; "assassination has never changed the history of the world" [Disraeli].

362. Corpse. — N. CORPSE, corse [*archaic*], carcass *or* carcase, cadaver, bones, skeleton, dry bones; defunct, relics, reliquiæ, remains, mortal remains, dust, ashes, earth, clay; mummy; carrion; food for -worms, – fishes; tenement of clay, "this mortal coil" [*Hamlet*]; "this too, too solid flesh" [*Hamlet*].

GHOST, shade, manes, phantom, specter *or* spectre, apparition, spirit, revenant, sprite [*archaic*], spook [*colloq.*].

ORGANIC REMAINS, fossils.

Adj. CADAVEROUS, cadaveric, corpse-like; unburied &c. 363.

363. Interment. — N. INTERMENT, burial, sepulture, entombment *or* in-tombment, inhumation, humation [*obs.*]; obsequies, exequies; funeral, wake.

CREMATION, burning; pyre, funeral pile.

FUNERAL RITE, funeral solemnity; knell, passing bell, death bell, funeral ring, tolling; dirge &c. (*lamentation*) 839; cypress; obit, dead march, muffled drum; elegy; funeral -oration, – sermon.

UNDERTAKER, mortician [*cant, U. S.*], funeral director.

MOURNER, mute, keener [*Ireland*], lamenter; pallbearer, bearer.

GRAVECLOTHES, shroud, winding sheet, cerecloth; cerements.

COFFIN, casket, shell, sarcophagus.

urn, cinerary urn; pall, bier, litter, hearse, catafalque.

BURIAL PLACE, grave, pit, sepulcher *or* sepulchre, tomb, vault, crypt, cata-comb, mausoleum, cenotaph, golgotha, house of death, narrow house, low green tent, low house, long home, last home; cemetery, necropolis; burial ground;

---

[1] Bentham, *Chrestomathia.*

graveyard, churchyard; God's acre; potter's field; cromlech, barrow, tumulus, cairn; ossuary; bonehouse, charnel-house, deadhouse; morgue, mortuary; lich gate; burning ghât *or* ghaut [*India*]; crematorium, crematory; mastaba *or* mastabah [*Egypt*], tope *or* stupa [*Buddhist*]; dokhma, Tower of Silence [*Parsee*].

GRAVEDIGGER, sexton, *fossoyeur* [*F.*].

MONUMENT, cenotaph, shrine; gravestone, headstone, tombstone; *memento mori* [*L.*]; hatchment, stone, marker, cross; epitaph, inscription.

NECROPSY, necroscopy, autopsy, *post mortem* examination *or post mortem* [*L.*].

EXHUMATION, disinterment.

V. INTER, bury; lay in –, consign to- the -grave, – tomb; entomb *or* intomb; inhume; hold –, conduct- a funeral; put to bed with a shovel [*colloq.*]; inurn; cremate.

lay out; embalm, mummify; toll the knell.

EXHUME, disinter, unearth.

Adj. FUNEREAL, funebrial [*now rare*], funeral, funerary, mortuary, sepulchral, cinerary; buried &c. *v.;* burial; elegiac; necroscopic *or* necroscopical.

Adv. *hic jacet* [*L.*], *ci-gît* [*F.*], *R. I. P.; in memoriam* [*L.*]; *post obit* [*L.*], *post mortem* [*L.*]; beneath the sod, under the sod, underground; at rest.

⁎⁎⁎ requiescat in pace; resurgam; "the lone couch of his everlasting sleep" [Shelley]; "without a grave — unknell'd, uncoffin'd, and unknown [Byron]; "in the dark union of insensate dust" [Byron]; "the deep cold shadow of the tomb" [Moore]; "like one that wraps the drapery of his couch about him, and lies down to pleasant dreams" [Bryant].

2. Special Vitality

364. Animality. — N. ANIMALITY, animalism, animal life; animation, animalization, animalness.

CORPOREAL NATURE, human system; breath; flesh, flesh and blood; physique; strength &c. 159.

V. ANIMALIZE; incarnate, incarn [*rare*], incorporate.

Adj. FLESHLY, carnal, human, corporeal.

366. Animal. — N. ANIMAL KINGDOM, fauna, brute creation.

ANIMAL, creature, created being; creeping thing, living thing; dumb animal, dumb friend, dumb creature; brute, beast.

mammal, quadruped, bird, reptile, fish, crustacean, shellfish, mollusk, worm, insect, zoöphyte; plankton, nekton, benthos; animalcule &c. 193.

beasts of the field, fowls of the air, denizens of the day; flocks and herds, live stock, domestic animals; wild animals, *feræ naturæ* [*L.*], game.

[DOMESTIC ANIMALS] horse &c. (*beast of burden*) 271; cattle, kine, ox; bull, bullock; cow, milch cow, Alderney, Jersey, calf, heifer, shorthorn, yearling, steer. stot [*prov. Eng.*]; sheep; lamb, lambkin, ewe lamb, pet lamb; ewe, ram, tup, wether, tag [*prov. Eng.*], teg [*prov.*

365. Vegetation. — N. VEGETATION, vegetable life, vegetability [*obs.*], vegetativeness, vegetism, vegetality [*rare*]; herbage, flowerage.

V. VEGETATE, germinate, sprout, grow, shoot up, luxuriate, fungate; grow -rank, – lush, – like a weed; flourish &c. 367; cultivate.

Adj. VEGETATIVE, vegetal, vegetable; leguminous &c. 367.

LUXURIANT, rank, dense, lush, wild, jungly.

367. Vegetable. — N. VEGETABLE, vegetable kingdom; flora.

organism, plant, tree, shrub, bush, creeper, vine; herb, seedling, plantlet, exotic, annual, perennial, biennial, triennial; legume, pulse, vetch, greens; asparagus &c. (*vegetables*) 298.

FOLIAGE, leafage, verdure, foliation, frondescence [*rare*]; prefoliation, vernation; branch, bough, ramage, stem, tigella *or* tigelle *or* tigellum *or* tigellus; leaf, spray, leaflet, frond, foliole, bract, bractlet, bracteole, cotyledon, pad [*U. S.*], flag, petal, needle, sepal; spray &c. 51; petiole, petiolule, bine; shoot, tendril.

FLOWER, blossom, bud, burgeon, blow, blowth [*rare*]; floweret, floret, floscule, flowering plant; inflorescence, flowerage.

TREE, sapling, seedling, stand, pollard, dryad [*fig.*]; oak, elm, beech, birch,

Eng.]; pig, swine, boar, hog, sow; yak, zebu, Indian buffalo.

DOG, hound, canine; pup, puppy; whelp, cur [*contemptuous*].

house –, watch –, sheep –, shepherd's –, sporting –, hunting –, fancy –, lap –, toy-dog; collie; mastiff; bulldog, English bulldog, Boston bull, bull terrier, French bull; police dog, bloodhound, greyhound, staghound, deer-hound, foxhound, coach dog, bandog, lurcher, Russian *or* Siberian wolfhound, boarhound, St. Bernard, husky *or* Eskimo dog; otter-hound; harrier, beagle, spaniel, pointer, setter, retriever, Newfoundland; water -dog, – spaniel; pug, poodle; turnspit; terrier; fox –, Airedale –, Yorkshire –, Irish –, Skye –, toy-terrier; Dandie Dinmont; dachshund, badger dog; brindle; Pomeranian, cocker spaniel, King Charles span-iel, toy spaniel, spitz dog; chow *or* chow-dog, Japanese poodle.

pariah dog, pye-dog *or* pie-dog [*India*]; mon-grel, mut *or* mutt [*slang*].

FEMALE, bitch, slut, brach, brachet, lady [*euphemistic*].

CAT, feline, puss, pussy, grimalkin, tomcat *or* tom, gib [*rare*], Angora, Persian, Maltese, tortoiseshell, mouser; tabby; kitten, kit, catling, kitling [*dial.*].

[WILD ANIMALS] DEER, buck, doe, fawn, stag, hart, hind, roe, roebuck, caribou, elk, moose, reindeer, sambar, wapiti *or* American elk, mule deer, black-tailed deer *or* Virginia deer, fallow deer, red deer.

ANTELOPE, gazelle, nilghau, eland, gnu, hartebeest, springbok *or* spring-buck, oryx, steinbok, ibex; American antelope *or* pronghorn, chamois, koodoo *or* kudu.

armadillo, peba, poyou, tatouay; wild ass' kiang, dziggetai, onager; bear, polar bear, grizzly bear, brown bear; beaver; bison, buffalo; musk ox, giraffe, okapi, tapir; wild boar; babiroussa *or* babirussa; ape, monkey, gorilla, marmoset, chimpanzee, lemur, baboon, orang-utan *or* orang-outang; kangaroo, opos-sum; wild horse, zebra; elephant, *hathi* [*Hind.*]; fox, reynard, Reynard, vixen [*fem.*], varmin *or* varmint [*dial.*], prairie fox, gray fox, red fox, arctic fox; dingo, coyote; wildcat, lynx, bobcat; skunk; hippopotamus, rhinoceros, lion, tiger &c. (*wild beast*) 913; squirrel, chipmunk, gopher, prairie dog, ferret, stoat, weasel, mongoose, raccoon *or* coon, bandicoot, rat, mouse; bat, flying mouse, flying phalanger, flying squirrel; flying fox, flying lemur, colugo.

LIZARD, saurian, iguana, eft, newt, chame-leon, gecko, Gila monster, dragon, horned toad, horned lizard.

CROCODILIAN, crocodile, mugger *or* magar [*India*], gavial [*India*], alligator, cayman, American crocodile.

whale, sperm whale, baleen whale; shark, porpoise, walrus, seal, octopus, devilfish; swordfish; pike; salmon &c. (*food*) 298.

timber tree, pine, palm, spruce, fir, hemlock, yew, larch, cedar, savin *or* savine, juniper, chestnut, maple, alder, ash, myrtle, magnolia, walnut, olive, poplar, willow, linden, lime; apple &c. (*fruit trees*) 298; arboretum &c. 371.

banyan, teak, acacia, deodar, pipal *or* pipal tree; fig tree, eucalyptus, gum tree.

WOODLANDS, virgin forest, forest primeval, forest, wood, timberland, timber, wood lot; hurst, frith, holt [*poetic or dial.*], weald, wold [*obs.*], park, chase [*Eng.*], greenwood, grove, copse, coppice, *bocage* [*F.*], tope [*India*], clump of trees, thicket, spinet [*obs.*], spinney [*Eng.*], bosk, chaparral, *ceja* [*Texas*], motte [*local, U. S.*]; jungle, bush.

UNDERGROWTH, underwood, brush-wood, brake, "the mid-forest brake" [Keats]; boscage, scrub, palmetto bar-rens, bosch [*Dutch*]; heath, heather, fern, bracken, furze, gorse, whin, broom, genista, sedge, rush, bulrush, bamboo; weed, moss, foggage [*Scot.*], lichen, Iceland moss, mushroom, toadstool, fungus; turf, turbary, mold *or* mould.

GRASS, fog, second growth, second crop; herbage.

alfalfa, lucern *or* lucerne, alfilaria, clover, bent *or* bent grass, timothy, redtop *or* English grass, switch grass *or* black bent, blue grass, Kentucky blue grass, ribbon grass, meadow grass, spear grass, wire grass, blue joint, crab grass, bunch grass, meadow fescue, meadow foxtail, grama *or* mesquite grass, gama *or* sesame grass, sheep's fescue; cereal, wheat, barley, buckwheat, maize *or* Indian corn, oats, rice, rye.

GRASSLAND, greensward, green, lawn, sward, common, maidan [*India*], mead, meadow, pasture, pasturage, prairie, pampas, steppe, llano, savanna, campo, plain, field, campus [*U. S.*].

SEAWEED, alga (*pl.* algæ), fucus, fucoid, conferva (*pl.* confervæ), confer-void, wrack, dulse, kelp, rockweed, sea lettuce, gulfweed, sargasso, sargassum; plankton, benthos; Sargasso Sea.

V. VEGETATE, grow, flourish, bloom, flower, blossom; bud &c. (*expand*) 194; timber, retimber, coppice, copse; bush, plant, trim, cut.

Adj. VEGETABLE, vegetal, vegetive [*obs.*], vegetative, vegetarian; legumi-nous, herbaceous, herbal, botanic *or* botanical; arborary, arboreous, arbores-cent, arborical [*obs.*], arboreal, arboral; silvan *or* sylvan, treelike, dendriform,

[BIRDS] feathered tribes, feathered songster, singing bird, warbler, dicky-bird [colloq.].

canary, vireo, linnet, finch, goldfinch, brown thrasher, siskin, crossbill, aberdevine, chewink, peewee, lapwing [Scot.], titmouse or chickadee, nightingale, lark; magpie, cuckoo, mocking bird, catbird, laughing jackass, starling, myna or mina; bobolink, reedbird, ricebird, cardinal bird, cowbird, crow, rook, jackdaw, raven; pigeon, dove, cushat, ringdove, wood pigeon; swan, cygnet, goose, gander, duck, drake, wild duck, mallard; flamingo, heron, crane, stork, kingfisher, sandpiper, lyre bird, robin, thrush, hermit thrush, veery, mavis, missel thrush, ouzel or ousel, blackbird, red-winged blackbird; kingbird, fly-catcher; woodpecker, flicker; sparrow, song sparrow, chipping sparrow, vesper sparrow; swallow, swift, martin, sand martin, oriole, bluebird, meadow lark; bird of paradise, parrot, parrakeet or parakeet; pen-guin, pelican; gull, sea gull, albatross, petrel, stormy petrel or Mother Carey's chicken, fulmar or Mother Carey's goose; ostrich, emu; owl, bird of night; hawk, vulture, buzzard, turkey buzzard; eagle, bird of freedom, bird of Jove.

dendritic or dendritical, dendroid; grassy, verdant, verdurous; floral, floreal [rare], lignose or lignous [rare], ligneous, lignescent, wooden, woody; bosky, cespitose, copsy; mossy, turfy, turf-like; fungous, fungiform, fungoid; tigellate, radiculose, radicular, radiciform, radiciflorous, rhizanthous, radicated; endogenous, exogenous; deciduous, evergreen.

NATIVE, domestic, indigenous, native-grown, home-grown.

ALGAL, fucoid, confervoid; planktonic, benthonic.

₊ "green-robed senators of mighty woods" [Keats]; "this is the forest primeval" [Longfellow]; "Poems are made by fools like me, But only God can make a tree" [Joyce Kilmer].

GAME, black game, black grouse, ruffed grouse, grouse, blackcock, duck, plover, rail, snipe; pheasant &c. 298.

POULTRY, fowl, cock, rooster, chanticleer, dunghill fowl, barndoor fowl, barnyard fowl, hen, Partlet, chicken, chick, chickabiddy; guinea fowl, guinea hen; peafowl, peacock, bird of Minerva, peahen.

[INSECTS] bee, honeybee, queen bee, drone; ant, white ant, termite; wasp, sawfly, locust, grasshopper, cicada, cicala, cricket; dragon fly, June fly, caddis fly; beetle; butterfly, moth; fly, May fly, thrips, aphid, bug; ant lion, hellgramite or hellgamite, earwig; springtail, podura, lepisma; buffalo bug, buffalo carpet beetle &c. (injurious insects) 913.

VERMIN, lice, cooties [slang], flies, fleas, cockroaches or roaches, water bugs or Croton bugs, bugs, bedbugs, Norfolk Howards [slang], mosquitoes; rats, mice, weasels.

SNAKE, serpent, viper; asp, adder, coral snake or harlequin snake, krait [India], cobra, cobra de capello, king cobra, rattlesnake or rattler, copperhead, constrictor, boa constrictor, boa, python, Kaa [Kipling], ophidian.

[MYTHOLOGICAL] dipsas (pl. dipsades), basilisk, cockatrice, amphiobæna, Python, Hydra.

salamander; griffin or griffon or gryfon; chimæra; Cerberus.

Adj. ANIMAL, zoic, zooid or zooidal, zoölogical.

equine; bovine, vaccine; canine; feline; fishy, piscatory, piscatorial; molluscous, vermicular; gallinaceous, rasorial, solidungulate, soliped; planktonic, nekteric, benthonic.

OPHIDIAN, ophiologic, ophiomorphous, reptilian, anguine, ophic [rare], snake-like, serpentiform [rare], viperine, colubrine.

₊ "The whole creation groaneth and travaileth" [Bible]; "Hark! hark! the lark at heaven's gate sings" [Cymbeline]; "the mavis singing Its love song to the morn" [Jefferys]; "those feathery things, the hounds" [Masefield]; "some crush-nosed human-hearted dog" [Browning].

---

368. [SCIENCE OF ANIMALS.] Zoölogy — N. zoölogy, zoönomy, zoögraphy, zoötomy; morphology, anatomy, histology, embryology; comparative anatomy, animal physiology, comparative physiology; mammalogy.

anthropology, anthropotomy, ornithology, ornithotomy, ichthyology, ich-

369. [SCIENCE OF PLANTS.] Botany. — N. BOTANY; physiological -, structural -, systematic- botany; phytography, phytology, phytotomy, phytobiology, phytogenesis or phytogeny, phytonomy, phytopathology; phytochemistry, phytochimy [obsoles.], vegetable chemistry; pomology; vegetable

thyotomy, herpetology, herpetotomy, ophiology, malæology, helminthology, entomology, entomotomy; oryctology [obs.], paleontology or palæontology; mastology, vermeology; taxidermy.

ZOÖLOGIST, zoögrapher, zoögraphist, zoötomist, anatomist, anthropotomist, morphologist, promorphologist, anthropologist, ornithologist, ornithotomist, ichthyologist, ichthyotomist, herpetologist, herpetotomist, ophiliologist, malacologist, helminthologist, entomologist, entomotomist; oryctologist [obs.], paleontologist or palæontologist; vermeologist, taxidermist.

[PRINCIPAL GROUPS] PROTOZOA (the simplest animals): Rhizopoda, rhizopod; Foraminifera, foraminifer; Radiolaria, radiolarian; Flagellata; Infusoria, infusorian; Gregarinæ, gregarine.

CŒLENTERA or CŒLENTERATA (sponges, corals, jellyfishes): Porifera, poriferan; Cnidaria, cnida; Spongiæ or Spongiaria or Spongiozoa, sponge, calcareous sponges, siliceous sponges; Anthozoa, anthozoan, coral polyps; Hydrozoa, hydrozoön, hydroid, medusa.

ECHINODERMATA (crinoids, starfishes, and sea urchins): Pelmatozoa, Asterozoa, Echinozoa; Cystidea or Cystoidea, cystid, cystidean; Crinoidea, stone lilies, crinoidean; Blastoidea, blastoid; Ophiuroidea or Ophiurioidea, brittle stars, ophiuroid or ophiurid; Asterioidea or Asteridea, starfishes, asteridian; Echinoidea, sea urchins, echinoid; Holothurioidea, sea cucumbers, holothurian, holothure.

VERMES (worms): Platyhelminthes or Plathelminthes, flatworms, platyhelminth; Rotifera, rotifer; Nemathelminthes or Nematelminthes, roundworms; Gephyrea, marine annelids, gephyrean, gephyreoid; Annelida, annelid, annelidan, anneloid.

MOLLUSCOIDEA (mollusk-like animals): Bryozoa or Polyzoa, sea mosses, bryozoan; Brachiopoda, lamp shells, brachiopod.

MOLLUSCA (mollusks): Pelecypoda or Lamellibranchia, bivalves, lamellibranch; Scaphopoda, tooth-shells or tusk-shells, scaphopod; Amphineura, chitons; Gastropoda, univalves, snails, gastropod; Cephalopoda, nautilus, cuttlefish, squid, octopus, cephalopod or cephalopode.

ARTHROPODA (articulates): Branchiata, Tracheata; Crustacea, crustacean; Trilobita, trilobite; Limuloidea or Xiphosura, horseshoe crab, limulus; Entomostraca, ostracoids, barnacles, entomostracan; Malacostraca, lobsters, crabs, malacostracan; Myriapoda, centipeds or centipedes, galleyworms, millipeds, myriapod; Arachnida or Arachnoidea, spiders, scorpions, mites, ticks, arachnid, arachnidan; Insecta, insects.

physiology, herborization, dendrology, mycology, fungology, algology; flora, Flora, Pomona; botanic garden &c. (garden) 371; hortus siccus [L.]; herbarium, herbal [obs.].

PHYTON, phytomer or phytomeron.

[PRINCIPAL GROUPS] THALLOGENS or THALLOPHYTES (thallus plants): algæ and algoid forms: Cyanophyceæ, blue-green algæ; Chlorophyceæ, green algæ; Phæophyceæ, brown algæ; Rhodophyceæ, red algæ.

fungi and fungoid forms: Schizomycetes, fission fungi, bacteria; Myxomycetes, slime molds; Phycomycetes, algæ fungi, water molds; Ascomycetes, sac fungi, lichen fungi; Basidiomycetes, basidium fungi, rusts, mushrooms.

BRYOPHYTES (moss plants): Hepaticæ, liverworts; Musci, mosses.

PTERIDOPHYTES (fern plants): Lycopodiales: Sigillaria, Stigmaria, Lepidodendra, fossil trees, lepidodendrid, lepidodendroid; Lycopodiaceæ; club mosses: Equisetales, calamites, Equisetaceæ, horsetails, equisetum; Filicales: Cycadofilices, cycad ferns; Filices, ferns, filicoid.

SPERMATOPHYTES (seed plants): Gymnospermæ (naked-seeded plants): gymnosperm. Cycadales, cycads; Gnetales, gnetums; Ginkgoales, ginkgo (pl. ginkgoes); Coniferæ, cone-bearing evergreens, conifer.

Angiospermæ (covered-seeded plants): angiosperm; Monocotyledones, monocotyledon, cereals, palms, lilies, orchids, banana, pineapple &c., endogens; Dicotyledones: oak, apple, sunflower, pea, dicotyledon.

BOTANIST, phytologist, phytotomist, phytobiologist, dendrologist; mycologist, fungologist; phytopathologist, horticulturist &c. 371; herbalist, herbist, herbarist [obs.], herborist, herbarian; pomologist.

V. BOTANIZE, herborize.

Adj. BOTANIC or botanical, phytoid, dendroid or dendroidal, herbose or herbous, dendriform, dendritic or dendritical, dendrologous, herby, herbal; fungoid, fungous, mycologic or mycological, mycetoid, phytobiological, phytochemical, phytogenetic or phytogenous, pomological, horticultural.

thalloid, thalline; hepatic, musciform, muscoid, lycopodiaceous, lepidodendroid, equisetaceous, equisetiform, filicoid, filiciform, gymnospermous, cycadaceous, coniferous, angiospermous, angiospermatous, monocotyledonous, endogenous, dicotyledonous.

VERTEBRATA (vertebrate animals): Cyclostomata or Cyclostoma, lampreys; Pisces, fishes; Selachii, sharks, rays, selachian; Holocephali or Holocephala, chimæras, spooks; Dipnoi, lungfishes; Teleostomi, ordinary fishes, ganoids, teleost, teleostean; Amphibia, amphibians, batrachians; Reptilia, reptiles; Aves, birds; Mammalia, mammals; Monotremata or Protototheria, monotremes; Marsupialia, marsupials, marsupialian or marsupian; Placentalia, placentals.

Adj. ZOÖLOGICAL, zoölogic; zoönomic; zoögraphical &c. *n.*

PROTOZOAN, rhizopodous; foraminiferous, foraminous, foraminated; radiolarian; flagellate; infusorial, infusory; gregarine.

CŒLENTERATE, poriferan, spongiose *or* spongious, spongoid, spongiform; anthozoan, anthozoic, corallaceous, coralliferous, coralliform, coralligenous, coralligerous, coralloid, coralloidal; polyparous, polypean; hydrozoal, hydroid; medusiform, medusoid.

ECHINODERMATOUS, echinodermal; pelmatozoan; crinoidal, crinoid; ophiuran, ophiuroid; asteridian; echinoid, holothurian.

VERMICIOUS, vermicular, vermiculate, vermiculose *or* vermiculous, vermiform; gephyrean, gephyreoid; annelid *or* annelidan, annelidous.

MOLLUSCOID, molluscoidal; bryozoan; brachiopod.

MOLLUSCAN, molluscoid, molluscous; lamellibranch, lamellibranchiate, bivalvular, bivalvous, bivalved; gastropodous, univalve *or* univalved, univalvular; cephalopodic, cephalopodous, nautiloid.

ARTHROPODAL, articulate; branchial, branchiate, branchiferous; tracheate; crustacean, crustaceous; arachnoid, arachnoidal, arachnidan, arachnidial; insectile, insected.

VERTEBRATE, vertebred, vertebral; cyclostome, cyclostomous; piscatorial *or* piscatory, pisciform, piscine; amphibian, amphibial [*rare*], amphibious; batrachian, batrachoid; reptilian; avicular; mammalian, mammiferous.

---

370. [ECONOMY OR MANAGEMENT OF ANIMALS.] **Cicuration. — N.** CICURATION [*obs.*], taming &c. *v.;* zoöhygiantics;[1] domestication, domesticity; manège *or* manege, veterinary art; farriery; breeding; pisciculture; apiculture.

menagerie, vivarium, zoölogical garden, zoo [*colloq.*]; bear pit; aviary; apiary, alvearium, alveary, beehive, hive; aquarium, fishery, fish hatchery, fish pond; swan pond, duck pond; incubator.

[DESTRUCTION OF ANIMALS] phthisozoics[2] &c. (*killing*) 361.

[KEEPER] herder, oxherd, neatherd, cowherd, grazier, drover, cowkeeper; shepherd, shepherdess; keeper, gamekeeper; trainer, breeder; bull whacker [*U. S.*], cowboy, cow puncher [*U. S.*], vaquero [*Sp. Amer.*]; horse trainer, broncho-buster [*slang*]; apiarian [*rare*], apiarist, apiculturist.

VETERINARIAN, veterinary surgeon, vet [*colloq.*], horse doctor, horse leech [*rare*]; farrier [*obsoles. as veterinarian*], horseshoer.

INCLOSURE, stable, barn, byre; cage &c. (*prison*) 752; hencoop, bird cage, coif, cauf; sheepfold &c. 232.

V. TAME, domesticate, domesticize, acclimatize, breed, tend, corral, round up, break in, gentle, cicurate [*obs.*], break, bust [*slang, U. S.*], break to harness, train; ride, drive &c. (*take horse*) 266; cage, bridle, &c. (*restrain*) 751; guide, spur, prick, lash, goad, whip; trot, gallop &c. (*move quickly*) 274; bolt; yoke, harness, harness up [*colloq.*], hitch, hitch up [*colloq.*], cinch [*U. S.*].

[1] Bentham.

371. [ECONOMY OR MANAGEMENT OF PLANTS.] **Agriculture. — N.** AGRICULTURE, cultivation, husbandry, farming; georgics, geoponics; agronomy, agronomics, tillage, tilth, gardening, spade husbandry, vintage; horticulture, arboriculture, silviculture, forestry; floriculture; landscape gardening; viticulture.

HUSBANDMAN, horticulturist, gardener, florist; agricultor [*rare*], agriculturist, agronomist, yeoman, farmer, cultivator, tiller of the soil, plowman *or* ploughman, reaper, sower; logger, lumberman [*U. S. & Can.*], lumberjack [*N. W. U. S.*], forester, woodcutter, pioneer, backwoodsman; granger [*U. S.*], habitant, vigneron [*F.*], vinicuiturist, vine-grower, vintager, viticulturist; Triptolemus.

GARDEN; botanic -, winter -, ornamental -, flower -, kitchen -, market -, truck -, hop- garden; nursery; greenhouse, hothouse; conservatory, forcing house, cold-frame; bed, border, seed plot; grassplot *or* grassplat, lawn; parterre; shrubbery, plantation, avenue, arboretum, pinery, pinetum, orchard; vineyard, vinery, orangery.

FIELD, meadow, mead, green, common, maidan [*India*]; park &c. (*pleasure ground*) 840; farm &c. (*abode*) 189.

V. CULTIVATE, till, till the soil, farm, garden, sow, plant; reap, mow, cut; manure, dress the ground, dig, spade, delve, dibble, hoe, plow *or* plough, harrow, rake, weed, lop and top; backset [*U. S.*]; force, seed, turf, transplant, thin out, bed, prune, graft.

[2] Bentham.

GROOM, rub down, brush, currycomb; water, feed, fodder; bed, bed down, litter; drench, embrocate.

TEND STOCK, milk, shear; water &c. (*groom*) *v.;* herd; raise, bring up, bring up by hand.

hatch, incubate, sit, brood, cover.

swarm, hive.

Adj. PASTORAL, bucolic, rural; agricultural &c. 371.

TAME, domestic, domesticated, broken, gentle, docile.

Adj. AGRICULTURAL, agronomic, geoponic, georgic, agrestical [*obs.*], agrestian, prædial *or* predial; horticultural, viticultural.

ARABLE, plowable *or* ploughable, tillable.

RURAL, rustic, country, agrarian, pastoral, bucolic, Arcadian.

⁎⁎ "The first farmer was the first man, and all historic nobility rests on possession and use of land" [Emerson].

---

372. Mankind. — N. MANKIND, man; human -race, – species, – kind. – nature; humanity, mortality, flesh, generation.

[SCIENCE OF MAN] anthropology, anthropogeny, anthropography, anthroposophy; ethnology, ethnography; anthropotomy, androtomy; humanitarianism.

HUMAN BEING; person, personage; individual, creature, fellow creature, mortal, body, somebody, one; such a one, some one; soul, living soul; earthling; party [*slang or vulgar*], head, hand; member, members of the cast, *dramatis personœ* [*L.*]; *quidam* [*L.*].

PEOPLE, persons, folk, public, society, world; community, – at large; general public; nation, nationality; state, realm; commonweal, commonwealth; republic, body politic; million &c. (*commonalty*) 876; population &c. (*inhabitant*) 188.

cosmopolite; lords of creation; ourselves.

Adj. HUMAN, mortal, personal, individual, national, civic, public, social; cosmopolitan; anthropoid.

⁎⁎ "am I not a man and a brother?" [Wedgwood].

---

373. Man. — N. MAN, male, he; manhood &c. (*adolescence*) 131; gentleman, sir, master, dan [*archaic*], don, huzur [*India*], sahib [*India*]; yeoman, chap [*colloq.*], wight [*now chiefly jocose*], swain, fellow, blade, beau, gaffer [*dial. Eng.*], goodman [*archaic*]; husband &c. (*married man*) 903; boy &c. (*youth*) 129.

MISTER, Mr., *monsieur* (*abbr.* M., *pl.* MM. *or* Messrs.) [*F.*], *Herr* [*Ger.*], *signor* [*It., used before name*], *signore* [*It.*], *signorino* [*It., dim. of signore*], signior [*Eng. form*], seignior, *señor* [*Sp.*], *senhor* [*Pg.*]

[MALE ANIMAL] cock, drake, gander, dog, boar, stag, hart, buck, horse, entire horse, stallion; gib [*rare*], tom, tomcat; he-goat, billy-goat [*colloq.*]; ram, tup; bull, bullock; capon; ox, gelding; steer, stot [*prov. Eng.*].

Adj. MALE, he, masculine; manly; virile; unwomanly, unfeminine.

⁎⁎ *hominem pagina nostra sapit* [Mar.]; *homo homini aut deus aut lupus* [Erasmus]; *homo vitœ commodatus non donatus est* [Syrus]; "When Adam dolve, and Eve span, Who was then the gentleman?" [John Ball].

374. Woman. — N. WOMAN, she, female, petticoat; skirt, jane [*both slang*].

FEMINALITY, femininity, femineity, feminacy, feminity, muliebrity; gynics.

WOMANKIND; womanhood &c. (*adolescence*) 131; the sex, the fair; fair sex, softer sex; weaker vessel.

dame [*archaic except as an elderly woman*], madam, mastress [Chaucer, *obs.*], lady, Donna, belle, matron, dowager, goody, gammer [*dial. Eng.*], memsahib [*Anglo-Ind.*], sahiba [*Hind.*], bibi [*Hind.*], frow, vrouw [*Du.*], good woman, goodwife [*archaic*]; squaw; wife &c. (*marriage*) 903; matronage, matronhood.

bachelor girl, new woman, suffragist, suffragette; spinster, old maid.

nymph, houri, wench, grisette; girl &c. (*youth*) 129.

MISTRESS, Mrs., *madame* (*pl. mesdames*) [*F.*], *Frau* [*Ger.*], *signora* [*It*], *señora* [*Sp.*], *senhora* [*Pg.*]; miss, *mademoiselle* (*pl. mesdemoiselles*) [*F.*], *Fräulein* [*Ger.*], *signorina* [*It.*], *señorita* [*Sp.*], *senhorita* [*Pg.*].

[EFFEMINACY] betty, cot betty [*U. S.*], cotquean, henhussy, molly, mollycoddle, muff, old woman, tame cat [*all contemptuous*].

[FEMALE ANIMAL] hen; bitch, slut, brach, brachet; sow, doe, roe, mare; she-goat, nanny-goat [*colloq.*], nanny [*colloq.*]; ewe, cow; lioness, tigress; vixen.

HAREM, gynæceum *or* gynæcium, seraglio, zenana [*India*], purdah [*India*].

Adj. FEMALE, she; feminine, womanly, ladylike, matronly, girlish, maidenly; womanish, effeminate, unmanly; gynecic *or* gynæcic.

⁎ "a perfect woman nobly planned" [Wordsworth]; "a lovely lady garmented in white" [Shelley]; *das Ewig-Weibliche zieht uns hinan* [Goethe]; "earth's noblest thing, a woman perfected" [Lowell]; *es de vidrio la mujer;* "she moves a goddess and she looks a queen" [Pope]; "the beauty of a lovely woman is like music" [G. Eliot]; *varium et mutabile semper femina* [Vergil]; "woman is the lesser man" [Tennyson].

2. SENSATION

1. Sensation in general

375. Physical Sensibility. — N. SENSIBILITY; sensitiveness &c. *adj.*; physical sensibility, feeling, impressibility, perceptivity, susceptibility, æsthetics *or* esthetics; moral sensibility &c. 822.

SENSATION, impression; consciousness &c. (*knowledge*) 490.

external senses.

V. BE SENSIBLE OF &c. *adj.*; feel, perceive; feel -keenly, - exquisitely.

RENDER SENSIBLE &c. *adj.*; sharpen, refine, excite, stir, cultivate, tutor.

IMPRESS, cause sensation; excite -, produce- an impression.

Adj. SENSIBLE, sensitive, sensuous; æsthetic *or* esthetic, perceptive, sentient; conscious &c. (*aware*) 490; alive, alive to impressions, answering quickly to, impressionable, responsive, easily affected, quick in response.

ACUTE, sharp, keen, vivid, lively, impressive, thin-skinned.

Adv. TO THE QUICK; on the raw [*slang*].

⁎ "the touch'd needle trembles to the pole" [Pope].

376. Physical Insensibility. — N. INSENSIBILITY, physical insensibility; obtuseness &c. *adj.*; palsy, paralysis, anæsthesia *or* anesthesia, narcosis, narcotization, hypnosis, stupor, coma; twilight sleep, *Dämmerschlaf* [*Ger.*]; sleep &c. (*inactivity*) 683; moral insensibility &c. 823; hemiplegia, motor paralysis.

ANÆSTHETIC *or* anesthetic, anæsthetic agent; local -, general- anæsthetic; opium, ether, chloroform, chloral; nitrous oxide, laughing gas; exhilarating gas, protoxide of nitrogen; cocaine, novocain; refrigeration.

V. BE INSENSIBLE &c. *adj.*; have a -thick skin, - rhinoceros hide.

RENDER INSENSIBLE &c. *adj.*; blunt, cloy, satiate, pall, obtund, benumb, numb, deaden, freeze, paralyze; anæsthetize *or* anesthetize, put under the influence of chloroform &c. *n.*; put to sleep, hypnotize, stupefy, stun.

Adj. INSENSIBLE, unfeeling, senseless, impercipient, callous, thick-skinned, pachydermatous; hard, hardened; case-hardened; proof; obtuse, dull; anæsthetic *or* anesthetic; paralytic, palsied, numb, dead.

⁎ "a dreary numbness pains My sense, as though of hemlock I had drunk" [Keats].

377. Physical Pleasure. — N. PLEASURE; physical -, sensual -, sensuous - pleasure; bodily enjoyment, animal gratification, delight, sensual delight, hedonism, sensuality; luxuriousness &c. *adj.*; dissipation, round of pleasure; titillation, gusto, creature comforts, comfort, ease; pillow &c. (*support*) 215; luxury, lap of luxury; purple and fine linen; bed of -down, - roses; velvet.

378. Physical Pain. — N. PAIN; suffering, sufferance [*rare*]; bodily -, physical- -pain, - suffering; mental suffering &c. 828; dolor *or* dolour, ache; aching &c. *v.*; smart; shoot, shooting; twinge, twitch, gripe, hurt, cut; sore, soreness; discomfort; headache, *malaise* [*F.*], megrim, migraine, cephalalgy, cephalalgia; otalgia, earache; ischiagra, lumbago, arthritis, neuritis, gout, podagra, rheu-

clover; cup of Circe &c. (*intemperance*) 954.

TREAT; diversion, entertainment, banquet, regalement, refreshment, regale; feast; delice [*obs*.]; dainty &c. 394; *bonne bouche* [*F*.].

SOURCE OF PLEASURE &c. 829; happiness, felicity, bliss, beatitude &c. (*mental enjoyment*) 827.

V. ENJOY, pleasure [*rare*]; feel –, experience –, receive- pleasure; relish; luxuriate –, revel –, riot –, bask –, swim –, wallow- in; feast on; gloat -over, – on; smack the lips; roll under the tongue.

live on the fat of the land, live in comfort &c. *adv.;* bask in the sunshine, *faire ses choux gras* [*F*.].

GIVE PLEASURE &c. 829; charm, delight, enchant.

Adj. ENJOYING &c. *v.;* luxurious, voluptuous, sensual, comfortable, cosy, snug, in comfort, at ease, in clover [*colloq*.].

AGREEABLE &c. 829; grateful, refreshing, comforting, cordial, genial; gratifying, titillative, sensuous; apolaustic, hedonic, hedonistic, palatable &c. 394; sweet &c. (*sugar*) 396; fragrant &c. 400; melodious &c. 413; lovely &c. (*beautiful*) 845.

Adv. IN COMFORT &c. *n.;* on a bed of roses &c. *n.;* at one's ease; on flowery beds of ease.

** *ride si sapis* [Martial]; *voluptates commendat rarior usus* [Juvenal]; "the man who finds most pleasure for himself is often the man who least hunts for it" [Chesterton].

matism, sciatica, ischialgia; neuralgia, tic douloureux, toothache, odontalgia; stiffneck, torticollis.

SPASM, cramp; nightmare, ephialtes; kink, crick, stitch; convulsion, throe; throb &c. (*agitation*) 315; pang; colic; tormina, gripes.

sharp –, piercing –, throbbing –, grinding –, stabbing –, shooting –, gnawing –, burning- pain.

TORMENT, torture, agony, anguish, lancination, rack, cruciation, crucifixion, martyrdom; vivisection.

martyr, sufferer; toad under a harrow.

V. SUFFER; feel –, experience –, suffer –, undergo- pain &c. *n.;* ache, smart, bleed; tingle, shoot; twinge, twitch, lancinate; writhe, wince, make a wry face; sit on -thorns, – pins and needles.

PAIN, give pain, inflict pain; lacerate; hurt, chafe, sting, bite, gnaw, stab, grind, gripe; pinch, tweak; grate, gall, fret, prick, pierce, wring, convulse; torment, torture; rack, agonize; crucify; cruciate [*obs*.], excruciate, break on the wheel, put to the rack; flog &c. (*punish*) 972; grate on the ear &c. (*harsh sound*) 410.

Adj. IN PAIN &c. *n.,* in a state of pain; under the harrow; pained &c. *v.;* gouty, podagric, torminous, terminal.

PAINFUL; aching &c. *v.;* poignant, pungent, torturous, baleful [*rare*], biting; with exposed nerves, sore, raw.

** "the foundation of all our pain is unbelief" [Amiel]; "like dull narcotics numbing pain" [Tennyson]; "pain pays the income of each precious thing" [Shakespeare].

2. Special Sensation

(1) Touch

379. [SENSATION OF PRESSURE.] **Touch.** — **N.** TOUCH; tact, taction, tactility; contact, tangency, tangence [*rare*], impact, attaint [*archaic*]; feeling, kiss, osculation, graze, glance, brush; lick, licking, lambency, palpation, palpability; contrectation [*rare*]; manipulation, palmation [*obs*.], contaction [*obs*.]; stereognosis; rubbing, kneading, massage.

[ORGAN OF TOUCH] hand, palm, finger, forefinger, thumb, paw, feeler, antenna; tongue, palpus.

V. TOUCH, feel, handle, finger, thumb, paw, fumble, grope, grabble; twiddle, tweedle [*obs. or dial*.]; pass –, run- the fingers over; stroke, palpate, palm, massage, rub, knead, manipulate, wield; throw out a feeler.

Adj. TACTUAL, tactile; tangible, palpable, tangent, contactual [*rare*], lambent; touching &c. *v.;* stereognostic.

380. Sensations of Touch. — N.
ITCHING &c. *v.;* formication; aura [*med.*].
TICKLING, titillation.

ITCH, scabies, psora, pruritus, prurigo
[*all med.*]; mange.

V. ITCH, tingle, creep, thrill, sting;
prick, prickle.

TICKLE, titillate.

Adj. ITCHING, tingling &c. *v.*

TICKLISH, titillative.

ITCHY, psoric, scabious, mangy;
creepy, crawly; prurient.

381. [INSENSIBILITY TO TOUCH.]
Numbness. — N. NUMBNESS &c. (*physical insensibility*) 376; anæsthesia *or*
anesthesia, narcosis, narcotization; pins
and needles [*colloq.*].

V. BENUMB &c. 376; stupefy, narcotize,
drug, deaden, paralyze.

Adj. NUMB; benumbed &c. *v.;* insensible, unfeeling, anæsthetic *or* anesthetic, deadened; intangible, impalpable; dazed, dazy [*rare*], comatose, torporific, narcotic, carotic.

(*2*) *Heat*

382. Heat. — N. HEAT, caloric; temperature, warmth, fervor, calidity [*obs.*],
torridity; incalescence *or* incalescency
[*rare*], incandescence; recalescence, decalescence; adiathermancy, athermancy,
diathermacy, diathermance *or* diathermancy *or* diathermaneity; phlogiston
[*old chem.*], phlogisis; thermogenesis;
liquation.

summer, dog days, canicule, canicular
days; baking &c. 384 –, white –, tropical
–, Afric –, Indian –, Bengal –, summer
–, blood- heat; sirocco, simoom *or*
simoon, hot wave, sun at noon, "the
bloody Sun, at noon" [Coleridge], vertical rays, broiling sun; insolation; warming &c. 384.

FLUSH, glow, blush, bloom, redness;
rubicundity; fever, hectic; febricity,
pyrexia.

FIRE, spark, scintillation, flash, flame,
blaze; bonfire; firework, pyrotechny;
wildfire; sheet of fire, lambent flame;
devouring element; pyrotechnics.

sun &c. (*luminary*) 423.

HOT SPRINGS, geysers; thermæ, hot
baths; Turkish –, electric –, Russianbath; steam.

FIRE WORSHIP, pyrolatry, sun worship, heliolatry, Sabæanism *or* Sabeanism
or Sabeism, Parsiism *or* Parseeism,
Zoroastrianism; pyrolator, heliolator,
Sabæan *or* Sabean, Parsi *or* Parsee,
Zoroastrian.

[SCIENCE OF HEAT] pyrology; thermology, thermotics; thermometer &c.
389.

V. BE HOT &c. *adj.;* glow, flush,
sweat, swelter, bask, smoke, reek, stew,
simmer, seethe, boil, burn, singe, scorch,
scald, grill, broil, blaze, flame; smolder
or smoulder; parch, fume, pant.

383. Cold. — N. COLD, coldness &c.
adj.; frigidity, gelidity, algidity, glaciation, gelidness [*rare*], frore [*poetic*], inclemency, fresco [*obs.*]; "a hard, dull
bitterness of cold" [Whittier].

winter; depth of –, hard- winter;
Siberia, Nova Zembla; Arctic, North
Pole; Antarctic, South Pole.

ICE; sleet; hail, hailstone; frost, rime,
hoarfrost; rime –, white –, hard –, black
–, sharp- frost; *barf* [*Hind.*], glaze [*U. S.*],
lolly [*N. Amer.*]; icicle, thick-ribbed ice;
iceberg, floe, berg, ice field, ice float *or*
ice floe, ice pack, glacier; *nevé* [*F.*],
sérac [*F.*]; *pruina* [*L. & It.*]; icequake.

SNOW, snowflake, snowdrift, fall of
snow, snowstorm, heavy fall; snowball,
snowslide, snowslip, snow avalanche.

[SENSATION OF COLD] chilliness &c.
adj.; chill; shivering &c. *v.;* goose flesh,
goose skin, rigor, horripilation, aching,
ache, chilblains, frostbite, chattering of
teeth.

V. BE COLD &c. *adj.;* shiver, starve
[*rare in U. S.*], quake, shake, tremble,
shudder, didder, quiver; perish with
cold; chill &c. (*render cold*) 385; horripilate, glaciate [*obs.*].

Adj. COLD, cool; chill, chilly; gelid,
frigid, frore [*poet.*], algid; fresh, keen,
bleak, raw, inclement, bitter, biting,
cutting, nipping, piercing, pinching;
clay-cold; starved &c. (*made cold*) 385;
shivering &c. *v.;* aguish, *transi de froid*
[*F.*], frostbitten, frost-bound, frost-nipped.

cold as - a stone, – marble, – lead, –
iron, – a frog, – charity, – Christmas;
cool as -a cucumber, – custard.

ICY, glacial, ice-built, frosty, freezing,
wintry, brumal, hibernal, boreal, arctic,
Siberian, hiemal *or* hyemal; hyper-

HEAT &c. (*make hot*) 384; insolate, incandesce, recalesce.

THAW, fuse, melt, liquate, liquefy; give.

Adj. WARM, mild, genial, tepid, luke-warm, unfrozen; calid; warm as -toast, - wool.

HOT, heated, fervid, fervent; roasting, sweltry; reeking &c. *v.;* ardent, aglow; baking &c. 384; sunny, sunshiny, æsti-val *or* estival, canicular, torrid, tropical; thermal, thermic; calorific.

red -, white -, smoking -, burning &c. *v.* -, piping- hot; like -a furnace, - an oven; hot as -fire, - pepper; hot enough to roast an ox.

CLOSE, sultry, stifling, stuffy, suffocating, oppressive.

FIERY; incandescent, incalescent [*rare*]; candent, ebullient, glowing, smoking; live; on fire; blazing &c. *v.;* in flames, in a blaze; alight, afire, ablaze; unquenched; unextinguished; smoldering *or* smouldering; in a -heat, - glow, - perspiration, - sweat; sudorific; sweltering, sweltered; blood-hot, blood-warm; recalescent, decalescent, thermogenic, thermogenous, thermogenetic, thermotic *or* thermotical; pyrotechnic *or* pyrotechnical; phlogotic *or* phlogistic; pyrological.

[TRANSMITTING RADIANT HEAT] diathermic, diathermal, diathermanous.

[NOT TRANSMITTING RADIANT HEAT] athermanous, adiathermal, adiather-manous, adiathermic.

VOLCANIC, plutonic, igneous.

ISOTHERMAL, isothermic, isothermical.

FEVERISH, febrile, febricose [*rare*], febrific, febrifacient, pyretic, pyrexic [*rare*], inflamed, burning; in a fever.

*** not a breath of air; "whirlwinds of tempestuous fire" [*P. L.*]; "the land where every weed is flaming and only man is black" [Chesterton].

borean, hyperboreal [*rare*]; snow-bound, ice-bound; frozen out.

UNWARMED, unheated; unthawed.

LUKEWARM, tepid; warm &c. *adj.* 382.

ISOCHEIMAL, isocheimenal, isocheimic.

Adv. COLDLY, bitterly &c. *adj.;* à pierre fendre [*F.*]; with chattering teeth.

*** "Ho! why dost thou shiver and shake, Gaffer Guy?" [Holcroft]; "Marian's nose looks red and raw" [*L. L. L.*].

---

384. Calefaction. — N. CALEFACTION,
tepefaction, torrefaction; increase of temperature; heating &c. *v.;* melting, fusion; liquefaction &c. 335; burning &c. *v.;* combustion; incension [*obs.*], accension [*archaic*]; concremation, cre-mation; scorification; cautery, cau-terization; ustulation [*rare*], calcination; incineration; carbonization; cupellation.

IGNITION, kindling, inflammation, adustion [*rare*], flagration [*obs.*], defla-gration, conflagration; empyrosis, in-cendiarism; arson; *auto-da-fé* [*Pg.*], *auto-de-fe* [*Sp.*], the stake, burning at the stake; suttee.

INCENDIARY, arsonist, arsonite, *pétro-leur* (*fem. pétroleuse*) [*F.*], pyromaniac, fire bug [*U. S.*].

BOILING &c. *v.;* coction, ebullition, ebullience *or* ebulliency, æstuation *or* estuation, elixation [*obs.*], decoction; ebullioscope, ebulliometer; hot spring, geyser.

385. Refrigeration. — N. REFRIGERA-
TION, infrigidation, reduction of tem-perature; cooling &c. *v.;* congelation, conglaciation [*obs.*], glaciation, regela-tion; ice &c. 383; solidification &c. (*density*),321; ice box, ice chest; refriger-ator &c. 387.

FIRE-EXTINGUISHER, *extincteur* [*F.*]; fire annihilator; amianthus, amianth, earth flax, mountain flax; asbestos, flexi-ble asbestos; fireman, fire brigade, fire department, fire engine.

incombustibility, incombustibleness &c. *adj.*

V. COOL, fan, refrigerate, infrigidate, refresh, ice; congeal, freeze, glaciate; benumb, starve [*rare in U. S.*], pinch, chill, petrify, chill to the marrow, regelate, nip, cut, pierce, bite, make one's teeth chatter.

DAMP, slack; quench; put out, stamp out; extinguish.

go out, burn out, die.

CREMATORY, crematorium, burning ghat [*India*], incinerator, calcinatory; cupel; furnace &c. 386.

WRAP, blanket, flannel, wool, fur; muff, mittens, wristers; muffler, fascinator, comforter [*U. S.*], comfortable; ear-muffs, ear-flaps; shawl; wadding &c. (*lining*) 224; clothing &c. 225.

CAUTERANT, scorifier; match &c. (*fuel*) 388; caustic, lunar caustic, apozem, moxa; aqua fortis, aqua regia; catheretic, nitric acid, nitrochlorohydric acid, nitromuriatic acid, radium.

SUNSTROKE, *coup de soleil* [*F.*]; insolation [*rare*], siriasis, [*med.*]; sunburn, burn, ambustion [*rare*].

POTTERY, ceramics, crockery, porcelain, china; earthenware, stoneware; pot, mug, terra cotta, brick.

[PRODUCTS OF COMBUSTION] cinder, ash, scoriæ; embers, slag, clinker, coke, carbon, charcoal.

INFLAMMABILITY, combustibility, accendibility.

[TRANSMISSION OF HEAT] diathermance *or* diathermancy &c. 382; transcalency.

V. HEAT, warm, chafe, foment; make hot &c. 382; sun oneself, bask in the sun.

FIRE, set fire to, set on fire; kindle, enkindle, light, ignite, strike a light; apply the -match, – torch- to; rekindle, relume; fan –, add fuel to- the flame; poke –, stir –, blow- the fire; make a bonfire of; build a campfire.

MELT, thaw, fuse; liquefy &c. 335.

BURN, inflame, roast, toast, fry, grill, singe, parch, bake, torrefy, scorch; brand, cauterize, sear, burn in; corrode, char, carbonize, calcine, incinerate, calefy, calcinate [*rare*], tepefy, cupel, cupellate [*rare*], deflagrate [*chem.*]; smelt, scorify; reduce to ashes; burn to a cinder; commit –, consign- to the flames.

take –, catch- fire; blaze &c. (*flame*) 382.

BOIL, digest, stew, cook, seethe, ebullate [*rare*], scald, parboil, simmer; do to rags [*colloq.*].

Adj. HEATED &c. *v.*; molten, sodden; *réchauffé* [*F.*]; heating &c. *v.*; adust; ambustial [*rare*], calefactive, deflagrable [*chem.*], ustulate; calcinatory, cauterant; æstuous [*rare*]; apozemial, scoriaceous; transcalent; burnt &c. *v.*; volcanic.

INFLAMMABLE, burnable, inflammatory, accendible, combustible.

DIATHERMIC, diathermal, diathermanous.

radioactive; salamandrine.

Adj. COOLED &c. *v.*; frozen out; cooling &c. *v.*; frigorific, infrigidative [*rare*], refrigerative [*rare*].

INCOMBUSTIBLE, asbestic, unflammable, uninflammable; fireproof; amianthine, amianthoid *or* amianthoidal.

---

386. Furnace. — N. FURNACE, stove; air-tight –, Franklin –, Dutch –, gas –, oil –, electric- stove; cookstove, cooker, oven, brick oven, tin oven, Dutch oven, range, kitchener [*Eng.*]; fireless- heater, – cooker; forge, fiery furnace; kiln, brickkiln, limekiln; tuyère, brasier, salamander, heater, warming pan, footstove, foot-warmer; radiator, register,

387. Refrigeratory. — N. REFRIGERATORY, refrigerator; frigidarium; cold storage; ice –, freezing –, refrigerating-machine; refrigerating plant; icehouse, ice pail, ice bag, ice box, ice chest, ice pack, cold pack; cooler, wine cooler.

REFRIGERANT, freezing mixture, ice, ammonia.

---

coil; boiler, caldron, seething caldron, pot; urn, kettle, frying-pan, stew-pan, spider, broiler, skillet, tripod, chafing-dish; retort, crucible, alembic, still; waffle irons; flatiron, sadiron; curling tongs; toasting fork, toaster.

galley, caboose *or* camboose; hothouse, conservatory, bakehouse, washhouse, laundry; athanor, hypocaust, reverberatory; volcano.

FIREPLACE, hearth, grate, firebox, andiron, firedog, fire-irons; poker, tongs, shovel, hob, trivet; damper, crane, pothooks, chains, turnspit, spit, gridiron.

HOT BATH; thermæ, calidarium, tepidarium, vaporarium, sudatorium [*all L.*]; sudatory; Turkish –, Russian – vapor –, electric –, sitz –, hip –, shower –, warm - bath; tub, lavatory.

388. Fuel. — **N.** FUEL, firing, combustible, coal, wallsend [*Eng.*], anthracite, blind coal, glance coal; bituminous –, egg –, stove –, nut –, pea- coal; culm, coke, carbon, briquette, slack, cannel coal *or* cannel, lignite, charcoal; turf, peat; oil, gas, natural gas, electricity; ember, cinder &c. (*products of combustion*) 384; ingle; port-fire; fire-barrel, fireball, firebrand.

LOG, backlog, yule log *or* yule clog, firewood, fagot *or* faggot, kindling wood, kindlings, brushwood, bavin [*dial. Eng.*].

TINDER, touchwood; punk, German tinder, amadou; smudge [*U. S. & Can.*], pyrotechnic sponge.

FUMIGATOR, incense, joss-stick; sulphur, brimstone, disinfectant.

[ILLUMINANTS] candle &c. (*luminary*) 423; oil &c. (*grease*) 356.

brand, torch, fuse *or* fuze, wick; spill, match, safety match, lights [*chiefly Eng.*], light, lucifer, congreve, vesuvian, vesta, fusee *or* fuzee, locofoco [*obs., U. S.*], linstock [*obs. or hist.*].

V. coal, stoke; feed, fire &c. 384.

Adj. carbonaceous; combustible, inflammable; slow-burning, free-burning.

389. Thermometer. — **N.** THERMOMETER, thermometrograph, thermopile, thermostat, thermoscope; differential thermometer, telethermometer, pyrometer, calorimeter, radiomicrometer.

(3) Taste

390. Taste. — **N.** TASTE, flavor, gust [*archaic*], gusto, savor; *goût* [*F.*], relish; sapor [*obs.*], sapidity; twang [*dial. Eng.*], smack, smatch [*dial. Eng.*]; aftertaste, tang.

TASTING; degustation, gustation.

palate; tongue; tooth; stomach.

V. TASTE, savor, smatch [*dial. Eng.*], smack, flavor; tickle the palate &c. (*savory*) 394; smack the lips.

391. Insipidity. — **N.** INSIPIDITY; tastelessness &c. *adj.*; jejuneness.

V. BE TASTELESS &c. *adj.*

Adj. INSIPID; void of taste &c. 390; tasteless, gustless [*obs.*], unsavory, un-flavored, jejune, savorless; ingustible [*obs.*], mawkish, milk and water, weak, stale, flat, vapid, *fade* [*F.*], wishy-washy [*colloq.*], mild; untasted.

Adj. SAPID, saporific, gustable, gustatory, gustative, tastable, savory, gustful, tasty; strong; flavored, spiced, tanged [*obs.*]; palatable &c. 394.

⁎ "behold this cordial julep here, That flames and dances in his crystal bounds, With spirits of balmy fragrant syrups mixed" [Milton].

392. Pungency. — **N.** PUNGENCY, piquancy, poignancy, *haut-goût* [*F.*], acrity [*obs.*], strong taste, twang [*dial. Eng.*], race, tang, nip, kick [*slang*].

SHARPNESS &c. *adj.*; acrimony, acridity; roughness &c. (*sour*) 392; unsavoriness &c. 395.

[PUNGENT ARTICLES] niter, saltpeter; mustard, cayenne, caviare; seasoning &c. (*condiment*) 393; brine; carbonate of ammonia; sal-ammoniac, sal-volatile; smelling salts; hartshorn.

DRAM, cordial, nip, toothful [*colloq.*], tickler [*colloq.*], bracer [*colloq.*], pick-me-up [*colloq.*], potion, liqueur, *pousse-café* [*F.*].

TOBACCO, Lady Nicotine, Nicotiana, nicotian [*rare*], nicotine; snuff, quid; cigar *or* segar, cigarette, fag [*slang*], cheroot, Trichinopoli cheroot, Trichi [*colloq.*], Havana *or* Habana [*Sp.*], Cuban tobacco; weed [*colloq.*]; fragrant –, Indian-weed; Cavendish, fid [*dial.*], niggerhead *or* negro head, rappee, stogy, old soldier [*slang*].

V. BE PUNGENT &c. *adj.*; bite the tongue.

RENDER PUNGENT &c. *adj.*; season, spice, bespice, salt, pepper, pickle, brine, devil, curry.

USE TOBACCO, smoke, chew, inhale, take snuff.

Adj. PUNGENT, strong; high-flavored, full-flavored; high-tasted, high-seasoned; gamy, high; sharp, stinging, rough, piquant, racy; biting, mordant; spicy;

seasoned &c. *v.;* hot, – as pepper; peppery vellicative, vellicating, escharotic, meracious [*obs.*]; acrid, acrimonious, bitter; rough &c. (*sour*) 397; unsavory &c. 395.

SALT, saline, brackish, briny; salt as -brine, – a herring, – Lot's wife.

** "For thy sake, tobacco, I Would do anything but die" [Lamb]; "the man who smokes thinks like a sage and acts like a Samaritan" [Lytton]; "to win the secret of a weed's plain heart" [Lowell]; "Heaven's last, best gift, my ever new delight" [*P. L.*]; "divine in hookas, glorious in a pipe" [Byron]; "come, look not pale! observe *me!*" [B. Jonson]; "O thou weed, Who art so lovely fair and smell'st so sweet" [*Othello*]; "sweet to the world and grateful to the skies " [Pope].

---

393. Condiment. — N. CONDIMENT, flavoring, salt, mustard, pepper, cayenne, cinnamon, nutmeg, curry, seasoning, sauce, spice, relish, *sauce piquante* [*F.*], *sauce tartare* [*F.*], caviare, pot herbs, onion, sauce-alone, hedge garlic, garlic, pickle; *achar* [*Hind.*], allspice, appetizer; bell –, Jamaica –, red- pepper; horse-radish, capsicum, chutney, tabasco sauce *or* tabasco; cubeb, pimento.

V. SEASON &c. (*render pungent*) 392.

** "Stewed in brine, smarting in lingering pickle" [*Antony and Cleopatra*]; "'tis the sour sauce to the sweet meat" [Dryden]; "spiced dainties, every one, From silken Samarcand to cedar'd Lebanon" [Keats].

---

394. Savoriness. — N. SAVORINESS &c. *adj.;* nectareousness; relish, zest.

APPETIZER, *apéritif* [*F.*], *hors d'œuvre* [*F.*]

DELICACY, titbit, dainty, ambrosia, nectar, delice [*obs.*], *bonne-bouche* [*F.*]; game, turtle, venison; delicatessen.

V. BE SAVORY &c. *adj.;* tickle the -palate, – appetite; tempt the appetite, taste good, taste of something; flatter the palate.

render palatable &c. *adj.*

relish, like, smack the lips.

Adj. SAVORY, to one's taste, tasty, good, palatable, good-tasting, pleasing, nice, dainty, delectable; toothful [*obs.*], toothsome; gustful, appetizing, lickerish *or* liquorish [*rare*], delicate, delicious, exquisite, rich, luscious, ambrosial, ambroisan, nectareous, distinctive.

Adv. *per amusare la bocca* [*It.*].

** *cela se laisse manger;* "lickerish baits, fit to ensnare a brute" [Milton].

395. Unsavoriness. — N. UNSAVORI-NESS &c. *adj.;* amaritude [*rare*], acrimony, acritude [*obs.*], acridity, acridness, roughness &c. (*sour*) 397; acerbity, austerity.

gall and wormwood, rue, quassia, aloes, asafetida *or* asafœtida; hemlock; sickener; Marah.

V. BE UNPALATABLE &c. *adj.;* sicken, disgust, nauseate, pall, turn the stomach.

Adj. UNSAVORY, unpalatable, unsweet; ill-flavored; bitter, bitter as gall; amarulent [*obs.*], acrid, acrimonious; rough.

OFFENSIVE, repulsive, nasty; sickening &c. *v.;* nauseous; loathsome, fulsome; unpleasant &c. 830.

** "it's a strong stomach that has no turning" [*Cynic's Calendar*].

---

396. Sweetness. — N. SWEETNESS, dulcitude, saccharinity.

SUGAR, saccharin *or* saccharine, saccharose, crystallose; cane –, beet –, loaf –, lump –; granulated- sugar.

preserve, conserve, confiture [*obs.*], jam, julep; sugar candy, sugarplum; marmalade.

SWEETS, confectionery, caramel, lolly [*colloq.*], lollipop, bonbon, licorice, jujube, comfit, sweetmeat, confection, confectionery; honey, manna; apple butter, glucose, sucrose, dulcin [*chem.*],

397. Sourness. — N. SOURNESS &c, *adj.;* acid, acetosity, acerbity, acidity. subacidity; acescence *or* acescency; acetous fermentation.

[SOUR ARTICLES] vinegar, acetum, tartar, verjuice, crab, alum; acetic acid; lime, lemon, crab apple, chokeberry, chokecherry; unripe –, green fruit.

V. BE SOUR, turn sour &c. *adj.;* set the teeth on edge.

RENDER SOUR &c. *adj.;* acidify, acidulate, acetify, acetize [*are*], tartarize. ferment.

dulcite [*chem.*]; sirup *or* syrup, treacle, molasses, maple sirup *or* syrup, maple sugar; *mithai* [*India*], sorghum, taffy, butterscotch.

[SWEET BEVERAGES] nectar; hydromel, mead, metheglin, liqueur, sweet wine, *eau sucrée* [*F.*].

PASTRY, cake, pie, tart, puff, pudding.

DULCIFICATION, dulcoration [*obs.*], saccharification, saccharization, edulcoration.

V. BE SWEET &c. *adj.*

RENDER SWEET &c. *adj.*; sweeten, sugar, saccharize, saccharify, sugar off [*local, U. S. & Can.*]; edulcorate; dulcorate [*obs.*], dulcify [*obs.*]; candy; mull.

Adj. SWEET, sugary, saccharine, sacchariferous, saccharoid *or* saccharoidal; dulcet, candied, honied, luscious, cloying, honey-sweet, nectarious [*rare*], nectareous, nectareal, nectarous, nectarean, nectarian; melliferous; sweetened &c. *v.* sweet as –sugar, – honey.

*** "sweets to the sweet" [*Hamlet*]; "the daintiest last to make the end most sweet" [*Richard II*]; "lucent syrops, tinct with cinnamon" [Keats]; "a wilderness of sweets" [*P. L.*].

Adj. SOUR; acid, acidulous, acidulated; tart, crab, crabbed; acetous, acetose, acerb, acetic; sour as vinegar, sourish; acescent, subacid; hard, rough, unripe, green; astringent, styptic.

*** "Every white will have its blacke, And every sweet its soure" [Percy].

(4) Odor

398. Odor. — N.
ODOR *or* odour, smell, odorament [*obs.*], scent, effluvium; emanation, exhalation; fume, essence, trail, nidor [*obs.*], redolence.

SCENT; sense of smell; act of smelling &c. *v.*; olfaction, olfactories.

V. HAVE AN ODOR &c. *n.*; smell, – of, – strong of; exhale, effluviate [*rare*]; give out a smell &c. *n.*; scent.

SMELL, scent; snuff, – up; sniff, nose, inhale.

Adj. ODOROUS, odorant [*rare*], odoriferous; smelling, strong-scented, effluvious, redolent, nidorous, pungent.

[RELATING TO THE SENSE OF SMELL] olfactory, olfactive, olfactible *or* olfactable; quick-scented.

*** "Sabean odours from the spicy shore Of Araby the Blest" [Milton]; "Smells are surer than sounds or sights To make your heart-strings crack" [Kipling].

399. Inodorousness. — N.
INODOROUSNESS; absence –, want- of smell. deodorization; deodorizer, deodorant.

V. BE INODOROUS &c. *adj.*; not smell. deodorize.

Adj. INODOROUS, inodorate [*obs.*], scentless; without –, wanting- smell &c. 398. deodorized, deodorizing.

400. Fragrance. — N.
FRAGRANCE, aroma, redolence, incensation, thurification [*rare*], perfume, bouquet; sweet smell, sweet odor *or* odour, aromatic perfume, scent.

[COMPARISONS] agalloch *or* agallochum, agal-wood, eaglewood, aloes wood, sandalwood, cedar, champak, calambac *or* calambour, lign-aloes, linaloa; bayberry, bay leaf, balsam, fir balsam; wild clove, wild cinnamon, Jamaica bayberry, oil of myrcia, bay rum; horehound, Marrubium, mint, musk root, muskrat, napha water, olibanum.

PERFUMERY; incense, frankincense; musk, pastil *or* pastille; myrrh, perfumes of Arabia; attar *or* ottar *or* otto; bergamot, balm, civet, potpourri, pulvil [*obs.*]; tuberose, hyacinth, heliotrope, rose, jasmine, lily, lily of the valley, violet,

401. Fetor. — N.
FETOR *or* fœtor; bad &c. *adj.* -smell, – odor *or* odour; stench, stink; foul odor, malodor *or* malodour, fetidness, mephitis, empyreuma; fustiness, mustiness &c. *adj.*; rancidity, reastiness *or* reasiness [*dial. Eng.*]; foulness &c. (*uncleanness*) 653.

[COMPARISONS] stoat, polecat, skunk, zoril; foumart *or* foulmart, fitchew, fitchet, peccary; asafetida *or* assafœtida; fungus, garlic, onion, leek, skunk cabbage; stinkpot, stinkball, stinker, stinkhorn, stinkbush, stinkstone, stinkweed, stinkwood.

V. HAVE A BAD SMELL &c. *n.*; smell, empyreumatize; stink, – in the nostrils, – like a polecat; smell strong &c. *adj.*; smell to heaven, stench [*obs.*], smell offensively.

Adj. FETID; strong-smelling; high,

arbutus, carnation, sweet pea, sweet grass, new-mown hay, lilac; pomade, pomatum, pomander, toilet water; *eau de cologne* [*F.*], cologne, cologne water.

BOUQUET, nosegay, posy [*archaic or colloq.*], boughpot *or* bowpot; *boutonnière* [*F.*], buttonhole [*colloq.*].

spray; wreath, garland, chaplet.

[SCENT CONTAINERS] smelling bottle, scent bottle, vinaigrette; scent bag, sachet; thurible, censer, incense burner, incensorium, incensory; atomizer, spray.

PERFUMER, *parfumeur* [*F.*]; thurifer.

V. BE FRAGRANT &c. *adj.;* have a perfume &c. *n.;* smell sweet, scent, perfume; embalm.

INCENSE, cense, thurificate, thurify [*rare*]; aromatize.

Adj. FRAGRANT, aromatic, redolent, spicy, balmy, scented; sweet-smelling, sweet-scented; perfumed, perfumatory [*rare*], perfumy, incense-breathing, thuriferous; fragrant –, sweet- as a rose, muscadine, ambrosial.

*** "a steam of rich-distilled perfumes" [Milton]; "die of a rose in aromatic pain" [Pope].

bad, strong, fulsome, offensive, graveolent, noisome, rank, rancid, reasty *or* reasy [*dial. Eng.*], moldy *or* mouldy, tainted, musty, frowsty [*dial. Eng.*], fusty, frowsy *or* frouzy; olid, olidous [*obs.*]; nidorous [*rare*], smelling, stinking; putrid &c. 653; suffocating, mephitic; empyreumatic *or* empyreumatical.

---

(5) *Sound*

(i) SOUND IN GENERAL

402. Sound. — N. SOUND, noise; sonority, sonorosity [*obs.*], sonification, strain; accent, twang, intonation, tune, cadence; sonorescence, sonorousness &c. *adj.;* audibility; resonance &c. 408; voice &c. 580; phonation; aspirate; phonogram, ideophone; rough breathing.

[SCIENCE OF SOUND] acoustics, acoumetry, diacoustics, catacoustics, diaphonics, cataphonics, polycoustics, phonics, phonetics, phonology, phonography; telephony, radiophony, photophony; polyphony, homophony; phonetism; acoustician.

V. PRODUCE SOUND; sound, make a noise; give out sound, emit sound; phonate, consonate [*rare*], resound &c. 408.

PHONETICIZE, phonetize [*rare*].

Adj. SOUNDING; soniferous; sonorous, sonorescent; sonorific [*rare*]; sonorant, sonoric; resonant, audible, distinct; auditory, acoustic, acoustical, diacoustic, polycoustic; stertorous, ear-splitting.

PHONIC, phonetic; homophonic *or* homophonous (*opp. to* polyphonic), monodic, monophonic; sonant; ideophonous; phonocamptic [*rare*].

*** "a thousand trills and quivering sounds" [Addison]; *forensis strepitus;* "sing With notes angelical, to many a harp" [Milton]; "with the sound Of dulcet symphonies and voices sweet" [Milton]; "the trembling notes ascend the sky" [Dryden]; "beauty born of murmuring sound" [Wordsworth].

403. Silence. — N. SILENCE; stillness &c. (*quiet*) 265; peace, hush, lull; rest [*music*]; muteness &c. 581; solemn –, awful –, dead –, deathlike- silence; silence of the -tomb, – grave.

V. BE SILENT &c. *adj.;* hold one's tongue &c. (*not speak*) 585; whist [*dial. Eng.*].

RENDER SILENT &c. *adj.;* silence, still, hush; stifle, muffle, gag, stop; muzzle; put to silence &c. (*render mute*) 581.

Adj. SILENT; still, stilly; noiseless, quiet, calm, hush [*archaic*], echoless, speechless, soundless; hushed &c. *v.;* aphonic, surd, mute &c. 581.

SOLEMN, soft, awful, deathlike; silent as the -tomb, – grave; inaudible &c. (*faint*) 405.

Adv. SILENTLY &c. *adj.; sub silentio* [*L.*]; in –, in dead –, in perfect- silence.

Int. HUSH! silence! soft! whist! mum! sh! chut! tut! *pax!* [*L.*], *tais-toi!* [*F.*], hold your tongue! shut up! [*colloq.*], be quiet! be silent! be still! *chup!* [*Hind.*], chup rao! [*Hind.*], tace! [*L.*].

*** one might hear a -feather, – pin- drop; *grosse Seelen dulden still; le silence est la vertu de ceux qui ne sont pas sages; le silence est le parti le plus sûr de celui qui se défie de soi-même;* "silence more musical than any song" [C. G. Rossetti]; *tacent satis laudant;* "Silence, like a poultice, comes To heal the blows of sound" [Holmes]; "quiet as a nun Breathless with adoration" [Wordsworth]; "its grand orchestral silences" [E. B. Browning]; "thunders of white silence" [*ibid.*].

404. Loudness. — N. LOUDNESS, power; vociferation, uproariousness.

DIN, loud noise, clang, clangor, clatter, noise, bombilation, roar, uproar, racket, clutter, hullabaloo, pandemonium, hell let loose; outcry &c. 411; hubbub; explosion, detonation; bobbery, fracas, charivari.

BLARE, trumpet blast, flourish of trumpets, fanfare, tintamarre [archaic]; blast; peal, swell, larum [archaic], alarum, boom; resonance &c. 408.

lungs; stentor; megaphone; calliope, steam siren, steam whistle; watchman's rattle.

[COMPARISONS] artillery, cannon, guns, bombs, shells, barrage; thunder.

V. BE LOUD &c. adj.; peal, swell, clang, boom, thunder, fulminate, bombilate [rare], roar; resound &c. 408; speak up, shout &c. (vociferate) 411; bellow &c. (cry as an animal) 412.

CLATTER, clutter, racket, uproar [rare].

REND THE AIR, rend the skies; fill the air; din -, ring -, thunder- in the ear; pierce -, split -, rend- the -ears, - head; deafen, stun; faire le diable à quatre [F.]; make one's windows shake; awake the echoes, startle the echoes; give tongue.

Adj. LOUD, sonorous; high-sounding, big-sounding; deep, full, powerful, noisy, blatant, clangorous, multisonous; thundering, deafening &c. v.; trumpet-tongued; ear-splitting, ear-rending, ear-deafening; piercing; shrill &c. 410; obstreperous, rackety, uproarious; enough to wake the -dead, - seven sleepers; clamorous &c. (vociferous) 411;

Adv. LOUDLY &c. adj.; aloud; with - voice; lustily, in full cry.

. the air rings with; "the deep dread-bolted thunder" [Lear]; "on their hinges grate Harsh thunder" [Milton]; "The trumpet's loud clangor excites us to arms" [Dryden].

405. Faintness. — N. FAINTNESS &c. adj.; faint sound, whisper, breath; undertone, underbreath; murmur, hum, buzz, purr, lap [of waves], plash; sough, moan, rustle, susurration [rare], tinkle; "still small voice."

HOARSENESS &c. adj.

SILENCER, muffler; soft pedal, damper; mute, sordino [It.], sordine [all music].

V. WHISPER, breathe; mutter &c. (speak imperfectly) 583; susurrate [rare].

MURMUR, purl, hum, gurgle, ripple, babble, flow; rustle, tinkle.

steal on the ear, melt in the air, float on the air.

MUFFLE, deaden, mute, subdue.

Adj. FAINT, scarcely -, barely -, just-audible; low, dull; stifled, muffled; inaudible; hoarse, husky; gentle, soft; floating; purling, flowing &c. v.; muttered; whispered &c. v.; liquid; soothing; dulcet &c. (melodious) 413; susurrant [rare], susurrous [rare].

Adv. IN A WHISPER, with bated breath, sotto voce [It.], between the teeth, aside; piano, pianissimo [both music], sordamente [It.], sordo [It.], à la sourdine [F.]; out of earshot; inaudibly &c. adj.

. "the mingled notes came softened from below" [Goldsmith]; "the beetle winds His small but sullen horn" [Collins]; "A little noiseless noise among the leaves, Born of the very sigh that silence heaves" [Keats]; "'Twas whispered in heaven, 'twas muttered in hell, And echo caught faintly the sound as it fell" [Fanshawe].

stentorian, stentorophonic [obs.]. one wild yell; at the top of one's -lungs,

(ii) SPECIFIC SOUNDS

406. [SUDDEN AND VIOLENT SOUNDS.] **Snap. — N.** SNAP &c. v.; toot, shout, yell, yap [dial.], yelp, bark; rapping &c. v.

REPORT, decrepitation, crepitation; thump, knock, clap, thud; burst, thunderclap, thunderburst, eruption, blowout [tire], explosion, discharge, detonation, firing, salvo, volley.

DETONATION, bomb, gun, rifle; torpedo, squib, cracker, firecracker, popgun, rattle.

407. [REPEATED AND PROTRACTED SOUNDS.] **Roll. — N.** ROLL &c. v.; drumming &c. v.; berloque [F.], ululation, howl, bombilation, bombination, rumbling; dingdong; tantara, rataplan, ratatat, rubadub, tattoo; pitapat; quaver, clutter, brustle [dial.], charivari, racket; cuckoo; repetition &c. 104; peal of bells, devil's tattoo; drum fire, barrage; whirr, rattle, drone; reverberation &c. 408.

V. ROLL, drum, rataplan, boom; whirr,

V. SNAP, rap, tap, knock; click; clash; crack, crackle; crash; pop; slam, bang, clap; thump, toot, yap [*dial.*], yelp, bark, fire, explode, rattle, burst on the ear; crepitate, flump.

Adj. rapping &c. *v.;* crepitant.

Adv. SLAP-BANG *or* slam-bang [*colloq.*], bang [*colloq.*].

Int. BANG! crash!

rustle, tootle, clutter, roar, drone, rumble, rattle, clatter, patter, clack; bombinate, bombilate [*rare*].

hum, trill, shake; chime, peal, toll; tick, beat.

DRUM IN THE EAR, din in the ear.

Adj. ROLLING, &c. *v.;* monotonous &c. (*repeated*) 104; like a bee in a bottle.

⁎⁎ "The double double double beat Of the thundering drum" [Dryden].

---

408. Resonance. — N. RESONANCE; ring &c. *v.;* ringing &c. *v.;* reflection *or* reflexion; clangor, bell-note, tintinnabulation, vibration, reverberation.

low -, base -, bass -, flat -, grave -, deep- note; bass; *basso* [*It.*], *basso profondo* [*It.*]; barytone *or* baritone, contralto; pedal point, organ point.

V. RESOUND, reverberate, reëcho; ring, sound, jingle *or* gingle, chink, clink; tink, tinkle; chime; gurgle &c. 405; plash, guggle, echo, ring in the ear.

408a. Nonresonance. — N. NONRESONANCE; mutescence; thud, thump, dead sound; muffled drums, cracked bell; damper, *sordino* [*It.*], sordine, mute; muffler, silencer.

V. MUFFLE, deaden, mute; sound dead; stop -, damp -, deaden-, the -sound, - reverberations; use *or* employ the *sordino* [*It.*] &c. *n.*

Adj. NONRESONANT, dead, mute; muffled &c. *v.*

Adj. RESONANT, reverberant, resounding &c. *v.;* tinnient [*obs.*], tintinnabula *or* tintinnabulary; deep -toned, -sounding, -mouthed; hollow, sepulchral; gruff &c. (*harsh*) 410.

⁎⁎ "as when hollow rocks retain The sound of blustering winds" [Milton]; "The tintinnabulation that so musically wells From the bells" [Poe].

---

409. [HISSING SOUNDS.**] Sibilation. — N.** SIBILATION; zip; hiss &c. *v.;* sternutation; high note &c. 410.

goose, serpent, snake.

V. HISS, buzz, whiz, rustle; fizz, fizzle; wheeze, whistle, snuffle; squash; sneeze; sizz [*colloq.*], sizzle, swish.

Adj. SIBILANT; hissing &c. *v.;* wheezy; sternutative.

---

410. [HARSH OR HIGH SOUNDS.**] Stridor. — N.** STRIDOR, harshness, roughness, sharpness &c. *adj.;* raucousness, raucity; creak &c. *v.;* creaking &c. *v.;* discord, &c. 414; cacophony; cacoëpy.

HIGH NOTE, acute note; soprano, treble, tenor, alto, falsetto; *voce di testa* [*It.*], head voice, head tone; shriek, yell; cry &c. 411.

penny trumpet, piccolo, fife, whistle; penny -, willow- whistle; Panpipes, syrinx; pipes, bagpipes, doodlesack [*Scot.*].

V. GRATE, creak, saw, snore, jar, burr, pipe, twang, jangle, clank, clink; scream &c. (*cry*) 411; yelp &c. (*animal sound*) 412; buzz &c. (*hiss*) 409.

set the teeth on edge, *écorcher les oreilles* [*F.*]; pierce -, split- the -ears, - head; offend -, grate upon -, jar upon- the ear.

Adj. GRATING, creaking &c. *v.;* stridulous, strident, harsh, coarse, hoarse, horrisonant [*obs.*], raucous, metallic, horrisonous [*obs.*], rough, rude, jangly [*rare*], gruff, grum, sepulchral, hollow.

HIGH, sharp, acute, shrill; trumpet-toned; piercing, ear-piercing, high-pitched, high-toned; cracked; discordant &c. 414; cacophonous.

⁎⁎ "with impetuous recoil and jarring sound" [Milton]; "Like sweet bells jangled, out of tune and harsh" [*Hamlet*].

411. Cry. — **N.** CRY &c. *v.;* voice &c. (*human*) 580; view halloo, yoicks [*both hunting*]; hubbub; bark &c. (*animal*) 412.

OUTCRY, vociferation, hullabaloo, chorus, clamor *or* clamour, hue and cry, plaint; lungs; Stentor, stentor.

V. CRY, roar, shout, bawl, brawl, halloo, halloa, yo-ho, yoick, whoop *or* hoop [*rare*], yell, bellow, howl, scream, screech, screak, shriek, shrill, squeak, squeal, squall, whine, pule, pipe, yap, yaup *or* yawp.

CHEER, huzza, hurrah; hoot.

MOAN, grumble, groan.

SNORT, snore; grunt &c. (*animal sounds*) 412.

VOCIFERATE; raise –, lift up- the voice; yell out, call out, sing out, cry out; exclaim; rend the air; make the welkin ring; split the -throat, – lungs; thunder -, shout- at the -top of one's voice, – pitch of one's breath; *s'égosiller* [*F.*]; strain the -throat, – voice, – lungs; give cry; give a cry &c.; clamor *or* clamour.

Adj. CLAMANT, clamorous; crying &c. *v.;* vociferous; stentorian &c. (*loud*) 404; open-mouthed; full-mouthed.

⁎⁎ "And with no language but a cry" [Tennyson]; "A solitary shriek, the bubbling cry Of some strong swimmer in his agony" [Byron].

412. [ANIMAL SOUNDS.] **Ululation.** — **N.** ULULATION, howling, mugiency [*obs.*], reboation [*rare*]; cry &c. *v.;* crying &c. *v.;* call, note, howl, bark, yelp, bow-wow, latration, belling; woodnote; insect cry, twittering, fritiniancy [*obs.*], drone; cuckoo.

V. ULULATE, howl, cry, roar, bellow, blare, rebellow, latrate, bark, yelp; bay, bay the moon; yap, growl, yarr [*obs.*], yawl [*dial.*], yaup *or* yawp, snarl, howl; grunt, gruntle; snort, squeak; neigh, bray; mew, mewl, purr, caterwaul, miaow; bleat, low, moo; troat [*rare*], croak, crow, screech, caw, coo, gobble, quack, cackle, gaggle, guggle; chuck, chuckle; cluck, clack; chirp, cheep, chirrup, chirk [*obs.*], peep, sing, pule, twitter, chatter, hoot, wail, cuckoo; hum, buzz; hiss, blatter, blat [*colloq.*].

Adj. ULULANT, crying &c. *v.;* blatant, latrant, remugient [*obs.*], mugient; deep-mouthed, full-mouthed; rebellowing, reboant [*rare*].

Adv. in full cry.

⁎⁎ "I will roar you as gently as any sucking dove; I will roar you, an 'twere any nightingale" [*M. N. D.*]; "Whose household words are songs in many keys" [Longfellow]; "With bark and whoop and wild halloo" [Scott].

(iii) MUSICAL SOUNDS

413. Melody. Concord. — **N.** MELODY, rhythm, measure; rime *or* rhyme &c. (*poetry*) 597.

[MUSICAL TERMS] pitch, timbre, intonation, tone, overtone.

orchestration, harmonization, modulation, phrasing, temperament, syncope, syncopation, preparation, suspension, solution, resolution.

staff *or* stave, line, space, brace; bar, rest; *appoggiato* [*It.*], *appoggiatura* [*It.*]; *acciaccatura* [*It.*], trill *or* shake, turn, *arpeggio* [*It.*].

NOTE, musical note, notes of a scale; sharp, flat, natural; high note &c. (*shrillness*) 410; low note &c. 408; interval; semitone; second, third, fourth &c.; diatessaron [*ancient music*].

breve, semibreve *or* whole note, minim *or* half note, crotchet *or* quarter note, quaver *or* eighth note, semiquaver *or* sixteenth note, demisemiquaver *or* thirty-second note; sustained note, drone, bourdon, burden.

SCALE, gamut; diapason; diatonic –, chromatic –, enharmonic- scale; key, clef, chords.

414. Discord. — **N.** DISCORD, discordance; dissonance, cacophony, want of harmony, caterwauling; harshness &c. 410; charivari, shivaree [*dial., U. S.*], racket; consecutive fifths.

[CONFUSED SOUNDS] Babel, pandemonium; Dutch concert, cat's concert, marrowbones and cleavers [*all colloq.*].

V. BE DISCORDANT &c. *adj.;* jar &c. (*sound harshly*) 410; shivaree [*dial., U. S.*].

Adj. DISCORDANT, dissonant, absonant; out of tune, tuneless; unmusical, untunable; immelodious, unmelodious, unharmonious, inharmonious, unsweet [*rare*], singsong; cacophonous; harsh &c. 410; jarring.

⁎⁎ "Like sweet bells jangled, out of tune and harsh" [*Hamlet*]; "chromatic tortures soon shall drive them hence" [Pope].

tonic; key –, leading –, fundamental- note; supertonic, mediant, dominant; pedal point, organ point; submediant, subdominant; octave, tetrachord; Dorian *or* Doric - mode, – tetrachord; major –, minor- -mode, – scale, – key; passage, phrase.

HARMONY, concord, emmeleia; euphony, euphonism; tonality; consonance; concent [*archaic*], concentus; part.

unison, unisonance; chime, homophony.

[SCIENCE OF HARMONY] harmony, harmonics; thorough bass, fundamental bass; counterpoint; faburden [*medieval music*].

OPUS (*pl. opera*) [*L.*], piece of music &c. 415.

COMPOSER, harmonist, contrapuntist.

V. HARMONIZE, chime, symphonize, transpose, orchestrate; blend, put in tune, tune, accord, string; be harmonious &c. *adj.*

Adj. HARMONIOUS, harmonic, harmonical; in concord &c. *n.*, in tune, in concert, in unison; unisonant, concentual *or* concentuous [*rare*], symphonizing, isotonic, homophonous, assonant; ariose, consonant.

MEASURED, rhythmic *or* rhythmical, diatonic, chromatic, enharmonic.

MELODIOUS, musical; melic; tuneful, tunable; sweet, dulcet, canorous; mellow, mellifluous; soft; clear, – as a bell; silvery; euphonious, euphonic *or* euphonical, symphonious; enchanting &c. (*pleasure-giving*) 829; fine-toned, silver-toned, full-toned, deep-toned.

Adv. HARMONIOUSLY &c. *adj.*

*** "the hidden soul of harmony" [Milton]; "we did keep time, sir, in our catches" [*Twelfth Night*]; "What harmony is this? My good friends, hark!" [*Tempest*]; "music is harmony, harmony is perfection, perfection is our dream, and our dream is heaven" [Amiel]; "From Harmony, from heavenly Harmony, This universal frame began" [Dryden].

---

415. Music. — N. MUSIC; strain, tune, air; melody &c. 413; piece of music, *morceau* [*F.*], rondo, rondeau, *pastorale* [*It.*], pastoral, cavatina, fantasia, *toccata* [*It.*], *toccatella* [*It.*], *toccatina* [*It.*], *capriccio* [*It.*], fugue, canon; potpourri, medley, incidental music; variations, roulade, cadenza, cadence, trill; serenade, *notturno* [*It.*], nocturne; *passamezzo* [*It.*]; staff *or* stave &c. 413.

INSTRUMENTAL MUSIC; orchestral score, full score; minstrelsy, tweedledum and tweedledee [*applied by Byrom to the feuds between Handel and Bononcini*]; band, orchestra &c. 416; composition, opus (*pl. opera*) [*L.*], movement, concert piece, concerted piece, symphony, *concerto* [*It.*], sonata, symphonic poem, tone poem; chamber music; overture, prelude, voluntary, *Vorspiel* [*Ger.*]; string quartet *or* quartette.

LIVELY MUSIC, polka, reel &c. (*dance*) 848; ragtime, jazz; syncopation; *allegro* &c. *adv.*

SLOW MUSIC, slow movement, Lydian measures; *adagio* &c. *adv.*; minuet; siren strains, soft music; lullaby, cradle song, *berceuse* [*F.*]; dump [*obs.*]; dirge &c. (*lament*) 839; pibroch, coronach [*Scot. & Ir.*], dead march, martial music, march; waltz &c. (*dance*) 840.

VOCAL MUSIC, vocalism; chaunt [*archaic*], chant; psalm, psalmody, hymnology; hymn; song &c. (*poem*) 597; oratorio, opera, operetta; canticle, cantata, lay, ballad, ditty, carol, pastoral, recitative *or* recitativo, *aria parlante* [*It.*], aria, arietta *or* ariette, canzonet; bravura, *coloratura* [*It.*], colorature; virtuoso music, cantabile.

solo, duet, *duo* [*It.*], trio, terzetto, quartet *or* quartette, quintet *or* quintette, sestet *or* sextet, septet, double quartet, chorus; part song, descant, glee, madrigal, catch, round, chorale; antiphon, antiphony; accompaniment; inside part, second, alto, tenor, bass; score, piano score, vocal score; burden, bourdon, drone.

CONCERT, musicale, musical [*colloq.*], recital, chamber concert, popular concert *or* pop [*colloq.*], open-air concert, serenade, *aubade* [*F.*]; community singing, singsong [*colloq.*].

METHOD, *solfeggio* [*It.*], tonic sol-fa, solmization; sight -singing, – reading; reading at sight.

COMPOSER &c. 413; MUSICIAN &c. 416.

V. COMPOSE, write, set to music, arrange &c. 416; attune.

PERFORM, execute, play &c. 416.

Adj. MUSICAL; instrumental, vocal, choral, lyric, melodic, pure, operatic; classic, modern, orchestral, symphonic, contrapuntal, program; imitative, falsetto; harmonious &c. 413; Wagnerian.

Adv. *adagio; largo, larghetto, andante, andantino; alla cappella; maestoso, moderato; allegro, allegretto; spiritoso, vivace, veloce; presto, prestissimo; con brio; capriccioso; scherzo, scherzando; legato, staccato, crescendo, diminuendo, rallentando, affettuoso; arioso, parlante, cantabile; obbligato; pizzicato; desto* [all *It.*].

⁎⁎ "a snapp of musique" [Pepys]; "in notes by distance made more sweet" [Collins]; "like the faint exquisite music of a dream" [Moore]; "the music arose with its voluptuous swell" [Byron]; "music is the universal language of mankind" [Longfellow]; "music's golden tongue" [Keats]; "the speech of angels" [Carlyle]; "will sing the savageness out of a bear" [Othello]; "music hath charms to soothe the savage breast" [Congreve]; "lap me in soft Lydian airs" [Milton]; "what a voice was here now!" [Beaumont and Fletcher]; "I am never merry when I hear sweet music" [*M. of V.*].

416. Musician. [PERFORMANCE OF MUSIC.] — **N.** MUSICIAN, *artiste* [*F.*], virtuoso, performer, player, minstrel; bard &c. (*poet*) 597; accompanist, instrumentalist, organist, pianist, violinist, tweedledee [*Scot.*], fiddler, catgut scraper [*slang*]; flutist *or* flautist; harpist *or* harper, fifer, trumpeter, cornetist, piper, drummer; accordionist.

ORCHESTRA; string -orchestra, – quartet; strings, woodwind, brass; band, brass band, military band, German band, jazz band; street musicians, waits.

VOCALIST, melodist, singer, warbler; songster, chanter *or* chaunter [*archaic*]; *cantatore* [*It.*], *cantatrice* [*F.*], improvisator, *improvvisatore* or *improvisatore* [*It.*]; *improvvisatrice* or *improvisatrice* [*It.*], songstress, chantress *or* chauntress [*archaic*]; chorister; chorus singer.

choir *or* quire [*archaic*]; chorus; *Liedertafel* [*Ger.*], *Liederkranz* [*Ger.*]; choral -club, – society; singing -club, – society; festival chorus, eisteddfod [*Welsh*].

SONG BIRD, nightingale, philomel, lark, ringdove, bulbul, cuckoo, thrush, mavis.

[PATRONS] Orpheus, Apollo, Apollo Musagetes, the Muses, Polyhymnia, Erato, Euterpe, Terpsichore; Pierides, sacred nine, tuneful nine, tuneful quire [*archaic*]; Siren.

COMPOSER &c. 413.

CONDUCTOR, choirmaster, bandmaster, concert master *or* Konzertmeister [*Ger.*], drum major, song leader, precentor.

PERFORMANCE, execution, touch, expression.

V. PLAY, tune, tune up, pipe, pipe up, strike up, sweep the chords, fiddle, scrape [*derog.*], strike the lyre, beat the drum; blow –, sound –, wind- the horn; doodle [*Scot. or colloq.*]; toot, tootle, grind the organ; touch the guitar &c. (*instruments*) 417; twang, pluck, pick, paw the ivories [*slang*]; pound, thump; drum, thrum, strum, beat time.

EXECUTE, perform; accompany; sing –, play- a second.

COMPOSE, set to music, arrange, harmonize, orchestrate.

SING, chant *or* chaunt [*archaic*], intone, hum, warble, carol, yodel, chirp, chirrup, lilt, purl, quaver, trill, shake, twitter, whistle; sol-fa; do-re-mi.

have an ear for music, have a musical ear, have a correct ear, have absolute pitch.

Adj. MUSICAL; lyric, dramatic; ˉcoloratura [*It.*], bravura, florid, brilliant; playing &c. *v*.

Adv. *adagio* [*It.*], *andante* [*It.*] &c. (*music*) 415.

⁎⁎ "At last divine Cecilia came, Inventress of the vocal frame" [Dryden]; "He raised a mortal to the skies, She drew an angel down" [*ibid.*]; "the little fellow stood keeping time " [Pepys]; "blows out his brains upon the flute" [Browning].

417. Musical Instruments. — **N.** MUSICAL INSTRUMENTS; orchestra, band; string band, military band, brass band; orchestrion, orchestrina.

[STRINGED INSTRUMENTS] polychord, harp, lyre, lute, archlute, theorbo, cithara, cither, cittern *or* cithern, gittern, zither, psaltery, guitar, banjo, banjo-zither; rebec *or* rebeck, mandola, mandolin *or* mandoline, **ukulele** [*Hawaii*]; *bandurria* [*It.*], samisen [*Jap.*]; bina, vina [*India*].

violin, Cremona, Stradivarius; fiddle, kit; viol, vielle; viola, - *d'amore*, - *di gamba;* tenor, violoncello, bass viol *or* base viol; double bass *or* double base, *contrabasso* [*It.*], *violone* [*It.*]; bow, fiddlestick, strings, catgut.

piano *or* pianoforte; grand -, concert-grand -, baby-grand -, square -, upright - piano; harpsichord, monochord [*hist.*], clavichord, clarichord, manichord *or* manichordon, clavier, spinet, virginals, dulcimer; hurdy-gurdy, street piano, piano organ; pianette, pianino, piano player, player piano, player; Æolian (*or* Eolian) harp.

[WIND INSTRUMENTS] organ; church -, pipe -, reed- organ; seraphine *or* seraphina, harmonium, cabinet organ, American organ; harmoniphon [*obs.*], barrel organ, hand organ, melodeon, accordion, concertina; humming top.

flute, fife, piccolo, flageolet, clarinet *or* clarionet, bass clarinet, basset horn, *corno di bassetto* [*It.*], musette, oboe *or* hautboy, *cor anglais* [*F.*], English horn, *corno inglese* [*It.*], bassoon, double bassoon, *contrafagotto* [*It.*], serpent, bag-pipes, union pipes, doodlesack [*Scot.*]; ocarina, Panpipes *or* Pandean pipes; reed instrument; pipe, pitch-pipe; whistle; willow -, penny- whistle; calliope, siren *or* sirene; catcall.

horn, bugle, cornet, cornet-à-pistons, cornopean [*obs.*], clarion [*now chiefly poetic*], trumpet, trombone, tuba, bombardon, bass tuba, ophicleide; French horn, bugle horn, post horn, saxhorn, *Flügelhorn* [*Ger.*], alt horn *or* althorn, tenor horn, sackbut [*archaic*], euphonium.

[VIBRATING SURFACES] cymbals, bell, gong; drum, tambour, snare drum, side drum, tabor *or* tabour, taboret *or* tabouret, kettle drum, timpano (*pl.* timpani), timbal *or* tymbal, tom-tom *or* tam-tam, timbrel, tambourine, castanet, bones; musical glasses, musical stones; mouth organ, harmonica; sounding-board, *abat-voix* [*F.*]; rattle, watchman's rattle; phonograph, graphophone, gramophone, victrola [*trade-mark name*]; *zambomba* [*Sp.*].

[VIBRATING BARS] reed, tuning fork, triangle, jew's-harp, music box *or* musical box, harmonicon, xylophone.

MUTE, sourdine, *sordino* [*It.*], sordine, sordet, sourdet.

⁎ "But that which did please me beyond anything in the whole world was the windmusick" [Pepys]; "the vile squeaking of the wry-necked fife" [*M. of V.*]; "Bugles that whinnied, flageolets that crooned, And strings that whined and grunted" [Masefield].

(iv.) PERCEPTION OF SOUND

418. [SENSE OF SOUND.] **Hearing.** — **N.** HEARING &c. *v.;* audition, auscultation; audibility; acoustics &c. 402; eavesdropping.

acute -, nice -, delicate -, quick -, sharp -, correct -, musical- ear; ear for music.

EAR, auricle, pinna, concha, labyrinth, lug [*Scot.*], lobule *or* lobe, acoustic organs, auditory apparatus, eardrum, tympanum; malleus, incus, stapes, vestibule, cochlea, auditory nerve, Eustachian tube.

EAR TRUMPET, speaking trumpet; telephone, phonograph, microphone;

419. Deafness. — **N.** DEAFNESS, hardness of hearing, surdity [*obs.*], deaf ears; inaudibility, inaudibleness.

adder, beetle, slowworm, blindworm; deaf-mute.

DACTYLOLOGY, deaf-and-dumb alphabet.

V. BE DEAF &c. *adj.;* have no ear; shut -, stop -, close- one's ears; turn a deaf ear to.

RENDER DEAF, stun, deafen; split the -ears, - eardrum.

Adj. DEAF, earless, surd; hard -, dull-of hearing; deaf-mute; stunned, deaf-

gramophone, phonograph, victrola [*trade-mark name*], megaphone, phonorganon; dictagraph *or* dictograph [*trade-mark name*], dictophone [*trade-mark name*], audiphone, dentiphone; stethoscope; telephone &c. 527.

HEARER, auditor, auditory, audience, listener, eavesdropper.

OTOLOGY, otoscopy, auriscopy; otoscope, auriscope; otopathy, otography, otoplasty; otorrhea, tympanitis; otologist, aurist.

V. HEAR, overhear; hark, harken; list, listen; give –, lend –, bend- an ear; strain one's ears, attend to, give attention, catch a sound, prick up one's ears; give ear, give a hearing to, give audience to.

hang upon the lips of, be all ear, listen with both ears.

BECOME AUDIBLE; meet –, fall upon –, catch –, reach- the ear; be heard; ring in the ear &c. (*resound*) 408.

Adj. HEARING &c. *v.;* auditory, otic, aural, acoustic, acoustical, phonic; auriculate, auricular; auricled, eared; auditive.

Adv. *arrectis auribus* [*L.*]; all ears.

Int. HARK! hark ye! hear! list! listen! oyez *or* oyes! attend! attention! lend me your ears!

⁎⁎ "he that hath ears to hear, let him hear" [*Bible*]; little pitchers have big ears; "And hear, like ocean on a western beach, The surge and thunder of the Odyssey" [Andrew Lang].

ened; stone deaf; deaf as -a post, – an adder, – a beetle, – a trunkmaker; inattentive &c. 458.

INAUDIBLE, out of -earshot, – hearing.

⁎⁎ none so deaf as those that will not hear.

---

(6) *Light*

(i) LIGHT IN GENERAL

420. Light. — N. LIGHT, ray, beam, stream, gleam, streak, pencil; sunbeam, moonbeam; aurora, dawn.

day; sunshine; light of -day, – heaven; sun &c. (*luminary*) 423, daylight, broad daylight, noontide light; noontide, noonday.

glow &c. *v.;* afterglow, sunset glow; glimmering &c. *v.;* glint; glare; play –, glare –, flood- of light; phosphorescence, lambent flame.

HALO, glory, nimbus, aureola, aureole, gloriole [*rare*], aura.

SPARK, scintilla; facula; sparkling &c. *v.;* emication [*obs.*], scintillation, flash, blaze, coruscation, fulguration [*now rare*]; flame &c. (*fire*) 382; lightning, levin; *ignis fatuus* [*L.*] &c. (*luminary*) 423.

LUSTER *or* lustre, sheen, shimmer, reflection *or* reflexion; gloss, tinsel, spangle, brightness, brilliancy, splendor *or* splendour, effulgence, refulgence; fulgor, fulgidity [*rare*]; dazzlement, resplendence *or* resplendency, transplendency [*rare*], luminousness &c. *adj.;* luminosity; lucidity; nitency [*rare*]; radiance, radiation; irradiation, illumination.

421. Darkness. — N. DARKNESS &c *adj.;* tenebrosity, umbrageousness, dunness [*rare*], caliginousness, lightlessness, sootiness; blackness &c. (*dark color*) 431; obscurity, gloom, murk *or* mirk, murkiness *or* mirkiness, darksomeness; dusk &c. (*dimness*) 422.

Cimmerian –, Stygian –, Egyptian-darkness; night; midnight; dead of –, witching hour of –, witching time of- night; darkness visible; "darkness which may be felt" [*Bible*]; "the palpable obscure" [Milton]; "embalméd darkness" [Keats]; Erebus; "the jaws of darkness" [*M. N. D.*]; "sable-vested Night" [Milton].

SHADOW, shade, umbra, penumbra; skiagraphy *or* sciagraphy; skiagram *or* sciagram, skiagraph *or* sciagraph; radiograph.

OBSCURATION; obumbration [*rare*]; obtenebration [*rare*], offuscation [*obs.*], caligation [*obs.*], adumbration; extinction; eclipse, total eclipse; gathering of the clouds.

SHADING; distribution of shade; *chiaroscuro* [*It.*] &c. (*light*) 420.

V. BE DARK &c. *adj.;* be in darkness &c. *n.*

[Science of light] optics; photology, photics; actinology, actinometry, radiology, heliology, radiometry, radioscopy, photometry, dioptrics, catoptrics; photography, photolithography, photomicography, phototelegraphy, radiotelegraphy; phototherapy, heliotherapy, radiotherapy; heliometry, heliography.

actinic rays, actinism; radioactivity, radium emanation, exradio; Röntgen rays, X-rays, ultra-violet rays; photometer &c. 445; heliometer, refractometer.

[Distribution of light] *chiaroscuro* or *chiaro-oscuro* [*It.*], clair-obscure, *clairobscur* [*F.*], mezzotint, mezzotinto, half tone *or* half-tone, demitint, half tint; breadth, light and shade, black and white, tonality.

reflection, refraction, dispersion; refractivity.

ILLUMINANT, artificial light; gas &c. 423.

V. SHINE, glow, beam, glitter; glister, glisten; twinkle, gleam; flare, flare up; glare, shimmer, glimmer, flicker, sparkle, scintillate, coruscate, flash, blaze; be bright &c. *adj.;* reflect light, daze, dazzle, bedazzle, radiate, shoot out beams; fulgurate, phosphoresce.

clear up, brighten.

LIGHTEN, enlighten; levin; light, light up; irradiate, shine upon; give –, hang out a – light; cast –, throw –, shed- -luster, – light- upon; illume, illumine, illuminate; relume, strike a light; kindle &c. (*set fire to*) 384.

Adj. LUMINOUS, luminiferous; shining &c. *v.;* lucid, lucent, luculent, luciferous [*rare*], lucific [*rare*]; illuminate [*archaic*], illuminant, light, lightsome; bright, vivid, splendent, nitid, lustrous, shiny, beamy, scintillant, fulgurant, radiant, lambent; sheen [*dial. or poetic*], sheeny; glossy, burnished, glassy, sunny, orient, meridian; noonday, noontide; cloudless, clear; unclouded, unobscured.

garish; resplendent, transplendent [*rare*]; refulgent, effulgent, fulgid, fulgent, relucent, splendorous *or* splendrous, splendid, blazing, in a blaze, ablaze, rutilant, meteoric, phosphorescent; aglow.

bright as silver; light –, bright- as -day, – noonday, – the sun at noonday.

[Scientific] actinic, radioactive; optic, optical, photologic *or* photological. helio-

DARKEN, obscure, shade; dim; tone down, lower; overcast, overshadow; cloud, cloud over, darken over, murk *or* mirk; eclipse; offuscate [*obs.*], obumbrate, obtenebrate [*rare*], obfuscate; adumbrate; cast into the shade; becloud, bedim, bedarken; cast –, throw –, spread- a -shade, – shadow, – gloom; "walk in darkness and in the shadow of death" [*Book of Common Prayer*].

EXTINGUISH, put out, blow out, snuff out, dout [*obs. or dial. Eng.*]

Adj. DARK, darksome, darkling; obscure, tenebrious, tenebrous, sombrous, pitch dark, pitchy; caliginous [*archaic*]; black &c. (*in color*) 431.

dark as -pitch, – the pit, – Erebus.

SUNLESS, lightless &c. (*see* sun, light, &c. 423); somber, dusky; unilluminated &c. (*see* illuminate &c. 420); nocturnal; dingy, lurid, gloomy; murky *or* mirky, murksome *or* mirksome, sooty, shady, umbrageous; overcast &c. (*dim*) 422; cloudy &c. (*opaque*) 426; darkened &c. *v.*

BENIGHTED; noctivagant, noctivagous.

Adv. in the -dark, – shade; at night, by night, through the night; darkling, darklings [*rare*].

. "in the dead vast and middle of the night" [*Hamlet*]; "brief as the lightning in the collied night" [*M. N. D.*]; "eldest Night and Chaos, ancestors of Nature" [*P. L.*]; "Empress of silence, and the queen of sleep" [Marlowe]; "Who could have thought such darkness lay concealed Within thy beams, O Sun" [J. Blanco White]; "the blackness of the noonday night" [Longfellow]; "the prayer of Ajax was for light" [*ibid.*].

422. Dimness. — N. DIMNESS &c. *adj.;* darkness &c. 421; paleness &c. (*light color*) 429.

HALF LIGHT, *demi-jour* [*F.*]; partial shadow, partial eclipse; "shadow of a shade" [Æschylus]; "shadows numberless" [Keats]; glimmer, glimmering; nebulosity, nebulousness, obnubilation [*rare*]; cloud &c. 353; eclipse.

TWILIGHT, aurora, dusk, nightfall, gloaming, gloam [*rare*], blind man's holiday, *entre chien et loup* [*F.*], *inter canem et lupem* [*L.*], shades of evening, crepuscule, cockshut time [*obs.*]; break of day, daybreak, dawn.

moonlight, moonbeam, moonglade, moonshine; owl's-light, starlight, candlelight, rushlight, firelight; farthing candle.

V. BE *or* GROW DIM &c. *adj.;* gloom; cloud over; flicker, twinkle, glimmer,

logical; photogenic, photographic; helio-graphic; heliophagous.

. "a day for gods to stoop and men to soar" [Tennyson]; "dark with excessive bright" [*P. L.*]; "Hail holy light! offspring of heav'n first-born" [*P. L.*]; "And noon lay heavy on flower and tree" [Shelley].

loom, lower; fade; pale, "pale his un-effectual fire" [*Hamlet*].

RENDER DIM &c. *adj.;* dim, bedim, obscure, shade, shadow; encompass with -gloom, - shadow; darken, dark [*archaic*], cloud, becloud, darkle.

Adj. DIM, dull, lackluster, dingy, darkish, dusky, shorn of its beams; dark &c. 421.

FAINT, shadowed forth; glassy; cloudy; misty &c. (*opaque*) 426; blear; fuliginous; nebulous, nebular, obnubilated [*rare*], obnubilous [*obs.*].

LURID, leaden, dun, dirty; overcast, muddy; looming &c. *v.*

TWILIGHT, crepuscular, crepusculous [*rare*], crepusculine [*rare*].

pale &c. (*colorless*) 429; confused &c. (*invisible*) 447.

. "now fades the glimmering landscape on the sight" [Gray]; "draw the gradual dusky veil" [Collins]; "the lengthening shadows wait The first pale stars of twilight" [Holmes]; "fade away into the forest dim" [Keats].

423. [SOURCE OF LIGHT.] **Luminary.** — N. LUMINARY; light &c. 420; flame &c. (*fire*) 382.

spark, scintilla; phosphorescence.

[HEAVENLY BODIES] sun, orb of day, day-star [*poetic*], Aurora; star, orb, meteor; falling star, shooting star; blazing star, dog star, canicula, Sirius, Aldebaran; constellation, galaxy, Milky Way; pole star, Polaris; Cynosure; anthelion; morning star, Lucifer, Phos-phor, Phosphorus; Venus, Hesperus, evening star; mock sun, parhelion, sun dog *or* sundog, moon &c. 318.

SUN GOD, Helios, Titan, Phaëthon, Phœbus, Apollo, Hyperion, Ra *or* Re [*Egypt*], Shamash [*Babylon & Assyria*].

LIGHTNING, levin; chain -, fork -, sheet -, summer- lightning.

PHOSPHORUS; *ignis fatuus* [*L.*]; Jack o' -, Friar's- lantern; will-o'-the-wisp, firedrake, Fata Morgana, St. Elmo's fire, Castor and Pollux [*naut.*], corposant.

glowworm, firefly.

POLAR LIGHTS, northern lights, *aurora borealis* [*L.*], *aurora australis* [*L.*]; aurora; zodiacal light.

[ARTIFICIAL LIGHT] gas, gaslight, electric light; headlight, searchlight, spotlight, flashlight, limelight, calcium light, lamplight, lamp; lantern, lanthorn [*archaic*]; electric torch, dark lantern, bull's-eye; candle; wax -, tallow -, bayberry- candle; farthing dip, tallow dip [*colloq.*]; bougie, taper, rushlight; oil &c. (*grease*) 356; wick, burner; Argand, moderator, duplex; torch, flambeau, link, brand; gaselier, chandelier, electrolier; candelabrum, girandole, sconce, luster *or* lustre, candlestick.

FIREWORK, Catherine wheel, Roman candle, fizgig; pyrotechnics.

SIGNAL LIGHT, rocket, balefire, beacon fire; lighthouse &c. (*signal*) 550.

PYRE, funeral pyre; death fire; corpse candle.

V. ILLUMINATE &c. (*light*) 420.

Adj. SELF-LUMINOUS; phosphoric, phosphorescent; radiant &c. (*light*) 420.

. "blossomed the lovely stars, the forget-me-nots of the angels" [Longfellow]; "the senti-nel stars set their watch in the sky" [Campbell]; "and with joy the stars perform their shining" [Arnold]; "the planets in their station list'ning stood" [*P. L.*]; "the Scriptures of the skies" [Bailey]; "that orbed continent, the fire that severs day from night" [*Twelfth Night*]; "that orbed maiden with white fire laden, Whom mortals call the Moon" [Shelley].

424. Shade. — N. SHADE; awning &c. (*cover*) 223; parasol, sunshade, umbrella.

SCREEN, curtain, chick [*India*], purdah [*India*], *portière* [*F.*]; shutter, blind, Venetian blind, *jalousie* [*F.*].

gauze, veil, mantle, mask, yashmak [*Turk.*].

cloud, mist; gathering of clouds; smoke screen [*mil.*].

umbrage [*archaic*], glade; shadow &c. 421; ambush, covert.

BLINKERS, blinders; smoked glasses, colored spectacles.

V. VEIL &c. *v.;* draw a curtain; put up -, close- a shutter; cast a shadow &c. (*darken*) 421.

Adj. SHADY, umbrageous, shadowy, bowery.

. "welcome, ye shades! ye bowery thickets, hail" [Thomson].

425. Transparency. — N. TRANSPAR-ENCY, transparence, translucence, trans-lucency, diaphaneity, diaphanousness; lucidity, pellucidity, limpidity; fluores-cence; transillumination, translumina-tion.

TRANSPARENT MEDIUM, glass, crystal, lymph, water, hyalite, hyaline.

V. BE TRANSPARENT &c. *adj.;* transmit light.

Adj. TRANSPARENT, pellucid, lucid, diaphanous; translucent, tralucent [*obs.*], limpid, clear, serene, crystalline, clear as crystal, pervious [*rare*], vitreous, tran-spicuous [*rare*], glassy, hyaline, hyaloid [*rare*], vitreform.

⁎⁎ "translucent syrops tinct with cinna-mon" [Keats].

426. Opacity. — N. OPACITY; opaque-ness &c. *adj.;* obfuscation, fuliginosity, nubilation.

film; cloud &c. 353.

V. BE OPAQUE &c. *adj.;* obstruct the passage of light; obfuscate, offuscate [*obs.*].

Adj. OPAQUE, impervious to light; adiaphanous; dim &c. 422; turbid, thick, muddy, opacous [*obs.*], obfuscated, fulig-inous, cloudy, nubilous, nubilose [*obs.*], foggy, vaporous, nubiferous.

SMOKY, fumid [*obs.*], murky *or* mirky, smeared, dirty.

427. Semitransparency. — N. SEMI-TRANSPARENCY, opalescence, milkiness, pearliness.

[COMPARISONS] gauze, muslin, cypress *or* cyprus [*hist.*], bombyx, thin silk; film; mica, mother-of-pearl, nacre, opal glass, opaline, frosted glass; mist &c. (*cloud*) 353.

Adj. SEMITRANSPARENT, semipellucid, semidiaphanous, semiopacous [*obs.*], semiopaque; opalescent, opaline; pearly, milky; frosted, nacreous; hazy, misty.

V. CLOUD, frost, cloud over, frost over; become -pearly, – milky, – misty.

be opalescent &c. *adj.;* opalesce.

(ii) SPECIFIC LIGHT

428. Color. — N. COLOR *or* colour, hue, tint, tinct [*archaic*], tinction, tinge, dye, complexion, shade, tincture, cast, livery, coloration, chromatism *or* chro-mism, glow, flush; tone, key.

pure –, positive –, primary –, primitive –, complementary- color; three prima-ries; spectrum, chromatic dispersion; broken –, secondary –, tertiary- color.

local color, coloring, keeping, tone, value, aërial perspective.

[SCIENCE OF COLOR] chromatics, spec-trum analysis; chromatography, chro-matology, chromatoscopy; chromato-graph, chromatometer, chromatoscope, chromoscope, chromatrope, chromom-eter, colorimeter; prism, spectroscope, kaleidoscope.

PIGMENT, coloring matter, paint, dye, wash, distemper, stain, chromogen; medium; mordant; oil paint &c. (*paint-ing*) 556.

V. COLOR *or* colour, dye, tinge, stain, tint, tinct [*archaic*], hue, tone, com-plexion [*rare*]; paint, wash, distemper, ingrain, grain. illuminate, emblazon, imbue; paint &c. (*fine art*) 556.

Adj. COLORED &c. *v.;* colorific, tingent [*rare*], tinctorial; chromatic, prismatic;

429. [ABSENCE OF COLOR.] **Achroma-tism. — N.** ACHROMATISM, achromatiza-tion; decoloration, decolorization, dis-coloration; pallor, pallidity; paleness &c. *adj.;* etiolation.

neutral tint, monochrome, black and white.

V. LOSE COLOR &c. 428; fade, fly, go, become colorless &c. *adj.;* turn pale; pale, fade out, bleach out; wan; fly, go.

DEPRIVE OF COLOR, decolor *or* decolour, decolorize *or* decolourize, whiten, bleach, tarnish, achromatize, blanch, etiolate, wash out, tone down.

Adj. COLORLESS; achromatic; un-colored &c. (*see* color &c. 428); etiolated; hueless, pale, pallid; pale-faced, anæmic *or* anemic, tallow-faced; faint, dull, cold, muddy, leaden, dun, wan, sallow, dead, dingy, ashy, ashen, ghastly, cadaverous, glassy, lackluster; discolored &c. *v.*

pale as -death, – ashes, – a witch, – a ghost, – a corpse.

LIGHT-COLORED, fair, blond, ash-blond; white &c. 430; tow-headed, tow-haired.

⁎⁎ "O pale, pale now those rosy lips I oft hae kissed sae fondly" [Burns].

full –, high –, rich –, deep- colored; double-dyed; polychromatic; chromatogenous; chromatophoric, chromatophorous; tingible.

BRIGHT, vivid, intense, deep; fresh, unfaded; rich, gorgeous; bright-colored, gay.

GAUDY, florid; garish; showy, flaunting; flashy; many-colored, party-colored or parti-colored, variegated; raw, crude; glaring, flaring; discordant, inharmonious.

MELLOW, harmonious, pearly, sweet, delicate, subtle, tender.

DULL, sad, somber or sombre, sad-colored, grave, gray, dark.

---

430. Whiteness. — N. WHITENESS &c. adj.; whitishness, canescence; argent, argentine.

ALBIFICATION, albication, albinism, albinoism; leucopathy, leucoderma or leucodermia [med.], dealbation, albescence, etiolation; lactescence.

[COMPARISONS] snow, paper, chalk, milk, lily, ivory, silver, alabaster; albata, eburin or eburine or eburite, German silver, white metal, barium sulphate, blanc fixe [F.], pearl white; white lead, ceruse, carbonate of lead, Paris white, zinc white, flake white, Chinese white.

WHITEWASH, whiting, whitening, calcimine.

V. BE WHITE &c. adj.

RENDER WHITE &c. adj.; whiten, bleach, blanch, etiolate, silver, besnow, dealbate [obs.], albify [rare], frost.

WHITEWASH, calcimine, white.

Adj. WHITE; snow-white; snowy, niveous; candent, candid [archaic], frosted, hoar, hoary; silvery, silver, argent, argentine; canescent, chalky, cretaceous; lactescent, milk-white, milky, marmoreal or marmorean; albificative, albicant, albescent; albinistic.

white as –a sheet, – driven snow, – a lily, – silver; like ivory &c. n.

WHITISH, creamy, pearly, ivory, fair, blond, ash-blond; blanched &c. v.; high in tone, light.

** "lawn as white as driven snow" [Shakespeare]; "the white radiance of eternity" [Shelley]; "the chief assertion of religious morality is that white is a colour" [Chesterton].

431. Blackness. — N. BLACKNESS &c. adj.; darkness &c. (want of light) 421; swarthiness, swartness; lividity; dark -color, – tone; chiaroscuro [It.] &c. 420.

nigrification [rare], nigrefaction [obs.], nigrescence, denigration, infuscation [rare].

[COMPARISONS] jet, ink, ebony, ebon [now poetic], coal, pitch, soot, charcoal, sloe; smut, smutch, smudge, smirch; raven, crow.

NEGRO, negress, blackamoor, man of color, colored man, colored woman, nigger [colloq., usually contemptuous], darky or darkey [colloq.], black, blacky [colloq.], Ethiop, Ethiopian, buck or buck nigger [colloq., U. S.], coon [slang, U. S.], sambo [colloq. or humorous], kala admi [Hind.], Melanesian, Hottentot, Pygmy, Bushman, Negrillo [African Pygmy], Negrito [Asiatic Pygmy], African, Mandingo, Senegambian, Sudanese, Papuan, blackfellow, Australian aborigine.

[PIGMENTS] lamp –, ivory –, blue-black; writing –, printing –, printer's –, Indian- ink.

V. BE BLACK &c. adj.

RENDER BLACK &c. adj.; black, blacken, infuscate [rare], denigrate, nigrify; blot, blotch, smut, smudge, smutch, smirch; darken &c. 421.

Adj. BLACK, sable, somber or sombre, livid, dark, inky, ebon, atramentous, jetty; coal-black, jet-black; fuliginous, pitchy, sooty; dhu [Ir. & Gaelic], swart, swarthy, dusky, dingy, murky or mirky; blotchy, smudgy, smutty; nigrine [rare], nigricant, nigrescent, Ethiopian, Ethi-

---

opic; low-toned, low in tone; of the deepest dye.

black as –jet &c. n., – my hat, – a shoe, – a tinker's pot, – November, – the ace of spades, – thunder, – midnight; nocturnal &c. (dark) 421; gray &c. 432; obscure &c. 421.

Adv. in mourning.

** "more black than ash-buds in the front of March" [Tennyson]; "cyprus black as e'er was crow" [Shakespeare].

432. Gray. — **N.** GRAY or grey &c. *adj.;* neutral tint, silver, dove-color, pepper and salt, *chiaroscuro* [*It.*], grisaille.

grayness or greyness &c. *adj.*

[PIGMENTS] Payne's gray; black &c. 431.

V. RENDER GRAY &c. *adj.;* gray or grey.

Adj. GRAY or grey; iron-gray, dun, drab, dingy, leaden, livid, somber, sad, pearly, calcareous, limy, silver, silvery, silvered; French –, steel –, Quaker –, dapple- gray; dappled; dove-colored, *gorge-de-pigeon* [*F.*]; ashen, ashy, favillous; cinereous, cineritious; grizzly, grizzled; slate-colored, stone-colored, mouse-colored, ash-colored; cool.

433. Brown. — **N.** BROWN &c. *adj.;* brownness.

[PIGMENTS] bister or bistre, brown ocher or ochre, mummy, sepia, Vandyke brown.

V. RENDER BROWN &c. *adj.;* brown, tan, embrown, imbrown, bronze.

Adj. BROWN, adust [*rare*], castaneous, toast-brown, nut-brown, seal-brown, cinnamon, hazel, fawn, puce, musteline, musteloid, écru, *feuille-morte* [*F.*], tawny, fuscous, chocolate, maroon, tan, brunette, whitey-brown; fawn-colored, snuff-colored, liver-colored; brown as -a berry, – mahogany, – oak leaves; khaki.

REDDISH-BROWN, terra cotta, rufous, russet, russety, russetish, ferruginous, rust, foxy, bronze, coppery, copperish, copper-colored; bay, bayard, roan, sorrel, henna, auburn, chestnut, mahogany; rubiginous, rubiginose, rust-colored; lurid.

sun-burnt; tanned &c. *v.*

Primitive Colors [1]

434. Redness. — **N.** RED, scarlet, cardinal, cardinal red, vermilion, carmine, crimson, pink, rose, cerise, cherry, rouge, coquelicot, salmon, lake, maroon, carnation, *couleur de rose* [*F.*], *rose du Barry* [*F.*]; magenta, solferino, damask, flesh -color, – tint; color; fresh –, high-color; warmth; gules [*her.*].

REDNESS &c. *adj.;* rubescence, rubicundity, ruddiness, rubefaction, rubrication, rubification; erubescence, blush.

[COMPARISONS] ruby, *grenat* [*F.*], garnet, carbuncle; rust, iron mold or mould; rose, cardinal flower, lobelia; cardinal-bird, – grosbeak; redstart.

[DYES AND PIGMENTS] cinnabar, cochineal, red ocher or ochre, stammel, fuchsine or fuchsin, vermilion; ruddle, madder; Indian red, palladium red, light red, Venetian red; red ink, annotto or annotto, realgar, minium, red lead.

V. BE or BECOME RED &c. *adj.;* blush, flush, color, color up, mantle, redden.

Complementary Colors

435. Greenness. — **N.** GREEN &c. *adj.;* blue and yellow; vert [*her.*].

GREENNESS, verdancy, verdure, viridescence, viridity.

[COMPARISONS] emerald, malachite, chrysoprase, jasper, chrysolite or olivine, beryl; verd antique, verdigris, aquamarine; reseda, mignonette, absinthe, *crême de menthe* [*F.*].

[PIGMENTS] *terre verte* [*F.*], viridian, bice, verditer, verdine, celadon.

V. RENDER GREEN &c. *adj.;* green.

Adj. GREEN, verdant; glaucous, olive; green as grass; verdurous, citrine or citrinous, porraceous, olivaceous, smaragdine [*rare*].

emerald –, pea –, grass –, apple –, sea –, olive –, cucumber –, leaf –, Irish –, Kelly –, bottle- green.

GREENISH, virent [*rare*], virescent, viridescent [*rare*], chlorine; aquamarine, blue-green.

RENDER RED &c. *adj.;* redden, rouge, crimson, encrimson [*rare*], empurple; rubify [*rare*], rubricate; incarnadine; ruddle, rust.

Adj. RED &c. *n.*, reddish; incarnadine, sanguine, sanguineous, bloody, gory; coral, coralline, rosy, roseate; stammel, blood-red, laky, wine-red, wine-colored, vinaceous; incarmined [*rare*], rubiform [*rare*], rufous, rufulous, murrey, bricky, lateritious [*rare*]; rubineous, rubious, rubricate, rubricose; Pompeiian red; reddish-brown &c. 433.

---

[1] Roget's classification of colors has been retained, though it does not entirely accord with the theories of modern science.

rose-, ruby-, cherry-, claret-, flame-, flesh-, peach-, salmon-, brick-, rust-colored.

red as -fire, – blood, – scarlet, – a turkey cock, – a lobster; warm, hot.

RED-COMPLEXIONED, red-faced, florid, burnt, rubicund, ruddy, red, blowzed, blowzy, glowing, sanguine, blooming, rosy, hectic, flushed, inflamed; blushing &c. *v.*; erubescent, rubescent; reddened &c. *v.*

[OF HAIR] sandy, carroty, brick-red, Titian red, auburn, chestnut.

₊ "like a lobster boil'd, the morn From black to red began to turn" [Butler]; "red as a rose is she" [Coleridge]; "And Marian's nose looks red and raw" [Shakespeare].

436. Yellowness. — N. YELLOW &c. *adj.;* or [*her.*]; yellowness &c. *adj.;* xanthocyanopia *or* xanthocyanopsia, xanthochroia.

[COMPARISONS] crocus, jonquil, saffron, topaz; xanthite; gold, gilding, gilt; yolk; jaundice, icterus; London fog.

[PIGMENTS] gamboge, fustic, massicot; cadmium –, chrome –, Indian –, king's –, lemon- yellow; orpiment, yellow ocher, Claude tint, aureolin; xanthein, xanthin; xanthophyll.

V. RENDER YELLOW &c. *adj.;* yellow, gild; jaundice.

Adj. YELLOW, aureate, golden, gold, gilt, gilded, flavous [*obs.*], citrine, citreous, lemon, fallow; fulvous, fulvescent, fulvid [*rare*]; sallow, lutescent, luteolous, luteous, tawny, cream, creamy, sandy; xanthic, xanthous; jaundiced; auricomous, ocherous *or* ochreous, ochery *or* ochry, flaxen, yellowish, buff, écru; icterine, icteritious *or* icteritous, icteroid; xanthochroid, yellow complexioned.

gold-, saffron-, citron-, lemon-, sulphur-, amber-, straw-, primrose-, cream-colored; xanthocarpous, xanthopous [*bot., rare*].

yellow as a -quincy, – guinea, – crow's foot; yellow as saffron.

437. Purple. — N. PURPLE &c. *adj.;* blue and red, bishop's purple; gridelin, amethyst; damson, heliotrope; purpure [*her.*].

LIVIDNESS, lividity.

V. RENDER PURPLE &c. *adj.;* purple, empurple.

Adj. PURPLE, violet, plum-colored, lavender, lilac, puce, mauve, purplish, purpurate [*archaic*], violaceous, hyacinthine, amethystine, magenta, solferino, heliotrope; livid.

438. Blueness. — N. BLUE &c. *adj.;* garter-blue; watchet [*obs.*]; blueness, bluishness; bloom.

[COMPARISONS] *lapis lazuli* [*L.*], sapphire, turquoise; indicolite.

[PIGMENTS] ultramarine, smalt, cobalt, cyanogen; Prussian –, syenite- blue; bice, indigo; zaffer.

V. RENDER BLUE &c. *adj.;* blue.

Adj. BLUE, azure, cerulean, cyanic; sky-blue, sky-colored, sky-dyed; navy blue, midnight blue, cadet blue, robin's-egg blue, baby blue, ultramarine, aquamarine, electric blue *or* electric, steel blue *or* steel; cerulescent; bluish; atmospheric, retiring; cold.

₊ "Oh, yellow's forsaken, and green is forsworn, But blue is the sweetest color that's worn"; "Blue, darkly, deeply, beautifully blue" [Southey]; "colour'd with the heaven's own blue" [Bryant].

439. Orange. — N. ORANGE, red and yellow; old gold; gold color &c. *adj.*

[PIGMENTS] ocher *or* ochre, Mars orange, cadmium.

V. GILD, engild, deaurate [*rare*], warm.

Adj. ORANGE; ocherous *or* ochreous, ochery *or* ochry; henna, burnt orange; orange-, gold-, brass-, apricot- colored; warm, hot, glowing, flame-colored.

440. Variegation. — N. VARIEGATION; dichroism, trichroism; iridescence, irisation, play of colors, polychrome, maculation, spottiness, striæ.

[COMPARISONS] spectrum, rainbow, iris, tulip, peacock, chameleon, butterfly, zebra, leopard, jaguar, panther, cheetah, ocelot, ophite, nacre, mother-of-pearl, tortoise shell; opal, cymophane, marble; mackerel, mackerel sky; harlequin; Joseph's coat; tricolor.

CHECK, plaid, tartan, patchwork; marquetry, parquet, parquetry, mosaic, tesseræ. tessellation, checkerwork; chessboard, checkers *or* chequers.

V. VARIEGATE, stripe, streak, checker *or* chequer, fleck, bespeckle, speckle, besprinkle, sprinkle; stipple, maculate, dot, bespot; tattoo, inlay, tessellate. damascene; embroider, braid, quilt.

be variegated &c. *adj.*

Adj. VARIEGATED &c. *v.;* many-colored, many-hued; divers-colored, party-colored *or* parti-colored, dichromatic, polychromatic; bicolor, tricolor, versi-color; of all the colors of the rainbow, of all manner of colors; kaleidoscopic, nævose *or* nevose, dædal.

IRIDESCENT, opaline, opalescent, prismatic, nacreous, pearly, shot, *gorge-de-pigeon* [*F.*], chatoyant; irised, irisated, pavonine; tortoise-shell.

MOTTLED, pied, piebald, skewbald; motley, marbled, pepper-and-salt, paned, dappled, clouded, cymophanous.

CHECKERED *or* chequered, mosaic, tessellated, plaid.

SPOTTED, spotty; punctate *or* punctated [*rare*], powdered; speckled &c. *v.;* freckled, flea-bitten, studded; flecked, fleckered.

STRIATED, barred, veined; brinded, brindled, tabby; watered; strigose, strigillose, strigate, striolate; listed; embroidered &c. *v.*

. "to paint the rainbow's varying hues" [Scott]; "iris all hues, roses and jessamin" [*P.L.*]; "'Fly pride,' says the peacock" (*Comedy of Errors*); "That royal bird, whose tail's a diadem" [Byron].

(iii) PERCEPTIONS OF LIGHT

441. Vision. — N. VISION, sight, optics, eyesight.

VIEW, look, espial, glance, ken, *coup d'œil* [*F.*]; glimpse, glint, peep, peek; gaze, stare, leer; perlustration [*rare*], contemplation [*obs.*], conspectuity [*obs.*]; regard, survey; inspection, introspection; reconnoissance, reconnaissance, speculation, watch, espionage, *espionnage* [*F.*]; autopsy; ocular -inspection, – demonstration; sight-seeing, globe-trotting [*colloq.*].

VIEWPOINT, standpoint, point of view; gazebo, loophole, belvedere, watch-tower.

FIELD OF VIEW; theater *or* theatre, amphitheater *or* amphitheatre, arena, vista, horizon; commanding view, bird's-eye view, panoramic view.

VISUAL ORGAN, organ of vision; eye; naked eye, unassisted eye; retina, pupil, iris, cornea, white; optics, orbs; saucer -, goggle -, gooseberry- eyes.

short sight &c. 443; clear -, sharp -, quick -, eagle -, piercing -, penetrating- -sight, – glance, – eye; perspicacity, discernment; catopsis.

[COMPARISON] eagle, hawk; cat, lynx, weasel; Argus.

EVIL EYE, blighting glance; basilisk, cockatrice.

[OPTICAL DEVICES] spectacles, eye-glass, lorgnette, monocle, reading glass, field glass, opera glass; telescope &c. 445; microscope, periscope.

V. SEE, behold, discern, perceive, have

442. Blindness. — N. BLINDNESS, sightlessness, benightedness, anopsia *or* anopsy, cecity, excecation [*obs.*], cataract, ablepsia *or* ablepsy [*rare*], prestriction [*obs.*]; dim-sightedness &c. 443; amaurosis, *gutta serena* ["drop serene" *of Milton*], teichopsia.

[TYPE FOR THE BLIND] Braille *or* Braille type, New York point, Gall's serrated type, Howe's American type *or* Boston type, Moon's type; Alston's Glasgow type, Lucas's type, Frere's type; string alphabet, writing stamps, noctograph.

V. BE BLIND &c. *adj.;* not see; lose sight of; have the eyes bandaged; grope in the dark.

NOT LOOK; close -, shut -, turn away -, avert- the eyes; look another way; wink &c. (*limited vision*) 443; shut the eyes to, be blind to; wink at, blink at.

RENDER BLIND &c. *adj.;* excecate [*obs.*], blind, blindfold; hoodwink, dazzle; put one's eyes out; throw dust into one's eyes; *jeter de la poudre aux yeux* [*F.*]; screen from sight &c. (*hide*) 528.

Adj. BLIND; eyeless, sightless, vision-less; dark; stone-blind, stark-blind, sand-blind [*archaic*]; undiscerning; dim-sighted &c. 443.

blind as -a bat, – a buzzard, – a beetle, – a mole, – an owl; wall-eyed.

BLINDED &c. *v.*

Adv. BLINDLY, blindfold; darkly.

. "O dark, dark, dark, amid the blaze of noon" [Milton].

in sight, descry, sight, make out, discover, distinguish, recognize, spy, espy, ken [*archaic*]; get –, have –, catch- a -sight, – glimpse -of; command a view of; witness, contemplate, speculate; cast –, set- the eyes on; be a spectator of &c. 444; look on &c. (*be present*) 186; see sights &c. 455; see at a glance &c. 498.

LOOK, view, eye; lift up the eyes, open one's eye; look -at, – on, – upon, – over, – about one, – round; survey, scan, inspect; run the eye -over, – through; reconnoiter *or* reconnoitre, glance- round, – on, – over; turn –, bend- one's looks upon; direct the eyes to, turn the eyes on, cast a glance.

observe &c. (*attend to*) 457; watch &c. (*care*) 459; see with one's own eyes; watch for &c. (*expect*) 507; peep, peek, peer, pry, take a peep; play at bopeep.

look full in the face, look hard at, look intently; strain one's eyes; fix –, rivet- the eyes upon; stare, gaze; pore over, gloat on, gloat over; leer, ogle, glare; goggle; cock the eye, squint, gloat, look askance *or* askant.

Adj. OCULAR; seeing &c. *v.;* visual, optic *or* optical; ophthalmic.

CLEAR-SIGHTED &c. *n.;* clear-eyed, far-sighted; eagle-, hawk-, lynx-, keen-, Argus- eyed.

VISIBLE &c. 446.

Adv. VISIBLY &c. 446; in sight of, with one's eyes open.

AT SIGHT, at first sight, at a glance, at the first blush; *primâ facie* [*L.*].

Int. LOOK! &c. (*attention*) 457.

*** the scales falling from one's eyes; "an eye like Mars to threaten or command" [*Hamlet*]; "her eyes are homes of silent prayer" [Tennyson]; "looking before and after" [*Hamlet*]; "thy rapt soul sitting in thine eyes" [*Milton*].

443. Dim-sightedness. — N. [IMPERFECT VISION] dim –, dull –, half –, short –, near –, long –, double –, astigmatic –, failing- sight; dim &c. -sightedness; purblindness, monocularity, blearedness, lippitude; myopia, presbyopia; confusion of vision; astigmatism; color blindness, chromato-pseudoblepsis, Daltonism; day blindness, hemeralopia; snow blindness; xanthocyanopia *or* xanthocyanopsia; ophthalmia; cataract; nyctalopia, moon blindness.

SQUINT, cross-eye, strabismus, strabism, nystagmus; cast in the eye, swivel eye, cockeye, goggle-eyes; obliquity of vision.

WINKING &c. *v.;* nictitation, nictation; blinkard, albino.

DIZZINESS, swimming, scotomy *or* scotoma [*med.*].

[LIMITATION OF VISION] blinker, blinder; screen &c. (*hider*) 530.

[FALLACIES OF VISION] *deceptio visûs* [*L.*]; refraction, distortion, illusion, false light, anamorphosis, virtual image, spectrum, mirage, looming, phasma [*obs.*]; phantasm, phantasma, phantom; vision; specter *or* spectre, apparition, ghost; *ignis fatuus* [*L.*] &c. (*luminary*) 423; specter of the Brocken; magic mirror; magic lantern &c. (*show*) 448; mirror, lens &c. (*instrument*) 445.

V. BE DIM-SIGHTED &c. *n.;* see double; "see men as trees walking" [*Bible*]; have a mote in the eye, have a mist before the eyes, have a film over the eyes; see through a -prism, – glass darkly; wink, blink, nictitate, nictate; squint; look askance *or* askant, screw up the eyes, glare, glower.

DAZZLE, glare, swim, blur, loom.

Adj. DIM-SIGHTED &c.; myopic, nearsighted, shortsighted; presbyopic; astigmatic; moon-, blear-, goggle-, gooseberry-, one- eyed; blind of one eye, monoculous *or* monocular *or* monoculate; half-blind, purblind; cockeyed [*colloq.*], dim--eyed, mole-eyed, mope-eyed [*obs.*]; dichroic.

blind as a bat &c. (*blind*) 442; winking &c. *v.*

444. Spectator. — N. SPECTATOR, beholder, observer, looker-on, onlooker, *assistant* [*F.*], viewer, gazer, witness, eye-witness, bystander, passer-by; sightseer; rubberneck [*slang, U. S.*].

spy, scout; sentinel &c. (*warning*) 668.

GRANDSTAND [*fig.*], bleachers [*fig., U. S.*], gallery, the gods [*slang*].

V. WITNESS, behold &c. (*see*) 441; look on &c. (*be present*) 186; rubber *or* rubberneck [*slang, U. S.*].

445. Optical Instruments. — N. OPTICAL INSTRUMENTS; lens, meniscus, magnifier; microscope, simple microscope *or* single microscope, compound microscope, projecting microscope, ultramicroscope; spectacles, glasses, barnacles [*colloq.*, *Eng.*], gig lamps [*slang*], goggles, eyeglass, *pince-nez* [*F.*]; periscopic lens; telescope, glass, teinoscope, prism telescope; lorgnette, binocular; spyglass, opera glass, field glass; burning glass, convex lens.

prism; camera, hand camera, kodak [*trade name*], moving-picture machine; camera-lucida, camera-obscura; magic lantern &c. (*show*) 448; megascope; stereopticon; chromatrope, thaumatrope; stereoscope, pseudoscope, polyscope, kaleidoscope, kaleidophon *or* kaleidophone.

photometer, optometer, eriometer, actinometer, lucimeter, radiometer; abdominoscope, gastroscope, helioscope, polariscope, polemoscope, spectroscope, spectrometer.

MIRROR, reflector, speculum; looking-glass, pier-glass, cheval-glass; hand mirror.

OPTICS, optician; photography, photographer; optometry, optometrist; abdominoscopy; gastroscopy; microscopy, microscopist.

446. Visibility. — N. VISIBILITY, perceptibility, perceivability; conspicuousness, distinctness &c. *adj.;* conspicuity [*rare*]; appearance &c. 448; basset [*geol.*]; exposure; manifestation &c. 525; ocular -proof, − evidence, − demonstration; field of view &c. (*vision*) 441; periscopism.

V. BE *or* BECOME VISIBLE &c. *adj.;* appear, open to the view; meet −, catch- the eye; basset [*geol.*], crop out; present −, show −, manifest −, produce −, discover −, reveal −, expose −, betray- itself; stand forth, stand out; materialize; show; arise; peep out, peer out; start up, spring up, show up [*colloq.*], turn up, crop up; glimmer, gleam, glitter, glow, loom; glare; burst forth; burst upon the -view, − sight; heave in sight [*naut. or colloq.*]; come in sight, come into view, come out, come forth, come forward; see the light of day; break through the clouds; make its appearance, show its face, appear to one's eyes, come upon the stage, float before the eyes, speak for itself &c. (*manifest*) 525; attract the attention &c. 457; reappear; live in a glass house.

expose to view &c. 525.

Adj. VISIBLE, perceptible, perceivable, discernible, apparent; in view, in full view, in sight; exposed to view, *en évidence* [*F.*]; unclouded.

447. Invisibility. — N. INVISIBILITY, invisibleness, nonappearance, imperceptibility; indistinctness &c. *adj.;* mystery, delitescence *or* delitescency.

CONCEALMENT &c. 528; latency &c. 526.

V. BE INVISIBLE &c. *adj.;* be hidden &c. (*hide*) 528; lurk &c. (*lie hidden*) 526; escape notice.

RENDER INVISIBLE &c. *adj.;* conceal &c. 528; put out of sight.

not see &c. (*be blind*) 442; lose sight of.

Adj. INVISIBLE, imperceptible; undiscernible, indiscernible; unapparent, nonapparent; out of sight, not in sight; *à perte de vue* [*F.*], behind the -scenes, − curtain; viewless, sightless; unconspicuous, inconspicuous; unseen &c. (*see* see &c. 441); covert &c. (*latent*) 526; eclipsed, under an eclipse.

INDISTINCT; dim &c. (*faint*) 422; mysterious, dark, obscure, confused; indistinguishable, undiscernible *or* undiscernable, shadowy, indefinite, undefined; ill-defined, ill-marked; blurred, blurry, fuzzy, out of focus; misty &c. (*opaque*) 426; veiled &c. (*concealed*) 528; delitescent.

⁎⁎ "full many a flower is born to blush unseen" [Gray].

DISTINCT, plain, clear, definite; obvious &c. (*manifest*) 525; well-defined, well-marked; in focus; recognizable, palpable, autoptic *or* autoptical; glaring, staring, conspicuous; stereoscopic *or* stereoscopical; in bold relief, in strong relief, in high relief.

PERISCOPIC *or* periscopical, panoramic.

Adv. BEFORE ONE; under one's -nose, − very eyes; before −, under- one's eyes; *à vue d'œil* [*F.*], in one's eye, *oculis subjecta fidelibus* [*L.*]; visibly &c. *adj.;* in sight of; *veluti in speculum* [*L.*].

448. Appearance. — N. APPEARANCE,
phenomenon, sight, spectacle, show, premonstration [obs.], scene, species, view, coup d'œil [F.]; lookout, outlook, prospect, vista, perspective, bird's-eye view, scenery, landscape, seascape, picture, tableau; display, exposure, mise en scène [F.], rising of the curtain.

PHANTASM, phantom &c. (fallacy of vision) 443.

SPECTACLE, pageant; peep show, raree-show, galanty (or gallanty) show; ombres chinoises [F.]; magic lantern, phantasmagoria, dissolving views; biograph, cinematograph, cinema [colloq., Brit.], moving pictures, movies [colloq.], photoplay, photodrama; panorama, diorama, cosmorama, georama; coup de théâtre [F.], jeu de théâtre [F.]; pageantry &c. (ostentation) 882; insignia &c. (indication) 550.

ASPECT, angle, phase, phasis, seeming; shape &c. (form) 240; guise, look, complexion, color, image, mien, air, cast, carriage, port, demeanor; presence, expression, first blush, face of the thing; point of view, light.

LINEAMENT, feature, trait, lines; outline, outside; contour, silhouette, face, countenance, visage, phiz [colloq.], cast of countenance, profile, tournure [F.], cut of one's jib [colloq.], outside &c. 220.

PHYSIOGNOMY, metoposcopy, phrenology; physiognomist, metoposcopist, phrenologist.

V. APPEAR; be or become visible &c., 446; seem, look, show; present –, wear –, carry –, have –, bear –, exhibit –, take –, take on –, assume- the -appearance, – semblance- of; look like; cut a figure, figure; present to the view; show &c. (make manifest) 525.

Adj. APPARENT, seeming, ostensible; on view.

Adv. APPARENTLY; to all seeming, to all appearance; ostensibly, seemingly, as it seems, on the face of it, primâ facie [L.]; at the first blush, at first sight; in the eyes of; to the eye.

⁎ editio princeps; "this insubstantial pageant" [Tempest]; "all the world's a stage, And all the men and women merely players" [As You Like It]; "Look here, upon this picture, and on this" [Hamlet].

449. Disappearance. — N. DISAPPEARANCE,
evanescence, eclipse, occultation; insubstantiality.

departure &c. 293; exit; vanishing, vanishment, vanishing point; dissolving views.

V. DISAPPEAR, vanish, dissolve, fade, melt away, pass, go, avaunt [obs.]; be gone &c. adj.; leave no trace, "leave not a rack behind" [Tempest]; go off the stage &c. (depart) 293; suffer –, undergo- an eclipse; retire from sight; be lost to view, be lost to sight, see no longer, fade away [slang], pass out of sight.

lose sight of.

efface &c. 552.

Adj. DISAPPEARING &c. v.; evanescent; missing, lost; lost to sight, lost to view; gone.

Int. VANISH! disappear! fade! [slang], beat it! [slang], avaunt! &c. (ejection) 297.

CLASS IV

WORDS RELATING TO THE INTELLECTUAL FACULTIES

DIVISION (I) FORMATION OF IDEAS

Section I. OPERATIONS OF INTELLECT IN GENERAL

450. Intellect. — N. INTELLECT, mind, understanding, reason, thinking principle; rationality; cogitative –, cognitive –, discursive –, reasoning –, intellectual-faculties; faculties, senses, consciousness, observation, percipience *or* percipiency, apperception, mentality, intelligence, intellection [*obs.*], intuition, association of ideas, instinct, conception, judgment, wits, parts, capacity, intellectuality, genius; brains, cognitive –, intellectual-powers; wit &c. 498; ability &c. (*skill*) 698; wisdom &c. 498; *Vernunft* [*Ger.*], *Verstand* [*Ger.*].

450a. Absence or **want of Intellect.** **—N.** ABSENCE OF INTELLECT, want of intellect &c. 450; apartments to let [*slang*], nobody home [*slang*], unintellectuality; imbecility &c. 499; brutality, brute instinct, brute force.

Adj. unendowed with –, void of-reason; unintelligent &c. (*imbecile*) 499.

EGO, soul, spirit, ghost [*archaic*], inner man, heart, breast, bosom, *penetralia mentis* [*L.*], *divina particula auræ* [*L.*], *anima divina* [*L.*], heart's core; psyche, pneuma, subconscious self, subliminal consciousness, supreme principle, the Absolute.

SEAT OF THOUGHT, organ of thought, sensorium, sensory, brain; head, headpiece; pate [*colloq.*], noddle [*colloq.*], skull, pericranium, cerebrum, cranium, brain pan, brain box, brain case, sconce [*colloq.*], upper story [*colloq.*].

[SCIENCE OF MIND] metaphysics; philosophy &c. 451; psychics; pneumatology, psychology, psychogenesis; noölogy, noöscopics, ideology; mental –, moral-philosophy; philosophy of the mind.

phrenology; craniology, cranioscopy; psychometry, psychophysics, psychanalysis *or* psycho-analysis.

IDEALITY, idealism; transcendentalism, immateriality &c. 317; universal -concept, – conception; mahat [*theos.*].

PSYCHICAL RESEARCH; telepathy, thought transference, thought reading; clairaudience; clairvoyance, mediumship; spiritualism &c. 992a.

metaphysician, philosopher, psychologist, psychometer, psychopath, psychophysicist; psychic, medium, spiritist; adept, mahatma, yogi [*Hinduism*].

V. REASON, understand, think, reflect, cogitate, excogitate, conceive. judge, contemplate, meditate; ruminate &c. (*think*) 451.

NOTE, notice, mark; take -notice, – cognizance- of; be aware of, be conscious of; realize; appreciate; fancy &c. (*imagine*) 515.

Adj. [RELATING TO INTELLECT] intellectual, mental, rational, endowed with reason; subjective, noöscopic, psychological; cerebral; percipient, appercipient, animastic; brainy [*colloq.*].

HYPERPHYSICAL, superphysical; subconscious, subliminal; telepathic, clairaudient, clairvoyant; psychic *or* psychical, spiritual, ghostly; metaphysical, transcendental.

IMMATERIAL &c. 317.

₊ *cogito ergo sum; ens rationis; frons est animi janua* [Cicero]; *locos y niños dicen la verdad; mens sola loco non exulat* [Ovid]; "my mind is my kingdom" [Campbell]; "stern men with empires in their brains" [Lowell]; "the mind, the music breathing from her face" [Byron]; "thou living ray of intellectual Fire" [Falconer]; "the mental condition of the modern world . . . the condition in which all natural explanations have broken down and no supernatural explanation has been established" [Chesterton]; "Friends, fellow mortals, bearers of the ghost That burns, and breaks its lamp, but is not lost" [Masefield].

451. Thought. — N. THOUGHT; exercitation –, exercise- of the intellect; intellection; reflection, cogitation, consideration, meditation, study, lucubration, speculation, deliberation, pondering; head work, brainwork; cerebration; mentation, deep reflection; close study, application &c. (*attention*) 457.

association –, succession –, flow –, train –, current- of -thought, – ideas.

MATURE THOUGHT; afterthought, reconsideration, second thoughts; retrospection &c. (*memory*) 505; excogitation; examination &c. (*inquiry*) 461; invention &c. (*imagination*) 515.

thoughtfulness &c. *adj.*

ABSTRACTION, abstract thought, contemplation, musing; brown study &c. (*inattention*) 458; reverie *or* revery, depth of thought, workings of the mind, thoughts, inmost thoughts; self-counsel, self-communing, self-consultation.

[PHILOSOPHY] philosophical -opinions, – systems, – schools; the handmaid of theology, *ancilla theologiæ* [*L.*].

452. [ABSENCE OR WANT OF THOUGHT]. **Incogitance. — N.** INCOGITANCE *or* incogitancy, vacancy, inunderstanding, vacancy of mind, poverty of intellect &c. 499; thoughtlessness &c. (*inattention*) 458; inanity, fatuity, vacuity.

V. NOT THINK &c. 451; not think of; dismiss from the -mind, – thoughts &c. 451.

indulge in reverie &c. (*be inattentive*) 458.

put away thought; unbend –, relax –, divert- the mind; make the mind a blank, let the mind lie fallow.

Adj. VACANT, inane, unintellectual, nonunderstanding, unideal, unoccupied, unthinking, incogitant, incogitative, unreasoning, inconsiderate, thoughtless; absent &c. (*inattentive*) 458; diverted; irrational &c. 499; narrow-minded &c. 481.

UNTHOUGHT OF, undreamt of, unconsidered; off one's mind; incogitable, inconceivable, not to be thought of.

₊ *absence d'esprit; pabulum pictura pascit inani.*

ORIENTAL PHILOSOPHY: Vedânta *or* Uttara-Mîmâmsâ ["later investigation"]; Pûrva-Mîmâmsâ ["prior investigation"]; Sâmkhyas-, Yoga –, Nyâya –, Vaisheshika- philosophy.

GREEK AND GRECO-ROMAN PHILOSOPHY: Ionian –, Pythagorean –, Eleatic- school; Atomism; Sophism *or* Sophistic philosophy.
Socratic –, Megarian *or* Eristic –, Elean- school; Cynic philosophy; Cyrenaic *or* Hedonistic school, Hedonism; Platonism; philosophy of the -Absolute, – Academy; Aristotelianism, philosophy of the Lyceum; Peripatetic school [historical formula: *concept, Idea, essence*].
Stoic philosophy, Stoicism, philosophy of the Porch; Epicureanism, philosophy of the Garden; Scepticism; Eclecticism.
Neo-Pythagoreanism; Neo-Platonism.
PATRISTIC PHILOSOPHY: Gnosticism, Manicheism; Alexandrian school; philosophy of the Ante-Nicene Fathers, philosophy of the Post-Nicene Fathers.
SCHOLASTIC PHILOSOPHY: Scholasticism; Eclecticism; Mysticism, Mystic philosophy; Pantheistic school, pantheism; Thomism, Scotism, voluntarism; Averroism.
MODERN PHILOSOPHY: Post-Reformation philosophy; Humanism, rationalism, political philosophy; Cartesianism; Spinozism; empiricism, moralism; idealistic philosophy, idealism; Leibnitzianism *or* Leibnizianism, Berkeleian philosophy, Berkeleyism; pan-phenomenalism.
modern German philosophy: Kantianism, Fichteanism, Schelling's philosophy, Hegelianism, Herbartianism, Schopenhauer's philosophy; neocriticism; Freudianism, Freudian theory; Einstein theory, relativism.
modern French philosophy: traditionalism; psychologico-spiritualistic school; Positivism; sociological school; Bergsonism.
modern English philosophy: associational psychology, utilitarianism, Darwinism, evolutionistic ethics; Spencerian philosophy; agnosticism, idealism, Neo-Hegelianism.
modern Italian philosophy: Vicoism, sensism, empiricism, criticism, idealism, ontologism, Neo-Scholasticism.
American philosophy: Transcendentalism, pragmatism, neo-voluntarism, new ethical movement; Neo-Hegelianism, Neo-Hegelian movement.

V. THINK, reflect, cogitate, excogitate, consider, reason, deliberate; bestow -thought, – consideration -upon; speculate, contemplate, meditate, ponder, muse, dream, ruminate; brood over, con over, study; mouse over [*U. S.*], mull over [*colloq., U. S.*], sweat over [*colloq.*]; bend –, apply- the mind &c. (*attend*) 457; digest, discuss, hammer at, hammer out, weigh, perpend [*archaic*]; realize, appreciate; fancy &c. (*imagine*) 515; trow [*archaic*].

rack –, ransack –, crack –, beat –, cudgel- one's brains; set one's -brain, – wits- to work; cerebrate, mentalize [*rare*].

harbor –, entertain –, cherish –, nurture- an idea &c. 453, take into one's head; bear in mind; reconsider.

TAKE INTO CONSIDERATION; take counsel &c. (*be advised*) 695; commune with oneself, bethink oneself; collect one's thoughts; revolve –, turn over –, run over- in the mind; chew the cud upon [*colloq.*], sleep upon; take counsel of –, advise with- one's pillow.

SUGGEST itself, present itself, occur; come –, get- into one's head; strike one, flit across the view, come uppermost, run in one's head; enter –, pass in –, cross, –, flash on –, flash across –, float in –, fasten itself on –, be uppermost in –, occupy- the mind; have in one's mind.

MAKE AN IMPRESSION; sink –, penetrate- into the mind; engross the thoughts.

Adj. THOUGHTFUL, pensive, meditative, reflective, cogitative, excogitative, museful, wistful, contemplative, speculative, deliberative, studious, sedate, introspective, Platonic, philosophical; thinking &c. *v.*

UNDER CONSIDERATION, in contemplation, under advisement.

ABSORBED, rapt; lost in thought &c. (*inattentive*) 458; engrossed in &c. (*intent*) 457.

Adv. all things considered, taking everything into -account, – consideration.

*** the mind being on the stretch; the -mind, – head- -turning, – running- upon; "divinely bent to meditation" [*Richard III*]; *en toute chose il faut considérer la fin;* "freshpluckt from bowers of never-failing thought" [O. Meredith]; "go speed the stars of Thought" [Emerson]; "in maiden meditation fancy-free" [*M. N. D.*]; "so sweet is zealous contemplation" [*Richard III*]; "the power of Thought is the magic of the Mind" [Byron]; "those that think must govern those that toil" [Goldsmith]; "thought is parent of the deed" [Carlyle]; "thoughts in attitudes imperious" [Longfellow]; "thoughts that breathe and words that burn" [Gray]; *vivere est cogitare* [Cicero]; *Volk der Dichter und Denker;* "thinking is the function; living is the functionary" [Emerson].

---

453. [OBJECT OF THOUGHT.] **Idea.** — **N.** IDEA, notion, conception, thought, apprehension, impression, perception, image, eidolon [*Gr.* εἰδωλον], sentiment, reflection, observation, consideration; abstract idea; archetype, formative notion; guiding –, organizing- conception; image in the mind, regulative principle.

VIEW &c. (*opinion*) 484; theory &c. 514; conceit, fancy; phantasy &c. (*imagination*) 515.

VIEWPOINT, point of view; aspect &c. 448; field of view.

*** "Like a poet hidden In the light of thought" [Shelley].

454. [SUBJECT OF THOUGHT, νοήματα]. **Topic.** — **N.** SUBJECT OF THOUGHT, material for thought; food for the mind, mental pabulum.

SUBJECT, subject matter; matter, *motif* [*F.*], theme, noemata [*Gr.* νοήματα], topic, what it is about, thesis, text, business, affair, matter in hand, argument; motion, resolution; head, chapter; case, point; proposition, theorem; field of inquiry; moot point, debatable point, point at issue, point in question; problem &c. (*question*) 461.

V. float –, pass- in the mind &c. 451.

Adj. THOUGHT OF; uppermost in the mind; *in petto* [*It.*].

Adv. UNDER CONSIDERATION, under advisement; in question, in the mind; at issue, up for discussion, before the house, on foot, on the docket, on the carpet, on the tapis, *sur le tapis* [*F.*]; relative to &c. 9.

Section II. Precursory Conditions and Operations

455. [Desire of knowledge.] **Curiosity.** — **N.** CURIOSITY, curiousness; interest, thirst for knowledge, mental acquisitiveness; newsmongery, inquiring mind; inquisitiveness.

QUESTIONER, *enfant terrible* [F.], walking interrogation point [*humorous*], quidnunc.

BUSYBODY, newsmonger; Peeping Tom, Paul Pry, eavesdropper; gossip &c. (*news*) 532.

SIGHT-SEER, rubberneck [*slang, U. S.*],

V. BE CURIOUS &c. *adj.;* take an interest in, stare, gape; prick up the ears, see sights, lionize; rubber *or* rubberneck [*slang, U. S.*].

PRY, nose, search, ferret out, poke one's nose into.

Adj. CURIOUS, inquisitive, burning with curiosity, overcurious, nosey [*colloq.*]; inquiring &c. 461; prying; inquisitorial; agape &c. (*expectant*) 507.

₊ what's the matter? what next? little pitchers have big ears; "Curiosity is mere vanity. Most people want to know only in order to talk" [Pascal].

456. [Absence of curiosity.] **Incuriosity.** — **N.** INCURIOSITY; incuriousness &c. *adj.;* apathy, insouciance &c. 866; indifference.

V. BE INCURIOUS &c. *adj.;* have no curiosity &c. 455; be bored by, take no interest in &c. 823; mind one's own business, pursue the even tenor of one's way, glance neither to the right hand nor to the left.

Adj. INCURIOUS, uninquisitive, indifferent; impassive &c. 823; uninterested, bored.

₊ "eyes and no-eyes."

457. Attention. — **N.** ATTENTION; mindfulness &c. *adj.;* intentness, intentiveness [*rare*]; alertness; thought &c. 451; advertence *or* advertency; observance, observation; consideration, reflection, perpension [*obs.*]; heed; heedfulness; particularity; notice, regard &c. *v.;* circumspection &c. (*care*) 459; study, scrutiny; inspection, introspection; revision, revisal.

active –, diligent –, exclusive –, minute –, close –, intense –, deep –, profound –, abstract –, labored –: deliberate- –thought, – attention, – application, – study.

absorption of mind &c. (*abstraction*) 458.

MINUTENESS, meticulosity, meticulousness, finicality, finicalness; circumstantiality, attention to detail.

INDICATION, calling attention to &c. *v.*

V. BE ATTENTIVE &c. *adj.;* attend, advert to, observe, look, see, view, remark, notice, regard, take notice, mark; give –, pay- -attention, – heed- to; know what o'clock it is [*colloq.*], know the time of day [*colloq.*]; incline –, lend- an ear to; trouble one's head about; give a thought to, animadvert; occupy oneself with; contemplate &c. (*think of*) 451; look -at, – to, – after, – into, – over; see to; turn –, bend –, apply –, direct –, give- the -mind, – eye, –attention -to;

458. Inattention. — **N.** INATTENTION, inconsideration, want of consideration; inconsiderateness &c. *adj.;* oversight; inadvertence *or* inadvertency, nonobservance, disregard.

supineness &c. (*inactivity*) 683; *étourderie* [F.]; want of thought; heedlessness &c. (*neglect*) 460; insouciance &c. (*indifference*) 866.

ABSTRACTION; absence of mind, absorption of mind; preoccupation, distraction, reverie *or* revery, brown study [*colloq.*], woolgathering, moonraking [*dial. Eng.*], pipe dream [*colloq.*], castle in the air, *château en Espagne* [F.], fancy, deep musing, fit of abstraction.

V. BE INATTENTIVE &c. *adj.;* overlook, disregard; pass by &c. (*neglect*) 460; not observe &c. 457; think little of.

close –, shut- one's eyes to; pay no attention to; dismiss –, discard –, discharge- from one's -thoughts, – mind; drop the subject, think no more of; set –, turn –, put- aside: turn away from, turn one's attention from, turn a deaf ear to, turn one's back upon.

ABSTRACT ONESELF, dream, be somewhere else, be absent, be woolgathering, indulge in reverie *or* revery.

ESCAPE NOTICE, escape attention; come in at one ear and go out at the other; forget &c. (*have no remembrance*) 506.

have an eye to, have in one's eye; bear in mind; take into -account, – consideration; keep in -sight, – view; have regard to, heed, mind, take cognizance of, entertain, recognize; make –, take- note of; note.

EXAMINE, – closely, – intently; scan, scrutinize, consider; give –, bend- one's mind to; overhaul, revise, pore over; inspect, review, pass under review; take stock of; get the gist of; fix –, rivet –, devote- the -eye, – mind, – thoughts, – attention- on *or* to; hear out, think out; mind one's business, attend to one's business.

EXAMINE CURSORILY; glance -at, – upon, – over; cast –, pass- the eyes over; run over, turn over the leaves, dip into, perstringe [*obs.*]; skim &c. (*neglect*) 460; take a cursory view of.

REVERT TO, hark back to; watch &c. (*expect*) 507, (*take care of*) 459; hearken *or* harken to, listen to; prick up the ears; have –, keep- the eyes open; come to the point.

MEET WITH ATTENTION; fall under one's -notice, – observation; be under consideration &c. (*topic*) 454.

catch –, strike- the eye; attract notice; catch –, awaken –, wake –, invite –, solicit –, attract –, claim –, excite –, engage –, occupy –, strike –, arrest –, fix –, engross –, absorb –, rivet- the -attention, – mind, – thoughts; be present to the mind, be uppermost in the mind.

CALL ATTENTION TO, bring under one's notice; point -out, – to, – at, –the finger at; lay the finger on, indigitate [*obs.*], indicate; direct attention to; show; put a mark upon &c. (*sign*) 550; call soldiers to "attention"; bring forward &c. (*make manifest*) 525.

Adj. ATTENTIVE, mindful, heedful, intentive [*rare*], advertent, all eyes and ears, observant, regardful; alive to, awake to; on the job [*colloq.*]; there with the goods [*colloq.*]; observing &c. *v.*; alert; taken up with, occupied with; engaged in, engrossed in, wrapped in; absorbed, rapt, breathless; preoccupied &c. (*inattentive*) 458; watchful &c. (*careful*) 459; intent on, open-eyed; breathless, undistracted, upon the stretch; on the watch &c. (*expectant*) 507.

steadfast &c. (*persevering*) 604a.

Int. SEE! look! look you! look to it! mark! lo! behold! soho! hark! hark ye! mind! look out! look alive! [*colloq.*]; look here! [*colloq.*]; halloo! observe! lo and behold! attention! *nota bene* [*L.*]; N.B.; *, †; I'd have you know! notice! O yes! Oyez! *dekko!* [*Hind.*], *ecco!* [*It.*], yo-ho! ho!

. this is –, these are- to give notice; *dictum sapienti sat est; finem respice;* "Give every man thy ear, but few thy voice" [*Hamlet*].

call off –, draw off –, call away –, divert –, distract- the -attention, – thoughts, – mind; put out of one's head.

CONFUSE, disconcert, discompose, put out, perplex, bewilder, moider [*dial. Eng.*], fluster, flurry, rattle [*colloq.*], muddle, dazzle.

Adj. INATTENTIVE; unobservant, unmindful, unheeding, undiscerning; inadvertent; mindless, regardless, respectless; listless &c. (*indifferent*) 866; blind, deaf; hen-headed [*colloq.*], flighty, giddy-pated, giddy-headed, bird-witted; hand over head [*rare*]; cursory, percursory [*rare*], volatile, scatter-brained, hare-brained; unreflecting, *écervelé* [*F.*], inconsiderate, offhand, thoughtless, dizzy, muzzy [*colloq.*], brainsick; giddy, – as a goose; wild, harum-scarum [*colloq.*], rantipole, heedless, careless &c. (*neglectful*) 460.

ABSTRACTED, absent, *distrait* [*F.*], woolgathering, moonraking [*dial. Eng.*], dazed, absent-minded, lost; lost –, wrapped- in thought; rapt, in the clouds, bemused, day-dreaming; dreaming of–, musing on- other things; preoccupied, engrossed &c. (*attentive*) 457; in a reverie &c. *n.;* off one's guard &c. (*inexpectant*) 508; napping; dreamy; caught napping.

DISCONCERTED, put out &c. *v.;* rattled [*colloq.*].

Adv. INATTENTIVELY, inadvertently &c. *adj.; per incuriam* [*L.*], *sub silentio* [*L.*].

Int. stand at ease, stand easy!

. the attention wanders; one's wits gone a -woolgathering, – bird's nesting; it never entered into one's head; the mind running on other things; one's thoughts being elsewhere; had it been a bear it would have bitten you; *aliquando bonus dormitat Homerus* [Hor.].

459. Care. — [VIGILANCE.] — **N.** CARE, solicitude, heed, concern, reck [*poetic*], heedfulness &c. *adj.;* scruple &c. (*conscientiousness*) 939.

VIGILANCE; watchfulness &c. *adj.;* surveillance, eyes of a lynx, eyes of Argus, watch, vigil, lookout, watch and ward, *l'œil du maître* [*F.*].

espionage &c. (*reconnoitering*) 461; invigilation, watching.

ALERTNESS &c. (*activity*) 682; attention &c. 457; prudence &c., circumspection &c. (*caution*) 864; anxiety; forethought &c. 510; precaution &c. (*preparation*) 673; tidiness &c. (*order*) 58, (*cleanliness*) 652; accuracy &c. (*exactness*) 494; minuteness, meticulousness, meticulosity, circumstantiality, attention to detail.

WATCHER, watchdog &c. 664.

V. BE CAREFUL &c. *adj.;* reck [*archaic*]; take care &c. (*be cautious*) 864; pay attention to &c. 457; take care of; look -, see- -to, –after; keep an eye upon, keep a sharp eye upon; chaperon, matronize, play gooseberry; keep watch, keep watch and ward; mount guard, set watch, watch; keep in -sight, – view; mind, mind one's business.

look sharp, look about one; look with one's own eyes; keep a -good, – sharplookout; have all one's -wits, – eyesabout one; watch for &c. (*expect*) 507; keep one's eyes open, have the eyes open, sleep with one eye open; catch a weasel asleep.

do one's best &c. 682; mind one's Ps and Qs [*colloq.*], speak by the card, pick one's steps.

TAKE PRECAUTIONS &c. 673; protect &c. (*render safe*) 664.

Adj. CAREFUL, regardful, heedful; taking care &c. *v.;* particular; prudent &c. (*cautious*) 864; considerate; thoughtful &c. (*deliberative*) 451; provident &c. (*prepared*) 673; alert &c. (*active*) 682; sure-footed.

GUARDED, on one's guard; on the -*qui vive* [*F.*], – alert, – watch, – lookout; awake, broad awake, vigilant; watchful, wakeful, Argus-eyed, lynx-eyed; wide awake &c. (*intelligent*) 498; on the watch for &c. (*expectant*) 507.

SCRUPULOUS &c. (*conscientious*) 939; tidy &c. (*orderly*) 58, (*clean*) 652; accurate &c. (*exact*) 494; *cavendo tutus* [*L.*] &c. (*safe*) 664.

460. Neglect. — **N.** ɴEGLECT; carelessness &c. *adj.;* trifling &c. *v.;* negligence; omission, laches [*obs.*], deferment, procrastination, default; supineness &c. (*inactivity*) 683; conspiracy of silence; inattention &c. 458; nonchalance &c. (*insensibility*) 823; imprudence, recklessness &c. 863; slovenliness &c. (*disorder*) 59, (*dirt*) 653; improvidence &c. 674; noncompletion &c. 730; inexactness &c. (*error*) 495.

PARALEIPSIS *or* paralipsis [*rhet.*].

TRIFLER, waiter on Providence; Micawber; waster [*colloq.*], wastrel [*dial. Eng.*], drifter [*colloq.*], bum [*slang*, *U. S.*], hobo [*U. S.*], tramp, Knight of the Road [*humorous*], down-and-outer [*colloq.*], dead one [*slang*], stiff [*slang*], roustabout [*U. S.*], sundowner [*Australia*]; slacker.

V. BE NEGLIGENT &c. *adj.;* take no care of &c. (take care of &c. 459); neglect; let slip, let go; lay -, set -, cast -, put- aside; keep -, leave- out of sight; lose sight of.

DELAY, defer, procrastinate, postpone, adjourn, pigeonhole, tie up with red tape, shelve, stay, suspend, table, lay on the table.

OVERLOOK, disregard; pass over, pass by; let pass; blink; wink at, connive at; gloss over; take no -note, – notice, – thought, – account- of; pay no regard to; *laisser aller* [*F.*].

SCAMP, trifle, fribble; do by halves; slight &c. (*despise*) 930; play with, trifle with; slur; skimp [*dial. & colloq.*]; skim, – the surface; *effleurer* [*F.*]; take a cursory view of &c. 457; slur -, slip -, skip -, jump- over; pretermit, miss, skip, jump, cut [*colloq.*], omit, give the go-by to [*slang*], push aside, throw into the background, sink.

IGNORE, refuse to notice, shut one's eyes to, refuse to hear, turn a deaf ear to, leave out of one's calculation; not attend to &c. 457, not mind; not trouble -oneself, – one's head- -with, – about; forget &c. 506.

BE CAUGHT NAPPING &c. (*not expect*) 508; leave a loose thread; let the grass grow under one's feet.

RENDER NEGLECTFUL &c. *adj.;* put *or* throw off one's guard.

Adj. NEGLECTING &c. *v.;* unmindful, negligent, neglectful; heedless, careless,

Adv. CAREFULLY &c. *adj.;* with care, gingerly.

** *quis custodiet istos custodes?* "care will kill a cat" [Wither]; *ni bebas agua que no veas;* "O polished perturbation! golden care!" [*Henry IV*]; "the incessant care and labor of his mind" [*Henry IV*]; Heaven helps those who help themselves.

enly &c. (*disorderly*) 59, (*dirty*) 653; inexact &c. (*erroneous*) 495; improvident &c. 674.

NEGLECTED &c. *v.;* unheeded, uncared for, unperceived, unseen, unobserved, unnoticed, unnoted, unmarked, unattended to, unthought of, unregarded, unremarked, unmissed; shunted, shelved.

UNEXAMINED, unstudied, unsearched, unscanned, unweighed, unsifted, unexplored.

ABANDONED; buried in a napkin; hid under a bushel.

Adv. NEGLIGENTLY &c. *adj.;* hand over head [*obs.*], in any old way [*colloq.*], anyhow; in an unguarded moment &c. (*unexpectedly*) 508; *per incuriam* [*L.*]; when the cat is away.

Int. NEVER MIND, no matter, let it pass; it will be all the same a hundred years hence; *mañana* [*Sp.*].

** "procrastination is the thief of time" [Young].

thoughtless, inconsiderate; perfunctory, remiss.

UNWARY, unwatchful, unguarded, incircumspect [*rare*], uncircumspect, off one's guard, offhand.

SUPINE &c. (*inactive*) 683; inattentive &c. 458; insouciant &c. (*indifferent*) 823; imprudent, reckless &c. 863; slov-

---

461. Inquiry. [SUBJECT OF INQUIRY. Question.] — **N.** INQUIRY; request &c. 765; search, research, quest; pursuit &c. 622.

EXAMINATION, review, scrutiny, investigation, indagation [*obs.*]; perquisition, perscrutation [*rare*], pervestigation [*obs.*]; inquest, inquisition; exploration; exploitation, ventilation.

sifting; calculation, analysis, dissection, resolution, induction; Baconian method.

strict –, close –, searching –, exhaustive- inquiry; narrow –, strict-search; study &c. (*consideration*) 451.

scire facias [*L.*], *ad referendum* [*L.*]; trial.

QUESTIONING &c. *v.;* interrogation, interrogatory; interpellation; challenge, examination, third degree [*colloq.*], cross-examination, catechism, catechesis; feeler, Socratic method, zetetic philosophy; leading question; discussion &c. (*reasoning*) 476.

RECONNOITERING, reconnaissance *or* reconnoissance, prying &c. *v.;* espionage, *espionnage* [*F.*]; domiciliary visit, peep behind the curtain; lantern of Diogenes.

QUESTION, query, problem, poser, desideratum, point to be solved, porism; subject –, field- of -inquiry, – controversy; point –, matter- in dispute;

462. Answer. — **N.** ANSWER, response, reply, replication, riposte *or* ripost, subjoinder, rejoinder, retort, repartee; rescript, rescription [*archaic*]; antiphon, antiphony; acknowledgment; password; echo; counterstatement, counterblast, countercharge, contradiction.

[LAW] defense, plea, surrebutter, surrejoinder, reply, rejoinder, rebutter.

SOLUTION &c. (*explanation*) 522; discovery &c. 480*a*; rationale &c. (*cause*) 153; clew *or* clue &c. (*indication*) 550.

Œdipus; oracle &c. 513; return &c. (*record*) 551.

V. ANSWER, respond, reply, rebut, riposte *or* ripost, retort, rejoin; give answer, return for answer; acknowledge, echo.

[LAW] defend, plead, surrebut, surrejoin, rebut, reply.

EXPLAIN &c. (*interpret*) 522; solve &c. (*unriddle*) 522; discover &c. 480*a;* fathom, hunt out &c. (*inquire*) 461; satisfy, set at rest, determine.

Adj. ANSWERING &c. *v.;* responsive, respondent; antiphonal; Œdipean, oracular; conclusive.

Adv. FOR THIS REASON; because &c. (*cause*) 153; on the scent, on the right scent.

Int. eureka.

moot point; issue, question at issue; bone of contention &c. (*discord*) 713; plain –, fair –, open- question; enigma &c. (*secret*) 533; knotty point &c. (*difficulty*) 704; *quodlibet* [*L.*]; threshold of an inquiry.

INQUIRER, investigator, inquisitor, inspector, querist, examiner, probator, catechist; scrutator, scrutineer, scrutinizer; analyst; quidnunc &c. (*curiosity*) 455.

V. INQUIRE, seek, search; make inquiry &c. *n.;* look -for, – about for, – out for; scan, reconnoiter *or* reconnoitre, explore, sound, rummage, ransack, pry, peer, look round; look –, go- -over, – through; give the once-over [*slang*]; spy, overhaul.

scratch the head, slap the forehead.

look –, peer –, pry– into every hole and corner; visit –, look- behind the scenes; nose, nose out, trace up; hunt out, fish out, ferret out; unearth; leave no stone unturned.

TRACK, seek a clew *or* clue; hunt, trail, shadow, mouse, dodge, trace; follow the -trail, – scent; pursue &c. 662; beat up one's quarters; fish for; feel for &c. (*experiment*) 463.

INVESTIGATE; take up –, institute –, pursue –, follow up –, conduct –, carry on –, prosecute- an inquiry &c. *n.;* look at, look into; preëxamine; discuss, canvass, agitate.

EXAMINE, mouse over [*U. S.*], study, consider, calculate; dip –, dive –, delve –, go deep- into; make sure of, probe, sound, fathom; probe to the -bottom, – quick; scrutinize, analyze, anatomize, dissect, parse, resolve, sift, winnow; view –, try- in all its phases; thresh out.

BRING IN QUESTION, subject to examination, pose; put to the proof &c. (*experiment*) 463; audit, tax, pass in review; take into consideration &c. (*think over*) 451; take counsel &c. 695.

QUESTION, ask, demand; put –, propose –, propound –, moot –, start –, raise –, stir –, suggest -, put forth –, ventilate –, grapple with –, go into- a question.

INTERROGATE, put to the question, catechize, pump; cross-question, cross-examine; roast [*colloq.*], grill [*colloq.*], put through the third degree [*colloq.*]; dodge; require an answer; pick –, suck- the brains of; feel the pulse.

BE IN QUESTION &c. *adj.;* undergo examination.

Adj. INQUIRING &c. *v.;* inquisitive &c. (*curious*) 455; requisitive [*obs.*], requisitory; catechetical, inquisitorial, analytic; in search of, in quest of; on the lookout for, interrogative, zetetic; all-searching.

UNDETERMINED, untried, undecided, tentative; in question, in dispute, in issue, in course of inquiry; under -discussion, – consideration, – investigation &c. *n.;* *sub judice* [*L.*], moot, proposed; doubtful &c. (*uncertain*) 475.

Adv. WHAT? why? wherefore? *pourquoi?* [*F.*], *warum?* [*Ger.*], whence? whither? where? *quære?* [*L.*]; how comes it? how does it happen? how is it? what is the reason? what's the matter? what's in the wind? what's afoot? what's up? what's in the air? what is it all about? what on earth? when? who? *nicht wahr?* [*Ger.*].

463. Experiment. — **N.** EXPERIMENT; essay &c. (*attempt*) 675; analysis &c. (*investigation*) 461; docimasy, trial, tentative method, *tâtonnement* [*F.*].

VERIFICATION, probation, *experimentum crucis* [*L.*], proof, criterion, diagnostic, test, crucial test; assay, ordeal.

REAGENT, crucible, check, touchstone, pyx *or* pix [*Brit. mint*], curcuma paper, turmeric paper.

EMPIRICISM, rule of thumb.

FEELER; pilot –, messenger- balloon; pilot engine; scout; straw to show the wind.

SPECULATION, random shot, leap in the dark.

EXPERIMENTER, experimentist, experimentalist, assayer, analyst, analyzer; prospecter *or* prospector, Forty-Niner [*U. S.*], adventurer; speculator, gambler, stock gambler, plunger [*slang*].

V. EXPERIMENT; essay &c. (*endeavor*) 675; try, assay; make an experiment, make trial of; give a trial to; put upon –, subject to- trial; experiment upon; rehearse;

put –, bring –, submit- to the -test, – proof; prove, verify, test, touch, practice upon, try one's strength.

GROPE; feel –, grope- -for, – one's way; fumble, *tâtonner* [F.], *aller à tâtons* [F.]; put –, throw- out a feeler; send up a pilot balloon; see how the -land lies, – wind blows; consult the barometer; feel the pulse; fish for, bob for; cast -, beat- about for; angle, trawl, cast one's net, beat the bushes.

VENTURE; try one's fortune &c. (*adventure*) 675; explore &c. (*inquire*) 461.

Adj. EXPERIMENTAL, probative, probatory, probationary; analytic, docimastic or docimastical, speculative, tentative; empirical.

TRIED, tested, proved.

ON TRIAL, on examination, on or under probation, "on suspicion" [Elbert Hubbard], under suspicion; on one's trial.

464. Comparison. — N. COMPARISON, collation, contrast, parallelism, balance; identification; comparative –, relative- estimate.

simile, similitude, parallelization [*rare*]; allegory &c. (*metaphor*) 521.

V. COMPARE, – to, – with; collate, confront; place side by side &c. (*near*) 197; set –, pit- against one another; contrast, balance.

compare notes; institute a comparison; *parva componere magnis* [L.].

PARALLEL, parallelize; draw a parallel.

Adj. COMPARATIVE, relative, contrastive; metaphorical &c. 521.

COMPARED WITH &c. *v.*; comparable; judged by comparison.

Adv. RELATIVELY &c. (*relation*) 9; as compared with &c. *v.*

₊ comparisons are odious; "comparisons are odorous" [*Much Ado*].

465. Discrimination. — N. DISCRIMINATION, distinction, differentiation, diagnosis, diorism; nice perception; perception –, appreciation- of difference; estimation &c. 466; nicety, refinement; taste &c. 850; critique, judgment; tact; discernment &c. (*intelligence*) 498; acuteness, penetration; *nuances* [F.].

TIP, pointer, dope [*slang*]; past performances, record.

V. DISCRIMINATE, distinguish, severalize [*obs.*]; separate; draw the line, sift; separate -, winnow- the chaff from the wheat; separate the wheat from the tares; separate the sheep from the goats; split hairs.

465a. Indiscrimination. — N. INDISCRIMINATION; indistinctness, indistinction; want of distinction, want of discernment, inability to discriminate; uncertainty &c. (*doubt*) 475.

V. NOT DISCRIMINATE &c. 465; overlook &c. (*neglect*) 460- a distinction; confound, confuse, jumble, jumble together, heap indiscriminately; swallow whole, judge in a lump, use loosely.

Adj. INDISCRIMINATE, indistinguishable, lacking distinction, undistinguished, undistinguishable; unmeasured; promiscuous, undiscriminating.

₊ *valeat quantum valere potest.*

estimate &c. (*measure*) 466; tip, tip off, sum up, criticize; know which is which, know what's what [*colloq.*], know one's way about, know a thing or two, know what o'clock it is, know the time of day, have cut one's eyeteeth, know the ways of the world [*all colloq.*]; "know a hawk from a handsaw" [*Hamlet*].

take into -account, – consideration; give –, allow- due weight to; weigh carefully.

Adj. DISCRIMINATING &c. *v.*; dioristic or dioristical [*obs.*], critical, diagnostic, perceptive, discriminative, distinctive; nice, acute.

₊ *il y a fagots et fagots; rem acu tetigisti; la critique est aisée et l'art est difficile;* "He could distinguish, and divide A hair 'twixt south and south-west side" [Butler].

466. Measurement. — N. MEASUREMENT, admeasurement, mensuration, metage, mete [*rare*] survey, valuation, appraisement, assessment, assize; estimate, estimation; dead reckoning [*naut.*]; reckoning &c. (*numeration*) 85; gauging &c. *v.*; horse power, candle power, candle foot, foot candle, volt ampere, kilowatt; foot pound, foot poundal, foot ton; velo

METROLOGY, weights and measures, compound arithmetic.

MEASURE, yard measure, standard, rule, foot rule, spirit level, plumb line; square, T-square, steel square, compass, dividers, calipers; gauge *or* gage, standard gauge, broad *or* wide gauge, narrow gauge; log, log-line, patent log [*naut.*]; meter, line, rod, check.

flood mark, high-water mark, load-line mark, Plimsoll mark; index &c. 550.

SCALE; graduation, graduated scale; nonius; vernier &c. (*minuteness*) 193; quadrant, theodolite, transit *or* transit theodolite, viagraph; scale, beam, steelyard, weighing machine, balance &c. (*weight*) 319; anemometer &c. (*wind*) 349; barometer &c. (*air*) 338; bathometer &c. (*depth*) 208; dynamometer &c. (*force*) 276; galvanometer &c. (*power*) 157; goniometer &c. (*angle*) 244; hyetometer &c. (*fluids in motion*) 348; landmark &c. (*limit*) 233; pedometer &c. (*length*) 200; photometer &c. (*optical instruments*) 445; radiometer &c. (*light*) 420; stethoscope &c. (*medical*) 662; thermometer &c. 389.

coördinates, ordinate and abscissa, polar coördinates, latitude and longitude, declination and right ascension, altitude and azimuth.

GEOMETRY, stereometry, planimetry, hypsometry, altimetry, hypsography, chorometry, chorography, topography, cartography; surveying, land surveying, geodesy, geodetics, geodæsia *or* geodesia, orthometry; cadastre *or* cadaster; cadastral survey, cadastration.

astrolabe, armillary sphere.

SURVEYOR, land surveyor; geometer, chorographer, topographer, cartographer.

V. MEASURE, meter, mete; value, assess, rate, appraise, estimate, form an estimate, set a value on; appreciate; standardize.

span, pace, step, inch, dial; caliper, divide, apply the compass &c. *n.*; gauge *or* gage; balance, poise, hold the scales, place in the beam, kick the beam; plumb, probe, sound, fathom; heave the -log, - lead; survey, plot, block in, block out, rule, draw to scale.

take an average &c. 29; graduate, calibrate.

Adj. MEASURING &c. *v.*; metric, metrical; measurable; geodetical, cadastral, hypsographic *or* hypsographical, hypsometric *or* hypsometrical, chorographic *or* chorographical, topographic *or* topographical, cartographic *or* car ographical.

*** "For 'Is' and 'Is-not' though with Rule and Line, And 'Up-and-Down' by Logic I define" [Omar Khayyám — Fitzgerald].

Section III. Materials for Reasoning

467. Evidence [ON ONE SIDE.] — N. EVIDENCE; facts, premises, data, præcognitum (*pl.* præcognita), grounds; indication &c. 550; criterion &c. (*test*) 463.

TESTIMONY, testification; attestation; affirmation, declaration; deposition &c. 535; examination.

AUTHORITY, warrant, credential, diploma, voucher, certificate, docket; *testamur* [*L.*]; record &c. 551; muniments; document; *pièce justificative* [*F.*]; deed, warranty &c. (*security*) 771; autograph, handwriting, signature, seal &c. (*identification*) 550; exhibit; citation, reference, quotation; admission &c. (*assent*) 488.

WITNESS, indicator, eyewitness, earwitness, deponent; sponsor; cojuror, oath-helper [*hist.*], compurgator [*hist.*].

EVIDENCE IN CHIEF; oral -, docu-

468. [EVIDENCE ON THE OTHER SIDE.] **Counterevidence.** — N. COUNTEREVIDENCE; evidence on the other -side, - hand; disproof; refutation &c. 479; negation &c. 536; conflicting evidence.

plea &c. 617; vindication &c. 937; counter-protest; *tu quoque* [*L.*] argument; other side -, reverse- of the shield; *reductio ad absurdum* [*L.*].

V. COUNTERVAIL, oppose; rebut &c. (*refute*) 479; subvert &c. (*destroy*) 162; check, weaken; contravene; run counter; contradict &c. (*deny*) 536; tell another story, turn the scale, alter the case; turn the tables; cut both ways; prove a negative.

audire alteram partem [*L.*].

Adj. COUNTERVAILING &c. *v.*; contradictory, in rebuttal.

UNATTESTED, unauthenticated, un-

mentary –, hearsay –, external –, extrinsic –, internal –, intrinsic –, circumstantial –, cumulative –, *ex parte* [*L.*] –, presumptive –, collateral –, constructive- evidence; proof &c. (*demonstration*) 478; finger print, thumb print.

SECONDARY EVIDENCE; confirmation, corroboration, support; ratification &c. (*assent*) 488; authentication; compurgation [*hist.*], wager of law [*hist.*], comprobation [*obs.*].

WRIT, summons &c. (*lawsuit*) 696.

V. BE EVIDENCE &c. *n.*; evince, show, betoken, tell of; indicate &c. (*denote*) 550; imply, involve, argue, bespeak, breathe.

HAVE WEIGHT, carry weight; tell, speak volumes; speak for itself &c. (*manifest*) 525.

REST UPON, depend upon; repose on.

BEAR WITNESS &c. *n.*; give evidence &c. *n.*; testify, depose, witness, vouch for; sign, seal, undersign, set one's hand and seal, sign and seal, deliver as one's act and deed, certify, attest; acknowledge &c. (*assent*) 488.

CONFIRM, make absolute, ratify, corroborate, indorse *or* endorse, countersign, support, bear out, vindicate, uphold, warrant.

ADDUCE, attest, evidence, cite, quote; refer to, appeal to; call, call to witness; bring forward, bring on, bring into court; allege, plead; produce –, confront- witnesses; collect –, bring together –, rake up- evidence.

ESTABLISH; have –, make out- a case; authenticate, circumstantiate, substantiate, verify, make good, quote chapter and verse; bring home to, bring to book, bring off.

supported by evidence; supposititious, trumped up.

Adv. CONVERSELY, on the other hand, on the other side, in opposition; *per contra* [*L.*].

469. Qualification. — N. QUALIFICATION, limitation, modification, coloring.

ALLOWANCE, grains of allowance, consideration, extenuating circumstances; mitigation.

CONDITION, proviso, exception; exemption; salvo [*rare*], saving clause; discount &c. 813; restriction.

V. QUALIFY, limit, modify, affect, leaven, take color from, give a color to, introduce new conditions, narrow, temper.

ALLOW FOR, make allowance for; admit exceptions, take into account; modulate.

TAKE EXCEPTION, file exceptions, object, raise objections, rise to a point of order.

Adj. QUALIFYING &c. *v.*; modificatory, extenuatory, mitigatory, lenitive, palliative; conditional; exceptional &c. (*unconformable*) 83.

HYPOTHETICAL &c. (*supposed*) 514; contingent &c. (*uncertain*) 475.

Adv. PROVIDED, – always; if, unless, but, yet; according as; conditionally, admitting, supposing; on the supposition of &c. (*theoretically*) 514; with the understanding, even, although, though, for all that, after all, at all events.

IF POSSIBLE &c. 470; with grains of allowance, *cum grano salis* [*L.*]; *exceptis excipiendis* [*L.*], wind and weather permitting.

SUBJECT TO; with this proviso &c. *n.*

Adj. EVIDENTIAL; showing &c. *v.*; indicative, indicatory; deducible &c. 478; grounded on, founded on, based on; first-hand, authentic, verificative, verifiable, veridical, cumulative, corroborative, confirmatory; significant, weighty, overwhelming, damning, conclusive.

oral, documentary, hearsay &c. (*evidence in chief*) *n.*

Adv. BY INFERENCE; according to, witness, *a fortiori* [*L.*]; still more, still less; *raison de plus* [*F.*]; in corroboration of &c. *n.*; *valeat quantum* [*L.*]; under seal, under one's hand and seal; at first hand, at second hand.

** *dictum de dicto;* "where are the evidence that do accuse me?" [*Richard III*]; "we must never assume that which is incapable of proof" [George Henry Lewes]; "litigious terms, fat contentions, and flowing fees" [Milton]; "I do not know the method of drawing up an indictment against an whole people" [Burke]; "Still you keep o' the windy side of the law" [*Twelfth Night*]; "Oh Sammy, Sammy, vy worn't there a alleybi!" [Dickens]; "A dog's obeyed in office" [*King Lear*].

Degrees of Evidence

470. Possibility. — N. POSSIBILITY, potentiality, potency; what may be, what is possible &c. *adj.;* compatibility &c. (*agreement*) 23.

PRACTICABILITY, feasibility, workability, workableness; practicableness &c. *adj.*

CONTINGENCY, chance &c. 156.

V. BE POSSIBLE &c. *adj.;* stand a chance; have a leg to stand on; admit of, bear.

RENDER POSSIBLE &c. *adj.;* put in the way of, bring to bear, bring together.

Adj. POSSIBLE; on the -cards, –dice; *in posse* [*L.*], within the bounds of possibility, conceivable, imaginable, credible; compatible &c. 23; likely.

PRACTICABLE, feasible, workable, performable, achievable; within -reach, – measurable distance; accessible, superable, surmountable; attainable, obtainable; contingent &c. (*doubtful*) 475.

Adv. POSSIBLY, by any possibility; perhaps, perchance, peradventure; may be, it may be, haply, mayhap.

IF POSSIBLE, wind and weather permitting, God willing, *Deo volente* [*L.*], D. V.; as luck may have it.

₊ *misericordia Domini inter pontem et fontem;* "the glories of the Possible are ours" [B. Taylor].

471. Impossibility. — N. IMPOSSIBILITY &c. *adj.;* what cannot be, what can never be; sour grapes; hopelessness &c. 859; infeasibility, infeasibleness, impracticality; discrepancy &c. (*disagreement*) 241.

[COMPARISONS] Canute (commanding the tide), Mrs. Partington (and her mop).

V. BE IMPOSSIBLE &c. *adj.;* have no chance whatever.

ATTEMPT IMPOSSIBILITIES; square the circle, find the elixir of life, discover the philosopher's stone, discover the grand panacea, find the fountain of youth, discover the secret of perpetual motion; wash a blackamoor white; skin a flint; make a silk purse out of a sow's ear, make bricks without straw; have nothing to go upon; weave a rope of sand, build castles in the air, *prendre la lune avec les dents* [*F.*], extract sunbeams from cucumbers, milk a he-goat into a sieve, catch a weasel asleep, *rompre l'anguille au genou* [*F.*], be in two places at once; gather grapes from thorns, fetch water in a sieve, catch wind in cabbage nets, fling eels by the tail, make cheese of chalk.

Adj. IMPOSSIBLE; not possible &c. 470; absurd, contrary to reason; at variance with the facts; unlikely; unbeyond the bounds of -reason, – possibility; from which reason recoils; visionary; inconceivable &c. (*improbable*) 473; prodigious &c (*wonderful*) 870; unimaginable, inimaginable [*obs.*], not to be thought of, unthinkable.

IMPRACTICABLE, unachievable; unfeasible, infeasible; insuperable; insurmountable *or* unsurmountable, unattainable, unobtainable; out of reach, out of the question; not to be had; beyond control; desperate &c. (*hopeless*) 859; incompatible &c. 24; inaccessible, uncomeatable [*colloq.*], impassable, impervious, innavigable, inextricable; self-contradictory.

out of –, beyond- one's -power, – depth, – reach, – grasp; too much for; *ultra crepidam* [*L.*].

₊ the grapes are sour; *non possumus; non nostrum tantas componere lites* [Vergil]; *chercher une aiguille dans une botte de foin; il a la mer à boire;* "few things are impossible to diligence and skill" [Johnson]; "it is not a lucky word, this same *impossible*" [Carlyle].

472. Probability. — N. PROBABILITY, likelihood; credibleness; likeliness &c. *adj.; vraisemblance* [*F.*], verisimilitude, plausibility; color, semblance, show of; presumption; presumptive –, circumstantial- evidence; credibility.

reasonable –, fair –, good –, favorable- -chance, – prospect; prospect, well-grounded hope; chance &c. 156.

473. Improbability. — N. IMPROBABILITY, unlikelihood; unfavorable –, bad –, ghost of a –, little –, small –, poor –, scarcely any –, no- chance; bare possibility; long odds; incredibility &c. 485.

V. BE IMPROBABLE &c. *adj.;* violate –, stretch- the probabilities; go beyond reason, strain one's credulity; run

V. BE PROBABLE &c. *adj.;* give –, lend-color to; point to; imply &c. *(evidence)* 467; bid fair &c. *(promise)* 511; stand fair for; stand –, run- a good chance; stand–, run- an even chance.

PRESUME, infer, venture, suppose, take for granted, think likely, dare say, flatter oneself; expect &c. 507; count upon &c. *(believe)* 484.

Adj. PROBABLE, likely, hopeful, to be expected, in a fair way.

PLAUSIBLE, specious, ostensible, color-able, *ben trovato* [*It.*], well-founded, reasonable, credible, easy of belief, presumable, presumptive, apparent.

Adv. PROBABLY &c. *adj.;* belike [*archaic*]; in all probability, in all likelihood; very –, most- likely; like enough; very like; ten &c. to one; apparently, seemingly, to all seeming, as like as not [*colloq.*], according to every reasonable expectation; *primâ facie* [*L.*]; to all appearance &c. *(to the eye)* 448.

⁎ the chances are, the odds are; appearances –, chances- are in favor of; there is reason to -believe, – think, – expect; I dare say; dollars to doughnuts [*U. S.*]; all Lombard Street to a China orange.

counter to the laws of nature; have a small chance &c. *n.;* stand a poor show [*colloq.*].

Adj. IMPROBABLE, unlikely, contrary to all reasonable expectation; contrary to -fact, – experience; implausible, rare &c. *(infrequent)* 137; unheard of, inconceivable; unimaginable, inimaginable [*obs.*]; incredible &c. 485; more than doubtful.

Int. NOT LIKELY! no fear! [*chiefly Eng.*]; I ask you! [*slang*]; catch me! [*slang*].

⁎ the chances are against; *aquila non capit muscas; pedir peras al olmo;* "Lest men suspect your tale untrue, Keep probability in view" [Gay].

---

474. Certainty. — N. CERTAINTY; necessity &c. 601; certitude, sureness, surety, assurance; dead –, moral- certainty; infallibleness &c. *adj.;* infallibility, reliability, reliableness; indubitableness, inevitableness, unquestionableness.

gospel, scripture, church, pope, court of final appeal; *res adjudicata,* [*L.*], *res judicata* [*L.*]; ultimatum.

FACT; positive fact, matter of fact; *fait accompli* [*F.*].

BIGOTRY, positiveness, dogmatism, dogmatization; fanaticism.

DOGMATIST, dogmatizer, doctrinaire, bigot, opinionist, Sir Oracle; dogmatic theorist; zealot, fanatic; *ipse dixit* [*L.*].

V. BE CERTAIN &c. *adj.;* stand to reason.

RENDER CERTAIN &c. *adj.;* insure *or* ensure, assure; clinch, make sure; determine, find out once for all, decide, set at rest, "make assurance double sure" [*Macbeth*]; know &c. *(believe)* 484; dismiss all doubt, admit of no doubt.

DOGMATIZE, lay down the law.

Adj. CERTAIN, sure; assured &c. *v.;* solid, well-founded.

UNQUALIFIED, absolute, positive, determinate, definite, clear, unequivocal, categorical, unmistakable, decisive, decided, ascertained.

475. Uncertainty. — N. UNCERTAINTY, incertitude, doubt; doubtfulness &c. *adj.;* dubiety, dubitation, dubitancy [*obs.*], dubiosity, dubiousness.

HESITATION, suspense, state of suspense; perplexity, embarrassment, dilemma, Morton's fork [*hist.*], bewilderment; botheration [*colloq.*]; puzzle, quandary; timidity &c. *(fear)* 860; vacillation &c. 605; aporia, diaporesis, indetermination; sealed orders.

VAGUENESS &c. *adj.;* haze, fog; obscurity &c. *(darkness)* 421; ambiguity &c. *(double meaning)* 520; contingency, double contingency, possibility upon a possibility; open question &c. *(question)* 461; *onus probandi* [*L.*], blind bargain, pig in a poke, leap in the dark, something or other; needle in a bottle of hay; roving commission.

FALLIBILITY; unreliability, unreliableness, untrustworthiness; precariousness &c. *adj.*

V. BE UNCERTAIN &c. *adj.;* wonder whether.

lose the -clew *or* clue, – scent; miss one's way, wander aimlessly, beat about, hang around.

not know -what to make of &c. *(unintelligibility)* 519, – which way to turn, – whether one stands on one's head or one's heels; float in a sea of doubt,

INEVITABLE, unavoidable, avoidless; ineluctable.

CONCLUSIVE, unimpeachable, undeniable, unquestionable; indefeasible, indisputable, incontestable, incontrovertible, indubitable; irrefutable &c. (*proven*) 478; without power of appeal, inappealable, final.

INDUBIOUS; without –, beyond a –, without a shade or shadow of- -doubt, – question; past dispute; clear as day; beyond all -question, – dispute; undoubted, uncontested, unquestioned, undisputed; questionless, doubtless.

AUTHORITATIVE, authentic, official, governmental, curule.

sure as -fate, – death and taxes, – a gun [*colloq.*].

EVIDENT, self-evident, axiomatic; clear, – as day, – as the sun at noonday; apparent &c. (*manifest*) 525.

INFALLIBLE, unerring; unchangeable &c. 150; to be depended on, trustworthy, reliable, bound.

DOGMATIC, opinionative, opinionated, dictatorial, doctrinaire; fanatical, bigoted.

Adv. CERTAINLY &c. *adj.;* for certain, certes [*archaic*], sure, no doubt, doubtless, and no mistake [*colloq.*], *flagrante delicto* [*L.*]; sure enough, to be sure, of course, as a matter of course, *a coup sûr* [*F.*], *sans doute* [*F.*], questionless [*rare*], for a certainty, of a certainty, to a certainty; in truth &c. (*truly*) 494; at any rate, at all events; without fail; *coûte que coûte* [*F.*], *coûte qu'il coûte* [*F.*]; whatever may happen, if the worse come to the worst; come what may, come what will, happen what may, happen what will; sink or swim; rain or shine, live or die.

* *cela va sans dire;* there is -no question, – not a shadow of doubt; the die is cast &c. (*necessity*) 601; "facts are stubborn things" [Smollett].

hesitate, flounder; lose oneself, lose one's head; muddle one's brains.

RENDER UNCERTAIN &c. *adj.;* put out, pose, puzzle, perplex, embarrass; muddle, confuse, confound; bewilder, bother, moider [*dial.*], rattle [*colloq.*], nonplus, addle the wits, throw off the scent, keep in suspense, keep one guessing.

DOUBT, &c. (*disbelieve*) 485; hang in the balance, tremble in the balance; depend.

Adj. UNCERTAIN, unsure; casual; random &c. (*aimless*) 621; changeable, changeful &c. 149.

DOUBTFUL, dubious; dazed; insecure, unstable, indecisive; unsettled, undecided, undetermined; in suspense, open to discussion; controvertible; in question &c. (*inquiry*) 461.

VAGUE; indeterminate, indefinite; ambiguous, equivocal; undefined, undefinable, confused &c. (*indistinct*) 447; mysterious, cryptic, veiled, obscure, oracular.

PERPLEXING &c. *v.;* enigmatic, paradoxical, apocryphal, problematical, hypothetical; experimental &c. 463.

FALLIBLE, questionable, precarious, slippery, ticklish, debatable, disputable; unreliable, untrustworthy.

UNAUTHENTIC, unauthenticated, unauthoritative; unascertained, unconfirmed; undemonstrated; untold, uncounted.

CONTINGENT, contingent on, dependent on; subject to; dependent on circumstances; occasional; provisional.

in a state of uncertainty, on the horns of a dilemma, in a cloud, in a maze; bushed, off the track; derailed; ignorant &c. 491; afraid to say; out of one's reckoning, out of one's bearings, astray, adrift; at sea, at fault, at a loss, at one's wit's end, at a non-plus; puzzled &c. *v.;* lost, abroad, *désorienté* [*F.*]; distracted, distraught.

Adv. UNCERTAINLY &c. *adj.;* at random, until things straighten out, while things are so uncertain, in this state of suspense; *pendente lite* [*L.*]; *sub spe rati* [*L.*].

* Heaven knows; who can tell? who shall decide when doctors disagree? *spargere voces in vulgum ambiguas* [Vergil]; "he is no wise man who will quit a certainty for an uncertainty" [Johnson]; "a little philosophy inclineth man's mind to atheism, but depth in philosophy bringeth men's minds about to religion" [Bacon]; *dum in dubio est animus paulo momento huc illuc impellitur* [Terence]; "To-morrow is, ah, whose?" [Mulock]; "Unborn To-morrow and dead Yesterday" [Omar Khayyám—Fitzgerald]; "Gather ye rose-buds while ye may" [Herrick]; "Uncertainty! Fell demon of our fears! The human soul, That can support despair, supports not thee" [Mallet]; "There is such a choice of difficulties, that I own myself at a loss how to determine" [General James Wolfe—*Dispatch to Pitt*].

Section IV. Reasoning Processes

476. Reasoning. — N. reasoning; ratiocination, rationalism; dialectics, dialecticism, induction, generalization.

discussion, comment; ventilation; inquiry &c. 461.

argumentation, controversy, debate; polemics, wrangling; contention &c. 720; logomachy, disputation, disceptation [*archaic*]; paper war.

logic, art of reasoning.

process –, train –, chain- of reasoning; deduction, induction; synthesis, analysis.

argument; case, plea, *plaidoyer* [*F.*], opening; premise *or* premiss; lemma, proposition, terms, premises; postulate, data, starting point, principle; inference &c. (*judgment*) 480.

prosyllogism, syllogism; enthymeme, sorites, dilemma, *a fortiori* reasoning, *a priori* reasoning, *reductio ad absurdum* [*L.*], horns of a dilemma, *argumentum ad hominem* [*L.*], comprehensive argument; empirema, epagoge.

logical sequence; good case; correct –, just –, sound –, valid –, cogent –, irrefutable –, logical –, forcible –, persuasive –, persuasory [*rare*] –, consectary [*obs.*] –, conclusive &c. 478 –, subtle-reasoning; force of argument; strong -point, – argument.

arguments, reasons, pros and cons.

reasoner, logician, dialectician; disputant; controversialist, controvertist; wrangler, arguer, debater, polemic, casuist, rationalist; scientist; eristic.

V. reason, argue, discuss, debate, dispute, wrangle; argufy *or* argify [*dial.*], bandy -words, – arguments; chop logic; hold –, carry on- an argument; controvert &c. (*deny*) 536; canvass; comment –, moralize- upon; consider &c. (*examine*) 461.

try conclusions; open a -discussion, - case; join –, be at- issue; moot; come to the point; stir –, agitate –, ventilate –, torture- a question; take up a -side, - case.

contend, take one's stand upon, insist, lay stress on; infer &c. 480.

follow from &c. (*demonstration*) 478.

Adj. reasoning &c. *v.*; rational, ratiocinative, rationalistic; argumentative, controversial, dialectic, polemical;

477. [Absence of reasoning.] Intuition. [Specious reasoning.] Sophistry. — N. intuition, instinct, association; presentiment; rule of thumb.

sophistry, paralogy, perversion, casuistry, jesuitry, equivocation, evasion, mental reservation; chicane, chicanery; quiddit [*obs.*], quiddity; mystification; special pleading; speciousness &c. *adj.*; nonsense &c. 497; word fence, tongue fence; overrefinement, hairsplitting, quibbling &c. *v.*

false –, fallacious –, specious –, vicious- reasoning; begging of the question, *petitio principii* [*L.*], *ignoratio elenchi* [*L.*]; *post hoc ergo propter hoc* [*L.*]; *non sequitur* [*L.*], *ignotum per ignotius* [*L.*].

misjudgment &c. 481; false teaching &c. 538.

sophism, solecism, paralogism; quibble, quirk, elench, elenchus, fallacy, *quodlibet* [*L.*], subterfuge, shift, subtlety, quillet [*archaic*]; inconsistency, antilogy; "a delusion, a mockery, and a snare" [Denman]; claptrap, mere words; "lame and impotent conclusion" [*Othello*].

meshes –, cobwebs- of sophistry; flaw in an argument; weak point, bad case.

sophist, casuist, paralogist.

V. judge intuitively, judge by intuition; hazard a proposition, talk at random.

pervert, quibble; equivocate, mystify, evade, elude; gloss over, varnish; misteach &c. 538; mislead &c. (*error*) 495; cavil, refine, subtilize, split hairs; misrepresent &c. (*lie*) 544.

reason ill, reason falsely &c. *adj.*; misjudge &c. 481; paralogize.

beg the question, reason in a circle, cut blocks with a razor, beat about the bush, play fast and loose, blow hot and cold, prove that black is white and white black, travel out of the record, *parler à tort et à travers* [*F.*], put oneself out of court, not have a leg to stand on.

Adj. intuitive, instinctive, impulsive; independent of –, anterior to- reason; gratuitous, hazarded; unconnected.

illogical, unreasonable, false, unsound, invalid; unwarranted, not following, incongruous, inconsequent, inconsequential; inconsistent; absonous

discursory, discursive; disputatious; logomachic or logomachical; Aristotelian, eristic or eristical.

DEBATABLE, controvertible.

LOGICAL; syllogistic, soritical, epagogic, inductive, deductive, synthetic or synthetical, analytic or analytical; relevant &c. 23.

Adv. FOR, because, hence, whence, seeing that, since, sith [archaic], then, thence, so; for -that, – this, – which- reason; for as much as or forasmuch as, in as much as or inasmuch as; whereas, ex concesso [L.], considering, in consideration of; therefore, argal [archaic], wherefore; consequently, ergo [L.], thus, accordingly; a priori [L.]; a fortiori [L.].

FINALLY, in conclusion, in fine; after all, au bout du compte [F.], on the whole, taking one thing with another; pro and con; rationally &c. adj.

[obs.], absonant, unscientific; untenable, inconclusive, incorrect; fallacious, fallible; groundless, unproved.

SPECIOUS, sophistic or sophistical, jesuitic or jesuitical, casuistic or casuistical, paralogistic, paralogical; deceptive, illusive, illusory; hollow, plausible, ad captandum [L.], evasive; irrelevant &c. 10.

WEAK, feeble, poor, flimsy, loose, vague, irrational; nonsensical &c. (absurd) 497; foolish &c. (imbecile) 499; frivolous, pettifogging, quibbling; finespun, overrefined.

at the end of one's tether, au bout de son latin [F.].

Adv. INTUITIVELY &c. adj.; by intuition.

ILLOGICALLY &c. adj.

‚ non constat; that goes for nothing; "My dear madam, nonsense can only be defended by nonsense" [Johnson — Boswell's Life.]

‚ ab actu ad posse valet consecutio; per troppo dibatter la verità si perde; troppo disputare la verità fa errare; "Remembrance and reflection, how allied; What thin partitions sense from thought divide" [Pope]; "And many a Knot unravelled by the Road, But not the Master-knot of Human Fate" [Omar Khayyám — Fitzgerald]; "logic is mainly valuable wherewith to exterminate logicians" [Chesterton].

478. Demonstration. — N. DEMONSTRATION, proof, irrefragability; conclusiveness &c. adj.; apodeixis or apodixis, probation, comprobation [obs.].

logic of facts &c. (evidence) 467; experimentum crucis [L.] &c. (test) 463; argument &c. 476; rigorous –, absolute- establishment.

V. DEMONSTRATE, prove, establish, make good; show, evince &c. (be evidence of) 467; verify &c. 467; settle the question, reduce to demonstration, set the question at rest.

make out, – a case; prove one's point, have the best of the argument; draw a conclusion &c. (judge) 480.

FOLLOW, – of course; stand to reason; hold good, hold water [colloq.].

Adj. DEMONSTRATING &c. v., demonstrative, demonstrable; probative, unanswerable, conclusive, convincing; apodeictic or apodictic, apodeictical or apodictical; irresistible, irrefutable, irrefragable, undeniable.

CATEGORICAL, decisive, crucial.

DEMONSTRATED &c. v.; proven; unconfuted, unanswered, unrefuted; evident &c. 474.

479. Confutation. — N. CONFUTATION, refutation; answer, complete answer; disproof, conviction, redargution, invalidation; exposure, exposition, exposé [F.], clincher [colloq.], retort, reductio ad absurdum [L.]; knock-down–; tu quoque- argument; sockdolager [slang, U. S.].

V. CONFUTE, refute; parry, negative, disprove, redargue, expose, show up, show the fallacy of, rebut, defeat; demolish &c. (destroy) 162; overthrow, overturn; scatter to the winds, explode, invalidate; silence; put –, reduce- to silence; clinch -an argument, – a question; give one a setdown [colloq.], stop the mouth, shut up; have, have on the hip, have the better of; confound [archaic], convince.

not leave a leg to stand on, cut the ground from under one's feet; smash all opposition; knock the bottom out of an argument [colloq.].

BE CONFUTED &c.; fail; expose –, show- one's weak point.

Adj. CONFUTABLE, confutative, refutable; confuting, confuted, &c. v.; capable of refutation.

DEDUCIBLE, consequential, consectary [obs.], inferential, following.

Adv. OF COURSE, in consequence, consequently, as a matter of course.

₊ *probatum est;* there is nothing more to be said, Q.E.D., it must follow; *exitus acta probat;* "For now the field is not far off Where we must give the world a proof Of deeds, not words" [Butler]; "a thing that nobody believes cannot be proved too often" [Shaw].

condemned –on one's own showing, – out of one's own mouth; "hoist with his own petar" [*Hamlet*].

₊ the argument falls to the ground; *cadit quæstio;* it does not hold water; *suo sibi gladio hunc jugulo* [Terence]; "thy speech bewrayeth thee" [*Bible*]; "Now, infidel, I have you on the hip" [*M. of V.*]; "Let us have faith that Right makes Might" [Lincoln].

Section V. RESULTS OF REASONING

480. Judgment. ¦CONCLUSION.] — **N.** JUDGMENT, decision, determination, finding, verdict, sentence, decree; *res adjudicata* [L.], *res judicata* [L.]; opinion &c. (*belief*) 484; good judgment &c. (*wisdom*) 498.

RESULT, conclusion, upshot; deduction, inference, ergotism [obs.], illation; corollary, porism; moral.

ESTIMATION, valuation, appreciation, judication; dijudication, adjudication; arbitrament, arbitrement, arbitration; assessment, ponderation [rare]; valorization.

ESTIMATE, award; review, criticism, critique, notice, report.

PLEBISCITE, plebiscitum, voice, casting vote; vote &c. (*choice*) 609.

ARBITER, arbitrator; judge, umpire; assessor, referee; inspector, inspecting officer; censor.

REVIEWER, critic; connoisseur; commentator &c. 524.

V. JUDGE, conclude, opine; come to –, draw –, arrive at- a conclusion; ascertain, determine, make up one's mind.

DEDUCE, derive, gather, collect, infer, draw an inference, make a deduction, weet [obs.], ween [archaic].

ESTIMATE, form an estimate, appreciate, value, count, assess, rate, rank, account; regard, consider, think of; look upon &c. (*believe*) 484; review; size up [colloq.].

DECIDE, settle; pass –, give- an opinion; try, pronounce, rule; pass -judgment, – sentence; sentence, doom, decree; find; give –, deliver- judgment; adjudge, adjudicate, judicate [rare]; arbitrate, award, report; bring in a verdict; make absolute, set a question at rest; confirm &c. (*assent*) 488.

hold the scales, sit in judgment; try a cause, hear a cause.

REVIEW, comment, criticize; pass

481. Misjudgment. — **N.** MISJUDGMENT, obliquity of judgment, warped judgment; miscalculation, miscomputation, misconception &c. (*error*) 495, hasty conclusion.

PRECONCEPTION, prejudgment, prejudication [rare], prejudice; foregone conclusion; prenotion, prevention [Gallicism], predilection, prepossession, preapprehension, presumption, presentiment, foreboding; fixed idea; *idée fixe* [F.], obsession, preconceived idea, *mentis gratissimus error* [L.]; fool's paradise.

PARTISANSHIP, *esprit de corps* [F.], party spirit, mob spirit, class prejudice, class consciousness, race prejudice, provincialism, clannishness, prestige.

QUIRK, shift, quibble, equivocation, evasion, subterfuge.

BIAS, warp, twist; hobby, whim, craze, fad, crotchet, partiality, infatuation, blind side, blind spot, mote in the eye.

one-sided –, partial –, narrow –, confined –, superficial- -views, – ideas, – conceptions, – notions; purblindness, *entêtement* [F.]; narrow mind; bigotry &c. (*obstinacy*) 606; *odium theologicum* [L.]; pedantry; hypercriticism.

DOCTRINAIRE &c. (*positive*) 474.

V. MISJUDGE, misestimate, misesteem, misthink, misconjecture, misconceive &c. (*error*) 495; fly in the face of facts; miscalculate, misreckon, miscompute.

overestimate &c. 482; underestimate &c. 483.

PREJUDGE, forejudge; presuppose, presume, prejudicate [rare], dogmatize; have a bias &c. *n.;* have only one idea; *jurare in verba magistri* [L.], run away with the notion; jump –, rush- to a conclusion; go off half-cocked [colloq.]; look only at one side of the shield; view with jaundiced eye, view through distorting spectacles; not see beyond one's nose;

under review &c. (*examine*) 457; investigate &c. (*inquire*) 461.

Adj. JUDGING &c. *v.;* judicious &c. (*wise*) 498; determinate, conclusive, confirmatory.

CRITICAL, hypercritical, hairsplitting, censorious.

Adv. ON THE WHOLE, all things considered, taking all this into consideration, this being so, *quæ cum ita sint* [*L.*], therefore, wherefore.

⁎ "a Daniel come to judgment" [*Merchant of Venice*]; "and stand a critic, hated yet caress'd" [Byron]; "it is much easier to be critical than to be correct" [Disraeli]; *la critique est aisée et l'art est difficile;* "nothing if not critical" [*Othello*].

dare pondus fumo [*L.*]; get the wrong sow by the ear &c. (*blunder*) 699.

BIAS, warp, twist; give a -bias, – twist; prejudice, prepossess.

Adj. MISJUDGING &c. *v.;* ill-judging, wrong-headed; prejudiced, prepossessed; jaundiced; shortsighted, purblind; partial, one-sided, superficial.

NARROW, narrow-minded, narrow-souled; provincial, parochial, insular; mean-spirited; confined, illiberal, intolerant, besotted, infatuated, fanatical, *entêté* [*F.*], positive, dogmatic, dictatorial; pragmatic *or* pragmatical, egotistical, conceited; opinioned, opinionated, opinionate [*rare*], opinionative [*rare*], opinative [*obs.*], opiniative [*obs.*];

self-opinionated; self-opinioned, wedded to an opinion, *opiniâtre* [*F.*]; bigoted &c. (*obstinate*) 606; crotchety, fussy, impracticable; unreasonable, stupid &c. 499; credulous &c. 486; warped.

MISJUDGED &c. *v.*

Adv. *ex parte* [*L.*].

⁎ nothing like leather; the wish is father to the thought; "O most lame and impotent conclusion" [*Othello*]; *poudre aux yeux* [*F.*]; "Stiff in opinions, always in the wrong" [Dryden].

480a. [RESULT OF SEARCH OR INQUIRY.] **Discovery.** — **N.** DISCOVERY, detection, disenchantment; ascertainment, disclosure, find, revelation.

TROVER &c. 775.

V. DISCOVER, find, determine, evolve; fix upon; find –, trace –, make –, hunt –, fish –, worm –, ferret –, dig –, root- out; fathom; bring out, draw out; educe, elicit, bring to light; dig up, grub up, fish up; unearth, disinter.

SOLVE, resolve; unriddle, unravel, ravel, ravel out, unlock; pick –, open- the lock; find a clew *or* clue to; interpret &c. 522; disclose &c. 529.

TRACE, get at; hit it, have it; lay one's -finger, – hands- upon; spot [*colloq.*], see through a millstone [*colloq.*]; get –, arrive- at the -truth &c. 494; put the saddle on the right horse, hit the right nail on the head.

SCENT, be near the truth, be warm [*colloq.*], burn [*colloq.*]; smoke, sniff, smell out, smell a rat [*colloq.*].

SEE THROUGH, see daylight, see in its true colors, see the cloven foot; open the eyes to; detect; catch, catch tripping.

MEET WITH; pitch –, fall –, light –, hit –, stumble –, pop- upon; come across; fall in with.

RECOGNIZE, realize, verify, make certain of, identify.

Int. eureka! I have it! at last!

482. Overestimation. — **N.** OVERESTIMATION &c. *v.;* exaggeration &c. 549; vanity &c. 880; optimism, pessimism.

much cry and little wool, much ado about nothing; storm in a teacup; fine talking; fine writing, rodomontade, gush [*colloq.*], hot air [*slang*].

EGOISM, egotism, bombast, conceit, swelled head [*slang*], megalomania.

EGOIST, egotist, megalomaniac; optimist, booster [*U. S.*], pessimist; Rodo-

483. Underestimation. — **N.** UNDERESTIMATION; depreciation &c. (*detraction*) 934; pessimism; self-detraction, self-depreciation; undervaluation, miosis, litotes [*rhet.*]; undervaluing &c. *v.;* modesty &c. 881.

PESSIMIST, depreciator, knocker [*slang*], crape-hanger [*slang*].

V. UNDERRATE, underestimate, undervalue, underreckon; depreciate; disparage &c. (*detract*) 934; not do justice to; misprize, disprize; ridicule &c 856:

mont, Braggadochio, braggart, boaster, braggadocio, swaggerer; hot-air artist [*slang*], gas-bag [*slang*], wind-bag [*slang*].

V. OVERESTIMATE, overrate, over-value, overprize, overweigh, overreckon, overstrain, overpraise; estimate too highly, attach too much importance to, make mountains of molehills, catch at straws; strain, magnify; exaggerate &c. 549; set too high a value upon; think –, make- -much, – too much- of; out-reckon.

have too high an opinion of oneself &c. (*vanity*) 880.

EULOGIZE, panegyrize, optimize, gush [*colloq.*], gush over [*colloq.*], boost [*U. S.*]; puff *or* puff up [*colloq.*]; extol, – to the skies; make the -most, – best, – worst- of; make two bites of a cherry.

Adj. overestimated &c. *v.;* oversensitive &c. (*sensibility*) 822.

INFLATED, puffed up; grandiose, stilted, pompous, pretentious, megalomaniacal, braggart, bombastic.

⁂ all his geese are swans; *parturiunt montes nascetur ridiculus mus* [*Horace*].

---

pessimize; slight &c. (*despise*) 930; neglect &c. 460; slur over.

make -light, – little, – nothing, – no account- of; belittle, knock [*slang*], slam [*slang*], run down [*colloq.*], minimize, think nothing of; set no store by, set at naught; shake off like water from a duck's back, shake off as dewdrops from the lion's mane.

Adj. DEPRECIATING &c. *v.;* depreciative, depreciatory.

DEPRECIATED &c. *v.;* unappreciated, unvalued, unprized.

⁂ "All pessimism has a secret optimism for its object" [Chesterton]; "pessimist — a man who thinks everybody as nasty as himself and hates them for it" [Shaw].

---

484. Belief. — N. BELIEF; credence; credit; assurance; faith, trust, troth, confidence, presumption, sanguine expectation &c. (*hope*) 858; dependence on, reliance on.

CONVICTION, persuasion, convincement, plerophory [*rare*], self-conviction; certainty &c. 474; opinion, mind, view; conception, thinking; impression &c. (*idea*) 453; surmise &c. 514; conclusion &c. (*judgment*) 480.

TENET, dogma, principle, persuasion, views, way of thinking; popular belief &c. (*assent*) 488.

firm –, implicit –, settled –, fixed –, rooted –, deep-rooted –, staunch –, unshaken –, steadfast –, inveterate –, calm –, sober –, dispassionate –, impartial –, well-founded- -belief, – opinion &c.; *uberrima fides* [*L.*].

DOCTRINE, system of opinions, school, articles, canons; article –, declaration –, profession- of faith; tenets, credenda, creed, credo, thirty-nine articles &c. (*orthodoxy*) 983a; gospel, gospel truth; catechism; assent &c. 488; propaganda &c. (*teaching*) 537.

CREDIBILITY &c. (*probability*) 472.

V. BELIEVE, credit; give -faith, – credit, – credence- to; see, realize; assume, receive; set down for, take for; have it, take it; consider, esteem, presume.

count –, depend –, calculate –, pin

---

485. Unbelief. Doubt. — N. UNBELIEF, disbelief, misbelief; discredit, miscreance *or* miscreancy [*archaic*]; infidelity &c. (*irreligion*) 989; wrangling, ergotism [*rare*]; dissent &c. 489; change of opinion &c. 484; retractation &c. 607.

DOUBT &c. (*uncertainty*) 475; skepticism *or* scepticism, misgiving, demur; distrust, mistrust; misdoubt, suspicion, jealousy, scruple, qualm; *onus probandi* [*L.*].

INCREDIBILITY, incredibleness, incredulity, unbelievability.

AGNOSTIC, skeptic *or* sceptic; unbeliever &c. 487.

V. DISBELIEVE, discredit; not believe &c. 484; misbelieve; refuse to admit &c. (*dissent*) 489; refuse to believe &c. (*incredulity*) 487.

DOUBT; be doubtful &c. (*uncertain*) 475; doubt the truth of; be skeptical as to &c. *adj.;* diffide [*obs.*], distrust, mistrust; suspect, smoke, scent, smell, smell a rat [*colloq.*], have –, harbor –, entertain- -doubts, – suspicions; have one's doubts.

throw doubt upon, raise a question; bring –, call- in question; question, challenge; dispute; deny &c. 536; cause –, raise –, start –, suggest –, awake- a -doubt, – suspicion; cavil, wrangle, ergotize [*rare*].

DEMUR, stick at, pause, hesitate, shy at, scruple; stop to consider, waver.

one's faith –, reckon –, lean –, build –, rely –, rest- upon; cast one's bread upon the waters; lay one's account for; make sure of.

make oneself easy -about, – on that score; take on -trust, – credit; take for -granted, – gospel; allow –, attach- some weight to.

KNOW, – for certain; be in the know [*slang*]; have –, make- no doubt; doubt not; be –, rest- -assured &c. *adj.*; per- suade –, assure –, satisfy- oneself; make up one's mind.

CONFIDE IN, believe in, put one's trust in; give one credit for; place –, repose- implicit confidence in; take one's word for, take at one's word; place reliance on, rely upon, swear by, regard to.

THINK, hold; take, take it; opine, be of opinion, conceive, trow [*archaic*], ween [*archaic*], fancy, apprehend; have –, hold –, possess –, entertain –, adopt –, imbibe –, embrace –, get hold of –, hazard –, foster –, nurture –, cherish- -a belief, – an opinion &c. *n.*

hang in suspense, hang in doubt. STAGGER, startle; shake –, stagger- one's -faith, – belief.

Adj. UNBELIEVING; skeptical *or* scepti- cal, incredulous –, skeptical- as to; dis- trustful of, shy of, suspicious of; doubt- ing &c. *v.*

DOUBTFUL &c. (*uncertain*) 475; dispu- table; unworthy –, undeserving- of -belief &c. 484; questionable; suspect [*archaic*], suspicious; open to -suspicion – doubt; staggering, hard to believe, incredible, unbelievable, not to be be- lieved, inconceivable.

FALLIBLE &c. (*uncertain*) 475; unde- monstrable; controvertible &c. (*untrue*) 495.

Adv. WITH CAUTION, *cum grano salis* [*L.*]; with grains of allowance.

*** *fronti nulla fides; nimium ne crede colori* [Vergil]; *timeo Danaos et dona ferentes* [Vergil]; *credat Judæus Apella* [Hor.]; let those believe who may; *ad tristem partem strenua est suspicio* [Syrus].

view as, consider as, take as, hold as, conceive as, regard as, esteem as, deem as, look upon as, account as, set down as; surmise &c. 514.

get –, take- it into one's head; come round to an opinion; swallow &c. (*cre- dulity*) 486.

PERSUADE; cause to be believed &c. *v.*; satisfy, bring to reason, have the ear of, gain the confidence of, assure; convince, convict, convert; wean, bring round; bring –, win- over; indoctrinate &c. (*teach*) 537; cram down the throat; produce –, carry- conviction; bring –, drive- home to.

FIND CREDENCE, go down, pass current; be received &c. *v.*, be current &c. *adj.*; possess –, take hold of –, take possession of- the mind.

Adj. BELIEVING &c. *v.*; certain, sure, assured, positive, cocksure [*colloq.*], satis- fied, confident, unhesitating, convinced, secure.

under the impression; impressed –, imbued –, penetrated- with.

CONFIDING, trustful, suspectless [*obs.*], unsuspecting, unsuspicious, void of sus- picion; credulous &c. 486; wedded to.

BELIEVED &c. *v.*; accredited, putative; unsuspected, trusted, undoubted.

worthy of –, deserving of –, commanding- -belief, – confidence; credible, reli- able, trustworthy, to be depended on; satisfactory; probable &c. 472; fiducial, fiduciary; persuasive, impressive.

DOCTRINAL, relating to belief.

Adv. IN THE OPINION OF, in the eyes of; *me judice* [*L.*]; meseems [*archaic*], methinks [*archaic*]; to the best of one's belief; in my opinion, in my judgment, according to my belief; I dare say, I doubt not, I have no doubt, I am sure; cocksure, sure enough &c. (*certainty*) 474; depend –, rely- upon it; be –, rest- assured; I'll warrant you &c. (*affirmation*) 535.

*** *experto credite* [Vergil]; *Fata viam invenient; Justitiæ soror incorrupta Fides;* "live to explain thy doctrine by thy life" [Prior]; "stands not within the prospect of belief" [*Macbeth*]; *tarde quæ credita lædunt credimus* [Ovid]; *vide et crede;* "One in whom persuasion and belief Had ripened into faith, and faith become A passionate intuition" [Wordsworth]; "faith, that lodestar of the ghost" [Masefield]; "Nothing is so firmly believed as that we least know" [Montaigne]; "Belief consists in accepting the affirmations of the soul; unbelief, in denying them" [Emerson].

486. Credulity. — N. CREDULITY, credulousness &c. *adj.;* gullibility, cullibility [*obs.*]; gross credulity, infatuation; self-delusion, self-deception; superstition; one's blind side; bigotry &c. (*obstinacy*) 606; hyperorthodoxy &c. 984; misjudgment &c. 481.

CREDULOUS PERSON &c. (*dupe*) 547.

V. BE CREDULOUS &c. *adj.; jurare in verba magistri* [*L.*]; follow implicitly; swallow, swallow whole, gulp down; take on trust; take for -granted, – gospel; take on faith; run away with -a notion, – an idea; jump –, rush- to a conclusion; think the moon is made of green cheese; take –, grasp- the shadow for the substance; catch at straws.

IMPOSE UPON &c. (*deceive*) 545.

Adj. CREDULOUS, gullible; easily deceived &c. 545; simple, green, soft, childish, silly, stupid; easily convinced; overcredulous, overconfident, overtrustful; easy to stuff [*slang*]; infatuated, superstitious; confiding &c. (*believing*) 484.

*.** the wish is father to the thought; *credo quia impossibile* [Tertullian]; all is not gold 'that glitters; *no es oro todo lo que reluce; omne ignotum pro magnifico;* "And still they gazed, and still the wonder grew That one small head could carry all he knew" [Goldsmith].

488. Assent. — N. ASSENT, assentment [*archaic*]; acquiescence, admission; nod; accord, concord, concordance; agreement &c. 23; affirmance, affirmation; recognition, acknowledgment, avowal, recognizance [*rare*], confession, confession of faith.

UNANIMITY, common consent, consensus, acclamation, chorus, *vox populi* [*L.*]; popular –, current- -belief, – opinion; public opinion; concurrence &c. (*of causes*) 178; coöperation &c. (*voluntary*) 709.

RATIFICATION, confirmation, corroboration, approval, acceptance, visa, *visé* [*F.*]; indorsement &c. (*record*) 551.

consent &c. (*compliance*) 762.

AFFIRMANT, assentant [*obs.*], professor [*esp. in relig.*], confirmist, consenter, covenantor, subscriber, indorser *or* endorser; upholder &c. (*auxiliary*) 711.

V. ASSENT; give –, yield –, nod-assent; acquiesce; agree &c. 23; receive, accept, accede, accord, concur, lend oneself to, consent, coincide, reciprocate, go with; be at one with &c. *adj.;* go along

487. Incredulity. — N. INCREDULITY. incredulousness; skepticism, freethought, Pyrrhonism; want of faith &c. (*irreligion*) 989; minimifidianism; unbelief &c. 485.

SUSPICIOUSNESS &c. *adj.;* scrupulosity; suspicion &c. (*unbelief*) 485; inconvincibility.

UNBELIEVER, skeptic *or* sceptic, miscreant [*archaic*], doubting Thomas, disbeliever, agnostic, infidel, misbeliever, nullifidian, minimifidian, zendik [*Oriental*], freethinker, Pyrrhonist &c. (*irreligion*) 989; heretic &c. (*heterodox*) 984.

V. BE INCREDULOUS &c. *adj.;* distrust &c. (*disbelieve*) 485; refuse to believe; shut one's eyes to, shut one's ears to; turn a deaf ear to; hold aloof; ignore, *nullius jurare in verba magistri* [*L.*].

Adj. INCREDULOUS, skeptical *or* sceptical, dissenting, unbelieving, inconvincible; hard of belief, shy of belief; suspicious, scrupulous, distrustful, disposed to doubt, indisposed to believe; heterodox.

*.** "I'm from Missouri and I want to be shown"; "You call me misbeliever, cutthroat dog" [*M. of V.*]; "knowledge of divine things, for the most part, as Heraclitus says, is lost to us by incredulity" [Plutarch].

489. Dissent. — N. DISSENT, nonconsent, discordance &c. (*disagreement*) 24; difference –, diversity- of opinion.

NONCONFORMITY &c. (*heterodoxy*) 984; protestantism, recusancy, schism; disaffection; secession &c. 624; recantation &c. 607.

DISSENSION &c. (*discord*) 713; discontent &c. 832; caviling, wrangling, ergotism [*rare*].

PROTEST; contradiction &c. (*denial*) 536; noncompliance &c. (*rejection*) 764.

DISSENTIENT, dissenter, noncontent *or* noncon *or* non con [*House of Lords*], nonjuror, nonconformist; sectary, separatist, recusant, schismatic, protestant; heretic &c. (*heterodoxy*) 984.

V. DISSENT, nonconsent, demur; call in question &c. (*doubt*) 485; differ in opinion, disagree, agree to differ; say no &c. 536; refuse -assent, – to admit; cavil, wrangle, ergotize [*rare*], protest, raise one's voice against, repudiate; contradict &c. (*deny*) 536.

have no notion of, differ *toto cælo* [*L.*], revolt at, revolt from the idea.

with, chime in with, strike in with, close with; echo, enter into one's views, agree in opinion; vote for, give one's voice for; recognize; subscribe –, conform –, defer to; say -yes, – ditto, – amen, – aye- to.

go –, float –, swim- with the stream; float with the current; get on the band wagon [*slang*]; be in the fashion, join in the chorus; be in every mouth.

arrive at –, come to- -an understanding, – terms, – an agreement.

ACKNOWLEDGE, own, admit, allow, avow, confess; concede &c. (*yield*) 762; come round to; abide by; permit &c. 760.

CONFIRM, affirm; ratify, approve, indorse, visa, *visé* [*F.*], countersign; corroborate &c. 467.

Adj. ASSENTING &c. *v.*; of one -accord, – mind; of the same mind, affirmant, assentaneous [*rare*], assentant [*obs.*], at one with, agreed, acquiescent, content; willing &c. 602.

UNCONTRADICTED, unchallenged, unquestioned, uncontroverted.

carried –, agreed- -*nem. con.* [*L.*] &c. *adv.*; unanimous; agreed on all hands, carried by acclamation.

affirmative &c. 535.

shake the head, shrug the shoulders; look askance *or* askant.

SECEDE; recant &c. 607.

Adj. DISSENTING &c. *v.*; negative &c. 536; dissident, dissentient; unconsenting &c. (*refusing*) 764; noncontent, nonjuring; protestant, recusant; unconvinced, unconverted.

UNAVOWED, unacknowledged; out of the question.

UNWILLING &c. 603; extorted; discontented &c. 832.

SECTARIAN, sectary [*rare*], denominational, schismatic; heterodox; intolerant.

Adv. NO &c. 536; at variance with, at issue with; under protest.

Int. GOD FORBID! not for the world! I'll be hanged if! [*colloq.*]; not another word! no, sirree! [*U. S.*]; not if I know it! I beg to differ; never tell me! your humble servant [*archaic*], pardon me.

⁂ many men, many minds; *quot homines tot sententiæ* [Terence]; *tant s'en faut; il s'en faut bien;* "the dissidence of dissent and the protestantism of the Protestant religion" [Burke]; "I had no taste for what is called popular art, no respect for popular morality, no belief in popular religion, no admiration for popular heroics" [Shaw].

Adv. YES, yea, aye *or* ay, true; good; well; how true, very -well, – true; well and good; granted; even so, just so; to be sure, as you say, sure, surely, assuredly, "thou hast said"; truly, exactly, precisely, that's just it, indeed, certainly, certes [*archaic*], *ex concesso* [*L.*], of course, unquestionably, no doubt, doubtless.

BE IT SO; so be it, so let it be; so mote it be, with all one's heart; amen; willingly &c. 602.

AFFIRMATIVELY, in the affirmative.

UNANIMOUSLY, *unâ voce* [*L.*], by common consent, in chorus, to a man; with one -consent, – voice, – accord; *nem. con.* [*L.*]; *nemine contradicente* [*L.*], *nemine dissentiente* [*L.*], without a dissentient voice; as one man, one and all, on all hands.

⁂ avec plaisir; chi tace acconsente; "the public mind is the creation of the Master-Writers" [Disraeli].

490. Knowledge. — N. KNOWLEDGE; cognizance, cognition, cognoscence [*obs.*]; acquaintance, experience, ken, privity, insight, familiarity; comprehension, apprehension; recognition; appreciation &c. (*judgment*) 480; intuition; conscience, consciousness; perception, apperception, precognition; acroamatics.

system –, body- of knowledge; science, philosophy, pansophism, pansophy; acroama; theory, ætiology *or* etiology; circle of the sciences; pandect, doctrine, body of doctrine; cyclopedia *or* cyclopædia, encyclopedia *or* encyclopædia,

491. Ignorance. — N. IGNORANCE, nescience, *tabula rasa* [*L.*], illiteracy, unlearnedness, crass ignorance, *ignorance crasse* [*F.*]; unacquaintance; unconsciousness &c. *adj.*; darkness, blindness; incomprehension, inexperience, simplicity.

sealed book, *terra incognita* [*L.*], virgin soil, unexplored ground; dark ages.

unknown quantities; x, y, z.

[IMPERFECT KNOWLEDGE] smattering, superficiality, half-learning, shallowness, sciolism, glimmering; bewilderment &c. (*uncertainty*) 475; incapacity.

circle of knowledge; school &c. (*system of opinions*) 484.

tree of knowledge; republic of letters &c. (*language*) 560.

ENLIGHTENMENT, light; glimpse, inkling, glimmer, glimmering, dawn; scent, suspicion; impression &c. (*idea*) 453; discovery &c. 480a.

LEARNING, erudition, lore, scholarship, reading, letters; literature; book madness; book learning, bookishness; bibliomania, bibliolatry; information, general information; store of knowledge &c.; education &c. (*teaching*) 537; culture, *Kultur* [*Ger.*], cultivation, menticulture, attainments; acquirements, mental acquisitions; accomplishments; proficiency; practical knowledge &c. (*skill*) 698; liberal education, higher education; dilettantism; rudiments &c. (*beginning*) 66.

deep –, profound –, solid –, accurate –, acroatic –, acroamatic –, vast –, extensive –, encyclopedical- -knowledge, -learning; omniscience, pantology.

march of intellect; progress –, advance- of -science, – learning; schoolmaster abroad.

V. KNOW, ken [*dial.*], scan, wot [*archaic*]; wot of [*archaic*], be aware of &c. *adj.*; ween [*archaic*], weet [*obs.*], trow [*archaic*]; have, possess.

conceive; apprehend, comprehend; take, realize, understand, savvy [*slang, U. S.*], be wise to [*slang*], appreciate; fathom, make out; recognize, discern, perceive, see, get a sight of, experience.

KNOW FULL WELL; have –, possess-some knowledge of; be *au courant* [*F.*] &c. *adj.*; have in one's head, have at one's fingers' ends; know by -heart, – rote; be master of; *connaître le dessous des cartes* [*F.*], know what's what [*colloq.*] &c. 698.

DISCOVER &c. 480a; see one's way.

LEARN, come to one's knowledge &c. (*information*) 527.

Adj. KNOWING &c. *v.*; cognitive; acroamatic *or* acroamatical, apperceptive, appercipient.

AWARE OF, cognizant of, conscious of; acquainted with, made acquainted with; privy to, no stranger to; *au fait* [*F.*], *au courant* [*F.*]; in the secret; up to [*colloq.*], alive to; behind the -scenes, – curtain; let into; apprized of, informed of; undeceived.

[AFFECTATION OF KNOWLEDGE] pedantry, charlatanry, charlatanism; Philistine, *Philister* [*Ger.*].

V. BE IGNORANT &c. *adj.*; not know &c. 490; know -not, – not what, – nothing of; have no -idea, – notion, – conception; not have the remotest idea; not know chalk from cheese; not know a B from a -bull's foot, – battledore, – broomstick.

ignore, be blind to; keep in ignorance &c. (*conceal*) 528.

see through a glass darkly; have a film over the eyes, have a glimmering &c. *n.;* wonder whether; not know what to make of &c. (*unintelligibility*) 519; not pretend to say, not take upon oneself to say.

Adj. IGNORANT; nescient; unknowing, unaware, unacquainted, unapprized, unwitting, unweeting [*obs.*], unconscious; witless, weetless [*obs.*]; a stranger to; unconversant.

UNINFORMED, uncultivated, unversed, uninstructed, untaught, uninitiated, untutored, unschooled, unscholarly, unguided, unenlightened; Philistine; behind the age.

SHALLOW, superficial, green, rude, empty, half-learned, half-baked [*colloq.*], low-brow [*slang*]; illiterate; unread, uninformed, uneducated, unlearned, unlettered, unbookish; empty-headed; pedantic.

IN THE DARK; benighted, belated; blinded, blindfold; hoodwinked; misinformed; *au bout de son latin* [*F.*], at the end of his tether, at fault; at sea &c. (*uncertain*) 475; caught tripping, caught napping.

UNKNOWN, unapprehended, unexplained, unascertained, uninvestigated, unexplored, unheard of, unperceived; concealed &c. 528; novel.

Adv. IGNORANTLY &c. *adj.;* unawares; for anything one knows, for aught one knows; not that one knows.

Int. God –, Heaven –, the Lord –, dear [*dial.*] –, nobody- knows!

* * "ignorance never settles a question" [Disraeli]; *quantum animis erroris inest!* [Ovid]; "small Latin and less Greek" [B. Jonson]; "that unlettered, small-knowing soul" [*Love's Labor's Lost*]; "there is no darkness but ignorance" [*Twelfth Night*]; "a little learning is a dangerous thing" [Pope]; "only are reputed wise For saying nothing" [*M. of V.*].

PROFICIENT IN, versed in, read in, forward in, strong in, at home in; conversant with, familiar with.

EDUCATED, erudite, instructed, learned, lettered; well-conned, well-informed, well-versed, well-read, well-grounded, well-educated; enlightened, shrewd, *savant* [*F.*], blue [*colloq.*], bluestocking, high-brow [*slang*], bookish, scholastic, solid, profound, deep-read, book-learned, ætiological *or* etiological, pansophic *or* pansophical; accomplished &c. (*skillful*) 698; omniscient; self-taught, self-educated, auto-didactic; self-made.

KNOWN &c. *v.*; ascertained, well-known, recognized, received, notorious, noted; proverbial; familiar, – as household words, – to every schoolboy; hackneyed, trite, commonplace.

KNOWABLE, cognizable, cognoscible.

Adv. to –, to the best of- one's knowledge; as every schoolboy knows.

** one's eyes being opened &c. (*disclosure*) 529; *comprendre tout c'est tout pardonner; empta dolore docet experientia;* γνῶθι σεαυτόν; "half our knowledge we must snatch not take" [Pope]; *Jahre lehren mehr als Bücher;* "knowledge comes but wisdom lingers" [Tennyson]; "knowledge is power" [Bacon]; *les affaires font les hommes; nec scire fas est omnia* [Horace]; "the amassed thought and experience of innumerable minds" [Emerson]; *was ich nicht weiss macht mich nicht heiss;* "knowledge and timber shouldn't be much used till they are seasoned" [Holmes]; "only so much do I know as I have lived" [Emerson]; "And I see all of it, Only, I'm dying!" [Browning]; "Beyond the bounds our staring rounds, Across the pressing dark" [Kipling].

---

492. Scholar. — N. SCHOLAR, *savant* [*F.*], pundit *or* pandit [*India*], schoolman, professor, graduate, wrangler [*Cambridge Univ., Eng.*], academician, academist [*obs.*], doctor, fellow, don [*Eng. Univ. cant*], graduate, postgraduate, clerk [*archaic*]; *Artium Magister* [*L.*], A.M. *or* M.A., master of arts; *Artium Baccalaureus*, A.B. *or* B.A., bachelor of arts; bookman [*rare*], classicist, licentiate, gownsman; philosopher, philomath; scientist, connoisseur, sophist, sophister; linguist; etymologist, philologist; philologer [*now rare*]; lexicographer, glossographer, glossologist, lexicologist, scholiast, commentator, annotator; grammarian; *littérateur* [*F.*], *literati* [*L.*], *dilettanti* [*It.*], illuminati; munshi *or* moonshee [*India*], mullah [*Moslem*], moolvi [*India*], guru [*India*]; Hebraist, Hellenist, Græcist, Sanskritist; sinologist, sinologue.

BOOKWORM, *helluo librorum* [*L.*], bibliophile, bibliophilist, bibliomaniac, blue-stocking [*colloq.*], *bas-bleu* [*F.*], high-brow [*slang*].

Admirable Crichton, Mezzofanti, "learned Theban" [*King Lear*], Dominie Sampson [*Guy Mannering*], Socrates.

LEARNED MAN, literary man; *homo multarum literarum* [*L.*]; man of -learning, – letters, – education, – genius; giant of learning, colossus of knowledge, prodigy.

ANTIQUARIAN, antiquary, archæologist, Assyriologist, Egyptologist, sage &c. (*wise man*) 500.

PEDANT, doctrinaire; pedagogue, Dr. Pangloss; pantologist; instructor &c. (*teacher*) 540.

STUDENT, learner, classman, senior, junior, sophomore, freshman, pupil, schoolboy &c. (*learner*) 541.

Adj. LEARNED &c. 490; brought up at the feet of Gamaliel.

** "he was a scholar, and a ripe and good one" [*Henry VIII*]; "the manifold linguist" [*All's Well That Ends Well*]; "the office of the scholar is to cheer, to raise, to guide men by showing them facts amidst appearances" [Emerson]; "if it were only for a vocabulary, the scholar would be covetous of action" [*ibid.*]; "the modern literary artist is compounded of almost every man except the orator" [Chesterton]; "This man decided not to Live but Know" [Browning].

---

493. Ignoramus. — N. IGNORAMUS, illiterate, dunce, duffer, woodenhead [*colloq.*], bonehead [*slang*], solid ivory [*slang*], numskull [*colloq.*], wooden spoon [*Cambridge Univ., Eng., cant*]; no scholar.

SCIOLIST, smatterer, dabbler, half scholar; charlatan; wiseacre.

NOVICE, tenderfoot; greenhorn &c. (*dupe*) 547; plebe *or* pleb [*cant, U. S.*]; tyro &c. (*learner*) 541; lubber &c. (*bungler*) 701; fool &c. 501.

Adj. BOOKLESS, shallow, simple, lump-ish, dull, dumb [*colloq., U. S.*], dense, crass, imbecile; wise in his own conceit; ignorant &c. 491.

** "a wit with dunces and a dunce with wits" [Pope]; "Oh! these deliberate fools!" [*M. of V.*].

494. [OBJECT OF KNOWLEDGE.] **Truth.**
— **N.** TRUTH, verity; fact, reality &c.
(*existence*) 1; plain matter of fact; nature &c. (*principle*) 5; gospel; orthodoxy &c. 983a; authenticity; veracity &c. 543.

plain –, honest –, sober –, naked –, unalloyed –, unvarnished –, unqualified –, stern –, exact –, intrinsic- truth; *nuda veritas* [*L.*]; the very thing; not an illusion &c. 495; real Simon Pure; unvarnished tale; the truth, the whole truth and nothing but the truth; just the thing.

ACCURACY, exactitude; exactness, preciseness &c. *adj.;* precision, delicacy; rigor, mathematical precision, fidelity; clockwork precision &c. (*regularity*) 80; conformity to rule; nicety.

orthology; *ipsissima verba* [*L.*], the very words; realism.

V. BE TRUE &c. *adj.*, be the case; stand the test; have the true ring; hold good, hold true, hold water.

RENDER TRUE, prove true &c. *adj.;* substantiate &c. (*evidence*) 467.

GET AT THE TRUTH &c. (*discover*) 480a.

Adj. TRUE, real, actual &c. (*existing*) 1; veritable; certain &c.; 474; substantially –, categorically- true &c.; true -to the letter, – as gospel, – as steel, – to life, – to the facts; unimpeachable; veracious &c. 543; unrefuted, unconfuted; unideal, unimagined; realistic.

EXACT, accurate, definite, precise, well-defined, just, right, correct, strict, severe; close &c. (*similar*) 17; orthological, literal; rigid, rigorous; scrupulous &c. (*conscientious*) 939; religiously exact, punctual, punctilious, mathematical, scientific; faithful, constant, unerring; curious, particular, nice, meticulous, delicate, fine; clean-cut, clear-cut.

AUTHENTIC, genuine, legitimate; orthodox &c. 983a; official, *ex officio* [*L.*].

PURE, natural, sound, sterling, true-blue; unsophisticated, unadulterated, Simon-Pure [*colloq.*], unvarnished, uncolored; in its true colors.

VALID, well-grounded, well-founded; solid, substantial, pucka *or* pakka [*Hind.*], tangible; undistorted, undisguised; unaffected, unexaggerated, unromantic, unflattering.

Adv. TRULY &c. *adj.;* verily, indeed, in reality; in very truth, in fact, as a matter of fact, to state the facts; beyond -doubt, - question; with truth &c.

495. Error. — **N.** ERROR, fallacy; misconception, misapprehension, misunderstanding; aberration, aberrance *or* aberrancy; inexactness &c. *adj.;* laxity; misconstruction &c. (*misinterpretation*) 523; anachronism; miscomputation &c. (*misjudgment*) 481; *non sequitur* [*L.*] &c. 477; misstatement, misreport; mumpsimus.

MISTAKE; miss, fault, blunder, cross-purposes, oversight, misprint, erratum, corrigendum, slip, blot, flaw, loose thread; trip, stumble &c. (*failure*) 732; botchery &c. (*want of skill*) 699; slip of the tongue, *lapsus linguæ* [*L.*]; slip of the pen, *lapsus calami* [*L.*], clerical error; bull &c. (*absurdity*) 497; Spoonerism, Malapropism, Leiterism [*U. S.*], Mrs. Partington; haplography.

DELUSION, illusion; false –, warped –, distorted- -impression, – idea; bubble; self-deceit, self-deception; mists of error; exploded -notion, – idea, – superstition.

heresy &c. (*heterodoxy*) 984; hallucination &c. (*insanity*) 503; false light &c. (*fallacy of vision*) 443; dream &c. (*fancy*) 515; fable &c. (*untruth*) 546; bias &c. (*misjudgment*) 481; misleading &c. *v.*

V. BE ERRONEOUS &c. *adj.*

MISLEAD, misguide; lead astray, lead into error; cause error; beguile, misinform &c. (*misteach*) 538; delude; give a false -impression, – idea; falsify, misstate; deceive &c. 545; lie &c. 544.

ERR; be in error &c. *adj.*, be mistaken &c. *v.;* be deceived &c. (*duped*) 547; mistake, receive a false impression, deceive oneself; fall into –, lie under –, labor under- an error &c. *n.;* be in the wrong, blunder; misapprehend, misconceive, misunderstand, misreckon, miscount, miscalculate &c. (*misjudge*) 481.

play -, be- at cross purposes &c. (*misinterpret*) 523.

TRIP, stumble; lose oneself &c. (*uncertainty*) 475; go astray; fail &c. 732; be in the wrong box; take the wrong sow by the ear &c. (*mismanage*) 699; put the saddle on the wrong horse; reckon without one's host; take the shadow for the substance &c. (*credulity*) 486; dream &c. (*imagine*) 515.

Adj. ERRONEOUS, untrue, false, devoid of truth, faulty, erring, fallacious, apocryphal, unreal, ungrounded, groundless; unsubstantial &c. 4; heretical &c. (*heterodox*) 984; unsound; illogical &c. 477.

(*veracity*) 543; certainly &c. (*certain*) 474; actually &c. (*existence*) 1; in effect &c. (*intrinsically*) 5.

exactly &c. *adj.*; *ad amussim* or *adamussim* [*L.*], verbatim, *verbatim et literatim* [*L.*]; word for word, literally, *literatim* [*L.*], *totidem verbis* [*L.*], *sic* [*L.*], to the letter, chapter and verse, *ipsissimis verbis* [*L.*]; *ad unguem* [*L.*]; to an inch; to a –nicety, – hair, – tittle, – turn, – T; *au pied de la lettre* [*F.*]; neither more nor less; in every respect, in all respects; *sous tous les rapports* [*F.*]; at any rate, at all events; strictly speaking.

⁎ the truth is, the fact is; *rem acu tetigisti; ⁕n suivant la verité; ex facto jus oritur; la verità è figlia del tempo; locos y niños dicen la verdad; nihil est veritatis luce dulcius* [Cicero]; *veritas nunquam perit* [Seneca]; *veritatem dies aperit* [Seneca]; "Tell the truth and shame the devil"; "Truth crushed to earth shall rise again, The eternal years of God are hers" [Bryant].

divine" [Pope]; "you lie — under a mistake" with a little aversion" [Sheridan]; "the village all have a half-warmed fish in our bosoms" [*Spoonerism*].

INEXACT, unexact, inaccurate, incorrect; indefinite &c. (*uncertain*) 475.

ILLUSIVE, illusory, delusive; mock, ideal &c. (*imaginary*) 515; spurious &c. 545; deceitful &c. 544; perverted.

CONTROVERTIBLE, unsustainable, unsustained, unauthentic, unauthenticated, untrustworthy.

EXPLODED, refuted, discarded.

MISTAKEN &c. *v.*; in error, under an error &c. *n.*; tripping &c. *v.*; out, out in one's reckoning; aberrant; beside –, wide of- -the mark, – the truth; astray &c. (*at fault*) 475; on -a false, – the wrong- -scent, – trail; in the wrong box; at cross-purposes, all in the wrong; all out [*colloq.*]; all abroad [*colloq.*], at sea, bewildered.

Adv. more or less.

⁎ *errare est humanum; mentis gratissimus error* [Horace]; "on the dubious waves of error tost" [Cowper]; "to err is human, to forgive" [Shelley]; "'tis safest in matrimony to begin that voted the earth was flat" [Kipling]; "we

---

496. Maxim. — N. MAXIM, aphorism;

apothegm *or* apophthegm; dictum, saying, adage, saw, proverb, epigram, gnomic saying, gnome, sentence, mot [*Gallicism*], motto, word, byword, bromidium [*slang*], commonplace, moral, phylactery, protasis [*rare*].

wise –, sage –, received –, admitted –, recognized- maxim &c.; true –, common –, hackneyed –, trite –, commonplace- saying &c.

AXIOM, theorem, scholium, truism, postulate.

PRINCIPLE, principia; profession of faith &c. (*belief*) 484; settled principle, formula; reflection &c. (*idea*) 453; conclusion &c. (*judgment*) 480; golden rule &c. (*precept*) 697.

Adj. APHORISTIC, aphorismic, aphorismatic, proverbial, phylacteric; axiomatic *or* axiomatical, gnomic *or* gnomical.

Adv. as the saying is, as they say, as it was said by them of old.

⁎ "Full of wise laws and modern instances" [*As You Like It*].

497. Absurdity. — N. ABSURDITY,

absurdness &c. *adj.*; imbecility &c. 499; alogy [*obs.*], comicality, nonsense, paradox, inconsistency; stultiloquy [*rare*], stultiloquence [*rare*], stultification, futility, nugacity.

BLUNDER, muddle, bull; Irishism, Hibernicism; anticlimax, bathos; sophism &c. 477.

FARCE, galimatias, burlesque, parody, fiddle-faddle [*colloq.*], amphigory *or* amphigouri, rhapsody; farrago &c. (*disorder*) 59; *bêtise* [*F.*]; extravagance, romance; sciamachy.

PUN, sell [*colloq.*], catch [*colloq.*], verbal quibble, macaronic composition, limerick, joke.

JARGON, slipslop [*colloq.*], gibberish, balderdash, bombast, claptrap, fustian, twaddle &c. (*no meaning*) 517; exaggeration &c. 549; moonshine, stuff; mare's-nest, quibble, self-delusion.

TOMFOOLERY, vagary, mummery, monkeyshine [*slang, U. S.*], monkey trick, *boutade* [*F.*], frisk, practical joke, escapade.

V. PLAY THE FOOL &c. 499; stultify, blunder, muddle; employ absurdity &c. *n.*; rhapsodize; romance, sell [*slang*], fiddle-faddle [*colloq.*]; talk nonsense, *parler à tort et à travers* [*F.*]; *battre la campagne* [*F.*]; *anemolia bazein* [*Gr.* ἀνεμώλια βάζειν]; be absurd &c. *adj.*; frisk, caper, joke, play practical jokes.

BE THE FOOL, be the goat [*colloq.*], bite [*colloq.*].

Adj. ABSURD, nonsensical, farcical, preposterous, egregious, senseless, inconsistent, stultiloquent [*rare*], stulty [*obs.*], ridiculous, extravagant, quibbling; self-annulling, self-contradictory; paradoxical, macaronic *or* maccaronic, punning.

burlesque, foolish &c. 499; sophistical &c. 477; unmeaning &c. 517; amphigoric; without rime or reason; fantastic *or* fantastical, rhapsodic *or* rhapsodical, bombastic, high-flown.

Int. fiddledeedee! pish! pho *or* phoh! [*rare*], pooh! pooh-pooh! bah! stuff and nonsense! fiddle-faddle! bosh! rats! [*slang*], come off! [*slang*], "in the name of the Prophet — figs!" [Horace Smith].

⁎ *credat Judæus Apella* [Horace]; tell it to the marines; "A little nonsense now and then Is relished by the wisest men" [*Anon.*]; "Say 'Boo!' to you — 'pooh-pooh!' to you" [Gilbert].

Faculties

498. Intelligence. Wisdom. — N.

INTELLIGENCE, capacity, comprehension, understanding; cuteness [*colloq.*], sabe [*slang, U. S.*], savvy [*slang, U. S.*]; intellect &c. 450; nous [*colloq.*], docity [*dial.*], parts, sagacity, mother wit, wit, *esprit* [*F.*], gumption [*colloq.*], quick parts, grasp of intellect; acuteness &c. *adj.*; acumen, longheadedness, arguteness, subtility, subtlety, penetration, perspicacy [*obs.*], perspicacity, discernment, due sense of, good judgment; discrimination &c. 465; cunning &c. 702; refinement &c. (*taste*) 850.

HEAD, brains, gray matter [*colloq.*], brain-stuff [*colloq.*], headpiece, upper story [*colloq.*], long head.

eagle -eye, – glance; eye of a lynx, eye of a hawk.

WISDOM, sapience, sense; good-, common -, horse – [*colloq., U. S.*], plain-sense; clear thinking, rationality, reason; reasonableness &c. *adj.*; judgment, solidity, depth, profundity, caliber *or* calibre; enlarged views; reach -, compass- of thought; enlargement of mind.

GENIUS, lambent flame of intellect, inspiration, *Geist* [*Ger.*], fire of genius, heaven-born genius, soul; talent &c. (*aptitude*) 698.

[WISDOM IN ACTION] prudence &c. 864; vigilance &c. 459; tact &c. 698; foresight &c. 510; sobriety, self-possession, *aplomb* [*F.*], ballast, mental poise, balance.

a bright thought, an inspiration, not a bad idea.

V. BE INTELLIGENT &c. *adj.*; have all one's wits about one; be brilliant, be witty, scintillate, coruscate; understand &c. (*intelligible*) 518; catch -, take in an idea; take a -joke, – hint.

499. Imbecility. Folly. — N.

IMBECILITY; want of intelligence &c. 498, want of intellect &c. 450; shallowness, unwisdom, silliness, foolishness &c. *adj.*; morosis, incapacity, vacancy of mind, poverty of intellect, clouded perception, poor head; apartments –, rooms –, space- to let [*all slang*]; nobody home [*slang*]; stupidity, insulsity [*rare*], stolidity; hebetude, dull understanding, meanest capacity, shortsightedness; incompetence &c. (*unskillfulness*) 699.

BIAS &c. 481; infatuation &c. (*insanity*) 503; one's weak side.

SIMPLICITY, puerility, babyhood; senility, dotage, anility, second childishness, fatuousness, fatuity; idiocy, idiotism, jobbernowlism [*colloq., Eng.*], driveling, driveling idiocy; senile dementia.

FOLLY, frivolity, irrationality, trifling, ineptitude, nugacity, futility, inconsistency, lip wisdom, conceit; sophistry &c. 477; giddiness &c. (*inattention*) 458; eccentricity &c. 503; extravagance &c. (*absurdity*) 497; rashness &c. 863.

act of folly &c. 699.

V. BE IMBECILE &c. *adj.*; have no -brains, – sense &c. 498; have a screw loose [*colloq.*].

TRIFLE, drivel, *radoter* [*F.*], dote; ramble &c. (*madness*) 503; play the -fool, – monkey; take leave of one's senses; not see an inch beyond one's nose; stultify oneself &c. 699; talk nonsense &c. 497.

Adj. [APPLIED TO PERSONS] UNINTELLIGENT, unintellectual, unreasoning; mindless, witless, reasonless, brainless; half-baked [*colloq.*], having no head &c. 498; not bright &c. 498; inapprehensive, thick [*colloq.*].

blockish, unteachable; Bœotian, Bœotic; bovine; ungifted, undiscerning, un-

PENETRATE; see through, see at a glance, see with half an eye, see far into, see through a millstone [colloq.]; discern &c. (descry) 441; foresee &c. 510.

DISCRIMINATE &c. 465; know what's what [colloq.] &c. 698; listen to reason.

Adj. [APPLIED TO PERSONS] INTELLI-GENT, quick of apprehension, keen, acute, alive, brainy [colloq.], awake, bright, quick, sharp; quick-, keen-, clear-, sharp- -eyed, -sighted, -witted; wide-awake; canny or cannie [archaic or dial.], sly, pawky [dial.], shrewd, astute; clear-headed; farsighted &c. 510; discerning, perspicacious, pene-trating, piercing; argute; nimble-witted, needle-witted; sharp as a needle; alive to &c. (cognizant) 490; clever &c. (apt) 698; arch &c. (cunning) 702; pas si bête [F.]; acute &c. 682.

WISE, sage, sapient [often in irony], sagacious, reasonable, rational, sound, in one's right mind, sensible, abnormis sapiens [L.], judicious, strong-minded.

IMPARTIAL, unprejudiced, unbiased, unbigoted, unprepossessed; undazzled, unperplexed; of unwarped judgment, equitable, fair.

COOL; cool-, long-, hard-, strong-headed; long-sighted, calculating, thoughtful, reflecting; solid, deep, pro-found.

PRUDENT &c. (cautious) 864; sober, staid, solid; considerate, politic, wise in one's generation; watchful &c. 459; provident &c. (prepared) 673; in ad-vance of one's age; wise as -a serpent, – Solomon, – Solon, – Nestor, –Mentor. oracular; heaven-directed, heaven-born.

[APPLIED TO ACTIONS] WISE, sensible, reasonable, judicious; well-judged, well-advised; prudent, politic; expedient &c. 646.

₊ aut regem aut fatuum nasci oportet; "but with the morning cool reflection came" [Scott]; flosculi sententiarum; les affaires font les hommes; más vale saber que haber; más vale ser necio que porfiado; nemo solus sapit [Plau-tus); nosce te; γνῶθι σεαυτόν; nullum magnum ingenium sine mixtura dementiæ fuit [Seneca, from Aristotle]; sapere aude [Horace]; victrix fortunæ sapientia [Juvenal]; "wisdom is the principal thing; therefore, get wisdom; and with all thy getting get understanding" [Bible]; "genius is always sufficiently the enemy of genius by over-influence" [Emerson]; "I may not deal with wisdom, being a king" [Masefield].

196

enlightened, unwise, unphilosophical; apish, simious, simian.

weak-, addle-, puzzle-, blunder-, muddle- [colloq.], jolter-, jolt-, chowder-, pig-, beetle-, buffle- [obs.], chuckle-, mutton-, gross- headed; maggot-pated [obs.], beef-headed, beef-witted, fat-headed, fat-witted.

WEAK-MINDED, feeble-minded; dull-, shallow-, lack- brained; rattle- brained, -headed; sap-head [colloq.], muddy-brained, addle-brained; half-, lean-, short-, shallow-, dull-, blunt- witted; shallow-, clod-, addle- pated; dim-, short- sighted; thick-skulled; thick-headed; weak in the upper story [colloq.], inapprehensible, nutty [slang]. batty [slang], balmy in the crumpet [slang], loony or luny [slang].

SHALLOW, borné [F.], weak, wanting, soft [colloq.], sappy, spoony or spooney [slang]; dull, – as a beetle.

STUPID, heavy, insulse [rare], obtuse, blunt, stolid, doltish; asinine; inapt &c. 699; prosaic &c. 843; hebetudinous, hebetate, hebete [rare].

CHILDISH, childlike; infantine, infantile, babyish, babish; puerile, senile, anile; simple &c. (credulous) 486; old-womanish.

IMBECILE, fatuous, idiotic, driveling; blatant, babbling; vacant; sottish; be-wildered &c. 475.

FOOLISH, silly, senseless, irrational, insensate, nonsensical, inept; maudlin.

NARROW-MINDED &c. 481; bigoted &c. (obstinate) 606; giddy &c. (thoughtless) 458; rash &c. 863; eccentric &c. (crazed) 503.

[APPLIED TO ACTIONS] FOOLISH, un-wise, injudicious, improper, unreason-able, without reason, ridiculous, silly, stupid, asinine; ill-imagined, ill-advised, ill-judged, ill-devised; mal entendu [F.]; inconsistent, irrational, unphilosophical; extravagant &c. (nonsensical) 497; sleeveless [obs.], idle; useless &c. 645; inexpedient &c. 647; frivolous &c. (trivial) 643.

₊ Davus sum non Œdipus; "a fool's bolt is soon shot" [Henry V]; clitellæ bovi sunt im-positæ [Cicero]; "fools rush in where angels fear to tread" [Pope]; il n'a ni bouche ni éperon; "the bookful blockhead, ignorantly read" [Pope]; "to varnish nonsense with the charms of sound" [Churchill]; "And duller should'st thou be than the fat weed That roots itself in ease on Lethe wharf" [Hamlet]; "men are so necessarily foolish that not to be a fool is merely a varied freak of folly" [Pascal].

500. Sage. — N. SAGE, wise man; master mind, master spirit of the age; longhead, thinker, philosopher.

AUTHORITY, oracle, mentor, luminary, shining light, *esprit fort* [*F.*], *magnus Apollo* [*L.*], Solon, Solomon, Buddha, Confucius, Mentor, Nestor, the Magi; Seven Wise Men of Greece, Seven Sages, Philosophical Pleiad; "second Daniel."

savant [*F.*], pundit &c. (*scholar*) 492; wiseacre [*archaic or ironical*]; expert &c. 700; wizard &c. 994.

Adj. VENERABLE, venerated, reverenced, revered, honored, looked up to; authoritative, wise, oracular; erudite &c. (*knowledge*) 490; *emeritus* [*L.*].

⁎⁎* *barbâ tenus sapientes;* "O wise young judge, how I do honor thee" [*M. of V.*].

501. Fool. — N. FOOL, idiot, tomfool, wiseacre, simpleton, Simple Simon, moron, gaby [*colloq.*], witling, dizzard [*obs.*], donkey, ass; ninny, ninny hammer, chowderhead [*dial.*], jolterhead *or* jolthead, mutt [*slang*], chucklehead [*colloq.*], dolt, booby, tomnoddy, loony *or* luny [*slang*], looby, hoddy-doddy [*obs.*], noddy, nonny [*dial.*], noodle, nizy [*obs.*], owl, goose, imbecile; *radoteur* [*F.*], nincompoop [*colloq.*], *badaud* [*F.*], zany [*Eng.*]; trifler, babbler; pretty fellow; natural, *niais* [*F.*].

child, baby, infant, innocent, milksop, sop.

oaf, lout, loon *or* lown [*dial.*]; bullhead, blunderhead, addle-pate, addlebrain, addlehead [*all colloq.*]; blockhead, dullhead, bonehead [*slang*], rattlepate, dullard, doodle [*obs.*], calf [*colloq.*], colt,

buzzard [*obs.*], block, put, stick [*colloq.*], stock, numps [*obs.*], tony [*obs.*]; loggerhead, beetlehead, grosshead [*obs.*], muttonhead [*colloq.*], noodlehead, giddyhead [*colloq.*], numskull [*colloq.*], thickhead [*colloq.*], thick skull; lackbrain, shallowbrain; halfwit, lackwit; dunderpate; lunkhead [*U. S.*].

sawney [*dial. Eng.*], clod, clodhopper; clodpoll, clodpate, clotpole *or* clotpoll [*obs.*], clotpate [*obs.*], soft *or* softy [*colloq. or slang*], saphead [*slang*], bull calf [*colloq.*], spoony *or* spooney [*slang*], gawk, gawky, gowk, Gothamite, lummox [*dial.*], rube [*U. S.*]; men of Bœotia, wise men of Gotham.

un sot à triple étage [*F.*], sot [*Scot.*], jobbernowl [*colloq., Eng.*], changeling [*archaic*], mooncalf, *gobe-mouches* [*F.*].

greenhorn &c. (*dupe*) 547; dunce &c. (*ignoramus*) 493; lubber &c. (*bungler*) 701; madman &c. 504; solid ivory.

one who -will not set the Thames on fire, – did not invent gunpowder, – does not exactly scintillate; *qui n'a pas inventé la poudre* [*F.*]; no conjuror; no Solomon.

DOTARD, driveler; old fogy *or* fogey [*colloq.*], old woman; crone, grandmother; cotquean [*archaic*], henhussy, betty [*contempt*].

⁎⁎* *fortuna favet fatuis; les fous font les festins et les sages les mangent; nomina stultorum parietibus hærent; stultorum plena sunt omnia* [Cicero]; "a fool and his money are soon parted"; "where ignorance is bliss, 'tis folly to be wise" [Gray]; "Cruel children, crying babies All grow up as geese and gabies, Hated, as their age increases, By their nephews and their nieces" [Stevenson]; "a rosebud need not have a mind" [Masefield]; "you may lead an ass to knowledge, but you cannot make him think" [*Cynic's Calendar*].

502. Sanity. — N. SANITY; soundness &c. *adj.;* rationality, normalcy, normality, sobriety, lucidity, lucid interval; senses, sober senses, common sense, horse sense [*colloq.*], sound mind, *mens sana* [*L.*].

V. BE SANE &c. *adj.;* retain one's senses, – reason.

BECOME SANE &c. *adj.;* come to one's senses, sober down, cool down, get things into proportion, see things in proper perspective.

RENDER SANE &c. *adj.;* bring to one's senses, sober, bring to reason.

Adj. SANE, rational, normal, whole-

503. Insanity. — N. INSANITY, lunacy; madness &c. *adj.,* mania, rabies, furor, mental alienation, aberration, amentia, paranoia; dementation, dementia, demency [*rare*], morosis, idiocy; *dementia a potu* [*L.*], delirium tremens, D. T.'s, the horrors [*colloq.*]; phrenitis, frenzy, raving, incoherence, wandering, delirium, calenture of the brain, delusion, hallucination; lycanthropy; brain storm.

DERANGEMENT; disordered -reason, – intellect; diseased –, unsound –, abnormal- mind; unsoundness.

VERTIGO, dizziness, swimming, sunstroke, *coup de soleil* [*F.*], siriasis.

some, right-minded, reasonable, *compos mentis* [*L.*], of sound mind; sound, sound-minded; lucid.

self-possessed; sober, sober-minded.

in one's -sober senses, – right mind; in possession of one's faculties.

Adv. SANELY &c. *adj.*; in reason, within reason, within bounds; according to the dictates of -reason, – common sense; in the name of common sense.

** *Quisnam igitur̄ sanus? Qui non stultus* [Horace].

ODDITY, eccentricity, twist, monomania; fanaticism, infatuation, craze; kleptomania, dipsomania; hypochondriasis &c. (*low spirits*) 837; melancholia, hysteria.

screw –, tile –, slate- loose; bee in one's bonnet, rats in the upper story, bats in the belfry, bee in the head [*all colloq.*].

dotage &c. (*imbecility*) 499.

V. BE *or* BECOME INSANE &c. *adj.*; lose one's senses, – reason, – faculties, – wits; go mad, run mad; rave, dote, ramble, wander; drivel &c. (*be imbecile*) 499; have a screw loose &c. *n.*, have a devil; *avoir le diable au corps* [*F.*]; lose one's head &c. (*be uncertain*) 475.

DERANGE; render *or* drive mad &c. *adj.*; madden, dementate [*rare*], addle the wits, derange the head, infatuate, befool; turn the brain, turn one's head.

Adj. INSANE, mad, lunatic; crazy, crazed, *aliéné* [*F.*], *non compos mentis* [*L.*], not right, dement [*rare*], dementate, cracked [*colloq.*], touched; bereft of reason; all-possessed, unhinged, unsettled in one's mind; insensate, reasonless, beside oneself, demented, maniacal, daft; frenzied, frenetic *or* frenetical; possessed, – with a devil; deranged, far gone, maddened, moonstruck; shatterpated, shatterbrained; madbrained, scatterbrained, crack-brained; off one's head.

Corybantic, dithyrambic; rabid, giddy, vertiginous, wild; haggard, mazed; flighty; distracted, distraught; bewildered &c. (*uncertain*) 475.

mad as a -March hare, – hatter; of unsound mind &c. *n.*; touched –, wrong –, not right- in one's -head, – mind, – wits, – upper story [*colloq.*]; out of one's -mind, – senses, – wits; not in one's right mind; nutty [*slang*].

ODD, fanatical, infatuated, eccentric; hypochondriac, hyppish [*rare*], hipped *or* hypped [*colloq.*], hippish [*colloq.*].

DELIRIOUS, light-headed, incoherent, rambling, doting, wandering; frantic, raving, stark mad, stark staring mad.

IMBECILE, silly, &c. 499.

Adv. like one possessed.

** the mind having lost its balance; the reason under a cloud; *tête exaltée; tête montée; ira furor brevis est; omnes stultos insanire* [Horace]; "great wits are sure to madness near allied" [Dryden]; "moping melancholy and moon-struck madness" [Milton]; "And moody madness laughing wild Amid severest woe" [Gray]; "Though this be madness, yet there is method in't" [Hamlet]; "no excellent soul is exempt from a mixture of madness" [Aristotle]; "Fetter strong madness in a silken thread" [*Much Ado About Nothing*]; "That he is mad, 'tis true, 'tis true, 'tis pity; And pity 'tis 'tis true [Hamlet]; "we are not ourselves When nature, being oppress'd, commands the mind To suffer with the body" [King Lear].

504. Madman. — N. MADMAN, lunatic, maniac, bedlamite, candidate for Bedlam, raver, phrenetic, madcap; energumen [*eccl. antiq.*]; automaniac, monomaniac, dipsomaniac, kleptomaniac, paranoiac; hypochondriac &c. (*low spirits*) 837; crank [*colloq.*], Tom o' Bedlam; nut [*slang*].

DREAMER &c. 515; rhapsodist, seer, highflyer *or* highflier [*obs.*], enthusiast, fanatic, *fanatico* [*It.*], *exalté* [*F.*], Don Quixote, Ophelia, Madge Wildfire.

IDIOT &c. 501.

** "The lunatic, the lover, and the poet Are of imagination all compact" [*M. N. D.*]; "There is a pleasure, sure, In being mad, which none but madmen know" [Dryden]; "O, what a noble mind is here o'erthrown!" [Hamlet]; "who knows of madness whether it is divine or whether it be of the pit" [Dunsany].

Section VI. EXTENSION OF THOUGHT

1. To the Past

505. Memory. — N. MEMORY, remembrance; retentivity, retention, retentiveness; tenacity; *veteris vestigia flammæ* [*L.*]; tablets of the memory; readiness.

retentive –, tenacious –, trustworthy –, capacious –, faithful –, correct –, exact –, ready –, prompt- memory; Memory's halls, Memory's pictures.

RECOLLECTION, reminiscence, recognition, recurrence, rememoration [*rare*], rememorance [*rare*]; retrospect, retrospection; "that inward eye" [Wordsworth]; afterthought.

REMINDER; suggestion &c. (*information*) 527; prompting &c. *v.*; hint, token of remembrance, memento, souvenir, keepsake, relic, memorandum (*pl.* memoranda); remembrancer, flapper; memorial &c. (*record*) 551; commemoration &c. (*celebration*) 883.

things to be remembered, memorabilia.

MNEMONICS; art of –, artificial- memory; *memoria technica* [*L.*]; mnemotechnics, mnemotechny; Mnemosyne.

AIDS TO MEMORY, jogger [*colloq.*], memorandum book, notebook, promptbook, engagement book.

FAME, celebrity, renown, reputation &c. (*repute*) 873.

V. REMEMBER, mind [*obsoles.*], rememorate [*rare*]; retain the -memory, - remembrance- of; keep in view.

have –, hold –, bear –, carry –, keep–, retain- in *or* in the -thoughts, – mind, – memory, – remembrance; be in –, live

506. Oblivion. — N. OBLIVION; forgetfulness &c. *adj.*; obliteration &c. (552) of –, insensibility &c. (823) to- the past.

short –, treacherous –, loose –, slippery –, failing- memory; decay –, failure –, lapse- of memory; mind –, memory- like a sieve; untrustworthy memory; waters of -Lethe, – oblivion; amnesia.

AMNESTY, general pardon.

V. FORGET; be forgetful &c. *adj.*; fall –, sink- into oblivion; have a short memory &c. *n.*, have no head.

forget one's own name, have on the tip of one's tongue, come in at one ear and go out at the other.

slip –, escape –, fade from –, die away from- the memory; lose, lose sight of.

EFFACE &c. (552) –, discharge- from the memory; unlearn; consign to -oblivion, – the tomb of the Capulets; think no more of &c. (*turn the attention from*) 458; cast behind one's back, wean one's thoughts from; let bygones be bygones &c. (*forgive*) 918.

Adj. FORGOTTEN &c. *v.*; unremembered, past recollection, bygone, out of mind; buried –, sunk- in oblivion; clean forgotten; gone out of one's -head, – recollection.

FORGETFUL, oblivious, mindless, Lethean; insensible &c. (823) to the past; heedless.

*** *non mi ricordo;* the memory -failing, – deserting one, – being at (*or* in) fault.

---

in –, remain in –, dwell in –, haunt –, impress- one's -memory, – thoughts, – mind.

sink in the mind; run in the head; not be able to get it out of one's head; be deeply impressed with; rankle &c. (*revenge*) 919.

recognize, bethink oneself, recall, call up, conjure up, retrace; look –, trace- -back, – backwards; think upon, look back upon; review; call –, recall –, bring- to -mind, – remembrance; carry one's thoughts back; rake up the past.

redeem from oblivion; keep the -memory. alive, – wound green; *tangere ulcus* [*L.*]; keep the memory green, keep up the memory of; commemorate &c. (*celebrate*) 883.

RECOLLECT, recur to the mind; flash on the mind, flash across the memory.

REMIND; suggest &c. (*inform*) 527; prompt; put –, keep- in mind; fan the embers; call up, summon up; renew; *infandum renovare dolorem* [*L.*]; task –, tax –, jog –, flap –, refresh – rub up –, awaken- the memory; pull by the sleeve; bring back to the memory, put in remembrance, memorialize.

MEMORIZE, commit to memory; con, – over; fix –, rivet –, imprint –, impress –, stamp –, grave –, engrave –, store –, treasure up –, bottle up –, embalm –, bury –, enshrine- in the memory; load –, store –, stuff –, burden- the memory

with; get –, have –, learn –, know –, say –, repeat- by -heart, – rote; get –,
drive- into one's head; bury in the mind; say one's lesson; repeat, – like a parrot;
have at one's fingers' ends.

make a note of &c. (*record*) 551.

Adj. REMEMBERING, remembered &c. *v.*; mindful, reminiscential; alive in memory; retained in the memory &c. *v.*; pent up in one's memory; fresh; green, – in remembrance; still vivid, rememorant [*rare*]; not –, never -to be erased, – to be forgotten; unforgettable *or* unforgetable; enduring, – in memory; unforgotten, present to the mind; within one's memory &c. *n.*; indelible; uppermost in one's thoughts; memorable &c. (*important*) 642; suggestive.

Adv. BY HEART, *par cœur* [*F.*], by rote; without book, *memoriter* [*L.*].

IN MEMORY OF; *in memoriam* [*L.*]; *memoriâ in æternâ* [*L.*].

** *manet altâ mente repostum* [Vergil]; *forsan et hæc olim meminisse juvabit* [Vergil]; *absens hæres non erit; beatæ memoriæ:* "briefly thyself remember" [*Lear*]; *mendacem memorem esse oportet* [Quintilian]; "memory, the warder of the brain" [*Macbeth*]; *parsque est meminisse doloris* [Ovid]; "To live in hearts we leave behind, Is not to die" [Campbell]; *vox audita perit littera scripta manet; monumentum ære perennius* [Horace]; "Music, when soft voices die, Vibrates in the memory; Odours, when sweet violets sicken, Live within the sense they quicken" [Shelley]; "Lest we forget" [Kipling]; "They flash upon that inward eye Which is the bliss of solitude" [Wordsworth].

2. To the Future

507. Expectation. — N. EXPECTATION, expectance, expectancy; anticipation, contingency, contingent, reckoning, calculation; foresight &c. 510; contemplation, prospection.

PROSPECT, lookout [*chiefly Eng.*], perspective, horizon, vista; destiny &c. 152; futures [*stock exchange*].

SUSPENSE, waiting, abeyance; curiosity &c. 455; anxious –, ardent –, eager –, breathless –, sanguine- expectation; torment of Tantalus.

ASSURANCE, confidence, presumption, reliance; hope &c. 858; trust &c. (*belief*) 484; prognosis [*med.*], prognostic, prognostication; auspices &c. (*prediction*) 511.

V. EXPECT; look -for, – out for, – forward to; hope for, anticipate; have in -prospect, – contemplation; keep in view; contemplate, promise oneself; not wonder at *or* if &c. 870.

WAIT FOR, tarry for, lie in wait for, watch for, bargain for; keep a -good, – sharp -lookout for; await; stand at "attention," abide, mark time, bide one's time, watch.

prick up one's ears, hold one's breath.

FORESEE &c. 510; prepare for &c. 673; forestall &c. (*be early*) 132; count upon &c. (*believe in*) 484; think likely &c. (*probability*) 472; bargain for; make one's mouth water.

PREDICT, prognosticate, forecast; lead one to expect &c. (*predict*) 511; have in store for &c. (*destiny*) 152.

508. Inexpectation. — N. INEXPECTATION [*rare*], nonexpectation; unforeseen contingency, the unforeseen; false expectation &c. (*disappointment*) 509; miscalculation &c. 481.

SURPRISE, sudden burst, thunderclap, blow, shock; bolt out of the blue; surprisement [*rare*], astoundment [*rare*], astonishment, mazement [*rare*], amazement; wonder &c. 870; eye opener.

V. NOT EXPECT &c. 507; be taken by surprise; start; miscalculate &c. 481; not bargain for; come –, fall- upon.

BE UNEXPECTED &c. *adj.*; come unawares &c. *adv.*; turn up, pop [*colloq.*], drop from the clouds; come –, burst –, flash –, bounce –, steal –, creep- upon one; come –, burst- like a -thunderclap, -thunderbolt; take –, catch- -by surprise, – unawares; catch napping, catch off one's guard; yach [*S. Africa*].

SURPRISE, startle, take aback [*colloq.*], electrify, stun, stagger, take away one's breath, throw off one's guard; pounce upon, spring, spring upon, spring a mine upon; stound [*archaic*], astound; astonish &c. (*strike with wonder*) 870.

Adj. NONEXPECTANT, inexpectant; surprised &c. *v.*; unwarned, unaware; off one's guard; inattentive &c. 458.

UNEXPECTED, unanticipated, unlooked for, unforeseen, unhoped for; dropped from the clouds; beyond –, contrary to –, against- expectation; out of one's reckoning; unheard of &c. (*exceptional*)

Adj. EXPECTANT; expecting &c. *v.;* in expectation &c. *n.;* on the watch &c. (*vigilant*) 459; open-eyed, open-mouthed; agape, gaping, all agog; on tenterhooks, on tiptoe, on the tiptoe of expectation; *aux aguets* [*F.*]; ready, prepared, provided for, provisional, provident; curious &c. 455; looking forward to; on the rack.

EXPECTED &c. *v.;* long expected, foreseen; in prospect &c. *n.;* prospective, future, forward [*com.*], coming; in one's eye, in view, on the horizon; impending &c. (*destiny*) 152.

Adv. EXPECTANTLY; on the watch &c. *adj.;* in the event of; as a possible contingency; with muscles tense, on edge [*colloq.*]; with eyes -, with ears -strained; with ears pricked forward; *arrectis auribus* [*L.*]; with breathless expectation &c. *n.,* with bated breath.

SOON, shortly, forthwith, anon [*archaic*], presently; prospectively &c. 121.

⁎ we shall see; *nous verrons;* "expectation whirls me round" [*Troilus and Cressida*].

83, startling; sudden &c. (*instantaneous*) 113.

Adv. UNEXPECTEDLY, abruptly, plump, pop, *à l'improviste* [*F.*], unawares; without -notice, – warning, – saying "by your leave"; like a thief in the night, like a thunderbolt; like a lightning flash; in an unguarded moment; suddenly &c. (*instantaneously*) 113.

Int. heydey! &c. (*wonder*) 870; do tell! [*colloq., U. S.*].

⁎ little did one -think, – expect; nobody would ever -suppose, – think, – expect; who would have thought? it beats the Dutch; it is the unexpected that happens.

---

509. [FAILURE OF EXPECTATION.] **Disappointment. — N.** DISAPPOINTMENT; blighted hope, disillusion, balk; blow; slip 'twixt cup and lip; nonfulfillment of one's hopes; sad -, bitter- disappointment; trick of fortune; afterclap; false –, vain-expectation; miscalculation &c. 481; fool's paradise; much cry and little wool.

V. BE DISAPPOINTED; look blank, look blue [*colloq.*]; look *or* stand aghast &c. (*wonder*) 870; find to one's cost; laugh on the wrong side of one's mouth [*colloq.*], laugh out of the other corner of the mouth [*colloq.*]; find one a false prophet.

DISAPPOINT; crush -, dash -, balk -, disappoint -, blight -, falsify -, defeat -, not realize- one's -hope, – expectation; balk, jilt, bilk; play one -false, – a trick; dash the cup from the lips; tantalize; dumfounder *or* dumbfounder, dumfound *or* dumbfound, disillusion, disillusionize; come short of; dissatisfy, make dissatisfied, disgruntle.

Adj. DISAPPOINTED &c. *v.;* disconcerted, aghast; disgruntled; out of one's reckoning; short of expectations.

⁎ the mountain brought forth a mouse; *parturiunt montes nascetur ridiculus mus* [Horace]; *dis aliter visum* [Vergil]; the bubble burst; one's countenance falling.

---

510. Foresight. — N. FORESIGHT, prospicience, prevision, long-sightedness, farsightedness; anticipation; providence &c. (*preparation*) 673.

FORETHOUGHT, forecast; predeliberation, presurmise; foregone conclusion &c. (*prejudgment*) 481; prudence &c. (*caution*) 864.

FOREKNOWLEDGE, precognition, prescience, prenotion, presentiment; second sight; sagacity &c. (*intelligence*) 498; antepast, prelibation; prophasis [*med.*], prognosis [*med.*].   -

PROSPECT &c. (*expectation*) 507; foretaste; prospectus &c. (*plan*) 626.

V. FORESEE; look -forwards to, – ahead, – beyond; scent from afar; feel it in one's bones [*colloq.*]; look -, pry -, peep- into the future.

see one's way; see how the -land lies, – wind blows, – cat jumps [*colloq.*].

ANTICIPATE; expect &c. 507; be beforehand &c. (*early*) 132; predict &c. 511; foreknow, forejudge, forecast; surmise; have an eye to the -future, – main chance; *respicere finem* [*L.*]; keep a sharp lookout &c. (*vigilance*) 459; forewarn &c. 668.

Adj. FORESEEING &c. *v.;* prescient, anticipatory; farseeing, farsighted, long-sighted; sagacious &c. (*intelligent*) 498; weatherwise; provident &c. (*prepared*) 673; on the lookout, – for; prospective &c. 507.

Adv. against the time when; for a rainy day.

⁎ *cernit omnia Deus vindex; mihi cura futuri.*

511. Prediction. — N. PREDICTION, announcement; program *or* programme
&c. (*plan*) 626; premonition &c. (*warning*) 668; prognosis, prognostic, presage,
presagement, precurse [*obs.*], prophecy, vaticination, mantology [*rare*], prognostication, premonstration [*obs.*]; augury, auguration [*obs.*], ariolation [*obs.*], hario-
lation [*obs.*], foreboding, aboding [*obs.*], abode [*obs.*], bode [*obs.*], bodement,
abodement; omniation [*obs.*], auspice (*pl.* auspices), forecast; omen &c. 512; horoscope, nativity; sooth [*obs.*], soothsaying, fortune-telling; divination.

adytum, oak of Dodona; cave of the Cumæan Sibyl, Sibylline leaves, Sibylline
books; tripod of the Pythia.

prefiguration, prefigurement; prototype, type.

[DIVINATION BY THE STARS] astrology, astromancy, horoscopy, genethlialogy,
judicial *or* mundane astrology.

ORACLE, prophet, seer &c. 513.

[MEANS OF DIVINATION] crystal, ink, tea leaves, cards; Hallowe'en -nuts,
mirror; divining-rod, wych-hazel *or* witch-hazel; hand of glory; wax image; tera-
phim; shadows &c. [*see footnote*]; spell, charm &c. 993.

sorcery, magic, necromancy &c. 992; heteroscopic divination.[1]

V. PREDICT, prognosticate, prophesy, vaticinate, divine, foretell, soothsay, augurate, tell fortunes; cast a horoscope, cast a nativity; advise; forewarn, prewarn
&c. 668.

presage, augur, bode, abode [*obs.*], forebode; foretoken, betoken; prefigure, pre-
figurate, augurate [*rare*], ariolate [*rare*], figure [*obs.*], forecast, precurse, portend;
preshow, foreshow, foreshadow; shadow forth, typify, pretypify, ominate [*obs.*],
signify, point to.

hold out -, raise -, excite- -expectation, - hope; bid fair, promise, lead one to
expect; be the precursor &c. 64.

HERALD, usher in, premise, announce; lower.

Adj. PREDICTING &c. *v.;* predictive, prophetic, fatidic *or* fatidical, precursal, pre-
current, presageful, vaticinal, oracular, fatiloquent [*rare*], haruspical; Sibylline;
weatherwise.

OMINOUS, portentous; augurous, augurial, augural, precursive, precursory, auspi-
cial, auspicious; prescious [*rare*], prescient, monitory, extispicious [*obs.*], premonitory, significant of, pregnant with, big with the fate of.

** "If you can look into the seeds of time, And say which grain will grow and which will
not" [Macbeth]; "coming events cast their shadows before" [Campbell]; *dicamus bona verba;*
"there buds the promise of celestial worth" [Young].

---

[1] The following terms, expressive of different forms of divination, have been collected from
various sources, and are here given as a curious illustration of bygone superstitions:

Divination *by oracles*, theomancy; *by the Bible*, Bibliomancy; *by ghosts*, psychomancy; *by
crystal gazing*, crystallomancy; *by shadows or manes*, sciomancy; *by appearances in the air*,
aëromancy, chaomancy; *by the stars at birth*, genethliacs; *by meteors*, meteoromancy; *by winds*,
austromancy; *by sacrificial appearances*, aruspicy (*or* haruspicy), hieromancy, hieroscopy; *by the
entrails of animals sacrificed*, extispicy, hieromancy; *by the entrails of a human sacrifice*, anthropomancy; *by the entrails of fishes*, ichthyomancy; *by sacrificial fire*, pyromancy; *by redhot iron*,
sideromancy; *by the smoke from the altar*, capnomancy; *by mice*, myomancy; *by birds*, orniscopy,
ornithomancy; *by a cock picking up grains*, alectryomancy (*or* alectoromancy); *by snakes*,
ophiomancy; *by herbs*, botanomancy; *by water*, hydromancy; *by fountains*, pegomancy; *by a wand*,
rhabdomancy; *by dough of cakes*, crithomancy; *by meal*, aleuromancy, alphitomancy; *by salt*,
halomancy; *by lead*, molybdomancy; *by dice*, cléromancy; *by arrows*, belomancy; *by a balanced hatchet*, axinomancy; *by a balanced sieve*, coscinomancy; *by a suspended ring*, dactyliomancy; *by dots made at random on paper*, geomancy; *by precious stones*, lithomancy; *by pebbles*,
pessomancy; *by pebbles drawn from a heap*, psephomancy; *by mirrors*, catoptromancy; *by writings
in ashes*, tephramancy; *by dreams*, oneiromancy; *by the hand*, palmistry, chiromancy; *by nails
reflecting the sun's rays*, onychomancy; *by finger rings*, dactylomancy; *by numbers*, arithmancy;
by drawing lots, sortilege; *by passages in books*, stichomancy; *by the letters forming the name of the
person*, onomancy, nomancy; *by the features*, anthroposcopy; *by the mode of laughing*, geloscopy;
by ventriloquism, gastromancy; *by walking in a circle*, gyromancy; *by dropping melted wax into
water*, ceromancy; *by currents*, bletonism; *by the color and peculiarities of wine*, œnomancy; *by the
shoulder blade*, scapulimancy *or* scapulomancy, omoplatoscopy.

512. Omen. — N. OMEN, portent, presage, prognostic, augury, auspice; sign &c. (*indication*) 550; harbinger &c. (*precursor*) 64; yule candle, yule log *or* clog.

bird of ill omen; halcyon birds; signs of the times; gathering clouds, thunder, lightning, rainbow, comet, shooting star; rain of blood, warning &c. 668.

prefigurement &c. 511; adytum &c. 511.

Adj. ILL-BODING, ill-omened, inauspicious.

*** *auspicium melioris ævi.*

513. Oracle. — N. ORACLE; prophet, seer, soothsayer, augur, medium, clairvoyant, palmist, fortune teller, prophetess, sibyl, witch, geomancer, haruspice *or* aruspice, haruspex *or* aruspex; Sibyl; python, pythoness, Pythia; Pythian oracle, Delphian (*or* Delphic) oracle; Monitor, Sphinx, Tiresias, Cassandra, Sibylline leaves; oak –, oracle- of Dodona; sorcerer &c. 994; interpreter &c. 524.

WEATHER PROPHET, weather sharp [*slang*], weather bureau, Old Probabilities *or* Old Prob. [*humorous nickname for U. S. weather bureau*]; Old Moore, Zadkiel.

*** "it is not enough for a prophet to believe in his message; he must believe in its acceptability" [Chesterton].

Section VII. CREATIVE THOUGHT

514. Supposition. — N. SUPPOSITION, assumption, supposal, supposableness [*rare*], suppositality [*obs.*], postulation [*rare*], condition, presupposition, hypothesis, postulate, postulatum, theory, data; proposition, position; thesis, theorem; proposal &c (*plan*) 626; assumed position.

bare –, vague –, loose- -supposition, – suggestion; conceit; conjecture; guess, guesswork; rough guess, shot [*colloq.*]; conjecturality [*rare*], suggestiveness, presurmise, surmise, suspicion, inkling, suggestion, association of ideas, hint; presumption &c. (*belief*) 484; divination, speculation.

THEORIST, theorizer, speculatist [*rare*], speculator, notionalist, hypothesist, hypothetist [*rare*], doctrinaire, doctrinarian.

V. SUPPOSE, conjecture, surmise, suspect, guess, divine; theorize; presume, presuppose; assume, fancy, wis [*archaic*], take it; give a guess, speculate, believe, dare say, take it into one's head, take for granted.

PROPOUND, propose, put forth; start, put a case, submit, move, make a motion; hazard –, venture –, throw out –, put forward- a -suggestion, – conjecture, – supposition; hypothesize.

SUGGEST, allude to, hint, put it into one's head.

suggest itself &c. (*thought*) 451; run in the head &c. (*memory*) 505; marvel - . wonder- -if, – whether.

Adj. SUPPOSING &c. *v.;* given, mooted, postulatory [*now rare*]; assumed &c. *v.;* suppositive, supposititious; gratuitous, speculative, conjectural, conjecturable, hypothetical, theoretical, academic, supposable, presumptive, putative; suppositional, suppositionary.

SUGGESTIVE, allusive, stimulating.

Adv. IF, if so be; an [*archaic*]; on the supposition &c. *n.; ex hypothesi* [*L.*], in case, in the event of; if that [*archaic*], so that, whether; quasi, as if, provided; perhaps &c. (*by possibility*) 470; for aught one knows.

515. Imagination. — N. IMAGINATION, originality, invention; fancy; inspiration; verve.

warm –, heated –, excited –, sanguine –, ardent –, fiery –, boiling –, wild –, bold –, daring –, playful –, lively –, fertile- -imagination, – fancy.

"mind's eye" [*Hamlet*]; "the mind's internal heaven" [Wordsworth]; "such stuff as dreams are made on " [*Tempest*].

IDEALITY, idealism; romanticism, utopianism, castle-building; dreaming; frenzy *or* phrensy, ecstasy; calenture &c. (*delirium*) 503; reverie *or* revery, brown study, pipe dream, daydream, trance; somnambulism.

conception, *Vorstellung* [*Ger.*], excogitation, "a fine frenzy" [*M. N. D.*]; cloudland, dreamland; flight –, fumes– of fancy; "thick-coming fancies" [*Macbeth*]; creation –, coinage– of the brain; imagery; word painting.

FANTASY, conceit, figment, myth, dream, vision, shadow, chimera; phantasm, phantasy, fancy; maggot, whim, whimwham, whimsey *or* whimsy, vagary, rhapsody, romance, gest *or* geste, extravaganza; "air-drawn dagger" [*Macbeth*], bugbear, nightmare; flying Dutchman, great sea serpent, man in the moon, castle in the air, castle in Spain, *château en Espagne* [*F.*], pleasure dome of Kubla Khan, Utopia; Heavenly City, New Jerusalem; Atlantis, Happy Valley [Johnson], millennium, fairyland; land of Prester John, kingdom of Micomicon; Estotiland *or* Estotilandia [Milton]; Laputa; Cockagne, Lubberland; Arabian nights; *le pot au lait* [*F.*]; pot of gold at the foot of the rainbow; dream of Alnaschar &c. (*hope*) 858; golden dream.

CREATIVE WORKS] work of fiction &c.(*novel*) 594; poetry &c. 597; play, tragedy, comedy &c. (*drama*) 599; sonata &c. (*music*) 415.

ILLUSION &c. (*error*) 495; phantom &c. (*fallacy of vision*) 443; *Fata Morgana* [*L.*] &c. (*ignis fatuus*) 423; vapor &c. (*cloud*) 353; stretch of the imagination &c. (*exaggeration*) 549; mythogenesis.

IDEALIST, romanticist, visionary; mopus [*slang*], romancer, daydreamer, dreamer; somnambulist; rhapsodist &c. (*fanatic*) 504; castle-builder, fanciful projector; "sweetest Shakespeare, Fancy's child" [Milton].

V. IMAGINE, fancy, conceive; idealize, realize; dream, – of; "gives to airy nothing a local habitation and a name" [*M. N. D.*].

set one's wits to work; strain –, crack– one's invention; rack –, ransack –, cudgel– one's brains; excogitate.

give –play, – the reins, – a loose [*obs.*]– to the– –imagination, – fancy; tilt at windmills; indulge in rêverie.

conjure up a vision; fancy –, represent –, picture –, figure– to oneself; *vorstellen* [*Ger.*]; "see visions and dream dreams" [*Bible*].

float in the mind; suggest itself &c. (*thought*) 451.

CREATE, originate, devise, invent, make up, coin, fabricate; improvise, strike out something new.

Adj. IMAGINED &c. *v.; ben trovato* [*It.*]; air-drawn, air-built.

IMAGINATIVE; imagining &c. *v.*; original, inventive, creative, fertile, productive, ingenious.

EXTRAVAGANT, romantic, high-flown, flighty, preposterous; rhapsodic *or* rhapsodical; fanatic, enthusiastic, Utopian, Quixotic.

IDEAL, unreal; in the clouds, *in nubibus* [*L.*]; unsubstantial &c. 4; illusory &c. (*fallacious*) 495; fictitious, theoretical, hypothetical.

fanciful; fabulous, legendary, mythic *or* mythical, mythological, chimerical; imaginary, visionary; dream-beset, dream-ridden, dreamy, entranced, notional, fancy, fantastical, high-fantastical, fantasied, maggoty, made of empty air, vaporous, whimsical; fairy, fairylike.

⁎ "a change came o'er the spirit of my dream" [Byron]; *ægri somnia vana; delphinum appingit sylvis in fluctibus aprum* [Horace]; "your old men shall dream dreams; your young men shall see visions" [*Bible*]; "fancy light from fancy caught" [Tennyson]; "imagination rules the world" [Napoleon]; *l'imagination gallope, le jugement ne va que le pas; musæo contingens cuncta lepore* [Lucretius]; "He is a dreamer; let us leave him: pass" [*Julius Cæsar*]; "For he on honeydew hath fed And drunk the milk of Paradise" [Coleridge]; "Forms more real than living man, Nurslings of immortality" [Shelley]; *tous songes sont mensonges; Wahrheit und Dichtung;* "magic casements, opening on the foam Of perilous seas, in faëry lands forlorn" [Keats]; "O sweet Fancy! let her loose" [*ibid.*]; "the centre cf every man's existence is a dream" [Chesterton]; "this is visionary mania" [Galsworthy].

Division (II) COMMUNICATION OF IDEAS

Section I. Nature of Ideas Communicated

516. [Idea to be conveyed.] **Meaning.** [Thing signified.] — N. mean-ing; signification, significance; sense, expression; import, purport; implication, connotation, essence, force; drift, tenor, spirit, bearing, coloring; scope.

allusion &c. (*latency*) 526; suggestion &c. (*information*) 527; interpretation, acceptation &c. 522; acceptance [*rare*].

general –, broad –, substantial –, colloquial –, literal –, primary –, accepted –, essential –, plain –, simple –, natural –, unstrained –, true &c. (*exact*) 494 –, honest &c. 543 –, *primâ facie* [*L.*] &c. (*manifest*) 525- meaning.

literality; literal –, obvious –, real- -meaning, – sense, – interpretation.

equivalent meaning; interchangeable word, figure of speech &c. 521; equivalent, synonym &c. 522.

thing signified, matter, subject, subject matter, substance, sum and substance; gist &c. 5; argument, text.

V. mean, signify, connote, denote, express; import, purport; convey, imply, breathe, indicate, bespeak, bear a meaning, bear a sense; tell of, speak of; touch on; point to, allude to; drive at; involve &c. (*latency*) 526; declare &c. (*affirm*) 535.

understand by &c. (*interpret*) 522.

synonymize, express by a synonym; paraphrase, state differently.

Adj. meaning &c. *v.;* expressive, suggestive, allusive; significant, significative, significatory; pithy; meaningful; full of –, pregnant with- meaning; explicit &c. 525.

declaratory &c. 535; intelligible &c. 518.

literal, metaphrastic *or* metaphrastical, word-for-word, verbatim; exact, real.

synonymous; tantamount &c.(*equivalent*) 27.

implied &c. (*latent*) 526; understood, tacit.

Adv. to that effect; that is to say &c. (*being interpreted*) 522.

verbatim, literally; evidently, apparently, from the context.

517. [Absence of meaning.] **Unmeaningness.** — N. unmeaningness &c. *adj.;* scrabble, scribble, scrawl, pothooks.

empty sound, dead letter, *vox et præterea nihil* [*L.*]; "a tale Told by an idiot, full of sound and fury, Signifying nothing" [*Macbeth*]; "weasel words" [Roosevelt]; "sounding brass or a tinkling cymbal" [*Bible*].

nonsense, jargon, gibberish, jabber, mere words, hocus-pocus, fustian, rant, bombast, balderdash, palaver, patter [*cant or colloq.*], flummery, verbiage, babble, *bavardage* [*F.*], *baragouin* [*F.*], platitude, *niaiserie* [*F.*]; inanity; flapdoodle [*colloq.*]; rigmarole, rodomontade; truism; *nugæ canoræ* [*L.*]; twaddle, twattle, fudge, trash; poppy-cock [*U.S.*]; stuff, – and nonsense; bosh [*colloq.*], rubbish, moonshine, wish-wash [*slang*], fiddle-faddle [*colloq.*]; absurdity &c. 497; imbecility, folly &c. 499; unintelligibleness, ambiguity, vagueness &c. (*unintelligibility*) 519.

V. mean nothing; be unmeaning &c. *adj.;* twaddle, quibble, jabber, rant, rodomontade, palaver, babble, fiddle-faddle [*colloq.*].

scribble, scrawl, scrabble, scratch.

Adj. unmeaning; meaningless, senseless; nonsensical &c. 497; void of sense &c. 516.

inexpressive, unexpressive; vacant; not significant &c. 516; insignificant.

trashy, washy, wishy-washy [*colloq.*], inane, wash [*obs.*], rubbishy, vague, trumpery, trivial, fiddle-faddle [*colloq.*], twaddling, quibbling.

unmeant, not expressed; tacit &c. (*latent*) 526.

inexpressible, undefinable, ineffable, unutterable, incommunicable.

Int. fudge! stuff! stuff and nonsense! bosh! fiddle-faddle! [*colloq.*]; poppy-cock! oh! la-la! [*F.*]; rubbish! fiddledee-dee! &c. 497.

** "To varnish nonsense with the charms of sound" [Churchill]; "the spirits of the wise sit in the clouds and mock us" [*II Henry IV*].

518. Intelligibility. — N. INTELLIGI-
BILITY; clearness, clarity, explicitness
&c. *adj.;* lucidity, comprehensibility,
perspicuity; legibility, plain speaking
&c. (*manifestation*) 525; precision &c.
494; *phonanta sunetoisi* [*Gr.* φωνᾶντα
συνετοῖσι], a word to the wise.

V. BE INTELLIGIBLE &c. *adj.;* speak
for itself, speak volumes; tell its own
tale, lie on the surface.

RENDER INTELLIGIBLE &c. *adj.;* popularize, simplify, clear up; elucidate &c.
(*explain*) 522.

UNDERSTAND, comprehend; take, – in;
catch, grasp, follow, collect, master,
make out; see with half an eye, see
daylight, see one's way [*all colloq.*];
enter into the ideas of; come to an understanding.

Adj. INTELLIGIBLE; clear, clear as
-day, – noonday, – crystal; lucid; perspicuous, transpicuous; luminous, transparent.

easily understood, easy to understand, for the million, intelligible to the
meanest capacity, popularized.

PLAIN, distinct, clear-cut, hard-hitting, to the point, explicit; positive;
definite &c. (*precise*) 494.

unambiguous, unequivocal, unmistakable &c. (*manifest*) 525, unconfused;
legible, recognizable; obvious &c. 525.

GRAPHIC, telling, vivid; expressive &c.
(*meaning*) 516; illustrative &c. (*explanatory*) 522.

Adv. in plain -terms, – words, – English; hitting the nail on the head.

** he that runs may read &c. (*manifest*)
525; "that wayfaring men, though fools, should
not err therein" [*Bible*].

519. Unintelligibility. — N. UNIN-
TELLIGIBILITY, incomprehensibility, im-
perspicuity [*rare*]; inconceivableness,
unknowability, unknowableness, vagueness &c. *adj.;* obscurity; ambiguity &c.
520; doubtful meaning; uncertainty &c.
475; perplexity &c. (*confusion*) 59;
spinosity; *obscurum per obscurius* [*L.*];
mystification &c. (*concealment*) 528;
latency &c. 526; transcendentalism.

pons asinorum [*L.*], asses' bridge;
double Dutch, high Dutch [*slang*],
Greek, Hebrew, Choctaw; jargon &c.
(*unmeaning*) 517.

ENIGMA, riddle &c. (*secret*) 533; paradox; *dignus vindice nodus* [*L.*]; sealed
book; steganography, cryptography,
freemasonry.

V. BE UNINTELLIGIBLE &c. *adj.;* require explanation &c. 522; have a doubtful meaning, pass comprehension.

RENDER UNINTELLIGIBLE &c. *adj.;*
conceal &c. 528; darken &c. 421; confuse &c. (*derange*) 61; mystify, perplex
&c. (*bewilder*) 475.

NOT UNDERSTAND &c. 518; lose, – the
clew; miss; not know what to make of,
be able to make nothing of, give it up;
not be able to -account for, – make
head or tail of; be at sea &c. (*uncertain*)
475; wonder &c. 870; see through a
glass darkly &c. (*ignorance*) 491.

not understand one another; play at
cross-purposes &c. (*misinterpret*) 523.

Adj. UNINTELLIGIBLE, unaccountable,
undecipherable, undiscoverable, unknowable, unfathomable; incognizable,
inexplicable, inscrutable; inapprehensible, incomprehensible; insolvable, insoluble; impenetrable.

PUZZLING, as Greek to one, unex-
plained, paradoxical, enigmatic *or* enigmatical, indecipherable, illegible.

OBSCURE, crabbed, imperspicuous [*rare*], dark, muddy, clear as mud [*colloq.*],
seen through a mist, dim, nebulous, shrouded in mystery; undiscernible &c. (*invisible*) 447; misty &c. (*opaque*) 426; hidden &c. 528; latent &c. 526; mysterious;
mystic, mystical, acroamatic *or* acroamatical, metempiric *or* metempirical; transcendental; occult, esoteric, recondite, abstruse.

INDEFINITE &c. (*indistinct*) 447; perplexed &c. (*confused*) 59; undetermined,
vague, loose, ambiguous.

INCONCEIVABLE, inconceptible [*obs.*]; searchless; above –, beyond –, past-
comprehension; beyond one's depth; unconceived.

INEXPRESSIBLE, unutterable, ineffable, undefinable, incommunicable.

520. [HAVING A DOUBLE SENSE.] **Equivocalness. — N.** EQUIVOCALNESS &c. *adj.;*
equivocation; double meaning &c. 516; ambiguity, *double entente* [*F., often erron.*
double-entendre], pun, paragram [*rare*], *calembour* [*F.*], quibble, equivoque *or* equi-
voke, anagram; conundrum &c. (*riddle*) 533; word play &c. (*wit*) 842; homonym,

homonymy; amphiboly, amphibologism, amphilogism *or* amphilogy [*rare*], anagrammatism, ambilogy, ambiloquy [*obs.*].

Sphinx, Delphic oracle.

EQUIVOCATION &c. (*duplicity*) 544; white lie, mental reservation &c. (*concealment*) 528; paltering.

V. EQUIVOCATE &c. (*palter*) 544; anagrammatize; be equivocal &c. *adj.;* have two meanings &c. 516.

Adj. EQUIVOCAL, ambiguous, amphibolous [*obs.*], doubtful, amphibolic, ambiloquent [*obs.*], ambiloquous, homonymic, homonymous; double-tongued &c. (*lying*) 544; enigmatical, indeterminate.

---

521. Metaphor. — N. FIGURE OF SPEECH; *façon de parler* [F.], way of speaking, colloquialism.

phrase &c. 566; figure, trope, metaphor, tralatition, metonymy, enallage, catachresis, synecdoche, antonomasia; satire, irony, figurativeness &c. *adj.;* image, imagery, metathesis, metalepsis, type, anagoge, simile.

PERSONIFICATION, prosopopœia, allegory, allegorization, apologue, parable, fable.

INFERENCE, implication, deduction, allusion, adumbration; euphemism, euphuism, application.

V. EMPLOY METAPHOR &c. *n.;* personify, allegorize, fable, adumbrate, shadow forth, apply, allude to.

Adj. METAPHORICAL, tropical, tralatitious, figurative, catachrestic *or* catachrestical, antonomastic *or* antonomastical, typical, parabolic *or* parabolical, allegoric *or* allegorical, allusive, referential, anagogic *or* anagogical; euphuistic *or* euphuistical, euphemistic *or* euphemistical, ironic, ironical; colloquial.

Adv. AS IT WERE; so to -speak, – say, – express oneself; in a manner of speaking [*colloq.*].

₊ *mutato nomine de te fabula narratur* [Horace].

---

522. Interpretation. — N. INTERPRETATION, definition; explanation, explication; solution, answer; rationale; plain –, simple –, strict- interpretation; meaning &c. 516; *mot d'énigme* [F.]; clew &c. (*indication*) 550.

symptomatology, semeiology *or* semiology, diagnosis, prognosis; metoposcopy, physiognomy; paleography &c. (*philology*) 560; oneirology.

TRANSLATION; rendering, rendition; reddition; literal –, free- translation; key; secret; *clavis* [L.], crib, pony [U. S.].

COMMENT, commentary; exegesis; expounding, exposition; hermeneutics; inference &c. (*deduction*) 480; illustration, exemplification; gloss, annotation, scholium, note; enucleation, elucidation, dilucidation [*obs.*]; *éclaircissement* [F.].

acception [*obs.*], acceptation, acceptance; light, reading, lection, construction, version.

EQUIVALENT, – meaning &c. 516; synonym, pœcilonym, polyonym [*rare*]; paraphrase, metaphrase; convertible terms, apposition.

523. Misinterpretation. — N. MISINTERPRETATION, misapprehension, misdoubt, misconception, misunderstanding, misacceptation [*obs.*], misconstruction, misapplication; catachresis; eisegesis; cross-reading, cross-purposes; mistake &c. 495.

MISREPRESENTATION, perversion, misstatement, exaggeration &c. 549; false -coloring, – construction; abuse of terms; play upon words, *jeu de mots* [F.], pun, parody, travesty; falsification &c. (*lying*) 544.

V. MISINTERPRET, misapprehend, misunderstand, misconceive, misjudge, misdeem, misdoubt, misspell, mistranslate, misconstrue, misapply; mistake &c. 495.

MISREPRESENT, pervert; explain wrongly, misstate; garble &c. (*falsify*) 544; distort, detort [*obs.*]; travesty, play upon words; stretch –, strain –, twist –, wrench –, wring –, wrest- the -sense, – meaning; explain away; put a -bad, – wrong, – erroneous, – false- construction on; give a false coloring; look through dark –, rose-colored- spectacles.

dictionary &c. 562; polyglot.

PREDICTION &c. 511; chiromancy *or* cheiromancy, palmistry; astrology.

V. INTERPRET, explain, define, construe, translate, render; do into, turn into; transfuse the sense of.

find out &c. (480*a*)- -the meaning of &c. 516; read; spell out, make out; decipher, unravel, disentangle; find the key of, enucleate, resolve, solve; consignify [*rare*]; read between the lines.

ELUCIDATE, account for; find –, tell the cause of &c. 153; throw –, shed--light, –new light, – fresh light- upon; clear up.

BE OUT; be –, play- at cross-purposes; be off [*slang*], be 'way off [*slang*].

Adj. MISINTERPRETED &c. *v.;* eisegetical, catachrestic *or* catachrestical; untranslated, untranslatable.

CONFUSED, tangled, snarled, mixed, dazed, perplexed, bewildered, rattled [*slang*], benighted.

Adv. AT CROSS-PURPOSES, at sixes and sevens [*colloq.*]; *à tort et à travers* [*F.*]; all balled up [*colloq.*], in a maze.

** "there are no secrets better kept than the secrets that everybody guesses" [Shaw].

illustrate, exemplify; unfold, expound, comment upon, annotate; popularize &c. (*render intelligible*) 518.

UNDERSTAND BY; take –, understand –, receive –, accept- in a particular sense; put a construction on, be given to understand.

Adj. EXPLANATORY, expository; explicative, explicatory; exegetical; construable; hermeneutic *or* hermeneutical, interpretive, interpretative, commentarial, commentatorial, inferential, illustrative, exemplificative, exemplificational, annotative, scholiastic, elucidative; symptomatological; paleographic *or* paleographical.

EQUIVALENT &c. 27; paraphrastic, consignificative [*rare*], consignificant, synonymous, pœcilonymic, polyonymal [*rare*], polyonymic [*rare*].

metaphrastic, literal &c. 516; polyglot.

Adv. IN EXPLANATION &c. *n.;* that is to say, *id est* [*L.*], *videlicet* [*L.*], to wit, namely, in other words.

LITERALLY, strictly speaking: in -plain, – plainer- -terms, – words, – English; more simply.

** "one must be an inventor to read well" [Emerson].

524. Interpreter. — N. INTERPRETER (*fem.* interpretress), translator, expositor, expounder, exponent, explainer; demonstrator.

COMMENTATOR, scholiast, annotator; metaphrast, paraphrast; glossarist, prolocutor.

SPOKESMAN, speaker, mouthpiece, foreman of the jury; mediator, delegate, exponent, representative, diplomatic agent, ambassador, plenipotentiary; advocate, judge, Supreme Court.

GUIDE, dragoman, courier, *valet de place* [*F.*], cicerone, showman, barker [*colloq.*], oneirocritic; Œdipus, Joseph; oracle &c. 513.

Section II. MODES OF COMMUNICATION

525. Manifestation. — N. MANIFESTATION, unfoldment, unfolding; plainness &c. *adj.;* plain speaking; expression; showing &c. *v.;* exposition, demonstration, séance, materialization; exhibition, production; display, show-down [*slang*], show, showing off [*colloq.*]; premonstration [*obs.*].

[THING SHOWN] exhibit, exhibition, exposition, show [*colloq.*], performance.

INDICATION &c. (*calling attention to*)

526. Latency. — N. LATENCY, inexpression; hidden –, occult- meaning; obscurity &c. (*unintelligibility*) 519; occultness, mystery, cabala *or* cabbala, cabalism, occultism, mysticism, symbolism, anagoge; silence &c. (*taciturnity*) 585; concealment &c. 528; more than meets the -eye, – ear; Delphic oracle; *le dessous des cartes* [*F.*], undercurrent; "something rotten in the state of Denmark" [*Hamlet*].

457; publicity &c. 531; disclosure &c. 529; openness &c. (*honesty*) 543, (*artlessness*) 703; *épanchement* [*F*.]; saliency, prominence.

V. MAKE *or* RENDER MANIFEST &c. *adj*.; materialize; bring -forth, - forward, - to the front, - into view; give notice; express; represent, set forth, evidence, exhibit; show, - up; expose; produce; hold up -, expose- to view; set -, place -, lay- before -one, - one's eyes; tell to one's face; trot out [*colloq*.], put through one's paces [*colloq*.], show one's paces, show off [*colloq*.]; show forth, unveil, bring to light, display, demonstrate, unroll; lay open; draw out, bring out; bring out in strong relief; call -, bring- into notice; hold up the mirror to; wear one's heart upon his sleeve; show one's -face, - colors; manifest oneself; speak out; make no -mystery, - secret- of; unfurl the flag; proclaim &c. (*publish*) 531.

indicate &c. (*direct attention to*) 457; disclose &c. 529; translate, transcribe, decipher, decode; elicit &c. 480a.

BE MANIFEST &c. *adj*.; appear &c. (*be visible*) 446; transpire &c. (*be disclosed*) 529; speak for itself, stand to reason; stare one in the face, loom large, appear on the horizon, rear its head; give -token, - sign, - indication of; tell its own tale &c. (*intelligible*) 518; go without saying, be self-evident.

Adj. MANIFEST, apparent; salient, striking, demonstrative, prominent, in the foreground, notable, pronounced.

FLAGRANT; notorious &c. (*public*) 531; arrant; stark-staring; unshaded, glaring.

PLAIN, clear, defined, definite, distinct, conspicuous &c. (*visible*) 446; obvious, evident, unmistakable, conclusive, indubitable, not to be mistaken, palpable, self-evident, autoptic *or* autoptical; intelligible &c. 518; clear as -day, - daylight, - noonday; plain as -a pikestaff [*colloq*.], - the sun at noonday, - the nose on one's face [*colloq*.], - way to parish church [*colloq*.].

ostensible; open, - as day; overt, patent, express, explicit; naked, bare, literal, downright, undisguised, exoteric.

UNRESERVED; frank, plain-spoken &c. (*artless*) 703.

BAREFACED, brazen, bold, shameless, daring, flaunting, *risqué* [*F*.], loud.

snake in the grass &c. (*pitfall*) 667; secret &c. 533.

darkness, invisibility, imperceptibility.

ALLUSION, insinuation, inference, implication; innuendo &c. 527; adumbration.

LATENT INFLUENCE, invisible government, power behind the throne, friend at court, wire-puller [*colloq*.], kingmaker; "a destiny that shapes our ends" [*Hamlet*].

V. BE LATENT &c. *adj*.; lurk, smolder *or* smoulder, underlie, make no sign; escape -observation, - detection, - recognition; lie hid &c. 528.

laugh in one's sleeve; keep back &c. (*conceal*) 528.

INVOLVE, imply, implicate, connote, import, understand, allude to, infer, leave an inference; mysticize [*rare*], symbolize; whisper &c. (*conceal*) 528.

Adj. LATENT; lurking &c. *v*.; secret, occult, anagogic *or* anagogical, cabalistic *or* cabalistical, symbolic, esoteric, recondite, veiled, symbolic, cryptic *or* cryptical; mystic, mystical; implied &c. *v*.; dormant; abeyant.

unapparent, unknown, unseen &c. 441; in the background; invisible &c. 447; indiscoverable, dark; impenetrable &c. (*unintelligible*) 519; unspied, unsuspected.

undeveloped, unsolved, unexplained, untraced, undiscovered &c. 480a, untracked, unexplored, uninvented.

UNEXPRESSED, unmentioned, unpronounced, unsaid, unwritten, unpublished, unbreathed, untalked of, untold &c. 527, unsung, unexposed, unproclaimed, undisclosed &c. 529, not expressed, tacit.

INDIRECT, crooked, inferential; by inference, by implication; implicit; constructive; allusive, covert, muffled; steganographic; understood, underhand, underground; concealed; under cover &c. 528; delitescent.

Adv. SECRETLY &c. 528; by a side wind; *sub silentio* [*L*.]; in the background; behind the scenes, behind one's back; on the tip of one's tongue; between the lines; by a mutual understanding; *sub rosa* [*L*.]; below the surface.

⁎⁎* "thereby hangs a tale" [*As You Like It*]; *tacitum vivit sub pectore vulnus* [Vergil].

MANIFESTED &c. *v.;* disclosed &c. 529; capable of being shown, producible; unconcealable.

Adv. MANIFESTLY, openly &c. *adj.;* before one's eyes, under one's nose [*colloq.*], under one's very eyes, to one's face, face to face, above board, cards on the table, *cartes sur table* [*F.*], on the stage, in open court, in the open streets, in plain sight, in the open, at the cross-roads, in the market place, in market overt; in the face of -day, – heaven; in- broad –, open- daylight; without reserve; at first blush, *primâ facie* [*L.*], on the face of; in set terms.

*** *cela saute aux yeux;* he that runs may read; you can see it with half an eye; it needs no ghost to tell us; the meaning lies on the surface; *cela va sans dire; res ipsa loquitur;* "clothing the palpable and familiar" [Coleridge]; *fari quæ sentiat; volto sciolto i pensieri stretti.*

---

527. Information. — N. INFORMATION, advisement [*archaic*], enlightenment, acquaintance, knowledge &c. 490; publicity &c. 531.

mention; acquainting &c. *v.;* instruction &c. (*teaching*) 537; outpouring; intercommunication, communicativeness.

INTIMATION, communication, notice, notification, enunciation, annunciation, announcement, *communiqué* [*F.*]; representation, round robin, presentment.

REPORT, advice, monition; news &c. 532; return &c. (*record*) 551; account &c. (*description*) 594; statement &c. (*affirmation*) 535; case, estimate, specification.

DISPATCH *or* despatch, message, wire [*colloq.*], cable [*colloq.*], telegram &c. (*news*) 532; telephone, phone [*colloq.*], radiophone, wireless telephone, telegraphone.

INFORMANT, authority, teller, annunciator, harbinger, herald, intelligencer [*now rare*], reporter, exponent, mouthpiece; spokesman &c. (*interpreter*) 524; informer, eavesdropper, delator, detective, bull [*slang, U. S.*], sleuth [*colloq.*]; *mouchard* [*F.*], spy, newsmonger; messenger &c. 534; *amicus curiæ* [*L.*].

GUIDE, *valet de place* [*F.*], cicerone, pilot, guidebook, handbook; *vade mecum* [*L.*], manual; map, plan, chart, gazetteer; itinerary &c. (*journey*) 266.

HINT, suggestion, innuendo, inkling, whisper, passing word, word in the ear, subaudition, subauditur, cue, byplay; gesture &c. (*indication*) 550; gentle –, broad- hint; *verbum sapienti* [*L.*]; word to the wise; insinuation &c. (*latency*) 526.

V. TELL; inform, – of; acquaint, – with; impart, – to; make acquainted with, apprise, advise, enlighten, awaken.

let fall, mention, express, intimate, represent, communicate, make known; publish &c. 531; notify, signify, specify,

528. Concealment. — N. CONCEALMENT; hiding &c. *v.;* occultation, mystification.

reticence, reserve, reservation; mental reservation, aside; *arrière pensée* [*F.*], suppression, evasion, white lie, misprision; silence &c. (*taciturnity*) 585; suppression of truth &c. 544; underhand dealing; closeness, secret veness &c. *adj.;* mystery.

seal of secrecy; freemasonry; screen &c. 530; disguise &c. 530; masquerade; masked battery; hiding place &c. 530.

CRYPTOGRAPHY, steganography; cipher, code, cable code; sympathetic ink, palimpsest.

STALKING, still-hunt, hunt.

STEALTH, stealthiness; obreption [*obs.*]; slyness &c. (*cunning*) 702.

SECRECY, latitancy [*rare*], latitation [*obs.*]; seclusion &c. 893; privacy, secretness, hugger-mugger [*archaic*]; disguise, incognito (*fem.* incognita).

MYSTICISM, occultism, supernaturalism; esotericism, esoterics, esotery.

LATENCY &c. 526; snake in the grass; secret &c. 533; stowaway; blind baggage [*slang*].

MASQUERADER, masker, mask, domino.

V. CONCEAL, hide, secrete, put out of sight; lock up, seal up, bottle up.

cover, screen, cloak, veil, shroud; cover up one's tracks; screen from -sight, – observation; draw the veil; draw –, close- the curtain; curtain, shade, eclipse, throw a veil over; becloud, bemask; mask, camouflage, disguise; ensconce, muffle; befog; whisper.

keep -from, – back, – to oneself; keep -snug, – close, – secret, – dark; bury; sink, suppress; keep -from, – out of- -view, – sight; keep in –, throw into- the -shade, – background; stifle, hush up, smother, withhold, reserve; fence with a question; ignore &c. 460.

convey the knowledge of; retail, render an account; give an account &c. (*describe*) 594; state &c. (*affirm*) 535.

let one know, have one know; give one to understand; give notice; set -, lay -, put- before; point out, put into one's head; put one in possession of; instruct &c. (*teach*) 537; direct the attention to &c. 457.

ANNOUNCE, annunciate; report, - progress; bring -, send -, leave -, write-word; telegraph, wire [*colloq.*], telephone, phone [*colloq.*].

DISCLOSE &c. 529; show cause; explain &c. (*interpret*) 522.

HINT; give an inkling of; give -, drop -, throw out- a hint; insinuate; allude to, make allusion to; glance at; tip off [*slang*], give one a tip [*colloq.*]; tip the wink [*slang*] &c. (*indicate*) 550; suggest, prompt, give the cue, breathe; whisper, - in the ear.

BERATE, scold, chide, strafe [*colloq.*], score [*colloq.*, *U. S.*], dress down [*colloq.*], reprove, trim [*slang*], rate; give one a -bit, -piece- of one's mind; tell one -plainly, - once for all; speak volumes.

UNDECEIVE, unbeguile; set right, correct, open the eyes of, disabuse.

BE INFORMED OF &c.; know &c. 490; learn &c. 539; get scent of, gather from; sleuth [*colloq.*]; awaken to, open one's eyes to; become -alive, - awake- to; hear, understand; come to one's -ears, - knowledge; reach one's ears; overhear &c. (*hear*) 418; get wise to [*slang*].

Adj. INFORMED &c. *v.*; *communiqué* [*F.*]; informational, advisory, intelligential; reported &c. *v.*; published &c. 531.

expressive &c. 516; explicit &c. (*open*) 525, (*clear*) 518; plain-spoken &c. (*artless*) 703.

DECLARATORY, declarative, enunciative, nunciative [*rare*], annunciative [*rare*], enunciatory, insinuant [*rare*]; oral, nuncupative [*said of oral wills*], nuncupatory [*obs.*]; expository; communicative, communicatory.

Adv. FROM INFORMATION RECEIVED; according to -reports, - suggestion, - rumor; from notice given; by the underground route; as a matter of -general information, - common report; in the air; according to -, from- what one can gather.

⁎⁎⁎ a little bird told me; "foul whisperings are abroad" [*Macbeth*].

CODE, codify; use a -code, - cipher.

KEEP A SECRET, keep one's own counsel; hold one's tongue &c. (*silence*) 585; make no sign, not let it go further; not breathe a -word, - syllable- about; not let the right hand know what the left is doing; hide one's light under a bushel, bury one's talent in a napkin.

HOODWINK; keep -, leave- in -the dark, - ignorance; blind, - the eyes; blindfold, mystify; puzzle &c. (*render uncertain*) 475; bamboozle &c. (*deceive*) 545.

BE CONCEALED &c. *v.*; suffer an eclipse; occult, retire from sight, couch; hide oneself; lie -hid, - in ambush, - perdu, - snug, - low [*colloq.*], - close; latitate [*obs.*]; seclude oneself &c. 893; lurk, sneak, skulk, slink, prowl, gumshoe [*slang*, *U. S.*]; steal -into, - out of, - by, - along; play at -bopeep, - hide and seek; hide in holes and corners; still-hunt.

Adj. CONCEALED &c. *v.*; hidden; secret, latitant [*rare*], recondite, mystic, mystical, cabalistic *or* cabalistical, occult, dark; cryptic *or* cyptical, private, privy, *in petto* [*It.*], auricular, clandestine, close, close-mouthed, inviolate; tortuous.

behind a screen &c. 530; under -cover, - an eclipse; in ambush, in hiding, in disguise; in a -cloud, - fog, - mist, - haze, - dark corner; in the -shade, - dark; clouded, wrapt in clouds; invisible &c. 447; buried, underground, perdu; secluded &c. 893.

UNDISCLOSED &c. 529, untold &c. 527; covert &c. (*latent*) 526; mysterious &c. (*unintelligible*) 519.

INVIOLABLE, irrevealable, confidential; esoteric; not to be spoken of.

FURTIVE, obreptitious, stealthy, feline; skulking &c. *v.*; surreptitious, underhand, hole and corner [*colloq.*]; sly &c. (*cunning*) 702; secretive, clandestine, evasive; reserved, reticent, uncommunicative, buttoned up; close, - as wax; taciturn &c. 585.

Adv. SECRETLY &c. *adj.*; in secret, in private, in one's sleeve, in holes and corners [*colloq.*]; in the dark &c. *adj.*

januis clausis [*L.*], with closed doors, *à huis clos* [*F.*]; hugger-mugger, in hugger-mugger [*archaic*], *à la dérobée* [*F.*], under the -cloak of, - rose, - table; *sub rosâ* [*L.*], *en tapinois* [*F.*], in the background, aside, on the sly [*colloq.*], with bated breath, sotto voce, in a whisper, without beat of drum, *à la sourdine* [*F.*].

BEHIND THE VEIL; beyond -mortal ken, – the grave, – the veil; hid from mortal vision; into the -eternal secret, – realms supersensible, – supreme mystery.

CONFIDENTIALLY &c. *adj.;* in –, in strict- confidence; between -ourselves, – you and me; *entre nous* [*F.*], *inter nos* [*L.*], under the seal of secrecy; *à couvert* [*F.*].

UNDERHAND, by stealth, like a thief in the night; stealthily &c. *adj.;* behind -the scenes, – the curtain, – one's back, – a screen &c. 530; incognito; *in camerâ* [*L.*].

. it must go no further, it will go no further; "tell it not in Gath" [*Bible*]; nobody the wiser; *alitur vitium vivitque tegendo;* "let it be tenable in your silence still" [*Hamlet*]; "but let concealment, like a worm i' the bud, Feed on her damask cheek" [*Twelfth Night*]; "mysticism . . . a transcendent form of common sense" [Chesterton].

---

529. Disclosure. — **N.** DISCLOSURE; retection [*obs.*]; unveiling &c. *v.;* deterration [*obs.*], revealment, revelation; divulgement, divulgation [*rare*], divulgence, exposition, exposure, publication, *exposé* [*F.*], whole truth; telltale &c. (*news*) 532.

bursting of a bubble; *dénouement* [*F.*].

ACKNOWLEDGMENT, avowance, avowal; confession, confessional; shrift.

NARRATOR &c. 594; talebearer &c. 532.

V. DISCLOSE, discover, dismask [*obs.*]; draw –, draw aside –, lift –, raise –, lift up –, remove –, tear- the -veil, – curtain; unmask, unveil, unfold, uncover, unseal, unkennel; take off –, break- the seal; lay open, lay bare; expose; open, – up; bare, bring to light; evidence; make -clear, – evident, – manifest; evince.

raise –, drop –, lift –, remove –, throw off- the mask; expose; lay open; undeceive, unbeguile; disabuse, set right, correct, open the eyes of; *désillusionner* [*F.*].

530. Ambush. [MEANS OF CONCEALMENT.] — **N.** AMBUSH, ambuscade; stalking-horse; lurking-hole, -place; secret path, back stairs; retreat &c. (*refuge*) 666.

HIDING PLACE, hidlings [*Scot. & dial. Eng.*]; secret -place, – drawer; recess, hole, cubbyhole, hidie-hole [*Scot.*], holes and corners; closet, crypt, adytum, abditory [*rare*], *oubliette* [*F.*]; safe, safe-deposit box, safety-deposit box.

SCREEN, cover, shade, blinker; veil, curtain, blind, purdah [*India*], cloak, cloud.

MASK, visor *or* vizor, vizard [*archaic*], disguise, masquerade dress, domino.

PITFALL &c. (*source of danger*) 667; trap &c. (*snare*) 545.

V. AMBUSH, ambuscade; lie in ambush &c. (*hide oneself*) 528; lie in wait for; set a trap for &c. (*deceive*) 545.

Adv. *aux aguets* [*F.*]; *januis clausis* [*L.*] &c. 528.

DIVULGE, reveal, break [*obs.*]; let into the secret; reveal the secrets of the prison house; tell &c. (*inform*) 527; squeal [*slang*]; breathe, utter, blab, peach [*slang*]; let -out, – fall, – drop, – slip, – the cat out of the bag [*colloq.*], come out with it [*colloq.*], come it [*slang*], betray; tell tales, – out of school; come out with; give vent to, give utterance to; open the lips, blurt out, vent, whisper about; speak out &c. (*make manifest*) 525; break the news; make public &c. 531; unriddle &c. (*find out*) 480a; split.

ACKNOWLEDGE, allow, concede, grant, admit, own, confess, avow, throw off all disguise, turn inside out, make a clean breast; show one's -hand, – cards; unburden –, disburden- one's mind, – conscience, – heart; open –, lay bare –, give one a piece of [*colloq.*]- one's mind; unbosom oneself, "own the soft impeachment" [Sheridan]; say –, speak- the truth; turn informer; turn -King's, – Queen's, – State's- evidence; acknowledge the corn [*slang, U. S.*].

BE DISCLOSED &c.; transpire, come to light; come in sight &c. (*be visible*) 446; become known, escape the lips; come out, ooze out, creep out, leak out, peep out, crop out, crop forth, crop up; show its -face, – colors; discover &c. itself; break through the clouds, flash on the mind; come to one's ears &c. 527.

Adj. DISCLOSED &c. *v.;* revelative, revelatory, revelational, expository, confessional, confessionary, confessory.

Int. out with it! 'fess up! [*slang*]; open up! [*colloq*].

. the murder is out; a light breaks in upon one; the scales fall from one's eyes; the eyes are opened; "do good by stealth, and blush to find it fame" [Pope].

531. Publication. — N. PUBLICATION; public announcement &c. 527; promulgation, propagation, proclamation, pronouncement, *pronunciamiento* [*Sp.*], pronunciamento, edict, encyclical; circulation, indiction [*rare*], edition, impression, imprint.

PUBLICITY, notoriety, currency, flagrancy, cry, hue and cry, *bruit* [*F.*]; bruit, oyez *or* oyes, *vox populi* [*L.*]; report &c. (*news*) 532; telegram, cable [*colloq.*] &c. 532; telegraphy; publisher &c. *v.*

THE PRESS, the Fourth Estate, public press, newspaper, journal, gazette, daily, weekly, monthly, quarterly, annual; magazine.

ADVERTISEMENT, ad., placard, bill, flyer [*cant*], leaflet, handbill, *affiche* [*F.*], broadside, broadsheet, poster; circular, – letter; manifesto; notice &c. 527; program *or* programme.

V. PUBLISH; make -public, – known &c. (*information*) 527; speak of, talk of; broach, utter; put forward; circulate, propagate, promulgate; spread, – abroad; rumor, diffuse, disseminate, evulgate [*obs.*]; put -, give –, send- forth; emit, edit, get out; issue; bring –, lay –, drag- before the public; give -out, – to the world; report, cover [*newspaper cant*]; put –, bandy –, hawk –, buzz –, whisper –, bruit –, blaze- about; drag into the -open day, – limelight [*colloq.*], throw the spotlight on [*colloq.*]; voice, bruit.

PROCLAIM, herald, blazon; blaze –, noise- abroad; sound a trumpet; trumpet –, thunder- forth; give tongue; announce with -beat of drum, – flourish of trumpets; proclaim -from the housetops, – at Charing Cross, – at the crossroads, – at the market cross.

raise a -cry, – hue and cry, – report; set news afloat.

telegraph, cable, wireless [*colloq.*], broadcast, wire [*colloq.*].

ADVERTISE, placard; post, – up; *afficher* [*F.*], publish in the Gazette, send round the crier, cry abroad.

BE PUBLISHED &c.; be *or* become public &c. *adj.;* come out; go –, fly –, buzz –, blow- about; get -about, – abroad, – afloat, – wind; find vent; see the light; go forth, take air, acquire currency, pass current; go the rounds, go the round of the newspapers, go through the length and breadth of the land; *virum volitare per ora* [*L.*]; pass from mouth to mouth; spread; run –, spread- like wildfire.

Adj. PUBLISHED &c. *v.;* current &c. (*news*) 532; in circulation, public; notorious; flagrant, arrant; open &c. 525; trumpet-tongued; encyclic *or* encyclical, proclamatory, annunciatory, promulgatory; exoteric.

TELEGRAPHIC, cabled, radiotelegraphic, telegraphed, wireless; radiophonic.

Adv. PUBLICLY &c. *adj.;* in public, in open court, with open doors; in the -limelight, – spotlight [*both colloq.*]; for publication.

Int. Oyez! Oyes! notice!

** notice is hereby given; this is –, these are- to give notice; *nomina stultorum parietibus hærent; semel emissum volat irrevocabile verbum;* "thou god of our Idolatry, the Press!" [Cowper]; "report me and my cause aright To the unsatisfied" [*Hamlet*]; "A chiel's amang ye takin' notes And, faith, he'll prent it!" [Burns].

532. News. — N. NEWS; information &c. 527; piece –, budget- of -news, – information; intelligence, tidings; beat *or* scoop [*newspaper cant*], story, copy [*cant*], print, letterpress.

fresh –, stirring –, old –, stale- news; glad tidings; old –, stale- story; chestnut [*slang*].

MESSAGE, word, advice, aviso, dispatch *or* despatch; telegram, cable [*colloq.*], wire [*colloq.*], radio [*colloq.*], radiogram, wireless telegram, wireless [*colloq.*], marconigram, pneumatogram, communication, errand, embassy; bulletin; broadcast.

533. Secret. — N. SECRET; dead –, profound- secret; arcanum, mystery; latency &c. 526; Asian mystery; sealed book, secrets of the prison house; *le dessous des cartes* [*F.*].

ENIGMA, riddle, puzzle, nut to crack, conundrum, charade, rebus, logogriph; monogram, anagram, anagrammatism; Sphinx; *crux criticorum* [*L.*].

MAZE, labyrinth, meander [*usually in pl.*], Hyrcynian wood; intricacy.

PROBLEM &c. (*question*) 461; paradox &c. (*difficulty*) 704; unintelligibility &c. 519; *terra incognita* [*L.*] &c. (*ignorance*) 491.

REPORT, rumor, hearsay, on-dit, flying rumor, news stirring, cry, buzz,
bruit, fame; talk, *oui-dire* [*F.*], scandal,
eavesdropping; town –, table- -talk, –
gossip; tittle-tattle; canard, topic of
the day, idea afloat.

NARRATOR &c. (*describe*) 594; newsmonger, scandalmonger; busybody,
talebearer, telltale, gossip, tattler, blab,
babbler, tattletale, chatterer; informer,
squealer [*slang*].

Adj. SECRET &c. (*concealed*) 528; involved &c. 248; labyrinthian, labyrinthine, labyrinthic *or* labyrinthical, mazy,
meandrous.

ENIGMATIC *or* enigmatical, anagram-
matic *or* anagrammatical, monogram-
matic, logogriphic, cryptic *or* cryptical.

** "she was more mystical than Woman"
[Dunsany].

V. TRANSPIRE &c. (*be disclosed*) 529; rumor &c. (*publish*) 531.

Adj. RUMORED; publicly –, currently- -rumored, – reported; many-tongued;
rife, current, floating, afloat, going about, in circulation, in every one's mouth,
all over the town.

HAVING NEWS VALUE, newsy [*colloq.*], snappy [*slang*].

Adv. AS THEY SAY; as the story -goes, – runs; it is said.

BY TELEGRAPH, by cable, by radio [*colloq.*], by wireless [*colloq.*].

** "airy tongues that syllable men's names" [Milton]; "Master! master! news, old news,
and such news as you never heard of" [*Taming of the Shrew*]; · Some tell, some hear, some
judge of news, some make it" [Dryden].

534. Messenger. — N. MESSENGER, angel, envoy, emissary, legate, delegate,
nuncio, internuncio, intermediary, go-between; ambassador &c. (*diplomatist*) 758.

Gabriel, Hermes, Mercury, Iris, Ariel.

marshal, flag bearer, herald, crier, trumpeter, bellman, pursuivant, *parlementaire*
[*F.*], apparitor.

COURIER, runner, dak *or* dawk [*India*], estafette *or* estafet, commissionaire; errand
boy, chore boy, newsboy.

MAIL; post, post office; letter bag, mail bag; postman, mail-man, letter carrier;
mail train, mail boat, mailer; aërial mail; carrier pigeon.

TELEGRAPH, cable [*colloq.*], wire [*colloq.*], radiotelegraph, wireless telegraph, wireless [*colloq.*], radio [*colloq.*].

TELEPHONE, phone [*colloq.*], radio-telephone, radiophone, wireless telephone.

REPORTER, newspaperman, journalist; gentleman –, representative- of the Press;
penny-a-liner; hack writer, special –, war –, own- correspondent; spy, scout; informer &c. 527.

535. Affirmation. — N. AFFIRMATION,
affirmance, statement, allegation, assertion, predication, predicate [*logic*], declaration, word, averment; confirmation.

ASSEVERATION, adjuration, swearing,
oath, affidavit; deposition &c. (*record*)
551; avouchment, avouch [*rare*], assurance; protest, protestation; profession;
acknowledgment &c. (*assent*) 488; legal
pledge, pronouncement; solemn -aver-
ment, – avowal, – declaration.

VOTE, voice; ballot, suffrage; *vox
populi* [*L.*].

REMARK, observation; position &c.
(*proposition*) 514; saying, dictum, sentence, *ipse dixit* [*L.*].

POSITIVENESS, emphasis, peremptori-
ness; dogmatism &c. (*certainty*) 474;
weight.

536. Negation. — N. NEGATION, abnegation; denial; disavowal, disclaimer;
abjuration; contradiction, contravention; recusation, protest; recusancy &c.
(*dissent*) 489; flat –, emphatic- -contra-
diction, – denial; *démenti* [*F.*].

QUALIFICATION &c. 469; repudiation
&c. 610; recantation, revocation; retractation &c. 607; rebuttal; confutation
&c. 479; refusal &c. 764; prohibition
&c. 761.

V. DENY; contradict, contravene; controvert, give denial to, gainsay, negative, shake the head.

deny -flatly, – peremptorily, – emphatically, – absolutely, – wholly, – entirely; give the lie to, belie.

DISCLAIM, disown, disaffirm, disavow,
abjure, forswear, abnegate, renounce;

DOGMATIST &c. 887.

V. ASSERT; make an assertion &c. *n.;* have one's say; say, affirm, predicate, declare, state; protest, profess; acknowledge &c. (*assent*) 488.

put forth, put forward; advance, allege, propose, propound; announce &c. 527; enunciate, broach, set forth, hold out, maintain, contend, pronounce, pretend.

DEPOSE, depone, aver, avow, avouch, asseverate, swear, rap [*archaic slang*], affirm; make –, take one's– oath; make –, swear –, put in– an affidavit; take one's Bible oath, kiss the book, vow, *vitam impendere vero* [*L.*]; swear till –one is black in the face, – all's blue [*both colloq.*]; be sworn, call Heaven to witness; vouch, warrant, certify, assure; swear by bell, book, and candle; attest &c. (*evidence*) 467; adjure &c. (*put to one's oath*) 768.

EMPHASIZE; swear by &c. (*believe*) 484; insist upon, take one's stand upon; lay stress on; assert -roundly, – positively; lay down, – the law; raise one's voice, dogmatize, have the last word; rap out; repeat; reassert, reaffirm.

recant &c. 607; revoke &c. (*abrogate*) 756.

DISPUTE, impugn, traverse, rebut, join issue upon; bring *or* call in question &c. (*doubt*) 485; give (one) the lie in his throat.

REPUDIATE &c. 610; set aside, ignore &c. 460; rebut &c. (*confute*) 479; qualify &c. 469; refuse &c. 764.

Adj. DENYING &c. *v.;* denied &c. *v.;* revocatory, abjuratory, abnegative [*rare*], contradictory; negative, negatory; recusant &c. (*dissenting*) 489; at issue upon.

Adv. NO, nay, not, nowise, noways; not a -bit, – whit, – jot; not at all, not in the least, not so; no such thing; nothing of the -kind, – sort; quite the contrary, *tout au contraire* [*F.*], far from it; *tant s'en faut* [*F.*]; on no account, in no respect; by no means, by no manner of means; negatively.

***** there never was a greater mistake; I know better; *non hæc in fœdera.*

Adj. AFFIRMATIVE; asserting &c. *v.;* declaratory, predicatory, predicative, predicational, pronunciatory, pronunciative, *soi-disant* [*F.*]; positive; unmistakable, clear; certain &c. 474; express, explicit &c. (*patent*) 525; absolute, emphatic, flat, broad, round, pointed, marked, distinct, decided, assertive, insistent, confident, trenchant, dogmatic, definitive, formal, solemn, categorical, peremptory; unretracted.

PREDICABLE, affirmable, attributable.

Adv. AFFIRMATIVELY &c. *adj.;* in the affirmative.

with emphasis, ex-cathedra, without fear of contradiction.

I must say, indeed, i' faith, let me tell you, why, give me leave to say, marry [*archaic*], you may be sure, I'd have you know; upon my -word, – honor; by my troth, egad [*euphemism*], I assure you; by jingo, by Jove, by George &c. [*all colloq.*]; troth, seriously, sadly [*obs.*]; in –, in sober- -sadness, – truth, – earnest; of a truth, truly, pardie *or* perdy [*archaic*]; in all conscience, upon oath; be assured &c. (*belief*) 484; yes &c. (*assent*) 488; I'll -warrant, – warrant you, – engage, – answer for it, – be bound, – venture to say, – take my oath; in fact, forsooth, joking -aside, – apart; in all -soberness, – seriousness; so help me God; not to mince the matter.

***** quoth he; *dixi.*

---

537. Teaching. — N. TEACHING &c. *v.;* pedagogics, pedagogy; instruction; edification; education; tuition; tutorship, tutorage, tutelage; direction, guidance; opsimathy [*rare*].

PREPARATION, qualification, training, schooling &c. *v.;* discipline; exercise, exercitation, drill, practice.

PERSUASION, proselytism, propagan-

538. Misteaching. — N. MISTEACHING, misinformation, misintelligence, misguidance, misdirection, mispersuasion [*archaic*], misinstruction, misleading &c. *v.;* perversion; false –, dangerousteaching; sophistry &c. 477; college of Laputa; the blind leading the blind.

V. MISINFORM, misteach, misdescribe, misdirect, misguide, misinstruct, mis-

dism, propaganda; indoctrination, inculcation, inoculation, initiation.

LESSON, lecture, sermon, homily, harangue, disquisition; apologue, parable; discourse, prelection *or* prælection, preachment; explanation &c. (*interpretation*) 522; chalk talk [*colloq.*].

Chautauqua -system, - course; lyceum [*U. S.*].

exercise, task; curriculum; course, - of study; grammar, three R's; A. B. C. &c. (*beginning*) 66.

[EDUCATION] elementary -, primary -, grammar school -, common school -, high school -, secondary -, technical -, college -, collegiate -, military -, university -, liberal -, classical -, academic -, religious -, denominational -, moral -, secular- education; propædeutics, moral tuition; the humanities, humanism, humane studies.

normal -, kindergarten- -course, - training; vocational -training, - therapeutics; Montessori system.

PHYSICAL EDUCATION, physical drill, gymnastics, calisthenics, eurythmics *or* eurhythmics; sloyd.

V. TEACH, instruct, edify, school, tutor; cram [*colloq.*], grind [*colloq.*], prime, coach; enlighten &c. (*inform*) 527.

inculcate, indoctrinate, inoculate, infuse, instill, infix, ingraft *or* engraft, infiltrate; imbue, impregnate, implant; graft, sow the seeds of, disseminate, propagate.

give an idea of; put up to [*slang*]; put in the way of; set right.

sharpen the wits, enlarge the mind; give new ideas, open the eyes, bring forward, "teach the young idea how to shoot" [Thomson]; improve &c. 658.

direct, guide; direct attention to &c. (*attention*) 457; impress upon the -mind, - memory; beat into, - the head; convince &c. (*belief*) 484.

EXPOUND &c. (*interpret*) 522; lecture; read -, give- a -lesson, - lecture, - sermon, - discourse; incept [*Cambridge Univ., Eng.*]; hold forth, preach; prelect *or* prælect, sermonize, moralize; point a moral.

TRAIN, discipline; bring up, - to; educate, form, ground, prepare, qualify, drill, exercise, practice, habituate, familiarize with, nurture, drynurse, breed, rear, take in hand; break, - in; tame;

correct; pervert; put on a false -, throw off the- scent; deceive &c. 545; mislead &c. (*error*) 495; misrepresent; lie &c. 544; *spargere voces in vulgum ambiguas* [Vergil], preach to the wise, teach one's grandmother to suck eggs [*colloq.*].

RENDER UNINTELLIGIBLE &c. 519; bewilder &c. (*uncertainty*) 475; mystify &c. (*conceal*) 528; unteach [*archaic*].

Adj. MISTEACHING &c. *v.;* unedifying.

⁂ *piscem natare doces.*

539. Learning. — N. LEARNING; acquisition of -knowledge &c. 490, - skill &c. 698; acquirement, attainment; mental cultivation, edification, scholarship, erudition; acquired knowledge, lore; wide -, general- information; wide reading; self-instruction; study, grind [*colloq.*], reading, perusal; inquiry &c. 461.

docility &c. (*willingness*) 602; aptitude &c. 698.

APPRENTICESHIP, prenticeship [*obs. or colloq.*], pupilage, tutelage, novitiate.

EXAMINATION, matriculation; responsions *or* smalls [*Oxford Univ.*], previous examination *or* little go [*Cambridge Univ., Eng.*], moderations *or* mods. [*Oxford Univ.*], final examination, finals, greats [*Oxford Univ.*], great go, tripos [*both Cambridge Univ., Eng.*].

TRANSLATION, crib [*student cant*]; pony, trot, horse [*all student slang, U. S.*].

V. LEARN; acquire -, gain -, receive -, take in -, drink in -, imbibe -, pick up -, gather -, get -, obtain -, collect -, glean- -knowledge, - information, - learning.

acquaint oneself with, master; make oneself -master of, - acquainted with; grind [*college slang*], cram *or* cram up [*colloq.*], get up, coach up [*colloq.*]; learn by -heart, - rote.

read, spell, peruse; con; run -, pore -, thumb- over; wade through, run through, plunge into, dip into; glance -, run the eye- -over, - through; turn over the leaves.

STUDY; be studious &c. *adj.;* consume -, burn- -the midnight oil; mind one's book, bury oneself in.

go to -school, - college, - the university, - the 'varsity [*colloq.*]; serve an (*or* one's) apprenticeship, serve one's time; learn one's trade; be informed &c. 527; be taught &c. 537.

preinstruct; initiate, graduate; inure &c. (*habituate*) 613.

put to nurse, send to school.

Adj. EDUCATIONAL; scholastic, academic, doctrinal; disciplinal, disciplinary, instructive, instructional, hortatory, homiletic *or* homiletical, pedagogic *or* pedagogical, didactic; teaching &c. *v.*; taught &c. *v.*; propædeutic *or* propædeutical; propagative; cultural, humanistic, humane; pragmatic *or* pragmatical, practical, utilitarian; naturalistic, psychological, scientific, sociological, eclectic, coeducational.

. the schoolmaster abroad; *a bovi majori discit arare minor; adeo in teneris consuescere multum est* [Vergil]; *docendo discimus; quœ nocent docent; qui docet discit;* "sermons in stones and good in everything" [*As You Like It*]; "We will our youth lead on to higher fields" [*II Henry IV*].

Adj. STUDIOUS; industrious &c. 682; scholastic, scholarly, well read, widely read, well posted [*colloq.*], erudite, learned; full of -information, - learning, - lore.

TEACHABLE; docile &c. (*willing*) 602; apt &c. 698.

Adv. at one's books; *in statu pupillari* [*L.*] &c (*learner*) 541.

. "a lumber-house of books in every head" [Pope]; *ancora imparo!* "hold high converse with the mighty dead" [Thomson]; "lash'd into Latin by the tingling rod" [Gay]; "the more a man looks at a thing, the less he can see it, and the more a man learns a thing the less he knows it" [Chesterton]; "Macaulay is like a book in breeches" [Sydney Smith]; "learning without thought is labor lost; thought without learning is perilous" [Confucius]; "words of learned length and thundering sound" [Goldsmith].

---

540. Teacher. — N. TEACHER, trainer, preceptor, instructor, institutor [*obs.*], master, tutor, director, coryphæus [*Oxford Univ.*], dry nurse [*slang*], coach [*colloq.*], crammer [*colloq.*], grinder [*college slang, Eng.*], don [*Univ. cant*]; governor [*obs.*], bear leader [*humorous*]; governess, duenna; disciplinarian.

professor, lecturer, reader, prelector *or* prælector, prolocutor, preacher; chalk talker, *khoja* [*Turk.*], munshi *or* moonshee [*Moham.*]; pastor &c. (*clergy*) 996; schoolmaster, dominie, usher [*Brit.*], pedagogue, abecedarian; schoolmistress, dame [*rare*], kindergartner, monitor, pupil teacher.

GUIDE; expositor &c. 524; guru [*Hindu*]; mentor &c. (*adviser*) 695; pioneer, apostle, missionary, propagandist; example &c. 22.

PROFESSORSHIP &c. (*school*) 542.

TUTELAGE &c. (*teaching*) 537.

Adj. PEDAGOGIC *or* pedagogical, preceptorial, tutorial, professorial; scholastic &c. 537.

. *qui docet discit.*

541. Learner. — N. LEARNER, scholar, student, alumnus (*fem.* alumna, *pl.* alumni), *élève* [*F.*], pupil, schoolboy, schoolgirl; questionist, questioner, inquirer; monitor, prefect; beginner, tyro, abecedarian, alphabetarian.

UNDERGRADUATE, undergrad. [*colloq.*], freshman, fresh *or* freshie [*slang*], plebe [*West Point cant*], sophomore, soph [*colloq.*], junior, senior; commoner; pensioner, sizar [*both Cambridge Univ., Eng.*]; exhibitioner, scholar [*winner of a scholarship*], fellow commoner [*Eng. Univ.*], demy [*Magdalene Coll., Oxford*]; junior, sophister *or* soph, senior sophister *or* soph, sophister, questionist [*all Eng. Univ.*].

graduate student, post-graduate student.

CLASS, form, grade, room; promotion, graduation, remove; pupilage &c. (*learning*) 539.

DISCIPLE, chela [*India*], follower, apostle, proselyte.

fellow student, *condiscipulus* [*L.*], condisciple, classmate, schoolmate, schoolfellow, fellow pupil.

NOVICE, recruit, tenderfoot [*slang or colloq.*], neophyte, inceptor, *débutant* [*F.*], catechumen, probationer; apprentice, prentice [*obs. or colloq.*], articled clerk.

Adj. *in statu pupillari* [*L.*], in leading strings, pupillary, monitorial; abecedarian, rudimentary; probationary, probatory, probational; sophomoric *or* sophomoral [*U. S.*].

. "schoolboy, with his satchel And shining morning face, creeping like snail Unwillingly to school" [*As You Like It*].

542. School. — N. SCHOOL, academy, lyceum, *Gymnasium* [*Ger.*], *lycée* [*F.*], palæstra *or* palestra, seminary, college, educational institution, institute; university, 'varsity [*colloq.*], *Alma Mater* [*L.*].

[GENERAL] day –, boarding –, preparatory *or* prep [*colloq., U. S.*] –, elementary –, common –, denominational –, secondary –, endowed –, free –, continuation –, convent –, art –, music –, military –, naval –, technical –, library –, secretarial –, business –, correspondence- school; kindergarten, nursery, day nursery, nursery school, *crèche* [*F.*]; Sunday –, Sabbath –, Bible- school; reform school, reformatory; teachers' training college; university extension -lectures, – course.

[BRITISH] primary –, infant –, dame [*hist.*] –, voluntary –, government –, Board –, higher grade –, National –, mission –, missionary –, British and Foreign –, state-aided –, grant-in-aid –, middle-class –, County Council –, training –, normal –, grammar –, collegiate –, high –, upper –, modern –, lower –, County –, County high –, Cathedral –, municipal secondary-, municipal technical –, Friends' –, coeducational *or* dual –, Polytechnic –, King Henry VIII's –, King Edward's –, Queen Elizabeth's –, Queen Mary's –, merchant guild –, Blue-Coat- school; Christ's Hospital; public school (*as* Eton, Harrow, Rugby &c.); school of art, school of arts and crafts, trade school; Royal Naval College, Royal Military Academy (Woolwich), Royal Military College (Sandhurst); training ship for -royal navy, – mercantile marine; College of Preceptors; Royal Academy –, London College –, Trinity College- of Music; Royal College of Organists.

[UNITED STATES] district –, grade –, parochial –, public –, primary –, grammar –, junior high –, high –, Latin- school; private –, technological –, normal –, kindergarten training- school; summer school; military academy (West Point); naval academy (Annapolis); college, fresh-water college [*colloq.* or *slang, U. S.*], State university; graduate school, post-graduate school.

CLASS, division, form &c. 541; seminar *or* seminary.

CLASS ROOM, room, school room, recitation room, lecture room, lecture hall, theater *or* theatre, amphitheater *or* amphitheatre.

DESK, reading desk, ambo, pulpit, forum, stage, rostrum, platform, hustings, tribune.

SCHOOLBOOK, textbook, hornbook; grammar, primer, abecedary [*rare*], abecedarium, New England Primer, rudiments, manual, *vade mecum* [*L.*]; encyclopedia *or* encyclopædia; cyclopedia *or* cyclopædia; Lindley Murray, Cocker; dictionary, lexicon, thesaurus.

PROFESSORSHIP, associate professorship, lectureship, readership, fellowship, tutorship, instructorship; chair.

DIRECTORATE, board, syndicate; College Board, Board of Regents (N. Y.), School Board, Council of Education; Board of Education; Board –, Prefect- of Studies; Textbook Committee; propaganda.

Adj. SCHOLASTIC, academic, collegiate; educational, palæstral *or* palestral, cultural; gymnastic, athletic, physical, eurythmic.

Adv. ex-cathedra.

---

543. Veracity. — N. VERACITY; truthfulness, frankness &c. *adj.*; truth, soothfastness [*archaic*], sooth [*archaic*], veridicality, sincerity, candor, honesty, fidelity; plain dealing, *bona fides* [*L.*]; love of truth; probity &c. 939; ingenuousness &c. (*artlessness*) 703.

the truth the whole truth and nothing but the truth; honest –, unvarnished –, sober- truth &c. (*fact*) 494; unvarnished tale; light of truth.

V. SPEAK THE TRUTH, tell the truth; speak on oath; speak without -equivocation, – mental reservation; speak by the card; paint in its –, show oneself in one's- true colors; make a clean breast

544. Falsehood. — N. FALSEHOOD, falseness; falsity, falsification; deception &c. 545; untruthfulness; untruth &c. 546; guile; lying &c. *v.*, misrepresentation; mendacity, perjury, false swearing; forgery, invention, fabrication; subreption; covin [*archaic*].

perversion –, suppression- of truth; *suppressio veri* [*L.*]; perversion, distortion, false coloring; exaggeration &c. 549; prevarication, equivocat on, shuffling, fencing, evasion, fraud; *suggestio falsi* [*L.*] &c. (*lie*) 546; mystification &c. (*concealment*) 528; simulation &c. (*imitation*) 19; dissimulation, dissembling; deceit; *blague* [*F.*].

&c. (*disclose*) 529; speak one's mind &c. (*be blunt*) 703; not lie &c. 544, not deceive &c. 545.

Adj. TRUTHFUL, true; veracious, veridical; scrupulous &c. (*honorable*) 939; sincere, candid, frank, open, straightforward, unreserved; open-, frank-, true-, simple- hearted; soothfast [*archaic*], truth-telling, honest, trustworthy; undissembling &c. (dissemble &c. 544); guileless, pure; truth-loving; unperjured; true-blue, as good as one's word; one's word one's bond; unaffected, unfeigned, *bonâ fide* [L.]; outspoken, ingenuous &c. (*artless*) 703; undisguised &c. (*real*) 494.

Adv. TRULY &c. (*really*) 494; in plain words &c. 703; in -, with -, of a -, in good- truth; as the dial to the sun, as the needle to the pole; honor bright [*colloq.*]; troth; in good -sooth, - earnest; soothfast [*archaic*], unfeignedly, with no nonsense, in sooth, sooth to say, *bonâ fide* [L.], *in foro conscientiæ* [L.]; without equivocation; *cartes sur table* [F.], from the bottom of one's heart; by my troth &c. (*affirmation*) 535.

⁎ *di il vero e affronterai il diavolo; Dichtung und Wahrheit; esto quod esse videris; magna est veritas et prævalet;* "that golden key that opes the palace of eternity" [Milton]; *veritas odium parit; veritatis simplex oratio est; verité sans peur.*

SHAM, pretense, pretending, malingering.

DUPLICITY, double dealing, insincerity, tartufism *or* tartuffism, hypocrisy, cant, humbug, fake [*colloq. or slang*]; casuistry, jesuitism, jesuitry; pharisaism; Machiavelism, "organized hypocrisy"; lip -homage, - service; mouth honor; hollowness; mere -show, - outside; crocodile tears, mealy-mouthedness, quackery; charlatanism, charlatanry; gammon [*colloq.*], buncombe *or* bunkum, flam: bam [*slang*], flimflam, cajolery, flattery; Judas kiss; perfidy &c. (*bad faith*) 940; *il volto sciolto i pensieri stretti* [It.].

UNFAIRNESS &c. (*dishonesty*) 940; artfulness &c. (*cunning*) 702; missatement &c. (*error*) 495.

V. BE FALSE &c. *adj.*, be a liar &c. 548; speak falsely &c. *adv.;* tell a lie &c. 546; lie, fib; lie like a trooper; swear falsely, forswear, perjure oneself, bear false witness.

FALSIFY, misstate, misquote, miscite, misreport, misrepresent; belie, pervert, distort; put a false construction upon &c. (*misinterpret*) 523.

PREVARICATE, equivocate, quibble; palter, - to the understanding; *répondre en Normand* [F.]; trim, shuffle, fence, mince the truth, beat about the bush, blow hot and cold [*colloq.*], play fast and loose.

GARBLE, gloss over, disguise, give a color to; give -, put- a -gloss, - false coloring- upon; color, varnish, cook [*colloq.*], doctor [*colloq.*], dress up, embroider; exaggerate &c. 549; *blague* [F.].

FABRICATE, invent, trump up, get up; forge, fake [*slang*], hatch, concoct; romance &c. (*imagine*) 515; cry "wolf!"

DISSEMBLE, dissimulate; feign, assume, put on, pretend, make believe; act the old soldier [*colloq.*], play possum; play -false, - a double game; coquet; act -, play- a part; affect &c. 855; simulate, pass off for; counterfeit, sham, make a show of; malinger; say the grapes are sour.

cant [*dial. Eng.*], play the hypocrite, sham Abram *or* Abraham, *faire pattes de velours* [F.], put on the mask, clean the outside of the platter, lie like a conjuror; hand out -, hold out -, sail under- false colors; "commend the poisoned chalice to the lips" [*Macbeth*]; *spargere voces in vulgum ambiguas* [Vergil]; deceive &c. 545.

Adj. FALSE, deceitful, mendacious, unveracious, fraudulent, dishonest; faithless, truthless, untruthful, trothless [*archaic*]; unfair, uncandid; hollow-hearted; evasive; uningenuous, disingenuous; hollow, insincere, *Parthis mendacior* [L.]; forsworn.

collusive, collusory [*obs.*]; artful &c. (*cunning*) 702; perfidious &c. 940; spurious &c. (*deceptive*) 545; untrue &c. 546; falsified &c. *v.;* covinous.

HYPOCRITICAL, canting, jesuitical, pharisaical; tartufish *or* tartuffish; Machiavellic, Machiavellian *or* Machiavelian; double, -tongued, -handed, -minded, -hearted, -dealing; two-faced, double-faced; Janus-faced; smooth -faced, -spoken, -tongued; plausible; mealy-mouthed; affected &c. 855.

Adv. FALSELY &c. *adj.; à la Tartufe* [*F.*], with a double tongue; slily &c. (*cunning*) 702.

*** *blandæ mendacia linguæ; falsus in uno falsus in omnibus;* "I give him joy that's awkward at a lie" [Young]; *la mentira tiene las piernas cortas* [*Sp.*]; "O what a goodly outside falsehood hath!" [*M. of V.*]; "look like the innocent flower, But be the serpent under 't" [*Macbeth*]; "a Hair perhaps divides the False and True" [Omar Khayyám – Fitzgerald]; "sin has many tools, but a lie is the handle which fits them all" [Holmes].

545. Deception. — N. DECEPTION; falseness &c. 544; untruth &c. 546; imposition, imposture; fraud, deceit, guile; fraudulence, fraudulency; covin [*archaic*]; knavery &c. (*cunning*) 702; misrepresentation &c. (*falsehood*) 544; bluff; straw-bail, straw-bid [*U. S.*]; spoof [*slang*]; hocus-pocus, *escamoterie* [*F.*], jockeyship; trickery, coggery [*obs.*], pettifoggery, sharp practice, chicanery; *supercherie* [*F.*], cozenage, circumvention, ingannation [*obs.*], collusiveness, collusion; treachery &c. 940; practical joke.

DELUSION, gullery [*archaic*]; juggling, jugglery; sleight of hand, legerdemain; prestigiation [*obs.*], prestidigitation; magic &c. 992; conjuring, conjuration.

TRICK, cheat, wile, blind, feint, plant [*slang*], bubble, fetch, catch [*dial.*], chicane, artifice, reach [*obs.*], bite [*obs., colloq.*], juggle, hocus [*archaic*]; thimble-rig, card sharping, artful dodge, swindle; tricks upon travelers; trapan *or* trepan [*archaic*], stratagem &c. (*artifice*) 702; fake [*colloq. or slang*], hoax; theft &c. 791; ballot-box stuffing [*U. S.*], barney [*slang*], bunko *or* bunco, bunko game; confidence -trick, – game; brace -, drop -, gum -, panel -, shell -, skin- game [*all slang*]; gold brick [*colloq., U. S.*].

SNARE, trap, pitfall, Cornish hug, decoy, gin; springe, springle [*obs.*]; noose, hook; bait, decoy duck, stool pigeon, tub to the whale, baited trap, *guet-apens* [*F.*]; cobweb, net, meshes, toils, mouse trap, birdlime; Dionæa, Venus's flytrap; ambush &c. 530; trapdoor, sliding panel, false bottom; spring net, spring gun; mask, masked battery; mine; flytrap; green goods [*U. S.*]; panel house.

DISGUISE, disguisement; false colors, masquerade, mummery, borrowed plumes; wolf in sheep's clothing &c. (*deceiver*) 548; *pattes de velours* [*F.*].

SHAM; mockery &c. (*imitation*) 19; copy &c. 21; counterfeit, make-believe, forgery, fraud; lie &c. 546; "a delusion, a mockery, and a snare" [Denman], hollow mockery; whited -, painted- sepulcher; jerry-building, jerryism [*builders' cant*]; man of straw.

TINSEL, paste, false jewelry, scagliola, ormolu, mosaic gold, brummagem, German silver, albata, paktong, white metal, Britannia metal, paint.

ILLUSION &c. (*error*) 495; *ignis fatuus* [*L.*] &c. 423; mirage &c. 443.

V. DECEIVE, take in, Machiavellize; defraud, cheat, jockey, do [*slang, Eng.*], *escamoter* [*F.*], cozen, diddle [*dial.*], nab [*slang*], chouse [*colloq.*], bite [*colloq.*], play one false, bilk, cully, jilt [*obs.*], pluck [*rare*], swindle, victimize; abuse; mystify; blind, – one's eyes; blindfold, hoodwink; throw dust into the eyes, "keep the word of promise to the ear and break it to the hope" [*Macbeth*].

impose -, practice -, play -, put -, palm -, foist- upon; snatch a verdict; bluff, – off; bunko *or* bunco, four-flush [*slang*]; gum [*slang, U. S.*], spoof [*slang*], stuff (a ballot box) [*U. S.*].

CIRCUMVENT, overreach; outreach, outwit, outmaneuver *or* outmanœuvre, steal a march upon, give the go-by to [*slang*], leave in the lurch.

INSNARE, ensnare; set -, lay- a -trap, – snare- for; bait the hook, forelay [*obs.*], spread the toils, lime; decoy, waylay, lure, beguile, delude, inveigle; trapan *or* trepan [*archaic*]; kidnap; let in, hook in; trick; entrap *or* intrap, nick, springe [*rare*], nousel *or* nousle [*obs.*]; blind a trail, enmesh *or* immesh; shanghai, crimp; catch, – in a trap; sniggle, entangle, illaqueate [*rare*], balk, trip up; throw a tub to a whale, hocus.

FOOL, befool, practice on one's credulity, dupe, gull, hoax, bamboozle [*colloq.*]; hum [*slang or colloq.*], humbug, gammon [*colloq.*], stuff up [*slang*], stuff [*slang*], sell [*slang*]; play a -trick, – practical joke- upon one; fool to the top of one's bent, send on a fool's errand; make -game, – a fool, – an April fool, – an ass- of; trifle with, cajole, flatter; come over &c. (*influence*) 615; gild the pill, make things pleasant, divert, put a good face upon; dissemble &c. 544.

LIVE BY ONE'S WITS; cog [*rare*], cog the dice; play at hide and seek; obtain money under false pretenses &c. (*steal*) 791; conjure, juggle, practice chicanery; deacon [*U. S.*]; jerry-build; pass by trickery, play off, palm off, foist off, fob off [*archaic*].

MISLEAD &c. (*error*) 495; lie &c. 544; misinform &c. 538; betray &c. 940.

BE DECEIVED &c. 547.

Adj. DECEPTIVE, deceptious [*rare*], deceitful, covinous [*law*]; delusive, delusory; illusive, illusory; deceived &c. *v.*; deceiving &c. *v.*; cunning &c. 702; prestigious [*obs.*], prestigiatory [*obs.*]; elusive, insidious, *ad captandum vulgus* [*L.*].

MAKE-BELIEVE; untrue &c. 546; mock, sham, counterfeit, snide [*slang*], pseudo, spurious, so-called, pretended, feigned, trumped-up, bogus [*colloq.*], scamped, fraudulent, tricky, factitious, artificial, bastard; surreptitious, illegitimate, contraband, adulterated, sophisticated; unsound, rotten at the core; colorable; disguised; meretricious; jerry-built, jerry [*builders' cant*]; tinsel, pinchbeck, plated; catchpenny; brummagem; simulated &c. 544.

Adv. under -false colors, – the garb of, – cover of; over the left [*slang*].

** *fronti nulla fides;* "ah that deceit should steal such gentle shapes" [*Rich. III*]; "a quick-sand of deceit" [*Henry VI*]; *decipimur specie recti* [Hor.]; *falsi crimen; fraus est celare fraudem; lupus in fabula;* "so smooth, he daubed his vice with show of virtue" [*Rich. III*]; "there are but two classes of men, the righteous, who think themselves to be sinners, and the sinners, who think themselves righteous" [Pascal].

546. Untruth. — N. UNTRUTH, falsehood, lie, story, thing that is not, fib, bounce, crammer [*slang*], tarradiddle *or* taradiddle [*colloq. or dial. Eng.*], whopper *or* whapper [*colloq.*], *jhuth* [*Hind.*].

FABRICATION, forgery, invention; misstatement, misrepresentation, perversion, falsification, gloss, *suggestio falsi* [*L.*]; exaggeration &c. 549.

fiction; fable, nursery tale; romance &c. (*imagination*) 515; absurd –, untrue –, false –, trumped up- -story, – statement; thing devised by the enemy; canard; shave [*slang, Eng.*], sell [*colloq.*], hum, [*slang*], yarn [*colloq.*], fish story [*colloq.*], traveler's tale, Canterbury tale, cock-and-bull story, fairy tale, fake, press-agent's yarn [*colloq.*], hot air [*slang*], claptrap.

myth, moonshine, bosh [*colloq.*], all my eye and Betty Martin [*colloq.*], all my eye [*colloq.*], mare's-nest, farce.

HALF TRUTH, white lie, pious fraud; mental reservation &c. (*concealment*) 528; irony.

PRETENSE, pretext; false plea &c. 617; subterfuge, evasion, shift, shuffle, make-believe; sham &c. (*deception*) 545; profession, empty words; Judas kiss &c. (*hypocrisy*) 544; disguise &c. (*mask*) 530.

V. RING UNTRUE; have a -false meaning, – hidden meaning, – false appearance; be an untruth &c. *n.*; lie &c. 544.

FEIGN, pretend, sham, counterfeit, gammon [*colloq.*], make-believe.

Adj. UNTRUE, false, trumped up; void of –, without- foundation; fictive, far from the truth, false as dicer's oaths; unfounded, *ben trovato* [*It.*], invented, fabulous, fabricated, fraudulent, forged; fictitious, factitious, suppositious, surreptitious; illusory, elusory; evasive, satiric *or* satirical, ironical; *soi-disant* [*F.*] &c. (*misnamed*) 565.

** *se non e vero e ben trovato;* "where more is meant than meets the ear" [Milton]; "a lie in time saves nine" [*Cynic's Calendar*].

547. Dupe. — N. DUPE, gull, gudgeon, *gobemouche* [*F.*], cully, victim, April fool; jay, sucker, pigeon, cull [*all slang*]; laughingstock &c. 857; simple Simon, flat [*colloq.*], greenhorn; fool &c. 501; puppet, cat's-paw.

V. BE DECEIVED &c. 545, be the dupe

548. Deceiver. — N. DECEIVER &c. (deceive &c. 545); dissembler, hypocrite; sophist, Pharisee, Jesuit, Mawworm, Pecksniff, Joseph Surface, Tartufe *or* Tartuffe, Janus; serpent, snake in the grass, cockatrice, Judas, wolf in sheep's clothing; jilt; shuffler.

of; fall into a trap; swallow -, nibble at- the bait; bite; catch a Tartar.

Adj. CREDULOUS &c. 486.

MISTAKEN &c. (*error*) 495.

liar &c. (*lie* &c. 544); Tom Pepper, Machiavel, Machiavelist; story-teller, perjurer, false witness, *menteur à triple étage* [*F.*], Scapin; bunko steerer, carpet-bagger, capper [*all slang, U. S.*], faker [*slang*], fraud, four-flusher [*slang*], confidence man, horse coper [*Eng.*], ringer [*slang*], spieler [*colloq., Australasia*]; straw bidder [*U. S.*]; crimp; decoy duck, stool pigeon; rogue, knave, cheat; swindler &c. (*thief*) 792; jobber, gypsy.

IMPOSTOR, pretender, malingerer, humbug; adventurer, adventuress; Cagliostro, Fernam Mendez Pinto; ass in lion's skin &c. (*bungler*) 701; actor &c. (*stage player*) 599.

QUACK, charlatan, mountebank, saltimbanco [*obs.*], *saltimbanque* [*F.*], *blagueur* [*F.*], empiric, quacksalver [*now rare*], medicaster.

CONJUROR, juggler, trickster, prestidigitator, necromancer, sorcerer, magician, wizard, mage [*archaic*], medicine man, shaman.

✻ "saint abroad and a devil at home" [Bunyan].

---

549. Exaggeration. — N. EXAGGERATION; expansion &c. 194; hyperbole, stretch, strain, coloring; high coloring, caricature, *caricatura* [*It.*]; extravagance &c. (*nonsense*) 497; Baron Munchausen; Munchausenism; men in buckram, yarn [*colloq.*], fringe, embroidery, traveler's tale; fish story [*colloq.*], gooseberry [*slang*].

storm -, tempest- in a teacup; much ado about nothing &c. (*overestimation*) 482; puffery &c. (*boasting*) 884; rant &c. (*turgescence*) 577.

false coloring &c. (*falsehood*) 544; aggravation &c. 835.

FIGURE OF SPEECH, *façon de parler* [*F.*]; stretch of -fancy, - the imagination; flight of fancy &c. (*imagination*) 515.

V. EXAGGERATE, magnify, pile up, aggravate; amplify &c. (*expand*) 194; optimize; overestimate &c. 482; hyperbolize; overcharge, overstate, overdraw, overlay, overshoot the mark, overpraise; make much of, make the most of; strain, - a point; stretch, - a point; go great lengths; spin a long yarn [*colloq.*]; draw -, pull -, use -, shoot with- a (*or* the) longbow [*colloq.*]; deal in the marvelous.

out-Herod Herod, run riot, talk at random.

OVERCOLOR, heighten; color -highly, - too highly; *broder* [*F.*], embroider, be flowery; flourish; color &c. (*misrepresent*) 544; puff &c. (*boast*) 884.

UNDERRATE, pessimize, underestimate &c. 483.

Adj. EXAGGERATED &c. *v.*; overwrought; bombastic &c. (*magniloquent*) 577; hyperbolical, on stilts; fabulous, extravagant, preposterous, egregious, *outré* [*F.*], highflying.

✻ *excitabat enim fluctus in simpulo* [Cicero]; "exaggeration is to paint a snake and add legs" [*Chinese proverb*]; "there is no one who does not exaggerate" [Emerson].

Section III. MEANS OF COMMUNICATING IDEAS

1. *Natural Means*

550. Indication. — N. INDICATION; symbolism, symbolization; symptomatology, semeiology *or* semiology, semeiotics *or* semiotics, pathognomy; *Zeitgeist* [*Ger.*], sign of the times.

MEANS OF RECOGNITION; lineament, feature, trait, trick, earmark, characteristic, diagnostic; divining rod; cloven hoof; footfall.

SIGN, symbol; index, indice [*obs.*], indicator, point, pointer; exponent, note, token, symptom; dollar mark; type, figure, emblem, cipher, device; representation &c. 554.

MOTTO, epigraph, epitaph, posy [*archaic*].

GESTURE, gesticulation; pantomime; wink, glance, leer; nod, shrug, beck; touch, nudge; grip, freemasonry; telegraphy, byplay, dumb show; cue; hint &c. 527.

TRACK, spoor, trail, footprint, scent; clew *or* clue, key.

DACTYLOLOGY, dactylography, dactylonomy, dactyliomancy, chirology [*rare*], chiromancy, palmistry; finger print, Bertillon system.

SIGNAL, signal post, rocket, blue light, red light; watch fire, watchtower; telegraph, semaphore, flagstaff; fiery cross; calumet, peace pipe; heliograph; guidon; headlight, searchlight, flashlight, spotlight.

MARK, line, stroke, score, stripe, streak, scratch, tick, dot, point, notch, nick, blaze; red letter, sublineation, underlining, jotting; print; imprint, impress, impression; note, annotation.

[MAP DRAWING] hachure, contour line; isobar, isopiestic line, isobaric line; isotherm, isothermal line; latitude, longitude, meridian, equator.

[TYPOGRAPHY] dash, hyphen, parentheses, brackets *or* crotchets, apostrophe, interrogation *or* interrogation point, exclamation *or* exclamation point; acute -, grave- accent; long *or* macron, short *or* breve, diæresis, caret, brace, ellipsis, leaders, asterisk, dagger *or* obelisk, double dagger, section, parallels, paragraph, index, asterism, cedilla, guillemets [*rare*], quotation marks *or* quotes [*colloq.*], tilde, circumflex.

[FOR IDENTIFICATION] badge, criterion; countercheck, countermark, countersign, counterfoil, stub, duplicate, tally; label, ticket, billet, letter, counter, check, chip, chop [*Oriental*], dib [*slang*]; broad arrow; government mark; totem; tessera, card, bill; witness, voucher; stamp; *cachet* [*F.*]; trade -, hall- mark; signature; address -, visiting- card; *carte de visite* [*F.*]; credentials &c. (*evidence*) 467; attestation; hand, handwriting, sign manual; cipher; monogram; seal, sigil, signet; autograph, autography; finger print; paraph, brand; superscription; indorsement *or* endorsement; title, heading, docket; tonsure, scalp lock; mortar board [*colloq.*], cap and gown, hood; caste mark; *mot de passe* [*F.*], *mot du guet* [*F.*]; passeparole *or* passparole [*obs.*], shibboleth; watchword, catchword, password; sign, countersign, pass, dueguard, grip; open-sesame; timbrology [*rare*].

INSIGNIA; banner, banneret; banderole, bandrol *or* bannerol; flag, colors, streamer, standard, eagle, vexillum, labarum, oriflamme *or* oriflamb; figurehead; ensign; pennant, whip *or* coach-whip, pennon, burgee, blue peter, jack, ancient [*rare*], gonfalon, union jack; "Old Glory" [*colloq.*, *U. S.*], quarantine flag; yellow flag, yellow jack; tricolor, *drapeau tricolore* [*F.*], stars and stripes; half-masted flag, union down; red flag; bunting.

HERALDRY, crest; arms, coat of arms; armorial bearings, hatchment; escutcheon *or* scutcheon, achievement, shield, supporters; livery, uniform; cockade, brassard, epaulet, chevron; garland, chaplet, fillet [*antiq.*], love knot, favor.

[OF LOCALITY] beacon, beacon fire, cresset, cairn, post, staff, flagstaff, hand, pointer, vane, cock, weathercock, weathervane; guide-, hand-, finger-, directing-, sign- post; pillars of Hercules, pharos; balefire, signal fire; *l'Etoile du Nord* [*F.*], North Star, polestar, Polaris; landmark, seamark; lighthouse, balize [*rare*], lodestar *or* loadstar; cynosure, guide; address, direction, name; sign, signboard.

[OF THE FUTURE] warning &c. 668; omen &c. 512; prefigurement &c. 511.

[OF THE PAST] trace, record &c. 551.

[OF DANGER] warning &c. 668; fire alarm, burglar alarm; alarm &c. 669.

[OF AUTHORITY] scepter &c. 747.

[OF TRIUMPH] trophy &c. 733.

[OF QUANTITY] gauge &c. 466.

[OF DISTANCE] milestone, milepost; mileage ticket; milliary [*Rom. antiq.*].

[OF DISGRACE] brand, fool's cap, mark of Cain, stigma, stripes, broad arrow.

[FOR DETECTION] check, time clock, telltale; test &c. (*experiment*) 463.

NOTIFICATION &c. (*information*) 527; advertisement &c. (*publication*) 531.

CALL, word of command; bugle call, trumpet call; bell, alarum, cry; battle -, rallying- cry; reveille, taps [*Brit.*], last post [*U. S.*]; sacring bell, Sanctus bell, angelus; pibroch, keen [*Ir.*], coronach [*Scot. & Ir.*], dirge.

V. INDICATE; be the sign of &c. *n.;* denote, betoken; argue, testify &c. (*evidence*) 467; bear the impress of &c. *n.;* connote, connotate, signify.

represent, stand for; typify &c. (*prefigure*) 511; symbolize.

MARK; put an indication, put a mark &c. *n.;* note, tick,¦ stamp, nick, earmark; blaze; label, ticket, docket; dot, spot, score, dash, trace, chalk.

PRINT, imprint, impress; engrave, stereotype, electrotype, lithograph; prove, pull, reprint.

MAKE A SIGN &c. *n.;* signalize; give –, hang out- a signal; beck [*archaic*], beckon; nod; wink, glance, leer, nudge, shrug, tip the wink [*slang*]; gesture, gesticulate; raise –, hold up- the -finger, – hand; saw the air, "suit the action to the word" [*Hamlet*].

wave –, unfurl –, hoist –, hang out- a banner &c. *n.;* wave -the hand, – a kerchief; give the cue &c. (*inform*) 527; show one's colors; give –, sound- an alarm; beat the drum, sound the trumpets, raise a cry.

sign, seal, attest &c. (*evidence*) 467; underscore, underline &c. (*give importance to*) 642; call attention to &c. (*attention*) 457; give notice &c. (*inform*) 527.

Adj. INDICATIVE, indicatory; indicating &c. *v .* connotative, denotative; diacritical, representative, typical, symbolic *or* symbolical, pantomimic, pathognomonic *or* pathognomonical, symptomatic, semeiotic *or* semiotic, sematic, ominous, characteristic, significant, significative, demonstrative, diagnostic, exponential, emblematic, armorial; individual &c. (*special*) 79.

KNOWN BY, recognizable by; indicated &c. *v.;* pointed, marked.

[CAPABLE OF BEING DENOTED] denotable; indelible.

Adv. SYMBOLICALLY &c. *adj.;* in token of; in dumb show, in pantomime.

*** *ecce signum; ex ungue leonem; ex pede Herculem; vide ut supra; vultus ariete fortior; vera incessu patuit dea* [Vergil].

551. Record. — N. TRACE, vestige, relic, remains; scar, cicatrix; footstep, footmark, footprint; pug [*India*], track, mark, wake, trail, scent, *piste* [*F.*].

MONUMENT, hatchment, achievement; escutcheon *or* scutcheon; slab, tablet, trophy, obelisk, pillar, column, monolith; memorial; memento &c. (*memory*) 505; testimonial, medal, Congressional medal; cross, Victoria cross *or* V. C., iron cross [*Ger.*]; ribbon, garter; commemoration &c. (*celebration*) 883.

RECORD, note, minute; register, registry; roll &c. (*list*) 86; chartulary *or* cartulary, diptych, Domesday book; *catalogue raisonné* [*F.*]; entry, memorandum, indorsement *or* endorsement, inscription, copy, duplicate, docket; notch &c. (*mark*) 550; muniments; deed &c. (*security*) 771; document; deposition, *procés verbal* [*F.*]; affidavit; certificate &c. (*evidence*) 467.

notebook, memorandum book, pocketbook, commonplace book, portfolio; bulletin, bulletin board, score board, score sheet, totalizator [*racing*]; card index, file, letter file, pigeonholes; *excerpta* [*L.*], excerpt, extract, adversaria, jottings, dottings.

newspaper, daily, gazette &c. (*publication*) 531; magazine.

calendar, ephemeris, diary, log, log book *or* logbook, journal, daybook, ledger, cashbook, petty cashbook.

ARCHIVE, scroll, state paper, return, bluebook *or* blue book; almanac *or* almanack, gazetteer, Almanach de Gotha, Statesman's Year-book, Whitaker's Almanack; census report; statistics &c. 86; *compte rendu* [*F.*]; Acts –, Transactions –, Proceedings- of; Hansard's Debates; Congressional Records: minutes, chronicle, annals; legend; history, biography &c. 594.

552. [SUPPRESSION OF SIGN.] **Obliteration. — N.** OBLITERATION, erasure, rasure [*rare*]; cancel, cancellation; circumduction [*rare*], deletion, blot; *tabula rasa* [*L.*]; effacement, extinction.

V. EFFACE, obliterate, erase, rase [*rare*], expunge, cancel, dele; blot –, take –, rub –, scratch –, strike –, wipe –, wash –, sponge- out; wipe off, rub off; wipe away; deface, render illegible; draw the pen through, rule out, apply the sponge.

BE EFFACED &c.; leave no trace &c. 550; "leave not a rack behind" [*Tempest*].

Adj. OBLITERATED &c. *v.;* leaving no trace; intestate; unrecorded, unregistered, unwritten; printless, out of print.

Int. dele; out with it!

*** *delenda est Carthago* [Cato].

REGISTRATION; registry, enrollment *or* enrolment, tabulation; entry, booking; signature &c. (*identification*) 550; recorder &c. 553; journalism.

MECHANICAL RECORD, recording instrument; gramophone, phonograph &c. 418; seismograph, seismometer; speedometer, pedometer, patent log [*naut.*]; ticker, tape; time clock; anemometer &c. (*measurement*) 466; turnstile; cash register; votograph.

V. RECORD; put –, place– upon record; chronicle, calendar, excerpt, hand down to posterity; keep up the memory &c. (*remember*) 505; commemorate &c. (*celerate*) 883; report &c. (*inform*) 527; commit to –, reduce to– writing; put –, set down– –in writing, – in black and white; put –, jot –, take –, write –, note –, set-down; note, minute, put on paper; take –, make– a –note, – minute, – memorandum; summarize, make a return; mark &c. (*indicate*) 550; sign &c. (*attest*) 467.

ENTER, book; post, post up; insert, make an entry of; mark off, tick off; register, list, docket, enroll, inscroll; file &c. (*store*) 636.

Adv. ON RECORD, on file; in one's –good books, – bad books.

₊ *exegi monumentum ære perennius* [Horace]; "read their history in a nation's eyes" [Gray]; "records that defy the tooth of time" [Young].

553. Recorder. — N. RECORDER, notary, clerk; registrar, registrary [*obs.*], register; prothonotary; amanuensis, secretary, recording secretary, stenographer, scribe, babu [*India*], remembrancer, bookkeeper, *custos rotulorum* [*L.*], Master of the Rolls.

ANNALIST, historian, historiographer, chronicler; biographer &c. (*narrator*) 594; antiquary &c. (*antiquity*) 122; memorialist.

JOURNALIST, newspaperman, reporter, interviewer, pressman [*cant*], publicist, author, editor.

₊ "the journalists are now the true kings and clergy" [Carlyle].

554. Representation. — N. REPRESENTATION, depiction, depicture; imitation &c. 19; illustration, delineation, depictment; imagery, portraiture, iconography; design, designing; art, fine arts; painting &c. 556; sculpture &c. 557; engraving &c. 558.

PHOTOGRAPHY; radiography, X-ray photography, skiagraphy; spectroheliography, photospectroheliography.

PERSONATION, personification; impersonation; drama &c. 599.

DRAWING, picture, sketch, draft *or* draught; tracing; copy &c. 21.

PHOTOGRAPH, photo [*colloq.*], daguerreotype, talbotype, calotype; heliotype, heliograph; print, cabinet, *carte de visite* (*pl. cartes de visite*) [*F.*], ping-pong [*cant*], snapshot.

IMAGE, likeness, icon, portrait; striking likeness, speaking likeness; very image; effigy, facsimile.

FIGURE, figurehead; puppet, doll, figurine, aglet *or* aiglet, manikin, mannequin, lay figure, model, marionette, fantoccini, waxwork, bust; statue, statuette, hieroglyph.

hieroglyphic, anaglyph, diagram, monogram.

MAP, plan, chart; ground plan, projection, elevation; atlas; outline, scheme; view &c. (*painting*) 556; ichnography, cartography.

RADIOGRAPH, radiogram, scotograph, skiagraph *or* sciagraph, skiagram *or* sciagram, X-ray photograph, X-ray [*colloq.*]; spectrogram, spectroheliogram, photospectroheliogram.

555. Misrepresentation. — N. MISREPRESENTATION, misstatement, falsification, caricatura [*obs.*], exaggeration; daubing &c. *v.;* bad likeness, daub, scratch; imitation, effigy.

DISTORTION, anamorphosis, anamorphoscope; Claude Lorrain –, concave –, convex– mirror.

BURLESQUE, travesty, parody, take-off, caricature, extravaganza.

V. MISREPRESENT, distort, overdraw, exaggerate, daub; falsify, understate, overstate, stretch.

BURLESQUE, travesty, parody, caricature.

Adj. MISREPRESENTED &c. *v.;* blue-sky [*U. S.*].

DELINEATOR, draftsman *or* draughtsman; artist &c. 559; photographer, radiographer, X-ray photographer, skiagrapher, daguerreotypist.

V. REPRESENT, delineate, depict, depicture, portray, picture, limn, take -, catch- a likeness &c. *n.;* hit off, photograph, daguerreotype; snapshot; figure; shadow -forth, - out; adumbrate; body forth; describe &c. 594; trace, copy; mold *or* mould.

illustrate, symbolize; paint &c. 556; carve &c. 557; engrave &c. 558.

PERSONATE, personify, impersonate, dress up [*colloq.*], assume a character, pose as, act; play &c. (*drama*) 599; mimic &c. (*imitate*) 19; hold the mirror up to nature.

Adj. REPRESENTING &c. *v.*, representative; illustrative; represented &c. *v.;* imitative, figurative; iconic, like &c. 17; graphic &c. (*descriptive*) 594.

Renaissance, trecento, quattrocento, cinquecento, Directoire, Moyen Age.

₊ "Passionless eyes, long dead, that judged and glared" [Masefield].

556. Painting and Black and White. — N. PAINTING; depicting; drawing &c. *v.;* design; perspective; *chiaroscuro* &c. (*light*) 420; composition; treatment; arrangement, values, atmosphere, tone, technique.

historical -, portrait -, miniature -, landscape -, marine -, flower -, poster -, interior -, scene- painting; scenography.

pallet, palette; easel; brush, pencil, stump; black lead, charcoal, crayons, chalk, pastel; paint &c. (*coloring matter*) 428; water-, body-, oil- color; oils, oil paint; varnish &c. 356a; priming; *gouache* [*F.*], tempera, distemper, fresco, water glass; enamel; encaustic painting; mosaic; tapestry, batik; sun painting.

STYLE, school; the grand style, high art, *genre* [*F.*], portraiture; futurist, cubist, vorticist; ornamental art &c. 847; monochrome, polychrome; grisaille.

[SCHOOLS OF PAINTING] Italian -, Bolognese -, Florentine -, Milanese -, Modena -, Parma -, Neapolitan -, Paduan -, Roman -, Umbrian -, Venetian -, British -, Dutch -, Flemish -, French -, German -, Spanish- School; School of Raphael &c.

PICTURE, painting, piece, tableau, canvas; oil painting &c.; fresco, cartoon; easel -, cabinet- picture; drawing, draft *or* draught; pencil &c. drawing, water-color drawing; still life; sketch, outline, study.

PORTRAIT &c. (*representation*) 554; whole -, full -, half- length; three-quarters profile; head; miniature; shade, silhouette; profile.

VIEW, landscape, seascape, sea view, seapiece; scene, prospect; interior; panorama, bird's-eye view, diorama.

PICTURE GALLERY, art gallery, art museum, pinacotheca; studio, *atelier* [*F.*].

PHOTOGRAPHY, skiagraphy, radiography &c. 554; photograph, radiograph &c. 554; scenograph.

V. PAINT, design, limn, draw, sketch, pencil, scratch, shade, stipple, hatch, dash off, chalk out, square up; color, dead color, wash, varnish; draw in pencil &c. *n.;* paint in oils &c. *n.;* stencil; depict &c. (*represent*) 554.

Adj. PICTORIAL, graphic; painted &c. *v.;* picturesque, genre; historical &c. *n.;* monochrome, polychrome; scenographic; futurist, cubist, vorticist; in the grand style; painty, pastose.

pencil, oil &c. *n.*

Adv. in pencil &c. *n.*

₊ *fecit, delineavit; mutum est pictura poema;* "art is the perfection of nature" [Sir Thomas Browne]; "the canvas glow'd beyond ev'n nature warm" [Goldsmith]; "greater completion marks the progress of art, absolute completion usually its decline" [Ruskin].

557. Sculpture. — N. SCULPTURE, insculpture [*obs.*]; carving &c. *v.;* statuary, anaglyptics, ceramics.

marble, bronze, terra cotta; ceramic ware, pottery, porcelain, china, earthenware; cloisonné, enamel, faïence, satsuma.

RELIEF, relievo; basso-relievo *or bassorilievo* [*It.*], low relief, bas-relief; alto-relievo *or alto-rilievo* [*It.*], high relief; mezzo-relievo *or mezzo-rilievo* [*It.*]; glyph, intaglio, anaglyph; medal, medallion; cameo.

[SCHOOLS OF SCULPTURE] Æginetan –, Attic –, Chian –, Pergamene –, Rhodian –, Samian –, Sicyonian- School.

STATUE &c. (*image*) 554; cast &c. (*copy*) 21; glyptotheca.

[STATUES] Apollo Belvedere, Venus of Melos *or* Milo, Cnidian Aphrodite, Venus de' Medici, Dying Gaul, Farnese Hercules, Laocoön, Niobe, Silenus and Infant Bacchus, Theseus, Centaur and Eros, Niké *or* Winged Victory of Samothrace, The Wrestlers, Michelangelo's David, Mercury taking Flight, Rodin's The Thinker.

V. SCULPTURE, carve, cut, chisel, model, mold; cast.

Adj. SCULPTURED &c. *v.;* in relief, glyptic, anaglyphic, anaglyptic, ceroplastic, ceramic; Parian; marble &c. *n.;* xanthian.

558. Engraving. — N. ENGRAVING, chalcography, glyptography; line –, mezzotint –, stipple –, chalk- engraving; dry point, bur; etching, aquatint *or* aquatinta; chiseling; plate –, copperplate –, steel –, half-tone –, process –, wood- engraving; xylography, lignography, glyptography, cerography, lithography, chromolithography, photolithography, zincography, glyphography.

graver, burin, etching point, style; plate, stone, wood block, negative; die, punch, stamp.

PRINTING; plate –, copperplate –, anastatic –, color –, lithographic- printing; type printing &c. 591; three-color process.

IMPRESSION, print, engraving, plate; steel-plate, copperplate; etching; aquatint, mezzotint, lithotint; cut, woodcut; stereotype, graphotype, autotype, heliotype; xylograph, lignograph, glyptograph, cerograph, lithograph, chromolithograph, photolithograph, zincograph, glyphograph; process.

illustration, illumination; half tone; photogravure; rotogravure [*trade name*]; vignette, initial letter, *cul de lampe* [*F.*], tailpiece.

V. ENGRAVE, grave, insculp [*rare*], stipple, scrape, etch; bite, bite in; lithograph &c. *n.;* print.

Adj. ENGRAVED &c. *v.;* insculptured, glyptographic; "insculp'd upon" [*Merchant of Venice*].

✱ *sculpsit; imprimit.*

559. Artist. — N. ARTIST; painter, limner, drawer, sketcher, designer, engrave chalcographer, glyptographer, graver, line engraver, draftsman *or* draughtsman copyist; enameler *or* enameller, enamelist *or* enamellist; cartoonist, caricaturist.

historical –, landscape –, marine –, flower –, portrait –, genre –, miniature –, scene- painter; carver, chaser, modeler, *figuriste* [*F.*], statuary, sculptor.

Phidias, Praxiteles, Apelles, Raphael, Michelangelo, Titian; Royal Academician.

✱ "Dead he is not, but departed, — for the artist never dies" [Longfellow]; "Around the mighty master come The marvels which his pencil wrought" [Whittier].

2. Conventional Means

1. Language generally

560. Language. — N. LANGUAGE; phraseology &c. 569; speech &c. 582; tongue, lingo [*chiefly humorous or contemptuous*], vernacular; mother –, vulgar –, native- tongue; household words; King's *or* Queen's English; dialect, brogue, patois &c. 563; idiom, idiotism.

confusion of tongues, Babel; *pasigraphie* [*F.*], pasigraphy; universal language, Volapük, Esperanto, Ido; pantomime &c. (*signs*) 550.

LINGUISTICS, lexicology, philology, glossology, glottology, comparative philology; Grimm's law, Verner's law; comparative grammar, phonetics; chrestomathy; paleology *or* palæology, paleography *or* palæography.

onomatopœia, betacism, mimmation, myatism, nunnation.

LITERATURE, letters, polite literature, *belles lettres* [*F.*], muses, humanities, *litteræ humaniores* [*L.*], republic of letters, dead languages, classics; genius –, spirit –, idiom- of a language; scholarship &c. (*knowledge*) 490.

LINGUIST &c. (*scholar*) 492.

V. EXPRESS, say, express by words &c. 566.

Adj. LINGUAL, linguistic; dialectic; vernacular, current; bilingual; diglot, hexaglot, polyglot; literary; colloquial, slangy.

*** "syllables govern the world" [Selden]; "Literature is the Thought of thinking Souls" [Carlyle].

561. Letter. — N. LETTER; character; hieroglyphic &c. (*writing*) 590; type &c. (*printing*) 591; capitals; digraph, trigraph; ideogram, ideograph; majuscule, *majusculæ* [*L.*]; minuscule, *minusculæ* [*L.*]; alphabet, ABC, abecedary, christcross-row *or* crisscross-row [*obs. or dial. Eng.*].

consonant, vowel; diphthong, triphthong; mute, surd, sonant, liquid, labial, palatal, cerebral, dental, guttural; guna, vriddhi [*Skr. gram.*].

SYLLABLE; monosyllable, dissyllable, polysyllable; affix, prefix, suffix.

SPELLING, orthography; phonography, phonetic spelling, phonetics; anagrammatism, metagrammatism.

CIPHER, monogram, anagram; acrostic, double acrostic.

V. spell, orthographize [*rare*]; gunate; transliterate.

CIPHER, decipher; code, decode; make –, construct- acrostics; design monograms; play anagrams; use –, invent- ciphers.

Adj. LITERAL; alphabetical, abecedarian; syllabic; majuscular, minuscular; uncial &c. (*writing*) 590.

PHONETIC, voiced, tonic, sonant; voiceless, surd; mute, labial, palatal, cerebral, dental, guttural, liquid.

562. Word. — N. WORD, term, vocable; name &c. 564; phrase &c. 566; root, etymon; derivative; part of speech &c. (*grammar*) 567; ideophone.

DICTIONARY, lexicon, vocabulary, word book, index, glossary, thesaurus, gradus, delectus, concordance; Rosetta stone.

[SCIENCE OF LANGUAGE] etymology, derivation, glottology *or* glossology, terminology, orismology; translation; pronunciation, orthoëpy; paleology &c. (*philology*) 560; lexicography.

LEXICOGRAPHER, lexicologist, etymologist, orthoëpist, verbarian; glossographer &c. (*scholar*) 492.

VERBOSITY, verbiage, wordiness; loquacity &c. 584.

V. vocalize; etymologize, derive, philologize; index; translate.

Adj. VERBAL, literal; titular, nominal. [SIMILARLY DERIVED] conjugate, paronymous; derivative.

VERBOSE, wordy &c. 573; loquacious &c. 584.

Adv. VERBALLY &c. *adj.; verbatim* [*L.*] &c. (*exactly*) 494.

*** "in the beginning was the Word" [*Bible*]; "the artillery of words" [Swift].

563. Neology. — N. NEOLOGY, neologism; newfangled expression; caconym; barbarism; archaism, black letter, monkish Latin; corruption, missaying, antiphrasis; pseudology; idioticon.

PLAY UPON WORDS, paronomasia; word play &c. (*wit*) 842; *double-entente* [*F.*] &c. (*ambiguity*) 520; palindrome, paragram, clinch [*now rare*], pun; abuse of -language, – terms.

DIALECT, brogue, patois, provincialism, broken English, Anglicism, Briticism, Gallicism, Scotticism, Hibernicism, Americanism; Gypsy lingo, Romany.

LINGUA FRANCA, pidgin *or* pigeon English; Chinook, Hindustani, kitchen Kaffir, Swahili, Haussa, Volapük, Esperanto, Ido.

JARGON, dog Latin, gibberish; confusion of tongues, Babel; babu English, chi-chi [*Anglo-India*].

colloquialism &c. (*figure of speech*) 521; byword; technicality, lingo, slang, cant, argot, *bat* [*Hind.*], macaronics, St. Giles's Greek, thieves' Latin, peddler's French, flash tongue, Billingsgate, Wall Street slang.

PSEUDONYM &c. (*misnomer*) 565; Mr.

So-and-so; "Sergeant What-is-name" [Kipling]; what d'ye call 'em, what's his name, thingummy, thingamabob, thingummybob [*all colloq.*]; *je ne sais quoi* [*F.*].

NEOLOGIST, coiner of words.

V. coin words; Americanize, Anglicize, Gallicize; sling the bat [*slang, Anglo-Ind.*].

Adj. neologic, neological; archaic, rare, obsolescent; obsolete &c. (*old*) 124; colloquial, dialectal, dialectic *or* dialectical; slang, cant, flash, barbarous; *Anglice* [*NL.*].

564. Nomenclature. — N. NOMEN-
CLATURE; naming &c. *v.*; nuncupation
[*obs.*], nomination [*obs.*], baptism; orismology; onomatopœia; antonomasia.

NAME; appellation, appellative; designation; title; head, heading; caption;
denomination; by-name; nickname &c.
565; epithet; what one may -well, -
fairly, - properly, - fitly- call.

style, proper name; prænomen, agnomen, cognomen; patronymic, surname;
cognomination; eponym; compellation,
description, synonym, antonym; empty
-title, - name; title, handle to one's
name; namesake.

TERM, expression, noun; byword; convertible terms &c. 522; technical term;
cant &c. 563.

V. NAME, call, term, denominate,
designate, style, entitle, clepe [*archaic*],
dub [*colloq. or humorous*], christen, baptize, nickname, characterize, specify,
define, distinguish by the name of;
label &c. (*mark*) 550.

BE CALLED &c. *v.*; take -, bear -, go
(*or* be known) by -, go (*or* pass) under -, rejoice in- the name of; hight [*archaic*],
yclept *or* ycleped [*archaic or humorous*].

Adj. NAMED &c. *v.*; known as; nuncupatory [*obs.*], nuncupative [*obs.*]; cog-
nominal, titular, nominal, orismological.

⁎ "beggar'd all description" [*Antony and Cleopatra*]; "what's in a name? That which
we call a rose By any other name would smell as sweet" [*Romeo and Juliet*].

565. Misnomer. — N. MISNOMER; *lucus a non lucendo* [*L.*]; Mrs. Malaprop;
what d'ye call 'em &c. (*neologism*) 563.

NICKNAME, *sobriquet* [*F.*] *or* soubri-
quet, pet name, little name, by-name;
assumed -name, - title; alias; *nom de
course* [*F.*], *nom de théâtre* [*F.*], stage
name; *nom de guerre* [*F.*], *nom de plume*
[*English formation*], pen name, pseudonym; pseudonymity, pseudonymous-
ness.

V. MISNAME, miscall, misterm; call
out of one's name [*colloq.*], nickname;
assume -a name, - an alias; take an
-alias, - assumed name.

Adj. MISNAMED &c. *v.*; pseudony-
mous; *soi-disant* [*F.*]; self-called, self-
styled, self-christened; so-called, quasi.

NAMELESS, anonymous; without a -,
having no- name; innominate, unnamed; unacknowledged; pseudo, bastard.

Adv. in no sense; by whatever name,
under any name.

---

566. Phrase. — N. PHRASE, expression, locution, set phrase; sentence, paragraph;
figure of speech &c. 521; idiom, idiotism; turn of expression; style.

paraphrase &c. (*synonym*) 522; euphemism; euphuism; periphrase &c. (*circumlocution*) 573; motto &c. (*proverb*) 496; phraseology &c. 569.

V. EXPRESS, phrase; word, word it; give -words, - expression -to; voice; arrange
in -, clothe in -, put into -, express by- words; couch in terms; find words to
express; speak by the card; call, denominate, designate, dub.

Adj. expressed &c. *v.*; idiomatic; stylistic.

Adv. in -round, - set, - good set- terms; in set phrases; by the card.

---

567. Grammar. — N. GRAMMAR, accidence, syntax, analysis, praxis, punctuation; parts of speech; jussive; syllabi-
cation *or* syllabification, paradigm,
syllepsis, synopsis; inflection, case, declension, conjugation; *jus et norma
loquendi* [*L.*]; Lindley Murray &c.
(*schoolbook*) 542; correct style, philology
&c. (*language*) 560.

V. parse, analyze *or* analyse, conjugate, decline; punctuate, syllabicate,
syllabize.

Adj. grammatical, syntactic *or* syn-
tactical, inflectional; synoptic.

568. Solecism. — N. SOLECISM; bad
-, false -, faulty- grammar; grammatical
blunder; *faux pas* [*F.*], error, slip; slip
of the pen, *lapsus calami* [*L.*]; slip of the
tongue, *lapsus linguæ* [*L.*]; slipslop; bull,
Hibernianism; barbarism, impropriety.

V. SOLECIZE *or* solecise, commit a
solecism; use -bad, - faulty- grammar;
murder the King's (*or* Queen's) English;
speak -, write- out of the idiom; break
Priscian's head.

Adj. UNGRAMMATICAL; incorrect, inaccurate, faulty; improper, incongruous;
solecistic *or* solecistical; slipslop.

569. Style. — N. STYLE, diction, phraseology, wording; manner, strain; composition; mode of expression, idiom, choice of words; mode of speech, literary power, ready pen, pen of a ready writer; grand style, grand manner; command of language &c. (*eloquence*) 582; authorship, artistry; *la morgue littéraire* [*F.*].

V. WORD; express by words &c. 566; write; apply –, employ– the file.

.*. *le style c'est de l'homme* [Buffon]; "style is the dress of thoughts" [Chesterfield].

Various Qualities of Style

570. Perspicuity. — N. PERSPICUITY &c. (*intelligibility*) 518; plain speaking &c. (*manifestation*) 525; definiteness, definition; exactness &c. 494; explicitness, lucidness, lucidity, limpidity, clearness.

Adj. LUCID &c. (*intelligible*) 518; limpid, pellucid, clear; explicit &c. (*manifest*) 525; exact &c. 494.

.*. "Clear conception leads naturally to clear and correct expression" [Boileau].

571. Obscurity.— N. OBSCURITY &c. (*unintelligibility*) 519; involution, crabbedness, confusion; hard words; ambiguity &c. 520; unintelligibility, unintelligibleness; vagueness &c. 475, inexactness &c. 495; what d'ye call 'em &c. (*neologism*) 563; darkness of meaning.

Adj. OBSCURE &c. *n.;* crabbed; involved, confused.

.*. "full of sound and fury, Signifying nothing" [*Macbeth*].

572. Conciseness. — N. CONCISENESS &c. *adj.;* brevity, "the soul of wit," laconicism *or* laconism; ellipsis; syncope; abridgment &c. (*shortening*) 201; compression &c. 195; epitome &c. 596; monostich; Spartans; Tacitus.

PORTMANTEAU-WORD [Lewis Carroll]; brunch [breakfast+lunch], squarson [squire+parson]; slithy, *adj.* [slimy+lithe], torrible, *adj.* [torrid+horrible], crowzy, *adj.* [crowded+cozy].

V. BE CONCISE &c. *adj.;* telescope, laconize; condense &c. 195; abridge &c. 201; abstract &c. 596; come to the point.

Adj. CONCISE, brief, short, terse, close; to the point, exact; neat, compact; compressed, condensed, pointed; laconic, curt, pithy, trenchant, summary; pregnant; compendious &c. (*compendium*) 596; succinct; elliptical, epigrammatic, crisp; sententious.

Adv. CONCISELY &c. *adj.;* briefly, summarily; in brief, in short, in a word, in few words; for the sake of brevity, for shortness' sake; to come to the point, to make a long story short, to cut the matter short, to be brief; it comes to this, the long and short of it is, the gist is.

.*. *brevis esse laboro obscurus fio* [Horace].

573. Diffuseness. — N. DIFFUSENESS &c. *adj.;* amplification &c. *v.;* dilating &c. *v.;* verbosity, wordiness; verbiage, cloud of words, *copia verborum* [*L.*]; flow of words &c. (*loquacity*) 584; looseness.

TAUTOLOGY, battology, polylogy [*obs.*], perissology [*obs.*]; pleonasm, exuberance, redundance; thrice-told tale; prolixity, longiloquence, longsomeness, circumlocution, ambages [*rare*], periphrase, periphrasis, roundabout phrases; episode; expletive; penny-a-lining; richness &c. 577; padding [*editor's cant*]; drivel, twaddle, drool.

V. BE DIFFUSE &c. *adj.;* run out on, descant, expatiate, enlarge, dilate, amplify, expand, inflate, pad [*editor's cant*], launch out, branch out; rant.

MAUNDER, prose; harp upon &c. (*repeat*) 104; dwell on, insist upon.

DIGRESS, ramble, *battre la campagne* [*F.*], beat about the bush, perorate, spin a long yarn, protract; spin –, swell –, draw– out; battologize *or* battalogize; drivel, twaddle, drool.

Adj. DIFFUSE, profuse; wordy, verbose, largiloquent [*obs.*], copious, exuberant, pleonastic, lengthy; long, longsome, long-winded, longspun, long drawn out; spun out, protracted, prolix, diffusive, prosing, maundering; circumlocutory, periphrastic, ambagious *or* ambaguious, ambagitory, roundabout; digressive; discursive, excursive; loose; rambling, episodic; flatulent, frothy.

Adv. DIFFUSELY &c. *adj.;* at large, *in extenso* [*L.*]; about it and about.

.*. "Thou sayest an undisputed thing In such a solemn way" [Holmes].

574. Vigor. — N. VIGOR, power, force; boldness, raciness &c. *adj.;* intellectual force; spirit, punch [*slang*], point, piquancy; verve, ardor, enthusiasm, glow, fire, warmth; strong language; gravity, weight, sententiousness.

LOFTINESS, elevation, sublimity, grandeur.

ELOQUENCE; command of words, command of language.

Adj. VIGOROUS, nervous, powerful, forcible, forceful, mordant, biting, trenchant, incisive, graphic, impressive; sensational.

SPIRITED, lively, glowing, sparkling, racy, bold, slashing, crushing; pungent, piquant, full of pep [*slang*], having punch [*slang*], full of point, pointed, pithy; sententious.

LOFTY, elevated, sublime, poetic, grand, weighty, ponderous; eloquent.

VEHEMENT, petulant, passionate, burning, impassioned.

Adv. in -glowing, – good set, – no measured- terms; with his heart on fire; like a ton of bricks [*colloq.*].

*** "thoughts that breathe and words that burn" [Gray].

575. Feebleness. — N. FEEBLENESS &c. *adj.;* enervation, flaccidity, vapidity, poverty, frigidity.

Adj. FEEBLE, bald, tame, meager *or* meagre, insipid, watery, nerveless, jejune, vapid, trashy, cold, frigid, poor, dull, dry, languid; colorless, enervated; prosing, prosy, prosaic, unvaried, monotonous, weak, washy, wishy-washy [*colloq.*], sloppy, sketchy, slight; careless, slovenly, loose, disjointed, disconnected, lax; slipshod, slipslop; inexact; puerile, childish; flatulent; rambling &c. (*diffuse*) 573.

---

576. Plainness. — N. PLAINNESS &c. *adj.;* simplicity, *simplex munditiis* [Hor.], lack of ornamentation, severity; plain -terms, – English; Saxon English; household words.

V. SPEAK PLAINLY, waste no words, call a spade a spade; plunge *in medias res* [L.]; come to the point.

Adj. PLAIN, simple; unornamented, unadorned, unvarnished; homely, homespun; neat; severe, chaste, pure, Saxon; commonplace, matter-of-fact, natural, prosaic, sober, unimaginative.

DRY, unvaried, monotonous &c. 575.

Adv. POINT-BLANK; in plain -terms, words, – English; in common parlance.

577. Ornament. — N. ORNAMENT; floridness &c. *adj.;* turgidity, turgescence *or* turgescency; altiloquence [*obs.*], grandiloquence, magniloquence, declamation, teratology [*obs.*]; well-rounded periods; elegance &c. 578; orotundity.

inversion, antithesis, alliteration, paronomasia; trope; figurativeness &c. (*metaphor*) 521.

flourish; flowers of -speech, – rhetoric; frills, – of style; euphuism, euphemism.

BOMBAST, big-sounding words, high-sounding words; macrology, *sesquipedalia verba* [L.], sesquipedalian words, sesquipedality, sesquipedalianism, Alexandrine; inflation, pretension; rant, fustian, highfalutin' [*slang, U. S.*], buncombe *or* bunkum [*U. S.*], balderdash; prose run mad; fine writing; purple patches; Minerva press.

PHRASEMONGER, euphuist, euphemist; word coiner.

V. ORNAMENT, overlay with ornament, overcharge, overload; euphuize, euphemize; buncomize [*colloq.*]; smell of the lamp.

Adj. ORNATE; ornamented &c. *v.;* beautified &c. 847; florid, rich, flowery; euphuistic, euphemistic; sonorous; high- big- sounding; inflated, swelling, tumid; turgid, turgescent; pedantic, pompous, stilted; orotund; high-flown, high-flowing, highfalutin' [*slang, U. S.*]; sententious, rhetorical, declamatory; grandiose; grandiloquent; magniloquent; altiloquent [*obs.*]; sesquipedal, sesquipedalian; Johnsonian, mouthy; bombastic; fustian; frothy, flashy, flamboyant.

antithetical, alliterative, figurative &c. 521; artificial &c. (*inelegant*) 579.

Adv. *ore rotundo* [L.], with rounded phrase.

*** "to gild refinéd gold, to paint the lily, to throw a perfume on the violet" [*King John*]; "make all the little fishes talk like big whales" [Goldsmith, of Johnson — *Boswell's Life*]; "in the end never died, but passed away at her residence" [Dunsany].

578. Elegance. — N. ELEGANCE, distinction, clarity, purity, grace, felicity, ease; gracefulness, readiness &c. *adj.;* concinnity, concinnation [*rare*], euphony; balance, rhythm, symmetry, proportion, taste, good taste, restraint, nice discrimination, propriety, correctness; Attic salt, Atticism, classicalism, classicism.

well-rounded –, well-turned –, flowing- periods; the right word in the right place; antithesis &c. 577.

PURIST, classicist, stylist.

V. FLOW -SMOOTHLY, – with ease; discriminate nicely, display elegance &c. *n.;* point an antithesis, round a period.

Adj. ELEGANT, polished, classic *or* classical, classicistic, concinnous [*rare*], correct, Attic, Ciceronian, artistic; chaste, pure, Saxon, academic *or* academical.

graceful, easy, readable, fluent, flowing, tripping; unaffected, natural, unlabored; mellifluous, euphonious; euphemistic; symmetrical, balanced, restrained; rhythmic *or* rhythmical.

579. Inelegance. — N. INELEGANCE, impurity, vulgarity; want of –, poor –, bad- taste; stiffness &c. *adj.;* "unlettered Muse" [Gray]; cacology, cacography, poor diction, poor choice of words; loose –, slipshod- construction; want of balance, ill-balanced sentences; barbarism; slang &c. 563; solecism &c. 568; mannerism &c (*affectation*) 855; euphuism, Marinism, Gongorism; fustian &c. 577; cacophony; words that -break the teeth, – dislocate the jaw.

CACOGRAPHER, barbarian; euphuist, Marinist, Gongorist.

V. BE INELEGANT &c. *adj.;* employ inelegance &c. *n.*

Adj. INELEGANT, graceless, ungraceful; harsh, abrupt; dry, stiff, cramped, formal, *guindé* [*F.*]; forced, labored; artificial, mannered, ponderous; awkward, uncourtly, unpolished; turgid &c. 577; affected, euphuistic; barbarous, uncouth, grotesque, rude, crude, halting, cacographic *or* cacographical; offensive to ears polite; vulgar, tasteless.

FELICITOUS, happy, neat; well –, neatly- -put, – expressed.

*** "true ease in writing comes from art, not chance" [Pope]; "whoever wishes to obtain an English style . . . must give his days and nights to the volumes of Addison" [Johnson – *Boswell's Life*]; "elegant as simplicity" [Cowper].

2. Spoken Language

580. Voice. — N. VOICE; vocality; organ, lungs, bellows; good –, fine –, powerful &c. (*loud*) 404 –, musical &c. 413- voice; intonation; tone &c. (*sound*) 402- of voice.

UTTERANCE; vocalization; cry &c. 411; strain, prolation [*archaic*]; exclamation, ejaculation, vociferation; ecphonesis; enunciation, articulation; articulate sound, distinctness; clearness, – of articulation; stage whisper; delivery, attack.

ACCENT, accentuation; emphasis, stress; broad –, strong –, pure –, native –, foreign- accent; pronunciation; orthoëpy; euphony &c. (*melody*) 413; polyphonism, polyphony.

[WORDS SIMILARLY PRONOUNCED] homonyms.

VENTRILOQUISM *or* ventriloquy, ventrilocution, gastriloquism *or* gastriloquy [*rare*]; ventriloquist, gastriloquist [*rare*].

[SCIENCE OF VOICE], phonology; &c. (*sound*) 402.

581. Aphonia. — N. APHONIA *or* aphony; dumbness &c. *adj.;* obmutescence [*rare*]; absence –, want- of voice; dysphonia *or* dysphony; silence &c. (*taciturnity*) 585; raucity; harsh voice &c. 410, unmusical voice &c. 414; quaver, quavering; falsetto, "childish treble"; deaf-mutism, deaf-muteness, deaf-dumbness, mute, dummy, deaf-mute.

V. SPEAK LOW, speak softly; whisper &c. (*faintness*) 405; keep silence &c. 585.

SILENCE; render -mute, – silent; muzzle, muffle, suppress, smother, gag, strike dumb, dumfound *or* dumbfound dumfounder *or* dumbfounder, mum [*obs.*], drown the voice, put to silence, stop one's mouth, cut one short.

stick in the throat.

Adj. APHONOUS, nonvocal, aphonic, dumb, mute, deaf and dumb, deafdumb; mum; obmutescent [*rare*], tonguetied; breathless, tongueless, voiceless, speechless, wordless; mute as a -fish,

V. SPEAK, utter, breathe; give utterance, give tongue; cry &c. (*shout*) 411; ejaculate, rap out; vocalize, prolate [*obs.*], articulate, enunciate, pronounce, accentuate, aspirate, deliver, emit; whisper, murmur, whisper in the ear; ventriloquize.

Adj. VOCAL, phonetic, oral; ejaculatory, articulate, articulated, distinct, enunciative, accentuated, aspirated; euphonious &c. (*melodious*) 413; whispered.

VENTRILOQUOUS, ventriloquistic, gastriloquial [*rare*], gastriloquous [*rare*].

⁎⁎ "how sweetly sounds the voice of a good woman" [Massinger]; "the organ of the soul" [Longfellow]; "thy voice is a celestial melody" [Longfellow]; "speak in a monstrous little voice" [*M. N. D.*]; "I was never so bethump'd with words" [*King John*].

582. Speech. — N. SPEECH, faculty of speech; locution, talk, parlance, verbal intercourse, prolation [*archaic*], oral communication, word of mouth, parole, palaver, prattle.

ORATION, recitation, delivery, say [*colloq.*], speech, lecture, prelection *or* prælection, harangue, sermon, tirade, formal speech, peroration; speechifying; soliloquy &c. 589; allocution &c. 586; interlocution &c. 588; salutatory [*U. S.*]; screed; valedictory [*U. S.*].

ORATORY, elocution, eloquence, rhetoric, declamation; grandiloquence, multiloquence, talkativeness; burst of eloquence; facundity [*obs.*]; flow –, command- of -words, – language; *copia verborum* [*L.*]; power of speech, gift of the gab [*colloq.*]; *usus loquendi L.*].

SPEAKER &c. *v.;* spokesman; prolocutor, interlocutor; mouthpiece, Hermes; orator, oratrix, oratress; Demosthenes, Cicero; rhetorician, lecturer, preacher, prelector *or* prælector; elocutionist, reciter, reader [*U. S.*]; spellbinder; stump –, platform- orator; speechmaker, patterer, monologist, monologuist, improvisator, *improvvisatore* or *improvisatore* [*It.*], *improvvisatrice* or *improvisatrice* [*It.*].

V. SPEAK, – of; say, utter, pronounce, deliver, give utterance to; utter –, pour-
rap out, blurt out; have on one's lips; have at the -end, – tip- of one's tongue.

soliloquize &c. 589; tell &c. (*inform*) 527; speak to &c. 586; talk together &c. 588.

BREAK SILENCE; open one's - lips, –mouth; lift –, raise- one's voice; give tongue, wag the tongue [*colloq.*]; talk, outspeak; put in a word or two.

– stockfish, – mackerel; silent &c. (*taciturn*) 585; muzzled; inarticulate, inaudible.

CROAKING, raucous, hoarse, husky, dry, hollow, sepulchral, hoarse as a raven; rough.

Adv. WITH BATED BREATH, with the finger on the lips; *sotto voce* [*It.*]; in a -low tone, – cracked voice, – broken voice; in broken tones, aside, in an aside.

Int. MUM! hush! sh! silence! whist! whisht! [*dial.*]; chut! &c. (*silence*) 403.

⁎⁎ *vox faucibus hæsit* [Vergil]; "there is a homely old adage which runs: 'Speak softly and carry a big stick; you will go far'" [Roosevelt].

583. [IMPERFECT SPEECH.] **Stammering. — N.** INARTICULATENESS; stammering &c. *v.;* hesitation &c. *v.;* impediment in one's speech; titubancy [*obs.*], traulism [*obs.*]; whisper &c. (*faint sound*) 405; lisp, drawl, tardiloquence [*rare*]; nasal -tone, – accent; twang; falsetto &c. (*want of voice*) 581; cacology, cacoëpy; broken -voice, – accents, – sentences; brogue &c. 563.

SLIP OF THE TONGUE, *lapsus linguæ* [*L.*].

V. STAMMER, stutter, hesitate, falter, hammer [*obs. or dial. Eng.*], balbutiate [*obs.*], balbucinate [*obs.*], haw, hum and haw, be unable to put two words together.

MUMBLE, mutter, maund [*obs.*], maunder; whisper &c. 405; mince, lisp; jabber, gabble, gibber; splutter, sputter; muffle, mump; drawl, mouth; croak; speak thick, speak through the nose; talk incoherently, quaver, snuffle, clip one's words.

MURDER THE LANGUAGE, murder the King's (*or* Queen's) English; mispronounce, missay [*rare*].

Adj. INARTICULATE; stammering &c. *v.;* guttural, throaty, nasal; tremulous; affected; stertorous; cacoëpistic.

Adv. *sotto voce* &c. (*faintly*) 405.

forth; breathe, let fall, come out with;

DECLAIM, hold forth; make –, deliver- a speech &c. *n.;* speechify [*derisive or humorous*], harangue, stump [*colloq., U. S.*], flourish, spout, rant, recite, lecture, prelect *or* prælect, sermonize, discourse, be on one's legs; have –, say- one's say; expatiate &c. (*speak at length*) 573; speak one's mind, go on the –, take the-stump [*U. S.*].

BE ELOQUENT &c. *adj.;* have a tongue in one's head, have the gift of the gab [*colloq.*] &c. *n.*

PASS ONE'S LIPS, escape one's lips; fall from the -lips, – mouth.

Adj. ORAL, lingual, phonetic, not written, nuncupative [*of wills*], unwritten; speaking &c., spoken &c. *v.;* outspoken, facund [*archaic*].

ELOQUENT, oratorical, rhetorical, elocutionary, declamatory; grandiloquent &c. 577; talkative &c. 584; Ciceronian, Tullian.

Adv. ORALLY &c. *adj.;* by word of mouth, *vivâ voce* [*L.*], from the lips of; from his own mouth.

****** quoth –, said- he &c.; "action is eloquence" [*Coriolanus*]; "pour the full tide of eloquence along" [Pope]; "she speaks poignards and every word stabs" [*Much Ado About Nothing*]; "speech is but broken light upon the depth of the unspoken" [G. Eliot]; "to try thy eloquence now 'tis time" [*Antony and Cleopatra*]; "Language most shows a man; speak that I may see thee" [B. Jonson].

584. Loquacity. — N. LOQUACITY,
loquaciousness, effusion; talkativeness &c. *adj.;* garrulity; multiloquence, much speaking.

GABBLE, gab [*colloq.*], jaw [*low*], hot air [*slang*]; jabber, chatter; prate, prat-tle, cackle, clack; twaddle, twattle, rattle, *caquet* [*F.*], *caqueterie* [*F.*], blab-ber, *bavardage* [*F.*], bibble-babble, gibble-gabble; small talk &c. (*converse*) 588; Babel.

FLUENCY, flippancy, volubility, flow-ing tongue; flow, – of words; *flux de -bouche, – mots* [*F.*]; *copia verborum* [*L.*], cacoëthes loquendi [*L.*]; *furor loquendi* [*L.*]; verbosity &c. (*diffuseness*) 573; gift of the gab &c. (*eloquence*) 582.

TALKER; chatterer, chatterbox; bab-bler &c. *v.;* rattle; "agreeable rattle" [Goldsmith]; ranter; sermonizer, proser, driveler *or* driveller, blatherskite [*colloq., U. S.*], blab, jaw-box [*slang*], gas-bag [*slang*], wind-bag [*slang*], hot-air artist [*slang*]; gossip &c. (*converse*) 588; mag-pie, jay, parrot, poll *or* polly; *moulin à paroles* [*F.*].

V. BE LOQUACIOUS &c. *adj.;* talk glibly, pour forth, patter; prate, palaver, prose, maunder, chatter, blab, gush, prattle, clack, jabber, jaw [*low*], shoot one's mouth off [*slang*]; blather, blatter, blether; rattle, – on; twaddle, twattle; babble, gabble; outtalk; talk oneself -out of breath, – hoarse; talk –, run on- like a mill race; have one's tongue hanging in the middle and wagging at both ends; talk the hind legs off a mule, talk one deaf and dumb, clack like a hen, go on forever; expatiate &c. (*speak at length*) 573; gossip &c. (*converse*) 588; din in the ears &c. (*repeat*) 104; talk at random, talk nonsense &c. 497; be hoarse with talking.

585. Taciturnity. — N. SILENCE,
muteness, obmutescence [*rare*], laconism, laconicism, taciturnity, pauciloquy, cos-tiveness [*obs.*], curtness; reserve, reti-cence &c. (*concealment*) 528.

MAN OF FEW WORDS; Spartan, Laco-nian.

V. BE SILENT &c. *adj.;* keep silence; hold one's -tongue, – peace; not speak &c. 582; say nothing; seal –, close –, put a padlock on the -lips, – mouth; put a bridle on one's tongue; keep one's tongue between one's teeth; make no sign, not let a word escape one; keep a secret &c. 528; have not a word to throw at a dog, not have a word to say; lay –, place- the finger on the lips; render mute &c. 581.

stick in one's throat.

Adj. SILENT, mute, mum; silent as a -post, – stone, – the grave &c. (*still*) 403; dumb &c. 581; unconversable.

TACITURN, laconic, pauciloquent, con-cise, sententious, sparing of words; close, close-mouthed, close-tongued; costive [*obs.*], inconversable [*obs.*], curt; reserved; reticent &c. (*concealing*) 528.

Int. SILENCE! tush! mum! hush! *chut!* [*F.*], hist! tut! not another word! stop right there! be still! *chup!* [*Hind.*].

****** *cave quid dicis quando et cui; volto sciolto i pensieri stretti.*

Adj. LOQUACIOUS, talkative, garrulous, linguacious [*obs.*], multiloquent *or* multiloquous; chattering &c. *v.;* chatty &c. (*sociable*) 892; declamatory &c. 582; open-mouthed.

FLUENT, voluble, glib, flippant; long-tongued, long-winded &c. (*diffuse*) 573.

Adv. GLIBLY &c. *adj.;* trippingly on the tongue.

⁎⁎ the tongue running -fast, – loose, – on wheels; all talk and no cider; "foul whisperings are abroad" [*Macbeth*]; "the parrot is forever polishing his beak, however clean it may be" [Pascal]; "what a spendthrift is he of his tongue!" [*Tempest*]; "a loose tongue is just as unfortunate an accompaniment for a nation as for an individual" [Roosevelt]; "His talk was like a charge of horse" [Masefield]; "Another flood of words! A very torrent" [B. Jonson]; "It would talk, — Lord! how it talked!" [Beaumont and Fletcher].

---

586. Allocution. — N. ALLOCUTION, alloquy [*obs.*], address; smoke talk, chalk talk [*both colloq.*]; speech &c. 582; apostrophe, interpellation, appeal, invocation, salutation, salutatory [*U. S.*]; word in the ear.

PLATFORM &c. 542; plank [*politics*].

AUDIENCE &c. (*interview*) 588.

[FEIGNED DIALOGUE] dialogism.

V. ADDRESS, speak to, accost, make up to [*colloq.*], apostrophize, appeal to, invoke; hail, salute; call to, halloo.

lecture &c. (*make a speech*) 582; preach, sermonize, harangue, spellbind.

TAKE ASIDE, take by the button; talk to in private.

Int. soho! halloo! hey! hist! hi!

---

587. Response &c. *see* ANSWER 462.

---

588. Interlocution. — N. INTERLOCUTION; collocution, colloquy, converse, conversation, confabulation, confab [*colloq.*], chin-music [*slang*], talk, discourse, verbal intercourse; oral communication, commerce; dialogue, duologue, trialogue.

"the feast of reason and the flow of soul" [Pope]; *mollia tempora fandi* [*L.*].

CHAT, causerie [*F.*], chitchat; small –, table –, tea-table –, town –, village –, idle-talk; tattle, gossip, tittle-tattle; babble, babblement; *tripotage* [*F.*], cackle, prittle-prattle, *on dit* [*F.*]; talk of the -town, – village.

CONFERENCE, parley, interview, audience, *pourparler* [*F.*]; *tête-à-tête* [*F.*]; reception, *conversazione* [*It.*]; congress &c. (*council*) 696; powwow [*U. S.*].

HALL OF AUDIENCE, durbar [*India*], auditorium, assembly room.

DEBATE, palaver, logomachy, war of words, controversy, newspaper war.

TALKER, gossip, tattler; Paul Pry; tabby [*colloq.*], chatterer &c. (*loquacity*) 584; interlocutor &c. (*spokesman*) 582; conversationist, conversationalist, dialogist.

V. CONVERSE, talk together, confabulate; dialogue, dialogize; hold –, carry on –, join in –, engage in- a conversation; put in a word; shine in conversation; bandy words; parley; palaver; chat, gossip, tattle; prate &c. (*loquacity*) 584; powwow [*U. S.*].

CONFER WITH, discourse with, commune with, commerce with; hold -converse, – conference, – intercourse; talk it over; be closeted with; talk with one in private, talk with one *tête-à-tête* [*F.*].

Adj. CONVERSING &c. *v.;* interlocutory; conversational, conversable; discursive *or* discoursive [*obs.*]; chatty &c. (*sociable*) 892; colloquial, confabulatory, *tête-à-tête* [*F.*].

⁎⁎ "with thee conversing I forget all time" [*Paradise Lost*]; "Discourse, the sweeter banquet of the mind" [Pope].

---

589. Soliloquy. — N. SOLILOQUY, monology, monologue, apostrophe; monology.

SOLILOQUIST, monologist, monologuist, monologian, soliloquizer; speaker &c. 582; Dr. Johnson, Coleridge.

V. SOLILOQUIZE, monologize, monologuize, say –, talk- to oneself; rehearse a speech, address an imaginary audience; address the four walls; say aside, think aloud, apostrophize.

Adj. SOLILOQUIZING &c. *v.;* monologic *or* monological; apostrophic, apostrophal [*rare*].

Adv. ASIDE, apart.

3. Written Language

590. Writing. — **N.** WRITING &c. *v.;* chirography, stelography [*rare*], monography, stylography, cerography, graphology; pencraft, penmanship; quill driving [*humorous*]; typewriting.

stroke –, dash- of the pen; *coup de plume* [*F.*]; line; headline; pen and ink.

MANUSCRIPT, MS., writing, *litteræ scriptæ* [*L.*]; these presents [*law*].

CHARACTER, letter &c. 561; uncial writing, cuneiform character, arrowhead, contraction; Ogham, runes; hieroglyphic, hieratic, demotic, Hebrew, Greek, Cyrillic, Roman; Arabic, Persian, Naskhi *or* Neskhi, Shikasta, Nasta'lik *or* Ta'lik; Brahmi, Devanagari, Nagari; Chinese; script.

SHORTHAND; stenography, brachygraphy, tachygraphy; secret writing, writing in cipher; cryptography, steganography; phonography, pasigraphy, polygraphy [*rare*], logography.

COPY; transcript, rescript; rough –, fair- copy; rough draft.

HANDWRITING; signature, sign manual, mark, autograph, monograph, holograph; hand, fist [*colloq.*].

CALLIGRAPHY; good –, running –, flowing –, cursive –, Italian –, slanting –, perpendicular –, round –, copybook –, fine –, legible –, bold- hand.

CACOGRAPHY, *griffonage* [*F.*], *barbouillage* [*F.*]; bad –, cramped –, crabbed –, illegible- hand; scribble &c. *v.; pattes de mouche* [*F.*], fly tracks; ill-formed letters; pothooks and hangers.

STATIONERY; pen, reed, quill, goose quill; pencil, style, stylograph, stylographic pen, fountain pen; paper, foolscap, parchment, vellum, papyrus, tablet, block, pad, notebook, memorandum book, copybook, commonplace-book; slate, marble, pillar, table; blackboard; ink-bottle, inkhorn, inkpot, inkstand, inkwell; typewriter.

COMPOSITION, authorship; *cacoëthes scribendi* [*L.*]; graphomania; lucubration, production, work, preparation; screed, article, paper, pamphlet; book &c. 593; essay, theme, thesis; novel, textbook, poem, book of poems, book of verse; compilation, anthology; piece of music, *morceau* [*F.*] &c. (*musical composition*) 415.

591. Printing. — **N.** PRINTING; block –, type- printing; linotype, monotype; plate printing &c. (*engraving*) 558; the press &c. (*publication*) 531; composition.

PRINT, letterpress, text, matter; live –, standing –, dead- matter; copy; context, page, column, note, section; catchword; running head, running title; signature; justification; dummy.

folio &c (*book*) 593; copy, impression. pull, proof, revise, advance sheets; author's –, galley –, page –, plate –, press- proof; press revise.

TYPOGRAPHY; stereotype, electrotype; matrix; font *or* fount; pi *or* pie; roman, italics; capitals &c (*letters*) 561, caps., small caps., upper case, lower case; logotype; type-bar. type-slug; type-body; em, en; type measure. type scale; type casting, type metal, type mold, typograph; type foundry, letter foundry; composing stick, stick; composing -frame. – rule, – stand; foot stick; chase, form, galley, measure, scale, case, boxes; gauge, gauge pin, feed gauge, guide, dabber, gutter, gutter stick; brayer, boss, batter, bank; bearer, guard; bed, blanket, tympan, turtle, platen, bevel, burr, frame, frisket, gripper; quadrat, quad; quoin, slug, slur, ratchet, reglet; guillotine, rounce, cylinder; overlay, underlay, sinkage, macule; platen press, perfecting machine; printing-press, printing-machine; presswork; sheet work; off-cut, off-print; set-off; off-set, smut; turn, turned letter; bookplate, bookstamp, colophon; composing room, press room.

SPACE, 3-em, thick space; 4-em, 5-em, thin space; 6-em, hair space; patent space.

METAL TYPE, body, shank, face, shoulder, counter, serif *or* ceriph, stem, beard, groove, feet.

STYLES OF TYPE: Old English, Black Letter, German Text, Gothic, Antique, Clarendon, Boldface *or* Full-face, French Elzevir, Caslon Old Style, Ionic, Script, Typewriter.

POINT SYSTEM: 4½ point (diamond), 5 pt. (pearl), 5½ pt. (agate *or* ruby), 6 pt. (nonpareil), 7 pt. (minion), 8 pt. (brevier), 9 pt. (bourgeois), 10 pt. (long primer), 11 pt. (small pica), 12 pt. (pica), 14 pt. (English), 16 pt. (Columbian), 18 pt. (great primer).

PRINTER, compositor, reader, proof reader; printer's devil; copyholder.

V. PRINT; compose; put –, go- to press; pass –, see- through the press; publish &c. 531; bring out; appear in –, rush into- print; set up, stick [*cant*], make-up, impose, justify, macule *or* mackle, mortise, offset, overrun, rout.

DISTRIBUTE, pi *or* pie, pi a form.

Adj. TYPOGRAPHICAL &c. *n.;* printed &c. *v.;* in type; solid in galleys; kerned, deckle-edged; boldfaced *or* full-faced; pied.

transcription &c. (*copy*) 21; inscription &c. (*record*) 551; superscription &c. (*indication*) 550.

WRITER, scribe, amanuensis, scrivener, secretary, clerk, penman, copyist, transcriber, quill driver [*humorous*]; stenographer, brachygrapher, tachygrapher, phonographer, logographer, cipherer, cryptographer *or* cryptographist, steganographist; typewriter, typist; writer for the press &c. (*author*) 593; chirographer, cerographist; monographist, graphomaniac; calligraphist, calligrapher; cacographer; graphologist.

V. WRITE, pen, typewrite, type [*colloq.*]; copy, engross; write out, – fair; transcribe; scribble, scrawl, scrabble, scratch; interline; take down in -shorthand, – longhand; spoil –, stain- paper [*humorous*]; note down; write down &c. (*record*) 551; sign &c. (*attest*) 467; enface.

COMPOSE, indite, draw up, draft, formulate; dictate; inscribe, throw on paper, dash off; manifold.

take up the pen, take pen in hand; shed –, spill –, dip one's pen in- ink.

Adj. writing &c. *v.;* written &c. *v.;* in writing, in black and white; under one's hand.

uncial, runic, cuneiform, hieroglyphic *or* hieroglyphical, arrowhead &c. *n.*

STENOGRAPHIC, phonographic, brachygraphic, cryptographic, pasigraphic, logographic, tachygraphic; stenographical &c.

Adv. *currente calamo* [*L.*]; pen in hand; with the pen of a ready writer; that "the wayfaring men, though fools, shall not err therein" [*Bible*].

⁎ *audacter et sincere; le style est l'homme même;* "nature's noblest gift — my gray goose quill" [Byron]; *scribendi recte sapere et principium et fons* [Horace]; "that mighty instrument of little men" [Byron]; "the pen became a clarion" [Longfellow].

---

592. Correspondence. —N. CORRESPONDENCE, letter, epistle, note, billet, written communication, post card *or* postcard, postal [*U. S.*], postal card; missive, circular, favor, *billet-doux* [*F.*]; chit *or* chitty [*India*], letter card [*Brit.*], picture post card; dispatch *or* despatch; bulletin, these presents [*law*]; rescript, rescription [*archaic*]; post &c. (*messenger*) 534.

LETTER WRITER, epistolarian, correspondent, writer, communicator; author, contributor.

V. CORRESPOND, – with; write to, send a letter to; drop a line to [*colloq.*]; start –, begin –, keep up- a correspondence; deluge with -letters, – post cards; communicate by -writing, – letter; let one know by -post, – mail; dispatch *or* despatch, circularize, follow up, bombard; reply, reply by return mail, communicate.

Adj. EPISTOLARY, epistolarian.

⁎ *furor scribendi.*

593. Book.— N. BOOK, booklet; writing, work, volume, tome, opuscule *or* opuscle, opusculum; tract, tractate, treatise, *livret* [*F.*], brochure, monograph, pamphlet, codex, libretto; handbook, manual, enchiridion; novel &c. (*composition*) 590; circular, publication; the press &c. 531; chapbook.

part, issue, number, *livraison* [*F.*]; album, portfolio; periodical, serial, magazine, ephemeris, annual, journal.

PAPER, bill, sheet, broadsheet; leaf, leaflet; fly leaf, page; quire, ream.

PASTEBOARD, cardboard, strawboard, millboard, binder's board; carton.

MAKE-UP, bastard title, title, printer's imprint, subtitles, dedication, preface, contents, list of plates *or* illustrations, errata, introduction, text; chapter, section, head, article, paragraph, passage, clause; recto, verso *or* reverso; supplement, appendix, index.

[SIZES] folio, quarto (4to *or* 4°); octavo (8vo); cap 8vo, demy 8vo, imperial 8vo, medium 8vo, royal 8vo, post 8vo, pott 8vo, crown 8vo, foolscap 8vo; duodecimo, twelvemo *or* 12mo; sextodecimo, sixteenmo *or* 16mo; octodecimo, eighteenmo *or* 18mo.

BOOKBINDING, bibliopegy; folding, stitching, wire-stitching; tooling; blind –, gold- tooling; binder's title; case, cover; quarter –, half –, three-quarters- bound book; full leather.

[BINDING MATERIALS] paper, paper boards, buckram, cloth, skiver, roan, pigskin, Russia, Turkey morocco, levant morocco, seal, parchment, vellum.

WORK OF REFERENCE, encyclopedia *or* encyclopædia, cyclopedia *or* cyclopædia, dictionary, thesaurus, concordance, anthology; compilation.

WRITER, author, *littérateur* [*F.*], essayist; pen, scribbler, the scribbling race;

literary hack, Grub-street writer; adjective jerker [*slang*], hack writer, hack, ghost [*cant*], ink slinger [*slang*]; journalist, publicist, writer for –, gentleman of –, representative of- the press; reporter, correspondent; war –, special- correspondent; knight of the -plume, – pen, – quill [*all humorous*]; penny-a-liner; editor, subeditor, reviser, diaskeuast; scribe &c. 590; playwright &c. 599; poet &c. 597.

THE TRADE, publisher, bookseller; book -salesman, – agent, – canvasser, – solicitor.

bibliopole, bibliopolist, book collector; bookbinder, bibliopegist; bookworm &c. 492; bibliologist, bibliographer, bibliophile, bibliognost, librarian, bibliothec.

bookstore, bookshop, bookseller's shop, *librairie* [*F.*], publishing house.

LIBRARY, bibliotheca, public library, lending library.

KNOWLEDGE OF BOOKS, bibliography, bibliology; book learning &c. (*knowledge*) 490; bookselling, bibliopolism.

. "among the giant fossils of my past" [E. B. Browning]; *craignez tout d'un auteur en courroux;* "for authors nobler palms remain" [Pope]; "I lived to write and wrote to live" [Rogers]; "look in thy heart and write" [Sidney]; "there is no Past so long as Books shall live" [Bulwer-Lytton]; "the public mind is the creation of the Master-Writers" [Disraeli]; "volumes that I prize above my dukedom" [*Tempest*]; "the true University of these days is a Collection of Books" [Carlyle].

594. Description. — N. DESCRIPTION, account, statement, report; *exposé* [*F.*] &c. (*disclosure*) 529; specification, particulars; summary of facts; brief &c. (*abstract*) 596; return &c. (*record*) 551; *catalogue raisonné* [*F.*] &c. (*list*) 86; guidebook &c. (*information*) 527.

delineation &c. (*representation*) 554; sketch, pastel, vignette, monograph; minute –, detailed –, particular –, circumstantial –, graphic- account; narration, recital, rehearsal, relation.

NARRATIVE, history; memoir, memorials; annals &c. (*chronicle*) 551; saga; tradition, legend, story, tale, historiette; personal narrative, journal, letters, biography, autobiography, life; obituary, necrology; adventures, fortunes, experiences, confessions; anecdote, ana.

historiography, chronography; historic Muse, Clio.

WORK OF FICTION, novel, romance, short story; detective -story, – yarn; "grue" [Stevenson]; fairy –, nursery- tale; fable, parable, apologue, allegory; dime novel, penny dreadful, shilling shocker [*slang*].

RELATOR &c. *v.; raconteur* [*F.*]; historiographer, chronographer, historian &c. (*recorder*) 553; biographer, fabulist, novelist, story-teller, romancer, spinner of yarns, teller of tales, anecdotist, word-painter; writer &c. 593.

V. DESCRIBE; set forth &c. (*state*) 535; draw a picture, picture; portray &c. (*represent*) 554; characterize, analyze, give words to, narrate, relate, recite, recount, sum up, run over, recapitulate, rehearse, fight one's battles over again; harrow up the soul, hold one breathless, novelize, romance.

unfold &c. (*disclose*) 529- a tale; tell; give –, render- an account of; report, make a report, draw up a statement; throw into -essay form, – book form; stick to the facts, show life as it is; historicize.

DETAIL, particularize, itemize; enter into –, descend to- -particulars, – details.

Adj. DESCRIPTIVE, graphic, narrative, epic, suggestive, well-drawn; historic *or* historical, historiographical, chronographic *or* chronographical, biographic *or* biographical, autobiographical; traditive [*esp., from ancestors to descendants*], traditional, traditionary; legendary, mythical, fabulous; anecdotic, storied; described &c. *v.;* romantic, idealistic; realistic, true to life; expository.

. *furor scribendi;* "to hold, as 'twere, the mirror up to nature" [*Hamlet*].

595. Dissertation. — N. DISSERTATION, treatise, essay; thesis, theme; tract, tractate, tractation [*obs.*]; discourse, memoir, disquisition, lecture, sermon, homily, pandect, digest; excursus.

investigation &c. (*inquiry*) 461; study &c. (*consideration*) 451; discussion &c. (*reasoning*) 476; exposition &c. (*explanation*) 522.

COMMENTARY, commentation, review, critique, criticism, article; leader, leading article; editorial; running commentary.

COMMENTATOR, critic, essayist, pamphleteer, publicist, reviewer, leader writer, editor, annotator.

V. COMMENT, explain, interpret, criticize, illuminate; dissert [*rare*] –, descant –, write –, touch- upon a subject; treat of –, take up –, ventilate –, discuss –, deal with –, go into –, canvass –, handle –, do justice to- a subject; show the true inwardness of.

Adj. DISQUISITIONAL, disquisitive, disquisitionary [*rare*]; expository, commentarial, commentatorial, critical.

DISCURSIVE, discoursive, digressive, desultory.

596. Compendium. — N. COMPENDIUM, compend, abstract, *précis* [*F.*], epitome, *multum in parvo* [*L.*], analysis, pandect, digest, sum and substance, brief, abridgment, *abrégé* [*F.*], summary, *aperçu* [*F.*], draft, minute, note; excerpt, extract; synopsis, textbook, conspectus, outlines, syllabus, contents, heads, prospectus.

ALBUM; scrap –, note –, memorandum –, commonplace- book.

FRAGMENTS, ana, extracts, *excerpta* [*L.*], cuttings; fugitive -pieces, – writings; *spicilegium* [*L.*], flowers, anthology, miscellany, collectanea, analects *or* analecta; compilation.

RECAPITULATION, *résumé* [*F.*], review.

ABBREVIATION, abbreviature; contraction; shortening &c. 201; compression &c. 195.

V. ABRIDGE, abstract, epitomize, summarize; make –, prepare –, draw –, compile- an abstract &c. *n.;* abbreviate &c. (*shorten*) 201; condense &c. (*compress*) 195.

COMPILE &c. (*collect*) 72; note down, collect, edit.

RECAPITULATE, review, skim, run over, sum up.

Adj. COMPENDIOUS, synoptic, analectic; *abrégé* [*F.*], abridged &c. *v.;* abbreviatory; analytic *or* analytical; variorum.

Adv. IN SHORT, in epitome, in substance, in few words.

⁎⁎ it lies in a nutshell; "infinite riches in a little room" [Marlowe]; "in small proportions we just beauties see" [Jonson].

597. Poetry. — N. POETRY, poetics, poesy, Muse, tuneful Nine, Apollo, Apollo Musagetes, Calliope, Parnassus, Helicon, Pierides, Pierian spring; inspiration, fire of genius, coal from off the altar.

POEM; epic, epic poem; epopee *or* epopœia, epos, ode, epode, idyl *or* idyll, lyric, eclogue, pastoral, bucolic, georgic, dithyramb *or* dithyrambus, anacreontic, sonnet, roundelay, rondeau, rondel, roundel, rondelet; triolet, sestina, virelay, ballade, cento, ghazal *or* ghazel, madrigal, monody, elegy; amœbæum, palinode.

598. Prose. — N. PROSE, prosaism, prosaicness, prosaicism [*rare*]; poetic prose; history &c. (*description*) 594.

PROSE WRITER, essayist, monographer, monographist, novelist; *raconteur* [*F.*] &c. 594.

V. PROSE; write -prose, – in prose.

Adj. PROSAIC, prosy, prosal [*obs.*]; unpoetical.

rimeless *or* rhymeless, unrimed *or* unrhymed, in prose, not in verse.

⁎⁎ "prose, — words in their best order" [Coleridge].

dramatic –, didactic –, narrative –, lyric –, satirical- poetry; satire, opera.

ANTHOLOGY, posy [*archaic*], garland, miscellany, *disjecta membra poetæ* [*L.*].

SONG, ballad, lay; love –, drinking –, war –, sea- song; lullaby, *aubade* [*F.*]; music &c. 415; nursery rhymes.

[BAD POETRY] doggerel, Hudibrastic verse; macaronics, macaronic verse; "not poetry, but prose run mad" [Pope].

VERSIFICATION, riming *or* rhyming, making verses; prosody; scansion, scanning, orthometry [*rare*].

canto, stanza, distich, verse, line, couplet, triplet, quatrain; strophe, antistrophe; refrain, chorus, burden; octave, sextet.

VERSE, rime or rhyme, assonance, crambo [contemptuous], meter, measure, foot,
numbers, strain, rhythm; ictus, beat, accent; accentuation &c. (voice) 580;
iambus, iambic, iamb; dactyl, spondee, trochee, anapest &c.; hexameter, pentameter; Alexandrine; anacrusis, antispast, blank verse, Leonine verse, runes,
alliteration; bout-rimé [F.].

elegiacs &c. adj.; elegiac &c. adj. -verse, – meter or metre, – poetry.

POET, minor poet; genius, maker [obs.], creator; poet laureate; laureate; bard,
lyrist, scald or skald, scop [hist.], idylist or idyllist, sonneteer, rhapsodist, epic
[obs.], epic poet, dithyrambic, satirist, troubadour, trouvère; minstrel; minnesinger,
Meistersinger; jongleur, improvisator or improvvisatore [It.] or improvisatore;
versifier, rimer or rhymer, rimester or rhymester; ballad monger, runer; poetaster; genus irritabile vatum [L.].

V. POETIZE, sing, "lisp in numbers" [Pope], build the stately rime, sing deathless songs, make immortal by verse; satirize; compose epic &c. adj.- poetry;
string verses together, cap rimes, poeticize, versify, make verses, rime or rhyme,
scan.

produce -lame verses, – limping meters, – halting rime.

Adj. POETIC or poetical; lyric or lyrical; tuneful; epic; dithyrambic &c. n.;
metrical; acatalectic, catalectic; elegiac, iambic, dactylic, spondaic or spondaical,
trochaic, anapestic; amœbæic, Melibean, scaldic or skaldic; Ionic, Sapphic, Alcaic,
Pindaric, Pierian.

₊ "a poem round and perfect as a star" [Alex. Smith]; Dichtung und Wahrheit; furor
poeticus; "his virtues formed the magic of his song" [Hayley]; "I do but sing because I
must" [Tennyson]; "I learnt life from the poets" [de Staël]; licentia vatum; mutum est
pictura poema; "O for a muse of fire!" [Henry V]; "sweet food of sweetly uttered knowledge"
[Sidney]; "the true poem is the poet's mind" [Emerson]; Volk der Dichter und Denker;
"wisdom married to immortal verse" [Wordsworth]; "Unlock my heart with a sonnet-key"
[Browning].

599. The Drama. — N. THE DRAMA, the stage, the theater or theatre, the play;
theatricals, dramaturgy, histrionic art, mimography, buskin, sock, cothurnus,
Melpomene and Thalia, Thespis.

PLAY, drama, stageplay, piece, five-act play, tragedy, comedy, opera, vaudeville,
comedietta, lever de rideau [F.], curtain raiser, interlude, afterpiece, exode [Rom.
antiq.], farce, divertissement [F.], extravaganza, burletta, harlequinade, pantomime,
burlesque, opéra bouffe [F.], ballet, spectacle, masque, drame [F.], comédie drame
[F.]; melodrama; comédie larmoyante [F.]; emotional -drama, – play; sensation
drama; tragi-comedy; light –, genteel –, low –, farce- comedy, comedy of manners,
farcical-comedy; monodrama, monodram or monodrame, monologue, duologue,
dialogue; trilogy; charade, proverbe [F.]; mystery, miracle play, morality play.

ACT, scene, tableau, curtain; introduction, induction [archaic], exposition, expository scenes; prologue, epilogue; libretto, book, text, prompter's copy.

PERFORMANCE, representation, show [colloq.], mise en scène [F.], stage setting,
stagery [obs.], stagecraft, jeu de théâtre [F.]; acting; gesture &c. 550; impersonation
&c. 554; stage business, gag, patter, slap-stick [slang], buffoonery.

THEATER or theatre, playhouse, opera house; music hall; amphitheater or amphitheatre, circus, hippodrome; moving-picture theater, moving pictures, movies [colloq.],
cinematograph or cinema [colloq., Brit.]; puppet show, fantoccini; marionettes.
Punch and Judy.

AUDITORY, auditorium, front of the house, front [colloq. and professional], stalls
[chiefly Eng.], orchestra seats or orchestra, pit [chiefly Eng.], parquet, orchestra
circle, boxes, balcony, gallery, peanut gallery [slang]; dressing rooms, greenroom.

SCENERY; back scene, flat; drop, drop scene; wing, screen, coulisse, side scene,
transformation scene, curtain, act drop; proscenium; fire curtain, asbestos curtain.

STAGE, movable stage, scene, the boards; trap, mezzanine floor; flies; floats, footlights; limelight, spotlight, colored light; orchestra.

theatrical costume, theatrical properties, props [theat. cant].

CAST, dramatis personæ [L.], persons in the play; rôle, part, character; repertoire, repertory, répertoire [F.].

ACTOR, player; stage -, strolling- player; barnstormer, stager [rare], old stager; masker, masquer [rare], mime, mimer, mimic, mimester [rare]; artiste [F.], performer, star, headliner; comedian, tragedian, tragédienne [F.], Thespian, Roscius, ham [slang], hamfatter [slang]; utility, general utility, utility man.

BUFFOON, pantomimist, clown, farceur [F.], buffo (pl. buffi) [It.], grimacer, pantaloon, harlequin, columbine; punch, punchinello, pulcinella [It.].

mummer, guiser [Eng. & Scot.], guisard [Scot.], gysart [obs.], masque [obs.], mask.

mountebank, Jack Pudding; tumbler, posture master, acrobat; contortionist; ballet dancer, ballet girl; coryphée [F.], danseuse [F.]; chorus girl, chorus singer.

COMPANY; first tragedian, prima donna, leading lady; lead; leading man, protagonist; jeune premier [F.], débutant (fem. débutante) [F.]; light -, genteel -, low- comedian; walking gentleman or lady [obsoles.], amoroso [It.], juvenile lead, juvenile; heavy lead, heavy; heavy father, ingénue [F.], jeune veuve [F.], soubrette, farceur (fem. farceuse) [F.].

MUTE, figurant, figurante, walking part, supernumerary, super [theat. cant], supe [theat. cant].

manager; stage -, actor -, acting- manager; entrepreneur [F.], impresario; angel [slang].

[THEATER STAFF] property man, prop [theat. cant]; costumer, costumier, wigmaker, make-up artist; sceneshifter, grip [U. S.], stage hand, stage carpenter, machinist, electrician, chief electrician; prompter, call boy; advance agent, publicity agent.

DRAMATIST, playwright, playwriter; dramatic -author, - writer; mimographer, mimist [obs.]; dramatic critic.

AUDIENCE, auditory, house; orchestra &c. n.; gallery, the gods [colloq.], gallery gods [colloq.].

V. ACT, play, perform; put on the stage, dramatize, stage, produce, set; personate &c. 554; mimic &c. (imitate) 19; enact; play -, act -, go through -, perform a part; rehearse, spout, gag [slang], patter [slang], rant; strut and fret one's hour upon the stage; tread the -stage, - boards; make one's début, take a part, come out; star; supe [slang].

Adj. DRAMATIC; theatric or theatrical; scenic, histrionic, comic, tragic, buskined, cothurned; farcical, tragi-comic, melodramatic, operatic; stagy or stagey; spectacular, stellar, all-star [cant]; stagestruck.

Adv. ON THE STAGE, on the boards; in the limelight, in the spotlight; before the floats, before the footlights, before the curtain, before an audience; behind the scenes.

₊ fere totus mundus exercet histrionem [Petronius Arbiter]; "suit the action to the word, the word to the action" [Hamlet]; "the play's the thing" [Hamlet]; "is there no play, To ease the anguish of a torturing hour?" [M. N. D.]; "If it be true that good wine needs no bush, 'tis true that a good play needs no epilogue" [As You Like It]; "Come, sit down, every mother's son, and rehearse your parts" [M. N. D.]; "let gorgeous Tragedy In sceptred pall come sweeping by" [Milton]; "There's a dearth of wit in this dull town, While silly plays so savourily go down" [Dryden]; "Thus they jog on, still tricking, never thriving, And murd'ring plays, which still they call reviving" [ibid.]; "the monuments of vanished minds" [ibid.]; "to wake the soul by tender strokes of art" [Pope]; "For we that live to please must please to live" [Johnson]; "the players are my pictures and their scenes my territories" [Steele]; " 'The world's a stage,' — as Shakespeare said one day; The stage a world — was what he meant to say" [Holmes].

CLASS V

Words relating to THE VOLUNTARY POWERS[1]

Division (I) INDIVIDUAL VOLITION

Section I. Volition in general

1. *Acts of Volition*

600. Will. — N. will, volition, conation, volitiency, velleity; *liberum arbitrium* [*L.*]; will and pleasure, free will; freedom &c. 748; discretion; choice, inclination, intent, purpose, voluntarism; option &c. (*choice*) 609; voluntariness; spontaneity, spontaneousness; originality.

wish, desire, pleasure, mind, frame of mind &c. (*inclination*) 602; intention &c. 620; predetermination &c. 611; self-control &c. determination &c. (*resolution*) 604; force of will, will power, autocracy, bossiness [*colloq., U. S.*].

V. will, list [*archaic*]; see fit, think fit; determine &c. (*resolve*) 604; enjoin; settle &c. (*choose*) 609; volunteer.

have a will of one's own; do what one chooses &c. (*freedom*) 748; have it all one's own way; have one's will, have one's own way; use –, exercise-one's discretion; take -upon oneself, - one's own course, – the law into one's own hands; do of one's own accord, do upon one's own authority, do upon one's own responsibility; take responsibility, boss [*colloq.*], take the bit between one's teeth; originate &c. (*cause*) 153.

Adj. voluntary, volitional, willful *or* wilful; free &c. 748; optional; discretional, discretionary; volitient, volitive; volunteer, voluntaristic; dictatorial, bossy [*colloq., U. S.*].

minded &c. (*willing*) 602; prepense &c. (*predetermined*) 611; intended &c. 620; autocratic; unbidden &c. (bid &c. 741); spontaneous; original &c. (*causal*) 153; unconstrained.

Adv. voluntarily &c. *adj.;* at will, at pleasure; *à volonté* [*F.*], *à discrétion*

601. Necessity. — N. involuntariness; instinct, blind impulse; inborn –, innate- proclivity; native –, natural-tendency; natural impulse, predetermination.

necessity, necessitation, necessitarianism, obligation; compulsion &c. 744; subjection &c. 749; stern –, hard –, dire –, imperious –, inexorable –, iron –, adverse- -necessity, – fate; *anagke* [*Gr.* ἀνάγκη], what must be.

destiny, destination; fatality, fate, kismet, doom, foredoom, election, predestination; preordination, foreordination; lot, fortune; fatalism; inevitableness &c. *adj.;* spell &c. 993.

Fates, Parcæ, Sisters three, book of fate; God's will, Heaven, will of Heaven; star, stars; planet, planets; astral influence; wheel of Fortune, Ides of March, Hobson's choice.

last shift, last resort; *dernier ressort* [*F.*]; *pis aller* &c. (*substitute*) 147; necessaries &c. (*requirement*) 630.

necessarian, necessitarian; fatalist; automaton, pawn.

V. lie under a necessity; be fated, be doomed, be destined &c., be in for, be under the necessity of; be obliged, be forced, be driven; have no -choice, – alternative; be one's fate to &c. *n.;* be pushed to the wall, be driven into a corner, be unable to help, be swept on, be drawn irresistibly.

destine, doom, foredoom, devote; predestine, preordain; cast a spell &c. 992; necessitate; compel &c. 744.

be decreed, be determined, be destined &c., be written; be written in the -book of fate, - stars.

[1] Conative powers or faculties as distinguished from cognition and feeling [Hamilton].

[F.]; *al piacere* [*It.*]; *ad libitum* [*L.*], *ad arbitrium* [*L.*]; as one thinks proper, as it seems good to; *a beneplacito* [*It*].

of one's own -accord, – free will; on one's own responsibility; *proprio –, suo –, ex mero- motu* [*L.*]; out of one's own head; by choice &c. 609; purposely &c. (*intentionally*) 620; deliberately &c. 611.

  * *stet pro ratione voluntas; sic volo sic jubeo; beneficium accipere libertatem est vendere; Deus vult; was man nicht kann meiden muss man willig leiden;* "Sir, we *know* the will is free, and there's an end on't" [Johnson].

Adj. NECESSARY, necessarian, necessitarian; needful &c. (*requisite*) 630.

FATED; destined &c. *v.;* fateful, big with fate; set apart, devoted, elect.

COMPULSORY &c. (*compel*) 744; uncontrollable, inevitable, unavoidable, indefeasible, irresistible, irrevocable, inexorable, binding; avoidless, resistless.

INVOLUNTARY, instinctive, automatic, blind, mechanical; unconscious, unwitting, unthinking; unintentional &c. (*undesigned*) 621; spellbound; impulsive &c. 612.

Adv. NECESSARILY &c. *adj.;* of necessity, of course; *ex necessitate rei* [*L.*]; needs must; perforce &c. 744; *nolens volens* [*L.*]; will he nil he, will I nill I, willy-nilly, *bon gré mal gré* [*F.*]; willing or unwilling, *coûte que coûte* [*F.*]; compulsorily, by compulsion, by force. *faute de mieux* [*F.*]; by stress of; if need be; *que faire?* [*F.*].

  * it cannot be helped; there is no -help for, – helping- it; it -will, – must, – must needs- be, – be so, – have its way; the die is cast; *jacta est alea; che sarà sarà;* "it is written"; one's days are numbered, one's fate is sealed; *Fata obstant; dis aliter visum; actus me invito factus, non est meus actus; aujourd'hui roi demain rien; quisque suos patimur manes* [Vergil]; "but helpless pieces of the game He plays Upon this chequer-board of nights and days" [Omar Khayyám — Fitzgerald]; "the ball no question makes of ayes and noes" [*ibid.*]; *necessità il c'induce e non diletto* [Dante]; "There's a divinity that shapes our ends, Rough-hew them how we will" [*Hamlet*].

602. Willingness. — N.
WILLINGNESS, voluntariness &c. *adj.;* willing mind, heart.

DISPOSITION, inclination, liking, turn, propensity, propension, propenseness, leaning, animus; frame of mind, humor, mood, vein; bent &c. (*turn of mind*) 820; *penchant* [*F.*] &c. (*desire*) 865; aptitude &c. 698.

DOCILITY, docibleness [*rare*], docibility [*rare*], appetency, tractability, tractableness, persuadability, persuadableness, persuasibleness, persuasibility; pliability &c. (*softness*) 324.

GENIALITY, cordiality; goodwill; alacrity, readiness, zeal, enthusiasm, earnestness, forwardness; eagerness &c. (*desire*) 865.

ASSENT &c. 488; compliance &c. 762; pleasure &c. (*will*) 600.

LABOR OF LOVE, self-appointed task, volunteering; gratuitous service; social service, welfare work.

VOLUNTEER, unpaid worker, amateur, voluntary [*rare*]; social worker, welfare worker.

V. BE WILLING &c. *adj.;* incline, lean to, mind, propend [*rare*], had as lief, would as lief; lend –, give –, turn- a willing ear; have -a, – half a, – a great- mind to; hold to, cling to; desire &c. 865.

603. Unwillingness. — N.
UNWILLINGNESS &c. *adj.;* indisposition, indisposedness, disinclination, aversation [*rare*], aversion; averseness &c. (*dislike*) 867; nolleity [*rare*], nolition [*rare*]; renitence *or* renitency; reluctance: indifference &c. 866; backwardness &c. *adj.;* slowness &c. 275; want of -alacrity, – readiness; indocility &c. (*obstinacy*) 606.

SCRUPULOUSNESS, scrupulosity; qualms –, twinge- of conscience; delicacy, demur, scruple, qualm, shrinking, recoil; hesitation &c. (*irresolution*) 605; fastidiousness &c. 868.

DISSENT &c. 489; refusal &c. 764.

FORCED LABOR, unwilling service, peonage; compulsion &c. 744; slacker.

V. BE UNWILLING &c. *adj.;* nill [*archaic*]; dislike &c. 867; grudge, begrudge; not find it in one's heart to, not have the stomach to.

DEMUR, stick at, scruple, stickle; hang fire, run rusty [*colloq.*], go stale; give up, let down [*slang*]; pull back, be a dead weight, be a passenger in the boat, not pull fair, shirk, slack, shy [*dial. Eng.*], fight shy of, get by [*slang*], duck [*slang*]; recoil, shrink, swerve; hesitate &c. 605; avoid &c. 623.

OPPOSE &c. 708; dissent &c. 489; refuse &c. 764.

ACQUIESCE &c. (*assent*) 488; see think- -good, – fit, – proper; comply with &c. 762.

swallow –, nibble at- the bait; swallow bait, hook, and sinker; swallow bait and all; gorge the hook; have –, make- no scruple of; make no bones of [*colloq.*]; jump at, catch at; go in for, go in at [*both colloq.*]; take up, plunge into, have a go at [*colloq.*]; meet halfway.

VOLUNTEER, offer, proffer; offer oneself &c. 763.

Adj. WILLING, minded, fain, disposed, inclined, favorable; favorably -minded, -inclined, -disposed; well-disposed, lief [*archaic*], nothing loth; in the -vein, – mood, – humor, – mind.

READY, forward, earnest, eager, zealous, enthusiastic; bent upon &c. (*desirous*) 865; predisposed, desirous, propense.

DOCILE; persuadable, persuasible; suasible, amenable, easily persuaded, facile, easy-going; tractable &c. (*pliant*) 324; genial, gracious, cordial, cheering, hearty; content &c. (*assenting*) 488.

VOLUNTARY, gratuitous, spontaneous; unasked &c. (ask &c. 765); unforced &c. (*free*) 748.

Adv. WILLINGLY &c. *adj.*; fain, freely, as lief, heart and soul; with pleasure, with all one's heart, with open arms; with good will, with right good will; *de bonne volonté* [*F.*], *ex animo* [*L.*], *con amore* [*It.*], heart in hand, nothing loath, without reluctance, of one's own accord, graciously, with a good grace; without demur.

à la bonne heure [*F.*]; by all means, by all manner of means; to one's heart's content; yes &c. (*assent*) 488.

Int. SURELY! sure! with pleasure! of course! delighted!

Adj. UNWILLING; not in the vein, loath or loth, shy of, disinclined, indisposed, averse, reluctant, not content; renitent, opposed; adverse &c. (*opposed*) 708; laggard, backward, remiss, slack, slow to; indifferent &c. 866; scrupulous; squeamish &c. (*fastidious*) 868; repugnant &c. (*dislike*) 867; restiff [*obs.*], restive; demurring &c. *v.*; unconsenting &c. (*refusing*) 764; involuntary &c. 601; grudging, forced; irreconcilable.

Adv. UNWILLINGLY &c. *adj.*; grudgingly, with a heavy heart; with -a bad, – an ill- grace; against –, sore against- -one's wishes, – one's will, – the grain; *invita Minerva* [*L.*]; *à contre cœur* [*F.*]; *malgré soi* [*F.*]; in spite of -one's teeth, – oneself; *nolens volens* [*L.*] &c. (*necessity*) 601; perforce &c. 744; under protest; no &c. 536; if I must I must; not if one can help it; not for the world; far be it from me.

---

604. Resolution.— N. DETERMINATION, will; iron will, unconquerable will; will of one's own, decision, resolution; backbone; clear grit, grit [*U. S. & Can.*]; sand [*slang*]; strength of -mind, – will; resolve &c. (*intent*) 620; intransigence or intransigency, *intransigeance* [*F.*]; firmness &c. (*stability*) 150; energy, manliness, vigor; resoluteness &c. (*courage*) 861; zeal &c. 682; desperation; devotion, devotedness.

SELF-CONTROL, *aplomb* [*F.*], mastery over self, self-mastery, self-command, self-possession, self-reliance, self-government, self-restraint, self-conquest, self-denial; moral -courage, – fiber, – strength.

TENACITY, perseverance &c. 604*a*; obstinacy &c. 606; game, pluck; fighting cock, game cock; bulldog; British lion.

IRRECONCILABLE, intransigent, *in-*

605. Irresolution. — N. IRRESOLUTION, infirmity of purpose, indecision, indetermination, undetermination [*rare*], instability; loss of will power, abulia, abulomania; unsettlement; uncertainty &c. 475; demur, suspense; hesitating &c. *v.*, hesitation, hesitancy; wabble or wobble; revocability, vacillation; changeableness &c. 149; fluctuation; alternation &c. (*oscillation*) 314; caprice &c. 608; lukewarmness, Laodiceanism.

FICKLENESS, levity, *légèreté* [*F.*]; pliancy &c. (*softness*) 324; weakness; timidity &c. 860; cowardice &c. 862; half measures.

WAVERER, shilly-shally, ass between two bundles of hay; shuttlecock, butterfly, feather, piece of thistledown; house built on sand; doughface [*U. S.*]; turncoat, opportunist, Vicar of Bray, Dite Deuchars; Laodicean; timeserver &c. 607.

transigeant [*F.*], bitter-ender [*colloq.*]; fighting minority, militant remnant.

V. HAVE DETERMINATION &c. *n.;* know one's own mind; be resolved &c. *adj.;* make up one's mind; will, resolve, determine; decide &c. (*judgment*) 480; form –, come to– a –determination, – resolution, – resolve; conclude, fix, seal, determine once for all, bring to a crisis, drive matters to an extremity; take a decisive step &c. (*choice*) 609; take upon oneself &c. (*undertake*) 676.

STEEL ONESELF, devote oneself to, give oneself up to; throw away the scabbard, kick down the ladder, nail one's colors to the mast, set one's back against the wall, burn one's bridges, grit one's teeth, set one's teeth, set one's jaw, take the bit in one's mouth, put one's foot down, take one's stand, stand firm &c. (*stability*) 150; stand no nonsense, not listen to the voice of the charmer; insist upon, make a point of; set one's heart upon, set one's mind upon.

BUCKLE TO; buckle oneself; put –, lay –, set– one's shoulder to the wheel; put one's heart into; run the gauntlet, make a dash at, take the bull by the horns; rush –, plunge– *in medias res* [*L.*]; go in for [*colloq.*].

STICK AT NOTHING; make short work of &c. (*activity*) 682; not stick at trifles; go all lengths, go the limit [*slang*], go the whole hog [*slang*], go it blind [*slang*]; go down with one's colors flying; die game; persist &c. (*persevere*) 604*a*; go through fire and water, "ride in the whirlwind and direct the storm" [Addison].

Adj. RESOLVED &c. *v.;* determined; strong-willed, strong-minded; resolute &c. (*brave*) 861; self-possessed, earnest, serious; decided, definitive, peremptory; unhesitating, unflinching, unshrinking; firm, iron, game, plucky, tenacious, gritty [*U. S.*], indomitable, game to the backbone, game to the last; inexorable, relentless, not to be –shaken, – put down; *tenax propositi* [*L.*]; obstinate &c. 606; steady &c. (*persevering*) 604*a*.

V. BE IRRESOLUTE &c.; *adj.;* hang –, keep– in suspense; leave *ad referendum;* think twice about, pause; dawdle &c. (*inactivity*) 683; remain neuter; dilly-dally, hesitate, boggle, hover, dacker *or* daiker [*dial. Eng. & Scot.*], wabble *or* wobble [*colloq.*], shilly-shally, hum and haw, demur, not know one's own mind; debate, balance; dally with, coquet with; will and will not, *chasser-balancer* [*F.*]; go halfway, compromise, make a compromise; be thrown off one's balance, stagger like a drunken man; be afraid &c. 860; let "I dare not" wait upon "I would" [*Macbeth*]; falter, waver.

VACILLATE &c. 149; change &c. 140; retract &c. 607; fluctuate; pendulate; alternate &c. (*oscillate*) 314; keep off and on, play fast and loose; blow hot and cold &c. (*caprice*) 608; turn one's coat.

SHUFFLE, palter, blink, shirk, trim.

Adj. IRRESOLUTE, infirm of purpose, palsied, drifting, double-minded, half-hearted; undecided, unresolved, undetermined; shilly-shally, wabbly *or* wobbly; fidgety, tremulous; hesitating &c. *v.;* off one's balance; abulic; at a loss &c. (*uncertain*) 475.

VACILLATING &c. *v.;* unsteady &c. (*changeable*) 149; unsteadfast, fickle, unreliable, irresponsible, unstable, unstable as water, without ballast; capricious &c. 608; volatile, frothy; light, lightsome, lightminded; giddy; fast and loose.

WEAK, feeble-minded, frail; timid &c. 860; cowardly &c. 862; dough-faced [*U. S.*]; facile; pliant &c. (*soft*) 324; unable to say "no," easy-going.

REVOCABLE, reversible.

Adv. IRRESOLUTELY &c. *adj.;* irresolvedly; in faltering accents; off and on; on the sands; from pillar to post; seesaw &c. 314.

*** "the brave man chooses while the coward stands aside" [Lowell]; "to have twa minds is as confusing as twins" [Barrie]; "how happy could I be with either!" [Gay].

UNBENDING, unyielding; set –, bent –, intent– upon; grim, stern; inflexible &c. (*hard*) 323; cast-iron, irrevocable, irreversible; not to be deflected; firm as Gibraltar.

steeled –, proof– against; *in utrumque paratus* [*L.*].

Adv. RESOLUTELY &c. *adj.;* in earnest, in good earnest; seriously, joking apart, earnestly, heart and soul; on one's mettle; manfully, like a man; with a high –heart, – courage, – hand; with a strong hand &c. (*exertion*) 686.

AT ALL RISKS, at all hazards, at all events; at any –rate, – risk, – hazard,

-price, - cost, - sacrifice; *à bis ou à blanc* [*F.*], cost what it may; *coûte que coûte* [*F.*]; *à tort et à travers* [*F.*]; once for all; neck or nothing; survive or perish, live or die; rain or shine.

⁎ *spes sibi quisque; celui qui veut celui-là peut; chi non s'arrischia non guadagna; frangas non flectes; manu forti; tentanda via est;* "that bent like perfect steel, to spring again and thrust" [Lowell — *of Lincoln*]; "free peoples can escape being mastered by others only by being able to master themselves" [Roosevelt]; "if the single man plant himself indomitably on his instincts and there abide, the huge world will come round to him" [Emerson]; "yours is a thoroughbred heart: you don't scream and cry every time it's pinched" [Shaw].

604a. Perseverance. — N. PERSEVERANCE; continuance &c. (*inaction*) 143; permanence &c. (*absence of change*) 141; firmness &c. (*stability*) 150.

constancy, steadiness; singleness -, tenacity- of purpose; persistence, plodding, patience; sedulity [*rare*] &c. (*industry*) 682; pertinacy [*obs.*], pertinacity, pertinaciousness; iteration &c. 104.

GRIT, bottom, game, pluck, stamina, backbone, sand [*slang*]; indefatigability, indefatigableness; tenacity, staying power, endurance; bulldog courage.

V. PERSEVERE, persist; hold -on, - out; die in the last ditch, be in at the death; stick to, cling to, adhere to; stick to one's text; keep on, carry on, hold on; keep to -, maintain- one's -course, - ground; go all lengths, go through fire and water; bear up, keep up, hold up; plod; stick to work &c. (*work*) 686; continue &c. 143; follow up; die in harness, die at one's post.

Adj. PERSEVERING, constant; steady, steadfast; undeviating, unwavering, unfaltering, unswerving, unflinching, unsleeping, unflagging, undrooping; steady as time; unintermitting, unremitting; plodding; industrious &c. 682; strenuous &c. 686; pertinacious; persisting, persistent.

solid, sturdy, stanch *or* staunch, true to oneself; unchangeable &c. 150; unconquerable &c. (*strong*) 159; indomitable, game to the last, indefatigable, untiring, unwearied, never tiring.

Adv. WITHOUT FAIL; through evil report and good report, through thick and thin, through fire and water; *per fas et nefas* [*L.*]; sink or swim, at any price, *vogue la galère* [*F.*]; rain or shine, fair or foul, in sickness and in health.

⁎ *never say die; vestigia nulla retrorsum; aut vincere aut mori; la garde meurt et ne se rend pas; tout vient à temps pour qui sait attendre;* "If you can force your heart and nerve and sinew To serve your turn long after they are gone, And so hold on when there is nothing in you Except the Will which says to them: 'Hold on!' . . . Yours is the Earth, and everything that's in it" [Kipling]; "Man, the marvellous thing, that in the dark Works with his little strength to make a light" [Masefield].

606. Obstinacy. — N. OBSTINATENESS &c. *adj.*; obstinacy, tenacity; cussedness [*U. S.*]; perseverance &c. 604*a*; immovability; old school; inflexibility &c. (*hardness*) 323; obduracy, obduration [*rare*], obdurateness, doggedness, dogged resolution; resolution &c. 604; ruling passion; blind side.

self-will, contumacy, perversity; pervicaciousness [*rare*], pervicacy [*obs.*], pervicacity [*obs.*]; indocility [*obs.*].

BIGOTRY, intolerance, dogmatism; opiniatry [*obs.*], opiniativeness [*rare*]; impersuasibility, impersuadableness; intractableness, incorrigibility; fixed idea &c. (*prejudgment*) 481; fanaticism, zealotry, infatuation, monomania; opinionatedness, opinionativeness.

BIGOT, opinionist [*obs.*], opinionatist [*obs.*], opiniator [*obs.*], opinator [*obs.*];

607. Tergiversation. — N. TERGIVERSATION, tergiversating, recantation; palinode, palinody [*rare*]; renunciation; abjuration, abjurement; defection &c. (*relinquishment*) 624; going over &c. *v.*; apostasy; retraction, retractation; withdrawal; disavowal &c. (*negation*) 536; revocation, revokement [*rare*], reversal; repentance &c. 950; *redintegratio amoris* [*L.*].

change of -mind, - intention, - purpose; afterthought.

coquetry, flirtation; vacillation &c. 605.

recidivism, recidivation, backsliding; *volte-face* [*F.*].

TURNCOAT, turn-tippet [*obs.*]; rat [*cant*], apostate, renegade, pervert, deserter, backslider; recidivist; crawfish [*slang, U. S.*], mugwump [*U. S.*]; black-

stickler, dogmatist, zealot, enthusiast, fanatic, bitter-ender [colloq.]; mule.

V. BE OBSTINATE &c. *adj.*; stickle, take no denial, fly in the face of facts; opinionate [*rare*], be wedded to an opinion, hug a belief; have one's own way &c. (*will*) 600; persist &c. (*persevere*) 604a; have –, insist on having- the last word.

DIE HARD, die fighting, fight to the last ditch, fight against destiny, not yield an inch, stand out.

Adj. obstinate, tenacious, stubborn, obdurate, casehardened; inflexible &c. (*hard*) 323; balky; immovable, not to be moved; inert &c. 172; unchangeable &c. 150; inexorable &c. (*determined*) 604; mulish, obstinate as a mule, pig-headed.

dogged; sullen, sulky; unmoved, uninfluenced, unaffected.

WILLFUL *or* wilful, self-willed, perverse; resty [*dial. Eng.*], restive, pervicacious [*rare*], ungovernable, wayward, refractory, unruly; heady, headstrong; *entêté* [*F.*]; contumacious; crossgrained.

arbitrary, dogmatic, positive, bigoted, opinionated, opinionative, opinionate [*obs.*], opinioned, opiniative [*rare*]; prejudiced &c. 481; creed-bound; prepossessed, infatuated; stiff-backed, stiff-necked, stiff-hearted; hard-mouthed, hidebound; unyielding; impervious, impracticable, impersuasible, impersuadable, unpersuadable; untractable, intractable; incorrigible, deaf to advice, impervious to reason; crotchety &c. 608.

Adv. obstinately &c. *adj.*; with set jaw, with sullen mouth; no surrender.

⁎⁎ *non possumus;* no surrender; *ils n'ont rien appris ni rien oublié;* other people are obstinate, I am firm; "lest any foreigner should alter their laws, which are bad, but not to be altered by mere aliens" [Dunsany].

leg, scab [*slang*]; proselyte, convert.

TIMESERVER, time-pleaser; timist [*obs.*], Vicar of Bray, trimmer, ambidexter; double dealer; weathercock &c. (*changeable*) 149; Janus; coquet, flirt.

V. TERGIVERSATE, veer round, wheel round, turn round; change one's- mind, – intention, – purpose, – note; abjure, renounce; withdraw from &c.(*relinquish*) 624; turn a pirouette; go over –, pass –, change –, skip- from one side to another; go to the right-about; box the compass, shift one's ground, go upon another tack.

APOSTATIZE, change sides, go over, rat [*cant*], *tourner casaque* [*F.*], recant, retract; revoke; rescind &c. (*abrogate*) 756; recall; forswear, unsay; come -over, – round- to an opinion.

BACK DOWN, draw in one's horns, eat one's words; eat –, swallow- the leek; swerve, flinch, back out of, retrace one's steps, crawfish, crawl [*both slang, U. S.*]; think better of it; come back –, return- to one's first love; turn over a new leaf &c. (*repent*) 950.

TRIM, shuffle, play fast and loose, blow hot and cold, coquet, flirt, be on the fence, straddle, hold with the hare but run with the hounds; *nager entre deux eaux* [*F.*], wait to see how the -cat jumps, – wind blows.

Adj. CHANGEFUL &c. 149; irresolute &c. 605; ductile, slippery as an eel, trimming, ambidextrous, timeserving; coquetting &c. *v.*

revocatory, reactionary.

⁎⁎ "a change came o'er the spirit of my dream" [Byron]; "They are not constant, but are changing still" [*Cymbeline*]; "Was ever feather so lightly blown to and fro as this multitude?" [*II Henry VI*].

---

608. Caprice. — N. CAPRICE, fancy, humor; whim, whimsey *or* whimsy, whimwham, crotchet, *capriccio* [*It.*], quirk, freak, maggot, fad, vagary, prank, fit, flimflam, escapade, boutade [*obs.*], wild-goose chase; capriciousness &c. *adj.*; kink.

V. BE CAPRICIOUS &c. *adj.*; have a maggot in the brain; take it into one's head, take the bit in one's teeth; strain at a gnat and swallow a camel; blow hot and cold; play fast and loose, play fantastic tricks; *tourner casaque* [*F.*].

Adj. CAPRICIOUS; erratic, eccentric, fitful, hysterical; full of whims &c. *n.*; maggoty; inconsistent, fanciful, fantastic, whimsical, crotchety, kinky [*U. S.*], particular, humorsome, freakish, skittish, wanton, wayward; contrary; captious; unreasonable, unrestrained, undisciplined, not amenable to reason, arbitrary; unconformable &c. 83; penny wise and pound foolish; fickle &c. (*irresolute*) 605; frivolous, sleeveless [*obs.*], giddy, volatile.

Adv. BY FITS, by fits and starts, without rime or reason, at one's own sweet will; without counting the cost.

⁎⁎ *nil fuit unquam sic impar sibi;* the deuce is in him.

609. Choice. — N. CHOICE, option; discretion &c. (*volition*) 600; preoption; alternative; dilemma, *embarras de choix* [*F.*]; adoption, coöptation; novation [*law*]; decision &c. (*judgment*) 480.

ELECTION, poll, ballot, vote, division, voice, suffrage, cumulative vote; plebiscitum, plebiscite, *vox populi* [*L.*], popular decision, referendum; electioneering; voting &c. *v.*; elective franchise; straight ticket, ticket [*U. S.*]; ballot-box.

SELECTION, excerption, gleaning, eclecticism; *excerpta* [*L.*]; gleanings, cuttings, scissors and paste; pick &c. (*best*) 650.

PREFERENCE, prelation [*rare*]; predilection &c. (*desire*) 865; Apple of Discord; choice of Hercules; Scylla and Charybdis; good and evil.

V. OFFER FOR ONE'S CHOICE, set before; hold out –, present –, offer- the alternative; put to the vote.

CHOOSE, elect; coöpt, coöptate [*rare*]; take –, make- one's choice; make choice of, fix upon; use –, exercise –, one's- -discretion, – option; adopt, take up, embrace, espouse.

settle; decide &c. (*adjudge*) 480; list &c. (*will*) 600; make up one's mind &c. (*resolve*) 604.

VOTE, poll, hold up one's hand, give a (*or* the) voting sign; divide.

SELECT; pick, – and choose; pick –, single- out; excerpt, cull, glean, winnow; sift –, separate –, winnow- the chaff from the wheat; pick up, pitch upon; pick one's way; indulge one's fancy.

set apart, mark out for; mark &c. 550.

PREFER; have rather, had (*or* would) as lief; fancy &c. (*desire*) 865; reserve, set one's seal upon; be persuaded &c. 615.

TAKE A DECIDED STEP, take a decisive step; commit oneself to a course; pass –, cross- the Rubicon; cast in one's lot with; take for better or for worse.

Adj. OPTIONAL; coöptative; discretional &c. (*voluntary*) 600; at choice, on approval.

CHOOSING &c. *v.*; eclectic; preferential.

CHOSEN &c. *v.*; choice &c. (*good*) 648; elect, select, popular.

Adv. OPTIONALLY &c. *adj.*; at pleasure &c. (*will*) 600; either, – the one or the other; or; at the option of; whether or not; once for all; for one's money.

BY CHOICE, by preference; in preference; rather, before.

609a. Absence of Choice. — N. NO CHOICE, Hobson's choice; first come first served; necessity &c. 601; not a pin to choose &c. (*equality*) 27; any, the first that comes; that or nothing.

NEUTRALITY, indifference; indecision &c. (*irresolution*) 605.

V. BE NEUTRAL &c. *adj.*; have no -preference, – choice; waive, not vote; abstain –, refrain, -from voting; leave undecided; "make a virtue of necessity" [*Two Gentlemen*].

Adj. NEUTRAL, neuter; indifferent; undecided &c. (*irresolute*) 605.

Adv. EITHER &c. (*choice*) 609.

⁎⁎ "The Ball no question makes of Ayes and Noes, But Right or Left, as strikes the Player, goes" [Omar Khayyám — Fitzgerald]; "hanging and wiving goes by destiny" [*Merchant of Venice*].

610. Rejection. — N. REJECTION, repudiation, exclusion; refusal &c. 764; declination, declinature, withdrawal; averseness.

V. REJECT; set –, lay- aside; give up; decline &c. (*refuse*) 764; exclude, except; pluck up, spurn, cast out.

REPUDIATE, scout, set at naught; fling –, cast –, throw –, toss- -to the winds, – to the dogs, – overboard, – away; send to the right-about; disclaim &c. (*deny*) 536; discard &c. (*eject*) 297, (*have done with*) 678.

Adj. REJECTED &c. *v.*; rejectaneous [*obs.*], rejectitious [*obs.*], declinatory; not chosen &c. 609, not to be thought of; out of the question; "declined with thanks."

Adv. NEITHER, neither the one nor the other; no &c. 536.

⁎⁎ *non hæc in fœdera.*

611. Predetermination. — N. PREDETERMINATION, predestination, preordination, premeditation, predeliberation; foregone conclusion; *parti pris* [*F.*];

612. Impulse. — N. IMPULSE, sudden thought; impromptu, improvisation; inspiration, flash, spurt.

IMPROVISOR, extemporizer, *improvvisa-*

resolve, propendency [*obs.*]; intention &c. 620; project &c. 626; fate, foredoom, necessity.

SCHEDULE, list, calendar, docket [*U. S.*], slate [*pol. cant, U. S.*], register, roster, poll, muster, draft, *cadre* [*F.*], panel.

V. PREDETERMINE, predestine, preordain, premeditate, preresolve, preconcert; resolve beforehand.

LIST, schedule, docket [*U. S.*], slate [*U. S.*], register, poll, empanel, draft.

Adj. PREMEDITATED &c. *v.;* predesigned; prepense, advised, studied, designed, calculated; aforethought; intended &c. 620; foregone.

WELL-LAID, well-devised, well-weighed; maturely considered; cut-and-dried, slated [*pol. cant, U. S.*]; cunning.

Adv. ADVISEDLY &c. *adj.;* with premeditation, deliberately, all things considered, with eyes open, in cold blood; intentionally &c. 620.

₊ "With Earth's first Clay They did the Last Man knead [Omar Khayyám — Fitzgerald].

tore or *improvisatore* [*It.*]; creature of impulse.

V. flash on the mind.

IMPROVISE, extemporize; say what comes uppermost, say what comes first into one's head; act on the spur of the moment, rise to the occasion; spurt.

Adj. EXTEMPORANEOUS, impulsive, indeliberate [*rare*]; snap; improvised, improvisate, improviso, improvisatory; unpremeditated; unmeditated, improvisatorial, improvisatory, *improvisé* [*F.*]; unprompted, unguided; natural, unguarded; spontaneous &c. (*voluntary*) 600; instinctive &c. 601.

Adv. EXTEMPORE, extemporaneously; offhand, impromptu, *a l'improviste* [*F.*]; on the spur of the -moment, - occasion.

₊ "To its own impulse every creature stirs" [Arnold].

---

613. Habit. — **N.** HABIT, habitude, habituation, assuetude [*obs.*], assuefaction [*obs.*]; wont; run, way; habitual attitude, habitual state of mind, habitual course.

common -, general -, natural -, ordinary- -course, - run, - state- of things; matter of course; beaten -path, - track, - ground.

cacoëthes; bad -, confirmed -, inveterate -, intrinsic &c. (5)- habit; addictedness, addiction, trick.

CUSTOM, use, usage, prescription, immemorial usage, practice; prevalence, observance; conventionalism, conventionality; mode, fashion, vogue; etiquette &c. (*gentility*) 852; order of the day, cry; conformity &c. 82; consuetude, dastur *or* dustoor [*India*].

one's old way, old school, *veteris vestigia flammæ* [*L.*]; *laudator temporis acti* [*L.*].

RULE, standing order, precedent, routine; red tape, red-tapism; pipe clay; rut, groove.

ADDICT, habitué, habitual [*colloq.*], frequenter, case [*slang*], hard case [*slang*], the limit [*slang*].

INUREMENT; training &c. (*education*) 537; seasoning, hardening; radication; second nature, acclimatization; knack &c. (*skill*) 698.

614. Desuetude. — **N.** DESUETUDE, disusage; obsolescence, disuse &c. 678; want of -habit, - use, - practice; inusitation [*rare*]; newness to; new brooms.

NONPREVALENCE; infraction of usage &c. (*unconformity*) 83; "a custom more honored in the breach than the observance" [*Hamlet*].

V. BE UNACCUSTOMED &c. *adj.;* leave off -, cast off -, break off -, cure oneself of -, wean oneself from -, shake off -, violate -, break through -, infringe- -a habit, - a custom, - a usage; break one's -chains, - fetters; do old things in a new way, give an original touch, give a new dress to old ideas; disuse &c. 678; wear off.

Adj. UNACCUSTOMED, unused, unwonted, unseasoned, uninured, unhabituated, untrained; new, fresh, original; impulsive &c. *adj.* 612; green &c. (*unskilled*) 699; unhackneyed.

UNCONVENTIONAL, unfashionable; dissident, protestant; unusual &c. (*unconformable*) 83; nonobservant; disused &c. 678.

Adv. CONTRARY TO -CUSTOM, - USAGE, - convention; for once, just once; "this time doesn't count."

₊ exceptions prove the rule.

V. BE WONT &c. *adj.*

fall into a custom &c. (*conform to*) 82; tread –, follow- the beaten -track, – path; *stare super antiquas vias* [L.]; move in a rut, run on in a groove, go round like a horse in a mill, go on in the old jog-trot way; get wound up in red tape.

HABITUATE, inure, harden, season, caseharden; accustom, familiarize; naturalize, acclimatize; keep one's hand in; train &c. (*educate*) 537.

get into the -way, – knack- of; learn &c. 539; cling to, adhere to; repeat &c. 104; acquire –, contract –, fall into- a -habit, – trick; addict oneself to, take to, accustom oneself to.

BE HABITUAL &c. *adj.;* prevail; come into use, become a habit, take root; gain upon one, grow upon one.

Adj. HABITUAL; accustomary, customary; prescriptive; accustomed &c. *v.;* of -daily, – everyday- occurrence; consuetudinary; wonted, usual, general, ordinary, common, frequent, every day, household, jog-trot; well-trodden, well-known; familiar, vernacular, trite, commonplace, conventional, regular, set, stock, established, stereotyped; prevailing, prevalent; current, received, acknowledged, recognized, accredited; of course, admitted, understood.

CONFORMABLE &c. 82; according to -use, – custom, – routine; in vogue, in fashion; fashionable &c. (*genteel*) 852.

WONT; used to, given to, addicted to, attuned to, habituated to &c. *v.;* in the habit of; *habitué* [F.]; at home in &c. (*skillful*) 698; seasoned; imbued with, soaked in, permeated with, never free from; devoted to, wedded to.

HACKNEYED, fixed, rooted, deep-rooted, ingrafted *or* engrafted, permanent, inveterate, besetting, naturalized; ingrained &c. (*intrinsic*) 5.

Adv. HABITUALLY &c. *adj.;* always &c. (*uniformly*) 16.

AS USUAL, as is one's wont, as things go, as the world goes, as the sparks fly upwards; as you were [mil.]; *more suo* [L.], *more solito* [L.]; *ex more* [L.].

AS A RULE, for the most part; generally &c. *adj.;* most -often, – frequently.

⁎ *cela s'entend; abeunt studia in mores; adeo in teneris consuescere multum est; consuetudo quasi altera natura* [Cicero]; *hoc erat in more majorum;* "how use doth breed a habit in a man!" [*Two Gentlemen*]; *magna est vis consuetudinis; morem fecerat usus* [Ovid]; "Custom, like Winter, is the king of all" [Masefield].

2. *Causes of Volition*

615. Motive. — N. MOTIVE, springs of action.

REASON, ground, call, principle; by-end, by-purpose; mainspring, *primum mobile* [L.], keystone; the why and the wherefore; *pro* and *con*, reason why; secret motive, ulterior motive; *arrière pensée* [F.]; intention &c. 620.

INDUCEMENT, consideration; attraction; loadstone; magnet, magnetism, magnetic force; allectation [obs.], allective [obs.], temptation, enticement, *agacerie* [F.], allurement, witchery; bewitchment, bewitchery; charm; spell &c. 993; fascination, blandishment, cajolery; seduction, seducement; honeyed words, voice of the tempter, song of the Sirens; forbidden fruit, golden apple.

PERSUASIBILITY, persuasibleness, persuadability, persuadableness; attract-

615a. Absence of Motive. — N. ABSENCE OF MOTIVE; caprice &c. 608; chance &c. (*absence of design*) 621.

V. SCRUPLE &c. (*be unwilling*) 603; have no motive.

Adj. AIMLESS &c. (*chance*) 621; without rime or reason.

Adv. CAPRICIOUSLY, out of mere caprice.

616. Dissuasion. — N. DISSUASION, dehortation [rare], expostulation, remonstrance; deprecation &c. 766.

DISCOURAGEMENT, dehortative [rare], monitory, damper, wet blanket; contraindicant.

CURB &c. (*means of restraint*) 752; constraint &c. (*restraint*) 751; check &c. (*hindrance*) 706.

RELUCTANCE &c. (*unwillingness*) 603; contraindication.

ability; impressibility, susceptibility; softness; persuasiveness, attractiveness; tantalization.

INFLUENCE, prompting, dictate, instance; impulse, impulsion; incitement, incitation; press, insistence, urge [*rare*], instigation; provocation &c. (*excitation of feeling*) 824; inspiration; persuasion, suasion; encouragement, advocacy; exhortation, hortation; advice &c. 695; solicitation &c. (*request*) 765; lobbyism; pull [*slang*].

INCENTIVE, stimulus, spur, fillip, whip, goad, ankus [*India*], rowel, provocative, whet, dram.

BRIBE, lure; decoy, decoy duck; bait, trail of a red herring; bribery and corruption; sop, sop to Cerberus.

TEMPTER, seducer, seductor, seductress; prompter, suggester, coaxer, wheedler, Siren, Circe, vampire [*colloq.*],

V. DISSUADE, dehort [*rare*], cry out against, remonstrate, expostulate, warn, contraindicate.

DISINCLINE, indispose, shake, stagger; dispirit; discourage, dishearten, disenchant; deter; hold back, keep back &c. (*restrain*) 751; render averse &c. 603; repel; turn aside &c. (*deviation*) 279; wean from; act as a drag &c. (*hinder*) 706; throw cold water on, damp, cool, chill, blunt, calm, quiet, quench; deprecate &c. 766.

Adj. DISSUADING &c. *v.*; dissuasive; dehortatory [*rare*], dehortative [*rare*], expostulatory: monitive [*obs.*], monitory, monitorial.

DISSUADED &c. *v.*; admonitory; uninduced &c. (induce &c. 615); unpersuadable &c. (*obstinate*) 606; averse &c. (*unwilling*) 603; repugnant &c. (*dislike*) 867.

vamp [*slang*]; instigator, *agent provocateur* [*F.*]; lobbyist; firebrand, incendiary.

V. INDUCE, move; draw, draw on; bring in its train, give an impulse to &c. *n.;* inspire; put up to [*slang*], prompt, call up; attract, beckon.

STIMULATE &c. (*excite*) 824; spirit, spirit up, inspirit; rouse, arouse, animate, incite, provoke, instigate, set on, actuate; act upon, work upon, operate upon; encourage; pat -, clap- on the -back, - shoulder.

set an example, set the fashion; keep in countenance, back up.

INFLUENCE, weigh with, bias, sway, incline, dispose, predispose, turn the scale, inoculate; lead, - by the nose; have -, exercise -, influence- -with, - over, - upon; go -, come- round one [*colloq.*]; turn the head, magnetize; lobby [*chiefly U. S.*].

PERSUADE; prevail -with, - upon; overcome, carry; bring round, bring to one's senses; draw -, win - , gain -, talk- over; come over [*colloq.*]; procure, enlist, engage; invite, court.

TEMPT, seduce, overpersuade, entice, allure, captivate, fascinate, bewitch, carry away, charm, conciliate, wheedle, coax, lure, vamp [*slang*]; inveigle; tantalize; cajole &c. (*deceive*) 545.

BRIBE, tamper with, suborn, grease the palm, bait with a silver hook, gild the pill, make things pleasant, put a sop into the pan, throw a sop to, bait the hook.

ENFORCE, force; impel &c. (*push*) 276; propel &c. 284; whip, lash, goad, spur, prick, urge; egg on, hound on, hurry on; drag &c. 285; exhort; advise &c. 695; call upon &c., press &c. (*request*) 765; advocate.

BE PERSUADED &c.; yield to temptation, come round [*colloq.*]; concede &c. (*consent*) 762; obey a call; follow -advice, - the bent, - the dictates of; act on principle.

Adj. IMPULSIVE, motive; persuasive, persuasory [*rare*], hortative, hortatory; protreptical [*obs.*]; inviting, tempting, &c. *v.;* suasive, suasory [*obs.*], irresistible, seductive, attractive; fascinating &c. (*pleasing*) 829; provocative &c. (*exciting*) 824.

INDUCED &c. *v.;* disposed; persuadable &c. (*docile*) 602; spellbound; instinct -, taken -, smitten- with; inspired by &c. *v.*

Adv. BECAUSE, therefore &c. (*cause*) 155; from this motive, from that motive; for this reason, for that reason; for; by reason of, for the sake of, on the score of, on account of; out of, from, as, forasmuch as.

for all the world; on principle.

⁎⁎ *fax mentis incendium gloriæ;* "temptation hath a music for all ears" [Willis]; "to beguile many and be beguiled by one" [*Othello*].

617. [OSTENSIBLE MOTIVE, GROUND, OR REASON.] **Plea.** — **N.** PLEA, pretext; allegation, advocation [*archaic*]; ostensible -motive, – ground, – reason; excuse &c. (*vindication*) 937; color; gloss, guise.

handle, peg to hang on; room, *locus standi* [*L.*]; stalking-horse, *cheval de bataille* [*F.*], cue.

LOOPHOLE, starting-hole [*obs.*]; hole to creep out of, come-off [*colloq.*], way of escape.

PRETENSE &c. (*untruth*) 546; put-off, subterfuge, dust thrown in the eye; blind; moonshine; mere –, shallow- pretext; lame -excuse, – apology; tub to a whale; false plea, sour grapes; makeshift, shift, white lie; special pleading &c. (*sophistry*) 477; soft sawder [*slang*] &c. (*flattery*) 933.

V. PLEAD, allege; shelter oneself under the plea of; creep out of; tell a white lie; excuse &c. (*vindicate*) 937; color, gloss over, lend a color to; furnish a handle &c. *n.*; make a pretext of, make a handle of; use as a plea &c. *n.*; take one's stand upon, make capital out of; pretend &c. (*lie*) 544.

Adj. advocatory [*rare*], excusing; OSTENSIBLE &c. (*manifest*) 525; alleged, apologetic; pretended &c. 545.

Adv. OSTENSIBLY; under the plea of, under the pretense of.

3. *Objects of Volition*

618. Good. — **N.** GOOD, benefit, advantage; improvement &c. 658; greatest –, supreme- good; interest, service, behoof, behalf; weal [*archaic*]; main chance, *summum bonum* [*L.*]; commonwealth [*now rare*], commonweal *or* common weal; "consummation devoutly to be wished" [*Hamlet*]; gain, boot [*archaic*]; profit, harvest.

BOON &c. (*gift*) 784; good turn; blessing, benison; world of good; piece of good -luck, – fortune; nuts [*now slang*], prize, windfall, godsend, waif, treasuretrove.

good fortune &c. (*prosperity*) 734; happiness &c. 827.

[SOURCE OF GOOD] goodness &c. 648; utility &c. 644; remedy &c. 662; pleasure giving &c. 829.

V. BENEFIT, profit, advantage, serve, help, avail, boot [*archaic*], good [*obs.*], do good to.

GAIN, prosper, flourish, thrive &c. 734.

Adj. COMMENDABLE &c. 931; useful &c. 644; good &c., beneficial &c. 648.

Adv. WELL, aright, satisfactorily, favorably, not amiss; all for the best; to one's advantage &c. *n.*; in one's favor, in one's interest &c. *n.*

⁎⁎* so far so good; *magnum bonum*; "so shines a good deed in a naughty world" [*M. of V.*]; "from seeming evil still educing good" [Thomson]; "And learn the luxury of doing good" [Goldsmith]; "worthiest by being good, Far more than great or high" [Milton].

619. Evil. — **N.** EVIL, ill, harm, hurt, mischief, nuisance; machinations of the devil, Pandora's box, ills that flesh is heir to; mental suffering &c. (*pain*) 828.

[EVIL SPIRIT] demon &c. 980.

[CAUSE OF EVIL] bane &c. 663.

[PRODUCTION OF EVIL] badness &c. 649; painfulness &c. 830; evildoer &c. 913.

BLOW, buffet, stroke, scratch, bruise, wound, gash, mutilation; mortal -blow, – wound; *immedicabile vulnus* [*L.*]; damage, loss &c. (*deterioration*) 659.

DISADVANTAGE, prejudice, drawback.

DISASTER, accident, casualty; mishap &c. (*misfortune*) 735; bad job [*colloq.*], devil to pay [*colloq.*]; calamity, bale [*chiefly poetic*], woe, fatal mischief, catastrophe, tragedy; ruin &c. (*destruction*) 162; adversity &c. 735.

OUTRAGE, wrong, injury, foul play; bad turn, ill turn; disservice; spoliation &c. 791; grievance, crying evil.

V. DISSERVE, do disservice to, harm, injure, hurt.

BE IN TROUBLE &c. (*adversity*) 735.

Adj. DISASTROUS, bad &c. 649; awry, out of joint; disadvantageous; disserviceable, injurious, harmful.

Adv. AMISS, wrong, ill, to one's cost.

⁎⁎* "man is born unto trouble as the sparks fly upward" [*Bible*]; "the evil that men do lives after them" [*Julius Cæsar*]; "broken with the storms of state" [*Henry VIII*]; "one only good, namely, knowledge; and one only evil, namely, ignorance" [Diogenes Laertius].

Section II. Prospective Volition[1]

1. *Conceptional Volition*

620. Intention. — N. intention, intent, intentionality; purpose; *quo animo* [*L.*]; project &c. 626; undertaking &c. 676; predetermination &c. 611; design, ambition.

contemplation, mind, animus, view, purview [*law*], proposal; study; lookout.

object, aim, end; final cause; *raison d'être* [*F.*]; *cui bono* [*L.*]; "the be-all and the end-all" [*Macbeth*]; drift &c. (*meaning*) 516; tendency &c. 176; destination, mark, point, butt, goal, target, bull's-eye, quintain; prey, quarry, game.

decision, determination, resolve; fixed –, set –, settled- purpose; ultimatum; resolution &c. 604; wish &c. 865; *arrière pensée* [*F.*]; motive &c. 615.

[Study of final causes] teleology.

V. intend, purpose, design, mean; have to; propose to oneself; harbor a design; have in -view, – contemplation, – one's eye; have *in petto* [*It.*]; have an eye to.

bid for, labor for; be after, aspire to *or* after, endeavor after; be at, aim at, drive at, point at, level at; take aim; set before oneself; study to.

contemplate, meditate; take upon oneself &c. (*undertake*) 676; take into one's head; think of, dream of, talk of; premeditate &c. 611; compass [*legal*], calculate; destine, destinate; propose.

project &c. (*plan*) 626; have a mind to &c. (*be willing*) 602; desire &c. 865; pursue &c. 622.

Adj. intended &c. *v.;* intentional, advised, express, determinate; prepense &c. 611; bound for; intending &c. *v.;* disposed, inclined, minded; bent upon &c. (*earnest*) 604; at stake; on the -anvil, – tapis; in view, in prospect, in the breast of; *in petto* [*It.*]; teleological.

Adv. intentionally &c. *adj.;* advisedly, wittingly, knowingly, designedly, purposely, on purpose, by design, studiously, pointedly; with intent &c. *n.;* deliberately &c. (*with premeditation*) 611; with one's eyes open, in cold blood.

for; with a view to, with an eye to; in order -to, – that; to the end that,

621. [Absence of purpose.] Chance.[2] **— N.** chance &c. 156; lot, fate &c. (*necessity*) 601; luck; good luck &c. (*good*) 618; hoodoo, jinx [*slang*], jadoo *or* jadu [*Hind.*]; voodoo, voodooism; swastika *or* swastica, fylfot, gammadion; wheel of chance, Fortune's wheel; mascot.

speculation, venture, mere –, random- shot; blind bargain, leap in the dark; pig in a poke &c. (*uncertainty*) 475; fluke [*sporting cant*], potluck, flyer [*slang*], flutter [*slang*]; futures.

gambling, game of chance; drawing lots; sortilegy, sortition [*obs.*]; *sortes, – Vergilianæ* [*L.*]; *rouge et noir* [*F.*], hazard, ante, chuck-a-luck *or* chuckluck, crack-loo [*U. S.*], craps; faro, faro bank; roulette, pitch and toss, chuckfarthing, cup tossing, heads or tails, cross and pile [*archaic*], dice, dice box, poker-dice; fan-tan [*Chinese*].

wager; gamble, risk, stake, pyramid, plunge; bet, betting; gambling; the turf.

gambling house, gaming house, gambling den, pool room, betting-house; bucket shop; joint [*slang*]; totalizator; totalizer; hell; betting ring; Wall Street, Stock Exchange, curb, curb market.

gambler, gamester, dicer, sport [*cant*], punter, plunger, speculator, hazarder, bookmaker, bookie [*colloq.*], man of the turf; pool shark [*colloq.*], adventurer.

V. chance &c. (*hap*) 156; stand a chance &c. (*be possible*) 470.

toss up; cast –, draw- lots; leave –, trust- -to chance, – to the chapter of accidents; tempt fortune; chance it, take one's chance; run –, incur –, encounter- the -risk, – chance; stand the hazard of the die.

speculate, try one's luck, set on a cast, raffle, put into a lottery, buy a pig in a poke, shuffle the cards.

risk, venture, hazard, stake; ante; lay, – a wager; make a bet, wager, bet, gamble, game, play for; play at chuckfarthing; play the ponies [*slang*]; play craps &c.

Adj. fortuitous &c. 156; uninten-

---

[1] That is, volition having reference to a future object.   [2] See note on 156.

with the intent that; for the purpose of, with the view of, in contemplation of, on account of.

in pursuance of, pursuant to; *quo animo* [*L.*]; to all intents and purposes.

⁎⁎ "hell is paved with good intentions" [Johnson]; *sublimi feriam sidera vertice* [Horace].

tional, unintended; accidental; not meant; undesigned, unpurposed; unpremeditated &c. 612; never thought of.

INDISCRIMINATE, promiscuous; undirected, random; aimless, driftless, designless, purposeless, causeless; without purpose.

POSSIBLE &c. 470.

Adv. CASUALLY &c. 156; unintentionally &c. *adj.;* unwittingly.

INCIDENTALLY, *en passant* [*F.*], by the way.

at random, at a venture, at haphazard; as luck would have it; in luck; out of luck; by chance, by good fortune; as it may happen.

Int. what luck! better luck next time!

⁎⁎ *acierta errando; dextro tempore;* "fearful concatenation of circumstances" [D. Webster]; "fortuitous combination of circumstances" [Dickens]; *le jeu est le fils d'avarice et le père du désespoir;* "the happy combination of fortuitous circumstances" [Scott]; "the fortuitous or casual concourse of atoms" [Bentley]; "a fool must now and then be right by chance" [Cowper]; "fortune is unstable, while our will is free" [Laertius].

---

622. [PURPOSE IN ACTION.] **Pursuit.**
— **N.** PURSUIT; pursuing &c. *v.;* prosecution; pursuance; enterprise &c. (*un-*dertaking) 676; business &c. 625; adventure &c. (*essay*) 675; quest &c. (*search*) 461; scramble, hue and cry, game; hobby; still-hunt.

CHASE, hunt, *battue* [*F.*], race, steeplechase, hunting, coursing; venation [*obs.*], venery; fox chase, fox hunting; sport, sporting; shooting, angling, fishing, hawking; shikar [*India*].

PURSUER; hunter, huntsman, the field; shikari [*India*], sportman, Nimrod; hound &c. 366.

V. PURSUE, prosecute, follow; run –, make –, be –, hunt –, prowl- after; shadow; carry on &c. (*do*) 680; be absorbed in; engage in &c. (*undertake*) 676; set about &c. (*begin*) 66; endeavor &c. 675; court &c. (*request*) 765; seek &c. (*search*) 461; aim at &c. (*intention*) 620; follow the trail &c. (*trace*) 461; fish for &c. (*experiment*) 463; press on &c. (*haste*) 684; run a race &c. (*velocity*) 274.

tread a path; take –, hold- a course; shape –, direct –, bend- one's -steps, – course; play a game; fight –, elbow-one's way; follow up; take to, take up; go in for; ride one's hobby.

CHASE, give chase, still-hunt, stalk, shikar [*India*], course, dog, hunt, hound; tread –, follow- on the heels of, &c. (*sequence*) 281; start game.

RUSH UPON; rush headlong &c. (*vio-lence*) 173; ride at, run full tilt at; make a leap at, jump at, snatch at; run down.

623. [ABSENCE OF PURSUIT.] **Avoidance.** — **N.** AVOIDANCE, evasion, elusion; seclusion &c. 893.

avolation [*obs.*], flight; escape &c. 671; retreat &c. 287; recoil &c. 277; departure &c. 293; rejection &c. 610.

ABSTENTION, abstinence; forbearance; refraining &c. *v.;* inaction &c. 681; neutrality.

SHIRKER &c. *v.;* slacker [*colloq.*], shirk, quitter [*U. S.*], eye servant, truant; fugitive, refugee, runaway, runagate, deserter, renegade, backslider; maroon.

V. ABSTAIN, refrain, spare, not attempt; not do &c. 681; maintain the even tenor of one's way.

ESCHEW, keep from, let alone, have nothing to do with; keep –, stand –, hold- -aloof, – off; take no part in, have no hand in.

AVOID, shun; steer –, keep- clear of; fight shy of; keep one's distance, keep at a respectful distance; keep –, get-out of the way; evade, elude, turn away from; set one's face against &c. (*oppose*) 708; deny oneself.

SHRINK; hang –, hold –, draw- back; recoil &c. 277; retire &c. (*recede*) 287; flinch, blink, blench, shy, shirk, dodge, parry, make way for, give place to.

BEAT A RETREAT; turn tail, turn one's back; take to one's heels; run, run away, run for one's life; maroon; cut and run [*colloq.*]; be off, – like a shot; fly, flee, fly –, flee –, run away- from; take flight, take to flight; desert, elope; make off, scamper off, sneak off, shuffle off, sheer

Adj. PURSUING &c. *v.;* in quest of &c. (*inquiry*) 461; in pursuit, in full cry, in hot pursuit; on the scent.

Adv. AFTER; in pursuance of &c. (*intention*) 620.

Int. tallyho! yoicks! soho!

off; break –, burst –, tear oneself –, slip –, slink –, steal- -away, – away from; slip cable, part company, turn on one's heel; sneak out of, play truant, give one the go-by [*slang*], give leg bail [*slang*], take French leave, slope [*slang*], decamp, flit, bolt, abscond, levant [*slang, Eng.*], skedaddle [*dial. or slang, U. S.*], absquatulate [*U. S.*], cut one's stick [*slang*], walk one's chalks [*slang*], show the heels, show a clean (*or* light) pair of heels, make oneself scarce [*slang*]; escape &c. 671; go away &c. (*depart*) 293; abandon &c. 624; reject &c. 610.

lead one a dance, lead one a pretty dance; throw off the scent, play at hide and seek.

Adj. AVOIDING &c. *v.;* neutral; unsought, unattempted; shy of &c. (*unwilling*) 603; elusive, evasive; fugitive, runaway; shy, wild.

Adv. LEST, in order to avoid.

Int. forbear! keep off! hands off! *sauve qui peut!* [*F.*], devil take the hindmost!

*** "things unattempted yet in prose or rhyme" [*Paradise Lost*].

624. Relinquishment. — N. RELINQUISHMENT, abandonment; desertion, defection, secession, withdrawal; cave of Adullam; *nolle prosequi* [*L.*].

discontinuance &c. (*cessation*) 142; renunciation &c. (*recantation*) 607; abrogation &c. 756; resignation &c. (*retirement*) 757; desuetude &c. 614; cession &c. (*of property*) 782.

V. RELINQUISH, give up, abandon, desert, forsake, leave in the lurch; go back on [*colloq.*]; depart –, secede – withdraw- from; back out of [*colloq.*], back down from [*colloq.*]; leave, quit, take leave of, bid a long farewell; vacate &c. (*resign*) 757.

RENOUNCE &c. (*abjure*) 607; forego, have done with, drop; nol-pros [*law*]; disuse &c. 678; discard &c. 782; wash one's hands of; drop all idea of.

BREAK OFF, leave off; desist; stop &c. (*cease*) 142; hold one's hand, stay one's hand; quit one's hold; give over, shut up shop; throw up the -game, – cards.

give up the -point, – argument; pass to the order of the day, move the previous question, table, table the motion.

Adj. UNPURSUED; relinquished &c. *v.;* relinquishing &c. *v.*

Int. avast! &c. (*stop*) 142.

*** *aufgeschoben ist nicht aufgehoben; entbehre gern was du nicht hast.*

625. Business. — N. BUSINESS, occupation, employment, undertaking; pursuit &c. 622; what one is doing, what one is about; affair, concern, matter, case.

TASK, matter in hand, irons in the fire; thing to do, agendum (*pl.* agenda), work, job, chore [*U. S.*], errand, commission, mission, charge, care; duty &c. 926.

exercise; work &c. (*action*) 680; avocation, hobby; press of business &c. (*activity*) 682.

FUNCTION, part, rôle, cue; province, lookout [*colloq.*], department, capacity, sphere, orb [*now rare*], field, line; walk, - of life; beat, round, routine; race, career.

OFFICE, place, post, chargeship, incumbency, living; situation, berth, billet, appointment, employ [*rare*], service &c. (*servitude*) 749; engagement; undertaking &c. 676.

VOCATION, calling, profession, cloth, faculty; industry, art; industrial arts; craft, mystery [*obs.*], handicraft; trade &c. (*commerce*) 794.

V. OCCUPY ONESELF WITH; pass –, employ –, spend- one's time in; employ oneself -in, – upon; concern oneself with; make it one's business &c. *n.;* undertake &c. 676; enter a profession; betake oneself to, turn one's hand to; have to do with &c. (*do*) 680.

be about, be doing, be engaged in, be employed in, be occupied with, be at work on; have one's hands in, have in hand; have on one's -hands, – shoulders; bear the burden; have one's hands full &c. (*activity*) 682.

PLY ONE'S TASK, ply one's trade; drive a trade; carry on –, do –, transact- -business, – a trade &c. *n.;* keep a shop; labor in one's vocation; pursue the even tenor of one's way; attend to business, attend to one's work.

OFFICIATE, serve, act; act one's part, play one's part; do duty; serve –, discharge –, perform- the -office, – duties, – functions- of; hold –, fill- -an office, – a place, – a situation; hold a portfolio.

BE IN THE HANDS OF, be on the stocks, be on the anvil; pass through one's hands.

Adj. BUSINESSLIKE; workaday; professional, vocational; official, functional; humming, busy &c. (*actively employed*) 682.

IN HAND, on hand; on *or* in one's hands; afoot; on foot, on the anvil; going on; acting.

Adv. IN THE COURSE OF BUSINESS, all in the day's work; professionally &c. *adj.*

*** "a business with an income at its heels" [Cowper]; *amoto quæramus seria ludo* [Horace]; *par negotiis neque supra* [Tacitus]; "why not have a bit of romance in business when it costs nothing?" [Shaw].

626. Plan. — **N.** PLAN, scheme, design, project, proposal, proposition, suggestion; resolution, motion; precaution &c. (*provision*) 673; deep-laid &c. (*premeditated*) 611- plan &c.; germ &c. (*cause*) 153.

SYSTEM &c. (*order*) 58; organization &c. (*arrangement*) 60.

OUTLINE, sketch, skeleton, draft *or* draught, *ébauche* [F.], *brouillon* [F.]; rough -cast, – draft *or* draught, – copy; copy; proof, revise.

forecast, program *or* programme, prospectus; *carte du pays* [F.]; card; bill, protocol; order of the day, memoranda, list of agenda; bill of fare &c. (*food*) 298; base of operations; platform, plank, slate [U. S.], ticket [U. S.].

rôle; policy &c. (*line of conduct*) 692.

CONTRIVANCE, invention, expedient, receipt, nostrum, artifice, device; pipelaying [U. S.]; stratagem &c. (*cunning*) 702; trick &c. (*deception*) 545; alternative, loophole; shift &c. (*substitute*) 147; last shift &c. (*necessity*) 601, gadget.

MEASURE, step; stroke, – of policy; masterstroke; trump, trump card, courtcard; *cheval de bataille* [F.], great gun; *coup,* – *d'état* [F.]; clever –, bold –, good- -move, – hit, – stroke; bright -thought, – idea; great idea.

INTRIGUE, cabal, plot, conspiracy, complot, machination; underplot, counterplot; mine, countermine.

SCHEMER, schemist [*rare*], schematist [*obs.*]; strategist, machinator; Machiavellian, Machiavellist, conspirator; intrigant &c. (*cunning*) 702.

PROJECTOR, promoter, designer &c. *v.;* organizer, founder (*fem.* foundress), author, artist, builder.

V. PLAN, scheme, design, frame, contrive, project, forecast, sketch; devise, invent &c. (*imagine*) 515; set one's wits to work &c. 515; spring a project; fall upon, hit upon; strike –, chalk –, cut –, lay –, map- out; lay down a plan; shape –, mark- out a course; predetermine &c. 611; concert, preconcert, preëstablish; prepare &c. 673; hatch, – a plot; concoct; take -steps, – measures.

SYSTEMATIZE, organize; cast, recast, arrange &c. 60; digest, mature.

PLOT; counterplot, mine, countermine, dig a mine; lay a train; intrigue &c. (*cunning*) 702.

Adj. PLANNED &c. *v.;* strategic *or* strategical.

PLANNING &c. *v.;* in course of preparation &c. 673; under consideration, on the tapis, on the carpet, on the table.

*** "a mighty maze! but not without a plan" [Pope]; "lofty designs must close in like effects" [Browning].

627. Method. [PATH.] — **N.** METHOD, way, manner, wise [*rare, exc. in phrases*], gait, form, mode, fashion, tone, guise; *modus operandi* [L.]; procedure &c. (*line of conduct*) 692.

PATH, road, route, course; line of way, line of road; trajectory, orbit, track, beat, tack.

STEPS; stair, staircase; flight of -steps, – stairs; ladder, stile; perron.

BRIDGE, footbridge, viaduct, pontoon, stepping-stone, plank, gangway; draw-bridge.

pass, ford, ferry, tunnel; pipe &c. 260.

MEANS OF ACCESS, adit, entrance, approach, passage, cloister, covered way, lobby, corridor, aisle; alley, lane, vennel [*Scot. & dial. Eng.*], avenue, artery, channel; gateway &c. (*opening*) 260; door, backdoor, backstairs; secret passage; covert way.

ROADWAY, express; thoroughfare; highway, macadam, parkway, boulevard; turnpike –, royal –, state –, coach- road; broad –, King's –, Queen's- highway; beaten -track, – path; horse –, bridle- -road, – track, – path; walk, *trottoir* [*F.*], footpath, pathway, pavement, flags, sidewalk, by-road, crossroad; by –, cross-path, – way; cut; short cut & (*mid-course*) 628; *carrefour* [*F.*]; private –, occupation- road; highways and byways; railroad, railway, trolley track, tramroad, tramway; towpath; causeway; street &c. (*abode*) 189; stairway, gangway; speedway; canal &c. (*conduit*) 350.

Adv. HOW; in what way, in what manner; by what mode; so, thus, in this way, after this fashion.

ONE WAY OR ANOTHER, anyhow; somehow or other &c. (*instrumentality*) 631; by way of; *viâ* [*L.*]; *in transitu* [*L.*] &c. 270; on the high road to, on the way to.

** *hœ tibi erunt artes;* "the noblest prospect which a Scotchman ever sees is the high-road that leads him to England" [Johnson].

---

628. Mid-course. — N.

MID-COURSE, midway [*rare*], middle way, middle course; moderation; mean &c. 29; middle &c. 68; *juste milieu* [*F.*], *mezzo termine* [*L.*], golden mean, *ariston metron* [*Gr.* ἄριστον μέτρον], *aurea mediocritas* [*L.*]; fifty-fifty [*colloq.*].

SHORTCUT, crosscut; straight &c. (*direct*) 278 -course, – path; great-circle sailing.

COMPROMISE, half measures, half-and-half measures; neutrality.

V. KEEP THE GOLDEN MEAN; keep in –, steer –, preserve- -a middle, – an even- course; avoid both Scylla and Charybdis; go straight &c. (*direct*) 278.

COMPROMISE, make a compromise, go fifty-fifty [*colloq.*], concede half, go halfway.

Adj. NEUTRAL, average, even, evenly balanced; impartial, moderate; straight &c. (*direct*) 278.

Adv. MIDWAY, in the mean; in moderation.

** *medium tenuere beati; est modus in rebus* [Horace]; "moderation is the virtue best adapted to the dawn of prosperity" [Pitt].

629. Circuit. — N.

CIRCUIT, roundabout way, digression, detour, circumbendibus [*humorous*], circumambience, circumambiency, circumambulation, ambages, loop; winding &c. (*circuition*) 311; zigzag &c. (*deviation*) 279.

V. GO ROUND ABOUT, circumambulate, perform a circuit, make a circuit, go out of one's way; make a detour; meander &c. (*deviate*) 279.

lead a pretty dance; beat about, – the bush; make two bites of a cherry.

Adj. CIRCUITOUS, circumambient, circumambulatory, indirect, roundabout; zigzag &c. (*deviating*) 279; backhanded.

Adv. IN A ROUNDABOUT WAY; by a side wind, by an indirect course; from pillar to post.

** the longest way round is the shortest way home.

---

630. Requirement. — N.

REQUIREMENT, need, wants, necessities; necessaries, – of life; stress, exigency, pinch, *sine quâ non* [*L.*], matter of necessity; case of need, case of life or death.

desideratum &c. (*desire*) 865; want &c. (*deficiency*) 640.

NEEDFULNESS, essentiality, necessity, indispensability, urgency, prerequisite; the least one can -do, – require.

REQUISITION &c. (*request*) 765 (*exaction*) 741; run; demand for, call for.

CHARGE, claim, command, injunction, mandate, order, precept, ultimatum.

V. REQUIRE, need, want, have occasion for; not be able to do without, not able to dispense with; prerequire.

BE NECESSARY &c. *adj.;* stand in need of; lack &c. 640; desiderate; desire &c. 865.

RENDER NECESSARY, necessitate, create a necessity for, call for, put in requisition; make a requisition &c. (*ask for*) 765, (*demand*) 741.

Adj. NECESSARY; required &c. *v.;* requisite, needful, imperative, essential, indispensable, prerequisite; called for; in demand, in request.

in want of; destitute of &c. 640.

URGENT, exigent, pressing, instant, crying, absorbing.

Adv. OF NECESSITY; *ex necessitate rei* [*L.*] &c. (*necessarily*) 601; out of -stern necessity, – bitter need; at a pinch.

*** there is no time to lose; it cannot be -spared, – dispensed with; *mendacem memorem esse oportet* [Quintilian]; *necessitas non habet legem; nec tecum possum vivere nec sine te* [Martial]; needs must when the devil drives; "necessity has no law" [Rabelais]; "necessity's sharp pinch" [*Lear*]; "Socrates said, 'those who want fewest things are nearer to the gods'" [Diogenes Laertius].

2. *Subservience to Ends*

1. *Actual Subservience*

631. Instrumentality.— N. INSTRUMENTALITY; aid &c. 707; subservience *or* subserviency, intermediacy, intermediation, mediation, intervention, medium, intermedium, intermediary, interagent, intermediate, mediating agency, vehicle, hand; agency &c. 170.

minister, handmaid; midwife, *accoucheur* [*F.*], *accoucheuse* [*fem., F.*], obstetrician; servant, slave, maid, valet; friend at court; go-between; cat's-paw; stepping-stone.

KEY, master –, pass –, latch- key; "open sesame"; passport, *passe-partout* [*F.*], safe-conduct; pull [*slang*], influence.

INSTRUMENT &c. 633; expedient &c. (*plan*) 626; means &c. 632.

V. SUBSERVE, minister, mediate, intervene, intermediate, come –, go- between; interpose; pull the -strings, – wires; use one's influence; be instrumental &c. *adj.;* pander to; officiate; tend.

Adj. INSTRUMENTAL; useful &c. 644; ministerial, subservient, serviceable; mediatorial, intermedial, intermediary, intermediate, intervening; conducive.

Adv. THROUGH, by, *per* [*L.*]; whereby, thereby, hereby; by the agency of &c. 170; by dint of; by *or* in virtue of; through the medium of &c. *n.;* along with; on the shoulders of; by means of &c. 632; by *or* with the aid of &c. (*assistance*) 707.

SOMEHOW; *per fas et nefas* [*L.*]; by fair means or foul; somehow or other; by hook or by crook.

*** "man is thy most awful instrument In working out a pure intent" [Wordsworth].

632. Means. — N. MEANS, resources, wherewithal, ways and means; capital &c. (*money*) 800; revenue, income; stock in trade &c. 636; provision &c. 637; reserve, remnant, last resource, a shot in the locker [*colloq.*]; appliances &c. (*machinery*) 633; means and appliances; conveniences; cards to play; expedients &c. (*measures*) 626; two strings to one's bow; wheels within wheels; sheet anchor &c. (*safety*) 666; aid &c. 707; medium &c. 631.

V. PROVIDE THE WHEREWITHAL; find –, have –, possess- means &c. *n.;* have something laid by, – for a rainy day; have powerful friends, have friends at court; have something to draw on; beg, borrow, or steal.

Adj. INSTRUMENTAL &c. 631; MECHANICAL &c. 633.

RELIABLE, trustworthy, efficient; honorable &c. (*upright*) 939.

Adv. BY MEANS OF, with; by -what, – all, – any, – some- means; wherewith, herewith, therewith; wherewithal.

how &c. (*in what manner*) 627; through &c. (*by the instrumentality of*) 631; with *or* by the aid of &c. (*assistance*) 707; by the agency of &c. 170.

*** "my extremest means Lie all unlock'd to your occasions" [*M. of V.*].

633. Instrument. — N. MACHINERY, mechanism, engineering.

INSTRUMENT, organ, tool, implement, utensil, machine, engine, lathe, gin, mill; air –, caloric –, heat –, steam –, internal-combustion- engine; motor.

EQUIPMENT, gear, tackle, tackling; rigging, apparatus, appliances; plant, *matériel* [*F.*]; harness, trappings, fittings, accouterments *or* accoutrements, impedimenta; equipment, equipage; appointments, furniture, upholstery; chattels; paraphernalia &c. (*belongings*) 780.

MECHANICAL POWERS; mechanical -advantage, – movements, – contrivances; leverage; fulcrum lever, crow, crowbar, gavelock [*Scot. & dial. Eng.*], jemmy, jimmy, marline spike *or* |marlinspike, handspike, arm, limb, wing; oar, paddle &c. (*navigation*) 267.

wheel and axle; wheelwork, clockwork; rolling contact; epicyclic train; revolving lever; wheels within wheels; pinion, crank, winch; cam; capstan &c. (*lift*) 307; wheel &c. (*rotation*) 312; bevel gearing, spur gearing, universal joint; fly wheel, governor, turbine, water wheel; pump, lift-pump, force-pump, hydraulic ram.

pulley, crane, derrick; belt, open belt, crossed belt; cone pulley, stepped speed pulley.

inclined plane; wedge; screw; jack; spring, mainspring; can hook, glut, heald, heddle, loom, shuttle, jenny, parbuckle, sprag.

[TOOLS &c.] hammer &c. (*impulse*) 276; edge tool &c. (*cut*) 253; turnscrew, screw driver *or* screwdriver; borer &c. 262; vise, teeth, &c. (*hold*) 781; nail, rope &c. (*join*) 45; peg &c. (*hang*) 214; support &c. 215; spoon &c. (*vehicle*) 272; arms &c. 727.

handle, hilt, haft *or* heft, shaft, shank, blade, trigger, tiller, rudder, helm, treadle, pedal, key; knocker.

Adj. INSTRUMENTAL &c. 631.

MECHANICAL, machinal [*rare*]; brachial; propulsive, driving, hoisting, elevating, lifting.

useful, labor-saving, ingenious; simple; complicated; well made, well fitted, sharp, in good order, well equipped.

*** "the tools to him that can handle them" [Carlyle]; "there is no jesting with edge tools" [Beaumont and Fletcher]; a good workman is known by his tools.

634. Substitute. — N. SUBSTITUTE &c. 147; proxy, alternate, understudy; deputy &c. 759; *badli* [*Hind.*].

*** "man, proud man, Drest in a little brief authority" [*M. for M.*]; "a substitute shines brightly as a king, until a king be by" [*M. of V.*].

635. Materials. — N. MATERIAL, raw material, stuff, stock, staple; ore.

[BUILDING MATERIAL] marble, granite, limestone, freestone, sandstone, brown stone; stone, metal, brick, bricks and mortar; chinking, mortar, lime, chunam [*India*], clay, plaster, daubing, concrete, cement, reënforced concrete; unburnt brick, adobe; composition, compo; slates, tiles; whitewash &c. 223.

wood, timber, clapboard, shingle, shake, puncheon, log, rafter, beam, joist; two-by-four, three-by-four; post, upright, stud, lath; wall board.

MATERIALS; supplies, munition, fuel, grist, household stuff; crockery &c. 384; pabulum &c. (*food*) 298; oilcloth, linoleum; ammunition &c. (*arms*) 727; contingents; relay, reënforcement; baggage &c. (*personal property*) 780; means &c. 632.

FABRICS, calico, cambric, cashmere, linen, cotton, wool, silk; muslin, lawn, voile, gingham, dimity, broadcloth, homespun, serge, tweed, crêpe de chine, chiffon, satin, velvet.

Adj. raw &c. (*unprepared*) 674; finished; wooden &c. *n.;* adobe.

*** "all the means of action — The shapeless masses, the materials — Lie everywhere about us" [Longfellow]; "The carpenter dresses his plank — the tongue of his fore-plane whistles its wild ascending lisp" [Whitman].

636. Store. — **N.** STOCK, fund, mine, vein, lode, quarry; spring; fount, fountain; well, wellspring [obs. exc. fig.]; orchard, garden, farm; milch cow; hen.

STOCK IN TRADE, supply; heap &c. (collection) 72; treasure; reserve, corps de réserve [F.], reserve fund, nest egg, savings, bonne bouche [F.].

CROP, harvest, vintage, yield, product, gleaning.

STORE, accumulation, hoard; mow, rick, stack; lumber; relay &c. (provision) 637.

STOREHOUSE, storeroom, store closet; depository, depot, cache, repository, reservatory [obs.], repertory; repertorium [rare]; promptuary, warehouse, godown [Oriental], entrepôt [F.], magazine; buttery, larder, spence [dial. Eng.]; garner, granary, grain elevator, silo; cannery, safe-deposit vault, stillroom, bank &c. (treasury) 802; armory; arsenal; dock; freight yard, train shed, car-barn, power station; stable, barn, byre, cowhouse; piggery; hen house; fish hatchery; hothouse, conservatory.

quiver, bandoleer; coffer &c. (receptacle) 191.

RESERVOIR, cistern, aljibar [Sp. Am.], tank, pond, mill pond; gasometer.

[COLLECTIONS] library, public library, library of Congress, British Museum, Bodleian, Bibliothek; gallery, art gallery, picture gallery, Louvre, museum, Madame Tussaud's, zoölogical garden, zoo [colloq.], aquarium, menagerie.

WORK OF REFERENCE, dictionary, lexicon, encyclopedia or encyclopædia, cyclopedia or cyclopædia, thesaurus, atlas, concordance, anthology.

CONSERVATION; storing &c. v.; storage.

file, letter file, card index, portfolio, budget; photographic -plate, - film; memory.

V. STORE; put by, lay by, set by; stow away; set apart, lay apart; store up, hoard up, treasure up, lay up, heap up, put up, garner up, save up; bank; cache; accumulate, amass, hoard, fund, garner, save.

RESERVE; keep back, hold back; husband, - one's resources.

DEPOSIT; stow, stack, load; harvest; heap, collect &c. 72; lay in store &c. adj.; keep, file [papers]; lay in &c. (provide) 637; preserve &c. 670.

Adj. STORED &c. v.; in store, in reserve, in ordinary; spare, supernumerary.

Adv. for a rainy day, for a nest egg, to fall back upon; on deposit.

⁎ adde parvum parvo magnus acervus erit; "cast thy bread upon the waters" [Bible].

---

637. Provision. — **N.** PROVISION, supply; grist, - to the mill; subvention &c. (aid) 707; resources &c. (means) 632; groceries, grocery.

providing &c. v.; purveyance; reënforcement; commissariat.

PROVENDER &c. (food) 298; ensilage; viaticum; ration; emergency -, iron-ration.

CATERER, purveyor, provider, commissary, quartermaster, steward; purser, housekeeper, manciple, feeder, batman, victualer or victualler, compradore or compradore [China]; innkeeper, landlord, innholder, mine host, khansamah [India], restaurateur [F.]; grocer, green grocer, huckster, fishmonger, provision merchant; sutler &c. (merchant) 797.

PROVISION SHOP, provision store, meat shop, fish store; market, public market; grocery [U. S.], - shop, - store.

V. PROVIDE; make -provision, - due provision for; lay in, - a stock, - a store.

638. Waste. — **N.** CONSUMPTION, expenditure, exhaustion; dispersion &c. 73; ebb; leakage &c. (exudation) 295; loss &c. 776; wear and tear; waste; prodigality &c. 818; misuse &c. 679; wasting &c. v.; rubbish &c. (useless) 645.

V. CONSUME, spend, expend, use, swallow up; exhaust; impoverish; spill, drain, empty, deplete; disperse &c. 73.

cast -, fool -, muddle -, throw -, fling -, fritter- away; burn the candle at both ends, waste; squander &c. 818.

LABOR IN VAIN &c. (useless) 645; "waste its sweetness on the desert air" [Gray]; cast pearls before swine; employ a steam engine to crack a nut, waste powder and shot, break a butterfly on a wheel; cut blocks with a razor, pour water into a sieve, tilt at windmills.

RUN TO WASTE; ebb; leak &c. (run out) 295; melt away, run dry, dry up; spoil.

SUPPLY, suppeditate [*obs.*]; furnish; find, find one in; arm.

cater, victual, provision, purvey, forage; beat up for; stock, – with; make good, replenish; fill, – up; recruit, feed.

STORE, have in -store, – reserve; keep, keep by one; have to fall back upon; store &c. 636; provide against a rainy day &c. (*economy*) 817; conserve, keep, preserve, lay by, gather into barns.

** "soul, thou hast much goods laid up for many years" [*Bible*].

639. Sufficiency. — N. SUFFICIENCY,
adequacy, enough, wherewithal, *quantum sufficit* [*L.*], satisfaction, competence; no less.

MEDIOCRITY &c. (*average*) 29.

FILL; fullness &c. (*completeness*) 52; plenitude, plenty; abundance; copiousness &c. *adj.*; amplitude, galore [*rare*], lots [*colloq.*], profusion; full measure; "good measure, pressed down, and shaken together, and running over" [*Bible*].

LUXURIANCE &c. (*fertility*) 168; affluence &c. (*wealth*) 803; fat of the land; "a land flowing with milk and honey" [*Bible*]; cornucopia; horn of -plenty, – Amalthæa; mine &c. (*stock*) 636.

OUTPOURING; flood &c. (*great quantity*) 31; tide &c. (*river*) 348; repletion &c. (*redundance*) 641; satiety &c. 869.

RICH MAN &c. (*wealth*) 803; financier, banker, creditor &c. 805; plutocrat.

V. BE SUFFICIENT &c. *adj.*; suffice; do, just do [*both colloq.*], satisfy, pass muster; have enough &c. *n.*; eat –, drink –, have- one's fill; roll in, swim in; wallow in &c. (*superabundance*) 641; wanton.

ABOUND, exuberate, teem, flow, stream, rain, shower down; pour, pour in; swarm; bristle with; superabound.

RENDER SUFFICIENT &c. *adj.*; replenish &c. (*fill*) 52.

Adj. SUFFICIENT, enough, adequate, up to the mark, commensurate, competent, satisfactory, valid, tangible.

MODERATE &c. (*temperate*) 953; measured.

AMPLE; full &c. (*complete*) 52; plenty, plentiful, plenteous; plenty as blackberries; copious, abundant; abounding &c. *v.*; replete, enough and to spare, flush; chock-full *or* choke-full; well-stocked, well-provided; liberal; unstinted, unstinting; stintless; without

Adj. WASTED &c. *v.*; gone to waste, useless, rendered useless, made unavailable; run to seed; dried up; at a low ebb.

WASTEFUL &c. (*prodigal*) 818; penny wise and pound foolish.

** *magno conatu magnas nugas; le jeu ne vaut pas la chandelle;* "idly busy rolls their world away" [Goldsmith]; "Time wasted is existence, used is life" [Young]; "O, call back yesterday, bid time return" [*Richard II*].

640. Insufficiency. — N. INSUFFI-
CIENCY, inadequacy, inadequateness; incompetence &c. (*impotence*) 158; deficiency &c. (*incompleteness*) 53; imperfection &c. 651; shortcoming &c. 304; paucity; stint; scantiness &c. (*smallness*) 32; none to spare; bare subsistence.

SCARCITY, dearth; want, need, lack, poverty, exigency; inanition, starvation, famine, drought *or* drouth.

DOLE, mite, pittance; short -allowance, – commons; half rations; banyan day; fast day, Lent.

DEPLETION, emptiness, poorness &c. *adj.*; vacancy, flaccidity; ebb tide; low water; "a beggarly account of empty boxes" [*Rom. and Jul.*]; indigence &c. 804; insolvency &c. (*nonpayment*) 808.

POOR MAN, pauper &c. 804; bankrupt &c. (*nonpayment*) 808.

MISER, niggard &c. (*parsimony*) 819.

V. BE INSUFFICIENT &c. *adj.*; not suffice &c. 639; kick the beam; come short of &c. 304; run dry.

WANT, lack, need, require; *caret* [*L.*]; be in want &c. (*poor*) 804; live from hand to mouth.

RENDER INSUFFICIENT &c. *adj.*; drain of resources; impoverish &c. (*waste*) 638; stint &c. (*begrudge*) 819; put on short -allowance, – commons.

do insufficiently &c. *adv.*; scotch the snake.

Adj. INSUFFICIENT, inadequate; too little &c. 32; not enough &c. 639; unequal to; incompetent &c. (*impotent*) 158; perfunctory &c. (*neglect*) 460; deficient &c. (*incomplete*) 53; wanting &c. *v.*; imperfect &c. 651; ill-furnished, ill-provided, ill-stored, ill-off.

SHORT OF, out of, destitute of, devoid of, bereft of &c. 789, denuded of; slack, at a low ebb; empty, vacant, bare; dry, drained.

stint; unsparing, unmeasured; lavish &c. 641; wholesale.

unexhausted, unwasted; exhaustless, inexhaustible.

RICH; luxuriant &c. (*fertile*) 168; affluent &c. (*wealthy*) 803; wantless; big with &c. (*pregnant*) 161.

Adv. SUFFICIENTLY, amply &c. *adj.;* full; in abundance &c. *n.;* with no sparing hand; to one's heart's content, *ad libitum* [*L.*], without stint; to the good.

*** "cut and come again" [Crabbe]; *das Beste ist gut genug;* "scatter plenty o'er a smiling land" [Gray].

UNPROVIDED, unsupplied, unfurnished; unreplenished, unfed; unstored, untreasured; empty-handed.

MEAGER *or* meagre, poor, thin, scrimp, sparing, stunted, spare, stinted; starved, starveling, emaciated, undernourished, underfed, half-starved, famine-stricken, famished; jejune.

SCARCE; not to be had, – for love or money, – at any price; scurvy; stingy &c. 819; at the end of one's tether; without resources &c. 632; in want &c. (*poor*) 804; in debt &c. 806; scant &c. (*small*) 32.

Adv. insufficiently &c. *adj.;* in default of, for want of; failing.

*** *semper avarus eget* [Horace]; "a needy, hollow-eyed, sharp-looking wretch" [*M. for M.*]; "thou art weighed in the balances, and art found wanting" [*Bible*].

---

641. Redundance. — N. REDUNDANCE; too much, too many; superabundance, superfluity, superfluence [*obs.*], supersaturation; nimiety [*rare*], transcendency, exuberance, profuseness; profusion &c. (*plenty*) 639; repletion, enough in all conscience, *satis superque* [*L.*], lion's share; more than enough &c. 639; plethora, engorgement, congestion, load, surfeit, sickener; turgescence &c. (*expansion*) 194; overdose, overmeasure, oversupply, overflow; inundation &c. (*water*) 348; avalanche, deluge.

pleonasm &c. (*diffuseness*) 573; too many irons in the fire; *embarras de richesses* [*F.*]; embarrassment of riches; money to burn [*colloq.*].

ACCUMULATION &c. (*store*) 636; heap &c. 72; drug, – in the market; glut; crowd; burden.

EXCESS, surplus, overplus; epact; margin; remainder &c. 40; duplicate; surplusage, expletive; work of supererogation; bonus, bonanza [*U. S.*].

LUXURY; extravagance &c. (*prodigality*) 818; exorbitance, lavishment; intemperance &c. 954.

V. SUPERABOUND, overabound; know no bounds, swarm; meet one at every turn; creep with, bristle with; overflow; run –, flow –, well –, brim- over; run riot; overrun, overstock, overlay, overcharge, overdose, overfeed, overburden , overload, overdo, overwhelm, overshoot the mark &c. (*go beyond*) 303; surcharge, supersaturate, gorge, glut, load, drench, whelm, inundate, deluge, flood; drug, – the market; hepatize.

send –, carry- –coals to Newcastle, – owls to Athens; teach one's grandmother to suck eggs [*colloq.*]; *pisces natare docere* [*L.*]; kill the slain, butter one's bread on both sides, put butter upon bacon; employ a steam engine to crack a nut &c. (*waste*) 638.

wallow in; roll in &c. (*plenty*) 639; remain on one's hands, hang heavy on hand, go a-begging *or* go begging; exaggerate &c. 549.

CLOY, choke, accloy [*archaic*], suffocate; pile up, lay on thick; lay it on, – with a trowel; impregnate with; lavish &c. (*squander*) 818.

Adj. REDUNDANT; too much, too many; exuberant, inordinate, superabundant, excess, overmuch, replete, profuse, lavish; prodigal &c. 818; exorbitant; overweening; extravagant; overcharged &c. *v.;* supersaturated, drenched, overflowing; running -over, – to waste, – down.

CRAMMED –, filled- to overflowing; gorged, stuffed, smothered, ready to burst; dropsical, turgid, plethoric; full-blooded, hæmatose *or* hematose; obese &c. 194.

SUPERFLUOUS, unnecessary, needless, supervacaneous [*obs.*], uncalled for, to spare, in excess; over and above &c. (*remainder*) 40; *de trop* [*F.*]; adscititious &c. (*additional*) 37; supernumerary &c. (*reserve*) 636; on one's hands, spare, duplicate, supererogatory, expletory, expletive; *un peu fort* [*F.*].

Adv. OVER AND ABOVE; over much, too much; too far; over, too; without –, beyond –, out of- measure; with . . . to spare; over head and ears; over one's head; up to one's -eyes, – ears; extra; beyond the mark &c. (*overrun*) 303; *acervatim* [*L.*].

. it never rains but it pours; *fortuna multis dat nimium nulli satis;* "to gild refined gold, to paint the lily, to throw a perfume on the violet" [Shakespeare].

2. Degree of Subservience

642. Importance. — N.
IMPORTANCE, consequence, moment, prominence, consideration, mark, materialness, materiality.

greatness &c. 31; superiority &c. 33; notability &c. (*repute*) 873; weight &c. (*influence*) 175; value &c. (*goodness*) 648; usefulness &c. 644.

IMPORT, significance, concern; emphasis, interest.

GRAVITY, seriousness, solemnity; no joke, no laughing matter; pressure, urgency, stress; matter of life and death.

MEMORABILIA, notabilia, great doings; red-letter day.

SALIENT POINT, outstanding feature; great -thing, – point; main chance, "the be-all and the end-all" [*Macbeth*]; cardinal point; substance, gist &c. (*essence*) 5; sum and substance, gravamen, head and front; important –, principal –, prominent –, essential- part; half the battle; *sine quâ non* [*L.*]; breath of one's nostrils &c. (*life*) 359; cream, salt, core, kernel, heart, nucleus; key, keynote; keystone; corner stone; trump card &c. (*device*) 626.

CHIEF, top sawyer, first fiddle, prima donna, triton among the minnows; "it" [*U. S.*]; the only pebble on the beach [*U. S.*]; burra (*or* bara) sahib [*India*]; bigwig &c. 875.

V. BE IMPORTANT &c. *adj.;* be somebody, be something; import, signify, matter, be an object; carry weight &c. (*influence*) 175; make a figure &c. (*repute*) 873; be in the ascendant, come to the front, lead the way, take the lead, play first fiddle, throw all else into the shade; lie at the root of; deserve –, merit –, be worthy of- -notice, – regard, – consideration.

VALUE; attach –, ascribe –, give- importance &c. *n.-* to; care for; set store -upon, – by; mark &c. 550; mark with a white stone, underline; write –, put –, print- in -italics, – capitals, – large letters, – large type, – bold-faced type,

643. Unimportance. — N.
UNIMPORTANCE, insignificance, nothingness, immateriality.

TRIVIALITY, levity, frivolity, fribble; paltriness &c. *adj.;* poverty; smallness &c. 32; vanity &c. (*uselessness*) 645; matter of indifference &c. 866; no object.

NOTHING, – to signify, – worth speaking of, – particular, – to boast of, – to speak of; small –, no great –, trifling &c. *adj.-* matter; mere joke, mere nothing; hardly –, scarcely- anything; nonentity, small beer, cipher; no great shakes [*colloq.*], *peu de chose* [*F.*]; child's play.

TOY, plaything, popgun, paper pellet, gimcrack, gewgaw, bauble, trinket, bagatelle, kickshaw, knickknack, whimwham, trifle, "trifles light as air" [*Othello*].

TRUMPERY, trash, rubbish, stuff, *fatras* [*F.*], frippery; "leather or prunello" [Pope]; fiddle-faddle [*colloq.*], finglefangle; chaff, drug, froth, bubble, smoke, cobweb; weed; refuse &c. (*inutility*) 645; scum &c. (*dirt*) 653.

JOKE, jest, snap of the fingers, snap of one's thumb; fudge &c. (*unmeaning*) 517; fiddlestick, pack of nonsense, mere farce.

TRIFLE, straw, pin, fig, fico [*archaic*], button, rush; bulrush, feather, halfpenny, farthing, brass farthing, doit, peppercorn, iota, tinker's dam (*or* damn), continental [*U. S.*], jot, mote, rap, pinch of snuff, old song; cent, mill, picayune [*colloq.*]; pai, pice [*both India*]; pistareen, red cent [*U. S.*].

nine days' wonder, *ridiculus mus* [*L.*]; flash in the pan &c. (*impotence*) 158; much ado about nothing &c. (*overestimation*) 482; tempest –, storm- in a teapot.

MINUTIÆ, details, minor details, small fry; dust in the balance, feather in the scale, drop in the ocean, fleabite, pin prick, molehill.

V. BE UNIMPORTANT &c. *adj.;* not matter &c. 642; go for –, matter –,

– letters of gold; accentuate, emphasize, lay stress on.

MAKE MUCH OF; make -a fuss, – a stir, – a piece of work, – much ado- about.

Adj. IMPORTANT; of importance &c. *n.;* momentous, material; to the point; not to be -overlooked, – despised, – sneezed at [*colloq.*]; egregious; weighty &c. (*influential*) 175; of note &c. (*repute*) 873; notable, prominent, salient, signal; memorable, remarkable; worthy of -remark, – notice; never to be forgotten; stirring, eventful.

in the front rank, first-rate, A1 *or* A number 1 [*colloq.*], first chop [*Anglo-Ind. & colloq.*]; superior &c. 33; considerable &c. (*great*) 31; marked &c. *v.;* rare &c. 137.

GRAVE, serious, earnest, noble, grand, solemn, impressive, commanding, imposing.

URGENT, pressing, critical, instant.

PARAMOUNT, essential, vital, all-absorbing, radical, cardinal, chief, main, prime, primary, principal, leading, capital, foremost, overruling; of vital &c. importance.

SIGNIFICANT, telling, trenchant, emphatic, pregnant; *tanti* [*L.*].

Adv. IN THE MAIN; materially &c. *adj.;* above all, in the first place, before everything else; *kat' exochen* [*Gr.* κατ' ἐξοχήν], *par excellence* [*F.*], to crown all.

₊ *expende Hannibalem!* [Juvenal]; *delenda est Carthago!* [Cato]; "first cast out the beam out of thine own eye" [*Bible*]; "we talked about all those great things for which literature is too small and only life large enough" [Chesterton].

signify- -little, – nothing, – little or nothing; not matter a straw &c. *n.*

make light of &c. (*underestimate*) 483; catch at straws &c. (*overestimate*) 482; tumble -, stumble- over one's shadow; make mountains out of molehills, make much ado about nothing.

Adj. UNIMPORTANT; of -little, – small, – no- -account, – importance &c. 642; immaterial; nonessential, unessential, irrelevant, not vital, uninteresting; indifferent, amateurish.

SUBORDINATE &c. (*inferior*) 34; mediocre &c. (*average*) 29; passable, fair, respectable, tolerable, commonplace; uneventful, mere, common; ordinary &c. (*habitual*) 613; inconsiderable, soso *or* so-so, insignificant, nugatory, inappreciable.

TRIFLING, trivial; slight, slender, light, flimsy, frothy, idle; puerile &c. (*foolish*) 499; airy, shallow; weak &c. 160; powerless &c. 158; frivolous, petty, niggling; peddling, piddling, fribbling, fribble, inane, ridiculous, farcical; finical, finicking *or* finicky *or* finikin, mincing, fiddle-faddle [*colloq.*], namby-pamby, wishy-washy [*colloq.*], milk and water, insipid.

PALTRY, poor, pitiful; contemptible &c. (*contempt*) 930; sorry, mean, meager *or* meagre, shabby, miserable, wretched, vile, scrubby, scrannel [*archaic*], weedy, niggardly, scurvy, beggarly, worthless, twopenny-halfpenny, two-for-a-cent, two-by-four [*colloq., U. S.*], cheap, trashy, catchpenny, gimcrack, trumpery; one-horse [*U. S.*].

not worth -the pains, – while, – mentioning, – speaking of, – a thought, – a curse, – a cent, – a rap, – a hair, – a straw &c. *n.;* beneath contempt, below par; not up to -sample, – specification; beneath-, unworthy of- -notice, – regard – consideration; *de lanâ caprinâ* [*L.*]; vain &c. (*useless*) 645.

Adv. SLIGHTLY &c. *adj.;* rather, somewhat, pretty well, fairly, fairly well, tolerably.

FOR AUGHT ONE CARES; it matters not, it does not signify; it is of no -consequence, – importance.

Int. NO MATTER! pish! tush! tut! pshaw! pugh! pooh, -pooh! fudge! bosh! humbug! fiddlestick, – end! fiddledeedee! never mind! *n'importe!* [*F.*]; what signifies! what matter! what boots it! what of that! what's the odds! a fig for! stuff! nonsense! stuff and nonsense!

₊ *magno conatu magnas nugas; le jeu ne vaut pas la chandelle; elephantus non capit murem; tempête dans un verre d'eau;* "why beholdest thou the mote that is in thy brother's eye?" [*Bible*]; "very trifles comfort, because very trifles grieve us" [Pascal]; "Come, gentlemen, we sit too long on trifles" [*Pericles*]; "These little things are great to little men" [Goldsmith]; "Seeks painted trifles and fantastic toys, And eagerly pursues imaginary joys" [Akenside]; "Trifles unconsciously bias us for or against a person from the very beginning" [Schopenhauer].

644. Utility. — N. UTILITY; usefulness &c. *adj.;* efficacy, efficiency, adequacy; service, use, stead, avail, boot [*archaic*]; help &c. (*aid*) 707; applicability &c. *adj.;* subservience &c. (*instrumentality*) 631; function &c. (*business*) 625; value; worth &c. (*goodness*) 648; money's worth; productiveness &c. 168; *cui bono* &c. (*intention*) 620; utilization &c. (*use*) 677; step in the right direction.

COMMONWEAL *or* common weal; commonwealth [*now rare*]; public -good, – service, – interest; utilitarianism &c. (*philanthropy*) 910; public servant.

V. BE USEFUL &c. *adj.;* avail, serve; subserve [*rare*] &c. (*be instrumental to*) 631; conduce &c. (*tend*) 176; answer –, serve- -one's turn, – a purpose.

ACT A PART &c. (*action*) 680; perform –, discharge -a function &c. 625; do –, render- -a service, – good service, – yeoman's service; bestead, stand one in good stead; be the making of; help &c. 707.

BENEFIT &c. (*do good*) 648; bear fruit &c. (*produce*) 161; bring grist to the mill; profit, remunerate.

find one's -account, – advantage- in; reap the benefit of &c. (*be better for*) 658.

RENDER USEFUL &c. (*use*) 677.

Adj. USEFUL; of use &c. *n.;* serviceable, proficuous [*obs.*], good for; subservient &c. (*instrumental*) 631; conducive &c. (*tending*) 176; subsidiary &c. (*helping*) 707.

ADVANTAGEOUS &c. (*beneficial*) 648; profitable, gainful, remunerative, worth one's salt; valuable; invaluable, beyond price, of general utility; prolific &c. (*productive*) 168.

ADEQUATE; efficient, efficacious; effective, effectual; expedient &c. 646.

APPLICABLE, usable, available, ready, handy, at hand, tangible; commodious, adaptable; of all work.

Adv. USEFULLY &c. *adj.*

FOR USE, for service; in the public service; for the good of the -people, – public, – service; *pro bono publico* [*L.*].

** "life, like every other blessing, derives its value from its use alone" [Johnson].

645. Inutility. — N. INUTILITY; uselessness &c. *adj.;* inefficacy, futility; ineptitude, inaptitude; inadequacy &c. (*insufficiency*) 640; unfitness; inefficiency &c. (*incompetence*) 158; unskillfulness &c. 699; disservice; unfruitfulness &c. (*unproductiveness*) 169; labor -in vain, – lost, – of Sisyphus; lost -trouble, – labor; work of Penelope; Penelope's web; sleeveless [*obs.*] –, bootless- errand; wild-goose chase, mere farce.

REDUNDANCE, supererogation &c. 641; tautology &c. (*repetition*) 104.

WORTHLESSNESS; vanity, *vanitas vanitatum* [*L.*], inanity, nugacity; triviality &c. (*unimportance*) 643.

worthless residue, *caput mortuum* [*L.*, *old chem.*]; waste paper, dead letter; blunt tool.

RUBBISH, junk, lumber, litter, odds and ends, cast-off clothes; button top; shoddy; rags, orts [*archaic*], leavings, dross, trash, refuse, sweepings, scourings, offscourings, waste, rubble, *débris* [*F.*]; chaff, stubble, broken meat; dregs &c. (*dirt*) 653; weeds, tares; rubbish heap, dust hole; *rudera* [*L.*], deads, slag.

IDLER; *fruges consumere natus* [Horace] &c. (*drone*) 683.

V. BE USELESS &c. *adj.;* go a-begging &c. (*redundant*) 641; fail &c. 732.

LABOR IN VAIN; seek –, strive- after impossibilities; use vain efforts, roll the stone of Sisyphus, beat the air, lash the waves, *battre l'eau avec un bâton* [*F.*], *donner un coup d'épée dans l'eau* [*F.*], fish in the air, milk the ram, drop a bucket into an empty well, pour water into a sieve, sow the sand; bay the moon; preach –, speak- to the winds; whistle jigs to a milestone; kick against the pricks, *se battre contre des moulins* [*F.*]; lock the stable door when the steed is stolen &c. (*too late*) 135; hold a farthing candle to the sun; cast pearls before swine &c. (*waste*) 638; carry coals to Newcastle &c. (*redundance*) 641; wash a blackamoor white &c. (*impossible*) 471.

RENDER USELESS &c. *adj.;* dismantle, dismast, dismount, disqualify, disable; unrig [*chiefly naut.*]; hamstring, hock *or* spike guns, clip the wings; put out of gear; throw a wrench in the machinery; throw a monkey-wrench into the works.

hough, cripple, lame &c. (*injure*) 659;

Adj. USELESS, inutile, nugatory, inefficacious, futile, unavailing, bootless; inoperative &c. 158; inadequate &c. (*insufficient*) 640; inservient [*obs.*], inept; inefficient &c. (*impotent*) 158; of no avail &c. (*use*) 644; ineffectual &c. (*failure*)

732; incompetent &c. (*unskillful*) 699; "weary, stale, flat, and unprofitable" [*Hamlet*]; superfluous &c. (*redundant*) 641; dispensable; thrown away &c. (*wasted*) 638; abortive &c. (*immature*) 674.

WORTHLESS, valueless, unsalable; not worth a straw &c. (*trifling*) 643; dear at any price.

VAIN, empty, inane; gainless, profitless, fruitless; unserviceable, unprofitable; ill-spent; effete, barren, sterile, impotent, worn out; unproductive &c. 169; *hors de combat* [*F.*], past work &c. (*impaired*) 659; obsolete &c. (*old*) 124; fit for the dust hole; good for nothing; of no earthly use; not worth -having, – powder and shot; leading to no end, uncalled for; unnecessary, unneeded, superfluous.

Adv. USELESSLY &c. *adj.*; to -little, – no, – little or no- purpose.

Int. *cui bono?* [*L.*]; what's the good! what's the use!

⁎ *actum ne agas; chercher une aiguille dans une botte de foin; tanto buon che val niente;* "like sending them ruffles, when wanting a shirt" [Sorbienne]; "one might as well expect the Astronomer Royal to tell the time in a catacomb" [Shaw].

646. [SPECIFIC SUBSERVIENCE.] **Expedience. — N.** EXPEDIENCE *or* expediency, desirability, desirableness &c. *adj.*; fitness &c. (*agreement*) 23; utility &c. 644; propriety; opportunism; advantage, opportunity; pragmatism, pragmaticism; a working proposition.

high time &c. (*occasion*) 134; suitable time *or* season, tempestivity [*obs.*].

V. BE EXPEDIENT &c. *adj.*; suit &c. (*agree*) 23; befit; suit –, befit- the -time, – season, – occasion; produce the goods [*colloq.*].

CONFORM &c. 82.

Adj. EXPEDIENT; desirable, advisable, acceptable; convenient; worth while, meet; fit, fitting; due, proper, eligible, seemly, becoming; befitting &c. *v.*; opportune &c. (*in season*) 134; *in loco* [*L.*]; suitable &c. (*accordant*) 23; applicable &c. (*useful*) 644.

PRACTICAL, practicable, effective, pragmatic, pragmatical.

Adv. CONVENIENTLY &c. *adj.*; in the nick of time; in the right place.

⁎ *operæ pretium est;* "the end must justify the means" [Prior]; "too fond of the Right to pursue the Expedient" [Goldsmith — *of Burke*]; "Principle is ever my motto, not expediency" [Disraeli]; "expediency is the science of exigencies" [Kossuth].

647. Inexpedience. — N. INEXPEDIENCE *or* inexpediency, undesirability, undesirableness &c. *adj.*; discommodity, impropriety; unfitness &c. (*disagreement*) 24; inutility &c. 645; disadvantage, disadvantageousness, inconvenience, inadvisability.

V. BE INEXPEDIENT &c. *adj.*; come amiss &c. (*disagree*) 24; embarrass &c. (*hinder*) 706; put to inconvenience.

Adj. INEXPEDIENT, undesirable; unadvisable [*rare*], inadvisable, unsuitable, troublesome, objectionable; inapt, ineligible, inadmissible, inconvenient; incommodious, discommodious; disadvantageous; inappropriate, unfit &c. (*inconsonant*) 24.

ILL-CONTRIVED, ill-advised; unsatisfactory; unprofitable &c., inept &c. (*useless*) 645; inopportune &c. (*unseasonable*) 135; out of –, in the wrong- place; improper, unseemly.

CLUMSY, awkward; cumbrous, cumbersome; lumbering, unwieldy, hulky; unmanageable &c. (*impracticable*) 704; impedient &c. (*in the way*) 706.

UNNECESSARY &c. (*redundant*) 641.

⁎ it will never do; it doesn't pay; the game is not worth the candle; "he has paid dear, very dear, for his whistle" [Franklin].

648. [CAPABILITY OF PRODUCING GOOD. GOOD QUALITIES.] **Goodness. — N.** GOODNESS &c. *adj.*; excellence, merit; virtue &c. 944; value, worth, price.

SUPEREXCELLENCE, supereminence, quintessence; superiority &c. 33; perfection &c. 650; *coup de maître* [*F.*]; masterpiece, *chef d'œuvre* [*F.*], prime, flower, cream, *élite* [*F.*], pick, nonesuch [*now rare*], A1 *or* A number 1 [*colloq.*], nonpareil

649. [CAPABILITY OF PRODUCING EVIL. BAD QUALITIES.] **Badness. — N.** HURTFULNESS &c. *adj.*; virulence.

BANE &c. 663; plague spot &c. (*insalubrity*) 657; evil star, ill wind; hoodoo [*colloq.*], jinx [*slang*], *jadu* [*Hind.*], Jonah; snake in the grass, skeleton in the closet; *amari aliquid* [*L.*]; thorn in the -side, – flesh.

MALIGNITY, damnability, damnifica-

[*F*], *crême de la crême* [*F.*], flower of the
flock, cock of the roost, salt of the earth;
champion; prodigy, wonder, best ever
[*colloq.*].

GEM, – of the first water; *bijou* [*F.*],
precious stone, jewel, pearl, diamond,
ruby, brilliant, treasure; tidbit, good
thing; *rara avis* [*L.*], one in a thousand.

BENEFICENCE &c. 906.

GOOD MAN &c. 948.

V. BE BENEFICIAL &c. *adj.;* produce *or*
do good &c. 618; profit &c. (*be of use*)
644; benefit; confer a benefit &c. 618.

produce a good effect; be the making
of, do a world of good, make a man of;
do a good turn, confer an obligation;
improve &c. 658.

do no harm, break no bones.

BE GOOD &c. *adj.;* be pure gold, be all
wool; be the real -thing, – article; look
good to [*colloq.*]; excel, transcend &c.
(*be superior*) 33; bear away the bell.

stand the -proof, – test; pass muster,
pass an examination.

VIE, challenge comparison, emulate,
rival.

Adj. BENEFICIAL, valuable, of value;
serviceable &c. (*useful*) 644; advantageous, profitable, edifying; salutary &c.
(*healthful*) 656.

HARMLESS, hurtless; unobnoxious; innocuous, innocent, inoffensive.

FAVORABLE; propitious &c. (*hope-
giving*) 858; fair.

GOOD, good as gold; excellent; better;
superior &c. 33; above par; nice, fine;
genuine &c. (*true*) 494.

CHOICE, best, select, picked, elect,
recherché [*F.*], rare, priceless; unparagoned [*rare*], matchless, peerless, unequaled *or* unequalled, unparalleled &c.
(*supreme*) 33; superlatively &c. (33)-
good; bully [*slang*], crackajack [*slang*],
gilt-edge *or* gilt-edged [*colloq.*]; superfine, superexcellent; of the first water;
first-rate, first-class; high-wrought,
exquisite, very best, crack [*colloq.*],
prime, tip-top [*colloq.*], capital, cardinal;
standard &c. (*perfect*) 650; inimitable.

ADMIRABLE, estimable; praiseworthy
&c. (*approve*) 931; pleasing &c. 829; *couleur de rose* [*F.*], precious, of great price;
costly &c. (*dear*) 814; worth -its weight
in gold, – a king's ransom; priceless,
invaluable, inestimable, precious as the
apple of the eye.

SATISFACTORY, up to the mark,

tion, damnifying; malevolence &c. 907;
tender mercies [*irony*].

ILL-TREATMENT, annoyance, molestation, abuse, oppression, persecution, outrage; misusage &c. 679; *damnum* [*L.*],
scathe; injury &c. (*damage*) 659; knock-
out drops [*U. S.*].

BADNESS &c. *adj.;* peccancy, abomination; painfulness &c. 830; pestilence &c.
(*disease*) 655; guilt &c. 947; depravity
&c. 945.

BAD MAN &c. 949; evildoer &c. 913.

V. BE HURTFUL &c. *adj.;* cause -, produce -, inflict -, work -, do- evil &c.
619; damnify, endamage, hurt, harm,
scathe; injure &c. (*damage*) 659; pain
&c. 830.

WRONG, aggrieve, oppress, persecute;
trample -, tread -, bear hard -, put-
upon; overburden; weigh -down, –
heavy on; victimize; run down, run
hard; thwart; molest &c. 830.

MALTREAT, abuse; ill-use, illtreat;
buffet, bruise, scratch, maul; smite &c.
(*scourge*) 972; do violence, do a mischief;
stab, pierce, outrage.

DO MISCHIEF, do harm, make mischief;
bring -, lead -, get- into trouble; hoodoo
[*colloq., U. S.*].

DESTROY &c. 162.

Adj. HURTFUL, harmful, scathful [*obs.
or dial.*], scatheful, baneful, baleful,
injurious, deleterious, detrimental, noxious, pernicious, mischievous, full of
mischief, mischief-making, malefic, malignant, nocuous, noisome; prejudicial;
disserviceable, disadvantageous; wide-
wasting.

UNLUCKY, sinister; obnoxious; untoward, disastrous.

OPPRESSIVE, burdensome, onerous;
malign &c. (*malevolent*) 907.

CORRUPTING &c. (*corrupt* &c. 659);
virulent, venomous, envenomed, corrosive; poisonous &c. (*morbific*) 657;
deadly &c. (*killing*) 361; destructive &c
(*destroying*) 162; inauspicious &c. 859.

BAD, ill, arrant, as bad as bad can be,
dreadful; horrid, horrible; dire; rank,
peccant, foul, fulsome; rotten, rotten
at the core.

UNSATISFACTORY, indifferent; injured
&c. deteriorated &c. 659; exceptionable, below par &c. (*imperfect*) 651; ill-
contrived, ill-disposed, ill-conditioned.

DEPLORABLE, wretched, sad, grievous,
lamentable, pitiful, pitiable, woeful &c.

267

unexceptionable, unobjectionable; tidy [*colloq.*].

in -good, - fair- condition; unspoiled, fresh; sound &c. (*perfect*) 650.

Adv. BENEFICIALLY &c. *adj.;* well &c. 618; for one's benefit.

_{*} "jewels five words long" [Tennyson]; "long may such goodness live!" [Rogers]; "the luxury of doing good" [Goldsmith]; "seek Virtue: she alone is free" [Milton]; "before virtue the immortal gods have put the sweat of man's brow" [Hesiod].

(*painful*) 830; mean &c. (*paltry*) 643.

EVIL, wrong; depraved &c. 945; shocking; reprehensible &c. (*disapproved*) 932.

HATEFUL, - as a toad; abominable, vile, base, villainous, detestable, execrable, cursed, accursed, confounded; damned, damnable, damnatory, damnific [*rare*]; infernal; diabolic &c. (*malevolent*) 907.

INADVISABLE, unadvisable [*rare*] &c. (*inexpedient*) 647; unprofitable &c. (*useless*) 645; incompetent &c. (*unskillful*) 699; irremediable &c. (*hopeless*) 859.

Adv. BADLY &c. *adj.;* wrong, ill; to one's cost; where the shoe pinches; with malignity &c. *n.*

_{*} bad is the best; if the worst come to the worst; *herba mala presto cresco;* "wrongs unredressed or insults unavenged" [Wordsworth]; "one only evil, namely, ignorance" [Socrates]; "the love of money is the root of all evil" [*Bible*].

---

650. Perfection. — N. PERFECTION; perfectness &c. *adj.;* indefectibility; impeccancy, impeccability.

PARAGON, pink, *beau ideal* [F.]; pink -, acme- of perfection; *ne plus ultra* [L.]; summit &c. 210.

[COMPARISONS] *cygne noir* [F.]; Phœnix or Phenix; black tulip, *tulipe noir* [F.]; philosopher's stone; Koh-i-noor.

MODEL, standard, pattern, mirror, Admirable Crichton; trump, brick, corker, caution, humdinger [*all slang*]; "the observed of all observers" [*Hamlet*], very prince of.

Bayard, *chevalier sans peur et sans reproche* [F.]; Roland, Sidney.

MASTERPIECE, masterstroke, prizewinner, prize; superexcellence &c. (*goodness*) 648; transcendence &c. (*superiority*) 33.

V. BE PERFECT &c. *adj.;* transcend &c. (*be supreme*) 33.

PERFECT, bring to perfection, ripen, mature; consummate, crown, put the finishing touch to (*or* upon); complete &c. 729; put in trim &c. (*prepare*) 673; maturate [*rare*].

Adj. PERFECT, faultless; indefective [*rare*], indeficient [*rare*], indefectible; immaculate, spotless, impeccable; free from imperfection &c. 651; unblemished, uninjured &c. 659; sound, - as a roach; in perfect condition; scathless [*obs. or dial.*], scatheless, intact, harmless; seaworthy &c. (*safe*) 644; right as a trivet; *in se ipso totus teres atque rotundus* [Hor.]; consummate &c. (*complete*) 52; finished &c. 729; complete in itself; well-rounded.

651. Imperfection. — N. IMPERFECTION; imperfectness &c. *adj.;* deficiency; inadequacy &c. (*insufficiency*) 640; peccability, defection, peccancy &c. (*badness*) 649; immaturity &c. 674.

FAULT, defect, "little rift within the lute" [Tennyson], weak point; screw loose; flaw &c. (*break*) 70; gap &c. 198; twist &c. 243; taint, attainder; *mésalliance* [F.], bar sinister; hole in one's coat; blemish &c. 848; weakness &c. 160; shortcoming &c. 304; drawback; seamy side.

HALF BLOOD, drop of black blood, touch of the tar-brush [*colloq.*].

MEDIOCRITY; no great -shakes, - catch [*both colloq.*]; not much to boast of; one-horse shay; one-horse town; peanut -politics, - policy.

V. BE IMPERFECT &c. *adj.;* rot before it ripens, bear within it the seeds of decay; have a defect &c. *n.;* lie under a disadvantage; spring a leak.

not pass muster, barely pass muster; fall short &c. 304.

Adj. IMPERFECT; not perfect &c. 650; deficient, defective; faulty, unsound, tainted, specked; mutilated; out of order; out of tune, cracked; leaky; sprung; warped &c. (*distort*) 243; lame; injured &c. (*deteriorated*) 659; peccant &c. (*bad*) 649; frail &c. (*weak*) 160; inadequate &c. (*insufficient*) 640; crude &c. (*unprepared*) 674; incomplete &c. 53; found wanting; below par; short-handed; below -, under- its full -strength, - complement.

BEST &c. (*good*) 648; model, standard; inimitable, unparagoned [*rare*], unparalleled &c. (*supreme*) 33; superhuman, divine; beyond all praise &c. (*approbation*) 931; *sans peur et sans reproche* [*F.*].

Adv. TO PERFECTION; perfectly &c. *adj.*; *ad unguem* [*L.*]; clean, – as a whistle; with a finish; to the limit.

, "let us go on unto perfection" [*Hebrews vi, 1*]; "the perfection of art is to conceal art" [Quintilian]; "the glass of fashion and the mould of form" [*Hamlet*].

INDIFFERENT, middling, ordinary, mediocre; average &c. 29; soso *or* so-so; *couci-couci* [*F.*], milk-and-water; tolerable, fair, passable; pretty -well, – good; rather –, moderately- good; good –, well- enough; decent; not bad, not amiss; unobjectionable, admissible, bearable, better than nothing.

SECONDARY, inferior; second-rate; second best; one-horse [*U. S.*]; two-by-four [*U. S.*].

Adv. ALMOST &c.; to a limited extent, rather &c. 32; pretty, moderately; only, might be worse.

considering, all things considered, enough;

, *surgit amari aliquid;* "with all my imperfections on my head" [*Hamlet*]; "Frailty, thy name is woman" [*ibid.*].

---

652. Cleanness. — N. CLEANNESS &c. *adj.*; purity; cleaning &c. *v.*; purification, defecation &c. *v.*; purgation, lustration; abstersion [*rare*], detersion; aspersion, asperges [*R. C. Ch.*]; epuration [*rare*], mundation [*obs.*], ablution, lavation, colature [*obs.*]; disinfection &c. *v.*; drainage, sewerage.

BATH, bathroom, swimming pool, natatorium, swimming bath, public bath, baths, bathhouse, hot bath &c. 386; lavatory; laundry, washhouse.

CLEANER, washerwoman, laundress, dhobi [*India*], laundryman, washerman; scavenger, sweeper; mehtar (*fem.* mehtrani), bhangi [*all India*]; mud lark [*slang*]; crossing –, street- sweeper, white wings [*local, U. S.*]; dustman; sweep.

brush; broom, besom, vacuum cleaner, carpet sweeper; mop, swab, hose; scraper; rake, shovel; sieve, riddle, screen, filter; blotter.

napkin, serviette, cloth, maukin [*obs.*], malkin [*obs.*], handkerchief, towel, sudary, sudarium, face cloth, wash cloth; doily *or* doyley, bib; carving cloth, tablecloth; duster, sponge.

MAT, doormat, rug, drugget, cover.

[CLEANSING AGENTS] wash, lotion, detergent, soap, purifier &c. *v.*; disinfectant; benzene, benzine, benzol, benzolin; bleaching powder, chloride of lime; lye, buck.

DENTIFRICE, tooth paste, tooth powder; mouth wash.

CATHARTIC, purgative, aperient, deobstruent, laxative.

V. BE *or* RENDER CLEAN &c. *adj.*

CLEAN, cleanse; mundify [*obs.*], rinse,

---

653. Uncleanness.— N. UNCLEANNESS &c. *adj.*; impurity; immundity [*rare*], immundicity [*rare*], mucidness, impurity &c. (of mind) 961.

DEFILEMENT, contamination &c. *v.*; defœdation [*obs.*]; soilure, soiliness [*obs.*]; abomination; taint, tainture [*obs.*]; fetor &c. 401.

LOUSINESS, pediculosis, pediculation, phthiriasis [*med.*].

DECAY; putrescence, putrefaction; corruption; mold *or* mould, must, mildew, dry rot, mucor [*rare*], caries [*med.*], rubigo [*obs.*].

SLOVENRY; slovenliness &c. *adj.*; squalor.

DOWDY, drab, slut, malkin *or* mawkin [*obs. or dial. Eng.*], slattern, sloven, slammerkin [*obs.*], slammock *or* slummock [*dial.*], drabble-tail, draggle-tail, mud lark [*slang*], dustman, sweep; beast, pig.

DIRT, filth, soil, slop; dust, cobweb, flue; smoke, soot, smudge, smut, grime, raff [*dial.*], riffraff; sossle *or* sozzle [*dial.*].

DREGS, sordes, grounds, lees; argol; sediment, settlement; heeltap; dross, drossiness; mother [*obs.*], precipitate, *scoriæ* [*L.*], ashes, cinders, recrement, slag; scum, froth.

USELESS REFUSE, hogwash [*colloq.*], swill, garbage, ditch water, dishwater, bilge-water; rinsings, cheeseparings; sweepings &c. 645; outscourings, offscourings, offscum; *caput mortuum* [*L.*], residuum, sprue, dross, clinker, draff; scurf, scurfiness; exuviæ; furfur, dandruff; tartar, fur.

spawn, offal, gurry [*U. S.*]; carrion;

wring, flush, full, wipe, mop, sponge, scour, swab, scrub.

wash, lave &c. (*water*) 337; launder, buck; absterge [*rare*], deterge; decrassify; clear, purify; depurate, spurate [*rare*], despumate, defecate; purge, expurgate, elutriate, lixiviate, edulcorate, clarify, refine, rack; percolate, separate, strain, filter, filtrate, drain.

SIFT, winnow, sieve, bolt, screen, riddle; pick, weed.

COMB, rake, scrape, rasp; hackle, heckle, card.

SWEEP, brush, brush up, whisk, broom, vacuum [*colloq.*].

rout –, clear –, sweep &c.- out; make a clean sweep of, clean house, spruce up [*colloq.*].

DISINFECT, fumigate, ventilate, deodorize; whitewash.

Adj. CLEAN, cleanly; pure; immaculate; spotless, stainless, taintless, trig [*dial.*], without a stain, unstained, unspotted, unsoiled, unsullied, untainted, uninfected; sweet, – as a nut.

NEAT, spruce, tidy, trim, jimp *or* gimp [*Scot. & dial. Eng.*], clean as a new penny, like a cat in pattens; cleaned &c. *v.;* kempt [*archaic*].

ABSTERGENT, detergent, depurative, abstersive [*rare*], cathartic, cleansing, purifying.

Adv. NEATLY &c. *adj.;* clean as a whistle.

₊ cleanliness is next to godliness; "I'll purge and leave sack and live cleanly" [Shakespeare]; "wash me and I shall be whiter than snow" [*Bible*]; "cleanliness is not next to godliness nowadays, for cleanliness is made an essential and godliness is regarded as an offence" [Chesterton].

slough, peccant humor, pus, matter, suppuration.

DUNG, ordure, lienteria; feces *or* fæces, excrement, feculence; excreta &c. 299; sewage, sewerage [*rare in this sense*]; fertilizer, muck; coprolite; guano, manure, compost.

[RECEPTACLES] dunghill, colluvies [*med.*]; mixen, midden [*both archaic or dial. Eng.*], bog, laystall [*obs.*]; cesspool; sump [*Scot. & dial. Eng.*], sough [*dial. Eng.*], cloaca, Cloaca Maxima; sink, drain, sewer, common sewer; Cloacina; dust hole; glory hole [*colloq.*].

WATER-CLOSET, w. c., toilet [*colloq.*], *cabinet d'aisance* [*F.*], latrine, backhouse, necessary, privy, jakes [*rare*], Mrs. Jones; head [*naval slang*].

STY, pigsty, lair, den, Augean stable, sink of corruption; slum, rookery.

MUD, mire, quagmire, alluvium, silt, sludge, slime, slush, slosh [*dial.*], sposh [*U. S.*].

VERMIN, louse, flea, nit, bug, chinch; lice &c. 366.

V. BE *or* BECOME UNCLEAN &c. *adj.;* rot, putrefy, fester, rankle, reek; stink &c. 401; mold *or* mould, molder *or* moulder; go bad &c. *adj.*

wallow in the mire; slobber, slabber.

RENDER UNCLEAN &c. *adj.;* dirt, dirty; soil, smoke, tarnish, slaver, spot, smear; daub, blot, blur, smudge, smutch, smirch; begrease; drabble, dabble, daggle, spatter, slubber [*dial.*]; besmear &c., bemire, beslime, begrime, befoul; splash, stain, distain [*archaic*], maculate, sully, pollute, defile, debase, contaminate, taint, leaven; corrupt &c. (*injure*) 659; cover with dust &c. *n.;* drabble in the mud; roil.

Adj. UNCLEAN, dirty, filthy, grimy; soiled &c. *v.;* not to be handled -without gloves, – with kid gloves; dusty, snuffy, smutty, sooty, smoky; thick, turbid, dreggy; slimy; mussy [*U. S.*].

LOUSY, pedicular, pediculous.

UNCLEANLY, slovenly, slatternly, untidy, sluttish, dowdy, draggle-tailed, drabble-tailed; uncombed, unkempt, unscoured, unswept, unwiped, unwashed, unstrained, unpurified; squalid; lutose, slammocky *or* slummocky [*dial.*], sossly *or* sozzly [*dial.*], sloppy [*colloq.*].

OFFENSIVE, nasty, coarse, foul, impure, abominable, beastly, reeky, reechy [*dial. Eng.*]; fetid &c. 401.

moldy *or* mouldy, musty, fusty, mildewed, rusty, moth-eaten, mucid, rancid, bad, gone bad, lentiginous *or* lentiginose, touched, reasty [*dial. Eng.*], rotten, corrupt, tainted, high, flyblown, maggoty; putrid, putrefactive, putrescent, putrefied; saprogenic *or* saprogenous; purulent, carious, peccant; fecal, feculent; stercoraceous, excrementitious; scurfy, impetiginous; gory, bloody; rotting &c. *v.;* rotten as -a pear, – cheese.

crapulous &c. (*intemperate*) 954; beastlike; gross &c. (*impure in mind*) 961; fimetarious, fimicolous.

Int. pah! faugh! ugh!

*** "they that touch pitch will be defiled" [*Much Ado About Nothing*]; "if dirt was trumps, what hands you would hold!" [Lamb]; "sluts are good enough to make a sloven's porridge" [*old proverb*].

---

654. Health. — N.
HEALTH, sanity; soundness &c. *adj.;* vigor; good –, perfect –, excellent –, rude –, robust- health; bloom, *mens sana in corpore sano* [*L.*]; Hygeia; incorruption, incorruptibility; valetude [*obs.*]; good state –, clean bill- of health; eupepsia *or* eupepsy, euphoria *or* euphory; convalescence, upgrade; strength, poise.

V. BE IN HEALTH &c. *adj.;* be bursting with -vigor, – pep [*slang*]; never feel better; bloom, flourish.

keep body and soul together, keep on one's legs; enjoy -good, – a good state of- health; have a clean bill of health.

RETURN TO HEALTH; recover &c. 660; get better &c. (*improve*) 658; take a -new, – fresh- lease of life; convalesce, be convalescent; add years to one's life; recruit; restore to health; cure &c. (*restore*) 660.

Adj. HEALTHY, healthful; in health &c. *n.;* well, sound, whole, strong, blooming, hearty, hale, fresh, green, florid, flush, hardy, stanch *or* staunch, brave, robust, vigorous, weatherproof.

on one's legs; sound as a -roach, – bell; fresh as -a daisy, – a rose, – April; walking on air; hearty as a buck; in -fine, – high- feather; in good case, in full bloom; pretty bobbish [*dial. or slang*]; bursting with -health, – vigor; in fine fettle; chipper [*colloq., U. S.*]; tolerably well, as well as can be expected.

UNSCATHED, uninjured, unmaimed, unmarred, untainted; sound of wind and limb, without a scratch, safe and sound.

SANITARY &c. (*health-giving*) 656; sanatory &c. (*remedial*) 662.

*** "health that snuffs the morning air" [Grainger]; *non est vivere sed valere vita* [Martial].

---

655. Disease. — N.
DISEASE; illness, sickness &c. *adj.;* ailing &c. *v.;* "the thousand natural shocks That flesh is heir to" [*Hamlet*]; "all ills that men endure" [Cowley]; morbidity, morbosity [*obs.*]; infirmity, ailment, indisposition; complaint, disorder, malady, distemperature [*archaic*]; valetudinarianism; loss of health, delicacy, delicate health, invalidity, invalidism, invalescence [*rare*]; malnutrition, want of nourishment, cachexia *or* cachexy; prostration, decline, collapse; decay &c. 659.

VISITATION, attack, seizure, stroke, fit, epilepsy, apoplexy, bloodstroke; palsy, paralysis, motor paralysis, sensory paralysis, hemiplegia, paraplegia *or* paraplegy; *paralysis agitans* [*L.*], shaking palsy, Parkinson's disease; shock; shell-shock [*common during World War*].

TAINT, virus, pollution, infection, contagion; septicæmia *or* septicemia, blood poisoning, pyæmia *or* pyemia, septicity; epidemic; sporadic, endemic; plague, pestilence.

FEVER, calenture; inflammation; ague; intermittent –, remittent –, congestive –, pernicious- fever; malaria, malarial fever; dengue *or* dandy fever, breakbone fever; yellow fever, yellow jack; typhoid *or* typhoid fever, enteric fever; typhus; eruptive fever; scarlet fever, scarlatina; smallpox, variola; varioloid; vaccinia, cow pox; varicella, chicken pox; rubeola, measles.

ERUPTION, rash, brash, breaking out; canker rash; dartre, exanthema *or* exanthem; scabies, itch, psora; pox; eczema, tetter, psoriasis; lichen, papular rash; lichen tropicus, prickly heat; impetigo; erythema; erysipelas, St. Anthony's fire; urticaria, hives, nettlerash; herpes; herpes zoster, shingles; herpes circinatus, ringworm; miliaria, pemphigus, rupia.

SORE, canker, ulcer, fester, boil, gumboil; pimple &c. (*swelling*) 250; carbuncle; gathering; abscess, impostume *or* imposthume [*obsoles.*], aposteme; Rigg's disease, pyorrhea *or* pyorrhœa; chancre; peccant humor; proud flesh; mortification, sphacelus, sphacelation; slough,

---

corruption; enanthem *or* enanthema, gangrene; caries, necrosis; cancer, carcinoma; tumor, leprosy.

HEART DISEASE, carditis, pericarditis, endocarditis, valvular lesion; hypertrophy –, dilatation –, atrophy –, fatty degeneration- of the heart; angina pectoris.

WASTING DISEASE, marasmus, emaciation, atrophy; consumption, white plague, tuberculosis, T.B. [*med. cant*], phthisis; pulmonary –, galloping- consumption; pulmonary phthisis, phthisipneumonia, pneumonia; chlorosis, green sickness; anæmia *or* anemia; leucocythænia *or* leucocythenia.

THROAT DISEASE, laryngitis, tonsillitis, quinsy, cynanche; bronchitis, diphtheria, whooping cough, pertussis; thrush, canker.

COLD, cough; rheum; catarrh, hay fever; influenza, grippe *or* grip; rose cold.

INDIGESTION, dyspepsia, poor digestion, pyrosis, water qualm; cardialgia, heartburn; seasickness, *mal de mer* [*F.*]; nausea; giddiness, vertigo; constipation, autointoxication.

EYE DISEASE, trachoma, conjunctivitis, pink eye; cataract, caligo, pin-and-web, *gutta serena* [*L.*].

VENEREAL DISEASE, pox, syphilis; gonorrhea *or* gonorrhœa, blennorrhea *or* blennorrhœa, blennorrhagia.

[VARIOUS DISEASES] headache &c. (*physical pain*) 378; goiter *or* goitre, bronchocele, struma, tracheocele; lockjaw, tetanus, trismus; diarrhea *or* diarrhœa, dysentery, bloody flux, flux, issue, hemorrhage; hemorrhoids, piles; cholera, cholera morbus, Asiatic cholera [*colloq.*, *Eng.*] cholera infantum, summer complaint; colic; jaundice, icterus; apnœa; asthma; king's evil, scrofula; rickets, rachitis; appendicitis; gall-stones, biliary calculus, stone; hernia, rupture; varicosis, varicose veins; arteriosclerosis, hardening of the arteries; neuritis; nervous prostration; St. Vitus's dance, chorea; neurasthenia; sciatica; rheumatism, arthritis, lumbago; dropsy, œdema *or* edema; elephantiasis; beriberi [*bo h tropical*]; locomotor ataxia; paresis, softening of the brain; bubonic plague; black death; leprosy, elephantiasis Græcorum; sleeping sickness.

fatal &c. (*hopeless*) 859 –disease &c.; dangerous illness, churchyard cough; general breaking up, break-up of the system.

[DISEASE OF MIND] idiocy &c. 499; insanity &c. 503.

MARTYR TO DISEASE; cripple; "the halt, the lame, and the blind"; valetudinary, valetudinarian; invalid, patient, case.

sick-room, sick-chamber; hospital &c. 662.

[SCIENCE OF DISEASE] pathology, pathogeny, etiology, nosology, nosography, nosogeny, therapeutics; diagnostics, symptomatology, semeiology, semeiography, prognosis, diagnosis; clinic, polyclinic.

[VETERINARY] anthrax, splenic fever, woolsorter's disease, charbon, milzbrand, malignant pustule, quarter evil, quarter ill, Texas fever, blackwater, murrain, bighead; blackleg, black quarter; cattle plague, glanders, milk sickness; rinderpest, foot-and-mouth disease, hog cholera; epizoötic; heaves, rot, sheep rot; scabies, mange, distemper.

V. BE *or* FEEL ILL &c. *adj.;* ail, suffer, labor under, be affected with, complain of; droop, flag, languish, halt; sicken, peak, pine, dwindle; gasp; drop down in one's tracks; waste away, fail, lose strength, lose one's grip.

keep one's bed; lay by, lay up; be laid by the heels; lie helpless, – on one's back.

fall a victim to –, be stricken by –, take –, catch- -a disease &c. *n.,* – an infection; break out.

MALINGER, feign sickness &c. (*falsehood*) 544.

Adj. AILING &c. *v.;* ill, ill of; taken ill, seized with; indisposed, unwell, sick, squeamish, poorly, seedy [*colloq.*]; affected –, afflicted- with illness; laid up, confined, bedridden, invalided, in hospital, on the sick list; out of health, out of sorts [*colloq.*], under the weather [*U. S.*]; valetudinary.

UNSOUND, unhealthy; morbose [*obs.*], healthless, infirm, chlorotic, unbraced, cranky [*dial. Eng.*], sickly, weakly, weakened &c. (*weak*) 160; drooping, flagging; lame, halt, crippled, halting; *hors de combat* [*F.*] &c. (*useless*) 645.

touched in the wind, broken-winded, spavined, gasping.

DISEASED, morbid, tainted, vitiated, peccant, contaminated, poisoned, septic, septical, tabetic, tabid, mangy, leprous, cankered; rotten, – to, – at- the core; withered; palsied, paralytic; dyspeptic; luetic, pneumonic, pulmonic, phthisic *or* phthisical, consumptive, tubercular, tuberculous, rachitic; syntectic *or* syntectical, varicose.

DECREPIT; decayed &c. (*deteriorated*) 659; incurable &c. (*hopeless*) 859; in declining health; in a bad way, in danger, prostrate; moribund &c. (*death*) 360.

EPIDEMIC, epizoötic [*of animals*]; zymotic, contagious; morbific &c. 657.

⁎⁎ "in sickness and in health" [*marriage service*]; "tie up the knocker; say I'm sick, I'm dead" [Pope]; "the whole head is sick, and the whole heart faint" [*Bible*]; "diseases desperate grown By desperate appliance are reliev'd, Or not at all" [*Hamlet*]; "this sickness doth infect The very life-blood of our enterprise" [*I Henry IV*]; "That dire disease, whose ruthless power Withers the beauty's transient flower" [Goldsmith]; "a malady Preys on my heart that med'cine cannot reach" [Maturin]; "The best of remedies is a beefsteak Against sea-sickness; try it, sir, before You sneer" [Byron].

656. Salubrity. — N. SALUBRITY, salubriousness, wholesomeness, healthfulness; healthiness &c. *adj.;* Hygeia, Æsculapius.

fine -air, – climate; eudiometer.

[PRESERVATION OF HEALTH] hygiene; valetudinarianism; pure air, exercise, nourishment, tonic; immunity; sanitarium, sanatorium; valetudinarian, sanitarian.

V. BE SALUBRIOUS &c. *adj.;* make for health, conduce to health; be good for, agree with; assimilate &c. 23.

Adj. SALUBRIOUS, salutary, salutiferous [*rare*]; wholesome; healthy, healthful; sanitary, prophylactic; benign, bracing, tonic, invigorating, good for, nutritious; hygeian, hygienic; Hygeian.

sanative &c. (*remedial*) 662; restorative &c. (*reinstate*) 660; useful &c. 644.

INNOXIOUS, innocuous, innocent; harmless, uninjurious, uninfectious; immune.

657. Insalubrity. — N. INSALUBRITY, insalubriousness; unhealthiness &c. *adj.;* plague spot; malaria &c. (*poison*) 663; death in the pot, contagion; poisonousness, toxicity.

V. BE INSALUBRIOUS &c. *adj.;* disagree with; shorten one's days.

Adj. INSALUBRIOUS; unhealthy, unwholesome; noxious, noisome; morbific *or* morbifical, morbiferous; mephitic, septic, azotic, deleterious; pestilent, pestiferous, pestilential; virulent, venomous; envenomed, poisonous, toxic, toxiferous, narcotic; deadly &c. (*killing*) 361.

INNUTRITIOUS, unnutritious [*rare*], undigestible [*rare*], indigestible, ungenial; uncongenial &c. (*disagreeing*) 24.

CONTAGIOUS, infectious, catching, taking, communicable, inoculable, epidemic, zymotic, sporadic, endemic, pandemic; epizoötic [*of animals*].

658. Improvement. — N. IMPROVEMENT, amelioration, melioration, betterment; mend, amendment, emendation; mending &c. *v.;* advancement; advance &c. (*progress*) 282; ascent &c. 305; promotion, preferment; elevation &c. 307; increase &c. 35.

CULTIVATION, culture, march of intellect, menticulture; race-culture, acculturation, civilization; culture zone; eugenics.

REFORM, reformation; revision, radical reform; second thoughts, correction, *limæ labor* [*L.*], refinement, elaboration; purification &c. 652; repair &c. (*restoration*) 660; recovery &c. 660.

REVISE, revised edition, new edition, new issue.

REFORMER, reformist, progressive, radical.

V. IMPROVE; be –, become –, get-better; mend, amend.

advance &c. (*progress*) 282; ascend &c. 305; increase &c. 35; fructify, ripen, mature; pick up, come about, rally, take a favorable turn; turn over a new leaf, turn the corner; raise one's head, have sown one's wild oats; recover &c. 660.

PROFIT BY; be better &c. *adj.*, be improved by; turn to -right, – good, – best- account; reap the benefit of; make good use of, make capital out of; place to good account.

659. Deterioration. — N. DETERIORATION, debasement; wane, ebb; recession &c. 287; retrogradation &c. 283; decrease &c. 36.

DEGENERACY, degeneration, degenerateness; degradation; depravation, depravement [*rare*], depravedness; devolution; depravity &c. 945; demoralization, retrogression; masochism.

IMPAIRMENT, inquination [*obs.*], injury, damage, loss, detriment, delaceration [*obs.*], outrage, havoc, inroad, ravage, scathe, scath [*dial.*], perversion, prostitution, vitiation, discoloration, pollution, defœdation, poisoning, venenation [*rare*], leaven, contamination, canker, corruption, adulteration, alloy.

DECLINE, declension, declination; decadence *or* decadency; falling off &c. *v.;* caducity [*rare*], senility, decrepitude.

DECAY, dilapidation, ravages of time, wear and tear; erosion, corrosion, moldiness *or* mouldiness; rottenness; moth and rust, dry rot, blight, marcescence, marasmus, atrophy, collapse; disorganization; *délabrement* [*F.*] &c. (*destruction*) 162; aphid, aphis (*pl.* aphides), plant louse; vine fretter, vine grub; gypsy (*or* gipsy) moth; buffalo carpet beetle &c. (*injurious insects*) 913.

WRECK, mere wreck, honeycomb, *magni nominis umbra* [*L.*], jade, rackabones [*U. S.*], skate [*U. S.*]; tacky *or*

RENDER BETTER, improve, mend, amend, better; ameliorate, meliorate, relieve; correct; repair &c. (*restore*) 660; doctor &c. (*remedy*) 662; purify &c. 652; decrassify.

improve –, refine- upon; rectify; enrich, mellow, elaborate, fatten.

REFRESH, revive; put –, infuse- new blood into; invigorate &c. (*strengthen*) 159; reinvigorate, recruit, renew, make over, revivify, freshen.

PROMOTE, cultivate, advance, forward, enhance; bring forward, bring on; foster &c. 707.

TOUCH UP, rub up, brush up, furbish up, bolster up, vamp up, brighten up, warm up; polish, cook, make the most of, set off to advantage; prune; put in order &c. (*arrange*) 60.

REVISE, edit, redact, digest, review, make corrections, make improvements &c. n.

REFORM, remodel, reorganize; build -afresh, – anew; reclaim, civilize; lift, uplift, inspire; new-model.

view in a new light, think better of, appeal from Philip drunk to Philip sober.

PALLIATE, mitigate; lessen &c. (36) an evil.

Adj. BETTER, – off, – for; all the better for; better advised; improving &c. v.; progressive, improved &c. v.

REFORMATORY, emendatory; reparatory &c. (*restorative*) 660; remedial &c. 662.

CORRIGIBLE, improvable, curable; accultural.

Adv. ON CONSIDERATION, on reconsideration, on second thoughts, on better advice; on the mend, on the upgrade; *ad melius inquirendum* [*L.*].

*** *urbem latericiam invenit marmoream reliquit;* "to look up and not down, to look forward and not back, to look out and not in, and to lend a hand" [Hale].

tackey [*Southern U. S.*], plug [*slang or colloq., U. S.*].

V. DETERIORATE; be –, become- -worse, – deteriorated &c. *adj.*; have seen better days, degenerate, fall off; wane &c. (*decrease*) 36; ebb; retrograde &c. 283; decline, droop; go down &c. (*sink*) 306; go downhill, go on from bad to worse, go farther and fare worse; jump out of the frying pan into the fire; avoid Scylla and fall into Charybdis.

run to -seed, – waste; swale [*obs.*], sweal [*obs.*]; lapse, be the worse for; sphacelate; break, break down; spring a leak, crack, start; shrivel &c. (*contract*) 195; fade, go off, wither, molder *or* moulder, rot, rankle, decay, go bad; go to –, fall into- decay; fall "into the sere, the yellow leaf" [*Macbeth*]; rust, crumble, shake; totter, – to its fall; perish &c. 162; die &c. 360.

[RENDER LESS GOOD] deteriorate; weaken &c. 160; put back; taint, infect, contaminate, poison, empoison, envenom, canker, corrupt, exulcerate [*obs.*], pollute, vitiate, inquinate [*obs.*], debase, embase [*obs.*]; denaturalize, leaven; deflower, debauch, defile, deprave, degrade; ulcerate; stain &c. (*dirt*) 653; discolor; alloy, adulterate, sophisticate, tamper with, prejudice.

PERVERT, prostitute, demoralize, brutalize; render vicious &c. 945.

EMBITTER, acerbate, exacerbate, aggravate.

INJURE, impair, labefy [*rare*], damage, harm, hurt, shend, scath [*dial.*], scathe, spoil, mar, despoil, dilapidate, waste; overrun; ravage; pillage &c. 791.

wound, stab, pierce, maim, lame, surbate [*obs.*], cripple, hock *or* hough, hamstring, hit between wind and water, scotch, mangle, mutilate, disfigure, blemish, deface, warp.

BLIGHT, rot; corrode, erode; wear away, wear out; gnaw, – at the root of; sap, mine, undermine, shake, sap the foundations of, break up; disorganize, dismantle, dismast; destroy &c. 162.

DAMNIFY &c. (*aggrieve*) 649; do one's worst; knock down; deal a blow to; play -havoc, – sad havoc, – the mischief [*colloq.*], – the deuce [*colloq.*], – the very devil [*colloq.*]- -with, – among; decimate.

Adj. DETERIORATED &c. v.; altered, – for the worse; unimproved &c. (improve &c. 658); injured &c. v.; sprung; withering, spoiling &c. v.; on the -wane, – decline; tabid; degenerate; worse; the –, all the- worse for; out of -repair, – tune; imperfect &c. 651; the worse for wear; battered; weathered, weather-beaten; stale, *passé* [*F.*], shaken, dilapidated, frayed, faded, wilted, shabby, secondhand, threadbare; worn, – to- -a thread, – a shadow, – the stump, – rags; reduced, – to a skeleton; far-gone; tacky [*colloq. or slang*].

DECAYED &c. *v.;* moth-eaten, worm-eaten; mildewed, rusty, moldy *or* mouldy, spotted, seedy [*colloq.*], time-worn, moss-grown; discolored; effete, wasted, crumbling, moldering *or* mouldering, rotten, cankered, blighted, marcescent, tainted; depraved &c. (*vicious*) 945; decrepit; broken-down; done, – for, – up [*all colloq.*]; worn-out, used up [*colloq.*]; fit for the -dust hole, – waste-paper basket; past work &c. (*useless*) 645.

AT A LOW EBB, in a bad way, on one's last legs; undermined, deciduous; nodding to its fall &c. (*destruction*) 162; tottering &c. (*dangerous*) 665; past cure &c. (*hopeless*) 859; washed out, run down; fatigued &c. 688; unprogressive, improgressive [*rare*], backward, stagnant, behind the times; retrograde &c. (*retrogressive*) 283; deleterious &c. 649.

Adv. ON THE DOWN GRADE, on the downward track; beyond hope.

.*. *ægrescit medendo;* "what a falling off was there!" [*Hamlet*]; "oh, what a fall was there, my countrymen!" *Julius Cæsar*]; *fuimus Troës, fuit Ilium* [Vergil].

660. Restoration. — N. RESTORATION,
restoral [*rare*], restorance [*obs.*]; reinstatement, replacement, rehabilitation, reëstablishment, reconstitution, reconstruction; reproduction &c. 163; renovation, renewal; revival, revivement [*rare*], reviviscence *or* revivescence; refreshment &c. 689; resuscitation, reanimation, revivification, reviction [*obs.*]; reorganization.

reaction; redemption &c. (*deliverance*) 672; restitution &c. 790; relief &c. 834.

recurrence &c. (*repetition*) 104; *réchauffé* [F.], *rifacimento* [It.].

RENAISSANCE, renascence, rebirth, second youth, rejuvenescence, rejuvenation, new birth; regeneration, regeneracy, regenerateness, regenesis, palingenesis, reconversion; resurgence, resurrection.

661. Relapse. — N. RELAPSE, lapse;
falling back &c. *v.;* retrogradation &c. (*retrogression*) 283; deterioration &c. 659.

[RETURN TO, OR RECURRENCE OF, A BAD STATE] backsliding, recidivation [*obs.*]; recidivism, recidivity; recrudescence.

V. RELAPSE, lapse; fall –, slide –, slip –, sink- back; have a relapse, be overcome, be overtaken, yield again to, fall again into; return; retrograde &c. 283; recidivate [*rare*]; fall off &c. 659- again.

Adj. BACKSLIDING, relapsing &c. *v.;* recidivous, recidivistic, recrudescent, retrograde.

REDRESS, retrieval, reclamation, recovery; convalescence; resumption, *résumption* [F.]; sanativeness.

CURE, recure [*obs.*], sanation [*obs.*]; healing &c. *v.;* redintegration; rectification; instauration; cicatrization; disinfection; delousing, delousement.

REPAIR, repairing, reparation, mending; recruiting &c. *v.;* tinkering.

MENDER, doctor, physician, surgeon; priest, clergyman, pastor; carpenter, joiner, plumber, tinker, cobbler; reviver, revivor [*rare*], renewer, *vis medicatrix* [L.] &c. (*remedy*) 662.

CURABLENESS, curability, reparability, restorableness, retrievability, recoverability, recoverableness.

V. RETURN TO THE ORIGINAL STATE; recover, rally, revive; come to, come round, come to oneself; pull through, weather the storm, be oneself again; get -well, – round, – the better of, – over – up, – about; rise from -one's ashes, – the grave; resurge, resurrect; survive &c. (*outlive*) 110; resume, reappear; come to, – life again; live again, rise again.

HEAL, heal over, skin over, cicatrize; right itself, heal itself.

RESTORE, put back, place *in statu quo* [L.]; reinstate, replace, reseat, rehabilitate, reëstablish, reëstate, reinstall.

RECONSTRUCT, rebuild, reorganize, reconstitute; convert, reconvert; recondition, renew, renovate; regenerate; rejuvenate.

REDEEM, reclaim, recover, retrieve; rescue &c. (*deliver*) 672.

CURE, heal, remedy, doctor, physic, medicate; redress, recure; break of; bring round, set on one's legs.

RESUSCITATE, revive, reanimate, revivify, recall to life; reproduce &c. 163; warm up; reinvigorate, refresh &c. 689.

REDINTEGRATE, make whole; recoup &c. 790; make good, make all square; rectify; put -, set- -right, - to rights, - straight; set up, correct; put in order &c. (*arrange*) 60; refit, recruit; fill up, - the ranks; reinforce.

REPAIR, mend; put in repair, put in thorough repair; retouch, botch, vamp, tinker, cobble; do up, patch up, plaster up, vamp up; darn, finedraw, heelpiece; stop a gap, stanch *or* staunch, calk *or* caulk, careen, splice, bind up wounds.

Adj. RESTORED &c. *v.;* redivivus, redivivous [*rare*], reviviscible, ccnvalescent; in a fair way; none the worse; rejuvenated; renascent.

RESTORING &c. *v.;* restorative, recuperative; sanative, sanatory; reparative, reparatory; curative, remedial.

RESTORABLE, recoverable, remediable, retrievable, curable, sanable [*rare*].

Adv. *in statu quo* [*L.*[; as you were.

** *revenons à nos moutons; vestigia nulla retrorsum* [Horace]; "physician, heal thyself" [*Bible*]; 'with healing in his wings" [*Bible*]; "Richard's himself again!" [Cibber].

---

662. Remedy. — N. REMEDY, help, redress; anthelmintic, vermifuge, helminthagogue; antifebrile, febrifuge; antipoison, antidote, mithridate [*old pharm.*], theriaca *or* theriac, counterpoison; antispasmodic; lithagogue; bracer, pick-me-up [*colloq.*], stimulant, tonic; abirritant, prophylactic, antiseptic, germicide, bactericide, corrective, restorative; alterant, alterative; cathartic &c. 652; specific; emetic, carminative.

MATERIA MEDICA, pharmacy, pharmacology, pharmaceutics, acology, posology, dosology [*rare*]; pathology &c. 655; pharmacopœia.

NARCOTIC, nepenthe *or* nepenthes, opium, morphine, cocaine, hashish, bhang, ganja, dope [*slang*]; sedative &c. 174.

CURE; partial -, attempted -, radical -, perfect -, certain- cure; sovereign remedy, panacea, cure-all, catholicon.

PHYSIC, medicine, simples, drug, potion, draft *or* draught, dose, pill, bolus, electuary; lincture *or* linctus; medicament; pharmacon.

NOSTRUM, recipe, receipt, prescription; elixir, *elixir vitæ* [*L.*], balm, balsam, cordial, tisane, ptisan.

agueweed, boneset; arnica, benzoin, cream of tartar, bitartrate of potash, calomel, mercurous chloride; catnip, catmint; Epsom salts; feverroot *or* feverwort, feverweed, friar's balsam, Indian sage; ipecac *or* ipecacuanha; Peruvian

663. Bane. —N. BANE, curse, hereditary evil, thorn in the flesh; *bête noir* [*F.*], bugbear; evil &c. 619; hurtfulness &c. (*badness*) 649; painfulness &c. (*cause of pain*) 830; scourge &c. (*punishment*) 975; *damnosa hereditas* [*L.*]; white elephant.

rust, worm, helminth, moth, "moth and rust " [*Bible*]; fungus, mildew; dry rot; canker, cankerworm; cancer; viper &c. (*evildoer*) 913; demon &c. 980.

STING, fang, thorn, tang [*dial. Eng.*], bramble, brier *or* br ar, nettle.

POISON, leaven, virus, venom; arsenic, Prussic acid, antimony, tartar emetic, strychnine, tannin *or* tannic acid, nicotine; miasma *or* miasm, effluvium, mephitis, stench; fetor &c. 401; malaria, azote [*rare*], nitrogen, coal gas, illuminating gas, natural gas, gas, poison gas, mustard gas, chlorine, tear gas, lachrymose gas; sewer gas; pest.

Albany hemp, arsenious -oxide, - acid; bichloride of mercury; carbonic acid, - gas; choke ˙damp, black damp, fire damp, afterdamp, marsh gas, methane; cyanide of potassium, carbolic acid, corrosive sublimate; hydrocyanic acid, hydrocyanide; nux vomica, ratsbane.

toxicant, intoxicant, deliriant, delirifacient, hemlock, hellebore, nightshade, deadly nightshade, belladonna, henbane, aconite; banewort, opium, bhang [*India*], ganja [*India*], hemp, cannabin, hashish; Upas tree.

bark, Jesuits' bark, cinchona, quinine *or* quinin, sassafras, yarrow.

SALVE, ointment, cerate, oil, lenitive, palliative, lotion, embrocation, liniment.

harquebusade *or* arquebusade, traumatic, vulnerary, pepastic, maturative, maturant, suppurative; eyewater, collyrium; cosmetic; depilatory.

POULTICE, cataplasm, vesicatory, plaster, *emplastrum* [*L.*], epithem, sinapism.

compress, pledget; bandage &c. (*support*) 215.

TREATMENT, medical treatment, regimen, diet; dietary, dietetics; *vis medicatrix* [*L.*]; *vis naturæ* [*L.*]; *médecine expectante* [*F.*]; bloodletting, bleeding, venesection, phlebotomy, cupping, sanguisuge, leeches; operation, the knife [*colloq.*], surgical operation; major operation; electrolysis, electrolyzation.

HEALING ART, leechcraft [*archaic*], practice of medicine, therapeutics; allopathy, homeopathy *or* homœopathy, osteopathy, eclecticism, heteropathy; gynecology, gyniatrics, gynecological therapeutics; pediatrics *or* pædiatrics; surgery, chirurgery [*archaic*]; orthopedics *or* orthopædics, orthopedia *or* orthopædia, orthopraxy, orthopraxis, orthopedic surgery; sarcology, organotherapy; hydrotherapy, hydropathy, cold-water cure; faith cure, faith healing, mind cure, psychotherapy, psychotherapeutics; Christian Science, Eddyism; radiotherapy, heliotherapy, serotherapy, serum therapy; aërotherapy, pneumatotherapy; vocational therapy; dentistry, surgical dentistry; midwifery, obstetrics, tocology.

HOSPITAL, infirmary, clinic, *hôpital* [*F.*], general hospital, *hotel-Dieu* [*F.*]; special hospital (cancer, children's, dental, fever, maternity *or* lying-in, ophthalmic &c); pesthouse, lazarhouse, lazaretto, lazaret; lock hospital [*Eng.*]; *maison de santé* [*F.*]; *Hôtel des Invalides* [*F.*]; sanatarium, sanitarium, sanatorium, springs, baths, spa, pump room, well; hospice; asylum, home; Red Cross; ambulance.

dispensary, dispensatory, drug store, chemist's shop [*Brit.*].

DOCTOR, physician, leech [*archaic*], medical man, disciple of Æsculapius; medical –, general– practitioner; medical attendant, specialist; surgeon, chirurgeon [*archaic*].

consultant, operator; interne, anæsthetist *or* anesthetist; aurist, oculist, dentist, dental surgeon; osteopath, osteopathist; orthopedist *or* orthopædist; gynecologist, obstetrician; Christian Science practitioner, faith healer; medical student, medic [*colloq. or slang, U. S.*]; *accoucheur* (*fem. accoucheuse*) [*F.*], midwife; nurse; graduate –, trained –, district –, practical –, monthly– nurse; sister, nursing sister; dresser, bonesetter, apothecary, druggist, chemist [*Brit.*], pharmacopolist, pharmaceutist, pharmacist, pharmaceutical chemist, pharmacologist; Æsculapius, Hippocrates, Galen; *masseur* (*fem. masseuse*) [*F.*], massagist, rubber.

[INSTRUMENTS] stethoscope, stethometer, stethograph, respirometer, spirometer, pneumometer, spirograph, pneumatograph, pneumatometer, pulmotor.

V. APPLY A REMEDY &c. *n.;* doctor [*colloq.*], dose, physic, nurse, minister to, attend, dress the wounds, plaster, poultice; strap, splint, bandage; prevent &c. 706; relieve &c. 834; palliate &c. 658; heal, cure, "kill or cure," work a cure, remedy, stay (disease), snatch from the jaws of death; restore &c. 660; drench with physic; consult, specialize, operate, anæsthetize *or* anesthetize; straighten, mold *or* mould; deliver; extract, fill, stop; transfuse, bleed, cup, let blood; electrolyze.

manicure; pedicure; shampoo; massage, rub.

Adj. REMEDIAL; restorative &c. 660; corrective, palliative, healing; sanatory, sanative; prophylactic; salutiferous &c. (*salutary*) 656; medical, medicinal; therapeutic, hypnotic, neurotic, chirurgical [*archaic*], surgical, epulotic [*obs.*], paregoric, tonic, corroborant, roborant; analeptic, balsamic, anodyne, narcotic, sedative, lenitive, demulcent, emollient; detersive, detergent; abstersive, disinfectant; febrifugal, antifebrile; alterative; traumatic, vulnerary.

allopathic, homeopathic *or* homœopathic, eclectic, hydropathic, heteropathic; aperient, laxative, cathartic, purgative; septic; aseptic, antiseptic; antiluetic,

---

[SCIENCE OF POISONS] toxicology.

Adj. BANEFUL &c. (*bad*) 649; poisonous &c. (*unwholesome*) 657.

** bibere venenum in auro; "my bane and antidote are both before me" [Addison]; "this even-handed justice Commends the ingredients of our poisoned chalice To our own lips" [*Macbeth*]; die "like a poisoned rat in a hole" [Swift].

antisyphilitic; anthelmintic, vermifugal; chalybeate, deobstruent; purifying, cleansing, depurative, depuratory; electrolytic *or* electrolytical.

DIETETIC, dietary, alimentary; nutritious, nutritive; digestive, digestible, peptic.

REMEDIABLE, curable; antidotal, alexipharmic, alexiteric.

** *aux grands maux les grands remèdes; temporis ars medicina fere est* [Ovid]; "physicians mend or end us, *Secundum artem*" [Byron]; "troubled with thick-coming fancies" [*Macbeth*]; "the remedy is worse than the disease" [Dryden]; "throw physic to the dogs, I'll none of it" [*Macbeth*]; "the best doctors in the world are Doctor Diet, Doctor Quiet, and Doctor Merryman" [Swift]; "Divine presenter of the healing rod" [Browning].

3. Contingent Subservience

664. Safety. — N. SAFETY, security, surety, impregnability; invulnerability, invulnerableness &c. *adj.;* danger -past, – over; storm blown over; coast clear; escape &c. 671; means of escape; blow-, safety-, snifting- valve; safeguard, palladium; sheet anchor; rock, tower.

GUARDIANSHIP, wardship, wardenship; tutelage, custody, safe-keeping; preservation &c. 670; guardship [*obs.*], protection, auspices.

PROTECTOR, guardian; warden, warder; preserver, life saver, custodian, duenna, chaperon, third person.

safe-conduct, escort, convoy; guard, shield &c. (*defense*) 717; guardian angel; tutelary -god, – deity, – saint; *genius loci* [*L.*].

WATCHDOG, bandog; Cerberus.

WATCHMAN, patrolman, policeman, police officer, officer [*colloq.*], "the finest" [*local, U. S.*]; cop, copper, peeler, bobby [*all slang*], blue coat [*colloq.*], constable, roundsman [*U. S.*], *gendarme* [*F.*], military police; detective,· tec [*slang*], bull [*slang, U. S.*], spotter [*slang*]; sheriff, deputy; sentinel, sentry, scout &c. (*warning*) 668.

ARMED FORCE, garrison, life guard, State guard, militia, regular army, navy; volunteer; marine &c. 726; battleship, man-of-war &c. 726.

[MEANS OF SAFETY] refuge &c., anchor &c. 666; precaution &c. (*preparation*) 673; guard, guard rail, hand rail; bulkhead, watertight compartment, safety appliance; bolt, hasp &c. (*pin*) 45; cyclone cellar, dugout, bombproof dug-out; quarantine, *cordon sanitaire* [*F.*].

[SENSE OF SECURITY] confidence &c. 858.

JUDGE, justice, judiciary, magistrate, beak [*slang, Eng.*], justice of the peace, J. P.; deemster [*Isle of Man*], hakim [*Oriental*]; chancellor &c. 967.

V. BE SAFE &c. *adj.;* keep one's head above water, tide over, save one's bacon [*colloq.*]; ride out –, weather- the storm; light upon one's feet; bear a

665. Danger. — N. DANGER, peril, insecurity, jeopardy, risk, hazard, venture, precariousness, slipperiness; instability &c. 149; defenselessness &c. *adj.*

exposure &c. (*liability*) 177; vulnerability; vulnerable point, heel of Achilles; forlorn hope &c. (*hopelessness*) 859.

[DANGEROUS COURSE] leap in the dark &c. (*rashness*) 863; road to ruin, *facilis descensus Averni* [Vergil], hairbreadth escape.

[APPROACH OF DANGER] cause for alarm; source of danger &c. 667; rock –, breakers- ahead; storm brewing; clouds -in the horizon, – gathering; warning &c. 668; alarm &c. 669.

[SENSE OF DANGER] apprehension &c. 860.

V. BE IN DANGER &c. *adj.;* be exposed to –, run into –, incur –, encounter- danger &c. *n.;* run a risk; lay oneself open to &c. (*liability*) 177; lean on –, trust to- a broken reed; feel the ground sliding from under one, have to run for it; have the -chances, – odds- against one.

hang by a thread, totter; tremble on the verge; totter on the brink; sleep –, stand- on a volcano; sit on a barrel of gunpowder, live in a glass house.

ENDANGER; bring –, place –, put- in -danger &c. *n.;* expose to danger, imperil; be proscribed; have one's name on the danger list; be overdue [*naut.*], be despaired of; be under sentence of death; jeopard, jeopardize; put one's head in the lion's mouth; beard the lion in his den; compromise; sail too near the wind &c. (*rash*) 863.

threaten &c. (909) danger; run one hard; lay a trap for &c. (*deceive*) 545.

ADVENTURE, risk, hazard, venture, stake, set at hazard; run the gauntlet &c. (*dare*) 861; engage in a forlorn hope.

Adj. IN DANGER &c. *n.;* endangered

charmed life; escape &c. 671; possess
nine lives.

PROTECT, watch over; make or render
safe &c. adj.; take care of &c. (care) 459;
preserve &c. 670; cover, screen, shelter,
shroud, flank, ward; take charge of;
guard &c. (defend) 717; garrison; man
the -garrison, - lifeboat; secure &c.
(restrain) 751; intrench or entrench,
mine, countermine; dig in; fence round
&c. (circumscribe) 229; house, nestle,
ensconce.

ESCORT, support, accompany, convoy.

WATCH, mount guard, patrol, go on
one's beat; do -, perform- sentry go;
scout, spy.

TAKE PRECAUTIONS &c. (prepare for)
673; "make assurance double sure"
[Macbeth] &c. (caution) 864; take up a
loose thread; reef, take in a reef, make all
snug, have an anchor to windward,
double reef topsails.

seek safety; take -, find- shelter &c.
666; run into port.

Adj. SAFE, secure, sure; in safety, in
security; in shelter, in harbor, in port;
in the shadow of a rock; on terra firma
[L.]; on the safe side; under the -shield
of, - shade of, - wing of, - shadow of
one's wing; under cover, under lock and
key; out of -danger, - the meshes, -
harm's way; on sure ground, at anchor,
high and dry, above water; unthreatened, unmolested; protected &c. v.;
cavendo tutus [L.]; panoplied &c. (defended) 717.

safe and sound &c. (preserved) 670;
harmless; scatheless &c. (perfect) 650;
unhazarded; not dangerous &c. 665.

snug, seaworthy, airworthy; watertight, weathertight, weatherproof, waterproof, fireproof; bombproof, shell-
proof.

DEFENSIBLE, tenable, proof against,
invulnerable; unassailable, unattackable; "founded upon a rock" [Bible],
impregnable, imperdible [obs.]; inex-
pugnable.

PROTECTING &c. v.; guardian, tutelary; preservative &c. 670; trustworthy
&c. 939.

&c. v.; fraught with danger; dangerous,
hazardous, perilous, periculous [obs.],
parlous [archaic], unsafe, unprotected
&c. (safe, protect &c. 664); insecure,
untrustworthy, unreliable; built upon
sand, on a sandy basis; unsound, speculative, wild-cat.

DEFENSELESS, guardless, fenceless
[archaic], harborless, unsheltered, unshielded; vulnerable, expugnable, exposed; open to &c. (liable) 177.

aux abois [F.], at bay, with one's back
to the wall; on the wrong side of the
wall, on a lee shore, on the rocks.

PRECARIOUS, critical, ticklish; slippery,
slippy; hanging by a thread &c. v.; with
a halter round one's neck; between -the
hammer and the anvil, - Scylla and
Charybdis, - two fires; on the edge,
brink, or verge of -a precipice, - a volcano, - an abyss, -a pit; in the lion's den,
on slippery ground, under fire; not out
of the wood; in the condemned cell,
under sentence of death; at stake, in
question.

UNWARNED, unadmonished, unadvised; unprepared &c. 674; off one's
guard &c. (inexpectant) 508.

TOTTERING, unstable, unsteady;
shaky, top-heavy, tumble-down, ram-
shackle, crumbling, water-logged; helpless, guideless; in a bad way; reduced to
-, at- the last extremity; trembling in
the balance; nodding to its fall &c.
(destruction) 162.

THREATENING &c. 909; ominous, ill-
omened; alarming &c. (fear) 860; explosive; poisonous; venomous &c. (insalubrious) 657; rotten at the core.

ADVENTUROUS &c. (rash) 863, (bold)
861.

Int. STOP! look! listen! look out! look
alive! look slippy! [colloq.]; below there!
'ware heads! beware! take care! prenez
garde! [F.].

₊ incidit in Scyllam qui vult vitare Charybdim; nam tua res agitur paries dum proximus
ardet; "out of this nettle, danger, we pluck
this flower, safety" [King Henry IV]; "pleased
with the danger, when the waves went high
He sought the storms" [Dryden].

Adv. ex abundante cautelâ [L.]; with impunity.

Int. ALL'S WELL! all clear! all serene! [slang]; safety first! at rest! at ease!

₊ salva res est; suave mari magno; à couvert; e terra alterius spectare laborem [Lucretius]; Dieu
vous garde; "safe through a thousand perils brought" [Montgomery]; "early and provident fear
is the mother of safety" [Burke]; "be of good cheer: it is I; be not afraid" [Bible]; "he who
fights and runs away May live to fight another day" [Goldsmith]; "Astoundingly tricephalate,
Waits Cerberus, the mutt of Hades" [Don Marquis].

666. [MEANS OF SAFETY.] **Refuge.** —
N. REFUGE, sanctuary, retreat, fastness,
stronghold, fortress, castle, acropolis;
keep, last resort; ward; prison &c. 752;
asylum, ark, home, refuge for the
destitute; almshouse; hiding place &.
(*ambush*) 530; *sanctum sanctorum* [L.]
&c. (*privacy*) 893.

ANCHORAGE, roadstead; breakwater,
mole, port, haven; harbor, – of refuge;
seaport; pier, jetty, embankment, quay,
wharf, landing place; bund, bunder
[*both Oriental*]; water wing [*arch.*].

COVERT,, shelter, screen, lee wall,
wing, shield, umbrella; dashboard,
dasher [*U. S.*], splashboard, mud guard
or mudguard, wheel guard.

wall &c. (*inclosure*) 232; fort &c.
(*defense*) 717.

ANCHOR, sheet anchor, sacred anchor
[*Gr. & Rom. antiq.*], kedge *or* kedge
anchor; Trotman's –, Martin's –, mush-
room- anchor; killick; grapnel, grappling
iron; mainstay; support &c. 215; check
&c. 706; ballast.

MEANS OF ESCAPE &c. (*escape*) 671;
lifeboat, swimming belt, cork jacket,
life preserver, buoy, breeches buoy;
parachute, plank, stepping-stone.

SAFEGUARD &c. (*protection*) 664.

667. [SOURCE OF DANGER.] **Pitfall.** —
N. rocks, reefs, coral reef, sunken rocks,
snags; sands, quicksands; syrt [*rare*],
syrtis [*rare*]; Goodwin sands, sandy
foundation; slippery ground; breakers,
shoals, shallows, bank, shelf, flat, lee
shore, ironbound coast, rockbound coast;
rock –, breakers- ahead; derelict.

ABYSS, abysm, pit, void, chasm,
crevasse.

WHIRLPOOL, eddy, vortex, gurge [*rare*],
rapids, undertow; current, tide gate,
tide race, maelstrom; eagre, bore, tidal
wave.

PITFALL; ambush &c. 530; trapdoor;
trap &c. (*snare*) 545; mine, masked
battery, spring-gun.

PEST, ugly customer, dangerous person, *le chat qui dort* [F.]; crouching tiger;
incendiary, firebug [*slang*]; firebrand;
hornet's nest.

sword of Damocles; wolf at the door,
snake in the grass, snake in one's bosom,
death in the -cup, – pot; latency &c. 526.

⁎ *latet anguis in herbâ* [Vergil]; *proximus
ardet Ucalegon* [Vergil]; "O Thou, who didst
with pitfall and with sin Beset the Road I was
to wander in" [Omar Khayyám — Fitzgerald].

jury mast; vent-peg; safety -valve, – lamp; lightning -rod, – conductor.

V. SEEK *or* FIND SAFETY &c. 664; seek –, take –, find- refuge &c. *n.*;
claim sanctuary; throw oneself into the arms of; break for the tall timber [*U. S.*],
break for the woods; fly to, reach in time; make port, make the harbor;
anchor in the roadstead; crouch in the lee of; reach -shelter, – home, – running
water.

BAR THE GATE, let the portcullis down; lock –, bolt –, make fast- the door;
raise the drawbridge.

⁎ *bibere venenum in auro; valet anchora virtus;* "*ein feste Burg ist unser Gott*" — a mighty
fortress is our God [Luther].

---

668. Warning. — N. WARNING, caution, caveat; notice &c. (*information*) 257;
premonition, premonishment [*rare*]; prediction &c. 511; symptom, contraindication, lesson, dehortation; admonition, monition; alarm &c. 669.

handwriting on the wall, *tekel upharsin* [*Heb.*], yellow flag; red flag, red light, fog-
signal, fog-horn; siren; monitor, warning voice, Cassandra, signs of the times,
Mother Cary's chickens, stormy petrel, bird of ill omen, gathering clouds, cloud no
bigger than a man's hand, clouds in the horizon, death watch, death lights &c.
(*premonitions*) 992a.

WATCHTOWER, beacon, signal post; lighthouse &c. (*indication of locality*) 550.

SENTINEL, sentry; watch, watchman; watch and ward; watchdog, bandog, house
dog; patrol, vedette, picket, bivouac, scout, spy, spial [*obs.*]; advanced –, rear-
guard; lookout, flagman.

CAUTIOUSNESS &c. 864.

V. WARN, caution; forewarn, prewarn; admonish, forebode, premonish [*rare*]; give
-notice, – warning; menace &c. (*threaten*) 909; put on one's guard; sound the alarm
&c. 669; croak.

BEWARE, ware [*dial.*]; take -warning, – heed at one's peril; look out, keep one's wits about one; keep watch and ward &c. (*care*) 459.

Adj. WARNING &c. *v.;* premonitory, monitory, cautionary, admonitory, admonitive [*rare*]; ominous, threatening, lowering, minatory &c. (*threat*) 909; symptomatic, sematic [*biol.*].

WARNED &c. *v.;* on one's guard &c. (*careful*) 459, (*cautious*) 864.

Adv. with alarm, on guard, after due warning, with one's eyes open; *in terrorem* [*L.*].

Int. BEWARE! ware! take care! mind –, take care– what you are about! mind! look out! watch your step!

₊ *ne reveillez pas le chat qui dort; fanum habet in cornu; caveat actor; le silence du peuple zst la leçon des rois; verbum sat sapienti; un averti en vaut deux;* "by the pricking of my thumbs, Something wicked this way comes" [*Macbeth*]; "cold-pausing Caution's lesson scorning" [Burns].

---

669. [INDICATION OF DANGER.] **Alarm.** — **N.** ALARM; alarum, larum [*archaic*], alarm bell, tocsin, *alerte* [*F.*], beat of drum, sound of trumpet, note of alarm, hue and cry, fiery cross; signal of distress; flag at -half-mast, – half-staff; blue lights; war cry, war whoop; warning &c. 668; fog signal, fog bell, fog horn, siren; yellow flag; danger signal; red light, red flag; fire bell, fire alarm, still alarm; burglar alarm; watchman's rattle, police whistle.

FALSE ALARM, cry of wolf; bugbear, bugaboo.

V. ALARM; give –, raise –, sound –, turn in –, beat- the *or* an -alarm &c. *n.;* warn &c. 668; ring the tocsin; *battre la générale* [*F.*]; cry wolf; half-mast.

Adj. ALARMED; warned; alarming &c. *v.*

Int. *sauve qui peut!* [*F.*]; *qui vive?* [*F.*]; who goes there?

₊ "the trumpet's loud clangor Excites us to arms" [Dryden].

---

670. Preservation. — **N.** PRESERVATION; safe-keeping; conservation &c. (*storage*) 636; maintenance, support, sustentation [*rare*], conservatism; economy; *vis conervatrix* [*L.*]; salvation &c. (*deliverance*) 672.

[MEANS OF PRESERVATION] prophylaxis; preserver, preservative; hygiastics, hygiantics [*both rare*]; hygiene, hygienics; cover, drugget; *cordon sanitaire* [*F.*]; ensilage; dehydration, anhydration, evaporation; drying, putting up, canning, pickling; tinned goods [*chiefly Brit.*], canned goods; kyanization.

[SUPERSTITIOUS REMEDIES] charm &c. 993.

V. PRESERVE, maintain, keep, sustain, support; keep -up, – alive; not willingly let die; nurse; cure &c. (*restore*) 660; save, rescue; be –, make- safe &c. 664; take care of &c. (*care*) 459; guard &c. (*defend*) 717; bank, bank up, shore up.

embalm, dry, cure, salt, pickle, season, kyanize, bottle, pot, tin [*chiefly Brit.*], can; dehydrate, anhydrate, evaporate; husband &c. (*store*) 636.

HOLD ONE'S OWN; *stare super antiquas vias* [Bacon]; hold –, stand- one's ground &c. (*resist*) 719.

Adj. PRESERVING &c. *v.;* conservative; prophylactic; preservatory, preservative; hygienic.

PRESERVED &c. *v.;* unimpaired, unbroken, uninjured, unhurt, unsinged, unmarred; safe, – and sound; intact, with a whole skin, without a scratch.

₊ *nolumus leges Angliæ mutari;* "thrift, thrift, Horatio" [*Hamlet*]; "the back door robs the house" [Herbert]; "a man he seems of cheerful yesterdays And confident tomorrows" [Wordsworth].

---

671. Escape. — **N.** ESCAPE, scape [*obs.*]; avolation [*obs.*], elopement, flight; evasion &c. (*avoidance*) 623; retreat; narrow –, hairbreadth- escape; close call [*colloq.*], close shave, near shave [*colloq.*]; come off, impunity.

[MEANS OF ESCAPE] loophole &c. (*opening*) 260; path &c. 627; secret -chamber, passage; refuge &c. 666; vent, – peg; safety valve; drawbridge, fire escape. reprieve &c. (*deliverance*) 672; liberation &c. 750.

REFUGEE &c. (*fugitive*) 623.

V. ESCAPE, scape [*archaic*]; make –, effect –, make good- one's escape; break jail; get off, get clear off, get well out of; *échapper belle* [*F.*], save one's bacon [*colloq.*], make a get-away [*slang*]; weather the storm &c. (*safe*) 664; escape scot-free.

ELUDE &c., make off &c. (*avoid*) 623; march off &c. (*go away*) 293; give one the slip; slip through the -hands, – fingers; slip the collar, wriggle out of; break loose, break from prison; break – slip –, get- away; find vent, find a hole to creep out of.

Adj. escaping, escaped &c. *v.;* stolen away, fled; scot-free.

*** the bird has flown; "I am escaped with the skin of my teeth" [*Bible*].

---

672. Deliverance. — N. DELIVERANCE, extrication, rescue, ransom; reprieve, reprieval [*rare*], respite; armistice, truce; liberation &c. 750; emancipation; redemption, redeemableness, salvation; exemption; day of grace; riddance; jail (*or* gaol) delivery.

V. DELIVER, extricate, rescue, save, free, liberate, set free, release, emancipate, redeem, ransom; bring -off, – through; *tirer d'affaire* [*F.*], get the wheel out of the rut, snatch from the jaws of death, come to the rescue; rid; retrieve &c. (*restore*) 660; be –, get- rid of.

Adj. saved &c. *v.;* extricable, redeemable, rescuable.

Int. to the rescue! a rescue! saved!

*** "in the course of justice, none of us Should see salvation: we do pray for mercy" [*Merchant of Venice*].

---

3. *Precursory Measures*

673. Preparation.— N. PREPARATION; providing &c. *v.;* provision, providence; anticipation &c. (*foresight*) 510; precaution, preconcertedness, preconcertion, predisposition; forecast &c. (*plan*) 626; rehearsal, note of preparation; dissemination, propaganda.

groundwork, first stone, cradle, stepping-stone; foundation, first rung, scaffold &c. (*support*) 215; scaffolding, *échafaudage* [*F.*].

ELABORATION; ripening &c. *v.;* maturation, evolution; perfection; concoction, digestion; gestation, hatching, incubation, sitting.

[PUTTING IN ORDER] arrangement &c. 60; clearance; adjustment &c. 23; tuning; equipment, outfit, accouterment *or* accoutrement, armament, array.

[PREPARATION OF MEN] training &c. (*education*) 537; inurement &c. (*habit*) 613; novitiate.

[PREPARATION OF FOOD] cooking, cookery, culinary art; brewing.

[PREPARATION OF THE SOIL] tilling, plowing *or* ploughing, sowing, semination, cultivation.

[STATE OF BEING PREPARED] preparedness, readiness, ripeness, mellowness, maturity; *un impromptu fait à loisir* [*F.*].

[PREPARER] preparer, trainer, coach; teacher &c. 540; pioneer; *avant-courrier* [*F.*], *avant-coureur* [*F.*]; *voortrekker*

674. Nonpreparation. — N. NONPREPARATION, unpreparedness; absence of –, want of- preparation; inculture [*obs.*], inconcoction [*obs.*], improvidence.

IMMATURITY, crudity; rawness &c. *adj.;* abortion; disqualification.

[ABSENCE OF ART] nature, state of nature; virgin soil, unweeded garden; rough diamond; neglect &c. 460.

rough copy &c. (*plan*) 626; germ &c. 153; raw material &c. 635.

improvisation &c. (*impulse*) 612.

V. BE UNPREPARED &c. *adj.;* want –, lack- preparation; lie fallow; *s'embarquer sans biscuits* [*F.*]; live from hand to mouth.

[RENDER UNPREPARED] dismantle &c. (*render useless*) 645; undress &c. 226.

EXTEMPORIZE, improvise; cook up, fix up, vamp.

SURPRISE, drop in upon [*colloq.*], pay a surprise visit, drop in [*colloq.*], give a surprise party, take potluck with; take –, catch- unawares; take by surprise, call informally.

Adj. UNPREPARED &c. (prepare &c. 673); without preparation &c. 673; incomplete &c. 53; rudimental, embryonic, abortive; immature, unripe, *kutcha* or *kachcha* [*Hind.*]; callow, unfledged, unhatched, unnurtured, raw, green, crude; coarse; rough, roughcast, roughhewn; in the rough; rough-edged, unhewn, un-

[*Dutch*]; prophet; forerunner &c. (*pre-cursor*) 64; sappers and miners, pavior, navvy; packer, stevedore, longshore-man; warming pan.

V. PREPARE; get –, make- ready; predispose, address oneself to, get under weigh; make preparations, settle pre-liminaries, get up, sound the note of preparation.

set *or* put in order &c. (*arrange*) 60; forecast &c. (*plan*) 626; prepare –, plow –, dress- the ground; till –, cultivate- the soil; sow the seed, lay a train, dig a mine; lay –, fix- the -foundations, – basis, – groundwork; dig the founda-tions, erect the scaffolding; lay the first stone &c. (*begin*) 66.

ROUGHHEW; cut out work; block out, hammer out; lick into shape &c. (*form*) 240.

ELABORATE, mature, ripen, mellow, season, bring to maturity; nurture &c. (*aid*) 707; hatch, cook, brew; temper, anneal, smelt; barbecue; dry, cure, salt, smoke, infumate [*rare*]; maturate.

EQUIP, arm, man; fit out, fit up; furnish, rig, dress, garnish, betrim, accouter *or* accoutre, array, fettle [*dial. Eng.*], fledge; dress up, furbish up, brush up, vamp up; refurbish; sharpen one's tools, trim one's -tackle, – foils; set, prime, attune; whet the -knife, – sword; wind up, screw up; adjust &c. (*fit*) 27; put in -trim, – train, – gear, – working order, – tune, – a groove for; – harness; pack, stow away, stow down, stow, load, store.

formed, unfashioned, unwrought, un-labored, unblown; indigested, undigested; unmellowed, unseasoned, unleavened; uncooked, unboiled, unconcocted; un-polished, uncut, deckle-edged.

UNTAUGHT, uneducated, untrained, untutored, undrilled, unexercised; un-licked; precocious, premature.

FALLOW, unsown, untilled, unculti-vated.

NATURAL, *in puris naturalibus* [*L.*], in a state of nature; undressed; in dis-habille, *en déshabillé* [*F.*], in negligee.

UNFITTED, disqualified, unqualified, ill-digested; unbegun, unready, un-arranged, unorganized, unfurnished, unprovided, unequipped, untrimmed; out of -gear. – kilter *or* kelter [*colloq.*], – order; dismantled &c. *v.*

SHIFTLESS, improvident, unthrifty, thriftless, thoughtless, unguarded; happy-go-lucky; slack, remiss; caught napping &c. (*inexpectant*) 508; unpre-meditated &c. 612.

Adv. INADVERTENTLY, by surprise, without premeditation; extempore &c. 612.

PREPARE FOR &c.; train &c. (*teach*) 537; inure &c. (*habituate*) 613; breed; rehearse; make provision for; take -steps, – measures, – precautions; provide, provide against; beat up for recruits; open the door to &c. (*facilitate*) 705.

set one's house in order, make all snug; clear decks, clear for action; close one's ranks; shuffle the cards.

PREPARE ONESELF; serve an apprenticeship &c. (*learn*) 539; lay oneself out for, get into harness, gird up one's loins, buckle on one's armor, *reculer pour mieux sauter* [*F.*], prime and load, shoulder arms, get up steam; put the horses to, harness, harness up [*colloq.*], hitch up [*colloq.*].

guard against, make sure against; forearm, make sure, prepare for the evil day, have a rod in pickle, have a bone to pick, provide against a rainy day, feather one's nest; lay in provisions &c. 637; make investments; keep on foot, keep going.

BE PREPARED, be ready &c. *adj.*; hold oneself in readiness, watch and pray, keep one's powder dry, lie in wait for &c. (*expect*) 507; anticipate &c. (*foresee*) 510; *principiis obstare* [*L.*]; *venienti occurrere morbo* [*L.*].

Adj. PREPARING &c. *v.*; in preparation, in course of preparation, in agitation, in embryo, in hand, in train; afoot, afloat; on foot, on the stocks, on the anvil; under consideration &c. (*plan*) 626; in consultation; brewing, hatching, forthcoming, brooding; in store for, in reserve.

precautionary, provident; preparative, preparatory; provisional, inchoate, under revision; under advisement; preliminary &c. (*precedent*) 62.

PREPARED &c. *v.*; in readiness; ready, – to one's hand, ready made; cut and dried; made to one's hand, ready cut, made to order, at one's elbow, ready for use, all ready; handy, on the table; in gear; running -smoothly, – sweetly; in working -order, – gear; snug; in practice.

in full feather, in best bib and tucker [*colloq.*]; in –, at- harness; in the saddle, in arms, in battle array, in war paint; up in arms; armed -at all points, – to the teeth, – *cap à pie* [*F.*]; sword in hand; booted and spurred.

in utrumque paratus [Vergil], *semper paratus* [*L.*]; on the alert &c. (*vigilant*) 459; at one's post.

RIPE, mature, mellow; pucka *or* pakka [*Hind.*]; practiced &c. (*skilled*) 698; labored, elaborate, high-wrought, smelling of the lamp, worked up.

Adv. IN PREPARATION, in anticipation of; afoot, astir, abroad; abroach.

⁎ *a bove majori discit arare minor;* "looking before and after"[*Hamlet*], *si vis pacem para bellum;* "there is a divinity that shapes our ends, Roughhew them how we will" [*Hamlet*].

---

675. Essay. — N. ESSAY, trial, endeavor, attempt; aim, struggle, venture, adventure, speculation, *coup d'essai* [*F.*], *début* [*F.*]; probation &c. (*experiment*) 463.

V. TRY, essay; experiment &c. 463; endeavor, strive; tempt, attempt, make an attempt; venture, adventure, speculate, take one's chance, tempt fortune; try one's -fortune, – luck, – hand; use one's endeavor; feel –, grope –, pick- one's way.

try hard, push, make a bold push, use one's best endeavor; do one's best &c. (*exertion*) 686.

Adj. ESSAYING &c. *v.*; experimental &c. 463; tentative, empirical, problematic *or* problematical, probationary.

Adv. EXPERIMENTALLY &c. *adj.*; on trial, at a venture; by rule of thumb.

if one may be so bold.

⁎ *aut non tentaris aut perfice* [Ovid]; *chi non s'arrischia non guadagna;* I'll try anything once.

---

676. Undertaking. — N. UNDERTAKING; compact &c. 769; adventure, venture; engagement &c. (*promise*) 768; enterprise, emprise *or* emprize [*archaic*]; pilgrimage; matter in hand &c. (*business*) 625; move; first move &c. (*beginning*) 66.

V. UNDERTAKE; engage –, embark- in; launch –, plunge- into; volunteer; apprentice oneself to; engage &c. (*promise*) 768; contract &c. 769; take upon -oneself, – one's shoulders; devote oneself to &c. (*determination*) 604.

TAKE UP, take on, take in hand; tackle [*colloq.*]; set –, go- about; set –, fall- -to, – to work; launch forth; break the ice; set up shop; put in -hand, – execution; set forward; break the neck of a -day's work, – business; be in for [*colloq.*]; put one's hand to; betake oneself to, turn one's hand to, go to do; be in the midst of; begin &c. 66; broach, institute &c. (*originate*) 153; put –, lay- one's -hand to the plow, – shoulder to the wheel.

have in hand &c. (*business*) 625; have many irons in the fire &c. (*activity*) 682.

Adj. UNDERTAKING &c. *v.*; on the anvil &c. 625; available, receptive; full of pep [*slang*], energetic; adventurous, venturesome.

Int. here goes! shoot! [*colloq.*].

⁎ "Nowher so besy a man as he ther n'as, And yet he semed besier than he was" [Chaucer]; "So many worlds, so much to do!" [Tennyson].

---

677. Use. — N. USE, employ; exercise, exercitation; application, appliance; adhibition, disposal; consumption; agency &c. (*physical*) 170; usufruct; usefulness &c. 644; benefit; recourse, resort, avail; pragmatism, pragmaticism.

[CONVERSION TO USE] utilization, utility, service, wear.

[WAY OF USING] usage, employment, *modus operandi* [*L.*].

678. Disuse. — N. DISUSE; forbearance, abstinence; relinquishment &c. 782; desuetude &c. (*want of habit*) 614; disusage.

V. NOT USE; do without, dispense with, let alone, not touch, forbear, abstain, spare, waive, neglect; keep back, reserve.

DISUSE; lay up, lay by, lay on the shelf, lay up in a napkin; shelve; set –,

USER, consumer, purchasing public, buying public; market, public demand, popular demand, demand.

V. USE, make use of, employ, put to use; apply; put in -action, – operation, – practice; set in motion, set to work.

PLY, work, wield, handle, manipulate; play, play off; exert, exercise, practice, avail oneself of, profit by; resort to, lay one's hand to, fall back upon, have recourse to, recur to, take to [*colloq.*], take up, betake oneself to; take up with, take advantage of; lay one's hands on, try.

RENDER USEFUL &c. 644; mold *or* mould; turn to -account, – use; convert to use, utilize; administer; work up; call –, bring- into play; put into requisition; call –, draw- forth; press –, enlist- into the service; task, tax, put to task; bring to bear upon, devote, dedicate, consecrate, apply, adhibit, dispose of; make a handle of, make a cat's-paw of.

FALL BACK UPON, make a shift with; make the most of, make the best of.

CONSUME, use up, devour, swallow up; absorb, expend; wear, outwear.

Adj. IN USE; used &c. *v.;* well-worn, well-trodden.

USEFUL &c. 644; subservient &c. (*instrumental*) 631; utilitarian, pragmatic *or* pragmatical.

** "busy people are never busybodies" *Cynic's Calendar*].

put –, lay- aside; leave off, have done with; supersede; discard &c. (*eject*) 297; dismiss, give warning.

THROW ASIDE &c. (*relinquish*) 782; make away with &c. (*destroy*) 162; cast –, heave –, throw- overboard; cast to the -dogs, – winds; dismantle &c. (*render usless*) 645.

lie –, remain- unemployed &c. *adj.*

Adj. NOT USED &c. *v.;* unemployed, unapplied, undisposed of, unspent, unexercised, untouched, untrodden, unessayed, ungathered, unculled; uncalled for, not required.

DISUSED &c. *v.;* done with, run down, worn out, not worth saving.

Int. no use!

679. Misuse. — N. MISUSE, misusage, misemployment, misapplication, misappropriation.

ABUSE, profanation, prostitution, desecration; waste &c. 638.

V. MISUSE, misemploy, misapply, misappropriate.

DESECRATE, abuse, profane, prostitute.

OVERTASK, overtax, overwork, overdrive; squander &c. 818; waste &c. 638.

cut blocks with a razor, employ a steam engine to crack a nut; catch at a straw.

Adj. MISUSED &c. *v.*

** *ludere cum sacris;* "who first misuse, then cast their toys away" [Cowper].

Section III. VOLUNTARY ACTION

1. *Simple Voluntary Action*

680. Action. — N. ACTION, performance; doing &c. *v.;* perpetration; exercise, exercitation; movement, operation, evolution, work, employment; labor &c. (*exertion*) 686; *praxis* [*L.*], execution; procedure &c. (*conduct*) 692; handicraft; business &c. 625; agency &c. (*power at work*) 170.

DEED, act, overt act, stitch, touch, gest *or* geste; transaction, job, doings, dealings, proceeding, measure, step, maneuver *or* maneuvre, manœuver *or* manœuvre, bout, passage, move, stroke, blow; *coup, – de main, – d'état* [*F.*]; *tour de force* [*F.*] &c. (*display*) 882; feat, exploit; achievement &c. (*completion*) 729; handiwork, craftsmanship, work-

681. Inaction. — N. INACTION, passiveness, abstinence from action; watchful waiting; noninterference; Fabian –, *laisser-aller* [*F.*] –, *laisser-faire* [*F.*] –, conservative- policy; neglect &c. 460.

INACTIVITY &c. 683; stagnation, vegetation, loafing, loaf; rest &c. (*repose*) 687; quiescence &c. 265; want of occupation, unemployment, inoccupation; idle hours, idle hands, time hanging on one's hands, *dolce far niente* [*It.*]; shore duty; interregnum; sinecure; soft snap, soft thing, cinch [*all three slang*].

V. NOT DO, not act, not attempt; be inactive &c. 683; abstain from doing, do nothing, hold, spare; not stir –, not move –, not lift- a -finger, – hand,

manship; manufacture; stroke of policy &c. (*plan*) 626.

ACTOR &c. (*doer*) 690.

V. DO, perform, execute; achieve &c. (*complete*) 729; transact, enact; commit, perpetrate, inflict; exercise, prosecute, carry on, work, practice, play.

EMPLOY ONESELF, ply one's task; officiate, have in hand &c. (*business*) 625; labor &c. 686; be at work; pursue a course; shape one's course &c. (*conduct*) 692.

ACT, operate; take action, take steps; strike a blow, lift a finger, stretch forth one's hand; take in hand &c. (*undertake*) 676; put oneself in motion; put in practice; carry into execution &c. (*complete*) 729; act upon.

BE AN ACTOR &c. 690; take –, act –, play –, perform- a part in; participate in; have a -hand in, – finger in the pie; have to do with; be a party to, be a participator in; bear –, lend- a hand; pull an oar, run in a race; mix oneself up with &c. (*meddle*) 682.

BE IN ACTION; come into operation &c. (*power at work*) 170.

Adj. IN ACTION; doing &c. *v.*; acting; in harness; up to one's ears in work; in the midst of things; on duty; at work; operative; in operation &c. 170.

Adv. in the -act, – midst of, – thick of; red-handed, *in flagrante delicto* [*L.*]; while one's hand is in; while one is at it.

*** "action is eloquence" [*Coriolanus*]; actions speak louder than words; *actum ne agas* [Terence]; "awake, arise, or be forever fall'n" [*Paradise Lost*]; *dii pia facta vident* [Ovid]; *faire sans dire; fare fac; fronte capillata post est occasio calva;* "our deeds are sometimes better than our thoughts" [Bailey]; "we live in deeds not years" [*ibid.*]; "the great end of life is not knowledge but action" [Huxley]; "thought is the soul of act" [R. Browning]; *vivre ce n'est pas respirer c'est agir;* "our nature is movement; absolute stillness is death" [Pascal].

– foot, – peg; fold one's -arms, – hands; leave –, let- alone; let be, let pass, let things take their course, let it have its way, let well alone, let well enough alone; *quieta non movere* [*L.*]; *stare super antiquas vias* [*L.*]; rest and be thankful, live and let live; lie –, rest- upon one's oars; *laisser aller* [*F.*], *laisser faire* [*F.*]; stand aloof; refrain &c. (*avoid*) 623; keep oneself from doing; remit –, relax- one's efforts; desist &c. (*relinquish*) 624; stop &c. (*cease*) 142; pause &c. (*be quiet*) 265.

WAIT, lie in wait, bide one's time, take time, tide it over.

cool –, kick- one's heels; while away the -time, – tedious hours; pass –, fill up –, beguile- the time; talk against time; waste time &c. (*inactive*) 683.

lie by, lie on the shelf, lie idle, lie to, lie fallow; keep quiet, slug [*obs.*]; have nothing to do, whistle for want of thought; twiddle one's thumbs.

UNDO, do away with; take down, take to pieces; destroy &c. 162.

Adj. NOT DOING &c. *v.*; not done &c. *v.*; undone; passive; unoccupied, unemployed; out of -employ, – work, – a job; uncultivated, fallow; *désœuvré* [*F.*].

Adv. AT A STAND, *re infectâ* [*L.*], *les bras croisés* [*F.*], with folded arms; with the hands -in the pockets, – behind one's back; *pour passer le temps* [*F.*].

Int. STOP! &c. 142; hands off! so let it be! enough! no more! *bas!* [*Hind.*].

*** *cunctando restituit rem;* "inaction is cowardice" [Emerson].

---

682. Activity. — N. ACTIVITY; briskness, liveliness &c. *adj.*; animation, life, vivacity, spirit, verve, pep [*slang*], dash, go [*colloq.*], energy; snap, vim.

SMARTNESS, nimbleness, agility; quickness &c. *adj.*; velocity &c. 274; alacrity, promptitude; dispatch *or* despatch, expedition; haste &c. 684; punctuality &c. (*early*) 132.

EAGERNESS, zeal, ardor, enthusiasm, *perfervidum ingenium* [*L.*], *empressement* [*F.*], earnestness, intentness; *abandon* [*F.*]; vigor &c. (*physical energy*) 171;

683. Inactivity. — N. INACTIVITY; inaction &c. 681; inertness &c. 172; obstinacy &c. 606.

lull &c. (*cessation*) 142; quiescence &c. 265; rust, rustiness.

IDLENESS, remissness &c. *adj.*; sloth, indolence, indiligence [*rare*]; dawdling &c. *v.*; ergophobia, otiosity, hoboism [*U. S.*].

dull work; pottering; relaxation &c. (*loosening*) 47; Castle of Indolence.

LANGUOR; dullness &c. *adj.*; segnity [*obs.*], segnitude [*obs.*], lentor; sluggish-

devotion &c. (*resolution*) 604; exertion &c. 686.

INDUSTRY, assiduity; assiduousness &c. *adj.*; sedulity [*rare*], sedulousness; laboriousness; drudgery &c. (*labor*) 686; painstaking, diligence; perseverance &c. 604*a*; indefatigation [*obs.*]; businesslike habits, habits of business.

VIGILANCE &c. 459; wakefulness; sleeplessness, restlessness; insomnia; pervigilium, *insomnium* [*L.*]; racketing.

BUSTLE, hustle [*colloq.*], movement, stir, fuss, ado, bother, fidget, fidgetiness; flurry &c. (*haste*) 684.

OFFICIOUSNESS; dabbling, meddling; interference, interposition, intermeddling; butting in [*slang*], horning in [*slang*], intrusiveness, minding others' business, not minding one's own business; tampering with, intrigue.

PRESS OF BUSINESS, no sinecure, plenty to do, a great deal doing [*colloq.*], a lot going on [*colloq.*], many irons in the fire, great doings, busy hum of men, the madding crowd, the thick of things, battle of life, thick of the action.

MAN OF ACTION, busy bee; new broom; sharp fellow, blade; devotee, enthusiast, fanatic, zealot, hummer [*slang*], hustler [*colloq.*], humdinger [*slang, U. S.*], rustler [*slang, U. S.*]; live wire, human dynamo [*both colloq.*], live man [*U. S.*].

MEDDLER, intermeddler, intriguer, intrigant *or* intriguant, telltale, busybody, pickthank [*archaic*].

V. BE ACTIVE &c. *adj.*; busy oneself in; stir, stir about, stir one's stumps [*colloq.*]; bestir –, rouse- oneself; speed, hasten, peg away, lay about one, bustle, fuss; raise –, kick up- a dust; push; make a -fuss, – stir; go ahead, push forward; fight –, elbow- one's way; make progress &c. 282; toil &c. (*labor*) 686; moil, drudge, plod, persist &c. (*persevere*) 604*a*; keep up the ball; keep the pot boiling.

look sharp; have all one's eyes about one &c. (*vigilance*) 459; rise, arouse oneself, hustle [*colloq.*], push [*colloq.*], get up early, be about, keep moving, steal a march, catch a weasel asleep, kill two birds with one stone; seize the opportunity &c. 134; lose no time, not lose a moment, make the most of one's time, not suffer the grass to grow under one's feet, improve the shining hour, make short work of; dash off; make haste &c.

ness &c. (*slowness*) 275; procrastination &c. (*delay*) 133; torpor, torpidity, torpescence; stupor &c. (*insensibility*) 823; somnolence; drowsiness &c. *adj.*; nodding &c. *v.*; oscitation, oscitancy; pandiculation, hypnotism, lethargy; statuvolence *or* statuvolism; sand in the eyes, heaviness, heavy eyelids.

SLEEP, slumber; sound –, heavy –, balmy- sleep; Morpheus; Somnus; coma, trance, catalepsy, hypnosis, ecstasis, dream; hibernation; nap, doze, snooze [*colloq. or dial.*], siesta, wink of sleep, forty winks [*colloq.*]; snore; hypnology.

[CAUSE OF INACTIVITY] lullaby, *berceuse* [*F.*], *Schlummerlied* [*Ger.*]; anæsthesia *or* anesthesia, anæsthetic *or* anesthetic, opiate, sedative &c. 174.

IDLER, drone, dawdle [*rare*], dawdler; stiff, dead one [*both slang*], mopus [*obs.*], do-little, *fainéant* [*F.*], dummy, sleeping partner; afternoon farmer; truant &c. (*runaway*) 623; bummer [*U. S.*], bum [*slang, U. S.*], Weary Willie [*colloq.*], tramp, sundowner [*slang, Austral.*], hobo [*U. S.*], fakir *or* fakeer [*Moham.*], sunyasi [*Hind.*]; beggar, cadger [*slang*], lounge lizard [*slang, U. S.*], lounger, lazzarone, loafer; lubber, lubbard [*rare*]; slow coach &c. (*slow*) 275; opium –, lotus- eater; slug; laggard, sluggard; slumberer, the Dustman, the Sandman; the Fat Boy in Pickwick; dormouse, marmot; waiter on Providence, *fruges consumere natus* [*L.*]; Mr. Micawber.

V. BE INACTIVE &c. *adj.*; do nothing &c. 681; move slowly &c. 275; let the grass grow under one's feet; take one's time, dawdle, drawl, lag, hang back, slouch; loll, lollop [*colloq., Brit.*], lounge, poke, loaf, loiter; go to sleep over; sleep at one's post, *ne battre que d'une aile* [*F.*].

take it easy, take things as they come; lead an easy life, vegetate, swim with the stream, eat the bread of idleness; loll in the lap of -luxury, – indolence; waste –, consume –, kill –, lose- time; burn daylight, waste the precious hours.

DALLY, dilly-dally; idle –, trifle –, fritter –, fool- away time; spend –, take- time in; peddle, piddle; potter, putter [*U. S.*], dabble, faddle [*dial. Eng.*], fribble, fiddle-faddle.

SLEEP, slumber, be asleep; hibernate; oversleep; sleep like a -top, – log, – dormouse; sleep -soundly, – heavily;

684; do one's best, take pains &c. (*exert oneself*) 686; do -, work- wonders; have a lot of -kick [*colloq.*], - pep [*slang*].

have many irons in the fire, have one's hands full, have much on one's hands; have other -things to do, - fish to fry; be busy; not have a moment -to spare, - that one can call one's own.

HAVE ONE'S FLING, run the round of; go all lengths, stick at nothing, run riot.

OUTDO; overdo, overact, overlay, weigh down, overshoot the mark; make a toil of a pleasure.

HAVE A HAND IN &c. (*act in*) 680; take an active part, put in one's oar, have a finger in the pie, mix oneself up with, trouble one's head about, intrigue; agitate.

MEDDLE, tamper with, intermeddle, interfere, interpose; obtrude; poke -, thrust- one's nose in; butt in, horn in [*both slang*].

Adj. ACTIVE, brisk, - as a lark, - as a bee; lively, animated, vivacious; alive, - and kicking [*colloq.*]; frisky, spirited, stirring.

nimble, - as a squirrel; agile; light-footed, nimble-footed; featly tripping.

QUICK, prompt, yare [*archaic*], instant, ready, alert, spry [*colloq.* & *dial.*], sharp, smart; fast &c. (*swift*) 274; capable, smart as a steel trap, no sooner said than done &c. (*early*) 132; quick as a lamplighter, expeditious; awake, broad awake; go-ahead, live [*U. S.*], hustling [*colloq.*]; wide-awake &c. (*intelligent*) 498.

FORWARD, eager, ardent, strenuous, zealous, enterprising, in earnest; resolute &c. 604.

INDUSTRIOUS, assiduous, diligent, sedulous, notable [*obsoles. in this sense*], painstaking; intent &c. (*attention*) 457; indefatigable &c. (*persevering*) 604a; unwearied, never weary, sleepless, unsleeping, never tired; plodding, hard-working &c. 686; businesslike.

BUSTLING; restless, - as a hyena; fussy, fidgety, pottering; busy as a hen with one chicken.

WORKING, at work, on duty, in harness; up in arms; on one's legs, at call; up and -doing, - stirring; laboring, workday, workaday.

BUSY, occupied; hard at work, hard at it; up to one's ears in, full of business; busy as a -bee, - housewife.

MEDDLING &c. *v.*; meddlesome, pushing, officious, overofficious, *intrigant* [*F.*].

doze, drowse, snooze [*colloq. or dial.*], nap; take a nap &c. *n.*; dream; snore; settle -, go -, go off- to sleep; drop off [*colloq.*]; fall asleep, drop asleep; close -, seal up- -the -eyes, - eyelids; weigh down the eyelids; get sleepy, nod, yawn; go to bed, turn in, hit the hay [*slang*], rest in the arms of Morpheus.

LANGUISH, expend itself, flag, hang fire; relax.

RENDER IDLE &c. *adj.*; sluggardize; mitigate &c. 174.

Adj. INACTIVE; motionless &c. 265; unoccupied &c. (*doing nothing*) 681.

INDOLENT, lazy, slothful, idle, lusk [*obs.*], remiss, slack, inert, torpid, torpescent, sluggish, otiose, languid, supine, heavy, dull, leaden, lumpish; drony, dronish; lazy as Ludlam's dog.

dilatory, laggard; lagging &c. *v.*; slow &c. 275; rusty, flagging; fiddle-faddle; pottering &c. *v.*; shilly-shally &c. (*irresolute*) 605.

exanimate [*now rare*], soulless; listless; lackadaisical, maudlin.

SLEEPING &c. *v.*; asleep; fast -, dead -, sound- asleep; in a sound sleep; sound as a top, dormant, comatose; in the -arms, - lap- of Morpheus.

SLEEPY, sleepful [*rare*], full of sleep, oscitant, dozy, drowsy, somnolent, torpescent; lethargic or lethargical, somnifacient; statuvolent, statuvolic; heavy, heavy with sleep; nappy, somnific, somniferous; soporose or soporous, soporific, soporiferous; hypnotic; balmy, dreamy; unawakened, unwakened.

sedative &c. 174.

Adv. INACTIVELY &c. *adj.*; at leisure &c. 685; with half-shut eyes, half asleep; in dreams, in dreamland.

*** the eyes begin to draw straws; "bankrupt of life yet prodigal of ease" [Dryden]; "better fifty years of Europe than a cycle of Cathay" [Tennyson]; "idly busy rolls their world away" [Goldsmith]; "the mystery of folded sleep" [Tennyson]; "the timely dew of sleep" [Milton]; "thou driftest gently down the tides of sleep" [Longfellow]; "tired Nature's sweet restorer, balmy sleep" [Young]; "slumber lay so deep Even her hands upon her lap Seemed saturate with sleep" [De La Mare].

ASTIR, stirring; agoing, afoot; on foot; in full swing; eventful; on the alert &c. (*vigilant*) 459.

Adv. ACTIVELY &c. *adj.;* featly [*archaic*]; with life and spirit, with might and main &c. 686, with haste &c. 684, with wings; full tilt, *in mediis rebus* [*L.*].

Int. be –, look- -alive, – sharp! move on! push on! keep moving! go ahead! stir your stumps! [*colloq.*]; *age quod agis!* [*L.*], *jaldi!* [*Hind.*], *jaldi karo!* [*Hind.*], step lively!

⁎⁎ *carpe diem* &c. (*opportunity*) 134; *nulla dies sine lineâ* [Pliny]; *nec mora nec requies* [Vergil]; the plot thickens; *veni vidi vici* [Suetonius]; *abends wird der Faule fleissig; dictum ac factum* [Terence]; *schwere Arbeit in der Jugend ist sanfte Ruhe im Alter;* "the busy hum of men" [Milton]; "they shall run and not be weary; they shall walk and not faint [*Bible*]; "Life, not the daily coil, but as it is Lived in its beauty in eternity" [Masefield].

---

684. Haste. — N. HASTE, urgency, dispatch *or* despatch, acceleration, spurt *or* spirt, forced march, rush, scurry *or* skurry, scuttle, dash; velocity &c. 274; precipitancy, precipitation, precipitousness &c. *adj.;* impetuosity; *brusquerie* [*F.*]; hurry, drive, scramble, bustle, fuss, fidget, flurry, flutter, splutter.

V. HASTE, hasten; make haste, make a dash &c. *n.;* hurry -, dash -, whip -, push -, press- -on, – forward; hurry, scurry *or* skurry, scuttle along, bundle on, dart to and fro, bustle, flutter, scramble; plunge, – headlong; dash off; rush &c. (*violence*) 173; express, railroad [*colloq., U. S.*].

BESTIR ONESELF &c. (*be active*) 682; lose -no time, – not a moment, – not an instant; make short work of; make the best of one's -time, – way.

685. Leisure. — N. LEISURE; convenience; spare -time, – hours, - moments; vacant hour; time, – to spare, – to burn [*slang, U. S.*], – on one's hands; holiday &c. (*rest*) 687; *otium cum dignitate* [*Cic.*]; ease.

V. HAVE LEISURE &c. *n.;* take one's -time, – leisure, – ease; repose &c. 687; move slowly &c. 275; while away the time &c. (*inaction*) 681; be master of one's time, be an idle man; *desipere in loco* [*L.*].

⁎⁎ time hanging heavy on one's hands; *eile mit Weile;* my time is at your disposal; "retiréd Leisure That in trim gardens takes his pleasure" [Milton]; "Shall I not take mine ease in mine inn?" [Shakespeare].

---

be precipitate &c. *adj.;* jump at, be in haste, be in a hurry &c. *n.;* have -no time -, have not a moment- -to lose, – to spare; work against time, work under pressure.

QUICKEN &c. 274; accelerate, expedite, put on, precipitate, urge, whip, spur, flog, goad.

Adj. HASTY, hurried, brusque; scrambling, cursory, precipitate, headlong, furious, boisterous, impetuous, hot-headed; feverish, fussy; pushing.

IN HASTE, in a hurry &c. *n.;* in hot haste, in all haste; breathless, pressed for time, hard pressed, urgent.

Adv. WITH HASTE, with all haste, with breathless speed; in haste &c. *adj.;* apace &c. (*swiftly*) 274; amain; all at once &c. (*instantaneously*) 113; at short notice &c., immediately &c. (*early*) 132; posthaste; by cable, by telegraph, by wireless [*colloq.*], by aëroplane, by return mail, by steam [*colloq.*], by forced marches.

HASTILY, precipitately &c. *adj.;* helter-skelter, hurry-skurry, holus-bolus; slap-dash, slap-bang; full-tilt, full-drive; heels over head, head and shoulders, headlong, *à corps perdu* [*F.*].

BY FITS AND STARTS, by spurts; hop skip and jump.

Int. RUSH! immediate! urgent! look alive! *jaldi karo!* [*Hind.*]; get a move on! [*colloq.*], get a wiggle on! [*colloq.*]; quickmarch! [*mil.*], double! [*mil.*]; gallop! charge! [*mil.*].

⁎⁎ *sauve qui peut,* devil take the hindmost, no time to be lost; sharp is the word; no sooner said than done &c. (*early*) 132; a word and a blow; *maggiore frétta minore átto; ohne Hast aber ohne Rast* [Goethe's motto]; "stand not upon the order of your going" [*Macbeth*]; "swift, swift, you dragons of the night" [*Cymbeline*].

686. Exertion. — **N.** EXERTION, effort, strain, tug, pull, stress, throw, stretch, struggle, spell, spurt *or* spirt; stroke –, stitch- of work.

"a long pull, a strong pull, and a pull all together"; dead lift; heft [*dial.*]; wear and tear; ado; toil and trouble; uphill –, hard –, warm- work; harvest time.

EXERCISE, exercitation, practice, play, gymnastics, field sports; breather [*colloq.*], racing, running, jumping, riding &c.

LABOR, work, toil, travail [*rare*], manual labor, sweat of one's brow, swink [*obs.*], operoseness, drudgery, slavery, fag [*colloq., Eng.*], faggery, fagging, hammering; *limæ labor* [*L.*]; operosity [*obs.*], operoseness.

trouble, pains, duty; resolution &c. 604; energy &c. (*physical*) 171.

WORKER, plodder, laborer, drudge, fagger, fag [*Eng. schools*], slave; man of action &c. 682; agent &c. 690; Samson, Hercules.

V. EXERT ONESELF; exert –, tax- one's energies; use exertion.

LABOR, work, toil, moil, sweat, fag, swink [*archaic*], toil and moil, drudge, slave, drag a lengthened chain, wade through, strive, strain; make –, stretch- a long arm; pull, tug, ply; ply –, tug at- the oar; do the work; take the laboring oar.

bestir oneself (*be active*) 682; take trouble, trouble oneself.

WORK HARD; rough it; put forth -one's strength, – a strong arm; fall to work, bend the bow; buckle to, set one's shoulder to the wheel &c. (*resolution*) 604; work like a -horse, – cart horse, – dog, – galley slave, – coal heaver, – Briton; labor –, work- day and night; redouble one's efforts; do double duty; work double -hours, – tides; sit up, burn the candle at both ends, burn the midnight oil; stick to &c. (*persevere*) 604a; work –, fight- one's way; lay about one, hammer at.

DO ONE'S BEST, do one's level best, do one's utmost; take pains; do the best one can, do all one can, do all in one's power, do as much as in one lies, do what lies in one's power; use one's -best, – utmost- endeavor; try one's- -best, – utmost; play one's best card; put one's -best, – right- leg foremost; put one's best foot foremost; have one's whole soul in his work, put all one's strength into, strain every nerve; spare no -efforts, –pains; go all lengths; go through fire and water &c. (*resolution*) 604; move heaven and earth, leave no stone unturned.

Adj. laboring &c. *v.*

LABORIOUS, hefty [*colloq., U. S.*], operose, elaborate; strained; toilsome, troublesome, wearisome, burdensome; uphill; herculean, gymnastic, palæstric *or* palestric, athletic.

HARDWORKING, painstaking, strenuous, energetic, never idle.

hard at work, on the stretch, on the move, on the jump, on the dead jump, on the run.

Adv. LABORIOUSLY &c. *adj.*; lustily; *pugnis et calcibus* [*L.*]; with might and main, with all one's might, with a strong hand, with sledge hammer, with much ado; to the best of one's abilities, *totis viribus* [*L.*], *vi et armis* [*L.*], *manibus*

687. Repose. — **N.** REPOSE, rest, silken repose; sleep &c. 683.

relaxation, breathing time; halt, stay, pause &c. (*cessation*) 142; respite.

DAY OF REST, *dies non* [*L.*], Sabbath, Lord's day, Sunday, First Day, holiday, red-letter day; gala day &c. (*amusement*) 840; vacation, recess.

V. REPOSE; rest, rest and be thankful; take rest, take one's ease.

lie down; recline, recline on a bed of down, recline on an easychair; go to -rest, – bed, – sleep &c. 683.

RELAX, unbend, slacken; take breath &c. (*refresh*) 689; rest upon one's oars; pause &c. (*cease*) 142; stay one's hand.

take a holiday, shut up shop; lie fallow &c. (*inaction*) 681.

Adj. REPOSING &c. *v.*; unstrained.

HOLIDAY, festal, ferial [*rare*]; sabbatic *or* sabbatical.

Adv. at rest.

** "the best of men have ever loved repose" [Thomson]; "to repair our nature with comforting repose" [*Henry VIII*]; "The nightly mercy of the eventide" [Masefield].

pedibusque [*L.*], tooth and nail, *unguibus et rostro* [*L.*], hammer and tongs, heart and soul; through thick and thin &c. (*perseverance*) 604a.

by the sweat of one's brow, *suo Marte* [*L.*].

. *aide-toi, le ciel t'aidera;* "and still be doing, never done" [Butler]; *buen principio la mitad es hecha; cosa ben fatta è fatta due volte;* "it is better to wear out than to rust out" [Bp. Horne]; *labor omnia vincit* [Vergil]; "labor, wide as the earth, hās its summit in Heaven" [Carlyle]; *le travail du corps délivre des peines de l'esprit; manu forti; ora et labora;* "I wish to preach . . . the doctrine of the strenuous life" [Roosevelt]; "Sorrow of soul in toil, that brings delight" [Masefield].

688. Fatigue. — N. FATIGUE; weariness &c. 841; yawning, drowsiness &c. 683; lassitude, tiredness, fatigation [*obs.*], sweat.

SHORTNESS OF BREATH; anhelation [*rare*], dyspnœa *or* dyspnea, panting, labored breathing.

FAINTNESS, fainting, swoon, goneness, exhaustion, collapse, prostration, deliquium, syncope, lipothymy.

V. BE FATIGUED &c. *adj.;* yawn &c. (*get sleepy*) 683; droop, sink, flag; lose breath, lose wind; gasp, pant, puff, blow, drop, swoon, faint, succumb.

FATIGUE, tire, bore, weary, irk [*chiefly impersonal, as,* it irks me], flag, jade, harass, exhaust, knock up, wear out, bleed white, prostrate.

TAX, task, strain; overtask, overwork, overburden, overtax, overstrain, fag, fag out.

Adj. FATIGUED &c. *v.;* weary &c. 841; drowsy &c. 683; drooping &c. *v.;* haggard; toilworn, wayworn; footsore, surbated [*obs.*], weather-beaten; faint; done, done up, used up, knocked up [*all colloq.*]; bushed [*slang or dial., Amer.*]; exhausted, prostrate, spent; overtired, overspent, overfatigued; unrefreshed, unrestored.

ready to drop, all in [*slang*], more dead than alive, dog-weary, dog-tired, walked off one's legs, tired to death, on one's last legs, played out, *hors de combat* [*F.*].

WORN, worn out; battered, shattered, pulled down, seedy [*colloq.*], enfeebled, altered.

BREATHLESS, windless; short of –, out of –breath, – wind; blown, puffing and blowing; short-breathed; anhelose; broken-winded, short-winded; dyspnœal *or* dyspneal, dyspnœic *or* dyspneic.

. "weary and old with service" [*Henry VIII*]; "the weariness, the fever, and the fret" [Keats]; "When Ajax strives some rock's vast weight to throw, The line too labours and the words move slow" [Pope].

689. Refreshment. — N. RECUPERATION; recovery of strength &c. 159; refreshing, bracing &c. *v.;* restoration, revival &c. 660; repair, refection, refocillation [*obs.*], refreshment, regale, regalement, bait; relief &c. 834.

V. REFRESH; brace &c. (*strengthen*) 159; reinvigorate; air, freshen up, recruit; repair &c. (*restore*) 660; fan, refocillate [*obs.*]; refresh the inner man; get better, raise one's head; recover –, regain –, renew- one's strength &c. 159; perk up.

BREATHE, respire; drink in the ozone; draw –, take –, gather –, take a long –, regain –, recover- breath.

RECUPERATE; come to oneself &c. (*revive*) 660; feel like a giant refreshed.

Adj. REFRESHING &c. *v.;* recuperative &c. 660.

REFRESHED &c. *v.;* untired, unwearied.

. "they that wait upon the Lord shall renew their strength; they shall mount up with wings as eagles" [*Bible*].

690. Agent. — N. AGENT, doer, actor, performer, perpetrator, operator; executor, executrix; practitioner, worker, old stager; mediary, medium, reagent.

minister &c. (*instrument*) 631; representative &c. (*commissioner*) 758, (*deputy*) 759; factor, steward.

SERVANT &c. 746; factotum, general, maid-of-all-work, servant-of-all-work, do-all [*colloq.*].

[COMPARISONS] bee, ant, working bee, termite, white ant; laboring oar; shaft horse.

WORKMAN, artisan; craftsman, handicraftsman; mechanic, operative; workingman, laboring man; hewers of wood and drawers of water, laborer, navvy [*Eng.*];

hand, man, day laborer, journeyman, hack; mere tool &c. 633; beast of burden, drudge, fag; lumper, stevedore, roustabout [U. S.].

maker, artificer, *artifex* [L.], artist, wright, manufacturer, architect, contractor, builder, mason, bricklayer, smith, forger, Vulcan; carpenter; platelayer; blacksmith, locksmith, sailmaker, tailor, cordwainer, wheelwright.

machinist, mechanician, engineer, electrician, plumber, gasfitter.

WORKWOMAN, charwoman, seamstress *or* sempstress, needlewoman, laundress, washerwoman, "Madonna of the tubs" [Phelps].

COWORKER, associate, fellow worker, coöperator, colleague, *confrère* [F.]; party to, participator in, *particeps criminis* [L.], *dramatis personæ* [L.]; *personnel* [F.].

. *quorum pars magna fui* [Vergil]; *faber est quisque fortunæ suæ.*

691. Workshop. — N. WORKSHOP, workhouse; laboratory, manufactory, armory, arsenal, mill, factory, *usine* [F.], mint, loom; cabinet, bureau, studio, *atelier* [F.]; hive, hive of industry; plant; hothouse, hotbed; kitchen; alveary, beehive; bindery, forcing pit, nailery, dock, dockyard, slip, yard, wharf; foundry *or* foundery, forge, furnace; vineyard, orchard, nursery, truck garden, truck farm, farm.

melting pot, crucible, caldron *or* cauldron, mortar, alembic; matrix.

2. *Complex Voluntary Action*

692. Conduct. — N. CONDUCT, behavior; deportment, comportment; carriage, *maintien* [F.], demeanor, guise, bearing, manner, observance.

course -, line- of -conduct, – action, – proceeding; rôle; process, ways, practice, procedure, *modus operandi* [L.]; method &c., path &c. 627.

DEALING, transaction &c. (*action*) 680; business &c. 625.

POLICY, polity; tactics, game, generalship, statesmanship, seamanship; strategy, strategics; plan &c. 626.

MANAGEMENT; government &c. (*direction*) 693; stewardship, husbandry; housekeeping, housewifery; ménage *or* menage; régime *or* regime, regimen, economy; economics; political economy.

CAREER, life, course, walk, province, race, record; execution, manipulation, treatment; campaign.

V. TRANSACT, execute; dispatch *or* despatch, proceed with, discharge; carry -on, – through, – out, – into effect; work out; go through, get through; enact; put into practice; officiate &c. 625.

bear -, behave -, comport -, demean -, carry -, conduct -, acquit- oneself.

run a race, lead a life, play a game; take -, adopt- a course; steer -, shape- one's course; play one's part, play one's cards; shift for oneself; paddle one's own canoe; bail one's own boat.

conduct; manage &c. (*direct*) 693.

DEAL WITH, have to do with; treat, handle a case; take -steps, – measures.

Adj. CONDUCTING &c. *v.*; directive, strategic *or* strategical, methodical, businesslike, practical, executive; economic.

. "it is their care that the wheels run truly" [Kipling].

693. Direction. — N. DIRECTION; management, managery [*obs.*]; government, gubernation [*obs.*], conduct, legislation, regulation, guidance; bossism [*slang, U. S.*]; legislature; steerage, pilotage; reins, – of government; helm, rudder, needle, compass; guiding star, lodestar *or* loadstar, polestar; cynosure.

ministry, ministration; administration; stewardship, proctorship; chair; agency.

SUPERVISION, superintendence; surveillance, oversight; eye of the master; control, charge; auspices; board of control &c. (*council*) 696; command &c. (*authority*) 737.

STATESMANSHIP; statecraft, kingcraft, queencraft; premiership, senatorship; director &c. 694; seat, portfolio.

V. DIRECT, manage, govern, conduct; order, prescribe, cut out work for; head, lead; lead the way, show the way; take the lead, lead on; regulate, guide, steer, pilot; take the helm, be at the helm; have –, handle –, hold –, take- the reins; drive, tool [*cant*], tackle.

SUPERINTEND, supervise; overlook, oversee, control, keep in order, look after, see to, legislate for; administer, ministrate [*obs*.]; matronize; patronize; have the -care, – charge- of; have –, take- the direction; pull the -strings, – wires; rule &c. (*command*) 737; be the guiding force; have –, hold- -office, – the portfolio; preside, – at the board; take –, occupy –, be in- the chair; pull the stroke oar.

Adj. DIRECTING &c. *v.;* executive, gubernatorial, supervisory; hegemonic *or* hegemonical; predominant; statesmanlike.

Adv. IN CHARGE OF, under the guidance of, under the auspices of; in control of, at the helm, at the head of.

694. Director. — N. DIRECTOR, manager, governor, rector [*rare*], controller, comptroller; superintendent, supervisor; intendant; overseer, overlooker; supercargo, husband [*archaic*], inspector, foreman, ganger [*Eng*.], visitor, ranger, surveyor, ædile *or* edile [*Rom. hist*.], moderator, monitor, taskmaster; master &c. 745; leader, ringleader, agitator, demagogue, corypheus, conductor, fugleman, precentor, bellwether; *caporal* [*F*.], choregus, collector, file leader, flugelman, linkboy.

GUIDING STAR &c. (*guidance*) 693; adviser &c. 695; guide &c. (*information*) 527; pilot; helmsman; steersman, steersmate [*obs*.]; wire-puller.

DRIVER, whip, jehu [*humorous*], charioteer; coachman, carman, cabman; postilion, *vetturino* [*It*.], muleteer, *arriero* [*Sp*.], teamster; whipper-in; chauffeur, motorman, engine-driver.

HEAD, headman, chief, principal, president, speaker; chair, chairman; captain &c. (*master*) 745; superior; mayor &c. (*civil authority*) 745; vice-president, prime minister, premier, vizier *or* vizir, grand vizier, eparch.

OFFICER, functionary, minister, official, red-tape, red-tapist, bureaucrat; Jack in office; office bearer, office holder; person in authority &c. 745.

STATESMAN, strategist, legislator, lawgiver, politician, statist [*rare*], statemonger; Minos, Draco; arbiter &c. (*judge*) 967; boss [*slang*, *U. S*.], political dictator, power behind the throne, kingmaker; secretary, – of state; Reis Effendi; vicar &c. (*deputy*) 759; board &c. (*council*) 696.

STEWARD, factor; agent &c. 758; bailiff, middleman; clerk of works; landreeve; factotum, major-domo, seneschal, housekeeper, shepherd; croupier; proctor, procurator, curator, librarian.

Adv. *ex officio.*

⁎⁎ "drest in a little brief authority" [Shakespeare]; "it is excellent To have a giant's strength; but it is tyrannous To use it as a giant" [*ibid*.].

695. Advice. — N. ADVICE, counsel, adhortation [*obs*.]; word to the wise; suggestion, submonition [*obs*.], recommendation, advocacy; advisement [*archaic*]; consultation.

EXHORTATION &c. (*persuasion*) 615; expostulation &c. (*dissuasion*) 616; admonition &c. (*warning*) 668; guidance &c. (*direction*) 693.

INSTRUCTION, charge, injunction; Governor's –, President's- message; King's –, Queen's- speech; message, speech from the throne.

ADVISER, prompter; counsel, counselor; monitor, mentor, Nestor, sage, wise man, wise woman; *magnus Apollo* [*L*.], senator; teacher &c. 540; yogi *or* yogin; physician, leech [*archaic*]; archiater; arbiter &c. (*judge*) 967.

GUIDE, manual, chart &c. (*information*) 527.

CONSULTATION, conference, *pourparler* [*F*.], parley, powwow [*U. S*.]; reference, referment.

V. ADVISE, counsel; give -advice, – counsel, – a piece of advice; suggest, prompt, submonish [*obs*.], recommend, prescribe, advocate; exhort &c. (*persuade*) 615.

ENJOIN, enforce, charge, instruct, call; call upon &c. (*request*) 765; dictate.

EXPOSTULATE &c. (*dissuade*) 616; admonish &c. (*warn*) 668.

ADVISE WITH; lay heads –,consult- together; compare notes; hold a council, deliberate, be closeted with.

CONFER, consult, refer to, call in; follow, follow implicitly; take –, follow- advice; be advised by, have at one's elbow, take one's cue from.

Adj. RECOMMENDATORY; hortative &c. (*persuasive*) 615; dehortatory &c. (*dissuasive*) 616; admonitory &c. (*warning*) 668; consultative; dictatory, dictatorial; didactic.

Int. go to!

***** "give every man thine ear but few thy voice" [*Hamlet*]; "I am Sir Oracle, And when I ope my lips, let no dog bark!" [*M. of V.*]; "I pray thee cease thy counsel" [*Much Ado About Nothing*]; "my guide, philosopher and friend" [Pope]; "'twas good advice and meant, my son be good" [Crabbe]; *verbum sat sapienti; vive memor lethi* (or *leti*); "we ask advice but we mean approbation" [Colton].

696. Council.— N. COUNCIL, committee, subcommittee, comitia [*Rom. hist.*], privy council, court, chamber, cabinet, board, bench, staff.

junta, divan, musnud, sanhedrin or sanhedrim [*Jewish antiq.*], amphictyonic council [*Gr. hist.*]; syndicate; court of appeal &c. (*tribunal*) 966; board of -control, – works; county council, local board, parish council, common council, town meeting; board of overseers; zemstvo [*Russ.*].

[ECCLESIASTICAL] convocation, synod, congregation, church, chapter, directory, vestry, consistory, conventicle, conclave, convention, classis.

LEGISLATURE, parliament, congress, national council, states-general, diet.

Duma [*Russia*], Storthing or Storting [*Norway*], Rigsdag [*Denmark*], Riksdag [*Sweden*], Cortes [Spain], Reichsrath or Reichsrat [*Austria*], Volksraad [*Dutch*]; Dail Eireann [*Sinn Fein*]; witan, witenagemot or witenagemote [*Anglo-Saxon hist.*].

UPPER HOUSE, upper chamber, first chamber, senate, *senatus* [*Rom. hist.*], legislative council, House of Lords, House of Peers; Bundesrath or Bundesrat [*Ger.*], federal council, Lagting [*Nor.*], Landsthing [*Den.*].

LOWER HOUSE, lower chamber, second chamber, house of representatives, House of Commons, the house, legislative assembly, chamber of deputies; Odelsting [*Nor.*], Folkething [*Den.*], Reichstag [*Ger.*].

ASSEMBLY, plenum, caucus, clique; meeting, sitting, séance, *camarilla* [*Sp.*], conference, hearing, session, palaver, *pourparler* [*F.*], durbar [*India*]; quorum; council fire [*N. Am.*], powwow [*U. S.*].

[REPRESENTATIVES] congressman, M. C., senator, representative; member, – of parliament, M. P.; representative of the people; assemblyman, councilor.

Adj. curule, congressional, senatorial, parliamentary; synodic or synodical.

697. Precept. — N. PRECEPT, direction, instruction, charge; prescript, prescription; recipe, receipt; golden rule; maxim &c. 496.

rule, canon, law, code, *corpus juris* [*L.*], *lex scripta* [*L.*], convention; unwritten law; canon law; act, statute, rubric, stage direction, regulation; model, form, formula, formulary; technicality; nice point, fine point, norm.

order &c. (*command*) 741.

698. Skill. — N. SKILL, skillfulness or skilfulness, address; dexterity, dexterousness or dextrousness, adroitness, expertness &c. *adj.*; proficiency, competence, craft; callidity [*rare*], callidness, facility, knack, trick, sleight; mastery, mastership; excellence, panurgy [*rare*]; ambidexterity, ambidextrousness; sleight of hand &c. (*deception*) 545.

seamanship, airmanship, marksmanship, horsemanship; rope-dancing; tightrope –, slack-rope- walking.

699. Unskillfulness. — N. UNSKILLFULNESS or unskilfulness &c. *adj.*; want of skill &c. 698; incompetence or incompetency; inability, infelicity, indexterity [*rare*], clumsiness, inaptitude &c. *adj.*; inexperience; disqualification, unproficiency; quackery.

FOLLY, stupidity &c. 499; indiscretion &c. (*rashness*) 863; thoughtlessness &c. (*inattention*) 458, (*neglect*) 460; sabotage [*F.*].

MISMANAGEMENT, misconduct, mis-

ACCOMPLISHMENT, acquirement, attainment; art, science; finish, finished execution, technique, technic, practical -, technical- knowledge; technology.

WORLD WISDOM, knowledge of the world, *savoir faire* [*F.*]; tact; mother wit &c. (*sagacity*) 498; discretion &c. (*caution*) 864; finesse; craftiness &c. (*cunning*) 702; management &c. (*conduct*) 692; self-help.

CLEVERNESS, talent, ability, ingenuity, capacity, parts, talents, faculty, endowment, forte, turn, gift, genius; intelligence &c. 498; sharpness, readiness &c. (*activity*) 682; invention &c. 515; aptness, aptitude; turn for, capacity for, genius for; felicity, capability, *curiosa felicitas* [*L.*], qualification, habilitation.

PROFICIENT, expert, adept &c. 700.

MASTERPIECE, masterwork, *coup de maître* [*F.*,] *chef d'œuvre* [*F.*], *tour de force* [*F.*]; good stroke &c. (*plan*) 626.

V. BE SKILLFUL &c. *adj.*; excel in, be master of; have a turn for &c. *n.*

KNOW WHAT'S WHAT, know- a hawk from a handsaw, - what one is about, - on which side one's bread is buttered, - what's o'clock is, - what o'clock it is, - the time of day, - a thing or two, - the ropes; have cut one's -eyeteeth, - wisdom teeth; see through a millstone; be up to [*all colloq.*].

see one's way, see where the wind lies, see which way the wind blows; have all one's wits about one, have one's hand in; *savoir vivre* [*F.*]; *scire quid valeant humeri quid ferre recusent* [*L*].

look after the main chance; cut one's coat according to one's cloth; live by one's wits; exercise one's discretion, feather the oar, sail near the wind; stoop to conquer &c. (*cunning*) 702; play one's cards well, play one's best card; hit the right nail on the head, put the saddle on the right horse.

TAKE ADVANTAGE OF, make the most of; profit by &c. (*use*) 677; make a hit &c. (*succeed*) 731; make a virtue of necessity; make hay while the sun shines &c. (*occasion*) 134.

Adj. SKILLFUL *or* skilful, dexterous *or* dextrous, adroit, expert, apt, handy, quick, deft, ready, slick [*slang*], smart &c. (*active*) 682; proficient, good at, up to, at home in, master of, a good hand at, *au fait* [*F.*[, thoroughbred, masterly,

feasance; inexpedience, bad policy, impolicy; maladministration; misrule, misgovernment, misapplication, misdirection.

ABSENCE OF RULE, rule of thumb; bungling &c. *v.;* failure &c. 732; screw loose; too many cooks.

BLUNDER &c. (*mistake*) 495; *étourderie* [*F.*], *gaucherie* [*F.*], act of folly, *balourdise* [*F.*], bungle, botch, botchery; bad job, sad work.

sprat sent out to catch a whale, butterfly broken on a wheel, tempest in a teacup, storm in a teacup, much ado about nothing, wild-goose chase.

BUNGLER &c. 701; fool &c. 501; hen with its head cut off [*colloq.*].

V. BE UNSKILLFUL *or* unskilful, &c. *adj.;* not see an inch beyond one's nose; blunder, bungle, muff [*esp., baseball*], boggle, fumble, botch, mar, spoil, bitch [*obs.*], flounder, stumble, trip; hobble &c. 275; put one's foot in it [*colloq.*]; make a -mess, - hash, - sad work- of [*all colloq.*]; overshoot the mark.

play tricks with, play Puck; mismanage, misconduct, misdirect, misapply, missend.

ACT FOOLISHLY; stultify -, make a fool of -, commit- oneself; play the fool; put oneself out of court; lose one's -head, - senses, - cunning; begin at the wrong end; do things by halves &c. (*not complete*) 730; make two bites of a cherry; play at cross-purposes; strain at a gnat and swallow a camel &c. (*caprice*) 608; put the cart before the horse; lock the stable door when the horse is stolen &c. (*too late*) 135.

not know what one is about, not know one's own interest, not know on which side one's bread is buttered; stand in one's own light, quarrel with one's bread and butter, throw a stone in one's own garden, kill the goose which lays the golden eggs, pay dear for one's whistle, cut one's own throat, burn one's fingers; knock -, run- one's head against a stone wall; bring the house about one's ears; have too many -eggs in one basket (*imprudent*) 863, - irons in the fire.

cut blocks with a razor; hold a farthing candle to the sun &c. (*useless*) 645; fight with -, grasp at- a shadow; catch at straws, lean on a broken reed, reckon without one's host, pursue a wild-goose chase; go on a fool's errand,

crack [*colloq.*], crackajack [*slang*], accomplished; conversant &c. (*knowing*) 490.

EXPERIENCED, practiced, skilled; up in, well up in; in practice; competent, efficient, qualified, capable, fitted, fit for, up to the mark, up and coming [*dial., U. S.*], trained, initiated, prepared, primed, finished.

CLEVER, cute [*colloq.*], able, ingenious, felicitous, gifted, talented, endowed; inventive &c. 515; shrewd, sharp &c. (*intelligent*) 498; cunning &c. 702; alive to, up to snuff [*slang*], not to be caught with chaff; discreet.

neat-handed, fine-fingered, nimble-fingered, ambidextrous, sure-footed; cut out for [*colloq.*], fitted for.

technical, artistic, scientific, dædalian, shipshapelike, workmanlike, business-like, statesmanlike.

Adv. SKILLFULLY *or* skilfully &c. *adj.*; well &c. 618; artistically; with skill, with fine techique, with consummate skill; *secundum artem* [*L.*], *suo Marte* [*L.*]; to the best of one's abilities &c. (*exertion*) 686; like a machine.

*** *ars celare artem; artes honorabit; celui qui veut celui-là peut; c'est une grande habileté que de savoir cacher son habileté; expertus metuit* [Horace]; *es bildet ein Talent sich in der Stille sich ein Charakter in dem Strom der Welt;* "heart to conceive, the understanding to direct, or the hand to execute" [Junius].

go on a sleeveless errand [*obs.*]; go further and fare worse; fail &c. 732.

MISTAKE &c. 495; take the shadow for the substance &c. (*credulity*) 486; bark up the wrong tree; be in the wrong box, aim at a pigeon and kill a crow; take –, get- -the wrong pig by the tail, – the wrong sow by the ear, – the dirty end of the stick [*all colloq.*]; put the saddle on the wrong horse, put a square thing into a round hole, put new wine into old bottles; lose one's way, miss one's way; fall into a trap, catch a Tartar.

Adj. UNSKILLFUL *or* unskilful &c. 698; unskilled, inexpert; bungling &c. *v.*; awkward, clumsy, unhandy, lubberly, *gauche* [*F.*], maladroit; left-handed, heavy-handed; slovenly, slatternly; gawky.

adrift, at fault.

INAPT, unapt; inhabile [*obs.*]; untractable, unteachable; giddy &c. (*inattentive*) 458; inconsiderate &c. (*neglectful*) 460; stupid &c. 499; inactive &c. 683; incompetent; unqualified, disqualified, ill-qualified; unfit; quackish; raw, green, inexperienced, rusty, out of practice.

UNACCUSTOMED, unused, untrained &c. 537, uninitiated, unconversant &c. (*ignorant*) 491; unbusinesslike, unpractical, shiftless; unstatesmanlike.

ILL-ADVISED, unadvised, misadvised; ill-devised, ill-imagined, ill-judged, ill-contrived, ill-conducted; unguided, misguided; misconducted, foolish, wild; infelicitous; penny wise and pound foolish &c. (*inconsistent*) 608.

*** one's fingers being all thumbs; the right hand forgets its cunning; *il se noyerait dans une goutte d'eau; incidit in Scyllam qui vult vitare Charybdim;* out of the frying pan into the fire; *non omnia possumus omnes* [Vergil].

700. Proficient. — **N.** PROFICIENT, expert, adept; dab, dabster [*both colloq. or dial.*], connoisseur &c. (*scholar*) 492; master, – hand; top sawyer, prima donna, *première danseuse* [*F.*], first fiddle, *chef de cuisine* [*F.*]; protagonist; past master; mahatma.

nice –, good –, clean- hand; practiced –, experienced- -eye, – hand; marksman; good –, dead –, crack- shot [*colloq.*]; ropedancer, ropewalker, funambulist; contortionist, acrobat; conjuror &c. (*deceiver*) 548; wizard &c. 994.

PICKED MAN; medallist, prizeman, honorsman.

701. Bungler. — **N.** BUNGLER; blunderer, blunderhead; marplot, fumbler, lubber, clown, lout, duffer [*colloq.*]; stick, poor stick, odd stick [*all colloq.*]; bad –, poor- -hand, – shot; butter-fingers [*colloq.*], fumble-fist [*colloq.*].

no conjuror; flat, muff, muffer, slow coach [*all colloq.*]; looby, swab [*slang & dial.*], doit, yokel [*Eng.*], clod; awkward squad, novice, greenhorn, *blanc-bec* [*F.*], galoot [*slang*].

fish out of water, ass in lion's skin, jackdaw in peacock's feathers; quack &c. (*deceiver*) 548; Lord of Misrule, Abbot of Unreason [*both obs. or hist.*].

VETERAN; old -stager, – campaigner, – soldier, – file, – hand; man of business, man of the world.

GENIUS; master -mind, – head, – spirit.

PANTOLOGIST, Admirable Crichton, Jack of all trades; prodigy of learning, walking encyclopedia, mine of information.

MAN OF CUNNING; cunning –, sharp- -blade, – fellow; diplomatist, diplomat, Machiavellian; politician, jobber; tactician, strategist.

PECULATOR, forger, coiner; cracksman &c. 792.

LANDLUBBER, fresh-water sailor, fair-weather sailor, horse marine.

SLOVEN, slattern, traipse or trapes [obs. or dial. Eng.], slut.

. il n'a pas inventé la poudre; he will never set the Thames on fire; acierta errando; aliquis in omnibus nullus in singulis; "They called us the seasick scull'ry maids, An' we called 'em the Ass-Marines" [Kipling].

---

702. Cunning. — N. CUNNING, craft; cunningness, craftiness &c. adj.; subtlety, subtilty, subtility [rare]; the cunning of the -serpent, – Old Boy [slang]; artificiality; maneuvering or manœuvring &c. v.; temporization; circumvention.

CHICANE, chicanery; sharp practice, knavery, jugglery; concealment &c. 528; guile, a nigger in the woodpile [colloq.], doubling, duplicity &c. (falsehood) 544; foul play.

DIPLOMACY, politics; Machiavellianism or Machiavellism; gerrymander, jobbery, back-stairs influence.

ARTIFICE, art, device, machination; plot &c. (plan) 626; maneuver, stratagem, dodge, artful dodge, wile; trick, trickery &c. (deception) 545; ruse, ruse de guerre [F.]; finesse, side blow, thin end of the wedge, shift, go-by [colloq.], subterfuge, evasion; white lie &c. (untruth) 546; juggle, tour de force [F.]; tricks -of the trade, – upon travelers; gold brick [colloq., U. S.], imposture, deception; espièglerie [F.]; net, trap &c. 545.

SCHEMER, trickster, keener [Western U. S.], Philadelphia lawyer [colloq., U. S.]; sly boots [humorous], fox, reynard; intriguer, intrigant; repeater [U. S. politics], floater [U. S.]; man of cunning &c. 700; horse trader; Indian giver [colloq., U. S.].

Ulysses, Machiavelli or Machiavel.

V. BE CUNNING &c. adj.; have cut one's eyeteeth; contrive &c. (plan) 626; live by one's wits; maneuver or manœuvre; intrigue, gerrymander, finesse, double, temporize, stoop to conquer, reculer pour mieux sauter [F.], circumvent, steal a march upon; outdo, get the better of, snatch a thing from under one's nose, have a nigger in the wood-pile [colloq.]; overreach &c. 545; throw off one's guard; surprise &c. 508; snatch a verdict; waylay, undermine, introduce the thin end of the wedge; be too much for, be too deep for, sell a gold brick to [colloq., U. S.], give the go-by to [slang];

703. Artlessness. — N. ARTLESSNESS &c. adj.; inartificiality, unsophistication; nature, simplicity; innocence &c. 946; bonhomie [F.], naiveté [F.], abandon [F.], candor, sincerity; singleness of -purpose, – heart; honesty &c. 939; plain speaking; épanchement [F.].

rough diamond, matter-of-fact man; le palais de vérité [F.]; enfant terrible [F.].

V. BE ARTLESS &c. adj.; be round with one [Shakespeare]; look one in the face; wear one's heart upon one's sleeve for daws to peck at; think aloud; speak -out, – one's mind; be free with one, call a spade a spade; tell the truth, the whole truth, and nothing but the truth.

Adj. ARTLESS, natural, pure, native, confiding, simple, plain, inartificial, untutored, unsophisticated, ingénu [F.], unaffected, naïve; sincere, frank; open, – as day; candid, ingenuous, guileless; unsuspicious, honest &c. 939; childlike; innocent &c. 946; Arcadian; undesigning, straightforward, unreserved, aboveboard; simple-minded, single-minded; frank-, open-, single-, simple- hearted.

MATTER-OF-FACT, free-spoken, plain-spoken, outspoken; blunt, downright, direct, unpoetical; unflattering, untrimmed, unvarnished.

Adv. IN PLAIN -WORDS, – English; without mincing the matter; not to mince the matter &c. (affirmation) 535.

. Davus sum non Œdipus [Terence]; libe-ravi animam meam; "as frank as rain on cherry-blossoms" [E. B. Browning].

play a deep game, play tricks with; flatter, make things pleasant; have an ax to grind.

Adj. CUNNING, crafty, artful; skillful or skilful &c. 698; subtle, subtile, feline, vulpine; cunning as a -fox, – serpent; deep, – laid; profound; designing, contriving; intriguing &c. *v.*; strategic, diplomatic, politic, Machiavellian *or* Machiavelian, timeserving; artificial; tricky, tricksy [*rare*], wily, sly, slim [*S. Africa*], insidious, stealthy; underhand &c. (*hidden*) 528; subdolous [*obs.*], double-faced, double-tongued, shifty, deceptive; deceitful &c. 545; crooked; arch, pawky [*Scot. & dial. Eng.*], shrewd, acute; sharp, – as a needle; canny *or* cannie, astute, leery [*slang*], knowing, up to snuff, [*slang*] too clever by half, not to be caught with chaff.

Adv. CUNNINGLY &c. *adj.*; slily, on the sly [*colloq.*], by a side wind.

⁎ diamond cut diamond; *à bis ou à blanc; fin contre fin;* "something is rotten in the state of Denmark" [*Hamlet*].

Section IV. ANTAGONISM

1. *Conditional Antagonism*

704. Difficulty. — N. DIFFICULTY; hardness &c. *adj.*; impracticability &c. (*impossibility*) 471; tough –, hard –, uphill- work; hard –, Herculean –, Augean- task; task of Sisyphus, Sisyphean labor, tough job [*colloq.*], tough proposition [*colloq.*], teaser [*colloq.*], rasper [*slang*], dead weight, dead lift.

DILEMMA, embarrassment; deadlock; perplexity &c. (*uncertainty*) 475; intricacy; entanglement &c. 59; cross fire; awkwardness, delicacy; delicate ground, thin ice, ticklish card to play, knot, Gordian knot, *dignus vindice nodus* [*L.*], net, meshes, maze; coil &c. (*convolution*) 248; crooked path; involvement; hard road to travel.

VEXED QUESTION, *vexata quæstio* [*L.*], poser; puzzle &c. (*riddle*) 533; nice –, delicate –, subtle –. knotty- point; paradox; hard –, nut to crack; bone to pick, crux, *pons asinorum* [*L.*], where the shoe pinches.

QUANDARY, nonplus, strait, pass, pinch, rub, pretty pass, stress, brunt; critical situation, crisis; trial, emergency, exigency, scramble.

scrape, hobble, slough, quagmire, hot water [*colloq.*], hornet's nest; sea –, peck- of troubles; pretty kettle of fish [*colloq.*]; pickle, stew, imbroglio, mess, muddle, botch, fuss, bustle, ado; false position; stand; deadlock, dead set; fix, horns of a dilemma, *cul de sac* [*F.*], blind alley; hitch; stumblingblock &c. (*hindrance*) 706.

V. BE DIFFICULT &c. *adj.*; run one hard, go against the grain, try one's patience, put one out; put to one's

705. Facility. — N. FACILITY, ease; easiness &c. *adj.*; capability; feasibility &c. (*practicability*) 470; flexibility, pliancy &c. 324; smoothness &c. 255; disencumbrance, disentanglement; deoppilation [*obs.*]; permission &c. 760.

plain –, smooth –, straight- sailing; mere child's play, holiday task; cinch, snap [*both slang, U. S.*].

ALL CLEAR, smooth water, fair wind; smooth –, royal- road; clear -coast, – stage, – course; straight course; *tabula rasa* [*L.*]; full play &c. (*freedom*) 748.

V. BE EASY &c. *adj.*; go on –, run- smoothly; have full play &c. *n.*; go –, run- on all fours [*colloq.*]; hit on all -four, – six, – eight, – twelve (cylinders) [*automobile cant*]; obey the helm, work well, work smoothly, work like a machine.

flow –, swim –, drift –, go- with the- -stream, –' tide; see one's way; have it all one's own way, have the game in one's own hands; walk over the course, win at a canter, win at a walk, win hands down [*colloq.*]; make little of, make light of, make nothing of; be at home in &c. (*skillful*) 698.

RENDER EASY &c. *adj.*; facilitate, smooth, ease, popularize; lighten, – the labor; free, clear; disencumber, disembarrass, disentangle, disengage; deobstruct, unclog, extricate, unravel, unknot, get the links out of; untie –, cut- the knot; disburden, unload, exonerate, emancipate, free from, deoppilate [*obs.*]; humor &c. (*aid*) 707; lubricate &c. 332; relieve &c. 834.

V. (I) iv   ANTAGONISM

-shifts, – wit's end; go hard with one, try one; pose, perplex &c. (*uncertain*) 475; pother, bother, nonplus, gravel [*colloq.*], bring to a deadlock; be impossible &c. 471; be in the way of &c. (*hinder*) 706.

BE IN DIFFICULTY &c. *n.*; meet with –, labor under –, get into –, plunge into –, struggle with –, contend with –, grapple with- difficulties; labor under a disadvantage; fish in troubled waters, buffet the waves; swim against the -current, – stream; scud under bare poles; have much ado with, have a hard time of it; come to the -push, – pinch; bear the brunt; grope in the dark, lose one's way, weave a tangled web, walk on eggshells, walk among eggs.

get into a scrape &c. *n.*; bring a hornet's nest about one's ears; be put to one's shifts; flounder, boggle [*local, U. S.*], struggle; not know which way to turn &c. (*uncertain*) 475; *perdre son latin* [*F.*]; stick -at, – in the mud, – fast; come to a -stand, – deadlock; get all -balled up [*slang*], – snarled up, – tangled up, – wound up; hold the wolf by the ears.

RENDER DIFFICULT &c. *adj.*; enmesh, encumber, embarrass, ravel, entangle; put a spoke in the wheel &c. (*hinder*) 706; spike one's guns; lead a wild-goose chase, lead a pretty dance.

leave a hole to creep out of, leave a loophole, leave the matter open; give the reins to, give full play, give full swing; make way for; open the -door to, – way; prepare –, smooth –, clear- the -ground, – way, – path, – road; make all clear for, pave the way, bridge over; permit &c. 760.

Adj. EASY, facile; feasible &c. (*practicable*) 470; easily -managed, – accomplished; within reach, accessible, easy of access, for the million, open to.

MANAGEABLE, wieldy [*rare*], toward, towardly, tractable; submissive; yielding, ductile; suant *or* suent [*local U. S. & prov. Eng.*]; tractable &c. (*docile*) 602, pliant &c. (*soft*) 324; glib [*obs.*], slippery; smooth &c. 255; on friction wheels, on velvet.

UNBURDENED, disburdened, disencumbered, disembarrassed; exonerated; unloaded, unobstructed, untrammeled; unrestrained &c. (*free*) 748; at ease, light.

at home, quite at home; in one's element, in smooth water.

Adv. EASILY &c. *adj.*; readily, smoothly, swimmingly, with no effort, on easy terms, single-handed, with one hand tied behind one's back.

*** touch and go; "Custom hath made it in him a property of easiness" [*Hamlet*].

Adj. DIFFICULT, not easy, hard, tough [*colloq.*]; troublesome, toilsome, irksome; operose, laborious, onerous, arduous, Herculean, formidable; sooner –, more easily-said than done; difficult –, hard- to deal with; ill-conditioned, crabbed; not to be handled with kid gloves, not made with rose water.

AWKWARD, unwieldy, unmanageable; intractable, stubborn &c. (*obstinate*) 606; perverse, refractory, plaguy [*colloq.*], trying, thorny, rugged; knotted, knotty; invious [*obs.*]; pathless, trackless; labyrinthine &c. (*convoluted*) 248; intricate, complicated &c. (*tangled*) 59; impracticable &c. (*impossible*) 471; not feasible &c. 470; desperate &c. (*hopeless*) 859.

EMBARRASSING, perplexing &c. (*uncertain*) 475; delicate, ticklish, critical, uncertain, thorny, set with thorns; beset with –, full of –, surrounded by –, entangled by –, encompassed with- difficulties.

UNDER A DIFFICULTY; in a box; in difficulty, in hot water [*colloq.*], in the suds [*colloq.*], in the soup [*slang*], in a cleft stick, in a fix [*colloq.*], in the wrong box, in a scrape &c. *n.*, in deep water, in a fine pickle [*colloq.*], *in extremis* [*L.*]; between -two stools, – Scylla and Charybdis; on the horns of a dilemma; on the rocks; surrounded by -shoals, – breakers, – quicksands; at cross-purposes; not out of the wood.

reduced to straits; hard –, sorely- pressed; run hard; pinched, put to it, straitened; hard up [*slang*]; hard put to it, hard set [*both colloq.*]; put to one's shifts; puzzled, at a loss, &c. (*uncertain*) 475; at the end of one's tether, at one's wits' end, at a nonplus, at a standstill; graveled, nonplused *or* nonplussed, stranded, aground; stuck –, set- fast; out, put out, out in one's reckoning; up a tree, at bay, *aux abois* [*F.*], driven -into a corner, – from post to pillar, – to extremity, –

to one's wit's end, – to the wall; *au bout de son Latin* [*F.*]; out of one's depth; thrown out.

ACCOMPLISHED WITH DIFFICULTY; hard-fought, hard-earned.

Adv. WITH DIFFICULTY, with much ado; hardly &c. *adj.*; uphill; upstream; against the -stream, – grain; *à rebours* [*F.*]; *invitâ Minervâ* [*L.*]; in the teeth of; at a pinch, upon a pinch; at long odds.

** "ay, there's the rub" [*Hamlet*]; *hic labor hoc opus* [Vergil]; things are come to a pretty pass; *ab inconvenienti; ad astra per aspera; aucun chemin de fleurs ne conduit à la gloire.*

2. Active Antagonism

706. Hindrance. — N. PREVENTION, preclusion, obstruction, stoppage; embolus, clot, embolism; interruption, interception, interclusion [*obs.*], hindrance, impedition [*obs.*]; retardment, retardation; embarrassment, oppilation [*obs.*], striction, constriction, coarctation, stricture, restriction; infarct, infarction; restraint &c. 751; inhibition &c. 761; blockade &c. (*closure*) 261.

INTERFERENCE, interposition; obtrusion; discouragement, discountenance; disapproval, disapprobation, opposition.

IMPEDIMENT, let [*archaic*], obstacle, obstruction, knot, knag; check, hitch, *contretemps* [*F.*], screw loose, grit in the oil; stumbling-block, stumbling-stone; lion in the path; snag; snags and sawyers [*U. S.*], sawyer [*U. S.*], planter [*local, U. S.*]

BAR, stile, barrier; turnstile, turnpike; gate, portcullis; beaver dam; barricade &c. (*defense*) 717; wall, dead wall, breakwater, groin *or* groyne; bulkhead, block, buffer; stopper &c. 263; boom, dam, weir.

CHECK; encumbrance *or* incumbrance; clog, skid, shoe, spoke, brake; drag anchor, drag sail, drag sheet, drift sail, sea anchor, floating anchor; anchor; mushroom –, sheet –, kedge- anchor; kedge, bower; checkrein, bearing rein; bit, snaffle, curb, curb bit; drag, – chain, – weight; load, burden, fardel [*obs.*], onus, millstone round one's neck, impedimenta; dead weight; lumber, pack; nightmare, ephialtes, incubus, old man of the sea; remora [*surg.*]; stay, stop; preventive, prophylactic.

DRAWBACK, objection; difficulty &c. 704; insuperable &c. (471) obstacle; trail of a red herring; estoppel [*law*]; ill wind; head wind &c. (*opposition*) 708; trammel, tether &c. (*means of restraint*) 752; holdback, counterpoise.

DAMPER, wet blanket, hinderer, marplot, kill-joy, crape-hanger [*slang*], dog

707. Aid. — N. AID, aidance, assistance, help, opitulation [*obs.*], succor; support, lift, advance, furtherance, promotion; coadjuvancy &c. (*coöperation*) 709.

PATRONAGE, auspices, championship, countenance, favor, interest, advocacy.

SUSTENANCE, sustentation [*rare*], maintenance, alimentation, nutrition, nourishment; eutrophy; manna in the wilderness; food &c. 298; means &c. 632; subsidy, bounty, subvention.

MINISTRY, ministration; subministration [*obs.*], accommodation.

RELIEF, rescue; help at a dead lift; supernatural aid; *deus ex machinâ* [*L.*].

SUPPLIES, reënforcements, succors, contingents, recruits; support &c. (*physical*) 215; adjunct, ally &c. (*helper*) 711.

V. AID, assist, help, succor, lend one's aid; come to the aid of &c. *n.*; contribute, subscribe to; bring –, give –, furnish –, afford –, supply aid &c. *n.*; give –, stretch –, lend –, bear –, hold out- a -hand, – helping hand; give one a -lift, – cast, – turn; take by the hand, take in tow; help a lame dog over a stile, lend wings to.

relieve, rescue; set up, set agoing, set on one's legs; bear –, pull- through; give new life to, be the making of; reënforce, recruit; set –, put –, push- forward; give -a lift, – a shove, – an impulse- to; promote, further, forward, advance; speed, expedite, quicken, hasten.

SUPPORT, sustain, uphold, prop, hold up, bolster.

NCURISH, nurture, nurse, cradle, dry nurse, suckle, foster, cherish, put out to nurse; manure, cultivate, force; foment; feed –, fan- the flame.

SERVE; do service to, tender to, pander to; administer to, subminister to [*obs.*], minister to; tend, attend, wait on; take care of &c. 459; entertain; smooth the bed of sickness.

in the manger, Buttinsky [*humorous*, *U. S.*]; usurper, interloper; opponent &c. 710; filibusterer [*U. S.*].

V. HINDER, impede, filibuster [*U. S.*], impedite [*obs.*], embarrass.

AVERT, keep off, stave off, ward off; obviate; antevert [*obs.*]; turn aside, draw off, prevent, forfend *or* forefend [*archaic*], nip in the bud; retard, slacken, check, let [*archaic*]; counteract, counter-check; preclude, debar, foreclose, estop [*law*]; inhibit &c. 761; shackle &c. (*restrain*) 751; restrict.

OBSTRUCT, stop, stay, bar, bolt, lock; block, – up; choke off; belay, barricade; block –, stop- the way; forlay *or* forelay [*obs.*], dam up &c. (*close*) 261; put on the brake &c. *n.*; scotch –, lock –, put a spoke in- the wheel; put a stop to &c. 142; traverse, contravene; interrupt, intercept; oppose &c. 708; hedge -in, – round; cut off; interclude [*obs.*].

INTERFERE, interpose, intermeddle &c. 682.

ENCUMBER *or* incumber; cramp, hamper; clog, – the wheels; cumber; handicap; choke; saddle with, load with; overload, overlay, overwhelm; lumber, trammel, tie one's hands, put to inconvenience; incommode, discommode; discompose; hustle [*colloq.*], corner, drive into a corner.

RUN FOUL OF, fall foul of; cross the path of, break in upon.

THWART, frustrate, disconcert, balk, foil; faze, feeze *or* feaze [*U. S.*]; baffle, snub, override, circumvent; defeat &c. 731; spike guns &c. (*render useless*) 645; spoil, mar, clip the wings of; cripple &c. (*injure*) 659; put an extinguisher on; damp; dishearten &c. (*dissuade*) 616;

OBLIGE, accommodate, consult the wishes of; humor, cheer, encourage.

SECOND, stand by; back, – up; pay the piper, abet; work for, make interest for, stick up for [*colloq.*], stick by, take up the cudgels for; take up –, espouse –, adopt- the cause of; advocate, beat up for recruits, press into the service; squire [*colloq.*], give moral support to, keep in countenance, countenance, patronize, take up; lend one's name to; lend oneself to, lend one's countenance to; smile upon, shine upon; favor, befriend, take in hand, enlist under the banners of; side with &c. (*coöperate*) 709.

be of use to; subserve &c. (*instrument*) 631; benefit &c. 648; render a service &c. (*utility*) 644; conduce &c. (*tend*) 176.

Adj. AIDING &c. *v.*; auxiliary, adjuvant, helpful; coadjuvant &c. 709; subservient, ministrant, ancillary, accessary, accessory, subsidiary.

FRIENDLY, amicable, favorable, propitious, well-disposed; neighborly; obliging &c. (*benevolent*) 906; at one's beck.

Adv. WITH *or* BY THE AID OF &c. *n.*; on –, in- behalf of; in aid of, in the service of, in favor of, in the name of, in furtherance of; on account of; for the sake of, on the part of; *non obstante* [*L.*].

Int. HELP! save us! to the rescue! this way! *à moi!* [*F.*].

** *alterum alterius auxilio eget* [Sallust]; "God befriend us as our cause is just" [*Henry IV*]; "God helps those who help themselves" [Sidney]; "put your trust in God; but mind to keep your powder dry" [*ascribed to* Cromwell].

discountenance, throw cold water on; steal one's thunder; cut the ground from under one, take the wind out of one's sails, undermine; be –, stand- in the way of; act as a drag; hang like a millstone round one's neck.

Adj. HINDERING &c. *v.*; obstructive, obstruent; intrusive, meddlesome; impeditive, impedient; intercipient [*obs.*]; prophylactic &c. (*remedial*) 662; impedimentary, impedimental.

in the way of, unfavorable; onerous, burdensome; cumbrous, cumbersome; obtrusive.

HINDERED &c. *v.*; windbound, water-logged, heavy laden; hard pressed.

UNASSISTED &c. (*see* assist &c. 707); single-handed, alone; deserted &c. 624; unseconded.

Adv. IN THE WAY, with everything against one, with one's wheels clogged, through all obstacles; with many difficulties, under many difficulties.

** *occurrent nubes;* "he that wrestles with us strengthens our nerves and sharpens our skill. Our antagonist is our helper" [Burke.]

708. Opposition. — N. OPPOSITION, antagonism; oppugnancy, oppugnation [*rare*]; impugnance, impugnment, contrariousness [*rare*], contrariness, contrariety; contravention; counteraction &c. 179; counterplot.

resistance &c. 719; restraint &c. 751; hindrance &c. 706; absence of aid &c. 707.

cross fire, cross current, undercurrent, head wind.

CLASHING, collision, conflict, discord, want of harmony; filibuster [*U. S.*], filibusterism.

COMPETITION, two of a trade, rivalry, emulation, race, contest; tug of war.

V. OPPOSE, counteract, run counter to; withstand &c. (*resist*) 719; control &c. (*restrain*) 751; hinder &c. 706; antagonize, oppugn, fly in the face of, go dead against, kick against, cross, kick at, fall out with, fall foul of; set –, pit- against; face, confront, cope with; make a -stand, – dead set- against; set -oneself, – one's face- against; protest –, vote –, raise one's voice- against; disfavor, turn one's back upon; set at naught, slap in the face, slam the door in one's face.

THWART, be –, play- at cross-purposes; counterwork, countermine; over-thwart.

ENCOUNTER, stem, breast; stem –, breast- the -tide, – current, – flood; buffet the waves; beat up against, make head against; grapple with; kick against the pricks &c. (*resist*) 719; contend with *or* against &c. 720; do battle with *or* against &c. (*warfare*) 722.

CONTRADICT, contravene; belie; go –, run –, beat –, militate- against; come in conflict with.

COMPETE, emulate &c., 720; rival, spoil one's trade, force out, drive one out of business.

Adj. OPPOSING, opposed &c. *v.*; adverse, antagonistic, oppugnant, overthwart; contrary &c. 14; at variance &c. 24; at issue, at war with, in controversy with, in opposition; "agin' the government."

in hostile array, front to front, with crossed bayonets, at daggers drawn; up in arms; resistant &c. 719.

UNFAVORABLE, unpropitious, unfriendly, hostile, inimical, cross; filibusterous.

302

709. Coöperation. — N. COÖPERATION; coadjuvancy, coadjutorship, coadjument [*rare*], coagency, coefficiency; concert, concurrence, complicity, coadministration, coaction; participation union &c. 43; coefficacy; combination &c. 48; collusion, collusiveness.

ASSOCIATION, alliance, colleagueship, joint stock, copartnership, pool, gentleman's agreement; cartel; confederation &c. (*party*) 712; coalition, federation, fusion; a long pull a strong pull and a pull all together; logrolling [*chiefly U. S.*], *quid pro quo* [*L.*], freemasonry.

UNANIMITY &c. (*assent*) 488; *esprit de corps* [*F.*], party spirit; clanship, partisanship; concord &c. 714; synergy, synergism.

V. COÖPERATE, concur; conduce &c. 178; combine, coadjute, coadjuvate; coact [*rare*], unite one's efforts; keep –, draw –, pull –, club –, hand –, hold –, league –, band –, be banded- together; pool; stand –, put- shoulder to shoulder; act in concert, join forces, fraternize, cling to one another; vote solidly, vote in blocks; conspire, concert, lay one's heads together; confederate, make an agreement with, be in league with; collude, understand one another, play into the hands of, hunt in couples.

SIDE WITH, take sides with, go along with, go hand in hand with, join hands with, make common cause with, strike in with, unite with, join with, mix oneself up with, take part with, cast in one's lot with; join –, enter intopartnership with; rally round, flock to, follow the lead of; come to, pass over to, come into the views of; be –, row –, sail- in the same boat; sail on the same tack.

PARTICIPATE, be a party to, lend oneself to; chip in [*colloq.*], have a -hand in, – finger in the pie; take –, bear- part in; second &c. (*aid*) 707; take the part of, play the game of; espouse a -cause, – quarrel.

Adj. COÖPERATING &c. *v.*; in coöperation &c. *n.*, in league &c. (*party*) 712; coadjuvant, coadjutant, coadjutive, coactive, coalitional, hand in glove with; dyed in the wool; synergetic, synergistic.

FAVORABLE TO &c. 707; unopposed &c. 708.

COMPETITIVE, emulous, cut-throat; in rivalry with, in friendly rivalry.

Adv. AGAINST, *versus* [*L.*], counter to, in conflict with, at cross-purposes, cross, contrariwise, unfavorably.

against the -grain, – current, – stream, – wind, – tide; with a head-wind; with the wind -ahead, – in one's teeth.

IN SPITE, in despite, in defiance; in the -way, – teeth, – face- of; across; athwart, overthwart; where the shoe pinches; in one's teeth.

THOUGH &c. 30; even; *quand même* [*F.*]; *per contra* [*L.*].

⁎ *nitor in adversum;* "take arms against a sea of troubles, And by opposing end them" [*Hamlet*]; "I have no words, My voice is in my sword" [*Macbeth*].

Adv. UNANIMOUSLY, as one man &c. 488; shoulder to shoulder, in coöpera-tion with.

⁎ *due teste valgono più che una sola;* "we must all hang together, or assuredly we shall all hang separately" [Franklin, July 4, 1776]; "I shall know that your good is mine; ye shall know that my strength is yours" [Kipling].

---

710. Opponent. — N. OPPONENT, antagonist, adversary, oppugnant [*rare*]; adverse party, opposition; enemy &c. 891; assailant.

OPPOSITIONIST, obstructive; brawler, wrangler, brangler [*rare*], disputant; filibuster [*U. S.*], filibusterer [*U. S.*], extremist, bitter-ender [*U. S.*], irrecon-cilable, obstructionist, "willful men."

MALCONTENT; demagogue, reactionist; anarchist, anarch; Jacobin, Fenian, Sinn Feiner, Red; Industrial Workers of the World, I. W. W.

RIVAL, competitor, contestant, en-trant; the field.

⁎ "each brave foe was in his heart a friend" [Homer]; "He that wrestles with us strengthens our nerves and sharpens our skill. Our antagonist is our helper" [Burke].

711. Auxiliary. — N. AUXILIARY; recruit; assistant; adjuvant, adjutant; *ayudante* [*Sp. Amer.*], co-aid; adjunct; help, helper, helpmate, helping hand; colleague, partner, mate, confrère, co-öperator; coadjuvant, coadjutant, coad-jutator [*rare*], coadjútor, coadjutrix, collaborator.

ALLY; friend &c. 890; confidant (*fem.* confidante), *fidus Achates* [*L.*], *alter ego* [*L.*], pal [*slang*], chum [*colloq.*], mate, comate.

aide-de-camp [*F.*], secretary, clerk, associate, marshal; right-hand, right-hand man; candleholder, bottle-holder [*colloq.*]; handmaid; servant &c. 746.

PUPPET, cat's-paw, creature, jack-straw, tool; jackal; *âme damnée* [*F.*]; satellite, adherent; parasite, dependent, client [*Rom. hist.*].

CONFEDERATE; complice [*archaic*], accomplice; accessory, – after the fact; *particeps criminis* [*L.*]; *socius criminis* [*L.*].

UPHOLDER; votary; sectarian, sectary; seconder, backer, supporter, abettor, advocate, partisan, champion, patron, friend at court, mediator; angel [*slang*].

FRIEND IN NEED, jack at a pinch, special providence, *deus ex machinâ* [*L.*], guardian angel, fairy godmother, tutelary genius.

⁎ a friend in need is a friend indeed; "of every friendless name the friend" [Johnson]; "the best-condition'd and unwearied spirit In doing courtesies" [*Merchant of Venice*.].

712. Party. — N. PARTY, faction, denomination, class, communion, side, crew, team; band, horde, posse, phalanx; caste, family, gens [*Rom. hist.*], clan &c. 166.

Confederates, Conservatives, Democrats, Federalists, Federals, Liberals, Radi-cals, Republicans, Socialists, Tories, Whigs &c.

COMMUNITY, body, fellowship, solidarity; freemasonry; party spirit &c. (*coöpera-tion*) 709; fraternity, sodality, confraternity, sorority; *familistère* [*F.*], familistery; brotherhood, sisterhood.

FRATERNAL ORDER, Freemasons, Knights Templars, Odd Fellows, Knights of Pythias; Royal Arcanum &c.

GANG, tong [*Chin.*]; Camorra, Kuklux, Kuklux Klan, Molly Maguires, Fenians, Sinn Feiners, Bolsheviki, Bolshevists, Industrial Workers of the World, I. W. W., Luddites; ring, machine; Tammany, – Hall [*U. S.*]; junto, cabal, camarilla, brigue [*obs.*].

CLIQUE, knot, circle, set, coterie; club, casino.

CORPORATION, corporate body, guild; establishment, company, copartnership, partnership, cahoot [*slang*]; firm, house; joint concern, joint-stock company; combine [*colloq.*, *U. S.*], trust; holding company, merger.

SOCIETY, association; institute, institution; union; trades union; league, syndicate, alliance; *Verein, Bund, Zollverein* [*all Ger.*]; combination; *Turnverein* [*Ger.*]; *Liedertafel* &c. (*singing societies*) 416; league -, alliance- offensive and defensive; coalition; federation; confederation, confederacy.

STAFF; cast, *dramatis personæ* [*L.*].

V. UNITE, join; band together; club together &c. (*coöperate*) 709; found a -firm, - house; cement -, form- a party &c. *n.;* associate &c. (*assemble*) 72; federate, federalize, go cahoots [*slang*], go fifty-fifty [*slang*].

Adj. IN LEAGUE, in partnership, in alliance &c. *n.*

bonded -, banded -, linked &c. (*joined*) 43- together; embattled; confederated, federative, joint, corporate, organized, enleagued, leagued, syndicated; clubbable *or* clubable, fraternal, Masonic, institutional, denominational; cliquish, cliquy *or* cliquey; union-made.

Adv. SIDE BY SIDE, hand in hand, shoulder to shoulder, *en masse* [*F.*], in the same boat.

* "to party gave up what was meant for mankind" [Goldsmith — *of Burke*]; "he left not faction, but of it was left" [Dryden — *of Buckingham*].

---

713. Discord. — N. DISCORD, disaccord, dissidence, dissonance; disagreement &c. 24; jar, clash, break, shock; jarring, jostling &c. *v.;* screw loose.

VARIANCE, difference, dissension, misunderstanding, cross-purposes, odds, *brouillerie* [*F.*]; division, split, rupture, disruption, division in the camp, house divided against itself, "rift within the lute" [*Tennyson*], disunion, breach; schism &c. (*dissent*) 489; feud, faction.

POLEMICS; litigation; strife &c. (*contention*) 720; warfare &c. 722; outbreak, open rupture, breaking off of negotiations, recall of ambassadors, declaration of war.

QUARREL, dispute, tiff, bicker, *tracasserie* [*F.*], squabble, altercation, barney [*slang*], *démêlé* [*F.*], snarl, spat [*colloq. or dial.*], towrow [*Scot. & dial Eng.*], words, high words; wrangling &c. *v.;* jangle, brabble [*archaic*], brabblement [*archaic*], cross questions and crooked answers, snip-snap [*rare*]; family jars.

BROIL, brawl, row [*colloq.*], racket, hubbub, rixation [*obs.*]; embroilment, embranglement, imbroglio, fracas, breach of the peace, piece of work, scrimmage, rumpus [*colloq.*]; breeze [*colloq.*], squall; riot, disturbance &c. (*disorder*) 59; commotion &c. (*agitation*) 315; bear garden, Donnybrook Fair.

SUBJECT OF DISPUTE, ground of quarrel, battle ground, disputed point; bone -of contention, - to pick; apple

714. Concord. — N. CONCORD, accord, harmony, symphony; homologue, homology, correspondence; agreement &c. 23; sympathy &c. (*love*) 897; response; union, unison, unity; bonds of harmony; peace &c. 721; unanimity &c. (*assent*) 488; league &c. 712; happy family.

rapprochement [*F.*], reunion; amity &c. (*friendship*) 888; alliance, *entente cordiale* [*F.*], good understanding, conciliation, arbitration.

PEACEMAKER, intercessor, interceder, propitiator, mediator.

V. AGREE &c. 23; accord, harmonize with, blend in with; fraternize; be concordant &c. *adj.;* go hand in hand; run parallel &c. (*concur*) 178; understand one another; pull together &c. (*coöperate*) 709; put up one's horses together, sing in chorus.

SIDE WITH, sympathize with, go with, chime in with, fall in with; come round [*colloq.*]; be pacified &c. 723; assent &c. 488; enter into the -ideas, - feelings- of; reciprocate.

hurler avec les loups [*F.*]; go -, swim- with the stream; get on the band wagon [*slang*].

SMOOTH, pour oil on the troubled waters; keep in good humor, render accordant, put in tune; come to an understanding, meet halfway; keep the peace, remain at peace; mediate, intercede.

of discord, *casus belli* [*L.*]; question at issue &c. (*subject of inquiry*) 461; vexed question, *vexata quæstio* [*L*], brand of discord.

CONTENTIOUSNESS &c. *adj.*; enmity &c. 889; hate &c. 898; troublous times; cat-and-dog life; Kilkenny cats; disputant &c. 710; strange bedfellows.

V. DISAGREE; be discordant &c. *adj.*; disaccord, come amiss &c. 24; clash, jar, jostle, pull different ways, conflict, have no measures with, misunderstand one another; live like cat and dog; differ; dissent &c. 489; have a bone to pick with, have a crow to pluck with.

QUARREL, fall out, dispute; litigate; controvert &c. (*deny*) 536; squabble, tiff, spat [*colloq. or dial.*], altercate, row

Adj. CONCORDANT, congenial; agreeing &c. *v.*; in accord &c. *n.*; harmonious, united, cemented; banded together &c. 712; allied; friendly &c. 888; fraternal; conciliatory; at one with; of one mind &c. (*assent*) 488.

at peace, in still water; tranquil &c. (*pacific*) 721.

Adv. UNANIMOUSLY, without a dissentient voice; with one voice &c. (*assent*) 488; in concert with, hand in hand; on one's side.

Int. make it unanimous! are you with us?

⁎ *commune periculum concordiam parit;* "every expansion of civilization makes for peace" [Roosevelt].

[*colloq.*], brabble, wrangle, jangle, brangle, bicker, nag; spar &c. (*contend*) 720; have words with &c. *n.*; fall foul of.

split; break –, break squares –, part company- with; declare war, try conclusions; join –, put in- issue; pick a quarrel, fasten a quarrel on; sow –, stir up- dissension &c. *n.*; embroil, entangle, disunite, widen the breach; rub one's fur the wrong way; get one all het up [*dial.*]; get one hot under the collar [*colloq.*]; set at odds, set together by the ears; set –, pit- against.

get into hot water, fish in troubled waters, brawl; kick up a -row, - dust [*colloq.*]; turn the house out of window.

Adj. DISCORDANT, dissident; disagreeing &c. *v.*; out of tune, dissonant, harsh, grating, jangling, unmelodious, inharmonious, ajar; on bad terms, dissentient &c. 489; unreconciled, unpacified; inconsistent, contradictory, incongruous, discrepant.

QUARRELSOME, unpacific; gladiatorial, controversial, polemic, disputatious; factious; litigious, litigant.

AT STRIFE, at odds, at loggerheads, at daggers drawn, at variance, at issue, at cross-purposes, at sixes and sevens, at feud, at high words; up in arms, heated, het up [*dial.*], hot under the collar [*colloq.*], together by the ears, in hot water, embroiled; torn, disunited.

⁎ *quot homines tot sententiæ* [Terence]; no love lost between them, *non nostrum tantas componere lites* [Vergil]; *Mars gravior sub pace latet* [Claudius]; "She was no sister to the hen, But fierce and minded to be queen" [Masefield]; "above the pitch, out of tune, and off the hinges" [Rabelais].

715. Defiance. — **N.** DEFIANCE; daring &c. *v.*; dare, defial, defi [*slang*]; "dare, dare, and double-dare" [*child's challenge*]; challenge, cartel; threat &c. 909; war cry, war whoop.

V. DEFY, dare, beard; brave &c. (*courage*) 861; bid defiance to; bite the thumb at; set at defiance, set at naught; hurl defiance at; dance the war dance; snap the fingers at, laugh to scorn; disobey &c. 742.

show -fight, – one's teeth, – a bold front; bluster, look big, stand with arms akimbo; double –, shake- the fist; threaten &c. 909.

CHALLENGE, call out; throw –, fling- down the -gauntlet, – gage, – glove.

Adj. DEFIANT; defying &c. *v.*; with arms akimbo; rebellious, bold, insolent, reckless, contemptuous, greatly daring, regardless of consequences.

Adv. IN DEFIANCE OF, in the teeth of; under one's very nose; in open rebellion.

Int. do your worst! come if you dare! come on! marry come up! [*archaic or dial.*], hoity toity!

⁎ *noli me tangere; nemo me impune lacessit;* "And dar'st thou then To beard the lion in his den, The Douglas in his hall?" [Scott].

716. Attack. — **N.** ATTACK; assault, – and battery; onset, onslaught, charge.

base of operations, point of attack; echelon; open order; close formation.

AGGRESSION, offense; incursion, inroad, invasion; irruption; outbreak; bucking, estapade [manège], ruade [F.], kicking, kick; punch &c. (impulse) 276; coup de main [F.]; sally, sortie, camisade or camisado [archaic], raid, foray; run at, run against; dead set at.

STORM, storming; boarding, escalade; siege, investment, obsession [obs.], bombardment, cannonade, barrage; zero hour.

battue [F.], razzia, dragonnade or dragoonade; devastation &c. 162; éboulement [F.].

FIRE, volley; direct –, ricochet –, plunging –, rolling –, horizontal –, vertical –, platoon –, file- fire; fusilade; fire of demolition, percussion fire; sharpshooting, broadside; raking –, crossfire; volley of grapeshot, feu d'enfer [F.].

CUT, THRUST, lunge, pass, passado [obs.], stoccado or stoccata [archaic], carte (or quarte) and tierce, home thrust; coup de bec [F.].

ASSAILANT, aggressor, invader; sharpshooter, dead shot, fusilier, dragoon, Uhlan.

V. ATTACK, assault, assail; set upon, fall upon; charge, impugn, break a lance with, enter the lists.

SHOW FIGHT, come on; assume –, take the offensive; be –, become- the aggressor; strike the first blow, throw the first stone at, fire the first shot; lift a hand –, draw the sword- against; take up the cudgels; advance –, march-against; march upon, invade, harry.

strike at, poke at, thrust at; aim –, deal- a blow at; give –, fetch- one a -blow, – kick; have a -cut, – shot, – fling, – shy- at; be down upon, pounce upon; fall foul of, pitch into [colloq.], launch out against; bait, slap on the face; make a -thrust, – pass, – set, – dead set- at; bear down upon.

close with, come to close quarters, bring to bay, come to blows.

ride full tilt against; let fly at, dash at, run a tilt at, rush at, tilt at, run at, fly at, hawk at, have at, let out at; make a -dash, – rush at; attack tooth and nail; strike home; drive –, press-

306

717. Defense. — **N.** DEFENSE or defence, protection, guard, ward; shielding &c. v.; propugnation [obs.]; preservation &c. 670; guardianship.

SELF-DEFENSE, self-preservation; resistance &c. 719.

SAFEGUARD &c. (safety) 664; screen &c. (shelter) 666, (concealment) 350; fortification; munition, muniment; bulwark, fosse, trench, mine, countermine, dugout; moat, ditch, intrenchment or entrenchment, vallation, rampart, scarp, escarp, counterscarp, vanfoss; dike or dyke; parapet, sunk fence, haha, embankment, mound, mole, bank; earthwork, fieldwork; fence, wall, dead wall, contravallation or countervallation; paling &c. (inclosure) 232; palisade, stockade, stoccado [obs.], laager [S. Africa], sangar [India]; barrier, barricade; boom; portcullis, chevaux de frise [F.]; abatis or abattis, barbed wire entanglements, vallum [Rom. antiq.], circumvallation, merlon, battlement, glacis; casemate; buttress, abutment; shore &c. (support) 215.

breastwork, banquette, mantelet or mantlet, tenaille or tenail, ravelin, curtain, demilune, half-moon; bastion, demibastion, redan; vauntmure [rare], faussebraie or faussebraye, advanced work, hornwork, lunette, outwork; barbican, redoubt, sconce, fortalice; lines.

machicolation, bartizan, loophole, balistraria [ancient fortification]; postern gate, sally port.

STRONGHOLD, hold, fastness; asylum &c. (refuge) 666; keep, donjon, citadel, capitol, castle; tower, – of strength; fortress, propugnaculum, fort, kila [India]; barracoon, barrack; pah or pa [N. Z.]; peel, peel tower, peelhouse; rath [Ir. antiq.]; martello tower, blockhouse, wooden walls.

[PROTECTIVE DEVICES] buffer, fender, cowcatcher [U. S.]; apron, mask, gauntlet, thimble; armor or armour, shield, buckler, scutum [Rom. antiq.], target, targe [archaic], ægis, breastplate, cuirass, backplate, habergeon, mail, coat of mail, brigandine, hauberk, lorica, helm [archaic], armet, basinet or bassinet, sallet or salade, greave, jambe, heaume, morion, cabasset, beaver, visor or vizor; face guard, helmet, casque, casquetel, siege cap, headpiece; steel helmet, tin -helmet, – hat [soldiers' cant];

one hard; be hard upon, run down,
strike at the root of.

lay about one, run amuck.

FIRE UPON, fire at, fire a shot at; draw
a bead on [*U. S.*]; shoot at, pop at, level
at, let off a gun at; open fire, pepper,
bombard, shell, pour a broadside into;
fire a volley, fire red-hot shot; spring a
mine.

STONE, lapidate, pelt; throw - a stone,
– stones - at; hurl -at, – against, – at
the head of; rock [*U. S.*].

BESET, besiege, beleaguer; lay siege
to, invest, open the trenches, plant a
battery, sap, mine; storm, board, scale
the walls, go over the top.

cut and thrust, bayonet, give one the
bayonet; butt; kick, strike &c. (*impulse*) 276; horsewhip, whip &c. (*punish*) 972.

Adj. ATTACKING &c. *v.*; aggressive,
offensive, incursive, invasive, irrup-
tive, obsidional.

up in arms; amuck.

Adv. ON THE OFFENSIVE, on the warpath, amuck, over the top; at bay.

Int. "up and at them!"

⁎ "the din of arms, the yell of savage
rage, the shriek of agony, the groan of death"
[*Southey*]; "their fatal hands no second stroke
intend" [*Paradise Lost*]; "thirst for glory
quells the love of life" [*Addison*].

camail, neckguard; *Pickelhaube* [*Ger.*];
spiked helmet; shako &c. (*dress*) 225;
bearskin; vambrace, rerebrace, cubitière;
sollerets, pédieux; panoply, caparison,
housings; chamfron or chamfrain; truncheon &c. (*weapon*) 727; carapace, shell;
spines, needles.

DEFENDER, protector; Defender of the
Faith, *fidei defensor* [*L.*], guardian &c.
(*safety*) 664; bodyguard, champion;
knight-errant, Paladin; propugnator or
propugner or propugnor [*obs.*]; picket;
garrison.

V. DEFEND, forfend or forefend [*archaic*], fend [*archaic*]; shield, screen,
shroud; engarrison, garrison, man; fence
round &c. (*circumscribe*) 229; fence,
intrench or entrench; arm, harness
[*archaic*], accouter or accoutre; guard &c.
(*keep safe*) 664; guard against; take care
of &c. (*vigilance*) 459; bear harmless;
fend –, keep –, ward –, beat- off; hinder
&c. 706.

REPEL, parry, propugn [*obs.*], put to
flight; give a warm reception to [*ironical*]; hold – keep- at -bay, – arm's
length.

RESIST INVASION, stand siege; be –,
stand –, act- on the defensive; show
fight; maintain –, stand- one's ground;
stand by; hold one's own; bear –, stand-
the brunt; fall back upon, hold, stand

in the gap.

Adj. DEFENDING &c. *v.*; defensive; mural; armed, – at all points, – cap-a-pie,
– to the teeth; panoplied; accoutered or accoutred, harnessed [*archaic*], "in complete steel" [*Hamlet*]; iron-plated, ironclad; loopholed, castellated, machicolated,
casemated; defended &c. *v.*; proof against, ball-proof, bullet-proof; protective.

Adv. DEFENSIVELY; on the defensive; in defense; in self-defense; at bay, *pro
aris et focis* [*L.*].

Int. NO SURRENDER! "*ils ne passeront pas!*" "they shall not pass!" [*the French
at Verdun*].

⁎ defense not defiance; *Dieu défend le droit;* "Millions for defence, but not a cent for
tribute" [*Pinkney*].

---

718. Retaliation. — N. RETALIATION,
reprisal, talion [*rare*], retort; counter-
stroke, counterblast, counterplot, coun-
terproject; retribution, *lex talionis* [*L.*];
reciprocation &c. (*reciprocity*) 12.

REQUITAL, desert; tit for tat, give and
take, blow for blow, *quid pro quo* [*L.*],
a Roland for an Oliver, measure for
measure, diamond cut diamond, an eye
for an eye, boomerang, the biter bit, a
game at which two can play; reproof
valiant, retort courteous.

recrimination &c. (*accusation*) 938;

719. Resistance. — N. RESISTANCE,
stand, front, oppugnation [*rare*], oppug-
nance, oppugnancy; opposition &c. 708;
renitency, renitence, reluctance [*archaic*],
reluctation [*rare*], recalcitrance or recal-
citrancy, recalcitration; repugnance, repulsion; kicking &c. *v.*

REPULSE, rebuff, snub.

INSURRECTION &c. (*disobedience*) 742;
strike; turnout [*colloq.*], lockout; barring-
out; *levée en masse* [*F.*], *Jacquerie* [*F.
hist.*]; rebellion; boycott; riot &c. (*disorder*) 59.

revenge &c. 919; compensation &c. 30; reaction &c. (*recoil*) 277.

V. RETALIATE, retort, turn upon; pay, pay off, pay back; pay in -one's own, - the same- coin; cap, match; reciprocate &c. 148; turn the tables upon, return the compliment; give a *quid pro quo* &c. *n.*, give as much as one takes; give as good as was sent; exchange blows; give and take, exchange fisticuffs; be quits, be even with; pay off old scores.

serve one right, be hoist on one's own petard, throw a stone in one's own garden, catch a Tartar.

Adj. RETALIATING &c. *v.*; retaliatory, retaliative, retributive, recriminatory, reciprocal; talionic [*rare*].

Adv. IN RETALIATION; *en revanche* [*F.*].

** *mutato nomine de te fabula narratur* [Horace]; *par pari refero* [Terence]; *tu quoque*; you're another; *suo sibi gladio hunc jugulo; à beau jeu beau retour; litem lite resolvere* [adap'ed from Horace]; "curses, like chickens, come home to roost."

V. RESIST; not submit &c. 725; repugn [*obs.*], reluctate [*rare*], oppugn, withstand; stand up -, strive -, bear up -, be proof -, make head- against; stand, - firm, - fast, - one's ground, - the brunt of, - out; hold -one's ground, - one's own, - out; stick it out [*colloq.*].

FACE, confront, breast the -wave, - current; stem the -tide, - torrent; grapple with; show a bold front &c. (*courage*) 861; present a front, make a stand, take one's stand.

OPPOSE &c. 708; kick, - against; recalcitrate, kick against the pricks; fly in the face of; lift the hand against &c. (*attack*) 716; withstand -an attack, - a siege, - the onset; rise up in arms &c. (*war*) 722; strike, turn out; draw up a round robin &c. (*remonstrate*) 932; put one's foot down; boycott; revolt &c. (*disobey*) 742; make a riot.

prendre le mors aux dents [*F.*], take the bit between the teeth; sell one's life dearly, die hard, keep at bay; repel, repulse.

Adj. RESISTING &c. *v.*; oppugnant, resistive, resistant; refractory &c. (*disobedient*) 742; repugnant; recalcitrant, renitent, repulsive, repellent; up in arms.

PROOF AGAINST; unconquerable &c. (*strong*) 159; stubborn, unconquered; indomitable &c. (*persevering*) 604a; unyielding &c. (*obstinate*) 606.

Int. HANDS OFF! keep off!

NEVER SAY DIE! stick it! [*colloq.*]; show what you're made of! give 'em hell! [*colloq.*]; "up, Guards, and at them!" [Wellington — *at Waterloo, as alleged*].

720. Contention. —N. CONTENTION, strife; contest, contestation; struggle; belligerency; opposition &c. 708.

CONTROVERSY, polemics; debate &c. (*discussion*) 476; war of words, logomachy, litigation; paper war; high words &c. (*quarrel*) 713; sparring &c. *v.*

COMPETITION, rivalry; corrivalry, corrivalship; agonism [*obs.*], *concours* [*F.*], match, race, tug of war, horse racing, heat, dash, steeple chase, point-to-point race, handicap; regatta; field day; sham fight, Derby day; turf, sporting, bullfight, tauromachy [*rare*], gymkhana [*orig. Anglo-Indian*]; boat race, torpids [*Oxford Univ.*].

pugilism, boxing, fisticuffs, spar, mill [*cant*], set-to [*colloq.*], round, bout, event; prize fighting; quarterstaff, single stick; gladiatorship, gymnastics; wrestling; catch-as-catch-can -, Greco-Roman (*or* Græco-Roman) -, Cornish -, Westmorland and Cumberland- style [of wrestling]; jujutsu (*also* jujitsu, jiujutsu, jiujitsu), *samo* [*Jap.*], *kooshti* [*Hind.*]; athletics, athletic sports; games of skill &c. 840.

721. Peace. — N. PEACE; amity &c. (*friendship*) 888; pacifism; harmony &c. (*concord*) 714; tranquillity &c. (*quiescence*) 265; truce &c. (*pacification*) 723; pipe of peace, calumet.

piping time of peace, quiet life; neutrality.

V. BE AT PEACE; keep the peace &c. (*concord*) 714; make peace &c. 723; pacify; be a pacifist.

Adj. PACIFIC; peaceable, peaceful; calm, tranquil, untroubled, halcyon; bloodless; neutral, pacifistic, "too proud to fight" [Woodrow Wilson].

** the storm blown over; the lion lies down with the lamb; "all quiet on the Potomac"; *paritur pax bello* [Nepos]; "peace hath her victories no less renowned than war" [Milton]; "the peace of fact is not the peace of principle" [Amiel]; "peace is a goddess only when she comes with sword girt on thigh" [Roosevelt].

FRACAS &c. (*discord*) 713; clash of arms; tussle, scuffle, broil, fray; affray;
affrayment [*obs.*]; velitation [*obs.*]; luctation [*rare*], colluctation [*obs.*], shindy
[*colloq.*], brigue [*obs.*], brabble, scramble, *mêlée* [*F.*], scrimmage, stramash [*dial. or
slang*], free-for-all [*cant*]; free –, stand up –, hand to hand –, running- fight.

CONFLICT, skirmish; encounter, rencounter, rencontre, collision, affair, brush,
fight; sharp contest, hard knocks; battle, – royal; combat, action, engagement,
just *or* joust, tournament; tilt, tilting; tourney, lists; pitched battle; guerrilla
(*or* guerilla) –, irregular- warfare; bush-fighting.

deeds –, feats- of arms; pugnacity; combativeness &c. *adj.*; bone of contention &c. 713.

death struggle, struggle for life or death, Armageddon.

NAVAL ENGAGEMENT, naumachia *or* naumachy, sea fight.

DUEL, duello [*rare*], single combat, *monomachia* [*L.*] *or* monomachy, satisfaction,
passage d'armes [*F.*], passage of arms, affair of honor; triangular duel; hostile
meeting, digladiation [*archaic*]; appeal to arms &c. (*warfare*) 722.

V. CONTEND; contest, strive, struggle, scramble, wrestle; spar, square [*colloq.*];
exchange -blows, – fisticuffs; fib [*slang, Eng.*], jostle *or* justle, tussle, tilt, box,
stave [*obs. or dial.*], fence; skirmish; pickeer [*obs.*]; fight &c. (*war*) 722; wrangle
&c. (*quarrel*) 713.

contend &c. with; grapple –, engage –, close –, buckle [*obs.*] –, bandy –, try conclusions –, have a brush &c. *n.* –, tilt- with; encounter, fall foul of, pitch into
[*colloq.*], clapperclaw [*archaic or dial.*], run a tilt at; oppose &c. 708; reluct.

compete –, cope –, vie –, race- with; outvie, emulate, rival; run a race.

contend &c. for, stipulate for, stickle for; insist upon, make a point of.

JOIN ISSUE, come to blows; be at –, fall to –, go to- loggerheads; set to,
come to the scratch, pull a gun [*slang*], exchange shots, measure swords, meet
hand to hand; take up the -cudgels, – glove, – gauntlet; tourney, just *or* joust,
enter the lists; couch one's lance; give satisfaction; appeal to arms &c. (*warfare*)
722.

lay about one; break the peace.

Adj. CONTENDING &c. *v.;* at loggerheads, at war, at issue.

CONTENTIOUS, combative, bellicose, belligerent, unpeaceful; warlike &c. 722;
quarrelsome &c. 901; pugnacious, pugilistic; tauromachian *or* tauromachic [*rare*];
gladiatorial.

ATHLETIC, gymnastic, palæstral *or* palestral, palæstric *or* palestric; competitive,
rival.

⁎ *a verbis ad verbera;* a word and a blow; "a very pretty quarrel as it stands" [Sheridan];
commune periculum concordiam parit; lis litem generat; "litigious terms, fat contentions, and
flowing fees" [Milton].

---

722. Warfare. — N. WARFARE; fighting &c. *v.;* hostilities; war, arms, the
sword; Mars, Bellona, grim-visaged war,
horrida bella [*L.*]; bloodshed.

appeal to -arms, – the sword; ordeal –,
wager- of battle; *ultima ratio regum* [*L.*],
arbitrament of the sword, declaration of
war.

battle array, campaign, crusade, expedition; mobilization; state of siege;
battlefield &c. (*arena*) 728; warpath.

ART OF WAR, rules of war, the war
game, tactics, strategy, castrametation;
generalship, soldiership; military evolu-
tions, ballistics, gunnery; aviation;
chivalry; gunpowder, shot, shell, poison
gas.

723. Pacification. — N. PACIFICA-
TION, conciliation; reconciliation, reconcilement, shaking of hands, calumet,
peace pipe; accommodation, arrangement, adjustment; terms, compromise;
amnesty, deed of release.

PEACE OFFERING; olive branch; calumet, – of peace; overture, preliminaries
of peace.

TRUCE, armistice; suspension of -arms,
– hostilities; truce of God; breathing
time; convention; *modus vivendi* [*L.*];
flag of truce, white flag, *parlementaire*
[*F.*], cartel.

hollow truce, *pax in bello* [*L.*]; drawn
battle.

V. PACIFY, tranquillize, compose;

battle, conflict &c. (*contention*) 720; service, campaigning, active service, tented field; kriegspiel *or Kriegsspiel* [*Ger.*], fiery cross, trumpet, clarion, bugle, pibroch, slogan; war cry, war whoop; battle cry, beat of drum, *rappel* [*F.*], tom-tom; word of command; password, watchword; *passage d'armes* [*F.*].

war to the -death, – knife; *guerre à -mort*, – *outrance* [*F.*]; open –, trench –, guerrilla (*or* guerilla) –, internecine –, civil- war (*or* warfare).

WAR MEDAL, military medal, Victoria Cross, V. C., *croix de guerre* [*F.*], *médaille militaire* [*F.*], iron cross [*Ger.*].

WAR NEWS, war bulletin, war extra; war correspondent.

V. ARM; prepare for war; raise –, mobilize- troops; raise up in arms; take up the udgels &c. 720; take up –, fly to –, appeal to- -arms, – the sword; draw –, unsheathe- the sword; dig up the -hatchet, – tomahawk.

WAR, make war, go to war, declare war, wage war, "let slip the dogs of war" [*Julius Cæsar*]; cry havoc; kindle

allay &c. (*moderate*) 174; reconcile, propitiate, placate, conciliate, meet halfway, hold out the olive branch, heal the breach, make peace, restore harmony, bring to terms.

MAKE UP A QUARREL; settle –, arrange –, accommodate- -matters, – differences; set straight; *tantas componere lites* [*L.*]; come to -an understanding, – terms; bridge over, hush up; make it up, make matters up; shake hands; mend one's fences [*U. S.*].

raise a siege; put up –, sheathe- the sword; bury the hatchet, lay down one's arms, turn swords into plowshares; smoke the calumet, close the temple of Janus; keep the peace &c. (*concord*) 714; be pacified &c.; come round.

Adj. CONCILIATORY, pacificatory; composing &c. *v.*; pacified &c. *v.*; accommodative.

*** *requiescat in pace;* "to see great Hector in his weeds of peace" [*Troilus and Cressida*]; "Health, peace, and many a bloodless year To fight his battles o'er" [Holmes].

-, light- the torch of war; raise one's banner, send round the fiery cross, hoist the black flag; throw –, fling- away the scabbard; take the field; take the law into one's own hands; do –, give –, join –, engage in –, go to- battle; flesh one's sword; set to, fall to, engage, measure swords with, draw the trigger, cross swords; come to -blows, – close quarters; fight; combat; contend &c. 720; battle with, break a lance with.

SERVE; enroll, enlist; see –, be on- -service, – active service; campaign; wield the sword, shoulder a musket, smell powder, be under fire; spill blood, imbrue the hands in blood; be on the warpath.

carry on -war, – hostilities; keep the field; fight the good fight; take by storm; go over the top [*colloq.*]; fight -it out, – like devils, – one's way, – hand to hand; cut one's way -out, – through; sell one's life dearly.

Adj. ARMED, – to the teeth, – cap-a-pie; sword in hand; contending, contentious &c. 720; in –, under –, up in- arms; at war with; bristling with arms; in battle array, in open arms, in the field; embattled; battled.

WARLIKE, belligerent, combative, armigerous, bellicose, martial, unpacific, unpeaceful; military, militant; soldier like, soldierly, chivalrous; strategical, civil, internecine; irregular, guerrilla *or* guerilla.

Adv. *flagrante bello* [*L.*], in the thick of the fray, in the cannon's mouth; at the sword's point, at the point of the bayonet.

Int. TO ARMS! *væ victis!* [*L.*]· to your tents O Israel! *c'est la guerre!* [*F.*].

*** the battle rages; *à la guerre comme à la guerre; bis peccare in bello non licet; jus gladii;* "my voice is still for war" [Addison]; "my sentence is for open war" [Milton]; "pride, pomp, and circumstance of glorious war" [*Othello*]; "the cannons have their bowels full of wrath" [*King John*]; "the cannons . . . spit forth their iron indignation" [*ibid.*]; "the fire-eyed maid of smoky war" [*I Henry IV*]; *silent leges inter arma* [Cicero]; "O war! thou son of hell Whom angry heavens do make their minister" [*II Henry VI*]; "So frowned the mighty combatants that hell Grew darker at their frown" [*P. L.*]; "Nothing except a battle lost can be half so melancholy as a battle won" [Wellington]; "Charge, Chester, charge! On, Stanley, on!" [Scott]; "There never was a good war or a bad peace" [Franklin]; "Battle's magnificently stern array!" [Byron]; "But stay, I do not like Undue assassination" [Gilbert]; *si vis pacem para bellum;* "hard hitting is the best parry" [Roosevelt]; "If I should die, think only this of me: That there's some corner of a foreign field That is for ever England" [Rupert Brooke].

724. Mediation. — **N.** MEDIATION, mediatorship, mediatization, mediatorialism; intervention, interposition, interference, intermeddling, intercession; parley, negotiation, arbitration; flag of truce &c. 723; good offices, peace offering; diplomatics [*rare*], diplomacy; compromise &c. 774.

MEDIATOR, intercessor, peacemaker, make-peace, negotiator, go-between; diplomatist &c. (*consignee*) 758; moderator; propitiator; umpire, arbitrator.

V. MEDIATE, mediatize; intercede, interpose, interfere, intervene; step in, negotiate; meet halfway; arbitrate, propitiate; agree to arbitration; submit; *componere lites* [*L.*].

Adj. MEDIATORY, mediatorial, negotiable; mediating &c. *v.*; propitiatory, diplomatic.

---

725. Submission. — **N.** SUBMISSION, yielding, acquiescence, compliance, submittal, submissiveness, deference, nonresistance; obedience &c. 743.

SURRENDER, cession, capitulation, resignation, backdown [*colloq.*]; passing under the yoke, laying down one's arms, delivering up the keys (of the city &c.), handing over one's sword.

OBEISANCE, homage, kneeling, genuflexion, curtsy *or* curtsey, kotow [*Chinese*], salaam *or* salam [*Oriental*], prostration.

V. SUBMIT, succumb, yield, bend, stoop, accede, relent, resign, defer to.

SURRENDER, – at discretion; cede, capitulate, come to terms, retreat, beat a retreat; lay down –, deliver up– one's arms; lower –, haul down –, strike– one's -flag, – colors; draw in one's horns &c. (*humility*) 879; give -way, – ground, – in, – up; cave in [*colloq.*]; suffer judgment by default; bend, – to one's yoke, – before the storm; reel back; bend –, knuckle- -down, – to, – under; knock under.

HUMBLE ONESELF; eat -dirt, – crow, – the leek, – humble pie; bite –, lick- the dust; be –, fall- at one's feet; crouch before, throw oneself at the feet of; swallow the -leek, – pill; kiss the rod; turn the other cheek; *avaler les couleuvres* [*F.*], gulp down.

pocket the affront; make the best of, make a virtue of necessity; grin and abide, grin and bear it, shrug the shoulders, resign oneself; submit with a good grace &c. (*bear with*) 826.

YIELD OBEISANCE; obey &c. 743; kneel to, bow to, pay homage to, cringe to, truckle to; bend the -neck, – knee; kneel, fall on one's knees, bow submission, curtsy *or* curtsey, kotow [*Chinese*].

Adj. SUBMISSIVE, resigned, crouching, prostrate; downtrodden; surrendering &c. *v.*; down on one's marrowbones [*slang*]; on one's bended knee; nonresisting, unresisting; pliant &c. (*soft*) 324; humble &c. 879; undefended.

UNTENABLE, indefensible, insupportable, unsupportable.

*** have it your own way; it can't be helped; amen &c. (*assent*) 488; *da locum melioribus; tempori parendum.*

---

726. Combatant. — **N.** COMBATANT; disputant, controversialist, polemic, litigant, belligerent; competitor, rival, corrival; fighter, assailant; champion, Paladin; moss-trooper, swashbuckler, fire eater, duelist, swordsman, *sabreur* [*F.*], *beau sabreur* [*F.*]; athlete, wrestler, boxer.

bully, bludgeon man, rough, rowdy, ruffian, tough [*colloq., U. S.*], gunman [*colloq., U. S.*], Thug *or* thug; terrorist &c. 887; fighting man, prize fighter, pugilist, bruiser, the fancy [*now rare*], gladiator, fighting-cock, gamecock.

SOLDIER, warrior, brave, man at arms, guardsman, *gendarme* [*F.*]; campaigner, veteran; redcoat, military man, Rajput; armiger, esquire, knight; Amazon.

Janizary *or* Janissary; myrmidon; Mameluke *or* Mamaluke, spahi *or* spahee, bashi-bazouk [*Turk.*], Cossack, Croat, Pandor; irregular, free lance, franc-tireur, tirailleur, guerrilla *or* guerilla, *condottiere* [*It.*], mercenary; bushwhacker, companion; Hessian.

private, – soldier; Tommy Atkins [*Brit.*], doughboy [*slang, U. S.*], rank and file, peon, sepoy [*India*], *légionnaire* [*F.*], legionary, food for powder, fodder for cannon, *Kannonenfutter* [*Ger.*]; spearman, pikeman; archer, bowman; halberdier; musketeer, carabineer, rifleman, sharpshooter, jäger *or* yager, skirmisher; grenadier, fusileer, infantryman, foot soldier, footman [*rare*], light infantryman, chasseur, zouave; artilleryman, gunner, cannoneer, bombardier [*hist.*], matross [*obs.*]; engineer; sapper, — and miner; cavalryman, trooper, sowar [*India*], dragoon; light —, heavy-dragoon; heavy, cuirassier, hussar, lancer; recruit, rookie [*slang, U. S.*], conscript, drafted man, enlisted man.

officer &c. (*commander*) 745; subaltern, ensign, standard bearer.

HORSE AND FOOT; cavalry, horse, light horse, mounted rifles; infantry, foot, light infantry, rifles; artillery, horse artillery, field artillery, gunners; military train.

ARMED FORCE, troops, soldiery, military, forces, Sabaoth, host, the army, standing army, regulars, the line, troops of the line, militia, national guard, state guard [*U. S.*], bodyguard, yeomanry, volunteers, trainband, fencibles [*hist.*]; auxiliary, *bersagliere* [*It.*]; *garde -nationale*, — *royale* [*F.*]; minuteman [*Am. hist.*]; auxiliary - reserve- forces; reserves, *posse comitatus* [*L.*], posse; guards, yeomen of the guard, beefeaters [*Eng.*], life guards, household troops, Horse Guards, Foot Guards; Swiss guards.

LEVY, draft *or* draught; raw levies, awkward squad; Landwehr, Landsturm.

ARMY, *corps d'armée* [*F.*], army corps; host, division, battalia [*rare*], sotnia [*Russ.*], column, wing, detachment, garrison, flying column, brigade, regiment, corps, battalion, squadron, company, battery, subdivision, section, platoon, squad; picket, guard, rank, file; legion, phalanx, cohort, maniple, manipulus [*Rom. hist.*]; cloud of skirmishers.

WAR HORSE, charger, destrer *or* destrier [*archaic*].

NAVY, first line of defense, wooden walls, naval forces, fleet, flotilla, armada, squadron; man-of-war's man &c. (*sailor*) 269; marines.

MAN-OF-WAR, line-of-battle ship, ship of the line, battleship, warship, ironclad, war vessel, war castle, H.M.S., U.S.S.; superdreadnought, dreadnought, cruiser; armored —, protected- cruiser; torpedo-boat, — destroyer; destroyer, torpedo-catcher, gunboat; submarine, submersible, U-boat; submarine chaser; mine layer, sweeper; turret ship, ram, monitor, floating battery; first-rate, frigate, sloop of war, corvet *or* corvette; bomb vessel; flagship, guard ship, privateer; troopship, transport, tender, store-ship, catamaran [*obs.*], fire boat.

AËROPLANE, airplane, aëro [*colloq.*], *avion* [*F.*], Fokker, dirigible, blimp [*cant*]; zeppelin &c. (*aëronautics*) 273.

⁎ "They left the peaceful river. The cricket field, the quad, The shaven lawns of Oxford, To seek a bloody sod" [W. M. Letts]; "They who to Glory's fanning This streamer have unfurled, The men whose joy is manning, The men who man the world!" [William Watson].

727. Arms. — N.

ARMS, arm, weapon, deadly weapon; armament, armature; panoply, stand of arms; armor &c. (*defense*) 717; armory &c. (*store*) 636; *apparatus belli* [*L.*]; gunnery; ballistics &c. (*propulsion*) 284.

SIDE ARMS, *armes blanches* [*F.*], sword; good-, trusty -, naked- sword; cold steel, naked steel, steel, blade, brand [*archaic*]; broadsword, Toledo, Ferrara, claymore, glaive [*archaic*] *or* glave [*obs.*]; saber *or* sabre, cutlass, hanger, bilbo, falchion, scimitar *or* cimeter [*obs.*], whinyard [*obs.*], rapier, tuck [*hist.*], foil, yataghan (*also* ataghan, attaghan); dagger, poniard, baselard, dirk, stiletto, katar *or* kuttar [*India*], stylet; skean, skean dhu [*Scot.*]; creese *or* kris; dudgeon [*archaic*], bowie knife; bayonet, sword bayonet, sword stick.

AX *or* AXE, battle ax, Lochaber ax, adaga, poleax *or* poleaxe, halberd *or* halbert, gisarme, tomahawk, bill, black bill, brown bill, partisan.

SPEAR, lance, pike, spontoon, assagai *or* assegai, javelin, jereed *or* jerid, dart, shaft, bolt, reed, arrow; harpoon, gaff, eelspear; weet-weet, womerah, throwing stick, throw stick, boomerang; oxgoad, ankus.

CLUB, war club, waddy [*Austral.*], mace, truncheon, staff, bludgeon, cudgel, shillalah *or* shillelagh, handstaff, quarterstaff; bat, cane, stick, walking-stick, knuckle duster; billy, life-preserver, blackjack, sandbag.

BOW, crossbow, arbalest, ballista *or* balista, balister [*obs.*], trebuchet *or* trebucket, catapult, sling; battering-ram &c. (*impulse*) 276.

FIREARMS; gun, piece; artillery, ordnance; siege -, battering- train; park, battery;

cannon, gun of position, heavy gun, fieldpiece, field gun, mountain gun, siege gun, seacoast gun; mortar, howitzer, carronade, culverin, basilisk [*obs.*]; falconet, jingal, swivel, swivel gun, pedrero *or* pederero, *bouche à feu* [*F.*], smooth bore, rifled cannon; Armstrong –, Lancaster –, Paixhans –, Whitworth –, Parrott –, Krupp –, Vickers –, Benet-Mercié –, Gatling –, Maxim –, machine- gun; pompom, *mitrailleuse* [*F.*]; "seventy-five" [*French rapid-fire 75 mm. field gun*]; Lewis gun; auto-rifle, tenpounder; flame-thrower, *Flammenwerfer* [*Ger.*], *lance-flamme* [*F.*].

SMALL ARMS; musketry; musket, firelock, fowling piece, rifle, fusil [*obs. or hist.*], escopette *or* escopet, carbine, blunderbuss, musketoon, Brown Bess, matchlock, harquebus *or* arquebus, caliver, hackbut *or* hagbut, shotgun, petronel [*hist.*]; small bore; breechloader, muzzle-loader; gunflint, gunlock; Minié –, Enfield –, Flobert –, Westley Richards –, Snider –, Martini-Henry –, Lee-Metford –, Lee-Enfield –, Mauser –, Mannlicher –, Springfield –, magazine- rifle; needle gun, *chassepot* [*F.*]; wind gun, air gun; automatic -gun, – pistol; automatic; revolver, repeater; shooting iron [*slang, U. S.*], shooter [*colloq., U. S.*], six-shooter [*U. S.*], gun [*U. S. and colloq. for revolver or pistol*], pistol, pistolet [*obs.*].

MISSILE, bolt, projectile, shot, ball; grape; grape –, canister –, bar –, cannon –, langrage *or* langrel –, round –, chain- shot; slung shot; shrapnel, *mitraille* [*F.*], grenade, hand grenade, rifle grenade; shell, high-explosive shell, *obus explosif* [*F.*], bomb, depth bomb, smoke bomb, gas bomb; bullet; dumdum –, man-stopping –, explosive –, expanding- bullet; petard; infernal machine, torpedo; carcass, rocket; congreve, – rocket; slug, stone, rock, brickbat.

thunderbolt, levin- -bolt, – brand; stroke, stroke of lightning, thunderstone [*obs. or dial. Eng.*].

AMMUNITION; powder, – and shot; explosive; gunpowder, "villanous saltpetre" [*Hen. IV.*]; guncotton, pyroxylin *or* pyroxyline, dynamite, melinite, cordite, gelignite, lyddite, nitroglycerin *or* nitroglycerine, trinitrotoluol, trinitrotoluine, T.N.T.; cartridge; ball cartridge, cartouche, fireball; poison gas, mustard gas, chlorine gas, tear gas &c.

*** *en flûte; nervos belli pecuniam infinitam;* "his sword which he called Mouse because it was swift and nimble" [Dunsany].

728. Arena. — N. ARENA, field, platform; scene of action, theater *or* theatre, walk, course; hustings; stage, boards &c. (*playhouse*) 599; amphitheater *or* amphitheatre, Coliseum, Colosseum; Flavian amphitheater, hippodrome, circus, race course, *corso* [*It.*], turf, cockpit, bear garden, gymnasium, palæstra *or* palestra, ring, lists; tilt-yard, tilting ground; *Campus Martius* [*L.*], *Champ de Mars* [*F.*]; campus [*U. S.*], playing field, playground.

BATTLE FIELD, battle ground; field of -battle, – slaughter; No Man's Land [*World War*]; "over there" [*used in America, esp. of the Western Front*], "out there" [*corresponding term in Eng.*]; theater –, seat- of war; Aceldama, camp; the enemy's camp.

TRYSTING PLACE &c. (*place of meeting*) 74.

*** "My race being run, I love to watch the race" [Masefield].

Section V. RESULTS OF VOLUNTARY ACTION

729. Completion. — N. COMPLETION; accomplishment, achievement, fulfillment *or* fulfilment; performance, execution; dispatch *or* despatch, consummation, culmination; finish, conclusion; limit, effectuation; close &c. (*end*) 67; terminus &c. (*arrival*) 292; winding up; *finale* [*It.*], *dénouement* [*F.*], catastrophe, issue, upshot, result; final –, last –, crowning –, finishing- -touch, – stroke;

730. Noncompletion. — N. NONCOMPLETION, nonfulfillment *or* nonfulfilment, shortcoming &c. 304; incompleteness &c. 53; drawn -battle, – game: work of Penelope; Sisyphean -labor, – toil, – task.

NONPERFORMANCE, inexecution; neglect of execution; neglect &c. 460.

V. NOT COMPLETE &c. 729; leave unfinished &c. *adj.*, leave undone; neglect

last finish, *coup de grâce* [*F.*]; crowning of the edifice; coping stone, copestone, keystone; missing link &c. 53; superstructure, *ne plus ultra* [*L.*], work done, *fait accompli* [*F.*].

elaboration; finality; completeness &c. 52.

V. COMPLETE, perfect; effect, effectuate; accomplish, achieve, compass, consummate, hammer out; bring to -maturity, – perfection; elaborate.

DO, execute, make; go –, get- through; work out, enact; bring -about, – to bear, – to pass, – through, – to a head.

dispatch *or* despatch, knock off [*colloq.*], finish off, polish off; make short work of; dispose of, set at rest; perform, discharge fulfill *or* fulfil, realize; put in -practice, – force; carry -out, – into effect, – into execution; make good; be as good as one's word.

DO THOROUGHLY, not do by halves, go the whole hog [*colloq.*]; drive home, be in at the death &c. (*persevere*) 604*a*; carry through, deliver the goods [*colloq.*, *U. S.*], play out, exhaust; fill the bill [*colloq.*, *U. S.*].

FINISH, bring to a close &c. (*end*) 67; wind up, stamp, clinch, seal, set the seal on, put the seal to; give the final touch &c. *n.* to; put the -last, – finishing-touch to; crown, crown all; cap.

ripen, culminate; come to a -head, – crisis; come to its end; die a natural death, die of old age; run its course, run one's race; touch –, reach –, attain-the goal; reach &c. (*arrive*) 292; get in the harvest.

Adj. COMPLETING, final; concluding, conclusive; crowning &c. *v.*; exhaustive, elaborate, complete, mature, perfect, consummate, thorough.

DONE, completed &c. *v.*; done for [*colloq.*], sped, wrought out; highly wrought &c. (*preparation*) 673; thorough &c. 52; ripe &c. (*ready*) 673.

Adv. COMPLETELY &c. (*thoroughly*) 52; to crown all, out of hand; with absolute -perfection, – finish; as a last stroke; as a fitting climax.

⁎⁎ the race is run; *actum est; finis coronat opus; consummatum est; c'en est fait;* it is all over; the game is played out, the bubble has burst; *aussitôt dit aussitôt fait; aut non tentaris aut perfice* [Ovid]; "Life is as just as Death; Life pays its debt" [Masefield].

---

731. Success. — **N.** SUCCESS, successfulness; speed; advance &c. (*progress*) 282.

trump card; hit, stroke; lucky –, fortunate –, good- -hit, – stroke; bold stroke, masterstroke; ten-strike [*colloq.*, *U. S.*]; *coup de maître* [*F.*], checkmate; half the battle, prize; profit &c. (*acquisition*) 775.

continued success; good fortune &c. (*prosperity*) 734; time well spent.

MASTERY, advantage over; upper hand, whip hand; ascendancy, expugnation [*obs.*], conquest, victory, walkover [*colloq.*], subdual; subjugation &c. (*subjection*) 749; triumph &c. (*exultation*) 884; proficiency &c. (*skill*) 698; a feather in one's cap [*colloq.*].

VICTOR, victress [*rare*], victrix [*rare*],

&c. 460; let alone, let slip; lose sight of.

FALL SHORT OF &c. 304; do things by halves, scotch the snake not kill it; hang fire; be slow to; collapse &c. 304.

Adj. INCOMPLETE &c. 53; not completed &c. *v.*; uncompleted, unfinished, unaccomplished, unperformed, unexecuted; sketchy; addle, muddled, sterile.

in progress, in hand, on the stocks, in preparation, moving, getting along, going on, proceeding; on one's hands; on the anvil.

Adv. *re infectâ* [*L.*]; without –, lacking--the final touches, – the finishing stroke.

---

732. Failure. — **N.** FAILURE, unsuccess, nonsuccess, nonfulfillment *or* nonfulfilment; dead failure, successlessness; abortion, miscarriage; *brutum fulmen* [*L.*] &c. 158; labor in vain &c. (*inutility*) 645; no go [*colloq.*]; inefficacy, inefficaciousness &c. *adj.*; vain –, ineffectual –, abortive- -attempt, – efforts; flash in the pan, "lame and impotent conclusion" [*Othello*]; frustration; slip 'twixt cup and lip &c. (*disappointment*) 509.

BLUNDER &c. (*mistake*) 495; fault, omission, miss, oversight, slip, trip, stumble, claudication [*obs.*]; footfall; false –, wrong- step; *faux pas* [*F.*], titubation, *bévue* [*F.*], *faute* [*F.*], lurch; botchery &c. (*want of skill*) 699; scrape, mess, muddle, botch, fiasco, breakdown; flunk [*colloq.*, *U. S.*].

conqueror, master, champion, winner; master of the -situation, – position.

V. SUCCEED; be successful &c. *adj.*; gain one's -end, – ends; crown with success.

gain –, attain –, carry –, secure –, win- -a point, – an object; get there [*slang*, *U. S.*]; manage to, contrive to; accomplish &c. (*effect*, *complete*) 729; do –, work- wonders; make a go of it [*colloq.*].

come off -well, – successfully, – with flying colors; make short work of; take –, carry- by storm; bear away the bell; win one's spurs, win the battle; win –, carry –, gain- the -day, – prize, – palm; have the best of it, have it all one's own way, have the game in one's own hands, have the ball at one's feet, have one on the hip; walk over the course; carry all before one, remain in possession of the field; score a success.

make progress &c. (*advance*) 282; win –, make –, work –, find- one's way; speed; strive to some purpose; prosper &c. 734; drive a roaring trade; make profit &c. (*acquire*) 775; reap –, gather- the -fruits, – benefit of, – harvest; strike oil [*slang*, *U. S.*], make one's fortune, get in the harvest, turn to good account; turn to account &c. (*use*) 677.

TRIUMPH, be triumphant; gain –, obtain- -a victory, – an advantage; chain victory to one's car.

surmount –, overcome –, get over- -a difficulty, – an obstacle &c. 706; *se tirer d'affaire* [*F.*]; make head against; stem the -torrent, – tide, – current; weather -the storm, – a point; turn a corner, keep one's head above water, tide over; master; get –, have –, gain- the -better of, – best of, – upper hand, – ascendancy, – whip hand, – start of; distance; surpass &c. (*superiority*) 33.

DEFEAT, conquer, vanquish, discomfit; euchre [*slang*]; overcome, overthrow, overpower, overmaster, overmatch, overset, override, overreach; outwit, outdo, outflank, outmaneuver *or* outmanœuvre, outgeneral, outvote; take the wind out of one's adversary's sails; beat, beat hollow [*colloq.*], lick [*colloq.*], rout, drub, floor, worst, lick to a frazzle [*colloq.*]; put -down, – to flight, – to the rout, – *hors de combat* [*F.*], – out of court.

settle [*colloq.*], do for [*colloq.*], break the -neck of, – back of; capsize, sink,

MISHAP &c. (*misfortune*) 735; split, collapse, smash, blow, explosion.

REPULSE, rebuff, defeat, rout, overthrow, discomfiture; beating, drubbing; quietus, nonsuit, subjugation; checkmate, stalemate, fool's mate.

losing game, *affaire flambée* [*F.*]

FALL, downfall, ruin, perdition; wreck &c. (*destruction*) 162; deathblow; bankruptcy &c. (*nonpayment*) 808.

VICTIM, prey; bankrupt; flunker [*colloq.*, *U. S.*], flunky *or* flunkey [*cant*, *U. S.*].

V. FAIL; be unsuccessful &c. *adj.*; not succeed &c. 731; make vain efforts &c. *n.*; do –, labor –, toil- in vain; flunk [*colloq.*, *U. S.*]; lose one's labor, take nothing by one's motion; bring to naught, make nothing of; wash a blackamoor white &c. (*impossible*) 471; roll the stone of Sisyphus &c. (*useless*) 645; do by halves &c. (*not complete*) 730; lose ground &c. (*recede*) 283; fall short of &c. 304; go to -the wall, – the dogs, – pot [*colloq.*], lick –, bite- the dust; be defeated &c. 731; have the worst of it, lose the day, come off second best, lose; not have a leg to stand on; fall a prey to; succumb &c. (*submit*) 725.

MISS, – one's aim, – the mark, – one's footing, – stays [*naut.*]; slip, trip, stumble; make a slip &c., *n.*; make a blunder &c. 495, make a mess of, make a botch of; bitch it [*obs.*], miscarry, abort, go up like a rocket and come down like the stick, reckon without one's host; get the wrong -pig by the tail, – sow by the ear [*colloq.*] &c. (*blunder*, *mismanage*) 699.

FLOUNDER, falter; limp, halt, hobble, titubate; fall, tumble; lose one's balance; fall to the ground, fall between two stools; stick in the mud, run aground, split upon a rock; run –, knock –, dash- one's head against a stone wall; break one's back; break down, sink, drown, founder, have the ground cut from under one; get into -trouble, – a mess, – a scrape; come to grief &c. (*adversity*) 735.

COME TO NOTHING, end in smoke; flat out [*colloq.*, *U. S.*]; fall -to the ground, – through, – dead, – stillborn, – flat; slip through one's fingers; hang fire, misfire, flash in the pan, collapse; topple down &c. (*descent*) 305; go to wrack and ruin &c. (*destruction*) 162.

shipwreck, drown, swamp; subdue; subjugate &c. (*subject*) 749; reduce; make
the enemy bite the dust; victimize, roll'
in the dust, trample under foot, put an
extinguisher upon.

CHECKMATE, silence, quell, nonsuit,
upset, confound, nonplus, stalemate,
trump; baffle &c. (*hinder*) 706; circumvent, elude; trip up, – the heels of; drive
–into a corner, – to the wall; run hard,
put one's nose out of joint [*colloq.*].

AVAIL; answer, – the purpose; prevail,
take effect, do, turn out well, work well,
take [*colloq.*], tell, bear fruit; hit it, hit
the mark, hit the right nail on the head;
nick it; turn up trumps, make a hit;
find one's account in.

Adj. SUCCESSFUL; prosperous &c. 734;
succeeding &c. *v.;* triumphant; flushed
–, crowned- with success; victorious;
set up [*colloq.*]; in the ascendant; unbeaten &c. (*see beat &c. v.*); well-spent;
felicitous, effective, in full swing.

Adv. SUCCESSFULLY &c. *adj.;* with flying colors, in triumph, swimmingly; *à
merveille* [*F.*], beyond all hope; to some
–, to good- purpose; to one's heart's
content.

*** *veni vidi vici;* the day being one's own;
one's star in the ascendant; *omne tulit punctum;
bis vincit qui se vincit in victoria; cede repugnanti cedendo victor abibis* [Ovid]; *chacun est
l'artisan de sa fortune; dies faustus; l'art de
vaincre est celui de mépriser la mort; omnia
vincit amor;* "peace hath her victories no less
renowned than war" [Milton]; "the race by
vigor not by vaunts is won" [Pope]; *vincit qui
patitur; vincit qui se vincit;* "Is there anything
in life so disenchanting as attainment?"
[Stevenson].

GO AMISS, go wrong, go cross, go hard
with, go on a wrong tack; go on –, come
off –, turn out –, work- ill; take a wrong
turn, take an ugly turn, be all over with,
be all up with; explode; dash one's
hopes &c. (*disappoint*) 509; defeat the
purpose; sow the wind and reap the
whirlwind, jump out of the frying pan
into the fire.

Adj. UNSUCCESSFUL, successless, stick-
it [*Scot.*]; failing, tripping &c. *v.;* at
fault; unfortunate &c. 735.

ABORTIVE, sterile, impotent, addle,
stillborn; fruitless, bootless; ineffectual,
ineffective; inefficient &c. (*impotent*)
158; inefficacious; lame, hobbling, *décousu* [*F.*]; insufficient &c. 640; unavailing &c. (*useless*) 645; of no effect.

STRANDED, aground, grounded,
swamped, cast away, wrecked, foun-
dered, capsized, shipwrecked, nonsuited;
foiled; defeated &c. 731; struck –,
borne –, broken- down; downtrodden;
overborne, overwhelmed; all up with
[[*colloq.*]; plowed *or* ploughed [*Eng.
Univ. cant*], plucked [*college cant*].

UNDONE, lost, ruined, broken; bankrupt &c. (*not paying*) 808; played out;
done up, done for [*both colloq.*]; dead-
beat [*colloq.*], ruined root and branch,
flambé [*F.*], knocked on the head; destroyed &c. 162.

FRUSTRATED, thwarted, crossed, unhinged, disconcerted, dashed; thrown
–off one's balance, – on one's back, –
on one's beam ends; unhorsed, in a
sorry plight; hard hit; stultified, befooled, dished [*colloq.*], hoist on one's
own petard; victimized, sacrificed.

wide of the mark &c. (*error*) 495; out of one's reckoning &c. (*inexpectation*)
508; left in the lurch; thrown away &c. (*wasted*) 638; unattained; uncompleted
&c. 730.

Adv. UNSUCCESSFULLY &c. *adj.;* to little or no purpose, in vain, *re infectâ* [*L.*].

*** the bubble has burst, "the game is up" [*Cymbeline*]; all is lost; the devil to pay; *parturiunt montes &c.* (*disappointment*) 509; *dies infaustus; tout est perdu hors l'honneur;* "Trust
still to Life, the day is not yet old" [Masefield].

733. Trophy. — N. TROPHY; medal, prize, palm, laurel, laurels, bays, crown,
chaplet, wreath, civic crown; insignia &c. 550; eulogy, citation; scholarship;
feather in one's cap &c. (*honor*) 873; garland; triumphal arch; Victoria Cross,
Congressional medal, *croix de guerre* [*F.*], *médaille militaire* [*F.*], Iron Cross; Carnegie medal, Nobel prize; blue ribbon; red ribbon of the Legion of Honor; decoration &c. 877.

TRIUMPH &c. (*celebration*) 883; flying colors &c. (*show*) 882.

*** *monumentum ære perennius* [Hor.]; "for valor"; "Now are our brows bound with victorious
wreaths" [*Richard III*]; "'Tis deeds must win the prize" [*Taming of the Shrew*]; "It is a conquest
for a prince to boast of" [*I Henry IV*].

734. Prosperity. — N. PROSPERITY, welfare, well-being; affluence &c. (*wealth*) 803; success &c. 731; thrift, roaring trade; good -, smiles of - fortune; blessings, godsend; bed of roses; fat of the land, milk and honey, loaves and fishes, fleshpots of Egypt.

LUCK; good -, run of- luck; sunshine; fair -weather, - wind; fair wind and no favor; palmy -, bright -, halcyondays; piping times, tide, flood, high tide.

GOLDEN AGE, golden time, *Saturnia regna* [*L.*], Saturnian age.

MAN OF SUBSTANCE, made man, lucky dog, *enfant gâté* [*F.*], spoiled child of fortune.

UPSTART, parvenu, *nouveau riche* [*F.*], *narikin* [*Jap.*], skipjack [*dial. Eng.*], mushroom.

V. PROSPER, thrive, flourish; be prosperous &c. *adj.;* drive a roaring trade; go on -well, - smoothly, - swimmingly; sail before the wind, swim with the tide; run -smooth, - smoothly, - on all fours [*colloq.*].

rise -, get on- in the world; work -, make- one's way; look up; lift -, raiseone's head, make one's fortune, feather one's nest, make one's pile [*slang*].

flower, blow, blossom, bloom, fructify, bear fruit, fatten, batten.

keep oneself afloat; keep -, holdone's head above water; light -, fallon one's -legs, - feet; drop into a good thing; bear a charmed life; bask in the sunshine; have a good (*or* fine) time of it; have a run, - of luck; have the good fortune &c. *n.* to; take a favorable turn; live -on the fat of the land, - in clover, - on velvet.

Adj. PROSPEROUS; thriving &c. *v.;* in a fair way, buoyant; well off, well to do, well to live [*archaic*], set up [*colloq.*], well to do in the world; at one's ease; rich &c. 803; in good case; in full feather, in high feather; fortunate, lucky, in luck; born with a silver spoon in one's mouth, born under a lucky star; on the sunny side of the hedge.

palmy, halcyon; agreeable &c. 829; *couleur de rose* [*F.*].

AUSPICIOUS, propitious, providential.

Adv. PROSPEROUSLY &c. *adj.;* swimmingly; as good luck would have it; beyond all -expectation, - hope; be-

735. Adversity. — N. ADVERSITY, evil &c. 619; failure &c. 732; bad - ill -, evil -, adverse -, hard- -fortune, - hap, - luck, - lot; frowns of fortune; evil -dispensation, - star, - genius; ups and downs of life; the sport of fortune; broken fortunes; hard -case, - lines, - life; sea -, peck- of troubles; hell upon earth; slough of despond.

pressure of the times, iron age, evil day, time out of joint; hard -, bad -, sad- times; rainy day, cloud, dark cloud, gathering clouds, ill wind; affliction &c. (*painfulness*) 830; bitter -pill, - draft (*or* draught), - cup; care.

TROUBLE, hardship, curse, blight, blast, load, pressure, humiliation.

MISFORTUNE, misventure [*archaic*], mishap, mischance, misadventure, disaster, calamity, catastrophe; accident, casualty, cross, blow, trial, sorrow, visitation, infliction, reverse, check, *contretemps* [*F.*], pinch, rub; backset, comedown, setback.

DOWNFALL, fall; losing game; falling &c. *v.;* ruination, ruinousness, undoing; extremity; ruin &c. (*destruction*) 162.

V. BE ILL OFF &c. *adj.;* go hard with; fall on evil, - days; go on ill; not prosper &c. 734.

COME TO GRIEF, go downhill, go to rack and ruin &c. (*destruction*) 162, go to the dogs [*colloq.*]; fall, - from one's high estate; decay, sink, decline, go down in the world; have seen better days; bring one's gray hairs with sorrow to the grave; be all over with, be all up with [*colloq.*]; bring a wasp's (*or* hornet's) nest about one's ears.

Adj. UNFORTUNATE, unblest, unhappy, unlucky, unprosperous, improsperous [*obs.*]; hoodooed [*colloq., U. S.*], Jonahed [*slang*], jinxed [*slang*], luckless, hapless; out of luck; in trouble, in a bad way, in an evil plight; under a cloud; clouded; ill off, badly off; in adverse circumstances; poor &c. 804; behindhand, down in the world, decayed, undone; on the road to ruin, on its last legs, on the wane; in one's utmost need.

ILL-FATED, ill-starred, ill-omened; planet-struck, devoted, doomed; inauspicious, unauspicious [*rare*], ominous, sinister, unpropitious; unfavorable; born -under an evil star, - with a wooden ladle in one's mouth.

yond one's deserts; beyond the dreams of avarice.

. one's star in the ascendant; all for the best; one's course runs smooth.

chacun est l'artisan de sa fortune; donec eris felix multos numerabis amicos [Ovid]; *felicitas multos habet amicos; felix se nescit amari* [Lucan]; "good luck go with thee" [*Henry V*]; *nulli est homini perpetuum bonum* [Plautus]; "the lines are fallen unto me in pleasant places; yea, I have a goodly heritage" [*Bible*].

"adversity's sweet milk, philosophy" [*Romeo and Juliet*]; *amici probantur rebus adversis; bien vengas mal si vienes solo;* εὐτυχῶν μὲν μέτριος ἴσθι ἀτυχῶν δὲ φρόνιμος [Periander]; *gaudet tentamine virtus; curæ leves loquuntur ingentes stupent; res est sacra miser* [Ovid]; *sempre il mal non vien per nuocere; væ victis* [Livy]; "sweet are the uses of adversity" [*As You Like It*]; "the man who complains of the crumpled rose leaf very often has his flesh full of thorns" [Chesterton]; "in the shadow of a great affliction" [Whittier].

ADVERSE, untoward; disastrous, calamitous, ruinous, dire, deplorable.

Adv. if the worst come to the worst, as ill luck would have it, from bad to worse, out of the frying pan into the fire.

. one's star is on the wane; one's luck turns, one's luck fails; the game is up, one's doom is sealed, the ground crumbles under one's feet, *sic transit gloria mundi, tant va la cruche à l'eau qu' à la fin elle se casse.*

---

736. Mediocrity. — **N.** MEDIOCRITY; golden mean &c. (*mid-course*) 628, (*moderation*) 174; moderate –, average- circumstances; respectability.

middle classes, *bourgeoisie* [*F.*].

V. strike the golden mean; preserve a middle course &c. 628.

jog on, get along [*colloq.*], get by [*slang*]; go –, get on- -fairly, – quietly,- peaceably, – tolerably, – respectably.

Adj. MIDDLING, *comme ci comme ça* [*F.*], soso or so-so, fair, fair to middling [*colloq.*], medium, moderate, mediocre, ordinary; second –, third –, fourth- rate.

Adv. with nothing to brag about.

. "High hopes die on a warm hearthstone" [Kipling]; "No characteristic trait had he Of any distinctive kind" [Gilbert]; "contentment is the smother of invention" [*Cynic's Calendar*].

Division (II) INTERSOCIAL VOLITION[1]

Section I. GENERAL INTERSOCIAL VOLITION

737. Authority. — **N.** AUTHORITY; influence, patronage, power, preponderance, credit, prestige, prerogative, jurisdiction; right &c. (*title*) 924.

divine right, dynastic rights, authoritativeness; royalty, regality, imperiality [*rare*]; absoluteness, absolutism, despotism, tyranny; *jus nocendi* [*L.*]; *jus divinum* [*L.*].

COMMAND, empire, sway, rule; dominion, domination; sovereignty, supremacy, suzerainty; kinghood, kingship; lordship, headship; chiefdom; patriarchy, patriarchate; leadership, hegemony; seigniory; mastery, mastership, masterdom; government &c. (*direction*) 693; dictation, control.

hold, grasp; grip, gripe; reach; iron sway &c. (*severity*) 739; fangs, clutches, talons; rod of empire &c. (*scepter*) 747.

REIGN, *régime* [*F.*], dynasty; directorship, dictatorship; protectorate, protec-

738. [ABSENCE OF AUTHORITY] Laxity. — **N.** LAXITY; laxness, looseness, slackness; toleration &c. (*lenity*) 740; freedom &c. 748.

ANARCHY, interregnum; relaxation; loosening &c. *v.;* remission; dead letter, *brutum fulmen* [*L.*], misrule; license, licentiousness; insubordination &c. (*disobedience*) 742; mob rule, mob law, mobocracy, ochlocracy; lynch law &c. (*illegality*) 964, nihilism, reign of violence.

[DEPRIVATION OF POWER] dethronement, impeachment, deposition, abdication; usurpation.

V. BE LAX &c. *adj.; laisser faire* [*F.*], *laisser aller* [*F.*]; hold a loose rein; give the reins to, give rope enough, give a loose to [*obs.*], give a free course to, give free rein to; tolerate; relax; misrule.

go beyond the length of one's tether; have one's -swing, – fling; act without -instructions, – authority; act on one's

[1] Implying the action of the will of one mind over the will of another.

torship; caliphate, pashalic, electorate; presidency, presidentship; administration; consulship, proconsulship; prefecture; seneschalship; magistrature, magistracy.

[GOVERNMENTS] empire; monarchy; limited -, constitutional- monarchy; aristarchy, aristocracy; oligarchy, democracy, demagogy; heteronomy; republic; thearchy; diarchy, duarchy, duumvirate; triarchy, triumvirate; heterarchy [obs.]; autocracy, monocracy.

representative government, constitutional government, *vox populi* [L.], home rule, dominion rule [Brit.], colonial government; self-government, autonomy, self-determination; republicanism, federalism; socialism; collectivism; pantisocracy; *imperium in imperio* [L.]; bureaucracy; beadledom, Bumbledom; stratocracy [rare], martial law; military -power, - government; feodality, feodatory, feudal system, feudalism.

GYNOCRACY, gynarchy, gynecocracy *or* gynæcocracy, matriarchy, matriarchate, metrocracy; petticoat government.

[VICARIOUS AUTHORITY] commission &c. 755; deputy &c. 759; permission &c. 760.

STATE, realm, commonwealth, country, power, polity, body politic, *posse comitatus* [L.]; toparchy.

RULER; person in authority &c. (*master*) 745; judicature &c. 965; cabinet &c. (*council*) 696; seat of -government, - authority; headquarters.

usurper, tyrant, jack-in-office.

[ACQUISITION OF AUTHORITY] accession; installation &c. 755; usurpation.

V. AUTHORIZE &c. (*permit*) 760; warrant &c. (*right*) 924; dictate &c. (*order*) 741; have -, hold -, possess -, exercise -, exert -, grasp -, seize -, wrest -, wield- -authority &c. *n.*

RULE, sway, command, control, administer; govern &c. (*direct*) 693; lead, preside over, reign; possess -, be seated on -, occupy -, seize- the throne; sway -, wield- the scepter *or* sceptre; wear the crown.

be at the head of &c. *adj.*; hold -, be in -, fill an- office; hold- , occupy- a post; be master &c. 745.

DOMINATE; have -, get- the -upper, - whip- hand; gain a hold upon, preponderate, dominate, rule the roast; boss [colloq., chiefly U. S.]; override, overrule, overawe; lord it over, hold in hand, keep under, make a puppet of, lead by the nose, turn round one's little finger, bend to one's will, hold one's own, wear the breeches [colloq.]; have the ball at one's feet, have it all one's own way, have the game in one's own hand, have on the hip, have under one's thumb; be master of the situation; take the lead, play first fiddle, set the fashion; give the law to; carry with a high hand; lay down the law; "ride in the whirlwind and direct the storm" [adapted from Addison]; rule with a rod of iron &c. (*severity*) 739.

ASSUME AUTHORITY &c. *n.*; ascend -, mount- the throne; take the reins, - into one's hand; assume the reins of government; take -, assume the- command.

BE GOVERNED BY, be in the power of; be under the -rule of, - dominion of.

Adj. RULING &c. *v.*; regnant, at the head, dominant, paramount, supreme, predominant, preponderant, in the ascendant, influential; gubernatorial; imperious; authoritative, executive, administrative, clothed with authority, official, bureaucratic, departmental, *ex officio* [L.], imperative, peremptory, overruling, absolute; hegemonic *or* hegemonical; arbitrary; compulsory &c. 744; stringent.

at one's command; in one's power, in one's grasp; under control; authorized &c. (*due*) 924.

SOVEREIGN; regal, royal, royalist, monarchical, kingly; dynastic, imperial,

---

own responsibility, usurp authority, undermine the authority of.

DETHRONE, depose; abdicate.

Adj. LAX, loose; slack; remiss &c. (*careless*) 460; weak.

RELAXED; licensed; reinless, unbridled; anarchic *or* anarchical, nihilistic; "agin the government"; unauthorized &c. (*unwarranted*) 925; adespotic, undespotic; not imperious &c. (*ruling*) 737.

⁎⁎⁎ "when the cat's away the mice will play" [prov.]; "Pleasant it is for the little tin gods When great Jove nods" [Kipling].

imperialistic; princely; feudal; aristocratic, autocratic; oligarchic &c. *n.;* demo-cratic, republican.

Adv. in the name of, by the authority of, at one's command, *de par le Roi* [*F.*], in virtue of; under the auspices of, in the hands of.

at one's pleasure; by a dash (*or* stroke) of the pen; at one's nod; by lifting one's finger; *ex mero motu* [*L.*]; *ex cathedrâ* [*L.*].

⁎⁎ the gray mare the better horse; "every inch a king" [*Lear*]; "a dog's obeyed in office" [*ibid.*]; *cada uno tiene su alguazil; le Roi le veut; regibus esse manus an nescis longas; regnant populi;* "the demigod Authority" [*Measure for Measure*]; "off with his head! so much for Buckingham" [Cibber]; "the right divine of kings to govern wrong" [Pope]; "uneasy lies the head that wears a crown" [*Henry IV*]; "government of the people, by the people, for the people" [Lincoln]; "quack remedies . . . are generally as noxious to the body politic as to the body corporal" [Roosevelt].

---

739. Severity. — N. SEVERITY; strictness, harshness &c. *adj.;* rigor, stringency, austerity; inclemency &c. (*pitilessness*) 914a; arrogance &c. 885; precisianism, formalism.

ARBITRARY POWER; absolutism, despotism; dictatorship, autocracy, tyranny, domineering, domination, oppression; assumption, usurpation; inquisition, reign of terror, martial law; iron -heel, – rule, – hand, – sway; tight grasp; brute -force, – strength; coercion &c. 744; strong -, tight- hand.

BUREAUCRACY, red-tapism, pipe-clay, officialism; hard -lines, – measure; tender mercies [*ironical*]; sharp practice.

TYRANT, disciplinarian, precisian, martinet, stickler, bashaw, despot, the Grand Panjandrum himself, hard master, Draco, oppressor, inquisitor, extortioner, harpy, vulture; Accipitres, Raptores, raptors [*obs.*], birds of prey.

V. BE SEVERE &c. *adj.*

ARROGATE, assume, usurp, take liberties; domineer, bully &c. 885; tyrannize; wrest the law to one's advantage; inflict, wreak, stretch a point, put on the screw; be hard upon; bear -, lay- a heavy hand on; be down upon [*slang*], come down upon [*colloq.*]; illtreat; deal hardly with, deal hard measure to; rule with a rod of iron, chastise with scorpions; dye with blood; oppress, override; trample -, tread- -down, – upon, – under foot; crush under an iron heel, ride roughshod over; rivet the yoke; hold -, keep- a tight hand; force down the throat; coerce &c. 744; give no quarter &c. (*pitiless*) 914a.

Adj. SEVERE; strict, hard, harsh, dour [*Scot.*], rigid, stiff, stern, rigorous, uncompromising, exacting, exigent, *exigeant* [*F.*], inexorable, inflexible, obdurate, austere, hard-headed, hard-shell [*colloq., U. S.*], relentless, Spartan, Draconian, stringent, strict, prudish, precise, puritanical, strait-laced, searching, unsparing, ironhanded, peremptory, absolute, positive, arbitrary, imperative; coercive &c. 744; tyrannical, extortionate, grinding, withering, oppressive, inquisitorial; inclement &c. (*ruthless*) 914a; cruel &c. (*malevolent*) 907; haughty, arrogant &c. 885; precisian, formal, punctilious.

Adv. SEVERELY &c. *adj.;* with a -high, – strong, – tight, – heavy- hand.

at the point of the -sword, – bayonet.

⁎⁎ *quidquid delirant reges plectuntur Achivi* [Horace]; *manu forti; ogni debole ha sempre il suo tiranno;* "the King's argument was that anything that had a head could be beheaded" [Carroll].

---

740. Lenity. — N. LENITY, lenitence, lenitency; moderation &c. 174; tolerance, toleration; mildness, gentleness; favor; indulgence, indulgency [*rare*], clemence [*obs.*], clemency, mercy, forbearance, quarter; compassion &c. 914.

V. BE LENIENT &c. *adj.;* tolerate, bear with; *parcere subjectis* [*L.*], spare the vanquished, give quarter.

INDULGE; allow one to -go his own gait, – have his own way, spoil.

Adj. LENIENT; mild, – as milk; gentle, soft; tolerant, indulgent, easy, moderate, complaisant, unconcerned, easy-going; clement &c. (*compassionate*) 914; forbearing; long-suffering.

⁎⁎ "lenity has almost always wisdom and justice on its side" [Ballou]; "He was the mildest manner'd man That ever scuttled ship or cut a throat" [Byron]; "Sweet mercy is nobility's true badge" [*Coriolanus*]; "Nothing emboldens sin so much as mercy" [*Timon of Athens*].

741. Command. — **N.** COMMAND, order, ordinance, act, fiat, *hukm* [*Hind.*], bidding, dictum, hest, behest, call, beck, nod.

DISPATCH *or* despatch, message, direction, injunction, charge, instructions; appointment, fixture.

DEMAND, exaction, imposition, requisition, claim, reclamation, revendication [*rare*]; ultimatum &c. (*terms*) 770; request &c. 765; requirement.

DECREE, dictate, dictation, mandate, caveat, *senatus consultum* [*L.*]; precept; prescript, rescript, writ, ordination, bull, edict, decretal, dispensation, prescription, brevet, placet, *placitum* [*L.*], ukase, firman, hatti-sherif, hatti-humayoun (*or* humayun), warrant, passport, mittimus, mandamus, summons, subpœna, *nisi prius* [*L.*], interpellation, citation; word, – of command; *mot d'ordre* [*F.*]; bugle –, trumpet- call; beat of drum, tattoo; order of the day; enactment &c. (*law*) 963; plebiscite &c. (*choice*) 609.

V. COMMAND, order, decree, enact, ordain, dictate, direct, give orders.

issue a command; make –, issue –, promulgate- -a requisition, – a decree, – an order &c. *n.;* give the -word of command, – word, – signal; call to order; give –, lay down- the law; assume the command &c. (*authority*) 737; remand.

PRESCRIBE, set, appoint, mark out; set –, prescribe –, impose- a task; set to work, put in requisition.

BID, enjoin, charge, call upon, instruct; require, – at the hands of; exact, impose, tax, task; demand; insist on &c. (*compel*) 744.

CLAIM, lay claim to, revendicate [*rare*], reclaim.

CITE, summon, avoke; call for, send for; subpœna; beckon.

BE ORDERED &c.; receive an order &c. *n.*

Adj. COMMANDING &c. *v.;* authoritative &c. 737; decretory, decretive, decretal; callable; imperative, jussive; decisive, final, without appeal; interpellative, demanded, commanded &c. *v.*

Adv. in a commanding tone; by a -stroke, – dash- of the pen; by order, at beat of drum, on the first summons, to order, at the word of command; by -command, – order, – decree- of; as required, as requested, as ordered, as commanded.

*** the decree is gone forth; *sic volo sic jubeo; le roi le veut; boutez en avant.*

---

742. Disobedience. — **N.** DISOBEDIENCE, insubordination, contumacy; infraction, infringement; violation, noncompliance; nonobservance &c. 773.

REVOLT, rebellion, mutiny, outbreak, rising, uprising, insurrection, *émeute* [*F.*], riot, tumult &c. (*disorder*) 59; strike &c. (*resistance*) 719; barring out; defiance &c. 715.

mutinousness &c. *adj.;* mutineering; sedition, treason; high –, petty –, misprision of- treason; præmunire *or* premunire; *lèse-majesté* [*F.*]; violation of law &c. 964; defection, secession, Sinn Fein; revolution; overthrow –, overturn- of -government, – authority; *sabotage* [*F.*], sans-culottism, bolshevism.

INSURGENT, mutineer, rebel, revolter, rioter, traitor, *Carbonaro* [*It.*], sans-culotte, red republican, *bonnet rouge* [*F.*], communist, Fenian, Sinn Feiner, Red, Bolshevist, *frondeur* [*F.*], seceder, Secessionist [*esp., U. S. hist.*] *or* Secesh [*colloq. or slang, U. S.*]; apostate, renegade, runaway, runagate; brawler, an-

---

743. Obedience. — **N.** OBEDIENCE; observance &c. 772; compliance; submission &c. 725; subjection &c. 749; nonresistance; passiveness, passivity, resignation.

ALLEGIANCE, loyalty, fealty, homage, deference, devotion; constancy, fidelity.

SUBMISSIVENESS, submissness [*obs.*]; ductility &c. (*softness*) 324; obsequiousness &c. (*servility*) 886.

V. BE OBEDIENT &c. *adj.;* obey, bear obedience to; submit &c. 725; comply, answer the helm, come at one's call; do one's bidding, do what one is told, do suit and service; attend to orders; serve -faithfully, – loyally, – devotedly, – without question; give -loyal, – devoted-service; be resigned to, be submissive to.

follow, – the lead of, – to the world's end; serve &c. 746; play second fiddle.

Adj. OBEDIENT, law-abiding, complying, compliant; loyal, faithful, devoted; at one's -call, – command, – orders, – beck and call; under beck and call, under control.

archist, demagogue; Spartacus, Masaniello, Wat Tyler, Jack Cade; ringleader.

V. DISOBEY, violate, infringe; shirk, slide out of, slack; set at defiance &c. (*defy*) 715; set authority at naught, run riot, fly in the face of; take the law into one's own hands; kick over the traces; refuse to support, bolt [*U. S. politics*].

turn -, run- restive; champ the bit; strike &c. (*resist*) 719; rise, - in arms; secede; mutiny, rebel.

Adj. DISOBEDIENT; uncomplying, uncompliant; unsubmissive, unruly, ungovernable; breachy, insubordinate, impatient of control; restive, restiff [*obs.*], refractory, contumacious; recusant &c. (*refuse*) 764; recalcitrant; resisting &c. 719; lawless, riotous, mutinous, seditious, insurgent, revolutionary, sansculottic, secessionist.

unobeyed, disobeyed; unbidden.

⁎ *seditiosissimus quisque ignavus* [Tacitus]; "unthread the rude eye of rebellion" [*King John*]; "revolution is the larva of civilization" [Hugo]; "there is little hope of equity where rebellion reigns" [Sidney]; "rebellion to tyrants is obedience to God" [*epitaph to John Bradshaw*].

restrainable; resigned, passive; submissive &c. 725; henpecked; pliant &c. (*soft*) 324.

unresisted, unresisting.

Adv. OBEDIENTLY &c. *adj.*; as you please, if you please; in compliance with, in obedience to; at your -command, - orders, - service.

⁎ to hear is to obey; "theirs not to make reply, theirs not to reason why" [Tennyson]; "Obedience, bane of all genius, virtue, freedom, truth" [Shelley]; "obedience is the mother of success" [Æschylus]; "And art made tongue-tied by authority" [Shakespeare].

744. Compulsion. — N. COMPULSION, coercion, coaction, constraint; restraint &c. 751; duress, enforcement, press, conscription; eminent domain.

force; brute -, main -, physical- force; the sword, *ultima ratio* [*L.*]; club -, lynch -, mob- law, *argumentum baculinum* [*L.*], *le droit du plus fort* [*F.*]; the force of -might, - right; martial law.

necessity &c. 601; *force majeure* [*F.*], spur of necessity, Hobson's choice.

V. COMPEL, force, make, drive, coerce, constrain, enforce, necessitate, oblige.

force upon, press; cram -, thrust -, force- down the throat; say it must be done, make a point of, insist upon, take no denial; put down, dragoon.

extort, wring from; put -, turn- on the screw; drag into; bind, - over; pin-, tie- down; require, tax, put in force; commandeer; restrain &c. 751.

Adj. COMPELLING &c. *v.*; coercive, coactive; inexorable &c. 739; compulsory, compulsatory; obligatory, stringent, peremptory, binding.

forcible, not to be trifled with; irresistible &c. 601; compelled &c. *v.*; fain to.

Adv. FORCIBLY; by force &c. *n.*, by force of arms; on compulsion, perforce; *vi et armis* [*L.*], under the lash; at the point of the -sword, - bayonet; by a strong arm.

under protest, in spite of, in one's teeth; against one's will &c. 603; *nolens volens* [*L.*] &c. (*of necessity*) 601; by stress of -circumstances, - weather; under press of; *de rigueur* [*F.*].

745. Master. — N. MASTER, *padrone* [*It.*], lord, - paramount; commander, commandant, captain, chief, chieftain; paterfamilias [*Rom. law*], patriarch; sahib [*India*], bara (*or* burra) sahib [*India*], sirdar, sheik; head, senior, governor, ruler, dictator; leader &c. (*director*) 694; boss, baas [*Dutch*]; cockarouse [*obs.*], sachem, sagamore, werowance.

lord of the ascendant; cock of the -walk, - loft, - midden [*archaic*], - roost; gray mare; mistress.

POTENTATE; liege, - lord; suzerain,

746. Servant. — N. SERVANT, retainer, follower, henchman, servitor, domestic, menial, help [*local*, *U. S.*], lady help [*Brit.*], employee *or* employé; *attaché* [*F.*], official.

SUBJECT, liege, liegeman; people, "my people."

RETINUE, suite, *cortège* [*F.*], staff, court; office force, clerical staff, clerical force, workers, associate workers, employees, the help [*esp.*, *U. S.*].

ATTENDANT, squire, usher, donzel [*obs.*], apprentice, prentice [*colloq. or dial.*]; page, buttons [*colloq.*], footboy;

overlord, overking, sovereign, monarch, autocrat, despot, tyrant, oligarch.

crowned head, emperor, king, anointed king, majesty, imperator, protector, president, stadholder *or* stadtholder, judge.

cæsar, kaiser, czar *or* tsar, sultan, soldan [*obs.*], grand Turk, caliph, imam *or* imaum, shah, padishah, sophi, mogul, great mogul, khan, lama, pendragon, tycoon, mikado, inca, cazique; voivode *or* waywode, hospodar, landamman; sayid *or* sayyid, cacique, czarevitch, grand seignior.

prince, duke &c. (*nobility*) 875; archduke, doge, elector; seignior; landgrave, margrave; maharajah, rajah, emir, nizam, nawab &c. (*Indian ruling chiefs*) 875.

empress, queen, sultana, czarina *or* tsarina, princess, infanta, duchess, margravine; czarevna *or* tsarevna, czarina; maharani, rani [*both Hindu*], begum [*Moham.*]; rectoress *or* rectress, rectrix.

REGENT, viceroy, exarch, palatine, khedive, beglerbeg *or* beylerbey, three-tailed bashaw, pasha *or* bashaw, bey *or* beg, dey, shereef *or* sherif, tetrarch, satrap, mandarin, nabob, burgrave; laird &c. (*proprietor*) 779; commissioner, deputy commissioner, collector, woon *or* wun [*Burmese*].

THE AUTHORITIES, the powers that be, the government, "them above" [Eliot]; staff, *état major* [*F.*], aga, official, man in office, person in authority; sirkar *or* sircar; Sublime Porte.

[MILITARY AUTHORITIES] marshal, field marshal, *maréchal* [*F.*], generalissimo; commander-in-chief, seraskier [*Turk.*], hetman [*Cossack*]; general, brigadier general, brigadier, lieutenant general, major general, colonel, lieutenant colonel, major, captain, ressaldar *or* risaldar [*India*], subahdar *or* subadar [*India*]; centurion, lieutenant, jemadar [*India*], sublieutenant, officer, staff officer, aide-de-camp, brigade major, adjutant, ensign, cornet, cadet, subaltern; non-commissioned officer; sergeant, -major; color sergeant; top-sergeant [*U. S.*], havildar [*India*]; corporal, -major; lance corporal, acting corporal; naik [*India*]; drum major; captain general, knight marshal.

[CIVIL AUTHORITIES] mayor, mayoralty; *maire* [*F.*], prefect, chancellor,

trainbearer, cupbearer; waiter, tapster, butler, livery servant, lackey, footman, flunky *or* flunkey [*colloq.*]; bearer [*Anglo-Ind.*], boy [*any colored male servant, as in the Orient, South Africa,* &c.]; hamal [*India*], scout [*Oxford Univ.*], gyp [*Camb. Univ.*], valet, *valet de chambre* [*F.*]; equerry, groom; jockey, hostler *or* ostler, orderly, messenger, gillie *or* gilly, caddie *or* caddy, herdsman, swineherd; barkeeper, bartender, barkeep [*U. S.*]; boots [*Brit.*]; cad [*Eng. Univ. cant*], bell boy, bell-hop [*slang*], tiger, chokra [*India*], boy; counterjumper [*colloq.*]; khansamah *or* khansaman [*India*], khitmutgar [*India*]; yardman, journeyman.

bailiff, castellan *or* castellain, seneschal, chamberlain, major-domo, groom of the chambers.

secretary; under –, assistant- secretary; stenographer, clerk; subsidiary; agent &c. 758; subaltern; underling, understrapper; man.

MAID, maidservant; girl, help [*local, U. S.*], handmaid; confidant (*fem. confidante*), *confident* (*fem. confidente*) [*F.*]; lady's maid, abigail, soubrette, amah [*Oriental*], biddy [*colloq.*], *bonne* [*F.*], ayah [*India*]; nurse-, nursery-, house-, parlor-, waiting-, chamber-, kitchen-, scullery- maid; *femme –, fille- de chambre* [*F.*]; *chef de cuisine* [*F.*], *cordon bleu* [*F.*], cook, scullion, Cinderella; pot-walloper; maid-, servant- of all work; slavey [*slang, Eng.*], general servant [*Brit.*], general housework maid [*U. S.*], general [*colloq.*]; washerwoman, laundress, bedmaker; charwoman &c. (*worker*) 690.

DEPENDENT *or* dependant, hanger-on, led friend [*obs.*], satellite; parasite &c. (*servility*) 886; led captain; *protégé* [*F.*], ward, hireling, mercenary, puppet, man of straw, creature; serf, vassal, slave, negro, helot; bondsman, bondswoman, bondslave; *âme damnée* [*F.*], odalisque *or* odalisk, ryot, *adscriptus glebæ* [*L.*], villein *or* villain [*hist.*], churl *or* ceorl [*hist.*]; beadsman *or* bedesman; sizar *or* sizer [*Camb. & Dublin Univs.*], pensioner, pensionary; client.

badge of slavery; bonds &c. 752.

V. SERVE, minister to, help, coöperate; wait –, attend –, dance attendance –, fasten oneself –, pin oneself- upon; squire, valet, tend, hang on the sleeve of; chore [*dial., U. S.*], do the chores

archon [Gr.], provost, magistrate, syndic; alcalde [Sp.], alcaide or alcaid; burgomaster, corregidor [Sp.], seneschal, alderman, warden, constable, portreeve; lord mayor; officer &c. (executive) 965; diwan or dewan [India]; hakim; fonctionnaire [F.].

[NAVAL AUTHORITIES] admiral, admiralty; rear-, vice-, port- admiral; commodore, captain, commander, lieutenant; skipper, master, mate, navarch [Gr. antiq.].

₊ da locum melioribus; der Fürst ist der erste Diener seines Staats; "lord of thy presence and no land beside" [King John]; "Duty, not joy, is all a prince's share" [Masefield].

[colloq.], char [dial. Eng.], do for [colloq.], fag.

Adj. SERVICEABLE, useful, helpful; coöperative.

SERVING &c. v.; in the train of; in one's -pay; – employ; at one's call &c. (obedient) 743; in bonds.

SERVILE, slavish, vernile [rare]; subject, thrall, bond; subservient, obsequious, base, fawning, truckling, sycophantic or sycophantical, sycophantish [rare], parasitic, cringing.

₊ "art thou less a slave because thy master lo es and caresses thee?" [Pascal]; "How happy is he born and taught That serveth not another's will" [Wotton].

---

747. [INSIGNIA OF AUTHORITY.] **Scepter.** — **N.** [REGAL] scepter or sceptre, rod of empire; orb; pall; robes of -state, – royalty; ermine, purple; crown, coronet, diadem, cap of maintenance; triple plume, Prince of Wales's feathers; uræus, flail [both Egyptian]; signet, seal.

[ECCLESIASTICAL] tiara, triple crown; ring, keys; miter or mitre, crozier, crook, staff; cardinal's hat; bishop's -apron, – sleeves, – lawn, – gaiters, – shovel hat; fillet.

[MILITARY] epaulet or epaulette, star, bar, eagle, crown [Brit.], oak leaf, Sam Browne belt; chevron, stripe.

caduceus; Mercury's -staff, – rod, – wand; mace, fasces, ax or axe, truncheon, staff, baton, wand, rod; staff –, rod- -of office, – of authority; insignia –, ensign –, emblem –, badge- of authority; flag &c. (insignia) 550; regalia; toga, mantle, decoration; title &c. 877; portfolio.

THRONE, Peacock throne [Chinese], musnud or masnad [Ar.]; raj-gaddi, gaddi or guddee [India], divan; wool-sack, chair; dais &c. (seat) 215.

TALISMAN, amulet, charm, sign.

HELM; reins &c. (means of restraint) 752.

---

748. Freedom. — **N.** FREEDOM, liberty, independence; license &c. (permission) 760; eleutherism [rare]; facility &c. 705.

SCOPE, range, latitude, play; free –, full- -play, – scope; free field and no favor; swing, full swing, elbowroom, margin, rope, wide berth; Liberty Hall.

FRANCHISE, denization; prerogative &c. (dueness) 924.

freeman, freedman, liveryman [London guilds], citizen, denizen.

IMMUNITY, exemption; emancipation &c. (liberation) 750; affranchisement, enfranchisement; right, privilege.

AUTONOMY, self-government, liberalism, free trade; self-determination; noninterference &c. 706; Monroe Doctrine [U. S.].

FREE LAND, freehold; alod or allod, alodium or allodium; frankalmoign or

749. Subjection. — **N.** SUBJECTION; dependence, dependency; subordination; thrall, thralldom or thraldom, enthrallment or enthralment, subjugation, bondage, serfdom; feudalism, feudality; vassalage, villenage or villeinage, slavery, enslavement, involuntary servitude; conquest.

SERVICE; servitude, servitorship; tendence, employ, tutelage, clientship; liability &c. 177; constraint &c. 751; oppression &c. (severity) 739; yoke &c. (means of restraint) 752; submission &c. 725; obedience &c. 743.

V. BE SUBJECT &c. adj.; be or lie at the mercy of; depend –, lean –, hangupon; fall a prey to, fall under; play second fiddle.

be a -mere machine, – puppet, – doormat, – football; not dare to say one's soul is his own; drag a chain.

frankalmoigne [*Eng. law*], tenure in (*or* by) free alms [*Eng. law*]; dead hand, mortmain [*law*].

INDEPENDENT, free lance, freethinker, free trader *or* freetrader; bushwhacker [*U. S.*].

V. BE FREE &c. *adj.;* have -scope &c. *n.,* – the run of, – one's own way, – a will of one's own, – one's fling; do what one -likes, – wishes, – pleases, – chooses; go at large, feel at home, paddle one's own canoe; stand on one's rights; stand on one's own legs; shift for oneself.

TAKE A LIBERTY; make free with, make oneself quite at home; use a free-dom; take leave, take French leave.

FREE, liberate, set free &c. 750; give the reins to &c. (*permit*) 760; allow –, give -scope &c. *n.* to; give a horse his head.

make free of; give the -freedom of, – franchise; enfranchise, affranchise.

laisser faire [*F.*], *laisser aller* [*F.*]; live and let live; leave to oneself; leave *or* let alone, mind one's own business.

Adj. FREE, – as air; out of harness, independent, at large, loose, scot-free; left -alone, – to oneself.

UNCONSTRAINED, unbuttoned, uncon-fined, unrestrained, unchecked, un-prevented, unhindered, unobstructed, unbound, uncontrolled, untrammeled, uncaught; in full swing.

UNSUBJECT, ungoverned, unenslaved, unenthralled, unchained, unshackled, unfettered, unreined, unbridled, un-curbed, unmuzzled, unvanquished.

UNRESTRICTED, unlimited, uncondi-ditional; absolute; with unlimited -power, – opportunity; discretionary &c. (*optional*) 600.

unassailed, unforced, uncompelled.

serve &c. 746; obey &c. 743; submit &c. 725.

SUBJUGATE, subject, tame, break in; master &c. 731; tread -down, – under foot; weigh down; drag at one's chariot wheel; reduce to -subjection, – slavery; enthrall *or* enthral, inthrall *or* inthral, bethrall, enslave, lead captive; take into custody &c. (*restrain*) 751; rule &c. 737; drive into a corner, hold at the sword's point; keep under; hold in -bondage, – leading strings, – swaddling clothes; have at one's -apron strings, – beck and call; have in one's pocket.

Adj. SUBJECT, dependent, subordi-nate; feudal, feudatory; in subjection to, servitorial [*rare*], under control; in leading strings, in harness; subjected, thrall [*archaic*]; servile, slavish &c. 746; enslaved &c. *v.;* constrained &c. 751; downtrodden; overborne, overwhelmed; under the lash, on the hip, led by the nose, henpecked; the -puppet, – sport, – plaything- of; under one's -orders, – command; – thumb; used as a doormat, treated like dirt under one's feet; a slave to; at the mercy of; in the -power, – hands, – clutches- of; at the feet of; in one's pocket; tied to one's apron strings; at one's beck and call &c. (*obedient*) 743; liable &c. 177; parasiti-cal; stipendiary.

Adv. UNDER; under -orders, – the heel, – command; at one's orders; with no -mind, – will, – soul- of one's own.

*** "slaves — in a land of light and law" [Whittier]; "base in kind, and born to be a slave" [Cowper]; "Subjection, but requir'd with gentle sway" [Milton]; "the parrot of other men's thinking" [Emerson]; "La Belle Dame sans Mercy Hath thee in thrall" [Keats].

UNBIASED, unprejudiced, uninfluenced; spontaneous.

FREE AND EASY; at –, at one's- ease; *dégagé* [*F.*], quite at home; beyond all bounds; wanton, rampant, irrepressible.

EXEMPT; freed &c. 750; freeborn; autonomous, freehold, alodial *or* allodial; eleutherian [*rare*].

GRATUITOUS, gratis &c. 815; for nothing, for love.

UNCLAIMED, going a-begging.

Adv. freely &c. *adj.;* ad libitum [*L.*] &c. (*at will*) 600; with no restraint &c. 751.

*** *ubi libertas ibi patria;* "For what avail the plough or sail, Or land or life, if freedom fail?" [Emerson]; "We must be free or die who speak the tongue That Shakespeare spake" [Wordsworth]; "Oh! let me live my own, and die so too!" [Pope]; "He is the freeman whom the truth makes free, And all are slaves besides" [Cowper]; "Where liberty dwells, there is my country" [Franklin]; "liberty exists in proportion to wholesome restraint" [Daniel Webster]; "The God who gave us life gave us liberty at the same time" [Thomas Jefferson].

325

750. Liberation. — N. LIBERATION, disengagement, release, enlargement, emancipation, disenthrallment or disenthrallment, Emancipation Proclamation; affranchisement, enfranchisement; manumission; discharge, dismissal.

DELIVERANCE &c. 672; redemption, extrication, acquittance, absolution; acquittal &c. 970; escape &c. 671.

V. LIBERATE, free; set free, set at liberty; render free, emancipate, release; enfranchise, affranchise; manumit; enlarge; demobilize, disband, discharge, disenthrall or disenthral, disinthrall or disinthral, dismiss; let go, let loose, let out, let slip; cast –, turn- adrift; deliver &c. 672; absolve &c. (acquit) 970.

UNFETTER &c. 751, untie &c. 43; loose &c. (disjoin) 44; loosen, relax; unbolt, unbar, unclose, uncork, unclog, unhand, unbind, unchain, unharness; disengage, disentangle; clear, extricate, unloose; reprieve.

BECOME FREE; gain –, obtain –, acquire- one's -liberty &c. 748; get rid of, get clear of; deliver oneself from; shake off the yoke, slip the collar; break loose, break prison; tear asunder one's bonds, cast off trammels; escape &c. 671.

Adj. LIBERATED &c. v.; out of harness &c. (free) 748; foot-loose; breathing free air again; one's own master again.

Adv. AT LARGE, at liberty; adrift.

Int. unhand me! let me go! reprieve! go in peace! free!

. "In giving freedom to the slave we assume freedom to the free" [Lincoln]; "Over my head his arm he flung Against the world" [Browning].

751. Restraint. — N. RESTRAINT; hindrance &c. 706; coercion &c. (compulsion) 744; cohibition [rare], constraint, repression; discipline, control.

limitation, restriction, protection, monopoly; prohibition &c. 761; economic pressure.

CONFINEMENT, restringency [obs.], durance, duress; imprisonment; incarceration, coarctation [obs.], entombment, mancipation [obs.], thrall; thralldom &c. (subjection) 749; durance vile, limbo, captivity; blockade; detention camp; quarantine station.

ARREST, arrestation [rare], arrestment, custody.

KEEP, care, charge, ward.

curb &c. (means of restraint) 752; lettres de cachet [F.].   .

REPRESSIONIST, monopolist, protectionist.

PRISONER &c. 754.

V. RESTRAIN, check; put –, lay- under restraint, put under arrest; enthrall or enthral, inthrall or inthral, bethrall or bethral; restrict; debar &c. (hinder) 706; constrain; coerce &c. (compel) 744· curb, control; hold –, keep- -back, –from, – in, – in check, – within bounds; hold in -leash, – leading strings; withhold.

repress, suppress ; keep under ; smother; pull in, rein in; hold, – fast; keep a tight hand on; prohibit &c. 761; inhibit, cohibit.

FASTEN &c. (join) 43; enchain, fetter, shackle; entrammel, trammel; bridle, muzzle, hopple, gag, pinion, manacle, handcuff, tie one's hands, hobble, bind, bind hand and foot; swathe, swaddle; pin down, tether; picket; tie, – up, – down; peg -out, – down; keep [archaic], secure; forge fetters.

CONFINE; shut -up, – in; clap up, lock up, box up, mew up, bottle up, cork up, seal up, button up; hem in, bolt in, wall in, rail in; impound, pen, coop; inclose &c. (circumscribe) 229; cage; incage or encage; close the door upon, cloister; imprison, jug [slang], immure; incarcerate, entomb; clap –, lay- under hatches; put in -irons, – a strait-waistcoat; throw –, cast- into prison; put into bilboes.

ARREST; take -up, – charge of, – into custody; restringe [rare], cohibit [rare]; take –, make- -prisoner, – captive; captivate [rare]; lead -captive, – into captivity; send –, commit- to prison; commit; give in -charge, – custody; subjugate &c. 749.

Adj. RESTRAINED, constrained; imprisoned &c. v.; pent up; jammed in, packed in, wedged in; under -restraint, – lock and key, – hatches; in swaddling clothes; on parole; serving –, doing- time [colloq. or slang]; in irons, in the guardhouse; in custody &c. (prisoner) 754; cohibitive [rare]; mancipatory [Rom. law]; coactive &c. (compulsory) 744.

icebound, windbound, weatherbound; "cabined, cribbed, confined" [Macbeth]; in lob's pound, laid by the heels.

STIFF, restringent [*obs.*], narrow, prudish, strait-laced, hidebound, barkbound.

Adv. UNDER RESTRAINT, under discipline; in prison, in jail, in durance vile, in confinement; behind bars; in captivity, during captivity; under arrest; under prohibition; within limits, within bounds.

⁎ "Checked like a bondman" [*Julius Cæsar*]; "you forget yourself To hem me in" [*ibid.*]; "her cabin'd ample spirit" [Arnold].

752. [MEANS OF RESTRAINT.] **Prison. — N.** PRISON, prisonhouse; jail *or* gaol, cage, coop, den, cell; stronghold, fortress, keep, donjon, dungeon, Bastille, *oubliette* [*F.*], bridewell [*Eng.*], jug [*slang*], house of correction, hulks, tollbooth, panopticon, penitentiary, state prison, guardroom, lockup, roundhouse [*archaic*], watch-house [*obs. or Scot.*], station house, station [*colloq.*]; sponging house; house of detention, black hole, pen [*also slang for penitentiary*], fold, pinfold *or* penfold, pound; inclosure &c. 232; penal settlement; bilboes, stocks, limbo *or* limbus, quod [*slang*]; calaboose [*local, U. S.*], choky *or* chokey [*Anglo-Ind. or slang, Eng.*]; *chauki, thana* [*both India*]; workhouse [*U. S.; in England, a workhouse is a poorhouse*], reformatory, reform school; debtor's prison, college [*slang, Eng.*].

Tower, Newgate, Fleet, Marshalsea; King's (*or* Queen's) Bench; Sing Sing, the Tombs.

[RESTRAINING DEVICES] shackle, bond, gyve, fetter, trammel, irons, pinion, manacle, handcuff, strait-waistcoat, hopples; vise *or* vice; bandage, splint, strap.

yoke, collar, halter, harness; muzzle, gag, bit, curb, snaffle, bridle; rein, reins; bearing rein; martingale; leading string; tether, picket, band, guy, chain; cord &c. (*fastening*) 45; cavesson, hackamore [*Western U. S.*], jaquima [*S. W. U. S.*], headstall, lines [*U. S. & dial. Eng.*], ribbons [*colloq.*]; brake.

BAR, bolt, lock, padlock; rail, paling, palisade; wall, fence, **barrier, barricade.** drag &c. (*hindrance*) 706.

Adj. imprisoned &c. (*restrained*) 751.

⁎ "I am forbid To tell the secrets of my prison house" [*Hamlet*]; "Brightest in dungeons, Liberty! thou art" [Byron]; "Stone walls do not a prison make Nor iron bars a cage" [Lovelace].

753. Keeper. — N. KEEPER, custodian, *custos* [*L.*], ranger, gamekeeper, warder, jailer *or* gaoler, turnkey, castellan, guard; watch, watchdog, watchman, night watchman, Charley *or* Charlie [*Brit.*]; chokidar [*Anglo-Ind.*], durwan [*Anglo-Ind.*], hayward; sentry, sentinel, watch and ward; *concierge* [*F.*], coastguard.

ESCORT, bodyguard; convoy.

GUARDIAN, protector, governor, duenna; governess &c. (*teacher*) 540; nurse, *bonne* [*F.*], amah [*Oriental*], ayah [*India*].

⁎ "Am I my brother's keeper?" [*Bible*].

755. [VICARIOUS AUTHORITY.] **Commission. — N.** COMMISSION, delegation; consignment, assignment; proxy, power of attorney, procuration; deputation, legation, mission, embassy; agency, agentship; clerkship.

errand, charge, brevet, diploma, exequatur, permit &c. (*permission*) 760.

APPOINTMENT, nomination, return; charter; ordination; installation, inauguration, investiture; accession, coronation, enthronement.

754. Prisoner. — N. PRISONER, convict, captive, *détenu* [*F.*], collegian [*slang, Eng.*], close prisoner.

JAILBIRD *or* gaolbird, ticket-of-leave man [*Brit.*], *chevronné* [*F.*].

V. stand committed; be imprisoned &c. 751.

Adj. IMPRISONED &c. 751; in prison, in quod [*slang*], in durance vile, in limbo, in custody, in charge, in chains; behind bars; under lock and key, under hatches. on parole.

⁎ "Dweller in yon dungeon dark" [Burns].

756. Abrogation. — N. ABROGATION, annulment, nullification; *vacatur* [*L.*]; *nolle prosequi* [*L., law*]; canceling &c. *v.*; cancel; revocation, revokement; repeal, rescission, defeasance.

DISMISSAL, *congé* [*F.*], demission [*obs.*]; bounce [*slang, U. S.*]; deposal, deposition; dethronement; disestablishment, disendowment; secularization, deconsecration; sack [*slang*], walking-papers, walking-ticket [*both colloq.*], yellow cover [*slang*].

REGENCY, regentship; vicegerency.

viceroy &c. 745; consignee &c. 758; deputy &c. 759.

V. COMMISSION, delegate, depute; consign, assign; charge; intrust or entrust; commit, – to the hands of; authorize &c. (*permit*) 760.

put in commission, accredit, engage, hire, bespeak, appoint, name, nominate, return, ordain; install, induct, inaugurate, invest, crown; enroll, enlist; give power of attorney to; employ, empower; set –, place- over; send out.

BE COMMISSIONED, be accredited; represent, stand for; stand in the -stead, – place, – shoes- of.

Adj. commissioned &c. *v.*

Adv. INSTEAD OF; in one's -stead, – place; as proxy for; *per procurationem* [*L.*], *in loco parentis* [*L.*].

abolition, abolishment; dissolution.

COUNTERORDER, countermand; repudiation, retractation; recantation &c. (*tergiversation*) 607.

abolitionist, prohibitionist.

V. ABROGATE, annul, cancel; destroy &c. 162; abolish; revoke, repeal, rescind, reverse, retract, recall; overrule, override; set aside; disannul, dissolve, quash, nullify, make void, nol-pros [*law*], declare null and void; disestablish, disendow; deconsecrate.

countermand, counterorder; do away with; sweep –, brush- away; throw overboard, throw to the dogs; scatter to the winds, cast behind.

DISCLAIM &c. (*deny*) 536; ignore, repudiate; recant &c. 607; divest oneself, break off.

DISMISS, discard; cast –, turn- -off, – out, – adrift, – out of doors, – aside, – away; send off, send away, send about one's business; discharge, get rid of &c. (*eject*) 297; bounce [*slang, U. S.*]; fire, fire out, sack [*all slang*].

cashier; break; oust; unseat, unsaddle; unthrone, dethrone, disenthrone, depose, uncrown; unfrock, strike off the roll; disbar, disbench.

BE ABROGATED &c.; receive its quietus.

Adj. ABROGATED &c. *v.; functus officio* [*L.*].

Int. get along with you! begone! go about your business! away with!.

757. Resignation. — N. RESIGNATION, retirement, abdication; renunciation, retractation, retraction, renunciance [*rare*], disclamation, disclaimer, abjuration; abandonment, relinquishment.

V. RESIGN; give up, throw up; lay down, throw up the cards, wash one's hands of, abjure, renounce, forego, disclaim, retract; deny &c. 536.

ABROGATE &c. 756; desert &c. (*relinquish*) 624; get rid of &c. 782.

VACATE, – one's seat; abdicate; accept the stewardship of the Chiltern Hundreds [*Eng.*]; retire; tender –, pass in –, hand in- one's resignation.

Adj. ABDICANT; resigning &c *v.;* renunciatory, renunciant [*rare*], abjuratory, disclamatory [*rare*], retractive.

*** "Othello's occupation's gone" [*Othello*]; "few die and none resign" [Jefferson].

758. Consignee. — N. CONSIGNEE, trustee, nominee; committee.

functionary, placeman, curator; treasurer &c. 801; agent, factor, reeve [*Eng. hist.*], steward, gomashta [*India*], bailiff, clerk, secretary, attorney, solicitor, proctor, broker, dalal [*India*], dubash [*India*]; insurer, underwriter, commission agent, auctioneer, one's man of business; factotum &c. (*director*) 694; caretaker; garnishee; under agent, employé; servant &c. 746.

negotiator, go-between; middleman; walking delegate [*trade-unions*].

DELEGATE; commissary, commissioner; emissary, envoy, commissionaire; messenger &c. 534.

DIPLOMATIST, diplomat or diplomate, *corps diplomatique* [*F.*], embassy; ambassador or embassador, diplomatic agent, representative, resident, consul, legate, nuncio, internuncio, *chargé d'affaires* [*F.*], *attaché* [*F.*]; vicegerent &c. (*deputy*) 759; plenipotentiary.

SALESMAN, traveler, bagman, *commis voyageur* [*F.*], traveling salesman, commercial traveler, drummer [*U. S.*], traveling man; agent for (firm or commodity); touter [*colloq.*], barker [*colloq.*]

REPORTER; newspaper –, own –, war –, special- correspondent.

*** "Diplomacy: lying in state" [*Cynic's Calendar*].

759. Deputy. — N. DEPUTY, substitute, proxy, *locum tenens* [*L.*], *badli* [*Hind.*], delegate, representative, next friend [*law*], *prochein ami* [*F. law*], surrogate, secondary; vice-president, vice-chairman, vice [*colloq.*].

regent, vicegerent, vizier, minister, vicar; premier &c. (*director*) 694; chancellor, prefect, provost, warden, lieutenant, archon [*antiq.*], consul, proconsul [*Rom. antiq.*]; viceroy &c. (*governor*) 745; ambassador; commissioner &c. 758; plenipotentiary, plenipotent; *alter ego* [*L.*].

TEAM, eight, nine, eleven; captain, champion.

V. BE DEPUTY &c. *n.;* stand –, appear –, hold a brief –, answer- for; represent; stand –, walk- in the shoes of; stand in the stead of.

DELEGATE, depute, empower, commission, substitute, ablegate [*R. C. Ch.*], accredit.

Adj. ACTING; vice, viceregal; accredited to; delegated &c. *v.;* representative, plenipotent [*rare*], consular, proconsular.

Adv. IN BEHALF OF, in the place of, as representing, by proxy.

Section II. SPECIAL INTERSOCIAL VOLITION

760. Permission. — N. PERMISSION, leave; allowance, sufferance; tolerance, toleration; liberty, law, license, concession, grace; indulgence &c. (*lenity*) 740; favor, dispensation, exemption, release; connivance; vouchsafement.

authorization, warranty [*law*], accordance, admission.

PERMIT, warrant, brevet, precept, sanction, authority, firman; *hukm* [*Hind.*]; pass, passport; furlough, license, *carte blanche* [*F.*], ticket of leave; grant, charter, patent.

V. PERMIT; give permission &c. *n.,* give power; let, allow, admit; suffer, bear with, tolerate, recognize; concede &c. 762; accord, vouchsafe, favor, humor, gratify, indulge, stretch a point; wink at, connive at; shut one's eyes to.

grant, empower, charter, enfranchise, privilege, confer a privilege, license, authorize, warrant; sanction; intrust &c. (*commission*) 755.

give *carte blanche* [*F.*], give the reins to, give scope to &c. (*freedom*) 748; leave -alone, – it to one, – the door open; open the -door to, – floodgates; give a loose to [*obs.*].

ask –, beg –, crave –, request- -leave, – permission.

LET OFF; absolve &c. (*acquit*) 970; release, exonerate, dispense with.

Adj. PERMITTING &c. *v.;* permissive, indulgent.

PERMITTED &c. *v.;* patent, chartered, permissible, allowable, lawful, legitimate, legal; legalized &c. (*law*) 963; licit; unforbid [*archaic*], unforbidden; unconditional.

Adv. PERMISSIBLY, licitly; by –, with –, on- leave &c. *n.;* *speciali gratiâ* [*L.*]; under favor of; *pace* [*L.*]; *ad libitum* [*L.*] &c. (*freely*) 748, (*at will*) 600; by all means &c. (*willingly*) 602; yes &c. (*assent*) 488.

761. Prohibition. — N. PROHIBITION, inhibition; veto, disallowance; interdict, interdiction; injunction; embargo, ban, taboo *or* tabu, proscription; *index expurgatorius* [*L.*], restriction &c. (*restraint*) 751; hindrance &c. 706; forbidden fruit; Maine law, Volstead Act, 18th amendment [*all U. S.*].

V. prohibit, inhibit; forbid, put one's veto upon, disallow; bar; debar &c. (*hinder*) 706, forfend *or* forefend [*archaic*].

RESTRAIN &c. 751; keep -in, – within bounds; cohibit [*rare*], withhold, limit, circumscribe, clip the wings of, restrict; interdict, taboo *or* tabu; put –, place- under -an interdiction, – the ban; proscribe; exclude, shut out; shut –, bolt –, show- the door; warn off; dash the cup from one's lips; forbid the banns.

Adj. PROHIBITIVE, prohibitory; proscriptive; restrictive, exclusive; forbidding &c. *v.*

PROHIBITED &c. *v.;* not permitted &c. 760; unlicensed, contraband, under the ban of, taboo *or* tabu; illegal &c. 964; unauthorized, not to be thought of.

Adv. on no account &c. (*no*) 536.

Int. forbid it heaven! &c. (*deprecation*) 766.

HANDS OFF! keep off! hold! stop! avast!

** that will never do; "I would fain die a dry death" [*Tempest*].

** *avec permission; brevet d'invention;* "Who has no will but by her high permission" [Burns].

762. Consent. — N. CONSENT; assent &c. 488; acquiescence; approval &c. 931; compliance, agreement, concession; yieldance [*obs.*], yieldingness; accession, acknowledgment, acceptance, agnition [*obs.*].

settlement, adjustment, ratification, confirmation.

permit &c. (*permission*) 760; promise &c. 768.

V. CONSENT; assent &c. 488; yield assent, admit, allow, concede, grant, yield; come over, come round; give into, acknowledge, agnize [*archaic*], give consent, comply with, acquiesce, agree to, fall in with, accede, accept, embrace an offer, close with, take at one's word, have no objection.

satisfy, meet one's wishes, settle, come to terms &c. 488; not refuse &c. 764; turn a willing ear &c. (*willingness*) 602; jump at; deign, vouchsafe; promise &c. 768.

Adj. CONSENTING &c. *v.*; compliant, agreeable [*colloq.*], willing, eager; agreed &c. (*assent*) 488; unconditional.

Adv. YES &c. (*assent*) 488; by all means &c. (*willingly*) 602; if you please, as you please; be it so, so be it, well and good, of course.

*** *chi tace acconsente;* "Barkis is willin" [Dickens]; "silence gives consent" [Goldsmith]; "And whispering, 'I will ne'er consent.' — consented" [Byron].

---

763. Offer. — N. OFFER, proffer, presentation, tender, bid, overture; proposal, proposition; motion, invitation; candidature, candidacy; offering &c. (*gift*) 784.

V. OFFER, proffer, present, tender; bid; propose, move; make a motion, make advances; start; invite, hold out, place in one's way; put –, place– at one's disposal; put in one's power, make possible, put forward.

hawk about; offer for sale &c. 796; press &c. (*request*) 765; go a-begging; lay at one's feet.

VOLUNTEER, come forward, be a candidate; offer –, present– oneself; stand for, bid for; seek; be at one's service.

BRIBE &c. (*give*) 784; grease the palm [*slang*].

Adj. OFFERING, offered &c. *v.*; in the market, for sale, to let, disengaged, on hire; at one's disposal.

*** "Take the goods the gods provide thee" [Dryden]; "The gods to-day stand friendly" [*Julius Cæsar*].

764. Refusal. — N. REFUSAL, rejection; noncompliance, incompliance; denial; declining &c. *v.*; declension; declinature; peremptory –, flat –, point blank– refusal; repulse, rebuff; discountenance, disapprobation.

NEGATION, recusancy, abnegation, protest, disclamation, renunciation, disclaimer; dissent &c. 489; revocation &c. 756.

V. REFUSE, reject, deny, decline; nill [*archaic*], turn down [*slang*], abnegate, negate, negative; refuse –, withhold– one's assent; shake the head; close the –hand, – purse; grudge, begrudge, be slow to, hang fire; pass [*at cards*].

STAND ALOOF, be deaf to; turn a deaf ear to, turn one's back upon; set one's face against, discountenance, not hear of, have nothing to do with, wash one's hands of, forswear, set aside, cast behind one; not yield an inch &c. (*obstinacy*) 606.

RESIST, cross; not grant &c. 762; repel, repulse; shut –, slam– the door in one's face; rebuff; send –back, – to the right about, – away with a flea in the ear [*colloq.*]; deny oneself, not be at home to; discard &c. (*repudiate*) 610; rescind &c. (*revoke*) 756; disclaim, protest; dissent &c. 489.

Adj. REFUSING &c. *v.*; restive, restiff [*obs.*]; recusant; uncomplying, noncompliant, incompliant, unconsenting; declinatory, uncomplaisant, disclamatory [*rare*], negatory, protestant; not willing to hear of, deaf to.

REFUSED &c. *v.*; ungranted, out of the question, not to be thought of, impossible.

Adv. NO &c. 536; on no account, not for the world; no thank you; your humble servant [*ironically*], bien obligé [*F.*], not on your life! [*U. S.*].

*** "one refusal no rebuff" [Byron]; "'Tis fine to see them scattering refusals And wild dismay" [*ibid.*]; "he who begs timidly courts a refusal" [Seneca].

765. Request. — **N.** REQUEST, requisition; claim &c. (*demand*) 741; petition, suit, prayer; begging letter, round robin.

motion, overture, application, canvass, address, appeal, apostrophe; imprecation; rogation [*eccl.*]; proposal, proposition.

orison &c. (*worship*) 990; incantation &c. (*spell*) 993.

mendicancy, mendicat on [*rare*]; asking, begging &c. *v.*; postulation, solicitation, invitation, entreaty, importunity, supplication, instance, impetration, imploration, obsecration, obtestation, invocation, interpellation.

V. REQUEST, ask, beg, crave, sue, pray, petition, solicit, invite, pop the question [*colloq.*], make bold to ask; beg leave, beg a boon; apply to, call to, put to; call upon, call for; make –, address –, p refer –, put up- a -request, – prayer, – petition; make -application, – a requisition; ask –, trouble- one for; claim &c. (*demand*) 741; offer up prayers &c. (*worship*) 990; whistle for [*colloq.*].

bespeak, canvass, tout [*cant, Eng.*], make interest, court; seek, bid for &c. (*offer*) 763; publish the banns.

ENTREAT, beseech, plead, supplicate, beg hard, implore; conjure, adjure; obsecrate [*rare*], apostrophize, obtest [*rare*]; cry to, kneel to, appeal to; invoke, evoke; impetrate, imprecate, ply, press, urge, beset, importune, dun, tax, clamor for; cry aloud, cry for help; fall on one's knees; throw oneself at the feet of; come down on one's marrowbones [*slang or humorous*].

beg from door to door, send the hat round, go a-begging; mendicate [*rare*], mump, cadge [*dial. or slang, Eng.*], beg one's bread.

dance attendance on, besiege, knock at the door.

Adj. REQUESTING &c. *v.*; precatory, suppliant, supplicant, supplicatory, invocative, invocatory, invitatory, imprecatory, rogatory; postulatory [*rare*], postulant; obsecratory [*rare*], obsecrationary [*rare*]; imploratory [*rare*], mendicant, mendicatory [*obs.*].

IMPORTUNATE, clamorous, urgent, solicitous; cap in hand; on one's -knees, – bended knees, – marrowbones [*slang or humorous*].

Adv. PLEASE, prithee, do, pray; be so good as, be good enough; have the goodness, vouchsafe, will you, I pray thee, if you please.

Int. for- God's, – heaven's – goodness', – mercy's- sake! we beseech thee to hear us! help! save me!

** *Dieu vous garde; dirige nos Domine;* "urge them while their souls Are capable of this ambition" [*King John*].

766. [NEGATIVE REQUEST.] **Deprecation.** — **N.** DEPRECATION, expostulation; intercession, mediation, protest, remonstrance.

V. DEPRECATE, protest, expostulate, enter a protest, intercede for; remonstrate.

Adj. DEPRECATORY, expostulatory, intercessory, mediatorial.

deprecated, protested.

UNSOUGHT, unbesought; unasked &c. (*see* ask &c. 765).

Int. GOD FORBID! cry you mercy! forbid it Hea ven! Heaven forfend (*or* forefend)! Hea ven forbid! far be it from! hands off! &c. (*prohibition*) 761.

** "Woodman, spare that tree! Touch not a single bough!" [Morris]; "Be to her virtues very kind; Be to her faults a little blind" [Prior].

767. Petitioner. — **N.** PETITIONER, solicitor, applicant, suppliant, supplicant, suitor, candidate, claimant, postulant, aspirant, competitor, bidder; place hunter, pothunter, prizer [*archaic*].

SALESMAN, drummer [*U. S.*]; bagman &c. 758; canvasser.

BEGGAR, mendicant, mumper, sturdy beggar, panhandler [*slang*], cadger.

HOTEL RUNNER [*cant, U. S.*], touter [*colloq.*], runner [*cant, U. S.*], steerer [*U. S.*], tout [*cant, Eng.*]; barker [*colloq.*].

SYCOPHANT, parasite &c. (*servility*) 886.

** "Homer himself must beg if he wants means" [Burton]; "A beggar through the world am I" [Lowell]; "His house was known to all the vagrant train" [Goldsmith]; "Beggars must be no choosers" [Beaumont and Fletcher]; "Of others take a sheaf, of me a grain! Of me a grain!" [*Anon.*].

Section III. Conditional Intersocial Volition

768. Promise. — N. PROMISE, undertaking, word, troth, plight, pledge, parole, word of honor, vow; oath &c. (*affirmation*) 535; profession, assurance, warranty, guarantee, insurance, obligation; contract &c. 769; stipulation.

ENGAGEMENT, preëngagement; affiance; betrothal, betrothment; marriage -contract, - vow; plighted faith, troth-plight [*Scot. or dial.*], gage d'amour [*F.*].

V. PROMISE; give a promise &c. *n.*; undertake, engage; make -, form- an engagement; enter into *or* on an engagement; bind -, tie -, pledge -, commit -, take upon- oneself; vow; swear &c. (*affirm*) 535, give -, pass -, pledge -, plight- one's -word, - honor, - credit, - troth; betroth, plight faith, take the vows, trothplight [*Scot. or dial.*].

ASSURE, warrant, guarantee; covenant &c. 769; avouch, vouch for; attest &c. (*bear witness*) 467.

hold out an expectation; contract an obligation; become bound to, become sponsor for; answer for, be answerable for; secure; give security &c. 771; underwrite.

ADJURE, administer an oath, put to one's oath, swear a witness.

Adj. PROMISING &c. *v.*; promissory; votive; under hand and seal, upon oath, upon the Book; upon -, on- affirmation.

PROMISED &c. *v.*; affianced, pledged, bound; committed, compromised; in for it [*colloq.*].

Adv. as true as I live; in all soberness; upon my honor; my word for it; my head upon it; I call God to witness; as one's head shall answer for; ex voto [*L.*].

⁎ his word is his bond; in for a penny in for a pound; "Indeed, indeed, Repentance oft before I swore — but, was I sober when I swore?" [Omar Khayyám — Fitzgerald]; "Thy promises are like Adonis' gardens, That one day bloom'd, and fruitful were the next" [*I Henry VI*].

768a. Release from engagement.— N. RELEASE &c. (*liberation*) 750.

Adj. ABSOLUTE; unconditional &c. (*free*) 748.

769. Compact. — N. COMPACT, contract, specialty, bundobast [*India*], deal [*colloq.*], agreement, bargain; affidation [*rare*], pact, paction [*chiefly Scot.*], bond, covenant, indenture [*law*].

stipulation, settlement, convention; compromise, cartel.

negotiation &c. (*bargaining*) 794; diplomacy &c. (*mediation*) 724; negotiator &c. (*agent*) 758.

TREATY, protocol, concordat, Zollverein [*Ger.*], Sonderbund [*Ger.*], charter, Magna Charta *or* Magna Carta, pragmatic sanction.

RATIFICATION, completion, signature, seal, sigil, signet, bond.

V. CONTRACT, covenant, agree for; engage &c. (*promise*) 768; indent.

NEGOTIATE, treat, stipulate, make terms; bargain &c. (*barter*) 794.

CONCLUDE, close, close with, complete; make -, strike- a bargain; come to -terms, - an understanding; compromise &c. 774; set at rest; settle; confirm, ratify, clinch *or* clench, subscribe, underwrite; indorse, endorse, put the seal to; sign, seal &c. (*attest*) 467; take one at one's word, bargain by inch of candle.

Adj. CONTRACTUAL, complete; agreed &c. *v.*; conventional; under hand and seal; signed, sealed, and delivered.

Adv. AS AGREED UPON, as promised, as contracted for; according to the -contract, - bargain, - agreement.

⁎ caveat emptor; "'Tis not in the bond" [*M. of V.*]; "an honest man's word is as good as his bond" [Cervantes].

770. Conditions. — N. CONDITIONS, terms; articles, - of agreement; memorandum; clauses, provisions; proviso &c. (*qualification*) 469; covenant, stipulation, obligation, ultimatum, sine quâ non [*L.*]; casus fœderis [*L.*].

V. CONDITION, make it a condition, stipulate, insist upon, make a point of; bind, tie up; fence in, hedge in, have a string to it [*colloq.*]; make –, come to- -terms &c. (*contract*) 769.

Adj. CONDITIONAL, provisional, guarded, fenced, hedged in.

Adv. CONDITIONALLY &c. (*with qualification*) 469; provisionally, *pro re natâ* [L.], on condition; with a string to it [*colloq.*], with a reservation.

771. Security. — N. SECURITY; guaranty, guarantee; gage, warranty, bond, tie, pledge, *vadium vivum* [L.], plight [*rare*], mortgage, *vadium mortuum* [L.], debenture, hypothec [*Rom. & civil law*], hypothecation, bill of sale, lien, pawn, pignoration; real security; vadium, collateral, bail; parole &c. (*promise*) 768.

stake, deposit, earnest, handsel *or* hansel, handsale, caution [*Scot. law*].

PROMISSORY NOTE; bill, – of exchange; I.O.U.; personal security, covenant.

ACCEPTANCE, indorsement *or* endorsement, signature, execution, stamp, seal.

SPONSOR, surety, bail, replevin; mainpernor, mainprise *or* mainprize [*hist. law*]; hostage; godchild, godfather, godmother; sponsion, sponsorship.

RECOGNIZANCE; deed –, covenant- of indemnity.

AUTHENTICATION, verification, warrant, certificate, voucher, docket *or* doquet [*obs.*]; record &c. 551; probate, attested copy.

acquittance, quittance; discharge, release; receipt.

MUNIMENTS, title deed, instrument; deed, deed poll, indenture; specialty; insurance; charter &c. (*compact*) 769; charter poll; paper, parchment, settlement, will, testament, last will and testament, codicil.

V. GIVE SECURITY, give bail, give substantial bail; go bail; handsel *or* hansel, pawn, put in pawn, pledge, put up the spout [*slang*], impawn *or* empawn [*obs.*], spout [*slang*], impignorate, mortgage, hypothecate.

GUARANTEE, warrant, assure; accept, indorse *or* endorse, underwrite, insure.

EXECUTE, stamp; sign, seal &c. (*evidence*) 467.

LET, set *or* sett [*Scot. law*]; grant –, take –, hold- a lease; hold in pledge; lend on security &c. 787.

Adj. PLEDGED, pawned &c. *v.*; secure; impignorate, pignorative [*rare*], in pawn, up the spout [*slang*]; at stake, on deposit, as earnest.

SPONSORIAL, sponsional [*rare*]; as sponsor &c. *n.*

LET, leased; held in pledge.

** *bonis avibus*; "gone where the woodbine twineth"; "where there's a will there's a lawsuit" *Cynic's Calendar*].

772. Observance. — N. OBSERVANCE, performance, compliance, acquiescence, concurrence; obedience &c. 743; fulfillment *or* fulfilment, satisfaction, discharge; acquittance, acquittal.

ADHESION, acknowledgment; fidelity &c. (*probity*) 939; exact &c. 494- observance; unswerving fidelity to.

V. OBSERVE, comply with, respect, acknowledge, abide by; cling to, adhere to, be faithful to, act up to; meet, fulfill *or* fulfil; carry out, carry into execution; execute, perform, keep, satisfy, discharge; do one's office.

KEEP FAITH WITH; perform –, fulfill –, discharge –, acquit oneself of- an obligation; make good; make good –, keep- one's -word, – promise; redeem one's pledge; stand to one's engagement.

Adj. OBSERVANT, faithful, true, loyal;

773. Nonobservance. — N. NONOBSERVANCE &c. 772; evasion, inobservance, failure, omission, neglect, laches [*law*], casualness, slackness, laxness, laxity, informality.

lawlessness; disobedience &c. 742; bad faith &c. 940.

INFRINGEMENT, infraction; violation, transgression; piracy.

RETRACTATION, repudiation, nullification; protest; forfeiture.

V. EVADE, fail, neglect, omit, elude, give the go-by to [*slang*], cut [*colloq.*], set aside, ignore; shut –, close- one's eyes to.

INFRINGE, transgress, violate, pirate, break, trample under foot, do violence to, drive a coach and four (*or* six) through.

DISCARD, protest, repudiate, fling to

honorable &c. 939; true as the dial to the sun, true as the needle to the pole; punctual, punctilious, scrupulous, meticulous; literal &c. (*exact*) 494; as good as one's word.

Adv. FAITHFULLY &c. *adj.*; to the letter.

*** *ignoscito sæpe alteri nunquam tibi; tempori parendum;* "to God, thy country, and thy friend be true" [Vaughan]; "he that sweareth to his own hurt, and changeth not" [*Bible*].

the winds, set at naught, nullify, declare null and void; cancel &c. (*wipe off*) 552.

RETRACT, go back from, be off, forfeit, go from one's word, palter; stretch a point, strain a point.

Adj. VIOLATING &c. *v.*; lawless, transgressive; elusive, evasive, slack, lax, casual, slippery; nonobservant.

unfilfilled &c. (*see* fulfill &c. 772).

774. Compromise. — N. COMPROMISE, commutation, composition; middle term, *mezzo termine* [*It.*]; compensation &c. 30; abatement of differences, adjustment, mutual concession.

V. COMPROMISE, commute, compound; take the mean; split the difference, meet one halfway, give and take; come to terms &c. (*contact*) 769; submit to arbitration, abide by arbitration; patch up, bridge over, arrange; straighten out, adjust, adjust differences; agree; make the best of, make a virtue of necessity; take the will for the deed.

*** "all government, — indeed every human benefit and enjoyment, every virtue and every prudent act, — is founded on compromise and barter" [Burke].

Section IV. POSSESSIVE RELATIONS[1]

1. *Property in general*

775. Acquisition. — N. ACQUISITION; gaining &c. *v.*; obtainment, procuration, procurement; purchase, descent, inheritance; gift &c. 784.

RECOVERY, retrieval, revendication [*rare*], replevin; redemption, salvage, trover; find, *trouvaille* [*F.*], foundling.

GAIN, thrift; money-making, money-grubbing; lucre, filthy lucre, loaves and fishes, fleshpots of Egypt, the main chance, pelf; emolument &c. (*remuneration*) 973.

PROFIT, earnings, winnings, innings, pickings, perquisite, accruement [*obs.*], net profit; avails; income &c. (*receipt*) 810; proceeds, produce, product; outcome, output; return, fruit, crop, harvest; second crop, aftermath; benefit &c. (*good*) 618.

PRIZE, sweepstakes, trick, pool; kitty, jack pot, pot; wealth &c. 803.

[FRAUDULENT ACQUISITION] subreption; obreption; stealing &c. 791.

V. ACQUIRE, get, gain, win, earn, obtain, procure, gather; collect &c. (*assemble*) 72; pick, pick up; glean.

find; come –, pitch –, light- upon; come across, come at; scrape -up, – together; get in, reap and carry, net, draw, get in the harvest.

get hold of, get between one's finger and thumb, get into one's hand, get at; take –, come into – possession.

776. Loss. — N. LOSS, perdition, deperdition [*archaic*]; forfeiture, lapse.

privation, bereavement; deprivation &c. (*dispossession*) 789; riddance; damage, squandering, waste.

V. LOSE; incur –, experience –, meet with- a loss; miss; mislay, let slip, allow to slip through the fingers; be deprived of; be without &c. (*exempt*) 777a; forfeit, pay with.

SQUANDER; get rid of &c. 782; waste &c. 638.

BE LOST, lapse.

Adj. LOSING &c. *v.*; not having &c. 777a.

DEPRIVED OF; shorn of, deperdite [*rare*], denuded, bereaved, bereft, minus [*colloq., exc. in math.*], cut off; dispossessed &c. 789; rid of, quit of; out of pocket.

LOST &c. *v.*; long lost; irretrievable &c. (*hopeless*) 859; off one's hands.

Int. FAREWELL TO! adieu to! good riddance.

*** "Farewell! a long farewell, to all my greatness!" [*Henry VIII*]; "by losing rendered sager" [Byron]; "all is lost save honor" [*misquoted remark of Francis I*].

bag, sack, bring home, secure; derive, enter into- possession.

PROFIT; make –, draw- profit; turn to -profit, – account; make capital out of, make money by; obtain a return, reap the fruits of; reap –, gain- an advantage; turn -a penny, – an honest penny: make the pot boil, bring grist to the mill; make –, coin –, raise- money; raise funds, raise the wind [*slang*]; fill one's pocket &c. (*wealth*) 803.

realize, clear; treasure up &c. (*store*) 636; produce &c. 161; take &c. 789.

receive &c. 785; come by, come in for; inherit; step into, – a fortune, – the shoes of; succeed to.

RECOVER, get back, regain, retrieve, revendicate [*rare*], replevin, replevy, redeem, come by one's own.

BE PROFITABLE &c. *adj.*; pay, answer.

accrue &c. (*be received*) 785.

Adj. ACQUISITIVE, productive, profitable, advantageous, gainful, remunerative, paying, lucrative, acquiring, acquired &c. *v.*

Adv. in the way of gain; for money; at interest.

⁎⁎* *lucri causa;* "Getting and spending we lay waste our powers" [Wordsworth]; "the greatest possession is self-possession" [*Cynic's Calendar*].

777. Possession. — N. POSSESSION, seizin *or* seisin; ownership &c. 780; occupancy; hold, holding; tenure, tenancy, feodality, feodatory, feud *or* feod, fief, fee, fee tail, fee simple; dependency; villenage *or* villeinage; socage, chivalry, knight service.

bird in hand, *uti possidetis* [*L.*], chose in possession [*rare*].

EXCLUSIVE POSSESSION, impropriation, monopoly, retention &c. 781; prepossession, preoccupancy; nine points of the law; corner, usucapion *or* usucaption [*Rom. law*], prescription.

FUTURE POSSESSION, heritage, inheritance, heirship, reversion, fee; primogeniture, ultimogeniture.

V. POSSESS, have, hold, occupy, enjoy; be possessed of &c. *adj.*; have in hand &c. *adj.*; own &c. 780; command.

INHERIT; come to, come in for.

MONOPOLIZE, engross, forestall, regrate, impropriate, appropriate, usucapt [*Rom. law*], have all to oneself; corner; have a firm hold of &c. (*retain*) 781; get into one's hand &c. (*acquire*) 775.

BELONG TO, appertain to, pertain to; be in one's possession &c. *adj.*; vest in.

Adj. POSSESSING &c. *v.*; worth; possessed of, seized of, master of, usucapient [*Rom. law*]; in possession of; endowed –, blest –, instinct –, fraught –, laden –, charged- with.

POSSESSED &c. *v.*; on hand, by one; in hand, in store, in stock; unsold, unshared; in one's -hands, – grasp, – possession; at one's command, at one's disposal; one's own &c. (*property*) 780.

⁎⁎* *entbehre gern was du nicht hast; meum et tuum; tuum est;* "possession is eleven points in the law" [Cibber].

777a. Exemption. — N. EXEMPTION; absence &c. 187; exception, immunity, privilege, release.

V. NOT HAVE &c. 777; be without &c. *adj.*; excuse.

Adj. DEVOID OF, exempt from, without, unpossessed of, unblest with; immune from.

NOT HAVING &c. 777; unpossessed; untenanted &c. (*vacant*) 187; without an owner. UNOBTAINED, unacquired.

778. [JOINT POSSESSION.] Participation. — N. PARTICIPATION; cotenancy, joint tenancy; occupancy –, possession –, tenancy- in common; joint –, common- stock; copartnership, partnership; communion; community of -possessions, – goods; communization, communalization; communism, communalism, collectivism, socialism; coöperation &c. 709.

snacks [*obs.*], coportion [*obs.*], picnic, hotchpot *or* hotchpotch, hodgepodge; coheirship, coparcenary *or* coparceny; gavelkind.

PARTICIPATOR, sharer, copartner, partner; shareholder; cotenant, joint tenant; tenants in common; coheir, coparcener.

COMMUNIST, communitarian, communalist, collectivist, socialist.

V. PARTICIPATE, partake; share, share in; come in for a share; go shares, go snacks [*obs.*], go cahoots [*slang*], halve; share and share alike.

join in; have a hand in &c. (*coöperate*) 709.

COMMUNIZE, communalize; have –, possess –, be seized- -in common, – as joint tenants &c. *n.*

Adj. PARTAKING &c. *v.*

COMMUNISTIC, communalistic, socialistic; coöperative, profit-sharing.

Adv. IN COMMON, share and share alike; on shares.

---

779. Possessor. — N. POSSESSOR, holder; occupant, occupier; tenant; person *or* man in possession &c. 777; renter, lodger, lessee, underlessee; zamindar *or* zemindar [*India*]; ryot [*India*]; tenant -on sufferance, – at will, – from year to year, – for years, – for life.

OWNER; proprietor, proprietress, proprietary; impropriator, master, mistress, lord.

LANDHOLDER, landowner, landlord, landlady; lord -of the manor, – paramount; heritor [*Scots law*], laird [*Scot.*], vavasor *or* vavasour [*feud. law*]; landed gentry, mesne lord; planter.

BENEFICIARY, *cestui que* (or *qui*) *trust* [*law*], mortgagor.

GRANTEE, feoffee, feoffee in trust, releasee, devisee; legatee, legatary [*rare*].

TRUSTEE; holder &c. of the legal estate; mortgagee.

right owner, rightful owner.

[FUTURE POSSESSOR] heir, – apparent, – presumptive; inheritor, reversioner; remainder-man; heiress, inheritress, inheritrix.

** " 'Twas mine, 'tis his, and has been slave to thousands" [*Othello*].

---

780. Property. — N. PROPERTY, possession, seizin *or* seisin; tenure &c. (*possession*) 777; *suum cuique* [*L.*], *meum et tuum* [*L.*].

OWNERSHIP, proprietorship, lordship; seigniory *or* seignory *or* seigneury, seignoralty; empire &c. (*dominion*) 737.

ESTATE, interest, stake, right, title, claim, demand, holding; vested –, contingent –, beneficial –, equitable- interest; use, trust, benefit; legal –, equitable- estate.

absolute interest, paramount estate, freehold; fee, – simple, – tail; estate -in fee, – in tail, – tail; estate in tail -male, – female, – general.

term, limitation, lease, settlement, strict settlement, particular estate; estate -for life, – for years, – *pur autre vie* [*F.*]; remainder, reversion, expectancy, possibility.

DOWER, dowry, jointure, appanage *or* apanage, inheritance, heritage, patrimony, alimony; legacy &c. (*gift*) 784; Falcidian law, paternal estate, thirds.

ASSETS, belongings, means, resources, circumstances; wealth &c. 803; money &c. 800; what one -is worth, – will cut up for [*colloq.*]; estate and effects.

REALTY, land, lands, *prædium* [*L.*]; landed –, real- -estate, – property; tenements; hereditaments; corporeal –, incorporeal- hereditaments; acres; ground &c. (*earth*) 342; acquest, mesestead [*archaic*], messuage, toft [*Scot. & dial. Eng.*].

manor, honor [*Eng. feudal law*], domain, demesne; farm, plantation, hacienda [*Sp. Am.*]; alodium *or* allodium &c. (*free*) 748; feoff, fief, feud *or* feod, zamindari *or* zemindari [*India*], arado [*S. W. U. S.*], rancho [*S. W. U. S.*], ranch.

freeholds, copyholds, leaseholds; folkland [*O. Eng. law*].

chattels real; fixtures, plant, heirloom; easement; right of -common, – user.

TERRITORY, state, kingdom, principality, realm, empire, protectorate, dependency, sphere of influence, mandate.

PERSONALTY; personal -property, – estate, – effects; chattels, goods, effects, movables; stock, – in trade; things, traps [*colloq.*], chattels personal, rattletraps, paraphernalia; equipage &c. 633; parcels [*Eng.*], appurtenances.

IMPEDIMENTA; luggage, baggage; bag and baggage; pelf; cargo, lading.

INCOME &c. (*receipts*) 810; rent roll; maul and wedges [*U. S.*].

patent, copyright; chose in action; credit &c. 805; debt &c. 806.

V. POSSESS &c. 777; be the possessor of &c. 779; own; have for one's -own, – very own; come in for, inherit; enfeoff.

savor of the realty.

BELONG TO; be one's property &c. *n.*; pertain to, appertain to.

Adj. ONE'S OWN; landed, prædial *or* predial, manorial, alodial *or* allodial; seigniorial *or* seigneurial; freehold, copyhold, leasehold; feudal *or* feodal; hereditary, entailed, real, personal.

Adv. TO ONE'S CREDIT, to one's account; to the good.

to one and -his heirs for ever, – the heirs of his body, – his heirs and assigns, – his executors, administrators and assigns.

*** "Is it not lawful for me to do what I will with mine own?" [*Bible*].

---

781. Retention. — N. RETENTION; retaining &c. *v.;* keep [*archaic*], detention, custody; tenacity, firm hold, grasp, gripe, grip, iron grip; bond &c. (*vinculum*) 45.

CLUTCHES, tongs, forceps, tenaculum, pincers, nippers, pliers, vise, hook.

fangs, teeth, claws, talons, nail, unguis, tentacle.

paw, hand, finger, wrist, fist, nieve *or* nief [*archaic or dial.*].

CAPTIVE &c. 754; bird in hand.

V. RETAIN, keep; hold, – fast, – tight, – one's own, – one's ground; clinch, clench, clutch, grasp, gripe, hug, have a firm hold of.

SECURE, withhold, detain; hold –, keep- back; keep close; husband &c. (*store*) 636; reserve; have –, keep- in stock &c. (*possess*) 777; entail, tie up, settle.

Adj. RETENTIVE, tenacious; retaining &c. *v.*

UNFORFEITED, undeprived, undisposed, uncommunicated.

INCOMMUNICABLE, inalienable; in mortmain; in strict settlement.

*** *uti possidetis.*

---

derelict; unowned, disowned, disinherited, divorced; unappropriated, unculled; left &c. (*residuary*) 40.

Int. away with!

*** "dismiss'd without a parting pang" [Cibber]; "He cast off his friends as a huntsman, his pack" [Goldsmith].

---

782. Relinquishment. — N. RELINQUISHMENT, abandonment &c. (*of a course*) 624; renunciation, expropriation, dereliction; cession, surrender, dispensation; resignation &c. 757; riddance.

DERELICT &c. *adj.;* jetsam *or* jettison; abandoned farm [*U. S.*]; waif, foundling.

V. RELINQUISH, give up, surrender, yield, cede; let go, let slip; spare, drop, resign, forego, renounce, abandon, expropriate, give away, dispose of, part with; lay -aside, – apart, – down, – on the shelf *&* (*disuse*) 678; set aside, put aside; make away with, cast behind; discard, cast off, dismiss; maroon.

cast -, throw -, pitch -, fling- -away, – aside, – overboard, – to the dogs; cast -, throw -, sweep- to the winds; put -, turn -, sweep- away; jettison.

quit one's hold.

SUPERSEDE, give notice to quit, give warning; be *or* get rid of; be *or* get quit of; eject &c. 297.

rid -, disburden -, divest -, dispossess- oneself of; wash one's hands of.

DIVORCE, unmarry [*rare*]; cut off, desert, disinherit; separate.

Adj. RELINQUISHED &c. *v.;* cast off,

---

2. *Transfer of Property*

783. Transfer. — N. TRANSFER, conveyance, assignment, alienation, abalienation; demise, limitation; conveyancing; transmission &c. (*transference*) 270; enfeoffment, bargain and sale, lease and release; exchange &c. (*interchange*) 148; barter &c. 794; substitution &c. 147.

SUCCESSION, reversion; shifting use, shifting trust; devolution.

V. TRANSFER, convey; alien, alienate; assign; enfeoff; grant &c. (*confer*) 784; consign; make over, hand over; pass, hand, transmit, negotiate; hand down; exchange &c. (*interchange*) 148.

CHANGE HANDS, change from one to another; devolve, succeed; come into possession &c. (*acquire*) 775.

DISINHERIT; abalienate [*rare*]; dispossess &c. 789; substitute &c. 147.

Adj. ALIENABLE, negotiable, transferable, reversional, transmissive; inherited.

Adv. BY TRANSFER &c. *n.*; on lease.

784. Giving. — N. GIVING &c. *v.*; bestowal, bestowment, donation; presentation, presentment; accordance; concession, cession; delivery, consignment, dispensation, communication, endowment; investment, investiture; award.

CHARITY, almsgiving, liberality, generosity.

[THING GIVEN] gift, donation, present, *cadeau* [*F.*]; fairing; free gift, boon, favor, benefaction, grant, offering, oblation, sacrifice, immolation.

GRACE, act of grace, bonus.

ALLOWANCE, contribution, subscription, subsidy, tribute, subvention.

BEQUEST, legacy, devise, will, dotation, dot, appanage *or* apanage, dowry, dower; voluntary -settlement, - conveyance &c. 783; amortization.

GRATUITY, lagniappe *or* lagnappe [*Louisiana*], pilon [*S. W. U. S.*]; alms, largess, bounty, dole, sportule [*obs.*], donative, help, oblation, offertory, honorarium, Peter pence, sportula, Christmas box, Easter offering, vails [*rare*], *douceur* [*F.*], drink money, tip, hand out [*slang*], *pourboire* [*F.*], *Trinkgeld* [*G*], baksheesh *or* bakshish, cumshaw [China], dash *or* dashee [Africa]; fee &c. (*recompense*) 973; consideration.

BRIBE, bait, ground bait; peace offering; handsel *or* hansel; boodle [*slang*], graft [*colloq.*], grease [*slang*].

785. Receiving. — N. RECEIVING &c. *v.*; acquisition &c. 775; reception &c. (*introduction*) 296; suscipiency [*rare*], acceptance, admission.

RECIPIENT, receiver, suscipient [*rare*], accipient; assignee, devisee; legatee, legatary; grantee, feoffee, donee, relessee, lessee.

BENEFICIARY, sportulary [*obs.*], stipendiary; pensioner, pensionary; almsman.

INCOME &c. (*receipt*) 810.

V. RECEIVE; take &c. 789; acquire &c. 775; admit.

POCKET; take in, catch, touch; put into one's -pocket, - purse; accept; take off one's hands.

BE RECEIVED; come in, come to hand; pass -, fall- into one's hand; go into one's pocket; fall to one's -lot, - share; come -, fall- to one; accrue; have given &c. (784) to one.

Adj. RECEIVING &c. *v.*; recipient, suscipient [*rare*]; stipendiary, stipendarian, pensionary.

RECEIVED &c. *v.*; given &c. 784; secondhand.

NOT GIVEN, unbestowed &c. (*see* give, bestow &c. 784).

※ "it is more blessed to give than to receive" [*Bible*]; "presents, I often say, endear absents" [Lamb].

GIVER, grantor &c. *v.*; donor, almoner, testator, feoffer, settlor [*law*]; investor, subscriber, contributor; Fairy Godmother [*or l. c.*].

V. DELIVER, hand, pass, put into the hands of; hand -, make -, deliver -, pass -, turn- over; assign dower.

PRESENT, give away, dispense, dispose of; give -, deal -, dole -, mete -, squeeze-out; fork out, shell out [*both slang*].

make a present; allow, contribute, subscribe, furnish its quota.

PAY &c. 807; render, impart, communicate.

CONCEDE, cede, yield, part with, shed, cast; spend &c. 809; sacrifice, immolate.

GIVE, bestow, donate [*chiefly U. S.*], confer, grant, accord, award, assign; offer &c. 763.

INTRUST, consign, vest in.

INVEST, endow, settle upon; bequeath, leave, devise.

FURNISH, supply, help; administer to, minister to; afford, spare; accommodate with, indulge with, favor with; shower down upon; lavish, pour on, thrust upon.

BRIBE, tip; tickle –, grease- the palm [*slang*].

Adj. GIVING &c. *v.*; given &c. *v.*; allowed, allowable; concessional; communicable.

CHARITABLE, eleemosynary, sportulary [*obs.*], tributary; gratis &c. 815; donative.

Adv. AS A FREE GIFT &c. *n.*; in charity; toward the endowment fund.

Int. don't mention it! not another word! glad to do it!

* *auctor pretiosa facit; ex dono; res est ingeniosa dare* [Ovid]; freely ye have received; freely give" [*Bible*]; "the gift without the giver is bare" [Lowell]; "rich gifts wax poor when givers prove unkind" [*Hamlet*]; "To him who gives is given Corn, water, wine, the world, the starry heaven" [Masefield]; "Money makes the mayor go" [*Cynic's Calendar*]; "But the jingling of the guinea helps the hurt that Honor feels" [Tennyson].

786. Apportionment. — N. APPORTIONMENT, allotment, consignment, assignment, allocation, appointment; appropriation; dispensation, distribution; division, deal; partition, repartition, administration.

PORTION, dividend, contingent, share, allotment, lot, measure, dose; dole, meed, pittance; *quantum* [*L.*], ration; ratio, proportion, quota, modicum, mess, allowance.

V. APPORTION, divide; distribute, administer, dispense; billet, allot, allocate, detail, cast, share, mete; portion –, parcel –, dole- out; deal, carve.

partition, assign, appropriate, appoint.

PARTICIPATE, come in for one's share &c. 778.

Adj. apportioning &c. *v.*; apportioned &c. *v.*; respective.

Adv. respectively, each to each; by lot; in equal shares.

---

787. Lending. — N. LENDING &c. *v.*; loan, advance, accommodation, feneration [*obs.*]; mortgage &c. (*security*) 771; investment.

PAWNSHOP, spout [*slang*], *mont de piété* [*F.*], my uncle's [*slang*].

LENDER, pawnbroker, money lender, usurer, Shylock.

V. LEND, advance, accommodate with; lend on security; loan; pawn &c. (*security*) 771.

INVEST; intrust; place –, put- out to interest; place, put; embark, risk, venture, sink, fund.

LET, lease, set *or* sett [*Scot. law*], sublet, sublease, underlet; demise.

Adj. LENDING &c. *v.*; lent &c. *v.*; come across (*or* down) with the needful [*slang*].

Adv. in advance; on loan, on security.

* "It is a very good world to live in, To lend, or to spend, or to give in" [*attributed to* Earl of Rochester]; "the ruthless usurer's gold" [Bulwer-Lytton].

788. Borrowing. — N. BORROWING, pledging, pawning, putting up the spout [*slang*].

borrowed plumes; plagiarism &c. (*thieving*) 791.

V. BORROW, desume [*obs.*]; pawn, put up the spout [*slang*], patronize my uncle [*slang*].

raise –, take up- money; raise the wind [*slang*]; get the -dough, – needful [*both slang*]; fly a kite, borrow of Peter to pay Paul; run into debt &c. (*debt*) 806.

HIRE, rent, farm; take a -lease, – demise; take –, hire- by the -hour, – mile, – year &c.

APPROPRIATE, adopt, apply, imitate, make use of, take; plagiarize, pirate.

replevy.

Adj. borrowed &c. *v.*

* "Neither a borrower nor a lender be" [*Hamlet*]; "borrowing dulls the edge of husbandry" [*ibid.*]; "Who goes a borrowing Goes a sorrowing" [Tusser].

---

789. Taking. — N. TAKING &c. *v.*; reception &c. (*taking in*) 296; deglutition &c. (*taking food*) 298; appropriation, prehension [*chiefly zoöl.*], prensation [*obs.*]; capture, caption; apprehension, deprehension [*obs.*]; abreption [*obs.*], seizure; abduction, ablation; subtraction &c. (*subduction*) 38; abstraction, ademption; androlepsia *or* androlepsy.

790. Restitution. — N. RESTITUTION, return; rendition, reddition; restoration, reinstatement, reinvestment, recuperation; rehabilitation &c. (*reconstruction*) 660; reparation, atonement; compensation, indemnification.

RECOVERY &c. (*getting back*) 775; release, replevin, replevy, redemption; reversion; remitter.

DISPOSSESSION; deprivation, deprivement; bereavement; divestment; disinheritance, disherison; distraint, distress, attachment, execution; sequestration, confiscation; eviction &c. 297.

RAPACITY, rapaciousness, extortion, predacity; bloodsucking, vampirism; theft &c. 791.

RESUMPTION; reprises [law], reprisal; recovery &c. 775.

CLUTCH, swoop, wrench; grip &c. (retention) 781; haul, take, catch; scramble.

TAKER, captor, capturer; extortioner or extortionist; vampire.

V. TAKE, catch, hook, nab [obs. or slang], bag, sack, pocket, put into one's pocket; receive; accept.

REAP, crop, cull, pluck; gather &c. (get) 775; draw.

V. RESTORE, return; give –, carry –, bring- back; render, – up; give up; let go, unclutch; disgorge, regorge; regurgitate; recoup, reimburse, compensate, indemnify, reinvest, reinstate, remit, rehabilitate; repair &c. (make good) 660.

RECOVER &c. (get back) 775; redeem; take back again; revest, revert.

Adj. RESTORING &c. v.; recuperative &c. 660; compensatory, indemnificatory; reversionary, redemptive, revertible.

Adv. in full restitution; as partial compensation; to atone for.

₊ suum cuique; "He was ever precise in promise-keeping" [M. for M.]; "words pay no debts" [Troilus and Cressida]; "Who never promiseth but he means to pay" [I Henry IV].

APPROPRIATE, impropriate [Eng. eccl. law]; assume, possess oneself of; take possession of; commandeer [colloq.]; lay –, clap- one's hands on [colloq.]; help oneself to; make free with, dip one's hands into, lay under contribution; intercept; scramble for; deprive of.

SEIZE, abstract; take –, carry –, bear- -away, – off; adeem [law]; hurry off –, run away- with; abduct; steal &c. 791; ravish; pounce –, spring- upon; swoop to, swoop down upon; take by -storm, – assault; snatch, reave [archaic].

snap up, nip up, whip up, catch up; kidnap, crimp, capture, lay violent hands on.

get –, lay –, take –, catch –, lay fast –, take firm- hold of; lay by the heels, take prisoner; fasten upon, grapple, embrace, grip, gripe, clasp, grab [colloq.], make away with, clutch, collar, throttle, take by the throat, claw, clinch, clench, make sure of.

CATCH AT, jump at, make a grab at, snap at, snatch at; reach, make a long arm [colloq.], stretch forth one's hand.

DISSEIZE or disseise; take from, take away from; deduct &c. 38; retrench &c. (curtail) 201; dispossess, ease one of, snatch from one's grasp; tear –, tear away –, wrench –, wrest –, wring- from; extort; deprive of, bereave; disinherit, cut off with a shilling; oust &c. (eject) 297; divest; levy, distrain, confiscate; sequester, sequestrate; accroach; usurp; despoil, strip, fleece, shear, displume.

ABSORB &c. (suck in) 296; draw off; suck, – like a leach, – the blood of; impoverish, eat out of house and home; drain, – to the dregs; gut, dry, exhaust, swallow up.

RETAKE, resume; recover &c. 775.

Adj. TAKING &c. v.; privative, prehensile; predacious or predaceous, predal [obs.], predatory, wolfish, lupine, rapacious, raptorial; ravening, ravenous; parasitic; all-devouring, all-engulfing.

bereft &c. 776.

Adv. at one fell swoop.

₊ give an inch and take an ell.

791. Stealing. — N. STEALING &c. v.; theft, thievery, robbery, direption [rare]; abstraction, appropriation; plagiary [rare], plagiarism, autoplagiarism; rape, depredation; kidnaping or kidnapping.

PILLAGE, spoliation, plunder, sack, sackage [rare], rapine, brigandage, latrociny [obs.], latrocinium [Rom. law], highway robbery, holdup [slang, U. S.]; raid, foray, razzia; piracy, privateering, buccaneering; filibustering, filibusterism; burglary, housebreaking; abaction, cattle stealing, cattle lifting [*colloq.*], horse stealing; auto-mobile -, car- stealing.

BLACKMAIL, badger game [*cant*], Black Hand [*U. S.*].

PECULATION, embezzlement; fraud &c. 545; larceny, petty larceny, pilfering, shoplifting.

THIEVISHNESS, rapacity, predacity, predaciousness; kleptomania.

Alsatia; Whitefriars; den of Cacus, den of thieves.

LICENSE TO PLUNDER, letters of marque.

V. STEAL, thieve, rob, purloin, pilfer, filch, prig [*cant*], bag, nim [*obs.*], crib [*colloq.*], cabbage, palm; abstract; appropriate, plagiarize.

disregard the distinction between *meum* and *tuum*.

ABDUCT, convey away, carry off, kidnap, crimp, impress, press [*rare*]; make -, walk -, run- off with; run away with; spirit away, seize &c. (*lay violent hands on*) 789.

PLUNDER, pillage, rifle, sack, loot, ransack, spoil, spoliate, despoil, strip, sweep, gut, forage, levy blackmail, pirate, pickeer [*obs.*], maraud, lift cattle [*colloq.*], poach, smuggle, run; badger [*cant*], bunko *or* bunco; hold up; bail up, stick up [*both colloq. or slang, Austral.*], filibuster.

SWINDLE, peculate, embezzle; sponge, mulct, rook, bilk, pluck, pigeon [*slang*], thimblerig; diddle [*colloq. or dial.*], fleece; defraud &c. 545; obtain under false pre-tenses; live by one's wits.

rob -, borrow of- Peter to pay Paul; set a thief to catch a thief.

Adj. THIEVING &c. *v.;* thievish, light-fingered, furacious [*rare*]; furtive; piratical; predacious *or* predaceous, predal [*obs.*], predatory; raptorial &c. (*rapacious*) 789.

STOLEN &c. *v.*

*** *sic vos non vobis.*

792. Thief. — N. THIEF, robber, *homo trium literarum* [*L.*], spoiler, depredator, pillager, marauder; pilferer, rifler, filcher, plagiarist; harpy, shark [*slang*], land rat [*cant*], land pirate, land shark, falcon; smuggler, poacher; abductor, badger [*cant*], kidnaper *or* kidnapper; *chor* [*Hind.*], crook [*slang*], lifter, skin [*slang*], contraband-ist, hawk; hold-up, jackleg, rustler [*all three slang, U. S.*]; spieler [*colloq., Austral.*], sandbagger, sneak thief, strong-arm man [*U. S.*].

PIRATE, corsair, viking, sea king, buccaneer, privateer; Paul Jones.

BRIGAND, bandit, freebooter, thug, dacoit [*India*]; rover, ranger, pickeerer [*obs.*], picaroon, filibuster, rapparee [*Ir.*]; cattle thief, abactor; bushranger, mosstrooper [*hist.*], Bedouin; wrecker; highwayman, footpad, sturdy beggar, knight of the road. Dick Turpin, Claude Duval, Jonathan Wild, Macheath, Nevison.

PICKPOCKET, dip [*slang*], cutpurse, pickpurse [*rare*], light-fingered gentry; sharper; card sharper, card cheat, Greek; thimblerigger; bunkoman *or* buncoman, rook [*slang*], welsher [*slang*], blackleg [*colloq.*], leg [*slang, Eng.*], diddler [*colloq. or slang*], defaulter; Autolycus, Jeremy Diddler, Robert Macaire, Artful Dodger, trickster; swell mob [*slang*], *chevalier d'industrie* [*F.*]; shoplifter.

SWINDLER, duffer [*Eng.*], peculator; forger, coiner, smasher [*cant, Eng.*], counter-feiter; fence, receiver of stolen goods.

BURGLAR, housebreaker, yeggman *or* yegg [*slang*], cracksman [*slang*], magsman [*slang*], sneak thief; second-story -thief, - man; Bill Sikes, Jack Sheppard.

*** "he stole nothing smaller than the moomoo's egg" [Dunsany]; "a promising young robber, the lieutenant of his band" [Gilbert].

793. Booty. — N. BOOTY, spoil, plunder, prize, loot, swag [*cant*]; perquisite, boodle [*polit. cant*], graft [*colloq.*], pork barrel [*polit. cant, U. S.*], pickings; *spolia opima* [*L.*], prey; blackmail; stolen goods.

Adj. LOOTING, plundering, spoliative, manubial [*obs.*].

3. *Interchange of Property*

794. Barter. — N. BARTER, exchange, scorse [*obs.*], truck system; interchange &c. 148.

a Roland for an Oliver, *quid pro quo* [*L.*], commutation, composition; Indian gift [*colloq., U. S.*].

TRADE, commerce, mercature [*obs.*], buying and selling, bargain and sale; traffic, business, nundination [*obs.*], custom, shopping; commercial enterprise, speculation, jobbing, stockjobbing, agiotage, brokery.

dealing, transaction, negotiation, bargain.

free trade [*opp. to* protection].

V. BARTER, exchange, truck, scorse [*obs.*], swap *or* swop [*colloq. & dial.*]; interchange &c. 148; commutate &c. (*sub titute*) 147; compound for.

TRADE, traffic, buy and sell, give and take, nundinate [*obs.*]; carry on –, ply –, drive- a trade; be in -business, – the city; keep a shop, deal in, employ one's capital in.

trade –, deal –, have dealings- with; put through a deal with; have truck with; transact –, do- business with; open –, have –, keep- an account with.

BARGAIN; drive –, make- a bargain; negotiate, bid for; haggle, stickle, – for; higgle, dicker [*U. S.*], chaffer, huckster, cheapen, beat down; underbid; outbid; ask, charge; strike a bargain &c. (*contract*) 769.

SPECULATE; give –, bait with- a sprat to catch a -herring, – mackerel; buy low and sell high, buy in the cheapest and sell in the dearest market; stag the market [*London Stock Exchange*], rig the market [*Exchange cant*].

Adj. COMMERCIAL, mercantile, trading; interchangeable, marketable, staple, in the market, for sale; at a bargain, marked down.

wholesale, retail.

Adv. across the counter; in the marts of trade; on the Rialto, on 'change.

⁎⁎ cambio non è furto: "a business with an income at its heels" [*Cowper*]; "bad is the trade that must play fool'to sorrow" [*King Lear*]; "Traffic's thy god; and thy god confound thee!" [*Timon of Athens*]; "What news on the Rialto?" [*Merchant of Venice*].

---

795. Purchase. — N. PURCHASE, emption [*rare*]; buying, purchasing, shopping; preëmption, refusal.

coemption [*Rom. law*]; bribery; slave trade.

BUYER, purchaser, emptor [*law*], coemptor, vendee; client, customer, clientele, clientage; patron, employer.

V. BUY, purchase, invest in, regrate, procure; rent &c. (*hire*) 788; repurchase, buy in.

make –, complete- a purchase; buy over the counter; pay cash for; charge, – to one's account.

shop, market, go a-shopping.

keep in one's pay, bribe, suborn; pay &c. 807; spend &c. 809.

Adj. purchased &c. *v.*; emptorial, coemptional, coemptive; cliental.

⁎⁎ caveat emptor.

796. Sale. — N. SALE, vent [*rare*], vend [*Eng.*], disposal; auction, roup [*Scot.*], outcry, vendue, Dutch auction; custom &c. (*traffic*) 794.

SALABLENESS, salability, marketability, vendibility, vendibleness.

SELLER, vender, vendor; consigner; *institor* [*L.*]; rouping wife [*Scot.*]; merchant &c. 797; auctioneer.

SALESMANSHIP, selling ability.

V. SELL, vend, dispose of, make a sale, effect a sale; sell over the count r, sell at [*esp. U. S.*] auction, sell by [*esp. Brit.*] auction, auction, roup [*Scot.*], outcry; put up to (*or* at) auction; bring to (*or* under) the hammer; offer –, put up- for sale; hawk, bring to market; wholesale [*colloq.*]; dump, unload, place; offer &c. 763; undersell; dispense, retail; deal in &c. 794; sell -off, – out; turn into money, realize.

let; mortgage &c. (*security*) 771.

Adj. FOR SALE, under the hammer, in the market.

SALABLE, marketable, vendible, staple, merchantable; in demand, popular.

UNSALABLE &c., unpurchased, unbought; on the shelves, shelved, on one's hands.

⁎⁎ chose qui plaît est à demi vendue.

797. Merchant. — N. MERCHANT, trader, dealer, monger, chandler, salesman; money changer, changer [*archaic*]; regrater; shopkeeper, shopman; tradesman, tradespeople, tradesfolk.

RETAILER; chapman, hawker, huckster, higgler; peddler *or* pedlar, colporteur, cadger, Autolycus; sutler, vivandière; costerman, costermonger; tallyman [*rare*], canvasser, solicitor [*U. S.*]; cheap Jack, *camelot* [*F.*]; faker [*slang*]; vintner; greengrocer, groceryman, haberdasher.

MONEY-LENDER, cambist, usurer, moneyer [*obs.*], banker; money-changer, money-broker.

JOBBER; broker &c. (*agent*) 758; buyer &c. 795; seller &c. 796; bear, bull [*Stock Exchange*].

CONCERN, house, corporation; firm &c. (*partnership*) 712.

. "a merchant of great traffic through this world" [*Taming of the Shrew*].

798. Merchandise. — N. MERCHANDISE, ware, commodity, effects, goods, article, stock, produce, staple commodity; stock in trade &c. (*store*) 636; cargo &c. (*contents*) 190.

. "I sometimes wonder what the vintners buy One half so precious as the stuff they sell" [Omar Khayyám — Fitzgerald].

799. Mart. — N. MART, market, marketplace; fair, bazaar, staple, exchange, stock exchange, Wheat Pit [*Chicago*]; 'change, bourse, curb, hall, guildhall; tollbooth [*Scot. & dial. Eng.*], customhouse; Tattersall's.

SHOP, stall, booth; wharf; office, chambers, countinghouse, bureau; counter *or* compter [*obs.*].

STORE &c. 636; department store, finding store [*U. S.*], grindery warehouse, warehouse, wareroom; depot, interposit [*rare*], *entrepôt* [*F.*], emporium, establishment.

market overt, open market.

. "To business that we love we rise betime, And go to't with delight." [*Antony and Cleopatra*].

4. *Monetary Relations*

800. Money. — N. MONEY, finance; money -matters, – market; accounts &c. 811; funds, treasure; capital, stock; assets &c. (*property*) 780; wealth &c. 803; supplies, ways and means, wherewithal *or* wherewith, sinews of war, almighty dollar, cash.

SOLVENCY, responsibility, reliability, solidity, soundness.

SUM, amount; balance, balance sheet; sum total; proceeds &c. (*receipts*) 810.

CURRENCY, circulating medium, specie, coin, piece, hard cash; dollar, sterling; pounds, shillings, and pence, £ s. d.; guinea; gold mohur [*India*]; eagle, double eagle; pocket, breeches pocket [*colloq.*], wallet, roll, purse; money in hand; *argent comptant* [*F.*], ready [*colloq.*], ready money; Federal –, fractional –, postal- currency; bottom dollar [*colloq.*]; checks, chips.

[SLANG TERMS] the needful, rhino, brass, blunt, dust, mopus, tin, salt, chink, dough, jack, moss, rock, dibs, slug [*Calif.* 1849]; buzzard dollar, spondulics, long green; barrel, pile, wad.

PRECIOUS METALS, gold, silver, copper, bullion, ingot, bar, nugget.

PETTY CASH, pocket money, pin money, spending money, change, small coin; long bit, short bit, two bits, quarter [*all U. S.*]; dime, nickel, cent, red cent [*colloq.*, *U. S.*]; doit, stiver, rap, mite, farthing, sou, penny, shilling, tester, groat, rouleau.

WAMPUM, wampumpeag, seawan *or* seawant, roanoke, cowrie.

GREAT WEALTH, money to burn [*colloq.*]; power –, mint –, barrel –, raft- of money [*all colloq.*]; good –, round –, lump- sum; plum (= £100,000) [*rare slang*]; million, millions, thousands; crore (= ten million rupees, written *Rs.* 1,00,00,000) [*India*]; lac *or* lakh, lac of rupees (= 100,000 rupees, written *Rs.* 1,00,000) [*India*].

[SCIENCE OF COINS] numismatics, numismatology, chrysology.

PAPER MONEY; money –, postal –, post office- order; note, – of hand; bank –, promissory- note; I O U, bond; bill, – of exchange; draft, check [*esp. U. S.*] or cheque [*esp. Brit.*], hundi [*India*], order, warrant, coupon, debenture, exchequer bill, assignat, greenback [*U. S.*]; blueback [*U. S.*], shinplaster [*slang, U. S.*].

remittance &c. (*payment*) 807; credit &c. 805; liability &c. 806.

drawer, drawee; obligor, obligee.

COUNTERFEIT –, false –, bad– money; queer [*slang*], base coin, flash note, slip [*obs.*], kite [*slang*]; fancy stocks; Bank of Elegance.

COUNTERFEITER, coiner, moneyer, forger.

V. TOTAL, amount to, come to, mount up to.

TOUCH THE POCKET; draw, draw upon; back; indorse &c. (*security*) 771; discount &c. 813.

ISSUE, utter, circulate; fiscalize, monetize, remonetize.

DEMONETIZE, deprive of standard value; cease to issue.

COIN, counterfeit, forge; circulate bad money, shove the queer [*slang*].

Adj. MONETARY, pecuniary, crumenal [*obs.*], fiscal, financial, sumptuary, numismatical; sterling; nummary.

SOLVENT, sound, substantial, good, reliable, responsible, solid, having a good rating; able to pay –20 shillings to the pound, – 100 cents to the dollar.

***⁎** barbarus ipse placet dummodo sit dives* [Ovid]; *argumentum ad crumenam; nervos belli pecuniam infinitam* [Cicero]; *redet Geld so schweigt die Welt; Geld regiert die Welt;* "this bank-note world" [Halleck]; "get to live; Then live and use it" [Herbert]; "Get money; still get money, boy; No matter by what means" [B. Jonson]; "Money brings honor, friends, conquest, and realms" [Milton]; "the image of it gives me content already" [*Measure for Measure*].

801. Treasurer. — **N.** TREASURER; bursar, purser, purse bearer; cash keeper, banker; depositary; questor *or* quæstor [*Rom.*], receiver, liquidator, steward, trustee, accountant, expert accountant, Accountant General, almoner *or* almner, paymaster, cashier, teller; cambist; money changer &c. (*merchant*) 797.

financier, Chancellor of the Exchequer, Secretary of the Treasury, minister of finance.

802. Treasury. — **N.** TREASURY, bank, exchequer, almonry, fisc *or* fiscus, hanaper; kutcherry *or* cutcherry *or* kachahri [*India*], bursary; strong box, stronghold, strong room; coffer; chest &c. (*receptacle*) 191; safe; depository &c. 636; cash register, cash box, money-box, till, tiller.

PURSE, money-bag, portemonnaie, pocketbook, wallet; purse strings; pocket, breeches pocket.

sinking fund; stocks; public –, parliamentary- -stocks, – funds, – securities; Consols, *crédit mobilier* [*F.*]; bonds, government bonds, Liberty bonds [*U. S.*], three per cents; gilt-edged securities.

803. Wealth. — **N.** WEALTH, riches, fortune, handsome fortune, opulence, affluence; good –, easy- circumstances; independence; competence &c. (*sufficiency*) 639; solvency &c. 800.

capital, money; round sum; great wealth &c. (*treasure*) 800; mint of money, mine of wealth, bonanza, El Dorado, Pactolus, Golconda, Potosi, Philosopher's Stone; the Golden Touch.

long –, full –, well lined –, heavy-purse; purse of Fortunatus; *embarras de richesses* [*F.*].

pelf, Mammon, lucre, filthy lucre; loaves and fishes, fleshpots of Egypt.

MEANS, resources, substance, command of money; property &c. 780; income &c. 810.

804. Poverty. — **N.** POVERTY, indigence, penury, pauperism, destitution, want; need, neediness; lack, necessity, privation, distress, difficulties, wolf at the door.

STRAITS; bad –, poor –, needy –, embarrassed –, reduced –, straightened-circumstances; slender –, narrow- means; hand-to-mouth existence, *res angusta domi* [*L.*], low water [*slang, U. S.*], impecuniosity.

MENDICITY, beggary, mendicancy; broken –, loss of- fortune; insolvency &c. (*nonpayment*) 808.

empty -purse, – pocket; light purse; "a beggarly account of empty boxes" [*Romeo and Juliet*].

POOR MAN, pauper, mumper, mendi-

PROVISION, maintenance, livelihood; dowry, alimony.

RICH MAN, moneyed man, warm man [old slang], man of substance; capitalist, millionaire, tippybob [slang], Nabob, Crœsus, Midas, Plutus, Dives, Timon of Athens; Danaë.

timocracy, plutocracy.

V. BE RICH &c. adj.; roll –, wallow-in -wealth, – riches; have money to burn [colloq.].

AFFORD, well afford; command -money, – a sum; make both ends meet, hold one's head above water.

BECOME RICH &c. adj.; fill one's pocket &c. (treasury) 802; feather one's nest, make a fortune; make money &c. (acquire) 775.

enrich, imburse [rare].

worship Mammon, worship the golden calf.

Adj. WEALTHY, rich, affluent, opulent, moneyed, worth a great deal; well-to-do, well off; warm [old slang]; well –, provided for.

made of money; rich as - Crœsus; rolling in -riches, – wealth; having a power of money &c. (great wealth) 800.

flush, – of -cash, – money, – tin [slang]; in funds, in cash, in full feather.

SOLVENT &c., 800; pecunious [rare], out of debt, all straight.

* one's ship coming in.

amour fait beaucoup mais argent fait tout; aurea rumpunt tecta quietem [Seneca]; *magna servitus ist magna fortuna;* "mammon, the least erected spirit that fell from Heaven" [*Paradise Lost*]; *opum furiata cupido* [Ovid]; *vera prosperità è non aver necessità; wie gewonnen so zerronnen; O senza brama sicura ricchezza!* [Dante]; "whose plenty made him pore" [Spenser]; "base wealth preferring to eternal praise" [Homer]; "an incarnation of fat dividends" [Sprague].

cant, beggar, starveling; *pauvre diable* [F.], fakir or fakeer [India], sunyasi [India], schnorrer [Yiddish].

V. BE POOR &c. adj.; want, lack, starve, live from hand to mouth, have seen better days, go down in the world, come upon the parish; go to -the dogs, – the almshouse, – the poorhouse, – rack and ruin; not have a -penny &c. (money) 800, – shot in one's locker; beg one's bread, – from door to door; *tirer le diable par la queue* [F.]; run into debt &c. (debt) 806.

RENDER POOR &c. adj.; impoverish; reduce, – to poverty; pauperize, fleece, ruin, bring on the parish.

Adj. POOR, indigent; poverty-stricken; badly –, poorly –, ill- off; poor as -a rat, – a church mouse, – Job, – Job's turkey [colloq.]; fortuneless, dowerless, moneyless, penniless; unportioned, unmoneyed; impecunious; out –, short-of -money, – cash; without –, not-worth- a rap &c. (money) 800; *qui n'a pas le sou* [F.], out of pocket, hard up; out at -elbows, – heels; seedy [colloq.], in rags, barefooted; beggarly, beggared, destitute : fleeced, stripped; bereft, bereaved; reduced.

IN WANT &c. n.; needy, necessitous, distressed, pinched, straitened; put to one's -shifts, – last shifts; unable to -keep the wolf from the door, – make both ends meet; embarrassed, under hatches; involved &c. (in debt) 806; insolvent &c. (not paying) 808.

Adv. in formâ pauperis [L.].

* zonam perdidit; "a penniless lass wi' a lang pedigree" [Lady Nairne]; á pobreza no hay vergüenza; "he that is down can fall no lower" [Butler]; poca roba poco pensiero; "steep'd . . . in poverty to the very lips" [Othello]; "the short and simple annals of the poor" [Gray]; "the beggarly last doit" [Cowper]; "I am as poor as Job, my lord, but that Fortune send A little more than I can spend" [Holmes]; "I enjoyed the immunities of impecuniosity with the opportunities of

not so patient" [II Henry IV]; "I only ask spend" [Holmes]; "I enjoyed the immunities a millionaire" [Shaw].

---

805. Credit. — N. CREDIT, trust, tick [colloq.], strap [slang], score, tally, account.

PAPER CREDIT, letter of credit, circular note; duplicate; mortgage, lien, debenture, floating capital; draft, *lettre de créance* [F.], securities.

CREDITOR, lender, lessor, mortgagee; dun, dunner; usurer.

806. Debt. — N. DEBT, obligation, liability, indebtment, debit, score.

ARREARS, deferred payment, deficit, default; insolvency &c. (nonpayment) 808; bad debt.

INTEREST; premium; usance [obs.], usury; floating -debt, – capital.

DEBTOR, debitor [obs.], mortgagor; defaulter &c. 808; borrower.

V. CREDIT, accredit, intrust *or* entrust; keep –, run up– an account with.

place to one's –credit, – account; give –, take– credit; fly a kite [*com. slang*]; have one's credit good for.

Adj. ACCREDITED; of good credit, of unlimited credit; well rated; credited, crediting.

Adv. on credit &c. *n;* to the account of, to the credit of; *à compte* [*F*].

⁎⁎⁎ "we think ourselves unsatisfied Till he hath found a time to pay us" [*I Henry IV*]; "doubt not of the day" [*III Henry VI*].

V. BE IN DEBT &c. *adj.;* owe; incur –, contract– a debt &c. *n.;* run up –a bill, – a score, – an account; go on tick [*colloq.*]; borrow &c. 788; run –, get– into debt; be over head and ears in debt; be in difficulties; outrun the constable.

ANSWER FOR, go bail for; back one's note.

Adj. LIABLE, chargeable, answerable for.

INDEBTED, in debt, in embarrassed circumstances, in difficulties; encumbered *or* incumbered, involved; involved –, plunged –, deep –, over head and ears– in debt; deeply involved; fast tied up; insolvent &c. (*not paying*) 808; minus [*colloq.*], out of pocket.

UNPAID; unrequited, unrewarded; owing, due, in arrear, outstanding.

⁎⁎⁎ *æs alienum debitorem leve gravius inimicum facit;* "neither a borrower nor a lender be" [*Hamlet*]; "he that has no credit owes no debts!" [Middleton]; "Knowing how the debt grows, I will pay it" [*Comedy of Errors*]; "My lord, vouchsafe me a word with you" [*Hamlet*].

---

807. Payment. — N. PAYMENT, defrayment; discharge; acquittance, quittance; settlement, clearance, liquidation, satisfaction, reckoning, arrangement.

ACKNOWLEDGMENT, release; receipt, – in full, – in full of all demands; voucher.

REPAYMENT, reimbursement, retribution; pay &c. (*reward*) 973; money paid &c. (*expenditure*) 809.

READY MONEY &c. (*cash*) 800; stake, remittance, installment *or* instalment.

PAYER, liquidator &c. 801.

V. PAY, defray, make payment; pay –down, – on the nail [*slang*], – ready money, – at sight, – in advance; cash, honor a bill, acknowledge; redeem; pay in kind.

pay one's –way, – shot, – footing; pay –the piper, – sauce for all [*both colloq.*], – costs; come down with the needful [*slang*]; shell –, fork– out [*both slang*]; come down with, – the dust [*both slang*]; tickle –, grease– the palm [*both colloq.*]; expend &c. 809; put down, lay down.

DISCHARGE, settle, quit [*archaic*], acquit oneself of; foot the bill [*colloq., U. S.*]; account with, reckon with, settle with, be even with, be quits with; strike a balance; settle –, balance –, square– accounts with; quit scores [*archaic*]; wipe –, clear– off old scores; satisfy; pay in full; satisfy –, pay in full– all demands; clear, liquidate; pay –up, – old debts.

REPAY, refund, reimburse, retribute [*obs.*]; make compensation &c. 30; disgorge, make repayment.

Adj. PAYING &c. paid &c. *v.;* owing nothing, out of debt, all straight, all

808. Nonpayment. — N. NONPAYMENT; default, defalcation; protest, repudiation; application of the sponge; whitewashing.

INSOLVENCY, bankruptcy, failure; insufficiency &c. 640; run upon a bank; overdrawn account.

waste paper bonds; dishonored –, protested– bills; bogus check *or* cheque.

DEFAULTER, bankrupt, insolvent debtor, lame duck [*slang*], man of straw; welsher *or* welcher, stag [*obs.*], levanter, absconder.

V. NOT PAY &c. 807; fail, break, stop payment; become –insolvent, – bankrupt; be gazetted; have one's check –dishonored, – protested.

pay under protest; button up one's pockets, draw the purse strings; apply the sponge; pay over the left shoulder [*colloq.*], get whitewashed; swindle &c. 791; run up bills, fly kites [*com. slang*].

PROTEST, dishonor, repudiate, nullify.

Adj. NOT PAYING; in debt &c. 806; behindhand, in arrear; beggared &c., (*poor*) 804; unable to make both ends meet, minus [*colloq.*], worse than nothing.

INSOLVENT, bankrupt, in the gazette, gazetted, ruined.

UNPAID &c. (*outstanding*) 806; gratis &c. 815; unremunerated.

clear, clear of encumbrance, clear of debt, above water; unowed, never indebted; solvent &c. 800.

Adv. to the tune of [colloq.]; on the nail [slang], money down, cash down, cash on delivery, C.O.D.

. "You'll pay me altogether? Will I live?" [II Henry IV]; "Defer no time, delays have dangerous ends" [I Henry VI]; "he . . . prays your speedy payment" [Timon of Athens].

---

809. Expenditure. — N. EXPENDI-TURE, money going out; outgoings, out-lay; expenses, disbursement; prime cost &c. (price) 812; circulation; run upon a bank.

[MONEY PAID] payment &c. 807; pay &c. (remuneration) 973; bribe &c. 973; fee, footing, garnish [obs.]; subsidy; trib-ute; contingent, quota; donation, gift &c. 784.

investment; purchase &c. 795.

DEPOSIT, pay in advance, earnest, handsel or hansel, installment or instal-ment.

V. EXPEND, spend; run –, get-through; pay, disburse; ante, ante up [both poker]; pony up [slang, U. S.]; open –, loose –, untie- the purse strings, lay out, shell out [slang], fork out [slang]; bleed; make up a sum, invest, sink money.

fee &c. (reward) 973; pay one's way &c. (pay) 807; subscribe &c. (give) 784; subsidize; bribe.

Adj. EXPENDING, expended &c. v.; sumptuary, lavish, free, free with one's money, liberal; beyond one's income.

EXPENSIVE, costly, dear, high-priced, precious, high.

. vectigalia nervos esse reipublicæ [Cicero].

810. Receipt. — N. RECEIPT, value received, money coming in; income, in-comings [rare], revenue, return, proceeds; gross receipts, net profit; earnings &c. (gain) 775; accepta [L.], avails.

RENT, rent roll; rental, rentage [obs.], rack-rent.

PREMIUM, bonus; sweepstakes, ton-tine, prize, drawings, hand-out [slang].

PENSION, annuity; jointure &c. (prop-erty) 780; alimony, pittance; emolument &c. (remuneration) 973.

V. RECEIVE &c. 785; get, have an income of, be in receipt of, have coming in; take money; draw from, derive from; acquire &c. 775; take &c. 789; have in prospect.

YIELD, bring in, afford, pay, return; accrue &c. (be received from) 785.

Adj. RECEIVING, received &c. v.; well-paying, remunerative, interest-bearing; well –, profitably- invested; profitable &c. (gainful) 775.

Adv. at interest; within one's income.

---

811. Accounts. — N. ACCOUNTS, accompts [archaic]; business –, commercial –, monetary- arithmetic; statistics &c. (numeration) 85; money matters, finance, bud-get, bill, score, reckoning, account.

BOOKKEEPING, audit, single entry, double entry; computation, calculation, casting up.

ACCOUNT BOOK, books, ledger; day –, cash –, petty-cash –, pass- book; journal; debtor and creditor –, cash –, running- account; account current; balance, – sheet; compte rendu [F.], account settled; acquit [F.], assets, expenditure, liabilities, out-standing accounts; profit and loss -account, – statement; receipts; receipt -in full, – in part, – on account.

ACCOUNTANT, auditor, actuary, bookkeeper; financier &c. 801; accounting party; chartered accountant [Eng.], expert accountant [U. S.], certified accountant [U. S.], bank examiner.

V. KEEP ACCOUNTS, enter, post, post up, book, credit, debit, carry over; take stock; tot up [colloq.], add, add up; balance –, make up –, square –, settle –, wind up –, cast up- accounts; make accounts square.

bring to book, audit, examine the books, tax.

FALSIFY, surcharge; falsify –, garble- an account; cook –, doctor- an account [both colloq.].

Adj. monetary &c. 800; accountable, accounting; statistical; entered &c. v.

812. Price. — N. PRICE, amount, cost, expense, prime cost, charge, figure, demand, damage [*colloq.*], fare, hire; wages &c. (*remuneration*) 973.

DUES, duty, toll, tax, impost, tariff, cess, sess [*obs.*], tallage *or* tailage [*Old Eng.law*],levy; *abkari* [*India*],capitation, capitation tax, poll tax; doomage [*U.S.*], *likin* [*Chinese*], gabel *or* gabelle, salt tax; gavel [*Old Eng. law*], *octroi* [*F.*], custom, excise, assessment, taxation, benevolence [*hist.*], forced loan; tenths [*hist.*], tithe, exactment, ransom, salvage, towage; brokerage, wharfage, freightage.

WORTH, rate, value, par value, valuation, appraisement, money's worth; penny &c. -worth; price current, market price, quotation, current quotation; what it will fetch &c. *v.*

bill &c. (*account*) 811; shot, scot, scot and lot.

V. PRICE; bear -, set -, fix- a price; appraise, assess, doom [*U. S.*], charge, demand, ask, require, exact, run up; distrain; run up a bill &c. (*debt*) 806; have one's price; liquidate.

AMOUNT TO, come to, mount up to; stand one in [*colloq.*], put one back [*slang*].
FETCH, sell for, cost, bring in, yield, afford.

Adj. PRICED &c. *v.*; to the tune of, *ad valorem* [*L.*]; dutiable, taxable, assessable; mercenary, venal.

٭٭٭ no penny no paternoster; *point d'argent point de Suisse;* no longer pipe no longer dance; no song no supper.

813. Discount. — N. DISCOUNT, abatement, concession, reduction, depreciation, allowance, qualification, set-off, drawback, poundage, agio, percentage; rebate, rebatement, backwardization [*Eng.*], backwardation [*Eng.*], contango [*Eng. Stock Exchange*]; salvage; tare [*com.*], tare and tret.

V. DISCOUNT, bate, rebate, abate, deduct, strike off, mark down, reduce, take off, allow, give, make allowance; depreciate.

Adj. DISCOUNTING &c. *v.*; concessional; marked down; depreciative.

Adv. AT A DISCOUNT, at a bargain, below par.

814. Dearness. — N. DEARNESS &c. *adj.*; high -, famine -, fancy- price; overcharge; extravagance; exorbitance, extortion; heavy pull upon the purse.

V. BE DEAR &c. *adj.*; cost much, cost a pretty penny [*colloq.*]; rise in price, look up.

OVERCHARGE, bleed [*colloq.*], skin [*slang*], fleece, extort.

pay too much, pay through the nose [*colloq.*], pay too dear for one's whistle [*colloq.*].

Adj. DEAR; high -, - priced; of great price, expensive, costly, precious, dear bought; unreasonable, extravagant, exorbitant, extortionate.

at a premium; not to be had, - for love or money; beyond price, above price; priceless, of priceless value.

Adv. DEAR, dearly; at great cost, at heavy cost, at a high price, *à grands frais* [*F.*].

٭٭ prices looking up; *le jeu ne vaut pas la chandelle; le coût en ôte le goût; vel prece vel pretio;* "Since you are dear-bought, I will love you dear" [*Merchant of Venice*]; "But bless you, it's dear — it's dear!" [Browning].

815. Cheapness. — N. CHEAPNESS, low price; depreciation; bargain, *bon marché* [*F.*]; good penny &c. -worth; drug in the market.

[ABSENCE OF CHARGE] gratuity; free -quarters, - seats, -admission; free lunch; run of one's teeth [*slang*]; nominal price, peppercorn rent; labor of love.

DEADHEAD [*colloq.*], dead beat [*slang*], beat [*slang*], sponger.

V. BE CHEAP &c. *adj.*; cost little; come down -, fall- in price; be marked down.

buy for a mere nothing, buy at a bargain, buy dirt-cheap, buy for an old song; have one's money's worth; beat down, cheapen.

Adj. CHEAP; low, - priced; moderate, reasonable; inexpensive *or* unexpensive; well -, worth the money; *magnifique et pas cher* [*F.*]; good -, cheap- at the price; dirt-cheap, dog-cheap; cheap as dirt, cheap and nasty [*colloq.*]; peppercorn; catchpenny.

REDUCED, half-price, depreciated, shopworn, marked down, unsalable.

GRATUITOUS, gratis, free, for nothing;

costless, expenseless; without charge, not charged, untaxed; scot-free, shot-free, rent-free; free of -cost, – expense; complimentary, honorary, unbought, unpaid for.

Adv. AT A BARGAIN, for a mere song; at cost price, at prime cost, at a reduction; on the cheap [*colloq.*, *Eng.*]; *bon marché* or *à bon marché* [*F.*].

⁎ "ill ware is never cheap" [Herbert]; "cheapest is the dearest" [*proverb*].

---

816. Liberality. — N. LIBERALITY, generosity, munificence; bounty, bounteousness, bountifulness; hospitableness, hospitality; charity &c. (*beneficence*) 906; open –, free- hand; open –, large– , free- heart; enough and to spare.

CHEERFUL GIVER, free giver, patron; benefactor &c. 912.

V. BE LIBERAL &c. *adj.;* spend –, bleed- freely; shower down upon; open one's purse strings &c. (*disburse*) 809; spare no expense, give *carte blanche* [*F.*]; give with both hands; give the coat off one's back; keep open house, fill one's house with guests.

Adj. LIBERAL, free, generous; charitable &c. (*beneficent*) 906; hospitable; bountiful, bounteous, ample, handsome; unsparing, ungrudging; unselfish; open-, free-, full- handed; open-, large-, free-hearted; munificent, princely.

Adv. LIBERALLY &c. *adj.;* ungrudgingly; with open hands, with both hands.

⁎ "handsome is that handsome does" [Goldsmith]; "good measure, pressed down, and shaken together, and running over" [*Bible*]; "it snewed in his hous of mete and drynke" [Chaucer]; " 'Tis Heaven alone that is given away, 'Tis only God may be had for the asking" [Lowell].

---

818. Prodigality. — N. PRODIGALITY, prodigence [*obs.*], wastefulness, wastry *or* wastrie [*Scot.*], unthriftiness, waste; profusion, profuseness; extravagance; squandering &c. *v.;* lavishness.

pound-foolishness, pound-folly, penny wisdom.

PRODIGAL, spendthrift, wastethrift, wastrel [*dial. Eng.*], waster, high roller [*slang*, *U. S.*], squanderer, spender, spendall, scattergood [*archaic*]; locust; Prodigal Son; Timon of Athens.

V. BE PRODIGAL &c. *adj.;* squander, lavish, sow broadcast; blow in [*slang*]; pay through the nose &c. (*dear*) 814; spill, waste, dissipate, exhaust, drain, eat out of house and home, overdraw, outrun the constable; run out, run through; misspend; throw good money after bad, throw the helve after the

---

817. Economy. — N. ECONOMY, frugality; thrift, thriftiness; care, husbandry, good housewifery, savingness, retrenchment.

SAVINGS; prevention of waste, save-all; parsimony &c. 819.

V. BE ECONOMICAL &c. *adj.;* practice economy, economize, save; retrench, cut down expenses; cut one's coat according to one's cloth, make both ends meet, keep within compass, meet one's expenses, keep one's head above water, pay one's way; husband &c. (*lay by*) 636; save –, invest- money; put out to interest; provide –, save-, -for, – against– a rainy day; feather one's nest; look after the main chance [*colloq.*].

Adj. ECONOMICAL, frugal, careful, thrifty, saving, chary, spare, sparing; parsimonious &c. 819; sufficient; plain.

Adv. SPARINGLY &c. *adj.; ne quid nimis* [*L.*].

⁎ *adde parvum parvo magnus acervus erit; magnum est vectigal parsimonia* [Cicero]; "though on pleasure she was bent, She had a frugal mind" [Cowper]; "Gars auld claes look amaist as weel's the new" [Burns].

---

819. Parsimony. — N. PARSIMONY, parcity [*obs.*]; parsimoniousness, stinginess &c. *adj.;* stint; illiberality, avarice, tenacity, avidity, rapacity, extortion, malversation, venality, cupidity; lack of prodigality &c. 818; selfishness &c. 943; *auri sacra fames* [*L.*]; cheeseparings and candle ends.

MISER, niggard, churl, screw, skinflint, skin [*slang*], codger [*dial. Eng.*], money-grub [*slang*], muckworm, scrimp [*colloq.*], pinchgut [*obs. or vulgar*], lickpenny, hunks [*colloq.*], curmudgeon, harpy, extortioner, usurer, Hessian[*U.S.*]; pinchfist, pinchpenny [*obs*].

Harpagon, Euclio, Silas Marner, Daniel Dancer.

V. BE PARSIMONIOUS &c. *adj.;* grudge, begrudge, stint, pinch, gripe, screw, dole out, hold back, withhold, starve, fam-

hatchet; burn the candle at both ends; make ducks and drakes of one's money; fool –, potter –, muddle –, fritter –, throw- away one's money; squander one's substance in riotous living; spend money like water; pour water into a sieve, kill the goose that lays the golden eggs; *manger son blé en herbe* [*F*.].

Adj. PRODIGAL, profuse, thriftless, unthrifty, improvident, wasteful, losel, extravagant, lavish, dissipated, over-liberal; full-handed &c. (*liberal*) 816; overpaid.

penny-wise and pound-foolish.

Adv. with an unsparing hand; money burning one's pocket.

Int. keep the change! hang expense!

⁂ amor nummi; facile largiri de alieno; wie gewonnen so zerronnen; les fous font les festins et les sages les mangent; "spendthrift alike of money and of wit" [Cowper]; "squandering wealth was his peculiar art" [Dryden]; "How pleasant it is to have money!" [Clough].

ish, live upon nothing, skin a flint [*colloq*.], pinch a sixpence till it squeaks.

drive a bargain, cheapen, beat down; stop one hole in a sieve; have an itching palm, grasp, grab.

Adj. PARSIMONIOUS, penurious, stingy, miserly, mean, shabby, peddling, penny wise, near, near as the bark on a tree, niggardly, close; close-handed, close-fisted, fast-handed [*obs*.], hard-fisted, straithanded [*obs*.], tight-fisted; tight [*colloq*.], sparing; chary; grudging, griping &c. *v.*; illiberal, ungenerous, churlish, hidebound, sordid, mercenary, venal, covetous, usurious, avaricious; greedy, extortionate, rapacious; underpaid.

Adv. with a sparing hand.

⁂ desunt inopiæ multa avaritiæ omnia [Syrus]; "hoards after hoards his rising raptures fill" [Goldsmith]; "the unsunn'd heaps of miser's treasures" [Milton]; "a crusty old fellow, as close as a vise" [Hawthorne]; "all these men have their price" [Walpole].

CLASS VI

Words relating to the SENTIENT and MORAL POWERS

Section I. AFFECTIONS IN GENERAL

820. Affections. — N. CHARACTER, qualities, disposition, affections, nature, spirit, tone; temper, temperament; diathesis, idiosyncrasy; cast -, habit -, frame- of -mind, - soul; predilection, turn; natural -, turn of mind; bent, bias, predisposition, proneness, proclivity, propensity, propenseness, propension, propendency [obs.]; vein, humor, mood, grain, mettle, backbone; sympathy &c. (love) 897.

SOUL, heart, breast, bosom, inner man; heart's -core, - strings, - blood; heart of hearts, *penetralia mentis* [L.]; secret and inmost recesses of the heart, cockles of one's heart; inmost- heart, - soul.

PASSION, pervading spirit; ruling -, master- passion; *furore* [It.], furor; fullness of the heart, heyday of the blood, flesh and blood, flow of soul.

ENERGY, fervor, fire, verve, force.

V. have *or* possess character &c. *n.;* be of a character &c. *n.;* be affected &c. *adj.;* breathe energy &c. *n.*

Adj. CHARACTERIZED, affected, formed, molded *or* moulded, cast; attemperate, attempered, tempered; framed.

PRONE, predisposed, disposed, inclined; having a bias &c. *n.;* tinctured -, imbued -, penetrated -, eaten up- with.

INBORN, inbred, ingrained; deep-rooted, ineffaceable, inveterate; congenital, dyed in the wool, implanted by nature, inherent, in the grain.

Adv. in one's heart &c. *n.;* at heart; heart and soul &c. 821; in the vein, in the mood.

⁎⁎* the ruling passion strong in death; "the Divinity that stirs within us" [Addison]; "that dread apocalypse of soul" [E. B. Browning]; "how paint to the sensual eye what passes in the holy-of-holies of man's soul?" [Carlyle]; "build thee more stately mansions, O my soul" [Holmes]; "character is an historical fruit, and the result of a man's biography" [Amiel]; "One master-passion in the breast. Like Aaron's serpent, swallows all the rest" [Pope].

821. Feeling. — N. FEELING; suffering &c. *v.;* endurance, tolerance, sufferance, experience, response; sympathy &c. (love) 897; impression, inspiration, affection, sensation, emotion, pathos, deep sense.

WARMTH, glow, unction, gusto, vehemence, fervor, fervency; heartiness, cordiality; earnestness, eagerness; *empressement* [F.], gush [colloq.], ardor, zeal, passion, enthusiasm, verve, *furore* [It.], furor, fanaticism; excitation of feeling &c. 824; fullness of the heart &c. (disposition) 820; passion &c. (state of excitability) 825; ecstasy &c. (pleasure) 827.

STATE OF EXCITEMENT; blush, suffusion, flush; hectic, hectic fever, hectic flush; tingling, thrill, turn, shock; agitation &c. (irregular motion) 315; quiver, heaving, flutter, flurry, fluster, twitter, tremor; throb, throbbing; pulsation, palpitation, panting; trepidation, perturbation, ruffle, hurry of spirits, pother, stew [colloq.], ferment.

V. FEEL; receive an impression &c. *n.;* be impressed with &c. *adj.;* entertain -, harbor -, cherish- -feeling &c. *n.*

RESPOND; catch the -flame, - infection; enter into the spirit of.

BEAR, suffer, support, sustain, endure, thole [obs. or dial.], aby *or* abye; brook;

abide &c. (*be composed*) 826; experience &c. (*meet with*) 151; taste, prove; labor –, smart- under; bear the brunt of, brave, stand.

BE AGITATED, be excited &c. 824; swell, glow, warm, flush, blush, crimson, change color, mantle; darken, whiten, pale; turn -color, – pale, – red, – black in the face; tingle, thrill, heave, pant, throb, palpitate, go pitapat, tremble, quiver, flutter, twitter; shake &c. 315; blench, stagger, reel; look -blue, – black; wince, draw a deep breath.

impress &c. (*excite the feelings*) 824.

Adj. FEELING &c. *v.;* sentient; sensuous, sensorial, sensory; emotive, emotional; of *or* with feeling &c. *n.*

LIVELY, quick, smart, strong, sharp, acute, cutting, piercing, incisive; keen, – as a razor; trenchant, pungent, racy, piquant, poignant, caustic.

IMPRESSIVE, deep, profound, indelible; deep-felt, homefelt, heart-felt; swelling, soul-stirring, heart-expanding, electric, thrilling, rapturous, ecstatic; pervading, penetrating, absorbing.

EARNEST, wistful, eager, breathless; fervent, fervid, gushing [*colloq.*], warm, passionate, warm-hearted, hearty, cordial, sincere, zealous, enthusiastic, glowing, ardent, burning, red-hot, fiery, flaming; boiling, – over.

RABID, raving, feverish, fanatical, hysterical; impetuous &c. (*excitable*) 825; overmastering.

IMPRESSED –, moved –, touched –, affected –, penetrated –, seized –, imbued &c. 820- with; devoured by; wrought up &c. (*excited*) 824; struck all of a heap [*colloq.*]; rapt; in a quiver &c. *n.;* enraptured &c. 829.

the heart -big, – full, – swelling, – beating, – pulsating, – throbbing, – thumping, – beating high, – melting, – overflowing, –bursting, – breaking.

Adv. HEARTILY, heart and soul, from the bottom of one's heart, *ab imo pectore* L.], *de profundis* [*L.*]; at heart, *con amore* [*It.*], devoutly, over head and ears.

** "We should count time by heart-throbs" [Bailey]; "give me that man That is not passion's slave, and I will wear him In my heart's core" [*Hamlet*].

---

822. Sensibility. — N. SENSIBILITY, sensibleness, sensitiveness; moral sensibility; impressibility, affectibility; susceptibleness, susceptibility, susceptivity; mobility; vivacity, vivaciousness; tenderness, softness; sentimentality, sentimentalism.

excitability &c. 825; fastidiousness &c. 868; physical sensibility &c. 375; sensitive plant.

SORE POINT, sore place; quick, raw; where the shoe pinches.

V. BE SENSIBLE &c. *adj.;* have a tender, – warm, – sensitive- heart; be all heart.

take to heart, treasure up in the heart; shrink, wince, blench, quiver.

"die of a rose in aromatic pain" [Pope]; touch to the quick; touch –, flick one- on the raw.

Adj. SENSIBLE, sensitive; impressible, impressionable; susceptive, susceptible; alive to, impassionable, gushing [*colloq.*]; warm-hearted, tender-hearted, soft-hearted; tender, soft, maudlin, sentimental, romantic; enthusiastic, impassioned, highflying, spirited, mettle-

823. Insensibility. — N. INSENSIBILITY, insensibleness; want of sensibility &c. 823; moral insensibility; inertness, inertia, *vis inertiæ* [*L.*]; impassibility, impassibleness; inappetency, apathy, phlegm, dullness, hebetude, supineness, insusceptibility, unimpressibility, lukewarmness.

COLDNESS; cold -fit, – blood, – heart; coolness; frigidity, *sang-froid* [*F.*], stoicism, imperturbation &c. (*inexcitability*) 826; nonchalance, unconcern, dry eyes; insouciance &c. (*indifference*) 866; recklessness &c. 863; callousness, callosity, obtundity, brutification; heart of stone, blood and iron, stock and stone, marble, deadness.

neutrality; quietism, vegetation.

TORPOR, torpidity; obstupefaction [*obs.*], lethargy, coma, trance; sleep &c. 683; inanimation [*rare*], suspended animation; stupor, stupefaction; paralysis, palsy; numbness &c. (*physical insensibility*) 376; analgesia.

stoic, Indian, man of iron, pococurante, pococurantist; the Fat Boy in Pickwick.

some, vivacious, lively, expressive, mobile, tremblingly alive; excitable &c. 825; oversensitive, without skin, thin-skinned; fastidious &c. 868.

Adv. SENSIBLY &c. adj.; to the quick, on the raw, to the inmost core.

₄ mens æqua in arduis; "let the galled jade wince" [Hamlet]; "the bravest are the tenderest" [Taylor]; "If she could weep, they said, She could love, they said" [Dunsany].

TRIFLER, dabbler, dilettante, sciolist &c. 493.

V. BE INSENSIBLE &c. adj.; have a rhinoceros hide; show insensibility &c. n.; not mind, not care, not be affected by; have no desire for &c. 866; have –, feel –, take- no interest in; nil admirari [L.]; not care a straw &c. (unimportance) 643 for; disregard &c. (neglect) 460; set at naught &c. (make light of) 483; turn a deaf ear to &c. (inattention) 458; vegetate.

RENDER INSENSIBLE, render callous; blunt, obtund, numb, benumb, paralyze, chloroform, deaden, hebetate, stun, stupefy; brutify, brutalize.

INURE; harden, harden the heart; steel, caseharden, sear.

Adj. INSENSIBLE, unconscious; impassive, impassible; blind to, deaf to, dead to; obtundent, insusceptible or unsusceptible, unimpressionable, unimpressible; passionless, spiritless, heartless, soulless, unfeeling; unmoral.

APATHETIC, unemotional, leucophlegmatic [obs.], phlegmatic; dull, frigid; cold cold-blooded, cold-hearted; cold as charity; flat, obtuse, inert, supine, sluggish, torpid, torpedinous [rare], torporific; sleepy &c. (inactive) 683; languid, half-hearted, tame; numb, numbed; comatose; anæsthetic &c. 376; stupefied, chloro-formed, palsy-stricken.

INDIFFERENT, lukewarm, Laodicean, careless, mindless, regardless; inattentive &c. 458; neglectful &c. 460; disregarding.

UNCONCERNED, nonchalant, pococurante, insouciant, sans souci [F.]; unam-bitious &c. 866.

UNAFFECTED, unruffled, unimpressed, uninspired, unexcited, unmoved, unstirred, untouched, unshocked, unstruck; unblushing &c. (shameless) 885; unanimated; vegetative.

CALLOUS, thick-skinned, pachydermatous, impervious; hard, hardened; inured, casehardened; steeled –, proof- against; imperturbable &c. (inexcitable) 826; unfelt.

Adv. INSENSIBLY &c. adj.; æquo animo [L.], without being -moved, – touched, – impressed; in cold blood; with dry eyes, with withers unwrung.

Int. never mind! it is of no consequence &c (unimportant) 642; it cannot be helped! it is all the same!

₄ "But och! it hardens a' within, And petrifies the feelin'" [Burns]; "that repose Which stamps the caste of Vere de Vere" [Tennyson]; "if he is content with a vegetable love" [Gilbert].

---

824. Excitation. — N. EXCITATION OF FEELING; mental –, excitement; suscitation [obs.], suscitability [obs.], galvanism, high pressure, stimulation, piquancy, provoca-tion, inspiration, calling forth, infection; animation, agitation, perturbation; subju-gation, fascination, intoxication, enravishment, ravishment, entrancement; unction, impressiveness &c. adj.

trial of temper, casus belli [L.], irritation &c. (anger) 900; passion &c. (state of excitability) 825; thrill &c. (feeling) 821; repression of feeling &c. 826.

emotional appeal, melodrama; great moment, crisis; sensationalism, yellow jour-nalism.

V. EXCITE, affect, touch, move, impress, strike, interest, animate, inspire, impas-sion, smite, infect; stir –, fire –, warm- the blood; set astir; awake, wake; awaken, waken; call forth; evoke, provoke; raise up, summon up, call up, wake up, blow up, get up, light up; raise; get up the steam, rouse, arouse, stir, fire, kindle, enkindle, illumine, illuminate, apply the torch, set on fire, inflame.

STIMULATE; exuscitate or exsuscitate [both obs.], suscitate [obs.]; inspirit; spirit up, stir up, work up; infuse life into, give new life to; bring –, introduce- new blood; quicken; sharpen, whet; work upon &c. (incite) 615; hurry on, give a fillip, fillip, put on one's mettle.

fan the -fire, - flame; blow the coals, stir the embers; fan, fan into a flame; foster, heat, warm, foment, raise to a fever heat; keep up, keep the pot boiling; revive, rekindle; rake up, rip up.

intoxicate, overwhelm, overpower, *bouleverser* [*F.*], upset, turn one's head; fascinate; enrapture &c. (*give pleasure*) 829.

PENETRATE, pierce; stir -, play on -, come home to- the feelings; touch -a string, - a chord, - the soul, - the heart; go to one's heart, go through one, open the wound, turn the knife in the wound; touch to the quick; possess -, pervade -, imbue -, penetrate -, imbrue [*obs.*] -, absorb -, affect -, disturb- the soul; rivet the attention; sink into the -mind, - heart; absorb; prey on the mind.

AGITATE, perturb, ruffle, fluster, flutter, flurry, shake, disturb, startle, shock, stagger; give one a -shock, - turn; strike all of a heap [*colloq.*], strike dumb, stun, astound, electrify, galvanize, petrify.

IRRITATE, sting; cut; cut to the -heart, - quick; try one's temper; fool to the top of one's bent, pique; infuriate, madden, make one's blood boil; lash into fury &c. (*wrath*) 900.

BE EXCITED &c. *adj.*; flash up, flare up; catch the infection; thrill &c. (*feel*) 821; mantle; work oneself up; seethe, boil, simmer, foam, fume, flame, rage, rave; run mad &c. (*passion*) 825; run amuck.

Adj. EXCITED &c. *v.*; wrought up, on the *qui vive*, astir, sparkling; in a -quiver &c. 821, - fever, - ferment, - blaze, - state of excitement; in hysterics; black in the face, overwrought; hot, red-hot, flushed, feverish; all of a -flutter, - twitter; all in a pucker [*colloq.*]; with quivering lips, with trembling lips, with twitching lips, with tears in one's eyes.

RAGING, flaming; boiling, - over; ebullient, seething; foaming, - at the mouth; fuming; stung to the quick; on one's high ropes; on one's high horse; carried away by passion, wild, raving, frantic, mad, amuck, distracted, beside oneself, out of one's wits, ready to burst, *bouleversé* [*F.*], demoniacal.

LOST, *éperdu* [*F.*], tempest-tossed; haggard; ready to sink.

EXCITING &c. *v.*; impressive, warm, glowing, fervid, swelling, imposing, spirit-stirring, thrilling; high-wrought; soul-stirring, soul-subduing; heart-stirring, heart-swelling, heart-thrilling; agonizing &c. (*painful*) 830; telling, sensational, melodramatic, hysterical; overpowering, overwhelming; more than flesh and blood can bear; yellow.

piquant &c. (*pungent*) 392; spicy, appetizing, stinging, provocative, *provoquant* [*F.*], tantalizing.

Adv. at a critical -moment, - period, - point; under a sudden strain; with heart-interest [*cant*]; with plenty of pep [*slang*], with a punch [*slang*]; till one is black in the face.

⁎⁎* the heart -beating high, -'going pitapat, - leaping into one's mouth; the blood -being up, - boiling in one's veins; the eye -glistening, - "in a fine frenzy rolling" [*M. N. D.*].

"the Powers That stir men's spirits, waking or asleep, To thoughts like planets and to acts like flowers" [Masefield]; "I ha' harpit ye up to the throne o' God" [Kipling]; "I tried to force a note that was beyond its power, that is why the harp-string is broken" [Tagore]; "my senses swooned in ecstasy" [*ibid.*].

---

825. [EXCESS OF SENSITIVENESS.]
Excitability. — **N.** EXCITABILITY, impetuosity, vehemence; boisterousness &c. *adj.*; turbulence; impatience, intolerance, non-endurance; irritability &c. (*irascibility*) 901; itching &c. (*desire*) 865; wincing; disquiet, disquietude; restlessness; fidgets, fidgetiness; agitation &c. (*irregular motion*) 315.

TREPIDATION, perturbation, ruffle, hurry, fuss, flurry, fluster, flutter; pother, stew [*colloq.*], ferment; whirl;

826. **Inexcitability.** — **N.** INEXCITABILITY, imperturbability, inirritability; even temper, tranquil mind, dispassion; toleration, tolerance, patience.

PASSIVENESS &c. (*physical inertness*) 172; hebetude, hebetation; impassibility &c. (*insensibility*) 823; stupefaction.

CALMNESS &c. *adj.*; composure, placidity, indisturbance, imperturbation, *sang-froid* [*F.*], coolness, tranquillity, serenity; quiet, quietude; peace of mind, mental calmness.

buck fever [*colloq.*]; stage fright; hurry-scurry *or* hurry-skurry; thrill &c. (*feeling*) 821; state -, fever- of excitement; transport.

PASSION, excitement, flush, heat; fever, fever-heat; fire, flame, fume, blood boiling; tumult; effervescence, ebullition; boiling, - over; whiff, gust, storm, tempest; scene, breaking out, burst, fit, paroxysm, explosion, outbreak, outburst; agony.

FURY; violence &c. 173; fierceness &c. *adj.*; rage, furor, *furore* [*It.*], desperation, madness, distraction, raving, delirium; frenzy *or* phrensy, hysterics; intoxication; tearing -, raging- passion; towering rage; anger &c. 900.

FIXED IDEA, *l'idée fixe* [*F.*], monomania; fascination, infatuation, fanaticism; Quixotism, Quixotry; *tête montée* [*F.*].

V. BE IMPATIENT &c. *adj.*; not be able to bear &c. 826; bear ill, wince, chafe, champ the bit; be in a stew [*colloq.*] &c. *n.*; be out of all patience, fidget, fuss, not have a wink of sleep; toss, - on one's pillow.

FUME, rage, foam; lose one's temper &c. 900; break out, burst out, fly out; go -, fly- -off, - off at a tangent; explode; flare up, flame up, fire up, burst into a flame, take fire, fire, burn; stew [*colloq.*]; boil, - over; rave, rant, tear; go -, run- -wild, - mad; go into hysterics; run riot, run amuck; *battre la campagne* [*F.*], *faire le diable à quatre* [*F.*]; play the deuce [*slang*]; raise -Cain, - the mischief, - the devil [*all slang*].

Adj. EXCITABLE, easily excited, in an excitable state; startlish, mettlesome, high-mettled, skittish; high-strung; irritable &c. (*irascible*) 901; impatient, intolerant; moody, maggoty-headed.

FEVERISH, febrile, hysterical; delirious, mad.

UNQUIET, mercurial, electric, galvanic, hasty, hurried, restless, fidgety, fussy; chafing &c. *v.*

VEHEMENT, demonstrative, violent, wild, furious, fierce, fiery, hot-headed, madcap.

OVERZEALOUS, enthusiastic, impassioned, fanatical; rabid &c. (*eager*) 865.

RAMPANT, clamorous, uproarious, turbulent, tempestuous, tumultuary, boisterous.

IMPULSIVE, impetuous, passionate,

EQUANIMITY, poise, staidness &c. *adj.*; gravity, sobriety, quietism, Quakerism; philosophy, stoicism, command of temper; self-possession, self-control, self-command, self-restraint; presence of mind.

RESIGNATION, submission &c. 725; sufferance, supportance, endurance, longsufferance, forbearance, longanimity, fortitude; patience of Job, "patience on a monument" [*Twelfth Night*], "patience sovereign o'er transmuted ill" [Johnson]; moderation; repression -, subjugation- of feeling; restraint &c. 751; tranquillization &c. (*moderation*)174.

V. BE COMPOSED &c. *adj.*

laisser faire [*F.*], *laisser aller* [*F.*]; take things -easily, - as they come; take it easy, rub on [*colloq.*], live and let live; take -easily, - coolly, - in good part; *æquam servare mentem* [*L.*].

ENDURE; bear, - well, - the brunt; go through, support, brave, disregard; tolerate, suffer, stand, bide; abide, aby *or* abye; bear with, put up with, take up with, abide with; acquiesce; submit &c. (*yield*) 725; submit with a good grace; resign -, reconcile- oneself to; brook, digest, eat, swallow, pocket, stomach; carry on, carry through; make light of, make the best of, make "a virtue of necessity" [Chaucer]; put a good face on, keep one's countenance; check &c. 751- oneself.

COMPOSE, appease &c. (*moderate*) 174; propitiate; repress &c. (*restrain*) 751; render insensible &c. 823; overcome -, allay -, repress- one's excitability &c. 825; master one's feelings; make -oneself, - one's mind- easy; set one's mind at -ease, - rest; calm -, cool- down; gentle, tame, thaw, grow cool.

BE BORNE, be endured, be swallowed; go down.

Adj. INEXCITABLE, imperturbable; unsusceptible &c. (*insensible*) 823; dispassionate, unpassionate, cold-blooded, unirritable, inirritable; enduring &c. *v.*; stoical, Platonic, philosophic, staid, stayed [*obs.*], sober, - minded; grave; sober -, grave- as a judge; sedate, demure, cool-headed, level-headed.

EASY-GOING, peaceful, placid, calm; quiet, - as a mouse; tranquil, serene; cool, - as -a cucumber, - custard [*both colloq.*]; undemonstrative.

COMPOSED, collected; temperate &c.

uncontrolled, uncontrollable, ungovernable, irrepressible, stanchless or staunch-
less, inextinguishable, burning, simmering, volcanic, ready to burst forth.

excited, exciting &c. 824.

Adv. in confusion, pell-mell; in trepidation &c. *n.*

Int. pish! pshaw! horrors!

. *noli me tangere;* "filled with fury, rapt,
inspir'd" [Collins]; *maggiore frétta minore átto;*
"For joy he was as a song" [Dunsany]; "on
with the dance! let joy be unconfined" [Byron];
"whispering with white lips, 'The foe! They
come! They come!' " [*ibid.*]; "quiet to quick
bosoms is a hell" [*ibid.*]; "all is not bold that
titters" [*Cynic's Calendar*].

(*moderate*) 174; unexcited, unstirred,
unruffled, undisturbed, unperturbed,
unimpassioned.

MEEK, tolerant; patient, – as Job;
unoffended; unresisting; submissive &c.
725; tame; content, resigned, chastened,
subdued, lamblike; gentle, – as a lamb;
suaviter in modo [*L.*]; mild, – as mother's
milk; soft as peppermint; armed with
patience, bearing with, clement, long-
suffering, forbearant, longanimous.

Adv. "like patience on a monument
smiling at grief" [*Twelfth Night*]; *œquo
animo* [*L.*], in cold blood &c. 823; more
in sorrow than in anger.

Int. patience! and shuffle the cards.

. it will all be the same one hundred years hence; this too will pass; "adversity's sweet
milk, philosophy" [*Romeo and Juliet*]; *mens œqua in arduis; philosophia stemma non inspicit*
[Seneca]; *quo me cumque rapit tempestas deferor hospes* [Horace]; "they also serve who only
stand and wait" [Milton]; "Patience, thou young and rose-lipp'd cherubin" [*Othello*]; "the
mildest curate going" [Gilbert].

SECTION II. PERSONAL AFFECTIONS[1]

1. PASSIVE AFFECTIONS

827. Pleasure. — **N.** PLEASURE, gratification, enjoyment, fruition, delectation, oblectation [*rare*]; relish, zest;
gusto &c. (*physical pleasure*) 377; satisfaction &c. (*content*) 831; complacency.

WELL-BEING; good &c. 618; snugness,
comfort, ease; cushion &c. 215; *sans
souci* [*F.*], mind at ease.

JOY, gladness, delight, glee, cheer,
sunshine; cheerfulness &c. 836.

TREAT, refreshment; amusement &c.
840; luxury &c. 377.

HAPPINESS, felicity, bliss; beatitude,
beatification; enchantment, transport,
rapture, ravishment, ecstasy; *summum
bonum* [*L.*]; paradise, elysium &c.
(*heaven*) 981; third –, seventh- heaven;
unalloyed happiness &c.; hedonics, hedonism.

mens sana in corpore sano [Juvenal].

honeymoon; palmy –, halcyon- days;
golden -age, – time; Eden, Paradise;
Dixie, Dixie land or Dixie's land;
Saturnia regna [*L.*], Arcadia, Cockaigne,
happy valley, Agapemone.

V. BE PLEASED &c. 829; oblectate
[*rare*]; feel –, experience- pleasure &c.
n.; joy; enjoy –, hug- oneself; be in
clover [*colloq.*] &c. 377, be in elysium
&c. 981; tread on enchanted ground;
fall –, go- into raptures.

828. Pain. — **N.** PAIN, mental suffering, dolor, suffering, sufferance [*rare*],
ache; smart &c. (*physical pain*) 378;
passion.

DISPLEASURE, dissatisfaction, discomfort, discomposure, disquiet; *malaise*
[*F.*], inquietude, uneasiness, vexation of
spirit; taking [*colloq.*]; discontent &c.
832.

DEJECTION &c. 837; weariness &c.
841; anhedonia.

ANNOYANCE, irritation, worry, infliction, visitation; plague, bore; bother,
botheration [*colloq.*], stew [*colloq.*], vexation, mortification, chagrin, *esclandre*
[*F.*]; *mauvais quart d'heure* [*F.*].

CARE, anxiety, solicitude, trouble,
trial, ordeal, fiery ordeal, shock, blow,
cark [*archaic*], dole [*archaic*], fret, burden,
load.

GRIEF, sorrow, distress, affliction,
woe, bitterness, heartache; carking
cares [*archaic*]; concern; heavy –, aching –, bleeding –, broken- heart; heavy
affliction, gnawing grief.

MISERY, unhappiness, infelicity, tribulation, wretchedness, desolation; despair
&c. 859; extremity, prostration, depth
of misery; slough of despond &c. (*adversity*) 735; peck –, sea- of troubles;
"the thousand natural shocks that

[1] Or those which concern one's own state of feeling.

feel at home, breathe freely, bask in the sunshine.

ENJOY, like, relish; be pleased with &c. 829; receive -, derive- pleasure &c. *n*.- from; take pleasure &c. *n*.- in; delight in, rejoice in, indulge in, luxuriate in; gloat over &c. (*physical pleasure*) 377; love &c. 897; take to, take a fancy to [*both colloq*.]; have a liking for; enter into the spirit of; take in good part; treat oneself to, solace oneself with.

Adj. PLEASED &c. 829; not sorry; glad, gladsome; pleased as Punch; pleased as a child with a new toy.

HAPPY, blest, blessed, blissful, beatified; happy as -a clam at high water [*U. S.*], - a king, - the day is long; thrice happy, *ter quaterque beatus* [*L.*]; enjoying &c. *v.*; joyful &c. (*in spirits*) 836; hedonic.

in a blissful state, in paradise &c. 981, in raptures, in ecstasies, in a transport of delight.

COMFORTABLE &c. (*physical pleasure*) 377; at ease; in clover [*colloq.*]; content &c. 831; *sans souci* [*F.*].

OVERJOYED, entranced, enchanted; raptured, enraptured, enravished, ravished, transported; fascinated, captivated.

with a joyful face, with sparkling eyes.

PLEASING &c. 829; ecstatic, beatific *or* beatifical; painless, unalloyed, without alloy, cloudless.

Adv. HAPPILY &c. *adj.*; with pleasure &c. (*willingly*) 602; with glee &c. *n*.

⁎⁎* one's heart leaping with joy.
"a wilderness of sweets" [*P. L.*]; "I wish you all the joy that you can wish" [*M. of V.*]; *jour de ma vie;* "joy ruled the day and love the night" [Dryden]; "joys season'd high and tasting strong of guilt" [Young]; "oh happiness, our being's end and aim!" [Pope]; "there is a pleasure that is born of pain" [O. Meredith]; "throned on highest bliss" [*P. L.*]; *vedi Napoli e poi muori; zwischen Freud und Leid ist die Brücke nicht weit.*

flesh is heir to" [*Hamlet*] &c. (*evil*) 616; miseries of human life; the iron entering the soul; "unkindest cut of all" [*Julius Cæsar*].

NIGHTMARE, ephialtes, incubus.

ANGUISH, pang, agony, torture, torment; crucifixion, martyrdom, rack; purgatory &c. (*hell*) 982; hell upon earth; iron age, reign of terror.

SUFFERER, victim, prey, martyr, object of compassion, wretch, shorn lamb.

V. SUFFER, ail; feel -, suffer -, experience -, undergo -, bear -, endure- pain &c. *n.*, smart, ache &c. (*physical pain*) 378; bleed; be the victim of.

labor under afflictions; bear -, stagger under -, take up- the cross; quaff the bitter cup, have a bad time of it; fall on evil days &c. (*adversity*) 735; go hard with, come to grief, fall a sacrifice to, drain the cup of misery to the dregs, "sup full of horrors" [*Macbeth*].

FRET, chafe, sit on thorns, be on pins and needles, wince, worry oneself, be in a taking [*colloq.*], fret and fume; take on [*colloq.*], take to heart; cark [*archaic*].

GRIEVE; mourn &c. (*lament*) 839; yearn, repine, pine, droop, languish, sink; give way; despair &c. 859; heartscald [*dial. Eng.*]; break one's heart; weigh upon the heart &c. (*inflict pain*) 830.

Adj. PAINED, afflicted; in -, in a state of -, full of- pain &c. *n.*; suffering &c. *v.*; worried, displeased &c. 830; aching, griped, sore &c. (*physical pain*) 378; on the rack, in limbo; between hawk and buzzard.

UNEASY, uncomfortable, ill at ease; in a taking, in a way [*both colloq.*]; disturbed; discontented &c. 832; out of humor &c. 901a; weary &c. 841.

UNFORTUNATE &c. (*hapless*) 735; to be pitied, doomed, devoted, accursed, undone, lost, stranded; fey [*obs.*]; victimized, a prey to, ill-used.

UNHAPPY, infelicitous, poor, wretched, miserable, woe-begone; cheerless &c. (*dejected*) 837; careworn; heavy laden, stricken, crushed.

concerned, sorry; sorrowing, sorrowful; cut up [*colloq.*], chagrined, horrified, horror-stricken; in -, plunged in -, a prey to- grief &c. *n.*; in tears &c. (*lamenting*) 839; steeped to the lips in misery; heartstricken, heartbroken, heart-scalded [*dial. Eng.*]; broken-hearted; in despair &c. 859.

⁎⁎* *hæret lateri lethalis arundo* [Vergil]; one's heart bleeding; "the iron entered into his soul" [*Book of Common Prayer*]; "down, thou climbing sorrow" [*Lear*]; "mirth cannot move a soul in agony" [*Love's Labor's Lost*]; *nessun maggior dolere che ricordarsi del tempo felice nella miseria;* "sorrow's crown of sorrow is remembering happier things" [Tennyson]; "the Niobe of Nations" [Byron].

829. [Capability of giving pleasure.] **Pleasurableness. — N.** pleasurableness, pleasantness, agreeable-
ness &c. *adj.*; pleasure giving, jucundity
[*rare*], jocundity, delectability; amusement &c. 840; goodness &c. 648; manna
in the wilderness, land flowing with
milk and honey, "the shadow of a great
rock in a weary land" [*Bible*]; flowery
beds of ease; fair weather.

treat; regale &c. (*physical pleasure*)
377; sweets &c. (*sugar*) 396; dainty,
bonne bouche [F.], titbit or tidbit; sweets,
sweetmeats, nuts, *sauce piquante* [F.],
salt, savor; a sight for sore eyes
[*colloq.*].

ATTRACTION &c. (*motive*) 615; attractiveness, attractability [*rare*], attract-
ableness; invitingness &c. *adj.*; charm,
fascination, captivation, enchantment,
witchery, seduction, winning ways,
amenity, amiability; winsomeness; loveliness &c. (*beauty*) 845; sunny side,
bright side.

V. DELIGHT, charm, becharm, impara-
dise; gladden &c. (*make cheerful*) 836;
win -, gladden -, rejoice -, warm the
cockles of- the heart; do one's heart
good; bless, beatify; take, captivate,
fascinate; enchant, entrance, enrapture,
transport, bewitch, ravish, enravish.

cause -, produce -, create -, give -,
afford -, procure -, offer -, present -,
yield- pleasure &c. 827.

PLEASE, satisfy, gratify, - desire &c.
865; slake, satiate, quench; indulge,
humor, flatter, tickle; tickle the palate
&c. (*savory*) 394; regale, refresh; enliven; treat; amuse &c. 840; take -,
tickle -, hit- one's fancy; meet one's
wishes.

ATTRACT, allure &c. (*move*) 615; stimulate &c. (*excite*) 824; interest.

MAKE THINGS PLEASANT, make everyone feel happy, popularize, gild the pill,
sweeten; smooth -, pour oil upon- the
troubled waters.

Adj. PLEASURABLE, causing pleasure
&c. *v.*; lætificant; pleasure-giving; pleasing, pleasant, amiable, agreeable, grateful, gratifying; lief or leef [*obs.*], acceptable; dear, beloved; welcome, - as the
roses in May; welcomed; favorite; to
one's taste, - mind, - liking; satisfactory &c. (*good*) 648.

REFRESHING; comfortable; cordial; genial; glad, gladsome; sweet, delectable,

830. [Capability of giving pain.]
Painfulness. — N. painfulness &c.
adj.; trouble, care &c. (*pain*) 828; trial,
affliction, infliction; cross, blow, stroke,
burden, load, curse; bitter -pill, -
draft or draught, - cup; cup -, waters-
of bitterness.

ANNOYANCE, grievance, nuisance, vexation, mortification, sickener [*rare*],
worry, bore, bother, pother, hot water,
"sea of troubles" [*Hamlet*], hornet's
nest, plague, pest.

source of -irritation, - annoyance;
wound, sore subject, skeleton in the
closet; thorn in -the flesh, - one's side;
where the shoe pinches, gall and wormwood; fly in the ointment; worm at the
heart of the rose; crumpled rose-leaf;
pea in the shoe.

cancer, ulcer, sting, thorn; canker &c.
(*bane*) 663; scorpion &c. (*evildoer*) 913;
dagger &c. (*arms*) 727; scourge &c.
(*instrument of punishment*) 975; carking
care [*archaic*], canker worm of care.

mishap, misfortune &c. (*adversity*)
735; *désagrément* [F.], *esclandre* [F.], rub.

sorry sight, heavy news, provocation;
affront &c. 929; "head and front of
one's offending" [*Othello*].

INFESTATION, molestation; malignity
&c. (*malevolence*) 907.

V. PAIN, hurt, wound; cause -, occasion -, give -, bring -, induce -, produce
-, create -, inflict- pain &c. 828.

pinch, prick, gripe &c. (*physical
pain*) 378; pierce, lancinate, cut.

hurt -, wound -, grate upon -, jar
upon- the feelings; wring -, pierce -,
lacerate -, break -, rend- the heart;
make the heart bleed; tear -, rend- the
heartstrings; draw tears from the eyes;
add a nail to one's coffin.

SADDEN; make unhappy &c. 828;
plunge into sorrow, grieve, fash [*Scot.*],
afflict, distress; cut up [*colloq.*], cut to
the heart.

ANNOY, incommode, displease, discompose, trouble, disquiet; faze [*U. S.*],
feeze or feaze [*colloq., U. S. & dial. Eng.*],
disturb, cross, thwart, perplex, molest;
tease, tire, irk, vex, mortify, wherret
[*obs.*], worry, plague, bother, pester,
bore, pother, harass, harry, badger,
heckle [*Brit.*], bait, beset, infest, persecute, importune.

TORMENT, wring, harrow, torture;
bullyrag; put to the -rack, - question;

nice, dainty; delicate, delicious; dulcet; luscious &c. 396; palatable &c. 394.

LUXURIOUS, voluptuous; sensual &c. 377.

ATTRACTIVE &c. 615; inviting, prepossessing, engaging; winning, winsome; taking, fascinating, captivating, killing [colloq.]; seducing, seductive; heart-robbing; alluring, enticing; appetizing &c. (exciting) 824; cheering &c. 836; bewitching; enchanting, entrancing, enravishing.

DELIGHTFUL, charming, felicitous, exquisite; lovely &c. (beautiful) 845; ravishing, rapturous; heartfelt, thrilling, ecstatic, beatific or beatifical, seraphic; empyrean; paradisaic or paradisaical; elysian &c. (heavenly) 981.

PALMY, halcyon, Saturnian.

Adv. TO ONE'S DELIGHT, to one's heart's content, in utter satisfaction; at one's ease; in clover; in heaven, in paradise, in elysium; from a full heart.

. decies repetita placebit; "charms strike the sight but merit wins the soul" [Pope]; "sweetness and light" [Swift]; "when you speak, sweet, I'd have you do it ever" [Winter's Tale].

break on the wheel, rack, scarify; cruciate [obs.], crucify; convulse, agonize; barb the dart; plant a - dagger in the breast, - thorn in one's side.

IRRITATE, provoke, sting, nettle, try the patience, pique, fret, roil, rile [colloq. & dial.], tweak the nose, chafe, gall; sting -, wound -, cut- to the quick; aggrieve, affront, enchafe [obs.], enrage, ruffle, sour the temper; give offense &c. (resentment) 900.

MALTREAT, bite, snap at, assail; smite &c. (punish) 972; bite the hand that feeds one.

REPEL, revolt; sicken, disgust, nauseate; disenchant, offend, shock, stink in the nostrils; go against -, turn- the stomach; make one sick, set the teeth on edge, go against the grain, grate on the ear; stick in one's -throat, - gizzard [colloq.]; rankle, gnaw, corrode, horrify, appal, freeze the blood; make the flesh creep, make the hair stand on end; make the blood -curdle, - run cold; make one shudder.

HAUNT, haunt the memory; weigh -, prey- on the -heart, - mind, - spirits; bring one's gray hairs with sorrow to the grave.

Adj. PAINFUL, causing pain, hurting &c. v.; hurtful &c. (bad) 649; dolorific or dolorifical, dolorous.

UNPLEASANT, unpleasing, displeasing, disagreeable, unpalatable, bitter, distasteful, unpleasing, uninviting, unwelcome, undesirable, undesired; obnoxious; unacceptable, unpopular, thankless.

UNTOWARD, unsatisfactory, unlucky, inauspicious, ill-starred, uncomfortable.

DISTRESSING; afflicting, afflictive; joyless, cheerless, comfortless, dismal, disheartening; depressing, depressive; dreary, melancholy, grievous, piteous, woeful, rueful, mournful; deplorable, pitiable, lamentable, sad, affecting, touching, pathetic.

IRRITATING, provoking, stinging, annoying, aggravating [colloq.], exasperating, mortifying, galling; unaccommodating, invidious, vexatious; troublesome, tiresome, irksome, wearisome; plaguing, plaguesome, plaguy [colloq.]; awkward.

IMPORTUNATE; teasing, pestering, bothering, harassing, worrying, tormenting, carking [archaic].

INSUFFERABLE, intolerable, insupportable, unbearable, unendurable; past bearing; not to be -borne, - endured; more than flesh and blood can bear; enough to -drive one mad, - provoke a saint, - make a parson swear [colloq.], - try the patience of Job.

SHOCKING, terrific, grim, appalling, crushing; dreadful, fearful, frightful; thrilling, tremendous, dire; heartbreaking, heart-rending, heart-wounding, heart-corroding, heart-sickening; harrowing, rending.

ODIOUS, hateful, execrable, repulsive, repellent, abhorrent; horrid, horrible, horrific, horrifying; offensive; nauseous, nauseating; disgusting, sickening, revolting; nasty; loathsome, loathful; fulsome; vile &c. (bad) 649; hideous &c. 846.

ACUTE, sharp, sore, severe, grave, hard, harsh, cruel, biting, caustic; cutting, corroding, consuming, racking, excruciating, searching, searing, grinding, grating, agonizing; envenomed; catheretic, pyrotic.

CUMBROUS, cumbersome, burdensome, onerous, oppressive.

DESOLATING, withering, tragical, disastrous, calamitous, ruinous.

Adv. PAINFULLY &c. *adj.;* with pain &c. 828; deuced *or* deucedly [*slang*]; under torture, in agony, out of the depths.

Int. woe's me! alas! that I had ever been born! *hinc illæ lacrimæ!* [Terence].

, *surgit amari aliquid;* the place being too hot to hold one; the iron entering into the soul; "he jests at scars that never felt a wound", [*Romeo and Juliet*]; "I must be cruel only to be kind" [*Hamlet*]; "what deep wounds ever closed without a scar?" [Byron]; "every despot must have one disloyal subject to keep him sane" [Shaw]; "Upon the bitter iron there is peace" [Masefield].

---

831. Content. — N. CONTENT, contentment, contentedness; complacency, satisfaction, entire satisfaction, ease, heart's ease, peace of mind; serenity &c. 826; cheerfulness &c. 836; ray of comfort; comfort &c. (*well-being*) 827.

PATIENCE, moderation, endurance; conciliation, reconciliation; resignation &c. (*patience*) 826; quietism.

waiter on Providence; quietist.

V. BE CONTENT &c. *adj.;* rest satisfied, rest and be thankful; take the good the gods provide, let well enough alone, feel oneself at home, hug oneself, lay the flattering unction to one's soul.

take up with, take in good part; assent &c. 488; be reconciled to, make one's peace with; get over it; take heart, take comfort; put up with &c. (*bear*) 826.

RENDER CONTENT &c. *adj.;* set at ease, comfort; set one's -heart, – mind- at -ease, – rest; speak peace; conciliate, reconcile, win over, propitiate, disarm, beguile; content, satisfy; gratify &c. 829.

BE TOLERATED &c. 826; go down, go down with [*colloq.*], do.

Adj. CONTENT, contented; satisfied &c. *v.;* at ease, at one's ease, at home; with the mind at ease, *sans souci* [*F.*], *sine curâ* [*L.*], easy-going, not particular; conciliatory; unrepining, of good comfort; resigned &c. (*patient*) 826; cheerful &c. 836.

SERENE &c. 826; unafflicted, unvexed, unmolested, unplagued; at rest; snug, comfortable; in one's element; not easily perturbed; imperturbable.

SATISFACTORY, adequate, commensurate, sufficient, ample, equal to; satisfying.

Adv. to one's heart's content; *à la bonne heure* [*F.*]; all for the best.

Int. amen &c. (*assent*) 488; very well!

832. Discontent. — N. DISCONTENT, discontentment; dissatisfaction; "the winter of our discontent" [*Henry VI*]; dissent &c. 489; querulousness &c. (*lamentation*) 839; hypercriticism.

DISAPPOINTMENT, mortification; cold comfort; regret &c. 833; repining, taking on [*colloq.*] &c. *v.;* inquietude, vexation of spirit, soreness; heartburning, heartgrief.

MALCONTENT, grumbler, growler, grouch [*slang*], croaker, *laudator temporis acti* [*L.*]; censurer, complainer, faultfinder, murmurer.

The Opposition; Bitter-Enders [*U. S. politics*], Die-Hards; cave of Adullam; indignation meeting.

V. BE DISCONTENTED &c. *adj.;* quarrel with one's bread and butter; repine; regret &c. 833; wish one to Jericho, wish one at the bottom of the Red Sea; take on [*colloq.*], take to heart; shrug the shoulders; make a wry face, pull a long face; knit one's brows; look blue, look black, look black as thunder, look blank, look glum.

GRUMBLE, take ill, take in bad part; fret, chafe, make a piece of work [*colloq.*], croak; lament &c. 839.

CAUSE DISCONTENT &c. *n.;* dissatisfy, disappoint, mortify, put out [*colloq.*], disconcert; cut up; dishearten.

Adj. DISCONTENTED; dissatisfied &c. *v.;* unsatisfied, ungratified; dissident; dissentient &c. 489; malcontent, exigent, exacting, hypercritical.

REPINING &c. *v.;* regretful &c. 833; down in the mouth &c. (*dejected*) 837.

GLUM, sulky; in high dudgeon, in a fume, in the sulks, in the dumps, in bad humor; sour, sour as a crab; sore as a crab [*colloq.*]; soured, sore; out of humor, out of temper.

DISAPPOINTING &c. *v.;* unsatisfactory.

Adv. FROM BAD TO WORSE, out of the

all the better! so much the better!
well and good! it will do! that will do!
it cannot be helped! done! content!
i' faith! [archaic]; better and better!
good! good for you! put it thar, pard!
[colloq.].

*** nothing comes amiss.

"a heart with room for every joy" [Bailey];
ich habe genossen das irdische Glück ich habe
gelebt und geliebet [Schiller]; "nor cast one longing, ling'ring look behind" [Gray]; "shut up in
measureless content" [Macbeth]; "swee are the
thoughts that savor of content" [R. Greene];
"their wants but few, their wishes all confined"
[Goldsmith]; "man wants but little here below"
[Bible]; "Little I ask; my wants are few; I only
wish a house of stone, (A very plain brown
stone will do,) That I may call my own
[Holmes]; "Too grateful for the blessing lent
Of simple tastes and mind content!" [ibid.].

frying pan into the fire, in the depths
of despair.

Int. so much the worse! that's bad!
couldn't be worse! worse and worse!

*** that –, it- will never do; curtæ nescio
quid semper abest rei [Horace]; ne Jupiter quidem
omnibus placet; "poor in abundance, famished
at a feast" [Young]; "no tears but o' my
shedding" [Merchant of Venice].

833. Regret. — N. REGRET, repining;
homesickness, nostalgia; mal du pays
[F.], maladie du pays [F.]; lamentation
&c. 839; penitence &c. 950.

BITTERNESS, heartburning.

laudator temporis acti [L.] &c. (discontent) 832.

V. REGRET, deplore; bewail &c.
(lament) 839; repine, cast a longing lin-
gering look behind; rue, rue the day; repent &c. 950; infandum renovare dolorem [L.].
prey –, weigh –, have a weight- on the mind; leave an aching void.

Adj. REGRETTING &c. v.; regretful; homesick.

REGRETTED &c. v.; much to be regretted, regrettable; lamentable &c. (bad) 649.
Int. what a pity! hang it or hang it all! [colloq.].

*** "'tis true 'tis pity; And pity 'tis 'tis true" [Hamlet]; 'sigh'd and look'd and sigh'd
again" [Dryden]; "bombazine would have shown a deeper sense of her loss" [Gaskell]; "I am a
lone, lorn creetur' and every think goes contrairy with me" [Mrs. Gummidge, in David
Copperfield].

834. Relief. — N. RELIEF; deliver-
ance; refreshment &c. 689; easement,
softening, alleviation, mitigation, palliation, soothing; lullaby, cradle-song, berceuse [F.].

SOLACE, consolation, comfort, encouragement; crumb of comfort, balm in
Gilead.

LENITIVE, palliative, restorative &c.
(remedy) 662; stupe, poultice, fomen-
tation, assuasive; cushion &c. 215.

V. RELIEVE, ease, alleviate, mitigate,
palliate, soothe; salve; soften, – down;
foment, stupe, poultice; assuage, allay,
abirritate.

remedy; cure &c. (restore) 660; refresh; pour balm into, pour oil on.

smooth the ruffled brow of care,
temper the wind to the shorn lamb, lay
the flattering unction to one's soul.

CHEER, comfort, console; enliven;

835. Aggravation. — N. AGGRAVA-
TION, heightening; exacerbation; exasperation; overestimation &c. 482; exaggeration &c. 549.

V. AGGRAVATE, render worse, heighten,
embitter, sour; exacerbate, acerbate,
exasperate, envenom; enrage, provoke,
tease.

add fuel to the -fire, – flame; fan the
flame &c. (excite) 824; go from bad to
worse &c. (deteriorate) 659.

Adj. AGGRAVATED &c. v.; worse, unrelieved; aggravable [obs.], aggravative,
aggravating &c. v.

Adv. out of the frying pan into the
fire, from bad to worse, worse and worse.

Int. so much the worse! tant pis! [F.].

*** "When sorrows come, they come not
single spies, But in battalions" [Hamlet];
"One woe doth tread upon another's heel,
So fast they follow" [ibid.].

encourage, bear up, pat on the back, give comfort, set at ease; gladden –, cheer-
the heart; inspirit, invigorate.

DISBURDEN &c. (free) 705; take off a load of care.

BE RELIEVED; breathe more freely, draw a long breath; take comfort; dry the
eyes, dry the tears, wipe the eyes, wipe away the tears; pull oneself together.

Adj. RELIEVING &c. v.; consolatory, soothing; assuaging, assuasive; balmy, balsamic; lenitive, palliative; anodyne &c. (remedial) 662; curative &c. 660.

*** "here comes a man of comfort" [Measure for Measure].

836. Cheerfulness. — N. CHEERFULNESS &c. *adj.;* geniality, gayety, *L'Allegro* [*It.*], cheer, good humor, spirits; high spirits, animal spirits, flow of spirits; glee, high glee, light heart; sunshine of the -mind, – breast; *gaieté de cœur* [*F.*], *bon naturel* [*F.*].

LIVELINESS &c. *adj.;* life, alacrity, vivacity, animation, *allégresse* [*F.*]; jocundity, joviality, jollity; levity; jocularity &c. (*wit*) 842.

MIRTH, merriment, hilarity, exhilaration; laughter &c. 838; merrymaking &c. (*amusement*) 840; heyday, rejoicing &c. 838; marriage bell.

nepenthe *or* nepenthes, lotus; Euphrosyne.

OPTIMISM &c. (*hopefulness*) 858; self-complacency; hedonics, hedonism.

V. BE CHEERFUL &c. *adj.;* have the mind at ease, smile, put a good face upon, keep up one's spirits; view the bright side of the picture, view things *en couleur de rose* [*F.*]; look through rose-colored spectacles; *ridentem dicere verum* [*L.*], cheer up, brighten up, light up, bear up; take heart, cast away care, drive dull care away, perk up; keep a stiff upper lip [*slang*].

REJOICE &c.; 838; carol, chirp, chirrup, lilt; frisk, rollic, give a loose to mirth [*obs.*].

CHEER, enliven, elate, exhilarate, gladden, inspirit, animate, raise the spirits, inspire; put in good humor; cheer –, rejoice- the heart; delight &c. (*give pleasure*) 829.

Adj. CHEERFUL; happy &c. 827; cheery, of good cheer, smiling; blithe; in spirits, in good spirits; breezy, bully [*slang*], chipper [*colloq., U. S.*]; in high -spirits, – feather; happy as -the day is long, – a king; gay, gay as a lark; *allegro* [*It.*]; debonair *or* debonaire, light, lightsome, lighthearted; buoyant, bright, free and easy, airy; jaunty *or* janty, rollicky [*colloq.*], canty [*Scot. & dial. Eng.*], "crouse an' canty" [Burns]; hedonic; riant; sprightly, sprightful; spry; spirited, spiritful [*rare*], lively, animated, vivacious; brisk, – as a bee; sparkling; sportive; full of -play, – spirit; all alive.

sunny, palmy; hopeful &c. 858.

MERRY, – as a -cricket, – grig, – marriage bell; joyful, joyous, jocund, jovial; jolly, – as a thrush, – as a sand-boy;

837. Dejection. — N. DEJECTION; dejectedness &c. *adj.;* depression, prosternation [*obs.*], mopishness, damp; lowness –, depression- of spirits; weight –, oppression –, damp- on the spirits; low –, bad –, drooping –, depressed- spirits; heart sinking; heaviness –, failure- of heart.

heaviness &c. *adj.;* infestivity, gloom; weariness &c. 841; *tædium vitæ* [*L.*], disgust of life; *mal du pays* [*F.*] &c. (*regret*) 833; anhedonia.

MELANCHOLY; sadness &c. *adj.; Il Penseroso* [*Old It.*], melancholia, blue devils [*colloq.*], blues [*colloq.*], mopes, lachrymals *or* lacrimals, mumps, dumps [*chiefly humorous*] doldrums, vapors [*archaic*], megrims, spleen [*obsoles.*], horrors, hypochondriasis, hypochondria, hyps [*colloq.*], jawfall [*rare*], pessimism; *la maladie sans maladie* [*F.*], despondency, slough of Despond; disconsolateness &c. *adj.;* hope deferred, blank despondency; voiceless woe.

PROSTRATION, prostration of soul; broken heart; despair &c. 859; cave of despair, cave of Trophonius.

GRAVITY; demureness &c. *adj.;* solemnity; long face, grave face.

HYPOCHONDRIAC, seek-sorrow, self-tormentor, *heautontimorumenos* [*Gr.*], *malade imaginaire* [*F.*], *médecin tant pis* [*F.*]; croaker, pessimist; mope, mopus [*dial. Eng. & slang*], damper, wet blanket crape-hanger [*slang*], Job's comforter.

[CAUSE OF DEJECTION] affliction &c. 830; sorry sight; *memento mori* [*L.*]; deathwatch, death's-head, skeleton at the feast.

V. BE DEJECTED &c. *adj.;* grieve; mourn &c. (*lament*) 839; take on [*colloq.*], give way, lose heart, despond, droop, sink.

LOWER, look downcast, frown, pout; hang down the head; pull –, make- a long face; laugh on the wrong side of the mouth; grin a ghastly smile; look blue, look like a drowned man; lay to heart, take to heart.

MOPE, brood over; fret; sulk; pine, pine away; yearn; repine &c. (*regret*) 833; despair &c. 859.

refrain from laughter, keep one's countenance; be *or* look grave &c. *adj.;* repress a smile, keep a straight face.

DEPRESS, discourage, dishearten, dispirit; damp, hyp [*colloq.*], dull, deject,

blithesome; gleeful, gleesome; hilarious, rattling [colloq.].

WINSOME, bonny, hearty, buxom.

PLAYFUL, playsome; folâtre [F.], playful as a kitten, tricksy, frisky, frolicsome; gamesome; jocose, jocular, waggish; mirth-loving, laughter-loving, abderian; mirthful, rollicking.

ELATE, elated; exulting, jubilant, flushed; rejoicing &c. 838; cock-a-hoop.

CHEERING, inspiriting, exhilarating; cardiac or cardiacal; pleasing &c. 829; palmy, flourishing, halcyon.

Adv. CHEERFULLY &c. adj.; cheerily, with good cheer; with a cheerful &c. heart; with relish, with zest; on the crest of the wave.

Int. NEVER SAY DIE! come! cheer up! hurrah! &c. 838; "hence loathed melancholy!" begone dull care! away with melancholy!

₊ "a merry heart goes all the day" [A Winter's Tale]; "as merry as the day is long" [Much Ado]; ride si sapis [Martial]; "as merry as cards, suppers, wine, and old women can make us" [Goldsmith].

lower, sink, dash, knock down, unman, prostrate, break one's heart; frown upon; cast a gloom on, cast a shade on; sadden; damp -, dash -, wither- one's hopes; weigh -, lie heavy -, prey- on the -mind, - spirits; damp -, dampen -, depress- the spirits.

Adj. CHEERLESS, joyless, spiritless, uncheerful, uncheery, unlively; unhappy &c. 828; melancholy, dismal, somber, dark, gloomy, triste [F.], clouded, murky, lowering, frowning, lugubrious, funereal, mournful, lamentable, dreadful.

DREARY, flat; dull, - as -a beetle, - ditchwater; depressing &c. v.; damp [archaic].

DOWNCAST, downhearted, mopy [colloq.], "melancholy as a gib cat" [I Henry IV]; a prey to melancholy; "besieged with sable-coloured melancholy" [L. L. L.]; down in the mouth [colloq.], down on one's luck [colloq.]; heavy-hearted; in the -dumps, - suds [colloq.], - sulks, - doldrums; in doleful dumps, in bad humor; sullen; mumpish, dumpish, mopish, moping; moody, glum; sulky &c. (discontented) 832; out of -sorts, - humor, - heart, - spirits; ill at ease, low-spirited, in low spirits, a cup too low; weary &c. 841; discouraged, disheartened, desponding, chapfallen or chopfallen, jawfallen [rare], hypped [colloq.], hyppish [rare]; crestfallen.

SAD, pensive, pensieroso [It.], tristful; dolesome, doleful; woe-begone, lachrymose, in tears, melancholic, hypochondriacal, bilious, jaundiced, atrabilious, saturnine, splenetic; lackadaisical.

SERIOUS, sedate, staid, earnest; grave, - as -a judge, - an undertaker, - a mustard pot [colloq.]; sober, solemn, demure; grim, grim-faced, grim-visaged; rueful, wan, long-faced.

DISCONSOLATE, inconsolable, forlorn, comfortless, desolate, désolé [F.], sick at heart; soul-sick, heartsick; au désespoir [F.]; in despair &c. 859; lost.

OVERCOME; broken-down, borne-down, bowed-down; heartstricken &c. (mental suffering) 828; cut up [colloq.], dashed, sunk; unnerved, unmanned; downfallen, downtrodden; broken-hearted; careworn.

Adv. SADLY &c. adj.; with a long face, with tears in one's eyes.

₊ the countenance falling; the heart failing one, the heart sinking within one; "a plague of sighing and grief" [Henry IV]; "thick-ey'd musing and curs'd melancholy" [Henry IV]; "melancholy is the pleasure of being sad" [Victor Hugo]; "the sickening pang of hope deferred" [Scott]; "Our sincerest laughter With some pain is fraught" [Shelley].

838. [EXPRESSION OF PLEASURE.] Rejoicing. — N. REJOICING, exultation, triumph, jubilation, heyday, flush, reveling or revelling; merrymaking &c. (amusement) 840; jubilee &c. (celebration) 883; pæan, Te Deum [L.] &c. (thanksgiving) 990; congratulation &c. 896.

SMILE, simper, smirk, grin; broad grin, sardonic grin.

LAUGHTER, giggle, titter, snicker,

839. [EXPRESSION OF PAIN.] Lamentation. — N. LAMENTATION, lament, wail, complaint, plaint, murmur, mutter, grumble, groan, moan, whine, whimper, sob, sigh, suspiration, deep sigh; frown, scowl.

CRY &c. (vociferation) 411; scream, howl; outcry, wail, wail of woe.

WEEPING &c. v.; tear; flood of tears, fit of crying, lachrymation [rare], crying;

snigger, crow, cheer, chuckle, shout;
Homeric laughter; horse –, hearty-
laugh; guffaw; burst –, fit –, shout –,
roar –, peal- of laughter; cachinnation;
Kentish fire.

risibility; derision &c. 856; "sport
that wrinkled Care derides" [Milton].

Momus; Democritus the Abderite;
rollicker.

CHEER, huzza, hurrah or hurra, cheering; shout, yell [U. S. & Can.], college
yell; tiger [colloq.].

V. REJOICE; thank –, bless- one's
stars; congratulate oneself, hug oneself;
rub –, clap- one's hands; smack the lips,
fling up one's cap; dance, skip; sing,
carol, chirrup, chirp; hurrah or hurra;
cry for joy, leap with joy, skip for joy;
exult &c. (boast) 884; triumph; hold
jubilee &c. (celebrate) 883; sing a Te
Deum, sing a pæan of triumph; make
merry &c. (sport) 840.

SMILE, simper, smirk; grin, – like a
Cheshire cat [colloq.]; mock, laugh in
one's sleeve.

LAUGH, – outright; giggle, titter,
snigger, snicker, crow, smicker [obs.],
chuckle, cackle; burst out; burst into
a roar of laughter, burst into a fit of
laughter; shout, split [colloq.], roar.

shake –, split –, hold both- cne's
sides; roar –, shake –, nearly die –, die-
with laughter.

raise laughter &c. (amuse) 840.

Adj. REJOICING &c. v.; jubilant, exultant, triumphant; flushed, elated;
laughing &c. v.; risible; ready to -burst,
– split, – die with laughte [all colloq.];
convulsed with laughter; shaking like
a jelly with -laughter, – suppressed
merriment [both colloq.].

laughable &c. (ludicrous) 853.

Adv. LAUGHINGLY; on a broad grin,
in fits of laughter, amid peals of laughter; in triumph; in mockery; with a
-roar, – peal, – outburst- of laughter.

Int. HURRAH! huzza! three cheers!
hip, hip, hurrah! aha! hail! tolderolloll!
Heaven be praised! tant mieux! [F.],
so much the better! good enough!
tra-la-la!

.*. the heart leaping with joy; "laugh?
I thought I should a' died!" [Chevalier]; ce n'est
pas être bien aisé que de rire; "Laughter holding
both his sides" [Milton]; θάλαττα! θάλαττα! le
roi est mort, vive le roi; "with his eyes in flood
with laughter" [Cymbeline].

melting mood; "weeping and gnashing
of teeth" [Bible].

plaintiveness &c. adj.; languishment;
condolence &c. 915.

MOURNING, weeds [colloq.], widow's
weeds, willow, cypress, crape, deep
mourning; sackcloth and ashes; lachrymatory, tear bottle, lachrymals or
lacrimals; knell &c. 363; dump [obs.],
death song, dirge, coronach [Scot. & Ir.],
nenia, requiem, elegy, epicedium; threne
[rare], menody, threnody; jeremiad or
jeremiade, ululation, keen [Ir.], ullalulla
[Ir.].

MOURNER, keener [Ir.]; grumbler &c.
(discontent) 832; Niobe; Heraclitus,
Jeremiah, Mrs. Gummidge.

V. LAMENT, mourn, deplore, grieve,
keen [Ir.], weep over; bewail, bemoan;
condole with &c. 915; fret &c. (suffer)
828; wear –, go into –, put on- mourning;
wear -the willow, – sackcloth and ashes;
infandum renovare dolorem [Vergil] &c.
(regret) 833; give sorrow words.

SIGH; give –, heave –, fetch- a sigh;
"waft a sigh from Indus to the pole"
[Pope]; sigh "like furnace" [As You
Like It]; wail.

CRY, weep, sob, greet [archaic or Scot.],
blubber, snivel, bibber, whimper, pule;
pipe, pipe one's eye [both slang, orig.
naut.]; drop –, shed- -tears, – a tear; melt
–, burst- into tears; fondre en larmes
[F.], cry oneself blind, cry one's eyes
out; yammer [dial.].

scream &c. (cry out) 411; mew &c.
(animal sounds) 412; groan, moan,
whine, yelp, howl, yell, ululate; roar;
roar –, bellow- like a bull; cry out lustily,
rend the air.

SHOW SIGNS OF GRIEF; frown, scowl,
make a wry face, gnash one's teeth,
wring one's hands, tear one's hair, beat
one's breast, roll on the ground, burst
with grief.

COMPLAIN, murmur, mutter, grumble,
growl, clamor, make a fuss about, croak,
grunt, maunder [obs.]; deprecate &c.
(disapprove) 932.

cry out before one is hurt, complain
without cause.

Adj. LAMENTING &c. v.; in mourning,
in sackcloth and ashes; ululant, ulula-
tive [obs.], clamorous; crying –, lament-
ing- to high heaven, sorrowing, sorrowful &c. (unhappy) 828; mournful, tear-
ful; lachrymose, lachrymal or lacrimal,

lachrymatory, plaintive, plaintful; querulous, querimonious; in the melting mood.

IN TEARS, with tears in one's eyes; with moistened eyes, with watery eyes; bathed –, dissolved- in tears; "like Niobe, all tears" [*Hamlet*].

elegiac, epicedial, threnetic or threnetical.

Adv. *de profundis* [L.], *les larmes aux yeux* [F.].

Int. ALAS! alack! heigh-ho! O dear! ah me! woe is me! lackadaisy! well a day! lack a day! alack a day! wellaway! alas the day! *O tempora, O mores!* [L.]; what a pity! *miserabile dictu!* [L.]; too true!

*** tears standing in the eyes, tears starting from the eyes; eyes -suffused, – swimming, – brimming, – overflowing- with tears; "if you have tears prepare to shed them now" [*Julius Cæsar*; *interdum lacrymæ pondera vocis habent* [Ovid]; "strangled his language in his tears" [*Henry VIII*]; "tears such as angels weep" [*Paradise Lost*]; "she wept, she blubbered, and she tore her hair" [Swift]; "laughter is at all ages the natural recognition of destruction, confusion, and ruin" [Shaw].

---

840. Amusement. — N. AMUSEMENT, entertainment, diversion, divertisement, *divertissement* [F.]; reaction, relaxation, solace; pastime, *passe-temps* [F.], sport; labor of love; pleasure &c. 827.

FUN, frolic, merriment, jollity, joviality, jovialness; heyday; laughter &c. 838; jocosity, jocoseness; drollery, buffoonery, tomfoolery; mummery, mumming, masquing, pageant; pleasantry; wit &c. 842; quip, quirk.

PLAY; game, game of romps; gambol, romp, prank, antic, frisk, rig [*obs. or dial.*], lark [*colloq.*], spree, skylarking, vagary, monkey trick, *fredaine* [F.], escapade, *échappée* [F.], bout, *espièglerie* [F.]; practical joke &c. (*ridicule*) 856.

[DANCE STEPS] *gambade* [F.], gambado, *pas* [F.]; pigeonwing, heel-and-toe, buck-and-wing, shuffle, double shuffle; *chassé* [F.], *coupé* [F.], grapevine, &c.

[DANCES] dance, hop [*colloq.*], stag dance, shindig [*slang*, U. S.]; ball; *bal, bal masqué, bal costumé* [*all* F.], masquerade, masquerade ball, cornwallis [U. S.]; mistletoe-bough dance; Dance of Death, *danse macabre* [F.]; interpretative dance, step dance, sand dance, *pas seul* [F.], skirt dance, folk dance; Morisco or morice [*obs.*], morris dance, saraband, fandango, bolero, tarantella, boutade, gavot or gavotte, minuet, *allemande* [F.], rigadoon, fling, Highland fling, Highland schottische, strathspey, reel, jig, hornpipe, sword dance, breakdown, cakewalk; kantikoy, snake dance; country dance, Scotch reel, Virginia reel, Sir Roger de Coverley, Portland fancy; ballet &c. (*drama*) 599; ragtime [*colloq.*] &c. (*music*) 415; jazz [*slang*]; nautch [*India*].

SQUARE DANCE, quadrille, Lancers, cotillion or *cotillon* [F.], German.

ROUND DANCE, waltz, *valse* [F.], polka, mazurka, galop, gallopade or galopade, schottische, one-step, two-step, fox-trot, turkey-trot; shimmy.

danse du ventre [F.], *chonchina* [*Jap.*], cancan.

---

841. Weariness. — N. WEARINESS, defatigation [*obs.*], ennui, boredom; lassitude &c. (*fatigue*) 688; drowsiness &c. 683.

DISGUST, nausea, loathing, sickness; satiety &c. 869; *tædium vitæ* [L.] &c. (*dejection*) 837.

TEDIUM, wearisomeness, tediousness &c. *adj.*; heavy hours, dull work, monotony, twice-told tale; "the enemy" [*time*].

BORE, buttonholer, proser, dry-as-dust, fossil [*colloq.*], wet blanket; pill, stiff [*both slang*].

V. WEARY; tire &c. (*fatigue*) 688; bore; bore –, weary –, tire- -to death, – out of one's life, – out of all patience; set –, send- to sleep; buttonhole.

PALL, sicken, nauseate, disgust; harp on the same string; drag its -slow, – weary- length along.

never hear the last of; be tired &c. *adj.* of or with; yawn; die with *ennui*.

Adj. WEARYING &c. *v.*; wearing; wearisome, tiresome, irksome; uninteresting, stupid, bald, devoid of interest, jejune, dry, monotonous, dull, arid, tedious, humdrum, mortal [*colloq.*], flat; prosy, prosing; slow; soporific, somniferous, dormitive, opiate.

DISGUSTING &c. *v.*; unenjoyed.

WEARY; tired &c. *v.*; drowsy &c. (*sleepy*) 683; uninterested, flagging, used up, worn out, *blasé* [F.], life-weary, weary of life; sick of.

Adv. WEARILY &c. *adj.*; *usque ad nauseam* [L.].

*** time hanging heavily on one's hands; *toujours perdrix; crambe repetita;* "Weary of myself and sick of asking What I am and what I ought to be" [Arnold].

DANCER, *danseur* (*fem. danseuse*) [*F.*], *première danseuse* [*F.*], ballet dancer; geisha [*Jap.*]; nautch girl, bayadere [*both India*]; clog -, step -, skirt -, figure-dancer; figurant (*fem.* figurante), Morisco [*obs.*], morris dancer; terpsichorean [*colloq.*]; Terpsichore.

FESTIVITY, merrymaking; party &c. (*social gathering*) 892; revels, revelry, reveling *or* revelling, carnival, Saturnalia, jollification [*colloq.*], junket, picnic.

fête champêtre [*F.*], lawn party, garden party, regatta, field day, *fête* [*F.*], festival, gala, gala day; feast, banquet &c. (*food*) 298; regale, symposium, high jinks [*colloq.*], carouse, carousal, brawl; wassail; wake; bust [*slang*], tear [*slang*]; *Turnerfest* [*Ger.*]; gymkhana [*orig. Anglo-Ind.*]; treat; *ridotto* [*It.*], drum [*obs. or hist.*], kettledrum [*colloq.*], rout [*archaic*]; tea party, tea, tea fight [*slang*]; *Kaffee-Klatsch* [*Ger.*]; concert &c. (*music*) 415; show [*colloq.*]; play &c. (*drama*) 599; randy [*dial.*]; clambake, fish fry, beefsteak fry, squantum, donation party [*all U. S.*]; bat, bum [*both slang, U. S.*], jamboree [*slang*].

ROUND OF PLEASURE, dissipation, a short life and a merry one, racketing, holiday making.

rejoicing &c. 838; jubilee &c. (*celebration*) 883.

FIREWORKS, *feu-de-joie* [*F.*], firecrackers, bonfire.

HOLIDAY; red-letter day, play day; high days and holidays; high holiday, Bank holiday [*Eng.*]; May day, Derby day [*Eng.*]; Easter Monday, Whitmonday, Twelfth Night, Halloween; Christmas &c. 138; Dewali [*Hindu*], Holi *or* Hoolee [*Hindu*]; Bairam, Muharram [*both Moham.*]; wayzgoose [*Printers*]; beanfeast [*Eng.*]; Arbor -, Declaration -, Independence -, Labor -, Memorial *or* Decoration -, Thanksgiving- Day; Washington's -, Lincoln's -, King's- birthday; Empire Day [*Brit.*]; Mardi gras, *mi-carême* [*F.*], feria [*S. W. U. S.*], fiesta [*Sp.*].

PLACE OF AMUSEMENT, theater *or* theatre; concert -hall, - room; ballroom, dance hall, assembly room; moving-picture -, cinema- theater; movies [*colloq.*]; music hall; vaudeville -theater, - show; circus, hippodrome.

park, pleasance *or* plaisance [*archaic*]; arbor; garden &c. (*horticulture*) 371; pleasure-, play-, cricket-, croquet- archery-, polo-, hunting- ground; tennis-, racket-, squash-, badminton- court; bowling- green, -alley; croquet lawn, rink, glaciarium, ice rink, skating rink; golf links, race course, athletic field, stadium; gymnasium, swimming -pool, - bath; billiard room, pool room, casino, shooting gallery; flying horses, roundabout, merry-go-round; swing; *montagne Russe* [*F.*]; aërial railway, scenic railway, roller coaster, chutes, flying boats, etc.

Vauxhall, Ranelagh, Hurlingham; Lord's, Epsom, Newmarket, Doncaster, Sandown Park, Henley, Cowes, Mortlake [*all in Eng.*]; Coney Island; Brooklands, Sheepshead Bay, Belmont Park, Saratoga; New London, Forest Hills, Longwood [*all in U. S.*]; Monte Carlo; Longchamps [*France*]; Flemington [*Melbourne, Australia*].

[SPORTS AND GAMES] athletic sports, track events, gymnastics; archery, rifle shooting; tournament, pugilism &c. (*contention*) 720; sporting &c. 622; horse racing, the turf; water polo; aquatics &c. 267.

skating, ice skating, roller skating, sliding; cricket, tennis, lawn tennis, pallone, rackets, squash, fives, trap bat and ball, badminton, battledore and shuttlecock, pall-mall, croquet, golf, curling, hockey, shinny *or* shinney; polo, football, Rugby, rugger [*colloq.*]; association, soccer [*colloq.*]; tent pegging, tilting at the ring, quintain, greasy pole; knur (*or* knurr) and spell [*Eng.*]; quoits, discus; hammer -, horseshoe- throwing; putting the -weight, - shot; hurdling; leapfrog; sack -, potato -, obstacle -, three-legged- race; hop skip and jump; French and English, tug of war; rounders, baseball, basket ball, pushball, captain ball; lacrosse; tobogganing.

blind-man's buff, hunt the slipper, hide and seek, kiss in the ring; snapdragon; cross questions and crooked answers, twenty questions, what's my thought? charades, crambo, dumb crambo, crisscross, proverbs, *bouts rimés* [*F.*]; hopscotch, jackstones, mumble-the-peg *or* mumblety-peg; ping-pong, tiddledywinks, tipcat.

billiards, pool, pyramids, bagatelle; bowls, skittles, ninepins, American bowls; tenpins [*U. S.*], tivoli.

chess, draughts, checkers *or* chequers, backgammon, dominoes, halma, dice, craps, crap shooting, crap game, "negro golf," "indoor golf" [*both humorous*]; merelles, nine men's morris, gobang, "the royal game of goose" [Goldsmith]; fox and geese; lotto *or* loto &c.[1]

CARDS; whist, rubber; round game; loo, cribbage, *bésique* [*F.*], euchre, cutthroat euchre, railroad euchre; drole, écarté, picquet, all fours, quadrille, omber *or* ombre, reverse, Pope Joan, commit; boston, *vingt et un* [*F.*], quinze, thirty-one, put, speculation, connections, brag, cassino, lottery, commerce, snip-snap-snorem, tit smoke, blind hookey, Polish bank, Earl of Coventry, napoleon *or* nap. [*colloq.*]; banker, penny-ante, poker, jack pot; blind -, draw -, straight -, stud-

---

[1] A curious list of games is given in Sir Thomas Urquhart's translation of Rabelais. — *Life of Gargantua*, book i, chapter 22.

poker; bluff; bridge, – whist; auction; monte, reversis, squeezers, old maid, fright, beggar-my-neighbor, goat, hearts, patience, solitaire, pairs.

court cards; ace, king, queen, knave, jack, joker; bower; right –, left- bower; dummy; hand; trump; face cards, diamonds, hearts, clubs, spades; pack, deck; flush, full-house, straight, three of a kind, pair, *misère* [*F.*] &c.

TOY, plaything, bauble; doll &c. (*puppet*) 554; teetotum; knickknack &c. (*trifle*) 643; magic lantern &c. (*show*) 448; peep-, puppet-, raree-, galanty *or* gallanty-, Punch-and-Judy- show; marionettes; toy-shop; "quips and cranks and wanton wiles, nods and becks and wreathed smiles" [Milton].

SPORTSMAN (*fem.* sportswoman), hunter, Nimrod.

archer, toxophilite; cricketer, footballer, ball-players &c.

GAMESTER (*fem.* gamestress), sport, gambler; dicer, punter, plunger.

REVELER *or* reveller, carouser; master of the -ceremonies, – revels; *arbiter elegantiarum* [*L.*]; *arbiter bibendi* [*L.*].

DEVOTEE, enthusiast, follower, fan [*slang, U. S.*], rooter [*slang or cant, U. S.*]; turfman.

V. AMUSE, entertain, divert, enliven; tickle, – the fancy; titillate, raise a smile, put in good humor; cause –, create –, occasion –, raise –, excite –, produce –, convulse with- laughter; set the table in a roar, be the death of one.

CHEER, rejoice; recreate, solace; please &c. 829; interest; treat, regale.

AMUSE ONESELF; game; play, – a game, – pranks, – tricks; sport, disport, toy, wanton, revel, junket, feast, carouse, banquet, make merry, drown care; drive dull care away; frolic, gambol, frisk, romp; caper; dance &c. (*leap*) 309; keep up the ball; run a rig, sow one's wild oats, have one's fling, take one's pleasure; paint the town red [*slang*]; see life; *desipere in loco* [Horace], play the fool.

make –, keep- holiday; go a-Maying.

while away –, beguile- the time; kill time, dally.

Adj. AMUSING, entertaining, diverting &c. *v.*; recreative, lusory; pleasant &c. (*pleasing*) 829; laughable &c. (*ludicrous*) 853; witty &c. 842; festive, festal; jovial, jolly, jocund, roguish, rompish; playful, – as a kitten; sportive, ludibrious [*obs.*].

AMUSED &c. *v.*; "pleased with a rattle, tickled with a straw" [Pope].

Adv. "on the light fantastic toe" [Milton], at play, in sport.

Int. *vive la bagatelle!* [*F.*], *vogue la galère!* [*F.*], come on fellows! "hail, hail, the gang's all here!" some party! [*slang*].

** *Deus nobis hæc otia fecit; dum vivimus vivamus; dulce est desipere in loco* [Horace]; "(every room) hath blazed with lights and brayed with minstrelsy" [*Timon of Athens*]; *misce stultitiam consiliis brevem* [Horace]; "Foot it featly here and there" [*Tempest*]; "The grass stoops not, she treads on it so light" [*Venus and Adonis*]; "He capers, he dances, he has eyes of youth" [*Merry Wives*]; "Fleet the time carelessly as they did in the golden world" [*As You Like It*]; "therefore put you in your best array!" [*ibid.*]; "A very merry, dancing, drinking, Laughing, quaffing and unthinking time" [Dryden]; "a clear fire, a clean hearth, and the rigour of the game" [Lamb]; "Patience, and shuffle the cards" [Cervantes]; "Lady, wherefore talk you so?" [*I Henry VI*]; "they laugh that win" [*Othello*].

---

842. Wit. — **N.** WIT, wittiness; Attic -wit, – salt; Atticism; salt, *esprit* [*F.*], point, fancy, whim, humor *or* humour, drollery, pleasantry.

BUFFOONERY, fooling, farce, tomfoolery; shenanigan [*slang, U. S.*], harlequinade &c. 599; broad -farce, – humor; fun, *espiéglerie* [*F.*]; *vis comica* [*L.*].

JOCULARITY; jocosity, jocoseness; facetiousness; waggery, waggishness; whimsicality; comicality &c. 853.

SMARTNESS, ready wit, banter, persiflage, *badinage* [*F.*], retort, repartee, *quid pro quo* [*L.*]; ridicule &c. 856.

FACETIÆ, quips and cranks; jest,

843. Dullness. — **N.** DULLNESS *or* dulness, heaviness, flatness; infestivity &c. 837, stupidity &c. 499; want of originality; dearth of ideas.

prose, matter of fact; heavy book, *conte à dormir debout* [*F.*]; commonplace, platitude.

V. BE DULL &c. *adj.*; hang fire, fall flat; platitudinize, prose, take *au sérieux* [*F.*], be caught napping.

RENDER DULL &c. *adj.*; damp, depress, throw cold water on, lay a wet blanket on; fall flat upon the ear.

Adj. DULL, – as ditch water; jejune, dry, unentertaining, uninteresting, un-

joke, capital joke; *canoræ nugæ* [*L.*];
standing -jest, – joke; conceit, quip,
quirk, crank, quiddity [*rare*], *concetto*
[*It.*], *plaisanterie* [*F.*], brilliant idea;
merry –, bright –, happy- thought;
sally; flash, – of wit, – of merriment;
scintillation; *mot*, – *pour rire* [*F.*];
witticism, smart saying, *bon mot* [*F.*],
jeu d'esprit [*F.*], epigram; jest book; dry
joke, *quodlibet* [*L.*], cream of the jest.

WORD-PLAY, *jeu de mots* [*F.*], play upon
words; pun, punning; *double entente*
[*F.*] &c. (*ambiguity*) 520; quibble,
verbal quibble; conundrum &c. (*riddle*)

lively, heavy-footed, elephantine; slow
of comprehension; insipid, tasteless,
slow as cold molasses [*colloq.*], logy
[*U. S.*]; unimaginative; insulse; dry as
dust; prosy, prosing, prosaic; matter-of-
fact, commonplace, platitudinous, pointless; "weary, stale, flat, and unprofitable" [*Hamlet*].

STUPID, slow, flat, humdrum, monotonous; melancholic &c. 837; stolid &c.
499; plodding.

⁎⁎ *Davus sum non Œdipus;* "fain would I
write but that I fear to pall" [*Cynic's Calendar*].

533; anagram, acrostic, double acrostic, trifling, idle conceit, turlupinade [*obs.*].

OLD JOKE, Joe Miller, chestnut [*slang*]; hoary-headed -joke, – jest; joke –, jest-
with whiskers [*humorous*].

V. JOKE, jest, cut jokes; crack a joke, get off a joke; pun; perpetrate a -joke,
– pun; make fun of, make merry with; set the table in a roar &c. (*amuse*) 840;
tell a good -story, – yarn.

RETORT, flash back, flash, scintillate; banter &c. (*ridicule*) 856; *ridentem dicere
verum* [*L.*]; joke at one's expense.

Adj. WITTY, Attic; clever, keen, keen-witted, brilliant, pungent; quick-witted,
nimble-witted; smart; jocular, jocose, funny, waggish, facetious, whimsical,
humorous; playful &c. 840; merry and wise; pleasant, sprightly, cute [*colloq.*],
spirituel [*F.*], sparkling, epigrammatic, full of point, *ben trovato* [*It.*]; comic &c.
853.

Adv. in joke, in jest, for the jest's sake, in sport, in play.

⁎⁎ *adhibenda est in jocando moderatio;* "gentle dullness ever loves a joke" [Pope]; "leave this
keen encounter of our wits" [*Richard III*].

844. Humorist. — N. HUMORIST, wag, wit, reparteeist, epigrammatist, punster;
bel esprit [*F.*], life of the party; joker, jester, Joe Miller, *drôle de corps* [*F.*], galliard
or gaillard [*archaic*], spark; *bon diable* [*F.*]; *persifleur* [*F.*], banterer, "Agreeable
Rattle" [Goldsmith].

buffoon, *farceur* [*F.*], merry-andrew, mime, tumbler, acrobat, mountebank, charlatan, posture master, harlequin, punch, punchinello, *pulcinella* [*It.*], Scaramouch,
clown; wearer of the -cap and bells, – motley; motley fool; pantaloon, gypsy; jack-
pudding [*archaic*], Jack-in-the-green; jack-a-dandy [*unconscious humorist*]; zany;
madcap, pickle-herring, witling, caricaturist, grimacer, grimacier.

⁎⁎ "I never dare to write As funny as I can" [Holmes].

2. DISCRIMINATIVE AFFECTIONS

845. Beauty. — N. BEAUTY, beautifulness, pulchritude; the beautiful, *to
kalon* [*Gr.* τὸ καλόν].

beauty unadorned; form, elegance,
grace, *belle tournure* [*F.*]; symmetry &c.
242; concinnity, delicacy, refinement,
charm, *je ne sais quoi* [*F.*], *nescio quid*
[*L.*], style.

comeliness, fairness &c. *adj.*; polish,
gloss; good effect, good looks; trigness.

BLOOM, brilliancy, radiance, splendor
or splendour, gorgeousness, magnificence; sublimity, sublimification [*obs.*].

846. Ugliness. — N. UGLINESS &c.
adj.; deformity, inelegance; acomia,
baldness, alopecia; disfigurement &c.
(*blemish*) 848; want of symmetry, inconcinnity [*rare*], "uglification" [Carroll];
distortion &c. 243; squalor &c. (*uncleanness*) 653.

FORBIDDING COUNTENANCE, vinegar
aspect, hanging look, wry face, face
that would stop a clock [*colloq.*]; *spretæ
injuria formæ* [Vergil].

EYESORE, object, figure, sight [*colloq.*],
fright, octopus, specter *or* spectre.

BEAU IDEAL, *le beau idéal* [*F*.]; Venus, Aphrodite, Hebe, the Graces, Peri, Houri, Cupid, Apollo, Hyperion, Adonis, Antinous, Narcissus, Astarte; Helen of Troy, Cleopatra; Venus of Milo, Apollo Belvedere.

[COMPARISONS] butterfly; flower, flow'ret gay; garden, anemone, asphodel, buttercup, crane's-bill, daffodil, lily, lily of the valley, ranunculus, rose, rhododendron, windflower.

the flower of, the pink of; *bijou* [*F*.]; jewel &c. (*ornament*) 847; work of art.

LOVELINESS, pleasurableness &c. 829.

BEAUTIFYING, beautification [*rare*]; landscape gardening; decoration &c. &c. 847; calisthenics, physical culture.

[SCIENCE OF THE PERCEPTION OF BEAUTY] callæsthetics.[1]

V. BE BEAUTIFUL &c. *adj.;* shine, beam, bloom; become one &c. (*accord*) 23; set off, become, grace.

RENDER BEAUTIFUL &c. *adj.;* beautify; polish, burnish; gild &c. (*decorate*) 847; set out.

"snatch a grace beyond the reach of art" [Pope].

Adj. BEAUTIFUL, beauteous, handsome; pretty; lovely, graceful, elegant, exquisite, flowerlike, delicate, dainty, refined.

COMELY, fair, personable, seemly [*obs*.], decent [*archaic*], proper [*archaic or dial*.], bonny, good-looking; well-favored, well-made, well-formed, well-proportioned, shapely; symmetrical &c. (*regular*) 242; harmonious &c. (*color*) 428; sightly, fit to be seen.

bright, bright-eyed; rosy-cheeked, cherry-cheeked; rosy, ruddy; blooming, in full bloom.

goodly, dapper, tight, jimp *or* gimp [*Scot. & dial. Eng*.], jaunty *or* janty, trig, natty [*orig. slang*], quaint [*archaic*], trim, tidy, neat, spruce, smart, tricksy [*rare*].

BRILLIANT, shining; beamy, beaming; sparkling, radiant, splendid, resplendent, dazzling, glowing; glossy, sleek; rich, gorgeous, superb, magnificent, grand, fine, sublime.

ARTISTIC *or* artistical, æsthetic; picturesque, pictorial; *fait à peindre* [*F*.], paintable, well-composed, well-grouped, well-varied; curious.

enchanting &c. (*pleasure-giving*) 829; attractive &c. (*inviting*) 615; becoming &c. (*accordant*) 23; ornamental &c. 847; of consummate art.

scarecrow, hag, harridan, satyr, witch, toad, baboon, monster, Caliban, Æsop; *monstrum horrendum informe ingens cui lumen ademptum* [Vergil].

V. BE UGLY &c. *adj.;* look ill, grin horribly a ghastly smile, grin through a horse collar [*colloq*.], make faces.

RENDER UGLY &c. *adj.;* deface; disfigure, defigure [*obs*.], deform, uglify [*rare*], spoil; distort &c. 243; blemish &c. (*injure*) 659; soil &c. (*render unclean*) 653.

Adj. UGLY, – as -sin, – a toad, – a scarecrow, – a dead monkey; plain, coarse; homely &c. (*unadorned*) 849; ordinary, unornamental, inartistic; unsightly, unseemly, uncomely, unshapely, unlovely; sightless [*obs*.], seemless [*obs*.], not fit to be seen; unbeauteous, unbeautiful, beautiless.

BALD, bald-headed, acomous, hairless, *chauve* [*F*.], depilous [*rare*], glabrous [*bot*.]; smooth-faced, beardless, whiskerless, clean-shaven.

MISSHAPEN, misproportioned; shapeless &c. (*amorphous*) 241; monstrous; gaunt &c. (*thin*) 203; dumpy &c. (*short*) 201; curtailed of its fair proportions; ill-made, ill-shaped, ill-proportioned; crooked &c. (*distorted*) 243.

UNPREPOSSESSING, hard-featured, hard-visaged; ill-favored, hard-favored, evil-favored; ill-looking; squalid, haggard; grim, grim-faced, grim-visaged; grisly, ghastly; ghostlike, deathlike; cadaverous, gruesome *or* grewsome.

uncouth, ungainly, graceless, inelegant; ungraceful, stiff; rugged, rough, gross, rude, awkward, clumsy, slouching, rickety, gawky, lumping, lumpish, lumbering, hulking *or* hulky, unwieldy.

REPELLENT, forbidding, frightful, hideous, odious, uncanny, repulsive; horrid, horrible; shocking &c. (*painful*) 830.

foul &c. (*dirty*) 653; dingy &c. (*colorless*) 429; gaudy &c. (*color*) 428; tarnished, smeared, besmeared, bedaubed; disfigured &c. *v.;* discolored, spotted, spotty.

SHOWY, specious, pretentious, garish &c. (*ostentatious*) 882.

[1] Whewell, *Philosophy of the Inductive Sciences*.

PERFECT, unspotted, spotless &c. 650; immaculate; undeformed, undefaced.

PASSABLE, presentable, tolerable, not amiss.

₊ *auxilium non leve vultus habet* [Ovid]; "beauty born of murmuring sound" [Wordsworth]; "flowers preach to us if we will hear" [C. G. Rossetti]; "Winter makes water solid, yet the spring, That is but flowers, is a stronger thing" [Masefield]; "butterflies, the souls of summer hours" [*ibid.*]; *gratior ac pulchro veniens in corpore virtus* [Vergil]; "none but the brave deserve the fair" [Dryden]; "thou who hast the fatal gift of beauty" [Byron]; "Was this the face that launch'd a thousand ships?" [Marlowe].

847. Ornament. — N.

ORNAMENT, ornamentation, ornamental art; ornature [*rare*], ornateness, ornation [*rare*], adornment, decoration, embellishment; architecture.

GARNISH, polish, varnish, French polish, gilding, japanning, lacquer, ormolu, enamel; *champlevé* ware, *cloisonné* ware; cosmetics.

[ORNAMENTATION] pattern, diaper, powdering, paneling, graining, inlaid work, pargeting; detail; texture &c. 329; richness; tracery, molding *or* moulding, fillet, listel, strapwork, *coquillage* [F.], flourish, *fleur-de-lis* [F.], arabesque, fret, anthemion; egg and -tongue, – dart; astragal, zigzag, acanthus, cartouche; pilaster &c. (*projection*) 250; bead, beading; frostwork, tooling; Moresque, Morisco.

embroidery, broidery [*archaic*], needlework, brocade, brocatel *or* brocatelle, bugles, beads, galloon, lace, fringe, border, insertion, *motif* [F.], edging, trimming; trappings; drapery, overdrapery, hanging, tapestry, arras; millinery, ermine; *drap d'or* [F.].

wreath, festoon, garland, chaplet, flower, nosegay, bouquet, posy [*archaic or colloq.*]; "daisies pied and violets blue" [L. L. L.].

tassel, knot; shoulder knot, epaulet *or* epaulette, aglet *or* aiglet, aigulet [*rare*], frog; star, rosette, bow; feather, plume, panache, aigret *or* aigrette; fillet, snood.

JEWELRY *or* jewellery, *bijouterie* [F.] *or* bijoutry; tiara, crown, coronet, diadem; jewel, *bijou* [F.], trinket, locket, necklace, bracelet, bangle; armlet, anklet, earring, nose-ring, carcanet [*archaic*], chain, chatelaine, brooch, torque.

GEM, precious stone; diamond, brilliant; pearl; sapphire, Oriental topaz, lapis lazuli; ruby, balas *or* balais *or* balas ruby; emerald, beryl, aquamarine, alexandrite; opal, fire opal, girasol *or* girasole; garnet, carbuncle; amethyst, plasma; turquoise *or* turquois; topaz; coral; chalcedony, agate, onyx, sard, sardonyx, chrysoprase, carnelian, cat's-eye, jasper; heliotrope, bloodstone; hyacinth, jacinth, zircon, jargon *or* jargoon; chrysolite, peridot; spinel *or* spinelle, spinel ruby; moonstone, sunstone.

848. Blemish. — N.

BLEMISH, disfigurement, deformity; adactylism; defect &c. (*imperfection*) 651; flaw, maculation; injury &c. (*deterioration*) 659; spots on the sun; eyesore.

stain, blot, spot, spottiness; speck, speckle, blur, freckle, mole, macula, macule, patch, blotch, birthmark; blobber lip, blubber lip, harelip; blain, tarnish, smudge; dirt &c. 653; scar, wem [*obs.*], wen; pustule; whelk; excrescence, pimple &c. (*protuberance*) 250; burn, blister, roughness.

V. DISFIGURE &c. (*injure*) 659; uglify [*rare*]; render ugly &c. 846.

Adj. DISFIGURED; discolored; imperfect &c. 651; blobber-lipped *or* blubber-lipped, harelipped; chapped, specked, speckled, freckled, pitted, bloodshot, bruised; injured &c. (*deteriorated*) 659.

849. Simplicity. — N.

SIMPLICITY, plainness, homeliness; undress, nudity; beauty unadorned; chasteness, chastity, restraint, severity, naturalness, unaffectedness.

V. BE SIMPLE &c. *adj.*

RENDER SIMPLE &c. *adj.*; simplify, reduce to simplicity, strip of ornament, chasten, restrain.

Adj. SIMPLE, plain, homelike, homish, homely, homespun [*fig.*], ordinary, household.

unaffected, natural, native; inartificial &c. (*artless*) 703; free from -affectation, – ornament; *simplex munditiis* [Horace]; *sans façon* [F.], *en déshabillé* [F.].

chaste, inornate, severe.

UNADORNED, unornamented, undecked, ungarnished, unarranged, untrimmed, unvarnished.

bald, flat, blank, dull.

SIMPLE-MINDED, childish, credulous &c. 486.

₊ *veritatis simplex oratio est;* "Nothing is more simple than greatness; indeed, to be simple is to be great" [Emerson].

FRIPPERY, finery, gewgaw, knickknack, gimcrack, tinsel, spangle, clinquant, pinchbeck, paste; excess of ornament &c. (*vulgarity*) 851; gaud, pride, show, ostentation.

illustration, illumination, vignette; *fleuron* [F.]; headpiece, tailpiece, *cul-de-lampe* [F.]; purple patches, flowers of rhetoric &c. 577.

VIRTU, article of virtu, piece of virtu, work of art, bric-a-brac, curio; rarity, a find.

V. ORNAMENT, embellish, enrich, decorate, adorn, beautify; adonize [*rare*], dandify.

garnish, furbish, polish, gild, varnish, whitewash, enamel, japan, lacquer, paint, grain.

spangle, bespangle, bead, embroider, work; chase, tool, emboss, fret; emblazon, blazon, illuminate; illustrate.

SMARTEN, trim, dizen, bedizen, prink, prank; trick up, trick out, fig out; deck, bedeck, dight [*archaic*], bedight [*archaic*], array; titivate or tittivate [*colloq.*], spruce up [*colloq.*]; smarten up, dress, dress up; powder.

become &c. (*accord with*) 23.

Adj. ORNAMENTED, beautified &c. *v.*; ornate, rich, gilt, begilt, tessellated, inlaid, festooned; *champlevé* [F.], *cloisonné* [F.], topiary [*rare*].

SMART, gay, tricksy [*rare*], flowery, glittering; new-gilt, new-spangled; fine; fine as -a Mayday queen, – fivepence, – a carrot fresh scraped, – a fiddle [*all colloq.*]; pranked out, bedight [*archaic*], well-groomed.

in full dress &c. (*fashion*) 852; *en grande -tenue*, – *toilette* [F.]; in one's best bib and tucker, in Sunday best, *endimanché* [F.]; dressed to advantage.

SHOWY, flashy; gaudy &c. (*vulgar*) 851; garish or gairish, splendiferous [*obs. or humorous*], gorgeous.

ORNAMENTAL, decorative; becoming &c. (*accordant*) 23.

⁎ "The first spiritual want of a barbarous man is Decoration" [Carlyle].

---

850. [GOOD TASTE.] **Taste.** — N. TASTE; good -, refined -, cultivated-taste; delicacy, refinement, fine feeling, gust, gusto, tact, finesse; nicety &c. (*discrimination*) 465; to *prepon* [*Gr.* τὸ πρέπον], polish, elegance, grace.

ARTISTIC QUALITY, virtu; dilettanteism, virtuosity, connoisseurship, fine art of living; fine art; culture, cultivation.

"caviare to the general" [*Hamlet*].

[SCIENCE OF TASTE] æsthetics.

MAN OF TASTE &c.; connoisseur, judge, critic, conoscente, virtuoso, amateur, dilettante; Aristarchus, Corinthian; Aristotle, Stagirite; Petronius, *arbiter elegantiæ* [L.], *arbiter elegantiarum* [L.].

euphemist, purist, precisian.

V. DISPLAY TASTE &c. *n.*; appreciate, judge, criticize, discriminate &c. 465.

Adj. IN GOOD TASTE, tasteful, unaffected, pure, chaste, classical, Attic, cultivated; attractive, charming, dainty; æsthetic, artistic.

refined, tasty [*colloq.*]; prim, precise, formal, prudish; elegant &c. 578; euphemistic.

TO ONE'S TASTE, to one's mind; after

851. [BAD TASTE.] **Vulgarity.** — N. VULGARITY, vulgarism; barbarism, Vandalism, Gothicism; *mauvais goût* [F.], bad taste; want of tact; ungentlemanliness, ungentlemanlikeness; ill-breeding &c. (*discourtesy*) 895.

coarseness &c. *adj.*; indecorum, loud behavior [*colloq.*], misbehavior; *gaucherie* [F.], awkwardness; boorishness &c. *adj.*; homeliness, rusticity.

LOWNESS, low life, *mauvais ton* [F.]; brutality; blackguardism, rowdyism, ruffianism; ribaldry; slang &c. (*neology*) 563.

BAD JOKE, *mauvaise plaisanterie* [F.], poor joke, joke in bad taste; practical joke.

[EXCESS OF ORNAMENT] gaudiness, tawdriness, gingerbread, false ornament, cheap jewelry; flashy -clothes, – dress; finery, frippery, trickery, tinsel, gewgaw, clinquant.

VULGARIAN, rough diamond; clown &c. (*commonalty*) 876; Goth, Vandal, Bœotian; snob, cad [*colloq.*], gent [*humorous or vulgar*]; parvenu &c. 876; frump [*colloq.*], dowdy; slut, slattern &c. 653; tomboy, hoyden, cub, unlicked cub

one's fancy; *comme il faut* [F.]; *tiré à quatre épingles* [F.].

Adv. ELEGANTLY &c. *adj.;* with quiet elegance; with elegant simplicity; without ostentation.

*** *nihil tetigit quod non ornavit* [from Johnson's epitaph on Goldsmith]; *chacun à son goût; oculi picturâ tenentur aures cantibus* [Cicero]; "Be not the first by whom the new are tried, Nor get the last to lay the old aside" [Pope]; "The life of man is stronger than good taste" [Masefield].

852. Fashion. — N. FASHION, style, *ton* [F.], *bon ton* [F.], society; good -, polite- society; *monde* [F.]; drawing-room, civilized life, civilization, town, *beau monde* [F.], high life, court; world; fashionable -, gay- world; height -, pink -, star -, glass- of fashion; "the glass of fashion and the mould of form" [*Hamlet*]; Vanity Fair; Mayfair; show &c. (*ostentation*) 822.

MANNERS, breeding &c. (*politeness*) 894; air, demeanor &c. (*appearance*) 448; *savoir faire* [F.]; gentlemanliness, gentility, decorum, propriety, *bienséance* [F.]; conventions of society; Mrs. Grundy; dictates of -Society, - Mrs. Grundy; convention, conventionality, the proprieties; punctiliousness, punctilio, form, formality; etiquette, point of etiquette.

MODE, vogue, style, the latest thing, *dernier cri* [F.], the go [*colloq.*], the rage &c. (*desire*) 865; prevailing taste; dress &c. 225; custom &c. 613.

LEADER OF FASHION; *arbiter elegantiarum* [L.] &c. (*taste*) 850; man -, woman- of -fashion, - the world; club-man, clubwoman; upper ten thousand &c. (*nobility*) 875; upper ten [*colloq.*]; *élite* [F.] &c. (*distinction*) 873; smart set [*colloq.*]; the four hundred [*U. S.*].

V. BE FASHIONABLE &c. *adj.*, be the rage &c. *n.;* have a run, pass current.

V. be vulgar &c. *adj.;* misbehave; talk -, smell of the- shop; show a want of -tact, - consideration; be a vulgarian &c. *n.*

Adj. IN BAD TASTE, vulgar, unrefined, coarse, indecorous, ribald, gross; unseemly, unbeseeming, unpresentable; *contra bonos mores* [L.]; ungraceful &c. (*ugly*) 846; dowdy; slovenly &c. (*dirty*) 653; ungenteel, shabby genteel; low &c. (*plebeian*) 876.

extravagant, monstrous, horrid; shocking &c. (*painful*) 830.

ILL-MANNERED, ill-bred, underbred, snobbish, uncourtly; uncivil &c. (*discourteous* 895; ungentlemanly, ungentlemanlike; unladylike, unfeminine; wild, wild as a hawk, wild as an unbacked colt.

UNCOUTH, unkempt, uncombed, untamed, unlicked, unpolished, plebeian; incondite [*rare*]; heavy, rude, awkward; homely, homespun, homebred; provincial, countrified, rustic; boorish, clownish; savage, brutish, blackguard, blackguardly, rowdyish, rowdy.

barbarous, barbaric, Gothic, heathenish, tramontane, outlandish; uncultivated; Bohemian; unclassical, doggerel *or* doggrel.

OBSOLETE &c. (*antiquated*) 124; out of fashion, old-fashioned, out of date, unfashionable.

NEWFANGLED &c. (*unfamiliar*) 83; fantastic, fantastical, odd &c. (*ridiculous*) 853; particular; affected &c. 855.

TAWDRY, gaudy, meretricious, brummagem [*slang*], bedizened, tricked out; obtrusive, flaunting, loud, crass, showy, flashy, garish.

*** "it is considered more withering to accuse a man of bad taste than of bad ethics" [Chesterton]; "On with the dance! Let joy be unrefined!" [*Cynic's Calendar*].

follow -, keep up with -, conform to -, fall in with- the fashion &c. *n.;* go with the stream &c. (*conform*) 82; be on (*or* get on) the band wagon [*slang*], be in the swim [*colloq.*]; *savior -vivre, - faire* [F.]; keep up appearances, behave oneself.

set the fashion, bring into fashion; give a tone to society, cut a figure in society [*colloq.*]; brush shoulders with -the nobility, - royalty; appear -, be presented- at court.

keep one's -automobile, - car, - carriage, - yacht, - house in town [*Eng.*], - cottage at Newport [*U. S.*]; be a member of the best clubs.

Adj. FASHIONABLE; in fashion &c. *n.; à la mode* [F.], *comme il faut* [F.]; admitted -, admissible- in society &c. *n.;* presentable; punctilious, decorous, conventional &c. (*customary*) 613; genteel; well-bred, well-mannered, well-behaved, well-spoken; gentlemanlike, gentlemanly; ladylike; civil, polite &c. (*courteous*) 894.

dashing, jaunty *or* janty, showy, spirited, fast.

POLISHED, refined, thoroughbred, gently bred, courtly; *distingué* [*F.*], distinguished, aristocratic *or* aristocratical; unselfconscious, self-possessed, poised, easy, frank, unconstrained, unembarrassed, *dégagé* [*F.*].

MODISH, stylish, swell [*slang*], *récherché* [*F.*]; newfangled &c. (*unfamiliar*) 83; all the rage, all the go [*colloq.*].

in -court, – full, – evening- dress; *en grande tenue* [*F.*] &c. (*ornament*) 847.

Adv. FASHIONABLY &c. *adj.*; for fashion's sake; in fear of Mrs. Grundy; in the latest -style, – mode.

Int. it isn't done!

₂ *à la française, à la parisienne; à l'anglaise, à l'américaine; autre temps autre mœurs; chaque pays a sa guise; il faut souffrir pour être belle;* "the fashion Doth wear out more apparel than the man" [*Much Ado*]; "Custom, the ass man rides, will plod for years, But laughter kills him and he dies at tears" [Masefield].

853. Ridiculousness. — N. RIDICULOUSNESS &c. *adj.*; comicality, oddity &c. *adj.*; drollery; farce, comedy; burlesque &c. (*ridicule*) 856; buffoonery &c. (*fun*) 840; frippery; amphigory *or* amphigouri, doggerel (*or* doggrel) verses; bull, Irish bull, Hibernicism, Hibernianism, Spoonerism; absurdity &c. 497.

fustian, extravagance, bombast &c. (*unmeaning*) 517; anticlimax, bathos; monstrosity &c. (*unconformity*) 83; laughingstock &c. 857; screamer *or* scream [*slang*].

V. BE RIDICULOUS &c. *adj.*; pass from the sublime to the ridiculous; make one laugh; play the fool, make a fool of oneself, commit an absurdity; ride –, play- the goat [*colloq.*].

MAKE RIDICULOUS, make a goat of [*colloq.*], make a fool of, play a joke on.

Adj. RIDICULOUS, ludicrous, comic *or* comical, drollish, waggish, quizzical, droll, funny, laughable, risible, farcical, screaming; serio-comic, serio-comical; tragi-comic, tragi-comical; *pour rire* [*F.*].

ODD, grotesque; whimsical, – as a dancing bear; fanciful, fantastic, queer, rum [*slang*], quaint, bizarre; eccentric &c. (*unconformable*) 83; strange, outlandish, out-of-the-way, baroque, rococo; awkward &c. (*ugly*) 846.

EXTRAVAGANT, *outré* [*F.*], monstrous, preposterous, absurd, bombastic, inflated, stilted, burlesque, mock heroic.

TRIVIAL, doggerel *or* doggrel, gimcrack, contemptible &c. (*unimportant*) 643.

DERISIVE, ironical &c. 856.

₂ *risum teneatis amici?* [Horace]; *rideret Heraclitus; du sublime au ridicule il n'y a qu'un pas* [Napoleon]; "Oh, let's be kings in a humble way" [Gilbert]; "I know it is a sin For me to sit and grin At him here" [Holmes].

854. Fop. — N. FINE GENTLEMAN, fop, swell [*colloq.*], dandy, exquisite, coxcomb, beau, macaroni [*hist.*]; blade, blood, buck [*archaic*], man about town, fast man, *roué* [*F.*]; fribble, jemmy [*obs.*], spark, popinjay, puppy [*contemptuous*], prig, *petit maître* [*F.*]; jackanapes, jack-a-dandy, jessamy [*obs.*], man milliner; carpet knight; masher [*vulgar or slang*], dude [*colloq.*].

FINE LADY, belle, flirt, coquette, toast.

855. Affectation. — N. AFFECTATION; affectedness &c. *adj.*; acting a part &c. *v.*; pretense &c. (*falsehood*) 544, (*ostentation*) 882; boasting &c. 884; charlatanism, quackery, shallow profundity.

pretension, airs, pedantry, pedantism, purism, precisianism, stiffness, formality, buckram; prunes and prisms; euphuism; teratology &c. (*altiloquence*) 577.

prudery, demureness, mock modesty, *minauderie* [*F.*], sentimentalism; *mauvaise honte* [*F.*], false shame.

mannerism, *simagrée* [*F.*], grimace.

FOPPERY, dandyism, man millinery, coxcombry, coquetry, puppyism, conceit.

AFFECTER *or* affector, performer, actor; pedant, pedagogue, doctrinaire, purist, euphuist, mannerist; grimacier [*rare*]; lump of affectation, *précieuse ridicule* [*F.*], bas

bleu [*F.*], blue stocking, poetaster; prig; charlatan &c. (*deceiver*) 548; *petit maître*
[*F.*] &c. (*fop*) 854; flatterer &c. 935; coquette, prude, puritan, precisian, formalist.

V. AFFECT, act a part, put on; give oneself airs &c. (*arrogance*) 885; boast &c.
884; coquet; simper, mince, attitudinize, pose; flirt a fan; languish; euphuize;
overact, overdo.

Adj. AFFECTED, full of affectation, pretentious, pedantic, stilted, stagy, theatrical,
big-sounding, *ad captandum* [*L.*]; canting, insincere; not natural, unnatural; self-
conscious; mannered, *maniéré* [*F.*]; artificial; overwrought, overdone, overacted;
euphuistic &c. 577.

STIFF, starch, formal, prim, smug, demure, *tiré à quatre épingles* [*F.*], quakerish,
puritanical, prudish, pragmatical.

PRIGGISH, conceited, coxcomical, foppish, dandified, finical, finicking *or* finicky
or finikin; mincing, simpering, namby-pamby, sentimental, languishing.

** "conceit in weakest bodies strongest works" [*Hamlet*].

856. Ridicule. — N. RIDICULE, derision; sardonic -smile, – grin; irrision [*obs.*],
snicker *or* snigger, grin, twit [*rare*]; scoffing &c. (*disrespect*) 929; mockery, quiz,
banter, irony, persiflage, raillery, chaff, *badinage* [*F.*]; quizzing &c. *v.*; asteism.

SQUIB, satire, skit, quip, quib [*obs.*].

BURLESQUE, parody, travesty, *travestie* [*F.*]; farce &c. (*drama*) 599; caricature.

BUFFOONERY &c. (*fun*) 840; practical joke, horseplay, roughhouse [*slang*].

V. RIDICULE, deride; laugh at, grin at, smile at; snicker *or* snigger; laugh in one's
sleeve; banter, rally, chaff, joke, twit, quiz, poke fun at, roast [*slang*], guy [*colloq.*,
U. S.], jolly [*colloq.*], rag [*slang*, *Eng.*]; haze [*U. S.*]; tehee *or* teehee; fleer; play
upon, play tricks upon; get the laugh on [*slang*]; fool, – to the top of one's bent;
show up.

turn into ridicule; make merry with; make -fun, – game, – a fool, – an April
fool- of; rally; scoff &c. (*disrespect*) 929.

BURLESQUE, satirize, parody, caricature, travesty.

BE RIDICULOUS &c. 853; raise a laugh &c. (*amuse*) 840; play the fool, make a
fool of oneself.

Adj. DERISIVE, derisory, mock; sarcastic, ironical, quizzical, burlesque, Hudibrastic, Rabelaisian; scurrilous &c. (*disrespectful*) 929.

Adv. IN RIDICULE &c. *n.*; as a joke, to raise a laugh.

Int. "What fools these mortals be!" [*M. N. D.*].

857. [OBJECT AND CAUSE OF RIDICULE.] **Laughingstock. — N.** LAUGHINGSTOCK,
jesting-stock, gazing-stock; butt, game, fair game; April fool &c. (*dupe*) 547,
original, oddity; queer -, odd- fish [*colloq.*], figure of fun [*colloq.*]; quiz, square
toes; old fogy *or* fogey [*colloq.*].

monkey; buffoon &c. (*jester*) 844; pantomimist &c. (*actor*) 599.

JEST &c. (*wit*) 842.

** *dum vitant stulti vitia in contraria currunt* [Horace].

3. PROSPECTIVE AFFECTIONS

858. Hope. — N. HOPE, hopes; desire
&c. 865; fervent hope, sanguine expectation, trust, confidence, reliance; faith
&c. (*belief*) 484; affiance, assurance;
secureness, security; reassurance.

good -omen, – auspices; promise,
well-grounded hopes; good -, bright-
prospect; clear sky.

HOPEFULNESS, buoyancy, optimism,
enthusiasm, heart of grace, aspiration;
assumption, presumption; anticipation
&c. (*expectation*) 507.

859. [ABSENCE, WANT, OR LOSS OF
HOPE.] **Hopelessness. — N.** HOPELESS-
NESS &c. *adj.*; despair, desperation;
despondency &c. (*dejection*) 837; pessimism.

hope deferred, dashed hopes; vain
expectation &c. (*disappointment*) 509.

airy hopes &c. 858; bad -job, – business; gloomy -, clouds on the -, black
spots in the- horizon; dark future;
slough of Despond, cave of Despair;
immedicabile vulnus [*L.*].

OPTIMIST, utopist [*rare*], utopian.

DAYDREAM, castles in the air, *châteaux en Espagne* [*F.*], *le pot au lait* [*F.*], Utopia, millennium; golden dream; dream of Alnaschar; airy hopes, fool's paradise; mirage &c. (*fallacies of vision*) 443; fond hope.

RAY OF HOPE; beam –, gleam –, glimmer –, dawn –, flash –, star- of hope; cheer; bit of blue sky, silver lining of the cloud, bottom of Pandora's box, balm in Gilead.

MAINSTAY, anchor, sheet anchor; staff &c. (*support*) 215; heaven &c. 981.

V. HOPE, trust, confide, rely on, put one's trust in, lean upon; pin one's hope upon, pin one's faith upon &c. (*believe*) 484.

feel –, entertain –, harbor –, indulge –, cherish –, feed –, foster –, nourish –, encourage –, cling to –, live in- hope &c. *n.*; see land; feel –, rest- -assured, – confident &c. *adj.*

hope for &c. (*desire*) 865; anticipate; presume; promise oneself; expect &c. (*look forward to*) 507.

BE HOPEFUL &c. *adj.*; look on the bright side of, view on the sunny side, *voir en couleur de rose* [*F.*], make the best of it, hope for the best; hope against hope; put -a good, – a bold, – the best-face upon; keep one's spirits up; take heart, – of grace; be of good -heart, – cheer; flatter oneself, "lay the flattering unction to one's soul" [*Hamlet*].

catch at a straw, hope against hope, count one's chickens before they are hatched.

ENCOURAGE, hearten, inspirit; give –, inspire –, raise –, hold out- hope &c. *n.*; raise expectations; encourage, cheer, assure, reassure, buoy up, embolden; promise, bid fair, augur well, be in a fair way, look up, flatter, tell a flattering tale.

Adj. HOPEFUL, confident; hoping &c. *v.*; in hopes &c. *n.*; secure &c. (*certain*) 484; sanguine, in good heart, buoyed up, buoyant, elated, flushed, exultant, enthusiastic; heartsome [*chiefly Scot.*]; utopian.

FEARLESS; free from –, exempt from--fear, – suspicion, – distrust, – despair; unsuspecting, unsuspicious, undespairing, self-reliant; dauntless &c. (*courageous*) 861.

PROPITIOUS, promising; probable, on

FORLORN HOPE, *enfant perdu* (*pl. enfants perdus*) [*F.*]; goner [*slang*]; gone -case, – coon [*slang, U. S.*].

PESSIMIST, Job's comforter; hypochondriac &c. 837; bird of bad omen, bird of ill omen.

V. DESPAIR; lose –, give up –, abandon –, relinquish- -all hope, – the hope of; give up, give over; yield to despair; falter; despond &c. (*be dejected*) 837; *jeter le manche après la cognée* [*F.*].

shatter one's hopes; inspire –, drive to- despair &c. *n.*; disconcert; dash –, crush –, destroy- one's hopes; dash the cup from one's lips; undermine one's foundation; take away one's last hope.

Adj. HOPELESS, desperate, despairing, gone, in despair, *au désespoir* [*F.*], forlorn; inconsolable &c. (*dejected*) 837; broken-hearted.

out of the question, not to be thought of; impracticable &c. 471; past -hope, – cure, – mending, – recall; at one's last gasp &c. (*death*) 360; given up, given over.

UNDONE, ruined; incurable, cureless, immedicable, remediless, beyond remedy; incorrigible; irreparable, irremediable, irrecoverable, irreversible, irretrievable, irreclaimable, irredeemable, irrevocable, immitigable.

UNPROPITIOUS, unpromising, inauspicious, ill-omened, threatening, clouded over, lowering, ominous.

*** "*lasciate ogni speranza voi ch' entrate*" [Dante]; its days are numbered; the worst come to the worst; "*no change, no pause, no hope, yet I endure*" [Shelley]; "*O dark, dark, dark. amid the blaze of noon*" [Milton].

860. Fear. — N. FEAR, timidity, diffidence, want of confidence; apprehensiveness, fearfulness &c. *adj.*; solicitude, anxiety, care, apprehension, misgiving; feeze [*colloq., U. S.*]; mistrust &c. (*doubt*) 485; suspicion, qualm; hesitation &c. (*irresolution*) 605.

TREPIDATION, flutter, fear and trembling, perturbation, tremor, quivering, shaking, trembling, throbbing heart, palpitation, ague fit, cold sweat; nervousness, restlessness &c. *adj.*; inquietude, disquietude, heartquake; abject fear &c. (*cowardice*) 862; mortal funk [*colloq.*], heartsinking, despondency; despair &c. 859.

batophobia, hypsophobia; claustrophobia; agoraphobia.

the high road to; within sight of -shore, – land; of –, full of- promise; of good omen; auspicious, *de bon augure* [*F.*]; reassuring; encouraging, cheering, inspiriting, looking up, bright, roseate, *couleur de rose* [*F.*], rose-colored.

Adv. hopefully &c. *adj.*

Int. God speed! good luck!

****** nil desperandum* [Horace]; never say die, *dum spiro spero, latet scintillula forsan,* all is for the best, *spero meliora;* "the wish being father to the thought" [*Henry IV*]; "hope told a flattering tale"; *rusticus expectat dum defluat amnis; at spes non fracta; ego spem pretio non emo* [Terence].

en Dieu est ma fiance; "hope! thou nurse of young desire" [Bickerstaff]; *in hoc signo spes mea; in hoc signo vinces; la speranza è il pan de' miseri; l'espérance est le songe d'un homme éveillé;* "the mighty hopes that make us men" [Tennyson]; "the sickening pang of hope deferred" [Scott].

FRIGHT, affright [*archaic*], affrightment [*archaic*], boof [*slang, U. S.*], alarm, dread, awe, terror, horror, dismay, consternation, panic, scare, panic fear, panic terror; "terror by night" [*Bible*]; chute [*N. U. S.*], stampede [*of horses*].

INTIMIDATION, terrorism, reign of terror; terrorist.

[OBJECT OF FEAR] bugbear, bugaboo, scarecrow; hobgoblin &c. (*demon*) 980; nightmare, Gorgon, mormo [*obs.*], ogre, Hurlothrumbo, raw head and bloody bones, fee-faw-fum, *bête noire* [*F.*], *enfant terrible* [*F.*].

ALARMIST &c. (*coward*) 862.

V. FEAR, stand in awe of; be afraid &c. *adj.;* have qualms &c. *n.;* apprehend, sit upon thorns, eye askance; distrust &c. (*disbelieve*) 485.

hesitate &c. (*be irresolute*) 605; falter, funk [*colloq.*], cower, crouch; skulk &c. (*cowardice*) 862; take fright, take alarm; start, wince, flinch, shy, shrink, blench; fly &c. (*avoid*) 623.

grow pale, turn pale, stand aghast; be in a daze; not dare to say one's soul is one's own.

TREMBLE, shake; shiver, – in one's shoes; shudder, flutter; shake –, tremble- -like an aspen leaf, – all over; quake, quaver, quiver, quail.

FRIGHTEN, fright, affright, terrify; inspire –, excite- -fear, – awe; raise apprehensions; bulldoze [*colloq., U. S.*], faze [*colloq. or dial.*], feeze *or* feaze [*dial. Eng. & colloq. U. S.*]; give –, raise –, sound- an alarm; alarm, startle, scare, cry "wolf," disquiet, dismay, astound; frighten from one's propriety; frighten out of one's -wits, – senses, – seven senses; awe; strike all of a heap [*colloq.*], strike an awe into, strike terror; harrow up the soul, appall *or* appal, unman, petrify, horrify; pile on the agony.

make one's -flesh creep, – hair stand on end, – blood run cold, – teeth chatter; take away –, stop- one's breath; make one tremble &c.

DAUNT, put in fear, intimidate, cow, daunt, overawe, abash, deter, discourage; browbeat, bully; threaten &c. 909; terrorize, put in bodily fear.

HAUNT, obsess, beset, besiege; prey –, weigh- on the mind.

Adj. AFRAID, fearful, timid, timorous, nervous, diffident, coy, faint-hearted, tremulous, shaky, afraid of one's shadow, apprehensive, restless, fidgety; more frightened than hurt.

fearing &c. *v.;* frightened &c. *v.;* in fear, in a fright &c. *n.;* haunted with the fear of &c. *n.;* afeard [*obs. or dial.*].

aghast; awe-struck, awe-stricken; horror-struck, horror-stricken; terror-struck, terror-stricken; panic-struck, panic-stricken; frightened to death, white as a sheet; pale, – as -death, – ashes, – a ghost; breathless, in hysterics.

INSPIRING FEAR &c. *v.;* alarming; formidable, redoubtable; perilous &c. (*danger*) 665; portentous; fearful, dread, dreadful, fell, dire, direful, shocking, frightful, terrible, terrific, tremendous; horrid, horrible, horrific, ghastly, awful, awe-inspiring; revolting &c. (*painful*) 830; Gorgonian, Gorgon-like.

Adv. *in terrorem* [*L.*].

Int. "angels and ministers of grace defend us!" [*Hamlet*].

****** ante tubam trepidat; horresco referens,* one's heart failing one, *obstupui steteruntque comæ et vox faucibus hæsit* [Vergil].

"a dagger of the mind" [*Macbeth*]; *expertus metuit* [Horace]; "letting 'I dare not' wait upon 'I would'" [*Macbeth*]; "fain would I climb but that I fear to fall" [Raleigh]; "fear is the parent of cruelty" [Froude]; "Gorgons and hydras and chimeras dire" [*Paradise Lost*], *omnia tuta timens* [Vergil]; "our fears do make us traitors" [*Macbeth*].

861. [ABSENCE OF FEAR.] **Courage.** —

N. COURAGE, bravery, valor or valour; resoluteness, boldness &c. adj.; spirit, daring, gallantry, intrepidity, prowess, heroism, chivalry; contempt -, defiance- of danger; derring-do [pseudo-archaic]; audacity; rashness &c. 863; dash; defiance &c. 715; confidence, self-reliance.

manhood, manliness, nerve, pluck, mettle, game; heart, - of grace; spunk [colloq.], grit, virtue, hardihood, fortitude; firmness &c. (stability) 150; heart of oak; bottom, backbone &c. (preseverance) 604a; resolution &c. (determination) 604; tenacity, bulldog courage.

EXPLOIT, feat, deed, act, achievement; heroic, -deed, - act; bold stroke.

BRAVE MAN, man of courage, man of mettle; a man; hero, demigod, paladin; Hercules, Theseus, Perseus, Achilles, Hector; Bayard, chevalier sans peur et sans reproche; Lancelot, Sir Galahad.

BRAVE WOMAN, heroine, Amazon, Joan of Arc.

[COMPARISONS] lion, tiger, panther, bulldog; gamecock, fighting-cock.

DARE-DEVIL, fire eater &c. 863.

V. BE COURAGEOUS &c. adj.; dare, venture, make bold; face -, front -, affront -, confront -, brave -, defy -, despise -, mock- danger; look in the face; look -full, - boldly, - danger- in the face; face; meet, meet in front; brave, beard; defy &c. 715.

bell the cat, take the bull by the horns, beard the lion in his den, march up to the cannon's mouth, go through fire and water, run the gantlet or gauntlet.

NERVE oneself; take -, muster -, summon up -, pluck up- courage; take heart; take -, pluck up- heart of grace; hold up one's head, screw one's courage to the sticking place; come -to, - up to- the scratch; stand, - to one's guns, - fire, - against; bear up, - against; hold out &c. (persevere) 604a.

put a bold face upon; show -, present- a bold front; show fight; face the music.

862. [EXCESS OF FEAR.] **Cowardice.** —

N. COWARDICE, pusillanimity; cowardliness &c. adj.; timidity, effeminacy.

poltroonery, baseness, dastardness, dastardy, abject fear, funk [colloq.]; Dutch courage [colloq.]; fear &c. 860; white feather, faint heart; cold feet [slang, U. S.], yellow streak [slang].

COWARD, poltroon, dastard, sneak, recreant; shy -, dunghill- cock; coistrel or coistril [archaic], milksop, white-liver [colloq.], nidget [obs.], one that cannot say "Bo" to a goose; slink [Scot. & dial. Eng.], cur [contemptuous], craven, caitiff; Bob Acres, Jerry Sneak.

ALARMIST, terrorist, pessimist; sheep in wolf's clothing.

SHIRKER, slacker; runagate &c. (fugitive) 623.

V. QUAIL &c. (fear) 860; be cowardly &c. adj., be a coward &c. n.; funk [colloq.], cower, skulk, sneak; flinch, shy, fight shy, slink, turn tail; run away &c. (avoid) 623; show the white feather.

Adj. COWARDLY, coward, fearful, shy, timid, timorous, skittish; poor-spirited, spiritless, soft, effeminate; weak-minded; infirm of purpose &c. 605; weak-, faint-, chicken-, hen-, pigeon- hearted; white-, lily-, milk- livered; smock-faced; unable to say "Bo" to a goose.

DASTARD, dastardly, base, craven, sneaking, dunghill, recreant; unwarlike, unsoldierlike; "in face a lion but in heart a deer"; "more like a rabbit than a robber."

UNMANNED; frightened &c. 860.

Adv. with fear and trembling, in fear of one's life, in a blue funk [colloq.]; "with groanings that cannot be uttered" [Bible].

Int. sauve qui peut! [F.], devil take the hindmost!

⁎ ante tubam trepidat, one's courage oozing out; degeneres animos timor arguit [Vergil]; "Thou wear a lion's hide! doff it for shame, And hang a calf's skin on those recreant limbs" [King John]; "the coward stands aside, Doubting in his abject spirit, till his Lord is crucified" [Lowell].

HEARTEN; give -, infuse -, inspire- courage; reassure, encourage, embolden, inspirit, cheer, nerve, put upon one's mettle, rally, raise a rallying cry; pat on the back, make a man of, keep in countenance.

Adj. COURAGEOUS, brave, valiant, valorous, gallant, intrepid, spirited, spiritful; high-spirited, high-mettled, mettlesome, plucky; manly, manful, resolute, stout, stout-hearted; iron-hearted, lion-hearted; heart of oak; Penthesilean.

bold, bold-spirited; daring, audacious; fearless, dauntless, aweless, dreadless [obs.]; undaunted, unappalled, undismayed, unawed, unblenched, unabashed, unalarmed, unflinching, unshrinking, unblenching, unapprehensive; confident, self-reliant; bold as -a lion, – brass [colloq.].

ENTERPRISING, adventurous, venturous, venturesome, dashing, chivalrous; soldierly &c. (warlike) 722; heroic.

FIERCE, savage; pugnacious &c. (bellicose) 720.

STRONG-MINDED, strong-willed, hardy, doughty [archaic or humorous]; firm &c. (stable) 150; determined &c. (resolved) 604; dogged, indomitable &c. (persevering) 604a.

upon one's mettle; up to the scratch; reassured &c. v.; unfeared, undreaded.

⁎ one's blood being up; courage sans peur; fortes fortuna adjuvat [Terence]; "have I not in my time heard lions roar" [Taming of the Shrew]; "I dare do all that may become a man" [Macbeth]; male vincetis sed vincite [Ovid]; omne solum forti patria; "self-trust is the essence of heroism" [Emerson]; stimulos dedit æmula virtus [Lucan]; "strong and great, a hero" [Longfellow]; teloque animus præstantior omni [Ovid]; "there is always safety in valor" [Emerson]; virtus ariete fortior; "the way to avoid death is not to have too much aversion to it" [Chesterton].

863. Rashness. — N. RASHNESS &c. adj.; temerity, want of caution, imprudence, indiscretion; overconfidence, presumption, audacity; precipitancy, precipitation, impetuosity; levity; foolhardihood, foolhardiness; heedlessness, thoughtlessness &c. (inattention) 458; carelessness &c. (neglect) 460; desperation; Quixotism, knight-errantry; fire eating.

gaming, gambling; blind bargain, leap in the dark, fool's paradise; too many eggs in one basket.

DESPERADO, rashling [obs.], madcap, daredevil, Hotspur, Hector; scapegrace, enfant perdu [F.]; Don Quixote, knighterrant, Icarus; adventurer; dynamiter or dynamitard; fire eater, bully, bravo.

GAMBLER, gamester &c. (chance) 621.

V. BE RASH &c. adj.; stick at nothing, play a desperate game; run into danger &c. 665; play with -fire, – edge tools; donner tête baissée [F.]; knock one's head against a wall &c. (be unskillful) 699; kick against the pricks; rush on destruction; tempt Providence, go on a forlorn hope.

carry too much sail, sail too near the wind, ride at single anchor, go out of one's depth; go to sea in a sieve.

take a leap in the dark; buy a pig in a poke; bet against a dead certainty.

count one's chickens before they are hatched; reckon without one's host; catch at straws; trust to -, lean on- a broken reed.

Adj. RASH, incautious, indiscreet, injudicious, imprudent, improvident, temerarious; uncalculating, impulsive; heedless; careless &c. (neglectful) 460;

864. Caution. — N. CAUTION; cautiousness &c. adj.; discretion, prudence, cautel [obs.], heed, circumspection, calculation, deliberation.

foresight &c. 510; vigilance &c. 459; warning &c. 668.

worldly wisdom; "safety first," Fabian policy, "watchful waiting."

COOLNESS &c. adj.; self-possession, self-command; presence of mind, sangfroid [F.], well-regulated mind.

V. BE CAUTIOUS &c. adj.; take -care, – heed, – good care; have a care; mind, mind what one is about; be on one's guard &c. (keep watch) 459; "make assurance double sure" [Macbeth].

think twice, look before one leaps, keep one's eye peeled [slang], keep one's weather eye open [colloq.]; count the cost, look to the main chance; cut one's coat according to one's cloth; feel one's -ground, – way; see how the land lies &c. (foresight) 510; pussy-foot [Roosevelt]; wait to see how the cat jumps; bridle one's tongue; reculer pour mieux sauter [F.] &c. (prepare) 673; let well enough alone, ne pas reveiller le chat qui dort [F.]; let sleeping dogs lie.

keep out of -harm's way, – troubled waters; keep at a respectful distance, stand aloof; keep –, be- on the safe side.

ANTICIPATE; bespeak &c. (be early) 132.

LAY BY; husband one's resources &c. 636.

WARN, caution &c. 668.

Adj. CAUTIOUS, wary, guarded, guardful [rare]; on one's guard &c. (watchful) 459; gingerly, precautious [rare], sus-

without ballast, head over heels, heels over head; giddy &c. (*inattentive*) 458.

RECKLESS, wanton, wild, madcap, desperate, devil-may-care, death-defying; hot-blooded, hot-headed, hotbrained; headlong, headstrong; breakneck, foolhardy, harebrained, precipitate.

overconfident, overweening; venturesome, venturous, adventurous, Quixotic; fire-eating.

UNEXPECTED; off one's guard &c. (*inexpectant*) 508.

Adv. posthaste, *à corps perdu* [*F.*], hand over head [*rare*], *tête baissée* [*F.*], headforemost; happen what may.

** neck or nothing, the devil being in one; *non semper temeritas est felix* [Livy]; *paucis temeritas est bono multis malo* [Phædrus]; "I am reckless what I do to spite the world" [*Macbeth*]; "I tell thee, be not rash; a golden bridge Is for a flying enemy" [Byron].

picious, leery [*slang*]; *cavendo tutus* [*L.*]; *in medio tutissimus* [*L.*]; vigilant; careful, heedful, cautelous [*obs.*], stealthy, chary, shy of, circumspect, prudent, canny [*Scot.*], safe, noncommittal, discreet, politic; sure-footed &c. (*skillful*) 698.

UNENTERPRISING, unadventurous, cool, steady, self-possessed; overcautious.

Adv. cautiously &c. *adj.*

Int. have a care! look out! danger! mind your eye! [*colloq.*]; stop! look! listen! *cave canem!* [*L.*].

** *timeo Danaos et dona ferentes* [Vergil]; *festina lente.*

ante victoriam ne canas triumphum; "give every man thine ear but few thy voice" [Hamlet]; *il rit bien qui rit le dernier; ni firmes carta que no leas ni bebas agua que no veas; nescit vox missa reverti* [Horace]; "love all, trust a few" [*All's Well*]; *noli irritare leones;* safe bind safe find; "the cautious seldom err" [Confucius].

---

865. Desire. — N. DESIRE, wish, fancy, fantasy; inclination, leaning, bent, mind, animus, partiality, *penchant* [*F.*], predilection; propensity &c. 820; willingness &c. 602; liking, love, fondness, relish.

longing, hankering, yearning, coveting; aspiration, ambition, vaulting ambition; eagerness, zeal, ardor, *empressement* [*F.*], breathless impatience, solicitude, anxiety, overanxiety; impetuosity &c. 825.

NEED, want, exigency, urgency, necessity.

APPETITE, appetition, appetence, appetency; sharp appetite, keenness, hunger, stomach, twist; thirst, thirstiness; drought *or* drouth, mouth-watering.

edge of -appetite, – hunger; torment of Tantalus; sweet tooth [*colloq.*], lickerish (*or* liquorish) tooth; longing –, wistful –, sheep's- eyes.

AVIDITY, greed, greediness, covetousness, ravenousness &c. *adj.*; grasping, craving, canine appetite, rapacity; voracity &c. (*gluttony*) 957.

PASSION, rage, furor, frenzy, mania, manie [*obs.*]; itching palm; inextinguishable desire; itch, itching, prurience, cacoëthes, cupidity, lust, concupiscence; kleptomania, dipsomania; monomania, *idée fixe* [*F.*].

[OF ANIMALS] heat, rut, œstrus.

[PERSON DESIRING] lover, amateur,

866. Indifference. — N. INDIFFERENCE, neutrality; unconcern, insouciance, nonchalance; want of -interest, – earnestness; anorexia *or* anorexy, inappetence *or* inappetency; apathy &c. (*insensibility*) 823; supineness &c. (*inactivity*) 683; disdain &c. 930; recklessness &c. 863; inattention &c. 458; coldness &c. *adj.*; anaphrodisia.

ANAPHRODISIAC *or* antaphrodisiac; lust-quencher, passion-queller.

V. BE INDIFFERENT &c. *adj.*; stand neuter; take no interest in &c. (*insensibility*) 823; have no desire for &c. 865, have no taste for, have no relish for; not care for; care nothing -for, – about; not care a -straw &c. (*unimportance*) 643 -about, – for; not mind.

set at naught &c. (*make light of*) 483; spurn &c. (*disdain*) 930.

Adj. INDIFFERENT, cold, frigid, lukewarm; cool, – as a cucumber; neutral, unconcerned, insouciant, phlegmatic, pococurantish, pococurante, easy-going, devil-may-care, careless, listless, lackadaisical; half-hearted, unambitious, unaspiring, undesirous, unsolicitous, unattracted, inappetent, all one to.

UNATTRACTIVE, unalluring, undesired, undesirable, uncared for, unwished, unvalued.

insipid &c. 391.

Adv. for aught one cares; with utter indifference.

votary, devotee, aspirant, solicitant, candidate; cormorant &c. 957; parasite, sycophant.

[OBJECT OF DESIRE] desideratum, desideration; want &c. (*requirement*) 630; "a consummation devoutly to be wish'd" [*Hamlet*]; attraction, magnet, loadstone, lure, allurement, fancy, temptation, seduction, fascination, prestige, height of one's ambition, idol; whim, whimsey *or* whimsy, whimwham; maggot; hobby, hobbyhorse [*rare*].

Fortunatus's cap; wishing -cap, − stone, − well; love potion; aphrodisiac.

V. DESIRE; wish, wish for; be desirous &c. *adj.*; have a longing &c. *n.*; hope &c. 858.

care for, affect, like, list [*archaic*]; take to, cling to, take a fancy to; fancy; prefer &c. (*choose*) 609; have an eye to, have a mind to; find it in one's heart &c. (*be willing*) 602; have a fancy for, set one's eyes upon; cast sheep's eyes upon, look sweet upon [*colloq.*]; take into one's head, have at heart, be bent upon; set one's cap at [*colloq.*], set one's heart upon, set one's mind upon; covet.

hunger −, thirst −, crave −, lust −, itch −, hanker −, run mad- after; raven for, die for; burn to; sigh −, cry −, gape −, gasp −, pine −, pant −, languish −, yearn −, long −, be on thorns −, hope- for; aspire after; catch at, grasp at, jump at.

woo, court, ogle, solicit; fish for, whistle for, put up for [*slang*].

WANT, miss, need, lack, desiderate, feel the want of; would fain -have, − do; would be glad of.

HUNGER; be hungry &c. *adj.*; have a good appetite, play a good knife and fork [*colloq.*].

ATTRACT, allure; cause −, create −, raise −, excite −, provoke- desire; whet the appetite; appetize, titillate, take one's fancy, tempt; hold out -temptation, − allurement; tantalize, make one's mouth water, *faire venir l'eau à la bouche* [*F.*].

GRATIFY DESIRE &c. (*give pleasure*) 829.

Adj. DESIROUS; desiring &c. *v.*; orectic, appetitive; inclined &c. (*willing*) 602; partial to [*colloq.*]; fain, wishful, longing, wistful; optative; anxious, curious; at a loss for, sedulous, solicitous.

380

Int. NEVER MIND! who cares! it's all one to me!

⁎⁎ "Let the world slide, let the world go; A fig for care, and a fig for woe!" [Heywood]; "I care for nobody, no, not I, If no one cares for me" [Bickerstaff].

867. Dislike. — N. DISLIKE, distaste, disrelish, disinclination, displacency [*rare*].

reluctance; backwardness &c. (*unwillingness*) 603.

REPUGNANCE, disgust, queasiness, nausea, loathing, loathfulness [*rare*], aversion, averseness, aversation [*obs.*], abomination, antipathy, abhorrence, horror; mortal −, rooted- -antipathy, − horror; hatred, detestation; hate &c. 898; animosity &c. 900.

hydrophobia, canine madness; xenophobia, batophobia &c. (*nervousness*) 860; Anglophobia, Germanophobia, Slavophobia &c.

sickener; gall and wormwood &c. (*unsavory*) 395; shuddering, cold sweat.

V. DISLIKE, mislike, disrelish; mind, object to; would rather not, not care for; have −, conceive −, entertain −, take- -a dislike, − an aversion- to; have no -taste, − stomach- for; shrug the shoulders at, shudder at, turn up the nose at, look askance at; make a -mouth, − wry face, − grimace; make faces.

shun, avoid &c. 623; eschew; withdraw −, shrink −, recoil - from; not be able to -bear, − abide, − endure.

LOATHE, nauseate, wamble [*obs. or dial. Eng.*], abominate, detest, abhor; hate &c. 898; take amiss &c. 900; have enough of &c. (*be satiated*) 869.

CAUSE DISLIKE, excite dislike; disincline, repel, sicken; make sick, render sick; turn one's stomach, nauseate, disgust, shock, stink in the nostrils; go against the -grain, − stomach; stick in the throat; make one's blood run cold &c. (*give pain*) 830; pall.

Adj. DISLIKING &c. *v.*; averse to, loath *or* loth, adverse; shy of, sick of, out of conceit with; disinclined; heartsick, dogsick; queasy.

DISLIKED &c. *v.*; uncared for, unpopular, out of favor; repulsive, repugnant, repellent; abhorrent, insufferable, fulsome, nauseous, loathsome, loathful [*rare*], offensive; disgusting &c. *v.*; disagreeable &c. (*painful*) 830.

eager, avid, keen; burning, fervent, ardent; agog; all agog; breathless; impatient &c. (*impetuous*) 825; bent –, intent –, set- -on, – upon; mad after, *enragé* [*F*.], rabid, dying for, devoured by desire.

aspiring, ambitious, vaulting, sky-aspiring, high-reaching.

CRAVING, hungry, sharp-set, peckish [*colloq*.], ravening, with an empty stomach, esurient, lickerish, thirsty, athirst, parched with thirst, pinched with hunger, famished, dry, droughty *or* drouthy; hungry as a -hunter, – hawk, – horse, – church mouse.

GREEDY, – as a hog; overeager, voracious; ravenous, – as a wolf; openmouthed, covetous, rapacious, grasping, extortionate, exacting, sordid, *alieni appetens* [*L*.]; insatiable, insatiate, unquenchable, quenchless; omnivorous.

unsatisfied, unsated, unslaked.

DESIRABLE; desired &c. *v.*; in demand, popular; pleasing &c. (*giving pleasure*) 829; appetizing, appetible; tantalizing.

Adv. FAIN; with eager appetite; wistfully &c. *adj.*

Int. would that! would it were! O for! if only! *esto perpetua!* [*L*.].

⁎ the wish being father to the thought; *sua cuique voluptas; hoc erat in votis*, the mouth watering, the fingers itching; *aut Cæsar aut nullus.*

"Cassius has a lean and hungry look" [*Julius Cæsar*]; "hungry as the grave" [Thomson]; "I was born to other things" [Tennyson]; "not what we wish but what we want" [Merrick]; "such joy ambition finds" [*P. L.*]; "the sea hath bounds but deep desire hath none" [*Venus and Adonis*]; *ubi mel ibi apes;* "let us pay with our bodies for our souls' desire" [Roosevelt].

UNEATABLE, inedible, inesculent [*rare*], unappetizing, unsavory.

Adv. TO SATIETY, to one's disgust; *usque ad nauseam* [*L*.].

Int. faugh! foh! ugh!

⁎ *non libet;* "more abhorr'd Than spotted livers in the sacrifice" [*Troilus and Cressida*]; "I find no abhorring in my appetite" [Donne].

868. Fastidiousness. — N. FASTIDIOUSNESS &c. *adj.;* nicety, meticulosity, hypercriticism, difficulty in being pleased; *friandise* [*F*.], epicurism, *omnia suspendens naso* [*L*.].

DISCRIMINATION, discernment, perspicacity, perspicaciousness [*rare*], keenness, sharpness, insight.

EPICURE, gourmet.

[EXCESS OF DELICACY] prudery, prudishness, primness.

V. BE FASTIDIOUS &c. *adj.;* split hairs; hunt for the crumpled rose-leaf. mince the matter; turn up one's nose at &c. (*disdain*) 930; look a gift horse in the mouth, see spots on the sun; see the mote in one's brother's eye.

DISCRIMINATE, have nice discrimination; have exquisite taste; be discriminative &c. *adj.*

Adj. FASTIDIOUS, nice, delicate, *délicat* [*F*.]; meticulous, finicking *or* finicky *or* finikin, exacting, finical; difficult, dainty, lickerish, squeamish, thinskinned; queasy; hard –, difficult- to please; querulous; particular, scrupulous; censorious &c. 932; hypercritical; overcritical.

PRUDISH, strait-laced, prim.

DISCRIMINATIVE, discriminating, discerning, discriminant [*rare*], judicious,

keen, sharp, perspicacious.

⁎ *noli me tangere;* "you are idle, shallow things: I am not of your element" [*Twelfth Night*].

869. Satiety. — N. SATIETY, satisfaction, saturation, repletion, glut, surfeit; cloyment [*obs*.], satiation; weariness &c. 841.

spoiled child; *enfant gâté* [*F*.]; too much of a good thing, *toujours perdrix* [*F*.]; a diet of cake; *crambe repetita* [Juvenal].

V. SATE, satiate, satisfy, saturate; cloy, quench, slake, pall, glut, gorge, surfeit; bore &c. (*weary*) 841; tire &c. (*fatigue*) 688; spoil.

have enough of, have quite enough of, have one's fill, have too much of; be satiated &c. *adj.*

Adj. SATIATED &c. *v.;* overgorged; gorged with plenty, overfed; *blasé* [*F*.], used up [*colloq*.], sick of, heartsick.

Int. ENOUGH! hold! *eheu jam satis!* [*L*.].

⁎ "mitigate the ennui of ˆa crushing satiety" [Shaw]; "I feel the old convivial glow (unaided) o'er me stealing" [Holmes].

4. Contemplative Affections

870. Wonder. — **N.** WONDER, marvel; astonishment, amazement, wonderment, bewilderment; amazedness &c. *adj.;* admiration, awe; stupor, stupefaction, stound [*obs.*], fascination; sensation; surprise &c. (*inexpectation*) 508.

note of admiration; thaumaturgy &c. (*sorcery*) 992.

V. WONDER, marvel, admire; be surprised &c. *adj.;* start; stare; open –, rub –, turn up- one's eyes; gloar [*obs.*]; gape, open one's mouth, hold one's breath; look –, stand- -aghast, – agog; look blank &c. (*disappointment*) 509; *tomber des nues* [*F.*]; not believe one's –eyes, – ears, – senses; not be able to account for &c. (*unintelligible*) 519; not know whether one stands on one's head or one's heels.

ASTONISH, surprise, amaze, astound; dumfound *or* dumbfound, dumfounder *or* dumbfounder, startle, dazzle; daze; strike, – with -wonder, – awe; electrify; stun, stupefy, petrify, confound, bewilder, flabbergast [*colloq.*]; stagger, throw on one's beam ends, fascinate, turn the head, take away one's breath, strike dumb; make one's -hair stand on end, – tongue cleave to the roof of one's mouth; make one stare.

TAKE BY SURPRISE, take unawares &c. (*be unexpected*) 508.

BE WONDERFUL &c. *adj.;* beggar –, baffle- description; stagger belief.

Adj. ASTONISHED, surprised &c. *v.;* aghast, all agog, breathless, agape; openmouthed; awe-, thunder-, moon-, planet- struck; spellbound; lost in -amazement, – wonder, – astonishment; struck all of a heap [*colloq.*], unable to believe one's senses; like a duck in -a fit, – thunder [*both colloq.*].

WONDERFUL, wondrous; surprising &c. *v.;* unexpected &c. 508; unheard of; mysterious &c. (*inexplicable*) 519; miraculous.

monstrous, prodigious, stupendous, marvelous; inconceivable, incredible, inimaginable [*obs.*], unimaginable; strange &c. (*uncommon*) 83; passing strange.

striking &c. *v.;* overwhelming; wonder-working.

INDESCRIBABLE, inexpressible, ineffable; unutterable, unspeakable.

Adv. WONDERFULLY &c. *adj.;* fearfully; for a wonder, in the name of wonder; strange to say; *mirabile dictu* [*L.*], *mirabile visu* [*L.*]; to one's great surprise.

WITH WONDER &c. *n.,* with gaping mouth, with open eyes, with upturned eyes; with the eyes starting out of one's head.

Int. LO! lo and behold! O! heyday! halloo! what! indeed! really! surely! humph! hem! good -lack, – heavens, – gracious! gad so! welladay! dear me! only think! lackadaisy! my stars! my goodness! gracious goodness! goodness gracious! mercy on us! heavens and earth! God bless me! bless us! bless my heart! odzookens! *O gemini!* adzooks! hoity-toity! strong! Heaven save –, bless- the mark! can such things be! zounds! 'sdeath! what on earth! what in the world! who would have thought it! &c. (*inexpectation*) 508; you don't say so! what do you say to that! *nous verrons!* [*F.*], how now! where am I? fancy! do tell! [*U. S.*], *Ciel!* [*F.*]; what do you know! [*slang, U. S.*]; what do you know about that! [*slang, U. S.*]; well, I'll be jiggered! [*colloq.*].

. *vox faucibus hæsit;* one's hair standing on end; "oppress'd with awe And stupid at the wondrous things he saw" [Dryden]; "this is wondrous strange" [*Hamlet*]; "all wonder is the effect of novelty upon ignorance" [Johnson]; "wonder is involuntary praise" [Young]; "That is ever the difference between the wise and the unwise: the latter wonders at what is unusual; the wise man wonders at the usual" [Emerson]; "the world will never starve for want of wonders, but only for want of wonder" [Chesterton].

871. [ABSENCE OF WONDER.] Expectance. — **N.** EXPECTANCE, expectancy &c. (*expectation*) 507.

IMPERTURBABILITY. imperturbableness, imperturbation, *sang-froid* [*F.*], calmness, unruffled calm, coolness, coldbloodedness, hardheadedness, steadiness, lack of nerves, want of imagination, practicality.

nothing out of the ordinary.

V. EXPECT &c. 507; not be surprised, not wonder &c. 870; *nil admirari* [*L.*], make nothing of; take it coolly; be unamazed &c. *adj.;* display imperturbability &c. *n.*

Adj. EXPECTING &c. *v.;* unamazed, astonished at nothing; *blasé* [*F.*] &c. (*weary*) 841; expected &c. *v.;* foreseen.

IMPERTURBABLE, nerveless, cool, coolheaded, unruffled, calm, steady, hardheaded, practical, unimaginative.

common, ordinary &c. (*habitual*) 613.

Int. no wonder! of course! why not?

872. Prodigy. — N. PRODIGY, phenomenon, wonder, wonderment, marvel, miracle; freak, freak of nature, *lusus naturœ* [*L.*], monstrosity; monster &c. (*unconformity*) 83; curiosity, infant prodigy, lion, sight, spectacle; *jeu –, coup- de théâtre* [*F.*]; gazingstock; sign; St. Elmo's -fire, – light; portent &c. 512.

what no words can paint; wonders of the world; *annus mirabilis* [*L.*]; *dignus vindice nodus* [*L.*].

DETONATION; bursting of a -shell, – bomb, – mine; volcanic eruption, peal of thunder; thunderclap, thunderbolt, thunderstone [*obs. or dial. Eng.*].

'' *⁎⁎⁎* *natura il fece e poi roppe la stampa;* "A schoolboy's tale, the wonder of an hour!" [Byron]; "Stones have been known to move and trees to speak" [*Macbeth*]; " 'Twas strange, 'twas passing strange; 'Twas pitiful, 'twas wondrous pitiful" [*Othello*].

5. EXTRINSIC AFFECTIONS[1]

873. Repute. — N. REPUTE, reputation; distinction, mark, name, figure; good –, high- repute; note, notability, notoriety, éclat, "the bubble reputation" [*As You Like It*], vogue, celebrity; fame, famousness; renown; popularity, *aura popularis* [*L.*]; approbation &c. 931; credit, *succès d'estime* [*F.*], prestige, talk of the town; name to conjure with.

account, regard, respect; reputability [*rare*], reputableness &c. *adj.;* respectability &c. (*probity*) 939; good -name, – report; fair name.

DIGNITY; stateliness &c. *adj.;* solemnity, grandeur, splendor, nobility, majesty, sublimity; glory, honor; luster &c. (*light*) 420; illustriousness &c. *adj.*

RANK, standing, brevet rank, precedence, *pas* [*F.*], station, place, status; position, – in society; order, degree, *locus standi* [*L.*], caste, condition.

graduation, university degree, baccalaureate, doctorate, doctorship; scholarship, fellowship.

EMINENCE; greatness &c. *adj.;* height &c. 206; importance &c. 642; preëminence, supereminence; high mightiness, primacy; top of the -ladder, – tree; elevation; ascent &c. 305; superexaltation, exaltation, dignification [*rare*], aggrandizement; dedication, consecration, enthronement.

CELEBRITY, worthy, hero, man of mark, great card, lion, *rara avis* [*L.*], notability, somebody; "the observed of all observers" [*Hamlet*]; classman; man of rank &c. (*nobleman*) 875; pillar of the -state, – church; "a mother in Israel" [*Bible*].

chief &c. (*master*) 745; first fiddle &c. (*proficient*) 700; scholar, *savant* [*F.*] &c. 492; cynosure, mirror; flower, pink,

874. Disrepute. — N. DISREPUTE, discredit; ill-, bad- -repute, -name, -odor, -favor; disapprobation &c. 932; ingloriousness, derogation, abasement, debasement; abjectness &c. *adj.;* degradation, dedecoration [*rare*]; "a long farewell to all my greatness" [*Henry VIII*]; odium, obloquy, opprobrium, ignominy.

dishonor, disgrace, shame, crying –, burning- shame; humiliation; scandal, baseness, vileness; turpitude &c. (*improbity*) 940; infamy.

STIGMA, brand, reproach, imputation, slur, stain, blot, spot, blur; *scandalum magnatum* [*L.*], badge of infamy, blot in one's escutcheon; bend sinister, bar sinister, champain, point champain [*her.*]; byword of reproach; object of scorn, hissing [*archaic*]; Ichabod.

tarnish, taint, defilement, pollution. *argumentum ad verecundiam* [*L.*]; sense of shame &c. 879.

V. BE INGLORIOUS &c. *adj.;* incur disgrace &c. *n.;* have –, earn- a bad name; put –, wear- a halter round one's neck; disgrace –, expose- oneself.

play second fiddle; lose caste; "pale his uneffectual fire" [*Hamlet*]; recede into the shade; fall from one's high estate; keep in the background &c. (*modesty*) 881; be conscious of disgrace &c. (*humility*) 879; look -blue, – foolish, – like a fool; cut a -poor, – sorry- figure; laugh on the wrong side of the mouth [*colloq.*]; make a sorry face, go away with a flea in one's ear [*colloq.*], slink away.

CAUSE SHAME &c. *n.;* shame, disgrace, put to shame, dishonor; throw –, cast –, fling –, reflect- dishonor &c. *n.* upon; be a reproach to &c. *n.;* derogate from.

tarnish, stain, blot, sully, taint; dis-

---

[1] Or personal affections derived from the opinions or feelings of others.

pearl; paragon &c. (*perfection*) 650; "the choice and master spirits of this age" [*Julius Cæsar*]; *élite* [*F*.]; star, sun, constellation, galaxy.

ORNAMENT, honor, feather in one's cap, halo, aureole, nimbus; halo –, blaze- of glory; "blushing honors" [*Henry VIII*]; laurels &c. (*trophy*) 733.

POSTHUMOUS FAME, memory, niche in the temple of fame; celebration, canonization, enshrinement, glorification; immortality, immortal name; *magni nominis umbra* [Lucan].

V. GLORY IN; be conscious of glory; be proud of &c. (*pride*) 878; exult &c. (*boast*) 884; be vain of &c. (*vanity*) 880.

BE DISTINGUISHED &c. *adj.*; shine &c. (*light*) 420; shine forth, figure; cut a figure, cut a dash [*colloq*.], make a splash [*colloq*.].

SURPASS, outshine, outrival, outvie, outjump, eclipse; throw –, cast- into the shade; overshadow.

RIVAL, emulate, vie with.

GAIN *or* ACQUIRE HONOR &c. *n.*; live, flourish, glitter; flaunt; play first fiddle &c. (*be of importance*) 642; bear the -palm, – bell; lead the way, take precedence, take the wall of [*obs*.]; gain –, win- -laurels, – spurs, – golden opinions &c. (*approbation*) 931; graduate, take one's degree, pass one's examination; win a -scholarship, – fellowship.

make -a, – some- -noise, – noise in the world; leave one's mark, exalt one's horn, star, have a run, be run after; be lionized, come into vogue, come to the front; raise one's head.

HONOR; give –, do –, pay –, render- honor to; accredit, pay regard to, dignify, glorify; sing praises to &c. (*approve*) 931; look up to; exalt, aggrandize, elevate, nobilitate [*archaic*]; enthrone, signalize, immortalize, deify, exalt to the skies; hand one's name down to posterity.

consecrate; dedicate to; devote to; enshrine, inscribe, blazon, lionize, blow the trumpet, crown with laurel.

confer *or* reflect honor on &c. *n.*; shed a luster on; redound to one's honor, ennoble.

Adj. DISTINGUISHED, *distingué* [*F*.], noted; of note &c. *n.*; honored &c. *v.*; remarkable &c. (*important*) 642; notable, notorious; celebrated, renowned, in every one's mouth, talked of, famous, famed, far-famed; conspicuous, to the front; foremost; in the -front rank, – ascendant.

credit; degrade, debase, defile; beggar; expel &c. (*punish*) 972.

STIGMATIZE, vilify, defame, slur, cast a slur upon, impute shame to, brand, post, hold up to shame, send to Coventry; tread –, trample- under foot; show up [*colloq*.], drag through the mire, heap dirt upon; reprehend &c. 932.

bring low, put down, snub; take down; take down a peg, – lower, – or two [*colloq*.].

OBSCURE, eclipse, outshine, take the shine out of [*colloq*.]; throw –, cast- into the shade; overshadow; leave –, put- in the background; push into a corner, put one's nose out of joint [*colloq*.]; put out, put out of countenance.

DISCONCERT, upset, throw off one's center, discompose; put to the blush &c. (*humble*) 879.

Adj. DISGRACED &c. *v.*; blown upon; "shorn of its beams" [Milton], shorn of one's glory; overcome, downtrodden; loaded with shame &c. *n.*; in bad repute &c. *n.*; out of -repute, – favor, – fashion, – countenance; at a discount; under -a cloud, – an eclipse; unable to show one's face; in the -shade, – background; out at elbows, down in the world, down on one's uppers [*colloq*.], down and out.

inglorious, nameless, renownless, obscure, unknown to fame, unnoticed, unnoted, unhonored, unglorified.

DISCREDITABLE, shameful, disgraceful, disreputable, despicable; questionable; unbecoming, unworthy, derogatory; degrading, humiliating, *infra dignitatem* [*L*.], dedecorous [*rare*]; scandalous, infamous, too bad, unmentionable, ribald, opprobrious; arrant, shocking, outrageous, notorious.

ignominious, scrubby, dirty, abject, vile, beggarly, pitiful, low, mean, petty, shabby; base &c. (*dishonorable*) 940.

Adv. to one's shame be it spoken.

Int. SHAME! fie! for shame! *proh pudor!* [*L*.]; *O tempora! O mores!* [*L*.]; ough! *sic transit gloria mundi!* [*L*.].

** fama malum quo non velocius ullum [Vergil].

popular; fashionable &c. 852;

in good odor; in favor, in high favor; reputable, respectable, creditable.

IMPERISHABLE, deathless, immortal, never fading, fadeless, *œre perennius* [L.], time-honored.

ILLUSTRIOUS, glorious, splendid, brilliant, radiant; bright &c. 420; full-blown; honorific.

EMINENT, prominent; high &c. 206; in the zenith; at the -head of, – top of the tree; peerless, of the first water; superior &c. 33; supereminent, preëminent.

great, dignified, proud, noble, honorable, worshipful, lordly, grand, stately, august, princely, imposing, solemn, transcendent, majestic, sacred, sublime, heaven-born, heroic, *sans peur et sans reproche* [F.]; sacrosanct.

Int. HAIL! all hail! *ave!* [L.], *viva!* [It.], *vive!* [F.], long life to! glory –, honorbe to!

*** one's name being in every mouth; one's name living for ever; *sic itur ad astra, fama volat, aut Cæsar aut nullus;* none but himself could be his parallel; *palmam qui meruit ferat* [Nelson's motto]; "above all Greek above all Roman fame" [Pope]; *cineri gloria sera est* [Martial]; "great is the glory for the strife is hard" [Wordsworth]; *honor virtutis præmium* [Cicero]; *immensum gloria calcar habet* [Ovid]; "the glory dies not and the grief is past" [Brydges]; *vivit post funera virtus;* "not to know me argues yourselves unknown" [Milton].

---

875. Nobility. — N. NOBILITY, rank, condition, distinction, optimacy [*rare*], blood, *pur sang* [F.], birth, high descent, order; quality, gentility; blue blood of Castile; "all the blood of all the Howards" [Pope]; caste of "Vere de Vere" [Tennyson]; *ancien régime* [F.].

high life, *haut monde* [F.]; upper classes, upper ten [*colloq.*], upper ten thousand; the four hundred [*U. S.*]; *élite* [F.], aristocracy, great folks; fashionable world &c. (*fashion*) 852.

personage –, man- of -distinction, – mark, – rank; notables, notabilities; celebrity, bigwig [*humorous*], magnate, great man, star; big bug, big gun, great gun [*colloq.*]; gilded rooster [*slang*, *U. S.*]; *magni nominis umbra* [Lucan]; "every inch a king" [*Lear*].

[THE NOBILITY] peerage, baronage; house of -lords, – peers; lords, – temporal and spiritual; noblesse; knightage.

peer, noble, nobleman; lord, lording [*archaic*], lordling; grandee, magnifico, hidalgo; daimio, samurai, *shizoku* [*Jap.*]; don; aristocrat, swell [*colloq.*], three-tailed bashaw; gentleman, squire, squireen [*humorous, Eng.*], patrician; laureate.

gentry, gentlefolk; squirarchy *or* squirearchy, better sort, magnates, primates, optimates; pantisocracy.

king &c. (*master*) 745; atheling [*hist.*]; prince, duke, marquis, earl, viscount, baron, thane [*hist.*], banneret, baronet, knight, chevalier, count, armiger, esquire, laird [*Scot.*]; signior, seignior; *signor* [*It.*], *señor* [*Sp.*], *senhor* [*Pg.*]; boyar *or* boyard [*Russ.*]; effendi, sheik

876. Commonalty. — N. COMMONALTY, democracy; obscurity; low -condition, – life, – society, – company; *bourgeoisie* [F.]; mass of -the people, – society; Brown, Jones, and Robinson; Tom, Dick, and Harry; "the four million" [O. Henry]; the peepul [*humorous*]; lower –, humbler- -classes, – orders; vulgar –, common- herd; rank and file, *hoc genus omne* [L.]; the -many, – general, – crowd, – people, – populace, – multitude, – million, – masses, – mobility [*humorous*], – other half, - peasantry; king Mob; proletariat; *fruges consumere nati* [L.], *demos* [Gr. δῆμος], *hoi polloi* [Gr. οἱ πολλοί], great unwashed; man in the street.

RABBLE, – rout; chaff, rout, horde, canaille; scum –, residuum –, dregs- of -the people, – society; mob, swinish multitude, *fæx populi* [L.]; trash; *profanum –, ignobile- vulgus* [L.]; vermin, raff, riffraff, rag-tag and bobtail; small fry.

COMMONER, one of the people, democrat, plebeian, republican, proletary, proletarian, proletaire, *roturier* [F.], John Smith, Mr. Snooks, *bourgeois* [F.], *épicier* [F.], Philistine, cockney; grisette, demimonde, demimondaine.

PEASANT, countryman, boor, carl *or* carle [*Scot. or archaic*], churl; villain *or* villein [*obs. or rare*], serf; *terræ filius* [L.], kern *or* kerne [*Ir.*], gossoon [*Anglo-Ir.*]; tike *or* tyke [*archaic or dial.*], ryot [*India*], fellah [*Ar. pl.* fellahin *or* fellaheen]; docker, stevedore, longshoreman; swain, clown, hind [*Eng.*], clod, clodhopper,

or sheikh, emir, shereef *or* sherif, pasha, sahib; palsgrave [*Ger. hist.*], waldgrave, margrave; vavasor [*feudal law*].

empress, queen, princess, duchess, marchioness, viscountess, countess; lady, doña [*Sp.*], dona [*Pg.*[; *signora* [*It.*], *señora* [*Sp.*], senhora [*Pg.*]; dame; memsahib.

[INDIAN RULING CHIEFS] raja, rana, rao, rawal, rawat, rai, raikwar, raikbar, raikat; maharaja, maharana, maharao &c.; Gaekwar [*lit.* cowherd; *Baroda*]; maharaja bahadur, raja bahadur, rai (*or* rao) bahadur; rai (*or* rao) sahib; jám, thakur [*all Hindu titles*].

nawab, wali, sultan, ameer *or* amir, mir, mirza, mian, khan; Nizam, nawab bahadur, khan bahadur, khan sahib [*all Moham. titles*].

sirdar *or* sardar, diwan *or* dewan [*both Hindu and Moham. titles*].

[HONORIFICS] shahzada ["King's son"], kumar *or* kunwar ["prince"]; mirza [*when appended it signifies* "prince"; *when prefixed,* "Mr."]; arbab ["lord"]; malik ["master"]; khanzada ["son of a khan"]; huzur *or* huzoor ["the presence"].

[FEMALE TITLES] rani, maharani [*Hindu*]; sultana, malikah, begum *or* begam [*Moham.*].

shahzadi, kumari *or* kunwari, raj-kumari, malikzadi, khanam [*all equivalent to* "princess"].

[RANK OR OFFICE] kingship, dukedom, marquisate, earldom; viscountship, viscounty, viscountcy; lordship, baronetcy, knighthood, donship.

V. be noble &c. *adj.*

Adj. NOBLE, exalted; of rank &c. *n.;* princely, titled, patrician, aristocratic; highborn, well-born; of gentle blood; genteel, *comme il faut* [*F.*], gentleman-like, courtly &c. (*fashionable*) 852; highly respectable.

Adv. in high quarters.

** *Adel sitzt im Gemüthe nicht im Geblüte; adelig und edel sind zweierlei; noblesse oblige.*

877. Title. — **N.** TITLE, honor; knighthood &c. (*nobility*) 875.

highness, excellency, grace, lordship, worship; reverence; reverend; esquire, sir, master, Mr., *signor* [*It.*], señor [*Sp.*], &c. 373; *Mein Herr* [*Ger.*], mynheer; your –, his- honor; serene highness.

madam, *madame* [*F.*] &c. (*mistress*) 374; empress, queen &c. 875.

DECORATION, laurel, palm, wreath, garland, bays, medal, ribbon, riband, blue ribbon, red ribbon, cordon, cross, crown, coronet, star, garter, fleece; feather, – in one's cap; epaulet *or* epaulette, chevron, *fourragère* [*F.*], colors, cockade; livery; order, arms, coat of arms, shield, escutcheon *or* scutcheon, crest; reward &c. 973; handle to one's name.

hobnail, yokel [*Eng.*], bogtrotter, bumpkin; plowman *or* ploughman, plowboy *or* ploughboy; chuff, hayseed [*slang*], rustic, lunkhead [*colloq., U. S.*], loon [*archaic*], rube [*slang, U. S.*], chawbacon [*slang*], tiller of the soil; hewers of wood and drawers of water; sons of Martha; groundling [*obs.*], gaffer, put, cub, Tony Lumpkin [Goldsmith], looby, lout, underling; gamin, street Arab, mudlark.

ROUGH, rowdy, roughneck [*slang*], ruffian, tough [*colloq., U. S.*], potwallopper [*slang*], scullion, slubberdegullion [*obs.*], vulgar –, low- fellow; cad.

UPSTART, parvenu, skipjack [*dial. Eng.*]; nobody, – one knows; *hesterni quirites* [*L.*], *pessoribus orti* [*L.*]; *bourgeois gentilhomme* [*F.*]; *novus homo* [*L.*], snob, gent [*vulgar or humorous*], mushroom, no one knows who, adventurer; *nouveau riche* (*pl. nouveaux riches; fem. nouvelles riches*) [*F.*].

VAGABOND, beggar, gaberlunzie [*Scot.*], beadsman *or* bedesman [*Scot.*], muckworm, *sans-culotte* [*F.*], tatterdemalion, caitiff, ragamuffin, pariah, outcast of society, tramp, bezonian [Shakespeare], panhandler [*slang*], sundowner [*Austral.*], bum [*slang, U. S.*], hobo [*U. S.*]; chiffonier *or* chiffonnier [*rare*], ragman, ragpicker, sweeper, sweep, scrub.

wench, slut, quean, Cinderella.

BARBARIAN, Goth, Vandal, Hottentot, Zulu, savage, Yahoo; unlicked cub, rough diamond.

barbarousness, barbarism, savagery; Bœotia; Philistinism; parvenuism, parvenudom.

V. BE IGNOBLE &c. *adj.*, be nobody &c. *n.;* be of (*or* belong to) the common herd &c. *n.*

Adj. IGNOBLE, common, mean, low, base, vile, sorry, scrubby, beggarly; below par; no great shakes &c. (*unimportant*) 643; homely, homespun, vulgar, low-minded; snobbish, parvenu, low bred; menial, underling, servile.

PLEBEIAN, proletarian; of -low, – mean- -parentage, – origin, – extraction; lowborn, baseborn, earthborn; mushroom, dunghill, risen from the ranks; unknown to fame, obscure, untitled.

RUSTIC, country, uncivilized; loutish, boorish, clownish, churlish, brutish, raffish; rude, unpolished, unlicked.

BARBAROUS, barbarian, barbaric, barbaresque [De Quincey].

COCKNEY, born within sound of Bow bells.

Adv. below the salt.

*** *dummodo sit dives Barbarus ipse placet* [Ovid]; "The play, I remember, pleased not the million; 'twas caviare to the general" [*Hamlet*]; "he who meanly admires mean things is a snob" [Thackeray].

878. Pride. — N. PRIDE; haughtiness

&c. *adj.;* high notions, hauteur; vainglory, crest; arrogance &c. (*assumption*) 885; self-importance, pomposity, pompousness; side [*slang*], swank [*dial. Eng.*], swagger, toploftiness [*colloq.*].

proud man, highflyer *or* highflier; fine gentleman; fine lady, *grande dame* [F.].

DIGNITY, self-respect, *mens sibi conscia recti* [Vergil].

V. BE PROUD &c. *adj.;* put a good face on; look one in the face; stalk abroad, perk, perk up, perk oneself up; think no small beer of oneself [*colloq.*]; think no small potatoes of oneself [*colloq.*]; presume, swagger, strut; rear –, lift up –, hold up– one's head; hold one's head high, look big, take the wall; "bear like the Turk no rival near the throne" [Pope]; carry with a high hand; ride the –, mount on one's– high horse; set one's back up, bridle, toss the head; give oneself airs &c. (*assume*) 885; boast &c. 884.

pride oneself on; glory in, take a pride in; pique –, plume –, hug– oneself; stand upon, be proud of; not hide one's light under a bushel; not put one's talent in a napkin; not think small beer of oneself [*colloq.*] &c. (*vanity*) 880.

Adj. DIGNIFIED; stately, proud-crested, lordly, baronial; lofty-minded, high-souled, high-minded, high-mettled, high-plumed, high-flown, high-toned.

PROUD, haughty, lofty, high, mighty, swollen, puffed up, flushed, blown; vainglorious; purse-proud, fine; proud as –a peacock, – Lucifer; bloated with pride.

SUPERCILIOUS, disdainful, bumptious, magisterial, imperious, high-handed, high and mighty, overweening, consequential; pompous, toplofty [*colloq.*]; arrogant &c. 885; unblushing &c. 880.

STIFF, stiff-necked, starched, perked up, stuck up [*colloq.*]; in buckram, strait-laced; prim &c. (*affected*) 855.

ON ONE'S DIGNITY; on one's -high horse, – tight ropes, – high ropes; on stilts; *en grand seigneur* [F.].

879. Humility. — N. HUMILITY,

humbleness, meekness, lowness, lowliness, lowlihood; abasement, self-abasement; submission &c. 725; resignation.

modesty, timidity &c. 881; verecundity [*obs.*], blush, suffusion, confusion; sense of -shame, – disgrace; humiliation, mortification; letdown, setdown.

CONDESCENSION; affability &c. (*courtesy*) 894.

V. BE HUMBLE &c. *adj.;* deign, vouchsafe, condescend; humble oneself, demean oneself [*colloq.*]; stoop, – to conquer; carry coals; submit &c. 725; submit with a good grace &c. (*brook*) 826; yield the palm.

lower one's -tone, – note; sing small [*colloq.*], draw in one's horns [*colloq.*], sober down; hide one's -face, – diminished head; not dare to show one's face, take shame to oneself, not have a word to say for oneself; feel –, be conscious of- -shame, – disgrace; be humiliated, be put out of countenance, be shamed, be put to the blush &c. *v.;* receive a snub; eat humble pie, eat crow, eat dirt; drink the cup of humiliation to the dregs.

blush for, blush up to the eyes; redden, change color; color up; hang one's head, look foolish, feel small.

RENDER HUMBLE; humble, humiliate; let –, set –, take –, tread –, frowndown; snub, abash, abase, make one sing small [*colloq.*], strike dumb; teach one his distance; take down a peg, – lower; throw –, cast- into the shade &c. 874; stare –, put– out of countenance; put to the blush; confuse, ashame [*rare*], shame, mortify, disgrace, crush; send away with a flea in one's ear [*colloq.*].

get a setdown.

Adj. HUMBLE ,lowly, meek; modest &c. 881; humble-minded, sober-minded; unoffended; submissive &c. 725; servile &c. 886.

CONDESCENDING; affable &c. (*courteous*) 894.

HUMBLED &c. *v.;* bowed down, resigned; abashed, ashamed, dashed; out

Adv. with head erect; *de haut en bas* [*F.*]; with nose in air, with nose turned up; with a sneer, with curling lip.

** *odi profanum vulgus et arceo* [Horace].

"a duke's revenues on her back" [*Henry VI*]; "disdains the shadow which he treads on at noon" [*Coriolanus*]; "pride in their port, defiance in their eye" [Goldsmith].

of countenance; down in the mouth; down on one's -knees, – marrowbones [*colloq.*], – uppers [*colloq.*]; humbled in the dust, brow-beaten; chapfallen, crestfallen; dumfoundered *or* dumbfoundered, flabbergasted [*colloq.*], struck all of a heap [*colloq.*]; shorn of one's glory &c. (*disrepute*) 874.

Adv. HUMBLY; with downcast eyes, with bated breath, on bended knee; on all fours; with one's tail between one's legs.

UNDER CORRECTION, with due deference.

** I am your -obedient, – very humble- servant; my service to you; *da locum melioribus* [Terence]; *parvum parva decent* [Horace]; "humility is a virtue all preach, none practice" [Selden].

---

880. Vanity. — N. VANITY; conceit, conceitedness; self-conceit, self-complacency, self-confidence, self-sufficiency, self-esteem, self-love, self-approbation, self-praise, self-glorification, self-laudation, self-gratulation, self-applause, self-admiration; *amour propre* [*F.*]; selfishness &c. 943.

PRETENSIONS, airs, affected manner, mannerism; egoism, egotism, priggism, priggishness; coxcombery, gaudery, vainglory, elation; pride &c. 878; ostentation &c. 882; assurance &c. 885.

vox et præterea nihil [*L*].

EGOIST, egotist; peacock; coxcomb &c. 854; Sir Oracle &c. 887.

V. BE VAIN &c. *adj.;* be vain of; pique oneself &c. (*pride*) 878; lay the flattering unction to one's soul.

have -too high, – an overweening- opinion of -oneself, – one's talents; blind oneself as to one's own merit; not think small beer of oneself [*colloq.*]; strut; put oneself forward; fish for compliments; give oneself airs &c. (*assume*) 885; boast &c. 884.

RENDER VAIN &c. *adj.;* inspire with vanity &c. *n.;* inflate, puff up, turn one's head.

Adj. VAIN, – as a peacock; conceited, overweening, pert, forward; vainglorious, high-flown; ostentatious &c. 882; puffed up, inflated, flushed.

self-satisfied, self-confident, self-sufficient, self-flattering, self-admiring, self-applauding, self-glorious, self-opinionated; *entêté* [*F.*] &c. (*wrong-headed*) 481; wise in one's own conceit, pragmatical [*rare*], overwise, pretentious, priggish; egotistic *or* egotistical; *soidisant* [*F.*] &c. (*boastful*) 884; arrogant &c. 885; assured.

UNABASHED, unblushing, unconstrained, unceremonious; free and easy.

Adv. VAINLY &c. *adj.*

** "how we apples swim!" [Swift]; "prouder than rustling in unpaid-for silk" [*Cymbeline*]; "the fuming vanities of earth" [Wordsworth]; "How many saucy airs we meet, From Temple Bar to Aldgate Street!" [Gay]; "Vain? Let it be so! Nature was her teacher" [Holmes].

881. Modesty. — N. MODESTY; humility &c. 879; diffidence, timidity; retiring disposition; unobtrusiveness; bashfulness &c. *adj.; mauvaise honte* [*F.*]; blush, blushing; verecundity [*obs.*]; self-knowledge.

reserve, constraint; demureness &c. *adj.;* "blushing honors" [*Henry VIII*]. [COMPARISON] violet.

V. BE MODEST &c. *adj.;* retire, reserve oneself; give way to; draw in one's horns &c. 879; hide one's face.

keep private, keep in the background, keep one's distance; pursue the noiseless tenor of one's way, "do good by stealth and blush to find it fame" [Pope], hide one's light under a bushel; cast sheep's eyes.

Adj. MODEST, diffident; humble &c. 879; timid, timorous, bashful; shy, nervous, skittish, coy, sheepish, shamefaced, blushing, overmodest.

unpretending, unpretentious; unobtrusive, unassuming, unostentatious, unboastful, unaspiring; poor in spirit; deprecative, deprecatory.

reserved, constrained, demure.

ABASHED, ashamed; out of countenance &c. (*humbled*) 879.

Adv. MODESTLY &c. *adj.;* quietly, privately; without -ceremony, – beat of drum; *sans façon* [*F.*].

** "not stepping o'er the bounds of modesty" [*Romeo and Juliet*]; "thy modesty's a candle to thy merit" [Fielding].

882. Ostentation. — N. OSTENTATION, display, show, *coup d' œil* [*F.*], flourish, parade, *étalage* [*F.*], pomp, magnificence, splendor, pageantry, array, state, solemnity; dash [*colloq.*], splash [*colloq.*], splurge [*colloq.*], glitter, strut, pomposity, pompousness; pretense, pretensions, showing off; fuss; grand doings.

DEMONSTRATION, flying colors; flourish of trumpets &c. (*celebration*) 883; pageant, spectacle, exhibition, exposition, procession, turnout [*colloq.*], set out; grand function; fête, gala, field day, review, march past, promenade, "insubstantial pageant" [*Tempest*].

coup de théâtre [*F.*], stage effect, stage trick; claptrap; *mise en scène* [*F.*], *tour de force* [*F.*], *chic* [*colloq.*, *F.*].

DRESS; court -, full -, evening -, ball -, fancy- dress; tailoring, millinery, man millinery, frippery; foppery, equipage.

CEREMONY, ceremonial, ritual, form, formality, etiquette, puncto [*obs.*], punctilio, punctiliousness, starchedness, stateliness.

mummery, solemn mockery, mouth honor; tomfoolery; attitudinarianism.

ATTITUDINARIAN; fop &c. 854; no modest violet.

V. BE OSTENTATIOUS &c. *adj.*; come forward, put oneself forward, attract attention, star; make -, cut- a -figure, - dash, - splash, - splurge [*all colloq.*]; strut; blow one's own trumpet; have no false modesty; figure; make a show, - display; glitter.

SHOW OFF, show one's paces; parade, march past; display, exhibit, put forward, hold up; trot out [*slang*], hand out; sport [*colloq.*], brandish, blazon forth; dangle, - before the eyes; cry up &c. (*praise*) 931; *prôner* [*F.*], flaunt, emblazon, prink, set off, mount, have framed and glazed.

put on the mask; put a -good, - smiling- face upon; clean the outside of the platter &c. (*disguise*) 544.

Adj. OSTENTATIOUS, showy, dashing, pretentious, jaunty *or* janty, grand, pompous, high-sounding; turgid &c. (*big-sounding*) 577; garish *or* gairish; gaudy, - as a -peacock, - butterfly, - tulip; flaunting, flashing, flaming, glittering; gay &c. (*ornate*) 847.

splendid, magnificent, sumptuous, palatial.

THEATRICAL, theatric, dramatic, spectacular, scenic, scenical; dramaturgic *or* dramaturgical.

CEREMONIAL, ritual, ritualistic; solemn, stately, majestic, formal, stiff, ceremonious, punctilious, starched, starchy.

en grande tenue [*F.*], in one's best bib and tucker [*colloq.*], in one's Sunday best, *endimanché* [*F.*], *chic* [*colloq.*, *F.*].

Adv. with flourish of trumpet, with beat of drum, with flying colors, with a brass band; at the head of the procession; with no false modesty.

ad captandum vulgus [*L.*].

*** *honores mutant mores;* "Hell is paved with big pretensions" [*Cynic's Calendar*].

883. Celebration. — N. CELEBRATION, solemnization, commemoration, ovation, triumph; lionization.

inauguration, installation, presentation; coronation; *début* [*F.*], coming out [*colloq.*]; Lord Mayor's show [*London, Eng.*]; harvest-home, husking bee, quilting bee; birthday, anniversary, biennial, triennial &c.; centenary, centennial; bicentennial; bicentennial; tercentenary, tercentennial &c.; "the day we celebrate"; red-letter day; trophy &c. 733; jubilation, laudation, pæan *or* pean; *Te Deum* &c. (*thanksgiving*) 990; festivity, festival; fête &c. 882; Forefathers' Day [*U. S.*], Independence Day, "the Glorious Fourth" [*U. S.*]; holiday &c. 840.

triumphal arch, bonfire; salute, salvo, salvo of artillery; *feu de joie* [*F.*], flourish of trumpets, fanfare, colors flying, illuminations.

[WEDDING ANNIVERSARIES] *wooden* wedding [5th], *tin* wedding [10th], *crystal* wedding [15th], *china* wedding [20th], *silver* wedding [25th], *golden* wedding [50th], *diamond* wedding [60th].

JUBILEE, 50th anniversary; diamond jubilee, 60th anniversary.

V. CELEBRATE, keep, signalize, do honor to, commemorate, solemnize, hallow; keep high festival, keep holiday; mark with a red letter.

PLEDGE, drink to, toast; hob and nob, hobnob with; present.

INAUGURATE, install, instate, induct, chair.

rejoice &c. 838; kill the fatted calf, hold jubilee; roast an ox, serve up the Thanksgiving turkey, serve up the Christmas goose; fire a salute, dip the colors, present arms; paint the town red [colloq.]; maffick [colloq., Eng.].

Adj. CELEBRATING &c. v.; commemorative, celebrated, immortal; solemn, jubilant; kept, kept in remembrance.

Adv. IN HONOR OF, in commemoration of, in celebration of, in memory of; as a toast.

Int. HAIL! all hail! "see the conquering hero comes!" "Hail! hail! the gang's all here!"

. "I drink to the general joy of the whole table" [Macbeth]; "God bless thy lungs, good Knight" [II Henry IV.]; "One flag, one land, one heart, one hand, One nation evermore!" [Holmes]; "A broadside for our Admiral, Load every crystal gun" [ibid.]; "ere we depart we'll share a bounteous time" [Timon of Athens]; "they are ever forward In celebration of this day" [Henry VIII]; "less noise, less noise!" [II Henry IV]; "The yearly course that brings this day about Shall never see it but a holiday" [King John]; "Lest we forget" [Kipling].

---

884. Boasting. — N. BOASTING &c. v.; boast, vaunt, crake [obs.], pretense, pretensions, cock-a-hoopness, braggadocio, braggadocianism, puff [colloq.], puffery; flourish, fanfaronade; gasconade, bluff, highfaluting or highfalutin, blague [F.]; side [slang, Eng.], swagger, jingoism, spread-eagleism [U. S.]; brag, braggartism or braggardism, braggartry, bounce, rant, bluster, bravado, buncombe or bunkum [cant or slang, U. S.]; jactation, jactitation, jactancy; venditation]obs.], vaporing, rodomontade, bombast, gas [slang], hot air [slang], fine talking, tall talk, tall story [both colloq.], fish story [humorous]; magniloquence, teratology [obs.], heroics; chauvinism; exaggeration &c. 549; vanity &c. 880; vox et præterea nihil [L.]; much cry and little wool, brutum fulmen [L.].

exultation, gloriation [obs.], glorification; flourish of trumpets; triumph &c. 883.

BOASTER, braggart, braggadocio, fanfaron, pretender, bluffer, blower [slang, U. S.], blower of his own trumpet, windbag [slang], hot-air artist [slang], Fourth of July orator; Thraso, Gascon; chauvinist, jingo, jingoist; blusterer, swaggerer &c. 887; charlatan, trumpeter; puppy &c. (fop) 854.

V. BOAST, make a boast of, brag, vaunt, puff, show off, flourish, crake [obs.], crack, trumpet, strut, swagger, blague [F.], gasconade, vapor; blow [slang], four-flush [slang], bluff; talk big, draw the long bow, speak for Buncombe; faire claquer son fouet [F.], blow one's own trumpet; put on side [slang, Eng.], swank [dial. Eng.]; let the American eagle scream, sing "Rule, Britannia," indulge in jingoism; se faire valoir [F.], take merit to oneself, make a merit of; holloa before one is out of the wood.

EXULT; crow, crow over [both colloq.], triumph, glory, jubilate, rejoice, maffick [colloq., Eng.], throw up one's cap, yell oneself hoarse, cheer.

gloat, gloat over; chuckle; neigh.

Adj. BOASTING &c. v.; magniloquent, flaming, thrasonic [rare], thrasonical, stilted, gasconading, braggart, boastful, pretentious; vainglorious &c. (conceited) 880; highfaluting or highfalutin; spread-eagle [colloq. & humorous, U. S.].

ELATE, elated, jubilant, triumphant, exultant; in high feather; flushed, – with victory; cock-a-hoop, cock-a-hoopish; on stilts [colloq.].

vaunted &c. v.

Adv. VAUNTINGLY &c. adj.; in triumph; with a blare of trumpets.

. "God, I thank thee that I am not as other men are" [Bible]; facta non verba; "The empty vessel makes the greatest sound" [Henry V]; "What cracker is this same, that deafs our ears With this abundance of superfluous breath?" [King John]; "every braggart shall be found an ass" [All's Well]; "Cæsar's thrasonical brag of 'I came, saw, and overcame'" [As You Like It]; "Where boasting ends, there dignity begins" [Young].

885. [UNDUE ASSUMPTION OF SUPE-RIORITY.] Insolence. — N. INSOLENCE, brashness, brazenness, malapertness; haughtiness &c. *adj.;* arrogance, airs; bumptiousness, toploftiness [*colloq.*], assumption, presumption; assumption of infallibility; contumely, disdain, insult; overbearance, domineering &c. *v.;* bluster, swagger, swaggering &c. *v.;* bounce; terrorism; tyranny &c. 739; beggar on horseback; usurpation.

impertinence, cheek [*colloq. or slang*], nerve [*slang*], nerviness [*slang*], sauce [*colloq.*], abuse; sauciness &c. *adj.;* flippancy, dicacity [*obs.*], petulance [*rare in this sense*], procacity [*rare*].

impudence, self-assertion, assurance, audacity, hardihood; front, face, brass, gall [*slang*]; shamelessness &c. *adj.;* effrontery, hardened front, face of brass.

JINGOISM, chauvinism; *Kultur* [Ger.], "might is right," *Macht ist Recht* [Ger.].

MALAPERT, saucebox &c. (*blusterer*) 887.

JINGO, jingoist, chauvinist; fire eater [*colloq.*]; boaster &c. 884.

V. BE INSOLENT &c. *adj.;* bluster, vapor, swagger, swell, give oneself airs, snap one's fingers, kick up a dust [*colloq.*]; swear &c. (*affirm*) 535; rap out oaths; roister.

arrogate, assume, presume; make bold, make free; take a liberty, give an inch and take an ell.

outface, outlook, outstare, outbrazen, outbrave; stare out of countenance; brazen out; lay down the law; teach one's grandmother to suck eggs [*colloq.*]; assume a lofty bearing; talk big, look big, put on big looks, act the *grand seigneur;* mount –, ride- the high horse; toss the head, carry with a high hand; tempt Providence; want snuffing [*colloq.*].

DOMINEER, bully, dictate, hector; lord it over; *traiter –, regarder- de haut en bas* [F.]; exact; snub, huff, beard, fly in the face of; put to the blush; bear –, beat- down; browbeat, intimidate; trample –, tread- -down, – under foot; dragoon, ride roughshod over; bulldoze [*colloq., U. S.*], terrorize.

Adj. INSOLENT, haughty, arrogant, imperious, magisterial, dictatorial, arbitrary; high-handed, high and mighty; contumelious, supercilious, overbearing, toplofty [*colloq.*], toploftical [*rare*], in-

886. Servility. — N. SERVILITY; slavery &c. (*subjection*) 749; obsequiousness &c. *adj.;* subserviency; abasement, prostration, prosternation [*obs.*]; genuflection &c. (*worship*) 990; toadeating; fawning &c. *v.;* tufthunting, timeserving, flunkyism *or* flunkeyism; sycophancy &c. (*flattery*) 933; humility &c. 879.

SYCOPHANT, parasite; toad, toady, toadeater, tufthunter; snob, flunky *or* flunkey, lapdog, spaniel, lick-spit, lickspittle, smell-feast, *Græculus esuriens* [L.], hanger on, cavalier (or *cavaliere*) *servente* [It.], led captain, carpet knight; timeserver, fortune hunter, Vicar of Bray, Sir Pertinax MacSycophant, pickthank; flatterer &c. 935; doer of dirty work; *âme damnée* [F.], tool; reptile; slave &c. (*servant*) 746; *homme de cour* [F.], courtier; beat [*slang*], dead beat [*slang*], doughface [*slang, U. S.*]; heeler, ward heeler [*both polit. cant, U. S.*]; jackal, sponge, sponger, sucker [*slang*], tagtail, truckler.

V. CRINGE, bow, stoop, kneel, bend the knee; fall on one's knees, prostrate oneself; worship &c. 990.

fawn, crouch, cower, sneak, crawl, sponge, truckle, toady, truckle to, grovel, lick the feet of, lick one's shoes, make a doormat of oneself, kiss the hem of one's garment; be servile &c. *adj.*

pay court to; feed on, fatten on, batten on, dance attendance on, follow at heel, pin oneself upon, hang on the sleeve of, *avaler les couleuvres* [F.], keep time to, fetch and carry, do the dirty work of.

go with the stream, follow the crowd, worship the rising sun, hold with the hare and run with the hounds; get on the band wagon; be a timeserver &c. *n.*

Adj. SERVILE, obsequious; supple, – as a glove; soapy [*slang*], oily, pliant, cringing, abased, dough-faced [*colloq.*], fawning, slavish, groveling, reptilian, sniveling, mealy-mouthed; beggarly, sycophantic, parasitical; abject, prostrate, down on one's marrowbones [*jocular or slang*]; base, mean, sneaking; crouching &c. *v.;* timeserving.

Adv. WITH SERVILITY &c. *n.;* hat –, cap- in hand; "in a bondman's key" [*M. of V.*]; "with bated breath and whispering humbleness" [*ibid*].

Int. so please you! as my lord wills! don't mind me!

tolerant, domineering, overweening, high-flown; precocious, assuming, would-be, bumptious.

pert, flippant, fresh [*slang, U. S.*], brash, cavalier, saucy, forward, impertinent, malapert; impudent, audacious, presumptuous.

BRAZEN, bluff, shameless, aweless, unblushing, unabashed; bold-faced, bare-faced, brazen-faced; dead –, lost- to shame.

BLUSTERING, swaggering, hectoring, rollicking, roistering, vaporing, free and easy, devil-may-care, jaunty *or* janty; thrasonic [*rare*], thrasonical, fire-eating [*colloq.*]; "full of sound and fury" [*Macbeth*].

JINGO, jingoistic, chauvinistic.

Adv. INSOLENTLY &c. *adj.*; with nose in air; with arms akimbo; *de haut en bas* [*F.*]; with a high hand; *ex cathedra* [*L.*].

₊ one's bark being worse than his bite; "beggars mounted run their horse to death" [*III Henry VI*]; *quid times? Cæsarem vehis* [Plutarch].

887. Blusterer. — N. BLUSTERER, swaggerer, vaporer, roisterer, brawler; fanfaron; braggart &c. (*boaster*) 884; bully, terrorist, rough, ruffian, rough-neck [*slang*], tough [*colloq., U. S.*], rowdy, bulldozer [*colloq., U. S.*], roarer [*slang, obs.*], slangwhanger [*slang*], larrikin [*Austral. & Eng.*]; hoodlum [*colloq.*], hooligan [*slang*], Mohock, Mohawk [*rare*], Drawcansir, swashbuckler, Captain Bobadil, Sir Lucius O'Trigger, Thraso, Pistol, Parolles, Bombastes Furioso, Hector, Chrononhotonthologos; jingo; desperado, dare-devil, fire eater [*colloq.*]; fury &c. (*violent person*) 173.

puppy &c. (*fop*) 854, jackanapes, bantam-cock; malapert, saucebox [*colloq.*]; minx, hussy.

DOGMATIST, doctrinaire, Sir Oracle, stump orator &c. 582; prig, Jack-in-office.

SECTION III. SYMPATHETIC AFFECTIONS

1. SOCIAL AFFECTIONS

888. Friendship. — N. FRIENDSHIP, amity; friendliness &c. *adj.*; brotherhood, fraternity, sodality, confraternity; sorority, sorosis, sisterhood; harmony &c. (*concord*) 714; peace &c. 721.

firm –, staunch –, intimate –, familiar –, bosom –, cordial –, tried –, devoted –, lasting –, fast –, sincere –, warm –, ardent- friendship.

cordiality, fraternization, association, *entente cordiale* [*F.*], good understanding, *rapprochement* [*F.*], sympathy, fellow-feeling, response, welcomeness; affection &c. (*love*) 897; partiality, favoritism; good will &c. (*benevolence*) 906.

acquaintance, introduction, familiarity, intimacy, intercourse, fellowship, knowledge of.

V. BE FRIENDLY &c. *adj.*, be friends &c. 890, be acquainted with &c. *adj.*; know; have the ear of; keep company

889. Enmity. — N. ENMITY, hostility, antagonism; unfriendliness &c. *adj.*; discord &c. 713; bitterness, rancor; heartburning; animosity &c. 900; malevolence &c. 907.

alienation, estrangement; dislike &c. 867; aversion, hate &c. 898.

V. BE UNFRIENDLY &c. *adj.*; keep –, hold- at arm's length; be at loggerheads; bear malice &c. 907; fall out; take umbrage &c. 900; harden the heart, alienate, estrange.

Adj. UNFRIENDLY, inimical, hostile; at enmity, at variance, at daggers drawn, at open war with; up in arms against; in bad odor with.

on bad terms, not on speaking terms; cool, cold, cold-hearted; estranged, alienated, disaffected, irreconcilable.

₊ "To be wroth with one we love Doth work like madness in the brain" [Coleridge].

with &c. (*sociality*) 892; hold communication with, have dealings with, sympathize with; have a leaning to; bear good will &c. (*benevolent*) 906; love &c. 897; make much of; befriend &c. (*aid*) 707; introduce to.

set one's horses together; have the latchstring out [*U. S.*]; hold out –, extend-the right hand of -friendship, – fellowship; become friendly &c. *adj.;* make friends &c. (890) with; break the ice, be introduced to; pick up acquaintance; make –, scrape- acquaintance with; get into favor, gain the friendship of.

shake hands with, strike hands with, fraternize, sororize [*rare*], embrace; receive with open arms, throw oneself into the arms of; meet halfway, take in good part.

Adj. FRIENDLY, amicable, amical; well-affected, unhostile, neighborly; brotherly, fraternal, sisterly, sororal [*rare*]; ardent, devoted, sympathetic, harmonious, hearty, cordial, warm-hearted.

friends with, at home with, hand in hand with; on -good, – friendly, – amicable, – cordial, – familiar, – intimate- -terms, – footing; on speaking terms, on visiting terms, on one's visiting list; in one's good -graces, – books.

acquainted, familiar, intimate, thick, hand and glove, hail fellow well met, free and easy; welcome.

Adv. AMICABLY &c. *adj.;* with open arms, *à bras ouverts* [*F.*]; *sans cérémonie* [*F.*]; arm in arm.

⁎⁎ *amicitia semper prodest* [Seneca]; "a mystic bond of brotherhood makes all men one" [Carlyle]; "friendship is love without either flowers or veil" [Hare]; *vulgus amicitias utilitate probat* [Ovid].

890. Friend. — N. FRIEND, – of one's bosom; *alter ego* [*L.*], other self; intimate, confidant (*masc.*), confidante (*fem.*), confident; best –, bosom –, fast-friend; *amicus usque ad aras* [*L.*], *fidus Achates* [*L.*]; *persona grata* [*L.*]; well-wisher; neighbor *or* neighbour, acquaintance.

favorer, fautor [*rare*], patron, backer, Mæcenas; tutelary saint, good genius, advocate, partisan, sympathizer; ally; friend in need &c. (*auxiliary*) 711.

ASSOCIATE, consociate, compeer, comrade, mate, companion, *camarade* [*F.*], mate *or* copesmate [*obs.*]; partner; side-partner, copartner, consort; old –, crony; chum [*colloq.*], pal [*slang*], buddy [*slang*, *World War*]; playfellow, playmate, schoolfellow; bedfellow, bunkie [*colloq.*, *U. S.*], bedmate, chamberfellow; class-fellow, classman, classmate; roommate, shopmate, shipmate, messmate; fellow –, boon –, pot- companion; fellow-man, stable companion; best man, bridesmaid, maid of honor.

[FAMOUS FRIENDSHIPS] Pylades and Orestes, Castor and Pollux, Achilles and Patroclus, Diomedes and Sthenalus, Hercules and Iolaus, Theseus and Pirithoüs, Epaminondas and Pelopidas, Nisus and Euryalus, Damon and Pythias, David and Jonathan, Christ and the beloved disciple; Soldiers Three, the Three Musketeers.

par nobile fratrum [*L.*, *often ironical*]; *Arcades ambo* [*L.*].

HOST, hostess (*fem.*), Amphitryon, Boniface.

GUEST, visitor, frequenter, habitué, *protégé* [*F.*].

COMPATRIOT; fellow –, countryman; fellow townsman, townie [*slang*].

Int. "Thank God for a trusty chum!" [Kipling].

⁎⁎ *amici probantur rebus adversis; ohne Bruder kann man leben nicht ohne Freund;* "best friend, my well-spring in the wilderness" [G. Eliot]; *conocidos muchos amigos pocos;* "friend more divine than all divinities" [G. Eliot]; *vida sin amigo muerte sin testigo;* "to each a man that knows his naked soul" [Kipling]; "friends who make salt sweet and blackness bright" [Masefield].

891. Enemy. — N. ENEMY; antagonist; foe, foeman; open –, bitter-enemy; opponent &c. 710; backfriend [*obs.*], copemate *or* copesmate [*obs.*], "dearest foe"; mortal -aversion, – antipathy; snake in the grass.

PUBLIC ENEMY, enemy to society; anarchist, seditionist, traitor, traitress (*fem.*).

⁎⁎ every hand being against one; "he makes no friend who never made a foe" [Tennyson].

892. Sociality. — N. SOCIALITY, sociability, sociableness &c. *adj.;* social intercourse, consociation, intercourse, intercommunion; consortship, companionship, comradeship, fellowship; urban-

893. Seclusion. Exclusion. — N. SECLUSION, privacy, retirement, eremitism, anchoretism, anchoritism, reclusion, recess; suspension; snugness &c. *adj.;* concealment, delitescence; rustication,

ity &c. (*courtesy*) 894; intimacy, familiarity; clubbability *or* clubability [*colloq.*], clubbism; *esprit de corps* [*F.*]; *morale* [*F.*].

CONVIVIALITY; good- fellowship, – company; joviality, jollity, *savoir vivre* [*F.*], *joie de vivre* [*F.*], festivity, festive board, walnuts and wine, merrymaking; loving cup; hospitality, heartiness; cheer; "the feast of reason and the flow of soul" [Pope].

WELCOME, welcomeness, greeting; hearty –, warm –, welcome- reception; hearty welcome; hearty –, warm-greeting; the glad hand [*slang*].

BOON COMPANION; good –, jolly-fellow; *bon enfant* [*F.*], bawcock [*archaic*], crony, *bon vivant* [*F.*]; a good mixer [*colloq., U. S.*]; a j'iner [*colloq., U. S.*].

social –, family- circle; family hearth; circle of acquaintance, coterie, society, company; club &c. (*association*) 712.

SOCIAL GATHERING, social reunion; assembly &c. (*assemblage*) 72; barbecue [*U. S.*]; bee; corn-husking [*U. S.*], corn-shucking [*U. S.*]; husking, husking-bee [*U. S.*]; hen party [*colloq.*]; house raising, house-warming, hanging of the crane; infare *or* infair [*Scot & dial., U. S.*]; smoker, – party [*both colloq.*]; Dutch treat [*colloq., U. S.*]; stag, – party [*both colloq.*]; sociable [*U. S.*], tamasha [*Hind.*], party, entertainment, reception, levee, at home, *conversazione* [*It.*], *soirée* [*F.*], matinée; evening –, morning –, afternoon –, garden –, coming-out [*colloq.*] –, surprise- party; *partie carrée* [*F.*]; kettledrum, drum, drum major, rout [*archaic*], tempest, hurricane; *ridotto* [*It.*]; ball, hunt ball, dance, dinner dance, festival &c. (*amusement*) 840.

[SOCIAL MEALS] breakfast, wedding breakfast, hunt breakfast; luncheon, lunch; picnic lunch, basket lunch, picnic; tea, afternoon tea, five o'clock tea, cup of tea, dish of tea [*esp. Brit.*], *thé dansant* [*F.*], coming-out tea [*colloq.*]; tea party, tea fight [*slang*]; dinner, potluck, bachelor dinner, stag dinner [*colloq.*], hunt dinner; church supper, high tea; banquet &c. 298.

VISIT, visiting; round of visits; call, morning call; interview &c. (*interlocution*) 588; assignation; tryst, trysting place; appointment.

V. be sociable &c. *adj.*; know; be acquainted &c. *adj.*; associate with, sort with, consort with, keep company with, walk hand in hand with; eat off the same trencher, club together, consort, bear one company, join; consociate [*rare*], intercommunicate, intercommune [*rare*], make acquaintance with &c. (*friendship*) 888; make advances, fraternize, embrace.

rus in urbe [*L.*], ruralism, rurality [*rare*], solitude; solitariness &c. (*singleness*) 87; isolation; "splendid isolation"; loneliness &c. *adj.*; estrangement from the world, voluntary exile; aloofness.

depopulation, desertion, desolation; wilderness &c. (*unproductive*) 169; howling wilderness; rotten borough, Old Sarum [*Eng.*].

RETREAT, cell, hermitage, cloister; convent &c. 1000; *sanctum sanctorum* [*L.*], study, library, den [*colloq.*].

EXCLUSION, excommunication, banishment, exile, ostracism, proscription; economic pressure; cut, cut direct; dead cut.

UNSOCIABILITY, unsociableness, dissociability, dissociality; inhospitality, inhospitableness &c. *adj.*; domesticity, self-sufficiency, Darby and Joan.

RECLUSE, hermit, eremite, anchoret *or* anchorite, anchorist [*obs.*]; santon; stylite, pillarist, pillar-saint [*all Ch. hist.*]; St. Simeon Stylites; caveman, cave-dweller, troglodyte, Timon of Athens, solitarian [*obs.*], solitaire, ruralist [*obs.*], disciple of Zimmermann, closet cynic, cynic, Diogenes.

OUTCAST, pariah, leper; outsider, rank outsider; castaway, pilgarlic [*low*], wastrel [*dial. Eng.*], losel, foundling; wilding.

V. BE *or* LIVE SECLUDED &c. *adj.*; keep –, stand –, hold oneself- -aloof, – in the background; keep snug; shut oneself up; deny oneself, seclude oneself; creep into a corner, rusticate, dissocialize; retire, – from the world; hermitize; take the veil; abandon &c. 624; sport one's oak [*Univ. slang, Eng.*].

EXCLUDE, repel; cut, – dead; refuse to -associate with, – acknowledge; send to Coventry, look cool –, turn one's back –, shut the door- upon; blackball, excommunicate, exile, expatriate; banish, outlaw, maroon, ostracize, proscribe, cut off from, keep at arm's length, draw a cordon round, boycott, embargo, blockade, isolate.

DEPOPULATE, dispeople, unpeople; desolate, devastate.

Adj. SECLUDED, sequestered, retired, delitescent, private, by; in a backwater; out of the world, out of the way; "the world forgetting by the world forgot" [Pope].

UNSOCIABLE, unsocial, dissocial, inhospitable, cynical, inconversable [*obs.*],

VISIT, pay a visit; interchange -visits, – cards; call at, call upon; leave a card; drop in, look in, look one up, beat up one's quarters [*colloq.*].

RECEIVE HOSPITALITY; be –, feel –, make oneself- at home with; make free with; crack a bottle with; take potluck with; live at free quarters; find the latchstring out [*U. S.*].

ENTERTAIN; give a party &c. *n.*; be at home, see one's friends, keep open house, do the honors; receive, – with open arms; welcome; give a warm reception &c. *n.* to; kill the fatted calf.

Adj. SOCIABLE, companionable, clubbable *or* clubable [*colloq.*], clubbish; conversable, cozy *or* cosy *or* cosey, chatty, conversational; convivial, festive, festal, jovial, jolly, hospitable.

welcome, – as roses in May; fêted, entertained.

free and easy, hail fellow well met, familiar, intimate, consociate, consociated; associated with &c. *v.*; on visiting terms, acquainted; social, neighborly.

international, cosmopolitan; gregarious.

Adv. SOCIABLY &c. *adj.*; *en famille* [*F.*], in the family circle; on terms of intimacy; in the social whirl; *sans*

unclubbable *or* unclubable [*colloq.*], *sauvage* [*F.*]; hermitical, eremitic *or* eremitical, anchoretic *or* anchoretical, anchoritic *or* anchoritical, anchoretish, anchoritish, troglodytic.

snug, domestic, stay-at-home.

EXCLUDED &c. *v.*; unfrequented, unvisited, unintroduced, uninvited, unwelcome; on the fringe of society; under a cloud, left to shift for oneself; deserted, – in one's utmost need; unfriended, friendless, kithless, homeless, desolate, lorn, forlorn; solitary, lonely, lonesome, isolated, single, estranged; derelict, outcast, outside the gates, "yammering at the bars"; banished &c. *v.*; under an embargo.

UNINHABITED, unoccupied, untenanted, tenantless, abandoned; uninhabitable.

** noli me tangere.

"among them but not of them" [Byron]; "and homeless near a thousand homes I stood" [Wordsworth]; "far from the madding crowd's ignoble strife" [Gray]; "makes a solitude and calls it peace" [Byron]; *magna civitas magna solitudo;* "never less alone than when alone" [Rogers]; "O sacred solitude! divine retreat!" [Young]; "Alone as the last man on earth" [Galsworthy].

-*façon*, – *cérémonie* [*F.*], arm in arm.

** "a crowd is not company" [Bacon]; "be bright and jovial among your guests to-night" [*Macbeth*]; "his worth is warrant for his welcome" [*Two Gentlemen*]; "let's be red with mirth" [*Winter's Tale*]; "welcome the coming speed the parting guest" [Pope]; "we have heard the chimes at midnight" [*II Henry IV*]; "'tis grievous parting with good company" [George Eliot]; "O go not yet!" [*II Henry VI*]; "and now subscribe your names" [*L. L. L.*]; "drink a health to me for I must hence" [*Taming of the Shrew*]; "Stand not upon the order of your going, But go at once" [*Macbeth*].

---

894. Courtesy. — N. COURTESY; respect &c. 928; good- manners, – behavior, – breeding; manners; politeness &c. *adj.*; *bienséance* [*F.*], urbanity, comity, gentility, breeding, gentle breeding, cultivation, culture, polish, presence; civility, civilization; amenity, suavity; good temper, good humor, amiability, easy temper, complacency, soft tongue, mansuetude [*archaic*]; condescension &c. (*humility*) 879; affability, complaisance, compliance, *prévenance* [*F.*], amiability, gallantry, chivalry; fine flower of -courtesy, – chivalry.

pink of courtesy, pink of politeness; flower of knighthood, *chevalier sans peur et sans reproche*, Bayard, Sidney, "a verray parfit gentil knight" [Chaucer], Chesterfield; Launcelot, Gawaine,

895. Discourtesy. — N. DISCOURTESY; ill-breeding; ill –, bad –, ungainlymanners; tactlessness; uncourteousness &c. *adj.*; rusticity, inurbanity; illiberality, incivility, displacency [*obs.*]; lack *or* want of courtesy &c. 894; disrespect &c. 929; procacity [*obs.*], impudence, misbehavior, barbarism, barbarity; brutality, brutishness, brutification, blackguardism, conduct unbecoming a gentleman, *grossièreté* [*F.*], *brusquerie* [*F.*], vulgarity &c. 851.

BAD TEMPER, ill temper; peevishness, surliness; churlishness &c. *adj.*; spinosity, perversity; moroseness &c. (*sullenness*) 901*a*.

sternness &c. *adj.*; austerity; moodishness, captiousness &c. 901; cynicism; tartness &c. *adj.*; acrimony, acerbity, virulence, asperity.

Colonel Newcome; "gentle Shakespeare" [Ben Jonson].

compliment; fair –, soft –, sweet-words; honeyed phrases, ceremonial; salutation, reception, presentation, introduction, *accueil* [*F.*], greeting, recognition; welcome, abord [*obs.*], respects, *devoir* [*F.*], duty [*archaic*], regards, remembrances; kind -regards, – remembrances; deference, love, best love, empty encomium, flattering remark, hollow commendation; salaams.

[FORMS OF GREETING] obeisance &c. (*reverence*) 928; bow, curtsy *or* curtsey, scrape, salaam, kotow *or* kowtow [*China*], bowing and scraping; kneeling; genuflection &c. (*worship*) 990; obsequiousness &c. 886; capping, pulling the forelock, making a leg [*colloq.*], shaking hands, &c. *v.*; grip of the hand; embrace, hug, squeeze, kiss, buss, smack; salute, accolade; loving cup, *vin d'honneur* [*F.*], pledge; love token &c. (*endearment*) 902.

mark of recognition, nod; "nods and becks and wreathed smiles" [Milton]; valediction &c. 293; condolence &c. 915.

V. BE COURTEOUS &c. *adj.*; show courtesy &c. *n.*

mind one's P's and Q's [*colloq.*], behave oneself, be all things to all men, conciliate, speak one fair, take in good part; do the amiable [*colloq.*]; look as if butter would not melt in one's mouth; mend –, mind- one's manners.

DO THE HONORS, usher, usher in, receive, greet, hail, bid welcome; welcome, – with open arms; shake hands; hold out –, press –, squeeze- the hand; bid Godspeed; speed the parting guest; cheer, serenade.

visit, wait upon, present oneself, pay one's respects, pay a visit &c. (*sociability*) 892; dance attendance on &c. (*servility*) 886; pay attentions to; do homage to &c. (*respect*) 928; give *or* send one's regards to &c. *n.*

SALUTE; embrace &c. (*endearment*) 902; kiss, – hands; drink to, pledge, hob and nob; move to [*colloq.*], nod to; smile upon.

uncover, cap; touch –, raise –, lift –, take off- the hat; doff the cap; tip the hat to [*slang*]; pull the forelock; present arms; make way for; bow, make one's bow, make a leg scrape, curtsy *or* curtsey,

scowl, black looks, frown; sulks, short answer, rebuff; hard words, contumely; unparliamentary language, personality.

bear, bruin, grizzly, grizzly bear; brute, blackguard, beast; unlicked cub; frump [*colloq.*], crosspatch [*colloq.*]; grouch, old grouch [*both slang*]; saucebox &c. 887; crooked stick.

V. BE RUDE &c. *adj.*; insult &c. 929; treat with discourtesy; take a name in vain; make bold with, make free with; take a liberty; stare out of countenance, ogle, point at, put to the blush.

CUT; turn one's back upon, turn on one's heel; give the cold shoulder; keep at -a distance, – arm's length; look -cool, – coldly, – black- upon; show the door to, send away with a flea in the ear [*colloq.*].

LOSE ONE'S TEMPER &c. (*reser.tment*) 900; mump [*dial.*], sulk &c. 9C1a; frown, scowl, glower, pout; snap, snarl, growl.

RENDER RUDE &c. *adj.*; brutalize, brutify.

Adj. DISCOURTEOUS, uncourteous, uncourtly; ill-bred, ill-mannered, ill-behaved, ill-conditioned, unbred; unmannerly, unmannered, impolite, unpolite; uncivil, ungracious, unceremonious, cool; unpolished, uncivilized, ungenteel; ungentlemanlike, ungentlemanly; unladylike; blackguard; vulgar &c. 851; dedecorous [*obs.*]; foul-mouthed, foulspoken; abusive.

pert, forward, obtrusive, impudent, rude, saucy, procacious [*archaic*], brash; flippant &c. (*insolent*) 885.

repulsive; uncomplaisant, unaccommodating, unneighborly, ungallant; inaffable; ungentle, ungainly, rough, rugged, bluff, blunt, gruff; churlish, boorish, bearish; brutal, brusque, stern, harsh, austere; cavalier.

BAD-TEMPERED, ill-tempered, ill-humored; out of -temper, – humor; crusty, tart, sour, crabbed, sharp, short, trenchant, sarcastic, biting, doggish, currish, caustic, virulent, bitter, acrimonious, venomous, contumelious; snarling &c. *v.*; surly, – as a bear; perverse; grim, sullen &c. 901a; peevish &c. (*irascible*) 901; bristling, thorny, spinose, spinous.

Adv. DISCOURTEOUSLY &c. *adj.*; with discourtesy &c. *n.*, with a bad grace.

** "You are rude; I pretend not to perceive it" [Martial].

bow and scrape, bob a curtsy, kneel; bow –, bend- the knee; salaam, kotow *or* kowtow [*China*]; prostrate oneself &c. (*worship*) 990.

RENDER POLITE &c. *adj.*; polish, rub off the -corners, – rough edges; cultivate, civilize, humanize.

Adj. COURTEOUS, polite, civil, mannerly, urbane; well-behaved, well-mannered, well-bred, well-brought up; gently bred; of gentle -manners, – breeding; good-mannered, polished, civilized, cultivated; refined &c. (*taste*) 850; gentlemanlike &c. (*fashion*)852; gallant, chivalrous, chivalric; on one's good (*or* best) behavior.

ingratiating, winning; gentle, mild; good-humored, cordial, gracious, amiable, tactful, affable, familiar; neighborly; obliging, complaisant, complacent, conciliatory.

BLAND, suave; fine –, fair –, soft- spoken; honey-mouthed, honey-tongued; oily, oily-tongued, unctuous; obsequious &c. 886.

Adv. COURTEOUSLY &c. *adj.*; with a good grace; with open arms, with outstretched arms, *à bras ouverts* [*F.*]; *suaviter in modo* [*L.*], with perfect courtesy, in good humor.

Int. HAIL! welcome! well met! *ave!* [*L.*]; all hail! good -day, – morrow, – morning, – evening, – afternoon, – night! sweet dreams! Godspeed! *pax vobiscum!* [*L.*]; all good go with you! may your shadow never be less!

*** *rien de plus estimable que la cerémonie;* "the very pink of courtesy" [*Romeo and Juliet*].

896. Congratulation. — N. CONGRATULATION, gratulation, felicitation; salute &c. 894; condolence &c. 915; compliments of the season; good wishes, best wishes.

V. CONGRATULATE, gratulate, felicitate; give joy, wish one joy; compliment; tender –, offer- one's congratulations; wish many happy returns of the day, wish a merry Christmas and a happy new year.

congratulate oneself &c. (*rejoice*) 838.

Adj. CONGRATULATORY, gratulatory.

*** "I wish you all the joy that you can wish" [*Merchant of Venice*].

897. Love. — N. LOVE, affection, sympathy, fellow-feeling; tenderness &c. *adj.*; heart, brotherly love; charity, good will; benevolence &c. 906; attachment; fondness &c. *adj.*; liking; inclination &c. (*desire*) 865; regard, dilection [*obs.*], admiration, fancy.

yearning, *eros* [*Gr.* ἔρως], tender passion, amour; gyneolatry; gallantry, passion, flame, devotion, fervor, enthusiasm, transport of love, rapture, enchantment, infatuation, adoration, idolatry.

mother love, maternal love, natural affection, *storge* [*Gr.* στοργή].

attractiveness, charm; popularity; idol, favorite &c. 899.

god of love, Cupid, Venus, Eros, Kama [*Hindu*]; myrtle; turtle dove, sparrow; cupid amoretto; true lover's knot; love -token, – suit, – affair, – tale, – story; the old story, plighted love; courtship &c. 902; amourette; free-love.

LOVER, suitor, *fiancé* [*F.*], follower [*colloq.*], admirer, adorer, wooer, amoret [*obs.*], amorist, beau, sweetheart, inamorato, swain, young man [*colloq.*], flame [*colloq.*], love, truelove: leman [*archaic*],

898. Hate. — N. HATE, hatred, vials of hate; "Hymn of Hate."

disaffection, disfavor; alienation, estrangement, coolness; enmity &c. 889; animosity &c. 900; malice &c. 907; implacability &c. (*revenge*) 919.

umbrage, pique, grudge, dudgeon, spleen, bitterness, bitterness of feeling; ill blood, bad blood; acrimony.

repugnance &c. (*dislike*) 867; odium, unpopularity; detestation, abhorrence, loathing, execration, abomination, aversion, antipathy; demonophobia, gynephobia, negrophobia; Anglophobia &c. 867.

OBJECT OF HATRED, an abomination, an aversion, *bête noire* [*F.*]; enemy &c. 891; bitter pill; source of annoyance &c. 830.

V. HATE, detest, abominate, abhor, loathe; recoil at, shudder at; shrink from, view with horror, hold in abomination, revolt against, execrate; scowl &c. 895; disrelish &c. (*dislike*) 867.

owe a grudge; bear spleen, bear a grudge, bear malice &c. (*malevolence*) 907; conceive an aversion to.

Lothario, gallant, paramour, captive; *amoroso, cavaliere servente, cicisbeo, caro sposo* [*all It.*].

LADYLOVE, sweetheart, mistress, inamorata, idol, darling, duck, Dulcinea, angel, goddess, *cara sposa* [*It.*]; betrothed, affianced, *fiancée* [*F.*].

flirt, coquette, amorette.

pair of turtledoves; abode of love; Agapemone [*Ch. hist.*].

V. LOVE, like, affect, fancy, care for, take an interest in, be partial to, sympathize with; affection; be in love with &c. *adj.*; have –, entertain –, harbor –, cherish- a love for &c. *n.*; regard, revere; take to, bear love to, be wedded to; set one's affections on; burn; adore, idolize, love to distraction, *aimer éperdument* [*F.*]; dote- on, – upon.

make much of, feast one's eyes on; hold dear, prize; hug, cling to, cherish, caress, fondle, pet.

take a fancy to, look sweet upon [*colloq.*]; become enamored &c. *adj.*; fall in love with, lose one's heart; desire &c. 865.

EXCITE LOVE; win –, gain –, secure –, engage- the -love, – affections, – heart; take the fancy of; have a place in –, wind round- the heart; attract, attach, endear, charm, fascinate, captivate, bewitch, seduce, enamor, enrapture, turn the head.

EXCITE HATRED, provoke hatred &c. *n.*; be hateful &c. *adj.*; stink in the nostrils; estrange, alienate, repel, set against, sow dissension, set by the ears, envenom, incense, irritate, rile [*dial. or colloq.*], ruffle, vex, roil; horrify &c. 830.

Adj. HATING &c. *v.*; abhorrent; averse from &c. (*disliking*) 867; set against; bitter &c. (*acrimonious*) 895; implacable &c. (*revengeful*) 919.

UNLOVED, unbeloved, unlamented, undeplored, unmourned, uncared for, unendeared, unvalued; disliked &c. 867.

crossed in love, forsaken, rejected, lovelorn, jilted.

HATEFUL, obnoxious, odious, abominable, repulsive, offensive, shocking; disgusting &c. (*disagreeable*) 830; reprehensible.

invidious, spiteful; malicious &c. 907. insulting, irritating, provoking.

[MUTUAL HATE] at daggers drawn; not on speaking terms &c. (*enmity*) 889; at loggerheads.

*** no love lost between; "In time we hate that which we often fear" [*Antony and Cleopatra*]; "I like a good hater" [Johnson]; "Heaven has no rage like love to hatred turned" [Congreve]; "There are glances of hatred that stab and raise no cry of murder" [G. Eliot].

get into favor; ingratiate –, insinuate –, worm- oneself; propitiate, curry favor with, pay one's court to, *faire l'aimable* [*F.*], set one's cap at [*colloq.*], coquet, flirt.

Adj. LOVING &c. *v.*; fond of; taken with [*colloq.*], struck with [*colloq.*], smitten, bitten [*colloq.*]; attached to, wedded to; enamored; charmed &c. *v.*; in love; lovesick; over head and ears in love.

affectionate, tender, sweet upon [*colloq.*], sympathetic, amorous, amatory; fond, erotic, uxorious, ardent, passionate, rapturous, devoted, motherly.

LOVED &c. *v.*; beloved, well beloved, dearly beloved; dear as the apple of one's eye, nearest to one's heart; dear, precious, darling, pet, little; favorite, popular.

congenial; to –, after- one's -mind, – taste, – fancy, – own heart; in one's good graces &c. (*friendly*) 888.

LOVABLE, adorable, lovely, sweet, attractive, seductive, winning, winsome, charming, engaging, interesting, enchanting, captivating, fascinating, bewitching, amiable; seraphic *or* seraphical, angelic, like an angel.

*** *amantes amentes* [Terence]; *credula res amor est* [Ovid]; *militat omnis amasius* [Ovid]; *omnia vincit amor* [Vergil]; *si vis amari ama* [Seneca]; "the sweetest joy, the wildest woe" [Bailey]; "Affection is a coal that must be cool'd; Else, suffer'd, it will set the heart on fire" [*Venus and Adonis*]; "Affection lights a brighter flame Than ever blazed by art" [Cowper].

899. Favorite. — N. FAVORITE, pet, fondling, cosset, minion [*rare*], idol, jewel; spoiled child, *enfant gâté* [*F.*]; led captain; crony; apple of one's eye, man after one's own heart; *persona grata* [*L.*].

love, dear, darling, duck, honey, jewel; mopsy *or* mopsey, moppet; sweetheart &c. (*love*) 897.

general –, universal- favorite; idol of the people; matinée idol.

900. Resentment. — N. RESENTMENT, displeasure, animosity, anger, wrath, ire, indignation; exasperation, vexation, bitter resentment, wrathful indignation.

pique, umbrage, huff, miff [*colloq.*], soreness, dudgeon, acerbity, virulence, bitterness, acrimony, asperity, spleen, gall; heartburning, heart-swelling; rankling.

ill –, bad- -humor, – temper; irascibility &c. 901; scowl &c. 895; sulks &c. 901*a*; ill blood &c. (*hate*) 898; revenge &c. 919.

IRRITATION; warmth, bile, choler, fume, pucker [*colloq.*], dander [*colloq.*], ferment, excitement, ebullition; angry mood, taking [*colloq.*], pet, tiff, passion, fit, tantrum [*colloq.*].

RAGE, fury; towering -rage, – passion; *acharnement* [*F.*], desperation, burst, explosion, paroxysm, storm; violence &c. 173; fire and fury; vials of wrath; gnashing of teeth, hot blood, high words.

FURIES, Erinyes (*sing.* Erinys), Eumenides; Alecto, Megæra, Tisiphone.

[CAUSE OF UMBRAGE] affront, provocation, offense; indignity &c. (*insult*) 929; grudge; crow to -pluck, – pick, – pull; red rag, last straw, sore subject, *casus belli* [*L.*]; ill turn, outrage.

buffet, blow, slap in the face, box on the ear, rap on the knuckles.

V. RESENT; take -amiss, – ill, – to heart, – offense, – umbrage, – huff, – exception; not take it as a joke; *ne pas entendre raillerie* [*F.*]; take in bad part, take in ill part.

pout, knit the brow, frown, scowl, lower, snarl, growl, gnarl, gnash, snap; redden, color; look black, look black as thunder, look daggers; bite one's thumb; show –, grind- one's teeth; champ the bit.

BE ANGRY; fly –, fall –, get- into a -rage, – passion; fly off the handle [*slang*], fly off at a tangent; let one's angry passions rise; bridle up, bristle up, froth up, fire up, flare up; foam at the mouth; open –, pour out- the vials of one's wrath.

chafe, mantle, fume, kindle, fly out, take fire; boil, – over; boil with- indignation, – rage; rage, storm, foam; hector, bully, bluster; vent one's -rage, spleen; lose one's temper; have a fling at; kick up a -row, – dust, – shindy [*all slang*]; cut up rough [*slang*], stand on one's hind legs, stamp the foot; stamp –, quiver –, swell –, foam- with rage; burst with anger; raise -Cain, – the devil, – Ned, – the mischief, – the roof [*all slang*]; breathe fire and fury; breathe revenge. '

bear malice &c. (*revenge*) 919.

CAUSE ANGER, raise anger; affront, offend; give -offense, – umbrage; anger; hurt the feelings; insult, discompose, fret, ruffle, roil, heckle [*Brit.*], nettle, huff, pique; excite &c. 824; irritate, stir the blood, stir up bile; sting, – to the quick; rile [*dial. or colloq.*], provoke, chafe, wound, incense, inflame, wrath [*obs.*], make one hot under the collar [*slang*], enrage, aggravate, add fuel to the flame, fan into a flame, widen the breach, envenom, embitter, exasperate, infuriate, kindle wrath; stick in one's crop *or* gizzard [*colloq.*]; rankle &c. 919; hit –, rub –, sting –, strike- on the raw.

put out of -countenance, – humor; put (*or* get) one's monkey up [*slang or colloq., Eng.*], put (*or* get) one's back up; raise one's -gorge, – dander [*colloq.*], – choler; work up into a passion, make one's blood boil, make the ears tingle, throw into a ferment, madden, drive one mad; lash into -fury, – madness; fool to the top of one's bent; set by the ears; bring a hornet's nest about one's ears.

Adj. ANGRY, wroth, irate, ireful, wrathful; cross &c. (*irascible*) 901; Achillean; sulky &c. 901*a;* bitter, virulent; acrimonious &c. (*discourteous*) &c. 895; offended &c. *v.;* waxy [*slang, Eng.*], wrought, worked up; indignant, hurt, sore; set against.

warm, burning; boiling, – over; fuming, raging, hot under the collar [*slang*]; *acharné* [*F.*]; foaming, – at the mouth; convulsed with rage; fierce, wild, rageful, furious, mad with rage, fiery, infuriate, rabid, savage; relentless &c. 919; violent &c. 173.

flushed with -anger, – rage; in a- huff, – stew [*colloq.*], – fume, – pucker [*dial. or colloq.*], – wax [*slang*], – passion, – rage, – fury, – taking [*colloq.*]; on one's high ropes [*colloq.*], up in arms; in high dudgeon.

Adv. ANGRILY &c. *adj.;* in the height of passion; in the heat of -passion, – the moment; in an ecstasy of rage.

Int. *tantæne animis cælestibus iræ*! [Vergil]; marry come up! zounds! 'sdeath!

. one's blood being up, one's back being up, one's monkey being up [*slang or colloq., Eng.*]; *fervens difficili bile jecur;* the gorge rising, eyes flashing fire; the blood -rising, – boiling; *hæret lateri lethalis arundo* [Vergil]; "beware the fury of a patient man" [Dryden]; *furor arma ministrat* [Vergil]; *ira furor brevis est* [Horace]; *quem Jupiter vult perdere dementat prius;* "What, drunk with choler? stay and pause awhile" [*I Henry IV*].

901. Irascibility. — N. IRASCIBILITY, irascibleness, temper; crossness &c. *adj.;* susceptibility, procacity [*rare*], petulance, irritability, tartness, acerbity, acrimony, asperity, protervity [*rare*]; huff &c. (*resentment*) 900; a word and a blow; pugnacity &c. (*contentiousness*) 720; excitability &c. 825; bad –, fiery –, crooked –, irritable &c. *adj.*- temper; *genus irritabile* [*L.*], hot blood.

ill humor &c. (*sullenness*) 901*a*; churlishness &c. (*discourtesy*) 895.

Sir Fretful Plagiary; brabbler, Tartar; shrew, vixen, virago, termagant, dragon, scold, Xanthippe *or* Xantippe, Kate the Shrew; porcupine; spitfire; fire eater &c. (*blusterer*) 887; fury &c. (*violent person*) 173.

V. BE IRASCIBLE &c. *adj.;* have a temper &c. *n.,* have a devil in one, be possessed of the devil, have the temper of a fiend; brabble [*archaic or dial.*]; fire up &c. (*be angry*) 900.

Adj. IRASCIBLE, bad-tempered, ill-tempered, irritable, susceptible; excitable &c. 825; thin-skinned &c. (*sensitive*) 822; fretful, fidgety; on the fret.

hasty, overhasty, quick, warm, hot, testy, touchy, techy *or* tetchy; like -touch-wood, – tinder, – a barrel of gunpowder; huffy, pettish, petulant, querulous, captious, moody, moodish; fractious, peevish, *acariâtre* [*F.*].

QUARRELSOME, contentious, disputatious; pugnacious &c. (*bellicose*) 720; cantankerous [*colloq.*], exceptious [*rare*], cross-grained; waspish, snappish, peppery, fiery, passionate, choleric, shrewish, "sudden and quick in quarrel" [*As You Like It*]; restive &c. (*perverse*) 901*a;* churlish &c. (*discourteous*) 895; cross, – as -crabs, – a bear with a sore head, – a cat, – a dog, – two sticks, – the tongs [*all colloq.*]; sore, sore as a crab [*colloq.*].

in a bad temper; sulky &c. 901*a;* angry &c. 900; resentful, resentive; vindictive &c. 919.

Int. pish!

. *à vieux comptes nouvelles disputes; quamvis tegatur proditur vultu furor* [Seneca]; *vino tortus et irâ* [Horace]; "What sudden anger's this?" [Henry VIII].

901a. Sullenness. — N. SULLENNESS &c. *adj.;* morosity, spleen; churlishness &c. (*discourtesy*) 895; irascibility &c. 901; moodiness &c. *adj.;* perversity; obstinacy &c. 606; torvity [*obs.*], thorniness, spinosity; crabbedness &c. *adj.*

ill –, bad- -temper, – humor; sulks, dudgeon, mumps, dumps [*humorous*], doleful dumps [*colloq. or humorous*], vapors [*archaic*], glooming, doldrums, fit of the sulks, bouderie, black looks, scowl; grouch [*slang*]; huff &c. (*resentment*) 900.

V. BE SULLEN &c. *adj.;* sulk; frown, scowl, lower, glower, pout, have a hangdog look, glout [*rare or dial.*], grouch [*slang*], grout [*U. S.*].

Adj. SULLEN, sulky; ill-tempered, ill-humored, ill-affected, ill-disposed; grouty [*colloq., U. S.*]; in -an ill, – a bad, – a shocking- -temper, – humor; out of -temper, – humor; naggy [*colloq.*], torvous [*obs.*], crusty, crabbed, sour, sore, sore as a crab; surly &c. (*discourteous*) 895.

moody, moodish, spleenish, spleeny, spleenful, splenetic, cankered; cross, cross-grained; perverse, wayward, humorsome; restive, restiff [*rare*], malignant, refractory, ungovernable, cantankerous, intractable, exceptious [*rare*], sinistrous [*obs.*], deaf to reason, unaccommodating, rusty [*dial. Eng.*], froward, cussed [*vulgar or euphemistic, U. S.*], curst [*archaic or dial.*].

grumpy, glum, grim, grum, morose, frumpish [*obs.*]; in the sulks &c. *n.;* out of sorts; scowling, glowering, growling, grouchy [*slang*]; peevish &c. (*irascible*) 901; dogged &c. (*stubborn*) 606.

. "Gathering her brows like gathering storm, Nursing her wrath to keep it warm" [Burns].

902. [EXPRESSION OF AFFECTION.] **Endearment.** — **N.** ENDEARMENT, caress, blandishment, blandiment [obs.]; épanchement [F.], fondling, billing and cooing, dalliance, caressing, embrace, salute, kiss, buss, smack, osculation, deosculation [obs.].

COURTSHIP, wooing, suit, addresses, the soft impeachment; love-making; calf love [colloq.]; amorous glances, ogle, side-glance, sheep's eyes, goo-goo eyes [slang, U. S.]; serenading, caterwauling.

flirting &c. v.; flirtation, gallantry; coquetry, spooning [slang].

true lover's knot, plighted love, engagement, betrothal; marriage &c. 903; honeymoon; love tale, love token; love letter, billet-doux [F.]; posy [archaic]; valentine. Strephon and Chloe, 'Arry and 'Arriet.

FLIRT, coquette; male flirt, philanderer; spoon [slang].

V. CARESS, fondle, pet, dandle; pat, – on the -head, – cheek; chuck under the chin, smile upon, coax, wheedle, cosset, coddle, cocker, make much of, cherish, foster, kill with kindness.

clasp, hug, cuddle; fold to the heart, press to the bosom; fold –, strain- in one's arms; take to one's arms; snuggle, nestle, nuzzle; embrace, kiss, buss, smack, blow a kiss; salute &c. (courtesy) 894.

MAKE LOVE, bill and coo, spoon [slang], toy, dally, flirt, coquet, gallivant or galavant; philander; pay one's -court, – addresses, – attentions- to; serenade; court, sweetheart [colloq. or dial.], woo; set one's cap at or for [colloq.]; be or look sweet upon [colloq.]; ogle, cast sheep's eyes upon, make goo-goo eyes at [slang, U. S.], faire les yeux doux [F.].

fall in love with, fall over head and ears in love with; win the affections &c. (love) 897; die for.

propose; make –, have- an offer; pop the question [colloq.]; become engaged, become betrothed; plight one's -troth, – faith.

Adj. CARESSING &c. v.; "sighing like furnace" [As You Like It]; love-sick, spoony or spooney [slang].

CARESSED &c. v.

⁎ "faint heart ne'er won fair lady"; "kisses honeyed by oblivion" [G. Eliot].

903. Marriage. — **N.** MARRIAGE, matrimony, wedlock, union, intermarriage, miscegenation, marriageability; vinculum matrimonii [L.], nuptial tie, nuptial knot; match; betrothment &c. (promise) 768

married state, coverture, bed, cohabitation.

WEDDING, nuptials, Hymen, bridal, espousals, spousals; leading to the altar &c. v.; nuptial benediction, epithalamium; sealing.

torch –, temple- of Hymen; saffron -veil, – robe; hymeneal altar; honeymoon.

bridesmaid, maid of honor, matron of honor; usher, best man, bridesman, groomsman; bride, bridegroom.

MARRIED MAN, neogamist [obs.], Benedict, partner, spouse, mate, yokemate, husband, man, consort, baron [old law & her.], goodman [archaic or dial.], old man.

MARRIED WOMAN, wife, wife of one's bosom, wedded wife, rib [dial. & sportive], helpmeet, helpmate, better half,

904. Celibacy. — **N.** CELIBACY, singleness, single blessedness; bachelorhood, bachelorship; misogamy, misogyny.

virginity, pucelage [rare], maidhood [rare], maidenhood, maidenhead.

UNMARRIED MAN, bachelor, Cœlebs, agamist, old bachelor; misogamist, misogynist; monk, priest, celibate, religious.

UNMARRIED WOMAN, spinster, maid, maiden; virgin, feme sole [law], old maid; bachelor-girl, girl-bachelor; nun, sister, vestal, vestal virgin; Diana, St. Agnes.

V. live single, enjoy single blessedness, keep bachelor hall.

Adj. UNMARRIED, unwedded; wifeless, spouseless; single, celibate, virgin.

⁎ "Is the single man therefore blessed? No!" [As You Like It]; "a man is all in the way in the house" [Gaskell].

905. Divorce. Widowhood. — **N.** DIVORCE, divorcement; separation, judicial separation, separate maintenance;

gray mare, goodwife [*archaic or dial.*], old woman [*vulgar*].

feme, – covert [*law*]; lady [*obs. or uncultivated*]; squaw; matron, matronship, matronage, matronhood.

MARRIED COUPLE, man and wife, wedded pair, wedded couple, Darby and Joan, Philemon and Baucis.

AFFINITY, soul-mate; spiritual wife, spiritual husband.

[KINDS OF MARRIAGE] monogamy, monogyny; bigamy, digamy, deuterogamy; trigamy; polygamy, polygyny, polyandry, polyandrism; Mormonism, spiritual wifery (*or* wifeism); levirate.

harem, seraglio; Mormon.

monogamist, monogynist, bigamist &c.; Turk, Bluebeard.

unlawful –, left-handed –, morganatic –, ill-assorted- marriage; *mésalliance* [*F.*], *mariage de convenance* [*F.*].

MARRIAGE BROKER, matchmaker, professional matchmaker, schatchen [*Yiddish*]; matrimonial -agency, – agent, – bureau.

V. MARRY, wive, take to oneself a wife; be married, be spliced [*colloq.*]; go off, go to the world [*obs.*], pair off; wed, espouse, lead to the hymeneal altar, take "for better for worse," give one's hand to, bestow one's hand upon.

marry, join, handfast [*archaic*]; couple &c. (*unite*) 43; be made one; tie the nuptial knot; give away, give in marriage; seal; affy, affiance; betroth &c. (*promise*) 768; publish –, call –, proclaim –, bid- the banns, be asked in church.

remarry, rewed; intermarry, interwed.

Adj. MARRIED &c. *v.;* one, one bone and one flesh.

MARRIAGEABLE, nubile.

ENGAGED, betrothed, affianced.

MATRIMONIAL, marital, conjugal, connubial, wedded; nuptial, hymeneal, spousal, bridal; monogamous &c.

⁎ the gray mare the better horse; "a world-without-end bargain" [*L. L. L.*]; "marriages are made in Heaven" [Tennyson]; "render me worthy of this noble wife" [*Julius Cæsar*]; *si qua voles apte nubere nube pari* [Ovid]; "He for God only, she for God in him" [Milton]; "Look down, you gods, And on this couple drop a blessed crown!" [*Tempest*]; "procure the vicar To stay for me at church twixt twelve and one" *Merry Wives*]; "good luck Shall fling her old shoe after" [Tennyson]; "Now sighs steal out and tears begin to flow!" [Pope].

separatio a -mensâ et thoro, – *vinculo matrimonii* [*L.*].

WIDOWHOOD, viduity [*rare*], viduage, viduation, weeds; viduate [*eccl.*].

widow, relict, dowager; divorcée; grass widow.

widower; grass widower; cuckold.

V. live separate; separate, divorce, disespouse [*obs.*], put away; wear the horns.

2. DIFFUSIVE SYMPATHETIC AFFECTIONS

906. Benevolence. — N. BENEVOLENCE, Christian charity; God's love, God's grace; good will; philanthropy &c. 910; unselfishness &c. 942.

good -nature, – feeling, – wishes; kindness, kindliness &c. *adj.;* lovingkindness, benignity, brotherly love, charity, humanity, kindly feelings, fellow-feeling, sympathy; goodness –, warmth- of heart; warm-heartedness, bonhomie *or* bonhommie, kind-heartedness; amiability, milk of human kindness, tenderness; love &c. 897; friendship &c. 888; toleration, consideration; mercy &c. (*pity*) 914.

CHARITABLENESS &c. *adj.;* bounty, almsgiving; good works, beneficence, generosity; "the luxury of doing good" [Goldsmith].

907. Malevolence. — N. MALEVOLENCE, bad intent, bad intention, unkindness, diskindness [*obs.*]; ill-nature, ill-will, ill-blood, bad blood; enmity &c. 889; hate &c. 898; malice, – prepense, – aforethought; malignance, malignancy, malignity; maliciousness &c. *adj.;* spite, despite; resentment &c. 900.

uncharitableness &c. *adj.;* incompassion [*rare*], incompassionateness [*rare*] &c. 914a; gall, venom, rancor, rankling, virulence, mordacity, acerbity; churlishness &c. (*discourtesy*) 895; hardness of heart, heart of stone, obduracy; evil eye, cloven -foot, – hoof.

ill turn, bad turn; affront &c. (*disrespect*) 929; bigotry, intolerance, tender mercies [*ironical*]; "unkindest cut of all" [*Julius Cæsar*].

acts of kindness, a good turn; good -, kind- -offices, - treatment.

PHILANTHROPIST, "one who loves his fellow-men" [Hunt], salt of the earth; good Samaritan, sympathizer, well-wisher, bon enfant [F.]; altruist.

V. BE BENEVOLENT &c. adj.; have one's heart in the right place, bear good will; wish well, wish Godspeed; view -, regard- with an eye of favor; take in good part; take -, feel- an interest in; be -, feel- interested- in; have a fellow-feeling for, sympathize with, feel for; fraternize &c. (be friendly) 888.

enter into the feelings of others, practice the Golden Rule, do as you would be done by, meet halfway.

treat well; give comfort, smooth the bed of death; do good, do a good turn; benefit &c. (goodness) 648; render a service, render assistance, give one a hand, be of use; aid &c. 707.

Adj. BENEVOLENT, kind, kindly, well-meaning, amiable, cordial; obliging, accommodating, indulgent, gracious, complacent, good-humored; tender, considerate; warm-hearted, kind-hearted, tender-hearted, large-hearted, broad-hearted, soft-hearted; merciful &c. 914.

good-natured, well-natured, spleenless [rare]; sympathizing, sympathetic; complaisant &c. (courteous) 894; well-meant, well-intentioned, kindly meant.

full of natural affection, fatherly, motherly, brotherly, sisterly; paternal, maternal, fraternal; sororal [rare]; friendly &c. 888.

CHARITABLE, beneficent, philanthropical, generous, humane, benignant, bounteous, bountiful.

Adv. WITH GOOD WILL, with a good intention [rare], with the best intentions; out of deepest sympathy; in a burst of generosity.

Int. GODSPEED! good luck! all good luck go with you! count on me!

₊ "act a charity sometimes" [Lamb]; "a tender heart, a will inflexible" [Longfellow]; de mortuis nil nisi bonum; "kind hearts are more than coronets" [Tennyson]; quando amigo pide no hay mañana; 'the social smile, the sympathetic tear" [Gray]; "in kindness preferring one another" [Bible]; "Who gives himself with his alms feeds three — Himself, his hungering neighbor, and Me" [Lowell].

CRUELTY, cruelness &c. adj.; brutality, savagery, ferity, ferocity; outrage, atrocity, ill-usage, persecution; barbarity, inhumanity, immanity [obs.], truculence, ruffianism; Inquisition, torture, vivisection.

V. BE MALEVOLENT &c. adj.; bear -, harbor- -spleen, - a grudge, -- malice; betray -, show- the cloven foot; hurt &c. (physical pain) 378; annoy &c. 830; injure, harm, wrong; do harm to, do an ill office to; outrage; disoblige, malign, plant a thorn in the breast; turn and rend one.

molest, worry, harass, haunt, harry, bait, tease; throw stones at; play the devil with; hunt down, dragoon, hound; persecute, oppress, grind, maltreat, ill-treat, ill-use, misuse.

wreak one's malice on, do one's worst, break a butterfly on the wheel; dip -, imbrue- one's hands in blood; show no quarter, have no mercy &c. 914a.

Adj. MALEVOLENT, unbenevolent, unbenign; ill-disposed, ill-intentioned, ill-natured, ill-conditioned, ill-contrived; evil-minded, evil-disposed, black-browed; malicious, malign, malignant; rancorous, spiteful, despiteful, treacherous, mordacious, caustic, bitter, envenomed, acrimonious, virulent; unamiable, uncharitable; maleficent, venomous, grinding, galling.

harsh, disobliging, unkind, unfriendly, ungracious, inofficious [obs.], invidious; churlish &c. (uncourteous) 895; surly, sullen &c. 901a.

COLD-BLOODED, cold-hearted; black-hearted, hard-hearted, flint-hearted, marble-hearted, stony-hearted, hard of heart, cold, unnatural; ruthless &c. (unmerciful) 914a; relentless &c. (revengeful) 919.

CRUEL, brutal, brutish, savage; savage as a -bear, - tiger; ferine, ferocious, feral, inhuman; barbarous, fell, untamed, tameless, truculent, incendiary; bloodthirsty &c. (murderous) 361; atrocious; bloody-minded; fiendish, fiendlike; demoniac or demoniacal; diabolic or diabolical, devilish, infernal, hellish, Tartarean or Tartareous, Satanic.

Adv. MALEVOLENTLY &c. adj.; with bad intent &c. n.; with the ferocity of a tiger.

₊ cruel as death; "hard unkindness' alter'd eye" [Gray]; homo homini lupus [Plautus]; mala mens malus animus [Terence]; "rich gifts wax poor when givers prove unkind" [Hamlet]; "sharp-tooth'd unkindness" [Lear].

908. Malediction. — N. MALEDICTION, malison, curse, imprecation, denunciation, execration; anathema, – maranatha; maranatha [*a misinterpretation*]; ban, proscription, excommunication, commination, thunders of the Vatican, fulmination; aspersion, disparagement, vilification, vituperation.

ABUSE; foul –, bad –, strong –, unparliamentary- language; billingsgate, sauce [*colloq.*]; blackguardism &c. (*discourtesy*) 895; evil speaking; cursing &c. v.; profane swearing, oath; foul invective, ribaldry, rude reproach, scurrility, threat &c. 909; more bark than bite; invective &c. (*disapprobation*) 932.

V. CURSE, accurse, imprecate, damn; curse with bell, book, and candle; invoke –, call down- curses on the head of; call down curses upon one's devoted head; devote to destruction.

execrate, beshrew [*archaic*], scold; anathematize &c. (*censure*) 932; hold up to execration, denounce, proscribe, excommunicate, fulminate, thunder against; curse up hill and down dale; threaten &c. 909.

SWEAR, curse and swear; swear like a trooper; fall a-cursing, rap out an oath, swear at, damn.

Adj. MALEDICTORY, imprecatory; cursing, cursed &c. v.

Int. woe to! beshrew! [*archaic*], *ruat cœlum!* [*L.*], woe betide! ill betide! confusion seize! damn! confound! blast! curse! devil take! hang! out with! a plague upon! out upon! aroynt! *honi soit!* [*F.*], *parbleu!* [*F.*].

** *delenda est Carthago;* "Ruin seize thee, ruthless king" [*Gray*].

909. Threat. — N. THREAT, menace; defiance &c. 715; abuse, minacity *rare*], minaciousness, intimidation; denunciation; fulmination; commination &c. (*curse*) 908; gathering clouds &c. (*warning*) 668.

V. THREATEN, threat, menace; snarl, growl, gnarl, mutter, bark, bully.

defy &c. 715; intimidate &c. 860; keep –, hold up –, hold out- *in terrorem* [*L.*]; shake –, double –, clinch- the fist at; thunder, talk big, fulminate, use big words, bluster, look daggers.

Adj. THREATENING, menacing, minatory, minacious, comminatory, abusive; *in terrorem* [*L.*]; ominous &c. (*predicting*) 511; defiant &c. 715; under the ban.

Int. *vœ victis!* at your peril! do your worst! look out!

** *nemo me impune lacessit;* "an eye like Mars, to threaten and command" [*Hamlet*].

910. Philanthropy. — N. PHILANTHROPY, altruism, humanity, humanitarianism, universal benevolence, eudæmonism *or* eudemonism, *deliciœ humani generis* [*L.*].

PUBLIC WELFARE, commonwealth [*now rare*], commonweal *or* common weal [*now rare*]; socialism, communism; Fourierism, phalansterism *or* phalansterianism, Saint Simonianism; cosmopolitanism, utilitarianism, the greatest happiness of the greatest number, social science, sociology.

PUBLIC SPIRIT, patriotism, civism, nationality, love of country, *amor patriœ* [*L.*].

CHIVALRY, knight errantry; generosity &c. 942.

PHILANTHROPIST, eudæmonist *or* eudemonist, utilitarian, Benthamite, socialist, communist, cosmopolite, citizen of the world, *amicus humani generis* [*L.*]; altruist &c. 906; "little friend of all the world" [*Kipling*]; knight errant; patriot.

Adj. PHILANTHROPIC, altruistic, humanitarian, utilitarian, cosmopolitan; public-

911. Misanthropy. — N. MISANTHROPY, incivism; egotism &c. (*selfishness*) 943; moroseness &c. 901a; cynicism; want of patriotism &c. 910.

MISANTHROPE, misanthropist, egotist, cynic, man hater, Timon, Diogenes.

woman hater, misogynist.

Adj. MISANTHROPIC, antisocial, unpatriotic; egotistical &c. (*selfish*) 943; morose &c. 901a.

** "no man is a true American who hates another country more than he loves his own" [*Roosevelt*]; "the worst thing about cynicism is its truth" [*Cynic's Calendar*].

spirited, patriotic; humane, large-hearted &c. (*benevolent*) 906; chivalric, chivalrous; generous &c. 942.

Adv. *pro bono publico* [*L.*]; *pro aris et focis* [Cicero].

.*. *humani nihil a me alienum puto* [Terence]; *omne solum forti patria* [Ovid]; *un bienfait
n'est jamais perdu;* "mine is that great country which shall never take toll from the weakness
of others" [Galsworthy].

---

912. Benefactor. — N. BENEFACTOR,
savior, protector, good genius, tutelary
saint, guardian angel, good Samaritan;
friend in need, "a very present help in
time of trouble" [*Bible*]; fairy godmother; *pater patriæ* [*L.*]; salt of the
earth &c. (*good man*) 948; auxiliary &c.
711.

---

bane &c. 963; torpedo, bomb, U-boat.

SAVAGE, brute, ruffian, barbarian, semibarbarian, caitiff, desperado; Apache,
gunman, hoodlum [*colloq.*], plug-ugly [*slang, U. S.*], Redskin, tough [*colloq., U. S.*],
Mohock, Mohawk [*rare*], bludgeon man, bully, rough, hooligan [*slang*], larrikin
[*Austral. & Eng.*], ugly customer, dangerous classes; thief &c. 792; butcher, hangman; cutthroat &c. (*killer*) 361.

WILD BEAST, tiger, leopard, panther, hyena, catamount [*U. S.*], catamountain,
lynx, cougar, jaguar, puma; bloodhound, hellhound, sleuth-hound; gorilla; vulture.

cockatrice, adder; snake, – in the grass; serpent, cobra, asp, rattlesnake, ana-
conda; boa; viper &c. (*snake*) 366; *alacrán* [*Sp. Amer.*], alligator, cayman, crocodile, mugger *or* magar [*Hind.*]; Gila monster; octopus.

[INJURIOUS INSECTS] buffalo carpet beetle, cucumber flea beetle, elm-tree beetle, striped
cucumber beetle, gypsy (*or* gipsy) moth, brown-tail moth, flat-headed apple-tree borer, peach-
tree borer, round-headed apple-tree borer, squash vine borer, bedbug, harlequin cabbage bug,
potato bug, buffalo bug, rose bug, squash bug, tent caterpillar; curculio, weevil, snout beetle,
billbeetle, billbug, plum curculio; horn fly, white grub, San José scale, onion maggot, clover-seed
midge, grain weevil, bollworm, cankerworm, cutworm, fall webworm, tobacco worm, tomato
worm, wireworm; white ant, scorpion, hornet, mosquito, locust, Colorado beetle.

HAG, hellhag, beldam, Jezebel.

MONSTER; fiend &c. (*demon*) 980; devil incarnate, demon in human shape;
Frankenstein's monster; cannibal, anthropophagus, anthropophagist; blood-
sucker, vampire, ogre, ghoul.

harpy, siren, vampire [*colloq.*], vamp [*slang*]; Furies, Eumenides.

.*. *fœnum habet in cornu;* "Tremble thou wretch, That hast within thee undivulged crimes,
Unwhipp'd of justice" [*King Lear*]; "From the fury of the Northmen, Good Lord, deliver us."

---

913. [MALEFICENT BEING.**] Evildoer
— N.** EVILDOER, evil worker, mal-
feasor; wrongdoer &c. 949; mischief-
maker, marplot; oppressor, tyrant; firebrand, incendiary, fire bug [*U. S.*],
pyromaniac, arsonist &c. 384; anarchist,
nihilist, destroyer, Vandal, iconoclast,
terrorist; Attila, scourge of the human
race.

---

3. SPECIAL SYMPATHETIC AFFECTIONS

914. Pity. — N. PITY, compassion,
commiseration; bowels, – of compassion; sympathy, fellow-feeling, tenderness, soft-heartedness, yearning, forbearance, humanity, mercy, clemency;
leniency &c. (*lenity*) 740; exorability,
exorableness; charity, ruth, long-suffering.

melting mood; *argumentum ad misericordiam* [*L.*]; quarter, grace, *locus pœnitentiæ* [*L.*].

SYMPATHIZER; advocate, friend, par-

914a. Pitilessness. — N. PITILESS-
NESS &c. *adj.;* inclemency, inexorability,
inflexibility, incompassion [*rare*], hardness of heart; want of pity &c. 914;
severity &c. 739; malevolence &c. 907.

V. BE PITILESS &c. *adj.;* turn a deaf
ear to; claim one's "pound of flesh"
[*M. of V.*]; have no –, shut the gates of-
mercy &c. 914; give no quarter.

Adj. PITILESS, merciless, ruthless,
bowelless; unpitying, unmerciful, inclement; grim-faced, grim-visaged; un-

tisan, patron, wellwisher, defender, champion.

V. PITY; have –, show –, take- pity &c. *n.;* commiserate, compassionate; condole &c. 915; sympathize; feel for, be sorry for, yearn over; weep, melt, thaw, enter into the feelings of.

forbear, relent, relax, give quarter, wipe the tears, *parcere subjectis* [*L.*]; give a *coup de grâce* [*F.*], put out of one's misery; be cruel to be kind.

RAISE *or* EXCITE PITY &c. *n.;* touch, soften, melt, melt the heart; appeal, – to one's better feelings; propitiate, disarm.

SUPPLICATE &c. (*request*) 765; ask for mercy &c. *n.;* cry for quarter, beg one's life, kneel; deprecate.

Adj. PITYING &c. *v.;* pitiful, compassionate, sympathetic, touched.

merciful, clement, ruthful; humane; humanitarian &c. (*philanthropic*) 910; tender, tender-hearted; soft, soft-hearted; unhardened; lenient &c. 740; exorable, forbearing; melting &c. *v.;* weak.

Int. for pity's sake! mercy! have –, cry you- mercy! God help you! poor -thing, – dear, – fellow! woe betide! *quis talia fando temperet a lachrymis!* [Vergil].

* one's heart bleeding for; *haud ignara mali miseris succurrere disco* [Vergil]; "a fellow feeling makes one wondrous kind" [Garrick]; *onor di bocca assai giova e poco costa;* "Taught by that Power that pities me, I learn to pity them" [Goldsmith].

compassionate, incompassionate [*rare*], uncompassioned; inflexible, relentless, inexorable; unrelenting &c. 919; harsh &c. 739; cruel &c. 907.

---

915. Condolence. — N. CONDOLENCE; lamentation &c. 839; sympathy, consolation.

V. CONDOLE WITH, console, sympathize; express –, testify- pity; afford–, supply-consolation; lament with &c. 839; express sympathy for, feel for, send one's condolences; feel -grief, – sorrow- in common with; share one's sorrow.

* "the human heart Finds nowhere shelter but in human kind" [G. Eliot]. "pity and need Make all flesh kin. There is no caste in blood" [Edwin Arnold].

---

4. RETROSPECTIVE SYMPATHETIC AFFECTIONS

916. Gratitude. — N. GRATITUDE, gratefulness, thankfulness; feeling of –, sense of- obligation.

acknowledgment, recognition, thanksgiving, giving thanks; thankful good will.

THANKS, praise, benediction; pæan; *Te Deum* &c. (*worship*) 990; grace, – before meat, – after meat; thank offering; requital.

V. BE GRATEFUL &c. *adj.;* thank; give –, render –, return –, offer –, tender-thanks &c. *n.;* acknowledge, requite.

feel –, be –, lie- under an obligation; *savoir gré* [*F.*]; not look a gift horse in the mouth; never forget, overflow with gratitude; thank –, bless- one's stars; fall on one's knees.

Adj. GRATEFUL, thankful, obliged, beholden, indebted to, under obligation

Int. THANKS! many thanks! gramercy! much obliged! thank you! thank Heaven! Heaven be praised!

917. Ingratitude. — N. INGRATITUDE, thanklessness, oblivion of benefits, unthankfulness.

"benefits forgot" [*As You Like It*]; thankless task, thankless office.

V. BE UNGRATEFUL &c. *adj.;* feel no obligation, owe one no thanks, forget benefits; look a gift horse in the mouth.

Adj. UNGRATEFUL, unmindful, unthankful; thankless, ingrate, wanting in gratitude, insensible of benefits.

forgotten; unacknowledged, unthanked, unrequited, unrewarded; ill-requited; ill-rewarded.

Int. thank you for nothing! *"et tu Brute!"* [*Julius Cæsar*].

* "ingratitude! thou marble-hearted fiend" [*Lear*]; "this was the most unkindest cut of all" [*Julius Cæsar*]; "hearts unkind, kind deeds With coldness still returning" [Wordsworth].

* "Now, God be praised, the day is ours" [Macaulay]; "the still small voice of gratitude" [Gray]; "Alas! the gratitude of men Hath often left me mourning" [Wordsworth]; "a lively sense of favors to come."

918. Forgiveness. — N. FORGIVE-NESS, pardon, condonation, grace, remission, absolution, amnesty, oblivion; indulgence; reprieve.

conciliation; reconcilement; reconciliation &c. (*pacification*) 723; propitiation.

longanimity, placability; *amantium iræ* [*L.*]; *locus pœnitentiæ* [*L.*]; forbearance.

EXONERATION, excuse, quittance, release, indemnity; bill -, act-, covenant -, deed- of indemnity; exculpation &c. (*acquittal*) 970.

V. FORGIVE, - and forget; pardon, condone, think no more of, let bygones be bygones, shake hands; forget an injury; bury the hatchet; drown all unkindness; start afresh, make a new start.

let off [*colloq.*], remit, absolve, give absolution; blot out one's -sins, - offenses, - transgressions, - debts; wipe the slate clean; reprieve; acquit &c. 970.

EXCUSE, pass over, overlook; wink at &c. (*neglect*) 460; bear with; allow for, make allowances for; let one down easily, not be too hard upon, pocket the affront.

CONCILIATE, propitiate, placate; beg -, ask -, implore- pardon &c. *n.*; make up a quarrel &c. (*pacify*) 723; let the wound heal.

Adj. FORGIVING, placable, conciliatory.

forgiven &c. *v.*; unresented, unavenged, unrevenged.

Int. have mercy! cry you mercy! forgive and forget!

⁎⁎ *veniam petimusque damusque vicissim* [Horace]; more in sorrow than in anger; *tout comprendre c'est tout pardonner;* "the offender never pardons" [Herbert]; "Good to forgive, Best to forget" [Browning]; "to err is human, to forgive, divine" [Pope]; "the sin That neither God nor man can well forgive" [Tennyson].

919. Revenge. — N. REVENGE, revengement [*rare*], vengeance; avengement, avengeance [*obs.*], sweet revenge, vendetta, death feud, blood for blood; eye for an eye, tooth for a tooth, retaliation &c. 718; day of reckoning.

rancor, vindictiveness, immitigability; implacability; malevolence &c. 907; ruthlessness &c. 914a.

AVENGER, vindicator [*obs.*], Nemesis, Eumenides.

V. REVENGE, avenge, vindicate [*obs.*]; take revenge, have one's revenge; breathe -revenge, - vengeance; wreak one's -vengeance, - anger; cry quittance; give no quarter, take no prisoners.

have accounts to settle, have a crow to pluck, have a rod in pickle.

keep the wound green; nurse one's revenge, harbor -revenge, - vindictive feeling; bear malice; rankle, rankle in the breast.

HAVE AT A DISADVANTAGE, have on the hip, have the upper hand, have at one's mercy.

Adj. REVENGEFUL, vengeful, vindictive, rancorous; pitiless &c. 914a; ruthless, rigorous, avenging, retaliative, grudgeful [*rare*].

unforgiving, unrelenting; inexorable, stony-hearted, implacable, relentless, remorseless.

RANKLING, immitigable; *æternum servans sub pectore vulnus* [*L.*].

⁎⁎ *manet cicatrix; manet altâ mente repostum; dies iræ dies illa;* "in high vengeance there is noble scorn" [G. Eliot ; *inhumanum verbum est ultio* [Seneca]; *malevolus animus abditos dentes habet* [Syrus]; "revenge is sweet — especially to women" [Byron]; "Revenge, at first though sweet, Bitter ere long back on itself recoils" [Milton]; 'Vengeance is in my heart, death in my hand" [*Titus Andronicus*]; "I will feed fat the ancient grudge I bear him" [*M. of V.*]; "vengeance is mine; I will repay, saith the Lord" [*Bible*].

---

920. Jealousy. — N. JEALOUSY, jealousness; jaundiced eye; distrust, mistrust, misdoubt, heartburn; envy &c. 921; doubt, envious suspicion, suspicion; "green-eyed monster" [*Othello*]; yellows; Juno.

V. BE JEALOUS &c. *adj.*; view with jealousy, view with a jealous eye, view with a jaundiced eye; grudge, begrudge.

doubt, distrust, mistrust, suspect, misdoubt, heartburn [*obs.*]; jealouse [*obs. or Scot. & dial. Eng.*].

Adj. JEALOUS, jealous as a Barbary pigeon; jaundiced, yellow-eyed, envious; beside oneself with -jealousy, - envy.

⁎⁎ "Jealousy is cruel as the grave" [*Bible*]; "in jealousy there is more self-love than love" [La Rochefoucauld]; "For jealousy dislikes the world to know it" [Byron]; "the injur'd lover's hell" [*Paradise Lost*].

921. Envy.— **N.** ENVY; enviousness &c. *adj.;* rivalry; *jalousie de métier* [*F.*]; ill-will, spite; jealousy &c. 920.

V. ENVY, covet, grudge, begrudge, burst with envy, break the tenth commandment.

Adj. ENVIOUS, invidious, covetous, grudging, begrudged; belittling; *alieni appetens* [*L.*].

. "base envy withers at another's joy" [Thomson]; *cæca invidia est* [Livy]; *multa petentibus desunt multa* [Horace]; *summa petit livor* [Ovid]; "for envy is a kind of praise" [Gay]; "Envy, to which th' ignoble mind's a slave, Is emulation in the learn'd or brave" [Pope].

SECTION IV. MORAL AFFECTIONS

1. MORAL OBLIGATIONS

922. Right.— **N.** RIGHT; what ought to be, what should be; what is fit &c. *adj.;* fitness &c. *adj.; summum jus* [*L.*].

JUSTICE, equity; equitableness &c. *adj.;* propriety; fair play, square deal [*colloq.*], impartiality, measure for measure, give and take, *lex talionis* [*L.*].

scales of justice, evenhanded justice, karma; *suum cuique* [*L.*]; clear stage –, fair field- and no favor; retributive justice, nemesis.

Astræa, Nemesis, Themis, Rhadamanthus.

morals &c. *(duty)* 926; law &c. 963; honor &c. *(probity)* 939; virtue &c. 944.

V. BE RIGHT &c. *adj.;* stand to reason.

see justice done, see one righted, see fair play; do justice to; recompense &c. *(reward)* 973; hold the scales even, give and take; serve one right, put the saddle on the right horse; give every one his due, give the devil his due; *audire alteram partem* [*L.*].

DESERVE &c. *(be entitled to)* 924.

Adj. RIGHT, good; just, reasonable; fit &c. 924; equal, equable, equitable; evenhanded, fair, square, fair and square.

LEGITIMATE, justifiable, rightful; as it should be, as it ought to be; lawful &c. *(permitted)* 760, *(legal)* 963.

DESERVED &c. 924.

Adv. RIGHTLY &c. *adj.; à* –, *au- bon droit* [*F.*], in justice, in equity, in reason.

without -distinction of, – regard to, – respect to- persons; upon even terms.

Int. all right!

. *Dieu et mon droit;* "in equal scale weighing delight and dole" [*Hamlet*]; *justitia suum cuique distribuit* [Cicero]; *justitiæ soror incorrupta fides; justitia virtutum regina;* "thrice is he armed that hath his quarrel just" [*II Henry VI*]; "Sir, I would rather be right than be president" [Henry Clay]; "Heaven itself has ordained the right" [Washington]; "righteousness is at the bottom of all things" [Phillips Brooks].

923. Wrong.— **N.** WRONG; what ought not to be, what should not be *malum in se* [*L.*]; unreasonableness grievance; shame.

INJUSTICE; unfairness &c. *adj.;* iniquity, foul play, partiality, leaning, favor, favoritism, nepotism; partisanship, party spirit; undueness &c. 925; unlawfulness &c. 964.

robbing Peter to pay Paul &c. *v.;* the wolf and the lamb; vice &c. 945.

V. BE WRONG &c. *adj.;* cry to heaven for vengeance.

DO WRONG &c. *n.;* be inequitable &c. *adj.;* favor, lean towards; encroach; impose upon; reap where one has not sown; give an inch and take an ell; rob Peter to pay Paul.

Adj. WRONG, wrongful; bad, too bad; unjust, unfair, inequitable, unequitable, unequal, partial, one-sided; injurious.

UNJUSTIFIABLE, unreasonable, unallowable, unwarrantable, objectionable, improper, unfit; unjustified &c. 925; illegal &c. 964; iniquitous; immoral &c. 945.

in the wrong, – box; in bad [*slang*], in wrong [*slang*].

Adv. WRONGLY &c. *adj.*

Int. this is too bad! it will not do!

. "a custom more honored in the breach than the observance" [*Hamlet*]; "Truth forever on the scaffold, Wrong forever on the throne" [Lowell]; "stiff in opinions, always in the wrong" [Dryden]; "To do a great right, do a little wrong" [*Merchant of Venice*].

924. Dueness. — N. dueness, right, droit [law], due, privilege, prerogative, prescription, title, claim, pretension, demand, birthright.

immunity, license, liberty, franchise; vested -interest, – right.

sanction, authority, warranty [law], charter, licitness, warrant &c. (permission) 760; constitution &c. (law) 963; tenure; bond &c. (security) 771.

deserts, merits, dues; all that is coming to one [colloq.].

claimant, appellant; plaintiff &c. 938.

V. be due to &c. adj.; be the due of &c. n.; have -right, – title, – claim- to; be entitled to; have a claim upon; belong to &c. (property) 780.

deserve, merit, be worthy of, richly deserve.

demand, claim; call upon one for, come upon one for, appeal to for; revendicate [rare], revindicate, reclaim; exact; insist -on, – upon; challenge; take one's stand, make a point of, require, lay claim to; assert, assume, arrogate.

make good; substantiate; vindicate a -claim, – right; fit –, qualify- for; make out a case.

use a right, assert, enforce, put in force, lay under contribution.

entitle; give or confer a right; authorize &c. 760; sanction, sanctify, legalize, ordain, prescribe, allot.

give every one his due &c. 922; pay one's dues; have one's -due, – rights; stand upon one's rights.

Adj. having a right to &c. v.; entitled to; claiming; deserving, meriting, worthy of.

privileged, allowed, sanctioned, warranted, authorized; ordained, prescribed, constitutional, chartered, enfranchised.

prescriptive, presumptive, absolute, indefeasible, unalienable, inalienable, imprescriptible, inviolable, unimpeachable, unchallenged; sacrosanct.

due to, merited, deserved, condign [archaic, except of punishment], richly deserved.

right, fit, fitting, correct, proper, meet, befitting, becoming, seemly; decorous; creditable, up to the mark, right as a trivet; just –, quite- the thing; selon les règles [F.]; square, unexceptionable, equitable &c. 922; due, en règle [F.].

lawful, licit, legitimate, legal; legalized &c. (law) 963; allowable &c. (permitted) 760.

Adv. duly; as is -right, – fitting, – just; unexceptionably; ex officio [L.], de jure [L.]; by right, by divine right; jure divino [L.], Dei gratiâ [L.], in the name of.

*** civis Romanus sum [Cicero]; à chaque saint sa chandelle; "render to Cæsar the things that are Cæsar's" [Bible].

925. [absence of right.**] Undueness. — N.** undueness &c. adj.; malum prohibitum [L.]; impropriety; illegality &c. 964.

falseness &c. adj.; emptiness –, invalidity- of title; illegitimacy.

loss of right, disfranchisement, forfeiture.

assumption, usurpation, tort [law], violation, breach, encroachment, presumption, seizure; stretch, exaction, imposition, lion's share.

usurper, pretender, impostor.

V. be undue &c. adj.; not be due &c. 924.

infringe, encroach, trench on, exact; arrogate, – to oneself; give an inch and take an ell; stretch –, strain- a point; usurp, violate, do violence to; get under false pretenses, sail under false colors.

disentitle, disfranchise, disqualify; invalidate.

relax &c. (be lax) 738; misbehave &c. (vice) 945; misbecome.

Adj. undue; unlawful &c. (illegal) 964; unconstitutional, illicit, unauthorized, unwarranted, unallowed, unsanctioned, unjustified; disentitled, unentitled; disqualified, unqualified; unprivileged, unchartered.

undeserved, unmerited, unearned; unfulfilled.

forfeited, disfranchised.

illegitimate, bastard, spurious, false; usurped, tortious [law].

improper; unmeet, unfit, unbefitting, unseemly, unbecoming, misbecoming, seemless [obs.]; contra bonos mores [L.]; not the thing, out of the question, not to be thought of; preposterous, pretentious, would-be.

*** filius nullius; "an honour snatch'd with boisterous hands" [II Henry VI].

926. Duty. — N. DUTY, what ought to be done, moral obligation, accountableness, liability, onus, responsibility; bounden –, imperative- duty; call, – of duty; accountability.

allegiance, fealty, tie; engagement &c. (*promise*) 768; part; function, calling &c. (*business*) 625.

OBSERVANCE, fulfillment, discharge, performance, acquittal, satisfaction, redemption; good behavior.

MORALITY, morals, decalogue; case of conscience; conscientiousness &c. (*probity*) 939; conscience, inward monitor, still small voice within, sense of duty, tender conscience; the hell within [*P. L.*].

PROPRIETY, fitness; dueness &c. 924; seemliness, amenableness, amenability, decorum, *to prepon* [*Gr.* τὸ πρέπον]; the thing, the proper thing; the -right, – proper- thing to do.

[SCIENCE OF MORALS] ethics, ethology [*obs. in this sense*]; deontology, aretology [*obs.*]; moral –, ethical- philosophy; casuistry, polity.

V. BE THE DUTY OF, be incumbent on &c. *adj.*; be responsible &c. *adj.*; behoove, become, befit, beseem; belong to, pertain to; fall to one's lot; devolve on; lie upon, lie on one's head, lie at one's door; rest with, rest on the shoulders of.

take upon oneself &c. (*promise*) 768; be –, become- -bound to, – sponsor for; incur a responsibility &c. *n.*; be –, stand –, lie- under an obligation; stand responsible for; have to answer for; owe it to oneself.

enter upon –, perform –, observe –, fulfill –, discharge –, adhere to –, acquit oneself of –, satisfy- -a duty, – an obligation; act one's part, redeem one's pledge, do justice to, be at one's post; do duty; do one's duty &c. (*be virtuous*) 944.

927. Dereliction of Duty. — N. DERELICTION OF DUTY; fault &c. (*guilt*) 947; sin &c. (*vice*) 945; nonobservance, nonperformance, noncoöperation; indolence, neglect, relaxation, infraction, violation, transgression, failure, evasion; eyeservice; dead letter.

SLACKER, loafer, time-killer; eyeserver, eyeservant; striker; noncoöperator.

V. VIOLATE; break, break through; infringe; set aside, set at naught; encroach upon, trench upon; trample -on, – under foot; slight, get by [*slang*], neglect, evade, renounce, forswear, repudiate; wash one's hands of; escape, transgress, fail.

call to account &c. (*disapprobation*) 932.

. "There never was a bad man that had ability for good service" [Burke].

927a. Exemption. — N. EXEMPTION, freedom, irresponsibility, immunity, liberty, license, release, quitclaim [*law*]; exoneration, excuse, dispensation, absolution, franchise [*obs.*], renunciation, discharge; exculpation &c. 970.

V. EXEMPT, release, acquit, discharge, quitclaim [*law*], remise, remit; free, set at liberty, let off [*colloq.*], pass over, spare, excuse, dispense with, give dispensation, license; stretch a point; absolve &c. (*forgive*) 918; exonerate &c. (*exculpate*) 970; save the necessity.

be exempt &c. *adj.*

Adj. EXEMPT, free, immune, at liberty, scot-free; released &c. *v.;* unbound, unencumbered; irresponsible, not responsible, unaccountable, not answerable; excusable.

. *bonis nocet quisquis pepercerit malis* [Syrus]; "The charter of thy worth gives thee releasing" [Shakespeare].

be on one's good behavior, mind one's P's and Q's; walk the straight path.

IMPOSE A DUTY &c. *n.;* enjoin, require, exact; bind, – over; saddle with, prescribe, assign, call upon, look to, oblige.

Adj. OBLIGATORY, binding; imperative, peremptory; stringent &c. (*severe*) 739; behooving &c. *v.;* incumbent on, chargeable on; under obligation; obliged by, bound by, tied by; saddled with.

due to, beholden to, bound to, indebted to; tied down; compromised &c. (*promised*) 768; in duty bound.

AMENABLE, liable, accountable, responsible, answerable.

RIGHT, meet &c. (*due*) 924; moral, ethical, casuistical, conscientious, ethological.

Adv. with a safe conscience, as in duty bound, on good behavior, on one's own responsibility, at one's own risk, *suo periculo* [L.]; *in foro conscientiæ* [L.]; *quamdiu se bene gesserit* [L.]; at one's post.

, *dura lex sed lex; dulce et decorum est pro patria mori; honos habet onus; leve fit quod bene fertur onus* [Ovid]; *loyauté m'oblige;* "simple duty hath no place for fear" [Whittier]; "stern daughter of the voice of God" [Wordsworth]; "there is a higher law than the Constitution" [Wm. Seward]; "So nigh is grandeur to our dust, So near is God to man, When Duty whispers low, *Thou must*, The youth replies, *I can!*" [Emerson]; "labor to keep alive in your breast that little spark of celestial fire — conscience" [George Washington]; "Thus conscience does make cowards of us all" [*Hamlet*]; "And voices that we thought were fled Arise and call us, and we come" [Noyes].

2. MORAL SENTIMENTS

928. Respect. — N. RESPECT, regard, consideration; courtesy &c. 894; attention, deference, reverence, honor, esteem, estimation, veneration, admiration; approbation &c. 931.

HOMAGE, fealty, obeisance, genuflection, kneeling, prostration; obsequiousness &c. 886; salaam, kotow or kowtow [*Chinese*], bow, presenting arms, salute.

RESPECTS, regards, duty, *devoirs* [F.], *égards* [F.].

devotion &c. (*piety*) 987.

V. RESPECT, regard; revere, reverence; hold in reverence, honor, venerate, hallow; esteem &c. (*approve of*) 931; think much of; entertain –, bear-respect for; look up to, defer to; have –, hold- a high opinion of; pay attention to, pay respect to &c. *n.;* do or render honor to; do the honors, hail; show courtesy &c. 894; salute, present arms.

do or pay homage to; pay tribute to, kneel to, bow to, bend the knee to; fall down before, prostrate oneself, kiss the hem of one's garment; worship &c. 990.

keep one's distance, make room, observe due decorum, stand upon ceremony.

COMMAND RESPECT, inspire respect; awe, impose, overawe, dazzle.

Adj. RESPECTING &c. *v.;* respectful, deferential, decorous, reverential, obsequious, ceremonious, bareheaded, cap in hand, on one's knees; prostrate &c. (*servile*) 886.

RESPECTED &c. *v.;* in high -esteem; - estimation; time-honored, venerable, *emeritus* [L.].

Adv. IN DEFERENCE TO; with all respect, with due respect, with the highest respect; with submission.

excusing the liberty; saving your -grace, – presence; *salva sit reverentia* [L.]; *pace tanti nominis* [L.].

929. Disrespect. — N. DISRESPECT, disesteem, disestimation; disfavor, disrepute, want of esteem, low estimation, disparagement &c. (*dispraise*) 932, (*detraction*) 934; irreverence; slight, neglect; *spretæ injuria formæ* [Vergil], superciliousness &c. (*contempt*) 930.

indignity, vilipendency [*obs.*], contumely, affront, dishonor, insult, outrage, discourtesy &c. 895; practical joking; scurrility, scoffing; sibilation, hiss, hissing, hoot, irrision [*rare*], derision; mockery; irony &c. (*ridicule*) 856; sarcasm.

GIBE or jibe, flout, jeer, scoff, gleek [*obs.*], fleer, taunt, sneer, quip, fling, twit, wipe [*dial. or slang*], slap in the face.

V. TREAT WITH DISRESPECT &c. *n.;* hold in disrespect &c. (*despise*) 930; misprize, disregard, slight, undervalue, humiliate, depreciate, trifle with, set at naught, pass by, push aside, overlook, turn one's back upon, laugh in one's sleeve; be disrespectful &c. *adj.;* be discourteous &c. 895; set down, browbeat.

dishonor, desecrate; insult, affront, outrage.

speak slightingly of; disparage &c. (*dispraise*) 932; vilipend, call names; throw –, fling- dirt; throw mud at; make ride the rail, drag through the mud, point at, indulge in personalities; make mouths [*archaic*], make faces; bite the thumb; take –, pluck- by the beard; toss in a blanket, tar and feather.

DERIDE, have or hold in derision; scoff, barrack [*dial. Eng. & Austral.*], sneer, laugh at, snigger, ridicule, gibe or jibe, mock, jeer, taunt, twit, niggle, gleek [*obs.*], gird, flout, fleer; roast [*colloq.*], guy [*colloq.*], rag [*dial. Eng. & college slang*], smoke [*old slang*]; turn into ridicule; burlesque &c. 856; laugh to scorn &c.

Int. hail! all hail! *hoch!* [*Ger.*]; *esto perpetua!* [*L.*], may your shadow never be less!

⁎ "and pluck up drowned honor by the locks" [*I Henry IV*]; "honor pricks me on" [*ibid.*]; "his honor rooted in dishonor stood" [Tennyson].

(*contempt*) 930; lead one a dance, have a fling at, scout, hiss, hoot, mob.

fool; make game of, make a fool of, make an April fool of; play a practical joke.

Adj. DISRESPECTFUL; aweless, irreverent; disparaging &c. 934; insulting &c. *v.;* supercilious &c. (*scornful*) 930; rude, derisive, sarcastic; scurrile, scurrilous, contumelious, contemptuous, insolent, disdainful.

UNRESPECTED, unworshiped, unenvied, unsaluted; unregarded, disregarded.

Adv. DISRESPECTFULLY &c. *adj.*

⁎ "old friends pass me as if I were a wall" [Galsworthy].

930. Contempt. — N. CONTEMPT, disdain, scorn, sovereign contempt; despisal [*rare*], despiciency [*obs.*], despisement [*rare*]; vilipendency [*obs.*], contumely; slight, sneer, spurn, byword; despect [*rare*].

contemptuousness &c. *adj.;* scornful eye; smile of contempt; derision &c. (*disrespect*) 929.

[STATE OF BEING DESPISED] despisedness.

V. DESPISE, contemn, scorn, disdain, feel contempt for, view with a scornful eye; disregard, slight, not mind; pass by &c. (*neglect*) 460; look down upon; hold -cheap, – in contempt, – in disrespect; think nothing of, think small beer of [*colloq.*]; make light of; underestimate &c. 483; esteem slightly, esteem of small or no account; take no account of, care nothing for; set no store by; not care a straw &c. (*unimportance*) 643; set at naught, laugh in one's sleeve, snap one's fingers at, shrug one's shoulders, turn up one's nose at, pooh-pooh, "damn with faint praise" [Pope].

sneeze at, whistle at, sneer at; curl up one's lip, toss the head, *traiter de haut en bas* [*F.*]; laugh at &c. (*be disrespectful*) 929; point the finger of –, hold up to –, laugh to- scorn; scout, hoot, flout, hiss, scoff at.

SPURN, turn one's back upon, turn a cold shoulder upon; tread –, trample- -upon, – under foot; kick; fling to the winds &c. (*repudiate*) 610; send away with a flea in the ear [*colloq.*].

Adj. CONTEMPTUOUS, disdainful, scornful, withering, contumelious, supercilious, cynical, haughty, cavalier; derisive; with the nose in air, *de haut en bas* [*F.*].

CONTEMPTIBLE, despicable; pitiable; pitiful &c. (*unimportant*) 643; despised &c. *v.;* downtrodden; unenvied.

Adv. CONTEMPTUOUSLY &c. *adj.*

Int. a fig for &c. (*unimportant*) 643; bah! pooh! pshaw! never mind! away with! hang it! fiddledeedee!

⁎ "a dismal universal hiss, the sound of public scorn" [*Paradise Lost*]; "I had rather be a dog and bay the moon than such a Roman" [*Julius Cæsar*]; "as if I was next door's dog" [Shaw]; "This is my private hell" [Galsworthy]; "there are many men who feel a kind of twisted pride in cynicism" [Roosevelt].

931. Approbation. — N. APPROBATION, approval, approvement [*obs.*], bepraisement, sanction, advocacy; nod of approbation; esteem, estimation, good opinion, golden opinions, admiration; love &c. 897; appreciation, regard, account, popularity, *kudos* [*Gr.* κῦδος], credit; repute &c. 873.

commendation, praise, laud, laudation; good word; meed –, tribute- of praise; encomium, eulogy, eulogium, *éloge* [*F.*], panegyric, blurb [*slang*];

932. Disapprobation. — N. DISAPPROBATION, disapproval, improbation [*obs.*], disesteem, displacency [*rare*]; odium; dislike &c. 867; black list, blackball, ostracism, boycott; index expurgatorius.

DISPARAGEMENT, depreciation, disvaluation, dispraise, discommendation; detraction &c. 934; denunciation; condemnation &c. 971; animadversion, reflection, stricture, objection, exception, criticism; blame, censure, obloquy; sar-

homage, hero worship; benediction, blessing, benison.

APPLAUSE, plaudit, clap; clapping, – of hands; acclaim, acclamation; cheer; pæan, hosanna; shout –, peal –, chorus –, thunders- of -applause &c.; prytaneum.

WINNER, prize winner, best seller, corker [slang], peach [slang], oner [slang], the real thing [colloq.], the goods [slang].

V. APPROVE, approbate,[1] think good of, think much of, think well of, think highly of; esteem, value, prize; set great store by.

honor, hold in esteem, look up to, admire; like &c. 897; be in favor of, wish Godspeed; hail, hail with satisfaction, do justice to, appreciate.

stand up for, stick up for [colloq.], uphold, hold up, countenance, sanction; clap –, pat- on the back; keep in countenance, indorse or endorse; give credit, recommend; mark with a white -mark, - stone.

COMMEND, belaud, praise, laud, compliment, pay a tribute, bepraise; clap, – the hands; applaud, cheer, acclaim, acclamate [rare], encore; panegyrize, eulogize, boost [colloq., U. S.], root for [slang, U. S.], cry up, prôner [F.], puff; extol, – to the skies; magnify, glorify, exalt, swell, make much of; flatter &c. 933; bless, give a blessing to; have –, say- a good word for; speak -well, – highly, – in high terms- of; sing –, sound –, chant –, resound- the praises of; sing praises to; cheer –, applaud- to the -echo, – very echo.

redound to the -honor, – praise, – credit- of; do credit to; deserve -praise &c. n.; recommend itself; pass muster.

BE PRAISED &c.; receive honorable mention; be in favor with, be in high favor with; ring with the praises of, win golden opinions, gain credit, find favor with, stand well in the opinion of; laudari a laudato viro [L.].

Adj. APPROVING &c. v.; in favor of; lost in admiration; commendatory, complimentary, benedictory, laudatory, panegyrical, eulogistic, encomiastic, acclamatory, lavish of praise, uncritical.

APPROVED, praised &c. v.; uncensured, unimpeached; popular, in good odor; in high esteem &c. (respected) 928; in favor, in high favor.

donic -grin, – laugh; sarcasm, satire, insinuation, innuendo; bad –, poor –, left-handed- compliment.

sneer &c. (contempt) 930; taunt &c. (disrespect) 929; cavil, carping, censoriousness; hypercriticism &c. (fastidiousness) 868.

REPREHENSION, remonstrance, expostulation, reproof, reprobation, admonition, increpation [archaic], reproach; rebuke, reprimand, castigation, jobation [colloq.], lecture, curtain lecture, blowup [colloq.]; blowing up, trimming, wigging, dressing, dressing down [all colloq.]; rating, scolding, correction, set down, rap on the knuckles, coup de bec [F.], rebuff; slap, slap oɴ the face; home thrust, hit; frown, scowl, black look.

diatribe, jeremiad or jeremiade, tirade, philippic.

chiding, upbraiding &c. v.; exprobration [rare], personal remarks, abuse, vituperation, invective, objurgation, contumely; hard –, cutting –, bitter-words; evil-speaking; bad language &c. 908; personality.

CLAMOR, outcry, hue and cry; hiss, hissing, sibilation, catcall; execration &c. 908.

V. DISAPPROVE; dislike &c. 867; lament &c. 839; object to, take exception to; be scandalized at, think ill of; view with -disfavor, – dark eyes, – jaundiced eyes; nil admirari [L.], disvalue, improbate [obs.].

frown upon, look grave; bend –, knit-the brows; shake the head at, shrug the shoulders; turn up the nose &c. (contempt) 930; look askance, look black upon; look with an evil eye; make a wry face at, make a mouth at [archaic], set one's face against.

BLAME; lay –, cast- blame upon; censure, fronder [F.], reproach, pass censure on, reprobate, impugn, impeach; disbar, unfrock.

accuse &c. 938; impeach, denounce; hold up to -reprobation, – execration; expose, brand, gibbet, stigmatize; show up, pull up [both colloq.]; take up; cry "shame" upon; be outspoken; raise a hue and cry against.

REPREHEND, chide, admonish; berate, betongue; bring –, call- -to account, – over the coals [colloq.], – to order; take

---

[1] Obsolete in England except in legal writings, but surviving in the United States chiefly in a technical sense for license. C. O. S. M.

PRAISEWORTHY, commendable, of estimation; deserving -, worthy of-praise &c. *n.*; good &c. 648; meritorious, estimable, creditable, unimpeachable; beyond all praise.

Adv. COMMENDABLY, with credit, to admiration; well &c. 618; with three times three.

Int. hear hear! good for you! do it again! bully for you! [*slang*], well done! fine! bravo! *bravissimo!* [*It.*], *euge!* [*Gr. & L.*], *macte virtute!* [*L.*], so far so good! that's right! quite right! one cheer more! may your shadow never be less! *esto perpetua!* [*L.*], long life to! *viva!* [*It.*], *evviva!* [*It.*], Godspeed! *valete et plaudite!* [*L.*], *encore!* [*F.*], *bis!* [*L. & F.*].

⁎ *probatum est; tacent satis laudant;* "servant of God, well done!" [*Paradise Lost*]; "I have bought Golden opinions from all sorts of people" [*Macbeth*]; "How his silence drinks up this applause!" [*Troilus and Cressida*]; "we are the Jasons, we have won the fleece" [*M. of V.*]; "O well done! I commend your pains" [*Macbeth*]; "right noble is thy merit" [*Richard II*].

to task, haul over the coals [*colloq.*], reprove, lecture, bring to book; read a -lesson, - lecture- to; rebuke, correct; reprimand, chastise, castigate, lash, trounce; trim, blow up, give it to, give one fits, give it to one, lay out [*all si₂ colloq.*]; *laver la tête* [*F.*], overhaul.

remonstrate, expostulate, recriminate.

execrate &c. 908; exprobate [*rare*], speak daggers, vituperate; abuse, - like a pickpocket; tongue-lash [*colloq.*], scold, rate, objurgate, upbraid, fall foul of; jaw [*low*]; rail, - at, - in good set terms; bark at, yelp at, anathematize, call names; call by -hard, - ugly- names; avile [*obs.*], revile, vilify, vilipend, bespatter; clapperclaw [*archaic*]; rave -, thunder -, fulminate- against; load with reproaches.

DECRY, cry down, run down, frown down; exclaim -, protest -, inveigh -, declaim -, cry out -, raise one's voice-against; clamor, hiss, hoot, catcall, mob; backbite; ostracize, blacklist, boycott, blackball; draw up -, sign- a round robin.

take down, set down; snub, snap one up, give a rap on the knuckles; throw a stone -at, - in one's garden; have a fling at, have a snap at; have words with, pluck a crow with; give one a wipe [*dial. or slang*]; give one a lick with the rough side of the tongue [*colloq.*].

animadvert upon, reflect upon; glance at; cast -reflection, - reproach - a slur-upon; insinuate, "damn with faint praise" [Pope]; "hint a fault and hesitate dislike" [Pope]; not to be able to say much for.

DISPARAGE, depreciate, knock [*colloq., U. S.*], dispraise, discommend [*rare*], deprecate, speak ill of, not speak well of; condemn &c. (*find guilty*) 971; scoff at, point at; twit, taunt &c. (*disrespect*) 929; sneer at &c. (*despise*) 230; satirize. lampoon; defame &c. (*detract*) 934; depreciate, find fault with, criticize, cut up; pull -, pick- to pieces; take exception; cavil; peck at, nibble at, carp at; be censorious &c. *adj.*; pick -holes, - a hole, - a hole in one's coat; make a fuss about.

INCUR BLAME, excite disapprobation, scandalize, shock, revolt; get a bad name, forfeit one's good opinion, be under a cloud, come under the ferule, bring a hornet's nest about one's ears.

take blame, stand corrected; have to answer for.

Adj. DISAPPROVING &c. *v.*; disparaging, condemnatory, damnatory, denunciatory, reproachful, abusive, objurgatory, clamorous, vituperative; defamatory &c. 934.

satirical, sarcastic, sardonic, cynical, dry, sharp, cutting, biting, severe, withering, trenchant, hard upon; censorious, critical, captious, carping, hypercritical; scandalized; fastidious &c. 868; sparing of -, grudging -praise.

DISAPPROVED, chid &c. *v.*; in bad odor, blown upon, unapproved; unblest; at a discount, exploded; weighed in the balance and found wanting.

unlamented, unbewailed, unpitied.

BLAMEWORTHY, reprehensible &c. (*guilt*) 947; to -, worthy of- blame; answerable, uncommendable, exceptionable, not to be thought of; bad &c. 649; vicious &c. 945.

Adv. REPROACHFULLY &c. *adj.*; with a wry face.

Int. it is too bad! it won't do! it will never do! it isn't done! marry come up! [*archaic or dial.*], Oh! come! 'sdeath! [*archaic*].

forbid it Heaven! God forbid! Heaven forbid! out upon it! fie upon it! away with! tut! *O tempora! O mores!* [*L.*]; shame! fie, – for shame! out on you!

tell it not in Gath!

.*. "The poorest way to face life is to face it with a sneer" [Roosevelt]; "defamed by every charlatan" [Tennyson]; "willing to wound, and yet afraid to strike" [Pope]; "Compound for sins they are inclined to By damning those they have no mind to" [Butler]; "Of whom to be disprais'd were no small praise" [Milton]; "Censure is the tax a man pays to the public for being eminent" [Swift]; "There is no defense against reproach except obscurity" [Addison].

---

933. Flattery. — N. FLATTERY, adulation, gloze [*rare*]; blandishment [*rare*], blandiloquence; cajolery; fawning, wheedling &c. *v.*; captation, coquetry, obsequiousness, sycophancy, flunkeyism, toadyism, toadeating, tufthunting; snobbishness.

incense, honeyed words, flummery, buncombe *or* bunkum [*cant or slang*]; blarney, butter, soft soap, soft sawder [*all colloq.*]; rose water.

voice of the charmer, mouth honor; lip homage; euphemism; unctuousness &c. *adj.*

V. FLATTER, praise to the skies, puff; wheedle, cajole, glaver [*obs. or dial.*], coax; fawn, – upon; humor, gloze [*now rare*], soothe, pet, coquet, slaver, butter [*colloq.*], jolly [*slang or colloq.*]; bespatter, beslubber, beplaster, beslaver; lay it on thick, overpraise; cog [*obs.*], collogue [*obs. in this sense*]; truckle to, pander *or* pandar to, pay court to; court; creep into the good graces of, curry favor with, hang on the sleeve of; fool to the top of one's bent; lick the dust.

lay the flattering unction to one's soul, gild the pill, make things pleasant.

overestimate &c. 482; exaggerate &c. 549.

Adj. FLATTERING &c. *v.*; adulatory; mealy-mouthed, honey-mouthed, honeyed, smooth, smooth-tongued; soapy [*slang*], oily, unctuous, blandiloquous, specious; fine-, fair- spoken; plausible, servile, sycophantic, fulsome; courtierly, courtierlike.

Adv. ad captandum.

.*. "for ne'er Was flattery lost on Poet's ear" [Scott]; "Lay not that flattering unction to your soul" [*Hamlet*]; "Flatter and praise, commend, extol their graces" [*Two Gentlemen*]; "Our praises are our wages" [*Winter's Tale*]; "The sweeter sound of woman's praise" [Macaulay]; "And wrinkles, the d——d democrats, won't flatter" [Byron].

934. Detraction. — N. DETRACTION, disparagement, depreciation, vilification, obloquy, scurrility, scandal, defamation, aspersion, traducement [*rare*], slander, calumny, obtrectation [*obs.*], evil-speaking, backbiting, *scandalum magnatum* [*L.*].

sarcasm, cynicism; criticism (*disapprobation*) 932; invective &c. 932; envenomed tongue; *spretæ injuria formæ* [*L.*].

PERSONALITY, libel, lampoon, skit [*Scot. & dial.*], squib, pasquil, pasquinade; *chronique scandaleuse* [*F.*], roorback [*U. S.*].

DETRACTOR &c. 936.

V. DETRACT, derogate, decry, depreciate, disparage; run down, cry down; back-cap [*U. S.*]; belittle; pessimize; sneer at &c. (*contemn*) 930; criticize, pull to pieces, pick a hole in one's coat, asperse, cast aspersions, blow upon, bespatter, blacken, vilify, vilipend, avile [*obs.*]; give a dog a bad name, brand, malign; backbite, libel, lampoon, traduce, slander, defame, calumniate, bear false witness against; speak ill of behind one's back.

muckrake; fling dirt &c. (*disrespect*) 929; anathematize &c. 932; dip the pen in gall, view in a bad light.

Adj. DETRACTING &c. *v.*; defamatory, traducent [*rare*], detractory, derogatory, disparaging, libelous; scurrile, scurrilous, abusive; foul-spoken, foul-tongued, foul-mouthed; slanderous, calumnious, calumniatory; sarcastic, sardonic, satirical, cynical.

.*. "Damn with faint praise, assent with civil leer; And without sneering, teach the rest to sneer" [Pope]; another lie nailed to the counter; "cut men's throats with whisperings" [B. Jonson]; "foul whisperings are abroad" [*Macbeth*]; "soft-buzzing slander" [Thomson]; "virtue itself 'scapes not calumnious strokes" [*Hamlet*]; "ill-will never said well" [*Henry V*].

935. Flatterer. — N. FLATTERER, adulator, eulogist, euphemist; optimist, encomiast, laudator, booster [*colloq.*, *U. S.*], whitewasher.

toady, toadeater, sycophant, courtier, flattercap [*obs. or dial. Eng.*], pickthank [*archaic or dial.*], Damocles, Sir Pertinax MacSycophant; *flatteur* [*F.*], *prôneur* [*F.*]; puffer, *claqueur* [*F.*], claquer; tout, touter [*both colloq.*], claw-back [*obs. or dial. Eng.*], slaverer; doer of dirty work; parasite, hanger-on &c. (*servility*) 886.

Adj. flattering &c. 933.

₊ *pessimum genus inimicorum laudantes* [Tacitus]; "But when I tell him he hates flatterers, He says he does, being then most flattered" [*Julius Cæsar*].

936. Detractor. — N. DETRACTOR, reprover; censor, censurer; cynic, critic, caviler, carper, word-catcher, *frondeur* [*F.*], barracker [*dial. Eng. & Austral.*].

defamer, knocker [*colloq., U. S.*], backbiter, slanderer, Sir Benjamin Backbite, lampooner, satirist, traducer, libeler, calumniator, dearest foe, Thersites; Zoilus; good-natured friend [*satirical*]; reviler, vituperator, castigator; shrew &c. 901; muckraker.

DISAPPROVER, *laudator temporis acti* [Horace].

Adj. black-mouthed, abusive &c. 934.

₊ "You know who the critics are? — the men who have failed in literature and art" [Disraeli]; "Oh, you chorus of indolent reviewers!" [Tennyson].

937. Vindication. — N. VINDICATION, justification, warrant; exoneration, exculpation, disculpation; acquittal &c. 970; whitewashing.

EXTENUATION, palliation, palliative, softening, mitigation.

PLEA &c. 617; apology, gloss, varnish; salvo [*rare*], excuse, extenuating circumstances; allowance, – to be made; *locus pœnitentiæ* [*L.*]; reply, defense *or* defence; recrimination &c. 938.

APOLOGIST, vindicator, justifier; defendant &c. 938.

TRUE BILL, justifiable charge.

V. JUSTIFY, warrant; be an excuse for &c. *n.;* lend a color, furnish a handle; vindicate, exculpate, disculpate [*rare*]; acquit &c. 970; clear, set right, exonerate, whitewash; clear the skirts of.

EXTENUATE, palliate, excuse, soften, apologize, varnish, slur, gloze; put a -gloss, – good face- upon; mince; gloss over, bolster up, help a lame dog over a stile.

ADVOCATE, defend, plead one's cause; stand up for, stick up for [*colloq.*], speak up for; contend for, speak for; bear out, keep in countenance, support; plead &c. 617; say in defense; plead ignorance; confess and avoid, propugn [*obs.*], put in a good word for.

take the will for the deed, make allowance for, do justice to; give one his due, give the Devil his due.

make good; prove the truth of, prove one's case; be justified by the event.

Adj. VINDICATIVE, vindicatory, vindicated, vindicating &c. *v.;* palliative;

938. Accusation. — N. ACCUSATION, charge, imputation, slur, inculpation, exprobration [*rare*], delation; crimination, incrimination, accrimination [*obs.*], recrimination; *tu quoque* argument; invective &c. 932.

denunciation, denouncement [*archaic*]; libel, challenge, citation, arraignment, impeachment, appeachment [*obs.*], indictment, bill of indictment, true bill; lawsuit &c. 969; condemnation &c. 971.

gravamen of a charge, head and front of one's offending, *argumentum ad hominem* [*L.*]; scandal &c. (*detraction*) 934; *scandalum magnatum* [*L.*].

ACCUSER, prosecutor, plaintiff, complainant, libelant, delator, informant, informer.

ACCUSED, defendant, prisoner, respondent, corespondent; litigant; panel.

V. ACCUSE, charge, tax, impute, twit, taunt with, reproach; brand with reproach; stigmatize, slur; cast a stone at, cast a slur on; criminate, incriminate, inculpate, implicate; call to account &c. (*censure*) 932; take to -blame, – task; put in the black book.

inform against, indict, denounce, arraign; impeach, appeach [*obs.*]; have up, show up [*colloq.*], pull up [*colloq.*]; challenge, cite, lodge a complaint; prosecute, bring an action against &c. 969; blow upon [*colloq.*], squeal [*slang*].

charge with, saddle with; lay to one's -door, – charge; lay the blame on, bring home to; cast -, throw- in one's teeth; cast the first stone at.

exculpatory, disculpatory, apologetic.

EXCUSABLE, defensible, pardonable; venial, veniable [obs.]; specious, plausible, justifiable.

₊ "honi soit qui mal y pense"; "good wine needs no bush" [As You Like It]; "The lady doth protest too much, methinks" [Hamlet]; "apologies only account for that which they do not alter" [Disraeli].

[slang], in stir [slang], in the house of detention.

ACCUSABLE, imputable, indefensible, inexcusable, unpardonable, unjustifiable; vicious &c. 845.

Int. look at home! tu quoque [L.] &c. (retaliation) 718.

₊ qui s'excuse s'accuse; "the breath of accusation kills an innocent name" [Shelley]; "thou canst not say I did it" [Macbeth].

have –, keep- a rod in pickle for; have a crow to pluck with.

trump up a charge.

Adj. ACCUSING &c. v.; accusatory, accusative, imputative, denunciatory, recriminatory, criminatory.

ACCUSED &c. v.; suspected; under -suspicion, – a cloud, – surveillance.

IN CUSTODY, in detention, in the lock-up, in the watch-house, in the jug

3. MORAL CONDITIONS

939. Probity. — N. PROBITY, integrity, rectitude; uprightness &c. adj.; honesty, faith; honor; bonne foi [F.], good faith, bona fides [L.]; purity, grace; clean hands.

constancy; faithfulness &c. adj.; fidelity, loyalty, incorruption [archaic], incorruptibility; trustworthiness &c. adj.; truth, candor, singleness of heart; veracity &c. 543; tender conscience &c. (sense of duty) 926.

fairness &c. adj.; fair play, justice, equity, impartiality, principle.

court of honor, a fair field and no favor; argumentum ad verecundiam [L.].

PUNCTILIOUSNESS, punctilio, delicacy, nicety, scrupulosity, scrupulousness &c. adj.; scruple; point, – of honor; punctuality [rare in this sense].

dignity &c. (repute) 873; respectability, respectableness &c. adj.

MAN OF HONOR, man of his word, gentleman, gentilhomme [F.], fidus Achates [L.], preux chevalier [F.], galantuomo [It.]; true-penny, trump [slang], brick [slang or colloq.], true Briton; white man [slang, U. S.].

V. BE HONORABLE &c. adj.; deal -honorably, – squarely, – impartially, – fairly; speak the truth &c. (veracity) 543; draw a straight furrow; tell the truth and shame the Devil, vitam impendere vero [L.]; show a proper spirit, make a point of; do one's duty &c. (virtue) 944; play the game [colloq.].

redeem one's pledge &c. 926; keep –, be as good as- one's -promise, – word; keep faith with, not fail.

940. Improbity. — N. IMPROBITY, dishonesty, dishonor; deviation from rectitude; disgrace &c. (disrepute) 874; fraud &c. (deception) 545; lying &c. 544; mouth honor &c. (flattery) 933; bad faith, mala fides [L.], Punic faith, Punica fides [L.]; infidelity; faithlessness &c. adj.; Judas kiss, betrayal; perfidy; perfidiousness &c. adj.; treachery, double dealing; unfairness &c. adj.

breach of -promise, – trust, – faith; prodition [obs.], disloyalty, divided allegiance, hyphenated allegiance [cant], treason, high treason; apostacy &c. (tergiversation) 607; nonobservance &c. 773.

shabbiness &c. adj.; villainy; baseness &c. adj.; abjection, debasement, degradation, turpitude, moral turpitude, laxity, trimming, shuffling.

KNAVERY, roguery, rascality, foulplay; jobbing, jobbery, graft [colloq.], venality, nepotism; corruption, job, shuffle, fishy transaction; barratry [law], sharp practice, heads I win tails you lose.

V. BE DISHONEST &c. adj.; play false; break one's -word, – faith, – promise; jilt, betray, forswear; shuffle &c. (lie) 544; play with marked cards, cheat at cards, live by one's wits, sail near the wind.

disgrace –, dishonor –, lower –, demean [colloq.] –, degrade- oneself; derogate, stoop, grovel, sneak, lose caste; sell oneself, squeal [slang], go back on [colloq.], go over to the enemy; seal one's infamy.

give and take, *audire alteram partem*
[*L.*], give the Devil his due, put the
saddle on the right horse.

redound to one's honor.

Adj. UPRIGHT; honest, – as daylight;
veracious &c. 543; virtuous &c. 944;
noble, honorable, reputable, respectable; fair, right, just, equitable, impartial, evenhanded, square; fair –, open-
and aboveboard; white [*slang*, *U. S.*].

inviolable, inviolate, unviolated, unbroken, unbetrayed; unbought, unbribed.

constant, – as the northern star; faithful, loyal, staunch; true, – blue, – to
one's colors, – to the core, – as the
needle to the pole; "marble-constant"
[*Antony and Cleopatra*]; true-hearted,
trusty, trustworthy; as good as one's
word, to be depended on, incorruptible,
honest as the day.

manly, straightforward &c. (*ingenuous*) 703; frank, candid, open-hearted.

CONSCIENTIOUS, tender-conscienced,
right-minded, high-principled, high-
minded, scrupulous, religious, strict;
nice, punctilious, overscrupulous, correct, punctual.

STAINLESS, unstained, untarnished,
unsullied, untainted, unperjured, uncor-
rupt, uncorrupted; innocent &c. 946;
pure, undefiled, undepraved, unde-
bauched; *integer vitæ scelerisque purus*
[*Horace*]; *justus et tenax propositi*
[*Horace*]; supramundane, unworldly.

chivalrous, jealous of honor, *sans peur
et sans reproche* [*F.*]; high-spirited.

Adv. HONORABLY &c. *adj.; bonâ fide*
[*L.*]; on the square [*colloq.*], in good
faith, in all honor, by fair means, *foro
conscientiæ* [*L.*], with clean hands.

Int. on my honor! honor bright! [*colloq.*]; by my faith!

⁎ "a face untaught to feign" [Pope]; *bene qui latuit bene vixit* [Ovid]; *mens sibi conscia
recti; probitas laudatur et alget* [Juvenal]; *fidelis ad urnam;* "his heart as far from fraud as heaven
from earth" [*Two Gentlemen*]; *loyauté m'oblige; loyauté n'a honte;* "what stronger breastplate than
a heart untainted?" [*Henry VI*]; "among the faithless, faithful only he" [Milton].

Adj. DISHONEST, dishonorable; uncon-
scientious, unscrupulous; fraudulent &c.
545; knavish; disgraceful &c. (*disreputable*) 974; wicked &c. 945.

false-hearted, disingenuous; unfair,
one-sided; double, double-hearted,
double-tongued, double-faced; timeserving, crooked, tortuous, insidious,
Machiavellian, dark, slippery; fishy
[*colloq.*], questionable.

INFAMOUS, arrant, foul, base, vile,
low, ignominious, blackguard, perfidious,
treacherous, perjured; hyphenated
[*cant*].

contemptible, abject, mean, shabby,
little, paltry, dirty, scurvy, scabby,
sneaking, groveling, scrubby, rascally,
barratrous [*law*], pettifogging; corrupt,
venal; debased, mongrel; beneath one.

low-minded, low-thoughted, base-
minded.

DEROGATORY, degrading, undignified,
indign [*obs.*], unbecoming, unbeseeming, unbefitting, *infra dignitatem* [*L.*],
ungentlemanly, ungentlemanlike; unknightly, unchivalric, unmanly, unhand-
some; recreant, inglorious.

FAITHLESS, of bad faith, false, unfaithful, disloyal; untrustworthy; trustless,
trothless [*archaic*], lost to shame, dead
to honor.

Adv. DISHONESTLY &c. *adj.; malâ fide*
[*L.*]; like a thief in the night, by crooked
paths, by foul means.

Int. *O tempora! O mores!* [Cicero].

⁎ *corruptissimâ republicâ plurimæ leges*
[Tacitus], "And seem a saint, when most I
play the devil" [*Richard III*]; "Crooked
counsels and dark politics" [Pope]; "Honor is
without profit — in most countries" [*Cynic's
Calendar*].

---

941. Knave. — N. KNAVE, rogue, villain; Scapin, rascal; Lazarillo de Tormes;
bad man &c. 949; blackguard &c. 949; barrator *or* barrater [*law*], shyster [*U. S.*].

TRAITOR, betrayer, archtraitor, conspirator, Judas, Catiline; reptile, serpent, snake
in the grass, wolf in sheep's clothing, sneak, Jerry Sneak, squealer [*slang*], telltale,
mischief-maker; trimmer, renegade &c. (*tergiversation*) 607; truant, recreant,
slacker; sycophant &. (*servility*) 886.

⁎ "O villain, villain, smiling, damned villain" [*Hamlet*]; "Thou little valiant, great in villainy!" [*King John*]; "he's been true to *one* party, and that is himself" [Lowell]; "Just for a
handful of silver he left us, Just for a riband to stick in his coat" [Browning]; "His honor rooted
in dishonor stood, And faith unfaithful left him falsely true" [Tennyson].

942. Disinterestedness. — N. DIS-INTERESTEDNESS &c. *adj.;* generosity; liberality, liberalism; altruism; benevolence &c. 906; elevation, loftiness of purpose, exaltation, magnanimity; chivalry, chivalrous spirit, heroism, sublimity.

SELF-DENIAL, self-abnegation, self-sacrifice, self-devotion, self-immolation, self-control &c. (*resolution*) 604; stoicism, devotion; martyrdom, suttee.

labor of love.

[COMPARISONS] Good Shepherd, Good Samaritan, Bishop Bienvenu [Victor Hugo], Great Heart.

V. BE DISINTERESTED &c. *adj.;* make a sacrifice, lay one's head on the block; put oneself in the place of others, do as one would be done by, do unto others as we would men should do unto us.

Adj. DISINTERESTED, unselfish, self-denying, self-sacrificing, self-devotional.

MAGNANIMOUS, noble-minded, high-minded; princely, handsome, great, high, elevated, lofty, exalted, spirited, stoical, great-hearted, large-hearted; generous, liberal; chivalrous, heroic, sublime.

unbought, unbribed; uncorrupted &c. (*upright*) 939.

⁎ *non vobis solum;* "Earth changes, but thy soul and God stand sure" [Browning]; "A courage terrible to see, And mercy for his enemy" [Masefield]; "Love took up the harp of Life, and smote on all the chords with might; Smote the chord of Self, that, trembling, pass'd in music out of sight" [Tennyson].

943. Selfishness. — N. SELFISHNESS &c. *adj.;* self-love, self-indulgence, self-worship, self-seeking, self-interest; egotism, egoism; *amour propre* [*F.*] &c. (*vanity*) 880; nepotism; charity that begins at home.

worldliness &c. *adj.;* world wisdom. illiberality; meanness &c. *adj.*

SELF-SEEKER, timeserver, time-pleaser, tuft-hunter, fortune hunter; jobber, worldling; egotist, egoist, monopolist, nepotist; dog in the manger, *canis in præsepi* [*L.*], "foes to nobleness," temporizer, hyphenate [*cant*], trimmer; hog, road-hog, end-seat hog [*colloq.*].

V. BE SELFISH &c. *adj.;* please -, indulge -, pamper -, coddle- oneself; consult one's own -wishes, - pleasure; look after one's own interest; feather one's nest; take care of number one, have an eye to the main chance, know on which side one's bread is buttered; give an inch and take an ell.

Adj. SELFISH, self-seeking, self-indulgent, self-interested; wrapt up in self, centered in self; egotistic *or* egotistical, egoistic *or* egoistical.

ILLIBERAL, mean, ungenerous, narrow-minded; mercenary, venal; covetous &c. 819.

WORLDLY, unspiritual, earthly, earthly -minded, mundane, worldly-minded, worldly-wise; timeserving.

interested; *alieni appetens sui profusus* [Sallust].

Adv. UNGENEROUSLY &c. *adj.;* to gain some private ends, from selfish motives, from interested motives.

⁎ *après nous le déluge;* "the fine Felicity and flower of wickedness" [Browning]; "I to myself am dearer than a friend" [*Two Gentlemen*]; "The wretch, concentred all in self" [Scott].

944. Virtue. — N. VIRTUE; virtuousness &c. *adj.;* morality; moral rectitude; integrity &c. (*probity*) 939; nobleness &c. 873.

merit, worth, desert, excellence, credit; self-control &c. (*resolution*) 604; self-denial &c. (*temperance*) 953.

well-doing; good actions, good behavior; discharge -, fulfillment -, performance- of duty; well-spent life; innocence &c. 946.

morals; ethics &c. (*duty*) 926; cardinal virtues.

[SCIENCE OF VIRTUE] aretaics (*contrasted with* eudemonism); aretology.

V. BE VIRTUOUS &c. *adj.;* practice vir-

945. Vice. — N. VICE; evildoing, evil courses; wrongdoing; wickedness, viciousness &c. *adj.;* hardness of heart; iniquity, peccability, demerit; sin, Adam, old Adam, offending Adam.

immorality, impropriety, indecorum, scandal, laxity, looseness of morals; want of -principle - ballast; knavery, &c. (*improbity*) 940; atrocity, brutality &c. (*malevolence*) 907; obliquity, backsliding, infamy.

DEPRAVITY, demoralization, pravity, pollution; corruption &c. (*debasement*) 659; profligacy; flagrancy, unnatural desires, unnatural habits, Sadism, Lesbianism, sodomy; lust &c. 961.

tue &c. *n.*; do –, fulfill –, perform –, discharge- one's duty; redeem one's pledge &c. 926; act well, – one's part; fight the good fight; acquit oneself well; command –, master- one's passions; keep in the right path, keep on the straight and narrow way.

set an example, set a good example; be on one's -good, – best- behavior.

Adj. VIRTUOUS, good; innocent &c. 646; meritorious, deserving, worthy, desertful [*rare*], correct; dutiful, duteous; moral, right, righteous, right-minded; well-intentioned, creditable, laudable, commendable, praiseworthy; above praise, beyond all praise; excellent, admirable; sterling, pure, noble; whole-souled.

exemplary; matchless, peerless; saintly, saintlike; heaven-born, angelic, seraphic, godlike.

Adv. VIRTUOUSLY &c. *adj.*; *e merito* [*L.*].

∗∗ *esse quam videri bonus malebat* [Sallust]; *Schönheit vergeht Tugend besteht;* "virtue the greatest of all monarchies" [Swift]; *virtus laudatur et alget* [Juvenal]; *virtus vincit invidiam;* "every noble life leaves the fibre of it in the work of the world" [Ruskin]; "the nobleness That lovely spirits gather from distress" [Masefield]; "He had the russet-apple mind That betters as the weathers worsen" [*ibid.*]; "Virtue is not the absence of vices or the avoidance of moral dangers; virtue is a vivid and separate thing, like pain or a particular smell" [Chesterton].

lowest dregs of vice, sink of iniquity, Alsatian den; *gusto picaresco* [*L.*].

CANNIBALISM, endocannibalism, endophagy; exocannibalism, exophagy; "long pig" [*humorous*].

WEAKNESS &c. *adj.*; infirmity, weakness of the flesh, frailty, imperfection, error; weak side; foible; failing, failure; crying sin, besetting sin; defect, deficiency; cloven foot.

fault, crime; criminality &c. (*guilt*) 947.

REPROBATE; sinner &c. 949.

[RESORTS] brothel &c. 961; gambling house &c. 621; joint [*slang*], opium den.

V. BE VICIOUS &c. *adj.*; sin, commit sin, do amiss, err, transgress; misdemean –, forget –, misconduct- oneself; misdo [*rare*], misbehave; fall, lapse, slip, trip, offend, trespass; deviate from the -line of duty, – path of virtue &c. 944; take a wrong course, go astray; hug a sin, hug a fault; sow one's wild oats.

RENDER VICIOUS &c. *adj.*; demoralize, brutalize; corrupt &c. (*degrade*) 659.

Adj.[1] VICIOUS; sinful; sinning &c. *v.*; wicked, iniquitous, immoral, unrighteous, wrong, criminal; unprincipled, lawless, disorderly, dissolute, profligate, scampish; worthless, desertless [*rare*], disgraceful, recreant, disreputable; demoralizing, degrading.

miscreated, misbegotten; demoralized, corrupt, depraved; Sadistic, degenerate.

evil-minded, evil-disposed; ill-conditioned; malevolent &c. 907; heartless, graceless, shameless, virtueless, abandoned, lost to virtue; unconscionable; sunk –, lost –, deep –, steeped- in iniquity.

BASE, sinister, scurvy, foul, gross, vile, black, grave, facinorous [*obs.*], felonious, nefarious, shameful, scandalous, infamous, villainous, of a deep dye, heinous; flagrant, flagitious, atrocious, incarnate, accursed.

DIABOLIC *or* diabolical, Mephistophelian, satanic, hellish, infernal, stygian, fiendlike, hellborn, demoniacal, devilish, fiendish.

INCORRIGIBLE, irreclaimable, obdurate, reprobate, past praying for; culpable, reprehensible &c. (*guilty*) 947.

UNJUSTIFIABLE, indefensible, inexcusable, inexpiable, unpardonable, irremissible.

IMPROPER, unseemly, indecorous, indiscreet, *contra bonos mores* [*L.*], unworthy, blameworthy, reprehensible, uncommendable, discreditable; naughty, incorrect, unduteous, undutiful.

WEAK, frail, lax, infirm, imperfect; spineless, invertebrate [*both fig.*]; dotty [*slang*].

Adv. wrong; sinfully &c. *adj.*; without excuse.

Int. fie upon! it smells to heaven!

∗∗ *alitur vitium vivitque tegendo* [Vergil]; *genus est mortis male vivere* [Ovid]; *mala mens malus animus* [Terence]; *nemo repente fuit turpissimus;* "the trail of the serpent is over them all" [Moore]; "to sanction vice and hunt decorum down" [Byron]; "wild oats make a bad autumn crop" [*Cynic's Calendar*].

[1] Most of these adjectives are applicable both to the act and to the agent.

946. Innocence. — N. INNOCENCE; guiltlessness &c. *adj.;* incorruption, impeccability, inerrability, inerrableness.

clean hands, clear conscience, *mens sibi conscia recti* [Vergil].

INNOCENT, new-born babe; lamb, dove.

V. BE INNOCENT &c. *adj.; nil conscire sibi nullâ pallescere culpâ* [Horace].

ACQUIT &c. 970; exculpate &c. *(vindicate)* 937.

Adj. INNOCENT, not guilty; unguilty; guiltless, faultless, sinless, stainless, bloodless, spotless; clear, immaculate; *rectus in curiâ* [L.]; unspotted, unblemished, unerring; undefiled &c. 939; unhardened, Saturnian; Arcadian &c. *(artless)* 703; paradisaic *or* paradisaical, paradisiac *or* paradisiacal.

inculpable, unculpable [*rare*], unblamed, unblamable, blameless, unfallen, inerrable, above suspicion, irreproachable, irreprovable [*rare*], irreprehensible; unexceptionable, unobjectionable, unimpeachable; salvable; venial &c. 937.

virtuous &c. 944; unreproved, unimpeached, unreproached.

HARMLESS, inoffensive, innoxious [*obs.*], innocuous; dovelike, lamblike; pure, harmless as doves; innocent as -a lamb, - the babe unborn; "more sinned against than sinning" [*Lear*].

Adv. INNOCENTLY &c. *adj.;* with clean hands; with a -clear, - safe- conscience.

** murus aëneus conscientia sana [Horace]; "He's armed without that's innocent within" [Horace, *trans. by* Pope]; "plain and holy innocence" [*Tempest*].

947. Guilt. — N. GUILT, guiltiness, culpability, criminality, criminousness [*obs.*]; deviation from rectitude &c. *(improbity)* 940; sinfulness &c. *(vice)* 945; peccability.

misconduct, misbehavior, misdoing, misdeed; fault, sin, error, transgression; dereliction, delinquency.

INDISCRETION, lapse, slip, trip, *faux pas* [F.], peccadillo; flaw, blot, omission, failing, failure; blunder, break *or* bad break [*colloq., U. S.*].

OFFENSE, trespass; misdemeanor, tort [*law*], delict, *delictum* [L.]; misfeasance [*law*], misprision, misprision of treason *or* felony [*law*]; malfeasance [*law*], official misconduct, nonfeasance [*law*]; malefaction, malversation, corruption, malpractice; crime, felony, capital crime.

enormity, atrocity, outrage; unpardonable sin, deadly sin, mortal sin; "deed without a name" [*Macbeth*].

corpus delicti [L.], body of the crime, substantial facts, fundamental facts, damning evidence.

Adj. GUILTY, blamable, culpable, peccable, in fault, censurable, reprehensible; blameworthy.

OBJECTIONABLE, exceptionable, uncommendable, illaudable; weighed in the balance and found wanting.

Adv. IN THE VERY ACT, *in flagrante delicto* [L.], red-handed.

** cui prodest scelus is fecit [Seneca]; *culpam pœna premit comes* [Horace]; "O would the deed were good!" [*Richard II*]; "responsibility prevents crimes" [Burke]; *se judice nemo nocens absolvitur* [Juvenal]; "so many laws argues so many sins" [*Paradise Lost*].

948. Good Man. [GOOD WOMAN.] — **N.** GOOD MAN, worthy.

model, paragon &c. *(perfection)* 650; good example; hero, demigod, seraph, angel; saint &c. *(piety)* 987; benefactor &c. 912; philanthropist &c. 910; Aristides; noble liver, pattern.

salt of the earth; one in ten thousand; a man among men, white man [*slang*]; brick [*slang*], trump [*slang*], rough diamond.

GOOD WOMAN, virgin, innocent; goddess, queen, Madonna, ministering angel, heaven's noblest gift; "a perfect woman, nobly planned" [Wordsworth].

** si sic omnes! "how few Know their own good, or knowing it, pursue" [Dryden]; "How near to good is what is fair!" [Ben Jonson]; "Only the young die good" [*Cynic's Calendar*].

949. Bad Man. [BAD WOMAN.] — **N.** BAD MAN, wrongdoer, worker of iniquity; evildoer &c. 913; sinner, transgressor; the wicked &c. 945; bad example.

rascal, scoundrel, villain, miscreant, budmash [*India*], caitiff, wretch, reptile, viper, serpent, cockatrice, basilisk; tiger, monster; devil &c. *(demon)* 980; devil incarnate; demon in human shape, Nana Sahib; hellhound, rakehell.

roué [F.], rake; Sadist, one who has sold himself to the devil, fallen angel, *âme damnée* [F.], *vaurien* [F.], *mauvais sujet* [F.], loose fish [*colloq.*], rounder [*slang*]; lost sheep, black sheep; castaway, recreant, defaulter; prodigal &c. 818.

BAD WOMAN, jade, Jezebel, hell-cat, quean, wench, slut; adultress &c. 962.

ROUGH, rowdy, ugly customer, ruffian, bully, tough [colloq., U. S.], hoodlum &c. 886; Jonathan Wild; hangman; incendiary, fire bug [U. S.]; thief &c. 792; murderer &c. 361.

CULPRIT, delinquent, criminal, malefactor, misdemeanant; felon; convict, jail-bird or gaolbird, ticket-of-leave man [Brit.]; outlaw.

RIFFRAFF, scum of the earth; blackguard, polisson [F.], loafer, sneak, rascalion or rascallion; cullion, mean wretch, varlet [archaic], kern [obs.], âme-de-boue [F.], drôle [F.]; cur, dog, hound, whelp, mongrel; losel [archaic or dial.], loon or lown [obs. or dial. variant], ronion or ronyon or runnion [obs. or rare]; outcast, vagabond, runagate; rogue &c. (knave) 941.

SCAMP, scapegrace, rip [colloq.], ne'er-do-well, good for nothing, reprobate, scala-wag or scallawag [colloq.], skeesicks or skeesix [colloq., U. S.], sad dog [colloq.], limb [colloq.], rapscallion [all the words in this paragraph are commonly applied jocularly or lightly].

Int. sirrah!

₊ Acherontis pabulum; gibier de potence; "We have done with Hope and Honour, we are lost to Love and Truth, We are dropping down the ladder rung by rung" [Kipling]; "Our towns of wasted honour, Our streets of lost delight" [ibid.].

---

950. Penitence. — N.

PENITENCE, contrition, compunction, repentance, remorse; regret &c. 833.

self-reproach, self-reproof, self-accu-sation, self-condemnation, self-humilia-tion; stings -, pangs -, qualms -, prick-ings -, twinge -, twitch -, touch -, voice- of conscience; "compunctious visitings of nature" [Macbeth].

acknowledgment, confession &c. (dis-closure) 529; apology &c. 952; recanta-tion &c. 607; penance &c. 952; resipis-cence [rare].

awakened conscience, deathbed re-pentance, locus pœnitentiæ [L.], stool of repentance, cutty stool [Scot.], mourners' bench [local, U. S.].

PENITENT, repentant [rare], Magdalen, prodigal son, returned prodigal, "a sadder and a wiser man" [Coleridge].

951. Impenitence. — N.

IMPENI-TENCE, irrepentance, recusancy, recu-sance; lack of contrition.

hardness of heart, heart of stone, seared conscience, induration, obduracy; deaf ears.

V. BE IMPENITENT &c. adj.; steel the heart, harden the heart; turn away from the light; die game, die and make no sign.

Adj. IMPENITENT, uncontrite, obdu-rate, hard, hardened, seared, recusant, unrepentant; relentless, remorseless, graceless, shriftless.

lost, incorrigible, irreclaimable.

unreclaimed, unreformed; unrepented, unatoned.

₊ "The good die first, And they whose hearts are dry as summer dust Burn to the socket" [Wordsworth].

V. REPENT, be sorry for; be penitent &c. adj.; rue; regret &c. 833; think better of; recant &c. 607; knock under &c. (submit) 725; plead guilty; sing -miserere, - de profundis [L.]; cry peccavi [L.]; say culpâ meâ [L.], own oneself in the wrong; acknowledge, confess &c. (disclose) 529; humble oneself; beg pardon &c. (apolo-gize) 952; turn over a new leaf, put on the new man, turn from sin; repent in sackcloth and ashes &c. (do penance) 952; learn by experience.

RECLAIM, reform, regenerate, redeem, convert, amend, set straight again, make a new man of, restore self-respect.

Adj. PENITENT; repenting &c. v.; repentant, contrite, softened, melted, touched; conscience-smitten, conscience-stricken; self-accusing, self-convicted.

penitential, penitentiary; reclaimed; not hardened: unhardened.

Adv. meâ culpâ [L.]; de profundis [L.].

₊ peccavi; erubuit; salva res est [Terence]; "Vous l'avez voulu, George Dandin" [Molière]; "and wet his grave with my repentant tears" [Richard III]; "Indeed, indeed, Repentance oft before I swore — but was I sober when I swore?" [Omar Khayyám — Fitzgerald]; "Amid the roses, fierce Repentance rears her snaky crest" [Thomson]; "he who is penitent is almost innocent" [Seneca].

952. Atonement. — N. ATONEMENT, reparation; compromise, composition; compensation &c. 30; quittance, quits [*rare*], expiation, redemption, reclamation, conciliation, propitiation; indemnification, redress.

AMENDS, apology, *amende honorable* [*F.*], satisfaction; peace -, sin -, burnt- offering; scapegoat, sacrifice.

PENANCE, fasting, maceration, sackcloth and ashes, white sheet, shrift, flagellation, lustration; purgation, purgatory.

V. ATONE, atone for; expiate; propitiate; make amends, make good; reclaim, redeem, repair, ransom, absolve, purge, shrive, do penance, stand in a white sheet, repent in sackcloth and ashes.

set one's house in order, wipe off old scores, make matters up; pay the forfeit, pay the penalty.

APOLOGIZE, express regret, beg pardon, *faire l'amende honorable* [*F.*], give satisfaction; get -, fall- down on one's knees, - marrowbones [*slang or jocular*].

Adj. PROPITIATORY, expiatory, sacrific, sacrificial, sacrificatory [*rare*]; piacular, piaculous [*rare*].

* * "when the scourge Inexorable, and the torturing hour Calls us to penance" [*Paradise Lost*].

4. MORAL PRACTICE

953. Temperance. — N. TEMPERANCE, moderation, sobriety, soberness.

forbearance, abnegation; self-denial, self-restraint, self-control &c. (*resolution*) 604.

ABSTINENCE, abstemiousness, asceticism; Encratism, prohibition; frugality; vegetarianism, teetotalism, total abstinence; system of -Pythagoras, -Cornaro; Pythagorism, Stoicism.

ABSTAINER, Pythagorean, gymnosophist; nephalist, teetotaler &c. 958; Encratite, vegetarian, fruitarian, hydropot [*rare*]; ascetic &c. 995.

V. BE TEMPERATE &c. *adj.;* abstain, forbear, refrain, deny oneself, spare; know when one has had enough; take the pledge; prohibit; control the -old Adam, - carnal man, - fleshly lusts; refrain from indulgence, look not upon the wine when it is red.

Adj. TEMPERATE, moderate, sober, frugal, sparing, abstemious, abstinent; within compass; measured &c. (*sufficient*) 639.

Pythagorean; vegetarian, fruitarian; teetotal.

*** *appetitus rationi obediant* [Cic.]; *l'abstenir pour jouir c'est l épicurisme de la raison* [Rousseau]; *trahit sua quemque voluptas* [Vergil]; "feed on pulse, Drink the clear stream, and nothing wear but frieze" [Milton]; "holy dictate of spare Temperance" [*ibid.*]; "At rich men's tables eaten bread and pulse" [Emerson].

954. Intemperance. — N. INTEMPERANCE, sensuality, rakery [*rare*], animalism, carnality; tragalism; pleasure; effiminacy, silkiness; luxury, luxuriousness; lap of -pleasure, - luxury; free-living.

indulgence; high living, inabstinence, self-indulgence; voluptuousness &c. *adj.;* epicurism, epicureanism, sybaritism.

dissipation; licentiousness &c. *adj.;* debauchery; crapulence.

REVEL, revels, revelry, orgy; drunkenness &c. 959; debauch, carousal, jollification [*colloq.*], high old time [*colloq.*], drinking bout, wassail, saturnalia, excess, too much.

DRUG HABIT; Circean cup; bhang, hashish, opium, hop [*slang*], dope [*slang*], cocaine; drug fiend, dope fiend [*slang*].

V. BE INTEMPERATE &c. *adj.;* indulge, exceed; live -well, - high, - on the fat of the land; eat drink and be merry, look upon the wine when it is red, dine not wisely but too well; give free rein to indulgence &c. *n.;* wallow in voluptuousness &c. *n.;* plunge into dissipation; sensualize, brutify, carnalize.

revel, rake, live hard, run riot, sow one's wild oats; slake one's -appetite, - thirst; swill; pamper.

Adj. INTEMPERATE, inabstinent, excessive; sensual, self-indulgent; voluptuous, licentious, wild, dissolute, rakish, fast, debauched; orgiastic, Corybantic,

Paphian.

BRUTISH, crapulous, swinish, piggish, hoggish, beastlike, theroid [*med.*].

LUXURIOUS, Epicurean, Sybaritical; bred –, nursed- in the lap of luxury; indulged, pampered; full fed, high fed.

INTOXICATED, drunk &c. 959.

*** "being full of supper and distempering draughts" [*Othello*]; "swinish gluttony Ne'er looks to Heaven amidst his gorgeous feast" [Milton]; "lickerish baits, fit to ensnare a brute" [*ibid.*]; "And damn'd be him that first cries 'Hold, enough!'" [*Macbeth*].

954a. Sensualist. — N. SENSUALIST, Sybarite, voluptuary, Sardanapalus, man of pleasure, carpet knight; epicure, epicurean, *gourmet* [*F.*]; gourmand; glutton &c. 957; pig, hog; votary –, swine- of Epicurus; Heliogabalus; free liver, hard liver; libertine &c. 962; hedonist; tragalist.

*** "the sons Of Belial, flown with insolence and wine" [Milton]; "Serenely full, the epicure would say, Fate cannot harm me — I have dined to-day" [Sydney Smith]; "Ah, make the most of what we yet may spend, Before we too into the Dust descend" [Omar Khayyám — Fitzgerald].

955. Asceticism. — N. ASCETICISM, puritanism, sabbatarianism; cynicism, austerity; total abstinence; nephalism; Yoga.

mortification, maceration, sackcloth and ashes, flagellation; penance &c. 952; fasting &c. 956; martyrdom.

ASCETIC, anchoret *or* anchorite, *Heautontimorumenos* [*Gr.*]; hermit &c. (*recluse*) 893; puritan, sabbatarian, cynic; bhikshu, sannyasi *or* sanyasi, yogi [*all Hindu*]; dervish, fakir [*both Moham.*]; martyr.

Adj. ASCETIC, austere, puritanical; cynical; over-religious; acerb, acerbic.

*** "clothed with camel's hair, and with a girdle of skin about his loins; and he did eat locusts and wild honey" [*Bible*].

956. Fasting. — N. FASTING; xerophagy; famishment, starvation.

FAST, *jour maigre* [*F.*]; fast day, banyan day; Lent, quadragesima; Ramadan *or* Ramazan [*Moham.*]; spare –, meager- diet; lenten -diet, – entertainment; *soupe maigre* [*F.*], short commons, Barmecide feast; short rations; punishment of Tantalus.

V. FAST, starve, clem [*obs.*], famish, perish with hunger; dine with Duke Humphrey; make two bites of a cherry; "keep the larder lean."

Adj. FASTING &c. *v.;* lenten, quadragesimal; unfed; starved &c. *v.;* half-starved; hungry &c. 865.

*** "Spare Fast, that oft with gods doth diet" [Milton].

957. Gluttony. — N. GLUTTONY; greed; greediness &c. *adj.;* voracity.

epicurism, gastronomy; good –, high-living; edacity, gulosity [*rare*], crapulence; guttling, guzzle [*rare*], guzzling; pantophagy.

FEAST &c. (*food*) 298; good cheer, blow out [*slang*]; *batterie de cuisine* [*F.*].

GLUTTON, gormandizer, cormorant, hog &c. (*sensualist*) 954a; guttler, pantophagist; belly-god, Apicius, gastronome.

EPICURE, *bon vivant* [*F.*], gourmand [*obs. as* glutton], *gourmet* [*F.*].

V. GORMANDIZE, gorge; overgorge oneself, overeat oneself, glut, satiate, engorge, eat one's fill, cram, stuff, guttle, guzzle, bolt, devour, gobble up; gulp &c. (*swallow food*) 298; raven, eat out of house and home; have the stomach of an ostrich; play a good knife and fork &c. (*appetite*) 865; have a capacious -gorge, – maw.

pamper [*obs. as* glut], indulge.

Adj. GLUTTONOUS, greedy; gormandizing &c. *v.;* edacious, omnivorous, pantophagic, pantophagous, voracious, devouring, all-devouring, crapulent, swinish. pampered [*obs. as* fed to excess]; overfed, overgorged, overindulged.

*** *jejunus raro stomachus vulgaria temnit* [Horace]; "His belly was upblown with luxury, And eke with fatness swollen were his eyne" [Spenser].

958. Sobriety. — N. SOBRIETY; tee-totalism, nephalism.

WATER-DRINKER; hydropot [*rare*], pro-hibitionist; teetotaler *or* teetotaller, abstainer, nephalist, Good Templar, band of hope, W. C. T. U. (Women's Christian Temperance Union).

V. take the pledge.

Adj. SOBER, - as a judge; temperate, moderate.

⁎ "Honest water, which ne'er left man in the mire" [*Timon of Athens*]; "a cup of cold Adam from the next purling spring" [*Tom Brown*]: "A Rechabite poor Will must live, And drink of Adam's ale" [Prior].

959. Drunkenness. — N. DRUNKEN-NESS &c. *adj.*; intemperance; drinking &c. *v.;* inebriety, inebriation, ebriety [*rare*], ebriosity [*rare*], insobriety, intoxi-cation; temulence [*rare*], bibacity, wine-bibbing; compotation, potation; deep potations, bacchanals, bacchanalia, bac-chanalianism, libations; bender [*slang, U. S.*].

alcoholism, oinomania, dipsomania; delirium tremens, D. T.'s [*colloq.*]; *mania a potu* [*L.*].

DRINK, alcoholic drinks, alcohol, blue ruin [*slang*], booze *or* bouse [*colloq.*], "the luscious liquor" [Milton]; grog, port wine, punch; punchbowl, cup, rosy wine, flowing bowl; drop, - too much; dram; beer &c. (*beverage*) 298; *aguardiente* [*Sp.*]; apple-brandy, apple-jack; brandy, brandy-smash [*U. S.*]; chain lightning [*slang*], champagne, cocktail; gin, gin-sling; highball [*U. S.*], peg [*slang, orig. India*]; burra (*or* bara) peg, chota peg [*both India*]; rum, schnapps [*U. S.*], sherry, xeres, sling [*U. S.*], usquebaugh, whisky *or* whiskey, rye; stirrup cup, parting cup, doch-an-dorrach *or* doch-an-dorris [*Scot.*].

ILLICIT DISTILLING; moonshining, moonshine *or* moonshine whisky [*dial. Eng. & colloq., U. S.*], hooch [*slang*], home-brew; moonshiner [*dial. Eng. & colloq., U. S.*]; bootlegger [*slang, U. S.*].

DRUNKARD, sot, toper, tippler, bibber, winebibber; hard -, gin -, dram- drinker; soaker [*slang*], sponge [*slang*], tun [*jocose*], love-pot, tosspot, guzzler, guzzle [*rare*], boozer *or* bouser [*colloq.*], bum [*slang, U. S.*], tavern haunter, thirsty soul, reveler, carouser, Bacchanal, Bacchanalian; Bacchæ, bacchante, mænad; devotee to Bacchus.

V. GET *or* BE DRUNK &c. *adj.;* see double; take a -drop, - glass- too much; drink, tipple, tope [*colloq.*], booze *or* bouse [*colloq.*], guzzle, swill [*slang*], soak [*slang*], sot [*rare*], bum [*slang, U. S.*], besot, have a jag on [*slang*], lush [*slang*], bib [*obs. or dial.*], swig [*dial. or colloq.*], carouse; sacrifice at the shrine of Bacchus; take to drinking; drink -hard, - deep, - like a fish; have one's swill [*slang*], drain the cup, splice the main brace [*slang*], take a hair of the dog that bit you.

liquor, liquor up [*both slang*], wet one's -whistle, - clay, - swallow [*colloq. or humorous*]; wet the red lane [*humorous*]; raise the elbow, raise the little finger, hit the booze [*slang*], take a whet; crack a -, pass the- bottle; toss off &c. (*drink up*) 298; go to the -alehouse, - public house, - saloon.

make one drunk &c. *adj.;* inebriate, fuddle [*colloq.*], befuddle, fuzzle [*obs.*], get into one's head.

SELL ILLICITLY, bootleg [*slang, U. S.*].

Adj. DRUNK, tipsy, intoxicated, bibacious, inebrious, inebriate, inebriated; in one's cups; in a state of intoxication &c. *n.;* temulent, temulentive [*both rare*]; fuddled [*colloq.*], mellow, cut [*slang*], boozy *or* bousy [*colloq.*], full [*vulgar*], fou [*Scot.*], lit up [*slang*], glorious [*humorous*], fresh [*slang*], merry, elevated; flush, flushed, flustered, disguised [*archaic*], groggy [*colloq.*], beery; top-heavy; pot-val-iant, potulent [*obs.*], squiffy [*slang*]; overcome, overtaken [*obs.*], whittled [*obs.*]; screwed, tight, primed, corned, raddled, sewed up, lushy [*all slang*], muzzy [*colloq.*], nappy [*rare*], muddled, obfuscated, maudlin; crapulous, blind drunk, dead drunk.[1]

inter pocula [*L.*], in liquor, the worse for liquor; having had a drop too much, half-seas over [*slang*], three sheets in the wind [*sailors' slang*], under the table.

[1] More than three hundred slang expressions coming under this category are given in Farmer and Henley's *Dictionary of Slang and Colloquial English*. C. O. S. M.

drunk as -a piper, – a fiddler, – a lord, – Chloe, – an owl, – David's sow, – a wheelbarrow [all colloq.].

DRUNKEN, bibacious, sottish; given –, addicted- to -drink, – the bottle; toping &c. v.; primed, – on the hip; heeled [slang].

. nunc est bibendum; "Bacchus ever fair and young" [Dryden]; "drink down all unkindness" [Merry Wives]; "O God, that men should put an enemy in their mouths to steal away their brains!" [Othello]; "Fetch me a quart of sack; put a toast in 't" Merry Wives]; "From Sabine jar bring forth the sparkling wine" [Horace]; "Drain we the cup. Friend, art afraid?" [Thackeray]; "What man dare, I dare!" [Macbeth]; "so gloz'd the tempter!" [Milton]; "Stands Scotland where it did?" [Macbeth]; "Once more unto the breach, dear friends, once more!" [Henry V]; "His devious course uncertain, seeking home" [Cowper].

---

960. Purity. — N. PURITY; decency, decorum, delicacy; continence, chastity, honesty, virtue, modesty, shame; pudicity, pucelage [rare], virginity.

virgin, vestal, prude; Lucretia, Diana, Athena Parthenos; Joseph, Hippolytus.

Adj. PURE, undefiled, modest, delicate, decent, decorous; virginibus puerisque [L.]; chaste, continent, virtuous, honest, Platonic.

. "as chaste as unsunn'd snow" [Cymbeline]; "a soul as white as heaven" [Beaumont and Fletcher]; "the sun-clad power of Chastity" [Milton]; "to the pure all things are pure" [Shelley].

961. Impurity. — N. IMPURITY; uncleanness &c. (filth) 653; immodesty; grossness &c. adj.; indelicacy, indecency, impudicity, obscenity, ribaldry, smut, bawdry, double entente, équivoque [F.]; pornography.

incontinence, debauchery, libertinism, libertinage, fornication, wenching, venery, dissipation.

concupiscence, lust, carnality, flesh, salacity; pruriency, lechery, lasciviousness, lewdness, lasciviency [obs.], lubricity; Sadism, Sapphism, Lesbianism, nymphomania, aphrodisia, satyriasis.

SEDUCTION; defloration, defilement, abuse, violation, stupration, rape; incest.

SOCIAL EVIL, harlotry, whoredom, concubinage, cuckoldom, adultery, advoutry [obs.], crim. con.; free-love.

INTRIGUE, amour, amourette, liaison [F.], faux pas [F.], entanglement; gallantry.

[RESORTS] brothel, bagnio, stew, bawdyhouse, lupanar, house of ill fame, bordel [obs.]; Yoshiwara [Jap.], red-light district.

HAREM, seraglio, zenana [India].

V. BE IMPURE &c. adj.; debauch, defile, seduce; prostitute; abuse, violate, rape, stuprate [rare], deflower; commit adultery &c. n.; intrigue.

Adj. IMPURE; unclean &c. (dirty) 653; not to be mentioned to ears polite; immodest, shameless, indecorous, indelicate, indecent, Fescennine; loose, risqué [F.], coarse, gross, broad, free, equivocal, smutty, fulsome, ribald, obscene, bawdy, pornographic.

concupiscent, prurient, lickerish, rampant, lustful; carnal, carnal-minded; lewd, lascivious, lecherous, libidinous, erotic, ruttish, must or musty [said of elephants]; salacious, Paphian, voluptuous; goatish, beastly, bestial, incestuous.

UNCHASTE, light, wanton, licentious, adulterous, debauched, dissolute; of loose character, of easy virtue; frail, gay, riggish [obs.], incontinent, meretricious, rakish, gallant, dissipated; no better than she should be; on the town, on the streets, on the pavé [F.], on the loose [colloq.].

---

962. Libertine. — N. LIBERTINE; voluptuary &c. 954a; rake, debauchee, loose fish [colloq.], rip [colloq.], rakehell, fast man; intrigant, gallant, seducer, fornicator, lecher, satyr, goat, whoremonger, paillard [F.], advocater [obs.], adulterer, gay deceiver, Lothario, Don Juan, Bluebeard; chartered libertine.

ADULTRESS, advoutress [obs.], courtesan, prostitute, strumpet, harlot, whore, punk [obsoles.], fille de joie [F.], woman, woman of the town, streetwalker, Cyprian, miss [obs.], piece [slang], demirep, wench, trollop, trull, baggage, hussy, drab, bitch [low], jade, skit [obs.], rig [obs.], quean, mopsy [dial. Eng.], slut, minx, harridan; unfortunate, – female, – woman; woman -of easy virtue &c. (unchaste)

961; wanton, fornicatress; *lorette* [F.], *cocotte* [F.], *petite dame* [F.], grisette; demi-mondaine; chippy [*slang*, U. S.]; Sapphist; white slave.

Jezebel, Messalina, Delilah, Thais, Phryne, Aspasia, Lais.
demimonde, erring sisters, fallen women, frail sisterhood.

MISTRESS, concubine, kept woman, doxy, *chère amie* [F.]; *bona roba* [It.]; spiritual wife.

PROCURER, pimp, pander *or* pandar, bawd, *conciliatrix* [L.], procuress, mackerel [*archaic*], wittol [*obs.*].

. "she may be a good sort but she is a bad lot" [Shaw]; "Ah, take the Cash and let the Credit go, Nor heed the rumble of a distant drum" [Omar Khayyám — Fitzgerald].

5. INSTITUTIONS

963. Legality. — N. LEGALITY, legitimacy, legitimateness; legitimatization, legitimization.

LAW, code, *corpus juris* [L.], constitution, pandect, charter, act, enactment, statute, rule; canon &c. (*precept*) 697; ordinance, institution, regulation; by-law *or* bye-law; rescript, decree &c. (*order*) 741; ordonnance; standing order; plebiscite &c. (*choice*) 609; legislature.

legal process; form, formula, formality, rite, arm of the law; *habeas corpus* [L.]; *fieri facias* [L.].

equity, common law; *lex scripta* [L.]; *lex non scripta* [L.], unwritten law; law of nations, *droit des gens* [F.], international law, *jus gentium* [L.]; *jus civile* [L.]; civil –, canon –, crown –, criminal –, statute –, ecclesiastical- law; *lex mercatoria* [L.].

constitutionalism, constitutionality; justice &c. 922.

[SCIENCE OF LAW] jurisprudence, nomology; legislation, codification, nomography.

V. LEGALIZE, legitimate, legitimize, legitimatize; enact, ordain; decree &c. (*order*) 741; pass a law, legislate; codify, formulate, formalize, regularize, authorize.

Adj. LEGAL, legitimate; according to law; vested, constitutional, chartered, legalized; lawful &c. (*permitted*) 760; statutable, statutory; legislatorial, legislative; judicial, juridical; nomistic, nomothetical.

Adv. LEGALLY &c. *adj.*; in the eye of the law; *de jure* [L.].

. *ignorantia legis neminem excusat;* "where law ends tyranny begins" [Earl of Chatham]; "the majesty and power of law and justice" [*II Henry IV*]; "The Law, our kingdom's golden chaine" [Dekker]; "there is a higher law than the Constitution" [Seward]; "the gladsome light of jurisprudence" [Coke]; "We must not make a scarecrow of the law" [*M. for M.*]; "the lawless science of our law" [Tennyson].

964. [ABSENCE OR VIOLATION OF LAW.] Illegality. — N. LAWLESSNESS; illicitness; breach –, violation- of law; disobedience &c. 742; unconformity &c. 83; arbitrariness &c. *adj.;* antinomy, violence, brute force, despotism, tyranny, outlawry.

mob –, lynch –, club –, Lydford –, martial –, drumhead- law; *coup d'état* [F.]; *le droit du plus fort* [F.]; *argumentum baculinum* [L.].

ILLEGALITY, informality, unlawfulness, illegitimacy, bar sinister.

trover and conversion; smuggling, bootlegging [*slang*, U. S.], illicit distilling &c. 959; poaching; simony.

V. VIOLATE THE LAW, offend against the law, set the law at defiance, ride roughshod over, drive a coach and six through a statute; make the law a dead letter, take the law into one's own hands.

smuggle, run, poach, bootleg [*slang*, U. S.].

Adj. ILLEGAL; prohibited &c. 761; not allowed, unlawful, illegitimate, illicit, contraband, actionable.

unchartered, unconstitutional; unwarranted, unwarrantable, unauthorized; informal, unofficial, injudicial [*rare*], extra-judicial.

LAWLESS, arbitrary, despotic, despotical; summary, irresponsible; unanswerable, unaccountable.

null and void; a dead letter.

Adv. ILLEGALLY &c. *adj.;* with a high hand, in violation of law.

. "Bleed, bleed, poor country! Great Tyranny! lay thou thy basis sure, For goodness dares not check thee!" [*Macbeth*].

427

965. Jurisdiction. [EXECUTIVE.] — N. JURISDICTION, judicature, administration of justice; soc, soke [both A. S. & early Eng. law]; executive, commission of the peace; magistracy &c. (authority) 737; judge &c. 967; tribunal &c. 966.

city government, municipal government, commission government, Oregon plan [U. S.]; municipality, corporation, bailiwick, shrievalty; police, police force; constabulary, Bumbledom.

EXECUTIVE OFFICER, officer, commissioner, lord lieutenant [Brit.], collector [India]; city manager, mayor, alderman, councilor or councillor, selectman; bailiff, tipstaff, bumbailiff [Eng.], catchpole or catchpoll, beadle; sheriff, shrieve [obs.], bailie [Scot.], constable; policeman, police constable, police sergeant, patrolman &c. 664; sbirro [It.], alguazil, gendarme [F.], kavass [Turk.], lictor, mace bearer, huissier [F.], tithingman; excise man, gauger or gager, customhouse officer, douanier [F.]; press gang or pressgang.

coroner, ædile or edile; reeve, portreeve [early Eng. hist.], paritor [obs.], posse comitatus [L.].

BUREAU, cutcherry [India], department, portfolio, secretariat.

V. JUDGE, sit in judgment; have jurisdiction over.

Adj. EXECUTIVE, administrative, judicative, municipal; inquisitorial, causidical; judicatory, judiciary, judicial, juridical.

Adv. coram judice [L.].

₊ "a dog's obeyed in office" [King Lear]; "Ill can he rule the great that cannot rule the small" [Spenser].

966. Tribunal. — N. TRIBUNAL, court, curia, board, bench, judicature, judicatory; court of -justice, – law, – arbitration; inquisition; guild; durbar [India], divan [Oriental], Areopagus.

justice –, judgment –, mercy- seat; woolsack; bar, bar of justice; dock; forum, hustings, bureau, drumhead; jury-box; witness box, witness stand.

senate-house, town hall, theater or theatre; House of Commons, House of Lords; statehouse [U. S.], townhouse, courthouse.

[BRITISH COURTS], sessions; petty –, quarter –, special –, general- sessions [Eng. law]; assizes; eyre, justices in eyre, wardmote, burghmote, barmote, courtleet, court-baron, court of piepoudre [all old Eng. law]; superior courts of Westminster; court of -record, – oyer and terminer, – assize, – appeal, – error; High court of -Judicature, – Appeal; Judicial Committee of the Privy Council; Star Chamber; Court of -Chancery, – King's or Queen's Bench, – Exchequer, – Common Pleas, – Probate, – Admiralty; Lords Justices' –, Rolls –, Vice Chancellor's –, Stannary –, Divorce –, Palatine –, county –, police- court; Court of Criminal Appeal; Court of Small Causes [India]; court of common council; board of green cloth.

[UNITED STATES COURTS] United States -Supreme Court, – District Court, – Circuit Court of Appeal; Federal Court of Claims, Court of Private Land Claims; Supreme Court, court of sessions, criminal court, police court, juvenile court.

COURT-MARTIAL (pl. courts-martial), drumhead court-martial.

ECCLESIASTICAL COURT, Rota or Rota Romana [R. C. Ch.]; Court of Arches [Eng.]. Papal Court, Curia.

Adj. JUDICIAL &c. 965; appellate; curial.

₊ die Weltgeschichte ist das Weltgericht; "Whoever fights, whoever fails, Justice conquers evermore" [Emerson]; "Justice discards party, friendship, kindred, and is therefore always represented as blind" [Addison]; "We have strict statutes and most biting laws" [Measure for Measure].

967. Judge. — N. JUDGE, justice; justiciar [Eng. & Scot. hist.]; justiciary [Eng. & Scot. hist.]; chancellor; justice –, judge- of assize; recorder, common serjeant; puisne –, assistant –, county court- judge; conservator –, justice- of the peace; J. P.; "the Great Unpaid" [Eng.]; court &c. (tribunal) 966; deemster [Isle of Man & archaic], moderator, bencher [archaic], jurat, magistrate, police magistrate, beak [slang]; his worship, his honor, his lordship; the court.

Lord Chancellor, Lord Justice; Master of the Rolls, Vice Chancellor; Lord Chief
Justice, – Baron; Chief Justice; Mr. Justice; Baron, – of the Exchequer.

assessor; arbiter, arbitrator, doomsman or domesman [obs.], umpire, referee, refer-
endary [rare]; revising barrister [Eng.], receiver, official receiver; censor &c. (critic)
480; barmaster [Eng.].

archon, tribune, prætor, ephor, syndic, podesta [It.]; mollah, ulema, hakim, mufti,
cadi or kadi [all Moham.]; alcalde [Sp.]; Rhadamanthus, Minos, Solomon.

JURY, grand jury, petty jury, inquest, panel, country; twelve men in a box.

JUROR, juryman, talesman; grand-juror, grand-juryman, recognitor; petty-juror,
petty-juryman.

LITIGANT &c. (accusation) 938.

V. ADJUDGE &c. (determine) 480; try a case, try a prisoner.

Adj. judicial &c. 965.

⁎ "a Daniel come to judgment" [Merchant of Venice]; "The law: it has honored us; may we
honor it" [Daniel Webster].

968. Lawyer. — N. LAWYER, jurist, legist, pundit [India], civilian, publicist,
jurisconsult, legal adviser, advocate; barrister, barrister-at-law; counsel, counselor
or counsellor, King's or Queen's counsel; K. C.; Q. C.; silk or silk gown; junior
counsel, stuff or stuff gown; leader, serjeant-at-law, bencher, pleader, special pleader;
tubman [Eng. law], judge &c. 967.

solicitor, attorney, vakil or vakeel [India], proctor; equity draftsman, conveyancer, notary, – public; scrivener, cursitor [Eng. law]; writer, – to the signet; S.S.C.;
limb of the law; pettifogger, shyster [U. S.].

BAR, legal profession, gentlemen of the long robe; junior –, outer –, inner- bar;
Inns of Court [Eng.].

V. PRACTICE LAW; practice at (or within) the bar, plead; call to (or within) the
bar, be called to (or within) the bar; admitted to the bar, take silk.

DISBAR, disbench [Eng. law], degrade.

Adj. learned in the law; at the bar; forensic.

⁎ banco regis; "Litigious terms, fat contentions, and flowing fees" [Milton]; "Oh 'tis a
blessed thing to have rich clients" [Beaumont and Fletcher]; "with promise of high pay and great
rewards" [III Henry VI]; "The first thing we do, let's kill all the lawyers" [II Henry VI].

969. Lawsuit. — N. LAWSUIT, suit, action, cause; litigation; suit in law; dispute
&c. 713.

WRIT, summons, subpœna, citation, latitat [Eng. law]; nisi prius, venire, venire
facias, habeas corpus [all L.].

ARRAIGNMENT, prosecution, impeachment; accusation &c. 938; presentment, true
bill, indictment.

ARREST, apprehension, committal, commitment; imprisonment &c. (restraint) 751.

PLEADINGS; declaration, bill, claim; procès-verbal [F.], bill of right, information,
corpus delicti [L.]; affidavit, state of facts, libel; answer, replication, plea, demurrer,
rebutter, rejoinder: surrebutter, surrejoinder.

suitor, libelant or libellant, party to a suit; litigant &c. 938.

HEARING, trial; judgment, sentence, finding, verdict &c. 480; appeal, – motion;
writ of error; certiorari.

CASE, decision, precedent; decided case, reports.

V. GO TO LAW, appeal to the law; bring to -justice, – trial, – the bar; put on
trial, pull up; accuse &c. 938; prefer or file a claim &c. n.; take the law of [colloq.],
inform against.

cite, summon, summons, serve with a writ, arraign, sue, prosecute, bring an action
against, indict, impeach, attach, distrain, commit; apprehend, arrest; give in charge
&c. (restrain) 751.

empanel a jury, challenge the jurors; implead, join issue; close the pleadings;
set down for hearing.

TRY, hear a cause; sit in judgment; adjudicate &c. 480.

Adj. LITIGIOUS &c. (*quarrelsome*) 713; *qui tam, coram judice, sub judice* [*all L.*].

Adv. *pendente lite* [*L.*].

⁎ *adhuc sub judice lis est; accedas ad curiam; transeat in exemplum;* "these nice sharp quillets of the law "[*I Henry VI*]; "we are for law; he dies" [*Timon of Athens*]; "No man e'er felt the halter draw, With good opinion of the law" [Trumbull]; "Strive mightily, but eat and drink as friends" [*Taming of the Shrew*].

970. Acquittal. — N. ACQUITTAL, acquitment [*obs.*]; exculpation, acquittance, clearance, exoneration; discharge &c. (*release*) 750; *quietus* [*L.*], absolution, compurgation, reprieve, respite; pardon &c. (*forgiveness*) 918.

[EXEMPTION FROM PUNISHMENT] impunity, immunity.

V. ACQUIT, exculpate, exonerate, clear; absolve, whitewash, assoil [*archaic*], assoilzie [*Scot.*]; discharge, release; liberate &c. 750.

reprieve, respite; pardon &c. (*forgive*) 918; let off, let off scot-free.

Adj. ACQUITTED &c. *v.;* uncondemned, unpunished, unchastised; recommended to mercy.

⁎ *nemo bis punitur pro eodem delicto;* "And earthly power doth then show likest God's When mercy seasons justice" [*M. of V.*].

971. Condemnation. — N. CONDEMNATION, conviction, judgment, penalty, sentence; proscription, damnation; death warrant.

attainder, attainture, attaintment.

V. CONDEMN, convict, cast [*obs. or dial.*], bring home to, find guilty, damn, doom, sign the death warrant, sentence, pass sentence on, attaint, confiscate, proscribe, sequestrate; nonsuit.

disapprove &c. 932; accuse &c. 938.

stand condemned, be convicted.

Adj. CONDEMNATORY, damnatory; condemned &c. *v.;* nonsuited &c. (*failure*) 732; self-convicted.

⁎ *mutato nomine de te fabula narratur;* "unrespited, unpitied, unreprieved" [*P. L.*]; "Beyond the infinite and boundless reach Of mercy" [*King John*]; "every crime destroys more Edens than our own" [Hawthorne].

972. Punishment. — N. PUNISHMENT, punition, chastisement, chastening, correction, castigation; discipline, infliction, trial; judgment; penalty &c. 974; retribution; thunderbolt, Nemesis, Eumenides, the Furies; requital &c. (*reward*) 973; retributive justice; penology.

[FORMS OF PUNISHMENT] lash, scaffold &c. (*instrument of punishment*) 975; imprisonment &c. (*restraint*) 751; transportation, banishment, expulsion, exile, involuntary exile, ostracism; penal servitude, hard labor; galleys &c. 975; beating &c. *v.;* flagellation, fustigation, cudgeling, gantlet, strappado, estrapade, bastinado, *argumentum baculinum* [*L.*], stick law, rap on the knuckles, box on the ear; blow &c. (*impulse*) 276; stripe, cuff, kick, buffet, pummel; slap, – in the face; wipe [*dial. or slang*], douse *or* dowse [*rare*]; torture, rack; rail-riding, scarpines; picket [*obs.*], picketing; dragonnade.

CAPITAL PUNISHMENT, execution; hanging, shooting &c. *v.;* electrocution, decapitation, decollation, dismemberment; strangling, strangulation, garrote *or* garrotte; crucifixion, impalement; martyrdom, *auto-da-fé* (*pl. autos-da-fé*) [*Pg.*], *auto-de-fe* [*Sp.*], *noyade* [*F.*], harakiri [*Jap.*], seppuku [*Jap.*], happy dispatch [*jocular*], lethal chamber, hemlock.

V. PUNISH, chastise, chasten, castigate, correct, inflict punishment, administer correction, deal retributive justice; tar and feather; masthead, keelhaul.

visit upon, pay; pay out [*colloq.*], serve out [*colloq.*], settle, settle with, do for [*colloq.*], get even with, get one's own back [*slang*], make short work of, give a lesson to, serve one right, make an example of; have a rod in pickle for; give it to, give it one [*both colloq.*].

STRIKE &c. 276; deal a blow to, administer the lash, smite; slap, – the face; smack, cuff, box the ears, spank, thwack, thump, beat, lay on, swinge, buffet; thresh, thrash, pummel, drub, leather [*colloq. or slang*], trounce, baste, belabor; lace, – one's jacket; dress, dress down, give a dressing, trim [*colloq.*], warm [*colloq. & dial.*], warm one's jacket [*colloq.*], wipe [*dial. or slang*], tund [*obs.*], cob [*dial., Eng.*], bang, strap, comb [*humorous*], lick, larrup [*both colloq.*], wallop [*Scot., dial. Eng. &*

colloq., *U. S*]., cowhide, lambaste [*slang*], lash, whop [*obs.*], flog, scourge, whip, birch, cane, give the stick, switch, flagellate, horsewhip, bastinado, towel [*slang or dial. Eng.*], rub down with an oaken towel [*slang*], ribroast [*slang*], dust one's jacket [*colloq. or slang*], fustigate, pitch into [*colloq.*], lay about one, beat black and blue; beat to a -mummy, – jelly; give a black eye; hit on the head, crack on the bean [*slang*], sandbag, blackjack, put away [*slang*]; pelt, stone, lapidate.

EXECUTE; bring to the -block, – gallows; behead, decapitate, decollate, guillotine; hang, turn off [*slang*]; gibbet, bowstring, dismember, hang draw and quarter; shoot; burn; break on the wheel, crucify; impale *or* empale, flay; lynch; electrocute.

TORTURE, agonize, rack, put on (*or* to) the rack, martyr, martyrize, picket [*obs. or hist.*]; prolong the agony, kill by inches.

BANISH, exile, transport, deport, expel, ostracize; rusticate; drum out; dismiss, disbar, disbench [*Eng. law*]; strike off the roll, unfrock; post.

SUFFER, suffer for, suffer punishment; be flogged, be hanged &c.; come to the gallows, dance upon nothing [*ironical*], die in one's shoes; be rightly served.

Adj. PUNISHING &c. *v.;* penal, punitory, punitive, inflictive, castigatory; punished &c. *v.*

Int. *à la lanterne!* [*F.*].

*** *culpam pœna premit comes* [Horace]; "eating the bitter bread of banishment" [*Richard II*]; *gravis ira regum est semper* [Seneca]; *sera tamen tacitis pœna venit pedibus* [Tibullus]; *suo sibi gladio hunc jugulo* [Terence]; "Thou shalt be whipp'd with wire, and stewed in brine, Smarting in ling'ring pickle" [*Antony and Cleopatra*]; "back to thy punishment, False fugitive, and to thy speed add wings" [*Paradise Lost*].

973. Reward. — N.

REWARD, recompense, remuneration, prize, meed, guerdon, reguerdon [*obs.*]; price; indemnity, indemnification; quittance, compensation, reparation, redress, retribution, reckoning, acknowledgment, requital, amends, sop; atonement; consideration, return, *quid pro quo* [*L.*]; salvage.

perquisite, perks [*slang*]; vail &c. (*donation*) 784; *douceur* [*F.*], tip; bribe, bait &c. 784; hush-money, smart-money, blackmail; carcelage [*obs.*]; solatium.

ALLOWANCE, salary, stipend, wages; pay, payment; emolument; tribute; batta [*India*], shot, scot; premium, fee, honorarium; hire; dasturi *or* dustoori [*India*]; mileage.

crown &c. (*decoration of honor*) 877.

V. REWARD, recompense, repay, requite; remunerate, munerate [*obs.*]; compensate; fee, tip, bribe; pay one's footing &c. (*pay*) 807; make amends, indemnify, atone; satisfy, acknowledge.

get for one's pains, reap the fruits of.

Adj. remunerative, remuneratory [*rare*], munerary [*obs.*], compensatory, retributive, reparatory [*rare*], reparative.

*** *fideli certa merces*; *honor virtutis prœmium* [Cicero]; *tibi seris tibi metis;* "Besides commends and courteous breath, Gifts of rich value" [*M. of V.*]; "'Tis deeds must win the prize" [*Taming of the Shrew*]; "A Muezzin from the Tower of Darkness cries, 'Fools, your Reward is neither Here nor There'" [Omar Khayyám — Fitzgerald]; "God shall repay: I am safer so" [Browning].

974. Penalty. — N.

PENALTY; retribution &c. (*punishment*) 972; pain, pains and penalties; wergild *or* weregild [*hist.*], bloodwite *or* bloodwit [*early Eng. law*]; *peine forte et dure* [*F.*]; penance &c. (*atonement*) 952; the devil to pay.

fine, mulct, amercement, sconce [*Oxford Univ., Eng.*], forfeit, forfeiture, escheat, damages, deodand, sequestration, confiscation, præmunire *or* premunire; doomage [*U. S.*].

V. PENALIZE, fine, mulct, amerce, sconce, confiscate, sequestrate, sequester, escheat, estreat, forfeit.

*** "some of us will smart for it" [*Much Ado*]; "I crave the law, The penalty and forfeit of my bond" [*Merchant of Venice*].

975. [INSTRUMENT OF PUNISHMENT.] Scourge. — N.

SCOURGE, whip, lash, strap, thong, cowhide, knout, cat, cat-o'-nine-tails; rope's end; azote [*Sp. Am.*], black-snake, bullwhack [*U. S.*], kurbash [*Turk.*], chabuk [*Hind.*], quirt, rawhide, sjambok [*S. Africa*].

ROD, cane, stick, rattan *or* ratan, birch, birch rod; rod in pickle; switch, ferule, cudgel, truncheon.

[VARIOUS INSTRUMENTS] pillory, stocks, whipping post; cucking stool, ducking stool, brank, trebuchet *or* trebucket; triangle, wooden horse, maiden; thumbscrew, boot, rack, wheel, iron heel; treadmill, crank, galleys; bed of Procrustes.

scaffold; block, ax, guillotine; stake; cross, gallows, gibbet, tree, drop; noose, rope, halter, bowstring; death chair, electric chair; *mecate* [*Sp.*].

PRISON, house of correction &c. 752; jailer *or* gaoler.

EXECUTIONER; electrocutioner; lyncher, garroter *or* garrotter, torturer; headsman, hangman, topsman *or* topping cove [*slang*], Jack Ketch.

MALEFACTOR, criminal, culprit, felon, evildoer, misdemeanant; victim, gallowsbird [*slang*], Jack Ketch's pippin [*old slang*].

. "Be ready, gods, with all your thunderbolts; Dash him to pieces" [*Julius Cæsar*]; "Nature knows best, and she says, *roar!*" [Edgeworth]; "whoso sheddeth man's blood, by man shall his blood be shed" [*Bible*].

Section V. RELIGIOUS AFFECTIONS

1. SUPERHUMAN BEINGS AND REGIONS

976. Deity. — N. DEITY, Divinity, Godhead, Godship, Omnipotence, Omniscience, Providence.

[QUALITY OF BEING DIVINE] divineness, divinity.

GOD, Lord, Jehovah, The King of Kings, The Lord of Lords, The Almighty, The Supreme Being, The Eternal Being, The Absolute Being, The First Cause; I AM, The All-Father, *Ens Entium* [*L.*], Author of all things, Creator of all things, Author of our being; Cosmoplast, Demiurge; The Infinite, The Eternal; The All-powerful, The Omnipotent, The All-wise, The All-merciful, The All-holy, The All-knowing, The Omniscient.

Deus [*L.*], *Theos* [*Gr.* Θεός], *Dieu* [*F.*], *Gott* [*Ger.*], *Dio* [*It.*], *Dios* [*Sp.*], *Deos* [*Pg.*], *Gud* [*Nor., Sw., & Dan.*], *God* [*Du.*], *Bog'* [*Russ.*], Brahmā [*Skr.*], *Deva* [*Skr.*], *Khuda* [*Hind.*], *Allah Ar.*], *Kami* [*Jap.*], *Ten-shu* [*Jap., Christian*].

[ATTRIBUTES AND PERFECTIONS] infinite -power, – wisdom, – goodness, – justice, – truth, – love, – mercy; omnipotence, omniscience, omnipresence; unity, immutability, holiness, glory, light, majesty, sovereignty; infinity, eternity &c. (*perpetuity*) 112.

THE TRINITY, The Holy Trinity, The Trinity in Unity, The Triune God, Triunity, Threefold Unity, "Three in One and One in Three."

I. GOD THE FATHER, The Maker, The Creator, The Preserver.

[FUNCTIONS] creation, preservation, divine government, Theocracy, Thearchy; Providence;-ways -, dealings -, dispensations -, visitations- of Providence.

II. GOD THE SON, Jesus Christ; The Messiah, The Anointed, The Saviour, The Redeemer, The Mediator, The Intercessor, The Advocate, The Judge; The Son of God, The Son of Man, The Son of David; The Only-Begotten, The Lamb of God, The Word, Logos; The Man of Sorrows, Jesus of Nazareth, King of the Jews, The Son of Mary, The Risen, Immanuel, Emmanuel, The King of Kings and Lord of Lords, The King of Glory, The Prince of Peace, The Good Shepherd, The Way, The Door, The Truth, The Life, The Bread of Life, The Light of the World, The Vine, The True Vine; The Lord our Righteousness, The Sun of Righteousness.

The Incarnation, The Hypostatic Union, The Word made Flesh.

[FUNCTIONS] salvation, redemption, atonement, propitiation, mediation, intercession, judgment; soteriology.

III. GOD THE HOLY GHOST, The Holy Spirit, Paraclete, The Comforter, The Consoler, The Intercessor, The Spirit of God, The Spirit of Truth, The Dove.

[FUNCTIONS] inspiration, unction, regeneration, sanctification, consolation, grace.

[THE DEITY IN OTHER RELIGIONS] BRAHMANISM *or* HINDUISM: Brahm *or* Brahmā (*neuter*), the Supreme Soul *or* Essence of the Universe; Trimurti *or* Hindu trinity *or* Hindu triad: (1) Prahma (*masc.*), the Creator; (2) Vishnu, the Preserver; (3) Siva *or* Shiva, the Destroyer and Regenerator. For other Hindu deities see 979.

BUDDHISM: the Protestantism of the East; Buddha, the Blessed One, the Teacher, the Lord Buddha.

ZOROASTRIANISM: Zerâna-Akerana, the Infinite Being; Ahuramazda *or* Ormazd, the Creator, the Lord of Wisdom, the Wise Lord, the Wise One, the King of Light, the Guardian of Mankind (*opposed by* Ahriman, the King of Darkness).

MOHAMMEDANISM *or* ISLAM: Allah.

V. CREATE, fashion, make, form, mold *or* mould, manifest.

PRESERVE, uphold, keep, perpetuate, immortalize.

ATONE, redeem, save, propitiate, expiate; intercede, mediate.

PREDESTINATE, predestine, foreordain, preordain; elect, call, ordain.

BLESS, sanctify, hallow, justify, absolve, glorify.

Adj. ALMIGHTY, all-powerful, omnipotent; omnipresent, all-wise, all-seeing, all-knowing, omniscient, supreme.

DIVINE, heavenly, celestial; holy, hallowed, sacred, sacrosanct.

SUPERNATURAL, superhuman, hyperphysical, superphysical, spiritual, ghostly, supramundane, supersensuous, supersensitive, supersensual, supernormal, unearthly.

theistic; theocratic; deistic; anointed; soterial.

Adv. UNDER GOD, by God's will, by God's help, *Deo volente* [*L.*], D. V., God willing; in Jesus' name, in His name, in His fear, to His glory; *jure divino* [*L.*], by divine right.

✱ *Domine dirige nos; en Dieu est ma fiance; et sceleratis sol oritur* [Seneca]; "He mounts the storm and walks upon the wind" [Pope]; "Thou great First Cause, least understood" [Pope]; *sans Dieu rien;* "naught but God Can satisfy the soul" [Bailey]; "God's in His Heaven — All's right with the world!" [Browning]; "The Somewhat which we name but cannot know" [William Watson]; "If there were no God, it would be necessary to invent him" [Voltaire].

---

977. [BENEFICENT SPIRITS.] **Angel.** —
N. ANGEL, archangel, Messenger of God, guardian angel, ministering spirits, invisible helpers, Choir Invisible, heavenly host, host of heaven, sons of God; morning star; saint.

[CELESTIAL HIERARCHY OF PSEUDO-DIONYSIUS] (1) Seraphim (*sing.* seraph, *E. pl.* seraphs), Cherubim (*sing.* cherub, *E. pl.* cherubs; cherubim *or* cherubin *are often treated as sing.*), Thrones; (2) Dominions, Virtues, Powers; (3) Principalities, Archangels, Angels.

Michael, Gabriel, Raphael, Uriel, Chamuel, Jophiel, Zadkiel; Abdiel, Azrael.

MADONNA, Our Lady, *Notre Dame* [*F.*], Holy Mary, The Virgin, The Blessed Virgin, The Virgin Mary; *Dei Mater* [*L.*]. Mother of God; *Regina Cœli* [*L.*], Queen of Heaven; *Regina Angelorum* [*L.*], Queen of Angels; *Stella Maris* [*L.*], Star of the Sea; *Mater Dolorosa* [*L.*]; Zion's Lily; *Alma Mater Redemptoris, Virgo Gloriosa, Virgo Sponsa Dei, Virgo Potens, Virgo Veneranda, Virgo Prœdicanda, Virgo Clemens, Virgo Sapientissima, Sanc'a Virgo Virginum* [*all L.*]; *La Vergine Gloriosa* [*It.*]; *La Grande Vierge* [*F.*].

Adj. ANGELIC, seraphic, cherubic, archangelic.

✱ "are they not all ministering spirits?" [*Bible*]; "And flights of angels sing thee to thy rest!" [*Hamlet*]; "Millions of spiritual creatures walk the earth Unseen, both when we wake and when we sleep" [*P. L.*]; "*Ave, maris stella, Dei Mater Alma, Atque semper Virgo, Felix cœli porta*" [*hymn*].

978. [MALEFICENT SPIRITS.] **Satan.** —
N. SATAN, the Devil, Lucifer, Belial, Beëlzebub, Eblis [*Ar.*], Ahriman [*Zoroastrianism*], Mephistopheles, Mephisto, Shaitan [*Hind.*], Samael, Asmodeus, Satanas [*archaic*], Abaddon [*Heb.*], Apollyon, *le Diable* [*F.*], Deil [*Scot.*], *Teufel* [*Ger.*], *Diabolus* [*L.*].

his Satanic Majesty, the Prince of the Devils, the Prince of Darkness, the Prince of this world, the Prince of the power of the air; the Tempter, the Adversary, the Evil One, the Evil Spirit, the Archenemy, the Archfiend, the Foul Fiend, the Devil Incarnate, the Father of Lies, the Author of Evil, the Father of Evil, the Old Serpent, the Wicked One, the Common Enemy, the angel of the bottomless pit.[1]

FALLEN ANGELS, unclean spirits, devils; the rulers of darkness, the powers of darkness; inhabitants of Pandemonium; demon &c. 980.

Moloch, Mammon, Azazel [*Milton*]; Belial [*P. L.*], Beëlzebub [*in P. L., the fallen angel next to Satan*], Loki [*Norse myth.*]

DIABOLISM, devil worship, devil lore, diablerie *or* diablery, diabolology *or* diabology, Satanism, devilism; devilship, devildom; demonry, demonism, demonology, Manichæism *or* Manicheism; Black Mass, Black Magic, demonolatry, demonomagy; witchcraft &c. (*sorcery*) 992; the cloven hoof; hoofs and horns; demonomy.

DIABOLIST, demonologist, demonol-

---

[1] The slang expressions "the Deuce, the Dickens, the Old Gentleman, Old Nick, Old Scratch, Old Horny, Old Harry, Old Gooseberry," have not been inserted in the text.

oger, demonolater, demonist, demonographer [*rare*], demonomist; Manichæan *or* Manichean.

V. DIABOLIZE [*rare*], demonize; bewitch, bedevil &c. (*sorcery*) 992; possess, obsess.

Adj. SATANIC, diabolic *or* diabolical, devilish, demoniac *or* demoniacal, infernal, hellborn.

. "Satan exalted sat, by merit raised To that bad eminence"[*P. L.*]; "from morn To noon he fell, from noon to dewy eve" [*P. L.*]; "The prince of darkness is a gentleman" [*King Lear*]; "The Devil, my friends, is a woman just now, 'Tis a woman that reigns in Hell" [Owen Meredith]; "Get thee behind me, Satan" [*Bible*].

979. Mythic and pagan deities. —

N. GOD, goddess; *deus* [*L.*], *dea* [*L.*]; deva (*fem.* devi) ["the shining ones," *Skr.*]; heathen gods and goddesses; pantheon; theogony.

[GREEK AND LATIN] Zeus, Jupiter *or* Jove (*King*); Apollon, Apollo (*the sun*); Ares, Mars (*war*); Hermes, Mercury (*messenger*); Poseidon, Neptune (*ocean*); Hephaistos, Vulcan (*smith*); Dionysus, Bacchus (*wine*); Pluton *or* Hades [*Gr.*], Pluto *or* Dis [*L.*] (*King of the lower world*); Kronos, Saturn (*time*); Eros, Cupid (*love*); Pan, Faunus (*flocks, herds, forests, and wild life*).

Hera, Juno (*Queen*); Demeter, Ceres (*fruitfulness*); Persephone, Proserpina *or* Proserpine (*Queen of the lower world*); Artemis, Diana (*the moon and hunting*); Athena, Minerva (*wisdom*); Aphrodite, Venus (*love and beauty*); Hestia, Vesta (*the hearth*); Rhea *or* Cybele ("Mother of the gods," *identified with* Ops, *wife of Saturn*); Gæa *or* Ge, Tellus (*earth goddess, mother of the Titans*).

[NORSE] Ymir (*primeval giant*), Reimthursen (*frost giants*), Bori (*fashioner of the world*), Bor (*father of Odin*), Odin *or* Woden (*the All-father,* =*Zeus*); the Æsir *or* Asas; Thor (*the Thunderer*), Balder *or* Baldr (=*Apo lo*), Freyr (*fruitfulness*), Tyr *or* Tyrr (*war*), Bragi (*poetry and eloquence*), Höder *or* Höär (*blind god of the winter*), Heimdall (*warder of Asgard*), Vidar (= *Pan*), Uller *or* Ullr (*the chase*), Forseti (*peacemaker*), Vali (*knowledge and eternal light*), Loki (*evil*).

the Vanir *or* Vans: Njorth *or* Njord (*the winds and the sea*), Frey *or* Freyr (*prosperity and love*), Freya *or* Freyja (*goddess of love and beauty,* = *Venus*).

Frigg *or* Frigga (*wife of Odin*), Hel (*goddess of death,* = *Persephone*), Sif (*wife of Thor*), Nanna (*wife of Balder*), Idun (*goddess of spring, wife of Bragi*), Sigyn (*wife of Loki*).

[HINDU] VEDIC GODS: Dyaus (*the Heaven*), Indra (*cloud-compeller*), Varuna (*the sky, also the waters*), Surya (*the sun,* =*Gr.* Helios), Savitar ("*the Inciter,*" *a sun god*), Soma (*the sus ainer*), Agni (*fire*), Vavu (*the winds*), the Marutas (*storm gods*), Ushas ("the Dawn," *goddess of wisdom*).

BRAHMANIC GODS: Brahmâ, Vishnu, Siva *or* Shiva &c. (*Brahmanism*) 976; avatars of

980. Evil Spirits. —

N. demon, fiend, devil &c. (*Satan*) 978; evil genius, familiar, familiar spirit; bad –, unclean-spirit; cacodæmon *or* cacodemon, incubus, succubus *and* succuba; dæva *or* deev, bad peri, afreet, lamia, barghest *or* barguest; ogre, ogress, ghoul, vampire, harpy; Fury, the Furies, the Erinyes, the Eumenides; Titan; Friar Rush.

imp, bad fairy, sprite, jinni *or* jinnee (*pl.* jin), genius (*pl.* genii), flibbertigibbet, ouphe, dwarf, troll, urchin, Cluricaune.

changeling, elf-child, auf, oaf; werewolf, *loup-garou* [*F.*]; satyr.

ELEMENTAL, sylph, gnome, salamander, nymph [*Rosicrucian*].

SIREN, nixie, undine, Lorelei.

BUGBEAR, bugaboo, bogy *or* bogey *or* bogie, bug [*obs.*], poker [*rare*], goblin, hobgoblin, boggart *or* boggard.

DEMONOLOGY, demonry &c. (*diabolism*) 978.

Adj. demoniac, demoniacal, fiendish, fiendlike, evil, ghoulish; pokerish [*colloq., U. S.*], bewitched.

. "For we wrestle not against flesh and blood, but against principalities, against powers, against the rulers of the darkness of this world" [*Bible*]; "to another [is given] discerning of spirits" [*Bible*]; "Whence and what art thou, execrable shape?" [*Paradise Lost*].

980a. Specter. —

N. SPECTER *or* spectre, ghost, revenant, apparition, spirit, sprite, shade, shadow, wraith, spook [*now humorous*], phantom, phantasm, fantasm [*rare*], idolum; materialization [*Spiritualism*], ectoplasmic manifestation; double, etheric body, etheric self, aura, auric egg, astral body, *mayavi rupa*, ego [*all Theos. and Occultism*]; vision, theophany.

banshee, White Lady, the White Ladies of Normandy, the White Lady of Avenel [Scott]; lemures, larva *or* larve [*Roman relig.*].

Vishnu: (1) Matsya, the fish; (2) Karma, the turtle; (3) Varah, the boar; (4) Narsinh, man-lion; (5) Vaman, the dwarf; (6) Parshuram, a Brahman; (7) Rama; (8) Krishna; (9) Buddha; (10) Kalki; Jagannath *or* Juggernaut (*Krishna*); Ganesha *or* Ganpati (*wisdom*), Hanuman (*monkey god*), Yama (*judge of the dead*).

Sarasvati (*sakti or wife of Brahmâ; goddess of poetry, wisdom, and fine art*), Lakshmi (*wife of Vishnu; goddess of wealth and prosperity*), Durga *or* Kali (*wife of Siva, conceived as a malignant deity*); Devi ("the goddess") *or* Uma ("light") *or* Gauri ("the brilliant") *or* Parvati ("the mountaineer," *wife of Siva, conceived as a beneficent deity*).

[EGYPTIAN] Ra *or* Amun-Ra (*the sun god*), Neph *or* Nef (*spirit or breath*), Pthah (*demiurge*), Khem (*reproduction*), Mut *or* Maut (= *Gr. Demeter*). Osiris (*judge of the dead*), Isis (*wife of Osiris*), Horus (*the morning sun; son of Osiris and Isis*), Anubis (*jackal-god, brother of Horus, a conductor of the dead*), Nephthys (*sister of Isis*). Set (*evil deity, brother of Osiris*), Thoth (*clerk of the under world*), Bast *or* Bubastis (*a goddess with head of a cat*), the Sphinx (*wisdom*).

[VARIOUS] Baal (*Heb. pl.* Baalim) [*Semitic*]; Astarte *or* Ashtoreth (*goddess of fertility and love*) [*Phœnician*]; Bel *Babylonian*]; The Great Spirit [*N. Amer Indian*]; Mumbo Jumbo [*Sudanese Negroes, an idol or bugaboo*].

NYMPH, dryad, hamadryad, alseid, wood nymph; naiad, fresh-water nymph; oread, mountain nymph; nereid, sea nymph; limoniad *or* leimoniad, meadow nymph *or* flower nymph; Oceanid, ocean nymph; napæa, glen nymph; potamid, river nymph; Pleiades *or* Atlantides, Hyades, Dodonides.

FAIRY, fay, sprite *or* spright [*archaic*]; nix (*fem.* nixie), water sprite; the Good Folk, brownie *or* browny, pixy, elf (*pl.* elves), banshee *or* banshie; the Fates *or* Mœræ, *Clotho* (Spinner), *Lachesis* (Disposer of Lots), *Atropos* (Inflexible One); gnome, kelpie; faun; peri, nis, kobold, sylph, sylphid; undine, sea maid, sea nymph, mermaid (*masc.* merman); Mab, Oberon, Titania, Ariel; Puck, Robin Goodfellow, Hobgoblin; Leprechaun; denizens of the air; afreet &c. (*bad spirit*) 980.

FAMILIAR SPIRIT, familiar, genius, guide, good genius, tutelary genius, daimon, demon *or* dæmon, guardian.

MYTHOLOGY, mythical lore, heathen mythology, folklore, fairyism, fairy mythology.

Adj. MYTHICAL, mythic, mythological, fabulous, legendary &c. 515.

FAIRYLIKE, sylphlike, sylphine, sylphish, sylphidine; elfin, elflike, elfish, nymph-like.

*** "Where'er he moves, the goddess shone before" [Homer — *Pope's trans.*]; "speak of the gods as they are" [Bias]; "You moonshine revelers and shades of night" [*Merry Wives*] "Where the bee sucks, there suck I; In a cowslip's bell I lie" [*Tempest*]; "Aërial spirits, by great Jove designed To be on earth the guardians of mankind" [Hesiod].

WILL-O'-THE-WISP, Friar's lantern &c. 423.

Adj. SPECTRAL, ghostly, ghostlike, spiritual, wraithlike, weird, uncanny, eerie *or* eery, spooky *or* spookish [*colloq.*], haunted; unearthly, supernatural.

*** "Is not this something more than fantasy!" [*Hamlet*]; "But soft! behold! lo! where it comes again" [*ibid.*]; "Of calling shapes, and beck'ning shadows dire" [Milton].

---

981. **Heaven.** — **N.** HEAVEN; kingdom of -heaven, – God; heavenly kingdom; heaven of heavens, God's throne, throne of God, presence of God; inheritance of the saints in light.

Paradise, Eden, Zion, Holy City, New Jerusalem, Heavenly City, City Celestial, abode of the blessed; celestial bliss, eternal bliss, unending bliss, glory, never-ending day.

[MYTHOLOGICAL HEAVEN OR PARADISE] Olympus; Elysium, Elysian fields, Islands (*or* Isles) of the Blessed, Happy Isles, Fortunate Isles, Arcadia, bowers

982. **Hell.** — **N.** HELL, bottomless pit, place of torment; habitation of fallen angels; Pandemonium, Abaddon, Domdaniel; *jahannan* [*Hind.*], Sheol.

hell fire; everlasting -fire, – torment; lake of fire and brimstone; fire that is never quenched, worm that never dies.

purgatory, limbo, gehenna, abyss, Tophet.

[MYTHOLOGICAL HELL] Tartarus, Hades, Avernus, Styx, Stygian creek, pit of Acheron, Cocytus; infernal regions, inferno, shades below, realms of Pluto.

of bliss, garden of the Hesperides, third heaven, seventh heaven; Valhalla *or* Walhalla [*Scandinavian*]; Nirvana [*Buddhist*]; happy hunting grounds [*N. Amer. Indian*]; *Alfardaws, Assama; Falak al aflak,* ("the highest heaven") [*Mohammedan*].

FUTURE STATE, life after death, eternal home, resurrection, translation; resuscitation &c. 660; apotheosis, deification.

Pluto, Rhadamanthus, Erebus, Charon, Cerberus; Persephone, Proserpina *or* Proserpine; Minos, Osiris.

RIVERS OF HELL: Styx, Acheron, Cocytus, Phlegethon, Lethe.

Adj. HELLISH, infernal, stygian.

⁎ *dies iræ dies illa;* "the hue of dungeons and the scowl of night" [*L. L. L.*]; "Hell the Shadow from a Soul on fire Cast on the Darkness" [Omar Khayyám — Fitzgerald].

[THEOSOPHY] Devachan *or* Devaloka, the land of the Gods.

Adj. HEAVENLY, celestial, supernal, unearthly, from on high, paradisaic *or* paradisaical, paradisiac *or* paradisiacal, beatific, elysian, Olympian, Arcadian.

⁎ "looks through Nature up to Nature's God" [Pope]; "the great world's altar stairs, That slope through darkness up to God" [Tennyson]; "the treasury of everlasting joy" [*Henry VI*]; *vigeur de dessus;* "Heav'n but the Vision of fulfil'd desire" [Omar Khayyám — Fitzgerald]; "that bright kingdom where the souls who strove Live now forever, helping living men" [Masefield]; "that goal That lies beyond the purchase of the world" [Presland].

2. RELIGIOUS DOCTRINES

983. [RELIGIOUS KNOWLEDGE.] **Theology.** — N. THEOLOGY (natural and revealed), theosophy, divine wisdom, divinity, hagiology, hagiography, hierography; Caucasian mystery; monotheism, theism, religion; religious -persuasion, - sect, - denomination, - affiliation; creed &c. (*belief*) 484; articles -, declaration -, profession -, confession- of faith.

THEOLOGIAN, theologue [*now rare*], scholastic, divine, schoolman, canonist, theologist [*now rare*], theologus; monotheist, theist; Homoousian (*opp. to* Homoiousian); the Fathers.

Adj. THEOLOGICAL, religious, divine, canonical; denominational; sectarian &c. 984.

983a. Orthodoxy. — N. ORTHODOXY; strictness, soundness, religious truth, true faith; truth &c. 494; soundness of doctrine.

Christianity, Christianism; Catholicism, Catholicity; "the faith once delivered to the saints"; hyperorthodoxy &c. 984.

THE CHURCH, Holy Church, Church Militant, Church Triumphant; Catholic -, Universal -, Apostolic -, Established- Church; the Bride of the Lamb; temple of the Holy Ghost; Church -, body -, members -, disciples -, followers- of Christ; Christians.

true believer; textualist, textuary; canonist &c. (*theologian*) 983; the Orthodox; Christian community; Christendom, collective body of Christians.

CANONS &c. (*belief*) 484; thirty-nine articles; Apostles' -, Nicene -, Athanasian- Creed; Church Catechism.

Adj. ORTHODOX, sound, strict, faithful, catholic, schismless, Christian, evangelical; scriptural, literal, divine, mono-

984. Heterodoxy. [SECTARIANISM.] — N. HETERODOXY; error &c. 495; false doctrine, heresy, schism, schismaticism, schismaticalness; recusancy, backsliding, apostasy; materialism, hylotheism; atheism &c. (*irreligion*) 989.

anthropomorphism, anthropopathism, anthropopathy; idolatry &c. 991; superstition &c. (*credulity*) 486.

BIGOTRY &c. (*obstinacy*) 606; fanaticism, iconoclasm; hyperorthodoxy, precisianism; bibliolatry, hagiolatry; sabbatarianism, puritanism.

SECTARIANISM, sectarism [*obs.*], nonconformity; dissent &c. 489; secularism; syncretism; religious sects, the clash of creeds.

protestantism, Arianism, Adventism, Jansenism, Stundism, Erastianism, Calvinism, Quakerism, Methodism, Anabaptism, Puseyism, tractarianism, ritualism, Origenism, Sabellianism, Socinianism, Gnosticism, Mormonism, Second Adventism, materialism, positivism, latitudinarianism, ethicism,

theistic, theistic; true &c. 494; true blue.

. of the true faith; "Ever the fiery Pentecost Girds with one flame the countless host" [Emerson]; "Odinism was valor; Christianism was humility, another kind of valor" [Carlyle]; "prove their doctrine orthodox By apostolic blows and knocks" [Butler]; "orthodoxy is my doxy; heterodoxy another man's doxy" [Warburton]; "orthodoxy is the Bourbon of the world of thought; it learns not, neither can it forget" [Huxley]; "The Church . . . the world-tree of the nations for so long!" [Carlyle].

deism, higher pantheism, henotheism; monism, philosophical unitarianism &c.; the isms.

Anglicanism; High –, Low –, Broad –, Free- Church; ultramontanism; monasticism, monkery; Catholicism, Romanism, popery, papism, papistry, papacy, Maryolatry [usually opprobrious], Scarlet Woman, Church of Rome; Greek Church. [Generally speaking, each sect is orthodox to itself and heterodox to others.]

Judaism; Mohammedanism, Islam, Islamism.

Theosophy, New Thought, ethical culture, mental science, mental healing; Christian Science, Eddyism; Spiritualism, Spiritism, occultism; Swedenborgianism.

PAGANISM, heathenism, heathendom; mythology; animism, polytheism, ditheism, tritheism, pantheism; dualism.

Gentilism, Babism, Sufiism, Neoplatonism, Brahmanism, Hinduism, Vedantism, Buddhism, Lamaism; Sikhism, Jainism; Confucianism, Taoism; Shintoism, Sabæanism or Sabeanism or Sabeism.

PAGAN, heathen, paynim; giaour [Turk.], Gheber or Ghebre, kafir, non-Mohammedan; gentile; pantheist, polytheist, animist.

MISBELIEVER, heretic, apostate; backslider; antichrist; idolater; skeptic &c. 989.

BIGOT &c. (obstinacy) 606; fanatic, abdal, dervish, iconoclast.

SECTARIAN, sectary, sectarist [rare], schismatic; seceder, separatist, recusant, dissenter, nonconformist, nonjuror.

Huguenot, Protestant, Episcopalian; Trinitarian; latitudinarian; limitarian· orthodox dissenter, Puritan, Unitarian, Congregationalist, Independent; Presbyterian; Lutheran, Ubiquitarian, Calvinist, Methodist, Wesleyan; Anabaptist, Baptist; Mormon, Latter-day Saint; Irvingite, Sandemanian, Glassite, Erastian, Sublapsarian, Supralapsarian; Gentoo, Antinomian, Swedenborgian; Adventist, Second Adventist, Bible Christian, Bryanite, Brownian, Dunker, Ebionite, Eusebian; Faith Curer, Faith Curist, Faith Healer, Mental Healer, Christian Scientist; Familist, Jovinianist, Libadist, Restitutionist, Quaker, Shaker, Quietist, Stundist, Tunker &c.

Catholic, Roman Catholic, Romanist, Papist, ultramontane; Anglican, Oxford School; tractarian, Puseyite, ritualist; High Churchman.

Jew, Hebrew, Rabbinist; Mohammedan, Mussulman, Moslem, Islamite, Osmanli, Motazilite, Shiah, Sunni, Wahabi; Brahman or Brahmin; Brahmo; Vedantist, Jain or Jaina, Sikh, Parsi or Parsee, fire worshiper, Zoroastrian [erron. called fire worshiper]; Sufi, Babist, Buddhist; Confucianist, Taoist, Shintoist; Magi, Gymnosophist, Sabian, henotheist, Gnostic, Sadducee, Rosicrucian, Mystic, Occultist, Theosophist, Spiritualist, Spiritist &c.

MATERIALIST, hylotheist; positivist, deist, agnostic, atheist &c. 989.

Adj. HETERODOX, heretical, unorthodox, unscriptural, uncanonical, unchristian, antiscriptural, apocryphal; antichristian; schismatic, recusant, iconoclastic; sectarian, dissenting, dissident [now rare]; Protestant &c. n.; secular &c. (lay) 997; deistic, agnostic, atheistic; skeptical &c. 989.

bigoted &c. (prejudiced) 481, (obstinate) 606; superstitious &c. (credulous) 486; fanatical; idolatrous &c. 991; visionary &c. (imaginative) 515.

Judaical; Mohammedan, Islamic or Islamitic, Moslem; Brahmanic or Brahmanical, Brahminic or Brahminical; Buddhist &c. n.

Popish, papish, papistic or papistical, Romish.

PAGAN, heathen, heathenish, ethnic, ethnical; gentile, paynim; polytheistic, pantheistic, animistic.

₊ "slave to no sect" [Pope]; *superstitione tollendâ religio non tollitur* [Cicero]; "our wishes ought not to determine what we shall accept as truth" [H. C. Örsted]; "Whatever creed be taught or land be trod, Man's conscience is the oracle of God" [Byron]; "A Pagan suckled in some creed outworn" [Wordsworth]; "There lives more faith in honest doubt Believe me, than in half the creeds" [Tennyson]; "The religion of Christ is peace and good-will, that of Christendom war and ill-will" [Landor]; "Now join your hands, and with your hands your hearts" [*III Henry VI*]; "With malice toward none, with charity for all, with firmness in the right, as God gives us to see the right" [Lincoln].

---

985. Revelation. [BIBLICAL.] — **N.** REVELATION, inspiration, *afflatus* [L.]; theophany, theopneusty.

THE BIBLE, the Book, the Book of Books, the Good Book, the Word, the Word of God, Scripture, the Scriptures, Holy Writ, Holy Scriptures, inspired writings, Gospel.

OLD TESTAMENT, Septuagint, Vulgate, Pentateuch; Octateuch; the Law, the Jewish Law; the Prophets; major -, minor- Prophets; Hagiographa, Hierographa; Apocrypha.

NEW TESTAMENT; Gospels, Evangelists, Synoptic Gospels, Acts, Epistles, Apocalypse, Revelation; Good Tidings, Glad Tidings.

[HEBREW] Talmud, Mishna, Gemara; Masora *or* Masorah.

INSPIRED WRITERS, inspired penmen; prophet &c. (*seer*) 513; evangelist, apostle, disciple, saint; the Fathers, the Apostolic Fathers; Holy Men of old.

Adj. SCRIPTURAL, biblical, sacred, prophetic; evangelical, evangelistic, apostolic, apostolical; inspired, theopneustic, theopneusted [*rare*], apocalyptic, revealed; ecclesiastical, canonical, textuary; Talmudic.

₊ "Out from the heart of nature rolled The burdens of the Bible old" [Emerson]; "The word unto the prophet spoken Was writ on tables yet unbroken" [*ibid.*]; "Within that awful volume lies The mystery of mysteries!" [Scott]; "A glory gilds the sacred page, Majestic like the sun, It gives a light to every age, It gives but borrows none" [Cowper].

---

986. Sacred Writings. [NON-BIBLICAL.] — **N.** The Vedas (Rig-Veda, Yajur-Veda, Sama-Veda, Atharva-Veda), the Upanishads, the Puranas, Sutras, Sastra *or* Shastra, Tantra, Bhagavad Gita [*all Brahmanic*]; Zendavesta, Avesta [*Zoroastrian*]; The Koran *or* Alcoran [*Mohammedan*]; Tripitaka, Dhammapada [*Buddhist*]; Granth, Adigranth [*Sikh*]; the Agamas [*Jain*]; the Kings [*Chinese*]; the Eddas [*Scandinavia*].

Arcana Coelestia &c. [*Swedenborgian*]; Book of Mormon; "Science and Health with Key to the Scriptures" [*Christian Science*].

[NON-BIBLICAL PROPHETS AND RELIGIOUS FOUNDERS] Gautama (Buddha); Zoroaster, Confucius, Lao-tse [*Taoism*], Mohammed, Nanak Shah [*Sikhism*], Vaddhamana, "Maha-vira" [*Jainism*], Mirza Ali Mohammed, "Bab-ud-Din" (*Per.* "Gate of the Faith") [*Babism*], Ram Mohun Roy [*Brahmo-Samaj*].

Swedenborg, Joseph Smith [*Mormonism*], Mary Baker Eddy [*Christian Science*].

₊ "In Faith and Hope the world will disagree, But all mankind's concern is Charity" [Pope]; "There is only one religion, though there are a hundred versions of it" [Shaw].

---

3. RELIGIOUS SENTIMENTS

987. Piety. — **N.** PIETY, religion, theism, faith; religiousness, religiosity; holiness &c. *adj.*; saintship; religionism; sanctimony &c. (*assumed piety*) 988; reverence &c. (*respect*) 928; humility, veneration, devotion; prostration &c. (*worship*) 990; grace, unction, edification; sanctity, sanctitude [*rare*]; consecration.

988. Impiety. — **N.** IMPIETY; sin &c. 945; irreverence; profaneness &c. *adj.*, profanity, profanation; blasphemy, desecration, sacrilege; scoffing &c. *v.*

[ASSUMED PIETY] hypocrisy &c. (*falsehood*) 544; pietism, cant, pious fraud; lip-devotion, lip-service, lip-reverence; misdevotion, formalism, austerity; sanctimony, sanctimoniousness &c. *adj.*;

spiritual existence, odor of sanctity, beauty of holiness.

theopathy, beatification, adoption, regeneration, conversion, justification, theodicy, sanctification, salvation, inspiration, bread of life; Body and Blood of Christ.

BELIEVER, convert, theist, Christian, devotee, pietist, Saint.

the -good, – righteous, – just, – believing, – elect; the children of -God, – Our Father, – the kingdom, – light.

V. BE PIOUS &c. *adj.;* have faith &c. *n.;* believe, receive Christ; venerate, adore, worship, perform the acts of devotion; revere &c. 928; be converted &c.; experience the divine illumination [*Mysticism*]; be at one with God, be on God's side, stand up for Jesus, fight the good fight, keep the faith, let one's light shine.

REGENERATE, convert, edify, sanctify, hallow, keep holy, beatify, inspire, consecrate, enshrine.

Adj. PIOUS, religious, devout, devoted, reverent, godly, heavenly-minded, humble, pure, pure in heart, holy, spiritual, pietistic, saintly, saintlike; seraphic, sacred, solemn.

believing, faithful, Christian, Catholic.

REGENERATED; inspired, consecrated, converted, unearthly, ʌot of the earth, in the world not of it.

elected, adopted, justified, sanctified.

*** *ne vile fano;* "pure-eyed Faith . . . thou hovering angel girt with golden wings" [Milton]; "To me religion is life before God and in God" [Amiel]; "See God's world through the rags of this" [Masefield].

pharisaism, precisianism; sabbatism, sabbatarianism; *odium theologicum* [*L.*], sacerdotalism; bigotry &c. (*obstinacy*) 606, (*prejudice*) 481; blue laws.

APOSTASY, recusancy, hardening, backsliding, declension, perversion, reprobation.

HYPOCRITE &c. (*dissembler*) 548; "Scribes and Pharisees" [*Bible*]; *Rawana-sannyasi* [*Hind.*]; Tartufe, Mawworm, Holy Willie [*Burns*].

BIGOT, saint [*ironical*]; Pharisee, sabbatarian, formalist, methodist, puritan, pietist, precisian, religionist, devotee, ranter, fanatic; juramentado [*Moro*].

SINNER &c. 949; scoffer, blasphemer, sacrilegist [*rare*], sabbath breaker; worldling.

the wicked, the evil, the unjust, the reprobate; sons of -men, – Belial, – the wicked one; children of -the devil, – darkness.

V. BE IMPIOUS &c. *adj.;* profane, desecrate, blaspheme, revile, scoff; swear &c. (*malediction*) 908; commit sacrilege.

DISSEMBLE, simulate, play the hypocrite, hypocrify [*obs.*], hypocrize [*rare*], snuffle, talk through the nose, talk nasally, hold up the hands in horror, turn up the whites of the eyes; sing psalms for a pretense, make long prayers.

Adj. IMPIOUS; irreligious &c. 989; desecrating &c. *v.;* profane, irreverent, sacrilegious, blasphemous.

unhallowed, unsanctified, unregenerate; hardened, perverted, reprobate.

HYPOCRITICAL &c. (*false*) 544; canting, pietistical, sanctimonious, unctuous, pharisaical, overrighteous, righteous over much.

BIGOTED, fanatical, hidebound, narrow, illiberal, prejudiced, little; provincial, parochial, insular; priest-ridden.

Adv. under the -mask, – cloak, – pretense, – form, – guise- of religion; in blasphemy.

*** *giovane santo diavolo recchio;* "Oh, for a *forty-parson power* to chant Thy praise, Hypocrisy!" [Byron]; "But all was false and hollow; though his tongue Dropped manna" [*P. L.*]; "O serpent heart, hid with a flowering face!" [*Romeo and Juliet*]; "Saint abroad, and a devil at home" [Bunyan].

989. Irreligion. — N. IRRELIGION, indevotion, impiety; ungodliness &c. *adj.;* laxity, apathy, indifference; quietism, passiveness, passivity.

SKEPTICISM, doubt; unbelief, disbelief, incredulity, incredulousness &c. *adj.;* want of -faith, – belief; pyrrhonism; doubt &c. 485; agnosticism, freethinking; deism; hylotheism; materialism, rationalism, positivism; nihilism.

INFIDELITY, antichristianity, antichristianism, atheism.

UNBELIEVER, infidel, atheist, antichristian; *giaour* [*Turk.*], heretic, miscreant [*archaic*], heathen, alien, gentile, Nazarene; *esprit fort* [*F.*], freethinker, skeptic, pyrrhonist, deist, latitudinarian, rationalist; materialist, positivist, nihilist, agnostic, somatist, theophobist.

V. BE IRRELIGIOUS &c. *adj.;* disbelieve, lack faith; doubt, question &c. 485.

dechristianize, antichristianize [*rare*]; serve Mammon, contend against the light, love darkness rather than light, deny the truth.

Adj. IRRELIGIOUS; indevout, undevout, devoutless, godless, graceless, ungodly; unholy, unsanctified, unhallowed; atheistic, without God.

SKEPTICAL, freethinking, unbelieving, unconverted; incredulous, faithless, lacking faith; deistic, deistical; antichristian, unchristian.

WORLDLY, mundane, earthly, carnal; worldly &c. worldly-minded, unspiritual.

Adv. IRRELIGIOUSLY &c. *adj.*

. "Unbelief is blind" [Milton]; "the fool hath said in his heart, There is no God" [*Bible*]; "no one is so much alone in the world as a denier of God" [Richter].

4. ACTS OF RELIGION

990. Worship. — N. WORSHIP, adoration, devotion, cult, aspiration, homage, service, humiliation; kneeling, genuflection, prostration; latria, dulia, hyperdulia.

PRAYER, invocation, supplication, rogation, intercession, orison, holy breathing, petition &c. (*request*) 765; collect, litany, Lord's prayer, paternoster; *Ave Maria* [*L.*]; Hail, Mary; rosary, bead-roll.

revival; anxious –, revival –, camp- meeting.

THANKSGIVING; giving –, returning- thanks; grace, praise, glorification, pæan, benediction, doxology, hosanna, hallelujah or halleluiah, alleluia or alleluiah; *Te Deum, non nobis Domine, nunc dimittis; O Salutaris* [*all L.*]; Sanctus, *Agnus Dei* [*L.*], *Kyrie Eleison* [*Gr.*], *Gloria* [*L.*], The Annunciation, Tersanctus, Trisagion.

psalm, psalmody; hymn, plain song, chant, chaunt [*archaic*], response, anthem, motet, antiphon, antiphony.

OBLATION, sacrifice, incense, libation, offering; burnt –, heave –, thank –, votive-offering; offertory, collection.

DISCIPLINE, self-discipline, self-examination, self-denial; fasting, penance, confession.

DIVINE SERVICE, office, duty; exercises; morning prayer; Mass, matins, nones, complin or compline, evensong, vespers, vigils, lauds; undersong, tierce; holyday &c. (*rites*) 998.

PRAYER BOOK, missal, breviary, Virginal; ritual &c. 998.

WORSHIPER, congregation, communicant, celebrant.

V. WORSHIP, lift up the heart, aspire; revere &c. 928; adore, do service, pay homage; humble oneself, kneel; bow –, bend- the knee; throw oneself on one's knees, fall down, fall on one's knees; prostrate oneself, bow down and worship; beat the breast.

intone, chant, deacon or deacon off [*colloq., U. S.*], lead the choir, sing.

PRAY, invoke, supplicate; put –, offer- up -prayers, – petitions; beseech &c. (*ask*) 765; say one's prayers, tell one's beads, recite the rosary.

GIVE THANKS, return thanks, say grace, bless, praise, laud, glorify, magnify, sing praises; give benediction.

propitiate, offer sacrifice, fast, deny oneself; vow, offer vows, give alms.

ATTEND SERVICE, attend Mass, go to church, attend divine service; communicate &c. (*rite*) 998; work out one's salvation.

Adj. WORSHIPING &c. *v.;* devout, devotional, reverent, pure, solemn; fervid &c. (*heartfelt*) 821.

Int. HALLELUJAH or halleluiah! alleluia or alleluiah! hosanna! glory be to God! *sursum corda* [*L.*], *Deo gratias* [*L.*].

O Lord! pray God that! God -grant, – bless, – save, – forbid!

. "making their lives a prayer" [Whittier]; *ora et labora;* "prayer ardent opens heaven" [Young]; "Be comforted, thou wouldst not seek Me if thou hadst not already found Me" [Pascal]; "what greater calamity can fall upon a nation than the loss of worship" [Emerson].

991. Idolatry.— N. IDOLATRY, idolatrousness, idololatry, idolism, idolodoulia, demonism, demonolatry, demonology; idol -, chthonian -, demon -, devil -, fire-worship; zoölatry, fetishism or fetichism; ecclesiolatry, heliolatry, bibliolatry, hierolatry [rare].

idolization, deification, apotheosis, canonization; hero worship.

SACRIFICE, idolothyte, hecatomb, holocaust; human sacrifices, immolation, mactation, infanticide, self-immolation, suttee.

IDOL, golden calf, graven image, fetish or fetich, eidolon, thakur [Hind.], joss [Chinese], lares et penates [L.]; god (or goddess) of one's idolatry; Baal, Moloch, Dagon, Juggernaut.

IDOLATER, idolatress, demonolater or demonolator, chthonian, fetishist or fetichist idolatrizer, idolizer, idolant [obs.], idolaster [obs.]; ecclesiolater, heliolater, zoölater, bibliolater.

V. IDOLATRIZE, idolize; adorer le veau d'or [F.]; worship -idols, – pictures, – relics; apotheosize, worship, put on a pedestal, prostrate oneself before; make sacrifice to, immolate before; deify, canonize.

Adj. IDOLATROUS, idololatric [rare], idolatric [rare], idolistic, chthonian, demonolatrous, fetishic [rare], fetishistic or fetichistic, idolothyte; worshiping or worshipping, prone before, prostrate before, in the dust before, at the feet of; heliolatrous, zoölatrous.

.•. "the idol is the measure of the worshipper" [Lowell]; "he who offers God a second place offers him no place" [Ruskin]; "condemnable idolatry is insincere idolatry — a human soul clinging spasmodically to an Ark of the Covenant, which it half feels is now a phantasm" [Carlyle].

992. Sorcery. — N. SORCERY; occult -art, – sciences; magic, black magic, the black art, necromancy, theurgy, thaumaturgy; demonology, demonomy [obs.], demonomancy, demonship; diablerie, bedevilment, witchcraft, witchery; fetishism or fetichism; ghost dance, hoodoo, voodoo, voodooism; fire worship, heliolatry; obi or obiism, shamanism, vampirism; conjuration, incantation, bewitchment, glamour, enchantment; obsession, possession; exorcism.

divination &c. (prediction) 511; sortilege, ordeal, sortes Vergilianæ; hocuspocus &c. (deception) 545.

V. PRACTICE SORCERY &c. n.; cast a nativity, cast a horoscope, conjure, exorcise or exorcize [rare in the sense of conjure], charm, enchant, bewitch, bedevil, overlook, look on with the evil eye, witch, voodoo, hoodoo [colloq.]; entrance, fascinate &c. (influence) 615; taboo or tabu; wave a wand; rub the -ring, – lamp; cast a spell; call up spirits; raise spirits from the dead; raise ghosts, lay ghosts; command jinn or genii.

Adj. MAGIC, magical; witching, weird, cabalistic, talismanic, phylacteric, incantatory; charmed &c. v.; Circean; voodoo.

992a. Psychical Research.— N. PSYCHICAL RESEARCH, psychical (or psychic) investigation; abnormal psychology; abnormal -, supernormal -, mediumistic-phenomena; mysticism; psychophysics; "psychologist's fallacy" [William James].

THE SUBCONSCIOUS, the subconscious self, the subliminal self, the higher self ego &c. 980a; subconsciousness, subliminal consciousness; dual personality, mental duality, secondary consciousness, intuition; multiple personality, mental dissociation, dissociation of personality, functional disintegration; impersonation, obsession, possession.

PSYCHOTHERAPY, psychotherapeutics, psychanalysis; hysteria, neurasthenia, psychasthenia; over-stimulation; dreams, visions, apparitions, hallucinations, veridical hallucinations; Freud's theory.

MESMERISM, animal magnetism; od, odyl or odylic force [obsoles.], electrobiology; mesmeric trance; hypnotism; hypnosis, hypnoidal state.

[PHENOMENA] TELEPATHY, thought transference, thought transmission, telepathic transmission; "malicious animal magnetism" or "M. A. P."; telepathic dreams; second sight, clairvoyance, clairaudience, psychometry.

PREMONITIONS, previsions, telepathic hallucinations; premonitory apparition, fetch, wraith, double; symbolic hallucinations; death lights, ominous dreams, ominous animals.

AUTOMATISM, automatic writing, planchette, ouija board, trance writing, spirit writing, psychography; trance speaking, inspirational speaking.

CRYSTAL GAZING, crystallomancy, crystal vision; hydromancy, lecanomancy, catoptromancy, onychomancy.

SPIRITUALISM, spiritism, spirit rapping, "Rochester knockings," table-turning, Poltergeist; spirit manifestations; ghost, specter &c. 980a; haunted houses; trance, spirit control, spirit possession; mediumistic communications; séance; materialization.

[THEOSOPHY AND OCCULTISM] astral body &c. 980a, *kamarupa* [*Skr.*], desire body; etheric body, *linga sharira* [*Skr.*]; dense body, *sthula sharira* [*Skr.*]; mental body; causal body; bliss body, Buddhic body.

SEVEN PRINCIPLES OF MAN: (1) spirit *or* atma [*Skr.*], (2) spiritual mind, (3) intellect, (4) instinctive mind, (5) prana *or* vital force, (6) astral body, (7) physical body [*Yogi philosophy*].

MEDIUM, ecstatica [*rare*], seer, clairvoyant, clairaudient, telepathist; guide, control; mesmerist, hypnotist.

V. PSYCHOLOGIZE; investigate the -abnormal, – suprarational, – supernormal, – the subconscious, – the subliminal; search beyond the threshold, traverse the borderland, know oneself.

MESMERIZE, magnetize, hypnotize, place under control, subject to suggestion, place in a trance, induce hypnosis.

HOLD A SÉANCE, call up spirits, summon familiar spirits, "call spirits from the vasty deep" [*I Henry IV*]; hold spirit communications; materialize.

Adj. PSYCHICAL, psychic, psychal [*rare*], psychological; spiritistic, spiritualistic, spiritual; subconscious, "coconscious" [Morton Prince], subliminal (*opp. to* supraliminal); supernormal, abnormal, suprarational; mystic *or* mystical.

mediumistic, clairvoyant, clairaudient, telepathic; psychometric; hypnoidal, hypnagogic.

*** "There exists in nature, in myriad activity, a *psychic element* the essential nature of which is still hidden to us" [Flammarion]; "There are more things in heaven and earth, Horatio, Than are dreamt of in your philosophy' [*Hamlet*]; "I give you an eye divine" [*Bhagavad Gita*]; "But often, in the world's most crowded streets, But often, in the din of strife. There rises an unspeakable desire After the knowledge of our buried life" [Arnold].

993. Spell. — N. SPELL, charm, incantation, exorcism, weird [*obs. or Scot.*], cabala *or* cabbala, exsufflation [*obs.*], cantrip *or* cantraip *or* contrap [*chiefly Scot.*], runes, abracadabra, open sesame, *or* open-sesame, hocus-pocus, counter-charm, Ephesian letters, bell book and candle, Mumbo Jumbo, evil eye.

talisman, amulet, madstone [*U. S.*], periapt, telesm [*archaic*], phylactery, philter *or* philtre, fetish *or* fetich, manito *or* manitou *or* manitu; furcula, furculum, wishbone, merrythought; mascot *or* mascotte, rabbit's foot, hoodoo [*colloq.*], jinx [*slang*], scarabæus *or* scarab; Om *or* Aum, *Om mani padme hum* [*Buddhist*]; sudarium, veronica, triskelion; swastika, fylfot, gammadion.

WAND, caduceus, rod, divining rod, witch hazel, Aaron's rod.

[MAGIC WISH-GIVERS] Aladdin's lamp, Aladdin's casket, magic casket, magic ring, magic belt, magic spectacles, wishing cap, Fortunatus's cap; seven-league boots; cap of darkness, Tarnkappe, Tarnhelm.

[FAIRY LORE] fairy ring, fairy circle, fairy round; fernseed, rowan tree, quicken tree [*dial. Eng.*].

994. Sorcerer. — N. SORCERER, magician, wizard, warlock, necromancer, conjuror, prestidigitator, *prestidigitateur* [*F.*], charmer, exorcist, voodoo, thaumaturge, thaumaturgist, theurgist, mage [*poetic*], Magi (*sing.* Magus); diviner, dowser.

sorceress, witch, hag.

medicine man *or* medicine, witch doctor, shaman, shamanist.

VAMPIRE, lamia, ghoul; siren, harpy; incubus &c. 980.

ASTROLOGER, figure caster [*obs.*], figure flinger [*obs.*]; soothsayer &c. 513.

Katerfelto, Cagliostro, Merlin, Comus; Circe, weird sisters, Grææ *or* Graiæ, witch of Endor.

*** "You secret, black, and midnight hags!" [*Macbeth*]; "Aroint thee, witch, aroint thee!" [*ibid.*].

5. RELIGIOUS INSTITUTIONS

995. Churchdom. — N. CHURCHDOM; church, ministry, apostleship, priesthood, prelacy, hierarchy, church government, pale of the church, christendom.

clericalism, sacerdotalism, episcopalianism, ultramontanism; ecclesiology; theocracy; priestcraft, *odium theologicum* [*L.*]; religious sects &c. 984.

MONASTICISM, monkhood, monachism; celibacy.

[ECCLESIASTICAL OFFICES AND DIGNITIES] cardinalate, cardinalship; primacy, archbishopric, archiepiscopacy; prelacy, bishopric, bishopdom, episcopate, episcopacy, see, diocese; deanery, stall; canonry, canonicate; prebend, prebendaryship, prebendal stall; benefice, incumbency, glebe, advowson, living, cure, charge, cure of souls; rectorship, vicariate, vicarship; pastorate, pastorship, pastoral charge; deaconry, deaconship; curacy; chaplaincy, chaplainship, chaplainry *or* chaplanry [*Scot.*]; abbacy, presbytery.

HOLY ORDERS, ordination, institution, consecration, induction, reading in [*Eng.*], preferment, translation, presentation.

PAPACY, pontificate, popedom, See of Rome, the Vatican, the apostolic see.

COUNCIL &c. 696; conclave, college of cardinals, convocation, conference [*Meth.*], session, synod, consistory, chapter, vestry, presbytery, standing committee; sanhedrim, *congé d'élire* [*F.*].

ECCLESIASTICAL COURTS, consistorial court, court of Arches.

V. CALL, ordain, induct, prefer [*rare*], translate, consecrate, present, elect, bestow take orders, take the veil, take vows.

Adj. ECCLESIASTICAL, ecclesiological; clerical, sacerdotal, priestly, prelatical, pastoral, ministerial, capitular, theocratic; hierarchical, archiepiscopal; episcopal, episcopalian; canonical; monastic, monachal, monkish; abbatial, abbatical; Anglican; Aaronic, levitical, pontifical, papal, apostolic; ultramontane; priestridden.

996. Clergy. — N. CLERGY, clericals, ministry, priesthood, presbytery, the cloth, the pulpit, the desk.

CLERGYMAN, divine, ecclesiastic, churchman, priest, presbyter, hierophant, pastor, shepherd, minister, clerk in holy orders, parson, sky pilot [*slang*]; father, - in Christ; padre, *abbé* [*F.*], *curé* [*F.*]; reverend; black coat; confessor.

997. Laity. — N. LAITY, flock, fold, congregation, assembly, brethren, people; society [*U. S.*]; class [*Meth.*].

LAYMAN, civilian [*obs.*], laic, parishioner, catechumen; secularist.

V. LAICIZE, secularize.

Adj. SECULAR, lay, laic *or* laical, congregational, civil, temporal, profane.

[DIGNITARIES OF THE CHURCH] ecclesiarch, sacrist, hierarch; patriarch [*Eastern Ch.*]; Abba Salamah, Abuna [*Abyssinian Ch.*]; eminence, reverence, primate, metropolitan, archbishop, bishop, angel [*as in the Cath. Apostolic Ch.*], prelate, diocesan, suffragan, bishop coadjutor, dean, subdean, archdeacon, prebendary, canon, rural dean, rector, vicar, perpetual curate, residentiary, beneficiary, incumbent, chaplain, curate; elder, deacon, deaconess; preacher, reader, Bible reader, lay reader, lecturer; capitular; missionary, propagandist, Jesuit, revivalist, field preacher, colporteur.

churchwarden, deacon, questman [*hist.*], sidesman; clerk, precentor, choir; almoner, *suisse* [*F.*], verger, beadle, sexton, sacristan; acolyte, thurifer, censorbearer; chorister, choir boy, member of the choir; soloist, quartet *or* quartette; organist.

[ROMAN CATHOLIC PRIESTHOOD] Pope, Holy Father, papa [*obs. or rare*], pontiff, high priest, cardinal; archbishop, bishop, bishop coadjutor; canon-regular, canon-secular, confessor, penitentiary, Grand Penitentiary, spiritual director.

RELIGIOUS, mo⁓astic, cenobite, conventual, abbot, prior, monk, friar, lay brother, beadsman or bedesman, mendicant, pilgrim, palmer; Jesuit, Franciscan, Friars minor, Minorites; Observant, Capuchin, Dominican, Carmelite; Augustinian; Gilbertine; Austin-, Black-, White-, Gray-, Crossed-, Crutched- Friars; Bonhomme, Carthusian, Benedictine, Cistercian, Trappist, Cluniac, Premonstratensian, Maturine; Templar, Hospitaler; Bernardine, Lorettine, pillarist, stylite; caloyer, hieromonach [both Eastern Ch.].

NUN, sister, religieuse [F.]; priestess, abbess, prioress, canoness; mother superior, superioress, the reverend mother; novice, postulant.

[JEWISH DISPENSATION] prophet, priest, high priest, Levite; Rabbi, Rabbin, scribe.

[MOHAMMEDAN] imam or imaum, kahin, kasis, sheik; mullah, murshid, mufti; hadji or haji, muezzin [all Ar.]; dervish or darvesh [Pers.], abdal (pl. abdali) [Pers.], fakir or faquir [Ar.], beshara [Hind.], bashara [Hind.], santon [Turkey].

[HINDU] Brahman or Brahmin, pujari, purohit [family priest]; pundit or pandit, guru; yogi, sannyasi or sanyasi; bhikshu, bhikhari, vairagi or bairagi, Ramwat, Ramanandi [all Hind.].

[BUDDHIST] poonghie or poonghee [Burma], talapoin [Ceylon & Indo-China], bonze; lama, Grand Lama or Dalai Lama [Tibet].

[VARIOUS] druid, druidess [ancient Celts]; flamen [Rom. relig. and ancient Britain]; hierus, hierophant [Gr. relig.]; daduchus or dadouchos, mystæ, epoptæ [Eleusinian Mysteries].

V. take orders &c. 995.

Adj. ORDAINED, in orders, in holy orders, called to the ministry; the Reverend, the very Reverend, the Right Reverend.

₊ "O most gentle pulpiter! what tedious homily of love have you wearied your parishioners withal!" As You Like It]; "The shepherd seeks the sheep and not the sheep the shepherd" [M. for M.]; "To have a thin stipend, and an everlasting parish, Lord, what a torment 'tis!" [Beaumont and Fletcher]; "Wait till you hear me from the pulpit, there you cannot answer me!" [Bishop Gilbert Haven].

998. Rite. — N. RITE, ceremony, ceremonial, ordinance, observance, function, duty; form, formulary; solemnity, sacrament; incantation &c. (spell) 993; service, ministry, ministration; liturgics.

SERMON, preaching, preachment, predication [obs. or Scot.], exhortation, religious harangue, homily, lecture, discourse, pastoral.

[SEVEN SACRAMENTS] BAPTISM, immersion, christening, chrism; baptismal regeneration; font.

CONFIRMATION, imposition of hands, laying on of hands.

EUCHARIST, Lord's supper, communion; the sacrament, the holy sacrament; consecrated elements, bread and wine; intinction; celebration, high celebration; missa cantata [L.]; asperges [L.]; offertory; introit; consecration; consul stantiation, impanation, subpanation, transubstantiation; real presence; elements; Mass; high –, low –, dry- mass; hunter's (or hunting) mass [obs.].

PENANCE &c. (atonem nt) 952; flagellation, maceration, fasting, sackcloth and ashes.

EXTREME UNCTION, last rites, viaticum.

HOLY ORDERS, ordination &c. (churchdom) 995.

MATRIMONY, marriage, wedlock &c. 903.

WORSHIP &c. 990; invocation of saints, canonization, transfiguration, auricular confession, the confessional; absolution; reciting the rosary, telling of beads; processional; thurification, incense, holy water, aspersion.

circumcision; purification; visitation of the sick; burial &c. 363.

[SACRED ARTICLES] relics, rosary, beads, reliquary, host, cross, rood, crucifix; pyx, pix [obs.]; pax, Agnus Dei [L.], censer, thurible, incensory, patera; urceus, urceole; prayer wheel, prayer machine; Sangraal or Sangrael, Holy Grail.

RITUAL, rubric, canon, ordinal, missal, breviary, Mass book, beadroll; farse; liturgy, prayer book, Book of Common Prayer, Pietà [It.], euchologion or euchology [Eastern Ch.], litany, lectionary.

psalter, psalm book, hymn book, hymnal; hymnology, psalmody.

ritualism, ceremonialism; sabbatism, sabbatarianism; ritualist, sabbatarian.

HOLYDAY, feast, fast; Sabbath, Passover, Pentecost; Advent, Christmas, Epiphany, Lent; Passion Week, Holy Week; Good Friday, Easter; Ascension Day, Holy Thursday; Whitsuntide, Whitsunday or Whit-Sunday [erroneously, Whitsun Day]; Trinity Sunday, Corpus Christi; All Saints or All Saints' Day, All Souls' Day; love feast, agape; Candlemas or Candlemas Day; Lammas, Lammas Day, Lammastide; Michaelmas, Martinmas.

V. PERFORM SERVICE, do duty, minister, officiate; baptize, dip, sprinkle; confirm, lay hands on; give –, administer –, take –, receive –, attend –, partake of- the -sacrament, – communion, – Holy Eucharist; communicate; celebrate Mass, celebrate; administer –, receive- extreme unction; anele [o s.], shrive, absolve; administer –, receive- absolution; confess, make confession; do –, perform –, receive –, inflict-penance; tell one's beads; genuflect; make the sign of the Cross.

EXCOMMUNICATE, ban with bell book and candle.

PREACH, sermonize, predicate, lecture, address the congregation.

Adj. RITUAL, ritualistic, ceremonial; liturgic or liturgical; baptismal, eucharistical; paschal.

₊ "what art thou, thou idol ceremony?" [Henry V].

999. Canonicals. — N. CANONICALS, vestments; robe, gown, Geneva gown, frock, pallium, surplice, cotta, cassock; communion cloth, eileton [Eastern Ch.], corporal [Western Ch.]; scapular or scapulary, cope, mozetta or mozzetta, amice, scarf, fanon or fannel, bands, chasuble, tunicle, dalmatic, alb or alba, stole; tonsure, cowl, hood, capuche, calotte; vagas or vakas or vakass; apron, lawn sleeves, pontificals, pall; miter or mitre, tiara, triple crown; shovel –, cardinal's- hat; biretta or berretta; crosier or crozier, cross staff, pastoral staff; Sanctus bell, sacring bell; seven-branched candlestick; monstrance; censer &c. 998; costume &c. 225.

1000. Temple. — N. TEMPLE, place of worship; house of God, house of prayer; cathedral, minster, church, kirk [Scot. & dial. Eng.], chapel, meeting-house, bethel, ebenezer [Eng.], conventicle, basilica, fane, holy place, chantry, oratory.

synagogue, tabernacle; mosque, masjid [Moham.]; dewal, kan-pati [both Hindu], girja [Hind., Christian]; pagoda, pagod [archaic], kiack [Buddhist]; Chinese temple, joss house [colloq.]; pantheon.

SHRINE, dagoba [India]; tope, stupa [Buddhist], Marabout [Moham.].

[INTERIOR] altar, sanctuary, Holy of Holies, sanctum sanctorum [L.], sacristy; sacrarium; communion –, holy –, Lord's- table; table of the Lord; pyx; baptistery, font; piscina; stoup; holy-water stoup, holy-water basin; ambry, aumbry [archaic]; sedile; reredos; rood screen, rood beam, chapel screen, jube; rood loft.

chancel, apse, choir, quire [archaic], nave, triforium, blindstory, aisle, transept, crypt, porch, cloisters; churchyard, golgotha; calvary, Easter sepulcher; stall, pew, seat, seating; pulpit, ambo, lectern, reading desk; confessional; prothesis, table (or altar) of prothesis, chapel of prothesis [Eastern Ch.]; credence, baldachin or baldaquin; belfry; vestry, chapter house; presbytery; diaconicon or diaconicum; mourners' bench, mourners' seat; anxious bench, anxious seat, penitent form.

MONASTERY, priory, abbey, friary, convent, nunnery, cloister.

PARSONAGE, rectory, vicarage, manse, deanery, clergy house; glebe; Vatican; bishop's palace; Lambeth.

Adj. CHURCHLY, claustral, cloistered, monastic, monasterial, monachal, conventual; cruciform.

₊ ne vile fano; "there's nothing ill can dwell in such a temple" [Tempest]; "The hand that rounded Peter's dome And groined the aisles of Christian Rome Wrought in a sad sincerity; Himself from God he could not free; He builded better than he knew; — The conscious stone to beauty grew" [Emerson]; "Whilst love and terror laid the tiles" [ibid.].

INDEX GUIDE

IMPORTANT NOTE

The numbers following all references in this Index Guide refer to the *section numbers* in the text, and *not* to pages. Thus "Aaronic 995" refers to *section* 995, "Churchdom," under which the citation will be found. For further ease of reference, the *section* numbers will be found in bold type at the *top* of every page.

INDEX GUIDE

The numbers refer to the headings under which the words or phrases occur. When the same word or phrase can be used in various senses, the several headings under which it, or its synonyms, will be found are indicated by *Italics*. These words in Italics are not intended to explain the meaning of the word or phrase to which they are annexed, but only to assist in the required reference.

Italicized references within parentheses are merely suggestive, the parentheses indicating that the term itself is not included in the list referred to.

When the word given in the Index Guide is itself the title or heading of a category, the reference number is printed in bold-face type, thus: **abode 189.**

To keep the Index Guide — necessarily very large — from becoming unwieldy, a considerable number of obsolete, rare, foreign, dialectic, and slang terms has been omitted; for such words, while useful in the text, are not the ones for which synonyms would ordinarily be sought.

Derivatives likewise have been sparingly admitted, since the allied or basic term will serve as a key to the various derived forms; thus, *cold* is given, but not *coldness* and *coldly*. By such means, unnecessary duplication is avoided.

A

around 227
- it and about 573
- to 121
- to be 152
be - *busy with* 625
  active 682
beat - 629
come - 658
get - *public* 531
  recover 660
go - *turn* 311
going - *news* 532
put - *turn round* 283
round - 311
set - 676
turn - *invert* 218
what it is - 454
what one is - 625
above 206
- all *superior* 33
  important 642
- board *manifest* 525
  artless 703
  fair 939
- comprehension 519
- ground *alive* 359
- par *great* 31
  good 648
- praise 944
- price 814
- stairs 206
- suspicion 946
- the mark 33
- water *safe* 664
above-mentioned
  preceding 62
  repeated 104
  prior 116
abra 198
abracadabra 993
abrade [see abrasion]
Abraham,
  sham - 544
abrasion *paring* 38
  filing 330, 331
abrasive 331
abreast 216, 236
abregé 596
abreption 789
abridge *lessen* 36
  shorten 201
- *in writing* 572, 596
abridger 201
abridgment
  compendium 596
abroach 673
abroad *extraneous* 57
  distant 196
  uncertain 475
  astir 673
  get - public 531
abrogation 756
abrupt *sudden* 113
  violent 173
  steep 217
  unexpected 508
  style 579
abruption 44
abscess 655
abscind 44
abscissa 466

abscission
  retrenchment 38
  division 44
abscond 623
absconder 808
absence
  nonpresence 187
- *d'esprit* 452
- of choice 609a
- of influence 175a
- of intellect 450a
- of mind 458
- of motive 615a
absent [see absence]
absentee 187
absent-minded 458
absinthe 435
absolute *not relative* 1
  great 31
  complete 52
  certain 474
  affirmative 535
  authoritative 737
  severe 739
  free 748
  unalienable 924
- establishment 478
- interest *property* 980
  make - *confirm* 467
  adjudge 480
Absolute, the 450
absolution 918
absolutism 739
absolve *liberate* 750
  forgive 918
  exempt 927a
  shrive 952, 998
  acquit 970
absonant
  discordant 414
  unreasonable 477
absorb *combine* 48
  take in 296
  consume 677
- the mind
  attention 457
  inattention 458
- the soul 824
absorbed 451
absorbent 296 [see
  absorb]
absorbing *exigent* 630
  impressive 821
absorption 296
absquatulate 623
abstain *refrain* 623
  disuse 678
  temperance 953
- from action 681
- from voting 609a
abstainer 953, 958
abstemious 953
abstention 623
absterge 652
abstersive 662
abstinence [see
  abstain]
  total - 953, 955
abstract *separate* 44
  abridge 596
  take 789

  steal 791
- idea 453
- oneself
  inattention 458
- thought 451
  attention 457
in the - *apart* 44
  alone 87
abstracted
  inattentive 458
abstraction [see
  abstract]
abstruse 519
absurd [see absurdity]
- statement 546
absurdity
  impossible 471
  nonsense **497**
  ridiculous 853
abulia 605
Abuna 996
abundance 639
  poor in - 832
abundant *great* 31
  enough 639
abuse *deceive* 545
  illtreat 649
  misuse 679
  insolence 885
  malediction 908
  threat 909
  upbraid 932
  violate 961
- of language 563
- of terms 523
abusive
  discourteous 895
  defamatory 934, 936
abut *adjoin* 197
  touch 199
  rest on 215
abutment *defense* 717
abutter 199
aby *remain* 141
  endure 821, 826
abysm 198
abysmal *deep* 208
abyss *space* 180
  interval 198
  depth 208
  pitfall 667
  hell 982
acacia 367
academic *theory* 514
  teaching 537, 542
academical *style* 578
academician 492
  Royal - 559
academy 542
acanaceous 253
acanthophorous 253
acanthus 847
acariâtre 901
acarpous 169
acatalectic 597
acatastasia 139
acaudal 38
acaudate 38
accede *assent* 488
  submit 725
  consent 762

accelerate *early* 132
  stimulate 173
  velocity 274
  hasten 684
accension 384
accent *sound* 402
  tone of voice 580
  rhythm 597
accentuate 642
accentuated 581
accentuation 580
accept *assent* 488
  consent 762
  receive 785
  take 789
accepta 810
acceptable
  expedient 646
  agreeable 829
acceptance *security* 771
acceptation
  meaning 516
  interpretation 522
acception 522
access *approach* 286
  easy of - 705
  means of - 627
accessible *possible* 470
  easy 705
accession *increase* 35
  addition 37
- to office 737, 755
  consent 762
accessory *extrinsic* 6
  additive 37
  adjunct 39
  accompanying 88
  aid 707
  auxiliary 711
acciaccatura 413
accidence 567
accident *event* 151
  chance 156
  disaster 619
  misfortune 735
- of an accident 156
  fatal - 361
accidental *extrinsic* 6
  irrelative 10
  occasional 134
  fortuitous 156
  undesigned 621
accidentalism 156
Accipitres 739
acclamation *assent* 488
  approbation 931
  acclamatory 931
acclimatize
  domesticate 370
  inure 613
acclivity 217
accloy 641
accolade 894
accommodate *suit* 23
  adjust 27
  aid 707
  reconcile 723
  give 784
  lend 787
- oneself to
  conform 82

accommodating
  kind 906
accommodation [see
  accommodate]
  space 180
  -train 272
accompaniment
  adjunct 39
  coexistence 88
  musical 415
accompanist 416
accompany add 37
  coexist 88
  concur 120
  music 416
  escort 664
accomplice 711
accomplish execute 161
  complete 729
  succeed 731
accomplishment
  learning 490
  talent 698
accompts 811
accord uniform 16
  agree 23
  music 413
  assent 488
  concord 714
  grant 760
  give 784
  of one's own - 600,
    602
accordance 23
according
  -as qualification 469
  -to evidence 467
  -to circumstances 8
  -to Gunter 82
  -to law 963
  -to rule
    conformably 82
accordingly
  logically 476
accordion 417
accordionist 416
accost 586
accouchement 161
accoucheur
  minister 631
  doctor 662
accoucheuse 662
account list 86
  adjudge 480
  description 594
  credit 805
  money - 811
  fame 873
  approbation 931
  -as deem 484
  -for attribution 155
  interpret 522
  -with trade 794
  pay 807
  call to -
    censure 932
  find one's - in
    useful 644
    success 731
  make no - of
    undervalue 483

despise 930
  not - for
    unintelligible 519
  on - of cause 155
  motive 615
  behalf 707
  on no - 536
  send to one's -
    kill 361
  small - 643
  take into -
    attend to 457
    qualify 469
  to one's -
    property 780
  turn to -
    improve 658
    use 677
    success 731
    gain 775
accountable liable 177
  debit 811
  duty 926
accountant
  treasurer 801
  auditor 811
  -general 801
accounting 811
accounts 811
accouple 43
accouter 717
accouterment
  dress 225
  appliance 633
  equipment 673
accoy 174
accredit
  commission 755, 759
  money 805
  honor 873
accredited believed 484
  recognized 613
  -to 755, 759
accretion increase 35
  coherence 46
accrimination 938
accroach 789
accrue add 37
  result 154
  acquire 775
  be received 785, 810
accruement 775
accubation 213
accueil 894
accultural 658
acculturation 658
accumbent 213
accumulate collect 72
  store 636
  redundance 641
accumulation
  [see accumulate]
  increase 35
accurate 494
  -knowledge 490
accurse 908
accursed
  disastrous 649
  undone 828
  vicious 945
accusation 938

accuse disapprove 932
  charge 938
  lawsuit 969
accustom habit 613
accustomary 613
ace small quantity 32
  unit 87
  aviator 269a
  cards 840
  within an - 197
aceldama kill 361
  arena 728
acephalous 59
acequiador 350
acerb 397
acerbate embitter 659
  aggravate 835
acerbic 955
acerbity acrimony 395
  sourness 397
  rudeness 895
  spleen 900, 901
  malevolence 907
acervate 72
acervatim 72, 102, 641
acescence 397
acetic 397
  -acid 397
acetify 397
acetosity 397
acetous 397
acetum 397
achar 393
acharne 900
Achates, fidus -
  friend 890
  faithful 939
ache cold 383
  physical 378
  mental 828
Acheron
  pit of - 982
achievable 470
achieve end 67
  produce 161
  do 680
  accomplish 729
achievement
  hatchment 550
  sign 551
  feat 861
Achillean 900
Achilles
  - absent 187
  heel of -
    vulnerable 665
aching 383
achromatism 429
achromatization 429
acicular 253
acid 397
acidify 397
aciform 253
acinaciform 253
acknowledge
  answer 462
  assent 488
  disclose 529
  avow 535
  consent 762
  observe 772

pay 807
  thank 916
  repent 950
  reward 973
  - the corn 529
acknowledged
  custom 613
acme 210
  - of perfection 650
acology 662
acolyte 996
acomia 846
aconite 663
acoumetry 602
acoustic 402, 418
  - organs 418
acoustician 402
acoustics sound 402
  hearing 418
acquaint
  - oneself with 539
  - with 527
acquaintance
  knowledge 490
  information 527
  friend 890
  make - with 888
acquest 780
acquiesce assent 488
  willing 488
  consent 762
  tolerate 826
acquiescence
  assent 488
  submission 725
  observance 772
acquire develop 161
  get 775
  receive 785
  - a habit 613
  - learning 539
acquirement
  knowledge 490
  learning 539
  talent 698
  receipt 810
acquisition
  knowledge 490
  gain 775
acquisitive 775
acquit liberate 750
  accounts 811
  exempt 927a
  vindicate 937
  innocent 946
  absolve 970
acquit oneself
  behave 692
  - of a debt 807
  - of a duty 926
  - of an obligation 772
acquittal 970
acquittance receipt 771
acreage 180
acres space 180
  land 342
  property 780
Acres, Bob
  coward 862
acrid pungent 392
  unsavory 395

451

acridity *causticity* 171
  pungency 392
  unsavoriness 395
acrimony *physical* 171
  discourtesy 895
  hatred 898
  anger 900
  irascibility 901
  malevolence 907
acritude 395
acroama 490
acroamatic 490, 519
acrobat *strength* 159
  actor 599
  proficient 700
  mountebank 844
acrobatism 159
acropolis 666
acrospire 167
across *transverse* 219
  opposite 708
acrostic *letter* 561
  wit 842
act *imitate* 19
  physical 170
  - *of a play* 599
  personate 599
  voluntary 680
  statute 697
  - a part *feign* 544
  - one's part
    business 625
    duty 926
  - upon *physical* 170
    mental 615
    take steps 680
  - up to 772
  - well one's part 944
  - without authority
    738
  in the - *doing* 680
    guilt 947
acting *deputy* 759
actinic 420
actinology 420
actinometer 445
action *physical* 170
  voluntary **680**
  battle 720
  law 969
  line of - 692
  mix with - 170
  put in - 677
  suit the - to the word
    550, 599
  thick of the - 682
actionable 964
activate 171
active *physical* 171
  voluntary 682
  - service 722
  - thought 457
activity 682
actor *impostor* 548
  player 599
  agent 690
  affectation 855
Acts *record* 551
  Apostolic 985
actual *existing* 1
  present 118

  real 494
  (*identical* 13)
actuality [*see* actual]
actualize 220
actuary 85, 811
actuate *influence* 175
  incite 615
acuity 253
aculeated 253
acumen 498
acuminated 253
acupuncture 260
acute *energetic* 171
  physically violent 173
  pointed 253
  physically sensible
    375
  musical tone 410
  discriminative 465
  perspicacious 498
  cunning 702
  strong feeling 821
  morally painful 830
  - angle 244
  - ear 418
  - note 410
acutely 31
acuteness 465
A. D. 106
adactylism 848
adaga 727
adage 496
adagio *music* 415
  slow 275
Adam *sin* 945
adamant *strong* 159
  hard 323
Adam's ale 337
Adam's needle 253
adapt *agree* 23
  equalize 27
  - oneself to
    conform 82
adaptable
  conformable 82
  useful 644
adaptation [*see* adapt]
add *increase* 35
  join 37
  numerically 85
  accounts 811
addendum 39
adder 366, 913
  deafness 419
addict *habit* 613
adding machine 85
additament 39
addition [*see* add]
  adjunction **37**
  thing added 39
  arithmetical 85
addle *barren* 169
  incomplete 730
  abortive 732
  - the wits
    bewilder 475
    craze 503
addle-head 501
addle-headed 499
address *compose* 54
  residence 189

  direction 550
  speak to 586
  skill 698
  request 765
addressee 188
addresses
  courtship 902
adduce *bring to* 288
  evidence 467
adduct 288
adeem 789
adelomorphous 83
ademption 789
adenology 329
  intellectual 450
  proficient 698, 700
adept
adequate *power* 157
  sufficient 639
  for a purpose 644
  content 831
adespotic 738
adhere *stick* 46
  - to *persevere* 604a
    habit 613
  - to a duty 926
  - to an obligation 772
adherent 65, 711
adhesive *sticking* 46
  tenacious 327
  sticky 352
adhibit 677
adhortation 695
adiaphanous 426
adiathermancy 382
adieu *departure* 293
  loss 776
adipocere 356
adipose 355
adit *orifice* 260
  conduit 350
  passage 627
adjacent 197
adjection 37
adjective 39
  - jerker 593
adjoin *near* 197
  contact 199
adjourn *postpone* 133
  neglect 460
adjudge 480
adjudicate 480
adjunct *addition* 37
  thing added **39**
  accompaniment 88
  aid 707
  auxiliary 711
adjuration
  affirmation 535
  negation 536
adjure *request* 765
  promise 768
adjust *adapt* 23
  equalize 27
  regulate 58
  prepare 673
  settle 723
  - differences 774
adjustment 762, 774
adjutant *auxiliary* 711
  military 745

adjuvant *helping* 707
  auxiliary 711
admeasurement 466
administer *utilize* 677
  conduct 693
  exercise authority 737
  distribute 786
  - correction 972
  - oath 768
  - sacrament 998
  - to *aid* 707
  give 784
administration of
  justice 965
administrative
  official 737
  judicial 965
admirable *excellent* 648
  virtuous 944
admiral 745
Admiralty, court of -
  966
admiration *wonder* 870
  love 897
  respect 928
  approval 931
admirer 897
admissible *relevant* 23
  receivable 296
  tolerable 651
  - in society 852
admission [*see* admit]
admit *composition* 54
  include 76
  let in 296
  assent 488
  acknowledge 529
  permit 760
  concede 762
  accept 785
  - exceptions 469
  - of 470
admitted
  customary 613
  - maxim &c. 496
admixture 41
admonish *warn* 668
  advise 695
  reprove 932
admonitory 616
ado *activity* 682
  exertion 686
  difficulty 704
  make much - about
    important 642
  much - about nothing
    overestimate 482
    unimportant 643
    unskillful 699
adobe 635
adolescence **131**
Adonis 845
adonize 847
adopt *naturalize* 184
  choose 609
  appropriate 788
  - a cause *aid* 707
  - a course 692
  - an opinion 484
adoption *religious* 987
adore *love* 897

worship 990
adorn 847
adown 207
adrift *unrelated* 10
  disjoined 44
  dispersed 73
  uncertain 475
  unapt 699
  liberated 750
  go - *deviate* 279
  turn - *disperse* 73
  liberate 750
  dismiss 756
adroit 698
adscititious *extrinsic* 6
  added 37
  redundant 641
adulation 933
adulator 935
Adullam, cave of -
  desertion 624
  discontent 832
adult 131
adulterate *mix* 41
  deteriorate 659
adulterated *sham* 545
adulterer 962
adultery 961
adulthood 131
adultism 131
adumbrate
  darkness 421
  allegorize 521
  represent 554
adumbration
  semblance 21
  darkness 421
  allusion 526
aduncate 245
aduncity 244
adust *arid* 340
  heated 384˝
  brown 433
adustion 384
advance *increase* 35
  course 109
  progress 282
  assert 535
  improve 658
  aid 707
  succeed 731
  lend 787
  - against 716
  - agent 599
  - guard 234
  - of learning &c. 490
  - upon 303
  in - *precedence* 62
  front 234
  precession 280
  in - of
  superior 33
  in - of one's age 498
advanced 282
  - in life 128
  - work 717
advancement [*see*
  advance]
  infringement 303
advances, make -
  offer 763

social 892
advantage
  superiority 33
  increase 35
  influence 175
  benefit 618
  expedience 646
  - over *success* 731
  dressed to - 847
  find one's - in 644
  gain an - 775
  mechanical - 633
  set off to - 658
  take - of *use* 677
   make the most of
   698
advantageous
  beneficial 648
  profitable 775
advene 37
Advent 998
advent *futurity* 121
  event 151
  approach 286
  arrival 292
Adventist 984
adventitious
  extrinsic 6
  casual 156
adventive 156
adventure *event* 151
  chance 156
  pursuit 622
  danger 665
  trial 675
  undertaking 676
adventurer
  traveler 268
  experimenter 463
  deceiver 548
  gambler 621
  rash 863
  ignoble 876
adventures
  history 594
adventuress 548
adventurous
  undertaking 676
  bold 861
  rash 863
adversaria 551
adversary 710
Adversary, the - 978
adverse *contrary* 14
  opposed 708
  unprosperous 735
  disliking 867
  - party 710
adversity 735
advert 457
advertent 457
advertise 531
advice *notice* 527
  news 532
  counsel **695**
  good - 695
advisable 646
advise *predict* 511
  inform 527
  counsel 695
  - with one's pillow 451

advised *predetermined*
  611
  intended 620
  better - 658
advisement *advice* 695
  [*see* advise]
  under - 453
adviser *teacher* 540
  counselor 695
advisory 527
advocacy
  approbation 931
advocate
  interpreter 524
  prompt 615
  recommend 695
  aid 707
  auxiliary 711
  friend 890, 914
  vindicate 937
  counselor 968
Advocate, the -
  Saviour 976
advocation *plea* 617
advoutress 962
advoutry 961
advowson 995
adynamic 160
adytum *room* 191
  prediction 511
  secret place 530
ædile 965
ægis 717
Æolian 349
  - harp 417
Æolus 349
æon 109, 110
aërate 334, 353
aëration 334
aërial *elevated* 206
  navigation 267, 273
  gas 334
  air 338
  - mail 534
  - mail-carrier 271
  - navigator 269
  - perspective 428
  - railway 840
aerie 189
aëriferous 334
aërification 334
aëriform 334
aërify 334
aëro 273
aëroboat 273
aërobus 273
aërodonetics 267
aërodrome 273
aërodynamics
  navigation 267
  gas 334
  wind 349
aërography 334, 349
aëro-hydroplane 273
aërolite 318
aërology *gaseity* 334
  air 338
  wind 349
aëromancy 511
aëromechanic 267, 334
aërometer 338

aërometric 338
aëronat 273
aëronaut 269a
aëronautic 273
  [*see* aëronautics]
aëronautics
  navigation 267
  air 338
aëroplane 273
  combatant 726
  by - 684
aëroplanist 269
aëroscope 338
aëroscopy 334
aërosphere 338
aërostat *balloon* 273
aërostatics 267 334
aërostation 338
aërotherapy 662
aëroyacht 273
aëry *gaseous* 334
  atmospheric 338
Æsculapius 662
Æsop 846
æsthetic *sensibility* 375
  beauty 845
  taste 850
æstival 125
æstivation 384
ætiology *causes* 155
  life 359
  knowledge 490
  disease 655
afar 196
afeard 860
affable
  condescending 879
  courteous 894
affair *event* 151
  topic 454
  business 625
  battle 720
  - of honor 720
affaires, chargé d' -
  758
affect *relate to* 9
  tend to 176
  qualify 469
  feign 544
  touch 824
  desire 865
  love 897
affectation 855
affected 583
  - manner 880
affected with
  feeling 821
  disease 655
affectibility 822
affecting *pathetic* 830
affection *feeling* 821
  love 897
affectionate 821, 897
affections 820
affettuoso *music* 415
affiance *promise* 768
  trust 858
affianced *love* 897
  marriage 903
affiche 531
affidation 769

affidavit
  affirmation 535
  record 551
  lawsuit 969
affiliation *relation* 9
  kindred 11
  attribution 155
affinal 11
affinitive 9
affinity *relation* 9
  similarity 17
affirmant 488
affirmation *evidence*
  467
  assent 488
  assert **535**
affirmative 535
affix *add* 37
  sequel 39
  fasten 43
  precedence 62
  letter 561
afflation 349
afflatus *wind* 349
  inspiration 985
afflict 830
  - with illness 655
affliction *pain* 828
  infliction 830
  adversity 735
affluence
  sufficiency 639
  prosperity 734
  wealth 803
affluent *river* 348
afflux 286
afford *supply* 784
  wealth 803
  yield 810
  sell for 812
  - aid &c. 707
affranchise
  make free of 748
  liberate 750
affray 720
affriction 331
affright 860
affront *molest* 830
  provocation 900
  insult 929
  - danger 861
affuse 337
affusion 73
afield 186
afire 382
afloat *extant* 1
  unstable 149
  going on 151
  ship 273
  navigation 267
  ocean 341
  news 532
  preparing 673
  keep oneself - 734
  set - *publish* 531
afoot *on hand* 625
  ready 673
  astir 682
afore 116
aforegoing 116
aforehand 116
  454

afore-mentioned 62, 116
aforesaid *preceding* 62
  repeated 104
  prior 116
aforesighted 116
aforethought 116, 611, 907
aforetime 116
a fortiori
  superiority 33
  evidence 467
  reasoning 476
afraid 860
  - to say *uncertain* 4
  be - *irresolute* 605
afreet 980
afresh *repeated* 104
  new 123
African 431
Afric *heat* 382
Afrikander 57
aft 235
after *in order* 63
  in time 117
  too late 135
  rear 235
  pursuit 622
  - all *for all that* 30
  qualification 469
  on the whole 476
  - time 133
  be - *intention* 620
  pursuit 622
  go - *follow* 281
after acceptance 516
after-age 124
afterbirth 63
afterburden 63
afterclap 63, 154, 509
aftercome 65, 154
aftercrop 63, 154, 168
afterdamp 663
afterdinner 117
afterglow *decrement* 40a
  sequence 63
  light 420
aftergrass 63
aftergrowth 65, 154
afterlife 152
aftermath *sequence* 63
  effect 154
  fertile 168
  profit 775
afternoon 126
  - farmer 683
afterpain 63
after-part *sequel* 65
  rear 235
afterpiece 63, 599
aftertaste 63, 390
afterthought
  thought 451
  memory 505
  change of mind 607
aftertime 121, 133
afterwards 117
aga 745
again *duplicate* 90
  repeated 104
  - and again 136

come - *periodic* 138
against
  counteraction 179
  anteposition 237
  voluntary opposition 708
  - one's expectation 508
  - one's will 744
  - one's wishes 603
  - the grain *difficult* 704
  painful 830
  dislike 867
  - the stream 704
  - the time when 510
  go - 708
agalloch 400
agamist 904
agape *opening* 260
  curious 455
  expectant 507
  wonder 870
agape *love feast* 998
Agapemone
  pleasure 827
  love 897
agate 847
age *time* 106
  period 108
  course 109
  long time 110
  present time 118
  oldness 124
  advanced life **128**
  from age to - 112
  of - 131
agency *physical* **170**
  instrumentality 631
  means 632
  employment 677
  voluntary action 680
  direction 693
  commission 755
agenda 625
  list of - 626
agent *physical* 153
  worker 686
  voluntary **690**
  consignee 758
  - *provocateur* 615
agentship 755
ages: - ago 122
  for - 110
agglomerate
  cohere 46
  assemble 72
agglutinate 46, 48
aggrandize
  in degree 35
  in bulk 194
  honor 873
aggravate
  increase 35
  vehemence 173
  exaggerate 549
  render worse 659
  distress 835
  exasperate 900
aggravating
  painful 830

aggravation 835
aggregate
  whole 50
  collect 72
  number 84
aggregation 46
aggression 716
aggrieve *injure* 649
  distress 830
aggroup 72
aghast
  disappointed 509
  fear 860
  wonder 870
agile *swift* 274
  active 682
agio 813
agiotage 794
agitate *move* 315
  inquire 461
  activity 682
  excite the feelings 824
  - a question 476
agitation [*see* agitate]
  changeableness 149
  energy 171
  motion **315**
  in - *preparing* 673
agitator
  leader 694
aglet 554
aglow *warm* 382
  shine 420
agnate 11
agnition 762
agnomen 564
agnostic 487
agnosticism 451, 989
agnus Dei 998
ago 122
agog *expectant* 507
  desire 865
  wonder 870
  (*envious* 455)
agoing 682
  set - 707
agone 122
agonism 720
agonistic 159
agonize 972
agonizing
  thrilling 824
  painful 830
agony
  physical 378
  mental 828
  - of death 360
  - of excitement 825
agora 182
agoraphobia 860
agostadero 344
agrarian 371
agree *accord* 23
  concur 178
  assent 488
  concord 714
  consent 762
  compact 769
  compromise 774
  - in opinion 488
  - with *salubrity* 656

agreeable
  consistent 82
  physically 377
  consenting 762
  mentally 829
agreeably to
  conformably 82
agreement 23   [*see*
  agree]
  compact 769
agrestic 189, 371
agriculture 342, **371**
agriculturist 342
agronomics 342, 371
agronomist 371
agronomy 342, 371
aground *fixed* 150
  in difficulty 704
  failure 732
agua 337
aguardiente 959
ague 655
ague fit 860
agueweed 662
aguish *cold* 383
aha! *rejoicing* 838
ahead *in front* 234
  procession 280
  go - *progression* 282
Ahriman 978
aid *help* **707**
  charity 906
  - to memory 505
  by the - of
  instrument 631
  means 632
aidance 707
aid-de-camp
  auxiliary 711
  officer 745
aider [*see* aid]
aidless 160
aigrette 847
aiguille 253
aigulet 847
ail *sick* 655
  pain 828
aileron 267, 273
ailment 655
aim *direction* 278
  purpose 620
  essay 675
  - a blow at 716
  - high 305
aimable 278
aimless *without design*
  59, 621
  without motive 615a
air *unsubstantial* 4
  broach 66
  lightness 320
  gas 334
  atmospheric **338**
  wind 349
  tune 415
  appearance 448
  refresh 689
  fashionable 852
  fill the - 404
  fine - *salubrity* 656
  take - 531

air balloon 273
air bladder 334
air bubble 250
aircraft 273
air cruiser 273
air-drawn 515
air engine 633
air gun 727
air hole 260, 351
airing 266
air line 278
airman 269
airmanship 267, 698
air pipe 349, **351**
airplane 273
air pump 349
airs *affectation* 855
  pride 878
  vanity 880
  arrogance 885
air shaft 351
airship 273
air-tight 261
air tube 351
airward 206
airway 351
airwoman 269a
airworthy 273, 664
airy [*see* air]
  windy 349
  unimportant 643
  gay 836
  - hopes 858, 859
  - tongues 532
aisle *passage* 260
  way 627
  in a church 1000
ait 346
aitchbone 235
ajar *open* 260
  discordant 713
ajee 217
ajutage *opening* 260
  pipe 350
akimbo *angular* 244
  stand - 715
akin *related* 11
  similar 17
alabaster *white* 430
alack! 839
alacran 913
alacrity *willing* 602
  active 682
  cheerful 836
Aladdin's lamp 993
alameda 189
alar 39
alarm *warning* 668
  notice of danger **669**
  fear 860
  cause for - 665
  give an - *indicate* 550
alarmist 862
alarum *loudness* 404
  indication 550
  notice of danger 669
alas! 839
alate 39
alb 999
alba 999
Albany beef 298

Albany hemp 663
albata 430, 545
albatross 366
albeit 30
alberca 343
albescence 430
albication 430
albification 430
albinism 430
albino 443
albinoism 430
Alborah 271
album *book* 593
  compendium 596
albumen
  semiliquid 352
  protein 161, 357
albumin 357
albuminoid 357
Alcaic 597
alcaid 745
alcalde 745, 967
alchemy 144
alcohol 959
alcoholism 959
Alcoran 986
alcove *bower* 191
  hollow 252
Aldebaran 423
alder 367
alderman 745
Alderney 366
ale 298
Alecto 173
alectromancy 511
alehouse 189
  go to the - 959
alembic *conversion* 144
  vessel 191
  furnace 386
  laboratory 691
alert *watchful* 459
  active 682
alerte 669
alertness 457
aleuromancy 511
Alexandrian school 451
Alexandrine
  ornate style 577
  verse 597
  (*length* 200)
alexandrite 847
alexipharmic 662
alexiteric 662
alfalfa 367
alfilaria 367
alfresco 220
algæ 367, 369
algebra 85
algebraist 85
algid 383
algidity 383
algology 369
algorism 85
algorithm 85
alguazil 965
alias 18, 565
alibi 187
alien *irrelevant* 10
  foreign 57
  transfer 783

gentile 989
alienable 783
alienage 57
alienate *disjoin* 44
  transfer 783
  estrange 889
  set against 898
alienation
  mental - 503
aliéné 503
alienism 57
alight *stop* 265
  arrive 292
  descend 306
  on fire 382
align *horizontal* 213
  direction 278
aligned 216
alike 17
aliment *food* 298
  (*materials* 635)
alimentary
  regimen 662
alimentation *aid* 707
alimony *property* 780
  provision 803
  income 810
aliquot *part* 51
  number 84
alive *living* 359
  sentient 375
  intelligent 498
  active 682
  cheerful 836
  - to *attention* 457
  cognizant 490
  informed 527
  able 698
  sensible 822
  - to impressions 375
  - with 102
  keep - *continue* 143
aljibar 636
alkahest 335
alkali 344
all *whole* 50
  complete 52
  generality 78
  - aboard 293
  - absorbing 642
  - agog 865
  - along 106
  - along of 154
  - at once 113
  - but 32
  - colors 440
  - considered
  thought 451
  judgment 480
  - day long 110
  - ears 418
  - eyes and ears 457
  - fours *easy* 705
  cards 840
  - hail! *welcome* 292
  honor to 873
  celebration 883
  courtesy 894
  - hands *everybody* 78
  - in 688
  - in all 50

- in good time 152
- in one's power 686
- manner of *different* 15
multiform 81
- one *equal* 27
indifferent 866
- out *completely* 52
error 495
- over *end* 67
universal 78
destruction 162
space 180
- powerful
mighty 159
God 976
completely 52
truly 494
- right! 922
- sorts *diverse* 16a
mixed 41
multiform 81
- talk 4
- the better 831
- the go 852
- the rage 852
- the time 106
- things to all men 894
- ways *distortion* 243
deviation 279
at - events *compensation* 30
qualification 469
true 494
resolve 604
at - points 52
at - times 136
in - ages 112
in - directions 278
in - quarters 180
on - hands 488
on - sides 227
Allah 976
allay *moderate* 174
pacify 723
relieve 834
- excitability 826
all-destroying 162
all-devouring 162
allective 615
allege *evidence* 467
assert 535
plea 617
allegiance
obedience 743
duty 926
allegorization 521
allegory
similitude 464
metaphor 521
allegresse 836
allegro *music* 415
cheerful 836
alleluia 990
all-embracing 56
all-engulfing 162
alleviate *moderate* 174
relieve 834
alley *court* 189
passage 260
way 627

Allhallowmas 138
alliance *relation* 9
kindred 11
physical coöperation 178
voluntary coöperation 709
party 712
union 714
allied 48
- to *like* 17
alligation 43
alligator 366, 913
- *pear* 298
alliteration
similarity 17
repetition 104
style in writing 577
all-knowing 976
allness 52
allocation 60, 786
allocution 586
allodium *free* 748
property 780
allopathy 662
alloquy 586
allot *arrange* 60
distribute 786
due 924
allow *assent* 488
admit 529
permit 760
consent 762
give 784
allowable
permitted 760
due 924
allowance
qualification 469
gift 784
allotment 786
discount 813
salary 973
make - for *forgive* 918
vindicate 937
with grains of - 485
alloy *mixture* 41
combine 48
solution 335
debase 659
all-possessed 503
All Saints' Day 138
all-searching 461
all-seeing 976
all-sided 52
All Souls' Day 138
allspice 393
all-star 599
all-sufficient 159
allude *hint* 514
mean 516
refer to 521
latent 526
inform 527
allure *move* 615
create desire 865
alluring
pleasurable 829
allusion 516
allusive 9
alluvial *level* 213

land 342
plain 344
alluvion 270, 348
alluvium *deposit* 40
land 342
soil 653
all-wise 976
ally *combine* 48
auxiliary 711
friend 890
Alma Mater 542
almanac
chronometry 114
record 86, 551
- de Gotha 86
almighty 157
Almighty, the - 976
almond 298
almoner *giver* 784
treasurer 801
church officer 996
almonry 801
almost *nearly* 32
not quite 651
- all 50
- immediately 132
alms *gift* 784
benevolence 906
worship 990
almshouse 189, 666
almsman 785
Alnaschar's dream
imagination 515
hope 858
alod 748
aloes 395
aloes wood 400
aloft 206
alogy 497
alone *single* 87
unaided 706
let - *not use* 678
not restrain 748
never less - 893
along 200
- with *added* 37
together 88
by means of 631
get - *progress* 282
go - *depart* 293
go - with *concur* 178
assent 488
coöperate 709
alongside *near* 197
parallel 216
laterally 216
aloof *distant* 196
high 206
secluded 893
stand - *inaction* 681
refuse 764
cautious 864
aloofness 893
alopecia 226
aloud 404
think - *soliloquy* 589
naïveté 703
Alp 206
alpenstock 215
Alpha 66
- and Omega 50

alphabet
beginning 66
letters 561
alphabetarian 541
alphabetize 60
alphitomancy 511
alpine *high* 206
Alpine Club
traveler 268
ascent 305
already
antecedently 116
even now 118
past time 122
Alsatia *thieving* 791
Alsatian *den* 945
also 37
altar *marriage* 903
church 1000
alter 140
emasculate 158
- one's course 279
- the case 468
alterable 149
alterant 662
alteration
correlation 12
difference 15
alterative
remedy 662
altercation 713
altered *worn* 688
- for the worse 659
alter ego *similar* 17
auxiliary 711
deputy 759
friend 890
alternacy 138
alternate
reciprocal 12
vary 20a
sequence 63
discontinuous 70
periodic 138
substitute 147, **634**
changeable 149
oscillate 314
alternation 148
alternative
substitute 147
choice 609
plan 626
although
compensation 30
counteraction 179
unless 469
(opposition 708)
altiloquence 577
altimeter 206
altimetry *height* 206
angle 244
measurement 466
altitude *height* 206
- and azimuth 466
alto 410, 415
hill 206
altogether
collectively 50
entirely 52
the - 50, 226
alto - rilievo

compendium 596
analyst
  investigator 461
  experimenter 463
analytical [see analysis]
analyze *grammar* 567
  describe 594
  [see analysis]
anamorphoscope 555
anamorphosis
  distortion 243
  optical 443
  misrepresentation
    555
anapest 597
anaphrodisia 174, 866
anarch 710
anarchist
  opponent 710
  insurgent 742
  enemy 891
  evil doer 913
anarchy *disorder* 59
  social 738
anastatic printing 558
anastomosis
  junction 43
  crossing 219
anastomotic 219
anastrophe 218
anathema 908
anathematize *curse* 908
  censure 932
  detract 934
anatomize *dissect* 44
  investigate 461
anatomy
  dissection 44
  leanness 203
  texture 329
  science 357
  comparative - 368
anatripsis 331
anatriptic 331
ancestor 69, 166
ancestral
  bygone 122
  old 124
  aged 128
ancestry 69, 166
anchor *connection* 45
  stop 265
  safeguard 666
  check 706
  hope 858
  at - *fixed* 150
  stationed 184
  safe 664
  cast - *settle* 184
  arrive 292
  sheet - *means* 632
anchorage
  location 184
  roadstead 189
  refuge 666
anchored *fixed* 150
anchoretic 893
anchorite *recluse* 893
  ascetic 955
ancien régime 875
ancient *old* 124
    458

flag 550
- *mariner* 269
- *times* 122
ancientness 122
ancillary 707
ancon 342
and *addition* 37
  accompaniment 88
andante 415
andiron 386
androgynous 83
androlepsia 789
androtomy 372
anecdote 594
anecdotist 594
anele 998
anemograph 349
anemography 349
anemology 349
anemometer
  wind 349
  measure 466
  record 551
anemometrograph 349
anemometry 349
anemone 845
anemoscope 349
anent 9
aneroid 338, 340
anew *again* 104
  newly 123
anfractuosity 248
angel *messenger* 534
  backer 599, 711
  object of love 897
  good person 948
  supernatural being
    977
  bishop 996
  - of death 360
  fallen - *bad man* 949
  devil 978
  guardian - *safety* 664
  auxiliary 711
  benefactor 912
angelic 944
angelus 550
anger 900
angina pectoris 655
angiology 329
angle 244
  point of view 448
  try 463
  at an - 217
angle rafter 215
Anglican *sectarian*
    984
  ecclesiastical 995
Anglicanism 984
Anglice 563
Anglicism 563
angling 622
Anglophobia 898
angry [see anger]
anguiform 248
anguilliform
  filament 205
  serpentine 248
anguilloid 248
anguillous 248
anguine 366

anguish *physical* 378
  moral 828
angular 244
- *velocity* 264
angularity 244
angustation 203
anhedonia 828, 837
anhelation 688
anhydrate 340, 670
anhydration 340
anhydric 340
anhydrous 340
anility *age* 128
  imbecility 499
anima 359
- *bruta* 359
- *divina* 359
- *mundi* 359
animadvert
  attend to 457
  reprehend 932
animal 366
- *cries* 412
- *economy* 359
- *gratification* 377
- *life* 364
- *magnetism* 992a
- *physiology* 368
- *spirits* 836
  female - 364
animalcular 193
animalcule
  minute 193
  animal 366
animalism
  animality 364
  sensuality 954
animality **364**
animalization 364
animastic 450
animate *induce* 615
  excite 824
  enliven 836
animation *life* 359
  animality 364
  activity 682
  vivacity 836
  suspended - 823
animative 359
animism 317, 984
animist 317
animosity *dislike* 867
  enmity 889
  hatred 898
  anger 900
animus
  willingness 602
  intention 620
  desire 865
ankle 244
- deep *deep* 208
  shallow 209
anklet 847
ankus 615
ankylosis 150
annalist
  chronologist 115
  recorder 553
annals *chronology* 114
  record 551
  account 594

annatto 434
anneal 673
annex *add* 37, 39
  join 43
annexationist 43
annexe 39
annihilate *extinguish* 2
  destroy 162
anniversary 138, 883
anno 106
annotation
  explanation 522
  note 550
annotator *scholar* 492
  interpreter 524
  commentator 595
annotto 434
announce *herald* 116
  predict 511
  inform 527
  publish 531
  assert 535
announcement
  [see announce]
annoy *molest* 649, 907
  disquiet 830
annoyance 828
  source of - 830
annual *periodic* 138
  plant 367
  book 593
annuity 810
annul *destroy* 162
  abolish 756
annular 247
annularity 249
annulet 247
annunciate *inform* 527
  (*publish* 531)
Annunciation, the - 990
annunciative 527
annunciator 527
annunciatory 531
anodyne *lenitive* 174
  remedial 662
  relief 834
anoint *coat* 223
  lubricate 332
  oil 355
Anointed, the 976
anointment
  lubrication 332
  oil 355
anomalous 241
anomaly *disorder* 59
  irregularity 83
anon 132
anonymous 565
anopsia 442
anorexy 866
another *different* 15
  repetition 104
- *time* 119
answer
  to an inquiry **462**
  confute 479
  solution 522
  succeed 731
  pecuniary profit 775
  pleadings 969
- for *deputy* 759

promise 768
  go bail 806
  - one's turn 644
  - the helm 743
  - the purpose 731
  - to *correspond* 9
  require an - 461
answerable
  agreeing 23
  liable 177
  bail 806
  duty 926
  censurable 392
ant 366, 690
Antæus *strength* 159
  size 192
antagonism
  difference 14
  physical 179
  voluntary 708
  enmity 889
antagonist 710
antagonistic 24
antaphrodisiac 866
antarctic 237, 383
ante 621
  expend 809
  - up 809
antecedence
  in order 62
  in time 116
antecedent 64
antechamber 191
antedate 115
antediluvian 124
antelope 274, 360
antemundane 124
antenna 379
antepast 510
anteposition 62
anterior
  in order 62
  in time 116
  in place 234
  - to *reason* 477
anteroom 191
antevert 706
anthelion 423
anthelmintic 662
anthem 990
anthemion 847
antherozoid 357
anthology *writing* 590
  book 593
  collection 596
  poem 597
  store 636
anthracite 388
anthrax 655
anthropod 193
anthropogeny 372
anthropoid 372
anthropology
  zoölogy 368
  mankind 372
anthropomancy 511
anthropomorphism 984
anthropophagus 913
anthroposcopy 511
anthroposophy 372
anthropotomy 372

antic 840
antichristian
  heterodox 984
  irreligious 989
antichronism 115
anticipant 120
anticipate
  anachronism 115
  priority 116
  future 121
  early 132
  expect 507
  foresee 510
  prepare 673
  hope 858
  caution 864
anticipation 120
  [see anticipate]
anticlimax
  decrease 36
  bathos 497, 853
anticlinal 217
anticyclone 265
antidote 662
antigropelos 225
antifebrile 662
antilogarithm 84
antilogy 477
antiluetic 662
antimacassar 223
antimony 663
Antinomian 984
antinomy 964
Antinous 845
antiorgastic 174
antiparallel 217
antipathy
  contrariety 14
  dislike 867
  hate 898
antiphon *music* 415
  answer 462
  worship 990
antiphonal 462
antiphrasis 563
antipodes
  difference 14
  distance 196
  contraposition 237
antipoison 662
antiquary
  past times 122
  scholar 492
  historian 553
antiquated *aged* 128
  (*out of fashion* 851)
antique 124
antiquity 122
antiscriptural 984
antiseptic 662
antisocial 911
antispasmodic 174, 662
antispast 597
antistrophe 597
antithesis *contrast* 14
  difference 15
  contraposition 237
  style 577
antithesize 14
antitype 22
antler 253

antonomasia
  metaphor 521
  nomenclature 564
antrum 252
anvil *conversion* 144
  support 215
  on the -
  intended 620
  in hand 625, 730
  preparing 673
anxiety *solicitude* 459
  pain 828
  fear 860
  desire 865
anxious [see anxiety]
  - bench 1000
  - expectation 507
  - meeting 1000
  - seat 1000
any *some* 25
  part 51
  no choice 609a
  at - rate *certain* 474
  true 494
  at all hazards 604
anybody 78
anyhow *careless* 460
  in some way 627
aorist 109, 119
aorta 350
apace *early* 132
  swift 274
Apache 913
apache *assassin* 361
aparejo 215
apart *irrelative* 10
  separate 44
  singleness 87
  soliloquy 589
  set - 636
  wide - 196
apartment 191
  - house 189
  -s to let
  imbecile 450a, 499
apathetic 275
apathy *incuriosity* 456
  insensibility 823
  irreligion 989
ape *monkey* 366
  imitate 19
aperient 652, 662
apéritif 394
aperture 260
apery 19
apex *height* 206
  summit 210
aphelion 196
aphid 366, 659
Aphis 659
aphonic 403, 581
aphonia 581
aphorism 496
aphrodisia 173, 961
aphrodisiac 865
Aphrodite 845
apiarism 370
apiarist 370
apiary 370
apical 210
apiculate 253

apiculture 370
apiece 79
apish 19, 499
apishamore 223
aplomb *stability* 150
  verticality 212
  self-possession 498
  resolution 604
Apocalypse 985
Apocrypha 985
apocryphal
  uncertain 475
  erroneous 495
  heterodox 984
apodeictic 478
apodeixis 478
apodosis 67
apograph 21
apolaustic 377
Apollo *sun* 318
  music 416
  luminary 423
  beauty 845
  - Musagetes 416
  magnus - *sage* 500
  adviser 695
apologue *metaphor* 521
  teaching 537
  description 594
apology *substitution* 147
  excuse 617
  vindication 937
  penitence 950
  atonement 952
apophthegm 496
apophysis 250
apoplexy 158
aporia 475
apostasy
  recantation 607
  dishonor 940
  heterodoxy 984
  impiety 988
apostate *convert* 144
  turncoat 607
  seceder 742
  heretic 984
  (*recreant* 941)
apostatize 607
apostle *teacher* 540
  disciple 541
  inspired 985
  -'s creed 983a
apostolic 985
  - church 983a
  - see 995
apostrophe
  typography 550
  address 586
  soliloquy 589
  appeal 765
apostrophize 765
apothecary 662
  -'s weight 319
apothegm 496
apotheosis
  resuscitation 163
  heaven 981
  hero worship 991
apozem *liquefy* 335
  fuse 384

apozemial 384
appal *pain* 830
  terrify 860
appanage
  property 780
  gift 784
apparatus 633
apparel 225
apparent
  visible 446
  appearing 448
  probable 472
  manifest 525
  heir - 779
apparition
  shade 362
  fallacy of vision 443
  spirit 980a
  psychical research
    992a
  (*appearance* 448)
apparitor *precursor* 64
  messenger 534
appeach 938
appeal *address* 586
  request 765
  - motion 969
  - to *call to witness* 467
  - to arms 722
  - to for (*claim*) 924
  court of - 966
appear *come in sight* 446
  show itself 525
  (*come into being* 1)
  - for 759
  - in print 591
appearance 448
  make one's -
    arrive 292
  to all - *to the eye* 448
  probable 472
appearances
  keep up - 852
appease 174
appellant
  claimant 924
appellate 966
appellation 564
append *add* 37
  sequence 63
  hang 214
appendage *addition* 37
  adjunct 39
  accompaniment 88
  rear 235
appendicitis 655
appendix 65, 67
apperception 450, 490
appercipient 450
appertain *related to* 9
  component 56
  belong 777
  property 780
appetence 865
appetency 602
appetite 865
  tickle the -
    savory 394
appetitive 865
appetizer 393, 394
appetizing 865
460

exciting 824
applaud 931
applause 931
apple 298, 369
  - brandy 959
  - butter 396
  - dumpling 298
  - fritters 298
  - jack 959
  - of discord 713
  - of one's eye *good* 648
    love 897
    favorite 899
  - pie 298
  - slump 298
  golden -
    allurement 615
apple green 435
apple-pie order 58
appliance *use* 677
  -s *means* 632
  machinery 633
applicable *revelant* 9, 23
  useful 644
  expedient 646
applicant 767
application *study* 457
  metaphor 521
  use 677
  request 765
apply *appropriate* 788
  - a match 384
  - the mind 457
  - a remedy 662
appoggiato 413
appoggiatura 413
appoint *prescribe* 741
  assign 786
appointment
  business 625
  order 741
  charge 755
  assignment 786
  interview 892
appointments *gear* 633
apportion *arrange* 60
  disperse 73
  allot 786
  (*portion* 51)
apportionment 786
apposition *relation* 9
  relevancy 23
  closeness 199
  paraphrase 522
appraise
  estimate 466
  value 812
appreciate
  realize 450, 451
  measure 466
  judge 480
  know 490
  taste 850
  approve 931
apprehend *believe* 484
  know 490
  fear 860
  seize 969
apprehension *idea* 453
  taking 789
apprehensive 860

apprentice 541
  servant 746
  - oneself 676
apprenticeship
  learning 539
  training 673
apprize 527
apprized of 490
approach
  of time 121
  impend 152
  nearness 197
  move **286**
  path 627
approbation **931**
appropinquation 286
appropinquity 197
appropriate *fit* 23
  peculiar 79
  possess 777
  assign 786
  borrow 788
  take 789
  steal 791
  (*expedient* 646)
appropriation
  allotment 786
  taking 789
  stealing 791
approval *assent* 488
  commend 931
approve 488, 931
approximate
  related to 9
  resemble 17
  in mathematics 85
  nearness 197
  approach 286
appulse *meeting* 199
  collision 276
  approach 286
  converge 290
appulsion 199, 276
appurtenance
  adjunct 88
  component 56
  belonging 780
  (*part* 51)
appurtenant
  relating 9
apricot *fruit* 298
  color 439
April
  - fool *dupe* 547
    laughingstock 857
  - showers 149
  make an - fool of 545
a priori *reasoning* 476
apron *clothing* 39, 225
  defense 717
  canonicals 999
à propos *relative* 9
  apt 23
  occasion 134
  (*expedient* 646)
apse 1000
apt *consonant* 23
  tendency 176, 177
  docile 539
  willing 602
  clever 698

(*intelligent* 498)
(*expedient* 646)
aqua 337
  - fortis 384
  - regia 384
aquamarine 435, 438
aquarium 370, 636
Aquarius *rain* 348
aquatic 267, 337
aquatics 267
aquatinta 558
aquatist 558
aqueduct 350
aqueous 337
aquiline 244
A. R. 106
Arab *wanderer* 268
  horse 271
araba 272
arabesque 847
Arabian - nights 515
  - perfumes 400
arable 371
arado 780
arbiter *critic* 480
  director 694
  adviser 695
  judge 967
  - bibendi 840
  - elegantiarum
    revels 840
    taste 850
    fashion 852
arbitrament
  judgment 480
  (*choice* 609)
  - of the sword 722
arbitrary
  without relation 10
  irregular 83
  willful 606
  capricious 608
  authoritative 737
  severe 739
  insolent 885
  lawless 964
  - power 739
arbitrate
  adjudicate 480
  mediate 724
arbitration
  concord 714
  compromise 774
  court of - 966
  submit to - 774
arbitrator 724
arbor *abode* 189
  summerhouse 191
  support 215
  rotation 312
  plaisance 840
Arbor Day 840
arboreal 367
arborescent
  ramifying 242
  rough 256
  trees 367
arboriculture 371
arboriform 242
arc 245
arcade *street* 189

mental reservation
528
motive 615
set purpose 620
arriero 694
arrish 168
arrival 292
arrive *happen* 151
reach 292
complete 729
(stop 142)
- at a conclusion 480
- at an understanding
488
- at the truth 480*a*
arroba 319
arrogance
[*see* arrogant]
arrogant *severe* 739
proud 878
insolent 885
arrogate *assume* 885
claim 924
- to oneself
undue 925
arrondissement 181
arrosion 331
arrow *swift* 274
missile 284
arms 727
arrowhead *form* 253
writing 590
arrow-shaped 253
arroyo 350
arsenal *store* 636
workshop 691
(arms 727)
arsenic 663
arsenious oxide 663
arson 384
art *representation* 554
business 625
skill 698
cunning 702
(deception 545)
- gallery 556
- museum 556
- school 542
fine - 850
perfection of - 650
work of -
beauty 845
ornament 847
arteriosclerosis 655
artery *conduit* 350
channel 627
artesian well 343
artful *deceitful* 544
cunning 702
- dodge 545, 702
arthritis 655
arthropoda 368
artichoke 298
article *thing* 3
part 51
matter 316
chapter 593
review 595
goods 798
articled clerk 541
articles

- of agreement 770
- of faith
belief 484
theology 983
thirty-nine - 983*a*
articulates 368
articulation
junction 43
speech 580
articulo, in-
transient 111
dying 360
artifice *plan* 626
cunning 702
(deception 545)
artificer 690
artificial
fictitious 545
cunning 702
affected 855
- language 579
- light 420
artillery
explosion 404
arms 727
- of words 562
artilleryman 726
artisan 690
artist *painter* &c. **559**
contriver 626
agent 690
artiste *music* 416
drama 599
artistic *skillful* 698
beautiful 845
taste 850
- language 578
artistry 569
Artium - Baccalaureus
492
- Magister 492
artless 703
artlessness
natural **703**
(veracious 543)
arundinaceous 253
aruspex 513
aruspicy 511
as *motive* 615
- broad as long 27
- can be 52
- good as 27
- if *similar* 17
suppose 514
- it may be
circumstance 8
event 151
chance 156
- it were *similar* 17
metaphor 521
- little as may be 32
- much again 90
- soon as 120
- they say
proverb 496
news 532
- things are 7
- things go *event* 151
habit 613
- to 9
- usual 82

- you were 283
- well as 37
asafetida 395, 401
asbestic 385
asbestos 385
ascend *be great* 31
increase 35
rise 305
improve 658
ascendancy
power 157
influence 175
success 731
ascendant
in the -
influence 175
important 642
success 731
authority 737
repute 873
lord of the - 745
one's star in the -
prosperity 734
ascension
[*see* ascend]
calefaction 384
Ascension Day 998
ascent [*see* ascend]
gradient 217
rise **305**
glory 873
ascertain *fix* 150
determine 480
ascertained
certain 474
known 490
ascertainment 480*a*
ascetic 955
asceticism 953, **955**
ascititious
intrinsic 6
additional 37
supplementary 52
ascribe 155
ascription [*see* ascribe]
aseptic 662
ash 367, 384
- blond 429
- colored 432
ashamed 879, 881
ash cake 298
ashen 429
ashes *corpse* 362
dirt 653
lay in - 162
pale as -
colorless 429
fear 860
ashore 342
go - *arrive* 292
Ash Wednesday 138
ashy 429
Asian mystery 533
aside *laterally* 236
whisper 405
private 528
- from the purpose 10
say - 589
set - *displace* 185
neglect 460
negative 536

reject 610
disuse 678
abrogate 756
discard 782
step - 279
asinine *ass* 271
fool 499
ask *inquire* 461
request 765
for sale 794
price 812
(invoke 990)
- leave 760
askance 217
eye - *fear* 860
look - *vision* 441, 443
dissent 489
dislike 867
disapproval 932
asked in church 903
askew *oblique* 217
distorted 243
asking [*see* ask]
aslant 217
asleep 683
aslope 217
Asmodeus 978
asomatous 317
asp *animal* 366
evil doer 913
asparagus 298, **367**
Aspasia 962
aspect *feature* 5
state 7
situation 183
appearance 448
aspen leaf
shake like an -
motion 315
fear 860
asperges 998
aspergillum 337
asperity
roughness 256
discourtesy 895
anger 900
irascibility 901
asperse 934
aspersion
nonassemblage 73
cleanness 652
malediction 908
rite 998
asphalt *smooth* 255
resin 356*a*
asphodel 845
asphyxia 360
asphyxiate 361
aspirant *candidate* 767
desire 865
aspirate 402, 580
aspirated 681
aspire *rise* 305
project 620
hope 858
desire 865
worship 990
asportation 270
asquint 217
ass *beast of burden* 271
fool 501

- 's bridge
unintelligible 519
cheat 548
bungler 701
make an - of
delude 545
assafetida 401
assagai 727
assail *attack* 716
pain 830
assailant *opponent* 710
attacker 726·
assassin, -ate 361
assault 716
take by - 789
assay 463
assayer 463
assemblage 72
assembly *council* 696
society 892·
religious 997
assemblyman 696
assembly room 189,
588
assent *belief* 484
agree **488**
willing 602
consent 762
content 831
assert *affirm* 535
claim as a right 924
assess *measure* 466
determine 480
tax 812
assessor *judge* 967
assets *property* 780
money 800
accounts 811
asseverate 535
assiduous 682
assign *commission* 755
transfer 783
give 784
allot 786
- a duty 926
- as cause 155
- dower 784
- places 60
assignable 270
assignat 800
assignation *tryst* 892
place of - 74
assignee *transfer* 270
donee 785
assignment 155
assimilate *uniform* 16
resemble 17
imitate 19
agree 23
transmute 144
assimilation 161
assist 707
assistant 711
assize *measure* 466
tribunal 966
justice of - 967
associate *mix* 41
unite 43
combine 48
collect 72
accompany 88

colleague 690
auxiliary 711
friend 890
- professorship 542
- with
sociality 892
association
[see associate]
relation 9
coöperation 709
partnership 712
friendship 888
- of ideas
intellect 450
thought 451
intuition 477
hint 514
associational psycholo-
gy 457
assoil *acquit* 970
(liberate 750)
assoilzie 970
assonance *agreement* 23
music 413
poetry 597
assort *arrange* 60
assortment
collection 72
class 75
assuage *moderate* 174
relieve 834
(- morally 826)
assuasive 174, 834
assuetude 613
assume *believe* 484
suppose 514
falsehood 544
take 789
insolent 885
right 924
- a character 554
- a form 144
- authority 737
- command 741
- the offensive 716
assumed
- name 565
- position 514
assuming *insolent* 885
assumption [see assume]
severity 739
hope 858
insolence 885
seizure 925
assurance
speculation 156
certainty 474
belief 484
confidence 507
assertion 535
promise 768
security 771
hope 858
vanity 880
insolence 885
make - double sure
safe 664
caution 864
assure *render certain*
474
believe 484

certify 535
promise 768
secure 771
give hope 858
assured *self -satisfied*
880
assuredly *assent* 488
astatic 320
asteism 856
asterisk 550
astern 235
fall - 283
asteroid 318
asthenia 160
astigmatism 443
astir *ready* 673
active 682
set - 824
astonish 870
astonishing *great* 31
astonishment 508, 870
astound *be unexpected*
508
excite 824
fear 860
surprise 870
astraddle 215
astragal 847
astral 318
- body 317, 992a
- influence 601
- plane 317
astray *at fault* 475
error 495
go - *deviate* 279
sin 945
astriction 43, 195
astride 215
astringent 195, 397
astrolabe 466
astrology 511, 522
astronomy 318
astute *wise* 498
cunning 702
asunder *separate* 44
distant 196
as poles - 237
asylum *hospital* 662
retreat 666
defense 717
asymptote 290
ataghan 727
atajo 72
atavism 145
atelier *studio* 556
workshop 691
athanasia 112
Athanasian creed 983a
athanor 386
atheism 989
atheist 984
atheling 875
athermancy 382
athirst 865
athlete *strong* 159
combatant 726
athletic *strong* 159
school 542
laborious 686
gymnastic 720
- sports

contest 720
games 840
athletics 720, 840
athwart *oblique* 217
crossing 219
opposing 708
Atkins, Tommy - 726
Atlantean *great* 31
strong 159
supporting 215
Atlantis 515
at large 750
atlas *arrangement* 60
list 86
maps 554
store 636
Atlas *strength* 159
support 215
atmosphere
circumambience 227
air 338
painting 556
atmospheric blue 438
atole 298
atoll 346
atom *small in degree*
32
small in size 193
atomism 451
atomize 336
atomizer 336, 400
atoms
crush to - 162
atomy 193, 203
atonement
restitution 790
expiation **952**
amends 973
religious 976
atonic 158
atony 158, 160
atrabilious 837
atramentous 431
atrium 191 ◄
atrocity *malevolence* 907
vice 945
guilt 947
atrophy *shrinking* 195
disease 655
decay 659
attach *add* 37
join 43
love 897
legal 969
- importance to 642
attaché *employé* 746
diplomatic 758
attachment [see attach]
dispossession 789
attack *voice* 580
disease 655
assault **716**
attaghan 727
attain *arrive* 292
succeed 731
- majority 131
attainable
possible 470
(easy 705)
attainder *taint* 651
at law 971

attainment *knowledge* 490
  learning 539
  skill 698
attar 400
attemper *mix* 41
  moderate 174
attempered
  affected 820
attempt 675
  - impossibilities 471
  vain - 732
attend *accompany* 88
  be present 186
  follow 117, 281
  apply the mind 457
  medically 662
  aid 707
  serve 746
  - to 418
  - to business 625
  - to one's business 457
  - to orders 743
attendance [*see* attend]
  dance - on 866
attendant [*see* attend]
attention 457
  care 459
  respect 928
  attract - 882
  call - to 550
  call to - 457
  pay -s to 894
  pay one's -s to 902
attentive *mindful* 457
  [*see* attend]
attenuate *decrease* 36
  impotent 158
  reduce 195
  rare 322
attenuated 203
attest
  bear testimony 467
  affirm 535
  adjure 768
attested copy 771
attic *garret* 191
  summit 210
Attic *homespun* 42
  style 578
  wit 842
  taste 850
  - salt 578, 842
Atticism 578
Attila 913
attire 225
attitude *circumstance* 8
  situation 183
  posture 240
attitudinarian 882
attitudinize 855
attollent 307
attorney *consignee* 758
  at law 968
  power of - 755
attract
  be powerful 157
  bring towards 288
  induce 615
  allure 865
  excite love 897
464

  - the attention 457
  visible 446
attraction [*see* attract]
  natural power 157
  bring towards **288**
attractive [*see* attract]
  pleasing 829
  beautiful 845
  taste 850
attractivity 288
attrahent 288
attribute *power* 157
  -s of the Deity 976
  - to 155
attribute
  accompaniment 88
attribution 155
attrite 330, 331
attrition 331
attritus 331
attune *music* 415
  prepare 673
attuned to *habit* 613
aubade 415
auburn 433, 434
auction 796
auctioneer *agent* 758
  seller 796
audacity *courage* 861
  rashness 863
  insolence 885
audible 402
  become - 418
  scarcely - 405
audience *hearing* 418
  conversation 588
  drama 599
  before an - 599
audiphone 418
audit *numeration* 85
  examination 461
  accounts 811
auditive 418
auditor *hearer* 418
  accountant 811
auditorium 189, 588
auditory *sound* 402
  hearing 418
  theater 599
  - apparatus 418
  - nerve 418
au fait *knowledge* 490
  skillful 698
Augean
  - stable 653
  - task 704
auger 262
aught 51
  for - one cares
    unimportant 643
    indifferent 866
  for - one knows
    ignorance 491
    conjecture 514
augment *increase* 35
  thing added 39
  expand 194
augur *soothsayer* 513
  - well 858
augural 511
augurate 511

augury 512
august 31, 873
Augustinian 996
auk 310
Aum 993
aumbry 1000
aunt 11
aura *wind* 349
  sensation 380
  light 420
  astral 980a
aural 418
aureate 436
aurelia 129
aureola 420
aureole 420, 873
aureolin 436
auricle 418
auricomous 436
auricular *hearing* 418
  clandestine 528
  - confession 998
auriculate 418
auriscope 418
auriscopy 418
aurist 418, 662
aurora *dawn* 125
  light 420, 423
  twilight 422
  - australis 423
  - borealis 423
auroral 236
auscultation 418
auspicate 66
auspice *omen* 512
auspices *influence* 175
  prediction 511
  protection 664
  supervision 693
  aid 707
  under the - of 737
auspicious
  opportune 134
  prosperous 734
  hopeful 858
  (*expedient* 646)
austere [*see* austerity]
austerity
  harsh taste 395
  severe 739
  discourteous 895
  ascetic 955
  pietism 988
Austral 237
austromancy 511
authentic
  well-founded 1
  evidential 467
  certain 474
  true 484
authentication
  evidence 467
  security 771
author *producer* 164
  designer 554
  writer 593
  projector 626
  - of evil 978
  - of our being 976
  -s proof 591
  dramatic - 599

authoritative
  influential 175
  certain 474
  oracular 500
  commanding 741
authority *influence* 175
  testimony 467
  sage 500
  informant 527
  power **737**
  permission 760
  right 924
  do upon one's own - 600
  ensign of - 747
  person in - 745
authorize *empower* 737
  permit 760
  entitle 924
  legalize 963
authorized *due* 924
authorship
  composition 54
  production 161
  style 569
  writing 590
auto 272
autobiography 594
autocar 272
autochthonous 188
autocracy *will* 600
  authority 737
  severity 739
autocrat 745
autocratic *will* 600
  ruling 737
auto-da-fe *burning* **384**
  execution 972
autodidactic 490
autograph
  evidence 467
  signature 550
  writing 590
autography 550
autointoxication 655
Autolycus *thief* 792
  peddler 797
automaniac 504
automatic 266, 601
  pistol 727
  - gun 727
  - writing 992a
automatism 992a
automaton 1
automobile 266, 272]
  - race 274
automobilist 268
automotive 266
autonomy *rule* 737
  free 748
autoplagiarism 791
autopsy
  post-mortem 363
  vision 441
autoptical *visible* 446
  manifest 525
auto-rifle 727
autotype 558
autumn 126
auxiliary 711
  extra 37

aid 707
- forces 726
avail *benefit* 618
   useful 644
   succeed 731
- oneself of 677
   of no - 645
available 676
avails 775, 810
avalanche *fall* 306
   redundance 641
avant-courier
   precursor 64
   pioneer 673
avarice 819
avast! *stop* 142, 265
   desist 624
   forbid 761
avatar *change* 140
   Vishnu 979
avaunt! *eject* 297
   disappear 449
ave! *honor* 873
   courtesy 894
Ave Maria 900
avenge 919
avenger 919
avenue *plantation* 371
   way 627
aver 535
average *mean* 29
   neutral 628
   mediocre 651
- circumstances 736
   take an - 466
Avernus 982
averruncate *eject* 297
   extract 301
averse *contrary* 14
   unwilling 603
averseness

unwillingness 603
   rejection 610
aversion *dislike* 867
   enmity 889
   hate 898
avert 706
- the eyes 442
Avesta 986
aviary 370
aviate 267
aviation 267
aviator 269
avidity *avarice* 819
   desire 865
avile 932, 934
avion 273, 726
aviso 532
avocado 298
avocation 625
avoid 623
avoidance 623
avoidless *certain* 474
   necessary 601
avoirdupois 319
avoke 741
avolation *avoid* 623
   escape 671
avouch 535
avow *assent* 488
   disclose 529
   assert 535
avowal [see avow]
avulsion *separation* 44
   extraction 301
await *future* 121
   be kept waiting 133
   impend 152
   expect 507
awake *attentive* 457
   careful 459
   intelligent 498

active 682
   excite 824
awaken *inform* 527
   excite 824
- the attention 457
- the memory 505
award *adjudge* 480
   give 784
aware 490
away *absent* 187
   distant 196
   depart 293
- from *unrelated* 10
- with! 930, 932
   break - 623
   do - with *undo* 681
   abrogate 756
   fly - 293
   get - 671
   move - 287
awayness 187
awe *fear* 860
   wonder 870
   respect 928
aweless *fearless* 861
   insolent 885
   disrespectful 929
awe-struck 870
awful *great* 31
   fearful 860
- silence 403
awhile 111
awkward *uncouth* 579
   inexpedient 647
   unskillful 699
   difficult 704
   painful 830
   ugly 846
   vulgar 851
   ridiculous 853
- squad 701, 726

awkwardness
   [see awkward]
awl 262
- shaped 253
awned 253
awning *tent* 223
   shade 424
awry *oblique* 217
   distorted 243
   evil 619
ax *edge tool* 253
   impulse 276
   weapon 727
   for beheading 975
axial 222
axinomancy 511
axiom 496
axiomatic 474
axis *support* 215
   center 222
   rotation 212
axle 312
   wheel and - 633
axletree 215
ay 488
ayah *servant* 746
   nurse 753
aye *ever* 112
   yes 488
ayudante 711
azimuth *horizontal* 213
   direction 278
   measurement 466
- circle 212
azoic 358
azote 663
   whip 975
azotic 657
Azrael 360
azure 438
azygous *single* 87

B

Baal *divinity* 979
   idol 986
baas *master* 745
babble *rivulet* 348
   faint sound 405
   unmeaning 517
   talk 584, 588
babbler 501, 532
babbling *foolish* 499
babe 129
Babel *confusion* 59
   discord 414
   tongues 560
   jargon 563
   loquacity 584
Babism 984
Babist 984
baboon 366, 846
babu 553
- English 563
Bab-ud-Din 986
baby *infant* 129
   posterity 167
   fool 501
- blue 438

- grand piano 417
- linen 225
babyhood 127
babyish 499
baccalaureate 873
baccarat 840
baccate 354
bacchanals 959
Bacchus *drink* 959
bachelor 904
bachelor girl 374, 904
back *rear* 235
   shoulder 250
   aid 707
   indorse 800
- and forth 148, 314
- down *recede* 283
   apostatize 607
- out *retire* 283
   change sides 607
   relinquish 624
- pedal 275
- to back 235
- up *support* 215
   aid 707

behind one's -
   latent 526
   hidden 528
   come - 292
   fall - *relapse* 661
   give - 790
   go - 283
   go - from *retract* 773
   have at one's - 215
   hold - *avoid* 623
   keep - *reserve* 636
   look - 505
   on one's - *impotent*
      158
   horizontal 213
   failure 732
   pat on the -
   incite 615
   encourage 861
   approve 931
   pay - *retaliate* 718
   put - *deteriorate* 659
   restore 660
   send - 764
   set one's - against the

   wall 604
   set one's - up
   pride 878
   some time - 122
   spring - 277
   take - again 790
   trace - 505
   turn - 283
   turn one's -
   retire 283
   turn one's - upon
   repel 289
   inattention 458
   avoid 623
   oppose 708
   seclusion 893
   discourtesy 895
   disrespect 929
   contempt 930
backbite *traduce* 932
   detract 934
backbiter 936
backbone *intrinsic* 5
   energy 171
   frame 215

abode 189
shed 223
jibe 929
defence 717
barracker 936
barracoon 717
barrage *loudness* 404
  drumming 407
  attack 716
barranco 198
barrator 941
barratrous 940
barratry 940
barred *crossed* 219
  striped 440
barrel *vessel* 191
  cylinder 249
  -*organ* 417
barrel house 189
barren 169
barricade *fence* 232
  obstacle 706
  defense 717
  prison 752
barrier [*see* barricade]
barring *save* 38
  excluding 55
  except 83
  -out *resist* 719
  disobey 742
barrister 968
  revising - 967
barrow *mound* 206
  vehicle 272
  grave 363
barter *reciprocate* 12
  interchange 148
  commerce **794**
barway 294
barytone 408
bas bleu *scholar* 492
  affectation 855
base *low* 207
  lowest part **211**
  support 215
  evil 649
  menial 746
  cowardly 862
  shameful 874
  servile 886
  dishonorable 940
  vicious 945
  -coin 800
  -note 408
  -of operations
  plan 626
  attack 716
baseball 840
baseboard 211
baseborn 876
based on *ground of belief* 467
baselard 727
baseless *unreal* 2
  unsubstantial 4
basement *cellar* 191
  lowest part 207, 211
baseness [*see* base]
  inferiority 34
bashaw *tyrant* 739
  ruler 745

bashful 881
bashfulness 881
bashi-bazouk 726
basilica 1000
basilisk
  unconformity 83
  sight 441
  cannon 737
  serpent 366, 949
basin *dock* 189
  vessel 191, 211
  hollow 252
  plain 344
basis *lowest part* 211
  support 215
  preparation 673
bask *physical enjoyment* 377
  warmth 382
  prosperity 734
  moral enjoyment 827
  - in the sun 384
basket 191
  - of 190
basket ball 840
bas-relief *convex* 250
  sculpture 557
bass *music* 415
  - clarinet 417
  - note 408
  - tuba 417
  - viol 417
basset 446
basset horn 417
bassinet *cradle* 191
  helmet 717
bassoon 417
basso profondo 408
basso-rilievo
  convex 250
  sculpture 557
bastard *spurious* 545
  nameless 565
  illegitimate 925
baste *beat* 276
  punish 972
Bastille 752
bastinado 972
bastion 717
bat *strike* 276
  club 727
  spree 840
batch *quantity* 25
  collection 72
bate *diminish* 36
  subtract 38
  reduce price 813
bateau 273
bated breath
  with-*faint sound* 405
  expecting 507
  hiding 528
  whisper 581
  humble 879
bath 337, 652
  -s *remedy* 662
  warm - 386
Bath chair 272
bathe *immerse* 300
  plunge 310
  water 337

bathhouse 652
bathometer 208, 341, 466
bathos *anticlimax* 497
  (*ridiculous* 853)
bathroom 191, 652
bathybic 341
bathycolpian 208
bathymeter 208
bathymetry 208
bathypelagic 208
bathysmal 208
batik 556
bating 55
batman 637
baton *support* 215
  scepter 747
batophobia 206, 860, 867
batrachians 368
batta 973
battalia 726
battalion 726
batten 298
  -on 886
batter *destroy* 162
  beat 276
  pulpiness 354
battered
  worse for wear 659
  tired 688
battering-ram 276
battering train **727**
battery *artillery* 726
  guns 727
  floating - 726
  plant a - 716
battle *killing* 361
  contention 720
  warfare 722
  - array *order* 60
  prepare 673
  war 722
  - ax 727
  - cruiser 273
  - cry *sign* 550
  war 722
  - field *arena* 728
  - ground *discord* 713
  - with *oppose* 708
  half the - 642
  win the - 731
battled 722
battledore 325
  - and shuttlecock
  interchange 148
  game 840
battlement
  embrasure 257
  defense 717
battleship 664, 726
battologize 573
battology *repeat* 104
  diffuse style 573
battue *kill* 361
  pursuit 622
  attack 716
bauble *trifle* 643
  toy 840
bavardage
  unmeaning 517

chatter 584
bavin 388
bawarchi-khana 191
bawcock 892
bawd 962
bawdy, -house 961
bawl 411
bawn 189
bay *concave* 252
  gulf 343
  cry 412
  brown 433
  at - *danger* 665
  difficulty 604
  defense 717, 719
  - leaf 400
  - the moon
  useless 645
  bring to - 716
bayadere 840
Bayard 271
bayard *bay* 433
bayberry 400
  - candle 423
baygall 345
bayonet *kill* 361
  attack 716
  weapon 727
  at the point of the -
  war 722
  severity 739
  coercion 744
  crossed -s 708
bayou 343
bay rum 400
bays *trophy* 733
  crown 877
bay salt 336
bay window 245, 260
bazaar 799
B. C. 106
be 1
  - alive with 102
  - all and end all
  whole 50
  intention 620
  importance 642
  - all up with 162
  - off *depart* 293
  eject 297
  retract 773
  - it so 488
  - that as it may 30
beach 342
beach comber 268, 348
beacon *sign* 550
  warning 668
  (light 423)
  - fire 423, 550
bead 249, 847
beading 847
beadle *janitor* 263
  law officer 965
  church 996
beadledom 737
beadroll *list* 86
  prayers 990
  ritual 998
beads 847
  tell one's - 990, 998

beadsman *servant* 746
  clergy 996
beagle 366
beak *face* 234
  nose 250
  magistrate 967
beaked 245
beaker 191
beam *support* 215
  quarter 236
  weigh 319
  light 420
  measurement 466
  on - ends
  powerless 158
  horizontal 213
  side 236
  fail 732
  wonder 870
beaming *beautiful* 845
beanfeast 840
beans 298
bear *produce* 161
  sustain 215
  carry 270
  animal 366
  admit of 470
  stock exchange 797
  suffer 821
  endure 826
- a hand 680
- a sense 516
- away 789
- away the bell
  best 648
  success 731
- company 88
- date 114
- down *violent* 173
  insolent 885
- down upon 716
- false witness 544
- fruit *produce* 161
  useful 644
  success 731
  prosper 734
- hard upon 649
- harmless 717
- ill 825
- off *deviate* 279
- on 215
- oneself 692
- out *evidence* 467
  vindicate 937
- pain 828
- the brunt
  difficult 704
  defense 717
- the burden 625
- the cross 828
- the palm *supreme* 33
- through 707
- up *approach* 286
  persevere 604a
  relieve 834
  cheerful 836
- up against *resist* 719
  brave 861
- upon *relevant* 9, 23
  influence 175
- with *tolerate* 740

  permit 760
  take coolly 826
  forgive 918
  bring to - 677
  more than flesh and
    blood can - 824
  unable to -
  excited 825
  dislike 867
bear *savage* 907
  surly 895
- garden *disorder* 59
  discord 713
  arena 728
- leader 540
- pit 370
- skin *cap* 225
  helmet 717
bearable 651
beard *hair* 205
  prickles 253
  rough 256
  defy 715
  brave 861
  insolence 885
  pluck by the -
  disrespect 929
bearded *hairy* 256
beardless 127, 226
bearer 271
  funeral 363
  servant 746
bear grass 253
bearing *relation* 9
  support 215
  direction 278
  meaning 516
  demeanor 692
- rein 706, 752
bearings
  circumstances 8
  situation 183
bearish 895
beast *animal* 366
  unclean 653
  discourteous 895
- of burden
  carrier 271
  laborer 690
beastlike *unclean* 653
beastly *unclean* 653
  impure 961
beat *be superior* 33
  periodic 138
  region 181
  impulse 276
  surpass 303
  oscillate 314
  agitation 315
  crush 330
  sound 407
  verse 597
  line of pursuit 625
  path 627
  overcome 731
  sponger 886
  strike 972
- about *circuit* 629
- about the bush
  try for 463
  evade the point 477

  prevaricate 544
  diffuse style 573
- against 708
- a retreat *retire* 283
  avoid 623
  submit 725
- down *destroy* 162
  cheapen 794, 815, 819
  insolent 885
- hollow 33
- into *teach* 537
- of drum *music* 416
  publish 531
  alarm 669
  war 722
  command 741
  pomp 882
- off 717
- one's breast 839
- the air 645
- the Dutch 508
- time *clock* 114
  music 416
- up *churn* 352
- up against
  oppose 708
- up for *cater* 637
- up for recruits
  prepare 673
  aid 707
- up one's quarters
  seek 461
  visit 892
beaten track
  habit 613
  way 627
  leave the - 83
  tread the - 82
beatific
  pleasing 827, 829
  heavenly 981
beatification *piety* 987
beating high
  the heart - 824
beau *man* 373
  fop 854
  admirer 897
- catcher 256
- idéal *perfect* 650
  beauty 845
- monde
  fashion 852
  (*nobility* 875)
beautiful 845
beautify 845, 847
beautiless 846
beauty 845
- of a lovely woman
  374
beaver *covering* 223
  hat 225
  animal 366
- dam 706
becalm 265
because *cause* 153
  attribution 155
  answer 462
  reasoning 476
  motive 615
bechance 151
becharm 829

  bêche de mer 298
beck *rill* 348
  sign 550
  mandate 741
  at one's - *aid* 707
  obey 743
beckon *sign* 550
  motive 615
  call 741
becloud *befog* 353
  dark 421
  dim 422
  hide 528
become
  change to 144
  accord with 23
  behove 926
- of 151
becoming
  accordant 23
  proper 646
  beautiful 845, 847
  due 924
becripple 158
bed *lodgment* 191
  layer 204
  base 211
  support 215
  for animals 370
  garden 371
  marriage 903
- bugs 366
- maker 746
- of down *repose* 687
- of Procrustes 975
- of roses *pleasure* 377
  prosperity 734
  brought to - 161
  death - 360
  go to - *quiet* 265
  sleep 683
  keep one's - *ill* 655
bedarken 421
bedaub *cover* 223
  dirt 653
  (*deface* 846)
bedazzle 420
bedding 215
bedeck 847
bedesman
  [*see* beadsman]
bedevil *derange* 61
  diabolize 978
  sorcery 992
bedew 339
bedfellow 890
bedgown 225
bedight 225, 847
bedim 421, 422
bedizen *invest* 225
  ornament 847
  vulgar 851
Bedlam
- broke loose 59
  candidate for - 504
bedog 63
Bedouin 792
bedridden 655
bed rock 211
bedroom 191
bedstead 215

bedtime 126
bedwarf 195
bee 690
  gathering 892
  - in a bottle 407
  - in one's bonnet 503
  busy - 682
  swarm like -s 102
beech *tree* 367
beef 298
beefeater 263, 726
beefheaded 499
beehive *convexity* 250
  for bees 370
  workshop 691
bee line 278
Beelzebub 978
beënt 1
beer 298
beery 959
beeswax 352
beetle *overhang* 206
  project 250
  insect 366
  deafness 419
  - head 501
  blind as a - 442
  Colorado - 913
beetling 214
beet root 298
beets 298
beet sugar 396
befall 151
befit *agree* 23
  expedient 646
  due 924, 926
befog *becloud* 353
  conceal 528
befool *mad* 503
  deceive 545
befooled
  victimized 732
before *in order* 62
  in time 116
  presence 186
  in space 234
  precession 280
  preference 609
  - Christ 106
  - everything 153
  - long 132
  - mentioned 62, 116
  - now 122
  - one's eyes
    visible 446
    manifest 525
  - one's time 132
  - the house 454
  set - one 525
beforehand *prior* 116
  early 132
  foresight 510
  resolve - 611
befoul 653
befriend *aid* 707
  friendship 888
befuddle 959
beg *Turkish title* 745
beg *ask* 765
  - leave 760
  - one's bread 765

poor 804
  - one's life 914
  - pardon 952
  - the question 477
beget 161
begetter 164, 166
beggar *idler* 683
  petitioner 767
  poor 804
  degrade 874
  low person 876
  - description
    unconformable 83
    nomenclature 564
    wonderful 870
  - my neighbor 840
  - on horseback 885
  -s mounted 885
  sturdy - 792
beggared
  bankrupt 808
beggar's-lice 253
beggarly *mean* 643
  vile 874
  vulgar 876
  servile 886
  - account of empty
    boxes
    insufficient 640
    poor 804
begging
  - letter 765
  go a - *too much* 641
    useless 645
    offered 763
    free 748
begilt 847
begin 66
  - again 104
beginner 541
beginning 66
  still ending and - 140
begird 227, 229
beglerbeg 745
begone *depart* 293
  ejection 297
  abrogate 756
  (*disappear* 440)
  - dull care 836
begrease 653
begrime 653
begrudge
  unwilling 603
  refuse 764
  stingy 819
  envy 921
beguile *mislead* 495
  deceive 545
  reconcile 831
  - the time
    inaction 681
    amusement 840
  to - many 615
begum 745, 875
behalf *advantage* 618
  aid 707
  in - of 759
behave oneself
  conduct 692
  fashion 852
  courtesy 894

behavior 692
  one's good –
    polite 894
    virtuous 944
behead *kill* 361
  execute 972
behemoth 192
behest 741
behind *in order* 63
  in space 235
  sequence 281
  - bars 754
  - one's back
    missing 187
  - the age *old* 124
    ignorant 491
  - the scenes
    cause 153
    unseen 447
    cognizant 490
    latent 526
    hidden 528
    playhouse 599
  - the veil 528
  - time 115, 133
behindhand *late* 133
  shortcoming 304
  adversity 735
  insolvent 808
behold *see* 441
  look 457
beholden *grateful* 916
  obligatory 926
beholder 444
behoof 618
behoove 926
being *abstract* **1**
  concrete 3
  created - 366
  human - 372
  time - 106
Bel 979
belabor *buffet* 276
  thump 972
belated *late* 133
  ignorant 491
belaud 931
belay *join* 43
  restrain 706
belch *eject* 297
  emit gas 349
beldam
  grandmother 130
  hag 173, 913
belduque 253
beleaguer, 227, 716
belfry 206, 1000
Belial 978
  sons of - 988
belie *deny* 536
  falsify 544
  contradict 708
belief *credence* **484**
  religious creed 983
  easy of - 472
  hug a - 606
believe [*see* belief]
  suppose 514
  - who may 485
  not - one's senses 870
  reason to - 472

believer *religious* 987
  true - 983a
belike 472
belittle *decrease* 36
  underestimate 483
  detract 934
belittling *envy* 921
bell *time* 106
  sound 417
  sign 550
  alarm - 669
  bear away the –
    goodness 648
    success 731
    repute 873
  - book, and candle
    swear 535
    curse 908
    spell 993
    rite 998
  - boy 746
  - mare 64
  - note 408
  - pepper 393
  - the cat 861
  cracked - 408a
  passing - 363
  peal of -s 407
belladonna 663
belle 374, 854
belles-lettres 560
bellicose
  contentious 720
  warlike 722
bellied 250
belligerent
  contentious 720
  warlike 722
  combatant 726
belling 412
bellman 534
Bellona 722
bellow *loud* 404
  cry 411
  animal cry 412
  wail 839
bellows *wind* 349
  lungs 580
bell-shaped
  globose 249
  concave 252
bellwether
  go first 64
  direct 694
belly *inside* 221
  convex 250
  - god 957
bellyful *complete* 52
  enough 639
belomancy 511
belong to *related* 9
  component 56
  included 76
  attribute 157
  property 777, 780
  duty 926
beloved 897
below 207
  - its full strength 651
  - par *inferior* 34
  at a low ebb 207

- itself *visible* 446
betrayer 941
betrim 673
betroth *promise* 768
  marriage 903
betrothal 902
  [see betroth]
betrothed 897
better *good* 648
  improve 658
- half 903
- sort
  beau monde 875
for - for worse
  choice 609
  marriage 903
get - *health* 654
  improve 658
  refreshment 689
  restoration 660
get the - of 731
seen - days
  deteriorate 659
  adversity 735
  poor 804
think - of
  correct 658
  repent 950
betting house 621
betty 374
between 228
- cup and lip 111
- ourselves 528
- the lines 526
- two fires 665
far - 198
lie - 228
betwixt 228
bevel 217
bever 298
beverage 298
bevue 732
bevy *assemblage* 72
  multitude 102
bewail *regret* 833
  lament 839
beware 668
bewilder *put out* 458
  uncertain 475
  astonish 870
bewildered 495, 523
bewitch *fascinate* 615
  please 829
  excite love 897
  diabolize 978
  hoodoo 992
bey 745
beyond *superior* 33
  distance 196
- compare 31, 33
- control 471
- expression 31
- hope 731, 734
- measure 641
- mortal ken 528
- one's depth
  deep 208
  unintelligible 519
- one's grasp 471
- possibility 471
- praise *perfect* 650
472

approbation 931
  virtue 944
- price 814
- question 474
- range 196
- reason 471
- remedy 859
- seas 57
- the grave 528
- the mark
  transcursion 303
  redundance 641
- the veil 528
- the verge 180
go - 303
bezel 217
bezonian 876
bhang 663, 954
bhangi 652
bhikshu 955
bias *influence* 175
  tendency 176
  slope 217
  prepossession 481
  disposition 820
  (*motive* 615)
bib *pinafore* 225
  drink 959
  cleanness 652
bibber *weep* 839
  tope 959
bibble-babble 584
Bible 985
- Christian 984
- oath 535
biblioclasm 162
biblioclast 165
bibliognost 593
bibliographer 593
bibliography 593
bibliolatry *learning* 490
  heterodoxy 984
  idolatry 991
bibliologist 593
bibliomancy 511
bibliomania 490
bibliomaniac 492
bibliopegist 593
bibliophile 492, 593
bibliopole 593
bibliotheca 593
bibulous 298
bice 435, 438
bicentenary, 98, 138, 883
bicentennial 98, 138, 883
bicephalous 90
bichhona 215
bichloride of mercury 663
bicipital 90
bicker *flutter* 315
  quarrel 713
  (*contend* 720)
bickering 24
bicolor 440
biconjugate 91
bicorn 245
bicuspid 91
bicycle 266, 272

bid *order* 741
  offer 763
- a long farewell 624
- defiance 715
- fair *tend* 176
  probable 472
  promise 511
  hope 858
- for *intend* 620
  offer 763
  request 765
  bargain 794
- the banns 903
bidder 767
bidding *command* 741
biddy 746
bide *wait* 133
  remain 141
  take coolly 826
- one's time 133
  watch 507
  inactive 681
bidental 90
bidet 271
biduous 89
biennial *periodic* 138
  plant 367
  celebration 883
bienséance *polish* 852
  manners 894
bier 363
bifacial 90
bifarious 90
bifid 91
bifold 90
biform *double* 90
  (*two* 89)
bifurcate *bisect* 91
  angle 244
big *in degree* 31
  in size 192
  wide 194
- bug 875
- gun 875
- sounding
  loud 404
  words 577
  affected 855
- with 161
- with the fate of 511
look - *defy* 715
  proud 878
  insolent 885
talk - 885
  threat 909
bigamist 903
bigamy 903
biggin 191
bighead 655
bight 343
bigot *positive* 474
  prejudice 481
  obstinate 606
  heterodox 984
  impious 988
bigwig 875
bijou *goodness* 648
  beauty 845
  ornament 847
bijouterie 847
bike 272

bilabiate 90
bilander 273
bilateral *two* 90
  side 236
bilbao 727
bilboes 752
  put into - 751
bile 900
bilge *base* 211
  convex 250
  yawn 260
- water 653
biliary calculus 655
bilingual 560
bilious 837
bilk *disappoint* 509
  cheat 545
  steal 791
bill *list* 86
  hatchet 253
  placard 531
  ticket 550
  paper 593
  plan 626
  weapon 727
  money order 800
  money account 811
  charge 812
  in law 969
- and coo 902
- of exchange
  security 771
- of fare *food* 298
  plan 626
- of indictment 938
- of sale 771
-s of mortality 360
true - 969
billet *locate* 184
  apportion 786
billet *ticket* 550
  epistle 592
  business 625
- doux 902
billhook 253
billiard - ball
  round 249
- room 191
- table *flat* 213
billiards 840
billingsgate
  slang 563
  curse 908
  (*censure* 932)
billion 98, 102
billow *sea* 348
billows *ocean* 341
billy *kettle* 191
  club 727
billycock 225
billy goat 373
bimonthly 138
bin 191
bina 417
binary 89
binate 89
bind *connect* 43
  cover 223
  compel 744
  condition 770
  obligation 926

darken 421
gorge 957
- over *past* 122
- the coals 824
- the fire 384
- the horn 416
- the trumpet 873
- up *destroy* 162
eruption 173
inflate 194
wind 349
excite 824
objurgate 932, 934
- upon *accuse* 938
- valve 664
come to -s 720, 722
deal a - at 716
deal a - to 972
death - 360, 361
blowhole 351
blower 884
blown [see blow]
fatigued 688
proud 878
- upon
disreputable 874
censured 932
- with restless violence 173
storm - over
safe 664
peace 721
blowpipe 144, 349
blowth 367
blowzy *swollen* 194
red 434
blubber *fat* 356
cry 830
- lip 848
Blucher boot 225
bludgeon *weapon* 727
(*strike* 276)
- man *fighter* 726
brute 913
blue *sky* 338
ocean 341
color 438
learned 490
bit of - *hope* 858
- and red 437
- and yellow 435
- blood 875
- book *list* 86
record 551
- devils 837
- green 435
- jacket 269
- laws 988
- light *signal* 550
alarm 669
- moon 110
- peter *flag* 550
set sail 293
- points 298
- ribbon 733, 877
- ruin 959
- serene 338
look -
disappointed 509
feeling 821
discontent 832

disrepute 874
out of the - 338, 508
true - *veracity* 543
probity 939
blueback 800
Bluebeard
marriage 903
libertine 962
blueberry 298
- pie 298
bluefish 298
blueness **438**
blues 837
bluestocking
pedant 491
scholar 492
affectation 855
bluff *violent* 173
high 206
cliff 212
blunt 254
deceive 545
brag 884
card game 840
insolent 885
discourteous 895
- off 545
bluffer *boaster* 884
blunder *error* 495
absurdity 497
awkward 699
failure 732
indiscretion 947
- upon 156
blunderbuss 727
blunderhead 701
blunderheaded 499
blunt *weaken* 160
inert 172
to moderate 174
obtuse 254
benumb 376
to damp 616
plain-spoken 703
cash 800
deaden feelings 823
discourteous 895
- tool 645
- witted 499
bluntness **254**
blur *dim* 443
dirt 653
blemish 848
stigma 874
blurb 931
blurred *invisible* 477
blurt out *disclose* 529
speak 582
blush *heat* 382
redden 434
feel 821
humbled 879
modest 881
at first - *see* 441
appear 448
manifest 525
put to the -
humble 879
browbeat 885
discourtesy 895
blushing honors

repute 873
modesty 881
bluster *violent* 173
defiant 715
insolent 885
resent 900
threaten 909
blusterer **887**
blustering [see bluster]
windy 349
Blut und Eisen 159
boa 225
- constrictor 366
boar *animal* 366
male 373
wild - 366
board *layer* 204
support 215
food 298
hard 323
directorate 542
council 696
attack 716
tribunal 966
- of education 542
- of Regents 542
- of studies 542
- school 542
festive - 892
go by the -
powerless 158
destruction 162
go on - 293
on - *present* 186
ship 273
preside at the - 693
boarder 188
boards *theater* 599
arena 728
board-walk 189
boast 884
not much to - of 651
boaster 884
jingo 885
boastful 884
boasting **884**
boat 273
- race 720
in the same -
accompany 88
party 712
boating 267
boatman 269
boat-shaped 245
boatswain 269
bob *depress* 308
leap 309
oscillate 314
agitate 315
- a courtesy 894
- for *fish* 463
Bobadil, Captain - 887
bobbery 404
bobbin 312
bobbish 654
bobcat 366
bobsled 272
bobtailed 53
bocage 367
bock beer 298
bode 511

bodice 225
bodiless 317
bodily *substantially* 3
wholly 50
material 316
- enjoyment 377
- fear 860
- pain 378
bodkin *go between* 228
perforator 262
body *substance* 3
whole 50
assemblage 72
matter 316
party 712
- and blood of Christ 987
- clothes 225
- color 556
- forth 554
- of doctrine 490
- of knowledge 490
- of water 348
- politic
mankind 372
authority 737
in a - *together* 88
keep - and soul together 654
body-guard *defense* **717**
combatant 726
keeper 753
Bœotian *small* 32
stupid 499
fool 501
vulgar 851
ignoble 876
bog *swamp* 345
dunghill 653
- trotter 876
boggart 980a
boggle *hesitate* 605
awkward 699
difficulty 704
bogie 980
bogle 980
bogus 545
- check 808
Bohemian
unconformity 83
traveler 268
ungenteel 851
boil *violence* 173
effervesce 315
bubble 353
heat 382, 384
ulceration 655
excitement 824, 825
anger 900
- down 195
boiled [see boil]
- beef 298
- eggs 298
boiler 386
boisterous *violent* **173**
hasty 684
excitable 825
bold *prominent* 250
unreserved 525
rigorous 574
defiant 715

brave 861
- push *essay* 675
- relief *visible* 446
- stroke *plan* 626
  success 731
make - with
  discourtesy 895
show a - front
  defy 715
  brave 861
bold face *type* 591
boldfaced *insolent* 885
  printing 591
bole 50
bolero 840
boldness [*see* bold]
bolshevism 146, 742
bolshevist 146, 712
bolster *support* 215
  repair 658
  aid 707
- up *vindicate* 937
bolt *sift* 42, 652
  fasten 43
  fastening 45
  close 261
  move rapidly 274
  propel 284
  run away 370, 623
  safety 664
  escape 671
  hindrance 706
  shaft 727
  shackle 752
- food *swallow* 298
  gormandize 957
- in 751
- out of the blue 508
- the door 761
- upright 212
bolthead 191
bolus *mouthful* 298
  remedy 662
bomb 404, 406, 727
- explosion 361
- vessel 726
bombard 716
  circularize 592
bombardier 726
bombardon 417
bombast
  overestimation 482
  absurdity 497
  unmeaning 517
  magniloquence 577
  ridiculous 853
  boasting 884
  (*exaggeration* 549)
bombastic
  [*see* bombast]
bomber 269*a*
bombilation 404, 407
bombinate 407
bombing cruiser 273
bombproof 664
bon: - diable 844
- enfant *social* 892
  kindly 906
- mot 842
- ton 852
- vivant 957
476

voyage 267
bona fides
  veracity 543
  probity 939
bonanza *extra* 641
  wealth 803
bonbon 396
bond *tie* 45
  servile 746
  compact 769
  security 771
  money 800
  right 924
- of union 9, 45
bondage 749
bonded together 712
bonds [*see* bond]
  fetters 752
  securities 802
- of harmony 714
in - *service* 746
bondsman 746
bone *dense* 321
  hard 323
  strength 159
- of contention 713, 720
- to pick *difficulty* 704
  discord 713
  bred in the - 5
  one - and one flesh 903
bonehouse 363
bones [*see* bone]
  corpse 362
  music 417
  break no - 648
  make no - *willing* 602
bonesetter 662
bonfire 382
  festivity 840
  celebration 883
  make a - of 384
bonhomie *candor* 703
  kindness 906
bonhomme 996
Boniface 890
bonne *servant* 746
  nurse 753
- bouche *treat* 377
  savory 394
  saving 636
  pleasant 829
bonnet 225
- rouge 742
bonny *cheerful* 836
  pretty 845
bonnyclabber 321
bonus *extra* 641
  gift 784
  money 810
bony 323
bonze 996
booby 501
boodle 784
boof 860
book *part* 51
  register 86
  record 551
  volume **593**
  libretto 599
  enter accounts 811

at one's -s 539
- collector 593
- learning 490
- madness 490
- of fate 601
- of poems 590
bring to -
  evidence 467
  account 811
  reprove 932
mind one's - 539
school - 542
without -
  by heart 505
bookbinder 593
bookbinding 593
bookcase 191
booked *dying* 360
bookish 490
bookkeeper 553
bookkeeping 811
bookless *unlearned* 493
bookmaker 156
bookmaking 156
bookseller 593
bookshop 593
bookstore 593
bookworm 492, 593
booly 268
boom *support* 215
  sail 267
  rush 274
  impulse 276
  sound 404
  roll 407
  obstacle 706
  defense 717
boomerang *recoil* 277
  weapon 727
boon 784
  beg a - 765
- companion 890
boor *clown* 876
boorish *ridiculous* 851
  uncourteous 895
boost *impulse* 276
  praise 931
booster 935
boot *box* 191
  dress 225
  advantage 618
  punishment 975
to - *added* 37
booted and spurred 673
bootee 225
booth *stall* 189
  shop 799
bootikin 225
bootleg *drunkenness* 959
bootlegging 964
bootless *useless* 645
  failing 732
boots *dress* 225
  servant 746
  what - it 643
booty 35, **793**
booze 959
bo-peep *peep* 441
  hide 528

bordel 961
border *contiguity* 199
  edge 231
  flank 236
  flower bed 371
  ornament 847
- upon 197, 199
borderer 197
bordering 233
- upon 197
bore *diameter* 202
  hole 260
  tide 348
  tidal wave 667
  trouble 828
  plague 830
  weary 841
Boreal *Northern* 237
  cold 383
borean 349
Boreas 349
boredom 841
borer 262
boresome 275
born 359
- so 5
- to other things 865
- under a lucky star 734
- under an evil star 735
borne 826
- down *failure* 732
  defection 837
borné 499
borough 189
  rotten - 893
borrow *imitate* 19
  receive 788
borrowed plumes
  deception 545
borrower 806
borrowing 788
boscage 367
bosh *absurdity* 497
  unmeaning 517
  untrue 546
  trifling 643
bosk 367
bosky 367
bosom *breast* 221
  mind 450
  affections 820
- friend 890
- of one's family 221
  in the - of 229
boss *knob* 250
  will 600
  politician 694
  rule 737
  master 745
bossiness 600
bossism 693
boston 840
Boston bag 191
botanic 369
- garden 369, 371
botanomancy 511
botany 367, **369**
botch *disorder* 59
  mend 660

unskillful 699
difficulty 704
fail 732
both 89
bother
  uncertainty 475
  bustle 682
  difficulty 704
  trouble 828
  harass 830
botheration 828
bothy 189
bottle *receptacle* 191
  preserve 670
  bee in a - 407
  - *green* 435
  - holder
    auxiliary 177
    mediator 724
  - up *remember* 505
  hide 528
  restrain 751
  crack a - 298
  pass the - 959
  smelling - 400
bottom *lowest part* 211
  support 215
  rear 235
  combe 252
  ship 273
  pluck 604a
  courage 861
  at - 5
  at the - of
    cause 153
  - dollar 67, 800
  - upwards 218
  from the - of one's
    heart *veracity* 543
  feeling 821
  go to the - 310
  probe to the - 461
bottomless 208
  - pit 982
bottoms 345
bouderie 901a
boudoir 191
  - cap 225
bouge 250
bough *part* 51
  curve 245
  tree 367
boughpot 400
bought *flexure* 245
bougie 423
bouilli 298
boulder 249
boulevards 227
bouleversement
  revolution 146
  destruction 162
  excite 824
bounce *eject* 297
  jump 309
  lie 546
  dismiss 756
  boast 884
  insolence 885
  - upon *arrive* 292
  surprise 508
bouncer *ejection* 297

bouncing *large* 192
bound
  circumscribe 229, 233
  swift 274
  leap 309
  certain 474
  - back *recoil* 277
  - by 926
  - for *direction* 278
  destination 620
  - to *promise* 768
  responsible 926
  I'll be - 535
boundary 233
bounden duty 926
boundless *infinite* 105
  space 180
bounds 233
  outline 230
  - of modesty 881
  - of possibility 470
  keep within -
    moderation 174
    shortcoming 304
    restrain 751
    prohibit 761
bountiful *liberal* 816
  benevolent 906
bounty *aid* 707
  gift 784
bouquet *fragrant* 400
  beauty 847
bourdon *staff* 215
  melody 413
  drone 415
bourgeois *medium* 29
  type 591
  commoner 876
bourgeon 161, 194
bourn 233, 292
bourse 799
bouse 959
bout *turn* 138
  job 680
  fight 720
  prank 840
  drinking - 954
boutade *absurdity* 497
  caprice 608
boutonnière 400
bovine *ox* 366
  beef-witted 499
bow *fore part* 234
  curve 245
  projection 250
  stoop 308
  fiddlestick 417
  weapon 727
  ornament 847
  servility 886
  reverence 894
  respect 928
  bend the - 686
  - down *worship* 990
  - out 297
  - submission 725
  - window 245, 260
Bow bells 876
bowed down
  lament 837
  humble 879

bowelless 914a
bowels *inside* 221
  conduit 350
  - full of wrath 722
  - of compassion 914
  - of the earth 208
bower *abode* 189
  alcove 191
  cards 840
  -s of bliss 981
bowery 424
bowie knife 253, 727
bowl *vessel* 191
  rotate 312
  - along *walk* 266
  swift 274
  flowing - 959
bowlder - 249
bow-legged 243
bowler *hat* 225
bowling green
  level 213
bowls 840
bowman 726
bowshot 197
bowsprit 234
bowstring
  execution 972, 975
bowwow 412
box *house* 189
  chest 191
  theater 599
  fight 720
  - car 272
  - pleat 258
  - the compass
    direction 278
    rotation 312
  - change *of mind* 607
  - the ear *anger* 900
  strike 972
  - up 751
  horse - 272
  in a - 704
  musical - 417
  wrong - *error* 495
  unskillful 699
  dilemma 704
boxer 726
boy 129
  servant 746
boyage 127
boyar 875
boycott *eject* 297
  resist 719
  seclude 893
  disapprove 893
boyhood 127
boylike 129
brabble *discord* 713
  contest 720
brabbler 901
brace *tie* 43
  fasten 45
  two 89
  strengthen 159
  support 215
  music 413
  typography 550
  refresh 689
  - game 545

bracelet *circle* 247
  ornament 847
bracer 392, 662
brachial 633
brachygraphy 590
bracing *salubrious* 656
bracken 367
bracket *tie* 43, 45
  couple 89
  support 215
  -s *typography* 550
brackish 392
bract 367
brad 45
bradawl 262
Bradshaw 266
brae 206
brag *cards* 840
  boast 884
braggadocio 482, 884
braggart 482, 884
Brahma 976
Brahman *religion* 984
  priest 996
Brahmanism 976
Brahmi 590
Brahmo 984
braid *tie* 43
  ligature 45
  net 219
  variegate 440
Braille 442
brain *kill* 361
  intellect 450
  skill 498
  rack one's -s 451, 515
  suck one's -s 461
brainless 499
brainpan 450
brainsick 458
brain storm 503
brainwork 451
brainy 450, 498
brake *slowness* 275
  copse 367
  check 706
  curb 752
  apply the - *slower* 275
  hinder 706
  put the -s on 265
  [see also break]
bramble *thorn* 253
  bane 663
bran 330
brancard 272
branch *member* 51
  posterity 167
  ramify 244
  stream 348
  tree 367
  - off *bifurcate* 91
  diverge 291
  - out *ramify* 91
  diffuse style 573
branchiæ 349
branching *ramous* 242
brand *burn* 384
  fuel 388
  torch 423
  mark 550
  sword 727

disrepute 874
censure 932
stigmatize 934
- new 123
- of discord 713
- with reproach 938
brandish
oscillate 314
flourish 315
display 882
brandy smash 959
brangle 713
brangler 710
brank 975
brash *brittle* 328
downpour 348
sickness 655
brashness 885
brasier 386
brass *alloy* 41
music 416
insolence 885
bold as - 861
- band 416, 417
- colored 439
- farthing 643
brassard 550
brassière 225
brat 129, 167
brattice 224, 228
bravado 884
brave *healthy* 654
defy 234, 715
warrior 726
bear 821, 826
courage 861
bravery [*see* brave]
bravo *assassin* 361
desperado 863
applause 931
bravura 415, 416
brawl *cry* 411
discord 713
revel 840
brawler *disputant* 710
rioter 742
blusterer 887
brawny *strong* 159
stout 192
bray *grind* 330
cry 412
Bray, Vicar of -
tergiversation 607
servility 886
braze 43
brazen *unreserved* 525
insolent 885
brazier 191
Brazil tea 298
breach *crack* 44
gap 198
quarrel 713
violation 925
- of faith 940
- of law
unconformity 83
illegal 964
- of the peace 713
custom honored in
the - 614
breachy 198

unruly 742
bread 298
beg - 765
selfish 943
- of idleness 683
- of life *Christ* 976
piety 987
- upon the waters 484
breadbasket 191
breadfruit 298
breadstuffs 298
breadth 202
chiaroscuro 420
break *fracture* 44
discontinuity 70
change 140
gap 198
carriage 272
deviate 279
crumble 328
train animals 370
disclose 529
discord 713
cashier 756
violate 773, 927
bankrupt 808
faux pas 947
- a habit 614
- a lance *attack* 716
battle 722
- a law 83
- away *depart* 293
avoid 623
- bread 298
- bulk 297
- camp 293
- down *destroy* 162
fall short 304
decay 659
fail 732
- for taller timber 666
- forth 295
- ground *begin* 66
depart 293
- in *ingress* 294
domesticate 370
teach 537
tame 749
- in upon *derange* 61
inopportune 135
hinder 706
- jail 671
- loose *escape* 671
get free 750
- no bones 648
- of 660
- of day *morning* 125
twilight 422
- off *cease* 70, 142
relinquish 624
abrogate 756
- one's neck
powerless 158
die 360
- on the wheel
physical pain 378
mental pain 830
punishment 972
- open 173
- out *begin* 66
violent 173

disease 655
excited 825
- Priscian's head 568
- prison 750
- short 328
- silence 582
- the heart *pain* 828, 830
dejection 837
- the ice 888
- the neck of *task* 676
success 731
- the peace *violence* 173
contest 720
- the ranks 61
- the teeth
hard words 579
- the thread 70
- through a custom 614
- through the clouds
visible 446
disclose 529
- up *disjoin* 44
decompose 49
end 67
revolution 146
destroy 162
- up of the system
death 360
disease 655
- with 713
- with the past 146
- word *deceive* 545
improbity 940
breakable 328
breakbone fever 655
breakdown 840
breaker *of horses* 268
wave 348
breakers *surf* 348
shallow 667
- ahead 665
surrounded by - 704
breakfast 298
breakneck
precipice 217
rash 863
breakwater *refuge* 666
obstruction 706
breast *interior* 221
confront 234
convex 250
meat 298
mind 450
oppose 708
soul 820
at the - 129
- high 206
- the current 719
in the - of 620
breastplate 717
breastwork 717
breath *instant* 113
breeze 349
life 359
animality 364
faint sound 405
- of accusation 938
hold - *quiet* 265

expect 507
wonder 870
in the same - 120
not a - of air *quiet* 265
hot 382
out of - 688
shortness of - 688
take away one's -
unexpected 508
fear 860
wonder 870
take - *rest* 265
refresh 689
with bated - 581
breathe *exist* 1
blow 349
live 359
faint sound 405
evince 467
mean 516
inform 527
disclose 529
utter 580
speak 582
refresh 689
- freely *pleasure* 827
relief 834
- one's last 360
- the vital air 359
not - a word 528
breathing *time* 106
air 349
- time *repose* 687
truce 723
breathing-hole 351
breathless
voiceless 581
out of breath 688
feeling 821
fear 860
eager 865
wonder 870
- attention 457
- expectation 507
- impatience 865
- speed 684
breech *invest* 225
rear 235
breeches 225
- maker 225
- pocket
money 800, 802
wear the - 737
breechloader 727
breed *race* 11
kind 75
multiply 161
progeny 167
animals 370
rear 537
(*prepare* 673)
breeding
production 161
style 852
politeness 894
- place 153
breeze *wind* 349
discord 713
breezy 836
brethren 997
breve 413

brevet *warrant* 741
  commission 755
  permit 760
  - rank 873
breviary 990, 998
brevier 591
brevipennate 193
brevity *short* 201
  concise 572
brew *mix* 41
  prepare 673
brewing
  impending 152
Briarean 102, 159
Briareus 159, 192
bribe *equivalent* 30
  tempt 615
  offer 763
  gift 784
  buy 795
  reward 809, 973
bribery [*see* bribe]
bric-a-brac 847
brick *hard* 323
  pottery 384
  material 635
  trump 939, 948
  - color 434
  - over 386
  - red 434
  make -s without straw 471
brickbat 727
brickkiln 386
bricklayer 690
bricky 434
bridal 903
bride 903
bridegroom 903
bridesmaid 890, 903
bridesman 903
bridewell 752
bridge
  intermedium 45
  way 627
  card game 840
  - of death 360
  - over *join* 43
  facilitate 705
  make peace 723
  compromise 774
bridle *depart* 293
  restrain 751
  rein 752
  - one's tongue
  silent 585
  cautious 864
  - road 627
  - up 900
brief *time* 111
  space 201
  concise 572
  compendium 596
  - case 191
  hold a - for 759
briefly *anon* 132
brier *sharp* 253
  bane 663
brig 273
brigade *arrange* 60
  military 726

brigadier 745
brigand 792
brigandage 791
brigandine 717
brigantine 273
bright *shine* 420
  color 428
  intelligent 498
  cheery 836
  beauty 845
  glory 873
  - colored 428
  - days 734
  - prospect 858
  - side 829
  - thought *sharp* 498
  good stroke 626
  wit 842
  look at the - side
  cheer 836
  hope 858
brighten up
  furbish 658
bright-eyed 845
brigue *party* 712
  contention 720
brilliant *shining* 420
  music 416
  good 648
  witty 842
  beautiful 845
  gem 847
  glorious 873
  be - *intellectual* 498
  - idea 842
brim 231
  - over 641
brimful 52
brimstone 388
brindled 440
brine *sea* 341
  salt 392
bring 270
  - about *cause* 153
  achieve 729
  - back 790
  - back to the memory 505
  - forth *produce* 161
  extract 301
  - forward
  evidence 467
  manifest 525
  teach 537
  improve 658
  - gray hairs to the grave
  adversity 735
  pain 830
  - grist to the mill 644
  - home 775
  - home to 155
  - in *receive* 296
  income 810
  price 812
  - in a verdict 480
  - in its train 88
  - in question 461
  - into being 161
  - into play 677
  - low 874

  - off 672
  - out *discover* 480a
  manifest 525
  publish 591
  - over *persuade* 484
  - round *persuade* 615
  restore 660
  - to *convert* 144
  halt 265
  - to a crisis 604
  - to a point 74
  - to bear 470
  - to bear upon
  relation 9
  action 170
  - together *assemble* 72
  - to life 359
  - to light 480a
  - to maturity
  prepare 673
  complete 729
  - to mind 505
  - to perfection 677
  - to terms 723
  - to trial 969
  - under one's notice 457
  - up *develop* 161
  vomit 297
  train 370
  educate 537
  - up the rear 235
  - word 527
brink 231
  - of the grave 360
  on the - *almost* 32
  coming 121
  near 197
briny 392
  - deep 341
brio *music* 415
briquette 388
brisk *prompt* 111
  energetic 171
  active 682
  cheery 836
bristle 253
  - up *stick up* 250
  angry 900
  - with *plenty* 639
  too much 641
  - with arms 722
bristling *thorny* 253
  discourtesy 895
bristly *rough* 256
Britannia metal 545
Briticism 563
British 188
  - courts 966
  - lion 604
Britisher 188
Briton 188
  true - 939
brittle 328
brittleness 328
britzka 272
broach *begin* 66
  found 153
  perforate 262
  tap 297
  publish 531

  assert 535
broad *general* 78
  space 202
  lake 343
  emphatic 535
  indelicate 961
  - accent 580
  - arrow 550
  - awake *vigilant* 459
  brisk 682
  - daylight *light* 420
  manifest 525
  - farce 842
  - gauge 466
  - grin 838
  - highway 627
  - hint 527
  - meaning 516
broadcast *disperse* 73. 291
  publish 531
  news 532
  sow - 818
broadcloth 219, 635
broaden 78
broadhearted 906
broadhorn 273
broadsheet 531, 593
broad-shouldered 159
broadside *lateral* 236
  publication 531
  cannonade 716
broadsword 727
Brobdingnagian 159, 192
brocade 847
brocatelle 847
brochure 593
broder 549
brogan 225
brogue *boot* 225
  dialect 560, 563
broidery 847
broil *heat* 382
  fry 384
  fray 713, 720
broiler *fowl* 298
broken *divided* 51
  discontinuous 70
  weak 160
  of horses 370
  - color 428
  - down *decrepit* 659
  failing 732
  dejected 837
  - English 563
  - fortune
  adversity 735
  poverty 804
  - heart *pain* 828
  dejected 837
  hopeless 859
  - meat 645
  - reed 665
  - voice 581, 583
  - winded *disease* 655
  fatigue 688
broker *agent* 758
  merchant 797
brokerage *pay* 812
brokery 794

bromide
  conventionalist 82
bromidium 496
bronchia 351
broncho 271
  - **buster** 370
bronchocele 655
bronze *brown* 433
  sculpture 557
brooch 847
brood *multitude* 102
  family 167
  hatch 370
  - **over** *think* 451
  mope 837
brooding *preparing* 673
brook *stream* 348
  bear 826
broom *undergrowth* 367
  sweep 652
broomstick 491
broth 298
brothel 945, 961
brother *kin* 11
  similar 17
  equal 27
  - **Jonathan** 188
brotherhood 712
brotherly
  friendship 888
  love 897
  benevolence 906
brougham 272
brought to bed 161
brouillerie 713
brouillon 626
brow *top* 210
  edge 231
  front 234
browbeat
  intimidate 860
  swagger 885
  disrespect 929
  -en *humbled* 879
brown **433**
  - **Bess** 727
  - **ocher** 433
  - **stone** 635
  - **stone house** 189, 831
  - **study** *thought* 451
  inattention 458
  imagination 515
Brownian 984
brownie 979
brownness 433
browse 298
bruin 895
bruise *powder* 330
  hurt 619
  injure 649
bruised *blemished* 848
bruiser 726
bruit 531, 532
brumal 383
brummagem 545
brunch 572
brunette 433
Brunswick black 356a
brunt *beginning* 66
  impulse 276
  bear the -

480

  difficulty 704
  defense 717
  endure 821, 826
  (*resist* 719)
brush *tail* 235
  rough 256
  rapid motion 274
  groom 370
  touch 379
  clean 652
  fight 720
  - **away** *reject* 297
  abrogate 756
  - **up** *clean* 652
  furbish 658
  prepare 673
  paint - 556
brushwood 367, 388
brusque *violent* 173
  haste 684
  discourtesy 895
Brussels sprouts 298
brustle 407
brutal *vulgar* 851
  rude 895
  savage 907
brutalize
  [see brutal]
  corrupt 659
  deaden 823
  vice 945
brute *animal* 366
  rude 895
  maleficent 913
  - **force** *strength* 159
  violence 173
  animal 450a
  severe 739
  compulsion 744
  lawless 964
  - **matter** *matter* 316
  inorganic 358
brutify 954
brutish [see brute]
  vulgar 851
  ignoble 876
  intemperate 954
Bryanite 984
bryophites 369
bubble
  unsubstantial 4
  transient 111
  little 193
  light 320
  water 348
  air **353**
  error 495
  deceit 545
  trifle 643
  - **burst**
  fall short 304
  disappoint 509
  fail 732
  - **reputation** 873
  - **up** *agitation* 315
bubbling 353
bubo 250
bubonic plague 655
buccaneer 791, 792
Bucephalus 271
buck *confront* 234

  leap 309
  stag 366
  male 373
  negro 431
  wash 652
  fop 854
  - **basket** 191
  - **fever** 825
  - **jump** 309
  - **nigger** 431
bucket *receptacle* 191
  load 270
  - **shop** 621
  kick the - 360
bucking *attack* 716
buckle *tie* 43
  fastening 45
  distort 243
  curl 248
  - **oneself** 604
  - **on one's armor** 673
  - **to** *resolution* 604
  exertion 686
  - **with** *grapple* 720
buckler 717
buckram
  affectation 855
  pride 878
  men in - 549
buckwheat 367
bucolic
  pastoral 370, 371
  poem 597
bud *beginning* 66
  germ 153
  expand 194
  graft 300
  blossom 367
  - **from** 154
Buddha 976, 986
Buddhism 976, 984
Buddhist 984
  - **priests** 996
  - **temple** 1000
budding *young* 127
  expansion 194
buddy *chum* 890
budge 264
budget *heap* 72
  bag 191
  store 636
  finance 811
  - **of news** 532
budmash 949
buff *skin* 223
  color 436
  native - 226
buffalo 366
  - **bug** 366
  - **robe** 223
  - **wallow** 343
buffer *hindrance* 706
  defense 717
buffet *strike* 276
  agitate 315
  evil 619
  bad 649
  affront 900
  smite 972
  - **the waves**
  difficulty 704

  opposition 708
buffet *bar* 189
  cupboard 191
buffle-headed 499
buffo 599
buffoon *actor* 599
  humorist 844
  butt 857
buffoonery
  amusement 840
  humor 842
bug *littleness* 193
  insect 366, 653
bugaboo *alarm* 669
  fear 860
bugbear *imaginary* 515
  alarm 669
  fear 860, 980
buggy 272
bugle *instrument* 417
  war cry 722
  - **call** *sign* 550
  command 741
bugles *ornament* 847
build *construct* 161
  form 240
  - **a campfire** 384
  - **up** *compose* 54
  - **upon** *belief* 484
  - **upon a rock** 150
builder 626, 690
building material 635
buildings 189
built on *basis* 211
bulb *knob* 249
  projection 250
bulbul 416
bulge 250
bulk *be great* 31
  whole 50
  size 192
bulkhead *covering* 223
  interjacence 228
  safety 664
  hindrance 706
bulky 31
bull *animal* 366
  male 373
  error 495
  absurdity 497
  solecism 568
  detective 664
  ordinance 741
  stock exchange 797
  - **in a china shop** 59
  take the - by the horns
  resolution 604
  courage 861
Bull, John - 188
bulla 250
bull calf 501
bulldog *animal* 327, 366
  pluck 604, 604a
  courage 861
bulldoze 860, 885
bulldozer 887
bullet *ball* 249
  arms 727
  (*missile* 284)
  - **proof** 717

bulletin *list* 86
  news 532
  record 551
  letter 592
  - board 551
bullfight 720
bullhead 501
bullion 800
bull's-eye *center* 222
  lantern 423
  aim 620
bullwhack 975
bullwhacker 370
bully *boat* 273
  first-rate 648
  fighter 726
  jovial 836
  frighten 860
  rashness 863
  bluster 885
  blusterer 887
  resent 900
  threaten 909
  evildoer 913
  bad man 949
  - for you 931
bullyrag 830
bulrush *worthless* 643
bulwark 717
bum *idler* 683
  spree 840
  beggar 876
  drink 959
bumbailiff 965
Bumbledom
  authority 737
  jurisdiction 965
bumboat 273
bummer 683
bump *projection* 250
  thump 276
bumper 52
bumpkin 876
bumptious *proud* 878
  insolent 885
bun 298
bunch *collection* 72
  protuberance 250
bunch-backed 243
buncombe *lie* 544
  bombast 577
  boast 884
  flattery 933
Bund 712
bund *quay* 666
bunder 292, 666
bunderboat 273
bundle *packet* 72
  go 266
  start 284
  - along 274
  - off 234
  - on *hurry* 274
  haste 684
  - out 297
bundobust 60, 769
bung 263, 351
  - up 261
bungalow 189
bunghole 351
bungle 699

bungler **701**'
bunk *reside* 186
  support 215
bunker 181
bunkie *bedfellow* 890
bunko 545,791
  - game 545
  - steerer 548
bunkoman 792
bunkum[*see* buncombe]
bunt 276
bunting 550
buoy *raise* 307
  float 320
  refuge 666
  hope 858
buoyant *floating* 305
  light 320
  elastic 325
  prosperous 734
  cheerful 836
  hopeful 858
bur *clinging* 46
  rough 256
  in engraving 558
burden *lading* 190
  weight 319
  melody 413
  music 415
  poetry 597
  too much 641
  clog 706
  oppress 828
  care 830
  - of a song
  repetition 104
  - the memory 505
burdensome
  [*see* burden]
  hurtful 649
  laborious 686
  cumbrous 830
bureau *chest* 191
  office 691
  shop 799
  tribunal 966
  department 965
bureaucracy 737
bureaucrat 694
bureaucratic 737
burgee 550
burgeon 161, 194
burgess 188
burgh 189
burgher 188
burghmote 966
burglar 792
  - alarm 550, 669
burglary 791
burgomaster 745
burgrave 745
burial 363
buried *deep* 208
  imbedded 229
  hidden 528
  - in a napkin 460
  - in oblivion 506
burin 558
burke 361
burlesque
  imitation 19

  travesty 21, 555
  absurdity 497
  drama 599
  comic 853
  ridicule 856
burletta 599
burly 192
burn *near* 197
  rivulet 348
  hot 382
  consume 384
  neglect 460
  near the truth 480a
  excited 825
  blemish 848
  love 897
  punish 972
  - daylight 683
  - in 384
  - one's fingers 699
  - out 385
  - the candle at both
    ends
  waste 638
  exertion 686
  prodigal 818
  - to 865
  - up the road 266
burner 423
burning [*see* burn]
  of a corpse 363
  passion 821
  angry 900
  - ghât 363, 384
  - glass 445
  - pain 378
  - shame 874
  - with curiosity 455
burnish *polish* 255
  shine 420
  beautify 845
burnoose 225
burnt [*see* burn]
  red 434
  - offering *atone* 952
  worship 990
  - orange 434
burr 253, 410
burra sahib 642, 745
burro 271
burrow *lodge* 184
  excavate 252
bursar 801
bursary 802
bursat 348
burst *disjoin* 44
  instantaneous 113
  explosion 173
  brittle 328
  sound 406
  paroxysm 825
  bubble -
  disclosure 529
  all over 729
  - away 623
  - forth *begin* 66
  expand 194
  be seen 446
  - in 294
  - into a flame 825
  - into tears 839

  - of anger 900
  - of eloquence 582
  - of envy 921
  - of laughter 838
  - out *violence* 173
  egress 295
  - upon *arrive* 292
  unexpected 508
  - with grief 839
  ready to -
  replete 641
  excited 824
burthen [*see* burden]
bury *inclose* 229
  inter 363
  conceal 528
  - one's talent 528
  - the hatchet 723
busby 225
bush *branch* 51
  lining 224
  jungle 344
  shrub 367
  beat about the - 629
  in the - 344
bushed 475, 688
bushel *much* 31
  multitude 102
  receptacle 191
  size 192
  hid under a - 460
  not hide light under a
    - 878
bushfighting 720
bushing 224
Bushman 431
bushranger 792
bushwhacker
  scythe 253
  guerrilla 726
  free lance 748
bushy 256
business *event* 151
  topic 454
  occupation **625**
  commerce 794
  full of - 682
  man of -
  proficient 700
  consignee 758
  mind one's -
  incurious 456
  attentive 457
  careful 459
  send about one's - 297
  stage - 599
businesslike
  orderly 58
  business 625
  active 682
  practical 692
  skillful 698
buskin *dress* 225
  drama 599
buss *boat* 273
  courtesy 894
  endearment 902
bust 554
  spree 840
bustee 189
bustle *energy* 171

dress 225
agitation 315
activity 682
haste 684
difficulty 704
bustling [see bustle]
eventful 151
busy 682
idly - 638, 683
busybody *curiosity* 455
newsmonger 532
activity 682
but *on the other hand* 30
except 83
limit 233
qualifying 469
- *now* 118
butcha 129, 167
butcher *kill* 361
evildoer 913
butchered 53
butler 746
butt *cask* 191
push 276
aim 620
attack 716
laughingstock 857
- *end* 67
- *in* 294
butte 206
butter 356
flattery 933
- *bread on both sides*
641

- *not melt in mouth*
894
buttercup 845
buttered side
know - skill 698
selfish 943
not know - 699
butter-fingers 701
butterfly *insect* 366
variegated 440
fickle 605
beauty 845
gaudy 882
break - on wheel
waste 638
spite 907
butterscotch 396
buttery 636
Buttinsky 294
buttock 235
button *fasten* 43
fastening 45
little 193
hanging 214
knob 250
trifle 643
- *up close* 261
restrain 751
- *up one's pockets* 808
take by the - 586
buttoned-up
reserved 528
buttonhole *flower* 400
bore 841

buttonholer 841
buttons *page* 746
button-top *useless* 645
buttress *strength* 159
support 215
defense 717
butyraceous 355
buxom 836
buy 795
- *and sell* 794
- *a pig in a poke* 621
buzz *hiss* 409
insect cry 412
publish 531
news 532
- *saw* 44
buzzard *bird* 366
fool 501
between hawk and -
agitation 315
worry 828
b[l]ind as a - 442
- *dollar* 800
by *alongside* 236
instrumental 631
sequestered 893
- *and by* 121, 132
- *itself* 87
- *means of* 632
- *my troth &c.* 535
- *no means* 32
- *telegraph* 532
- *the by* 134
- *the card* 82

- *the hour &c.*
hire 788
- *the way à propos* 9
beside the purpose 10
parenthetical 134
- *wireless* 532
go - pass 303
_*have - one*
provide 637
possess 777
bye *departure* 293
by-end 615
bygone *past* 122
forgotten 506
let -s be bygones 918
bylaw 963
byname 565
by-pass 287
bypast 122
bypath 279
byplay *hint* 527
gesture 550
by-purpose 615
byre 189, 370, 636
byroad 278, 627
by-room 191
byssus 256
bystander *near* 197
spectator 444
byway 627
byword *maxim* 496
cant term 563, 564
reproach 874
contempt 930

C

cab 272
cabal *plan* 626
confederacy 712
cabala *latency* 526
spell 993
cabalism 526
cabalistic *hidden* 528
sorcery 992
cabane 273
cabaret 189
cabasset 717
cabbage 298, 791
cabestro 45
cabin *room* 189
receptacle 191
cabined 751
cabinet *receptacle* 191
workshop 691
council 696
- *picture* 556
cable *link* 45
dispatch 527
news 531, 532
telegraph 534
by - 684
- *code* 528
slip - 623
telegraphic - 534
cabled *telegraphic* 531
cabman *traveler* 268
director 694
caboose 386
482

cabriolet 272
cacation 299
cachalot 192
cache 636
cachet 550
lettre de - 751
cachexia *weakness* 160
disease 655
cachinnation 838
cacique 745
cackle *of geese* 412
chatter 584
talk 588
laugh 838
cacodemon 980
cacoëpy 410, 583
cacoëthes *habit* 613
itch 865
- *loquendi* 584
- *scribendi* 590
cacographer 579
cacographic 579
cacography 590
cacology 579, 583
caconym 563
cacophonous
[see cacophony]
cacophony *stridor* 410
discord 414
style 579
Cacus, den of - 791
cad *servant* 746

vulgar 851
plebeian 876
cadastral survey 466
cadastration 466
cadastre *list* 86
measurement 466
cadaverous *corpse* 362
pale 429
hideous 846
caddy 191
cadeau 784
cadence *pace* 264
fall 306
sound 402
music 415
cadenza 415
cadet *junior* 129
soldier 726
officer 745
- *blue* 438
cadge 765
cadger *beggar* 767
huckster 797
cadi 967
cadmium 439
caduceus *insignia* 747
wand 215, 993
caducity *fugacity* 111
age 128
impotence 158
decay 659
caducous 111

cæcal 261
cæcum 221, 350
Cæsar 745
cæsura *disjunction* 44
discontinuity 70
cessation 142
interval 198
café 189
caftan 225
cafuzo 41
cage *receptacle* 191
restrain 751
prison 752
Cagliostro *impostor* 548
sorcerer 994
cahoot 712
cahot 250, 315
cahotage *disorder* 59
agitation 315
Cain 361
caique 273
cairn *grave* 363
sign 550
caisson 191, 252
caitiff *churl* 876
ruffian 913
villain 949
cajole *flatter* 933
[see cajolery]
cajolery
imposition 544, **545**
_*persuasion* 615

candlestick 423
seven-branched - 999
candor *veracity* 543
artlessness 703
honor 939
candy *dense* 321
sweet 396
cane *weapon* 727
punish 972
scourge 975
- sugar 396
canescent 430
can hook 633
Canicula 423
canicule 382
canicular 382
caniculated 259
canine 366
- appetite 865
- madness 867
canister 191
canker *disease* 655
deterioration 659
bane 663
pain 830
cankered *sullen* 901a
cankerworm 663
evildoer 913
care 830
canned goods 670
cannel coal 388
cannery 636
cannibal 913
cannibalism 945
cannikin 191
canning 670
cannon *collision* 276
loud 404
arms 727
-'s mouth *war* 722
courage 861
cannonade 716
cannonball *round* 249
swift 274
cannoneer 726
cannot 471
cannular 260
canny *wise* 498
cunning 702
canoe 273
paddle one's own -
748
canon *regularity* 80
music 415
belief 484
precept 697
priest 996
rite 998
- law 697
canon *ravine* 198, 350
canonical *regular* 82
inspired 985
ecclesiastical 995
canonicals 999
canonist 983
canonization *repute* 873
deification 991
rite 998
canonize 991
canonry 995
canopy 223

- of heaven 318
canorous 413
cant *oblique* 217
jerk 276
hypocrisy 544
neology 563
impiety 988
cantabile 415
cantankerous 901, 901a
cantata 415
cantatore 416
cantatrice 416
canteen 189, 191
canter *move* 266
gallop 274
win at a - 705
canterbury
receptacle 191
Canterbury tale 546
cantharides 171
cant hook 276
canticle 415
cantilever 215
canting 855
cantle 51
cantlet *small* 32
piece 51
canto 597
canton *partition* 44
area 181
cantonment
location 184
abode 189
cantrap 993
canty 836
Canuck 188
canvas *sail* 267
picture 556
under press of - 274
canvass
investigate 461
discuss 476
dissert 595
solicit 765
canvasser 767, 797
canzonet *song* 415
caoutchouc 325
cap *be superior* 33
height 206
summit 210
cover 223
hat 225
retaliate 718
complete 729
salute 894
- and bells 844
- and gown 550
- fits 23
- in hand
request 765
servile 886
respect 928
- of maintenance 747
fling up one's - 838
Fortunatus's - 993
set one's - at 897, 902
capability
endowment 5
power 157
skill 698
facility 705

capable *quick* 682
[see capability]
capacious *space* 180
- memory 505
capacity
endowment 5
power 157
space 180
size 192
intellect 450
wisdom 498
office 625
talent 698
meanest - 499, 518
cap-a-pie
complete 52
armed -
prepared 673
defense 717
war 722
caparison 225
cape *height* 206
cloak 225
projection 250
(*land* 342)
Cape cart 272
caper *leap* 309
absurdity 497
dance 840
capful *quantity* 25
small 32
- of wind 349
capillament 205
capillary *hairlike* 205
(*thin* 203)
capital *city* 189
top 210
letter 561
important 642
excellent 648
money 800
wealth 803
- crime 947
- punishment 972
make - out of
pretext 617
acquire 775
capitalist 803
capitals 591
print in -s 642
capitation 85
- tax 812
capitol 717
capitular *rule* 80
churchdom 995
clergy 996
capitulate 725
capnomancy 511
capon 298, 373
caponize 38, 158
caporal 694
capote 225
capper 548
capriccio *music* 415
whim 608
caprice **608**
out of - 615a
capricious
irregular 139
changeable 149
irresolute 605

whimsical 608
capriciously
without motive 615a
[see capricious]
capriole 309
capsheaf 210
capsicum 393
capsize
inversion 218
wreck 731
capsized 732
capstan *lift* 307
machine 633
capstone 210
capsular *concave* 252
capsule *vessel* 191
tunicle 223
captain *mariner* 269
master 745
captation 933
caption 789
heading 66, 564
captious
capricious 608
irascible 901
censorious 932
captivate *induce* 615
restrain 751
please 829
captivated
fascinated 827
captivating
pleasing 829
lovable 897
captivation
attraction 829
captive *prisoner* 754
adorer 897
- balloon 273
lead - 749
make - 751
captivity 751
captor 789
capture 789
capturer 789
Capuchin 996
caquet 584
car 272
carabineer 726
carack 273
caracole 309
caracoler 266
carafe 191
caramel 396
carapace 717
carat 319
caravan
company 72
journey 266
vehicle 272
caravansary 189
caravel 273
car-barn 636
carbine 727
carbolic acid 663
carbon 388
carbonaceous 388
Carbonaro 742
carbonate
- of ammonia **392**
- of lead 430

carbonic acid 663
carbonization 384
carbonize 384
carboy 191
carbuncle *red* 434
  abscess 655
  jewel 847
carburetor 272
carcanet 847
carcass *structure* 329
  corpse 362
  bomb 727
carcelage 973
carcinoma 655
card *unravel* 60
  ticket 550
  plan 626
  comb 652
  address – 550
  by the – 82
  – cheat 792
  – index
    arrangement 60
    list 86
    record 551
    store 636
  –s to play 632
  great – 873
  house of –s 328
  leave a – 892
  on the –s *liable* 177
    destiny 152
    possible 470
  playing –s 840
  play one's best – 686
  play one's – 692
  play one's –s well 698
  shuffle the –s
    begin again 66
    change 140
    chance 621
    prepare 673
  speak by the –
    care 459
    veracity 5..
    phrase 566
  throw up the –s 757
  trump – 626
cardboard 593
cardcase 191
cardiac 836
cardialgia 655
Cardigan *jacket* 225
cardinal *dress* 225
  red 434
  bird 434
  important 642
  excellent 648
  priest 995, 996
  – bird 434
  – flower 434
  – grosbeak 434
  – points *compass* 278
  – virtues 944
cardinalate 995
cardioid 245
carditis 655
card-sharper 792
card-sharping 545
care *attention* **459**
  business 625

adversity 735
  custody 751
  economy 817
  pain 828
  fear 860
  – for *important* 642
  desire 865
  love 897
  – will kill a cat 459
  drive – away 840
  for aught one –s
    unimportant 643
    indifferent 866
  have the – of 693
  take – 864
  take – of 459
careen *slope* 217
  repair 660
career *business* 625
  conduct 692
careful *heedful* 459
  frugal 817
careless
  inattentive 458
  neglectful 460
  feeble 575
  insensible 823
  indifferent 866
carelessness
  [*see* careless]
caress 902
caret *incomplete* 53
  typography 550
  want 640
caretaker 758
careworn *pain* 828
  dejection 827
cargador 271
cargo
  large quantity 31
  contents 190
  shipment 270
  property 780
  goods 798
caribou 366
caricature *likeness* 19
  copy 21
  exaggerate 549
  misrepresent 555
  ridicule 856
caricaturist 559, 844
caries 49, 655
cariole 272
carious 653
cark 828
carking 828
  – care 830
carle 876
carlock 352
carman 694
Carmelite 996
carminative 174, 662
carmine 434
carnage 361
carnal *fleshly* 364
  intemperate 954
  impure 961
  irreligious 989
carnalize 954
carnation 434
Carnegie medal 733

carnival 840
carnivore 298
carnivorism 298
carnivorous 298
carol *music* 415, 416
  cheerful 836
  rejoice 838
carom 276
carouse *feast* 298
  festivity 840
  intemperance 954
  drinking 959
carp at 932
carpenter 690
carper 936
carpet 211
  – knight *fop* 854
  servile 886
  sybarite 954a
  – sweeper 652
  on the – *topic* 454
  project 626
carpetbagger 548
carphology 315
carrefour 627
carriage *gait* 264
  transference 270
  vehicle 272
  aspect 448
  conduct 692
  keep one's – 852
carried [*see* carry]
  – away by passion 824
  – by acclamation 488
carrier **271**
  – pigeon 534
carriole 272
carrion *carcass* 362
  foul 653
carrom 276
carronade 727
carroty 434
carry *conduce to* 176
  support 215
  transfer 270
  induce 615
  – all before one 731
  – a point
  succeed 731
  – by storm 731
  – coals 879
  – conviction 484
  – in the mind 505
  – into execution
  complete 729
  observe 772
  – off *take* 789
  steal 791
  – on [*see below*]
  – oneself 692
  – out *conduct* 692
  complete 729
  – over *transfer* 270
  accounts 811
  – through 692, 729
  – weight
  influence 175
  evidence 467
  importance 642
  – with a high hand
  authority 737

pride 878
  insolence 885
  reap and – 775
  carry on *continue* 143
  persevere 604a
  pursue 622
  do 680
  conduct 692
  – an argument 476
  – an inquiry 461
  – a trade 794
  – business 625
  – war 722
cart 272
  – away 185
  – before the horse
  disorder 59
  inversion 218
  bungling 699
  – horse 271
  – load *much* 31
  contents 190
cartage 270
carte *list* 86
  – and tierce 716
  – blanche *power* 157
  permit 760
  liberal 816
  – de visite 550, 554
cartel *defiance* 715
  truce 723
  compact 709. 769
carter 268
Cartesianism 451
Carthusian 996
cartilage *dense* 321
  hard 323
  tough 327
cartilaginous *hard* 323
  tenacious 327
cartographer 466
cartography 466, 554
carton 593
cartoon 21, 556
cartoonist 558
cartouche
  ammunition 727
  ornament 847
cartridge 727
cartulary *list* 86
  record 551
caruncle 250
caruncular 250
carunculation 250
carve *cut* 44
  make 161
  form 240
  furrow 259
  sculpture 557
  apportion 786
  – one's way 282
carvel 273
carver 559
Caryatides 215
casa 189
cascade 348
case *state* 7
  box 191
  sheath 223
  topic 454
  argument 476

485

long time 110
cephalalgia 378
ceramic 384
  - ware 557
ceramics 557
cerate 355, 662
Cerberus *janitor* 263
  custodian 664
  sop for - 615
cereal 298, 367
cereals 369
cerebral *phonetic* 561
cerebrate 451
cerebration 451
cerebrum 450
cerecloth 223, 363
cerement *covering* 223
  wax 356
  burial 363
ceremonious 928
ceremony *parade* 882
  courtesy 894
  rite 998
cerise 434
cerograph 558
cerography
  engraving 558
  writing 590
ceromancy 511
ceroplastic 557
certain *special* 79
  indefinite number 100
  sure 474
  belief 484
  true 494
  make - of 480*a*
  of a - age 128
  to a - degree 32
certainly *yes* 488
certainty 474
certes *surely* 474
  yes 488
certificate
  evidence 467
  record 551
  security 771
certify *evince* 467
  affirm 535
certiorari 969
certitude 474
cerulean 438
cerulescent 438
ceruse 430
cespitose 367
cess *tax* 812
cessation 142
cession *surrender* 725
  of property 782
  gift 784
cesspool 653
cest 247
cestus *ligtaure* 45
  girdle 247
chabuk 975
chafe *physical pain* 378
  warm 384
  irritate 825
  mental pain 828, 830
  discontent 832
  incense 900
chaff *trash* 643

rubbish 645
ridicule 856
vulgar 876
not to be caught with-
  clever 698
  cunning 702
winnow - from wheat
  609
chaffer 794
chafing-dish 386
chagrin 828
chain *fasten* 43
  vinculum 45
  series 69
  measure 200
  interlinking 219
  imprison 752
  ornament 847
  adamantine -s 360
  - lightning 423
  drink 959
  -s *fireplace* 386
  drag a - 749
  drag a lengthened -
    686
  in -s *prisoner* 754
chain shot 727
chair *support* 215
  vehicle 272
  professorship 542
  throne 747
  celebration 883
  president 694
  - *car* 272
  in the - 693
chairman 694
chaise 272
chalcedony 847
chalcography 558
chalet 189
chalice 191
chalk *earth* 342
  white 430
  mark 550
  drawing 556
  - out *plan* 626
  - talk 537, 584
  - talker 540
  not know - from
    cheese 491
chalky 430
challenge
  question 461
  doubt 485
  claim 924
  defy 715
  accuse 938
  - *comparison* 648
  - the jurors 969
chalybeate 662
chamber *room* 191
  council 696
  mart 799
  - concert 415
  - fellow 890
  - music 415
  sick - 655
chamberlain 746
chambermaid 746
chameleon *lizard* 366
  changeable 149

variegated 440
chamfer 259
chamois
  smoothness 255
  leap 306
  animal 366
champ 298
  - the bit *disobedient*
    742
  chafe 825
  angry 900
champagne 959
champaign 344
champain 874
champak 400
champion *best* 648
  auxiliary 711
  defense 717
  combatant 726
  victor 731
  representative 759
  pity 914
championship 707
champlevé 847
chance
  absence of cause 156
  liability 177
  absence of aim 621
  as - would have it 152
  be one's - 151
  -s against one *danger*
    665
  game of - 840
  great - 472
  small - 473
  stand a - *liable* 177
  possible 470
  take one's - 675
chanceable 156
chanceful 156
chancel 1000
chancellor *judge* 664,
  967
  president 745
  deputy 759
  - of the exchequer 801
chancery
  - suit *delay* 133
  court of - 966
chandelier 214, 423
chandler 797
change *alteration* 140
  interchange 148
  mart 799
  small coin 800
  - about 149
  - color 821
  - for 147
  - hands 783
  - of mind 607
  - of opinion 485
  - of place 264
  radical - 146
  sudden - 146
changeable 149
changeableness
  mutable 149
  irresolute 605
changeful 607
changeling
  substitute 147

fool 501
changer 797
channel *base* 211
  furrow 259
  opening 260
  conduit 350
  artery 627
chant *song* 415
  sing 416
  worship 990
chanter 416
chanticleer 366
chantress 416
chantry 1000
chaomancy 511
chaos 59
chap *crack* 198
  jaw 231
  fellow 373
chaparajos 225
chaparral 367
chap book 593
chapeau 225
chapel 189, 1000
chaperon
  accompany 88
  guard 459
  safety 664
chapfallen 837, 878
chaplain 996
chaplaincy 995
chaplet *circle* 247
  fragrance 400
  favor 550
  trophy 733
  ornament 847
chapman 797
chaps *chaparajos* 225
chapter *partition* 44
  part 51
  topic 454
  book 593
  council 696
  church 995
  - and verse
    evidence 467
    exact 494
  - of accidents 156, 621
chapter house 1000
chaqueta 225
char 384
char-à-bancs 272
character *nature* 5
  state 7
  class 75
  oddity 83
  letter 561
  drama 599
  disposition 820
characteristic
  intrinsic 5
  special 79
  mark 550
characterize *name* 564
  describe 594
characterized 820
charade *riddle* 533
  drama 599
charcoal *fuel* 384, 388
  black 431
  drawing 556

charge *fill* 52
　contents 190
　business 625
　mandate 630
　direction 693
　advice 695
　precept 697
　attack 716
　order 741
　custody 751
　commission 755
　bargain for 794
　price 812
　accusation 938
　churchdom 995
　- d with
　possessed of 777
　- on *attribute* 155
　in - *prisoner* 754
　justifiable - 937
　take - of *safe* 664
　take in - 751
chargeable *debt* 806
　- on *duty* 926
chargé d'affaires 758
charger *carrier* 271
　fighter 726
chargeship 625
chariot 272
　drag at one's - wheels
　749
charioteer
　driver 268
　pilot 694
charitable [*see* charity]
charity *give* 784
　liberal 816
　benefi: ent 906
　pity 914
　- that begins at home
　943
　cold as - *insensible* 823
charivari *loud* 404
　clatter 407
　discord 414
charlatan
　ignoramus 493
　impostor 548
　mountebank 844
　boaster 884
charlatanism
　ignorance 491
　falsehood 544
　affectation 855
Charles's wain 318
Charley 753
charm *draw* 288
　motive 615
　talisman 747
　please 829
　beauty 845
　love 897
　attraction 928
　conjure 992
　spell 993
　bear a -d life
　safe 664
　prosperous 734
charmer *sorcerer* 994
　voice of the -
　flattery 933

charming *taste* 850
　[*see* charm]
charnel house 363
chart *inform* 527
　represent 554
charter
　commission 755
　permit 760
　compact 769
　security 771
　privilege 924
chartered *legal* 963
　- accountant 811
　- libertine 962
chartulary 86
charwoman
　worker 690
　servant 746
chary *economical* 817
　stingy 819
　cautious 864
Charybdis
　whirlpool 312, 346
　danger 665
chase *emboss* 250
　drive away 289
　killing 361
　forest 367
　pursue 622
　ornament 847
　wild goose - 645
chaser 559
chasm *interval* 198
　opening 260
　gully 350
　abyss 667
　(*discontinuity* 70)
chassepot 727
chasser 297
　- balancer 605
chasseur 726
chassis 272
chaste *shapely* 242
　language 576, 578
　simple 849
　good taste 850
　pure 960
chasten *moderate* 174
　punish 972
chastened
　subdued spirit 826
chasteness [*see* chaste]
chastise *censure* 932
　punish 972
　- with scorpions 739
chastity 960
chasuble 999
chat 588
château 189
châtelaine 847
chatoyant 440
chattels *furniture* 633
　property 780
chatter 412, 584
chatterbox 584
chattering of teeth
　cold 383
chatti 191
chatty *talkative* 584
　sociable 892
chauffeur 268, 271, 694

chauki 752
chaunt [*see* chant]
chaussé 225
Chautauqua 537
chauvinism 884, 885
chauvinist 885
chawbacon 876
cheap *worthless* 643
　low price 815
　hold - 930
cheapen *haggle* 794
　begrudge 819
cheapness **815**
cheat *deceive* 545
　deceiver 548
check *numerical* 85
　cessation 142
　moderate 174
　counteract 179
　slacken 275
　plaid 440
　experiment 463
　measure 466
　evidence 468
　ticket 550
　dissuade 616
　hinder 706
　misfortune 735
　restrain 751
　money order 800
　- in full career 142
　- oneself 829
　- the growth 201
checkered
　diversified 16a
　changeable 149
　variegated 440
checkers 440
　game 840
checkmate
　deadlock 142
　success 731
　failure 732
checkrein 706
checkroll 86
checkstring
　pull the - 142
cheek *side* 236
　- by jowl *with* 88
　near 197
cheeks *dual* 89
cheep 412
cheer *repast* 298
　cry 411
　aid 707
　pleasure 827
　relief 834
　mirth 836
　rejoicing 838
　amusement 840
　courage 861
　exult 884
　sociality 892
　welcome 894
　applaud 931
　(*please* 829)
　good - *hope* 858
　high living 957
cheerful 836
　- giver 816
cheerfulness **836**

cheering 602
cheerless
　unpleasing 830
　dejected 837
cheese 298
cheesecake 298
cheeseparings
　remains 40
　dirt 653
　parsimony 819
cheetah 440
chef de cuisine
　proficient 700
　servant 746
chef-d'œuvre
　masterpiece 648
　master stroke 698
cheiromancy 522
chela 541
chemical 144
chemise 225
chemisette 225
chemistry 144
　organic - 357
cheque 800
chequer 440
　- roll 86
cherish *aid* 707
　love 897
　endearment 902
　- a belief 484
　- an idea &c. 451
　- feelings &c. 821
cheroot 392
cherry 298, 434
　two bites of a -
　overrate 482
　roundabout 629
　clumsy 699
cherry-cheeked 845
cherry-colored 434
chersonese 342
cherub 167,977
Cherubim 977
Cheshire cat 838
chess 840
chessboard 440
chest *box* 191
　money coffer 802
chestnut
　stale joke 105, **532**
　fruit 367
　red 434
chestnut-color 433
cheval-de-bataille
　plea 617
　plan 626
cheval glass 445
chevalier 875
　-d'industrie 792
chevaux de frise
　spikes 253
　defense 717
chevron *obliquity* 217
　rank 550, 747, 877
chevronné 754
chew 298
　tobacco 392
　- the cud 451
chiaroscuro *light* 420
　gray 432

chthonian 991
chubby 192
chuck *throw* 284
  beef 298
  animal cry 412
  - under chin 902
chucker-out 297
chuck farthing 621
chuckle *animal cry* 412
  laugh 838
  exult 884
chucklehead 501
chuddar 225
chuff 876
chum 711, 890
chummery 189
chunk 51
chunky 201
chupatty 298
Church *building* 189
  infallible 474
  orthodox 983a
  Christendom 995
  temple 1000
  - of Christ 983a
  dignitaries of - 996
  go to - 990
  High -, Low -, &c. 984
churchdom **995**
churchman 996
churchwarden 996
churchyard *burial* 363
  church 1000
  - cough 655
churl *boor* 876
churlish *niggard* 819
  rude 895
  sulky 901a
  malevolent 907
churn *agitate* 315
  butter 352
chute 348
chutney 393
chyle 333
chylification 333
chylous 333
cibarious 298
cicada 366
cicatrix 551
cicatrize 660
Cicero 582
cicerone 524, 527
Ciceronian 578, 582
cicisbeo 897
cicuration **370**
cider 298
cienaga 345
cigar 392
cilia *hairs* 205
  rough 256
ciliolum 205
timeter 727
Cimmerian 421
cinch *girth* 45, 370
  facility 705
cinchona 662
cinct 229
cincture 247
cinder *combustion* 384
  dirt 653
  (*remains* 40)

Cinderella *servant* 746
  commonalty 876
cinema 448, 840
cinematograph 448, 559
cinerary 363
cineration 384
cinereous 432
cingle 230
cinnabar 434
cinnamon 393, 433
cinque 98
cinquecento 114, 554
cipher *unsubstantial* 4
  number 84
  compute 85
  zero 101
  concealment 528
  mark 550
  letter 561
  unimportant 643
  writing in - 590
Circe *seductor* 615
  sorcerer 994
Circean 992
  - cup *pleasure* 377
  intemperance 954
circination 312
circle *region* 181
  encompass 227
  form 247
  party 712
  (*assemblage* 72)
  - of acquaintance 892
  - of the sciences 490
  describe a - 311
  great - sailing 628
  in - s 312
circling
  convolution 248
circuit *region* 181
  outline 230
  winding 248
  tour 266
  indirect path 311
  indirect course **629**
circuition **311**
circuitous
  winding 248
  devious 279
  indirect 311
  - method 629
circular *round* 247
  publication 531
  letter 592
  pamphlet 593
  - note 805
  - saw 44
circularity 247
circulate
  circuit 311
  rotate 312
  publish 531
  money 800
circulating medium
  800
circulation
  [*see* circulate]
  - of money 809
  in - *news* 532
circumambience 629
  [*see* circumambient[

circumambient   227,
  229, 311
circumambulate
  travel 266
  go round 311
circumambulation 629
circumbendibus
  winding 248
  indirect method 629
  (*circuition* 311)
circumcinct 229
circumcision 44, 998
circumduction 552
circumference 230
circumferential   227,
  230
circumflex *turn* 311
circumflexion 311
circumfluent
  tie round 227
  move round 311
circumforaneous
  traveling 266
  circuition 311
circumfuse 73, 312
circumgyration 312
circumjacence **227**
circumlocution
  periphrase 573
  (*phrase* 566)
  - court 133
  - office 133
circumlocutory 573
circummigration 311
circumnavigate
  navigation 267
  circuition 311
circumnutation 314
circumrotation 312
circumscribe
  surround 229
  limit 233
  circle 311
  limit 761
circumscription **229**
circumspection
  attention 457
  care 459
  caution 459
circumstance
  phase **8**
  event 151
  blows of - 151
  - of glorious war 722
circumstances
  property 780
  bad - 804
  depend on - 475
  good - 803
  under the - 8
circumstantial 8
  - account 594
  - evidence 467
  probability 472
circumstantiality   457,
  459
circumstantiate 467
circumvallation
  inclosure 229, 232
  defense 717
  line of - 233

circumvent
  environ 227
  move round 311
  cheat 545
  cunning 702
  hinder 706
  checkmate 731
circumvest 225
circumvolant 311
circumvolute 312
circumvolution
  winding 248
  rotation 312
circus *buildings* 189
  drama 599
  arena 728
cirrocumulus 353
cirrose 353
cirrostratus 353
cirrous 353
cirrus 205, 353
Cistercian 996
cistern *receptacle* 191
  store 636
cit 188
citadel *defense* 717
  (*refuge* 666)
citation *summons* 467
  trophy 733
cite *quote as example* 82
  as evidence 467
  summon 741
  accuse 938
  arraign 969
cithern 417
citizen *inhabitant* 188
  freeman 748
  (*man* 373)
  - of the world 910
citreous 436
citrine 435, 436
city 189
  in the - 794
civet 400
civic 372
  - crown 733
civil *warfare* 722
  courteous 894
  laity 997
  - authorities 745
  - crown 733
  - law 963
  - service list 86
  - war 722
civilian *lawyer* 968
  layman 997
civility 894
civilization
  improvement 658
  fashion 852
  courtesy 894
civilize 658
civilized life 852
civism 910
clabber 321
clack *clatter* 407
  animal cry 412
  talkative 584
clad 225
claim *mandate* 630
  demand 741

property 780
right 924
lawsuit 969
- the attention 457
claimant petitioner 767
right 924
clairaudience 450, 992a
clairaudient 450
clair-obscur 420, 421
clairvoyance 450, 992a
clairvoyant 450, 513, 992a
clam 298
clamant 411
clambake 840
clamber 305
clammy 352
clamor cry 411
wail 839
- against 932
- for 765
clamorous
[see clamor]
loud 404
excitable 825
clamp fasten 43
fastening 45
clan race 11
class 75
family 166
party 712
clandestine 528
clang 404
clangor 404, 508
clank 410
clannishness 481
clanship 709
clap shut 261
explosion 406
applaud 931
- on the back 931
- on the shoulder 615
- the hands rejoice 838
- together 43
- up imprison 751
thunder - prodigy 872
clapboard 223, 635
clapperclaw
contention 720
censure 932
claptrap absurdity 497
pretense 546
display 882
claque 72
claquer 935
clarence 272
claret 298
- color 434
clarify 652
clarinet 417
clarion music 417
war 722
clarity clearness 518
elegance 578
clash disagree 24
cross 179
concussion 276
sound 406
oppose 708
discord 713
- of arms 720
492

clashing
contrariety 14
wrangle 24
clasp fasten 43
fastening 45
stick 46
come close 197
belt 230
embrace 902
class arrange 60
category 75
learners 541
school 542
party 712
laity 997
- fellow 890
classfellow 890
classic old 124
symmetry 242
music 415
classical
elegant writing 578
taste 850
- education 537
classicism 578
classicist 578
classics 560
classification 60
classify 60
classis 696
classman 873
associate 890
classmate 492, 541, 890
class room 542
clatter noise 404
rattle 407
claudication
slowness 275
failure 732
clause part 51
passage 593
condition 770
claustral 1000
claustrophobia 860
clavate 250
clavichord 417
clavier 417
claviform 250
clavis opening 260
interpretation 522
claw tenacity 327
hook 781
grasp 789
- back 935
clawhammer coat 225
clay soft 324
earth 342
corpse 362
material 635
clay-cold 383
clayey 324
claymore 727
clean entirely 52
perfect 650
unstained 652
- bill of health 654
- breast
disclose 529
- cut 494
- forgotten 506

- hand
proficient 700
- out empty 297
- sweep
revolution 146
destruction 162
with - hands
honesty 939
innocence 946
cleanly 652
cleanness 652
cleanse 652
cleansing 652
clean-up 35
clear simple 42
leap 309
sound 413
light 420
transparent 425
visible 446
certain 474
intelligible 518
manifest 525
distinct 535
perspicuous 570
easy 705
liberate 750
profit 775
vindicate 937
innocent 946
acquit 970
- articulation 580
- as day 474
- conscience 946
- for action
prepare 673
- grit 604
- of distant 196
- off pay 807
- out empty 297
clean 652
- sky hope 858
- stage
occasion 134
easy 705
right 922
- the course 302
- the ground
facilitate 705
- the skirts of 937
- the throat 297
- up light 420
intelligible 518
interpret 522
coast - 664
get - off 671
keep - of 623
clearance 970
clear-cut true 494
plain 518
clear-eyed 441
clear-headed 498
clear-sighted vision 441
shrewd 498
clearing 181, 184
clearness [see clear]
clear-thinking 498
cleavage cutting 44
structure 329
cleave sunder 44
adhere 46

bisect 91
cleaver 253
cledge 342
clef 413
cleft disjoined 44
bisected 91
chink 198
in a - stick
difficulty 704
clem 956
clement lenient 740
long-suffering 826
compassionate 914
clench compact 769
retain 781
take 789
clepe 564
clepsydra 114
clerestory 191
clergy 996
- list 86
clerical 995, 996
- error 495
- staff 746
clericalism 995
clerk scholar 492
recorder 553
writer 590
helper 711
servant 746
agent 758
clergy 996
articled - 541
- of works 694
clerkship
commission 755
cleromancy 511
clever intelligent 498
skillful 698
witty 842
too - by half 702
clew ball 249
inquiry 461
answer 462
interpretation 522
indication 550
seek a - 461
click 406
client follower 65
dependent 711, 746
customer 795
clientele 795
clientship
subjection 749
cliff height 206
vertical 212
steep 217
climacteric 128
climate region 181
weather 338
fine - 656
climatology 338
climatometer 338
climax supremacy 33
summit 210
turning point 283
climb 305
fain would I - 860
thou -ing sorrow 828
clime 181
clinal 217

clinch *fasten* 43
 close 261
 certify 474
 pun 563
 complete 729
 clutch 781
 snatch 789
 - an argument 479
 - the fist at 909
clincher 479
cling *adhere* 46
 - to *near* 197
 willing 602
 persevere 604a
 habit 613
 observe 772
 desire 865
 love 897
 - to *hope* 858
 - to one another 709
clinic *disease* 655
 remedy 662
clink *resonance* 408
 stridor 410
clinker *brick* 384
 dirt 653
clinometer
 oblique 217
 angle 244
 (*measurement* 466)
clinquant
 ornament 847
 vulgar 851
Clio 594
clip *shorten* 201
 pace 264
 blow 276
 - one's words 583
 - the wings
 powerless 158
 slow 275
 useless 645
 hinder 706
 prohibit 761
 (*prune* 38)
 (*contract* 195)
clipper 273
clipping *small piece* 51
clique *class* 75
 conclave 696
 party 712
 (*sociality* 892)
cliquish 712
clivers 253
cloaca *conduit* 350
 foul 653
Cloacina 653
cloak *dress* 225
 conceal 528
 disguise 530
 (*pretense* 546)
clock 114
clockwise 312
clockwork 633
 by - *uniform* 16
 order 58
 regular 80
clod *lump* 192
 earth 342
 fool 501
 bungler 701

clodhopper 876
clodpated *stupid* 499
clog *shoe* 225
 hinder 706
cloisonné 557, 847
cloister *arcade* 189
 passage 627
 restraint 751
 seclusion 893
 convent 1000
 (*seclusion* 893)
close *similar* 17
 copy 21
 tight 43
 end 67
 field 181
 court 189
 near 197
 narrow 203
 shut 261
 dense 321
 warm 382
 hidden 528
 concise 572
 taciturn 585
 complete 729
 conclude 769
 stingy 819
 - at hand
 to-morrow 121
 imminent 152
 near 197
 - call 671
 - formation 716
 - in upon
 converge 290
 - inquiry 461
 - one's eyes to
 not attend 458
 set at naught 773
 - one's ranks 673
 - prisoner 754
 - quarters 197
 approach 286
 attack 716
 battle 722
 - study *thought* 451
 attention 457
 - the door upon
 restrain 751
 - the ears 419
 - the eyes *die* 360
 not see 442
 - the hand *refuse* 764
 - with *cohere* 46
 assent 488
 attack 716
 contend 720
 consent 762
 compact 769
 keep - *hide* 528
 retain 781
closely [see close]
 - packed 72
closet *receptacle* 191
 ambush 530
closeted with
 conference 588
 advice 695
closure 261
 stopping 142

clot *solidify* 321
 earth 342
 hindrance 706
 (*cohere* 46)
cloth *vocation* 625
 napkin 652
 clergy 996
clothe 225
clothes 225
 - basket 191
 - horse 215
 - press 191
 grave - 363
clothier 225
clothing 225
clotpoll 501
clotted 352
 - cream 321, 354
cloture 142
cloud *assemblage* 72
 multitude 102
 wind 349
 mist 353
 darken 421
 dim 422
 shade 424
 semitransparency 427
 screen 520
 break through the -s
  446
 - capt 206
 - of dust 330
 - of skirmishers 726
 - of smoke 333
 - of words 573
 - over 421, 422
 -s gathering *dark* 421
 danger 665
 warning 668
 - topped 206
 drop from the -s 508
 in a - *uncertain* 475
 hidden 528
 in the -s *lofty* 206
 inattentive 458
 dreaming 515
 under a -
 insane 503
 adversity 735
 disrepute 874
 secluded 893
 censured 932
 accused 938
cloud-built 4
cloudburst 348
clouded *variegated* 440
 dejected 837
 hopeless 859
 - perception 499
cloudland 515
cloudless *light* 420
 happy 827
cloudy *dim* 422
 opaque 426
clough 206
clove 198
cloven 91
cloven foot *mark* 550
 malevolence 907
 vice 945
 Satan 978

 see the - 480a
 show the - 907
clover *grass* 367
 luxury 377
 prosperity 734
 comfort 827
 in - 377, 827
clown *pantomime* 599
 buffoon 844
 vulgar 851
 rustic 876
cloy *pall* 376
 redundance 641
 satiety 869
cloying 396
cloyment 869
club *combine* 48
 place of meeting 74
 house 189
 association 712
 weapon 727
 sociality 892
 - law
 compulsion 744
 lawless 964
 - together
 coöperate 709
clubbability 892
clubbable 712
club-footed 243
clubman 852
club-shaped 250
clubwoman 852
cluck 412
clue [see clew]
clump *assemblage* 72
 projecting mass 250
 - of trees 367
clumsiness
 [see clumsy]
clumsy *unfit* 647
 awkward 699
 ugly 846
Cluniac 996
cluricaune 980
cluster 72
clutch *automobile* 272
 retain 781
 seize 789
clutches 737
 in the - of 749
clutter *be loud* 404
 roll 407
clypeate 245
clypeiform 245
clyster 300
coacervation 72
coach *carriage* 272
 teach 537
 tutor 540, 673
 - road 627
 - up 539
 drive a - and six
  through 964
coach house 191
coachman *travel* 268
 pilot 694
coaction
 concurrence 178
 coöperation 709
 compulsion 744

coactive 709
coadjutant 709, 711
coadjutive 709
coadjutor 711
coadjuvancy 709
coadjuvant 711
coadjuvate 709
coadministration 709
coadunate 178
coagency *concur* 178
  coöperate 709
coagmentation 72
coagulate *cohere* 46
  densify 321
  thicken 352
  pulpy 354
coagulum 321, 352
co-aid 711
coal 388
  carry -s 879
  carry -s to Newcastle
    641
  haul over the -s 932
coal - black 431
coalesce *identity* 13
  combine 48
coalheaver
  work like a - 686
coalition *coöperate* 709
  party 712
coaptation 23
coarctate 195, 203
coarctation
  decrease 36
  contraction 195
  narrow 203
  impede 706
  restraint 751
  (*compulsion* 744)
coarse *harsh* 410
  dirty 653
  unpolished 674
  vulgar 851
  impure 961
  - grain 329
coast *border* 231
  glide 266
  navigate 267
  land 342
  - line 230
coaster 273
coastguard 753
coat *layer* 204
  paint 223
  habit 225
  (*surface* 220)
  - of arms 550
  - of mail 717
  cut - according to
    cloth 698
coatee 225
coating, inner - 224
coax *persuade* 615
  endearment 902
  flatter 933
coaxer 615
cob *horse* 271
  punish 972
cobalt 438
cobble *mend* 660
cobbler *shoemaker* 225
494

coble 273
cobra 366, 913
cobweb *filament* 205
  light 320
  fiction 545
  flimsy 643
  dirt 653
  -s of antiquity 124
  -s of sophistry 477
cocaine 376, 662, 954
cochineal 434
cochlea 418
cochleate 248
cock *vane* 338
  bird 366
  male 373
  - and - bull story 546
  - of the roost
  best 648
  master 745
  - the eye 441
  - up *vertical* 212
  convex 250
  game - 861
cockade *badge* 550
  title 877
cock-a-hoop *gay* 836
  exulting 884
cockarouse 745
cockatrice *monster* 83
  serpent 366
  piercing eye 548
  evildoer 913
  miscreant 949
cockboat 273
cockcrow 125
Cocker *school book* 542
  according to - 82
cocker *fold* 258
  dog 366
  caress 902
cock-eyed 443
cockle *pucker* 195
  fold 258
  -s of one's heart 820
cockleshell 273
cockloft 191
cockney *Londoner* 188
  plebeian 876
cockpit *hold* 191
  arena 728
cockroach 366
cockshut *evening* 126
  dusk 422
cocksure 484
cockswain 269
cocktail 959
cocoa 298
co-conscious 992*a*
coconut - butter
  - oil 356
cocoon 129
cocotte 962
coction 384
Cocytus 982
C. O. D. *receipt* 810
cod *fish* 298
  shell 223
coddle 902
  - oneself 943
code *concealment* 528

cipher 561
  precept 697
  law 963
  (*compendium* 596)
codex 593
codger 819
codicil *addition* 37
  sequel 65
  testament 771
  (*adjunct* 39)
codification 60
codify *arrange* 60
  conceal 528
  legalize 963
codlin 129
cœcum 261
coeducational 537
coefficacy 709
coefficient *factor* 84
  accompany 88
  coöperate 709
Cœlebs 904
Cœlentera 368
cœliac 221
  - flux 299
coemption 795
coequal 27
coequality 27
coerce *compel* 744
  restrain 751
coetaneous 120
coeternal *perpetual* 112
  synchronous 120
coeternity 110, 112
coeval 120
  - with birth 5
coevality 27
coexist *exist* 1
  accompany 88
  synchronism 120
  contiguity 199
coexistence
  [*see* coexist]
coextension *equality* 27
  parallelism 216
  symmetry 242
coextensive 216, 242
coffee 298
coffeepot 191
coffeehouse 189
coffer *chest* 191
  store 636
  money chest 802
cofferdam 55 ⸜
coffin 363
  add a nail to one's -
    830
cog *tooth* 253
  boat 273
  deceive 545
  flatter 933
cogency 157
cogent *powerful* 157
  - reasoning 476
coggery 545
cogitate 450, 451
cogitative 451
  - faculties 450
cognate *related* 9
  consanguineous 11
  similar 17

cognation 11
cognition 490
cognitive
  - faculties 450
cognizance 490
  take - of
  intellect 490
  attention 457
cognomen 564
cognoscence 490
cogwheel 312
cohabitation
  location 184
  marriage 903
coheir 778
cohere 46
coherence *unite* 46
  stability 150
  dense 321
coherent 23
cohesion 46
cohesive 46, 327
cohibit *restrain* 751
  prohibit 761
  (*counteract* 179)
cohobation 336
cohort 726
cohue 72
coif 225, 370
coiffure 225
coign 244
coil *disorder* 59
  convolution 248
  circuition 311
  radiator 386
  shuffle off this mortal
    - 360
coin *fabricate* 161
  imagine 515
  money 800
  - money 775
  - words 563
coincide
  [*see* coincidence]
coincidence
  identity 13
  in time 120
  in place 199
  in opinion 488
coincident 13, 178
coiner *thief* 792
  counterfeiter 800
coinstantaneous 120
coistril 862
coition 43
cojuror 467
coke 388
colander 60, 260
colature 652
cold *frigid* 383
  color 429, 438
  style 575
  insensible 823
  indifferent 866
  - comfort 832
  - feet *cowardice* 862
  - shoulder
  discourtesy 895
  contempt 930
  - steel 727
  - storage 387

- sweat *fear* 860
  dislike 867
- water cure 662
in - blood
  premediated 611
  purposely 620
  unfeeling 823
  dispassionate 826
throw - water on
  dissuade 616
  hinder 706
  dull 843
coldbloodedness 871
cold-frame 371
cold-hearted
  unfeeling 823
  hostile 889
  malevolent 907
cold-short 328
coleslaw 298
colic 378
Coliseum 728
collaboration 178
collaborator 711
collapse
  prostration 158
  contract 195
  shortcoming 304
  disease 655
  deteriorate 659
  fatigue 688
  failure 732
collar *dress* 225
  circlet 247
  shackle 752
  seize 789
  slip the - 750
collate 54, 464
collateral *relative* 9
  relation 11
  synchronous 120
  parallel 216
  lateral 236
- evidence 467
collation *repast* 298
  comparison 464
colleague
  accompany 88
  associate 690
  coöperation 709
  auxiliary 711
  friend 890
collect *assemble* 72
  opine 480
  understand 518
  compile 596
  acquire 775
  prayer 990
  (*take* 789)
- evidence 467
- knowledge 539
- one's thoughts 451
collectanea
  assemblage 72
  compendium 596
collected *calm* 826
collection
  assemblage 72
  store 636
  offertory 990
collective 78

collectively *whole* 50
  generality 78
  together 88
collectivism 737, 778
collectivist 778
collector
  director 694, 745
colleen 129
college 542
- board 542
- education 537
- yell 838
go to - 539
collide 276
collie 366
collier 273
colliery 252
colligate 72
collimate 216
collimation 216, 278
colliquation 335
collision *clash* 179
  percussion 276
  opposition 708
  encounter 720
collocate *arrange* 60
  assemble 72
  place 184
collocution 588
collogue
  wheedle 933
collop 51
colloquial
  figure of speech 521
  language 560
  neology 563
  conversation 588
- meaning 516
colluctation 720
collusion *deceit* 545
  conspiring 709
collusive 544
colluvies 653
collyrium 662
cologne 400
colon *punctuation* 142
  intestine 350
colonel 745
colonial 188
colonist 188, 294, 295
colonization 184
colonize 184
colonnade *series* 69
  houses 189
colony *region* 181, 184
  settlement 188
colophon 65
colophony 356a
color *hue* 428
  tone 431
  redden 434
  appearance 448
  probability 472
  disguise 544
  paint 556
  plead 615
  plea 617
  be angry 900
all -s 440
change -
  shame 879

- too highly 549
- up *redden* 434
  blush 879
give a - to
  change 140
  qualify 469
  probable 472
  falsehood 544
lend a - to
  plea 617
  vindicate 937
man of - 431
show in true -s 543
colorable
  ostensible 472
  deceptive 545
Colorado beetle 913
coloration 428
coloratura 415, 416
color-blindness 443
colored [see color]
- man 431
- spectacles 424
colorimeter 428
coloring [see color]
  meaning 516
- matter 428
false - 523
colorless
  weak 160
  pale 429
  feeble 575
color-printing 558
colors *ensign* 550
  decoration 877
false - 544, 545
flying - *display* 882
  celebration 883
lower one's - 735
nail one's - to the
  mast 604
show one's -
  manifest 525
  disclose 529
true to one's - 939
color-sergeant 745
colossal 192
Colosseum 728
colossus *strength* 159
  size 192
  height 206
colporteur 797, 996
colt *young* 129
  horse 271
  fool 501
colter 253
colubrine 366
columbarium 189
columbine 599
columella 215
columelliform 215
column *series* 69
  height 206
  support 215
  cylinder 249
  caravan 266
  monument 551
  printing 591
  troop 726
colures 318
coma *inactive* 683

insensible 376, **823**
comate 711, 890
comb *teeth* 253
  clean 652
  punish 972
combat 720, 722
- plane 273
combatant **726**
combative 720, 722
combe 252
comber *wave* 348
combination **48**
  arithmetical 84
  party 712
- of fortuitous cir-
  cumstances 621
combine *unite* 48
  component 56
  concur 178
  partnership 712
  coöperate 709
combustible 388
combustion 384
come *happen* 151
  approach 286
  arrive 292
  cheer up! 836
  out upon! 932
- about 658
- across *discover* 480a
- after *sequence* 63
  posterior 117
- amiss
  disagreeable 24
  ill-timed 135
- and go 314
- at one's call 743
- back 283
- before 116
- by 775
- down with 807
- first *superior* 33
  precede 62
- forth *egress* 295
  appear 446
- forward 763
- from *follow* 154
  hail from 292
- in *ingress* 294
  receipt 785
- in for
  property 778, 780
- into existence *be* 1
  begin 66
- into operation 170
- into the views of
  coöperate 709
- into the world 359
- into use 613
- into view 446
- near 286
- of 154
- of age 131
- off *loose* 44
  event 151
  escape 671
- off well 731
- on *future* 121
  destiny 152
  I defy you 715
  attack 716

495

- singing 415
commutation
  difference 15
  compensation 30
  substitution 147
  interchange 148
  compromise 774
  barter 794
commuter 268
commutual 12
compact *joined* 43
  united 87
  compressed 195
  compendious 201
  dense 321
  bargain **769**
compactness [*see* com-
  pact]
compages *whole* 50
  structure 329
compagination 43
companion *match* 17
  accompaniment 88
  stairway 305
  friend 890
companionable 892
companionless 87
companionship 892
companionway 305
company *assembly* 72
  actors 599
  party,partnership 712
troop 726
  sociality 892
  (*merchants* 791)
  bear - 88
  in - with 88
comparable 9
comparative *degree* 26
  compare 464
  - anatomy 368
  - estimate 464
comparatively 32
compare 464
  - notes 695
comparison **464**
compartition 44
compartment *part* 51
  region 181
  place 182
  cell 191
  carriage 272
compass *degree* 26
  space 180
  surround 227
  circumscribe 233
  circuition 311
  measure 466
  intent 620
  guidance 693
  achieve 729
  box the - *azimuth* 278
  rotation 312
  - about 229
  - of thought 498
  in a small - 193
  keep within -
  moderation 174
  fall short 304
  economy 817
  points of the - 236

compassion 914
  object of - 828
compassionate 914
compatible
  consentaneous 23
  possible 470
compatriot
  inhabitant 188
  friend 890
compeer *equal* 27
  friend 890
compel 744
compellation 564
compelled 744
compendious
  inclusive 56
  short 201
compendium **596**
compensate
  make up for 30
  restore 790
  requite 973
compensation **30**
compensatory 30, 790
compete 708, 720
competence
  power 157
  sufficiency 639
  skill 698
  wealth 803
competition
  opposition 708
  contention 720
competitor
  opponent 710
  combatant 726
  candidate 767
compilation
  composition 54
  collect 72
  writing 590
  book 593
  compendium 596
compile 54, 72
complacent
  pleased 827
  content 831
  courteous 894
  kind 906
complain 839
  - without cause 839
complainant 938
complainer 832
complaint
  illness 655
  murmur 839
  lodge a - 938
complaisant
  lenient 740
  courteous 894
  kind 906
complanate 251
complement
  counterpart 14
  adjunct 39
  remainder 40
  part 52
  arithmetic 84
complemental 12
complementary color
  428

complete
  entire 52
  accomplish 729
  conclude 769
  - answer 479
  - circle 311
  in a - degree 31
completeness **52**
  unity 87
completion **729**
complex 59
complexion *state* 7
  color 428
  appearance 448
complexity 59
complexus 50, 59
compliance
  conformity 82
  submission 725
  obedience 743
  consent 762
  observance 772
  courtesy 894
compliant [*see* compli-
  ance]
complicate *derange* 61
complicated *disorder*
  59
  convolution 248
  mechanical 633
complice 711
complicity 709
compliment
  courtesy 894
  congratulate 896
  praise 931
  -s of season 896
  poor - 932
complimentary 815
complot 626
comply [*see* compli-
  ance]
compo *coating* 223
  material 635
component **56**
comport
  - oneself 692
  - with 23
compos 502
compose
  make up 54, 56
  arrange 60
  produce 161
  moderate 174
  music 416
  write 590
  printing 591
  pacify 723
  assuage 826
composed
  self-possessed 826
composer *music* 413
composing
  - frame 591
  - room 591
  - rule 591
composite 41
composition **54**
  [*see* compose]
  combination 48
  piece of music 415

  picture 556
  style 569
  writing 590
  building material **635**
  compromise 774
  barter 794
  atonement 952
compositor 591
compost 653
composure 826
compotation 298, 959
compote 298
compound *mix* 41
  combination 48
  yard 232
  compromise 774
  - arithmetic 466
  - for *substitute* 147
  barter 794
  (*stipulate* 769)
comprador 637
comprehend
  compose 54
  include 76
  know 490
  understand 518
comprehensibility **518**
comprehension
  [*see* comprehend]
  intelligence 498
comprehensive
  wholesale 50
  inclusive 56, 76
  general 78
  wide 192
  - argument 476
compress
  contract 195
  curtail 201
  condense 321
  remedy 662
compressed 572
compressible 322
comprise 76
comprised
  be - in 1
comprobation
  evidence 467
  demonstration **478**
compromise
  dally with 605
  mid-course 628
  danger 665
  pacify 723
  compact 769
  compound **774**
  atone 952
compromised
  promised 768
compter 799
compte rendu
  record 551
  accounts 811
  (*abstract* 596)
comptroller
  director 694
  (*master* 745)
compulsion **744**
  forced labor 603
compulsory 601, **744**
compunction 950

confessional
 disclosure 529
 rite 998
 temple 1000
confessions
 biography 594
confessor 996
confidant
 auxiliary 711
 maid 746
 friend 890
confidante
 servant 746
 friend 890
confidence *trust* 484
 expectation 507
 deception 545
 hope 858
 courage 861
 - *man* 548
 - *trick* 545
 in - 528
confident [*see* confi-
 dence]
 affirm 535
confidential 528
confiding 703
configuration 240
confine *place* 182
 circumscribe 229
 border 231
 limit 233
 imprison 751
confined
 narrow judgment 481
 ill 655
confinement
 childbed 161
confines of
 on the - 197
confirm
 corroborate 467
 assent 488
 consent 762
 compact 769
 rite 998
confirmation 535
confirmatory 480
confirmed 150
 - *habit* 613
confirmist 488
confiscate *take* 789
 condemn 971
 penalty 974
confiture 298, 396
conflagration 384
conflation 54
conflexure 245
conflict
 disagreement 24
 opposition 708
 discord 713
 contention 720
 warfare 722
conflicting
 contrary 14
 counteracting 179
 - *evidence* 468
confluence
 junction 43
 convergence 290

 river 348
confluent 290
conflux
 assemblage 72
 convergence 290
conform *assent* 488
conformable
 agreeing 23
 concurrent 178
conformation 240
conformity 82
 concurrence 178
 - *to rule* 494
confound *disorder* 61
 destroy 162
 not discriminate 465a
 perplex 475
 confute 479
 defeat 731
 astonish 870
 curse 908
confounded *great* 31
 bad 649
confraternity *party* 712
 friendship 888
confrère *colleague* 711
 friend 890
confrication 331
confront *face* 234
 compare 464
 oppose 708
 resist 719
 - *danger* 861
 - *witnesses* 467
Confucius 986
confuse *derange* 61
 perplex 458
 obscure 519
 not discriminate 465a
 abash 879
confused *disorder* 59
 invisible 447
 uncertain 475
 perplexed 523
 style 571
 harmoniously - 81
confusion [*see* confuse]
 obscurity 571
 - *of tongues* 560, 563
 - *of vision* 443
 - *seize* 908
 - *worse confounded*
  59
 in - *excited* 825
confutation 479
confute 479
congé *departure* 293
 abrogation 756
 - *d'elire* 995
congeal *dense* 321
 cold 385
congener *similar* 17
 included 76
congeneric *similar* 17
congenerous 9, 17
congenial *agreeing* 23
 concord 714
 love 897
 (*expedient* 646)
congenital 5
 inborn 820

congenite 5
Congeries 72
congestion 641
conglaciation 385
conglobation 72
conglomerate *cohere* 46
 assemblage 72
 dense 321
conglutinate 46
congratulate 896
 - *oneself* 838
congratulation 896
congregation
 assemblage 72
 worshipers 990
 laity 997
congregational 995
Congregationalist 984
congress *assembly* 72
 convergence 290
 conference 588
 council 696
congressional 696
 - *medal* 551
congressman 696
congreve *fuel* 388
 - *rocket* 727
congruence 23
congruous
 agreeing 23
 (*expedient* 646)
conical *round* 249
 pointed 25
conifer 369
conjectural 514
conjecture 514
conjoin 43
conjoint 48
conjointly 37
conjugal 903
conjugate *combined* 48
 words 562
 grammar 567
 - *in all its tenses &c.*
  104
conjugation
 junction 43
 pair 89
 phase 144
 contiguity 199
 grammar 567
conjunction
 junction 43
 contiguity 199
 in - *with* 37
conjunctive 48
conjuncture
 contingency 8
 occasion 134
conjure *deceive* 545
 entreat 765
 sorcery 992
 - *up* 506
 - *up a vision* 515
 name to - *with* 873
conjuror *deceiver* 548
 sorcerer 994
connate *intrinsic* 5
 related 9
 kindred 11
 cause 153

connation 11
connatural *related* **9**
 uniform 16
 similar 17
connaturality 13
connature 13, 16
connect *relate* 9
 link 43
connection *kin* 11
 coherence 46
connective 45
conned, well - 490
connivance 760
connive *overlook* 460
 coöperate 709
 allow 760
connivent 286
connoisseur *critic* 480
 scholar 492
 taste 850
connoisseurship 850
connotate 550
connotation 516
connote *mean* 516
 indicate 550
connubial 903
conoscente 850
conquer 731
conquered (*failure* 732)
conqueror 731
conquest 749
consanguinity 11
conscience
 knowledge 490
 moral sense 926
 awakened - 950
 clear - 946
 in all - *great* 31
 affirmation 535
 qualms of - 603
 stricken - 950
 tender - 926
 honor 939
conscientious 926
 faithful 21
 scrupulous 939
 (*veracious* 543)
 (*virtuous* 944)
conscious
 intuitive 450
 knowledge 490
 - *of disgrace* 874
 - *of glory* 873
consciousness 450
 subliminal - 992a
conscript 726
conscription 744
consecrate *use* 677
 dedicate 873
 sanctify 987
 holy orders 995
consecration *rite* 998
consectary 478
 - *reasoning* 476
consecution 63
consecutive
 following 63
 continuous 69
 posterior 117
 - *fifths* 414
consecutively

contend *reason* 476
  assert 535
  fight 720
  - for *vindicate* 937
  - with difficulties 704
content *assenting* 488
  willing 602
  calm 826
  satisfied **831**
  to one's heart's -
  sufficient 639
  success 731
contention **720**
contentious 901
contents
  ingredients 56
  list 86
  components **190**
  book 593
  synopsis 596
conterminate *end* 67
  limit 233
conterminous 199
contesseration 72
contest 708, 720
contestant 710
context 591
contexture 329
  (*state* 7)
contiguity **199**
contiguous 197
continence 960
continent 342
continental *trifle* 643
continentals 225
contingency
  junction 43
  event 151
  uncertainty 475
  expectation 507
contingent
  extrinsic 6
  conditional 8
  casual 156
  liable 177
  possible 470
  uncertain 475
  supply 635
  aid 707
  allotted 786
  donation 809
  - duration **108a**
  - interest 780
continual
  perpetual 112
  frequent 136
continuance 117, **143**
continuation
  affix 37
  adjunct 39
  sequence 63
  sequel 65
  - school 542
continuations
  trousers 225
continue *exist* 1
  endure 106, 110
  persist 143
continued 69
  - existence 112
  - success 731

continuing 143
continuity 16, **69**
continuous 69
contortion
  distortion 243
  convolution 248
  (*ugliness* 846)
contortionist 599
contortuosity 243
contour *outline* 230
  appearance 448
  - line 550
contra 14
  per - 708
contraband
  deceitful 545
  prohibited 761
  illicit 964
contrabandist 792
contrabasso 417
contraclockwise 283
contract *shrink* 195
  narrow 203
  promise 768
  bargain 769
  (*decrease* 36)
  (*curtail* 201)
  - a debt 806
  - a habit 613
  - an obligation 768
contractible 195
contractility 195
  (*elasticity* 325)
contraction **195**
  shorthand 590
  compendium 596
contractive 36, 464
contractor 690
contractual 769
contradict
  contrary 14
  dissent 489
  deny 536
  oppose 708
contradiction
  difference 15
  answer 462
contradictoriness 15
contradictory
  evidence 468
  discordant 713
contradistinction 15
contrafagotto 417
contraindicant 616
contraindicate
  dissuade 616
  warning 668
contralto 408
contraposition
  inversion 218
  reversion **237**
contrapuntal 415
contrapuntist 413
contrariety **14**, 15, 708
contrariness 708
contrariwise 148, 708
contrary *opposite* 14
  antagonistic 179
  captious 608
  opposing 708
  - to expectation

  improbable 473
  unexpected 508
  - to reason 471
  quite the - 536
contrast
  contrariety 14
  difference 15
  comparison 464
contrastive 15
contrate wheel 247
contravallation 717
contravene
  contrary 14
  counteract 179
  counterevidence 468
  deny 536
  hinder 706
  oppose 708
contre-coup 277
contrectation 379
contretemps
  ill timed 135
  hindrance 706
  misfortune 735
contribute *cause* 153
  tend 176
  concur 178
  aid 707
  give 784
contribution 784
  lay under -
  take 789
  due 924
contributor
  correspondent 592
  giver 784
contributory *extra* 37
contrition *abrasion* 331
  penitence 950
contrivance 626
contrive *produce* 161
  plan 626
  - to succeed in 731
contriving
  cunning 702
control *power* 157
  influence 175
  aviation 273
  regulate 693
  authority 737
  restrain 751
  board of - 696
  get - of 175
  under -
  obedience 743
  subjection 749
controller 694
controversial
  discussion 476
  discordant 713
controversialist 476,
  726
controversy
  discussion 476
  interlocution 588
  contention 720
controvert *deny* 536
controvertible
  uncertain 475
  debatable 476
  untrue 495

contumacy
  obstinacy 606
  disobedience **742**
contumely
  arrogance 885
  rudeness 895
  disrespect 929
  scorn 930
  reproach 932
contund 330
contuse 330
conundrum *pun* 520
  riddle 533
  wit 842
  (*problem* 461)
convalesce 654
convalescence 654, 660
convection 270
convene 72
convenience 685
conveniences 632
convenient 646
convent 1000
  - school 542
conventicle
  assembly 72
  council 696
  chapel 1000
convention
  assembly 72
  canon 80
  council 696
  law 697
  treaty of peace **723**
  compact 769
  - of society 852
conventional
  customary 613
conventionalism 613
conventionalist 82
conventionality 613
conventionalize 82
conventual *monk* 996
  convent 1000
converge 290
convergence **290**
convergent 286, 290
conversable *talk* 588
  sociable 892
conversant
  know 490
  skillful 698
conversation 588
conversational 588
  sociable 892
conversationist 588
conversazione
  interlocution 588
  social gathering 892
converse
  reverse 14, 237
  talk 588
  hold high - 539
conversely 148, 168
conversible 144
conversion **144**
  trover and - 964
convert *change* 140
  change to 144
  opinion 484
  tergiversation 607

penitent 950
religion 987
- to use 677
convertible
identical 13
equal 27
- terms 522
convex 250
- lens 445
- mirror 555
convexity 250
convey *transfer* 270
mean 516
assign 783
- away 791
- the knowledge of
527
conveyable 270
conveyance [*see* con-
vey]
vehicle 272
conveyancer 968
conveyancing 783
convict *convince* 484
prisoner 754
condemned 949
condemn 971
conviction
confutation 479
belief 484
prove guilty 971
convince *confute* 479
belief 484
teach 537
easily - d 486
convincing
conclusive 478
convivial 892
convocate 72
convocation
assemblage 72
council 696
church 995
convoke 72
convolution
coil 248
rotation 312
convoy *transfer* 270
accompany 88
guard 664
escort 753
convulse
derange 61
violent 173
agitate 315
bodily pain 378
mental pain 830
convulsed with
- laughter 838
- rage 900
convulsion [*see* con-
vulse]
disorder 59
revolution 146
in -s 315
coo 412
cook *heat* 384
falsify 544
improve 658
prepare 673
servant 746
502

- accounts 811
too many - s 699
cooker *range* 386
cookery 673
cook house 191
cookie 298
cookshop 189
cookstove 386
cool *moderate* 174
cold 383
refrigerate 385
gray 432
dissuade 616
inexcitable 826
cautious 864
indifferent 866
imperturbable 871
unfriendly 889
discourteous 895
- down *become sane*
502
be composed 826
- one's heels
kept waiting 133
inaction 681
look - upon
unsocial 893
take -ly 826
cooler 387
cool-headed
judicious 498
unexcitable 826
coolie *bearer* 271
cooling 385
coolness [*see* cool]
insensibility 823
estrangement 898
coomb 252
coon 431
coon's age 110
coop *abode* 189
restrain 751
prison 752
coöperate 709
coöperation
physical 178
voluntary **709**
participation 778
coöperative
concurring 178
coöperating 709
helpful 746
coöperator 690, 711
coöptative 609
coöptation 609
coordinate *equal* 27
arrange 60
measure 466
cop 664
copal 356*a*
coparcener 778
copartner
accompanying 88
participator 778
associate 890
copartnership
coöperation 709
party 712
participation 778
cope *equal* 27
oppose 708

contend 720
canonicals 999
copemate *enemy* 891
coping 204, 210
- stone *top* 210
completion 729
copious *productive* 168
diffuse style 573
abundant 639
coportion 778
copper *money* 800
copper-colored 433
copperhead 366
copperish 433
copperplate
engraving 558
coppery 433
coppice 367
coprolite 653
copse 367
copula 45
copulation 43
copy *imitate* 19
facsimile 21
prototype 22
duplicate 90
record 561
represent 554
write 590
for the press 591
plan 626
copyhold 780
copyholder 591
copyist *imitator* 19
artist 559
writer 590
copyright 780
coquelicot 434
coquet *lie* 544
change the mind 607
affected 855
love 897
endearment 902
flattery 938
- with *irresolute* 605
coquette
affected 854, 855
flirt 897, 902
coquillage 847
coracle 273
coral *animal* 368
red 434
ornament 847
- reef 667
coralline 434
cor Anglais 417
corbeille 191
corbel 215
cord *tie* 45
size 192
filament 205
cordage 45, 192
cordate 245
cordial
pleasure 377
dram 392
willing 602
remedy 662
feeling 821
grateful 829
friendly 888

courteous 894
benevolent 906
cordiality *goodwill* 602
fervor 821
friendship 888
cordiform 245
cordite 727
cordon *inclosure* 232
circularity 247
decoration 877
- bleu 746
- sanitaire *safety* 664
preservation 670
corduroy 259
- road 259
cordwain 223
cordwainer
shoemaker 225
artificer 690
core *center* 222
gist 5, 642
true to the - 939
corespondent 938
coriaceous 327
Corinthian 850
corium 223
corival [*see* corrival]
cork *plug* 263
lightness 320
- jacket 666
- up *close* 261
restrain 751
corking pin 45
corkscrew *spiral* 248
perforator 262
circuition 311
corky *shriveled* 195
dry 340
cormorant *desire* 865
gluttony 957
corn *projection* 250
food 298
- fed 192
- husk 223
- husking 892
- shuck 223
Cornaro 953
corncake 298
corndabs 298
corndodgers 298
cornea 441
corned 959
corneous 323
corner *plight* 7
place 182
receptacle 191
angle 244
discommode 706
monopoly 777
creep into a - 893
drive into a - 706
in a dark - 528
push into a - 874
rub off - s 82
turn a - 311
turn the - 658
cornerstone *support* 215
importance 642
cornet *music* 417
officer 745
cornetist 416

cornice 210
corniculate 253
cornification 323
Cornish hug 545
corno 417
cornopean 417
cornstarch 298
cornucopia 639
cornute
   projecting 250
   sharp 253
cornwallis 840
corollary
   adjunct 39
   deduction 480
corona *summit* 210
   circularity 247
coronach 415, 550, 839
coronation
   enthronement 755
   celebration 883
coroner 965
coronet *hoop* 247
   insignia 747
   jewel 847
   title 877
corporal
   corporeal 316
   officer 745
corporate *joined* 43
   combine 48
   party 712
   - *body* 712
corporation *bulk* 192
   convex 250
   association 712
   merchants 797
   jurisdiction 965
corporeal 3, 316
   - *hereditaments* 780
   - *nature* 364
corporeity 3, 316
corposant 423
corps *assemblage* 72
   troops 726
   - *de reserve* 636
corpse 362
   - *candle* 423
corpulence 192
corpulent 192, 194
corpus 316
   - *delicti*
      guilt 947
      lawsuit 969
   - *juris*
      precept 697
      law 963
corpuscle *small* 32
   little 193
corradiation
   focus 74
   convergence 290
corral
   circumscribe 229
   inclosure 232
   round up 370
correct *orderly* 58
   true 494
   inform 527
   disclose 529

   improve 658
   repair 660
   due 924
   censure 932
   honorable 939
   virtuous 944
   punish 972
   - *ear* 416, 418
   - *memory* 505
   - *reasoning* 476
   - *style*
      grammatical 567
      elegant 578
correction [*see* correct]
   house of - 752
   under - 879
corrective 662
correctness [*see* correct]
   elegance 578
corregidor 745
correlation
   relation 9
   reciprocity **12**
correlative 9, 17
correspond *agree* 23
   write 592
correspondence
   correlation 12
   similarity 17
   agreement 23
   writing **592**
   concord 714
correspondent
   reciprocal 12
   messenger 534
   letter writer 592
   journalist 593
   consignee 758
corresponsive 178
corridor *place* 191
   passage 627
   - *s of time* 109
   - *train* 272
corrigendum 495
corrigible 658
corrival 726
corrivalry 720
corrivation 348
corroborant 662
corroboration
   evidence 467
   assent 488
corrode *burn* 384
   erode 659
   afflict 830
corrosion [*see* corrode]
corrosive [*see* corrode]
   acrid 171
   destructive 649
   - *sublimate* 663
corrugate
   derange 61
   constrict 195
   roughen 256
   rumple 258
   furrow 259
corrupt
   [*see* corruption]
corrupting
   noxious 649

corruption
   decomposition 49
   neology 563
   foulness 653
   disease 655
   deterioration 659
   improbity 940
   vice 945
   guilt 947
corsage 225
corsair *boat* 273
   pirate 792
corse 362
corselet 225
corset 225
corso 728
cortège *adjunct* 39
   continuity 69
   accompaniment 88
   journey 266
   suite 646
cortes 696
cortex *cortical* 223
coruscate 420, 498
corvet *ship* 273
   man-of-war 726
corvette [*see* corvet]
Corybantic 503, 954
coryphée 599
Corypheus *teacher* 540
   director 694
coscinomancy 511
cosey 892
cosine 217
cos lettuce 298
cosmetic *remedy* 662
   ornament 847
cosmical 318
cosmogony 318
cosmography 318
cosmology 318
cosmoplast 976
cosmopolitan
   abode 189
   mankind 372
   sociality 892
   philanthropic 910
cosmorama 448
cosmos 60, 318
Cossack 726
cosset *darling* 899
   caress 902
cost 812
   - *price* 815
   - *what it may* 604
   pay -s 807
   to one's - *evil* 619
      badness 649
costate 259
costermonger 797
costive *compact* 321
   taciturn 855
costless 815
costly 809, 814
costume 225
   theatrical - 599
costumé 225
   bal - 840
costumer 225, 599
costumier 225
   theatrical 599

cosy *snug* 377
   sociable 892
cot *abode* 189
   bed 215
   - *betty* 374
cotangent 217
cote 189
cotenancy 778
coterie *class* 75
   junto 712
   society 892
coterminous 120
cothurnus 599
cotidal 341
cotillon 840
cotquean 374, 501
cottage 189
cottager 188
cotter 188
cotton 205, 635
cottonseed oil 356
cotyledon 367
couch *lie* 213
   bed 215
   stoop 308
   lurk 528
   - *in terms* 566
   - *one's lance* 720
   lone - *of everlasting sleep* 360, 363
couchant 213
couci-couci 651
cougar 913
cough 349
   churchyard - 655
coulee 211, 350
couleur de rose
   good 648
   prosperity 734
   view en - 836
coulisse 599
council *senate* **696**
   church 995
   cease thy - 695
   - fire 696
   - of education 542
   hold a - 695
councilor 696
counsel *advice* 695
   lawyer 968
   keep one's own - 528
   take - *think* 451
   inquire 461
   be advised 695
count *clause* 51
   item 79
   compute 85
   estimate 480
   lord 875
   - the cost 864
   - upon *believe* 484
   expect 507
countable 85
countenance
   face 234
   appearance 448
   favor 707
   approve 931
   - falling
      disappointment 509
      dejection 837

coverlet 223
Coverley, Sir Roger
de - 840
covert *abode* 189
  shade 424
  invisible 447
  latent 526
  refuge 666
  - *way* 627
  feme - e 903
coverture 903
covet *desire* 865
  envy 921
covetous *miserly* 819
covey *assemblage* 72
  multitude 102
covin 544, 545
cow *animal* 366
  female 374
  intimidate 860
  - *pony* 271
coward 862
cowardice **862**
cowardly 862
cowboy 370
cowcatcher 717
cower *stoop* 308
  fear 860
  cowardice 862
  servile 886
cowherd 370
cowhide *lash* 972
  whip 975
cowhouse 189
cowkeeper 370
cowl *sacerdotal* 999
  (*dress* 225)
cowled 223
cowlstaff 215
coworker 690
coworking 178
cow-puncher 370
coxcomb 854
coxcombry
  affectation 855
  vanity 880
coxswain 269
coy *timid* 860
  modest 881
coyote 366
cozen 545
crab *crustacean* 298, 368
  sourness 397
  - like motion
  deviation 279
  regression 283
crab apple 397
crabbed *sour* 397
  unintelligible 519
  obscure style 571
  difficult 704
  uncivil 895
  sulky 901a
crabmeat 298
crack *split* 44
  discontinuity 70
  instantaneous 113
  fissure 198
  furrow 259
  brittle 328
  sound 406

excellent 648
injure 659
skillful 698
boast 884
- a bottle
  food 298
  social 892
  drunken 959
- a joke 842
- of doom
  end 67
  future 121
  destruction 162
- one's invention 515
- shot 700
crackajack 33, 648, 698
crack-brained
  insane 503
  (*foolish* 499)
cracked
  unmusical 410
  mad 503
  faulty 651
  - bell 408a
  - voice 581
cracker *biscuit* 298
  firework 406
crackle 406
crack-loo 621
cracksman 792
cradle *beginning* 66
  infancy 127
  origin 153
  placing 184
  bed 215
  crossing 219
  training 673
  aid 707
  - hole 259
  - song 415, 834
  in the - 129
craft *shipping* 273
  business 625
  skill 698
  cunning 702
craftsman 690
craftsmanship 680
crag *cliff* 212
  pointed 253
  hard 323
  land 342
craggy *rough* 256
craichy 160
craig *height* 206
crake 884
cram *crowd* 72
  stuff 194
  choke 261
  teach 537
  learn 539
  gorge 957
  - down the throat
  compel 744
crambo 597
crammed 52
  - to overflowing 641
crammer *teacher* 540
  lie 546
cramp *fastening* 45
  paralyze 158
  weaken 160

little 193
  compress 195
  spasm 315, 378
  hinder 706
cramped *style* 579
cramp iron 45
cran 191
cranberry 298
cranch [*see* craunch]
crane *angle* 244
  elevate 307
  bird 366, 386
  - neck 245
crane's-bill 845
craniology &c. 450
cranium 450
crank *fanatic* 504
  instrument 633
  wit 842
  treadmill 975
  - shaft 272
crankle *fold* 258
crankling *rough* 256
cranky *weak* 160
  ill health 655
cranny 198
crape *crinkle* 248
  mourning 839
craps 621
crapulence
  intemperance 954
  gluttony 957
  drunken 959
crash *destruction* 162
  collision 276
  brittle 328
  sound 406
crasis *nature* 5
  coherence 48
  composition 54
crass *great* 31
  dense 321
  semifluid 352
  unintelligent 493
  bad taste 851
  - ignorance 491
crassamentum 321,
  352
crassitude
  breadth 202
  density 321
  thickness 352
crate *receptacle* 191
crater *deep* 208
  hollow 252
craunch *shatter* 44
  chew 298
  pulverize 330
cravat 225
crave *ask* 765
  desire 865
craven *cowardly* 862
craw 191
crawfish 298
  recede 283
  apostatize 607
crawl *elapse* 109
  creep 275
  withdraw 283
  apostatize 607
  servile 886

crawly 380
crayon 556
crazy *weak* 160
  mad 503
creak 410
creaking 410
cream *emulsion* 352
  oil 356
  yellow 436
  important part 642
  best 648
  - color *white* 430
  yellow 436
  - of tartar 662
  - of the jest 842
creamy 352
crease 258
create *cause* 153
  produce 161
  imagine 515
created *being* 366
creation [*see* create]
  effect 154
  world 318
creative 20, 153
creativeness 18, 20
Creator 976
creator *producer* 164
  poet 597
creature *thing* 3
  effect 154
  animal 271, 366
  man 372
  slave 746
  - comforts
  food 298
  pleasure 377
  the - *food* 298
crèche 542
credence *belief* 484
  church 1000
credenda 484
credential 467
credible *possible* 470
  probable 472
  belief 484
credit *belief* 484
  influence 737
  pecuniary **805**
  account 811
  repute 873
  approbation 931
  desert 944
  to one's -
  property 780
creditable *right* 924
credit mobilier 802
creditor 639, 805
credulity **486**
  (*heterodoxy* 984)
credulous 486, 849
  - person *dupe* 547
creed *belief* 484
  theology 983
  Apostles' - 983a
  - bound 606
creek *interval* 198
  water 343
creel 191
creep *crawl* 275
  tingle 380

cullion 949
cully *deceive* 545
  dupe 547
culm 388
culminate
  maximum 33
  height 206
  top 210
  complete 729
culpability *vice* 945
  guilt 947
culprit 949, 975
cult 990
cultivate *till* 365, 371
  sharpen 375
  improve 658
  prepare 673
  aid 707
  courtesy 894
cultivated
  courteous 894
  - taste 850
cultivation [*see* culti-
  vate]
  knowledge 490
cultivator 371
cultural 537, 542
culture
  knowledge 490
  improvement 658
  taste 850
  courtesy 894
culverin 727
culvert 350
cumber *load* 319
  obstruct 706
cumbersome
  incommodious 647
  disagreeable 830
cumbrous 830
cummerbund 225
cumshaw 784
cumulative
  assembled 72
  evidential 467
  - evidence 467
  - vote 609
cumulous 353
cumulus 353
cunctation *delay* 133
  (*inactivity* 683)
cuneate 244
cuneiform 244
  - character 590
cunning *prepense* 611
  sagacious 698
  artful **702**
  · - fellow 700
cup *vessel* 191
  hollow 252
  beverage 298
  remedy 662
  tipple 959
  between - and lip 111
  bitter - 828
  - of humiliation 879
  - that cheers &c. 298
  - too low 837
  - tossing 621
  dash the - from one's
    lips 509

in one's -s 959
cupbearer 746
cupboard 191
cupel 384
cupellation 336, 384
Cupid *beauty* 845
  love 897
cupidity *avarice* 819
  desire 865
cupola *height* 206
  dome 223, 250
cupping 662
cup-shaped 252
cur *dog* 366
  sneak 949
curable 658, 660, 662
curacy 995
curate 996
curative 660
curator 694, 758
curb *moderate* 174
  slacken 275
  dissuade 616
  chance 621
  check 706
  restrain 751
  shackle 752
  mart 799
  - bit 706
  - roof 244
curcuma paper 463
curd *density* 321
  pulp 354
  (*cohere* 46)
curdle *condense* 321
  make the blood - 830
curdled 352
cure *reinstate* 660
  remedy 662
  preserve 670
  benefice 995
curé 996
cure-all 662
cureless 859
curfew 126
curia 966
curio 847
curiosity
  unconformity 83
  inquiring **455**
  phenomenon 872
curious
  exceptional 83
  inquisitive 455
  true 494
  beautiful 845
  desirous 865
curiously *very* 31
curl *bend* 245
  convolution 248
  hair 256
  cockle up 258
  - cloud 353
  - paper 256
  - up one's lip 930
curling *game* 840
curling tongs 386
curly 248
curmudgeon
  miser 819
currants 298

currency
  publicity 531
  money 800
current *existing* **1**
  general 78
  present 118
  happening 151
  of water 348
  of air 349
  rife 531, 532
  language 560
  habit 613
  danger 667
  account - 811
  against the - 708
  - belief 488
  - of events 151
  - of ideas 451
  - of time 109
  go with the - 82
  pass - *believed* 484
  fashion 852
  stem the - 708
curricle 272
curricular 272
curriculum 537
currish 895
curry *rub* 331
  condiment 393
  - favour with
    love 897
    flatter 933
currycomb 370
curse *bane* 663
  adversity 735
  painful 830
  malediction 908
  (*evil* 619)
cursed *bad* 649
cursitor 968
cursive 573
cursory *transient* 111
  inattentive 458
  hasty 684
  take a - view of 457
  neglect 460
curst *sullen* 901a
curt *short* 201
  concise 572
  taciturn 585
curtail *retrench* 38
  shorten 201
  (*decrease* 36)
  (*deprive* 789)
  -ed of its fair propor-
    tions
  distorted 243
  ugly 846
curtailment *decrease* 36
  [*see* curtail]
curtain *shade* 424
  hide 528, 530
  theater 599
  fortification 717
  behind the -
    invisible 447
    inquiry 461
    knowledge 490
  close the - 528
  - lecture 932
  - raiser *drama* 66, 599

raise the - 529
rising of the - 448
curtal 201
curtate 201
curtsy *stoop* 308, 314
  submit 725
  polite 894
curule 474, 696
curvate 245
curvature **245**
curve 245
curved 245
curvet *leap* 309
  turn 311
  oscillate 314
  agitate 315
curvilinear 245
  - motion 311
cushat 366
cushion *pillow* 215
  soft 324
  relief 834
cusp *angle* 244
  sharp 253
cuspidor 191
cussed 901a
cussedness 606
custard pie 298
custodian 753
custody *safe* 664
  captive 751
  retention 781
  in - *prisoner* 754
  accused 938
  take into - 751
custom *old* 124
  habit 613
  barter 794
  sale 796
  tax 812
  fashion 852
  - honored in breach
    614
customary
  [*see* custom]
  regular 80
customer 795
customhouse 799
  - officer 965
custos 753
  - rotulorum 553
cut *geld* 38
  divide 44
  bit 51
  discontinuity 70
  absent 187
  interval 198
  curtail 201
  layer 204
  form 240
  notch 257
  blow 276
  depart 293
  eject 297
  reap 371
  physical pain 378
  cold 385
  neglect 460
  carve 557
  engraving 558
  road 627

D

order of the - 613
red letter - 642
see the light of - 446
day-bed 215
day-blindness 443
daybook *record* 551
  accounts 811
daybreak *morning* 125
  dim 422
daydream *fancy* 515
  hope 858
daydreamer 515
daydreaming 458
day-laborer 690
daylight *morning* 125
  light 420
see - *intelligible* 518
daypeep 125
dayspring 125
day-star 318, 423
daze 420, 870
  in a - 860
dazed *inattentive* 458
  uncertain 475
  confused 523
dazzle *light* 420
  blind 422, 443
  put out 458
  astonish 870
  awe 928
dazzling [see dazzle]
  beautiful 845
deacon 996
  juggle 545
  intone 990
deaconry 995
dead *complete* 52
  obsolete 124
  inert 172
  colorless 429
  lifeless 360
  insensible 376
- against *contrary* 14
  oppose 708
- asleep 683
- beat *powerless* 158
  sponger 886
- certainty 474
- color 556
- cut 893
- drunk 959
- failure 732
- flat 213
- heat 27
- languages 560
- letter *impotent* 158
  unmeaning 517
  useless 645
  laxity 738
  exempt 927
  illegal 964
- lift *exertion* 686
  difficulty 707
- march 275, 363, 415
- of night
  midnight 126
  dark 421
- one 460
- reckoning
  numeration 85
  measurement 466

- secret 533
- set against 708
- set at *attack* 716
- shot 284, 700, 716
- silence 403
- slow 275
- sound 408a
- stop 142
- to 823
- wall *hindrance* 706
  defense 717
- water 142, 343
- weight 706
more - than alive 688
deaden *weaken* 158
  moderate 174
  insensible 376
  muffle 405, 408a
  benumb 823
deadened 381
deadhead 815
deadhouse 363
deadlock *cease* 142
  stoppage 265
  difficulty 704
deadly *killing* 361
  pernicious 649
  unhealthy 657
- sin 947
- weapon 361, 727
deads 645
deaf 419
  inattentive 458
- and dumb 581
- and - dumb alphabet
  419
- ears 419
- to *insensible* 823
- to advice 606
- to reason 901a
turn - ear to
  neglect 460
  unbelief 487
  refuse 764
deafen *loud* 404
deaf-mute 419, 581
deaf-mutism 581
deafness 419
deal *much* 31
  arrange 60
  compact 769
  allot 786
- a blow *injure* 659
  attack 716
  punish 972
- board 323
- in 794
- out *scatter* 73
  give 784
- with *treat of* 595
  handle 692
  barter 794
dealbation 430
dealer 797
dealings *action* 680
have - with
  trade - 794
  friendly 888
dean *age* 128
  clergyman 996
deanery *office* 995

house 1000
dear *expending* 809
  high priced 814
  loved 897
  favorite 899
- at any price 646
- me *wonder* 870
O - ! *lament* 839
dearborn 272
dearness 814
dearth 640
- of ideas 843
death 360
be the - of one
  amuse 840
- defying 863
- in the pot
  unhealthy 657
  hidden danger 667
do to - 361
house of - 363
in at the - *arrive* 292
  persevere 604a
pale as - *colorless* 429
  fear 860
put to - 361
still as - 265
violent - 361
deathbed 360
- repentance 950
death bell 363
deathblow *end* 67
  killing 361
  failure 732
death chair 975
death fire 423
deathless
  perpetual 112
  fame 873
deathlike *silent* 403
  hideous 846
death's-head 837
death-song 839
death-struggle 720
death-warrant 971
deathwatch 668, 837
debacle
  revolution 146
  destruction 162
  violence 173
  downfall 306
  torrent 348
debar *hinder* 706
  restrain 751
  prohibit 761
debark 292, 342
debarment 55
debase *depress* 308
  foul 653
  deteriorate 659
  degrade 874
debased *lowered* 207
  dishonored 940
debatable 475
- point 454
debate *reason* 476
  talk 588
  hesitate 605
  dispute 720
debauch *spoil* 659
  intemperance 954

impurity 961
debauchee 962
debenture *security*
  771
  money 800
  credit 805
debility 160
debit *debt* 806
  accounts 811
debitor 806
debonair 836
debouch 293, 295
debouchment 293
débris *fragments* 51
  crumbled 330
  useless 645
debt 806
- of nature 360
get out of - 807
out of - 803
debtor 806
- and creditor 811
début *beginning* 66
  essay 675
débutant *learner* 541
  drama 599
decade *ten* 98
  period 108
  celebration 883
decadence 659
decagon 98, 244
decagonal 98
decahedral 98
decalescence 382
decalogue 926
decamp *go away* 293
  run away 623
decant 270
decanter 191
decapitate *kill* 361
  punish 972
decarbonized iron 323
decare 98
decarnate 317
decastyle 98
decasyllable 98
decay *decrease* 36
  decomposition 49
  shrivel 195
  unclean 653
  disease 655
  spoil 659
  adversity 735
- of memory 506
  natural - 360
decayed [see decay]
  old 124
  rotten 160
decease 360
deceit *falsehood* 544
  deception 545
  cunning 702
deceitful [see deceit]
deceive 545
deceived *in error* 495
  duped 547
deceiver 548
  gay - 962
decemvir 98
decennial 138
decennium 108

defensive alliance 712
defer *put off* 133
  neglect 460
  - to *assent* 488
  submit 725
  respect 928
deference
  submission 725
  obedience 743
  humility 879
  courtesy 894
  respect 928
deferment 460
defial 715
defiance **715**
  threat 909
  - of *danger* 861
  in - *opposition* 708
  set at - *disobey* 742
defiant 715
deficiency
  [see deficient]
  vice 945
  - of *blood* 160
deficient *inferior* 34
  incomplete 53
  shortcoming 304
  insufficient 640
  imperfect 651
deficit
  incompleteness 53
  debt 806
defigure 846
defile *interval* 198
  march 266
  dirt 653
  spoil 659
  shame 874
  impure 961
define *limit* 233
  explain 522
  name 564
definite *special* 79
  limited 233
  visible 446
  certain 474
  exact 494
  intelligible 518
  manifest 525
  perspicuous 570
definition
  interpretation 521
definitive *final* 67
  affirmative 535
  decided 604
deflagration 384
deflate 195
deflect *curve* 245
  deviate 279
deflower *spoil* 659
  violate 961
defluent 348
defluxion *egress* 295
  flowing 348
defœdation 653, 659
deform 241, 846
deformed 243
deforming 241
deformity
  distortion 243
  ugliness 846

blemish 848
defraud *cheat* 545
  swindle 791
defray 807
defrayment 807
deft *suitable* 23
  clever 698
defunct 360, 362
defy *confront* 234
  set at defiance 715
  disobey 742
  threaten 909
  - *danger* 861
dégagé *free* 748
  fashion 852
degeneracy 659
degenerate
  deteriorate 659
  vice 945
deglutition 298
degradation
  deterioration 659
  shame 874
  dishonor 940
degrade *disbar* 968
  [see degradation]
degree 26
  term 71
  honor 873
  by -s 26
  by slow -s 275
  in no - 107
  no - 4
degustation 390
dehisce 260
dehiscence 260
dehort *dissuade* 616
  advise 695
dehydrate 340, 670
dehydration 340, 670
deification 981
deify *honor* 873
  idolatry 991
deign *condescend* 762
  consent 879
deism
  heterodoxy 984
  irreligion 989
deistic 976, 989
Deity **976**
  tutelary - 664
dejection
  excretion 299
  melancholy **837**
déjeûner 298
dejudication 480
dekko 457
delaceration 659
delaminate 204
delation 133, 938
delator 527, 938
delay 133, 460
dele 162, 552
delectable *savory* 394
  agreeable 829
delectation 827
delectus 552
delegate *transfer* 270
  interpreter 524
  messenger 534
  commission 755

consignee 758
  deputy 759
delegated *acting* 759
delegation 755
delete 162
deleterious
  pernicious 649
  unwholesome 657
deletion 552
deletory *destructive* 162
deliberate *slow* 275
  think 451
  attentive 457
  leisure 685
  advise 695
  cautious 864
deliberately
  [see deliberate]
  late 133
  with *premeditation* 611
deliberation
  [see deliberate]
delicacy *weak* 160
  slender 203
  dainty 298
  texture 329
  savory 394
  delicate ear 418
  exact 494
  scruple 603
  ill health 655
  difficult 704
  pleasing 829
  beauty 845
  taste 850
  fastidious 868
  honor 939
  pure 960
delicate [see delicacy]
  color 428
  brittle 328
delicatessen 394
délice 377
delicious *taste* 394
  pleasing 829
delict 947
delictum 947
delight *pleasure* 377, 827
  pleasing 829
Delilah 962
delimit 233
delineate *outline* 230
  represent 554
  describe 594
delineavit 556
delinquency 304, 947
delinquent 949
deliquation 335
deliquesce 36, 335
deliquescent 335, 348
deliquium
  paralysis 158
  fatigue 688
deliriant 663
delirifacient 663
delirious 503, 825
delirium *raving* 503
  passion 825
  - tremens 959

delitescence
  invisible 447
  latency 526
  seclusion 893
deliver *transfer* 270
  utter 580, 582
  remedy 662
  rescue 672
  liberate 750
  give 784
  relieve 834
  - as one's *act and deed* 467
  - a *speech* 582
  - *judgment* 480
  - the *goods* 729
deliverance **672**
delivery [see deliver]
  bring forth 161
dell 252
Delphic oracle
  prophetic 513
  equivocal 520
  latent 526
delta *triad* 92
  land 342
delude *error* 495
  deceive 545
deluge *crowd* 72
  water 337
  flood 348
  redundance 641
delusion [see delude]
  insane 503
  self - *credulous* 486
delve *dig* 252
  till 371
  - into *inquire* 461
demagogue
  director 694
  malcontent **710**
  rebel 742
demagogy 737
demand
  inquire 461
  user 677
  order 741
  ask 765
  price 812
  claim 924
  in - *require* 630
  salable 795
  desire 865
  public - 677
demarcate 233
demarcation 233
dematerialize 317
demean oneself
  conduct 692
  humble 879
  dishonor 940
demeanor *aid* 448
  conduct 692
  fashion 852
demency 503
dement 61
dementate 503
démenti 536
dementia 503
demerit 945
demesne *abode* 189

dejection 837
dullness 843
deprivation 789
deprive *subduct* 38
   take 789
   - of life 361
   - of power 158
   - of property 789
   - of strength 160
deprived of 776
de profundis
   lamentation 839
   penitence 950
depth *physical* **208**
   mental 498
   - beyond depth 104
   - bomb 208, 727
   - of misery 828
   - of thought 451
   - of winter 383
   out of one's - 304, 310
depthless 209
depurate *clean* 652
   improve 658
depurative 652
depuratory 662
deputation 755
depute 755, 759
deputies, chamber of - 696
deputy 759
   police 664
   - commissioner 745
dequantitate 36
deracinate 2
derail 142
derange *insane* 503
deranged 503
derangement 61
   mental - 503
derby *hat* 225
Derby-day 720
derelict *ship* 273
   land 342
   source of danger 667
   relinquished 782
   outcast 893
dereliction
   relinquishment 624, 782
   guilt 947
   - of duty **927**
deride *ridicule* 856
   disrespect 929
   contempt 930
derisive 582, 853
   [see deride]
derivate 155
derivation
   origin 153, 154, 155
   verbal 562
derivative 562
derive *attribute* 155
   deduce 480
   word 562
   acquire 775
   income 810
derm 223
dermal 223
dermatogen 223
dermatography 223

dermatoid 223
dermatology 223
dermatopathy 223
dermatophyte 223
dermatoplasty 223
dermic 223
dermis 223
dermoid 223
dernier cri 123
derogate
   underrate 483
   disparage 934
   dishonor 940
   - from 874
derogatory
   shame 874
   dishonor 940
derrick 307, 633
derring-do 861
dervish 955, 984, 996
descant *precursor* 64
   music 415
   diffuseness 573
   loquacity 584
   dissert 595
descend *slope* 217
   go down 306
   - to particulars
   special 79
   describe 594
descendant 120, 167
descent 69
   lineage 166
   fall **306**
   inheritance 775
describe 594
description *kind* 75
   name 564
   narration **594**
descriptive 594
descry 441
desecrate *misuse* 679
   disrespect 929
   profane 988
desert
   unproductive 169
   space 180
   empty 187
   plain 344
   run away 623
   relinquish 624
   retaliation 718
   divorce 782
   merit 924, 944
deserted *outcast* 893
deserter 607, 623
desertion
   [see desert]
desertless 945
deserve
   be entitled to 924
   merit 944
   - belief 484
   - notice 642
deserving 924
déshabille
   [see dishabille]
desiccate 340
desiccator 340
desiderate *need* 630
   desire 865

desideratum
   inquiry 461
   requirement 630
   desire 865
design
   prototype 22
   composition 54
   delineation 554
   painting 556
   intention 620
   plan 626
designate *specify* 79
   call 564
   express 566
designation
   kind 75
designed
   aforethought 611
designer 559, 626
designing
   cunning 702
designless 621
desinence *end* 67
   discontinuance 142
desirability 646
desirable 646
desire **865**
   will 600
   have no - for 866
desirous *ready* 602
   desiring 865
desist *discontinue* 142
   relinquish 624
   inaction 681
desk *box* 91
   support 215
   school 542
   pulpit 1000
   the - 996
désobligeant
   carriage 272
desolate *alone* 87
   ravage 162
   afflicted 828
   dejected 837
   secluded 893
desolating
   painful 830
desolation
   [see desolate]
despair *grief* 828
   hopeless 859
despatch
   [see dispatch]
despect 930
desperado
   rash 863
   blusterer 887
   evil doer 913
desperate *great* **31**
   violent 173
   impossible 471
   resolved 604
   difficult 704
   excitable 825
   hopeless 859
   rash 863
   anger 900
despicable *trifling* 643
   shameful 874
   contemptible 930

despise 930
   - danger 861
despite 30, 907
   in - 708
despoil *injure* 659
   take 789
   rob 791
despond *dejected* 837
   fear 860
despot 745
despotism
   authority 737
   severity 739
   arbitrary 964
despumate 652
desquamate 226
desquamation 223, 226
dess 204
dessert 298
destination *end* 67
   arrival 292
   intention 620
destine 620
destiny *chance* **152**
   fate 601
   fight against - 606
destitute
   insufficient 640
   poor 804
   refuge for - 666
desto 415
destrier 726
destroy *demolish* 162
   injure 659
   - hopes 859
   - life 361
destroyed
   [see destroy]
   inexistent 2
   failure 732
destroyer **165**
   naval 726
   evil doer 913
destruction
   [see destroy]
destructive *bad* 649
   mutually - 361
destructor 165
desuetude **614**
   disuse 678
desultory
   disordered 59
   fitful 70
   multiform 81
   irregular in time **139**
   changeable 149
   deviating 279
   agitated 315
   discursive 595
desume 788
detach 44
detached *irrelated* 10
   loose 47
detachment *part* 51
   army 726
detail *item* 79
   describe 594
   allot 786
   ornament 847
   attention to - 457, 459
   in - 51

515

detailed
  circumstantial 8
details *minuti ɛ* 32
  unimportant 643
detain 781
detect 480a
detective 527, 664
detent 45
detention 781
  - camp 751
  house of - 752
  in house of - 938
deter *dissuade* 616
  alarm 860
deterge *clean* 652
detergent 652, 662
deteriorate 659
deterioration 659
determinable 278
determinate
  special 79
  exact 474
  conclusive 480
  intended 620
determinative 67
determine *end* 67
  define 79
  cause 153
  direction 278
  satisfy 462
  make sure 474
  judge 480
  discover 480a
  resolve 604
determined
  resolute 604
deterration 529
detersion 652
detersive 662
detest
  dislike 876
  hate 898
detestable 649
dethronement
  anarchy 738
  abrogation 756
detonate *explode* 173
  sound 406
detonation   404, 406,
  872
detortion *form* 243
  meaning 523
détour *curve* 245
  circuit 629
detract *subduct* 38
  underrate 483
  defame 934
  slander 938
detraction 934
detractor 936
detrain 292
detriment *evil* 619
  deterioration 659
detrimental 649
detrital 330
detrition 330
detritus *fragments* 51
  transference 270
  powder 330
detrude
  cast out 297
  516

  cut down 308
detruncate 38
detrusion
  [*see* detrude]
detrusive 308
deuce *two* 89
  devil 978
  - is in him 608
  play the - 825
deuced *great* 31
  painful 830
deus ex machina
  aid 707
  auxiliary 711
deuterogamy 903
deva 979
Devanagari 590
devastate *destroy* 162
  havoc 659
  depopulate 893
devastation 162
develop *increase* 35
  produce 161
  expand 194
  evolve 313
development 194
devexity *bending* 217
  curvature 245
deviate *vary* 20a
  change 140
  turn 279
  diverge 291
  circuit 629
  - from 15
  - from rectitude 940
  - from virtue 945
deviation 279
deviatory 311
device *motto* 550
  expedient 626
  artifice 702
devil
  seasoned food 392
  evil doer 913
  bad man 949
  Satan 978
  demon 980
  - in one
  headstrong 863
  temper 901
  - may care *rash* 863
  indifferent 866
  insolent 885
  -'s tattoo 407
  - take 908
  - take the hindmost
  run away 623
  haste 684
  cowardice 862
  - to pay *disorder* 59
  violence 173
  evil 619
  failure 732
  penalty 974
  - worship 978
  fig't like -s 722
  give the - his due
  right 922
  vindicate 937
  fair 939
  have a - 503

  machinations of the -
  619
  play the - with
  injure 659
  malevolent 907
  printer's - 591
devil-dog 269
devilish *great* 31
  bad 649
  malevolent 907
  vicious 945
devious *curved* 245
  deviating 279
  circuitous 311
devisable 270
devise *imagine* 515
  plan 626
  bequeath 784
  -d by the enemy 546
devisee
  transference 270
  possess 779
  receive 785
deviser 164
devitalize 158
devoid *absent* 187
  empty 640
  not having 777a
devoir *courtesy* 894
  respect 928
devolution 659, 783
devolve 783
  - on 926
Devonshire cream 321
devote *destine* 601
  employ 677
  consecrate 873
  - oneself to 604
  - the mind to 457
  - to destruction 908
devoted *habit* 613
  ill-fated 735
  obedient 743
  undone 828
  love 897
devotee *zealot* 682
  sports 840
  aspirant 865
  pious 987
  fanatic 988
devotion
  [*see* devotee,
  devoted]
  love 897
  piety 987
  worship 990
  self - 942
devour *destroy* 162
  eat 298
  gluttony 957
devoured by
  feeling 821
devouring element 382
devout 987, 990
devoutless 989
devoutly 821
dew 339
Dewali 138
dewan 745
dewy 339
  - eve 126

dexter 238
dexterous 238, 698
dextrality **238**
dextrorsal 238
dey 745
dhobi 652
dhoti 225
dhow 273
dhu 431
diablerie 992
diabolic *bad* 649
  malevolent 907
  wicked 945
  satanic 978
diabolist 978
diabolology 978
diacaustic 245
diaconicum 1000
diacoustics 402
diacritical 15, 550
diadem 747, 847
diæresis 49, 550
diagnosis 465, 522, 655
diagnostic
  distinguishable 15
  special 79
  experiment 463
  discriminative 465
  indication 550
  (*intrinsic* 5)
diagnostics 655
diagonal 217
diagram 554
dial 114
  measure 466
  as the - to the sun
  veracious 543
  faithful 772
dialect 563
dialectic *argument* 476
  language 56
dialogism 586
dialogue 588, 599
diameter 202
diametrical 237
  - ly opposite
  contrariety 14
  contraposition 237
diamond
  lozenge 244
  goodness 648
  ornament 847
  - cut diamond
  cunning 702
  retaliation 718
  - wedding 883
  rough - 703
Diana *moon* 318
  chaste 960
diapason 413
diaper 847
diaphanous 425
diaphonics 402
diaphoresis 299
diaphragm *middle* 68
  partition 228
diaporesis 475
diarrhea 290
diary *journal* 114
  record 551
diaskenast 593

diastase 320
diastatic 320
diaster 161
diastole 194
diatessaron 413
diathermancy 384
diathermic 384
diathesis *nature* 5
  state 7
  temperament 820
diatom 193
diatomic 193
diatonic 413
diatribe 932
dib 550
dibble *perforator* 262
  till 371
dibs 800
dicacity 885
dice *chance* 156, 621
  on the - 470
dicer 621, 840
dichotomy *bisect* 91
  angle 244
dichroic 443
dichroism 440
dickens 978
dicker *ten* 98
  haggle 794
dictagraph 418
dictate *write* 590
  enjoin 615
  advise 695
  authority 737
  command 741
dictator 745
dictatorial *certain* 474
  narrow 481
  willful 600
  insolent 885
dictatorship 737, 739
diction 560
dictionary *list* 542
  words 562
  book 593
  store 636
dictophone 418
dictum *maxim* 496
  affirmation 535
  command 741
didactic 537
didder 383
diddle 545
dido 309
diduction 44
die *mould* 22
  expire 360
  burn out 385
  engraving 558
- and make no sign
  951
- a violent death 361
- away *dissolve* 4
  decrease 36
  cease 142
- for *desire* 865
  endearment 902
- for one's country
  360
- from the memory
  536

- game 951
- hard *obstinate* 606
  resist 719
- in harness
  continue 143
  persevere 604a
- in one's shoes 972
- in the last ditch
  604a
- of a rose in aro-
  matic pain 822
- out *pass away* 2
  vanish 4
- with ennui 841
- with laughter 838
hazard of the - 621
never say - 604a
not willingly let - 670
the - is cast 601
dies - faustus 731
- infaustus 732
- iræ 919, 982
- non *never* 107
  rest 687
diet *food* 298
  remedy 662
  council 696
  spare - 956
dietetics 662
differ 15
  discord 713
- in opinion 489
- toto cœlo
  contrary 14
  dissimilar 18
difference 15
  [*see* differ]
  numerical 84
- engine 85
perception of - 465
split the - 774
different 15
  multiform 81
- time 119
differentia 15
differential
  differing 15
  number 84
  gear 272
- calculus 85
- thermometer 389
differentiate 79
differentiation
  calculation 85
  discrimination 465
differentiative 15
difficult 704
- to please 868
difficulties
  poverty 804
  in - 806
difficulty 704
  question 461
diffide 485
diffident *fearful* 860
  modest 881
diffluent 348
diffuse *mix* 41
  disperse 73
  publish 531
  style 573

  (*permeate* 186)
diffuseness 104, **573**
diffusion 73
diffusive *dispersed* 73
  verbose 573
dig *deepen* 208
  excavate 252
  till 371
- in *intrench* 664
- the foundations 673
- up 480a
- up the tomahawk
  722
digamy 903
digenesis 161
digest *arrange* 60
  boil 384
  think 451
  dissertation 595
  compendium 596
  plan 626
  improve 658
  prepare 673
  brook 826
digestible 662
digestion 673
digestive 662
diggings 189
dight *dress* 225
  ornament 847
digit 84
  morsel 32
digitated 253
digladiation 720
diglot 560
dignified 31
dignify 873
dignitary *clergy* 996
dignity *greatness* 31
  glory 873
  pride 878
  honor 939
digraph 561
digress *deviate* 279
  style 573
digression *circuit* 629
digressive 595
dijudication 480
dike *gap* 198
  fence 232
  furrow 259
  gulf 343
  conduit 350
  defense 717
dilaceration 44
dilapidation 659
dilation [*see* dilate]
dilate *increase* 35
  swell 194
  widen 202
  rarefy 322
  expatiate 573
dilation 194
dilatory *slow* 275
  inactive 683
dilection 897
dilemma *state* 7
  uncertain 475
  logic 476
  choice 609
  difficulty 704

dilettante
  connoisseur 492
  dabbler 823
  taste 850
dilettantism
  knowledge 490
  taste 850
diligence *coach* 272
diligent *active* 682
- thought 457
dilly-dally
  irresolution 605
  inactivity 683
dilogy 104
dilucidation 522
diluent 335
dilute *weaken* 160
  water 337
diluvian 124
dim *dark* 421
  faint 422
  invisible 447
  unintelligible 519
- eyed 443
dime 800
- novel 594
dimension 192
dimidiate 91
diminish *lessen* 36
  reduce 103
  contract 195
- the number 103
diminuendo
  music 415
diminution 36, 195
diminutive *degree* 32
  size 193
dimity 635
dimness **422**
dimple *concavity* 252
  notch 257
dim-sightedness **443**
  unwise 499
din 404
- in the ear
  repeat 104
  drum 407
  loquacity 584
- of arms 716
dine 298
- with Duke Hum-
  phrey 956
dingdong *repeat* 104
  chime 407
dinghy 273
dingle 252
  door 232
dingy *dark* 421, 422
  colorless 429
  black 431
  gray 432
dining room 191
dinner 298
- jacket 225
dint *power* 157
  concavity 252
  blow 276
by - of
  instrumentality **631**
diocesan 996
diocese 181, 995

Diogenes *recluse* 893
  cynic 911
lantern of -
  inquiry 461
Dionæa 545
dioptrics 420
diorama *view* 448
  painting 556
diorism 465
dip *slope* 217
  concavity 252
  load 270
  direction 278
  insert 300
  descent 306
  depression 308
  plunge 310
  water 337
  baptize 998
- into *glance at* 457
  inquire 461
  learn 539
- one's hands into
  take 789
diphthong 561
diphyletic 89, 167
diploma *evidence* 467
  commission 755
diplomacy
  artfulness 702
  mediation 724
  negotiation 769
diplomatic
  [*see* diplomacy]
- agent 758
diplomatist
  messenger 534
  consignee 758
dipper 191
Dipper 318
dipsomania
  insanity 503
  desire 865
  drunkenness 959
dipsomaniac 504
diptych *list* 86
  record 551
dire *hateful* 649
  disastrous 735
  grievous 830
  fearful 860
direct *straight* 246
  teach 537
  artless 703
  command 741
- attention to 457
- one's course
  motion 278
  pursuit 622
- the eyes to 441
directable 278
direction [*see* direct]
  tendency **278**
  indication 550
  management **693**
  precept 697
directive 692
directly *soon* 132
director *teacher* 540
  college 542
  manager **694**
518

  master 745
directorship 737
directory *list* 86
  council 696
diremption 44
direption 791
dirge *funeral* 363
  song 415
  lament 839
dirigible
  balloon 273, 726
  direction 278
dirk 727
dirt 653
- cheap 815
throw - *defame* 874
  disrespect 929
dirtiness [*see* dirty]
dirty *dim* 222
  opaque 426
  unclean 653
  disreputable 874
  dishonorable 940
- end of stick 699
- sky 353
- weather 349
do - work
  servile 886
  flatterer 935
diruption 162
disability
  impotence 158
disable 158
  weaken 160
disabled 158
disabuse *inform* 527
  disclose 529
disaccord 713
- with 15
disadvantage *evil* 619
  inexperience 647
at a - 34
lie under a - 651
disadvantageous
  disastrous 619
  inexpedient 647
  bad 649
disaffection *dissent* 489
  enmity 889
  hate 898
disaffirm 536
disagree
  [*see* disagreement]
disagreeable
  unpleasing 830
  dislike 867
disagreement
  difference 15
  incongruity 24
  dissent 489
  discord 713
disallow 761
disannul 756
disappear 449
disappearance **449**
disappointment
  balk **509**
  fail 732
  discontent 832
disapprobation
  hindrance 706

  refusal 764
  disapproval **932**
disapprove 932
disapprover 936
disarm *disable* 158
  weaken 160
  reconcile 831
  propitiate 914
disarrange 61
disarray *disorder* 59
  undress 226
disaster *killing* 361
  evil 619
  failure 732
  adversity 735
  calamity 830
disastrous *bad* 649
disavow 536
disband *separate* 44
  disperse 73
  liberate 750
disbar *abrogate* 756
  disapprove 932
  punish 968, 972
disbelief 485
  religious 989
disbelieve 485, 989
disbench *abrogate* 756
  disbar 968
  punish 972
disbowel 297
disbranch 44
disburden
  facilitate 705
- oneself of 782
- one's mind 529
disburse 809
disc *surface* 220
  front 234
discard *eject* 297
  relinquish 624
  disuse 678
  abrogate 756
  refuse 764
  repudiate 773
  surrender 782
- from one's thoughts
  458
discarded 495
discarnate 317
disceptation 476
discern *see* 441
  know 490
discernible 446
discerning 498
discernment 498, 868
disceptible 51
discerption 44
discharge *violence* 173
  propel 284
  emit 297
  excrete 299
  sound 406
  acquit oneself 692
  complete 729
  liberate 750
  abrogate 756
  pay 807
  exempt 927a
  acquit 970
- a duty 926, 944

- a function
  business 625
  utility 644
- an obligation 772
- from the memory
  506
- from the mind 458
- itself *egress* 295
  river 348
discind 44
disciple *pupil* 541
  Christian 985
disciplinarian
  master 540
  martinet 739
discipline *order* 58
  follower 65
  teaching 537
  training 673
  restraint 751
  punishment 972
  religious 990
disclaim *deny* 536
  repudiate 756
  objure 757
  refuse 764
disclaimer 536
disclamation
  [*see* disclaim]
disclose 529
disclosure **529**
  discovery 480a
discoid *broad* 202
  layer 204
  frontal 220
  flat 251
discoloration 429
discolored *shabby* 659
  ugly 846
  blemish 848
discomfit 731
discomfiture 732
discomfort
  physical 378
  mental 828
discommend 932
discommode
  hinder 706
discommodious
  useless 645
  inexpedient 647
discompose
  derange 61
  put out 458
  hinder 706
  pain 830
  disconcert 874
  anger 900
discomposure 828
disconcert *derange* **61**
  distract 458
  disappoint 509
  hinder 706
  discontent 832
  confuse 874
disconcerted
  hopeless 859
  (*failure* 732)
disconformity 83
discongruity 15, 24
disconnect 44, 70

dissonant 15, 713
dissuade 616
dissuasion **616**
dissuitable 24
dissyllable 561
distain *dirty* 653
  ugly 846
distal 196
distance **196**
  overtake 282
  go beyond 303
  defeat 731
  angular - 244
  - of time
  long time 110
  past 122
  keep at a -
  discourtesy 895
  keep one's -
  avoid 623
  modest 881
  respect 928
  teach one his - 879
distant 196
distaste 867
distasteful 830
distemper *color* 428
  painting 556
  disease 655
distend 194
distended 192
distich 89, 597
distichous 91
distill *come out* 295
  extract 301
  evaporate 336
  drop 348
distillation 336
distinct *disjoined* 44
  audible 402
  visible 446
  intelligible 518
  manifest 525
  express 535
  articulate 580
distinction
  difference 15
  greatness 31
  discrimination 465
  elegance 578
  fame 873
  rank 875
  - without a difference
  27
  lacking - 465a
distinctive
  different 15
  savory 394
  - feature 79
distingué
  fashion 852
  repute 873
distinguish
  perceive 441
  discriminate 465
  - by the name of 564
distinguishable 15
distinguished
  superior 33
  repute 873
distinguishing 15

distort
  [see distortion]
distortion
  obliquity 217
  twist **243**
  of vision 443
  misinterpret 523
  falsehood 544
  misrepresent 555
  ugly 846
  (*misjudge* 481)
distract 458
distracted *confused* 475
  insane 503
  excited 824
distraction *passion* 825
  love to - 897
distrain *take* 789
  appraise 812
  attach 969
distrait 458
distraught 475, 503
distress *distraint* 789
  poverty 804
  affliction 828
  cause pain 830
  signal of - 669
distribute *arrange* 60
  disperse 73
  type 591
  allot 786
distribution
  [see distribute]
distributor
  electrical 272
district *to partition* 44
  area 181
  - court 966
distrust *disbelief* 485
  fear 860
.distrustful 487
disturb *derange* 61
  change 140
  displace 185
  agitate 315
  excite 824
  distress 828, 830
disturbance
  disorder 59
disunion
  disagreement 24
  separation 44
  disorder 59
  discord 713
disunite *separate* 44
  break with 713
disunity 24
disuse *desuetude* 614
  relinquish 624
  unemploy **678**
disused 124, 678
disvaluation 932
disvalue 932
ditch *inclosure* 232
  hollow 252
  trench 259
  water 343
  conduit 350
  defense 717
ditch water 653
ditheism 984

dithyramb
  poetry 597
dithyrambic *wild* 503
ditto *iden ity* 13
  repe ition 104
  say - to 488
ditty 415
  - bag 191
diurnal 138
diuturnal 110
diuturnity 110'
divagate 279
divan *sofa* 215
  council 696
  throne 747
  tribunal 966
divaricate *differ* 15
  bifurcate 91
  fork 244
  diverge 291
divarication 16a
dive *resort* 189
  swim 267
  plunge 310
  - into *inquire* 461
divellicate 44
diverge
  [see divergence]
divergence
  nonuniformity 16a
  difference 15
  dissimilarity 18
  variation 20a
  disagreement 24
  deviation 279
  separation **291**
divers *different* 15
  multiform 81
  many 102
  - colored 440
diverse 15
diversiform 81
diversify
  [see diversity]
  vary 20a
  change 140
diversion *change* 140
  deviation 279
  pleasure 377
  amusement 840
diversity
  difference 15
  irregular 16a
  dissimilar 18
  multiform 81
  - of opinion 489
divert *turn* 279
  deceive 545
  amuse 840
  - the mind 452, 458
divertissement
  drama 599
  amusement 840
Dives 803
divest *denude* 226
  take 789
  - oneself of
  abrogate 756
  relinquish 782
divestment **226**
divide *separate* 44

  part 51
  arrange 60
  arithmetic 85
  bisect 91
  measure 466
  vote 609
  apportion 786
dividend *part* 51
  number 84
  portion 786
dividers 466
divination
  prediction 511
  sorcery 992
divine *predict* 511
  guess 514
  perfect 650
  of God 976, 983, 983a
  clergyman 996
  - right
  authority 737
  due 924
  - service 990
diviner 994
diving 267
  - bird 310
divining rod
  sign 550
  magic 993
Divinity *God* 976
  theology 983
divisible
  [see divide]
  number 84
division [see divide]
  part 51
  class 75
  arithmetic 85
  school 542
  election 609
  discord 713
  military 726
divisor 84
divorce
  separation 44
  relinquish 782
  matrimonial **905**
Divorce Court 966
divorcée 905
divulge 529
divulsion 44
diwan 745
dixi 535
Dixie's land 827
dizen 225, 847
dizzard 501
dizziness
  [see dizzy]
dizzy *dim-sighted* 443
  confused 458
  vertigo 503
  - height 206
  - round 312
do *fare* 7
  suit 23
  produce 161
  cheat 545
  act 680
  complete 729
  succeed 731
  I beg 765

all one can - 686
- as done by 906, 942
- a service *useful* 644
  aid 707
- as one pleases 748
- as others do 82
- away with
  destroy 162
  eject 297
  abrogate 756
- battle 722
- business 625
- for *destroy* 162
  kill 261
  conquer 731
  punish 972
- good 906
- harm 907
- honor 873
- into *translate* 522
- justice to 595
- like 19
- little 683
- no harm 648
- nothing 681
- nothing but 136
- one's bidding 743
- one's office 772
- over 223
- tell 508
- the work 686
- up 660
- without 678
- wrong 923
have to - with 680, 692
plenty to - 682
thing to - 625
doch-an-dorrach 959
docile *of horses* 370
  learning 539
  willing 602
docimastic 463
docimasy 463
dock *diminish* 36
  cut off 38
  port 189
  shorten 201
  store 636
  tribunal 966
- walloper 269
docked *incomplete* 53
docket *list* 69, 86
  evidence 467
  note 550
  record 551
  schedule 611
  security 771
on the - 454
dockyard 691
doctor *learned man* 492
  prevaricate 544
  improve 658
  restore 660
  remedy 662
after death the - 135
- accounts 811
when -s disagree 475
doctorate 873
doctorship 873
522

doctrinaire
  positive 474
  pedant 492
  theorist 514
  affectation 855
  blusterer 887
doctrinal 537
doctrine *tenet* 484
  knowledge 490
document 551
documentary 467
- evidence 467
dodder 160
dodecahedron 244
dodge *follow* 63
  change 140
  shift 264
  deviate 279
  oscillate 314
  pursue 461
  avoid 623
  stratagem 702
  (*deceive* 545)
doe *swift* 274
  deer 366
  female 374
doer *originator* 164
  agent 690
doff 226
- the cap 894
dog *follow* 63, 281
  animal 366
  male 373
  pursue 622
  wretch 949
cast to the -s
  destroy 162
  reject 610
  disuse 678
  abrogate 756
  relinquish 782
- in manger 943
- in office 737
-s of war 722
go to the -s
  destruction 162
  fail 732
  adversity 735
  poverty 804
hair of - that bit you 959
dogcart 272
dog-cheap 815
dog days 382
doge 745
dogged *obstinate* 606
  valor 861
  sullen 901a
doggedness 606
  [*see* dogged]
dogger 273
doggerel *verse* 597
  ridiculous 851, 853
doggish 895
doghole 189
dog Latin 563
dogma *tenet* 484
  theology 983
dogmatic
  certain 474
  positive 481

  assertion 535
  obstinate 606
dogmatism
  [*see* dogmatic]
dogmatist 887
dogmatization 474
dog's age 110
dog's-ear 258
dogsick 867
dog star 423
dogtrot 275
dog-weary 688
doily 852
doing
up and - 682
what one is - 625
doings *events* 151
  actions 680
  conduct 692
doit *trifle* 643
  coin 800
dokhma 363
dolce far niente 681
doldrums
  dejection 837
  sulks 901a
dole *mite* 32
  scant 640
  give 784
  allot 786
  parsimony 819
  grief 828
doleful 837
doll *small* 193
  image 554
dollar 800
- mark 550
dollish 129
dolor *physical* 378
  moral 828
dolorous 830
dolphin 341
dolt 501
doltish 499
domain *class* 75
  region 181
  property 780
dome *high* 206
  covering 223
  convex 250
Domesday book
  list 86
  record 551
domesman 967
domestic
  inhabitant 188
  home 189
  interior 221
  servant 746
  secluded 893
- animals 366
domesticate
  locate 184
  acclimatize 613
- animals 370
domesticize 370
domicile 189
domiciled
  inhabiting 186
domiciliary 188
- visit 461

dominant
  influence 175
  note in music 413
dominate *influence* 175
  rule 737
domination 175, **737**, 939
domineer
  tyrannize 739
  insolence 885
Dominican 996
Dominie 540
dominion 181, 737
- rule 737
domino *dress* 225
  mask 530
  concealment 528
  game 840
don *put on* 225
  man 373
  scholar 492
  tutor 540
  noble 875
Doña 875
donate 784
donation
  compensation 30
  gift 784
- party 840
donative 784
done *finished* 729
- for *impotent* 158
  spoilt 659
  failure 732
- up *impotent* 158
  tired 688
have - with *cease* **142**
  relinquish 624
  disuse 678
work - 729
donee 270, 785
donga 252
donjon
  defense 717
  prison 752
donkey *ass* 271
  fool 501
Donna 374
Donnybrook Fair
  disorder 59
  discord 713
donor 784
donship 875, 877
donzel 746
doodle 501
  music 416
doodlesack 410, 417
dooly 272
doom *end* 67
  fate 152
  destruction 162
  death 360
  judgment 480
  necessity 601
  assess 812
  sentence 971
- sealed *death* 360
  adversity 735
doomage 812, 974
doomed 735, 828
doomsday *end* 67

future 121
till - 112
door *entrance* 66
  cover 223
  brink 231
  barrier 232
  opening 260
  passage 627
  at one's - 197
  beg from door to - 765
  close the - upon 751
  death's - 360
  keep within -s 265
  lie at one's - 926
  open a - to
   liable 177
  open the - to
   receive 296
   facilitate 705
   permit 760
  show the - to
   eject 297
   discourtesy 895
   (*prohibit* 761)
doorkeeper 263
doormat 652
doorway 260
dope 465, 662
Dorado, El 803
dormancy 172
dormant *inert* 172
  latent 526
  asleep 683
dormer 260
dormeuse 272
dormitive 841
dormitory 191
dormouse 683
dorp 189
dorsal 235
dorser 191
dorsigerous 215
dorsum *back* 235
  hump 250
dory 273
dose *quantity* 25
  part 51
  medicine 662
  apportion 786
dosser 191
dossil *cover* 223
  stopper 263
dot *small* 32
  point 180a
  place 182
  little 193
  variegate 440
  mark 550
dot *dowry* 784
dotage *age* 128
  imbecility 499
dotard *old* 130
  foolish 501
dotation 784
dote *drivel* 499, 503
  - upon 897
dotted 440
douanier 965
double *similar* 17
  increase 35
  duplex 90

substitute 147
  fold 258
  turn 283
  finesse 702
  specter 980a
  wraith 992a
  - acrostic *letters* 561
  wit 842
  - a point 311
  - eagle 800
  - entry 811
  - meaning 520
  - quartet 415
  - reef topsails 664
  - sure 474
  - the fist 909
  - up
   render powerless 158
  in quick time 274
  march at the - 274
  see - *dim sight* 443
   drunk 959
  work - tides 686
double bass 417
double-dealer 607
double-dealing *lie* 544
  cunning 940
double-distilled 171
double-dyed 428
double-edged 171
double entente
  ambiguity 520
  impure 961
double-faced *lie* 544
  cunning 702
  dishonorable 940
double-handed 544
double-headed 90
double-hearted 940
double-minded 605
double-ripper 272
double-runner 272
double-shot 171
double-shotted 171
doublet 225
doublets 89
double-tongued
  lie 544
  cunning 702, 940
doubling 702
doubt *uncertain* 475
  disbelieve **485**
  skeptic 989
doubtful *uncertain* 475
  equivocal 520
  - meaning
   unintelligible 519
   (*equivocal* 520)
  more than - 473
doubtless *certain* 474
  belief 484
  assent 488
douceur *gift* 784
  reward 973
douche 337
dough *inelastic* 324
  pulp 354
  money 800
doughboy 726
doughface 605, 886
doughnut 298

doughty 159, 861
dour 739
douse *blow* 276, 972
  immerse 310
  splash 337
Dove *Holy Ghost* 976
dove *bird* 366
  innocent 946
  roar like sucking - 174
dove-color 432
dovecote 189
dovetail *agree* 23
  join 43
  intersect 219
  intervene 228
  angle 244
  insert 300
dowager *lady* 374
  widow 905
dowdy *dirty* 653
  vulgar 851
dower *property* 780
  bequest 784
  wealth 803
dowerless 804
down *upland* 180
  below 207
  sleep 306
  cast down 308
  light 320
  bear - upon 716
  bed of - *pleasure* 377
   repose 687
  be - upon *attack* 716
   severe 739
  come - 306
  - in price 815
  - in the mouth 837
  - on one's marrow-
   bones 886
  - on one's uppers 879
  get - 306
  go - *sink* 306
   calm 826
  go - like a stone 310
  money - 807
  take - *lower* 308
   rebuff 874
   humble 879
downcast
  descendent 306
  dejected 837
  - eyes 879
downcome 306
down-easter 188
downfall
  destruction 162
  fall 306
  earth 342
  failure 732
  misfortune 735
down-grade 306
down-hearted 837
downhill *sloping* 217
  descent 306
  go - *adversity* 735
downpour 348
down-reaching 208
downright *absolute* 31
  manifest 525
  sincere 703

downs *uplands* **180**
  heights 206
  wolds 344
down-trodden
  submission 725
  vanquished 732
  subject 749
  dejected 837
  disrepute 874
  contempt 930
downwards 306
downy *smooth* 255
  plumose 256
  soft 324
dowry *property* 780
  bequest 784
  provision 803
dowse 276
dowser 994
doxology 990
doxy 962
doyen 128, 130
doyley 652
doze 683
dozen 98
drab *color* 432
  slut 59, 653
  hussy 962
drabble 653
drachm 319
Draco *ruler* 694
  severe 739
draff 653
draft [*see also* draught]
  decrement 40a
  traction 285
  drawing 554, 556
  write 590
  abstract 596
  list 611
  plan 626
  physic 662
  combatant 726
  cheque 800, 805
  - off *displace* 185
  transfer 270
drafted man 726
draft-horse 271
drag *elapse* 109
  carriage 272
  crawl 275
  traction 285
  impediment 706
  - a chain *tedious* 110
  exertion 686
  subjection 749
  - along 106
  - anchor 706
  - into *implicate* 54
  compel 744
  - into open day 531
  - on *endure* 106, 110
  continue 143
  - sail *check* 706
  - sheet 706
  - slow length
   long 200
   weary 841
  - through mire
   disrepute 874
   disrespect 929

- towards *attract* 288
put on the - 275
draggle 285, 653
draggle-tail 59
drag-net *all sorts* 78
dragoman 524
dragon *monster* 83, 366
  violent 173
  irascible 901
dragon fly 366
dragonnade *attack* 716
  punish 972
dragoon *attack* 716
  soldier 726
  compel 744
  insolent 885
  worry 907
drain *dike* 232
  flow out 295
  empty 297
  dry 340
  conduit 350
  waste 638
  clean 652
  unclean 653
  exhaust 789
  dissipate 818
  - into 348
  - of resources 640
  - the cup *drink* 298
  drunken 959
  - the cup of misery 828
drainage [*see* drain]
drake *male* 373
  fire - 423
dram *drink* 298
  weight 319
  pungent 392
  stimulus 615
  - drinking 959
drama **599**
dramatic
  musician 416
  drama 599
  ostentation 882
  - author 599
  - poetry 597
dramatis personæ
  mankind 372
  play 599
  agents 690
  party 712
dramatist 599
dramatize 599
dramaturgic 882
dramaturgy 599
drap d' or 847
drape 225
draper 225
drapery 225
drastic 171
draught
  [*see also* draft]
  depth 208
  traction 285
  drink 298
  stream of air 349
  delineation 554, 556
  plan 626
  physic 662

  troops 726
  - off 73
draughts *game* 840
draughtsman
  artist 559
draw *compose* 54
  pull 285
  delineate 554, 556
  money 800
  - a bead on 716
  - a curtain 424
  - and quarter 972
  - an inference 480
  - a parallel 9
  - a picture 594
  - aside 279
  - a straight furrow 939
  - back *regret* 283
  avoid 623
  - breath *refresh* 689
  feeling 821
  relief 834
  - down 153
  - forth *extract* 301
  use 677
  - from 810
  - in 195
  - in one's horns
  tergiversation 607
  humility 879
  - lots 621
  - near *time* 121
  approach 286
  - off *eject* 297
  hinder 706
  take 789
  - off the attention 458
  - on *time* 121
  event 151
  induce 615
  - on futurity 132
  - out *protract* 110
  late 133
  prolong 200
  extract 301
  discover 480a
  exhibit 525
  diffuse style 573
  - over *induce* 615
  - poker 840
  - profit 775
  - the line 465
  - the pen through 552
  - the sword *attack* 716
  war 722
  - the teeth of 158
  - the veil 528
  - together
  assemble 72
  coöperate 709
  - towards 288
  - up *order* 58
  stop 265
  write 590
  - up a statement 594
  - upon *money* 800
drawback
  decrement 40a
  evil 619
  imperfection 651

  hindrance 706
  discount 813
drawbridge *way* 627
  escape 671
drawcansir 887
drawee 800
drawer *receptacle* 191
  artist 559
  - of water 690
drawers *garment* 225
drawing
  delineation 554, 556
drawing knife 253
drawing-room
  assembly 72
  room 191
  fashion 852
  - car 272
drawl *prolong* 200
  creep 275
  in speech 583
  sluggish 683
drawn *equated* 27
  - battle
  pacification 723
  incomplete 730
dray 272
dray horse 271
drayman 268
dread 860
dreadful *great* 31
  bad 649
  dire 830
  depressing 837
  fearful 860
dreadless 861
dreadnought *coat* 225
  battleship 726
dream *unsubstantial* 4
  error 495
  fancy 515
  sleep 683
  psychotherapy 992a
  - of *think* 451
  intend 620
  - on other things 458
  golden - 858
dreamer *madman* 504
  imaginative 515
dreamlike 4
dreamy
  unsubstantial 4
  inattentive 458
  imaginative 515
  sleepy 683
drear 16
drearisome 16
dreary *uniform* 16
  solitary 87
  melancholy 830, 837
dredge *collect* 72
  extract 301
  raise 307
dredging machine 307
dregs *remainder* 40
  density 321
  refuse 645
  dirt 653
  - of the people 876
  - of vice 945
drench *drink* 298

  water 337
  physic 370
  redundance 641
  - with physic 662
drencher 348
drenching 337
  - rain 348
dress *uniformity* 16
  agree 23
  equalize 27
  clothes 225
  prepare 673
  ornament 847
  ostentation 882
  - down *berate* 527
  - the ground 371
  - to advantage 847
  - up *falsehood* 544
  represent 554
  - wounds 662
  full - 852
dress clothes 225
dress coat 225
dress suit 225
dresser *sideboard* 215
  surgeon 662
dressing
  reprimand 932
  punish 972
dressing gown 225
dressmaker 225
dribble *flow out* 295
  drop 348
dribbling 32
driblet 25, 32
dried 340
drier 340
drift *accumulate* 72
  distance 196
  tunnel 260
  motion 264
  float 267
  transfer 270
  direction 278
  deviation 279
  approach 286
  air 338
  wind 349
  meaning 516
  intention 620
  - sail 706
  snow - 383
drifter *neglecter* 460
drifting *irresolute* 605
driftless 621
drill *crossing* 219
  bore 260
  auger 262
  teach 537
  prepare 673
drink *swallow* 296
  liquor 298
  tipple 959
  - in *imbibe* 296, 298
  - in learning 539
  - in the ozone 689
  - one's fill
  enough 639
  - to *celebrate* 883
  courtesy 894
drinkable 298

drinker 959
drinking bout 954
drinking song 597
drink money 784
drip *ooze* 295
  flow 348
dripping *wet* 339
  fat 356
drive *assemblage* 72
  airing 266
  impel 276
  propel 284
  urge 615
  haste 684
  direct 693
  compel 744
  - a bargain
  barter 794
  parsimony 819
  - a coach and six
   through 83
  - ahead *progress* 282
  - at *mean* 516
  intend 620
  - care away 836
  - from *repel* 289
  - home 729
  - in 300
  - into a corner
  difficult 704
  hinder 706
  defeat 731
  subjection 749
  - matters to an ex-
   tremity 604
  - on *progress* 282
  - one hard 716
  - out 297
  - to despair 859
  - to the last 133
  - trade *business* 625
  barter 794
drive gate 260
drivel *slobber* 297
  imbecile 499
  mad 503
  diffuseness 573
driveler *fool* 501
  loquacious 584
driver *coachman* 268
  director 694
driveway 260
driving rain 348
drizzle 348
drizzly 348
drogher 273
drole *cards* 840
drollery
  amusement 840
  wit 842
  ridiculous 853
dromedary 271
drone *slow* 275
  sound 407, 412, 413
  music 415
  inactive 683
drool *drivel* 297
  diffuseness 573
droop *weak* 160
  pendency 214
  sink 306

  disease 655
  decline 659
  flag 688
  sorrow 828
  dejection 837
drop *small quantity* 32
  discontinue 142
  powerless 158
  bring forth 161
  fell 213
  pendent 214
  spherule 249
  emerge 295
  fall 306
  trickle 348
  relinquish 624
  discard 782
  gallows 975
  - a hint 527
  - all idea of 624
  - asleep 683
  - astern 283
  - by drop
  by degrees 26
  in parts 51
  - dead 360
  - from the clouds 508
  - game 545
  - in *arrive* 292
  immerse 300
  sociality 892
  - in one's tracks 361
  - in the ocean
  trifling 643
  - into a good thing
   734
  - into the grave 360
  - off *decrease* 36
  die 360
  sleep 683
  - serene 442
  - the mask 529
  - the subject 458
  - too much 959
  let - 308
  ready to - *fatigue* 688
dropping fire 70
drop scene 599
dropsical *swollen* 194
  redundant 641
droshki 272
dross *remainder* 40
  trash 643
  rubbish 645
  dirt 653
drought *dryness* 340
  insufficiency 640
  thirst 865
droughty 340
drouk 337
droukit 339
drove *assemblage* 72
  multitude 102
drover 370
drown *affusion* 337
  kill 361
  ruin 731, 732
  - care 840
  - the voice 581
drowsy *slow* 275
  sleepy 683

  weary 841
drub *defeat* 731, 732
  punish 972
drudge *plod* 682
  labor 686
  worker 690
drudgery 686
drug *superfluity* 641
  trash 643
  remedy 662
  - habit 954
  - in the market 815
  - store 662
drugget *cover* 223
  clean 652
  preserve 670
druggist 662
druid 996
drum *repeat* 104
  cylinder 249
  sound 407
  musician 416
  music 417
  party 892
  beat of - *signal* 550
  alarm 669
  war 722
  command 741
  parade 882
  - fire 407
  - out 972
  ear - 418
  muffled - *funeral*
   363
  nonresonance 408a
drumhead *lawless* 964
  tribunal 966
drum major 416, 745
drummer 416
  traveler 758, 767
drunk 959
  - with choler 900
drunkard 959
drunken 959
  reel like a - man 315
drunkenness **959**
dry *arid* 340
  style 575, 576, 579
  hoarse 581
  scanty 640
  preserve 670
  exhaust 789
  tedious 841
  thirsty 865
  cynical 932
  - as dust *dull* 843
  - goods 329
  - joke 842
  - land 342
  - the tears 834
  - up 340
  waste 638
  on - land 342
  run - 640
  with - eyes 823
dryad *tree* 367
  nymph 979
Dryasdust
  antiquarian 122
dry land 342
dryness **340**

dry nurse *teach* 537
  teacher 540
  aid 707
dry point 558
dry rot *dirt* 653
  decay 659
  bane 663
duad 89
dual 89, 90
  - personality 992a
dualism 984
duality 89
duarchy 737
dub 564, 566
dubash 758
dubiosity 475
dubious 475
dubitation
  uncertainty 475
  (*unbelief* 485)
duchess *mistress* 745
  nobility 875
duchy 181
duck *zero* 101
  stoop 308
  plunge 310
  bird 298, 366
  water 337
  darling 897, 899
  - in thunder 870
  play -s and drakes
  recoil 277
  prodigality 818
ducking stool 975
duckling 129
duck pond 370
duct 350
ductibility 324
ductile *tractile* 285
  flexible 324
  trimming 607
  easy 705
  docile 743
ductility
  [*see* ductile]
dud 304
dude 854
dudgeon *dagger* 727
  discontent 832
  churlishness 895
  hate 898
  anger 900
  sullenness 901a
duds 225
due *expedient* 646
  owing 806
  proper 924, 926
  - respect 928
  - sense of 498
  - time *soon* 132
  - to c*ause and effect*
   154, 155
  give - weight 465
  give his - to
  right 922
  vindication 937
  fair 939
  in - course 109
  occasion 134
dueguard 550
duel 720

duelist 726
duello 720
dueness **924**
duenna *teacher* 540
 guardian 664
 keeper 753
dues 812
duet 415
duffer
 ignoramus 493
 bungler 701
 smuggler 792
dug 250
dugout *dwelling* 189
 trench 232
 boat 273
 safety 664
 defense 717
duke *ruler* 745
 noble 875
dukedom 877
dulcet *sweet* 396
 sound 405
 melodious 413
 agreeable 829
dulcify 174, 324, 396
dulcimer 417
dulcin 396
Dulcinea 897
dulcorate 396
dulia 990
dull *weak* 160
 unintelligent 32, 493
 inert 172
 moderate 174
 blunt 254
 slow 275
 insensible 376
 sound 405
 dim 422
 color 428
 colorless 429
 stolid 499
 style 575
 inactive 683
 unapt 699
 callous 823
 dejected 837
 weary 841
 prosing 843
 simple 849
 - of hearing 419
 - sight 443
dullard 501
dullish *blunt* 254
dullness **843**
duly 924
dulse 367
duma 696
dumb *ignorant* 493
 voiceless 581
 - animal 366
 - friend 366
 - show 550

strike - *astonish* 870
 humble 879
dumb-waiter 307
dumdum bullet 727
dumfound
 disappoint 509
 silence 581
 astonish 870
 humble 879
dummy *substitute* 147
 impotent 158
 speechless 581
 printing 591
 inactive 683
 cards 840
dump *unload* 297
 music 415
 sale 796
 lament 839
 - cart 272
dumps *discontent* 832
 dejection 837
 sulk 901a
dumpy *little* 193
 short 201
 thick 202
dun *din* 422
 colorless 429
 gray 432
 importune 765
 creditor 805
dunce *ignoramus* 493
 fool 501
dunderhead 501
dune 206
dung 653
dungeon 752
dunghill *dirt* 653
 cowardly 862
 baseborn 876
 - cock 366
Dunker 984
duo 415
duodecimal 99
duodecimo *little* 193
 book 593
duodenal 221
duodenary 98
duodenum 221, 350
duologue
 interlocution 588
 drama 599
dupe *credulous* 486
 deceive 545
 deceived **547**
duplex 90
 - house 189
duplicate *copy* 21
 double 90
 repetition 104
 tally 550
 record 551
 redundant 641
 pawn 805

duplication
 imitation 19
 doubling **90**
 repetition 104
duplicature *fold* 258
duplicity *duality* 89
 falsehood 544
durability 141
durable *long time* 110
 permanent 141
 stable 150
durance 751
 in - 754
duration 106
 contingent - **108a**
durbar *conference* 588
 council 696
 tribunal 966
dure 106
duress *compulsion* 744
 restraint 751
Durga 979
Durham boat 273
during 106
 - pleasure &c. 108a
durity 323
durwan 263, 753
dusk *evening* 126
 half-light 422
dusky *dark* 421
 dim 422
 black 431
dust *levity* 320
 powder 330
 corpse 362
 trash 643
 dirt 653
 money 800
 come to - *die* 360
 - in the balance 643
 - one's jacket 972
 humbled in the - 879
 kick up a - 885
 level with the - 162
 lick the - *submit* 725
 fail 732
 make to bite the - 731
 throw - in the eyes
 blind 442
 deceive 545
 plead 617
 turn to -
 deorganized 358
 die 360
duster 652
dust hole 519
 fit for the -
 useless 645
 dirty 653
 spoilt 659
dustman
 cleaner 652
dustoor 613
dustoori 973

dust storm 330
dusty *powder* 330
 dirt 653
Dutch - auction 796
 - cap 225
 - courage 862
 - oven 386
 - treat 892
 high - 519
 it beats the - 508
Dutchman 57
 flying - 515
dutiable 812
dutiful 944
duty *business* 625
 work 686
 tax 812
 courtesy 894
 obligation **926**
 respect 928
 worship 990
 rite 998
 do one's - *virtue* 944
 on - 680, 682
duumvirate 737
Duval, Claude - 792
D. V. 470
dwarf *lessen* 36
 small 193
 elf 980
dwell *reside* 186
 abide 265
 - upon *descant* 573
dweller 188
dwelling *location* 184
 abode **189**
dwindle *lessen* 36
 shrink 195
 droop 655
dyad 193
dyadic 89
dye 428
 -d in the wool 709,
 820
dying 360
dyke [*see* dike]
dynamic 157
 - energy 157
dynamics 276
dynamitard 863
dynamite 727
dynamize 171
dynamo 157
dynamograph 276
dynamometer 276, 466
dynasty 737
dysentery 299
dysmerogenesis 161
dysmeromorph 357
dyspepsia 655
dyspeptic 655
dysphonia 581
dysphoria 149
dyspnœa 688

partial - *dim* 422
total - *dark* 421
under an - *invisible* 447
  out of repute 874
ecliptic 318
eclogue 597
ecology 357
economic 692
  - pressure 751
economical 817
economics 692
economize 817
economy *order* 58
  preservation 670
  conduct 692
  frugality **817**
  (*plan* 626)
  animal - 359
ecphonesis 580
ecrhythmic 139
ecrhythmus 139
écru 426, 433
ecstasis 683
ecstasy *frenzy* 515
  transport 821
  rapture 827
ecstatic 829
ecstatica 992a
ecteron 223
ectoderm 223
ectogenous 161
ectropic 218
ectype 21
ecumenical 78
edacity 957
Edda 986
eddish 168
Eddy, Mary Baker - 986
eddy *whirlpool* 348
  current 312
  danger 667
Eden *heaven* 827
  (*pleasure* 827)
edentate 254
edge *energy* 171
  height 206
  brink **231**
  deviate 279
  cutting - 253
  - in 228
  - of hunger 865
  - one's way 282
  set on - 256
  take the - off 174
edge tools 253
  play with - 863
edgewise 217
edging *obliquity* 217
  border 231
  ornament 847
edible 298
edict 531, 741
edification
  building 161
  teaching 537
  learning 539
  piety 987
edifice 161
edifying *good* 648
528

edile 965
edit *publication* 531
  compile 596
  revise 658
  (*printing* 591)
edition 531
  new - 658
editor *recorder* 553
  book 593
  commentator 595
editorial 595
edomorphic 221
educate *teach* 537
  (*prepare* 673)
educated 490
education *teaching* 537
  knowledge 490
  man of - 492
educational 537
  school 542
educe *extract* 301
  discover 480a
educt 40
eduction 40a
edulcorate
  sweeten 396
  clean 652
eel *convolutions* 248
  fish 298
  - spear 727
  wriggle like an - 315
efface *destroy* 162
  disappear 449
  obliterate 552
  - from the memory 506
effect *consequence* **154**
  complete 729
  carry into - 692
  in - 5
  take - 731
  to that - 516
  with crushing - 162
effective
  substantial 3
  capable 157
  influential 175
  useful 644
  practical 646
effects *property* 780
  goods 798
effectual
  influential 175
  success 731
effectually 52
effectuate 729
effeminacy
  [*see* effeminate]
effeminate *weak* 160
  womanlike 374
  timorous 862
  sensual 954
effeminize 158
effendi 875
effervesce *energy* 171
  violence 173
  agitate 315
  bubble 353
  excited 825
effervescent
  [*see* effervesce]

aërated 338
effete *old* 128
  weak 160
  useless 645
  spoiled 659
efficacious
  [*see* efficient]
efficient *power* 157
  agency 170
  reliable 632
  utility 644
  skill 698
effigy *copy* 21
  representation 554
efflation 349
efflorescence 330
effluence *egress* 295
  flow 348
effluent 295
effluvious 398
effluvium *vapor* 334
  odor 398
efflux *egress* 295
  (*flow* 348)
efformation 240
effort 686
effrontery 885
effulgence 420
effuse
  pour out 295, 297
  excrete 299
  speech 582
effusion [*see* effuse]
  loquacity 584
  - of blood 361
effusive 295
eft 366
eftsoon 113, 117, 132
egad 535
egest 297
egesta 299
egestion 297
egestive 297
egg *beginning* 66
  cause 153
  food 298
  - and dart
  ornament 847
  - on 615
  too many -s in one basket
  unskillful 699
  (*imprudent* 863)
  walk among -s 704
eggplant 298
egg-shaped 247, 249
eggshell 223
ego *intrinsic* 5
  immaterial 317
  astral body 980a
  non - 6
egohood 5
egoism 880
egoist 880
egotism
  overestimation 482
  vanity 880
  cynicism 911
  selfishness 943
egotist 482
egotistical [*see* egotism]

narrow 481
egregious
  exceptional 83
  absurd 497
  exaggerated 549
  important 642
egregiously *greatly* 31
  supremely 33
egress **295**
egurgitate 295
Egyptian
  - darkness 421
  - deities 979
eiderdown 223, 324
eidoloclast 165
eidolon 453, 991
eidouranion 318
eight *number* 98
  boat 273
  representative 759
eighty 98
eileton 999
Einstein theory 451
eisegesis 523
eisteddfod 72
either *choice* 609
  happy with - 605
ejaculate *propel* 284
  utter 580
eject 297
ejecta 299
ejection *displace* 185
  emit **297**
  excretion 299
ejective 297, 299
ejector 349
eke *also* 37
  - out *complete* 52
  spin out 110
ekka 272
elaborate *improve* 658
  prepare 673
  laborious 686
  work out 729
elaboration
  [*see* elaborate]
elaine 356
élan 276
elapse *flow* 109
  pass 122
elastic
  [*see* elasticity]
  - fluid 334
elasticity *power* 157
  strength 159
  energy 171
  spring **325**
elate *cheer* 836
  rejoice 838
  hope 858
  vain 880
  boast 884
elbow *angle* 244
  projection 250
  push 276
  at one's - *near* **197**
  advice 695
  - one's way
  progress 282
  pursuit 622
  active 682

epitaph 363, 550
epithalamium 903
epithelium 223
epithem 662
epithet 564
epitome *miniature* 193
  short 201
  concise 572
  compendium 596
epitomist 201
epitomization 201
epitomizer 201
epizoötic 655, 657
epoch *time* 106
  period 108
  instant 113
  date 114
  present time 118
epochal 108
epode 597
eponym 564
epopœa 597
Epsom salts 662
epulation 298
epulotic 662
epuration 652
equable *uniform* 16
  equitable 922
equal *even* 27
  be parallel 216
  equitable 922
  - *chance* 156
  - *times* 104
  - *to power* 157
equality **27**
  identity 13
equalize 213
equanimity 826
equate 27
  compensate 30
equation 37, 85
equator *middle* 68
  world 318, 550
equatorial 68
equerry 746
equestrian 268
equestrienne 268
equibalanced 27
equidistant 68, 216
equilibration 27
equilibrium 27
equine *carrier* 271
  horse 366
equinox *spring* 125
  autumn 126
equip *dress* 225
  prepare 673
equipage *vehicle* 272
  instruments 633
  display 882
equiparable 9
equiparant 9, 27
equiparate 27
equipment *gear* 633
  [*see* equip]
equipoise 27
equipollence 27
equiponderant 27
equitable *wise* 498
  just 922
  due 924

honorable 939
- *interest* 780
equitation 266
equity *right* 922
  honor 939
  law 963
  - *draftsman* 968
  in - 922
equivalent
  correlated 12
  identical 13
  equal 27
  compensation 30
  substitute 147
  translation 522
equivocalness
  dubious 475
  double meaning **520**
  impure 961
equivocate
  sophistry 477
  palter 520
  lie 544
equivocation
  [*see* equivocate]
  quirk 481
  without - 543
équivoque
  double meaning 520
  impure 961
era *time* 106
  period 108
  date 114
  - *of indiction* 108
eradicate *destroy* 162
  eject 297
  extract 301
eradication 103
erase *destroy* 162
  rub out 331
  obliterate 552
Erastian 984
erasure [*see* erase]
Erato 416
ere 116
  - *long* 132
  - *now* 116
  past 122
  - *then* 116
Erebus *dark* 421
  hell 982
erect *build* 161
  vertical 212
  straight 246
  raise 307
  - *the scaffolding* 673
  with head - 878
erection *building* 161
  elevation 307
eremite 893
erewhile 116, 122, 132
ergo 476
ergophobia 683
ergotism 480, 489
ergotize 485
Erinyes 173
eriometer 445
eristic 476
ermine *covering* 223
  badge of authority 747
  ornament 847

erode 36, 659
erosion [*see* erode]
erotic *amorous* 897
  impure 961
err - *in opinion* 495
  - *morally* 945
  to - *is human* 495
errand *message* 532
  business 625
  commission 755
errand boy 534
errant 279
erratic *irregular* 139
  changeable 149
  wandering 279
  capricious 608
erratum 495
errhine 349
erroneous 495
error *fallacy* **495**
  vice 945
  guilt 947
  court of - 966
  writ of - 969
erst 66, 122
erstwhile 122
erubescence 434
eructate 297
eructation 297, 349
erudite 490, 500, 539
erudition
  knowledge 490
  learning 539
erumpent 295
eruption *revolution* 146
  violence 173
  egress 295
  ejection 297
  explosion 406
  disease 655
  volcanic - 872
eruptive
  [*see* eruption]
eruptivity 297
erysipelas 655
erythroblast 357
escalade *mounting* 305
  attack 716
escalator 305, 307
escalop 248
escamoter 545
escapade *absurdity* 497
  freak 608
  prank 840
escape *flight* **671**
  liberate 750
  evade 927
  - *notice &c.*
  invisible 447
  inattention 458
  latent 526
  - *the lips a*
  disclosure 529
  speech 582
  - *the memory* 506
  means of - 664, 666
escarp *fortification* 717
escarpment
  stratum 204
  height 206
  oblique 217

eschar 204
escharotic
  caustic 171
  pungent 392
eschatology 67
escheat 145, 974
eschew *avoid*
  dislike 867
esclandre 828, 830
escopet 727
escort *accompany* 88
  safeguard 664
  keeper 753
escritoire 191
esculent 298
escutcheon 550, 551
esophagus 350
esoteric *private* 79
  unintelligible 519
  concealed 528
esotericism 528
espalier 232
especial 79
especially *more* 33
Esperanto 560, 563
espial 441
espionage *looking* 441
  inquiry 461
esplanade *houses* 189
  flat 213 (*plain* 344)
espousals 903
espouse *choose* 609
  marriage 903
  - *a cause aid* 707
  coöperate 709
esprit *shrewdness* **498**
  wit 842
  bel - 844
  - *de corps*
  bias 481
  coöperation **709**
  sociality 892
  (*party* 712)
  - *fort thinker* 500
  irreligious 989
espy 441
esquire *rank* 875
  title 877
essay *experiment* 463
  writing 590
  dissertation 595
  endeavor **675**
essayist
  author 593, 595
esse 1
essence *being* 1
  nature 5
  scent 398
  meaning 516
  (*important part* **642**)
essential
  real 1
  intrinsic 5
  great 31
  required 630
  important 642
  - *nature* 3
essentially
  substantially 3
establish *settle* **150**
  create 161

in - respect 194
on - side 22
everybody 78
every one 78
- his due 922
- in his turn 148
everywhere *space* 180
presence 186
evict 297
evidence **467**
manifestation 525
disclosure 529
ocular - 446
evident *visible* 446
certain 474
manifest 525
evidential 467
evil *harm* **619**
badness 649
demoniac 980
impious 988
- day *adversity* 735
- eye *vision* 441
malevolence 907
disapprobation 932
spell 993
- favored 846
- fortune 735
- genius 980
- hour 135
- one 978
- plight 735
- spirits **980**
- star 649
prepare for - 673
through - report &c.
604a
evildoer **913**, 975
evildoing 945
evil-minded
malevolent 907
vicious 945
evil speaking
malediction 908
censure 932
detraction 934
evince *show* 467
prove 478
disclose 529
evirate 158
eviscerate *eject* 297
extract 301
eviscerated 4
eviternal 112
evoke *cause* 153
call upon 765
excite 824
evolution
numerical 85
production 161
motion 264
circuition 311
turning out **313**
organization 357
training 673
action 680
military -s 722
evolutionary 264, 313
evolve *discover* 480a
evolved from 154
[*and see* evolution]

evolvement 313
evulgate 531
evulsion 301
evviva! 931
ewe *sheep* 366
female 374
ewer 191
ex - *animo* 602
- dono 784
- more 613
- officio *officer* 694
authority 737
duty 924
- parte 467
- post facto 122, 133
- tempore *instant* 113
occasion 134
- voto 768
exacerbate
increase 35
exasperate 173
pervert 659
aggravate 835
exact *similar* 17
copy 21
true 494
literal 516
style 572
require 741
tax 812
insolence 885
claim 924, 926
- meaning 516
- memory 505
- observance 772
- truth 494
exacting *severe* 739
discontented 832
grasping 865
exaction [*see* exact]
undue 925
exactly *literally* 19
just so 488
exactness [*see* exact]
exaggeration
increase 35
expand 194
overestimate 482
magnify **549**
misrepresent 555
exalt *increase* 35
elevate 307
extol 931
(*boast* 884)
- one's horn 873
exalté 504
exalted *high* 206
repute 873
noble 875
magnanimous 942
examination
[*see* examine]
evidence 467
on - 463
undergo - 461
examine
attend to 457
inquire 461
- the books
accounts 811
example *pattern* 22

instance 82
bad - 949
good - 948
make an - of 974
set a good - 944
exanimate *dead* 360
supine 683
exanthema 655
exarch 745
exasperate
exacerbate 173
aggravate 835
enrage 900
excavate 252
excavation 252
execration 442
exceed *surpass* 33
remain 40
transgress 303
intemperance 954
exceedingly (*greatly* 31)
excel *surpass* 33
- in *skillful* 698
excellence
goodness 648
virtue 944
excellency *title* 877
excelsior 305
except *subduct* 38
exclude 55
reject 610
exception
unconformity 83
qualification 469
exemption 777a
disapproval 932
take - *qualify* 469
resent 900
exceptionable *bad* 649
guilty 947
exceptional
unimitated 20
extraneous 57
unconformable 83
in an - degree 31
exceptions 901, 901a
excern 297
excerpt 551, 609
excerpta *parts* 51
compendium 596
selections 609
exception 609
excess *remainder* 40
redundance 641
intemperance 954
excessive *great* 31
exchange
reciprocity 12
interchange 148
saloon 189
transfer 783
barter 794
mart 799
bill of - 771
- blows &c.
retaliation 718
battle 720
Exchequer 802
Baron of - 967
Court of - 966
- bill 800

excise 812
exciseman 965
excision 38
excitability
excitement **825**
irascibility 901
excitant 171
excitation **824**
excitative 171
excite *energy* 171
violence 173
impassion 824
- an impression **375**
- attention 457
- desire 865
- hope 811
- love 897
excited 173
- fancy 515
excitement 824, 825
anger 900
exclaim 411
- against 932
exclamation
typography 550
utterance 580
exclude *sift* 42
leave out 55
reject 610
prohibit 761
banish 893
exclusion **55, 57**
exclusive *simple* 42
omitting 55
special 79
irregular 83
forbidding 761
- of 38
- possession 777
- thought 457
excogitate
ruminate 450
thought 451
imagination 515
excommunicate
banish 893
curse 908
rite 998
(*exclude* 55)
excoriate 226
excrement
excretion 299
dirt 653
excrescence
projection 250
blemish 848
excreta *excretion* 299
dirt 653
excretion 297, **299**
excretory 295, 299, 350
excruciating
physical pain 378
mental pain 830
exculpate *forgive* 918
vindicate 937
acquit 970
excursion 266, 311
excursionist 268
excursive
deviating 279
- *style* 573

535

excursus 595
excuse *plea* 617
  exempt 777a
  forgive 918
  exempt 927a
  vindicate 937
execrable *bad* 649
  offensive 830
execrate *hate* 898
  curse 908
execute *kill* 361
  [*see* execution]
execution *music* 416
  action 680
  conduct 692
  signing 771
  observance 772
  punishment 972
  carry into –
    complete 729
  put in –
    undertaking 676
executioner 975
executive *conduct* 692
  directing 693
  authority 737
  judicature 965
executor 690
  to one and his –s &c.
    property 780
exegesis 522
exegetical 522
exemplar 22
exemplary 944
exemplify *quote* 82
  illustrate 522
exempt *free* 748
  dispensation 927a
  – from *absent* 187
  unpossessed 777a
exemption *exception* 83
  qualification 469
  deliverance 672
  permission 760
  nonpossession **777a**
  nonliability **927a**
exenterate 297
exequatur 755
exequies 363
exercise *operation* 170
  teach 537
  task 625
  use 677
  act 680
  exert 686
  (*prepare* 673)
  – *authority* 737
  – *discretion* 600
  – *power* 157
  – the *intellect* 451
exercises 990
exercitation
  [*see* exercise]
exergue 231
exert *use* 677
  – *authority* 737
  – *oneself* 686
exertion *physical* 171
  effort **686**
exertive 170
exfoliate 226

exhalation
  ejection 297
  excretion 299
  vapor 336
  breathing 349, 353
  odor 398
exhale 349
exhaust *paralyze* 158
  deflate 195
  of an *automobile* 272
  waste 638
  fatigue 688
  complete 729
  drain 789
  squander 818
exhausted
  inexistent 2
exhaustion
  [*see* exhaust]
exhaustive
  complete 52
  – *inquiry* 461
exhaustless
  infinite 105
  enough 639
exhibit
  evidence 467
  show 525
  display 882
exhibition
  [*see* exhibit]
  scholarship 541
exhilarate 836
exhilarating gas 376
exhort *persuade* 615
  advise 695
exhortation
  sermon 998
  [*see* exhort]
exhume *past times* 122
  disinter 363
exigeant 739
exigency *crisis* 8
  requirement 630
  dearth 640
  difficulty 704
  need 865
exigent *exacting* 739
  discontented 832
exiguity 193
exiguous 193
exile *transport* 185
  banish 893
  punish 972
  (*eject* 297)
  voluntary – 893
exility 203
existence *being* 1
  thing 3
  – in *time* 118
  destiny 152
  – in *space* 186
  come into – 151
exit *departure* 293
  egress 295
  disappear 449
  give – to 297
exode 599
exodus 293
exogenous 367
exomorphic 220

exonerate
  disburden 705
  release 760
  forgive 918
  exempt 927a
  vindicate 937
  acquit 970
exophagy 945
exorable 914
exorbitant
  enormous 31
  redundant 641
  dear 814
exorcism 992, 993
exorcist 994
exordium 64, 66
exosmose 302
exosmosis 302
exostosis 250
exoteric *open* 525
  public 531
exotic *alien* 10
  exceptional 83
  plant 367
expand *increase* 35
  swell 194
  – in *breadth* 202
  rarefy 322
  – in *writing* 573
expanse *space* 180
  size 192
  plain 344
expansion **194**
expansive 194
expatiate *range* 266
  – in *writing* &c. 573
  – in *discourse* 584
expatriate *deport* 295
  banish 893
expect
  look forward to 507
  hope 858
  not wonder 871
  (*future* 121)
  reason to – 472
expectance **871**
expectancy 780, 871
expectant 121, 507
expectation **507**
  beyond – 508
  hold out an – 768
expected 507
  as well as can be – 654
expectorate 297
expedience **646**
expedient *plan* 626
  means 632
  useful 646
expedite *early* 132
  quickening 274
  hasten 684
  aid 707
expedition
  [*see* expedite]
  march 266
  activity 682
  war 722
expel *push* 284
  eject 297
  punish 972
  (*displace* 185)

expend *waste* 638
  use 677
  pay 809
  – itself 683
expenditure **809**
  accounts 811
expense *price* 812
  joke at one's – 842
  spare no – 816
expenseless 815
expenses 809
expensive 809, 814
experience
  meet with 151
  knowledge 490
  undergo 821
  learn by – 950
experienced 698
  – *eye* &c. 700
experiences
  narrative 594
experiment *trail* **463**
  endeavor 675
experimental 463
  – *philosophy* 316
expert *skillful* 698
  proficient 700
  – *accountant* 801
expiate 952, 976
expiration
  [*see* expire]
expire *end* 67
  run. its course 109
  breathe 349
  die 360
expired *past* 122
explain *exemplify* 82
  answer 462
  interpret 522
  comment 595
  (*inform* 527)
  (*teach* 537)
  – away 523
  – wrongly 523
explainer 524
explanation
  [*see* explain]
expletive *diffuse* 573
  redundant 641
expletory 641
explication 522
explicit *meaning* 516
  clear 518
  potent 525
explicitness 570
explode *burst* 173
  sound 406
  confute 479
  failure 732
  passion 825
exploded *past* 122
  antiquated 124
  error 495
  blown upon 932
  [*see* explosion]
exploit *action* 680
  courage 861
exploitation 461
exploration 461
explore *investigate* 461
  experiment 463

explorer 268
explosion
　[see explode]
　revolution 146
　violence 173
　loudness 404
　sound 406
　anger 900
explosive 727
　dangerous 665
exponent numerical 84
　interpreter 524
　informant 527
　index 550
export 295
expose denude 226
　confute 479
　disclose 529
　censure 932
　- oneself
　disreputable 874
　- to danger 665
　- to view visible 446
　manifest 525
exposé confutation 479
　disclosure 529
　description 594
exposed bare 226
　- to liable 177
exposition
　[see expose]
　explanation 522
　indication 550
　drama 599
　exhibition 882
expositor
　interpreter 524
　teacher 540
expository
　explaining 522
　informing 527
　disclosed 529
　disserting 595
expostulate
　dissuade 616
　advise 695
　deprecate 766
　reprehend 932
exposure
　[see expose]
　appearance 448
　- to weather 338
expound interpret 522
　teach 537
expounder 524
express carrier 268,
　271
　rapid 274
　squeeze out 301
　mean 516
　declare 525
　inform 527
　language 560
　intentional 620
　transit 627
　haste 684
　- by words 566
　- car 272
　- regret 952
　- sympathy for 915
　- train 272

expressed 566
　well - 578
expression
　[see express]
　musical - 416
　aspect 448
　nomenclature 564
　phrase 566
　mode of - 569
　new fangled - 563
expressive
　meaning 516
　sensibility 822
expressman 271
exprobation
　censure 932
　accusation 938
expropriation 782
expugnable 665
expugnation
　success 731
　(taking 789)
expuition 297
expulsion [see expel]
　exclusion 55
expunge destroy 162
　efface 552
expurgate 652
exquisite savory 394
　excellent 648
　pleasurable 829
　beautiful 845
　fop 854
exquisitely very 31
exradio 420
exsiccate 340
exspuition 297
exsudation 299
exsufflation 993
extant 1
extasy [see ecstasy]
extemporaneous
　[see extempore]
　transient 111
extempore
　instant 113
　early 132
　occasion 134
　offhand 612
　unprepared 674
extemporize 612
extemporizer 612
extend expand 194
　prolong 200
　(increase 35)
　- to 196
extended
　spacious 180
　long 200
　broad 202
extendibility 324
extensibility 324, 325
extensile 324
extension
　[see extend]
　increase 35
　continuance 143
　space 180
　- of time 110
extensive great 31
　wide 180

- knowledge 490
extent degree 26
　space 180
　length 200
extenuate
　decrease 36
　weaken 160
　excuse 937
extenuated 203
extenuating 937
　- circumstances
　qualification 469
　excuse 937
extenuatory 469
exterior 57, 220
exteriority 220
exterminate 162
extermination 301
exterminator 165
extern 220
external 220
　- evidence 467
　- senses 375
externalize 220
exterritorial 220
extinct inexistent 2
　past 122
　old 124
　destroyed 162
　darkness 421
extincteur 385
extinction
　obliteration 552
　- of life 360
extinguish
　destroy 162
　blow out 385
　darken 421
extinguisher 165
　put an - upon
　hinder 706
　defeat 731
extinguishment 2
extirpate 2, 301
extispicious 511
extispicy 511
extol
　overestimate 482
　praise 931
extort extract 301
　compel 744
　despoil 789
extorted dissent 489
extortion dearness 814
　rapacity 819
extortionate severe 739
　dear 814
　rapacious 819
　grasping 865
extortioner 789, 819
extra additional 37
　supernumerary 641
　ab - 220
extract take out 301
　record 551
　quotation 596
　remedy 662
extraction 301
　paternity 166
　- of roots 85
extractor 301

extradition
　deportation 270
　expulsion 297
extrados 220
extrajudicial 964
extralimitary 220
extramundane 220, 317
extramural 220
extraneous extrinsic 6
　not related 10
　foreign 57
　exterior 220
extraneousness 57
extraordinary great 31
　exceptional 83
extraregarding 220
extraterrene 220
extraterrestrial 220
extraterritorial 220
extravagance
　[see extravagant]
extravagant
　inordinate 31
　violent 173
　absurd 497
　foolish 499
　fanciful 515
　exaggerated 549
　excessive 641
　high-priced 814
　prodigal 818
　vulgar 851
　ridiculous 853
extravaganza
　fanciful 515
　misrepresentation
　555
　drama 599
extravagation 303
extravasate egress 295
　ejection 297
extreme
　inordinate 31
　end 67
　- unction 998
extremist 710
extremity end 67
　adversity 735
　tribulation 828
　at the last - 665
　drive matters to an -
　604
extricate take out 301
　deliver 672
　facilitate 705
　liberate 750
extrinsicality 6
extrinsic evidence 467
extrusion eject 297
　excrete 299
extrusive 297
exuberant
　- style 573
　redundant 639
exudation egress 295
　excretion 299
exudative 295
exude 295
exulcerate 659
exult rejoice 838
　boast 884

537

exultant *hopeful* 858
exulting *cheerful* 836
exunge 356
exuviæ 223, 653
  (*remains* 40)
exuvial 226
exuv.ate 226
eye *circle* 247
  opening 260
  organ of sight 441
  appear to one's - 446
  before one's -s
    front 234
    visible 446
    manifest 525
  cast the -s on
    see 441
  cast the -s over
    attend to 457
  catch the - 457
  close the -s
    blind 442

death 360
sleep 683
dry -s 823
- askance 860
- disease 655
- glistening 824
- like Mars 441
- of a needle 260
- of the master 693
-s draw straws 683
-s of a lynx 459
-s open
  attention 457
  care 459
  intention 620
-s opened
  disclosure 529
-s out 442
fix the -s on 457
have an - to
  attention 457
  intention 620

desire 865
have one's -s about
  one 459
in one's - *visible* 446
  expectant 507
in the - of the law
  963
in the -s of
  appearance 448
  belief 484
keep an - upon 459
look with one's own -s
  459
mind's - 515
open the -s to 480a
set one's -s upon 865
shut one's -s to
  inattention 458
  permit 760
to the -s 448
under the -s of 186
up to one's -s 641

with moistened -s 839
with open -s 870
eyeglass 445
eyelashes 256
eyeless 442
eyelet 260
eye opener 508
eyesight 441
eyesore *ugly* 846
  blemish 848
eyeteeth
  have cut one's -
    adolescence 131
    skill 698
    cunning 702
eyewater 662
eyewitness
  spectator 444
  evidence 467
eyot 346
eyre 966
eyrie 189

F

Fabian policy
  delay 133
  inaction 681
  caution 864
fable *error* 495
  metaphor 521
  fiction 546
  description 594
fabric *state* 7
  effect 154
  texture 329
  -s 635
fabricate *compose* 54
  form 56
  make 161
  invent 515
  falsify 544
fabrication *lie* 546
fabulist 594
fabulous
  enormous 31
  imaginary 515
  untrue 546
  exaggerated 549
  descriptive 594
  mythical 979
faburden 413
façade 234
face *exterior* 220
  covering 223
  line 224
  front 234
  aspect 448
  oppose 708
  resist 719
  impudence 885
  change the - of 146
  - about 279
  - of the country 344
  - of the thing
    appearance 448
  - the music 861
  - to face *front* 234
    contraposition 237
538

manifest 525
fly in the - of
  disobey 742
in the - of
  presence 186
  opposite 708
look in the - *see* 441
  proud 878
make -s *distort* 243
  ugly 846
  disrespect 929
not show -
  disreputable 874
  bashful 879
on the - of
  manifest 525
on the - of the earth
  space 180
  world 318
put a good - upon
  sham 545
  calm 826
  cheerful 836
  hope 858
  pride 878
  display 882
  vindicate 937
set one's - against 708
show - *present* 186
  visible 446
to one's - 525
wry - 378
face cloth
  cleanness 652
face guard 717
facet 220
facetiæ 842
facetious 842
facia 234
facile *willing* 602
  irresolute 605
  easy 705
facile princeps 33
facilitate 705

facility *skill* 698
  easy **705**
facing *covering* 223
  lining 224
facinorous 945
façon de parler
  figure of speech 521
  exaggeration 549
facsimile *copy* 21
  duplication 90
  representation 554
fact *existence* 1
  event 151
  certainty 474
  truth 494
  in - 535
faction *company* 72
  party 712
  feud 713
factious 24, 713
factit.ous 545, 546
factor *numerical* 84
  agent 690
  director 694
  consignee 758
  (*merchant* 797)
factory 691
factotum *agent* 690
  manager 694
  employé 758
facts *evidence* 467
  summary of - 594
factual 1
facula 420
faculties 450
  in possession of one's
    - 502
faculty *power* 157
  profession 625
  skill 698
facundity 582
fad *bias* 481
  caprice 608
faddle 683

fade *vanish* 4
  transient 111
  become old 124
  droop 160
  grow dim 422
  lose color 429
  disappear 449
  spoil 659
  - away *cease* 142
  disappear 449
  - from the memory
    506
  - out 129
fadeless 873
fadge 23
fæces [*see* feces]
fag *labor* 686
  fatigue 688
  drudge 690
  - end *remainder* 40
    end 67
fagot *bundle* 72
  fuel 388
  - voter 4
faïence 557
fail *droop* 160, 655
  shortcoming 304
  be confuted 479
  not succeed 732
  not observe 773
  not pay 808
  dereliction 927
failing [*see* fail]
  incomplete 53
  insufficient 640
  vice 945
  guilt 947
  - heart 837
  - luck 735
  - memory 506
  - sight 443
  - strength 160
failure **732**
fain *willing* 602

misrepresent 555
- accounts 811
- one's hope 509
falsity [see false]
falter slow 275
  stammer 583
  hesitate 605
  slip 732
  hopeless 859
  fear 860
fame greatness 31
  memory 505
  renown 873
familiar known 490
  habitual 613
  sociable 892
  affable 894
  spirit 979, 980
  on - terms 888
familiarity
  [see familiar]
familiarize teach 537
  habit 613
Familist 984
familistery 712
family kin 11
  pedigree 69
  class 75
  ancestors 166
  posterity 167
  domestic 221
  party 712
  - circle 892
  - jars 713
  - likeness 17
  - tie 11
  - tree 166
  happy - 714
  in the bosom of one's
   - 221
  in the - way 161
famine 640
  - price 814
famine-stricken 640
famish stingy 819
  fasting 956
famished
  insufficient 640
  hungry 865
famous 873
famously much 31
fan
  strike 276
  blow 349
  cool 385
  refresh 689
  stimulate 824
  enthusiast 840
  - into a flame
  anger 900
  - the embers 505
  - the flame
  violence 173
  heat 384
  aid 707
  excite 824
  flirt a - 855
fanatic dogmatist 474
  madman 504
  imaginative 515
  zealot 682

religious - 988
fanatical
  dogmatic 474
  misjudging 481
  insane 503
  emotional 821
  excitable 825
  heterodox 984
  overrighteous 988
fanaticism
  dogmatism 474
  obstinacy 606
  [see fanatical]
fanciful
  imaginative 515
  capricious 608
  ridiculous 853
  - projector 515
fancy think 451
  idea 453
  believe 484
  suppose 514
  imagine 515
  caprice 608
  choice 609
  pugilism 726
  wit 842
  desire 865
  love 897
  after one's - 850
  - dog 366
  - price 814
  - stocks 800
  indulge one's - 609
  take a - to
  delight in 827
  desire 865
  take one's - please 829
fandango 840
fane 1000
fanfare loudness 404
  celebration 883
fanfaron 887
fanfaronade 884
fangs venom 663
  rule 737
  retention 781
fanlight 260
fanlike 202
fannel 999
fanon 999
fan-shaped 194
fantasia 415
fantastic odd 83
  absurd 497
  imaginative 515
  capricious 608
  bad taste 851
  ridiculous 853
fantasy
  imagination 515
  desire 865
fantoccini
  representation 554
  drama 599
faquir [see fakir]
far
  - and near 180
  - and wide 31, 180, 196
  - as the eye can see 180

- away 196
- be it from
  unwilling 603
  deprecation 766
- between
  disjunction 44
  few 103
  interval 198
- from it unlike 18
  shortcoming 304
  no 536
- from the truth 546
- off 196
farce absurdity 497
  untruth 546
  drama 599
  wit 842
  ridiculous 853
  mere -
  unimportant 643
  useless 645
farceur actor 599
  humorist 844
farcical absurd 497
  ridiculous 853
fardel bundle 72
  hindrance 706
fare state 7
  food 298
  price 812
  bill of - list 86
farewell
  departure 293
  relinquishment 624
  loss 776
  - to greatness 874
far-famed 31, 873
far-fetched 10
far-flung 180
far-gone much 31
  insane 503
  spoiled 654
farina 330
farinaceous 330
farm till 371
  productiveness 636
  property 780
  rent 788
farmer 371
  afternoon - 683
farmhouse 189
faro 621
  - bank 621
farrago 59
farrier 370
farrow
  produce 161
  litter 167
  multitude 102
farse 998
far-sighted vision 441
  foresight 510
farther 196
  [see further]
farthing quarter 97
  worthless 643
  coin 800
  - candle 422
farthingale 225
fasces 747
fascia band 205

circle 247
fasciate 247
fascicle 51, 72
fasciculated 72
fascinate
  influence 615
  excite 824
  please 829
  astonish 870
  love 897
  conjure 992
fascinated pleased 827
fascination [see fas-
  cinate]
  infatuation 825
  desire 870
  (spell 993)
fascinator wrap 384
fascine 72
fash 830
fashion state 7
  form 240
  custom 613
  method 627
  ton 852
  create 976
  after a - middling 32
  after this - 627
  be in the - 488
  follow the - 82
  for - 's sake 852
  man of - 852
  set the - influence 175
  authority 737
fast joined 43
  steadfast 150
  rapid 274
  fashionable 852
  intemperate 954
  not eat 956
  worship 990
  rite 998
  - and loose
  sophistry 477
  falsehood 544
  irresolute 605
  tergiversation 607
  caprice 608
  - asleep 683
  - by 197
  - day 640, 956
  - friend 890
  - man fop 854
  libertine 962
  stick - 704
fasten join 43
  hang 214
  restrain 751
  - a quarrel upon 713
  - on the mind 451
  - upon 789
fastening 45
fast-handed 819
fastidious 868
  censorious 932
fastidiousness 868
fastigium 210
fasting
  worship 990
  penance 952
  abstinence 956

fives *game* 840
fix *dilemma* 7
  join 43
  arrange 60
  establish 150
  place 184
  immovable 265
  solidify 321
  resolve 604
  difficulty 704
  - the eyes upon 441
  - the foundations 673
  - the memory 505
  - the thoughts 457
  - the time 114
  - upon *discover* 480a
    choose 609
fixed *intrinsic* 5
  durable 110
  permanent 141
  stable 150
  quiescent 265
  habitual 613
  - idea 481, 825
  - opinion 484
  - periods 138
  - purpose 620
fixity 141, 265
fixture
  appointment 741
  property 780
fizgig 423
fizz 409
fizzle 304, 353
  - out 304
fizzy 353
flabbergast
  astonish 870
flabbergasted
  humbled 879
flabby 324
flabelliform 194
flabellum 349
flaccid
  weak 160
  soft 324
  empty 640
flaccidity
  [see flaccid]
  feeble style 575
flag *weak* 160
  flat stone 204
  floor 211
  smoothness 255
  slow 275
  plant 367
  sign 550
  path 627
  infirm 655
  inactive 683
  tired 688
  insignia 747
  weary 841
  - of truce 723
  - ship 726
  lower one's - 725
  red - *alarm* 669
  yellow -
    warning 668
    alarm 669
flag bearer 534

flagellation
  penance 952
  asceticism 955
  flogging 972
  rite 998
flagelliform 205
flageolet 417
flagitious 945
flagman 668
flagon 191
flagrant *great* 31
  manifest 525
  notorious 531
  atrocious 945
flagration 384
flagstaff *tall* 206
  signal 550
flagstone 204
flail 276
flake 204
  snow - 383
flam 544
flambé 732
flambeau 423
flamboyant 577
flame *fire* 382
  light 420
  luminary 423
  passion 824, 825
  love 897
  add fuel to the - 173
  catch the -
    emotion 821
  consign to the -s 384
  - colored *red* 434
    orange 439
  - thrower 727
  - up 825
  in -s 382
flamen 996
flaming *violent* 173
  feeling 821
  excited 824
  ostentatious 882
  boasting 884
flamingo 366
flange
  support 215
  rim 231
  projection 250
flank *side* 236
  protect 664
flannel 384
flap *adjunct* 39
  hanging 214
  move to and fro 315
  - the memory 505
flapdoodle 517
flapjack 298
flapper *girl* 129
flapping *loose* 47
flare *violent* 173
  glare 420
  - up *excited* 824, 825
  angry 900
flaring *color* 428
flash *instant* 113
  violent 173
  fire 382
  light 420
  wit 842

eyes - fire 900
  - across the memory 505
  - back 842
  - in the pan
    unsubstantial 4
    impotent 158
    unproductive 169
    failure 732
  - note 800
  - of wit 842
  - on the mind
    thought 451
    disclose 529
    impulse 612
  - tongue 563
  - up *excited* 824
  - upon *unexpected* 508
flashing *ostentatious* 882
flashlight 423, 550
flashy
  gaudy color 428
  - *style* 577
  ornament 847
  tawdry 851
flask 191
flat *inert* 172
  story 191
  low 207
  horizontal 213
  paint 223
  vapid 391
  low tone 408
  musical note 413
  positive 535
  dupe 547
  back-scene 599
  shoal 667
  bungler 701
  insensible 823
  dejected 837
  weary 841
  dull 843
  simple 849
  fall - 732
  - contradiction 536
  - house 189
  - out 304, 732
  - refusal 764
flatboat 273
flatiron 255, 386
flatness 251
flatsided 203
flatten 251
flatter *deceive* 545
  cunning 702
  please 829
  encourage 858
  approbation 931
  adulation 933
  - oneself *probable* 472
  hope 858
  - the palate 394
flatterer **935**
flattering
  - remark 894
  - tale *hope* 858
  - unction to one's soul
    content 831
    vain 880

flattery 933
flattery *falsehood* 544
  adulation **933**
flattish 251
flatulent *gaseous* 334
  air 338
  wind 349
  - *style* 573, 575
flatus *gas* 334
  wind 349
flaunt *flourish* 873
  display 882
flaunting *gaudy* 428
  unreserved 525
  ridiculous 853
flautist 416
flavor 390
flavoring 393
flavous 436
flaw *break* 70
  crack 198
  error 495
  imperfection 651
  blemish 848
  fault 947
  - in an argument 477
flax comb 253
flaxen 436
flay *divest* 226
  punish 972
flea *jumper* 309
  insect 366
  dirt 653
  - in one's ear
    repel 289
    eject 297
    refuse 764
    disrepute 874
    abashed 879
    discourteous 895
    contempt 930
flea-bite 643
flea-bitten 440
fleck 440
flecked 440
flection 279
fled *escaped* 671
fledge 673
flee *avoid* 623
fleece *tegument* 223
  strip 789
  rob 791
  impoverish 804
  surcharge 814
fleer *ridicule* 856
  insult 929
fleet *unsubstantial* 4
  transient 111
  ships 273
  swift 274
  navy 726
Fleet *prison* 752
fleeting 111
flesh *bulk* 192
  animal 364
  mankind 372
  carnal 961
  - and blood
    substance 3
    materiality 316
    animality 364

545

fluidity **333**
fluke *chance* 156, 621
  hook 244
flume 350
flummery
  unmeaning 517
  flattery 933
flump 406
flunk 732
flunker 732
flunky *servant* 746
  servile 886
flunkyism 933
fluorescence 425
flurry *disconcert* 458
  hurry 684
  agitation 821, 824
  excitability 825
flush *flat* 251
  flood 348
  heat 382
  light 420
  color 428
  red 434
  abundant 639
  wash 652
  health 654
  feeling 821
  passion 825
  rejoicing 838
  cards 840
  in liquor 959
  - *of cash* 803
flushed [*see* flush]
  red 434
  excited 824
  cheerful 836
  hopeful 858
  proud 878
  vain 880
  - *with rage* 900
  - *with success* 731
  - *with victory* 884
fluster *distract* 458
  move 821
  excite 824, 825
flustered *tipsy* 959
flute *furrow* 259
  music 417
flutist 416
flutter *variable* 149
  agitation 315, 824
  hurry 684
  emotion 821
  excite 825
  fear 860
fluvial 348
fluviograph 348
fluvio-marine 344
fluviometer 348
fluvioterrestrial 318
flux *conversion* 144
  motion 264
  liquefaction 335
  flow 348
  - *and reflux* 314
  - *of time* 109
fluxion 84
fluxions 85
fly *vanish* 4
  flap 39

time 109
transient 111
  burst 173
  minute 193
  wings 267
  vehicle 272
  swift 274
  depart 293
  break 328
  insect 366
  lose color 429
  shun 623
  - *aloft* 305
  - *at* 716
  - *back* 277
  - *from* 623
  - *in the face of*
    oppose 708
    resist 719
    disobey 742
    insolence 885
  - *in the face of facts*
    misjudge 481
    obstinate 606
  - *kites borrow* 788
    credit 805
    not pay 808
  - *off* 291
  - *open* 260
  - *out violent* 173
    excitable 825
    angry 900
  - *to arms* 722
  - *tracks writing* 590
flyblown 653
flyboat 273
flyer *aviator* 269a
  advertisement 531
flying [*see* fly]
  - *boat* 273
  - *colors success* 731
    display 882
    celebrate 883
  - *column* 726
  - *fish* 83
  - *rumor* 532
Flying Dutchman 269
fly leaf *interjacent* 228
  book 593
flytrap 545
fly wheel 312, 633
foal *young* 129
  horse 271
foam *violent* 173
  boil 315
  spray 353
  excitement 824, 825
  - *with rage* 900
foamy 320
fob 191
  - *off* 545
focal 222
focus **74**
  nucleus 153
  center 222
  bring into a -
    collect 72
    convergence 290
  in - *visible* 446
  out of - *dim* 447
| fodder *food* 298

  for animals 370
  (*provision* 637)
  - *for cannon* 726
foe 891
  -s *to nobleness* 943
fœhn 349
fœticide 361
fœtor 401
fœtus [*see* fetus]
fog *mist* 353
  uncertainty 475
  in a - *hidden* 528
  London - *yellow* 436
fog bell 669
foggy *opaque* 426
fog horn 669
fog signal 668, 669
fogy *fool* 501
  laughingstock **857**
foible 945
foil *contrast* 14
  lamina 204
  baffle 706
  weapon 727
  defeat 731
foiled 732
foin 276
foist *ship* 273
  - *in* 228
  - *upon* 545
Fokker *combatant* 726
folâtre 836
fold *bisect* 91
  inclosure 232
  plait **258**
  prison 752
  congregation 997
  - *in one's arms* 902
  - *one's arms* 681
  - *to the heart* 902
  - *up* 225
foliaceous 204
foliage 367
foliate *page* 85
foliated 204
foliation 204
folio 593
foliole 367
folk 372
folkland 780
folklore 124, 979
follicle *cyst* 191
  hollow 252
follicular 260
follow *be similar* 17
  - *in order* 63
    conform to 82
  - *in time* 117
  - *in motion* 281
    understand 518
    pursue 622
    obey 743
  - *advice* 695
  - *from result from* 154
    be proved by 478
  - *implicitly* 486
  - *the dictates of* 615
  - *the example of* 19
  - *the lead of*
    coöperate 709
  - *suit imitate* 19

  - *the trail* 461
  - *up continue* 143
    circularize 592
    persevere 604a
follower [*see* follow]
  sequel 65
  learn 541
  servant 746
  lover 897
  escort 988
folly *building* 189
  irrationality **499**
  act of -
    mismanagement 699
foment *stimulate* 173
  warm 384
  promote 707
  excite 824
  relieve 834
fonctionnaire 745
fond 897
  - *hope* 858
fondle 902
fondling *favorite* 899
  endearment 902
fondness *desire* 865
font *origin* 153
  type 591
  rite 998
  altar 1000
fontanel 260
food *eatables* **298**
  (*materials* 635)
  (*provision* 637)
  - *for powder* 726
  - *for the mind* 454
  preparation of - 673
fool 501
  deceive 545
  ridicule 856
  disrespect 929
  a -s *bolt* 499
  - *away* 638
  - *away money* 818
  - *away time* 683
  -'s *errand*
    deceived 545
    unskillful 699
  -'s *mate* 732
  -'s *paradise*
    unsubstantial 4
    misjudgment 481
    disappoint 509
    hope 858
    rash 863
  -s *rush in* 499
  - *to the top of one's*
    bent
    excite 824
    anger 900
    flatter 933
  make a - *of oneself*
    bungle 699
    ridiculous 853
    motley - 844
  play the - *folly* 499
    amusement 840
foolhardy 863
fooling *humor* 842
foolish 499
  act -ly 699

547

look - *disrepute* 874
shame 879
foolscap *sign* 550
  paper 590
foot *length* 200
  stand 211
  meter 579
at -'s pace 275
at the - of 207
- by foot 51
- it *journey* 266
  dance 309
- the bill 807
keep on - *continue* 143
  support 215
  prepare 673
not stir a - 681
on - *existing* 1
  during 106
  event 151
  action 170
  journey 266
  topic 454
  business 625
  preparing 673
  active 682
one - in the grave *age* 128
  death 360
put one's - down
  resolved 604
put one's - in
  bungle 699
set - on land 342
trample under - 930
football *subjection* 749
  game 840
footballer 840
footboy 746
footbridge 627
foot candle 466
footfall *motion* 264
  indication 550
  stumble 732
foot guards 726
footing
  circumstances 8
  addition 37
  rank 71
  influence 175
  situation 183
  foundation 211
  support 215
  payment 809
be on a - *state* 7
friendly - 888
get a - *location* 184
pay one's - 807
footlights *stage* 599
foot-loose *liberated* 750
footman 746
footmark 551
footpad 792
foot passenger 268
footpath 627
foot pound 466
footprint 550, 551
foot soldier 726
foot-sore 688
footstep *trace* 551
footstool 215

548

foot-stove 386
foot ton 466
foot-warmer 386
fop **854**
foppery *display* 882
foppish *affected* 855
for *cause* 155
  tendency 176
  reason 476
  motive 615
  intention 620
- all that
  notwithstanding 30
  qualification 469
- a season 106
- a time 111
- aught one knows 156
- better for worse 78
- ever 16, 112
- example 82
- form's sake 82
- good *complete* 52
  diuturnity 110
  permanence 141
- nothing 815
- the most part
  great 31
  general 78
  special 79
- the nonce 118
- the time being 106
have - *price* 812
forage *food* 298
  provision 637
  steal 791
forage cap 225
foramen 260
foraminous 260
forasmuch as
  relating to 9
  cause 155
  reason 476
  motive 615
foray *attack* 716
  robbery 791
forbear *avoid* 623
  spare 678
  lenity 740
  sufferance 826
  pity 914
  abstain 953
forbearance 918
forbid 761
  God - *dissent* 489
  deprecation 766
  censure 932
  prayer 990
forbidden fruit
  seduction 615
  prohibition 761
forbidding
  prohibitive 761
  ugly 846
force *assemblage* 72
  power 157
  strength 159
  agency 170
  energy 171
  violence 173
  cascade 348
  agriculture 371

  significance 516
- of style 574
  urge 615
  cultivate 707
  compulsion 744
  passion 820
armed - 726
brute - 964
- down the throat
  severe 739
  compel 744
- majeure 744
- of argument 476
- of arms 744
- of will 600
- one's way
  progression 282
  passage 302
- open 173
put in - 924
forced *irrelative* 10
- style 579
  unwilling 603
- labor 603
- loan 812
- march 744
forceful 171, 574
forceless 175a
forcemeat 298
forceps *extraction* 301
  grip 781
forces 726
forcible [see force]
- separation 301
forcing house 371
forcing pit 691
ford *passage* 302
  way 627
fore 116, 234
fore-and-aft
  complete 52
  lengthwise 200
- schooner 273
fore-and-after 273
forearm 673
forebears 166
forebode 511, 668
forecast *foresight* 510
  prediction 507, 511
  plan 626
  (*prepare* 673)
foreclose 706
foreday 125
foredoom 152, 601, 611
forefathers
  ancestors 166
  (*veteran* 130)
Forefathers' Day 883
forefend *prohibit* 761
  (*hinder* 706)
  (*guard* 717)
forefinger 379
forefront 66, 234
forego *relinquish* 624
  renounce 757
  surrender 782
foregoing
  preceding 62
  prior 116
foregone *past* 122
- conclusion

  prejudged 481
  predetermined 611
foreground 234
  in the - *manifest* 525
forehead 234
foreign *alien* 10
  extraneous 57
- accent 580
- parts 196
foreigner 57
forejudge *prejudge* 481
  foresight 510
foreknow 510
foreknowledge 510
foreland *height* 206
  projection 250
forelay 706
forelock
  take time by the -
  early 132
  occasion 134
forelooper 64
foreman 694
foremost *superior* 33
  beginning 66
  front 234
  in advance 280
  important 642
  reputed 873
forenoon 125
forensic 968
foreordain *destine* 152
  predestinate 976
foreordination
  necessity 601
fore part 234
forerun *precede* 62
  prior 116
  go before 280
forerunner *precursor* 64
  preparer 673
  (*omen* 512)
foresee *expect* 507
  foreknow 510
foreseen 871
foreshadow 511
foreshorten 201
foreshow 511
foresight **510**
  caution 864
forest 367
- primeval 367
forestall *prior* 116
  early 132
  possession **777**
  (*expect* 507)
  (*prepare* 673)
forester 371
forestry 371
foretaste 510
foretell 511
forethought 510
  vigilance 459
foretoken 511
forever 16, 112
forewarn *predict* 511
  warn 668
foreword 64
forfeit *fail* 773
  lose 776
  penalty 974

- one's good opinion 932

forfeiture
  disfranchisement 925
forfend *hinder* 706
  defend 717
forgather 72
forge *imitate* 19
  produce 161
  furnace 368
  trump up 544
  foundry 691
  - ahead 282
  - fetters 751
forged *false* 546
forger *maker* 690
  thief 792
  counterfeiter 800
forgery *deception* 545
forget 506
  - benefits 917
  - injury 918
  - oneself 945
  hand - cunning 699
forgetful 506
forgive 918
forgiveness 918
forgo [see forego]
forgotten *past* 122
  ingratitude 917
  - by the world 893
fork *bifid* 91
  pointed 244
  - lightning 423
  - out *give* 784
  pay 807
  expenditure 809
forking 291
forlay 706
forlorn *dejected* 837
  hopeless 859
  deserted 893
  - hope *danger* C65
  hopelessness 859
  rashness 863
form *state* 7
  likeness 21
  make up 54
  order 58
  arrange 60
  convert 144
  produce 161
  bench 215
  shape **240**
  organization 357
  educate 537
  pupils 541
  school 542
  manner 627
  beauty 845
  fashion 852
  etiquette 882
  law 963
  create 976
  rite 998
  - a party 712
  - a resolution 604
  - part of 56
formal [see form]
  regular 82
  definitive 535

style 579
  severe 739
  taste 850
  affected 855
  stately 882
  - speech 582
formalism 739, 988
formalist 82, 988
formality [see formal]
  ceremony 852
  affectation 855
  law 963
formalize 963
formation
  composition 54
  production 161
  shape 240
formative *causal* 153
  form 240
  - notion 453
formed [see form]
  attempered 820
former *in order* 62
  prior in time 116
  past 122
formerly 66, 119
formication 380
formidable
  difficult 704
  terrible 860
formless 241
formula *rule* 80
  arithmetic 84
  maxim 496
  precept 697
  law 963
formulary 998
formulate 590
fornication 961
fornicator 962
forsake 624
forsaken 898
forsooth 535
forswear *deny* 536
  lie 544
  tergiversation 607
  refuse 764
  transgress 927
  improbity 940
fort *refuge* 666
  defense 717
fortalice 717
forte 698
forth 282
  come - *egress* 295
  visible 446
  go - *depart* 293
forthcoming
  destiny 152
  preparing 673
forthright 113, 132
forthwith 132, 507
fortification
  defense 717
fortify
  strengthen 159
fortitude
  endurance 826
  courage 861
fortnightly 138
fortress *refuge* 666

defense 717
  prison 752
fortuitous
  adventitious 6
  chance 156
  undesigned 621
  - combination of circumstances 621
  - concourse of atoms 59
fortuity 156
fortunate
  opportune 134
  successful 731
  prosperous 734
Fortunatus's - cap
  wish 865
  spell 993
  - purse 803
fortune *chance* 156
  fate 601
  wealth 803
  be one's - 151
  evil - 735
  -s *narrative* 594
  good - 734
  make one's -
  succeed 731
  wealth 803
  tempt - *hazard* 621
  essay 675
  trick of - 509
  try one's - 675
  wheel of - 601
fortune hunter
  servile 886
  selfish 943
fortuneless 804
fortune teller 513
fortune telling 51
forty 98
  - winks 683
Forty-Niner 463
forum *place* 182
  school 542
  tribunal 966
forward *early* 132
  front 234
  transmit 270
  advance 282
  interjection 286
  willing 602
  improve 658
  active 682
  help 707
  vain 880
  insolent 885
  uncourteous 895
  bend - 234
  come - in sight 446
  offer 763
  display 882
  - in knowledge 490
  move - 282
  press - haste 684
  put - aid 707
  offer 763
  put oneself - 88
  set - 676
foss 348
fosse *inclosure* 232

ditch 259
  defense 717
  (interval 198)
fossil *remains* 40
  ancient 124
  hard 323
  organic 357
  dry bones 362
fossilization 357
fossilize 357
foster *aid* 707
  excite 824
  caress 902
  - a belief 484
fou 959
foul *collide* 276
  bad 649
  dirty 653
  ugly 846
  base 940
  vicious 945
  fall - of *oppose* 708
  quarrel 713
  attack 716
  fight 720
  censure 932
  - fiend 978
  - invective 908
  - language
  malediction 908
  - odor 401
  - play *evil* 619
  cunning 702
  wrong 923
  improbity 940
  run - of *impede* 706
foul-mouthed
  uncourteous 895
foulness [see foul]
foul-spoken
  detraction 934
foumart 401
found *cause* 153
  support 215
foundation
  stability 150
  base 211
  support 215
  lay the -s 673
  sandy - 667
  shake to its -s 315
founded
  - on *base* 211
  evidence 467
  well - 472
founder
  originator 164
  sink 310
  projector 626
  fail 732
  religious -s 986
foundling *trover* 775
  derelict 782
  outcast 893
foundry 691
fount *type* 591
fountain *source* 153
  river 348
  store 636
  - pen 590
fountainhead 210

549

four 95
- in hand 272
- score &c. 98
- times 96
from the - winds 278
on all -s *identity* 13
  agreement 23
  horizontal 213
  easy 705
  prosperous 734
  humble 879
four-flush 545, 884
fourfold 96
Four Hundred 852, 875
Fourierism 910
four-oar 273
four-poster 215
fourragère 877
foursquare 244
fourth 96, 97
  musical 413
Fourth Estate 531
four-wheeler 272
fowl 298, 366
fowling piece 727
fox *animal* 366
  cunning 702
  - chase 622
  - hunting 622
foxhound 366
foxy *brown* 433
fox terrier 366
fox trot *dance* 840
fracas *disorder* 59
  noise 404
  discord 713
  contention 720
fraction *part* 51
  numerical 84
  less than one **100a**
Foxy Quiller 804
fractional 100a
  - *currency* 800
fractious 901
fracture
  disjunction 44
  discontinuity 70
  fissure 198
fragile *weak* 160
  brittle 328
fragment *small* 32
  part 51
  little 193
  extract 596
fragmentary 100a
fragrance **400**
fragrant 400
  - *weed* 392
frail *weak* 160
  brittle 328
  irresolute 605
  imperfect 651
  failing 945
  impure 961
  - *sisterhood* 962
frailty [*see* frail]
frame *intrinsicality* 5
  condition 7
  make 161
  support 215
  border 231

form 240
  substance 316
  structure 329
  contrive 626
  - of *mind*
  inclination 602
  disposition 820
  have -d and glazed 822
frame house 189
framework *support* 215
  structure 329
franchise *freedom* 748
  right 924
  exemption 927a
Franciscan 996
franc-tireur 726
frangible 328
frank *open* 525
  sincere 543
  artless 703
  honorable 939
  - as rain 703
frankalmoigne 748
Frankenstein 913
Frankfurter 298
frankincense 400
frantic *violent* 173
  delirious 503
  excited 824
fraternal *brother* 11
  leagued 712
  concord 714
  friendly 888
  (*benevolent* 906)
  - *order* 711
fraternity *brothers* 11
  party 712
  friends 888
fraternize
  combine 48
  coöperate 709
  agree 714
  sympathize 888
  associate 892
fratricide 361
Frau 374
fraud *falsehood* 544
  deception 545
  impostor 548
  dishonor 940
  pious - 988
fraudulent
  [*see* fraud]
  untruth 546
fraught *full* 52
  pregnant 161
  possessing 777
  (*sufficient* 639)
  - with *danger* 665
fray *rub* 331
  battle 720
  in the thick of the - 722
frayed *worn* 659
freak 608
  - of *nature* 83
freckle 848
freckled 440, 848
fredaine 840
free *detached* 44, 47

unconditional 52
deliver 672
unobstructed 705
liberate 748, 750
expending 809
gratis 815
liberal 816
insolent 885
exempt 927a
impure 961
- and easy
  cheerful 836
  vain 880
  insolent 885
  friendly 888
  sociable 892
- companion 726
- fight 720
- from *simple* 42
- from imperfection 650
- gift 784
- giver 816
- lance 726, 748
- land 748
- liver 954a
- living 954
- love 897, 961
- lunch 815
- play 170, 748
- quarters *cheap* 815
  hospitality 892
- space 180
- stage 748
- trade *commerce* 794
- translation 522
- will 600
make - of 748
make - with
  frank 703
  take 789
  sociable 892
  uncourteous 895
freebooter 792
freeborn 748
free-burning 388
freedman 748
freedom **748**
free-handed 816
freehold 780
freely *willingly* 602
freeman 748
Freemason 711
freemasonry
  unintelligible 519
  secret 528
  sign 550
  coöperation 709
  party 712
free-spoken 703
freestone 635
freethinker 487, 748, 989
free thought 487
free trader 748
freeze 376, 385
- the blood 830
freezing 383
- machine 387
- mixture 387
freight *lade* 184

cargo 190
  transfer 270
  - train 272
  - yard 636
freightage 270, 812
freighter *carrier* 271
  vessel 273
French 188
- beans 298
- gray 432
- horn 417
- leave *avoid* 623
  freedom 748
- philosophy 451
- polish 847
  peddler's - 563
Frenchman 188
frenetic 503
frenzy *madness* 503
  imagination 515
  excitement 825
frequency **136**
frequent
  in number 104
  in time 136
  in space 186
  habitual 613
frequenter 613
fresco *cold* 383
  painting 556
al - *out of doors* 220
  in the air 338
fresh *extra* 37
  new 123
  flood 348
  cold 383
  color 428
  remembered 505
  novice 541
  unaccustomed 614
  good 648
  healthy 654
  pert 885
  tipsy 959
  - breeze 349
  - color 434
  - news 532
freshen 689
freshet 348
freshman 492, 541
freshness [*see* fresh]
fresh-water
  - college 542
  - sailor 701
fret *suffer* 378
  grieve 828
  gall 830
  discontent 832
  sad 837
  ornament 847
  irritate 900
  - and fume 828
fretful 901
fretwork 219
Freud's theory 992a
friable *brittle* 328
  pulverulent 330
friandice 868
friar 996
  Black -s 996
  - Rush 980

-'s balsam 662
-'s lantern 423
friary 1000
fribble *slur over* 460
  trifle 643
  dawdle 683
  fop 854
fricassee 298
frication 331
friction *force* 157
  obstacle 179
  rubbing **331**
on - wheels 705
fried - brains 298
  - eggs 298
  - sole 298
friend *auxiliary* 711
  wellwisher **890**
  sympathizer 914
be -s 888
  - at court 631
next - 759
see one's -s 892
friendless 893
friendliness 888
friendly *amicable* 714
friendship **888**
frieze 210, 329
frigate *man-of-war* 726
  (*ship* 273)
fright *cards* 840
  alarm 860
frighten 860
frightful *dreadful* 830
  ugly 846
frightfully *much* 31
frigid *cold* 383
  - *style* 575
  callous 823
  indifferent 866
frigidarium 387
frigorific 385
frill *border* 231
  convolution 248
frills 577
  - of style 577
fringe *border* 231
  lace 256
  exaggeration 549
  ornament 847
frippery *trifle* 643
  ornament 847
  finery 851
  ridiculous 853
  ostentation 882
  (*dress* 225)
friseur 225
frisk *prance* 266
  leap 309
  absurdity 497
  gay 836
  amusement 840
frisky *brisk* 682
  in spirits 836
frith *chasm* 198
  strait 343
  forest 367
fritiniancy 412
fritter *small* 32
  - away *lessen* 36
  waste 638

(*misuse* 679)
  - away time 683
frivolity [*see* frivolous]
frivolous *unreasonable* 477
  foolish 499
  capricious 608
  trivial 643
friz *curl* 245, 248
  fold 258
frock *dress* 225
  canonicals 999
  - coat 225
frog *leaper* 309
  ornament 847
frolic 840
frolicsome 836
from *motive* 615
  - day to day 106, 138
  - end to end 52
  - that time 117
  - this cause 155
  - time   immemorial 122
  - time to time 136
frond 367
fronder *censure* 932
frondeur *disobey* 742
  detract 936
front *first* 66
  wig 225
  fore part **234**
  resist 719
  insolence 885
  bring to the -
  manifest 525
  come to the -
  surpass 303
  important 642
  repute 873
  - danger 861
  - of the house 599
  - rank 234
  - to front 708
  in - 280
  in the - rank
  important 642
  repute 873
  present a - 719
frontage 234
frontal 220
frontier *vicinity* 199
  limit 233
fronting *opposite* 237
frontispiece 64
frost *cold* 383
  semitransparent 427
  whiten 430
  - over 427
frost-bite 383
frosted 427, 430
  - glass 427
frost *smoke* 353
frostwork 847
froth *bubble* 353
  trifle 643
  dirt 653
  - up *angry* 900
frothy 353
  - *style* 573, 577
  irresolute 605

frounce 258
frow 374
froward 901*a*
frown *lower* 837
  scowl 839
  discourteous 895
  angry 900
  sulky 901*a*
  disapprove 932
  - down *abash* 879
  -s of fortune 735
frowzy 401
frozen 383, 385
fructiferous 168
fructify *produce* 161
  be productive 168
  improve 658
  prosper 734
fructuous 168
frugal *economical* 817
  temperate 953
fruit *result* 154
  produce 161
  profit 775
  forbidden - 615
  - tree 367
  reap the -s
  succeed 731
  reward 973
fruitarian 953
fruit-bearing 168
fruitful 168
fruition 161, 827
fruitless
  unproductive 169
  useless 645
  failure 732
frumenty 298
frump *vulgar* 851
  unmannerly 895
frumpish *sulky* 901*a*
frustrate
  counteract 179
  prevent 706
  (*defeat* 731)
frustrated 732
frustum 51
fry *shoal* 102
  child 129
  heat 384
  small -
  unimportant 643
  commonalty 876
frying pan 386
  out of - into fire
  worse 659
  clumsy 699
  failure 732
  misfortune 735
  aggravation 835
fuchsine 434
fucoid 367
fuddled 959
fudge *unmeaning* 517
  trivial 643
  (*nonsense* 497)
fuel *combustible* **388**
  materials 635
  add - to the flame
  increase 35
  heat 384

  aggravate 835
  anger 900
fugacious 111
fugitive *transient* 111
  emigrant 268
  avoiding 623
  (*escape* 671)
  - writings 596
fugleman *pattern* 22
  director 694
fugue 415
fulciment 215
fulcrum *support* 215
  mechanical   power 633
  (*leverage* 175)
fulfill *complete* 729
  - a duty 926
  - an obligation 772
fulgent 420
fulgurant 420
fulgurite 260
fuliginosity 426
fuliginous *dim* 422
  opaque 426
  black 431
full *circumstantial* 8
  much 31
  complete 52
  large 192
  loud 404
  abundant 639
  cleanse 652
  - age 131
  - bloom *health* 654
  beauty 845
  - colored 428
  - cry *aloud* 404
  bark 412
  pursuit 622
  - dress *dress* 225
  ornament 847
  fashion 852
  show 882
  - drive 274
  - feather
  prepared 673
  - force 159
  - gallop 274
  - heart 820
  - house *cards* 840
  - many 102
  - measure 639
  - of business 682
  - of incident 151
  - of meaning 516
  - of people 186
  - of point 842
  - of whims 608
  - play *facility* 705
  freedom 748
  - scope 748
  - score 415
  - size 192
  - speed 274
  - steam ahead **282**
  - stop *cease* 142
  rest 265
  - swing *strong* 159
  active 682
  successful 731

girl *young* 129
  female 374
  servant 746
girl bachelor 904
girleen 129
girlhood 127
girlish 374
girllike 129
girt 229
girth *bond* 45
  circumference 230
gisarme 727
gist *essence* 5
  meaning 516
  important 642
gite 265
gittern 417
give *yield* 324
  melt 382
  bestow 784
  discount 813
- a horse his head 748
- and take
  compensation 30
  interchange 148
  retaliation 718
  compromise 774
  barter 794
  equity 922
  honor 939
- attention 418
- a turn to 140
- away 782, 784
  in marriage 903
- back 790
- birth to 161
- chase 622
- consent 762
- cry 411
- ear 418
- expression to 566
- forth 531
- in *submit* 725
- in charge
  restrain 751
- in custody 751
- in to *consent* 762
- it one *censure* 932
  punish 972
- light 420
- notice *inform* 527
  warn 668
- one credit for 484
- one the slip 671
- one to understand
  527
- out *emit* 297
  publish 531
  bestow 784
- over *cease* 142
  relinquish 624
  lose hope 859
- place to
  substitute 147
  avoid 623
- play to the imagina-
  tion 515
- points to 27
- quarter 740
- rise to 153
- security 771

- the go-by 623
- the lie 536
- the mind to 457
- the once-over 461
- tongue 531
- up
  not understand 519
  reject 610
  relinquish 624
  submit 725
  resign 757
  surrender 782
  restore 790
  hopeless 859
- up the ghost 360
- way *weak* 160
  brittle 328
  submit 725
  pine 828
  despond 837
  modest 881
given [see give]
  circumstances 8
  supposition 514
  received 785
- over *dying* 360
- time 143
- to 613
- up 360
giver 784
giving 784
gizzard 191
  stick in one's - 900
glabrate 226
glabrous 226, 255
glacial 383
glaciarum 840
glaciate 385
glaciation 383
glacier 383
glacis 217, 717
glad *pleased* 827
  pleasing 829
- rags 225
- tidings 532
  would be - of 865
gladden 834, 836
glade *hollow* 252
  opening 260
  shade 424
gladiate 253
gladiator 726
gladiatorial 713, 720
- combat 361
gladsome 827, 829
glair 352
glaive 727
glamour 992
glance *touch* 379
  look 441
  sign 550
- at *take notice of* 457
  allude to 527
  censure 932
- off *deviate* 279
  diverge 291
- coal 388
  see at a - 498
gland 221
- cell 221
glanders 655

glandule 221
glare *light* 420
  stare 441
  imperfect vision 443
  visible 446
glaring [see glare]
  great 31
  color 428
  visible 446
  manifest 525
glass *vessel* 191
  smooth 255
  brittle 328
  transparent 425
  lens 445
- of fashion 852
- too much 959
live in a - house
  brittle 328
  visible 446
  danger 665
  musical -es 47
see through a - darkly
  491
glass-coach 272
Glassite 984
glassy [see glass]
  shining 420
  colorless 429
glaucous 435
glave 727
glaver 933
glaze 255
  ice 383
gleam *small* 32
  light 420
  visibility 446
glean *choose* 609
  acquire 775
glebe *land* 342
  ecclesiastical 995
  church 1000
glee *music* 415
  satisfaction 827
  merriment 836
gleek 929
glen 252
glib *voluble* 584
  facile 705
glide *lapse* 109
  move 264
  travel 266
  aviation 267
  (*slow* 275)
- into *conversion* 144
glimmer *light* 420
  dim 422
  visible 446
  slight knowledge 490,
  491
glimpse *sight* 441
  knowledge 490
glint 420, 441
glissade 306
glisten 420
glitter *shine* 420
  be visible 446
  illustrious 882
glittering
  ornament 847
  display 882

gloaming 126, **422**
gloar *look* 441
  wonder 870
gloat - on
  look 441
- over *pleasure* 377
  look 441
  delight 827
globated 249
globe *sphere* 249
  world 318
  on the face of the -
  318
globe-trotter 268
globe-trotting 441
globoid 249
globularity 249
globule *small* 32
  spherule 249
glochidiate 253
glomeration 72
gloom *darkness* 421
  dimness 422
  sadness 837
gloomy *dark* 421
  sad 837
- horizon 859
gloriation 884
glorification
  [see glorify]
glorify *honor* 873
  approve 931
  worship 990
glorious
  illustrious 873
  tipsy 959
glory *light* 420
  honor 873
  heaven 981
- be to God 990
- dies not 873
- in 878
  King of - 976
gloss *smooth* 255
  sheen 420
  interpretation 522
  falsehood 546
  plea 617
  beauty 845
- of novelty 123
- over *neglect* 460
  sophistry 477
  falsehood 544
  plead 615
  vindicate 937
glossarist 524
glossary *list* 86
  dictionary 562
  (*interpretation* 522)
glossographer 492
glossologist 492
glossology 560, 562
glossy [see gloss]
glottology 560, 562
glout 901a
glove 225
  take up the - 720
  throw down the - 715
glover 225
glow *warm* 382
  shine 420

goiter 655
Golconda 803
gold *yellow* 436
  orange 439
  money 800
  all is not - 486
  - brick 545, 702
  - mohur 800
  worth its weight in - 648
  write in letters of - 642
golden [*see* gold]
  - age *prosperity* 734
  pleasure 827
  - apple 615
  - calf *wealth* 803
  idolatry 991
  - dream
  imagination 515
  hope 858
  - mean
  moderation 174
  mid-course 628
  - opinions 931
  - opportunity 134
  - rule *precept* 697
  - season of life 127
  - wedding 883
  music's - tongue 415
golf 840
Golgotha *burial* 363
  churchyard 1000
Goliath *strength* 159
  size 192
gomashta 758
gondola 273
gondolier 269
gone [*see* go]
  past 122
  absent 187
  dead 360
  hopeless 859
  - bad 653
  - by *antiquated* 124
  - case 859
  - coon 859
  - out of one's recollection 506
  - where the woodbine twineth 771
goneness 688
goner 859
gonfalon 550
gong 417
goniometer *angle* 244
  measure 466
gonorrhea 655
good *complete* 52
  palatable 394
  assent 488
  benefit **618**
  beneficial 648
  right 922
  virtuous 944
  pious 987
  as - as 197
  be - enough 765
  be so - as 765
  do - 906
  for - *diuturnal* 110

  permanent 141
  - actions 944
  - as one's word
  veracity 543
  observance 772
  probity 939
  - at 698
  - at the price 815
  - auspices 858
  - behavior
  contingent 108a
  duty 926
  virtue 944
  - bye 293
  - chance 472
  - cheer *food* 298
  cheerful 826
  - circumstances 803
  - condition 192
  - day *arrival* 292
  departure 293
  courtesy 894
  - effect *goodness* 648
  beauty 845
  - enough
  not perfect 651
  - fellow 892
  - fight *war* 722
  virtue 944
  - for *useful* 644
  salubrious 656
  - fortune 734
  - Friday 138, 998
  - genius *friend* 890
  benefactor 912
  god 979
  - hand 700
  - humor *concord* 714
  cheerfulness 836
  amuse 840
  courtesy 894
  kindly 906
  - intention 906
  - judgment 498
  - lack! 870
  - living *food* 298
  gluttony 957
  - look out 459
  - looks 845
  - luck 734
  - man *man* 373
  husband 903
  worthy **948**
  - manners 894
  - morrow 292
  - name 873
  - nature 906
  - offices
  mediation 724
  kind 906
  - old time 122
  - omen 858
  - opinion 931
  - pennyworth 815
  - repute 873
  - sense 498
  - society 852
  - taste 850
  - tasting 394
  - temper 894
  - thing 648

  - time *early* 132
  opportune 134
  prosperous 734
  - turn *kindness* 906
  - understanding 714
  - wife *woman* 374
  spouse 903
  - will *willingness* 602
  benevolence 906
  - woman 948
  - word *approval* 931
  vindication 927
  - works 906
  in - case 192
  in - odor *repute* 873
  approbation 931
  in one's - books 888
  in one's - graces 888
  make - *evidence* 467
  provide 637
  restore 660
  complete 729
  substantiate 924
  vindicate 937
  atone for 952
  put a - face upon
  cheerful 836
  proud 878
  so far so - 931
  take in - part
  pleased 827
  courteous 894
  kind 906
  think - 931
  to - purpose 731
  to the - 780
  turn to - account 731
  what's the - 645
good-for-nothing
  impotence 158
  useless 645
good-looking 845
goodly *great* 31
  large 192
  handsome 845
good-natured 906
goodness
  [*see* good] **648**
  virtue 944
  - gracious! 870
  - of heart 906
  have the - *request* 765
goods *effects* 780
  merchandise 798
Goodwin sands 667
goody 374
goose *bird* 298, 366
  hiss 409
  game of - 840
  giddy as a - 458
  - egg *zero* 101
  - flesh 383
  - grass 253
  kill the - with golden eggs
  bungler 699
  prodigal 818
gooseberry *fruit* 298
  yarn 549
  - eyes 441, 443
  old - 978

goosecap 501
goosequill 590
goose-skin 383
Gordian knot
  tangled 59
  difficulty 704
  (*problem* 461)
gore *gusset* 43
  stab 260
  blood 361
gorge *ravine* 198, 350
  fill 641
  satiety 869
  gluttony 957
  (*eat* 298)
  - the hook 602
  raise one's - 900
gorge-de-pigeon 432, 440
gorgeous *color* 428
  beauty 845
  ornament 847
Gorgon 860
gorilla 366, 913
gormandize *eat* 298
  gluttony 957
gorse 367
gory *murderous* 361
  red 434
  unclean 653
gospel *certainty* 474
  doctrine 484
  truth 494
  take for - 484
Gospels 985
gossamer *filament* 205
  light 320
  texture 329
gossamery
  unsubstantial 4
  weak 160
  light 320
gossip *news* 532
  babbler 584
  conversation 588
gossoon 876
Goth *vulgar* 851
  barbarian 876
gothamite 501
Gotham, wise men of 501
gothic *amorphous* 241
Gothicism 851
gouache 556
gouge *concave* 252
  perforator 262
goulash 298
gourmand
  sensualist 954a
  glutton 957
gourmet
  fastidious 868
  sybarite 954a
gout 378
goût 390
govern *direct* 693
  authority 737
governess 540
government
  [*see* govern]
  ruling power 745

divine - 976
- bonds 802
- mark 550
-s authority 737
- school 542
petticoat - 699
governor father 166
  tutor 540
  director 694
  ruler 745
  keeper 753
-'s message 695
gowk 501
gown dress 225
  canonicals 999
gownsman 492
grab take 789
  miser 819
grabble 379
grace style 578
  permission 760
  concession 784
  elegance 845
  polish 850
  title 877
  pity 914
  forgiveness 918
  honor 939
  piety 987
  worship 990
act of - 784
God's - 906
- before meat 916
heart of - 861
in one's good -s 888
say - 990
submit with a good -
    826
with a bad - 603
with a good -
  willing 602
  courteous 894
graceful elegant 578
  beautiful 845
  tasteful 850
graceless inelegant 579
  ugly 846
  vicious 945
  impenitent 951
  irreligious 989
Graces 845
gracile 203
gracious willing 602
  courteous 894
  kind 906
good - 870
gradatim in order 58
  continuous 69
  slow 275
gradation degree 26
  order 58
  continuity 69
gradatory 26
grade degree 26
  classify 60
  term 71
  obliquity 217
  ascent 305
  class 541, (75)
at - 219
- crossing 219

gradient 217, 305
gradual degree 26
  continuous 69
  slow 275
graduate adjust 23
  degree 26
  divide 44
  arrange 60
  series 69
  measure 466
  scholar 492
  teaching 537
  rank 873
- school 542
graduated scale 466
graduation class 541
  rank 873
gradus 86, 562
Græcist 492
graft join 43
  locate 184
  insert 300
- a plant 371
  teach 537
  bribe 784
  improbity 940
grain essence 5
  small 32
  tendency 176
  little 193
  rough 256
  weight 319
  texture 329
  powder 330
  paint 428
  temper 820
  ornament 847
against the -
  rough 256
  unwilling 603
  opposing 708
- elevator 636
- oil 356
-s of allowance
  qualification 469
  doubt 485
in the - 820
like -s of sand
  incoherent 47
grallatory 267
gramercy 916
gram-fed 192
graminivorous 298
grammar
  beginning 66
  teaching 537
  school 542
  language 567
bad - 568
  comparative - 560
- school 537
grammarian 492
grammatical 567
- blunder 568
grammatism 561
gramophone 417, 418,
    551
granary 636
grand august 31
  vigor 574
  important 642

handsome 845
  glorious 873
  ostentatious 882
- climacteric 128
- doings 882
- juror 967
- manner solecism 568
- piano 417
- seignior 745
- style 556, 568
- tour 266
- Turk 745
- vizier 694
grandam 130
grandchildren 167
grandee 875
grandeur greatness 31
  vigor 574
  repute 873
grandfather
  veteran 130
  paternity 166
grandiloquent 577
grandiose 482, 577
grandmother
  maternal 166
  simple 501
teach - 538
grandness [see grand]
grandsire veteran 130
  paternity 166
grandstand 444
grange 189
granger 371
granite 323, 635
granivorous 298
  qualification 469
  unbelief 485
granny 130
granolithic pavement
    255
grant admit 529
  permit 760
  consent 762
  confer 784
God - 990
- a lease 771
- in-aid school 542
granted 488
take for - believe 484
  suppose 514
grantee
  transference 270
  possessor 779
  receiver 785
grantor 784
granular 330
granulate 330
granulated 330
- sugar 386
granule 32
grapefruit 298
grapes 298
sour -
  unattainable 471
  falsehood 544
  excuse 617
grapeshot attack 716
  arms 727
graphic intelligible 518
  painting 556

vigorous 574
  descriptive 594
graphology 590
graphomania 590
graphomaniac 590
graphometer 244
graphophone 417
graphotype 558
grapnel 666
grapple fasten 43
  clutch 789
- with
  - a question 461
  - difficulties 704
  oppose 708
  resist 719
  contention 720
grappling iron
  fastening 45
  safety 666
grasp comprehend 518
  power 737
  retain 781
  seize 789
- at 865
- of intellect 498
in one's - 737
  possess 777
tight - severe 739
grasping miserly 819
  covetous 856
grass fell 213
  vegetation 367
- widow 905
let the - grow under
  one's feet
  neglect 460
  inactive 683
not let the - &c.
  active 682
grasshopper 309, 366
grassland 367
grassplot 371
grassy 367
grate arrangement 60
  rub 330
  physical pain 378
  stove 386
- on the ear
  harsh sound 410
- on the feelings 830
grated barred 219
grateful
  physically pleasant
    377
  agreeable 829
  thankful 916
grater 330
gratification
  animal - 377
  moral - 827
gratify permit 760
  please 829
gratifying 377, 829
grating [see grate]
  lattice 219
  stridor 410
gratis 815
gratitude 916
gratuitous
  inconsequent 477
    559

supposititious 514
voluntary 602
free 748
　payless 815
－ service 602
gratuity *gift* 784
　gratis 815
gratulate 896
gravamen 642
－ of a charge 938
grave *great* 31
　furrow 259
　tomb 363
　somber 428
　engrave 558
　important 642
　composed 826
　distressing 830
　sad 837
　heinous 945
－ in the memory 505
－ note 408
　look － *disapprove* 932
　on this side of the －
　　359
　rise from the － 660
　silent as the － 403
　sink into the － 360
　without a － 363
gravel *earth* 342
　puzzle 704
graven image 991
graveolent 401
graver 558
gravestone 363
gravitate
　descend 306
　weigh 319
－ towards 176
gravity *force* 157
　weight **319**
　vigor 574
　importance 642
　sedateness 826
　seriousness 827
　center of － 222
　specific － *weight* 319
　density 321
gravy 298, 333
gray *color* 428, **432**
　bring － hairs to the
　　grave
　adversity 735
　harass 830
－ friar 996
－ hairs 128
－ mare *ruler* 737
　master 745
　wife 903
graybeard 130
graze *touch* 199
　browze 298
　rub 331
　touch 379
grazier 370
grease *lubricate* 332
　oil 355, 356
　graft 784
－ the palm *tempt* 615
　give 784
　pay 807
560

greasy 355
great *much* 31
　big 192
　glorious 873
　magnanimous 942
　(*important* 642)
－ bear 318
－ circle sailing 628
－ coat 225
－ doings
　importance 642
　bustle 682
－ First Cause 153
－ folks 875
－ gun 626, 875
－ hearted 942
－ is the glory 873
－ Mogul 745
－ moment 824
－ number 102
－ quantity 31
－ Spirit 979
　the － adventure
　death 360
greater 33
－ number 102
－ part 31
　nearly all 50
greatest 33
－ good 618
greatness **31**
greave 225
grebe 310
Greco-Roman
－ philosophy 450
greed *desire* 865
　gluttony 957
greedy
　avaricious 819
Greek *Grecian* 188
　unintelligible 519
　sharper 792
－ Church 984
－ deities 979
－ Kalends 107
－ philosophy 451
　St. Giles's － 563
green *new* 123
　young 127
　lawn 344
　grass 367, 371
　sour 397
　color 435
　credulous 486
　novice 491
　unused 614
　healthy 654
　immature 674
　unskilled 699
　board of － cloth 966
－ goods 545
－ old age 128
－ peas 298
－ sickness 655
greenback 800
green-eyed monster
　920
greengrocer 797
greenhorn *novice* 493
　dupe 547
　bungler 701

greenhouse
　receptacle 191
　horticulture 371
greenish 435
greenness **435**
greenroom 599
greens 298, 367
greensward 344, 367
greenwood 367
greet *weep* 839
　hail 894
greeting *sociality* 892
gregarious 892
grenade 727
grenadier *tall* 206
　soldier 726
grey [*see* gray]
greyhound *swift* 274
　animal 366
griddlecake 298
gridelin 437
gridiron *crossing* 219
　stove 386
grief 828
　come to － 735
grievance *evil* 619
　painful 830
　wrong 923
grieve *mourn* 828
　pain 830
　dejected 837
　complain 839
grievous *bad* 649
　painful 830
grievously *very* 31
griffe 41
griffin *newcomer* 57
　monster 83
griffonage 590
grig *merry* 836
grill 382, 384
　question 461
grille 219
grill room 189
grim *resolute* 604
　painful 830
　doleful 837
　ugly 846
　discourteous 895
　sullen 901a
－ faced 914a
－ visaged war 722
grimace *distortion* 243
　affectation 855
grimacer
　actor 599
　humorist 844
　affected 855
grimalkin 366
grimy 652
grin *laugh* 838
　ridicule 856
－ a ghastly smile
　dejected 837
　ugly 846
－ and abide 725
grind *reduce* 195
　sharpen 253
　pulverizer 330
　pain 378
　teaching 537

learn 539
　oppress 907
- one's teeth 900
- the organ 416
grinder *teacher* 330
grindery warehouse
　799
grinding *severe* 739
　distressing 830
grindstone
　sharpener 253
　pulverizer 330
grip *bag* 191
　paroxysm 315
　indication 550
　sceneshifter 599
　power 737
　retention 781
　clutch 789
- of the hand 894
gripe [*see* grip]
　pain 378
　parsimony 819
gripes 378
grippe 655
gripsack 191
grisaille *gray* 432
　painting 556
grisard 130
grisette *woman* 374
　commonalty 876
　libertine 962
grisly 846
grist *quantity* 25
　materials 635
　provision 637
- to the mill
　useful 644
　acquire 775
gristle *dense* 321
　tough 327
gristmill 330
grit *strength* 159
　powder 330
　resolution 604
　stamina 604a
- in the oil
　hindrance 706
gritty *hard* 323
grizzled *gray* 432
　variegated 440
grizzly 895
groan *cry* 411
　lament 839
groat 800
grocer 637
groceries 637
groceryman 797
grog *drink* 298
　intoxicating 959
groin 244
groom
　tend a horse 370
　servant 746
groomed, well - 847
groomsman 903
groove
　furrow 259
　habit 613
　move in a - 82
　put in a - for 673

H

- to one's name
  name 564
  honor 877
make a - of 677
handmaid
  instrumentality 631
  auxiliary 711
  servant 746
hand mirror 445
hand post 550
handsel *begin* 66
  security 771
  gift 784
  pay 809
handsome *liberal* 816
  beautiful 845
  disinterested 942
- fortune 803
- is that handsome
  does 816
handspike 633
handstaff 727
handwriting
  evidence 467
  signature 550
  autograph 590
- on the wall
  warning 668
handy *near* 197
  useful 644
  ready 673
  dexterous 698
hang *lateness* 133
  pendency 214
  kill 361
  curse 908
  execute 972
- about 133, 197
- back 133, 623
- by a thread 665
- down the head 837
- fire *late* 133
  cease 142
  unproductive 169
  inert 172
  slow 275
  reluctance 603
  inactive 683
  not finish 730
  fail 732
  refuse 764
- in doubt 485
- in suspense 605
- in the balance 133
- it! *regret* 833
  contempt 930
- on *accompany* 88
- on hand 641
- on the sleeve of
  servant 746
  servility 886
  flattery 933
- out *display* 882
- out a light 420
- out a signal 550
- out one's shingle 184
- over *destiny* 152
  height 206
  project 250
  (futurity 121)
- over the head 152

- together *joined* 43
  cohere 46
  concur 178
  coöperate 709
- up *delay* 133
- up the fiddle 67
- upon *effect* 154
  dependency 749
- upon the lips of 418
hangar 191, 273
hang-dog look 901a
hanger *weapon* 727
hanger-on
  accompaniment 88
  servant 746
  servile 886
  pothooks and -s 590
hanging [see hang]
  oblique 217
  elevated 307
  ornament 847
- look 846
hangman *evildoer* 913
  bad man 949
  executioner 975
hangnail 214
hank *tie* 45
hanker 865
Hansard 551
hansom 272
hap 156
haphazard
  chance 156, 621
hapless
  unfortunate 735
  (miserable 828)
  (hopeless 859)
haplography 495
haply *possibly* 470
  (by chance 156)
happen 151
- as it may
  chance 621
- what may
  certain 474
  reckless 863
happening 151
happiness
  [see happy]
  the greatest - of the
  greatest number
  910
happy *fit* 23
  opportune 134
  style 578
  glad 827
  cheerful 836
- as a clam 827
- dispatch 972
- go lucky 674
- hunting grounds 981
- release 360
- returns of the day
  896
- thought 842
- valley 515, 827
  imagination 515
  delight 827
harakiri 361, 972
harangue *teaching* 537
  speech 582

  allocution 586
harass *fatigue* 688
  vex 830
  worry 907
harbinger *precursor* 64
  omen 512
  informant 527
harbor *abode* 189
  haven 292
  refuge 666
  cherish 821
- a design 620
- an idea 451
- revenge 919
  natural - 343
harborless 185, 665
hard *strong* 159
  dense 323
  physically insensible
  376
  sour 397
  difficult 704
  severe 739
  morally insensible
  823
  grievous 830
  impenitent 951
  blow - 349
  go - *difficult* 704
  failure 732
  adversity 735
  pain 828
- a-lee 273
- and fast rule 80
- a-port 273
- at it 682
- at work 682
- bargain 819
- by 197
- case 735
- cash 800
- earned 704
- fought 704
- frost 383
- heart
  malevolent 907
  vicious 945
  impenitent 951
- hit 732
- knocks 720
- life 735
- lines *adversity* 735
  severity 739
- liver 954a
- lot 735
- master 739
- measure 739
- names 932
- necessity 601
- nut to crack 704
- of belief 487
- of hearing 419
- pressed *haste* 684
  difficulty 704
  hindrance 706
- put to it 704
- set 704
- tack 298
- task 703
- time 704
- to believe 485

- to please 868
- up *difficulty* 704
  poor 804
- upon *nearness* 197
  attack 715
  severe 739
  censure 932
- winter 383
- words *obscure* 571
  rude 895
  censure 932
- work 686
hit - 276
look - at 441
not be too - upon 918
strike - *energy* 171
  impulse 276
try - 675
work - 686
harden [see hard]
  strengthen 159
  accustom 613
- the heart
  insensible 823
  enmity 889
  impenitence 951
hardened *impious* 988
- front *insolent* 885
hardening *habit* 613
hard-favored 846
hard-featured 846
hard-fisted 819
hard-handed 739
hard-headed 498, 871
hard-hitting 518
hardihood
  courage 861
  insolence 885
hardiness [see hardy]
hardly *scarcely* 32
  deal - with 739
- any *few* 103
- anything *small* 32
  unimportant 643
- ever 137
hard-mouthed 606
hardness 323
hardpan 211
hard-shell 739
hardship 735
hard-visaged 846
hardware 323
hardy *strong* 159
  healthy 654
  brave 861
hare 274, 298
  hold with the - and
  run with the
  hounds
  fickle 607
  servile 886
harebrained *giddy* 458
  rash 863
  (foolish 499)
  (mad 503)
harelip 243, 848
harem *household* 189
  woman 374
  marriage 903
  impurity 961
haricot 298

hellhound
evildoer 913
bad man 949
hellish *malevolent* 907
vicious 945
hell 982
(*bad* 649)
helm *handle* 633
scepter 747
(*authority* 737)
answer the - 743
at the - 693
obey the - 705
take the - 693
helmet *hat* 225
armor 717
helminth 663
helminthagogue 662
helminthology 368
helmsman 269, 694
helot 746
help *benefit* 618
utility 644
remedy 662
aid 707
servant **746**
give 784
- oneself to 789
it can't be -ed
submission 725
never mind 823
content 831
God - you 914
so - me God 535
helper 711
helpful 746
helpless
incapable 158
exposed 665
helpmate
auxiliary **711**
wife 903
helpmeet 903
helter-skelter
disorder 59
haste 684
hem *edge* 231
fold 258
indeed! 870
- in *inclose* 229
restrain 751
kiss the - of one's garment 886
hemeralopia 443
hemi- 91
hemiplegia 376
hemisphere 181
hemispheric 250
hemlock *herb* 367
unsavoriness 395
bane 663
punishment 972
hemorrhage 299
hemorrhoids 655
hemp
filament 205
poison 663
hen *bird* 366
female 374
source of supply 636
- party 892

- with one chicken
busy 682
henbane 663
hence *arising from* 155
departure 293
deduction 476
henceforth 121
henchman 746
hencoop 370
hen-headed 458
hen-hearted 862
henhussy 374, 501
henna 433, 439
henotheism 984
henpecked
obedient 743
subject 749
hepatize 641
heptad 98, 193
heptagon 98, 244
heptahedral 98
heptamerous 98
heptangular 98
herald *precursor* 64
precede 116
precession 280
predict 511
informant 527
proclaim 531
messenger 534
heraldry 550
herb 367
herbaceous 367
herbage 367
herbal 369
Herbartianism 451
herbivore 298
herbivorous 298
herborize 369
herculean *great* 31
strong 159
exertion 686
difficult 704
Hercules *strength* 159
size 192
support 215
pillars of - *limit* 233
mark 550
herd *assemblage* 72
multitude 102
herder 370
herdsman 746
here *situation* 183
presence 186
arrival 292
come -! 286
- and there
dispersed 73
few 103
place 182, 183
- below 318
- goes 676
- there and everywhere
diversity 16a
space 180
omnipresence 186
- to-day and gone to-morrow 111
hereabouts *site* 183
near 197

hereafter 121
destiny 152
hereby 631
hereditament 780
hereditary
intrinsic 5
derivative 154, 167
property 780
heredity 154, 167
herein 221
heresy *error* 495
religious 984
heretic 489, 984
heretical 495, 984
heretofore 122
hereupon 106
herewith
accompanying 88
means 632
heritage *futurity* 121
possession 777
property 780
heritor 779
hermaphrodite 83
- brig 273
hermeneutics 522
Hermes 582
hermetically 261
hermit *recluse* 893
ascetic 955
hermitage *house* 189
cell 191
seclusion 893
hermitize 893
hernia 655
hero *brave* 861
glory 873
good man 948
- worship
approbation 931
idolatry 991
Herod, out-Herod-549
heroic [*see* hero]
magnanimous 942
mock - 853
heroics 884
heroism 861
heron 366
herpes 655
herpetology 368
herring *fish* 298
pungent 392
- pond 341
trail of a red - 615, 706
herring-gutted 203
hesitate *uncertain* 475
skeptical 485
stammer 583
reluctant 603
irresolute 605
fearful 860
Hesperian 236
Hesperides
garden of the - 981
Hesperus 423
Hessian 726, 819
Hessian boot 225
hest 741
heterarchy 737

heteroclite 83, 139
heterodox 487, 489
heterodoxy **984**
heterogamy 161, 357
heterogeneity 15, 16a
heterogeneous
unrelated 10
different 15
mixed 41
multiform 81
exceptional 83
heterogenesis 161
heteromorphism 16a
heteronomy 737
heteropathy 662
heterotopy 185
hetman 745
hew *cut* 44
shorten 201
fashion 240
- down 213, 308
hewers of wood
workers 690
commonalty 876
hexad 98, 193
hexaglot 560
hexagon 98, 244
hexahedral 98
hexahedron 98, 244
hexameter 98, 597
hexangular 98
hexastyle 98
heyday
exultation 836, 838
festivity 840
wonder 870
- of the blood 820
- of youth 127
hiation 260
hiatus *interval* 198
(*discontinuity* 70)
hibernal 383
hibernate 683
Hibernian 188
Hibernicism
absurdity 497
neology 563
hiccup 349
hickory shirt 225
hid
- under a bushel 460
hidalgo 875
hidden 528
- meaning 526
hide *skin* 223
conceal 528
- and seek
deception 545
avoid 623
game 840
- diminished head
inferior 34
decrease 36
humility 879
- one's face
modesty 881
hidebound |
strait-laced 751
stingy 819
bigoted 988
hideous 846

hang 214
  jerk 315
  - *a horse* 370
  difficulty 704
  hindrance 706
hither *direction* 278
  arrival 292
  come - 286
hitherto 122
hive *multitude* 102
  location 184
  abode 189
  apiary 370
  workshop 691
H. M. S. 726
hoar *aged* 128
  white 430
  - frost 383
hoard 636
  -s after -s 819
hoarse *husky* 405
  harsh 410
  voiceless 581
  talk oneself - 584
hoary [*see* hoar]
  old 124
hoax 545
hob *support* 215
  stove 386
  - and nob
  celebration 883
  courtesy 894
hobble *limp* 275
  awkward 699
  difficulty 704
  fail 732
  shackle 751
hobbledehoy 129
hobby *crotchet* 481
  pursuit 622
  avocation 625
  desire 865
hobbyhorse 272
hobgoblin *fearful* 860
  demon 980
hobnail 876
hobo *tramp* 268
  neglect 460
  idler 683
  vagabond 876
hoboism 266, 683
Hobson's choice
  necessity 601
  no choice 609a
  compulsion 744
hock *maim* 645
hockey 840
hocus 545
hocus-pocus
  interchange 148
  unmeaning 517
  cheat 545
  conjuration 992
  spell 993
hod *receptacle* 191
  vehicle 272
hoddy-doddy 501
hodgepodge 41, 59
hoe *vehicle* 272
  agriculture 371
hoecake 298

hog *animal* 366
  selfishness 943
  sensualist 954a
  glutton 957
  go the whole - 604
  greedy as a - 865
hog's back 206
hog wallow 343
hog wash 653
hoist 307
  - a flag 550
  - on one's own petard
  retaliation 718
  failure 732
  - the black flag 722
hoity-toity *defiance* 715
  wonder 870
hold *cohere* 46
  contain 54
  remain 141
  cease 142
  go on 143
  happen 151
  receptacle 191
  cellar 207
  base 211
  support 215
  halt 265
  believe 484
  be passive 681
  defend 717
  power 737
  restrain 751
  prohibit 761
  possess 777
  retain 781
  enough! 869
  gain a - upon 737
  get - of 789
  have a firm - 781
  have a - upon 175
  - a council 695
  - a high opinion of 928
  - a lease 771
  - aloof *absence* 187
  distrust 487
  avoid 623
  - a meeting 72
  - an argument 476
  - a situation 625
  - authority 737
  - back *avoid* 623
  store 636
  restrain 751
  retain 781
  miserly 819
  - both one's sides 838
  - converse 588
  - fast *restrain* 751
  retain 781
  - forth *teach* 537
  speak 582
  - good
  demonstration 478
  truth 494
  - hard 265
  - in hand 737
  - in remembrance 505
  - in solution 335
  - off 623
  - office 693

- on *continue* 141, 143
  persevere 604a
  - one's breath
  wonder 870
  - oneself in readiness
  673
  - oneself up 307
  - one's ground 141
  - one's hand
  cease 142
  relinquish 624
  - one's own
  preserve 670
  defend 717
  resist 719
  - one's tongue 585
  - out [*see below*]
  - the scales 466
  - to 602
  - together
  junction 43
  coöperate 709
  - up [*see below*]
  - up one's head 861
  quit one's - 782
  take - 175
holdback 706
holder 779
holdfast 45
holding *tenancy* 777
  property 780
  - company 712
hold out *continue* 106
  affirm 535
  persevere 604a
  resist 719
  offer 763
  brave 861
  - expectation
  predict 511
  promise 768
  - temptation 865
hold up *continue* 143
  support 215
  not rain 340
  aid 707
  display 882
  extol 931
  - one's hand *sign* 550
  threat 600
  - the mirror 525
  - to execration
  curse 908
  censure 932
  - to scorn 930
  - to shame 874
  - to view 525
hold-up 791, 792
hole *state* 7
  place 182
  hovel 189
  receptacle 191
  cave 251
  opening 260
  ambush 530
  - and corner
  place 182
  peer into - 461
  hiding 528, 530
  - in one's coat 651
  - to creep out of

plea 617
  escape 671
  facility 705
Holi 138
holiday *leisure* 685
  repose 687
  amusement 840
  celebration 883
  - task *easy* 705
holiness *God* 976
  piety 987
holloa 411
  - before one is out of
  the wood 884
hollow
  unsubstantial 4
  completely 52
  incomplete 53
  depth 208
  concavity 252
  - sound 408
  gruff 410
  specious 477
  voiceless 581
  beat - 731
  - commendation 894
  - truce 723
hollow-hearted 544
hollowness
  [*see* hollow]
holm 345, 346
holocaust *kill* 361
  sacrifice 991
  (*destruction* 162)
holograph 590
holt 367
holus-bolus 684
Holy *of God* 976
  pious 987
  - breathing 990
  - day 998
  - Ghost 976
  - Grail 998
  - men of old 985
  - orders 995
  - place 1000
  - Scriptures 985
  - Spirit 976
  - Thursday 998
  - water 998
  - week 998
  keep - 987
  temple of the - **Ghost**
  983a
homage
  submission 725
  fealty 743
  reverence 928
  approbation 931
  worship 990
homaloid 251
home *focus* 74
  habitation 189
  near 197
  interior 221
  arrival 292
  country 342
  hospital 662
  refuge 666
  at - *party* 72
  present 186

horse *hang on* 214
  stand 215
  carrier 271
  animal 366
  male 373
  translation 539
  cavalry 726
- and foot 726
- artillery 726
- box 272
- car 272
- cloth 225
- coper 548
- doctor 370
- guards 726
- laugh 838
- leech 370
- litter 272
- marine 268, 701
- racing *pastime* 840
  contention 720
- sense 498
- soldier 726
- stealing 791
- track 627
- trainer 370
like a - in a mill 613
put the -s to 673
put up one's -s at 184
put up one's -s to-
  gether
  concord 714
  friendship 888
ride the high - 885
take - 266
war - 726
work like a - 686
horseback 266
horseman 268
horsemanship
  riding 266
  skill 698
horseplay 856
horse power 466
horse-radish 298, 393
horseshoe 245
- crab 368
horseshoer 370
horsewhip 972
horsewoman 268
hortation
  persuasion 615
  advice 695
hortatory 537, 615
horticulture 371
horticulturist 369
hosanna *praise* 931
  worship 990
hose *stockings* 225
  pipe 350
  cleanness 652
hosier 225
hospice *house* 189
  hospital 662
hospitable
  liberal 816
  social 892
hospital 662
in - 655
hospitality
  [*see* hospitable]
572

Hospitaller 996
hospodar 745
host *collection* 72
  multitude 102
  army 726
  friend 890
  rite 998
- in himself 175
- of heaven 977
reckon without one's -
  error 495
  unskillful 699
  rash 863
hostage 771
hostel 189
hostelry 189
hostile *disagreeing* 24
  opposed 708
  enmity 889
- meeting 720
in - array 708
hostilities 722
hostility 889
hostler 746
hot *violent* 173
  warm 382
  pungent 392
  red 434
  orange 439
  excited 824
  irascible 901
blow - and cold
  inconsistent 477
  falsehood 544
  tergiversation 607
  caprice 608
- air *bombast* 884
- bath 382, 386
- blood *rash* 863
  angry 900
  irascible 901
- dog *sausage* 298
- springs 382, 384
- water *difficulty* 704
  quarrel 713
  painful 830
- wave 382
in - haste 684
in - pursuit 622
make - 384
hotbed *cause* 153
  center 222
  workshop 691
hot-brained 863
hotchpot *mixture* 41
  confusion 59
  participation 778
hotel 189
- keeper 188
- runner 767
Hotel des Invalides
  662
hot-headed *hasty* 684
  excitable 825
hothouse
  conservatory 371
  furnace 386
  store 636
  workshop 691
hotpress 255
Hotspur 863

Hottentot 431, 876
hough 659
hound *follow* 63
  animal 366
  hunt 622
  persecute 907
  wretch 949
hold with the hare
  but run with the
  -s 607
- on 615
hour *period* 108
  point of time 113
  present time 118
- after hour 110
improve the shining -
  682
one's - is come
  occasion 134
  death 360
the long -s 106
hourglass
  chronometer 114
  contraction 195
  narrow 203
Houri 845
hourly *time* 106
  frequent 136
  periodical 138
house *lineage* 69
  assembly 72
  family 166
  locate 184
  abode 189
  theater 599
  make safe 664
  council 696
  firm 712
  merchant 797
bring the - about
  one's ears 699
eat out of - and home
  prodigal 818
  gluttony 957
- built on sand 160
- divided against it-
  self 713
- of cards 160
- of Commons 966
- of correction
  prison 752
  punishment 975
- of death 363
- of detention 752
- of God 1000
- of Lords 875, 966
- of peers 875
- of prayer 1000
- of Representatives
  696
keep - 184
set one's - in order 952
turn - out of window
  713
turn out of - and
  home 297
housebreaker 792
housebreaking 791
house dog 366
household
  inhabitants 188

abode 189
- gods 189
- stuff 635
- troops 726
- words *known* 490
  language 560
  plain 576, 849
householder 188
housekeeper 637, 694
housekeeping 692
houseless 185
housemaid 746
house raising 892
houseroom 180
housetop *summit* 210
  proclaim from - 531
housewarming 892
housewife 682
  bag 191
housewifery
  conduct 692
  economy 817
housing *lodging* 189
  covering 223
  horse-cloth 225
hovel 189
hover *impend* 152
  high 206
  rove 266
  soar 267
  ascend 305
  air 338
  irresolute 605
- about *move* 264
- over *near* 197
how *way* 627
  means 632
- comes it?
  attribution 155
  inquiry 461
- now 870
howbeit 30
however *degree* 26
  notwithstanding 30
  except 83
howitzer 727
howker 273
howl *blow* 349
  protracted sound 407
  human cry 411
  animal cry 412
  lamentation 839
howling 412
- wilderness
  unproductive 169
  secluded 893
hoy 273
hoyden *girl* 129
  rude 851
hub *centrality* 222
  circularity 247
  convexity 250
hubbub *stir* 315
  noise 404
  outcry 411
  discord 713
hubby 250
huckleberry 298
huckster *provision* 637
  barter 794
  merchant 797

huddle *disorder* 59
  derange 61
  collect 72
  hug 197
  - on 225
Hudibrastic 856
  - verse 597
hue 428
  - and cry *cry* 411
  proclaim 531
  pursuit 622
  alarm 669
  - of dungeons 982
  raise a - and cry 932
hueless 429
huff *insolence* 885
  anger 900
huffy 901
hug *cohere* 46
  border on 197
  retain 781
  courtesy 894
  love 897
  endearment 902
  - a belief 606
  - a sin 945
  - oneself *pleasure* 827
  content 831
  rejoicing 338
  pride 878
  - the shore
  navigation 267
  approach 286
huge *in degree* 31
  in size 192
hugger-mugger 59, 528
Huguenot 984
huissier 965
huke 225
hukm 741, 760
hulk *body* 50
  ship 273
hulking 193
hulks 752
hulky *big* 192
  unwieldy 647
  ugly 846
hull 50
hullabaloo *noise* 404
  shout 411
hum *faint sound* 405
  continued sound 407
  animal sound 412
  sing 416
  deceive 545, 546
  busy- of men 682
  - and haw
  stammer 583
  irresolute 605
human 372
  - face divine 234
  - race 372
  - sacrifices 991
  - system 364
humane
  benevolent 906
  philanthropic 910
  merciful 914
  - studies 537
  - teaching 537
humanism 451, 537

humanistic 537
humanitarian 910
humanitarianism 372
humanities
  letters 560
humanize 894
humation 363
humble *inferior* 34
  meek 879
  modest 881
  pious 987
  eat - pie 725
  - oneself *meek* 879
  penitent 950
  worship 990
  - r classes 876
  your - servant
  dissent 489
  refusal 764
humble-minded 879
humbug *falsehood* 544
  deception 545
  deceiver 548
  trifle 643
humdinger 682
humdrum *weary* 841
  dull 843
  (prose 598)
humectate *water* 337
  moisture 339
humid 339
humiliate *humble* 879
  disrespect 929
humiliation
  adversity 735
  disrepute 874
  sense of shame 879
  worship 990
  self - 950
humility *meekness* 879
  piety 987
hummer 682
humming top 417
hummock *hill* 206
  hump 250
humor *essence* 5
  tendency 176
  liquid 333
  disposition 602
  caprice 608
  aid 707
  indulge 760
  affections 820
  please 829
  wit 842
  flatter 933
  (fun 840)
  in the - 602
  out of - 901a
  peccant - *unclean* 653
  disease 655
humorist 844
humorous 842
humorsome
  capricious 608
  sulky 901a
hump 250
humpbacked 243
Hun *destroyer* 165
hunch 250
hunchbacked 243

hundi 800
hundred *number* 98
  many 102
  region 181
hundredth 99
hundredweight 319
hunger 865
hungry 865
hunks 819
hunt *follow* 63
  inquiry 461
  pursuit 622
  - after 622
  - down 907
  - in couples 17, 709
  - out *inquiry* 461
  discover 480a
  - the slipper 840
hunter *horse* 271
  killer 361
  pursuer 622
  sportsman 840
  place - 767
hunting *killing* 361
  sporting 622
hunting ground 840
huntsman 268, 361
hurdle 272
hurdy-gurdy 417
hurl 284
  - against 716
  - defiance 715
hurly-burly 315
hurrah 411, 836, 838
hurricane *tempest* 349
  (violence 173)
  - deck 210
hurry *haste* 684
  excite 825
  - forward 684
  - off with 789
  - of spirits 821
  - on 615
  - skurry 825
hurst 367
hurt *physical pain* 378
  evil 619
  maltreat 649
  injure 659
  - the feelings
  pain 830
  anger 900
  more frightened than
    - 860
hurtful 649
hurtle 276
hurtless 648
husband *store* 636
  director 694
  spouse 903
husbandman 371
husbandry
  agriculture 371
  conduct 692
  economy 817
hush *moderate* 174
  stop 265
  silence 403
  taciturn 585
  - up *conceal* 528
  pacify 723

hush money
  compensation 30
  reward 973
husk *covering* 223
  strip 226
husking bee 892
husky *strong* 159
  dry 340
  dog 366
  faint sound 405
  hoarse 581
hussar 726
hussif 191
hussy *girl* 129
  blusterer 887
  libertine 962
hustings *school* 542
  arena 728
  tribunal 966
hustle *perturb* 61
  push 276
  agitate 315
  activity 682
  hinder 706
hustler 682
hustling 682
hut 189
hutch 189
huzur 373
huzza 411, 838
hyacinth *jewel* 847
hyacinthine 437
Hyades 318
hyaline *ocean* 318, 341
  transparency 425
hyalite 425
hyaloid 425
hybernation 683
hybrid *mixture* 41
  exception 83
hydra *monster* 83, 366
  productive 168
hydra-headed 163
hydrant 348
hydrargyrum 274
hydrate of amyl 356
hydraulics 348
hydrocephalus 194
hydrocyanic acid 663
hydrocyanide 663
hydrocycle 272
hydrodynamics
  fluid 333
  stream 348
hydrodynamometer
  348
hydrography 341
hydrokinetics 333, 348
hydrology 333
hydrolysis 49
hydromancy 511, 992
hydromechanics 348
hydromel 396
hydrometer 321, 333,
  348
hydrometrograph 348
hydrometry 333
hydropathy 662
hydrophobia 867
hydrophone 333
hydrophthalmus 194

I

ileum 221, 350
ilk 13
ill *evil* 619
  badness 649
  sick 655
  as - luck would have
    it 135
  bird of - *omen* 668
  do an - *office to* 907
  go on - *fail* 732
    adversity 735
  house of - *fame* 961
  - at ease *pain* 828
    dejection 837
  - betide 908
  - blood *hate* 898
    malevolence 907
  - humor *anger* 900
    sullenness 901a
  - luck 735
  - name 874
  - off *insufficient* 640
    adversity 735
    poor 804
  - repute 874
  -s that flesh is heir to
    evil 619
    disease 655
  - temper 900
  - turn *evil* 619
    affront 900
    spiteful 907
  - usage 907
  - will 907, 921
  - wind *bad* 649
    hindrance 706
    adversity 735
  look - 846
  take - *discontent* 832
    anger 900
ill-adapted 24
ill-advised *foolish* 499
  inexpedient 647
  unskillful 699
ill-affected 901a
illapse *conversion* 144
  ingress 294
illaqueate 545
ill-assorted 24
illation 480
illaudible 947
ill-behaved 895
ill-boding 512
ill-bred *vulgar* 851
  rude 895
ill-conditioned *bad* 649
  difficult 704
  discourteous 895
  malevolent 907
  vicious 945
ill-conducted
  unskillful 699
ill-contrived
  inexpedient 647
  bad 649
  unskillful 699
  malevolent 907
ill-defined 447
ill-devised *foolish* 499
  unskillful 699
ill-digested 674

ill-disposed *bad* 649
  sullen 901a
  spiteful 907
illegality **964**
illegible 519
  render - 552
  - hand 590
illegitimate
  deceitful 545
  undue 925
  illegal 964
ill-fated 135, 735
ill-favored 395
ill-furnished 640
illiberal
  narrow-minded 481
  stingy 819
  uncourteous 895
  selfish 943
  bigoted 988
illicit *undue* 925
  illegal 964
ill-imagined
  foolish 499
  unskillful 699
illimited 105
ill-intentioned 907
illiteracy 491
illiterate 491, 493
ill-judged *foolish* 499
  unskillful 699
ill-judging 481
ill-made *distorted* 243
  ugly 846
ill-mannered
  vulgar 851
  rude 895
ill-marked *invisible* 447
ill-natured 907
illogical
  sophistical 477
  erroneous 495
ill-omened
  untoward 135
  danger 605
  adverse 735
  hopeless 859
ill-proportioned 243
ill-provided 640
ill-qualified 699
ill-requited 917
ill-rewarded 917
ill-shaped *ugly* 846
ill-spent 646
ill-starred 135, 735
ill-tempered 901
ill-timed 135
illtreat *bad* 649
  severe 739
  malevolent 907
illuminant 388, 420
illuminate
  enlighten 420
  color 428
  comment 595
  ornament 847
illuminati 492
illumination
  [see illuminate]
  book illustration 558
  celebration 883

illumine *lighten* 420
  excite 824
ill-use 907
ill-used 828
illusion
  fallacy of vision 443
  error 495
illusive
  unsubstantial 4
  sophistical 477
  erroneous 495
  deceitful 545, 546
illusory [see illusive]
illustrate
  exemplify 82
  interpret 522
  represent 554
  engravings 558
  ornament 847
illustrious 873
image *likeness* 17
  appearance 448
  idea 453
  metaphor 521
  representation 554
  graven - *idol* 991
  - in the mind 453
imagery *fancy* 515
  metaphor 521
  representation 554
imaginable 470
imaginary
  non-existing 2
  fancied 515
  - *quantity* 84
imagination **515**
imaginative 515
imaum *prince* 745
  priest 996
imbecile *incapable* 158
  ignorant 493
  foolish 499
  fool 501
imbecility
  impotence 158
  folly **499**
  unmeaningness 517
imbed *locate* 184
  base 215
  insert 300
imbedded 229
imbibe 296
  - learning 539
imbibitory 296
imbrangle 61
imbricate 223
imbrication 223
imbroglio *disorder* 59
  difficulty 704
  discord 713
imbrue *impregnate* 300
  moisten 339
  - one's hands in blood
    killing 361
    war 722
  - the soul 824
imbue *mix* 41
  impregnate 300
  moisten 339
  tinge 428
  teach 537

imbued
  combination 48
  affections 820
  - with *belief* 484
  habit 613
  feeling 821
imburse 803
imitate *copy* 19
  appropriate 788
imitation *copying* **19**
  copy 21
  representation 554
  misrepresentation
    555
imitative *imitating* 19
  music 415
imitator 19
immaculate
  perfect 650, 847
  clean 652
  innocent 946
  (*excellent* 648)
immanence 5
immanent 5, 132
Immanity 907
immanuel 976
immaterial
  unsubstantial 4
immaterialist 317
immateriality
  spiritual **317**
  trifling 643
immaterialize 317
immature *new* 123
  unprepared 674
immeasurable
  great 31
  infinite 105
immediate
  continuous 69
immediately
  instantly 113
  early 132
immedicable 859
immelodious 414
immemorial 124
  from time - 122
  - usage 613
immense *great* 31
  infinite 105
  - *size* 192
immensity
  infinity 105
  size 192
immerge *introduce* 300
  dip 337
immerse *insert* 300
  submerge 310
  dip 337
immersed in 229
immersion
  [see immerse]
  baptism 998
immesh 545
immethodical 59, 139
immigrant *alien* 57
  traveler 268
  entering 294
immigration
  migration 266
  entrance 294

incage 751
incalculable *much* 31
  infinite 105
incalescence 382
incandescence 382
incantation
  invocation 765
  spell 993
incantatory 992
incapable
  impotent 158
  (*weak* 160)
incapacious 203
incapacitate 158
incapacity
  impotence 158
  ignorance 491
  stupidity 499
  (*weakness* 160)
incarcerate
  imprison 751
  (*surround* 229)
incarnadine 434
incarnate
  intrinsic 5
  materiality 316
  to incorporate 364
  vicious 945
  devil - *bad man* 949
  Satan 978
incarnation 316, 976
incase *cover* 223
  surround 229
incautious *rash* 863
  (*neglect* 460)
incendiary *destroy* 162
  burn 384
  influence 615
  pitfall 667
  malevolent 907
  evildoer 913
  bad man 949
incensation 400
incense *fuel* 388
  fragrant 400
  hate 898
  anger 900
  flatter 933
  worship 990
  rite 998
  - *breathing* 400
  - *burner* 400
incension *burning* 384
incensorium 400
incentive 615
incept 66, 537
inception 66
inceptive *beginning* 66
  causal 153
  generative 168
inceptor 541
incertitude 475
incessant *repeated* 104
  ceaseless 112
  frequent 136
incest 961
inch *small* 32
  length 200
  move slowly 275
  measure 466
by - es 275

give an - and take an
  ell 789
  - *by inch*
  by degrees 26
  in parts 51
  slowly 275
  not see an - beyond
  one's nose 699
  not yield an - 606
  to an - 494
inchoation
  beginning 66
  preparation 673
incide 44
incidence 278
incident 151
  full of - 151
incidental *extrinsic* 6
  circumstance 8
  irrelative 10
  occurring 151
  casual 156
  liable 177
  chance 621
  - *music* 415
incinerate 384
incinerator 384
incipience 66
incircumspect 460
incise *cut* 44
  furrow 259
incision *cut* 44
  furrow 259
incisive *energy* 171
  vigor 574
  feeling 821
incite *exasperate* 173
  urge 615
incitement [*see* incite]
incivility 895
incivism 911
inclasp 229
inclement *violent* 173
  cold 383
  severe 739
  pitiless 914a
inclination [*see* incline]
  descent 306
  will 600
  affection 820
  desire 865
  love 897
incline *tendency* 179
  slope 217
  direction 278
  willing 602
  induce 615
  - an ear to 457
inclined *oblique* 217
  intended 620
  - *plane* 633
inclose
  place within 221
  surround 227
  hem in 229
inclosure *region* 181
  envelope **232**
  fence 752
include
  composition 54
  - *in a class* 76

inclusion **76**
inclusive *additive* 37
  component 56
  class 76
inclusory 56
incogitance **452**
incognito 528
incognizable 519
incoherence
  physical **47**
  mental 503
incombustible 385
income *means* 632
  profit 775
  property 780
  wealth 803
  receipt 810
incomer
  immigrant 294
incoming *ingress* 294
  receipt 810
incommensurable
  irrelation 10
  (*disagreeing* 24)
  - *quantity* 84, 85
incommode *hinder* 706
  (*trouble* 830)
  (*incommodious* 647)
incommodious 647
incommunicable
  unmeaning 517
  unintelligible 519
  retention 781
incommutable 150
incomparable
  superior 33
  (*good* 648)
incompassionate 914a
incompatibility 15
incompatible 24
incompetence
  inability 158
  incapacity 499
  unskillful 699
incomplete
  fractional 51
  not complete 53, 730
incompleteness **53**
  noncompletion 730
incomplex 42
incompliance 764
incomprehensible
  infinite 105
  unintelligible 519
incomprehension 491
incompressible 321
inconceivable
  unthought of 452
  impossible 471
  improbable 473
  incredible 485
  unintelligible 519
  wonder 870
inconceptible 519
inconcinnity
  disagreement 24
  ugliness 846
inconclusive 477
inconcoction 674
incondite 851
inconformity 15

incongruous
  differing 15
  disagreeing 24
  faulty 568
  discordant 713
inconnection
  irrelation 10
  disjunction 44
inconsequence
  irrelation 10
inconsequential
  illogical 477
inconsiderable
  small 32
  fractional 100a
  unimportant 643
inconsiderate
  thoughtless 452
  inattentive 458
  neglectful 460
  foolish 699
inconsistent
  contrary 14
  disagreeing 24
  illogical 477
  absurd 497
  foolish 499
  discordant 713
  capricious 608
inconsolable 837
inconsonant
  disagreeing 24
  fitful 149
inconspicuous 447
inconstant 149
incontestable
  strong 159
  certain 474
incontiguous 196
incontinent 961
incontinently 132
incontrollable 173
incontrovertible
  certain 474
  (*stable* 150)
inconvenience 647
  put to - 706
inconvenient 135, 647
inconversable
  taciturn 585
  unsociable 893
inconvertible
  continuing 143
  (*stable* 150)
inconvincible 487
incorporality 317
incorporate *combine* 48
  include 76
  materialize 316
  immaterial 317
  animality 364
incorporation
  [*see* incorporate]
incorporeal 317
  - *hereditaments* 780
incorrect *illogical* 477
  erroneous 495
  solecism 568
  vicious 945
incorrigible
  obstinate 606

hopeless 859
vicious 945
impenitent 951
incorruptible
    honorable 939
incorruption
    probity 939
    innocence 946
    (*health* 654)
incrassate
    increase 194
    density 321
    - *fluids* 352
    (*thick* 202)
increase
    - *in degree* **35**
    - *in number* 102
    - *in size* 194
incredible *great* 31
    impossible 471
    improbable 473
    doubtful 485
    wonderful 870
incredulity
    unbelief **487**
    religious - 989
increment *increase* 35
    addition 37
    adjunct 39
    expansion 194
increpation 932
incriminate 938
incrust *coat* 223
    line 224
incubate 370
incubation 673
incubus *hindrance* 706
    pain 828
    demon 980
inculcate 537
inculcated 6
inculpable 946
inculpate 938
inculture 674
incumbency
    business 625
    churchdom 995
incumbent
    inhabitant 188
    high 206
    weight 319
    duty 926
    clergyman 996
incumber 706
incumbered 806
incumbrance 706
incunabula 66, 127
incur 177
    - *a debt* 806
    - *a loss* 776
    - *blame* 932
    - *danger* 665
    - *disgrace* 874
    - *the risk* 621
incurable *ingrained* 5
    disease 655
    hopeless 859
incuriosity **456**
incursion
    ingress 294
    attack 716

incurvation 245
incus 418
indagation 461
indebted *owing* 806
    gratitude 916
    duty 926
indecent 961
indeciduous 150
indecipherable 519
indecision 605
indecisive 475
indeclinable 150
indecorous *vulgar* 851
    vicious 945
    impure 961
indeed *existing* 1
    very 31
    assent 488
    truly 494
    assertion 535
    wonder 870
indefatigable
    persevering 604a
    active 682
indefeasible *stable* 150
    certainty 474
    necessity 601
    due 924
indefectible 650
indefensible
    powerless 158
    submission 725
    accusable 938
    wrong 945
indeficient 650
indefinite *great* 31
    every 78
    infinite 105
    aoristic 119
    misty 447
    uncertain 475
    inexact 495
    vague 519
indeliberate 612
indelible *stable* 150
    memory 505
    mark 550
    feeling 821
indelicate 961
indemnification 790,
    952
indemnificatory 30
indemnity
    compensation 30
    forgiveness 918
    reward 973
    deed of - 771
indent *list* 86
    scallop 248
indentation 252, 257
indenture *compact* 769
    security 771
    (*evidence* 467)
    (*record* 551)
independence
    irrelation 10
    freedom 748
    wealth 803
Independence   Day
    138, 840
Independent 984

independent
    [*see* independence]
indescribable
    great 31
    wonderful 870
indesinent 112
indestructible 150
indeterminate
    chance 156
    uncertain 475
    equivocal 520
    irresolute 605
indevotion 989
index *arrangement* 60
    exponent 84
    list 86
    sign 550
    words 562
index   expurgatorius
    761
indexterity 699
Indian
    - *file* 69
    - *gift* 794
    - *giver* 702
    - *rubber* 325
    - *ruling chiefs* 875
    - *sage* 662
    - *summer* 126
    - *weed* 392
indicate *specify* 79
    direct attention to 457
    mean 516
    mark 550
indication 75, **550**
indicative
    evidence 467
    indicating 550
indicatory 550
indicolite 438
indict *accuse* 938
    arraign 969
indiction 108, 531
indifference
    incuriosity 456
    unwillingness 603
    no choice 609a
    insensibility 823
    unconcern **866**
    irreligion 989
    matter of - 643
indifferent
    [*see* indifference]
    unimportant 643
    bad 649
indigence
    insufficiency 640
    poverty 804
indigene 188
indigenous
    intrinsic 5
    inhabitant 188
indigested 674
indigestible 657
indigestion 655, 657
indigitate 457
indign 940
indignation 900
    - *meeting* 832
    iron - 722
indignity *affront* 900

insult 929
indigo 438
indiligence 683
indirect *oblique* 217
    devious 279
    latent 526
    circuitous 629
indiscernible 447
indiscerptible *whole* 50
    unity 87
    dense 321
indiscoverable 526
indiscreet *rash* 863
    blamable 945
    (*neglectful* 460)
    (*unskillful* 699)
indiscrete 48
indiscretion *guilt* 947
    [*see* indiscreet]
indiscriminate
    mixed 41
    unarranged 59
    multiform 81
    casual 621
indiscrimination **465a**
indispensable 630
indispose
    dissuade 616
indisposed
    unwilling 603
    sick 655
    - *to believe* 487
indisputable 474
indissoluble
    joined 43
    whole 50
    stable 150
    dense 321
indissolvable
    [*see* indissoluble]
indistinct *dim* 447
    (*vague* 519)
indistinction 465a
indistinguishable
    identical 13
    invisible 447
    indiscriminate 465**a**
indisturbance
    quiescence 265
    inexcitation 826
indite 54, 590
individual *whole* 50
    special 79
    unity 87
    person 372
individuality
    speciality 79
    unity 87
individualize 79
indivisible *whole* 50
    dense 321
indocility
    incapacity 158
    obstinacy 606
indoctrinate 537
indolence 683, 927
indomitable *strong* 159
    determined 604
    persevering 604a
    resisting 719
    courage 861

581

inofficious 907
inoperative
  powerless 158
  unproductive 169
  useless 645
inopportune
  untimely 135
  inexpedient 647
inordinate *great* 31
  excessive 641
inorganic 358
inorganization **358**
inornate 849
inosculate *join* 43
  combined 48
  intersect 219
  convoluted 248
inquest 461, 967
inquietude
  changeable 149
  uneasy 828
  discontent 832
  apprehension 860
  (*motion* 264)
inquinate 659
inquire 461
  - into 595
inquirer 461, 541
inquiring 461
  - mind 455
inquiry **461**
inquisition
  inquiry 461
  severity 739
  tribunal 966
inquisitive 455
inquisitorial
  prying 455
  inquiry 461
  severe 739
  jurisdiction 965
inroad *ingress* 294
  trespass 303
  devastation 659
  invasion 716
insalubrity **657**
insanity 61, **503**
insatiable 865
inscribe *write* 590
  blazon 873
inscription
  [see inscribe]
  interment 363
  record 551
inscroll 551
inscrutable 519
insculpture 557
insculptured 558
insecable *junction* 43
  unity 87
insect 366, 368
  minute 193
  injurious -s 913
  - cry 412
insecure *danger* 665
  (*uncertain* 475)
insensate
  foolish 499
  insane 503
insensibility *slow* 275
  physical **376**

moral **823**
- of benefits 917
- to the past 506
insensible *numb* 381
  [see insensibility]
inseparable
  junction 43
  coherence 46
insert *locate* 184
  interpose 228
  enter 294
  put in 300
  record 551
  - itself 300
insertion **300**
  ornament 847
inservient 645
insessorial 206
inseverable
  junction 43
  unity 87
inside 221
  - out 218
  - part *music* 415
  turn - out 529
insidious *deceitful* 545
  cunning 702
  dishonorable 940
insight 490, 868
insignia 550
  - of authority 747
insignificant
  unmeaning 517
  unimportant 643
insincere 544, 855
insinuate *intervene* 228
  ingress 294
  insert 300
  latency 526
  hint 527
  ingratiate 897
  blame 932
  (*suppose* 514)
  (*mean* 516)
insipid *tasteless* 391
  style 575
  trifling 643
insipidity
  tasteless **391**
  indifferent 866
insist *argue* 476
  command 741
  - upon *affirm* 535
  dwell on 573
  be determined 604
  contend 720
  compel 744
  conditions 770
  due 924
insistence [see insist]
  influence 615
insnare 545
insobriety 959
insolation 340, 382, 384
insolence **885**
insolent *defiant* 715
  arrogant 885
  disrespectful 929
insoluble *dense* 321
  unintelligible 519
insolvable 519

insolvent *poverty* 804
  debt 806
  nonpayment 808
insomnia 682
insouciance
  thoughtlessness 458
  supineness 823
  indifference 866
inspan 293
inspect *look* 441
  attend to 457
inspector
  inquisitor 461
  judge 480
  director 694
inspiration
  breathing 349
  wisdom 498
  imagination 515
  impulse 612
  motive 615
  feeling 821
  Deity 976
  revelation 985
  religious - 987
inspirator 349
inspire *breathe* 349
  prompt 615
  improvement 658
  animate 824
  cheer 836
  - courage 861
  - hope 858
  - respect 928
inspired 615
  - writers 985
inspirit *incite* 615
  animate 824
  cheer 834
  hope 858
  encourage 861
inspiriting *hopeful* 858
inspissate *dense* 321
  semiliquid 352
instability 149, 605
install *locate* 184
  commission 755
  celebrate 883
installment *portion* 51
  payment 807, 809
instance *example* 82
  motive 615
  solicitation 765
instant *moment* 113
  present 118
  destiny 152
  required 630
  importance 642
  active 682
  lose not an - 684
  on the - 132
instantaneity **113**
instanter 113, 132
instate 883
instauration 660
instead 147
instigate 615
instigator 615
instill *imbue* 41
  introduce 296
  insert 300

teach 537
instinct *intellect* 450
  intuition 477
  impulse 601
  brute - 450a
  - with *motive* 615
  possession 777
instinctive *inborn* 5
institute *begin* 66
  cause 153
  produce 161
  academy 542
  society 712
  - an inquiry 461
institution
  academy 542
  society 712
  political - 963
  church 995
institutional 712
institutor 540
instruct *teach* 537
  advise 695
  precept 697
  order 741
instructed 490
instruction
  [see instruct]
instructional 537
instructive 537
instructor 540
instructorship 542
instrument
  implement **633**
  security 771
  musical - 417
  optical - 445
instrumental 631
  - music 415
instrumentalist 416
instrumentality **631**
instrumentation 54, 60
insubordinate 742
insubstantial
  inexistent 2
  unsubstantial 4
  immaterial 317
  - *pageant* 882
insubstantiality
  disappearance 449
  [see insubstantial]
insufferable
  painful 830
  dislike 867
insufficiency **640**
insufflation 349
insular *unrelated* 10
  detached 44
  single 87
  region 181
  island 346
  narrow 481
  bigoted 988
insulate 44, 346
insulse *stupid* 499
  dull 843
insult *insolence* 885
  rudeness 895
  offense 900
  disrespect 929
insulting 898

interpenetration
  interjacence 228
  ingress 294
  passage 302
interplanetary 228
interpolar 228
interpolation
  analytical 85
  interpose 228
  insertion 300
interpose
  intervene 228
  act 682
  hinder 706
  mediate 724
interposit 799
interposition
  [*see* interpose]
interpret 522, 595
interpretation 516, **522**
  (*answer* 462)
interpreter **524**
interradial 228
interregnum
  intermission 106
  transient 111
  discontinuance 142
  interval 198
  inaction 681
  laxity 738
  (*discontinuity* 70)
interrelation 9, 12
interrenal 228
interrogate 461
interrogation 461
  typography 550
interrupt
  discontinuity 70
  cessation 142
  hinder 706
interruption
  derangement 61
  interval 198
interscapular 228
interscholastic 148
intersect 219
intersection 198, 219
interseptal 228
interspace *interval* 198
  interior 221
intersperse *diffuse* 73
  interpose 228
  (*music* 41)
interstate 148
interstellar 228
interstice 198
interstitial *internal* 221
  interjacent 228
intertanglement 41
intertexture
  mixture 41
  intersection 219
  tissue 329
intertribal 148
intertwine *unite* 43
  cross 219
intertwist 43, 219
interurban 148
interval *degree* 26
  - *of time* 106
  - *of space* **198**
584

  - *in music* 413
at -s
  discontinuously 70
  at regular -s 138
intervalvular 228
intervascular 228
intervene
  - *in order* 70
  - *in time* 106
  - *in space* 228
  be instrumental 631
  mediate 724
  (*agent* 758)
intervener 228
interventricular 228
intervert *change* 140
  deviate 279
intervertebral 228
interview
  conference 588
  society 892
interviewer 553, 554
intervolved 43
interweave *join* 43
  cross 219
  interjacence 228
interwork 148
interworking 170
intestate 552
intestine 221, 350
inthrall *subjection* 749
  restraint 751
intimacy 888
intimate *special* 79
  close 197
  tell 527
  friendly 888
  friend 890
intimately *joined* 43
intimation 527
intimidate *frighten* 860
  insolence 885
  threat 909
intinction 998
into go - 294
  put - 300
  run - 300
intolerable 830
intolerance
  prejudice 481
  obstinacy 606
  impatience 825
  insolence 885
  malevolence 907
intolerant 489
intomb 363
intonation *sound* 402
  musical 413
  voice 580
intone *sing* 416
  worship 990
intort 248
intoxicant *bane* 663
intoxicated 959
intoxication
  excitement 824, 825
  inebriation 959
intracanal 221
intracellular 221
intractable
  obstinate 606

  difficult 704
  sullen 901a
intrados 221
intralobular 221
intramarginal 221
intramolecular 221
intramundane 221
intramural 221
intransient 110
intransigence 604
intransigent 604
intransitive 110
intransmutable
  diuturnal 110
  stable 150
intraocular 221
intrap 545
intraregarding 221
intraseptal 221
intratelluric 221
intrauterine 221
intravascular 221
intravenous 221
intraventricular 221
intrench *safety* 664
  defend 717
  - *on* 303
intrepid 861
intricacy 533
intricate *confused* 59
  convoluted 248
  difficult 704
intrigant
  meddlesome 682
  cunning 702
  libertine 962
intrigue *plot* 626
  activity 682
  cunning 702
  licentiousness 961
intriguer *activity* 682
  cunning 702
intrinsic 5
  forming 56
  - *evidence* 467
  - *habit* 613
  - *truth* 494
intrinsicality **5**
introception 296
introduce *lead* 62
  interpose 228
  precede 280
  insert 300
  - *new blood* 140
  - *new conditions* 469
  - *to* 888
introducer 164
introduction
  [*see* introduce]
  preface 64
  reception 296
  drama 599
  friendship 888
  courtesy 894
introductory
  precursor 64
  beginning 66
  priority 116
  receptive 296
introgression 294
introit 296, 998

intromissive 296
intromit *receive* 296
intromittent 296
introspection
  look into 441
  attend to 457
introspective 451
introvert 218
intrude *interfere* 24
  inopportune 135
  intervene 228
  enter 294
  trespass 303
intruder 57 j
intrusion [*see* intrude]
intrusive 706
intrusiveness 682
intrust *commit* 755
  lend 787
intuition *mind* 450
  unreasoning **477**
  knowledge 490
  subconsciousness 992a
intumescence
  swell 194
  convex 250
intussuscept 14, 218
intwine *join* 43
  twist 248
inunction 223
inundate *effusion* 337
  flow 348
  redundance 641
inurbanity 895
inure *habituate* 613
  train 673
inured *insensible* 823
inurn 363
inusitate 20
inusitation 614
inutility **645**
invade *ingress* 294
  trespass 303
  attack 713
invaginate 14, 218
invagination 218, 357
invalid *powerless* 158
  illogical 477
  diseased 655
  undue 925
invalidate *disable* 158
  weaken 160
  confute 479
invalidity *disease* 655
invaluable 644, 648
invariable *intrinsic* 5
  uniform 16
  conformable 82
  stable 150
invasion
  ingress 294
  attack 716
invective 932
inveigh 932
inveigle *deceive* 545
  seduce 615
invent *imagine* 515
  lie 544
  devise 626
invented *untrue* 546

invention [*see* invent]
  composition 54
inventive *skillful* 698
inventor 164
inventory 86
inverse *contrary* 14
  upside down 218
inversion
  derangement 61
  change 140
  of position **218**
  contraposition 237
  reversion 145
  language 577
invertebracy 158
invertebrate
  impotent 158
  frail 945
invest *impower* 157
  clothe 225
  surround 227
  besiege 716
  commission 755
  give 784
  lend 787
  expend 809
  - in *locate* 184
  purchase 795
  - money 817
  - with *ascribe* 155
investigate 461
investiture
  appointment 755
investment
  clothing 225
  [*see* invest]
  make -s 673
investor 784
inveterate *old* 124
  established 150
  inborn 820
  - belief 484
  - habit 613
invidious *painful* 830
  hatred 898
  spite 907
  envy 921
invigilation 459
invigorate
  strengthen 159
  improve 658
  inspirit 834
invigorating
  healthy 656
invincible 159
inviolable *secret* 528
  right 924
  honor 939
inviolate *permanent* 141
  secret 528
  honorable 939
invious *closed* 261
  pathless 704
invisibility **447**
invisible *small* 193
  not to be seen 447
  concealed 526
  - government 526
  - helpers 977
invitation [*see* invite]
invitatory 765

invite *induce* 615
  offer 763
  ask 765
  - the attention 457
inviting [*see* invite]
  pleasing 829
invocation [*see* invoke]
invocative 765
invoice 86
invoke *address* 586
  implore 765
  pray 990
  - curses 908
  - saints 998
involucrum 223
involuntary
  necessary 601
  unwilling 603
  - servitude 749
involution [*see* involve]
  algebra 85
involve *include* 54
  derange 61
  wrap 225
  evince 467
  mean 516
  latency 526
involved *disorder* 59
  convoluted 248
  secret 533
  obscure style 571
  in debt 806
involvement 61, 704
invulnerable 664
inward *intrinsic* 5
  inside 221
  incoming 294
  - monitor 926
inweave 219, 300
inwrap 225
inwrought 5
Ionian school 451
Ionic 597
iota *small* 32
  trifle 643
  (*minute* 193)
I O U *security* 771
  money 800
ipecacuanha 662
ipse dixit
  certainty 474
  affirmation 535
ipso facto 1
irascibility **901**
irate 900
ire 900
iridescent 440
iridosmine 323
Iris *traveler* 268
  messenger 534
iris *rainbow* 440
  eye 441
irisated 440
irisation 440
Irish 188
  - green 435
Irishism 497
Irishman 188
irk 688, 830
irksome
  tiresome 688

  difficult 704
  painful 830
  weary 841
iron *strength* 159
  smooth 255
  hard 323
  resolution 604
  - age *adversity* 735
  pain 828
  - cross 551, 733
  - entering into the
    soul 828, 830
  - gray 432
  - grip 159
  - gripe 781
  - heel 739
  - necessity 601
  - rule 739
  - sway 739
  - will 604
  rule with a rod of -
    739
iron-bound coast
  land 342
  danger 667
ironclad *covering* 223
  defense 717
  man of war 726
iron-handed 739
iron-hearted 861
ironic [*see* irony]
iron mold 434
irons 752
  fire - 386
  - in the fire
  business 625
  redundance 641
  active 682
  unskillful 699
  put in - 751
irony
  figure of speech 521
  untruth 546
  ridicule 856
irradiate 420
irrational *number* 84
  illogical 477
  silly 499
irreclaimable
  hopeless 859
  vicious 945
  impenitent 951
irreconcilable
  unrelated 10
  discordant 24
  unwilling 603
  intransigent 604
  opponent 710
  enmity 889
irrecoverable *past* 122
  hopeless 859
  (*lost* 776)
irredeemable
  hopeless 859
  (*lost* 776)
irreducible
  discordant 24
  out of order 59
  unchangeable 150
irrefragable 478
irrefutable *certain* 474

  proved 478
irregular *diverse* 16a
  out of order 59
  multiform 81
  against rule 83
  - in recurrence 139
  distorted 243
  guerrilla 722
  combatant 726
irregularity **139**
irrelation 10
irrelevant *unrelated* 10
  unaccordant 24
  sophistical 477
  unimportant 643
irreligion **989**
irremediable *bad* 649
  hopeless 859
  (*spoiled* 659)
  (*lost* 776)
irremissible 945
irremovable 141, 150
irreparable
  hopeless 859
  (*bad* 649)
  (*spoiled* 659)
  (*lost* 776)
irrepentance 951
irreprehensible 946
irrepressible
  violent 173
  free 748
  excitable 825
irreproachable 946
irreprovable 946
irresilient 326
irresistible *strong* 159
  demonstration 478
  necessary 601
  impulsive 615
irresoluble 150
irresolution **605**
irresolvable 87
irresolvedly 605
irrespective 10
irresponsible
  vacillating 605
  exempt 927a
  arbitrary 964
irretrievable *stable* 150
  lost 776
  hopeless 859
irrevealable 528
irreverence
  disrespect 929
  impiety 988
irreversible
  stable 150
  resolute 604
  hopeless 859
  (*past* 122)
irrevocable *stable* 150
  necessary 601
  resolute 604
  hopeless 859
irrigate 337
irriguous 339
irrision *ridicule* 856
  disrespect 929
irritable *excitable* 825
  irascible 901

irritate *violent* 173
  excite 824
  pain 830
  provoke 898
  incense 900
irritating
  [*see* irritate]
  stringent 171
irritation
  [*see* irritate]
  pain 828
  source of - 830
irruption *ingress* 294
  invasion 716
Irvingite 984
is - to be 152
  that - 118
ischiagra 378
ischialgia 378
Ishmael 83
isinglass 352
Isis 979
Islam 976
Islamism 984
island 44, **346**
islander 188

isle 346
isobar 338, 550
isobath 27
isocheimal 383
isochronal 27, 114
isochronize 120
isochronous 114, 120
isogamy 17, 161, 357
isolate *detach* 44
  seclude 893
isolated
  unrelated 10
  single 87
isomorph 240
isomorphism 240
isonomy 27
isoperimetric 27
isopiestic line 338, 550
isopolity 27
isotherm 550
isothermal 382
isotonic 413
isotropy 27
issue *distribute* 73
  focus 74
  event 151

effect 154
  posterity 167
  depart 293
  egress 295
  stream 348, 349
  inquiry 461
  publication 531
  book 593
  ulcer 655
  dénouement 729
  money 800
  at - *discussion* 476
  dissent 489
  negation 536
  opposition 708
  discord 713
  contention 720
  in - 461
  - a command 741
  join - *lawsuit* 969
issueless 169
isthmus
  connection 45
  narrow 203
  land 342
it *importance* 642

italics *mark* 550
  printing 591
  put in -
    importance 642
itch *titillation* 380
  disease 655
  desire 865
itching 380
  - palm 819
item *addition* 37, 39
  part 51
  speciality 79
  integer 87
itemize, 79, 594
iterance 104
iteration 104
itinerant
  moving 266
  traveler 268
itinerary
  journey 266
  guidebook 527
ivory 430
ivy
  cling like - 46
Ixion 312

J

jab 276
jabber *unmeaning* 517
  stammer 583
  chatter 584
jacal 189
jacent 213
jacet, hic - 363
jacinth 847
jack *rotation* 312
  ensign 550
  cards 840
Jack *sailor* 269
  - at a pinch 711
  - Cade 742
  - in office *director* 694
  bully 887
  - Ketch 975
  - of all trades 700
  - o' lantern 423
  - Pudding *actor* 599
  humorist 844
  - tar 269
jack-a-dandy
  buffoon 844
  fop 854
jackal *auxiliary* 711
  sycophant 886
jackanapes *fop* 854
  blusterer 887
jackass 271
jack boot 225
jackeroo 57
jacket 225
  cork - 666
jackleg 792
jackpot 775, 840
jackstones 840
Jacobin 710
Jacob's ladder 305
Jacquerie *tumult* 719
586

jactation 315
jactitation *tossing* 315
  boasting 884
jaculation 284
jade *horse* 271
  worn-out 659
  fatigue 688
  low woman 876
  scamp 949
  drab 962
jadu 621, 649
jag 257
  burden 190
  dent 257
jäger 726
jagged 244, 256
jaguar 440, 913
jail 767
jailbird *prisoner* 754
  bad man 949
jailer *keeper* 753
  punisher 975
jakes 653
jalousie 351, 424
jam *squeeze* 43
  pulp 354
  sweet 298, 396
  - in *interpose* 228
Jamaica
  - bayberry 400
  - pepper 393
jamb 215
jamboree 840
jammed in
  restraint 751
jampan 272
jane *woman* 374
jangle *harsh sound* 410
  quarrel 713
janissary 726

janitor 263
Jansenist 984
janty [*see* jaunty]
January 138
Janus *deceiver* 607
  tergiversation 607
  close the temple of -
    723
Janus-faced 544
japan *coat* 223
  resin 356a
  ornament 847
jaquima 752
jar *clash* 24
  vessel 191
  agitation 315
  stridor 410
  discord 713
  - upon the feelings 830
jardinière 191
jargon *absurdity* 497
  no meaning 517
  unintelligible 519
  neology 563
jarring 24, 414
jasper 435, 847
jaundice 436
jaundiced *yellow* 436
  prejudiced 481
  dejected 837
  jealous 920
  view with - eyes
    disapprove 932
jaunt 266
jaunting car 272
jaunty *gay* 836
  pretty 845
  stylish 852
  showy 882
  insolent 885

javelin 727
jaw *chatter* 584
  scold 932
jaw-fallen 837
jaws *mouth* 231
  eating 298
  - of death 360
jay 584
  dupe 547
jazz *music* 415
  dance 840
  - band 416
jealous 920
  - of honor 939
jealousy **920**
  suspicion 485
jeer *flout* 929
  (*joke* 842)
  (*banter* 856)
Jehovah 976
Jehu *traveler* 268
  director 694
jejune *incomplete* 53
  unproductive 169
  insipid 391
  style 575
  scanty 640
  wearying 841
  dull 843
jejunum 221, 350
jell 352
jellify 352
jelly 352
  beat to a - 972
jellyfish 368
jemadar 745
jemmy *lever* 633
  dandy 854
jennet 271
jenny **633**

jeopardy 665
jerboa 309
jereed 727
jeremiad *lament* 839
  invective 932
  (accusation 938)
Jericho, send to - 297
jerk *start* 146
  throw 284
  pull 285
  agitate 315
jerkin 225
jerks, by - 70
  the - 315
jerky 315
jerry *deceived* 545
jerry-build 545
jerry-building 545
jerry-built 160, 545
Jerry Sneak
  coward 862
  knave 941
Jersey *cow* 366
jersey *clothing* 225
jessamy *affectation* 855
jest *trifle* 643
  wit 842
jest book 842
jester 844
jesting stock 857
Jesuit *deceiver* 548
  priest 996
jesuitical
  sophistical 477
  deceitful 544
Jesus 976
jet *stream* 348
  - black 431
jetsam 782
jettison 782
jetty *projection* 250
  harbor 666
jeu - de mots 842
  - d'esprit 842
  - de theatre 599
Jew. In the original
  edition Roget includ-
  ed the word Jew in
  several groups of syn-
  onyms. In this print-
  ing all uncompliment-
  ary racial allusions
  have been omitted.
jewel *gem* 648
  ornament 847
  favorite 899
  -s five words long 648
jewelry 847
  false - 545
jew's-harp 417
Jezebel *wicked* 913
  wretch 949
  courtesan 962
jhil 345
jhilmil 351
jib *reverse* 140
  front 234
  recoil 276
  regression 283
  cut of one's -
  form 240

appearance 448
jibe *concur* 178
jiffy 113
jig *dance* 840
  (music 415)
jigger 215, 272
jilt *disappoint* 509
  deceive 545
  deceiver 548
  dishonor 940
jilted 898
jimp 845
jingal 727
jingle 408
jingo *boaster* 884
  insolence 885
  blusterer 887
jingoism 884, 885
jinks, high - 840
jinn 980
jinrikisha 266, 272
jitney 272
jiujitsu 720
jiva 157
job *business* 625
  action 680
  unfair 940
  tough - 704
Job
  -'s comforter
  dejection 837
  hopeless 859
  patience of - 826
  poor as - 804
jobation 932
jobber *deceiver* 548
  tactician 700
  merchant 797
  trickster 943
jobbernowl 501
jobbery *cunning* 702
  improbity 940
jobbing *barter* 794
jockey *rider* 268
  deceive 545
  servant 746
jocose *gay* 836
  witty 842
jocoseness *fun* 840
jocular *gay* 636
  droll 842
jocund *gay* 836
  sportive 840
Joe Miller *wit* 842
  humorist 844
jog *push* 276
  shake 315
  - on *continue* 143
  trudge 266
  slow 275
  advance 282
  mediocrity 736
  - the memory 505
jogger *memory aid* 505
joggle 315
jog-trot *uniformity* 16
  trudge 266
  slow 275
  habit 613
John Doe and Richard
  Roe 4

Johnsonian 577
join *connect* 43
  assemble 72
  contiguous 199
  arrive 272
  party 712
  sociality 892
  marry 903
  - battle 722
  - forces 708
  - hands 708
  - in 778
  - in the chorus 488
  - issue *discuss* 476
  deny 536
  quarrel 713
  contend 720
  lawsuit 969
  - the choir invisible
    360
  - the majority 360
  - with 709
joining *meeting* 292
joint *junction* 43
  part 51
  accompanying 88
  concurrent 178
  meat 298
  low resort 621, 945
  - concern 712
joint stock
  coöperation 709
  participation 778
joint tenancy 778
jointure 780
joist 215
joke *absurdity* 497
  trifle 643
  wit 842
  ridicule 856
  in - 842
  mere - 643
  no - *existing* 1
  important 642
  practical -
  deception 545
  ridicule 856
  disrespect 929
  take a - 498
joker 844
  cards 840
joking apart
  affirmation 535
  resolution 604
jole 236
jollification
  amusement 840
  intemperance 954
jollity
  amusement 840
  sociality 892
jolly *plump* 192
  marine 269
  gay 836
  flattery 933
  - boat 273
  - fellow 892
jolt *impulse* 276
  agitation 315
jolthead 501
Jonah 621, 649

Jones
  Davy -'s locker 360
  Paul - 792
jongleur 597
jonquil 436
Jordan 360
jornada 200
jorum 191
Joseph 960
  -'s coat 440
joss 991
joss-house 1000
joss-stick 388
jostle *rush* 276
  jog 315
  clash 713
  contend 720
  (disagree 24)
jot *small* 32
  unimportant 643
jotting
  indication 550
  record 551
jounce 315
journal *annals* 114
  newspaper 531
  record 551
  magazine 593
  narrative 594
  accounts 811
journalism 551
journalist *recorder* 553
  representation 554
  author 593
journey 266
  -'s end 292
journeyman
  artisan 690
  servant 746
joust 720
Jove 979
  sub - *out of doors* 220
  air 338
jovial *gay* 836
  amusement 840
  social 892
Jovinianist 984
jowl 236
joy 827
  give one - 896
  - rider 274
joyful 836
joyless *painful* 830
  sad 837
J. P. 967
Juan, Don - 962
jubbah 225
jube 1000
jubilant *gay* 836
  rejoicing 838
  celebrating 883
  boastful 884
jubilate 884
jubilee *anniversary* 138
  celebration 883
jucundity 829
Judaism 984
Judas *deceiver* 548
  knave 941
  - kiss *hypocrisy* 544
  base 940

587

K

L

destitute 804
want 865
- faith 989
- of contrition 951
- preparation 674
- wit 501
lackadaisical
inactive 683
melancholy 837
indifferent 866
lackadaisy!
lament 839
wonder 870
lackaday 839
lackbrain 499, 501
lacker [*see* lacquer]
lackey 746
lackluster 422, 429
laconic 572, 585
laconicism 572
laconize 572
lacquer
covering 223
resin 356a
adorn 847
lacrosse 840
lacteal 352
lactescence 352, 430
lacuna *gap* 198
pit 252
lacustrine 343
- dwelling 189
lad 129
ladder *ascent* 305
way 627
kick down the - 604
laddie 129
lade *load* 184
transfer 185, 270
contents 190
- out 297
laden 52
heavy - 828
- with 777
lading *contents* 190
property 780
bill of - *list* 86
ladino 41, 271
ladle *receptacle* 191
transfer 270
vehicle 272
lady *woman* 374
rank 875
wife 903
- help 746
Lady day 138
ladylike *womanly* 374
fashionable 852
(*courteous* 894)
ladylove 897
lady's maid 746
lætificant 829
lag *linger* 275
follow 281
dawdle 683
lager-beer 298
laggard
unwilling 603
inactive 683
lagoon 343
lagniappe 784

laical 997
laicize 997
laid - by the heels 751
- low 160
- on one's back 158
- up 655
lair *den* 189
sty 653
laird *master* 745
proprietor 779
nobility 875
Lais 962
laisser - aller, - faire
permanence 141
neglect 460
inaction 681
laxity 738
freedom 748
inexcitable 826
laity 997
lake *water* **343**
pink 434
- dwelling 189
- of fire and brim-
stone 982
lakh 98
laky *red* 434
Lama *ruler* 745
prince 996
Lamarckism 357
lamb *infant* 129
food 298
animal 366
gentle 826
innocent 946
go out like a - 174
lion lies down with-
721
lamba-chauki 215
lambaste 972
lambency 379
lambent *touching* 379
- flame *heat* 382
light 420
Lambeth 1000
lambkin 167, 223
Lamb of God 976
lame *incomplete* 53
impotent 158
weak 160
imperfect 651
disease 655
injury 659
failing 732
(*bad* 649)
(*lax* 738)
help a - dog over a
stile *aid* 707
vindicate 937
- conclusion
illogical 477
failure 732
- duck 808
- excuse 617
lamellar 204
lamentable *bad* 649
painful 830
sad 837
lamentably *very* 31
lamentation **839**
(*regret* 833)

lamenter 363
lamia *demon* 980
sorcerer 994
lamina *part* 51
layer 204
laminate 204
Lammas 998
lamp 423
- shells 368
rub the - 992
safety - 666
smell of the -
style 577
prepared 673
lamplight 423
lamplighter
quick 682
lampoon *censure* 932
detraction 934
lampooner 936
lampreys 368
lanate 255, 256
lance *pierce* 260
throw 284
spear 727
break a - with
attack 716
warfare 722
couch one's - 720
- corporal 745
lanceolate 253
lancer 726
lancet *sharp* 253
piercer 262
lanciform 253
lancinate
bodily pain 378
mental pain 830
land *arrive* 267, 292
ground **342**
estate 780
how the - lies
circumstances 8
experiment 463
foresight 510
hug the - 286
in the - of the living
359
- flowing with milk
and honey 168
make the - 286
on - 342
see - 858
landamman 745
landau 272
landed *property* 780
- gentry 779
- estate 780
landgrave 745
landholder 779
landing place
stage 215
arrive 292
refuge 666
landlady 779
landlocked 229
landloper 268
landlord *innkeeper* 637
possessor 779
landlubber 268, 342,
701

landmark *limit* 233
measurement 466
indication 550
landowner 779
landreeve 694
landscape *prospect* 448
- gardening
agriculture 371
beauty 845
- painter 559
- painting 556
landshark 792
landslide 306
landslip 306
landsman 268, 342
Landsturm 726
landsurveying 466
Landwehr 726
lane *street* 189
opening 260
way 627
langrage shot 727
langrel 727
langsyne 122
language **560**
command of - 582
strong -
vigor 574
malediction 908
languid *weak* 160
inert 172
slow 275
- *style* 575
inactive 683
torpid 823
languish *decrease* 36
ill 655
inactive 683
repine 828
affect 855
- for 865
languishing 160
languishment
lament 839
languor [*see* languid]
laniate 162
lank *long* 200
lanky *thin* 203
tall 200, 206
lantern *window* 260
lamp 423
- jaws 203
- of Diogenes 461
magic - 448
lanuginous 256
Laocoön 557
Laodicean 823
lap *flap* 39
abode 189
eager 204
support 215
interior 221
wrap 225
encompass 227, 229
drink 298
circuition 311
- *of waves* 405
- of luxury
pleasure 377
inactivity 683
voluptuousness 954

take the - into one's
 own hands
 war 722
 disobedience 742
 lawless 964
take the - of 969
law-abiding 743
lawful *permitted* 760
 due 924
 legal 963
lawgiver *director* 694
 (*master* 745)
lawless *irregular* 83
 mutinous 742
 nonobservant 773
 vicious 945
 arbitrary 964
lawn *plain* 344
 sward 367
 agriculture 371
 fabric 635
 - sleeves 999
 - tennis 840
lawsuit **969**
lawyer **968**
lax *incoherent* 47
 soft 324
 error 495
 - *style* 575
 remiss 738
 nonobservant 773
 dishonorable 940
 licentious 945
 irreligious 989
laxative 652
 remedial 662
laxity **738**
laxness 738, 773
lay *arrangement* 60
 moderate 174
 place 184
 ley 344
 music 415
 poetry 597
 bet 621
 secular 997
 - about one *active* 682
 exertion 686
 attack 716
 content 720
 punish 972
 - apart *exclude* 55
 relinquish 782
 - aside *neglect* 460
 reject 610
 disuse 678
 give up 782
 - at one's feet 763
 - at the door of 155
 - bare 529
 - before 527
 - brother 996
 - by *store* 636
 provide 637
 sickness 655
 disuse 678
 - by the heels 162
 - claim to 924
 - down [see below]
 - eggs 161
 - figure

thing of naught 4
model 22
representation 554
- hands on *use* 677
take 789
rite 998
- heads together
advise 695
coöperaie 709
- in *eat* 298
store 336
provide 637
- in ruins 162
- in the dust 162
- it on thick *cover* 223
too much 641
flatter 933
- on 972
- one's account for
 484
- oneself open to 177
- oneself out for 673
- one's finger upon
 480a
- one's head on the
 block 942
- on the table 133
- open *divest* 226
opening 260
show 525
disclose 529
- out *destroy* 162
horizontal 213
- *corpse* 363
plan 626
expend 809
- over 133
- siege to 716
- stress on 642
- the ax at the root
 of tree 162
- the first stone 66
- the flattering unc-
 tion to one's soul
content 831
relief 834
- the foundations
originate 153
prepare 673
- to *attribute* 155
rest 265
- together 43
- to one's charge 938
- train 626
- under hatches 751
- under restraint 751
- up *store* 636
sickness 655
disuse 678
- waste 162
lay down *locate* 184
horizontal 213
assert 535
renounce 757
relinquish 782
pay 807
- a plan 626
- one's arms
passification 723
submission 725
- one's life 360

- the law *certain* 474
assert 535
command 741
insolence 885
layer **204**
layette 225
layman **997**
laystall 653
lazar house 662
lazy *inactive* 683
 (*slow* 275)
lazzarone 683
lb. 319
lea *land* 342
 plain 344
leach 295, 335
leachy 335
lead *supremacy* 33
 in order 62
 influence 175
 tend 176
 soundings 208
 - *in motion* 280
 heavy 319
 induce 615
 direct 693
 authority 737
heave the - 466
- a dance
 run away 623
 circuit 629
 difficulty 704
 disrespect 929
- a life 692
- astray 495
- by the nose 737
- captive *subject* 749
 restraint 751
- on 693
- one to expect 511
- the choir 990
- the dance 280
- the way
 precedence 62
 begin 66
 precession 280
 importance 642
 direction 693
 repute 873
- to no end 645
- to the altar 903
red - 434
take the -
 influence 175
 importance 642
 authority 737
leadable 298
leaden *dim* 422
 colorless 429
 gray 432
 inactive 683
leader *precursor* 64
 dissertation 595
 director 694
 counsel 968
 - *writer* 595
leaders *typography* 550
leadership **737**
leading *beginning* 66
 important 642
 - article 595

- lady *actress* 599
- note *music* 413
- part 175
- question 461
- strings *childhood* 127
 child 129
 pupil 541
 subject 749
 restraint 751, 752
leads 223
leaf *part* 51
 layer 204
 plant 367
 - *of a book* 593
 - green 435
turn over a new - 65⁸
leafage 367
leafless 226
leaflet 531
leafy 256
league *combine* 48
 length 200
 coöperation 709
 party 712
leak *crack* 198
 dribble 295
 waste 638
 - out *disclosure* **529**
spring a-
 injury 659
leakage [see leak]
leaky *oozing* 295
 imperfect 651
lean *thin* 203
 oblique 217
 - on 215
 - to *shed* 191
 willing 602
 - towards *favor* 923
 - upon *belief* 484
 subjection 749
 hope 858
leaning *tendency* 176
 willingness 602
 desire 865
 friendship 888
 favoritism 923
lean-witted 499
leap *sudden change* 146
 ascent 305
 jump **309**
by -s and bounds **274**
- in the dark
 experiement 463
 uncertain 475
 chance 621
 rash 863
- with joy 838
make a - at 622
leapfrog 840
leaping 309
leap year 138
learn 539
- by experience 950
- by heart 505
learned 490, 539
- man 492
learner 492, **541**
learning
 knowledge 490
 acquisition of - **539**

lease *property* 270, 780
  lending 787
  grant a - 771
  - and release 783
  take a new - of life 654
leasehold 780
leash *tie* 43
  three 92
  hold in - 751
least
  - *in quantity* 34
  - *in size* 193
  at the - 32
leather *skin* 223
  tough 327
  beat 972
  - or prunello 643
  nothing like - 481
leave *remainder* 40
  part company 44
  relinquish 624
  permission 760
  bequeath 784
  French - 623
  give me - to say 535
  - alone *inaction* 681
  freedom 748
  permit 760
  - a loophole 705
  - an inference 526
  - a place 293
  - in the lurch
  pass 303
  decisive 545
  - it to one 760
  - no trace
  disappear 449
  obliterate 552
  - off *cease* 142
  desuetude 614
  relinquish 624
  disuse 678
  - out 55
  - out of one's calcula-
    tion 460
  - the beaten track 83
  - to chance 621
  - to oneself 748
  - undecided 609a
  - undone 730
  - void *regret* 833
  - word 527
  take - *depart* 293
  freedom 748
leaven *component* 56
  cause 153
  lighten 320
  qualify 469
  deterioration 659
  bane 663
leavings *remainder* 40
  useless 645
lecher 962
lechery 961
lectern 1000
lection *special* 79
  interpretation 522
lectionary 998
lecture *teach* 537
  speak 582
  dissertation 595

censure 932
  sermon 998
  - room 542
lecturer *teacher* 540
  speaker 582
  preacher 996
lectureship 542
led - captain
  follower 746
  servile 886
  favorite 899
  - by the nose 749
ledge *height* 206
  horizontal 213
  shelf 215
  projection 250
ledger *list* 86
  record 551
  accounts 811
lee *front* 234
  side 236
leech *remedy* 662
  physician 695
Lee Enfield rifle 727
leef 829
leek 401
  eat the - *recant* 607
  submit 725
Lee-Metford rifle 727
leer *stare* 441
  dumb show 550
leery 702
lees 321, 653
lee shore
  danger 665, 667
leet, court - 966
lee wall 666
leeward 236
leeway *tardy* 133
  space 180
  navigation 267
  progression 282
  shortcoming 304
left *residuary* 40
  sinistral 239
  - alone 748
  - bower 840
  - in the lurch 732
  - to shift for oneself
    893
  over the - 545
  pay over the - shoul-
    der 808
left-handed *clumsy* 699
  - compliment 932
  - marriage 903
leg *support* 215
  walker 266
  food 298
  thief 792
  best - foremost 686
  fast as - s will carry
    274
  keep on one's - s 654
  last - s *spoiled* 659
  fatigue 688
  - bail 623
  light on one's - s 734
  make a - 894
  not a - to stand on
  illogical 477

confuted 479
  failure 732
off one's - s
  propulsion 284
on one's - s
  upright 212
  elevation 307
  speaking 582
  in health 654
  active 682
  free 748
  set on one's - s 660
legacy *transference* 270
  property 780
  gift 784
legadero 45
legal *permitted* 760
  legitimate 924
  relating to law 963
  - adviser 968
  - estate 780
  - pledge 535
legality **963**
legalize 963
legate 534
legatee *transferee* 270
  possessor 779
  receiver 785
legation 755
legato 415
legend *record* 551
  description 594
legendary
  imaginary 515
  mythical 979
legerdemain
  change 146
  trick 545
  (*cunning* 702)
leggings 225
leghorn 225
legible 518
  - hand 590
legion *multitude* 102
  army 726
legionary 726
legislation
  government 693
  legality 963
legislative
  - assembly 696
legislator 694
legislature 72, 696
legist 968
legitimate *true* 494
  permitted 760
  right 922
  due 924
  legal 963
legume 298, 367
legumin 321
leguminous 365, 367
Leibnitzianism 451
leiodermatous 255
leisure
  spare time **685**
  (*opportunity* 134)
  at one's - *late* 133
leisurely *slowly* 275
leman 897
lemma 476

lemon *fruit* 298
  sour 397
  color 436
  - pie 298
lemures 980
lend 787
  - a hand 680
  - aid 707
  - countenance 707
  - oneself to
  assent 488
  - coöperate 709
  - on security 789
  - wings to 707
lender *creditor* 805
lending **787**
  - library 593
length **200**
  at - *in time* 133
  full - *portrait* 556
  go all - s
  resolution 604
  activity 682
  exertion 686
  go great - s 549
  - and breadth of 50
  - and breadth of the
    land
  space 180
  publication 531
  - of time 110
lengthen *increase* 35
  make long 200
  - out *diuturnity* 110
  late 133
lengthwise 200, 251
lengthy *long* 200
  diffuse 573
lenient *moderate* 174
  mild 740
  compassionate 914
lenify 174
lenitive
  moderating 174
  lubricant 332
  qualification 469
  remedy 662
  relieving 834
lenity **740**
lens 445
lens-shaped 245
Lent *fasting* 956
  rite 998
lenten 956
lenticular *curved* 245
  convex 250
lentiginous 330, 653
lentor *slowness* 275
  spissitude 352
  inactivity 683
  (*inertness* 172)
lentous 352
leonine verses 597
leopard *variegated* 440
  - 's spots
  unchanging 150
leper *outcast* 892
lepidote 330
Leprechaun 979
leprosy 655
lerret 273

length 200
no breadth 203
string 205
lining 224
outline 230
straight 246
direction 278
music 26, 413
appearance 448
measure 466
mark 550
writing 590
verse 597
vocation 625
army and navy 726
between the -s 526
boundary - 233
draw the - 465
in a - continuous 69
straight 246
in a - with 278
- engraving 558
- of action 692
- of battle 69
- of battle ship 726
- of march 278
- of road 627
- of steamers 273
-s cue 51
read between the -s
522
sounding - 208
straight - 246
troops of the - 726
lineage kindred 11
series 69
ancestry 166
posterity 167
lineament outline 230
feature 240
appearance 448
mark 550
linear continuity 69
pedigree 166
length 200
linen 225, 635
linen draper 225
liner 273
lines fortification 717
reins 752
hard - adversity 735
severity 739
linger protract 110
delay 133
loiter 275, 291
- on time 106
lingo language 560
neology 563
linguacious 584
lingua franca 563
lingual language-560
speech 582
linguiform 245
linguist scholar 492
linguistics 560
lingulate 245
liniment ointment 356
remedy 662
lining 224
link relation 9
connect 43

connecting - 45
part 51
term 71
crossing 219
torch 423
missing - wanting 53
completing 729
linkboy 694
linked together
party 712
linn 343, 348
linoleum 223, 635
linotype 591
linseed oil 356
linsey-woolsey 41, 329
linstock 388
lint 223
lintel 215
lion animal 366
courage 861
prodigy 872
repute 873
come in like a - 173
heard -s roar 861
in the -'s den 665
- in the path 706
- lies down with the
lamb 721
-'s share more 33
chief part 50
too much 641
undue 925
lioness 374
lion-hearted 861
lionize curiosity 455
repute 873
lip beginning 66
edge 231
side 236
prominence 250
between cup and -
111
finger on the -s
silent 581
speechless 585
hang on the -s of 418
- homage flattery 933
- service falsehood 544
hypocrisy 988
- wisdom 499
open one's -s
speak 582
seal the -s 585
smack the - taste 390
savory 394
lipothymy 688
lipotype 187
lippitude 443
liquation 382
liquefaction 333, 335
- by heat 384
liquefy 382, 335
liquescence 335
liqueur drink 298, 392
sweet 396
liquid fluid 333
sound 405
letter 561
- diet 298
liquidate pay 807
assess 812

liquidator 801
liquidity 333
liquor potable 298
fluid 333
in - 959
- up 959
liquorish [see lickerish]
lisp 583
lissom 324
list arrange 69
catalogue 86
strip 205
leaning 217
fringe 231
hear 418
record 551
will 600
choose 609
schedule 611
arena 728
desire 865
enter the -s attack 716
contend 720
listed 440
listel 847
listen 418
be -ed to 175
- to 457
- to reason 498
listless inattentive 458
inactive 683
indifferent 866
litany worship 990
rite 998
literal imitated 19
exact 494
- meaning 516
manifest 525
letter 561
word 562
- meaning 516
- translation 522
literary 560
- hack 593
- man 492
- power 569
literati 492
literatim [see literal]
literature learning 490
language 560
lithagogue 662
lithe 324
lithic 323
lithify 323
lithograph 550, 558
lithoidal 358
lithology 358
lithomancy 511
lithotint 558
litigant litigious 713
combatant 726
accusation 938
litigation quarrel 713
contention 730
lawsuit 969
litigious 713
litotes 483
litter disorder 59
derange 61
multitude 102
brood 167

support 215
vehicle 266, 272
bedding for cattle 370
useless 645
littérateur scholar 492
author 593
Little - Bear 318
- Mary 191
little - in degree 32
- in size 193
darling 897
mean 940
bigoted 988
cost - 815
do - 683
- by little degree 26
slowly 275
- did one think 508
- name 565
- one 129
make - of 483
signify - 643
think - of 458
to - purpose
useless 645
failure 732
littleness 193
littoral 342
liturgics 998
liturgy 998
lituus 215
live exist 1
continue 141
dwell 186
life 359
glowing 382
activity 682
repute 873
- again 660
- and let live
inaction 681
freedom 748
inexcitability 826
- by one's wits 545
- circuit 157
- from hand to mouth
674
- hard 954
- in hope 858
- in the memory 505
- man 682
- matter 591
- on 298
- rail 157
- to explain 485
- to fight again 110
- upon nothing 819
- wire hustler 682
we - in deeds 680
livelihood 803
liveliness [see lively]
livelong 110
lively leap 309
keen 375
- style 574
active 682
acute 821
sensitive 822
sprightly 836
- imagination 515
- pace 274

597

M

malgre 179
malice *hate* 898
  spite 907
  bear - *revenge* 919
  - prepense 907
malign *bad* 649
  malevolent 907
  detract 934
malignant 649, 901*a*, 907
malignity 173, 907
malinger 544, 548, 655
malison 908
malkin *mop* 652
  slattern 653
mall *walk* 189
  opening 260
  club 276
malleable *soft* 324
  (*facile* 705)
mallet 276
malleus 418
malnutrition 655
malodor 401
malpractice 974
malt liquor 298
maltreat *injure* 649
  aggrieve 830
  molest 907
malversation
  rapacious 819
  guilt 947
mamelon 250
Mameluke 726
mamma 166
mammal 366, 368
mammalogy 368
mammiform 250
mammilla 250
Mammon 803
mammoth 192
man *adult* 131
  mankind 372
  male **373**
  prepare 673
  workman 690
  defend 717
  servant 746
  courage 861
  husband 903
make a - of *good* 648
  brave 861
- among men 948
- and a brother 372
- and wife 903
- at-arms 726
- in office 745
- in the street 876
- of action 682, 686
- of letters 271
- of straw 545, 746
-'s estate 131
one's - of business 758
Son of - 976
to a - 488
manacle *restraint* 751
  fetter 752
manage *influence* 175
  direct 693
- to *succeed* 731
manageable *easy* 705

management
  conduct 692
  skill 698
manager *stage* - 599
  director 694
managery 693
man bird 269
mancipation 751
manciple 637
mandamus 741
mandarin 745
mandate
  requirement 630
  command 741
mandible 298
mandola 417
mandolin 417
mandragora 174
mandrel 312
manducation 298
mane 256
man-eater 361
manège *riding* 266
  equestration 370
manes 362
maneuver
  operation 680
  stratagem 702
  (*scheme* 626)
manful *strong* 159
  resolute 604
  brave 861
mange 380, 655
manger 191
mangle *separate* 44
  smooth 255
  injure 659
mangled 53
  [*see* mangle]
mango 298
mangosteen 298
mangy 380, 655
man hater 911
manhood 131, 861
mania *insanity* 503
  desire 865
- a potu 959
maniac 504
Manichæism 451, 978
manichord 417
manicure 662
manie 865
manifest *list* 86
  visible 446
  obvious 525
  disclosure 529
  (*appear* 448)
  (*intelligible* 518)
manifestation **525**
manifesto 531
manifold *multiform* 81
  multitude 102
  automobile 272
  writing 590
- linguist 492
manikin *dwarf* 193
  image 554
manipulate *handle* 379
  use 677
  conduct 692
manito 993

mankind **372**
manlike 131
manly *adolescent* 131
  strong 159
  male 373
  brave 861
  upright 939
manna *food* 396
- in the wilderness
  aid 707
  pleasing 829
mannequin 554
manner *kind* 75
  style 569
  way 627
  conduct 692
by all - of means 536
by no - of means 602
in a - 32
to the - born 5
mannered 579
mannerism *special* 79
  unconformity 83
  affectation 855
  vanity 880
mannerly 894
manners *breeding* 852
  politeness 894
man-of-war
  ship 273, 664
  combatant 726
man-of-war's man 269
manor 780
lord of the - 779
- house 189
manorial 780
mansard 223
- roof 244
manse 1000
mansion 189
manslaughter 361
mansuetude 894
mantelpiece 215
mantilla 225
mantle *spread* 194
  dress 225
  foam 353
  shade 424
  redden 434
  robes 747
  flush 821, 824
  anger 900
mantlet *cloak* 225
  defense 717
mantology 511
manual *guide* 527
  schoolbook 542
  book 593
  advice 695
- labor 686
manubial 793
manufactory 691
manufacture 161, 680
manufacturer 690
manu forti 604, 686, 739
manumission 750
manumotor 272
manure *agriculture* 371
  dirt 653
  aid 707

manuscript 21, 590
many 102
  frequency 136
  for - a day 110
- irons in the fire 682
- men many minds 489
- times *repeated* 104
  frequent 136
the - 876
many-colored 428, 440
manyplies 191
many-sided
  multiform 81
  sides 236
many-tongued 532
map *information* 527
  representation 554
- of days outworn 236
- out 626
maple 367
- sugar 396
- syrup 396
mar *deface* 241
  spoil 659
  botch 699
  obstruct 706
marabou 41
Marabout 1000
marah 395
maranatha 908
marasmus
  shrinking 195
  atrophy 655
  deterioration 659
Marathon race 274
maraud 791
marauder 792
marble *ball* 249
  hard 323
  sculpture 557
  tablet 590
  materials 635
  insensible 823
marble-constant 939
marbled 440
marble-hearted 907
marcescence 659
march *region* 181
  journey 266
  progression 282
  music 415
dead - 363
forced - 684
- against 716
- of events 151
- off 293
- of intellect
  knowledge 490
  improvement 658
- of time 109
- on a point 278
- past 882
- with 199
on the - 264
steal a - *advance* 280
  go beyond 303
  deceive 545
  active 682
  cunning 702
March, Ides of - 601

marches 233
marchioness 875
marchpane 298
marcid 203
marconigram 532
marcor 203
Mardi gras 840
mare *horse* 271
  female 374
marechal 745
mare's-nest 497, 546
mare's-tail *wind* 349
  cloud 353
margin *space* 180
  edge 231
  redundance 641
  latitude 748
marginate 231
margrave
  master 745
  nobility 875
mariage de convenance 903
marigraph 348
marinate 337
marine *fleet* 273
  sailor 269
  oceanic 341
  safety 664
  soldier 726
  -painter 559
  - painting 556
  tell it to the -s 497
mariner 269
Marinism 579
Mariolatry 991
marionette
  representation 554
  drama 599
marish 345
marital 903
maritime
  navigation 267
  ship 273
  oceanic 241
mark *degree* 26
  term 71
  take cognizance 450
  attend to 457
  measurement 466
  indication 550
  record 551
  writing 590
  object 620
  importance 642
  repute 873
  beyond the - 303
  leave one's - 873
  man of -
    repute 873
    rank 875
  - of Cain 550
  - off 551
  - of recognition 894
  - out *choose* 609
    plan 626
    command 741
  - time
    chronometry 114
    halt 265
    expectation 507
  604

- with a red letter 883
- with a white stone 931
near the - 197
overshoot the - 699
put a - upon 457
save the - 870
up to the -
  enough 639
  good 648
  skill 698
  due 924
wide of the -
  distant 196
  error 495
within the - 304
marked [*see* mark]
  great 31
  special 79
  affirmed 535
in a - degree 31
- down *cheap* 815
well - 446
marker *interment* 363
market *provision* 637
  consumer 677
  buy 795
  mart 799
  bring to - 796
  buy in the cheapest &c. - 794
  in the - *offered* 763
    barter 794
    sale 796
  - garden 371
  - overt *manifest* 525
  - place *street* 189
    mart 799
  - price 812
  public - 637
  rig the - 794
marketable 794, 796
marksman 700
marksmanship 698
marl 342
marmalade 396
marmoreal 430
marmot 683
maroon *brown* 433
  red 434
  fugitive 623
  abandon 782
  outlaw 893
marplot *bungler* 701
  obstacle 706
  malicious 913
marque, letters of - 791
marquee 223
marquetry
  variegated 440
marquis 875
marquisate 877
marriable 131
marriage 903
  ill-assorted - 904
  - bell 836
  - broker 903
marriageable
  adolescent 131
  nubile 903

married
  903
- man 903
- woman 903
marrow *essence* 5
  interior 221
  central 222
  (*meaning* 516)
  (*importance* 642)
  chill to the - 385
marrowbones, on one's -
  submit 725
  beg 765
  humble 879
  servile 886
  atonement 952
marrowless 158
Marrubium 400
marry *combine* 48
  assertion 535
  wed 903
  - come up
    defiance 715
    anger 900
    censure 932
Mars 722
  - orange 439
marsh 345
  - gas 663
marshal *arrange* 60
  messenger 534
  auxiliary 711
  officer 745
Marshalsea 752
marshy 345
marsupial 191, 368
mart 799
martello tower 206, 717
martial 722
  court - 966
  - law *severe* 739
    compulsory 744
    illegal 964
  - music 415
martinet 739
martingale 752
Martinmas 998
martyr
  bodily pain 378
  mental pain 828
  ascetic 955
  punishment 972
  - to disease 655
martyrdom *killing* 361
  agony 378, 828
  unselfish 942
  punishment 972
marvel *wonder* 870
  prodigy 872
  - whether 514
marvelous *great* 31
  wonderful 870
  deal in the - 549
Masaniello 742
mascot 621, 993
masculine *strong* 159
  male 373
mash *mix* 41
  disorder 59
  soft 324

  semiliquid 352
  pulpiness 354
masher 854
masjid 1000
mask *dress* 225
  shade 424
  concealment 528
  ambush 530
  deceit 545
  shield 717
  put on the - 544
masked *concealed* 528
  - battery 667
masker 599
masochism 659
mason 690
Masonic 712
Masorah 985
masque 599
masquerade
  dress 225
  concealment 528
  deception 545
  frolic 840
  - dress 530
masquerader 528
Mass *worship* 990
  Eucharist 998
  - book 998
mass *quantity* 25
  much 31
  whole 50
  heap 72
  size 192
  gravity 319
  density 321
  in the - 50
  - of society 876
massacre 361
massage 324, 331, 379, 662
masses, the - 876
masseur 331, 662
massicot 436
massive *huge* 192
  heavy 319
  dense 321
mast 206
mastaba 363
master, Master
  boy 129
  influence 175
  man 373
  know 490
  understand 518
  learn 539
  teacher 540
  director 694
  proficient 698, 700
  succeed, conquer 731
  ruler **745**
  possession 777
  possessor 779
  title 877
  eye of the - 693
  hard - 739
  - hand 700
  - key *open* 260
    instrument 631
  - mariner 269
  - mind *sage* 500

proficient 700
- of Arts 492
- of one's time 685
- of self 604
- of the position 731
- of the revels 840
- of the Rolls
  recorder 553
  judge 967
- of the situation
  success 731
  authority 737
- one's feelings 826
- one's passions 944
- passion 820
- spirit of the age
  sage 500
  repute 873
past - 700
masterdom 737
masterpiece *good* 648
  perfect 650
  skill 698
masterstroke *plan* 626
  masterpiece 650
  success 731
masterwork 698
mastery *success* 731
  authority 737
get the - of 175
masthead
  punish 972
mastic *viscid* 352
  resin 356a
masticate 298, 354
mastiff 366
mastology 368
mat *support* 215
  woven 219
  roughness 256
  doormat 652
matador 361
match *similar* 17
  copy 19
  equal 27
  fuel 388
  retaliate 718
  contest 720
  marriage 903
matchless *unequal* 28
  supreme 33
  virtuous 944
  best 648
  (*perfect* 650)
matchlock 727
matchmaker
  marriage 903
mate *similar* 17
  equal 27
  duality 89
  auxiliary 711
  master 745
  friend 890
  wife 903
check - 732
maté 298
mater, alma - 542
- familias 166
material *substance* 316
  stuff 635
  important 642

- existence 316
- for thought 454
- point 32
materialism *matter* 316
  heterodoxy 984
  irreligion 989
materiality
  substantiality 3
  matter **316**
  importance 642
materialization
  materiality 316
  manifestation 525
  spiritualism 992a
materialize 316, 446
materials **635**
materia medica 662
matériel 316, 633
maternal *parental* 166
  benevolent 906
- love 897
maternity 166
mathematical
  precise 494
- point 193
mathematician 85
mathematics 25
mathesis 25
matin 125
matinée 892
- idol 899
matins 125, 990
matrass 191
matriarch 166
matriarchy 737
matriculate 86
matriculation 539
matrimonial 903
- agency 903
matrimony *mixture* 41
  wedlock 903
matrix *mold* 22
  printing 591
  workshop 691
matron *woman* 374
  married 903
- of honor
  marriage 903
matronize 459, 693
matronly *age* 128
  adolescent 131
matross 726
matter *substance* 3
  copy 21
  material world 316
  topic 454
  meaning 516
  printing 591
  business 625
  importance 642
  pus 653
in the - of 9
- in dispute 461
- in hand *topic* 454
  business 625
- nothing 643
- of course
  conformity 82
  certain 474
  habitual 613
- of fact *event* 151

certainty 474
  truth 494
- of indifference 866
- of no consequence 4
-s *affairs* 151
no - 460
  the wreck of - 59
  what - 643
  what's the -
  curiosity 455
  inquiry 461
matter-of-fact
  prosaic 576
  artless 703
  dull 843
mattock 253
mattress 215
maturate 650, 673
maturative 662
mature *old* 124
  adolescent 131
  conversion 144
  scheme 626
  perfect 650
  improve 658
  prepare 673
  completing 729
- thought 451
Maturine 996
maturity
  [see *mature*]
  bring to - 729
matutinal
  morning 125
  (*early* 132)
matzo 298
maudlin *inactive* 683
  sentimental 822
  drunk 959
mauger 30, 179
maukin 652
maul *hammer* 276
  hurt 649
- and wedges 780
maund *basket* 191
  mumble 583
maunder
  diffuse style 573
  mumble 583
  loquacity 584
  lament 839
Maundy Tuesday 138
Mauser *rifle* 727
mausoleum 363
mauvais
- goût 851
- quart d'heure 828
- sujet 949
- ton 851
mauve 437
mavis 366, 416
maw 191
mawkish 391
mawworm
  deceiver 548
  sham piety 988
maxim 80, **496**
maximal 33
Maxim gun 727
maximum *supreme* 33
  summit 210

may be 470
  as it - 156
May Day 840
May fly 111
mayhap 470
mayor 745
maypole 206
May queen 847
mazard 298
maze *convolution* 248
  enigma 533
  difficulty 704
  (*ignorance* 491)
  in a - *uncertain* 475
mazed 503
mazurka 840
mazy 533
me 317
mead *plain* 344
  field 367
  sweet 396
meadow *plain* 344
- land 371
meager *small* 32
  incomplete 53
  thin 203
- style 575
  scanty 640
  poor 643
- diet 956
meal *repast* 298
  powder 330
mealy-mouthed
  falsehood 544
  servile 886
  flattering 933
mean *average* **29**
  small 32
  middle 68
  interjacent 228
  signify 516
  intend 620
  contemptible 643
  stingy 819
  shabby 874
  ignoble 876
  sneaking 886
  base 940
  selfish 943
  golden - 174
- nothing 517
- parentage 876
- wretch 949
  take the - 774
meander
  convolution 248
  deviate 279
  circuition 311
  river 348
  maze 533
meandering
  diffuse 573
meaning **516**
meaningless 517
meanness
  inferiority 34
  [see *mean*]
means *appliances* **632**
  property 780
  wealth 803
  by all - 602

mendicity 804
menial *servant* 746
  rustic 876
meniscal 245
meniscus 245, 445
menses 138, 299
menstrual 138
menstruum 335
mensuration 466
mental 450
 - acquisitiveness 455
 - calm 826
 - cultivation 539
 - excitement 824
 - healing 984
 - pabulum 454
 - philosophy 450
 - poise 498
 - reservation 528, 543
 - suffering 828
mentality 450
mentalize 451
mentation 451
menticulture 490, 658
mention 527
 above -ed 104
 not worth -ing 543
mentor *sage* 500
 teacher 540
 adviser 695
mentum 234
menu *list* 86
 food 298
Mephistopheles 978
Mephistophelian 945
mephitic *fetid* 401
 deleterious 654
mephitis 663
meracious 392
mercantile 794
mercatoria, lex - 963
mercature 794
mercenary *soldier* 726
 servant 746
 price 812
 parsimonious 819
 selfish 943
mercer 225
merchandise **798**
merchant **797**
merchantable 795
merchantman 273
merciful 914
merciless 914a
mercurial
 changeable 149
 mobile 264
 quick 274
 excitable 825
mercurouschlorid⸗662
Mercury *traveler* 268
 quick 274
 messenger 534
 -'s rod 747
mercy *lenity* 740
 pity 914
 at the - of *liable* 177
 subject 749
 cry you - 766
 for -'s sake 765
 have no - 914a

 - on us! 870
 - seat 966
mere *simple* 32
 lake 343
 trifling 643
 buy for a - nothing 815
 - nothing *small* 32
 trifle 643
 - pretext 617
 - words 477
 - wreck 659
merelles 840
meretricious
 false 495
 vulgar 851
 licentious 961
merge *combine* 48
 include 76
 insert 300
 plunge 337
 - in 56
 - into *become* 144
merged 228
merger 712
meridian *region* 181
 room 125
 summit 210
 light 420
 map drawing 550
 - of life 131
meridional 125, 237
meringue 298
merit *goodness* 648
 due 924
 virtue 944
 make a - of 884
 - notice 642
merito, e - 944
meritorious 931
mermaid *monster* 83
 ocean 341
 mythology 979
merman 341
meroblast 357
merogenesis 161
merriment
 cheerful 836
 amusement 840
merry *cheerful* 836
 drunk 959
 make - *sport* 840
 make - with *wit* 842
 ridicule 856
 - and wise 842
 - as the day is long 836
 - heart 836
 wish a - Christmas &c. 896
merry-andrew 844
merry-go-round 840
merrymaking *revel* 840
 sociality 892
merrythought 842, 993
mersion 337
mesa 344
mésalliance
 ill-assorted 24
 marriage 903
meseems 484

mesh *interstices* 198
 crossing 219
meshes *trap* 545
 difficulty 704
 - of sophistry 477
mesial *middle* 68
 (central 222)
mesilla 344
mesmerism 992
mesmerist 992a
mesne 228
 - lord 779
mesoblast 357
mess *mixture* 41
 disorder 59
 derangement 61
 meal 298
 difficulty 704
 portion 786
 make a - *unskillful* 699
 fail 732
message *dispatch* 527
 intelligence 532
 command 741
Messalina 962
messenger *traveler* 268
 cloud 353
 envoy **534**
 servant 746
 - balloon 463
Messiah 976
messmate 890
messuage 189, 780
mestee 41
mestizo 41
metabatic 264
metabola 140
metabolism 140, 357
metabolize 140
metacenter 222
metachronism 115
metage 466
metagenesis 140
metagrammatism 561
metal 635
 Britannia - 545
metalepsis 521
metallic *harsh* 410
metallurgy 358
metamorphosis 140
metamorphotic 81
metaphor
 comparison 464
 figure **521**
 (analogy 17)
metaphrase 522
metaphrast 524
metaphrastic 516
metaphysics 450
metaplasm 357
metasomatism 140
metastasis *change* 140
 inversion 218
 displacement 270
metathesis *change* 140
 inversion 218
 displacement 270
 metaphor 521
mete *measure* 466
 distribute 786
 - out *give* 784

metempirical 519
metempsychosis 140
meteor
 heavenly body 318, 353
 luminary 423
meteoric *transient* 111
 violent 173
 light 420
meteorite 318
meteorology 338, 353
meteoromancy 466
meter *length* 200
 measure 333, 466
 versification 597
methane 663
metheglin 396
methinks 484
method *order* 58
 way **627**
 want of - 59
methodical *arranged* 60
 regular 80, 138
 businesslike 692
Methodist 984
methodist *formalist* 988
methodize 58, 60
Methuselah 130
 old as - 128
 since the days of - 124
metic 57
meticulosity 457, 459, 868
meticulous *exact* 494
 observant 772
 fastidious 868
métis 83
metogenesis 161
metonymy 521
metopic 234
metoposcopist 234, 448
metoposcopy
 front 234
 appearance 448
 interpret 522
metrical *measured* 466
 verse 597
metrocracy 737
metrology 466
metropolis 189, 222
metropolitan
 archbishop 996
mettle *energy* 171
 spirit 820
 courage 861
 man of - 861
 on one's -
 resolved 604
 put on one's -
 excite 824
 encourage 861
mettlesome
 energetic 171
 sensitive 822
 excitable 825
 brave 861
meum et tuum 777, 780
 disregard distinction between - 791

mew *molt* 226
  cry 412
  - up 751
mewed up 229
mewl 412
mews 189
mezzanine floor
  house 191
  theater 599
Mezzofanti 492
mezzo rilievo
  convex 250
  sculpture 557
mezzotint 259, 421, 558
miasm 663
miasma 663
mica 527
micaceous 204
mi-careme 840
M'cawber 460
Michaelmas 998
mickle 31
Micomicon 519
microbe 193
microbic 193
microcosm 193
microgamete 357
micrography 193
micrometer 193
micromorph 193
micron 193
microörganism 193
microphone 418
microphyte 193
microscope *little* 193
  vision 441
  optics 445
microscopic 32, 193
microspore 357
microzoa 193
microzyme 193
mid 68
Midas 803
mid-course 29, **628**
midday 125
midden 653
middle
  - *in degree* 29
  - *in order* **68**
  - *in space* 222
  interjacent 228
  - age 131
  - classes 736
  - constriction 203
  - course 628
  - man *director* 694
  agent 758
  - state 29
  - term 68
  compromise 774
middle-aged 131
middleman 328
middlemost 222
middling *small* 32
  imperfect 651
  mediocre 736
middy 269
  - blouse 225
Midgard 318
midge 193
midland 342

608

midmost 68
midnight *night* 126
  dark 421
  - blue 438
  - oil 539
midriff *middle* 68
  interjacence 228
midshipman 269
midships 68
midst - *in order* 68
  central 222
  interjacent 228
  in the - of
  mixed with 41
  doing 680
midsummer 125
  - day 138
midway 68, 628
midwife
  instrument 631
  remedy 662
midwifery
  production 161
  surgery 662
mien 448
miff 900
might *power* 157
  violence 173
  energy 686
mightless 158
mighty *much* 31
  strong 159
  large 192
  haughty 878
mignonette 435
migraine 378
migrate 266
mikado 745
milch cow
  productive 168
  animal 366
  store 636
mild *moderate* 174
  warm 382
  insipid 391
  lenient 740
  calm 826
  courteous 894
milden 324
mildew *dirt* 653
  bane 663
mildewed
  spoiled 659
mile 200
mileage 200, 973
  - ticket 550
milestone 50
  whistle jigs to a - 645
militant 722
military 722
  warfare
  soldiers 726
  - authorities 745
  - band 416, 417
  - education 537
  - power 737
  - school 542
  - time 132
  - train 726
militate against 708
militia 664, 726

milk *moderate* 174
  semiliquid 352
  - cows 370
  white 430
  mild 740
  flow with - and honey
  plenty 639
  prosperity 734
  pleasant 829
  - a he-goat into a
  sieve 471
  - and water *weak* 160
  insipid 391
  unimportant 643
  imperfect 651
  - of human kindness
  906
  - sickness 655
  - the ram 645
  - white 430
milk-livered 862
milksop *impotent* 158
  fool 501
  coward 862
milky [*see* milk]
  semitransparent 427
  white 430
  become - 427
Milky Way 318, 423
mill *indent* 257
  pulverize 330
  machine 633
  unimportance 643
  workshop 691
  fight 720
  like a horse in a - 312
millboard 593
millenary 98, 120
millennium *number* 98
  period 108
  futurity 121
  utopia 515
  hope 858
millesimal 99
millet seed 193
milliard 98
milliary 550
milliner 225
  man - 854
millinery *dress* 225
  ornament 847
  display 882
  man - 855
million 98
  multitude 102
  people 372
  populace 876
  for the -
  intelligible 518
  easy 705
millionaire 803
mill pond *level* 213
  pond 343
  store 636
mill race 343, 348
millstone 330
mime *player* 599
  buffoon 844
mimeography 19
mimic *imitate* 19
  actor 599

mimmation 560
mimography 599
minacity 909
minaret 206
minatory 668
minauderie 855
mince *cut up* 44
  slow 275
  food 298
  stammer 583
  affected 855
  extenuate 937
  - the matter 868
  - the truth 544
  not - the matter
  affirm 525
  artless 703
mincemeat 298
  make - of 162
mince pie 298
mincing 855
  - steps 275
mind *intellect* 450
  attend to 457
  take care 459
  believe 484
  remember 505
  will 600
  willing 602
  purpose 620
  warning 668
  desire 865
  dislike 867
  bear in - *thought* 451
  attention 457
  bit of one's - 527
  food for the - 454
  give one a piece of
  one's - 529
  give the - to 457
  have a - to *willing* 602
  desire 865
  in the - *thought* 451
  topic 454
  willing 602
  make one's - easy 826
  make up one's -
  opinion 484
  resolve 604
  - at ease 827
  - cure 662
  - one's book 539
  - one's business
  incurious 456
  attentive 457
  -'s eye 515
  - what one is about
  864
  never - *neglect* 460
  unimportant 643
  not know one's own -
  605
  not - 866
  out of - 506
  set one's - upon 604
  speak one's - *say* 582
  blunt 703
  to one's - *taste* 850
  love 897
  the public - 488
  willing - 602

minded *willing* 602
  intending 620
mindful *attentive* 457
  memory 505
mindless
  inattentive 458
  imbecile 499
  forgetful 506
  insensible 823
mine *sap* 162
  hollow 252
  open 260
  snare 545
  intrigue 626
  store 636
  abundance 639
  damage 659
  intrench 664
  pitfall 667
  attack 716
  defense 717
dig a - *plan* 626
  prepare 673
  - layer 726
  - of wealth 803
spring a -
  unexpected 508
  attack 716
miner 252
  sapper and - 726
mineral 358
  - oil 356
mineralize 358
mineralogy 358
Minervâ invitâ
  unwilling 603
  difficult 704
Minerva press
  fustian 577
mingle 41
miniature *small* 32, 193
  portrait 556
  - painter 559
Minié rifle 727
minikin 32, 193
minim *small* 32
  music 413
minimifidian 487
minimize 36, 483
minimum *small* 32
  inferior 34
minion 899
minister
  instrumentality 631
  remedy 662
  agent 690
  director 694
  aid 707
  deputy 759
  give 784
  clergy 996
  rites 998
  - to *help* 746
ministerial
  clerical 995
ministering - angel 948
  - spirit 977
ministration
  direction 693
  aid 707
  rite 998

ministry *direction* 693
  aid 707
  church 995
  clergy 996
  rite 998
minium 434
miniver 223
minnesinger 597
minnow 193
minor *inferior* 34
  infant 129
  - key 413
  - poet 597
Minorites 996
minority *few* 103
  youth 127
Minos 694
minotaur 83
minster 1000
minstrel *musician* 416
  poet 597
minstrelsy 415
mint *mold* 22
  fragrance 400
  workshop 691
  wealth 803
  - julep 298
minuend 38
minuet *music* 415
  dance 840
minus *inexistent* 2
  less 34
  subtracted 38
  absent 187
  deficient 304
  loss 776
  in debt 806
  nonpayment 808
minusculæ 561
minute
  circumstantial 8
  - in degree 32
  special 79
  - of time 108
  instant 113
  - in size 193
  record 551
  compendium 596
  (*unimportant* 643)
  - account 594
  - attention 457
  to the - 132
minutemen 726
minuteness *care* 459
minutiæ *small* 32
  details 79
  unimportant 643
minx *girl* 129
  malapert 887
  wanton 962
miosis 483
mir 188
miracle *exceptional* 83
  prodigy 872
  - play 599
miraculous
  wonderful 870
mirage 443
mire 653
mirror *imitate* 19
  reflector 445

  perfection 650
  glory 873
  hold the - up to na-
    ture 554
  hold up the - 525
  magic - 443
mirth 836
misacceptation 523
misadventure
  contretemps 135
  adversity 735
  (*evil* 619)
  (*failure* 732)
misadvised 699
misanthropy **911**
misapply
  misinterpret 523
  misuse 679
  mismanage 699
misapprehend
  mistake 495
  misinterpret 523
misappropriate 679
misarrange 61
misbecome 925
misbegotten
  crooked 243
  vicious 945
misbehave *vulgar* 851
  vice 945
misbehavior
  discourtesy 895
  guilt 947
misbelief 485
misbeliever 487, 984
miscalculate
  misjudge 481
  err 495
  disappoint 509
miscall 565
miscarry 732
miscegenation 41, 903
miscellany
  mixture 41
  collection 72
  generality 78
  compendium 596
  poetry 597
mischance *evil* 619
  misfortune 735
  (*failure* 732)
mischief 619
  do - 649
  make - 649
mischief-maker
  evildoer 9'3
  knave 941
mischievous 649
miscible 41
miscite 544
miscompute
  misjudge 481
  mistake 495
misconceive
  mistake 495
  misinterpret 523
misconception 495, 523
misconduct
  bungling 699
  guilt 947
  - oneself 945

misconjecture 481
misconstrue 523
miscorrect 538
miscount 495
miscreance 485
miscreant 487, 949
miscreated 945
misdate 115
misdeed 947
misdemean 945
misdemeanant 949, 975
misdemeanor 947
misdescribe 538
misdevotion 988
misdirect *misteach* 538
  unskillful 699
misdo 945
misdoing 947
misdoubt 485, 523
mise en scène
  appearance 448
  drama 599
  display 882
misemploy 679
miser 640, 819
miserable *small* 32
  contemptible 943
  unhappy 828
miserably *very* 31
misère 840
miserere *sing* - 950
misericordia Domini
    470
miserly 819
misery 828
  put out of one's - 914
misesteem 481
misestimate
  misjudge 481
  (*mistake* 495)
misfeasance
  bungling 699
  guilt 947
misfire 732
misfortune
  adversity 735
  unhappiness 830
  (*evil* 619)
  (*failure* 732)
misgiving *doubt* 485
  fear 860
misgovern 699
misguide *error* 495
  misteaching 538
misguided 699
mishap *evil* 619
  failure 732
  misfortune 735
  painful 830
mishmash 59
Mishna 985
misinform 538
misinformed 491
misinstruct 538
misintelligence 538
misinterpretation **523**
misjoined 24
misjudgment
  sophistry 477
  misjudge **481**
  (*error* 495)

mislay *derange* 61
  lose 776
mislead *error* 495
  misteach 538
  deceive 545
mislike 867
mismanage 699
mismatch
  difference 15
  disagreement 24
misname 565
misnomer **565**
misogamist
  celibacy 904
  misanthropy 911
misogyny 904
mispersuasion 538
misplace *derange* 61
  displace 185
misplaced
  intrusive 24
  unconformable 83
  displaced 185
  (*disorder* 59)
misprint 495
misprision
  concealment 528
  guilt 947
  - of treason 742
misprize
  underrate 483
  disrespect 929
mispronounce 583
misproportion 241
misproportioned
  distortion 243
  ugly 846
misquote 544
misreckon
  misjudge 481
  mistake 495
misrelation 10
misrelish 867
misreport *err* 495
  falsify 544
misrepresent
  misinterpret 523
  misteach 538
  lie 544
misrepresentation 555
  untruth 546
misrule *misconduct* 699
  laxity 738
  Lord of - 701
miss *girl* 129
  neglect 460
  error 495
  unintelligible 519
  fail 732
  lose 776
  want 865
  courtesan 962
  - one's aim 732
  - one's way
    uncertain 475
    unskillful 699
  - stays 304
missa cantata 998
missal 990, 998
missay *neology* 563
  stammering 583

missend 699
misshapen
  shapeless 241
  distorted 243
  ugly 846
missile 727
missing *nonexistent* 2
  absent 187
  disappear 449
  - link *wanting* 53
  completing 729
mission *business* 625
  commission 755
missionary
  teacher 540
  clergyman 996
  - school 542
missive 592
misspell 523
misspend 818
misstate *mistake* 495
  misrepresent 523
  falsify 544
misstatement *error* 495
  untruth 546
  misrepresentation 555
mist *cloud* 353
  dark 424
  semitransparency 427
  (*dim* 422)
  in a - 528
  - before the eyes 443
  -s of error 495
  seen through a - 519
mistake *error* 495
  misconstrue 523
  mismanage 699
  failure 732
  lie under a - 495
misteaching **538**
mister 373
misterm 565
misthink 481
mistime 135
mistral 349
mistranslate 523
mistress *lady* 374
  master 745
  possessor 779
  love 897
  concubine 962
mistrust 485
misty [see *mist*]
  become - 427
misunderstand
  misinterret 523
misunderstanding
  disagreement 24
  error 495
  discord 713
misuse **679**
misventure 135
mite *bit* 32
  infant 129
  small 193
  arachnid 368
  dole 640
  money 800
miter *junction* 43
  angle 244
  crown 747, 999

mithai 396
mithridate 662
mitigate *abate* 174
  improve 658
  relieve 834
  (*calm* 826)
mitigation
  [see mitigate]
  qualification 469
  extenuation 937
mitosis *production* 161
mitraille 727
mitrailleuse 727
mitten 225, 384
mittimus 741
mix 41
  disorder 59
  - oneself up with
    meddle 682
    coöperate 709
mixed *confused* 523
  [see *mix*]
mixen 653
mixture **41**
  mere - *disorder* 59
mizzen 235
  - mast 235
mizzle 293, 348
mnemonics 505
mnemotecnhics 505
Mnemosyne 505
moan *faint sound* 405
  cry 411
  lament 839
moat *inclosure* 232
  ditch 259
  canal 350
  defense 717
mob *crowd* 72
  vulgar 876
  hustle 929
  scold 932
  king - 876
  - cap 225
  - law *authority* 738
    compulsion 744
    illegality 964
mobcap 225
mobile *inconstant* 149
  movable 264
  sensitive 822
mobility the - 876
mobilization 72, 264,
  722
mobilize 264
  - troops 722
mobocracy 738
moccasin 225
mock *imitate* 17, 19
  repeat 104
  erroneous 495
  deceptive 545
  chuckle 838
  ridicule 856
  desrespect 929
  - danger 861
  - modesty 855
  - sun 423
  - turtle soup 298
mockery [see *mock*]
  unsubstantial 4

- delusion and snare
  sophistry 477
  deception 545
solemn - 882
mocking bird 19
modal 6, 7, 8
mode *state* 7
  music 413
  habit 613
  method 627
  fashion 852
  - of expression 569
model *copy* 21
  prototype 22
  rule 80
  form 240
  representation 554
  sculpture 557
  perfection 650
  good man 948
  - after 19
  - condition 80
  new - 658
modeler 559
moderate *small* 32
  allay 174
  slow 275
  neutral 628
  sufficient 639
  lenient 740
  cheap 815
  temperate 953
  - circumstances
    mediocrity 736
moderately
  imperfect 651
moderation **174**
  inexcitability 826
  patience 831
  [see *moderate*]
moderato *music* 415
moderator
  moderation 174
  lamp 423
  director 694
  mediator 724
  judge 967
modern 123
  - philosophy 451
modernist 123
modernity 123
modernization 123
modest *small* 32
modesty *humility* **881**
  purity 960
  mock - 855
modicum *little* 32
  allotment 786
modification
  difference 15
  variation 20a
  change 140
  qualification 469
modillion 215
modiolus 215
modish 852
modiste 225
modulate 469
modulation *change* 140
  music 413
module 22

modulus 84
modus operandi 627, 692
modus vivendi 723
mofussil 181
mogul 745
Mohammed 986
Mohammedan 984
 - priests 996
 - temples 1000
Mohammedanism 976
Mohawk
 swaggerer 887
 evildoer 913
moider *inattention* 458
 uncertain 475
moiety 51, 91
moil *plod* 682
 exertion 686
moisture *wet* 337
 humid **339**
moke 219
molar 250
molasses 352, 396
mold *condition* 7
 matrix 22
 convert 144
 form 240
 structure 329
 earth 342
 vegetation 367
 model 554
 carve 557
 decay 653
 remedy 662
 turn to account 677
 create 976
molded 820
 - on 19
molder *decay* 653
 deteriorate 659
molding 847
moldy *fetid* 401
 unclean 653
 deteriorated 659
mole *wound* 206
 prominence 250
 refuge 666
 defense 717
 spot 848
molecular 32
molecule 193
mole-eyed 443
molehill *little* 193
 low 207
 trifling 643
molest *trouble* 830
molestation
 damage 649
 malevolence 907
mollah *judge* 967
mollescence 324
mollify *allay* 174
 soften 324
 (*mental calm* 826)
mollusca 368
mollusk 366, 368
mollycoddle 158, 372
Moloch *slaughter* 361
 demon 978
 heathen deity 991

molt 226
molten *liquefied* 384
 (*heated* 335)
molybdomancy 511
moment - *of time* 113
 importance 642
for the - 111
lose not a - 684
not have a - 682
on the spur of the - 612
momentous 151
momentum 276
Momus 838
monachal 1000
monachism 995
monad 87, 193
monarch 745
monarchical 737
monarchy 737
monastery 1000
monastic 995
monasticism 995
monde 852
monetary 800
 - arithmetic 811
monetize 800
money 800
 wealth 803
 bad - 800
 command of - 803
 for one's - 609
 made of - 803
 make - 775
 - burning one's pocket 818
 - coming in 810
 - down 807
 - going out 809
 - market 800
 - matters 811
 - paid 809
 -'s worth *useful* 644
 price 812
 cheap 815
 raise - 788
 save - 817
 throw away one's - 818
money bag 802
money box 802
money broker 797
money changer
 merchant 797
 treasurer 801
moneyed 803
money-grubbing 775
moneyless 804
monger 797
mongoose 366
mongrel
 mixture 41
 anomalous 83
 dog 366
 base 949
moniliform 249
monism 984
monition
 information 527
 warning 668
 (*advice* 695)

monitor *oracle* 513
 pupil teacher 540, 541
 director 694
 adviser 695
 war ship 726
inward - 926
 - building 189
monitory
 prediction 511
 dissuasion 616
 warning 668
monk 904, 996
monkery 984
monkey *imitative* 19
 support 215
 catapult 276
 animal 366
 ridiculous 857
 - trick *absurdity* 497
 sport 840
 - up 900
 play the - 499
monkeyshine 497
monkhood 995
monkish Latin 553
monochord 417
monochrome
 no color 429
 painting 556
monoclinous 83
monocracy 737
monoculous 443
monocycle 272
monodic 402
monodrame 599
monody *poem* 597
 lament 839
monogamist 903
monogamy 903
monogram *cipher* 533
 indication 550
 diagram 554
 letter 561
monograph
 writing 590
 description 594
monographer 598
monolith 551
monolithic 983a
monologist 582, 589
monologue
 soliloquy 589
 drama 599
monomachy 720
monomania
 insanity 503
 obstinacy 606
 excitability 825
monomaniac 504
monophonic 402
monoplane 273
monoplanist 269a
monopolist 751, 943
monopoly *restraint* 751
 possession 777
monospermous 87
monostich 572
monosyllable 561
monotheism 983
monotone 104

monotonous
 uniform 16
 equal 27
 repetition 104
 permanent 141
 - *style* 575
 weary 841
 dull 843
monotony
 [see monotonous]
monotype 591
Monroe Doctrine 748
monsoon 348, 349
monster *exception* 83
 large 192
 ugly 846
 prodigy 872
 evildoer 913
 ruffian 949
monstrance 191, 999
monstrosity
 [see monster]
 distortion 243
monstrous *excessive* 31
 exceptional 83
 huge 192
 ugly 846
 vulgar 851
 ridiculous 853
 wonderful 870
montagne Russe
 slope 217
 sport 840
mont de piété 787
monte 840
Montgolfier 273
month 108
monthly 138
 - nurse 662
monticle 206
monticoline 206
monument *tall* 206
 tomb 363
 record 551
monumentalize 112
moo 412
mood *nature* 5
 state 7
 change 140
 tendency 176
 willingness 602
 temper 820
moodish *rude* 895
 irascible 901
 sullen 901a
moods and tenses
 difference 15
 variation 20a
moody *furious* 825
 sad 837
 sullen 901a
moolvi 492
moon *period* 108
 changes 149
 world 318
 bay the - 645
 jump over the - 309
 man in the - 515
 - blindness 443
 - glade 422
 - of green cheese

motor bus 272
motor car 272
motorcycle 266, 272
motorial 264
motorist 268
motorium 264
motorize 266
motorman 268, 694
motory 264
motte 367
mottled 440
motto *maxim* 496
  device 550
  phrase 566
mouchard 527
mould [*see* mold]
mound *large* 192
  hill 206
  defense 717
mount *greatness* 31
  increase 35
  hill 206
  ascend 305
  raise 307
  display 882
  - guard *care* 459
  safety 664
  - up to *money* 800
  price 812
mountain *large* 192
  hill 206
  weight 319
  make -s of molehills
    482
  - brought forth mouse
  disappoint 509
  - flax 385
mountaineer 268
mountainous 206
mountebank
  quack 548
  drama 599
  buffoon 844
mounted rifles 726
mourn *grieve* 828
  lament 839
mourner 839
mourners' bench 1000
mournful *afflicting* 830
  sad 837
  lamentable 839
mourning *dress* 225
  in - *black* 431
  lament 839
mouse *little* 193
  animal 366
  search 461
  mountain brought
    forth - 509
  - over 451, 461
  not a - stirring 265
mouse-colored 432
mousehole 260
mouser 366
mouse trap 545
mousseux 353
mouth *entrance* 66
  receptacle 191
  brink 231
  opening 260
  eat 298

estuary 343
  drawl 583
  down in the - 879
  make -s 929
  - honor *falsehood* 544
  show 882
  flattery 933, 940
  - wash 652
  - watering 865
  open one's - 582
  pass from - to mouth
    531
  stop one's - 581
  word of - 582
mouthful *quantity* 25
  small 32
  food 298
mouthpiece
  speaker 534
  information 527
  speech 582
mouthy *style* 577
moutonné 250
movable *motion* 26
  transference 270
movables 780
move *begin* 66
  motion 264
  propose 514
  induce 615
  undertake 676
  act 680
  offer 763
  excite 824
  good - 626
  - back 287
  - forward 282
  - from 287
  - heaven and earth
    686
  - in a groove 82
  - off 293
  - on *progress* 282
  activity 682
  - out of 295
  - quickly 274
  - slowly 275
  - to 894
  on the - 293
moved with 821
moveless 265
movement
  motion 264
  music 415
  action 680
  activity 682
mover 164
movies
  theater 448, 599, 840
moving 185
  keep - 682
  - pictures 448, 599
  - picture machine 445
mow *shorten* 201
  smooth 255
  agriculture 371
  store 636
  - down *destroy* 162
  level 213
moxa 384
mozetta 999

M. P. 696
Mr. *man* 373
  gentleman 877
Mrs. 374
M. S. 590
much 31
  make - of
  important 642
  friends 888
  love 897
  endearment 902
  approval 931
  - ado *exertion* 686
  difficulty 704
  - ado about nothing
  overestimate 482
  exaggerate 549
  unimportant 643
  unskillful 699
  - cry and little wool
    884
  - speaking 584
  - the same *identity* 13
  similarity 17
  equality 27
  not say - for 932
  think - of *respect* 928
  approbation 931
muchness 31
mucid *semiliquid* 352
  unclean 653
mucilage 352
muck 653
muckle 31
muckrake 934
muckraker 936
muckworm *miser* 819
  lowborn 876
mucor 653
mucosity 352
mucous 352
mucronate 253
mucronulate 253
muculent 352
mucus 352
mud *marsh* 345
  semiliquid 352
  dirt 653
  clear as - 519
  stick in the - 704
muddle *disorder* 59
  derange 61
  inattention 458
  render uncertain 475
  absurd 497
  difficulty 704
  blunder 732
  - away 638
  - one's brains 475
muddled 730, 959
muddle-headed 499
muddy *moist* 339
  dim 422
  opaque 426
  color 429
mudguard 666
mud lark *dirty* 653
  commonalty 876
muezzin 996
muff *incapable* 158
  dress 225

effeminacy 374
  warmth 384
  bungle 699
  bungler 701
muffer *bungler* 701
muffle *wrap* 225
  silent 403
  faint 405
  nonresonant 408a
  conceal 528
  voiceless 581
  stammer 583
muffled *faint* 405
  latent 526
  - drums *funeral* 363
  nonresonance 408a
muffler *dress* 225
  wrap 384
  silencer 405, 408a
mufti *undress* 225
  judge 967
  priest 996
mug *cup* 191
  face 234
  pottery 384
mugger 913
muggy *moist* 339
mughouse 189
mugient 412
mugwump 607
Muharram 138
mulada 72
mulatto *mixture* 41
  exception 83
mulct *steal* 791
  fine 974
mule *mongrel* 83
  beast of burden 271
  obstinate 606
muleteer 694
muliebrity 374
mulish 606
mull *prominence* 250
  sweeten 396
  - over 451
mullah 492, 996
mulligatawny 298
mullion 215
multangular 244
multifarious
  irrelevant 10
  diverse 16a
  multiform 81
multifid *divided* 51
multifold 81, 102
multiformity 81
multigenerous 81
multilateral *sides* 236
  angles 244
multilocular 191
multiloquence
  speech 582
  loquacity 584
multinominal 102
multiparity 168
multiparous 168
multipartite 44
multiphase 81
multiple *product* 84
  numerous 102
multiplex 81

multiplicand 84
multiplication
  arithmetic 85
  multitude 102
  reproduction 163
  productiveness 168
multiplicator 84
multiplicity 102
multiplier 84
multiply
  [*see* multiplication]
multipotent 157
multisonous 404
multitude *number* **102**
  (*assemblage* 72)
many-headed - 102
the - 876
multum in parvo 596
multure 330
mum *mute* 581
  taciturn 585
mumble *chew* 298
  mutter 583
mumble peg 840
mumblety 840
Mumbo Jumbo
  god 979
  spell 993
mummer 599
mummery
  absurdity 497
  imposture 545
  masquerade 840
  parade 882
  (*ridicule* 856)
mummify 357, 363
mumming 840
mummy *dry* 340
  corpse 362
  brown 433
  beat to a - 972
mump *mutter* 583
  beg 765
mumper *beggar* 767
  pauper 804
mumpish *sad* 837
mumps *dejection* 837
  sullenness 901a
mumpsimus 495
munch 298
Munchausen 549
munchil 272
mundane *world* 318
  selfish 943
  irreligious 989
mundation 652
mundivagant 266
munerary 973
munerate 973
municipal 965
munificent 816
muniment
  evidence 467
  record 551
  defense 717
  security 771
munition
  materials 635
  defense 717

munshi
  learned man 493
  teacher 540
mural 717
murder 361
  - the King's English
  solecism 568
  stammering 583
  the - is out 529
murderer 361
muricated 253
murky *dark* 421
  opaque 426
  black 431
  gloomy 837
murmur *purl* 348
  sound 405
  voice 580
  complain 839
murmurer 832
murrain 655
Murray *travel* 266
  Lindley - 542
murrey 434
muscadine 400
muscle 159
muscular 159
muse 451
  [*see* musing]
Muse *poetry* 597
  historic - 594
  - of fire 597
  unlettered - 579
museology 72
Muses, the - 416
musette 417
museum
  collection 72
  store 636
mush *food* 298
mushroom
  unsubstantial 4
  new 123
  fungus 367
  upstart 734
  lowborn 876
  - anchor 706
  -s *food* 298
  fungi 369
  spring up like -s 163
music **415**
  - box 417
  - of the spheres
  order 58
  universe 318
  set to - 416
musical 413, 415, 416
  - ear *musician* 416
  hearing 418
  - instruments **417**
  - note 413
  - voice 580
musicale 415
music hall
  playhouse 599
  amusement 840
musician **416**
musing *thought* 451
  - on other things 458

thick-eyed - 837
musk 400
musket 727
  shoulder a - 722
musketeer 726
musketry 727
musk ox 366
muskrat 400
musk root 400
muslin
  semitransparent 427
  fabric 635
musnud *support* 215
  council 696
  scepter 747
muss 59, 61
mussuk 191, 348
Mussulman 984
mussy 61, 653
must *necessity* 601
  mucor 653
  compulsion 744
mustache 256
mustang 271
mustard *pungent* 392
  condiment 393
  after meat - 135
mustard gas 663, 737
mustard seed 193
musteline 433
muster *collect* 72
  numeration 85
  schedule 611
  - courage 861
  not pass - 651
  pass - 639
muster roll *list* 86
  (*record* 551)
musty 961
  smelling 401
  foul 653
mutable
  changeable 149
  (*irresolute* 605)
mutation 140
mutatis mutandis
  correlation 12
  change 140
  interchange 148
mute *funeral* 363
  silent 403
  sordine 405, 408a, 417
  letter 561
  speechless 581
  taciturn 585
  drama 599
  deaf - 419
  render - 581
mutescence 408a
mutilate *retrench* 38
  deform 241
  injure 659
mutilated
  incomplete 53
  imperfect 651
mutilation *evil* 619
mutineer 742
mutiny *revolution* 146
  disobedience 742

(*resistance* 719)
mutter *faint sound* 405
  imperfect speech 583
  grumble 839
  threaten 909
mutton 298
  - chop 298
muttonhead 501
mutton-headed 499
mutual *correlative* 12
  interchange 148
  - concession 774
  - understanding 23
muzzle *powerless* 158
  edge 231
  opening 260
  silence 403
  render speechless 581
  restrain 751
  gag 752
muzzle-loader 727
muzzy *confused* 458
  in liquor 959
myatism 560
mycologist 369
mycology 369
mynheer 877
myology 329
myomancy 511
myopia 443
myriad
  ten thousand 98
  multitude 102
myrmidon 726
myrrh 400
myrtle *tree* 367
  love 897
myself *I* 79
  immateriality 317
mysterious
  invisible 447
  uncertain 475
  obscure 519
  concealed 528
mystery
  [*see* mysterious]
  latency 526
  secret 533
  play 599
  craft 625
  into the supreme - 528
mystic *obscure* 519
  concealed 528
  psychic 992a
mysticism *thought* 451
  latency 526
  concealment 528
mystify *falsify* 477
  unintelligible 519
  hide 528
  misteach 538
  deceive 545
myth *fancy* 515
  untruth 546
mythic deities **979**
mythical *descriptive* 594
mythogenesis 515
mythology *gods* 979
  heathen 984

nab *deceive* 545
  seize 789
Nabob *master* 745
  wealthy 803
nacreous 440
nadir 211
nævose 440
nag *horse* 271
  quarrel 713
Nagari 590
naggy 901a
Naiad *ocean* 341
  mythology 979
naik 745
nail *fasten* 43
  fastening 45
  measure of length 200
  peg 214
  hard 323
  retain 781
  hit the right - on the
    head
  discover 480a
  skill 698
  on the - *present* 118
  pay 807
nailery 691
naïveté 703
naked *denuded* 226
  manifest 525
  - *eye* 441
  - *fact* 151
  - *sword* 727
  - *truth* 494
namby-pamby
  trifling 643
  affected 855
name *indication* 550
  appellation 564
  appoint 755
  celebrity 873
  assume a - 565
  call -s *disrespect* 929
  disapprobation 932
  fair - 873
  good - 873
  in the - of *aid* 707
  authority 737
  due 924
  - to conjure with 873
nameless
  anonymous 565
  obscure 874
namely *special* 79
  interpretation 522
namesake 564
nanny goat 374
nap *down* 256
  texture 329
  sleep 683
nape *back* 235
napha water 400
naphtha 356
napiform 245
napkin 652
  buried in a - 460
  lay up in a - 678
napless 226
napoleon *cards* 840
napping
  inattentive 458

  inexpectant 508
  dull 843
  - catch - 508
nappy *frothy* 353
  tipsy 959
Narcissus 845
narcosis 376, 381
narcotic
  unhealthy 657
  remedy 662
  (*bad* 649)
narcotization 381
narikin 123
Narraganset 271
narration 594
narrator 529
narrow *contract* 195
  thin 203
  qualify 469
  constrained 751
  bigoted 988
  - end of the wedge 66
  - escape 671
  - gauge 466
  - house 363
  - means 804
  - search 461
narrow-minded
  bigoted 481
  selfish 943
narrowness 203
narrows 343
narrow-souled 481
nasal 349
  - accent 583
nascent 66
nasty *unsavory* 395
  foul 653
  offensive 830
  cheap and - 815
natal *birth* 66
  indigenous 188
  - day 138
natation 267
natatorium 652
nathless 30
nation 372
  law of -s 963
national 372
  - guard 726
nationality *nation* 372
  patriotism 910
nationwide 78
native *inhabitant* 188
  indigenous 367
  artless 703
  - accent 580
  - land 189
  - soil 189
  - tendency 601
  - tongue 560
nativity *birth* 66
  cast a - *predict* 511
  sorcery 992
natty 845
natural *intrinsic* 5
  musical note 413
  true 494
  fool 501
  plain 576
  - *style* 578

  spontaneous 621
  not prepared 674
  artless 703
  simplicity 849
  - affection 897
  - course of things 613
  - death *death* 360
  completion 729
  - gas 388
  - history 357
  - impulse 601
  - meaning 516
  - order of things 82
  - philosophy 316
  - state 80
  - theology 983
  - turn 820
naturalist 357
naturalistic 537
naturalization
  conformity 82
  conversion 144
  location 184
naturalize *habit* 613
naturalized
  inhabitant 188
naturally 154
nature *essence* 5
  rule 80
  tendency 176
  world 318
  reality 494
  artlessness 703
  affections 820
  animated - 357
  in -'s garb 226
  organized - 357
  second - 613
  state of - *naked* 226
  raw 674
naught *nothing* 4
  zero 101
  bring to - 732
  set at -
  make light of 483
  opposition 708
  disobey 742
  not observe 773
  disrespect 929
  contempt 930
naughty 945
naumachia 720
nausea *weariness* 841
  disgust 867
nauseate
  unsavory 395
  give pain 830
nauseous
  unsavory 395
  unpleasant 830
  disgusting 867
nautch 840
nautch girl 840
nautical 267, 273
  -almanac 86
nautilus 368
naval 267, 273
  - authorities 745
  - engagement 720
  - forces 627
  - school 542

navarch 745
nave *middle* 68
  center 222
  circularity 247
  church 1000
navel *middle* 68
  center 222
navicular 245
naviform 245
navigation 267
navigator 269
navvy *pioneer* 673
  laborer 690
navy *ships* 273
  fighters 664, 726
  - blue 438
  - list 86
nawab 745, 875
nay 536
  - rather 14
Nazarene 989
naze 250
ne plus ultra
  supreme 33
  complete 52
  distance 196
  summit 210
  limit 233
  perfection 650
  completion 729
neap *going down* 195
  low 207
  - tide 36
near *like* 17, 19
  - *in space* 197
  - *in time* 121
  soon 132
  impending 152
  approach 286
  stingy 819
  bring - 17
  come - 286
  draw - 197
  - at hand 132
  - one's end 360
  - run 32
  - side 239
  - sight 443
  - the mark 32
  - the truth 480a
  - upon 32
  sail - the wind
  skillful 698
  rash 863
nearly 32
  - all 50
nearness 9, 197
nearsighted 443
neat *simple* 42
  order 58
  form 240
  in writing 572, 576,
    578
  clean 652
  spruce 845
  -'s foot oil 356
neat-handed 698
neatherd 370
neb 250
nebula *stars* 318
  mist 353

nebular *dim* 422
nebulous *misty* 353
  obscure 519
necessarian 601
necessaries 630
necessarily
  cause and effect 154
necessary
  [see necessity]
necessitarianism 601
necessitate 630
necessity *fate* 601
  predetermination 611
  requirement 630
  compulsion 744
  indigence 804
  need 865
  make a virtue of - 698
neck *contraction* 195
  narrow 203
  break one's - 360
  - and crop
  completely 52
  turn out - 297
  - and neck 27
  - of land 342
  - or nothing
  resolute 604
  rash 863
neckcloth 225
necklace *circle* 247
  ornament 847
necrology *obituary* 360
  biography 594
necromancer 548, 994
necromancy 511, 992
necropolis 363
necropsy 363
necroscopic 363
necrosis 655
nectar *savory* 394
  sweet 396
nectareous 394, 396
need *necessity* 601
  requirement 630
  insufficiency 640
  indigence 804
  desire 865
  friend in - 711
  in one's utmost - 735
needful *necessary* 601
  requisite 630
  money 800
  do the - *pay* 807
needle *sharp* 253
  perforator 262
  compass 693
  foliage 367
  as the - to the pole
  veracity 543
  observance 772
  honor 939
  - in a bottle of hay 475
needle gun 727
needle-shaped 253
needless 641
needle-witted 498
needlewoman 690
needlework 847
ne'er 107

ne'er-do-well 949
nefarious 945
negation **536,** 764
negatory 764
negative *inexisting* 2
  contrary 14
  prototype 22
  quantity 84
  confute 479
  deny 536
  photograph 558
  refuse 764
  prove a - 468
neglect **460**
  disuse 678
  leave undone 730
  omit 773
  evade 927
  disrespect 929
  - of time 115
négligé 225
negligence 460
negligent 460
negotiable
  transferable 270
  mediatory 724
negotiate *leap* 309
  mediate 724
  bargain 769
  transfer 783
  traffic 794
negotiator
  go-between 724
  agent 758
negress 431
Negrillo 193, 431
Negrito 193, 431
negro *black* 431
  slave 746
negro head 392
negrophobia 898
negus 298
neif 781
neigh *cry* 412
  boast 884
neighbor *near* 197, 199
  friend 890
neighborhood 197, 227
neighborly *aid* 707
  friendly 888
  social 892
  courteous 894
neither 610
  - here nor there
  irrelevant 10
  absent 187
  - more nor less
  equal 27
  true 494
  - one thing nor another 83
nekton 366
nem. con. 488
Nemesis
  vengeance 919
  justice 922
  punishment 972
nenia 839
neo-criticism 451
neogamist 903
Neo-Hegelianism 451

Neo-Lamarckism 357
neologism 123
neologist 123
neology **563**
neophyte 144, 541
Neoplatonism 451, 984
neoteric 123
neo-voluntarism 451
nepenthe *remedy* 662
  cheer 836
nephalism 953, 955
nephelognosy 353
nephelometer 353
nephew 11
nephograph 353
nephology 353
nephoscope 353
nepotism *nephew* 11
  wrong 923
  dishonest 940
  selfish 943
Neptune 341
Nereid *ocean* 341
  mythology 979
nerve *strength* 159
  courage 861
  with exposed -s 378
nerveless *impotent* 158
  - style 575
  imperturbable 871
nervous *weak* 160
  style 574
  timid 860
  modest 881
nescience 491
ness 250
nest *cradle* 153
  lodging 189
  - of boxes 204
nest egg 636
nestle *lodge* 186
  safety 664
  endearment 902
nestling 129, 167
Nestor *veteran* 130
  sage 500
  advice 695
net *remainder* 40
  receptacle 191
  intersection 219
  inclosure 232
  snare 545
  difficulty 704
  gain 775
  - profit *gain* 775
  receipt 810
nether 207
nethermost 207, 211
netlike 219
netting 219
nettle *bane* 663
  sting 830
  incense 900
network *disorder* 59
  crossing 219
neural 235
neuralgia 378
neurasthenia 158, 655, 992a
neurology 329
neurotic 662

neuter *matter* 316
  no choice 609a
  remain - *irresolute* 605
  stand - *indifferent* 866
neutral *mean* 29
  no choice 609a
  avoidance 623
  mid-course 628
  pacific 721
  indifferent 866
  - tint *colorless* 429
  gray 432
neutrality
  mid-course 628
  peace 721
  insensibility 823
  indifference 866
neutralize
  compensate 30
  counteract 179
nevée 383
never 107
  it will - do
  inexpedient 647
  prohibit 761
  discontent 832
  disapprobation 932
  - a one 4
  - dying 112
  - ending 112
  - fading *perpetual* 112
  glory 873
  - forget 916
  - hear the last of 841
  - indebted 807
  - mind *neglect* 460
  unimportant 643
  insensible 823
  indifferent 866
  contempt 930
  - more 107
  - otherwise 16
  - say die
  persevere 604a
  cheerful 836
  hope 858
  - so 31
  - tell me 489
  - thought of 621
  - tired *active* 682
  - tiring
  persevering 604a
  - to be forgotten 642
  - to return 122
  - was seen the like 83
neverness **107**
nevertheless 30
ne vile fano 987, 1000
new *different* 18
  extra 37
  novel 123
  unaccustomed 614
  give - life to
  aid 707
  stimulate 824
  - birth 660
  - blood *change* 140
  improve 658
  excite 824
  - brooms
  desuetude 614

active 682
- chum 57
- conditions 469
- departure 66
- edition
  repetition 104
  reproduction 163
  imyrovement 658
- ethical movement
  451
- ideas 537
- woman 374
put on the - man 950
turn over a - leaf
  change 140
  repent 950
view in a - light 658
newborn *new* 123
  infant 129
**Newcastle, carry coals
  to -** 641
newcomer 57, 294
New England Primer
  542
newfangled
  unfamiliar 83
  new 123
  change 140
  neology 563
newfashioned 123
new-fledged 129
Newfoundland dog 366
Newgate 572
new-gilt 847
new-model
  convert 144
  revolutionize 146
  improve 658
newness 123
news 532
newsboy 534
newsmonger
  curious 455
  informant 527
  news 532
newsmongery 455
newspaper
  publish 531
  record 551
- correspondent 758
- war 588
newspaperman 554
newsy 532
newt 366
New Thought 984
New Year's Day 138
next *following* 63
  later 117
  future 121
  near 197
- friend 759
- of kin 11
- to nothing 32
- world 152
Niagara 348
niasis 501
niaiserie 517
nib *cut* 44
  end 67
  summit 210
  point 253

nibble *eat* 298
- at *censure* 932
- at the bait
  dupe 547
  willing 602
nice *savory* 394
  discriminative 465
  exact 494
  good 648
  pleasing 829
  fastidious 868
  honorable 939
  (*taste* 850)
- ear 418
- hand 700
- perception 465
- point 697, 704
nicely *completely* 52
Nicene Creed 983*a*
niceness [see nice]
nicety 494
niche *recess* 182
  receptacle 191
  angle 244
- in the temple of
  fame 873
nick *notch* 257
  deceive 545
  mark 550
- it 731
- of time 134
nickel 800
Nick, Old - 978
nicknack 643
nickname 564, 565
nicotine *pungent* 392
  poison 663
nictate 443
nictitate 443
nidget 862
nidification 189
nidor 398
nidorous 401
nidus *cradle* 153
  nest 189
niece 11
niggard
  insufficiency 640
  miser 819
  (*trifling* 643).
nigger 57, 431
niggerhead 392
niggle *mock* 929
niggling *trifling* 643
nigh 197
nighness 197
night 421
  labor day and - 686
- and day 136
- watchman 753
  orb of - 318
nightcap 225
nightfall 126, 422
nightgown 225
nightingale 366, 416
nightmare
  bodily pain 378
  dream 515
  incubus 706
  mental pain 828
  alarm 860

nightshade 663
nightshirt 225
nighttide 126
nightwalker 268
nightwalking 266
nigrescence 431
nigricant 431
nigrification 431
nihilism 738, 989
nihilist 165, 913
nihilistic 738
nihility *inexistence* 2
  unsubstantiality 4
nil *inexistence* 2
  unsubstantiality 4
nill *unwilling* 603
  refuse 764
nilometer 348
nim 791
nimble *swift* 274
  active 682
  (*skillful* 698)
nimble-fingered 698
nimble-footed 274
nimble-witted
  intelligence 498
  wit 842
nimbus *cloud* 353
  halo 420
  glory 873
nimiety 641
Nimrod *slayer* 361
  hunter 622
nincompoop 501
nine 98
  team 759
- day's wonder
  transient 111
  unimportant 643
- lives 359
- men's morris 840
- points of the law 777
  tuneful - *music* 416
  poetry 597
ninefold 98
ninepins 840
ninety 98
ninny 501
Niobe *all tears* 839
- of nations 828
nip *cut* 44
  destroy 162
  shorten 201
  dram 298
  freeze 385
  pungent 392
- in the bud
  kill 361
  hinder 706
- up 789
nipperkin 191
nippers 327, 781
nipple 250
Nirvana 2, 981
nis 979
nisi prius
  summons 741
  lawsuit 969
nisus 176
nitency 420
niter 392

nitric acid 384
nitrogen 663
nitroglycerin 727
nitrous oxide 376
niveous *white* 430
nix *nothing* 101
  absence 187
  fairy 979
nixie *fairy* 979
nizam 745
nizy 501
no *zero* 101
  dissent 489
  negation 536
  refusal 764
and - mistake 474
at - great distance 197
at - hand 32
at - time 107
have - business there
  83
have - end
  perpetual 112
in - degree 32
- chicken *aged* 128
  grown up 131
- choice *necessary* 601
  neutral 609*a*
- conjuror *fool* 501
  bungler 701
- consequence 643
- doubt *certain* 474
  assent 488
- end of *great* 31
  multitude 102
  length 200
- go *shortcoming* 304
  failure 732
- less 639
- longer 122
- man's land
  arena 728
- matter *neglect* 460
  unimportant 643
- more *inexistent* 2
  past 122
  dead 360
- more than 32
- object 643
- one 4
- one knows who 876
- other *same* 13
  one 87
- scholar 493
- sooner said than
  done
  instantaneous 113
  early 132
- stranger to 490
- such thing
  nonexistent 2
  unsubstantial 4
  contrary 14
  dissimilar 18
- thank you 764
- wonder 871
on - account 761
unable to say - 605
with - interval 199
Noah's ark *mixture* 41
  assemblage 72

nostrum
contrivance 626
remedy 662
not *negation* 536
(dissent 489)
it will - do 923
- a bit 536
- a few 102
- a leg to stand on 158
- a little 31
- allowed 964
- amiss *good* 618
mediocre 651
pretty 845
- any 101
- a particle 4
- a pin to choose 27
- a soul 101
- at all 32
- bad 651
- bargain for 508
- come up to 34
- expect 508
- fail 939
- far from 197
- fit to be seen 846
- following 477
- for the world
unwilling 603
refusal 764
- grant 764
- guilty 946
- hardened 950
- having *absent* 187
exempt 777a
- hear of 764
- included 55
- know what to make
of 519
- matter
unimportant 643
- mind *insensible* 823
contempt 930
- often 137
- of the earth 987
- one 101
]- on speaking terms
889
- on your life 764
- particular 831
- pay 808
- quite 32
- reach 304
- right 503
- seldom 136
- sorry 827
- the thing 925
- to be borne 830
- to be despised 642
- to be had
impossible 471
insufficient 640
- to mention
together with 37
- to be put down 604
- to be thought of
incogitancy 452
impossible 471
refusal 764
hopeless 859
undue 925

disapprobation 932
- trouble oneself
about 460
- understand 519
- vital
unimportant 643
- vote 609a
- within previous ex-
perience 137
- wonder 871
- worth *trifling* 643
useless 645
what is - 546
what ought - 923
nota bene 457
notabilia 642
notabilities 875
notable *great* 31
manifest 525
important 642
active 682
distinguished 873
notables 875
notably 31
notary *recorder* 553
lawyer 968
notation 85
notch *gully* 198
nick **257**
mark 550
note *music* 413
take cognizance 450
remark 457
explanation 522
sign 550
record 551
printing 591
epistle 592
minute 596
money 800
fame 873
change one's - 607
make a - of 551
- of admiration 870
- of alarm 669
- of preparation 673
of - 873
take - of 457
notebook *record* 551
compendium 569
writing 590
noted *known* 490
famous 873
noteworthy *great* 31
exceptional 83
important 642
nothing *nihility* 4
zero 101
trifle 643
come to -
fall short 304
fail 732
do - 681
for - 815
go for - 643
good for - 646
make - of
underestimate 483
fail 732
- comes amiss 831
- in it 4

- loth 602
- more to be said 478
- of the kind *unlike* 18
negation 536
- on 226
- to do 681
- to do with 764
- to go upon 471
- to signify 643
take - by 732
think of - 930
worse than - 808
nothingness 2
notice *intellect* 450
observe 457
review 480
information 527
warning 668
bring into - 525
deserve - 642
give - *manifest* 525
inform 527
indicate 550
- is hereby given
publication 531
- to quit 782
short - 111
take - of 450
this is to give - 457
worthy of - 642
noticeable 31
notification
information 527
(publication 531)
notion *idea* 453
(belief 484)
(knowledge 490)
have no - of 489
notional *fanciful* 515
notionalist 514
notoriety
publication 531
fame 873
notorious *known* 490
public 531
famous 873
infamous 874
Notre Dame 977
notturno 415
notwithstanding 30,
179
nought
unsubstantiality 4
[see *naught*]
noun 564
nourish 707
nourishment *food* 298
aid 707
nous 498
nousle 545
nouveau riche 123
novaculite 253
novation 140, 609
Nova Zembla 383
novel *dissimilar* 18
new 123
unknown 491
tale 594
(romance 515)
(fiction 546)
novelist 594, 598

novelize 594
novena 98, 108
novenary 98
novice *ignoramus* 493
learner 541
bungler 701
religious 996
novitiate *learning* 539
training 673
novocain 376
novus homo
stranger 57
upstart 876
now 118
- and then 136
- or never 134
noways 32, 536
nowhere 187
nowise *small* 32
negation 536
noxious *bad* 649
unhealthy 657
noyade *kill* 361
punish 972
nozzle *projection* 250
opening 260
for water 337
air pipe 351
nuance *difference* 15
discrimination 465
nubiferous 353, 426
nubilation 426
nubile *adolescent* 131
marriage 903
nubilous 426
nuclear 222
nucleolus 357
nucleus *middle* 68
cause 153
center 222
kernel 642
nudation 226
nude 226
nudge 550
nudity 226, 849
nugacity *absurdity* 497
folly 499
inutility 645
nugatory
powerless 158
useless 645
nuggar 273
nugget *mass* 192
money 800
nuisance *evil* 619
annoyance 830
null *inexistent* 2
unsubstantial 4
absent 187
declare - and void
abrogation 756
nonobservance 773
- and void
powerless 158
unproductive 169
illegal 964
(inexistence 2)
nullah 198, 252
nullibiety 187
nullicity 187
nullifidian 487

O

obnubilated 422
oboe 417
obovate 247
obreption 528, 775
obscene *dirty* 653
  indecent 961
obscure *dark* 421
  dim 422
  unseen 447
  uncertain 475
  unintelligible 519
  eclipse 874
  ignoble 876
obscurity
  [see obscure]
  unsubstantiality 4
  latency 526
  style **571**
obsecration 765
obsecratory 765
obsequies 363
obsequious
  servile 746, 886
  courteous 894
  respectful 928
obsequiousness 933
observance *rule* 82
  attention 457
  habit 613
  practice 692
  fulfillment **772**
  duty 926
  rite 998
Observant *friar* 996
observation
  intellect 450
  idea 453
  attention 457
  assertion 535
observatory 318
observe [see observ-
  ance, observation]
  - a duty 926
  - rules 82
observer *aviator* 269a
  spectator 444
obsess *haunt* 860
  bedevil 978
  sorcery 992
obsession [see obsess]
  siege 716
obsidional 716
obsolescence 614
obsolescent 563
obsolete *old* 124
  words 563
  effete 645
obstacle *moral* - 706
  (*physical* - 179)
obstetrician 631
obstetrics
  production 161
  surgery 662
obstinacy **606**
  prejudice 481
obstipation 261
obstreperous
  violent 173
  loud 404
obstruct *close* 261
  hinder 706

- the passage of light
  426
obstructionist 710
obstructive
  opponent 710
obstruent 706
obstupefaction 823
obtain *exist* 1
  get 775
- under false pretense
  791
obtainable 470
obtenebration 421
obtestation
  entreaty 765
obtrectation 934
obtrude *interfere* 228
  insert 300
  meddle 682
  (*obstruct* 706)
obtruncate 201
obtrusion
  interference 228
  obstruction 706
obtrusive
  interfering 228
  vulgar 851
  rude 895
obtund *mitigate* 174
  blunt 254
  deaden 376
  paralyze 823
obtundent 823
obtundity 823
obtuse *blunt* 253
  insensible 376
  imbecile 499
  dull 823
- angle 244
obumbrate 421
obverse 234
obviate 706
obvious *visible* 446
  clear 518
  manifest 525
ocarina 417
occasion *juncture* 8
  opportunity 134
  cause 153
  befit the - 646
  have - for 630
  on the present - 118
  on the spur of - 612
occasional 134, 475
occasionally 136
Occident 236
occiput 235
occision 361
occlusion 261
occult
  unintelligible 519
  latent 526
  hidden 528
- art 992
occultation
  disappearance 449
  concealment 528
occultism *latency* 526
  concealment 528
  heterodoxy 984
  psychic 992a

occupancy
  presence 186
  possession 777
  (*property* 780)
- in common 778
occupant
  inhabitant 188
  proprietor 779
occupation
  business 625
  in the - of 188
- road 627
occupied 682
- by 188
- with *attention* 457
  business 625
occupier *dweller* 188
  possessor 779
occupy *presence* 186
  possess 777
- a post 737
- oneself with
  attend 457
  business 625
- the chair 693
- the mind *thought* 451
  attention 457
- time 106
occur *exist* 1
  follow 117
  happen 151
- in a place 186
- to the mind 451
occurrence 151
  circumstance 8
  of daily - 613
occursion 276
ocean **341**
- basin 341
- greyhound 273
- lane 341
- of dreams 4
  plow the - 267
ocean-going 273
oceanography 341
Oceanus 341
ocelot 440
ocher *brown* 433
  orange 439
  yellow - 436
ocherous 436, 439
ochlocracy 738
o'clock 114
  know what's - 698
octad 193
octagon 98, 244
octahedron 244
octangular 98
octastyle 98
Octateuch 985
octave *eight* 98
  period 108
  music 413
  poetry 597
octavo 98, 593
octennial 138
octodecimo 593
octogenarian 130
octonary 98
octopus
  mollusk 366, 368

  monster 846, 913
octoroon 41
octroi 812
octuple 98
ocular 441
- demonstration
  see 441
  visible 446
- inspection 441
oculist 662
odalisque 746
odd *remaining* 40
  exception 83
  single 87
  insane 503
  vulgar 851
  ridiculous 853
- fish 857
Odd Fellows 712
oddity
  laughingstock 857
oddments 51
odds *inequality* 28
  chance 156
  discord 713
at - *disagreement* 24
  discord 713
  long - 704
- against one 665
- and ends
  remainder 40
  mixture 41
  part 51
  useless 645
  the - are 472
  what's the - 643
ode 597
od force 992
Odin 979
odious *disagreeable* 830
  ugly 846
  hateful 898
odi profanum vulgus
  878
odium *disgrace* 874
  hatred 898
  blame 932
odium theologicum
  pedantry 481
  pietism 988
  church 995
odograph 200
odometer 200
odontalgia 378
odontoid
  prominent 250
  sharp 253
odor **398**
  in bad - 932
- of sanctity 987
O. D. shirt 225
odylic force 992
œcology 357
œcumenical 78
œdematous
  swollen 194
  soft 324
Œdipus
  answer 462
  expounder 524
  Davus sum non - 703

œnomancy 511
o'er [*see* over]
œstrus 865
œuvres 161
of - all things 33
- a piece *uniform* 16
similar 17
agreeing 23
- course
conformity 82
effect 154
- late 123
- no effect 169
- old 122
- one mind 23
off 196
be - 623
keep - 623
make - with 791
move - 287
- and on
periodical 138
changeable 149
irresolute 605
- one's balance 605
- one's guard
neglect 260
inexpectant 508
- one's hands 776
- one's head 503
- one's legs
carry one - 284
dance one - 309
- one's mind 452
- side 238
- the track 475
- with you 297
sheer - 287
stand - 287
start - 293
take - one's hands 785
throw - one's center 874
throw - the scent
uncertain 475
avoid 623
offal 653
offend *pain* 830
vice 945
- against the law 964
offender
- never pardons 918
offense *attack* 716
anger 900
guilt 947
offensive *unsavory* 395
fetid 401
foul 653
aggressive 716
displeasing 830
distasteful 867
obnoxious 898
- and defensive alliance 712
- to ears polite 579
offer *volunteer* 602
proposal **763**
give 784
- a choice 609
- for sale 796
- of marriage 902

622

- oneself 763
- sacrifice 990
- the alternative 609
- up prayers 990
offering *gift* 784
burnt - 990
sin - 952
offertory *gift* 784
worship 990
rite 998
offhand *soon* 132
inattentive 458
careless 460
spontaneous 612
(*unprepared* 674)
office *doing* 170
room 191
business 625
mart 799
worship 990
do an ill - 907
do one's - 772
good -s
mediate 724
kind 906
hold - 693
kind -s 906
man in - 694
- force 746
- holder 694
officer *director* 694
soldier 726
commander 745
constable 965
offices *kitchen* &c. 191
official *certain* 474
true 494
business 625
man in office 694
authoritative 737
master 745
servant 746
- receiver 967
officialism 739
officiate *business* 625
instrumentality 631
act 680
conduct 692
religious 998
officious 682
offing *distance* 196
ocean 341
offprint 21
offsaddle 292
offscourings *useless* 645
dirt 653
offscum 653
offset
compensation 30
offspring 167
counteract 179
printing 591
offshoot *adjunct* 39
part 51
effect 154
offspring 167
offspring *posterity* 167
offtake 40a
offuscate *dark* 421
opaque 426
often *repeated* 104

frequent 136
most - 613
Ogham 590
ogle *look* 441
desire 865
rude 895
endearment 902
ogre *bugbear* 860
evildoer 913
demon 980
oil *lubricate* 332
grease 355, **356**
fuel 388
- on the troubled waters 174
- stove 386
pour - on *relieve* 834
oilcloth 223, 635
oil painting 556
oilskins 225
oily *smooth* 255
greasy 355
servile 886
courteous 894
flattery 933
oinomania 959
ointment
lubrication 332
grease 356
remedy 662
old 124
die of - *age* 729
- of - 122
- age 128
- bachelor 904
- clothes 225
- fogy *fool* 501
laughingstock 857
- glory 550
- gold 439
- joke 842
- maid *cards* 840
spinster 374, 904
- man *veteran* 130
husband 903
- man of the sea 706
- Nick 978
- school
antiquated 124
obstinate 606
habit 613
- soldier 392
- song *repetition* 104
trifle 643
cheap 815
- stager *veteran* 130
proficient 700
- story *repetition* 104
stale news 532
love 897
- stuff *repetition* 104
- times 122
- woman *fool* 501
effeminacy 374
wife 903
- womanish 499
- world 124
one's - way 613
pay off - *scores* 718
older 128
old-fangled 124

old-fashioned 124
oldness **124**
oldster 130
oldwife 130
oleagine 356
oleaginous 355
olein 356
olfactible 398
olfactory 398
- organ 250
olibanum 400
olid 401
oligarch 745
oligarchy 737
olio 41
olivaceous 435
olive 367
olive branch
infant 129
offspring 167
pacification 723
olive drab 225
olive green 435
olivine 435
olla podrida 41
Olympus 981
Om 993
omasum 191
omber 840
ombrometer 348
omega *end* 67
omelet 298
omen **512**
ominate 511
ominous
predicting 511
danger 665
warning 668
adverse 735
hopeless 859
omission
incomplete 53
exclusion 55
neglect 460
failure 732
nonobservance 773
guilt 947
omit [*see* omission]
omitted *inexistent* 2
absent 187
omnibus 272
omnifarious 81
omnific 168
omniform 81
omnigenous 81
omnipotence *power* 157
God 976
omnipresence
presence 186
God 976
omniscience
knowledge 490
God 976
omnium-gatherum
mixture 41
confusion 59
assemblage 72
omnivorous *eating* 298
desire 865
gluttony 957
omophagic 298

overborne *failure* 732
  subjection 749
overburden
  redundant 641
  bad 649
  fatigue 688
overcast *cloudy* 353
  dark 421
  dim 422
overcautious 864
overcharge
  exaggerate 549
  style 577
  redundance 641
  dearness 814
overcloud 353
overcoat 225
overcolor 549
overcome
  counteract 179
  induce 615
  conquer 731
  sad 837
  disgraced 874
  tipsy 959
  - an obstacle 731
overconfident
  credulous 486
  rash 863
overcredulous 486
overcurious 455
overdate 115
overdistention 194
overdo *redundance* 641
  bustle 682
  affectation 855
overdone - *meat* 298
overdose 641
overdraw
  exaggerate 549
  misrepresent 555
  prodigal 818
overdrawn account
  808
overdrive *misuse* 679
overdue 115, 133
overeager 865
overeat oneself 957
overestimation **482**
overfatigued 688
overfed 869, 957
overfeed 641
overflow *stream* 348
  redundance 641
  - with gratitude 916
overgo 303
overgorged *satiety* 869
  gluttony 957
overgrown *much* 31
  large 192
  expanded 194
overhang *high* 206
  pendency 214
overhanging *destiny* 152
  pendency 214
overhasty 901
overhaul *count* 85
  attend to 457
  inquire 461
  censure 932
overhead 206

overhear *hear* 418
  be informed 527
overjoyed 827
overjump 303
overlap *inwrap* 225
  go beyond 303
overlay *layer* 204
  cover 223
  exaggerate 549
  excess 641
  overdo 682
  hinder 706
  - with ornament
    writing 577
overleap 303
overliberal 818
overlie 223
overload *ornament* 577
  redundance 641
  hinder 706
overlook *slight* 458
  neglect 460
  superintend 693
  forgive 918
  disparage 929
  bewitch 992
overlooked 642
  not to be - 642
overlooker 694
overlord 745
overlying 206
overman 33
overmaster 731
overmastering 821
overmatch
  unequal 28
  superior 33
  strength 159
  conquer 731
overmeasure 641
overmodest 881
overmost 210
overmuch 641
overnight 122
overofficious 682
overpaid 816
overpass
  exceed 33
  transgress 303
overpersuade 615
overplus *remainder* 40
  excess 641
overpoise 179
overpower
  counteract 179
  subdue 731
  emotion 824
overpowering
  strong 159
overpraise
  overrate 482
  exaggerate 549
  flatter 933
overprize 482
overrate 482
overreach *pass* 303
  deceive 545
  baffle 545
overreckon 482
overrefinement 477
over-religious 955

override *superior* 33
  influence 175
  pass 303
  hinder 706
  defeat 731
  authority 737
  severity 739
  abrogate 756
overrighteous 988
overrule *control* 737
  cancel 756
overruling
  important 642
overrun *presence* 186
  spread 194
  motion beyond **303**
  printing 591
  redundance 641
  despoil 659
overscrupulous 939
oversea 57, 341
overseas *cap* 225
oversee 693
overseer 694
oversensitive 822
overset *invert* 218
  level 308
  subvert 731
overshadow
  darken 353, 421
  repute 873
  disrepute 874
overshoot the mark
  go beyond 303
  exaggerate 549
  overdo 682
  clumsy 699
oversight
  inattention 458
  error 495
  superintendence 693
  failure 732
overskip 303
oversleep 683
overspent 688
overspread *disperse* 73
  be present 186
  cover 223
overstate 549, 555
overstep 303
overstock 641
overstrain *extol* 482
  fatigue 688
oversupply 641
overt 525
  - act 680
overtake 292
overtaken *tipsy* 959
overtask *misuse* 679
  fatigue 688
overtax 679, 688
overthrow
  revolution 146
  destroy 162
  level 308
  confute 479
  vanquish 751
overthrown
  vanquished 732
overthwart 708
overtired 688

overtone 413
overtop *surpass* 33
  height 206
  (perfection 650)
overtrustful 486
overture
  precursor 62, 64
  music 415
  offer 763
  request 765
overturn *revolution* 146
  destroy 162
  invert 218
  level 308
  confute 479
overvalue 482
overweening
  excess 641
  rash 863
  pride 878
  conceit 880
  insolence 885
overweigh *exceed* 33
  influence 175
  overrate 482
overwhelm *ruin* 162
  redundant 641
  thwart 706
  affect 824
overwhelmed
  defeated 732
  subjection 749
overwhelming
  strong 159
  wonderful 870
overwise 880
overwork *misuse* 679
  fatigue 688
overwrought
  exaggerated 549
  emotion 824
  affectation 855
overzealous 825
ovicell 357
oviform 249
ovo, in - 153
ovoid 247, 249
ovule 247
ovum 357
owe 806
  - it to oneself 926
owelty 27
owing *debt* 806
  attribution 155
owl *bird* 366
  fool 501
  -'s light 422
  -s to Athens 641
  screech - 412
own *assent* 488
  divulge 529
  possess 777
  property 780
  act on one's - respon-
    sibility 738
  after one's - heart 897
  at one's - risk 926
  come by one's - 775
  condemned   out of
    one's - mouth 479
  hold one's - 737

look after one's - interest 943
look with one's - eyes 459
out of one's - head 600
- flesh and blood
  consanguinity 11

owner *possessor* 779
  without an - 777*a*
ownership
  property 780
ox *animal* 366
  male 373
  hot enough to roast
  an - 382

Oxford school 984
Oxford shoe 225
oxgoad 727
oxidation 357
oxreim 45
ox-tail soup 298
oxygen 359
oxygon 244

oyer and terminer,
  court of - 966
oyes 531
oyez! *hear* 418
  publication 531
oyster 298
  - plant 298
  - stew 298

P

P
mind one's -'s and Q's
  care 459
  polite 894
  duty 926
pabulum *food* 298
  material 316
  mental - 454
pace *walk* 264
  journey 266
  measure 466
  keep - with
  concur 178
  velocity 274
  - up and down 266
  put through one's -s 525
  show one's -s
  ostentation 882
pace *permission* 760
  - tanti nominis 928
pachydermatous
  physically - 376
  morally - 823
pacific 721
pacification **723**
pacifism 721
pacify *allay* 174
  (*compose* 823)
  (*forgive* 918)
pack *arrange* 60
  assemblage 72
  locate 184
  squeeze 195
  prepare 673
  burden 706
  - off *depart* 293
  eject 297
  - of nonsense 643
  - up 229
  send -ing 297
package
  assemblage 72
packer 673
packet *assemblage* 72
  ship 273
pack horse 271
pack saddle 215
pack thread 205
pact 769
Pactolus 803
pad *thicken* 194
  line 224
  horse 271
  diffuseness 573
  writing 590
padding *lining* 224
  stopper 263
628

soft 324
  diffuseness 573
paddle *walk* 266
  row 267
  oar 633
  - one's own canoe
  conduct 692
  free 748
  - *steamer* 273
paddock 232
Paddy *Irishman* 188
paddy *rice* 330
padishah 745
padlock *fastening* 45
  fetter 752
  put a - on one's lips 585
padre 996
padrone 745
pæan *rejoicing* 838
  celebration 883
  gratitude 916
  approbation 931
  worship 990
pagan 984
  - deities **979**
paganism 984
page *numeration* 85
  printing 591
  book 593
  attendant 746
pageant *spectacle* 448
  amusement 840
  show 882
pagination 85
pagoda 206, 1000
pagri 225
pah 717
pai 643
pail 191
paillard 962
paillasse 215
pain *physical* - **378**
  moral - **828**
  penalty 974
painfulness **830**
painfully *very* 31
painless 827
pains 686
  get for one's - 973
  - and penalties 974
  take - 686
painstaking *active* 682
  laborious 686
paint *coat* 223
  color 428
  deceive 545
  delineate 556

ornament 847
  - the lily 641
  - the town red 840
painter *rope* 45
  artist 559
painting 54, **556**
painty 556
pair *similar* 17
  combine 48
  couple 89
  - *horses* 272
  - off *average* 29
  marry 903
pair-oar 273
pairs *cards* 840
pajamas 225
pakka [see pucka]
paktong 545
pal *ally* 711
  chum 890
palace **189**
  bishop's - 1000
  - *car* 272
Paladin *defense* 717
  combatant 726
palæocrystic 124
palæology
  [see paleology &c.]
palæstra *school* 542
  arena 728
palæstral *strength* 159
  school 542
  contention 720
palæstric *exertion* 686
  [see palæstral]
palang 215
palanquin 266, 272
palatable *savory* 394
  pleasant 829
palatal *phonetic* 561
palate 390
  tickle the - 394
palatial *palace* 189
  ostentatious 882
palatinate 181
palatine 745
Palatine Court 966
palaver *unmeaning* 517
  speech 582
  loquacity 584
  colloquy 588
  council 696
pale *region* 181
  inclosure 232
  limit 233
  dim 422
  colorless 429
  frightened 860

- its ineffectual fire
  dim 422
  out of repute 874
  - of the church 995
  turn - *lose color* 429
  emotion 821
  fear 860
pale-faced 429
paleoanthropic 124
paleography *past* 122
  philology 560
paleology *past* 122
  language 160
paleontology 357, 368
paleozoic 124
paleozoölogy 357
palestra
  [see palæstra &c.]
paletot 225
palette 556
palfrey 271
palimpsest 147, 528
palindrome
  inversion 218
  neology 563
paling *fence* 232
  prison 752
palingenesis 163, 660
palinody 607
palisade *defense* 717
  prison 752
  -s *cliff* 212
palki 272
pall *mantle* 225
  funeral 363
  disgust 395
  insignia 747
  weary 841
  dislike 867
  satiety 869
  canonicals 999
  - bearer 363
palladium
  safety 664
  (*defense* 717)
pallet *support* 215
  painter's - 556
palliament 225
palliate *moderate* 174
  mind 658
  relieve 834
  extenuate 937
  moderation 174
palliative 174
  qualification 469
  remedy 662
pallid 429
pallium 999

pall-mall 840
pallone 840
pallor 429
palm
 measure of length 200
 tree 367, 369
 touch 379
 trophy 733
 steal 791
 laurel 877
 bear the - 873
 grease the - *induce* 615
 give 784
 itching - 865
 - off 545
 - upon 545
 win the - 731
palmated 257
palmer *traveler* 268
 clergy 996
palmiped 219
palmist 513
palmistry 500, 511, 522
palm oil 356
palmy *prosperous* 734
 pleasant 829
 joyous 836
 - days *prosperity* 734
 pleasure 827
palpable *material* 316
 tactile 379
 obvious 446
 manifest 525
 (*intelligible* 518)
 - obscure 421
palpate 379
palpation 379
palpitate *tremble* 315
 emotion 821
 fear 860
palpus 379
palsgrave 875
palsied [see palsy]
 irresolute 605
palsy *impotence* 158
 physical insensibility 376
 disease 655
 mental insensibility 823
 (*weakness* 160)
palter *falsehood* 544
 shift 605
 elude 773
paltering 520
paltry *small* 32
 unimportant 643
 mean 940
paludal 345
pampas 344, 367
pamper *indulge* 954
 gorge 957
pamphlet 590, 593
pamphleteer 595
pan 191
panacea 662
panache *plume* 256
 ornament 847
panama *hat* 225
Pan-American 78
Pan-Anglican 78

pancake 298
pancratiast 159
pandar [see pander]
Pandean pipes 417
pandect
 knowledge 490
 dissertation 595
 compendium 596
 code 963
pandemic 657
Pandemonium 982
 inhabitants of - 978
pandemonium 59, 404, 414
pander *pimp* 962
 - to *instrument* 631
 help 707
 flatter 933
pandiculation
 expansion 194
 opening 260
 sleepy 683
Pandoor 726
Pandora's box 619
 bottom of - 858
pan-dowdy 298
paned 440
panegyric 931
panegyrize 482
panel *list* 86
 partition 228
 accused 938
 jury 967
 - game 545
 sliding - 545
paneling 847
pang *physical* - 378
 moral 828
Pan-Germanic 78
Pangloss 492
panhandler 876
panharmonic 78
Pan-Hellenic 78
pani 337
panic 860
 - fear 860
panier 225
pannel 213
pannier 191
panoply 490
 defense 717
 arms 727
panopticon 752
panorama *view* 448
 painting 556
panoramic 78, 446
 - view 441
pan-phenomenalism 451
Panpipes 417
Panslavic 78
pansophism 490
pant *heat* 382
 fatigue 688
 emotion 821
 - for 865
pantaloon
 old man 130
 pantomimist 599
 buffoon 844
pantaloons 225

pantheism 451, 984
Pantheon *gods* 979
 temple 1000
panther *variegation* 440
 courage 861
pantile *roof* 223
 conduit 350
pantisocracy 737, 875
pantologist
 scholar 492
 proficient 700
pantology 490
pantometer 244
pantomime
 signs 550
 drama 599
pantophagous 298
pantophagy 298, 957
pantry 191
pants 225
panurgy 698
pap *mamma* 250
 pulp 354
papa *father* 166
Papa *pope* 996
papacy 984
papal 995 -
paper *cover* 223
 white 430
 writing 590
 book 593
 security 771
 (*record* 551)
 - credit 805
 - money 800
 - pellet 643
 - war *discussion* 476
 contention 720
papery *weak* 160
Paphian
 intemperate 954
 impure 961
papilionaceous 242
papilla 250
papillote 256
papistry 984
papoose 129, 167
pappous 256
Papuan 431
papula 250
papule 250
papulose 250
papyrus 590
par 27
 above - 648
 below - *low* 207
 imperfect 651
 - excellence 33
 - value 812
parable *metaphor* 521
 teaching 537
 description 594
parabola *curve* 245
parabolic
 metaphorical 521
paracentesis 297
parachronism 115
parachute *balloon* 273
 means of safety 666
Paraclete 976
paracme 63

parade *procession* 69
 walk 189
 journey 266
 ostentation 882
paradigm 22, 567
paradisaic 829, 946
Paradise *bliss* 827
 heaven 981
 in - 827
paradox *absurdity* 497
 obscurity 519
 difficulty 704
 (*mystery* 528)
paradoxical
 uncertain 475
 absurd 497
 unintelligible 519
paraffin 356
paragon *perfect* 650
 glory 873
 good man 948
paragram
 ambiguous 520
 neology 563
paragraph *part* 51
 indication 550
 phrase 566
 article 593
paraleipsis 460
parallax 196
parallel *similarity* 17
 imitate 19
 - position 216
 symmetry 242
 draw a - 464
 - s *indication* 550
 run - 178
parallelism 216
 agreement 23
 equality 27
 comparison 464
parallelize 464
parallelogram 244
paralogism 477
paralysis *impotence* 158
 physical insensibility 376
 disease 655
 moral insensibility 823
paralyze 158, 376, 823
paramount *supreme* 33
 important 642
 authority 737
 lord - *master* 745
 possessor 779
 - estate 780
paramour 897
paranoia 503
paranoiac 504
parapet 717
paraph 550
paraphernalia
 machinery 633
 belonging 780
paraphrase
 imitation 19
 copy 21
 meaning 516
 synonym 522
 phrase 566

629

perversion
  sophistry 477
  misinterpretation 523
  misteaching 538
  falsehood 544
  untruth 546
  injury 659
  impiety 988
perversity
  [*see* perverse]
pervert
  [*see* perversion]
  convert 144
  recant 607
perverted *in error* 495
pervestigation 461
pervicacious 606
pervigilium 682
pervious 260, 295
pessimism *overrate* 482
  underrate 483
  dejection 837
  hopeless 859
pessimist 482, 862, 859
pessimize 549, 934
pessomancy 511
pest *bane* 663
  painfulness 830
pester 830
pesthouse 662
pestiferous 657
pestilence 655
pestle 330
pet *love* 897
  favorite 899
  anger 900
  fondle 902
  flatter 933
petal 367
petard 727
  hoist on one's own -
  retaliation 718
  failure 732
Peter pence 784
petiole 367
petition *ask* 765
  pray 990
petitioner 767
petitio principii 477
petit maitre 854
petname 565
petrel *warning* 668
petrify *dense* 321
  hard 323
  organization 357
  freeze 385
  thrill 824
  affright 860
  astonish 870
petrol 356
petroleum 356
pétroleur 384
petrology 358
petronel 727
petticoat *dress* 225
  woman 374
  - government 737
pettifogger 968
pettifogging
  sophistry 477
  dishonorable 940

pettish 901
petty *shallow* 32
  little 193
  unimportant 643
  - cash 800, 811
  - cashbook 551
  - larceny 791
  - sessions 966
  - treason 742
petulance
  insolence 885
  irascibility 901
petulant
  - *language* 574
pew *cell* 191
  church 1000
pewter 41
phaeton 272
Phaëthon 306, 423
phalansterism 910
phalanx *party* 712
  army 726
  (*assemblage* 72)
phantasm
  illusion 443
  appearance 448
  imagination 515
phantasmagoria 448
phantasy *idea* 453
  imagination 515
phantom *unreal* 4
  corpse 362
  fallacy of vision 443
  imaginary 515
  specter 980a
pharisaical
  falsehood 544
  false piety 988
Pharisee *deceiver* 548
  pietist 988
pharmaceutist 662
pharmacology 662
pharmacopœia 662
pharmacopolist 662
pharmacy 662
pharos 550
phase *aspect* 8
  transition 144
  form 240
  appearance 448
  assume a new - 144
  have many -s 149
  view in all its -s 461
phasis 448
phasma 443
pheasant 298
phenix [*see* phœnix]
phenomenon *event* 151
  appearance 448
  prodigy 872
phial 191
  [*see* vial]
Phidias 559
philander 902
philanderer 902
philanthropical 906, 910
philanthropy **910**
philippic 932
Philistine
  conformity 82

  unintellectual 491
  bourgeois 876
philologist 492
philologize 562
philology 560
philomath 492
philomel 416
philosopher
  intellect 450
  scholar 492
  sage 500
  -'s stone 650
philosophical
  thoughtful 451
  calm 826
  - unitarianism 984
philosophy *intellect* 450
  thought 451
  knowledge 490
  calmness 826
  moral - 450
  - of the mind 450
philter 993
phiz *face* 234
  look 448
phlebotomy
  ejection 297
  remedy 662
phlegm *viscid* 352
  insensibility 823
phlegmatic *dull* 32
  slow 275
  indifferent 866
phlogiston 382
pho! 497
Phœbe 318
Phœbus *sun* 318
  luminary 423
phœnix *exception* 83
  reproduction 163
  paragon 650
  restoration 660
phone *telephone* 534
phonetic *sound* 402
  tonic 561
  voice 580
  speech 582
  - spelling 561
phonetics 560, 561
phonic 402, 418
phonics 402
phonocamptic 402
phonograph 417, 418, 551
phonography *sound* 402
  letter 561
  writing 590
phonorganon 418
phosphorescence
  light 420
  luminary 423
phosphorus 423
photics 420
photodrama 448
photogenic 420
photograph *like* 17
  picture 556
photographer 445
photography *light* 420
  optical instruments 445

  representation 554
  painting 556
photogravure 558
photolithograph 558
photolithography 420
photology 420
photometer *light* 420
  optical instrument 445, 466
photometry 420
photomicrography 420
photophony 402
photoplay 448
photospectroheliog-
  raphy 554
photosphere 318
phototelegraphy 420
phototherapy 420
phragma 228
phrase *music* 413
  language **566**
phrasemonger 577
phraseology 569
phrenetic
  deranged 503
  madman 504
phrenitis 503
phrenologist 448
phrenology 448, 450
phrensy
  imagination 515
  passion 825
Phryne 962
phthiriasis 653
phthisis 655
phthisozoics 361
phylacteric
  sorcery 992
phylactery
  maxim 496
  spell 993
phyletic 166
phylogeny 161, 357
phylum 75
physic *cure* 660
  remedy 662
  throw - to the dogs
  662
physical 316, 542
  - culture 845
  - drill 537
  - education
  material 316
  teaching 537
  - force *strength* 159
  compulsion 744
  - pain **378**
  - pleasure **377**
  - science 316
physician 662, 695
physicism 316
physics 316
physiogeny 161
physiognomy
  face 234
  appearance 448
  interpret 522
physiology
  organization 357
  life 359
  vegetable - 369

physique *strength* 159
 animality 364
phytivorous 298
phytobiology 369
phytology 369
phyton 369
phytopathologist 369
phytotomy 369
phytozoaria 193
pi 591
piacular 952
pianino 417
pianissimo 415
pianist 416
piano *gentle* 174
 slow 275
 music 415
 - player 417
 - score 415
pianoforte 417
piazza 182, 189, 191
pibroch *music* 415
 indication 550
 war 722
pica 591
picacho 206
picaroon 792
picayune 643
piccolo 410, 417
pick *arr* 253
 eat 298
 select 609
 best 648
 clean 652
 gain 775
 - a quarrel 713
 - holes *censure* 932,934
 - one's steps 459
 - one's way 675
 - out *extract* 301
 select 609
 - the brains of 461
 - the lock 480a
 - to pieces *separate* 44
 destroy 162
 find fault 932
 - up *learn* 539
 get better 658
 gain 775
pickaninny 129
pickax 253
picked 648
 - men 700
pickeer 720
pickeerer 792
pickelhaube 717
picket *join* 43
 locate 184
 fence 229
 guard 668
 defense 717
 soldiers 726
 restrain 751
 imprison 752
 torture 972
pickings *gain* 775
 booty 793
pickle *condition* 7
 macerate 337
 pungent 392
 condiment 393

preserve 670
 difficulty 704
 have a rod in - 673
pickle-herring 844
pick-me-up 392, 662
pickpocket 792
 abuse like a - 932
pickthank *busy* 682
 servile 886
picnic *food* 298
 participation 778
 amusement 840
picot edge 257
picquet 840
pictorial *painting* 556
 beauty 845
picture *appearance* 448
 representation 554
 painting 556
 description 594
 - post card 592
 - to oneself 515
picture gallery 556
picturesque
 painting 556
 beauty 845
piddle *dawdle* 683
piddling 643
pidgin English 563
pie *food* 298
 sweet 396
 printing 591
piebald 440
piece *adjunct* 39
 bit 51
 change 140
 painting 556
 drama 599
 cannon 727
 coin 800
 courtesan 962
 fall to -s 162
 give a - of advice 695
 in -s 330
 make a - of work
  about 642
 of a - 42
 - of a good fortune
  618
 - of music 415
 - of news 532
 - of work *discord* 713
 - out 52
 - together 43
 pull to -s 162
pièce
 - de résistance 298
 - justificative 467
piecemeal 51
pied 440
pier 666
pierce *perforate* 260
 insert 300
 bodily pain 378
 chill 385
 hurt 649
 wound 659
 affect 824
 mental pain 830
 - the head 410
 - the heart 830

piercer 262
piercing *cold* 383
 loud 404
 shrill 410
 intelligent 498
 feeling 821
 - eye 441
 - pain 378
pier glass 445
Pierian spring 597
Pierides 416
pietas 998
pietism 988
pietist 987, 988
piety 987
pig *animal* 366
 sensual 954a
 - in a poke
 uncertain 475
 chance 621
 rash 863
 - together 72
pigeon *bird* 298, 366
 dupe 547
 steal 791
 gorge de - 440
pigeon-hearted 862
pigeonhole
 receptacle 191
 hole 260
 shelve 460
piggery 636
piggin 191
piggish 954
pig-headed *foolish* 499
 obstinate 606
pigment 428
pigmy [*see* pygmy]
pignoration 771
pig-sticking 361
pigsty 653
pigtail 214
Pigwiggen 193
pike *hill* 206
 sharp 253
 fish 366
 weapon 727
pikeman 726
pikestaff *tall* 206
 plain 525
pilaster
 support 215
 projection 250
 ornament 847
pile *heap* 72
 multitude 102
 edifice 161
 velvet 256
 store 636
 money 800
 (*house* 189)
 funeral - 363
 - on the agony 860
 - up *exaggeration* 549
 redundance 641
pile-driver 276
pile-dwelling 189
pileous 256
piles 655
pilfer *steal* 791
pilferer 792

pilgarlic *outcast* 893
pilgrim *traveler* 268
 palmer 996
pilgrimage *journey* 266
 undertaking 676
pill *sphere* 249
 medicine 662
 bore 841
 bitter - 735
pillage *injury* 659
 theft 791
pillager 792
pillar *stable* 150
 lofty 206
 support 215
 monument 551
 tablet 590
 from - to post
 transfer 270
 agitation 315
 irresolute 505
 circuit 629
 - of the state &c. 873
 -s of Hercules 550
pillarist 996
pillion 215
pillory 975
pillow *support* 215
 soft 324
 consult one's -
 temporize 133
 reflect 451
pillowcase 223
pilon 784
pilose 256
pilot *mariner* 269
 inform 527
 guide 693
 director 694
pilot balloon
 experiment 463
pilot boat 273
pilot bread 298
pilot jacket 225
Pilsener beer 298
pimento 393
pimp 962
pimple *tumor* 250
 blemish 848
pin *fasten* 43
 fastening 45
 locate 184
 sharp 253
 axis 312
 trifle 643
 might hear a - drop
  403
 not a - to choose
 equal 27
 no choice 609a
 - down *compulsion* 744
 restraint 751
 - oneself upon
 serve 746
 servile 886
 - one's faith upon **484**
 point of a - 193
pinacotheca 556
pinafore 225
pince-nez 445
pincers 781

pleasant
 agreeable 829
 amusing 840
 witty 842
 make things –
  deceive 545
  induce 615
  please 829
  flatter 933
pleasantry 840, 842
please 829
 as you –
  obedience 743
 do what one –s 748
 if you – *obedience* 743
  consent 762
  request 765
 – oneself 943
pleasing 394, 829
pleasurableness 829
pleasure *physical* – 377
  will 600
  moral – **827**
  dissipation 954
  at – 600
 at one's – 737
 during – 108a
 give – 829
 make toil of – 682
 man of – 954a
 take one's – 840
 will and – 600
 with – *willingly* 602
pleasure-giving 829
pleasure ground
  demesne 189
  amusement 840
pleat 219, 258
plebe 493, 541
plebeian 851, 876
plebiscite
  judgment 480
  choice 609
pledge *promise* 768
  security 771
  borrow 788
  drink to 883, 894
 hold in – 771
 – oneself 768
 – one's word 768
 take the –
  temperance 771
  sobriety 958
pledget *lining* 224
  stopper 263
  remedy 662
Pleiades *cluster* 72
  stars 318
plenary *full* 31
  complete 52
plenipotent *power* 157
plenipotentiary
  interpreter 524
  consignee 758
  deputy 759
plenitude 639
 in the – of power 159
plenteous 168, 639
plenty *multitude* 102
  sufficient 639
 – to do 682

plenum *substance* 3
  space 180
  matter 316
pleonasm
  repetition 104
  diffuseness 573
  redundance 641
plerophory 484
plethora 641
plexiform 219
plexure 219
plexus 219
pliable 324
pliant *soft* 324
  irresolute 605
  facile 705
  servile 886
plicature 258
pliers *extractor* 301
  holder 781
plight *state* 7
  circumstance 8
  promise 768
  security 771
 evil – 735
 – one's faith 902
 – one's troth 768, 902
plighted love *love* 897
  endearment 902
Plimsoll mark 466
plinth *base* 211
  rest 215
plod *journey* 266
  slow 275
  persevere 604a
  work 682
plodder *worker* 686
plodding 604a, 682
  dull 843
plot – *of ground* 181
  plain 344
  measure 466
  plan 626
 the – thickens
  assemblage 72
  events 682
plough [see plow]
plover 366
plow *furrow* 259
  agriculture 371
 – in 228
 – one's way 266
 – the ground
  prepare 673
 – the waves 267
plowable 371
plowboy 876
plowed *failure* 732
plowman 371
plowshare 253
pluck *music* 416
  cheat 545
  resolution 604
  persevere 604a
  take 789
  steal 791
  courage 861
 – a crow with 932
 – out 301
 – up *reject* 610
 – up courage 861

plucked 732
plucky 604
plug *close* 261
  stopper 263
  blow 276
  deterioration 659
plugugly 913
plum *number* 98
  money 800
 – pudding 298
plumage 256
plumb *vertical* 212
  straight 246
  close 261
  measure 466
plumber 690
plumb line 212
plum-colored 437
plume *feather* 256
  ornament 847
 borrowed –s 788
 – oneself 878
plumigerous 256
plummet *depth* 208
  verticality 212
plumose 256
plump
  instantaneous 113
  fat 192
  tumble 306
  plunge 310
  unexpected 508
 – down 306
 – upon 292
plumper *expansion* 194
  vote 609
plumpness
 [*see* plump]
plumule 167
plunder *gain* 35
  steal 791
  booty 793
  (*ravage* 659)
plunge *revolution* 146
  insert 300
  dive **310**
  immerse 337
  chance 621
  hurry 684
 – headlong 684
 – in medias res
  plain language 576
  resolute 604
 – into *adventure* 676
 – into difficulties 704
 – into dissipation 954
 – into sorrow 830
plunged – in debt 806
 – in grief 828
plunger
  gambler 463, 621, 840
pluperfect 122
plurality 33, **100**
plus 37
plush 256
Pluto ? 82
 realms of – 982
plutocracy 803
plutocrat 803
plutonic 382
Plutus 803

pluvial 348
pluviograph 348
pluviometer 348
pluviometry 348
ply *layer* 204
  fold 258
  use 677
  exert 686
  request 765
 – a trade 794
 – one's task 680
 – one's trade 625
plytophagous 298
p. m. 126
pneuma 450
pneumatics 334, 338
pneumatogram 532
pneumatograph 662
pneumatology 334, 450
pneumatolytic 334
pneumatometer 334,
  662
pneumatonomy 334
pneumatoscope 334
pneumatoscopic 317
pneumatotherapy 662
pneumometer 662
pneumonia 655
poach *steal* 791
  illegality 964
poached eggs 298
poacher 792
poachy 345
pock 250
pocket *place* 184
  pouch 191
  diminutive 193
  receive 785
  take 789
  money 800
  treasury 802
  brook 826
 button up one's – 808
 out of – *loss* 776
  debt 806
 – the affront
  submit 725
  forgive 918
 touch the – 800
pocketbook 551
  purse 802
pocket   handkerchief
  225
pocket money 800
pocket pistol *bottle* 191
pococurante
  insensible 823
  indifferent 866
pod *receptacle* 191
  covering 223
podagra 378
podesta 967
poem 597
poesy 597
poet 597
poetaster *poet* 597
  affectation 855
poetic *style* 574
 – vigor 574
 – prose 598
poetize 597

poncho 225
pond *lake* 343
  store 636
  fish - 370
ponder 451
ponderable *matter* 316
  weight 319
ponderation
  weighing 319
  judgment 480
ponderous *heavy* 319
  - *style* 574, 579
poniard 727
pons asinorum
  unintelligible 519
  difficulty 704
pontiff 996
pontifical 995
pontificals 999
pontificate 995
pontoon *vehicle* 272
  boat 273
  way 627
pony 271
  translation 522, 539
  - *up expend* 809
poodle 366
pooh, pooh!
  absurd 497
  unimportance 643
  contempt 930
pool *lake* 343
  coöperate 709
  prize 775
  billiards 840
  - room 621
  - shark 621
poonghie 996
poop 235
poor *incomplete* 53
  weak 160
  emaciated 203
  - *reasoning* 477
  - *style* 575
  insufficient 640
  trifling 643
  indigent 804
  unhappy 828
  cut a - *figure* 874
  - hand 701
  - head 499
  - in spirit 881
  - man 640, 804
  - thing 914
poorhouse 189
poorly 655
  - off 804
poorness [*see* poor]
  inferiority 34
poor-spirited 862
pop *bubble* 353
  noise 406
  concert 415
  unexpected 508
  - a question 461
  - at 716
  - in *ingress* 294
  insertion 300
  - off *die* 360
  - the question
  request 765

  endearment 902
  - upon *arrive* 292
  discover 480a
pope *infallibility* 474
  priest 996
popedom 995
Pope Joan 840
popery 984
popgun *trifle* 643
popinjay 854
poplar *tall* 206
  tree 367
poppy *sedative* 174
poppy-cock 517
populace 876
popular *choosing* 609
  salable 795
  desirable 865
  celebrated 873
  favorite 897
  approved 931
  - concert 415
  - demand 677
  - opinion 488
popularize
  render intelligible 518
  facilitate 705
  make pleasant 829
population
  inhabitants 188
  mankind 372
populous
  crowded 72
  multitude 102
  presence 186
porcelain *baked* 384
  sculpture 557
porch *entrance* 66
  lobby 191
  mouth 231
  opening 260
  (*way* 627)
porcupine *prickly* 253
  touchy 901
pore *opening* 260
  egress 295
  conduit 350
  - over *look* 441
  apply the mind 457
  learn 539
porism *inquiry* 461
  judgment 480
pork 298
pornographic 961
porous *open* 260
  outgoing 295
  spongy 322
  liquescent 335
porpoise 192, 366
porraceous 435
porridge 298, 352
porringer 191
port *abode* 189
  sinistral 239
  gait 264
  arrival 292
  carriage 448
  harbor 666
  - admiral 745
  - fire 388
  - wine 959

portable *small* 193
  transferable 270
  light 320
portage 270
portal *entrance* 66
  mouth 231
  opening 260
  (*way* 627)
portamento 270
portative *small* 193
  transferable 270
  (*light* 320)
portcullis
  hindrance 706
  defense 717
portemonnaie 802
portend 511
portent 512
portentous
  prophetic 511
  fearful 860
porter *janitor* 263
  carrier 271
porterage 270
porterhouse steak 298
portfolio *case* 191
  book 593
  file 636
  direction 693
  authority 747
  jurisdiction 965
porthole 260
portico *entrance* 66
  room 191
portière 424
portion *part* 51
  allotment 786
  - out 786
portional 100a
portly 192
portmanteau 191
  - word 572
portrait 554
  - painter 559
  - painting 556
portraiture 554, 556
portray 554
portreeve *master* 745
  functionary 965
portress 263
posada 189
pose *situation* 183
  form 240
  inquiry 461
  puzzle 475
  difficulty 704
  affectation 855
  - as 554
poser 461
Poseidon 341
posited 184
position
  circumstances 8
  term 71
  situation 183
  proposition 514
  assertion 535
  - in society 873
positive *real* 1
  great 31
  strict 82

  certain 474
  narrow-minded 481
  belief 484
  unequivocal 518
  assertion 535
  obstinate 606
  absolute 739
  (*precise* 494)
  Philosophie - 316
  - color 428
  - degree 31
  - fact 474
  - quantity 84
Positivism 451
positivism
  heterodoxy 984
  irreligion 989
posnet 191
posology 662
posse *collection* 72
  party 712
  in - 470
  - comitatus
  collection 72
  army 726
  authority 737
  jurisdiction 965
possess 777
  bedevil 978
  - a state 7
  - knowledge 490
  - oneself of 789
  - the mind 484
  - the soul 824
possessed 777
  - with a devil 503
possession **777**, 780
  sorcery 992
  come into - 775, 783
  in one's - 777
  person in - 779
  put one in - of 527
  remain in - of the field
  731
possessor **779**
possibility *chance* 156
  liability 177
  may be **470**
  property 780
  - upon a possibility
  475
possible
  [*see* possibility]
post *fastening* 45
  list 86
  situation 183
  location 184
  support 215
  send 270
  swift 274
  publish 531
  mail 534
  beacon 550
  record 551
  employment 625
  accounts 811
  stigmatize 874
  punish 972
  at one's - *persist* 604a
  prepared 673
  on duty 926

practiced *skilled* 698
- eye 700
- hand 700
practitioner
  medical - 662
  doer 690
præcognita 467
prædial 342, 371
præmunire 742, 974
prænomen 564
prætor 967
pragmatic *narrow* 481
  teaching 537
  practical 646
  - sanction 769
pragmatical
  pedantic 855
  vain 880
pragmatism
  philosophy 451
  expedience 646
  use 677
prahu 273
prairie *space* 180
  plain 344
  vegetation 367
  - dog 366
  - schooner 272
praise *thanks* 916
  commendation 931
  worship 990
praiseworthy
  commendable 931
  virtue 944
prance *move* 266
  leap 309
  dance 315
prank *caprice* 608
  amusement 840
  adorn 847
prate 584
prattle *talk* 582
  chatter 584
pravity 945
prawns 298
praxis *grammar* 567
  action 680
Praxiteles 559
pray *beg* 765
  worship 990
prayer *request* 765
  worship 990
  house of - 1000
  - of Ajax 421
prayer book 990, 998
prayer wheel 998
preach *teach* 537
  allocution 586
  predication 998
  - to the winds 645
  - to the wise 538
preacher *teacher* 540
  speaker 582
  priest 996
preachment 998
preadamite *antique* 124
  veteran 130
preamble 62, 64
preapprehension 481
prebend 995
prebendary 996

precarious *transient* 111
  uncertain 475
  dangerous 665
precatory 765
precaution *care* 459
  expedient 626
  safety 664
  preparation 673
precede *superior* 33
  - in order 62
  - in time 116
  - in motion 280
precedence 62
  rank 873
  [see precede]
precedent
  [see precede]
  prototype 22
  precursor 64
  priority 116
  habit 613
  legal decision 969
  follow -s 82
precentor *musician* 416
  leader 694
  priest 996
precept
  requirement 630
  maxim **697**
  order 641
  permit 760
preceptor 540
precession
  - in order 62
  - in motion **280**
précieuse *ridicule* 855
precinct *region* 181
  place 182
  environs 227
  boundary 233
precious *great* 31
  excellent 648
  expending 809
  valuable 814
  beloved 897
  - metals 800
  - stone *goodness* 648
  ornament 847
precipice *vertical* 212
  slope 217
  dangerous 667
  on the verge of a - 665
precipitancy *haste* 684
  rashness 863
precipitate *early* 132
  sink 308
  consolidate 321
  refuse 653
  haste 684
  rash 863
  - oneself 306
precipitous 217
précis 596
precise *exact* 494
  severe 739
  taste 850
precisely *imitation* 19
  assent 488
precisian 739, 850
precisianism
  affectation 855

  heterodoxy 984
  overreligious 988
preclude 706
preclusion 55
preclusive 55
precocious *early* 132
  immature 674
  pert 885
precognition
  forethought 490
  knowledge 510
precompose 56
preconception 481
preconcert
  predetermination 611
  plan 626
precursal 511
precurse 511
precursor
  - in order 62, **64**
  - in time 116
  (*predict* 511)
  (*presage* 512)
predacious 789, 791
predacity 789
predatory *taking* 789
  thieving 791
predecessor 64
predeliberation
  foresight 510
  predetermination 611
predella 215
predesigned 611
predestination *fate* 152
  necessity 601
  predetermination 611
  Deity 976
predetermination 601,
  611
predial *land* 342
  agriculture 371
  manorial 780
predicament *state* 7
  circumstances 8
  junction 43
  character 75
predicate *forecast* 507
  affirm 535
  preach 998
predict 511
prediction **511**
predilection *bias* 481
  affection 820
  desire 865
  (*love* 897)
predispose
  motive 615
  prepare 673
predisposed
  willing 602
predisposition
  tendency 176
  affection 820
predominance 157
  [see predominant]
predominant
  influence 175
  directing 693
  authority 737
predominate
  superior 33

preëminent *superior* 33
  celebrated 873
preëmption 795
preëngage *early* 132
preëngagement 768
preëstablish 626
preëxamine 461
preëxist *existence* 1
  priority 116
  (*past* 122)
preface *precedence* 62
  precursor 64
  book 593
prefect *learner* 541
  ruler 745
  deputy 759
  - of studies 542
prefecture 737
prefer *choose* 609
  - a claim 969
  - a petition 765
preference 62
preferment
  improvement 658
  ecclesiastical - 995
prefigure
  prediction 511
  (*indication* 550)
prefix 62, 64
preglacial 124
pregnable 158]
pregnant *producing* 161
  productive 168
  predicting 511
  - style 572
  important 642
  - with meaning 516
prehensile 789
prehension 789
prehistoric 124
preinstruct 537
prejudge 481
prejudicate 481
prejudice *misjudge* 481
  evil 619
  detriment 659
prejudicial 649
prelacy 995
prelate 996
prelation 609
prelect *expound* 531
  teach 537
  speech 582
prelection 537, 582
prelector 540, 582
prelibation 510
preliminaries
  - of peace 723
  settle - 673
preliminary
  preceding 62
  precursor 64
  reception 296
  (*prior* 116)
prelude *prefix* 62
  precursor 64
  beginning 66
  music 415
  (*priority* 116)
premature *early* 132
  unripe 674

premeditate
  predetermine 611
  intend 620
premices 154
premier *director* 694
  vicegerent 759
  - *pas* 66
premiership 693
premise *prefix* 62
  announce 511
premises *precursor* 64
  prior 116
  ground 182
  evidence 467
  logic 476
premium *debt* 806
  receipt 810
  reward 973
  at - 814
premonish 668
premonition 668, 992*a*
premonitory
  prediction 511
  warning 668
Premonstratensian
  996
premonstration
  appearance 448
  prediction 511
  manifestation 525
premunire
  [*see* præmunire]
prenotion
  misjudgment 481
  foresight 510
prensation 789
prentice 541
prenticeship 539
preoccupancy
  possession 777
preoccupation
  inattention 458
preoption 609
preordain 611
  destiny 152
  necessity 601
  Deity 976
preparation **673**
  music 413
  instruction 537
  writing 590
  in course of - *plan* 626
preparatory *preceding*
  62
prepare 673
  - the way 705
prepared *predict* 507
  deft 698
preparedness 673
preparing *destined* 152
prepense
  spontaneous 600
  predetermined 611
  intended 620
  malice - 907
prepollence 157
preponderance
  superiority 33
  influence 175
  dominance 737
  (*importance* 642)

prepossessed
  obstinate 606
prepossessing 829
prepossession
  prejudice 481
  possession 777
preposterous *great* 31
  absurd 497
  imaginative 515
  exaggerated 549
  ridiculous 853
  undue 925
prepotency 157
Pre-Raphaelite 122,
  124
prerequire 630
prerequisite 630
preresolve 611
prerogative
  authority 737
  right 924
presage *predict* 511
  omen 512
presbyopia 443
presbyter 996
Presbyterian 984
presbytery 995, 996,
  1000
prescience 510
prescient 510, 511
prescious 511
prescribe *direct* 693
  advice 695
  order 741
  entitle 924
  enjoin 926
prescript *precept* 697
  decree 741
prescription
  remedy 662
prescriptive *old* 124
  unchanged 141
  habitual 613
  due 924
presence *in space* **186**
  appearance 448
  breeding 894
  in the - of *near* 197
  - chamber 191
  - of God 981
  - of mind *calm* 826
  cautious 864
  real - 998
  saving one's - 928
present
  - *in time* 118
  - *in space* 186
  offer 763
  give 784
  church preferment 995
  at - 118
  - a bold front 861
  - a front 719
  - arms *courtesy* 894
  respect 928
  - in spirit 187
  - itself *event* 151
  visible 446
  thought 451
  - oneself *presence* 186
  offer 763

  courtesy 894
  - time **118**
  instant 113
  - to the mind
  attention 457
  memory 505
  - to the view 448
  these -s *writing* 590
  epistle 592
presentable 845, 852
presentation
  [*see* present]
  celebration 883
  courtesy 894
presentiment
  instinct 477
  prejudgment 481
  foresight 510
presently 132
presentment
  information 527
  law proceeding 969
preservation
  continuance 141
  conservation **670**
  Divine attributes 976
preserve *sweets* 396
  provision 637
  [*see* preservation]
  - a middle course 628
preserver
  safeguard 664
preshow 511
preside
  - at the board
  direction 693
  - over *authority* 737
presidency 737
president
  director 694
  master 745
  -'s message 695
press *crowd* 72
  closet 191
  weight 319
  public - 531
  printing 591
  book 593
  move 615
  compel 744
  offer 763
  solicit 765
  go to - 591
  - agent's yarn 546
  - in 300
  - into the service
  use 677
  aid 707
  - of business 682
  - on *course* 109
  progression 282
  haste 684
  - one hard 716
  - out 301
  - proof 591
  - to the bosom 902
  under - of 744
  writer for the - 593
pressed, hard - 704
  - for time 684
pressgang 965

pressing *need* 630
  urgent 642
pressman 554
press room 591
pressure *power* 157
  influence 175
  weight 319
  urgency 642
  adversity 735
  center of - 222
  high - 824
presswork 591
Prester John 515
prestidigitation 545
prestidigitator 548
prestige *bias* 481
  authority 737
  fascination 865
  fame 873
prestigiation 545
prestissimo 415
presto *instantly* 113
  music 415
prestriction 442
presumable 472
presume
  probability 472
  misjudge 481
  believe 484
  suppose 514
  hope 858
  pride 878
presumption
  [*see* presume]
  probability 472
  expectation 607
  rashness 863
  arrogance 885
  unlawfulness 925
presumptive
  probable 472
  supposed 514
  due 924
  heir - 779
  - evidence
  evidence 467
  probability 472
presumptuous 885
presuppose
  misjudge 481
  suppose 514
presurmise *foresee* 510
  suppose 514
pretend *assert* 535
  simulate 544
  untruth 546
pretended 545
pretender *deceiver* 548
  braggart 884
  unentitled 925
pretending 544
pretense *imitation* 19
  falsehood 544
  untruth 546
  excuse 617
  ostentation 882
  boast 884
pretension
  ornament 577
  affectation 855
  due 924

pretentious
  inflated 482
  specious 846
  affected 855
  vain 880
  ostentatious 882
  boasting 884
  undue 925
preterience 111
preterit 122
preterition **122**
preterlapsed 122
pretermit 460
preternatural 83
pretext *untruth* 546
  plea 617
pretty *much* 31
  imperfectly 651
  beautiful 845
  - fellow 501
  - good 651
  - kettle of fish, pass,
    &c.
  disorder 59
  difficulty 704
  - quarrel 720
  - well *much* 31
  little 32
  trifling 643
preux chevalier 939
prevail *exist* 1
  superior 33
  general 78
  influence 175
  habit 613
  succeed 731
  - upon 615
prevailing 78
  - taste 852
prevalence
  [see prevail]
prevaricate
  falsehood 544
  (*equivocate* 520)
prévenance 894
prevene 116
prevenient
  precedent 62
  early 132
prevent 706
prevention
  prejudice 481
  hindrance 706
  - of waste 817
preventive 55
previous
  - in time 116
  (- *in order* 62)
  move the - question
    624
  not within - experi-
    ence 137
prevision 510
prewarn 668
prey *food* 298
  quarry 620
  booty 793
  victim 828
  fall a - to
  be defeated 732
  subjection 749

- on the mind
  excite 824
  regret 833
  fear 860
- on the spirits 837
- to grief 828
- to melancholy 837
price *consideration* 147
  value 648
  money **812**
  at any - 604a
  beyond - 814
  cheap at the - 815
  have one's - 812
  of great - *good* 648
  dear 814
  reward 973
price current 812
priceless *valuable* 648
  dear 814
prick *sharp* 253
  hole 260
  sting 378
  sensation of touch 380
  incite 615
  mental suffering 830
  kick against the -s
  useless 645
  resistance 719
  - up one's ears *hear*
    418
  curiosity 455
  attention 457
  expect 507
prickle *sharp* 253
  sensation of touch 380
prickly 253
pride *ornament* 847
  loftiness **878**
  take a - in 878
prie-dieu 215
priest 904, 996
priestcraft 995
priestess 996
priesthood 995, 996
priest-ridden
  false piety 988
  churchdom 995
prig *steal* 791
  puppy 854
  affected 855
priggish *affected* 855
  vain 880
prim *taste* 850
  affected 855
  proud 878
prima donna
  actress 599
  important 642
  proficient 700
primacy
  superiority 33
  celebrity 873
  church 995
prima facie *sight* 441
  appearance 448
  probable 472
  - *meaning* 516
  manifest 525
primal 66

primary *initial* 66
  cause 153
  important 642
  - color 428
  - education 537
primate 996
primates 875
prime *initial* 66
  primeval 124
  early 132
  teach 537
  important 642
  excellent 648
  prepare 673
  in one's - 131
  - and load 673
  - cost *price* 812
  cheap 815
  - minister 694
  - mover 153, 164
  - number 84
  - of life *youth* 127
  adolescence 131
  - of the morning 125
primed *skilled* 698
  tipsy 959
primer *automobile* 272
  schoolbook 542
primeval 124
primices 154
primigenous 124
priming 556
primitive *old* 124
  cause 153
  - color 428
primogenial
  beginning 66
primogeniture *old* 124
  age 128
  posterity 167
  heritage 777
primordial *original* 20
  old 124
  cause 153
primordiate 124
primordium 153
primrose-colored 436
prince *perfection* 650
  master 745
  nobility 875
  - of darkness 978
Prince Albert coat 225
princely
  authoritative 737
  liberal 816
  famous 873
  noble 875
  generous 942
princess 745, 875
principal *important* 642
  director 694
  - part *great* 31
  whole 50
principality *region* 181
  property 780
principally 33
principia 66, 496
principle *intrinsic* 5
  rule 80
  cause 153
  element 316

  reasoning 476
  tenet 484
  maxim 496
  motive 615
  probity 939
  on - 615
  want of - 945
prink *adorn* 847
  show off 882
print *news* 532
  mark 550
  engraving 558
  letterpress 591
  out of - 552
printer 591
printing **591**
  - press 591
prior - *in order* 62
  - *in time* 116
  clergy 996
priority **116,** 234
priory 1000
prism *angularity* 244
  optical instrument 445
  see through a - 443
prismatic *color* 428
  variegated 440
prison **752**
  cast into - 751
  in - 751, 754
prisoner *restraint* 751
  captive **754**
  accused 938
  take - *restrain* 751
  seize 789
pristine 122
prithee 765
prittle-prattle 588
privacy *conceal* 528
  seclude 893
private *special* 79
  hidden 528
  secluded 893
  in - 528
  keep - 881
  - road 627
  - soldier 726
  talk to in - 586, 588
  to gain some - ends 943
privateer *combatant* 726
  robber 792
privateering 791
privately 881
privation *loss* 776
  poverty 804
privative 789
privilege *freedom* 748
  permission 760
  exemption 777a
  due 924
privity *relation* 9
  knowledge 490
privy *hidden* 528
  latrines 653
  - to 490
Privy Council
  tribunal 966
prize *good* 618
  masterpiece 650
  palm 733
  gain 775

prolegomena 64
prolepsis *precursor* 64
  anachronism 115
proletarian 876
proliferous 163, 168
prolific 168
proligerous 163
prolix 573
prolixity 573
prolocutor
  interpreter 524
  teacher 540
  speaker 582
prologue
  precursor 64
  drama 599
  what's past is - 122
prolong *protract* 110
  late 133
  continue 143
  lengthen 200
prolongation
  sequence 63
  protraction 110
  posterity 117
  continuance 143
prolusion 64
promenade *walk* 266
  display 882
Promethean 359
  - spark 359
prominence
  [*see* prominent]
prominent *convex* 250
  manifest 525
  important 642
  eminent 873
prominently *much* 31
  more 33
promiscuous *mixed* 41
  irregular 59
  indiscriminate 465a
  casual 621
promise *predict* 511
  engage **768**
  hope 858
  keep one's - 939
  keep - to ear and
    break to hope 545
  - of celestial worth
    511
  - oneself *expect* 507
  hope 858
promissory 768
  - note *security* 771
  money 800
promontory *height* 206
  projection 250
  land 342
promorphology 357
promote *improve* 658
  aid 707
promoter *planner* 626
promotion *class* 541
  improvement 658
prompt *early* 132
  remind 505
  tell 527
  induce 615
  active 682
  advise 695

(*quick* 274)
  - book 505
  - memory 505
prompter *theater* 599
  tempter 615
  adviser 695
promptuary 636
promulgate 531
  - a decree 741
pronation and supina-
  tion 218
prone *horizontal* 213
proneness *tendency* 176
  disposition 820
prôner *ostentation* 882
  praise 931
prôneur 935
prong 91
pronounce *judge* 480
  assert 535
  voice 580
  speak 582
pronounced 31, 525
pronouncement 531,
  535
pronunciation 562, 580
pronunciative 535
proof *hard* 323
  insensible 376
  test 463
  demonstration 478
  indication 550
  printing 591
  draft 626
  ocular - 446
  - against *strong* 159
  resolute 604
  safe 664
  defense 717
  resistance 719
  insensible 823
proof reader 591
prop *support* 215
  help 707
propædeutic 537
propædeutics 537
propagable 168
propaganda
  teaching 537
  school 542
  preparation 673
propagandism 537
propagandist
  teacher 540
  priest 996
propagate *produce* 161
  be productive 168
  publish 531
  teach 537
propel 284
propeller 284, 312
propend 602
propendency
  predetermination 611
  inclination 820
propense 602
propension 820
propensity
  tendency 176
  willingness 602
  inclination 820

proper *special* 79
  expedient 646
  handsome 845
  due 924
  (*right* 922)
  in its - place 58
  - name 564
  - time 134
  show a - spirit 939
  the - thing *duty* 926
properties, theatrical -
  costume 225
  drama 599
property *power* 157
  possessions **780**
  wealth 803
property-man 599
prophasis 510
prophecy 511
prophet *oracle* 511
  seer 513
  preparer 673
  priest 996
  non-Biblical -s 986
prophetess 513
prophetic *predict* 511
  revelation 985
Prophets, the - 985
prophylactic
  healthful 656
  remedy 662
  preservative 670
  hindrance 706
prophylaxis 670
propinquity 197
propitiate *pacify* 723
  mediate 724
  calm 826
  content 831
  love 897
  pity 914
  forgive 918
  atone 952
  worship 990
propitiator 714, 724
propitious *timely* 134
  beneficial 648
  helping 707
  prosperous 734
  auspicious 858
proplasm 22
proportion *relation* 9
  mathematical 84
  sum 85
  symmetry 242
  elegance 578
  allotment 786
proportionate
  agreeing 23
proportions *space* 180
  size 192
proposal 765
  plan 626
propose *suggest* 514
  broach 535
  intend 620
  offer 763
  offer marriage 902
  - a question 461
proposition
  supposition 454

reasoning 476
project 626
suggestion 514
offer 763
request 765
propound *suggest* 514
  broach 535
  - a question 461
proprietary 779
proprietor 779
proprietorship 780
propriety
  agreement 23
  elegance 578
  expedience 646
  fashion 852
  right 922
  duty 926
propugn *resist* 717
  vindicate 937
propugnaculum 717
propulsion **284**
propulsive 276, 284,
  633
propylon 66
prore 234
prorogue 133
proruption 295
prosaic *usual* 82
  slow 275
  - *style* 575
  dry 576
  dull 843
prosaism *prose* 598
prosal 598
proscenium *front* 234
  theater 599
proscribe *interdict* 761
  banish 893
  curse 908
  condemn 971
  (*exclude* 77)
prose *diffuse style* 573
  prate 584
  not verse **598**
  - run mad *ornate* 577
  poetical 597
  - writer 598
prosecute *pursue* 622
  act 680
  accuse 938
  arraign 969
  - an inquiry 461
prosecutor 938
proselyte
  conversion 144
  learner 541
  convert 607
proselytism 537
proser 841
prosody 597
prosopopœia 521
prospect *futurity* 121
  view 448
  probability 472
  expectation 507
  landscape painting
  556
  good - 858
  in - *intended* 620
prospector 463

Q

R

exaggerate 549
loquacity 584
- *experiment* 463
chance 621
randy 840
range *extent* 26
collocate 60
series 69
term 71
class 75
space 180
distance 196
nearness 197
roam 266
direction 278
stove 386
freedom 748
long - 196
- *itself* 58
- *under*, - *with* 76
within - 177
ranger *director* 694
keeper 753
thief 792
rangy *long* 200
rani 745, 875
rank *prevalent* 1
degree 26
thorough 31
collocate 60
precede 62
row 69
term 71
vegetation 365
fetid 401
estimate 480
bad 649
soldiers 726
glory 873
nobility 875
fill up the -s 660
man of - 875
- and file
continuity 69
soldiers 726
commonalty 876
- *outsider outcast* 893
risen from the -s 876
rankle *unclean* 653
corrupt 659
painful 830
animosity 900
malevolence 907
revenge 919
ransack *seek* 461
deliver 672
plunder 791
price 812
atonement 952
- *one's brains*
thought 451
imagination 515
ransom 672, 952
rant *unmeaning* 517
exaggeration 549
diffuse style 573
turgescence 577
speech 582
acting 599
excitement 825
boasting 884

654

ranter *talker* 584
false piety 988
rantipole 458
ranunculus 845
rap *blow* 276
sound 406
trifle 643
money 800
not worth a - 804
- on the knuckles
angry 900
censure 932
punish 972
- *out affirm* 535
voice 580
speak 582
- out oaths
insolence 885
malediction 908
rapacity *taking* 789
stealing 791
avarice 819
greed 865
rape *seizure* 791
violation 961
rape oil 356
rapid 274
- *slope* 217
- *strides progress* 282
velocity 274
- *succession* 136
rapids 348, 667
rapier 727
rapine 791
rapparee 792
rappee 392
rappel 722
rapport 9, 23
rapprochement
concord 714
friendship 888
rapscallion 949
rapt *thought* 451
attention 457
inattention 458
emotion 821
raptorial *taking* 789
stealing 791
raptors 739
rapture *bliss* 827
love 897
rapturous 221, 827
rara avis
exceptional 83
good 648
famous 873
rare *unique* 20
exceptional 83
few 103
infrequent 137
underdone 298
tenuous 322
neologic 563
choice 648
raree show
appearance 448
amusement 840
rarefaction
expand 194
render light 322
rari nantes 103

rarity 322, 847
rascal *knave* 941
bad man 949
rascality 940
rase *obliterate* 552
rash *skin disease* 655
reckless 863
(*careless* 460)
rasher 204
rashness 863
rasorial 366
rasp *powder* 330
rub 331
clean 652
raspberry 298
rasper *difficult* 704
rasure 552
rat *animal* 366
recant 607
-s in the upper story
503
smell a -
discover 480a
doubt 485
rataplan 407
ratatat 407
ratchet 253
rate *quantity* 25
degree 26
motion 264
measure 466
estimation 480
berate 527
price, tax 812
abuse 932
at a great - 274
rath *early* 132
fort 717
rather *a little* 32
trifling 643
have - 609
have - not 867
- *good* 651
ratification *confirm* 467
affirm 488
consent 762
compact 769
ratio *relation* 9
degree 26
proportion 84
apportionment 786
ratiocination 476
ration *food* 298
provision 637
allotment 786
rational - *quantity* 84
intellectual 450
reasoning 476
judicious 498
sane 502
rationale *cause* 153
attribution 155
answer 462
interpretation 522
rationalism
philosophy 451
reasoning 476
irreligion 989
ratlings 215
ratsbane 663
rattan 975

ratten 158
rattle *noise* 406, **407**
music 417
confuse 458
prattle 584
death - 360
- on 584
rattle-brained 499
rattled *inattentive* 458
confused 523
rattle-headed 499
rattlesnake 366, 913
rattletraps 780
rattling 836
- *pace* 274
raucity 410
raucous *strident* 410
hoarse 581
ravage *destroy* 162
despoil 659
-s of time 659
rave *madness* 503
excitement 824, 825
- *against* 932
ravel *untwist* 60
derange 61
entangle 219
solve 480a
difficulty 704
raveled 59
ravelin 717
raven *bird* 366
black 431
hoarse 581
gorge 957
- *for* 865
ravening *violent* 173
desire 865
ravenous *grasping* 789
desirous 865
raver 504
ravine *interval* 198
narrow 203
dike 259, 350
raving *mad* 503
feeling 821
excitement 824, 825
ravish *seize* 789
please 829
ravished *pleased* 827
ravishment 824
raw *immature* 123
sensitive 378
cold 383
color 428
unprepared 674
unskilled 699
sensibility 822
on the - 375
- head and bloody
bones 860
- *levies* 726
- *material* 635
rawboned 203
rawhide 975
ray *fish* 368
light 420
- *of comfort* 831
thou living - 450
rayah 745
rayless 421

raze *destroy* 162
  level 213
  friction 331
  - to the ground
    lower 308
razor 253
  cut blocks with a -
    waste 638
  misuse 679
  unskillful 699
  keen as a - 821
razzia *destruction* 162
  attack 716
  plunder 791
reabsorb 296
reach *degree* 26
  equal 27
  distance 196
  fetch 270
  arrive at 292
  plain 344
  river 348
  deceive 545
  grasp 737
  take 789
  - of thought 498
  - the ear *hearing* 418
  information 527
  - to *distance* 196
  length 200
  within - *near* 197
  possible 470
reaction
  compensation 30
  counteraction 179
  recoil 277
  restoration 660
reactionary
  reversion 145
  tergiversation 607
reactionist
  opponent 710
read *interpret* 522
  learn 539
  - a lecture 537
  well - 490
readable 578
reader *teacher* 540
  speaker 582
  printer 591
  clergyman 996
readership 542
readily 705
reading *specialty* 79
  knowledge 490
  interpretation 522
  learning 539
  - at sight *music* 415
  - in 995
reading desk 1000
readjust *agree* 23
  equalize 27
readmit 296
ready *expecting* 507
  willing 602
  useful 644
  prepare 673
  active 682
  skillful 698
  cash 800
  get - 673

make - 673
  - made 673
  - memory 505
  - money 800
  - pen 569
  - to burst forth 825
  - to sink 824
  ~ wit 842
reaffirm 535
reagent 463, 690
real *existing* 1
  - *number* 84
  true 494
  liberal 516
  property 780
  - estate 780
  - *property* 780
  - security 771
realgar 434
realism 494
realistic 494, 594
realize *speciality* 79
  intellect 450
  think 451
  discover 480a
  believe 484
  conceive 490
  imagine 515
  accomplish 729
  acquire 775
  sell 796
really *wonder* 870
  (*very* 31)
realm *region* 181
  people 372
  government 737
  property 780
realty 342, 780
ream 593
reamer 262
reanimate
  reproduce 163
  life 359
  resuscitate 660
reap *shorten* 201
  agriculture 371
  take 789
  - and carry 775
  - the benefit of
    be better for 658
  - the fruits *succeed* 731
  acquire 775
  reward 973
  - the whirlwind
    product 154
    failure 732
  - where one has not
    sown 154, 923
reaper 371
reappear *repetition* 104
  reproduce 163
  visible 446
  restore 660
  (*frequent* 136)
rear *sequel* 65
  end 67
  bring up 161
  erect 212
  back **235**
  elevate 307
  teach 537

in the - 281
  - its head *manifest* 525
  - one's head *pride* 878
rear admiral 745
reason *cause* 153
  intellect 450
  thought 451
  argue 476
  wisdom 498
  motive 615
  by - of 615
  feast of - 588
  for this - 462
  in - *moderate* 174
  sanity 502
  right 922
  listen to - 498
  - in a circle 477
  - why *cause* 153
  motive 615
  stand to - *certain* 474
  proof 478
  manifest 525
  what's the - ? 461
  without rime or - 615a
reasonable
  moderate 174
  probable 472
  judicious 498
  sane 502
  cheap 815
  right 922
  - prospect 472
reasoner 476
reasoning **476**
  - faculties 450
reasonless 499
reasons 476
reassemble 72
reassert 535
reassure *hope* 858
  courage 861
reasty *fetid* 401
  unclean 653
reave 789
rebate *deduction* 38
  discount 40a
  moderate 174
  discount 813
rebatement 36, 813
rebec 417
rebel *revolution* 146
  disobedience 742
  (*resistance* 719)
rebellion *revolution* 146
  insurrection 719
  revolt 742
rebellious *defiant* 715
  [*see* rebellion]
rebellow 412
rebirth 660
reboation 412
rebound *recoil* 277
  regression 283
  (*counteraction* 179)
  on the - 145
rebuff *recoil* 277
  resist 719
  repulse 732
  refuse 764
  discourtesy 895

  censure 932
rebuild 660
rebuke 932
rebus 533
rebut *answer* 462
  counter evidence 468
  confute 479
  deny 536
rebuttal [*see* rebut]
rebutter *answer* 462
  law pleadings 969
recalcitrance 719
recalcitrant 742
recalcitrate *recoil* 277
  resist 719
recalesce 382
recall *recollect* 505
  recant 607
  cancel 756
  - to life 660
recant *deny* 536
  retract 607
  resign 756
recapitulate
  enumerate 85
  repeat 104
  describe 594
  summarize 596
recast *revolution* 146
  scheme 626
recede *move back* 283
  move from 287
  - into the shade 874
receipt *scheme* 626
  prescription 662
  precept 697
  security 771
  payment 807
  - *of money* **810**
  - in full 807
  -s *accounts* 811
receive *include* 76
  admit 296
  belief 484
  assent 488
  acquire 775
  take in 785
  take 789
  - *money* 810
  welcome 892, 894
  - Christ 987
received *known* 490
  habitual 613
  (*conformable* 82)
  - *maxim* 496
receiver *vessel* 191
  assignee 785, 967
  treasurer 801
  - of stolen goods 792
receiving **785**
recension 85
recent *lately* 122
  new 123
receptacle **191**
  (*storehouse* 636)
reception
  comprehension 54
  inclusion 76
  arrival 292
  ingestion **296**
  interview 588

receiving 785
welcome 892, 894
warm - 892
reception room 191
receptive
  undertaking 676
  [see reception]
recess receptacle 191
  corner 244
  regression 283
  ambush 530
  vacation 687
  retirement 893
recesses interior 221
  secret - of one's heart
    820
recession
  motion from **287**
recessive 287
réchauffé copy 21
  repetition 104
  food 298
  made hot 384
  restored 660
recherché
  unimitated 20
  good 648
  fashionable 852
recidivation
  regression 283
  relapse 661
recidivism 607
recidivist 607
recipe remedy 662
  precept 697
recipient receptacle 191
  receiving 785
reciprocal mutual 12
  - quantity 84
  retaliation 718
reciprocate
  correlation 12
  interchange 148
  assent 488
  concord 714
  retaliate 718
reciprocitist 12
reciprocity 12, 148
recision 38
recital music 415
recitation [see recite]
recitativo 415
recite enumerate 85
  speak 582
  narrate 594
reciter 582
reck 459
reckless careless 460
  defiant 715
  rash 863
reckon count 85
  - among 76
  - upon believe 484
  expect 507
  - with 807
  - without one's host
    unskillful 699
    fail 732
    rash 863
reckoning
  numeration 85
656

measure 466
expectation 507
payment 807
accounts 811
reward 973
day of - 919
reclaim improve 658
  restore 660
  command 741
  due 924
  atonement 952
reclaimed
  penitent 950
reclamation land 342
  [see reclaim]
recline lie flat 213
  depress 308
  repose 687
  - on 215
reclivate 248
recluse 893
recognition
  [see recognize]
  courtesy 894
  thanks 916
  means of - 550
recognitor 967
recognizable
  visible 446
  intelligible 518
  - by 550
recognizance 771
recognize see 441
  attention 457
  discover 480a
  assent 488
  know 490
  remember 505
  permit 760
  (affirm 535)
recognized
  influential 175
  customary 613
  (conformable 82)
  - maxim 496
recoil reaction 179
  repercussion **277**
  reluctance 603
  shun 623
  'rom which reason -s
    471
  - at hate 898
  - from dislike 867
recollect 505
recommence 66
recommend advise 695
  approve 931
  (induce 15)
  - itself approbation 931
recompense reward 973
  (pay 809)
recompose combine 56
reconcile agree 23
  pacify 723
  content 831
  forgive 918
  - oneself to 826
recondite obscure 519
  hidden 528
recondition 660
reconnoissance 441

reconnoiter see 441
  inquire 461
reconsideration 451
  on - 658
reconstitute 660
reconstruct 660
reconvert 660
record **551**
  discrimination 465
  career 692
  break the - 33
  Congressional -s 551
  court of - 966
recorder **553**
  judge 967
recording
  - instrument 551
  - secretary 554
recount 594
recoup 30, 790
recourse 677
recovery
  improvement 658
  reinstatement 660
  getting back 775
  restitution 790
  - of strength 689
recreant coward 862
  base 940
  knave 941
  vicious 945
  bad man 949
recreation 840
recrement 653
recriminate 932
recrimination 938
recriminatory 718, 938
recrudescence 661
recruit alien 57
  strength 159
  learner 541
  provision 637
  health 654
  repair 658
  reinstate 660
  refresh 689
  aid 707
  auxiliary 711
  soldier 726
  beat up for -s
  prepare 673
  aid 707
rectal 221
rectangle 244
rectangular
  perpendicular 212
  angle 244
rectify degree 26
  straighten 246
  improve 658
  reëstablish 660
rectilinear 246
rectitude probity 939
  virtue 944
rector director 694
  clergyman 996
rectorship 995
rectory 1000
rectrix 745
rectum 221, 350
recubant 213, 217

recueil 54
recumbent
  horizontal 213
  oblique 217
recuperation 689, 790
recuperative 660
recur repeat 104
  frequent 136
  periodic 138
  - to 677
  - to the mind 505
recure 660
recurrence [see recur]
recursion 292
recurvity 245
recusancy impiety 988
  [see recusant]
recusant dissenting 489
  denying 536
  disobedient 742
  refusing 764
  impenitent 951
  heterodox 984
  (unwilling 603)
Red anarchist 146, 710
red 434
  - and yellow 439
  - book list 86
  - cap porter 271
  - cent 643, 800
  - cross 662
  - flag 550, 668
  - hot great 31
  violent 173
  hot 382
  emotion 821
  excited 824
  - lead 434
  - letter mark 550
  celebrate 883
  - letter day
  important 642
  rest 687
  amusement 840
  celebration 883
  - light 550, 668
  - light district 961
  - ocher 434
  - pepper 393
  - republican 742
  - tape 613, 694
  - with mirth 892
  turn - feeling 821
redact 54, 658
redan 717
redargue 479
redcoat 726
red-complexioned 434
redden color 434
  humble 879
  angry 900
reddish-brown 433, 434
reddition
  interpretation 522
  restitution 790
redeem compensate 30
  substitute 147
  reinstate 660
  deliver 672
  regain 775
  restore 790

retrieve *restore* 660
  acquire 775
retriever *dog* 366
retroaction
  counteraction 179
  recoil 277
  regression 283
retroactive *past* 122
retrocession
  reversion 145
  regression 283
  recession 287
retroflexion 218
retrograde *contrary* 14
  moving back 283
  recession 287
  deteriorated 659
  relapsing 661
retrogression
  regression 283
  deterioration 659
  relapse 661
retrorse 145
retrospection *past* 122
  reversion 145
  thought 451
  memory 505
retroussé 201, 307
retroversion 218
retrude 289
return *list* 86
  repeat 104
  periodic 138
  reverse 145
  recoil 277
  regression 283
  arrival 292
  answer 462
  report 551
  relapse 661
  appoint 755
  profit 775
  restore 790
  proceeds 810
  reward 973
  in - *compensation* 30
  - thanks *gratitude* 916
  worship 990
  - the compliment
    interchange 148
    retaliate 718
  - to the original state
    660
reunion *junction* 43
réunion *assemblage* 72
  concord 714
  point de - 74
  social - 892
reveal 529
  - itself 446
reveille 550
revel *amuse* 840
  dissipation 954 ˉ
  - in *enjoy* 377
revelation
  discovery 480a
  disclosure 529
  theological 985
Revelation 985
reveler 840
  drunkard 959

reveling
  disorder 59
  rejoicing 838
revelry 954
revenant 361, 980a
revendicate *claim* 741
  acquisition 775
  due 924
revenge **919**
  breathe - *anger* 900
revenue 810
  means 632
  - cutter 273
reverberate *recoil* 277
  sound 408
reverbatory 386
revere *love* 897
  respect 928
  piety 987
revered *sage* 500
reverence *title* 877
  respect 928
  piety 987
  clergy 996
reverenced 500
reverend *title* 877
  clergy 996
  - sir 130
reverent *pious* 987
  worship 990
reverential
  respectful 928
reverie
  train of thought 451
  inattention 458
  imagination 515
reversal *inversion* 218
  revolution 607
  irresolute 605
reverse *contrary* 14
  return 145
  inversion 218
  - of a medal 235
  anteposition 237
  adversity 735
  abrogate 756
  cards 840
  - of the shield 468
reverseless 150
reversible
reversion [*see* reverse]
  posteriority 117
  return **145**
  possession 777
  property 780
  succession 783
  remitter 790
reversioner 779
reversis 840
revert *repeat* 104
  return 145
  turn back 283
  revest 790
  - to 457
revest 790
reviction 660
review *consider* 457
  inquiry 461
  judge 480
  recall 505
  dissertation 595

compendium 596
revise 658
  parade 882
reviewer 480, 595
revile *abuse* 932
  blaspheme 988
reviler 936
revise *copy* 21
  consider 457
  printing 591
  plan 626
  edit 658
revising barrister 967
revision 658
  under - 673
revisit 186
revival
  reproduction 163
  life 359
  restoration 660
  worship 990
revivalist 996
revive *reproduce* 163
  refresh 658
  resuscitate 660
  excite 824
revivify *reproduce* 163
  life 359
  resuscitate 660
revocable 605
revocation 536
revoke *recant* 607
  cancel 756
  (*deny* 536)
  (*refuse* 764)
revolt *contrariety* 14
  revolution 146
  resist 719
  disobey 742
  shock 830
  disapproval 932
  - against *hate* 898
  - at the idea
    dissent 489
revolting *painful* 830
revolution
  periodicity 138
  change **146**
  rotation 312
revolutionary 146, 742
revolutionize 140, 146
revolve
  [*see* revolution]
  - in the mind 451
revolver 727
revulsion *reversion* 145
  revolution 146
  inversion 218
  recoil 277
revulsive 276
revulsively 145
reward 30, **973**
reword 104
rewriting 21
Reynard *animal* 366
  cunning 702
rez de chaussée
  room 191
  low 207
rhabdology 85
rhabdomancy 511

rhadamanthus
  judge 967
  hell 982
rhamphoid 245
rhapsodical
  irregular 139
rhapsodist *fanatic* 504
  poet 597
rhapsodize 497
rhapsody
  discontinuity 70
  nonsense 497
  fancy 515
rheometer 157
rhetoric *speech* 582
  flowers of - 577
rheum *excretion* 299
  fluidity 333
rheumatism 378
rhino 800
rhinoceros 366
  - hide *physically in-
    sensible* 376
  morally insensible
    823
rhipidate 194
rhizanthous 367
rhododendron 845
rhomb 244
rhomboid 244
rhubarb 298
rhumb 278
rhyme [*see* rime &c.]
rhythm *periodicity* 138
  melody 413
  elegance 578
  verse 597
rhythmic 413, 578
rhythmical
  - *style* 578
riant 836
rib *support* 215
  ridge 250
  wife 903
ribald *vulgar* 851
  disreputable 874
  impure 961
ribaldry 908
ribband [*see* ribbon]
ribbed *furrowed* 259
ribbon *tie* 45
  filament 205
  record 551
  decoration 877
ribbons *reins* 752
ribroast 972
rice 330, 367
ricebird 298
rich *savory* 394
  color 428
  language 577
  abundant 639
  wealthy 803
  beautiful 845
  ornament 847
  - gifts wax poor 907
  - man 639, 803
riches 803
richly *much* 31
  - deserve 924
rick *accumulation* 72

roofless 226
rook *steal* 791
   thief 792
rookery *nests* 189
   dirt 653
room *occasion* 134
   space 180
   presence 186
   chamber 191
   class 541
   classroom 542
   plea 617
   assembly - 840
   in the - of 147
   make - for
      opening 260
      respect 928
roomer 188
roommate 890
roomy 180
roorback 934
roost *abode* 189
   bed 215
rooster 366
root *algebraic* - 84
   cause 153
   place 184
   abide 186
   base 211
   etymon 562
   cut up - and branch
      162
   lie at the - of 642
   pluck up by the -s 301
   - and branch 52
   - for *applaud* 931
   - out *eject* 297
      extract 301
      discover 480a
   strike at the - of 716
   [take - *influence* 175
      locate 184
      habit 613
rooted *old* 124
   firm 150
   located 184
   habit 613
   (*permanent* 141)
   deep - 820
   - antipathy 867
   - belief 484
rooter *sports* 840
rope *fastening* 45
   cord 205
   freedom 748
   scourge 975
   give - enough 738
   - of sand
      incoherence 47
      weakness 160
      impossible 471
   -'s end 975
ropedancer 700
ropedancing 698
ropy 352
roquelaure 225
roric 339
rorid 339
rosâ, sub - 528
rosary 990, 998
roscid 339

Roscius 599
rose *pipe* 350
   fragrant 400
   red 434
   beauty 845
   bed of -s
      pleasure 377
      prosperity 734
   couleur de - *red* 434
      good 648
      prosperity 734
      hope 858
   under the - 528
   welcome as the - s in
      June *pleasing* 829
      sociality 892
roseate *red* 434
   hopeful 858
rose-colored *hope* 858
rosehead 350
rosette 847
rose water
   moderation 174
   flattery 933
   not made with - 704
Rosicrucian 984
rosin *rub* 331
   resin 356a
Rosinante 271
roster 69, 86
rostrate 245
rostriferous 245
rostrum *beak* 234
   pulpit 542
rosy 434
   - wine 959
rosy-cheeked 845
rot *decay* 49
   putrefy 653
   disease 655
   decay 659
rota *list* 86
   period 138
   court 966
rotation *periodicity* 138
   motion round **312**
rote, by - 505
   know - 490
   learn - 539
roti 298
rotogravure 558
rotten *weak* 160
   bad 649
   foul 653
   decayed 659
   (*fetid* 401)
   - at the core
      deceptive 545
      diseased 655
   - borough 893
   - in state of Denmark
      702
rotund 249
rotunda 189
rotundity **249**
roturier 876
roué 949
rouge 434
rouge et noir 621
rough *violent* 173
   shapeless 241

uneven 256
pungent 392
unsavory 395
sour 397
sound 410
raucous 581
unprepared 674
fighter 726
ugly 846
low fellow 876
bully 887
churlish 895
evildoer 913
bad man 949
in the - 241
- and tumble 59
- breathing 402
- copy *writing* 590
   unprepared 674
- diamond
   amorphism 241
   artless 703
   vulgar 851
   commonalty 876
   good man 948
- draft 590, 626
- guess 514
- it 686
- sea 348
- side of the tongue
   censure 932
- weather *violent* 173
   wind 349
roughcast *covering* 223
   shape 240
   roughness 256
   scheme 626
   unpolished 674
roughhew *form* 240
   prepare 673
rough-house 173
roughly *nearly* 197
roughness **256**
   blemish 848
   [see rough]
roughrider 268
roulade 415
rouleau *assemblage* 72
   cylinder 249
   money 800
roulette 621
round *series* 69
   revolution 138
   - of a ladder 215
   curve 245
   circle 247
   rotund 249
   music 415
   fight 720
   all - *circumjacent* 227
   bring - *restore* 660
   come - *periodic* 138
      recant 607
      persuade 615
   dizzy - 312
   get - 660
   go - 311
   go one's -s 266
   go the -
      publication 531
   go the same - 104

in - numbers
   mean 29
   nearly 197
make the - of 311
- a corner 311
- and round
   periodic 138
   rotation 312
- assertion 535
- game 840
- like a horse in a mill
   613
- number *number* 84
   multitude 102
- of life 151
- of pleasures
   pleasure 377
   amusement 840
- of the ladder 71
- of visits 892
- pace 274
- robin
   information 527
   petition 765
   censure 932
- sum 800
- terms 566
- trot 274
- up *cattle* 370
run the - of *active* **682**
turn - *invert* 218
   retreat 283
   revolve 311
roundabout
   circumjacent 227
   deviation 279
   circuit 311
   amusement 840
   - phrases 573
   - way 629
rounded 247
   - periods 577, 578
roundelay 597
rounder 949
rounders 840
roundhouse 752
roundlet 247
round-shouldered 243
round-up 72
roup 796
rouse *stimulate* 615
   excite 824
   - oneself 682
rouser 83
rousing 171
roustabout 460, 690
rout *agitation* 315
   printing 591
   overcome 731
   discomfit 732
   rabble 876
   assembly 892
   put to the - 731
   - out 652
route 627
   en - 270
   en - for 282
routine *uniform* 16
   order 58
   rule 80
   periodic 138

custom 613
business 625
rove *travel* 266
  deviate 279
rover *traveler* 268
  pirate 792
roving commission 475
row *disorder* 59
  series 69
  violence 173
  street 189
  navigate 267
  discord 713
  - in the same boat 88
rowdy *rough* 726
  vulgar 851
  blusterer 887
  bad man 949
rowel *sharp* 253
  stimulus 615
rowen 168
rower 269
rowlock 215
royal 737
  - *road way* 627
  easy 705
Royal   Academician
  559
royalist 737
royalty 737
royne 298
ruade *impulse* 276
  attack 716
rub *friction* 331
  touch 379
  massage 662
  difficulty 704
  adversity 735
  painful 830
  - down *lessen* 195
  powder 330
  - *a horse* 370
  - down with an oaken
    towel 972
  - off 552
  - off corners 82
  - on *slow* 275
  progress 282
  inexcitable 826
  - one's eyes 870
  - one's hands 838
  - on the raw 900
  - out 552
  - up 658
  - up the memory 505
rubadub 407
rubber *eraser* 331
  masseur 662
  whist 840
rubberneck 444, 455
rubbers 225
rubbing 379
rubbish *unmeaning* 517
  trifling 643
  useless 645
rubble 645
rube 501, 876
rubefaction 434
rubeola 655
rubescence 434
Rubicon *limit* 233
666

pass the - *begin* 66
  cross 303
  choose 609
rubicose 434
rubicund 434
rubicundity 382, 434
rubiform 434
rubify 434
rubiginous 433
rubigo 653
rubious 434
rubric *precept* 697
  liturgy 998
rubricate *redden* 434
ruby *red* 434
  gem 648
  ornament 847
ruck 258
ructation 297
rudder 273, 633, 693
rudderless 158
ruddle 434
ruddy *red* 434
  beautiful 845
rude *violent* 173
  shapeless 241
  strident 410
  ignorant 491
  inelegant 579
  ugly 846
  vulgar 851
  uncivilized 876
  uncivil 895
  disrespect 929
  - health 654
  - reproach 908
rudera 645
rudiment *beginning* 66
  cause 153
rudimental *small* 193
  immature 674
rudimentary *small* 193
  learner 541
rudiments
  knowledge 490
  school 542
rue *bitter* 395
  regret 833
  repent 950
rueful *painful* 830
  sad 837
ruff 225
ruffian *combatant* 726
  maleficent 913
  scoundrel 949
ruffianism 851, 907
ruffle *disorder* 59
  derange 61
  roughen 256
  fold 258
  feeling 821
  excite 824, 825
  pain 830
  irritate 898
  anger 900
rufous 433, 434
rufulous 434
rug *support* 215
  covering 223
rugged *shapeless* 241
  rough 256

difficult 704
  ugly 846
  churlish 895
rugose 256
rugulose 256
ruin *destruction* 162
  evil 619
  failure 732
  adversity 735
  poverty 804
  (*decay* 659)
ruined *nonpayment* 808
  hopeless 859
ruinous *painful* 830
ruins *remains* 40
rule *normal* 29
  regularity **80**
  influence 175
  length 200
  measure 466
  decide 480
  custom 613
  precept 697
  government 737
  law 963
  absence of - 699
  as a - 613
  by - 82
  golden - 697
  obey -s 82
  - of three 85
  - of thumb
  experiment 463
  unreasoning 477
  essay 675
  unskilled 699
ruler 737, 745
ruling passion
  obstinacy 606
  character 820
rum *queer* 853
  drink 959
rumal 225
rumble 407
rumen 191
ruminate *chew* 298
  think 450, 451
rummage 461
rummer 191
rumor *publicity* 531
  report 532
rumored 531
  publicly - 532
rump *remainder* 40
  rear 235
  beef 298
rumple *disorder* 59
  derange 61
  roughen 256
  fold 258
rumpus *confusion* 59
  violence 173
  discord 713
  (*contention* 720)
run *rule* 29
  generality 78
  repetition 104
  time 106
  course 109
  continuance 143
  eventuality 151

motion 264
  speed 274
  trend 278
  cards 281
  liquefy 335
  flow 348
  habit 613
  demand 630
  smuggle 791
  contraband 964
  have a - *fashion* 852
  repute 873
  have - of 748
  he that -s may read
    525
  near - 197
  race is - 729
  - abreast 27
  - a chance
  probable 472
  chance 621
  - after *pursue* 622
  in repute 873
  - against *impact* 276
  oppose 708
  attack 716
  - amuck *violent* 173
  kill 361
  attack 716
  - a race *speed* 274
  conduct 692
  contend 720
  - a rig 840
  - a risk 665
  - at 716
  - a tilt at *attack* 716
  contend 720
  - away *avoid* 623
  (*escape* 671)
  - away with *take* 789
  steal 791
  - away with a notion
  misjudge 481
  credulous 486
  - back 283
  - counter 468
  - counter to 708
  - down *pursue* 622
  bad 649
  attack 716
  depreciate 932
  detract 934
  - dry *waste* 638
  insufficient 640
  - foul of 276
  - hard *danger* 665
  difficult 704
  success 731
  - high *great* 31
  violent 173
  - in *introduce* 228
  - in a race *act* 680
  - in couples 17
  - in the head
  think 451
  remember 505
  - into *conversion* 144
  insert 300
  - into danger 665
  - into debt 806
  - its course *course* 109

S

bad 649
  painful 830
  dejected 837
  - disappointment 509
  - dog 949
  - times 735
  - work 699
sadden 830, 837
saddle *attribute* 155
  support 215
  meat 298
  in the - 673
  - blanket 223
  - on *add* 37
  join 43
  - on the right horse
  discovery 480a
  skill 698
  right 922
  fair 939
  - on the wrong horse
  mistake 495
  bungle 699
  - with *add* 37
  quarter on 184
  clog 706
  impose a duty 926
  accuse 938
saddlebags 191
saddle-shaped 250
Sadducee 984
sadiron 253, 386
sadism 945, 961
sadist 949
sadness 837
  in - *without joking* 535
safe *cupboard* 191
  ambush 530
  secure 664
  treasury 802
  caution 864
  on the - side
  cautious 864
  - and sound
  health 654
  - bind, safe find 864
  - conscience *duty* 926
  innocent 946
safe-conduct 631
safe-keeping 670
safety 664
  - bicycle 272
  - first 864
  - in valor 861
  - match 388
  - valve 666
saffron *color* 436
sag *oblique* 217
  curve 245
saga 594
sagacious
  intelligent 498
  foresight 510
  (*skillful* 698)
sagamore 745
sage *wise* 498
  wise man 500
  adviser 695
  - maxim 496
sagittary 83
sagittate 253
668

sagum 225
Sahara 169
sahib 373, 745, 875
saic 273
said *preceding* 62
  repeated 104
  prior 116
  it is - 532
  more easily - than
  done 704
  thou hast - 488
sail *navigate* 267
  ship 273
  set out 293
  easy - 174
  full - 274
  press
  press of - 274
  - before the wind 734
  - near the wind 698
  - too near the wind 863
  shorten - 275
  take in - 174
  take the wind out of
  one's -s 706
  too much - 863
  under - 267
sailing, plain - 705
  - vessel 273
sailor 269
  fair weather - 701
saint *angel* 977
  revelation 985
  piety 987
  false piety 988
  - abroad 548
  tutelary - 664
Saint
  - Anthony's fire 655
  - Bernard *dog* 366
  - Elmo's fire 423, 872
  - Martin's summer
  126
  - Swithin, reign of -
  348
  - Swithin's day 138
  - Tib's eve 107
  - Vitus's dance 315,
  655
saintly *virtuous* 944
  pious 987
Saint's day 138
Saint Simonianism 910
sake
  for goodness'- 765
  for the - of
  motive 615
  aid 707
salaam *obeisance* 725
  courtesy 894
  respect 928
salable 796
salacity 961
salad 41
  - oil 356
salade 717
salamander
  elemental 83, 980
  furnace 386
  salamandrine 384
sal ammoniac 392

salary 973
sale 796
  bill of - 771
  for - *offer* 763
  barter 794
salebrosity 256
salesman 758, 767, 797
salesmanship 796
salient *projecting* 250
  sharp 253
  manifest 525
  important 642
  - angle 244
  - point 642
saline 392
saliva *excretion* 299
  lubrication 332
salivant 297
salivate 297, 332
salle-à-manger 191
sallow *colorless* 429
  yellow 436
sally *issue* 293
  attack 716
  wit 842
sally port *egress* 295
  fortification 717
salmagundi 41
salmis 298
salmon *fish* 298
  red 434
salmon-colored 434
salon 191
saloon 191
  bar 189
salsify 298
salt *sailor* 269
  pungent 392
  condiment 393
  importance 642
  preserve 670
  money 800
  wit 842
  below the - 876
  - of the earth
  goodness 648
  goodman 948
  - tax 812
  - water 341
  worth one's - 644
saltant 315
saltation 309
saltatory 315
saltimbanco 548
saltpeter *pungent* 392
  gunpowder 727
salubrity 656
salutary *healthful* 656
  (*remedial* 662)
salutation [*see* salute]
salutatory 582, 587
salute *allocution* 586
  celebration 883
  courtesy 894
  kiss 902
  respect 928
salutiferous
  [*see* salutary]
salvable 946
salvage *acquisition* 775
  tax 812

discount 813
reward 973
salvation
  preservation 670
  deliverance 672
  religious 976
  piety 987
  work out one's - 990
salve
  lubrication 332, 355
  remedy 662
  relieve 834
salver 191
salvo *exception* 83
  explosion 406
  qualification 469
  excuse 937
  (*condition* 770)
  - of artillery
  celebration 883
sal-volatile 392
Samaol 978
Samaritan, good
  benevolent 906
  benefactor 912
sambar 366
sambo 41, 431
Sam Browne belt 747
same 13
  all the - to 823
  at the - time
  compensatory 30
  synchronous 120
  go over the - ground
  104
  in the - boat 709
  in the - breath
  instantaneous 113
  synchronous 120
  of the - mind 488
  on the - tack 709
sameness 16
samiel 349
samisen 417
samo 720
samovar 191
samp 298
sampan 273
sample 82
Samson 159
samurai 875
sanation
  restoration 660
sanative
  remedial 662
sanatorium 189, 662
sanctification 976
sanctify *authorize* 920
  piety 987
sanctimony 988
sanction
  permission 760
  dueness 924
  approbation 931
  to - vice 945
sanctitude 987
sanctity 987
sanctuary *refuge* 666
  altar 1000
  claim - 666
sanctum *chamber* 191

- sanctorum
abode 189
privacy 893
temple 1000
sanctus 900
- bell 550, 999
sand *powder* 330
resolution 604
built upon - 665
sow the - 645
sandal 225
sandalwood 400
sandbag 727, 972
sandbagger 792
sand-blind 442
Sandemanian 984
sandpaper 255
sands *danger* 667
- on the seashore
multitude 102
sand storm 330
sandstone 635
sandwich-wise 228
sandy *yellow* 436
red 434
sane 502
sangar 717
sang-froid
insensibility 823
inexcitability 826
presence of mind 864
sangraal 998
sanguinary 361
sanguine *red* 434
hopeful 858
- expectation
expect 507
hope 858
- imagination 515
sanguineous 434
sanguisage 662
sanhedrim
council 696
churchdom 995
sanies 333
sanious 333
sanitarian 656
sanitarium 189, 656, 662
sanitary 656
sanity *mental* **502**
bodily - 654
sannyasi 804, 955, 996
sans 187
- cérémonie
friendly 888
social 892
- façon *simple* 849
modest 881
social 892
- pareil 33
- peur et sans re-
proche
perfect 650
heroic 873
honorable 939
- souci *insensible* 823
pleasure 827
content 831
sans-culotte *revel* 742
commonalty 876

sans-culottic 146
sans-culottism 146
sans Dieu rien 976
Sanskrit 124
Sanskritist 492
santon *hermit* 893
priest 996
sap *essence* 5
destroy 162
excavate 252
juice 333
damage 659
attack 716
- the foundations 162, 659
sap-headed 499
sapid 390
sapient 498
sapless *weak* 160
dry 340
sapling 129, 367
saponaceous 355
saporific 390
sapper *excavator* 252
soldier 726
sappers and miners
preparers 673
Sapphic 597
sapphire *blue* 438
gem 847
sapphism 961
sapphist 962
sappy *young* 127
juicy 333
foolish 499
saprogenic 653
saraband 840
sarcasm *disrespect* 929
censure 932
detraction 934
sarcastic *ridicule* 856
discourteous 895
sarcology 662
sarcoma 250
sarcophagus 363
sarculation 103
sard 847
Sardanapalus 954a
sardines 298
sardonic *censure* 932
detraction 934
- grin *laughter* 838
ridicule 856
discontent 932
sardonyx 847
sargasso 367
Sargasso Sea 367
sark 225
sarmentum 51
sartorial 225
sash 247
sassafras 662
Sastra 986
Satan **978**
satanic *malevolent* 907
vicious 945
diabolic 978
satchel 191 *i*
sate 869
satellite *companion* 88
follower 281

heavenly body 318
auxiliary 711
servant 746
satiate 52, 376
satiety *sufficient* 639
pleasant 829
cloy **869**
(*redundance* 641)
satin 219, 329, 635
smoothness 255
satire *metaphor* 521
poetry 597
ridicule 856
censure 932
satiric *untruth* 546
satirical 932
detraction 934
satirist *poet* 597
detractor 936
satirize 597
satisfaction
[*see* satisfy]
duel 720
pleasure 827
atonement 952
hail with - 931
satisfactorily 618
satisfactory
[*see* satisfy]
good 648
satisfy *answer* 462
convince 484
sufficient 639
consent 762
observance 772
pay 807
gratify 829
content 831
satiate 869
reward 973
- an obligation 926
- oneself 484
satisfying 831
satrap *governor* 745
(*deputy* 759)
satsuma 557
saturate *fill* 52
moisten 339
satiate 869
saturnalia *disorder* 59
games 840
intemperance 954
- of blood 361
Saturnian *pleasing* 829
innocent 946
- age 734
Saturnia regna
prosperity 734
pleasure 827
saturnine 837
satyr *ugly* 846
libertine 962
demon 980
sauce *adjunct* 39
mixture 41
condiment 393
abuse 908
pay - for all 807
what is - for the goose 27
saucebox *blusterer* 887

saucepan 191
sauce piquante
condiment 393
pleasing 829
saucer 191
- eyes 441
saucy *insolent* 885
flippant 895
sauerkraut 298
saunter *ramble* 266
dawdle 275
sausage 298
sauvage 893
sauve qui peut
run away 623
alarm 669
haste 684
cowardice 862
savage *violent* 173
vulgar 851
brave 861
boorish 876
angry 900
malevolent 907
evildoer 913
savagery
[*see* savage]
savanna 344, 367
savant *knowledge* 490
learned man 492
sage 500
save *subduct* 38
exclude 55
except 83
store 636
preserve 670
deliver 672
economize 817
God - 990
- and except 83
- money 817
- one's bacon 671
- the necessity 927a
- us 707
save-all 817
saving 817
- clause 469
- one's presence 928
savings *store* 636
economy 817
savior *benefactor* 912
Saviour 976
savoir faire
skill 698
fashion 852
savoir vivre *skill* 698
fashion 852
sociality 892
savor 390
- of *resemble* 17
- of the reality 780
savoriness **394**
savorless 391
savory 390, 394
savvy 490, 498
saw *cut* 44
jagged 257
maxim 496
- the air *gesture* 550
sawder, soft -
flattery 933

scientist *reasoner* 476
  learned man 492
scimitar 727
  - shaped 253
scintilla *small* 32, 193
  spark 420, 423
scintillate
  [*see* scintillation]
  intelligence 498
scintillation *heat* 382
  light 420
  wit 842
sciolism 491
sciolist 493
sciomancy 511
scion *part* 51
  child 129
  posterity 167
scission 44
scissors 253
  - and paste 609
scissure 198
sclerotics 195
scobs 330
scoff *ridicule* 856
  deride 929
  impiety 988
  - at *despise* 930
  censure 932
scold *berate* 527
  shrew 901
  malediction 908
  censure 932
  (*detractor* 936)
scolecoid 248
scollop *convolution* 248
  notch 257
sconce *top* 210
  candlestick 423
  brain 450
  defense 717
  mulct 974
scone 298
scoop *depression* 252
  perforator 262
scop 597
scope *degree* 26
  occasion 134
  extent 180
  meaning 516
  freedom 748
  (*intention* 620)
scorch 382, 384
scorcher 268, 274
scorching *violent* 173
score *compose* 54
  arrangement 60
  count 85
  list 86
  twenty 98
  indent 257
  furrow 259
  music 415
  berate 527
  mark 550
  credit 805
  debt 806
  accounts 811
  on the - of
  relation 9
  motive 615

- a success 731
- board 551
- sheet 551
scores *many* 102
scoriaceous 384
scoriæ *ash* 384
  dirt 653
  (*useless* 645)
scorify 384
scorn 930
scorpion *insect* 368
  painful 830
  evildoer 913
  (*bane* 663)
  chastise with -s 739
scorse 794
scot *reward* 973
scotch *notch* 257
  injure 659
  - the snake *maim* 158
  insufficient 640
  noncompletion 730
  - the wheel 706
Scotchman 188

scot-free *escape* 671
  free 748
  cheap 815
  exempt 927a
  escape -
  escape 671
  let off - 970
scotograph 554
scotomy 443
Scotsman 188
Scotticism 563
scoundrel 949
scour *run* 274
  rub 331
  clean 652
  - the country 266
  - the plain 274
scourge *bane* 663
  painful 830
  punish 972
  instrument of punishment **975**
  - of the human race 913
scourings 645
scout *vanguard* 234
  aviator 269a
  spectator 444
  feeler 463
  messenger 534
  reject 610
  patrol 664
  warning 668
  servant 746
  disrespect 929
  disdain 930
  (*looker* 444)
  (*underrate* 483)
  (*ridicule* 856)
scow 273
scowl *complain* 839
  frown 895
  anger 900
  sullen 901a
  disapprobation 932
  - of night 982

scrabble
  unmeaning 517
  scribble 590
scrag 203
scraggy *lean* 193
  amorphous 241
  rough 256
  (*ugly* 846)
scramble *confusion* 59
  climb 305
  pursue 622
  haste 684
  difficulty 704
  contend 720
  seize 789
scrambled eggs 298
scranch 330
scrannel 643
scrap *small* 32
  piece 51
  child 129
  (*minute* 193)
scrapbook 596
scrape *subduct* 38
  reduce 195
  pulverize 330
  abrade 331
  - the fiddle 416
  mezzotint 558
  clean 652
  difficulty 704
  mischance 732
  bow 894
  - together
  assemble 72
  acquire 775
scraper 652
scratch *groove* 259
  abrade 331
  unmeaning 517
  mark 550
  daub 555
  draw 556
  write 590
  hurt 619
  wound 649
  come to the -
  contention 720
  courage 861
  mere - 209
  old - 978
  - out 552
  - the head 461
  up to the - 861
  without a - 670
scrawl *unmeaning* 517
  write 590
scrawny 203
screak 411
scream *blow* 349
  cry 411
  wail 839
screaming 853
screech 411, 412
screed 86, 590
screen *sift* 60
  crossing 219
  sieve 260
  shade 424
  hide 528
  hider 530

  side scene 599
  sift 652
  safety 664
  shelter 666
  defense 717
  - from sight 442
screw *fasten* 43
  fastening 45
  distortion 243
  oar 267
  propeller 284
  rotation 312
  instrument 633
  miser 819
  put on the -
  severity 739
  compel 744
  - loose *insane* 503
  imperfect 651
  unskillful 699
  hindrance 706
  attack 713
  - one's courage to the
    sticking place 861
  - up *fasten* 43
  strengthen 159
  prepare 673
  - up the eyes 443
screw-driver 633
screwed *drunk* 959
screw-shaped 248
screw steamer 273
scribble *compose* 54
  unmeaning 517
  write 590
scribbler 593
scribe *recorder* 553
  writer 590, 593
  priest 996
scrimmage *discord* 713
  contention 720
scrimp *short* 201
  insufficient 640
  stingy 819
scrip 191
script 590
scriptural
  orthodox 983a
Scripture *certain* 474
  revelation 985
scrivener *writer* 590
  lawyer 968
scrofula 655
scroll *list* 86
  record 551
scrub *short* 201
  rub 331
  bush 367
  clean 652
  dirty person 653
  commonalty 876
scrubby *small* 193
  trifling 643
  disreputable 874
  vulgar 876
  shabby 940
scruple
  small quantity 32
  weight 319
  doubt 485
  reluctance 603

semicircular 245
semicolon 142
semidiaphanous 427
semifluid 352
semiliquidity 352
semilunar 245
seminal *causing* 153
seminar 542
seminary 542
semination
  preparation 673
semiopaque 427
semipellucid 427
semiquaver 413
semitone 413
semitransparency **427**
sempervirid 110, 123
sempiternal 112
sempiternity 110, 112
sempstress
  dressmaker 225
  workwoman 690
senary 98
senate 72, 696
senate house 966
senator *counsel* 695
  councillor 696
senatorship 693
send *transfer* 270
  propel 284
- about one's business
  289
- adrift 597
- a letter to 592
- away *repel* 289
  eject 297
  refuse 764
- for 741
- forth *propel* 284
  publish 531
- off 284
- out *eject* 297
  commission 755
- word 527
seneca-oil 356
senectitude 128
senescence 128
seneschal *director* 694
  master 745
  servant 746
seneschalship 737
senile 128, 158, 499
- dementia 499
senior *age* 128
  student 492
  master 745
seniority *oldness* 124
  age 128
señor 877
sensation
  physical sensibility
  375
  emotion 821
  wonder 870
sensational
  language 574
  exciting 824
sensation drama 599
sensations of touch 380
sense *wisdom* 498
  meaning 516

accept in a particular
  - 522
deep - 821
in no - 565
- of duty 926
senseless
  insensible 376
  absurd 497
  foolish 499
  unmeaning 517
senses *external* - 375
  intellect 450
  sanity 502
sensibility
  physical - **375**
  moral **822**
sensible *material* 316
  wise 498
sensitive 375, 822
- plant 822
sensorial 821
sensorium 450
sensual *pleasure* 377
  intemperate 954
sensualist 954*a*
sensualize 954
sensuous
  sensibility 375
  pleasure 377
  feeling 821
sentence *decision* 480
  maxim 496
  affirmation 535
  phrase 566
  lawsuit 969
  condemnation 971
my - is for war 722
sententious
  concise 572
  - *language* 574, 577
  taciturn 585
sentient
  - *physically* 375
  - *morally* 821
sentiment *idea* 453
  (*opinion* 484)
  (*maxim* 496)
sentimental
  sensitive 822
  affected 855
sentinel *guard* 263
  guardian 664
  watch 668
  keeper 753
sentry 664, 668, 753
sepal 367
separable 44
separate *disjoin* 44
  exclude 55
  bisect 91
  diverge 291
  clean 652
  divorce 782, 905
- into elements 49
- maintenance 905
- the chaff from the
  wheat
  discriminate 465
  select 609
separation
  [*see* separate]

separatist 489, 984
  disjunction 44
separative 49
sepia 433
seposition
  disjunction 44
  exclusion 55
sepoy 726
seppuku 972
sept *kin* 11
  class 75
  clan 166
septal 228
septenary 98
septennial 138
Septentrional 237
septet 415
septic 655, 657, 662
septicæmia 655
septicity 655
septimal 98
septuagenary 98
septuagesimal 98
Septuagint 985
septulum 228
septum 228
septuple 98
sepulcher 363
  whited - 545
sepulchral
  interment 363
  resonance 408
  stridor 410
  hoarse 581
sepulture 363
sequacious 63, 117
sequacity *soft* 324
  tenacity 327
sequel *following* **65**
  - *in time* 117
  sequence 281
  (*addition* 39)
sequela 63, 65
sequence
  - *in order* **63**
  - *in time* 117
  motion **281**
  logical - 476
sequent 63, 117
sequester *take* 789
  confiscate 974
  (*hide* 528)
sequestered
  secluded 893
sequestrate *seize* 789
  condemn 971
  confiscate 974
sérac 383
seraglio *abode* 189
  woman 374
  marriage 903
  impurity 961
seraph *saint* 948
  angel 977
seraphic *blissful* 829
  virtuous 944
  pious 987
Seraphim 977
seraphina 417
seraskier 745
sere [*see* sear]

- and yellow leaf **128**
serein *dew* 339
  rain 348
serenade *music* 415
  compliment 894
  endearment 902
serene *pellucid* 425
  calm 826
  content 831
- highness 877
serf *slave* 746
  clown 876
serfdom 749
serge 635
sergeant 745
serial *continuous* 69
  periodic 138
  book 593
seriatim *in order* 58
  continuously 69
  each to each 79
  slowly 275
series *continuity* 69
  number 84
serif 591
serio-comic 853
serious *great* 31
  resolved 604
  important 642
  dejected 837
seriously 535
serjeant
  common - 967
  -at-law 968
sermon *lesson* 537
  speech 582
  dissertation 595
  pastoral 998
  funeral - 363
sermonize 586
sermonizer 584
serosity *fluid* 333
serotherapy 662
serotine 133
serpent *tortuous* 248
  snake 366
  hiss 409
  wind instrument 417
  wise 498
  deceiver 548
  cunning 702
  evildoer 913
  knave 941
  demon 949
  great sea - 515
  the old - 978
serpentine 248
serrated *angular* 244
  notched 257
serried *crowded* 72
  dense 321
serum *lymph* 333
  water 337
servant *minister* 631
  agent 690
  help 711
  retainer **746**
- of all work 690
serve *benefit* 618
  business 625
  utility 644

aid 707
warfare 722
obey 743
servant 746
(*work* 680)
- an apprenticeship 539
- as a substitute 147
- faithfully 743
- one right
retaliation 718
right 922
punish 972
- one's turn 644
- out 972
- with a writ 969
service *good* 618
utility 644
use 677
warfare 722
servitude 749
worship 990
rite 998
at one's - 763
press into the - 677
render a - *utility* 644
benevolence 906
serviceable
instrumental 631
useful 644
good 648
servant 746
servile *servant* 746
subject 749
ignoble 876
obsequious 886
servility
obsequious **886**
(*flattery* 933)
[see servile]
servitor 746
servitorship 749
servitude 749
penal - 972
sesame, open -
opening 260
watchword 550
spell 993
sesqui - 87
sesquipedalian
long 200
sess 812
sessile 46
session *council* 696
churchdom 995
sessions *law* 966
sestet 415
set *condition* 7
join 43
coherence 46
compose 54
group 72
class 75
firm 150
tendency 176
situation 183
place 184
form 240
sharpen 253
direction 278
go down 306

dense 321
stage 599
habit 613
prepare 673
gang 712
impose 741
make a dead - at 716
- about *begin* 66
undertake 676
- abroach 73
- afloat *originate* 153
publish 531
oppose 708
quarrel 713
hate 898
angry 900
(*counteract* 179)
- against one another 464
- agoing *impulse* 276
propulsion 284
aid 707
- an example *model* 22
motive 615
- apart *separate* 44
exclude 55
select 609
- a price 812
- aside *displace* 185
disregard 458
neglect 460
negative 536
reject 610
disuse 678
annul 756
refuse 764
not observe 773
relinquish 782
dereliction 927
- at ease 831
- at hazard 665
- at naught
make light of 483
reject 610
oppose 708
defy 715
disobey 742
not observe 773
dereliction 927
- a trap for 545
- at rest *end* 67
answer 462
adjudge 480
complete 729
compact 769
- before *inform* 527
choice 609
- before oneself 620
- by 636
- by the ears 898
- down [see below]
- foot on 294
- forth *show* 525
assert 535
describe 594
- forward 293
- free 750
- going [see - agoing]
- in *begin* 66
rain 348
- in motion

move 264
use 677
- in order 60
- in towards 286
- no store by
make light of 483
despise 930
- off *compensation* 30
depart 293
improve 658
discount 813
adorn 845
display 882
- on 615
- on a cast 621
- one's affections on 897
- one's back up 878
- one's cap at *love* 897
endearment 902
- one's face against
oppose 708
refuse 764
disapprove 932
- one's hand to 467
- one's heart upon
resolve 604
desire 865
- one's seal to 467
- one's teeth 604
- one's wits to work
think 451
imagine 515
plan 626
- on fire *ignite* 384
excite 824
- on foot 66
- on its legs
establish 150
- on one's legs
strengthen 159
restore 669
- out *arrange* 60
begin 66
depart 293
decorate 845
display 882
- over 755
- phrase 566
- purpose 620
- right *inform* 527
disclose 529
teach 537
reinstate 660
vindicate 937
- sail 293
- store by 642
- straight
straighten 246
pacify 723
- terms *manifest* 525
phrase 566
style 574
- the eyes on 441
- the fashion
influence 175
authority 737
fashion 852
- the seal on 729
- the table in a roar 840

- to *contend* 720
war 722
- to music 416
- too high a value upon 482
- to rights 60
- to work
undertake 676
impose 741
- up *originate* 153
strengthen 159
produce 161
upright 212
raise 307
successful 731
prosperous 734
- upon *resolved* 604
attack 716
desirous 865
(*intending* 620)
- up shop 676
- watch 459
setaceous 256
setarious 253
setback 306, 735
set down *record* 551
humiliate 879
slight 929
censure 932
give one a -
confute 479
- a cause for hearing 969
- as 484
- for 484
- in writing 551
- to 155
setiferous 256
set-off *printing* 591
setose 256
sett *lease* 771, 787
settee 215
setter 366
settle *regulate* 60
establish 150
be located 184
bench 215
come to rest 265
subside 306
kill 361
decide 480
choose 609
vanquish 731
consent 762
compact 769
pay 807
- accounts *pay* 807
accounts 811
- down *adolescence* 131
stability 150
moderate 174
locate oneself 184
- into 144
- matters 723
- preliminaries 673
- property 781
- the question 478
- to sleep 683
- upon *give* 784
- with *pay* 807
settled [see settle]

probability 472
- off *display* 882
boast 884
- one's cards 529
- one's colors 550
- one's face
  presence 186
  manifest 525
  disclose 529
- one's hand 529
- one's teeth 715
- up *visible* 446
  manifest 525
  ridicule 856
  degrade 874
  censure 932
  accuse 938
show-down 525
shower *assemblage* 72
  shower bath 337
  rain 348
- bath 337, 386
- down
  abundance 639
- down upon
  give 784
  liberal 816
showman 524
showy *color* 428
  ugliness 846
  ornament 847
  tawdry 851
  fashionable 852
  ostentatious 882
shrapnel 727
shred *small* 32
  filament 205
  (*part* 51)
shrew 901
shrewd *knowing* 490
  wise 498
  cunning 702
  (*clever* 698)
shriek 410, 411
shrievalty 965
shrieve 965
shrift *confession* 529
  absolution 952
shriftless 951
shrill *loud* 404, 410
  cry 411
shrimp 193, 298
shrine *receptacle* 191
  tomb 363
  temple 998, 1000
shrink *decrease* 36
  shrivel 195
  go back 283, 287
  unwilling 603
  avoid 623
  sensitive 822
  - from *fear* 860
  dislike 867
  hate 898
shrive 952
shrivel *contract* 195
  fold 258
  (*decrease* 36)
shriveled *thin* 203
  (*small* 193)
shroud *covering* 223

invest 225
  funeral 363
  hide 528
  safety 664
  defend 717
-ed in mystery 519
shrub *plant* 367
  plantation 371
shrug *sign* 550
  (*hint* 527)
- the shoulders
  dissent 489
  submit 725
  discontent 832
  dislike 867
  contempt 930
  disapprobation 932
shrunk *little* 193
  shrink 195
shudder *cold* 383
  fear 860
make one -
  painful 830
- at *aversion* 867
  hate 898
shuffle *mix* 41
  derange 61
  change 140
  interchange 148
  changeable 149
  move slowly 275
  agitate 315
  falsehood 544
  untruth 546
  irresolute 605
  recant 607
  improbity 940
  patience and - the
    cards 826
- off *run away* 623
- off this mortal coil
  360
- on 266
- the cards
  begin again 66
  change 140
  chance 621
  prepare 673
shuffler 548
shun *avoid* 623
  dislike 867
shunt *transfer* 270
  deviate 279
  remove 287
shunted *shelved* 460
shut 261
- in 751
- one's ears *deaf* 419
  not believe 487
- oneself up 893
- one's eyes to
  not attend to 458
  neglect 460
  not believe 487
  permit 760
  not observe 773
- out *exclude* 55
  prohibit 761
- the eyes 442
- the door 761
- the door in one's

face 764
- the door upon 893
- the gates of mercy
  914*a*
- up *close* 261
  confute 479
  imprison 751
  (*inclose* 229)
- up shop *end* 67
  cease 142
  relinquish 624
  repose 687
shutter 424
shuttle *correlation* 12
  oscillate 314
  instrument 633
shuttlecock 605
shuttlewise 314
shy *deviate* 279
  draw back 283
  propel 284
  avoid 623
  fearful 860
  cowardly 862
  modest 881
fight - of 623
have a - at 716
- cock 862
- of *doubtful* 485
  unwilling 603
  cautious 864
  dislike 867
- of belief 487
Shylock 787
shyster 941, 968
Siamese twins 89
sib 11
Siberia 383
sibilation *hiss* 409
  disrespect 929
  disapprobation 932
sibyl *oracle* 513
  ugly 846
sibylline 511
- leaves 513
sic *imitation* 19
  exact 494
siccation 340
siccity 340
sick *ill* 655
make one -
  painful 830
  aversion 867
- at heart 837
- of *weary* 841
  dislike 867
  satiated 869
visitation of the - 998
sick chamber 655
sicken *nauseate* 395
  disease 655
  pain 830
  weary 841
  disgust 867
sickener *too much* 641
sickle *pointed* 244
  sharp 253
sickle-shaped 245
sickly *weak* 160
sickness 655
sick room 655

side *consanguinity* 11
  edge 231
  laterality 236
  party 712
at one's - 197
from - to side 314
look only at one - of
  the shield 481
on every - 227
on one - 243
on one's - 714
pass from one - to
  another 607
- by side
  accompaniment 88
  near 197
  laterality 236
  party 712
- issue 39
- with *aid* 707
  coöperate 709
  concord 714
take up a - 476
wrong - up 218
side arms 727
side blow 702
sideboard 191
side dish 298
side drum 417
sideling 237, 279
sidelong 236, 237, 279
side partner 891
sideration 318
sidereal 318
siderite 288
sideromancy 511
sidesaddle 215
side scene 599
sidesman 996
sidetrack 279, 287
sidewalk 627
sideways *oblique* 217
  lateral 236
side wind *oblique* 217
  circuit 629
  cunning 702
sidewinder 276
sidewipe 276
sidewise 237
sidle *oblique* 217
  lateral 236
  deviate 279
siege 716
lay - to 716
state of - 722
siege cap 717
siege gun 727
siege train 727
siesta 683
sieve *sort* 60
  crossing 219
  perforate 260
  sift 552
pour water into a -
  waste 638
  lavish 818
stop one hole in a -
  819
sift *simplify* 42
  sort 60
  inquire 461

discriminate 465
clean 652
- the chaff from the
  wheat 609
sifter 219
sigh 839
- for 865
sighing 839
- like furnace 902
sight *much* 31
  multitude 102
  vision 441
  appearance 448
  ugly 846
  prodigy 872
  at - *soon* 132
  seeing 441
  dim - 443
  in - 446
  in - of *near* 197
  seen 441
  keep in - 457
  within - of shore 858
sightless *blind* 442
  invisible 447
  ugly 846
sightly 845
sight-reading
  music 415
sights, see - 455
sight-seeing 441
sight-seer
  spectator 444
  curiosity 455
sight-singing 415
sigil *seal* 550
  evidence 769
sigmoid 245, 248
sign *attest* 467
  omen 512
  indication 550
  record 551
  write 590
  talisman 747
  compact 769
  prodigy 872
  give - of 525
  make no - 585
  -s of the times
  omen 512
  warning 668
  -s of the zodiac 318
signal *great* 31
  eventful 151
  sign 550
  important 642
  give the - 741
  -of distress 669
signalize *indicate* 550
  glory 873
  celebrate 883
signally 31
signal light 423
signal post 550, 668
signature
  mark, identification
  550
  writing 590
  printing 591
  compact 769
  security 771

signboard 550
signet
  mark, identification
  550
  sign of authority 747
  compact 769
  (*evidence* 467)
  writer to the - 968
significant
  [*see signify*]
  evidence 467
  importance 642
  (*clear* 518)
signifies, what - 643
signify *forebode* 511
  mean 516
  inform 527
  indication 550
signior 875
sign manual 550, 590
signor 877
sign painting 555
signpost 550
sike 348
Sikes, Bill - 792
silence *disable* 158
  no sound **403**
  confute 479
  latency 526
  concealment 528
  aphony 581
  taciturn 585
  check 731
silencer 405, 408a
silent [*see silence*]
silhouette *outline* 230
  appearance 448
  portrait 556
siliquose 191
silk *texture* 219, 329,
  635
  smooth 255
  soft 324
  make a - purse out of
    a sow's ear 471
  - gown *barrister* 968
silken 255
  - repose 687
silkiness
  voluptuousness 954
sill 215
silly *credulous* 486
  imbecile 499
  insane 503
silo 636
silt *dirt* 653
  (*remainder* 40)
silvan 367
silver *bright* 420
  white 430
  gray 432
  money 800
  bait with a - hook 615
  German - 545
  - footed queen 318
  - lining of the cloud
    858
  - wedding 883
silver-toned 413
silviculture 371
simagrée 855

simian 499
similarity 17
- of form 240
simile *similarity* 17
  comparison 464
  metaphor 521
similitude *likeness* 17
  copy 21
simious 499
simmer *agitation* 315
  boil 382, 384
  excitement 824
simmering 825
Simon, Simple - 547
Simon Pure
  the real - 494
Simon Stylites 893
simony 964
simoon 349, 382
simous 243
simper *smile* 838
  affectation 855
simple *mere* 32
  unmixed 42
  credulous 486
  ignorant 493
  silly 499
  - *language* 576
  instrumental 633
  herb 662
  artless 703
  unadorned 849
  - *duty* 926
  - *meaning* 516
simple-hearted 543
simple-minded 849
simpleness 42
Simple Simon 501, 547
simpleton 501
simplicity 849
  ignorance 491
  [*see simple*]
simplify [*see simple*]
  elucidate 518
simply *little* 32
  singly 87
  more - *interpreted* 522
simulate *resemble* 17
  imitate 19
  cheat 544
  impiety 988
simultaneous 120
sin *vice* 945
  guilt 947
Sinæan 188
sinapism 662
since *under the circumstances* 8
  after 117
  cause 155
  reason 476
sincere *veracious* 543
  ingenuous 703
  feeling 821
sine 217
sine die *never* 107
  defer 133
sine quâ non
  required 630
  important 642
  condition 770

sinecure 681
  no - 682
sinew 159
sinewless 158
sinews of war
  money 800
sinewy 159
sinful 945
sing *blow* 349
  bird cry 412
  music 416
  poetry 597
  rejoice 838
  - in the shrouds 349
  - out 411
  - praises *approve* 931
  worship 990
  - small 879
singe 382, 384
singer *musician* 416
  poet 597
singing club 416
single *unmixed* 42
  unit 87
  secluded 893
  unmarried 904
  ride at - anchor 863
  - combat 720
  - entry 811
  - file 69
  - out 609
single-foot 275
single-handed *one* 87
  easy 705
  unassisted 706
single-minded 703
singleness [*see single*]
  - of heart *artless* 703
  probity 939
  - of purpose
  perseverance 604a
  artless 703
single-seater 273
singlestick 720
singsong 16, 414
singular *special* 79
  exceptional 83
  one 87
singularly *very* 31
  nonconformity 83
sinister *left* 239
  bad 649
  adverse 735
  vicious 945
  bar - *imperfect* 651
  disrepute 874
sinistrality 239
sinistrorsal 239
sinistrous
  sullen 901a
sink *disappear* 4, 111
  destroy 162
  descend 306
  lower 308
  submerge 310
  neglect 460
  conceal 528
  cloaca 653
  fatigue 688
  vanquish 731
  fail 732

snakestone 248
snap *break* 44
  time 106
  shut 261
  eat 298
  brittle 328
  noise **406**
  impulse 612
  activity 682
  cheapness 815
  rude 895
  - at *seize* 789
  bite 830
  censure 932
  - of the fingers
  trifle 643
  - one's fingers at
  defy 715
  insolence 885
  despise 930
  - one up *censure* 932
  - the thread 70
  - up *seize* 789
snapdragon 840
snappish 901
snappy *news* 532
snap shot 554
snare *deception* 545
  (*source of danger* 667)
snare drum 417
snarl *growl* 412
  discord 713
  rude 895
  angry 900
  threaten 909
snarled *confused* 523
snatch
  small quantity 32, 51
  seize 789
  by -es 70
  - at *pursue* 622
  seize 789
  - a verdict *deceive* 545
  cunning 702
  - from one's grasp 789
  - from the jaws of death 672
sneak *hide* 528
  coward 862
  servile 886
  base 940
  knave 941
  bad man 949
  - off, - out of 623
  - thief 792
sneakers *shoes* 225
sneer *disparage* 929
  contempt 930
  blame 932
sneeze *blow* 349
  snuffle 409
  not to be -d at 642
  - at *despise* 930
snick *small quantity* 32
  part 51
snicker *rejoicing* 838
  ridicule 856
snide 545
sniff *blow* 349
  odor 398

discovery 480a
sniffle 349
snifting valve 664
snigger *laugh* 838
  ridicule 856
  disrespect 929
sniggle 545
snip *small quantity* 32
  cut 44
  tailor 225
snipe 298, 366
snippet 32
snip-snap 713
snivel *weep* 839
sniveling *servile* 886
snob *vulgar* 851
  plebeian 876
  servile 886
snobbishness
  flattery 933
snood *headdress* 225
  circle 247
snooze 683
snore *noise* 441
  sleep 683
snort 411, 412
snorter 83
snout 250
snow *ship* 273
  ice 383
  white 430
snow avalanche 383
snowball 72, 383
snow blindness 443
snow-bound 383
snowdrift 72
snowshoes 225, 266, 272
snowslide 306, 383
snowslip 306, 383
snowstorm 383
snub *short* 201
  hinder 706
  cast a slur 874
  humiliate 879
  bluster 885
  censure 932
snub-nosed
  distortion 243
  (*ugly* 846)
snuff *blow* 349
  pungent 392
  odor 398
  go out like the - of a candle 360
  - out *destroy* 162
  dark 421
  - up *inhale* 296
  smell 398
  up to - *skillful* 698
  cunning 702
snuff-color 433
snuffle *blow* 349
  hiss 409
  stammer 583
  hypocrisy 988
snuffy 653
snug *closed* 261
  comfortable 377
  safe 664
  prepared 673

content 831
  secluded 893
  keep - *conceal* 528
  seclude 893
  make all - *prepare* 673
snuggery 189
snuggle 902
snugness 827
so *similar* 17
  very 31
  therefore 476
  method 627
  - be it *assent* 488
  consent 762
  - far so good 618
  - let it be 681
  - much the better
  content 831
  rejoicing 838
  - much the worse
  discontent 832
  aggravation 835
  - to speak *similar* 17
  metaphor 521
soak *immerse* 300
  water 337
  moist 339
  drunkenness 959
  - up 340
soap *lubricate* 332
  oil 356
soapy *unctuous* 355
  service 886
  flattery 933
soar *great* 31
  height 206
  fly 267
  rise 305
  air 338
sob 839
sober *substantial* 3
  moderate 174
  wise 498
  sane 502
  plain 576
  grave 837
  temperate 953
  abstinent 958
  in - sadness
  affirmation 535
  - down 174, 502
  humility 879
  - senses 502
  - truth *fact* 494
sober-minded 502
  calm 826
  humble 879
soberness 953
sobriety **958**
sobriquet 565
soc *jurisdiction* 965
socage 777
so-called
  deception 545
  misnomer 565
sociable *carriage* 272
  sociality 892
social *mankind* 372
  sociable 892
  - circle 892
  - evil 961

  - gathering 892
  - science 910
  - service 602
  - smile 906
  - worker 602
socialism
  government 737
  participation 778
  philanthropy 910
Socialists 712
sociality **892**
society *mankind* 372
  party 712
  fashion 852
  sociality 892
  laity 997
  position in - 873
sociological 537
  - school 451
sociology 910
socinianism 984
socius criminis 711
sock *hosiery* 225
  drama 599
sockdolager 67, 479
socket *receptacle* 191
  concave 252
socle 215
Socratic method 461
Socratic school 451
sod 344
  beneath the - 363
sodality *party* 712
  friendship 888
  (*sociality* 892)
sodden *moist* 339
  boiled 384
sofa 215
soft *stop!* 142
  weak 160
  moderate 174
  smooth 255
  not hard 324
  moist 339
  marsh 345
  silence! 403
  - *sound* 405
  dulcet 413
  credulous 486
  silly 499
  lenient 740
  tender 822
  timid 862
  (*docile* 602)
  (*irresolute* 605)
  own the - *impeach-ment* 529
  - buzzing *slander* 934
  - music 415
  - pedal 405
  - sawder *plea* 617
  flattery 933
  - snap 681
  - soap *oil* 356
  flattery 933
  - thing 681
  - tongue, - words 894
soften [see *soft*]
  moderate 174
  relieve 834
  pity 914

sorites 476
sororal 906
sorority 712, 888
sorosis 888
sorrel 433
sorrow 828
  give - words 839
  more in - than anger
   patient 826
   forgiveness 918
sorry *trifling* 643
  grieved 828
  mean 876
  (*small* 32)
  (*bad* 649)
  be - for *pity* 914
  repent 750
  cut a - figure 874
  in a - plight
   failure 732
  make a - face 874
  - sight *painful* 830
  sad 837
sort *degree* 26
  arrange 60
  kind 75
  - with *sociality* 892
sortable 23
sortes
  chance 156, 621
  - Virgilianæ
   sorcery 992
sortie 716
sortilege
  prediction 511
  sorcery 992
sortilegy 621
sortition 621
sorts, out of -
  ill health 655
  sulky 901a
so-so *small* 32
  trifling 643
  imperfect 651
sossle 653
sot *fool* 501
  drunkard 959
soterial 976
soteriology 976
sotnia 726
sotto voce
  faint sound 405
  conceal 528
  voiceless 581
sou *money* 800
soubrette 599, 746
soufflé 298
sough *conduit* 350
  faint sound 405
  cloaca 653
soul *essence* 5
  person 372
  intellect 450
  genius 498
  affections 820
  (*whole* 50)
  (*important* 642)
  flow of - 588
  have one's whole - in
   his work 686
  not a - 187
686

not dare to say one's
  - is his own
   subjection 749
  fear 860
  - of wit 572
soulless *inactive* 683
  insensible 823
soul-mate 903
soul-sick 837
soul-stirring
  emotion 821
  excitement 824
sound *great* 31
  conformable 82
  stable 150
  strong 159
  fathom 208
  - of a fish 334
  bay 343
  noise **402**
  resonance 408
  investigate 461
  measure 466
  true 494
  wise 498
  sane 502
  good 648
  perfect 650
  healthy 654
  solvent 800
  orthodox 983a
  catch a - 418
  full of - and fury
   unmeaning 517
  insolent 885
  safe and - *health* 654
  preserved 670
  - a retreat 283
  - asleep 683
  - a trumpet
   publish 531
   alarm 669
  - mind 502
  - of limb 654
  - of wind 654
  - reasoning 476
  - sleep 683
  - the alarm
   indication 550
   warning 668
   alarm 669
   fear 860
  - the horn 416
  - the note of prepara-
   tion 673
  - the praises of 931
soundable 310
sounding 402
  big - 577
  - brass 517
sounding-board 417
soundings 208
soundless
  unfathomable 208
  silent 403
soundness
  - of doctrine 983a
soup *food* 298
  semiliquid 352
soupcon *small* 32
  mixture 41

sour *acid* 397
  discontented 832
  embitter 835
  uncivil 895
  sulky 901
  - grapes
   impossibls 471
   excuse 617
  - the temper 830
source *beginning* 66
  cause 153
sourdet 417
sourdine 417
  à la - *noiseless* 405
  concealed 528
soured 832
  discontented 832
sourness **397**
souse *plunge* 306, 310
  water 337
south *direction* 278
  north and -
   opposite 237
Southern 237
  - Cross 318
south paw 239
South Pole 383
southward 237
souvenir 505
sovereign *superior* 33
  all-powerful 159
  authoritative 737
  ruler 745
  - contempt 930
  - remedy 662
sovereignty 737
  [*see* sovereign]
sow *scatter* 73
  pig 366
  agriculture 371
  female 374
  get the wrong - by
   the ear
   misjudgment 481
   error 495
   mismanage 699
   fail 732
  - broadcast 818
  - dissension
   discord 713
   hate 898
  - one's wild oats
   improve 658
   amusement 840
   vice 945
   intemperance 954
  - the sand 645
  - the seed *prepare* 673
  - the seeds of *cause* 153
   teach 537
sowar 726
sower 371
sozzle 653
spa *town* 189
  sanatorium 662
space *music* 26, 413
  arrange 60
  time 106
  occasion 134
  extension **180**
  printing 591

  celestial -s 318
spaddle 272
spade 272
  call a - a spade
   plain language 576
   straightforward 703
spade husbandry 371
spahi 726
span *similarity* 17
  join 43
  link 45
  duality 89
  time 106
  transient 111
  small 193
  distance 196
  near 196
  length 200
  short 201
  - of horses 272
  measure 466
spangle *spark* 420
  ornament 847
spaniel *dog* 366
  servile 886
  (*flatterer* 935)
Spanish fly 171
spank *swift* 274
  flog 792
spanking *large* 192
  - pace 274
span-new 123
spar *beam* 214
  quarrel 713
  contend 720
spare *small* 193
  meager 203
  refrain 623
  store 636
  scanty 640
  redundant 641
  disuse 678
  inaction 681
  relinquish 782
  give 784
  economy 817
  exempt 927a
  temperate 953
  enough and to - 639
  not a moment to - 682
  - diet 956
  - no expense 816
  - no pains 686
  - room 180
  - time 685
  to - 641
spared, be - *live* 359
  it cannot be - 630
sparge 337
spargefaction
  scatter 73
  wet 337
sparger 337
sparing [*see* spare]
  small 32
  economy 817
  parsimony 819
  temperate 953
  - of praise 932
  - of words 585
  with a - hand 819

lavish 818
(*misuse* 679)
- and pelt 59
- blood 722
spin *journey* 266
  aviation 267
  rotate 312
  - a long yarn
  exaggerate 549
  - out *protract* 110
  late 133
  prolong 200
  diffuse style 573
spinach 298
spinal 222, 235
spindle 312
spindle-shanks 203
spindle-shaped 253
spindrift 353
spine 253
spinel 847
spineless *weak* 945
spinet *copse* 367
  harpsichord 417
spinney 367
spinosity
  unintelligible 519
  discourtesy 895
  sullenness 901a
spinous *prickly* 253
Spinozism 451
spinster 374, 904
spinuliferous 253
spiny 253
spiracle 260, 351
spiral 248, 311
spire *height* 206
  peak 253
  soar 305
spiriferous 248
spirit *essence* 5
  immateriality 317
  intellect 450
  meaning 516
  vigorous language 574
  stimulate 615
  activity 682
  affections 820
  courage 861
  ghost 361, 980
  evil - **980a**
  keep one's - up
  hope 858
  - away 791
  - control 992a
  - of my dream 515
  - of myrcia 400
  - up *induce* 615
  excite 824
  unclean - 978
  with life and - 682
Spirit, the Holy - 976
spirited *language* 574
  active 682
  sensitive 822
  cheerful 836
  dashing 852
  brave 861
  generous 942
spiritism 317, 992a
spiritist 317, 450

spiritistic 317
spiritless
  insensible 823
  sad 837
  cowardly 862
spiritoso *music* 415
spirit rapping 992a
spirits *drink* 298
  cheer 836
spirit-stirring 824
spiritual
  immaterial 317
  psychical 450
  divine 976
  pious 987
  - director 996
  - existence 987
  - wife 903, 962
spiritualism
  immateriality 317
  intellect 450
  heterodoxy 984
  psychical research 992a
spiritualist 317
spiritualize 317
spirituel 842
spiroid 248
spirograph 662
spirometer 662
spirt *eject* 297
  stream 348
  haste 684
  exertion 686
spirtle *disperse* 73
  splash 348
spissitude *dense* 321
  viscid 352
spit *pointed* 253
  perforate 260
  eject 297, 299
  rain 348
  - fire *irascible* 901
spite 907
  envy 921
  in - of *disagreement* 24
  counteraction 179
  opposition 708
  in - of one's teeth
  unwilling 603
spiteful
  malevolent 907
  hating 898
spittle 299
spittoon 191
splanchnic 221, 329
splanchnology 221, 329
splash *affuse* 337
  stream 348
  spatter 653
  parade 882
  make a - *fame* 873
  display 882
splashboard 666
splayfooted 243
spleen *melancholy* 837
  hatred 898
  anger 900
  sullen 901a
  harbor - 907
spleenless 906

splendiferous 851
splendor *bright* 420
  beautiful 845
  glorious 873
  display 882
splenetic *sad* 837
  morose 901a
splice *join* 43
  cross 219
  interjacent 228
  repair 660
  - the main brace
  tipsy 959
spliced, be -
  marriage 903
splint 215, 662, 752
splinter *small piece* 32
  divide 44
  filament 205
  brittle 328
  (*part* 51)
split *divide* 44
  bisect 91
  brittle 328
  divulge 529
  quarrel 713
  fail 732
  laugh 838
  - hairs
  discriminate 465
  sophistry 477
  - one's sides 838
  - the difference
  mean 29
  compromise 774
  - the ears *loud* 404
  stridor 410
  deafness 419
  - the lungs 411
  - upon a rock 732
splurge 882
splutter *energy* 171
  spit 297
  stammer 583
  haste 684
spoil *waste* 638
  vitiate 659
  botch 699
  hinder 706
  lenity 740
  plunder 791
  booty 793
  satiate 869
  (*bad* 649)
  -s of time 106
  - sport 706
  - trade 708
spoiled child
  satiated 869
  favorite 899
  - of fortune 734
spoiler 792
spoke *radius* 200
  tooth 253
  obstruct 706
  put a - in one's wheel
  render powerless 158
  hinder 706
spokesman
  interpreter 524
  speaker 582

spoliate 791
spoliative 793
spondee 597
sponge *stopper* 263
  moisten 339
  dry 340
  pulpiness 354
  marine animal 368
  clean 652
  despoil 791
  drunkard 959
  apply the -
  obliterate 552
  nonpayment 808
  - out 552
sponger 886
sponging-house 752
spongy *porous* 252
  soft 324
  squashy 345
sponsion 771
sponsor *witness* 467
  security 771
  be - for *promise* 768
  obligation 926
sponsorship 771
spontaneous
  voluntary 600
  willing 602
  impulsive 612
  - generation 357
spontoon 727
spoof 545
spook 361, 980a
  fish 368
spool 312
spoon *receptacle* 191
  ladle 272
  bill and coo 902
  born with a silver -
  in one's mouth 734
spoondrift 353
Spoonerism 495
spoonful *some* 25
  small quantity 32
spoon-meat 298
spoony *foolish* 499
  lovesick 902
spoor 550
sporaceous 330
sporadic
  unassembled 73
  infrequent 137
  disease 655, 657
spore 330
sporogenous 161
sporophyte 357
sporous 330
sport *killing* 361
  chase 622
  amusement 840
  show off 882
  (*enjoyment* 827)
  in - *pastime* 840
  humor 842
  - of fortune 735
  - one's oak 893
  the - of 749
sporting *killing* 361
  contention 720
  amusement 840

- dog 366
sportive *gay* 836
  frolicsome 840
sportsman 361, 622, 840
sportswoman 840
sportulary 784, 785
sportule 784
sporule 330
sposh 653
spot *inextension* 180a
  place 182
  discover 480a
  mark 550
  dirt 653
  blemish 848
  blot 874
  (*decoloration* 429)
  (*sully* 846)
  (*disgrace* 940)
  on the - *instantly* 113
  present time 118
  soon 132
  in one's presence 186
spotless *perfect* 650
  clean 652
  innocent 946
  (*beautiful* 845)
spotlight 423, 550, 599
spotted *variegated* 440
  damaged 659
  ugly 846
spotter *aviator* 269a
spousal 903
spouse *companion* 88
  married 903
spouseless 904
spout *egress* 295
  flow out 348
  conduit 350
  speak 582
  act 599
  pawn 771
  (*lend* 787)
sprag 633
sprain *powerless* 158
  weak 160
sprat
  - to catch a herring
  barter 794
  - to catch a whale
  bungling 699
sprawl *length* 200
  horizontal 213
  descend 306
spray *sprig* 51
  atomizer 336
  foam 353
  foliage 367
  flowers 400
spread *enlarge* 35
  disperse 73
  universalize 78
  expanse 180
  expand 194
  diverge 291
  meal 298
  publish 531
  - abroad 531
  - a shade 421
  - canvas 267

- out 194
- sail 267
- the toils 545
- to 196
spread-eagle 884
spree 840
sprig *branch* 51
  infant 129
sprightly
  cheerful 836
  witty 842
spring *early* 125
  source 153
  strength 159
  velocity 274
  recoil 277
  fly 293
  leap 309
  elasticity 325
  rivulet 348
  instrument 633
  store 636
  remedy 662
- a leak *imperfect* 651
  damage 659
- a mine *destroy* 162
  unexpected 508
  attack 716
- a project 626
- back 277
- from 154
- of life 131
-s of action 615
- tide *flood* 31, 35, 52
  high 206
  water 337
  wave 348
  (*abundance* 639)
- to one's feet 307
- up *begin* 66
  event 151
  grow 194
  ascend 305
  visible 446
- upon 508, 789
spring balance 319
springe 545
Springfield rifle 727
spring gun 545, 667
springle 545
spring-net 545
springtide *youth* 127
springy 325
sprinkle *add* 37
  mix 41
  scatter 73
  wet 337, 348
  variegate 440
  baptize 998
sprinkler 337
sprinkling
  small quantity 32
sprint 274
sprit *sprout* 167
  support 215
sprite *good spirit* 979
  demon 980
sprout *grow* 35, 365
  offspring 167
  expand 194
  - from *result* 154

spruce *tree* 367
  neat 652
  beautiful 845
  - up 652, 847
sprue 653
sprung *imperfect* 651
  damaged 659
spry *active* 682
  cheerful 836
  (*skillful* 698)
spud 272
spume 353
spunk 861
spun out
  long time 110
  diffuse style 573
spur *pointed* 250
  sharp 253
  - a horse 370
  incite 615
  quicken 684
  on the - of the moment
  instantly 113
  now 118
  soon 132
  opportune 134
  impulse 612
  win -s *succeed* 731
  glory 873
spurious *erroneous* 495
  false 544
  deceptive 545
  illegitimate 925
spurn *reject* 610
  disdain 930
spurred 253
spurt *transient* 111
  swift 274
  gush 348
  impulse 612
  haste 684
  exertion 686
spurtle 73
sputum 299
sputter *emit* 297
  splash 348
  stammer 583
spy *see* 441
  spectator 444
  inquire 461
  informer 527
  emissary 534
  scout 664
  warning 668
spyglass 445
squab *large* 192
  short 201
  broad 202
  bench 215
  nestling 298
squabble 713
squad *assemblage* 72
  soldiers 726
squadron *fighters* 726
  (*crowd* 72)
  (*ships* 273)
squalid *dirty* 653
  unsightly 846
squall *violent* 173
  wind 349

  cry 411
  quarrel 713
squalor 653
squamate 223
squamiferous 223
squamous *layer* 204
  skin 223
squander *waste* 638
  misuse 679
  lose 776
  prodigal 818
squandering 776
squantum 840
square *congruous* 23
  compensate 30
  four 95
  place 182
  houses 189
  perpendicular 212
  form 244
  measure 466
  sparring 720
  justice 924
  honorable 939
  make all - 660
  on the - 939
  - accounts
  pay 807
  account 811
  put a - thing into a
  round hole 699
  - deal 922
  - inches 180
  - piano 417
  - the circle 471
  - up 556
  - with 23
  - yards 180
square-toes 857
squash *destroy* 162
  flatten 251
  blow 276
  fruit 298
  soft 324
  marsh 345
  semiliquid 352
  pulpiness 354
  hiss 409
  - pie 298
squashy 345, 352
squat *locate oneself* 184
  little 193
  short 201
  thick 202
  low 207
  sit 308
  (*ugly* 846)
squatter 188
squaw *woman* 374
  wife 903
squeak *human cry* 411
  animal cry 412
  disclosure 529
  (*weep* 839)
squeal [see squeak]
squealer 532, 941
squeamish
  unwilling 603
  sick 655
  fastidious 868
  (*censorious* 932)

silent 403
remedy 662
inaction 681
hinder 706
prohibit 761
put a - to 142
- a flow 348
- a gap *repair* 660
- payment 808
- short
  discontinue 142
  cease to move 265
- short of 304
- the breath 361
- the ears 419
- the mouth
  confute 479
  gag 581
- the sound 408a
- the way 706
- to consider 485
- up 261
stopcock 263
stop-gap
  substitute 147
  stopper 263
stoppage *end* 67
  cessation 142
  hindrance 706
stopper 263
store *location* 184
  stock **636**
  shop 799
  (*collection* 72)
  (*abundance* 639)
in - *destiny* 152
  preparing 673
lay in a - 637
set no - 483
set - by
  important 642
  commend 931
- away 184
- in the memory 505
- of knowledge 490
storehouse 636
storeroom 636
storeship *ship* 273
  ship of war 726
storge *love* 897
storied
  descriptive 594
stork 366
storm *crowd* 72
  convulsion 146
  violence 173
  agitation 315
  wind 349
  attack 716
  passion 825
  anger 900
ride the - 267
- brewing 665
- in a teacup
  overrate 482
  exaggerate 549
  unimportance 643
  blunder 699
- is up 349
take by - *conquer* 731
  seize 789

694

storthing 696
story *rooms* 191
  layer 204
  lie 546
  history 594
as the - goes 532
the old - 897
story-teller 548, 594
stot 366
stound 870
stoup *cup* 191
  altar 1000
stour 59
  large 192
stout *strong* 159
stout-hearted 861
stove *fireplace* 386
- in 252
stow *locate* 184
  pack close 195
  store 636
stowage *space* 180
  location 184
stowaway 528
strabismus 443
straddle 266
  tergiversation 607
Stradivarius 417
strafe 527
straggle *stroll* 266
  deviate 279
straggler 268
straggling
  disjunction 44
  disorder 59
straight *vertical* 212
  rectilinear 246
  direction 278
  cards 840
all - *rich* 803
  solvent 807
- course 628
- descent 167
- lined 246
- poker 840
- sailing 705
- shot 278
- ticket 609
- up *vertical* 212
straighten
  make straight 246
  remedy 662
- out 774
straightforward 278
  truthful 543
  artless 703
  honorable 939
straightness 246
straightway 132
strain *race* 11
  continuity 69
  weaken 160
  operation 170
  violence 173
  percolate 295
  transgress 303
  sound 402
  melody 415
  overrate 482
  exaggerate 549
  style 569

voice 580
poetry 597
clean 652
effort 686
fatigue 688
- a point
  go beyond 303
  exaggerate 549
  not observe 773
  undue 925
- at a gnat and swal-
  low a camel 608
- every nerve 686
- in the arms 902
- one's ears 418
- one's eyes 441
- one's invention 515
- the meaning 523
- the throat 411
strainer *sieve* 260
strait *interval* 198
  water 343
  difficulty 704
-s *poverty* 804
straitened *poor* 804
strait-handed 819
strait-laced *severe* 739
  restraint 751
  fastidious 868
  haughty 878
strait-waistcoat
  restrain 751
  means of restraint
  752
stramash 720
strand *thread* 205
  land 342
stranded
  stuck fast 150
  in difficulty 704
  failure 732
  pain 828
strange *unrelated* 10
  exceptional 83
  ridiculous 853
  wonderful 870
- bedfellows 713
- to say 870
strangely *much* 31
stranger *extraneous* 57
a - to *ignorant* 491
strangle
  render powerless 158
  contract 195
  kill 361
strangulation
  [see strangle]
  punishment 972
strap *fasten* 43
  fastening 45, 752
  remedy 662
  punish 972
  *instrument of pun-
  ishment* 975
strappado 972
strapping *strong* 159
  big 192
- pace 274
strapwork 847
stratagem
  deception 545

plan 626
artifice 702
strategic *plan* 626
  artifice 702
strategist *planner* 626
  director 694
  proficient 700
strategy *conduct* 692
  warfare 722
  (*skill* 698)
strath 252
strathspey 840
stratification
  layers 204
  structure 329
stratocracy 737
stratum 204
stratus 353
straw *scatter* 73
  light 320
  unimportant 643
catch at -s
  overrate 482
  credulous 486
  misuse 679
  unskillful 699
  hope 858
  rash 863
care not a -
  indifference 866
  despise 930
in the - 161
man of -
  unsubstantial 4
  cheat 548
  insolvent 808
  low person 876
not worth a -
  trifling 643
  useless 645
- bail 545
- bid 545
- bidder 548
- to show the wind
  463
the eyes drawing -s
  683
strawberry 298
strawboard 593
straw-colored 436
stray *dispersion* 73
  exceptional 83
  traveler 268
  deviate 279
  (*stroll* 266)
streak *long* 200
  narrow 203
  furrow 259
  light 420
  stripe 440
  mark 550
streaked *crossed* 219
  variegated 440
stream *assemble* 72
  move 264
- of fluid **347**
- of water 348
- of air 349
- of light 420
  abundance 639
against the - 708

suffragan 996
suffrage 609
  vote 535
suffragette 374
suffragist 609
suffusion *mixture* 41
  feeling 821
  blush 879
Sufi *religious sect* 984
Sufism 984
sugar 396
sugar loaf *pointed* 253
sugary 396
suggest *suppose* 514
  inform 527
  advise 695
  - itself *thought* 451
  fancy 515
  - a question 461
suggester *tempter* 615
suggestion *plan* 626
  advice 695
suggestive
  reminder 505
  significant 516
  descriptive 594
suicidal
  destructive 162
suicide *killing* 361
sui generis 20, 83
suigenetic 163
suisse *beadle* 996
Suisse point d'argent
  point de - 812
suit *accord* 23
  series 69
  class 75
  clothes 225
  expedient 646
  petition 765
  courtship 902
  do - and service 743
  follow - 19
  law - 969
  love - 897
  - in law 969
  - the action to the
    word 550
  - the occasion 646
suitable 23, 646
  - season 134
suit case 191
suite *sequel* 65
  series 69
  retinue 746
  - of rooms 191
suitor *petitioner* 767
  lover 897
  lawsuit 969
sulcated 259
sulcus 259
sulkiness [*see* sulky]
  discourtesy 895
sulky *carriage* 272
  obstinate 606
  discontented 832
  dejected 837
  sullen 901a
sulks 895
sullen *obstinate* 606
  gloomy 837
  698

discourteous 895
sulky 901a
sullenness **901a**
sully *dirty* 653
  dishonor 874
  (*deface* 846)
sulphite 83
sulphur 388
sulphur-colored 436
sultan 745
sultry 382
sum *add* 37
  number 84
  money 800
  - and substance
    meaning 516
    synopsis 596
    important part 642
  - total 800
  - up *reckon* 85
    discriminate 465
    description 594
    compendium 596
sumless 105
summarize 551, 596
summation 37, 85
summary *transient* 111
  early 132
  short 201
  concise 572
  compendious 596
  illegal 964
  - of facts 594
summer *season* 125
  support 215
  heat 382
  - lightning 423
  - school 542
summerhouse 191
summerset 218
summit *top* **210**
  (*superiority* 33)
summon *command* 741
  lawsuit 969
  (*accuse* 938)
  - up *memory* 505
    excite 824
  - up *courage* 861
summons *evidence* 467
  command 741
  lawsuit 969
sump *base* 211
  inlet 343
  slough 345
  cess 653
sumpter-horse 271
sumptuary
  money 800
  expenditure 809
sumptuous 882
sum total 50
sun *heavenly body* 318
  luminary 423
  glory 873
  as the - at noonday
    bright 420
    certain 474
    plain 525
  bask in the - 377
  farthing candle to the
    - 645

going down of the -
  126
  - oneself 384
  under the - *space* 180
    world 318
Sun of Righteousness
  976
sunbeam 420
  -s from cucumbers
    471
sunburn 384
sunburnt 433
Sunday 138, 687
  - best *ornament* 847
    show 882
  - school 542
sunder 44
sundial 114
sun dog 423
sundown 126
sundowner 460, 876
sundry 102
sunflower 369
sunk [*see* sink]
  deep 208
  - fence 717
  - in iniquity 945
  - in oblivion 508
sunken rocks 667
sunless 421
sunlight 420
Sunni 984
sunny *warm* 382
  luminous 420
  cheerful 836
sunny side 829
  - of hedge 734
  view the - 858
sun painting 556
sunrise 125, 236
sunset 126, 236.
  at - 133
  - glow 420
sunshade *cover* 223
  shade 424
sunshine *light* 420
  prosperity 734
  happy 827
  cheerful 836
sunshiny 382
sunstone 847
sunstroke *heat* 384
  madness 503
sun-up 125
sun worship 382
sunyasi [*see* sannyasi]
  retaliation 718
  punishment 972
sup *small quantity* 32
  feed 298
  - full of horrors 828
supawn 298
super *theatrical* 599
superable *possible* 470
  (*easy* 705)
superabound 641
  sufficiency 639
superadd 37
superannuated 128,
  158
superb 845

supercargo 694
supercherie 545
supercilious *proud* 878
  insolent 885
  disrespectful 929
  scornful 930
superdreadnought 726
supereminence
  goodness 648
  repute 873
supererogation
  redundant 641
  useless 645
  (*activity* 682)
superexaltation 873
superexcellence 648
superfetation
  added 37
  productive 168
superficial *shallow* **209**
  outside 220
  misjudging 481
  ignorant 491
  - extent 180
superficies 220
superfine 648
superfluitant 305
superfluity
  remainder 40
  redundance 641
superfluous
  remaining 40
  redundant 641
  useless 645
superhuman
  perfect 650
  godlike 976
superimpose 233
superimposed 206
superincumbent
  above 206
  heavy 319
superinduce
  change 140
  cause 153
  produce 161
superintend 693
superintendent 694
superior *greater* 33
  - in size 194
  high 206
  important 642
  good 648
  director 694
superiority **33**
superjunction 37
superlative 33
superman 33
supernal *height* 206
  summit 210
  heavenly 981
supernatant *high* 206
  ascent 305
supernatural *deity* **976**
  spectral 980a
  - aid 707
supernaturalism 528
supernormal 20, **976**
supernumerary
  adjunct 39
  theatrical 599

reserve 636
redundant 641
(remainder 40)
superphysical 450, 976
superplus 40
superpose *add* 37
cover 223
supersaturate 641
superscription
mark 550
writing 590
(evidence 467)
supersede
substitute 147
disuse 678
relinquish 782
supersensible
- regions 317, 318
supersensitive 976
supersensual 976
supersensuous 976
superstition 486
religious - 984
superstitious 486, 984
- remedies 670
superstratum 220
superstructure 729
supertonic 413
supervacaneous
redundant 641
(useless 645)
supervene *be added* 37
succeed 117
happen 151
supervise 693
supervisor 694
supervisory 693
supination 213
supine *horizontal* 213
inverted 218
sluggish 683
mentally torpid 823
suppeditate 637
supper 298
full of - 954a
supplant 147
supple *soft* 324
servile 886
supplement *addition* 37
adjunct 39
completion 52
suppletory 37
suppliant *begging* 765
beggar 767
supplicate *beg* 765
pity 914
worship 990
supplies *materials* 635
aid 707
money 800
supply *store* 636
provide 637
give 784
- aid 707
- deficiencies 52
- the place of 147
support *perform* 170
sustain 215
evidence 467
escort 664
preserve 670

aid 707
feel 821
endure 826
vindicate 937
- life 359
supporter
auxiliary 711
supporters
heraldic 550
suppose 472, 514
supposing *provided* 469
supposition 514
supposititious
unattested 468
untrue 546
suppress *destroy* 162
conceal 528
silent 581
restrain 751
suppression
[see suppress]
- of truth 544
suppuration 653
suppurative 663
suppute 85
supralapsarian 984
supramundane 939
supremacy
superior 33
authority 737
supreme 33
summit 210
authority 737
almighty 976
in a - degree 31
- good 618
- principle 450
Supreme Being 976
surbate 659
surbated 688
surcease 142
surcharge
redundance 641
(dear 814)
falsify 811
surcingle 45
surcost 225
surd *number* 84
silent 403
deaf 419
phonetic 561
sure *certain* 474
belief 484
assent 488
safe 664
make - against 673
make - of *inquire* 461
take 789
on - ground 664
security 771
to be - *assent* 488
you may be -
affirmation 535
sure-footed
careful 459
skillful 698
cautious 864
surely 870
sureness [see sure]
surety *certainty* 474
safety 664

surf *tide* 348
foam 353
surface *outside* 220
texture 329
lie on the -
intelligible 518
manifest 525
skim the -
slur over 460
- car 272
surfeit
redundance 641
satiety 869
surge *swarm* 72
swell 305
rotation 312
wave 348
surgeon 662
surgery 662
surly *gruff* 895
sullen 901a
unkind 907
surmise 510, 514
surmount *tower* 206
summit 210
transcursion 303
ascent 305
- a difficulty 731
surmountable 470
surname 564
surpass
be superior 33
grow 194
go beyond 303
outshine 873
surplice 999
surplus *remainder* 40
redundance 641
surplusage 641
surprise
nonexpectation 508
take unawares 674
wonder 870
- party 892
surprisingly 31
surrebut 462
surrebutter
answer 462
pleadings 969
surrejoin 462
surrejoinder 462
surrender *submit* 725
relinquish 782
(obey 743)
no - *obstinate* 606
defense 717
- one's life 360
surreptitious
furtive 528
deceptive 545
untrue 546
surrogate 147, 759
surround
circumjacent 227
circumscribe 229
surroundings 227
surtout *coat* 225
surveillance *care* 459
direction 693
under - 938
survene 151

survey *view* 441
measure 466
surveyor 466, 694
survive *remain* 40
long time 110
permanent 141
susceptibility
power 157
tendency 176
liability 177
sensibility 375
motive 615
impressibility 822
irascibility 901
susceptive 177
suscipient 785
suscitate *cause* 153
produce 161
stir up 173
excite 824
suspect *doubt* 485
suppose 514
suspected *accused* 938
suspectless 484
suspend *defer* 133
discontinue 142
hang 214
neglect 460
suspended   animation
823
suspenders 45
suspense *cessation* 142
uncertainty 475
expectation 507
irresolution 605
in - *inert* 172
suspension
lateness 133
cessation 142
hanging 214
music 413
seclusion 893
- of arms 723
suspicion *doubt* 485
incredulity 487
knowledge 490
supposition 514
fear 860
cautious 864
jealousy 920
under - 938
suspiration 839
suspire 359
sustain *continue* 143
strength 159
perform 170
support 215
preserve 670
aid 707
endure 821
sustained note 413
sustaining power 170
sustenance 298, 707
sustentation
[see sustain]
food 298
sustentative 215
sustention 215
susurration 405
sutler *purveyor* 637
merchant 797

699

suttee *killing* 361
  burning 384
  unselfishness 942
  idolatry 991
sutteeism 361
suture 43
suzerain 745
suzerainty 737
swab *dry* 340
  clean 652
  lubber 701
swaddle *clothe* 225
  restrain 751
swaddling clothes
  in - *infant* 129
  subjection 749
swag *hang* 214
  lean 217
  curve 245
  drop 306
  oscillate 314
  booty 793
swage 174
swagger *pride* 878
  boast 884
  bluster 885
swaggerer 482, 884, 887
swagsman 268
swain *man* 373
  rustic 876
  lover 897
swale 659
swallow *swift* 274
  gulp 296
  eat 298
  bird 366
  believe 484
  credulous 486
  brook 826
  - flight 274
  - the bait *dupe* 547
  willing 602
  - the leek *recant* 607
  submit 725
  - up *destroy* 162
  store 636
  use 677
  take 789
  - whole 465a
swallow-tailed coat 225
swamp *destroy* 162
  marsh 345
  defeat 731
swamped *failure* 732
swampy *moist* 339
swan 366
  - bath 341
  - road 341
  - song 360
swap *exchange* 148
  blow 276
  barter 794
sward 344, 367
swarm *crowd* 72
  multitude 102
  climb 305
  bees 370
  sufficiency 639
  redundance 641
swarthy 431
700

swartness 431
swash *affuse* 337
  spurt 348
swashbuckler
  fighter 726
  blusterer 887
swashy 339
swastika 621, 993
swath 72
swathe *fasten* 43
  clothe 225
  restrain 751
sway *power* 157
  influence 175
  lean 217
  oscillate 314
  agitation 315
  induce 615
  authority 737
  - to and fro 149
sweal 659
swear *affirm* 535
  promise 768
  curse 908
  just enough to - by 32
  - at 908
  - a witness 768
  - by *believe* 484
  - false 544
sweat *exude* 295
  excretion 299
  heat 382
  exertion 686
  fatigue 688
  cold - 860
  in a - 382
  - of one's brow 686
  - over 451 .
sweater 225
Swedenborg 986
Swedenborgian
  religious sect 984
sweep *space* 180
  curve 245
  navigation 267
  rapid 274
  bend 279
  clean 652
  dirty fellow 653
  steal 791
  make a clean - of 297
  - along 264
  - away *destroy* 162
  eject 297
  abrogate 756
  relinquish 782
  - off 297
  - of time 109
  - out *eject* 297
  clean 652
  - the chords 416
sweeper
  cleaner 652, 876
  war vessel 726
sweeping *whole* 50
  complete 52
  inclusive 76
  general 78
  - change 146
sweepings
  useless 645

  dirt 653
  (*trifle* 643)
sweepstakes
  gain 775
  receipt 810
sweet *saccharine* 396
  melodious 413
  color 428
  clean 652
  agreeable 829
  lovely 897
  look - upon *desire* 865
  love 897
  endearment 902
  - potatoes 298
  - smell 400
  - tooth *desire* 865
  - wine 396
  - words 894
sweeten 396, 829
sweetheart 897, 902
sweetmeat 396, 829
sweetness 396
  - and light 829
sweets *pastry* 298
  sugar 396
  treat 829
sweet-scented 400
swell *increase* 35
  expand 194
  convexity 250
  wave 348
  sound 404
  emotion 821
  fop 854
  nobility 875
  swagger 885
  extol 931
  (*increase* 35)
  ground - *agitation* 315
  - out *diffuse style* 573
  - over 250
  - the ranks of 37
  - with rage 900
swelling *expansion* 194
  prominence 250
  - *style* 577
  excitement 824
swell mob 792
swelter 382
sweltry 382
swerve *variation* 20a
  change 140
  deviate 279
  demur 603
  tergiversation 607
  - from 287
swift 274
swig *drink* 298
  drunkenness 959
swill *drink* 298
  uncleanness 653
  intemperance 954
  drunkenness 959
swim *navigate* 267
  float 305
  light 320
  dim-sightedness 443
  - against the stream 704
  - in *pleasure* 377

  abundance 639
  - with the stream
  conformity 82
  inactivity 683
  - with the tide
  prosperity 734
swimming
  - *eyes* 443
  - *head* 503
  - *bath* 652
  - *belt* 666
  - *bladder* 334
  - *pool* 652
swimmingly *easily* 705
  success 731
  prosperity 734
swindle *cheat* 545
  peculate 791
swindler *cheat* 548
  thief 792
swine 366
  cast pearls before 638
  - of Epicurus 954a
swineherd 746
swing *operation* 170
  space 180
  hang 214
  oscillate 314
  freedom 748
  amusement 840
  full - *active* 682
  success 731
  give full -
  facilitate 705
  have one's - 738
swinge 972
swinging *great* 31
swinish
  intemperance 954
  gluttony 957
  - *multitude* 876
swink 686
swirl 312, 348
swish 409
switch *deviate* 279
  recede 287
  flog 972
  rod 975
swivel *hinge* 312
  cannon 727
swivel-eye 443
swollen *expanded* 194
  proud 878
swoon *powerless* 158
  fatigue 688
swoop *descend* 274, 306
  seize 789
  at one fell - 173
swop 794
sword *weapon* 727
  at the point of the - 722
  severity 739
  compulsion 744
  subjection 749
  draw the - *war* 722
  flesh one's - *war* 722
  measure -s 720, 722
  put to the - 361
  - of Damocles 667

T

tænia 205
tæniate 205
taffeta 255
taffy 396
tag *small* 32
  addition 37
  fastening 45
  follow 63, 235
  sequel 65
  end 67
  point 253
  animal 366
  game 840
  (*adjunct* 39)
tagtail 886
tail *sequel* 65
  end 67
  pendent 214
  rear 235
  aëronautics 273
  estate - 780
  - off *decrease* 36
  turn - 623
tail coat 225
tailless 38
tailor *clothier* 225
  workman 690
tailoress 225
tailoring *clothes* 225
  finery 882
tailpiece *sequel* 65, 235
  engraving 558
  ornament 847
tailrace 350
taint *imperfection* 651
  dirt 653
  decay 659
  disgrace 874
tainted *fetid* 401
  diseased 655
taintless 652
taj 225
tajo 259
take *eat* 298
  believe 484
  know 490
  understand 518
  succeed 731
  receive 785
  appropriate 788, 789
  captivate 829
give and - 718
  - aback *unexpected* 508
  astonish 870
  - a back seat 34
  - a course 692
  - action 680
  - a disease 655
  - advice 695
  - after 17
  - a hint 498
  - a leaf out of an-
    other's book 19
  - a lease 788
  - a liberty 748
  - a likeness 554
  - an account of
    enumerate 85
  - an ell 885
  - an infection 655
  - a peep 441

- aside 586
- a turn 140
- away *annihilate* 2
  subtract 38
  remove 185
  seize 789
- away life 361
- back again 790
- by [*see below*]
- care *warning* 668
  cautious 864
- care of 459
- comfort *constant* 831
  relief 834
- coolly 826
- down *swallow* 298
  depress 308
  record 551
  dismantle 681
  humiliate 874
  censure 932
- easily 826
- effect *event* 151
  act 170
- exception 932
- fire 384
- flight 623
- for [*see below*]
- from *subtract* 38
  seize 789
- heart *contented* 831
  cheerful 836
- heed 864
- hold of *cohere* 46
  seize 789
- hold of the mind 484
- ill 832
- in [*see below*]
- into [*see below*]
- it *believe* 484
  suppose 514
- its course
  continue 143
  event 151
- its rise *begin* 66
  result 154
- leave of 624
- measures 626
- money 810
- no care of 460
- no denial
  obstinate 606
  compel 744
- no interest in 823
- no note of 460
- no note of time 115
- notice 457
- off [*see below*]
- on [*see below*]
- one at one's word
  769
- one's chance
  chance 621
  essay 675
- one's choice 609
- oneself off 293
- one's fancy
  pleasing 829
  desire 865
- one's oath 535
- one with another 29

- on trust 484
- out *extract* 301
  obliterate 552
- part with 709
- pattern by 19
- pen in hand 590
- place 151
- possession of 789
- precedence
  superior 33
  precede 62
- root *firm* 150
  located 184
- ship 267
- steps *prepare* 673
  act 680
- stock 85
- the air line 278
- the back track 283
- the cake 33
- the consequences
  154
- the field 722
- the good the gods
  provide 831
- the lead 62
- the place of 147
- the shine out of 33
- the stump 582
- things as they come
  inactivity 683
  inexcitable 826
  relief 834
- time *duration* 106
  late 133
  leisure 685
- time by the forelock
  132
- to *habit* 613
  pursuit 622
  use 677
  like 827
  desire 865
  love 897
- to heart *pain* 828
  discontent 832
- to pieces
  disjoin 44
  dismantle 681
- up [*see below*]
- upon onself
  undertake 676
  promise 768
- warning 668
- wing 293
take by
- surprise 508
- the button 586
- the hand *aid* 707
take for 484
- better for worse 609
- gospel 486
- granted 472, 484
take in *include* 54
  shorten 201
  admit 295
  understand 518
  deceive 545
  receive money 785
- an idea 498
- good part

be calm 826
be pleased 827
content 831
- hand *teach* 537
  undertake 676
  aid 707
- sail 275
take into - account
  include 76
  discriminate 465
  qualify 469
- consideration 451
- custody 751
- one's head
  suppose 514
  caprice 608
taken
  be - *die* 360
- ill 655
- with 897
take off *mimic* 19
  destroy 162
  remove 185
  divest 226
  burlesque 555
  discount 813
- one's hands 785
- the hat 894
take on
  discontent 832
  melancholy 837
- credit 484
- trust 484
taker 789
take up *elevate* 307
  inquire 461
  dissent 595
  choose 609
  undertake 676
  arrest 751
  borrow 788
  censure 932
- a case 476
- an inquiry 461
- arms 722
- money 788
- one's abode 184
- one's pen 590
- the cudgels
  attack 716
  contend 720
- with *attention* 457
  use 677
  content 831
taking 789
  infectious 657
  in a - *pained* 828
  angry 900
- off *death* 360
talapoin 996
talbotype 554
tale *counting* 85
  narrative 594
  thereby hangs a - 526
  twice-told -
    diffuse style 573
    weary 841
talebearer 529, 532
talent 264, 698
  bury one's - in a nap-
    kin 528

this 79
  at - time of day 118
  - that or the other 15
thistle *prickly* 253
thistledown *light* 320
thither 278
thole 821
thole pin 215
thong *fastening* 45
  scourge 975
Thor 979
thorn *sharp* 253
  bane 663
  painful 830
  plant a - 830
  spiteful 907
  - in the flesh 830
  - in the side
  badness 649
  annoyance 830
  on -s for *longing* 865
  sit on -s
  physical pain 378
  moral pain 828
  fear 860
thorniness [see thorny]
  sullenness 901a
thorny *prickly* 253
  difficult 704
  discourteous 895
thorough 52, 729
thoroughbass 413
thoroughbred
  intrinsic 5
  horse 271
  skill 698
  fashionable 852
thoroughfare
  opening 260
  way 627
  (*passage* 302)
thoroughgoing 52
thoroughly do - 729
thoroughpaced 31
thorp 189
though *compensation* 30
  qualification 469
  opposition 708
  (*counteraction* 179)
thought *little* 32
  reflection **451**
  idea 453
  (*maxim* 496)
  give a - to 457
  not to be - of
  reject 610
  prohibit 761
  organ of - 450
  quick as - 274
  seat of - 450
  subject of - 454
  the power of - 451
  - of 454
  - reading 450
  - transference 450, 992a
  want of - 458
  who could have 508
thoughtful
  reflecting 451
  wise 498

thoughtless
  incogitant 452
  inattentive 458
  careless 460
  improvident 674
thousand *number* 98
  many 102
  one in a - *good* 648
  good man 948
thrall 746, 751
thralldom 749
thrash *punish* 972
Thraso 887
Thrasonic 884, 885
thrawn 217
thread *arrange* 60
  series 69
  weak 160
  filament 205
  pass through 302
  hang by a - 665
  life hangs by a - 360
  not have a dry - 339
  - one's way
  journey 266
  passage 302
  worn to a - 659
threadbare *bare* 226
  deteriorated 659
threadlike 205
thread paper 203
threat 909
threaten *future* 121
  destiny 152
  danger 665
  (*alarm* 669)
threatening
  warning 668
  unhopeful 859
three 93
  sisters - 601
  - color process 558
  - per cent 802
  - R's 537
  - sheets in the wind 959
  - times three
  number 98
  approbation 931
three-decker *house* 189
threefold 93
three-score 98
  - years and ten 128
three-tailed bashaw
  master 745
  nobility 875
threne 839
threnetic 838
threnody 839
thresh 972
  - out 461
threshold *beginning* 66
  edge 231
  at the - *near* 197
  - of an inquiry 461
thrice 93
  - happy 827
  - is he armed 922
  - told tale 573
thrid 302
thrift *prosperity* 734

  gain 775
  economy 817
thriftless 674, 818
thrill *touch* 380
  feeling 821
  excitation 824
thrilling *pleasing* 829
  painful 830
thrive *prosper* 73
  gain 618
  (*succeed* 732)
throat *opening* 260
  air pipe 350, 351
  cut the - 361
  force down the - 739
  stick in one's -
  voiceless 581
  speechless 585
  take by the - 789
  - disease 655
throaty 583
throb *oscillate* 314
  agitate 315
  emotion 821
throbbing' - heart 860
  - pain 378
throe *revolution* 146
  violence 173
  agitation 315
  physical pain 378
  (*moral pain* 828)
  birth - 161
throne *abode* 189
  seat 215
  emblem of authority 747
  ascend the - 737
  occupy the - 737
  - of God 981
throng 72
throttle
  render powerless 158
  close 261
  kill 361
  seize 789
  - down 275
through *owing to* 154
  via 278
  by means of 631
  (*passage* 302)
  get - 729
  go - one 824
  - thick and thin
  complete 52
  violence 173
  perseverance 604a
throughout *totality* 50
  completeness 52
  - the world 180
throw *impel* 276
  propel 284
  exertion 686
  - a tub to catch a whale 545
  - a veil over 528
  - away *eject* 297
  reject 610
  waste 638
  relinquish 782
  - away the scabbard 722

  - cold water on 616
  - doubt upon 485
  - down *destroy* 162
  lower 308
  - good money after bad 818
  - in 228
  - into the shade
  superior 33
  lessen 36
  surpass 303
  important 642
  (*repute* 873)
  - off [see below]
  - of the dice 156
  - oneself at the feet of 725
  - oneself into the arms of
  safety 664
  - on paper 590
  - open *open* 260
  admit 296
  - out [see below]
  - over *destroy* 162
  - overboard *exclude* 55
  destroy 162
  eject 297
  abrogate 756
  - up [see below]
throwback 145
throw off 297
  - all disguise 529
  - one's guard
  inexpectation 508
  cunning 702
  - the mask 529
  - the scent
  misdirect 538
  avoid 623
throw out *propel* 284
  eject 297
  - a feeler 379
  - a hint 527
  - a suggestion 514
  - of gear *disjoin* 44
  derange 61
thrown out 704
throw up *eject* 297
  resign 757
  - one's cap 884
  - the game 624
thrum 416
thrush 366, 416
thrust *push* 276
  attack 716
  - down one's throat 744
  - in *insert* 300
  (*interpose* 228)
  - one's nose in 682
  - upon 784
thud 406, 408a
thug *murderer* 361, 726
  bandit 792
thuggee 361
thuggery 361
thumb *touch* 379
  bite the - 929
  one's fingers all -s 699
  rule of -

true - 113
waste - 683
timeful 134
time-honored *old* 124
  repute 873
  respected 928
timekeeper 114
timeless 135
timely *early* 132
  opportune 134
timeous 134
timepiece 114
timepleaser 607, 943
times *present* 118
  events 151
  hard - 735
  many - 136
timeserver 607, 943
timeserving
  tergiversation 607
  cunning 702
  servility 886
  improbity 940
  selfishness 943
time-worn *old* 124
  age 128
  deteriorated 659
timid *fearful* 860
  cowardly 862
  humble 881
timidity [see timid]
  humility 879
timist 607
timocracy 803
Timon of Athens
  wealth 803
  seclusion 893
  misanthrope 911
timorous [see timid]
timothy 367
timpano 417
tin *preserve* 670
  money 800
  - oven 386
  - wedding 883
tinct 428
tinction 428
tinctorial 428
tincture
  small quantity 32
  mixture 41
  color 428
tinctured
  disposition 820
tinder *fuel* 388
  irascible 901
tine 253
tinge *small quantity* 32
  mix 41
  color 428
tingent 428
tingible 428
tingle *pain* 378
  touch 380
  emotion 821
  make the ears - 900
tink 408
tinker *repair* 660
  (*improve* 658)
tinkle *faint sound* 405
  resonance 408

tinkling cymbal 517
tinned goods 670
tinnient 408
tinsel *glitter* 420
  sham 545
  ornament 847
  frippery 851
tint 428
tintamarre 404
tintinnabulary 408
tintinnabulation 408
tiny 193
tip *end* 67
  summit 210
  cover 223
  discrimination 465
  give 784
  (*pay* 807)
  on - toe *high* 206
  expect 507
  - off 465
  - the wink 550
tipcat 840
tippet 214, 225
tipple *drink* 298
  tope 959
tippler 959
tippybob 803
tipstaff 965
tipsy 959
tiptop *summit* 210
  good 648
tirade *speech* 582
  censure 932
tirailleur 726
tire *invest* 225
  automobile 272
  fatigue 688
  worry 830
  weary 841
tiresome [see tire]
tisane 662
Tisiphone 173
tissue *whole* 50
  assemblage 72
  matted 219
  texture 329
tit *small* 193
  pony 271
Titan *strength* 159
  size 192
  sun god 423
  demon 980
Titaness 192
Titanic 159
titanic 31, 192
titbit *savory* 394
  pleasing 829
tit for tat 718
tithe *tenth* 99
  tax 812
tithing 181
tithingman 965
Titian red 434
titillate *amuse* 840
  provoke desire 865
titillation *pleasure* 377
  touch 380
titivate 847·
title *indication* 550
  name 564

  book 593
  authority 747
  right to property 780
  distinction **877**
  right 924
titled 875
title deed 771
title-page 66
titter 838
tittle *small quantity* 32
  inextension 180a
  to a - 494
tittle-tattle *news* 532
  small talk 588
titubancy 583
titubate *fall* 306
  fail 732
titular *word* 562
  nomenclature 564
tivoli 840
tmesis 218
T.N.T. 727
to *direction* 278
  lie - 681
  - a certain degree 32
  - a great extent 31
  - all intents and pur-
    poses
  equally 27
  whole 52
  - a man 78
  - and fro 12, 148, 314
  - a small extent 32
  - be sure 488
  - come *future* 121
  destiny 152
  - crown all 33, 642
  - do 59
  - some extent 26
  - the credit of 805
  - the end of the chap-
    ter 52
  - the end of time 112
  - the full 52
  - the letter 19
  - the point 23
  - the purpose 23
  - this day 118
  - wit 79
toad *hateful* 649
  ugly 846
  - under a harrow 378
toadeater *servile* 886
  sycophant 935
toadeating *flattery* 933·
toadstool 367
toadying 886
toadyism 933
toast *roast* 384
  celebrate 883
  - brown 433
toaster 386
tobacco 392
toboggan 272
tobogganing 840
toby 191
toccata 415
tocogony 161
tocology 161, 662
tocsin 669
tod 319

to-day 118
toddle *walk* 266
  limp 275
toddy 298
toe 211
  on the light fantastic -
    jump 309
  dance 840
toes turn up the -
  die 360
toft 189, 780
toga *coat* 225
  robes 747
  assume the - virilis
    131
together
  accompanying 88
  same time 120
  come - 290
  get - 72
  hang - 709
  lay heads - 695
  - with added to 37
  accompanied by 88
toggery 225
toil *activity* 682
  exertion 686
  - of a pleasure 682
  -s *trap* 545
  (*danger* 667)
  (*wile* 702)
toilet 225
  - water 400
toilette 225
  en grande - 847
toilsome 686
  difficult 704
toilworn 688
token 550
  give - *manifest* 525
  - of remembrance 505
tolderolloll 838
Toledo 727
tolerable *a little* 32
  trifling 643
  not perfect 651
  passable 845
toleration *laxity* 738
  lenity 740
  permission 760
  feeling 821
  calmness 826
  benevolence 906
toll *sound* 407
  tax 812
  - the knell 363
tollbooth *prison* 752
  market 799
tom *male* 373
tomahawk 727
tomato 298
tomb 363
  lay in the - 363
  - of the Capulets **506**
tombola 156
tomboy 129, 851
tombstone 363
tomcat 373
tome 593
tomentose 256
tomfool 501

- upon *badness* 649
  severity 739
tramway 627
trance *dream* 515
  sleep 683
  lethargy 823
tranquil *calm* 174
  quiet 265
  peaceful 721
  - *mind* 826
tranquillize
  moderate 174
  pacify 723
  soothe 826
transact *act* 680
  conduct 692
  - *business* 625
  - *business with* 794
transaction
  event 151
  action 680
  -s *of record* 551
transalpine 196
transanimation 140
transatlantic 196
transcalency 384
transcend *great* 31
  superior 33
  go beyond 303
transcendency 641
transcendent
  unequal 28
  superior 33
  glorious 873
  (*perfect* 650)
transcendental
  intellectual 450
  unintelligible 519
transcendentalism 450,
  451
transcolate
  exude 295
  (*stream* 348)
transcribe *copy* 19
  manifest 525
  write 590
transcript *copy* 21
  writing 590
transcursion 303
transept *church* 1000
transeunt 111
transfer *copy* 21
  displace 185
  - *of things* 270
  - *of property* **783**
transferable 270, 783
transferee 270
transference **270**
transfiguration
  change 140
  divine - 908
transfix 260
transfixed *firm* 150
transforation 260
transform 140
transformation scene
  599
transfuse *mix* 41
  transfer 270
  remedy 662
  - the sense of 522
     712

transgress
  go beyond 303
  infringe 773
  violate 927
  sin 945
transgression *guilt* 947
transgressor 949
transience 111
transient *time* 109, 111
  changeable 149
  traveler 268
transilience
  revolution 146
  transcursion 303
transit *conversion* 144
  angularity 244
  motion 264
  transference 270
  measurement 466
transition 144, 270
transitional *change* 140
transitory 111
translate *interpret* 522
  manifest 525
  word 562
  promote 995
translation
  transference 270
  crib 539
  word 562
  resurrection 981
translator 524
transliterate 561
translocate 185
translocation 270
translucence 425
translumination 425
transmarine 196
transmigration
  change 140
  conversion 144
transmission
  moving 270
  automobile 272
  passage 302
  - *of property* 783
transmit 270, 302
  transfer 783
  - *light* 425
transmogrify 140
transmorphism 140
transmutation
  change 140
  conversion 144
transom 215, 349
transparency **425**
transparent
  transmitting light 425
  obvious 518
transpicuous
  transmitting light 425
  obvious 518
transpierce 260
transpire *evaporate* 336
  appear 525
  be disclosed 529
transplace 270
transplant 270, 371
transplendent 420
transpontine 196
transport *transfer* 270

  ship 273
  war vessel 726
  excitement 825
  delight 827
  please 829
  punish 972
  (*emotion* 821, 824)
  - *of love* 897
transportation 144
transported
  overjoyed 827
transposal 148, 218
transpose *invert* 14, 218
  exchange 148
  displace 185
  transfer 270
  - *music* 413
transshape 140
transshipment 185
transubstantiation
  change 140
  sacrament 998
transudatory 295
transude *ooze* 295
  pass 302
  (*stream* 348)
transume *change* 140
transumption
  transfer 270
transverse *change* 140
  oblique 217
  crossing 219
tranter 271
trap *closure* 261
  gig 272
  snare 545
  stage - 599
  pitfall 667
  fall into a - *dupe* 547
  clumsy 699
  lay a - for 545
trapan 545
trapdoor *opening* 260
  snare 545
  pitfall 667
trapes 701
trappings *adjunct* 39
  clothes 225
  equipment 633
  ornament 847
Trappist 996
traps *clothes* 225
  baggage 780
trash *unmeaning* 517
  trifling 643
  useless 645
  riffraff 876
trashy - *style* 575
traulism 583
traumatic 662
travail *childbirth* 161
  labor 686
trave 215
travel 266
  - *out of the record* 10,
    477
traveler **268**
  bagman 758
  tricks upon -s
  deception 545
  cunning 702

  -'s *tale* *untruth* 546
  exaggeration 549
traveling 266
  - bag 191
  - salesman 758
traverse *contravene* 179
  move 266
  pass 302
  negative 536
  obstruct 706
travestie *copy* 21
  ridicule 856
travesty *imitate* 19
  misinterpret 523
  burlesque 555
  ridicule 856
travis 215
trawl 285, 463
trawler 273
tray 191
treacherous 907, 940
  - *memory* 506
treachery
  deception 545
  dishonesty 940
treacle *thick* 352
  sweet 396
tread *motion* 264
  walk 266
  - a path *journey* 266
  pursuit 622
  - down *harsh* 739
  humble 879
  - in the steps of 19
  - on the heels of 281
  - the beaten track
  conformity 82
  habit 613
  - the boards 599
  - the stage 599
  - under foot
  destroy 162
  subjection 749
  disrepute 874
  insolence 885
  contempt 930
  - upon *persecute* 649
treadle 633
treadmill 312, 975
treason *revolt* 742
  treachery 940
treasure *store* 636
  goodness 648
  money 800
  - trove 618
  - up in the memory
    505
treasurer **801**
treasury **802**
treat
  physical pleasure 377
  manage 692
  bargain 769
  delight 827, 829
  amusement 840
  - of 595
  - oneself to 827
  - well 906
treatise 593, 595
treatment
  painting 556

trippingly 584
tripsis 330
Triptolemus 371
triquetral 94
trireme 92, 273
Trisagion 900
triseme 92
trisection 94
triskelion 92, 993
trismus 655
triste 837
tristful 837
trisula 92
trisulcate *trisected* 94
　furrow 259
trite *known* 490
　conventional 613
　- *saying* 496
tritheism 984
Triton *sea* 341
　- among the minnows
　　superior 33
　huge 192
　important 642
trituration 330
triumph *procession* 69
　success 731
　trophy 733
　exult 838
　celebrate 883
　boast 884
triumvirate 92, 737
triune 93
Triune God 976
triunity 92
trivet *support* 215
　stove 386
　right as a -
　　perfect 650
　　due 924
trivial *unmeaning* 517
　trifling 643
　useless 645
　ridiculous 853
　(*small* 32)
troat 412
trocar 262
trochaic 597
trochee 597
trochilic 312
trodden down - 749
　well - *habitual* 613
　used 677
troglodyte 893
troll *roll* 312
　fairy 980
trolley 266, 271, 273
　- *car* 272
trollibus 273
trollop 59, 962
trombone 417
troop *assemblage* 72
　soldiers 726
　raise -s 722
trooper 726
　lie like a - 544
　swear like a - 908
troopship 726
trope 521
Trophonius, cave of
　- 837

trophoplasm 357
trophy *record* 551
　palm **733**
tropical 382
　metaphorical 521
trot *run* 266, 370
　velocity 274
　translation 539
　- out *manifest* 525
　display 882
troth *belief* 484
　veracity 543
　promise 768
　by my - 535
　plight one's - 902
trothless *false* 544
　dishonorable 940
trotters 266, 298
trottoir 627
troubadour 597
trouble *disorder* 59
　derange 61
　exertion 686
　difficulty 704
　adversity 735
　pain 828
　painful 830
　bring into - 649
　get into - 732
　in - *evil* 619
　　adversity 735
　take - 686
　- one for 765
　- oneself 686
　- one's head about
　　682
troubled [*see* trouble]
　fish in - waters 704
troublesome
　inexpedient 647
　exertion 686
　difficult 704
　painful 830
troublous 59
　violent 173
　- times 713
trough *hollow* 252
　trench 259
　conduit 350
trounce *censure* 932
　punish 972
troupe 72
trousers 225
　put on long - 131
trousseau 225
trout 298
trouvaille 775
trouvère 597
trover *acquisition* 775
　unlawful 964
trow *think* 451
　believe 484
　know 490
trowel 191
troy weight 319
truant *absent* 187
　runaway 623
　idle 682
　apostate 941
truce *lateness* 133
　cessation 142

　deliverance 672
　peace 721
　pacification 723
flag of - 724
　- of God 142
trucidation 361
truck *summit* 210
　vehicle 272
　barter 794
　- driver 268, 271
　- farm 691
　- garden 371, 691
truckle-bed 215
truckler 886
truckle to *submit* 725
　servile 886
　flatter 933
truckling *servile* 746
truckman 268
truculent 907
trudge *walk* 266
　move slowly 275
true *real* 1
　straight 246
　assent 488
　accurate 494
　veracious 543
　faithful 772
　honorable 939
　orthodox 983a
　see in its - colors 480a
　- bill *vindicate* 937
　　accuse 938
　　lawsuit 969
　- faith 983a
　- meaning 516
　- to nature 17
　- to oneself 604a
　- saying 496
true-blue 494
true-hearted 543, 939
truelove 897
truelover's knot
　love 897
　endearment 902
trueness [*see* true]
true-penny 939
truffles 298
truism *axiom* 496
　unmeaning 517
trull 962
truly *very* 31
　assent 488
　really 494
　indeed 535
trump *perfect* 650
　cards 840
　honorable 939
　good man 948
　- card *device* 626
　　success 731
　- up *falsehood* 544
　　accuse 938
　turn up -s 731
trumped up
　counterevidence 468
　deception 545
　untruth 546
trumpery
　unmeaning 517
　trifling 643

,trumpet *music* 417
　war cry 722
　boast 884
　ear - 418
　flourish of -s
　　ostentation 882
　　celebration 883
　　boasting 884
　penny - *skill* 410
　sound of - *alarm* 669
　speaking - 418
　- blast 404
　- call *signal* 550
　　command 741
　- forth 531
trumpeter
　musician 416
　messenger 534
　boaster 884
trumpet-toned
　shrill 410
trumpet-tongued
　loud 404
　public 531
truncate *shorten* 201
　formless 241
truncated
　incomplete 53
truncheon *weapon* 727
　staff of office 747
　*instrument of pun-
　　ishment* 975
trundle *propel* 284
　roll 312
　- bed 215
trunk *whole* 50
　origin 153
　paternity 166
　box 191
trunk hose 225
trunnion *support* 215
　projection 250
truss *tie* 43
　pack, packet 72
　support 215
trust *belief* 484
　property 780
　credit 805
　hope 858
　- to a broken reed 699
　- to the chapter of
　　accidents 621
trusted 484
trustee *consignee* 758
　possessor 779
　treasurer 801
trustful 484
trustless 940
trustworthy
　certain 474
　belief 484
　- *memory* 505
　veracious 543
　reliable 632
　honorable 939
truth *exactness* **494**
　veracity 543
　probity 939
　arrive at the - 480a
　in - *certainly* 474
　love of - 543

of a - *affirmation* 535
veraciously 543
prove the - of 937
religious - 983a
speak the - *disclose* 529
veracity 543
Truth, Spirit of - 976
truthless 544
truth-loving 543
truth-telling 543
trutination 319
try *experiment* 463
adjudge 480
endeavor 675
use 677
lawsuit 969
- a case 967
- a cause 480
- a prisoner 967
- conclusions
discuss 476
quarrel 713
contend 720
- one *difficulty* 704
- one's hand 675
- one's luck 621
- one's temper 824
- one's utmost 686
- the patience 830
trying *fatigue* 688
difficulty 704
tryst 74, 892
trysting place 74
tsar 745
tub 191, 386
- to a whale
deception 545
excuse 617
tuba 417
tubate 260
tubby 201
tube 260
tubercle 250
tubercular 655
tuberculosis 655
tuberosity 250
tubman 968
tubular 260
tubulated 260
tubule 260
tuck *adjunct* 39
fold 258
dagger 727
- in *locate* 184
eat 298
insert 300
tucker 225
tuft *collection* 72
rough 256
tufted 256
tufthunter *servile* 886
selfish 943
tufthunting
servility 886
flattery 933
tug *ship* 273
pull 285
effort 686
- of war 720
athletic sport 840

tuition 537
tulip *variegated* 440
gaudy 882
Tullian 582
tumble *derange* 61
destruction 162
fall 306
agitate 315
fail 732
rough and - 59
tumble-down
weak 160
tottering 665
tumbler *glass* 191
actor 599
buffoon 844
tumbrel 272
tumefaction 194
tumid *expanded* 194
- style 577
(*big* 192)
tumor *expansion* 194
prominence 250
tump 206
tumult *disorder* 59
agitation 315
revolt 742
emotion 825
tumultuous
[*see* tumult]
violent 173
tumulus 363
tun *receptacle* 191
large 192
drunkard 959
tuna 298
tunable 413
tund 972
tundra 344
tune *music* 415, 416
in - 413
out of -
unmusical 414
imperfect 651
deteriorated 659
put in - *prepare* 673
concord 714
to the - of *quantity* 25
payment 807
price 812
- up 416
tuneful *music* 413
poetry 597
- nine *musician* 416
poet 597
tuneless 414
tunic 225
tunicle 999
tuning fork 417
tunker 984
tunnage 192
tunnel
ncave 252
opening 260
passage 627
tup *sheep* 366
male 373
tu quoque 718
- argument
counterevidence 468
confutation 479

accuse 938
turban 225
turbary 367
turbid *opaque* 426
foul 653
turbinal 248
turbinated
convoluted 248
rotation 312
turbine 267, 284, 312, 633
- steamer 273
turbiniform 245, 248
turbinoid 248
turbulence
violence 173
agitation 315
excitation 825
(*disorder* 59)
turbulent
[*see* turbulence]
disorderly 59
Turcism 984
tureen 191
turf *elasticity* 325
lawn 344
grass 367, 371
fuel 388
gambling 621
races 720
race course 728
amusement 840
turfman 840
turgid
expanded 194
- style 577
redundant 641
ostentatious 882
(*exaggerated* 549)
Turk *polygamist* 903
grand - 745
turkey 298
- trot 840
Turkish bath 386
turlupinade 842
turmeric paper 463
turmoil
confusion 59
violence 173
agitation 315
turn *state* 7
crisis 134
period of time 138
change 140
tendency 176
form 240
curve 245
blunt 254
stroll 266
deviate 279
recession 287
circulation 311
rotate 312
music 413
willingness 602
aptitude 698
affections 820
emotion 821
trepidation 860
by -s *periodic* 138
interchange 148

come in its - 138
do a good - *good* 648
benevolent 906
each in its - 148
give one a - *aid* 707
excite 824
ill - 907
in - *order* 58
periodic 138
in his - 148
meet one at every - 641
one's luck -s 735
serve one's - 644
take a favorable - 658
take a wrong - 732
to a - 494
- about *interchange* 148
- a corner *go round* 311
succeed 731
- a deaf ear to *deaf* 419
refuse 764
- adrift *disperse* 73
eject 297
- and turn about
interchange 148
changeable 149
- and twist 248
- a penny 775
- aside *change* 140
deviate 279
hinder 706
- away *eject* 297
not look 442
avoid 623
dismiss 756
relinquish 782
- back *reversion* 145
regression 283
- color 821
- down 258
- end for end 14
- for 698
- from *repent* 950
- in *go to bed* 683
- in an alarm 669
- inside out 529
- into *conversion* 144
translate 522
- money 796
- ridicule 856
- off 972
- of mind 820
- of the cards 156
- of the table 156
- of the tide *reverse* 145
invert 218
- one's attention from 458
- one's back upon
oppose 708
refuse 764
disrespect 929
contempt 930
- one's hand to 625
- on one's heel *avoid* 623
discourtesy 895
- on the tap 297

715

letter 561
printing 591
- for the blind 442
typescript 21
typesetting 54
typewrite 590
typewriting 590

typhonic 349
typhoon *wind* 349
　(violent 173)
typical *special* 79
　conformable 82
　metaphorical 521
　significant 550

typify 511
typist 590
typography 591
tyranny
　authority 737
　severity 739
　illegality 964

tyrant *authority* 737
　severe 739
　ruler 745
　evildoer 913
tyre 230
tyro *ignoramus* 493
　learner 541

U

uberty *luxuriance* 168
　(*sufficiency* 639)
ubiety 186
ubiquitarian 984
ubiquity 186
U-boat 208, 726
udder 191
udometer 348
ugh! 867
uglification 846
ugliness **846**
ugly 846
　call by - names 932
　take an - turn 732
　- customer
　　source of danger 667
　evildoer 913
　bad man 949
uhlan 716, 726
ukase 741
ukulele 417
ulcer *disease* 655
　care 830
ulcerate 659
ulema *judge* 967
uliginous 352
ullalulla 839
ulster 225
ulterior *extra* 37
　extraneous 57
　- in time 121
　- in space 196
ultima ratio 744
　- regum 722
ultimate 67
　- cause 153
ultimately *difference* 15
　future 121
　latest 133
ultima Thule 196
ultimatum *definite* 474
　intention 620
　requirement 630
　terms 770
ultimeter 244
ultimo 122
ultimogeniture 777
ultra *great* 31
　superior 33
ultramarine 438
ultramicroscope 445
ultramontane
　foreign 57
　distant 196
　heterodox 984
　church 995
ultramundane 196
ultra-violet rays 420
ululate 412, 839

ululation 407, **412**
Ulysses 702
umbilicus 222
umbra 421
umbrage *shade* 424
　hatred 898
　take - *anger* 900
umbrageous 421
umbrageousness 421
umbrella *covering* 223
　shade 424
　protection 666
umpire *judgment* 480
　mediator 724
　judge 967
unabashed *bold* 861
　vain 885
　insolent 885
unabated 31
unable 158
　- to say "No" 605
unacceptable 830
unaccommodating
　disagreeing 24
　disagreeable 830
　discourteous 895
　sulky 901a
unaccompanied 87
unaccomplished 730
unaccountable
　exceptional 83
　unintelligible 519
　irresponsible 927a
　arbitrary 964
　(*wonderful* 870)
unaccustomed
　unusual 83
　unused 614
　unskillful 699
unachievable 471
unacknowledged
　ignored 489
　nameless 565
　unrequited 917
unacquainted 491
unacquired 777a
unactuated (616)
unadmonished 665
unadorned *style* 576
　simple 849
　beauty - 845
unadulterated
　simple 42
　genuine 494
　(*good* 648)
unadventurous 864
unadvisable 647
unadvised
　dangerous 665

unskillful 699
unaffected *genuine* 494
　sincere 543
　- style 578
　obstinate 606
　artless 703
　insensible 823
　simple 849
　taste 850
　(*physically callous* 376)
unafflicted 831
unaided *weak* 160
　(*unsupported* 706)
unalarmed 861
unalienable 924
unallayed 159
unallied 10
unallowable 923
unallowed 925
unalloyed 42
　- *happiness* 827
　- *truth* 494
unalluring 866
unalterable 150
unaltered *identical* 13
　stable 150
　(*unchanged* 141)
unamazed 871
unambiguous 518
unambitious 866
unamiable 907
unanimated 823
unanimity
　agreement 23
　assent 488
　accord 714
unannexed 44
unanswerable
　demonstrative 478
　irresponsible 927a
　arbitrary 964
　(*certain* 474)
unanswered 478
unanticipated 508
unappalled 861
unappareled 226
unapparent *latent* 526
　(*invisible* 447)
unappeasable 173
unappetizing 867
unapplied 678
unappreciated 483
unapprehended 491
unapprehensive 861
unapprized 491
unapproachable
　great 31
　infinite 105

distant 196
unapproached
　unequal 28
　superior 33
unappropriated 782
unapproved 932
unapt *incongruous* 24
　impotent 158
　unskillful 699
　(*inexpedient* 647)
unarmed 158
unarranged
　disorder 59
　unprepared 674
unarrayed 226, 849
unartificial 849
unascertained
　uncertain 475
　ignorant 491
unasked *voluntary* 602
　not asked 766
unaspiring
　indifferent 866
　modest 881
unassailable 664
unassailed 748
unassembled 73
unassisted *weak* 160
　unaided 706
　- eye 441
unassociated 44
unassuming 881
unatoned 951
unattached 44
unattackable 664
unattainable 471
unattained 732
unattempted 623
unattended 87
　- to 460
unattested
　not evidence 468
　(*unrecorded* 552)
unattracted
　indifferent 866 (616)
unattractive 866
unauthenticated
　improved 468
　uncertain 475
　inexact 495
unauthoritative
　uncertain 475
unauthorized
　prohibited 761
　undue 925
　lawless 964
unavailing *useless* 645
　failure 732
unavenged 918

unavoidable *certain* 474
    necessary 601
unavowed 489
unawakened 683
unaware *ignorant* 491
    unexpecting 508
unawed 861
unbalanced 28
unbar 750
unbearable 830
unbeaten 123
unbeauteous 846
unbecoming
    incongruous 24
    disreputable 874
    undue 925
    dishonorable 940
    - a gentleman 895
unbefitting *inapt* 24
    undue 925
    improbity 940
    [*see* unbecoming]
unbegotten 2
unbeguile *inform* 527
    disclose 529
unbegun
    unprepared 674
unbeheld (447)
unbelief **485**
    irreligion 989
    (*incredulity* 487)
unbelievable 485
unbeliever *infidel* 989
unbelieving 485
unbeloved 898
unbend *straighten* 246
    repose 687
    - the mind 452
unbending *hard* 323
    resolute 604
unbenevolent 907
unbenign 907
unbent 246
unbeseeming
    vulgar 851
    dishonorable 940
unbesought
    not ask 766
    (*spontaneous* 602)
unbestowed (785)
unbetrayed 939
unbewailed 932
unbiased *wise* 498
    free 748
    (*spontaneous* 602a)
unbidden *willful* 600
    disobedient 742
unbigoted 498
unbind *detach* 44
    release 750
unblamable 946
unblamed 946
unblemished
    perfect 650
    innocent 946
unblenching 861
unblended 42
unblest
    unfortunate 735
    not approved 932
    - with 777a

unblown 674
unblushing *proud* 878
    vain 880
    imprudent 885
unboastful 881
unbodied 317
unboiled 674
unbolt *liberate* 750
    (*unfasten* 44)
unbookish 491
unborn *not existing* 2
    destined 152
    (*future* 121)
unbosom oneself 529
unbought
    not bought 796
    honorary 815
    honorable 939
    unselfish 942
unbound *free* 748
    exempt 927a
unbounded
    infinite 105
    (*great* 31)
    (*large* 192)
    (*space* 180)
unbrace *weaken* 160
    relax 655
unbreathed 526
unbred 895
unbribed
    honorable 939
    disinterested 942
unbridled *violent* 173
    lax 738
    free 748
unbroken *entire* 50
    continuous 69
    preserved 670
    unviolated 939
    - extent 69
unbruised 50
unbuckle 44
unburden
    - one's mind 529
unburdened 705
unburied 362
unbuttoned 748
uncalculating 863
uncalled for
    redundant 641
    useless 645
    not used 678
uncandid *insincere* 544
    morose 907
uncanny *ugly* 846
    spectral 980a
uncanonical 984
uncared for
    neglected 460
    indifferent 866
    disliked 867
    hated 898
uncase (226)
uncate 245
uncaught *free* 748
uncaused 156
unceasing 112, 143
uncensured 931
unceremonious
    vain 880

discourteous 895
uncertain
    irregular 139
    not certain 475
    doubtful 485
    embarrassing 704
    in an - degree 32
uncertainty **475**
unchain *unfasten* 44
    liberate 750
unchained *free* 748
unchallenged   *assent*
    488
    due 924
unchangeable
    stable 150
    persevering 604a
unchanged 16, 141
unchangingly 136
uncharitable 907
unchartered *undue* 925
    illegal 964
unchaste 961
unchastised 970
unchecked 748
uncheerful 837
unchequered 141
unchivalric 940
unchristian
    heterodox 984
    irreligious 989
uncial 590
unciform 245
uncinated 244
uncircumscribed 180
uncircumspect 460
uncivil *vulgar* 851
    rude 895
uncivilized *low* 876
    uncourteous 895
unclad 226
unclaimed 748
unclassed (59)
unclassical 851
unclassified (59)
uncle *kin* 11
    my -'s *pawnshop* 787
unclean 653
    - spirit 978, 980
uncleanness **653**
Uncle Sam **188**
unclipped 50
unclog *facilitate* 705
    liberate 750
unclose *open* 260
    liberate 750
unclothed 226
unclouded *light* 420
    visible 446
    (*joyful* 827)
unclubbable 893
unclutch 790
uncoif 226
uncoil *evolve* 313
    (*straighten* 246)
uncollected (73)
uncolored
    achromatic 429
    true 494
    (*veracious* 543)
uncombed *dirty* 653

vulgar 851
uncombined
    simple 42
    incoherent 47
uncomeatable 471
uncomely 846
uncomfortable
    annoyed 828
    annoying 830
uncommendable
    blamable 932
    bad 945
    guilt 947
uncommensurable 24
uncommon
    unimitated 20
    exceptional 83
    infrequent 137
uncommonly 31
uncommonness 137
uncommunicated 781
uncommunicative 528
uncompact 322
uncompassionate 914a
uncompelled 748
uncomplaisant 764
    (895)
uncompleted
    incomplete 53
    unfinished 730
    failure 732
uncomplying
    disobedient 742
    refusing 764
uncompounded 42
uncompressed *light* 320
    rare 322
uncompromising
    conformable 82
    severe 739
unconcealable 525
unconceived
    uncreated 12
    unintelligible 519
unconcern
    insensible 823
    indifferent 866
unconcerned *tolerant*
    740
    [*see* unconcern]
unconcocted 674
uncondemned 970
unconditional
    complete 52
    free 748
    permission 760
    consent 762
    release 768a
unconducive 175a
unconfined 748
unconfirmed 475
unconformity
    disagreement 24
    irregularity **83**
unconfused
    methodical 58
    clear 518
unconfuted
    demonstrated 478
    true 494
uncongealed 333

uninformed 491
uningenuous 544
uninhabit *absence* 187
  secluded 893
uninhabitable 187, 893
uninhabited 187, 893
uninitiated
  ignorant 491
  unskillful 699
uninjured *perfect* 650
  healthy 654
  preserved 670
uninjurious 656
uninquisitive 456
uninspired
  unexcited 823
  (*unactuated* 616)
uninstructed 491
unintellectual
  incogitant 452
  imbecile 499
unintellectuality 450a
unintelligent 32, 499
unintelligibility **519**,
  571
unintelligible 519
  - *style* 571
  render - 538
unintended 621
unintentional
  necessary 601
  undesigned 621
uninterested
  incurious 456
  weary 841
  dull 843
uninteresting 643
unintermitting
  unbroken 69
  durable 110
  continuing 143
  persevering 604a
uninterrupted
  continuous 69
  perpetual 112
  unremitting 893
  - *existence* 112
unintroduced 893
uninured
  unaccustomed 614
  (*unprepared* 674)
uninvented 526
uninvestigated 491
uninvited 893
uninviting 830
union *agreement* 23
  junction 43
  combination 48
  concurrence 178
  party 712
  concord 714
  marriage 903
  - *down flag* 550
union jack 550
union pipes 417
unique *dissimilar* 18
  original 20
  unequal 28
  exceptional 83
  alone 87
unirritable 826

722

unirritating 174
unison *agreement* 23
  melody 413
  concord 714
  (*uniform* 16)
  in - *melody* 413
unisulcate 259
unit 87
Unitarian 984
unitary 87
unite *join* 43
  combine 48
  component 56
  assemble 72
  concur 178
  converge 290
  party 712
  (*agree* 23)
  - in pairs 89
  - one's efforts 709
  - with *coöperate* 709
united *coherent* 46
  concord 714
United States courts
  966
unity *identity* 13
  uniformity 16
  whole 50
  complete 52
  single **87**
  concord 714
  - of time 120
Unity, Trinity in - 976
universal 78
  - Church 983a
  - concept 450
  - favorite 899
  - joint 272, 633
  - language 560
  -ly present 186
  - predicament 25
universality 52
universalize 78
universe 318
university 542
  go to the - 539
  - degree 873
  - education 537
unjust *wrong* 923
  impious 988
unjustifiable
  wrong 923
  inexcusable 938
  wicked 945
unjustified 923
  undue 925
unkempt *rough* 256
  unclean 653
  vulgar 851
unkennel *eject* 297
  disclose 529
unkind 907
  -est cut of all 828
unkindness hard - 907
unknightly 940
unknit (44)
unknot 705
unknowable 519
unknowing 491
unknown
  ignorant 491

  latent 526
  - quantities 491
  - to fame
  inglorious 874
  lowborn 876
unlabored
  - *style* 578
  unprepared 674
unlace (44)
unlade 297
unladylike
  vulgar 851
  rude 895
unlamented
  hated 898
  disapproved 932
unlatch 44
unlawful *undue* 925
  illegal 964
unlearn 506
unlearned 491
unleavened 674
unless
  circumstances 8
  except 83
  qualification 469
  (*condition* 770)
unlettered 491
  - Muse 579
unlicensed 761
unlicked
  unprepared 674
  vulgar 851
  clownish 876
  - cub *shapeless* 241
  unmannerly 895
unlike 18
unlikely 471, 473
unlimber 323
unlimited *great* 31
  infinite 105
  free 748
  - space 180
unlink (44)
unliquefied 321
unlively *grave* 837
  dull 843
unload *displace* 185
  eject 297
  disencumber 705
  sell 796
unlock *unfasten* 44
  discover 480a
  (*explain* 462)
unlooked for 508
unloose *unfasten* 44
  liberate 750
unloved 898
unlovely 846
unlucky
  inopportune 135
  bad 649
  unfortunate 735
  in pain 830
unmade 2
unmaimed 654
unmake 145
unman *castrate* 38
  render powerless 158
  madden 837
  frighten 860

unmanageable
  unwieldy 647
  perverse 704
unmanly
  effeminate 374
  dishonorable 940
unmanned
  dejected 837
  cowardly 862
unmannered 895
unmannerly 895
unmarked 460
unmarred *sound* 654
  preserved 670
unmarried 904
unmask *disclose* 529
  (*show* 525)
unmatched
  different 15
  dissimilar 18
  unparalleled 20
  unequal 28
unmeaningness **517**
unmeant 517
unmeasured
  infinite 105
  undistinguished 465a
  abundant 639
unmeditated
  impulsive 612
  (*undesigned* 621)
unmeet 925
unmellowed 674
unmelodious 414, 713
unmelted 321
unmentionable 874
unmentionables 225
unmentioned 526
unmerciful
  pitiless 914a
  (*malevolent* 907)
unmerited 925
unmethodical 59
unmindful
  inattentive 458
  neglectful 460
  ungrateful 917
unmingled 42
unmissed 460
unmistakable
  certain 474
  intelligible 518
  manifest 525
  affirmation 535
  (*visible* 446)
unmitigable 173
unmitigated *great* 31
  complete 52
  violent 173
unmixed 42
unmodified (141)
unmolested *safe* 664
  content 831
unmoneyed 804
unmoral 823
unmourned 898
unmoved *quiescent* 265
  obstinate 606
  insensible 823
  (*resolute* 604)
  (*uninduced* 616)

unmusical 414
- voice 581
unmuzzle 748
unnamed 565
unnatural
exceptional 83
affected 855
spiteful 907
unnecessary
redundant 641
useless 645
inexpedient 647
unneeded 645
unneighborly 895
unnerved *powerless* 158
weak 160
dejected 837
unnoted *neglected* 460
ignoble 874
unnoticed 460, 874
unnumbered 105
unnurtured 674
unobeyed 742
unobjectionable
good 648
pretty good 651
innocent 946
unobnoxious 648
unobscured 420
unobservant 458
unobserved 460
unobstructed *clear* 705
free 749
(*unopposed* 709)
unobtainable 471
unobtained 777a
unobtrusive 881
unoccupied *vacant* 187
unthinking 452
doing nothing 681
inactive 683
leisured 685
secluded 893
unoffended
enduring 826
humble 879
unofficial 964
unoften 137
unopened 261
unopposed 709
unordinary 20, 83
unorganized 358
unprepared 674
- matter 358
unornamental 846
unornamented
- *style* 576
simple 849
unorthodox 984
unostentatious 881
unowed 807
unowned 782
unpacific
discordant 713
warfare 722
unpacified 713
unpack *unfasten* 44
take out 297
unpaid *debt* 806
honorary 815
- worker *volunteer* 602

unpalatable
unsavory 395
disagreeable 830
(*dislike* 867)
unparagoned
supreme 33
best 648
perfect 650
unparalleled
unimitated 20
unequaled 28
supreme 33
exceptional 83
best 648
unpardonable
inexcusable 938
wicked 945
**unparliamentary
language**
discourteous 895
cursing 908
unpassable 261
unpassionate 826
unpatriotic 911
unpatterned 28
unpeaceful
contention 720
war 722
unpeered 28
unpeople
emigration 297
banishment 893
(*displace* 185)
unperceived
neglected 460
unknown 491
(*latent* 526)
unperformed 730
unperjured
truthful 543
honorable 939
unperplexed 498
unpersuadable
obstinate 606
unpersuaded 616
unperturbed 826
unphilosophical 499
unpierced 261
unpin (44)
unpitied 932
unpitying *pitiless* 914a
(*angry* 900)
(*malevolent* 907)
unplaced 185
unplagued 831
unpleasant 830
unpleasing 830
unplumbed 104
unpoetical *prose* 598
matter of fact 703
unpointed *blunt* 254
unpolished *rough* 256
inelegant 579
unprepared 674
vulgar 851
rude 895
unpolite 895
unpolluted *good* 648
perfect 650
unpopular
disagreeable 830

dislike 867
unpopularity
hatred 898
unportioned 804
unpossessed 777a
unpracticed (699)
unprecedented
exceptional 83
rare 137
unprejudiced 498, 748
unpremeditated
impulsive 612
undesigned 621
unprepared 674
unprepared 674
unprepossessed 498
unprepossessing 846
unpresentable 851
unpretending 881
unpretentious 881
unprevented 748
unprincipled 945
unprivileged 925
unprized 483
unproclaimed 526
unproduced
inexistent 2
unproductive
useless 645
unproductiveness 169
unproficiency 699
unprofitable
unproductive 169
useless 645
inexpedient 647
bad 649
unprogressive 659
unprolific 169
unpromising 859
unprompted 612
unpronounced
latent 526
unpropitious
ill-timed 135
opposed 708
adverse 735
hopeless 859
unproportioned
(*disagreeing* 24)
unprosperous 735
unprotected 665
unproved 477
unprovided
scanty 640
unprepared 674
unprovoked (616)
unpublished 526
unpunctual *tardy* 133
untimely 135
irregular 139
unpunished 970
unpurchased 796
unpurified 653
unpurposed 621
unpursued 624
unqualified
incomplete 52
impotent 158
certain 474
unprepared 674
inexpert 699

unentitled 925
- *truth* 494
unquelled 173
unquenchable
strong 159
desire 865
unquenched
violence 173
heat 382
unquestionable
certain 474
unquestionably
assent 488
unquestioned 474
agreed upon 488
unquiet *motion* 264
agitation 315
excitable 825
unravel *untie* 44
arrange 60
straighten 246
evolve 313
discover 480a
interpret 522
disembarrass 705
(*solve* 462)
unreached 304
unread *ignorant* 491
unready 674
unreal *not existing* 2
unsubstantial 4
erroneous 495
imaginary 515
unreasonable
impossible 471
illogical 477
misjudging 481
foolish 499
capricious 608
exorbitant 814
unjust 923
unreasoning 452
unreclaimed 951
unrecognizable 146
unreconciled 713
unrecorded 552
unrecounted 55
uncumbent 212
unreduced 31
unrefined 851
unreflecting 458
unreformed 951
unrefreshed 688
unrefuted *proved* 478
true 494
unregarded
neglected 460
unrespected 929
unregenerate 988
unregistered 552
unreined 748
unrelated 10
unrelenting
pitiless 914a
revengeful 919
(*malevolent* 907)
unreliable
uncertain 475
vacillating 605
insecure 665
unrelieved 835

unremarked 460
unremembered 506
unremitting
  continuous 69, 143
  continuing 110
  persevering 604a
  (industrious 682)
unremoved 184
unremunerated 808
unrenewed 141
unrepaid (806)
unrepealed 141
unrepeated single 87
  few 103
unrepentant 951
unrepining 831
unreplenished 640
unreported (526)
unrepressed 173
unreproached 946
unreproved 946
unrequited owing 806
  ingratitude 917
unresented
  forgiven 918
unresenting
  enduring 826
unreserved
  manifest 525
  veracious 543
  artless 703
unresisted 743
unresisting 725
unresolved 605
unrespected 929
unrespited 971
unrest changeable 149
  moving 264
unrestored fatigue 688
unrestrained
  capricious 608
  unencumbered 705
  free 748
unrestricted
  undiminished 31
  free 748
unretracted 535
unrevealed (528)
unrevenged 918
unreversed 143
unrevoked 143
unrewarded
  unpaid 806
  ingratitude 917
unrhymed 598
unriddle
  find out 480a
  disclose 529
  (interpret 522)
unrig 645
unrighteous 945
unrip 260
unripe youth 127
  sour 397
  unprepared 674
  - fruit 397
unrivaled
  unequaled 28
  supreme 33
  (good 648)
unrivet (44)

unrobe (226)
unroll evolve 313
  display 525
  (unravel 47)
  (straighten 246)
unromantic 494
unroof (226)
unroot extract 301
  (destroy 162)
unruffled calm 174
  quiet 265
  unaffected 823
  placid 826
  imperturbable 871
  (in order 58)
unruly violent 173
  obstinate 606
  disobedient 742
unsaddle 756
unsafe 665
unsaid 526
unsalable
  useless 645
  selling 796
  cheap 815
unsaluted 929
unsanctified
  impiety 988
  irreligion 989
unsanctioned 925
unsated 865
unsatisfactory
  inexpedient 647
  bad 649
  displeasing 830
  discontent 832
unsatisfied
  discontented 832
  desirous 865
unsavoriness 395
unsavory insipid 391
  not savory 395
  inedible 867
unsay recant 607
  (negation 536)
unscanned 460
unscathed 654
unscattered (72)
unscholarly 491
unschooled
  ignorant 491
  (unskillful 699)
unscientific
  illogical 477
  (erroneous 495)
unscoured 653
unscreened (665)
unscrew (44)
unscriptural 984
unscrupulous 940
unseal 529
unsearched 460
unseasonable
  inappropriate 24
  ill-timed 135
  (inexpedient 647)
unseasoned
  unaccustomed 614
  unprepared 674
unseat displace 185
  abrogate 756

unseconded
  unassisted 706
unseemly
  inexpedient 647
  ugly 846
  vulgar 851
  undue 925
  vicious 945
unseen invisible 447
  neglected 460
  latent 526
unsegmentic 357
unseldom 136
unselfconscious 852
unselfish 816, 942
unseparated 46
unserviceable 645
unservient 645
unsettle derange 61
unsettled mutable 149
  displaced 185
  uncertain 475
  - in one's mind 503
unsevered 50
unsex 146
unshackle (untie 44)
  (liberate 750)
unshackled (free 748)
unshaded
  manifest 525
unshaken strong 159
  (resolute 604)
  - belief 484
unshapely 241, 846
unshapen
  amorphous 241
  (ugly 846)
unshared 777
unsheathe
  (uncover 226)
  - the sword war 722
unsheltered 665
unshielded 665
unshifting 143
unship 297
unshipment 185
unshocked 823
unshorn 50
unshortened 200
unshrinking
  determined 604
  courageous 861
unsifted 460
unsightly 846
unsinged 670
unskilled 699
unskillfulness 699
unslaked 865
unsleeping
  persevering 604a
  active 682
unsmooth 256
unsociable 893
unsocial 893
unsoiled 652
unsold 777
unsolder (disjoin 44)
  (incoherence 47)
unsoldierlike 862
unsolicitous 866
unsolved 526

unsophisticated
  simple 42
  genuine 494
  artless 703
  (good 648)
unsorted 59
unsought avoided 623
  unrequested 766
unsound weak 160
  illogical 477
  erroneous 495
  deceptive 545
  imperfect 651
  speculative 665
  (unhealthy 655)
  - mind 503
unsown 674
unsparing
  abundant 639
  severe 739
  liberal 816
  with an - hand 818
unspeakable great 31
  wonderful 870
unspecified 78
unspent 678
unspied 526
unspiritual 316
unspoiled good 648
unspoken (581)
unspotted clean 652
  beautiful 845
  innocent 946
unstable
  changeable 149
  inverted 218
  vacillating 605
  precarious 665
  - equilibrium 149
unstaid 149
unstained clean 652
  honorable 939
unstatesmanlike 699
unsteadfast 605
unsteady mutable 149
  irresolute 605
  in danger 665
  (fickle 607)
unstinted 639
unstirred 823, 826
unstopped
  continuing 143
  open 260
unstored 640
unstrained turbid 653
  relaxed 687
  - meaning 516
unstrengthened 160
unstruck 823
unstrung 160
unstudied 460
unsubject 748
unsubmissive 742
unsubstantial 4
  weak 160
  immaterial 317
  rare 322
  erroneous 495
  imaginary 515
unsubstantiality 4
unsuccess 732

unsuccessful 732
unsuccessive 70
unsuitable
  incongruous 24
  inexpedient 647
  - time 135
unsullied *clean* 652
  honorable 939
  (*guiltless* 946)
unsung 526
unsupplied 640
unsupported
  weak 160
  (*unassisted* 706)
  - by evidence 468
unsuppressed 141
unsurmountable 471
unsurpassed 33
unsusceptible 823
unsuspected *belief* 484
  latent 526
unsuspecting
  hopeful 858
unsuspicious *belief* 484
  artless 703
  hope 858
unsustainable
  erroneous 495
unsustained *error* 495
  (*weak* 160)
  (*unassisted* 706)
unswayed (616)
unsweet 395, 414
unswept 653
unswerving
  straight 246
  direct 278
  persevering 604a
unsymmetric
  unconformable 83
unsymmetrical
  irregular 59
  shapeless 241
  distorted 243
unsympathetic 24
unsystematic 59, 139
untack (44)
untainted *pure* 652
  healthy 654
  honorable 939
untalked of 526
untamed *rude* 851
  ferocious 907
untangled (58)
untarnished
  honorable 939
  (*innocent* 946)
untasted 391
untaught *ignorant* 491
  untrained 674
untaxed 815
unteach 538
unteachable
  foolish 499
  unskillful 699
untempted (616)
untenable
  powerless 158
  illogical 477
  undefended 725
  secluded 893

untenanted 187
unthanked 917
unthankful 917
unthankfulness 915
unthawed *solid* 321
  cold 383
unthinkable 471
unthinking
  unconsidered 452
  involuntary 601
unthought of
  unconsidered 452
  neglected 460
unthreatened 664
unthrifty
  unprepared 674
  prodigal 818
unthrone 756
untidy *in disorder* 59
  slovenly 653
untie *liberate* 750
  (*loose* 44)
  - the knot 705
until 106 (108)
  - now 118
untilled 674
untimely 135
  - end 360
untinged *simple* 42
  (*uncolored* 429)
untired 689
untiring 604a
untitled 876
untold *countless* 105
  uncertain 475
  latent 526
  secret 528
untouched *disused* 678
  insensible 823
untoward *ill-timed* 135
  bad 649
  unprosperous 735
  unpleasant 830
untraced 526
untracked 526
untractable
  obstinate 606
  unskillful 699
untrained
  unaccustomed 614
  unprepared 674
  unskilled 699
untrammeled
  easy 705
  free 748
untranslatable 523
untranslated 20, 523
untraveled 265
untreasured 640
untried *new* 123
  not decided 461
untrimmed
  unprepared 674
  matter-of-fact 703
  simple 849
untrodden *new* 123
  impervious 261
  not used 678
untroubled *calm* 174
  peaceful 721
untrue *erroneous* 495

  unveracious 546
untrustworthy
  uncertain 475
  erroneous 495
  danger 665
  dishonorable 940
untruth **546**
untruthfulness 544
untunable 414
unturned 246
untutored *ignorant* 491
  unprepared 674
  artless 703
untwine 313
untwist *evolve* 313
  (*separate* 44, 47)
  (*straighten* 246)
unused
  unaccustomed 614
  unskillful 699
unusual 83
unusually *very* 31
unutterable *great* 31
  unmeaning 517
  wonderful 870
unvalued
  underrated 483
  undesired 866
  disliked 898
unvanquished 748
unvaried *uniform* 16
  monotonous 104
  continuing 143
  - *style* 575, 576
unvarnished
  true 494, 543
  - *style* 576
  matter-of-fact 703
  simple 849
  - tale *true* 494
  veracious 543
unvarying 143
unveil *manifest* 525
  disclose 529
  (*manifest* 525)
unventilated 261
unveracious 544
unversed *ignorant* 491
  (*unskilled* 699)
unvexed 831
unviolated 939
unvisited 893
unvitiated (648)
unwakened 683
unwarlike 862
unwarmed 383
unwarned
  unexpected 508
  danger 665
unwarped judgment
  498
unwarrantable
  wrong 923
unwarranted 923
  illogical 477
  undue 925
  illegal 964
unwary *neglectful* 460
  (*rash* 863)
unwashed 653
  great - 876

unwaste (639)
unwatchful 460
unwavering 604a
unweakened 159
unwearied
  persevering 604a
  indefatigable 682
  refreshed 689
unweave 60
unwedded 904
unweeded garden 674
unweeting 491
unweighed 460
unwelcome
  disagreeable 830
  unsocial 893
unwell 655
unwept 831
unwholesome 657
unwieldy *large* 192
  heavy 319
  cumbersome 647
  difficult 704
  ugly 846
unwilling *dissent* 489
  - service 603
unwillingness **603**
unwind *evolve* 313
  (*straighten* 246)
unwiped 653
unwisdom 499
unwise 499
unwished 866
unwithered 159
unwitnessed (526)
unwitting
  ignorant 491
  involuntary 601
unwittingly
  undesignedly 621
unwomanly 373
unwonted
  unimitated 20
  unusual 83
  unaccustomed 614
unworldly 939
unworn 159
unworshiped 929
unworthy
  shameful 874
  vicious 945
  - of belief 485
  - of notice 643
unwrap 246
unwrinkled 255
unwritten *old* 124
  latent 526
  obliterated 552
  spoken 582
  - law 697, 963
unwrought 674
unyielding *stable* 150
  tough 323
  unbending 604
  obstinate 606
  resisting 719
unyoke (44)
up *aloft* 206
  vertical 212
  ascent 305
  effervescing 353

excited 824
all - with
  destruction 162
  failure 732
  adversity 735
  prices looking - 814
  the game is - 735
  time - 111
  - and at them 716
  - and coming 698
  - and doing 682
  - and down 314
  - for discussion 454
  - in 698
  - in arms
    prepared 673
    active 682
    opposition 708
    attack 716
    resistance 719
    warfare 722
  - on end 212
  - to [*see below*]
Upanishads 986
upas tree 663
upbear *support* 215
  raise 307
upbraid 932
upcast 305, 307
upgrade 305, 654
upgrow 206
upgrowth
  expansion 194
  ascent 305
upheaval 146, 307
upheave 307
uphill *acclivity* 217
  ascent 305
  laborious 686
  difficult 704
uphoist 307
uphold *continue* 143
  support 215
  evidence 467
  aid 707
  praise 931
  preserve 976
upholder 488, 711
upholstery 633
upland 180
uplands 206, 344
uplift *elevation* 307
  improvement 658
upon - my honor 535
  - oath 535
  - which *after* 117
  future 121
upper 206
  - case *printing* 591
  - classes 875
  - hand *influence* 175
  success 731
  sway 737
  - story *summit* 210
  intellect 450
  wisdom 498

- ten thousand 875
uppermost *summit* 210
  say what comes - 612
  - in one's thoughts
    memory 505
  - in the mind
    thought 451
    topic 454
    attention 457
upraise 307
uprear 307
upright *vertical* 212
  straight 246
  honest 939
  - piano 417
uprise 305
uprising 146, 742
uproar *disorder* 59
  violence 173
  noise 404
uproarious
  excitable 825
uproariousness   404,
  825
uproot
  extract 301
  (*destroy* 162)
ups and downs of life
  events 151
  adversity 735
upset *destroy* 162
  invert 218
  throw down 308
  defeat 731
  excite 824
  disconcert 874
upshot *result* 154
  judgment 480
  completion 729
  (*end* 67)
upside down 218
upstairs 206
upstart *newness* 123
  prosperous 734
  plebeian 876
upstream
  with difficulty 704
up to *time* 106
  power 157
  knowing 490
  skillful 698
  - one's ears 641
  - one's eyes 641
  - snuff 702
  - the brim 52
  - the mark *equal* 27
  sufficient 639
  good 648
  due 924
  - the scratch 861
  - this time *time* 106
  past 122
upturn 210
upturned 305, 307
upward 305
  - flight 305

upwards 206
  - of *more* 33
  plurality 100
uranic 318
uranography 318
uranolite 318
uranology 318
uranometry 318
urban 189
urbane 894
urceole 998
urceus 191, 998
urchin *child* 129, 167
  small 193
  wretch 949
urge *violence* 173
  impel 276
  incite 615
  hasten 684
  beg 765
urgency *need* 865
  [*see* urgent]
urgent *required* 630
  important 642
  haste 684
  request 765
urn *vase* 191
  funeral 363
  heater 386
  cinerary - 363
Ursa Major 318
Ursa Minor 318
usable 644
usage *custom* 613
  use 677
  (*rule* 80)
usance 806
use *habit* 613
  waste 638
  utility 644
  employ 677
  property 780
  be of - to *aid* 707
  benevolence 906
  in - 677
  make good - of 658
  - a right 924
  - loosely 465a
  - one's discretion 600
  - one's endeavor 675
  - up 677
  used to 613
used up *deteriorated* 659
  fatigue 688
  weary 841
  satiated 869
useful *instrumental* 633
  utility 644
  serviceable 746
  render - 677
useless   *unproductive*
  169
  wasted 638
  inutility 645
user 677
  right of - 780

Ushas 979
usher *attendant* 263
  receive 296
  teacher 540
  servant 746
  courtesy 894
  marriage 903
  - in *precedence* 62
  begin 66
  herald 116
  precession 280
  announce 511
  - into the world 161
usine 691
usquebaugh 959
ustulate 384
ustulation 384
usual *ordinary* 82
  customary 613
usucapion 777
usufruct 677
usurer *lender* 787
  merchant 797
  credit 805
  miser 819
usurious 819
usurp *assume* 739
  seize 789
  illegal 925
  - authority 738
usurpation
  [*see* usurp]
  authority 737
  insolence 885
usurper 706, 737
usury 806
utensil *recipient* 191
  instrument 633
utilitarian *teaching* 537
  useful 677
  philanthropy 910
utilitarianism 451
utility 644
  general - *actor* 599
utilize 677
utmost 33
  do one's - 686
  - height 210
Utopia *visionary* 515
  hopeful 858
utricle 191
utter *extreme* 31
  distribute 73
  disclose 529
  publish 531
  speak 580, 582
  money 800
utterance [*see* utter]
utterly *completely* 52
uttermost 31
  to the - parts of the
    earth
  space 180
  distance 196
uxoricide 361
uxorious 897

vaulted *curved* 245
  concave 252
vaulting *superior* 33
  aspiring 865
vaunt 884
vauntmure 717
vaurien 949
vavasour *possessor* 779
  nobleman 875
veal 298
vection 270
Vedanta 451
Vedantism 984
Vedas 986
vedette 668
Vedic 124
veer *change* 140
  deviate 279
  go back 283
  change intention 607
vega 344
vegetability 365
vegetable 298, **367**
  - kingdom 367
  - life 365
  - oil 356
  - physiology 369
vegetality 365
vegetarian 298, 367, 953
vegetarianism 298
vegetate *exist* 1
  grow 194, 365, 367
  inactive 683
  insensible 823
vegetation **365**
  inaction 681
vegetative 365, 367
vegetism 365
vehemence
  violence 173
  feeling 821
  emotion 825
vehement
  - language 574
vehicle *carriage* **272**
  instrument 631
vehicular 272
veil *covering* 225
  shade 424
  conceal 528
  ambush 530
  draw aside the - 529
  take the - *seclude* 893
  church 995
veiled 475
  (*invisible* 447)
vein *intrinsicality* 5
  tendency 176
  thin 203
  thread 205
  conduit 350
  humor 602
  mine 636
  affections 820
  in the - 602
  not in the - 603
veined 440
veinlet 205
veldt 344
veldtschoen 225
728

velitation 720
velleity 600
vellicate 315
vellicating 392
vellicative 315, 392
vellum 590
velo 466
veloce *music* 415
velocimeter 274
velocipede 272
velocity
  rate of motion 264
  swiftness **274**
  angular - 244
velumen 255
velutinous 255
velvet *smooth* 255
  pile 256
  pleasure 377
  fabric 635
  on - *easy* 705
velveteen 255
vena 350
venal *price* 812
  stingy 819
  dishonest 940
  selfish 943
venation 622
vend 796
vendaval 349
vendee 795
vender 796
vendetta 919
vendible 796
venditation 884
vendor 796
vendue 796
veneer *layer* 204
  covering 223
venenation 659
venerable *old* 124
  aged 128
  sage 500
  respected 928
venerated 500
veneration *respect* 928
  piety 987
venereal disease 655
venery *killing* 361
  hunting 622
  impurity 961
venesection
  ejection 297
  remedy 662
Venetian blinds 351, 424
vengeance 919
  cry to heaven for - 923
  with a - *greatly* 31
  violent 173
vengeful 919
venial 937
venire 969
  - facias 969
venison 298, 394
vennel 627
venom *bane* 663
  malignity 907
venomous *bad* 649
  poisonous 657

  dangerous 666
  rude 895
  maleficent 907
venose 205
vent *opening* 260
  egress 295
  air pipe 351
  disclose 529
  escape 671
  sale 796
  find - *egress* 295
  passage 302
  publish 531
  escape 671
  give - to *emit* 297
  disclose 529
  - one's rage 900
  - one's spleen 900
ventage 351
venter 191
venthole 260, 351
ventiduct 351
ventilabrum 349
ventilate *begin* 66
  air 338
  wind 349
  discuss 595
  - a question
  inquiry 461
  reasoning 476
ventilative 349
ventilator *wind* 349
  air pipe 351
ventose 349
ventosity 349
vent peg *stopper* 263
  safety 666
  escape 671
ventricle 191
ventricose 250
ventriloquism 580
ventriloquist 580
venture *experiment* 463
  presume 472
  chance 621
  danger 665
  try 675
  undertaking 676
  invest 787
  courage 861
  I'll - to say 535
venturesome
  undertaking 676
  brave 861
  rash 863
venue 74, 183
venula 205
Venus
  luminary 318, 423
  -'s flytrap 545
  beauty 845
  love 897
veracity **543**
veranda 191
verbal 562
  - intercourse
  speech 582
  interlocution 588
  - quibble
  absurdity 497
  wit 842

verbarian 562
verbatim *imitation* 19
  exact 494
  literal 516
  words 562
  - report 551
verbiage
  unmeaning 517
  words 562
  diffuse 573
  (*absurdity* 497)
verbosity *words* 562
  diffuse 573
  loquacity 584
verdant
  vegetation 367
  green 435
verd antique 435
verdict *opinion* 480
  lawsuit 969
  snatch a - *cheat* 545
  cunning 702
verdigris 435
verdine 435
verditer 435
verdure *vegetation* 367
  green 435
verecundity
  humility 879
  modesty 881
Verein 712
verge *tendency* 176
  near 197
  edge 231
  limit 233
  direction 278
vergent 67
verger 996
veridical 467, 543
  - hallucination 992a
veriest 31
verification *test* 463
  warrant 771
verificative 467
verify 463
  evidence 467
  demonstrate 478
  find out 480a
verily *truly* 494
  (*positively* 32)
verisimilitude 472
veritable 1, 494
verity 494
verjuice 397
vermeology 368
vermes 368
vermicelli 298
vermicular
  convoluted 248
  worm 366
vermiculation 221
vermiform 248, 249
vermifuge 662
vermilion 434
vermin *animal* 366
  unclean 653
  base 876
vernacular *native* 188
  internal 221
  language 560
  habitual 613

vinaigrette 400
vincible *impotent* 158
  (*weak* 160)
vincture 43
vinculum **45**
vindicate
  evidence 467
  avenge 919
  justify 937
  - a right 924
vindication **937**
vindicator *revenge* 919
vindictive
  irascible 901
  revengeful 919
vine 367
vinegar 397
  - aspect 846
vine-grower 371
vinegrub 659
vineyard *tillage* 371
  workshop 691
vingt et un 840
viniculturist 371
vintage
  agriculture 371
  store 636
vintner 797
viol 417
violaceous 437
violate *disobey* 742
  nonobservance 773
  undue 925
  dereliction 927
  ravish 961
  - a law 83
  - a usage 614
  - the law 964
violence **173**
  arbitrary 964
  do - to *bad* 649
  nonobservance 773
  undue 925
violent 173
  excitable 825
  in a - degree 31
  lay - hands on 789
  - death *death* 360
  kill 361
violet 437
  modesty 881
violin 417
violinist 416
violoncello 417
violone 417
viper *snake* 366
  bane 663
  evildoer 913
  bad man 949
viperine 366
virago 901
virent 435
virescence 435
virgate 246
virgin *new* 123
  girl 129
  spinster 904
  good woman 948
  pure 960
  - soil *ignorance* 491
  untilled 674
730

virginal 900
virginals 417
Virginia
  crooked as - fence 243
  - reel 840
viridian 435
viridity 435
virile *adolescent* 131
  strong 159
  manly 373
virtu 847, 850
virtual *inexistent* 2
  unsubstantial 5
  - image 443
virtually 5
  (*truly* 494)
virtue *power* 157
  courage 86¹
  goodness 94̶
  purity 960
  by - of *power* 157
  instrumentality 631
  in - of *authority* 737
  make a - of necessity
  no choice 609a
  skill 698
  submit 725
  compromise 774
  bear 826
virtueless 945
virtuosity *taste* 850
virtuoso 415, 416, 850
virtuous *virtue* 944
  purity 960
virulence *energy* 171
  noxiousness 649
  insalubrity 657
  discourtesy 895
  anger 900
  malevolence 907
virus *disease* 655
  poison 663
vis inertiæ *power* 157
  inertness 172
  insensibility 823
visa 488
visage *front* 234
  appearance 448
vis-à-vis *contrariety* 14
  front 234
  opposite 237
  carriage 272
viscera 221
visceral 221, 329
viscid 327, 352
viscidity 327
viscount 875
viscountship 877
viscous 352
viscum 45
vise 327, 752, 781
Vishnu 979
visibility **446**
visible 446
  (*intelligible* 518)
  become - 448
  be - 448
  darkness - 421
vision *sight* **441**
  phantasm 443
  dream 515

specter 980a
psychical research 992a
  organ of - 441
visionary *inexistent* 2
  unsubstantial 4
  impossible 471
  imaginary 515
  heterodox 984
  (*untrue* 495)
visionless 442
visit *arrival* 292
  social 892
  courtesy 894
  - behind the scenes 461
  - upon 972
visitation *disease* 655
  adversity 735
  suffering 828
  (*evil* 619)
  - of the sick 998
  -s of Providence 976
visiting 892
  on - terms
  friendship 888
  sociality 892
  - card 550
visitor
  immigrant 294
  director 694
  friend 890
visor 530
vista *convergence* 260
  sight 441
  appearance 448
  expectation 507
  - of time 109
visual 441
  - organ 441
visualize 220
vitability 359
vital *life* 359
  important 642
  - air 359
  - force 359
  - part 3
  - principle 1
vitalic 359
vitality *stability* 150
  strength 159
  life 359
vitalize 359
vitals 221
vitiate *deteriorate* 659
vitiated *diseased* 655
viticulture 371
vitreform 425
vitreous *hard* 323
  transparent 425
vitrescent 323
vitrics 191
vitrify 323
vitrine 191
vituperate 932
vituperation 908
vituperator 936
viva! *glory* 873
  praise 931
vivace *music* 415
vivacious *active* 682

sensitive 822
  cheerful 836
vivandière 797
vivarium 370
vivâ voce 582
vive *glory be to* 873
  on the qui - 824
vivid *energetic* 171
  sensibility 375
  light 420
  color 428
  graphic 518
  (*powerful* 157)
  still -
  remembering 506
vivify *strength* 159
  life 359
vivisection *pain* 378
  cruelty 907
vixen *fox* 366
  female 374
  shrew 901
viz. [*see* videlicet]
vizier *director* 694
  deputy 759
vizor *mask* 530
  shield 717
vlei 345
vocable 562
vocabulary 562
vocal *music* 415
  voice 580
  - score 415
vocalist 416
vocalize 562, 580
vocation *business* 625
  (*duty* 926)
vocational 625
  - therapy 662
  - training 537
vociferation *loud* 404
  cry 411
  voice 580
vogue *custom* 613
  fashion 852
  fame 873
voice *sound* 402
  cry 411
  judgment 480
  promulgate 531
  affirmation 535
  express 566
  human - **580**
  choice 609
  (*belief* 484)
  give one's - for 488
  make one's - heard 175
  raise one's - *shout* 411
  speak 582
  still small -
  faint sound 405
  conscience 926
  want of - 581
  warning - 668
  - against *dissent* 489
  oppose 708
  - of the charmer 933
  - of the tempter 615
voiceless 561, 581
  - woe 837

W

succeed 731
- the earth 359
walker 268
walking delegate 758
walking gentleman 599
walking papers 756
walking-stick 727
walk-over
success 731
wall vertical 212
parietes 224
inclosure 232
refuge 666
obstacle 706
defense 717
prison 752
driven to the -
difficulty 704
go to the -
destruction 162
fail 732
pushed to the -
necessity 601
take the - repute 873
pride 878
- eyed 442
- in circumscribe 229
restrain 751
wooden -s 726
wallaby 309
wallet 191, 800
wallop 315, 972
wallow low 207
plunge 310
rotate 312
pool 343
- in pleasure 377
superabundance 641
- in riches 803
- in the mire 653
- in voluptuousness 954
wallsend 388
Wall Street chance 621
- slang 563
walnut 298, 367
across the -s 299
walrus 366
waltz music 415
dance 840
wamble vacillate 149
slowness 275
oscillate 314
dislike 867
(irresolute 605)
wampum 800
wan pale 429
sad 837
wand scepter 747
magic 993
wave a - 992
wander move 264
journey 266
deviate 279
delirium 503
the attention -s 458
wanderer 268
wandering
exceptional 83
- Jew 268
Wanderjahr 266
732

wanderlust 266
wane decrease 36
age 128
contract 195
decay 659
one's star on the - 735
wax and - 140
wanigan 273
want inferiority 34
incompleteness 53
shortcoming 304
requirement 630
insufficiency 640
poverty 804
desire 865
their -s but few 831
- of consideration 458
- of discernment 465a
- of distinction 465a
- of esteem 929
wanting
incomplete 53
absent 187
imbecile 499
found - imperfect 651
disapproval 932
guilt 947
wantless 639
wanton
uncomfortable 83
capricious 608
sufficiency 639
unrestrained 748
amusement 840
rash 863
impure 961
harlot 962
(inconsiderate 460)
wapentake 181
war 361, 722
at - disagreement 24
contention 720
at - with
opposed 708
fighting 722
declare - 713
man of - 727
seat of - 728
- correspondent 722
- news 722
- of words
talk 588
contention 720
warble 416
war castle 726
war cry alarm 669
defiance 715
war 722
ward part 51
parish 181
safety 664
asylum 666
dependent 746
restraint 751
- heeler 886
- off hindrance 706
defense 717
watch and - care 459
keeper 753
war dance
defiance 715

warden guardian 664
master 745
deputy 759
warder porter 263
guardian 664
keeper 753
- of the brain 505
wardmote 966
wardrobe 225
wardship 664
ware warning 668
merchandise 798
warehouse store 636
mart 799
warfare 361, **722**
discord 713
war horse 726
warlike 722
warlock 994
warm violent 173
near 197
hot 382
make hot 384
red 434
orange 439
wealthy 803
ardent 821
excited 824
angry 900
irascible 901
flog 972
- bath 386
- imagination 515
- man 803
- reception
repel 717
welcome 892
- the blood 824
- the cockles of the
heart 829
- up improve 658
resuscitate 660
- work 686
warmed up
repeated 104
war medal 722
warm-hearted
feeling 821
sensibility 822
friendship 888
benevolence 906
warming 384
warming pan
locum tenens 147
heater 386
preparation 673
warmth
vigorous language 574
warn dissuade 616
caution 668
(forebode 511)
- off 761
warning omen 512
caution **668**
(advice 695)
give - dismiss 678
relinquish 782
- voice alarm 669
warp change 140
tendency 176
contract 195

distort 243
navigate 267
deviate 279
prejudice 481
deteriorate 659
- and weft 329
war paint
preparation 673
warpath 722
warped
narrow-minded 481
imperfect 651
warrant evidence 467
protest 535
order 741
permit 760
promise 768
security 771
money order 800
justify 937
death - die 360
kill 361
condemn 971
I'll - you 535
warranted 924
warranty
permission 760
promise 768
security 771
sanction 924
warren 168
warrior 726
warship 726
wart 250
war whoop 715, 722
wary cautious 864
(careful, vigilant 459)
wash cover 223
water 337
marsh 345
color 428
faint 556
cleanse 652
- down 298
- one's hands of
relinquish 624
depute 757
refuse 764
part with 782
dereliction 927
- out discolor 429
obliterate 552
wash cloth 652
washerman 652
washerwoman 652, 690
washhouse furnace 386
cleansing 652
washout 162, 348
washy weak 160
unmeaning 517
feeble style 575
wasp insect 366
narrow 203
bring a -'s nest about
one's ears 735
waspish violent 173
irascible 901
(discourteous 895)
wassail beverage 298
feast 840
drunkenness 954

waste *decrease* 36
  decrement 40a
  destroy 162
  unproductive 169
  space 180
  contract 195
  plain 344
  consumption **638**
  useless 645
  spoiled 659
  misuse 679
  loss 776
  prodigality 818
  run to -
  superfluity 641
  deteriorate 659
  - away 655
  - of years 151
  - time *inactive* 683
  watery - 341
wasted *weak* 160
  deteriorated 659
wasteful 818
waste paper
  of no force 158
  - bonds 808
waste pipe 350
waster *neglect* 460
  prodigal 818
wastethrift 818
wasting 638
  wide - 649
wastrel *vagrant* 268
  neglect 460
  outcast 893
watch *company* 72
  clock 114
  observe 441
  attend to 457
  take care of 459
  expect 507
  guardian 664
  warning 668
  keeper 573
  death - *death* 360
  warning 668
  on the - *vigilant* 459
  expectant 507
  - and ward *care* 459
  keeper 573
  - for 507
watchdog *guardian* 664
  warning 668
  keeper 753
watcher 459
watchet 438
watch fire 550
watchful 459
  - waiting
  inaction 681
  caution 864
watchhouse 752
  in the - 938
watchman
  guardian 664
  sentinel 668
  keeper 753
watchman's rattle 417
watchtower *view* 441
  signal 550
  warning 668

watchword *sign* 550
  military 722
water **337**
  - animals 370
  transparent 425
  back - 283
  cast one's bread upon
    the -s 638
  depth of - 208
  great -s 341
  hold - *proof* 478
  truth 494
  [keep one's head
    above] - 664
  land covered with -
    343
  of the first - 648
  pour - into a sieve 638
  running - 348
  spend money like -
    818
  throw cold - on 174
  walk the -s 267
water carrier 348
water color 556
water course 350
water cress 298
water cure 662
water dog 269, 361
water drinker 958
watered
  variegated 440
waterfall 348
water gap 350
water glass 556
water gruel 160
watering - cart 348
  - place 189
  - pot 348
waterless 340
water-logged
  powerless 158
  danger 665
  hindrance 706
waterman 269
watermelon 298
water nymph 979
water pipe 350
water polo 840
waterproof *dress* 225
  dry 340
  protection 664
water qualm 655
waters
  on the face of the -
    180
  - of bitterness 830
  - of oblivion 506
watershed 210
water spaniel 366
waterspout 348
water-tight
  closed 261
  dry 340
  protection 664
water wheel 633
waterworks 350
watery *wet* 337
  moist 339
  feeble style 575
  - eyes 839

- grave 360
wattle 219
wattmeter 157
Wat Tyler 742
wave *sinuous* 248
  oscillate 314
  - of water 348
  [see waive]
  - a banner 550
  - a wand 992
waver *changeable* 149
  doubt 485
  irresolute 605
waverer 605
waves 341
  buffet the -
  navigate 267
  difficult 704
  oppose 708
  lash the - 645
  plow the - 267
waveson 73
wavy 248
wax *increase* 35
  become 144
  expand 194
  soft 324
  lubrication 332
  viscid 352
  substance 356
  close as - 528
  - and wane 140
wax candle 423
waxed 356a
waxwork 554
waxy *unctuous* 355
  irate 900
way *degree* 26
  space 180
  habit 613
  road 627
  by the -
  in transitu 270
  accidental 621
  by - of *direction* 278
  method 627
  fall in the - of 186
  fight one's -
  pursue 622
  warfare 722
  find its - 302
  gather - 267
  get into the - of 613
  go one's - 293
  go your - 297
  have one's own -
  will 600
  easy 705
  succeed 731
  authority 737
  freedom 748
  havc - on 267
  in a bad - 655
  in a - *pained* 828
  in the - *near* 197
  in the - of
  hinder 706
  oppose 708
  it must have its - 601
  let it have its - 681
  long - off 196

  make one's -
  journey 266
  progression **282**
  passage 302
  prosperity 734
  make - 302
  make - for
  substitution 147
  opening 260
  turn aside 279
  avoid 623
  facilitate 705
  courtesy 894
  not know which - to
    turn 475
  on the - 282
  place in one's -
  offer 763
  put in the - of
  enable 470
  teach 537
  see one's - 490
  show the - 693
  under - *move* 264
  sail 267
  progression **282**
  depart 293
  - in 294
  - of escape 617
  - of speaking 521
  - of thinking 484
  - out 295
  wing one's - 267
Way, the - 976
wayfarer 268
wayfaring 266
waylay *deception* 545
  cunning 702
wayless 261
ways 692
  inall manner of - 278
  - and means
  means 632
  money 800
wayward
  changeable 149
  obstinate 606
  capricious 608
  sullen 901a
wayworn
  journey 266
  fatigue 688
wayzgoose 840
weak *feeble* 160
  water 337
  insipid 391
  illogical 477
  foolish 499
  - style 575
  irresolute 605
  trifling 643
  lax 738
  compassionate 914
  vicious 945
  (small 32)
  expose one's - point
  confute 479
  - point *illogical* 477
  imperfection 651
  - side *folly* 499
  vice 945

weaken *decrease* 36
  diminish 38
  enfeeble 160
  refute 468
weakened
  unhealthy 655
weaker vessel 374
weak-headed 499
weak-hearted 862
weakly *unhealthy* 655
weak-minded 499
weakness 160
 - of the flesh 945
weal 618
  common - 644
weald 367
wealth *property* 780
  riches **803**
wean
  change opinion 484
  change habit 614
  - from *dissuade* 616
  - one's thoughts from
    506
weanling 129
weapon *arms* 727
  (*instrument* 633)
weaponless 158
wear *decrease* 36
  clothes 225
  deflect 279
  use 677
  better to - out 686
  - and tear *waste* 638
  injury 659
  exertion 686
  - away *cease* 142
  deteriorate 659
  - off *cease* 142
  desuetude 614
  - on 109
  - out *deteriorate* 659
  tire 688
  - the breeches 737
weariness *ennui* **841**
wearing *wearisome* 841
  - apparel 225
wearisome *slow* 275
  laborious 686
  fatiguing 688
  painful 830
weary *fatigue* 688
  painful 828
  sad 837
  ennuyant 841
  - flat, stale, and un-
    profitable 843
  - waste 344
weasand *throat* 260
  pipe 351
weasel 366, 441
  catch a - asleep
    impossible 471
  active 682
  - words 517
weather 338
  rough &c. - *violent* 173
  wind 349
  - the storm
  stability 150
  recover 660
    734

safe 664
  succeed 731
under the - 655
  - bureau 513
  - permitting 469, 470
  - prophet 513
  - vane 149
weather-beaten
  weak 160
  damaged 659
  fatigue 688
weather-bound 751
weathercock
  changeable 149
  wind 349
  indication 550
  fickle 607
weathered 659
weather gauge 338
weatherglass 338
weatherproof
  healthy 654
  safe 664
weathertight 664
weather vane
  [*see* vane]
weatherwise 338
  foresight 510
  indication 550
  (*prediction* 511)
weave *compose* 54
  produce 161
  interlace 219
  - a tangled web 704
weazen 193, 195
web *intersection* 219
  texture 329
web-footed 219
webwork 59
wed 903
wedded 903
  - pair 903
  - to *belief* 484
  habit 613
  loving 897
  - to an opinion
  misjudgment 481
  obstinacy 606
wedding 903
  - anniversaries 883
wedge *join* 43
  angular 244
  sharp 253
  instrument 633
  thin edge of the -
  begin 66
  insinuate 228
  cunning 702
  - in 228
wedged in
  imprisoned 751
wedlock 903
wee 193
  - sma' hours 125
weed *exclude* 55
  few 103
  plant 367
  agriculture 371
  cigar 392
  trifle 643
  clean 652

 - out *eject* 297
  extract 301
weeds *dress* 225
  useless 645
  mourning 839
  widowhood 905
weedy *thin* 203
  trifling 643
week 108
weekly 138
ween *judge* 480
  believe 484
  know 490
weep *lament* 839
  pity 914
weet *judgment* 480
  knowledge 490
weetless 491
weet-weet 727
weft 329
weigh *influence* 175
  lift 307
  heavy 319
  ponder 451
  under - [*see* way]
  - anchor 267, 293
  - carefully
  discriminate 465
  - down *aggrieve* 649
  subjection 749
  - on the heart 830
  - heavy on 649
  - on the mind
  regret 833
  dejection 837
  fear 860
  - with 615
weighbridge 319
weighed [*see* weigh]
  - and found wanting
  inferior 34
  disapproved 932
weighing machine 466
weight *influence* 175
  contents 190
  gravity 319
  affirmation 535
  vigor 574
  importance 642
  attach - to 484
  carry - 175
  drag - 706
  have - *evidence* 467
  throw one's - into the
    scale 175
weightless 320
weights and measures
  466
weighty [*see* weight]
  evidence 467
weir *inclosure* 232
  conduit 350
  hindrance 706
weird *spectral* 980a
  mystic 992
  spell 993
  - sisters 994
Weismannism 357
welcome *arrival* 292
  grateful 829
  friendly 888

  sociality 892
  reception 894
weld *join* 43
  cohere 46
welfare 734
  - work 602
  - worker 602
welkin *worlds* 318
  air 338
  make the - ring 411
well *much* 31
  origin 153
  deep 208
  exude 295
  pool 343
  flow 348
  assent 488
  good 618
  store 636
  healthy 654
  spa 662
  act - 944
  all's - 664
  drop a bucket into an
    empty - 645
  get - 660
  go on - 734
  let - alone
  quiescence 265
  inaction 681
  think - of 931
  treat - 906
  turn out - 731
  - and good *assent* 488
  consent 762
  content 831
  - done! 931
  - enough *not much* 32
  imperfect 651
  - out 295
  - over 641
  - up in 698
  - with 888
  work - 731
welladay *lament* 839
  wonder 870
well-advised 498
well-affected 888
well-behaved
  genteel 852
  courteous 894
well-being
  prosperous 734
  happy 827
well-beloved 897
well-born 875
well-bred *genteel* 852
  (*courteous* 894)
well-composed 845
well-defined
  visible 446
  exact 494
  predetermined 611
  (*plan* 626)
well-devised 611
well-disposed 602, 707
well-doing 944
well-done *cooked* 298
well-favored 845
well-formed 240, 845
well-fed 192

well-founded
existent 1
probable 472
certain 474
- *belief* 484
true 494
well-grounded
existent 1
informed 490
- *hope* 858
well-grouped 845
wellhead 153
well-informed 490
Wellington boots 225
well-intentioned
benevolent 906
virtuous 944
well-knit *strong* 159
well-known
knowledge 490
habitual 613
well-laid 611
well-made *form* 240
beauty 845
well-mannered 894
well-marked 446
well-meaning 906
well-meant 906
well-met 894
well-natured 906
well-nigh *almost* 32
near 197
well-off *prosperous* 734
rich 803
well-proportioned 240,
845
well-provided 639
well-regulated
order 58
conformity 82
circumspect 864
well-set 242
well-spent
successful 731
virtuous 944
wellspring 153, 636
well-timed 134
well-to-do
prosperous 734
rich 803
well-turned   periods
578
well-weighed 611
wellwisher 890, 906,
914
Welsh 188
- *rabbit* 298
welsher *swindler* 792
nonpayment 808
welt 321
welter *plunge* 310
roll 311
- *in one's blood* 361
wem 848
wen 250, 848
wench *girl* 129
woman 374
peasant 876
impure 962
wenching 961
wend 266

were, as you - 660
wergild 974
werewolf 980
werowance 745
Wesleyan 984
west *lateral* 236
direction 278
westing 196
Westminster
superior   courts   of -
966
westward 236
wet *water* 337, 348
moist 339
just enough to - *one's*
feet 209
- *blanket*
dissuade 616
hindrance 706
sadden 837
weary 841
dull 843
- *one's whistle*
drink 298
tipple 959
wether 366
whack 276
whacking *large* 31, 192
whale *large* 192
mammal 366
sprat to catch a - 699
tub to a -
deception 545
excuse 617
whalebone 325
whaler 273
whap 276
wharf *houses* 189
refuge 666
workshop 691
mart 799
wharfage 812
wharf boat 273
what *inquiry* 461
wonder 870
and - *not* 81
know -'s *what*
discriminate 465
intelligent 498
skill 698
- *d'ye call 'em* 563
- *in the world*
singular 83
wonderful 870
- *is the reason?* 461
- *next* 455
- *on earth singular* 83
-'s *his name* 563
- *signifies* 643
whatever 78
- *may happen* 474
wheal 250
wheat 367
winnow   the   chaff
from the - 609
Wheat Pit *mart* 799
wheedle *coax* 615
endearment 902
flatter 933
wheedler 615
wheel *circle* 247

convexity 250
bicycle 272
deviate 279
turn back 283
circuition 311
rotation 312
rack 975
break on the -
pain 478
punish 972
get the - *out of the*
rut 672
scotch the - 706
- *about* 279
- *and axle* 633
- *guard* 666
- *of Fortune*
changeable 149
chance 156
rotation 312
necessity 601
- *round inversion* 218
tergiversation 607
-s *within wheels*
entangled 59
machinery 633
wheelbarrow 272
wheel chair 272
wheelman 268, 269
wheelwork 633
wheelwright 690
wheeze *blow* 349
hiss 409
wheezy 409
whelk 250, 848
whelm 641
whelp *infant* 129
production 161
dog 366
rogue 949
when *inquiry* 461
(different time 119)
in the time - 106
whence
attribution 155
departure 293
inquiry 461
reasoning 476
where
presence 186
inquiry 461
- *am I?* 870
whereabouts
place 182
situation 183
near 197
whereas *relating to* 9
because 476
whereby 631
wherefore
attribution 155
inquiry 461
reasoning 476
judgment 480
motive 615
wherein 221
whereness 186
whereupon *time* 106
different time 119
after 121
wherever 180, 182

wherewith *means* 632
money 800
wherewithal 639
wherret 830
wherry 273
whet *sharpen* 253
meal 298
incite 615
excite 824
take a - *tipple* 959
- *the appetite* 865
- *the knife* 673
whether 514
- *or not* 609
whetstone 253
which *at* - *time* 119
know - *is which* 465
whiff *wind* 349
excitement 825
whiffet 129, 349
whiffle 349
Whig 274, 712
while *time* 106
(same time 120)
in a - 132
- *away time time* 106
inaction 681
pastime 840
worth - 646
whilom 122
whilst 106
whim *fancy* 515
caprice 608
wet 842
desire 865
whimper 839
whimsical [*see* whim]
ridiculous 853
whimsey *fancy* 515
caprice 608
desire 865
whimwham
imagination 515
caprice 608
unimportance 643
whin 367, 407
whine *cry* 411
complain 839
whinyard 727
whip *coachman* 268
strike 276
stir up 315
- *a horse* 370
indication 550
urge 615
hasten 684
director 694
flog 972
scourge 975
- *and spur swift* 274
- *away depart* 293
- *hand success* 731
authority 737
- *in* 300 *collect* 72
- *on* 684
- *off* 293
- *up* 789
whipcord 205
whipped cream 298
whipper-in 694
whippersnapper 129

at one's -'s end
 uncertain 475
 difficulty 704
mother - 498
soul of - 572
to - 522
witan 696
witch oracle 513
 ugly 846
 sorceress 994
 (proficient 700)
witchcraft 978, 992
witchery
 attraction 615
 pleasing 829
 sorcery 992
witching time
 midnight 126
 dark 421
wit-cracker 844
witenagemote 696
with added 37
 mixed 41
 ligature 45
 accompanying 88
 means 632
 (joined 43)
 go - 178
 - all its parts 52
 - a sting to it 770
 - a vengeance
 great 31
 complete 52
 - a witness 31
 - regard to 9
withal in addition 37
 accompanying 88
withdraw subduct 38
 absent 187
 turn back 283
 recede 287
 depart 293
 - from rezant 607
 relinquish 624
 dislike 867
withdrawal
 [see withdraw]
 rejection 610
withe 45
wither shrink 195
 decay 659
 - one's hopes 837
withered weak 160
 disease 655
withering harsh 739
 painful 830
 contempt 930
 censure 932
withers 250
 - unwrung strong 159
 insensible 323
withhold hide 528
 restrain 751
 prohibit 761
 retain 781
 stint 819
 - one's assent 764
within 221
 derived from - 5
 keep - 221
 place - 221
738

- an ace 32
- bounds small 32
 shortcoming 304
 restraint 751
- call 197
- ccmpass
 shortcoming 304
 temperate 953
- one's memory 505
- reach near 197
 easy 705
- the mark 304
without unless 8
 subduction 38
 exception 83
 absence 187
 exterior 220
 circumjacent 227
 exemption 777a
 derived from - 6
 not be able to do -
 630
- a dissentient voice
 488
- a leg to stand on 158
- alloy 827
- a rap 804
- a shadow of turning
 141
- ballast irresolute 605
 unprincipled 945
- ceasing 136
- ceremony 881
- charge 815
- end infinite 105
 perpetual 112
- exception 16
- excuse 945
- fail certain 474
 persevering 604a
- fear of contradiction
 535
- God 989
- limit 105
- measure 105
- notice 508
- number 105
- parallel 33
- reason 499
- regard to 10
- reluctance 602
- reserve 525
- rime or reason 615a
- stint 639
- warning 508
withstand oppose 708
 resist 719
 (counteract 179)
withy 45
witless 491
witling fool 501
 wag 844
witness see 441
 spectator 444
 evidence 467
 voucher 550
 call to - 467
witness box 966
wits 450
 all one's - about one
 care 459

intelligence 498
 skin 698
live by one's -
 deceive 545
 skill 698
 cunning 702
 steal 791
 dishonorable 940
 one's - gone a wool-
 gathering 458
 set one's - to work
 think 451
 invent 515
 plan 626
witsnapper 844
witticism 842
wittingly 620
wittol 962
witty 842, 844
 be - 498
wive 903
wivern 83
wizard sage 500
 deceiver 548
 proficient 700
 sorcerer 994
 - of the air 269
wizen wither 195
 throat 260
woe pain 828
 evil 619
- betide
 malediction 908
 pity 914
- is me 839
- to⸱ 908
woebegone 828
 sad 837
woeful bad 649
 painful 830
woefully very 31
wold 344
wolf ravenous 865
 cry - false 544
 alarm 669
 fear 860
 hold the - by the ears
 704
 keep the - from the
 door 359
 unable to keep the -
 from the door 804
- and the lamb 923
- at the door
 source of danger 667
 poverty 804
- in sheep's clothing
 deceiver 548
 knave 941
wolfish 789
woman adult 131
 human 374
- of the town 962
- perfected 374
- the lesser man 374
woman hater 911
womanhood 131, 374
womanish 374
womankind 374
womanly
 adolescent 131

feminine 374
womb cause 153
 interior 221
- of time future 121
 destiny 152
womerah 727
wonder exception 83
 superexcellence 646
 astonishment 870
 prodigy 872
 do -s activity 682
 succeed 731
 for a - 870
 nine days' - 643
 not - 507
 -s of the world 872
- whether
 uncertain 475
 ignorant 491
 suppose 514
wonderfully
 greatly 31
wonderworking 870
wondrous 870
wont habitual 613
 (conformity 82)
won't do, it -
 disapproval 932
woo desire 865
 courtship 902
wooer 897
wood trees 367
 material 635
 not out of the -
 danger 665
 difficulty 704
- lot 232
woodbine
 gone where the -
 twineth 771
woodchuck day 138
woodcut 558
woodcutter 371
wooded, well - 256
wooden 635
- horse 975
- spoon 493
- walls defense 717
 men-of-war 726
wood engraving 558
woodlands 367
wood-note 412
wood nymph 979
wood pavement 255
wood pigeon 366
woodwind 416
woody 367
woof 329
wool flocculent 256
 warm 382
 wrap 384
 fabric 635
 much cry and little -
 482
woolgathering 458
woolly 255, 256
woolpack cloud 353
woolsack pillow 215
 authority 747
 tribunal 966
woon 745

Wop 57
word *maxim* 496
  intelligence 532
  assertion 535
  volable 562
  phrase 566
  command 741
  promise 768
  give the - 741
  good as one's -
  veracious 543
  complete 729
  probity 939
  in a - 572
  keep one's - 939
  man of his - 939
  not a - to say
  silent 585
  humble 879
  pass - 550
  put in a - 582
  take at one's -
  believe 484
  consent 762
  upon my - 535
  watch - *military* 722
  - and a blow
  hasty 684
  contentious 720
  irascible 901
  - for word
  imitction 19
  truth 494
  - it 566
  - of command
  indication 550
  military 722
  command 741
  - in the ear
  information 527
  allocution 586
  - of honor 768
  - of mouth 582
  - to the wise
  intelligible 518
  advice 695
Word *Deity* 573
  - of God £85
wordbook 86
word-catcher 936
wordiness 562, 573
wording 569
wordless 581
word painter 594
word painting 515
word play
  equivocal 520
  neology 563
  wit 842
words *quarrel* 713
  bandy - 588
  bitter - 932
  choice of - 569
  command of - 574
  express by - 566
  flow of - *eloquence* 582
  loquacity 584
  mere - *sophistry* 477
  unmeaning 517
  no - can paint 872
  play of - 842

  put into - 566
  war of - *interlocution*
    588
  contest 720
  - that burn 574
  - with *censure* 932
wordy 562, 573
work *product* 154
  operation 170
  pass and repass 302
  ferment 320
  writing 590
  book 593
  business 625
  use 677
  action 680
  exertion 686
  ornament 847
  at - *in operation* 170
  business 625
  doing 680
  active 682
  earth - 717
  field - 717
  hard - *exertion* 686
  difficulty 704
  piece of -
  importance 642
  discord 713
  stick to - 604a
  stitch of - 686
  stroke of - 686
  - a change 140
  - against time 684
  - for 707
  - hard *exertion* 686
  difficult 704
  - ill 732
  - in 228
  - of art *beauty* 845, 847
  (*painting* 556)
  (*sculpture* 557)
  (*engraving* 558)
  - of fiction 594
  - of reference 636
  - one's way
  progress 282
  ascent 305
  exertion 686
  succeed 731
  - towards *tend* 176
  - up [see below]
  - upon *influence* 175
  incite 615
  excite 824
  - out *conduct* 692
  complete 729
  - out cne's salvation
    990
  - well *easy* 705
  successful 731
  - wonders *active* 682
  succeed 731
workability 490
workable 490
workableness 470
workaday *business* 625
  active 682
worker 686, 690, 746
workhouse 691
  prison 752

working *acting* 170
  active 682
  - bee 690
  - man 690
  - order 673
  - towards 176
workman 690
workmanlike 698
workmanship
  production 161
  action 680
works [see **work**]
  board of - 696
  good - 906
  - of the mind 451
workshop 691
work up
  prepare 673
  use 677
  excite 824
  - into *form* 240
  - into a passion 900
workwoman 690
world *great* 31
  events 151
  space 180
  universe **318**
  mankind 372
  fashion 852
  (*events* 151)
  all the - over 180
  as the - goes 613
  a - of 102
  citizen of the - 910
  come into the - 359
  follow to the -'s end
    743
  for all the - 615
  give to the - 531
  knowledge of the - 698
  man of the -
  proficient 700
  fashion 852
  not for the -
  dissent 489
  refusal 764
  organized - 357
  pendent - 173
  Prince of this - 978
  rise in the - 734
  throughout the - 180
  - and his wife 102
  - beyond the grave
    152
  - forgetting, by the
    world forgot 893
  - of good *good* 618
  do good 648
  - principle 359
  - soul 359
  - spirit 359
  - to come 152
  - wisdom *skill* 698
  caution 864
  selfishness 943
  - without end 112
worldling *selfish* 943
  impious 988
worldly *selfish* 943
  irreligious 989
  - wisdom 864

world-wide *great* 31
  universal 78
  space 180
worm *small* 193
  spiral 248
  animal 366, 368
  bane 663
  food for -s 362
  - in 228
  - oneself *ingress* 294
  love 897
  - one's way *slow* 275
  passage 302
  - out 480a
  - that never dies 982
worm-eaten 659
wormwood
  gall and - 395
worn *weak* 160
  damage 659
  fatigue 688
  well - *used* 677
worn-out 659
  weary 841
worry *vexation* 828
  tease 830
  harass 907
worse
  deteriorated 659
  aggravated 835
  - for wear 160
worship *title* 877
  servility 886
  venerate 987
  religious **990**
  idolize 991
  demon - 991
  idol - 991
  fire - 991
  his - 967
  place of - 1000
  - Mammon 803
  - the rising sun 886
worshiper 990
worshipful 873
worst *defeat* 731
  do one's - *injure* 659
  spite 907
  do your - *defiance* 715
  threat 909
  have the - of it 732
  make the - of 482
  worst come to the -
  certain 474
  bad 649
  hopeless 859
worth *value* 644
  goodness 648
  possession 777
  price 812
  virtue 944
  penny - 812
  what one is - 780
  - a great deal 803
  - one's salt 644
  - the money 815
  - while 646
worthless *trifling* 643
  useless 645
  profligate 945
  - residue 645

X

Z

SPECIAL SUPPLEMENTS
FOR STUDENTS

The following categories of scientific words and phrases offer terms in nine basic fields of study: botany, zoology, psychology and psychotherapy, anthropology, mathematics, physics, chemistry, geology, and astronomy. The unique arrangement of these categories, which follows many textbooks now used in college freshman survey courses, permits a systematic scrutiny of the vocabulary of each science. Moreover, this section is a true thesaurus, with a separate index for quick and effortless location of terms needed in writing assignments.

A THESAURUS OF
BASIC SCIENTIFIC WORDS

1. BOTANY

1. botany, plant biology, phytology, systematic botany *or* taxonomy, plant morphology, plant anatomy *or* structural botany, phytography, plant physiology, phytopathology, phytoecology, phytogeography, plant sociology, economic botany, paleobotany, floristics.

2. agrostology, algology *or* phycology, bacteriology, bryology, dendrology, mycology, pteridology.

3. kingdom, division, subdivision, class, subclass, order, family, genus, species, variety.

4. Chlorophyta; Euglenophyta; Pyrrophyta; Chrysophyta; Phaeophyta; Cyanophyta; Rhodophyta; Schizomycophyta; Myxomycophyta; Eumycophyta, Phycomycetae, Ascomycetae, Lichenes, Basidiomycetae, Deuteromycetae; Bryophyta, Hepaticae, Marchantiales, Jungermanniales, Anthocerotae, Anthocerotales, Musci, Sphagnales, Andreaeales, Bryales; Tracheophyta, Psilopsida, Psilophytinae, Psilophytales, Psilotales, Lycopsida, Lycopodinae, Lepidodendrales, Lycopodiales, Selaginellales, Isoetales, Sphenopsida, Equisetinae, Sphenophyllales, Calamitales, Equisetales, Pteropsida, Filicinae, Ophioglossales, Marattiales, Filicales, Gymnospermae, Cycadophyteline (Cycadofilicales *or* Pteridosperms, Bennettitales, Cycadales), Coniferophyteline (Cordaitales, Ginkgoales, Coniferales, Gnetales), Angiospermae, Dicotyledonae, Ranales, Rosales, Geraniales, Monocotyledonae, Graminales, Liliales.

5. metabolism, anabolism, catabolism; photosynthesis, chemosynthesis; irritability; contractility; digestion, absorption, diffusion, osmosis; respiration; assimilation; regulation; imbibition, guttation, transpiration; excretion; growth; differentiation; reproduction.

6. autotrophic plant, heterotrophic plant; parasitism, parasite, host; saprophytism, saprophyte; symbiosis.

7. (plant movements) autonomic movement, paratonic movement; taxies, nasties; tropism, geotropism, heliotropism, hydrotropism, thermotropism, phototropism, chemotropism, thigmotropism.

8. cell; protoplast; protoplasm; nucleus, nuclear membrane, nucleolus, chromatin; cytoplasm, cytosome, plasma membrane (ectoplast), endoplast, plastids (leucoplasts, chromoplasts, chloroplasts; chlorophyll, carotin, xanthophyll); mitochondria or chondriosomes; vacuole; cell wall, cellulose, hemicellulose, lignin, cutin.

9. tissue; meristematic tissue; parenchyma, chlorenchyma, collenchyma, sclerenchyma; stele; pith; procambium; vascular tissue, vascular bundle, vascular ray; sieve tube; phloem; cambium; xylem, annual ring, heartwood, sapwood; cortex; pericycle; endodermis, epidermis; bark, cork.

10. root, primary root, taproot; root cap, root hair; adventitious root, climbing root, storage root, aerial root, prop root.

11. bud, apical meristem; terminal bud, axillary bud *or* lateral bud, accessory bud, adventitious bud; node, internode; leaf scar; lenticel.

12. stem; underground stem, rhizome, bulb, tuber, corm; prostrate stem, runner; climbing stem; columnar (unbranched) stem; branching stem, excurrent branching, deliquescent branching.

13. herb, shrub, tree; annual, biennial, perennial; evergreen, deciduous plant.

14. leaf, leaflet; tendril; stipule; bud scale; petiole; blade *or* lamina; simple leaf, compound leaf, pinnately compound leaf, palmately compound leaf; whorled leaves, spiral leaves, opposite leaves; vein, venation, midrib; stomata.

15. flower, staminate flower, pistillate flower; monoecious plant, dioecious plant; peduncle; pedicel; receptacle; perianth; sepals (calyx); petals (corolla); stamens (androecium), filament, anther; pistils (gynoecium), ovary, style, stigma; carpel; inflorescence; mixed inflorescence; indeterminate inflorescence, spike, catkin *or* ament, head, spadix, raceme, panicle, umbrel, corymb; determinate inflorescence, cyme, scorpioid cyme.

16. fruit, simple fruit, aggregate fruit, multiple fruit, accessory fruit; indehiscent fruit, dehiscent fruit; fleshy fruit, dry fruit; pericarp, exocarp, mesocarp, endocarp; legume, follicle, capsule, achene, caryopsis *or* grain, samara, schizocarp, nut, pome, drupe *or* stone fruit, berry.

17. seed; seed coat *or* testa, hilum, micropyle, raphe; embryo, plumule, cotyledon, hypocotyl, radicle; dormancy; germination; seedling; monocotyledon, dicotyledon.

18. reproduction; sexual reproduction; pollination, self-pollination; fertilization, self-fertilization; meiosis; conjugation; alternation of generations, gametophyte, sporophyte; isogamy, heterogamy; antheridium, sperm *or* male gamete; archegonium, oögonium, egg *or* female gamete; gametangium, gamete, heterogametes; zygote; sporangium, spore, zoospore, zygospore; asexual reproduction, cell division, mitosis, fission; gemma.

19. genetics; heredity; Mendel's laws; phenotype, genotype; homozygous plant, heterozygous plant; chromosome, homologous chromosomes; haploid cell, diploid cell, polyploid cell; chromatids; linkage, synapsis, crossing over; gene, allelic genes, dominant gene, recessive gene; dominant character, recessive character, allele; F_1 generation (first filial generation), F_2 generation (second filial generation); hybridization, hybrid; mutation, mutant.

2. ZOOLOGY

1. zoology, animal biology; morphology, anatomy, histology, cytology, physiology, embryology, taxonomy, ecology, zoogeography, genetics, organic evolution, anthropology, paleontology; entomology, helminthology, herpetology, ichthyology, ornithology, parasitology, protozoology.

2. (taxonomy) kingdom, subkingdom, phylum, subphylum, class, subclass, order, family, genus, species, subspecies; animal kingdom; animal subkingdoms, Protozoa *or* one-celled animals, Metazoa *or* many-celled animals.

3. Protozoa: Plasmodroma (Mastigophora, Sarcodina, Sporozoa); Ciliophora (Ciliata). Porifera (Calcarea, Hexactinellida, Demospongiae). Coelenterata (Hydrozoa, Scyphozoa, Anthozoa). Ctenophora (Tentacula, Nuda). Platyhelminthes (Turbellaria, Trematoda, Cestoda). Mesozoa. Nemertinea. Acanthocephala. Aschelminthes (Nematoda, Nematomorpha, Rotifera, Gastroricha, Kinorhyncha or Echinodera). Entoprocta. Bryozoa. Brachiopoda. Phoronidea. Sipunculoidea. Echiuroidea. Priapuloidea. Annelida (Archiannelida, Polychaeta, Oligochaeta, Hirudinea). Mollusca (Amphineura, Monoplacophora, Scapopoda, Gastropoda, Pelecypoda, Cephalopoda). Chaetognatha. Echinodermata (Asteroidea, Ophiuroidea, Echinoidea, Holothuroidea, Crinoidea). Onychophora. Linguatulida. Tardigrada. Arthropoda (Crustacea, Chilopoda, Diplopoda, Insecta, Arachnoidea). Brachiata. Chordata: Hemichordata; Urochordata; Cephalochordata; Vertebrata (Pisces: Agnatha, Chondrichthyes, Osteichthyes; Tetrapoda: Amphibia, Reptilia, Aves, Mammalia).

4. cell; cell membrane; protoplast; protoplasm; cytoplasm, plasma membrane, vacuole, mitochondria *or* chondriosomes, Golgi network, centrosome, centriole, centrosphere, cytoplasmic inclusions; nucleus, nucleolus, chromatin, achromatin, chromosome, nuclear sap, nuclear membrane; flagellum, cilia.

5. mitosis, interphase, prophase, prometaphase, metaphase, anaphase, telophase; meiosis; amitosis.

6. tissue; epithelium *or* epithelial tissue, simple epithelium, stratified epithelium, squamous epithelium, cuboidal epithelium, columnar epithelium, ciliated epithelium, flagellated epithelium; connective *or* supporting tissue, fibrillar connective tissue (ligaments, tendons), areolar connective tissue, chondroid connective tissue (bone, cartilage), me-

senchyme, blood *or* vascular tissue, fat *or* adipose tissue, muscular tissue, nervous tissue.

7. symmetry, spherical symmetry, radial symmetry, biradial symmetry, bilateral symmetry; ventral surface, dorsal surface, lateral surface; anterior end, posterior end; proximal end, distal end.

8. pericardial cavity, pleural cavity, peritoneal cavity; coelom; coelomate animal, acoelomate animal.

9. skeleton; endoskeleton *or* internal skeleton, exoskeleton *or* external skeleton *or* dermal skeleton (scales, horny plates, feathers, hair); appendicular skeleton (limbs, girdles), axial skeleton (trunk, head).

10. (bones) skull, cranium *or* brain case, occipital, frontal, parietal, temporal, zygomatic, maxilla, mandible; vertebral column *or* backbone, cervical vertebrae, thoracic vertebrae, lumbar vertebrae, sacral vertebrae, caudal vertebrae, coccyx; sternum *or* breastbone, ribs; pectoral girdle *or* shoulder girdle, scapula *or* shoulder blade, clavical *or* collarbone; pectoral appendage *or* arm bones, humerus, radius, ulna, carpals *or* wristbones, metacarpals *or* palm bones, phalanges (fingers); pelvic girdle *or* hip girdle, ilium, ischium, pubis; pelvic appendage *or* leg bones, femur *or* thigh, patella *or* kneecap, tibia *or* shinbone, fibula, tarsals, metatarsals, phalanges (toes).

11. muscle, smooth muscle *or* nonstriated muscle *or* visceral muscle, striated muscle *or* skeletal muscle, cardiac muscle; masseter, biceps, triceps, deltoid, pectoralis major, gastrocnemius.

12. metabolism, anabolism, catabolism, basal metabolic rate.

13. ingestion, salivation, mastication, digestion, peristalsis, hydrolysis, absorption, assimilation, defecation; digestive system, alimentary canal; mouth, esophagus, crop, gizzard, stomach, intestine, caecum, rectum, anus, cloaca.

14. excretion, excretory system; kidney, nephridium, ureter, urinary bladder, urethra, flame cell.

15. respiration, cell respiration *or* internal respiration; breathing; inspiration, expiration; pharynx, larynx, glottis, epiglottis, trachea, bronchi, bronchial tubes, alveoli, lung, pleura,

diaphragm; gills, pharyngeal gill slits.

16. (circulation) pulmonary circulation, systemic circulation; heart, right auricle, left auricle, right ventricle, left ventricle, bicuspid valve *or* mitral valve, tricuspid valve, semilunar valve; artery, aorta, pulmonary artery, carotid artery; capillary; vein; blood, plasma, corpuscles, erythrocytes *or* red blood corpuscles, leucocytes *or* white blood corpuscles, thrombocytes *or* blood platelets; lymphatic system, lymphatic capillaries, lymph, lymphocytes, spleen.

17. nervous system; peripheral nervous system; autonomic nervous system, parasympathetic nervous system, sympathetic nervous system; central nervous system; brain, cerebrum, cerebellum, medulla; spinal cord; nerve, nerve cell *or* neuron, ganglia, dendrites, axon, medullary sheath, end plates, synapse.

18. sense organs, receptors; sight, eye, cornea, iris, pupil, lens, retina, optic nerve; hearing, ear, pinna *or* outer ear, tympanic membrane *or* eardrum, tympanum, cochlea, semicircular canals, auditory nerve, Eustachian tube; taste, tongue, taste buds; smell, olfactory nerves; touch, tactile receptors; antenna.

19. glands, digestive glands, endocrine glands; pituitary glands *or* hypophysis, thyroid glands, parathyroid glands, pancreas, adrenal glands, gonads, mammary glands, sweat glands, lachrymal glands *or* tear glands, scent glands, salivary glands.

20. asexual reproduction; fission, binary fission, multiple fission *or* sporulation, budding *or* gemmation.

21. sexual reproduction; gametogenesis; gonad; gamete; female gamete, ovum, egg cell, oögenesis; male gamete, sperm cell, sperm, spermatogenesis; copulation, fertilization; zygote, cleavage; reproductive organs; scrotum, testes, interstitial cells, epididymis, *vas deferens*, seminal vesicle, prostate gland, penis; ovary, oviducts *or* Fallopian tubules, uterus, vagina; oviparous animal, viviparous animal, ovoviviparous animal; monoecious animal, dioecious animal; hermaphroditism, protandrous hermaphroditism, hermaphrodite; parthenogenesis; pedogenesis.

22. embryology; embryogeny; embryo, fetus *or* mammalian embryo;

metamorphosis; larva, nymph, pupa, chrysalis, adult.

3. PSYCHOLOGY AND PSYCHOTHERAPY

1. psychology, psychonomics, abnormal psychology, applied psychology, animal psychology, child psychology, clinical psychology, comparative psychology, differential psychology, dynamic psychology, experimental psychology, existential psychology, faculty psychology, functional psychology, genetic psychology, individual psychology, industrial psychology, parapsychology, rational psychology, self-psychology, structural psychology; physiological psychology, psychobiochemistry, psychobiology, psychophysics; psychoasthenics, psychostatics, psychogenetics; psychotechnics, psychotechnology.

2. (systems) Freudian psychology; Gestalt psychology or configurationism; behavior psychology or Watson's psychology; association psychology, mental chemistry.

3. psychiatry, psychiatrics, neuropsychiatry; prophylactic psychiatry, mental hygiene; psychosomatic medicine; psychosocial medicine.

4. psychotherapy; group therapy; occupational therapy; recreational therapy; narcotherapy, narcoanalysis, amytal or pentothal interview; hypnotherapy, hypnoanalysis; psychosurgery; suggestion therapy; hypnotic suggestion, posthypnotic suggestion; autosuggestion; sleep treatment; shock therapy, electroshock therapy, protein shock therapy, metrazol shock therapy, hypoglycemic shock therapy, insulin shock therapy, insulin coma therapy, convulsive shock therapy; psychoanalysis, depth interview; psychoanalytic therapy, depth psychology; psychognosis; dream analysis, interpretation of dreams, dream symbolism.

5. psychological test; aptitude test, Oseretsky test, Stanford scientific aptitude test; personality test, Bernreuter personality inventory, Minnesota multiplastic personality inventory; association test, controlled association test, free association test; apperception test, card test; Rorschach test, ink-blot test; intelligence test, I.Q. test; alpha test, beta test, Babcock-Levy test, Binet-Simon test, Goldstein-Sheerer test, Kent mental test, aussage test; Wechsler-Bellevue intelligence scale, Gesell's development schedule, Minnesota preschool scale, Cattell's infant intelligence scale.

6. psyche, mind; preconscious, foreconscious, coconscious; subconscious, unconscious, submerged mind; libido, libidinal energy, libidinal object; id, ego, superego; ego-ideal, ego-id conflict.

7. (pathological personality types) neurotic, psychoneurotic, neuropath; maladjusted personality, hostile personality; antisocial personality, sociopath; escapist; psychotic personality; mental defective, ament; hypochondriac; alcoholic.

8. neurosis, psychoneurosis, functional nervous disorder; pathoneurosis, actual neurosis, anxiety neurosis, blast neurosis, fright neurosis, traumatic neurosis, transference neurosis; compulsion neurosis, obsessional neurosis, obsessive-compulsion neurosis; occupational neurosis, professional neurasthenia; combat or war neurosis, battle fatigue, shellshock; nervous breakdown.

9. psychosis, psychopathy, psychopathic condition; schizophrenia, functional disintegration, dissociation of personality, split personality, multiple personality; dementia praecox, paranoia, catatonia; hebephrenia, paraphrenia, schizophasia, schizothymia; melancholia, manic-depressive insanity, affective psychosis, cyclothymia; Korsakoff's psychosis, polyneuritic psychosis; amentia, fugue; dementia paralytica; senile dementia, senile psychosis, degenerative psychosis; presenile dementia; psychopathia sexualis, psychosexuality; pharmacopsychosis; arteriosclerotic psychosis, climacteric psychosis, exhaustive psychosis, gestational psychosis, involuntary psychosis, involutional psychosis, metabolic psychosis, organic psychosis, postinfectious psychosis, psychasthenia, psycholepsy, psychokinesia, psychorhythmia, toxic psychosis; moral insanity, psychopathic personality; rabies, hydrophobia.

10. (neurotic symptoms) anxiety, precordial anxiety, free-floating anxiety; asthenia; hysteria, conversion hysteria, anxiety hysteria; dissociation, emotional instability, flight reaction, immaturity; depression; detachment; passive aggres-

sion, passive dependence; phobia, morbid fear, astraphobia (lightning and thunder), acrophobia (heights), agoraphobia (open places), ailurophobia (cats), claustrophobia (confined places), hematophobia (blood), hydrophobia (water), pyrophobia (fire), scotophobia (darkness), toxiphobia (being poisoned), xenophobia (strangers); unresponsiveness, apathy; stupor, catatonic stupor, euphoria, elation.

11. (psychosomatic disorders) anesthesia, analgesia; bulimia, neurasthenia, paresthesia, parorexia, psychalgia, psychesthesia, psychoepilepsy, stereotypy.

12. (thought disturbances) mental block; psychotaxis; paralogia, mental confusion; flight of ideas; delusion, delusion of persecution, delusion of grandeur, nihilistic delusion; hallucinosis; delirium; (psychomotor disturbances) convulsion, jerk, tremor, twitching, chorea, tic; (speech abnormalities) dysarthria, stammering, stuttering, lisping, incoherence; echolalia, verbigeration, aphasia, jargon aphasia, paraphasia, mutism, aphonia, hysterical aphonia.

13. (amnesic states) amnesia; fugue; disorientation, amnesic dissociation, word deafness or blindness, auditory or verbal amnesia, alexia; aphrasia, amnesic aphrasia; apraxia, amnesic apraxia; agnosia, agraphia; paranomia; confabulation; catalepsy, catalepsis, cataplexy; trance, dream state; somnambulism.

14. mania, obsession, compulsion; megalomania, monomania, kleptomania, pyromania, erotomania, dipsomania.

15. complex, inferiority complex, superiority complex, Oedipus or nuclear complex, Electra complex, persecution complex, castration complex; fixation, libido fixation, arrested development; infantile fixation, pregenital fixation; regression.

16. perversion; coprophilia, necrophilia; paraphilia, psychosexuality, sexual abnormality; aphrodisia, bestiality, exhibitionism, fetishism, narcissism, nymphomania, satyrism, satyriasis, pedophilia, psycholagny, scopophilia, voyeurism, sadism, masochism, cannibalism.

17. defense mechanism, psychological or sociological adjustive reaction; negativism; escape mechanism; withdrawal; isolation, emotional insulation; autistic thinking; compensation, overcompensation, decompensation; substitution; sublimation; projection; displacement; rationalization; suppression, repression, inhibition, reaction formation.

18. adjustment, adjustive reaction; readjustment, rehabilitation, psychosynthesis, integration of personality.

19. catharsis, purgation, abreaction; acting out, psychodrama; transference, emotional attachment; identification, introjection; positive transference, negative transference, countertransference.

20. cathexis, desire concentration; charge, energy charge, cathectic energy; anticathexia, countercharge; hypercathexis, overcharge.

4. ANTHROPOLOGY

1. anthropology; physical anthropology, anthropometry, human evolution, human paleontology; cultural anthropology or social anthropology, ethnology, ethnography, archaeology, linguistics.

2. (eras of recent life) Cenezoic era; Tertiary period or Age of Mammals (Paleocene epoch, Eocene epoch, Oligocene epoch, Miocene epoch, Pliocene epoch), Quaternary period or Age of Man (Pleistocene epoch, Holocene epoch).

3. (fossil primates) Parapithecus; Propliopithecus; Dryopithecus, Dryopithecus fontani, Dryopithecus rhenanus, Dryopithecus darwini; Proconsul africanus; Pliopithecus; Australopithecus africanus, Paranthropus robustus, Plesianthropus transvaalensis.

4. (fossil races of man) Gigantanthropus or Gigantopithecus blacki, Meganthropus paleojavanicus; Pithecanthropus robustus, Pithecanthropus erectus, Pithecanthropus modjokertensis; Sinanthropus pekinensis or Peking man; Homo soloensis or Solo man; Homo Africanthropus; Homo heidelbergensis or Heidelberg man; Homo neanderthalensis or Neanderthal man, Rhodesian group, Mousterian group, Ehringsdorf group (Ehringsdorf forms, Tabun Mt. Carmel forms, Steinheim forms), Skhul Mt. Carmel forms, Galilee forms; Homo Sapiens, Galley Hill man, London man, Swanscombe man, Fontechevade man; Cro-Magnon man, Grimaldi man, Predmost man, Brünn man, Chancelade

man, Ofnet man; Wadjak man, Keilor man, Talgai man; Oldoway man, Boskop man, Springbok man, Fish Hoek man; Eoanthropus dawsoni *or* Piltdown "man."

5. (prehistorical cultural eras) Eolithic *or* Dawn Stone Age; Paleolithic *or* Old Stone Age, Lower Paleolithic Age (pre-Chellean stage, Chellean stage, Acheulean stage), Middle Paleolithic Age *or* Mousterian stage, Upper Paleolithic Age (Aurignacian stage, Solutrean stage, Magdalenian stage); Epipaleolithic *or* Mesolithic Age *or* Azilian-Tardenoisian stage; Neolithic or New Stone Age; Metal Age; Bronze Age, Early Bronze Age, Middle Bronze Age, Late Bronze Age; Iron Age.

6. (prehistorical technological levels) core biface work (Abbevillian industries, Acheulean industries, Mousterian industries); flake work (Clactonian industries, Levalloisian industries, Tayacian industries); blade work (Chatelperronian industries, Aurignacian industries, Gravettian industries, Solutrean industries, Magdalenian industries, Hamburgian industries).

7. (races) Caucasoid (Ainu, Australoid, Dravidian, Vedda; Alpine, Armenoid, Mediterranean, Nordic; Dinaric, East Baltic, Polynesian); Mongoloid (Asiatic, Indonesian-Malay, American Indian); Negroid (Forest Negro, Negrito; Hottentot-Bushman, Nilote *or* Nilotic Negro, Oceanic Negro).

8. index, acrocranic index, acromio-cristal index, bodily fullness index, brachial index, cephalic index (dolichocephalic index, mesocephalic index, brachycephalic index), cranial index, cranial breadth-height index, cranial length-height index, crural index, facial index (euryprosopic index, mesoprosopic index, leptoprosopic index), femoro-humeral index, forearm-hand index, gnathic index, hand index, intermembral index, ischium-pubis index, length-breadth sacral index, lower leg-foot index, maxillo-alveolar index, morphological *or* Naccarati's index, nasal index (platyrrhine index, mesorrhine index, leptorrhine index), orbital index, palatal index, pelvic breadth-height index, pelvic inlet index, pilastric index, platycnemic index, platymeric index, sicklemia index, stem-leg length *or* Manouvrier's

skelic index, thoracic index, tibio-femoral index, tibio-radial index, total facial index, transverse fronto-parietal index, trunk index, upper facial index, vertical lumbar index; Frankfort line *or* Frankfort plane; Mongoloid eye; epicanthic *or* Mongoloid fold, external epicanthic fold, internal epicanthic fold; Negroid lip; prognathism; peppercorn hair; steatopygy *or* steatopygia; genotype, phenotype; blood type *or* group; constitutional type, pyknic type, leptosome type, athletic type; ectomorphy, mesomorphy, endomorphy.

9. culture; culture pattern, ideal pattern, behavioral pattern; integration of culture; function, theme, configuration, drive, postulate, affirmation; Apollonian configuration, Dionysian configuration; culture trait *or* element; trait complex *or* culture complex; age area, culture area, culture center *or* nucleus, marginal area; cultural evolution, savagery, barbarism, civilization; invention, discovery; convergence, parallelism; cultural transmission *or* borrowing; diffusion, stimulus diffusion; assimilation; acculturation, antagonistic acculturation, marginal acculturation, planitational acculturation; evolutionism, diffusionism (heliolithic diffusionism, culture-historical diffusionism), Kulturkreis, functionalism.

10. etiquette, folkway; custom; mos; moral; law; collective responsibility; tort *or* private wrong crime *or* public wrong; sanction, legal *or* organized sanction; oath, compurgation; ordeal.

11. status, ascribed status, achieved status; role; class, caste; patriarchate, matriarchate; age grade, age set *or* class; association, voluntary association; kin group; society, secret society (leopard society, medicine society, military society), graded society; brotherhood; club; sodality.

12. kinship *or* descent, kin group; consanguine kinship, affinal kinship; unilateral kinship *or* descent, bilateral kinship *or* descent, mixed kinship *or* descent; patrilineal *or* agnatic kinship, matrilineal *or* uterine kinship; sibling; cross-cousin, parallel cousin *or* ortho-cousin; family; nuclear family, stem family, elementary family, composite family, extended family, joint family (patrilocal joint family, matrilocal joint

family); conjugal *or* biological *or* small family, consanguineal family; patriarchal family; paternal family, maternal family; sib; clan; complex *or* genealogical clan, equalitarian clan; patrilineal clan, matrilineal clan; gens; lineage, unilocal lineage, multilocal lineage; phratry; moiety, simple moiety, compound moiety; tribe; familiarity *or* privileged familiarity, kin familiarity (avunculate, amitate), joking relationship; kin avoidance.

13. mating, preferential mating, random mating; agamy; marriage; primary marriage, secondary marriage; monogamy *or* pair marriage, polygamy (polygyny, polandry); sororate, levirate, cross-cousin marriage, symmetrial cross-cousin marriage, avuncular marriage, affinal marriage, extended affinal marriage, interfamilial exchange marriage; group marriage; marriage by capture, mock capture, marriage by exchange; child marriage; fictive marriage; half marriage; preferential marriage; term marriage; endogamy, royal endogamy; exogamy; incest, dynastic incest; bride price, dowry; divorce.

14. (political organization) horde; band, unilineal band, patrilineal band; community, village community, endogamous community *or* local group; tribe; confederacy, Iroquois Confederacy *or* League; nation; state; oligarchy, gerontocracy, theocracy; monarchy; headman; chief, dual chief, war chief, peace chief, talking chief; sachem; cacique; king.

15. (artifacts) core *or* biface, flake, chopper; eolith, microlith; percussion-flaked tool, pressure-flaked tool; *coup de poing* (fist ax); blade tool, backed blade, shouldered point, notched blade, borer *or* awl, burin; polished stone tool, adze, maul, quern, mano, metate; dibble, digging stick, hoe, spade, plow; spear, spear thrower *or* rigid spear thrower, flexible spear thrower, harpoon, bow and arrow, throwing-stick, sling, bola, boomerang; gourd, net bag, parfleche; basket; pottery, potsherd *or* shard.

16. mound, conical mound, effigy mound, platform mound, symbolic mound; kitchen midden; megalith; menhir *or* monolith, cromlech; dolmen, barrow, long barrow, round barrow; alignment; bilithon, trilithon; Stonehenge;

lake *or* pile dwelling; cliff dwelling, pueblo; pit house; long house; communal house, bachelor's house, men's house; tent, tipi *or* tepee, yurt *or* yourta.

17. food-gathering *or* food-collecting; fishing; hunting, fire hunting, higher hunting; cultivation, dry cultivation, wet cultivation, shifting cultivation; horticulture; agriculture, hoe agriculture, plow agriculture, maize agriculture; slash-and-burn; pastoralism *or* stock rearing, extensive stock rearing, intensive stock rearing.

18. economy, subsistence economy, collecting economy, handicraft economy; property, real property, incorporeal *or* intangible property, communal property, joint property; exchange, gift exchange *or* covert exchange; trade, symbiotic trade, silent trade *or* dumb barter; kula ring; barter, gift barter, pure barter; money, brick tea money, dog tooth money, feather money, moon money, paper money, pig money, ring money, token money; wealth, surplus wealth; potlatch.

19. (religion) mana, manitou, orenda, wakonda *or* wakan; preanimism; animism; animatism *or* vitalism; anthropomorphism; monotheism, polytheism; diabolism, eidolism, totemism, fetishism, shamanism, sacerdotalism; worship, nature worship, sun worship, animal worship, serpent worship, devil worship, hero worship, mother worship; cult, ancestor cult, hero cult, mystery cult, individual cult; vodun; god, high god, finite god, tribal god, momentary god; mother goddess; spirit; ghost; shaman, witch doctor, talking doctor; medicine man; Druid; priest; apotropaism; reverence, cajoling, scolding; prayer; hospitality; sacrifice, human sacrifice, child sacrifice; austerities; magic, sympathetic *or* imitative magic, envoûtement, contagious magic; divination; necromancy; augury; sorcery; witchcraft; fetish; amulet; tabu *or* taboo; rite *or* ritual, rite of passage (rite of separation, rite of transition, rite of incorporation), rite of intensification, rite of purification, initiation rite, increase rite, fertility rite; birth rite, puberty rite, marriage rite; ceremony, seasonal ceremony; soul, external soul, ghost soul; cremation; burial, extended burial, contracted burial *or* position, flexed burial, water burial,

secondary burial; suttee *or* sati; afterlife, afterworld.

20. (linguistic families *or* stocks) Indo-European: Indo-Iranian, Armenian, Tocharian, Hellenic, Albanian, Italic, Celtic, Germanic *or* Teutonic, Balto-Slavic, Hittite; Ural-Altaic: Turkish, Mongolian, Tungus-Manchu, Uralic *or* Finno-Ugric; Sinitic *or* Sino-Tibetan: Chinese, Tibetan, Thai *or* Siamese, Burmese; Dravidian; Japanese; Malay-Polynesian: Malay, Javanese, Tagalog; Semitic: Hebrew, Arabic, Ethiopian, Phoenician, Babylonian, Assyrian; Hamitic: Egyptian, Berber (Tuareg, Kabyle), Galla, Somali; Sudanic; Bantu; Eskimo-Aleut; Athapaskan *or* Nadéné; Algonkian; Siouan; Uto-Aztecan; Carib and Arawak; Tupi-Guarani; Araucanian; Quechuan.

21. language, formless language, analytic language, flectional language (agglutinative language, amalgamating language), inflective *or* synthetic language, polysynthetic *or* incapsulating language; word form; phoneme, allophone; morpheme, bound morpheme, free morpheme; phonetics; grammar, morphology, syntax; semantics; writing, picture writing, ideographic writing, alphabetic writing; pictograph, ideograph, rebus; hieroglyphic, hieratic, demotic; cuneiform.

22. (primitive arts) motif; folklore, folktale; mythology, myth, sacred myth, trickster myth, culture hero myth; tradition; riddle; superstition; survival; primitive music; membranophone, drum, membrane drum, single membrane drum, double membrane drum, talking drum, fontomfrom drum; idiophone, gong, slit gong, xylophone, single xylophone, compound xylophone; dance, character dance, play dance, solstice dance, puberty dance, courtship dance, fertility dance (phallic dance, sun dance), death dance; art, decorative art, art mobilier, parietal art, cave *or* Cro-Magnon art; painting, dry *or* sand painting.

5. MATHEMATICS

1. mathematics, elementary mathematics, higher mathematics, pure mathematics, abstract mathematics, applied mathematics, mixed mathematics; arithmetic, algebra, geometry, plane geometry, solid geometry, spherical geometry, analytical geometry, graphical geometry, trigonometry, plane trigonometry, analytical trigonometry, spherical trigonometry, calculus.

2. number; unit; digit; whole number *or* integer, positive integer, zero integer (zero, cipher), negative integer; natural number; mixed number; fraction, proper fraction, improper fraction, common fraction, complex fraction, numerator, denominator, lowest common denominator; decimal *or* decimal fraction; rational number, irrational number; real number, imaginary number, complex number; prime number, composite number; concrete number; ordinal number, cardinal number.

3. calculation; addition, augend, addend, sum; subtraction, minuend, subtrahend, remainder; division, dividend, divisor, quotient; multiplication, multiplicand, multiplier, product; factoring, factor, common factor, lowest common multiple; average *or* arithmetical mean.

4. power, index, base, exponent, radicand; square, root, square root, cube root, nth root, surd.

5. quantity, unknown quantity, constant, variable, dependent variable, independent variable, argument; coefficient, numerical coefficient, literal coefficient, detached coefficient, undetermined coefficient; algebraic sum, expression, linear expression, symmetrical expression, algebraic equivalent, monomial expression, binomial expression, polynomial expression *or* multinomial expression, fractional expression; term, element, dimension.

6. (sequence of numbers) series; sequence, convergent sequence, infinite sequence; arithmetical progression, arithmetic means, common difference; geometrical progression, geometric means, common ratio; harmonic progression; permutation; combination; probability, probable number, expectation.

7. ratio, antecedent, consequent; inverse ratio; analogy; proportion, means, extremes.

8. equation, simple equation, quadratic equation, biquadratic equation, determinate equation, fractional equation; binomial theorem; formula; analysis, solution, verification.

9. graph, rectangular co-ordinate sys-

tem; quadrant; x-axis, y-axis, co-ordinates; vertical co-ordinate, ordinate; horizontal co-ordinate, abscissa; cartesian co-ordinates; polar co-ordinates; vector, radius vector; locus; x-intercept, y-intercept.

10. line, straight line *or* right line, horizontal line, vertical line, gradient, transversal, median; chord, tangent; vertex, apex, cusp, orthocenter; point, locus, focus, centric; pencil, intersection, trace; curve, envelope, node.

11. plane, surface, plane surface, area, perimeter, diagonal; geometrical figure, congruent figures.

12. angle, right angle, oblique angle (acute angle, obtuse angle), straight angle, reflex angle, adjacent angle, alternate angles, corresponding angles, conjugate angles, opposite angles, vertical angles, interior angle, exterior angle, complementary angle, supplementary angle, positive angle, negative angle, variable angle; degree, minute, second, radian; initial side, terminal side.

13. triangle, right triangle, equilateral triangle, isosceles triangle, scalene triangle, acute triangle, obtuse triangle, oblique triangle; base, hypotenuse, altitude.

14. circle, arc, circumference, diameter, radius, centroid, segment, semicircle, quadrant, sector, tangent, pole.

15. polygon, irregular polygon, rectangle *or* orthogon, rhombus, parallelogram, rhomboid, square, quadrilateral, trapezium *or* trapezoid; pentagon, hexagon, heptagon, etc.

16. solid, geometrical solid, regular solid; sphere, spheroid, small circle, great circle, spherical triangle, spherical polygon; cube, hexahedron; parallelepiped; octahedron; tetrahedron; prism; cylinder; pyramid; cone.

17. (conic sections) frustrum, parabola, hyperbola, ellipse; center, focus, vertex, directrix, eccentricity, latus rectum, axis of symmetry, semimajor axis, major axis, minor axis, semiminor axis, transverse axis.

18. sine, cosine, tangent, cotangent, secant, cosecant; arcsin x; trigonometric table; interpolation; trigonometrical identities, reciprocal relations, quotient relations, Pythagorean relations; trigonometrical functions; inverse trigonometric functions; trigonometrical ratios;

trigonometrical equation; sine curve, tangent curve.

19. logarithm, antilogarithm, decimal logarithm, common logarithm; characteristic *or* index, mantissa; radix.

6. PHYSICS

1. physics, classical physics, modern physics; mechanics (kinematics, dynamics, statics, hydrostatics, hydrodynamics, hydraulics), heat (thermometry, calorimetry, thermodynamics), sound, acoustics, light, optics, spectroscopy, electricity (electrostatics, electronics), magnetism; high-energy physics *or* elementary-particle physics, nuclear physics, atomic physics, molecular physics, solid-state physics, physics of liquids, physics of gases, plasma physics, biophysics, low-temperature physics, mathematical physics, theoretical physics, space physics.

2. atom, neutral atom, ion, nucleus, atomic number, atomic weight, mass number, isobar, isotope; elementary particles *or* subatomic particles; hyperons, nucleons, mesons, leptons, photons; proton, neutron, electron, positron; element; molecule; chemical change, nuclear change, physical change.

3. matter; solid, liquid, gas, extension *or* volume, mass, weight, density, fluid; specific gravity, impenetrability; elasticity, stress, strain, elastic limit; malleability, ductility; adhesion, cohesion, surface tension, capillarity, diffusion, osmosis, Brownian movement, buoyancy, viscosity; pressure, atmospheric pressure, air pressure; Hooke's law, kinetic theory of matter *or* molecular theory of matter, Pascal's law, Archimedes' principle, Bernoulli's principle; pycnometer, hydrometer, barometer, aneroid barometer, barograph, altimeter, manometer.

4. fusion, heat of fusion, melting, melting point; freezing, freezing point; regelation; vaporization, heat of vaporization; boiling, boiling point; evaporation, dew point, humidity, absolute humidity, relative humidity; sublimation, volatile liquid *or* solid; condensation *or* liquefaction, critical temperature, critical pressure, vapor; distillation, fractional distillation, distillate.

5. motion, rectilinear motion, curvi-

linear motion, circular motion, projectile motion, rotation *or* rotary motion, precession, revolution; velocity, terminal velocity, acceleration, speed, momentum, impulse, inertia; Newton's laws of motion; projectile, trajectory; pendulum, simple pendulum, compound pendulum, compensation pendulum, seconds pendulum; center of percussion; oscillation *or* vibration, amplitude, period, frequency.

6. force, centrifugal force, centripetal force, parallel forces, couple, component forces, effective component, ineffective component, resultant force; friction, coefficient of friction; equilibrant, equilibrium; resolution of forces, composition of forces, moment of force *or* torque; vector, vector quantity, scalar quantity; dyne, poundal, slug, newton; gravitation, gravity; free fall; Newton's law of universal gravitation.

7. work; foot-pound, foot-poundal; gram-centimeter, kilogram-meter; erg, joule; power, horsepower; energy, potential energy, kinetic energy; law of conservation of energy.

8. machines, simple machine, compound machine; inclined plane, screw, wedge, lever and fulcrum, wheel and axle, pulley; mechanical advantage, ideal mechanical advantage, actual mechanical advantage; efficiency, input, output.

9. (heat) conduction, conductor, conductometer; insulator, convection; radiation; law of heat exchange, Newton's law of cooling; expansion, linear expansion, coefficient of linear expansion, differential expansion; bimetallic bar, compound bar, thermostat; pressure coefficient of gases, general gas law, Boyle's law, Charles's law, Gay-Lussac's law; standard conditions, standard pressure, standard temperature; absolute zero; heat engine, internal-combustion engine, external-combustion engine, turbine; Joule's equivalent; temperature, degree; thermometer, absolute scale, Kelvin scale, Fahrenheit scale, centigrade scale; foot-pound-second system, centimeter-gram-second system; British thermal unit, btu; calorie, kilogram-caloric; specific heat.

10. (sound) wave, wavelength, sound wave, longitudinal wave (condensation, rarefaction); transverse wave (crest, trough); pitch, intensity, loudness; bel, decibel; beat, echo, reverberation; interference, resonance; frequency, audio frequency, ultrasonic frequency, infrasonic frequency.

11. (musical sound) tone, fundamental tone, overtone, quality, major chord, musical interval; consonance, dissonance; noise; musical scale, chromatic scale *or* tempered scale, diatonic scale; standing wave, node, antinode, loop, segment.

12. (light) luminosity, incandescence, fluorescence, illuminated body; opaque body, translucent body, transparent body; shadow, umbra, penumbra; photometry, photometer; luminous intensity, candle power, candle, foot-candle, lumen, illumination; quantum, quantum theory; Einstein's special theory of relativity, Einstein's general theory of relativity; Doppler effect.

13. reflection, diffusion, angle of reflection, angle of incidence; image, real image, virtual image; magnification; mirror, concave mirror, convex mirror; center of curvature, radius of curvature, principal axis; focus, virtual focus, focal length, principal focus, focal plane; spherical aberration.

14. refraction, angle of refraction, index of refraction, critical angle; diffraction; convex lens *or* positive lens, concave lens *or* negative lens; optical center, optical density; achromatic lens, chromatic aberration; diopter.

15. color, primary colors, complementary colors; pigments, primary pigments; complementary pigments; monochromatic light, polychromatic light, polarized light, polarization; polarizer, analyzer.

16. spectrum; dispersion; electromagnetic spectrum, electromagnetic radiations (infrared rays, ultraviolet rays, X-rays, gamma rays); angstrom; continuous spectrum, absorption spectrum (Fraunhofer lines); bright-line spectrum, dark-line spectrum; spectroscope.

17. magnetism, induced magnetism, residual magnetism; magnet, saturated magnet, temporary magnet, permanent magnet; lodestone, magnetic compass, dipping needle; magnetic retentivity; magnetic poles, south-seeking pole, north-seeking pole; magnetic line of force, magnetic field, magnetic flux,

magnetic permeability, magnetic transparency; magnetic delination, isogonic line, agonic line; magnetic inclination, isoclinic line, magnetic equator, aclinic line.

18. electricity, static electricity; electric current, direct current, D.C., alternating current, A.C.; induced current; eddy current; electromagnetism; electric field; circuit, parallel circuit, series circuit; electromotive force or e.m.f.; resistance, specific resistance or resistivity; reactance, inductive reactance, capacitive reactance; impedance; conduction, conductance, conductor; induction, electromagnetic induction, inductance; self-inductance; capacitance; electrolysis; dissociation; electroplating; electrolyte, nonelectrolyte, Ohm's law, Coulomb's law, inverse-square law, Lenz's law.

19. generator, motor; armature or keeper, commutator, brush, slip rings; electrophorus; capacitor or condenser; insulator or dielectric; transformer; primary coil, secondary coil; rectifier; rheostat, galvanoscope; oscillator, relay; shunt; electrode, anode or plate, cathode; electrolytic cell; Leyden jar, voltaic cell, storage cell.

20. coulomb, ohm, ampere, volt, henry, farad, watt; watt-hour, kilowatt-hour; electroscope, ammeter, galvanometer, voltmeter.

21. diode, triode, vacuum tube; cathode-ray tube, cathode rays; photoelectric cell, photoelectric effect; transistor.

22. radioactivity, alpha particle, beta particle, gamma rays, cosmic rays; isotope, radioactive isotope; transmutation of elements; particle accelerator or atom smasher, betatron, cyclotron, synchrotron; nuclear reactor, uranium-graphite pile; atomic energy, nuclear energy; fission, chain reaction, critical mass; fusion, thermonuclear reaction.

7. CHEMISTRY

1. chemistry, general chemistry, inorganic chemistry, organic chemistry, analytical chemistry (qualitative analysis, quantitative analysis), biological chemistry or biochemistry, radiochemistry or nuclear chemistry, theoretical chemistry or physical chemistry.

2. matter, organic matter, inorganic matter; homogeneous matter, substance, stable substance, unstable substance, volatile substance, amorphous substance, crystalline substance; element, active element, inactive element, nonmetal, metal, alkali metal, alkaline earth metal, amphoteric element; free state, combined state; allotropic forms, allotropy.

3. (chemical notation) symbol, coefficient, subscript, radical; formula, equation, word equation, skeleton equation, balanced equation, ionic equation; molecular weight, formula weight; valence, negative valence, positive valence, zero valence.

4. mixture; compound, binary compound, ternary compound, electrovalent compound, ionic compound, chain compound, covalent compound; covalent linkage; law of definite proportions; heat of formation, heat of neutralization.

5. chemical change, chemical reaction, chemical combination, decomposition, displacement, double decomposition; irreversible reaction, completion, reversible reaction, complete reaction, incomplete reaction; endothermic reaction, exothermic reaction, photochemical reaction; dynamic equilibrium, equilibrium constant, ionization constant, solubility product constant; common ion effect; catalyst or catalytic agent; law of conservation of matter, law of mass action.

6. ionization or dissociation, nonionization, electrolytic dissociation; electrolyte, nonelectrolyte; electrolysis; ion, positive ion or cation, negative ion or anion; positive electrode or anode, negative electrode or cathode; Ionization Theory or Theory of Electrolytic Dissociation; activity coefficient.

7. acid, binary acid, ternary acid, monobasic acid, dibasic acid, tribasic acid; weak acid (or base), strong acid (or base); base, alkali, monoacid base, diacid base, triacid base; salt, binary salt, ternary salt, acid salt, basic salt, normal salt, double salt, complex salt; neutralization, hydrolysis, titration; indicators, litmus, phenolphthalein, methyl orange, methyl violet, alizarin yellow; hydrogen ion concentration or pH.

8. ascorbic acid, benzoic acid, boric acid, butyric acid, carbolic acid, citric acid, formic acid, gallic acid, hydrochloric acid, hydrofluoric acid, lactic acid,

malic acid, nitric acid, oleic acid, oxalic acid, phosphoric acid, picric acid, prussic acid, salicylic acid, stearic acid, sulfuric acid, tannic acid, tartaric acid; (bases) ammonium hydroxide, calcium hydroxide, magnesium hydroxide, potassium hydroxide, sodium hydroxide; (salts) ammonium chloride, bismuth subnitrate, calcium carbonate, potassium chloride, potassium nitrate, sodium acetate, sodium acid phosphate, sodium bicarbonate, sodium bisulfite, sodium chloride.

9. solution, gaseous solution, liquid solution, solid solution, dilute solution, concentrated solution, unsaturated solution, supersaturated solution; molar solution, molal solution, normal solution, standard solution; solute, solvent; seeding, precipitate, filtration; suspension.

10. crystal, ionic crystal, atom crystal, molecule crystal; crystal symmetry, isometric crystal (cube), hexagonal crystal, tetragonal crystal, orthorhombic crystal, monoclinic crystal, triclinic crystal; water of crystallization or water of hydration; hydrate, anhydrous compound; decrepitation, sublimation; deliquescent substance, hygroscopic substance, efflorescent substance.

11. oxide, metallic oxide or basic anhydride, nonmetallic oxide or acid anhydride, amphoteric oxide, neutral oxide, suboxide, saline oxide, peroxide; oxidation, rapid oxidation, combustion, spontaneous combustion, slow oxidation, organic oxidation, inorganic oxidation; oxidizing agent; reduction, reducing agent; kindling temperature, temperature of combustion, heat of combustion.

12. hydrocarbons; aliphatic hydrocarbons, saturated or methane series (methane, ethane, propane), unsaturated series, ethylene series (ethylene, propylene, butylene), acetylene series (acetylene, allylene); aromatic hydrocarbons, benzene series (benzene, toluene, xylene), naphthalene series (naphthalene), anthracene series (anthracene).

13. (hydrocarbon derivatives) halogen substitution products (chloroform or trichloromethane); alcohols, monohydroxy alcohols, dihydroxy alcohols (methyl alcohol, ethyl alcohol); aldehydes (formaldehyde, acetaldehyde); ketones (acetone, butanone); organic acids; ethers (diethyl ether); esters (methyl acetate); carbohydrates (sugars,

starches, cellulose); proteins (albumin, globulin, glutelin).

14. colloid, natural colloid, lyophobic colloid, hydrophobic colloidal system, lyophilic colloid, hydrophilic colloidal system; sol, gel; dispersed medium, dispersing medium; condensation or coagulation method, dispersion method (mechanical disintegration, peptization, emulsification); emulsion, temporary emulsion, permanent emulsion; emulsifying agent or protective colloid; miscible liquids, nonmiscible liquids; dialysis, adsorption, flotation process, Cottrell process, cataphoresis, electroendosmosis.

15. (periodic table of the elements) first series: 1 hydrogen (H), 2 helium (He); second series: 3 lithium (Li), 4 beryllium (Be), 5 boron (B), 6 carbon (C), 7 nitrogen (N), 8 oxygen (O), 9 fluorine (F), 10 neon (Ne); third series: 11 sodium (Na), 12 magnesium (Mg), 13 aluminum (Al), 14 silicon (Si), 15 phosphorus (P), 16 sulfur (S), 17 chlorine (Cl), 18 argon (A); fourth series: 19 potassium (K), 20 calcium (Ca), 21 scandium (Sc), 22 titanium (Ti), 23 vanadium (V), 24 chromium (Cr), 25 manganese (Mn), 26 iron (Fe), 27 cobalt (Co), 28 nickel (Ni), 29 copper (Cu), 30 zinc (Zn), 31 gallium (Ga), 32 germanium (Ge), 33 arsenic (As), 34 selenium (Se), 35 bromine (Br), 36 krypton (Kr); fifth series: 37 rubidium (Rb), 38 strontium (Sr), 39 yttrium (Y), 40 zirconium (Zr), 41 niobium (Nb), 42 molybdenum (Mo), 43 technetium (Tc), 44 ruthenium (Ru), 45 rhodium (Rh), 46 palladium (Pd), 47 silver (Ag), 48 cadmium (Cd), 49 indium (In), 50 tin (Sn), 51 antimony (Sb), 52 tellurium (Te), 53 iodine (I), 54 xenon (Xe); sixth series: 55 cesium (Cs), 56 barium (Ba), 57 lanthanum (La), [lanthanide series 58–71] 58 cerium (Ce), 59 praseodynium (Pr), 60 neodymium (Nd), 61 promethium (Pm), 62 samarium (Sm), 63 europium (Eu), 64 gadolinium (Gd), 65 terbium (Tb), 66 dysprosium (Dy), 67 holmium (Ho), 68 erbium (Er), 69 thulium (Tm), 70 ytterbium (Yb), 71 lutecium or lutetium (Lu), 72 hafnium (Hf), 73 tantalum (Ta), 74 tungsten or wolfram (W), 75 rhenium (Re), 76 osmium (Os), 77 iridium (Ir), 78 platinum (Pt), 79 gold (Au), 80 mercury (Hg), 81 thallium (Tl), 82 lead (Pb), 83 bismuth (Bi), 84

polonium (Po), 85 astatine (At), 86 radon (Rn); seventh series: 87 francium (Fr), 88 radium (Ra), 89 actinium (Ac), [actinide series 90–102] 90 thorium (Th), 91 protactinium (Pa), 92 uranium (U), 93 neptunium (Np), 94 plutonium (Pu), 95 americium (Am), 96 curium (Cm), 97 berkelium (Bk), 98 californium (Cf), 99 einsteinium (Es), 100 fermium (Fm), 101 mendelevium (Md), 102 nobelium (No).

16. (apparatus and instruments) alembic, aspirator, blowpipe, Büchner funnel, Bunsen burner, burette or buret, crucible, desiccator, distiller, etna, Kipp apparatus, matrass, mortar, pestle, reagent bottle, receiver, retort, ring, ring stand, still, test tube.

8. GEOLOGY

1. geology, mineralogy, petrology, stratigraphy, paleontology, structural geology, glacial geology, geomorphology, oceanography, meteorology, geophysics, terrestrial magnetism, seismology, geodesy, geochemistry, petroleum geology, economic geology, engineering geology, hydrology.

2. crystal, crystallization; euhedral crystal, subhedral crystal, anhedral crystal; crystal symmetry, isometric system, hexagonal system, tetragonal system, orthorhombic system, monoclinic system, triclinic system.

3. minerals, amphibole group, feldspar group, mica group, pyroxene group; hornblende, apatite, azurite, bauxite, bornite, calcite, carnotite, cassiterite, chalcopyrite, chert, chlorite, chromite, copper, corundum, diamond, dolomite, epidote, microcline, orthoclase, albite, labradorite, anorthite, fluorite, galena, garnet, gold, graphite, gypsum, halite, hematite, kyanite, limonite, magnetite, malachite, biotite, lepidolite, muscovite, olivine, pyrite, augite, pyrrhotite, quartz, serpentine, sillimanite, sphalerite, staurolite, sulfur, talc, tourmaline.

4. (properties of minerals) specific gravity, cleavage, hardness, fracture, luster (adamantine luster, vitreous luster, resinous luster, greasy luster, pearly luster, silky luster), color, streak, taste, radio-activity, magnetism, opalescence, fluorescence; twinning.

5. (gross features of earth's crust) continent, continental shield, young folded mountain belt; zone of transition, continental margin, continental shelf, continental slope, continental rise; island arcs; ocean basin, deep oceanic crust, mid-ocean ridges; ocean currents; drift, tide, tidal current, wave, breaker, surf, sea, ground swell.

6. earthquake, shallow earthquake, intermediate earthquake, deep earthquake, volcanic earthquake; seismism; elastic rebound, foreshock, aftershock; shock wave, P wave or dilational wave or compressional wave or longitudinal wave, S wave or shear wave or transverse wave; Rayleigh wave; seismograph, seismometer, seismogram, accelerograph.

7. (deformation of earth's crust) isostasy; epeirogeny, uplifting, downwarping; orogeny, mountain building; diastrophism, confining pressure, stress, strain; fold, anticline, sycline, dome, basin, monocline; fault, fault plane, slickensides, hanging-wall side, foot-wall side, strike-slip movement, dip-slip movement, oblique-slip movement, normal fault, reverse fault, scissors fault, transverse fault, thrust fault, fault scarp, graben, horst, klippe, nappe or decke; fracture, tension fracture, shear fracture, rock cleavage; unconformity.

8. metamorphism, rock flowage, granulation, recrystallization, recombination; contact metamorphism, dynamic metamorphism; foliated metamorphic rock, nonfoliated metamorphic rock; slates, schists, gneisses, phyllites, marble, quartzite, hornfels, amphiboles.

9. volcano, cinder cone, lava cone, composite cone; shield volcano, flood basalt; vent, fumarole, solfatara, spatter cone, caldera; volcanism, eruption, explosion, expulsion, lava flow; (pyroclastic materials) blocks, bombs, lapilli, ash, volcanic dust; gases; lava, basalt lavas, rhyolite lavas, andesite lavas.

10. igneous rock, magmas, basaltic magma, granitic magma; (discordant igneous intrusions) batholith, stock, dike; (concordant igneous intrusions) sill, laccolith, lopolith; aphanitic rock, phaneritic rock, porphyritic rock, glassy rock; granite, graphic granite, granite pegmatite, orbicular granite, syenite, diorite, gabbro, peridotite, dunite, pyroxene, hornblendite, felsite, basalt,

dolerite, obsidian, pitchstone, pumice, scoria; pyroclastic debris, tuff, agglomerate, volcanic breccia.

11. sedimentary rock; marine environment, transitional environment, continental environment; residual deposits, transported deposits; mechanical deposition, chemical deposition, organic deposition; rudaceous rocks, arenaceous rocks, silty rocks, argillaceous rocks, chemically deposited siliceous rocks, carbonate rocks, chemically deposited ferruginous rocks, salt rocks, organically deposited siliceous rocks, calcareous rocks, phosphatic rocks, organically deposited ferruginous rocks, carbonaceous rocks; conglomerate, breccia; sandstone, arkose, graywacke; siltstone, loess; mudstone, shale; sinter, chert-flint; tufa, travertine, oölitic limestone, dolostone, lithographic limestone; ironstone, caliche, gypsum, anhydrite, halite; radiolarian ooze, diatom ooze; fossiliferous limestone, chalk, marl; rock phosphates, guano; bog iron ore; coal.

12. erosion, weathering; mechanical weathering, thermal contraction *and* expansion, unloading, crystal growth, freezing; chemical weathering, oxidation, hydration, carbonation; (specialized erosion) deflation, corrasion, abrasion, impact, corrosion, hydraulicking, quarrying, plucking, solution, slump, rolling, sliding, dislodgement, falling; transportation; deposition.

13. (wind erosion) undercut hill, cave rock, table, mushroom rock, ventifact, desert pavement, lag gravel; (running water erosion) river valley, pediment, peneplain, river terrace, wadi, pothole; (glacial erosion) striation, groove, drumlin, crescentic mark, u-shaped valley, truncated spur, hanging valley, cirque, fiord, col, arête, horn; (ground water erosion) cave, sinkhole, karst topography; (mass movement erosion) slide scar, surface subsidence; (ocean erosion) cliff, terrace, guyot, stack, arch, sea cave, notch.

14. (transportation methods) saltation, suspension, rolling, solution, pushing, dragging, slump, sliding, plastic flow, creep.

15. (wind deposits) loess, volcanic ash, volcanic dust, dune, Barchan dune, longitudinal dune, transverse dune, seif dune, parabolic dune; (running water deposits) alluvial fan, bar, channel fill, alluvial terrace, delta, levee, flood plain deposits; (glacial deposits) lateral moraine, terminal moraine, recessional moraine, medial moraine, ground moraine, esker, kame, terrace, outwash, varved lake clay, erratic; (ground water deposits) spring terrace, stalactite, stalagmite, pore fillings, vein *and* cavity filling, petrified wood; (mass movement deposits) talus cone, talus sheet, rock glacier, mud flow, felsenmeer; (ocean deposits) offshore beach, foreshore beach, backshore beach, barrier reef, atoll; shore line.

16. geologic time, era, period, epoch, age; rock system, rock series, rock stage; Precambrian Era; Paleozoic Era, Cambrian Period, Ordovician Period, Silurian Period, Devonian Period, Mississippian Period, Pennsylvanian Period, Permian Period; Mesozoic Era, Triassic Period, Jurassic Period, Cretaceous Period; Cenozoic Era, Paleogene Period, Paleocene Epoch, Eocene Epoch, Oligocene Epoch, Neogene Period, Miocene Epoch, Pliocene Epoch, Pleistocene Epoch.

9. ASTRONOMY

1. astronomy, cosmogony, interpretational astronomy, observational astronomy, descriptive astronomy, astrometry, geometrical astronomy, celestial mechanics; astrophysics, astrionics, radio astronomy, solar radio astronomy; astrobiology; planetology, heliography, actinometry, areography, cometography, astrography; celestial navigation, astrogation, nautical astronomy.

2. Ptolemaic system; Copernican system; evolutionary theory of the universe, expanding universe hypothesis, nebular hypothesis, collision hypothesis; planetismal hypothesis, protoplanet hypothesis; Lorentz-Fitzgerald contraction theory; infinity of the universe; Newton's universal laws of motion; Bode's law; Kepler's laws; Fechner's law; fission theory.

3. universe, cosmos, metagalaxy; firmament, space, deep space, interplanetary space, intergalactic space, interstellar space; lunar space, solar space.

4. solar system; planet; inner planets, outer planets; minor planets, major planets; inferior planets, superior plan-

ets; Mercury, Venus, Earth, Mars, Jupiter, Saturn, Uranus, Neptune, Pluto; evening star, morning star; satellite; asteroid, planetoid; comet (nucleus, coma, tail), periodic comets (Encke, Giacobini-Zinner, Pons-Winnecke, Biela, Faye, Arend, Westphal, Olbers, Halley, Herschel-Rigollet), comet group, comet family.

5. meteor, fire ball, bolide; meteor shower, Aquarids, Arietids, Draconids, Geminids, Leonids, Perseids; micrometeorite; meteorite, aerolite, achrondite, siderite, ataxite, siderolite.

6. sun; photosphere, sunspots, granules, faculae, plages, maculae; M regions; reversing layer; chromosphere, flocculi, spicules; corona, K corona, F corona; prominences, jets; limb; aureole; halo; Zeeman effect.

7. moon, new moon, first quarter, crescent moon, half-moon, last quarter gibbous moon, full moon; harvest moon, hunter's moon; lunar plains *or* maria *or* seas (Mare Foecunditatis, Mare Nectaris, Mare Crisium, Mare Tranquillitatis, Mare Serenitatis, Mare Imbrium, Oceanus Procellarum, Mare Nubium, Mare Humorum), lunar mountain ranges, lunar rays, lunar rills, lunar craters (Alphonsus, Archimedes, Aristarchus, Aristoteles, Arzachel, Bullialdus, Catharina, Clavius, Copernicus, Cyrillus, Eratosthenes, Furnerius, Gassendi, Grimaldi, Kepler, Langrenus, Maginus, Maurolycus, Petavius, Plato, Proclus, Ptolemaeus, Schickard, Theophilus, Tycho).

8. star, circumpolar star, double star, binary star, lucid star, lucida, faint companion star, astrometric companion, multiple star, nova, supernova, Kepler's star; Population I stars, Population II stars; main sequence stars; dwarf, subdwarf, white dwarf, subgiant, giant, red giant, blue giant, supergiant; variable star, Cepheid variables, RR Lyrae variables, irregular variables, eclipsing variables, Mira-type stars; high velocity stars; star cluster, galactic cluster, globular cluster, moving cluster; Hertzsprung-Russell diagram, color-magnitude diagram, color index; magnitude, apparent magnitude, absolute magnitude, bolometric magnitude; absolute luminosity, period-luminosity relation; Messier number.

9. (stars) Achernar, Acrux, Adhara, Albireo, Alcor, Aldebaran, Algol, Alioth, Alkaid, Alphard, Alphecca, Alpheratz, Altair, Antares, Arcturus, Bellatrix, Benetnasch, Betelgeuse, Canopus, Capella, Caph, Castor, Cor Caroli, Deneb, Deneb Kaitos, Denebola, Dubhe, Fomalhaut, Hamal, Kaus Australis, Kochab, Marfak, Markab, Megrez, Merak, Mira, Mizar, Phad, Polaris, Pollux, Procyon, Rasalhague, Regulus, Rigel, Rigil Kentaurus, Saiph, Shaula, Sirius, Spica, Thuban, Vega; (constellations) Andromeda, Aquarius, Aquila, Ara, Aries, Auriga, Boötes, Canes Venatici, Canis Major, Canis Minor, Capricornus, Carina, Cassiopeia, Centaurus, Cepheus, Cetus, Columba, Corona Borealis, Corvus, Crux, Cygnus, Delphinus, Draco, Eridanus, Gemini, Grus, Hercules, Hydra, Hydrus, Leo, Lepus, Libra, Lupus, Lyra, Musca, Ophiuchus, Orion, Pavo, Pegasus, Perseus, Phoenix, Puppis, Sagitta, Sagittarius, Scorpius, Serpens, Taurus, Triangulum, Triangulum Australe, Tucana, Ursa Major, Ursa Minor, Vela, Virgo.

10. nebulae, galactic nebulae, bright nebulae, dark nebulae, planetary nebulae, diffuse nebulae; Orion Nebula, Coal Sack Nebula, Loop Nebula; extragalactic nebulae, external galaxy, galaxy, spiral galaxy, barred spiral galaxy, elliptical galaxy, irregular galaxy; galactic cluster; galactic window; Milky Way; Magellanic Clouds, Andromeda Nebula.

11. celestial sphere; celestial equator, celestial poles, celestial meridian, antimeridian, zenith, nadir, vertical circle, diurnal circle, horizon, azimuth; hour angle, hour circle; amplitude; altitude, altitude circle, altitude difference; declination; apex, antapex; culmination; astronomical latitude, celestial latitude, astronomical longitude, celestial longitude; ecliptic; right ascension; equinox, autumnal equinox, vernal equinox; solstice, summer solstice, winter solstice.

12. celestial motion; proper motion; rotation; revolution; orbit, perihelion, aphelion, apogee, perigee; inclination, perturbation; libration; precession, nutation; acceleration, deceleration; antecedence; arc of progression, arc of retrogression; anomaly; inequality; daily aberration, annual aberration.

13. transit; occultation; immersion;

eclipse, annular eclipse, partial eclipse, total eclipse, umbra, penumbra; conjunction, inferior conjunction, synodic period, sidereal period.

14. gravity; acceleration of gravity, g; antigravity; barycenter; galactic center; atmospheric tides.

15. (instruments) accelerometer; astrolabe; astronomical triangle; barograph, barometer; chronometer, chronograph, astronomical clock; helioscope, spectrohelioscope, spectroheliograph, coronagraph, heliometer, magnetograph; illuminometer; sextant; thermocouple; spectroscope, spectrograph, spectrobolometer, micrometer; telescope, astronomical telescope, meridian circle telescope, equatorial telescope; reflecting telescope, Newtonian telescope, coelostat; refracting telescope; radio telescope; astronomical observatory; planetarium.

INDEX TO
SCIENTIFIC THESAURUS

anhydrite 8.11
anhydrous compound 7.10
animal biology 2.1
animal kingdom 2.2
animal psychology 3.1
animal subkingdoms 2.2
animal worship 4.19
animatism 4.19
animism 4.19
anion 7.6
Annelida 2.3
annual 1.13
annual aberration 9.12
annual ring 1.9
annular eclipse 9.13
anode physics 6.19
  chemistry 7.6
anomaly 9.12
anorthite 8.3
antagonistic
  acculturation 4.9
antapex 9.11
Antares 9.9
antecedence 9.12
antecedent 5.7
antenna 2.18
anterior end 2.7
anther 1.15
antheridium 1.18
Anthocerotae 1.4
Anthocerotales 1.4
Anthozoa 2.3
anthracene 7.12
anthracene series 7.12
anthropology 2.1; 4
anthropometry 4.1
anthropomorphism 4.19
anticathexia 3.20
anticline 8.7
antigravity 9.14
antilogarithm 5.19
antimeridian 9.11
antimony 7.15
antinode 6.11
antisocial personality 3.7
anus 2.13
anxiety 3.10
anxiety hysteria 3.10
anxiety neurosis 3.8
aorta 2.16
apathy 3.10
apatite 8.3
apex mathematics 5.10
  astronomy 9.11
aphanitic rock 8.10
aphasia 3.12
aphelion 9.12
aphonia 3.12
aphrasia 3.13
aphrodisia 3.16
apical meristem 1.11
apogee 9.12
Apollonian
  configuration 4.9
apotropaism 4.19
apparatus, chemical 7.16

apparent magnitude 9.8
appendicular skeleton 2.9
apperception test 3.5
applied mathematics 5.1
applied psychology 3.1
apraxia 3.13
aptitude test 3.5
Aquarids 9.5
Aquarius 9.9
Aquila 9.9
Ara 9.9
Arabic 4.20
Arachnoidea 2.3
Araucanian 4.20
Arawak 4.20
arc mathematics 5.14
  - of progression 9.12
  - of retrogression 9.12
arch 8.13
archegonium 1.18
archaeology 4.1
Archiannelida 2.3
Archimedes 9.7
Archimedes'
  principle 6.3
arcsin x 5.18
Arcturus 9.9
area mathematics 5.11
  culture 4.9
arenaceous rocks 8.11
Arend 9.4
areography 9.1
areolar connective
  tissue 2.6
arête 8.13
argillaceous rocks 8.11
argon 7.15
argument 5.5
Aries 9.9
Arietids 9.5
Aristarchus 9.7
Aristoteles 9.7
arithmetic 5.1
arithmetical mean 5.3
arithmetical
  progression 5.6
arithmetic means 5.6
arkose 8.11
armature 6.19
arm bones 2.10
Armenian 4.20
Armenoid 4.7
aromatic hydrocarbons 7.12
arrested development 3.15
arsenic 7.15
arteriosclerotic
  psychosis 3.9
artery 2.16
Arthropoda 2.3
artifacts 4.15
art mobilier 4.22
arts, primitive 4.22
Arzachel 9.7
Aschelminthes 2.3
Ascomycetae 1.4
ascorbic acid 7.8

ascribed status 4.11
asexual reproduction
  botany 1.18
  zoology 2.20
ash 8.9
Asiatic 4.7
aspirator 7.16
assimilation botany 1.5
  zoology 2.13
  anthropology 4.9
association 4.11
association psychology 3.2
association test 3.5
Assyrian 4.20
astatine 7.15
asteroid 9.4
Asteroidea 2.3
asthenia 3.10
astraphobia 3.10
astrionics 9.1
astrobiology 9.1
astrogation 9.1
astrography 9.1
astrolabe 9.15
astrometric companion 9.8
astrometry 9.1
astronomical
  observatory 9.15
astronomical
  telescope 9.15
astronomy 9
astrophysics 9.1
ataxites 9.5
Athapaskan 4.20
athletic type 4.8
atmospheric pressure 6.3
atmospheric tides 9.14
atoll 8.15
atom 6.2
atom crystal 7.10
atomic energy 6.22
atomic number 6.2
atomic physics 6.1
atomic weight 6.2
atom smasher 6.22
audio frequency 6.10
auditory amnesia 3.13
auditory nerve 2.18
augend 5.3
augite 8.3
augury 4.19
aureole 9.6
Auriga 9.9
Aurignacian industries 4.6
Aurignacian stage 4.5
aussage test 3.5
austerities 4.19
Australoid 4.7
Australopithecus
  africanus 4.3
autistic thinking 3.17
autonomic movement 1.7
autonomic nervous
  system 2.17
autosuggestion 3.4

autotrophic plant 1.6
autumnal equinox 9.11
average 5.3
Aves 2.3
avuncular marriage 4.13
avunculate 4.12
awl 4.15
axial skeleton 2.9
axillary bud 1.11
axis of symmetry 5.17
axon 2.17
Azilian-Tardenoisian
  stage 4.5
azimuth 9.11
azurite 8.3

B

Babcock-Levy test 3.5
Babylonian 4.20
bachelor's house 4.16
backbone 2.10
backed blade 4.15
backshore beach 8.15
bacteriology 1.2
balanced equation 7.3
Balto-Slavic 4.20
band 4.14
Bantu 4.20
bar 8.15
barbarism 4.9
Barchan dune 8.15
barium 7.15
bark 1.9
barograph 6.3; 9.15
barometer 6.3; 9.15
barred spiral galaxy 9.10
barrier reef 8.15
barrow 4.16
barter 4.18
barycenter 9.14
basal metabolic rate 2.12
basalt 8.10
basaltic magma 8.10
basalt lavas 8.9
base number 5.4
  - of a triangle 5.13
  chemistry 7.7, 8
basic anhydride 7.11
basic salt 7.7
Basidiomycetae 1.4
basin 8.7
basket 4.15
batholith 8.10
battle fatigue 3.8
bauxite 8.3
beat 6.10
behavioral pattern 4.9
behavior psychology 3.2
bel 6.10
Bellatrix 9.9
Benetnasch 9.9
Bennettitales 1.4
benzene 7.12
benzene series 7.12
benzoic acid 7.8
Berber 4.20

berkelium 7.15
Bernoulli's principle 6.3
Bernreuter personality inventory 3.5
berry 1.16
beryllium 7.15
bestiality 3.16
beta particle 6.22
beta test 3.5
betatron 6.22
Betelgeuse 9.9
biceps 2.11
bicuspid valve 2.16
Biela 9.4
biennial 1.13
biface 4.15
bilateral descent 4.12
bilateral kinship 4.12
bilateral symmetry 2.7
bilithon 4.16
bimetallic bar 6.9
binary acid 7.7
binary compound 7.4
binary fission 2.20
binary salt 7.7
binary star 9.8
Binet-Simon test 3.5
binomial expression 5.5
binomial theorem 5.8
biochemistry 7.1
biological chemistry 7.1
biological family 4.12
biology, plant 1.1
    animal 2.1
biophysics 6.1
biotite 8.3
biquadratic equation 5.8
biradial symmetry 2.7
birth rite 4.19
bismuth 7.15
bismuth subnitrate 7.8
blade 1.14
blade tool 4.15
blade work 4.6
blast neurosis 3.8
blocks 8.9
blood 2.6, 16
blood group 4.8
blood platelets 2.16
blood type 4.8
blowpipe 7.16
blue dwarf 9.8
blue giant 9.8
Bode's Law 9.2
bodily fullness index 4.8
bog iron ore 8.11
boiling 6.4
boiling point 6.4
bola 4.15
bolide 9.5
bolometric magnitude 9.8
bombs 8.9
bone 2.6, 10
boomerang 4.15
Boötes 9.9

borer 4.15
boric acid 7.8
bornite 8.3
boron 7.15
borrowing, cultural 4.9
Boskop man 4.4
botany 1
bound morpheme 4.21
bow and arrow 4.15
Boyle's Law 6.9
brachial index 4.8
Brachiata 2.3
Brachiopoda 2.3
brachycephalic index 4.8
brain 2.17
brain case 2.10
branching stem 1.12
breaker 8.5
breastbone 2.10
breathing 2.15
breccia 8.11
brick tea money 4.18
bride price 4.13
bright-line spectrum 6.16
bright nebulae 9.10
British thermal unit 6.9
bromine 7.15
bronchi 2.15
bronchial tubes 2.15
Bronze Age 4.5
brotherhood 4.11
Brownian movement 6.3
Brünn man 4.4
brush 6.19
Bryales 1.4
bryology 1.2
Bryophyta 1.4
Bryozoa 2.3
btu 6.9
Büchner funnel 7.16
bud 1.11
budding 2.20
bud scale 1.14
bulb 1.12
bulimia 3.11
Bulliardus 9.7
Bunsen burner 8.16 7.16
buoyancy 6.3
burette, buret 7.16
burial 4.19
burin 4.15
Burmese 4.20
butanone 7.13
butylene 7.12
butyric acid 7.8

C

cacique 4.14
cadmium 7.15
caecum 2.13
cajoling 4.19
Calamitales 1.4
Calcarea 2.3
calcareous rocks 8.11
calcite 8.3

calcium 7.15
calcium carbonate 7.8
calcium hydroxide 7.8
calculation 5.3
calculus 5.1
caldera 8.9
caliche 8.11
californium 7.15
calorie 6.9
calorimetry 6.1
calyx 1.15
cambium 1.9
Cambrian Period 8.16
candle 6.12
candle power 6.12
Canes Venatici 9.9
Canis Major 9.9
Canis Minor 9.9
cannibalism 3.16
Canopus 9.9
capacitance 6.18
capacitive reactance 6.18
capacitor 6.19
Capella 9.9
Caph 9.9
capillarity 6.3
capillary 2.16
Capricornus 9.9
capsule 1.16
carbohydrates 7.13
carbolic acid 7.8
carbon 7.15
carbonaceous rocks 8.11
carbonate rocks 8.11
carbonation 8.12
cardiac muscle 2.11
cardinal number 5.2
card test 3.5
Carib 4.20
Carina 9.9
carnotite 8.3
carotid artery 2.16
carotin 1.8
carpals 2.10
carpel 1.15
cartesian coordinates 5.9
cartilage 2.6
caryopsis 1.16
Cassiopeia 9.9
cassiterite 8.3
caste 4.11
Castor 9.9
castration complex 3.15
catabolism botany 1.5
    zoology 2.12
catalepsis 3.13
catalepsy 3.13
catalyst 7.5
catalytic agent 7.5
cataphoresis 7.14
cataplexy 3.13
catatonia 3.9
catatonic stupor 3.10
Catharina 9.7
catharsis 3.19
cathectic energy 3.20
cathexis 3.20

cathode 6.19; 7.6
cathode rays 6.21
cathode-ray tube 6.21
cation 7.6
catkin 1.15
Cattell's infant intelligence scale 3.5
Caucasoid 4.7
caudal vertebrae 2.10
cave 8.13
cave art 4.22
cave rock 8.13
cavity filling 8.15
celestial equator 9.11
celestial sphere 9.11
cell botany 1.8
    zoology 2.4
cell respiration 2.15
cellulose botany 1.8
    chemistry 7.13
Celtic 4.20
Cenozoic era
    anthropology 4.2
    geology 8.16
Centaurus 9.9
center
    culture 4.9
    of a conic section 5.17
    - of percussion 6.5
    - of curvature 6.13
centigrade scale 6.9
centimeter-gram-second system 6.9
central nervous system 2.17
centric 5.10
centrifugal force 6.6
centriole 2.4
centripetal force 6.6
centroid 5.14
centrosome 2.4
centrosphere 2.4
cephalic index 4.8
Cephalochordata 2.3
Cephalopoda 2.3
Cepheid variables 9.8
Cepheus 9.9
cerebellum 2.17
cerebrum 2.17
ceremony 4.19
cerium 7.15
cervical vertebrae 2.10
cesium 7.15
Cestoda 2.3
Cetus 9.9
Chaetognatha 2.3
chain compound 7.4
chain reaction 6.22
chalcopyrite 8.3
chalk 8.11
Chancelade man 4.4
channel fill 8.15
character dance 4.22
characteristic 5.19
charge 3.20
Charles' law 6.9
Chatelperronian industries 4.6
Chellean stage 4.5
chemical apparatus 7.16

corrasion 8.12
corresponding angles 5.12
corrosion 8.12
cortex 1.9
corundum 8.3
Corvus 9.9
corymb 1.15
cosecant 5.18
cosine 5.18
cosmic rays 6.22
cosmogony 9.1
cosmos 9.3
cotangent 5.18
Cottrell process 7.14
cotyledon 1.17
coulomb 6.20
Coulomb's Law 6.18
countercharge 3.20
countertransference 3.19
coup de poing 4.15
couple 6.6
courtship dance 4.22
covalent compound 7.4
covalent linkage 7.4
covert exchange 4.18
cranial index 4.8
cranium 2.10
craters, lunar 9.7
creep 8.14
cremation 4.19
crescentic mark 8.13
crescent moon 9.7
crest 6.10
Cretaceous Period 8.16
crime 4.10
Crinoidea 2.3
critical angle 6.14
critical mass 6.22
critical pressure 6.4
critical temperature 6.4
Cro-Magnon art 4.22
Cro-Magnon man 4.4
cromlech 4.16
crop 2.13
cross-cousin 4.12
cross-cousin marriage 4.13
crossing over 1.19
crucible 7.16
crural index 4.8
Crustacea 2.3
Crux 9.9
crystal chemistry 7.10
geology 8.2
crystal growth 8.12
crystalline substance 7.2
crystallization 8.2
Ctenophora 2.3
cube mathematics 5.16
chemistry 7.10
cube root 5.4
cuboidal epithelium 2.6
culmination 9.11
cult 4.19
cultivation 4.17

cultural anthropology 4.1
culture 4.9
culture hero myth 4.22
culture-historical diffusionism 4.9
cuneiform 4.21
curium 7.15
curve 5.10
curvilinear motion 6.5
cusp 5.10
custom 4.10
cutin 1.8
Cyanophyta 1.4
Cycadales 1.4
Cycadofilicales 1.4
Cycadophyte line 1.4
cyclothymia 3.9
cyclotron 6.22
Cygnus 9.9
cylinder 5.16
cyme 1.15
Cyrillus 9.7
cytology 2.1
cytoplasm botany 1.8
zoology 2.4
cytoplasmic inclusions 2.4
cytosome 1.8

D

daily aberration 9.12
dance 4.22
dark-line spectrum 6.16
dark nebulae 9.10
Dawn Stone Age 4.5
D. C. 6.18
death dance 4.22
deceleration 9.12
decibel 6.10
deciduous plant 1.13
decimal 5.2
decimal fraction 5.2
decimal logarithm 5.19
decke 8.7
declination 9.11
magnetic- 6.17
decompensation 3.17
decomposition 7.5
decorative art 4.22
decrepitation 7.10
deep earthquake 8.6
deep oceanic crust 8.5
deep space 9.3
defecation 2.13
defense mechanism 3.17
deflation 8.12
degenerative psychosis 3.9
degree mathematics 5.12
heat 6.9
dehiscent fruit 1.16
deliquescent branching 1.12
deliquescent substance 7.10

delirium 3.12
Delphinus 9.9
delta 8.15
deltoid 2.11
delusion 3.12
- of grandeur 3.12
- of persecution 3.12
dementia paralytica 3.9
dementia praecox 3.9
Demospongiae 2.3
demotic 4.21
dendrites 2.17
dendrology 1.2
Deneb 9.9
Deneb Kaitos 9.9
Denebola 9.9
denominator 5.2
density 6.3
dependent variable 5.5
deposition 8.12
depression 3.10
depth interview 3.4
depth psychology 3.4
dermal skeleton 2.9
descent 4.12
descriptive astronomy 9.1
desert pavement 8.13
desiccator 7.16
desire concentration 3.20
detached coefficient 5.5
detachment 3.10
determinate equation 5.8
determinate inflores-cence 1.15
Deuteromycetae 1.4
devil worship 4.19
Devonian Period 8.16
dew point 6.4
diabolism 4.19
diacid base 7.7
diagonal 5.11
dialysis 7.14
diameter 5.14
diamond 8.3
diaphragm 2.15
diastrophism 8.7
diatom ooze 8.11
diatonic scale 6.11
dibasic acid 7.7
dibble 4.15
dicotyledon 1.17
Dicotyledonae 1.4
dielectric 6.19
diethyl ether 7.13
differential expansion 6.9
differential psychology 3.1
differentiation 1.5
diffraction 6.14
diffuse nebulae 9.10
diffusion botany 1.5
anthropology 4.9
- of molecules 6.3
- of light 6.13
diffusionism 4.9

digestion botany 1.5
zoology 2.13
digestive glands 2.19
digestive system 2.13
digging stick 4.15
digit 5.2
dihydroxy alcohols 7.13
dike 8.10
dilational wave 8.6
dilute solution 7.9
dimension 5.5
Dinaric 4.7
diode 6.21
dioecious animal 2.21
dioecious plant 1.15
Dionysian configuration 4.9
diopter 6.14
diorite 8.10
diploid cell 1.19
Diplopoda 2.3
dipping needle 6.17
dip-slip movement 8.7
dipsomania 3.14
direct current 6.18
directrix 5.17
discordant igneous intrusions 8.10
discovery 4.9
dislodgement 8.12
disorientation 3.13
dispersed medium 7.14
dispersing medium 7.14
dispersion 6.16
dispersion method 7.14
displacement psychology 3.17
chemistry 7.5
dissociation psychology 3.9, 10, 13
physics 6.18
chemistry 7.6
dissonance 6.11
distal end 2.7
distillate 6.4
distillation 6.4
distiller 7.16
diurnal circle 9.11
dividend 5.3
divination 4.19
division taxonomy 1.3
cell 1.18
mathematics 5.3
divisor 5.3
divorce 4.13
dog tooth money 4.18
dolerite 8.10
dolichocephalic index 4.8
dolmen 4.16
dolomite 8.3
dolostone 8.11
dome 8.7
dominant character 1.19
dominant gene 1.19
Doppler effect 6.12
dormancy 1.17
dorsal surface 2.7

double decomposition
7.5
double membrane
drum 4.22
double salt 7.7
double star 9.8
downwarping 8.7
dowry 4.13
Draco 9.9
Draconids 9.5
dragging 8.14
Dravidian race 4.7
linguistic stock 4.20
dream analysis 3.4
dream state 3.13
dream symbolism 3.4
drift 8.5
drive 4.9
Druid 4.19
drum 4.22
drumlin 8.13
drupe 1.16
dry cultivation 4.17
dry fruit 1.16
Dryopithecus 4.3
Dryopithecus darwini
4.3
Dryopithecus fontani
4.3
Dryopithecus
rhenanus 4.3
dry painting 4.22
dual chief 4.14
Dubhe 9.9
ductility 6.3
dumb barter 4.18
dune 8.15
dunite 8.10
dwarf 9.8
dynamic equilibrium
7.5
dynamic
metamorphism 8.8
dynamic psychology
3.1
dynamics 6.1
dynastic incest 4.13
dyne 6.6
dysarthria 3.12
dysprosium 7.15

E

ear 2.18
eardrum 2.18
Early Bronze Age 4.5
Earth 9.4
earthquake 8.6
East Baltic 4.7
eccentricity 5.17
Echinodera 2.3
Echinodermata 2.3
Echinoidea 2.3
Echiuroidea 2.3
echo 6.10
echolalia 3.12
eclipse 9.13
eclipsing variable 9.8
ecliptic 9.11
ecology 2.1
economic botany 1.1

economic geology 8.1
economy 4.18
ectomorphy 4.8
ectoplast 1.8
eddy current 6.18
effective component
6.6
efficiency 6.8
effigy mound 4.16
efflorescent substance
7.10
egg 1.18
egg cell 2.21
ego 3.6
ego-id conflict 3.6
ego-ideal 3.6
Egyptian 4.20
Ehringsdorf forms 4.4
Ehringsdorf group 4.4
eidolism 4.19
einsteinium 7.15
Einstein's general
theory of relativity
6.12
Einstein's special
theory of relativity
6.12
elasticity 6.3
elastic limit 6.3
elastic rebound 8.6
elation 3.10
Electra complex 3.15
electric current 6.18
electric field 6.18
electricity science 6.1
energy 6.18
electrode 6.19
electroendosmosis
7.14
electrolysis 6.18; 7.6
electrolyte 6.18; 7.6
electrolytic cell 6.19
electrolytic
dissociation 7.6
electromagnetic
induction 6.18
electromagnetic
radiations 6.16
electromagnetic
spectrum 6.16
electromagnetism 6.18
electromotive force
6.18
electron 6.2
electronics 6.1
electrophorus 6.19
electroplating 6.18
electroscope 6.20
electroshock therapy
3.4
electrostatics 6.1
electrovalent
compound 7.4
element mathematics
5.5
physics 6.2
chemistry 7.2
culture- 4.9
elementary family 4.12
elementary
mathematics 5.1

elementary-particle
physics 6.1
elementary particles
6.2
ellipse 5.17
elliptical galaxy 9.10
embryo botany 1.17
zoology 2.22
embryogeny 2.22
embryology 2.1, 22
e.m.f. 6.18
emotional attachment
3.19
emotional instability
3.10
emotional insulation
3.17
emulsification 7.14
emulsifying agent 7.14
emulsion 7.14
Encke 9.4
endocarp 1.16
endocrine glands 2.19
endodermis 1.9
endogamous
community 4.14
endogamy 4.13
endomorphy 4.8
endoplast 1.8
endoskeleton 2.9
endothermic reaction
7.5
end plates 2.17
energy 6.7
energy charge 3.20
engineering geology
8.1
entomology 2.1
Entoprocta 2.3
envelope 5.10
environment, marine
8.11
envoûtement 4.19
Eoanthropus dawsoni
4.4
Eocene epoch
anthropology 4.2
geology 8.16
eolith 4.15
Eolithic Age 4.5
epeirogeny 8.7
epicanthic fold 4.8
epidermis 1.9
epididymis 2.21
epidote 8.3
epiglottis 2.15
Epipaleolithic Age 4.5
epithelial tissue 2.6
epithelium 2.6
epoch 8.16
equalitarian clan 4.12
equation mathematics
5.8
chemistry 7.3
equator
magnetic- 6.17
celestial- 9.11
equatorial telescope
9.15
equilateral triangle
5.13

equilibrant 6.6
equilibrium 6.6
equilibrium constant
7.5
equinox 9.11
Equisetales 1.4
Equisetinae 1.4
era 8.16
Eratosthenes 9.7
erbium 7.15
erg 6.7
Eridanus 9.9
erosion 8.12
erotomania 3.14
erratic 8.15
eruption 8.9
erythrocytes 2.16
escape mechanism
3.17
escapist 3.7
esker 8.15
Eskimo-Aleut 4.20
esophagus 2.13
esters 7.13
ethane 7.12
ethers 7.13
Ethiopian 4.20
ethnography 4.1
ethnology 4.1
ethyl alcohol 7.13
ethylene 7.12
ethylene series 7.12
etiquette 4.10
etna 7.16
Euglenophyta 1.4
euhedral crystal 8.2
Eumycophyta 1.4
euphoria 3.10
europium 7.15
euryprosopic index 4.8
Eustachian tube 2.18
evaporation 6.4
evening star 9.4
evergreen 1.13
evolutionary theory of
the universe 9.2
evolution, cultural 4.9
evolutionism 4.9
exchange 4.18
excretion botany 1.5
zoology 2.14
excretory system 2.14
excurrent branching
1.12
exhaustive psychosis
3.9
exhibitionism 3.16
existential psychology
3.1
exocarp 1.16
exogamy 4.13
exoskeleton 2.9
exothermic reaction
7.5
expanding universe
hypothesis 9.2
expansion 6.9
expectation 5.6
experimental
psychology 3.1
expiration 2.15

Geraniales 1.4
Germanic 4.20
germanium 7.15
germination 1.17
gerontocracy 4.14
Gesell's development
  schedule 3.5
Gestalt psychology 3.2
gestational psychosis
  3.9
ghost, ghost soul 4.19
Giacobini-Zinner9
gibbous moon .74.9
gift barter 4.18
gift exchange 4.18
Gigantanthropus 4.4
Gigantopithecus blacki
  4.4
gills 2.15
Ginkgoales 1.4
girdles 2.9
gizzard 2.13
glacial deposits 8.15
glacial erosion 8.13
glacial geology 8.1
glands 2.19
glassy rock 8.10
globular cluster 9.8
globulin 7.13
glottis 2.15
glutelin 7.13
gnathic index 4.8
gneisses 8.8
Gnetales 1.4
god 4.19
gold chemistry 7.15
  geology 8.3
Goldstein-Sheerer test
  3.5
Golgi network 2.4
gonads 2.19, 21
gong 4.22
gourd 4.15
graben 8.7
graded society 4.11
gradient 5.10
grain 1.16
gram-centimeter 6.7
Graminales 1.4
grammar 4.21
granite 8.10
granite pegmatite 8.10
granitic magma 8.10
granulation 8.8
granules 9.6
graph 5.9
graphical geometry 5.1
graphic granite 8.10
graphite 8.3
Gravettian industries
  4.6
gravitation 6.6
gravity physics 6.6
  astronomy 9.14
graywacke 8.11
greasy luster 8.4
great circle 5.16
Grimaldi 9.7
Grimaldi man 4.4
groove 8.13
ground moraine 8.15

ground swell 8.5
ground water deposits
  8.15
ground water erosion
  8.13
group marriage 4.13
group therapy 3.4
growth 1.5
Grus 9.9
guano 8.11
guttation 1.5
guyot 8.13
Gymnospermae 1.4
gynoecium 1.15
gypsum 8.3, 11

H

hafnium 7.15
hair 2.9
half marriage 4.13
half-moon 9.7
halite 8.3, 11
Halley 9.4
hallucinosis 3.12
halo 9.6
halogen substitution
  products 7.13
Hamal 9.9
Hamburgian
  industries 4.6
Hamitic 4.20
handicraft economy
  4.18
hand index 4.8
hanging valley 8.13
hanging-wall side 8.7
haploid cell 1.19
hardness 8.4
harmonic progression
  5.6
harpoon 4.15
harvest moon 9.7
head botany 1.15
  zoology 2.9
headman 4.14
hearing 2.18
heart 2.16
heartwood 1.9
heat 6.1, 9
  - of fusion 6.4
  - of vaporization 6.4
  - of neutralization 7.4
  - of formation 7.4
  - of combustion 7.11
heat engine 6.9
hebephrenia 3.9
Hebrew 4.20
Heidelberg man 4.4
heliography 9.1
heliolithic diffusionism
  4.9
heliometer 9.15
helioscope 9.15
heliotropism 1.7
helium 7.15
Hellenic 4.20
helminthology 2.1
hematite 8.3
hematophobia 3.10
hemicellulose 1.8

Hemichordata 2.3
henry 6.20
Hepaticae 1.4
heptagon 5.15
herb 1.13
Hercules 9.9
heredity 1.19
hermaphrodite 2.21
hermaphroditism 2.21
hero cult 4.19
hero worship 4.19
herpetology 2.1
Herschel-Rigollet 9.4
Hertzsprung-Russell
  diagram 9.8
heterogametes 1.18
heterogamy 1.18
heterotrophic plant 1.6
heterozygous plant
  1.19
Hexactinellida 2.3
hexagon 5.15
hexagonal crystal 7.10
hexagonal system 8.2
hexahedron 5.16
hieratic 4.21
hieroglyphic 4.21
high-energy physics
  6.1
higher hunting 4.17
higher mathematics
  5.1
high god 4.19
high velocity stars 9.8
hilum 1.17
hip girdle 2.10
Hirudinea 2.3
histology 2.1
Hittite 4.20
hoe 4.15
hoe agriculture 4.17
hydrophobia 3.10
hybridization 1.19
holmium 7.15
Holocene epoch 4.2
Holothuroidea 2.3
Homo Africanthropus
  4.4
homogeneous matter
  7.2
Homo heidelbergensis
  4.4
homologous
  chromosomes 1.19
Homo neanderthal-
  ensis 4.4
Homo Sapiens 4.4
Homo soloensis 4.4
homozygous plant 1.19
Hooke's law 6.3
horde 4.14
horizon 9.11
horizontal coordinate
  5.9
horizontal line 5.10
horn 8.13
hornblende 8.3
hornblendite 8.10
hornfels 8.8
horny plates 2.9
horsepower 6.7

horst 8.7
horticulture 4.17
hospitality 4.19
host 1.6
hostile personality 3.7
Hottentot-Bushman
  4.7
hour angle 9.11
hour circle 9.11
human evolution 4.1
human paleontology
  4.1
human sacrifice 4.19
humerus 2.10
humidity 6.4
hunter's moon 9.7
hunting 4.17
hybrid, hybridization
  1.19
Hydra 9.9
hydrate 7.10
hydration 8.12
hydraulicking 8.12
hydraulics 6.1
hydrocarbon
  derivatives 7.13
hydrocarbons 7.12
hydrochloric acid 7.8
hydrodynamics 6.1
hydrofluoric acid 7.8
hydrogen 7.15
hydrogen ion
  concentration 7.7
hydrology 8.1
hydrolysis zoology
  2.13
  chemistry 7.7
hydrometer 6.3
hydrophilic colloidal
  system 7.14
hydrophobia 3.9, 10
hydrophobic colloidal
  system 7.14
hydrostatics 6.1
hydrotropism 1.7
Hydrozoa 2.3
Hydrus 9.9
hygiene, mental 3.3
hygroscopic substance
  7.10
hyperbola 5.17
hypercathexis 3.20
hyperons 6.2
hypnoanalysis 3.4
hypnotherapy 3.4
hypnotic suggestion
  3.4
hypochondriac 3.7
hypocotyl 1.17
hypoglycemic shock
  therapy 3.4
hypophysis 2.19
hypotenuse 5.13
hysteria 3.10
hysterical aphonia 3.12

I

ichthyology 2.1
id 3.6

ideal mechanical
    advantage 6.8
ideal pattern 4.9
identification 3.19
ideograph 4.21
ideographic writing
    4.21
idiophone 4.22
igneous rock 8.10
ilium 2.10
illuminated body 6.12
illumination 6.12
illuminometer 9.15
image 6.13
imaginary number 5.2
imbibition 1.5
imitative magic 4.19
immaturity 3.10
immersion 9.13
impact 8.12
impedance 6.18
impenetrability 6.3
improper fraction 5.2
impulse 6.5
inactive element 7.2
incandescence 6.12
incapsulating language
    4.21
incest 4.13
inclination, magnetic
    6.17
    astronomy 9.12
inclined plane 6.8
incoherence 3.12
incomplete reaction 7.5
incorporation, rite of
    4.19
incorporeal property
    4.18
increase rite 4.19
indehiscent fruit 1.16
independent variable
    5.5
indeterminate
    inflorescence 1.15
index anthropology 4.8
    mathematics 5.4, 19
    - of refraction 6.14
indicators 7.7
indium 7.15
individual cult 4.19
individual psychology
    3.1
Indo-European 4.20
Indo-Iranian 4.20
Indonesian-Malay 4.7
induced current 6.18
induced magnetism
    6.17
inductance 6.18
induction 6.18
inductive reactance
    6.18
industrial psychology
    3.1
ineffective component
    6.6
inequality 9.12
inertia 6.5
infantile fixation 3.15

inferior conjunction
    9.13
inferiority complex
    3.15
inferior planets 9.4
infinite sequence 5.6
infinity of the universe
    9.2
inflective language
    4.21
inflorescence 1.15
infrared rays 6.16
infrasonic frequency
    6.10
ingestion 2.13
inhibition 3.17
initial side 5.12
initiation rite 4.19
ink-blot test 3.5
inner planets 9.4
inorganic chemistry
    7.1
inorganic matter 7.2
inorganic oxidation
    7.11
input 6.8
Insecta 2.3
inspiration 2.15
instruments
    astronomical- 9.15
    chemical- 7.16
insulator heat 6.9
    electricity 6.19
insulin coma therapy
    3.4
insulin shock therapy
    3.4
intangible property
    4.18
integer 5.2
integration of culture
    4.9
integration of
    personality 3.18
intelligence test 3.5
intensification, rite of
    4.19
intensity 6.10
intensive stock
    rearing 4.17
interfamilial exchange
    marriage 4.13
interference 6.10
intergalactic space 9.3
interior angle 5.12
intermediate
    earthquake 8.6
intermembral index
    4.8
internal-combustion
    engine 6.9
internal epicanthic fold
    4.8
internal respiration
    2.15
internal skeleton 2.9
internode 1.11
interphase 2.5
interplanetary space
    9.3
interpolation 5.18

interpretational
    astronomy 9.1
interpretation of
    dreams 3.4
intersection 5.10
interstellar space 9.3
interstitial cells 2.21
intestine 2.13
introjection 3.19
invention 4.9
inverse ratio 5.7
inverse-square law
    6.18
inverse trigonometric
    functions 5.18
involuntary psychosis
    3.9
involutional psychosis
    3.9
iodine 7.15
ion physics 6.2
    chemistry 7.6
ionic compound 7.4
ionic crystal 7.10
ionic equation 7.3
ionization 7.6
ionization constant 7.5
Ionization Theory 7.6
I.Q. test 3.5
iridium 7.15
iris 2.18
iron 7.15
Iron Age 4.5
ironstone 8.11
Iroquois Confederacy
    4.14
Iroquois League 4.14
irrational number 5.2
irregular galaxy 9.10
irregular polygon 5.15
irregular variables 9.8
irreversible reaction
    7.5
irritability 1.5
ischium 2.10
ischium-pubis index
    4.8
island arcs 8.5
isobar 6.2
isoclinic line 6.17
Isoetales 1.4
isogamy 1.18
isogonic line 6.17
isolation 3.17
isometric crystal 7.10
isometric system 8.2
isosceles triangle 5.13
isostasy 8.7
isotope 6.2, 22
Italic 4.20

J

Japanese 4.20
jargon aphasia 3.12
Javanese 4.20
jerk 3.12
jets 9.6
joint family 4.12
joint property 4.18

joking relationship
    4.12
joule 6.7
Joule's equivalent 6.9
Jungermanniales 1.4
Jupiter 9.4
Jurassic Period 8.16

K

Kabyle 4.20
kame 8.15
karst topography 8.13
Kaus Australis 9.9
K corona 9.6
keeper 6.19
Keilor man 4.4
Kelvin scale 6.9
Kent mental test 3.5
Kepler 9.7
Kepler's laws 9.2
Kepler's star 9.8
ketones 7.13
kidney 2.14
kilogram-calorie 6.9
kilogram-meter 6.7
kilowatt-hour 6.20
kin avoidance 4.12
kindling temperature
    7.11
kinematics 6.1
kinetic energy 6.7
kinetic theory of
    matter 6.3
kin familiarity 4.12
king 4.14
kingdom botany 1.3
    zoology 2.2
kin group 4.11, 12
Kinorhyncha 2.3
kinship 4.12
Kipp apparatus 7.16
kitchen midden 4.16
kleptomania 3.14
klippe 8.7
kneecap 2.10
Kochab 9.9
Korsakoff's psychosis
    3.9
krypton 7.15
kyanite 8.3
kula ring 4.18
Kulturkreis 4.9

L

labradorite 8.3
laccolith 8.10
lachrymal glands 2.19
lactic acid 7.8
lag gravel 8.13
lake dwelling 4.16
lamina 1.14
Langrenus 9.7
language 4.21
lanthanide series 7.15
lanthanum 7.15
lapilli 8.9
larva 2.22
larynx 2.15
last quarter 9.7

niobium 7.15
nitric acid 7.8
nitrogen 7.15
nobelium 7.15
node botany 1.11
  mathematics 5.10
  physics 6.11
noise 6.11
nonelectrolyte
  physics 6.18
  chemistry 7.6
nonfoliated meta-
  morphic rock 8.8
nonionization 7.6
nonmetal 7.2
nonmetallic oxide 7.11
nonmiscible liquids
  7.14
nonstriated muscle
  2.11
Nordic 4.7
normal fault 8.7
normal salt 7.7
normal solution 7.9
north-seeking pole
  6.17
notch 8.13
notched blade 4.15
nova 9.8
nth root 5.4
nuclear change 6.2
nuclear chemistry 7.1
nuclear complex 3.15
nuclear energy 6.22
nuclear family 4.12
nuclear membrane
  botany 1.8
  zoology 2.4
nuclear physics 6.1
nuclear reactor 6.22
nuclear sap 2.4
nucleolus botany 1.8
  zoology 2.4
nucleons 6.2
nucleus botany 1.8
  zoology 2.4
  culture- 4.9
  physics 6.2
  astronomy 9.4
Nuda 2.3
number 5.2
numerator 5.2
numerical coefficient
  5.5
nut 1.16
nutation 9.12
nymph 2.22
nymphomania 3.16

O

oath 4.10
oblique angle 5.12
oblique-slip
  movement 8.7
oblique triangle 5.13
observational
  astronomy 9.1
observatory,
  astronomical 9.15
obsession 3.14

obsessional neurosis
  3.8
obsessive-compulsion
  neurosis 3.8
obsidian 8.10
obtuse angle 5.12
obtuse triangle 5.13
occipital 2.10
occulation 9.13
occupational neurosis
  3.8
occupational therapy
  3.4
ocean basin 8.5
ocean currents 8.5
ocean deposits 8.15
ocean erosion 8.13
Oceanic Negro 4.7
oceanography 8.1
Oceanus Procellarum
  9.7
octahedron 5.16
Oedipus complex 3.15
offshore beach 8.15
Ofnetman 4.4
ohm 6.20
Ohm's law 6.18
Olbers 9.4
Oldoway man 4.4
Old Stone Age 4.5
oleic acid 7.8
olfactory nerves 2.18
oligarchy 4.14
Oligocene epoch
  anthropology 4.2
  geology 8.16
Oligochaeta 2.3
olivine 8.3
one-celled animals 2.2
Onychophora 2.3
oögenesis 2.21
oögonium 1.18
oölitic limestone 8.11
opalescence 8.4
opaque body 6.12
Ophioglossales 1.4
Ophiuchus 9.9
Ophiuroidea 2.3
opposite angles 5.12
opposite leaves 1.14
optical center 6.14
optical density 6.14
optic nerve 2.18
optics 6.1
orbiscular granite 8.10
orbit 9.12
orbital index 4.8
ordeal 4.10
order botany 1.3
  zoology 2.2
ordinal number 5.2
ordinate 5.9
Ordovician Period 8.16
orenda 4.19
organic acids 7.13
organic chemistry 7.1
organic deposition 8.11
organic evolution 2.1
organic matter 7.2
organic oxidation 7.11
organic psychosis 3.9

organized sanction
  4.10
Orion 9.9
Orion Nebula 9.10
ornithology 2.1
orogeny 8.7
orthocentre 5.10
orthoclase 8.3
ortho-cousin 4.12
orthogon 5.15
orthorhombic crystal
  7.10
orthorhombic system
  8.2
oscillation 6.5
oscillator 6.19
Oseretsky test 3.5
osmium 7.15
osmosis botany 1.5
  physics 6.3
Osteichthyes 2.3
outer ear 2.18
outer planets 9.4
output 6.8
outwash 8.15
ovary botany 1.15
  zoology 2.21
overcharge 3.20
overcompensation 3.17
overtone 6.11
oviducts 2.21
oviparous animal 2.21
ovoviviparous animal
  2.21
ovum 2.21
oxalic acid 7.8
oxidation chemistry
  7.11
  geology 8.12
oxide 7.11
oxidizing agent 7.11
oxygen 7.15

P

painting 4.22
pair marriage 4.13
palatal index 4.8
paleobotany 1.1
Paleocene epoch
  anthropology 4.2
  geology 8.16
Paleogene Period 8.16
Paleolithic Age 4.5
paleontology
  zoology 2.1
  geology 8.1
Paleozoic Era 8.16
palladium 7.15
palmately compound
  leaf 1.14
palm bones 2.10
pancreas 2.19
panicle 1.15
paper money 4.18
parabola 5.17
parabolic dune 8.15
parallel circuit 6.18
parallel cousin 4.12
parallelepiped 5.16

parallel forces 6.6
parallelism 4.9
parallelogram 5.15
paralogia 3.12
paranoia 3.9
paranomia 3.13
Paranthropus robustus
  4.3
paraphasia 3.12
paraphilia 3.16
paraphrenia 3.9
Parapithecus 4.3
parapsychology 3.1
parasite 1.6
parasitism 1.6
parasitology 2.1
parasympathetic
  nervous system 2.17
parathyroid glands
  2.19
paratonic movement
  1.7
parenchyma 1.9
paresthesia 3.11
parfleche 4.15
parietal 2.10
parietal art 4.22
parorexia 3.11
parthenogenesis 2.21
partial eclipse 9.13
particle accelerator
  6.22
Pascal's law 6.3
passage, rite of 4.19
passive aggression
  3.10
passive dependence
  3.10
pastoralism 4.17
patella 2.10
paternal family 4.12
pathological personal-
  ity types 3.7
pathoneurosis 3.8
patriarchal family 4.12
patriarchate 4.11
patrilineal band 4.14
patrilineal clan 4.12
patrilineal kinship 4.12
patrilocal joint family
  4.12
pattern, culture 4.9
Pavo 9.9
peace chief 4.14
pearly luster 8.4
pectoral appendage
  2.10
pectoral girdle 2.10
pectoralis major 2.11
pedicel 1.15
pediment 8.13
pedogenesis 2.21
pedophilia 3.16
peduncle 1.15
Pegasus 9.9
Peking man 4.4
Pelecypoda 2.3
pelvic appendage 2.10
pelvic breadth-height
  index 4.8
pelvic girdle 2.10

primitive arts 4.22
primitive music 4.22
principal axis 6.13
principal focus 6.13
prism 5.16
private wrong 4.10
privileged familiarity 4.12
probability 5.6
probable number 5.6
procambium 1.9
Proclus 9.7
Proconsul africanus 4.3
Procyon 9.9
product 5.3
professional neurasthenia 3.8
prognathism 4.8
projectile 6.5
projectile motion 6.5
projection 3.17
prometaphase 2.5
promethium 7.15
prominences 9.6
propane 7.12
proper fraction 5.2
proper motion 9.12
property 4.18
prophase 2.5
prophylactic psychiatry 3.3
Propliopithecus 4.3
proportion 5.7
prop root 1.10
propylene 7.12
prostate gland 2.21
prostrate stem 1.12
protactinium 7.15
protandrous hermaphroditism 2.21
protective colloid 7.14
proteins 7.13
protein shock therapy 3.4
proton 6.2
protoplanet hypothesis 9.2
protoplasm botany 1.8
  zoology 2.4
protoplast botany 1.8
  zoology 2.4
Protozoa 2.2, 3
protozoology 2.1
proximal end 2.7
prussic acid 7.8
Psilophytales 1.4
Psilophytinae 1.4
Psilopsida 1.4
Psilotales 1.4
psychalgia 3.11
psychasthenia 3.9
psyche 3.6
psychesthesia 3.11
psychiatrics 3.3
psychiatry 3.3
psychoanalysis 3.4
psychoanalytic therapy 3.4
psychoasthenics 3.1

psychobiochemistry 3.1
psychobiology 3.1
psychodrama 3.19
psychoepilepsy 3.11
psychogenetics 3.1
psychognosis 3.4
psychokinesia 3.9
psycholagny 3.16
psycholepsy 3.9
psychological adjustive reaction 3.17
psychological test 3.5
psychology 3
psychomotor disturbances 3.12
psychoneurosis 3.8
psychoneurotic 3.7
psychonomics 3.1
psychopathia sexualis 3.9
psychopathic condition 3.9
psychopathic personality 3.9
psychopathy 3.9
psychophysics 3.1
psychorhythmia 3.9
psychosexuality 3.9, 16
psychosis 3.9
psychosocial medicine 3.3
psychosomatic disorders 3.11
psychosomatic medicine 3.3
psychostatics 3.1
psychosurgery 3.4
psychosynthesis 3.18
psychotaxis 3.12
psychotechnics 3.1
psychotechnology 3.1
psychotherapy 3.4
psychotic personality 3.7
pteridology 1.2
Pteridosperms 1.4
Pteropsida 1.4
Ptolemaeus 9.7
Ptolemaic system 9.2
puberty dance 4.22
puberty rite 4.19
pubis 2.10
public wrong 4.10
pueblo 4.16
pulley 6.8
pulmonary artery 2.16
pulmonary circulation 2.16
pumice 8.10
pupa 2.22
pupil 2.18
Puppis 9.9
pure barter 4.18
pure mathematics 5.1
purgation 3.19
purification, rite of 4.19
pushing 8.14
P wave 8.6
pycnometer 6.3

pyknic type 4.8
pyramid 5.16
pyrite 8.3
pyroclastic debris 8.10
pyroclastic materials 8.9
pyromania 3.14
pyrophobia 3.10
pyroxene 8.10
pyroxene group 8.3
pyrrhotite 8.3
Pyrrophyta 1.4
Pythagorean relations 5.18

Q

quadrant 5.9, 14
quadratic equation 5.8
quadrilateral 5.15
qualitative analysis 7.1
quality 6.11
quantitative analysis 7.1
quantity 5.5
quantum theory 6.12
quarrying 8.12
quartz 8.3
quartzite 8.8
Quaternary period 4.2
Quechuan 4.20
quern 4.15
quotient 5.3
quotient relations 5.18

R

rabies 3.9
raceme 1.15
races 4.7
radial symmetry 2.7
radian 5.12
radiation 6.9
radical 7.3
radicand 5.4
radicle 1.17
radioactive isotope 6.22
radioactivity
  physics 6.22
  geology 8.4
radio astronomy 9.1
radiochemistry 7.1
radiolarian ooze 8.11
radio telescope 9.15
radium 7.15
radius zoology 2.10
  mathematics 5.14
  - of curvature 6.13
radius vector 5.9
radix 5.19
radon 7.15
Ranales 1.4
random mating 4.13
raphe 1.17
rapid oxidation 7.11
rarefaction 6.10
Rasalhague 9.9
ratio 5.7
rationalization 3.17
rational number 5.2

rational psychology 3.1
Rayleigh wave 8.6
rays, lunar 9.7
reactance 6.18
reaction formation 3.17
readjustment 3.18
reagent bottle 7.16
real image 6.13
real number 5.2
real property 4.18
rebus 4.21
receiver 7.16
receptacle 1.15
receptors 2.18
recessional moraine 8.15
recessive character 1.19
recessive gene 1.19
reciprocal relations 5.18
recombination 8.8
recreational therapy 3.4
recrystallization 8.8
rectangle 5.15
rectangular coordinate system 5.9
rectifier 6.19
rectilinear motion 6.5
rectum 2.13
red blood corpuscles 2.16
red giant 9.8
reducing agent 7.11
reduction 7.11
reflecting telescope 9.15
reflection 6.13
reflex angle 5.12
refracting telescope 9.15
refraction 6.14
regelation 6.4
regression 3.15
regular solid 5.16
regulation 1.5
Regulus 9.9
rehabilitation 3.18
relative humidity 6.4
relay 6.19
remainder 5.3
repression 3.17
reproduction 1.5, 18
reproductive organs 2.21
Reptilia 2.3
residual deposits 8.11
residual magnetism 6.17
resinous luster 8.4
resistance 6.18
resistivity 6.18
resolution of forces 6.6
resonance 6.10
respiration botany 1.5
  zoology 2.15
resultant force 6.6
retentivity, magnetic 6.17
retina 2.18

retort 7.16
reverberation 6.10
reverence 4.19
reverse fault 8.7
reversible reaction 7.5
reversing layer 9.6
revolution physics 6.5
  astronomy 9.12
rhenium 7.15
rheostat 6.19
rhizome 1.12
Rhodesian group 4.4
rhodium 7.15
Rhodophyta 1.4
rhomboid 5.15
rhombus 5.15
rhyolite lavas 8.9
ribs 2.10
riddle 4.22
Rigel 9.9
right angle 5.12
right ascension 9.11
right auricle 2.16
right line 5.10
right triangle 5.13
right ventricle 2.16
rigid spear thrower
  4.15
Rigil Kentaurus 9.9
rills, lunar 9.7
ring 7.16
ring money 4.18
ring stand 7.16
rise, continental 8.5
rite 4.19
ritual 4.19
river terrace 8.13
river valley 8.13
rock cleavage 8.7
rock flowage 8.8
rock glacier 8.15
rock stage 8.16
role 4.11
rolling 8.12, 14
root botany 1.10
  mathematics 5.4
root cap 1.10
root hair 1.10
Rorschach test 3.5
Rosales 1.4
rotary motion 6.5
rotation physics 6.5
  astronomy 9.12
Rotifera 2.3
round barrow 4.16
royal endogamy 4.13
RR Lyrae variables 9.8
rubidium 7.15
rudaceous rocks 8.11
runner 1.12
running water deposits
  8.15
running water erosion
  8.13
ruthenium 7.15

S

sacerdotalism 4.19
sachem 4.14
sacral vertebrae 2.10

sacred myth 4.22
sacrifice 4.19
sadism 3.16
Sagitta 9.9
Sagittarius 9.9
Saiph 9.9
salicylic acid 7.8
saline oxide 7.11
salivary glands 2.19
salivation 2.13
salt 7.7, 8
saltation 8.14
salt rocks 8.11
samara 1.16
samarium 7.15
sanction 4.10
sand painting 4.22
sandstone 8.11
saprophyte 1.6
saprophytism 1.6
sapwood 1.9
Sarcodina 2.3
satellite 9.4
sati 4.19
saturated magnet 6.17
saturated series 7.12
Saturn 9.4
satyriasis 3.16
satyrism 3.16
savagery 4.9
scalar quantity 6.6
scalene triangle 5.13
scales 2.9
scandium 7.15
Scaphopoda 2.3
scapula 2.10
scent glands 2.19
Schickard 9.7
schists 8.8
schizocarp 1.16
Schizomycophyta 1.4
schizophasia 3.9
schizophrenia 3.9
schizothymia 3.9
scissors fault 8.7
sclerenchyma 1.9
scolding 4.19
scopophilia 3.16
scoria 8.10
scorpioid cyme 1.15
Scorpius 9.9
scotophobia 3.10
screw 6.8
scrotum 2.21
Scyphozoa 2.3
sea 8.5
sea cave 8.13
seas, lunar 9.7
seasonal ceremony
  4.19
secant 5.18
second 5.12
secondary burial 4.19
secondary coil 6.19
secondary marriage
  4.13
second filial generation
  1.19
seconds pendulum 6.5
secret society 4.11
sector 5.14

sedimentary rock 8.11
seed 1.17
seed coat 1.17
seeding 7.9
seedling 1.17
segment mathematics
  5.14
  physics 6.11
seif dune 8.15
seismism 8.6
seismogram 8.6
seismograph 8.6
seismology 8.1
seismometer 8.6
Selaginellales 1.4
selenium 7.15
self-fertilization 1.18
self-inductance 6.18
self-pollination 1.18
self-psychology 3.1
semantics 4.21
semicircle 5.14
semicircular canals
  2.18
semilunar valve 2.16
semimajor axis 5.17
semiminor axis 5.17
seminal vesicle 2.21
Semitic 4.20
senile dementia 3.9
senile psychosis 3.9
sense organs 2.18
sepals 1.15
separation, rite of 4.19
sequence 5.6
series mathematics 5.6
  rock- 8.16
series circuit 6.18
Serpens 9.9
serpentine 8.3
serpent worship 4.19
sextant 9.15
sexual abnormality
  3.16
sexual reproduction
  botany 1.18
  zoology 2.21
shadow 6.12
shale 8.11
shallow earthquake 8.6
shaman 4.19
shamanism 4.19
shard 4.15
Shaula 9.9
shear fracture 8.7
shear wave 8.6
shellshock 3.8
shield, continental 8.5
shield volcano 8.9
shifting cultivation
  4.17
shinbone 2.10
shock therapy 3.4
shock wave 8.6
shore line 8.15
shoulder blade 2.10
shouldered point 4.15
shoulder girdle 2.10
shrub 1.13
shunt 6.19
Siamese 4.20

sib 4.12
sibling 4.12
sicklemia index 4.8
sidereal period 9.13
siderite 9.5
siderolite 9.5
sieve tube 1.9
sight 2.18
silent trade 4.18
silicon 7.15
silky luster 8.4
sill 8.10
sillimanite 8.3
siltstone 8.11
silty rocks 8.11
Silurian Period 8.16
silver 7.15
simple epithelium 2.6
simple equation 5.8
simple fruit 1.16
simple leaf 1.14
simple machine 6.8
simple moiety 4.12
simple pendulum 6.5
Sinanthropus
  pekinensis 4.4
sine 5.18
sine curve 5.18
single membrane
  drum 4.22
single xylophone 4.22
Sinitic 4.20
sinkhole 8.13
Sino-Tibetan 4.20
sinter 8.11
Siouan 4.20
Sipunculoidea 2.3
Sirius 9.9
skeletal muscle 2.11
skeleton 2.9
skeleton equation 7.3
Skhul Mt. Carmel
  forms 4.4
skull 2.10
slash-and-burn 4.17
slates 8.8
sleep treatment 3.4
slickensides 8.7
slide scar 8.13
sliding 8.12, 14
sling 4.15
slip rings 6.19
slit gong 4.22
slope, continental 8.5
slow oxidation 7.11
slug 6.6
slump 8.12, 14
small circle 5.16
small family 4.12
smell 2.18
smooth muscle 2.11
social anthropology 4.1
society 4.11
sociological adjustive
  reaction 3.17
sociopath 3.7
sodality 4.11
sodium 7.15
sodium acetate 7.8
sodium acid phosphate
  7.8

FOREIGN WORDS AND PHRASES
TRANSLATED INTO ENGLISH

A

a, ab (*L*) From, by.

ab actu ad posse valet consecutio (*L*) [Law] From what has been done to what may be done the conclusion is valid.

abandon (*F*) Abandonment, easy style in speech, forgetfulness.

a bas! (*F*) Down, down with!

abat-jour (*F*) Lampshade, screen.

à bâtons rompus (*F*) With starts and stops, by fits and starts.

abattoir (*F*) Slaughterhouse.

abat-voix (*F*) Sounding board in a church.

abbé (*F*) Abbot, ecclesiastic.

abdal (*Hind.*) Religious person, devotee.

à beau jeu beau retour (*F*) To a good turn a good return, tit for tat.

abends wird der Faule fleissig (*G*) By evening the idler becomes industrious.

a beneplacito (*It.*) At one's pleasure.

Aberglaube (*G*) Superstition.

abest (*L*) He is absent.

abeunt studia in mores (*L*) Practices become habits. Ovid — *Heroides*, *XV, 83*.

ab extra (*L*) From without.

ab hoc et ab hac et ab illa (*L*) From this man and from this woman and from that woman, gossipy.

ab imo pectore (*L*) From the bottom of the heart.

ab inconvenienti (*L*) From inconvenience.

ab incunabulis (*L*) From swaddling clothes, from childhood.

ab initio (*L*) From the beginning.

ab intra (*L*) From within.

a bisogni si conoscon gli amici (*It.*) In need friends are recognized; a friend in need is a friend indeed.

à bis ou à blanc (*F*) To gray or white, in some way or other.

abkari (*Pers.*) (India) Manufacture of liquors, tax on liquors.

abnormis sapiens (*L*) Abnormally wise. Horace — *Satires*, *II, 2, 3*.

à bon chat, bon rat (*F*) To a good cat a good rat; well attacked well defended.

à bon compte (*F*) Cheaply.

à bon droit (*F*) With good right.

à bon entendeur demi-mot suffit (*F*) A word to the wise is sufficient.

à bon marché (*F*) At good bargain, cheaply.

ab origine (*L*) From the beginning.

a bove majore discit arare minor (*L*) From the ox the steer learns to plow; one learns from one's elders. Proverb.

ab ovo (*L*) From the egg.

ab ovo usque ad mala (*L*) From egg to apples, from soup to nuts. Horace — *Satires, I, 3, 6*.

abra (*Sp.*) Cove, dale.

à bras ouverts (*F*) With open arms.

abrégé (*F*) Abridgment.

abri (*F*) Protection, shelter.

abricot (*F*) Apricot.

abricot-pêche (*F*) Peach-apricot.

absence d'esprit (*F*) Absence of mind.

absens hæres non erit (*L*) The absent one will not be the heir.

absenti nemo ne nocuisse velit (*L*) Let no one wish to have harmed the absent. Propertius — *Elegies, II, 19, 32*.

absit invidia (*L*) Let envy keep away.

ab uno disce omnes (*L*) From one learn to know all. Vergil — *Æneid, II, 65*.

ab urbe condita (*L*) From the founding of the city (Rome), 753 B. C., A. U. C. Compare *anno urbis conditæ*.

a capite ad calcem (*L*) From head to foot.

acariâtre (*F*) Cross, disagreeable.

accedas ad curiam (*L*) You may approach the court.

accepta (*L*) Credits.

acciaccatura (*It.*) [Mus.] Grace note.

accouchement (*F*) Childbed.

accoucheur (*F*) Obstetrical assistant.

accoucheuse (*F*) Midwife.

accueil (*F*) Welcome, reception.

aceite (*Sp.*) Oil.

acequia (*Sp.*) Drain, canal.

acequiador (*Sp.*) Constructor.

acervatim (*L*) In heaps.

à chaque saint sa chandelle (*F*) To each saint his candle; honor to whom honor is due.

achar (*Pers.*) (India) Pickle, relish.

acharné (*F*) Furious, raging.

acharnement (*F*) Blind ardor, animosity.

Acherontis pabulum (*L*) Food for Acheron, marked for death. Plautus — *Casina, II, 1, 11*.

à cheval (*F*) On horseback.

à compte (*F*) On account.

à contre cœur (*F*) Against a person's will.

à corps perdu (*F*) Impetuously, headlong.

à coup sûr (*F*) Surely, certainly.

à couvert (*F*) Under cover.

acqua (*It.*) Water.

acquit (*F*) Receipt.

actum aiunt ne agas (*L*) The saying goes that you shouldn't do what has already been done. Terence — *Phormio, II, 3, 72.*

actum est (*L*) It is finished.

actum ne agas (*L*) Don't do a thing already done. Terence — *Phormio, II, 3, 72.* Compare *actum aiunt ne agas.*

actus (*L*) Act, deed.

actus me invito factus non est meus actus (*L*) [Law] An act done against my will is not my act.

adaga (*Port.*). (Short sword), Asiatic weapon consisting of a blade attached transversely to a staff.

adagio (*It.*) Slowly, [mus.] slowly, leisurely.

ad amussim (*L*) According to a rule, by a level.

ad arbitrium (*L*) At will.

ad astra per aspera (*L*) Through hardships to the stars. *Motto of Kansas.*

ad calendas Græcas (*L*) See *ad kalendas Græcas.*

ad captandum (*L*) For captivating.

ad captandum vulgus (*L*) For attracting the rabble.

adde parvum parvo magnus acervus erit (*L*) Add little to little and there will be a great heap. Ovid.

addio (*It.*) Good-bye.

additum (*L*) Something added.

adelig und edel sind zweierlei (*G*) Noble birth and noble soul are different things.

Adel sitzt im Gemüthe nicht im Geblüte (*G*) True nobility lies in worth not birth.

adeo in teneris consuescere multum est (*L*) Thus training is of great importance in the early years. Vergil — *Georgics, II, 272.*

ad eundem (*L*) To the same (degree).

adeus (*Port.*) Good-bye.

à deux (*F*) Of two, for two, two at a time.

ad finem (*L*) To the finish, at the end.

adhibenda est in jocando moderatio (*L*) One should be moderate in his jests. Cicero — *De Oratore, II, 59.*

ad hoc (*L*) For this thing, for this purpose.

ad hominem (*L*) To the man.

adhuc sub judice lis est (*L*) The case is still before the court. Horace — *Ars Poetica, 78.*

ad infinitum (*L*) To infinity.

ad instar (*L*) In the likeness of, after the fashion of.

ad instar omnium (*L*) In the likeness of all.

ad interim (*L*) In the meantime.

adios (*Sp.*) Good-bye.

à discrétion (*F*) At discretion, at will.

ad kalendas Græcas (*L*) At the Greek calends, never.

ad libitum (*L*) At will, at pleasure.

ad melius inquirendum (*L*) For finding a better method.

ad nauseam (*L*) To the point of nausea, to the point of disgust.

adorer le veau d'or (*F*) To worship the golden calf.

ad quem (*L*) To whom, to which.

ad referendum (*L*) To be referred, for consideration.

ad rem (*L*) To the point, relevant.

à droite (*F*) On the right, to the right.

adscriptus glebæ (*L*) Attached to the soil, serf.

adsum (*L*) I am present.

ad tristem partem strenua est suspicio (*L*) Among the less fortunate faction suspicion is strong. Publius Syrus.

ad unguem (*L*) To the finger nail, to a hair. Horace — *Satires, I, 5, 32*

ad valorem (*L*) According to value.

ad verbum (*L*) To a word, verbatim.

ad vitam aut culpam (*L*) For life or until fault, during good behavior.

advocatus diaboli (*L*) Devil's advocate, one who argues against canonization.

ægrescit medendo (*L*) He grows worse by the remedy. Vergil — *Æneid, XII, 46.*

ægri somnia vana (*L*) A sick man's delusions. Horace — *Ars Poetica, 7.*

æquam servare mentem (*L*) To preserve one's equanimity. Horace — *Odes, II, 3, 1.*

æquo animo (*L*) With a calm spirit.

ære perennius (*L*) More enduring than bronze. Horace — *Odes, III, 30, 1.*

æs alienum debitorem leve gravius inimicum facit (*L*) A small loan makes the debtor a more troublesome enemy. Laberius.

æternum servans sub pectore vulnus (*L*) Nursing an everlasting sore in the breast. Vergil — *Æneid, I, 36.*

ἀετὸς ἐν νεφέλαισι (*Gr.*) An eagle in the clouds, something unattainable.

affaire d'amour (*F*) Love affair.

affaire de cœur (*F*) Affair of the heart.

affaire d'honneur (*F*) Affair of honor, duel.

affaire flambée (*F*) Business ruined.

affettuoso (*It.*) Tender, kind [mus.] in a sentimental manner.

affiche (*F*) Placard, notice.

afficher (*F*) To post a placard.

afflatus (*L*) Breath, breeze, inspiration.

afflatus montium (*L*) Mountain air.

affogare in un bicchier d'acqua (*It.*) To drown in a goblet of water.

à fleur d'eau (*F*) At water-level.

à fond (*F*) At bottom, thoroughly.

a fortiori (*L*) With all the stronger reason, all the more.

a fresco (*It.*) (Painting) in fresco, painted in fresco.

aga, see *agha*

agacerie (*F*) Allurement, enticement.

à gauche (*F*) On the left, to the left.

agent provocateur (*F*) A person hired by the police to incite a suspect.

age quod agis! (*L*) Do what you do well; anything worth doing is worth doing well.

agha (*Turk.*) Lord, chief. Also *aga*.

Agnus Dei (*L*) Lamb of God, image of a lamb emblematical of Christ.

agora (ἀγορά, *Gr.*) Market place, central square.

agostadero (*Sp.*) Summer pasture.

à grands frais (*F*) At great expense.

agua (*Sp.*) Water.

aguardiente (*Sp.*) Brandy.

agua viva (*Sp.*) Running water.

aguerri (*F*) Hardened to war.

à haute voix (*F*) Aloud.

à huis clos (*F*) Behind closed doors.

aide-de-camp (*F*) Officer in the personal service of a commander.

aide-toi, le ciel t'aidera (*F*) Help yourself and Heaven will help you; God helps them who help themselves. La Fontaine — *Fables*.

αἰδὼς ὀυκ ἀγαθή (*Gr.*) False shame. Hesiod.

aimer éperdument (*F*) To be desperately in love.

à la (*F*) In the manner of.

à l'abandon (*F*) In disorder.

à la belle étoile (*F*) In the open, under the sky.

à la bonne heure (*F*) At the right moment, well done.

à la carte (*F*) According to the menu, of a meal to be ordered with a stated price for each dish. Compare *table d'hôte*.

alacrán (*Sp.*) Scorpion.

à la dérobée (*F*) Secretly, furtively.

à la française (*F*) In the French manner.

à la grâce de quelqu'un (*F*) At the mercy of some one.

à la guerre comme à la guerre (*F*) War must be war.

à la lanterne! (*F*) To the lamp-post, lynch him!

alameda (*Sp.*) Poplar grove, public promenade.

à l'américaine (*F*) In the American manner.

à la mode (*F*) According to fashion, in current style.

à l'anglaise (*F*) In the English manner.

à la parisienne (*F*) In the Parisian manner.

à la sourdine (*F*) With the mute, noiselessly.

à la Tartufe (*F*) Like Tartufe, hypocritically.

alberca (*Sp.*) Pool, drain.

albergo (*It.*) Inn, hotel.

alcaide (*Sp.*) Governor of a castle, warden. Also *alcaid*.

alcalde (*Sp.*) Burgomaster, mayor.

alentours (*F*) Environs, associates.

alerte (*F*) Alarm.

al fresco (*It.*) In the open air.

aliéné (*F*) Crazy, lunatic.

alieni appetens (*L*) Eager for another's property. Sallust — *Catiline*, V.

alieni appetens sui profusus (*L*) Eager for another's property prodigal of his own. Sallust — *Catiline*, V.

à l'improviste (*F*) Suddenly, unexpectedly.

aliquando bonus dormitat Homerus (*L*) Sometimes the good Homer falls asleep; the greatest make mistakes. After Horace — *Ars Poetica, 359*.

aliquis in omnibus nullus in singulis (*L*) A somebody in general, a nobody in particular. Scaliger.

alitur vitium vivitque tegendo (*L*) Vice is nourished by secrecy. Vergil — *Georgics, III, 454*.

aljibar (*Sp. Amer.*) Reservoir, cistern.

alla cappella (*It.*) [Mus.] In old church style, unaccompanied.

allégresse (*F*) Great joy, gaiety.

allegretto (*It.*) [Mus.] Merry, sprightly.

allegro (*It.*) [Mus.] Lively.

allemande (*F*) [Mus.] A lively dance in two-three time.

aller Anfang ist schwer (*G*) Every beginning is difficult.

aller Anfang ist heiter (*G*) Every beginning is cheerful. Goethe.

aller à tâtons (*F*) To walk gropingly.

aller au fait (*F*) To get to the point.

aller planter ses choux (*F*) To go plant one's cabbages, to retire into the country.

allez-vous-en! (*F*) Go away!

alma mater (*L*) Foster mother.

Alma Mater Redemptoris (*L*) Fostering Mother of the Redeemer.

Almanach de Gotha (*F*) Gotha Almanac, genealogical manual of the titled families of Europe.

al piacere (*It.*) At pleasure, at one's will.

alter ego (*L*) The other I, one's second self.

alterum alterius auxilio eget (*L*) One thing needs the help of another.

alto (*It.*) High, high tenor or contralto voice.

alto-rilievo (*It.*) [Sculp.] High relief.

amah (*Oriental*) Nurse, lady's maid. Portuguese *ama* — *nurse*.

amantes amentes (*L*) Lovers are lunatics. Terence — *Andria, I, 3, 13*.

amantium iræ (*L*) Lovers' quarrels. Terence — *Andria, III, 3, 23*.

amari aliquid (*L*) Something bitter.

a maximis ad minima (*L*) From the greatest things to the least.

âme damnée (*F*) Damned soul, unscrupulous henchman.

âme de boue (*F*) Soul of mud, low-down creature.

amende honorable (*F*) Public confession of a crime.

a mensa et thoro (*L*) [Law] From bed and board.

âme qui vive (*F*) Living soul.

à merveille (*F*) Marvelously.

amici probantur rebus adversis (*L*) Friends are proved by adversity. Cicero — *De Amicitia*.

amicitia semper prodest (*L*) Friendship is always helpful. Seneca — *Epistles, XXXV*.

amicus curiæ (*L*) Friend of the court, impartial adviser.

amicus humani generis (*L*) A friend of the human race.

amicus usque ad aras (*L*) A friend as far as the altars, a friend as far as conscience will permit.

à moi! (*F*) (To me), help!

amor (*L*) Love, desire.

amor nummi (*L*) Love of money, Scotch thrift.

amoroso (*It.*) Lover, gallant.

amor patriæ (*L*) Love of country, patriotism.

amoto quæramus seria ludo (*L*) Let us put joking aside and treat of serious matters. Horace — *Satires, I, 1, 27*.

amour fait beaucoup mais argent fait tout (*F*) Love does much but money does everything.

amour propre (*F*) Self-love, egotism.

anagke (ἀνάγκη, *Gr.*) Necessity, constraint.

ancien régime (*F*) Old rule, government of France prior to 1789.

ancilla theologiæ (*L*) Hand-maid of theology, philosophy.

anconada (*Sp.*) Open bay.

ancora imparo (*It.*) I still learn. Motto of Michelangelo.

ancora una volta (*It.*) Again.

andante (*It.*) [Mus.] Slow.

andantino (*It.*) [Mus.] Rather slow.

anemolia bazein (ἀνεμώλια βάζειν, *Gr.*) To speak idle words.

anerithmon gelasma (ἀνήριθμον γέλασμα, *Gr.*) Numberless smiles (of the waves). Æschylus — *Prometheus, 90*.

Anglice (*L*) In English.

anguille (*F*) Eel.

anguille de mer (*F*) Conger.

anguis in herba (*L*) Snake in the grass, hidden danger. Compare *latet anguis in herba*.

anima (*L*) Breath, life, spirit, soul.

anima bruta (*L*) Crude spirit, vital principle.

anima divina (*L*) Divine life.

anima mundi (*L*) Spirit of the world.

animum pictura pascit inani (*L*) He feasts his mind on an empty painting. Vergil — *Æneid, I, 464*.

ankus (*Hind.*) A hook for driving elephants.

anno (*L*) A year ago, the past year, yearly.

anno ætatis suæ (*L*) In the year of his age.

anno Domini (*L*) In the year of the Lord, counting from the birth of Christ, A.D.

anno hejiræ (*L*) In the year of Mahomet's *hejirah*, or flight from Mecca, 622 A.D.

anno regni (*L*) In the year of the reign, A.R.

anno urbis conditæ (*L*) Since the year of the founding of the city, 753 B.C. Compare *A. U. C.*

annus magnus (*L*) Great year, [astron.] that period when the constellations return to their original positions.

annus mirabilis (*L*) Wonderful year.

ante bellum (*L*) Before the war.

ante Christum (*L*) Before Christ, A. C.

ante meridiem (*L*) Before noon, A. M.

ante tubam trepidat (*L*) He trembles before the trumpet (sounds). Vergil — *Æneid, XI, 424*.

ante victoriam ne canas triumphans (*L*) Do not celebrate the victory before you have conquered. Proverb.

ἄνθρωπος ἀνθρώπῳ δαιμόνιον (*Gr.*) Man is a divinity to man.

à outrance (*F*) To the utmost.

apage Satanas (*L*) Begone, Satan.

aparejo (*Sp.*) Tackle, apparatus.

à pas de géant (*F*) With a giant's strides.

aperçu (*F*) First sight of anything, sketch, glance, survey, hint.

apéritif (*F*) Appetizer.

à perte de vue (*F*) Out of sight.

à peu près (*F*) Almost, nearly.

a piacere (*It.*) At pleasure, at will.

à pied (*F*) On foot.

à pierre fendre (*F*) To split a stone.

à plomb (*F*) Perpendicularly.

aplomb (*F*) Perpendicularity, equilibrium, assurance.

á pobreza no hay vergüenza (*Sp.*) Poverty has no shame.

a posteriori (*L*) From the subsequent, from effect to cause.

apparatus belli (*L*) Apparatus of war, munitions.

appetitus rationi obediant (*L*) Let the passions be amenable to reason. Cicero— *De Officiis, I, 29*.

appliqué (*F*) Applied, something applied.

appoggiato (*It.*) Sustained, [mus.] of notes to be elided one into the other.

appogiatura (*It.*) [Mus.] Grace note.

après coup (*F*) Too late.

après nous le déluge (*F*) After us the deluge. Louis XV.

a priori (*L*) From the former, from cause to effect.

à propos (*F*) Regarding, opportunely.

à propos de bottes (*F*) Speaking of boots, without connection.

à propos de rien (*F*) A propos of nothing at all.

aqua (*L*) Water.

aquila (*L*) Eagle.

aquila non capit muscas (*L*) Eagles don't catch flies.

aquilam volare doces (*L*) You are teaching the eagle to fly; you are carrying coals to Newcastle. Proverb.

a quo (*L*) From which, from whom.

araba (*Hind. and Pers.*) Heavy springless vehicle used in Tatar countries.

arada (*Sp.*) Plowed land, arable ground.

arado (*Sp.*) Plow, [S. W. U. S.] ploughed land.

arbiter bibendi (*L*) Master of revels, toastmaster. Horace — *Odes, II, 7, 25.*

arbiter elegantiarum (*L*) Master of elegancies, judge of good taste.

Arcades ambo (*L*) Both Arcadians, two of a kind. Vergil — *Eclogues, VII, 4.*

arcana imperii (*L*) State secrets.

archon (ἄρχων, *Gr.*) Chief, magistrate.

à (au) rebours (*F*) Wrong way, against the grain.

à reculons (*F*) Backwards.

arête (*F*) Narrow ridge of rock separating two precipices.

argent (*F*) Silver, money.

argent comptant (*F*) Ready money.

argumentum ad crumenam (*L*) Address to the purse.

argumentum ad hominem (*L*) Argument to the man, argument stressing the personal.

argumentum ad ignorantiam (*L*) Argument addressed to ignorance, argument based on the opponent's ignorance.

argumentum ad misericordiam (*L*) Argument addressed to pity.

argumentum ad populum (*L*) Appeal to the people, argument addressed to popular sympathies.

argumentum ad verecundiam (*L*) Argument to reverence, appeal to authority.

argumentum baculinum (*L*) Argument of the cudgel.

aria parlante (*It.*) Speaking aria, recitative.

arioso (*It.*) Airy, [mus.] flowing, vocal.

ariston metron (ἄριστον μέτρον, *Gr.*) Moderation is best. Cleobulus.

a rivederci (*It.*) Till we see each other again, good-bye.

a rivederla (*It.*) Good-bye, till we meet again.

armes à feu (*F*) Firearms.

armes blanches (*F*) (White arms), sidearms.

armet (*F*) Helmet used by cavalry troops from the fifteenth to the seventeenth century.

arpeggio (*It.*) [Mus.] Notes played in succession instead of simultaneously, broken chord.

arrectis auribus (*L*) With ears pricked up.

arrêtez! (*F*) Stop!

arrière-pensée (*F*) Mental reservation.

arriero (*Sp.*) Muleteer, driver of a packhorse.

arrondissement (*F*) Ward, divisions of a French *département.*

ars artium (*L*) The art of arts.

ars artium omnium conservatrix (*L*) The art which is the saver of all arts, printing.

ars longa vita brevis (*L*) Art is long, life is short.

artes honarabit (*L*) He will adorn the arts.

art est celare artem (*L*) Art is the concealing of art. Proverb.

artifex (*L*) Artisan, artist, skilled workman.

artiste (*F*) Artist, one who practices a liberal profession.

Artium Baccalaureus (*L*) Bachelor of Arts.

Artium Magister (*L*) Master of Arts.

Art Nouveau (*F*) New Art, style of decoration which appeared in the latter part of the nineteenth century.

aruspex (*L*) Soothsayer. Also *haruspex.*

ascenseur (*F*) Elevator.

a se (*L*) Of or by itself.

asinus ad lyram (*L*) An ass at the lyre, an awkward fellow. Proverb.

asperges (*L*) Thou shalt sprinkle. (Sung at High Mass.)

assistant (*F*) Witness, onlooker.

assister (*F*) To be present, to assist, to witness.

ataghan, see *yataghan.*

atajo (*Sp.*) String of mules.

atelier (*F*) Studio.

atma (*Sansk.*) [Hinduism] Soul, life principle.

atole (*Sp.*) Gruel made of Indian corn.

à tort et à travers (*F*) At random, inconsiderately.

à toute force (*F*) At any cost, absolutely.

à toute outrance (*F*) To the very utmost.

atqui vivere militare est (*L*) To live as a soldier is to live indeed. Seneca — *Epistles, XCVI.*

at spes non fracta (*L*) But my hope is not broken.

attaché (*F*) Member of the staff of an embassy.

attroupement (*F*) Mob, assemblage.

aubade (*F*) Early morning song, serenade.

au beau milieu (*F*) In the very middle.

auberge (*F*) Inn.

au bon droit (*F*) By good right.

au bout de son latin (*F*) At the end of his Latin, at his wits' end. Proverb.

au bout du compte (*F*) At the end of one's reckoning, all things considered.

A. U. C. (*L*) *Anno urbis conditæ*, from the year of the founding of the city (Rome), 753 B.C. Also *ab urbe condita*.

au contraire (*F*) On the contrary.

au courant (*F*) In the current, well-informed, up to date.

auctor pretiosa facit (*L*) It is the giver who makes gifts most dear. Ovid —*Heroides, XVII, 70, 71.*

aucun chemin de fleurs ne conduit à la gloire (*L*) No flowery road leads to glory. La Fontaine — *Fables, X, 14.*

audacter et sincere (*L*) Frankly and boldly.

au désespoir (*F*) In despair.

audire alteram partem (*L*) To listen to the other side.

au fait (*F*) To the act, capable, up to the mark.

aufgeschoben ist nicht aufgehoben (*G*) Postponed is not abandoned.

Aufklärung (*G*) Enlightenment, philosophical movement of the eighteenth century.

au fond (*F*) At bottom, in reality.

auf Wiedersehen (*G*) Good-bye, till we meet again.

au grand sérieux (*F*) In all seriousness.

au gratin (*F*) With a crust of bread crumbs.

aujourd'hui roi demain rien (*F*) King today, nothing tomorrow.

au naturel (*F*) Naturally, in a natural state.

au pied de la lettre (*F*) Down to the foot of the letter, literally, thoroughly.

au pis aller (*F*) At the worst event.

au plaisir de vous revoir (*F*) To the pleasure of seeing you again

aura (*L*) Wind, breeze.

aura popularis (*L*) Breath of popular favor. Cicero — *De Haruspicum Responsis, XX, 43.*

aurea mediocritas (*L*) Golden moderation. Horace — *Odes, II, 10, 5.*

aurea rumpunt tecta quietem (*L*) Gilded palaces disturb the sleep. Seneca — *Hercules Œtœus, 646.*

au reste (*F*) For the rest, moreover.

au revoir (*F*) Good-bye, till we meet again.

auri sacra fames (*L*) Accursed hunger for gold. Vergil — *Æneid, III, 57.*

aurora australis (*L*) (Southern dawn), luminous phenomena at the South Pole.

aurora borealis (*L*) (Northern dawn), northern lights.

au secours! (*F*) To the rescue, help!

au sérieux (*F*) In a serious way.

auspicium melioris ævi (*L*) Omen of a better age.

aussitôt dit aussitôt fait (*F*) No sooner said than done.

autant d'hommes, autant d'avis (*F*) As many opinions as people.

aut Cæsar aut nullus (*L*) Either Cæsar or no one, either emperor or nothing.

aut non tentaris aut perfice (*L*) Either finish it or don't try at all. Ovid — *Ars Amatoria, I, 389.*

auto-da-fé (*Port.*) Act of faith, punishment of a heretic. Spanish *auto-de-fe.*

aut regem aut fatuum nasci oportet (*L*) One should be born either a king or a fool. Seneca — *De Morte Claudii Cæsaris.*

autres temps, autres mœurs (*F*) Other times other customs; customs change with the times.

aut vincere aut mori (*L*) Either conquer or die. Motto of Duke of Kent.

aux abois (*F*) At bay, in desperate straits.

aux absents les os (*F*) To those absent, the bones. Compare *sero venientibus ossa.*

aux aguets (*F*) On the watch.

aux armes! (*F*) To arms!

aux grands maux les grands remèdes (*F*) Great remedies for great evils.

auxilia humilia firma consensus facit (*L*) Unanimity makes humble help strong. Publius Syrus.

auxilium non leve vultus habet (*L*) The face is no little help. Ovid — *Letters from Pontus, II, 8, 54.*

avaler les couleuvres (*F*) To swallow the adders, to swallow an insult.

avant-coureur (*F*) Forerunner, herald.

avant-courrier (*F*) Herald, harbinger.

avant-propos (*F*) Preface; introduction.

ave! (*L*) Hail!

avec permission (*F*) With permission, with authorization.

avec plaisir (*F*) With pleasure.

ave et vale! (*L*) Hail and farewell!

ave, Imperator, morituri te salutamus (*L*) Hail, Emperor, we who are about to die salute thee. Suetonius — *Claudius, XXI.*

Ave Maria! (*L*) Hail, Mary!

Ave, maris stella, Dei Mater Alma, Atque semper Virgo, Felix cœli porta (*L*) Hail, star of the sea, Fostering Mother of the Lord, and forever Virgin, blessed gate of Heaven.

a verbis ad verbera (*L*) From words to blows.

à vieux comptes nouvelles disputes (*F*) New quarrels over old accounts.

a vinculo matrimonii (*L*) [Law] From the bonds of matrimony.

avi numerantur avorum (*L*) Ancestors of ancestors are reckoned; one follows back through a long line of ancestors.

avion (*F*) Airplane.

avion de chasse (*F*) Pursuit plane.

avoir le diable au corps (*F*) To have the devil in the body, to be ill-tempered.

avoir le pas (*F*) To hold precedence.

avoir les armes belles (*F*) To fence skilfully.

à volonté (*F*) At will.

a vostro beneplacito (*It.*) At your good pleasure.

à votre santé (*F*) To your health.

à vue d'œil (*F*) In sight.

ayah (*Ang.-Ind.*) Native nurse, lady's maid. Portuguese *aia*.

ayudante (*Sp.*) Adjutant, aide-de-camp.

azote (*Sp.*) Whip, lash, calamity.

B

baas (*S. African Dut.*) (Uncle), boss, master.

babu (*Hind.*) [India] A native clerk who can write English. Also *baboo*.

baccarat (*F*) A card-game.

bacha (*Hind.*) Child, young animal. Also *butcha*.

badaud (*F*) Simpleton.

badinage (*F*) Pleasantry, banter.

badli (*Hind.*) Substitute.

baignoire (*F*) Place for bathing, theatre box.

bain-marie (*F*) Double-boiler.

bairagi (*Hind.*) Hindu beggar mendicant. Also *vairagi*.

bakshish (*Oriental*) Tip, gratuity. Also *baksheesh*. Persian *bakhshish*.

bal (*F*) Ball, party.

bal costumé (*F*) Fancy-dress ball, masquerade.

baldacchino (*It.*) Baldachin, brocade, canopy.

ballerina (*It.*) Professional female dancer.

ballista (*L*) Military engine for throwing stones.

ballon d'essai (*F*) Trial balloon, something tentative, "feeler."

bal masqué (*F*) Masked ball.

balourdise (*F*) Dullness, stupid blunder.

bambino (*It.*) Baby, child.

banco regis (*L*) [Law] On the King's Bench.

banco di rei (*It.*) Prisoners' dock.

bandobast (*Ang.-Ind.*) Binding, settlement. Also *bundobust*.

bandurria (*Sp.*) Bandore, stringed musical instrument.

banlieue (*F*) Suburb.

barachois (*F*) Small rock-bound harbor.

baragouin (*F*) Unintelligible language, confused speech.

bara hazri (*Hind.*) Big breakfast.

bara khana (*Hind.*) Big dinner, feast.

barbæ tenus sapientes (*L*) Men wise as far as their beards. Proverb.

barbarus ipse placet dummodo sit dives (*L*) Even the crude person pleases if only he have money. Ovid — *Ars Amatoria*, *II, 276.*

barbouillage (*F*) Scrawl, daub.

barf (*Hind.*) Ice, snow

barranca (*Sp.*) Gully.

bas bleu (*F*) Blue-stocking, woman of literary pretensions.

bashaw, see *pasha*.

bashi bazouk (*Turk.*) Irregular soldier in the Turkish army.

bassinet (*F*) Sixteenth century helmet.

basso (*It.*) [Mus.] Bass.

basso profondo (*It.*) [Mus.] Deep bass, male voice of the lowest range.

basso-rilievo (*It.*) [Sculp.] Bas relief, low relief.

basti (*Hind.*) Abode, village. Anglo-Indian *bustee*.

bâton (*F*) Thin round stick.

batterie de cuisine (*F*) Set of kitchen dishes.

battre la campagne (*F*) To beat about the country, to beat around the bush.

battre la générale (*F*) To sound a general alarm.

battre l'eau avec un bâton (*F*) To beat the water with a stick, to make useless efforts.

battre le fer pendant qu'il est chaud (*F*) To strike the iron while it is hot.

battre le fer sur l'enclume (*F*) To pound the iron on the anvil, to accomplish anything in the right way.

battue (*F*) Animal hunt, beating for game.

bavardage (*F*) Idle chatter, nonsense.

bawarchi khana (*Hind.*) Cook-house, kitchen.

beatæ memoriæ (*L*) Of blessed memory.

beau idéal (*F*) Ideal perfection, ideal beauty.

beau monde (*F*) High society.

beau sabreur (*F*) Dashing cavalryman.

beauté du diable (*F*) Zest of youth.

beaux yeux (*F*) Beautiful eyes.

bec-à-bec (*F*) Face to face.

bêche de mer (*F*) Polynesian shellfish.

beg (*Turk.*) Prince. Also *bey*.

beglerbeg (*Turk.*) Prince of princes, governor-general of an Ottoman province. Also *beylerbey*.

begum (*Pers.*) Princess, lady of rank in India.

beignet de pommes (*F*) Apple-fritter.

bel esprit (*F*) Man of wit, wit.

belles-lettres (*F*) Polite literature.

belle montre et peu de rapport (*F*) Great show and small result.

belle tournure (*F*) Fine figure.

benedetto è quel male che vien solo (*It.*) Blessed is the misfortune that comes alone.

beneficium accipere est libertatem vendere (*L*) To accept a favor is to sell one's liberty. Publius Syrus.

bene qui latuit bene vixit (*L*) He who has lived a retired life has lived well. Ovid — *Tristia, III, 4, 25*.

benêt (*F*) Simpleton.

ben trovato (*It.*) Well invented.

berceuse (*F*) Cradle song.

berretta (*It.*) Square cap worn by church clerics. Also *biretta*.

bersagliere (*It.*) Sharpshooter.

bésigue (*F*) Besique, a card-game.

bête comme un chou (*F*) As stupid as a cabbage, as stupid as an owl.

bête noire (*F*) Black beast, bugbear, aversion.

bêtise (*F*) Piece of stupidity.

bévue (*F*) Misunderstanding, blunder.

bey, see *beg.*

beylerbey, see *beglerbeg.*

bhangi (*Hind.*) Caste of sweepers.

bhikhari (*Hind.*) Mendicant, beggar.

bhikshu (*Sansk.*) Buddhist monk. Pali *bhikku.*

bibere venenum in auro (*L*) To drink poison from a golden cup.

bibi (*Hind.*) Lady.

bibliothécaire (*F*) Librarian.

bibliothèque (*F*) Library.

bichana (*Hind.*) Bedding.

bien cuit (*F*) Well cooked.

bien entendu (*F*) Well understood, of course.

bien obligé (*F*) Much obliged, no thank-you.

bien perdu bien connu (*F*) Well lost well known, fortune flown fortune known.

bienséance (*F*) Correctness, propriety.

bien vengas, mal, si vienes solo (*Sp.*) Welcome, misfortune, if thou comest alone. Cervantes — *Don Quixote.*

bienvenue (*F*) Welcome.

bifteck (*F*) Beefsteak.

bijou (*F*) Jewel, pretty child, graceful person.

bijouterie (*F*) Jewelry.

billet (*F*) Note, handbill, ticket.

billet-doux (*F*) Love letter.

biplace (*F*) Two-seater.

biretta, see *berretta.*

bis (*L and F*) Again, once more!

bis dat qui cito dat (*L*) He gives twice who gives without hesitation.

bise (*F*) North wind.

bis peccare in bello non licet (*L*) To blunder twice in war is not permissible.

bis pueri senes (*L*) Old men are boys twice over; there's no fool like an old fool.

bis vincit qui se vincit in victoria (*L*) He conquers twice who conquers himself in victory. Publius Syrus — *Maxims.*

bizarrerie (*F*) Oddness, whim.

blague (*F*) Lie, humbug, boast.

blagueur (*F*) Hoaxer.

blanc-bec (*F*) White-beak, greenhorn, young fellow.

blanc fixe (*F*) Sulphate of barium, white substance.

blandæ mendacia linguæ (*L*) The lies of a glozing tongue.

blasé (*F*) Palled, tired of everything.

Blut und Eisen (*G*) Blood and iron.

bocage (*F*) Grove, bit of woodland.

bolero (*Sp.*) [Mus.] Spanish dance in three-four time.

bona fide (*L*) In good faith, genuine. Compare *mala fide.*

bona fide polliceor (*L*) I promise in good faith. Cicero.

bona fides (*L*) Good faith.

bon ami (*F*) Good friend, lover.

bona mors (*L*) Death is good, kind.

bonanza (*Sp.*) Fair weather, prosperity.

bona roba (*It.*) (Good goods), courtesan.

bon diable (*F*) Good devil, good fellow, fine chap.

bon enfant (*F*) Good child, good fellow.

bon gré mal gré (*F*) Willingly or unwillingly, willy nilly.

bonhomie (*F*) Goodness of heart, geniality.

bonis avibus (*L*) With favorable omens.

bonis nocet quisquis pepercerit malis (*L*) Whoever spares the bad injures the good. Publius Syrus — *Maxims.*

bonis quod benefit haud perit (*L*) That which is done for good men never perishes. Plautus — *Rudens, IV, 3.*

bonjour (*F*) Good day, good morning.

bon marché (*F*) Good buy, bargain.

bon mot (*F*) (Good word), witty saying, epigram.

bon naturel (*F*) Good-nature.

bonne (*F*) Nurse, sewing-maid.

bonne bouche (*F*) Choice morsel, finishing titbit.

bonne foi (*F*) Good faith, sincerity, honesty.

bonnet rouge (*F*) Red cap, revolutionist.

bono ingenio me esse ornatum, quam auro multo malo (*L*) I prefer to be adorned with a good disposition than with much gold. Plautus — *Pœnulus, I, 2, 90.*

786

bon ton (*F*) Good tone, good taste, refined society. Compare *mauvais ton*.

bon vivant (*F*) Good liver, epicure, boon companion.

bon voyage (*F*) Good voyage, farewell.

borné (*F*) Limited, unintelligent.

bosch (*Dut.*) Bush.

bouche à feu (*F*) Cannon, howitzer, gun.

bouderie (*F*) Sulkiness, ill-humor.

bouillabaisse (*F*) Provençal stew.

bouilli (*F*) Boiled, meat cooked in water.

bouillon (*F*) Clear broth.

bouleversé (*F*) Overturned, upset.

bouleversement (*F*) Upsetting, trouble, agitation.

bouleverser (*F*) To overturn, to upset.

bourdon (*F*) Pilgrim's staff, great bell, bumblebee.

bourgeois (*F*) Middle-class citizen, well-to-do but not aristocratic person, Babbitt.

bourgeois gentilhomme (*F*) Would-be gentleman.

bourgeoisie (*F*) Middle-class, merchant or burgher class.

boutade (*F*) Caprice, whim, old French dance.

boutez en avant (*F*) Push forward.

boutique (*F*) Shop.

bout-rimé (*F*) Verses made to fit given rhymes.

boutonnière (*F*) Buttonhole, buttonhole bouquet.

boyau (*F*) [Mil.] Zigzag trench.

brassière (*F*) Under-bodice.

bravissimo (*It.*) Very good.

bravo (*It.*) Hired assassin, cut-throat; (as exclamation) good.

breloque (*F*) [Mil.] Drumbeat as a signal to break ranks.

brevet d'invention (*F*) Certificate of invention, patent.

brevis esse laboro, obscurus fio (*L*) I strive to be brief, I become obscure. Horace — *Ars Poetica, 25.*

briller par son absence (*F*) To be conspicuous by one's absence.

brio (*It.*) Vivacity, life, fire.

brocatelle (*F*) Material of many colors.

broder (*F*) To embroider, to amplify, to embellish.

broder n'est pas mentir, mais farder la verité (*F*) To embellish is not to lie but to disguise the truth.

brouillerie (*F*) Dissension, misunderstanding, falling-out.

brouillon (*F*) Rough copy, draft.

bruit (*F*) Confusion, sedition, news, sensation.

brûler le pavé (*F*) To burn the pavement, to go like the wind.

brusquerie (*F*) Bluntness, rudeness, abruptness.

brutum fulmen (*L*) Senseless thunderbolt, vain display of force.

budmash (*Ang.-Ind.*) Scoundrel, good-for-nothing.

buen principio, la mitad es hecha (*Sp.*) Good beginning, half is done; well begun is half done.

buffi (*It.*) Debts.

buffo (*It.*) Comic actor, buffoon.

Bund (*G*) Confederation, alliance.

bundobast. see *bandobast.*

C

cabasset (*F*) Sixteenth century helmet resembling a *bassinet* without vizor.

cabello luengo y corto el seso (*Sp.*) Long hair and short wits.

cabestro (*Sp.*) Halter.

cabinet d'aisance (*F*) Toilet, water-closet.

cabotage (*F*) Coasting trade.

cachet (*F*) Small seal.

cacoëthes loquendi (*L*) Mania for talking.

cacoëthes scribendi (*L*) Mania for writing. Juvenal — *Satires, VII, 51.*

cacolet (*F*) Mule-litter, double pannier.

cadastre (*F*) Register, census of landed property.

cada uno es artífice de su ventura (*Sp.*) Each one is the maker of his own fortune. Cervantes — *Don Quixote.*

cada uno tiene su alguazil (*Sp.*) Everyone has his own monitor.

cadi (*Arab.*) Village judge.

cadit quæstio (*L*) The question drops, the case is dismissed.

cadre (*F*) Frame, list.

cæca invidia est (*L*) Envy is blind. Livy *Annals, XXXVIII, 49.*

cælitus mihi vires (*L*) My strength is of heaven.

cælum non animum mutant qui trans mare currunt (*L*) They who cross the sea change their skies but not their natures. Horace — *Epistles, I, 11, 27.*

cætera desunt (*L*) The other things are lacking.

cæteris paribus (*L*) Other things being equal.

cahotage (*F*) Jolt, lurch. Also *cahotement.*

caille (*F*) Quail.

caïque (*F*) Long narrow boat used on the Bosporus. Turkish *kaik.*

calèche (*F*) Open four-wheeled carriage.

calembour (*F*) Pun.

calotte (*F*) Skull-cap worn by ecclesiastics.

camarade (*F*) Comrade, companion.

camaraderie (*F*) Companionship, good-fellowship.

camarilla (*Sp.*) King's privy council.

camarista (*Sp.*) Chamberlain, member of the supreme council of the *Camara*.

cambio non è furto (*It.*) Exchange is not theft.

camelot (*F*) Petty merchant, shop-keeper.

camera lucida (*It.*) (Light room), drawing instrument employing a prism.

camera obscura (*L*) (Dark room), camera.

campo santo (*It.*) (Sacred field), cemetery.

Campus Martius (*L*) Field of Mars, assembly-place of the Roman people.

canaille (*F*) Rabble.

canapé (*F*) (Couch), titbit of bread spread with some delicacy.

cancelli (*L*) Railing, railing in a church.

candelia (*Sp.*) Cold wind.

candida pax (*L*) Shining peace. Ovid — *Ars Amatoria, III, 502.*

canis in præsepi (*L*) A dog in the manger.

canoræ nugæ (*L*) Graceful trifles, mere jingles. Horace — *Ars Poetica, 322.*

cantabile (*It.*) Able to be sung, [mus.] easy-flowing.

cantata (*It.*) (Sung), [mus.] choral composition.

cantatore (*It.*) Reciter, elocutionist, male singer.

cantatrice (*It.*) Female singer, songstress.

cantilenam eandem canis (*L*) You are singing the same song; you are giving us the same old stuff. Terence — *Phormio, III, 2, 10.*

cantus planus (*N. L.*) Plain song, Gregorian chant.

canzone (*It.*) Song, lyric.

cap-à-pie (*F*) Head-to-foot, completely.

caporal (*F*) Corporal.

capote (*F*) Cape.

capriccio (*It.*) Caprice, [mus.] light piece.

capriccioso (*It.*) Capricious, [mus.] lightly, capriciously.

capuche (*F*) Hood, cowl.

caput (*L*) Head.

caput mortuum (*L*) Deadhead, worthless residue.

caquet (*F*) Cackle, gabble, gossip.

caquet bon bec (*F*) Chattering malicious person. La Fontaine — *Fables, XII.*

caqueterie (*F*) Cackling, gabbling.

caracoler (*F*) To prance.

cara sposa (*It.*) Dear wife.

carbonaro (*It.*) Charcoal burner, member of anti-Austrian political society.

caro sposo (*It.*) Dear husband.

carpe diem (*L*) Pluck the day, seize time by the forelock. Horace — *Odes, I, 11, 8.*

carrefour (*F*) Crossroads.

carte blanche (*F*) Blank paper, unlimited power.

carte de visite (*F*) Visiting card.

carte du pays (*F*) Map of the country, full knowledge of a country.

cartes sur table (*F*) Cards on table, exposed.

casa (*It., Sp. and Port.*) House, home, family.

casaque tourner (*F*) To turn coat, to change sides.

casque (*F*) Helmet.

casus belli (*L*) Grounds for war.

casus fœderis (*L*) Condition stipulated in a treaty.

catalogue raisonné (*F*) (Reasoned catalogue), classified catalogue.

causa causans (*L*) Causing cause, primary cause.

causa latet vis est notissima (*L*) While the cause is hidden the force is very well known. Ovid — *Metamorphoses, IV, 287.*

cause célèbre (*F*) Famous case, noted lawsuit.

causerie (*F*) Intimate conversation.

causeuse (*F*) Small sofa for two people.

cavaliere servente (*It.*) Serving cavalier, devoted lover.

cavatina (*It.*) [Mus.] Short simple air.

caveat actor (*L*) Let the doer beware.

caveat emptor (*L*) Let the purchaser beware; let the buyer look out for himself.

cavendo tutus (*L*) Safe by taking precautions.

cave quid dicis quando et cui (*L*) Take care what you say, when and to whom.

cavo-rilievo (*It.*) [Sculp.] Hollow relief.

cedant arma togæ (*L*) Let arms yield to the toga; let military power give way to civil.

cede repugnanti cedendo victor abibis (*L*) Give way to him who resists, by yielding you will go away the victor. Ovid — *Ars Amatoria, II, 197.*

ceja (*Sp.*) Eyebrow, (S. W. U. S.) strip of scrub growth.

cela m'importe peu (*F*) That matters little to me.

cela saute aux yeux (*F*) That leaps to the eyes; that is very evident.

cela se laisse manger (*F*) That is good to eat.

cela s'entend (*F*) That is understood, of course.

cela va sans dire (*F*) That goes without saying; that is a matter of course.

celui qui veut, celui-là peut (*F*) Who wills can; who has the will has the skill.

cénacle (*F*) The room in which the Last Supper took place, coterie of like-minded people.

c'en est fait (*F*) It is all over; it is all up with him.

ce n'est pas être bien aise que de rire (*F*) To laugh is no proof of being happy.

cento (*It.*) One hundred, medley of poetical extracts.

cérémonie (*F*) Pomp, ceremony.

cernit omnia Deus vindex (*L*) An avenging God sees all things.

certum est quia impossible est (*L*) It is certain because it is impossible. Tertullian — *De Carne Christi, 5.*

c'est-à-dire (*F*) That is to say.

c'est autre chose (*F*) That is another matter.

c'est égal (*F*) (It is equal), it is all the same.

c'est la guerre (*F*) That's war.

c'est là le diable (*F*) There is the devil; there's the rub.

cestui que trust (*A.-F.*) [Law] He who trusts, one for whom property is held.

c'est une grande habileté que de savoir cacher son habileté (*F*) It requires great ability to be able to hide one's ability. La Rochefoucauld — *Maxims, 247.*

chabuk (*Hind.*) Horsewhip, whip used for flogging. Also *chabouk.*

chacun à son goût (*F*) Everyone to his own taste.

chacun est l'artisan de sa fortune (*F*) Each one is the architect of his own fortune.

chadar (*Hind.*) A kind of woollen shawl. Also *chuddar.*

χαῖρε, χαίρετε (*Gr.*) Good-bye, farewell, rejoice.

chaise longue (*F*) (Long chair), reclining chair.

chalet (*F*) Swiss cottage, country house in Swiss style.

champak (*Hind.*) Magnolia sacred in India.

Champ de Mars (*F*) Field of Mars, large square in the Grenelle section of Paris.

champlevé (*F*) Grooved, a ware bearing designs set in grooves.

Champs Élysées (*F*) Elysian Fields, an avenue in Paris.

chanson (*F*) Song.

chant (*F*) Song.

chantage (*F*) Blackmail.

chant du cygne (*F*) Swan song, last work of a poet or musician.

chaparajos (*Mex. Sp.*) Leather breeches worn by cowboys, chaps.

chapeau (*F*) Hat.

chaque pays à sa guise (*F*) Each country in its own way.

chaqueta (*Sp.*) Woman's short jacket.

char-à-bancs (*F*) A large sight-seeing bus.

chargé d'affaires (*F*) Diplomat, aide.

charmeuse (*F*) Enchantress, charming woman.

charrette (*F*) Heavy two-wheeled cart.

chassé (*F*) Dance-step involving a gliding movement.

chasse-marée (*F*) Three-masted coasting vessel.

chassepot (*F*) A breech-loading gun.

chasser (*F*) To chase, to hunt, to drive out.

chasser-balancer (*F*) To vacillate.

chasseur (*F*) Hunter.

chat (*F*) Cat.

château (*F*) Royal castle, country residence.

châteaux en Espagne (*F*) Castles in Spain, air-castles.

châtelaine (*F*) Necklace, pendant.

chatoyant (*F*) Gleaming like the eye of a cat.

chat qui dort (*F*) Sleeping cat.

chatti (*Ang.-Ind.*) Earthen pot. Tamil *shaki.*

chaudron (*F*) Caldron, kettle.

chauki (*Hind.*) Watch, guard.

chaussé (*F*) Shod.

chaussure (*F*) Footwear.

chef de cuisine (*F*) Kitchen chief, head cook.

chef-d'œuvre (*F*) Masterpiece.

chela (*Hind.*) Pupil, disciple.

chemin de fer (*F*) Railway.

chemin faisant (*F*) Making one's way, on the way.

cher ami (*F*) Dear friend.

chercher la petite bête (*F*) To search for the little beast, to be exceedingly cautious.

chercher une aiguille dans une botte de foin (*F*) To look for a needle in a haystack.

cherchez la femme (*F*) Look for the woman (as the source of trouble).

chère amie (*F*) Dear friend, mistress.

che sarà sarà (*It.*) What will be will be. Proverb.

cheval de bataille (*F*) War-horse, mainstay.

chevalier d'industrie (*F*) Man who lives by his wits, sharper.

chevalier sans peur et sans reproche (*F*) Fearless and irreproachable gentleman.

cheveaux de frise (*F*) Pieces of timber armed with spikes for keeping away an enemy.

chevreuil (*F*) Deer, roebuck.

chevronné (*F*) [Her.] Shield covered with chevrons.

chiaroscuro (*It.*) Light dark, [painting] disposition of light and shade.

chic (*F*) Smart, stylish.

chick (*Ang.-Ind.*) Cane blind. Hindustani *chik.*

chicote (*Sp.*) (S. W. U. S.) whip for driving cattle.

chi erra in fretta, si pente a bel'agio (*It.*) He who makes a hasty error repents at leisure.

chiffonière (*F*) Small bureau.

chiffonnier (*F*) Rag-picker, scavenger.

chignon (*F*) Back of the neck, knot of hair.

chi non s'arrischia non guadagna (*It.*) Who risks nothing gains nothing.

chi si scusa s'accusa (*It.*) He accuses himself who excuses himself.

chit (*Ang.-Ind.*) Note, memorandum. Hindustani *chitti.*

chi tace acconsente (*It.*) He who is silent gives consent.

chi tace confessa (*It.*) He who is silent confesses.

chokidar (*Ang.-Ind.*) Watchman. Hindustani *chaukidar.*

chokra (*Ang.-Ind.*) Boy, servant.

choky (*Ang.-Ind.*) Lockup, customs-station. Also *chokey.* Hindustani *chauki — watch.*

chor (*Hind.*) Thief, robber.

chose jugée (*F*) Affair already decided, closed proposition.

chose qui plaît est a demi vendue (*F*) Anything that pleases is half sold.

chota hazri (*Hind.*) Small breakfast.

chou (*F*) Cabbage.

χρήματα ἀνήρ (*Gr.*) Money makes the man. Pindar.

chronique scandaleuse (*F*) Scandal history.

chuddar, see *chadar.*

chup! (*Hind.*) Silence!

chup raho! (*Hind.*) Remain quiet!

chut! (*F*) Hush, silence!

cicatrix (*L*) Scar.

cicatrix manet (*L*) The scar remains.

cicerone (*It.*) Guide.

cicisbeo (*It.*) Gallant, recognized lover.

ci-devant (*F*) Previous, former.

ciénaga (*Sp.*) Puddle, marsh.

cierge (*F*) Candle, church candle.

ci-gît (*F*) Here lies.

cineri gloria sera est (*L*) Glory for one's ashes is rather late. Martial — *Epigrams, VI, 1, 28.*

cinque (*It.*) Five.

cinquecento (*It.*) (Five hundred), sixteenth century.

circa (*L*) About.

circulus in probando (*L*) A circle in proving, [log.] a faulty form of reasoning in which the conclusion itself serves as a premise.

civet (*F*) A stew.

civis Romanus sum (*L*) I am a Roman citizen. Cicero — *Against Verres, V, 57, 147.*

clair-obscur (*F*) [Painting] disposition of light and shade. Same as *chiaroscuro.*

claquer (*F*) To snap.

claqueur (*F*) Hired applauder.

clavis (*L*) Key, glossary.

cliché (*F*) (Stereotyped), trite expression.

clientèle (*F*) Clients, patronage.

clitellæ bovi sunt impositæ (*L*) Pack-saddles are placed upon the ox; people receive tasks for which they are not fitted. Proverb.

cloison (*F*) Partition.

cloisonné (*F*) Partitioned, a ware in which the design is made of metal strips or partitions.

clôture (*F*) Ending, finishing.

cocher (*F*) Coachman.

cochero (*Sp.*) Hackney-coachman.

cocotte (*F*) Casserole, woman of easy virtue.

codex rescriptus (*L*) Parchment cleaned and used again.

cogito ergo sum (*L*) I think, therefore I am. Descartes.

cognoscente (*It.*) Connoisseur.

cohue (*F*) Noisy assembly, crowd, confusion.

coiffeur (*F*) Hairdresser.

coiffure (*F*) Mode of wearing the hair.

col (*F*) Neck.

collectanea (*L*) Collected passages, extracts, miscellany.

coloratura (*It.*) [Mus.] Runs, trills, embellishments.

comédie larmoyante (*F*) Tear-compelling comedy, sentimental comedy.

comme ci comme ça (*F*) So so, indifferently well.

comme deux gouttes d'eau (*F*) Like two drops of water, almost identical.

comme il faut (*F*) As it ought to be, suitable, according to the best social usage.

commencement de la fin (*F*) Beginning of the end.

commissionnaire (*F*) Commission agent.

commis-voyageur (*F*) Commercial traveler, traveling agent.

commune periculum concordiam parit (*L*) A common peril brings agreement. Proverb.

communi consensu (*L*) With common consent.

communibus annis (*L*) In average years.

communiqué (*F*) Official communication, announcement.

compagnon de voyage (*F*) Traveling companion.

complexus (*L*) Embrace, compass.

componere lites (*L*) To settle lawsuits. Horace — *Epistles, I, 2, 11.*

compos mentis (*L*) In control of one's mind, sane.

compote (*F*) Fruit cooked with sugar.

compte rendu (*F*) Report rendered, review of a work.

con amore (*It.*) With love, zealously.

con brio (*It.*) [Mus.] With dash and noise.

concerto (*It.*) [Mus.] Composition for instruments with orchestral accompaniments.

concetto (*It.*) Conception, idea, maxim.

concierge (*F*) Door-keeper, porter.

conciliatrix (*L*) Woman conciliator, procuress.

concordia discors (*L*) Inharmonious harmony. Horace — *Epistles, I, 12, 19.*

concours (*F*) Concourse, gathering, concurrence.

concours hippique (*F*) Horse-show.

condamné (*F*) Condemned man.

condiscipulus (*L*) Schoolfellow, classmate.

condottiere (*It.*) Driver, leader.

confident (*F*) Confidant, bosom-friend.

confiture (*F*) Jam, preserve.

confrère (*F*) Colleague, fellow-member.

congé (*F*) Holiday, leave, permission.

congé d'élire (*F*) Authorization to elect.

connaître le dessous des cartes (*F*) To know the under side of the cards, to know the secret.

connaître son monde (*F*) To know one's associates.

conocidos muchos amigos pocos (*Sp.*) Many acquaintances, few friends.

consommé (*F*) A soup.

consuetudo quasi altera natura (*L*) Habit is almost second nature.

consummatum est (*L*) It is finished. Vulgate — *John, XIX, 30.*

conte à dormir debout (*F*) A story that would put you to sleep standing up, wearisome tale.

contentement passe richesse (*F*) Happiness surpasses wealth.

contrabasso (*It.*) (Counter to bass), double-bass.

contra bonos mores (*L*) Contrary to good manners.

contrafagotto (*It.*) Double bassoon.

contre-coup (*F*) Rebound, repercussion.

contretemps (*F*) Mischance. mishap.

conversazione (*It.*) Conversation, evening party, reception.

copia verborum (*L*) Abundance of words, prolixity.

coquillage (*F*) Shellfish, [arch.] shell adornment.

coram (*L*) In the presence of.

coram judice (*L*) Before the judge.

coram populo (*L*) Before the people.

cor anglais (*F*) English horn.

corbeau (*F*) Crow.

corbeille (*F*) Basket.

cordon bleu (*F*) Blue ribbon, distinction, person of distinction.

cordon sanitaire (*F*) Official guard of sanitation.

cornet-à-pistons (*F*) Cornet with keys.

corno (*It.*) Horn.

corno di bassetto (*It.*) Bass horn.

corno inglese (*It.*) English horn.

corona lucis (*L*) Crown of light, circular chandelier used in churches.

corpora lente augescunt cito extinguuntur (*L*) Bodies grow slowly (and) quickly expire. Tacitus — *Agricola, 3.*

corps d'armée (*F*) Army corps.

corps de reserve (*F*) Troops in reserve.

corps diplomatique (*F*) Diplomatic staff.

corpus (*L*) Body, flesh.

corpus delicti (*L*) [Law.] Body of a crime, essential nature.

corpus juris (*L*) Body of laws, code of laws.

corpus omnis Romani juris (*L*) Compendium of all Roman Law. Livy.

corregidor (*Sp.*) Chief magistrate in a Spanish town.

corrigendum (*L*) To be corrected, error.

corruptissima re publica plurimæ leges (*L*) In the most corrupt state the most laws. Tacitus — *Annals, III, 27.*

corso (*It.*) Course, race, wide street.

cortège (*F*) Train of attendants, accompanying throng.

cortile (*It.*) Small court inclosed by a building.

coryphée (*F*) Coryphæus, chief ballet dancer.

cosa ben fatta è fatta due volte (*It.*) A thing well done is twice done.

costumé (*F*) In costume.

cotillon (*F*) (Petticoat), French figure dance.

couci-couci (*F*) So so, fairly well.

coulée (*Am. from F*) Ravine, stream-bed.

couleur de rose (*F*) Rose color, optimism.

couloir (*F*) Corridor, narrow gorge.

coup (*F*) Shock, blow, stroke, wound.

coup de bec (*F*) Peck.

coup de foudre (*F*) Thunderclap.

coup de grâce (*F*) Blow of mercy, finishing stroke, death-blow.

coup de main (*F*) Bold stroke, sudden attack.

coup de maître (*F*) Master-stroke.

coup de pied (*F*) Blow of the foot, kick.

coup de plume (*F*) Pen-stroke.

coup de poing (*F*) Blow of the fist.

coup de soleil (*F*) Sunstroke.

coup d'essai (*F*) First attempt, draft.

coup d'état (*F*) Sudden political revolution.

coup de tête (*F*) Desperate deed.

coup de théâtre (*F*) Unexpected stage effect.

coup d'œil (*F*) Quick glance, view.

coupé (*F*) A salutation in dancing.

coupure (*F*) Cut, bank-note.

courage sans peur (*F*) Fearless courage.

coûte que coûte (*F*) Cost what it costs, cost what it may.

couturière (*F*) Dressmaker.

craignez tout d'un auteur en courroux (*F*) Fear everything from a wrathful writer.

crambe repetita (*L*) Cabbage repeatedly, distasteful repetition. Juvenal — *Satires, VII, 154.* Compare δὶς χράμβη θάνατος.

crèche (*F*) Manger, nursery.

credat Judæus Apella (*L*) Let the Jew Apella believe it (— not I). Horace — *Satires, I, 5, 100.*

credenda (*L*) Things to be believed.

crédit mobilier (*F*) Movable credit, loan based on personal property.

credo quia absurdum (*L*) I believe it because it is absurd.

credo quia impossible (*L*) I believe it because it is impossible.

credula res amor est (*L*) Love is a credulous thing. Ovid — *Metamorphoses, XII, 82.*

crème de la crème (*F*) Cream of the cream, the best.

crème de menthe (*F*) Cream of mint, a cordial.

crème fouettée (*F*) Whipped cream.

crêpé (*F*) Ruffled like crape.

crescendo (*It.*) [Mus.] Increasing in power, growing louder.

crimen falsi (*L*) Crime of falsification, crime of forgery.

critique (*F*) Criticism, correction of text.

croix de guerre (*F*) War cross, decoration for bravery.

crore (*Ang.-Ind.*) Ten millions. Hindustani *kror.*

crux criticorum (*L*) A puzzle for critics.

cubitière (*F*) Elbow-piece in medieval armor.

cui bono? (*L*) For what advantage, for whose good?

cui prodest scelus is fecit (*L*) The crime was committed by the one whom it would benefit. Seneca — *Medea, 500.*

cuisine (*F*) Kitchen, art of cooking.

culbute (*F*) Somersault, fall, ruin.

culbuter (*F*) To overturn violently, to conquer.

cul-de-lampe (*F*) [Arch.] Ceiling ornament resembling the base of a church lamp.

cul-de-sac (*F*) Bottom of a sack, dead-end street.

culpa mea (*L*) My fault.

culpam pœna premit comes (*L*) Punishment presses close upon the fault like a companion. Horace — *Odes, IV, 5, 24.*

cum grano salis (*L*) With a grain of salt, with a reservation.

cummerbund (*Ang.-Ind.*) Sash, belt. Hindustani *kamarband — loin band.*

cum multis aliis (*L*) With many others.

cumshaw (*Oriental*) Bonus, gift.

cunctando restituit rem (*L*) By delaying he regained the advantage. Quintus Ennius.

curæ leves loquuntur ingentes stupent (*L*) Trivial troubles are voluble, severe ones are silent. Seneca — *Hippolitus, II, 3, 607.*

curé (*F*) Priest, curate.

curiosa felicitas (*L*) Assiduous felicity of expression. Petronius Arbiter.

currente calamo (*L*) With a running reed, with an easy style.

curtæ nescio quid semper abest rei (*L*) Something is always lacking to one's fortune. Horace — *Odes, III, 24, 64.*

custos (*L*) Guard, custodian.

custos morum (*L*) Custodian of morals.

custos rotulorum (*L*) Keeper of the records, chief officer of an English county.

cygne noir (*F*) Black swan, rarity.

cyma recta (*L*) [Arch.] Beak-molding, molding concave at the top and convex at the bottom.

cyma reversa (*L*) [Arch.] Molding convex at the top and concave at the bottom.

D

da capo (*It.*) [Mus.] From the beginning.

d'accord (*F*) In accord, in sympathy.

dacoit (*Ang.-Ind.*) Member of an armed robber-band. Hindustani *dakait.*

daduchus (δᾳδοῦχος, *Gr.*) Torch-bearer in the Eleusinian Mysteries. Also *dadouchos.*

daimio (*Jap.-Chin.*) (Great name), Japanese feudal lord.

dak (*Hind. and Mahratti.*) Post-office, relay of men for carrying letters. Also *dawk.*

da locum melioribus (*L*) Give place to your betters. Terence — *Phormio, III, 2, 37.*

Dämmerschlaf (*G*) Twilight sleep.

damnosa hereditas (*L*) Cursed inheritance.

damnum (*L*) Damage.

dandi (*Hind.*) (Ganges boatman), hammock-like conveyance for passengers. Also *dandy.*

danke *or* **danke schön** (*G*) Thank you, thank you very much.

danse du ventre (*F*) Belly-dance, lewd dance.

danse macabre (*F*) Death-dance.

danseuse (*F*) Professional female dancer.

dare pondus idonea fumo (*L*) Fit to give weight to smoke, fit to give importance to trifles. Persius — *Satires, V, 20.*

das Beste ist gut genug (*G*) The best is good enough; the best is none too good.

das Ewig-Weibliche zieht uns hinan (*G*) The ever-womanly draws us upward. Goethe — *Faust, II, 5.*

dash (*African*) Gift, to give a gift.

da svidanya (*Rus.*) Good-bye.

Davus sum non Œdipus (*L*) I am Davus not Œdipus; I can't answer your riddles. Terence — *Andria, 194.*

dawk, see *dak.*

débâcle (*F*) Breaking-up of ice, ruin, rout.

de bona fide (*L*) On one's honor, by conscience.

de bon augure (*F*) Of good omen.

débonnaire (*F*) Airily gay, light-hearted.

de bonne grâce (*F*) With good grace.

de bonne volonté (*F*) Of good will, willingly, with pleasure.

débouché (*F*) Opening, outlet.

débris (*F*) Fragments, rubbish.

début (*F*) Beginning, entrance into society.

débutant (*F*) Youth beginning a career, new performer.

débutante (*F*) Girl or woman beginning a career, young woman entering social life.

deceptio visus (*L*) Deception of vision, optical illusion.

decies repetita placebit (*L*) It will please though ten times repeated. Horace — *Ars Poetica, 365.*

decipimur specie recti (*L*) We are deceived by an appearance of right. Horace — *Ars Poetica, 25.*

décolletée (*F*) Low-necked, low-cut.

décousu (*F*) Ripped, [log.] disconnected.

de die in diem (*L*) From day to day.

de facto (*L*) In fact, actually.

deficit omne quod nascitur (*L*) Everything when is born passes away. Quintillian — *De Institutione Oratoria, V, 10.*

de fond en comble (*F*) From foundation to roof, from bottom to top, completely.

dégagé (*F*) Free, easy.

degeneres animos timor arguit (*L*) Fear betrays ignoble souls. Vergil — *Æneid, IV, 13.*

de gustibus non est disputandum (*L*) Concerning tastes there is no disputing. Proverb.

de haut en bas (*F*) From top to bottom.

Dei gratia (*L*) By the grace of God.

de integro (*L*) Anew.

déjeuner (*F*) Luncheon.

déjeuner à la fourchette (*F*) Fork breakfast, meat breakfast.

de jure (*L*) By law, lawfully.

dekko! (*Ang.-Ind.*) Hello there, hail!

délabrement (*F*) State of ruin.

de lana caprina (*L*) About goat's wool, about some trifle. Horace — *Epistles, I, 18, 15.*

delenda est Carthago (*L*) Carthage must be destroyed. Cato the Censor.

deliberando sæpe perit occasio (*L*) With deliberation the opportunity often dies. Publius Syrus.

délicat (*F*) Delicate, fastidious, nice.

deliciæ humani generis (*L*) The delight of the human race.

delictum (*L*) Fault, offense.

delineavit (*L*) He drew (it).

delirant reges plectuntur Achivi (*L*) When their kings are foolish the Achæans get the punishment. Horace — *Epistles, I, 2, 14.*

delphinum appingit sylvis in fluctibus aprum (*L*) He portrays a dolphin in the forest, a wild boar in the waves. Horace — *Ars Poetica, 30.*

de mauvais augure (*F*) Of bad omen, portentous.

démêlé (*F*) Quarrel, dispute.

démenti (*F*) Denial.

dementia (*L*) Insanity.

dementia a potu (*L*) Insanity from drinking, delirium tremens.

demi (*F*) Half-

demi-jour (*F*) Half-day, dark day.

demi-monde (*F*) (Half-world), woman of low character, common woman.

de mortuis nil nisi bonum (*L*) (Say) nothing but good of the dead.

demos (δῆμος, *Gr.*) Land, people.

de multis grandis acervus erit (*L*) A great heap will be made of many things. Ovid — *Remedy for Love, 424.*

de nihilo nihil (*L*) Nothing from nothing, nothing can come from nothing. Persius — *Satires, III, 84.*

dénouement (*F*) Issue, unraveling of a plot.

de novo (*L*) Anew, afresh.

Deo gratias (*L*) Thanks (be) to God.

de omnibus rebus et quibusdam aliis (*L*) Concerning all things and some besides.

deos fortioribus adesse (*L*) The gods assist the stronger. Tacitus — *Annals, IV, 17.*

Deo volente (*L*) God willing.

de par le roi (*F*) By order of the king.

de profundis (*L*) From out of the depths. Vulgate — *Psalms, CXXX, 1.*

de règle (*F*) Required by custom.

der Fürst ist der erste Diener seines Staats (*G*) The prince is the first servant of his state. Frederick the Great — *Memoirs of Brandebourg.*

de rigueur (*F*) Rigorously required, absolutely necessary.

der kranke Mann (*G*) The sick man.

dernier cri (*F*) Latest cry, last word.

dernier ressort (*F*) Last resort, last resource.

désagrément (*F*) Unpleasantness, cause of displeasure.

desideratum (*L*) Something needed, something desired.

désillusionner (*F*) To disillusion.

desipere in loco (L) To trifle in the right place. Horace — *Odes, IV, 12, 28.* Compare *dulce est desipere in loco.*

désobligeant (F) A carriage for two persons.

désœuvré (F) Unemployed, unoccupied.

désolé (F) Deeply afflicted, exceedingly sorry.

désorienté (F) Lost, disconcerted, bewildered.

desto (It.) Lively, [mus.] in a sprightly manner.

desunt inopiæ multa avaritiæ omnia (L) Many things are wanting to poverty, everything to avarice. Publius Syrus — *Maxims, 441.*

de te fabula narratur (L) The story is told of thee. Horace — *Satires, I, 1, 69.*

détenu (F) (Detained), person in prison.

détour (F) Curve, indirect route.

de trop (F) Superfluous.

deus (L) A god.

deus ex machina (L) A god from a machine, [Greek and Roman theatre] supernatural intervention usually through a mechanical contrivance, [drama] outside means for hastening the dénouement. Same as θεὸς ἐκ μηχανῆς.

deus nobis hæc otia fecit (L) A god has conferred this leisure upon us. Vergil — *Eclogues, I, 6.*

Deus vult (L) God wills it.

devoir (F) Duty.

dewal (Hind.) Temple, pagoda.

dewan, see *diwan.*

dextro tempore (L) At the right time, at the favorable moment. Horace — *Satires, II, 1, 18.*

dey (F) Commander of Janizaries in Algiers. Turkish *dai — uncle.*

dhobi (Hind.) Washerwoman.

dhoti (Hind.) Loin-cloth.

dhu (for *Ir. and Gael. dubh*) Black.

diable (F) Devil, the Devil.

diable à quatre (F) Devil in four, confusion.

diablerie (F) Devilry, malice.

Diabolus (L) The Devil.

diaconicum (L) Depository for sacred objects, sacristy. Greek διακόνικον.

di baldacchino (It.) (Of brocade), pre-eminent, superior.

dicamus bona verba (L) Let us speak words of good omen. Tibullus — *Elegies, II, 2, 1.*

dic bona fide (L) Tell me in good faith. Plautus.

dicitur (L) It is said, they say.

dictum ac factum (L) No sooner said than done. Terence — *Andria, 381.*

dictum de dicto (L) A report from a report, a second-hand story, gossip.

dictum factum (L) Said and done. Terence — *Heauton Timorumenos, V, 1, 31.*

dictum sapienti sat est (L) A word to the wise is sufficient. Plautus — *Persa, IV, 7, 19.*

Dichtung und Wahrheit (G) Poetry and truth.

die geistige Welt (G) The intellectual world, the intelligentsia.

die Kunst ist lang, das Leben kurz, die Gelegenheit flüchtig (G) Art is long, life brief, opportunity fleeting. Goethe —*Wilhelm Meister.*

die lustige Wittwe (G) The gay widow.

die Saiten hoch spannen (G) To tune the strings high, to make pretensions.

dies faustus (L) Fortunate day.

dies infaustus (L) Inauspicious day, unfortunate day.

dies iræ (L) Day of wrath, Judgment Day.

dies non (for *dies non juridicus*, L). A day when no business is transacted.

Dieu défend le droit (F) God defends the right.

Dieu et mon droit (F) God and my rights. Royal motto of England.

Dieu vous garde (F) May God protect you.

die Weltgeschichte ist das Weltgericht (G) Earth is but the frozen echo of the silent voice of God.

difficile (F) Difficult.

difficilia quæ pulchra (L) Things which are pretty are difficult.

di fresco (It.) Recently.

dignus vindice nodus (L) A knotty problem worthy of a disentangler. Horace — *Ars Poetica, 191.*

di grado in grado (It.) From step to step, step by step.

di il vero e affrontara il diavolo (It.) Speak the truth and shame the devil.

dii pia facta vident (L) The gods see virtuous deeds. Ovid — *Fasti, II, 117.*

diis aliter visum (L) To the gods it seemed otherwise. Vergil — *Æneid, II, 428.*

dilettante (It.) Lover of the fine arts, superficial amateur, dabbler.

diligence (F) Stagecoach.

di majores (L) Greater gods, greater figures.

dimidium facti qui cœpit habet (L) He who has begun has the work half done. Horace — *Epistles, I, 2, 40.*

di minores (L) Lesser gods, lesser figures.

diminuendo (It.) [Mus.] Diminishing, growing softer.

di novello tutto par bello (It.) Everything new appears beautiful.

Diós que da la llaga da la medicina (Sp.) God who gives the wound gives the medicine. Cervantes — *Don Quixote.*

dirige nos Domine (*L*) Guide us, O Lord!

di salto in salto (*It.*) From leap to leap, precipitately.

discors concordia (*L*) Inharmonious harmony. Ovid.

δὶς χράμβη θάνατος (*Gr.*) Cabbage twice is death. Proverb.

disjecta membra (*L*) Scattered limbs. Ovid — *Metamorphoses, III, 724.*

disjecti membra poetæ (*L*) Scattered remains of a poet. Horace — *Satires, I, 4, 62.*

distingué (*F*) Distinguished, remarkable, eminent.

distrait (*F*) Inattentive, absent-minded.

diva (*It.*) Goddess, prima donna.

divertissement (*F*) Diversion, amusement, [drama] interlude.

divide et impera (*L*) Divide and rule.

divina particula auræ (*L*) Divine particle of life.

divitiæ virum faciunt (*L*) Means make the man.

divorcé (*F*) Divorced man.

divorcée (*F*) Divorced woman.

diwan (*Pers.*) (India) State council, minister of finance. Anglo-Indian *dewan.*

dixi (*L*) I have spoken.

docendo discimus (*L*) We learn by teaching.

dolce far niente (*It.*) Sweet idleness.

Domine dirige nos (*L*) Oh Lord, guide us.

Dominus vobiscum (*L*) The Lord be with you.

donec eris felix multos numerabis amicos (*L*) As long as you are fortunate you will number many friends. Ovid — *Tristia, I, 9, 5.*

donga (*S. African*) Gully, watercourse.

donner tête baissée (*F*) To go at anything with the head down.

donner un coup de bec (*F*) To peck, to make a harsh remark.

donner un coup de chapeau (*F*) To take off one's hat.

donner un coup de l'épée dans l'eau (*F*) To stab water, to misdirect one's efforts.

dooly (*Ang.-Ind.*) A litter lighter than the palanquin. Also *doolie.* Hindustani *duli.*

dormeuse (*F*) Carriage with sleeping accommodations.

δός μοι ποῦ στῶ καὶ κινῶ τὴν γῆν (*Gr.*) Give me the place to stand and I will move the earth. Archimedes.

douanier (*F*) Customs official.

double entente (*F*) Double meaning, pun.

douceur (*F*) Sweetness, flattering remark, tip.

doyen (*F*) Elder, senior.

dramatis personæ (*N. L.*) Masks of the drama, cast of a play.

drame (*F*) Drama, tragi-comedy.

drame comédie (*F*) Comedy in verse.

drap d'or (*F*) Cloth woven in gold thread.

drapeau tricolore (*F*) Tricolor, the blue, white, and red flag of France.

droit des gens (*F*) Law of nations, international law.

drôle (*F*) Rogue, scoundrel.

drôle de corps (*F*) Comical person, jester.

dubash (*Ang.-Ind.*) Native interpreter. Hindustani *dubashi.*

dubh, see *dhu.*

duce (*It.*) Leader.

duello (*It.*) Duel.

due teste valgono più che una sola (*It.*) Two heads are better than one.

du fort au faible (*F*) From the strong to the weak, average.

dulce domum (*L*) It is sweet to go home.

dulce est desipere in loco (*L*) It is pleasant to act foolishly in the right place. Horace — *Odes, IV, 12, 28.*

dulce et decorum est pro patria mori (*L*) It is a sweet and seemly thing to die for one's country. Horace — *Odes, III, 2, 13.*

dum in dubio est animus paulo momento huc illuc impellitur (*L*) While the mind is in doubt it is driven this way and that by a slight impulse. Terence — *Andria, I, 5, 32.*

dum loquimur fugerit invida ætas (*L*) Even while we are chatting churlish time will have flown. Horace — *Odes I, 11, 7.*

dummodo sit dives barbarus ipse placet (*L*) So long as he is rich even a barbarian is attractive. Ovid — *Ars Amatoria, II, 276.*

dum Roma deliberat Saguntum perit (*L*) Even while Rome is deliberating Saguntum is perishing.

dum spiro spero (*L*) While I breathe I hope; while there's life there's hope.

dum vitant stulti vitia in contraria currunt (*L*) Fools in avoiding vices run into opposite extremes. Horace — *Satires, I, 2, 24.*

dum vivimus vivamus (*L*) While we are alive let us live. Doddridge family motto.

duo (*It.*) [Mus.] Duet.

duomo (*It.*) Cathedral.

dura lex sed lex (*L*) A hard law but still a law.

durbar (*Ang.-Ind.*) Audience hall, formal reception. Urdu and Persian *darbar — court.*

durwaun (*Hind.*) Door-keeper. Persian *darwan.*

du sublime au ridicule il n'y a qu'un pas (*F*) From the sublime to the ridiculous it is but a step. Napoleon.

E

eau (*F*) Water.

eau de Cologne (*F*) Cologne water, cologne.

eau sucrée (*F*) Sweetened water.

ébauche (*F*) First sketch of an art work.

éboulement (*F*) Landslide.

écarté (*F*) (Discarded), a card-game.

Ecce Homo (*L*) Behold the man. Vulgate — *John, XIX, 5.*

ecce iterum Crispinus (*L*) There is that fellow Crispinus again. Juvenal — *Satires, IV, 1.*

ecce signum (*L*) Behold the sign.

ecco (*It.*) Behold, there, lo.

eccum tibi lupus in sermone (*L*) Here is the wolf we were talking about; here is the very person we were talking about.

écervelé (*F*) Stupid, lacking in judgment.

échafaudage (*F*) Scaffold, scaffolding.

échappée (*F*) Escape, escapade.

échapper belle (*F*) To make a fortunate escape.

echar el mango tras el destral (*Sp.*) To throw the helve after the hatchet.

éclaircissement (*F*) Explanation, elucidation.

éclat (*F*) Blaze of light, burst of noise.

écorcher les oreilles (*F*) To skin the ears, to make a disagreeable impression.

écrasez l'infâme (*F*) Crush the infamous thing. Voltaire.

édition de luxe (*F*) Elegant edition.

editio princeps (*L*) First edition.

effigies (*L*) Effigy, likeness.

effleurer (*F*) To touch lightly, to touch upon.

égard (*F*) Marks of regard, esteem.

ego spem pretio non emo (*L*) I do not purchase hope for a price. Terence — *Adelphi II, 2, 12 (219).*

eheu! fugaces labuntur anni (*L*) Alas, the fleeting years glide by. Horace — *Odes, II, 14, 1.*

eheu jam satis! (*L*) Alas, enough now!

eidolon (εἴδωλον, *Gr.*) Image, shape, phantom.

eigner Herd ist goldes Werth (*G*) One's own hearth is worth gold.

eile mit Weile (*G*) Hasten deliberately; haste makes waste.

eileton (εἰλητον, *Low Gr.*) Communion cloth in the Eastern Church.

einen hohen Geist haben (*G*) To be haughty.

einer Frau und einem Glas drohet jede Stunde was (*G*) Every hour threatens a woman and a piece of glass.

ein fester Burg ist unser Gott (*G*) A solid citadel is our God. Martin Luther.

einmal keinmal (*G*) ·Once not at all, once does not count.

ein starker Geist (*G*) A powerful mind.

εἰς ὄνυχα (*Gr.*) To a hair.

ejectamenta (*L*) That which is cast out, ejecta.

ekka (*Hind.*) One-horse vehicle. Also *yakka.*

élan (*F*) Sudden impulsive movement, vivacity.

el comenzar las cosas es tenerlas medio acabadas (*Sp.*) To begin things is to have them half finished. Cervantes — *Don Quixote.*

elegantiæ arbiter (*L*) Judge of manners. Tacitus — *Annals, XVI, 18.*

elephantus non capit murem (*L*) The elephant does not catch mice.

ἐλεφας μῦν οὐκ ἁλίσκει (*Gr.*) The elephant does not catch mice.

élève (*F*) Pupil.

élite (*F*) Choicest part, select group of society.

elixir vitæ (*L*) Elixir of life.

éloge (*F*) Eulogy, panegyric.

embarras de choix (*F*) Embarrassment of choices.

embarras de richesses (*F*) Embarrassment of wealth, too much money.

embonpoint (*F*) Fatness, corpulence.

è meglio cader dalle finestre che dal tetto (*It.*) It is better to fall from the window than from the roof.

è meglio tardi che mai (*It.*) Better late than never.

è meglio una volta che mai (*It.*) Better once than never.

è meglio un buon amico che cento parenti (*It.*) Better one good friend than a hundred relatives.

emeritus (*L*) Retired with honor.

e merito (*L*) From merit, by merit.

émeute (*F*) Riot, insurrection.

émigré (*F*) One who has emigrated, one who has left his native country.

emir (*Arab.*) Military commander.

ἐμοῦ θανόντος γαῖα μιχθήτω πυρί (*Gr.*) After I am dead let the earth dissolve in air.

emplastrum (*L*) Plaster, salve.

empressement (*F*) Zeal, ardor.

empta dolore docet experientia (*L*) Experience bought by pain teaches. Proverb.

emptor (*L*) Purchaser.

en alerte (*F*) On the alert.

en avant! (*F*) Forward!

en avant de (*F*) In front of.

en bloc (*F*) Wholesale, in the mass.

en cada tierra su uso (*Sp.*) Each land has its own customs. Cervantes — *Don Quixote.*

enceinte (*F*) Pregnant, inclosure, ramparts.

encore (*F*) Again.

en couleur de rose (*F*) In rose-color, hopefully.

en courroux (*F*) In frowns, angrily.

en désespoir de cause (*F*) As a last resource.

en déshabillé (*F*) In partial attire, carelessly dressed.

en diable (*F*) Exceedingly.

en Dieu est ma fiance (*F*) In God is my trust.

endimanché (*F*) In Sunday best.

en effet (*F*) In fact, as a matter of fact.

en évidence (*F*) In evidence, in sight, in public.

en famille (*F*) With the family, informally.

enfant (*F*) Child.

enfant gâté (*F*) Spoiled child.

enfant perdu (*F*) Lost child, soldier sent on a desperate mission, (pl.) forlorn hope.

enfant terrible (*F*) Naughty child.

enfant trouvé (*F*) Found child, foundling.

enfer (*F*) Hell.

enfin (*F*) At last, finally.

en foule (*F*) In great quantity, in crowds.

en grande tenue (*F*) In full dress.

en grande toilette (*F*) In full evening dress.

en grand seigneur (*F*) Like a great lord.

en habiles gens (*F*) After the manner of skilled people.

en masse (*F*) In a mass, all together.

ennui (*F*) Boredom.

ennuyé (*F*) Bored.

en passant (*F*) In passing, by the way.

en plein jour (*F*) In full daylight.

enragé (*F*) Mad, violent, irritated.

en rapport (*F*) In relation, in sympathy.

en règle (*F*) According to rule, in due form.

en revanche (*F*) In revenge, in requital.

en route (*F*) On the way.

ens (*L*) Being, entity of a thing.

ensemble (*F*) Together, whole.

Ens Entium (*L*) The Being of beings, the Creator.

ens rationis (*L*) Being of reason, product of the mind.

en suite (*F*) In series.

en suivant la vérité (*F*) In following the truth.

en tapinois (*F*) Secretly, furtively.

entbehre gern was du nicht hast (*G*) Forego willingly that which thou hast not.

entbehren sollst du! sollst entbehren (*G*) Thou must refrain, refrain thou must! Goethe — *Faust, I, 4.*

entente (*F*) Agreement, understanding.

entente cordiale (*F*) Cordial understanding.

entêté (*F*) Headstrong, obstinate.

entourage (*F*) Surroundings, social environment.

en tout cas (*F*) In any case.

en toute chose il faut considérer la fin (*F*) In every affair it is necessary to consider the end.

entr'acte (*F*) Between the acts, intermission.

entre chien et loup (*F*) Between dog and wolf, at twilight.

entre deux âges (*F*) Between two ages, middle-aged.

entre dos aguas (*Sp.*) Between two waters, in doubt.

entremets (*F*) Side-dish, light course before dessert.

entremetteuse (*F*) Go-between.

entre nous (*F*) Between ourselves.

entrepôt (*F*) Storehouse, warehouse.

entrepreneur (*F*) Contractor, organizer.

entresol (*F*) A floor between the first and the second floors.

en vérité (*F*) In truth, really.

épanchement (*F*) Pouring out, effusion.

épanchement de cœur (*F*) Confession from the heart.

éperdu (*F*) Agitated, troubled, excited.

éperdu d'amour (*F*) Madly in love.

épicier (*F*) (Grocer), vulgar fellow.

e pluribus unum (*L*) One out of many. Motto of the United States.

epopœia (ἐποποιία, *Gr.*) Epic poetry.

epoptæ (ἐπόπται, *Gr.*) Second-year votaries of the Eleusinian Mysteries.

eppur si muove (*It.*) Nevertheless it does move. Galileo.

éprouvette (*F*) Testing apparatus, test-tube.

équivoque (*F*) Equivocal, of double meaning.

ergo (*L*) Therefore, consequently.

eripuit cælo fulmen sceptrumque tyrannis (*L*) He snatched the thunderbolt from heaven and the scepter from the tyrants. Houdon, of Benjamin Franklin.

ἔρως (*Gr.*) Love, passion, god of love.

errare humanum est (*L*) To err is human.

erubuit; salva res est (*L*) He blushed, the affair is safe. Terence — *Adelphi, IV, 5, 9, (643).*

es bildet ein Talent sich in der Stille, sich ein Charakter in dem Strom der Welt (*G*) A talent is developed in quiet, a character in the stream of the world. Goethe — *Torquato Tasso, I, 2, 66.*

escadrille (*F*) Squadron.

escamoterie (*F*) Slight-of-hand feat, sneak-theft.

esclandre (*F*) Scandal, uproar, fracas.

es de vidrio la mujer (*Sp.*) A woman is made of glass. Cervantes — *Don Quixote.*

è sempre l'ora (*It.*) It is always the hour it is always the right time.

es gibt für die Kammerdiener keine Helden (*G*) Valets have no heroes. Goethe.

es ist nicht alles Gold was glänzt (*G*) All is not gold that glitters.

espièglerie (*F*) Mischief, trickery, roguish trick.

espionnage (*F*) Spying, cozenage.

esposa (*Sp.*) Wife.

espressivo (*It.*) [Mus.] Expressively.

esprit (*F*) Spirit, shrewdness, wit.

esprit borné (*F*) Person of small intelligence.

esprit de corps (*F*) Uniting spirit.

esprit fort (*F*) Master-mind, free-thinker.

esse (*L*) To be, existence. Compare *non esse.*

esse quam videri bonus malebat (*L*) He preferred to be rather than to seem good. Sallust — *Catiline, 54.*

estafette (*F*) Courier with dispatches.

estaminet (*F*) Café, coffee-house, smoking-room.

estancia (*Sp.*) (Stay), cattle-ranch.

est modus in rebus (*L*) There is a mean in (all) things. Horace — *Satires, I, 1, 106.*

esto perpetua (*L*) Let her be everlasting. Paul Sarpi.

esto perpetuum (*L*) Let it be everlasting.

esto quod esse videris (*L*) Be what you seem to be. Proverb.

étagère (*F*) Shelf-cupboard.

étalage (*F*) Display, affectation, show.

étape (*F*) Stopping-place, distance between stopping-places.

état-major (*F*) Staff of an army, headquarters.

et hoc genus omne (*F*) And all this kind of people. Horace — *Satires, I, 2, 2.*

etiam sanato volnere cicatrix manet (*L*) After the wound is healed the scar remains. Proverb.

étourderie (*F*) Thoughtlessness, lack of reflection, blunder.

être entre le marteau et l'enclume (*F*) To be between the anvil and the hammer, to be between the devil and the deep sea.

et sceleratis sol oritur (*L*) And the sun rises on the wicked too. Seneca — *De Beneficiis, III, 25.*

et sic de similibus (*L*) And so concerning like things.

et tu, Brute (*L*) Thou too, Brutus. Julius Cæsar.

euge! (*L*) Well done, bravo!

εὐτυχῶν μὴ ἴσθι ὑπερήφανος· ἀπορήσας μὴ ταπεινοῦ (*Gr.*) Be not puffed up by good fortune nor cast down by bad fortune. Cleoboulos.

εὐτυχῶν μὲν μέτριος ἴσθι ἀτυχῶν δὲ φρόνιμος (*Gr.*) In good fortune learn moderation, in bad fortune learn to be prudent. Periander.

evviva! (*It.*) Hurrah!

Ewigkeit (*G*) Eternity.

Ewig-Weibliche (*G*) Eternal feminine.

ex abundantia (*L*) Out of abundance.

ex abundanti cautela (*L*) Out of excessive caution.

exalté (*F*) Excited, inspired.

ex animo (*L*) From the heart, sincerely.

ex animo effluere (*L*) To escape from the mind, to be forgotten.

ex bona fide (*L*) On one's honor.

ex cathedra (*L*) From the chair, with authority.

exceptis excipiendis (*L*) With the necessary exceptions made.

excerpta (*L*) Selections, excerpts.

excitabat enim fluctus in simpulo (*L*) For he made waves in a ladle; he raised a tempest in a tea-pot. Cicero — *De Legibus, III, 16.*

ex concesso (*L*) From what has been conceded.

ex curia (*L*) [Law] Out of court.

excusatio non petita fit accusatio manifesta (*L*) A voluntary excuse becomes a manifest accusation.

ex dono (*L*) Out of a gift, the gift of.

exegi monumentum ære perennius (*L*) I have reared a monument more enduring than bronze. Horace — *Odes, III, 30, 1.*

exempla sunt odiosa (*L*) Examples are odious.

exempli gratia (*L*) For the sake of example, e.g.

exeunt (*L*) They go out; they leave the stage.

exeunt omnes (*L*) All go out.

ex facto jus oritur (*L*) From the fact arises the law; actions originate laws. Blackstone.

ex hypothesi (*L*) According to the hypothesis.

exigeant (*F*) Exacting, demanding too much.

exit (*L*) He goes out; he leaves the stage.

exitus acta probat (*L*) The outcome justifies the act. Ovid — *Heroides, II, 85.*

ex libris (*L*) From the books, in the library.

ex mero motu (*L*) From a purely personal motive, out of mere whim.

ex more (*L*) According to custom.

ex necessitate rei (*L*) From the necessity of the matter.

ex nihilo nihil (*L*) Nothing from nothing, nothing comes from nothing.

ex officio (*L*) By virtue of office, officially.

ex parte (*L*) From one side, for the sake of only one party.

ex parvis sæpe magnarum momenta rerum pendent (*L*) Events of great moment often hang on trifling things.

ex pede Herculem (*L*) From the foot (one may judge) Hercules; the part is an index to the whole.

expende Hannibalem (*L*) Weigh Hannibal. Juvenal — *Satires, X, 147.*

experimentum crucis (*L*) Test by the cross, crucial experiment.

experto crede (*L*) Trust in a person well tried. Vergil — *Æneid, XI, 283.*

expertus metuit (*L*) The man of experience is full of fear. Horace — *Epistles, I, 18, 87.*

exposé (*F*) Statement, account, outline.

ex post facto (*L*) After the offense has been committed.

ex quovis ligno non fit Mercurius (*L*) Mercury is not made of any block of wood. Apuleius from Pythagoras.

ex tempore (*L*) Extemporaneously, off-hand.

extincteur (*F*) Fire-extinguisher.

extortor bonorum legumque contortor (*L*) A blackmailer and wrester of laws. Terence — *Phormio, II, 3, 27.*

extra muros (*L*) Outside the walls, beyond the city limits.

ex ungue lionem (*L*) From its claw (one may know) the lion; the part is index to the whole.

ex uno disce omnes (*L*) From one learn to know all. Proverb.

ex vi termini (*L*) By the force of the term.

ex voto (*L*) From a vow, as fulfilment of a vow.

F.

faber est quisque fortunæ suæ (*L*) Each one is the maker of his own fortune. Sallust — *De Republica, I, 1.*

faber est quisque ingeni sui (*L*) Each one is the maker of his own talent.

facies non omnibus una nec diversa tamen (*L*) The features not alike in all respects nor yet different. Ovid — *Metamorphoses, II, 13.*

facile largiri de alieno (*L*) It is easy to be generous with another's goods. Proverb.

facile princeps (*L*) Easily first.

facilis descensus Averni (*L*) Easy is the descent to Hell, the downward path is smooth. Vergil — *Æneid, VI, 126.*

facinus quos inquinat æquat (*L*) A crime brings to a common level those whom it defiles. Lucan — *Pharsalia, V, 287.*

façon de parler (*F*) Manner of speaking.

facta non verba (*L*) Deeds not words.

facteur (*F*) Agent, postman.

fade (*F*) Insipid, stale, mawkish.

fæces (*L*) Dregs, filth, dung.

fænum habet in cornu (*L*) He has hay on his horns; he is a dangerous fellow. Horace — *Satires, I, 4, 34.*

fæx populi (*L*) The dregs of the populace. Cicero.

fainéance (*F*) Doing nothing, idleness.

fainéant (*F*) Do-nothing, idler.

faire accueil (*F*) To welcome.

faire antichambre (*F*) To force one's self upon a person.

faire claquer son fouet (*F*) To make one's whip crack, to blow one's own horn.

faire l'aimable (*F*) To play the amiable one.

faire l'amende honorable (*F*) To make honorable amends, to ask pardon.

faire la moue (*F*) To make a grimace.

faire le diable à quatre (*F*) To make great confusion, to play the devil.

faire les yeux doux (*F*) To make sweet eyes, to ogle.

faire l'ingenu (*F*) To affect simplicity.

faire pattes de velours (*F*) To play velvet paws, to be deceptively ingratiating.

faire sans dire (*F*) To act without talking.

faire ses choux gras (*F*) To make his cabbages fat, to make profit.

faire son coup (*F*) To make one's success.

faire un esclandre (*F*) To make a scene.

faire venir l'eau à la bouche (*F*) To make the mouth water.

fait accompli (*F*) Deed accomplished.

fait à peindre (*F*) Made to paint, fit to paint.

fallacia consequentis (*L*) Fallacy of the consequent, illogical conclusion.

falsi crimen (*L*) The crime of falsification.

falsus in uno falsus in omnibus (*L*) False in one thing, false in everything. Proverb.

fama malum quo non velocius ullum (*L*) Rumor is an evil than which there is nothing swifter. Vergil — *Æneid, IV, 174.*

fama volat (*L*) The report flies. Vergil — *Æneid, III, 121.*

familistère (*F*) Community, after the system of Fourier.

fanatico (*It.*) Fanatic, visionary.

fandango (*Sp.*) Lively dance popular in Spain and Spanish America.

farceur (*F*) Actor in a farce, professional humorist.

fare, fac (*L*) Speak, do. Motto.

fare un bel trovato (*It.*) To come upon something opportunely.

fari quæ sentiat (*L*) To say what one feels. Horace — *Epistles, I, 4, 9.*

far la parte del diavolo (*It.*) To play the devil's advocate.

fasces (*L*) Bundles of rods, symbol of power.

fasti (*L*) List of court days, calendar.

fata Morgana (*It.*) The fairy Morgana, mirage, optical illusion.

Fata obstant (*L*) The Fates oppose. Vergil — *Æneid, IV, 440.*

Fata regunt homines (*L*) The Fates rule men's destiny.

Fata viam invenient (*L*) The Fates will find the way. Vergil — *Æneid, X, 113.*

fatihah (*Arab.*) Beginning, opening sura of the Koran.

fatras (*F*) Confused medley, rubbish.

faubourg (*F*) Suburbs, part of a city outside the walls.

faute (*F*) Fault, lack, blunder.

faute de mieux (*F*) For lack of something better.

fauteuil (*F*) Arm-chair, easy-chair.

faux pas (*F*) False step, mistake, blunder.

fax mentis incendium gloriæ (*L*) The fire of glory is the torch of the mind.

fecit (*L*) He made (it).

felicitas multos habet amicos (*L*) Prosperity has many friends. Proverb.

felix qui potuit rerum cognoscere causas (*L*) Happy he who has been able to know the reasons for things. Vergil — *Georgics, II, 490.*

felix se nescit amari (*L*) The prosperous man does not know whether he is loved or not. Lucan — *Pharsalia, VII, 727.*

fellah (*Arab.*) Peasant, plowman.

felo de se (*L*) [Law] Felon to one's self, suicide.

felucca (*It.*) Long narrow sailboat used in the Mediterranean.

feme (*O.F.*) Woman.

feme coverte (*O.F.*) Married woman under covert of her husband.

feme sole (*O.F.*) Unmarried woman.

femme (*F*) Woman, wife.

femme de chambre (*F*) Chamber-maid, waiting-maid.

feræ naturæ (*L*) Of wild nature.

fere totus mundus exercet histrionem (*L*) Almost the entire world plays a part. Petronius Arbiter.

feria (*It.*) Feast, holiday.

fervens difficili bile tumet jecur (*L*) My hot liver swells with angry bile. Horace — *Odes, I, 13, 4.*

festina lente (*L*) Make haste slowly.

fête (*F*) Ceremony in honor of a saint or an important event.

fête champêtre (*F*) Rural festival, lawn party.

feu de joie (*F*) Bonfire in celebration.

feu d'enfer (*F*) Fire of hell, violent firing.

feuille-morte (*F*) Dead leaf, pale yellow color.

feuilleton (*F*) Daily article of criticism at the foot of a French newspaper.

fiacre (*F*) Cab, hackney coach.

fiancé (*F*) Betrothed man.

fiancée (*F*) Betrothed woman.

fiat justitia, ruat cælum (*L*) Let justice be done though the sky fall.

fiat lux (*L*) Let there be light. Vulgate — *Genesis, I, 3.*

fidei defensor (*L*) Defender of the faith.

fideli certa merces (*L*) To the faithful a sure reward.

fidelis ad urnam (*L*) Faithful up to the urn, faithful unto death.

fides Punica (*L*) Punic faith, treachery. Sallust — *Jugurtha, 108, 3.*

fidus Achates (*L*) Faithful Achates, trusted friend. Vergil — *Æneid, VI, 158.*

fieri facias (*L*) Have it done, [law] a writ to execute judgment.

fiesta (*Sp.*) Feast, entertainment, church holiday.

figlie e vetri son sempre in pericolo (*It.*) Girls and windows are in constant danger.

figurante (*It.*) Figure-dancer, one who plays a mute part.

figuriste (*F*) Modeler in plaster.

filius nullius (*L*) Son of no one, bastard son.

filius terræ (*L*) Son of the earth, low-born person.

fille (*F*) Girl, daughter.

fille de chambre (*F*) Waiting-maid, chamber-maid.

fille de joie (*F*) Prostitute.

fils (*F*) Son.

finale (*It.*) End, last part of a play or composition.

fin contre fin (*F*) End against end, object opposed to object.

fin de siècle (*F*) Century's end, (adj.) progressive, ultra-modern.

finem respice (*L*) Look to the end.

finis coronat opus (*L*) The end crowns the work.

fioritura (*It.*) (Flowering), embellishment.

flabellum (*L*) Fan. Terence — *Eunuchus, III, 5, 47.*

flagrante bello (*L*) With the war raging.

flagrante delicto (*L*) With the crime flaming, in the very act.

flambé (*F*) Burned, ruined.

Flammenwerfer (*G*) Flame-thrower.

flânerie (*F*) Idling, lounging.

flâneur (*F*) Idler, lounger, stroller.

flatteur (*F*) Flatterer.

flèche (*F*) Arrow, church spire.

flecti non frangi (*L*) To be bent, not broken.

fleur d'eau (*F*) Level of the water.

fleur de lis (*F*) Flower of the lily, royal insignia of France.

fleuron (*F*) Architectural or typographical ornament in the form of a flower.

flosculi sententiarum (*L*) Flowerets of thought.

Flügelhorn (*G*) Military bugle.

flux de bouche (*F*) Flow of mouth, loquacity.

flux de mots (*F*) Flow of words.

flux de paroles (*F*) Flow of words.

folâtre (*F*) Gay, lively, frivolous.

fonctionnaire (*F*) Functionary, public official.

fondre en larmes (*F*) To dissolve in tears.

fons et origo (*L*) Fount and origin.

forçat (*F*) Criminal condemned to hard labor.

force majeure (*F*) Superior force, irresistible force.

forensis strepitus (*L*) Din of the forum.

formosa facies muta commendatio est (*L*) Beautiful features are a mute commendation. Publius Syrus — *Maxims.*

foro conscientiæ (*L*) In the court of conscience, conscientiously.

forsan et hæc olim meminisse juvabit (*L*) And perhaps sometime it will be pleasant to recall these things. Vergil — *Æneid, I, 203.*

fortes fortuna adjuvat (*L*) Fortune favors the brave. Terence — *Phormio, I, 4, 26.*

fortis cadere cedere non potest (*L*) The brave man may fall, but not yield. Proverb.

fortiter in re (*L*) Boldly in deed. Aquaviva — *Industriæ ad Curandos Animæ Morbos.* Compare *suaviter in modo fortiter in re.*

fortuna favet fatuis (*L*) Fortune favors fools.

fortuna magna magna domino est servitus (*L*) A great fortune is a great bondage to its master. Proverb.

fortuna multis dat nimium, nulli satis (*L*) Fortune gives many too much, no one enough. Martial — *Epigrams, XII, 10.*

forum (*L*) Public square.

fossoribus orti (*L*) To spring from ditch-diggers, to be of humble origin.

fossoyeur (*F*) Grave-digger, sexton.

fougade (*F*) Sudden whim, caprice.

fougasse (*F*) Mine-shaft.

fourgon (*F*) Wagon for heavy loads, supply wagon.

franc-tireur (*F*) Mercenary soldier, hireling.

frangas non flectes (*L*) You may break, not bend. Motto of Leveson-Gower families.

frater (*L*) Brother.

Frau (*G*) Woman, wife.

Fräulein (*G*) Miss, unmarried woman.

fraus est celare fraudem (*L*) [Law] It is a fraud to conceal a fraud.

fredaine (*F*) Youthful folly.

friandise (*F*) Taste for delicacies.

friseur (*F*) Hair-dresser.

fronder (*F*) To grumble.

frondeur (*F*) Faultfinder, partisan of the Fronde.

frons est animi janua (*L*) The forehead is the door to the mind. Cicero — *Oratio de Provinciis Consularibus, XI.*

front à front (*F*) Forehead to forehead, face to face.

fronte capillata post est occasio calva (*L*) Opportunity with hair in front is bald behind. Dionysius Cato — *Disticha de Moribus, II, 26.*

fronti nulla fides (*L*) No faith is to be put in outward appearances. Juvenal — *Satires, II, 8.*

fruges consumere nati (*L*) Born to eat the fruits of the earth. Horace — *Epistles, I, 2, 27.*

fugit hora (*L*) The hour flies by. Ovid — *Amorum, I, 11, 15.*

fuimus Troes (*L*) We have been Trojans. Vergil — *Æneid, II, 325.*

fuit Ilium (*L*) Troy used to be. Vergil — *Æneid, II, 325.*

functus officio (*L*) Having fulfilled duty, retired from office.

furor arma ministrat (*L*) Rage furnishes weapons. Vergil — *Æneid, I, 150.*

furore (*It.*) Rage, passion, fury.

furor loquendi (*L*) Passion for speaking.

furor poeticus (*L*) Poetic frenzy.

furor scribendi (*L*) Passion for writing.

Fürsten haben lange Hände und viele Ohren (*G*) Princes have long hands and many ears.

G

gaddi (*Hind.*) Cushion, throne. Also *gadi* and *guddee.*

gage d'amour (*F*) Token of love.

gaieté de cœur (*F*) Gaiety of heart.

galantuomo (*It.*) Upright man, well-bred person.

galbe (*F*) Outline, contour.

galimatias (*F*) Confused talk, jumble.

Gallice (*L*) In Gallic, in French.

gamache (*F*) Leather leggings.

gambade (*F*) Gambol.

gametangium (*L*) One of the gametes.

garçon (*F*) Boy, waiter.

garde nationale (*F*) National guard.

garde royale (*F*) Royal guard.

gare (*F*) Railway station.

gari (*Hind.*) Cart or carriage of two wheels. Also *gharry* and *gharri.*

gari-wala (*Hind.*) Gharry-wallah, carriage-runner.

Gasthof (*G*) (Guest court), inn, public house.

gâteau (*F*) Cake.

gauche (*F*) Left, awkward, tactless.

gaucherie (*F*) Awkwardness, blunder.

gaudeamus igitur (*L*) Therefore let us rejoice. Author unknown.

gaudet tentamine virtus (*L*) Courage delights in a trial.

gavotte (*F*) Gavot, old French dance in quick time.

geisha (*Jap.*) Singing and dancing girl.

Geist (*G*) Spirit, mind, wit.

geistig (*G*) Spiritual, intellectual, witty.

Geld regiert die Welt (*G*) Money rules the world.

gelée de groseilles (*F*) Currant jelly.

gendarme (*F*) Armed policeman.

genius loci (*L*) Guardian deity of a place.

genre (*F*) Kind, [painting] intimate scenes.

gens d'armes (*F*) Men at arms.

gens de guerre (*F*) Men of war, soldiers.

gens de même famille (*F*) Folk of the same family, kin.

gentilhomme (*F*) Nobleman, gentleman.

gentilhomme de lièvre (*F*) Petty country squire.

genus est mortis male vivere (*L*) It is a kind of death to lead an evil life. Ovid — *Letters from Pontus, III, 4, 75.*

genus irritabile vatum (*L*) The excitable race of poets. Horace—*Epistles,II, 2,102.*

Germanice (*N. L.*) In German, in the German style.

Gesundheit! (*G*) Your health!

geta (*Jap.*) Sandal used in Japan in rainy weather.

gharri, see *gari.*

gharry, see *gari.*

ghat (*Hind.*) Mountain pass. Also *ghaut.*

ghazal (*Arab.*) Oriental love poem.

ghurry (*Ang.-Ind.*) Water clock, hour.

giallo antico (*It.*) Antique yellow, marble of a golden color found in Roman ruins.

giaur (*Turk. and Pers.*) Infidel.

gibier de potence (*F*) Game for the gibbet, gallows-bird.

giovane santo diavolo vecchio (*It.*) Young saint, old devil.

girja (*Ang.-Ind.*) Christian church.

gîte (*F*) Resting-place, lair.

glacé (*F*) Smooth, iced.

Gloria in excelsis Deo (*L*) Glory be to God on high. First words of the *greater doxology.*

Gloria Patri (*L*) Glory be to the Father. First words of the *lesser doxology.*

Gloria Tibi, Domine (*L*) Glory be to Thee, Lord. (Liturgical response.)

glückliche Reise (*G*) Pleasant journey, bon voyage.

γνῶθι σεαυτόν (*Gr.*) Know thyself.

gobe-mouches (*F*) Sparrow, dupe, gull.

gomashta (*Ang.-Ind.*) Agent, clerk. Hindustani and Persian *gumashta.*

gooroo, see *guru.*

gorge-de-pigeon (*F*) Pigeon's throat.

gossoon (*Ang.-Ir.*) Lad, man servant.

gouache (*F*) Painting in paste.

gourmand (*F*) Glutton.

gourmet (*F*) Connoisseur of wines or foods.

goût (*F*) Taste, savor.

grâce (*F*) Grace, favor.

grâce à Dieu (*F*) Thanks to God.

gradatim (*L*) Step by step, gradually.

gradino (*It.*) Step, altar shelf.

Græculus esuriens (*L*) Starving little Greek. Juvenal — *Satires, III, 78.*

grande passion (*F*) Great passion, violent love.

grande toilette (*F*) Full dress.

grand seigneur (*F*) Great nobleman, lord.

grand tour (*F*) Great tour, conventional tour of Europe.

gratificacion (*Sp.*) Gratuity.

gratior ac pulchro veniens in corpore virtus (*L*) Valor displayed by a handsome body is more pleasing. Vergil — *Æneid, V, 344.*

gratis dictum (*L*) Mere statement.

gravis ira regum est semper (*L*) The wrath of kings is always heavy. Seneca — *Medea, III, 494.*

grazie (*It.*) Thank-you.

grenat (*F*) Garnet.

griffonage (*F*) Illegible handwriting, scribbling.

grisette (*F*) Shop-girl, girl of easy virtue.

groseille (*F*) Currant.

grosse Seelen dulden still (*G*) Great souls suffer in silence.

grossièreté (*F*) Grossness, rudeness, vulgarity.

guardacoste (*It.*) Coast-guard.

guéris-toi toi-même (*F*) Heal thyself.

guerre à mort (*F*) War to the death.

guerre à outrance (*F*) War to the last extremity.

guerre de plume (*F*) War of the pen.

guet-apens (*F*) Ambush.

guindé (*F*) Affected, stilted.

guna (*Sansk.*) Quality, [gram.] lengthen.ing the simple vowels by prefixing an *a* element.

guru (*Hind.*) Teacher, priest. Also *gooroo.*

gusto picaresco (*Sp.*) Rogue's taste.

gutta serena (*It.*) (Drop serene), amauroses, eye-disease.

gymkhana (*Ang.-Ind.*) Racquet house. Urdu *gendkhana — ball house.*

Gymnasium (*G*) Grammar school.

H

habeas corpus (*L*) That you have the body, [law] writ to produce a prisoner at court.

habet! (*L*) He has it; he is wounded! Compare *hoc habet.*

habitué (*F*) Frequenter, regular customer.

hacienda (*Sp.*) Estate, property, (Spanish America) farming or manufacturing establishment in the country.

hackery (*Ang.-Ind.*) Two-wheeled cart. Hindustani *chhakra.*

hac urget lupus hac canis (*L*) A wolf menaces you on this side, a dog on that. Horace — *Satires, II, 2, 64.*

hadj, see *hajj.*

hærit lateri lethalis arundo (*L*) The death-bearing arrow sticks in his side. Vergil — *Æneid, IV, 73.*

hæ tibi erunt artes (*L*) These arts shall be thine. Vergil — *Æneid, VI, 852.*

haji (*Arab.*) Mohammedan who has made his *hajj* or pilgrimage to Mecca. Also *hadji.*

hajj (*Arab.*) Pilgrimage, esp. pilgrimage to Mecca. Also *hadj.*

hakim (*Arab.*) Sage, judge, ruler.

haruspex (*L*) Soothsayer.

haud ignara mali miseris succurrere disco (*L*) Not inexperienced in misfortune, I have learned to aid the wretched. Vergil — *Æneid, I, 630.*

haud passibus æquis (*L*) With unequal steps. Vergil — *Æneid, II, 724.*

haute comédie (*F*) Comedy of life and manners.

hauteur (*F*) (Hight), haughtiness.

haut goût (*F*) High flavor.

haut monde (*F*) High life, upper circles.

haut ton (*F*) High tone, in the manner of high society.

havildar (*Ang.-Ind.*) Sepoy sergeant. Hindustani *hawaldar.*

heaume (*F*) Large helmet chiefly of the thirteenth century.

heautontimorumenos (ἑαυτὸν τιμωρού-μενος, *Gr.*) Self-tormenter. Menander and Terence.

Heimweh (*G*) Homesickness.

helluo librorum (*L*) Glutton of books, bookworm.

herba mala presto cresce (*It.*) Ill weeds grow apace.

herbarium (*L*) Museum of plants.

Herr (*G*) Mr., sir.

hesterni quirites (*L*) Citizens made yesterday. Persius — *Satires, III, 106.*

hetman (*Pol. and Little Rus.*) (Poland) commander of an army, (Russia) captain of the Cossacks.

hiatus maxime (valde) deflendus (*L*) An omission to be seriously deplored.

hic et ubique (*L*) Here and everywhere.

hic jacet (*L*) Here he lies.

hidalgo (*Sp.*) Noble, excellent, nobleman of the lower class.

hiems (*L*) Winter.

hierus (ἱερεύς, *Gr.*) Priest.

hinc illæ lacrimæ (*L*) Hence those tears. Terence — *Andria, I, 1, 126.*

ὁ βίος μὲν βραχὺς ἡ δὲ τέχνη μακρά (*Gr.*) Life is short, art is long.

hoc erat in more majorum (*L*) This was in the manner of our ancestors. Proverb.

hoc erat in votis (*L*) This used to be in my prayers. Horace — *Satires, II, 6, 1.*

hoc genus omne (*L*) All this class. Horace — *Satires, I, 2, 2.*

hoch! (*G*) Hurrah!

hoc habet! (*L*) He has it; he is wounded!

hoc opus hic labor (*L*) This is labor, this is toil. Vergil — *Æneid, VI, 129.*

hoc opus, hoc studium (*L*) This work, this pursuit. Horace — *Epistles, I, 3, 28.*

hodie mihi, cras tibi (*L*) Today for me, tomorrow for thee. Proverb.

hoi polloi (οἱ πολλοί, *Gr.*) The many, the masses.

homard (*F*) Lobster.

hombre bueno no le busquen abolengo (*Sp.*) One does not inquire too closely into a good man's ancestry.

hominem pagina nostra sapit (*L*) Our page reveals the man. Martial — *Epigrams, X, 4, 10.*

homme de cœur (*F*) Man of heart, man of feeling.

homme de cour (*F*) Man of the court, courtier.

homme d'esprit (*F*) Man of wit.

homo (*L*) Man, human being.

homo homini aut deus aut lupus (*L*) Man is to man either a god or a wolf. Erasmus.

homo homini dæmon (*L*) Man is a divinity to man.

homo homini lupus (*L*) Man is a wolf to man. Plautus — *Asinaria, II, 4, 88.*

homo multarum litterarum (*L*) A man of many letters, a learned man.

Homo sapiens (*L*) (Wise man), man, the human species.

homo trium litterarum (*L*) A man of three letters, i.e. F U R (thief). Plautus— *Aulularia, II, 4, 46.*

homo vitæ commodatus non donatus est (*L*) A man is lent not given to life. Publius Syrus — *Maxims.*

honesta mors turpi vita potior (*L*) An honorable death is more significant than a shameful life. Tacitus — *Agricola, XXXIII.*

honi soit qui mal y pense (*F*) Shame be to him who thinks evil of it. Motto of the Order of the Garter.

honores mutant mores (*L*) Honors change manners. Margaret More—*Diary, October, 1524.*

honor virtutis præmium (*L*) Honor is the reward of valor. Cicero — *Brutus, 82.*

honos habet onus (*L*) Honor has its burden.

hôpital (*F*) Free hospital, refuge.

horresco referens (*L*) I shudder to recall (it). Vergil — *Æneid, II, 204.*

horribile dictu (*L*) Horrible to relate.

horrida bella (*L*) Savage wars.

hors concours (*F*) Out of the running, out of competition.

hors de combat (*F*) Out of the battle, unable to fight.

hors-d'œuvre (*F*) Appetizer.

803

hortus siccus (*L*) Dry garden, herbarium.

hospodar (*Roum.*) Ottoman governor.

ὅταν δὲ δαίμων ἀνδρὶ προσύνῃ κακὰ τὸν νοῦν ἔβλαψε πρῶτον (*Gr.*) When a divinity would inflict evils on a man, he first strikes him mad. Euripides.

Hôtel des Invalides (*F*) Hospital for invalid soldiers in Paris.

hôtel de ville (*F*) Town hall.

hotel-Dieu (*F*) Chief hospital in a French city.

ὁ τοῦ δεσπότου ὀφθαλμός (*Gr.*) The master's eye. Aristotle.

houppelande (*F*) Ulster, great-coat.

ὕδωρ (*Gr.*) Water.

huissier (*F*) Royal door-keeper, usher.

huître (*F*) Oyster, stupid person

hukm (*Hind.*) Order, command.

humani nihil a me alienum puto (*L*) I regard nothing human as alien to me. Terence — *Heauton Timorumenos, I, 1, 25.*

humano capiti cervicem jungere equinam (*L*) To fit a horse's neck with a human head.

hurler avec les loups (*F*) To howl with the wolves, to conform.

huzur (*Arab.*) (Presence), term of respectful address.

hysterica passio (*L*) Hysterical passion, hysteria.

hysteron proteron (ὕστερον πρότερον, *Gr.*) The last first, figure of speech involving inversion.

I

ibidem (*L*) In the same place, ibid.

ich dien (*G*) I serve. Motto of the Prince of Wales.

ich habe genossen das irdische Glück ich habe gelebt und geliebt (*G*) I have enjoyed earthly bliss; I have lived and loved. Schiller — *Piccolomini, III, 7, 9.*

ici on parle français (*F*) Here French is spoken.

idée fixe (*F*) Fixed idea, obsession.

idem (*L*) The same.

id est (*L*) That is, i.e., viz.

ignis fatuus (*L*) Foolish fire, will-o-the-wisp, illusion.

ignobile vulgus (*L*) Ignoble crowd, vulgar herd.

ignorance crasse (*F*) Crass ignorance.

ignorantia legis neminem excusat (*L*) [Law] Ignorance of the law excuses no one.

ignoratio elenchi (*L*) Ignoring the pearl, leaving out the point.

ignoscito sæpe alteri nunquam tibi (*L*) Pardon the other person often, yourself never. Decimus Ausonius Magnus.

ignotum per ignotius (*L*) The unknown by the more unknown, (to explain) an obscurity by something still more obscure.

il a la mer à boire (*F*) He has the sea to drink up; he has an impossible task.

il faut souffrir pour être belle (*F*) To be beautiful it is necessary to suffer.

il frappe toujours sur la même enclume (*F*) He always strikes on the same anvil; he is always harping on the same string.

Ilias malorum (*L*) An Iliad of woes.

illam perditissimam atque infimam fæcem populi (*L*) That lowest and most degraded refuse of society.

il n'a ni bouche ni éperon (*F*) He has neither mouth nor spur; he feels no curb.

il n'a pas inventé la poudre (*F*) He did not invent gunpowder; he'll never set the Thames afire.

il ne faut pas s'endormir sur le roti (*F*) One must not fall asleep·over the roast; one should keep his wits about him.

il n'y a pas de quoi (*F*) Nothing at all; don't mention it.

il n'y a que le premier pas qui coûte (*F*) It is only the first step which costs; the beginning is hardest.

il penseroso (*O.It.*) The melancholy man.

il rit bien qui rit le dernier (*F*) He laughs well who laughs last.

il s'en faut bien (*F*) It is greatly lacking.

il se noyerait dans une goutte d'eau (*F*) He would drown in a drop of water.

ils ne passeront pas (*F*) They shall not pass.

ils n'ont rien appris et rien oublié (*F*) They have learned nothing and forgotten nothing.

il tondrait un œuf (*F*) He would shave an egg; he is a skin-flint.

il volto sciolto i pensieri stretti (*It.*) The face open the thoughts sly.

il y a fagots et fagots (*F*) There are fagots and fagots; things which look similar may be quite different.

il y a quelque anguille sous le rocher (*F*) There is some eel under the rock; there is some mischief afoot.

imaginem in pariete carbone delineavit (*L*) He sketched a portrait on the wall with charcoal. Pliny — *XXV, 10, 36.*

imago animi vultus est, indices oculi (*L*) The countenance is the reflection of the soul; the eyes, the informers. Cicero— *De Oratore, III, 59.*

imam (*Arab.*) Mohammedan priest, sovereign prince. Also *imaum.*

i matti fanno le feste e i savi le godono (*It.*) Madmen give the feasts and the wise men enjoy them.

immedicabile vulnus (*L*) Incurable wound. Ovid — *Metamorphoses, I, 190.*

immensum gloria calcar habet (L) Glory has an enormous stimulus. Ovid— *Letters from Pontus, IV, 36.*

impasse (F) Blind alley, deadlock.

impayable (F) Invaluable, inestimable.

imperium in imperio (L) An empire in an empire.

imprimis (L) Chiefly, especially.

imprimit (L) He printed (this).

improvisé (F) Improvised.

improvvisatore (*It.*) Extemporaneous versifier. Also *improvisatore.*

improvvisatrice (*It.*) Woman versifier. Also *improvisatrice.*

in æternum (L) For eternity, forever.

in articulo (L) At the point.

in articulo mortis (L) At the point of death.

inca (*Peruv.*) Lord, king (of Peru).

in camera (L) In a chamber, in private.

in casa (*It.*) At home.

incidit in Scyllam qui vult vitare Charybdem (L) He falls upon Scylla who wishes to avoid Charybdis.

incipit (L) It begins (here).

Index Expurgatorius (L) List expurgatory, catalogue of books which must be expurgated before they may be read by Catholics.

Index Librorum Prohibitorum (L) List of forbidden books, catalogue of books forbidden to Catholic readers.

in equilibrio (L) In equilibrium.

in esse (L) In actuality.

in extenso (L) At full length.

in extremis (L) In the extremes, near death.

infandum renovare dolorem (L) To renew an unspeakable sorrow. Vergil— *Æneid, II, 3.*

in flagrante delicto (L) In the very act. — *Code of Justinian.*

in forma pauperis (L) In the guise of a pauper.

in foro conscientiæ (L) In the forum of conscience, with one's conscience as judge.

infra dignitatem (L) Beneath one's dignity.

ingénu (F) Innocent, naïve.

ingénue (F) [Theater] Rôle of an innocent girl.

in hoc signo spes mea (L) In this sign is my hope.

in hoc signo vinces (L) In this sign you will conquer.

inhumanum verbum est ultio (L) A cruel word is revenge. Seneca— *De Ira, II, 32.*

in limine (L) On the threshold, in the beginning.

in limine belli (L) At the outbreak of the war. Livy.

in loco (L) In the place, in the right place.

in loco parentis (L) [Law] In the place of a parent.

in medias res (L) Into the midst of things. Horace — *Ars Poetica, 148.*

in mediis rebus (L) In the midst of things.

in medio tutissimus (L) In the middle safest, the middle course is the most safe. Ovid — *Metamorphoses, II, 137.*

in memoriam (L) In memory.

in nomine (L) In the name of.

in nubibus (L) In the clouds.

in omnia paratus (L) Prepared for everything.

in ovo (L) In the egg, unhatched.

in petto (*It.*) In the heart, secretly.

in posse (L) Within possibility, what may be.

in præsenti (L) At present.

in propria persona (L) In one's own person, personally.

in puris naturalibus (L) In an absolutely natural state.

in re (L) In the matter, concerning.

in rerum natura (L) In the nature of things.

in sæcula sæculorum (L) For ages of ages, forever. Vulgate — *Galatians, I, 5.*

insculpsit (L) He engraved (it).

in se ipso totus teres atque rotundus (L) Complete in himself, polished and well-rounded. Horace—*Satires, II, 7, 86.*

in situ (L) In place.

insomnium (L) Dream.

insouciance (F) Heedlessness, listlessness.

instar omnium (L) Like all, the type of all.

in statu pupillari (L) In the status of a ward or pupil.

in statu quo (L) In the same state as.

in statu quo ante bellum (L) In the same state as before the war.

insulaire (F) Islander.

intaglio rilevato (*It.*) [Sculp.] Hollow relief.

in tauros Libyci ruunt leones; non sunt papilionibus molesti (L) Libyan lions attack bulls, they do not harm butterflies. Martial — *Epigrams, XII, 62, 5.*

integer vitæ scelerisque purus (L) Blameless in life and pure of crime. Horace — *Odes, I, 22, 1.*

inter alia (L) Among other things.

inter alios (L) Among other people.

inter canem et lupum (L) Between the dog and the wolf, twilight.

interdum lachrymæ pondera vocis habent (L) Sometime tears have the significance of the voice. Ovid — *Epistles from Pontus, III, 1, 158.*

inter gladium et jugulum (L) Between the sword and the throat.

inter nos (*L*) Among ourselves.

inter pocula (*L*) Among the cups, while drinking.

in terrorem (*L*) For a terror, warning.

inter se (*L*) Among themselves.

in totidem verbis (*L*) In so many words.

in toto (*L*) In the whole, entirely.

intra muros (*L*) Within the walls.

intransigeance (*F*) Uncompromisingness, ultraradicalism.

intransigeant (*F*) Uncompromising, ultra-radical.

in transitu (*L*) In transit, on the way.

in utrumque paratus (*L*) Prepared for either course. Vergil — *Æneid, II, 61*

in vacuo (*L*) In a vacuum.

in vino veritas (*L*) In wine truth; wine brings out the truth. Proverb.

in virtute summum bonum ponunt (*L*) They consider virtue the ideal. Cicero.

invita Minerva (*L*) With Minerva unwilling, against the will of Minerva. Horace — *Ars Poetica, 385.*

io triumphe! (*L*) Hail the victor!

ipse dixit (*L*) He himself said so.

ipsissima verba (*L*) The very words.

ipsissimis verbis (*L*) In the precise words.

ipso facto (*L*) By the very deed, by the very fact.

ipso jure (*L*) By the law itself.

ira furor brevis est (*L*) Wrath is a transient madness. Horace — *Epistles, I, 2, 62.*

J

Jacquerie (*F*) The peasant insurrection of 1358, any revolt.

jacta est alea (*L*) The die is cast. Suetonius — *Cæsar, 32.*

jadu (*Hind. and Pers.*) Magic, fortune telling. Also *jadoo.*

jahannam (*Hind.*) Hell. Also *jahannan.*

Jahre lehren mehr als Bücher (*G*) Years teach more than books.

jaldi (*Hind.*) Quickness, rashness.

jaldi karo (*Hind.*) Make haste.

jalousie (*F*) Jealousy, fear.

jalousie de métier (*F*) Anxious love.

jamais de ma vie (*F*) Never in my life, never in the world.

jampan (*E. Ind.*) Sedan-chair borne by four men.

jam satis (*L*) Enough already.

januis clausis (*L*) With closed doors.

jao (*Hind.*) Go, go away.

jardin (*F*) Garden.

jardinière (*F*) Flower-stand, two or four wheeled cart.

jejunus raro stomachus vulgaria temnit (*L*) The empty stomach rarely scorns simple food. Horace — *Satires, II, 2, 38.*

jemadar (*Angl.-Ind.*) Native officer. Hindustani and Persian *jam'dar.*

je ne sais quoi (*F*) I don't know what, something or other.

jet d'eau (*F*) Spurt of water, fountain.

jeter de la poudre aux yeux (*F*) To throw dust into one's eyes, to dazzle, to deceive.

jeter la manche après la cognée (*F*) To throw the helve after the hatchet, to throw good money after bad.

jeu de mots (*F*) Play on words, pun, jest.

jeu d'esprit (*F*) Play of wit, witticism.

jeu de théâtre (*F*) Stage-business, stage-trick.

jeune premier (*F*) Player of lover's parts, actor of youthful parts.

jeunesse dorée (*F*) Gilded youth, fashionable young people.

jeune veuve (*F*) Young widow.

jhil (*Ind.*) Pond filled with water-weeds.

jhilmil (*Hind.*) Shutter, Venetian blind.

jhuth (*Hind.*) False.

joie de vivre (*F*) Joy of living.

jornada (*Sp.*) Day's journey.

jouer cartes sur table (*F*) To play an open hand, not to hide one's actions.

jouer les ingénues (*F*) To play juvenile parts.

jour de ma vie (*F*) Day of my life.

jour maigre (*F*) Fast-day, fish-day.

journal intime (*F*) Private diary, private papers.

jubba (*Hind.*) A long vest resembling a shirt. Also *jubbah.*

jubilate Deo (*L*) Rejoice in God. Vulgate — *Psalms, XCVII, 4.*

Judenhetze (*G*) Persecution of the Jews.

julienne (*F*) A vegetable soup.

juramentado (*Sp.*) Bound by an oath.

jurare in verba magistri (*L*) To swear to the words of a master. Horace — *Epistles, I, 1, 14.*

jure divino (*L*) By divine law.

jure humano (*L*) By human law.

jus civile (*L*) Civil law. Cicero — *De Officiis, III, 17.*

jus divinum (*L*) Divine law.

jus et norma loquendi (*L*) The rule and pattern of speech. Horace — *Ars Poetica, 72.*

jus gentium (*L*) Law of nations, international law. Cicero — *De Officiis, III, 17.*

jus gladii (*L*) Law of the sword.

jus nocendi (*L*) The right to inflict injury.

juste-milieu (*F*) Fair mean, golden mean.

justitiæ soror incorrupta fides (*L*) Faith uncorrupted, the sister of justice. Horace — *Odes, I, 24, 6.*

justitia suum cuique distribuit (*L*) Justice renders to every one what is due to him. Cicero — *De Legibus, I, 15.*

justitia virtutum regina (*L*) Justice is queen of the virtues. Proverb.

j'y suis et j'y reste (*F*) Here I am and here I stay.

K

kachcha (*Hind.*) Unripe, crude, silly. Also *kucha*.

kadi (*Arab.*) Village judge.

Kaffeeklatsch (*G*) Coffee-party, reunion.

kaffiyeh (*Syrian*) Scarf worn about the head.

kahin (*Hind.*) Priest, prophet, astrologer.

kal (*Hind.*) Time, death.

kala admi (*Hind.*) Black man.

kala jagah (*Hind.*) Dark place, shady spot.

kala pani (*Hind.*) Dark water.

kama rupa (*Sansk.*) [Theos.] Love-shape, astral likeness of a person living after his death.

kantikoy (*Algonkin*) Indian tribal dance.

Kapelle (*G*) Chapel, band or orchestra.

Kapellmeister (*G*) Conductor of an orchestra.

karma (*Sansk.*) Effects of one's acts upon his after-life.

kasis (*Hind.*) Presbyter, priest. Also *kisis*.

katar (*Hind.*) Short dagger. Also *kuttar*.

kat' exochen (κατ' ἐξοχήν, *Gr.*) According to prominence.

kavass (*Turk.*) Armed attendant, armed policeman.

keddah (*Hind.*) (Bengal) Enclosure for trapping elephants.

képi (*F*) Military cap.

khan (*Arab.*) Inn, caravanserai.

khan (*Turk.*) Prince, chief.

khansamah (*Ang.-Ind.*) Consumer, house steward. Hindustani *khansaman*.

khedive (*Turk.*) Governor of Egypt, governor.

khitmutgar (*Ang.-Ind.*) Table-servant, butler. Hindustani *khidmatgar*.

khoja (*Turk.*) Teacher in a Mohammedan school.

khudd (*Hind.*) Hillside, deep valley.

kiack (*Burmese*). Buddhist temple.

kibitka (*Rus.*) Tilt wagon, covered wagon.

kila (*Hind.*) Fort, palace.

Kinder und Narren sagen die Wahrheit (*G*) Children and fools speak the truth.

Klangfarbe (*G*) Tone color.

Klatsch (*G*) Gossip, chatter.

Konzertmeister (*G*) Concert-master, subleader of an orchestra.

kooshti (*Hind.*) Wrestling. Also *kushti*.

kos (*Hind.*) Measure of distance, about two miles.

kotow (*k'o-t'ou*, *Chin.*) (Knock-head), bow of obeisance.

kraal (*S. African Dut.*) Enclosed village.

kraken (*Norw.*) Monster of the sea.

Kriegsspiel (*G*) War-game, military manœuvres.

kris (*Malay*) Curved knife.

kudos (κῦδος, *Gr.*) Glory, fame, pride.

Kultur (*G*) Culture, civilization.

κύριε ἐλέησον(*Gr.*) Lord, have mercy.

kutcha (*Ang.-Ind.*) Crude, raw. Compare *pukka*. Hindustani *kachcha*.

kuttar. see *katar*.

L

laager (*S. African Dut.*) Camp equipped with a defensive barrier.

labitur et labetur (*L*) It flows and will flow. Compare *labitur et labetur in omne volubilis ævum*.

labitur et labetur in omne volubilis ævum (*L*) Gliding on it flows and will flow forever. Horace — *Epistles, I, 2, 43.*

labora et ora (*L*) Work and pray.

laborare est orare (*L*) To work is to pray. Medieval proverb.

labor omnia vincit (*L*) Hard work conquers all things. Vergil — *Georgics, I, 145.*

l'abstenir pour jouir, c'est l'épicurisme de la raison (*F*) To abstain in order to enjoy is the epicureanism of reason. Rousseau.

lac (*Ang.-Ind.*) One hundred thousand. Hindustani *lakh*.

lachrimis oculos suffusa nitentes (*L*) Her shining eyes suffused with tears. Vergil — *Æneid, I, 228.*

la critique est aisée et l'art est difficile (*F*) Criticism is easy and art is difficult. Destouches.

lagniappe (*Louisiana F.*) Trifling present between tradesmen, gratuity. Also *lagnappe*.

La Grande Vierge (*F*) The Great Virgin.

laisser aller (*F*) To neglect, negligence.

laisser faire (*F*) To leave things as they are.

l'allegro (*It.*) The cheerful man.

lama (*Tibetan*) Celibate priest of Lamaism.

la maladie sans maladie (*F*) Sickness without being sick, hypochondria.

lamba chauki (*Hind.*) Long chair, easy chair.

lamba kursi (*Hind.*) Chair, throne.

la mentira tiene las piernas cortas (*Sp.*) A lie has short legs.

la morgue littéraire (*F*) Literary arrogance.

lance-flamme (*F*) Flame-thrower.

langage de carrefour (*F*) Trivial talk.

la pierre souvent remuée n'amasse pas volontiers mousse (*F*) A rolling stone gathers no moss.

lapis lazuli (*L*) Stone of azure, blue semiprecious stone.

la plus grande habileté consiste souvent à n'en pas montrer (*F*) The greatest ability often consists in not showing it.

lapsus calami (*L*) Slip of the pen.

lapsus linguæ (*L*) Slip of the tongue.

lapsus memoriæ (*L*) Slip of the memory.

lar (*L*) Household god.

lares et penates (*L*) Tutelary family gods.

lar familiaris (*L*) Family household god.

larghetto (*It.*) [Mus.] Rather broad and full, rather slow.

largo (*It.*) [Mus.] Slow and full.

larigo (*Sp. Amer.*) Ring at each end of a saddle cinch.

l'art de vaincre est celui de mépriser la mort (*F*) The art of conquering consists in scorn of death.

lasciate ogni speranza voi ch'entrate (*It.*) All hope abandon, ye who enter here. Dante — *Inferno, III, 1, 9.*

la speranza è il pan de' miseri (*It.*) Hope is the food of the wretched.

latet anguis in herba (*L*) The snake hides in the grass; there lurks a hidden danger. Vergil — *Eclogues, III, 93.*

latet scintillula forsan (*L*) Perhaps a little spark still lingers. Motto of the Royal Humane Society of England.

lathi (*Hind.*) Stick, bludgeon.

latrocinium (*L*) Highway robbery, looting.

laudari a laudato viro (*L*) To be praised by one praised. Cicero.

laudator (*L*) Lauder, praiser.

laudator temporis acti (*L*) Praiser of times past.

laus Deo (*L*) Praise to God.

l'avenir (*F*) The future.

La Vergine Gloriosa (*It.*) The Glorious Virgin.

la verità è figlia del tempo (*It.*) Truth is daughter of Time; truth will out.

la vérité est le secret de l'éloquence (*F*) Truth is the secret of eloquence. Amiel.

laver la tête (*F*) (To wash the head), to reprimand.

lazzarone (*It.*) Beggar of Naples.

le beau idéal (*F*) The ideal perfection, the ideal beauty.

le beau monde (*F*) The fashionable world.

lebe wohl (*G*) (Live well), farewell, good-bye.

le concours de deux époques (*F*) The meeting of two eras.

le coût en ôte le goût (*F*) Its cost takes away its taste.

le diable (*F*) The Devil.

le diable à quatre (*F*) The devil in four, confusion.

le droit du plus fort (*F*) The right of the most strong.

legadero (*Mex. Sp.*) Stirrup strap.

le garde meurt et ne se rend pas (*F*) The guard dies but does not surrender.

legato (*It.*) [Mus.] Smoothly.

légèreté (*F*) Lightness, levity.

légionnaire (*F*) Member of the Legion of Honor.

le grand Monarque (*F*) The Great Monarch, Louis XIV.

Leitmotiv (*G*) [Mus.] Recurring theme, leitmotiv.

le jeu est le fils d'avarice et le père du désespoir (*F*) Gaming is the son of avarice and the father of despair.

le jeu ne vaut pas la chandelle (*F*) The game is not worth the candle.

lemma (λῆμμα, *Gr.*) [Log.] Subsidiary proposition.

le monde (*F*) The world, society.

le palais de verité (*F*) The palace of truth.

le pas (*F*) Precedence, the superiority.

le pot au lait (*F*) (The milk-pot), a milkmaid's dreams.

le premier pas (*F*) The first step.

le premier pas qui coûte (*F*) The first step which costs.

le roi est mort, vive le roi (*F*) The king is dead, long live the king!

le roi le veut (*F*) The king wills it.

le roi s'avisera (*F*) The king will consider.

les affaires font les hommes (*F*) Business makes men.

les alentours de la vérité (*F*) The environs of truth.

les badauds de Paris (*F*) Idlers of Paris, gaping idlers.

les bons comptes font les bons amis (*F*) Short reckonings make long friends.

les bras croisés (*F*) The arms crossed.

les choses commencent à prendre mauvaise tournure (*F*) Matters are beginning to look bad.

les dessous des cartes (*F*) The undersides of the cards, inside facts.

lèse-majesté (*F*) Lese majesty, high treason.

les fous font les festins et les sages les mangent (*F*) Fools give banquets and wise men eat them.

le silence du peuple est la leçon des rois (*F*) The silence of the people is the lesson of their kings.

le silence est la vertu de ceux qui ne sont pas sages (*F*) Silence is the virtue of those who are not wise.

le silence est le parti le plus sûr de celui qui se defie de soi-même (*F*) Silence is the safest way for one who lacks self-confidence.

le silence est l'esprit des sots et une des vertus du sage (*F*) Silence is the wit of fools and one of the virtues of the sage. Bonnard.

les larmes aux yeux (*F*) Tears in the eyes.

l'espérance est le songe d'un homme éveillé (*F*) Hope is the waking man's dream.

les petits ruisseaux font les grandes rivières (*F*) Little streams make great rivers; great oaks from little acorns grow.

le style c'est de l'homme (*F*) A man's style is a part of him. Buffon.

le style est l'homme même (*F*) His style is the man himself. Buffon.

l'état, c'est moi (*F*) The state is myself. Voltaire of Louis XIV.

l'Etoile du Nord (*F*) North Star.

le tout ensemble (*F*) The whole considered in its entirety.

le travail du corps délivre des peines de l'esprit (*F*) Physical labor frees from mental pains.

lettre de créance (*F*) Letter announcing a diplomat's arrival.

lettres de cachet (*F*) Royal orders of imprisonment.

leurs chiens ne chassent pas ensemble (*F*) Their hounds do not hunt together; they are not congenial.

levée (*F*) (Rising), reception.

levée en masse (*F*) General rising.

leve fit quod bene fertur onus (*L*) Lightly lies the load that is well carried. Ovid — *Amores, I, 2, 10.*

lever de rideau (*F*) Curtain-raiser, introductory piece.

le véritable Amphitryon est l'Amphitryon où l'on dine (*F*) The true Amphitryon is the Amphitryon with whom one dines. Molière — *Amphitryon, III, 5.*

lex loci (*L*) Law of the place, local law.

lex mercatoria (*L*) Mercantile law.

lex non scripta (*L*) Unwritten law.

lex scripta (*L*) Written law.

lex talionis (*L*) The law of retaliation.

l'homme propose, et Dieu dispose (*F*) Man proposes and God disposes.

liaison (*F*) Union, love-affair.

liberavi animam meam (*L*) I have freed my soul; I have spoken my mind.

liberum arbitrium (*L*) Free-will.

librairie (*F*) Book store.

licentia vatum (*L*) Poetic license.

Lied (*G*) Song, lyric.

Liederkranz (*G*) (Garland of songs), men's singing club.

Liedertafel (*G*) (Song-table), singing society.

likin (*Chin.*) Provincial tax.

limæ labor (*L*) Labor of the file. Horace — *Ars Poetica, 291.*

limæ probationem (*L*) The test of the file. Pliny.

l'imagination galope, le jugement ne va que le pas (*F*) The imagination gallops, judgment only walks.

l'inconnu (*F*) The unknown.

linga sharira (*Sansk.*) [Theos.] Astral counterpart of the physical body.

lingerie (*F*) Linen articles, underclothing.

lis litem generat (*L*) One quarrel begets another. Proverb.

litem lite resolvit (*L*) It settles a quarrel with a quarrel. Horace — *Satires, II, 3, 103.*

literæ humaniores (*L*) Very cultivated letters, polite literature.

literæ sciptæ (*L*) Written letters, documents.

literati (*L*) Literati, men of letters.

literatim (*L*) Letter by letter.

littera scripta manet (*L*) The written letter remains.

littérateur (*F*) Literary man, professional writer.

livraison (*F*) Serial part of a book or magazine.

livre jaune (*F*) Yellow book, governmental publication.

livret (*F*) Booklet, explanatory catalogue.

llano (*Sp.*) Plain, treeless steppe.

locale (*F*) Region, place.

l'occhio del padrone ingrassa il cavallo (*It.*) The eye of the master fattens the horse.

loco citato (*L*) In the place cited.

locos y niños dicen la verdad (*Sp.*) Fools and children speak the truth.

locum tenens (*L*) One holding a place, substitute.

locus classicus (*L*) Classical passage.

locus pœnitentiæ (*L*) Place for repentance.

locus sigilli (*L*) The place for the seal.

locus standi (*L*) Standing-place, right to a place in court.

l'œil du maître (*F*) The master's eye.

l'œil du maître engraisse le cheval (*F*) The master's eye maketh fat the horse.

loger le diable dans la bourse (*F*) To keep the devil in one's purse, not to have a cent.

loma (*Sp.*) Hillock.

longo intervallo (*L*) With a long interval.

longs cheveux, courte cervelle (*F*) Long hair, short wits.

loquitur (*L*) He speaks.

lorcha (*Port.*) Chinese coasting vessel.

l'ordre du jour (*F*) [Mil.] The order of the day.

lorette (*F*) Woman of fine manners and easy virtue.

lorgnon (*F*) Eyeglass, monocle.

lorica (*L*) Leather cuirass.

lota (*Hind.*) Round pot used in bathing. Also *lotah.*

loup-garou (*F*) Were-wolf.

loyauté m'oblige (*F*) Loyalty compels me.

loyauté n'a honte (*F*) Loyalty has no shame.

lucidus ordo (*L*) Clear arrangement. Horace — *Ars Poetica, 41.*

lucri causa (*L*) For the sake of lucre.

lūcus a non lucendo (*L*) A grove from not being light, an absurd conclusion.

ludere cum sacris (*L*) To trifle with sacred things.

Lügen haben kurze Beine (*G*) Lies have short legs.

lumen naturale (*L*) Natural insight, natural intelligence.

lungi (*Burmese*) Narrow strip of cloth, loin cloth.

lupus in fabula (*L*) The wolf in the proverb, of a person appearing at his being mentioned. Terence — *Adelphi, IV, 1, 21.*

l'usage du monde (*F*) The way of the world.

lusus naturæ (*L*) Sport of nature, freak of nature.

lycée (*F*) Secondary school.

M

mabap (*Hind.*) Mother-father, parents.

macte virtute (*L*) Go forward in virtue. Livy — *Annals, VII, 36.*

macula (*L*) Spot, blemish.

madame (*F*) Madam.

mademoiselle (*F*) Miss, unmarried woman.

maestoso (*It.*) [Mus.] Majestically, solemnly.

maestro (*It.*) [Mus.] Master, eminent musician.

ma foi! (*F*) My faith, my word!

magar (*Hind.*) Crocodile. Also *mugger.*

magasin (*F*) Store, warehouse.

maggiore frétta, minore átto (*It.*) The greater the haste, the less accomplished.

magna civitas, magna solitudo (*L*) A great city, great loneliness.

magna est veritas et prævalet (*L*) Great is truth and it prevails. Vulgate — *1 Esdras, IV, 41.*

magna est vis consuetudinis (*L*) Mighty is the force of habit. Cicero — *Tusculan Disputations, II, 15.*

magna servitus est magna fortuna (*L*) A great fortune is a great slavery. Seneca — *De Consolatione, 2, 6.*

magnifique et pas cher (*F*) Magnificent and not expensive.

magni nominis umbra (*L*) Ghost of a great name. Lucan — *Pharsalia, I, 135.*

magno conatu magnas nugas (*L*) Great trifles at great effort. Terence — *Heauton Timorumenos, IV, 1, 8.*

magnos homines virtute metimur non fortuna (*L*) We estimate men as great not by their wealth but by their virtue. Cornelius Nepos — *Dives.*

magnum bonum (*L*) Great good, prosperity.

magnum est vectigal parsimonia (*L*) Thrift is a great revenue. Cicero — *Paradoxes, VI, 3, 49.*

magnum opus (*L*) Great work, one's most important undertaking.

magnus ab integro sæclorum nascitur ordo (*L*) The great cycle of the ages is born anew. Vergil — *Eclogues, IV, 5.*

magnus annus (*L*) The great year, [astrol.] the time when the constellations return to their starting-places.

magnus Apollo (*L*) Great Apollo, mighty oracle.

maharaja (*Sansk.*) Indian prince. Also *maharajah.*

maharani (*Hind.*) Queen in her own right.

mahatma (*Sansk.*) Buddhist of the highest order.

maidan (*Pers.*) Indian market-place, grassy plain.

maintien (*F*) Maintenance, behavior.

maire (*F*) Mayor.

maison (*F*) House, company.

maison de santé (*F*) Health house, hospital receiving paying patients.

maître d'hôtel (*F*) House master, steward.

majusculæ (*L*) Majuscules, capital letters.

malade imaginaire (*F*) A person imagining himself ill.

maladie du pays (*F*) Homesickness, nostalgia.

mala fide (*L*) In bad faith, fraudulently. Compare *bona fide.*

mala fides (*L*) Bad faith. Compare *bona fides.*

malaise (*F*) Physical or mental discomfort.

mala mens malus animus (*L*) Evil mind, evil spirit. Terence — *Andria, I, 1, 137.*

mal à propos (*F*) Inopportune.

mal de mer (*F*) Seasickness.

mal du pays (*F*) Homesickness, nostalgia.

malentendu (*F*) Misunderstanding, misinterpretation.

male vincetis sed vincite (*L*) You will conquer badly, but conquer. Ovid — *Metamorphoses, VIII, 509.*

malevolus animus abditos dentes habet (*L*) A malevolent nature has hidden teeth. Publius Syrus — *Maxims.*

malgré nous (*F*) In spite of us.

malgré soi (*F*) In spite of one's self.

malheur ne vient jamais seule (*F*) Misfortune never comes alone.

malignum spernere vulgus (*L*) To disdain the noxious crowd. Horace — *Odes, II, 16, 40.*

malum in se (*L*) Wrong in itself, inherently wrong.

malum prohibitum (*L*) A thing prohibited as wrong.

mañana (*Sp.*) Tomorrow.

mancia (*It.*) Gratuity.

mandamus (*L*) We command, [law] order of court.

mandola (*It.*) [Mus.] Older and larger mandolin.

manège (*F*) Horse-training, hippodrome.

manet alta mente repostum (*L*) It remains deeply stored in the mind. Vergil — *Æneid, I, 26.*

manet cicatrix (*L*) The scar remains.

mangee, see *manjhi.*

manger son blé en herbe (*F*) To eat one's wheat before it is ripe.

mania a potu (*L*) Madness from drinking, delirium tremens.

manibus pedibusque (*L*) With hands and feet, with might and main.

manie (*F*) Mania, obsession.

manière (*F*) Manner, method.

maniéré (*F*) Affected person.

manipulus (*L*) (Handful), detachment of sixty or a hundred and twenty men.

manito (*Algonkin*) Spirit.

manjhi (*Hind.*) Master of a vessel, sailor. Also *mangee.*

man sagt (*G*) They say.

manu forti (*L*) With a strong hand.

maquereau (*F*) Mackerel.

Märchen (*G*) Fairy-tale, folk tale.

marcher à reculons (*F*) To walk backwards.

Mardi gras (*F*) (Fat Tuesday), Shrove Tuesday, day before Ash Wednesday.

mare clausum (*L*) Closed sea, sea within the jurisdiction of one nation.

mariage de convenance (*F*) Marriage for advantage.

Mars gravior sub pace latet (*L*) A graver war lurks beneath the peace. Claudius Claudianus — *Panegyric on Honorius Augustus, 307.*

masjid (*Arab.*) Mohammedan mosque.

masnad (*Hind. and Arab.*) Draped cushion as a seat of honor. Also *musnud.*

massepain (*F*) Cake of almonds and spice.

masseur (*F*) One who massages.

mastaba (*Arab.*) Ancient tomb.

más vale saber que haber (*Sp.*) It is worth more to know than to have.

más vale ser necio que porfiado (*Sp.*) It is better to be ignorant than stubborn.

maté (*Sp.*) Paraguay tea.

Mater dolorosa (*L*) Sorrowing Mother, the Virgin Mary in sorrow.

mater familias (*L*) Mother of a family.

Materia Medica (*L*) Medical material, drugs.

materiam superabat opus (*L*) The workmanship was superior to the material. Ovid — *Metamorphoses, II, 5.*

matériel (*F*) Material, working-stock.

Mater Redemptoris (*L*) Mother of the Redeemer.

mauvaise honte (*F*) Excessive modesty, timidity.

mauvaise plaisanterie (*F*) Poor joke, unpleasant jest.

mauvais goût (*F*) Bad taste, vulgarity.

mauvais quart d'heure (*F*) Bad quarter hour, unpleasant experience.

mauvais suj{c}t (*F*) Poor subject, worthless fellow.

mauvais ton (*F*) Bad tone, bad taste, vulgarity. Compare *bon ton.*

mazurka (*Pol.*) (Woman of the province of Mazovia), Polish dance in triple time.

mea culpa (*L*) Through my fault.

mecate (*Mex. Sp.*) Rope of fiber or hair.

médaille militaire (*F*) Military decoration.

médécine expectante (*F*) Waiting medicine, cure by doing nothing.

médecin guéris-toi toi-même (*F*) Doctor heal yourself.

médecin tant pis (*F*) Makeshift doctor.

meden agan (μηδὲν ἄγαν, *Gr.*) Nothing to excess.

medio tutissimus ibis (*L*) You will go most safely in the middle course.

medium tenuere beati (*L*) Happy are they who have held to the middle course.

mehr Licht (*G*) More light. Last words of Goethe.

mehtar (*Pers. and Hind.*) (Prince), groom, stable-boy.

Mein Herr (*G*) Sir.

Meistersinger (*G*) Mastersinger, German guild musician of the fourteenth to sixteenth centuries.

me judice (*L*) I being the judge. Juvenal — *Satires, XIII, 1.*

mélange (*F*) Mixture, medley.

mêlée (*F*) Pitched battle.

memento mori (*L*) Remember that you must die, emblem of death.

memorabilia (*L*) Memorable things, things to be remembered.

memoria in æterna (*L*) In perpetual remembrance.

memoria technica (*L*) Technical memory, scientific assistance to the memory.

memoriter (*L*) In memory, by heart.

memsahib (*Ang.-Ind.*) (Madam-master), mistress of a household.

ménage (*F*) Administration of a household.

mendacem memorem esse oportet (*L*) A liar must have a good memory. Quintilian — *IV, 2, 91.*

mens æqua in arduis (*L*) An even mind in adversities. Horace — *Odes, II, 3, 1.*

mens sana in corpore sano (*L*) A sound mind in a sound body. Juvenal — *Satires, X, 356.*

mens sibi conscia recti (*L*) A mind conscious of rectitude. Vergil — *Æneid, I, 604.*

mens sola loco non exulat (*L*) Only the mind cannot be exiled. Ovid — *Epistles from Pontus, IV, 9, 41.*

menteur à triple étage (*F*) Third story liar, consummate liar.

mentis gratissimus error (*L*) A very pleasant mental distraction. Horace — *Epistles, II, 2, 140.*

meo periculo (*L*) At my own peril.

merci (*F*) Thank you.

merlan (*F*) Whiting.

mesa (*Sp.*) Table-land.

mésalliance (*F*) Marriage with an inferior.

métayage (*F*) Coöperative renting system.

métier (*F*) Trade, calling.

métis (*F*) Hybrid, cross.

mettre à la lanterne (*F*) To hang a person on the lamp-post.

mettre aux oubliettes (*F*) To consign to oblivion.

mettre de l'eau dans son vin (*F*) To put water in one's wine, to be abstemious.

mettre quelqu'un au desespoir (*F*) To drive anyone to despair.

meum et tuum (*L*) Mine and yours.

mezzo cammin (*It.*) Mid-path.

mezzo-rilievo (*It.*) [Sculp.] Half-relief.

mezzo termine (*It.*) Middle term, compromise.

mi-carême (*F*) Mid-Lent.

mihi cura futuri (*L*) I shall take care of the future.

mikado (*Jap.*) (Reverend door), emperor.

milieu (*F*) Middle, means, environment, atmosphere.

militat omnis amans (*L*) Every lover is a fighter. Ovid — *Amores, I, 9, 1.*

minauderie (*F*) Affectation of manner, simpering.

minimum decet libere cui multum licet (*L*) He to whom much is permitted should take least advantage of it. Seneca — *Troades, 336.*

Minnesinger (*G*) Love-singer, German lyric poet of the twelfth and thirteenth centuries.

minusculæ (*L*) Lower-case letters.

minutiæ (*L*) Trivialities, particulars.

mir (*Rus.*) Peasant community.

mirabile dictu (*L*) Wonderful to relate. Vergil — *Georgics, II, 30.*

mirabile visu (*L*) Wonderful to behold.

miscebit sacra profanis (*L*) He will mingle sacred things with profane. Horace — *Epistles, I, 16, 54.*

misce stultitiam consiliis brevem (*L*) Mix some small folly with your wisdom. Horace — *Odes, IV, 12, 27.*

mise en scène (*F*) Stage-setting.

miserabile dictu (*L*) Mournful to relate.

misère (*F*) A declaration in solo-whist.

miserere (*L*) Have mercy, a plea for mercy.

misericordiam Domini inter pontem et fontem (*L*) The mercy of God between bridge and stream, salvation at the last minute.

missa cantata (*L*) Sung Mass, High Mass.

mithai (*Hind.*) Sweetmeat, sweetness.

mitraille (*F*) Grape-shot.

mitrailleur (*F*) Machine-gunner.

mitrailleuse (*F*) Machine-gun.

mittimus (*L*) We send, [law] order of commitment to prison.

moderato (*It.*) Moderate, [mus.] in moderate tempo.

modiste (*F*) Milliner.

modus operandi (*L*) Manner of working.

modus vivendi (*L*) Way of merely living, temporary adjustment.

mofussil (*Ang.-Ind.*) Provincial districts, country. Hindustani *mufassil.*

moglie (*It.*) Wife.

mollah (*Turk. and Pers.*) Judge of the Mohammedan sacred law. Compare *mullah.*

mollia tempora (*L*) Favorable times.

mollia tempora fandi (*L*) Agreeable times for speaking.

mollissima fandi tempora (*L*) The most favorable times for speaking. Vergil — *Æneid, IV, 293.*

mon ami (*F*) My friend.

mon cher (*F*) My dear fellow.

monde (*F*) World, society.

monomachia (*L*) Single combat. Greek μονομαχία.

monoplace (*F*) Single-seater.

mon petit chou (*F*) My little darling.

monsieur (*F*) Sir, Mr.

monstrum horrendum informe ingens cui lumen ademptum (*L*) Immense, formless terrible monster, whose eye is out. Vergil — *Æneid, III, 658.*

montagne russe (*F*) Artificial mound.

mont-de-piété (*F*) Pawnshop.

monte di pietà (*It.*) Charity bank.

monte (*Sp.*) (Mountain), game of chance played with cards.

monumentum ære perennius (*L*) A monument more lasting than bronze. Horace — *Odes, III, 30, 1.*

moolvee (*Ang.-Ind*) Mohammedan doctor of law Also *moolvi.*

moonshee (*Ang.-Ind.*) Native teacher. Urdu and Arabic *munshi.*

morceau (*F*) Morsel, piece, [mus.] short piece often a part of another.

more majorum (*L*) After the manner of the ancestors.

morem fecerat usus (*L*) Practice had made a habit. Ovid — *Metamorphoses, II, 345.*

more solito (*L*) In the usual manner.

more suo (*L*) In one's own way.

morgue (*F*) Haughtiness, disdain.

morì in concetto di santo (*It.*) He died with the reputation of a saint.

morion (*F*) Open hat-like helmet of the sixteenth century.

morisco (*Sp.*) Moorish.

morituri te salutamus (*L*) We who are about to die salute thee. Address of Roman gladiators to the emperor.

morra (*It.*) Finger game.

mors ultima linea rerum est (*L*) Death is the last boundary of things. Horace — *Epistles, I, 16, 79.*

mot (*F*) Word, witticism.

mot à mot (*F*) Word for word.

mot d'énigme (*F*) Subject of a puzzle.

mot de passe (*F*) Password, countersign.

mot d'ordre (*F*) Password, countersign.

mot du guet (*F*) Watchword.

motif (*F*) Theme.

mot pour rire (*F*) Clever, appropriate remark

motu proprio (*L*) Of its own motion, of its own accord.

mouchard (*F*) Police spy.

mouillé (*F*) Wet, dampened, softened in sound.

moulin à paroles (*F*) Word mill, talkative person.

mousseux (*F*) Foamy.

mouton (*F*) Sheep, mutton.

moutonné (*F*) Fluffy.

moyen âge (*F*) Middle Ages.

mozzetta (*It.*) Hood, cape worn by the Pope.

muchos pocos hacen un mucho (*Sp.*) Many littles make a much. Cervantes — *Don Quixote.*

mufti (*Arab.*) Magistrate, Mohammedan law-officer.

mugger, see *magar.*

mullah (*Hind.*) Judge of the Mohammedan sacred law. Compare *mollah.*

multa acervatim frequentans(*L*) Crowding many thoughts in one passage. Cicero — *De Oratore, 25, 85.*

multa petentibus desunt multa (*L*) Many things are lacking to those who seek many. Horace — *Odes, III, 16, 42.*

multum in parvo (*L*) Much in little.

murshid (*Arab.*) Mohammedan religious teacher.

murus æneus conscientia sana (*L*) A sound conscience is a wall of brass. Proverb.

musæo contigens cuncta lepore (*L*) Touching all th ngs with a musical charm. Lucretius — *De Rerum Natura, IV, 9.*

musette (*F*) Rustic bag-pipe.

musnud, see *masnad.*

mussuk (*E. Ind.*) Skin for carrying water. Also *mussuck.*

mutatis mutandis (*L*) Necessary changes having been made.

mutato nomine de te fabula narratur (*L*) The name changed the story is told of you. Horace — *Satires, I, 1, 69.*

mutum est pictura poema (*L*) A picture is a silent poem.

mynheer (*mijn heer, Dut.*) Sir.

mystæ (μύσται, *Gr.*) Initiates in the Lesser Eleusinia.

N

nacré (*F*) Pearly.

nager entre deux eaux (*F*) To swim between two waters, to belong to two parties.

naik (*Ang.-Ind.*) Leader, chief. Hindustani *nayak.*

naïve (*F*) Ingenuous, simple.

naïveté (*F*) Ingenuousness, simplicity.

nam tua res agitur paries dum proximus ardet (*L*) For your property is in peril while the next house is burning. Horace — *Epistles, I, 18, 84.*

narikin (*Jap.*) Upstart.

narren bauen Häuser, der Kluge kauft sie (*G*) Fools build houses and the wise man buys them.

natura il fece e poi roppe la stampa (*It.*) Nature made him and then broke the mold. Ariosto — *Orlando Furioso, X, 84.*

natura non facit saltum (*L*) Nature makes no leap.

naumachia (ναυμαχία, *Gr.*) Naval combat.

nautch (*Ang.-Ind.*) Ballet-dance performed by professional dancers. Hindustani *nach.*

nawab (*Hind.*) Nabob, governor.

ne battre que d'une aile (*F*) To flap with only one wing, to be handicapped.

necessità 'l c'induce e non diletto (*It.*) Necessity brings him here and not his pleasure. Dante — *Inferno, XII, 87.*

necessitas non habet legem (*L*) Necessity has no law.

nec mora nec requies (*L*) Neither rest nor respite. Vergil — *Georgics, III, 110.*

nec scire fas est omnia (*L*) It is not permitted to know all things. Horace — *Odes, IV, 4, 22.*

nec tecum possum vivere nec sine te (*L*) I can live neither with you nor without you. Martial — *Epigrams, XII, 47.*

née (*F*) Born (used of a woman to indicate her maiden name).

ne e quovis ligno Mercurius fiat (*L*) Let Mercury be not carved from every stick; fit the subject to your eloquence. Erasmus.

négligé (*F*) Morning costume, informal dress.

ne Jupiter quidem omnibus placet (*L*) Not even Jupiter pleases everyone.

nemine contradicente (*L*) No one contradicting, unanimously.

nemine dissentiente (*L*) No one dissenting.

nemo bis punitur pro eodem delicto (*L*) No one is punished twice for the same offence.

nemo me impune lacessit (*L*) No one attacks me with impunity. Motto of the Scottish order of the Thistle.

nemo repente fuit turpissimus (*L*) No one ever became wicked all of a sudden. Juvenal — *Satires, II, 83*.

nemo solus sapit (*L*) No one is wise by himself. Plautus — *Miles Gloriosus, III, 3, 12*.

ne pas entendre raillerie (*F*) Not to take a joke.

ne pas réveiller le chat qui dort (*F*) Don't awaken the sleeping cat.

ne plus ultra (*L*) No more beyond, the highest degree.

ne quid nimis (*L*) Nothing to excess.

nervi belli pecunia infinita (*L*) Plenty of money is the sinews of war. Cicero — *Philippics, V, 2, 5*.

nescio quid (*L*) I know not what, something or other.

nescit vox missa reverti (*L*) The word once spoken cannot be called back. Horace — *Ars Poetica, 390*.

nessun maggior dolore che ricordarsi del tempo felice nella miseria (*It.*) No greater pain than to remember happy days in the midst of wretchedness. Dante — *Inferno, V, 123*.

n'est-ce pas? (*F*) Isn't that true?

ne sutor supra crepidam judicaret (*L*) Let not the cobbler criticize beyond the last. Pliny — *Natural History, XXXV, 36*.

neue Besen kehren gut (*G*) New brooms sweep well.

névé (*F*) Mass of frozen snow.

ne vile fano (*L*) Bring nothing cheap to the temple. Proverb.

niais (*F*) Dunce.

niaiserie (*F*) Foolishness, bagatelle.

ni bebas agua que no veas (*Sp.*) Drink no water which you do not see. Compare *ni firmes carta que no leas ni bebas agua que no veas*.

nichts (*G*) Nothing.

nicht wahr? (*G*) Isn't that true?

nidor (*L*) Odor, savor.

nie kommt das Unglück ohne seinem Gefolge (*G*) Misfortune never comes without others in its train.

ni firmes carta que no leas ni bebas agua que no veas (*Sp.*) Sign no paper without reading it and drink no water before seeing it.

nigaud (*F*) Booby.

niger cycnus (*L*) Black swan, prodigy. Juvenal — *Satires, VI, 165*.

nihil (*L*) Nothing. Also *nil*.

nihil ad rem (*L*) Nothing to the point, irrelevant.

nihil est veritatis luce dulcius (*L*) Nothing is sweeter than the light of truth.

nihil tetigit quod non ornavit (*L*) He touched nothing which he did not adorn. Samuel Johnson — *Epitaph on Oliver Goldsmith*.

nil (*L*) Nothing. Also *nihil*.

nil admirari (*L*) To be moved at nothing. Horace — *Epistles, I, 6, 1*.

nil agit exemplum litem quod lite resolvit (*L*) One instance accomplishes nothing which settles a quarrel with another. Horace — *Satires, 2, 3, 103*.

nil conscire sibi nulla pallescere culpa (*L*) To be conscious of no wrong-doing, to pale at no crime. Horace — *Epistles, I, 1, 61*.

nil desperandum (*L*) Never despair.

nil fuit unquam sic impar sibi (*L*) Nothing was ever so unlike itself. Horace — *Satires, I, 3, 18*.

nimium ne crede colori (*L*) Don't trust too much in appearance. Vergil — *Eclogues, II, 17*.

n'importe (*F*) No matter.

nisi Dominus, frustra (*L*) Except the Lord (keep the city, the watchman waketh but) in vain. Vulgate — *Psalms, CXXVII, 1*.

nisi prius (*L*) Unless before, [law] authority to try cases.

nisus (*L*) Endeavor.

nisus formativus (*L*) Creative effort.

nitor in adversum (*L*) I strive against opposition. Ovid — *Metamorphoses, II, 72*.

nizam (*Hind.*) Ruler of Hyderabad.

noblesse (*F*) Nobility, rank.

noblesse oblige (*F*) Rank imposes obligations.

Noël (*F*) Christmas.

noemata (*νοήματα, Gr.*) Thoughts, purposes.

no es oro todo lo que reluce (*Sp.*) All is not gold that glitters.

noix (*F*) Walnut.

nolens volens (*L*) Willy, nilly.

noli irritare leones (*L*) Do not stir up lions. Proverb.

noli me tangere (*L*) Touch me not. Vulgate — *John, XX, 17*.

nolle prosequi (*L*) [Law] To be unwilling to proceed, discontinuance of suit.

nolo episcopari (*L*) I do not wish to become a bishop; I do not wish the office.

nolumus leges Angliæ mutari (*L*) We refuse to have the laws of England changed.

nom de course (*F*) Pseudonym.

nom de guerre (*F*) War name, assumed name.

nom de plume (*F*) Pen-name, author's pseudonym.

nom de théâtre (*F*) Theatre name, stage name.

nomina stultorum parietibus hærent (*L*) Fools' names stick to walls; fools' names are seen in public places.

nominis umbra (*L*) The shadow of a name.

non compos mentis (*L*) Not in control of one's mind, insane.

non constat (*L*) [Law] It is not sure.

non deficit alter (*L*) The second is not lacking. Vergil — *Æneid, VI, 143.*

non ego (*L*) The not I, the world outside.

non ens (*L*) The non-existent.

non è oro ciò che luce (*It.*) All is not gold that glitters.

non esse (*L*) Not to be, non-existence. Compare *esse.*

non est (*L*) It is not.

non est inventus (*L*) [Law] He has not been found.

non est meus actus (*L*) [Law] It is not my act. Compare *actus me invito factus non est meus actus.*

non est vivere sed valere vita (*L*) Life is not living but being well. Martial — *Epigrams, VI, 70.*

non è vero? (*It.*) Isn't that true?

non hæc in fœdera (*L*) Not into these stipulations.

non libet (*L*) It is not agreeable.

non liquet (*L*) [Law] It is not clear; it does not appear.

non mi ricordo (*It.*) I do not remember.

non multa sed multum (*L*) Not many things but much.

non nobis, Domine (*L*) Not unto us, O Lord. Vulgate — *Psalms, 115, 1.*

non nostrum tantas componere lites (*L*) It is not for me to settle such great controversies. Vergil — *Eclogues, III, 108.*

non numero hæc judicantur sed pondere (*L*) These things are judged by weight, not by number. Cicero.

non obstante (*L*) Notwithstanding.

non omne quod mitet aurum est (*L*) All is not gold that glitters.

non omnia possumus omnes (*L*) Not all of us can do all things. Vergil — *Eclogues, VIII, 63.*

non omnis moriar (*L*) I shall not die altogether. Horace — *Odes, III, 30, 6.*

nonpareil (*F*) Without equal.

non passibus æquis (*L*) With steps not equal. Vergil — *Æneid, II, 724.*

non possumus (*L*) We cannot.

non semper erit æstas (*L*) It will not always be summer.

non semper temeritas est felix (*L*) Rashness is not always fortunate. Livy — *Annals, XXVIII, 42.*

non sequitur (*L*) It does not follow; it is illogical.

non sum qualis eram (*L*) I am not what I used to be. Horace — *Odes, IV, 1, 3.*

nonum prematur in annum (*L*) Let it be kept until the ninth year. Horace — *Ars Poetica, 388.*

non vobis solum (*L*) Not for you alone.

norma loquendi (*L*) The measure of speaking.

nosce te (*L*) Know thyself.

nosce tempus (*L*) Know the time. Proverb.

noscitur a sociis (*L*) A person is known by the company he keeps. Proverb.

no se conoce el bien hasta que se ha perdido (*Sp.*) One never recognizes something good until he has lost it. Cervantes — *Don Quixote.*

nota bene (*L*) Note well.

Notre Dame (*F*) Our Lady, the Virgin Mary.

notturno (*It.*) Nightly, by night, [mus.] nocturne.

nous (νοῦς, *Gr.*) Mind, intelligence.

nous avons changé tout cela (*F*) We have changed all that. Molière — *Le Médecin Malgré Lui, II, 6.*

nous verrons (*F*) We shall see.

nouveau riche (*F*) Newly rich person.

novena (*L*) Nine days' devotion.

novus homo (*L*) New man, upstart.

noyade (*F*) Drowning.

noyer (*F*) Walnut-tree.

nuages moutonnés (*F*) Fluffy clouds.

nuance (*F*) Shade, shade of meaning.

nuda veritas (*L*) The naked truth. Horace — *Odes, I, 24, 7.*

nugæ (*L*) Trifles.

nugæ canoræ (*L*) Pleasant jingles. Horace — *Ars Poetica, 322.*

nuggar (*Egyptian*) Broad boat used on the Nile.

nulla dies sine linea (*L*) Not a day without a line. Pliny.

nulla fere causa est in qua non femina litem moverit (*L*) There is scarcely ever a law-suit in which a woman will not be the prime mover. Juvenal — *Satires, VI, 242.*

nullah (*Ang.-Ind.*) Ravine, gully. Hindustani *nala.*

nulli est homini perpetuum bonum (*L*) No man has never-failing good fortune. Plautus — *Curculio, I, 3, 33.*

nulli secundus (*L*) Second to no one.

nullius jurare in verba magistri (*L*) To swear allegiance to the words of no master. Horace — *Epistles, I, 1, 14.*

nullum est jam dictum quod non dictum sit prius (L) Nothing is said which has not been said before. Terence — *Eunuchus, Prologue, 41*.

nullum magnum ingenium sine mixtura dementiæ fuit (L) There was never a great genius without a mixture of madness. Seneca — *De Tranquillitate Animi, XVII, 10*.

nunc aut nunquam (L) Now or never.

nunc dimittis (L) Now thou sendest away. Vulgate — *Luke, II, 29*.

nunc dimittis servum tuum, Domine, in pace (L) Lord, now lettest Thou Thy servant depart in peace. Vulgate — *Luke, II, 29*.

nunc est bibendum (L) Now it is time to drink. Horace — *Odes, I, 37, 1*.

nusquam enim est qui ubique est (L) For he who is everywhere is nowhere. Seneca — *Epistles, II*.

O

obbligato (*It.*) [Mus.] Instrumental accompaniment.

obi (*West African*) A system of sorcery.

obit (L) (He dies), death.

obiter (L) On the way, in passing.

obiter dictum (L) Said in passing.

objet d'art (F) Object of art.

obscurum per obscurius (L) (To explain) the obscure by something more obscure.

obstupui steteruntque comæ et vox faucibus hæsit (L) I was dazed, my hair stood on end, and my voice stuck in my throat. Vergil — *Æneid, II, 774*.

occasionem cognosce (L) Recognize your chance. Proverb.

occurrent nubes (L) Clouds will appear.

octroi (F) City duty on merchandise.

oculi pictura tenentur aures cantibus (L) The eyes are held enthralled by a picture, the ears by songs. Cicero.

oculis subjecta fidelibus (L) Subjected to faithful eyes.

odalisque (F) Harem attendant.

odi profanum vulgus et arceo (L) I hate the uninitiated rabble and I keep it at a distance. Horace — *Odes, III, 1, 1*.

odium (L) Hate.

odium theologicum (L) Theological hatred, hatred among theologians.

œil-de-bœuf (F) Bull's-eye, small round or oval window.

œuf (F) Egg.

œuvre (F) Work.

O Gemini! (L) Oh, by the twins, by Castor and Pollux!

ogni debolo ha sempre il suo tiranno (*It.*) Every weakling always has his tyrant.

ogni medaglia ha il suo rovescio (*It.*) Every medal has its reverse.

ohne Bruder kann man leben, nicht ohne Freund (G) One can live without a brother, but not without a friend.

ohne Hast, ohne Rast (G) Without haste but without rest. Motto of Goethe.

oleum addere camino (L) Pour oil on the fire; make it worse. Horace — *Satires, II, 3, 321*.

ombres chinoises (F) Chinese shadows, shadow silhouettes.

Om mani padme hum (*Sansk.*) Oh, the Jewel in the Lotus, Amen.

omne ignotum pro magnifico (L) Every thing unknown (is taken to be) magnificent. Tacitus — *Agricola, 30*.

omnem movere lapidem (L) To move every stone, to leave no stone unturned.

omne solum forti patria (L) Every land is a fatherland to the brave man. Ovid — *Fasti, I, 493*.

omnes stultos insanire (L) That all foolish people are crazy. Horace — *Satires, III, 3*.

omne tulit punctum (L) He has gained every point. Horace — *Ars Poetica, 343*.

omnia mors æquat (L) Death levels all things. Claudianus.

omnia mutantur nos et mutamur in illis (L) All things change and we change with them.

omnia suspendens naso (L) Suspending all things from his nose, treating everything with a sneer. Horace — *Satires, II, 8, 64*.

omnia tuta timens (L) Fearing all things, even though they are safe. Vergil — *Æneid, IV, 298*.

omnia vincit amor (L) Love conquers all things. Vergil — *Eclogues, X, 69*.

omnium rerum principia parva sunt (L) The beginnings of all things are small. Cicero — *De Finibus, V, 21, 58*.

omphalos (ὀμφαλος, *Gr.*) Boss of a shield, middle point.

on dit (F) They say.

onor di bocca assai giova e poco costa (*It.*) Lip-homage is rather helpful and costs little.

onus (L) Weight, burden.

onus probandi (L) [Law] The burden of the proof.

opéra bouffe (F) Comic opera.

operæ pretium est (L) There is reward for the work. Terence — *Andria, 217*,

opere citato (L) In the work cited.

opiniâtre (F) Opinionated, obstinate.

optima fides (L) Absolutely good faith, best of faith.

optima mors Parca quæ venit apta die
(*L*) The best death is that which comes
on the day fixed by Fate. Propertius —
Elegies, III, 5, 18.

optime! (*L*) Very good, most excellent!

opum furiata cupido (*L*) A mad desire
for wealth. Ovid — *Fasti, I, 211.*

opus (*L*) Work, usually literary or musical.

ora e sempre (*It.*) Now and forever.

ora et labora (*L*) Pray and work.

ora pro nobis (*L*) Pray for us.

ὅρα τέλος μακροῦ βίον (*Gr.*) Consider the
end of a long life. Solon to Crœsus.

orator fit, poeta nascitur (*L*) The orator
is made, the poet born.

**ordo est parium dispariumque rerum
sua loca tribuens dispositio** (*L*) Order
is the arrangement of like and unlike
things giving to each its proper place.
St. Augustine.

ore rotundo (*L*) In well-rounded speech.
Horace — *Ars Poetica, 323.*

O Salutaris (*L*) Oh Savior.

O senza brama sicura ricchezza! (*It.*)
Oh wealth secure without eagerness!
Dante — *Paradise, XXVII, 8.*

O si sic omnia! (*L*) Oh, if all things were
thus!

o si tacuisses philosophus mansisses
(*L*) Oh, if thou hadst held thy tongue
thou wouldst have remained a wise man.
Boëthius.

O tempora, O mores! (*L*) What times,
what customs! Cicero — *Catiline, II, 1.*

otiosa sedulitas (*L*) Leisurely diligence.

otium cum dignitate (*L*) Leisure with
dignity. Cicero — *For Publius Sextius,
XLV, 98.*

oubliette (*F*) Dungeon.

**οὐδὲν οὕτω πιαίνει τὸν ἵππον ὡς βασιλέως
ὀφθαλμός** (*Gr.*) Nothing so fattens the
horse as the king's eye. Plutarch —
Morals, I.

οὐ γὰρ δοκεῖν ἄριστος ἀλλ' εἶναι θέλει (*Gr.*)
He does not wish to seem the best but to
be the best. Æschylus — *Seven Against
Thebes, 592.*

ouï-dire (*F*) Hearsay.

οὐρανος (*Gr.*) Sky.

outré (*F*) Exaggerated, odd.

outre mer (*F*) Across the sea.

ouvrage de longue haleine (*F*) Long-
winded work.

ovis (*L*) Sheep.

oyez! (*F*) Hear ye! (opening of court).

P

pabulum (*L*) Food.

pace (*L*) By leave of.

pace tanti nominis (*L*) By permission of
so great a personage.

pace tua (*L*) By your leave.

padishah (*Turk.*) Protecting lord.

padre (*It.*) Father, ecclesiastic.

padrone (*It.*) Master, employer.

pagri (*Hind.*) Turban. Also *puggree.*

pah (*Maori*) Native fort. Also *pa.*

paillard (*F*) Tramp, wanton.

paillasse (*F*) Bed of straw.

paktong (*Cantonese*) Chinese alloy.

palabra y piedra suelta no tiene vuelta
(*Sp.*) Word and stone once gone never
come back.

palæstra (*L*) Gymnasium, school. Greek
παλαίστρα.

palafitte (*F*) Lake-dwelling built upon
piles.

palais de vérité (*F*) Palace of truth.

palang (*Hind.*) Bed, bedstead.

palki (*Hind.*) Palanquin, litter.

pallium (*L*) Cloak.

palmam qui meruit ferat (*L*) Let him
win the palm who has deserved it.
Proverb.

pani (*Hind.*) Water.

πάντα λίθον κινεῖν (*Gr.*) To move every
stone, to leave no stone unturned.

παντ' ἄνδρα πάντων χρημάτων μέτρον (*Gr.*)
That every man is a measure of all
things.

Papa (*It.*) Pope.

paralysis agitans (*L*) Shaking palsy.

**para todo hay remedio sino para la
muerte** (*Sp.*) There is a remedy for
everything except death. Cervantes —
Don Quixote.

parbleu (*F*. for *par Dieu*) By God.

parc (*F*) Park.

Parcæ (*L*) The Fates.

parcere subjectis (*L*) To spare the conquered. Vergil — *Æneid, VI, 853.*

pardonnez-moi (*F*) Excuse me.

par excellence (*F*) Of the highest degree.

par exemple (*F*) For example.

par hasard (*F*) By chance.

pariah (*Tamil*) (Drummer), low-caste
person, outcast.

pari mutuel (*F*) Mutual wager, system of
betting in which the winners divide the
total stakes less a small percentage.

pari passu (*L*) With equal step, at the
same rate.

paritur pax bello (*L*) Peace is the offspring of war.

parlando (*It.*) [Mus.] In a speaking or declamatory style. Also *parlante.*

parler à tort et à travers (*F*) To speak
unjustly and foolishly.

parlimentaire (*F*) Negotiator of truce
proceedings.

par negotiis neque super (*L*) Equal to
his business and not above it. Tacitus —
Annals, VI, 39.

par nobile fratrum (*L*) A noble pair of brothers. Horace — *Satires, II, 3, 243.*

parole d'honneur (*F*) Word of honor.

par parenthèse (*F*) By way of parenthesis, incidentally.

par pro pari refero (*L*) I return like for like, tit for tat. Terence — *Eunuchus, III, 1, 55.*

parsque est meminisse doloris (*L*) It is part of grief to remember. Ovid.

parterre (*F*) (On the ground), flower garden, ground-floor.

Parthis mendacior (*L*) More untruthful than the Parthians. Horace — *Epistles, II, 1, 112.*

particeps criminis (*L*) [Law] An accomplice in crime.

partie carrée (*F*) Two couples.

parti pris (*F*) Part taken, preconceived opinion.

parturiunt montes (*L*) The mountains are in labor. Horace — *Ars Poetica, 139.*

parturiunt montes; nascetur ridiculus mus (*L*) The mountains are in labor; a ridiculous mouse will be born. Horace — *Ars Poetica, 139.*

parva componere magnis (*L*) To compare small things with great ones. Vergil — *Georgics, IV, 176.*

parva sæpe scintilla contempta magnum excitavit incendium (*L*) A small spark neglected has often started a great conflagration. Quintus Curtius Rufus — *Alexander the Great.*

parvenu (*F*) Upstart.

parvum parva decent (*L*) Humble things befit a humble person. Horace — *Epistles, I, 7, 44.*

pas (*F*) Step, pace, precedence.

pasha (*Turk.*) Honorary title for high ranks. Also *bashaw.*

pasigraphie (*F*) Universal writing.

passado (*Sp.*) [Fencing] Thrust, lunge.

passage d'armes (*F*) Passage of arms.

passamezzo (*It.*) Pass through the middle, [mus.] old Italian dance.

passé (*F*) Out of date, unfashionable.

passe-partout (*F*) Master-key.

passer la plume par le bec (*F*) To frustrate hopes.

passer l'arme à gauche (*F. slang*) To be killed.

passe-temps (*F*) Pastime.

pas si bête (*F*) Not so stupid, not so bad.

passim (*L*) Here and there.

pasticcio (*It.*) Pie, [mus.] medley.

pastiche (*F*) Imitative artistic or literary work, [mus.] medley.

pastorale (*It.*) Pastoral, [mus.] idyllic or rustic music.

pâté (*F*) Meat pasty.

pâté de foie gras (*F*) Patty of fattened liver, goose liver patty.

patella (*L*) Small dish.

patera (*L*) Libation dish.

pater familias (*L*) Father of a family, head of a household.

paternoster (*L*) (Our Father), the Lord's Prayer.

pater patriæ (*L*) Father of his country.

patio (*Sp.*) Enclosed court.

pâtisserie (*F*) Pastry, pastry making.

patois (*F*) Dialect, regional idiom.

patron (*F*) Captain of a small boat.

patte (*F*) Paw, claw.

pattes de mouche (*F*) (Fly paws), illegible handwriting.

pattes de velours (*F*) Velvet paws, false front, hidden guile.

paucis temeritas est bona multis mala (*L*) Rashness is good for a few, bad for many. Phædrus — *Fables, V, 4, 12.*

paucis verbis (*L*) In a few words.

paulo post futurum (*L*) A little after the future, remote.

pauvre diable (*F*) Poor devil, miserable wretch.

pavé (*F*) Pavement.

pax! (*L*) Peace, hold your tongue! Plautus — *Miles Gloriosus, III, 1, 211.*

pax in bello (*L*) Peace in war.

pax vobiscum (*L*) Peace (be) with you.

paysage (*F*) Landscape, landscape painting.

peccavi (*L*) I have sinned.

pédieux (pertaining to the foot, *F.*) Elaborate foot-piece of sixteenth century armor.

pedir peras al olmo (*Sp.*) To ask pears of the elm, to ask figs from thistles. Cervantes — *Don Quixote.*

peignoir (*F*) Wrapper, dressing-gown.

peine forte et dure (*F*) Strong and harsh punishment.

pelure (*F*) Peel, skin, rind.

peña (*Sp.*) (S. W. U. S.) Rock, cliff.

pena de azote (*Sp.*) Public flogging.

penchant (*F*) Leaning, propensity.

pendeloque (*F*) Pendant, ear-drop.

pendente lite (*L*) [Law] While the suit is pending.

pendule (*F*) Pendulum clock.

penetralia mentis (*L*) The inner recesses of the mind.

pensée (*F*) Thought, idea.

pensieroso (*It.*) Thoughtful.

pensionnat (*F*) Boarding-school.

per (*L*) Through, for.

per annum (*L*) By the year, yearly.

per capita (*L*) By the heads, for each person.

per contra (*L*) On the contrary.

per diem (*L*) By the day, daily.

perdre son latin (*F*) To lose one's Latin, to fail to understand.

père (*F*) Father.

per fas et nefas (*L*) Through right and wrong, by fair means and foul.

perfervidum ingenium (*L*) Very fervid temperament.

peri (*Pers.*) Fairy descended from fallen angels.

per incuriam (*L*) Through carelessness.

per mensem (*L*) By the month, monthly.

per procurationem (*L*) Through administrative means.

per saltum (*L*) By a leap, without intermediate steps.

per se (*L*) By itself alone, intrinsically.

persiflage (*F*) Banter, irony.

persifleur (*F*) Mocker, banterer.

persona grata (*L*) Acceptable person.

persona non grata (*L*) A person not acceptable. Compare *persona grata*.

personnel (*F*) The group of persons employed in a given place.

per troppo dibatter la verità si perde (*It.*) Through too much debating the truth is lost.

pessimum genus inimicorum laudantes (*L*) The flatterers are the worst kind of enemies. Tacitus — *Agricola, 41.*

petit (*F*) Little, insignificant, dainty.

petit à petit l'oiseau fait son nid (*F*) Little by little the bird builds her nest.

petite dame (*F*) Little lady, vain fashionable woman.

petite noblesse (*F*) Petty nobility.

petitio principii (*L*) Begging the question, taking for granted a thing is true.

petit maître (*F*) Little master, dude, fop.

petit souper (*F*) Little supper, informal gathering.

petits soins (*F*) Little attentions.

petit verre (*F*) Little glass, liqueur glass.

pétroleur (*F*) Incendiary who uses oil.

peu à peu (*F*) Little by little.

peu de chose (*F*) A little thing, trifle.

peu de gens savent être vieux (*F*) Few people know how to grow old. La Rochefoucauld — *Maxims, 423.*

peu s'en faut (*F*) It lacks little, almost.

Pfahlbauten (*G*) Pile buildings, lake dwellings.

Philister (*G*) Philistine, vulgarian.

philosophia stemma non inspicit (*L*) Philosophy pays no heed to pedigree. Seneca — *Epistles, XLIV.*

philosophie positive (*F*) Positive philosophy, system of Compte.

phonanta sunetoisi (φωνᾶντα συνετοῖσι, *Gr.*) Words to the wise. Pindar — *Olympian Odes, II, 152.*

pianino (*It.*) Little piano, [mus.] upright piano.

pianissimo (*It.*) [Mus.] Very soft.

piano (*It.*) [Mus.] Soft.

piazza (*It.*) Public square, market-place.

picacho (*Sp.*) Summit of a mountain.

pice (*Ang.-Ind.*) Copper coin, one-quarter anna. Hindustani *paisa.*

Pickelhaube (*G*) Spiked helmet.

pièce de résistance (*F*) Chief dish of a dinner, most important feature.

pièce justicative (*F*) Instrument in proof.

pied (*F*) Foot.

pied-à-terre (*F*) Temporary lodging.

Pietà (*It.*) [Painting] Representation of Mary mourning over the dead body of Christ.

pietra mossa non fa muschio (*It.*) A moved stone makes no moss; a rolling stone gathers no moss.

pilon (*Sp.*) Sugar loaf, (S. W. U. S.) small gratuity given by tradesmen to their patrons.

pinacotheca (πινακοθήκη, *Gr.*) Picture-gallery.

pince-nez (*F*) (Pinch-nose), pair of eye-glasses.

pincette (*F*) Small pincers, tweezers.

pinxit (*L*) He painted (it).

piragua (*W. Ind. Sp.*) Dugout, canoe made from a tree-trunk.

pis aller (*F*) (To go worse), makeshift.

pisces (*L*) Fishes.

pisces natare docere (*L*) To teach fishes to swim, to overdo something.

piscina (*L*) Fish-pond, reservoir.

piste (*F*) Footprint, race-track.

pizzicato (*It.*) [Mus.] Played by plucking the strings.

place (*F*) City square.

place aux dames (*F*) Make way for the ladies, ladies first.

placebo (*L*) (I shall please), vesper for the dead.

placitum (*L*) Pleased, [law] judgment, decree.

plafond (*F*) Ceiling.

plaidoyer (*F*) Plea of the lawyer for the defense.

plaisance (*F*) Pleasure, means of pleasure.

plaisanterie (*F*) Pleasantry, jest.

plat (*F*) Dish, dish of food.

playa (*Sp.*) Shore, strand.

plaza (*Sp.*) Public square.

plenus annis abiit plenus honoribus (*L*) He passed away, with great honors and many years. Pliny the Younger — *Epistles.*

plus royaliste que le Roi (*F*) More royalist than the king, to take another's interests more to heart than one's own.

poca favilla gran fiamma seconda (*It.*) A small spark starts a great flame. Dante — *Paradiso, I, 34.*

poca roba poco pensiero (*It.*) Small estate, little care.

poco a poco (*It.*) Little by little.

pococurante (*It.*) Little-caring, heedless person.

podárok (*Rus.*) Gratuity.

podestà (*It.*) Power, mayor.

poetis mentiri licet (*L*) Poets are allowed to lie. Pliny — *Epistles, VI, 21.*

pogrom (*Rus.*) Organized massacre.

poilu (*F*) Hairy fellow, [slang] brave soldier, World War soldier.

point d'appui (*F*) Resting-point, fulcrum

point d'argent point de Suisse (*F*) No money no servants.

point de réunion (*F*) Point of reunion, hyphen.

poisson d'avril (*F*) April fish, April fool trick.

polacca (*It.*) Small vessel used in the Mediterranean.

polisson (*F*) Vagabond child, reprobate.

polka (*Pol.*) (Polish woman), lively dance of Bohemian origin.

pons asinorum (*L*) (The bridge of asses), fifth proposition of first book of Euclid, something difficult.

pontificalia (*L*) Pontificals, pontifical vestments.

portamento (*It.*) Bearing, [mus.] sliding from one note to another.

porte-cochère (*F*) Carriage entrance.

portefeuille (*F*) Portfolio.

porte-monnaie (*F*) Money-carrier, pocketbook.

portière (*F*) Carriage door, curtain before a door.

posada (*Sp.*) Home, dwelling.

pose (*F*) Attitude, affectation.

poseur (*F*) Poser, affected person.

posse comitatus (*L*) [Law] Armed force raised by a sheriff.

poste restante (*F*) (Post remaining), notice in addressing mail equivalent to *Hold until called for.*

post hoc, ergo propter hoc (*L*) After this, therefore on account of this.

post meridiem (*L*) Afternoon, P.M.

post mortem (*L*) After death, anything occurring after death.

post-obit (*L*) After death.

post obitum (*L*) After death.

potage (*F*) Soup.

poudre aux yeux (*F*) Dust in the eyes, misled.

poularde (*F*) Fattened fowl.

pour acquit (*F*) Received payment.

pourboire (*F*) Tip, gratuity.

pour faire rire (*F*) To excite laughter.

pourparler (*F*) Diplomatic conference.

pour passer le temps (*F*) To pass away the time.

pour prendre congé (*F*) To take leave.

pourquoi? (*F*) Why?

pour rire (*F*) For laughing, in fun.

pour tout potage (*F*) For every soup, for all possible advantage.

pousse-café (*F*) After-coffee cordial.

pou sto (πού στῶ, *Gr.*) Where I may stand, fulcrum. Compare δός μοι πού στῶ καὶ κινῶ τὴν γῆν.

præcognita (*L*) Things known in advance.

prahu (*Malay*) Small boat. Also *proa.*

pram (*Dan.*) Flat-bottomed lighter used in Baltic ports.

praxis (πρᾶξις, *Gr.*) Business, practice.

préciate más de ser humilde virtuoso que pecador soperbio (*Sp.*) Realize that it is better to be virtuous and humble than to be a sinner and proud. Cervantes — *Don Quixote.*

précieuse (*F*) Affected over-refined woman.

précieuse ridicule (*F*) Ridiculously affected woman.

précis (*F*) Abstract, summary.

première (*F*) Leading woman, leading actress; first performance.

première danseuse (*F*) First dancer, leading lady in a ballet.

prendre la balle au bond (*F*) To catch the ball on the bounce, to profit by an opportunity.

prendre la lune avec les dents (*F*) To seize the moon with one's teeth, to do the impossible.

prendre le mors aux dents (*F*) To take the bit in the teeth.

prenez garde (*F*) Take care; be careful.

prestance (*F*) Noble bearing, commanding appearance.

prestidigitateur (*F*) Prestidigitator, magician.

prestissimo (*It.*) [Mus.] In very rapid tempo.

presto (*It.*) [Mus.] In rapid tempo.

preux chevalier (*F*) Brave knight.

prévenance (*F*) Ingratiating manner.

pri dengakh Panfil vsyem lindom mil (*Rus.*) When he has money, Pamfil (the muzhik) is liked by all.

prie-dieu (*F*) Pray-God, rest for the knees in church.

prima donna (*It.*) First lady, principal singer in opera.

prima facie (*L*) [Law] At first sight.

primas partes agere (*L*) To play the leading rôles.

primeur (*F*) Novelty, first fruits of the season.

primo (*L*) In the beginning, in the first place.

primum mobile (*L*) The first movable, Ptolemaic sphere.

primus inter pares (*L*) First among equals.

principia non homines (*L*) Principles not men.

principiis obstare (*L*) To block the beginnings.

prior tempore prior jure (L) First in time, first in law.

Privatdozent (G) Private teacher recognized by the faculty.

pro (L) For, in behalf of.

proa (*Malay*) Small boat. Also *prahu*.

pro aris et focis (L) For altars and hearths, for home and religion.

probatum est (L) It has been tested.

probitas laudatur et alget (L) Integrity is praised and dies of the cold. Juvenal — *Satires, I, 74.*

pro bono publico (L) For the public good.

procès-verbal (F) A detailed statement of a crime.

prochein ami [French law] Next friend.

prodromos (πρόδρομος, *Gr.*) Forerunner.

pro et contra (L) For and against, pro and con.

profanum vulgus (L) The vulgar herd. Horace — *Odes, III, 1, 1.*

pro forma (L) In behalf of form, for form's sake.

pro hac vice (L) For this occasion.

proh pudor! (L) Oh shame! Petronius Arbiter.

prôner (F) To praise, to recommend.

prôneur (F) One who recommends, radio-announcer.

pronunziamento (*It.*) Pronouncement, proclamation.

pro patria (L) For one's fatherland.

proprio motu (L) Of one's own accord.

propter hoc (L) On account of this.

pro rata (L) In proportion, proportionally.

pro re nata (L) As occasion may arise.

proscrit (F) Proscribed person, outlaw.

prosit! (L) May it be for your good, your health!

pro tanto (L) For so much, to such an extent.

protégé (F) Person who is protected or cared for.

pro tempore (L) For the time, for the time being, pro tem.

proverbe (F) Saying, short comedy based upon a proverb.

provoquant (F) Provoking, exciting.

proxime accessit (L) He came nearest.

proximo (L) Of the next (month).

proximus ardet Ucalegon (L) Ucalegon's house nearest of all is on fire. Vergil — *Æneid, II, 311.*

pruina (L) Hoar-frost.

pruneaux (F) Dried plums.

pudor malus (L) False shame.

pug (*Ang.-Ind.*) Spoor, footprint.

pugnis et calcibus (L) With fists and heels. Cicero — *Tusculan Disputations, V, 27, 77.*

pujari (*Hind.*) Priest having charge of an idol temple.

pukka (*Ang.-Ind.*) Solid, good. Also *pucka* and *pakka*.

pulcinella (*It.*) Punchinello, punch.

pulmo (L) Lung.

Punica fides (L) Punic faith, unreliability. Sallust — *Jugurtha, 108.*

punkah (*Ang.-Ind.*) Large fan worked by a rope.

pur autre vie [French law] During the life of another.

purdah (*Ang.-Ind.*) Screen for secluding women. Hindustani and Persian *parda.*

purée (F) A thick soup.

pur et simple (F) Pure and simple, absolutely.

purohit (*Hind.*) Family priest.

pur sang (F) Pure-blooded, thoroughbred.

Q

quæ cum ita sint (L) Since these things are so.

quæ fuit durum pati meminisse dulce est (L) What was hard to bear is sweet to remember. Seneca — *Hercules Furens, III, 656.*

quæ nocent docent (L) The things which hurt teach.

quære (L) Ask, inquire.

qualis ab incepto (L) As it was in the beginning. Horace — *Ars Poetica, 127.*

qualis rex talis grex (L) Like king like people.

quamdiu se bene gesserit (L) As long as he may have behaved well, during good behavior.

quamvis tegatur proditur vultu furor (L) However much it may be concealed, anger is always betrayed in the face. Seneca — *Hippolytus, 363.*

quand même (F) Even if, nevertheless

quando amigo pide no hay mañana (*Sp.*) When a friend asks a favor there is no tomorrow.

quantum (L) How much, quantity, unit.

quantum animis erroris inest (L) How much error there is in human minds. Ovid.

quantum libet (L) As much as one pleases.

quantum mutatus (L) How changed! Vergil — *Æneid, II, 274.*

quantum placet (L) As much as one pleases.

quantum sufficit (L) As much as suffices, enough.

quantum vis (L) As much as you wish.

quaquaversum (L) On every side.

quasi (L) As if, nearly.

quattrocento (*It.*) (Four hundred), fifteenth century.

quelque chose (L) Something, trifle.

quem Jupiter vult perdere dementat prius (*L*) Whom Jupiter wishes to destroy he first makes mad.

quidam (*L*) Some one, a certain person.

qui docet discit (*L*) He who teaches is learning.

quid pro quo (*L*) Something for something, exchange.

quid sit futurum cras fuge quærere (*L*) Do not seek to find out what the morrow will bring. Horace — *Odes, I, 9, 13.*

quid times? Cæsarem vehis (*L*) What are you afraid of? You are carrying Cæsar. Julius Cæsar, to his pilot.

quid valeant humeri quid ferre recusent (*L*) What the shoulders may carry and what they would refuse to carry. Horace — *Ars Poetica, 38.*

quién sabe? (*Sp.*) Who knows?

quien te cubre te descubre (*Sp.*) Whoever covers you discovers you.

quieta non movere (*L*) Do not disturb quiet things; leave things as they are.

qui n'a pas inventé la poudre (*F*) Who didn't invent gunpowder, a fellow who will never set the Thames afire.

qui n'a pas le sou (*F*) Not having a sou, penniless.

quis custodiet istos custodes? (*L*) Who will guard those very guards. Juvenal — *Satires, VI, 347.*

qui s'excuse s'accuse (*F*) He accuses himself who excuses himself.

quisnam igitur sanus? qui non stultus (*L*) Who therefore is sound in mind? He that is not a fool. Horace — *Satires, II, 3, 158.*

quisque suos patimur manes (*L*) We each suffer our own destinies. Vergil — *Æneid, VI, 743.*

quis separabit? (*L*) Who shall separate? Motto of the Order of Saint Patrick.

quis talia fando temperet a lachrymis? (*L*) Who could refrain from tears in relating such things? Vergil — *Æneid, II, 6.*

qui tacet consentire videtur (*L*) He who is silent seems to consent.

qui tam (*L*) Who as well, [law] action brought by an informer.

qui va là? (*F*) Who goes there?

qui vive? (*F*) Who lives, who goes there?

quoad (*L*) As to, as regards.

quoad hoc (*L*) Concerning this.

quoad minus (*L*) As to the lesser matter.

quo animo? (*L*) With what purpose?

quod erat demonstrandum (*L*) Which was to be demonstrated, Q.E.D.

quod erat faciendum (*L*) Which was to be done, Q. E. F.

quodlibet (*L*) Whatever you please, argument, [mus.] medley.

quod vide (*L*) Which see, q. v.

quo jure? (*L*) By what right?

quo me cumque rapit tempestas deferor hospes (*L*) Wherever the wind blows me I am taken as a welcome guest. Horace — *Epistles, I, 1, 15.*

quondam (*L*) At one time, formerly.

quorum pars magna fui (*L*) Of which I was a great part. Vergil — *Æneid, II, 6.*

quot homines tot sententiæ (*L*) As many opinions as men. Terence — *Phormio, II, 3, 14.*

quot servi tot hostes (*L*) As many enemies as slaves. Cato.

R

rabat (*F*) Neckpiece worn by clergymen and professors.

raccroc (*F*) Fortunate outcome, fluke.

raconteur (*F*) Person given to telling stories.

radoter (*F*) To tell foolish stories.

radoteur (*F*) Teller of foolish stories driveler.

rafale (*F*) Squall, fusillade.

raison de plus (*F*) Still more reason.

raison d'état (*F*) Reason of state.

raison d'être (*F*) Reason for being.

raisonner comme une huître (*F*) To reason like an oyster, to argue stupidly.

raja (*Hind.*) Indian prince. Also *rajah.*

rajput (*Hind.*) Son of a rajah, Hindu aristocrat. (supposedly descended from the Kshatriyas or warrior caste).

rallentando (*It.*) [Mus.] Growing slower in tempo.

rancho (*Sp Amer.*) (Mess room), collection of huts, ranch.

rani (*Hind.*) Queen, reigning princess.

ranz des vaches (*Swiss.*) Pastoral air played by mountain shepherds.

rappel (*F*) Recall, call to arms.

rapport (*F*) Relation, sympathy.

rapprochement (*F*) Reconciliation.

rara avis (*L*) Rare bird, unusual person. Juvenal — *Satires, VI, 164.*

rari nantes (*L*) Occasional swimmers. Vergil — *Æneid, I, 118.*

razzia (*F.-Algerian*) Military raid.

Realschule (*G*) Technical school, nonclassical secondary school.

réchauffé (*F*) Warmed-over, an old idea or thing presented as new.

recherché (*F*) Uncommon, choice.

réclame (*F*) Publicity, advertisement.

rectus in curia (*L*) Correct in court, blameless.

reculade (*F*) Hesitation, falling back.

reculer pour mieux sauter (*F*) To draw back in order to make a better leap, to deliberate before making a decision.

redet Geld, so schweigt die Welt (*G*) When money speaks the world keeps silent.

redintegratio amoris (*L*) Renewal of love.

redivivus (L) Renewed.

reductio ad absurdum (L) A reduction to the absurd, showing a thing to be true by proving its contrary absurd.

reduire à l'hôpital (F) To reduce to the alms-house, to ruin.

regarder de haut en bas (F) To regard scornfully.

regibus esse manus an nescio longas (L) Am I not aware that kings have long arms? Ovid — Heroides, XVII, 166.

régime (F) Governmental authority, the laws of a government.

Regina Cœli (L) Queen of Heaven, the Virgin Mary.

règlement (F) Regulation.

regnant populi (L) The people rule. Motto of Arkansas.

re infecta (L) With the matter unfinished.

relevé (F) A dinner-course following the soup.

religieuse (F) Woman attached to a monastic order, nun.

religio loci (L) Sacred character of a place.

reliquiæ (L) Remains.

remuda (Sp.) Saddle-horses, relay of horses.

rencontre (F) Meeting, encounter.

rente (F) Rent, annual revenue.

rentier (F) Receiver of rents, property holder.

répertoire (F) The plays of a troupe, stock parts.

répondez s'il vous plaît (F) Please reply, R. S. V. P.

répondre en Normand (F) To reply in Norman, to give an evasive answer.

repoussage (F) Repoussé work, beaten work.

repoussé (F) Beaten, of metal veneer beaten over a form of resin.

requiescat in pace (L) May he rest in peace.

res adjudicata (L) A matter settled.

res angusta domi (L) Poverty at home. Juvenal — Satires, III, 165.

res est ingeniosa dare (L) To give is a thing which requires genius. Ovid — Amores, I, 8, 62

res est sacra miser (L) A wretched man is a sacred object. Seneca.

res gestæ (L) Things done, acts, deeds.

res ipsa loquitur (L) The matter speaks for itself.

res judicata (L) A matter settled in court.

respicere finem (L) To look to the end.

ressaldar, see risaldar.

restaurateur (F) Keeper of a restaurant.

résumé (F) Summary, digest.

resurgam (L) I shall rise again.

retenue (F) Discretion, modesty.

retroussé (F) Turned up.

réunion social (F) Social reunion, party.

revanche (F) Revenge, retaliation.

revenons à nos moutons (F) Let us return to our sheep; let us resume our subject.

revue (F) Review, survey.

rex bibendi (L) King of the revels.

rez-de-chaussée (F) Ground floor.

rhythmus (L) Rhythm.

ride bene che ride l'ultimo (It.) He laughs well who laughs last.

ridentem dicere verum (L) To tell the truth while laughing. Horace — Satires, I, 1, 24.

rideret Heraclitus (L) Heraclitus would laugh.

ride si sapis (L) Laugh if you are wise. Martial — Epigrams, II, 41.

ridiculus mus (L) Absurd mouse. Compare parturiunt montes; nascetur ridiculus mus.

ridotto (It.) Retreat, fashionable resort.

rien de plus estimable que la cérémonie (F) Nothing more estimable than ceremony.

rifacimento (It.) Re-making, restoration.

rigor mortis (L) Stiffness of death, rigidity of a corpse.

rilievo (It.) Relief, embossed work.

risaldar (Hind.) Commander of a cavalry detachment. Also ressaldar.

risqué (F) Risky, slightly indelicate.

risum teneatis amici? (L) Would you refrain from laughing, my friends? Horace — Ars Poetica, 5.

ritardando (It.) [Mus.] Becoming slower.

ritornello (It.) [Mus.] Chorus of a song.

Romanus sedendo vincit (L) The Roman conquers by sitting still.

rondeau (F) A poem of fixed form, two rhymes, and certain repetitions, [mus.] air with several variations. Italian rondo.

rose du Barry (F) Color named after Madame du Barry.

roti (F) Roasted meat.

roturier (F) Peasant, commoner.

roué (F) Broken on the wheel, reprobate.

rouge et noir (F) Red and black, game of chance.

roulade (F) [Mus.] Run of notes on one syllable, flourish.

rouleau (F) Roll, pile of money.

ruade (F) Sudden, unexpected attack.

ruat cœlum (L) Let the heavens fall.

Rucksack (G) Loose knapsack.

rudera (L) Rubbish, débris.

rudis indigestaque moles (L) Rough and disorderly mass. Ovid — Metamorphoses, I, 7.

rumal (Hind. and Pers.) Shawl.

rusé (F) Artful, cunning.

ruse de guerre (F) Stratagem of war.

rus in urbe (*L*) The country in the city, solitude in the city. Martial — *Epigrams, XII, 57, 21.*

rusticus expectat dum defluat amnis (*L*) A peasant waits until the river run out. Horace — *Epistles, I, 2, 42.*

ryot (*Ang.-Ind.*) Peasant, tenant. Hindustani *raiyat.*

S

sabot (*F*) Wooden shoe.

sabotage (*F*) (Shoe-making), malicious destruction of property by discontented workmen.

sabreur (*F*) User of the sabre, brutal soldier.

sabr karo (*Hind.*) Be patient, wait.

sac (*F*) Bag, sack.

sac de nuit (*F*) Night bag, traveling bag.

sæpe creat molles aspera spina rosas (*L*) Often the sharp thorn produces delicate roses. Ovid — *Epistles from Pontus, II, 2, 34.*

sagouin (*F*) Species of monkey, slovenly person.

sahib (*Hind.*) (Friend), sir.

sahiba (*Hind.*) Madam, mistress, lady.

saignant (*F*) Bleeding, underdone (of meat).

salade (*F*) Light helmet common in the sixteenth century.

salam (*Arab.*) (Peace), ceremonious salutation. Also *salaam.*

salle à manger (*F*) Dining room.

salle d'attente (*F*) Waiting-room.

salon (*F*) Drawing-room, fashionable circle.

saltimbanco (*It.*) Mountebank, ballad-singer.

saltimbanque (*F*) Professional gymnast, charlatan.

salva res est (*L*) The matter is safe. Terence — *Eunuchus, II, 2, 37.*

salva sit reverentia (*L*) May your reverence be safe; save your reverence.

saman (*Hind.*) Equipment, furniture.

samisen (*Jap.*) Three-stringed banjo-like instrument.

samo (*Jap.*) Wrestling.

sampan (*Chin.*) (Three board), skiff used in the Orient.

samurai (*Jap.*) Military class of feudal Japan, army officer.

Sancta Virgo Virginum (*L*) Holy Virgin of Virgins.

sanctum sanctorum (*L*) Holy of holies, innermost part of Jewish tabernacle.

Sand in die Augen werfen (*G*) To throw sand into the eyes, to dazzle, to deceive.

sangar (*Ang.-Ind.*) Breastwork of stone.

sang-de-bœuf (*F*) Ox-blood, deep red color.

sang-froid (*F*) Cold blood, coolness.

sannyasi (*Sansk.*) Abandoner, [Hinduism] person devoted to asceticism and meditation. Also *sanyasi* and *sannyasin.*

sans cérémonie (*F*) Without ceremony, informal.

sans-culotte (*F*) (Without breeches), French revolutionary of 1789.

sans Dieu rien (*F*) Without God nothing.

sans doute (*F*) Without doubt, doubtless.

sans façon (*F*) Without ceremony, informal.

sans-gêne (*F*) Coolness, indifference.

sans le sou (*F*) Without a sou, penniless.

sans mélange (*F*) Pure, unmixed.

sans pareil (*F*) Without equal, unequaled.

sans peur et sans reproche (*F*) Without fear and without reproach.

sans phrase (*F*) Without (formal) speech, in plain language.

sans-souci (*F*) Without care.

sans tache (*F*) Without blemish.

santon (*Sp.*) Turkish monk.

saper dove il diavolo tien la coda (*It.*) To know where the devil keeps his tail, to be very crafty.

sapere aude (*L*) Dare to be wise. Horace — *Epistles, I, 2, 40.*

sapiens (*L*) Wise, knowing.

sarmentum (*L*) Twigs, brushwood.

sartor resartus (*L*) The tailor retailored.

satis superque (*L*) Enough and over, enough and more than enough.

satis verborum (*L*) Enough of words.

Saturnia regna (*L*) The Saturnian rule, the Golden Age. Vergil — *Eclogues, IV, 6.*

sauce piquante (*F*) Sharp sauce.

saumon (*F*) Salmon, salmon color.

sauté (*F*) (Jumped), fried quickly.

sauter le pas (*F*) To take a resolution.

sauvage (*F*) Wild, savage, uncultivated.

sauve qui peut (*F*) Each one save himself, disorderly retreat.

savant (*F*) Scholar, sage.

savoir-faire (*F*) To know how to do, skill, sophistication.

savoir gré (*F*) To feel satisfied.

savoir-vivre (*F*) To know how to live, philosophy of life.

saxum volutum non obducitur musco (*L*) A rolling stone gathers no moss.

sayonara (*Jap.*) (If that be so), good-bye.

sbirro (*It. slang*) Bailiff, constable.

scandalum magnatum (*L*) Slander of magnates.

schatchen (*Yid.*) Marriage-broker, go-between.

scherzando (*It.*) [Mus.] Playful, mocking.

scherzo (*It.*) Jest, play, [mus.] light piece.

schnell genug wär's genug (*G*) Quick enough is good enough.

Schönheit vergeht Tugend besteht (*G*) Beauty fades virtue stays.

schwere Arbeit in der Jugend ist sanfte Ruhe im Alter (*G*) Hard work in youth is gentle rest in age.

scintilla (*L*) Spark.

scire facias (*L*) Let it be known, [law] writ to enforce the execution of a judgment.

scire quid valeant humeri quid ferre recusent (*L*) To know what the shoulders may carry and what they would refuse to carry.

scoriæ (*L*) Cinders, dross.

scribendi recte sapere et principium et fons (*L*) Accurate thinking is the beginning and the fountain of writing. Horace — *Ars Poetica, 309.*

scripsit (*L*) He wrote (it).

sculpsit (*L*) He sculptured (this).

scutum (*L*) Shield.

séance (*F*) Deliberation, session.

se battre contre des moulins (*F*) To fight against windmills.

secrétaire (*F*) Secretary, writing-desk.

secundis avibus (*L*) Under favorable auguries.

secundum artem (*L*) According to art.

secundum naturam (*L*) According to nature, naturally.

secundum quid (*L*) According to something, in some respect only.

se defendre du bec (*F*) To defend one's self by word of mouth.

seditiosissimus quisque ignavus (*L*) Everyone of a depraved and most turbulent nature. Tacitus — *Annals, IV, 34.*

se faire valoir (*F*) To assert one's self.

s'égosiller (*F*) To yell loud and long.

se judice nemo nocens absolvitur (*L*) No delinquent is acquitted when he himself is judge. Juvenal — *Satires, XIII, 1.*

selon les règles (*F*) According to the regulations.

s'embarquer sans bisquits (*F*) To embark without bisquits, to undertake an enterprise without sufficient preparation.

semel emissum volat irrevocabile verbum (*L*) A word once spoken flies away never to be called back. Horace — *Epistles, I, 18, 71.*

semper avarus eget (*L*) The avaricious man is always in want. Horace — *Epistles, I, 2, 56.*

semper eadem (*L*) Always the same. Motto of Queen Elizabeth.

semper et ubique (*L*) Always and everywhere.

semper fidelis (*L*) Forever faithful.

semper idem (*L*) Forever the same.

semper paratus (*L*) Always ready.

semplice (*It.*) Simple.

sempre il mal non vien per nuocere (*It.*) Misfortune never comes to harm anyone.

senatus consultum (*L*) Decree of the senate.

senatus populusque Romanus (*L*) The senate and people of Rome, S. P. Q. R.

senhor (*Port.*) Sir, Mr.

senhora (*Port.*) Madam, lady.

senhorita (*Port.*) Miss, unmarried woman.

se nicher (*F*) To nest, to hide.

seniores priores (*L*) The elders first.

se non è vero è molto ben trovato (*It.*) If it is not true it is very well invented. Giordani Bruno — *Degli Eroici Furori.*

señor (*Sp.*) Sir, Mr.

señora (*Sp.*) Madam, lady.

señorita (*Sp.*) Miss, unmarried woman.

sens dessus dessous (*F*) Topsy-turvy, upside-down.

sensu bono (*L*) In a good sense.

sensu malo (*L*) In a bad sense.

separatio a mensa et thoro (*L*) Separation from bed and board.

separatio a vinculo matrimoni (*L*) Freedom from the bonds of matrimony.

sepoy (*Ang.-Ind.*) Native soldier. Urdu and Persian *sipahi*.

seppuku (*setsu puku, Jap.*) Cut-the-belly, suicide, hari-kiri.

sérac (*Swiss F*) Heap of ice-blocks.

sera tamen tacitis pœna venit pedibus (*L*) Punishment though late comes nevertheless on noiseless feet. Tibullus — *Carmina, I, 9, 4.*

serein (*F*) Mist arising after sunset.

seriatim (*N. L*) In series.

seron (*Sp.*) Pannier, hamper.

sero venientibus ossa (*L*) To the latecomers, bones. Proverb.

sesqui- (*L*) One and a half.

sesquipedalia verba (*L*) Words a foot and a half long.

se tirer d'affaire (*F*) To get out of a difficulty.

sforzando (*It.*) Forcing, [mus.] with sudden force.

sfumato (*It.*) Smoked, [painting] blended, of vague outlines.

sgraffito (*It.*) Designs scratched through plaster on a differently covered ground. Also *graffito.*

shah (*Pers.*) Ruler.

shaitan (*Arab.*) Evil spirit, devil.

shamianah (*Pers.*) Awning, flat tent roof.

sherif (*Arab.*) Noble, Arab chieftain. Also *shereef.*

shikari (*Hind.*) Hunter, sportsman.

shizoku (*Jap.-Chin.*) Japanese warrior class, gentry.

sic (*L*) Thus.

sic itur ad astra (*L*) Thus the way leads to the stars. Vergil — *Æneid, IX, 641.*

sic passim (*L*) Thus here and there, so in different places.

sic transit gloria mundi (*L*) Thus passes the glory of the world.

sicut ante (*L*) Just as before.

sic volo sic jubeo (*L*) Thus I will thus I command. Juvenal — *Satires, VI, 223.*

sic vos non vobis (*L*) Thus you (work) but not for yourselves. Vergil — *Lines on Bathyllus.*

siesta (*Sp.*) After-dinner nap.

signor (*It.*) Sir, Mr.

signora (*It.*) Madam, lady.

signorina (*It.*) Miss, unmarried woman.

si jeunesse savait! si vieillesse pouvait! (*F*) If youth knew; if age could!

silent leges inter arma (*L*) Laws are silent in the midst of arms. Cicero — *For Milo, IV, 10.*

s'il vous plaît (*F*) If you please, please.

simagrée (*F*) False show.

similia similibus curantur (*L*) Like things are cured by like.

simplex munditiis (*L*) Of simple smartness. Horace — *Odes, I, 5, 5.*

sine cura (*L*) Without cure (of souls; said of a *benefice*).

sine die (*L*) Without any day (being set).

sine ictu (*L*) Without a blow.

sine prole (*L*) Without offspring, childless.

sine qua non (*L*) Without which not, something absolutely necessary.

sinistra (*It.*) Left.

sinistra mano (*It.*) [Mus.] Left hand.

sinistra manu (*L*) With the left hand.

si peccavi, insciens feci (*L*) If I have sinned I have done so unwittingly. Terence — *Heauton Timorumenos, IV, 1, 18, (63).*

si qua voles apte nubere nube pari (*L*) If you wish to marry well, marry an equal. Ovid — *Heroides, IX, 32.*

sirkar (*Ang.-Ind.*) Supreme authority, (Bengal) steward. Also *sircar.*

si sic omnes! (*L*) If all (did) thus!

siste, viator (*L*) Stop, traveler.

sit pro ratione voluntas (*L*) Let will stand for reason. Juvenal — *Satires, VI, 223.*

sit tibi terra levis (*L*) May the earth be light upon thee.

si vis amari ama (*L*) If you wish to be loved, love. Seneca — *Epistles, IX.*

si vis pacem para bellum (*L*) If you wish peace, prepare for war. After Vegetius.

sjambok (*S. African Dut.*) Heavy leather whip. Compare *chabuk.*

sobriquet (*F*) Derisive nickname.

socius criminis (*L*) Accomplice in crime.

soi-disant (*F*) Self-styled, pretended.

soirée (*F*) Evening, evening party.

sola topi (*Bengali and Hind.*) Pith helmet.

solfeggio (*It.*) [Mus.] Singing exercise in sol-fa system.

sollerets (*F*) Flexible steel shoes in medieval armor. Also *solerets.*

solus (*L*) Alone, sole.

somnus (*L*) Sleep.

sonata (*It.*) [Mus.] Instrumental composition of several movements.

Sonderbund (*G*) Separate league, League of the Roman Catholic Cantons of Switzerland.

σοφός (*Gr.*) Wise, knowing.

sordamente (*It.*) Dully, [mus.] in a muffled manner.

sordes (*L*) Dirt, filth.

sordino (*It.*) [Mus.] Mute.

sordo (*It.*) Deaf, dull, [mus.] muffled with a mute.

s'orienter (*F*) To orient one's self, to get one's bearings.

soror (*L*) Sister.

sortes (*L*) Lots.

sortes Vergilianæ (*L*) Vergilian lots, book divination out of Vergil.

sostenuto (*It.*) [Mus.] Sustained, in a sustained manner.

sot à triple étage (*F*) Stupid to the third degree, utterly fatuous .

sotnia (*Rus.*) Hundred, division of a hundred men.

sotto voce (*It.*) Under the voice, whispered.

sou (*F*) Five centimes, farthing.

soubrette (*F*) Chamber-maid, particularly as a character in comedy.

soufflé (*F*) Blown up, light pastry-like dish.

soupçon (*F*) Suspicion, trace, very small quantity.

soupe maigre (*F*) Thin soup, meatless soup.

sourdine (*F*) [Mus.] Mute. Also *sourdet.*

sous tous les rapports (*F*) In all respects.

sowar (*Ang.-Ind.*) Horseman. Urdu and Persian *sawar.*

spahi (*F*) Irregular Turkish cavalryman, Algerian cavalryman of the French army. Turkish *sipahi.*

spargere voces in vulgum ambiguas (*L*) To spread deceptive reports among the people. Vergil — *Æneid, II, 98.*

sparsim (*L*) Scattered here and there.

speciali gratia (*L*) By special favor.

spécialité (*F*) Specialty.

spero meliora (*L*) I hope for better things. Cicero.

spes sibi quisque (*L*) Let each be a hope unto himself. Vergil — *Æneid, II, 309.*

σπεῦδε βραδέως (*Gr.*) Make haste slowly. Proverb.

spicelegium (*L*) Gleaning.

spiritoso (*It.*) [Mus.] With spirit, lively.

spirituel (*F*) Spiritual, witty.

spiritus (*L*) Breath of life, spirit.

splendide mendax (*L*) Nobly untruthful. Horace — *Odes, III, 11, 35.*

spolia opima (*L*) Richest spoils. Livy.

sportula (*L*) Lawyer's fee, gratuity.

sposare Gesu (*It.*) To wed Jesus Christ, to become a nun.

spretæ injuria formæ (*L*) Insult to beauty despised. Vergil — *Æneid, I, 27.*

staccato (*It.*) [Mus.] Disconnected, with distinct pauses between notes.

stafetta (*It.*) Express messenger.

stare fresco (*It.*) To be in a fix.

stare super antiquas vias (*L*) To stand on ancient ways, to be conservative.

status quo (*L*) The state in which, unchanged.

status quo ante bellum (*L*) The state in which (matters were) before the war.

stet (*L*) Let it stand.

sthula sharira (*Sansk.*) [Theos.] Physical body.

stiacciato (*It.*) [Sculp.] Very low relief.

stimulos dedit æmula virtus (*L*) Valor stirred by rivalry applies the spurs. Lucan — *Pharsalia, I, 120.*

stoep (*S. African Dut.*) Porch, roofed platform before a house.

storge (στοργή, *Gr.*) Affection.

striæ (*L*) Grooves, furrows.

strictum jus (*L*) Strict law, letter of the law.

strigæ (*L*) Furrows, bristles.

stultorum plena sunt omnia (*L*) Fools everywhere. Cicero — *Letters, IX, 22.*

stupa (*Sansk.*) Tope, Buddhist monument.

Sturm und Drang (*G*) Storm and stress.

sua cuique utilitas (*L*) To everything its own use. Tacitus — *History, I, 15.*

sua cuique voluptas (*L*) Each to his own pleasure.

suave mari magno (*L*) It is pleasant, on the open sea. Lucretius — *De Rerum Natura, II, 1.*

suaviter in modo (*L*) Gently in manner. Aquaviva — *Industriæ ad Curandos Animæ Morbos.*

suaviter in modo, fortiter in re (*L*) Gently in manner, boldly in deed. Aquaviva — *Industriæ ad Curandos Animæ Morbos.*

subahdar (*Hind.*) Ruler of a *subah*, local commandant. Also *subadar.*

subaudi (*L*) Supply the missing words; read between the lines.

sub die (*L*) Under the day, out-of-doors.

subito (*It.*) Immediately, suddenly.

sub Jove (*L*) Beneath Jove, in the open air.

sub judice (*L*) Under the judge, under judicial consideration.

sublimi feriam sidera vertice (*L*) I shall strike the stars with my exalted head. Horace — *Odes, I, 1, 36.*

subpœna (*L*) Under penalty, [law] a writ exacting presence at court.

sub rosa (*L*) Under the rose, secretly.

sub silentio (*L*) In silence.

sub specie (*L*) Under the form of.

sub spe rati (*L*) In the hope of a decision.

sub voce (*L*) Under the word, under the heading, s. v.

succès d'estime (*F*) Success critically rather than financially.

suerte (*Sp.*) Chance, lot.

suerte está echada (*Sp.*) The die is cast.

suggestio falsi (*L*) A suggestion of the false. Compare *suppressio veri suggestio falsi.*

sui generis (*L*) Of its own kind, unique.

suisse (*F*) Swiss guard, Swiss footman, head beadle of a church.

suivre son penchant (*F*) To follow one's bent.

summa petit livor (*L*) Envy seeks the highest things of all. Ovid — *Remedy for Love, 369.*

summum bonum (*L*) The greatest good.

summum jus (*L*) The supreme law.

sumo (*Jap.*) Japanese wrestling.

sunyasi (*Ang.-Ind.*) [Hinduism] Person devoted to asceticism and meditation. Compare *sannyasi.* Also *sunyasee.*

suo Marte (*L*) By one's own exertions.

suo motu (*L*) Of its own motion.

suo periculo (*L*) At one's own peril.

suo sibi gladio hunc jugulo (*L*) I cut this man's throat with his own sword; I beat him at his own game. Terence— *Adelphi, V, 8, 35.*

supercherie (*F*) Calculated deceit.

superstitione tollenda religio non tollitur (*L*) Religion is not removed by the removal of superstition. Cicero — *De Divinatione, II, 72.*

suppressio veri (*L*) Suppression of the truth.

suppressio veri suggestio falsi (*L*) Suppressing the truth is suggesting the false.

surgit amari aliquid (*L*) Something bitter arises. Lucretius — *De Rerum Natura, IV, 1133.*

sur le pavé (*F*) On the street, homeless.

sur le tapis (*F*) On the cloth, under consideration.

sursum corda (*L*) Lift up your hearts.

surveillance (*F*) Watch, watchfulness.

suttee (*Ang.-Ind.*) The act of self-immolation on the funeral pyre of one's husband. Hindustani *sati — faithful wife.*

suum cuique (*L*) To each his own.

syce (*Ang.-Ind.*) Groom. Hindustani and Arabic *sais.*

T

tabes (*L*) Wasting away.

tableau (*F*) Painting, list, live picture.

tableau vivant (*F*) Living picture, tableau.

table d'hôte (*F*) (Host's table), fixed price in serving meals. Compare *à la carte*.

tablier (*F*) Apron.

tablinum (*L*) Balcony, recess for archives.

tabula rasa (*L*) Smooth tablet, clean slate.

tace! (*L*) Be silent, hush!

tacent satis laudant (*L*) They are silent, they give sufficient praise; their silence is praise enough. Terence — *Eunuchus, III, 2, 23*.

tacitum vivit sub pectore vulnus (*L*) The wound rankles in the breast unknown. Vergil — *Æneid, IV, 67*.

tædium vitæ (*L*) Tediousness of life. Aulus Gellius — *VII, 18, 11*.

tailleur (*F*) Cutter, tailor.

tais-toi! (*F*) Keep still!

talapoin (*Port.*) (Ceylon and Indo-China) Buddhist priest.

talmouse (*F*) A sort of pastry.

tamasha (*Ang.-Ind.*) Entertainment, pageant.

tangere ulcus (*L*) To touch a sore spot. Terence — *Phormio, IV, 4, 19*.

tantæne animis cælestibus iræ? (*L*) Can celestial minds (harbor) such wrath? Vergil — *Æneid, I, 11*.

tantas componere lites (*L*) To settle such great quarrels.

tante (*F*) Aunt.

tanti (*L*) Of so much (importance).

tant mieux (*F*) So much the better.

tanto buon che val niente (*It.*) What is worth nothing is just so good; what costs nothing is worth nothing.

tant pis (*F*) So much the worst.

tant s'en faut (*F*) (So much is lacking), far from it.

tant soit peu (*F*) Ever so little.

tantus amor scribendi (*L*) Such a passion for writing. Horace — *Satires, II, 1, 10*.

tant va la cruche à l'eau qu'à la fin elle se brise (*F*) However many times the jug goes for water it is broken at last.

tapis (*F*) Carpet.

tarantella (*It.*) Neapolitan dance of a whirling type.

tardamente (*It.*) [Mus.] Slowly.

tarde quæ credita lædunt credimus (*L*) We are slow to believe what when believed hurts. Ovid — *Heroides, II, 9*.

tartane (*F*) Single-masted boat used in the Mediterranean.

tâtonner (*F*) To grope.

Taubenpost (*G*) Pigeon post.

Tausch ist kein Raub (*G*) Fair exchange is no robbery.

tavarishch (*Rus.*) Comrade.

tazza (*It.*) Cup.

Te Deum (*L*) Thee, Lord. (From ancient hymn *Te Deum laudamus — Thee, Lord, we praise.*)

tekel upharsin (*Heb.*) Found wanting. Compare *mene, mene, tekel upharsin — weighed, weighed, and found wanting.* (Translation uncertain.) *Daniel, V, 25*.

tel maître tel valet (*F*) Like master, like valet.

teloque animus præstantior omni (*L*) A mind is more excellent than every weapon; brain is better than brawn. Ovid — *Metamorphoses, III, 54*.

tel père tel fils (*F*) Like father, like son.

telum imbelle (*L*) Missile unfit for war.

tempête dans un verre d'eau (*F*) Tempest in a glass of water, tempest in a teapot.

tempi passati (*It.*) Times past, days gone by.

tempora mutantur nos et mutamur in illis (*L*) Times change and we change with them. Emperor Lothaire I — *Delitiæ Poetarum Germanorum*.

tempori parendum (*L*) One must yield to his time. Theodosius II.

temporis ars medecina fere est (*L*) The art of medicine is usually a matter of time. Ovid — *Remedy for Love, 131*.

tempus edax rerum (*L*) Time (is) the devourer of things. Ovid — *Metamorphoses, XV, 234*.

tempus fugit (*L*) Time flies. Vergil — *Georgics, III, 284*.

tenax propositi (*L*) Steadfast of purpose. Horace — *Odes, III, 3, 1*.

tenez! (*F*) Hold, wait a minute!

tenir quelqu'un le bec dans l'eau (*F*) To offer anyone false hopes.

tenir quelqu'un sur le tapis (*F*) To make anyone a subject of conversation.

tentanda via est (*L*) The way must be tried. Vergil — *Georgics, III, 8*.

tente d'abri (*F*) Shelter-tent.

teres atque rotundus (*L*) Polished and well-rounded. Horace — *Satires, II, 7, 83*. Compare *in se ipso totus teres atque rotundus*.

terminus ad quem (*L*) The limit to which.

terminus a quo (*L*) The limit from which, starting-point.

ter quaterque beatus (*L*) Thrice and four times blessed. Vergil — *Æneid, I, 94*.

terra (*L*) Ground, earth.

terræ filius (*L*) Son of the soil.

terra firma (*L*) Solid earth, dry land.

terra incognita (*L*) Unknown land, unexplored country.

terre verte (*F*) Green earth.

tertium quid (*L*) A third something.

terzetto (*It.*) [Mus.] Vocal trio

tesseræ (*L*) Small stone blocks, markers, tickets, dice.

testamur (*L*) We bear witness, we testify.

tête-à-tête (*F*) Head to head, confidential chat between two persons.

tête baissée (*F*) Head lowered, impetuous.

tête exaltée (*F*) Over-excited.

tête montée (*F*) Excited.

tetigisti acu (*L*) You have touched it with a needle; you have hit the nail on the head. Plautus — *Rudens, V, 2, 19.*

thakur (*Hind.*) Idol.

θάλαττα! θάλαττα! (*Gr.*) The sea, the sea! Xenophon—*Anabasis, IV, 7.*

thana (*Hind.*) Police station.

thé dansant (*F*) Tea-dance.

θεὸς ἐκ μηχανῆς (*Gr.*) A God from the machine, [drama] mechanical contrivance in supernatural effects.

tibi seris tibi metis (*L*) You sow for yourself, you reap for yourself; as ye sow, so shall ye reap. Cicero.

Tiergarten (*G*) Zoölogical garden, public park.

tiers état (*F*) The third estate of France, commonalty.

tige (*F*) Stem, shaft.

timeo Danaos et dona ferentes (*L*) I fear the Greeks bringing gifts. Vergil — *Æneid, II, 49.*

tirailleur (*F*) Rifleman, sniper.

tiré à quatre épingles (*F*) Drawn to four pins, dressed with extreme care.

tirer d'affaire (*F*) To rescue from a difficulty.

tirer le diable par la queue (*F*) To pull the devil by the tail, to find it hard going.

toccata (*It.*) (Touched), [mus.] improvisation.

toccatella (*It.*) [Mus.] Short *toccata.* Also *toccatina.*

toga virilis (*L*) Toga of manhood worn only by adults.

toile (*F*) Cloth, fabric.

to kalon (τὸ καλόν, *Gr.*) The beautiful.

tombé des nues (*F*) Fallen from the clouds, supernatural.

ton (*F*) Tone, style.

tong (*Chin.*) Chinese secret society.

tonga (*Ang.-Ind.*) Light two-wheeled vehicle.

tope (*Ang.-Ind.*) Clump of trees. Telugu *topu.*

topi (*Hind.*) Hat, esp. sun-helmet.

to prepon (τὸ πρέπον, *Gr.*) The seemly, propriety.

Totentanz (*G*) Death-dance.

totidem verbis (*L*) In so many words.

toties quoties (*L*) As often as.

totis viribus (*L*) With all one's forces.

toto cœlo (*L*) By the whole sky.

toujours perdrix (*F*) Always partridge, too much of a good thing.

tour de force (*F*) Feat of strength.

tourner casaque (*F*) To turn cloak, to change parties.

tournure (*F*) Way in which a person is made, figure.

tous frais faits (*F*) All expenses paid.

tous songes sont mensonges (*F*) All dreams are lies.

tout à fait (*F*) Altogether, entirely.

tout à l'heure (*F*) Presently.

tout au contraire (*F*) Quite the contrary, wholly opposite.

tout à vous (*F*) All to you, sincerely yours.

tout bien ou rien (*F*) Everything well or nothing at all.

tout comprendre c'est tout pardonner (*F*) To understand everything is to pardon everything. Madame de Staël.

tout court (*F*) Absolutely short, briefly.

tout de suite (*F*) Immediately.

tout ensemble (*F*) All together.

tout est perdu hors l'honneur (*F*) All is lost save honor.

tout le monde (*F*) All the world, everyone.

tout vient à temps pour qui sait attendre (*F*) All comes in time to him who knows how to wait. Also *tout vient à point à qui sait attendre.*

tracasserie (*F*) Bother, worry.

tragédien (*F*) Tragedian, player of tragic parts.

trahit sua quemque voluptas (*L*) Each one is carried away by his own desire. Vergil — *Eclogues, II, 65.*

traiter de haut en bas (*F*) To treat scornfully.

tranchant (*F*) Cutting, decisive.

tranchée (*F*) Trench, ditch.

transeat in exemplum (*L*) Let it pass for an example.

transi de froid (*F*) Overcome with cold.

trecento (*It.*) (Three hundred), fourteenth century.

trek (*S. African Dut.*) To journey by wagon.

trekker (*S. African Dut.*) A traveler by wagon.

tria juncta in uno (*L*) Three joined in one. Motto of the Order of the Bath.

τρικυμία (*Gr.*) Third wave, largest wave.

Trinkgeld (*G*) Drink-money, tip.

tripotage (*F*) Senseless jumble.

tripsis (τρῦψις, *Gr.*) Rubbing, pulverizing.

triste (*F*) Sad, gloomy.

trocha (*Sp.*) Path across a highway.

troppo disputare la verità fa errore (*It.*) It is a mistake to argue too much about the truth.

trottoir (*F*) Sidewalk.

trou de loup (*F*) Wolf den, [mil.] trapholes containing pointed stakes.

trouvaille (*F*) Find, discovery.

trouvère (*F*) Medieval poet.

truditur dies die (*L*) The day is pushed on by a day; one day makes way for another. Horace — *Odes, II, 18, 15*.

tsarevna (*Rus.*) Daughter of the Czar of Russia.

tuba (*L*) Trumpet.

tulipe noir (*F*) Black tulip, rarity.

tu quoque (*L*) You too.

Turnerfest (*G*) Gymnastic meeting.

Turnverein (*G*) Gymnastic society.

tutamen (*L*) Defence, protection.

tutto di novello par bello (*It.*) Everything new seems beautiful.

tuum est (*L*) It is yours.

tuyère (*F*) Entrance for the blast pipes in a furnace.

tympani (*It.*) [Mus.] Drums, percussion instruments.

U

u babui volos dolog, da um korotok (*Rus.*) A woman's hair is long but her understanding is short.

uberrima fides (*L*) Most copious faith.

ubi libertas ibi patria (*L*) Where there is freedom there is one's fatherland.

ubi mel ibi apes (*L*) Where the honey is there are the bees. Plautus.

ubi supra (*L*) Where above, in the place mentioned above.

ulema (*Arab.*) (One who knows), Moslem doctors of sacred law.

ultima ratio (*L*) The final argument, force.

ultima ratio regum (*L*) The final argument of kings, force.

ultima Thule (*L*) Farthest Thule, farthest limit. Vergil — *Georgics, I, 30*.

ultimo (*L*) In the last month.

ultimus Romanorum (*L*) The last of the Romans.

ultra (*L*) Beyond, farther, more.

ultra crepidam (*L*) Beyond the last, beyond one's depth. Compare *ne sutor supra crepidam judicaret*.

ultra vires (*L*) Beyond one's power.

umbra (*L*) Shade.

una nuova scopa spazza bene (*It.*) A new broom sweeps clean.

un à-propos (*F*) Something said or done, opportunely.

un averti en vaut deux (*F*) A person warned is equal to two; forewarned is forearmed.

una voce (*L*) With one voice.

un bienfait n'est jamais perdu (*F*) A kindness is never lost.

und so weiter (*G*) And so forth, et cetera, u. s. w.

unguibus et rostro (*L*) With claws and beak.

un homme de bonne foi (*F*) An honest man, a man of fair dealing.

un impromptu fait à loisir (*F*) An impromptu composed at leisure.

uno animo (*L*) With one mind, with one accord.

uno saltu (*L*) At one leap, abruptly.

un petit brouillon et troublefeste (*F*) A little meddlesome killjoy. Paul Scarron — *Sagesse*.

un peu fort (*F*) A little strong.

un pur sang (*F*) A pedigreed horse, a thoroughbred.

urbem latericiam invenit marmoream reliquit (*L*) He found the city built of brick, left it built of marble. Suetonius — *Augustus Cæsar, 28*.

urbi et orbi (*L*) To the city (Rome) and to the world, (form of issue of papal documents).

urceus (*L*) Pitcher, urn.

usine (*F*) Factory.

usque ad nauseam (*L*) Even to nausea.

usus loquendi (*L*) Practice of speaking.

utile dulci (*L*) The useful with the agreeable. Horace — *Ars Poetica, 343*.

ut infra (*L*) As below, u. i.

uti possidetis (*L*) As you now possess, [law] interdict allowing actual possessor to retain property.

V

vache (*F*) Cow, cow-hide traveling trunk.

vade in pace (*L*) Go in peace. Vulgate — *Exodus, IV, 18*.

vade mecum (*L*) Go with me, manual.

vadium mortuum (*L*) (Dead bail), [law] mortgage.

væ victis! (*L*) Woe to the vanquished! Plautus — *Pseudolus, V, 2, 35*.

vairagi, see *bairagi*.

vakass (*Armenian.*) Eucharistic vestment in the Armenian Church. Also *vakas* and *vagas*.

vakil (*Hind.*) Native commissioner. Also *vakeel*.

vale (*L*) Farewell.

valeat quantum (*L*) How much it may be worth.

valeat quantum valere potest (*L*) Let it be valued at what it may be worth. Proverb.

valet ancora virtus (*L*) Virtue serves as an anchor.

valet de chambre (*F*) Valet, personal servant.

valet de place (*F*) Local guide, courier.

valete et plaudite (*L*) Farewell and applaud.

vallum (*L*) Rampart.

valse (*F*) Waltz.

va, mouche, laisse-moi tranquille (*F*) Shoo, fly, don't bother me.

vanitas vanitatum (*L*) Vanity of vanities. Vulgate — *Ecclesiastes, I, 2.*

vaquero (*Mex. Sp.*) Herdsman, cowboy.

vara (*Sp. and Port.*) (Pole), yard.

vargueno (*Sp.*) Box-like cabinet.

varia lectio (*L*) Variant reading.

variorum notæ (*L*) Notes of various commentators.

varium et mutabile semper femina (*L*) Woman is ever a fickle and changeable thing. Vergil — *Æneid, IV, 569.*

varuna (*Sansk.*) Heaven, sky.

va-t'en! (*F*) Go away, get out!

vaurien (*F*) Good-for-nothing.

veau (*F*) Calf, veal.

vectigalia nervos esse rei publicæ (*L*) Revenues are the sinews of the state. Cicero — *Manilian Law, VII.*

vedi Napoli e poi muori (*It.*) See Naples and then die.

vega (*Sp.*) Open plain, meadow.

veilleuse (*F*) Small night lamp.

veldtschoen (*S. African Dut.*) Footgear worn in the African plains.

velis et remis (*L*) With sails and oars, with all speed.

veloce (*It.*) [Mus.] In fast tempo.

vel prece vel pretio (*L*) By either prayer or bribe.

velumen (*L*) Fleece.

veluti in speculum (*L*) As in a glass.

vendaval (*Sp.*) Gale, strong wind.

vendetta (*It.*) Revenge, feud.

venenum in auro bibitur (*L*) Poison is drunk from golden cups. Seneca — *Thyestes, III, 453.*

veniam petimusque damusque vicissim (*L*) We seek pardon for ourselves and in turn give it (to others).

venienti occurrere morbo (*L*) To meet the disease as it comes. Persius — *Satires, III, 64.*

venire (*L*) To come.

venire facias (*L*) Have them come, [law] writ to summon a jury.

veni, vidi, vici (*L*) I came, I saw, I conquered. Suetonius — *Julius Cæsar, 37.*

ventilabrum (*L*) Winnowing fan.

ventre à terre (*F*) Belly to the ground, with all speed.

vera incessu patuit dea (*L*) The true goddess was revealed by her gait. Vergil — *Æneid, I, 405.*

vera prosperità è non aver necessità (*It.*) True prosperity is not to feel need.

verbatim et literatim (*L*) Word for word and letter for letter.

verbis ad verbera (*L*) From words to blows.

verbum inane perit (*L*) The empty word perishes.

verbum sapienti (*L*) A word to the wise.

verbum sat sapienti (*L*) A word to the wise is sufficient.

Verein (*G*) Society, club.

veritas nunquam perit (*L*) Truth never dies.

veritas odium parit (*L*) Truth bears hate. Ausonius — *Bias, 3.*

veritatem dies aperit (*L*) Time reveals the truth.

veritatis simplex oratio est (*L*) The language of truth is simple. Seneca — *Letters, XLIX.*

vérité sans peur (*F*) Truth without fear.

Vernunft (*G*) Reason.

verre (*F*) Glass.

vers libre (*F*) Free verse.

Verstand (*G*) Understanding, intelligence.

versus (*L*) Against.

vesica piscis (*L*) (Fish bladder), [painting] oval auriole enclosing a sacred personage.

vestigia nulla retrorsum (*L*) No steps backward. Horace — *Epistles, I, 1, 74.*

vetera extollimus recentium incuriosi (*L*) Neglectful of recent events we praise what is old. Tacitus — *Annals, II, 298.*

veteris vestigia flammæ (*L*) Vestiges of the old flame. Vergil — *Æneid, IV, 23.*

vettura (*It.*) Traveling carriage.

vetturino (*It.*) Coachman.

vexata quæstio (*L*) Mooted question.

via (*L*) Way, road.

via lactea (*L*) The Milky Way.

via media (*L*) Middle course.

via trita, via tuta (*L*) The beaten path, the safe path.

vice versa (*L*) With the course changed, conversely, in reverse order.

victrix fortunæ sapientia (*L*) Wisdom is the victor over fortune. Juvenal — *Satires, XIII, 20.*

vida sin amigo muerte sin testigo (*Sp.*) Life without a friend, death without a witness.

vide ante (*L*) See before.

vide et crede (*L*) See and believe.

vide infra (*L*) See below, v. i.

videlicet (*L*) It may be seen, evidently.

vide post (*L*) See after, see the following.

vide supra (*L*) See above, v. s.

vide ut supra (*L*) See as above.

vielle (*F*) Viol, medieval predecessor of the violin.

vi et armis (*L*) By force of arms.

vigneron (*F*) Vine culturist.

vigoroso (*It.*) [Mus.] Vigorous, with vigor.

vigueur de dessus (*F*) Strength from above.

villeggiatura (*It.*) Sojourn at a villa, country visit.

vina (*Hind.*) Guitar-like instrument. Also *bina.*

vincet amor patriæ laudumque immensa cupido (*L*) Love of country and thirst for praise will prevail. Vergil — *Æneid, VI, 823.*

vincit qui patitur (*L*) He conquers who endures.

vincit qui se vincit (*L*) He conquers who conquers himself. Proverb.

vinculum matrimonii (*L*) Bond of matrimony.

vin d'honneur (*F*) Wine of honor, wine presented officially to a distinguished guest.

vingt et un (*F*) (Twenty-one), card game. Also *vingt-un.*

vin ordinaire (*F*) Ordinary wine, cheap wine.

vino tortus et ira (*L*) Racked by wine and anger. Horace — *Epistles, I, 18, 38.*

viola d'amore (*It.*) Viol of love, bass viol of the seventeenth century.

viola da gamba (*It.*) "Leg" viol, six-stringed forerunner of violoncello.

violone (*It.*) Double-bass viol.

vires acquirit eundo (*L*) It gains strength as it goes. Vergil — *Æneid, IV, 175.*

virginibus puerisque (*L*) For maids and boys. Horace — *Odes, III, 1, 4.*

Virgo Clemens (*L*) Virgin Most Merciful.

Virgo Gloriosa (*L*) Virgin Most Glorious.

Virgo Potens (*L*) Virgin Most Powerful.

Virgo Prædicanda (*L*) Virgin Most Renowned.

Virgo Sapientissima (*L*) Virgin Most Wise.

Virgo Sponsa Dei (*L*) Virgin Bride of the Lord.

Virgo Veneranda (*L*) Virgin Most Venerable.

virtus (*L*) Virtue, valor.

virtus ariete fortior (*L*) Valor is stronger than a battering ram.

virtus laudatur et alget (*L*) Virtue is praised and freezes.

virtus vincit invidiam (*L*) Virtue conquers envy. Proverb.

virtutis fortuna comes (*L*) Good fortune is the comrade of virtue.

virum volitare per ora (*L*) To fly in the mouths of men. Ennius.

vis a fronte (*L*) Force from in front.

vis a tergo (*L*) Force from behind.

vis-à-vis (*F*) Facing, opposite; two-seated carriage.

vis comica (*L*) Comic power, talent for comedy. Suetonius — *Caius Cæsar.*

vis conservatrix (*L*) Preserving force.

visé (*F*) Visa, consular endorsement of passport.

vis inertiæ (*L*) Power of inertia.

vis medicatrix (*L*) Power to heal.

vis medicatrix naturæ (*L*) The healing power of nature.

vis mortua (*L*) Dead force, counteracted energy.

vis naturæ (*L*) Strength of nature.

vis vitæ (*L*) Force of life.

vis viva (*L*) Living force.

vitam impendere vero (*L*) To devote one's life to the truth. Juvenal — *Satires, IV, 91.*

viva! (*It.*) Hurrah, long life!

vivace (*It.*) Vivacious, [mus.] in a brisk manner.

vivandier (*F*) Military provisioner, sutler.

vivandière (*F*) Female military provisioner.

vivat regina! (*L*) Long live the queen!

vivat rex! (*L*) Long live the king!

viva voce (*L*) With the living voice, out loud.

vive! (*F*) Live, long live!

vivè et crede! (*F*) Live and believe!

vive la bagatelle! (*F*) Long live nonsense!

vive le roi! (*F*) Long live the king!

vive memor leti (*L*) Live mindful of death. Persius — *Satires, V, 153.*

vivendi causa (*L*) Cause of living, source of life.

vivere est cogitare (*L*) To think is to live. Cicero — *Tusculan Disputations, V, 30.*

vive valeque (*L*) Live and farewell, good-bye. Horace — *Satires, II, 5, 110.*

vivit post funera virtus (*L*) Virtue lives after death. Tiberius Cæsar.

vivre ce n'est pas respirer c'est agir (*F*) Living is not breathing but doing. J. J. Rousseau.

vlei (*S. African.*) Depression, swamp.

voce di testa (*It.*) Head voice, high voice.

vogue la galère (*F*) Row the galley on, let come what may.

voilà! (*F*) There, there you are, look!

voilà tout (*F*) That's all.

voir en couleur rose (*F*) To see in rose color, to be optimistic.

voir le dessous des cartes (*F*) To see the under side of the cards, to be in the secret.

voiture (*F*) Carriage, vehicle.

voiturier (*F*) Driver, coachman.

volant (*F*) Flying.

volat hora per orbem (*F*) Time flies through the world.

vol-au-vent (*F*) Patty shell.

Volk der Dichter und Denker (*G*) Folk of writers and thinkers.

volte-face (*F*) About face.

voltigeur (*F*) Loose-rope walker.

voluptates commendat rarior usus (*L*) A more rare indulgence in pleasures enhances them. Juvenal — *Satires, XI, 208.*

voodoo (*Creole F.*) A system of sorcery.

voorlooper (*Dut.*) Forerunner.

voortrekker (*Dut.*) Forerunner.

Vorspiel (*G*) Fore-play, prelude.

vorstellen (*G*) To perform, to represent.

Vorstellung (*G*) Presentation, performance.

vouloir prendre la lune avec les dents (*F*) To wish to seize the moon with one's teeth, to attempt the impossible.

vouloir rompre l'anguille au genou (*F*) To try to break the eel over the knee, to attempt the impossible.

Vous l'avez voulu, George Dandin (*F*) You wished it upon yourself, George Dandin. Molière — *George Dandin.*

vox audita perit littera scripta manet (*L*) The spoken word dies, the written letter remains.

vox et præterea nihil (*L*) A voice and nothing more.

vox faucibus hæsit (*L*) His voice stuck in his throat. Vergil — *Æneid, II, 774.*

vox populi (*L*) Voice of the people.

vox populi vox Dei (*L*) The voice of the people is the voice of God.

voyageur (*F*) Traveler, Canadian trapper.

vraisemblance (*F*) Appearance of truth, probability.

vriddhi (*Sansk.*) Increase, [gram.] lengthening the *guna* forms by prefixing an *a* element.

vrouw (*Dut.*) Woman, madam.

vulgo (*L*) Among the rabble, commonly.

vulgus amicitias utilitate probat (*L*) The common herd values friendships for their utility. Ovid — *Epistles from Pontus, II, 3, 8.*

vultus ariete fortior (*L*) Expression stronger than a battering ram.

vultus est index animi (*L*) The face is the index of the mind.

W

Wahrheit und Dichtung (*G*) Truth and poetry.

Wanderjahr (*G*) Year of wandering.

Wanderlust (*G*) Joy of wandering.

warum? (*G*) Why?

was ich nicht weiss macht mich nicht heiss (*G*) What I don't know doesn't bother me.

was man nicht kann meiden muss man willig leiden (*G*) One must bear willingly what he cannot avoid.

Wasser (*G*) Water.

Weltanschauung (*G*) View of the world, world philosophy.

Weltgeschichte (*G*) History of the world.

Weltschmerz (*G*) World-pain, idealistic dissatisfaction with the state of the world.

wer zuletzt lacht, lacht am besten (*G*) Who laughs last laughs best.

wie gewonnen so zerronnen (*G*) As won so lost, "easy come easy go."

Wirtshaus (*G*) Public house, inn.

womerah (*native word of New South Wales*). Throwing-stick.

Wörterbuch (*G*) Word-book, dictionary.

wun (*Burmese.*) (Burden), governor. Also *woon.*

Y

yashmak (*Arab.*) Veil of Moslem women.

yataghan (*Turk.*) Dagger-like sword. Also *ataghan.*

yogi (*Hind.*) Hindu ascetic, practiser of Yoga.

Z

zambomba (*Sp.*) Drum-like instrument.

zamindar (*Pers.*) (India) native landlord. Also *zemindar.*

zamindari (*Pers.*) (India) land belonging to a zamindar. Also *zemindari.*

Zeitgeist (*G*) Spirit of the times.

zenana (*Pers.*) Belonging to women, (India) portion of the house reserved for women.

zingaro (*It.*) Gypsy.

Zollverein (*G*) Customs-union.

zonam perdidit (*L*) He has lost his money-belt. Horace — *Epistles, II, 2, 40.*

zum Beispiel (*G*) For example, z. B.

zwischen Freud und Leid ist die Brücke nicht weit (*G*) Between joy and sorrow the bridge is not wide.

zwischen uns sei Wahrheit (*G*) Let there be truth between us. Goethe — *Iphigenie.*

BASIC SYNONYMS

A

to ABANDON, desert, forsake, relinquish.
to ABANDON, resign, forego, give up.
to ABANDON, resign, renounce, abdicate.
ABANDONED, reprobate, profligate.
to ABASE, humble, degrade, disgrace, debase.
to ABASH, confound, confuse.
to ABATE, intermit, subside.
to ABATE, lessen, diminish, decrease.
ABATEMENT, deduction.
to ABDICATE, abandon, resign, renounce.
ABETTOR, accessary, accomplice.
to ABHOR, detest, abominate, loathe.
to ABIDE, sojourn, dwell, live, reside, inhabit.
ABILITY, capacity.
ABILITY, dexterity, address.
ABILITY, faculty, talent.
ABJECT, low, mean.
to ABJURE, recant, retract, revoke, recall.
ABLE, capable, capacious.
to ABOLISH, abrogate, repeal, revoke, annul, cancel.
ABOMINABLE, detestable, execrable.
to ABOMINATE, loathe, abhor, detest.
ABORTION, failure, miscarriage.
ABOVE, over, upon, beyond.
to ABRIDGE, curtail, contract.
to ABRIDGE, deprive, debar.
ABRIDGMENT, compendium, epitome, digest, summary, abstract.
to ABROGATE, repeal, revoke, annul, cancel, abolish.
ABRUPT, rugged, rough.
to ABSCOND, steal away, secrete one's self.
ABSENT, abstracted, abstract, diverted, distracted.
ABSOLUTE, despotic, arbitrary, tyrannical.
ABSOLUTE, peremptory, positive.
to ABSOLVE, acquit, clear.
to ABSOLVE, remit, forgive, pardon.
to ABSORB, swallow up, engulf, engross, imbibe.
to ABSTAIN, forbear, refrain.
ABSTEMIOUS, temperate, abstinent, sober.
ABSTINENCE, fast.
ABSTINENT, sober, abstemious, temperate.
to ABSTRACT, separate, distinguish.
ABSTRACT, abridgment, compendium, epitome, digest, summary.
ABSTRACT, diverted, distracted, absent, abstracted.
ABSTRACTED, abstract, diverted, distracted, absent.

ABSTRACTION, alienation, estrangement.
ABSURD, preposterous, irrational, foolish.
ABUNDANT, copious, ample, plentiful, plenteous.
to ABUSE, misuse.
ABUSE, invective.
ABUSIVE, scurrilous, reproachful.
ABYSS, gulf.

ACADEMY, school.
to ACCEDE, consent, comply, acquiesce, agree.
to ACCELERATE, speed, expedite, dispatch, hasten.
ACCENT, stress, strain, emphasis.
to ACCEPT, take, receive.
ACCEPTABLE, grateful, welcome.
ACCEPTANCE, acceptation.
ACCEPTATION, acceptance.
ACCESS, admittance, approach.
ACCESSARY, accomplice, abettor.
ACCESSION, augmentation, increase, addition.
ACCIDENT, adventure, occurrence, event, incident.
ACCIDENT, chance.
ACCIDENT, contingency, casualty.
ACCIDENTAL, incidental, casual, contingent.
ACCLAMATION, applause.
to ACCOMMODATE, adjust, fit, suit, adapt.
ACCOMPANIMENT, companion, concomitant.
to ACCOMPANY, attend, escort.
ACCOMPLICE, abettor, accessary.
ACCOMPLICE, confederate.
to ACCOMPLISH, effect, execute, achieve.
to ACCOMPLISH, realize, fulfill.
ACCOMPLISHED, perfect.
ACCOMPLISHMENT, qualification.
to ACCORD, suit, agree.
ACCORDANCE, melody, harmony.
ACCORDANT, consistent, consonant.
ACCORDINGLY, therefore, consequently.
to ACCOST, salute, address, greet, hail, welcome.
to ACCOUNT, count, number, reckon.
ACCOUNT, narrative, description.
ACCOUNT, reason, purpose, end, sake.
ACCOUNT, reckoning, bill.
ACCOUNTABLE, amenable, answerable, responsible.
to ACCUMULATE, amass, heap, pile.
ACCURATE, correct.
ACCURATE, exact, precise.
ACCUSATION, complain.

to ACCUSE, censure.
to ACCUSE, charge, impeach, arraign.
to ACHIEVE, accomplish, effect, execute.
ACHIEVEMENT, feat, deed, exploit.
to ACKNOWLEDGE, own, confess, avow.
ACKNOWLEDGE, recognize.
to ACQUAINT, apprize, inform, make known.
ACQUAINTANCE, familiarity, intimacy.
to ACQUIESCE, agree, accede, consent, comply.
to ACQUIRE, attain.
to ACQUIRE, obtain, gain, win, earn.
ACQUIREMENT, acquisition.
ACQUISITION, acquirement.
to ACQUIT, clear, absolve.
ACRIMONY, tartness, asperity, harshness.
to ACT, do, make.
to ACT, work, operate.
ACT, action, deed.
ACTION, agency.
ACTION, battle, combat, engagement.
ACTION, deed, act.
ACTION, gesture, gesticulation, posture, attitude.
ACTIVE, brisk, agile, nimble.
ACTIVE, busy, officious.
ACTIVE, diligent, industrious, assiduous, laborious.
ACTOR, agent.
ACTOR, player, performer.
ACTUAL, real, positive.
to ACTUATE, impel, induce.
ACUTE, keen, sharp.
ACUTE, keen, shrewd.
ACUTENESS, sagacity, penetration.

ADAGE, proverb, byword, saw, axiom, maxim, aphorism, apophthegm, saying.
to ADAPT, accommodate, adjust, fit, suit.
to ADD, join, unite, coalesce.
to ADDICT, devote, apply.
ADDITION, accession, augmentation, increase.
to ADDRESS, apply.
to ADDRESS, greet, hail, welcome, accost, salute.
ADDRESS, ability, dexterity.
ADDRESS, speech, harangue, oration.
ADDRESS, superscription, direction.
to ADDUCE, allege, assign, advance.
ADEQUATE, proportionate, commensurate.
to ADHERE, attach.
to ADHERE, stick, cleave.
ADHERENCE, adhesion.
ADHERENT, partisan, follower.
ADHESION, adherence.
ADJACENT, adjoining, contiguous.
ADJECTIVE, epithet.
ADJOINING, contiguous, adjacent.
to ADJOURN, prorogue.
to ADJUST, fit, suit, adapt, accommodate.
to ADMINISTER, contribute, minister.
ADMINISTRATION, government.

to ADMIRE, surprise, astonish, amaze, wonder.
ADMISSION, admittance.
to ADMIT, allow, grant.
to ADMIT, allow, permit, suffer, tolerate.
to ADMIT, receive.
ADMITTANCE, admission.
ADMITTANCE, approach, access.
to ADMONISH, advise.
ADMONITION, warning, caution.
to ADORE, reverence, venerate, revere.
to ADORE, worship.
to ADORN, decorate, embellish.
ADROIT, clever, skillful, expert, dexterous.
to ADULATE, flatter, compliment.
to ADVANCE, adduce, allege, assign.
to ADVANCE, proceed.
to ADVANCE, promote, prefer, forward, encourage.
ADVANCE, advancement, progress, progression.
ADVANCEMENT, progress, progression, advance.
ADVANTAGE, benefit, utility.
ADVANTAGE, good, benefit.
ADVANTAGE, profit.
ADVENTURE, occurrence, event, incident, accident.
ADVENTUROUS, enterprising.
ADVENTUROUS, rash, foolhardy.
ADVERSARY, opponent, antagonist, enemy, foe.
ADVERSE, averse.
ADVERSE, contrary, opposite.
ADVERSE, inimical, hostile, repugnant.
ADVERSITY, distress.
to ADVERTISE, publish.
ADVICE, counsel, instruction.
ADVICE, information, intelligence, notice.
to ADVISE, admonish.
ADVOCATE, pleader, defender.

AFFABLE, courteous.
AFFAIR, business, concern.
to AFFECT, assume.
to AFFECT, concern.
to AFFECT, pretend to.
AFFECTED, disposed.
AFFECTING, pathetic, moving.
AFFECTION, inclination, attachment.
AFFECTION, love.
AFFECTIONATE, kind, fond.
AFFINITY, alliance.
AFFINITY, consanguinity, kindred, relationship.
to AFFIRM, assert.
to AFFIRM, asseverate, assure, vouch, aver, protest.
to AFFIX, subjoin, attach, annex.
to AFFLICT, distress, trouble.
AFFLICTION, grief, sorrow.
AFFLUENCE, riches, wealth, opulence.

to AFFORD, give.
to AFFORD, spare.
to AFFORD, yield, produce.
AFFRAY, fray, quarrel.
AFFRONT, insult, outrage.
AFFRONT, offence, trespass, transgression, misdemeanor, misdeed.
AFRAID, fearful, timorous, timid.
AFTER, behind.

AGE, date, era, epoch, time, period.
AGE, generation.
AGED, old, elderly.
AGENCY, action.
AGENT, actor.
AGENT, factor.
AGENT, minister.
to AGGRAVATE, heighten, raise.
to AGGRAVATE, irritate, provoke, exasperate, tantalize.
AGGRESSOR, assailant.
AGILE, nimble, active, brisk.
to AGITATE, toss, shake.
AGITATION, trepidation, tremor, emotion.
AGONY, anguish, pain, pang.
AGONY, distress, anxiety, anguish.
to AGREE, accede, consent, comply, acquiesce.
to AGREE, accord, suit.
to AGREE, coincide, concur.
AGREEABLE, pleasant, pleasing.
AGREEABLE, suitable, conformable.
AGREEMENT, contract, covenant, compact, bargain.
AGRICULTURIST, farmer, husbandman.

to AID, succour, relieve, help, assist.
to AIM, aspire.
to AIM, point, level.
to AIM, strive, struggle, endeavor.
AIM, tendency, drift, scope.
AIM, object, end, view.
AIR, aspect, appearance.
AIR, manner.
AIR, mien, look.

ALACRITY, alertness.
ALARM, terror, fright, consternation.
ALERTNESS, alacrity.
ALIEN, stranger, foreigner.
ALIENATION, estrangement, abstraction.
ALIKE, like, uniform, equal, even, equable.
ALL, every, each.
ALL, whole.
to ALLAY, soothe, appease, mitigate, assuage.
to ALLEGE, assign, advance, adduce.
ALLEGORY, emblem, symbol, type, figure, metaphor.
ALLEGORY, parable.
to ALLEVIATE, relieve.
ALLIANCE, affinity.
ALLIANCE, league, confederacy.

to ALLOT, appoint, destine.
to ALLOT, assign, apportion, distribute.
to ALLOW, consent, permit.
to ALLOW, grant, admit.
to ALLOW, grant, bestow.
to ALLOW, permit, suffer, tolerate, admit.
ALLOWANCE, stipend, salary, wages, hire, pay.
to ALLUDE, refer, hint, suggest.
to ALLUDE To, glance at.
to ALLURE, invite, engage, attract.
to ALLURE, tempt, seduce, entice, decoy.
ALLUREMENTS, charms, attractions.
ALLY, confederate.
ALMANAC, ephemeris, calendar.
ALONE, solitary, lonely.
ALSO, likewise, too.
to ALTER, vary, change.
ALTERCATION, quarrel, difference, dispute.
ALTERNATE, successive.
ALWAYS, at all times, ever.

to AMASS, heap, pile, accumulate.
to AMAZE, wonder, admire, surprise, astonish.
AMBASSADOR, envoy, plenipotentiary, deputy.
AMBIGUOUS, equivocal.
AMENABLE, answerable, responsible, accountable.
to AMEND, correct, emend, improve, mend, better.
AMENDS, restoration, restitution, reparation.
AMENDS, satisfaction, recompense, remuneration, requital, reward, compensation.
AMIABLE, lovely, beloved.
AMICABLE, friendly.
AMOROUS, loving, fond.
AMPLE, plentiful, plenteous, abundant, copious.
AMPLE, spacious, capacious.
to AMUSE, beguile.
to AMUSE, divert, entertain.
AMUSEMENT, entertainment, diversion, sport, recreation, pastime.

ANATHEMA, malediction, curse, imprecation, execration.
ANCESTORS, forefathers, progenitors.
ANCIENT, antique, antiquated, old-fashioned, obsolete, old.
ANCIENTLY, in ancient times, formerly, in times past, in old times, in days of yore.
(IN) ANCIENT TIMES, anciently, formerly, in times past, in old times, in days of yore.
ANECDOTE, story.
ANECDOTES, memoirs, chronicles, annals.
ANGER, choler, rage, fury.
ANGER, disapprobation, displeasure.
ANGER, resentment, wrath, ire, indignation.
ANGLE, corner.

ANGRY, passionate, hasty.

ANGUISH, agony, distress, anxiety.

ANGUISH, pain, pang, agony.

ANIMADVERSION, criticism, stricture.

to ANIMADVERT, criticize, censure.

ANIMAL, brute, beast.

to ANIMATE, incite, impel, urge, stimulate, instigate, encourage.

to ANIMATE, inspire, enliven, cheer, exhilarate.

ANIMATION, life, vivacity, spirit.

ANIMOSITY, hostility, enmity.

ANNALS, anecdotes, memoirs, chronicles.

to ANNEX, affix, subjoin, attach.

ANNOTATION, commentary, remark, observation, comment, note.

to ANNOUNCE, proclaim, publish.

to ANNOY, molest, inconvenience.

ANSWER, reply, rejoinder, response.

ANSWERABLE, responsible, accountable, amenable.

ANSWERABLE, suitable, correspondent.

ANTAGONIST, enemy, foe, adversary, opponent.

ANTECEDENT, preceding, foregoing, previous, anterior, prior, former.

ANTERIOR, prior, former, antecedent, preceding, foregoing, previous.

to ANTICIPATE, prevent.

ANTIPATHY, dislike, hatred, repugnance, aversion.

ANTIQUATED, old-fashioned, obsolete, old, ancient, antique.

ANTIQUE, antiquated, old-fashioned, obsolete, old, ancient.

ANXIETY, anguish, agony, distress.

ANXIETY, care, solicitude.

ANY, some.

APARTMENTS, lodgings.

APATHY, indifference, insensibility.

to APE, mock, imitate, mimic.

APERTURE, cavity, opening.

APHORISM, apophthegm, saying, adage, proverb, byword, saw, axiom, maxim.

to APOLOGIZE, defend, justify, exculpate, excuse, plead.

APOPHTHEGM, saying, adage, proverb, byword, saw, axiom, maxim, aphorism.

to APPALL, dismay, daunt.

APPAREL, attire, array.

APPARENT, visible, clear, plain, obvious, evident, manifest.

APPARITION, phantom, spectre, ghost, vision.

to APPEAR, look.

to APPEAR, seem.

APPEARANCE, air, aspect.

APPEARANCE, semblance, show, outside.

to APPEASE, calm, pacify, quiet, still.

to APPEASE, mitigate, assuage, allay, soothe.

APPELLATION, title, denomination, name.

to APPLAUD, extol, praise, commend.

APPLAUSE, acclamation.

APPLICATION, study, attention.

to APPLY, addict, devote.

to APPLY, address.

to APPOINT, depute, constitute.

to APPOINT, destine, allot.

to APPOINT, order, prescribe, ordain.

to APPORTION, distribute, allot, assign.

to APPRAISE, appreciate, estimate, esteem.

to APPRECIATE, appraise, estimate, esteem.

to APPREHEND, conceive, suppose, imagine.

to APPREHEND, fear, dread.

to APPRIZE, inform, make known, acquaint.

APPRIZED, conscious, aware, on one's guard.

to APPROACH, approximate.

APPROACH, access, admittance.

APPROBATION, concurrence, assent, consent.

to APPROPRIATE, usurp, arrogate, assume, ascribe.

APPROPRIATE, particular, peculiar.

to APPROXIMATE, approach.

APT, meet, fit.

APT, prompt, ready.

ARBITER, arbitrator, judge, umpire.

ARBITRARY, tyrannical, absolute, despotic.

ARBITRATOR, judge, umpire, arbiter.

ARCHITECT, builder.

ARDENT, hot, fiery, burning.

ARDOR, fervor.

ARDUOUS, hard, difficult.

to ARGUE, dispute, debate.

to ARGUE, evince, prove.

ARGUMENT, reason, proof.

to ARISE, rise, mount, ascend, climb, scale.

to ARISE, rise, proceed, issue, spring, flow, emanate.

ARMS, weapons.

ARMY, host.

to ARRAIGN, accuse, charge, impeach.

to ARRANGE, digest, dispose.

to ARRANGE, range, class.

ARRAY, apparel, attire.

to ARRIVE, come.

ARROGANCE, assumption, presumption.

ARROGANCE, haughtiness, disdain.

to ARROGATE, assume, ascribe, appropriate, usurp.

ART, business, trade, profession.

ART, cunning, deceit.

ARTFUL, artificial, fictitious.

ARTICLE, condition, term.

to ARTICULATE, pronounce, utter, speak.

ARTIFICE, trick, finesse, stratagem.

ARTIFICER, mechanic, artist, artisan.

ARTIFICIAL, fictitious, artful.

ARTISAN, artificer, mechanic, artist.

ARTIST, artisan, artificer, mechanic.

to ASCEND, climb, scale, arise, rise, mount.

ASCENDANCY, ascendant, sway, influence, authority.

ASCENDANT, ascendancy, sway, influence, authority.

to ASCRIBE, appropriate, usurp, arrogate, assume.

to ASCRIBE, impute, attribute.

to ASK, ask for, claim, demand.

to ASK, beg, request.

to ASK, inquire, question, interrogate.

to ASK FOR, ask, claim, demand.

ASPECT, appearance, air.

ASPERITY, harshness, acrimony, tartness.

to ASPERSE, detract, defame, slander, calumniate.

to ASPIRE, aim.

to ASSAIL, assault, encounter, attack.

ASSAILANT, aggressor.

to ASSASSINATE, slay, slaughter, kill, murder.

to ASSAULT, encounter, attack, assail.

ASSAULT, encounter, onset, charge, attack.

ASSEMBLAGE, group, collection, assembly.

to ASSEMBLE, convene, convoke.

to ASSEMBLE, muster, collect.

ASSEMBLY, assemblage, group, collection.

ASSEMBLY, company, meeting, congregation, parliament, diet, congress, convention, synod, convocation, council.

ASSENT, consent, approbation, concurrence.

to ASSERT, affirm.

to ASSERT, maintain, vindicate.

ASSESSMENT, tax, rate.

to ASSEVERATE, assure, vouch, aver, protest, affirm.

ASSIDUOUS, laborious, active, diligent, industrious.

ASSIDUOUS, sedulous, diligent.

to ASSIGN, apportion, distribute, allot.

to ASSIST, aid, succour, relieve, help.

ASSISTANT, coadjutor.

ASSOCIATE, companion.

ASSOCIATION, combination.

ASSOCIATION, society, company, partnership.

to ASSUAGE, allay, soothe, appease, mitigate.

to ASSUME, affect.

to ASSUME, ascribe, appropriate, usurp, arrogate.

ASSUMPTION, presumption, arrogance.

ASSURANCE, confidence.

ASSURANCE, impudence.

to ASSURE, vouch, aver, protest, affirm, asseverate.

to ASTONISH, amaze, wonder, admire, surprise.

ASTROLOGY, astronomy.

ASTRONOMY, astrology.

ASYLUM, refuge, shelter, retreat.

(AT) ALL TIMES, ever, always.

to ATONE FOR, expiate.

ATROCIOUS, heinous, flagrant, flagitious.

to ATTACH, adhere.

to ATTACH, annex, affix, subjoin.

ATTACHMENT, affection, inclination.

to ATTACK, assail, assault, encounter.

to ATTACK, impugn.

ATTACK, assault, encounter, onset, charge.

to ATTAIN, acquire.

ATTEMPT, trial, endeavor, effort, essay.

ATTEMPT, undertaking, enterprise.

to ATTEND TO, mind, regard, heed, notice.

to ATTEND, escort, accompany.

to ATTEND, hearken, listen.

to ATTEND, wait on.

ATTENTION, application, study.

ATTENTION, heed, care.

ATTENTIVE, careful.

ATTIRE, array, apparel.

ATTITUDE, action, gesture, gesticulation, posture.

to ATTRACT, allure, invite, engage.

ATTRACTIONS, allurements, charms.

to ATTRIBUTE, ascribe, impute.

ATTRIBUTE, quality, property.

AUDACITY, effrontery, hardihood, hardiness, boldness.

AUGMENTATION, increase, addition, accession.

to AUGUR, presage, forbode, betoken, portend.

AUGUST, dignified, magisterial, majestic, stately, pompous.

AUSPICIOUS, propitious.

AUSTERE, rigid, severe, rigorous, stern.

AUTHOR, writer.

AUTHORITATIVE, commanding, imperative, imperious.

AUTHORITY, ascendancy, ascendant, sway, influence.

AUTHORITY, dominion, power, strength, force.

to AUTHORIZE, empower, commission.

to AVAIL, signify.

AVAIL, utility, use, service.

AVARICE, covetousness, cupidity.

AVARICIOUS, miserly parsimonious, niggardly.

to AVENGE, revenge, vindicate.

to AVER, protest, affirm, asseverate, assure, vouch.

AVERSE, adverse.

AVERSE, unwilling, backward, loath, reluctant.

AVERSION, antipathy, dislike, hatred, repugnance.

AVIDITY, greediness, eagerness.

to AVOID, eschew, shun, elude.

to AVOW, acknowledge, own, confess.

to AWAIT, look for, expect, wait, wait for.

to AWAKEN, excite, provoke, rouse, stir up.

AWARE, on one's guard, apprized, conscious.
AWE, reverence, dread.
AWKWARD, clumsy.
AWKWARD, cross, untoward, crooked, froward, perverse.
AWRY, bent, curved, crooked.

AXIOM, maxim, aphorism, apophthegm, saying, adage, proverb, byword, saw.

B

to BABBLE, chatter, chat, prattle, prate.
BACK, backward, behind.
BACKWARD, behind, back,
BACKWARD, loath, reluctant, averse, unwilling.
BAD, wicked, evil.
BADGE, stigma, mark.
BADLY, ill.
to BAFFLE, defeat, disconcert, confound.
to BALANCE, poise.
BALL, globe.
BAND, company, crew, gang.
BAND, shackle, chain, fetter.
BANE, pest, ruin.
to BANISH, exile, expel.
BANKRUPTCY, insolvency, failure.
BANQUET, carousal, entertainment, treat, feast.
to BANTER, deride, mock, ridicule, rally.
BARBAROUS, brutal, savage, cruel, inhuman.
BARE, mere.
BARE, naked, uncovered.
BARE, scanty, destitute.
BAREFACED, glaring.
to BARGAIN, cheapen, buy, purchase.
BARGAIN, agreement, contract, covenant, compact.
to BARTER, substitute, change, exchange.
to BARTER, truck, commute, exchange.
BASE, vile, mean.
BASHFUL, diffident, modest.
BASIS, foundation, ground.
BATTLE, combat, engagement, action.

to BE, become, grow.
to BE, exist, subsist.
to BE ACQUAINTED WITH, know.
to BE DEFICIENT, fail, fall short.
to BE RESPONSIBLE, warrant, guarantee, be security.
to BE SECURITY, be responsible, warrant, guarantee.
to BE SENSIBLE, be conscious, to feel.
BEAM, gleam, glimmer, ray.
to BEAR, carry, convey, transport.
to BEAR, suffer, endure, support.
to BEAR, yield.
to BEAR DOWN, overpower, overwhelm, subdue, overbear.
BEAST, animal, brute.

to BEAT, defeat, overpower, rout, overthrow.
to BEAT, strike, hit.
BEATIFICATION, canonization.
BEATITUDE, happiness, felicity, bliss, blessedness.
BEAU, spark, gallant.
BEAUTIFUL, fine, handsome, pretty.
to BECOME, grow, be.
BECOMING, comely, graceful.
BECOMING, decent, seemly, fit, suitable.
to BEDEW, sprinkle.
to BEG, beseech, solicit, entreat, supplicate, implore, crave.
to BEG, desire.
to BEG, request, ask.
to BEGIN, commence, enter upon.
BEGINNING, rise, source, origin, original.
to BEGUILE, amuse.
BEHAVIOR, conduct, carriage, deportment, demeanor.
BEHIND, after.
BEHIND, back, backward.
to BEHOLD, view, eye, look, see.
BEHOLDER, observer, looker-on, spectator.
BELIEF, credit, trust, faith.
to BELIEVE, deem, think, suppose, imagine.
BELOVED, amiable, lovely.
BELOW, beneath, under.
to BEMOAN, lament, bewail.
to BEND, lean, incline.
to BEND, twist, distort, wring, wrest, wrench, turn.
BEND, bent.
BENEATH, under, below.
BENEFACTION, donation.
BENEFICE, living.
BENEFICENCE, benevolence.
BENEFICENT, bountiful, bounteous, munificent, generous, liberal.
BENEFIT, advantage, good.
BENEFIT, favor, kindness, civility.
BENEFIT, service, good office.
BENEFIT, utility, advantage.
BENEVOLENCE, beneficence.
BENEVOLENCE, benignity, humanity, kindness, tenderness.
BENIGNITY, humanity, kindness, tenderness, benevolence.
BENT, bend.
BENT, bias, inclination, prepossession.
BENT, curved, crooked, awry.
BENT, turn.
BENUMBED, torpid, numb.
to BEQUEATH, devise.
to BEREAVE, deprive, strip.
to BESEECH, solicit, entreat, supplicate, implore, crave, beg.
BESIDES, except.
BESIDES, moreover.
to BESTOW, allow, grant.
to BESTOW, confer.

to BESTOW, give, grant.
BETIMES, soon, early.
to BETOKEN, portend, augur, presage, forebode.
to BETTER, amend, correct, emend, improve, mend.
to BEWAIL, bemoan, lament.
BEYOND, above, over, upon.

BIAS, inclination, prepossession, bent.
BIAS, prepossession, prejudice.
to BID, summon, call, invite.
to BID, tender, propose, offer.
to BID ADIEU, bid farewell, leave, take leave.
to BID FAREWELL, bid adieu, leave, take leave.
BIG, great, large.
BILL, account, reckoning.
BILLOW, surge, breaker, wave.
to BIND, oblige, engage.
to BIND, tie.
BISHOPRIC, diocese.

to BLAME, censure, condemn, reprove, reproach, upbraid.
to BLAME, object to, find fault with.
BLAMELESS, irreproachable, unblemished, unspotted, spotless.
BLAST, gust, storm, tempest, hurricane, breeze, gale.
BLAZE, flash, flare, glare, flame.
BLEMISH, stain, spot, speck, flaw.
BLEMISH, defect, fault.
to BLEND, confound, mix, mingle.
BLESSEDNESS, beatitude, happiness, felicity, bliss.
BLIND, veil, cloak, mask.
BLISS, blessedness, beatitude, happiness, felicity.
BLOODY, bloodthirsty, sanguinary.
BLOODTHIRSTY, sanguinary, bloody.
to BLOT OUT, expunge, raze, erase, efface, cancel, obliterate.
BLOW, stroke.
BLUNDER, error, mistake.

to BOAST, vaunt, glory.
BOATMAN, ferryman, waterman.
BODILY, corporal, corporeal.
BODY, corpse, carcass.
BOISTEROUS, vehement, impetuous, violent, furious.
BOLD, daring.
BOLD, fearless, intrepid, undaunted.
BOLD, strenuous.
BOLDNESS, audacity, effrontery, hardihood, hardiness.
BOMBASTIC, turgid, tumid.
BONDAGE, servitude, slavery.
BOOTY, spoil, prey.

BORDER, boundary, frontier, confine, precinct.
BORDER, edge, rim, brim, brink, margin, verge.
to BORE, penetrate, pierce, perforate.
to BOUND, limit, confine, circumscribe, restrict.
BOUNDARY, bounds.
BOUNDARY, frontier, confine, precinct, border.
BOUNDARY, term, limit.
BOUNDLESS, unbounded, unlimited, infinite.
BOUNDS, boundary.
BOUNTEOUS, bountiful, munificent, generous, liberal, beneficient.
BOUNTIFUL, bounteous, munificent, generous, liberal, beneficient.

BRACE, couple, pair.
to BRAVE, defy, dare, challenge.
BRAVE, gallant.
BRAVERY, courage, valor.
BREACH, break, gap, chasm.
to BREAK, bruise, squeeze, pound, crush.
to BREAK, burst, crack, split.
to BREAK, rack, rend, tear.
BREAK, gap, chasm, breach.
BREAKER, wave, billow, surge.
to BREED, engender.
BREED, race, generation.
BREEDING, education, instruction.
BREEZE, gale, blast, gust, storm, tempest, hurricane.
BRIEF, concise, succinct, summary, short.
BRIGHT, vivid, clear, lucid.
BRIGHTNESS, lustre, splendor, brilliancy.
BRILLIANCY, brightness, lustre, splendor.
BRILLIANCY, radiance.
BRIM, rim, brink, margin, verge, border, edge.
to BRING, fetch, carry.
BRINK, margin, verge, border, edge, rim, brim.
BRISK, agile, nimble, active.
BRITTLE, fragile, frail.
BROAD, large, wide.
BROIL, feud, quarrel.
to BRUISE, squeeze, pound, crush, break.
BRUTAL, savage, cruel, inhuman, barbarous.
BRUTE, beast, animal.

to BUD, sprout.
BUFFOON, fool, idiot.
to BUILD, erect, construct.
to BUILD, found, ground, rest, build.
BUILDER, architect.
BULK, size, magnitude, greatness.
BULKY, massive.
BURDEN, freight, cargo, lading, load.
BURDEN, load, weight.
BURDENSOME, weighty, ponderous, heavy.

BURIAL, interment, sepulture.
BURLESQUE, wit, humor, satire, irony.
BURNING, ardent, hot, fiery.
to BURST, crack, split, break.
BUSINESS, concern, affair.
BUSINESS, office, duty.
BUSINESS, occupation, employment, engagement, vocation.
BUSINESS, trade, profession, art.
BUSTLE, tumult, uproar.
BUSY, officious, active.
BUTCHERY, carnage, slaughter, massacre.
BUTT, mark.
to BUY, purchase, bargain, cheapen.

BYWORD, saw, axiom, maxim, aphorism, apophthegm, saying, adage, proverb.

C

CABAL, plot, conspiracy, combination.
to CAJOLE, fawn, coax, wheedle.
CALAMITY, disaster, misfortune, mischance, mishap.
to CALCULATE, reckon, compute, count.
CALENDAR, almanac, ephemeris.
to CALL, cry, exclaim.
to CALL, invite, bid, summon.
to CALL, name.
CALLOUS, hardened, obdurate, hard.
to CALM, pacify, quiet, still, appease.
CALM, composed, collected.
CALM, placid, serene.
CALM, tranquillity, peace, quiet.
to CALUMNIATE, asperse, detract, defame, slander.
CAN, may.
to CANCEL, abolish, abrogate, repeal, revoke, annul.
to CANCEL, obliterate, blot out, expunge, raze, erase, efface.
CANDID, ingenuous, free, open, plain, frank.
CANDID, open, sincere.
CANONIZATION, beatification.
CAPABLE, capacious, able.
CAPACIOUS, able, capable.
CAPACIOUS, ample, spacious.
CAPACIOUSNESS, capacity.
CAPACITY, ability.
CAPACITY, capaciousness.
CAPRICE, humor.
CAPRICIOUS, humorsome, humorous.
CAPTIOUS, cross, peevish, petulant, fretful.
to CAPTIVATE, charm, enchant, fascinate, enrapture.
to CAPTIVATE, enslave.
CAPTIVITY, confinement, imprisonment.
CAPTURE, seizure, prize.
CARCASS, body, corpse.
CARE, attention, heed.
CARE, charge, management.
CARE, concern, regard.

CARE, solicitude, anxiety.
CAREFUL, attentive.
CAREFUL, cautious, provident.
CARELESS, indolent, supine, listless.
CARELESS, thoughtless, heedless, inattentive, negligent, remiss.
to CARESS, fondle.
CARGO, lading, load, burden, freight.
CAROUSAL, entertainment, treat, feast, banquet.
CARNAGE, slaughter, massacre, butchery.
to CARP, cavil, censure.
CARRIAGE, deportment, demeanor, behavior, conduct.
CARRIAGE, gait, walk.
to CARRY, bring, fetch.
to CARRY, convey, transport, bear.
CASE, cause.
CASE, situation, condition, state, predicament, plight.
CASH, money.
to CAST, throw, hurl.
CAST, turn, description.
CASUAL, contingent, accidental, incidental.
CASUAL, occasional.
CASUALTY, accident, contingency.
CATALOGUE, register, list, roll.
to CATCH, seize, snatch, grasp, grip, lay hold of, take hold of.
to CAUSE, occasion, create.
CAUSE, case.
CAUSE, reason, motive.
CAUTION, admonition, warning.
CAUTIOUS, provident, careful.
CAUTIOUS, wary, circumspect.
to CAVIL, censure, carp.
CAVITY, opening, aperture.

to CEASE, leave off, discontinue.
to CEDE, concede, give up, deliver, surrender, yield.
to CELEBRATE, commemorate.
CELERITY, rapidity, velocity, quickness, swiftness, fleetness.
to CENSURE, accuse.
to CENSURE, animadvert, criticize.
to CENSURE, carp, cavil.
to CENSURE, condemn, reprove, reproach, upbraid, blame.
CEREMONIAL, formal, ceremonious.
CEREMONIOUS, ceremonial, formal.
CEREMONY, rite, observance, form.
CERTAIN, sure, secure.
CESSATION, stop, rest, intermission.

CHACE, park, forest.
to CHAFE, fret, gall, rub.
CHAGRIN, vexation, mortification.
CHAIN, fetter, band, shackle.
to CHALLENGE, brave, defy, dare.
CHAMPION, combatant.
to CHANCE, happen.

CHANCE, accident.
CHANCE, fortune, fate.
CHANCE, hazard.
CHANCE, probability.
to CHANGE, alter, vary.
to CHANGE, exchange, barter, substitute.
CHANGE, variation, vicissitude.
CHANGEABLE, mutable, variable, inconstant, fickle, versatile.
CHARACTER, letter.
CHARACTER, reputation.
to CHARACTERIZE, name, denominate, style, entitle, designate.
to CHARGE, impeach, arraign, accuse.
CHARGE, attack, assault, encounter, onset.
CHARGE, cost, expense, price.
CHARGE, function, office, place.
CHARGE, management, care.
to CHARM, enchant, fascinate, enrapture, captivate.
CHARM, grace.
CHARM, pleasure, joy, delight.
CHARMING, delightful.
CHARMS, attractions, allurements.
CHASE, hunt.
CHASM, breach, break, gap.
to CHASTEN, to chastise.
to CHASTISE, to chasten.
CHASITY, continence.
to CHAT, prattle, prate, babble, chatter.
CHATTELS, moveables, effects, goods, furniture.
to CHATTER, chat, prattle, prate, babble.
to CHEAPEN, buy, purchase, bargain.
to CHEAT, defraud, trick.
to CHECK, chide, reprimand, reprove, rebuke.
to CHECK, curb, control.
to CHECK, stop.
to CHEER, encourage, comfort.
to CHEER, exhilarate, animate, inspire, enliven.
CHEERFUL, glad, pleased, joyful.
CHEERFUL, merry, sprightly, gay.
to CHERISH, harbor, indulge, foster.
to CHERISH, nourish, nurture.
to CHIDE, reprimand, reprove, rebuke, check.
CHIEF, leader, chieftain, head.
CHIEF, principal, main.
CHIEFLY, especially, particularly, principally.
CHIEFTAIN, head, chief, leader.
CHILDISH, infantine.
CHILL, cold.
CHOICE, option.
to CHOKE, suffocate, stifle, smother.
CHOLER, rage, fury, anger.
to CHOOSE, elect.
to CHOOSE, pick, select.
to CHOOSE, prefer.
CHRONICLES, annals, anecdotes, memoirs.

CHURCH, temple.

CIRCLE, sphere, orb, globe.
CIRCUIT, tour, round.
to CIRCULATE, propagate, disseminate, spread.
to CIRCUMSCRIBE, enclose.
to CIRCUMSCRIBE, restrict, bound, limit, confine.
CIRCUMSPECT, cautious, wary.
CIRCUMSTANCE, incident, fact.
CIRCUMSTANCE, situation.
CIRCUMSTANTIAL, particular, minute.
to CITE, quote.
to CITE, summon.
CIVIL, obliging, complaisant.
CIVIL, polite.
CIVILITY, benefit, favor, kindness.
CIVILIZATION, refinement, cultivation, culture.

to CLAIM, demand, ask, ask for.
CLAIM, pretension.
CLAIM, privilege, right.
CLAMOR, noise, cry, outcry.
CLAMOROUS, loud, noisy, high-sounding.
CLANDESTINE, secret.
to CLASP, hug, embrace.
to CLASS, arrange, range.
CLASS, order, rank, degree.
CLEAN, cleanly, pure.
CLEANLY, pure, clean.
to CLEAR, absolve, acquit.
CLEAR, fair.
CLEAR, lucid, bright, vivid.
CLEAR, plain, obvious, evident, manifest, apparent, visible.
CLEARLY, distinctly.
CLEARNESS, perspicuity.
to CLEAVE, adhere, stick.
CLEMENCY, lenity, mercy.
CLERGYMAN, parson, priest, minister.
CLEVER, skillful, expert, dextrous, adroit.
to CLIMB, scale, arise, rise, mount, ascend.
CLOAK, mask, blind, veil.
to CLOG, load, encumber.
CLOISTER, convent, monastery.
to CLOSE, conclude, finish.
to CLOSE, end, terminate.
to CLOSE, shut.
CLOSE, compact.
CLOSE, near, nigh.
CLOSE, sequel.
CLOWN, countryman, peasant, swain, hind, rustic.
to CLOY, satisfy, satiate, glut.
CLUMSY, awkward.

COADJUTOR, assistant.
to COALESCE, add, join, unite.
COARSE, gross.
COARSE, rough, rude.

to COAX, wheedle, cajole, fawn.
to COERCE, restrain.
COEVAL, contemporary.
COGENT, forcible, strong.
to COINCIDE, concur, agree.
COLD, chill.
COLD, frigid, cool.
COLLEAGUE, partner.
to COLLECT, assemble, muster.
to COLLECT, gather.
COLLECTED, calm, composed.
COLLECTION, assembly, assemblage, group.
COLLOQUY, conversation, dialogue, conference.
to COLOR, dye, tinge, stain.
COLOR, hue, tint.
COLORABLE, specious, ostensible, plausible, feasible.
COLUMN, pillar.
to COMBAT, oppose.
COMBAT, contest, conflict.
COMBAT, engagement, action, battle.
COMBATANT, champion.
COMBINATION, association.
COMBINATION, cabal, plot, conspiracy.
to COMBINE, unite, connect.
to COME, arrive.
COMELY, elegant, graceful.
COMELY, graceful, becoming.
to COMFORT, cheer, encourage.
to COMFORT, console, solace.
COMFORT, pleasure.
COMIC, comical, droll, laughable, ludicrous, ridiculous.
COMICAL, comic, droll, laughable, ludicrous, ridiculous.
COMMAND, order, injunction, precept.
COMMANDING, imperative, imperious, authoritative.
to COMMEMORATE, celebrate.
to COMMENCE, enter upon, begin.
to COMMEND, applaud, extol, praise.
COMMENDABLE, laudable, praiseworthy.
COMMENSURATE, adequate, proportionate.
COMMENT, note, annotation, commentary, remark, observation.
COMMENTARY, remark, observation, comment, note, annotation.
COMMERCE, intercourse, communication, connection.
COMMERCE, traffic, dealing, trade.
COMMERCIAL, mercantile.
COMMISERATION, condolence, sympathy, compassion.
to COMMISSION, authorize, empower.
to COMMIT, entrust, consign.
to COMMIT, perpetrate.
COMMODIOUS, convenient.
COMMODITY, goods, merchandise, ware.
COMMON, vulgar, ordinary, mean.
COMMONLY, generally, frequently, usually.
COMMONWEALTH, state, realm.

COMMOTION, disturbance.
to COMMUNICATE, impart.
COMMUNICATION, connection, commerce, intercourse.
COMMUNION, converse.
COMMUNION, sacrament, Lord's Supper, eucharist.
COMMUNITY, society.
to COMMUTE, exchange, barter, truck.
COMPACT, bargain, agreement, contract, covenant.
COMPACT, close.
COMPANION, associate.
COMPANION, concomitant, accompaniment.
COMPANY, crew, gang, band.
COMPANY, meeting, congregation, parliament, diet, congress, convention, synod, convocation, council, assembly.
COMPANY, partnership, association, society.
COMPANY, troop.
COMPARISON, contrast.
COMPARISON, simile, similitude.
COMPASSION, commiseration, condolence, sympathy.
COMPASSION, pity.
COMPATIBLE, consistent.
to COMPEL, force, oblige, necessitate.
to COMPEL, impel, constrain, restrain.
COMPENDIUM, epitome, digest, summary, abstract, abridgment.
COMPENSATION, amends, satisfaction, recompense, remuneration, requital, reward.
COMPETENT, fitted, qualified.
COMPETITION, emulation, rivalry.
to COMPLAIN, lament, regret.
to COMPLAIN, murmur, repine.
COMPLAINT, accusation.
COMPLAISANCE, deference, condescension.
COMPLAISANT, civil, obliging.
COMPLAISANT, courtly, courteous.
to COMPLETE, finish, terminate.
COMPLETE, perfect, finished.
COMPLETE, total, integral, whole, entire.
COMPLIANT, yielding, submissive.
COMPLETION, consummation.
COMPLEX, compound.
COMPLEXITY, complication, intricacy.
COMPLICATION, intricacy, complexity.
to COMPLIMENT, adulate, flatter.
to COMPLY, acquiesce, agree, accede, consent.
to COMPLY, conform, yield, submit.
to COMPOSE, compound.
to COMPOSE, constitute, form.
to COMPOSE, settle.
COMPOSED, collected, calm.
COMPOSED, sedate.
to COMPOUND, compose.
COMPOUND, complex.
to COMPREHEND, conceive, understand.
to COMPREHEND, embrace, contain, include, comprise.

COMPREHENSIVE, extensive.

to COMPRISE, comprehend, embrace, contain, include.

COMPULSION, constraint.

COMPUNCTION, remorse, repentance, penitence, contrition.

to COMPUTE, count, calculate, reckon.

to COMPUTE, rate, estimate.

to CONCEAL, dissemble, disguise.

to CONCEAL, hide, secrete.

CONCEALMENT, secrecy.

to CONCEDE, give up, deliver, surrender, yield, cede.

CONCEIT, fancy.

CONCEIT, pride, vanity.

CONCEITED, egoistical, opinionated, opinionative.

to CONCEIVE, suppose, imagine, apprehend.

to CONCEIVE, understand, comprehend.

CONCEPTION, notion, perception, idea.

to CONCERN, affect.

CONCERN, affair, business.

CONCERN, interest.

CONCERN, regard, care.

to CONCERT, contrive, manage.

to CONCILIATE, reconcile.

CONCISE, succinct, summary, short, brief.

to CONCLUDE, finish, close.

to CONCLUDE UPON, decide, determine.

CONCLUSION, inference, deduction.

CONCLUSIVE, decisive, convincing.

CONCLUSIVE, final.

CONCOMITANT, accompaniment, companion.

CONCORD, harmony.

to CONCUR, agree, coincide.

CONCURRENCE, assent, consent, approbation.

CONCUSSION, shock.

to CONDEMN, reprobate.

to CONDEMN, reprove, reproach, upbraid, blame, censure.

to CONDEMN, sentence, doom.

CONDESCENSION, complaisance, deference.

CONDITION, state, predicament, plight, case, situation.

CONDITION, station.

CONDITION, term, article.

CONDOLENCE, sympathy, compassion, commiseration.

to CONDUCE, contribute.

to CONDUCT, guide, lead.

to CONDUCT, manage, direct.

CONDUCT, carriage, deportment, demeanor, behavior.

CONFEDERACY, alliance, league.

CONFEDERATE, accomplice.

CONFEDERATE, ally.

to CONFER, bestow.

CONFERENCE, colloquy, conversation, dialogue.

to CONFESS, avow, acknowledge, own.

to CONFIDE, trust.

CONFIDENCE, assurance.

CONFIDENCE, hope, expectation, trust.

CONFIDENT, dogmatical, positive.

to CONFINE, circumscribe, restrict, bound, limit.

CONFINE, precinct, border, boundary, frontier.

CONFINED, narrow, contracted.

CONFINEMENT, imprisonment, captivity.

to CONFIRM, corroborate.

to CONFIRM, establish.

CONFLICT, combat, contest.

to CONFORM, yield, submit, comply.

CONFORMABLE, agreeable, suitable.

CONFORMATION, form, figure.

to CONFOUND, baffle, defeat, disconcert.

to CONFOUND, to confuse.

to CONFOUND, mix, mingle, blend.

to CONFRONT, face.

to CONFUSE, abash, confound.

CONFUSED, indistinct.

CONFUSION, disorder.

to CONFUTE, refute, disprove, oppugn.

to CONGRATULATE, felicitate.

CONGREGATION, parliament, diet, congress, convention, synod, convocation, council, assembly, company, meeting.

CONGRESS, convention, synod, convocation, council, assembly, company, meeting, congregation, parliament, diet.

to CONJECTURE, divine, guess.

CONJECTURE, supposition, surmise.

CONJUNCTURE, crisis.

to CONNECT, combine, unite.

CONNECTION, commerce, intercourse, communication.

CONNECTION, relation.

to CONQUER, vanquish, subdue, overcome, surmount.

CONQUEROR, victor.

CONSANGUINITY, kindred, relationship, affinity.

CONSCIENTIOUS, scrupulous.

CONSCIOUS, aware, on one's guard, apprized.

to CONSECRATE, hallow, dedicate, devote.

to CONSENT, comply, acquiesce, agree, accede.

to CONSENT, permit, allow.

CONSENT, approbation, concurrence, assent.

CONSEQUENCE, effect, result, issue, event.

CONSEQUENCE, weight, moment, importance.

CONSEQUENTLY, accordingly, therefore.

CONSEQUENTLY, of course, naturally, in course.

to CONSIDER, reflect.

to CONSIDER, regard.

CONSIDERATE, deliberate, thoughtful.

CONSIDERATION, reason.

to CONSIGN, commit, entrust.

CONSISTENT, compatible.

Consistent, consonant, accordant.

to Console, solace, comfort.

Consonant, accordant, consistent.

Conspicuous, noted, eminent, illustrious, distinguished.

Conspicuous, prominent.

Conspiracy, combination, cabal, plot.

Constancy, stability, steadiness, firmness.

Constant, continual, perpetual.

Constant, durable.

Consternation, alarm, terror, fright.

to Constitute, appoint, depute.

to Constitute, form, compose.

Constitution, frame, temper, temperament.

Constitution, government.

to Constrain, restrain, compel, impel.

Constraint, compulsion.

Constraint, restraint.

to Construct, build, erect.

to Consult, deliberate.

to Consume, waste, destroy.

Consummation, completion.

Consumption, decay, decline.

Contact, touch.

Contagion, infection.

Contagious, epidemical, pestilential.

to Contain, hold.

to Contain, include, comprise, comprehend, embrace.

to Contaminate, defile, pollute, taint, corrupt.

to Contemn, despise, scorn, disdain.

to Contemplate, meditate, muse.

Contemporary, coeval.

Contemptible, despicable, pitiful.

Contemptuous, scornful, disdainful.

to Contend, contest, dispute.

to Contend, vie, strive.

Contention, discord, dissension.

Contention, strife.

Contentment, satisfaction.

to Contest, dispute, contend.

Contest, conflict, combat.

Contiguous, adjacent, adjoining.

Continence, chastity.

Contingency, casualty, accident.

Contingent, accidental, incidental, casual.

Continual, continued.

Continual, perpetual, constant.

Continuance, continuation, duration.

Continuation, continuity.

Continuation, duration, continuance.

to Continue, persevere, persist, pursue, prosecute.

to Continue, remain, stay.

Continued, continual.

to Contract, abridge, curtail.

Contract, covenant, compact, bargain, agreement.

Contracted, confined, narrow.

to Contradict, deny, oppose.

Contrary, opposite, adverse.

Contrast, comparison.

to Contribute, conduce.

to Contribute, minister, administer.

Contribution, tax, duty, custom, toll, impost, tribute.

Contrition, compunction, remorse, repentance, penitence.

to Contrive, devise, invent.

to Contrive, manage, concert.

to Control, check, curb.

to Controvert, dispute.

Contumacious, stubborn, headstrong, heady, obstinate.

Contumacy, rebellion.

Contumely, obloquy, reproach.

to Convene, convoke, assemble.

Convenient, commodious.

Convenient, suitable.

Convent, monastery, cloister.

Convention, synod, convocation, council, assembly, company, meeting, congregation, parliament, diet, congress.

Conversable, pleasant, jocular, jocose, facetious.

Conversant, familiar.

Conversation, dialogue, conference, colloquy.

to Converse, discourse, speak, talk.

Converse, communion.

Convert, proselyte.

to Convey, transport, bear, carry.

to Convict, convince, persuade.

to Convict, detect.

Convict, criminal, culprit, malefactor, felon.

to Convince, persuade, convict.

Convincing, conclusive, decisive.

Convivial, social.

Convocation, council, assembly, company, meeting, congregation, parliament, diet, congress, convention, synod.

to Convoke, assemble, convene.

Cool, cold, frigid.

Cool, dispassionate.

Copious, ample, plentiful, plenteous, abundant.

Copiously, fully, largely.

to Copy, counterfeit, imitate.

to Copy, transcribe.

Copy, model, pattern, specimen.

Coquet, jilt.

Cordial, hearty, warm, sincere.

Corner, angle.

Corporal, corporeal, bodily.

Corporeal, bodily, corporal.

Corporeal, material.

Corpse, carcass, body.

Corpulent, stout, lusty.

to Correct, emend, improve, mend, better, amend.

to Correct, rectify, reform.

CORRECT, accurate.
CORRECTION, discipline, punishment.
CORRECTNESS, justness.
CORRESPONDENT, answerable, suitable.
to CORROBORATE, confirm.
to CORRUPT, contaminate, defile, pollute, taint.
to CORRUPT, rot, putrefy.
CORRUPTION, depravity, depravation.
COST, expense, price, charge.
COSTLY, valuable, precious.
COUNCIL, assembly, company, meeting, congregation, parliament, diet, congress, convention, synod, convocation.
COUNSEL, instruction, advice.
to COUNT, account, number, reckon.
to COUNT, calculate, reckon, compute.
to COUNTENANCE, sanction, support.
COUNTENANCE, visage, face.
to COUNTERFEIT, imitate, copy.
COUNTERFEIT, spurious, supposititious.
COUNTRY, land.
COUNTRYMAN, peasant, swain, hind, rustic, clown.
COUPLE, pair, brace.
COURAGE, fortitude, resolution.
COURAGE, valor, bravery.
(IN) COURSE, consequently, of course, naturally.
(OF) COURSE, naturally, in course, consequently.
COURSE, means, way, manner, method, mode.
COURSE, race, passage.
COURSE, route, road.
COURSE, series.
COURT, homage, fealty.
COURTEOUS, affable.
COURTEOUS, complaisant, courtly.
COURTLY, courteous, complaisant.
COVENANT, compact, bargain, agreement, contract.
to COVER, hide.
COVER, shelter, screen.
COVERING, tegument.
to COVET, desire, wish, long for, hanker after.
COVETOUSNESS, cupidity, avarice.

to CRACK, split, break, burst.
CRAFTY, subtle, sly, wily, cunning.
to CRAVE, beg, beseech, solicit, entreat, supplicate, implore.
to CREATE, cause, occasion.
to CREATE, make, form, produce.
CREDIT, favor, influence.
CREDIT, name, reputation, repute.
CREDIT, trust, faith, belief.
CREED, faith.
CREW, gang, band, company.
CRIME, misdemeanor.
CRIME, vice, sin.

CRIMINAL, culprit, malefactor, felon, convict.
CRIMINAL, guilty.
CRISIS, conjuncture.
CRITERION, standard.
CRITICISM, stricture, animadversion.
to CRITICIZE, censure, animadvert.
CROOKED, awry, bent, curved.
CROOKED, froward, perverse, awkward, cross, untoward.
CROSS, peevish, petulant, fretful, captious.
CROSS, untoward, crooked, froward, perverse, awkward.
CROWD, throng, swarm, multitude.
CRUEL, inhuman, barbarous, brutal, savage.
CRUEL, unmerciful, merciless, hardhearted.
to CRUSH, break, bruise, squeeze, pound.
to CRUSH, overwhelm.
CRUTCH, staff, stick.
to CRY, exclaim, call.
to CRY, scream, shriek.
to CRY, weep.
CRY, outcry, clamor, noise.

CULPABLE, faulty.
CULPRIT, malefactor, felon, convict, criminal.
CULTIVATION, culture, civilization, refinement.
CULTIVATION, tillage, husbandry.
CULTURE, civilization, refinement, cultivation.
CUNNING, crafty, subtle, sly, wily.
CUNNING, deceit, art.
CUPIDITY, avarice, covetousness.
to CURB, control, check.
to CURE, heal, remedy.
CURE, remedy.
CURIOUS, inquisitive, prying.
CURRENT, tide, stream.
CURSE, imprecation, execration, anathema, malediction.
CURSORY, hasty, slight, desultory.
to CURTAIL, contract, abridge.
CURVED, crooked, awry, bent.
CUSTODY, keeping.
CUSTOM, fashion, manner, practice.
CUSTOM, habit.
CUSTOM, prescription, usage.
CUSTOM, toll, impost, tribute, contribution, tax, duty.

D

DAILY, diurnal.
DAINTY, delicacy.
DAMAGE, detriment, loss.
DAMAGE, hurt, harm, mischief, injury.
DAMPNESS, moisture, humidity.
DANGER, peril, hazard.
to DARE, challenge, brave, defy.
DARING, bold.
DARK, obscure, dim, mysterious.

Dark, opaque.
to Dart, shoot.
Date, era, epoch, time, period, age.
to Daub, smear.
to Daunt, appall, dismay.
(In) Days Of Yore, anciently, in ancient times, formerly, in times past, in old times.

Dead, inanimate, lifeless.
Deadly, mortal, fatal.
Deal, quantity, portion.
Dealing, trade, commerce, traffic.
Dearth, scarcity.
Death, departure, decease, demise.
to Debar, abridge, deprive.
to Debase, abase, humble, degrade, disgrace.
to Debate, argue, dispute.
to Debate, deliberate.
to Debilitate, enervate, invalidate, weaken, enfeeble.
Debility, infirmity, imbecility.
Debt, due.
to Decay, perish, die.
Decay, decline, consumption.
Decease, demise, death, departure.
Deceit, art, cunning.
Deceit, deception.
Deceit, duplicity, double-dealing.
Deceit, fraud, guile.
to Deceive, delude, impose upon.
Deceiver, impostor.
Decency, decorum.
Deceitful, fraudulent, fallacious.
Decent, seemly, fit, suitable, becoming.
Deception, deceit.
to Decide, determine, conclude upon.
Decided, decisive.
Decided, determined, resolute.
Decisive, convincing, conclusive.
Decisive, decided.
Declaim, inveigh.
to Declare, discover, manifest.
to Declare, profess.
to Declare, publish, proclaim.
to Declare, signify, testify, utter, express.
to Decline, reject, repel, rebuff, refuse.
Decline, consumption, decay.
to Decorate, embellish, adorn.
Decorum, decency.
to Decoy, allure, tempt, seduce, entice.
to Decrease, abate, lessen, diminish.
Decree, edict, proclamation.
to Decry, disparage, detract, traduce, depreciate, degrade.
to Dedicate, devote, consecrate, hallow.
to Deduce, derive, trace.
to Deduct, subtract.
Deduction, abatement.
Deduction, conclusion, inference.
Deed, act, action.

Deed, exploit, achievement, feat.
to Deem, think, suppose, imagine, believe.
to Deface, disfigure, deform.
to Defame, slander, calumniate, asperse, detract.
to Defeat, disconcert, confound, baffle.
to Defeat, foil, disappoint, frustrate.
to Defeat, overpower, rout, overthrow, beat.
Defect, fault, blemish.
Defect, fault, vice, imperfection.
Defection, revolt.
Defective, deficient.
to Defend, justify, exculpate, excuse, plead, apologize.
to Defend, protect, vindicate.
to Defend, watch, guard.
Defendant, defender.
Defender, advocate, pleader.
Defender, defendant.
Defensible, defensive.
Defensive, defensible.
to Defer, postpone, procrastinate, prolong, protract, retard, delay.
Deference, condescension, complaisance.
Deficient, defective.
to Defile, pollute, taint, corrupt, contaminate.
Definite, positive.
Definition, explanation.
to Deform, deface, disfigure.
to Defraud, trick, cheat.
to Defy, dare, challenge, brave.
to Degrade, decry, disparage, detract, traduce, depreciate.
to Degrade, disgrace, debase, abase, humble.
to Degrade, disparage, derogate.
to Degrade, humble, humiliate.
Degree, class, order, rank.
Deity, divinity.
Dejection, depression, melancholy.
to Delay, defer, postpone, procrastinate, prolong, protract, retard.
to Delegate, depute.
Delegate, deputy.
to Deliberate, consult.
to Deliberate, debate.
Deliberate, thoughtful, considerate.
Delicacy, dainty.
Delicate, nice, fine.
Delight, charm, pleasure, joy.
Delightful, charming.
to Delineate, sketch.
Delinquent, offender.
to Deliver, liberate, free, set free.
to Deliver, rescue, save.
to Deliver, surrender, yield, cede, concede, give up.
Deliverance, delivery.
Delivery, deliverance.
to Delude, impose upon, deceive.

to DELUGE, overflow, inundate.
DELUSION, illusion, fallacy.
to DEMAND, ask, ask for, claim.
to DEMAND, require.
DEMEANOR, behavior, conduct, carriage, deportment.
DEMISE, death, departure, decease.
to DEMOLISH, raze, dismantle, destroy.
DEMON, devil.
to DEMONSTRATE, evince, manifest, prove.
to DEMUR, hesitate, pause.
DEMUR, doubt, hesitation, objection.
TO DENOMINATE, style, entitle, designate, characterize, name.
DENOMINATION, name, appellation, title.
to DENOTE, signify.
DENSE, thick.
to DENY, disown, disavow.
to DENY, oppose, contradict.
to DENY, refuse.
DEPARTURE, decease, demise, death.
DEPARTURE, exit.
DEPENDENCE, reliance.
to DEPICT, paint.
to DEPLORE, lament.
DEPONENT, evidence, witness.
DEPORTMENT, demeanor, behavior, conduct, carriage.
DEPOSIT, pledge, security.
DEPRAVATION, corruption, depravity.
DEPRAVITY, depravation, corruption.
to DEPRECIATE, degrade, decry, disparage, detract, traduce.
DEPREDATION, robbery.
DEPRESSION, melancholy, dejection.
to DEPRIVE, debar, abridge.
to DEPRIVE, strip, bereave.
DEPTH, profundity.
to DEPUTE, constitute, appoint.
to DEPUTE, delegate.
DEPUTY, delegate.
to DERANGE, disconcert, discompose, disorder.
DERANGEMENT, insanity, lunacy, madness, mania.
to DERIDE, mock, ridicule, rally, banter.
to DERIVE, trace, deduce.
to DEROGATE, degrade, disparage.
to DESCRIBE, relate, recount.
DESCRIPTION, account, narrative.
DESCRIPTION, cast, turn.
to DESCRY, find, find out, discover, espy.
to DESERT, forsake, relinquish, abandon.
DESERT, desolate, solitary.
DESERT, merit, worth.
to DESIGN, purpose, intend, mean.
DESIGN, plan, scheme, project.
to DESIGNATE, characterize, name, denominate, style, entitle.
to DESIRE, beg.
to DESIRE, wish, long for, hanker after, covet.

to DESIST, leave off.
DESOLATE, solitary, desert.
DESOLATION, devastation, ravage.
DESPAIR, desperation, despondency.
DESPERATE, hopeless.
DESPERATION, despondency, despair.
DESPICABLE, pitiful, contemptible.
to DESPISE, scorn, disdain, contemn.
DESPONDENCY, despair, desperation.
DESPOTIC, arbitrary, tyrannical, absolute.
DESTINATION, destiny.
to DESTINE, allot, appoint.
DESTINY, destination.
DESTINY, fate, lot, doom.
DESTITUTE, bare, scanty.
DESTITUTE, forsaken, forlorn.
to DESTROY, consume, waste.
to DESTROY, demolish, raze, dismantle.
DESTRUCTION, ruin.
DESTRUCTIVE, ruinous, pernicious.
DESULTORY, cursory, hasty, slight.
to DETACH, separate, sever, disjoin.
to DETAIN, retain, hold, keep.
to DETECT, convict.
to DETECT, discover.
to DETER, discourage, dishearten.
to DETERMINE, conclude upon, decide.
to DETERMINE, resolve.
to DETERMINE, settle, limit, fix.
DETERMINED, resolute, decided.
to DETEST, abominate, loathe, abhor.
to DETEST, hate.
DETESTABLE, execrable, abominable.
to DETRACT, defame, slander, calumniate, asperse.
to DETRACT, traduce, depreciate, degrade, decry, disparage.
DETRIMENT, loss, damage.
DETRIMENT, prejudice, disadvantage, injury, hurt.
DEVASTATION, ravage, desolation.
to DEVELOP, unfold, unravel.
to DEVIATE, digress.
to DEVIATE, wander, swerve, stray.
DEVIL, demon.
to DEVISE, bequeath.
to DEVISE, invent, contrive.
DEVOID, empty, vacant, void.
to DEVOTE, apply, addict.
to DEVOTE, consecrate, hallow, dedicate.
DEVOUT, religious, holy, pious.
DEXTERITY, address, ability.
DEXTEROUS, adroit, clever, skillful, expert.

DIALECT, language, tongue, speech, idiom.
DIALOGUE, conference, colloquy, conversation.
to DICTATE, prescribe.
DICTATE, suggestion.
DICTION, style, phrase, phraseology.
DICTIONARY, encyclopaedia.

DICTIONARY, lexicon, vocabulary, glossary, nomenclature.
to DIE, decay, perish.
to DIE, expire.
DIET, congress, convention, synod, convocation, council, assembly, company, meeting, congregation, parliament.
DIET, regimen, food.
to DIFFER, vary, disagree, dissent.
DIFFERENCE, dispute, altercation, quarrel.
DIFFERENCE, distinction.
DIFFERENCE, variety, diversity, medley.
DIFFERENT, distinct, separate.
DIFFERENT, several, divers, sundry, various.
DIFFERENT, unlike.
DIFFICULT, arduous, hard.
DIFFICULTIES, embarrassments, troubles.
DIFFICULTY, exception, objection.
DIFFICULTY, obstacle, impediment.
DIFFIDENCE, distrust, suspicion.
DIFFIDENT, modest, bashful.
to DIFFUSE, spread, expand.
DIFFUSE, prolix.
to DIGEST, dispose, arrange.
DIGEST, summary, abstract, abridgment, compendium, epitome.
DIGNIFIED, magisterial, majestic, stately, pompous, august.
DIGNITY, honor.
DIGNITY, pride, haughtiness, loftiness.
to DIGRESS, deviate.
to DILATE, expand.
DILATORY, tardy, tedious, slow.
DILIGENT, assiduous, sedulous.
DILIGENT, expeditious, prompt.
DILIGENT, industrious, assiduous, laborious, active.
DIM, mysterious, dark, obscure.
to DIMINISH, decrease, abate, lessen.
DIMINUTIVE, little, small.
DIOCESE, bishopric.
to DIRECT, conduct, manage.
to DIRECT, regulate, dispose.
DIRECT, straight, right.
DIRECTION, address, superscription.
DIRECTION, order.
DIRECTLY, immediately, instantly, instantaneously.
DISABILITY, inability.
DISADVANTAGE, injury, hurt, detriment, prejudice.
DISAFFECTION, disloyalty.
to DISAGREE, dissent, differ, vary.
to DISAPPEAR, vanish.
to DISAPPOINT, frustrate, defeat, foil.
DISAPPROBATION, displeasure, anger.
to DISAPPROVE, dislike.
DISASTER, misfortune, mischance, mishap, calamity.
to DISAVOW, deny, disown.
DISBELIEF, unbelief.
to DISCARD, dismiss, discharge.

to DISCERN, distinguish, perceive.
DISCERNMENT, penetration, discrimination, judgment.
to DISCHARGE, discard, dismiss.
DISCIPLE, scholar.
DISCIPLINE, punishment, correction.
to DISCLAIM, disown.
to DISCLOSE, publish, promulgate, divulge, reveal.
to DISCLOSE, uncover, discover.
to DISCOMPOSE, disorder, derange, disconcert.
to DISCONCERT, confound, baffle, defeat.
to DISCONCERT, discompose, disorder, derange.
to DISCONTINUE, cease, leave off.
DISCORD, dissension, contention.
DISCORD, strife.
to DISCOURAGE, dishearten, deter.
to DISCOURSE, speak, talk, converse.
to DISCOVER, detect.
to DISCOVER, disclose, uncover.
to DISCOVER, espy, descry, find, find out.
to DISCOVER, invent, find, find out.
to DISCOVER, manifest, declare.
DISCREDIT, discharge, reproach, scandal.
DISCRETION, prudence, judgment.
to DISCRIMINATE, distinguish.
DISCRIMINATION, judgment, discernment, penetration.
to DISCUSS, examine.
to DISDAIN, contemn, despise, scorn.
DISDAIN, haughtiness, arrogance.
DISDAINFUL, contemptuous, scornful.
DISEASE, distemper, malady, disorder.
DISEASED, morbid, sick, sickly.
to DISENGAGE, disentangle, extricate.
to DISENTANGLE, extricate, disengage.
to DISFIGURE, deform, deface.
to DISGRACE, debase, abase, humble, degrade.
DISGRACE, reproach, scandal, discredit.
DISGRACE, shame, dishonor.
to DISGUISE, conceal, dissemble.
DISGUST, dislike, displeasure, dissatisfaction, distaste.
DISGUST, loathing, nausea.
to DISHEARTEN, deter, discourage.
DISHONOR, disgrace, shame.
DISHONEST, knavish.
DISINCLINATION, dislike.
to DISJOIN, detach, separate, sever.
to DISJOINT, dismember.
to DISLIKE, disapprove.
DISLIKE, disinclination.
DISLIKE, displeasure, dissatisfaction, distaste, disgust.
DISLIKE, hatred, repugnance, aversion, antipathy.
DISLOYALTY, disaffection.
DISMAL, dull, gloomy, sad.
to DISMANTLE, destroy, demolish, raze.

to DISMAY, daunt, appall.
to DISMEMBER, disjoint.
to DISMISS, discharge, discard.
to DISORDER, derange, disconcert, discompose.
DISORDER, confusion.
DISORDER, disease, distemper, malady.
DISORDERLY, inordinate, intemperate, irregular.
to DISOWN, disavow, deny.
to DISOWN, disclaim.
to DISPARAGE, derogate, degrade.
to DISPARAGE, detract, traduce, depreciate, degrade, decry.
DISPARITY, inequality.
DISPASSIONATE, cool.
to DISPATCH, hasten, accelerate, speed, expedite.
to DISPEL, disperse.
to DISPENSE, distribute.
to DISPERSE, dispel.
to DISPERSE, spread, scatter.
to DISPLAY, show, exhibit.
to DISPLEASE, offend, vex.
DISPLEASURE, anger, disapprobation.
DISPLEASURE, dissatisfaction, distaste, disgust, dislike.
DISPOSAL, disposition.
to DISPOSE, arrange, digest.
to DISPOSE, direct, regulate.
to DISPOSE, order, place.
DISPOSED, affected.
DISPOSITION, disposal.
DISPOSITION, inclination.
DISPOSITION, temper.
to DISPROVE, oppugn, confute, refute.
to DISPUTE, contend, contest.
to DISPUTE, controvert.
to DISPUTE, debate, argue.
DISPUTE, altercation, quarrel, difference.
to DISREGARD, neglect, slight.
DISSATISFACTION, distaste, disgust, dislike, displeasure.
to DISSEMBLE, disguise, conceal.
DISSEMBLER, hypocrite.
to DISSEMINATE, spread, circulate, propagate.
DISSENSION, contention, discord.
to DISSENT, differ, vary, disagree.
DISSENTER, nonconformist, heretic, schismatic, sectarian, sectary.
DISSERTATION, essay, treatise, tract.
DISSIMULATION, simulation.
to DISSIPATE, squander, spend, expend, waste.
DISSOLUTE, licentious, loose, vague, lax.
DISTANT, far, remote.
DISTASTE, disgust, dislike, displeasure, dissatisfaction.
DISTEMPER, malady, disorder, disease.
DISTINCT, separate, different.
DISTINCTION, difference.

DISTINCTLY, clearly.
(OF) DISTINCTION, of fashion, of quality.
to DISTINGUISH, abstract, separate.
to DISTINGUISH, discriminate.
to DISTINGUISH, perceive, discern.
to DISTINGUISH, signalize.
DISTINGUISHED, conspicuous, noted, eminent, illustrious.
to DISTORT, wring, wrest, wrench, turn, bend, twist.
DISTRACTED, absent, abstracted, abstract, diverted.
to DISTRESS, harass, perplex.
to DISTRESS, trouble, afflict.
DISTRESS, adversity.
DISTRESS, anxiety, anguish, agony.
to DISTRIBUTE, allot, assign, apportion.
to DISTRIBUTE, dispense.
to DISTRIBUTE, share, divide.
DISTRICT, region, tract, quarter.
DISTRUST, suspicion, diffidence.
to DISTURB, interrupt.
to DISTURB, molest, trouble.
DISTURBANCE, commotion.
DIURNAL, daily.
to DIVE, plunge.
to DIVE INTO, pry, scrutinize.
DIVERS, sundry, various, different, several.
DIVERSION, sport, recreation, pastime, amusement, entertainment.
DIVERSITY, medley, difference, variety.
to DIVERT, entertain, amuse.
DIVERTED, distracted, absent, abstracted, abstract.
to DIVIDE, distribute, share.
to DIVIDE, separate, part.
to DIVINE, guess, conjecture.
DIVINE, heavenly, godlike.
DIVINE, holy, sacred.
DIVINE, theologian, ecclesiastic.
DIVINITY, deity.
DIVISION, portion, share, part.
to DIVULGE, reveal, disclose, publish, promulgate.

to DO, make, act.
DOCILE, tractable, ductile.
DOCTRINE, dogma, tenet.
DOCTRINE, precept, principle.
DOGMA, tenet, doctrine.
DOGMATICAL, positive, confident.
DOLEFUL, woeful, rueful, piteous.
DOMESTIC, menial, drudge, servant.
DOMINEERING, overbearing, imperious, lordly.
DOMINION, empire, reign.
DOMINION, power, strength, force, authority.
DOMINION, territory.
DONATION, benefaction.
DONATION, gift, present.
to DOOM, condemn, sentence.

Doom, destiny, fate, lot.
to Doubt, question.
Doubt, hesitation, objection, demur.
Doubt, suspense.
Doubtful, dubious, uncertain, precarious.
Double-dealing, deceit, duplicity.
Downfall, ruin, fall.
to Doze, drowse, nap, sleep, slumber.

to Drag, haul, hale, pull, pluck, tug, draw.
to Drain, spend, exhaust.
to Draw, drag, haul, hale, pull, pluck, tug.
to Dread, apprehend, fear.
Dread, awe, reverence.
Dreadful, frightful, tremendous, terrible,
  terrific, horrible, horrid, fearful.
Dreadful, terrible, shocking, formidable.
Dream, reverie.
Dregs, sediment, dross, scum, refuse.
to Drench, steep, soak.
Drift, scope, aim, tendency.
Droll, laughable, ludicrous, ridiculous,
  comical, comic.
to Droop, languish, pine, flag.
to Droop, sink, tumble, fall, drop.
to Drop, droop, sink, tumble, fall.
Dross, scum, refuse, dregs, sediment.
to Drowse, nap, sleep, slumber, doze.
Drowsy, heavy, dull.
Drowsy, lethargic, sleepy.
Drudge, servant, domestic, menial.
Drudgery, task, work, labor, toil.
Drunkenness, infatuation, intoxication.

Dubious, uncertain, precarious, doubtful.
Ductile, docile, tractable.
Due, debt.
Dull, drowsy, heavy.
Dull, flat, insipid.
Dull, gloomy, sad, dismal.
Dull, stupid.
Dumb, mute, speechless, silent.
Duplicity, double-dealing, deceit.
Durable, constant.
Durable, lasting, permanent.
Duration, continuance, continuation.
Duration, time.
Dutiful, obedient, respectful.
Duty, business, office.
Duty, custom, toll, impost, tribute, con-
  tribution, tax.
Duty, obligation.

to Dwell, live, reside, inhabit, abide, sojourn.

to Dye, tinge, stain, color.

E

Each, all, every.
Eager, earnest, serious.

Eagerness, avidity, greediness.
Early, betimes, soon.
to Earn, acquire, obtain, gain, win.
Earnest, pledge.
Earnest, serious, eager.
Ease, easiness, facility, lightness.
Ease, quiet, rest, repose.
Easiness, facility, lightness, ease.
Easy, ready.

Ebullition, effervescence, fermentation,
  ferment.

Eccentric, strange, particular, singular,
  odd.
Ecclesiastic, divine, theologian.
to Eclipse, obscure.
Economical, saving, sparing, thrifty, pe-
  nurious, niggardly.
Economy, frugality, parsimony.
Economy, management.
Ecstasy, rapture, transport.

Edge, rim, brim, brink, margin, verge, bor-
  der.
Edict, proclamation, decree.
Edifice, structure, fabric.
Education, instruction, breeding.

to Efface, cancel, obliterate, blot out, ex-
  punge, raze, erase.
to Effect, execute, achieve, accomplish.
to Effect, produce, perform.
Effect, result, issue, event, consequence.
Effective, efficient, effectual, efficacious.
Effects, goods, furniture, chattels, move-
  ables.
Effectual, efficacious, effective, efficient.
Effeminate, female, feminine.
Effervescence, fermentation, ferment,
  ebullition.
Efficacious, effective, efficient, effectual.
Efficient, effectual, efficacious, effective.
Effigy, likeness, picture, image.
Effort, essay, attempt, trial, endeavor.
Effort, exertion, endeavor.
Effrontery, hardihood, hardiness, bold-
  ness, audacity.
Effusion, ejaculation.

Egoistical, opinionated, opinionative, conceited.

Ejaculation, effusion.

Elder, older, senior.
Elderly, aged, old.
to Elect, choose.
Elegant, graceful, comely.
to Elevate, exalt, lift, raise, erect.
Eligible, preferable.
Elocution, eloquence, oratory, rhetoric.

ELOQUENCE, oratory, rhetoric, elocution.
to ELUCIDATE, explain, illustrate.
to ELUDE, avoid, eschew, shun.
to ELUDE, evade, escape.

to EMANATE, arise, rise, proceed, issue, spring, flow.
to EMBARRASS, perplex, entangle.
EMBARRASSMENTS, troubles, difficulties.
to EMBELLISH, adorn, decorate.
EMBLEM, symbol, type, figure, metaphor, allegory.
to EMBOLDEN, encourage.
to EMBRACE, clasp, hug.
to EMBRACE, contain, include, comprise, comprehend.
EMBRYO, foetus.
to EMEND, improve, mend, better, amend, correct.
to EMERGE, rise, issue.
EMERGENCY, exigency.
EMINENT, illustrious, distinguished, conspicuous, noted.
EMISSARY, spy.
to EMIT, exhale, evaporate.
EMOLUMENT, lucre, gain, profit.
EMOTION, agitation, trepidation, tremor.
EMPHASIS, accent, stress, strain.
EMPIRE, kingdom.
EMPIRE, reign, dominion.
to EMPLOY, use.
EMPLOYMENT, engagement, vocation, business, occupation.
to EMPOWER, commission, authorize.
EMPTY, hollow.
EMPTY, vacant, void, devoid.
EMULATION, rivalry, competition.

to ENCHANT, fascinate, enrapture, captivate, charm.
to ENCIRCLE, surround, encompass, environ.
to ENCLOSE, circumscribe.
to ENCLOSE, include.
ENCOMIUM, eulogy, panegyric.
to ENCOMPASS, environ, encircle, surround.
to ENCOUNTER, attack, assail, assault.
ENCOUNTER, onset, charge, attack, assault.
to ENCOURAGE, advance, promote, prefer, forward.
to ENCOURAGE, animate, incite, impel, urge, stimulate, instigate.
to ENCOURAGE, comfort, cheer.
to ENCOURAGE, embolden.
to ENCROACH, intrench, intrude, invade, infringe.
to ENCUMBER, clog, load.
ENCYCLOPAEDIA, dictionary.
to END, terminate, close.
END, extremity.
END, sake, account, reason, purpose.
END, view, aim, object.
to ENDEAVOR, aim, strive, struggle.

ENDEAVOR, effort, essay, attempt, trial.
ENDEAVOR, effort, exertion.
ENDLESS, everlasting, eternal.
to ENDOW, endue, invest.
ENDOWMENT, talent, gift.
to ENDUE, endow, invest.
ENDURANCE, resignation, patience.
to ENDURE, support, bear, suffer.
ENEMY, foe, adversary, opponent, antagonist.
ENERGY, force, vigor.
to ENERVATE, invalidate, weaken, enfeeble, debilitate.
to ENFEEBLE, debilitate, enervate, invalidate, weaken.
to ENGAGE, attract, allure, invite.
to ENGAGE, bind, oblige.
ENGAGEMENT, action, battle, combat.
ENGAGEMENT, vocation, business, occupation, employment.
ENGAGEMENT, word, promise.
to ENGENDER, breed.
ENGRAVING, picture, print.
to ENGROSS, imbibe, absorb, swallow up, engulf.
to ENGULF, engross, imbibe, absorb, swallow up.
ENJOYMENT, fruition, gratification.
to ENLARGE, increase, extend.
to ENLIGHTEN, illuminate, illumine.
to ENLIST, list, register, record, enroll.
to ENLIVEN, cheer, exhilarate, animate, inspire.
ENMITY, animosity, hostility.
ENMITY, ill-will, rancor, hatred.
ENORMOUS, huge, immense, vast.
ENORMOUS, prodigious, monstrous.
ENOUGH, sufficient.
to ENRAPTURE, captivate, charm, enchant, fascinate.
to ENROLL, enlist, list, register, record.
ENSAMPLE, example, pattern.
to ENSLAVE, captivate.
to ENSNARE, entrap, entangle, inveigle.
to ENSUE, follow, succeed.
to ENTANGLE, embarrass, perplex.
to ENTANGLE, inveigle, ensnare, entrap.
to ENTER UPON, begin, commence.
ENTERPRISE, attempt, undertaking.
ENTERPRISING, adventurous.
to ENTERTAIN, amuse, divert.
ENTERTAINMENT, diversion, sport, recreation, pastime, amusement.
ENTERTAINMENT, treat, feast, banquet, carousal.
ENTHUSIAST, fanatic, visionary.
to ENTICE, decoy, allure, tempt, seduce.
to ENTICE, prevail upon, persuade.
ENTIRE, complete, total, integral, whole.
to ENTITLE, designate, characterize, name, denominate, style.
to ENTRAP, entangle, inveigle, ensnare.

to ENTREAT, supplicate, implore, crave, beg, beseech, solicit.
ENTREATY, suit, prayer, petition, request.
to ENTRUST, consign, commit.
ENVIOUS, invidious.
to ENVIRON, encircle, surround, encompass.
ENVOY, plenipotentiary, deputy, ambassador.
ENVY, suspicion, jealousy.

EPHEMERIS, calendar, almanac.
EPICURE, sensualist, voluptuary.
EPIDEMICAL, pestilential, contagious.
EPISTLE, letter.
EPITHET, adjective.
EPITOME, digest, summary, abstract, abridgment, compendium.
EPOCH, time, period, age, date, era.

EQUABLE, like, alike, uniform, equal, even.
EQUAL, even, equable, like, alike, uniform.
to EQUIP, prepare, qualify, fit.
EQUITABLE, reasonable, fair, honest.
EQUITY, justice.
EQUIVOCAL, ambiguous.
to EQUIVOCATE, prevaricate, evade.

to ERADICATE, extirpate, exterminate.
to ERASE, raze, efface, cancel, obliterate, blot out, expunge.
to ERECT, construct, build.
to ERECT, elevate, exalt, lift, raise.
to ERECT, institute, establish, found.
ERRAND, message.
ERROR, fault.
ERROR, mistake, blunder.
ERUDITION, knowledge, science, learning.
ERUPTION, explosion.

to ESCAPE, elude, evade.
to ESCHEW, shun, elude, avoid.
to ESCORT, accompany, attend.
ESPECIALLY, particularly, principally, chiefly.
to ESPY, descry, find, find out, discover.
ESSAY, attempt, trial, endeavor, effort.
ESSAY, treatise, tract, dissertation.
ESSENTIAL, requisite, necessary, expedient.
to ESTABLISH, confirm.
to ESTABLISH, fix, settle.
to ESTABLISH, found, erect, institute.
to ESTEEM, appraise, appreciate, estimate.
to ESTEEM, value, prize.
ESTEEM, respect, regard.
to ESTIMATE, compute, rate.
to ESTIMATE, esteem, appraise, appreciate.
ESTRANGEMENT, abstraction, alienation.

ETERNAL, endless, everlasting.

EUCHARIST, communion, sacrament, Lord's Supper.
EULOGY, panegyric, encomium.

to EVADE, equivocate, prevaricate.
to EVADE, escape, elude.
to EVAPORATE, emit, exhale.
EVASION, shift, subterfuge.
EVEN, equable, like, alike, uniform, equal.
EVEN, smooth, level, plain.
EVENT, consequence, effect, result, issue.
EVENT, incident, accident, adventure, occurrence.
EVER, always, at all times.
EVERLASTING, eternal, endless.
EVERY, each, all.
EVIDENCE, testimony, proof.
EVIDENCE, witness, deponent.
EVIDENT, manifest, apparent, visible, clear, plain, obvious.
EVIL, bad, wicked.
EVIL, ill, misfortune, harm, mischief.
to EVINCE, manifest, prove, demonstrate.
to EVINCE, prove, argue.

EXACT, extort.
EXACT, nice, particular, punctual.
EXACT, precise, accurate.
to EXALT, lift, raise, erect, elevate.
EXAMINATION, search, inquiry, research, investigation, scrutiny.
to EXAMINE, discuss.
to EXAMINE, search, explore.
EXAMPLE, instance.
EXAMPLE, pattern, ensample.
EXAMPLE, precedent.
to EXASPERATE, tantalize, aggravate, irritate, provoke.
to EXCEED, excel, surpass, transcend, outdo.
to EXCEL, surpass, transcend, outdo, exceed.
EXCELLENCE, superiority.
EXCEPT, besides.
EXCEPT, unless.
EXCEPTION, objection, difficulty.
EXCESS, superfluity, redundancy.
EXCESSIVE, immoderate, intemperate.
to EXCHANGE, barter, substitute, change.
to EXCHANGE, barter, truck, commute.
EXCHANGE, reciprocity, interchange.
to EXCITE, incite, provoke.
to EXCITE, provoke, rouse, stir up, awaken.
to EXCLAIM, call, cry.
to EXCULPATE, excuse, plead, apologize, defend, justify.
to EXCULPATE, exonerate.
EXCURSION, ramble, tour, trip, jaunt.
to EXCUSE, pardon.
to EXCUSE, plead, apologize, defend, justify, exculpate.
EXCUSE, pretense, pretension, pretext.
EXECRABLE, abominable, detestable.
EXECRATION, anathema, malediction, curse, imprecation.
to EXECUTE, achieve, accomplish, effect.
to EXECUTE, fulfill, perform.

Exempt, free.

Exemption, immunity, privilege, prerogative.

to Exercise, exert.

to Exercise, practise.

to Exert, exercise.

Exertion, endeavor, effort.

to Exhale, evaporate, emit.

to Exhaust, drain, spend.

to Exhibit, display, show.

to Exhibit, give, present, offer.

Exhibition, representation, sight, spectacle, show.

to Exhilarate, animate, inspire, enliven, cheer.

to Exhort, persuade.

Exigency, emergency.

to Exile, expel, banish.

to Exist, live.

to Exist, subsist, be.

Exit, departure.

to Exonerate, exculpate.

to Expand, diffuse, spread.

to Expand, dilate.

to Expect, wait, wait for, await, look for.

Expectation, trust, confidence, hope.

Expedient, essential, requisite, necessary.

Expedient, fit.

Expedient, resource.

to Expedite, dispatch, hasten, accelerate, speed.

Expeditious, prompt, diligent.

to Expel, banish, exile.

to Expend, spend, waste, dissipate, squander.

Expense, price, charge, cost.

Experience, experiment, trial, proof, test.

Experiment, trial, proof, test, experience.

Expert, dexterous, adroit, clever, skillful.

to Expiate, atone for.

to Expire, die.

to Explain, expound, interpret.

to Explain, illustrate, elucidate.

Explanation, definition.

Explanatory, explicit, express.

Explicit, express, explanatory.

Exploit, achievement, feat, deed.

to Explore, examine, search.

Explosion, eruption.

Exposed, obnoxious, subject, liable.

to Expostulate, remonstrate.

to Expound, interpret, explain.

to Express, declare, signify, testify, utter.

Express, explanatory, explicit.

Expression, word, term.

Expressive, significant.

to Expunge, raze, erase, efface, cancel, obliterate, blot out.

to Extend, enlarge, increase.

to Extend, stretch, reach.

Extensive, comprehensive.

Extent, limit.

to Extenuate, palliate.

Exterior, outward, external.

to Exterminate, eradicate, extirpate.

External, exterior, outward.

to Extirpate, exterminate, eradicate.

to Extol, praise, command, applaud.

Extort, exact.

Extraneous, extrinsic, foreign.

Extraordinary, remarkable.

Extravagant, prodigal, lavish, profuse.

Extreme, extremity.

Extremity, end.

Extremity, extreme.

to Extricate, disengage, disentangle.

Extrinsic, foreign, extraneous.

Exuberant, luxuriant.

to Eye, look, see, behold, view.

F

Fable, tale, novel, romance.

Fabric, edifice, structure.

to Fabricate, forge, invent, feign, frame.

Fabrication, falsehood, fiction.

to Face, confront.

Face, countenance, visage.

Face, front.

Facetious, conversable, pleasant, jocular, jocose.

Facility, lightness, ease, easiness.

Fact, circumstance, incident.

Faction, party.

Factious, seditous.

Factor, agent.

Faculty, talent, ability.

to Fail, fall short, be deficient.

Failing, failure.

Failing, foible, imperfection, weakness, fraility.

Failure, bankruptcy, insolvency.

Failure, failing.

Failure, miscarriage, abortion.

Faint, languid.

Fair, clear.

Fair, honest, equitable, reasonable.

Faith, belief, credit, trust.

Faith, creed.

Faith, fidelity.

Faithful, trusty.

Faithless, perfidious, treacherous.

to Fall, drop, droop, sink, tumble.

Fall, downfall, ruin.

to Fall Short, be deficient, fail.

Fallacious, deceitful, fraudulent.

Fallacy, delusion, illusion.

Falsehood, falsity, lie, untruth.

Falsehood, fiction, fabrication.

Falsity, lie, untruth, falsehood.

to Falter, stammer, stutter, hesitate.

Fame, report, rumor, hearsay.

Fame, reputation, renown.

FAMILIAR, conversant.
FAMILIAR, free.
FAMILIARITY, intimacy, acquaintance.
FAMILY, house, lineage, race.
FAMOUS, celebrated, renowned, illustrious.
FANATIC, visionary, enthusiast.
FANCIFUL, fantastical, whimsical, capricious.
FANCY, conceit.
FANCY, imagination.
FANTASTICAL, whimsical, capricious, fanciful.
FAR, remote, distant.
FARE, provision.
FARMER, husbandman, agriculturist.
to FASCINATE, enrapture, captivate, charm, enchant.
to FASHION, mold, shape, form.
FASHION, manner, practice, custom.
(OF) FASHION, of quality, of distinction.
FAST, abstinence.
to FASTEN, stick, fix.
FASTIDIOUS, squeamish.
FATAL, deadly, mortal.
FATE, chance, fortune.
FATE, lot, doom, destiny.
FATIGUE, weariness, lassitude.
FAULT, blemish, defect.
FAULT, error.
FAULT, vice, imperfection, defect.
FAULTY, culpable.
FAVOR, grace.
FAVOR, influence, credit.
FAVOR, kindness, civility, benefit.
to FAWN, coax, wheedle, cajole.

FEALTY, court, homage.
to FEAR, dread, apprehend.
FEARFUL, dreadful, frightful, tremendous, terrible, terrific, horrible, horrid.
FEARFUL, timorous, timid, afraid.
FEARLESS, intrepid, undaunted, bold.
FEASIBLE, colorable, specious, ostensible, plausible.
FEAST, banquet, carousal, entertainment, treat.
FEAST, festival, holiday.
FEAT, deed, exploit, achievement.
FEEBLE, infirm, weak.
to FEEL, be sensible, be conscious.
FEELING, sense, sensation.
FEELING, sensibility, susceptibility.
to FEIGN, frame, fabricate, forge, invent.
to FEIGN, pretend.
to FELICITATE, congratulate.
FELICITY, bliss, blessedness, beatitude, happiness.
FELLOWSHIP, society.
FELON, convict, criminal, culprit, malefactor.
FEMALE, feminine, effeminate.
FEMININE, effeminate, female.

FENCE, guard, security.
FERMENT, ebullition, effervescence, fermentation.
FERMENTATION, ferment, ebullition, effervescence.
FEROCIOUS, fierce, savage.
FERRYMAN, waterman, boatman.
FERTILE, fruitful, prolific.
FERVOR, ardor.
FESTIVAL, holiday, feast.
FESTIVITY, mirth.
to FETCH, carry, bring.
FETTER, band, shackle, chain.
FEUD, quarrel, broil.

FICKLE, versatile, changeable, mutable, variable, inconstant.
FICTION, fabrication, falsehood.
FICTITIOUS, artful, artificial.
FIDELITY, faith.
FIERCE, savage, ferocious.
FIERY, burning, ardent, hot.
FIGURE, conformation, form.
FIGURE, metaphor, allegory, emblem, symbol, type.
FINAL, conclusive.
FINAL, ultimate, last, latest.
to FIND, find out, discover, espy, descry.
to FIND, find out, discover, invent.
to FIND FAULT WITH, blame, object to.
to FIND OUT, discover, espy, descry, find.
to FIND OUT, discover, invent, find.
FINE, delicate, nice.
FINE, handsome, pretty, beautiful.
FINE, mulct, penalty, forfeiture.
FINESSE, stratagem, artifice, trick.
FINICAL, spruce, foppish.
to FINISH, close, conclude.
to FINISH, terminate, complete.
FINISHED, complete, perfect.
FINITE, limited.
FIRE, heat, warmth, glow.
FIRM, fixed, solid, stable.
FIRM, solid, hard.
FIRMNESS, constancy, stability, steadiness.
to FIT, equip, prepare, qualify.
to FIT, suit, adapt, accommodate, adjust.
FIT, apt, meet.
FIT, expedient.
FIT, proper, right, just.
FIT, suitable, becoming, decent, seemly.
FITTED, qualified, competent.
to FIX, determine, settle, limit.
to FIX, fasten, stick.
to FIX, settle, establish.
FIXED, solid, stable, firm.

to FLAG, droop, languish, pine.
FLAGITIOUS, atrocious, heinous, flagrant.
FLAGRANT, flagitious, atrocious, heinous.
FLAME, blaze, flash, flare, glare.
FLARE, glare, flame, blaze, flash.

FLASH, flare, glare, flame, blaze.
FLAT, insipid, dull.
FLAT, level.
to FLATTER, compliment, adulate.
FLATTERER, sycophant, parasite.
FLAVOR, relish, savor, taste.
FLAW, blemish, stain, spot, speck.
FLEETING, temporary, transient, transitory.
FLEETNESS, celerity, rapidity, velocity, quickness, swiftness.
FLEXIBLE, pliable, pliant, supple.
FLIGHTINESS, volatility, giddiness, lightness, levity.
FLIMSY, superficial, shallow.
to FLOURISH, thrive, prosper.
to FLOW, stream, gush.
to FLOW, emanate, arise, rise, proceed, issue, spring.
to FLUCTUATE, waver.
FLUID, liquid.
to FLUTTER, pant, gasp, palpitate.

FOE, adversary, opponent, antagonist, enemy.
FOETUS, embryo.
FOIBLE, imperfection, weakness, fraility, failing.
to FOIL, disappoint, frustrate, defeat.
FOLKS, people, persons.
to FOLLOW, imitate.
to FOLLOW, pursue.
to FOLLOW, succeed, ensue.
FOLLOWER, adherent, partisan.
FOLLY, foolery.
FOND, affectionate, kind.
FOND, amorous, loving.
FOND, indulgent.
FOOD, diet, regimen.
FOOL, idiot, buffoon.
FOOLERY, folly.
FOOLHARDY, adventurous, rash.
FOOLISH, absurd, preposterous, irrational.
FOOLISH, simple, silly.
FOOTSTEP, track, mark, trace, vestige.
FOPPISH, finical, spruce.
to FORBEAR, refrain, abstain.
to FORBID, prohibit, interdict.
to FORCE, oblige, necessitate, compel.
FORCE, authority, dominion, power, strength.
FORCE, strain, sprain, stress.
FORCE, vigor, energy.
FORCE, violence.
FORCIBLE, strong, cogent.
to FOREBODE, betoken, portend, augur, presage.
FORECAST, premeditation, foresight, forethought.
FOREFATHERS, progenitors, ancestors.
to FOREGO, give up, abandon, resign.
FOREGOING, previous, anterior, prior, former, antecedent, preceding.

FOREIGN, extraneous, extrinsic.
FOREIGNER, alien, stranger.
FORERUNNER, precursor, messenger, harbinger.
FORESIGHT, forethought, forecast, premeditation.
FOREST, chace, park.
to FORETELL, predict, prophesy, prognosticate.
FORETHOUGHT, forecast, premeditation, foresight.
FORFEITURE, fine, mulct, penalty.
to FORGE, invent, feign, frame, fabricate.
FORGETFULNESS, oblivion.
to FORGIVE, pardon, absolve, remit.
FORLORN, destitute, forsaken.
to FORM, compose, constitute.
to FORM, fashion, mold, shape.
to FORM, produce, create, make.
FORM, ceremony, rite, observance.
FORM, figure, conformation.
FORMAL, ceremonious, ceremonial.
FORMER, antecedent, preceding, foregoing, previous, anterior, prior.
FORMERLY, in times past, in old times, in days of yore, anciently, in ancient times.
FORMIDABLE, dreadful, terrible, shocking.
to FORSAKE, relinquish, abandon, desert.
FORSAKEN, forlorn, destitute.
to FORSWEAR, perjure, suborn.
to FORTIFY, invigorate, strengthen.
FORTITUDE, resolution, courage.
FORTUITOUS, prosperous, successful, fortunate, lucky.
FORTUNATE, lucky, fortuitous, prosperous, successful.
FORTUNE, fate, chance.
to FORWARD, encourage, advance, promote, prefer.
FORWARD, progressive, onward.
to FOSTER, cherish, harbor, indulge.
to FOUND, erect, institute, establish.
to FOUND, ground, rest, build.
FOUNDATION, ground, basis.
FOUNTAIN, source, spring.

FRACTION, rupture, fracture.
FRACTURE, fraction, rupture.
FRAGILE, frail, brittle.
FRAGRANCE, smell, scent, odor, perfume.
FRAIL, brittle, fragile.
FRAILTY, failing, foible, imperfection, weakness.
to FRAME, fabricate, forge, invent, feign.
FRAME, temper, temperament, constitution.
FRANK, candid, ingenuous, free, open, plain.
FRAUD, guile, deceit.
FRAUDULENT, fallacious, deceitful.
FRAY, affray, quarrel.
FREAK, whim.
to FREE, set, free, deliver, liberate.
FREE, exempt.

FREE, familiar.
FREE, liberal.
FREE, open, plain, frank, candid, ingenuous.
FREEDOM, liberty.
FREIGHT, cargo, lading, load, burden.
FRENZY, rage, fury, madness.
to FREQUENT, resort to, haunt.
FREQUENTLY, often.
FREQUENTLY, usually, commonly, generally.
FRESH, recent, new, novel, modern.
to FRET, gall, rub, chafe.
FRETFUL, captious, cross, peevish, petulant.
FRIENDLY, amicable.
FRIENDSHIP, love.
FRIGHT, consternation, alarm, terror.
to FRIGHTEN, intimidate.
FRIGHTFUL, tremendous, terrible, terrific, horrible, horrid, fearful, dreadful.
FRIGID, cool, cold.
FRIVOLOUS, futile, trifling, trivial, petty.
FROLIC, gambol, prank.
FRONT, face.
FRONTIER, confine, precinct, border, boundary.
FROWARD, perverse, awkward, cross, untoward, crooked.
FRUGALITY, parsimony, economy.
FRUITFUL, prolific, fertile.
FRUITION, gratification, enjoyment.
FRUITLESS, vain, ineffectual.
to FRUSTRATE, defeat, foil, disappoint.

to FULFILL, accomplish, realize.
to FULFILL, keep, observe.
to FULFILL, perform, execute.
FULLY, largely, copiously.
FULLNESS, plentitude.
FUNCTION, office, place, charge.
FUNERAL, obsequies.
FURIOUS, boisterous, vehement, impetuous, violent.
to FURNISH, supply, provide, procure.
FURNITURE, chattels, moveables, effects, goods.
FURY, anger, choler, rage.
FURY, madness, frenzy, rage.
FUTILE, trifling, trivial, petty, frivolous.

G

to GAIN, obtain, procure, get.
to GAIN, win, earn, acquire, obtain.
GAIN, profit, emolument, lucre.
GAIT, walk, carriage.
GALE, blast, gust, storm, tempest, hurricane, breeze.
to GALL, rub, chafe, fret.
GALLANT, beau, spark.
GALLANT, brave.
GAMBOL, prank, frolic.
GAME, sport, play.
GAMESOME, sportive, playful.

GANG, band, company, crew.
GAP, chasm, breach, break.
to GAPE, stare, gaze.
GARRULOUS, talkative, loquacious.
to GASP, palpitate, flutter, pant.
to GATHER, collect.
GAUDY, gay, showy.
GAY, cheerful, merry, sprightly.
GAY, showy, gaudy.
to GAZE, gape, stare.

GENDER, sex.
GENERAL, universal.
GENERALLY, frequently, usually, commonly.
GENERATION, age.
GENERATION, breed, race.
GENEROUS, liberal, beneficent, bountiful, bounteous, munificent.
GENIUS, talent, intellect.
GENIUS, taste.
GENTEEL, polite.
GENTILE, heathen, pagan.
GENTLE, meek, soft, mild.
GENTLE, tame.
GENUINE, native, intrinsic, real.
GESTICULATION, posture, attitude, action, gesture.
GESTURE, gesticulation, posture, attitude, action.
to GET, gain, obtain, procure.

GHASTLY, grim, grisly, hideous.
GHOST, vision, apparition, phantom, spectre.
GHOSTLY, spirituous, spirited, spiritual.

to GIBE, jeer, sneer, scoff.
GIDDINESS, lightness, levity, flightiness, volatility.
GIFT, endowment, talent.
GIFT, present, donation.
to GIVE, afford.
to GIVE, grant, bestow.
to GIVE, present, offer, exhibit.
to GIVE UP, abandon, resign, forego.
to GIVE UP, deliver, surrender, yield, cede, concede.

GLAD, pleased, joyful, cheerful.
GLADNESS, mirth, joy.
GLANCE, glimpse.
GLANCE, look.
to GLANCE AT, allude to.
to GLARE, sparkle, radiate, shine, glitter.
GLARE, flame, blaze, flash, flare.
GLARING, barefaced.
GLEAM, glimmer, ray, beam.
to GLIDE, slip, slide.
GLIMMER, ray, beam, gleam.
GLIMPSE, glance.
to GLITTER, glare, sparkle, radiate, shine.
GLOBE, ball.

GLOBE, circle, sphere, orb.
GLOOM, heaviness.
GLOOMY, sad, dismal, dull.
GLOOMY, sullen, morose, splenetic.
to GLORY, boast, vaunt.
GLORY, honor.
to GLOSS, varnish, palliate.
GLOSSARY, nomenclature, dictionary, lexicon, vocabulary.
GLOW, fire, heat, warmth.
to GLUT, cloy, satisfy, satiate.

GODLIKE, divine, heavenly.
GODLY, righteous.
GOLD, golden.
GOLDEN, gold.
GOOD, benefit, advantage.
GOOD, goodness.
GOOD HUMOR, good nature.
GOOD NATURE, good humor.
GOOD OFFICE, benefit, service.
GOODNESS, good.
GOODS, furniture, chattels, moveables, effects.
GOODS, merchandise, ware, commodity.
to GOVERN, rule, regulate.
GOVERNMENT, administration.
GOVERNMENT, constitution.

GRACE, charm.
GRACE, favor.
GRACEFUL, becoming, comely.
GRACEFUL, comely, elegant.
GRACIOUS, merciful, kind.
GRAND, noble.
GRAND, sublime, great.
GRANDEUR, magnificence.
to GRANT, admit, allow.
to GRANT, bestow, allow.
to GRANT, bestow, give.
to GRASP, grip, lay hold of, take hold of, catch, seize, snatch.
GRATEFUL, welcome, acceptable.
GRATIFICATION, enjoyment, fruition.
to GRATIFY, indulge, humor.
to GRATIFY, satisfy, please.
GRATITUDE, thankfulness.
GRATUITOUS, voluntary.
GRATUITY, recompense.
GRAVE, serious, solemn.
GRAVE, sober.
GRAVE, tomb, sepulchre.
GRAVITY, weight, heaviness.
GREAT, grand, sublime.
GREAT, large, big.
GREATNESS, bulk, size, magnitude.
GREEDINESS, eagerness, avidity.
to GREET, hail, welcome, accost, salute, address.
GREETING, salute, salutation.
GRIEF, sorrow, affliction.
GRIEVANCE, hardship.

to GRIEVE, mourn, lament.
GRIEVED, hurt, sorry.
GRIM, grisly, hideous, ghastly.
to GRIP, lay hold of, take hold of, catch, seize, snatch, grasp.
to GRIPE, press, squeeze, pinch.
GRISLY, hideous, ghastly, grim.
to GROAN, moan.
GROSS, coarse.
GROSS, total.
to GROUND, rest, build, found.
GROUND, basis, foundation.
GROUP, collection, assembly, assemblage.
to GROW, be, become.
to GROW, increase.
GRUDGE, pique, malice, rancor, spite.

to GUARANTEE, be security, be responsible, warrant.
to GUARD, defend, watch.
GUARD, guardian.
GUARD, security, fence.
GUARD, sentinel.
to GUARD AGAINST, take heed.
GUARDIAN, guard.
to GUESS, conjecture, divine.
GUEST, visitor, visitant.
to GUIDE, lead, conduct.
GUIDE, rule.
GUILE, deceit, fraud.
GUILTLESS, innocent, harmless.
GUILTY, criminal.
GUISE, habit.
GULF, abyss.
to GUSH, flow, stream.
GUST, storm, tempest, hurricane, breeze, gale, blast.

H

HABIT, custom.
HABIT, guise.
to HAIL, welcome, accost, salute, address, greet.
to HALE, haul, pull, pluck, tug, draw, drag.
to HALLOW, dedicate, devote, consecrate.
HANDSOME, pretty, beautiful, fine.
to HANKER AFTER, covet, desire, wish, long for.
to HAPPEN, chance.
HAPPINESS, felicity, bliss, blessedness, beatitude.
HAPPINESS, well-being, welfare, prosperity.
HAPPY, fortunate.
HARANGUE, oration, address, speech.
to HARASS, perplex, distress.
to HARASS, weary, tire, jade.
HARBINGER, forerunner, precursor, messenger.
to HARBOR, indulge, foster, cherish.
to HARBOR, shelter, lodge.
HARBOR, haven, port.
HARD, callous, hardened, obdurate.

HARD, difficult, arduous.
HARD, firm, solid.
HARD, hardy, insensible, unfeeling.
HARDENED, obdurate, hard, callous.
HARDHEARTED, cruel, unmerciful, merciless.
HARDIHOOD, hardiness, boldness, audacity, effrontery.
HARDINESS, hardihood, boldness, audacity, effrontery.
HARDLY, scarcely.
HARDSHIP, grievance.
HARDY, insensible, unfeeling, hard.
HARM, mischief, evil, ill, misfortune.
HARM, mischief, injury, damage, hurt.
HARMLESS, guiltless, innocent.
HARMLESS, unoffending, inoffensive.
HARMONY, accordance, melody.
HARMONY, concord.
HARSH, rough, severe, rigorous.
HARSHNESS, acrimony, tartness, asperity.
to HASTEN, accelerate, speed, expedite, dispatch.
to HASTEN, hurry.
HASTINESS, precipitancy, rashness, temerity.
HASTY, angry, passionate.
HASTY, slight, desultory, cursory.
to HATE, detest.
HATEFUL, odious.
HATRED, enmity, ill-will, rancor.
HATRED, repugnance, aversion, antipathy, dislike.
HAUGHTINESS, disdain, arrogance.
HAUGHTINESS, loftiness, dignity, pride.
HAUGHTY, high, high-minded.
to HAUL, hale, pull, pluck, tug, draw, drag.
to HAUNT, frequent, resort to.
HAVEN, port, harbor.
to HAZARD, risk, venture.
HAZARD, chance.
HAZARD, danger, peril.

HEAD, chief, leader, chieftain.
HEADSTRONG, heady, obstinate, contumacious, stubborn.
HEADY, obstinate, contumacious, stubborn, headstrong.
to HEAL, remedy, cure.
HEALTHY, sound, sane.
HEALTHY, wholesome, salubrious, salutary.
to HEAP, pile, accumulate, amass.
to HEAR, hearken, overhear.
to HEARKEN, listen, attend.
to HEARKEN, overhear, hear.
HEARSAY, fame, report, rumor.
HEARTY, warm, sincere, cordial.
HEAT, warmth, glow, fire.
HEATHEN, pagan, gentile.
to HEAVE, hoist, lift.
to HEAVE, swell.
HEAVENLY, godlike, divine.

HEAVINESS, gloom.
HEAVINESS, gravity, weight.
HEAVY, burdensome, weighty, ponderous.
HEAVY, dull, drowsy.
to HEED, notice, attend to, mind, regard.
HEED, care, attention.
HEEDLESS, inattentive, negligent, remiss, careless, thoughtless.
to HEIGHTEN, raise, aggravate.
HEINOUS, flagrant, flagitious, atrocious.
to HELP, assist, aid, succour, relieve.
HERESY, heterodoxy.
HERETIC, schismatic, sectarian, sectary, dissenter, nonconformist.
to HESITATE, falter, stammer, stutter.
to HESITATE, pause, demur.
to HESITATE, waver, scruple.
HESITATION, objection, demur, doubt.
HETERODOXY, heresy.

HIDDEN, latent, occult, mysterious, secret.
to HIDE, cover.
to HIDE, secrete, conceal.
HIDE, peel, rind, skin.
HIDEOUS, ghastly, grim, grisly.
HIGH, high-minded, haughty.
HIGH, tall, lofty.
HIGH-MINDED, haughty, high.
HIGH-SOUNDING, clamorous, loud, noisy.
HILARITY, mirth, merriment, joviality, jollity.
HIND, rustic, clown, countryman, peasant, swain.
to HINDER, prevent, impede, obstruct.
to HINDER, retard.
to HINDER, stop.
to HINT, suggest, allude, refer.
to HINT, suggest, intimate, insinuate.
HIRE, pay, allowance, stipend, salary, wages.
HIRELING, mercenary.
to HIT, beat, strike.

to HOARD, treasure.
to HOIST, lift, heave.
to HOLD, contain.
to HOLD, keep, detain, retain.
to HOLD, occupy, possess.
to HOLD, support, maintain.
HOLIDAY, feast, festival.
HOLINESS, sanctity.
HOLLOW, empty.
HOLY, pious, devout, religious.
HOLY, sacred, divine.
HOMAGE, fealty, court.
HONEST, equitable, reasonable, fair.
HONEST, true, plain, sincere.
HONESTY, honor.
HONESTY, probity, uprightness, integrity.
to HONOR, reverence, respect.
HONOR, dignity.
HONOR, glory.

HONOR, honesty.
HOPE, expectation, trust, confidence.
HOPELESS, desperate.
HORRIBLE, horrid, fearful, dreadful, frightful, tremendous, terrible, terrific.
HORRID, fearful, dreadful, frightful, tremendous, terrible, terrific, horrible.
HOST, army.
HOSTILE, repugnant, adverse, inimical.
HOSTILITY, enmity, animosity.
HOT, fiery, burning, ardent.
HOUSE, lineage, race, family.
HOWEVER, yet, nevertheless, notwithstanding.

HUE, tint, color.
to HUG, embrace, clasp.
HUGE, immense, vast, enormous.
HUMAN, humane.
HUMANE, human.
HUMANITY, kindness, tenderness, benevolence, benignity.
to HUMBLE, humiliate, degrade.
HUMBLE, lowly, low.
HUMBLE, modest, submissive.
HUMIDITY, dampness, moisture.
to HUMILIATE, degrade, humble.
to HUMOR, gratify, indulge.
to HUMOR, qualify, temper.
HUMOR, caprice.
HUMOR, liquid, liquor, juice.
HUMOR, satire, irony, burlesque, wit.
HUMOR, temper, mood.
HUMOROUS, capricious, humorsome.
HUMORSOME, humorous, capricious.
HUNT, chase.
to HURL, cast, throw.
HURRICANE, breeze, gale, blast, gust, storm, tempest.
to HURRY, hasten.
HURT, detriment, prejudice, disadvantage, injury.
HURT, harm, mischief, injury, damage.
HURT, sorry, grieved.
HURTFUL, pernicious, noxious, noisome.
HUSBANDMAN, agriculturist, farmer.
HUSBANDRY, cultivation, tillage.

HYPOCRITE, dissembler.

I

IDEA, conception, notion, perception.
IDEA, thought, imagination.
IDEAL, imaginary.
IDIOM, dialect, language, tongue, speech.
IDIOT, buffoon, fool.
IDLE, lazy, indolent.
IDLE, at leisure, vacant.
IDLE, vain.

IGNOMINY, opprobrium, infamy.
IGNORANT, illiterate, unlearned, unlettered.

ILL, badly.
ILL, evil, misfortune, harm, mischief.
ILLITERATE, unlearned, unlettered, ignorant.
ILLNESS, indisposition, sickness.
to ILLUMINATE, illumine, enlighten.
to ILLUMINE, enlighten, illuminate.
ILLUSION, fallacy, delusion.
to ILLUSTRATE, elucidate, explain.
ILLUSTRIOUS, distinguished, conspicuous, noted, eminent.
ILLUSTRIOUS, famous, celebrated, renowned.
ILL WILL, rancor, hatred, enmity.

IMAGE, effigy, likeness, picture.
IMAGINARY, ideal.
IMAGINATION, fancy.
IMAGINATION, idea, thought.
to IMAGINE, apprehend, conceive, suppose.
to IMAGINE, believe, deem, think, suppose.
IMBECILITY, debility, infirmity.
to IMBIBE, absorb, swallow up, engulf, engross.
to IMITATE, copy, counterfeit.
to IMITATE, follow.
to IMITATE, mimic, ape, mock.
IMMATERIAL, inconsiderable, unimportant, insignificant.
IMMATERIAL, spiritual, incorporeal, unbodied.
IMMEDIATELY, instantly, instantaneously, directly.
IMMENSE, vast, enormous, huge.
IMMINENT, impending, threatening.
IMMODERATE, intemperate, excessive.
IMMODEST, impudent, shameless.
IMMODEST, indelicate, indecent.
IMMUNITY, privilege, prerogative, exemption.
to IMPAIR, injure.
to IMPART, communicate.
IMPASSABLE, inaccessible, impervious.
to IMPEACH, arraign, accuse, charge.
to IMPEDE, obstruct, hinder, prevent.
IMPEDIMENT, difficulty, obstacle.
to IMPEL, constrain, restrain, compel.
to IMPEL, induce, actuate.
to IMPEL, urge, stimulate, instigate, encourage, animate, incite.
IMPENDING, threatening, imminent.
IMPERATIVE, imperious, authoritative, commanding.
IMPERFECTION, defect, fault, vice.
IMPERFECTION, weakness, frailty, failing, foible.
IMPERIOUS, authoritative, commanding, imperative.
IMPERIOUS, lordly, domineering, overbearing.
IMPERTINENT, rude, saucy, impudent, insolent.
IMPERVIOUS, impassable, inaccessible.

IMPETUOUS, violent, furious, boisterous, vehement.

IMPIOUS, irreligious, profane.

IMPLACABLE, unrelenting, relentless, inexorable.

to IMPLANT, ingraft, inculcate, instill, infuse.

to IMPLICATE, involve.

to IMPLORE, crave, beg, beseech, solicit, entreat, supplicate.

to IMPLY, signify.

IMPORT, sense, signification, meaning.

IMPORTANCE, consequence, weight, moment.

IMPORTUNATE, pressing, urgent.

IMPORTUNITY, solicitation.

to IMPOSE UPON, deceive, delude.

IMPOST, tribute, contribution, tax, duty, custom, toll.

IMPOSTER, deceiver.

IMPRECATION, execration, anathema, malediction, curse.

IMPRESSION, stamp, mark, print.

IMPRISONMENT, captivity, confinement.

to IMPROVE, mend, better, amend, correct, emend.

IMPROVEMENT, progress, proficiency.

IMPUDENCE, assurance.

IMPUDENT, insolent, impertinent, rude, saucy.

IMPUDENT, shameless, immodest.

to IMPUGN, attack.

to IMPUTE, attribute, ascribe.

INABILITY, disability.

INACCESSIBLE, impervious, impassable.

INACTIVE, inert, lazy, slothful, sluggish.

INADEQUATE, incapable, insufficient, incompetent.

INADVERTENCY, inattention, oversight.

INANIMATE, lifeless, dead.

INANITY, vacancy, vacuity.

INATTENTION, oversight, inadvertency.

INATTENTIVE, negligent, remiss, careless, thoughtless, heedless.

INBORN, innate, inherent, inbred.

INBRED, inborn, innate, inherent.

INCAPABLE, insufficient, incompetent, inadequate.

INCESSANTLY, unceasingly, uninterruptedly, without intermission.

INCIDENT, accident, adventure, occurrence, event.

INCIDENT, fact, circumstance.

INCIDENTAL, casual, contingent, accidental.

to INCITE, impel, urge, stimulate, instigate, encourage, animate.

to INCITE, provoke, excite.

INCLINATION, attachment, affection.

INCLINATION, disposition.

INCLINATION, prepossession, bent, bias.

INCLINATION, tendency, propensity, proneness.

to INCLINE, bend, lean.

to INCLUDE, comprise, comprehend, embrace, contain.

to INCLUDE, enclose.

INCOHERENT, inconsistent, incongruous.

INCOMPETENT, inadequate, incapable, insufficient.

INCONGRUOUS, incoherent, inconsistent.

INCONSIDERABLE, unimportant, insignificant, immaterial.

INCONSISTENT, incongruous, incoherent.

INCONSTANT, fickle, versatile, changeable, mutable, variable.

INCONTROVERTIBLE, irrefragable, indubitable, unquestionable, indisputable, undeniable.

to INCONVENIENCE, annoy, molest.

INCORPOREAL, unbodied, immaterial, spiritual.

to INCREASE, extend, enlarge.

to INCREASE, grow.

INCREASE, addition, accession, augmentation.

INCREDULITY, unbelief, infidelity.

to INCULCATE, instill, infuse, implant, ingraft.

INCURSION, irruption, inroad, invasion.

INDEBTED, obliged.

INDECENT, immodest, indelicate.

INDELICATE, indecent, immodest.

to INDICATE, show, point out, mark.

INDICATION, mark, sign, note, symptom, token.

INDIFFERENCE, insensibility, apathy.

INDIFFERENT, unconcerned, regardless.

INDIGENCE, need, poverty, want, penury.

INDIGENOUS, natal, native.

INDIGNATION, anger, resentment, wrath, ire.

INDIGNITY, insult.

INDISCRIMINATE, promiscuous.

INDISPOSITION, sickness, illness.

INDISPUTABLE, undeniable, incontrovertible, irrefragable, indubitable, unquestionable.

INDISTINCT, confused.

INDIVIDUAL, particular.

INDOLENT, idle, lazy.

INDOLENT, supine, listless, careless.

INDUBITABLE, unquestionable, indisputable, undeniable, incontrovertible, irrefragable.

to INDUCE, actuate, impel.

to INDULGE, foster, cherish, harbor.

to INDULGE, humor, gratify.

INDULGENT, fond.

INDUSTRIOUS, assiduous, laborious, active, diligent.

INEFFABLE, unutterable, inexpressible, unspeakable.

INEFFECTUAL, fruitless, vain.

INEQUALITY, disparity.

INERT, lazy, slothful, sluggish, inactive.

INEXORABLE, implacable, unrelenting, relentless.

INEXPRESSIBLE, unspeakable, ineffable, unutterable.

INFAMOUS, scandalous.

INFAMY, ignominy, opprobrium.

INFANTINE, childish.

INFATUATION, intoxication, drunkenness.

INFECTION, contagion.

INFERENCE, deduction, conclusion.

INFERIOR, second, secondary.

INFERIOR, subservient, subject, subordinate.

INFIDELITY, incredulity, unbelief.

INFINITE, boundless, unbounded, unlimited.

INFIRM, weak, feeble.

INFIRMITY, imbecility, debility.

INFLUENCE, authority, ascendancy, ascendant, sway.

INFLUENCE, credit, favor.

to INFORM, instruct, teach.

to INFORM, make known, acquaint, apprize.

INFORMANT, informer.

INFORMATION, intelligence, notice, advice.

INFORMER, informant.

INFRACTION, infringement.

to INFRINGE, encroach, intrench, intrude, invade.

to INFRINGE, violate, transgress.

INFRINGEMENT, infraction.

INFUSE, implant, ingraft, inculcate, instill.

INGENUITY, wit.

INGENUOUS, free, open, plain, frank, candid.

to INGRAFT, inculcate, instill, infuse, implant.

to INGRATIATE, insinuate.

to INHABIT, abide, sojourn, dwell, live, reside.

INHERENT, inbred, inborn, innate.

INHUMAN, barbarous, brutal, savage, cruel.

INIMICAL, hostile, repugnant, adverse.

INIQUITOUS, nefarious, wicked.

INJUNCTION, precept, command, order.

to INJURE, impair.

INJURY, damage, hurt, harm, mischief.

INJURY, hurt, detriment, prejudice, disadvantage.

INJURY, wrong, injustice.

INJUSTICE, injury, wrong.

INNATE, inherent, inbred, inborn.

INNER, interior, inward, internal.

INNOCENT, harmless, guiltless.

INOFFENSIVE, harmless, unoffending.

INORDINATE, intemperate, irregular, disorderly.

to INQUIRE, question, interrogate, ask.

INQUIRY, research, investigation, scrutiny, examination, search.

INQUISITIVE, prying, curious.

INROAD, invasion, incursion, irruption.

INSANITY, lunacy, madness, mania, derangement.

INSCRUTABLE, unsearchable.

INSENSIBILITY, apathy, indifference.

INSENSIBLE, unfeeling, hard, hardy.

INSIDE, interior.

INSIDIOUS, treacherous.

INSIGHT, inspection.

INSIGNIFICANT, immaterial, inconsiderable, unimportant.

to INSINUATE, hint, suggest, intimate.

to INSINUATE, ingratiate.

INSINUATION, reflection.

INSIPID, dull, flat.

to INSIST, persist.

INSOLENT, impertinent, rude, saucy, impudent.

INSOLVENCY, failure, bankruptcy.

INSPECTION, insight.

INSPECTION, superintendency, oversight.

to INSPIRE, enliven, cheer, exhilarate, animate.

INSTANCE, example.

INSTANT, moment.

INSTANTLY, instantaneously, directly, immediately.

INSTANTANEOUSLY, directly, immediately, instantly.

to INSTIGATE, encourage, animate, incite, impel, urge, stimulate.

INSTILL, infuse, implant, ingraft, inculcate.

to INSTITUTE, establish, found, erect.

to INSTRUCT, teach, inform.

INSTRUCTION, advice, counsel.

INSTRUCTION, breeding, education.

INSTRUMENT, tool.

INSUFFICIENT, incompetent, inadequate, incapable.

INSULT, indignity.

INSULT, outrage, affront.

INSUPERABLE, insurmountable, invincible, unconquerable.

INSURMOUNTABLE, invincible, unconquerable, insuperable.

INSURRECTION, sedition, rebellion, revolt.

INTEGRAL, whole, entire, complete, total.

INTEGRITY, honesty, probity, uprightness.

INTELLECT, genius, talent.

INTELLECT, intelligence, understanding.

INTELLECTUAL, intelligent, mental.

INTELLIGENCE, notice, advice, information.

INTELLIGENCE, understanding, intellect.

INTELLIGENT, mental, intellectual.

INTEMPERATE, excessive, immoderate.

INTEMPERATE, irregular, disorderly, inordinate.

to INTEND, mean, design, purpose.

INTENSE, intent.

INTENT, intense.

to INTERCEDE, interpose, mediate, interfere, intermeddle.

INTERCHANGE, exchange, reciprocity.

INTERCOURSE, communication, connection, commerce.

to INTERDICT, forbid, prohibit.

INTEREST, concern.

to INTERFERE, intermeddle, intercede, interpose, mediate.
INTERIOR, inside.
INTERIOR, inward, internal, inner.
INTERLOPER, intruder.
to INTERMEDDLE, intercede, interpose, mediate, interfere.
INTERMEDIATE, intervening.
INTERMENT, sepulture, burial.
INTERMISSION, cessation, stop, rest.
to INTERMIT, subside, abate.
INTERNAL, inner, interior, inward.
to INTERPOSE, mediate, interfere, intermeddle, intercede.
INTERPOSITION, intervention.
to INTERPRET, explain, expound.
to INTERROGATE, ask, inquire, question.
to INTERRUPT, disturb.
INTERVAL, respite.
INTERVENING, intermediate.
INTERVENTION, interposition.
INTIMACY, acquaintance, familiarity.
to INTIMATE, insinuate, hint, suggest.
to INTIMIDATE, frighten.
INTOXICATION, drunkenness, infatuation.
to INTRENCH, intrude, invade, infringe, encroach.
INTREPID, undaunted, bold, fearless.
INTRICACY, complexity, complication.
INTRINSIC, real, genuine, native.
to INTRODUCE, present.
INTRODUCTORY, previous, preliminary, preparatory.
to INTRUDE, invade, infringe, encroach, intrench.
to INTRUDE, obtrude.
INTRUDER, interloper.
to INUNDATE, deluge, overflow.
to INVADE, infringe, encroach, intrench, intrude.
INVALID, patient.
to INVALIDATE, weaken, enfeeble, debilitate, enervate.
INVASION, incursion, irruption, inroad.
INVECTIVE, abuse.
INVEIGH, declaim.
to INVEIGLE, ensnare, entrap, entangle.
to INVENT, contrive, devise.
to INVENT, feign, frame, fabricate, forge.
to INVENT, find, find out, discover.
to INVERT, reverse, overturn, overthrow, subvert.
to INVEST, endue, endow.
INVESTIGATION, scrutiny, examination, search, inquiry, research.
INVIDIOUS, envious.
to INVIGORATE, strengthen, fortify.
INVINCIBLE, unconquerable, insuperable, insurmountable.
to INVITE, bid, summon, call.
to INVITE, engage, attract, allure.

to INVOLVE, implicate.
INWARD, internal, inner, interior.

IRE, indignation, anger, resentment, wrath.
IRKSOME, vexatious, troublesome.
IRONY, burlesque, wit, humor, satire.
IRONY, sarcasm, ridicule, satire.
IRRATIONAL, foolish, absurd, preposterous.
IRREFRAGABLE, indubitable, unquestionable, indisputable, undeniable, incontrovertible.
IRREGULAR, disorderly, inordinate, intemperate.
IRRELIGIOUS, profane, impious.
IRREPROACHABLE, unblemished, unspotted, spotless, blameless.
to IRRITATE, provoke, exasperate, tantalize, aggravate.
IRRUPTION, inroad, invasion, incursion.

to ISSUE, emerge, rise.
to ISSUE, spring, flow, emanate, arise, rise, proceed.
ISSUE, event, consequence, effect, result.
ISSUE, offspring, progeny.

J

to JADE, harass, weary, tire.
to JANGLE, jar, wrangle.
to JAR, wrangle, jangle.
JAUNT, excursion, ramble, tour, trip.

JEALOUSY, envy, suspicion.
to JEER, sneer, scoff, gibe.
to JEST, joke, sport.

JILT, coquet.

JOCOSE, facetious, conversable, pleasant, jocular.
JOCULAR, jocose, facetious, conversable, pleasant.
JOCUND, lively, sprightly, vivacious, sportive, merry.
to JOIN, unite, coalesce, add.
to JOKE, sport, jest.
JOLLITY, hilarity, mirth, merriment, joviality.
JOURNEY, travel, voyage.
JOVIALITY, jollity, hilarity, mirth, merriment.
JOYFUL, cheerful, glad, pleased.
JOY, delight, charm, pleasure.
JOY, gladness, mirth.

JUDGE, umpire, arbiter, arbitrator.
JUDGMENT, discernment, penetration, discrimination.
JUDGMENT, discretion, prudence.
JUDGMENT, sense.
JUICE, humor, liquid, liquor.
JUST, fit, proper, right.

JUSTICE, equity.
to JUSTIFY, exculpate, excuse, plead, apologize, defend.
JUSTNESS, correctness.
JUVENILE, puerile, youthful.

K

KEEN, sharp, acute.
KEEN, shrewd, acute.
to KEEP, detain, retain, hold.
to KEEP, preserve, save.
to KEEP, observe, fulfill.
KEEPING, custody.

to KILL, murder, assassinate, slay, slaughter.
KIND, fond, affectionate.
KIND, gracious, merciful.
KIND, species, sort.
KINDNESS, civility, benefit, favor.
KINDNESS, tenderness, benevolence, benignity, humanity.
KINGDOM, empire.
KINDRED, relation, relative, kinsman.
KINDRED, relationship, affinity, consanguinity.
KINGLY, royal, regal.
KINSMAN, kindred, relation, relative.

KNAVISH, dishonest.
to KNOW, be acquainted with.
KNOWLEDGE, science, learning, erudition.

L

to LABOR, take pains, take trouble.
LABOR, toil, drudgery, task, work.
LABORIOUS, active, diligent, industrious, assiduous.
LABYRINTH, maze.
to LACK, want, need.
LADING, load, burden, freight, cargo.
to LAG, saunter, linger, tarry, loiter.
to LAMENT, bewail, bemoan.
to LAMENT, deplore.
to LAMENT, grieve, mourn.
to LAMENT, regret, complain.
LAND, country.
LANDSCAPE, view, prospect.
LANGUAGE, tongue, speech, idiom, dialect.
LANGUID, faint.
to LANGUISH, pine, flag, droop.
LARGE, big, great.
LARGE, wide, broad.
LARGELY, copiously, fully.
LASSITUDE, fatigue, weariness.
LAST, latest, final, ultimate.
(AT) LAST, at length, lastly.
LASTING, permanent, durable.
LASTLY, at last, at length.
LATENT, occult, mysterious, secret, hidden.

LATEST, final, ultimate, last.
LAUDABLE, praiseworthy, commendable.
to LAUGH AT, ridicule.
LAUGHABLE, ludicrous, ridiculous, comical, comic, droll.
LAVISH, profuse, extravagant, prodigal.
LAW, maxim, precept, rule.
LAWFUL, legal, legitimate, licit.
LAX, dissolute, licentious, loose, vague.
to LAY, set, put, place.
to LAY HOLD OF, take hold of, catch, seize, snatch, grasp, grip.
LAZY, indolent, idle.
LAZY, slothful, sluggish, inactive, inert.

to LEAD, conduct, guide.
LEADER, chieftain, head, chief.
LEAGUE, confederacy, alliance.
to LEAN, incline, bend.
LEAN, meagre.
LEARNING, erudition, knowledge, science.
LEARNING, letters, literature.
to LEAVE, quit, relinquish.
to LEAVE, suffer, let.
to LEAVE, take leave, bid farewell, bid adieu.
LEAVE, liberty, permission, license.
to LEAVE OFF, desist.
to LEAVE OFF, discontinue, cease.
LEAVINGS, remains.
LEGAL, legitimate, licit, lawful.
LEGITIMATE, licit, lawful, legal.
(AT) LEISURE, vacant, idle.
(AT) LENGTH, lastly, at last.
LENITY, mercy, clemency.
to LESSEN, diminish, decrease, abate.
to LET, leave, suffer.
LETHARGIC, sleepy, drowsy.
LETTER, character.
LETTER, epistle.
LETTERS, literature, learning.
to LEVEL, aim, point.
LEVEL, flat.
LEVEL, plain, even, smooth.
LEVITY, flightiness, volatility, giddiness, lightness.
LEXICON, vocabulary, glossary, nomenclature, dictionary.

LIABLE, exposed, obnoxious, subject.
LIBERAL, beneficent, bountiful, bounteous, munificent, generous.
LIBERAL, free.
to LIBERATE, free, set free, deliver.
LIBERTY, freedom.
LIBERTY, permission, license, leave.
LICENSE, leave, liberty, permission.
LICENTIOUS, loose, vague, lax, dissolute.
LICIT, lawful, legal, legitimate.
LIE, untruth, falsehood, falsity.
LIFE, vivacity, spirit, animation.
LIFELESS, dead, inanimate.

to LIFT, heave, hoist.
to LIFT, raise, erect, elevate, exalt.
LIGHTNESS, ease, easiness, facility.
LIGHTNESS, levity, flightiness, volatility, giddiness.
LIKE, alike, uniform, equal, even, equable.
LIKENESS, picture, image, effigy.
LIKENESS, resemblance, similarity, similitude.
LIKEWISE, too, also.
LIMB, member.
to LIMIT, confine, circumscribe, restrict, bound.
to LIMIT, fix, determine, settle.
LIMIT, boundary, term.
LIMIT, extent.
LIMITED, finite.
LINEAGE, race, family, house.
to LINGER, tarry, loiter, lag, saunter.
LIQUID, fluid.
LIQUID, liquor, juice, humor.
LIQUOR, juice, humor, liquid.
to LIST, enlist, register, record, enroll.
LIST, roll, catalogue, register.
to LISTEN, attend, hearken.
LISTLESS, careless, indolent, supine.
LITERATURE, learning, letters.
LITTLE, small, diminutive.
to LIVE, exist.
to LIVE, reside, inhabit, abide, sojourn, dwell.
LIVELIHOOD, living, subsistence, maintenance, support, sustenance.
LIVELY, sprightly, vivacious, sportive, merry, jocund.
LIVING, benefice.
LIVING, subsistence, maintenance, support, sustenance, livelihood.

to LOAD, encumber, clog.
LOAD, burden, freight, cargo, lading.
LOAD, weight, burden.
to LOATH, abhor, detest, abominate.
LOATH, reluctant, averse, unwilling, backward.
LOATHING, nausea, disgust.
to LODGE, harbor, shelter.
LODGINGS, apartments.
LOFTINESS, dignity, pride, haughtiness.
LOFTY, high, tall.
to LOITER, lag, saunter, linger, tarry.
LONELY, alone, solitary.
to LONG FOR, hanker after, covet, desire, wish.
to LOOK FOR, expect, wait, wait for, await.
to LOOK, appear.
to LOOK, see, behold, view, eye.
LOOK, air, mien.
LOOK, glance.
LOOKER-ON, spectator, beholder, observer.
LOOSE, slack.
LOOSE, vague, lax, dissolute, licentious.

LOQUACIOUS, garrulous, talkative.
LORDLY, domineering, overbearing, imperious.
LORD'S SUPPER, eucharist, communion, sacrament.
to LOSE, miss.
LOSS, damage, detriment.
LOT, doom, destiny, fate.
LOUD, noisy, high-sounding, clamorous.
LOVE, affection.
LOVE, friendship.
LOVELY, beloved, amiable.
LOVER, suitor, wooer.
LOVING, fond, amorous.
LOW, humble, lowly.
LOW, mean, abject.
to LOWER, reduce.
LOWLY, low, humble.

LUCID, bright, vivid, clear.
LUCKY, fortuitous, prosperous, successful, fortunate.
LUCRE, gain, profit, emolument.
LUDICROUS, ridiculous, comical, comic, droll, laughable.
LUNACY, madness, mania, derangement, insanity.
LUSTRE, splendor, brilliancy, brightness.
LUSTY, corpulent, stout.
LUXURIANT, exuberant.

M

MADNESS, frenzy, rage, fury.
MADNESS, mania, derangement, insanity, lunacy.
MAGISTERIAL, majestic, stately, pompous, august, dignified.
MAGNIFICENCE, grandeur.
MAGNIFICENCE, splendor, pomp.
MAGNITUDE, greatness, bulk, size.
to MAIM, mangle, mutilate.
MAIN, chief, principal.
to MAINTAIN, hold, support.
to MAINTAIN, sustain, support.
to MAINTAIN, vindicate, assert.
MAINTENANCE, support, sustenance, livelihood, living, subsistence.
MAJESTIC, stately, pompous, august, dignified, magisterial.
to MAKE, act, do.
to MAKE, form, produce, create.
to MAKE KNOWN, acquaint, apprize, inform.
MALADY, disorder, disease, distemper.
MALEDICTION, curse, imprecation, execration, anathema.
MALEFACTOR, felon, convict, criminal, culprit.
MALEVOLENT, malicious, malignant.
MALICE, rancor, spite, grudge, pique.
MALICIOUS, malignant, malevolent.

MALIGNANT, malevolent, malicious.
to MANAGE, concert, contrive.
to MANAGE, direct, conduct.
MANAGEMENT, care, charge.
MANAGEMENT, economy.
MANFUL, manly.
to MANGLE, mutilate, maim.
MANIA, derangement, insanity, lunacy, madness.
to MANIFEST, declare, discover.
to MANIFEST, prove, demonstrate, evince.
MANIFEST, apparent, visible, clear, plain, obvious, evident.
MANLY, manful.
MANNER, air.
MANNER, method, mode, course, means, way.
MANNER, practice, custom, fashion.
MANNERS, morals.
MARGIN, verge, border, edge, rim, brim, brink.
MARINE, naval, nautical, maritime.
MARINER, seaman, waterman, sailor.
MARITIME, marine, naval, nautical.
to MARK, indicate, show, shew, point out.
to MARK, note, notice.
MARK, badge, stigma.
MARK, butt.
MARK, print, impression, stamp.
MARK, sign, note, symptom, token, indication.
MARK, trace, vestige, footstep, track.
MARRIAGE, matrimony, wedlock.
MARRIAGE, wedding, nuptials.
MARTIAL, warlike, military, soldier-like.
MARVEL, prodigy, monster, wonder, miracle.
MASK, blind, veil, cloak.
MASSACRE, butchery, carnage, slaughter.
MASSIVE, bulky.
MASTER, possessor, proprietor, owner.
MATERIAL, corporeal.
MATERIALS, subject, matter.
MATRIMONY, wedlock, marriage.
MATTER, materials, subject.
MATURE, ripe.
MAXIM, aphorism, apophthegm, saying, adage, proverb, byword, saw, axiom.
MAXIM, precept, rule, law.
MAY, can.
MAZE, labyrinth.

MEAGRE, lean.
to MEAN, design, purpose, intend.
MEAN, base, vile.
MEAN, common, vulgar, ordinary.
MEAN, abject, low.
MEAN, medium.
MEAN, pitiful, sordid.
MEANING, import, sense, signification.
MEANS, way, manner, method, mode, course.
MECHANIC, artist, artisan, artificer.

to MEDIATE, interfere, intermeddle, intercede, interpose.
MEDIOCRITY, moderation.
to MEDITATE, muse, contemplate.
MEDIUM, mean.
MEDLEY, difference, variety, diversity.
MEDLEY, miscellany, mixture.
MEEK, soft, mild, gentle.
MEET, fit, apt.
MEETING, congregation, parliament, diet, congress, convention, synod, convocation, council, assembly, company.
MEETING, interview.
MELANCHOLY, dejection, depression.
MELODY, harmony, accordance.
MEMBER, limb.
MEMOIRS, chronicles, annals, anecdotes.
MEMORABLE, signal.
MEMORIAL, remembrancer, monument.
MEMORY, remembrance, recollection, reminiscence.
MENACE, threat.
to MEND, better, amend, correct, emend, improve.
MENIAL, drudge, servant, domestic.
MENTAL, intellectual, intelligent.
to MENTION, notice.
MERCANTILE, commercial.
MERCENARY, hireling.
MERCENARY, venal.
MERCHANDISE, ware, commodity, goods.
MERCIFUL, kind, gracious.
MERCILESS, hardhearted, cruel, unmerciful.
MERCY, clemency, lenity.
MERCY, pity.
MERE, bare.
MERIT, worth, desert.
MERRIMENT, joviality, jollity, hilarity, mirth.
MERRY, jocund, lively, sprightly, vivacious, sportive.
MERRY, sprightly, gay, cheerful.
MESSAGE, errand.
MESSENGER, harbinger, forerunner, precursor.
to METAMORPHOSE, transfigure, transform.
METAPHOR, allegory, emblem, symbol, type, figure.
METHOD, mode, course, means, way, manner.
METHOD, rule, order.
METHOD, system.

MIEN, look, air.
MIGHTY, powerful, potent.
MILD, gentle, meek, soft.
MILITARY, soldier-like, martial, warlike.
to MIMIC, ape, mock, imitate.
to MIND, regard, heed, notice, attend to.
MIND, soul.
MINDFUL, regardful, observant.
to MINGLE, blend, confound, mix.

to MINISTER, administer, contribute.
MINISTER, agent.
MINISTER, clergyman, parson, priest.
MINUTE, circumstantial, particular.
MIRTH, festivity.
MIRTH, joy, gladness.
MIRTH, merriment, joviality, jollity, hilarity.
MISCARRIAGE, abortion, failure.
MISCELLANY, mixture, medley.
MISCHANCE, mishap, calamity, disaster, misfortune.
MISCHIEF, evil, ill, misfortune, harm.
MISCHIEF, injury, damage, hurt, harm.
to MISCONSTRUE, misinterpret.
MISDEED, affront, offense, trespass, transgression, misdemeanor.
MISDEMEANOR, crime.
MISDEMEANOR, misdeed, affront, offence, trespass, transgression.
MISERABLE, wretched, unhappy.
MISERLY, parsimonious, niggardly, avaricious.
MISFORTUNE, harm, mischief, evil, ill.
MISFORTUNE, mischance, mishap, calamity, disaster.
MISHAP, calamity, disaster, misfortune, mischance.
to MISINTERPRET, misconstrue.
to MISS, lose.
MISTAKE, blunder, error.
to MISUSE, abuse.
to MITIGATE, assuage, allay, soothe, appease.
to MIX, mingle, blend, confound.
MIXTURE, medley, miscellany.

to MOAN, groan.
MOB, mobility, people, populace.
MOBILITY, people, populace, mob.
to MOCK, imitate, mimic, ape.
to MOCK, ridicule, rally, banter, deride.
MODE, course, means, way, manner, method.
MODEL, pattern, specimen, copy.
MODERATION, mediocrity.
MODERATION, temperance, sobriety, modesty.
MODERN, fresh, recent, new, novel.
MODEST, bashful, diffident.
MODEST, submissive, humble.
MODESTY, moderation, temperance, sobriety.
MOISTURE, humidity, dampness.
to MOLD, shape, form, fashion.
to MOLEST, inconvenience, annoy.
to MOLEST, trouble, disturb.
MOMENT, importance, consequence, weight.
MOMENT, instant.
MONARCH, sovereign, potentate, prince.
MONASTERY, cloister, convent.
MONEY, cash.

MONSTER, wonder, miracle, marvel, prodigy.
MONSTROUS, enormous, prodigious.
MONUMENT, memorial, remembrancer.
MOOD, humor, temper.
MORALS, manners.
MORBID, sick, sickly, diseased.
MOREOVER, besides.
MOROSE, splenetic, gloomy, sullen.
MORTAL, fatal, deadly.
MORTIFICATION, chagrin, vexation.
MOTION, movement.
MOTIVE, cause, reason.
MOTIVE, principle.
to MOUNT, ascend, climb, scale, arise, rise.
to MOURN, lament, grieve.
MOURNFUL, sad.
to MOVE, stir.
MOVEABLES, effects, goods, furniture, chattels.
MOVEMENT, motion.
MOVING, affecting, pathetic.

MULCT, penalty, forfeiture, fine.
MULTITUDE, crowd, throng, swarm.
MUNIFICENT, generous, liberal, beneficent, bountiful, bounteous.
to MURDER, assassinate, slay, slaughter, kill.
to MURMUR, repine, complain.
to MUSE, contemplate, meditate.
to MUSE, think, reflect, ponder.
to MUSTER, collect, assemble.
MUTABLE, variable, inconstant, fickle, versatile, changeable.
MUTE, speechless, silent, dumb.
to MUTILATE, maim, mangle.
MUTINOUS, tumultuous, turbulent, seditious.
MUTUAL, reciprocal.

MYSTERIOUS, dark, obscure, dim.
MYSTERIOUS, mystic.
MYSTERIOUS, secret, hidden, latent, occult.
MYSTIC, mysterious.

N

NAKED, uncovered, bare.
to NAME, call.
to NAME, denominate, style, entitle, designate, characterize.
to NAME, nominate.
NAME, appellation, title, denomination.
NAME, reputation, repute, credit.
to NAP, sleep, slumber, doze, drowse.
NARRATION, narrative, relation, recital.
NARRATIVE, description, account.
NARRATIVE, relation, recital, narration.
NARROW, contracted, confined.
NARROW, strait.
NATAL, native, indigenous.

NATION, people.
NATIVE, indigenous, natal.
NATIVE, intrinsic, real, genuine.
NATIVE, natural.
NATURAL, native.
NATURALLY, in course, consequently, of course.
NAUSEA, disgust, loathing.
NAUTICAL, maritime, marine, naval.
NAVAL, nautical, maritime, marine.

NEAR, nigh, close.
NECESSARIES, necessities.
NECESSARY, expedient, essential, requisite.
to NECESSITATE, compel, force, oblige.
NECESSITIES, necessaries.
NECESSITY, need.
NECESSITY, occasion.
to NEED, lack, want.
NEED, necessity.
NEED, poverty, want, penury, indigence.
NEFARIOUS, wicked, iniquitous.
to NEGLECT, omit.
to NEGLECT, slight, disregard.
NEGLIGENT, remiss, careless, thoughtless, heedless, inattentive.
to NEGOTIATE, treat for, transact.
NEIGHBORHOOD, vicinity.
NEVERTHELESS, notwithstanding, however, yet.
NEW, novel, modern, fresh, recent.
NEWS, tidings.

NICE, fine, delicate.
NICE, particular, punctual, exact.
NIGGARDLY, avaricious, miserly, parsimonious.
NIGGARDLY, economical, saving, sparing, thrifty, penurious.
NIGH, close, near.
NIGHTLY, nocturnal.
NIMBLE, active, brisk, agile.

NOBLE, grand.
NOCTURNAL, nightly.
NOISE, cry, outcry, clamor.
NOISOME, hurtful, pernicious, noxious.
NOISY, high-sounding, clamorous, loud.
NOMENCLATURE, dictionary, lexicon, vocabulary, glossary.
to NOMINATE, name.
NONCONFORMIST, heretic, schismatic, sectarian, sectary, dissenter.
to NOTE, notice, mark.
NOTE, annotation, commentary, remark, observation, comment.
NOTE, symptom, token, indication, mark, sign.
NOTED, eminent, illustrious, distinguished, conspicuous.
NOTED, notorious.
to NOTICE, attend to, mind, regard, heed.

to NOTICE, mark, note.
to NOTICE, mention.
to NOTICE, remark, observe.
NOTICE, advice, information, intelligence.
NOTION, opinion, sentiment.
NOTION, perception, idea, conception.
NOTORIOUS, noted.
NOTWITHSTANDING, however, yet, nevertheless.
to NOURISH, nurture, cherish.
NOVEL, modern, fresh, recent, new.
NOVEL, romance, fable, tale.
NOXIOUS, noisome, hurtful, pernicious.

NUMB, benumbed, torpid.
to NUMBER, reckon, count, account.
NUMERAL, numerical.
NUMERICAL, numeral.
NUPTIALS, marriage, wedding.
to NURTURE, cherish, nourish.

O

OBDURATE, hard, callous, hardened.
OBEDIENT, respectful, dutiful.
OBEDIENT, submissive, obsequious.
OBJECT, end, view, aim.
to OBJECT To, find fault with, blame.
to OBJECT To, oppose.
OBJECTION, demur, doubt, hesitation.
OBJECTION, difficulty, exception.
OBLATION, offering.
OBLIGATION, duty.
to OBLIGE, engage, bind.
to OBLIGE, necessitate, compel, force.
OBLIGED, indebted.
OBLIGING, complaisant, civil.
to OBLITERATE, blot out, expunge, raze, erase, efface, cancel.
OBLIVION, forgetfulness.
OBLOQUY, reproach, contumely.
OBNOXIOUS, offensive.
OBNOXIOUS, subject, liable, exposed.
to OBSCURE, eclipse.
OBSCURE, dim, mysterious, dark.
OBSEQUIES, funeral.
OBSEQUIOUS, obedient, submissive.
OBSERVANCE, form, ceremony, rite.
OBSERVANCE, observation.
OBSERVANT, mindful, regardful.
OBSERVATION, comment, note, annotation, commentary, remark.
OBSERVATION, observance.
to OBSERVE, fulfill, keep.
to OBSERVE, notice, remark.
to OBSERVE, see, perceive.
to OBSERVE, watch.
OBSERVER, looker-on, spectator, beholder.
OBSOLETE, old, ancient, antique, antiquated, old-fashioned.
OBSTACLE, impediment, difficulty.

OBSTINATE, contumacious, stubborn, headstrong, heady.
to OBSTRUCT, hinder, prevent, impede.
to OBTAIN, gain, win, earn, acquire.
to OBTAIN, procure, get, gain.
to OBTRUDE, intrude.
to OBVIATE, preclude, prevent.
OBVIOUS, evident, manifest, apparent, visible, clear, plain.

to OCCASION, create, cause.
OCCASION, necessity.
OCCASION, opportunity.
OCCASIONAL, casual.
OCCULT, mysterious, secret, hidden, latent.
OCCUPANCY, occupation.
OCCUPATION, employment, engagement, vocation, business.
OCCUPATION, occupancy.
to OCCUPY, possess, hold.
OCCURRENCE, event, incident, accident, adventure.

ODD, eccentric, strange, particular, singular.
ODD, uneven.
ODIOUS, hateful.
ODOR, perfume, fragrance, smell, scent.

OFFENCE, trespass, transgression, misdemeanor, misdeed, affront.
to OFFEND, vex, displease.
OFFENDER, delinquent.
OFFENDING, offensive.
OFFENSIVE, obnoxious.
OFFENSIVE, offending.
to OFFER, bid, tender, propose.
to OFFER, exhibit, give, present.
OFFERING, oblation.
OFFICE, duty, business.
OFFICE, place, charge, function.
OFFICIOUS, active, busy.
OFFSPRING, progeny, issue.
OFTEN, frequently.

OLD, ancient, antique, antiquated, old-fashioned, obsolete.
OLD, elderly, aged.
OLDER, senior, elder.
OLD-FASHIONED, obsolete, old, ancient, antique, antiquated.
(IN) OLD TIMES, in times past, in days of yore, anciently, in ancient times, formerly.

OMEN, prognostic, presage.
to OMIT, neglect.

ONE, single, only.
(ON) ONE'S GUARD, apprized, conscious, aware.
ONLY, one, single.

ONLY, single, solitary, sole.
ONSET, charge, attack, assault, encounter.
ONWARD, forward, progressive.

OPAQUE, dark.
OPEN, plain, frank, candid, ingenuous, free.
OPEN, sincere, candid.
OPENING, aperture, cavity.
to OPERATE, act, work.
OPINION, sentiment, notion.
OPINIONATED, opinionative, conceited, egoistical.
OPINIONATIVE, opinionated, conceited, egoistical.
OPPONENT, antagonist, enemy, foe, adversary.
OPPORTUNITY, occasion.
to OPPOSE, combat.
to OPPOSE, contradict, deny.
to OPPOSE, object to.
to OPPOSE, resist, withstand, thwart.
OPPOSITE, adverse, contrary.
OPPROBRIUM, infamy, ignominy.
to OPPUGN, confute, refute, disprove.
OPTION, choice.
OPULENCE, affluence, riches, wealth.

ORAL, verbal, vocal.
ORATION, address, speech, harangue.
ORATORY, rhetoric, elocution, eloquence.
ORB, globe, circle, sphere.
to ORDAIN, appoint, order, prescribe.
to ORDER, place, dispose.
to ORDER, prescribe, ordain, appoint.
ORDER, direction.
ORDER, injunction, precept, command.
ORDER, method, rule.
ORDER, rank, degree, class.
ORDER, succession, series.
ORDINARY, mean, common, vulgar.
ORIFICE, perforation.
ORIGIN, original, beginning, rise, source.
ORIGINAL, beginning, rise, source, origin.
ORIGINAL, primary, primitive, pristine.

OSTENSIBLE, plausible, feasible, colorable, specious.
OSTENTATION, show, parade.

OUTCRY, clamor, noise, cry.
to OUTDO, exceed, excel, surpass, transcend.
OUTLINES, sketch.
to OUTLIVE, survive.
OUTRAGE, affront, insult.
OUTSIDE, appearance, semblance, show.
OUTWARD, external, exterior.
to OUTWEIGH, preponderate, overbalance.

OVER, upon, beyond, above.
to OVERBALANCE, outweigh, preponderate.
to OVERBEAR, bear down, overpower, overwhelm, subdue.

OVERBEARING, imperious, lordly, domineering.

to OVERCOME, surmount, conquer, vanquish, subdue.

to OVERFLOW, inundate, deluge.

to OVERHEAR, hear, hearken.

to OVERPOWER, overwhelm, subdue, overbear, bear down.

to OVERPOWER, rout, overthrow, beat, defeat.

to OVERRULE, supersede.

OVERRULING, predominant, prevailing, prevalent, ruling.

to OVERRUN, ravage, overspread.

OVERSIGHT, inadvertency, inattention.

OVERSIGHT, inspection, superintendency.

to OVERSPREAD, overrun, ravage.

to OVERTHROW, beat, defeat, overpower, rout.

to OVERTHROW, subvert, invert, reverse, overturn.

to OVERTURN, overthrow, subvert, invert, reverse.

to OVERWHELM, crush.

to OVERWHELM, subdue, overbear, bear down, overpower.

to OWN, confess, avow, acknowledge.

OWNER, master, possessor, proprietor.

P

PACE, step.

PACIFIC, peaceable, peaceful.

to PACIFY, quiet, still, appease, calm.

PAGAN, gentile, heathen.

PAIN, pang, agony, anguish.

to PAINT, depict.

PAIR, brace, couple.

PALATE, taste.

PALE, pallid, wan.

to PALLIATE, extenuate.

to PALLIATE, gloss, varnish.

PALLID, wan, pale.

to PALPITATE, flutter, pant, gasp.

PANEGYRIC, encomium, eulogy.

PANG, agony, anguish, pain.

to PANT, gasp, palpitate, flutter.

PARABLE, allegory.

PARADE, ostentation, show.

PARASITE, flatterer, sycophant.

to PARDON, absolve, remit, forgive.

to PARDON, excuse.

PARDONABLE, venial.

to PARE, peel.

PARK, forest, chace.

PARLIAMENT, diet, congress, convention, synod, convocation, council, assembly, company, meeting, congregation.

PARSIMONIOUS, niggardly, avaricious, miserly.

PARSIMONY, economy, frugality.

PARSON, priest, minister, clergyman.

to PART, divide, separate.

PART, division, portion, share.

PART, piece, patch.

to PARTAKE, participate, share.

to PARTICIPATE, share, partake.

PARTICULAR, individual.

PARTICULAR, minute, circumstantial.

PARTICULAR, peculiar, appropriate.

PARTICULAR, punctual, exact, nice.

PARTICULAR, singular, odd, eccentric, strange.

PARTICULAR, special, specific.

PARTICULARLY, principally, chiefly, especially.

PARTISAN, follower, adherent.

PARTNER, colleague.

PARTNERSHIP, association, society, company.

PARTY, faction.

PASSAGE, course, race.

PASSIONATE, hasty, angry.

PASSIVE, submissive, patient.

PASTIME, amusement, entertainment, diversion, sport, recreation.

PATCH, part, piece.

PATHETIC, moving, affecting.

PATIENCE, endurance, resignation.

PATIENT, invalid.

PATIENT, passive, submissive.

PATTERN, ensample, example.

PATTERN, specimen, copy, model.

PAUPER, poor.

to PAUSE, demur, hesitate.

PAY, allowance, stipend, salary, wages, hire.

PEACE, quiet, calm, tranquillity.

PEACEABLE, peaceful, pacific.

PEACEFUL, pacific, peaceable.

PEASANT, swain, hind, rustic, clown, countryman.

PECULIAR, appropriate, particular.

to PEEL, pare.

PEEL, rind, skin, hide.

PEEVISH, petulant, fretful, captious, cross.

PELLUCID, transparent.

PENALTY, forfeiture, fine, mulct.

to PENETRATE, pierce, perforate, bore.

PENETRATION, acuteness, sagacity.

PENETRATION, discrimination, judgment, discernment.

PENITENCE, contrition, compunction, remorse, repentance.

PENMAN, scribe, writer.

PENURIOUS, niggardly, economical, saving, sparing, thrifty.

PENURY, indigence, need, poverty, want.

PEOPLE, nation.

PEOPLE, persons, folks.

PEOPLE, populace, mob, mobility.

to PERCEIVE, discern, distinguish.

to PERCEIVE, observe, see.

PERCEPTIBLE, sensible.
PERCEPTION, idea, conception, notion.
PERCEPTION, sentiment, sensation.
PEREMPTORY, positive, absolute.
PERFECT, accomplished.
PERFECT, finished, complete.
PERFIDIOUS, treacherous, faithless.
to PERFORATE, bore, penetrate, pierce.
PERFORATION, orifice.
to PERFORM, effect, produce.
to PERFORM, execute, fulfill.
PERFORMANCE, work, production.
PERFORMER, actor, player.
PERFUME, fragrance, smell, scent, odor.
PERIL, hazard, danger.
PERIOD, age, date, era, epoch, time.
PERIOD, phrase, sentence, proposition.
to PERISH, die, decay.
to PERJURE, suborn, forswear.
PERMANENT, durable, lasting.
PERMISSION, license, leave, liberty.
to PERMIT, allow, consent.
to PERMIT, suffer, tolerate, admit, allow.
PERNICIOUS, destructive, ruinous.
PERNICIOUS, noxious, noisome, hurtful.
to PERPETRATE, commit.
PERPETUAL, constant, continual.
to PERPLEX, distress, harass.
to PERPLEX, entangle, embarrass.
to PERSEVERE, persist, pursue, prosecute, continue.
to PERSIST, insist.
to PERSIST, pursue, prosecute, continue, persevere.
PERSONS, folks, people.
PERSPICUITY, clearness.
to PERSUADE, convict, convince.
to PERSUADE, entice, prevail upon.
to PERSUADE, exhort.
PERTINACIOUS, tenacious.
PERVERSE, awkward, cross, untoward, crooked, froward.
PEST, ruin, bane.
PESTILENTIAL, contagious, epidemical.
PETITION, request, entreaty, suit, prayer.
PETTY, frivolous, futile, trifling, trivial.
PETULANT, fretful, captious, cross, peevish.

PHANTOM, spectre, ghost, vision, apparition.
PHRASE, phraseology, diction, style.
PHRASE, sentence, proposition, period.
PHRASEOLOGY, diction, style, phrase.

to PICK, select, choose.
PICTURE, image, effigy, likeness.
PICTURE, print, engraving.
PIECE, patch, part.
to PIERCE, perforate, bore, penetrate.
to PILE, accumulate, amass, heap.
PILLAGE, rapine, plunder.
PILLAR, column.

to PINCH, gripe, press, squeeze.
to PINE, flag, droop, languish.
PIOUS, devout, religious, holy.
PIQUE, malice, rancor, spite, grudge.
PITEOUS, doleful, woeful, rueful.
PITEOUS, pitiful, pitiable.
PITIABLE, piteous, pitiful.
PITIFUL, contemptible, despicable.
PITIFUL, pitiable, piteous.
PITIFUL, sordid, mean.
PITY, compassion.
PITY, mercy.

to PLACE, dispose, order.
to PLACE, lay, set, put.
PLACE, charge, function, office.
PLACE, spot, site.
PLACE, station, situation, position, post.
PLACID, serene, calm.
PLAIN, even, smooth, level.
PLAIN, frank, candid, ingenuous, free, open.
PLAIN, obvious, evident, manifest, apparent, visible, clear.
PLAIN, sincere, honest, true.
PLAN, scheme, project, design.
PLAUSIBLE, feasible, colorable, specious, ostensible.
PLAY, game, sport.
PLAYER, performer, actor.
PLAYFUL, gamesome, sportive.
to PLEAD, apologize, defend, justify, exculpate, excuse.
PLEASANT, jocular, jocose, facetious, conversable.
PLEASANT, pleasing, agreeable.
to PLEASE, gratify, satisfy.
PLEASED, joyful, cheerful, glad.
PLEASING, agreeable, pleasant.
PLEASURE, comfort.
PLEASURE, joy, delight, charm.
PLEDGE, earnest.
PLEDGE, security, deposit.
PLENIPOTENTIARY, deputy, ambassador, envoy.
PLENTEOUS, abundant, copious, ample, plentiful.
PLENTIFUL, plenteous, abundant, copious, ample.
PLENTITUDE, fullness.
PLIABLE, pliant, supple, flexible.
PLIANT, supple, flexible, pliable.
PLIGHT, case, situation, condition, state, predicament.
PLOT, conspiracy, combination, cabal.
to PLUCK, tug, draw, drag, haul, hale, pull.
PLUNDER, pillage, rapine.
to PLUNGE, dive.

to POINT, level, aim.
to POINT OUT, mark, indicate, show.
to POISE, balance.
POISON, venom.

POLISHED, refined, polite.
POLITE, civil.
POLITE, genteel.
POLITE, polished, refined.
POLITIC, political.
POLITICAL, politic.
to POLLUTE, taint, corrupt, contaminate, defile.
POMP, magnificence, splendor.
POMPOUS, august, dignified, magisterial, majestic, stately.
to PONDER, muse, think, reflect.
PONDEROUS, heavy, burdensome, weighty.
POOR, pauper.
POPULACE, mob, mobility, people.
PORT, harbor, haven.
to PORTEND, augur, presage, forebode, betoken.
PORTION, deal, quantity.
PORTION, share, part, division.
POSITION, post, place, station, situation.
POSITION, posture.
POSITION, tenet.
POSITIVE, absolute, peremptory.
POSITIVE, actual, real.
POSITIVE, confident, dogmatical.
POSITIVE, definite.
to POSSESS, have.
to POSSESS, hold, occupy.
POSSESSOR, proprietor, owner, master.
POSSIBLE, practicable, practical.
POST, place, station, situation, position.
to POSTPONE, procrastinate, prolong, protract, retard, delay, defer.
POSTURE, attitude, action, gesture, gesticulation.
POSTURE, position.
POTENT, mighty, powerful.
POTENTATE, prince, monarch, sovereign.
to POUND, crush, break, bruise, squeeze.
to POUR, spill, shed.
POVERTY, want, penury, indigence, need.
POWER, strength, force, authority, dominion.
POWERFUL, potent, mighty.

PRACTICABLE, practical, possible.
PRACTICAL, possible, practicable.
PRACTICE, custom, fashion, manner.
to PRACTISE, exercise.
to PRAISE, commend, applaud, extol.
PRAISEWORTHY, commendable, laudable.
PRANK, frolic, gambol.
to PRATE, babble, chatter, chat, prattle.
to PRATTLE, prate, babble, chatter, chat.
PRAYER, petition, request, entreaty, suit.
PRECARIOUS, doubtful, dubious, uncertain.
PRECEDENCE, prominence, preference, priority.
PRECEDENT, example.
PRECEDING, foregoing, previous, anterior, prior, former, antecedent.

PRECEPT, command, order, injunction.
PRECEPT, principle, doctrine.
PRECEPT, rule, law, maxim.
PRECINCT, border, boundary, frontier, confine.
PRECIOUS, costly, valuable.
PRECIPITANCY, rashness, temerity, hastiness.
PRECISE, accurate, exact.
to PRECLUDE, prevent, obviate.
PRECURSOR, messenger, harbinger, forerunner.
PREDICAMENT, plight, case, situation, condition, state.
to PREDICT, prophesy, prognosticate, foretell.
PREDOMINANT, prevailing, prevalent, ruling, overruling.
PREËMINENCE, preference, priority, precedence.
PREFACE, prelude.
to PREFER, choose.
to PREFER, forward, encourage, advance, promote.
PREFERABLE, eligible.
PREFERENCE, priority, precedence, preëminence.
PREJUDICE, bias, prepossession.
PREJUDICE, disadvantage, injury, hurt, detriment.
PRELIMINARY, preparatory, introductory, previous.
PRELUDE, preface.
PREMEDITATION, foresight, forethought, forecast.
to PREMISE, presume.
PREPARATORY, introductory, previous, preliminary.
to PREPARE, qualify, fit, equip.
to PREPONDERATE, overbalance, outweigh.
PREPOSSESSION, bent, bias, inclination.
PREPOSSESSION, prejudice, bias.
PREPOSTEROUS, irrational, foolish, absurd.
PREROGATIVE, exemption, immunity, privilege.
to PRESAGE, forbode, betaken, portend, augur.
PRESAGE, omen, prognostic.
to PRESCRIBE, dictate.
to PRESCRIBE, ordain, appoint, order.
PRESCRIPTION, usage, custom.
to PRESENT, introduce.
to PRESENT, offer, exhibit, give.
PRESENT, donation, gift.
to PRESERVE, protect, save, spare.
to PRESERVE, save, keep.
to PRESS, squeeze, pinch, gripe.
PRESSING, urgent, importunate.
to PRESUME, premise.
PRESUMING, presumptive, presumptuous.
PRESUMPTION, arrogance, assumption.
PRESUMPTIVE, presumptuous, presuming.
PRESUMPTUOUS, presuming, presumptive.

to PRETEND, feign.
to PRETEND To, affect.
PRETENSE, pretension, pretext, excuse.
PRETENSION, claim.
PRETENSION, pretext, excuse, pretense.
PRETEXT, excuse, pretense, pretension.
PRETTY, beautiful, fine, handsome.
to PREVAIL UPON, persuade, entice.
PREVAILING, prevalent, ruling, overruling, predominant.
PREVALENT, ruling, overruling, predominant, prevailing.
to PREVARICATE, evade, equivocate.
to PREVENT, anticipate.
to PREVENT, impede, obstruct, hinder.
to PREVENT, obviate, preclude.
PREVIOUS, anterior, prior, former, antecedent, preceding, foregoing.
PREVIOUS, preliminary, preparatory, introductory.
PREY, booty, spoil.
PRICE, charge, cost, expense.
PRICE, value, worth, rate.
PRIDE, haughtiness, loftiness, dignity.
PRIDE, vanity, conceit.
PRIEST, minister, clergyman, parson.
PRIMARY, primitive, pristine, original.
PRIMITIVE, pristine, original, primary.
PRINCE, monarch, sovereign, potentate.
PRINCIPAL, main, chief.
PRINCIPALLY, chiefly, especially, particularly.
PRINCIPLE, doctrine, precept.
PRINCIPLE, motive.
PRINT, engraving, picture.
PRINT, impression, stamp, mark.
PRIOR, former, antecedent, preceding, foregoing, previous, anterior.
PRIORITY, precedence, preëminence, preference.
PRISTINE, original, primary, primitive.
PRIVACY, retirement, seclusion.
PRIVILEGE, prerogative, exemption, immunity.
PRIVILEGE, right, claim.
PRIZE, capture, seizure.
to PRIZE, esteem, value.
PROBABILITY, chance.
PROBITY, uprightness, integrity, honesty.
to PROCEED, advance.
to PROCEED, issue, spring, flow, emanate, arise, rise.
PROCEEDING, transaction.
PROCESSION, train, retinue.
to PROCLAIM, declare, publish.
to PROCLAIM, publish, announce.
PROCLAMATION, decree, edict.
to PROCRASTINATE, prolong, protract, retard, delay, defer, postpone.
to PROCURE, furnish, supply, provide.
to PROCURE, get, gain, obtain.
PRODIGAL, lavish, profuse, extravagant.

PRODIGIOUS, monstrous, enormous.
PRODIGY, monster, wonder, miracle, marvel.
to PRODUCE, afford, yield.
to PRODUCE, create, make, form.
to PRODUCE, perform, effect.
PRODUCE, product, production.
PRODUCT, production, produce.
PRODUCTION, performance, work.
PRODUCTION, produce, product.
PROFANE, impious, irreligious.
to PROFESS, declare.
PROFESSION, art, business, trade.
PROFICIENCY, improvement, progress.
PROFIT, advantage.
PROFIT, emolument, lucre, gain.
PROFLIGATE, abandoned, reprobate.
PROFUNDITY, depth.
PROFUSE, extravagant, prodigal, lavish.
PROFUSENESS, profusion.
PROFUSION, profuseness.
PROGENITORS, ancestors, forefathers.
PROGENY, issue, offspring.
PROGNOSTIC, presage, omen.
to PROGNOSTICATE, foretell, predict, prophesy.
PROGRESS, proficiency, improvement.
PROGRESS, progression, advance, advancement.
PROGRESSION, advance, advancement, progress.
PROGRESSIVE, onward, forward.
to PROHIBIT, interdict, forbid.
PROJECT, design, plan, scheme.
PROLIFIC, fertile, fruitful.
PROLIX, diffuse.
to PROLONG, protract, retard, delay, defer, postpone, procrastinate.
PROMINENT, conspicuous.
PROMISCUOUS, indiscriminate.
PROMISE, engagement, word.
to PROMOTE, prefer, forward, encourage, advance.
PROMPT, diligent, expeditious.
PROMPT, ready, apt.
to PROMULGATE, divulge, reveal, disclose, publish.
PRONENESS, inclination, tendency, propensity.
to PRONOUNCE, utter, speak, articulate.
PROOF, argument, reason.
PROOF, evidence, testimony.
PROOF, test, experience, experiment, trial.
PROP, support, staff, stay.
to PROPAGATE, disseminate, spread, circulate.
PROPENSITY, proneness, inclination, tendency.
PROPER, right, just, fit.
PROPERTY, attribute, quality.
to PROPHESY, prognosticate, foretell, predict.
PROPITIOUS, auspicious.

PROPORTION, ratio, rate.
PROPORTION, symmetry.
PROPORTIONATE, commensurate, adequate.
PROPOSAL, proposition.
to PROPOSE, offer, bid, tender.
to PROPOSE, purpose.
PROPOSITION, proposal.
PROPOSITION, period, phrase, sentence.
PROPRIETOR, owner, master, possessor.
to PROROGUE, adjourn.
to PROSECUTE, continue, persevere, persist, pursue.
PROSELYTE, convert.
PROSPECT, landscape, view.
PROSPECT, view, survey.
to PROSPER, flourish, thrive.
PROSPERITY, happiness, well-being, welfare.
PROSPEROUS, successful, fortunate, lucky, fortuitous.
to PROTECT, save, spare, preserve.
to PROTECT, vindicate, defend.
to PROTEST, affirm, asseverate, assure, vouch, aver.
to PROTRACT, retard, delay, defer, postpone, procrastinate, prolong.
to PROVE, argue, evince.
to PROVE, demonstrate, evince, manifest.
PROVERB, byword, saw, axiom, maxim, aphorism, apophthegm, saying, adage.
to PROVIDE, procure, furnish, supply.
PROVIDENCE, prudence.
PROVIDENT, careful, cautious.
PROVISION, fare.
to PROVOKE, exasperate, tantalize, aggravate, irritate.
to PROVOKE, excite, incite.
to PROVOKE, rouse, stir up, awaken, excite.
PRUDENCE, judgment, discretion.
PRUDENCE, providence.
PRUDENCE, wisdom.
PRUDENT, prudential.
PRUDENTIAL, prudent.
to PRY, scrutinize, dive into.
PRYING, curious, inquisitive.

to PUBLISH, advertise.
to PUBLISH, announce, proclaim.
to PUBLISH, proclaim, declare.
to PUBLISH, promulgate, divulge, reveal, disclose.
PUERILE, youthful, juvenile.
to PULL, pluck, tug, draw, drag, haul, hale.
PUNCTUAL, exact, nice, particular.
PUNISHMENT, correction, discipline.
to PURCHASE, bargain, cheapen, buy.
PURE, clean, cleanly.
to PURPOSE, intend, mean, design.
to PURPOSE, propose.
PURPOSE, end, sake, account, reason.
to PURSUE, follow.
to PURSUE, prosecute, continue, persevere, persist.

to PUSH, shove, thrust.
to PUT, place, lay, set.
to PUTREFY, corrupt, rot.

Q

to QUAKE, shake, tremble, shudder, quiver
QUALIFICATION, accomplishment.
QUALIFIED, competent, fitted.
to QUALIFY, fit, equip, prepare.
to QUALIFY, temper, humor.
QUALITY, property, attribute.
(OF) QUALITY, of distinction, of fashion.
QUANTITY, portion, deal.
QUARREL, affray, fray.
QUARREL, broil, feud.
QUARREL, difference, dispute, altercation.
QUARTER, district, region, tract.
QUERY, question.
to QUESTION, doubt.
to QUESTION, interrogate, ask, inquire.
QUESTION, query.
QUICKNESS, swiftness, fleetness, celerity, rapidity, velocity.
to QUIET, still, appease, calm, pacify.
QUIET, calm, tranquillity, peace.
QUIET, rest, repose, ease.
to QUIT, relinquish, leave.
to QUIVER, quake, shake, tremble, shudder.
to QUOTE, cite.

R

RACE, family, house, lineage.
RACE, generation, breed.
RACE, passage, course.
to RACK, rend, tear, break.
RADIANCE, brilliancy.
to RADIATE, shine, glitter, glare, sparkle.
RAGE, fury, anger, choler.
RAGE, fury, madness, frenzy.
to RAISE, aggravate, heighten.
to RAISE, erect, elevate, exalt, lift.
to RALLY, banter, deride, mock, ridicule.
to RAMBLE, rove, roam, range, wander, stroll.
RAMBLE, tour, trip, jaunt, excursion.
RANCOR, hatred, enmity, ill-will.
RANCOR, spite, grudge, pique, malice.
to RANGE, class, arrange.
to RANGE, wander, stroll, ramble, rove, roam.
RANK, degree, class, order.
to RANSOM, redeem.
RAPACIOUS, ravenous, voracious.
RAPIDITY, velocity, quickness, swiftness, fleetness, celerity.
RAPINE, plunder, pillage.
RAPTURE, transport, ecstasy.
RARE, scarce, singular.
RASH, foolhardy, adventurous.

RASHNESS, temerity, hastiness, precipitancy.
to RATE, estimate, compute.
RATE, assessment, tax.
RATE, price, value, worth.
RATE, proportion, ratio.
RATIO, rate, proportion.
RATIONAL, reasonable.
to RAVAGE, overspread, overrun.
RAVAGE, desolation, devastation.
RAVENOUS, voracious, rapacious.
RAY, beam, gleam, glimmer.
to RAZE, dismantle, destroy, demolish.
to RAZE, erase, efface, cancel, obliterate, blot out, expunge.

REACH, extend, stretch.
READY, apt, prompt.
READY, easy.
REAL, genuine, native, intrinsic.
REAL, positive, actual.
to REALIZE, fulfill, accomplish.
REALM, commonwealth, state.
REASON, consideration.
REASON, motive, cause.
REASON, proof, argument.
REASON, purpose, end, sake, account.
REASONABLE, fair, honest, equitable.
REASONABLE, rational.
REBELLION, contumacy.
REBELLION, revolt, insurrection, sedition.
to REBOUND, reverberate, recoil.
to REBUFF, refuse, decline, reject, repel.
to REBUKE, check, chide, reprimand, reprove.
to RECALL, adjure, recant, retract, revoke.
to RECANT, retract, revoke, recall, adjure.
to RECAPITULATE, repeat, recite, rehearse.
to RECEDE, retreat, retire, withdraw, secede.
RECEIPT, reception.
to RECEIVE, accept, take.
to RECEIVE, admit.
RECENT, new, novel, modern, fresh.
RECEPTION, receipt.
RECIPROCAL, mutual.
RECIPROCITY, interchange, exchange.
RECITAL, narration, narrative, relation.
to RECITE, rehearse, recapitulate, repeat.
to RECKON, compute, count, calculate.
to RECKON, count, account, number.
RECKONING, bill, account.
to RECLAIM, reform.
to RECLINE, repose.
RECOGNIZE, acknowledge.
to RECOIL, rebound, reverberate.
RECOLLECTION, reminiscence, memory, remembrance.
RECOMPENSE, remuneration, requital, reward, compensation, amends, satisfaction.
to RECONCILE, conciliate.
to RECORD, enroll, enlist, list, register.
RECORD, register, archive.

to RECOUNT, describe, relate.
to RECOVER, retrieve, repair, recruit.
RECOVERY, restoration.
RECREATION, pastime, amusement, entertainment, diversion, sport.
to RECRUIT, recover, retrieve, repair.
to RECTIFY, reform, correct.
RECTITUDE, uprightness.
to REDEEM, ransom.
REDRESS, relief.
to REDUCE, lower.
REDUNDANCY, excess, superfluity.
to REEL, totter, stagger.
to REFER, hint, suggest, allude.
to REFER, relate, respect, regard.
REFINED, polite, polished.
REFINEMENT, cultivation, culture, civilization.
to REFLECT, consider.
to REFLECT, ponder, muse, think.
REFLECTION, insinuation.
to REFORM, correct, rectify.
to REFORM, reclaim.
REFORM, reformation.
REFORMATION, reform.
REFRACTORY, unruly, ungovernable.
to REFRAIN, abstain, forbear.
to REFRESH, renovate, renew, revive.
REFUGE, shelter, retreat, asylum.
to REFUSE, decline, reject, repel, rebuff.
to REFUSE, deny.
REFUSE, dregs, sediment, dross, scum.
to REFUTE, disprove, oppugn, confute.
REGAL, kingly, royal.
to REGARD, consider.
to REGARD, heed, notice, attend to, mind.
to REGARD, refer, relate, respect.
REGARD, care, concern.
REGARD, esteem, respect.
REGARDFUL, mindful, observant.
REGARDLESS, indifferent, unconcerned.
REGIMEN, food, diet.
REGION, tract, quarter, district.
to REGISTER, record, enroll, enlist, list.
REGISTER, archive, record.
REGISTER, list, roll, catalogue.
to REGRET, complain, lament.
to REGULATE, dispose, direct.
to REGULATE, govern, rule.
to REHEARSE, recapitulate, repeat, recite.
REIGN, dominion, empire.
to REJECT, repel, rebuff, refuse, decline.
REJOINDER, response, answer, reply.
to RELATE, recount, describe.
to RELATE, respect, regard, refer.
RELATION, connection.
RELATION, recital, narration, narrative.
RELATION, relative, kinsman, kindred.
RELATIONSHIP, affinity, consanguinity, kindred.
RELATIVE, kinsman, kindred, relation.
to RELAX, remit.

RELENTLESS, inexorable, implacable, unrelenting.

RELIANCE, dependence.

RELICS, remains.

RELIEF, redress.

to RELIEVE, alleviate.

to RELIEVE, help, assist, aid, succour.

RELIGIOUS, holy, pious, devout.

to RELINQUISH, abandon, desert, forsake.

to RELINQUISH, leave, quit.

RELISH, savor, taste, flavor.

RELUCTANT, averse, unwilling, backward, loath.

to REMAIN, stay, continue.

REMAINDER, remnant, residue, rest.

REMAINS, leavings.

REMAINS, relics.

to REMARK, observe, notice.

REMARK, observation, comment, note, annotation, commentary.

REMARKABLE, extraordinary.

to REMEDY, cure, heal.

REMEDY, cure.

REMEMBRANCE, recollection, reminiscence, memory.

REMEMBRANCER, monument, memorial.

REMINISCENCE, memory, remembrance, recollection.

REMISS, careless, thoughtless, heedless, inattentive, negligent.

to REMIT, forgive, pardon, absolve.

to REMIT, relax.

REMNANT, residue, rest, remainder.

to REMONSTRATE, expostulate.

REMORSE, repentance, penitence, contrition, compunction.

REMOTE, distant, far.

REMUNERATION, requital, reward, compensation, amends, satisfaction, recompense.

to REND, tear, break, rack.

to RENEW, revive, refresh, renovate.

to RENOUNCE, abdicate, abandon, resign.

RENOWN, fame, reputation.

RENOWNED, illustrious, famous, celebrated.

to REPAIR, recruit, recover, retrieve.

REPARATION, amends, restoration, restitution.

REPARTEE, retort.

to REPAY, restore, return.

to REPEAL, revoke, annul, cancel, abolish, abrogate.

to REPEAT, recite, rehearse, recapitulate.

to REPEL, rebuff, refuse, decline, reject.

REPENTANCE, penitence, contrition, compunction, remorse.

REPETITION, tautology.

to REPINE, complain, murmur.

REPLY, rejoinder, response, answer.

REPORT, rumor, hearsay, fame.

to REPOSE, recline.

REPOSE, ease, quiet, rest.

REPREHENSION, reproof.

REPRESENTATION, sight, spectacle, show, exhibition.

to REPRESS, restrain, suppress.

REPRIEVE, respite.

to REPRIMAND, reprove, rebuke, check, chide.

REPRISAL, retaliation.

to REPROACH, upbraid, blame, censure, condemn, reprove.

REPROACH, contumely, obloquy.

REPROACH, scandal, discredit, disgrace.

REPROACHFUL, abusive, scurrilous.

to REPROBATE, condemn.

REPROBATE, profligate, abandoned.

REPROOF, reprehension.

to REPROVE, rebuke, check, chide, reprimand.

to REPROVE, reproach, upbraid, blame, censure, condemn.

REPUGNANT, adverse, inimical, hostile.

REPUGNANCE, aversion, antipathy, dislike, hatred.

REPUTATION, character.

REPUTATION, renown, fame.

REPUTATION, repute, credit, name.

REPUTE, credit, name, reputation.

to REQUEST, ask, beg.

REQUEST, entreaty, suit, prayer, petition.

to REQUIRE, demand.

REQUISITE, necessary, expedient, essential.

REQUITAL, reward, compensation, amends, satisfaction, recompense, remuneration.

REQUITAL, retribution.

to RESCUE, save, deliver.

RESEARCH, investigation, scrutiny, examination, search, inquiry.

RESEMBLANCE, similarity, similitude, likeness.

RESENTMENT, wrath, ire, indignation, anger.

RESERVATION, reserve.

to RESERVE, retain.

RESERVE, reservation.

to RESIDE, inhabit, abide, sojourn, dwell, live.

RESIDUE, rest, remainder, remnant.

to RESIGN, forego, give up, abandon.

to RESIGN, renounce, abdicate, abandon.

RESIGNATION, patience, endurance.

to RESIST, withstand, thwart, oppose.

RESOLUTE, decided, determined.

RESOLUTION, courage, fortitude.

to RESOLVE, determine.

to RESOLVE, solve.

to RESORT TO, haunt, frequent.

RESOURCE, expedient.

to RESPECT, honor, reverence.

to RESPECT, regard, refer, relate.

RESPECT, regard, esteem.

RESPECTFUL, dutiful, obedient.

RESPITE, interval.

RESPITE, reprieve.

RESPONSE, answer, reply, rejoinder.
RESPONSIBLE, accountable, amenable, answerable.
to REST, build, found, ground.
to REST, stagnate, stand, stop.
REST, intermission, cessation, stop.
REST, remainder, remnant, residue.
REST, repose, ease, quiet.
RESTITUTION, reparation, amends, restoration.
RESTORATION, recovery.
RESTORATION, restitution, reparation, amends.
to RESTORE, return, repay.
to RESTRAIN, coerce.
to RESTRAIN, compel, impel, constrain.
to RESTRAIN, restrict.
to RESTRAIN, suppress, repress.
RESTRAINT, constraint.
to RESTRICT, bound, limit, confine, circumscribe.
to RESTRICT, restrain.
RESULT, issue, event, consequence, effect.
to RETAIN, hold, keep, detain.
to RETAIN, reserve.
RETALIATION, reprisal.
to RETARD, delay, defer, postpone, procrastinate, prolong, protract.
to RETARD, hinder.
RETINUE, procession, train.
to RETIRE, withdraw, secede, recede, retreat.
RETIREMENT, seclusion, privacy.
RETORT, repartee.
to RETRACT, revoke, recall, abjure, recant.
to RETREAT, retire, withdraw, secede, recede.
RETREAT, asylum, refuge, shelter.
RETRIBUTION, requital.
to RETRIEVE, repair, recruit, recover.
RETROSPECT, review, survey.
to RETURN, repay, restore.
to RETURN, revert.
to REVEAL, disclose, publish, promulgate, divulge.
to REVENGE, vindicate, avenge.
to REVERBERATE, recoil, rebound.
to REVERE, adore, reverence, venerate.
to REVERENCE, respect, honor.
to REVERENCE, venerate, revere, adore.
REVERENCE, dread, awe.
REVERIE, dream.
to REVERSE, overturn, overthrow, subvert, invert.
to REVERT, return.
REVIEW, survey, retrospect.
to REVILE, vilify.
REVISAL, revision, review.
REVISION, review, revisal.
to REVIVE, refresh, renovate, renew.
to REVOKE, annul, cancel, abolish, abrogate, repeal.

to REVOKE, recall, abjure, recant, retract.
REVOLT, defection.
REVOLT, insurrection, sedition, rebellion.
REWARD, compensation, amends, satisfaction, recompense, remuneration, requital.

RHETORIC, elocution, eloquence, oratory.

RICHES, wealth, opulence, affluence.
to RIDICULE, laugh at.
to RIDICULE, rally, banter, deride, mock.
RIDICULE, satire, irony, sarcasm.
RIDICULOUS, comical, comic, droll, laughable, ludicrous.
RIGHT, claim, privilege.
RIGHT, direct, straight.
RIGHT, just, fit, proper.
RIGHTEOUS, godly.
RIGID, severe, rigorous, stern, austere.
RIGOROUS, harsh, rough, severe.
RIGOROUS, stern, austere, rigid, severe.
RIM, brim, brink, margin, verge, border, edge.
RIND, skin, hide, peel.
RIPE, mature.
to RISE, arise, mount, ascend, climb, scale.
to RISE, arise, proceed, issue, spring, flow, emanate.
to RISE, issue, emerge.
RISE, source, origin, original, beginning.
to RISK, venture, hazard.
RITE, observance, form, ceremony.
RIVALRY, competition, emulation.

ROAD, course, route.
to ROAM, range, wander, stroll, ramble, rove.
ROBBERY, depredation.
ROBUST, sturdy, strong.
ROLL, catalogue, register, list.
ROMANCE, fable, tale, novel.
ROOM, space.
to ROT, putrefy, corrupt.
ROTUNDITY, roundness.
ROUGH, abrupt, rugged.
ROUGH, rude, coarse.
ROUGH, severe, rigorous, harsh.
ROUND, circuit, tour.
ROUNDNESS, rotundity.
to ROUSE, stir up, awaken, excite, provoke.
to ROUT, overthrow, beat, defeat, overpower.
ROUTE, road, course.
to ROVE, roam, range, wander, stroll, ramble.
ROYAL, regal, kingly.

to RUB, chafe, fret, gall.
RUDE, coarse, rough.
RUDE, saucy, impudent, insolent, impertinent.
RUEFUL, piteous, doleful, woeful.

Rugged, rough, abrupt.
Ruin, bane, pest.
Ruin, destruction.
Ruin, fall, downfall.
Ruinous, pernicious, destructive.
to Rule, regulate, govern.
Rule, guide.
Rule, law, maxim, precept.
Rule, order, method.
Ruling, overruling, predominant, prevailing, prevalent.
Rumor, hearsay, fame, report.
Rupture, fracture, fraction.
Rural, rustic.
Rustic, clown, countryman, peasant, swain, hind.
Rustic, rural.

S

Sacrament, Lord's Supper, eucharist, communion.
Sacred, divine, holy.
Sad, dismal, dull, gloomy.
Sad, mournful.
Safe, secure.
Sagacious, sapient, sage.
Sagacity, penetration, acuteness.
Sage, sagacious, sapient.
Sailor, mariner, seaman, waterman.
Sake, account, reason, purpose, end.
Salary, wages, hire, pay, allowance, stipend.
Salubrious, salutary, healthy, wholesome.
Salutary, healthy, wholesome, salubrious.
Salutation, greeting, salute.
to Salute, address, greet, hail, welcome, accost.
Salute, salutation, greeting.
to Sanction, support, countenance.
Sanctity, holiness.
Sane, healthy, sound.
Sanguinary, bloody, bloodthirsty.
to Sap, undermine.
Sapient, sage, sagacious.
Sarcasm, ridicule, satire, irony.
to Satiate, glut, cloy, satisfy.
Satire, irony, burlesque, wit, humor.
Satire, irony, sarcasm, ridicule.
Satisfaction, contentment.
Satisfaction, recompense, remuneration, requital, reward, compensation, amends.
to Satisfy, please, gratify.
to Satisfy, satiate, glut, cloy.
Saucy, impudent, insolent, impertinent, rude.
to Saunter, linger, tarry, loiter, lag.
Savage, cruel, inhuman, barbarous, brutal.
Savage, ferocious, fierce.
to Save, deliver, rescue.
to Save, keep, preserve.
to Save, spare, preserve, protect.

Saving, sparing, thrifty, penurious, niggardly, economical.
Savor, taste, flavor, relish.
Saw, axiom, maxim, aphorism, apophthegm, saying, adage, proverb, byword.
to Say, tell, speak.
Saying, adage, proverb, byword, saw, axiom, maxim, aphorism, apophthegm.

to Scale, arise, rise, mount, ascend, climb.
Scandal, discredit, disgrace, reproach.
Scandalous, infamous.
Scanty, destitute, bare.
Scarce, singular, rare.
Scarcely, hardly.
Scarcity, dearth.
to Scatter, disperse, spread.
Scent, odor, perfume, fragrance, smell.
Scheme, project, design, plan.
Schismatic, sectarian, sectary, dissenter, nonconformist, heretic.
Scholar, disciple.
School, academy.
Science, learning, erudition, knowledge.
to Scoff, gibe, jeer, sneer.
Scope, aim, tendency, drift.
to Scorn, disdain, contemn, despise.
Scornful, disdainful, contemptuous.
to Scream, shriek, cry.
Screen, cover, shelter.
Scribe, writer, penman.
to Scruple, hesitate, waver.
Scrupulous, conscientious.
to Scrutinize, dive into, pry.
Scrutiny, examination, search, inquiry, research, investigation.
Scum, refuse, dregs, sediment, dross.
Scurrilous, reproachful, abusive.

Seal, stamp.
Seaman, waterman, sailor, mariner.
to Search, explore, examine.
to Search, seek.
Search, inquiry, research, investigation, scrutiny, examination.
Season, time.
Seasonable, timely.
to Secede, recede, retreat, retire, withdraw.
Seclusion, privacy, retirement.
to Second, support.
Second, secondary, inferior.
Secondary, inferior, second.
Secrecy, concealment.
Secret, clandestine.
Secret, hidden, latent, occult, mysterious.
to Secrete, conceal, hide.
to Secrete One's Self, abscond, steal away.
Sectarian, sectary, dissenter, nonconformist, heretic, schismatic.

SECTARY, sectarian, dissenter, nonconformist, heretic, schismatic.
SECULAR, temporal, worldly.
SECURE, certain, sure.
SECURE, safe.
SECURITY, deposit, pledge.
SECURITY, fence, guard.
SEDATE, composed.
SEDIMENT, dross, scum, refuse, dregs.
SEDITION, rebellion, revolt, insurrection.
SEDITIOUS, factious.
SEDITIOUS, mutinous, tumultuous, turbulent.
to SEDUCE, entice, decoy, allure, tempt.
SEDULOUS, diligent, assiduous.
to SEE, behold, view, eye, look.
to SEE, perceive, observe.
to SEEK, search.
to SEEM, appear.
SEEMLY, fit, suitable, becoming, decent.
to SEIZE, snatch, grasp, grip, lay hold of, take hold of, catch.
SEIZURE, prize, capture.
to SELECT, choose, pick.
SELF-CONCEIT, self-sufficiency, self-will.
SELF-SUFFICIENCY, self-will, self-conceit.
SELF-WILL, self-conceit, self-sufficiency.
SEMBLANCE, show, outside, appearance.
SENIOR, elder, older.
SENSATION, feeling, sense.
SENSATION, perception, sentiment.
SENSE, judgment.
SENSE, sensation, feeling.
SENSE, signification, meaning, import.
SENSIBILITY, susceptibility, feeling.
SENSIBLE, perceptible.
SENSIBLE, sensitive, sentient.
SENSITIVE, sentient, sensible.
SENSUALIST, voluptuary, epicure.
to SENTENCE, doom, condemn.
SENTENCE, proposition, period, phrase.
SENTENTIOUS, sentimental.
SENTIENT, sensible, sensitive.
SENTIMENT, notion, opinion.
SENTIMENT, sensation, perception.
SENTIMENTAL, sententious.
SENTINEL, guard.
to SEPARATE, distinguish, abstract.
to SEPARATE, part, divide.
to SEPARATE, sever, disjoin, detach.
SEPARATE, different, distinct.
SEPULCHRE, grave, tomb.
SEPULTURE, burial, interment.
SEQUEL, close.
SERENE, calm, placid.
SERIES, course.
SERIES, order, succession.
SERIOUS, eager, earnest.
SERIOUS, solemn, grave.
SERVANT, domestic, menial, drudge.
SERVICE, avail, utility, use.
SERVICE, good office, benefit.

SERVITUDE, slavery, bondage.
to SET, put, place, lay.
to SET FREE, deliver, liberate, free.
to SETTLE, compose.
to SETTLE, establish, fix.
to SETTLE, limit, fix, determine.
to SEVER, disjoin, detach, separate.
SEVERAL, divers, sundry, various, different.
SEVERE, rigorous, harsh, rough.
SEVERE, rigorous, stern, austere, rigid.
SEVERE, strict.
SEX, gender.

SHACKLE, chain, fetter, band.
SHADE, shadow.
SHADOW, shade.
to SHAKE, agitate, toss.
to SHAKE, tremble, shudder, quiver, quake.
SHALLOW, flimsy, superficial.
SHAME, dishonor, disgrace.
SHAMELESS, immodest, impudent.
to SHAPE, form, fashion, mold.
to SHARE, divide, distribute.
to SHARE, partake, participate.
SHARE, part, division, portion.
SHARP, acute, keen.
to SHED, pour, spill.
to SHELTER, lodge, harbor.
SHELTER, retreat, asylum, refuge.
SHELTER, screen, cover.
SHIFT, subterfuge, evasion.
to SHINE, glitter, glare, sparkle, radiate.
SHOCK, concussion.
SHOCKING, formidable, dreadful, terrible.
to SHOOT, dart.
SHORT, brief, concise, succinct, summary.
to SHOVE, thrust, push.
to SHOW, exhibit, display.
to SHOW, point out, mark, indicate.
SHOW, exhibition, representation, sight, spectacle.
SHOW, outside, appearance, semblance.
SHOW, parade, ostentation.
SHOWY, gaudy, gay.
SHREWD, acute, keen.
to SHRIEK, cry, scream.
to SHRINK, spring, start, startle.
to SHUDDER, quiver, quake, shake, tremble.
to SHUN, elude, avoid, eschew.
to SHUT, close.

SICK, sickly, diseased, morbid.
SICKLY, diseased, morbid, sick.
SICKNESS, illness, indisposition.
SIGHT, spectacle, show, exhibition, representation.
SIGN, note, symptom, token, indication, mark.
SIGN, signal.
SIGNAL, sign.
SIGNAL, memorable.
to SIGNALIZE, distinguish.

SIGNIFICANT, expressive.
SIGNIFICATION, meaning, import, sense.
to SIGNIFY, avail.
to SIGNIFY, denote.
to SIGNIFY, imply.
to SIGNIFY, testify, utter, express, declare.
SILENCE, taciturnity.
SILENT, dumb, mute, speechless.
SILENT, tacit.
SILLY, foolish, simple.
SIMILE, similitude, comparison.
SIMILITUDE, comparison, simile.
SIMILITUDE, similarity, likeness, resemblance.
SIMPLE, silly, foolish.
SIMPLE, single, singular.
SIMULATION, dissimulation.
SIN, crime, vice.
SINCERE, candid, open.
SINCERE, cordial, hearty, warm.
SINCERE, honest, true, plain.
SINGLE, singular, simple.
SINGLE, only, one.
SINGLE, solitary, sole, only.
SINGULAR, odd, eccentric, strange, particular.
SINGULAR, rare, scarce.
SINGULAR, simple, single.
to SINK, tumble, fall, drop, droop.
SITE, place, spot.
SITUATION, circumstance.
SITUATION, condition, state, predicament, plight, case.
SITUATION, position, post, place, station.
SIZE, magnitude, greatness, bulk.

to SKETCH, delineate.
SKETCH, outlines.
SKILLFUL, expert, dexterous, adroit, clever.
SKIN, hide, peel, rind.

SLACK, loose.
to SLANDER, calumniate, asperse, detract, defame.
to SLANT, slope.
to SLAUGHTER, slay, kill, murder, assassinate.
SLAUGHTER, massacre, butchery, carnage.
to SLAY, slaughter, kill, murder, assassinate.
to SLEEP, slumber, doze, drowse, nap.
SLEEPY, drowsy, lethargic.
SLENDER, slight, slim, thin.
to SLIDE, glide, slip.
to SLIGHT, disregard, neglect.
SLIGHT, desultory, cursory, hasty.
SLIGHT, slim, thin, slender.
SLIM, thin, slender, slight.
to SLIP, slide, glide.
to SLOPE, slant.
SLOTHFUL, sluggish, inactive, inert, lazy.
SLOW, dilatory, tardy, tedious.
SLUGGISH, inactive, inert, lazy, slothful.

to SLUMBER, doze, drowse, nap, sleep.
SLY, wily, cunning, crafty, subtle.

SMALL, diminutive, little.
to SMEAR, daub.
SMELL, scent, odor, perfume, fragrance.
SMOOTH, level, plain, even.
to SMOTHER, choke, suffocate, stifle.
to SMOTHER, stifle, suppress.

to SNATCH, grasp, grip, lay hold of, take hold of, catch, seize.
to SNEER, scoff, gibe, jeer.

to SOAK, drench, steep.
SOBER, abstemious, temperate, abstinent.
SOBER, grave.
SOBRIETY, modesty, moderation, temperance.
SOCIABLE, social.
SOCIAL, convivial.
SOCIAL, sociable.
SOCIETY, community.
SOCIETY, company, partnership, association.
SOCIETY, fellowship.
SOFT, mild, gentle, meek.
to SOIL, sully, tarnish, stain.
to SOJOURN, dwell, live, reside, inhabit, abide.
to SOLACE, comfort, console.
SOLDIER-LIKE, martial, warlike, military.
SOLE, only, single, solitary.
SOLEMN, grave, serious.
to SOLICIT, entreat, supplicate, implore, crave, beg, beseech.
SOLICITATION, importunity.
SOLICITUDE, anxiety, care.
SOLID, hard, firm.
SOLID, stable, firm, fixed.
SOLID, substantial.
SOLITARY, desert, desolate.
SOLITARY, lonely, alone.
SOLITARY, sole, only, single.
to SOLVE, resolve.
SOME, any.
SOON, early, betimes.
to SOOTHE, appease, mitigate, assuage, allay.
SORDID, mean, pitiful.
SORROW, affliction, grief.
SORRY, grieved, hurt.
SORT, kind, species.
SOUL, mind.
SOUND, sane, healthy.
SOUND, tone.
SOURCE, origin, original, beginning, rise.
SOURCE, spring, fountain.
SOVEREIGN, potentate, prince, monarch.

SPACE, room.
SPACIOUS, capacious, ample.
to SPARE, afford.

to SPARE, preserve, protect, save.
SPARING, thrifty, penurious, niggardly, economical, saving.
SPARK, gallant, beau.
to SPARKLE, radiate, shine, glitter, glare.
to SPEAK, articulate, pronounce, utter.
to SPEAK, say, tell.
to SPEAK, talk, converse, discourse.
SPECIAL, specific, particular.
SPECIES, sort, kind.
SPECIFIC, particular, special.
SPECIMEN, copy, model, pattern.
SPECIOUS, ostensible, plausible, feasible, colorable.
SPECK, flaw, blemish, stain, spot.
SPECTACLE, show, exhibition, representation, sight.
SPECTATOR, beholder, observer, looker-on.
SPECTRE, ghost, vision, apparition, phantom.
SPECULATION, theory.
SPEECH, harangue, oration, address.
SPEECH, idiom, dialect, language, tongue.
SPEECHLESS, silent, dumb, mute.
to SPEED, expedite, dispatch, hasten, accelerate.
to SPEND, exhaust, drain.
to SPEND, expend, waste, dissipate, squander.
SPHERE, orb, globe, circle.
to SPILL, shed, pour.
SPIRIT, animation, life, vivacity.
SPIRITED, spiritual, ghostly, spirituous.
SPIRITUAL, ghostly, spirituous, spirited.
SPIRITUAL, incorporeal, unbodied, immaterial.
SPIRITUOUS, spirited, spiritual, ghostly.
SPITE, grudge, pique, malice, rancor.
SPLENDOR, brilliancy, brightness, lustre.
SPLENDOR, pomp, magnificence.
SPLENETIC, gloomy, sullen, morose.
to SPLIT, break, burst, crack.
SPOIL, prey, booty.
SPONTANEOUSLY, willingly, voluntarily.
to SPORT, jest, joke.
SPORT, game, play.
SPORT, recreation, pastime, amusement, entertainment, diversion.
SPORTIVE, merry, jocund, lively, sprightly, vivacious.
SPORTIVE, playful, gamesome.
SPOT, site, place.
SPOT, speck, flaw, blemish, stain.
SPOTLESS, unspotted, blameless, irreproachable, unblemished.
to SPOUT, spurt.
SPRAIN, stress, force, strain.
to SPREAD, circulate, propagate, disseminate.
to SPREAD, expand, diffuse.
to SPREAD, scatter, disperse.
SPRIGHTLY, gay, cheerful, merry.

SPRIGHTLY, vivacious, sportive, merry, jocund, lively.
to SPRING, flow, emanate, arise, rise, proceed, issue.
to SPRING, start, startle, shrink.
SPRING, fountain, source.
to SPRINKLE, bedew.
to SPROUT, bud.
SPRUCE, foppish, finical.
SPURIOUS, supposititious, counterfeit.
to SPURT, spout.

to SQUANDER, spend, expend, waste, dissipate.
SQUEAMISH, fastidious.
to SQUEEZE, pinch, gripe, press.
to SQUEEZE, pound, crush, break, bruise.

STABILITY, steadiness, firmness, constancy.
STABLE, firm, fixed, solid.
STAFF, stay, prop, support.
STAFF, stick, crutch.
to STAGGER, reel, totter.
to STAGNATE, stand, stop, rest.
to STAIN, color, dye, tinge.
to STAIN, soil, sully, tarnish.
STAIN, spot, speck, flaw, blemish.
to STAMMER, stutter, hesitate, falter.
STAMP, mark, print, impression.
STAMP, seal.
to STAND, stop, rest, stagnate.
STANDARD, criterion.
to STARE, gaze, gape.
to START, startle, shrink, spring.
to STARTLE, shrink, spring, start.
STATE, predicament, plight, case, situation, condition.
STATE, realm, commonwealth.
STATELY, pompous, august, dignified, magisterial, majestic.
STATION, condition.
STATION, situation, position, post, place.
to STAY, continue, remain.
STAY, prop, support, staff.
STEADINESS, firmness, constancy, stability.
to STEAL AWAY, secrete one's self, abscond.
to STEEP, soak, drench.
STEP, pace.
STERN, austere, rigid, severe, rigorous.
to STICK, cleave, adhere.
to STICK, fix, fasten.
STICK, crutch, staff.
to STIFLE, smother, choke, suffocate.
to STIFLE, suppress, smother.
STIGMA, mark, badge.
to STILL, appease, calm, pacify, quiet.
to STIMULATE, instigate, encourage, animate, incite, impel, urge.
STIPEND, salary, wages, hire, pay, allowance.
to STIR, move.
to STIR UP, awaken, excite, provoke, rouse.

STOCK, store.
to STOP, check.
to STOP, hinder.
to STOP, rest, stagnate, stand.
STOP, rest, intermission, cessation.
STORE, stock.
STORM, tempest, hurricane, breeze, gale, blast, gust.
STORY, anecdote.
STORY, tale.
STOUT, lusty, corpulent.
STRAIGHT, right, direct.
STRAIN, emphasis, accent, stress.
STRAIN, sprain, stress, force.
STRAIT, narrow.
STRANGE, particular, singular, odd, eccentric.
STRANGER, foreigner, alien.
STRATAGEM, artifice, trick, finesse.
to STRAY, deviate, wander, swerve.
to STREAM, gush, flow.
STREAM, current, tide.
STRENGTH, force, authority, dominion, power.
to STRENGTHEN, fortify, invigorate.
STRENUOUS, bold.
STRESS, force, strain, sprain.
STRESS, strain, emphasis, accent.
STRETCH, reach, extend.
STRICT, severe.
STRICTURE, animadversion, criticism.
STRIFE, contention.
STRIFE, discord.
to STRIKE, hit, beat.
to STRIP, bereave, deprive.
to STRIVE, contend, vie.
STROKE, blow.
to STROLL, ramble, rove, roam, range, wander.
STRONG, cogent, forcible.
STRONG, robust, sturdy.
STRUCTURE, fabric, edifice.
to STRUGGLE, endeavor, aim, strive.
STUBBORN, headstrong, heady, obstinate, contumacious.
STUDY, attention, application.
STUPID, dull.
STURDY, strong, robust.
to STUTTER, hesitate, falter, stammer.
to STYLE, entitle, designate, characterize, name, denominate.
STYLE, phrase, phraseology, diction.

SUAVITY, urbanity.
to SUBDUE, overbear, bear down, overpower, overwhelm.
to SUBDUE, overcome, surmount, conquer, vanquish.
to SUBDUE, subject, subjugate.
to SUBJECT, subjugate, subdue.
SUBJECT, liable, exposed, obnoxious.
SUBJECT, matter, materials.

SUBJECT, subordinate, inferior, subservient.
to SUBJOIN, attach, annex, affix.
to SUBJUGATE, subdue, subject.
SUBLIME, great, grand.
SUBMISSIVE, compliant, yielding.
SUBMISSIVE, humble, modest.
SUBMISSIVE, obsequious, obedient.
SUBMISSIVE, patient, passive.
to SUBMIT, comply, conform, yield.
SUBORDINATE, inferior, subservient, subject.
to SUBORN, forswear, perjure.
SUBSERVIENT, subject, subordinate, inferior.
to SUBSIDE, abate, intermit.
to SUBSIST, be, exist.
SUBSISTENCE, maintenance, support, sustenance, livelihood, living.
SUBSTANTIAL, solid.
to SUBSTITUTE, change, exchange, barter.
SUBTERFUGE, evasion, shift.
SUBTLE, sly, wily, cunning, crafty.
to SUBTRACT, deduct.
to SUBVERT, invert, reverse, overturn, overthrow.
to SUCCEED, ensue, follow.
SUCCESSFUL, fortunate, lucky, fortuitous, prosperous.
SUCCESSION, series, order.
SUCCESSIVE, alternate.
SUCCINCT, summary, short, brief, concise.
to SUCCOUR, relieve, help, assist, aid.
to SUFFER, endure, support, bear.
to SUFFER, let, leave.
to SUFFER, tolerate, admit, allow, permit.
SUFFICIENT, enough.
to SUFFOCATE, stifle, smother, choke.
SUFFRAGE, voice, vote.
to SUGGEST, allude, refer, hint.
to SUGGEST, intimate, insinuate, hint.
SUGGESTION, dictate.
to SUIT, adapt, accommodate, adjust, fit.
to SUIT, agree, accord.
SUIT, prayer, petition, request, entreaty.
SUITABLE, becoming, decent, seemly, fit.
SUITABLE, conformable, agreeable.
SUITABLE, convenient.
SUITABLE, correspondent, answerable.
SUITOR, wooer, lover.
SULLEN, morose, splenetic, gloomy.
to SULLY, tarnish, stain, soil.
SUMMARY, abstract, abridgment, compendium, epitome, digest.
SUMMARY, short, brief, concise, succinct.
to SUMMON, call, invite, bid.
to SUMMON, cite.
SUNDRY, various, different, several, divers.
SUPERFICIAL, shallow, flimsy.
SUPERFICIES, surface.
SUPERFLUITY, redundancy, excess.
SUPERINTENDENCY, oversight, inspection.
SUPERIORITY, excellence.
SUPERSCRIPTION, direction, address.
to SUPERSEDE, overrule.

Supine, listless, careless, indolent.
Supple, flexible, pliable, pliant.
to Supplicate, implore, crave, beg, beseech, solicit, entreat.
to Supply, provide, procure, furnish.
to Support, bear, suffer, endure.
to Support, countenance, sanction.
to Support, maintain, hold.
to Support, maintain, sustain.
to Support, second.
Support, staff, stay, prop.
Support, sustenance, livelihood, living, subsistence, maintenance.
to Suppose, imagine, apprehend, conceive.
to Suppose, imagine, believe, deem, think.
Supposition, surmise, conjecture.
Supposititious, counterfeit, spurious.
to Suppress, repress, restrain.
to Suppress, smother, stifle.
Sure, secure, certain.
Surface, superficies.
Surge, breaker, wave, billow.
Surmise, conjecture, supposition.
to Surmount, conquer, vanquish, subdue, overcome.
to Surpass, transcend, outdo, exceed, excel.
to Surprise, astonish, amaze, wonder, admire.
to Surrender, yield, cede, concede, give up, deliver.
to Surround, encompass, environ, encircle.
Survey, prospect, view.
Survey, retrospect, review.
to Survive, outlive.
Susceptibility, feeling, sensibility.
Suspense, doubt.
Suspicion, diffidence, distrust.
Suspicion, jealousy, envy.
to Sustain, support, maintain.
Sustenance, livelihood, living, subsistence, maintenance, support.

Swain, hind, rustic, clown, countryman, peasant.
to Swallow Up, engulf, engross, imbibe, absorb.
Swarm, multitude, crowd, throng.
Sway, influence, authority, ascendancy, or ascendant.
to Swell, heave.
to Swerve, stray, deviate, wander.
Swiftness, fleetness, celerity, rapidity, velocity, quickness.

Sycophant, parasite, flatterer.
Symbol, type, figure, metaphor, allegory, emblem.
Symmetry, proportion.
Sympathy, compassion, commiseration, condolence.
Symptom, token, indication, mark, sign, note.

Synod, convocation, council, assembly, company, meeting, congregation, parliament, diet, congress, convention.
System, method.

T

Tacit, silent.
Taciturnity, silence.
to Taint, corrupt, contaminate, defile, pollute.
to Take, receive, accept.
to Take Heed, guard against.
to Take Hold Of, lay hold of, catch, seize, snatch, grasp, grip.
to Take Leave, bid farewell, adieu, leave.
to Take Pains, take trouble, labor.
to Take Trouble, take pains, labor.
Tale, novel, romance, fable.
Tale, story.
Talent, ability, faculty.
Talent, gift, endowment.
Talent, intellect, genius.
to Talk, converse, discourse, speak.
Talkative, loquacious, garrulous.
Tall, lofty, high.
Tame, gentle.
to Tantalize, aggravate, irritate, provoke, exasperate.
to Tantalize, torment, tease, vex, taunt.
Tardy, tedious, slow, dilatory.
to Tarnish, stain, soil, sully.
to Tarry, loiter, lag, saunter, linger.
Tartness, asperity, harshness, acrimony.
Task, work, labor, toil, drudgery.
Taste, flavor, relish, savor.
Taste, genius.
Taste, palate.
to Taunt, tantalize, torment, tease, vex.
Tautology, repetition.
Tax, duty, custom, toll, impost, tribute, contribution.
Tax, rate, assessment.

to Teach, inform, instruct.
to Tear, break, rack, rend.
to Tease, vex, taunt, tantalize, torment.
Tedious, slow, dilatory, tardy.
Tedious, wearisome, tiresome.
Tegument, covering.
to Tell, speak, say.
Temerity, hastiness, precipitancy, rashness.
to Temper, humor, qualify.
Temper, disposition.
Temper, mood, humor.
Temper, temperament, constitution, frame.
Temperament, constitution, frame, temper.
Temperament, temperature.
Temperance, sobriety, modesty, moderation.
Temperate, abstinent, sober, abstemious.
Temperature, temperament.

TEMPEST, hurricane, breeze, gale, blast, gust, storm.
TEMPLE, church.
TEMPORAL, worldly, secular.
TEMPORARY, transient, transitory, fleeting.
TEMPORIZING, timeserving.
to TEMPT, seduce, entice, decoy, allure.
to TEMPT, try.
TENACIOUS, pertinacious.
TENDENCY, drift, scope, aim.
TENDENCY, propensity, proneness, inclination.
to TENDER, propose, offer, bid.
TENDERNESS, benevolence, benignity, humanity, kindness.
TENET, doctrine, dogma.
TENET, position.
TERM, article, condition.
TERM, expression, word.
TERM, limit, boundary.
to TERMINATE, close, end.
to TERMINATE, complete, finish.
TERRIBLE, shocking, formidable, dreadful.
TERRIBLE, terrific, horrible, horrid, fearful, dreadful, frightful, tremendous.
TERRIFIC, horrible, horrid, fearful, dreadful, frightful, tremendous, terrible.
TERRITORY, dominion.
TERROR, fright, consternation, alarm.
TEST, experience, experiment, trial, proof.
to TESTIFY, utter, express, declare, signify.
TESTIMONY, proof, evidence.

THANKFULNESS, gratitude.
THEOLOGIAN, ecclesiastic, divine.
THEORY, speculation.
THEREFORE, consequently, accordingly.
THICK, dense.
THIN, slender, slight, slim.
to THINK, reflect, ponder, muse.
to THINK, suppose, imagine, believe, deem.
THOUGHT, imagination, idea.
THOUGHTFUL, considerate, deliberate.
THOUGHTLESS, heedless, inattentive, negligent, remiss, careless.
THREAT, menace.
THREATENING, imminent, impending.
THRIFTY, penurious, niggardly, economical, saving, sparing.
to THRIVE, prosper, flourish.
THRONG, swarm, multitude, crowd.
to THROW, hurl, cast.
to THRUST, push, shove.
to THWART, oppose, resist, withstand.

TIDE, stream, current.
TIDINGS, news.
to TIE, bind.
TILLAGE, husbandry, cultivation.
TIME, duration.
TIME, period, age, date, era, epoch.
TIME, season.

TIMELY, seasonable.
(IN) TIMES PAST, in old times, in days of yore, anciently, in ancient times, formerly.
TIMESERVING, temporizing.
TIMID, afraid, fearful, timorous.
TIMOROUS, timid, afraid, fearful.
to TINGE, stain, color, dye.
TINT, color, hue.
to TIRE, jade, harass, weary.
TIRESOME, tedious, wearisome.
TITLE, denomination, name, appellation.

TOIL, drudgery, task, work, labor.
TOKEN, indication, mark, sign, note, symptom.
to TOLERATE, admit, allow, permit, suffer.
TOLL, impost, tribute, contribution, tax, duty, custom.
TOMB, sepulchre, grave.
TONE, sound.
TONGUE, speech, idiom, dialect, language.
TOO, also, likewise.
TOOL, instrument.
TORMENT, torture.
to TORMENT, tease, vex, taunt, tantalize.
TORPID, numb, benumbed.
TORTURE, torment.
to TOSS, shake, agitate.
TOTAL, integral, whole, entire, complete.
to TOTTER, stagger, reel.
TOUCH, contact.
TOUR, round, circuit.
TOUR, trip, jaunt, excursion, ramble.

to TRACE, deduce, derive.
TRACE, vestige, footstep, track, mark.
TRACK, mark, trace, vestige, footstep.
TRACT, dissertation, essay, treatise.
TRACT, quarter, district, region.
TRACTABLE, ductile, docile.
TRADE, commerce, traffic, dealing.
TRADE, profession, art, business.
to TRADUCE, depreciate, degrade, decry, disparage, detract.
TRAFFIC, dealing, trade, commerce.
TRAIN, retinue, procession.
TRAITOROUS, treasonable, treacherous.
TRANQUILLITY, peace, quiet, calm.
to TRANSACT, negotiate, treat for.
TRANSACTION, proceeding.
to TRANSCEND, outdo, exceed, excel, surpass.
to TRANSCRIBE, copy.
to TRANSFIGURE, transform, metamorphose.
to TRANSFORM, metamorphose, transfigure.
to TRANSGRESS, infringe, violate.
TRANSGRESSION, misdemeanor, misdeed, affront, offence, trespass.
TRANSIENT, transitory, fleeting, temporary.
TRANSITORY, fleeting, temporary, transient.
TRANSPARENT, pellucid.

to TRANSPORT, bear, carry, convey.
TRANSPORT, ecstasy, rapture.
TRAVEL, voyage, journey.
TREACHEROUS, faithless, perfidious.
TREACHEROUS, insidious.
TREACHEROUS, traitorous, treasonable.
TREASONABLE, treacherous, traitorous.
to TREASURE, hoard.
to TREAT FOR, transact, negotiate.
TREAT, feast, banquet, carousal, entertainment.
TREATISE, tract, dissertation, essay.
TREATMENT, usage.
to TREMBLE, shudder, quiver, quake, shake.
TREMBLING, tremor, trepidation.
TREMENDOUS, terrible, terrific, horrible, horrid, fearful, dreadful, frightful.
TREMOR, emotion, agitation, trepidation.
TREMOR, trepidation, trembling.
TREPIDATION, trembling, tremor.
TREPIDATION, tremor, emotion, agitation.
TRESPASS, transgression, misdemeanor, misdeed, affront, offence.
TRIAL, endeavor, effort, essay, attempt.
TRIAL, proof, test, experience, experiment.
TRIBUTE, contribution, tax, duty, custom, toll, impost.
to TRICK, cheat, defraud.
TRICK, finesse, stratagem, artifice.
TRIFLING, trivial, petty, frivolous, futile.
TRIP, jaunt, excursion, ramble, tour.
TRIVIAL, petty, frivolous, futile, trifling.
TROOP, company.
to TROUBLE, afflict, distress.
to TROUBLE, disturb, molest.
TROUBLES, difficulties, embarrassments.
TROUBLESOME, irksome, vexatious.
to TRUCK, commute, exchange, barter.
TRUE, plain, sincere, honest.
to TRUST, confide.
TRUST, confidence, hope, expectation.
TRUST, faith, belief, credit.
TRUSTY, faithful.
TRUTH, veracity.
to TRY, tempt.

to TUG, draw, drag, haul, hale, pull, pluck.
to TUMBLE, fall, drop, droop, sink.
TUMID, bombastic, turgid.
TUMULT, uproar, bustle.
TUMULTUARY, tumultuous.
TUMULTUOUS, tumultuary.
TUMULTUOUS, turbulent, seditious, mutinous.
TURBULENT, seditious, mutinous, tumultuous.
TURGID, tumid, bombastic.
to TURN, bend, twist, distort, wring, wrest, wrench.
to TURN, wind, whirl, twirl, writhe.
TURN, bent.
TURN, description, cast.

to TWIRL, writhe, turn, wind, whirl.
to TWIST, distort, wring, wrest, wrench, turn, bend.

TYPE, figure, metaphor, allegory, emblem, symbol.
TYRANNICAL, absolute, despotic, arbitrary.

U

ULTIMATE, last, latest, final.

UMPIRE, arbiter, arbitrator, judge.

UNBELIEF, disbelief.
UNBELIEF, infidelity, incredulity.
UNBLEMISHED, unspotted, spotless, blameless, irreproachable.
UNBODIED, immaterial, spiritual, incorporeal.
UNBOUNDED, unlimited, infinite, boundless.
UNCEASINGLY, uninterruptedly, without intermission, incessantly.
UNCERTAIN, precarious, doubtful, dubious.
UNCONCERNED, regardless, indifferent.
UNCONQUERABLE, insuperable, insurmountable, invincible.
to UNCOVER, discover, disclose.
UNCOVERED, bare, naked.
UNDAUNTED, bold, fearless, intrepid.
UNDENIABLE, incontrovertible, irrefragable, indubitable, unquestionable, indisputable.
UNDER, below, beneath.
to UNDERMINE, sap.
to UNDERSTAND, comprehend, conceive.
UNDERSTANDING, intellect, intelligence.
UNDERTAKING, enterprise, attempt.
UNDETERMINED, unsettled, unsteady, wavering.
UNEVEN, odd.
UNFEELING, hard, hardy, insensible.
to UNFOLD, unravel, develop.
UNGOVERNABLE, refractory, unruly.
UNHAPPY, miserable, wretched.
UNIFORM, equal, even, equable, like, alike.
UNIMPORTANT, insignificant, immaterial, inconsiderable.
to UNITE, coalesce, add, join.
to UNITE, connect, combine.
UNIVERSAL, general.
UNINTERRUPTEDLY, without intermission, incessantly, unceasingly.
UNLEARNED, unlettered, ignorant, illiterate.
UNLESS, except.
UNLETTERED, ignorant, illiterate, unlearned.
UNLIKE, different.
UNLIMITED, infinite, boundless, unbounded.
UNMERCIFUL, merciless, hardhearted, cruel.
UNOFFENDING, inoffensive, harmless.
UNQUESTIONABLE, indisputable, undeniable, incontrovertible, irrefragable, indubitable.
to UNRAVEL, develop, unfold.

UNRELENTING, relentless, inexorable, implacable.
UNRULY, ungovernable, refractory.
UNSEARCHABLE, inscrutable.
UNSETTLED, unsteady, wavering, undetermined.
UNSPEAKABLE, ineffable, unutterable, inexpressible.
UNSPOTTED, spotless, blameless, irreproachable, unblemished.
UNSTEADY, wavering, undetermined, unsettled.
UNTOWARD, crooked, froward, perverse, awkward, cross.
UNTRUTH, falsehood, falsity, lie.
UNUTTERABLE, inexpressible, unspeakable, ineffable.
UNWILLING, backward, loath, reluctant, averse.
UNWORTHY, worthless.

to UPBRAID, blame, censure, condemn, reprove, reproach.
UPON, beyond, above, over.
UPRIGHTNESS, integrity, honesty, probity.
UPRIGHTNESS, rectitude.
UPROAR, bustle, tumult.

URBANITY, suavity.
to URGE, stimulate, instigate, encourage, animate, incite, impel.
URGENT, importunate, pressing.

USAGE, custom, prescription.
USAGE, treatment.
to USE, employ.
USE, service, avail, utility.
USUALLY, commonly, generally, frequently.
to USURP, arrogate, assume, ascribe, appropriate.

UTILITY, advantage, benefit.
UTILITY, use, service, avail.
to UTTER, express, declare, signify, testify.
to UTTER, speak, articulate, pronounce.

V

VACANCY, vacuity, inanity.
VACANT, idle, at leisure.
VACANT, void, devoid, empty.
VACUITY, inanity, vacancy.
VAGUE, lax, dissolute, licentious, loose.
VAIN, idle.
VAIN, ineffectual, fruitless.
VALOR, bravery, courage.
VALUABLE, precious, costly.
to VALUE, prize, esteem.
VALUE, worth, rate, price.
to VANISH, disappear.
VANITY, conceit, pride.

to VANQUISH, subdue, overcome, surmount, conquer.
VARIABLE, inconstant, fickle, versatile, changeable, mutable.
VARIATION, variety.
VARIATION, vicissitude, change.
VARIETY, diversity, medley, difference.
VARIETY, variation.
VARIOUS, different, several, divers, sundry.
to VARNISH, palliate, gloss.
to VARY, change, alter.
to VARY, disagree, dissent, differ.
VAST, enormous, huge, immense.
to VAUNT, glory, boast.

VEHEMENT, impetuous, violent, furious, boisterous.
VEIL, cloak, mask, blind.
VELOCITY, quickness, swiftness, fleetness, celerity, rapidity.
VENAL, mercenary.
to VENERATE, revere, adore, reverence.
VENIAL, pardonable.
VENOM, poison.
to VENTURE, hazard, risk.
VERACITY, truth.
VERBAL, vocal, oral.
VERGE, border, edge, rim, brim, brink, margin.
VERSATILE, changeable, mutable, variable, inconstant, fickle.
VESTIGE, footstep, track, mark, trace.
to VEX, displease, offend.
to VEX, taunt, tantalize, torment, tease.
VEXATION, mortification, chagrin.
VEXATIOUS, troublesome, irksome.

VICE, imperfection, defect, fault.
VICE, sin, crime.
VICINITY, neighborhood.
VICISSITUDE, change, variation.
VICTOR, conqueror.
to VIE, strive, contend.
to VIEW, eye, look, see, behold.
VIEW, aim, object, end.
VIEW, prospect, landscape.
VIEW, survey, prospect.
VIGILANT, wakeful, watchful.
VIGOR, energy, force.
VILE, mean, base.
to VILIFY, revile.
to VINDICATE, assert, maintain.
to VINDICATE, avenge, revenge.
to VINDICATE, defend, protect.
to VIOLATE, transgress, infringe.
VIOLENCE, force.
VIOLENT, furious, boisterous, vehement, impetuous.
VISAGE, face, countenance.
VISIBLE, clear, plain, obvious, evident, manifest, apparent.

VISION, apparition, phantom, spectre, ghost.
VISIONARY, enthusiast, fanatic.
VISITANT, visitor, guest.
VISITOR, visitant, guest.
VIVACIOUS, sportive, merry, jocund, lively, sprightly.
VIVACITY, spirit, animation, life.
VIVID, clear, lucid, bright.

VOCABULARY, glossary, nomenclature, dictionary, lexicon.
VOCAL, oral, verbal.
VOCATION, business, occupation, employment, engagement.
VOICE, vote, suffrage.
VOID, devoid, empty, vacant.
VOLATILITY, giddiness, lightness, levity, flightiness.
VOLUNTARILY, spontaneously, willingly.
VOLUNTARY, gratuitous.
VOLUPTUARY, epicure, sensualist.
VORACIOUS, rapacious, ravenous.
VOTE, suffrage, voice.
to VOUCH, aver, protest, affirm, asseverate, assure.
VOYAGE, journey, travel.

VULGAR, ordinary, mean, common.

W

WAGES, hire, pay, allowance, stipend, salary.
to WAIT, wait for, await, look for, expect.
to WAIT FOR, await, look for, expect, wait.
to WAIT ON, attend.
WAKEFUL, watchful, vigilant.
WALK, carriage, gait.
WAN, pale, pallid.
to WANDER, stroll, ramble, rove, roam, range.
to WANDER, swerve, stray, deviate.
to WANT, need, lack.
WANT, penury, indigence, need, poverty.
WARE, commodity, goods, merchandise.
WARLIKE, military, soldier-like, martial.
WARM, sincere, cordial, hearty.
WARMTH, glow, fire, heat.
WARNING, caution, admonition.
to WARRANT, guarantee, be security, be responsible.
WARY, circumspect, cautious.
to WASTE, destroy, consume.
to WASTE, dissipate, squander, spend, expend.
to WATCH, guard, defend.
to WATCH, observe.
WATCHFUL, vigilant, wakeful.
WATERMAN, boatman, ferryman.
WATERMAN, sailor, mariner, seaman.
WAVE, billow, surge, breaker.
to WAVER, fluctuate.

to WAVER, scruple, hesitate.
WAVERING, undetermined, unsettled, unsteady.
WAY, manner, method, mode, course, means.

WEAK, feeble, infirm.
to WEAKEN, enfeeble, debilitate, enervate, invalidate.
WEAKNESS, frailty, failing, foible, imperfection.
WEALTH, opulence, affluence, riches.
WEAPONS, arms.
WEARINESS, lassitude, fatigue.
WEARISOME, tiresome, tedious.
to WEARY, tire, jade, harass.
WEDDING, nuptials, marriage.
WEDLOCK, marriage, matrimony.
to WEEP, cry.
WEIGHT, burden, load.
WEIGHT, heaviness, gravity.
WEIGHT, moment, importance, consequence.
WEIGHTY, ponderous, heavy, burdensome.
to WELCOME, accost, salute, address, greet, hail.
WELCOME, acceptable, grateful.
WELFARE, prosperity, happiness, well-being.
WELL-BEING, welfare, prosperity, happiness.

to WHEEDLE, cajole, fawn, coax.
WHIM, freak.
WHIMSICAL, capricious, fanciful, fantastical.
to WHIRL, twirl, writhe, turn, wind.
WHOLE, all.
WHOLE, entire, complete, total, integral.
WHOLESOME, salubrious, salutary, healthy.

WICKED, evil, bad.
WICKED, iniquitous, nefarious.
WIDE, broad, large.
to WILL, wish.
WILLINGLY, voluntarily, spontaneously.
WILY, cunning, crafty, subtle, sly.
to WIN, earn, acquire, obtain, gain.
to WIND, whirl, twirl, writhe, turn.
WISDOM, prudence.
to WISH, long for, hanker after, covet, desire.
to WISH, will.
WIT, humor, satire, irony, burlesque.
WIT, ingenuity.
to WITHDRAW, secede, recede, retreat, retire.
WITHOUT INTERMISSION, incessantly, unceasingly, uninterruptedly.
to WITHSTAND, thwart, oppose, resist.
WITNESS, deponent, evidence.

WOEFUL, rueful, piteous, doleful.
to WONDER, admire, surprise, astonish, amaze.

WONDER, miracle, marvel, prodigy, monster.
WOOER, lover, suitor.
WORD, promise, engagement.
WORD, term, expression.
to WORK, operate, act.
WORK, labor, toil, drudgery, task.
WORK, production, performance.
WORLDLY, secular, temporal.
to WORSHIP, adore.
WORTH, desert, merit.
WORTH, rate, price, value.
WORTHLESS, unworthy.

to WRANGLE, jangle, jar.
WRATH, ire, indignation, anger, resentment.
to WRENCH, turn, bend, twist, distort, wring, wrest.
to WREST, wrench, turn, bend, twist, distort, wring.
WRETCHED, unhappy, miserable.

to WRING, wrest, wrench, turn, bend, twist, distort.
WRITER, author.
WRITER, penman, scribe.
to WRITHE, turn, wind, whirl, twirl.
WRONG, injustice, injury.

Y

YET, nevertheless, notwithstanding, however.

to YIELD, bear.
to YIELD, cede, concede, give up, deliver, surrender.
to YIELD, produce, afford.
to YIELD, submit, comply, conform.
YIELDING, submissive, compliant.

YOUTHFUL, juvenile, puerile.

TABULAR SYNOPSIS OF CATEGORIES

4. DISTRIBUTIVE...............	75. Class	
	76. Inclusion	77. Exclusion
	78. Generality	79. Speciality
5. CATEGORICAL...............	80. Rule	81. Multiformity
	82. Conformity	83. Unconformity

V. NUMBER

1. ABSTRACT..................	84. Number	
	85. Numeration	
	86. List	
	87. Unity	88. Accompaniment
	89. Duality	
	90. Duplication	91. Bisection
2. DETERMINATE...............	92. Triality	
	93. Triplication	94. Trisection
	95. Quaternity	
	96. Quadruplication	97. Quadrisection
	98. Five, &c.	99. Quinquesection, &c.
	100. Plurality	100a. Fraction
		101. Zero
3. INDETERMINATE.............	102. Multitude	103. Fewness
	104. Repetition	
	105. Infinity	

VI. TIME

	106. Time	107. Neverness
	Definite	*Indefinite*
1. ABSOLUTE.................	108. Period	109. Course
	108a. Contingent Duration	
	110. Diuturnity	111. Transience
	112. Perpetuity	113. Instantaneity
	114. Chronometry	115. Anachronism

	1. to Succession ...	116. Priority	117. Posteriority
		118. Present time	119. Different time
		120. Synchronism	
		121. Futurity	122. Preterition
		123. Newness	124. Oldness
2. RELATIVE	*2. to a Period.....*	125. Morning	126. Evening
		127. Youth	128. Age
		129. Infant	130. Veteran
		131. Adolescence	
	3. to an Effect or Purpose.....	132. Earliness	133. Lateness
		134. Occasion	135. Intempestivity
3. RECURRENT.................		136. Frequency	137. Infrequency
		138. Periodicity	139. Irregularity

VII. CHANGE

1. SIMPLE	140. Change	141. Permanence
	142. Cessation	143. Continuance
	144. Conversion	
		145. Reversion
	146. Revolution	
	147. Substitution	148. Interchange
	149. Changeableness	150. Stability
2. COMPLEX..................	*Present*	*Future*
	151. Eventuality	152. Destiny

VIII. CAUSATION

1. CONSTANCY OF SEQUENCE.....	153.	*Constant Antecedent* Cause	154.	*Constant Sequent* Effect
		Assignment of Cause		*Absence of Assignment*
	156.	Attribution		Chance
2. CONNECTION BETWEEN CAUSE AND EFFECT...............	157. Power		158. Impotence	
	Degrees of Power			
	159. Strength		160. Weakness	
	161. Production		162. Destruction	
	163. Reproduction			
	164. Producer		165. Destroyer	
3. POWER IN OPERATION........	166. Paternity		167. Posterity	
	168. Productiveness		169. Unproductiveness	
	170. Agency			
	171. Energy		172. Inertness	
	173. Violence		174. Moderation	

4. Indirect Power	175. Influence	175a. Absence of Influence
	176. Tendency	
	177. Liability	
5. Combination of Causes	178. Concurrence	179. Counteraction

Class II. SPACE

1. SPACE IN GENERAL

1. Abstract Space	180. { *Indefinite* Space }	180a. Inextension
		181. { *Definite* Region }
		182. { *Limited* Place }
2. Relative Space	183. Situation	
	184. Location	185. Displacement
	186. Presence	187. Absence
3. Existence in Space	188. Inhabitant	189. Abode
	190. Contents	191. Receptacle

II. DIMENSIONS

1. General	192. Size	193. Littleness
	194. Expansion	195. Contraction
	196. Distance	197. Nearness
	198. Interval	199. Contiguity
	200. Length	201. Shortness
	202. { Breadth Thickness }	203. { Narrowness Thinness }
	204. Layer	205. Filament
	206. Height	207. Lowness
2. Linear	208. Depth	209. Shallowness
	210. Summit	211. Base
	212. Verticality	213. Horizontality
	214. Pendency	215. Support
	216. Parallelism	217. Obliquity
	218. Inversion	
	219. Crossing	
	220. Exteriority	221. Interiority
	222. Centrality	
	223. Covering	224. Lining
	225. Investment	226. Divestment
1. General	227. Circumjacence	228. Interjacence
	229. Circumscription	
	230. Outline	
	231. Edge	
3. Centrical	232. Inclosure	
	233. Limit	
	234. Front	235. Rear
2. Special	236. Laterality	237. Contraposition
	238. Dextrality	239. Sinistrality

III. FORM

1. General	240. Form	241. Amorphism
	242. Symmetry	243. Distortion
	244. Angularity	
2. Special	245. Curvature	246. Straightness
	247. Circularity	248. Convolution
	249. Rotundity	
	250. Convexity	252. Concavity
	251. Flatness	
	253. Sharpness	254. Bluntness
	255. Smoothness	256. Roughness
3. Superficial	257. Notch	
	258. Fold	
	259. Furrow	
	260. Opening	261. Closure
	262. Perforator	263. Stopper

IV. MOTION

1. MOTION IN GENERAL........	264. Motion	265. Quiescence
	266. Journey	267. Navigation
	268. Traveler	269. Mariner
		269a. Aëronaut
	270. Transference	
	271. Carrier	
	272. Vehicle	273. Ship
2. DEGREES OF MOTION........	274. Velocity	275. Slowness
3. CONJOINED WITH FORCE......	276. Impulse	277. Recoil
4. WITH REFERENCE TO DIRECTION	278. Direction	279. Deviation
	280. Precession	281. Sequence
	282. Progression	283. Regression
	284. Propulsion	285. Traction
	286. Approach	287. Recession
	288. Attraction	289. Repulsion
	290. Convergence	291. Divergence
	292. Arrival	293. Departure
	294. Ingress	295. Egress
	296. Reception	297. Ejection
	298. Food	299. Excretion
	300. Insertion	301. Extraction
	302. Passage	
	303. Overrun	304. Shortcoming
	305. Ascent	306. Descent
	307. Elevation	308. Depression
	309. Leap	310. Plunge
	311. Circuition	
	312. Rotation	313. Evolution
	314. Oscillation	
	315. Agitation	

CLASS III. MATTER

I. MATTER IN GENERAL.......	316. Materiality	317. Immateriality
	318. World	
	319. Gravity	320. Levity

II. INORGANIC MATTER

1. SOLIDS.....................		321. Density	322. Rarity
		323. Hardness	324. Softness
		325. Elasticity	326. Inelasticity
		327. Tenacity	328. Brittleness
		329. Texture	
		330. Pulverulence	
		331. Friction	332. Lubrication
2. FLUIDS	1. In General......	333. Fluidity	334. Gaseity
		335. Liquefaction	336. Vaporization
	2. Specific..........	337. Water	338. Air
		339. Moisture	340. Dryness
		341. Ocean	342. Land
		343. Gulf	
		Lake	344. Plain
		345. Marsh	346. Island
		347. Stream	
	3. In Motion......	348. River	349. Wind
		350. Conduit	351. Air Pipe
3. IMPERFECT FLUIDS...........		352. Semiliquidity	353. Bubble Cloud
		354. Pulpiness	355. Unctuousness
			356. Oil
			356a. Resin

III. ORGANIC MATTER

1. VITALITY	1. In General.....	357. Organization	358. Inorganization
		359. Life	360. Death
			361. Killing
			362. Corpse
			363. Interment
	2. Special........	364. Animality	365. Vegetation
		366. Animal	367. Vegetable
		368. Zoölogy	369. Botany
		370. Cicuration	371. Agriculture
		372. Mankind	
		373. Man	374. Woman

TABULAR SYNOPSIS OF CATEGORIES

1. General . . . .

375. Sensibility	376. Insensibility
377. Pleasure	378. Pain

(1) Touch . . . .

379. Touch	
380. Sensations of Touch	381. Numbness

(2) Heat . . . .

382. Heat	383. Cold
384. Calefaction	385. Refrigeration
386. Furnace	387. Refrigeratory
388. Fuel	
389. Thermometer	

(3) Taste . . . .

390. Taste	391. Insipidity
392. Pungency	
393. Condiment	
394. Savoriness	395. Unsavoriness
396. Sweetness	397. Sourness

(4) Odor . . . .

398. Odor	399. Inodorousness
400. Fragrance	401. Fetor

2. Sensation

2. Special

(5) Sound . . . .

(i) *Sound in General*

402. Sound	403. Silence
404. Loudness	405. Faintness

(ii) *Specific Sounds*

406. Snap	407. Roll
408. Resonance	408a. Nonresonance
	409. Sibilation
410. Stridor	
411. Cry	412. Ululation

(iii) *Musical Sounds*

413. { Melody / Concord	414. Discord
415. Music	
416. Musician	
417. Musical Instruments	

(iv) *Perception of Sound*

418. Hearing	419. Deafness

(6) Light . . . .

(i) *Light in General*

420. Light	421. Darkness
	422. Dimness
423. Luminary	424. Shade
425. Transparency	426. Opacity
	427. Semitransparency

(ii) *Specific Light*

428. Color	429. Achromatism
430. Whiteness	431. Blackness
432. Gray	433. Brown
434. Redness	435. Greenness
436. Yellowness	437. Purple
438. Blueness	439. Orange
440. Variegation	

(iii) *Perceptions of Light*

441. Vision	442. Blindness
	443. Dim-sightedness
444. Spectator	
445. Optical Instruments	
446. Visibility	447. Invisibility
448. Appearance	449. Disappearance

CLASS IV. INTELLECT
Division (I). FORMATION OF IDEAS

I. OPERATIONS OF INTELLECT IN GENERAL . . . .

450. Intellect	450a. Absence of Intellect
451. Thought	452. Incogitance
453. Idea	454. Topic
455. Curiosity	456. Incuriosity
457. Attention	458. Inattention
459. Care	460. Neglect

II. PRECURSORY CONDITIONS AND OPERATIONS . . . .

461. Inquiry	462. Answer
463. Experiment	
464. Comparison	
465. Discrimination	465a. Indiscrimination
466. Measurement	

893

TABULAR SYNOPSIS OF CATEGORIES

	467. Evidence 468. Counterevidence
	469. Qualification
III. MATERIALS FOR REASONING.....	*Degrees of Evidence*
	470. Possibility 471. Impossibility
	472. Probability 473. Improbability
	474. Certainty 475. Uncertainty
IV. REASONING PROCESSES.........	476. Reasoning 477. { Intuition / Sophistry
	478. Demonstration 479. Confutation
	480. Judgment 481. Misjudgment
	480a. Discovery
	482. Overestimation 483. Underestimation
	484. Belief 485. { Unbelief / Doubt
	486. Credulity 487. Incredulity
	488. Assent 489. Dissent
	490. Knowledge 491. Ignorance
V. RESULTS OF REASONING.........	492. Scholar 493. Ignoramus
	494. Truth 495. Error
	496. Maxim 497. Absurdity
	Faculties
	498. { Intelligence / Wisdom 499. { Imbecility / Folly
	500. Sage 501. Fool
	502. Sanity 503. Insanity
	504. Madman

VI. EXTENSION OF THOUGHT.....	*1. To the Past ..*	505. Memory 506. Oblivion
		507. Expectation 508. Inexpectation
		509. Disappointment
	2. To the Future	510. Foresight
		511. Prediction
		512. Omen
		513. Oracle
VII. CREATIVE THOUGHT...........		514. Supposition
		515. Imagination

Division (II). COMMUNICATION OF IDEAS

	516. Meaning 517. Unmeaningness
	518. Intelligibility 519. Unintelligibility
I. NATURE OF IDEAS COMMUNICATED	520. Equivocalness
	521. Metaphor
	522. Interpretation 523. Misinterpretation
	524. Interpreter
	525. Manifestation 526. Latency
	527. Information 528. Concealment
	529. Disclosure 530. Ambush
	531. Publication
	532. News 533. Secret
	534. Messenger
	535. Affirmation 536. Negation
II. MODES OF COMMUNICATION	537. Teaching { 538. Misteaching / 539. Learning
	540. Teacher 541. Learner
	542. School
	543. Veracity 544. Falsehood
	545. Deception
	546. Untruth
	547. Dupe 548. Deceiver
	549. Exaggeration

III. MEANS OF COMMUNICATION

	550. Indication
	551. Record 552. Obliteration
	553. Recorder
1. *Natural Means*...............	554. Representation 555. Misrepresentation
	556. { Painting / Black and white
	557. Sculpture
	558. Engraving
	559. Artist

894

	560. Language	
	561. Letter	
	562. Word	563. Neology
	564. Nomenclature	565. Misnomer
	566. Phrase	
	567. Grammar	568. Solecism
1. Language Generally	569. Style	

Qualities of Style

570. Perspicuity	571. Obscurity
572. Conciseness	573. Diffuseness
574. Vigor	575. Feebleness
576. Plainness	577. Ornament
578. Elegance	579. Inelegance
580. Voice	581. Aphonia
582. Speech	583. Stammering

2. Conventional Means

2. Spoken Language	584. Loquacity	585. Taciturnity
	586. Allocution	587. Response
	588. Interlocution	589. Soliloquy
	590. Writing	591. Printing
	592. Correspondence	593. Book
	594. Description	
3. Written Language	595. Dissertation	
	596. Compendium	
	597. Poetry	598. Prose
	599. The Drama	

Class V. VOLITION

Division (I). Individual Volition

	600. Will	601. Necessity
	602. Willingness	603. Unwillingness
	604. Resolution	605. Irresolution
	604a. Perseverance	
1. Acts..........	606. Obstinacy	607. Tergiversation
		608. Caprice
	609. Choice	609a. Absence of Choice
		610. Rejection
	611. Predetermination	612. Impulse
	613. Habit	614. Desuetude

I. Volition in General

2. Causes........	615. Motive	615a. Absence of Motive
	617. Plea	616. Dissuasion
3. Objects........	618. Good	619. Evil
	620. Intention	621. Chance
	622. Pursuit	623. Avoidance
		624. Relinquishment
1. Conceptional ...	625. Business	
	626. Plan	
	627. Method	
	628. Mid-course	629. Circuit
	630. Requirement	

II. Prospective Volition

1. Actual Subservience

	631. Instrumentality	
	632. Means	
	633. Instrument	
	634. Substitute	
	635. Materials	
	636. Store	
	637. Provision	638. Waste

639. Sufficiency

2. Subservience to Ends........	641. Redundance	640. Insufficiency

2. Degree of Subservience

642. Importance	643. Unimportance
644. Utility	645. Inutility
646. Expedience	647. Inexpedience
648. Goodness	649. Badness
650. Perfection	651. Imperfection
652. Cleanness	653. Uncleanness
654. Health	655. Disease
656. Salubrity	657. Insalubrity

II. PROSPECTIVE VOLITION—*continued*		658. Improvement	659. Deterioration
		660. Restoration	661. Relapse
		662. Remedy	663. Bane

3. *Contingent Subservience*

	2. *Subservience to Ends*—*cont.*	664. Safety	665. Danger
		666. Refuge	667. Pitfall
		668. Warning	
		669. Alarm	
		670. Preservation	
		671. Escape	
		672. Deliverance	
	3. *Precursory Measures*	673. Preparation	674. Nonpreparation
		675. Essay	
		676. Undertaking	
		677. Use	678. Disuse
			679. Misuse

III. ACTION	1. *Simple*	680. Action	681. Inaction
		682. Activity	683. Inactivity
		684. Haste	685. Leisure
		686. Exertion	687. Repose
		688. Fatigue	689. Refreshment
	2. *Complex*	690. Agent	
		691. Workshop	
		692. Conduct	
		693. Direction	
		694. Director	
		695. Advice	
		696. Council	
		697. Precept	
		698. Skill	699. Unskillfulness
		700. Proficient	701. Bungler
		702. Cunning	703. Artlessness

IV. ANTAGONISM	1. *Conditional*	704. Difficulty	705. Facility
		706. Hindrance	707. Aid
		708. Opposition	709. Coöperation
		710. Opponent	711. Auxiliary
		712. Party	
		713. Discord	714. Concord
	2. *Active*	715. Defiance	
		716. Attack	717. Defense
		718. Retaliation	719. Resistance
		720. Contention	721. Peace
		722. Warfare	723. Pacification
		724. Mediation	
		725. Submission	
		726. Combatant	
		727. Arms	
		728. Arena	

V. RESULTS OF ACTION	729. Completion	730. Noncompletion
	731. Success	732. Failure
	733. Trophy	
	734. Prosperity	735. Adversity
	736. Mediocrity	

Division (II). INTERSOCIAL VOLITION

I. GENERAL	737. Authority	738. Laxity
	739. Severity	740. Lenity
	741. Command	
	742. Disobedience	743. Obedience
	744. Compulsion	
	745. Master	746. Servant
	747. Scepter	
	748. Freedom	749. Subjection
	750. Liberation	751. Restraint
		752. Prison
	753. Keeper	754. Prisoner
	755. Commission	756. Abrogation
		757. Resignation
	758. Consignee	
	759. Deputy	

CLASS VI. AFFECTIONS

2. DISCRIMINATIVE—*continued*....		853. Ridiculousness
		854. Fop
		855. Affectation
		856. Ridicule
		857. Laughingstock
	858. Hope	859. Hopelessness
		860. Fear
	861. Courage	862. Cowardice
	863. Rashness	864. Caution
3. PROSPECTIVE	865. Desire	867. Dislike
	866. Indifference	
		868. Fastidiousness
		869. Satiety
4. CONTEMPLATIVE	870. Wonder	871. Expectance
	872. Prodigy	
	873. Repute	874. Disrepute
	875. Nobility	876. Commonalty
	877. Title	
	878. Pride	879. Humility
5. EXTRINSIC	880. Vanity	881. Modesty
	882. Ostentation	
	883. Celebration	
	884. Boasting	
	885. Insolence	886. Servility
	887. Blusterer	

III. SYMPATHETIC

	888. Friendship	889. Enmity
	890. Friend	891. Enemy
	892. Sociality	893. Seclusion
	894. Courtesy	895. Discourtesy
	896. Congratulation	
1. SOCIAL	897. Love	898. Hate
	899. Favorite	
		900. Resentment
		901. Irascibility
		901a. Sullenness
	902. Endearment	
	903. Marriage	904. Celibacy
		905. Divorce
		Widowhood
	906. Benevolence	907. Malevolence
		908. Malediction
2. DIFFUSIVE		909. Threat
	910. Philanthropy	911. Misanthropy
	912. Benefactor	913. Evildoer
3. SPECIAL	914. Pity	914a. Pitilessness
	915. Condolence	
	916. Gratitude	917. Ingratitude
4. RETROSPECTIVE	918. Forgiveness	919. Revenge
		920. Jealousy
		921. Envy

IV. MORAL

	922. Right	923. Wrong
1. OBLIGATIONS	924. Dueness	925. Undueness
		927. Dereliction
	926. Duty	927a. Exemption
	928. Respect	929. Disrespect
		930. Contempt
2. SENTIMENTS	931. Approbation	932. Disapprobation
	933. Flattery	934. Detraction
	935. Flatterer	936. Detractor
	937. Vindication	938. Accusation
	939. Probity	940. Improbity
		941. Knave
	942. Disinterestedness	943. Selfishness
3. CONDITIONS	944. Virtue	945. Vice
	946. Innocence	947. Guilt
	948. Good Man	949. Bad Man
	950. Penitence	951. Impenitence
	952. Atonement	

4. PRACTICE ....
- 953. Temperance
- 955. Asceticism
- 956. Fasting
- 958. Sobriety
- 960. Purity

- 954. Intemperance
- 954a. Sensualist
- 957. Gluttony
- 959. Drunkenness
- 961. Impurity
- 962. Libertine

5. INSTITUTIONS ....
- 963. Legality
- 965. Jurisprudence
- 966. Tribunal
- 967. Judge
- 968. Lawyer
- 969. Lawsuit
- 970. Acquittal
- 973. Reward

- 964. Illegality
- 971. Condemnation
- 972. Punishment
- 974. Penalty
- 975. Scourge

V. RELIGIOUS

1. SUPERHUMAN BEINGS AND REGIONS ....
- 976. Deity
- 977. Angel
- 979. Mythic and Pagan Deities
- 981. Heaven

- 978. Satan
- 980. Evil Spirits
- 982. Hell

2. DOCTRINES ....
- 983. Theology
- 983a. Orthodoxy
- 985. Revelation (Biblical)

- 984. Heterodoxy
- 986. Sacred Writings (non-Biblical)

3. SENTIMENTS ....
- 987. Piety

- 988. Impiety
- 989. Irreligion

4. ACTS ....
- 990. Worship

- 991. Idolatry
- 992. Sorcery
- 992a. Psychical Research
- 993. Spell
- 994. Sorcerer

5. INSTITUTIONS ....
- 995. Churchdom
- 996. Clergy
- 998. Rite
- 999. Canonicals
- 1000. Temple

- 997. Laity

HOW TO USE ROGET IN CONVERSATION, WRITING, AND PUBLIC SPEAKING

ORDINARY conversationalists require *words*; and we admire a participant in social intercourse whose speech is rich, varied, and delicately accurate in distinguishing meanings. Unfortunately, the words with which many conversations are carried on are definitely commonplace, trite, and conventional. This is true even among so-called intelligent people: how many of the latter, for example, today in certain circles describe everything and anything good by one poor adjective — "swell"? Mental laziness, in conversation as in writing, takes refuge in tags, overworked slang phrases, fashionable locutions, clichés of all kinds.

A man's conversation is in fact often an index to his writing. If he is slovenly in speech, he can seldom make sure of exactness and strength in his written discourse. Inasmuch, too, as our opportunities for oral speech far exceed those for writing, it is all the more necessary to be constantly on our guard to secure the best expression of which we are capable.

This excellence of expression depends to a large extent on our vocabulary — its exactness and its strength. In speech as in writing, one must learn to make nice distinctions and to increase the wealth of one's vocabulary. Palmer well says that "good English is exact English"; and he gives the wise counsel that "something like what we mean must never be counted equivalent to what we mean. And if we are not sure of our meaning or of our word, we must pause until we are sure."

In reaching this state of certainty, Roget's THESAURUS is again an ever-present help in time of trouble. It can be employed in improving our discourse on all kinds of topics. Even in so ordinary a subject of conversation as the weather, Roget offers a host of substitutes for pleasant, violent, or indifferent conditions in the air and sky (Nos. 173 and 174). One's power of criticizing a book or a play may be improved by examining what the pages of Roget offer in the realm of literature (Nos. 560, 593, 597) or drama (No. 599); and it would repay an ambitious conversationalist to master terms suggested in these sections. Again, it is highly useful to find ways of avoiding such overworked words as *get* (No. 144) and *put* (No. 184) and *nice* (see Index); or to enlarge one's vocabulary of business with the help of such words as *barter* (No. 794), *purchase* (No. 795), *sale* (No. 796), *merchant* (No. 797), *merchandise* (No. 798), *money* (No. 800), *wealth* (No. 803), *credit* (No. 805), etc., or of politics, as in the amusing group of words under *cunning* (No. 702), or the appreciation of beautiful things, as in *beauty* (No. 845), *ornament* (No. 847), *taste* (No. 850), *fashion* (No. 852), etc. Much conversation, moreover, consists of the reporting of some other conversation, and one is often irked by the unpleasing repetition of a long string of "He said's" and "She said's." Roget gives the opportunity for finding a whole series of equivalents for the verb of *saying* (Nos. 535, 560, 582).

The outstanding merit of Roget is the immense wealth of such possible equivalents that his book provides, an advantage that H. W. Fowler emphatically pointed out in his article on *Synonyms* in his famous *Dictionary of Modern English Usage*. Fowler, speaking of lists of synonyms as "a blessed refuge," went on to say: "Such lists, to be of much use, must be voluminous, and those who need them should try Roget's THESAURUS."

Such study of *synonymy* demands keen powers of discrimination, and is therefore useful in developing these powers. Synonyms are, supposedly, words of the same meaning; for example, *begin* and *commence*, *humble* and *lowly*. But Lord Chesterfield well observed that "those who study a language attentively will find that there is no such thing." It was shown by George C. Loane that even the pairs cited are not exact synonyms. *Commence* is much less colloquial than *begin*, and careful writers avoid using an infinitive after it. No one, moreover, ever signed himself "Your lowly servant." Synonyms, to be accurate, are therefore definable as words of similar but not identical meaning. Often the shade of distinction is what marks the careful and the capable writer.

It is, moreover, true that as such a writer composes a particular passage, he may write down a word that, for the moment, seems to express his meaning exactly. Then, on reflection, he finds that it fails to do so; and there begin to float around in his mind a whole series of possible substitutes. But none of them fits the occasion or is sufficiently accurate and appropriate. The writer is certain, however, that the right, the inevitable word exists, if only he can find it. It is at such moments that Roget's THESAURUS is of inestimable value. Locating the proper passage by means of the index, the perplexed writer finds before him practically all the words in the English language which revolve around the idea he wishes to express; and if the term that he believes is the best one actually exists, there he will find it — to his great relief.

Naturally, in view of this characteristic of so-called synonyms, students of the art of writing will anticipate such problems and difficulties by investigating the lists in Roget beforehand, setting themselves such investigation as a definite project. An analysis of related words, furthermore, invariably turns out to be an analysis of ideas — just as Roget's THESAURUS itself is really a classification of thought. One cannot, for example, take a group like that headed *Wit* (No. 842) without sharpening the mind and increasing one's stock of ideas and information. Such an analysis, if confined entirely to Roget, would provide a considerable number of words of varying meaning, several expressions in other languages, colloquial and proverbial expressions, and a useful group of antonyms in No. 843. If the analysis were continued, as it should be, in other authorities, it would lead one to the useful discrimination between *wit* and *humor* furnished in Webster's *New International Dictionary* and to the table dealing keen-mindedly with humor, wit, satire, sarcasm, invective, irony, cynicism, and the sardonic that may be found in Fowler's *Dictionary* under the first-named term.

Fowler may again be cited as follows: "No one who does not expend, whether expressly and systematically or as a half-conscious accompaniment of his reading and writing, a good deal of care upon points of synonymy is likely to write well." Perhaps Francis Bacon had the same point in mind when he declared that "writing maketh an *exact* man."

Yet it is not merely exactness for which Roget offers the prescription; his book is every bit as useful in providing the material for what many might regard as an even more important quality of good conversation — *expressiveness*. Possibly if a choice were to be offered a first-rate writer or speaker, he would prefer, if one of these had to be sacrificed, to take expressiveness rather than accuracy in language, and particularly in the vigorous give-and-take that marks the speech of hearty and amusing conversationalists. A dull accord with usage must not be made an excuse for sacrificing the picturesque, the imaginative, and the forceful elements of language. Words must, of course, be used so that they can be readily understood: the first object of language is naturally to communicate. But a meticulous correctness may strip one's language of all life, and a full knowledge of grammar and of the laws of language often reveals the fact that the so-called rules by which some seek to bind speech have no warrant in fact; the rule, for example, that to end a sentence with a preposition is wrong. As Palmer forcibly puts it, "What stamps a man as great is not freedom from faults, but abundance of powers."

But this "audacious accuracy," as Palmer calls it, can be practised rightly and successfully only by those who command a wide range of words; and here, once more, Roget offers assistance such as can nowhere else be equalled. It is precisely through a full and intelligent use of Roget that one's expressiveness can be immensely increased. In Roget we start with the one poor word that formed our sole means of communicating an idea, and with that as a clue we proceed to the tremendous wealth of the English language. It is assembled for us in Roget so that we may find it and use it when we need it. "It's a lie," says the hasty and angry man; but Roget would teach him — if he were to cool down long enough to consult *untruth* (No. 546) — how many effective fashions English provides of saying the same thing more graciously, more forcefully, more variedly, more dramatically, more humorously. We are telling a story, and need to mention a weapon. Possibly only two or three alternatives occur to us, but under *arms* (No. 727) Roget has a whole army of equivalent words, from which we may choose the one best suited to us. We are discussing style, and we may find in Roget long lists of suggestive words dealing with perspicuity (No. 570), conciseness (No. 572), diffuseness (No. 573), plainness (No. 576), ornament (No. 577), and scores of other qualities.

Similarly, Roget may help us to avoid that most detestable fault of all writing — the *cliché*, the hackneyed or trite term. Some people have a positive genius for finding and using all the outworn terms, all the phrases shiny with overmuch circulation that can be found in the language. Jane Austen once wrote to a niece with literary ambitions: "I wish you would not let him 'plunge into a vortex of dissipation.' I do not object to the thing, but I cannot bear the expression; it is such thorough novel slang; and so old that I daresay Adam met with it in the first novel he opened."

Leigh Hunt observed that Addison's *Cato* was full of such phrases: "plant daggers in my heart; ripe for a revolt; towers above her sex; courting the yoke; straining every nerve." Webster gives as examples of the trite these phrases: "a downy couch; a deadly missile; the worse for wear; a seething mass of humanity." Walter Savage Landor objected to "palmy days" and "at the eleventh hour."

But the best list of hackneyed expressions is to be found in *Crowell's Dictionary of English Grammar*, prepared by Maurice H. Weseen. Professor Weseen gives a two-page, double-column inventory of such expressions, citing first those employed in business letters, then those that occur frequently in general composition. As we glance over his list, each one of us will, doubtless, recognize sins of his own. Among the hackneyed business expressions Professor Weseen ranges from "above subject" to "writer wishes to state." In his other list he goes from "along this line" to "worse for wear." In this catalogue one may meet the blushing bride and the happy benedict, the downy couch and the groaning board, the golden locks and the marble brow, the motley crew and the motley throng, the blush of shame and the lean and hungry look, the arms of Morpheus and the sleep of the just.

Roget offers four lines of words under the heading of *bed* (No. 215) and two groups of words that are the equivalents of *downy* — *smooth* (No. 255) and *soft* (No. 324). *Assemblage* (No. 72) is unusually full (for *crew* and *throng*), and it will be an extraordinary writer indeed who does not find new verbal riches when he looks up *lean*, is referred to *narrowness, thinness* (No. 203), and finds in the second group of adjectives a list of words descriptive of a skeletal condition that includes such rarities as *coarctate, augustate, tabic,* and *marcid*. This section, moreover, closes with a quotation from Shakespeare; and how much better it would be to use this line rather than the stale, moth-eaten, insipid "lean and hungry look":

"Pinch, a hungry, lean-faced villain, a mere anatomy."

The objections to hackneyed expressions such as we have been discussing may be summed up as twofold: they are, in the first place, offensive to readers because they are so commonplace and outworn; they affect many people in the way that old and crumpled dollar bills do or coins thin and smooth from too much use. In the second place, they frequently fail to express exact shades of meaning: because of their very age they are dubious as means of telling exactly what is in one's mind at the present time.

The same is true in business letters where words must be as carefully analyzed as the article or service which they describe. There must be avoidance of a constantly repeated term. Adjectives must be fresh and vigorous. Verbs must catch and hold attention. Phrases of courtesy must be agreeably varied. With the help of Roget's THESAURUS it is possible to gain in one's business correspondence such an access of new and striking terms as to make one's letters a pleasure to read. To the wide-awake dictator of letters the volume becomes indispensable.

One suspects, too, that the good copywriter in a successful advertising agency has a copy of Roget's THESAURUS at his right hand. One of the most valuable books ever issued on methods of writing effective advertisements is *The Written Word*, composed by three copywriters in a great American agency: H. A. Batten, Maurice Goodrich, and Granville Toogood. This is called "a study of the art of advertising," and it is in the amusing and instructive pages of this volume that one finds this striking passage from William Blake:

"I have heard many people say, 'Give me the ideas, it does not matter what words you put them into.' These people knew enough of artifice, but nothing of art. Ideas cannot be given but in their minutely appropriate words."

In the same volume Aldous Huxley is cited as saying: "The problem presented by the sonnet is child's play compared with the problem of the advertisement."

According to these authors, the most interesting (and therefore effective) copy is that which finds the least hackneyed approach, the freshest and most vital expression, and the most dramatic idea. Given the last, certainly Roget is a good road to travel towards the other two.

All that has been said of conversation and writing applies in even greater measure to public speaking. Everyone admires the public speaker with a rich and flowing vocabulary and endowed with an eloquence that carries his audience along with him. We notice that he has a phrase ready for every idea, and that he sometimes says the same thing in two or three different ways, so that those who are slow to comprehend or who have not been paying the most careful attention may know what he has been saying.

This richness of vocabulary and this eloquence are rarely matters of chance, although undoubtedly some men are born with greater powers of speech than others. For even where the native ability is present, it must be fostered and improved by study; and to the orator the study of words is every whit as important as the study of the psychology of audiences or the study of society.

From a study of Roget can be obtained highly valuable assistance in the acquisition of oral adroitness. For from Roget the student of public speaking will particularly learn one important secret of the orator as of other users of words who play upon words: the necessity for discriminating skilfully and artistically between the *denotation* and the *connotation* of the terms we employ. The exact significance of a word, we soon discover, is of less import than its suggestiveness, the aura of meaning that hangs around it. Here is a realm in which Roget is of special, almost unique value. We start out, presumably, with the denotation; Roget goes on to supply other words, the connotation of which may be far superior to the word with which we first started. From among these other words we may choose those of most potent connotation, and so immensely increase the power of our discourse.